# ASPLOS XIX

## Nineteenth International Conference on Architectural Support for Programming Languages and Operating Systems

I0882249

**March 1–5, 2014**

**Salt Lake City, Utah, USA**

**Sponsored by:**

**SIGARCH**

**SIGOPS**

**SIGPLAN**

Association for Computing Machinery

**In co-operation with: SIGBED**

**With Support from:**

**NSF, Microsoft Research, ARM, AMD, Google, Hewlett-Packard, Intel, VMware, Facebook, Oracle Labs, EMC$^2$, and IBM Research**

Association for
Computing Machinery

*Advancing Computing as a Science & Profession*

**The Association for Computing Machinery**
**2 Penn Plaza, Suite 701**
**New York, New York 10121-0701**



**Notice to Past Authors of ACM-Published Articles**
ACM intends to create a complete electronic archive of all articles and/or other material previously published by ACM. If you have written a work that has been previously published by ACM in any journal or conference proceedings prior to 1978, or any SIG Newsletter at any time, and you do NOT want this work to appear in the ACM Digital Library, please inform permissions@acm.org, stating the title of the work, the author(s), and where and when published.

**ISBN:** 978-1-4503-2305-5 (Digital)

**ISBN:** 978-1-4503-3100-5 (Print)

Additional copies may be ordered prepaid from:

**ACM Order Department**
PO Box 30777
New York, NY 10087-0777, USA

Phone: 1-800-342-6626 (USA and Canada)
+1-212-626-0500 (Global)
Fax: +1-212-944-1318
E-mail: acmhelp@acm.org
Hours of Operation: 8:30 am – 4:30 pm ET

Printed in the USA

# ASPLOS 2014 General Chairs' Welcome

It is our great pleasure to welcome you to the *2014 ACM International Conference on Architectural Support for Programming Languages and Operating Systems – ASPLOS-XIX* in Salt Lake City, UT on March 1-5, 2014.

This year's ASPLOS finds a home in beautiful Salt Lake City, a thriving technology hub that is surrounded by snow-capped mountains and a handful of geologically diverse national parks. In fact, the large number of technology start-ups in the Salt Lake valley has inspired the moniker "Silicon Slopes". Visitors can choose among a wide array of activities while in town – skiing or snowboarding in one of eight nearby world-class ski resorts, hiking on numerous local trails, visiting Historic Temple Square in downtown, or taking the five-hour drive to national parks in Utah and surrounding states. As the site of the 2002 Winter Olympic games, there are numerous Olympic class facilities nearby. The conference banquet will be held at the Olympic Oval, site of both the long and short track speed skating events. Apollo Anton Ohno appeared on the world stage as the gold medalist in the 1500 meter short-track event in the 2002 Olympics. We hope the banquet will not only provide the usual social opportunity to mingle with colleagues but also give you all the chance to feel some of the spirit that lies behind the Winter Olympic Games.

This year's conference continues the ASPLOS tradition of being the premiere venue for reporting integrative research comprising computer architecture, programming languages, and operating systems. The conference represents the hard work of the organizing committee, reviewers, and in particular the contributing authors. Particular thanks goes to Sarita Adve for the amazing effort she put in to create the technical program. Her organization and diligence in every aspect was simply spectacular. The Program Chair message details her many innovative approaches to improving our peer review process. We also thank the other organizing committee members who worked hard behind the scenes to make this conference possible: Gabe Loh (AMD Research) for his efforts on fund-raising; Venkatesh Akella (UC Davis) for organizing the workshops; Ioanna Baldini and Livio Soares (IBM TJ Watson) for putting together a great set of tutorials; Matt Might (U. Utah) for managing the many complexities of the student travel grant process; John Regehr (U. Utah) for organizing the lightning and poster sessions; Ani Udipi (ARM) for handling registration; Luis Ceze and Karin Strauss for enthusiastically leading the WACI session; Niti Madan (Oracle) for taking care of publicity; Rakesh Komuravelli and Hyojin Sung (UIUC) for managing the submission site; Manju Shevgoor (U. Utah) for developing and maintaining the conference website; and the ASPLOS Steering Committee for their wise input throughout the past year. Sarita's message will acknowledge a number of others who significantly contributed to the technical program.

We are grateful for our many supporters. Their support goes a long way to reducing registration fees, and defrays student costs. This year's supporters are: Microsoft Research, ARM, Google, AMD, HP, VMWARE, Facebook, Intel, Oracle, IBM, and EMC. We also receive generous sponsorship from ACM SIGARCH, SIGOPS, SIGPLAN and NSF for student travel grants.

Finally, thanks to the attendees. You are the lifeblood of the conference. We sincerely hope that you find the program exciting as well as thought provoking. We have a packed program with 49 technical papers, a reception, banquet, business meeting, two keynotes, a debate, and a WACI session. We hope this provides a stimulating platform for several rewarding interactions.

**Rajeev Balasubramonian**
*ASPLOS 2014 General co-Chair*

**Al Davis**
*ASPLOS 2014 General co-Chair*

# Program Chair's Message

It has been a privilege to serve as the program chair for ASPLOS 2014. I am inspired and humbled by the breadth and quality of the work submitted and the commitment of the organizing team to an excellent conference.

The broad goal of a conference is to move the field forward. I was fortunate that recent PC chairs of ASPLOS led very successful conferences, and I mostly followed in their footsteps. Nevertheless I identified two narrower goals for additional efforts: (1) to continue to enhance the image of ASPLOS as a broad, multidisciplinary conference, and (2) to continue to raise the bar for quality and fairness in our review process. This document describes the processes I used, summarizes the program, and acknowledges those who made this program possible.

**Scope of ASPLOS**

The call for papers emphasized that ASPLOS is a broad multidisciplinary conference open to new and non-traditional systems related topics. I reached out to "non-traditional" SIGs and other organizations to advertise the call. One concrete outcome is that ASPLOS is "in-cooperation" with SIGBED this year. I hope our ties with SIGBED continue to strengthen in the coming years.

The call also said that papers should emphasize synergy of at least two ASPLOS disciplines (broadly defined) and the submission form explicitly asked authors to identify these areas.

We received 217 submissions, a 12% increase from last year and a new record. About 147 papers identified architecture as one of their areas, 89 identified PL or compilers, and 94 identified OS. Many papers identified other broad areas, including verification, graphics, big data, networks, cloud computing, mobile computing, embedded systems, software engineering, and more.

For specific research topics, again there was a large diversity. The following were listed by more than 20 submissions: power/energy/thermal management (34 papers), parallel architecture (31), heterogeneous architectures and accelerators (28), caches (27), high-performance computing (26), OS scheduling and resource management (26), compiler optimization (23), software reliability (23), virtualization (22), parallel programming languages (21), and programming models (21). The accepted papers constitute a similarly diverse set of topics.

In summary, ASPLOS continues to live up to its vision of a multidisciplinary conference, attracting a broad range of systems related researchers.

**The Review Process: Setting the Stage**

I was fortunate to have an excellent program committee (PC) of 35 members and external review committee (ERC) of 69 members. An additional 43 reviewers contributed to the process.

*Review process overview:* I used a two phase process similar to recent ASPLOS conferences. Unlike ASPLOS'13 but like other ASPLOS conferences, I obtained phase 2 reviews for only a subset of papers. The two review phases were followed by an author response period, an intense 2-week long online discussion period, and a 1-day in-person PC meeting. ERC reviewers were required to participate in all parts of this process except for the PC meeting.

*Aids for reviewer assignments:* I assigned all reviews. To help find the best reviewers, I used the following aids new to ASPLOS. (1) The submission instructions allowed unlimited pages for the bibliography and required all citations to include all authors (i.e., no et al.). This borrows from NSF and makes it easier to identify potential reviewers from related work. (2) I asked reviewers to suggest other reviewers as part of their review, borrowed from ISCA'13. (3) I allowed authors to (optionally) suggest reviewers.

I required all reviewers to write their assigned reviews themselves. Consulting with others for small aspects was allowed if it brought clear added value (after checking with me for conflicts), but the assigned reviewers needed to write the bulk of the review and give their own scores.

*System enhancements for conflicts:* I used double-blind reviewing and handled conflicts of interest using community norms. Sandhya Dwarkadas handled the 20 papers with which I had a conflict using the same process described here. I requested Eddie Kohler, the author of the HotCRP reviewing software, to add a new mechanism to handle PC chair conflicts. This mechanism allows the PC chair to yield (most) chair privileges to a different "manager" for a given paper, and allows reviewers to email paper-specific issues to the (anonymous) paper manager. This system (1) significantly streamlined handling the review process for Sandhya, (2) was better at hiding sensitive information from me than alternatives I had previously used, and (3) was better at hiding the conflict from assigned reviewers, preventing inadvertent guessing of author identity. I am grateful to Eddie for implementing such an intrusive change at very short notice.

*Tone:* I consistently set a tone that encouraged reviewers to not look for perfection but to focus on moving the field forward while being constructive and fair to all authors. I emphasized that there was no target acceptance rate and all worthy papers would be accepted. Accepting many papers implies multitrack sessions and potentially reduced interaction. To mitigate these downsides, the first day of the conference features lightning presentations and the second day features a poster session for all papers, borrowed from MICRO'12. Although I used numeric scores in the review forms, decisions were made based on the review texts.

**Phase 1 Reviews**

I assigned 2 PC and 1 ERC reviewers for each paper in phase 1. I received virtually all reviews within two days of the completion deadline (I learned to nag). Unlike ASPLOS'13 (but like other conferences), I did not move all papers to phase 2. An important benefit of two phase reviewing is to relieve reviewers of the burden of reviewing clearly weak papers. On the other hand, a process that rejects papers on the basis of just three reviews risks inadequately informed decisions and inadequate author feedback. I put significant effort to balance these opposing demands.

I classified papers with at least one accept score for overall merit to move to phase 2 by default. Papers with all reject scores with high confidence levels were candidates to not move to phase 2. I highlighted the remaining 38 papers (no accepts, but some undecided and/or low confidence scores) for online discussion among reviewers, using the HotCRP comments system which provides a persistent record. Many reviewers voluntarily discussed many other papers as well.

In parallel, I read most reviews and every review of every paper that was a candidate for terminating at phase 1 or under discussion. For each review that did not provide adequate justification for a low score (e.g., a subjective claim that the paper was incremental without adequate citations of prior work), I used a HotCRP comment to request the reviewer to update their review or risk the paper moving to phase 2. I ensured all score changes were accompanied with justifications in the review text and not just an easy reaction to adjust to the majority. I used the HotCRP color tags feature extensively to help reviewers and myself distinguish different paper categories and track online discussion results.

After this process, all papers with at least one accept or undecided score proceeded to phase 2. A few papers with all reject scores also moved to phase 2 if the review text did not justify the reject scores or had low confidence scores (when in doubt, I took the authors' perspective and moved the paper to phase 2). 30% of the papers did not move to phase 2.

**Phase 2 Reviews**

The phase 1 discussions and reviewer suggestions were very helpful in assigning reviewers for phase 2. All phase 2 papers had at least 5 total reviews, with at least 3 from the PC. The maximum total number of reviews for a PC or ERC member was 19 or 7 respectively.

Mid-phase 2, I used a tool by Andrew Myers[1] to calibrate excessive negativity or exuberance among reviewers. I sent each reviewer their estimated bias score and an anonymized list of all reviewers' scores. A positive (negative) bias indicated a tendency to give scores that are higher (lower) than others who reviewed the same paper. I believe (hope) this calibration motivated some reflection as reviewers moved to the critical decision-making stages.

The phase 2 reviews were due three days before the author response period. I wanted to ensure high quality reviews to facilitate responses focused on substantive issues. Since there was limited time, I distributed the quality assurance task among all reviewers. The last reviewer that submitted the review on a paper was asked to do a *review sufficiency check (RSC)* to ensure that (1) the reviews provided sufficient information to make an informed decision for the paper and (2) the reviews provided sufficient feedback to the authors. If the paper passed the RSC, the reviewer colored the paper purple (using HotCRP color tags); otherwise, they noted the problems.

The RSC mechanism significantly enhanced my ability to find the problem papers and focus my attention on them. Many reviews were updated and we identified 18 papers for additional reviews. When the author response started, *all* reviews from phase 2 had already been received (I got good at nagging). All post-phase2 (post-RSC) reviews had been requested and some were already received! The authors were notified that all pending reviews were late requests and they wouldn't be penalized for not responding to them. At the end, we received a total of 902 reviews.

**Online Discussion After Author Response**

This was the most critical phase of the review process. The goal for the online discussion phase was to triage papers into preliminary accept (tagged green, to be presented quickly at the PC meeting), preliminary reject (tagged red, not to be presented at the PC meeting), and discuss (tagged yellow, and the focus of most of the PC meeting).

Each paper was assigned a lead from the PC or ERC to initiate discussion among its reviewers (tagging the paper purple) and lead it towards a **consensus** (unanimous agreement) for green (accept) or red (reject). If significant discussion did not lead to a unanimous agreement, the paper was marked yellow (discuss). For these, the discussion was expected to reconcile as many differences among the reviewers as possible, leaving only a few substantive differences for a focused PC meeting discussion. That is, tagging yellow was not simply a way to duck work during this phase. These decisions assumed liberal use of shepherding, but not for adding new results.

I monitored discussions for all papers, nagging reviewers, clarifying policies, reminding philosophies, and obtaining yet more reviews as needed, while paying extra attention to papers turning red and those leaning to yellow.

---

[1] http://www.cs.cornell.edu/andru/reviewAdj/

Although this phase required significant effort, it played a critical role in running a smooth PC meeting with well-informed decisions. No system is perfect, but I identify the following advantages of having an online discussion phase with mandatory participation from all reviewers.

(1) It ensured non-PC reviewers' opinions were adequately represented during the PC meeting. In a conference as broad as ASPLOS, often the non-PC reviewers provide key expertise. We accepted some papers where the only champions were ERC reviewers because they forcefully argued for the paper during the online discussion phase.

(2) It allowed reviewers to reflect on each others' opinions in ways not possible when the first discussion is at the PC meeting; e.g., by reading previous work or confirming an opinion from another expert. These reflections resolved many differences among reviewers that could have become unhelpful sticking points in the limited time of a PC meeting.

(3) It allowed me to provide clarifications on matters of policy and philosophy that sometimes needlessly take up too much PC meeting time (e.g., does a prior workshop submission constitute prior art or does the paper meet the multidisciplinary criteria of ASPLOS).

(4) Mandatory participation (and judicious nagging) reduced (hopefully eliminated) the number of PC members arriving at the meeting without reading author responses and other reviews.

(5) It resulted in a more effective PC meeting with more engagement from all members. I reminded the PC that most of the meeting was focused on papers where ≥ 5 reviewers had failed to reach consensus after significant deliberation, elevating the importance of their input with clear issues to debate.

This phase identified 23 green and 65 yellow papers for the PC meeting.

**PC Meeting**

The PC meeting took place at the O'Hare Hilton on October 30th (a week day) from 8am to 6:15pm. One PC member could not attend due to an injury. I made all papers and reviews available to all PC members (sans conflicts), assigned a PC lead to each green and yellow paper, and sent all meeting procedures two days before the meeting. A PC member was allowed to turn any paper to yellow to discuss in the meeting.

The guiding philosophy for the PC discussion was to seek consensus rather than make decisions through narrow majority votes and to give the reviewers (who had read the papers) priority in making the final decision.

For discussion order, within each color, I mostly used the average overall merit score, but I interleaved sessions of green and yellow papers in the morning. We covered about 50 papers before lunch, with the green papers taking little time. For the yellow papers, if about 5 minutes of discussion did not reveal a path to consensus among the reviewers, then we took a full PC (without the reviewers) vote. This vote was advisory input for the reviewers and was recorded in HotCRP. In many cases, the PC vote changed some reviewers' minds and resulted in an immediate consensus decision among the reviewers. In 9 cases, the differences remained and the paper was tabled.

For tabled papers, the reviewers and any interested PC members got together during the ample breaks (with food!) to attempt a consensus. I nudged these small-group discussions along as needed; many were long and intense. A late afternoon session revisited these papers with the full PC. If the reviewers had reached the same agreement as the majority in the previously recorded PC vote, then this result was simply recorded as the final decision. If the new reviewer consensus was different from the PC vote, then the reviewers provided their rationale, entertained questions from the PC, and the new consensus vote was recorded as the final decision. If the reviewers could not reach a consensus even after all the deliberation, then we used the majority vote among them as the final decision. A tie among reviewers used the earlier full PC majority vote for the decision.

During the meeting, a PC member conflicted with a paper left the room for that paper (Sandhya led the discussion for my conflicts). Papers of PC members were handled similar to the others.

We accepted 49 papers, 12 of which were shepherded. The acceptance rate of 23% was coincidentally the same as last year. 10 accepted papers were co-authored by a PC member out of 24 PC submissions. For most papers and all rejected papers that had an author response, the lead for the paper included a brief summary of the online and PC meeting discussions with the review.

**Reflections**

In the last several years, our reviewing processes have come a long way, but there appears to still be scope for improvement. My review checks and the distributed review sufficiency checks (RSCs) resulted in many reviews being updated. The mandatory online discussions, adopted by some but not all recent conferences, clarified many misunderstandings and changed opinions. I believe the high quality of these pre-PC meeting deliberations and the consensus-driven approach led to more informed (and efficient) decisions during the PC meeting. For the papers where consensus was hardest, the face-to-face, small group deliberations during the PC meeting provided opportunity for more reflection before a final decision.

I would like to credit all past PC chairs from whom I liberally borrowed many ideas. Specifically, Ras Bodik (ASPLOS'13) first exposed me to a review process that employed intensive online discussion and was consensus-driven. The ASPLOS'14 process was mostly based on his framework. I also benefited from discussions with Vikram Adve (ASPLOS'10), Christos Kozyrakis (MICRO'13), Margaret Martonosi (ISCA'13), and Onur Mutlu (MICRO'12).

**The Program**

The 49 accepted technical papers are organized in two tracks. Monday morning will feature two lightning sessions with overviews of all papers to help you choose the sessions to attend. For closer interaction with authors, Tuesday afternoon features a poster session with all papers.

Several plenary sessions complement the technical papers. Monday morning kicks off with a keynote by Brad Calder (Microsoft) describing his experiences with a modern commercial cloud operating system, a topic that directly resonates with many ASPLOS submissions. Tuesday morning starts with a keynote by Jeff Gehlhaar (Qualcomm) describing a brain-inspired processor that overcomes the obstacles of post-Dennard scaling but creates new challenges that could inspire many future ASPLOS submissions. Tuesday ends with the ASPLOS tradition of a "Wild and Crazy Ideas (WACI)" session. The WACI team, ably led by Luis Ceze and Karin Strauss, has done a remarkable job attracting frontier ideas that are sure to inspire, with a cornerstone invited WACInote by Josh Smith (U Washington) on RF-powered computing and communication. Wednesday will start with a debate on whether specialized systems will supplant general-purpose alternatives, moderated by David Wood, again a hot topic touching many ASPLOS submissions.

This year, ASPLOS will have a business meeting and an awards lunch for the first time. Also new is that the technical papers will be openly available in the ACM digital library about a week before the conference. In spite of the packed program, we have included many breaks and a one-of-a-kind excursion – we hope these enable serendipitous interactions leading to technical inspirations and collaborations that make some of the most memorable conference experiences.

**Acknowledgements**

The program is the result of the hard work of many people, several of whom went above and beyond the call of duty. The general co-chairs, Rajeev Balasubramonian and Al Davis, were an absolute pleasure to work with. I started to imagine them with a magic wand in their hands – no matter what I asked of them, they said yes, even though it meant more fund raising and attention to more countless details.

I benefitted throughout from the wisdom and quick response times of the steering committee, and earlier mentioned my gratitude to past PC chairs. The submission chairs, my students Rakesh Komuravelli and Hyojin Sung, tirelessly and cheerfully took care of the submission web site. They also attended the PC meeting, recording decisions, moving conflicts in and out, and handling numerous logistics required for a smooth meeting. The review process I described would not be possible without HotCRP and the generosity of its author, Eddie Kohler. Sandhya Dwarkadas handled my conflicts, diligently following all the details of this year's review process. I was originally undecided on whether to have a WACI session, but the infectious enthusiasm of Luis Ceze and Karin Strauss and their volunteering to lead the charge enabled me to make the right decision. David Wood agreed to organize the debate even though I interrupted his vacation. Manju Shevgoor diligently kept the conference web site up to date and Niti Madan contacted many places new to ASPLOS as publicity chair. Michelle Osborne, my assistant, helped with logistics for the PC meeting.

Finally, none of this would be possible without the tireless efforts of the PC, ERC, and other reviewers and the work of the authors. Many of these were truly inspiring.

**Sarita Adve**
*ASPLOS'14 Program Chair*
*University of Illinois at Urbana-Champaign*

# Table of Contents

## Session 3A: Software Reliability and Testing I

Session Chair: Santosh Nagarakatte *(Rutgers University)*



## Session 3B: Heterogeneous Computing

Session Chair: Debbie Marr *(Intel Corp.)*



## Keynote

Session Chair: Rajeev Balasubramonian *(University of Utah)*



## Session 4A: Virtualization

Session Chair: Carl A. Waldspurger *(independent)*

## Session 4B: Transactional Memory and Consistency

Session Chair: Sandhya Dwarkadas *(University of Rochester)*



## Session 5A: Storage Systems

Session Chair: Martha Kim *(Columbia University)*



## Session 5B: Parallelism I

Session Chair: Josep Torrellas *(University of Illinois at Urbana-Champaign)*



## Session 6A: Parallelism II

Session Chair: Babak Falsafi *(École Polytechnique Fédérale de Lausanne)*

## Session 6B: Compilers, Optimization, and Co-design

Session Chair: Keshav Pingali *(University of Texas at Austin)*



## Debate

Session Chair: David A. Wood *(University of Wisconsin-Madison)*



## Session 7A: Software Reliability and Testing II

Session Chair: Shan Lu *(University of Wisconsin-Madison)*



## Session 7B: Caches and TLBs

Session Chair: Kathryn S. McKinley *(Microsoft Research)*

# ASPLOS 2014 Organization

**General Chairs:** Rajeev Balasubramonian, University of Utah
Al Davis, University of Utah

**Program Chair:** Sarita Adve, University of Illinois at Urbana-Champaign

**Finance Chair:** Gabriel Loh, AMD Research

**Workshop Chair:** Venkatesh Akella, University of California, Davis

**Tutorial Chairs:** Ioana Baldini, IBM TJ Watson Research Center
Livio Soares, IBM TJ Watson Research Center

**WACI Chairs:** Luis Ceze, University of Washington
Karin Strauss, Microsoft Research

**Travel Grant Chair:** Matthew Might, University of Utah

**Poster/Lightning Session Chair:** John Regehr, University of Utah

**Registration Chair:** Aniruddha Udipi, ARM

**Publicity Chair:** Niti Madan, Oracle

**Web Chair:** Manjunath Shevgoor, University of Utah

**Submissions Chair:** Rakesh Komuravelli, University of Illinois at Urbana-Champaign
Hyojin Sung, University of Illinois at Urbana-Champaign

**Steering Committee:** Ras Bodik, UC Berkeley
Doug Burger, Microsoft
George Candea, EPFL
Timothy Harris, Microsoft
Jeremy Gibbons, Oxford University
Vivek Sarkar, Rice University
Michael Scott, University of Rochester
David Wood, University of Wisconsin

**Program Committee:** Sarita Adve, University of Illinois at Urbana-Champaign
David F. Bacon, IBM Research
Emery Berger, University of Massachusetts, Amherst
Francois Bodin, Irisa
Calin Cascaval, Qualcomm
Luis Ceze, University of Washington
Brad Chen, Google
Trishul Chilimbi, Microsoft Research
Sandhya Dwarkadas, University of Rochester
Krisztian Flautner, ARM

**Program Committee (continued):** Tim Harris, Oracle Labs
Mark Hill, University of Wisconsin
Mary Jane Irwin, Pennsylvania State University
Ravi Iyer, Intel Corp.
Martha Kim, Columbia University
Eddie Kohler, Harvard University
John Kubiatowicz, University of California, Berkeley
David Lie, University of Toronto
Shan Lu, University of Wisconsin
Debbie Marr, Intel Corp.
Margaret Martonosi, Princeton University
Kathryn S. McKinley, Microsoft Research
Santosh Nagarakatte, Rutgers University
Satish Narayanasamy, University of Michigan
Vijay Pai, Purdue University
Keshav Pingali, University of Texas at Austin
Parthasarathy Ranganathan, Google
Karin Strauss, Microsoft Research/University of Washington
Martin Vechev, ETH
Carl Waldspurger, independent
Tom Wenisch, University of Michigan
Emmett Witchel, Univerity of Texas at Austin
Lin Zhong, Rice University
Yuanyuan Zhou, University of California, San Diego
Willy Zwaenepoel, EPFL

**External Review Committee:** Ole Agesen, VMware
Anastassia Ailamaki, EPFL
Krste Asanovic, University of California, Berkeley
Tom Ball, Microsoft Research
Luiz Barroso, Google
Rajeev Barua, University of Maryland
Ricardo Bianchini, Rutgers University
Rob Bocchino, Jet Propulsion Laboratory
Hans Boehm, HP Labs
Greg Bronevetsky, Lawrence Livermore National Laboratory
David Brooks, Harvard University
Angela Demke Brown, University of Toronto
Mihai Budiu, Microsoft Research
Stephen Chong, Harvard University
Albert Cohen, INRIA
Srini Devadas, MIT
Dave Dice, Oracle Labs
Chen Ding, University of Rochester
Mattan Erez, University of Texas at Austin
Babak Falsafi, EPFL
Stephen Freund, Williams College
Xin Fu, University of Kansas

**External Review Committee (continued):**

Maria J. Garzaran, University of Illinois at Urbana-Champaign
Ada Gavrilovska, Georgia Tech
Robert Geva, Intel Corp.
Ashvin Goel, University of Toronto
Steven Gribble, University of Washington
Dan Grossman, University of Washington
Gernot Heiser, NICTA and University of New South Wales
Tony Hosking, Purdue University
Wilson Hsieh, Google
Chris Hughes, Intel Corp.
Hillery Hunter, IBM T. J. Watson Research Center
Rebecca Isaacs, Microsoft Research
Mahmut Kandemir, Pennsylvania State University
Orran Krieger, Boston University
Rakesh Kumar, University of Illinois at Urbana-Champaign
E. Christopher Lewis, VMware
Kai Li, Princeton University
Geoff Lowney, Intel Corp.
Evangelos Markatos, University of Crete
Milo Martin, University of Pennsylvania
Jonathan McCune, Google
Maged M. Michael, IBM T. J. Watson Research Center
Todd Millstein, University of California, Los Angeles
Tipp Moseley, Google
Onur Mutlu, Carnegie Mellon University
Andrew Myers, Cornell University
Edmund Nightingale, Microsoft Research
Li-Shiuan Peh, MIT
Milos Prvulovic, Georgia Tech
Feng Qin, Ohio State University
Ravi Rajwar, Intel Corp.
Pradeep Ramachandran, Intel Corp., India
Lawrence Rauchwerger, Texas A&M University
Mendel Rosenblum, Stanford University
Karu Sankaralingam, University of Wisconsin-Madison
Simha Sethumadhavan, Columbia University
Mark Silberstein, Technion
Anand Sivasubramanian, Pennsylvania State University
Edward Suh, Cornell University
Steve Swanson, University of California, San Diego
Josep Torrellas, University of Illinois at Urbana-Champaign
Eric Tune, Google
Amit Vasudevan, Carnegie Mellon University
Kaushik Veeraraghavan, Facebook
TN Vijaykumar, Purdue University
Adam Welc, Oracle
Xiaolan Zhang, IBM T. J. Watson Research Center

**Additional Reviewers:** Tor Aamodt, University of British Columbia
Parosh Abdulla, Uppsala University
Alaa R. Alameldeen, Intel Corp.
Erik Altman, IBM Research
Christopher Batten, Cornell University
Pradip Bose, IBM Research
Robert Cameron, Simon Fraser University
David Christie, AMD
Chita Das, Pennsylvania State University
Nikil Dutt, University of California, Irvine
Jason Flinn, University of Michigan
Ali Ghodsi, University of California, Berkeley
Tony Givargis, University of California, Irvine
Daniel Gmach, HP Labs
Engin Ipek, University of Rochester
Xiaofan Jiang, Intel Labs
Ian Kash, Microsoft Research
Steve Keckler, University of Texas at Austin/Nvidia
Hyesoon Kim, Georgia Tech
David Levinthal, Google
Steve Lumetta, University of Illinois at Urbana-Champaign
Haohui Mai, Hortonworks
John Mellor-Crummey, Rice University
Klara Nahrstedt, University of Illinois at Urbana-Champaign
Dhabaleswar Panda, Ohio State University
Sungwoo Park, Pohang University of Science and Technology
Avi Pfeffer, Charles River Analytics
Eric Phipps, Sandia National Laboratories
Moinuddin Qureshi, Georgia Tech
Vijay Raghunathan, Purdue University
Christian Renner, Hamburg University of Technology
Chris Rossbach, Microsoft Research
Michael L. Scott, University of Rochester
Martin Schulz, Lawrence Livermore National Laboratory
Dan Sorin, Duke University
Herb Schwetman, Oracle Labs
Kai Shen, University of Rochester
Michael Spear, Lehigh University
Petar Tsankov, ETH
Vincent Vanhoucke, Google
Nalini Venkatasubramanian, University of California, Irvine
Vincent Weaver, University of Maine
Yuan Xie, Pennsylvania State University

# ASPLOS 2014 Sponsors & Supporters

**Sponsors:** SIGARCH, SIGOPS (ACM SIG on Operating Systems), SIGPLAN

**In co-operation with:** SIGBED

**Supporters:** NSF, Microsoft Research, ARM, AMD, Google, HP Labs, Intel, VMware, Facebook, Oracle, EMC², IBM

# Inside Windows Azure: The Challenges and Opportunities of a Cloud Operating System

Brad Calder
Microsoft

## Abstract

Cloud operating systems provide on-demand, scalable compute and storage resources. They allow service developers to focus on their business logic by simplifying many portions of their service, including resource management, provisioning, monitoring, and application lifecycle management. This talk describes some of the technical challenges faced, as well as emergent opportunities created, by Microsoft's cloud operating system Windows Azure.

***Categories and Subject Descriptors*** D.4.7 Software; OPERATING SYSTEMS; Organization and Design: Distributed systems

***Keywords*** Cloud; Cloud Operating System; Windows Azure.

## Bio

Brad Calder is a Corporate Vice President at Microsoft leading the development of Windows Azure Storage. In 2006 he joined Microsoft and started the Windows Azure Storage team. Windows Azure Storage provides massively scalable, durable, and available cloud storage. The service stores trillions of objects and processes millions of requests per second. This allows customers to store and access NoSQL Tables, Blobs, Queues, and VM Disks when using Microsoft's cloud operating system.

Before coming to Microsoft, Brad was a Professor at the University of California, San Diego in the Department of Computer Science and Engineering where he graduated 14 PhD students, published over 100 papers in the areas of systems, architecture and compilers, and was a recipient of an NSF CAREER award. Before joining UC San Diego in 1997, he worked as a Principal Engineer at Digital Equipment Corporation's Western Research Lab. He is also a co-founder of two startup companies: Entropia Inc. (high performance computing) and Trace Point Inc. (program analysis tools for x86).

Brad received a B.S. in Computer Science and a B.S. in Mathematics from University of Washington in 1991, and his Ph.D. from University of Boulder, Colorado in 1995.


*ASPLOS'14,* March 1–5, 2014, Salt Lake City, Utah, USA.
ACM 978-1-4503-2305-5/14/03.
http://dx.doi.org/10.1145/2541940.2560008

# Scale-Out NUMA

Stanko Novaković Alexandros Daglis Edouard Bugnion Babak Falsafi Boris Grot†
EcoCloud, EPFL
†University of Edinburgh

## Abstract

Emerging datacenter applications operate on vast datasets that are kept in DRAM to minimize latency. The large number of servers needed to accommodate this massive memory footprint requires frequent server-to-server communication in applications such as key-value stores and graph-based applications that rely on large irregular data structures. The fine-grained nature of the accesses is a poor match to commodity networking technologies, including RDMA, which incur delays of 10-1000x over local DRAM operations.

We introduce Scale-Out NUMA (soNUMA) – an architecture, programming model, and communication protocol for low-latency, distributed in-memory processing. soNUMA layers an RDMA-inspired programming model directly on top of a NUMA memory fabric via a stateless messaging protocol. To facilitate interactions between the application, OS, and the fabric, soNUMA relies on the *remote memory controller* – a new architecturally-exposed hardware block integrated into the node's local coherence hierarchy. Our results based on cycle-accurate full-system simulation show that soNUMA performs remote reads at latencies that are within 4x of local DRAM, can fully utilize the available memory bandwidth, and can issue up to 10M remote memory operations per second per core.

***Categories and Subject Descriptors*** C.1.4 [*Computer System Organization*]: Parallel Architectures—Distributed Architectures; C.5.5 [*Computer System Organization*]: Computer System Implementation—Servers

***Keywords*** RDMA, NUMA, System-on-Chips

## 1. Introduction

Datacenter applications are rapidly evolving from simple data-serving tasks to sophisticated analytics operating over enormous datasets in response to real-time queries. To minimize the response latency, datacenter operators keep the data in memory. As dataset sizes push into the petabyte range, the number of servers required to house them in memory can easily reach into hundreds or even thousands.

Because of the distributed memory, applications that traverse large data structures (e.g., graph algorithms) or frequently access disparate pieces of data (e.g., key-value stores) must do so over the datacenter network. As today's datacenters are built with commodity networking technology running on top of commodity servers and operating systems, node-to-node communication delays can exceed 100$\mu s$ [50]. In contrast, accesses to local memory incur delays of around 60ns – a factor of 1000 less. The irony is rich: moving the data from disk to main memory yields a 100,000x reduction in latency (10ms vs. 100ns), but distributing the memory eliminates 1000x of the benefit.

The reasons for the high communication latency are well known and include deep network stacks, complex network interface cards (NIC), and slow chip-to-NIC interfaces [21, 50]. RDMA reduces end-to-end latency by enabling memory-to-memory data transfers over InfiniBand [26] and Converged Ethernet [25] fabrics. By exposing remote memory at user-level and offloading network processing to the adapter, RDMA enables remote memory read latencies as low as 1.19$\mu s$ [14]; however, that still represents a $>$10x latency increase over local DRAM.

We introduce Scale-Out NUMA (soNUMA), an architecture, programming model, and communication protocol for distributed, in-memory applications that reduces remote memory access latency to within a small factor ($\sim$4x) of local memory. soNUMA leverages two simple ideas to minimize latency. The first is to use a stateless request/reply protocol running over a NUMA memory fabric to drastically reduce or eliminate the network stack, complex NIC, and switch gear delays. The second is to integrate the protocol controller into the node's local coherence hierarchy, thus avoiding state replication and data movement across the slow PCI Express (PCIe) interface.

soNUMA exposes the abstraction of a partitioned global virtual address space, which is useful for big-data applications with irregular data structures such as graphs. The programming model is inspired by RDMA [37], with applica-


*ASPLOS '14*, March 1–4, 2014, Salt Lake City, Utah, USA.

ACM 978-1-4503-2305-5/14/03.
http://dx.doi.org/10.1145/2541940.2541965

tion threads making explicit remote memory read and write requests with copy semantics. The model is supported by an architecturally-exposed hardware block, called the *remote memory controller* (RMC), that safely exposes the global address space to applications. The RMC is integrated into each node's coherence hierarchy, providing for a frictionless, low-latency interface between the processor, memory, and the interconnect fabric.

Our primary contributions are:

- the RMC – a simple, hardwired, on-chip architectural block that services remote memory requests through locally cache-coherent interactions and interfaces directly with an on-die network interface. Each operation handled by the RMC is converted into a set of stateless request/reply exchanges between two nodes;
- a minimal programming model with architectural support, provided by the RMC, for one-sided memory operations that access a partitioned global address space. The model is exposed through lightweight libraries, which also implement communication and synchronization primitives in software;
- a preliminary evaluation of soNUMA using cycle-accurate full-system simulation demonstrating that the approach can achieve latencies within a small factor of local DRAM and saturate the available bandwidth;
- an soNUMA emulation platform built using a hypervisor that runs applications at normal wall-clock speeds and features remote latencies within 5x of what a hardware-assisted RMC should provide.

The rest of the paper is organized as follows: we motivate soNUMA (§2). We then describe the essential elements of the soNUMA architecture (§3), followed by a description of the design and implementation of the RMC (§4), the software support (§5), and the proposed communication protocol (§6). We evaluate our design (§7) and discuss additional aspects of the work (§8). Finally, we place soNUMA in the context of prior work (§9) and conclude (§10).

## 2. Why Scale-Out NUMA?

In this section, we discuss key trends in datacenter applications and servers, and identify specific pain points that affect the latency of such deployments.

### 2.1 Datacenter Trends

***Applications.*** Today's massive web-scale applications, such as search or analytics, require thousands of computers and petabytes of storage [60]. Increasingly, the trend has been toward deeper analysis and understanding of data in response to real-time queries. To minimize the latency, datacenter operators have shifted hot datasets from disk to DRAM, necessitating terabytes, if not petabytes, of DRAM distributed across a large number of servers.

The distributed nature of the data leads to frequent server-to-server interactions within the context of a given computation, e.g., Amazon reported that the rendering of a single page typically requires access to over 150 services [17]. These interactions introduce significant latency overheads that constrain the practical extent of sharding and the complexity of deployed algorithms. For instance, latency considerations force Facebook to restrict the number of sequential data accesses to fewer than 150 per rendered web page [50].

Recent work examining sources of network latency overhead in datacenters found that a typical deployment based on commodity technologies may incur over 100$\mu s$ in round-trip latency between a pair of servers [50]. According to the study, principal sources of latency overhead include the operating system stack, NIC, and intermediate network switches. While 100$\mu s$ may seem insignificant, we observe that many applications, including graph-based applications and those that rely on key-value stores, perform minimal computation per data item loaded. For example, read operations dominate key-value store traffic, and simply return the object in memory. With 1000x difference in data access latency between local DRAM (100ns) and remote memory (100$\mu s$), distributing the dataset, although necessary, incurs a dramatic performance overhead.

***Server architectures.*** Today's datacenters employ commodity technologies due to their favorable cost-performance characteristics. The end result is a *scale-out* architecture characterized by a large number of commodity servers connected via commodity networking equipment. Two architectural trends are emerging in scale-out designs.

First, System-on-Chips (SoC) provide high chip-level integration and are a major trend in servers. Current server SoCs combine many processing cores, memory interfaces, and I/O to reduce cost and improve overall efficiency by eliminating extra system components, e.g., Calxeda's ECX-1000 SoC [9] combines four ARM Cortex-A9 cores, memory controller, SATA interface, and a fabric switch [8] into a compact die with a 5W typical power draw.

Second, system integrators are starting to offer *glueless fabrics* that can seamlessly interconnect hundreds of server nodes into fat-tree or torus topologies [18]. For instance, Calxeda's on-chip fabric router encapsulates Ethernet frames while energy-efficient processors run the standard TCP/IP and UDP/IP protocols as if they had a standard Ethernet NIC [16]. The tight integration of NIC, routers and fabric leads to a reduction in the number of components in the system (thus lowering cost) and improves energy efficiency by minimizing the number of chip crossings. However, such glueless fabrics alone do not substantially reduce latency because of the high cost of protocol processing at the end points.

***Remote DMA.*** RDMA enables memory-to-memory data transfers across the network without processor involvement on the destination side. By exposing remote memory and re-

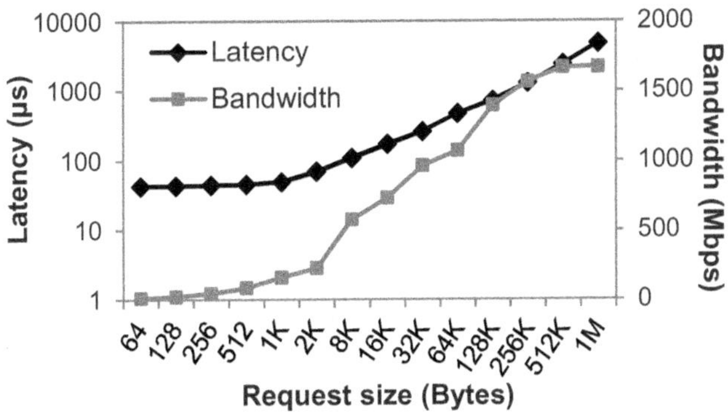


Figure 1: Netpipe benchmark on a Calxeda microserver.

liable connections directly to user-level applications, RDMA eliminates all kernel overheads. Furthermore, one-sided remote memory operations are handled entirely by the adapter without interrupting the destination core. RDMA is supported on lossless fabrics such as InfiniBand [26] and Converged Ethernet [25] that scale to thousands of nodes and can offer remote memory read latency as low as 1.19$\mu s$ [14].

Although historically associated with the high-performance computing market, RDMA is now making inroads into web-scale data centers, such as Microsoft Bing [54]. Latency-sensitive key-value stores such as RAMCloud [43] and Pilaf [38] are using RDMA fabrics to achieve object access latencies of as low as 5$\mu s$.

### 2.2 Obstacles to Low-Latency Distributed Memory

As datasets grow, the trend is toward more sophisticated algorithms at ever-tightening latency bounds. While SoCs, glueless fabrics, and RDMA technologies help lower network latencies, the network delay per byte loaded remains high. Here, we discuss principal reasons behind the difficulty of further reducing the latency for in-memory applications.

***Node scalability is power-limited.*** As voltage scaling grinds to a halt, future improvements in compute density at the chip level will be limited. Power limitations will extend beyond the processor and impact the amount of DRAM that can be integrated in a given unit of volume (which governs the limits of power delivery and heat dissipation). Together, power constraints at the processor and DRAM levels will limit the server industry's ability to improve the performance and memory capacity of scale-up configurations, thus accelerating the trend toward distributed memory systems.

***Deep network stacks are costly.*** Distributed systems rely on networks to communicate. Unfortunately, today's deep network stacks require a significant amount of processing per network packet which factors considerably into end-to-end latency. Figure 1 shows the network performance between two directly-connected Calxeda EnergyCore ECX-1000 SoCs, measured using the standard `netpipe` benchmark [55]. The fabric and the integrated NICs provide 10Gbps worth of bandwidth.

Despite the immediate proximity of the nodes and the lack of intermediate switches, we observe high latency (in excess of 40$\mu s$) for small packet sizes and poor bandwidth scalability (under 2 Gbps) with large packets. These bottlenecks exist due to the high processing requirements of TCP/IP and are aggravated by the limited performance offered by ARM cores.

***Large-scale shared memory is prohibitive.*** One way to bypass complex network stacks is through direct access to shared physical memory. Unfortunately, large-scale sharing of physical memory is challenging for two reasons. First is the sheer cost and complexity of scaling up hardware coherence protocols. Chief bottlenecks here include state overhead, high bandwidth requirements, and verification complexity. The second is the fault-containment challenge of a single operating system instance managing a massive physical address space, whereby the failure of any one node can take down the entire system by corrupting shared state [11]. Sharing caches even within the same socket can be expensive. Indeed, recent work shows that partitioning a single many-core socket into multiple coherence domains improves the execution efficiency of scale-out workloads that do not have shared datasets [33].

***PCIe/DMA latencies limit performance.*** I/O bypass architectures have successfully removed most sources of latency except the PCIe bus. Studies have shown that it takes 400-500ns to communicate short bursts over the PCIe bus [21], making such transfers 7-8x more expensive, in terms of latency, than local DRAM accesses. Furthermore, PCIe does not allow for the cache-coherent sharing of control structures between the system and the I/O device, leading to the need of replicating system state such as page tables into the device and system memory. In the latter case, the device memory serves as a cache, resulting in additional DMA transactions to access the state. SoC integration alone does not eliminate these overheads, since IP blocks often use DMA internally to communicate with the main processor [5].

***Distance matters.*** Both latency and cost of high-speed communication within a datacenter are severely impacted by distance. Latency is insignificant and bandwidth is cheap within a rack, enabling low-dimensional topologies (e.g., 3-D torus) with wide links and small signal propagation delays (e.g., 20ns for a printed circuit board trace spanning a 44U rack). Beyond a few meters, however, expensive optical transceivers must be used, and non-negotiable propagation delays (limited by the speed of light) quickly exceed DRAM access time. The combination of cost and delay puts a natural limit to the size of tightly interconnected systems.

## 3. Scale-Out NUMA

This work introduces soNUMA, an architecture and programming model for low-latency distributed memory.

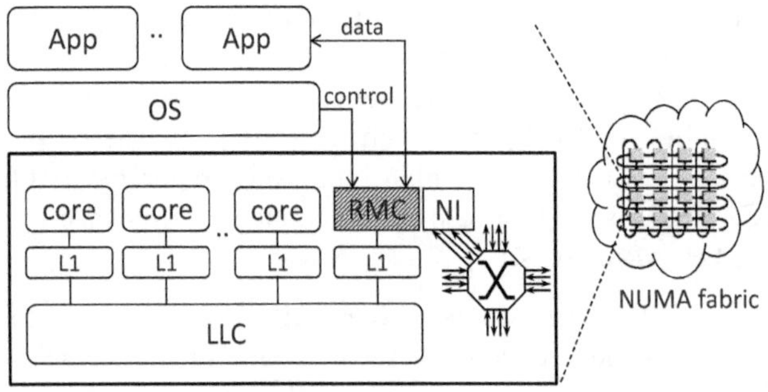


Figure 2: soNUMA overview.

soNUMA addresses each of the obstacles to low-latency described in §2.2. soNUMA is designed for a scale-out model with physically distributed processing and memory: (i) it replaces deep network stacks with a lean memory fabric; (ii) eschews system-wide coherence in favor of a global partitioned virtual address space accessible via RMDA-like remote memory operations with copy semantics; (iii) replaces transfers over the slow PCIe bus with cheap cache-to-cache transfers; and (iv) is optimized for rack-scale deployments, where distance is minuscule. In effect, our design goal is to borrow the desirable qualities of ccNUMA and RDMA without their respective drawbacks.

Fig. 2 identifies the essential components of soNUMA. At a high level, soNUMA combines a lean memory fabric with an RDMA-like programming model in a rack-scale system. Applications access remote portions of the global virtual address space through remote memory operations. A new architecturally-exposed block, the *remote memory controller* (RMC), converts these operations into network transactions and directly performs the memory accesses. Applications directly communicate with the RMC, bypassing the operating system, which gets involved only in setting up the necessary in-memory control data structures.

Unlike traditional implementations of RDMA, which operate over the PCI bus, the RMC benefits from a tight integration into the processor's cache coherence hierarchy. In particular, the processor and the RMC share all data structures via the cache hierarchy. The implementation of the RMC is further simplified by limiting the architectural support to one-sided remote memory read, write, and atomic operations, and by unrolling multi-line requests at the source RMC. As a result, the protocol can be implemented in a stateless manner by the destination node.

The RMC converts application commands into remote requests that are sent to the *network interface* (NI). The NI is connected to an on-chip low-radix router with reliable, point-to-point links to other soNUMA nodes. The notion of fast low-radix routers borrows from supercomputer interconnects; for instance, the mesh fabric of the Alpha 21364 connected 128 nodes in a 2D torus using an on-chip router with a pin-to-pin delay of just 11ns [39].

soNUMA's memory fabric bears semblance (at the link and network layer, but not at the protocol layer) to the QPI and HTX solutions that interconnect sockets together into multiple NUMA domains. In such fabrics, parallel transfers over traces minimize pin-to-pin delays, short messages (header + a payload of a single cache line) minimize buffering requirements, topology-based routing eliminates costly CAM or TCAM lookups, and virtual lanes ensure deadlock freedom. Although Fig. 2 illustrates a 2D-torus, the design is not restricted to any particular topology.

## 4. Remote Memory Controller

The foundational component of soNUMA is the RMC, an architectural block that services remote memory accesses originating at the local node, as well as incoming requests from remote nodes. The RMC integrates into the processor's coherence hierarchy via a private L1 cache and communicates with the application threads via memory-mapped queues. We first describe the software interface (§4.1), provide a functional overview of the RMC (§4.2), and describe its microarchitecture (§4.3).

### 4.1 Hardware/Software Interface

soNUMA provides application nodes with the abstraction of globally addressable, virtual address spaces that can be accessed via explicit memory operations. The RMC exposes this abstraction to applications, allowing them to safely and directly copy data to/from global memory into a local buffer using remote write, read, and atomic operations, without kernel intervention. The interface offers atomicity guarantees at the cache-line granularity, and no ordering guarantees within or across requests.

soNUMA's hardware/software interface is centered around four main abstractions directly exposed by the RMC: (i) the context identifier (`ctx_id`), which is used by all nodes participating in the same application to create a global address space; (ii) the context segment, a range of the node's address space which is globally accessible by others; (iii) the queue pair (QP), used by applications to schedule remote memory operations and get notified of their completion; and (iv) local buffers, which can be used as the source or destination of remote operations.

The QP model consists of a work queue (WQ), a bounded buffer written exclusively by the application, and a completion queue (CQ), a bounded buffer of the same size written exclusively by the RMC. The CQ entry contains the index of the completed WQ request. Both are stored in main memory and coherently cached by the cores and the RMC alike. In each operation, the remote address is specified by the combination of `<node_id, ctx_id, offset>`. Other parameters include the length and the local buffer address.

### 4.2 RMC Overview

The RMC consists of three hardwired pipelines that interact with the queues exposed by the hardware/software in-

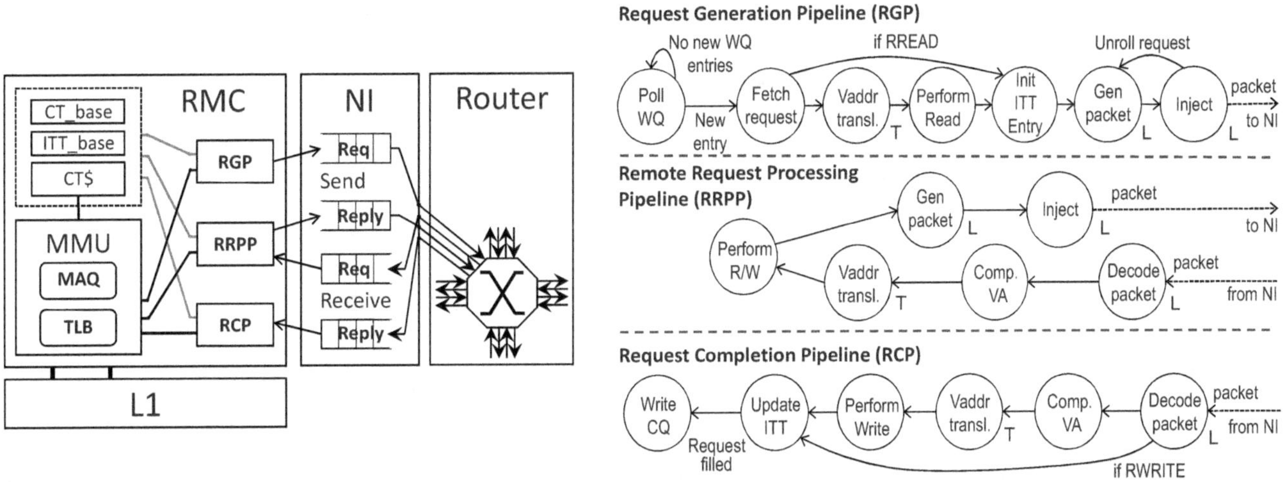


(a) RMC's internals: all memory requests of the three pipelines access the cache via the MMU. The CT_base register, the ITT_base register, and the CT$ offer fast access to the basic control structures.

(b) Functionality of the RMC pipelines. States with an '*L*' next to them indicate local processing in combinational logic; '*T*' indicates a TLB access; the rest of the states access memory via the MMU.

Figure 3: RMC internal architecture and functional overview of the three pipelines.

terface and with the NI. These pipelines are responsible for request generation, remote request processing, and request completion, respectively. They are controlled by a configuration data structure, the *Context Table* (CT), and leverage an internal structure, the *Inflight Transaction Table (ITT)*.

The CT is maintained in memory and is initialized by system software (see §5.1). The CT keeps track of all registered context segments, queue pairs, and page table root addresses. Each CT entry, indexed by its `ctx_id`, specifies the address space and a list of registered QPs (WQ, CQ) for that context. Multi-threaded processes can register multiple QPs for the same address space and `ctx_id`. Meanwhile, the ITT is used exclusively by the RMC and keeps track of the progress of each WQ request.

Fig. 3a shows the high-level internal organization of the RMC and its NI. The three pipelines are connected to distinct queues of the NI block, which is itself connected to a low-radix router block with support for two virtual lanes. While each of the three pipelines implements its own datapath and control logic, all three share some common data structures and hardware components. For example, they arbitrate for access to the common L1 cache via the MMU.

Fig. 3b highlights the main states and transitions for the three independent pipelines. Each pipeline can have multiple transactions in flight. Most transitions require an MMU access, which may be retired in any order. Therefore, transactions will be reordered as they flow through a pipeline.

***Request Generation Pipeline (RGP).*** The RMC initiates remote memory access transactions in response to an application's remote memory requests (reads, writes, atomics). To detect such requests, the RMC polls on each registered WQ. Upon a new WQ request, the RMC generates one or more network packets using the information in the WQ entry. For remote writes and atomic operations, the RMC accesses the local node's memory to read the required data, which it then encapsulates into the generated packet(s). For each request, the RMC generates a transfer identifier (`tid`) that allows the source RMC to associate replies with requests.

Remote transactions in soNUMA operate at cache line granularity. Coarser granularities, in cache-line-sized multiples, can be specified by the application via the `length` field in the WQ request. The RMC unrolls multi-line requests in hardware, generating a sequence of line-sized read or write transactions. To perform unrolling, the RMC uses the ITT, which tracks the number of completed cache-line transactions for each WQ request and is indexed by the request's `tid`.

***Remote Request Processing Pipeline (RRPP).*** This pipeline handles incoming requests originating from remote RMCs. The soNUMA protocol is stateless, which means that the RRPP can process remote requests using only the values in the header and the local configuration state. Specifically, the RRPP uses the `ctx_id` to access the CT, computes the virtual address, translates it to the corresponding physical address, and then performs a read, write, or atomic operation as specified in the request. The RRPP always completes by generating a reply message, which is sent to the source. Virtual addresses that fall outside of the range of the specified security context are signaled through an error message, which is propagated to the offending thread in a special reply packet and delivered to the application via the CQ.

***Request Completion Pipeline (RCP).*** This pipeline handles incoming message replies. The RMC extracts the `tid` and uses it to identify the originating WQ entry. For reads and atomics, the RMC then stores the payload into the application's memory at the virtual address specified in the request's WQ entry. For multi-line requests, the RMC computes the target virtual address based on the buffer base address specified in the WQ entry and the offset specified in the reply message.

The ITT keeps track of the number of completed cache-line requests. Once the last reply is processed, the RMC signals the request's completion by writing the index of the completed WQ entry into the corresponding CQ and moving the CQ head pointer. Requests can therefore complete out of order and, when they do, are processed out of order by the application. Remote write acknowledgments are processed similarly to read completions, although remote writes naturally do not require an update of the application's memory at the source node.

### 4.3 Microarchitectural Support

The RMC implements the logic described above using a set of completely decoupled pipelines, affording concurrency in the handling of different functions at low area and design cost. The RMC features two separate interfaces: a coherent memory interface to a private L1 cache and a network interface to the on-die router providing system-level connectivity. The memory interface block (MMU) contains a TLB for fast access to recent address translations, required for all accesses to application data. TLB entries are tagged with address space identifiers corresponding to the application context. TLB misses are serviced by a hardware page walker. The RMC provides two interfaces to the L1 cache – a conventional word-wide interface as well as a cache-line-wide interface. The former is used to interact with the application and to perform atomic memory operations. The latter enables efficient atomic reads and writes of entire cache lines, which is the granularity of remote memory accesses in soNUMA.

The RMC's integration into the node's coherence hierarchy is a critical feature of soNUMA that eliminates wasteful data copying of control structures, and of page tables in particular. It also reduces the latency of the application/RMC interface by eliminating the need to set up DMA transfers of ring buffer fragments. To further ensure high throughput and low latency at high load, the RMC allows multiple concurrent memory accesses in flight via a *Memory Access Queue* (MAQ). The MAQ handles all memory read and write operations, including accesses to application data, WQ and CQ interactions, page table walks, as well as ITT and CT accesses. The number of outstanding operations is limited by the number of miss status handling registers at the RMC's L1 cache. The MAQ supports out-of-order completion of memory accesses and provides store-to-load forwarding.

Each pipeline has its own arbiter that serializes the memory access requests from the pipeline's several stages and forwards the requests to the MAQ. The latter keeps track of each request's originating arbiter, and responds to that once the memory access is completed. Upon such a response, the arbiter feeds the data to the corresponding pipeline stage.

Finally, the RMC dedicates two registers for the CT and ITT base addresses, as well as a small lookaside structure, the *CT cache (CT$)* that caches recently accessed CT entries to reduce pressure on the MAQ. The CT$ includes the context segment base addresses and bounds, PT roots, and the queue addresses, including the queues' head and tail indices. The base address registers and the CT$ are read-only-shared by the various RMC pipeline stages.

## 5. Software Support

We now describe the system and application software support required to expose the RMC to applications and enable the soNUMA programming model. §5.1 describes the operating system device driver. §5.2 describes the lower-level wrappers that efficiently expose the hardware/software interface to applications. Finally, §5.3 describes higher-level routines that implement unsolicited communication and synchronization without additional architectural support.

### 5.1 Device Driver

The role of the operating system on an soNUMA node is to establish the global virtual address spaces. This includes the management of the context namespace, virtual memory, QP registration, etc. The RMC device driver manages the RMC itself, responds to application requests, and interacts with the virtual memory subsystem to allocate and pin pages in physical memory. The RMC device driver is also responsible for allocating the CT and ITT on behalf of the RMC.

Unlike a traditional RDMA NIC, the RMC has direct access to the page tables managed by the operating system, leveraging the ability to share cache-coherent data structures. As a result, the RMC and the application both operate using virtual addresses of the application's process once the data structures have been initialized.

The RMC device driver implements a simple security model in which access control is granted on a per `ctx_id` basis. To join a global address space `<ctx_id>`, a process first opens the device `/dev/rmc_contexts/<ctx_id>`, which requires the user to have appropriate permissions. All subsequent interactions with the operating system are done by issuing `ioctl` calls via the previously-opened file descriptor. In effect, soNUMA relies on the built-in operating system mechanism for access control when opening the context, and further assumes that all operating system instances of an soNUMA fabric are under a single administrative domain.

Finally, the RMC notifies the driver of failures within the soNUMA fabric, including the loss of links and nodes. Such transitions typically require a reset of the RMC's state, and may require a restart of the applications.

### 5.2 Access Library

The QPs are accessed via a lightweight API, a set of C/C++ inline functions that issue remote memory commands and synchronize by polling the completion queue.

We expose a synchronous (blocking) and an asynchronous (non-blocking) set of functions for both reads and writes. The asynchronous API is comparable in terms of functionality to the Split-C programming model [15].

Fig. 4 illustrates the use of the asynchronous API for the implementation of the classic PageRank graph algorithm [45]. `rmc_wait_for_slot` processes CQ events (calling `pagerank_async` for all completed slots) until the head of the WQ is free. It then returns the freed slot where the next entry will be scheduled. `rmc_read_async` (similar to Split-C's `get`) requests a copy of a remote vertex into a local buffer. Finally, `rmc_drain_cq` waits until all outstanding remote operations have completed while performing the remaining callbacks.

This programming model is efficient as: (i) the callback (`pagerank_async`) does not require a dedicated execution context, but instead is called directly within the main thread; (ii) when the callback is an inline function, it is passed as an argument to another inline function (`rmc_wait_for_slot`), thereby enabling compilers to generate optimized code without any function calls in the inner loop; (iii) when the algorithm has no read dependencies (as is the case here), asynchronous remote memory accesses can be fully pipelined to hide their latency.

To summarize, soNUMA's programming model combines true shared memory (by the threads running within a cache-coherent node) with explicit remote memory operations (when accessing data across nodes). In the PageRank example, the `is_local` flag determines the appropriate course of action to separate intra-node accesses (where the memory hierarchy ensures cache coherence) from inter-node accesses (which are explicit).

Finally, the RMC access library exposes atomic operations such as compare-and-swap and fetch-and-add as inline functions. These operations are executed atomically within the local cache coherence hierarchy of the destination node.

```
float *async_dest_addr[MAX_WQ_SIZE];
Vertex lbuf[MAX_WQ_SIZE];

inline void pagerank_async(int slot, void *arg) {
  *async_dest_addr[slot] += 0.85 *
    lbuf[slot].rank[superstep%2] / lbuf[slot].out_degree;
}

void pagerank_superstep(QP *qp) {
  int evenodd = (superstep+1) % 2;
  for(int v=first_vertex; v<=last_vertex; v++) {
    vertices[v].rank[evenodd] = 0.15 / total_num_vertices;
    for(int e=vertices[v].start; e<vertices[v].end; e++) {
      if(edges[e].is_local) {
        // shared memory model
        Vertex *v2 = (Vertex *)edges[e].v;
        vertices[v].rank[evenodd] += 0.85 *
              v2->rank[superstep%2] / v2->out_degree;
      } else {
        // flow control
        int slot = rmc_wait_for_slot(qp, pagerank_async);
        // setup callback arguments
        async_dest_addr[slot] = &vertices[v].rank[evenodd];
        // issue split operation
        rmc_read_async(qp, slot,
              edges[e].nid,      //remote node ID
              edges[e].offset,   //offset
              &lbuf[slot],       //local buffer
              sizeof(Vertex));   //len
      }
    }
  }
  rmc_drain_cq(qp, pagerank_async);
  superstep++;
}
```

Figure 4: Computing a PageRank superstep in soNUMA through a combination of remote memory accesses (via the asynchronous API) and local shared memory.

### 5.3 Messaging and Synchronization Library

By providing architectural support for only read, write and atomic operations, soNUMA reduces hardware cost and complexity. The minimal set of architecturally-supported operations is not a limitation, however, as many standard communication and synchronization primitives can be built in software on top of these three basic primitives. In contrast, RDMA provides hardware support (in adapters) for unsolicited send and receive messages on top of reliable connections, thus introducing significant complexity (e.g., per-connection state) into the design [47].

***Unsolicited communication.*** To communicate using `send` and `receive` operations, two application instances must first each allocate a bounded buffer from their own portion of the global virtual address space. The sender always writes to the peer's buffer using `rmc_write` operations, and the content is read locally from cached memory by the receiver. Each buffer is an array of cache-line sized structures that contain header information (such as the length, memory location, and flow-control acknowledgements), as well as an optional payload. Flow-control is implemented via a credit scheme that piggybacks existing communication.

For small messages, the sender creates packets of predefined size, each carrying a portion of the message content as part of the payload. It then *pushes* the packets into the peer's buffer. To receive a message, the receiver polls on the local buffer. In the common case, the send operation requires a single `rmc_write`, and it returns without requiring any implicit synchronization between the peers. A similar messaging approach based on remote writes outperforms the default send/receive primitives of InfiniBand [32].

For large messages stored within a registered global address space, the sender only provides the base address and size to the receiver's bounded buffer. The receiver then *pulls* the content using a single `rmc_read` and acknowledges the completion by writing a zero-length message into the sender's bounded buffer. This approach delivers a direct memory-to-memory communication solution, but requires synchronization between the peers.

At compile time, the user can define the boundary between the two mechanisms by setting a minimal message-size threshold: push has lower latency since small messages complete through a single `rmc_write` operation and also allows for decoupled operations. The pull mechanism leads to higher bandwidth since it eliminates the intermediate packetization and copy step.

***Barrier synchronization.*** We have also implemented a simple barrier primitive such that nodes sharing a `ctx_id` can synchronize. Each participating node broadcasts the arrival at a barrier by issuing a `write` to an agreed upon offset on each of its peers. The nodes then poll locally until all of them reach the barrier.

## 6. Communication Protocol

soNUMA's communication protocol naturally follows the design choices of the three RMC pipelines at the protocol layer. At the link and routing layers, our design borrows from existing memory fabric architectures (e.g., QPI or HTX) to minimize pin-to-pin delays.

***Link layer.*** The memory fabric delivers messages reliably over high-speed point-to-point links with credit-based flow control. The message MTU is large enough to support a fixed-size header and an optional cache-line-sized payload. Each point-to-point physical link has two virtual lanes to support deadlock-free request/reply protocols.

***Routing layer.*** The routing-layer header contains the destination and source address of the nodes in the fabric (<`dst_nid, src_nid`>). `dst_nid` is used for routing, and `src_nid` to generate the reply packet.

The router's forwarding logic directly maps destination addresses to outgoing router ports, eliminating expensive CAM or TCAM lookups found in networking fabrics. While the actual choice of topology depends on system specifics, low-dimensional k-ary n-cubes (e.g., 3D torii) seem well-matched to rack-scale deployments [18].

***Protocol layer.*** The RMC protocol is a simple request-reply protocol, with exactly one reply message generated for each request. The WQ entry specifies the `dst_nid`, the command (e.g., `read`, `write`, or `atomic`), the `offset`, the length and the local buffer address. The RMC copies the `dst_nid` into the routing header, determines the `ctx_id` associated with the WQ, and generates the `tid`. The `tid` serves as an index into the ITT and allows the source RMC to map each reply message to a WQ and the corresponding WQ entry. The `tid` is opaque to the destination node, but is transferred from the request to the associated reply packet.

Fig. 5 illustrates the actions taken by the RMCs for a remote read of a single cache line. The RGP in the requesting side's RMC first assigns a `tid` for the WQ entry and the

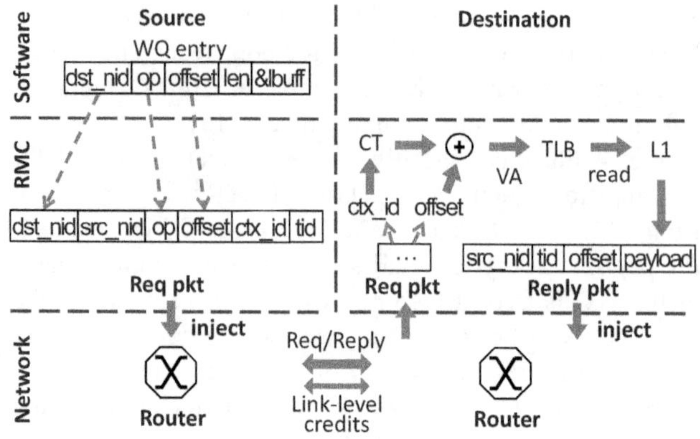


Figure 5: Communication protocol for a remote read.

`ctx_id` corresponding to that WQ. The RMC specifies the destination node via a `dst_nid` field. The request packet is then injected into the fabric and the packet is delivered to the target node's RMC. The receiving RMC's RRPP decodes the packet, computes the local virtual address using the `ctx_id` and the `offset` found in it and translates that virtual address to a physical address. This stateless handling does not require any software interaction on the destination node. As soon as the request is completed in the remote node's memory hierarchy, its RMC creates a reply packet and sends it back to the requesting node. Once the reply arrives to the original requester, the RMC's RCP completes the transaction by writing the payload into the corresponding local buffer and by notifying the application via a CQ entry (not shown in Fig. 5).

## 7. Evaluation

### 7.1 Methodology

To evaluate soNUMA, we designed and implemented two platforms: (i) development platform – a software prototype of soNUMA based on virtual machines used to debug the protocol stack, formalize the API, and develop large-scale applications; and (ii) cycle-accurate model – a full-system simulation platform modeling the proposed RMC.

***Development platform.*** Our software soNUMA prototype is based on the Xen hypervisor [3] and a conventional cc-NUMA server, on top of which we map (pin) multiple virtual machines to distinct NUMA domains. This includes both virtual CPUs and memory page frames. The server we use for the prototype is a modern AMD Opteron server with 4 CPU sockets (12 cores each, three-level cache hierarchy, 16MB LLC) and 256GB of RAM. The memory subsystem provides us with 8 NUMA domains (2 per socket).

Fig. 6 shows our setup. Each individual VM represents an independent soNUMA node, running an instance of the full software stack. The stack includes all user-space libraries, applications, the OS kernel, as well as the complete RMC device driver inside it. The driver is a Linux kernel mod-

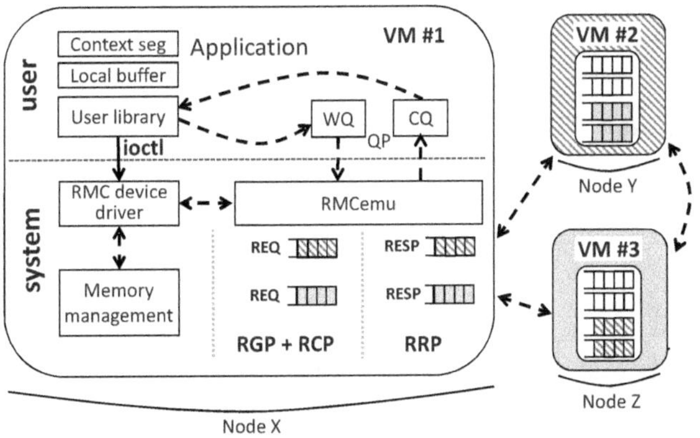


Figure 6: soNUMA development platform. Each node is implemented by a different VM. `RMCemu` runs on dedicated virtual CPUs and communicates with peers via shared memory.

ule that responds to user library commands through `ioctl`, enabling WQ/CQ registration, buffer management, and security context registration.

In this platform, we have implemented an RMC emulation module (RMCemu), which runs in kernel space. RMCemu implements the RMC logic and the soNUMA wire protocol (for a total of 3100LOC). The module exposes the hardware/software interface described in §4.1 to the RMC device driver and applications. RMCemu runs as a pair of kernel threads pinned to dedicated virtual CPUs, one running RGP and RCP, the other RRPP of Fig. 3b. All of the user-level data structures and buffers get memory-mapped by the device driver into the kernel virtual address space at registration time, and thus become visible to the RMCemu threads.

We emulate a full crossbar and run the protocol described in §6. Each pair of nodes exchanges protocol request/reply messages via a set of queues, mapped via the hypervisor into the guest physical address spaces of the VMs (there are two queue pairs per VM pair, emulating virtual lanes). To model the distributed nature of an soNUMA system, we pin each emulated node to a distinct NUMA domain such that every message traverses one of the server's chip-to-chip links. However, for the 16-node configuration, we collocate two VMs per NUMA domain.

| Core | ARM Cortex-A15-like; 64-bit, 2GHz, OoO, 3-wide dispatch/retirement, 60-entry ROB |
|---|---|
| L1 Caches | split I/D, 32KB 2-way, 64-byte blocks, 2 ports, 32 MSHRs, 3-cycle latency (tag+data) |
| L2 Cache | 4MB, 2 banks, 16-way, 6-cycle latency |
| Memory | cycle-accurate model using DRAMSim2 [49]. 4GB, 8KB pages, single DDR3-1600 channel. DRAM latency: 60ns; bandwidth: 12GBps |
| RMC | 3 independent pipelines (RGP, RCP, RRPP). 32-entry MAQ, 32-entry TLB |
| Fabric | Inter-node delay: 50ns |

Table 1: System parameters for simulation on Flexus.

***Cycle-accurate model.*** To assess the performance implications of the RMC, we use the Flexus full-system simulator [59]. Flexus extends the Virtutech Simics functional simulator with timing models of cores, caches, on-chip protocol controllers, and interconnect. Flexus models the SPARC v9 ISA and is able to run unmodified operating systems and applications. In its detailed OoO timing mode with the RMCs implemented, Flexus simulates "only" 5000 instructions per second, a slowdown of about six orders of magnitude compared to real hardware.

We model simple nodes, each featuring a 64-bit ARM Cortex-A15-like core and an RMC. The system parameters are summarized in Table 1. We extend Flexus by adding a detailed timing model of the RMC based on the microarchitectural description in §4. The RMC and its private L1 cache are fully integrated into the node's coherence domain. Like the cores, the RMC supports 32 memory accesses in flight. Fig. 3b illustrates how the logic is modeled as a set of finite state machines that operate as pipelines and eliminate the need for any software processing within the RMC. We model a full crossbar with reliable links between RMCs and a flat latency of 50ns, which is conservative when compared to modern NUMA interconnects, such as QPI and HTX.

### 7.2 Microbenchmark: Remote Reads

We first measure the performance of remote read operations between two nodes for both the development platform and the Flexus-based simulated hardware platform. The microbenchmark issues a sequence of read requests of varying size to a preallocated buffer in remote memory. The buffer size exceeds the LLC capacity in both setups. We measure (i) remote read latency with synchronous operations, whereby the issuing core spins after each read request until the reply is received, and (ii) throughput using asynchronous reads, where the issuing core generates a number of non-blocking read requests before processing the replies (similar to Fig. 4).

Fig. 7 plots the latency and bandwidth of remote read operations. Because of space limitations, we only show the latency graph on the emulation side. We run the microbenchmark in both single-sided (only one node reads) and double-sided (both nodes read from each other) mode.

Fig. 7a shows the remote read latency on the simulated hardware as a function of the request size. For small request sizes, the latency is around 300ns, of which 80ns are attributed to accessing the memory (cache hierarchy and DRAM combined) at the remote node and 100ns to round-trip socket-to-socket link latency. The end-to-end latency is within a factor of 4 of the local DRAM access latency. In the double-sided mode, we find that the average latency increases for larger message sizes as compared to the single-sided case. The reason for the drop is cache contention, as each node now has to both service remote read requests and write back the reply data.

Fig. 7b plots the bandwidth between two simulated soNUMA nodes using asynchronous remote reads. For 64B

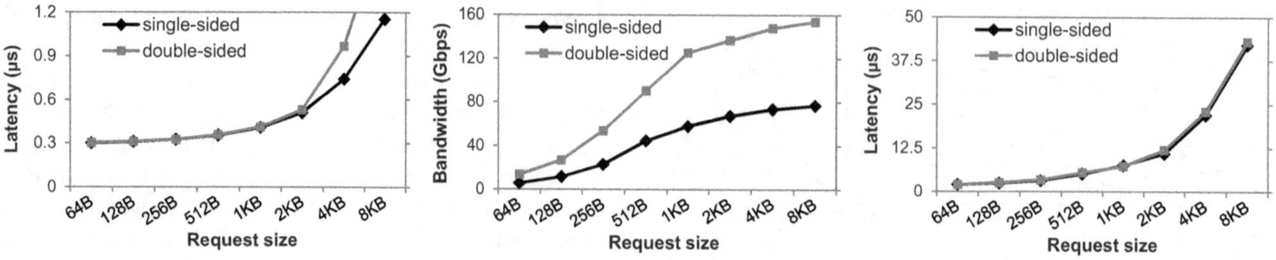


(a) Remote read latency (sim'd HW). (b) Remote read throughput (sim'd HW). (c) Remote read latency (dev. platform).

Figure 7: Remote read performance on the sim'd HW (latency and bandwidth) and the development platform (latency only).

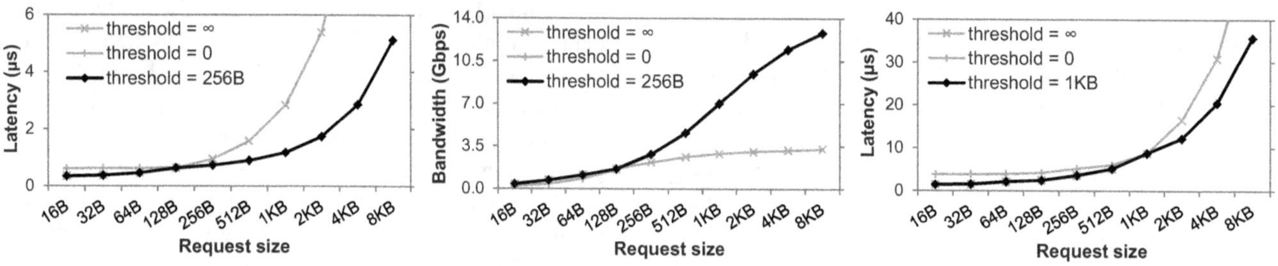


(a) Send/receive latency (sim'd HW). (b) Send/receive throughput (sim'd HW). (c) Send/receive latency (dev. platform).

Figure 8: Send/receive performance on the sim'd HW (latency and bandwidth) and the development platform (latency only).

requests, we can issue 10M operations per second. For page-sized requests (8KB), we manage to reach 9.6GBps, which is the practical maximum for a DDR3-1600 memory channel. Thanks to the decoupled pipelines of the RMC, the double-sided test delivers twice the single-sided bandwidth.

Fig. 7c shows the latency results on the development platform. The baseline latency is $1.5\mu s$, which is 5x the latency on the simulated hardware. However, we notice that the latency increases substantially with larger request sizes. On the development platform, the RMC emulation module becomes the performance bottleneck as it unrolls large WQ requests into cache-line-sized requests.

### 7.3 Microbenchmark: Send/Receive

We build a Netpipe [55] microbenchmark to evaluate the performance of the soNUMA unsolicited communication primitives, implemented entirely in software (§5.3). The microbenchmark consists of the following two components: (i) a ping-pong loop that uses the smallest message size to determine the end-to-end one-way latency and (ii) a streaming experiment where one node is sending and the other receiving data to determine bandwidth.

We study the half-duplex latency (Fig. 8a) and bandwidth (Fig. 8b) on our simulation platform. The two methods (`pull`, `push`) expose a performance tradeoff: `push` is optimized for small messages, but has significant processor and packetization overheads. `pull` is optimized for large transfers, but requires additional control traffic at the beginning of each transfer. We experimentally determine the optimal boundary between the two mechanisms by setting the threshold to 0 and $\infty$ in two separate runs. The black curve shows the performance of our unsolicited primitives with the threshold set to the appropriate value and both mechanisms enabled at the same time. The minimal half-duplex latency is 340ns and the bandwidth exceeds 10Gbps with messages as small as 4KB. For the largest request size evaluated (8KB), the bandwidth achieved is 12.8 Gbps, a 1.6x increase over Quad Data Rate InfiniBand for the same request size [24]. To illustrate the importance of having a combination of `push` and `pull` mechanisms in the user library, we additionally plot in grey their individual performance.

We apply the same methodology on the development platform. The minimal half-duplex latency (see Fig. 8c) is $1.4\mu s$, which is only 4x worse than the simulated hardware. However, the threshold is set to a larger value of 1KB for optimal performance, and the bandwidth is 1/10th of the simulated hardware. Again, we omit the bandwidth graph for the emulation platform due to space limitations. The relatively low bandwidth and a different threshold are due to the overheads of running the fine-grain communication protocol entirely in software (§7.2).

### 7.4 Comparison with InfiniBand/RDMA

To put our key results in perspective, Table 2 compares the performance of our simulated soNUMA system with an industry-leading commercial solution that combines the Mellanox ConnectX-3 [36] RDMA host channel adapter connected to host Xeon E5-2670 2.60Ghz via a PCIe-Gen3 bus. In the Mellanox system [14], the servers are connected back-to-back via a 56Gbps InfiniBand link. We consider four

| Transport | soNUMA | | RDMA/IB |
|---|---|---|---|
| | Dev. Plat. | Sim'd HW | [14] |
| Max BW (Gbps) | 1.8 | 77 | 50 |
| Read RTT ($\mu s$) | 1.5 | 0.3 | 1.19 |
| Fetch-and-add ($\mu s$) | 1.5 | 0.3 | 1.15 |
| IOPS (Mops/s) | 1.97 | 10.9 | 35 @ 4 cores |

Table 2: A comparison of soNUMA and InfiniBand.

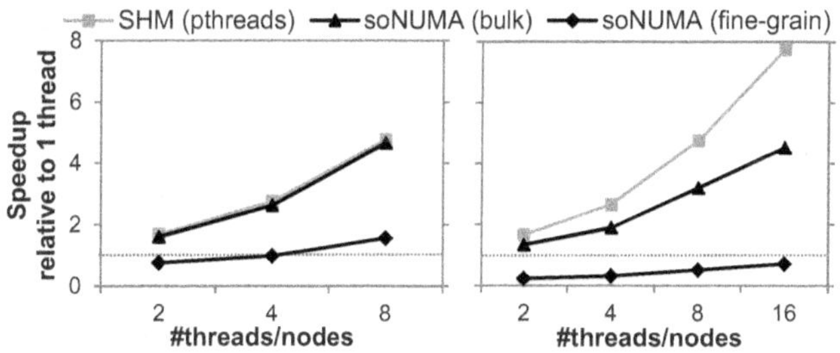


Figure 9: PageRank speedup on simulated HW (left) and on the development platform (right).

metrics – read bandwidth, read latency, atomic operation latency, and IOPS.

As Table 2 shows, compared to the state-of-the-art RDMA solution, soNUMA reduces the latency to remote memory by a factor of four, in large part by eliminating the PCIe bus overheads. soNUMA is also able to operate at peak memory bandwidth. In contrast, the PCIe-Gen3 bus limits RDMA bandwidth to 50 Gbps, even with 56Gbps InfiniBand. In terms of IOPS, the comparison is complicated by the difference in configuration parameters: the RDMA solution uses four QPs and four cores, whereas the soNUMA configuration uses one of each. Per core, both solutions support approximately 10M remote memory operations.

We also evaluate the performance of atomic operations using fetch-and-add, as measured by the application. For each of the three platforms, the latency of fetch-and-add is approximately the same as that of the remote read operations on that platform. Also, soNUMA provides more desirable semantics than RDMA. In the case of RDMA, fetch-and-add is implemented by the host channel adapter, which requires the adapter to handle all accesses, even from the local node. In contrast, soNUMA's implementation within the node's local cache coherence provides global atomicity guarantees for any combination of local and remote accesses.

### 7.5 Application Study

Large-scale graph processing engines, key-value stores, and on-line graph query processing are the obvious candidate applications for soNUMA. All of them perform very little work per data item (if any) and operate on large datasets, and hence typically require large scale-out configurations to keep all the data memory resident. Most importantly, they exhibit poor locality as they frequently access non-local data.

For our application study, we picked graph processing and the canonical PageRank algorithm [45], and compared three parallel implementations of it. All three are based on the widely used Bulk Synchronous Processing model [57], in which every node computes its own portion of the dataset (range of vertices) and then synchronizes with other participants, before proceeding with the next iteration (so-called superstep). Our three implementations are:

(i) `SHM(pthreads)`: The baseline is a standard pthreads implementation that assumes cache-coherent memory rather than soNUMA. For the simulated hardware, we model an eight-core multiprocessor with 4MB of LLC per core. We provision the LLC so that the aggregate cache size equals that of the eight machines in the soNUMA setting. Thus, no benefits can be attributed to larger cache capacity in the soNUMA comparison. For the development platform, we simply run the application on our ccNUMA server described in §7.1, but without a hypervisor running underneath the host OS. In this implementation, the application stores two rank values for each vertex: the one computed in the previous superstep and the one currently being computed. Barrier synchronization marks the end of each superstep.

(ii) `soNUMA(bulk)`: This implementation leverages aggregation mechanisms and exchanges ranks between nodes at the end of each superstep, after the barrier. Such an approach is supported by Pregel [35] as it amortizes high inter-node latencies and makes use of wide high-capacity links. In this implementation we exploit spatial locality within the global address space by using multi-line requests at the RMC level. At the end of each superstep, every node uses multiple `rmc_read_async` operations (one per peer) to pull the remote vertex information from each of its peers into the local memory. This allows a concurrent shuffle phase limited only by the bisection bandwidth of the system.

(iii) `soNUMA(fine-grain)`: This variant leverages the fine-grain memory sharing capabilities of soNUMA, as shown in Fig. 4. Each node issues one `rmc_read_async` operation for each non-local vertex. This implementation resembles the shared-memory programming model of `SHM(pthreads)`, but has consequences: the number of remote memory operations scales with the number of edges that span two partitions rather than with the number of vertices per partition.

We evaluate the three implementations of PageRank on a subset of the Twitter graph [29] using a naive algorithm that randomly partitions the vertices into sets of equal cardinality. We run 30 supersteps for up to 16 soNUMA nodes on the development platform. On the simulator, we run a single superstep on up to eight nodes because of the high execution time of the cycle-accurate model.

Fig. 9 (left) shows the speedup over the single-threaded baseline of the three implementations on the simulated hardware. Both `SHM(pthreads)` and `soNUMA(bulk)` have near identical speedup. In both cases, the speedup trend is determined primarily by the imbalance resulting from the graph partitioning scheme, and not the hardware. However, `soNUMA(fine-grain)` has noticeably greater overheads, primarily because of the limited per-core remote read rate (due to the software API's overhead on each request) and the fact that each reference to a non-local vertex results in a remote read operation. Indeed, each core can only issue up to 10 million remote operations per second. As shown in Fig. 7b, the bandwidth corresponding to 64B requests is a small fraction of the maximum bandwidth of the system.

Fig. 9 (right) shows the corresponding speedup on the software development platform. We identify the same general trends as on the simulated hardware, with the caveat that the higher latency and lower bandwidth of the development platform limit performance.

## 8. Discussion

We now discuss the lessons learned so far in developing our soNUMA prototype, known open issues, possible killer applications, and deployment and packaging options.

***Lessons learned.*** During our work, we appreciated the value of having a software development platform capable of running at native speeds. By leveraging hardware virtualization and dedicating processing cores to emulate RMCs, we were able to run an (emulated) soNUMA fabric at wall-clock execution time, and use that platform to develop and validate the protocol, the kernel driver, all user-space libraries, and applications.

***Open issues.*** Our design provides the ability to support many variants of remote memory operations that can be handled in a stateless manner by the peer RMC. This includes read, write, and atomic operations. A complete architecture will probably require extensions such as the ability to issue remote interrupts as part of an RMC command, so that nodes can communicate without polling. This will have a number of implications for system software, e.g., to efficiently convert interrupts into application messages, or to use the mechanisms to build system-level abstractions such as global buffer caches.

***Killer applications.*** Our primary motivation behind soNUMA is the conflicting trend of (i) large dataset applications that require tight and unpredictable sharing of resources; and (ii) manycore designs, which are optimized for throughput rather than resource aggregation. Our soNUMA proposal aims to reconcile these two trends. In our evaluation, we chose a simple graph application because it allows for multiple implementation variants that expose different aspects of the programming model, even though the regular, batch-oriented nature of that application is also a good fit for coarse-grain, scale-out models. Implementing these variants using the RMC API turned out to be almost as easy as using the conventional shared-memory programming abstractions. Many applications such as on-line graph processing algorithms, in-memory transaction processing systems, and key-value stores demand low latency [50] and can take advantage of one-sided read operations [38]. These applications are designed to assume that both client and server have access to a low-latency fabric [38, 43], making them killer applications for soNUMA. Beyond these, we also see deployment opportunities in upper application tiers of the datacenter. For example, Oracle Exalogic today provides a flexible, low-latency platform delivered on a rack-scale InfiniBand cluster [44]. Such deployments are natural candidates for tighter integration using SoC and soNUMA.

***System packaging options.*** The evaluation of the impact of system scale and fabric topologies is outside of the scope of this paper since we focused on the end-behavior of the RMC. To be successful, soNUMA systems will have to be sufficiently large to capture very large datasets within a single cluster, and yet sufficiently small to avoid introducing new classes of problems, such as the need for fault containment [11]. Industry solutions today provide rack-insert solutions that are ideally suited for soNUMA, e.g., HP's Moonshot with 45 cartridges or Calxeda-based Viridis systems with 48 nodes in a 2U chassis. Beyond that, rack-level solutions seem like viable near-term options; a 44U rack of Viridis chassis can thus provide over 1000 nodes within a two-meter diameter, affording both low wire delay and massive memory capacity.

***Research directions.*** This work has demonstrated the benefits on simple microbenchmarks and one application. We plan to evaluate the impact of soNUMA on latency-sensitive applications such as in-memory transaction processing systems and on-line query processing. We also see research questions around system-level resource sharing, e.g., to create a single-system image or a global filesystem buffer cache, or to rethink resource management in hypervisor clusters. Multikernels, such as Barrelfish [4], could be an ideal candidate for soNUMA.

We plan to investigate the micro-architectural aspects of the RMC. This includes further latency-reducing optimizations in the RMC and the processor, a reassessment of the RMC's design for SoC's with high core counts, and investigation of the flow-control, congestion and occupancy issues in larger fabrics.

Our study focused on data sharing within a single soNUMA fabric. For very large datasets, datacenter deployments would likely interconnect multiple rack-scale soNUMA systems using conventional networking technologies. This opens up new systems-level research questions in the areas of resource management (e.g., to maximize locality) and networking (e.g., how to use the soNUMA fabric to run network protocols).

## 9. Related Work

Many of the concepts found in remote memory architectures today and our soNUMA proposal originate from research done in the '80s and '90s. In this section we look at the relationship between soNUMA and several related concepts. We group prior work into six broad categories.

***Partitioned global address space.*** PGAS relies on compiler and language support to provide the abstraction of a shared address space on top of non-coherent, distributed memory [13]. Languages such as Unified Parallel C [13, 61] and Titanium [61] require the programmer to reason about data partitioning and be aware of data structure non-uniformity. However, the compiler frees the programmer from the burden of ensuring the coherence of the global address space by automatically converting accesses to remote portions into one-sided remote memory operations that correspond to soNUMA's own primitives. PGAS also provides explicit asynchronous remote data operations [7], which also easily map onto soNUMA's asynchronous library primitives. The efficiency of soNUMA remote primitives would allow PGAS implementations to operate faster.

***Software distributed shared memory.*** Software distributed shared memory (DSM) provides global coherence not present in the memory hierarchies of PGAS and soNUMA. Pure software DSM systems such as IVY [31], Munin [10] and Threadmarks [2] expose a global coherent virtual address space and rely on OS mechanisms to "fault in" pages from remote memory on access and propagate changes back, typically using relaxed memory models. Similarly, software DSM can be implemented within a hypervisor to create a cache-coherent global guest-physical address space [12], or entirely in user-space via binary translation [51]. Like software DSM, soNUMA operates at the virtual memory level. Unlike software DSM, soNUMA and PGAS target fine-grained accesses whereas software DSM typically operates at the page level. Shasta [51] and Blizzard [52] offer fine-grain DSM through code instrumentation and hardware assistance, respectively, but in both cases with non-negligible software overheads.

***Cache-coherent memory.*** ccNUMA designs such as Alewife [1], Dash [30], FLASH [28], Fugu [34], Typhoon [48], Sun Wildfire [42], and today's Intel QPI and AMD HTX architectures create a compute fabric of processing elements, each with its own local memory, and provide cache-coherent physical memory sharing across the nodes. FLASH and Sun's Wildfire also provide advanced migration and replication techniques to reduce the synchronization overheads [19].

soNUMA shares the non-uniform aspect of memory with these designs and leverages the lower levels of the ccNUMA protocols, but does not attempt to ensure cache coherence. As a result, soNUMA uses a stateless protocol, whereas ccNUMA requires some global state such as directories to ensure coherence, which limits its scalability. The ccNUMA designs provide a global physical address space, allowing conventional single-image operating systems to run on top. The single-image view, however, makes the system less resilient to faults [11]. In contrast, soNUMA exposes the abstraction of global virtual address spaces on top of multiple OS instances, one per coherence domain.

***User-level messaging.*** User-level messaging eliminates the overheads of kernel transitions by exposing communication directly to applications. Hybrid ccNUMA designs such as FLASH [23], Alewife [1], Fugu [34], and Typhoon [20] provide architectural support for user-level messaging in conjunction with cache-coherent memory. In contrast, soNUMA's minimal design allows for an efficient implementation of message passing entirely in software using one-sided remote memory operations.

SHRIMP [6] uses a specialized NIC to provide user-level messaging by allowing processes to directly write the memory of other processes through hardware support. Cashmere [56] leverages DEC's Memory Channel [22], a remote-write network, to implement a software DSM. Unlike SHRIMP and Cashmere, soNUMA also allows for direct reads from remote memory.

Fast Messages [46] target low latency and high bandwidth for short user-level messages. U-Net [58] removes the entire OS/Kernel off the critical path of messaging. These systems all focus on the efficient implementation of a message send. In soNUMA, the RMC provides architectural support for both one-sided read and write operations; messaging is implemented on top of these basic abstractions.

***Remote memory access.*** Unlike remote write networks, such as SHRIMP and DEC Memory Channel, Remote Memory Access provides for both remote reads and remote writes. Such hardware support for one-sided operations, similar to soNUMA's, was commercialized in supercomputers such as Cray T3D [27] and T3E [53]. Remote memory access can also be implemented efficiently for graph processing on commodity hardware by leveraging aggressive multithreading to compensate for the high access latency [41]. soNUMA also hides latency but uses asynchronous read operations instead of multithreading.

Today, user-level messaging and RDMA is available in commodity clusters with RDMA host channel adapters such as Mellanox ConnectX-3 [36] that connect into InfiniBand or Converged Ethernet switched fabrics [25]. To reduce complexity and enable SoC integration, soNUMA only provides a minimal subset of RDMA operations; in particular, it does not support reliable connections, as they require keeping per-connection state in the adapter.

***NI integration.*** One advantage of soNUMA over prior proposals on fast messaging and remote one-sided primitives is the tight integration of the NI into the coherence domain. The advantage of such an approach was previously demonstrated in Coherent Network Interfaces (CNI) [40], which leverage the coherence mechanism to achieve low-latency communication of the NI with the processors, using cacheable work queues. More recent work showcases the advantage of integration, but in the context of kernel-level TCP/IP optimizations, such as a zero-copy receive [5]. Our RMC is fully integrated into the local cache coherence hierarchy and does not depend on local DMA operations. The simple design of the RMC suggests that integration into the local cache-coherence domain is practical. Our evaluation shows that such integration can lead to substantial benefits by keeping the control data structures, such as the QPs and page tables, in caches. soNUMA also provides global atomicity by implementing atomic operations within a node's cache hierarchy.

## 10. Conclusion

Scale-Out NUMA (soNUMA) is an architecture, programming model, and communication protocol for low-latency big-data processing. soNUMA eliminates kernel, network stack, and I/O bus overheads by exposing a new hardware block –the remote memory controller– within the cache coherent hierarchy of the processor. The remote memory controller is directly accessible by applications and connects directly into a NUMA fabric. Our results based on cycle-accurate full-system simulation show that soNUMA can achieve remote read latencies that are within 4x of local DRAM access, stream at full memory bandwidth, and issue up to 10M remote memory operations per second per core.

## Acknowledgments

The authors thank Dushyanth Narayanan and Aleksandar Dragojevic from Microsoft Research for many inspiring conversations on rack-scale computing requirements and applications early in the project. We thank Amitabha Roy, Ryan Stutsman, David Wood, and the anonymous reviewers for their precious feedback on the manuscript. Patrick Tae ran netpipe between Calxeda nodes.

This work has been partially funded by the *EuroCloud* project of the 7th Framework Program of the European Commission, and by the *Workloads and Server Architectures for Green Datacenters* project of the Swiss National Science Foundation.

## References

[1] A. Agarwal, R. Bianchini, D. Chaiken, K. L. Johnson, D. A. Kranz, J. Kubiatowicz, B.-H. Lim, K. Mackenzie, and D. Yeung. The MIT Alewife Machine: Architecture and Performance. In *Proceedings of the 22nd International Symposium on Computer Architecture (ISCA)*, 1995.

[2] C. Amza, A. L. Cox, S. Dwarkadas, P. J. Keleher, H. Lu, R. Rajamony, W. Yu, and W. Zwaenepoel. Treadmarks: Shared Memory Computing on Networks of Workstations. *IEEE Computer*, 29(2):18–28, 1996.

[3] P. Barham, B. Dragovic, K. Fraser, S. Hand, T. L. Harris, A. Ho, R. Neugebauer, I. Pratt, and A. Warfield. Xen and the Art of Virtualization. In *Proceedings of the 19th ACM Symposium on Operating Systems Principles (SOSP)*, 2003.

[4] A. Baumann, P. Barham, P.-É. Dagand, T. L. Harris, R. Isaacs, S. Peter, T. Roscoe, A. Schüpbach, and A. Singhania. The Multikernel: a New OS Architecture for Scalable Multicore Systems. In *Proceedings of the 22nd ACM Symposium on Operating Systems Principles (SOSP)*, 2009.

[5] N. L. Binkert, A. G. Saidi, and S. K. Reinhardt. Integrated Network Interfaces for High-Bandwidth TCP/IP. In *Proceedings of the 12th International Conference on Architectural Support for Programming Languages and Operating Systems (ASPLOS-XII)*, 2006.

[6] M. A. Blumrich, K. Li, R. Alpert, C. Dubnicki, E. W. Felten, and J. Sandberg. Virtual Memory Mapped Network Interface for the SHRIMP Multicomputer. In *Proceedings of the 21st International Symposium on Computer Architecture (ISCA)*, 1994.

[7] D. Bonachea. Proposal for Extending the UPC Memory Copy Library Functions and Supporting Extensions to GASNet, Version 2.0. 2007.

[8] Calxeda Inc. Calxeda Energy Core ECX-1000 Fabric Switch. `http://www.calxeda.com/architecture/fabric/`, 2012.

[9] Calxeda Inc. ECX-1000 Technical Specifications. `http://www.calxeda.com/ecx-1000-techspecs/`, 2012.

[10] J. B. Carter, J. K. Bennett, and W. Zwaenepoel. Implementation and Performance of Munin. In *Proceedings of the 13th ACM Symposium on Operating Systems Principles (SOSP)*, 1991.

[11] J. Chapin, M. Rosenblum, S. Devine, T. Lahiri, D. Teodosiu, and A. Gupta. Hive: Fault Containment for Shared-Memory Multiprocessors. In *Proceedings of the 15th ACM Symposium on Operating Systems Principles (SOSP)*, 1995.

[12] M. Chapman and G. Heiser. vNUMA: A Virtual Shared-Memory Multiprocessor. In *Proceedings of the 2009 conference on USENIX Annual Technical Conference*, 2009.

[13] C. Coarfa, Y. Dotsenko, J. M. Mellor-Crummey, F. Cantonnet, T. A. El-Ghazawi, A. Mohanti, Y. Yao, and D. G. Chavarría-Miranda. An Evaluation of Global Address Space Languages: Co-Array Fortran and Unified Parallel C. In *Proceedings of the ACM SIGPLAN Symposium on Principles and Practice of Parallel Programming (PPOPP)*, 2005.

[14] D. Crupnicoff. Personal communication (Mellanox Corp.), 2013.

[15] D. E. Culler, A. C. Arpaci-Dusseau, S. C. Goldstein, A. Krishnamurthy, S. Lumetta, T. von Eicken, and K. A. Yelick. Parallel Programming in Split-C. In *Proceedings of the 1993 ACM/IEEE Conference on Supercomputing (SC)*, 1993.

[16] M. Davis and D. Borland. System and Method for High-Performance, Low-Power Data Center Interconnect Fabric. WO Patent 2,011,053,488, 2011.

[17] G. DeCandia, D. Hastorun, M. Jampani, G. Kakulapati, A. Lakshman, A. Pilchin, S. Sivasubramanian, P. Vosshall, and W. Vogels. Dynamo: Amazon's Highly Available Key-Value Store. In *Proceedings of the 21st ACM Symposium on Operating Systems Principles (SOSP)*, 2007.

[18] A. Dhodapkar, G. Lauterbach, S. Li, D. Mallick, J. Bauman, S. Kanthadai, T. Kuzuhara, G. S. M. Xu, and C. Zhang. SeaMicro SM10000-64 Server: Building Datacenter Servers Using Cell Phone Chips. In *Proceedings of the 23rd IEEE HotChips Symposium*, 2011.

[19] B. Falsafi and D. A. Wood. Reactive NUMA: A Design for Unifying S-COMA and CC-NUMA. In *Proceedings of the 24th International Symposium on Computer Architecture (ISCA)*, 1997.

[20] B. Falsafi, A. R. Lebeck, S. K. Reinhardt, I. Schoinas, M. D. Hill, J. R. Larus, A. Rogers, and D. A. Wood. Application-Specific Protocols for User-Level Shared Memory. In *Proceedings of the 1994 ACM/IEEE Conference on Supercomputing (SC)*, 1994.

[21] M. Flajslik and M. Rosenblum. Network Interface Design for Low Latency Request-Response Protocols. In *Proceedings of the 2013 USENIX Annual Technical Conference*, 2013.

[22] R. Gillett. Memory Channel: An Optimized Cluster Interconnect. *IEEE Micro*, 16(2):12–18, 1996.

[23] J. Heinlein, K. Gharachorloo, S. Dresser, and A. Gupta. Integration of Message Passing and Shared Memory in the Stanford FLASH Multiprocessor. In *Proceedings of the 6th International Conference*

on Architectural Support for Programming Languages and Operating Systems (ASPLOS-VI)*, 1994.

[24] HPC Advisory Council. Interconnect Analysis: 10GigE and InfiniBand in High Performance Computing. `http://www.hpcadvisorycouncil.com/pdf/IB_and_10GigE_in_HPC.pdf`, 2009.

[25] *IEEE 802.1Qbb: Priority-Based Flow Control.* IEEE, 2011.

[26] InfiniBand Trade Association. *InfiniBand Architecture Specification: Release 1.0.* 2000.

[27] R. Kessler and J. Schwarzmeier. Cray T3D: A New Dimension for Cray Research. In *Compcon Spring '93, Digest of Papers*, 1993.

[28] J. Kuskin, D. Ofelt, M. Heinrich, J. Heinlein, R. Simoni, K. Gharachorloo, J. Chapin, D. Nakahira, J. Baxter, M. Horowitz, A. Gupta, M. Rosenblum, and J. L. Hennessy. The Stanford FLASH Multiprocessor. In *Proceedings of the 21st International Symposium on Computer Architecture (ISCA)*, 1994.

[29] H. Kwak, C. Lee, H. Park, and S. B. Moon. What is Twitter, a Social Network or a News Media? In *Proceedings of the 19th International Conference on World Wide Web (WWW)*, 2010.

[30] D. Lenoski, J. Laudon, K. Gharachorloo, W.-D. Weber, A. Gupta, J. L. Hennessy, M. Horowitz, and M. S. Lam. The Stanford Dash Multiprocessor. *IEEE Computer*, 25(3):63–79, 1992.

[31] K. Li and P. Hudak. Memory Coherence in Shared Virtual Memory Systems. *ACM Trans. Comput. Syst.*, 7(4):321–359, 1989.

[32] J. Liu, J. Wu, and D. K. Panda. High Performance RDMA-Based MPI Implementation over InfiniBand. *International Journal of Parallel Programming*, 32(3):167–198, 2004.

[33] P. Lotfi-Kamran, B. Grot, M. Ferdman, S. Volos, Y. O. Koçberber, J. Picorel, A. Adileh, D. Jevdjic, S. Idgunji, E. Özer, and B. Falsafi. Scale-Out Processors. In *Proceedings of the 39th International Symposium on Computer Architecture (ISCA)*, 2012.

[34] K. Mackenzie, J. Kubiatowicz, A. Agarwal, and F. Kaashoek. Fugu: Implementing Translation and Protection in a Multiuser, Multimodel Multiprocessor. In *Proceedings of the 1994 Workshop on Shared Memory Multiprocessors*, 1994.

[35] G. Malewicz, M. H. Austern, A. J. C. Bik, J. C. Dehnert, I. Horn, N. Leiser, and G. Czajkowski. Pregel: A System for Large-Scale Graph Processing. In *Proceedings of the ACM International Conference on Management of Data (SIGMOD)*, 2010.

[36] Mellanox Corp. ConnectX-3 Pro Product Brief. `http://www.mellanox.com/related-docs/prod_adapter_cards/PB_ConnectX-3_Pro_Card_EN.pdf`, 2012.

[37] Mellanox Corp. RDMA Aware Networks Programming User Manual, Rev 1.4. `http://www.mellanox.com/related-docs/prod_software/RDMA_Aware_Programming_user_manual.pdf`, 2013.

[38] C. Mitchell, Y. Geng, and J. Li. Using One-Sided RDMA Reads to Build a Fast, CPU-Efficient Key-Value Store. In *Proceedings of the USENIX Annual Technical Conference*, 2013.

[39] S. Mukherjee, P. Bannon, S. Lang, A. Spink, and D. Webb. The Alpha 21364 Network Architecture. In *Hot Interconnects IX*, 2001.

[40] S. S. Mukherjee, B. Falsafi, M. D. Hill, and D. A. Wood. Coherent Network Interfaces for Fine-Grain Communication. In *Proceedings of the 23rd International Symposium on Computer Architecture (ISCA)*, 1996.

[41] J. Nelson, B. Myers, A. H. Hunter, P. Briggs, L. Ceze, C. Ebeling, D. Grossman, S. Kahan, and M. Oskin. Crunching Large Graphs with Commodity Processors. In *Proceedings of the 3rd USENIX Conference on Hot Topics in Parallelism (HotPar)*, 2011.

[42] L. Noordergraaf and R. van der Pas. Performance Experiences on Sun's WildFire Prototype. In *Proceedings of the ACM/IEEE Conference on Supercomputing (SC)*, 1999.

[43] D. Ongaro, S. M. Rumble, R. Stutsman, J. K. Ousterhout, and M. Rosenblum. Fast Crash Recovery in RAMCloud. In *Proceedings of the 23rd ACM Symposium on Operating Systems Principles (SOSP)*, 2011.

[44] Oracle Corp. Oracle Exalogic Elastic Cloud X3-2 (Datasheet). `http://www.oracle.com/us/products/middleware/exalogic/overview/index.html`, 2013.

[45] L. Page, S. Brin, R. Motwani, and T. Winograd. The PageRank Citation Ranking: Bringing Order to the Web. *Stanford InfoLab Technical Report*, 1999.

[46] S. Pakin, M. Lauria, and A. Chien. High performance messaging on workstations: Illinois Fast Messages (FM) for Myrinet. In *Proceedings of the 1995 ACM/IEEE Conference on Supercomputing*. ACM, 1995.

[47] R. Recio, B. Metzler, P. Culley, J. Hilland, and D. Garcia. A Remote Direct Memory Access Protocol Specification. RFC 5040, 2007.

[48] S. K. Reinhardt, J. R. Larus, and D. A. Wood. Tempest and Typhoon: User-Level Shared Memory. In *Proceedings of the 21st International Symposium on Computer Architecture (ISCA)*, 1994.

[49] P. Rosenfeld, E. Cooper-Balis, and B. Jacob. DRAMSim2: A Cycle Accurate Memory System Simulator. *Computer Architecture Letters*, 10(1):16–19, 2011.

[50] S. M. Rumble, D. Ongaro, R. Stutsman, M. Rosenblum, and J. K. Ousterhout. It's Time for Low Latency. In *Proceedings of the 13th USENIX Conference on Hot Topics in Operating Systems*, 2011.

[51] D. J. Scales, K. Gharachorloo, and C. A. Thekkath. Shasta: A Low Overhead, Software-Only Approach for Supporting Fine-Grain Shared Memory. In *Proceedings of the 7th International Conference on Architectural Support for Programming Languages and Operating Systems (ASPLOS-VII)*, 1996.

[52] I. Schoinas, B. Falsafi, A. R. Lebeck, S. K. Reinhardt, J. R. Larus, and D. A. Wood. Fine-Grain Access Control for Distributed Shared Memory. In *Proceedings of the 6th International Conference on Architectural Support for Programming Languages and Operating Systems (ASPLOS-VI)*, 1994.

[53] S. L. Scott and G. M. Thorson. The Cray T3E Network: Adaptive Routing in a High Performance 3D Torus. In *Hot Interconnects IV*, 1996.

[54] S. Shelach. Mellanox wins $200m Google, Microsoft deals. `http://www.globes.co.il/serveen/globes/docview.asp?did=1000857043&fid=1725`, 2013.

[55] Q. O. Snell, A. R. Mikler, and J. L. Gustafson. Netpipe: A Network Protocol Independent Performance Evaluator. In *IASTED International Conference on Intelligent Information Management and Systems*, volume 6, 1996.

[56] R. Stets, S. Dwarkadas, N. Hardavellas, G. C. Hunt, L. I. Kontothanassis, S. Parthasarathy, and M. L. Scott. Cashmere-2L: Software Coherent Shared Memory on a Clustered Remote-Write Network. In *Proceedings of the 16th ACM Symposium on Operating Systems Principles (SOSP)*, 1997.

[57] L. G. Valiant. A Bridging Model for Parallel Computation. *Communications of the ACM*, 33(8):103–111, 1990.

[58] T. von Eicken, A. Basu, V. Buch, and W. Vogels. U-Net: A User-Level Network Interface for Parallel and Distributed Computing. In *Proceedings of the 15th ACM Symposium on Operating Systems Principles (SOSP)*, 1995.

[59] T. Wenisch, R. Wunderlich, M. Ferdman, A. Ailamaki, B. Falsafi, and J. Hoe. SimFlex: Statistical Sampling of Computer System Simulation. *IEEE Micro*, 26:18 –31, 2006.

[60] WinterCorp. Big Data and Data Warehousing. http://www.wintercorp.com/.

[61] K. A. Yelick, D. Bonachea, W.-Y. Chen, P. Colella, K. Datta, J. Duell, S. L. Graham, P. Hargrove, P. N. Hilfinger, P. Husbands, C. Iancu, A. Kamil, R. Nishtala, J. Su, M. L. Welcome, and T. Wen. Productivity and Performance Using Partitioned Global Address Space Languages. In *Workshop on Parallel Symbolic Computation (PASCO)*, 2007.

# Rhythm: Harnessing Data Parallel Hardware for Server Workloads

Sandeep R Agrawal
Duke University
sandeep@cs.duke.edu

Valentin Pistol
Duke University
pistol@cs.duke.edu

Jun Pang
Duke University
pangjun@cs.duke.edu

John Tran
NVIDIA
johntran@nvidia.com

David Tarjan *
NVIDIA

Alvin R Lebeck
Duke University
alvy@cs.duke.edu

## Abstract

Trends in increasing web traffic demand an increase in server throughput while preserving energy efficiency and total cost of ownership. Present work in optimizing data center efficiency primarily focuses on the data center as a whole, using off-the-shelf hardware for individual servers. Server capacity is typically increased by adding more machines, which is cheap, though inefficient in the long run in terms of energy and area.

Our work builds on the observation that server workload execution patterns are not completely unique across multiple requests. We present a framework—called Rhythm—for high throughput servers that can exploit similarity across requests to improve server performance and power/energy efficiency by launching data parallel executions for request cohorts. An implementation of the SPECWeb Banking workload using Rhythm on NVIDIA GPUs provides a basis for evaluating both software and hardware for future cohort-based servers. Our evaluation of Rhythm on future server platforms shows that it achieves 4× the throughput (reqs/sec) of a core i7 at efficiencies (reqs/Joule) comparable to a dual core ARM Cortex A9. A Rhythm implementation that generates transposed responses achieves 8× the i7 throughput while processing 2.5× more requests/Joule compared to the A9.

* Now with Samsung Electronics, d.tarjan@samsung.com



*ASPLOS '14*, March 1–4, 2014, Salt Lake City, Utah, USA.

http://dx.doi.org/10.1145/2541940.2541956

***Categories and Subject Descriptors*** C.5.5 [*Computer System Implementation*]: Servers

***Keywords*** high throughput; power efficiency; execution similarity

## 1. Introduction

Data centers provide the computational and storage infrastructure required to meet today's ever increasing demand for Internet content. For example, Facebook utilizes more than 100,000 servers to provide approximately one trillion page views per month (about 350K per second) and 1.2 million photo views per second. Meeting the increasing demand for content often requires adding more machines to existing data centers and building more data centers. Although content distribution networks can offload some of the demand for static content, state-of-the-art data centers house vast numbers of servers and require 2-6 Mega Watts of power. Therefore server performance, scaling and energy efficiency (throughput/Watt) are crucial factors in reducing total cost of ownership (TCO) in today's server-based industries [4, 11, 16, 17, 39, 41].

For example, at Facebook, the majority of the traffic goes through front-end web servers and the majority of the data center servers (and thus power) are devoted to this front-end [25]. Reducing CPU load inspired the design of HipHop, which translates PHP to native code thereby increasing throughput per server by > 5× [15].

Current system designs based on commodity multicore processors may not be the most power/energy efficient for all server workloads. There is ongoing debate over which architecture is best suited for specific workloads [17, 31, 32, 39, 43]. Figure 1 shows an overview of the server design space based on throughput normalized to an x86 core versus energy efficiency (performance/Watt) normalized to an ARM core. An ideal design would achieve throughput at or above an x86 core with energy efficiency at or above an ARM core.

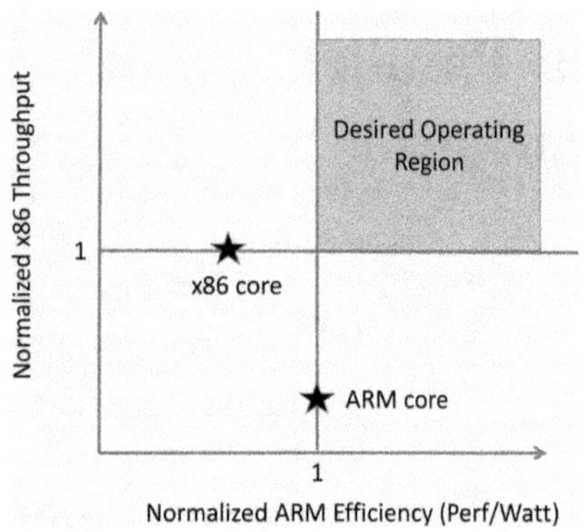


**Figure 1.** Server Design Space

Recent highly-threaded accelerators (i.e., NVIDIA Kepler [44], Intel Xeon Phi [30]) achieve >1 teraflop of performance within a 225W power envelope, achieving >5 gigaflops/W. This efficiency arises from several factors, including the amortization of overheads (e.g., instruction fetch) due to extensive use of vector (SIMD) and multi-threaded (SIMT) hardware, and simpler designs enabled by supporting a more restricted programming model; these accelerators excel at executing regular data-parallel programs, but are often considered unsuitable for arbitrary multi-threaded applications.

Nonetheless, as GPU-like hardware becomes increasingly general purpose, the potential advantages of highly-threaded, yet somewhat restricted hardware, are compelling. Even servers based on low power cores (e.g., ARM, Atom) could further benefit from amortizing microarchitecture power overheads (e.g., instruction fetch) over multiple requests, or utilizing heterogeneous System-on-Chip solutions (e.g., Tegra [45], AMD Fusion [8], or many core systems [35]) for servers. The challenge is to determine if traditional task parallel request-based server workloads can exploit the efficiencies of highly threaded data-parallel hardware in future server platforms.

This paper takes the first steps toward meeting this challenge by building on several observations about technology trends and server workloads. In a typical data center server environment, requests may be distributed to a set of servers based on information within the request (e.g., based on a hash of the user ID, URL), on the type of service requested (e.g., login, static image, database query), or other sharding methods. In this scenario, many of the requests perform the same task(s), such as login or search query. *The key insight is, given an incoming stream of requests, a server could delay some requests in order to align the execution of similar requests—allowing them to execute concurrently.* Our goal is to trade an increase in response time for improvement in server throughput per Watt by exploiting similarity across requests using cohort scheduling [34] to launch data parallel executions.

The contributions of this work include:

- *Rhythm*, a software architecture for high throughput SIMT-based servers. (*Rhythm* derives from the Greek word *rhythmos*, meaning any regular recurring motion or symmetry)
- A prototype implementation of *Rhythm* and the SPECWeb Banking service on NVIDIA GPUs that demonstrates it is possible to run server workloads on a GPU.[1]
- Evaluation of future server platform architectures. Our prototype achieves 1.5M requests/sec on an NVIDIA GTX Titan GPU card for an idealized environment that removes network and storage I/O limitations. This is 4× the throughput of a Core i7 running 8 threads at efficiencies comparable to a dual core ARM Cortex A9. Furthermore, approximately 192 1.2GHz, 1W ARM cores are required to achieve the same throughput with less than 40 Watts (21% overall) in available power to support the massively scaled system. We also demonstrate that array transpose offload can increase *Rhythm* throughput to over 3M reqs/sec.
- Standalone C and C+CUDA implementations of the SPECWeb2009 Banking workload that we plan to release publicly.

The remainder of this paper is organized as follows. Section 2 examines technology trends and workload characteristics that motivate our work. We present our overall server architecture (*Rhythm*) in Section 3 and provide implementation details in Section 4. Sections 5 and 6 describe our methodology and evaluates our prototype's potential performance on future server platforms. Related work is discussed in Section 7, while Section 8 concludes and discusses future work.

## 2. Motivation

This section motivates our work by first reviewing GPU-style accelerator efficiencies and then discussing several networking and system architecture trends that remove constraints of existing systems. We conclude this section with a study that demonstrates the existence of similarity across requests.

### 2.1 Accelerator Efficiency

GPU-style accelerators achieve efficiency through two primary mechanisms: hardware multithreading and SIMD execution. First, for high throughput computing, hardware multithreading enables significant latency tolerance by overlapping the execution of multiple threads. Second, by utilizing a single instruction multiple thread (SIMT) model, properly aligned threads exploit data parallel execution and amortize instruction fetch and decode overhead. Recent research indicates instruction fetch and decode can be as high as 40%-

[1] Our initial prototype targets GPUs, but our ideas are applicable to a broad class of accelerators. Without loss of generality, we use GPU or device to refer to this broad class.

50% of overall core power [49]. Amortizing this power over more operations can provide benefits across nearly all types of microarchitectures, from complex out-of-order cores to simple in-order cores. Although in this paper we focus on GPU-style accelerators, our work is broadly applicable to data parallel architectures.

The potential efficiencies available with emerging GPU-style accelerators is compelling. However, several aspects of current systems may limit the ability to exploit these efficiences. These limitations include PCIe bandwidth and latency, network bandwidth and the potential lack of similarity across requests. Below we address these potential limitations.

### 2.2 Enabling Trends

Current systems may introduce bottlenecks that limit the overall server throughput possible with a highly threaded accelerator. Here we identify three trends that can remove or mitigate these bottlenecks enabling scale-up solutions for high throughput servers.

#### 2.2.1 Increasing Bandwidth

Current systems may have bandwidth bottlenecks at either the network or the PCIe bus that limit overall throughput. Today's systems utilize 10 Gbps - 40 Gbps networking infrastructure and PCIe 3.0 for the system interconnect. A single 10 Gbps link limits throughput to approximately 1M req/sec for 1KB requests, and is lower for larger messages. However, efforts are underway to create 100 Gbps and 400 Gbps network standards [1] and announced systems claim to sustain these bandwidths [29]. Furthermore, research is exploring techniques to achieve $10^{12}$ bps to $10^{15}$ bps using novel multicore fiber optics [47].

Once network bandwidth increases, the PCIe bus may become the bottleneck. Fortunately, PCIe 4.0 doubles bandwidth to 16G Transfers/sec [3] and as discussed below, system on chip architectural changes can eliminate/reduce system bus bandwidth limitations. We believe that future server platforms can exploit these progressive enhancements in network and system bandwidth to sustain significant throughput per node.

#### 2.2.2 System on Chip

Another trend in processor and system architecture is heterogeneous computing where specialized accelerators and general purpose cores are combined in a system-on-chip (SoC) design (e.g., Tegra [45], AMD Fusion [8]). SoCs can reduce latency, improve bandwidth and reduce power by avoiding off-chip latency and exploiting on-chip density for a high bandwidth interconnect. Recent analysis [35, 36] shows overall benefits to data center design by using SoC architectures to reduce TCO, and mention the possibility of integrated accelerators for servers.

#### 2.2.3 Operating System and Backend Services

A final enabling trend is support for high throughput access to OS services. Recent research is exploring both high throughput and clean abstractions for parallel access to OS services. GPUfs [50] provides a filesystem abstraction that enables access from the GPU. Similar in spirit is the recent development of vector interfaces [55] that can provide 1M input/output operations per second to a high performance solid state disk (SSD). There is also recent work on providing high throughput backend services by exploiting GPUs [6, 28, 57] or constructing specialized hardware for key-value (e.g., memcached [19]) servers [10, 36].

### 2.3 Request Similarity

The potential efficiencies of parallel accelerators is compelling, and the above trends expose the opportunity to exploit those efficiences in future high throughput server designs. However, it remains to be determined if server workloads can exploit those efficiencies. As a first step toward answering this question we performed preliminary analysis of the SPECWeb2009 Banking workload [51]. This workload is a PHP web site representative of typical web-based banking.

We use Pin [40] to obtain x86 dynamic basic block traces for 61 individual dynamic web content (PHP) requests from the SPECWeb2009 Banking workload. These requests access 14 distinct top-level PHP files served by the Apache web server.[2] We use the UNIX utility *diff* to merge traces and obtain a measure of similarity between request traces based on the length of the merged trace. Minimal differences between traces indicates the two executions followed the same control paths during their execution.

The opportunity for exploiting GPU-style hardware for server workloads is obtained by examining the length of merged traces (e.g., shorter merged traces implies faster execution time). The resulting merge is an approximation of the actual execution order for all the batched requests executing on data parallel hardware. Note that our analysis is performed offline, and thus assumes a very high request arrival rate.

We merge traces for independent requests that access the same initial PHP file, resulting in 14 distinct merged traces. Execution speedup is approximated as the sum of traces (in number of basic blocks) divided by the merged trace size (i.e., cohort execution on idealized SIMD hardware). In our experiments between 2 and 6 traces per request (PHP file) are merged, with most requests having 5 unique traces. Figure 2 shows per request speedup normalized to ideal (linear) speedup. From these results we observe nearly linear speedup (i.e., nearly identical executions) for each request type.

[2] There are a total of 16 requests in this workload, but our experiments only exercised 14 of them.

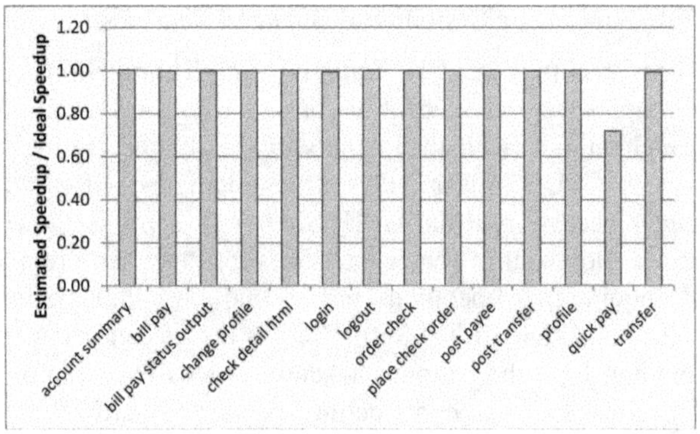


**Figure 2.** Potential Speedup of SPECWeb2009 Banking Workload on Data Parallel Hardware Relative to Ideal Speedup

We performed a similar study using Facebook's HipHop PHP to C++ system [15]. This experiment removes any potential affects of online PHP interpreting in Apache/Zend. We observed qualitatively similar results (not shown) with significant similarity among requests of the same type. Furthermore, on average there are approximately 33,000 instructions between system calls with 97% of them related to filesystem or network I/O and could utilize the high throughput interfaces described above (i.e., GPUfs and vector interfaces).

The above results quantitatively demonstrate the intuitive result that similar instruction control flow exists in a server workload for requests of the same type. Similar control flow is just one aspect required to efficiently utilize GPU-style compute accelerators. Other additional challenges include, but are not limited to: 1) scheduling, 2) data divergence, 3) copy overheads, and 4) current platform limitations.

## 3. *Rhythm* Server Software Architecture

*Rhythm* is a software architecture that extends event-based staged servers and cohort scheduling [34, 52, 56] to support high throughput servers on emerging highly threaded data parallel accelerators. Conceptually, *Rhythm* pipelines the processing of request *cohorts*—a set of requests that require similar computation. In this section we first provide an overview of the *Rhythm* design, including our core design goals. This is followed by a more detailed description of the *Rhythm* pipeline and the requisite data structures. *Rhythm* is a general architecture that could be implemented in many ways; Section 4 describes a specific implementation. Furthermore, *Rhythm* can be used to implement a variety of services, but in this work we focus on its use for web servers.

### 3.1 Overview

Figure 3 shows the typical pattern for processing requests in web servers. Requests arrive over the network and are dispatched for processing, generally based on the type of request (e.g., a particular PHP file or query type). Request

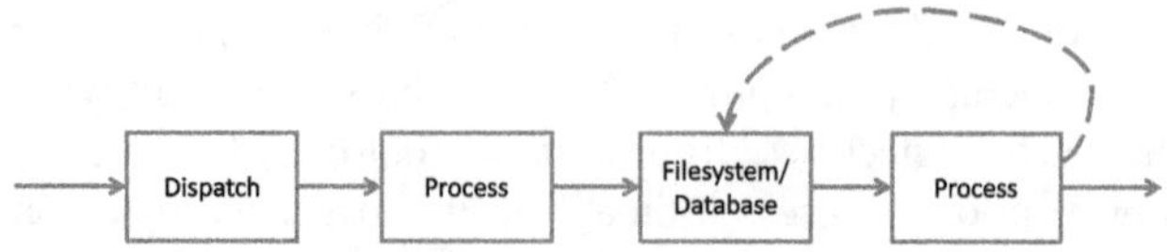


**Figure 3.** Typical Web Server Request Processing Overview

processing may be followed by access to a backend database (e.g., SQL or memcached), and the results from that query can lead to further processing before a response is sent back to the client. Conventional servers process requests individually, using a thread per request [18] or a staged event-based server [34, 52, 56].

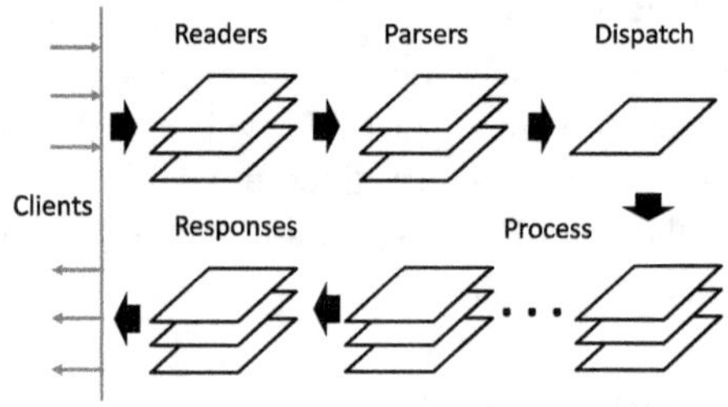


**Figure 4.** *Rhythm* Pipeline (Each stage can have multiple instances)

*Rhythm* extends event-based staged servers by providing a pipelined architecture for processing cohorts of requests on data parallel hardware. The *Rhythm* pipeline is composed of five stages, as shown in Figure 4: 1) Reader, 2) Parser, 3) Dispatch, 4) Process, 5) Response. For each of these stages there may be one or more instances, allowing for parallelism across and within stages. For a given service, the process stage is composed of $n$ backend stages and $n+1$ process stages. A specific implementation of the *Rhythm* pipeline can map each of these stages to either a general purpose CPU or an SIMT accelerator. We defer discussion of a specific implementation to Section 4.

The overall goal of *Rhythm* is to enable high throughput server implementations that can exploit the efficiencies of GPU-style accelerators. To achieve this, our design goals for *Rhythm* include: 1) Asynchronous, 2) Event driven, 3) Lock free & wait free, and 4) Utilize the most efficient computational resource (general purpose core or accelerator). The first three guidelines are well-known for high throughput server design on commodity general purpose processors (e.g., nginx [52]). The last design guideline is unique to an accelerator-based design and reflects our desire to exploit the efficiency of the accelerator as much as possible, but some requests that do not conform to a data parallel model may be executed more efficiently on a general purpose CPU.

The *Rhythm* pipeline is controlled by an event-based server with a single thread (see Figure 5) that provides cohort scheduling [34]. The server thread is generally responsible for delaying requests an appropriate amount of time to form

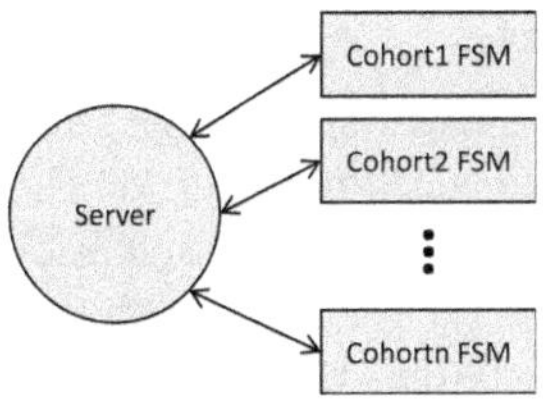


**Figure 5.** *Rhythm* Event-based Server: Each Finite State Machine (FSM) is associated with a cohort of requests.

cohorts, determining when a cohort is ready to launch on the accelerator, launching cohorts onto the accelerator, managing cohort context transitions, and sending responses back to the originating clients.

Requests can be delayed for a limited amount of time and still achieve acceptable response times [41]. *Rhythm* includes a timeout so that requests are not delayed indefinitely during cohort formation. Setting a specific timeout value is a policy decision that depends on particular service level agreements, *Rhythm* simply provides the mechanism. A similar timeout mechanism could be used to ensure that stragglers (e.g., long backend accesses) do not delay other requests in a cohort during execution. Furthermore, since cohort formation can occur after each stage, the set of requests in a cohort may change. Straggler responses from the backend can either be executed on the host CPU or added to a subsequent cohort.

The *Rhythm* pipeline stalls only when insufficient resources are available (i.e., structural hazards such as memory buffers or device execution units). The single threaded control avoids thread switching overheads, is lock-free, wait-free and fully asynchronous. The design also allows for multiple instances of each stage (reader, parser, process and response) and each of the stages can be tuned for optimal concurrency. *Rhythm* maintains state that allows it to efficiently schedule cohorts on the host or the accelerator based on the current state of the system.

***Cohort Management*** A cohort context contains information necessary to identify the specific request type and other properties of a cohort. *Rhythm* uses a cohort pool to track the availability of cohort contexts and manages their allocation throughout the pipeline. A cohort context can be *Free*, *Partially_Full*, *Full* or *Busy*. A *Free* context can be used to form a new cohort. Requests are added to a context by either the Reader or the Parser. The first request added to a *Free* cohort context transitions the context to *Partially_Full* where it can continue to accumulate requests until it becomes *Full*. When a cohort context begins execution, either because it was *Full* or a timeout occurred, it becomes *Busy*. A cohort context is *Busy* while the requests transition through the various process stages. A cohort context is *Free*d after the responses are sent to their respective clients.

### 3.2 The *Rhythm* Pipeline

We now elaborate more on the design and function of the individual stages of the *Rhythm* pipeline. An implementation would provide resources (execution units and memory) to support one or more instances of each stage.

***Reader*** The reader accumulates requests from the network to form a cohort, based purely on the request order. When a sufficient number of requests arrive, the reader passes the cohort to the next stage of the pipeline—the parser. The reader latency is primarily limited by the request arrival rate or network bandwidth. If all parsers are busy, the reader stalls.

***Parser*** Request parsing follows a standard protocol defined by the HTTP Specification [20], making it an ideal candidate for SIMT execution. The parser extracts the method (GET or POST), the request type (PHP file or image), the content length, cookie information, the client file descriptors and the query string parameters for each request in the cohort. This information is then composed into a *request* structure and added to the cohort. Cohorts are formed based on the file accessed or any other metric of similarity. The parser then signals dispatch if a cohort becomes *Full*.

***Dispatch*** Dispatch is performed on the host and determines if a request should be executed on the host or the device. Some requests that simply access the file system are best processed on the host rather than the device. GPU access to the file system (e.g., GPUfs [50]) would enable dispatch execution on the device and decrease transfer overheads, but we leave exploring this option to future work. A *Full* cohort context is ready for dispatch if the requisite resources on the device are available. Based on the resource requested (e.g., specific PHP file), the appropriate process stage is executed and the cohort context is updated to *Busy* to prevent redundant dispatch.

***Process*** The process phase is defined by the different request types supported by the server and is generally composed of $n$ backend stages and $n + 1$ process stages. Typically, a web service response contains the HTTP header, static HTML content, database content, and dynamic HTML generated based on the database content. The overall process phase alternates between content generation and backend access. For a typical remote backend, individual threads in a given process stage generate request strings which are sent to the backend, and the backend response is then passed on to the next stage of content generation (i.e., another process stage). We note that it is easy to incorporate a portion of the backend, such as a cache lookup, as part of a process stage. When the response is ready, an event is raised to signal process completion.

***Response*** The response stage sends the responses to the respective clients and frees the associated cohort context. Its latency is primarily limited by available network bandwidth.

The *Rhythm* pipeline is general and could be implemented entirely on a single machine or distributed across several machines. For example, read and parse could be implemented on a front-end machine, processing of specific request types on separate machines, and response formation on yet another machine. The next section presents an implementation on a single machine; we leave exploring alternative implementations as future work.

# 4. Rhythm Server Implementation

We implement a prototype version of *Rhythm* to evaluate its potential on existing NVIDIA GPU hardware. We apply several implementation specific optimizations to the *Rhythm* design. Many of these optimizations are well known software constructions and *Rhythm* exploits them for its goals of maximum throughput on accelerator hardware.

## 4.1 Pipeline Control

***Event loop*** *Rhythm* is single threaded by design, therefore it uses a central event loop based on *epoll* to process all I/O events and device interactions. These include requests for new connections, backend responses, service requests for existing clients, and file system responses. Asynchronous stage execution (i.e., transitions in the cohort FSM) is managed using callbacks and local unix *pipes*. Callbacks are maintained as a linked list that is traversed on each iteration of the event loop.

***Callbacks*** We use callbacks to track stage completion and transitions. The pipeline stages execute asynchronously on the device, and we need a mechanism to detect completion. Unfortunately, our current platform does not support interrupts from the device, therefore we use callbacks to implement a polling mechanism in the event loop. At the beginning of each stage, a callback is added to the callback list. We execute this callback to poll the stage and only remove it from the list if the stage is complete. When a stage completes, it adds another callback to start execution of the next stage in the pipeline. Although this approach doesn't appear to limit throughput, it introduces unnecessary power consumption for polling many inflight stages.

***Cohort context synchronization*** Our current implementation uses the host for cohort dispatch, and thus requires maintaining cohort context on both the host and the device. We synchronize these two copies of the context at the parser since it is the only stage that modifies device contexts (setting them to *Partially_Full* and *Full*) by populating cohorts with requests. The host contexts are copied to the device at parser launch, and the device contexts are copied to the host at parser termination for use in dispatch. Dispatch and response both execute on the host and modify the host cohort context by setting it to *Busy* or *Free*, respectively.

## 4.2 Pipeline Stages

***Reader/Parser*** The reader is double buffered to overlap request processing and accumulation. When a cohort becomes full, the reader swaps the front and back buffers, signals the parser to begin processing, and resumes reading requests into the new front buffer. If the back buffer is not free, the reader stalls, waiting for the parser. The reader and parser are low latency stages, and a single instance of each is sufficient to achieve high throughput in our experiments.

***Process/Backend*** The overall processing of a request is divided into one or more process stages separated by backend accesses. In our current implementation we preallocate pipeline resources (i.e., memory) for all process stages (including the backend when appropriate) and the response stage at the first process stage launch. Each stage is a computational unit on the device, called a *kernel*. Kernel progress and termination is tracked by the event loop. The overall process phase is latency bound depending on the specific request type. We provide multiple instances of process and response resources to maintain as many cohorts in flight as possible, allowing us to hide the latency of individual kernels and increase throughput. Exploring alternatives that do not preallocate resources is part of our future work.

***Response*** The final process stage adds a callback upon termination, and the response stage is invoked at the next iteration of the event loop. The callback is removed after the responses for the cohort are sent to the respective clients. All resources used by this cohort become available for reuse by subsequent cohorts.

## 4.3 Data Structures

*Rhythm* uses four primary data structures to support the web server: a cohort pool and the associated cohort contexts, a session array, a request buffer and a response buffer, each optimized to enable efficient data parallel execution. The cohort pool and contexts are implemented as static arrays to avoid allocation and synchronization overheads.

### 4.3.1 HTTP Session Array/Cookies

The session array is a device only structure that stores HTTP session state for the clients handled by the server. Sessions are created at login and destroyed upon logout. Since the session array is accessed for every request, its performance is critical to server throughput. To ensure conflict-free access for a cohort, the session array is implemented as a hash table with the number of buckets equal to the cohort size. Each request thread accesses a unique bucket, and insertion into a bucket is performed randomly based on a hash of the userid. The session identifier is a hash of the node index and the bucket index, ensuring O(1) time lookup for a session node. Collisions upon insertion are handled using a linear search for a free node, resulting in O(1) for collision free insertion, and O(n) time in the case of a collision. Since lookups are constant time and the array is static, deletions are O(1) time.

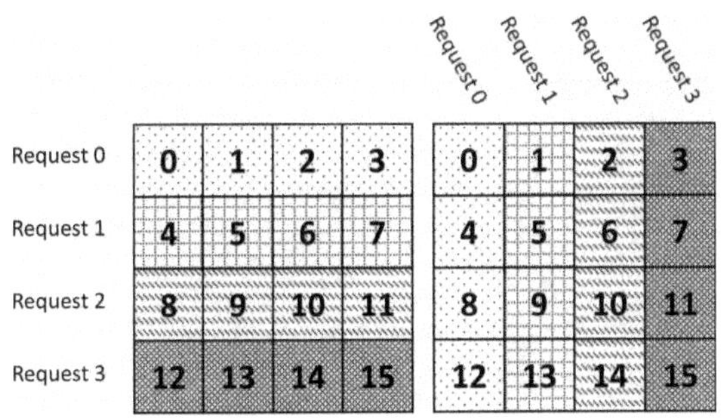


**Figure 6.** Request Buffer Layout (for illustrative purposes)

#### 4.3.2 Request and Response Buffer Layout

In a typical server application each request is allocated contiguous buffers for incoming and outgoing data. Unfortunately, when executing on a GPU this data layout can undermine the potential benefits of executing multiple requests simultaneously. Specifically, GPU memory systems work best when memory references of the co-scheduled threads (referred to as a *warp*) exhibit good spatial locality (often called *coalesced* memory accesses). While a single thread has good spatial locality, across threads the memory locations accessed are separated by large distances.

To overcome this challenge we explore several methods. One approach utilizes the GPU threads to cooperatively perform the operations of a single request (intra-request concurrency). Unfortunately, this approach does not exploit the similarity in instruction control flow across requests (inter-request concurrency) and performs poorly. Therefore, we use a second approach that performs a data transformation on the buffers by transposing them to improve spatial locality. We also insert whitespaces in the generated HTML content to tolerate control divergence in the response generation stages.

***Buffer Transpose*** We view the buffers per cohort as a 2D array with each row representing the contiguous buffer for a given request, as shown in Figure 6. Initially these buffers are in row-major layout. To improve spatial locality within a cohort, we need the array in column-major layout so that thread buffers are interleaved in the sequential address space. To achieve this, we perform a simple array transpose operation and leverage existing techniques to optimize the transpose [48]. When the requests are finished processing we perform an additional transpose to convert the responses back to row-major layout, with each buffer occupying contiguous locations in the linear address space. Other server workloads may require similar data structure design/transformations to fully utilize the hardware capabilities available. Our ongoing work is exploring other server workloads.

***Whitespace Padding in HTML Content*** Transposing buffers can provide coalesced memory accesses if the individual thread buffer pointers are aligned (i.e., each thread uses the same row index value). However, the web pages in our system are dynamically generated with data returned from the backend database; differences in returned data (i.e., string lengths) can result in unaligned buffer pointers. Fortunately, we can exploit the HTML specification, which allows an arbitrary number of linear white spaces in the response body, to embed the appropriate number of whitespace characters after newline characters for each buffer to realign the buffer pointers.

***Whitespace Padding in HTML Headers*** The HTTP response header requires the *Content-length* field whose value can only be known after the response is generated. Conventional servers can generate the header after the entire response content is created and use separate *send()* system calls for the header and response. For our *Rhythm* implementation, we avoid the overhead of an additional header generation stage by integrating header creation with response content creation. This creates an issue since the header is located near the beginning of the response buffer. To overcome this and ensure buffer pointer alignment we again exploit the HTML specification which allows white spaces after a header field. We reserve a fixed amount of space in the buffer by inserting white space characters (10 for a 32-bit content length), and replace whitespace with the actual content length value after the response is generated.

### 4.4 Error Handling

*Rhythm* maintains per request error state information to guarantee correctness. Request errors create control divergence among threads in a cohort; however, we assume that these scenarios are rare and do not impact throughput.

### 4.5 Request Flow in *Rhythm*

Figure 7 shows an overview of the request flow through the *Rhythm* pipeline. The ovals represent execution on the host and the boxes represent execution on the accelerator. The event-based server on the CPU copies request information into buffers on the device (step 1). When a sufficient number of requests arrive or the oldest request reaches a preset timeout, the parser is launched (steps 2-3) to identify and sort requests so that requests of the same type (PHP file) are contiguous in memory. The next stage (step 4) dispatches cohorts (and possibly processes some requests on the host CPU). Subsequent stages in the server include accessing backend storage services (step 7), handling backend responses (steps 8-10), and generating final HTML responses (steps 11-13).

### 4.6 CUDA Specifics

Our *Rhythm* prototype is implemented using CUDA on NVIDIA GPUs. A *stream* is defined as a sequence of dependent requests (memory copies or kernels) to the device, and different streams can execute concurrently on the device. We use asynchronous streams to implement the parser, the various process stages and the response stage of the

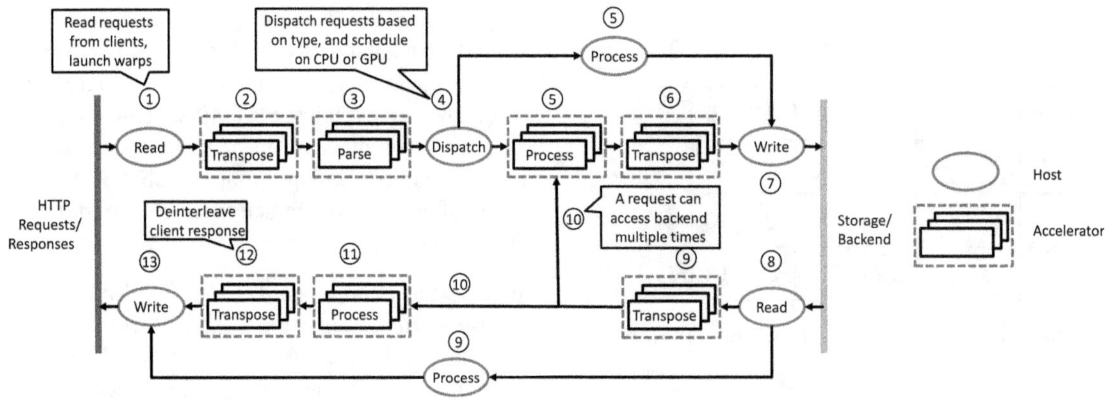


**Figure 7.** Rhythm Web Server Request Processing Overview

*Rhythm* pipeline. Memory pools are created at startup to avoid allocation and synchronization overheads, and memory is recycled. We use atomics to perform lock-free insertion and deletion into the session and cohort pools. We also perform several optimizations to *Rhythm* based on CUDA features, including:

- For padding in HTML content we perform a max butterfly reduction across a warp that uses CUDA shared memory to calculate the padding amount for each thread.
- We use CUDA constant memory where possible to store static HTML content for pages.
- We store frequently used pointers in CUDA constant memory instead of local memory to optimize register usage and enable more inflight *Rhythm* cohorts.

*Rhythm* is designed from the ground up keeping high throughput in mind, ideally with request arrival rate as the only limiter. Our implementation is guided by our experience with SPECWeb Banking, and there are nearly endless opportunities for continued optimization. We evaluate the benefits and pitfalls of *Rhythm* on existing platforms, and explore its potential to serve as a guideline for future server architectures.

## 5. Methodology

### 5.1 Platforms

Table 1 shows the various platforms we use to test workload performance. We use the quad-core Core i5 and Core i7 to represent the x86 family, and the dual-core Cortex A9 to represent the ARM family. The NVIDIA GTX Titan is used for our GPU measurements.

We use the SPECWeb Banking benchmark [51] for our studies. For general purpose processors we implement a standalone event-based C version and for the GPU we implement a *Rhythm* C+CUDA version. We implement 14 out of 16 Banking requests, and normalize the request percentages to sum to 100%. We skip the *quick pay* and *check detail images* benchmarks. *Quick pay* uses a variable number of

| Platform | GHz | Description |
|---|---|---|
| Core i5 | 3.4 | Core i5 3570, 22 nm, 4 cores (4 threads), 8GB DDR3 RAM, 1Gbps NIC |
| Core i7 | 3.4 | Core i7 3770, 22 nm, 4 cores (8 threads), 16GB DDR3 RAM, 1Gbps NIC |
| ARM A9 | 1.2 | OMAP 4460, 45 nm, Panda board, 2 cores, 1GB LPDDR2 RAM |
| Titan | 0.8 | GTX Titan, 28 nm, 14 Streaming Multiprocessors, 6GB GDDR5 Memory |

**Table 1.** Experimental System Platforms

kernel launches based on backend data, making it difficult to implement, and *check detail images* is completely disk bound, requiring GPUfs integration to allow us to process it on the GPU. We plan to address both these requests in future work. Table 2 summarizes characteristics about the Banking workload. The second column is the dynamic instruction count for our standalone C implementation and is the average across 100 random requests, and when combined with the third column we see a diverse mix of requests with varying compute/response byte ratios.

We use Ubuntu 12.04 with CUDA 5.5RC on our x86 platform and Linaro 13.01 for our ARM platform. All code is compiled using gcc with -O3 enabled. We test our server against the SPECWeb client validator to guarantee correctness. The X server is shut down for all our benchmark runs. We unplug the GPU for the baseline x86 test runs. For the CUDA version, we allocate 1KB per backend request and 4KB per backend response. We use the next higher power of two for the HTML response size (Table 2), since powers of two allow us to easily divide work on the hardware for the response transpose.

We implement support for static images, however, image throughput is primarily dictated by network bandwidth since there is no processing involved. The parser groups image requests into an image cohort, these cohorts bypass the process stage and the image responses are sent to the respective clients. Image cohorts can be processed on the device

| Request Type | x86 Instructions per Request | Response Size (KB) | | Fraction of Requests (%) | Backend Requests |
|---|---|---|---|---|---|
| | | SPECWeb | Rhythm | | |
| login | 132,401 | 4 | 8 | 28.17 | 2 |
| account summary | 392,243 | 17 | 32 | 19.77 | 1 |
| add payee | 335,605 | 18 | 32 | 1.47 | 0 |
| bill pay | 334,105 | 15 | 32 | 18.18 | 1 |
| bill pay status output | 485,176 | 24 | 32 | 2.92 | 1 |
| change profile | 560,505 | 29 | 32 | 1.60 | 1 |
| check detail html | 240,615 | 11 | 16 | 11.06 | 1 |
| order check | 433,352 | 21 | 32 | 1.60 | 1 |
| place check order | 466,283 | 25 | 32 | 1.15 | 1 |
| post payee | 638,598 | 34 | 64 | 1.05 | 1 |
| post transfer | 334,267 | 16 | 32 | 1.60 | 1 |
| profile | 590,816 | 32 | 64 | 1.15 | 1 |
| transfer | 277,235 | 13 | 16 | 2.24 | 1 |
| logout | 792,684 | 46 | 64 | 8.06 | 0 |
| Average | 429,563 | 15.5 | 26.4 | 100 | 1.2 |

**Table 2.** SPECWeb Banking Workload

as well using GPUfs [50], however, we leave that to future work. Static images can also be served at high throughputs via Content Delivery Networks (CDNs) like Akamai [46]. We do not evaluate image throughput for our prototype.

## 5.2 Metrics

Our metrics of interest include 1) throughput, 2) power, 3) latency, and 4) throughput/watt. We obtain throughput using the unix *clock_gettime()* interface to measure end-to-end time to process a set number of requests. Latency is calculated by logging the time that a request arrives and subtracting the request completion time, and we compute an average latency over all requests. Power is measured at the wall outlet using a Kill-A-Watt meter. We measure the idle and test power for each of our runs. Subtracting the two gives us the dynamic[3] power consumed by the workload. We examine throughput/Watt for both wall power and dynamic power as both of these represent different viewpoints on system efficiency. A system's cost of ownership is effectively based on wall power, whereas dynamic power measures the marginal costs incurred due to load.

## 5.3 Modeling Future Systems

SPECWeb's default test harness is based on Java and is quite slow, rendering it unusable for our system. We create our own test harness and use various optimizations to allow us to efficiently model future high bandwidth networks and datacenter-level throughputs.

### 5.3.1 Input Generation

We use the C *rand()* function to randomly generate input request data. For request types other than *login*, we randomly generate session identifiers and populate the session array with random user ids. We test each request type in isolation and process 48M requests. Using the request distributions from Table 2, we compute a weighted harmonic mean of request efficiency(throughput/watt) to obtain the efficiency for the entire workload.

[3] We use dynamic to represent the non-idle power under load. This is distinct from dynamic/static power used for circuit analysis.

### 5.3.2 Emulation

Our test system uses a 1Gbps NIC, and for an average response size of 16KB, cannot support more than $\sim$ 8K requests/sec. Similarly, PCIE bandwidth may artificially limit throughput. To explore future system architectures, we model three different *Rhythm* systems that progressively add capabilities: Titan A, Titan B, and Titan C.

**x86 and ARM platforms** run our C version of the Banking workload. For maximum throughput, we eliminate network and PCI limitations by generating requests from and copying responses to main memory and implement the backend as a function call.

**Titan A** models a high bandwidth network by generating requests locally and not sending responses across the network. We run the backend locally as one or more threads on the host to emulate the requisite backend throughput. We pre-generate requests into a buffer, and read them from memory on the fly to emulate high arrival rates.

**Titan B** extends the above design to eliminate the PCIe bandwidth bottleneck by implementing the SPECWeb Besim backend on the GPU. This emulates the effect of an SoC style approach with an integrated general purpose core and NIC. A local device backend also avoids the need to transpose the backend request and response data, potentially further improving performance.

**Titan C** further extends our system to emulate specialized hardware that performs the final transpose on the device after response generation, just prior to sending the response on the network. The response transpose could be performed on the host, on the NIC while reading data to send to the clients, or by a specialized logic unit associated with the memory controller (e.g., the logic layer of a 3D DRAM [2]). The latter is a general approach that could be used for other transpose operations in the *Rhythm* pipeline.

All of our optimizations are validated for correctness since we run on real hardware, and we can examine the output. Eliminating the network only eliminates the overheads of the *read()* and *write()* system calls and the network stack, and optimizing them is an important, but orthogonal issue to our work. A local or device backend emulates a high throughput key-value store [55], or the use of a database cache [19] on the local machine, which is commonly used to tolerate backend latencies.

## 6. Evaluation

*Rhythm* is designed as a free-flowing pipeline that serves to maximally utilize the underlying accelerator hardware to achieve optimal efficiency. This section presents our experimental results that confirm the expected limitations of current system bottlenecks on throughput. We then show how removing these bottlenecks enables *Rhythm* on a GPU to operate at high throughput with high efficiency. We also demonstrate that replicating general purpose cores to achieve high throughput cannot match the efficiency of *Rhythm* on today's GPUs. However, we caution that our results represent an initial exploration of the overall server design space primarily to gauge where *Rhythm* sits with respect to potential alternative platforms. A more comprehensive study, which is beyond the scope of this paper, would account for many differences such as technology node, different accelerators, etc. and include additional workloads. Nonetheless, our results point towards the design of future data parallel accelerators specialized for server workloads.

### 6.1 Overall Results

Table 3 shows the throughput, latency, wall and dynamic power of the banking workload for our various modeled platforms. More worker threads is always more beneficial for the general purpose cores since it amortizes the fixed costs associated with powering on the chip. For our evaluation we only consider the higher worker threads since they represent the best operating point for each platform.

To gain better insight into the results we utilize a throughput-efficiency plot that normalizes throughput to the Core i7 eight worker threads and efficiency to the ARM A9 two worker threads. Figure 8 shows the throughput-efficiency for the various platforms. Considering both wall power(Figure 8a) and dynamic power (Figure 8b), the Core i5 is more power efficient than the i7, with efficiencies comparable to the ARM, while delivering 75% of the i7's throughput. On the other hand, the ARM achieves only 4% of the i7's throughput, and 6% of the i5's throughput. The results also show that Titan A performs poorly in terms of efficiency, and provides only marginal throughput improvements. In contrast, Titan C provides massive gains in both throughput and power efficiency, processing $\sim 1.5\times$ more requests per Joule compared to the ARM and delivering $7\times$ more requests per second compared to the Core i7. Titan B provides more than $4\times$ the throughput of the i7, though at 91% dynamic efficiency and 124% wall efficiency of the ARM.

The Core i7 and i5 both exhibit low response latency, and even the ARM chip manages latencies of a few hundred microseconds. Titan A exhibits high response latencies, rendering it unusable for real server applications. Titan B and C perform relatively well, with latencies in 10s of milliseconds. We also measured the 99th percentile latency for our workloads, however it did not differ substantially from the average latency. The 99th percentile latency for different request types varies from 18%-40% of the average latency for Titan B, and varies from 7%-34% of the average for Titan C. These latencies are tolerable [13], and expected, since *Rhythm* sacrifices latency to achieve massive gains in throughput and efficiency. We now evaluate the nature of each Titan platform and their potential as exposed by *Rhythm*.

#### 6.1.1 Titan A: Emulated Remote Backend

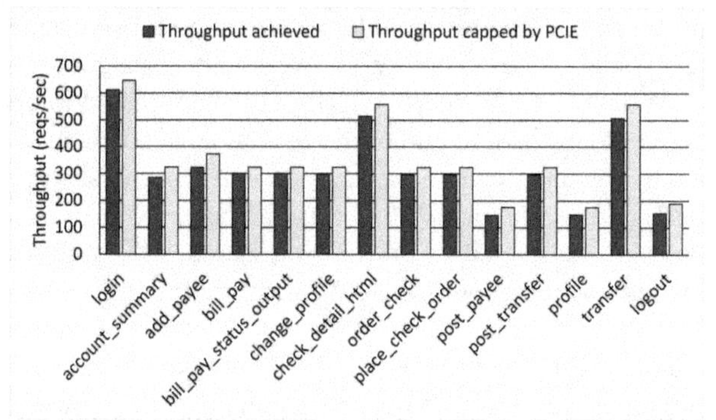


**Figure 9.** PCIe 3.0 Limitations in Titan A for various request types

Running with an emulated remote backend involves copies over the PCI Express bus for requests to, and responses from the backend. On current platforms, this limits overall throughput. *Rhythm* transfers 1KB for the request buffers, 1KB for the backend request, 4KB for the backend response and 26.4KB on an average for the response over the PCIe bus. We can calculate the throughput bound of the PCIe 3.0 bus by taking the ratio of the peak bandwidth (12GB/s) and the data transferred per request. Figure 9 shows the achieved throughput and throughput bounded by the available PCIe 3.0 bandwidth for the different request types. We can see that all requests achieve throughputs ranging from 83% to 95% of the PCI bounds. The minor difference between the two is expected since we transfer data in smaller chunks, which does not allow us to reach peak PCIe

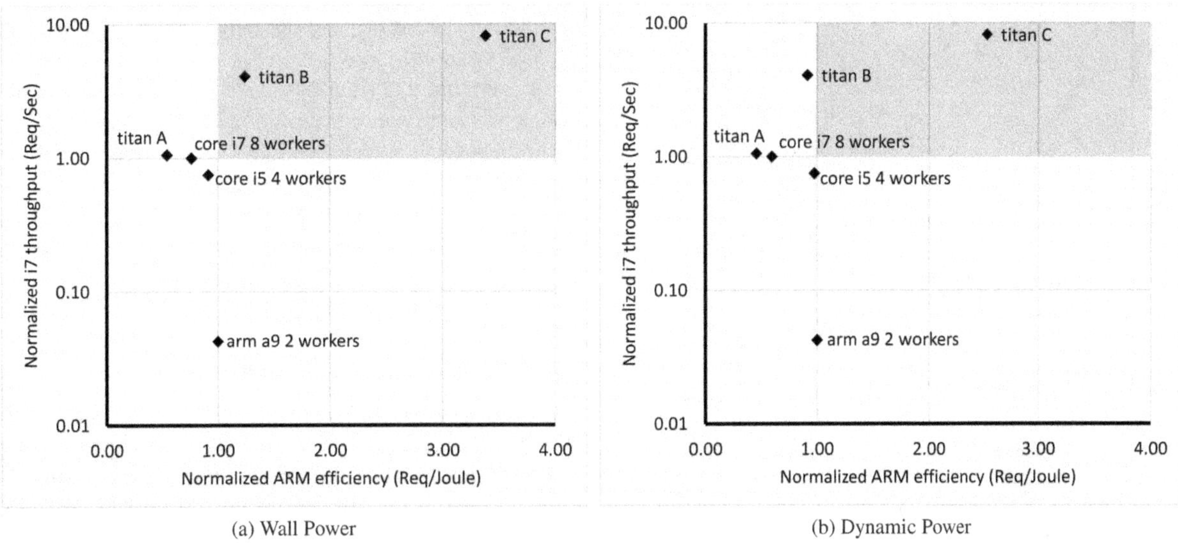


**Figure 8.** Throughput-Efficiency for Wall Power (a) and Dynamic Power (b). Throughput (y-axis) is normalized to Core i7 8 workers and efficiency (x-axis) to ARM A9 2 workers. The shaded region represents the desired operating range.

| Platform | Power (Watts) | | | Latency | Throughput | Reqs/Joule (Efficiency) | |
|---|---|---|---|---|---|---|---|
| | Idle | Wall | Dynamic | (ms) | (KReqs/s) | Wall | Dynamic |
| Core i5 1 worker | 47 | 67 | 20 | 0.016 | 75 | 972 | 3283 |
| Core i5 4 workers | 47 | 98 | 51 | 0.016 | 282 | 2447 | 4712 |
| Core i7 4 workers | 45 | 147 | 102 | 0.014 | 331 | 1901 | 2735 |
| Core i7 8 workers | 45 | 156 | 111 | 0.014 | 377 | 2042 | 2873 |
| ARM a9 1 worker | 2 | 3.4 | 1.4 | 0.176 | 8 | 1672 | 4061 |
| ARM a9 2 workers | 2 | 4.5 | 2.5 | 0.176 | 16 | 2683 | 4830 |
| Titan A | 74 | 226 | 152 | 86 | 398 | 1469 | 2193 |
| Titan B | 74 | 306 | 232 | 24 | 1535 | 3329 | 4410 |
| Titan C | 74 | 285 | 211 | 10* | 3082 | 9070 | 12264 |

**Table 3.** SPECWeb Banking Experimental Results. *Titan C Latency is for transposed response

bandwidth. We can see that *Rhythm* on Titan A is primarily limited by the PCIe 3.0 bandwidth, which creates a structural hazard in the *Rhythm* pipeline, leading to stalls and a loss in power efficiency.

A potential enabling trend is the PCIe 4.0 standard, which doubles usable bandwidth to 24 GB/s. This could increase Titan A's throughput to 864K reqs/s and a commensurate increase in efficiency that may bring it near the ARM A9's efficiency (depending on the PCIe 4.0 power). However, even at 25 GB/s, the PCIe bus is still a bottleneck for *Rhythm* on a Titan.

### 6.1.2 Titan B: Integrated NIC and Device Backend

Titan B increases *Rhythm*'s average throughput to more than 4$\times$ that of the core i7 achieving more than 1.5M reqs/sec, at 91% dynamic efficiency and 124% wall efficiency of the ARM chip.

We note that Titan B's throughput and efficiency could improve if we used a better response padding method. Many request types incur significant overhead due to excessive padding since their total response size is just beyond one power of two and we simply round up to the next power of two. This introduces exponentially more overhead for transposes for larger response sizes. Cross-referencing response sizes in Table 2 with dynamic efficiency in Figure 10 for different requests, we observe that for small responses (i.e., *login*) or where *Rhythm* uses a response buffer close to the size of the original response (e.g., *change_profile* and *transfer*), Titan B achieves throughput 3.5$\times$-5$\times$ higher than the core i7, with dynamic efficiencies of 105% to 120% of the ARM, showing room for further optimization. We further analyze this difference and observe that the response transpose takes up a significant fraction of device time, and creates bubbles in the *Rhythm* pipeline. Titan C removes this limitation.

### 6.1.3 Titan C: Increasing Device Utilization

Titan C tries to push the *Rhythm* pipeline to its limits by increasing GPU utilization and offloading the response trans-

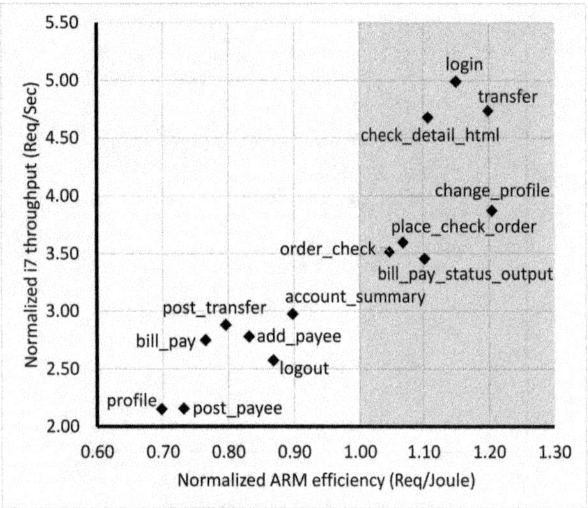


**Figure 10.** Throughput-Efficiency for different request types on Titan B (dynamic power). *Rhythm* buffer sizes that are close to required sizes perform well (shaded area represents the desired operating range).

pose. With these optimizations, Titan C achieves more than 3M reqs/sec on an average, or more than 8× the throughput of the Core i7. Increasing GPU utilization amortizes the fixed power overheads, achieving a dynamic efficiency of more than 2.5× that of the ARM, and a wall efficiency of more than 3.3×. These numbers ignore power to perform the transpose, and as we show in the next section, with an ample power budget for the transpose, *Rhythm* can still outperform the ARM in efficiency while achieving far greater throughputs.

### 6.2 Scaling Many Core Processors

A natural comparison for achieving high throughput is to scale the number of general purpose cores to match the throughput of *Rhythm* on both Titan B and Titan C. We use single thread throughput for the general purpose cores and idealistically assume linear performance scaling. The scaled systems incur additional *uncore* overhead to support scaling, such as additional chip I/Os, on chip interconnect, additional memory controllers and memory, etc. We use the i5 for scaling instead of the i7 due to its higher dynamic efficiency (Table 3). Based on our measurements, and other studies [35], we assume a dynamic power of 1W per ARM core and 10W per i5 core. The power available for the *uncore* overhead is the difference between the idealized scaled system's power and the Titan platform's power.

With respect to Titan B (dynamic power), we need 192 ARM cores and 21 i5 cores to match throughput, requiring 192W and 210W, respectively. Titan B uses 232W, leaving only 40W for the ARM (21%) or 22W (10%) for the i5 available for uncore scaling overhead. Compared to Titan C, we need 385 ARM cores and 41 i5 cores to match throughput. This results in 385W for the ARM system and 410W for the i5 system, and Titan C has more than 170W in which to implement the transpose operation and still outperform the scaled systems.

Given that the Titan-based systems also have room to reduce overall power consumption (e.g., lower power DRAM, eliminate GPU specific features, etc.) it appears difficult for simple replicated designs to match the overall throughput and throughput/watt of *Rhythm* on GPU-style accelerators. However, a more detailed analysis of complete server design, including specialized data parallel accelerators, is required, and we leave that to future work.

### 6.3 System Resource Requirements

***Network Bandwidth*** We perform our experiments on *Rhythm* for a request size of 512B, a backend request size of 1KB and a 4KB backend response size. Using the average value of the response size of the SPECWeb Banking workload (Table 2), and the average number of backend responses, we can easily calculate the network bandwidth requirements of our Titan platforms. At an average throughput of 398K reqs/s, Titan A requires a N/W bandwidth of 67 Gbps, Titan B requires 258 Gbps and Titan C requires 517 Gbps. All of these numbers assume raw uncompressed data. Most modern web browsers support compression and research has demonstrated more than 80% compression of HTML content in pages for popular websites [37]. A compression ratio of 80% means that Titan C can easily be operated on a 100Gbps link, already defined by the IEEE 802.3bj standard [1].

***Memory Capacity*** We are currently limited by the memory on the device. For our experiments, we emulate 16M active sessions on the GPU, and at 40B per session, this requires 640MB of memory. The session array is implemented as a hash table using random insertion, and we allocate memory for 64M sessions to reduce the chance of a collision to 25%, but this requires 2.5GB of device memory. Since all memory is preallocated in pools, we also need to allocate enough memory for the process phase, backend data, request buffers, response buffers and transpose buffers to avoid structural hazards in the pipeline. The memory required for buffers increases linearly with cohort size, therefore, we are limited to 8 cohorts in flight of size 4096 requests each on the GTX Titan.

### 6.4 Miscellaneous

***CPU based SIMD implementations*** Web service workloads and data parallel hardware are a great match, and *Rhythm* provides a way to bring the two together by exploiting similarity amongst requests to enable SIMD processing. The GPU's throughput oriented SIMT architecture provides a good platform to test this approach. A SIMD based implementation on current CPUs would provide a useful data point in this design space as well. We leave this exploration to future work.

***Cohort Size sensitivity*** We performed experiments on *Rhythm* for cohort sizes ranging from 256 to 8192, and found 4096 to provide the right balance between high throughput and memory limitations. Larger cohort sizes are better for throughput since they allow more work to be launched on the GPU, however, they require more memory. Larger cohort sizes also impact response latency, since it takes more time to form a cohort. However, for arrival rates of the order of a million reqs/sec, cohort formation times are negligible.

***Parser divergence*** Our current experiments run the same type for requests on the parser, however, this reduces control divergence in the parser. In a real world system, multiple request types would arrive at the parser, increasing control divergence and reducing single parser throughput. We measured parser latency for a real Specweb Banking Trace containing a mix of requests and images. On an average, the parser takes 556us including the request buffer tranpose, giving a throughput of 7.4M reqs/sec for a cohort size of 4096. Therefore, the parser is fast enough even when it is processing cohorts of different types. The *Rhythm* design also allows for multiple parsers to be launched concurrently, and for higher throughputs, this would further help in hiding parser latency.

***HyperQ*** We performed our experiments on a NVIDIA GTX690 as well, however, a single work queue between the host and device created false dependencies among process kernels, limiting throughput. The GTX Titan supports 32 simultaneous work queues (HyperQ), allowing for much higher throughput and GPU utilization. *Rhythm* can expose significant concurrency and the hardware must be capable of exploiting it. Emulating future platforms with integrated high bandwidth devices exposed the benefit of having HyperQ scheduling on the GPU.

## 7. Related Work

This paper touches on topics across a broad spectrum of computer systems related topics, including, but not limited to: server design, operating system design and implementation, system and processor architecture, and data layout optimizations. For brevity, we focus on some of the most closely related research.

At the application mapping level, several researchers have explored general purpose use of GPUs [9, 12, 27] and mapping non-traditional workloads onto GPUs, such as MIMD programs [14], database queries (e.g., [6, 24, 57], etc.) and memcached [28], and software routers [26]. Other work explores the potential opportunities created by delaying server requests for either improved memory hierarchy performance [34] or energy management [33, 41], and allocating compute resources dynamically based on load in staged servers [56].

Recent microarchitecture work [54] shows the benefits of data-triggered threads and methods for eliminating redundant computation, while other work (MMT [38] and Thread Fusion [23]) shows the benefit of exploiting identical instructions in SMT processors to remove redundant operations (i.e., fetch, execute, etc.). Our work focuses on coarser grain identification of cohorts and targets different applications, but may benefit from the addition of these methods. STREX [5] improves transaction processing by aligning instructions to reduce cache misses. Other work [7] explores data similarity and memory hierarchies that can merge identical content used by different cores into a single cache line. Thread scheduling on GPUs has been addressed in the context of reducing the impact of control divergence [21, 22, 42, 53]. More generally, several researchers are exploring processor design for data center workloads [10, 17, 31, 32, 35, 36, 39, 43].

## 8. Conclusion

A dramatic increase in the number of data centers in the last decade and their multi-megawatt power budgets has sharply brought into focus the energy economics of web services. We propose the use of data parallel accelerators and a software architecture called *Rhythm* to address throughput and efficiency demands of future server workloads. *Rhythm* is based on the insight that maximal power efficiency of an accelerator comes from maximizing utilization since it amortizes fixed system costs. We show *Rhythm* achieves throughput $4\times$ to $8\times$ of an 8 thread core i7 at efficiencies (requests/joule) comparable to or higher than a dual core ARM Cortex A9.

This work serves as a milestone that demonstrates that Web Servers and data parallel accelerators are a great match. Even on current generation GPU hardware, *Rhythm* outperforms both the x86 and ARM architectures. We plan to explore ways to increase the efficiency of *Rhythm* by designing data parallel processors specialized for server workloads. Currently, we test *Rhythm* on GPUs, and other accelerators like the Xeon Phi, NEON and Tegra also provide interesting possibilities. Programming for accelerators involves a significant amount of effort, and we are working on creating a language for regaining programmer productivity. We are also exploring other workloads like Search, Email and Chat, and deploying them using *Rhythm*. This paper is just a first step in exploring an exciting and varied design space.

## Acknowledgments

We would like to thank the Duke Computer Architecture Group, Mark Silberstein and Emmett Witchel for their support, and the reviewers for their valuable time and feedback. This work was supported in part by the National Science Foundation (CCF-1335443) and NVIDIA.

## References

[1] http://www.ieee802.org/3/.

[2] Hybrid memory cube. `http://hybridmemorycube.org`.

[3] Pci express 4.0 faq. http://www.pcisig.com/news_room/faqs/FAQ_PCI_Express_4.0/.

[4] D. G. Andersen, J. Franklin, M. Kaminsky, A. Phanishayee, L. Tan, and V. Vasudevan. Fawn: a fast array of wimpy nodes. In *Proceedings of the ACM SIGOPS 22nd symposium on Operating systems principles*, SOSP '09, pages 1–14, New York, NY, USA, 2009. ACM. ISBN 978-1-60558-752-3. . URL http://doi.acm.org/10.1145/1629575.1629577.

[5] I. Atta, P. Tözün, X. Tong, A. Ailamaki, and A. Moshovos. Strex: Boosting instruction cache reuse in oltp workloads through stratified transaction execution. In *Proceedings of the 40th Annual International Symposium on Computer Architecture*, ISCA '13, pages 273–284, New York, NY, USA, 2013. ACM. ISBN 978-1-4503-2079-5. . URL http://doi.acm.org/10.1145/2485922.2485946.

[6] P. Bakkum and K. Skadron. Accelerating sql database operations on a gpu with cuda. In *Proceedings of the 3rd Workshop on General-Purpose Computation on Graphics Processing Units*, GPGPU '10, pages 94–103, New York, NY, USA, 2010. ACM. ISBN 978-1-60558-935-0. . URL http://doi.acm.org/10.1145/1735688.1735706.

[7] S. Biswas, D. Franklin, A. Savage, R. Dixon, T. Sherwood, and F. T. Chong. Multi-Execution: Multicore Caching for Data-Similar Executions. In *Proceedings of the 36th annual international symposium on Computer architecture*, ISCA '09, pages 164–173, New York, NY, USA, 2009. ACM. ISBN 978-1-60558-526-0. .

[8] A. Branover, D. Foley, and M. Steinman. Amd fusion apu: Llano. *Micro, IEEE*, 32(2):28 –37, march-april 2012. ISSN 0272-1732. .

[9] I. Buck. GPU computing with NVIDIA CUDA. In *SIGGRAPH '07: ACM SIGGRAPH 2007 courses*, page 6, New York, NY, USA, 2007. ACM. .

[10] S. R. Chalamalasetti, K. Lim, M. Wright, A. AuYoung, P. Ranganathan, and M. Margala. An fpga memcached appliance. In *Proceedings of the ACM/SIGDA international symposium on Field programmable gate arrays*, FPGA '13, pages 245–254, New York, NY, USA, 2013. ACM. ISBN 978-1-4503-1887-7. . URL http://doi.acm.org/10.1145/2435264.2435306.

[11] J. S. Chase, D. C. Anderson, P. N. Thakar, A. M. Vahdat, and R. P. Doyle. Managing energy and server resources in hosting centers. In *Proceedings of the eighteenth ACM symposium on Operating systems principles*, SOSP '01, pages 103–116, New York, NY, USA, 2001. ACM. ISBN 1-58113-389-8. . URL http://doi.acm.org/10.1145/502034.502045.

[12] S. Che, M. Boyer, J. Meng, D. Tarjan, J. Sheaffer, S. Lee, and K. Skadron. Rodinia: A Benchmark Suite for Heterogeneous Computing. In *Proceedings of the IEEE International Symposium on Workload Characterization*, IISWC, pages 44–54. IEEE, 2009. .

[13] J. Dean and L. A. Barroso. The tail at scale. *Commun. ACM*, 56(2):74–80, Feb. 2013. ISSN 0001-0782. . URL http://doi.acm.org/10.1145/2408776.2408794.

[14] H. G. Dietz and B. D. Young. Mimd interpretation on a gpu. In *Proceedings of the 22nd international conference on Languages and Compilers for Parallel Computing*, LCPC'09, pages 65–79, Berlin, Heidelberg, 2010. Springer-Verlag. ISBN 3-642-13373-8, 978-3-642-13373-2. . URL http://dx.doi.org/10.1007/978-3-642-13374-9_5.

[15] Facebook. Hiphop-php. https://github.com/facebook/hiphop-php/wiki.

[16] X. Fan, W.-D. Weber, and L. A. Barroso. Power provisioning for a warehouse-sized computer. In *Proceedings of the 34th annual international symposium on Computer architecture*, ISCA '07, pages 13–23, New York, NY, USA, 2007. ACM. ISBN 978-1-59593-706-3. . URL http://doi.acm.org/10.1145/1250662.1250665.

[17] M. Ferdman, A. Adileh, O. Kocberber, S. Volos, M. Alisafaee, D. Jevdjic, C. Kaynak, A. D. Popescu, A. Ailamaki, and B. Falsafi. Clearing the clouds: a study of emerging scale-out workloads on modern hardware. In *Proceedings of the seventeenth international conference on Architectural Support for Programming Languages and Operating Systems*, ASPLOS XVII, pages 37–48, New York, NY, USA, 2012. ACM. ISBN 978-1-4503-0759-8. . URL http://doi.acm.org/10.1145/2150976.2150982.

[18] R. Fielding and G. Kaiser. The Apache HTTP Server Project. *IEEE Internet Computing*, 1(4):88–90, 1997. ISSN 1089-7801. .

[19] B. Fitzpatrick. Distributed caching with memcached. *Linux J.*, 2004(124):5–, Aug. 2004. ISSN 1075-3583. URL http://dl.acm.org/citation.cfm?id=1012889.1012894.

[20] T. I. E. T. Force. Hypertext transfer protocol – http/1.1. http://www.ietf.org/rfc/rfc2616.txt.

[21] W. Fung and T. Aamodt. Thread Block Compaction for Efficient SIMT Control Flow. In *17th IEEE International Symposium on High-Performance Computer Architecture*, HPCA-17, 2011.

[22] W. W. L. Fung, I. Sham, G. Yuan, and T. M. Aamodt. Dynamic Warp Formation and Scheduling for Efficient GPU Control Flow. In *Proceedings of the 40th Annual IEEE/ACM International Symposium on Microarchitecture*, MICRO 40, pages 407–420, Washington, DC, USA, 2007. IEEE Computer Society. ISBN 0-7695-3047-8. .

[23] J. González, Q. Cai, P. Chaparro, G. Magklis, R. Rakvic, and A. González. Thread Fusion. In *Proceeding of the 13th international symposium on Low power electronics and design*, ISLPED '08, pages 363–368, New York, NY, USA, 2008. ACM. ISBN 978-1-60558-109-5. .

[24] N. K. Govindaraju, B. Lloyd, W. Wang, M. Lin, and D. Manocha. Fast computation of database operations using graphics processors. In *Proceedings of the 2004 ACM SIGMOD international conference on Management of data*, SIGMOD '04, pages 215–226, New York, NY, USA, 2004. ACM. ISBN 1-58113-859-8. . URL http://doi.acm.org/10.1145/1007568.1007594.

[25] M. Hachman. How facebook will power graph search. http://slashdot.org/topic/datacenter/how-facebook-will-power-graph-search/.

[26] S. Han, K. Jang, K. Park, and S. Moon. Packetshader: a gpu-accelerated software router. In *Proceedings of the ACM*

*SIGCOMM 2010 conference*, SIGCOMM '10, pages 195–206, New York, NY, USA, 2010. ACM. ISBN 978-1-4503-0201-2. . URL `http://doi.acm.org/10.1145/1851182.1851207`.

[27] J. Hensley. AMD CTM Overview. In *ACM SIGGRAPH 2007 courses*, SIGGRAPH '07, New York, NY, USA, 2007. ACM. .

[28] T. H. Hetherington, T. G. Rogers, L. Hsu, M. O'Connor, and T. M. Aamodt. Characterizing and evaluating a key-value store application on heterogeneous cpu-gpu systems. In *Proceedings of the 2012 IEEE International Symposium on Performance Analysis of Systems & Software*, ISPASS '12, pages 88–98, Washington, DC, USA, 2012. IEEE Computer Society. ISBN 978-1-4673-1143-4. . URL `http://dx.doi.org/10.1109/ISPASS.2012.6189209`.

[29] http://netronome.com.

[30] Intel Corp. Intel xeon phi coprocessor. `http://www.intel.com/content/www/us/en/processors/xeon/xeon-phi-coprocessor-datasheet.html`.

[31] V. Janapa Reddi, B. C. Lee, T. Chilimbi, and K. Vaid. Web search using mobile cores: quantifying and mitigating the price of efficiency. In *Proceedings of the 37th annual international symposium on Computer architecture*, ISCA '10, pages 314–325, New York, NY, USA, 2010. ACM. ISBN 978-1-4503-0053-7. . URL `http://doi.acm.org/10.1145/1815961.1816002`.

[32] T. Kgil, A. Saidi, N. Binkert, S. Reinhardt, K. Flautner, and T. Mudge. Picoserver: Using 3d stacking technology to build energy efficient servers. *J. Emerg. Technol. Comput. Syst.*, 4(4):16:1–16:34, Nov. 2008. ISSN 1550-4832. . URL `http://doi.acm.org/10.1145/1412587.1412589`.

[33] W. Lang and J. Patel. Towards Eco-friendly Database Management Systems. In *4th Biennial Conference on Innovative Data Systems Research*, Asilomar, California, USA, January 4-7 2009.

[34] J. R. Larus and M. Parkes. Using Cohort Scheduling to Enhance Server Performance (Extended Abstract). In *LCTES '01: Proceedings of the ACM SIGPLAN workshop on Languages, compilers and tools for embedded systems*, pages 182–187, New York, NY, USA, 2001. ACM. ISBN 1-58113-425-8. .

[35] S. Li, K. Lim, P. Faraboschi, J. Chang, P. Ranganathan, and N. P. Jouppi. System-level integrated server architectures for scale-out datacenters. In *Proceedings of the 44th Annual IEEE/ACM International Symposium on Microarchitecture*, MICRO-44 '11, pages 260–271, New York, NY, USA, 2011. ACM. ISBN 978-1-4503-1053-6. . URL `http://doi.acm.org/10.1145/2155620.2155651`.

[36] K. Lim, D. Meisner, A. G. Saidi, P. Ranganathan, and T. F. Wenisch. Thin servers with smart pipes: designing soc accelerators for memcached. In *Proceedings of the 40th Annual International Symposium on Computer Architecture*, ISCA '13, pages 36–47, New York, NY, USA, 2013. ACM. ISBN 978-1-4503-2079-5. . URL `http://doi.acm.org/10.1145/2485922.2485926`.

[37] Z. Liu, Y. Saifullah, M. Greis, and S. Sreemanthula. Http compression techniques. In *Wireless Communications and Networking Conference, 2005 IEEE*, volume 4, pages 2495–2500 Vol. 4, 2005. .

[38] G. Long, D. Franklin, S. Biswas, P. Ortiz, J. Oberg, D. Fan, and F. T. Chong. Minimal Multi-threading: Finding and Removing Redundant Instructions in Multi-threaded Processors. In *Proceedings of the 2010 43rd Annual IEEE/ACM International Symposium on Microarchitecture*, MICRO '43, pages 337–348, Washington, DC, USA, 2010. IEEE Computer Society. ISBN 978-0-7695-4299-7. .

[39] P. Lotfi-Kamran, B. Grot, M. Ferdman, S. Volos, O. Kocberber, J. Picorel, A. Adileh, D. Jevdjic, S. Idgunji, E. Ozer, and B. Falsafi. Scale-out processors. In *Proceedings of the 39th Annual International Symposium on Computer Architecture*, ISCA '12, pages –, Washington, DC, USA, 2012. IEEE Computer Society. ISBN 978-1-4503-1642-2. . URL `http://dx.doi.org/10.1145/2337159.2337217`.

[40] C.-K. Luk, R. Cohn, R. Muth, H. Patil, A. Klauser, G. Lowney, S. Wallace, V. J. Reddi, and K. Hazelwood. Pin: Building Customized Program Analysis Tools with Dynamic Instrumentation. In *Proceedings of the 2005 ACM SIGPLAN conference on Programming language design and implementation*, PLDI '05, pages 190–200, New York, NY, USA, 2005. ACM. ISBN 1-59593-056-6. .

[41] D. Meisner and T. F. Wenisch. Dreamweaver: architectural support for deep sleep. In *Proceedings of the seventeenth international conference on Architectural Support for Programming Languages and Operating Systems*, ASPLOS XVII, pages 313–324, New York, NY, USA, 2012. ACM. ISBN 978-1-4503-0759-8. . URL `http://doi.acm.org/10.1145/2150976.2151009`.

[42] J. Meng, D. Tarjan, and K. Skadron. Dynamic Warp Subdivision for Integrated Branch and Memory Divergence Tolerance. In *Proceedings of the 37th annual International Symposium on Computer Architecture*, ISCA '10, pages 235–246, New York, NY, USA, 2010. ACM. ISBN 978-1-4503-0053-7. .

[43] T. Mudge and U. Holzle. Challenges and opportunities for extremely energy-efficient processors. *IEEE Micro*, 30(4):20–24, July 2010. ISSN 0272-1732. . URL `http://dx.doi.org/10.1109/MM.2010.61`.

[44] NVIDIA. Tesla k20 gpu accelerator board specification. `http://www.nvidia.com/content/PDF/kepler/Tesla-K20-Passive-BD-06455-001-v05.pdf`, .

[45] NVIDIA. Nvidia tegra mobile processors. `http://www.nvidia.com/object/tegra-3-processor.html`, .

[46] E. Nygren, R. K. Sitaraman, and J. Sun. The akamai network: a platform for high-performance internet applications. *SIGOPS Oper. Syst. Rev.*, 44(3):2–19, Aug. 2010. ISSN 0163-5980. . URL `http://doi.acm.org/10.1145/1842733.1842736`.

[47] D. J. Richardson, J. M. Fini, and L. E. Nelson. Space-division multiplexing in optical fibres. *Nat Photon*, 7(5):354–362, 05 2013. URL `http://dx.doi.org/10.1038/nphoton.2013.94`.

[48] G. Ruetsch and P. Micikevicius. Optimizing matrix transpose in cuda. `http://docs.nvidia.com/cuda/samples/6_Advanced/transpose/doc/MatrixTranspose.pdf`.

[49] J. Sartori, B. Ahrens, and R. Kumar. Power balanced pipelines. In *High Performance Computer Architecture (HPCA), 2012 IEEE 18th International Symposium on*, pages 1–12, 2012. .

[50] M. Silberstein, B. Ford, I. Keidar, and E. Witchel. Gpufs: integrating file systems with gpus. In *Proceedings of the Eighteenth International Conference on Architectural Support for Programming Languages and Operating Systems*, ASPLOS '13. ACM, 2013.

[51] Standard Performance Evaluation Corporation. SPECweb2009. `http://www.spec.org/web2009/`.

[52] I. Sysoev. Nginx introduction and architecture overview. `http://nginx.org/en/docs/introduction.html`.

[53] D. Tarjan, J. Meng, and K. Skadron. Increasing memory miss tolerance for simd cores. In *Proceedings of the Conference on High Performance Computing Networking, Storage and Analysis*, SC '09, pages 22:1–22:11, New York, NY, USA, 2009. ACM. ISBN 978-1-60558-744-8. .

[54] H. Tseng and D. Tullsen. Data-Triggered Threads: Eliminating Redundant Computation. In *Proceedings of 17th International Symposium on High Performance Computer Architecture*, HPCA-17, 2011.

[55] V. Vasudevan, M. Kaminsky, and D. G. Andersen. Using vector interfaces to deliver millions of iops from a networked key-value storage server. In *Proceedings of the Third ACM Symposium on Cloud Computing*, SoCC '12, pages 8:1–8:13, New York, NY, USA, 2012. ACM. ISBN 978-1-4503-1761-0. . URL `http://doi.acm.org/10.1145/2391229.2391237`.

[56] M. Welsh, D. Culler, and E. Brewer. SEDA: An Architecture for Well-Conditioned, Scalable Internet Services. In *SOSP '01: Proceedings of the eighteenth ACM symposium on Operating systems principles*, pages 230–243, New York, NY, USA, 2001. ACM. ISBN 1-58113-389-8. .

[57] H. Wu, G. Diamos, S. Cadambi, and S. Yalamanchili. Kernel weaver: Automatically fusing database primitives for efficient gpu computation. In *Proceedings of the 2012 45th Annual IEEE/ACM International Symposium on Microarchitecture*, MICRO '12, pages 107–118, Washington, DC, USA, 2012. IEEE Computer Society. ISBN 978-0-7695-4924-8. . URL `http://dx.doi.org/10.1109/MICRO.2012.19`.

# Paraprox: Pattern-Based Approximation for Data Parallel Applications

Mehrzad Samadi, Davoud Anoushe Jamshidi, Janghaeng Lee, and Scott Mahlke

Advanced Computer Architecture Laboratory
University of Michigan - Ann Arbor, MI
{mehrzads, ajamshid, jhaeng, mahlke}@umich.edu

## Abstract

*Approximate computing is an approach where reduced accuracy of results is traded off for increased speed, throughput, or both. Loss of accuracy is not permissible in all computing domains, but there are a growing number of data-intensive domains where the output of programs need not be perfectly correct to provide useful results or even noticeable differences to the end user. These soft domains include multimedia processing, machine learning, and data mining/-analysis. An important challenge with approximate computing is transparency to insulate both software and hardware developers from the time, cost, and difficulty of using approximation. This paper proposes a software-only system, Paraprox, for realizing transparent approximation of data-parallel programs that operates on commodity hardware systems. Paraprox starts with a data-parallel kernel implemented using OpenCL or CUDA and creates a parameterized approximate kernel that is tuned at runtime to maximize performance subject to a target output quality (TOQ) that is supplied by the user. Approximate kernels are created by recognizing common computation idioms found in data-parallel programs (e.g., Map, Scatter/Gather, Reduction, Scan, Stencil, and Partition) and substituting approximate implementations in their place. Across a set of 13 soft data-parallel applications with at most 10% quality degradation, Paraprox yields an average performance gain of 2.7x on a NVIDIA GTX 560 GPU and 2.5x on an Intel Core i7 quad-core processor compared to accurate execution on each platform.*

***Categories and Subject Descriptors*** D.3.4 [*Programming Languages*]: Processors—Code generation, Compilers



*ASPLOS'14*, March 01–05 2014, Salt Lake City, UT, USA.

ACM 978-1-4503-2305-5/14/03... $15.00.
http://dx.doi.org/10.1145/2541940.2541948

***General Terms*** Design, Performance

***Keywords*** Approximation; Accuracy-aware computing; Data parallel; GPU

## 1. Introduction

Over the past few years, the information technology industry has experienced a massive growth in the amount of data that it collects from consumers. Analysts reported that in 2011 alone the industry gathered a staggering 1.8 zettabytes of information, and they estimate that by 2020, consumers will generate 50 times this figure [10]. Most major businesses that host such large-scale data-intensive applications, including Google, Amazon, and Microsoft, frequently invest in new, larger data centers containing thousands of multi-core servers. However, it seems that such investments in new hardware alone may not translate to the computation capability required to keep up with the deluge of data. Rather, it may be necessary to consider using alternative programming models that exploit the data parallel computing abilities of existing servers in order to address this problem. This paper focuses on applying one such model, approximate computing, where the accuracy of results is traded off for computation speed, to solve the problem of processing big data.

Approximation is applicable in domains where some degree of variation or error can be tolerated in the result of computation. For domains where some loss of accuracy during computation may cause catastrophic failure, e.g. cryptography, approximation should not be applied. However, there are many important domains where approximation can greatly improve application performance, including multimedia processing, machine learning, data analysis, and gaming. Video processing algorithms are prime candidates for approximation as occasional variation in results do not cause the failure of their overall operation. For example, a consumer using a mobile device can tolerate occasional dropped frames or a small loss in resolution during video playback, especially when this allows video playback to occur seamlessly. Machine learning and data analysis applications also provide opportunities to exploit approximation to improve performance, particularly when such programs are operat-

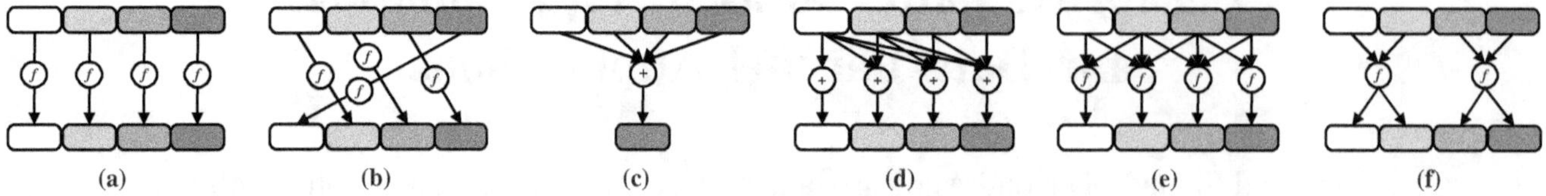

**Figure 1:** The data parallel patterns that Paraprox targets: (a) Map (b) Scatter/Gather (c) Reduction (d) Scan (e) Stencil (f) Partition.

ing on massive data sets. In this situation, processing the entire dataset may be infeasible, but by sampling the input data, programs in these domains can produce representative results in a reasonable amount of time.

Improving performance by applying approximation has been identified as an important goal by prior works [2, 4, 5, 11, 12, 23, 25, 28]. These works have studied this topic and proposed new programming models, compiler systems, and runtime systems to systematically manage approximation. However, these approaches have three critical limitations. We categorize the prior works based on these limitations:

- **Programmer-based [4, 5]:** In these systems, the programmer must write different approximate versions of a program and a runtime system decides which version to run. Although the programmer may best understand how his code works, writing different versions of the same program with varying levels of approximation is neither easy nor practical to be applied generally.
- **Hardware-based [11, 12, 28]:** These approaches introduce hardware modifications such as imprecise arithmetic units, register files, or accelerators. Although these systems work for general algorithms, they cannot be readily utilized without manufacturing new hardware. Furthermore, having both exact and approximate versions of the same hardware increases the hardware design complexity and the difficulty of validating and verifying such hardware.
- **Software-based [2, 23, 25, 27]:** Previous software-based approximation techniques do not face the problems of the other two categories as they (a) remove the burden of writing several versions of the program from the programmer, and (b) can be used with existing, commodity systems. However, with past approaches, *one solution does not fit all applications*. Each of these solutions works only for a small set of applications. They either cannot achieve a desired amount of performance improvement or generate unacceptable computation errors for applications that they were not explicitly built to handle.

To address these issues, this paper proposes a software framework called *Paraprox*. Paraprox identifies common patterns found in data-parallel programs and uses a custom-designed approximation technique for each detected pattern. Paraprox enables the programmer to write software once and run it on a variety of modern processors, without manually tuning code for different hardware targets. It is applicable to a wide range of applications as it determines the proper approximation optimizations that can be applied to each input program. Because Paraprox does not apply a single solution to all programs, it overcomes the aforementioned limitation of prior software-based approaches.

In this work, we identify different patterns commonly found in data parallel workloads and we propose a specialized approximation optimization for each pattern. We closely study data parallel programs because they are well-fitted for execution on prevalent multi-core architectures such as CPUs and GPUs. Paraprox is capable of targeting any data parallel architecture, provided that the underlying runtime supports such hardware.

Overall, Paraprox enables the programmer to implement a kernel once using the OpenCL or CUDA data parallel languages and, depending on the *target output quality (TOQ)* specified for the kernel, tradeoff accuracy for performance. To control the efficiency, accuracy, and performance of the system, each optimization allows some variables to be dynamically varied. After Paraprox generates the approximate kernels, a runtime system tunes the aforementioned variables to get the best performance possible while meeting the constraints of the $TOQ$.

To automatically create approximate kernels, Paraprox utilizes four optimization techniques which target six data parallel patterns: Map, Scatter/Gather, Reduction, Scan, Stencil, and Partition. Paraprox applies approximate memoization to map and scatter/gather patterns where computations are replaced by memory accesses. For reduction patterns, Paraprox uses sampling plus adjustment to compute the output by only computing the reduction of a subset of the data. The stencil & partition approximation algorithm is based on the assumption that adjacent locations in an input array are typically similar in value for such patterns. Therefore, Paraprox accesses a subset of values in the input array and replicates that subset to construct an approximate version of the array. For scan patterns, Paraprox only performs the scan operation on a subset of the input array and uses the results to predict the results for the rest of the array.

The specific contributions of this work are as follows:

- Pattern based compilation system for approximate execution.
- Automatic detection of data parallel patterns in OpenCL and CUDA kernels.
- Four pattern-specific approximation optimizations which are specifically designed for six common data parallel computation patterns.
- The ability to control performance and accuracy tradeoffs for each optimization at runtime using dynamic tuning parameters.

The rest of the paper is organized as follows. Section 2 explains how the Paraprox framework operates. Approximate optimizations used by Paraprox are discussed in Section 3. The results of using Paraprox for various benchmarks and architectures are presented in Section 4. Limitations of Paraprox's framework are discussed in Section 5. Section 6 discusses the related work in this area and how Paraprox is different from previous work. Section 7 concludes this paper and summarizes its contributions and findings.

## 2. Paraprox Overview

In order to generate approximate programs, Paraprox must detect data parallel patterns for optimization. As shown in Figure 1, these patterns have distinct characteristics that require specialized optimizations in order to create fast, approximate versions. In the following list, we describe the characteristics of the six patterns that Paraprox targets:

- ***Map:*** In the map pattern, a function operates on every element of an input array and produces one result per element as shown in Figure 1(a). To process all the input elements in parallel, a map function should be *pure*. A pure function always generates the same result for the same input, and its execution does not have any side-effects, e.g., it cannot read or write mutable state. Since there is no need to synchronize between two threads and no sharing of data is necessary, the map pattern is perfectly matched to data parallel, many-core architectures. In parallel implementations of map patterns, each thread executes one instance of a map function and generates its corresponding result. This pattern is used in many domains, including image processing and financial simulations.
- ***Scatter/Gather:*** Scatter and gather patterns are similar to map patterns but their memory accesses are random as illustrated in Figure 1(b). Based on McCool's definition [15], scatter is a map function that writes to random locations, and gather is the combination of a map function with memory accesses that read from random input elements. The parallel implementations of scatter/gather patterns are similar to map implementations. This pattern is commonly found in statistics applications.
- ***Reduction:*** When a function combines all the elements of an input array to generate a single output, it is said to be performing a reduction (Figure 1(c)). If the function used by the reduction pattern is both associative and commutative, e.g., XOR, the order in which the reduction operation is applied to its inputs is unimportant. In this case, tree-based implementations can be used to parallelize such a reduction. Reductions can be found in many domains, such as machine learning, physics, and statistics.
- ***Scan:*** The all-prefix-sums operation, more commonly termed *scan*, applies an associative function to an input array and generates another array. Every $N^{th}$ element of the output array is the result of applying the scan function on the first $N$ (inclusive scan) or $N-1$ (exclusive scan) input elements. An inclusive scan example is shown in Figure 1(d). The scan pattern is common in the signal processing, machine learning, and search domains.
- ***Stencil:*** In a stencil pattern, each output element is computed by applying a function on its corresponding input array element and its neighbors as shown in Figure 1(e). This pattern is common in image processing and physics applications.
- ***Partition:*** The partition (or tile) pattern is similar to the stencil pattern. The input array is divided into partitions and each partition is processed separately. Each partition is wholly independent of the others as shown in Figure 1(f). Partitioning is commonly used in data parallel applications to efficiently utilize the underlying architecture's memory hierarchy to improve performance. This pattern is common in domains such as image processing, signal processing, and physics modeling.

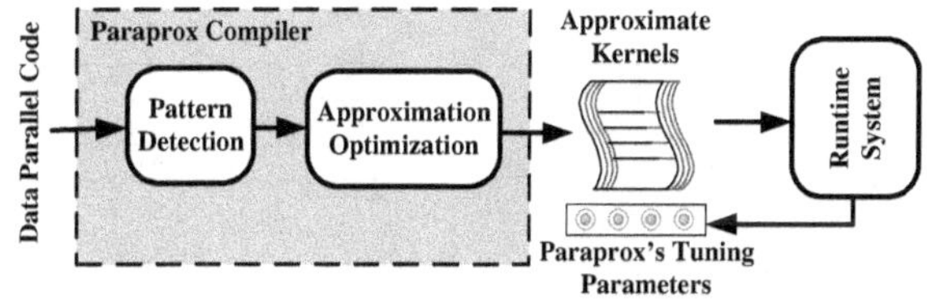


**Figure 2:** Approximation system framework.

In order to manage the output quality during execution, the Paraprox compilation framework should be used in tandem with a runtime system like Green [5] or SAGE [27] as shown in Figure 2. After Paraprox detects the patterns in the program and generates approximate kernels with different tuning parameters, the runtime profiles the kernels and tunes the parameters so that it provides the best performance. If the user-defined *target output quality (TOQ)* is violated, the runtime system will adjust by retuning the parameters and/or selecting a less aggressive approximate kernel for the next execution.

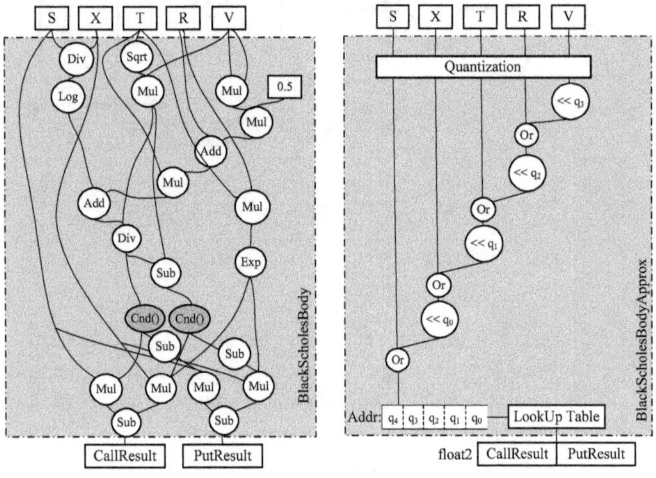


(a) (b)

**Figure 3:** (a) illustrates the dataflow graph of the main function of the *BlackScholes* benchmark. The function $Cnd()$ is a pure function. (b) shows the approximate kernel created using the map and scatter/gather technique described in 3.1.

# 3. Approximation Optimizations

We will now discuss the approximation optimizations that are applied to each data parallel pattern. For each pattern, we describe the intuition behind the optimization, the algorithm used to detect such a pattern, the implementation of the optimization, and tuning parameters that are used by a runtime to control the performance and accuracy of an approximate kernel during execution.

## 3.1 Map & Scatter/Gather

### 3.1.1 Idea:

Paraprox applies *approximate memoization* to optimize map and scatter/gather patterns. This technique replaces a function call with a query into a lookup table which returns a precomputed result. Since the size of this lookup table is limited by the size of memory and by performance considerations, there are situations in which the exact result is not stored in the table. In such cases, Paraprox finds the element nearest to the input present in the lookup table and returns that element instead. Consequently, the quality of the output is inversely proportional to the size of the lookup table (a.k.a. the number of quantization levels). As this optimization replaces the computations done by map and scatter/gather functions with a memory access, the unoptimized code should have more latency due to computation than that of one memory operation in order to achieve speedup.

To fill the lookup table with precomputed data, Paraprox computes the output of the map or scatter/gather function for a number of representative input sets (quantization levels) offline. During runtime, the launched kernel's threads use this lookup table to find the output for all input values.

### 3.1.2 Detection:

To detect map or scatter/gather patterns, Paraprox checks all functions in the input program to look for functions that can be replaced by a lookup table. There are two requirements for such functions. First, these functions should be pure. Pure functions do not have side effects and their output is only dependent on their inputs. To meet these constraints, pure functions should not:

- read or write any global or static mutable state.
- call an impure function.
- perform I/O.

In addition to being pure, these functions should not access global memory during execution, and their outputs should not be dependent on the thread ID. Therefore, Paraprox looks for functions which do not contain global/shared memory accesses, atomic operations, computations involving thread or block IDs, or calls to impure functions. If a function meets all these conditions, Paraprox marks it as a candidate for approximate memoization.

It should be noted that although Paraprox works at a function granularity, it is possible to find pure sections of code within a function. Detection of such map or scatter/gather sections within a function is left for future research.

As Paraprox will replace computation with memory accesses, this optimization should only be applied to computationally intensive map and scatter/gather patterns in order to achieve high performance improvements. To determine which functions to optimize, Paraprox computes the sum of the latencies of each instruction in the function as a metric to estimate the function's computation cycles as follows:

$$cycles\_needed = \sum_{inst \in f} latency(inst) \quad (1)$$

Instruction latency values are passed to Paraprox in a table based on the target architecture. Paraprox uses this latency table to compute the $cycles\_needed$ for all map and scatter/gather functions found in the program. For GPUs, we used microbenchmarks from Wong et al. [35] to measure the $latency$ of all instructions. We found that if a function's $cycles\_needed$ is at least one order of magnitude greater than the L1 read latency, it can benefit from this approximation. Therefore, Paraprox only applies the approximation on such functions.

### 3.1.3 Implementation:

Approximate memoization is accomplished in three steps: quantizing the inputs, joining these bit representations of inputs together to create an address, and accessing a lookup table using that address to get the final result. Figure 3(a) shows the dataflow in the BlackScholesBody function of the *BlackScholes* benchmark. This function meets all the candidacy conditions described in Section 3.1.2. Figure 3(b) shows the approximate version of the same function.

Paraprox quantizes the function's inputs to generate an address into the lookup table. For a quantized input $i$, Paraprox can control the output quality of the approximate function by altering the number of bits ($q_i$) used to represent that input. If a pattern has multiple input variables, e.g. $i$ and $i+1$, each input has its own quantization bits ($q_i$ and $q_{i+1}$). When concatenated together, these quantization bits form the address into the lookup table. The table's size is thus equal to $2^Q$, where $Q = \sum_{i=0}^{n} q_i$ for all $n$ inputs.

Using fewer bits reduces the number of quantization levels ($2^{q_i}$) that represent an input value, thus limiting the input's accuracy. Conversely, increasing the number of bits will permit more quantization levels, which will increase the accuracy of the input representation. If the pattern's output is very sensitive to small changes in the input and there are not enough bits allocated to adequately represent this, Paraprox detects that the output quality is deteriorating and increases $q_i$. On the other hand, if the output is not very sensitive to changes in the input or the input's dynamic range is very small, Paraprox can reduce $q_i$.

***Bit tuning:*** The process of determining $q_i$ for inputs is called *bit tuning* and is performed offline. For each input argument to the function, Paraprox computes the range of the function's output by applying training data to the function and storing the results in memory. If an input at runtime is not within this precomputed range, it will map to the nearest value present in the lookup table.

If a function has multiple inputs, naively dividing the quantization bits equally amongst all inputs does not necessarily yield ideal results, so Paraprox can unevenly divide the bits of the quantized input to favor some inputs over others. For example, in Figure 3, the BlackScholesBody function has five inputs, two of which ($R$ and $V$) are always constant during profiling. When Paraprox detects this, it chooses to allot all quantized bits to represent the other three variable inputs.

Our experiments show that the overall speedup of this optimization is dependent on the size of the lookup table but not the number of bits in $q_i$ assigned to each input. However, the quantization bits still need to be distributed carefully amongst inputs to guarantee satisfactory output quality.

To reduce output quality loss for a given lookup table size, bit tuning uses a tree algorithm. Each node in the tree corresponds to an approximate kernel with a specific $q_i$ bits per input. The root node divides bits equally between the inputs. Figure 4 shows the tree for the example shown in Figure 3(b). In this example, the lookup table size is 32768, which implies that the address into the table is 15 bits wide. The root of the tree shows that this address initially is evenly

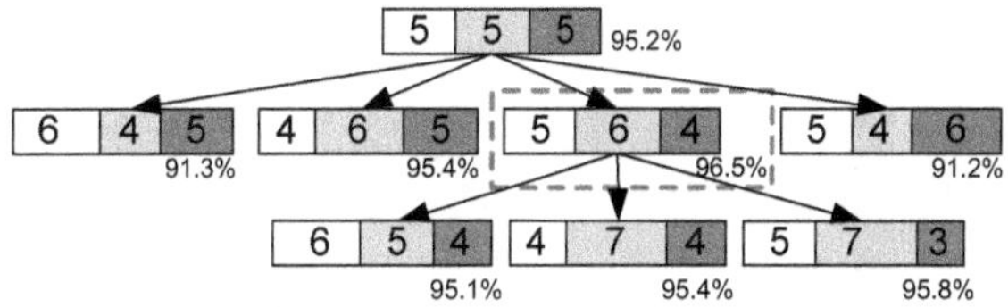


**Figure 4:** An example of how Paraprox's bit tuning finds the number of bits assigned to each input for the BlackScholesBody function. The lookup table has 32768 entries and its address is 15 bits wide. The output quality is printed beside each node. Bit tuning's final selection is outlined with a dotted box.

split into five bits each for the three variable inputs. Each child node is different from its parent such that one bit is reassigned from one input to an adjacent input.

The bit tuning process starts from the root and uses a steepest ascent hill climbing algorithm to reach a node with the highest output quality. Paraprox checks all the children of each node and selects the one with the best output quality. This process will continue until it finds a node for which all of its children have lower output quality than itself. In the example shown in Figure 4, Paraprox starts from node ($q_1 = 5$, $q_2 = 5$, $q_3 = 5$) and checks all its children. Among them, node (5,6,4) has the best output quality. Since all children of node (5,6,4) have a lower output quality than itself, node (5,6,4) is selected, and Paraprox assigns 5, 6, and 4 quantization bits to the first, second, and third inputs, respectively. Paraprox uses this process to find a configuration that returns the highest output quality for the specified lookup table size.

As bit tuning aims to control quality loss, it needs to determine how much error is introduced for each bit configuration it considers. To do so, bit tuning first quantizes the inputs using the division of bits specified by the current tree node under inspection. It then calculates the results of the exact and approximate functions and compares the two to compute a percent difference. Figure 4 shows these quality metrics for the BlackScholesBody example. It should be noted that bit tuning does not need to use an actual lookup table as it computes the approximate result that it is currently investigating.

To determine the size of the lookup table, Paraprox starts with a default size of 2048. For each lookup table size, Paraprox performs bit tuning to find the output quality. If the quality is better than the $TOQ$, Paraprox decreases the size of lookup table to see if it can further improve performance. If the quality is worse than the $TOQ$, Paraprox doubles the lookup table's size, as larger tables improve accuracy. This process stops when Paraprox finds the smallest table size that has an output quality that satisfies the $TOQ$.

After computing the size of the lookup table and assigning quantization bits for each input, Paraprox populates the lookup table. For each quantization level of each input, Paraprox computes the output and stores it in the lookup table. After filling the lookup table, Paraprox passes the approxi-

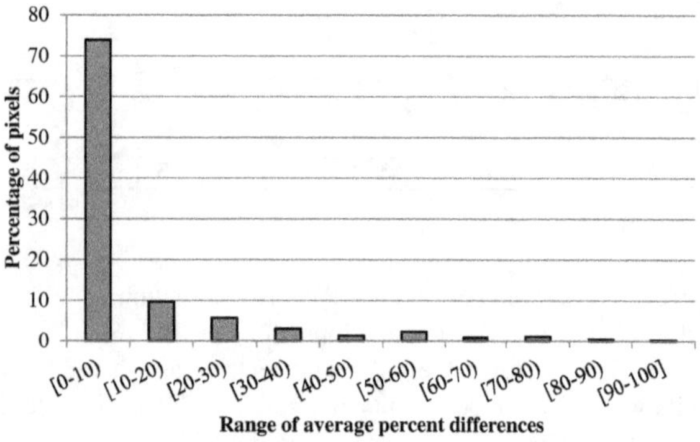


**Figure 5:** The average percent differences between adjacent pixels in ten images. More than 75% of pixels are less than 10% different from their neighbors.

mate kernel a pointer to the lookup table. The lookup table can be allocated in the global memory, or if a target has fast access memories, like the constant cache or shared memory in GPUs, those can be utilized instead of the global memory. Section 4.4.2 investigates these different options and compares their impacts on performance. Should the output quality change during runtime, Paraprox can accelerate the process of switching between different sized lookup tables by storing multiple tables in memory and changing the pointer passed to the kernel at runtime to reflect this decision. Paraprox can generate as many tables as it can fit in memory. However, in our experiments we found that no more than three tables are needed for our benchmarks.

#### 3.1.4 Tuning Parameter:

To tune the output quality and performance, Paraprox allows the runtime to select amongst lookup tables of different sizes.

### 3.2 Stencil & Partition

#### 3.2.1 Idea:

The stencil and partition approximation algorithm is based on the assumption that adjacent elements in the input array usually are similar in value. This is often the case for domains such as image and video processing, where neighboring pixels tend to be similar if not the same. To evaluate this assumption, Figure 5 shows the average percent difference of each pixel with its eight neighbors, which constitute a tile, for all pixels in 10 different images. As the figure shows, on average, more than 70% of the each image's pixels have less than 10% difference from their neighbors. Therefore, most of the neighbors of each pixel have similar values.

Under this assumption, rather than access all neighbors within a tile, Paraprox accesses only a subset of them and assumes the rest of the neighbors have the same value.

#### 3.2.2 Detection:

To detect stencil/partition patterns, Paraprox checks the load accesses to the arrays and looks for a constant number of affine accesses to the same array, indicating a tile size. These accesses can be found in loops with a constant loop trip or in manually unrolled loops. After finding these accesses, Paraprox computes the tile's size and dimensionality. Paraprox detects stencil/partition patterns based on the array access indices $((f + i) * w + g + j)$. Parameters $f$, $g$, and $w$ are the same (loop invariant) for all accesses that are examined. Parameters $i$ and $j$ can be hand-coded constants or loop induction variables. The size of a tile can be determined by looking at the dynamic range of $i$ and $j$.

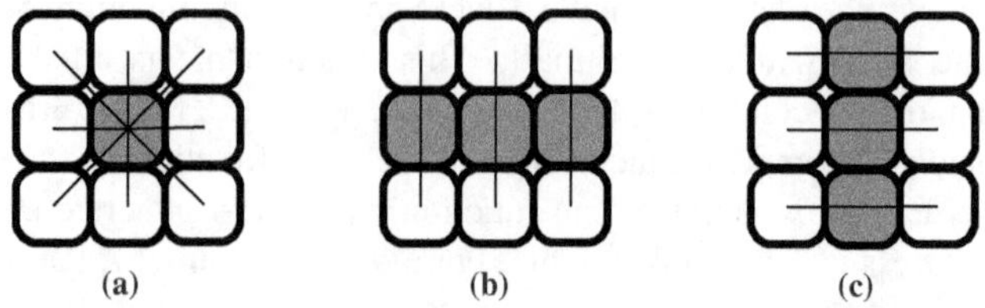


**Figure 6:** The three different schemes Paraprox uses to approximate the stencil pattern. (a) illustrates how the value at the center of the tile approximates all neighboring values. (b) and (c) depict how one row/column's values approximate the other rows/columns in the tile.

#### 3.2.3 Implementation:

To approximate stencil/partition patterns, Paraprox uses three different approximation schemes: center, row, and column based. For each approximation, a *reaching distance* parameter controls the number of memory elements that Paraprox accesses. In the center based approach, the element at the center of a tile is accessed and Paraprox assumes that all its neighbors have the same value. When Paraprox accesses an element, its neighbors, whose distances from the accessed element are less than the reaching distance, will not be accessed as shown in Figure 6(a).

Figures 6(b) and 6(c) illustrate the row and column based approximation schemes. In these schemes, one row/column within a tile is accessed, and all other rows/columns within a reaching distance from it are assumed to be the same and are left unaccessed.

#### 3.2.4 Tuning Parameter:

To control performance and output quality, Paraprox allows a runtime to select from various approximate kernels and tune each kernel's reaching distance.

### 3.3 Reduction

#### 3.3.1 Idea:

To approximate reduction patterns, Paraprox aims to predict the final result by computing the reduction of a subset of the input data in a way similar to loop perforation [2]. Figure 7 illustrates how this concept is applied. The assumption here is that the data is distributed uniformly, so a subset of the

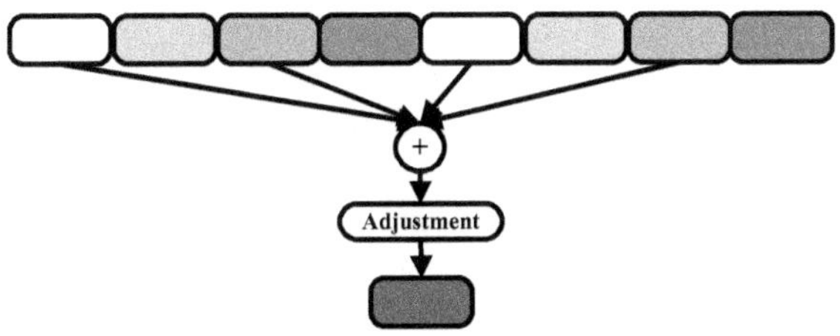


**Figure 7:** An illustration of how Paraprox approximates the reduction pattern. Instead of accessing all input elements, Paraprox accesses a subset of the input array and adds adjustment code to improve the accuracy.

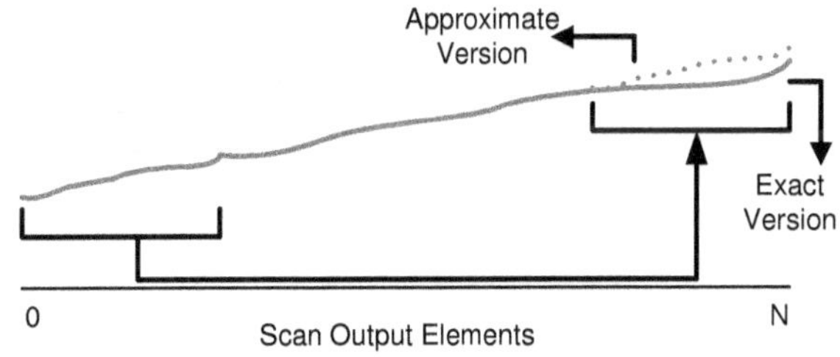


**Figure 8:** An example of how Paraprox uses the first elements of the scan results to approximate the end of the output array.

data can provide a good representation of the entire array. For example, instead of finding the minimum of the original array, Paraprox finds the minimum within one half of the array and returns it as the approximate result. If the data in both subarrays have similar distributions, the minimum of these subarrays will be close to each other and approximation error will be negligible.

Some reduction operations like addition need some adjustment to produce more accurate results. For example, after computing the sum of half of an array, if the result is doubled it more closely resembles the results of summing the entire array, thus the output quality is improved. In this case of addition, Paraprox assumes that the other half of the array has the exact same sum as the first half, so it doubles the approximated reduction result.

### 3.3.2 Detection:

Reduction recognition has been studied extensively by previous works [26, 36]. To detect reduction patterns, Paraprox searches for accumulative instructions that perform an operation like $a = a + b$, where $a$ is called the reduction variable and addition is the reduction operation. Reduction loops have the following two characteristics: *a)* they contain an accumulative instruction; and *b)* the reduction variable is neither read nor modified by any other instruction inside the loop.

In order to parallelize a reduction loop for a data parallel architecture, tree-based reduction implementations are often used. These reductions have three phases. In the first phase (Phase I), each thread performs a reduction on a chunk of input data. In the next phase (Phase II), each block accumulates the data generated by its threads and writes this result to the global memory. The final phase (Phase III) then accumulates the results of all the blocks to produce the final results. All of the phases contain a reduction loop that Paraprox optimizes, creating approximate kernels for each loop. The runtime determines which approximate version to execute.

Atomic operations can also be used to write data parallel reductions. An atomic function performs a read-modify-write atomic operation on one element residing in global or shared memory. For example, CUDA's *atomicInc()* and OpenCL's *atomic_inc()* both read a 32-bit word at some address in the global or shared memory, increment it, and write the result back to the same address [13, 19]. Among atomic operations, the atomic add, min, max, inc, and, or, and xor operations can be used in a reduction loop. Paraprox searches for and marks loops containing these operations as reduction loops.

### 3.3.3 Implementation:

After detecting a reduction loop, Paraprox modifies the loop step size to skip iterations of the loop. In order to execute every $N^{th}$ iteration and skip the other $N - 1$ iterations, Paraprox multiplies the loop step by $N$. We call $N$ the *skipping rate*. For example, if Paraprox multiplies the loop step size by four, only a quarter of the original iterations are executed and the rest are skipped.

If the reduction operation is addition, Paraprox inserts adjustment code after the loop. This code multiplies the result by the skipping rate. To make the adjustment more accurate, the reduction variable's initial value should be equal to zero before the reduction loop. Otherwise, by multiplying the result, the initial value is multiplied as well which produces an unacceptable output quality. In order to address this, Paraprox replaces the loop's reduction variable with a temporary variable set to zero just before the loop's entrance. After adjustment, Paraprox then adds the scaled temporary variable back to the original reduction variable to produce the final result.

### 3.3.4 Tuning Parameter:

Paraprox allows a runtime to change the skipping rate in order to tune the speedup and accuracy of the kernels.

## 3.4 Scan

### 3.4.1 Idea:

To approximate scan patterns, Paraprox assumes that differences between elements in the input array are similar to those in other partitions of the same input array. Parallel implementations of scan patterns break the input array into subarrays and computes the scan result for each of them. In order to approximate, Paraprox only applies the scan to a sub-

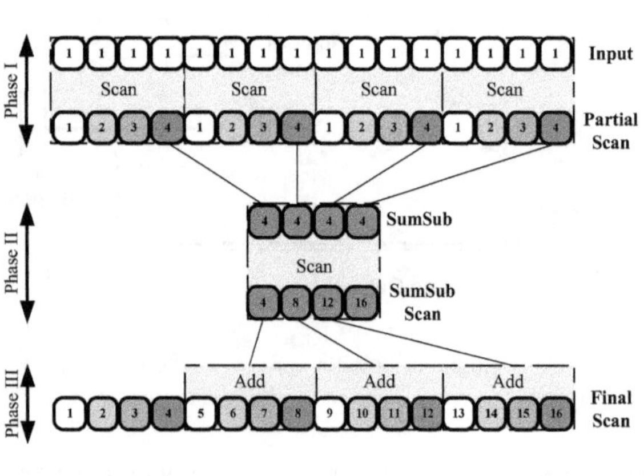


**Figure 9:** A data parallel implementation of the scan pattern has three phases. Phase I scans each subarray. Phase II scans the sum of all subarrays. Phase III then adds the result of Phase II to each corresponding subarray in the partial scan to generate the final result. This figure depicts how the scan is computed for an input array of all ones.

set of these subarrays and uses its results for the rest of the subarrays.

As the $N^{th}$ element of the scan result is the sum of the first $N$ elements of its input array, any change to the $N^{th}$ element modifies the $N^{th}$ output element and all elements afterwards. Therefore, if Paraprox applies approximation to one of the early input elements, any approximation error will propagate to the results for all the following elements, resulting in an unacceptable output quality. This effect is studied in Section 4.4.3.

In order to avoid this cascading error, rather than uniformly skipping loop iterations, Paraprox predicts the last elements of the scan results by examining the first output elements. Figure 8 presents an example of how Paraprox copies the first elements of the result to the end of the array to approximate the last elements.

#### 3.4.2 Detection:

The data parallel implementation of the scan pattern is traditionally composed of three phases as illustrated in Figure 9. As an example, this figure shows how these phases compute the scan results for an input array containing all ones. In the first phase, the input is divided into many subarrays and each block of threads performs a scan on one subarray and stores results in a partial scan array. The sum of each subarray is also written to another array called *sumSub*. The second phase then runs a scan on the *sumSub* array. The $i^{th}$ element of *sumSub*'s scan result is equal to the sum of elements in subarrays 0 to $i$. In the third phase, every $i^{th}$ element of *sumSub*'s scan result is added to the scan results of the $i+1$ partial scan subarray to produce the final scan results.

Because of its complicated implementation, detecting a scan pattern is generally difficult. A programmer can mark scan patterns for the compiler using pragmas, or the compiler can use template matching to find scan kernels used in benchmarks [20]. Paraprox uses the second approach by performing a recursive post order traversal of the abstract syntax tree of the kernel and comparing it with the template. If they match, Paraprox assumes that the kernel contains a scan pattern.

#### 3.4.3 Implementation:

The first phase of the scan pattern takes the longest time to execute, so approximation techniques should target this phase. As mentioned before, Paraprox approximates the results for the last subarrays to prevent the propagation of error through all of the results. In this approximation, Paraprox assumes that last subarrays have similar scan results to the first subarrays. Therefore, instead of computing scan results for all subarrays, Paraprox *skips* some and uses the first multiple subarrays' scan results in place of the scan results for the skipped subarrays.

In order to skip the last $N$ subarrays, Paraprox skips some of the computations in Phases I and II. In Phase I, Paraprox launches fewer blocks to skip the last $N$ subarrays. In Phase II, Paraprox changes the argument containing the number of subarrays that is passed to the kernel.

In Phase III, threads that are responsible for adding to generate the first $N$ subarrays add their scan results to the last element of Phase II's results (the *sumSub* scan array) and write these results as the scan's output for the last skipped subarrays. Figure 8 shows how these threads copy an early portion of the results to generate the result's last elements.

#### 3.4.4 Tuning Parameter:

A runtime can control the number of subarrays Paraprox skips in order to tune output quality and performance.

## 4. Experimental Evaluation

### 4.1 Methodology

The Paraprox compilation phases are implemented in the Clang compiler version 3.3. Paraprox's output codes are then compiled into GPU binaries using the NVIDIA nvcc compiler release 5.0. GCC 4.6.3 is used to generate the x86 and OpenCL binaries for execution on the host processor. To run OpenCL code on the CPU, we used the Intel OpenCL driver. We evaluated Paraprox using a system with an Intel Core i7 965 CPU and a NVIDIA GTX 560 GPU with 2GB GDDR5 global memory. We selected 13 applications from various domains and different patterns as benchmarks. We ran each application 110 times with different input sets. We ran the first 10 executions to train and detect the best kernel, and then we measured and averaged the runtimes of the next 100 executions. A summary of each application's characteristics is shown in Table 1.

***Compilation flow in Paraprox:*** This section describes Paraprox's compilation flow as illustrated in Figure 10. First,

| Applications | Domain | Input Size | Patterns | Error Metric |
|---|---|---|---|---|
| **BlackScholes [20]** | Financial | 4M elements | Map | L1-norm |
| **Quasirandom Generator [20]** | Statistics | 1M elements | Map | L1-norm |
| **Gamma Correction** | Image Processing | 2048x2048 image | Map | Mean relative error |
| **BoxMuller [20]** | Statistics | 24M elements | Scatter/Gather | L1-norm |
| **HotSpot [9]** | Physics | 1024x1024 matrix | Stencil-Partition | Mean relative error |
| **Convolution Separable [20]** | Image Processing | 2048x2048 image | Stencil-Reduction | L2-norm |
| **Gaussian Filter** | Image Processing | 512x512 image | Stencil | Mean relative error |
| **Mean Filter** | Image Processing | 512x512 image | Stencil | Mean relative error |
| **Matrix Multiply [20]** | Signal Processing | 2560x2560 matrix | Reduction-Partition | Mean relative error |
| **Image Denoising [20]** | Image Processing | 2048x2048 image | Reduction | Mean relative error |
| **Naive Bayes [32]** | Machine Learning | 256K elements with 32 features | Reduction | Mean relative error |
| **Kernel Density Estimation [16]** | Machine Learning | 256K elements with 32 features | Reduction | Mean relative error |
| **Cumulative Frequency Histograms** | Signal Processing | 1M elements | Scan | Mean relative error |

**Table 1:** Details of applications used in this study.

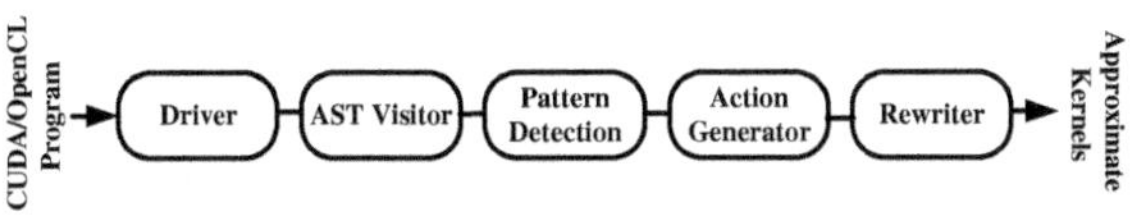


**Figure 10:** Paraprox's compilation flow.

Clang's *driver* generates the abstract syntax tree (AST) of the input code and sends it to the AST visitor. The *AST visitor* traverses the AST and runs the *pattern detector* on each kernel. The *pattern detector* identifies the parallel patterns within each kernel, and informs the action generator which kernels contain what patterns. The *action generator* then creates a list of actions for each approximate kernel, where an action represents a modification to the output CUDA code for each optimization applied. These actions include: adding, deleting, and substituting an expression in the final code. For each list of actions, the *rewriter* copies the input kernel and applies all actions on the copied version and generates the approximate kernel. To evaluate the impact of Paraprox's optimizations on the CPU, we created a CUDA-to-OpenCL script that converts Paraprox's generated CUDA code to an equivalent OpenCL version.

## 4.2 Results

In this section, we analyze how Paraprox's optimizations affect the execution time and accuracy of different applications. Figure 11 presents the results for the benchmarks run separately on a CPU and a GPU. The speedup is relative the exact execution of each program on the same architectures. As seen in the figure, Paraprox achieves an average speedup of ~2.5x for approximated code run on either the CPU or GPU with a target output quality of 90%.

***Output Quality:*** To assess the quality of each application's output, we used application-specific evaluation metrics as listed in Table 1. For benchmarks that already contained a specific evaluation metric, the included metric was used. Otherwise, we used the mean relative error as an evaluation metric. For all benchmarks, we compare the output of the unmodified, exact application to the output of the approximate kernel created by Paraprox.

A case study by Misailovic et al. [18] shows that users will tolerate quality loss in applications such as video decoding provided it does not exceed ~10%. Similar works [5, 12, 27, 28] cap quality losses for their benchmarks at around 10%. SAGE [27] verified this threshold using the experiments in the LIVE image quality assessment study [31]. Images in LIVE's database have different levels of distortion and were evaluated by 24 human subjects, who classified the quality of the images using a scale equally divided amongst the following ratings: "Bad," "Poor," "Fair," "Good," and "Excellent." SAGE [27] showed that more than 86% of images with quality loss less than 10% were evaluated as "Good" or "Excellent" by human subjects in the LIVE study. Therefore, we used 90% as the minimum target output quality ($TOQ$) in our experiments.

## 4.3 Performance Improvement

Paraprox applied map approximation to the *BlackScholes*, *Quasirandom Generator*, *Gamma Correction*, and *BoxMuller* benchmarks. For *BlackScholes*, Paraprox detects two map functions: *Cnd()* and *BlackScholesBody()*. Since the estimated cycle count for Cnd() is low, Paraprox only applies the optimization on BlackScholesBody() which has a high estimated cycle count. As a result, *BlackScholes* achieves ~60% improvement in performance with <10% loss in output quality. *BoxMuller* has a scatter/gather functionwith two inputs and two outputs. *Gamma Correction* is very resilient to quality losses caused by approximation, as its output quality remains at 99% while it achieves >3x speedup on the GPU. When reducing the lookup table size, however, its output quality drops suddenly to <90%. *BlackScholes* and *Quasirandom Generator* get better results on the CPU but *Gamma Correction* and *BoxMuller* perform better on the GPU. The reason is that for benchmarks that can retain good output quality with smaller lookup tables, the GPU achieves better performance. However, as the size of lookup table increases, the number of cache misses increases. In such cases,

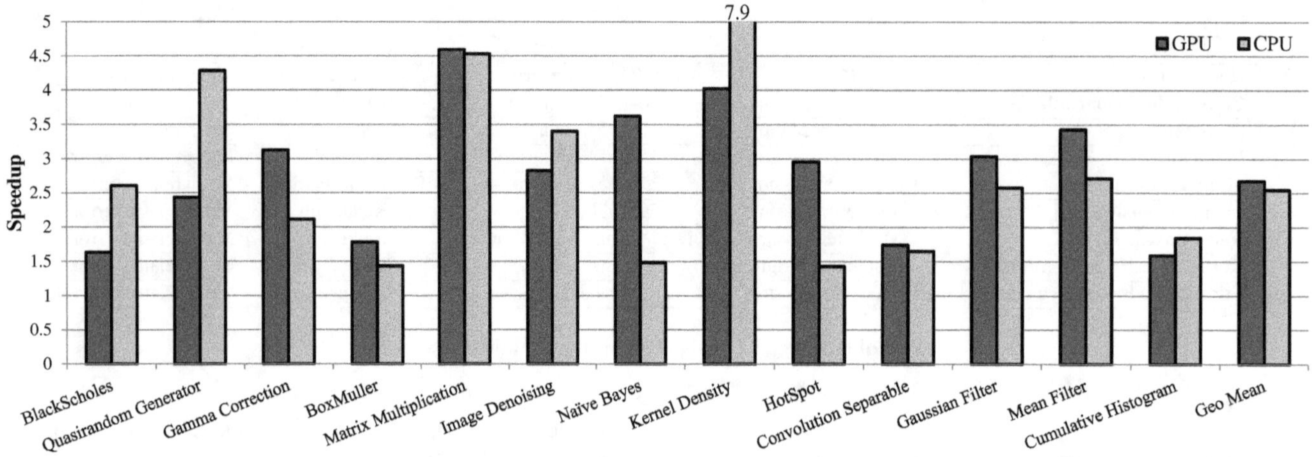


**Figure 11:** The performance of all applications approximated by Paraprox for both CPU and GPU code. The baseline is the exact execution of each application on the same architecture. In these experiments, the target output quality ($TOQ$) is 90%.

execution on a CPU is preferable to that on a GPU as cache misses have a lower impact on the performance for CPUs.

The reduction approximation is applied to the *Matrix Multiplication*, *Naive Bayes trainer*, *Image Denoising*, and *Kernel Density Estimation* applications. *Matrix Multiplication* and *Image Denoising* show similar performance on both the CPU and GPU. On the other hand, *Naive Bayes* achieves better speedup on the GPU. The approximated *Naive Bayes* performs very well on a GPU (>3.5x vs ~1.5x on a CPU) since this benchmark uses atomic operations, which are more expensive for GPU architectures with many threads running concurrently. By skipping a subset of atomic operations, great speedups in execution time are achieved on a GPU. Since the main component of *Kernel Density Estimation* is an exponential instruction and there is hardware support for such transcendental operations on a GPU (i.e. the special function unit on a CUDA device), skipping these operations provides better performance improvements for CPUs than it does for GPUs.

The *HotSpot*, *Convolution Separable*, *Gaussian filter*, and *Mean Filter* applications contain stencil patterns. *HotSpot*, *Gaussian filter*, and *Mean filter* use 3x3 tiles and *Convolution Separable* has two stencil loops with 1x17 tiles. Since the loop in *Mean Filter* is unrolled manually by the programmer and memory accesses are kept outside the function while computations are inside, there is no reduction loop and the reduction optimization is not applied. Paraprox just applies the stencil optimization on this application. On the other hand, *Convolution Separable* has both stencil and reduction patterns. Paraprox applies both optimizations on this application. The stencil optimization returns a 1.7x performance speedup while maintaining 90% output quality while the reduction optimization results in a 1.6x speedup. On the other hand, the reduction optimization's performance is better than stencil optimization for CPU. Therefore, when targeting a GPU Paraprox only used the results of the stencil optimization in its final kernel, and when targeting a CPU it used the reduction optimization. Because the partition and stencil optimizations primarily optimize memory accesses, speedups are greater for GPU approximated code as memory accesses are more costly on this platform.

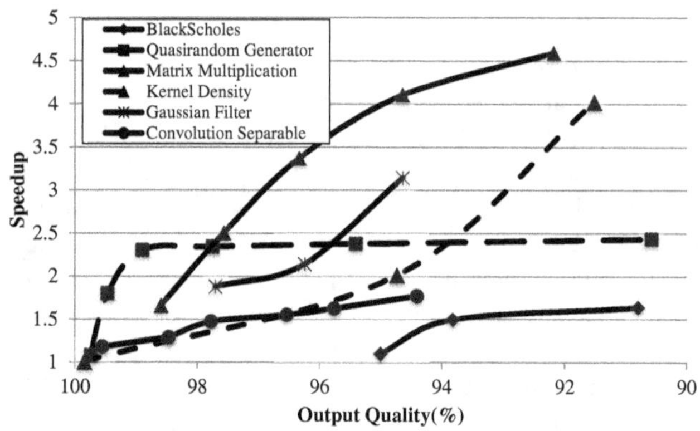


**Figure 12:** Controlling the speedup and output quality by varying an optimization's tuning parameters for six benchmarks.

The *Cumulative Histogram* benchmark contains a scan pattern. This application is another resilient application — even when skipping half of the subarrays, the output quality stays at ~99%. For this pattern, the speedup is similar for both CPU and GPU approximated kernels.

***Performance-Quality Tradeoffs:*** Figure 12 illustrates how Paraprox manages the performance-accuracy tradeoff for six benchmarks. The map approximated *BlackScholes* starts with 95% output quality and performance similar to the exact version, but as the size of the lookup table decreases, the speedup increases to 1.6x speedup with only ~4% more loss

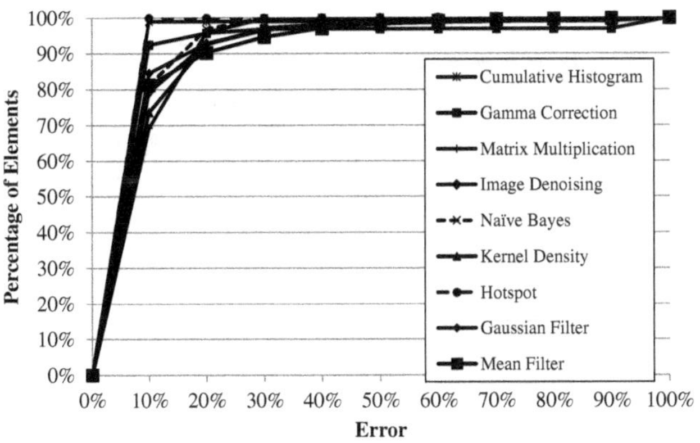


**Figure 13:** The CDF of final error for each element of an application's output with the $TOQ = 90\%$. The majority of output elements (>70%) have <10% error.

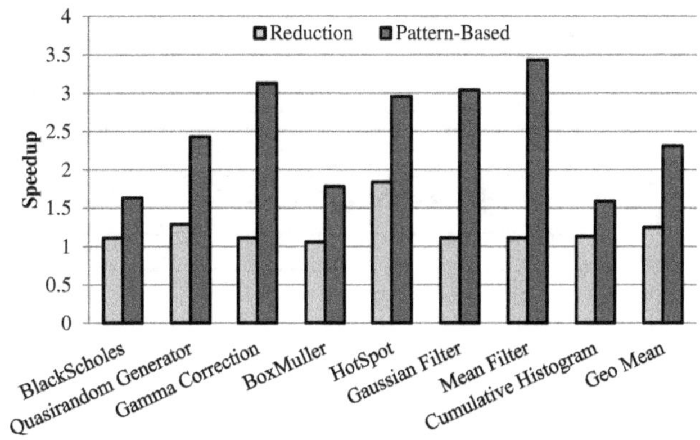


**Figure 14:** A performance comparison of the reduction optimization vs. specific pattern-based optimizations on benchmarks that do not contain a reduction pattern. In these experiments, the code targets a GPU, and the $TOQ = 90\%$.

in quality. Similar behavior is observed for the *Quasirandom Generator*. When the table size is small enough to fit in the cache, the speedup gains begin to saturate for these map optimized kernels. Both *Matrix Multiplication* and *Kernel Density Estimation* contain reduction patterns. As Paraprox doubles the skipping rate for these kernels, the difference between two consecutive nodes grows, thus causing both the speedup and quality loss to grow. The performance of *Gaussian Filter* and *Convolution Separable* rises as output quality degrades. For *Convolution Separable*, Paraprox changes the reaching distances of both loops in the kernel to control the output quality. Since *Gaussian Filter* applies a 2D filter to an image, Paraprox uses row, column, and center stencil patterns to control the output quality. For this benchmark, Paraprox gets >2x speedup with <4% quality loss.

***Error Distribution:*** To study each application's quality losses in more detail, Figure 13 shows the cumulative distribution function (CDF) of the error for each element of the application's output with the $TOQ = 90\%$. The CDF illustrates the distribution of output errors amongst an application's output elements. The figure shows that only a modest number of output elements see large output error. The majority (70%-100%) of each approximated application's output elements have an error of <10%.

## 4.4 Case Studies

### 4.4.1 Specialized Optimizations Achieve Better Results:

To show that one optimization does not work well when generally applied, we apply only the reduction optimization to benchmarks that do not contain such a pattern. We chose this optimization as it is most similar to a well-known approximation technique, loop perforation [2], where loop iterations are skipped to accelerate execution. Figure 14 compares the reduction optimization's performance with Paraprox's results on a GPU with the $TOQ = 90\%$. For benchmarks containing map and stencil patterns, skipping iterations results in unmodified output elements. Therefore, the output quality rapidly decreases, severely limiting the speedup. For benchmarks with scan patterns, the cascading error will reduce the output quality and speedup is similarly limited. On average, the reduction optimization alone achieves only ~25% speedup, compared to the 2.3x speedup that Paraprox achieves by matching patterns to specialized optimizations.

### 4.4.2 Design Considerations for the Map Optimization:

To fully investigate the impact of map approximation on both accuracy and performance, we used four common computationally intensive map functions from different domains:

- **Credit card balance equation [1]:** This equation finds the number of months it will take to pay off credit card debt.

$$N(i) = \frac{-1}{30}\frac{ln(1+\frac{b_0}{p}(1-(1+i)^{30}))}{ln(1+i)} \quad (2)$$

- **Shifted Gompertz distribution [21]:** This equation gives the distribution of the largest of two random variables.

$$F(x) = (1-e^{-bx})e^{-\eta e^{-bx}} \quad (3)$$

- **Log gamma [6]:** This equation calculates the logarithm of the gamma function. To implement this equation, we used the CUDA *lgammaf* [19] function.

$$LG(z) = log(\Gamma(z)) \quad (4)$$

- **Bass diffusion model [7]:** This equation describes how new products get adopted as an interaction between users

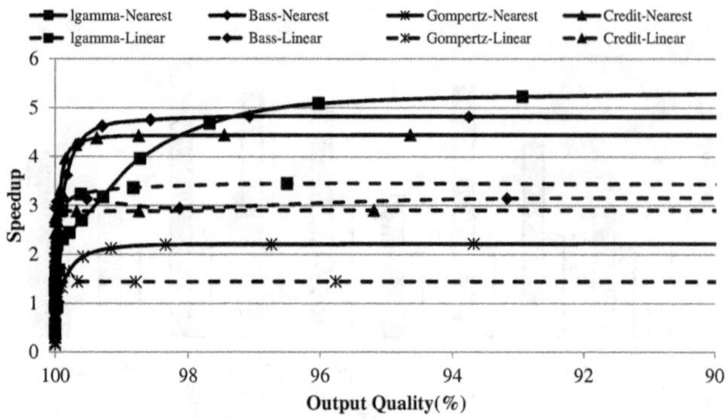


**Figure 15:** The impact of approximate memoization on four functions on a GPU. Two schemes are used to handle inputs that do not map to precomputed outputs: *nearest* and *linear*. *Nearest* chooses the nearest value in the lookup table to approximate the output. *Linear* uses linear approximation between the two nearest values in the table. For all four functions, *nearest* provides better speedups than *linear* at the cost of greater quality loss.

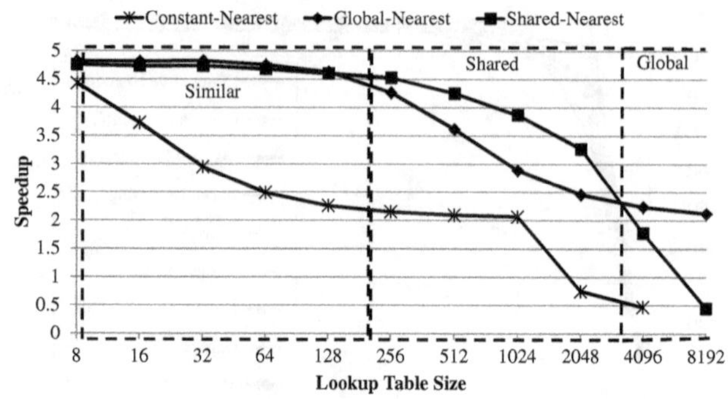


**Figure 16:** A comparison of the performance of approximate memoization when the lookup table is allocated in the constant, shared, and global memories on a GPU.

and potential users.

$$S(t) \quad = \quad m\frac{(p+q)^2}{p}\frac{e^{-(p+q)t}}{(1+\frac{p}{q}e^{-(p+q)t})^2} \qquad (5)$$

For all of these equations, all parameters other than the input variable are constant.

***Selecting an Output for an Unrepresented Input:*** As discussed in Section 3.1.3, there are a limited number of quantization levels based on the size of the lookup table. It is possible that there are inputs that do not directly map to a precomputed output. In such cases, Paraprox can either select the *nearest* precomputed output, or it can apply *linear* approximation to the two nearest values in the table to generate a result in between these values. Figure 15 shows the performance-quality curve for all four equations using the *nearest* and *linear* methods on the GPU. For all four equations, *nearest* gives better performance compared to *linear* but with lower output quality. Even though the same lookup table size is used, *linear* generates more accurate output, but the overhead of adding another memory access and more computation is overwhelming. On the other hand, *linear* is better at achieving higher output quality (~99%). In this experiment, the lookup table is allocated in the GPU's global memory.

As seen in Figure 15, the shifted Gompertz distribution achieves a lower speedup than the other functions. This is due to it having many low latency instructions. Both the Bass and Credit equations execute floating point divisions, which translate to subroutine calls to code with high latency and low throughput for GPUs [35]. On the other hand, the Gompertz equation uses several exponential instructions, which are not high latency as they are handled by a special functional unit on a GPU [19].

***Location of the Lookup Table:*** To find which memory location is best for storing lookup tables, we created approximate versions of the Bass function that used the constant, shared, and global memories of the GPU to store the lookup table. Figure 16 shows the performance versus the table size for these three versions of Bass on the GPU. For lookup tables stored in global and constant memory, we set the L1 cache size to 32KB and size of the shared memory to 16KB. When the lookup table is stored in shared memory, we set the size of the shared memory to 32KB and the L1 cache to 16KB.

Using constant memory never gives optimal results regardless of the cache size. The reason is that for larger table sizes, using shared memory or the global L1 cache will have a lower read latency [35].

To compare global and shared memory, we divided the figure into three regions. When the cache size is small, both global and shared memory show similar speedups. Since it takes time to warm up the L1 cache for global memory, shared memory outperforms the global memory in the second region. In the third region, however, by increasing the size of the lookup table, the overhead of transferring data from global to shared memory is increased and the global memory outperforms the shared memory.

Based on these results, Paraprox generates both shared and global approximate kernels, and the runtime system will choose one based on the performance, output quality, and the lookup table size. If the lookup table is larger than the size of the shared memory, the lookup table must be stored in global memory.

***Lookup Table Size vs. Performance:*** Figure 16 shows that speedup drops when increasing the size of the lookup table. Using the CUDA profiler, we found that the number of uncoalesced memory accesses is primarily responsible for this. As the lookup table's size increases, the number of uncoalesced accesses also increases, thus resulting in lower speedups as shown in Figure 17. This figure shows that the number of instructions that get serialized increases as the

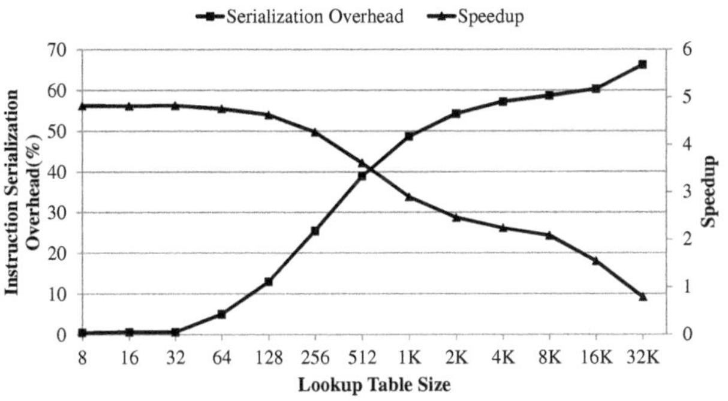


**Figure 17:** The impact of the lookup table size on the percentage of uncoalesced accesses on the GPU.

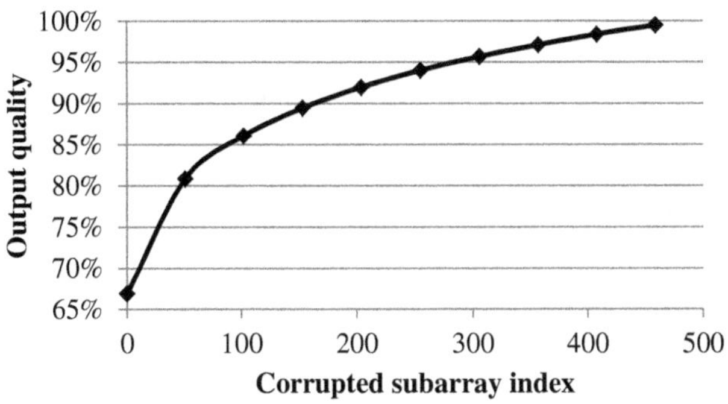


**Figure 18:** The impact of the starting point of the data corruption on an approximated scan pattern's final output.

size of the lookup table grows. This serialization is caused by more uncoalesced accesses.

### 4.4.3 Cascading Error in Scan Patterns:

Paraprox approximates the last subarrays of the results for scan patterns. To illustrate why this is done, we use the *Cumulative frequency histogram* benchmark with one million random input data points. For our first run, we "corrupt" the first input subarray (10% of the input elements) by setting its elements to zero. We then move this section of all zeroed data to the next subarray of elements, and rerun the scan. For each test modifying the first to the last input subarray, we record the output quality. Figure 18 shows the impact of the starting point of the data corruption on the final output result. When the first subarray of the input is zeroed, the overall output quality will be ~67%. This is caused by the error propagating through the rest of the results. However, if the error happens at the end of the input array, the output quality will be ~99%. Therefore, Paraprox only approximates the last elements of the final scan results to ensure a high output quality.

## 5. Limitations

Paraprox is a research prototype and it has some limitations. Below, we discuss some of these limitations which will be addressed in future work.

**Runtime System:** In this work, our main focus is automatically generating approximate kernels and providing tuning knobs for a runtime system. Paraprox generates approximate kernels, and a separate runtime system will decide which one to use and how tune the selected kernel's parameters. In our results, we did not consider runtime overhead. However, as shown in SAGE [27] and Green [5], it is not necessary to constantly monitor the quality, so checks are performed every $N^{th}$ invocation. Based on the experiments done in [27], checking the output quality every 40-50 invocations during runtime has less than 5% overhead. This would reduce our reported performance but only by a modest level.

**Pattern Recognition:** Since we used the AST to detect patterns, variations in code can make the pattern recognition process difficult, especially when detecting scan patterns. However, pattern recognition for other patterns like reduction or detecting pure functions for map and scatter-gather patterns are stable techniques which can detect patterns across a wide variety of implementations. It is also possible to enhance pattern detection by getting hints from the programmer or using higher level languages.

**Compiler Optimizations:** It is possible that approximation eliminates some other compiler optimization opportunities such as auto-vectorization. In these cases, an approximate kernel might not perform as well as expected. Fortunately, the runtime system chooses which approximate kernel to run based on their speedup and quality. Therefore, if the approximate kernel does show great performance improvement, the runtime system will choose the original kernel which is highly optimized.

**Safety of Optimizations:** It is possible that execution of approximate code causes raising exceptions or segmentation faults. There are compiler analyses that detect the possibility of crashing to prevent the compiler from applying the optimizations. For example, for a division that uses an approximated output and may raise a divide by zero exception, it is possible to instrument the code to skip this calculation where the approximated divisor is zero. However, improving the safety of approximation techniques is beyond the scope of this work and it is left for future study.

## 6. Related Work

Pattern-based programming is well-explained by McCool [15]. This book introduces various parallel patterns. Our focus is on the detection and approximation of data parallel patterns.

The concept of trading accuracy for improved performance or energy consumption is well-studied [2–5, 11, 12, 14, 17, 23, 25, 27, 28]. Previous approximation techniques can be categorized in three categories:

***Software-based:*** Using software approximation, SAGE's [27] framework accelerates programs on GPUs. SAGE's goal is to exploit the specific microarchitectural characteristics of the GPU to achieve higher performance. Although these optimization performs better than general methods, their applicability is limited compared to Paraprox's approximation methods. SAGE also has a runtime system which Paraprox can use to tune and calibrate the output quality during runtime.

Rinard et al. [23, 25] present a technique for automatically deriving probabilistic distortion and timing models that can be used to manage the performance-accuracy tradeoff space of a given application. Given a program that executes a set of tasks, these models characterize the effect of skipping task executions on the performance and accuracy. Agarwal et al. [2] use code perforation to improve performance and reduce energy consumption. They perform code perforation by discarding loop iterations. Paraprox uses a similar method for reduction patterns, but while loop perforation is applied only to sequential loops, Paraprox applies it to *all* loops in such patterns. Skipping iterations, however is not suitable for all data parallel patterns, so Paraprox only applies it to loops with reduction patterns. For example, by skipping iterations of a map loop, a subset of the output array will be left unmodified which results in an unacceptable output quality. A variation of approximate memoization is utilized in a work by Chadhuri [8] for sequential loops. Our approach is different in that it is designed for data parallel applications and it detects when to apply memoization to achieve performance improvement. Previous work by Sartori et. al. [30] targets control divergence on the GPU. Rinard et. al. [23] also proposes an optimization for parallel benchmarks that do not have balanced workloads. Misailovic et. al. [17] propose probabilistic guarantees for approximate applications using loop perforation. Relaxed synchronization is also used as an approximation method to improve performance [22, 24]. Although these approaches perform well for their target applications, their applicability is far more limited than tools that can identify and finely optimize kernels based on the varied data parallel patterns they may contain, which is one of Paraprox's key contributions.

***Programmer-based:*** Green [5] is a flexible framework that developers can use to take advantage of approximation opportunities to improve performance or energy efficiency. This framework requires the programmer to provide approximate kernels or annotate their code using C/C++ extensions. In contrast to these techniques, Paraprox automatically generates different approximate kernels for each application. Ansel et. al. [4] also propose language extensions to allow the programmer to mark parts of code as approximate. They use a genetic algorithm to select the best approximate version to run. Unlike these approaches, Paraprox chooses the approximation optimization based on the patterns detected in the input code and generates approximate versions automatically for each pattern without programmer annotation. Paraprox, however, can be utilized by the runtime systems introduced in these works to optimize performance.

***Hardware-based:*** EnerJ [28] uses type qualifiers to mark approximate variables. Using this type system, EnerJ automatically maps approximate variables to low power storage and uses low power operations to save energy. EnerJ also guarantees that the approximate part of a program cannot affect the precise portion of the program. Esmaeilzadeh et al. [11] demonstrated dual-voltage operation, with a high voltage for precise operations and a low voltage for approximate operations. Another work by Esmaeilzadeh [12] designs a neural processing unit (NPU) accelerator to accelerate approximate programs. Alvarez et al. [3, 14] introduced hardware-based fuzzy memoization and tolerant region reuse techniques for multimedia applications. Other works [33, 34] also designed different approximate accelerators. Sampson et. al. [29] show how to improve memory array lifetime using approximation. These approximate datatype optimizations and special accelerators require hardware support. Our approach, however, can be used by current architectures without hardware modification.

## 7. Conclusion

Approximate computing, where computation accuracy is traded for better performance or higher data throughput, provides an efficient mechanism for computation to keep up with the exponential growth of information. However, approximation can often be time consuming and tedious for programmers to implement, debug, and tune to achieve the desired results. This paper proposes a software-only framework called *Paraprox* that identifies common computation patterns found in data-parallel programs and uses a custom-designed approximation template to replace each pattern. Paraprox enables the programmer to write software once and run it on a variety of commodity processors, without manual tuning for different hardware targets, input sets, or desired levels of accuracy.

For 13 data-parallel applications, Paraprox yields an average of 2.7x and 2.5x speedup with less than 10% quality degradation compared to an accurate execution on a NVIDIA GTX 560 GPU and Intel Core i7 965 CPU, respectively. We also show that Paraprox is able to control the accuracy and performance by varying template configuration parameters at run-time. Our results show that pattern-specific optimizations yield nearly twice the performance improvement compared to naively applying a single, well-known approximation technique to all benchmarks.

## 8. Acknowledgement

Much gratitude goes to the anonymous referees who provided excellent feedback on this work. This research was supported by ARM Ltd. and the National Science Foundation under grants CNS-0964478 and CCF-0916689. We would like to thank Armin Alaghi and Gaurav Chadha for their comments.

## References


[1] The credit card equation, 2013. http://faculty.bennington.edu/~jzimba/CreditCardEquationDerivation.pdf.

[2] A. Agarwal, M. Rinard, S. Sidiroglou, S. Misailovic, and H. Hoffmann. Using code perforation to improve performance, reduce energy consumption, and respond to failures. Technical Report MIT-CSAIL-TR-2009-042, MIT, Mar. 2009.

[3] C. Álvarez, J. Corbal, and M. Valero. Fuzzy memoization for floating-point multimedia applications. *IEEE Transactions on Computers*, pages 922–927, 2005.

[4] J. Ansel, Y. L. Wong, C. Chan, M. Olszewski, A. Edelman, and S. Amarasinghe. Language and compiler support for autotuning variable-accuracy algorithms. In *Proc. of the 2011 International Symposium on Code Generation and Optimization*, pages 85 –96, 2011.

[5] W. Baek and T. M. Chilimbi. Green: a framework for supporting energy-conscious programming using controlled approximation. In *Proc. of the '10 Conference on Programming Language Design and Implementation*, pages 198–209, 2010.

[6] D. H. Bailey. *Experimental mathematics in action.* A.K. Peters, 2007.

[7] F. Bass. A new product growth for model consumer durables. *Management Science*, pages 215–227, 1969.

[8] S. Chaudhuri, S. Gulwani, R. L. Roberto, and S. Navidpour. Proving programs robust. In *Proc. of the 19th ACM SIGSOFT symposium and the 13th European conference on Foundations of software engineering*, pages 102–112, 2011.

[9] S. Che, M. Boyer, J. Meng, D. Tarjan, , J. W. Sheaffer, S.-H. Lee, and K. Skadron. Rodinia: A benchmark suite for heterogeneous computing. In *Proc. of the IEEE Symposium on Workload Characterization*, pages 44–54, 2009.

[10] EMC Corporation. Extracting value from chaos, 2011. www.emc.com /collateral/analyst-reports/idc-extracting-value-from-chaos-ar.pdf.

[11] H. Esmaeilzadeh, A. Sampson, L. Ceze, and D. Burger. Architecture support for disciplined approximate programming. In *17th International Conference on Architectural Support for Programming Languages and Operating Systems*, pages 301–312, 2012.

[12] H. Esmaeilzadeh, A. Sampson, L. Ceze, and D. Burger. Neural acceleration for general-purpose approximate programs. In *Proc. of the 45th Annual International Symposium on Microarchitecture*, pages 449–460, 2012.

[13] KHRONOS Group. OpenCL - the open standard for parallel programming of heterogeneous systems, 2013.

[14] C. A. Martinez, J. C. S. Adrian, and M. Cortes. Dynamic tolerance region computing for multimedia. *IEEE Transactions on Computers*, pages 650–665, 2012.

[15] M. McCool, J. Reinders, and A. Robison. *Structured Parallel Programming: Patterns for Efficient Computation.* Morgan Kaufmann, 2012.

[16] P. D. Michailidis and K. G. Margaritis. Accelerating kerne stimation on the GPU using the CUDA framework. *Journal of Applied Mathematical Science*, 7(30):1447–1476, 2013.

[17] S. Misailovic, D. M. Roy, and M. C. Rinard. Probabilistically accurate program transformations. In *Proc. of the 18th Static Analysis Symposium*, pages 316–333, 2011.

[18] S. Misailovic, S. Sidiroglou, H. Hoffmann, and M. Rinard. Quality of service profiling. In *Proc. of the 32nd ACM/IEEE conference on Software Engineering*, pages 25 –34, 2010.

[19] NVIDIA. *CUDA C Programming Guide*, Oct. 2012.

[20] NVIDIA. NVIDIA's next generation CUDA compute architecture: Kepler GK110, 2012. www.nvidia.com/content/PDF/NVIDIA_Kepler_GK110_Architecture_Whitepaper.pdf.

[21] K. Ohishi, H. Okamura, and T. Dohi. Gompertz software reliability model: Estimation algorithm and empirical validation. *Journal of Systems and Software*, pages 535 – 543, 2009.

[22] L. Renganarayana, V. Srinivasan, R. Nair, and D. Prener. Programming with relaxed synchronization. In *Proc. of the 2012 ACM Workshop on Relaxing Synchronization for Multicore and Manycore Scalability*, pages 41–50, 2012.

[23] M. Rinard. Probabilistic accuracy bounds for fault-tolerant computations that discard tasks. In *Proc. of the 2006 International Conference on Supercomputing*, pages 324–334, 2006.

[24] M. Rinard. Parallel synchronization-free approximate data structure construction. In *Proc. of the 5th USENIX Workshop on Hot Topics in Parallelism*, pages 1–8, 2013.

[25] M. C. Rinard. Using early phase termination to eliminate load imbalances at barrier synchronization points. In *Proc. of the 22nd annual ACM SIGPLAN conference on Object-Oriented Systems and applications*, pages 369–386, 2007.

[26] D. Roger, U. Assarsson, and N. Holzschuch. Efficient stream reduction on the GPU. In *Proc. of the 1st Workshop on General Purpose Processing on Graphics Processing Units*, pages 1–4, 2007.

[27] M. Samadi, J. Lee, D. A. Jamshidi, A. Hormati, and S. Mahlke. SAGE: Self-tuning approximation for graphics engines. In *Proc. of the 46th Annual International Symposium on Microarchitecture*, pages 13–24, 2013.

[28] A. Sampson, W. Dietl, E. Fortuna, D. Gnanapragasam, L. Ceze, and D. Grossman. EnerJ: approximate data types for safe and general low-power computation. *Proc. of the '11 Conference on Programming Language Design and Implementation*, 46(6):164–174, June 2011.

[29] A. Sampson, J. Nelson, K. Strauss, and L. Ceze. Approximate storage in solid-state memories. In *Proc. of the 46th Annual International Symposium on Microarchitecture*, pages 25–36, 2013.

[30] J. Sartori and R. Kumar. Branch and data herding: Reducing control and memory divergence for error-tolerant GPU applications. In *IEEE Transactions on on Multimedia*, pages 427–428, 2012.

[31] H. Sheikh, M. Sabir, and A. Bovik. A statistical evaluation of recent full reference image quality assessment algorithms. *IEEE Transactions on Image Processing*, 15(11):3440–3451, 2006.

[32] A. K. Sujeeth, H. Lee, K. J. Brown, H. Chafi, M. Wu, A. R. Atreya, K. Olukotun, T. Rompf, and M. Odersky. OptiML: an implicitly parallel domain specific language for machine learning. In *Proc. of the 28th International Conference on Machine learning*, pages 609–616, 2011.

[33] O. Temam. A defect-tolerant accelerator for emerging high-performance applications. In *Proc. of the 39th Annual International Symposium on Computer Architecture*, pages 356–367, 2012.

[34] S. Venkataramani, V. K. Chippa, S. T. Chakradhar, K. Roy, and A. Raghunathan. Quality programmable vector processors for approximate computing. In *Proc. of the 46th Annual International Symposium on Microarchitecture*, pages 1–12, 2013.

[35] H. Wong, M. M. Papadopoulou, M. Sadooghi-Alvandi, and A. Moshovos. Demystifying GPU microarchitecture through microbenchmarking. In *Proc. of the 2010 IEEE Symposium on Performance Analysis of Systems and Software*, pages 235–246, 2010.

[36] X.-L. Wu, N. Obeid, and W.-M. Hwu. Exploiting more parallelism from applications having generalized reductions on GPU architectures. In *Proc. of the 2010 10th International Conference on Computers and Information Technology*, pages 1175–1180, 2010.

# Uncertain<T>: A First-Order Type for Uncertain Data


James Bornholt
Australian National University
u4842199@anu.edu.au

Todd Mytkowicz
Microsoft Research
toddm@microsoft.com

Kathryn S. McKinley
Microsoft Research
mckinley@microsoft.com



## Abstract

Emerging applications increasingly use estimates such as sensor data (GPS), probabilistic models, machine learning, big data, and human data. Unfortunately, representing this *uncertain data* with discrete types (floats, integers, and booleans) encourages developers to pretend it is not probabilistic, which causes three types of *uncertainty bugs*. (1) Using estimates as facts ignores random error in estimates. (2) Computation compounds that error. (3) Boolean questions on probabilistic data induce false positives and negatives.

This paper introduces *Uncertain*$\langle T\rangle$, a new programming language abstraction for uncertain data. We implement a Bayesian network semantics for computation and conditionals that improves program correctness. The runtime uses sampling and hypothesis tests to evaluate computation and conditionals lazily and efficiently. We illustrate with sensor and machine learning applications that *Uncertain*$\langle T\rangle$ improves expressiveness and accuracy.

Whereas previous probabilistic programming languages focus on experts, *Uncertain*$\langle T\rangle$ serves a wide range of developers. Experts still identify error distributions. However, both experts and application writers compute with distributions, improve estimates with domain knowledge, and ask questions with conditionals. The *Uncertain*$\langle T\rangle$ type system and operators encourage developers to expose and reason about uncertainty explicitly, controlling false positives and false negatives. These benefits make *Uncertain*$\langle T\rangle$ a compelling programming model for modern applications facing the challenge of uncertainty.



***Categories and Subject Descriptors*** D.3.3 [*Programming Languages*]: Language Constructs and Features—Data types and structures

***Keywords*** Estimates; Statistics; Probabilistic Programming





*ASPLOS '14*, March 1–5, 2014, Salt Lake City, Utah, USA.
Copyright © 2014 ACM 978-1-4503-2305-5/14/03...$15.00.
http://dx.doi.org/10.1145/2541940.2541958


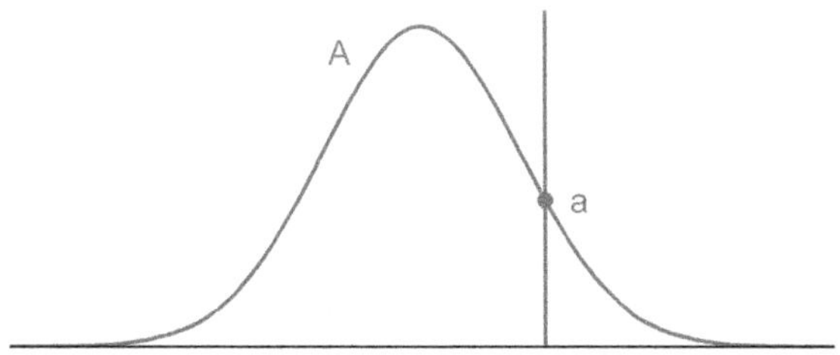


**Figure 1.** The probability distribution $A$ quantifies potential errors. Sampling $A$ produces a single point $a$, introducing uncertainty, but $a$ does not necessarily represent the true value. Many programs treat $a$ as the true value.

## 1. Introduction

Applications that sense and reason about the complexity of the world use estimates. Mobile phone applications estimate location with GPS sensors, search estimates information needs from search terms, machine learning estimates hidden parameters from data, and approximate hardware estimates precise hardware to improve energy efficiency. The difference between an estimate and its true value is *uncertainty*. Every estimate has uncertainty due to random or systematic error. Random variables model uncertainty with probability distributions, which assign a probability to each possible value. For example, each flip of a biased coin may have a 90% chance of heads and 10% chance of tails. The outcome of one flip is only a sample and not a good estimate of the true value. Figure 1 shows a sample from a Gaussian distribution which is a poor approximation for the entire distribution.

Most programming languages force developers to reason about uncertain data with discrete types (floats, integers, and booleans). Motivated application developers reason about uncertainty in ad hoc ways, but because this task is complex, many more simply ignore uncertainty. For instance, we surveyed 100 popular smartphone applications that use GPS and find only one (Pizza Hut) reasons about the error in GPS measurements. Ignoring uncertainty creates three types of *uncertainty bugs* which developers need help to avoid:

***Using estimates as facts*** ignores random noise in data and introduces errors.

***Computation compounds errors*** since computations on uncertain data often degrade accuracy significantly.

***Conditionals ask boolean questions*** of probabilistic data, leading to false positives and false negatives.

While probabilistic programming [6, 13, 15, 24, 25] and domain-specific solutions [1, 2, 11, 18, 28–30] address parts of this problem, they demand expertise far beyond what client applications require. For example in current probabilistic programming languages, domain experts create and query distributions through generative models. Current APIs for estimated data from these programs, sensors, big data, machine learning, and other sources then project the resulting distributions into discrete types. We observe that the probabilistic nature of estimated data does not stop at the API boundary. Applications using estimated data are probabilistic programs too! Existing languages do not consider the needs of applications that consume estimated data, leaving their developers to face this difficult problem unaided.

This paper introduces the *uncertain type*, *Uncertain*$\langle T\rangle$, a programming language abstraction for arbitrary probability distributions. The syntax and semantics emphasize simplicity for non-experts. We describe how expert developers derive and expose probability distributions for estimated data. Similar to probabilistic programming, the uncertain type defines an algebra over random variables to propagate uncertainty through calculations. We introduce a Bayesian network semantics for computations and conditional expressions. Instead of eagerly evaluating probabilistic computations as in prior languages, we lazily evaluate *evidence* for the conditions. Finally, we show how the uncertain type eases the use of prior knowledge to improve estimates.

Our novel implementation strategy performs lazy evaluation by exploiting the semantics of conditionals. The *Uncertain*$\langle T\rangle$ runtime creates a Bayesian network that represents computations on distributions and then samples it at conditional expressions. A sample executes the computations in the network. The runtime exploits hypothesis tests to take only as many samples as necessary for the particular conditional, rather than eagerly and exhaustively producing unnecessary precision (as in general inference over generative models). These hypothesis tests both guarantee accuracy bounds and provide high performance.

We demonstrate these claims with three case studies. (1) We show how *Uncertain*$\langle T\rangle$ improves accuracy and expressiveness of speed computations from GPS, a widely used hardware sensor. (2) We show how *Uncertain*$\langle T\rangle$ exploits prior knowledge to minimize random noise in digital sensors. (3) We show how *Uncertain*$\langle T\rangle$ encourages developers to explicitly reason about and improve accuracy in machine learning, using a neural network that approximates hardware [12, 26]. In concert, the syntax, semantics, and case studies illustrate that *Uncertain*$\langle T\rangle$ eases probabilistic reasoning, improves estimates, and helps domain experts and developers work with uncertain data.

Our contributions are (1) characterizing uncertainty bugs; (2) *Uncertain*$\langle T\rangle$, an abstraction and semantics for uncertain data; (3) implementation strategies that make this semantics practical; and (4) case studies that show *Uncertain*$\langle T\rangle$'s potential to improve expressiveness and correctness.

## 2. Motivation

Modern and emerging applications compute over uncertain data from mobile sensors, search, vision, medical trials, benchmarking, chemical simulations, and human surveys. Characterizing uncertainty in these data sources requires domain expertise, but non-expert developers (perhaps with other expertise) are increasingly consuming the results. This section uses Global Positioning System (GPS) data to motivate a correct and accessible abstraction for uncertain data.

On mobile devices, GPS sensors estimate location. APIs for GPS typically include a position and estimated error radius (a confidence interval for location). The Windows Phone (WP) API returns three fields:

```
public double Latitude, Longitude;  // location
public double HorizontalAccuracy;   // error estimate
```

This interface encourages three types of *uncertainty bugs*.

***Interpreting Estimates as Facts*** Our survey of the top 100 WP and 100 Android applications finds 22% of WP and 40% of Android applications use GPS for location. Only 5% of the WP applications that use GPS read the error radius and only one application (Pizza Hut) acts on it. All others treat the GPS reading as a fact. Ignoring uncertainty this way causes errors such as walking through walls or driving on water.

Current abstractions encourage this treatment by obscuring uncertainty. Consider the map applications on two different smartphone operating systems in Figure 2, which depict location with a point and horizontal accuracy as a circle. Smaller circles *should* indicate less uncertainty, but the left larger circle is a 95% confidence interval (widely used for statistical confidence), whereas the right is a 68% confidence interval (one standard deviation of a Gaussian). The smaller circle has a higher standard deviation and is less accurate! (We reverse engineered this confidence interval detail.) A single accuracy number is insufficient to characterize the underlying error distribution or to compute on it. The horizontal accuracy abstraction obscures the true uncertainty, encouraging developers to ignore it completely.

***Compounding Error*** Computation compounds uncertainty. To illustrate, we recorded GPS locations on WP while walk-

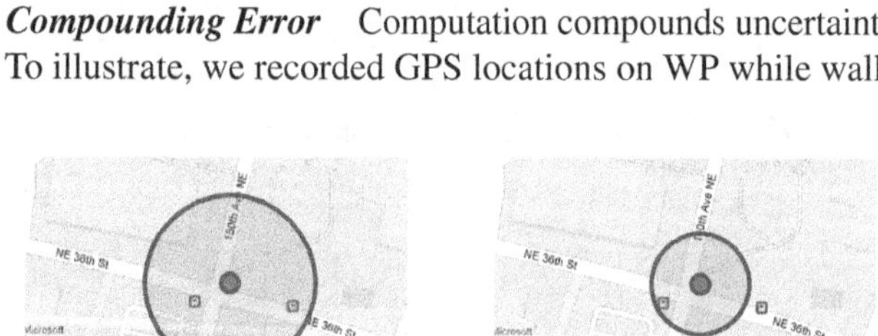

**(a)** 95% CI, $\sigma = 33$ m    **(b)** 68% CI, $\sigma = 39$ m

**Figure 2.** GPS samples at the same location on two smartphone platforms. Although smaller circles *appear* more accurate, the WP sample in (a) is actually more accurate.

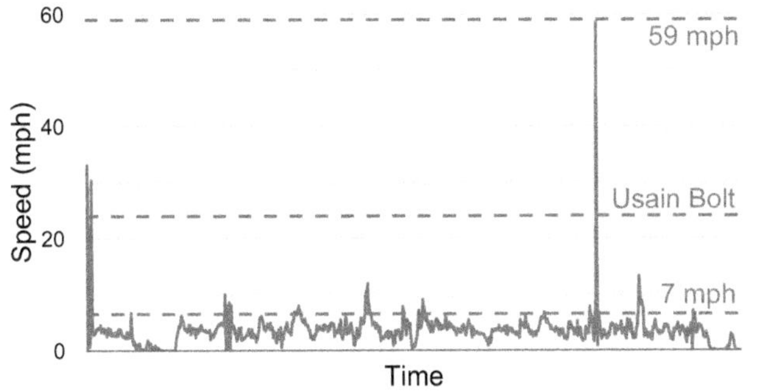


**Figure 3.** Speed computation on GPS data produces absurd walking speeds (59 mph, and 7 mph for 35 s, a running pace).

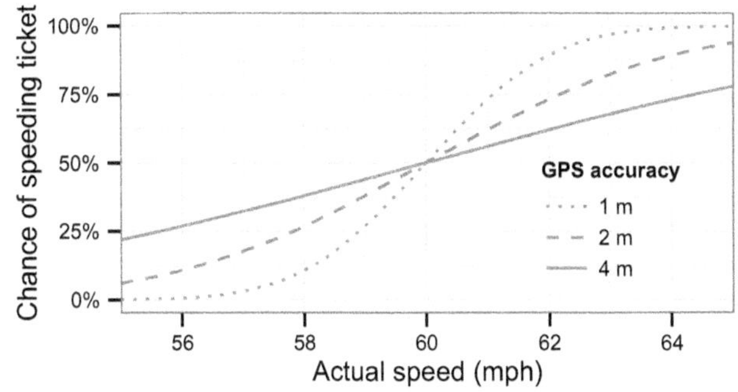


**Figure 4.** Probability of issuing a speeding ticket at a 60 mph speed limit. With a true speed of 57 mph and GPS accuracy of 4 m, there is a 32% chance of issuing a ticket.

ing and computed speed each second. Our inspection of smartphone applications shows this computation on GPS data is very common. Figure 3 plots speed computed by the code in Figure 5(a) using the standard GPS API. Whereas Usain Bolt runs 100 m at 24 mph, the average human walks at 3 mph. This experimental data shows an average of 3.5 mph, 35 s spent above 7 mph (running speed), and absurd speeds of 30, 33, and 59 mph. These errors are significant in both magnitude and frequency. The cause is compounded error, since speed is a function of *two* uncertain locations. When the locations have a 95% confidence interval of 4 m (the best that smartphone GPS delivers), speed has a 95% confidence interval of 12.7 mph. Current abstractions do not capture the compounding of error because they do not represent the distribution nor propagate uncertainty through calculations.

***Conditionals*** Programs eventually act on estimated data with conditionals. Consider using GPS to issue tickets for a 60 mph speed limit with the conditional *Speed* $> 60$. If your actual speed is 57 mph and GPS accuracy is 4 m, this conditional gives a 32% probability of a ticket due to random noise alone. Figure 4 shows this probability across speeds and GPS accuracies. Boolean questions ignore the potential for random error, leading to false positives and negatives. Applications instead should ask probabilistic questions; for example, only issuing a ticket if the probability is very high that the user is speeding.

> *Without an appropriate abstraction for uncertain data, propagation of errors through computations, and probabilistic semantics for conditionals, correctness is out of reach for many developers.*

## 3. A First-Order Type for Uncertain Data

We propose a new generic data type *Uncertain*$\langle T\rangle$ and operations to capture and manipulate uncertain data as probability distributions. The operations propagate distributions through computations and conditionals with an intuitive semantics that help developers program with uncertain data. The *uncertain type* programming language abstraction is broadly applicable to many languages and we implemented prototypes in C#, C++, and Python. Unlike existing probabilistic programming approaches, which focus on statistics and machine learning experts, *Uncertain*$\langle T\rangle$ focuses on creating an accessible interface for non-expert developers, who are increasingly encountering uncertain data.

This section first overviews *Uncertain*$\langle T\rangle$'s syntax and probabilistic semantics and presents an example. It then describes the syntax and semantics for specifying distributions, computing with distributions by building a Bayesian network representation of computations, and executing conditional expressions by evaluating evidence for a conclusion. We then describe how *Uncertain*$\langle T\rangle$ makes it easier for developers to improve estimates with domain knowledge. Section 4 describes our lazy evaluation and sampling implementation strategies that make these semantics efficient.

***Overview*** An object of type *Uncertain*$\langle T\rangle$ encapsulates a random variable of a numeric type $T$. To represent computations, the type's overloaded operators construct *Bayesian networks*, directed acyclic graphs in which nodes represent random variables and edges represent conditional dependences between variables. The leaf nodes of these Bayesian networks are known distributions defined by expert developers. Inner nodes represent the sequence of operations that compute on these leaves. For example, the following code

```
Uncertain<double> a = new Gaussian(4, 1);
Uncertain<double> b = new Gaussian(5, 1);
Uncertain<double> c = a + b;
```

results in a simple Bayesian network

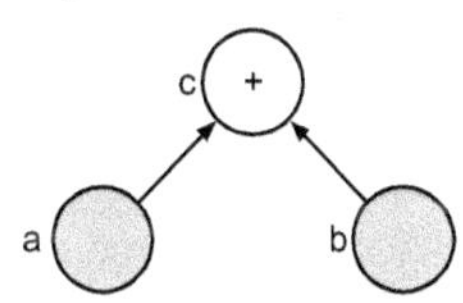


with two leaf nodes (shaded) and one inner node (white) representing the computation `c = a + b`. *Uncertain*$\langle T\rangle$ evaluates this Bayesian network when it needs the distribution of `c`, which depends on the distributions of `a` and `b`. Here the distribution of `c` is more uncertain than `a` or `b`, as Figure 6 shows, since computation compounds uncertainty.

This paper describes a runtime that builds Bayesian networks dynamically and then, much like a JIT, compiles those

```
double dt = 5.0;  // seconds
GeoCoordinate L1 = GPS.GetLocation();

while (true) {
  Sleep(dt);  // wait for dt seconds
  GeoCoordinate L2 = GPS.GetLocation();
  double Distance = GPS.Distance(L2, L1);
  double Speed = Distance / dt;
  print("Speed: " + Speed);
  if (Speed > 4) GoodJob();
  else           SpeedUp();
  L1 = L2; // Last Location = Current Location;
}
```

**(a)** Without the uncertain type

```
double dt = 5.0;  // seconds
Uncertain<GeoCoordinate> L1 = GPS.GetLocation();

while (true) {
  Sleep(dt);  // wait for dt seconds
  Uncertain<GeoCoordinate> L2 = GPS.GetLocation();
  Uncertain<double> Distance = GPS.Distance(L2, L1);
  Uncertain<double> Speed = Distance / dt;
  print("Speed: " + Speed.E());
  if (Speed > 4)                    GoodJob();
  else if ((Speed < 4).Pr(0.9)) SpeedUp();
  L1 = L2;  // Last Location = Current Location;
}
```

**(b)** With the uncertain type

**Figure 5.** A simple fitness application (GPS-Walking), encouraging users to walk faster than 4 mph, implemented with and without the uncertain type. The type `GeoCoordinate` is a pair of `doubles` (latitude and longitude) and so is numeric.

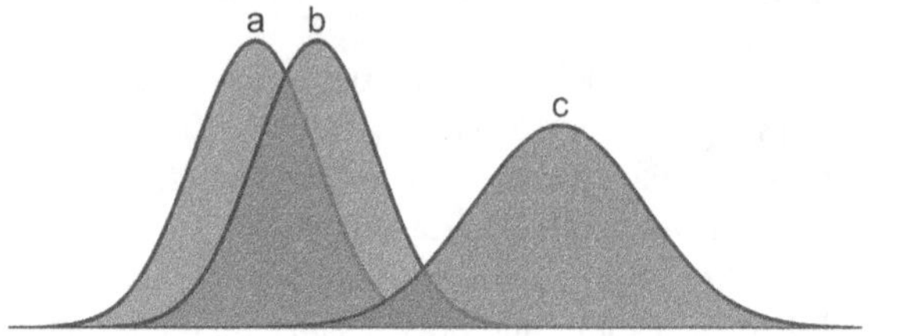


**Figure 6.** The sum $c = a + b$ is more uncertain than $a$ or $b$.

expression trees to executable code at conditionals. The semantics establishes hypothesis tests at conditionals. The runtime samples by repeatedly executing the compiled code until the test is satisfied.

***Example Program*** Figure 5 shows a simple fitness application (GPS-Walking) written in C#, both without (left) and with (right) *Uncertain*$\langle T\rangle$. GPS-Walking encourages users to walk faster than 4 mph. The *Uncertain*$\langle T\rangle$ version produces more accurate results in part because the type encourages the developer to reason about false positives and negatives. In particular, the developer chooses not to nag, admonishing users to `SpeedUp` only when it is very confident they are walking slowly. As in traditional languages, *Uncertain*$\langle T\rangle$ only executes one side of conditional branches. Some probabilistic languages execute both sides of conditional branches to create probabilistic models, but *Uncertain*$\langle T\rangle$ makes concrete decisions at conditional branches, matching the host language semantics. We demonstrate the improved accuracy of the *Uncertain*$\langle T\rangle$ version of GPS-Walking in Section 5.1.

This example serves as a good pedagogical tool because of its simplicity, but the original embodies a real-world uncertainty problem because *many* smartphone applications on all major platforms use the GPS API exactly this way. *Uncertain*$\langle T\rangle$'s simple syntax and semantics result in very few changes to the program: the developer only changes the variable types and the conditional operators.

### 3.1 Syntax with Operator Overloading

Table 1 shows the operators and methods of *Uncertain*$\langle T\rangle$. *Uncertain*$\langle T\rangle$ defines an algebra over random variables to propagate uncertainty through computations, overloading the usual arithmetic operators from the base numeric type $T$.

| **Operators** | |
|---|---|
| Math ($+ - * /$) | $op :: U\langle T\rangle \to U\langle T\rangle \to U\langle T\rangle$ |
| Order ($< > \leq \geq$) | $op :: U\langle T\rangle \to U\langle T\rangle \to U\langle Bool\rangle$ |
| Logical ($\wedge \vee$) | $op :: U\langle Bool\rangle \to U\langle Bool\rangle \to U\langle Bool\rangle$ |
| Unary ($\neg$) | $op :: U\langle Bool\rangle \to U\langle Bool\rangle$ |
| Point-mass | $Pointmass :: T \to U\langle T\rangle$ |
| **Conditionals** | |
| Explicit | $Pr :: U\langle Bool\rangle \to [0,1] \to Bool$ |
| Implicit | $Pr :: U\langle Bool\rangle \to Bool$ |
| **Evaluation** | |
| Expected value | $E :: U\langle T\rangle \to T$ |

$U\langle T\rangle$ is shorthand for *Uncertain*$\langle T\rangle$.

**Table 1.** *Uncertain*$\langle T\rangle$ operators and methods.

Developers may override other types as well. Developers compute with *Uncertain*$\langle T\rangle$ as they would with $T$, and the Bayesian network the operators construct captures how error in an estimate flows through computations.

*Uncertain*$\langle T\rangle$ addresses two sources of random error: *domain* error and *approximation* error. Domain error motivates our work and is the difference between an estimate and its true value. Approximation error is created because *Uncertain*$\langle T\rangle$ must approximate distributions. Developers ultimately make concrete decisions on uncertain data through conditionals. *Uncertain*$\langle T\rangle$'s conditional operators enforce statistical tests at conditionals, mitigating both sources of error.

### 3.2 Identifying Distributions

The underlying probability distribution for uncertain data is specific to the problem domain. In many cases expert library developers already know these distributions, and sometimes they use them to produce crude error estimates such as the GPS horizontal accuracy discussed in Section 2. *Uncertain*$\langle T\rangle$ offers these expert developers an abstraction to expose these distributions while preserving the simplicity of their current API. The non-expert developers who consume this uncertain data program against the common *Uncertain*$\langle T\rangle$ API, which is very similar to the way they already program with uncertain data today, but aids them in avoiding uncertainty bugs.

The expert developer has two broad approaches for selecting the right distribution for their particular problem.

***(1) Selecting a theoretical model.*** Many sources of uncertain data are amenable to theoretical models which library writers may adopt. For example, the error in the mean of a data set is approximately Gaussian by the Central Limit Theorem. Section 5.1 uses a theoretical approach for the GPS-Walking case study.

***(2) Deriving an empirical model.*** Some problems do not have or are not amenable to theoretical models. For these cases, expert developers may determine an error distribution empirically by machine learning or other mechanisms. Section 5.3 uses an empirical approach for machine learning.

#### Representing Distributions

There are a number of ways to store probability distributions. The most accurate mechanism stores the probability density function exactly. For finite domains, a simple map can assign a probability to each possible value [30]. For continuous domains, one might reason about the density function algebraically [4]. For example, a Gaussian random variable with mean $\mu$ and variance $\sigma^2$ has density function

$$f(x) = \frac{1}{\sigma\sqrt{2\pi}} \exp\left\{-\frac{(x-\mu)^2}{2\sigma^2}\right\}.$$

An instance of a Gaussian random variable need only store this formula and values of $\mu$ and $\sigma^2$ to represent the variable exactly (up to floating point error).

Exact representation has two major downsides. First, the algebra quickly becomes impractical under computation: even the sum of two distributions requires evaluating a convoluted *convolution integral*. Second, many important distributions for sensors, road maps, approximate hardware, and machine learning do not have closed-form density functions and so cannot be stored this way.

To overcome these issues, *Uncertain*$\langle T\rangle$ represents distributions through approximate *sampling functions*. Approximation can be arbitrarily accurate given sufficient space and time [31], leading to an efficiency-accuracy trade-off. Many possible approximation schemes might be appropriate for *Uncertain*$\langle T\rangle$, including fixed vectors of random samples, Chebyshev polynomials [16], or sampling functions [23]. We use sampling functions because they implement a principled solution for balancing accuracy and efficiency.

### 3.3 Computing with Distributions

Developers combine uncertain data by using the usual operators for arithmetic, logic, and comparison, and *Uncertain*$\langle T\rangle$ manages the resultant uncertainty. *Uncertain*$\langle T\rangle$ overloads such operators from the base type $T$ to work over distributions. For example, the example program in Figure 5(b) calculates the user's speed by division:

```
Uncertain<double> Speed = Distance / dt;
```

```
D = A / B
E = D - C
```

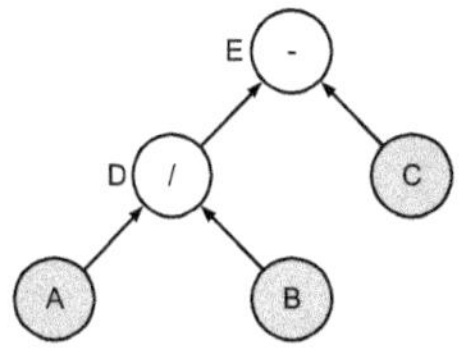


**Figure 7.** Bayesian network for a simple program with independent leaves.

The type *Double* has a division operator of type

$$/ :: Double \rightarrow Double \rightarrow Double.$$

The type *Uncertain*$\langle$*Double*$\rangle$ lifts this operator to work over random variables, providing a new operator

$$/ :: U\langle Double\rangle \rightarrow U\langle Double\rangle \rightarrow U\langle Double\rangle.$$

Note given $x$ of type $T$, the semantics coerces $x$ to type *Uncertain*$\langle T\rangle$ with a pointmass distribution centered at $x$, so the denominator `dt` is cast to type *Uncertain*$\langle$*Double*$\rangle$. The same lifting occurs on other arithmetic operators of type $T \rightarrow T \rightarrow T$, as well as comparison operators (type $T \rightarrow T \rightarrow Bool$) and logical operators (type $Bool \rightarrow Bool \rightarrow Bool$). A lifted operator may have any type. For example, we can define real division of integers as type $Int \rightarrow Int \rightarrow Double$, which *Uncertain*$\langle T\rangle$ lifts without issue.

Instead of executing operations instantaneously, the lifted operators construct Bayesian network representations of the computations. A Bayesian network is a *probabilistic graphical model* and is a directed acyclic graph whose nodes represent random variables and whose edges represent conditional dependences between those variables [5]. Figure 7 shows an example of this Bayesian network representation. The shaded leaf nodes are known distributions (such as Gaussians) specified by expert developers, as previously noted. The final Bayesian network defines a joint distribution over all the variables involved in the computation:

$$\Pr[A,B,C,D,E] = \Pr[A]\Pr[B]\Pr[C]\Pr[D \mid A,B]\Pr[E \mid C,D].$$

The incoming edges to a node in the Bayesian network graph specify the other variables that the node's variable depends on. For example, `A` has no dependences while `E` depends on `C` and `D`. Since we know the distributions of the leaf nodes `A`, `B`, and `C`, we use the joint distribution to infer the marginal distributions of the variables `D` and `E`, even though their distributions are not explicitly specified by the program. The conditional distributions of inner nodes are specified by their associated operators. For example, the distribution of $\Pr[D \mid A = a, B = b]$ in Figure 7 is simply a pointmass at $a/b$.

#### Dependent Random Variables

Two random variables $X$ and $Y$ are independent if the value of one has no bearing on the value of the other. *Uncertain*$\langle T\rangle$'s Bayesian network representation assumes that leaf nodes are independent. This assumption is common in probabilistic programming, but expert developers can override it by specifying the joint distribution between two variables.

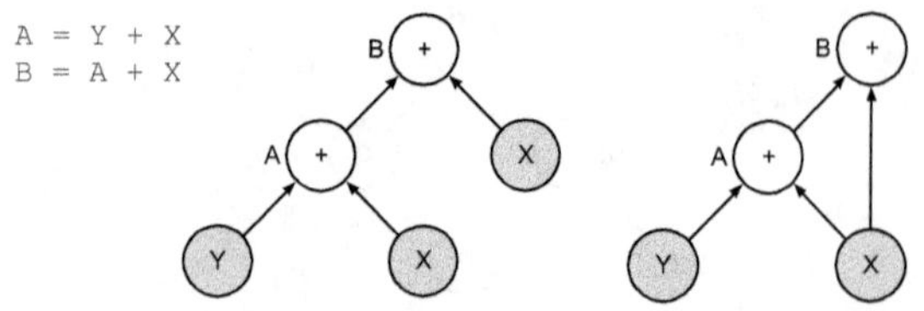


**(a)** Wrong network **(b)** Correct network

**Figure 8.** Bayesian networks for a simple program with dependent leaves.

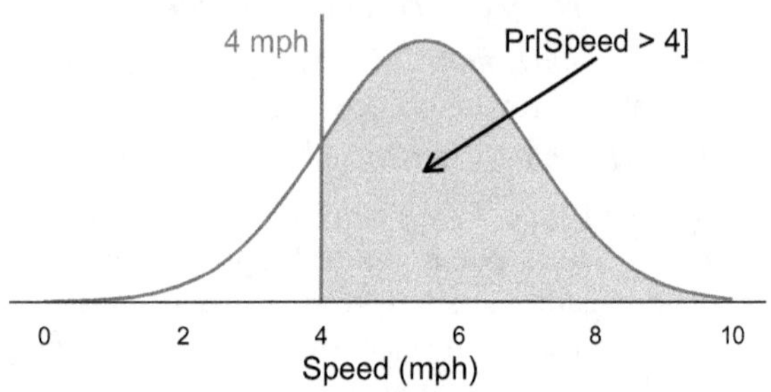


**Figure 9.** Uncertainty in data means there is only a *probability* that *Speed* > 4, not a concrete boolean value.

The *Uncertain*⟨*T*⟩ semantics automatically addresses program-induced dependences. For example, Figure 8(a) shows a simple program with a naive incorrect construction of its Bayesian network. This network implies that the operands to the addition that defines `B` are independent, but in fact both operands depend on the same variable `X`. When producing a Bayesian network, *Uncertain*⟨*T*⟩'s operators echo static single assignment by determining that the two `X` occurrences refer to the same value, and so `A` depends on the same `X` as `B`. Our analysis produces the correct Bayesian network in Figure 8(b). Because the Bayesian network is constructed dynamically and incrementally during program execution, the resulting graph remains acyclic.

### 3.4 Asking the Right Questions

After computing with uncertain data, programs use it in conditional expressions to make decisions. The example program in Figure 5 compares the user's speed to 4 mph. Of course, since speed is computed with uncertain estimates of location, it too is uncertain. The naive conditional $Speed > 4$ incorrectly asks a deterministic question of probabilistic data, creating uncertainty bugs described in Section 2.

*Uncertain*⟨*T*⟩ defines the semantics of conditional expressions involving uncertain data by computing *evidence* for a conclusion. This semantics encourages developers to ask appropriate questions of probabilistic data. Rather than asking "is the user's speed faster than 4 mph?" *Uncertain*⟨*T*⟩ asks "how much evidence is there that the user's speed is faster than 4 mph?" The evidence that the user's speed is faster than 4 mph is the quantity $\Pr[Speed > 4]$; in Figure 9, this is the area under the distribution of the variable `Speed` to the right of 4 mph. Since we are considering probability distributions, the area $A$ satisfies $0 \le A \le 1$.

When the developer writes a conditional expression

```
if (Speed > 4) ...
```

the program applies the lifted version of the > operator

$$> :: Uncertain\langle T\rangle \to Uncertain\langle T\rangle \to Uncertain\langle Bool\rangle.$$

This operator creates a Bernoulli distribution with parameter $p \in [0,1]$, which by definition is the probability that $Speed > 4$ (i.e., the shaded area under the curve). Unlike other probabilistic programming languages, *Uncertain*⟨*T*⟩ executes only a single branch of the conditional to match the host language's semantics. The *Uncertain*⟨*T*⟩ runtime must therefore convert this Bernoulli distribution to a concrete boolean value. This conditional uses the implicit conditional operator, which compares the parameter $p$ of the Bernoulli distribution to 0.5, asking whether the Bernoulli is more likely than not to be true. This conditional therefore evaluates whether $\Pr[Speed > 4] > 0.5$, asking whether it is more likely that the user's speed is faster than 4 mph.

Using an explicit conditional operator, developers may specify a threshold to compare against. The second comparison in Figure 5(b) uses this explicit operator:

```
else if ((Speed < 4).Pr(0.9)) ...
```

This conditional evaluates whether $\Pr[Speed < 4] > 0.9$. The power of this formulation is reasoning about false positives and negatives. Even if the mean of the distribution is on one side of the conditional threshold, the distribution may be very wide, so there is still a strong likelihood that the opposite conclusion is correct. Higher thresholds for the explicit operator require stronger evidence, and produce fewer false positives (extra reports when ground truth is false) but more false negatives (missed reports when ground truth is true). In this case, the developer chooses to favor some false positives for encouraging users (`GoodJob`), and to limit false positives when admonishing users (`SpeedUp`) by demanding stronger evidence that they are walking slower than 4 mph.

#### Hypothesis Testing for Approximation Error

Because *Uncertain*⟨*T*⟩ approximates distributions, we must consider approximation error in conditional expressions. We use statistical hypothesis tests, which make inferences about population statistics based on sampled data. *Uncertain*⟨*T*⟩ establishes a hypothesis test when evaluating the implicit and explicit conditional operators. In the implicit case above, the null hypothesis is $H_0 : \Pr[Speed > 4] \le 0.5$ and the alternate hypothesis $H_A : \Pr[Speed > 4] > 0.5$. Section 4.3 describes our sampling process for evaluating these tests in detail.

Hypothesis tests introduce a ternary logic. For example, given the code sequence

```
if (A < B) ...
else if (A >= B) ...
```

neither branch may be true because the runtime may not be able to reject the null hypothesis for either conditional at the required confidence level. This behavior is not new: just

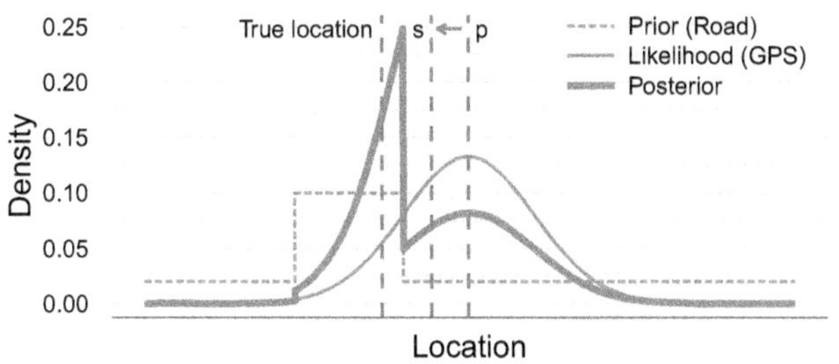


**Figure 10.** Domain knowledge as a prior distribution improves the quality of GPS estimates.

as programs should not compare floating point numbers for equality, neither should they compare distributions for equality. However, for problems that *require* a total order, such as sorting algorithms, *Uncertain*⟨*T*⟩ provides the expected value operator $E$. This operator outputs an element of type $T$ and so it preserves the base type's ordering properties.

### 3.5 Improving Estimates

Bayesian statistics represents the state of the world with degrees of belief and is a powerful mechanism for improving the quality of estimated data. Given two random variables, $B$ representing the target variable to estimate (e.g., the user's location), and $E$ the estimation process (e.g., the GPS sensor output), Bayes' theorem says that

$$\Pr[B=b|E=e] = \frac{\Pr[E=e|B=b]\cdot\Pr[B=b]}{\Pr[E=e]}.$$

Bayes' theorem combines evidence from estimation processes (the value $e$ of $E$) with hypotheses about the true value $b$ of the target variable $B$. We call $\Pr[B=b]$ the *prior* distribution, our belief about $B$ before observing any evidence, and $\Pr[B=b|E=e]$ the *posterior* distribution, our belief about $B$ after observing evidence.

*Uncertain*⟨*T*⟩ unlocks Bayesian statistics by encapsulating entire data distributions. Abstractions that capture only single point estimates are insufficient for this purpose and force developers to resort to ad-hoc heuristics to improve estimates.

#### Incorporating Knowledge with Priors

Bayesian inference is powerful because developers can encode their domain knowledge as prior distributions, and use that knowledge to improve the quality of estimates. For example, a developer working with GPS can provide a prior distribution that assigns high probabilities to roads and lower probabilities elsewhere. This prior distribution achieves a "road-snapping" behavior [21], fixing the user's location to nearby roads unless GPS evidence to the contrary is very strong. Figure 10 illustrates this example – the mean shifts from $p$ to $s$, closer to the road the user is actually on.

Specifying priors, however, requires a knowledge of statistics beyond the scope of most developers. In our current implementation, applications specify domain knowledge with *constraint abstractions*. Expert developers add preset prior distributions to their libraries for common cases. For example, GPS libraries would include priors for driving (e.g., roads and driving speeds), walking (walking speeds), and being on land. Developers combine priors through flags that select constraints specific to their application. The library applies the selected priors, improving the quality of estimates without much burden on developers. This approach is not very satisfying because it is not compositional, so the application cannot easily mix and match priors from different sources (e.g., maps, calendars, and physics for GPS). We anticipate future work creating an accessible and compositional abstraction for prior distributions, perhaps with the Bayes operator $P \sharp Q$ for sampled distributions by Park et al. [23].

## 4. Implementation

This section describes our practical and efficient C# implementation of the *Uncertain*⟨*T*⟩ abstraction. We also implemented prototypes of *Uncertain*⟨*T*⟩ in C++ and Python and believe most high-level languages could easily implement it.

### 4.1 Identifying Distributions

*Uncertain*⟨*T*⟩ approximates distributions with *sampling functions*, rather than storing them exactly, to achieve expressiveness and efficiency. A sampling function has no arguments and returns a new random sample, drawn from the distribution, on each invocation [23]. For example, a pseudo-random number generator is a sampling function for the uniform distribution, and the Box-Mueller transform [8] is a sampling function for the Gaussian distribution.

In the GPS-Walking application in Figure 5(b), the variables `L1` and `L2` are distributions obtained from the GPS library. The expert developer who implements the GPS library derives the correct distribution and provides it to *Uncertain*⟨*T*⟩ as a sampling function. Bornholt [7] shows in detail the derivation for the error distribution of GPS data. The resulting model says that the posterior distribution for a GPS estimate is

$$\Pr[\mathbf{Location} = p \mid \mathbf{GPS} = \mathit{Sample}] = \mathrm{Rayleigh}(\|\mathit{Sample} - p\|; \varepsilon/\sqrt{\ln 400})$$

where *Sample* is the raw GPS sample from the sensor, $\varepsilon$ is the sensor's estimate of the 95% confidence interval for the location (i.e., the horizontal accuracy from Section 2), and the Rayleigh distribution [22] is a continuous non-negative single-parameter distribution with density function

$$\mathrm{Rayleigh}(x;\rho) = \frac{x}{\rho^2}\exp\left\{-\frac{x^2}{2\rho^2}\right\}, \quad x \geq 0.$$

Figure 11 shows the posterior distribution given a particular value of $\varepsilon$. Most existing GPS libraries return a coordinate (the center of the distribution) and present $\varepsilon$ as a confidence parameter most developers ignore. Figure 11 shows that the true location is *unlikely* to be in the center of the distribution and more likely to be some fixed radius from the center.

We built a GPS library that captures error in its estimate with *Uncertain*⟨*T*⟩ using this distribution. Figure 12 shows our library function `GPS.GetLocation`, which returns an instance of *Uncertain*⟨*GeoCoordinate*⟩ by implementing a

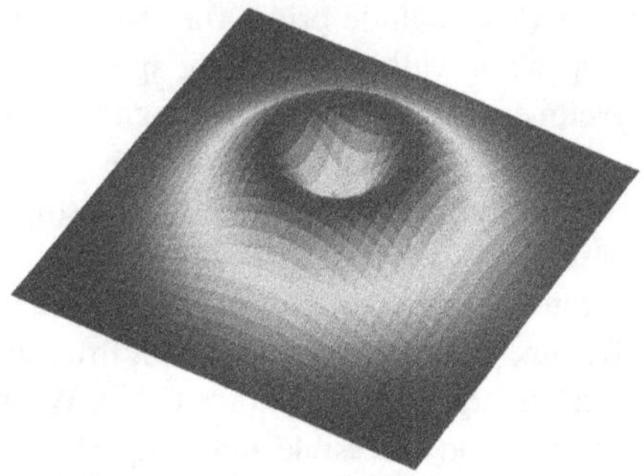

**Figure 11.** The posterior distribution for GPS is a distribution over the Earth's surface.

```
Uncertain<GeoCoordinate> GetLocation() {
    // Get the estimates from the hardware
    GeoCoordinate Point = GPS.GetHardwareLocation();
    double Accuracy = GPS.GetHardwareAccuracy();
    // Compute epsilon
    double epsilon = Accuracy / Math.Sqrt(Math.Log(400));
    // Define the sampling function
    Func<GeoCoordinate> SamplingFunction = () => {
        double radius, angle, x, y;
        // Samples the distribution in Figure 11 using
        // polar coordinates
        radius = Math.RandomRayleigh(epsilon);
        angle  = Math.RandomUniform(0, 2*Math.PI);
        // Convert to x,y coordinates in degrees
        x = Point.Longitude;
        x += radius*Math.Cos(angle)*DEGREES_PER_METER;
        y = Point.Latitude;
        y += radius*Math.Sin(angle)*DEGREES_PER_METER;
        // Return the GeoCoordinate
        return new GeoCoordinate(x, y);
    }
    // Return the instance of Uncertain<T>
    return new Uncertain<GeoCoordinate>(SamplingFunction);
}
```

**Figure 12.** The $Uncertain\langle T\rangle$ version of `GPS.GetLocation` returns an instance of $Uncertain\langle GeoCoordinate\rangle$.

sampling function to draw samples from the posterior distribution. The sampling function captures the values of `Point` and `Accuracy`. Although the sampling function is later invoked many times to draw samples from the distribution, the GPS hardware functions `GetHardwareLocation` and `GetHardwareAccuracy` are only invoked once for each call to `GetLocation`.

### 4.2 Computing with Distributions

$Uncertain\langle T\rangle$ propagates error through computations by overloading operators from the base type $T$. These lifted operators dynamically construct Bayesian network representations of the computations they represent as the program executes. However, an alternate implementation could statically build a Bayesian network and only dynamically perform hypothesis tests at conditionals. We use the Bayesian network to define the sampling function for a computed variable in terms of the sampling functions of its operands. We only evaluate the sampling function at conditionals and so the root node of a network being sampled is always a comparison operator.

The computed sampling function uses the standard *ancestral sampling* technique for graphical models [5]. Because the Bayesian network is directed and acyclic, its nodes can be topologically ordered. We draw samples in this topological order, starting with each leaf node, for which sampling functions are explicitly defined. These samples then propagate up the Bayesian network. Each inner node is associated with an operator from the base type, and the node's children have already been sampled due to the topological order, so we simply apply the base operator to the operand samples to generate a sample from an inner node. This process continues up the network until reaching the root node of the network, generating a sample from the computed variable. The topological order guarantees that each node is visited exactly once in this process, and so the sampling process terminates.

In the GPS-Walking application in Figure 5(b), the user's speed is calculated by the line

```
Uncertain<double> Speed = Distance / dt;
```

The lifted division operator constructs a Bayesian network for this computation:

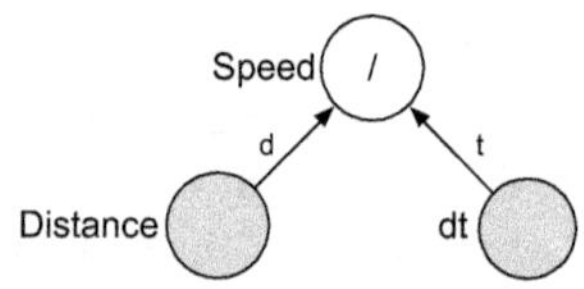


Here shaded nodes indicate leaf distributions, for which sampling functions are defined explicitly.

To draw a sample from the variable `Speed`, we draw a sample from each leaf: a sample $d$ from `Distance` (defined by the GPS library) and $t$ from `dt` (a pointmass distribution, so all samples are equal). These samples propagate up the network to the `Speed` node. Because this node is a division operator, the resulting sample from `Speed` is simply $d/t$.

### 4.3 Asking Questions with Hypothesis Tests

$Uncertain\langle T\rangle$'s conditional and evaluation operators address the domain error that motivates our work. These operators require concrete decisions under uncertainty. The conditional operators must select one branch target to execute. In the GPS-Walking application in Figure 5(b), a conditional operator

```
if (Speed > 4)...
```

must decide whether or not to enter this branch. Section 3.4 describes how $Uncertain\langle T\rangle$ executes this conditional by comparing the probability $\Pr[Speed > 4]$ to a default threshold 0.5, asking whether it is more likely than not that $Speed > 4$. To control approximation error, this comparison is performed by a hypothesis test, with null hypothesis $H_0 : \Pr[Speed > 4] \leq 0.5$ and alternate hypothesis $H_A : \Pr[Speed > 4] > 0.5$.

Sampling functions in combination with this hypothesis test control the efficiency-accuracy trade-off that approximation introduces. A higher confidence level for the hypothesis test leads to fewer approximation errors but requires more samples to evaluate. We perform the hypothesis test using Wald's *sequential probability ratio test* (SPRT) [32] to dynamically choose the right sample size for a particular conditional, only taking as many samples as necessary to obtain a statistically significant result.

We specify a step size, say $k = 10$, and start by drawing $n = k$ samples from the Bernoulli distribution $Speed > 4$. We then apply the SPRT to these samples to decide if the parameter $p$ of the distribution (i.e., the probability $\Pr[Speed > 4]$) is significantly different from 0.5. If so, we can terminate immediately and take (or not take) the branch, depending on in which direction the significance lies. If the result is not significant, we draw another batch of $k$ samples, and repeat the process with the now $n = 2k$ collection of samples. We repeat this process until either a significant result is achieved or a maximum sample size is reached to ensure termination. The SPRT ensures that this repeated sampling and testing process still achieves overall bounds on the probabilities of false positives (significance level) and false negatives (power).

Sampling functions and a Bayesian network representation may draw as many samples as we wish from any given variable. We may therefore exploit sequential methods, such as the SPRT, which do not fix the sample size for a hypothesis test in advance. Sequential methods are a principled solution to the efficiency-accuracy trade-off. They ensure we draw the minimum necessary number of samples for a sufficiently accurate result for each specific conditional. This goal-oriented sampling approach is a significant advance over previous random sampling approaches, which compute with a fixed pool of samples. These approaches do not efficiently control the effect of approximation error.

Wald's SPRT is optimal in terms of average sample size, but is potentially unbounded in any particular instance, so termination is not guaranteed. The artificial maximum sample size we introduce to guarantee termination has a small effect on the actual significance level and power of the test. We anticipate adapting the considerable body of work on group sequential methods [17], widely used in medical clinical trials, which provide "closed" sequential hypothesis tests with guaranteed upper bounds on the sample size.

We cannot apply the same sequential testing approach to the evaluation operator $E$, since there are no alternatives to compare against (i.e., no goal to achieve). Currently for this operator we simply draw a fixed number of samples and return their mean. We believe a more intelligent adaptive sampling process, sampling until the mean converges, may improve the performance of this approach.

## 5. Case Studies

We use three case studies to explore the expressiveness and correctness of *Uncertain*⟨*T*⟩ on uncertain data. (1) We show how *Uncertain*⟨*T*⟩ improves accuracy and expressiveness of speed computations from GPS, a widely used hardware sensor. (2) We show how *Uncertain*⟨*T*⟩ exploits prior knowledge to minimize random noise in digital sensors. (3) We show how *Uncertain*⟨*T*⟩ encourages developers to explicitly reason about and improve accuracy in machine learning, using a neural network that approximates hardware [12, 26].

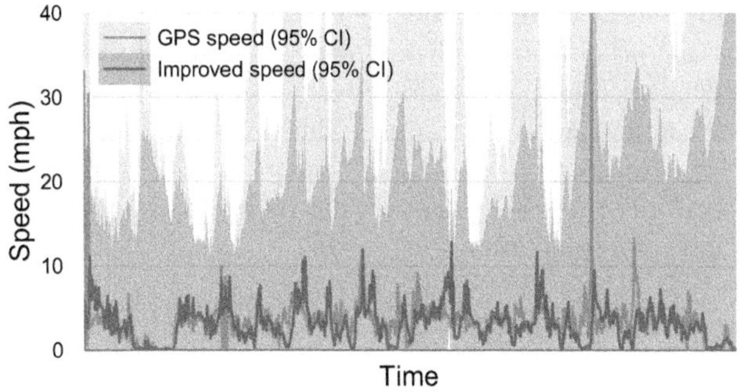


**Figure 13.** Data from the GPS-Walking application. Developers improve accuracy with priors and remove absurd values.

### 5.1 Uncertain<T> on Smartphones: GPS-Walking

The modern smartphone contains a plethora of hardware sensors. Thousands of applications use the GPS sensor, and many compute distance and speed from GPS readings. Our walking speed case study serves double duty, showing how uncertainty bugs occur in practice as well as a clear pedagogical demonstration of how *Uncertain*⟨*T*⟩ improves correctness and expressiveness. We wrap the Windows Phone (WP) GPS location services API with *Uncertain*⟨*T*⟩, exposing the error distribution. The GPS-Walking application estimates the user's speed by taking two samples from the GPS and computing the distance and time between them. Figure 5 compares the code for GPS-Walking with and without the uncertain type.

***Defining the Distributions*** Our *Uncertain*⟨*T*⟩ GPS library provides the function

```
Uncertain<GeoCoordinate> GPS.GetLocation();
```

which returns a distribution over the user's possible locations. Section 4.1 overviews how to derive the GPS distribution, and Figure 12 shows the implementation.

***Computing with Distributions*** GPS-Walking uses locations from the GPS library to calculate the user's speed, since $Speed = \Delta Distance/\Delta Time$. Of course, since the locations are estimates, so too is speed. The developer must change the line

```
print("Speed: " + Speed);
```

from the original program in Figure 5(a), since `Speed` now has type *Uncertain*⟨*Double*⟩. It now prints the expected value `Speed.E()` of the speed distribution.

We tested GPS-Walking by walking outside for 15 minutes. Figure 13 shows the expected values `Speed.E()` measured each second by the application (*GPS speed*). The uncertainty of the speed calculation, with extremely wide confidence intervals, explains the absurd values.

***Conditionals*** GPS-Walking encourages users to walk faster than 4 mph with messages triggered by conditionals. The original implementation in Figure 5(a) uses naive conditionals, which are susceptible to random error. For example, on our test data, such conditionals would report the user to be walking faster than 7 mph (a running pace) for 30 seconds.

The *Uncertain⟨T⟩* version of GPS-Walking in Figure 5(b) evaluates evidence to execute conditionals. The conditional

```
if (Speed > 4)                    GoodJob();
```

asks if it is *more likely than not* that the user is walking fast. The second conditional

```
else if ((Speed < 4).Pr(0.9)) SpeedUp();
```

asks if there is at least a 90% chance the user is walking slowly. This requirement is stricter than the first conditional because we do not want to unfairly admonish the user (i.e., we want to avoid false positives). Even the simpler *more likely than not* conditional improves the accuracy of GPS-Walking: such a conditional would only report the user as walking faster than 7 mph for 4 seconds.

***Improving GPS Estimates with Priors*** Because GPS-Walking uses *Uncertain⟨T⟩*, we may incorporate prior knowledge to improve the quality of its estimates. Assume for simplicity that users only invoke GPS-Walking when walking. Since humans are incredibly unlikely to walk at 60 mph or even 10 mph, we specify a prior distribution over likely walking speeds. Figure 13 shows the improved results (*Improved speed*). The confidence interval for the improved data is much tighter, and the prior knowledge removes the absurd results, such as walking at 59 mph.

***Summary*** Developers need only make minimal changes to the original GPS-Walking application and are rewarded with improved correctness. They improve accuracy by reasoning correctly about uncertainty and eliminating absurd data with domain knowledge. This complex logic is difficult to implement without the uncertain type because a developer must know the error distribution for GPS, how to propagate it through calculations, and how to incorporate domain knowledge to improve the results. The uncertain type abstraction hides this complexity, improving programming productivity and application correctness.

### 5.2 Uncertain<T> with Sensor Error: SensorLife

This case study emulates a binary sensor with Gaussian noise to explore accuracy when ground truth is available. For many problems using uncertain data, ground truth is difficult and costly to obtain, but it is readily available in this problem formulation. This case study shows how *Uncertain⟨T⟩* makes it easier for non-expert developers to work with noisy sensors. Furthermore, it shows how expert developers can simply and succinctly use domain knowledge (i.e., the fact that the noise is Gaussian with known variance) to improve these estimates.

We use Conway's Game of Life, a cellular automaton that operates on a two-dimensional grid of cells that are each dead or alive. The game is broken up into generations. During each generation, the program updates each cell by (i) sensing the state of the cell's 8 neighbors, (ii) summing the binary value (dead or alive) of the 8 neighbors, and (iii) applying the following rules to the sum:

1. A live cell with 2 or 3 live neighbors lives.
2. A live cell with less than 2 live neighbors dies.
3. A live cell with more than 3 live neighbors dies.
4. A dead cell with exactly 3 live neighbors becomes live.

These rules simulate survival, underpopulation, overcrowding, and reproduction, respectively. Despite simple rules, the Game of Life provides complex and interesting dynamics (e.g., it is Turing complete [3]). We focus on the accuracy of sensing if the neighbors are dead or alive.

***Defining the Distributions*** The original Game of Life's discrete perfect sensors define our ground truth. We view each cell as being equipped with up to eight sensors, one for each of its neighbors. Cells on corners and edges of the grid have fewer sensors. Each perfect sensor returns a binary value $s \in \{0,1\}$ indicating if the associated neighbor is alive.

We artificially induce zero-mean Gaussian noise $N(0,\sigma)$ on each of these sensors, where $\sigma$ is the amplitude of the noise. Each sensor now returns a real number, not a binary value. We define three versions of this noisy Game of Life:

**NaiveLife** reads a single sample from each noisy sensor and sums the results directly to count the live neighbors.

**SensorLife** wraps each sensor with *Uncertain⟨T⟩*. The sum uses the overloaded addition operator and each sensor may be sampled multiple times in a single generation.

**BayesLife** uses domain knowledge to improve SensorLife, as we describe below.

Our construction results in some negative sensor readings, but choosing a non-negative noise distribution, such as the Beta distribution, does not appreciably change our results.

***Computing with Distributions*** Errors in each sensor are independent, so the function that counts a cell's live neighbors is almost unchanged:

```
Uncertain<double> CountLiveNeighbors(Cell me) {
  Uncertain<double> sum = new Uncertain<double>(0.0);
  foreach (Cell neighbor in me.GetNeighbors())
    sum = sum + SenseNeighbor(me, neighbor);
  return sum;  }
```

Because each sensor now returns a real number rather than a binary value, the count of live neighbors is now a distribution over real numbers rather than an integer. Operator overloading means that no further changes are necessary, as the addition operator will automatically propagate uncertainty into the resulting sum.

***Conditionals*** The Game of Life applies its rules with four conditionals to the output of `CountLiveNeighbors`:

```
bool IsAlive = IsCellAlive(me);
bool WillBeAlive = IsAlive;
Uncertain<double> NumLive = CountLiveNeighbors(me);
if (IsAlive && NumLive < 2)
    WillBeAlive = false;
else if (IsAlive && 2 <= NumLive && NumLive <= 3)
    WillBeAlive = true;
else if (IsAlive && NumLive > 3)
    WillBeAlive = false;
else if (!IsAlive && NumLive == 3)
    WillBeAlive = true;
```

Each comparison involving `NumLive` implicitly performs a hypothesis test.

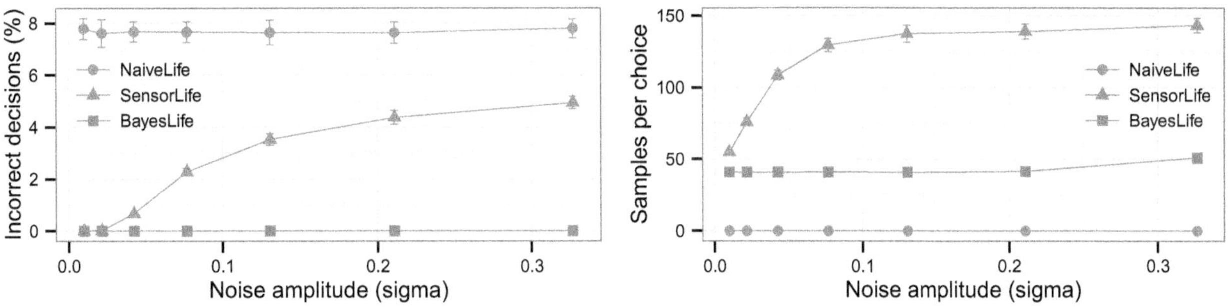

(a) Rate of incorrect decisions

(b) Samples required for each cell

**Figure 14.** SensorLife uses *Uncertain⟨T⟩* to significantly decrease the rate of incorrect decisions compared to a naive version, but requires more samples to make decisions. BayesLife incorporates domain knowledge into SensorLife for even better results.

***Evaluation*** We compare the noisy versions of the Game of Life to the precise version. We perform this comparison across a range of noise amplitude values $\sigma$. Each execution randomly initializes a $20 \times 20$ cell board and performs 25 generations, evaluating a total of 10000 cell updates. For each noise level $\sigma$, we execute each Game of Life 50 times. We report means and 95% confidence intervals.

Figure 14(a) shows the rate of incorrect decisions ($y$-axis) made by each noisy Game of Life at various noise levels ($x$-axis). NaiveLife has a consistent error rate of 8%, as it takes only a small amount of noise to cross the integer thresholds in the rules of the Game of Life. SensorLife's errors scale with noise, as it considers multiple samples and so can correct smaller amounts of noise. At all noise levels, SensorLife is considerably more accurate than NaiveLife.

Mitigating noise has a cost, as *Uncertain⟨T⟩* must sample each sensor multiple times to evaluate each conditional. Figure 14(b) shows the number of samples drawn for each cell update ($y$-axis) by each noisy Game of Life at various noise levels ($x$-axis). Clearly NaiveLife only draws one sample per conditional. The number of samples for SensorLife increases as the noise level increases, because noisier sensors require more computation to reach a conclusion at the conditional.

***Improving Estimates*** SensorLife achieves better results than NaiveLife despite not demonstrating any knowledge of the fact that the underlying true state of a sensor must be either 0 or 1. To improve SensorLife, an expert can exploit knowledge of the distribution and variance of the sensor noise. We call this improved version BayesLife.

Let $v$ be the raw, noisy sensor reading, and $s$ the underlying true state (either 0 or 1). Then $v = s + N(0,\sigma)$ for some $\sigma$ we know. Since $s$ is binary, we have two *hypotheses* for $s$: $H_0$ says $s = 0$ and $H_1$ says $s = 1$. The raw sensor reading $v$ is evidence, and Bayes' theorem calculates a *posterior probability*

$$\Pr[H_0|v] = \Pr[v|H_0]\Pr[H_0]/\Pr[v]$$

for $H_0$ given the evidence, and similarly for $H_1$. To improve an estimate, we calculate which of $H_0$ and $H_1$ is more likely under the posterior probability, and fix the sensor reading to be 0 or 1 accordingly.

This formulation requires (i) the prior likelihoods $\Pr[H_0]$ and $\Pr[H_1]$; and (ii) a likelihood function to calculate $\Pr[v|H_0]$ and $\Pr[v|H_1]$. We assume no prior knowledge, so both $H_0$ and $H_1$ are equally likely: $\Pr[H_0] = \Pr[H_1] = 0.5$. Because we know the noise is Gaussian, we know the likelihood function is just the likelihood that $N(0,\sigma) = s - v$ for each of $s = 0$ and 1, which we calculate trivially using the Gaussian density function. We need not calculate $\Pr[v]$ since it is a common denominator of the two probabilities we compare.

To implement BayesLife we wrap each sensor with a new function `SenseNeighborFixed`. Since the two likelihoods $\Pr[v|H_0]$ and $\Pr[v|H_1]$ have the same variance and shape and are symmetric around 0 and 1, respectively, and the priors are equal, the hypothesis with higher posterior probability is simply the closer of 0 or 1 to $v$. The implementation is therefore trivial:

```
Uncertain<double>
SenseNeighborFixed(Cell me, Cell neighbor) {
  Func<double> samplingFunction = () => {
    Uncertain<double> Raw = SenseNeighbor(me, neighbor);
    double Sample = Raw.Sample();
    return Sample > 0.5 ? 1.0 : 0.0;
  };
  return new Uncertain<double>(samplingFunction);  }
```

***Evaluation of BayesLife*** Figure 14(a) shows that BayesLife makes no mistakes at all at these noise levels. At noise levels higher than $\sigma = 0.4$, considering individual samples in isolation breaks down as the values become almost completely random. A better implementation could calculate joint likelihoods with multiple samples, since each sample is drawn from the same underlying distribution. Figure 14(b) shows that BayesLife requires fewer samples than SensorLife, but of course still requires more samples than NaiveLife.

### 5.3 Uncertain<T> for Machine Learning: Parakeet

This section explores using *Uncertain⟨T⟩* for machine learning, inspired by *Parrot* [12], which trains neural networks for approximate hardware. We study the Sobel operator from the Parrot evaluation, which calculates the gradient of image intensity at a pixel. Parrot creates a neural network that approximates the Sobel operator.

Machine learning algorithms estimate the true value of a function. One source of uncertainty in their estimates is generalization error, where predictions are good on training data but poor on unseen data. To combat this error, Bayesian machine learning considers *distributions* of estimates, reflecting how different estimators would answer an unseen input. Figure 15 shows for one such input a distribution of neural network outputs created by the Monte Carlo method described below, the output from the single naive neural network Parrot trains, and the true output. The one Parrot value is significantly different from the correct value. Using a distribution helps mitigate generalization error by recognizing other possible predictions.

Computation amplifies generalization error. For example, edge-detection algorithms use the Sobel operator to report an edge if the gradient is large (e.g., $s(p) > 0.1$). Though Parrot approximates the Sobel operator well, with an average root-mean-square error of 3.4%, using its output in such a conditional is a computation. This computation amplifies the error and results in a 36% false positive rate. In Figure 15, by considering the entire distribution, the evidence for the condition $s(p) > 0.1$ is only 70%. To accurately consume estimates, developers must consider the effect of uncertainty not just on direct output but on computations that consume it.

We introduce Parakeet, which approximates code using Bayesian neural networks, and encapsulates the distribution with *Uncertain*$\langle T \rangle$. This abstraction encourages developers to consider uncertainty in the machine learning prediction. We evaluate Parakeet by approximating the Sobel operator $s(p)$ and computing the edge detection conditional $s(p) > 0.1$.

***Identifying the Distribution*** We seek a *posterior predictive distribution* (PPD), which tells us for a given input how likely each possible output is to be correct, based on the training data. Intuitively, this distribution reflects predictions from *other* neural networks that also explain the training data well.

Formally, a neural network is a function $y(\mathbf{x}; \mathbf{w})$ that approximates the output of a target function $f(\mathbf{x})$. The weight vector $\mathbf{w}$ describes how each neuron in the network relates to the others. Traditional training uses example inputs and outputs to learn a single weight vector $\mathbf{w}$ for prediction. In a Bayesian formulation, we learn the PPD $p(t|\mathbf{x}, \mathcal{D})$ (the distribution in Figure 15), a distribution of predictions of $f(\mathbf{x})$ given the training data $\mathcal{D}$.

We adopt the *hybrid Monte Carlo* algorithm to create samples from the PPD [20]. Each sample describes a neural network. Intuitively, we create multiple neural networks by perturbing the search. Formally, we sample the posterior distribution $p(\mathbf{w}|\mathcal{D})$ to approximate the PPD $p(t|\mathbf{x}, \mathcal{D})$ using Monte Carlo integration, since

$$p(t|\mathbf{x}, \mathcal{D}) = \int p(t|\mathbf{x}, \mathbf{w}) p(\mathbf{w}|\mathcal{D}) \, d\mathbf{w}.$$

The instance of *Uncertain*$\langle T \rangle$ that Parakeet returns draws samples from this PPD. Each sample of $p(\mathbf{w}|\mathcal{D})$ from hybrid Monte Carlo is a vector $\mathbf{w}$ of weights for a neural network.

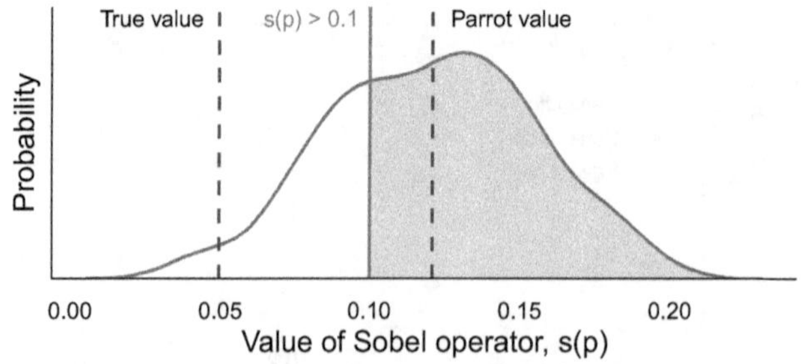


**Figure 15.** Error distribution for Sobel approximated by neural networks. Parrot experiences a false positive on this test, which Parakeet eliminates by evaluating the *evidence* that $s(p) > 0.1$ (the shaded area).

To evaluate a sample from the PPD $p(t|\mathbf{x}, \mathcal{D})$, we execute a neural network using the weights $\mathbf{w}$ and input $\mathbf{x}$. The resulting output is a sample of the PPD.

We execute hybrid Monte Carlo offline and capture a fixed number of samples in a training phase. We use these samples at runtime as a fixed pool for the sampling function. If the sample size is sufficiently large, this approach approximates true sampling well. As with other Markov chain Monte Carlo algorithms, the next sample in hybrid Monte Carlo depends on the current sample, which improves on pure random walk behavior that scales poorly in high dimensions. To compensate for this dependence we discard most samples and only retain every $M^{\text{th}}$ sample for some large $M$.

Hybrid Monte Carlo has two downsides. First, we must execute multiple neural networks (one for each sample of the PPD). Second, it often requires hand tuning to achieve practical rejection rates. Other PPD approximations strike different trade-offs. For example, a Gaussian approximation [5] to the PPD would mitigate all these downsides, but may be an inappropriate approximation in some cases. Since the Sobel operator's posterior is approximately Gaussian (Figure 15), a Gaussian approximation may be appropriate.

***Evaluation*** We approximate the Sobel operator with Parakeet, using 5000 examples for training and a separate 500 examples for evaluation. For each evaluation example we compute the ground truth $s(p) > 0.1$ and then evaluate this conditional using *Uncertain*$\langle T \rangle$, which asks whether $\Pr[s(p) > 0.1] > \alpha$ for varying thresholds $\alpha$.

Figure 16 shows the results of our evaluation. The $x$-axis plots a range of conditional thresholds $\alpha$ and the $y$-axis plots precision and recall for the evaluation data. Precision is the probability that a detected edge is actually an edge, and so describes false positives. Recall is the probability that an actual edge is detected, and so describes false negatives. Because Parrot does not consider uncertainty, it locks developers into a particular balance of precision and recall. In this example, Parrot provides 100% recall, detecting all actual edges, but only 64% precision, so 36% of reported edges are false positives. With a conditional threshold, developers select their own balance. For example, a threshold of $\alpha = 0.8$ (i.e., eval-

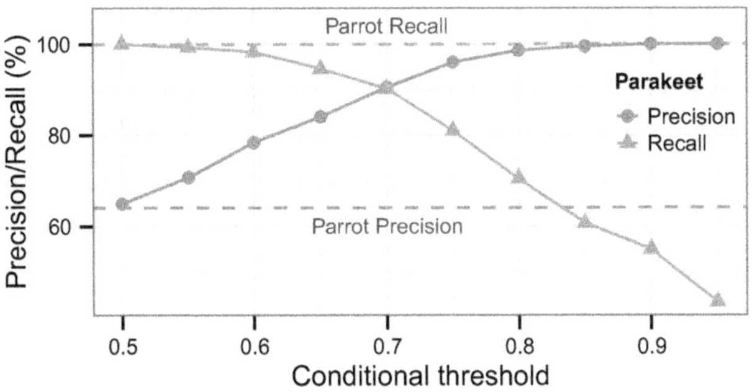


**Figure 16.** Developers choose a balance between false positives and negatives with Parakeet using *Uncertain*$\langle T\rangle$.

uating $\Pr[s(p) > 0.1] > 0.8$) results in 71% recall and 99% precision, meaning more false negatives (missed edges) but fewer false positives. The ideal balance of false positives and negatives depends on the particular application and is now in the hands of the developer.

***Summary*** Machine learning approximates functions and so introduces uncertainty. Failing to consider uncertainty causes uncertainty bugs; even though Parrot approximates the Sobel operator with 3.4% average error, using this approximation in a conditional results in a 36% false positive rate. Parakeet uses *Uncertain*$\langle T\rangle$, which encourages the developer to consider the effect of uncertainty on machine learning predictions. The results on Parakeet show that developers may easily control the balance between false positives and false negatives, as appropriate for the application, using *Uncertain*$\langle T\rangle$. Of course, *Uncertain*$\langle T\rangle$ is not a panacea for machine learning. Our formulation leverages a probabilistic interpretation of neural networks, which not all machine learning techniques have, and only addresses generalization error.

These case studies highlight the need for a programming language solution for uncertainty. Many systems view error in a local scope, measuring its effect only on direct output, but as all the case studies clearly illustrate, the effect of uncertainty on programs is inevitably global. We cannot view estimation processes such as GPS and machine learning in isolation. *Uncertain*$\langle T\rangle$ encourages developers to reason about how local errors impact the entirety of their programs.

## 6. Related Work

This section relates our work to programming languages with statistical semantics or that support solving statistical problems. Because we use, rather than add to, the statistics literature, prior sections cite this literature as appropriate.

***Probabilistic Programming*** Prior work has focused on the needs of experts. Probabilistic programming creates generative models of problems involving uncertainty by introducing random variables into the syntax and semantics of a programming language. Experts encode generative models which the program queries through inference techniques. The foundation of probabilistic programming is the monadic structure of

```
earthquake = Bernoulli(0.0001)
burglary = Bernoulli(0.001)
alarm = earthquake or burglary
if (earthquake)
  phoneWorking = Bernoulli(0.7)
else
  phoneWorking = Bernoulli(0.99)

observe(alarm)          # If the alarm goes off...
query(phoneWorking)     # ...does the phone still work?
```

**Figure 17.** A probabilistic program. To infer the probability of `phoneWorking` requires exploring both branches [10].

probability distributions [14, 25], an elegant representation of joint probability distributions (i.e., generative models) in a functional language. Researchers have evolved this idea into a variety of languages such as BUGS [13], Church [15], Fun [6], and IBAL [24].

Figure 17 shows an example probabilistic program that infers the likelihood that a phone is working given that an alarm goes off. The program queries the posterior distribution of the Bernoulli variable `phoneWorking` given the observation that `alarm` is true. To infer this distribution by sampling, the runtime must repeatedly evaluate both branches. This program illustrates a key shortcoming of many probabilistic programming languages: inference is very expensive for poor rejection rates. Since there is only a 0.11% chance of `alarm` being true, most inference techniques will have high rejection rates and so require many samples to sufficiently infer the posterior distribution. Using Church [15], we measured 20 seconds to draw 100 samples from this model [7].

*Uncertain*$\langle T\rangle$ is a probabilistic programming language, since it manipulates random variables in a host language. Unlike other probabilistic languages, *Uncertain*$\langle T\rangle$ only executes one side of a conditional branch, and only reasons about conditional distributions. For example, air temperature depends on variables such as humidity, altitude, and pressure. When programming with data from a temperature sensor, the question is not whether temperature can ever be greater than 85° (which a joint distribution can answer), but rather whether the current measurement from the sensor is greater than 85°. This measurement is inextricably conditioned on the current humidity, altitude, and pressure, and so the conditional distribution that *Uncertain*$\langle T\rangle$ manipulates is appropriate. For programs consuming estimated data, problems are not abstract but concrete instances and so the conditional distribution is just as useful as the full joint distribution. *Uncertain*$\langle T\rangle$ exploits this restriction to achieve efficiency and accessibility, since these conditional distributions are specified by operator overloading and evaluated with ancestral sampling.

Like the probability monad [25], *Uncertain*$\langle T\rangle$ builds and later queries a computation tree, but it adds continuous distributions and a semantics for conditional expressions that developers must implement manually using the monad. *Uncertain*$\langle T\rangle$ uses sampling functions in the same fashion as Park et al. [23], but we add accessible and principled conditional operators. Park et al. do not describe a mechanism for choosing how many samples to draw from a sampling function; instead their query operations use a fixed runtime-specified sample size. We exploit hypothesis testing in conditional expressions to dynamically select the appropriate sample size. Sankaranarayanan et al. [27] provide a static analysis for checking assertions in probabilistic programs. Their `estimateProbability` assertion calculates the probability of a conditional expression involving random variables being true. While their approach is superficially similar to *Uncertain*$\langle T \rangle$'s conditional expressions, `estimateProbability` handles only simple random variables and linear arithmetic operations so that it can operate without sampling. *Uncertain*$\langle T \rangle$ addresses arbitrary random variables and operations, and uses hypothesis testing to limit the performance impact of sampling in a principled way.

***Domain-Specific Approaches*** In robotics, CES [30] extends C++ to include probabilistic variables (e.g., `prob<int>`) for simple distributions. Instances of `prob<T>` store a list of pairs $(x, p(x))$ that map each possible value of the variable to its probability. This representation restricts CES to simple discrete distributions. *Uncertain*$\langle T \rangle$ adopts CES's idea of encapsulating random variables in a generic type, but uses a more robust representation for distributions and adds an accessible semantics for conditional expressions.

In databases, Barbara et al. incorporate uncertainty and estimation into the semantics of relational operators [1]. Benjelloun et al. trace provenance back through probabilistic queries [2], and Dalvi and Suciu describe a "possible worlds" semantics for relational joins [11]. Hazy [18] asks developers to write Markov logic networks (sets of logic rules and confidences) to interact with databases while managing uncertainty. These probabilistic databases must build a model of the entire joint posterior distribution of a query. In contrast, *Uncertain*$\langle T \rangle$ reasons only about conditional distributions.

Interval analysis represents an uncertain value as a simple interval and propagates it through computations [19]. For example, if $X = [4, 6]$, then $X/2 = [2, 3]$. Interval analysis is particularly suited to bounding floating point error in scientific computation. The advantage of interval analysis is its simplicity and efficiency, since many operations over real numbers are trivial to define over intervals. The downside is that intervals treat all random variables as having uniform distributions, an assumption far too limiting for many applications. By using sampling functions, *Uncertain*$\langle T \rangle$ achieves the simplicity of interval analysis when defining operations, but is more broadly applicable.

In approximate computing, EnerJ [26] uses the type system to separate exact from approximate data and govern how they interact. This type system encourages developers to reason about approximate data in their program. *Uncertain*$\langle T \rangle$ builds on this idea with a semantics for the quantitative impact of uncertainty on data. Rely is a programming language that statically reasons about the quantitative error of a program executing on unreliable hardware [9]. Developers use Rely to express assertions about the accuracy of their code's output, and the Rely analyzer statically verifies whether these assertions could be breached based on a specification of unreliable hardware failures. In contrast to *Uncertain*$\langle T \rangle$, Rely does not address applications that compute with random variables and does not reason dynamically about the error in a particular instance of uncertain data.

## 7. Conclusion

Emerging applications solve increasingly ambitious and ambiguous problems on data from tiny smartphone sensors, huge distributed databases, the web, and simulations. Although practitioners in other sciences have principled ways to make decisions under uncertainty, only recently have programming languages begun to assist developers with this task. Because prior solutions are either too simple to aid correctness or too complex for most developers to use, many developers create bugs by ignoring uncertainty completely.

This paper presents a new abstraction and shows how it helps developers to correctly operate on and reason with uncertain data. We describe its syntax and probabilistic semantics, emphasizing simplicity for non-experts while encouraging developers to consider the effects of random error. Our semantics for conditional expressions helps developers to understand and control false positives and false negatives. We present implementation strategies that use sampling and hypothesis testing to realize our goals efficiently. Compared to probabilistic programming, *Uncertain*$\langle T \rangle$ gains substantial efficiency through goal-specific sampling. Our three case studies show that *Uncertain*$\langle T \rangle$ improves application correctness in practice without burdening developers.

Future directions for *Uncertain*$\langle T \rangle$ include runtime and compiler optimizations that exploit statistical knowledge; exploring accuracy, efficiency, and expressiveness for more substantial applications; and improving correctness with models of common phenomena, such as physics, calendar, and history in uncertain data libraries.

Uncertainty is not a vice to abstract away, but many applications and libraries try to avoid its complexity. *Uncertain*$\langle T \rangle$ embraces uncertainty while recognizing that most developers are not statistics experts. Our research experience with *Uncertain*$\langle T \rangle$ suggests that it has the potential to change how developers think about and solve the growing variety of problems that involve uncertainty.

## Acknowledgments

We thank Steve Blackburn, Adrian Sampson, Darko Stefanovic and Ben Zorn for comments on earlier versions of this work and the anonymous reviewers for their helpful feedback.

## References

[1] D. Barbara, H. Garcia-Molina, and D. Porter. The management of probabilistic data. *IEEE Transactions on Knowledge and Data Engineering*, 4(5):487–502, 1992.

[2] O. Benjelloun, A. D. Sarma, A. Halevy, and J. Widom. ULDBs: Databases with uncertainty and lineage. In *ACM International Conference on Very Large Data Bases (VLDB)*, pages 953–964, 2006.

[3] E. R. Berlekamp, J. H. Conway, and R. K. Guy. *Winning Ways for Your Mathematical Plays*, volume 4. A K Peters, 2004.

[4] S. Bhat, A. Agarwal, R. Vuduc, and A. Gray. A type theory for probability density functions. In *ACM Symposium on Principles of Programming Languages (POPL)*, pages 545–556, 2012.

[5] C. M. Bishop. *Pattern Recognition and Machine Learning*. Springer, 2006.

[6] J. Borgström, A. D. Gordon, M. Greenberg, J. Margetson, and J. Van Gael. Measure transformer semantics for Bayesian machine learning. In *European Symposium on Programming (ESOP)*, pages 77–96, 2011.

[7] J. Bornholt. *Abstractions and techniques for programming with uncertain data*. Honors thesis, Australian National University, 2013.

[8] G. E. P. Box and M. E. Muller. A note on the generation of random normal deviates. *The Annals of Mathematical Statistics*, 29(2):610–611, 1958.

[9] M. Carbin, S. Misailovic, and M. C. Rinard. Verifying quantitative reliability of programs that execute on unreliable hardware. In *ACM Conference on Object-Oriented Programming Systems, Languages, and Applications (OOPSLA)*, pages 33–52, 2013.

[10] A. T. Chaganty, A. V. Nori, and S. K. Rajamani. Efficiently sampling probabilistic programs via program analysis. In *Proceedings of the 16th international conference on Artificial Intelligence and Statistics, AISTATS 2013, Scottsdale, AZ, USA, April 29 - May 1, 2013*, pages 153–160. JMLR, 2013.

[11] N. Dalvi and D. Suciu. Management of probabilistic data: Foundations and challenges. In *ACM Symposium on Principles of Database Systems (PODS)*, pages 1–12, 2007.

[12] H. Esmaeilzadeh, A. Sampson, L. Ceze, and D. Burger. Neural acceleration for general-purpose approximate programs. In *IEEE/ACM International Symposium on Microarchitecture (MICRO)*, pages 449–460, 2012.

[13] W. R. Gilks, A. Thomas, and D. J. Spiegelhalter. A language and program for complex Bayesian modelling. *Journal of the Royal Statistical Society. Series D (The Statistician)*, 43(1): 169–177, 1994.

[14] M. Giry. A categorical approach to probability theory. In *Categorical Aspects of Topology and Analysis*, volume 915 of *Lecture Notes in Mathematics*, pages 68–85. 1982.

[15] N. D. Goodman, V. K. Mansinghka, D. M. Roy, K. Bonawitz, and J. B. Tenenbaum. Church: A language for generative models. In *Conference in Uncertainty in Artificial Intelligence (UAI)*, pages 220–229, 2008.

[16] S. Jaroszewicz and M. Korzeń. Arithmetic operations on independent random variables: A numerical approach. *SIAM Journal on Scientific Computing*, 34:A1241–A1265, 2012.

[17] C. Jennison and B. W. Turnbull. *Group sequential methods with applications to clinical trials*. Chapman & Hall, 2000.

[18] A. Kumar, F. Niu, and C. Ré. Hazy: Making it Easier to Build and Maintain Big-data Analytics. *ACM Queue*, 11(1):30–46, 2013.

[19] R. E. Moore. *Interval analysis*. Prentice-Hall, 1966.

[20] R. M. Neal. *Bayesian learning for neural networks*. PhD thesis, University of Toronto, 1994.

[21] P. Newson and J. Krumm. Hidden Markov map matching through noise and sparseness. In *ACM International Conference on Advances in Geographic Information Systems (GIS)*, pages 336–343, 2009.

[22] A. Papoulis and S. U. Pillai. *Probability, random variables, and stochastic processes*. New York, NY, 4th edition, 2000.

[23] S. Park, F. Pfenning, and S. Thrun. A probabilistic language based on sampling functions. In *ACM Symposium on Principles of Programming Languages (POPL)*, pages 171–182, 2005.

[24] A. Pfeffer. IBAL: a probabilistic rational programming language. In *International Joint Conference on Artificial Intelligence (IJCAI)*, pages 733–740, 2001.

[25] N. Ramsey and A. Pfeffer. Stochastic lambda calculus and monads of probability distributions. In *ACM Symposium on Principles of Programming Languages (POPL)*, pages 154–165, 2002.

[26] A. Sampson, W. Dietl, E. Fortuna, D. Gnanapragasam, L. Ceze, and D. Grossman. EnerJ: Approximate data types for safe and general low-power computation. In *ACM Conference on Programming Language Design and Implementation (PLDI)*, pages 164–174, 2011.

[27] S. Sankaranarayanan, A. Chakarov, and S. Gulwani. Static analysis for probabilistic programs: inferring whole program properties from finitely many paths. In *ACM Conference on Programming Language Design and Implementation (PLDI)*, pages 447–458, 2013.

[28] J. Schwarz, J. Mankoff, and S. E. Hudson. Monte Carlo methods for managing interactive state, action and feedback under uncertainty. In *ACM Symposium on User Interface Software and Technology (UIST)*, pages 235–144, 2011.

[29] R. Thompson. Global positioning system: the mathematics of GPS receivers. *Mathematics Magazine*, 71(4):260–269, 1998.

[30] S. Thrun. Towards programming tools for robots that integrate probabilistic computation and learning. In *IEEE International Conference on Robotics and Automation (ICRA)*, pages 306–312, 2000.

[31] F. Topsøe. On the Glivenko-Cantelli theorem. *Zeitschrift fr Wahrscheinlichkeitstheorie und Verwandte Gebiete*, 14:239–250, 1970.

[32] A. Wald. Sequential Tests of Statistical Hypotheses. *The Annals of Mathematical Statistics*, 16(2):117–186, 1945.

# Using ARM TrustZone to Build a Trusted Language Runtime for Mobile Applications

Nuno Santos†1, Himanshu Raj‡2, Stefan Saroiu‡3, Alec Wolman‡4

†INESC-ID / Instituto Superior Técnico, University of Lisbon
‡Microsoft Research

1nuno.santos@inesc-id.pt, 2rhim@microsoft.com, 3ssaroiu@microsoft.com, 4alecw@microsoft.com

## Abstract

This paper presents the design, implementation, and evaluation of the Trusted Language Runtime (TLR), a system that protects the confidentiality and integrity of .NET mobile applications from OS security breaches. TLR enables separating an application's security-sensitive logic from the rest of the application, and isolates it from the OS and other apps. TLR provides runtime support for the secure component based on a .NET implementation for embedded devices. TLR reduces the TCB of an open source .NET implementation by a factor of 78 with a tolerable performance cost. The main benefit of the TLR is to bring the developer benefits of managed code to trusted computing. With the TLR, developers can build their trusted components with the productivity benefits of modern high-level languages, such as strong typing and garbage collection.

***Categories and Subject Descriptors*** D.4.6 [*Security and Protection*]: Security Kernels

***Keywords*** Mobile Computing; Trusted Computing; ARM TrustZone; Language Runtime

## 1. Introduction

*E-wallet* and *e-health* mobile apps have already started to revolutionize the way people make purchases, and how they handle their health records. As mobile apps start to handle security-sensitive data, smartphones become an attractive target for attacks. In particular, data such as personal photos, location trails, and online banking information have a high value to spammers and identity thieves. As a result, mobile applications have emerged recently with questionable practices [20] as well as outright malware [24].

Unfortunately, protecting data on mobile devices is far from trivial. Typically, mobile apps rely on ad-hoc OS and application-level mechanisms to protect sensitive data and prevent leaks. However, the Trusted Computing Base (TCB) code that mobile apps depend upon is very complex: popular mobile platforms based on iOS [3], Android [1], or Windows 8 [11] comprise a full blown OS, local services, and system libraries, consisting of millions of lines of code (LOC). Therefore it is difficult to ensure the absence of exploitable code vulnerabilities that could be used to disable security checks and retrieve sensitive data.

To improve this situation, the research community has studied the design of trusted computing systems with small TCBs. Flicker [28] and TrustVisor [29] provide confidentiality and integrity protection of application code and data while depending on a small TCB. These systems allow application developers to execute parts of the application logic in a trusted environment isolated from the OS. Because only a few basic services are offered in the trusted environment, in their minimal setup these systems can be built with a TCB on the order of tens of thousands of lines of code.

However, while this prior research has managed to explore the limits in shrinking the TCB of trusted computing systems, the functionality of these systems may be too restrictive for mobile applications. Mobile apps are typically written in high-level languages and compiled to intermediate code (e.g., Dalvik *bytecode* [2] or .NET *managed code* [5]). Flicker and TrustVisor can only execute small pieces of application logic written in native code; they have no built-in runtime engine and are unable to interpret intermediate code.

This paper presents the Trusted Language Runtime (TLR), a small runtime engine capable of interpreting .NET managed code inside a trusted environment. While adding this runtime increases the TCB size, TLR is carefully crafted to avoid a bloated TCB and keep it significantly smaller than a full-blown .NET framework and a full-featured OS. TLR uses three techniques to keep the TCB small: (i) allow application developers to factor out the security-sensitive app



*ASPLOS '14*, March 1–5, 2014, Salt Lake City, Utah, USA.

ACM 978-1-4503-2305-5/14/03. . . $15.00.
http://dx.doi.org/10.1145/2541940.2541949

logic into classes that transparently run in a trusted environment, (ii) isolate the TLR and the trusted app code from the bulk of the system software by using ARM TrustZone technology [14], and (iii) borrow parts of the runtime engine design from the .NET Micro Framework (NETMF) [6], a small .NET implementation designed for embedded devices.

Although we presented the basic TLR design in an earlier workshop paper [34], this paper goes beyond the original TLR proposal and makes the following contributions. First, we provide a complete design of the TLR architecture describing the components running in the trusted environment, in the OS, and in the untrusted application. We handle issues such as the arbitration of resource management between both the TLR and the native OS (i.e., how to securely share memory, CPU, and handle interrupts across domains) and include low-level mechanisms that coordinate the execution flow of the applications between the trusted and the untrusted domains (e.g., transparently bind the native-code processes of the OS with managed-code threads in the TLR).

Second, we describe our TLR prototype implementation on real TrustZone hardware, rather than in an ARM simulator. We present the challenges related to the TrustZone compatibility and portability issues of a large OS, namely Linux.

Third, we present a thorough evaluation of the TLR. We describe the performance overhead due to running interpreted code rather than native code. However, this overhead does not hurt the user experience for the use cases and benchmarks we tested. To illustrate that the TLR can be useful for realistic applications, we implemented several financial and e-health mobile apps. This experience shows that the TLR is easy to program because of its tight integration with .NET that offers the productivity benefits of modern high-level languages and rich software development tools. Our results show that, although the TCB size of the TLR is larger than existing trusted computing systems (namely, it is 6× larger than TrustVisor), the TLR's TCB reduction when targeting an open source .NET setup based on Mono [4] and Linux is substantial, namely by a factor of 78.

## 2. Background

This section provides background on ARM TrustZone and the .NET Micro Framework (NETMF), which are the key technologies used in the design of the TLR.

### 2.1 ARM TrustZone

TrustZone [14] is a hardware security technology incorporated into recent ARM processors. It consists of security extensions to an ARM System-On-Chip (SoC) covering the processor, memory, and peripherals. These mechanisms can be leveraged by system designers to run secure services in isolation from the operating system (OS). The secure services that can be built range from a simple library to a complete OS [14]. We briefly describe the relevant TrustZone mechanisms.

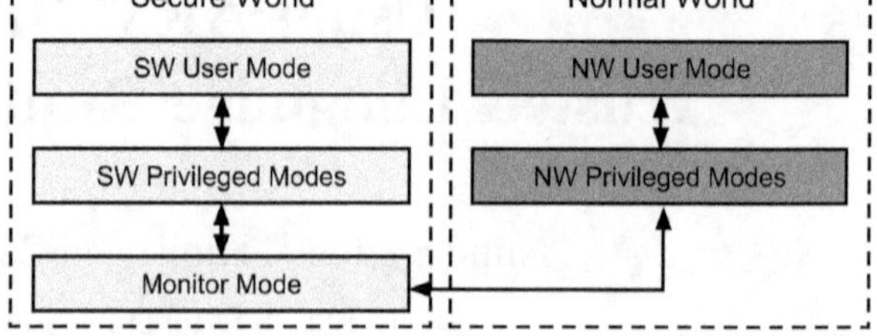


**Figure 1.** Processor modes of ARM-based device with TrustZone extensions.

With TrustZone, the processor can execute instructions in one of two possible security modes, referred to as the *normal world*, where untrusted code executes, and the *secure world*, where secure services run (see Figure 1). These processor modes have independent memory address spaces and different privileges. While code running in the normal world cannot access the secure world address space, code running in the secure world can access the normal world address space in certain conditions. A special processor bit, the *NS* bit, indicates which world the processor is currently executing in, and this bit is sent over the memory bus and certain I/O buses for peripherals. This enables the system designer to allocate memory solely to the secure world, and to control which devices are accessible from the different worlds. Hardware interrupts can trap directly into the secure world interrupt handler, which then enables flexible routing of those interrupts to either world.

Because the processor executes in one security mode at a time, to execute software in another security mode the processor must switch worlds. World switch is done via a special instruction called the Secure Monitor Call (*smc*). When the CPU executes the *smc* instruction, the hardware switches into the secure monitor, which (i) performs a secure context switch into the secure world, and (ii) enables sharing data by copying data across worlds.

### 2.2 Microsoft .NET Micro Framework

We use the .NET Micro Framework (NETMF) [6] as a starting point for the TLR design. The NETMF is a lightweight implementation of Microsoft's .NET optimized for embedded systems, such as sensor networks, robotics, and wearable devices [13].

The NETMF design was driven by three main tenets. First, an emphasis was put on offering a user-friendly and robust programming environment. To this end, NETMF enables application programmers to use fully featured development tools like Microsoft Visual Studio, high-level languages like C#, and a collection of code libraries to program embedded systems. Applications are compiled into *managed code*, an intermediate language comparable to Java bytecodes, and interpreted by a CLR runtime (the equivalent version of the Java virtual machine in .NET terminology). The CLR included in NETMF provides a type system, code execution safety, and garbage collection. Second, NETMF was

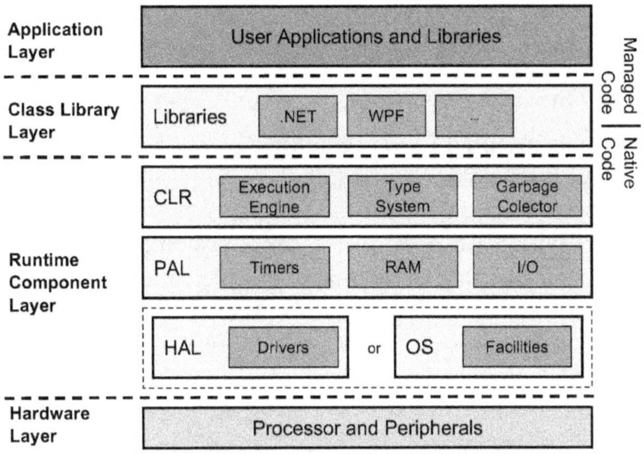


**Figure 2.** Architecture of the .NET Micro Framework.

tailored for resource constrained devices. For improved efficiency, NETMF precludes the existence of an underlying OS and runs directly on metal. Internally, NETMF owns all execution and it includes only the bare system functionality for managing memory, CPU, and peripherals. To optimize resources, some .NET features are not currently supported (e.g., no support for multidimensional arrays, and no templates). Third, NETMF was geared towards customizability for a wide variety of devices. For this reason, it includes a hardware abstraction layer (HAL) and a platform abstraction layer (PAL).

Figure 2 shows the NETMF hardware and software architecture in more detail. The hardware layer consists of the processor and peripherals. The runtime layer includes the CLR, the HAL, and the PAL. The CLR contains modules for managed code execution, thread scheduling, memory management, and other system services. The HAL and PAL manage the underlying hardware components. The class library layer is an object-oriented collection of classes implemented in C# that application developers can use to program embedded applications. The application layer contains the managed code of apps.

## 3. Goals, Assumptions, and Threat Model

TLR was designed to meet the following three goals:

1. **Small TCB size:** The TCB of the TLR should not include the OS nor any untrusted application code.
2. **Ease of programming:** Programming the TLR should be as simple as programming any of today's managed code environments such as Java or .NET.
3. **Compatible with legacy software environments:** Deploying the TLR should not require a radical redesign of today's legacy operating systems or other legacy software running on the mobile device.

We require that mobile devices where the TLR is deployed support the TrustZone security extensions, and that their hardware behaves correctly. We assume the existence of external *trusted parties*, such as offline certification authorities or online services with which security-sensitive apps deployed on the TLR can communicate over secure channels. Lastly, we rely on the correctness of cryptographic primitives and algorithms. Note that we make no assumptions about the correctness of the operating system on the mobile platform.

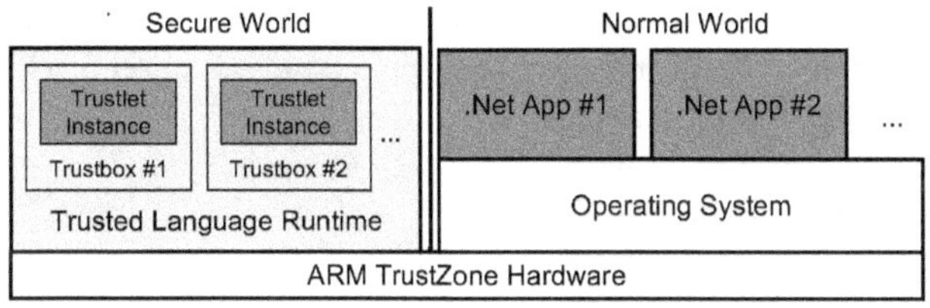


**Figure 3.** TLR high-level architecture.

TLR protects the application state against the following adversary. The attacker can compromise the OS and have access to the TLR interface, which is provided through specific TrustZone mechanisms. The attacker can reboot the mobile platform and gain access to data residing on persistent storage. She can eavesdrop the network and interfere with the communication between the TLR and any third party trusted components outside the device. However, we do not consider side-channel attacks nor physical attacks that fall outside the defense capabilities of TrustZone technology, namely those that require disassembling the chip packages of application processors or memory modules.

## 4. Overview of Trusted Language Runtime

Figure 3 illustrates the TLR's high-level architecture. TLR provides two execution environments: an *untrusted* one where the smartphone's OS and most application software run, and a *trusted* one, where the TLR code and security-sensitive application components run. These environments map to TrustZone's normal and secure worlds, respectively. Code running in the trusted environment is isolated via TrustZone from all code running in the untrusted one. TLR provides a secure communication channel between the two environments.

With the TLR, a mobile application must be partitioned into two components: a small trusted component running in the secure world, and a larger untrusted component implementing most of the application's functionality. This partitioning technique is similar to privilege separation [17] and to partitioning of applications for improved security in distributed systems [19].

In the trusted world, TLR provides a language runtime based on NETMF. Application code running in the TLR can only perform computations and has no access to peripherals, which are all managed by the untrusted OS. We deliberately limit TLR's access to peripherals to keep a small TCB. Adding I/O access requires building drivers inside the TrustZone, that may have large codebases. Even without access to peripherals, TLR offers enough functionality to meet the security needs of many mobile applications. Section 5 will describe four such applications.

### 4.1 TLR Primitives

**1. Trustbox.** A trustbox is an isolation runtime environment that protects the integrity and confidentiality of code and data. The smartphone's OS (or any untrusted application code) cannot tamper with code running in a trustbox nor inspect its state.
**2. Trustlet.** A trustlet is a class within an application designated to run inside a trustbox. The trustlet specifies an interface that defines what data can cross the boundary between the trustbox and the untrusted world. The .NET runtime's use of strong types ensures that the data crossing this boundary is clearly defined.
**3. Platform identity.** Each device that supports the TLR must provide a unique cryptographic platform identity used for platform authentication and for protection of any trusted code and data deployed on the platform (using encryption). We use a public key pair as the platform ID, and the TLR ensures that the private key is never revealed to any external component.
**4. Seal/Unseal data.** The *seal* primitive encrypts data and binds it to a particular trustlet and platform identity. The trustlet's identity is based on a secure hash of its code (e.g., SHA-2). The *unseal* primitive yields the data contained in the sealed envelope only if this operation is performed (i) inside a trustbox, and (ii) by the trustlet and platform ID originally specified upon seal. To recover sealed data, unseal decrypts it and checks that the hash of the requesting trustlet matches the hash of the trustlet that sealed the data. Seal and Unseal serve two roles: (i) allowing a trustlet to persist state across reboots, and (ii) enabling a remote trusted party (e.g., a trusted server) to encrypt data so that only a designated trustlet can decrypt it.

***Typical development scenario.*** To build a trusted mobile application with the TLR, a developer typically performs the following four steps: (i) partition off a small part of the application that needs to handle sensitive data into a trustlet, (ii) deploy the trustlet on the designated platform, (iii) ensure that sensitive data can only be accessed on a designated platform by sealing the data to the trustlet running on the designated platform, and (iv) deploy the sealed data to the designated platform to run it inside its trustbox, thereby ensuring that the trustlet state is protected at runtime.

## 5. Use Cases

To illustrate TLR's practicality, we show how to implement four common security use cases in TLR: storing one-time passwords, user authentication, secure mobile transactions, and access control to sensitive data. We describe these use cases in the context of four applications. While our description is done at a high-level, more details of these applications' security protocols can be found in Appendix A.

### 5.1 One-time Passwords

A commonly used form of one-time passwords is *Transaction Authentication Numbers* (TANs) [8] for online banking purposes. Today, some banks send paper cards to their customers with a list of TANs. When a customer initiates an online transfer, the bank specifies an index into the TAN list and asks for the associated TAN. The customer, in addition to typing their personal password, must respond with the correct TAN, otherwise the transaction is aborted. Each TAN is used once; when all TANs are used, the bank sends a new TAN list to the customer.

To avoid the burden of carrying a physical TAN list, banks can use the TLR to provide secure storage of *digital* TAN lists. A mobile app using the TLR keeps track of the TAN list on the customer's smartphone, and provides an interface for querying a TAN based on a TAN index. The TAN indices are not simply sequential integers, instead they are capabilities: hard-to-guess numbers chosen from a large address space.

The bank seals TAN lists on a per-customer basis such that it can only be unsealed by the bank's trustlet running on the customer's smartphone. When the customer initiates a bank transfer, the bank sends a TAN index challenge to the trustlet, and the trustlet unseals the TAN list, finds the index, and responds to the bank with the appropriate TAN value that authorizes the transfer. Because TAN indices are only used once, there is no opportunity for man-in-the-middle replay attacks. Because TAN indices are hard-to-guess, there is no opportunity for a malicious entity to obtain the TAN list. The trustlet interface only requires two methods: `LoadTanLst`, and `GetTan` (see Figure 5 for code excerpts).

### 5.2 User Authentication

Our second use case shows how to use the TLR for user authentication purposes by implementing a mobile ticketing app. Unlike existing digital ticket mechanisms that reveal the ticket during validation (e.g., QR codes), user authentication can be done by a TLR app without disclosing the ticket details. Apps that only send proof of ticket possession reduce the possibility of ticket theft by malware.

We illustrate how mobile ticketing could be done for a public transit company. There are three actors: a ticket issuer (the public transit service), a mobile ticketing app with a trustlet, and ticket verifiers (terminals at the entrance to the bus or subway). The issuer sends sealed tickets to the trustlet at purchase time. To obtain access, the user validates the digital ticket by asking the trustlet to issue a ticket proof to the terminal. If the proof is valid, the terminal produces a visual or audio output reflecting the verification result.

### 5.3 Secure Mobile Transactions

Our third use case uses the TLR to perform secure transactions. The mobile app enables payments at *point of sale*

(POS) terminals by simply waving a smartphone in front of the POS. A trustlet stores the customer's credit card details and engages in a payment protocol with the POS (e.g., via Near Field Communication (NFC) wireless technology). The TLR's role is to secure the runtime state of the mobile app.

We illustrate this mobile payment scenario involving three actors: a *bank*, which issues credit card information, the *mobile payment trustlet*, which keeps track of the credit card details, and the POS vending terminal. The bank seals the credit card information to the trustlet. To perform a transaction, the POS terminal issues a sealed challenge to the trustlet that includes the transaction amount. If the user authorizes the transaction, the trustlet answers the challenge, otherwise it aborts. Possibly at a later point in time, the trustlet communicates with the banks to record the transactions.

### 5.4 Access Control to Sensitive Data

Our final use case describes enforcing access control policies for security-sensitive data in the context of an *e-health* app. The app's goal is to store a personal clinical history on the smartphone and to give health providers secure access to this information during patient visits.

Because giving health providers unrestricted access to health records could raise serious privacy concerns, the TLR can restrict health providers' privileges to this data. Assuming that a central Health Care Authority (HCA) defines a user's access control policy for their clinical history, the TLR can enforce these policies and regulate access to health record information stored on mobile devices.

Our e-health app involves three actors: the *HCA*, the *health providers*, and the *e-health trustlet*. The HCA seals the health records and access control policies to the e-health trustlet. When a health provider asks for a record, the request is sealed to the trustlet. The trustlet unseals it, checks whether the provider's permissions meet the access control policy, and returns the relevant information if the policy is met.

## 6. Detailed Design

This section describes the internals and key design features of the TLR.

### 6.1 TLR Components

Figure 4 shows a detailed view of the TLR architecture. TLR spans the two TrustZone security worlds: the *TLR-domain* running in the secure world and the *OS-domain* running in the normal world. The TLR-domain hosts the TCB of the system: the *TLR core* components and the application trustlets. The OS-domain hosts the untrusted system components: the OS, the *TLR stubs*, and the untrusted application partitions. The TLR stack consists of four layers:

**1. Application layer:** corresponds to the logic of a mobile app split between a trustlet and an untrusted partition.

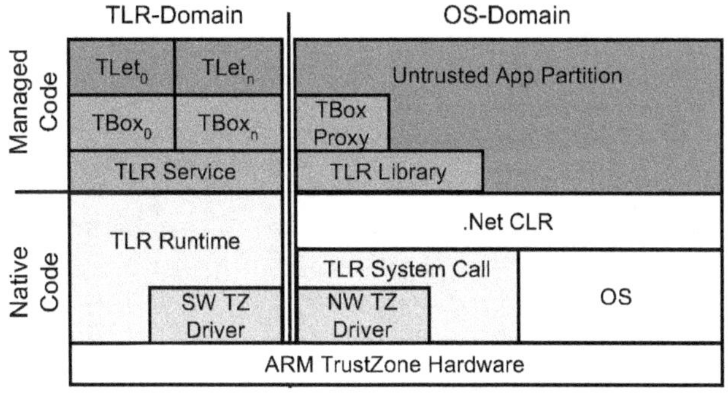


**Figure 4.** Component diagram of the entire TLR system. Components in each layer use the same color.

**2. Trustbox layer:** manages the state of the trustlet instances living in trustboxes. In the TLR-domain, dedicated service threads host the runtime state of trustlets. In the OS-domain, the TLR libraries and proxies contain the logic that bridges the untrusted app partition with the trustlet logic.

**3. Runtime layer:** executes the managed code of trustlet instances and serves their memory allocation needs. In the TLR-domain, the TLR runtime manages the service threads, interprets trustlets' managed code, and manages trustbox resources. In the OS-domain, a a TLR-specific system call bridges the trustbox requests coming from the local application processes (running the untrusted app code) and the TLR.

**4. Trustzone layer:** consists of drivers providing the low-level TrustZone mechanisms responsible for world switching, interrupt handling, communication, and protection.

### 6.2 Programming Model

To implement a trusted application with the TLR, a developer performs the following five steps. As we explain each step, we refer to Figure 5 which contains code snippets of the TAN-based e-banking application previously described in Section 5.1.

***1. Specify the security-sensitive logic:*** The security-sensitive app logic must be enclosed in a trustlet class. The developer creates a trustlet by defining its interface, implementing the class, and creating a meta-data file—the *manifest* (see Figure 5). The trustlet interface must inherit from the `IEntrypoint` interface, and the trustlet main class must inherit from the `Trustlet` class and implement the trustlet interface. The public methods that implement the trustlet interface enable data to cross the barrier between the trusted and untrusted worlds. The programmer must be careful not to let any sensitive data protected by the trustbox leak out into the untrusted world. The manifest's role is to specify the trustlet's class and interface.

***2. Instantiate a trustlet inside a trustbox container:*** The developer must instantiate the trustlet class inside a TLR trustbox. To create a TLR trustbox, an application invokes

**Trustlet Interface**

```
public interface ITanWallet : IEntrypoint
{
   public void Load(Envelope tanLst);
   public Tan GetTan(long id);
}
```

**Trustlet Main Class**

```
public class TanWallet: ITanWallet, Trustlet
{
   private TanList _tanLst = null;

   public void Load(Envelope tans) {
      try {
         _tanLst = (TanList) this.Unseal(tans);
      } catch(Exception e) {
         throw new Exception("Cannot unseal TAN list.");
      }
   }

   public Tan GetTan(long id) {
      Tan tan = _tanLst.Search(id);
      if (tan == null) {
         throw new Exception("ID invalid.");
      } else {
         return tan;
      }
   }
}
```

**Trustlet Manifest**

```
<trustlet name="TanWallet">
   <interface name="ITanWallet" />
   <implementation name="TanWallet" />
</trustlet>
```

**Snippet of Main Class**

```
// setup the TAN wallet trustlet in a trustbox
Trustbox tbox = Trustbox.Create("TanWallet.pkg");

// obtain a reference to trustbox entrypoint
ITanWallet twallet = (ITanWallet) tbox.Entrypoint();

// load the TAN list issued and sealed by bank
twallet.Load(myTanLst);

// obtain a TAN with id requested by bank
Tan tan = twallet.GetTan(id);
```

**Snippet of Third Party Service**

```
// the bank generats TAN list for customer
TanList newLst = customer.GenTanLst();

// seal the list
Envelope sealedLst = Trustlet.Seal(customer.PlatformID(),
   Trustlet.Hash("TanWallet.pkg"), newLst);
```

**Figure 5.** Code sample of a TLR application that manages Transaction Authentication Numbers (TAN) for online banking services (written in C#).

the `Create` method, which takes as input the manifest describing the trustlet class to be instantiated. The role of the `Destroy` method is to clean up the trustbox and release all its resources.

***3. Interact with the trustlet instance:*** The untrusted app partition interacts with the trustlet by invoking its methods. Because the trustlet instance and the untrusted application partition reside in separate domains, the calls must be routed across domains. To make this process transparent to the developer, the TLR library returns a proxy object with a method interface compatible with the trustlet.

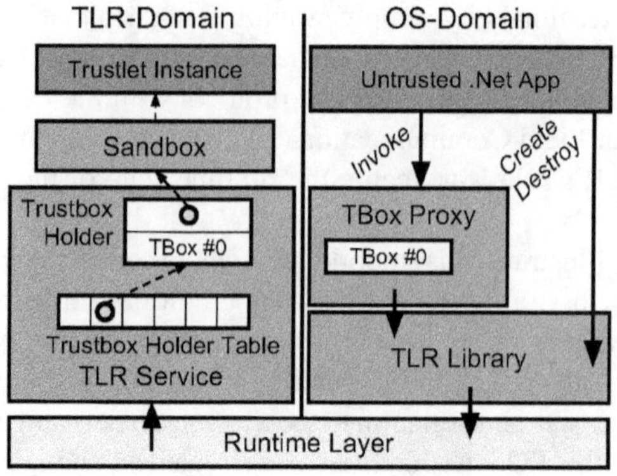


**Figure 6.** Details of the trustbox layer.

***4. Validate trustlet identity and integrity:*** Because arbitrary trustlet code can be instantiated inside trustboxes, third parties must validate the identity and integrity of the trustlet instances before uploading security-sensitive data into the trustbox. For this, the TLR provides the `Seal` and `Unseal` primitives, whose behavior is presented in Section 4.

***5. Compiling and packaging the application:*** In addition to the standard compilation and linking operations, two additional steps are required. First, using a pre-compilation tool, we generate transparent proxies for trustlet instances. Proxies marshal the parameters and return values of the trustlet method call invocation, and encode them into messages exchanged with the TLR. Second, using a packaging tool, we bundle the manifest and the code of all trustlet classes into a single package. This package is signed so that the trustlet's identity and integrity can be verified during unseal.

### 6.3 Trustbox Management

After compiling and packaging an app, users can execute it on a smartphone. The TLR automatically manages the trustboxes created by the app, loads and instantiates trustlet code in the trustboxes, and routes method calls across worlds. All these tasks are performed by the trustbox layer (see Figure 4).

The trustbox layer handles three issues. First, trustbox requests submitted by different applications must be properly routed to the intended trustboxes. Second, trustlet instances residing in trustboxes must be isolated from each other. Third, the runtime state of trustboxes and respective trustlet instances must be consistent across world changes.

To satisfy these requirements, the TLR maintains dedicated *service threads* for servicing the trustboxes owned by each application. Each service thread uses *trustbox holder* data structures (see Figure 6) that contain a trustbox ID and a sandbox object. The sandbox object is a container for the state of a trustlet instance: it handles loading of trustlet classes into memory, enforces isolation across trustbox domains, and provides an interface for invoking the methods of the trustlet instance. In .NET, the sandbox object is implemented using `AppDomain` objects.

Based on these mechanisms, the trustbox layer handles the three main events of the trustbox lifecycle as follows:

**1. Trustbox creation:** When the application requests creation of a trustbox, the TLR library sends a request to the respective service thread running in the TLR-domain. This service thread then: (i) creates a new trustbox holder, containing a new ID and a sandbox; (ii) computes the hash of the trustlet code specified in the manifest; (iii) loads the trustlet classes into the sandbox; and (iv) creates an instance of the trustlet's main class.

**2. Trustbox invocation:** When the application calls the `Entrypoint` method, the TLR library creates a transparent proxy and returns it to the untrusted part of the application. When the untrusted application invokes a method on the proxy, it forwards this invocation request to the TLR-domain service thread. There, the request is decoded and the corresponding method is invoked on the corresponding trustlet instance.

**3. Trustbox destruction:** Finally, destroying a trustbox triggers a request to the service thread for releasing all resources associated with the respective trustbox holder. To persist state across instances, the developer can use he seal primitive to encrypt the relevant state and store it persistently.

### 6.4 Runtime Support

The runtime layer must handle the following three issues. First, because trustlets are managed rather than native code, the TLR must be able to interpret managed code. Second, because multiple applications can execute concurrently, the TLR runtime must be multitasked. Thus, each trustlet service thread is bound to the respective application process running in the OS-domain. Finally, because the runtime layer provides a message delivery to the trustbox layer, an appropriate interface must be devised for this service, preferably without requiring significant OS changes.

To address these issues, the runtime layer implements several mechanisms In the TLR-domain, the TLR runtime includes subcomponents that allow managed code to execute: a managed code interpreter, a type system enforcer, and a garbage collector. The TLR runtime waits for incoming requests from the OS-domain and interprets the managed code required for servicing them. To enable service threads to execute trustlets, service threads are implemented as managed code threads scheduled by the TLR runtime. A service thread is bound to an application process by annotating the service thread descriptor with the PID of the application process.

In the OS-domain, the OS coordinates the service of trustbox requests by the TLR runtime via a special TLR system call added to the OS. Because the TLR runtime is not aware of application processes' lifetimes, the OS instructs the TLR runtime to create and destroy service threads as application processes are created and killed, respectively.

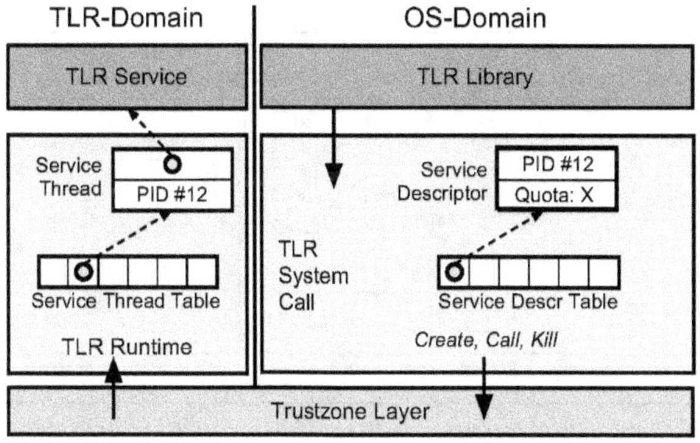


**Figure 7.** Details of the system layer.

The OS can exchange the following three messages with the TLR runtime:

**1. Create service thread:** The first time a TLR system call is issued by an application, no service thread for that process exists, and so it must be created. To keep track of the binding between service threads and application processes the OS maintains a descriptor table. To bind an application process, the OS issues a "create service thread" request to the TLR runtime. The TLR runtime creates a new service thread and annotates it with the caller's PID contained in the request.

**2. Call service thread:** This operation forwards the trustbox message requests received via the system call interface to the calling application process. After validating that the calling process is bound, the OS dispatches the request to the TLR runtime. The TLR runtime retrieves the trustbox message from the payload of the request, queues the message, and resumes the execution of the respective service thread. The service thread dequeues the request and processes it in the trustbox layer.

**3. Kill service thread:** This operation is issued by the OS to terminate a service thread and free its resources. This operation can be issued explicitly by an application or, alternatively, the OS periodically kills service threads of terminated applications. To kill a service thread, the OS simply sends a request to the TLR runtime and updates the local OS data structures.

### 6.5 Cross-world Communication and Interrupt Handling

Communication between the TLR-domain and the OS-domain is handled by the TLR's TrustZone layer (see Figure 8). This layer implements: (i) context save and restore for switching between normal and secure world; (ii) a simple message passing interface for exchanging data between the two worlds; and (iii) interrupt handling and re-routing if an interrupt arrives destined for a normal world device driver when the secure world is executing.

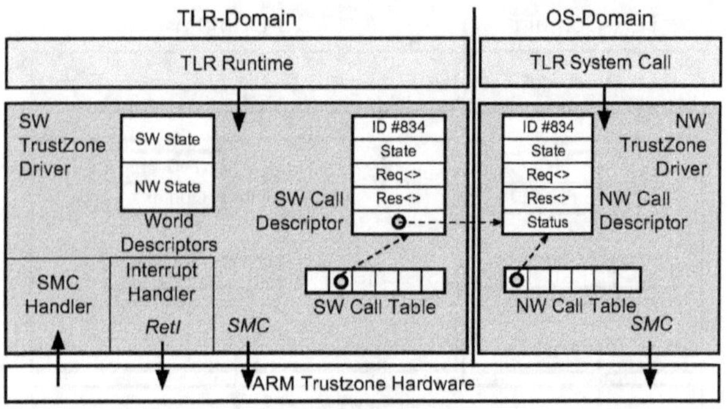


**Figure 8.** Details of the TrustZone layer.

To implement world switching, the secure world TrustZone driver maintains two *world descriptors*, each of which contains a snapshot of the processor state (CPU registers). The secure monitor implements world switching by detecting the direction of the transition, saving and restoring processor state from the corresponding world descriptors, and then toggling the processor mode bit. To ensure security, the world descriptors are stored in SW memory. A world switch can be activated in one of two ways: (i) a synchronous world-switch is caused when the *smc* instruction is issued, and (ii) an asynchronous world-switch is caused when a hardware interrupt fires in the secure world destined for a normal world device driver. Interrupts generated while the processor is executing in the NW do not cause a world switch.

To provide cross-world communication, the *secure monitor* implements data copying between the two worlds. This secure monitor must execute in the secure world so it can simultaneously address memory in both worlds.

One challenge is the support for interrupt handling and re-routing. Interrupts can be triggered while the processor is executing in the secure world, yet the normal-world OS retains control of system resources and contains all the I/O device drivers. Therefore, whenever an interrupt fires in the secure world, the secure world interrupt handler should switch worlds and hand control to the OS.

Because interrupts can fire in the middle of TLR runtime calls, the normal world OS must detect whether the secure world exiting is caused by TLR call completion or by an interrupt. If a TLR call completes, the OS can fetch the return parameters and schedule the application process. If any TLR calls are in progress, the OS must periodically switch worlds to continue executing those calls. When re-entering the secure world, the TLR decides if it should resume executing a prior service thread, or switch to a different service thread.

The TrustZone layer keeps track of the state of all ongoing TLR runtime calls. For each call, the TrustZone drivers maintain a descriptor that contains the call ID, input parameters, output parameters, and the current status of the call. Because this state must be accessible in both worlds, this descriptor table is replicated in both worlds (see Figure 8), and synchronized upon world transitions. Figure 9 shows the state machine for an individual TLR call.

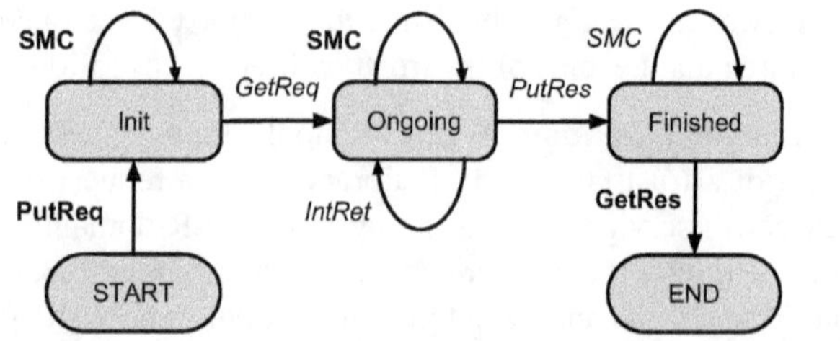


**Figure 9.** State machine of a TLR call as implemented in the TrustZone layer. Events in bold take place in the NW, and events in italic in the SW.

**Init state:** When the OS initiates a new TLR runtime request, the call status field is set to the `Init` value. On transition into the secure world, the input parameters are copied from the normal world and the call status is changed to `Ongoing`.

**Ongoing state:** This state indicates that a TLR call is in progress. This indicates to the OS that it should continue scheduling re-entry into the secure world until the call status changes to `Finished`.

**Finished state:** When a call is finished, the secure world TrustZone driver copies the output results to the normal world, and initiates a world switch.

### 6.6 Memory Management

To serve its memory needs, the TLR requires physical RAM dedicated to the secure world. The secure world bootloader uses low-level system firmware to statically allocate a fixed quantity of physically contiguous system RAM for secure world memory. TrustZone ensures that the normal world cannot address or otherwise access any of this RAM. The TLR then uses an internal memory allocator for all its internal state needs. In future work, we are considering allowing the OS to fine-tune how the TLR allocates memory to trustlets. Because the OS already controls allocation of system resources in the normal world, we can allow it to specify quotas to the TLR for trustlets, and balance those requests with fairness constraints.

### 6.7 System Boot

When an ARM SoC supports TrustZone, the processor initializes in secure mode and runs the secure world bootloader. This bootloader copies the TLR image into secure world memory and checks its integrity using a hash value signed with the platform ID. Next, the bootloader initializes the TLR runtime, and then performs the first world switch into the normal world, at which point the untrusted bootloader begins the standard OS boot sequence.

### 6.8 Platform Identity

The TLR requires a single, persistent per-device public key pair. This key pair constitutes a unique platform identity, similar to the role that the Endorsement Key (EK) plays for TPMs [22]. The device manufacturer must certify the platform ID in the same way that TPM manufacturers issue EK certificates.

To protect the platform ID, the key pair is provisioned by the device manufacturer for each TrustZone-enabled smartphone and tablet. The result of provisioning is writing the platform ID into secure fuses (a write-once persistent memory) accessible only from the secure world. The TLR offers methods for trustlets to obtain the public part of the platform ID, and makes sure that the private key is never leaked.

To preserve users' privacy, TLR also borrows ideas from solutions developed for TPMs. First, is the notion of a privacy CA [32]: the device attests its identity to the trusted privacy CA, which in turn issues new platform credentials signed by the privacy CA. These new credentials improve anonymity because the device can now have multiple trusted identities, and can choose which one to use depending on which entity the trustlet is communication with. An alternative design borrows ideas from group signatures (similar to TPM Direct Anonymous Attestation [16]). The device could be equipped with a shared platform ID, and others could not distinguish between different devices sharing their IDs.

### 6.9 Seal and Unseal Primitives

Seal and Unseal use the device platform ID for cryptographic operations. Sealing a piece of data to a trustlet *T* running on device *D* consists of encrypting the data with a symmetric key, and then encrypting the symmetric key and *T*'s hash with *D*'s public key. Unsealing is the reverse: using *D*'s private key to decrypt the symmetric key and the hash of *T*, validating the hash of the running trustlet matches, and finally decrypting the data using the symmetric key.

Sealed data is made persistent in encrypted form, but the TLR does not have direct access to the disk. Instead the TLR passes encrypted blobs to the disk managed by the untrusted OS. To prevent rollback attacks and enforce state continuity [31], we adopt the following defense. TrustZone-enabled devices use an eMMC storage controller that offers a security feature called replay-protected memory blocks (RPMB) (see [38]). The RPMB is a storage partition where operations from the secure world are authenticated and protected against rollback attacks. To achieve this, a key derived from the platform ID is also injected at manufacturing time into the eMMC controller. This key, shared between the secure world and the storage controller, is used to authenticate writes and a secure counter is also used to prevent rollbacks.

### 6.10 Trusted I/O Path

The TLR support for a trusted I/O path is limited to the storage functionality described above. TLR also adapts the same protocol to enable authenticated and replay-protected communication with external cloud services, even though all network communication is handled by the untrusted OS.

If we were to enable trusted I/O to the device's peripherals from the secure world, this would enable broader functionality within trustlets. For example, trustlets could directly interact with the device's sensors and directly display screen output. However, the cost of this approach would be a much larger TCB that incorporates device-specific drivers. In contrast, the current TLR design is generic – it works with all TrustZone-equipped devices.

Instead, we envision a future in which manufacturers equip their sensing hardware and other I/O peripherals with a secret key shared between the peripheral and the secure world. For input data, this allows sensors to gather and encrypt data before passing it to the untrusted OS, and only the TLR in the secure world can decrypt and use the data. For output, and it allows the I/O device to authenticate the data sent from the secure world before performing the output operation. This alternative allows the TLR to remain generic and eliminates driver code from its TCB.

## 7. Implementation

We implemented a TLR prototype for a TrustZone hardware testbed and leveraged existing open source software.

### 7.1 Hardware Testbed

Finding a TrustZone-compatible hardware testbed was not easy. Although the ARM TrustZone technology is prevalent in modern ARM-based SoCs, in most devices this technology is locked and cannot be used by application developers. We bypassed this limitation using a development board: NVidia's Tegra 250 Dev Kit [9].

The Tegra 250 board is equipped with dual-core 1 GHz Cortex A9 processors, 1 GB of RAM, 512 MB of flash memory, and multiple peripherals. Because the processor boots the OS in secure world, we can override the secure world environment and boot TLR. However, this board disallows flashing a unique key into the boards secure fuses, preventing us from implementing the platform ID in hardware. Moreover, the primary boot loader is closed-source, preventing us from modifying the secure world setup code in the first stage bootloader.

We address the first limitation by hard-coding the platform ID credentials in software. To address the second limitation, we boot the TLR using a customized second-level bootloader (u-boot [10]). This results in the unnecessary inclusion of the first-level bootloader in the TCB. These shortcomings are not fundamental and could be overcome with source access to a full-featured TrustZone board.

### 7.2 Software Implementation

In the OS-domain, we use Linux and Mono [4] v2.6.7 (an open source .NET framework implementation). We implement the TLR library for Mono and modify the Linux kernel in two ways: (i) implement the TLR system call, and (ii) change the kernel to eliminate all dependencies on resources only available in the secure world. In particular, we (i) modify the interrupt masks appropriately, (ii) disable certain cache control initialization code, and (iii) remove some

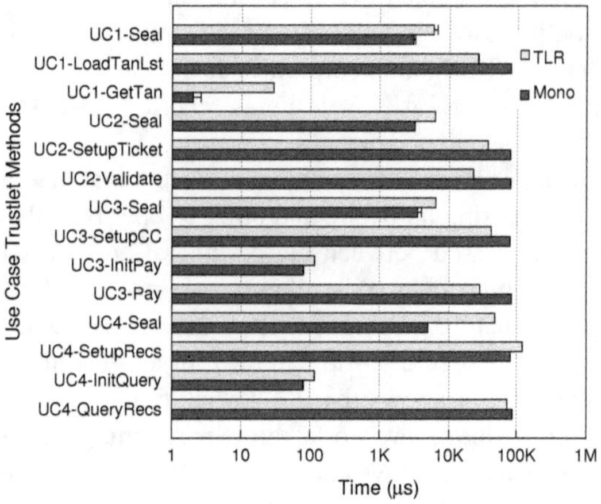


**Figure 10.** Execution time of trustlet methods from our use case prototypes.

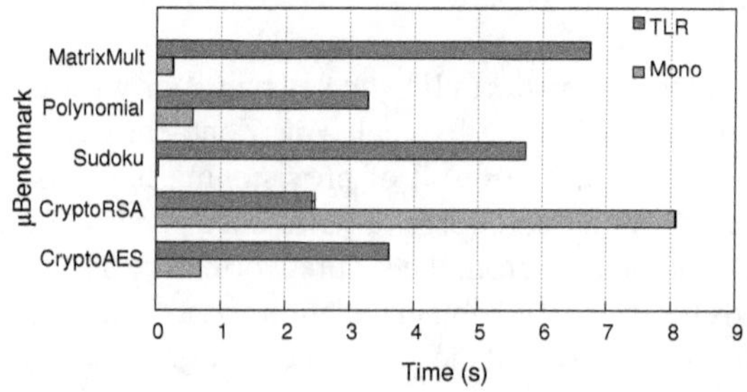


**Figure 11.** Performance of our benchmark suite executed on the TLR and on Mono.

processor initialization code. The goal of all these changes is to enable Linux to boot correctly in the normal world.

In the TLR-domain, our implementation covers the TLR and the bootloader. To build the TLR we leverage the codebase of NETMF v4.1 [6]. We borrow the CLR and PAL code from the NETMF and implement the remaining components in the HAL and application layers (see Figure 2). To customize the NETMF, we use the NETMF porting kit [12]. We also customize u-boot to initialize the TLR in the secure world, and to yield to the OS in the normal world.

# 8. Evaluation

This section presents a performance evaluation of the TLR and an analysis of its TCB size, programming complexity, and security.

## 8.1 Performance

We evaluate two sources of performance overhead for TLR applications when compared to standard .NET applications: (i) the overhead due to NETMF, a less efficient .NET stack than full-blown .NET, and (ii) the overhead due to executing additional TLR primitives.

***Methodology.*** To evaluate the performance of trustlet code and TLR primitives, we run multiple experiments based on micro-benchmarks. We run our experiments in the hardware testbed described in Section 7. In all our measurements, we run ten trials and report the mean time and standard deviation.

We use our four use case applications as well as a specific benchmark suite. The use case prototypes allow us to measure the TLR performance with realistic apps. In total, we evaluate 14 methods: three for Use Case 1 (online banking transfers), three for Use Case 2 (mobile ticketing), four for Use Case 3 (mobile payments), and four for Use Case 4 (e-health application). For an in-depth description of these methods' roles see Appendix A. In addition, we implemented a specific benchmark suite to help discover the source of inefficiencies of the TLR runtime. This benchmark suite consists of five CPU-intensive programs: *MatrixMult*, which is a straightforward $O(n^3)$ matrix multiplication program; *Poly*, which computes the value of a 100-degree polynomial using floating point match; *Sudoku*, which is a sudoku solver; *CryptoRSA*, which performs RSA cryptographic operations (signatures, encryptions, and decryptions) using 1024-bit keys; and *CryptoAES*, which performs AES cryptographic operations (encryptions and decryptions) with 256-bit keys. We run each test both on the TLR and on an efficient .NET runtime (Mono) and then compute the difference.

***Performance of trustlet code execution.*** Figure 11 plots the evaluation results of our use case prototypes, showing the execution time of all trustlet methods on the TLR and on Mono. The results show that Mono slightly outperforms the TLR: 57% of the methods execute on average 4.27× faster in Mono, whereas 43% of the methods execute on average 2.34× faster in the TLR. We find these numbers quite surprising, because we expected Mono to significantly outperform the TLR. Our expectation is justified by the fact that, in Mono, the trustlets' managed code is pre-compiled by a built-in jitter into native code, which runs on bare metal. In contrast, in the TLR, all the managed code is interpreted by the TLR, with the exception of certain libraries, such as the cryptographic library, which are implemented in native code.

To investigate why TLR's overhead is not more pronounced, we ran additional experiments using our specific benchmark suite. Figure 11 shows that, with the exception of *CryptoRSA*, all other programs of the benchmark run on average 54× slower on the TLR. This difference is particularly large for programs whose code the TLR must entirely interpret, such as *Sudoku*, where the difference reaches a factor of 176. However, this difference is clearly inverted in the *CryptoRSA*, which runs 3.3× faster on the TLR. This suggests that Mono's implementation of RSA is particularly inefficient.

We infer that, in the evaluation of our use case prototypes (see Figure 10), the TLR outperforms Mono when the trust-

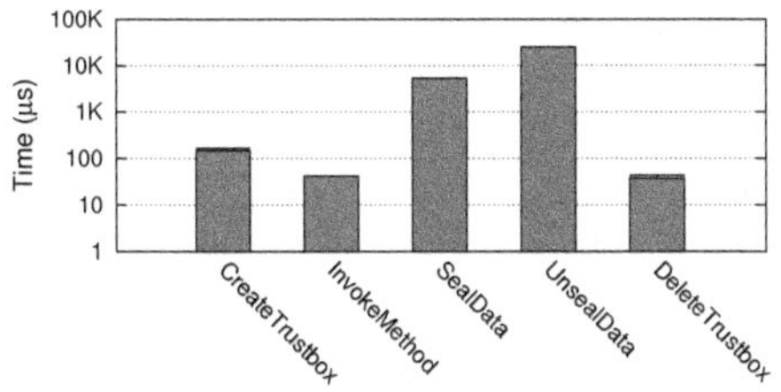


**Figure 12.** Baseline execution time of TLR primitives.

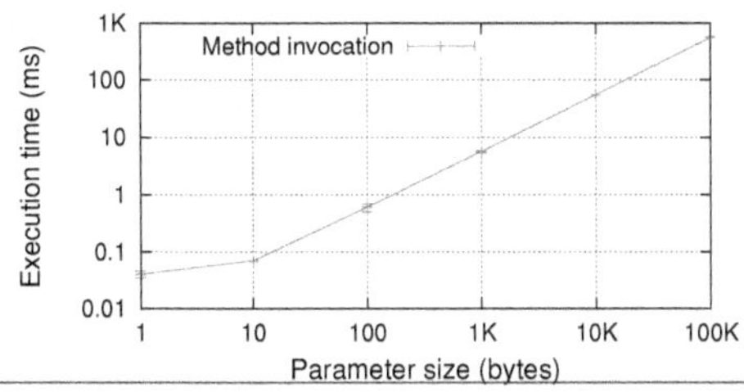


**Figure 13.** Performance of cross world method invocation varying the size of the method parameters.

let code makes heavy use of RSA. Since Mono's inefficiency is not fundamental, in general we should expect the TLR's performance slowdown to be more pronounced.

***Performance of the TLR primitives.*** We implemented micro-benchmarks that stress each of the five operations related to the trustbox lifecycle: *trustbox creation*, *trustlet method invocation*, *data seal*, *data unseal*, and *trustbox deletion*. Because these operations' durations depend on their parameter sizes, we further measure the factors responsible for such variation, namely the cross world communication (relevant in trustbox creation and trustlet method invocation) and cryptographic computations (relevant in seal and unseal).

Figure 12 shows the minimum execution time of the TLR primitives. While seal and unseal take on average 15.2ms, the remaining primitives execute on average in 75.8$\mu$s. This difference is explained by the heavy use of cryptographic operations in seal and unseal. With the exception of delete trustbox, which executes in a constant time of 38$\mu$s, the duration of the TLR primitives depends on their input parameters, namely 1) the amount of data that needs to be transferred across worlds, or 2) the amount of data that needs to be encrypted or decrypted.

Figure 13 plots the execution time of method invocation while varying the size of the parameters transferred between worlds. The method execution time increases linearly at an approximate rate of 5.6ms/KB. This overhead is explained by the need to marshal the parameters and pass them by value to the TLR. In fact, the parameters cannot be transferred across worlds by reference (which would take a constant time) because TLR's internal data structures inherited from NETMF are incompatible with Mono's.

Lastly, to shed some light on the impact of cryptographic operations on the performance of TLR primitives, Figure 14 plots our evaluation results of seal and unseal as we vary the

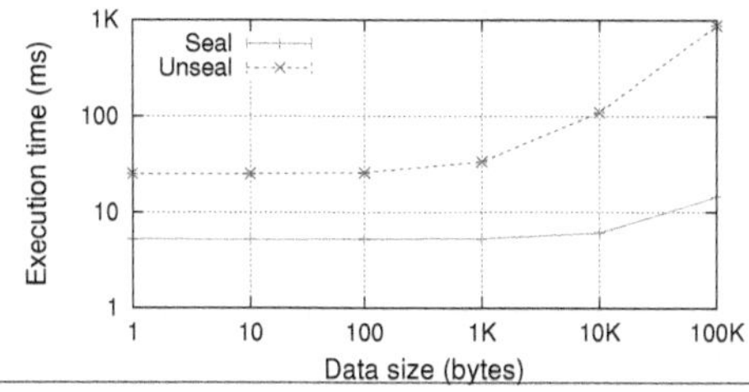


**Figure 14.** Performance of seal and unseal primitives varying the size of sealed and unsealed data, respectively.

size of the data to be sealed and the size of the envelope to be unsealed, respectively. Sealing 1KB takes 5.3ms and unsealing the same amount of data takes 33.6ms; these operations are dominated by the time complexity of the RSA algorithm used in their implementation. Seal and unseal are efficient, because the TLR makes use of the OpenSSL library, which implements cryptographic operations in native code.

### 8.2 TCB Size

To evaluate the TLR's TCB reduction, we compare its TCB size against that of two representative systems: TrustVisor v0.2 [29], and a setup based on Mono v2.6.7 and Linux v3.5.1 (Mono+Linux). While the former gives us an idea of the minimum TCB size achieved by a state-of-the-art system for securing native code apps, the latter points to the TCB size required by managed code .NET apps.

Table 1 presents the TCB sizes of the TLR, TrustVisor, and Mono+Linux. This table indicates which part of the codebase corresponds to native code (typically in C or C++) and which part to managed code (typically C#). The table also indicates which code belongs to the core versus to libraries of the system. To measure the TCB size, we use the metric of *lines of code* (LOC), which counts all lines of a system's codebase (including comments and empty lines).

Comparing TLR with TrustVisor, we see that TLR is approximately 6 times larger than TrustVisor: the TLR and TrustVisor comprise, respectively, 152.7 KLOC and 25.3 KLOC. This difference can be explained by the fact that, unlike the TLR, TrustVisor neither needs to implement a managed code runtime nor to include managed code libraries.

Comparing the TLR with the Mono+Linux setup, we see that the TLR drastically shrinks the TCB. While the TCB size of Mono+Linux is 11.9 MLOC [1], the TLR's is 152.7 KLOC, i.e., approximately 78 times smaller. The TLR cuts down the TCB size due to its design, which limits the services offered to trustlets and blends the OS and runtime functionality into a compact single system.

### 8.3 Programming Complexity

Since assessing the complexity of programming applications for the TLR is difficult, we mostly make an account of our experience with building the use case prototypes and bench-

[1] Appendix B explains how this number was obtained.

| Code (LOC) | TrustVisor | TLR | Mono+Linux |
|---|---|---|---|
| Managed Libs | N/A | 19.9K (C#) | 3,305.3K (C#) |
| Native Libs | 18.1K (C) | 80.5K (C++) | 1,308.6K (C) |
| Native Core | 7.2K (C) | 52.3K (C++) | 7,302.9K (C) |
| **Total** | 25.3K | 152.7K | 11,916.8K |

**Table 1.** TCB size of the TLR, TrustVisor, and Mono+Linux.

| Use Case | Code Size (LOC) | # Methods |
|---|---|---|
| Online banking | 179 | 3 |
| Mobile ticketing | 450 | 3 |
| Mobile payments | 754 | 4 |
| E-health app | 974 | 4 |

**Table 2.** Programming complexity of the use case prototypes measured in code size and number of methods.

mark programs. In our experience, programming with TLR apps is relatively easy. Once we sketched the security protocols for the four use cases (see Appendix A), programming their respective trustlets was done by a grad student in 3.5 days. Table 1 shows the codebase size and the number of methods implemented by each trustlet. These numbers show that the average code size is relatively small, consisting of 590 LOC in C#, and the trustlet interfaces are simple, consisting of three to four methods. Although real world applications would likely demand a bigger programming effort, our intuition is that such an effort is comparable to app development for standard .NET.

### 8.4 Security Analysis

The attack surface of the TLR comprises the `smc` instruction exposed to the OS and the managed code interface exposed to the trustlets. The `smc` interface is relatively narrow, which limits the exposure of code vulnerabilities. The managed code interface offers a larger attack surface: an attacker could exploit a bug in the TLR runtime by injecting carefully crafted code sequences in the trustlet code.

TLR can only provide limited protection against physical attacks: an attacker with the capability of tampering with the hardware could disable the TrustZone protections and bypass TLR. However, such attacks require a high degree of sophistication: since the core of the system (the SoC) is packaged in a single die, an attacker would need to break into the SoC and tamper with the TrustZone hardware.

## 9. Related Work

TLR borrows many concepts from previous work on building trusted execution environments (TEE). Some previous systems such as XOM [26] and AEGIS [36] require specific hardware that is not yet available on commodity processors.

For x86 platforms, a typical TEE system is based upon a Trusted Platform Module (TPM) and a trusted kernel [21]. The TPM is used to bootstrap trust in the system, and the trusted kernel provides runtime state protection for trusted application code. Because the security of such systems depends on the correctness of the trusted kernel, a lot of effort has been put into reducing the TCB size. In the first generation of these systems, the trusted kernel consisted of a full blown Virtual Machine Monitor (VMM) as in Terra [21], Proxos [37], and Overshadow [18]. Researchers also proposed systems based on microkernels, as in Nizza [23] and Nova [35]. Currently, the state of the art consists of tiny kernels implemented using late launch technology as in Flicker [28], hardware virtualization as in TrustVisor [29], and the handler code of the System Management Mode (SMM) as in SICE [15]. Reducing the TCB size, however, makes these systems difficult to program. In contrast, TLR aims to provide richer programming abstractions while keeping the TCB small.

For ARM TrustZone, the closest piece of work to TLR is Nokia's OnBoard Credentials (ObC) [25]. ObC can execute programs written in a modified variant of the LUA scripting language running in an isolated environment protected by TrustZone. TLR's primary benefit over ObC is bringing the trustbox and trustlet concepts to a mature managed-code environment, as well as providing a richer set of abstractions. Developers will find trusted computing primitives easier to program with .NET because it offers the productivity benefits of modern high-level languages, such as strong typing and garbage collection, to application developers.

Other previous systems leverage ARM TrustZone to implement specific security services. One system uses TrustZone to implement trusted sensors [27], which enable mobile apps to obtain guarantees of authenticity and integrity of sensor readings. In the commercial sphere, Proxama uses ARM TrustZone to enable secure mobile payments [7].

There is a large body of work on improving the security of OSes and mobile apps. In particular, researchers have paid considerable attention to protecting personal user data (e.g., address book, user photos, password information, GPS location) and preventing its unauthorized access and leakage by proposing novel techniques, such as new access control mechanisms [33] and information flow analysis [20]. This work, however, is complementary to ours: TLR does not need to trust the OS unlike this previous work.

Another research area uses privilege separation for partitioning an application into security-sensitive and security-insensitive components. These systems expose a partitioning interface at the level of the programming language, and enforce this separation by using a runtime [30], or the OS itself [17]. Such approaches still depend on a large TCB, which includes the OS and the runtime. TLR offers a coarser-grained privilege separation by compartmentalizing an application, but has a smaller TCB.

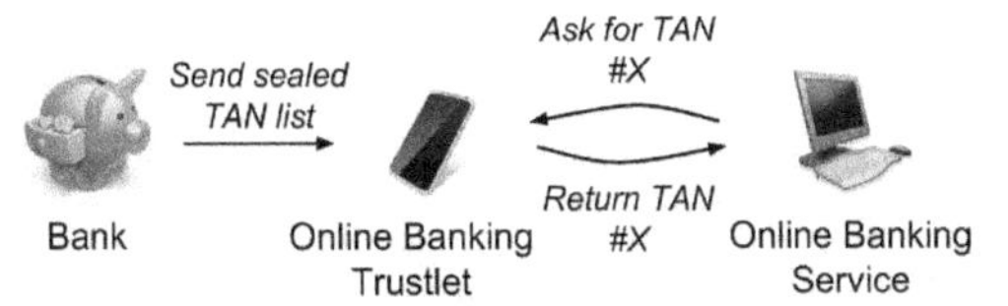


Setup: 1. Bank→Device $\text{seal}_{T,D}$([TANLST])

Query: 1. Svc→Device: *index*
2. Device→Svc: TANLST(*index*)

**Figure 15.** Use Case 1: Online banking transfers.

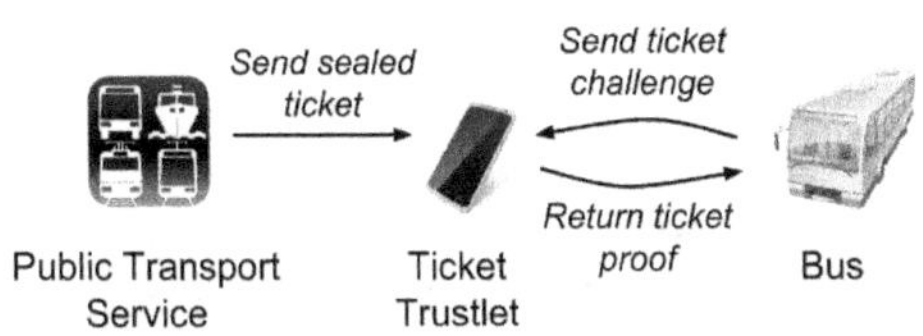


Purchase: 1. PTS→Device:
$\text{seal}_{T,D}([tinfo, KT, \text{cert}_{PTS}(KT)])$

Validate: 1. Bus→Device: $n_b$, *time*
2. Device→Bus: $[\{n_b\}_{KT}, \text{cert}_{PTS}(KT)]$ | fail

**Figure 16.** Use Case 2: Mobile ticketing.

## 10. Conclusions

This paper presents the design, implementation, and evaluation of the Trusted Language Runtime (TLR), a system for running security-sensitive applications on mobile devices. TLR offers programming primitives that allow small application components to execute within a trusted environment isolated from the operating system and other applications. The TLR protects the integrity and confidentiality of application code and data within the trusted environment. TLR provides these features using the ARM TrustZone hardware support for trusted computing found in ARM SoCs. Our evaluation shows that the TLR achieves a significant reduction in the TCB of mobile apps with an acceptable performance cost.


## Acknowledgments

We are grateful to the anonymous reviewers for their comments. This work was partly supported by national funds through FCT (Fundação para a Ciência e Tecnologia) under project PEst-OE/EEI/LA0021/2013, and by PCAS project (co-financed by the European Commission through the contract no. 610713).


## Appendix A: Use Case Protocols

This section presents a brief description of the security protocols that implement the use cases presented in Section 5.

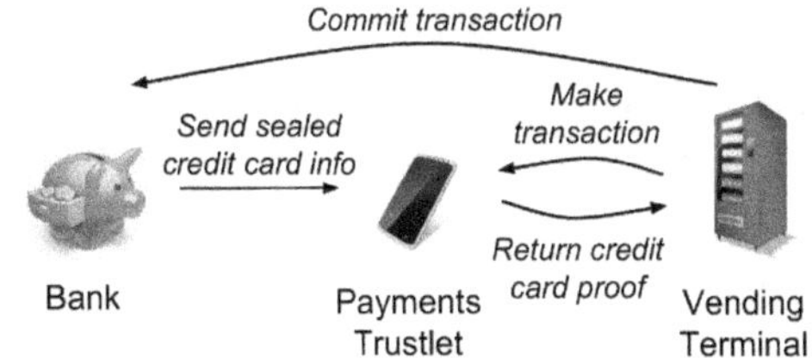


Setup: 1. Bank→Device:
$\text{seal}_{T,D}([CC, PIN, KT, KT_{ID}, \text{cert}_B(KT), \text{cert}_M(VT)])$

Pay: 1. Device→VT: $n_d$
2. VT→Device: $VT_{ID}$, *amount*, *date*, $n_d$, $n_v$, $h(PIN, n_d, amount)$, $\sigma_{VT}$, $\text{cert}_M(VT)$
3. Device→VT: $[VT_{ID}$, *amount*, *date*, $KT_{ID}$, $n_v$, $\sigma_{KT}$, $\text{cert}_B(KT)]$ | abort

Commit: 1. VT→Bank: $VT_{ID}$, *amount*, *date*, $n_v$, $KT_{ID}$, $\sigma_{KT}$

**Figure 17.** Use Case 3: Mobile payments.

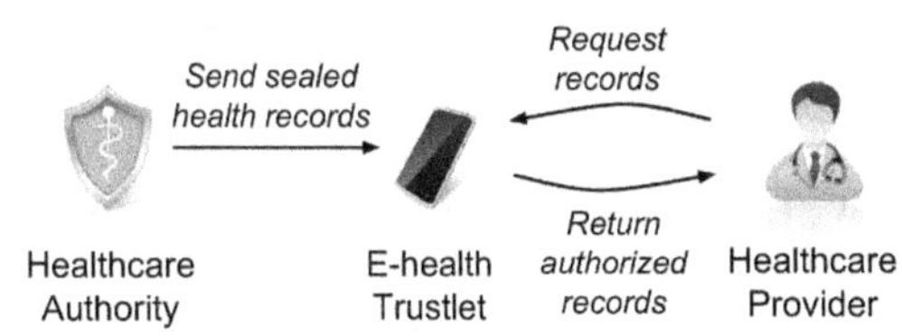


Deploy: 1. HA→Device:
$\text{seal}_{T,D}([[R_0, \ldots, R_n], \text{ACPOL}, KT, \text{cert}_{HA}(KT)])$

Query: 1. Device→HP: $n_d$
2. HP→Device: $[R_k^{ID}]$, $n_h$, $\{n_d\}_{KH}$, $\text{cert}_{HA}(KH)$
3. Device→HP: $[\langle R_i \ldots R_j\rangle_K$, $\{K, n_h\}_{KT}$, $\text{cert}_{HA}(KT)]$ | fail

**Figure 18.** Use Case 4: E-health application.

To represent cryptographic operations, we use following notation. For asymmetric cryptography, $K$ and $K^P$ denote private and public keys, respectively. For symmetric keys, we drop the superscript. Notation $\langle x \rangle_K$ indicates data $x$ encrypted with key $K$, and $\{y\}_K$ indicates data $y$ signed with key $K$. We represent nonces as $n$.

The protocols implementing each of our four use cases are represented in Figures 15–18, respectively.

## Appendix B: TCB of Mono+Linux Setup

The Linux+Mono TCB includes part of the Linux kernel (6.9 MLOC), Mono's runtime (471 KLOC), native code libraries, such as Glib2 (1.3 MLOC), and managed code libraries shipped with Mono (3.3 MLOC). Since real Linux deployments do not include all device drivers shipped in the kernel, to avoid reporting an artificially bloated Linux kernel, we conservatively exclude the drivers' source code.

## References


[1] Android. http://www.android.com.

[2] Dalvik VM Internals. https://sites.google.com/site/io/dalvik-vm-internals.

[3] Apple iOS 6. http://www.apple.com/ios.

[4] Mono. http://www.mono-project.com/Main_Page/.

[5] Common Language Runtime (CLR), . http://msdn.microsoft.com/en-us/library/8bs2ecf4.aspx.

[6] .NET Micro Framework, . http://www.microsoft.com/netmf/default.mspx.

[7] Proxama. http://www.proxama.com/products-and-services/trustzone.

[8] Transaction authentication number. http://www.wikipedia.org/wiki/Transaction_authentication_number.

[9] Tegra 250 Dev Board. https://developer.nvidia.com/tegra-250-development-board-features/.

[10] U-boot Bootloader. http://www.denx.de/en/News/WebHome/.

[11] Microsoft Windows 8. http://windows.microsoft.com/en-us/windows-8/meet.

[12] Porting the .NET Micro Framework. Microsoft Technical White Paper, 2007. http://msdn.microsoft.com/en-us/netframework/bb267253.aspx.

[13] Understanding .NET Micro Framework Architecture, 2010. http://msdn.microsoft.com/en-us/library/cc533001.aspx.

[14] ARM. ARM Security Technology – Building a Secure System using TrustZone Technology. ARM Technical White Paper, 2009. http://infocenter.arm.com/help/topic/com.arm.doc.prd29-genc-009492c/PRD29-GENC-009492C_trustzone_security_whitepaper.pdf.

[15] A. M. Azab, P. Ning, and X. Zhang. SICE: A Hardware-Level Strongly Isolated Computing Environment for x86 Multi-core Platforms. In *Proc. of CCS*, 2011.

[16] Brickell, Ernie and Camenisch, Jan and Chen, Liqun. Direct Anonymous Attestation. In *Proc. of CCS*, 2004.

[17] D. Brumley and D. Song. Privtrans: automatically partitioning programs for privilege separation. In *Proc. of USENIX Security '04*, 2004.

[18] X. Chen, T. Garfinkel, E. C. Lewis, P. Subrahmanyam, C. A. Waldspurger, D. Boneh, J. Dwoskin, and D. R. K. Ports. Overshadow: A Virtualization-Based Approach to Retrofitting Protection in Commodity Operating Systems. In *Proc. of ASPLOS*, 2008.

[19] S. Chong, J. Liu, A. C. Myers, X. Qi, K. Vikram, L. Zheng, and X. Zheng. Secure web applications via automatic partitioning. In *Proc. of SOSP '07*, 2007.

[20] W. Enck, P. Gilbert, B.-G. Chun, L. P. Cox, J. Jung, P. McDaniel, and A. N. Sheth. TaintDroid: an information-flow tracking system for realtime privacy monitoring on smartphones. In *Proc of OSDI'10*, 2010.

[21] T. Garfinkel, B. Pfaff, J. Chow, M. Rosenblum, and D. Boneh. Terra: A Virtual Machine-Based Platform for Trusted Computing. In *Proc. of SOSP*, 2003.

[22] T. C. Group. TPM Main Specification Level 2 Version 1.2, Revision 130, 2006.

[23] H. Härtig, M. Hohmuth, N. Feske, C. Helmuth, A. Lackorzynski, F. Mehnert, and M. Peter. The Nizza Secure-System Architecture. *CollaborateCom*, 2005.

[24] M. Hypponen. Malware goes Mobile. *Scientific American*, November 2006.

[25] K. Kostiainen, J.-E. Ekberg, N. Asokan, and A. Rantala. Onboard Credentials with Open Provisioning. In *Proc. of ASIACCS*, 2009.

[26] D. Lie, C. A. Thekkath, M. Mitchell, P. Lincoln, D. Boneh, J. C. Mitchell, and M. Horowitz. Architectural Support for Copy and Tamper Resistant Software. In *Proc. of ASPLOS*, 2000.

[27] H. Liu, S. Saroiu, A. Wolman, and H. Raj. Software Abstractions for Trusted Sensors. In *Proc. of Mobisys*, 2012.

[28] J. M. McCune, B. Parno, A. Perrig, M. K. Reiter, and H. Isozaki. Flicker: An Execution Infrastructure for TCB Minimization. In *Proc. of EuroSys*, 2008.

[29] J. M. McCune, Y. Li, N. Qu, Z. Zhou, A. Datta, V. D. Gligor, and A. Perrig. TrustVisor: Efficient TCB Reduction and Attestation. In *Proc. of IEEE S&P*, 2010.

[30] A. C. Myers. JFlow: Practical Mostly-Static Information Flow Control. In *Proc. of POPL '99*, 1999.

[31] B. Parno, J. R. Lorch, J. R. Douceur, J. Mickens, and J. M. Mccune. Memoir: Practical State Continuity for Protected Modules. In *Proc. of IEEE S&P*, 2011.

[32] PrivacyCA. PrivacyCA. http://privacyca.com.

[33] F. Roesner, T. Kohno, A. Moshchuk, B. Parno, H. J. Wang, and C. Cowan. User-Driven Access Control: Rethinking Permission Granting in Modern Operating Systems. In *Proc. of IEEE S&P*, 2012.

[34] N. Santos, H. Raj, S. Saroiu, and A. Wolman. Trusted Language Runtime (TLR): Enabling Trusted Applications on Smartphones. In *Proc. of HotMobile*, 2011.

[35] U. Steinberg and B. Kauer. Nova: A microhypervisor-based secure virtualization architecture. In *Eurosys*, 2010.

[36] G. E. Suh, D. Clarke, B. Gassend, M. van Dijk, and S. Devadas. AEGIS: Architecture for Tamper-Evident and Tamper-Resistant Processing. In *Proc. of ICS*, 2003.

[37] R. Ta-Min, L. Litty, and D. Lie. Splitting Interfaces: Making Trust Between Applications and Operating Systems Congurable. In *Proc. of OSDI*, 2006.

[38] V. Tsai. eMMC v4.41 and v4.5. http://www.jedec.org/sites/default/files/Victor_Tsai.pdf.

# Virtual Ghost: Protecting Applications from Hostile Operating Systems

John Criswell
University of Illinois at Urbana-Champaign
criswell@illinois.edu

Nathan Dautenhahn
University of Illinois at Urbana-Champaign
dautenh1@illinois.edu

Vikram Adve
University of Illinois at Urbana-Champaign
vadve@illinois.edu

## Abstract

Applications that process sensitive data can be carefully designed and validated to be difficult to attack, but they are usually run on monolithic, commodity operating systems, which may be less secure. An OS compromise gives the attacker complete access to all of an application's data, regardless of how well the application is built. We propose a new system, *Virtual Ghost*, that protects applications from a compromised or even hostile OS. Virtual Ghost is the first system to do so by combining compiler instrumentation and run-time checks on operating system code, which it uses to create *ghost memory* that the operating system cannot read or write. Virtual Ghost interposes a thin hardware abstraction layer between the kernel and the hardware that provides a set of operations that the kernel must use to manipulate hardware, and provides a few trusted services for secure applications such as ghost memory management, encryption and signing services, and key management. Unlike previous solutions, Virtual Ghost does *not* use a higher privilege level than the kernel.

Virtual Ghost performs well compared to previous approaches; it outperforms InkTag on five out of seven of the LMBench microbenchmarks with improvements between 1.3x and 14.3x. For network downloads, Virtual Ghost experiences a 45% reduction in bandwidth at most for small files and nearly no reduction in bandwidth for large files and web traffic. An application we modified to use ghost memory shows a maximum additional overhead of 5% due to the Virtual Ghost protections. We also demonstrate Virtual Ghost's efficacy by showing how it defeats sophisticated rootkit attacks.



*ASPLOS '14,* March 1–5, 2014, Salt Lake City, Utah, USA.

ACM 978-1-4503-2305-5/14/03. . . $15.00.
http://dx.doi.org/10.1145/2541940.2541986

***Categories and Subject Descriptors*** D.4.6 [*Operating Systems*]: Security and Protection

***General Terms*** Security

***Keywords*** software security; inlined reference monitors; software fault isolation; control-flow integrity; malicious operating systems

## 1. Introduction

Applications that process sensitive data on modern commodity systems are vulnerable to compromises of the underlying system software. The applications themselves can be carefully designed and validated to be impervious to attack. However, all major commodity operating systems use large monolithic kernels that have complete access to and control over all system resources [9, 25, 32, 34]. These operating systems are prone to attack [21] with large attack surfaces, including large numbers of trusted device drivers developed by numerous hardware vendors and numerous privileged applications that are as dangerous as the OS itself. A compromise of any of these components or of the kernel gives the attacker complete access to all data belonging to the application, whether in memory or offline. Developers of secure applications running on such a system generally have no control over any of these components and must trust them implicitly for their own security.

Several previous projects [11, 16, 22, 37] have created systems that protect applications from a compromised, or even a hostile, operating system. These systems have all used hardware page protection through a trusted hypervisor to achieve control over the operating system capabilities. They rely on a technique called *shadowing* or *cloaking* that automatically encrypts (i.e., shadows or cloaks) and hashes any application page that is accessed by the operating system, and then decrypts it and checks the hash when it is next accessed by the application. System call arguments must be copied between secure memory and memory the OS is allowed to examine. While these solutions are effective, they have several drawbacks. First, they rely upon encrypting any of an application's memory that is accessed by the OS; an application cannot improve performance by protecting only a selected subset of data, or requesting only integrity checks on data but not confidentiality (i.e., only using hashing and not encryption). Second, they assume the OS runs as a guest on a standard hypervisor, which may not be attractive in certain settings, such as energy-constrained mobile devices. Third, they require that all system call arguments must always be copied, even if the data being transferred is not security-sensitive, which is the common case in many applications. Fourth, these solutions do not provide any security benefits to the kernel itself; for example, control flow integrity or memory safety for the operating system kernel cannot reuse the mechanisms developed for shadowing.

We propose a new approach we call *ghosting* that addresses all these limitations. Our system, *Virtual Ghost*, is the first to enforce application security from a hostile OS using compiler instrumentation of operating system code; this is used to create secure memory called *ghost memory*, which cannot be read or modified *at all* by the operating system (in contrast, previous systems like Overshadow [11] and InkTag [16] do not prevent such writes and only guarantee that the tampering will be detected before use by the application). Virtual Ghost introduces a thin hardware abstraction layer that provides a set of operations the kernel must use to manipulate hardware, and the secure application can use to obtain essential trusted services for ghost memory management, encryption, signing, and key management. Although the positioning of, and some of the mechanisms in, this layer are similar to a hypervisor, Virtual Ghost is unique because (a) unlike a traditional hypervisor, there is *no* software that runs at a higher privilege level than the kernel – in particular, the hardware abstraction layer runs at the same privilege level; (b) Virtual Ghost uses (simple, reliable) compiler techniques rather than hardware page protection to secure its own code and data; and (c) Virtual Ghost completely denies OS accesses to secure memory pages, not just encrypting and signing the pages to detect OS tampering.

Moreover, the compiler instrumentation in Virtual Ghost inherently provides strong protection against external exploits of the OS. First, traditional exploits, such as those that inject binary code, are not even expressible: all OS code *must* first go through LLVM bitcode form and be translated to native code by the Virtual Ghost compiler. Second, attacks that leverage existing native code, like return-oriented programming (ROP) [31], require control-flow hijacking, which Virtual Ghost explicitly prevents as well. In particular, Virtual Ghost enforces Control Flow Integrity (CFI) [3] on kernel code in order to ensure that the compiler instrumentation of kernel code is not bypassed. CFI automatically defeats control-flow hijacking attacks, including the latter class of external exploits. Together, these protections provide an additional layer of defense for secure applications on potentially buggy (but non-hostile) operating systems.

Another set of differences from previous work is in the programming model. First, applications can use ghost memory selectively for all, some, or none of their data. When using it for all their data, the secure features can be obtained transparently via a modified language library (e.g., libc for C applications), just as in previous work. Second, applications can pass non-ghost memory to system calls without the performance overheads of data copying. Third, when sending sensitive data through the operating system (e.g., for I/O), ghost applications can choose which encryption and/or cryptographic signing algorithms to use to obtain desired performance/security tradeoffs, whereas previous systems generally baked this choice into the system design. Finally, a useful point of similarity with previous work is that the usability features provided by previous systems (e.g., secure file system services in InkTag) are orthogonal to the design choices in Virtual Ghost and can be directly incorporated.

We have developed a prototype of Virtual Ghost and ported the FreeBSD 9.0 kernel to it. To evaluate its effectiveness, we ported three important applications from the OpenSSH application suite to Virtual Ghost, using ghost memory for the heap: `ssh`, `ssh-keygen`, and `ssh-agent`. These three can exchange data securely by sharing a common application key, which they use to encrypt the private authentication keys used by the OpenSSH protocols.

Since exploiting a kernel that runs on Virtual Ghost via an external attack is difficult, we evaluated the effectiveness of Virtual Ghost by adding a malicious module to the FreeBSD kernel, replacing the `read` system call handler. This module attempted to perform two different attacks on `ssh-agent`, including a sophisticated one that tries to alter application control flow via signal handler dispatch. When running without Virtual Ghost, both exploits successfully steal the desired data from `ssh-agent`. Under Virtual Ghost, both exploits fail and `ssh-agent` continues execution unaffected.

Our performance results show that Virtual Ghost outperforms InkTag [16] on five out of seven of the LMBench microbenchmarks, with improvements between 1.3x and 14.3x. The overheads for applications that perform moderate amounts of I/O (thttpd and sshd) is negligible, but the overhead for a completely I/O-dominated application (postmark) was high. We are investigating ways to reduce the overhead of postmark.

The rest of the paper is organized as follows. Section 2 describes the attack model that we assume in this work. Section 3 gives an overview of our system, the programmer's view when using it, including the security guarantees the system provides. Section 4 describes our design in detail, and Section 5 describes the implementation of our prototype. Section 6 describes our modifications to secure OpenSSH applications with our system. Sections 7 and 8 evaluate the security and performance of our system. Section 9 describes related work, Section 10 describes future work, and Section 11 concludes the paper.

## 2. System Software Attacks

In this section, we briefly describe our threat model and then describe the attack vectors that a malicious operating system might pursue within this threat model.

### 2.1 Threat Model

We assume that a user-space (i.e., unprivileged) application wishes to execute securely and perform standard I/O operations, but without trusting the underlying operating system kernel or storage and networking devices. Our goal is to preserve the application's integrity and confidentiality. Availability is outside the scope of the current work; we discuss the consequences of this assumption further, below. We also do not protect against side-channel attacks or keyboard and display attacks such as stealing data via keyboard loggers or from graphics memory; previous software solutions such as Overshadow [11] and InkTag [16] do not protect against these attacks either, whereas hardware solutions such as ARM's TrustZone [6] and Intel's SGX [24] do.

We assume that the OS, including the kernel and all device drivers, is malicious, i.e., may execute arbitrary hostile code with maximum privilege on the underlying hardware. We *do not assume that a software layer exists that has higher privilege than the OS*. Instead, we assume that the OS source code is *ported* to a trusted run-time library of low-level functions that serve as the interface to hardware (acting as a hardware abstraction layer) and supervise all kernel-hardware interactions. The OS is then compiled using a modified compiler that instruments the code to enforce desired security properties, described in later sections.[1] We assume that the OS can load and unload arbitrary (untrusted) OS modules dynamically, but these modules must also be compiled by the instrumenting compiler. Moreover, we assume that the OS has full read and write access to persistent storage, e.g., hard disk or flash memory.

We do *not* prevent attacks against the application itself. In practice, we expect that a secure application will be carefully designed and tested to achieve high confidence in its own security. Moreover, in practice, we expect that a secure application (or the secure subsets of it) will be much smaller than the size of a commodity OS, together with its drivers and associated services, which typically run into many millions of lines of code. For all these reasons, the developers and users of a secure application will not have the same level of confidence in a commodity OS as they would in the application itself.

Application availability is outside the scope of the current work. The consequence, however, is only that an attacker could deny a secure application from making forward progress (which would likely be detected quickly by users or system administrators); she could not steal or corrupt data produced by the application, even by subverting the OS in arbitrary ways.

[1] It is reasonable to expect the OS to be ported and recompiled because, in all the usage scenarios described in Section 1, we expect OS developers to make it an explicit design goal to take the OS out of the trusted computing base for secure applications.

### 2.2 Attack Vectors

Within the threat model described in Section 2.1, there are several attack vectors that malicious system software can take to violate an application's confidentiality or integrity. We describe the general idea behind each attack vector and provide concrete example attacks.

#### 2.2.1 Data Access in Memory

The system software can attempt to access data residing in application memory. Examples include:

- The system software can attempt to read and/or write application memory directly via load and store instructions to application virtual addresses.
- Alternatively, the OS may attempt to use the MMU to either map the physical memory containing the data into virtual addresses which it can access (reading), or it may map physical pages that it has already modified into the virtual addresses that it cannot read or write directly (writing).
- The system software can direct an I/O device to use DMA to copy data to or from memory that the system software cannot read or write directly and memory that the system software can access directly.

#### 2.2.2 Data Access through I/O

A malicious OS can attempt to access data residing on I/O devices or being transferred during I/O operations. Examples include:

- The OS can read or tamper with data directly from any file system used by the application.
- The OS can read or tamper with data being transferred via system calls to or from external devices, including persistent storage or networks.
- The OS can map unexpected blocks of data from I/O devices into memory on an `mmap` system call, effectively substituting arbitrary data for data expected by the application.

#### 2.2.3 Code Modification Attacks

A malicious OS may attempt to change the application code that operates upon application data, in multiple ways, so that the malicious code would execute with the full memory access and I/O privileges of the application. Some examples:

- The OS can attempt to modify the application's native code in memory directly.
- The OS could load a malicious program file when starting the application.

- The OS could transfer control to a malicious signal handler when delivering a signal to the application.
- The OS could link in a malicious version of a dynamically loaded library (such as libc) used by the application.

#### 2.2.4 Interrupted Program State Attacks

A malicious OS can attempt to modify or steal architectural state of an application while the application is not executing on the CPU. Examples include:

- Malicious system software could attempt to read interrupted program state to glean sensitive information from program register values saved to memory.
- Alternatively, it could modify interrupted program state (e.g., the PC) and put it back on to the processor on a return-from-interrupt or return-from-system call to redirect application execution to malicious code.

#### 2.2.5 Attacks through System Services

A more subtle and complex class of attacks is possible through the higher-level (semantic) services an OS provides to applications [10, 28]. While these attacks are still not well understood, our solution addresses an important subset of them, namely, memory-based attacks via the `mmap` system call (the same subset also addressed by InkTag). Examples include the following:

- The OS is the source of randomness used by pseudorandom number generators to create random seeds, e.g., via the device /dev/random. The OS can compromise the degree of randomness and even give back the same random value on different requests, violating fundamental assumptions used for encrypting application data.
- The OS could return a pointer into the stack via `mmap` [10], thereby tricking the application into corrupting its stack to perform arbitrary code execution via return-to-libc [35] or return-oriented programming [31].
- The OS could grant the same lock to two different threads at the same time, introducing data races with unpredictable (and potentially harmful) results.

It is important to note that the *five categories of attack vectors* listed above are intended to be comprehensive but the specific examples within each category are not: there may be several other ways for the OS to attack an application within each category. Nevertheless, our solution enables applications to protect themselves against *all attacks* within the first four categories and a subset of attacks from the fifth.

## 3. Secure Computation Programming Model

The key feature we provide to a secure application is the ability to compute securely using secure memory, which we refer to as *ghost memory*, and to exchange data securely with external files and network interfaces. Applications do *not* have to be compiled with the SVA-OS compiler or instrumented in any particular way; those requirements only apply to the OS. In this section, we discuss the programmer's interface to secure computation. In Section 4, we show how our system, which we call *Virtual Ghost*, prevents the operating system from violating the integrity or confidentiality of an application that uses secure computation.

### 3.1 Virtual Ghost Memory Organization

Virtual Ghost divides the address space of each process into three partitions. The first partition holds traditional, user-space application memory while a second partition, located at the high end of the virtual address space, holds traditional kernel-space memory. The kernel space memory is mapped persistently and is common across all processes, while the user-space memory mappings change as processes are switched on and off the CPU. Operating systems such as Linux and BSD Unix already provide this kind of user-space/kernel-space partitioning [9, 25].

A new third partition, the ghost memory partition, is application-specific and is accessible only to the application and to Virtual Ghost. Physical page frames mapped to this partition hold application code, thread stacks, and any data used by secure computation. These page frames logically belong to the process and, like anonymous `mmap()` memory mappings, are unmapped from/mapped back into the virtual address space as the process is context switched on and off the processor.

Some applications may choose not to protect any of their memory, in which case the Ghost memory partition would go unused (their code and thread stacks would be mapped into ordinary application memory). Others may choose to protect *all* of their memory except a small portion used to pass data to or from the operating system. The latter configuration is essentially similar to what Overshadow provides, and Virtual Ghost provides this capability in the same way – by interposing wrappers on system calls. This is described briefly in Section 6.

### 3.2 Ghost Memory Allocation and Deallocation

An application wishing to execute securely without trusting the OS would obtain one or more chunks of ghost memory from Virtual Ghost; this memory is allocated and deallocated using two new "system calls" shown in Table 1. The instruction `allocgm()` asks Virtual Ghost to map one or more physical pages into the ghost partition starting at a specific virtual address. Virtual Ghost requests physical page frames from the operating system, verifies that the OS has removed all virtual to physical mappings for the frames, maps the frames starting at the specified address within the application's ghost partition, and zeroes out the frames' contents. The instruction `freegm()` tells Virtual Ghost that the block of memory at a specified virtual address is no longer needed and can be returned to the OS. Virtual Ghost unmaps the

| Name | Description |
|---|---|
| `allocgm(void * va, uintptr_t num)` | Map num page frames at the virtual address va (which must be within the ghost memory region). |
| `freegm(void * va, uintptr_t num)` | Free num page frames of ghost memory starting at va (which must be previously allocated via `allocgm`) |

**Table 1.** Ghost Memory Management Instructions

frames, zeroes their contents, and returns them to the operating system.

These instructions are not designed to be called directly by application-level code (although they could). A more convenient way to use these instructions is via a language's run-time library (e.g., the C standard library), which would use them to create language allocation functions that allocate ghost memory, e.g., using a modified version of `malloc`.

Note that ghost memory pages cannot be initialized using demand-paging from persistent storage into physical memory. Ghost Memory is like anonymous `mmap` memory, which Virtual Ghost can provide to an application at startup and when the application allocates it via `allocgm()`. To get data from the network or file system into ghost memory, the application must first read the data into traditional memory (which is OS accessible) and then copy it (or decrypt it) into ghost memory. Other systems (e.g., InkTag [16]) perform the decrypt/copy operation transparently via the demand-paging mechanism. By requiring the application to decrypt data explicitly, Virtual Ghost avoids the complications of recovering encrypted application data after a crash (because the encryption keys are visible to the application and not hidden away within the Virtual Ghost VM). It also gives the application more flexibility in choosing different encryption algorithms and key lengths. Furthermore, this approach simplifies the design and reduces the size of Virtual Ghost, thus keeping Virtual Ghost's Trusted Computing Base (TCB) small.

### 3.3 I/O, Encryption, and Key Management

Applications that use ghost memory require secure mechanisms for communicating data with the external world, including local disk or across a network. Duplicating such I/O services in Virtual Ghost would significantly increase the size and complexity of the system's TCB. Therefore, like Overshadow [11] and InkTag [16], we let the untrusted OS perform all I/O operations. Applications running on Virtual Ghost must use cryptographic techniques (i.e., encryption, decryption, and digital signatures) to protect data confidentiality and detect potential corruption when writing data to or reading data from the OS during I/O.

Upon startup, applications need encryption keys to access persistently stored data (such as files on a hard drive) stored during previous executions of the application. Virtual Ghost provides each application with an application-specific public-private key pair that is kept secure from the OS and all other applications on the system. The application is responsible for encrypting (decrypting) secret data using this key pair before passing the data to (after receiving the data from) explicit I/O operations. Wrappers for widely used I/O operations such as `read()` and `write()` can make it largely transparent for applications to do the necessary encryption and decryption.

Using encryption for local IPC, network communication, and file system data storage allows applications to protect data confidentiality and to detect corruption. For example, to protect data confidentiality, an application can encrypt data with its public key before asking the OS to write the data to disk. To detect file corruption, an application can compute a file's checksum and encrypt and store the checksum in the file system along with the contents of the file. When reading the file back, it can recompute the checksum and validate it against the stored value. The OS, without the private key, cannot modify the file's contents and update the encrypted checksum with the appropriate value.

Unlike programmed I/O, swapping of ghost memory is the responsibility of Virtual Ghost. Virtual Ghost maintains its own public/private key pair for each system on which it is installed. If the OS indicates to Virtual Ghost that it wishes to swap out a ghost page, Virtual Ghost will encrypt and checksum the page with its keys before providing the OS with access. To swap a page in, the OS provides Virtual Ghost with the encrypted page contents; Virtual Ghost will verify that the page has not been modified and place it back into the ghost memory partition in the correct location. This design not only provides secure swapping but allows the OS to optimize swapping by first swapping out traditional memory pages.

### 3.4 Security Guarantees

An application that follows the guidelines above on a Virtual Ghost system obtains a number of strong guarantees, even in the presence of a hostile or compromised operating system or administrator account. All these guarantees apply to application data allocated in ghost memory. By "attacker" below, we mean an entity that controls either the OS or any process other than the application process itself (or for a multi-process or distributed application, the set of processes with which the application explicitly shares ghost memory or explicitly transfers the contents of that memory).

1. An attacker cannot read or write application data in memory or in CPU registers.
2. An attacker cannot read or write application code and cannot subvert application control flow at any point during the application execution, including application startup, signal delivery, system calls, or shutdown.

3. An attacker cannot read data that the application has stored unencrypted in ghost memory while the data is swapped out to external storage, nor can it modify such data without the corruption being detected before the data is swapped back into memory.
4. An attacker cannot read the application's encryption key, nor can it modify the application's encryption key or executable image undetected. Such modifications will be detected when setting the application up for execution and will prevent application startup.
5. By virtue of the application's encryption key being protected, data encrypted by the application cannot be read while stored in external storage or in transit via I/O (e.g., across a network). Likewise, any corruption of signed data will be detected.

# 4. Enforcing Secure Computation

In this section, we show how Virtual Ghost is designed to prevent the operating system from violating the integrity or confidentiality of secure applications. Section 5 describes implementation details of this design.

## 4.1 Overview of Virtual Ghost

Our approach for protecting ghost memory is conceptually simple: we instrument (or "sandbox") memory access instructions in the kernel to ensure that they cannot access this memory. Virtual Ghost also instruments kernel code with control-flow integrity (CFI) checks to ensure that our sandboxing instrumentation is not bypassed [3, 38].

While sandboxing prevents attacks that attempt to access ghost memory directly, it does not prevent the other attacks described in Section 2.2. Our design additionally needs a way to restrict the interactions between the system software and both the hardware and applications. For example, our system must be able to verify (either statically or at runtime) that MMU operations will not alter the mapping of physical page frames used for ghost memory, and it must limit the types of changes that system software can make to interrupted program state.

To achieve these goals, our system needs a framework that provides both compiler analysis and instrumentation of operating system kernel code as well as a way of controlling interactions between the system software, the hardware, and applications. The Secure Virtual Architecture (SVA) framework [12, 13] meets these requirements, and we modify and extend it to support Virtual Ghost. A high-level overview of our approach, built on SVA, is shown in Figure 1.

## 4.2 Background: Secure Virtual Architecture

As Figure 1 shows, SVA interposes a compiler-based virtual machine (VM)[2] between the hardware and the operating system. All operating system software, including the kernel and device drivers, is compiled to the virtual instruction set implemented by SVA. The SVA VM translates code from the virtual instruction set to the native instruction set of the hardware, typically ahead-of-time, and caches and signs the translations (although it could also be done just-in-time while the kernel is running) [14].

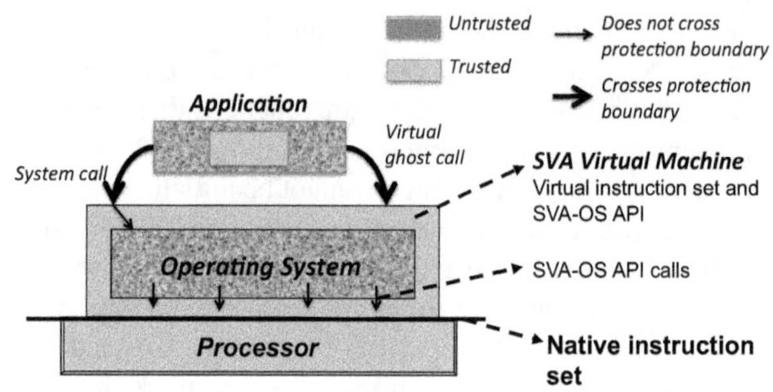


**Figure 1.** System Organization with Virtual Ghost

The core SVA virtual instruction set is based on the LLVM compiler intermediate representation (IR) [19], which is used in many popular systems (e.g., MacOS X, iOS, and Android) for static and/or just-in-time compilation. The LLVM IR enables efficient and precise compiler analyses at compile time, link time, install time, and run time for arbitrary languages [19].

SVA adds a set of instructions to LLVM called SVA-OS; these instructions replace the hardware-specific operations used by an OS to communicate with the hardware and to do low-level state manipulation [12–14]. SVA-OS handles operations such as saving and restoring processor state, signal handler dispatch, MMU configuration, and primitive reads and writes to I/O devices. System calls from an application are first fielded by SVA-OS, which saves processor state and performs minor bookkeeping, before passing the system call on to the OS as an ordinary function call. Modifying an OS to use the SVA-OS instructions is essentially like porting the OS to a new architecture, albeit with a clean, higher-level function interface that simplifies the port.

SVA-OS appears to the kernel as an ordinary run-time library; in particular, the OS can use these operations as direct function calls without crossing a protection boundary. The SVA compiler translates software from the virtual instruction set to the native instruction set. Moreover, the SVA-OS instructions are designed so that the SVA VM can perform run-time checks on all kernel-hardware interactions. *This combination of two capabilities in SVA is unique: it combines the compiler capabilities of a high-level language with the supervisory control of a hypervisor.*

Together, this combination allows SVA to enforce security policies on both application and kernel code [12, 13]. For

[2] We use the term "virtual machine" to mean a virtual architecture implemented via a translator and run-time system, similar to a language virtual machine, and not a guest operating system instance.

example, SVA has previously been used to provide memory safety to the Linux kernel, including the assurance that, even with dangling pointer and MMU configuration errors, SVA would enforce a strong set of safety guarantees and sound points-to analysis [12, 13]. In the present work, we do *not* require either memory safety or sound points-to analysis from SVA. Instead, we use the combination of SVA capabilities to provide secure computation and I/O with ghost memory.

### 4.3 Preventing Data Accesses in Memory

In this and the next few subsections, we discuss how Virtual Ghost addresses each of the five attack vectors described in Section 2.2.

#### 4.3.1 Controlling Direct Memory Accesses

The SVM VM must perform two kinds of instrumentation when generating native code for the kernel (both the core kernel and dynamically loaded kernel modules). First, it must instrument loads and stores to prevent them from accessing ghost memory and the SVA VM internal memory. Recall that application pages are usually left mapped in the kernel's address space when entering the kernel on a system call, interrupt or trap. By instrumenting loads and stores, we avoid the need to unmap the ghost memory pages or (as Overshadow and Inktag do) to encrypt them before an OS access. Second, it must ensure that the instrumentation cannot be skipped via control-flow hijacking attacks [3].

By strategically aligning and sizing the SVA VM and ghost memory partitions, the load/store instrumentation can use simple bit-masking to ensure that a memory address is outside these partitions. The control-flow integrity instrumentation places checks on all returns and indirect calls to ensure that the computed address is a valid control-flow target. To support native code applications, our control-flow integrity checks also ensure that the address is within the kernel address space. A side benefit of our design is that the operating system kernel gets strong protection against control flow hijacking attacks.

#### 4.3.2 MMU Protections

To prevent attacks that use illegal MMU page table entries, Virtual Ghost extends the MMU configuration instructions in SVA-OS to perform additional checks at run-time, which ensure that a new MMU configuration does not leave ghost memory accessible to the kernel. Specifically, Virtual Ghost does not permit the operating system to map physical page frames used by ghost memory into any virtual address. Virtual Ghost also prevents the operating system from modifying any virtual to physical page mapping for virtual addresses that belong to the ghost memory partition.

Virtual Ghost also protects other types of memory in addition to ghost memory. The SVA VM internal memory has the same restrictions as ghost memory. Native code is similarly protected; Virtual Ghost prevents native code pages from being remapped or made writable. This prevents the OS from bypassing the instrumentation or inserting arbitrary instructions into application code. Native code, unlike ghost memory or SVA internal memory, is made executable.

#### 4.3.3 DMA Protections

Ghost Memory should never be the target of a legitimate DMA request. If Virtual Ghost can prevent DMA transfers to or from ghost physical page frames, then it can prevent DMA-based attacks.

SVA requires an IOMMU [4] and configures it to prevent I/O devices from writing into the SVA VM memory [12, 13]. It further provides special I/O instructions for accessing processor I/O ports and memory-mapped I/O devices. Both SVA and Virtual Ghost must prevent the OS from reconfiguring the IOMMU to expose ghost memory to DMA transfers. How this is done depends on whether the hardware uses I/O ports or memory-mapped I/O to configure the IOMMU. If the hardware uses I/O ports, then SVA uses run-time checks within the I/O port read and write instructions [12]. If the hardware uses memory-mapped I/O, then SVA and Virtual Ghost simply use the MMU checks described above to prevent the memory-mapped physical pages of the IOMMU device from being mapped into the kernel or user-space virtual memory; instead, it is only mapped into the SVA VM memory, and the system software needs to use the I/O instructions to access it.

### 4.4 Preventing Data Accesses During I/O

Virtual Ghost relies on application-controlled encryption and hashing to prevent data theft or tampering during I/O operations, and uses automatic encryption and hashing done by the Virtual Ghost VM for page swapping, as described in Section 3.3.

The main design challenge is to find a way to start the application with encryption keys that cannot be compromised by a hostile OS. As noted earlier, Virtual Ghost maintains a public/private key pair for each system on which it is installed. We assume that a Trusted Platform Module (TPM) coprocessor is available; the storage key held in the TPM is used to encrypt and decrypt the private key used by Virtual Ghost. The application's object code file format is extended to contain a section for the application encryption keys, which are encrypted with the Virtual Ghost public key. Each time the application is started up, Virtual Ghost decrypts the encryption key section with the Virtual Ghost private key and places it into its internal SVA VM memory before transferring control to the application. An application can use the `sva.getKey()` instruction to retrieve the key from the Virtual Ghost VM and store a copy in its ghost memory. If an application requires multiple private keys, e.g., for communicating with different clients, it can use its initial private key to encrypt and save these additional keys in persistent storage. Thus, Virtual Ghost and the underlying hardware together enable a *chain of trust* that cannot be compromised by the OS or other untrusted applications:

TPM storage key ⇒ Virtual Ghost private key ⇒
Application private key ⇒ Additional application keys.

The use of a separate section in the object code format allows easy modification of the keys by trusted tools. For example, a software distributor can place unique keys in each copy of the software before sending the software to a user. Similarly, a system administrator could update the keys in an application when the system is in single-user mode booted from trusted media.

### 4.5 Preventing Code Modification Attacks

Virtual Ghost prevents the operating system from loading incorrect code for an application, modifying native code after it is loaded, or repurposing existing native code instruction sequences for unintentional execution (e.g., via return-oriented programming).

To prevent the system software from loading the wrong code for an application, Virtual Ghost assumes that the application is installed by a trusted system administrator (who may be local or remote). The application's executable, including the embedded, encrypted application key described in Section 3.3, is signed by Virtual Ghost's public key when the application binary is installed. If the system software attempts to load different application code with the application's key, Virtual Ghost refuses to prepare the native code for execution. The same mechanism is used to authenticate dynamically loaded native code libraries before they are linked in to the application.

To prevent native code modification in memory, Virtual Ghost ensures that the MMU maps all native code into non-writable virtual addresses. It also ensures that the OS does not map new physical pages into virtual page frames that are in use for OS, SVA-OS, or application code segments.

Virtual Ghost prevents repurposing existing instruction sequences or functions simply because the Control Flow Integrity (CFI) enforcement (for ensuring that sandboxing instructions are not bypassed) prevents all transfers of control not predicted by the compiler. For example, a buffer overflow in the kernel could overwrite a function pointer, but if an indirect function call using that function pointer attempted to go to any location other than one of the predicted callees of the function, the CFI instrumentation would detect that and terminate the execution of the kernel thread.

Finally, Virtual Ghost also prevents the OS from subverting signal dispatch to the application, e.g., by executing arbitrary code instead of the signal handler in the application context. Although this is essentially a code modification attack, the mechanisms used to defend against this are based on protecting interrupted program state, described next.

### 4.6 Protecting Interrupted Program State

An attacker may attempt to read interrupted program state (the program state that is saved on a system call, interrupt, or trap) to glean confidential information. Alternatively, she may modify the interrupted program state to mount a control-hijack or non-control data attack on the application. Such an attack could trick the application into copying data from ghost memory into traditional memory where the operating system can read or write it. Note that such an attack works even on a completely memory-safe program. We have implemented such an attack as described in Section 7.

The SVA framework (and hence Virtual Ghost) calls this interrupted program state the *Interrupt Context*. The creation and maintenance of the Interrupt Context is performed by the SVA virtual machine. While most systems save the Interrupt Context on the kernel stack, Virtual Ghost saves the Interrupt Context within the SVA VM internal memory. Virtual Ghost also zeros out registers (except registers passing system call arguments for system calls) after saving the Interrupt Context but before handing control over to the OS. With these two features, the OS is unable to read or modify the Interrupt Context directly or glean its contents from examining current processor state.

The OS does need to make controlled changes to the Interrupt Context. For example, process creation needs to initialize a new Interrupt Context to return from the `fork()` system call [9], and signal handler dispatch needs to modify the application program counter and stack so that a return-from-interrupt instruction will cause the application to start executing its signal handler [9, 25].

SVA provides instructions for manipulating the Interrupt Context, and Virtual Ghost enhances the checks on them to ensure that they do not modify the Interrupt Context in an unsafe manner, as explained below.

#### 4.6.1 Secure Signal Handler Dispatch

Virtual Ghost provides instructions for implementing secure signal handler dispatch. Signal handler dispatch requires saving the Interrupt Context, modifying the interrupted program state so that the signal handler is invoked when the interrupted application is resumed, and then reloading the saved Interrupt Context back into the interrupted program state buffer when the `sigreturn()` system call is called.

Virtual Ghost pushes and pops a copy of the Interrupt Context on and off a per-thread stack within the SVA VM internal memory, whereas the original SVA let this live on the kernel stack for unprivileged applications [12, 13] (because SVA did not aim to protect application control flow from the OS, whereas Virtual Ghost does). This enhancement to the original SVA design ensures that the OS cannot modify the saved state *and* ensures that the OS restores the correct state within the correct thread context.

SVA provides an operation, `sva.ipush.function()`, which the operating system can use to modify an Interrupt Context so that the interrupted program starts execution in a signal handler. The OS passes in a pointer to the application function to call and the arguments to pass to this function, and Virtual Ghost modifies the Interrupt Context on the operating system's behalf. For efficiency, we allow sva.ipush.function() to modify the application stack even though the stack may be within ghost memory. Since Virtual Ghost only adds a function frame to the stack, it cannot read or overwrite data that the application is using.

To ensure that the specified function is permissible, Virtual Ghost provides an operation, sva.permitFunction(), which the *application* must use to register a list of functions that can be "pushed"; sva.ipush.function() refuses to push a function that is not in this list. To simplify application development, we provide wrappers for the signal and sigaction system calls, which register the signal handlers transparently, without needing to modify the application.

#### 4.6.2 Secure Process Creation

A thread is composed of two pieces of state: an Interrupt Context, which is the state of an interrupted user-space program, and a kernel-level processor state that Virtual Ghost calls *Thread State* that represents the state of the thread before it was taken off the CPU.[3] Creating a new thread requires creating a new Interrupt Context and Thread State.

While commodity operating systems create these structures manually, Virtual Ghost provides a single function, sva.newstate(), to create these two pieces of state. This function creates these new state structures within the SVA VM internal memory to prevent tampering by the system software. The newly created Interrupt Context is a clone of the Interrupt Context of the current thread. The new Thread State is initialized so that, on the next context switch, it begins executing in a function specified by the operating system. In order to maintain kernel control-flow integrity, Virtual Ghost verifies that the specified function is the entry point of a kernel function.

Any ghost memory belonging to the current thread will also belong to the new thread; this transparently makes it appear that ghost memory is mapped as shared memory among all threads and processes within an application.

Executing a new program (e.g., via the execve() system call) also requires reinitializing the Interrupt Context [9]: the program counter and stack pointer must be changed to execute the newly loaded program image, and, in the case of the first user-space process on the system (e.g., init), the processor privilege level must be changed from privileged to unprivileged. Virtual Ghost also ensures that the program counter points to the entry of a program that has previously been copied into SVA VM memory. (Section 4.5 describes how Virtual Ghost ensures that this program is not tampered with by the OS before or during this copy operation.)

Finally, any ghost memory associated with the interrupted program is unmapped when the Interrupt Context is reinitialized. This ensures that newly loaded program code does not have access to the ghost memory belonging to the previously executing program.

[3] SVA divided Thread State into Integer State and Floating Point State, as an optimization. Virtual Ghost does not do that.

### 4.7 Mitigating System Service Attacks

System service attacks like those described in Section 2.2.5 are not yet well understood [10]. However, Virtual Ghost provides some protection against such attacks that are known.

First, Virtual Ghost employs an enhanced C/C++ compiler that instruments system calls in ghosting applications to ensure that pointers passed into or returned by the operating system are not pointing into ghost memory. This instrumentation prevents accidental overwrites of ghost memory. This protects private data and prevents stack-smashing attacks (because the stack will be located in ghost memory).

Second, the Virtual Ghost VM provides an instruction for generating random numbers. The random number generator is built into the Virtual Ghost VM and can be trusted by applications for generating random numbers. This defeats Iago attacks that feed non-random numbers to applications [10].

While these protections are far from comprehensive, they offer protection against existing system service attacks.

## 5. Implementation

To create Virtual Ghost, we implemented a new version of the SVA-OS instructions and run-time for 64-bit x86 processors, reusing code from the original 32-bit, single-core implementation [12, 13]. Our implementation runs 64-bit code only. The Virtual Ghost instructions are implemented as a run-time library that is linked into the kernel.

We ported FreeBSD 9.0 to the Virtual Ghost/SVA-OS instruction set. We used FreeBSD instead of Linux (which we had used before with SVA-OS) because FreeBSD compiles with the LLVM compiler out of the box.

Virtual Ghost builds on, modifies, and adds a number of SVA-OS operations to implement the design described. We briefly summarize them here, omitting SVA-OS features that are needed for hosting a kernel and protecting SVA itself, but not otherwise used by Virtual Ghost for application security. We first briefly describe the compiler instrumentation and end with a brief summary of features that are not yet implemented.

***Compiler Instrumentation:*** The load/store and CFI instrumentation is implemented as two new passes in the LLVM 3.1 compiler infrastructure. The load/store instrumentation pass transforms code at the LLVM IR level; it instruments mid-level IR loads, stores, atomic operations, and calls to memcpy(). The CFI instrumentation pass is an updated version of the pass written by Zeng et. al. [38] that works on x86_64 machine code. It analyzes the machine code that LLVM 3.1 generates and adds in the necessary CFI labels and checks. It also masks the target address to ensure that it is not a user-space address. We modified the Clang/LLVM 3.1 compiler to use these instrumentation passes when compiling kernel code. To avoid link-time interprocedural analysis, which would be needed for precise call graph construction, our CFI instrumentation uses a very conservative call graph: we use one label both for call sites (i.e., the targets of returns) and for the first address of every function. While conservative, this call graph allows us to measure the performance overheads and should suffice for stopping advanced control-data attacks.

We placed the ghost memory partition into an unused 512 GB portion of the address space (`0xffffff0000000000` – `0xffffff8000000000`). The load/store instrumentation determines whether the address is greater than or equal to `0xffffff0000000000` and, if so, ORs it with $2^{39}$ to ensure that the address will not access ghost memory. While our design would normally use some of this 512 GB partition for SVA internal memory, we opted to leave the SVA internal memory within the kernel's data segment; we added new instrumentation to kernel code, which changes an address to zero before a load, store, or `memcpy()` if it is within the SVA internal memory. This additional instrumentation adds some overhead but simplifies development.

To defend against Iago attacks through the `mmap` system call, a separate mid-level LLVM IR instrumentation pass performs identical bit-masking instrumentation to the return values of `mmap()` system calls for user-space application code.[4] This instrumentation moves any pointer returned by the kernel that points into ghost memory out of ghost memory. In this way, Iago attacks using `mmap()` [10] cannot trick an application into writing data into its own ghost memory. If an application stores its stack and function pointers in ghost memory, then our defense should prevent Iago attacks from subverting application control flow integrity.

***Memory Management:*** SVA-OS provides operations that the kernel uses to insert and remove page table entries at each level of a multi-level page table and ensures that they do not violate internal consistency of the page tables or the integrity of SVA code and data. Virtual Ghost augments these operations to also enforce the MMU mapping constraints described in Section 4.3.2.

***Launching Execution:*** Virtual Ghost provides the operation, `sva.reinit.icontext()`, to *reinitialize* an Interrupt Context with new application state. This reinitialization will modify the program counter and stack pointer in the Interrupt Context so that, when resumed, the program will begin executing new code.

Virtual Ghost uses the x86_64 Interrupt Stack Table (IST) feature [2] to protect the Interrupt Context. This feature instructs the processor to always change the stack pointer to a known location on traps or interrupts regardless of whether a change in privilege mode occurs. This allows the SVA VM to direct the processor to save interrupted program state (such as the program counter) within the SVA VM internal memory so that it is never accessible to the operating system.

***Signal Delivery:*** Virtual Ghost implements the `sva.icontext.save()` and `sva.icontext.load()` instructions to save and restore the Interrupt Context before and after signal handler dispatch. These instructions save the Interrupt Context within SVA memory to ensure that the OS cannot read or write it directly.

***What Is Not Yet Implemented:*** Our implementation so far does not include a few features described previously. (1) While explicit I/O is supported, the key management functions are only partially implemented: Virtual Ghost does not provide a public/private key pair; does not use a TPM; and application-specific keys are not embedded in application binaries (instead, a 128-bit AES application key is hard-coded into SVA-OS for our experiments). (2) Swapping of ghost memory is not implemented. (3) The system does not yet include the DMA protections. We believe that IOMMU configuration is rare, and therefore, the extra protections for DMA should not add noticeable overhead. (4) Finally, some operations in the FreeBSD kernel are still handled by inline assembly code (e.g., memory-mapped I/O loads and stores), but we do not believe that these unported operations will significantly affect performance once they are ported properly.

***Trusted Computing Base:*** Since the Virtual Ghost implementation is missing a few features, measuring the size of its Trusted Computing Base (TCB) is premature. However, the vast majority of the functionality has been implemented, and the current code size is indicative of the approximate size of the TCB. Virtual Ghost currently includes only 5,344 source lines of code (ignoring comments, whitespace, etc.). This count includes the SVA VM run-time system and the passes that we added to the compiler to enforce our security guarantees. Overall, we believe that the complexity and attack surface of Virtual Ghost are far smaller than modern production hypervisors like XenServer but approximately comparable to a minimal hypervisor.

## 6. Securing OpenSSH

To demonstrate that our system can secure real applications, we modified three programs from the OpenSSH 6.2p1 application suite to use ghost memory: `ssh`, `ssh-keygen`, and `ssh-agent`. The `ssh-keygen` program generates public/private key pairs which `ssh` can use for password-less authentication to remote systems. The `ssh-agent` server stores private encryption keys which the `ssh` client may use for public/private key authentication. We used a single private "application key" for all three programs so that they could share encrypted files.

We modified `ssh-keygen` to encrypt all the private authentication key files it generates with the application key; our `ssh` client decrypts the authentication keys with the application private key upon startup and places them, along with all other heap objects, into ghost memory. Since the OS cannot gain access to the application key, it cannot decrypt the authentication keys that are stored on disk, and it cannot read the cleartext versions out of `ssh`'s or `ssh-keygen`'s ghost memory.

[4] An alternative implementation method would be to implement a C library wrapper function for `mmap()`.

We modified the FreeBSD C library so that the heap allocator functions (`malloc()`, `calloc()`, `realloc()`) allocate heap objects in ghost memory instead of in traditional memory; the changes generate a 216 line patch. To ease porting, we wrote a 667-line system call wrapper library that copies data between ghost memory and traditional memory as necessary. This wrapper library also provides wrappers for `signal()` and `sigaction()` that register the signal handler functions with Virtual Ghost before calling the kernel's `signal()` and `sigaction()` system calls. The compiler and linker did not always resolve system calls to our wrapper functions properly, so we made some manual modifications to the programs. We also modified the programs to use traditional memory (allocated via `mmap()`) to store the results of data to be sent to `stdout` and `stderr` to reduce copying overhead. In total, our changes to OpenSSH can be applied with a patch that adds 812 and deletes 68 lines of code (OpenSSH contains 9,230 source lines of code).

We tested our applications on the system used for our experiments (see Section 8). We used `ssh-keygen` to generate a new private and public key for DSA authentication; the generated private key was encrypted while the public key was not encrypted. We then installed the public key on another system and used `ssh` to log into that system using DSA authentication.

For `ssh-agent`, we added code to place a secret string within a heap-allocated memory buffer. The rootkit attacks described in Section 7 attempt to read this secret string. The goal of adding this secret string is that `ssh-agent` treats it identically to an encryption key (it can use the string internally but never outputs it to another program). We used a secret string as it is easier to find in memory and easier to identify as the data for which our attack searches.

Our enhanced OpenSSH application suite demonstrates that Virtual Ghost can provide security-critical applications with in-memory secrets (e.g., the keys held by `ssh-agent`) and secure, long-term storage (e.g., the authentication keys created by `ssh-keygen` and read by `ssh`). It also demonstrates that a suite of cooperating applications can securely share data on a hostile operating system via a shared application key.

## 7. Security Experiments

To evaluate the security of our system, we built a malicious kernel module that attempts to steal sensitive information from a victim process. This module, based on the code from Joseph Kong's book [18], can be configured by a non-privileged user to mount one of two possible attacks – direct memory access or code injection – on a given victim process. The malicious module replaces the function that handles the `read()` system call and executes the attack as the victim process reads data from a file descriptor.

In the first attack, the malicious module attempts to directly read the data from the victim memory and print it to the system log.

In the second attack, the malicious module attempts to make the victim process write the confidential data out to a file. The attack first opens the file to which the data should be written, allocates memory in the process's address space via `mmap()`, and copies exploit code into the memory buffer. The attack then sets up a signal handler for the victim process that calls the exploit code. The malicious module then sends a signal to the victim process, triggering the exploit code to run in the signal handler. The exploit code copies the data into the `mmap`'ed memory and executes a `write()` system call to write the secret data out to the file opened by the malicious module.

We used both attacks on our ssh-agent program, described in Section 6. When we install the malicious module without instrumenting its code and run ssh-agent with `malloc()` configured to allocate memory objects in traditional memory, both attacks succeed.

We then recompiled our malicious module using our modified Clang compiler to insert the instrumentation required for Virtual Ghost. We reran both attacks on ssh-agent with `malloc()` configured to allocate memory objects in ghost memory. The first attack fails because the load/store instrumentation changes the pointer in the malicious module to point outside of ghost memory; the kernel simply reads unknown data out of its own address space. The second attack is thwarted because `sva.ipush.function()` recognizes that the exploit code isn't one of the functions registered as a valid target of `sva.ipush.function()`.

Note that a number of other possible attacks from within kernel code *are simply not expressible in our system*, e.g., anything that requires using assembly code in the kernel (such as to access CPU registers), or manipulating the application stack frames, or modifying interrupted application state when saved in memory. The second attack above illustrates that much more sophisticated multi-step exploits are needed to get past the basic protections against using assembly code or accessing values saved in SVA VM memory or directly reading or writing application code and data (as in the first attack). Virtual Ghost is successfully able to thwart even this sophisticated attack.

## 8. Performance Experiments

We ran our performance experiments on a Dell Precision T1650 workstation with an Intel® Core™ i7-3770 processor at 3.4 GHz with 8 MB of cache, 16 GB of RAM, an integrated PCIE Gigabit Ethernet card, a 7200 RPM 6 Gb/s 500 GB SATA hard drive, and a 256 GB Solid State Drive (SSD). Files in `/usr` were stored on the SSD. For network experiments, we used a dedicated Gigabit Ethernet network. The client machine was an iMac with a 4-core hyper-threaded Intel® Core™ i7 processor at 2.6 GHz with 8 GB of RAM.

We evaluated our system's performance on microbenchmarks as well as a few applications. We used microbenchmarks to see how Virtual Ghost affects primitive OS operations, `thttpd` and `sshd` for network applications, and Postmark [30] for a file system intensive program.

We conducted our experiments by booting the machine into single-user mode to minimize noise from other processes running on the system. Our baseline, unless otherwise noted, is a native FreeBSD kernel compiled with the LLVM 3.1 compiler and configured identically to our Virtual Ghost FreeBSD kernel.

### 8.1 Microbenchmarks

In order to understand how our system affects basic OS performance, we measured the latency of various system calls using LMBench [26] from the FreeBSD 9.0 ports tree. For those benchmarks that can be configured to run the test for a specified number of iterations, we used 1,000 iterations. Additionally, we ran each benchmark 10 times.

| Test | Native | Virtual Ghost | Overhead | InkTag |
|---|---|---|---|---|
| null syscall | 0.091 | 0.355 | 3.90x | 55.8x |
| open/close | 2.01 | 9.70 | 4.83x | 7.95x |
| mmap | 7.06 | 33.2 | 4.70x | 9.94x |
| page fault | 31.8 | 36.7 | 1.15x | 7.50x |
| signal handler install | 0.168 | 0.545 | 3.24x | - |
| signal handler delivery | 1.27 | 2.05 | 1.61x | - |
| fork + exit | 63.7 | 283 | 4.40x | 5.74x |
| fork + exec | 101 | 422 | 4.20x | 3.04x |
| select | 3.05 | 10.3 | 3.40x | - |

**Table 2.** LMBench Results. Time in Microseconds.

| File Size | Native | Virtual Ghost | Overhead |
|---|---|---|---|
| 0 KB | 166,846 | 36,164 | 4.61x |
| 1 KB | 116,668 | 25,817 | 4.52x |
| 4 KB | 116,657 | 25,806 | 4.52x |
| 10 KB | 110,842 | 25,042 | 4.43x |

**Table 3.** LMBench: Files Deleted Per Second.

| File Size | Native | Virtual Ghost | Overhead |
|---|---|---|---|
| 0 KB | 156,276 | 33,777 | 4.63x |
| 1 KB | 97,839 | 18,796 | 5.21x |
| 4 KB | 97,102 | 18,725 | 5.19x |
| 10 KB | 85,319 | 18,095 | 4.71x |

**Table 4.** LMBench: Files Created Per Second.

As Table 2 shows, our system can add considerable overhead to individual operations. System call entry increases by 3.9 times. We compare these relative slowdowns with InkTag, which has reported LMBench results as well [16]. Our slowdowns are nearly identical to or better than InkTag on 5/7 microbenchmarks: all except `exec()` and file deletion/creation. Our file deletion/creation overheads (shown in Tables 3 and 4) average 4.52x and 4.94x, respectively, across all file sizes, which is slower than InkTag. System calls and page faults, two of the most performance critical OS operations, are both considerably faster on Virtual Ghost than on InkTag.

While Virtual Ghost adds overhead, it provides double benefits for the cost: in addition to ghost memory, it provides protection to the OS itself via control flow integrity.

### 8.2 Web Server Performance

We used a statically linked, non-ghosting version of the `thttpd` web server [29] to measure the impact our system had on a web server. We used ApacheBench [1] to measure the bandwidth of transferring files between 1 KB and 1 MB in size. Each file was generated by collecting random data from the `/dev/random` device and stored on the SSD. We configured ApacheBench to make 100 simultaneous connections and to perform 10,000 requests for the file for each run of the experiment. We ran each experiment 20 times.

Figure 2 shows the mean performance of transferring a file of each size and displays the standard deviation as error bars. The data show that the impact of Virtual Ghost on the Web transfer bandwidth is negligible.

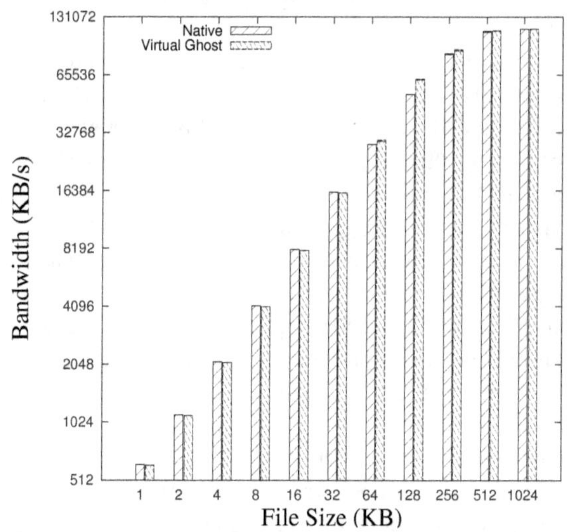


**Figure 2.** Average Bandwidth of thttpd

### 8.3 OpenSSH Performance

To study secure bulk data transfer performance, we measured the bandwidth achieved when transferring files of various sizes using the OpenSSH server and client [36]. We measured the performance of the `sshd` server without ghosting and our ghosting `ssh` client described in Section 6. Files were created using the same means described in Section 8.2.

#### 8.3.1 Server Performance Without Ghosting

We ran the pre-installed OpenSSH server on our test machine and used the standard Mac OS X OpenSSH `scp` client to measure the bandwidth achieved when transferring files.

We repeated each experiment 20 times and report standard deviation bars. The baseline system is the original FreeBSD 9.0 kernel compiled with Clang and configured identically to our Virtual Ghost FreeBSD kernel.

Figure 3 shows the mean bandwidth for the baseline system and Virtual Ghost. We observe bandwidth reductions of 23% on average, with a worst case of 45%, and negligible slowdowns for large file sizes.

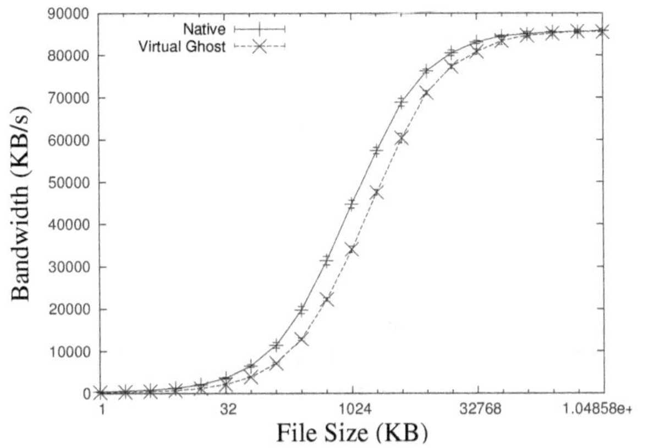


**Figure 3.** SSH Server Average Transfer Rate

### 8.4 Client Performance With Ghosting

To measure the effect of using ghost memory, we measured the average bandwidth of transferring file sizes of 1 KB to 1 MB using both the unmodified OpenSSH `ssh` client and our ghosting `ssh` client described in Section 6. We transferred files by having `ssh` run the `cat` command on the file on the server. We ran both on the Virtual Ghost FreeBSD kernel to isolate the performance differences in using ghost memory. We transferred each file 20 times. Figure 4 reports the average of the 20 runs for each file size as well as the standard deviation using error bars. (The numbers differ from those in Figure 3 because this experiment ran the ssh client on Virtual Ghost, instead of the sshd server.)

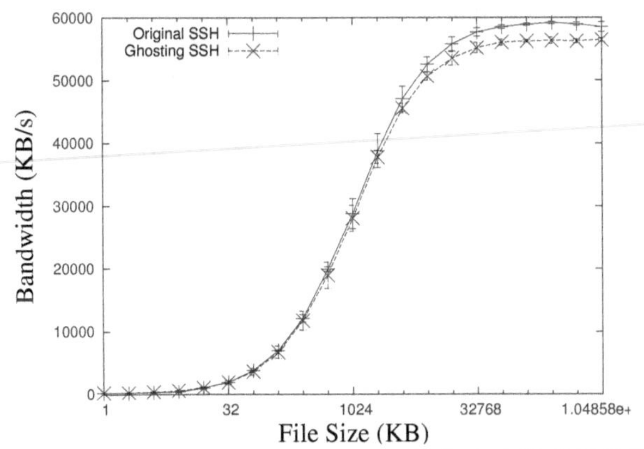


**Figure 4.** Ghosting SSH Client Average Transfer Rate

As Figure 4 shows, the performance difference between using traditional memory, which is accessible to the OS, and ghost memory is small. The maximum reduction in bandwidth by the ghosting `ssh` client is 5%.

### 8.5 Postmark Performance

In order to test a file system intensive benchmark, we ran Postmark [30]. Postmark mimics the behavior of a mail server and exercises the file system significantly.

| Native (s) | Std. Dev. | Virtual Ghost (s) | Std. Dev. | Overhead |
|---|---|---|---|---|
| 14.30 | 0.46 | 67.50 | 0.50 | 4.72x |

**Table 5.** Postmark Results

We configured Postmark to use 500 base files with sizes ranging from 500 bytes to 9.77 KB with 512 byte block sizes. The read/append and create/delete biases were set to 5, and we configured Postmark to use buffered file I/O. All files were stored on the SSD. Each run of the experiment performed 500,000 transactions.

We ran the experiment 20 times on both the native FreeBSD kernel and the Virtual Ghost system. Table 5 shows the results. As Postmark is dominated by file operations, the slowdown of 4.7x is similar to the LMBench open/close system call overhead of 4.8x. Due to its file system intensive behavior, Postmark represents the worst case for the application benchmarks we tried.

## 9. Related Work

Several previous systems attempt to protect an application's code and data from a malicious operating system. Systems such as Overshadow [11, 28], SP3 [37], and InkTag [16] build on a full-scale commercial hypervisor (e.g., VMWare Server or XenServer). The hypervisor presents an encrypted view of the application's memory to the OS and uses digital signing to detect corruption of the physical pages caused by the OS. These systems do *not* prevent the OS from reading or modifying the encrypted pages. To simplify porting legacy applications, such systems include a shim library between the application and the operating system that encrypts and decrypts data for system call communication.

Hypervisor-based approaches offer a high level of compatibility with existing applications and operating systems, but suffer high performance overhead. Additionally, they add overhead to the common case (when the kernel reads/writes application memory correctly via the system call API). They also do not provide additional security to the operating system and do not compose as cleanly with other kernel security solutions that use hypervisor-based approaches.

Virtual Ghost presents a different point in the design space for protecting applications from an untrusted OS. First, it uses compiler instrumentation ("sandboxing" and control-flow integrity) instead of page protections to protect both application ghost memory pages as well as its own code and metadata from the OS (similar to systems such as SPIN [8], JavaOS [33], and Singularity [15, 17]).

Second, it completely prevents the OS from reading and writing ghost memory pages rather than allowing access to the pages in encrypted form. Third, although Virtual Ghost introduces a hardware abstraction layer (SVA-OS) that is somewhat similar to a (minimal) hypervisor, SVA-OS does not have higher privilege than the OS; instead, it appears as a library of functions that the OS kernel code can call directly. Fourth, system calls from the secure application to the OS need not incur encryption and hashing overhead for non-secure data. Fifth, Virtual Ghost gives the application considerably more control over the choices of encryption and hashing keys, and over what subset of data is protected. Finally, the compiler approach hardens the OS against external exploits because it prevents both injected code and (by blocking control-flow hijacking) exploits that use existing code, such as return-oriented programming or jump-oriented programming. Moreover, the compiler approach can be directly extended to provide other compiler-enforced security policies such as comprehensive memory safety [12, 13].

In addition to isolation, InkTag [16] also provides some valuable usability improvements for secure applications, including services for configuring access control to files. These features could be provided by SVA-OS in very similar ways, at the cost of a non-trivial relative increase in the TCB size.

Other recent efforts, namely TrustVisor [22], Flicker [23], and Memoir [27], provide special purpose hypervisors that enable secure execution and data secrecy for pieces of application logic. They obtain isolated execution of code and data secrecy via hardware virtualization. These approaches prevent the protected code from interacting with the system, which limits the size of code regions protected, and data must be sealed via trusted computing modules between successive invocations of the secure code. In contrast, Virtual Ghost provides continuous isolation of code and data from the OS without the need for secure storage or monopolizing system wide execution of code.

Several systems provide hardware support to isolate applications from the environment, including the OS. The XOM processor used by XOMOS [20] encrypts all instructions and data transferred to or from memory and can detect tampering of the code and data, which enables a secure application on XOMOS to trust nothing but the processor (not even the OS or the memory system). HyperSentry [7] uses server-class hardware for system management (IPMI and SMM) to perform stealthy measurements of a hypervisor without using software at a higher privilege level, while protecting the measurements from the hypervisor. These mechanisms are designed for infrequent operations, not for more extensive computation and I/O.

ARM Security Extensions (aka TrustZone) [6] create two virtual cores, operating as two isolated "worlds" called the Secure World and the Normal World, on a single physical core. Applications running in the Secure World are completely isolated from an OS and applications running in the Normal World. Secure World applications can use peripheral devices such as a keyboard or display securely. Virtual Ghost and any other pure-software scheme would need complex additional software to protect keyboard and display I/O. Intel Software Guard eEtensions (SGX) provide isolated execution zones called enclaves that are protected from privileged software access including VMMs, OS, and BIOS [24]. The enclave is protected by ISA extensions and hardware access control mechanisms and is similar to Virtual Ghost in that it protects memory regions from the OS. Additionally, SGX provides both trusted computing measurement, sealing, and attestation mechanisms [5]. Unlike TrustZones and SGX, Virtual Ghost requires no architectural modifications and could provide a secure execution environment on systems that lack such hardware support.

## 10. Future Work

We have several directions for future work. First, we plan to investigate how applications can use Virtual Ghost's features along with cryptographic protocols to protect themselves from sophisticated attacks. For example, how should applications ensure that the OS does not perform replay attacks by providing older versions of previously encrypted files? How should applications share keys and authenticate themselves to each other? Second, while Virtual Ghost provides applications with great flexibility in protecting their data, taking advantage of this flexibility can be tedious. We plan to investigate library support that will make writing secure applications with Virtual Ghost more convenient.

## 11. Conclusion

In this paper, we present Virtual Ghost, which provides application security in the face of untrusted operating systems. Virtual Ghost does not require a higher-privilege layer, as hypervisors do; instead, it applies compiler instrumentation combined with runtime checks on operating system code to provide ghost memory to applications. We ported a suite of real-world applications to use ghost memory and found that Virtual Ghost protected the applications from advanced kernel-level malware. We observe comparable performance, and much better in some instances, than the state of the art in secure execution environments, while also providing an additional layer of protection against external attacks on the operating system kernel itself.

## Acknowledgments

The authors would like to thank Bin Zeng, Gang Tan, and Greg Morrisett for sharing their x86 CFI code with us. The authors also thank the anonymous reviewers for their comments and feedback.

This material is based on work supported by the AFOSR under MURI award FA9550-09-1-0539, and by NSF Grant CNS 07-09122.

## References


[1] Apachebench: A complete benchmarking and regression testing suite. http://freshmeat.net/projects/ apachebench/, July 2003.

[2] *Intel 64 and IA-32 architectures software developer's manual*, volume 3. Intel, 2012.

[3] M. Abadi, M. Budiu, U. Erlingsson, and J. Ligatti. Control-flow integrity principles, implementations, and applications. *ACM Trans. Inf. Syst. Secur.*, 13:4:1–4:40, November 2009.

[4] Advanced Micro Devices. AMD64 architecture programmer's manual volume 2: System programming, September 2006.

[5] I. Anati, S. Gueron, S. Johnson, and V. Scarlata. Innovative technology for cpu based attestation and sealing. In *Proceedings of the 2nd International Workshop on Hardware and Architectural Support for Security and Privacy*, page 10. ACM, 2013.

[6] ARM Limited. ARM security technology: Building a secure system using trustzone technology. http://infocenter.arm.com/help/topic/com.arm.doc.prd29-genc-009492c/PRD29-GENC-009492C_trustzone_security_whitepaper.pdf, 2009.

[7] A. M. Azab, P. Ning, Z. Wang, X. Jiang, X. Zhang, and N. C. Skalsky. Hypersentry: enabling stealthy in-context measurement of hypervisor integrity. In *Proceedings of the 17th ACM conference on Computer and communications security*, CCS '10, pages 38–49, New York, NY, USA, 2010. ACM.

[8] B. Bershad, S. Savage, P. Pardyak, E. G. Sirer, D. Becker, M. Fiuczynski, C. Chambers, and S. Eggers. Extensibility, Safety and Performance in the SPIN Operating System. In *Proc. ACM SIGOPS Symp. on Op. Sys. Principles*, pages 267–284, Copper Mountain, CO, USA, 1995.

[9] D. P. Bovet and M. Cesati. *Understanding the LINUX Kernel.* O'Reilly, Sebastopol, CA, $2^{nd}$ edition, 2003.

[10] S. Checkoway and H. Shacham. Iago attacks: why the system call API is a bad untrusted RPC interface. In *Proceedings of the eighteenth international conference on Architectural support for programming languages and operating systems*, ASPLOS '13, pages 253–264, New York, NY, USA, 2013. ACM.

[11] X. Chen, T. Garfinkel, E. C. Lewis, P. Subrahmanyam, C. A. Waldspurger, D. Boneh, J. Dwoskin, and D. R. Ports. Overshadow: a virtualization-based approach to retrofitting protection in commodity operating systems. In *Proceedings of the 13th international conference on Architectural support for programming languages and operating systems*, ASPLOS XIII, pages 2–13, New York, NY, USA, 2008. ACM.

[12] J. Criswell, N. Geoffray, and V. Adve. Memory safety for low-level software/hardware interactions. In *Proceedings of the Eighteenth Usenix Security Symposium*, August 2009.

[13] J. Criswell, A. Lenharth, D. Dhurjati, and V. Adve. Secure Virtual Architecture: A Safe Execution Environment for Commodity Operating Systems. In *Proc. ACM SIGOPS Symp. on Op. Sys. Principles*, pages 351–366, Stevenson, WA, USA, October 2007.

[14] J. Criswell, B. Monroe, and V. Adve. A virtual instruction set interface for operating system kernels. In *Workshop on the Interaction between Operating Systems and Computer Architecture*, pages 26–33, Boston, MA, USA, June 2006.

[15] M. Fahndrich, M. Aiken, C. Hawblitzel, O. Hodson, G. C. Hunt, J. R. Larus, and S. Levi. Language support for fast and reliable message-based communication in Singularity OS. In *Proceedings of EuroSys*, 2006.

[16] O. S. Hofmann, S. Kim, A. M. Dunn, M. Z. Lee, and E. Witchel. Inktag: secure applications on an untrusted operating system. In *Proceedings of the eighteenth international conference on Architectural support for programming languages and operating systems*, ASPLOS '13, pages 265–278, New York, NY, USA, 2013. ACM.

[17] G. C. Hunt and J. R. Larus. Singularity Design Motivation (Singularity Technical Report 1). Technical Report MSR-TR-2004-105, Microsoft Research, Dec 2004.

[18] J. Kong. *Designing BSD Rootkits.* No Starch Press, San Francisco, CA, USA, 2007.

[19] C. Lattner and V. Adve. LLVM: A compilation framework for lifelong program analysis and transformation. In *Proc. Conf. on Code Generation and Optimization*, pages 75–88, San Jose, CA, USA, Mar 2004.

[20] D. Lie, C. A. Thekkath, and M. Horowitz. Implementing an untrusted operating system on trusted hardware. In *Proceedings of the nineteenth ACM symposium on Operating systems principles*, SOSP '03, pages 178–192, New York, NY, USA, 2003. ACM.

[21] LMH. Month of kernel bugs (MoKB) archive, 2006. http://projects.info-pull.com/mokb/.

[22] J. M. McCune, Y. Li, N. Qu, Z. Zhou, A. Datta, V. Gligor, and A. Perrig. Trustvisor: Efficient tcb reduction and attestation. In *Proceedings of the 2010 IEEE Symposium on Security and Privacy*, SP '10, pages 143–158, Washington, DC, USA, 2010. IEEE Computer Society.

[23] J. M. McCune, B. J. Parno, A. Perrig, M. K. Reiter, and H. Isozaki. Flicker: an execution infrastructure for tcb minimization. In *Proceedings of the 3rd ACM SIGOPS/EuroSys European Conference on Computer Systems 2008*, Eurosys '08, pages 315–328, New York, NY, USA, 2008. ACM.

[24] F. McKeen, I. Alexandrovich, A. Berenzon, C. V. Rozas, H. Shafi, V. Shanbhogue, and U. R. Savagaonkar. Innovative instructions and software model for isolated execution. In *Proceedings of the 2nd International Workshop on Hardware and Architectural Support for Security and Privacy*, page 10. ACM, 2013.

[25] M. K. McKusick, K. Bostic, M. J. Karels, and J. S. Quarterman. *The Design and Implementation of the 4.4 BSD Operating System.* Addison-Wesley Publishing Company, Inc., Redwood City, CA, 1996.

[26] L. McVoy and C. Staelin. lmbench: portable tools for performance analysis. In *Proceedings of the 1996 annual conference on USENIX Annual Technical Conference*, ATEC '96, pages 23–23, Berkeley, CA, USA, 1996. USENIX Association.

[27] B. Parno, J. R. Lorch, J. R. Douceur, J. Mickens, and J. M. McCune. Memoir: Practical state continuity for protected modules. In *Proceedings of the 2011 IEEE Symposium on

*Security and Privacy*, SP '11, pages 379–394, Washington, DC, USA, 2011. IEEE Computer Society.

[28] D. R. K. Ports and T. Garfinkel. Towards application security on untrusted operating systems. In *Proceedings of the 3rd conference on Hot topics in security*, HOTSEC'08, pages 1:1–1:7, Berkeley, CA, USA, 2008. USENIX Association.

[29] J. Poskanze. thttpd - tiny/turbo/throttling http server, 2000. http://www.acme.com/software/thttpd.

[30] Postmark. Email delivery for web apps, July 2013.

[31] R. Roemer, E. Buchanan, H. Shacham, and S. Savage. Return-oriented programming: Systems, languages, and applications. *ACM Trans. Inf. Syst. Secur.*, 15(1):2:1–2:34, Mar. 2012.

[32] M. E. Russinovich and D. A. Solomon. *Microsoft Windows Internals, Fourth Edition: Microsoft Windows Server(TM) 2003, Windows XP, and Windows 2000 (Pro-Developer).* Microsoft Press, Redmond, WA, USA, 2004.

[33] T. Saulpaugh and C. Mirho. *Inside the JavaOS Operating System.* Addison-Wesley, Reading, MA, USA, 1999.

[34] A. Singh. *Mac OS X Internals.* Addison-Wesley Professional, 2006.

[35] Solar Designer. return-to-libc attack, August 1997. http://www.securityfocus.com/archive/1/7480.

[36] The OpenBSD Project. Openssh, 2006. http://www.openssh.com.

[37] J. Yang and K. G. Shin. Using hypervisor to provide data secrecy for user applications on a per-page basis. In *Proceedings of the fourth ACM SIGPLAN/SIGOPS international conference on Virtual execution environments*, VEE '08, pages 71–80, New York, NY, USA, 2008. ACM.

[38] B. Zeng, G. Tan, and G. Morrisett. Combining control-flow integrity and static analysis for efficient and validated data sandboxing. In *Proceedings of the 18th ACM conference on Computer and communications security*, CCS '11, pages 29–40, New York, NY, USA, 2011. ACM.

# Sapper: A Language for Hardware-Level Security Policy Enforcement

Xun Li∗
Facebook
xun@fb.com

Vineeth Kashyap
University of California, Santa Barbara
vineeth@cs.ucsb.edu

Jason K. Oberg
University of California, San Diego
jkoberg@cs.ucsd.edu

Mohit Tiwari∗
University of Texas, Austin
tiwari@austin.utexas.edu

Vasanth Ram Rajarathinam∗
AMD
vasanthram.rajarathinam@amd.com

Ryan Kastner
University of California, San Diego
kastner@cs.ucsd.edu

Timothy Sherwood
University of California, Santa Barbara
sherwood@cs.ucsb.edu

Ben Hardekopf
University of California, Santa Barbara
benh@cs.ucsb.edu

Frederic T. Chong
University of California, Santa Barbara
chong@cs.ucsb.edu

## Abstract

Privacy and integrity are important security concerns. These concerns are addressed by controlling *information flow*, i.e., restricting how information can flow through a system. Most proposed systems that restrict information flow make the implicit assumption that the hardware used by the system is fully "correct" and that the hardware's instruction set accurately describes its behavior in all circumstances. The truth is more complicated: modern hardware designs defy complete verification; many aspects of the timing and ordering of events are left totally unspecified; and implementation bugs present themselves with surprising frequency. In this work we describe Sapper, a novel hardware description language for designing security-critical hardware components. Sapper seeks to address these problems by using static analysis at compile-time to automatically insert dynamic checks in the resulting hardware that provably enforce a given information flow policy at execution time. We present Sapper's design and formal semantics along with a proof sketch of its security. In addition, we have implemented a compiler for Sapper and used it to create a non-trivial secure embedded processor with many modern microarchitectural features. We empirically evaluate the resulting hardware's area and energy overhead and compare them with alternative designs.

***Categories and Subject Descriptors*** B.6.3 [*Design Aids*]: Hardware Description Languages

***Keywords*** Hardware Description Language, Non-interference



*ASPLOS '14*, March 1–4, 2014, Salt Lake City, Utah, USA.

http://dx.doi.org/10.1145/10.1145/2541940.2541947

## 1. Introduction

Security has become a first-order priority in many system designs. High assurance and life-critical systems, such as aircraft control systems and implantable cardioverter-defibrillators and also systems used in banking and the military, all require strong guarantees about their security properties. However, designing systems with provably strong security properties can be extremely challenging and costly; just assessing the assurance of the resulting system can cost upwards of \$10,000 per line of code [3]. Our goal is to enable the design of provably-secure hardware systems such that (1) the designs are easily expressed by hardware designers, and (2) the resulting secure systems have low overhead in terms of chip area, performance, and power consumption.

Information flow security [10] is an important category of security properties that encompasses *confidentiality* (confidential information cannot leak into unclassified chan-

∗ The work is done when Xun Li, Mohit Tiwari and Vasanth Ram Rajarathinam are graduate students at University of California, Santa Barbara.

nels) and *integrity* (critical system components cannot be affected or tampered with by untrusted parties). Information flow control mechanisms associate *security labels* with the resources and data contained in a system. A *security policy* is specified by ordering the security labels in a lattice, such that data with labels higher in the lattice are more restricted (i.e., can flow to fewer places) than data with labels lower in the lattice. For example, secret data would be labeled with a high label, and an unsecured output port would be labeled with a low label—this policy specifies that the secret data (or any data directly or indirectly derived from the secret data) should not be sent on the publically-visible port. The goal is to ensure that a principal who can observe all data at some security level $\ell$ cannot deduce any information about data at a security level that is higher than or noncomparable to $\ell$. A system that meets this goal is said to enforce *non-interference* [11]. Many approaches have been previously attempted to enforce non-interference at the software or ISA level, yet the resulting systems are still left vulnerable to timing channels and bugs in the hardware implementation.

The core of our approach to this problem is a novel security-aware hardware design synthesis language called Sapper. The Sapper language is an extension of a synthesizable subset of Verilog; the Sapper compiler translates Sapper code into synthesizable Verilog that is guaranteed to meet a specified security policy. It does so by automatically deriving and inserting dynamic security checks into the Verilog hardware design. The semantics of Sapper ensures that the security properties of the resulting system are *statically guaranteed*, even though these security checks are executed dynamically. During the generated system's execution, these dynamic checks intercept any information flow that violates the security policy and replaces the offending operation with one that is guaranteed to be secure (though potentially changing the intended functionality of the system).

The intended design process makes use of the dynamic checks in two phases. First, during testing but before fabrication[2], these dynamic checks will ensure that security violations are revealed to the hardware designers as functionality bugs, which the modern design process already has many techniques for detecting and dealing with. In other words, Sapper transforms the problem of detecting security violations during testing (for which there is little support and experience in the modern design process) into the problem of detecting functionality bugs during testing (for which there is a great deal of support and experience). Through careful design iteration, the hardware designers can detect and fix security problems to ensure that the system will operate as intended in the vast majority of cases, including all common cases, even with these dynamic checks in place.

Once testing is complete and the hardware is deployed, the second function of these checks comes into play, because the checks will remain in the final hardware design. The checks serve as the last line of defense against run-time violations in conditions never encountered during testing and verification. Both undiscovered hardware bugs and rarely occurring combinations of events may provide opportunity to attack an unprotected system. In contrast to this, hardware designed with Sapper will automatically capture and prevent any runtime violations.

We describe the design of Sapper and provide a formal semantics and proof sketch of soundness. We demonstrate the expressiveness of Sapper by implementing a fully-featured secure embedded processor with a MIPS ISA and an array of modern microarchitectural features; the processor is complete enough to run real-world benchmarks. We empirically evaluate the overhead of the system generated by Sapper and show that it has only a 4% hardware overhead and no performance loss compared to an insecure baseline version of the same processor.

## 2. Background

There are many ways in which a hardware/software system might be compromised. We begin by describing our specific threat model and assumptions, and then present related work.

### 2.1 Threat Model

Sapper focuses specifically on the information-flow policy of noninterference.[3] In this work we do not consider other security properties of hardware systems.

For our purposes, a *system* consists of a set of input ports, a set of output ports, a hardware implementation, and an initial configuration. The input and output ports are assumed to have a set of security labels (for example, a set of high input "pins" and a set of low input "pins", which may be separate physical components or time multiplexed on the same physical component). An information flow policy is specified as a lattice over those labels. Sapper can enforce policies specified by any finite security lattice. For clarity, the discussion in the following sections assumes a simple security lattice with two labels *high* and *low* such that $low < high$. We evaluate the effect of a more complex security lattice in Section 4. We assume that the initial configuration of the machine is labeled conservatively (i.e., no high state is labeled as low). This initial configuration may include both high and low bits, and those bits may represent anything from executable code, to initial memory states, to the start states for various microarchitectural state machines.

The attacker is assumed to have *complete control* over (1) all low inputs to the device; and (2) all of the bits in the initial state labeled as low. The first assumption models an

[2] Typically such tests are performed through a combination of hardware simulation and prototyping on reconfigurable hardware.

[3] Noninterference is perhaps too strong a property for general purpose systems, but is useful both in the context of crypto systems and safety critical designs and matches closely with the existing design goals expressed by both Intel [7] and ARM [6].

active attacker. The second assumption models any way in which an attacker might take advantage of access to low data used by the system, including but not limited to malicious or compromised software running on the system. We do not assign intent to the hardware; it simply transforms the state of the system as directed by the hardware design and (after our modifications) subject to the security policy. We assume that hardware is fabricated as specified by our tools, and we do not attempt to address the trusted fabrication problem [5, 13, 35, 36], although we do *not* assume that the hardware has been *designed* correctly or securely.

Using Sapper, we create hardware that ensures the data flowing to any output port conforms to the information flow policy specified by a security lattice given at design time, e.g., that no untrusted information contaminates a trusted port, and no secret information leaks to a non-secret port. This threat model includes *both explicit and implicit* information flows, timing and storage channels, and any other digital form of information flow, but does not include the use of physical or analog phenomena such as EM emission, temperature, or power draw. A system is said to be strictly enforcing a policy if it can be shown that the policy can never be violated regardless of the actions of the attacker subject to this model.

### 2.2 Related Work

Denning and Denning are one of the first to show how programming language techniques and static analysis can be used to enforce information flow policies [10]. This approach was later formalized by Volpano [34] and subsequently implemented as various language extensions [20, 27]. A more comprehensive study of programming language techniques related to information flow security can be found in the survey by Sabelfeld and Myers [25].

While language level techniques provide strong guarantees inside application implementations, security enforcement between applications relies on an underlying operating system. Here too there are many related approaches [14, 16, 17, 24, 28, 39]. Security mechanisms at the OS level cannot provide full hardware/software system security guarantees in the face of adversaries that take advantage of information leakage in the underlying hardware implementation, such as through caches [23] and branch predictors [4]. Specific secure hardware component designs have been proposed to defend against existing covert channel attacks [32, 37, 38]. More systematic approaches have also been proposed to control hardware timing channels through software/hardware contracts [40], quantitative measurements [9], or fuzzing mechanisms [19]. Designing a hardware Trusted Computing Base (TCB) with minimum complexity while providing strong security guarantees is also an active research area [22, 33, 41].

Towards this end, various approaches have been proposed in previous work towards analyzing and enforcing information flow security in hardware designs, including Gate Level Information Flow Tracking (GLIFT) [31] (and its extension Star Logic [30]) and Caisson [18]. While these past approaches represent a first generation of secure hardware design languages, both the expressiveness of those languages (the class of hardware systems that could be shown to be secure) and the efficiency of their implementations (the amount of extra logic required to perform checks) can be prohibitively poor.

GLIFT tracks every single bit of information in the system through each logic gate. Every bit in the system is associated with a shadow bit to represent its security label, and for every logic gate, a shadow logic circuit is used to calculate the output's security level. The values of the gate's inputs are used to achieve precise tracking, e.g. when a low input of an AND gate is known to be 0, the output should be labeled as low even the other input can be high. This feature is extremely important for implementing a practical system in which trusted and untrusted components can be securely multiplexed [29]. Despite GLIFT's pure dynamic nature, the tracking technique is guaranteed to be complete, i.e. it covers both implicit flows and timing channels, since all forms of information flow become explicit at the gate level. Note that GLIFT itself *does not* provide any enforcement mechanism, but rather works as a foundation for information flow tracking. Later work on Execution Leases [29] builds upon GLIFT and enforces noninterference (*by construction*) through memory and timing boundaries. To reduce the substantial overhead of GLIFT, the authors reworked their method as a static analysis in the form of *Star Logic* [30]. As a verification tool, Star Logic takes a given hardware design, augments it with GLIFT tracking logic, loads a given piece of trusted computing base (e.g., the system kernel) and uses abstract interpretation to explore the execution space and detect potential violations. The tracking logic is removed from the final design before fabrication. It is important to see that Star Logic does not provide assistance to or early feedback for hardware designers attempting to create secure hardware; instead it allows for the *after-the-fact static verification of a coordinated processor and kernel design*, which is not the same problem that Sapper is solving. Hence throughout this work, references to GLIFT are regarding the dynamic tracking technique originally shown by Tiwari et al. [29, 31] and not with reference to Star Logic.

Caisson is another attempt to use programming language techniques to enable secure hardware design [18]. Caisson takes techniques from information flow security type systems at the programming language level and applies them at the hardware level. The Caisson language syntax is very similar to that of Sapper, and in fact Sapper borrows the concept of nested states from Caisson. However, since Caisson uses a purely static type system, all registers must be duplicated for different security levels and multiplexers are used to choose the corresponding register based on the current security context. The advantage of this approach is that (1) there is no runtime overhead due to the storage or manipulation of labels as labels are never tracked during execution; and (2) the programmer need never worry about the effects of a security violation because, by construction, there can never be one. It does come with two big problems however: (1) statically typing everything requires that resources be hard-partitioned or even duplicated, and then multiplexed at runtime, resulting in large area overheads; and (2) there is no way for the system to ever examine, react to, or affect the flow of program metadata (a.k.a. labels). Labels are strictly a concept used for analysis, and have no physical manifestation in the final design.

## 3. The Sapper Language

We propose Sapper, a hardware description language that enforces noninterference security policies through statically-inserted logic for dynamic tracking and enforcement. Instead of enforcing security policies completely statically via a type system as in our previous work [18], Sapper dynamically tracks security tags runtime, increasing the expressiveness and decreasing the overhead required for security. Importantly, designers do not need to manually insert dynamic tracking or enforcement logic. Instead, the Sapper compiler automatically does so in a provably sound manner. The tracking and enforcement logic is generated based on static analysis of Sapper programs to cover explicit, implicit, and timing based information flows.

Furthermore, Sapper (unlike any prior formally sound hardware approach) enables hardware systems to be aware of, and react to, the security tags of the data that they operate upon. Hardware designers have complete freedom to choose how the system responds to runtime security violations. Despite this flexibility, Sapper does all of this in a way that allows the security properties of the system to be *statically verified* by the Sapper compiler.

### 3.1 Language Overview

Sapper extends upon a core subset of Verilog and requires minimal changes to existing Verilog source code. A typical Verilog program consists of three parts: *signal declarations* that define registers and wires, a *synchronous block*, and a *combinational logic block.* We refer registers here as flip-flops that store data, and wires as communication channels between flip-flops and logic gates. The synchronous block is responsible for writing data back to flip-flops (i.e. registers) at clock edges. The combinational logic block contains computation that will always be executed within one clock cycle. Commands in combinational logic block are similar to those in software programming languages, including assignments, branches and switch/cases. Although in practice hardware designs can be more complicated, most of them can be reduced to such a simple model. In order to make hardware designs less ambiguous, Sapper simplifies

$$r \in \mathit{Register} \qquad n \in \mathbb{Z} \qquad \oplus \in \mathit{Operator}$$
$$t \in \mathit{SecurityLabel} \qquad \ell \in \mathit{ProgramLabel}$$

$$\begin{aligned}
\mathit{prog} \in \mathit{Prog} &::= \textbf{prog}\ \ell = \vec{r}, \vec{a}\ \textbf{in}\ d \\
d \in \mathit{Def} &::= \textbf{let}\ \vec{s}\ \textbf{in}\ c \mid c \\
s \in \mathit{State} &::= \textbf{state}\ \ell = d \\
e \in \mathit{Exp} &::= n \mid r \mid a[e] \mid e \oplus e \\
a \in \mathit{RegisterArray} &::= n \mapsto r \\
te \in \mathit{TagExp} &::= t \mid \textbf{tag}(u) \\
u \in \mathit{TaggedEntity} &::= r \mid \ell \mid a[e] \\
c \in \mathit{Cmd} &::= \textbf{skip} \mid x := e \mid c\,;c \mid \textbf{fall}_\ell \\
&\mid \textbf{goto}_{\ell_1}\ \ell_2 \mid \textbf{setTag}(u, te) \\
&\mid \textbf{if}_\ell\ e\ \textbf{then}\ c\ \textbf{else}\ c\textbf{; endif} \\
&\mid c\ \textbf{otherwise}\ c \\
p \in \mathit{Phrase} &::= \mathit{prog} \mid d \mid s \mid e \mid c
\end{aligned}$$

*Figure 1:* Abstract Syntax of Sapper

the syntax by having designers to only write a single combinational logic block. All writes to regsiters will be automatically compiled into a synchronous block by the Sapper compiler, while computation will remain in the combinational logic block.

Figure 1 describes the abstract syntax of Sapper. We have chosen the core subset such that all the interesting features of the full language are covered. Other language clauses are omitted either because their formal properties are trivial to reason about (e.g., unary operations such as $\sim x$) or they can be expressed equivalently using the syntax discussed in this section (e.g., `case/switch`).

In the rest of the section, we start with a list of basic definitions and assumptions; then describe how Sapper implements tracking and checking of security tags; how state machines are an integral Sapper abstraction for precise tracking and enforcement; and finally how Sapper enables runtime security tag manipulation and how Sapper enables configurable yet secure reactions to runtime security violations. The formal semantics of Sapper will be presented in the end of the setion.

### 3.2 Definitions and Assumptions

We define some terms used in the remainder of the section:

- **Variables:** We refer to the set of registers, wires, inputs and outputs in the hardware design as variables.
- **Join:** Given a security lattice, the operation $\sqcup$ takes two security levels as operands and calculates their least upper bound in the lattice, e.g., $high \sqcup low = high$
- **Security Context:** The security context of a statement in a Sapper program is informally defined as the maximum security level among all implicit information flowing into that statement. Sapper models the hardware design as a state machine, and the system can only be in one state at any given cycle. Hence the security context of

```
1: state S = {                          |  SC_2 = S.tag
2:     if ( a == 0 ) then {             |
3:         if ( b == 0 ) then           |  SC_3 = SC_5 = join(S.tag, a.tag)
4:             x := 0;                  |
5:         y := 0;                      |  SC_4 = join(S.tag, a.tag, b.tag)
6:     }                                |
7: }
              (a)                                     (b)
```

*Figure 2:* Example showing how to compute security context.

any statement is determined by the security context of the current state as well as any conditionals guarding the statement. The default security context of any statement inside a state is the same as the security context of the state itself. The security context of a statement inside a branch is calculated by taking the join of the default security context and the security level of the branch condition. Figure 2 illustrates how the security context is determined.

We assume that the security tags of data are public information, i.e., that only knowing the security level of data (but not the data's value) will not leak any information. This assumption is commonly used in previous work for enforcing information flow security. Without this assumption, the system would not be able to react to any runtime security violations, and hence could not enforce the security policy. It is important to note that, Sapper does ensure that security tags cannot be changed based upon data's value in a way that might violate security policies. More details are given in Section 3.5.

We further assume that the set of security tags are based on a statically-known (i.e., defined at design time) security lattice of arbitrary but finite size. Extending Sapper with dynamically-defined lattices rather than using a statically-known lattice would allow different processes in a system to define their own lattices for the hardware to enforce. This can be done through efficient protocols to encode and decode security policies in the hardware. The Raksha architecture proposed by Dalton et al. [8] demonstrates one way to achieve this. Supporting programmable lattices in Sapper is left to future work.

### 3.3 Security Tags

Variables (i.e., signals, wires, etc.) in Sapper are associated with security tags that are tracked and checked for security policy violations at runtime. Checking *every* data movement in hardware for violations of noninterference would be extremely expensive, both in terms of additional hardware and performance overhead. We observe that in most hardware designs only certain outputs are exposed and observable by software/programmers, and thus only these outputs require strict enforcement. Many variables, such as internal pipeline registers and wires used to hold intermediate results, are only used for temporary storage and are not directly observable. These non-observable variables only require security tags to be tracked dynamically so that their security level is correctly reflected at runtime; no enforcement is required. As such, Sapper allows designers to declare data variables as one of the following two categories: **Enforced Tagged** variables of which information flow will always be checked for non-interference, and **Dynamic Tagged** variables whose security tags will be automatically tracked and propagated at runtime. By default, a variable declared in Sapper is dynamic tagged. Designers can explciitly declare a enforced tagged variable by giving it a initial security type.

This dichotomy requires designers to make decisions on what data should be tracked versus enforced, but it is often an easy decision to make since typical architectures only consist of a small portion of components exposed to users or central to data movement. In many architectures, selecting enforced tags for all the bus output ports, the memory and the cache will be sufficient. Note that as long as the I/O ports are enforced, not enforcing policies on some of the other components does not lead to unsoundness, but rather makes the system less precise and thus potentially harder to use. The Sapper compiler is responsible for generating dynamic tracking logic and inserting dynamic checks for enforcement depending on the tag of the target variable. Below we describe the details of tracking and enforcement.

#### 3.3.1 Tracking Tags

Assignments to dynamic tagged variables will trigger the propagation of security tags: the maximum security level over all information that may affect the assigned value (directly or indirectly) shall be propagated to the target variable's tag (rule *ASSIGN-DYN-REG* in Figure 6(a)). Without careful consideration, simply tracking information at a fine granularity can lead to significant overhead, as in previous work. In general, tracking overhead consists of two parts: extra hardware bits needed to store security labels and extra hardware logic needed to perform tag propagations. Sapper aims at achieving the flexibility of dynamic tracking with minimum overhead. Instead of generating tracking logic for every single logic gate as in some previous work [31], Sapper takes advantage of static analysis on the HDL code and inserts tracking logic aggregately at the granularity of expressions and code blocks. Potential implicit flows (i.e., information flows arising from conditionals) are also derived by the compiler, which inserts logic to ensure sound security tag propagation. Purely dynamic tracking cannot handle implicit flows, and thus the static analysis is required to make this possible.

Sapper also uses simple logic to compute security levels: the security level of the output is the least upper bound of the security levels of the inputs. Sapper tracks security labels and tags data appropriately at the register level; [4] each variable has an $n$-bit tag independent of that variable's width,

[4] Note that we do not mean only architectural registers here (like %eax), we mean register-transfer-level registers, which is any set of bits used as a group in the hardware description language.

where $n$ depends on the size of the security lattice. The cache and main memory are each treated as a continuous array of $m$-bit registers (where $m$ is the width of the hardware being designed), with a $n$-bit label for each $m$ bits.

In theory, Sapper may be less precise (but still sound) compared to bit- and gate-level tracking due to the coarser tracking granularity and relaxed tag propagation. However we observe that the major purpose of using precise fine-grained tracking in previous work is to avoid label creep[5] and allow a secure switch from a high to low security context. In the next section we will describe how the "nested states" feature we use in Sapper provides exactly what is needed to satisfy this requirement. In fact, there is nothing that prohibits bit-level tracking in Sapper, but we believe this is not necessary because the state transforms can be expressed in the language itself rather than needing to be inferred from the generated logic. Hence Sapper achieves sufficient precision for security enforcement with significantly less overhead while retaining a high degree of flexibility.

### 3.3.2 Enforcing Policy

Any assignment to a variable with enforced tags needs to be checked for noninterference and violations must be dealt with in a secure way (rule *ASSIGN-ENF-REG* in Figure 6(a)). Specifically, the security level of the target variable must be higher than or equal to the maximum security level of information that may affect the assigned value. The necessary enforcement conditions will be derived by the compiler and the security checks will be automatically inserted into the resulting logic. Therefore, these assignments will take effect only when they are guaranteed to be secure. Sapper also provides flexibility for designers to specify how the system should handle violations, which will be described in Section 3.6. Figure 3 shows the generated Verilog code for an *8-bit-and* design written in Sapper. There are two different cases shown in the figure, one with enforcement (CHECK) while another with tracking (TRACK) only. Note that both the tracking and enforcement logic are automatically generated by the compiler and there is no need for designers to manually specify anything except the initial enforced tags.

|  | Sapper | Verilog |
|---|---|---|
| CHECK | reg[7:0] a : L,<br>reg[7:0] b, c;<br>a <= b & c; | reg[7:0] a,b,c;<br>reg a_tag,b_tag,c_tag;<br>if (a_tag>=(b_tag\|c_tag))<br>  a <= b & c; |
| TRACK | reg[7:0] a, b, c;<br>a <= b & c; | reg[7:0] a,b,c;<br>reg a_tag,b_tag,c_tag;<br>a <= b & c;<br>a_tag <= b_tag \| c_tag; |

*Figure 3:* An 8-bit adder written in Sapper along with the generated Verilog code. There are two cases: in the first case register $a$ is enforced tagged hence the assignment needs to be checked for noninterference; in the second case $a$ is dynamic tagged hence only tracking is needed.

## 3.4 A State Machine-based Language

Timing in synchronous hardware designs is strictly aligned to clock edges; for example, registers are only updated at clock edges. To capture the notion of hardware timing, the Sapper language explicitly models hardware designs as *state machines*. During a clock cycle the hardware can only be in one of the state machine's logical states,[6] and all of the program logic from that state will be executed within that clock cycle. State transitions (indicated by **goto** in the Sapper program) always take effect at clock edges. Another important motivation behind modeling hardware as state machines is that state machines are a common pattern used by hardware designers, and most hardware designs are already written as or can be easily transformed to state machines.

Because state transitions can be conditional, they open up the possibility of implicit leaks, i.e., information flow due to conditional execution. Therefore states must also have security tags, and these tags must be correctly propagated or checked during state transitions just like tags for variable. In the same manner as variables, states can be declared with enforced or dynamic tags. The security level of states with dynamic tags will be tracked dynamically at runtime, while states with enforced tags will be enforced for noninterference and their security level will not change unless it is explicitly modified. An immediate advantage of Sapper is that a single dynamic tagged state can safely act at different security levels at runtime, and hence that state can be reused between different security levels instead of requiring the design to duplicate states in order to have one per security level.

To properly enforce noninterference in the presence of conditional execution, a transition from some state $A$ to some state $B$ should only occur if A's tag is lower than B's tag. In the case of a state machine diagram that is strongly connected (i.e., every state can reach every other state), the existence of any high state will eventually require all states to be high. This problem is known as label creep. Sapper uses the concept of *nested states* proposed in Caisson [18] to solve this problem. States can be organized hierarchically as a tree structure. Within each clock cycle, before executing the logic of some state $S$, the logic of $S$'s parent state must be executed first; this rule is recursively applied until the root of the tree. To give parent states complete control over the execution of child states, **fall** commands are used to explicitly indicate transfer of control from the parent state to the child state. By having parent states with low security levels and child states with high security levels, low states

[5] Label creep happens when a large portion of the system has to be conservatively marked as tainted due to inability of a more precise analysis

[6] In the following discussion, *state* will always mean a state of the finite state machine specified by a Sapper program.

have the freedom to decide when to terminate high states without violating security.

Figure 4 shows an example of a state machine diagram for a secure hardware design based on TDMA (Time Division Multiple Access), which is a common design pattern used by secure systems. A trusted timer (low) is used to control the execution of untrusted components. In particular, the Master state (trusted, labeled with low, enforced tagged) sets up a timer and transits to the Slave state (also trusted, low), which falls into its child state (potentially untrusted, dynamic tagged) and executes the computation logic. At the beginning of every cycle, the Slave State is always executed first and the timer is checked. If the timer expires then control will transfer back to the Master State. The security level of the child state (i.e., Pipeline State in the diagram) can be either high or low at runtime depending on the data it is dealing with at the time. No matter what level it is, it will never affect the behavior of the parent states, thus enforcing noninterference. The corresponding implementation in Sapper is also shown on the side. When the code is compiled down to Verilog, tracking and checking logic will be generated based on the Sapper formal semantics. Although the runtime security level of the Pipeline State is dynamically changing, the generated checking logic will guarantee that the Master State is always trusted.

To ensure that state transitions and falls are securely performed, Sapper provides the following rules for **goto** commands and **fall** commands:

- **goto** *to enforced tagged state (GOTO-ENFORCED):* For a state transition **goto** $S$ in which $S$ is a enforced tagged state, it is required that the security context of the **goto** command be lower than the security level of $S$, otherwise information can leak implicitly.
- **goto** *to dynamic tagged state (GOTO-DYNAMIC):* For a state transition **goto** $S$ in which $S$ is a dynamic tagged state, no enforcement is required. Instead, the security tag of the target state $S$ will be updated to the security context of the **goto** command. Furthermore, if a **goto** command is guarded by conditionals (i.e., the system can transit to different states based on the value of conditions), implicit flows exist from the current state to all reachable states via the conditional **goto** commands. To precisely capture such implicit flows statically, the security tags of all dynamic registers that are assigned in all **goto**-reachable states need to be updated to the security context of the **goto**. This rule is the major cause of label creep in most designs, and Sapper provides nested states to contain states with higher security level in the child group, leaving parent states unaffected by the **goto**s from child states.
- **fall** *to enforced tagged state (FALL-ENFORCED):* **fall** to a enforced tagged state has the same rule as **goto** to a enforced tagged state.

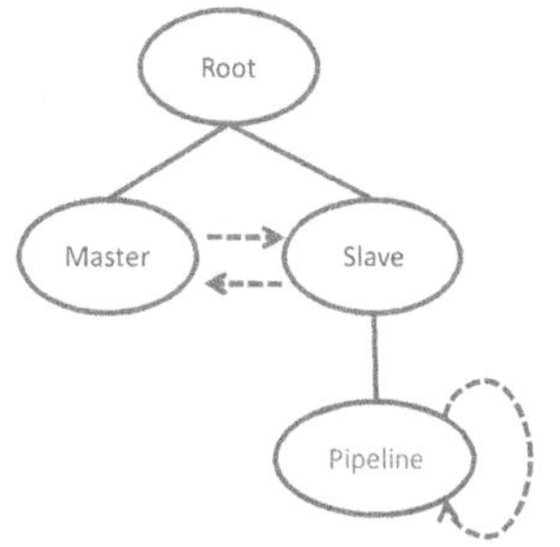


```
reg[31:0] timer : L;

state Master:L = {
    timer = 100;
    goto Slave;
}

state Slave:L = {
    let state pipeline = {
        // Pipeline logic
        goto pipeline;
    }
    in
        if (timer == 0) begin
            goto Master;
        end else begin
            timer <= timer - 1;
            fall;
        end
}
```

*Figure 4:* State Machine Diagram example of a secure hardware controller, along with its corresponding implementation in Sapper. Noninterference is achieved by having a trusted timer controlling the behavior of the computation logic.

- **fall** *to dynamic tagged state (FALL-DYNAMIC):* When there is a **fall** from a state $A$ to its child state $B$, the security tag of $B$ will be updated to the join of the context of the **fall** and the current security level of $B$. The reason we need to take the current security level of $B$ into consideration is as follows: when we have a **goto** from one state to another, their ancestor states will be executed first along with a series of **fall** commands. Hence before a **fall** to state $B$, there can exist a **goto** $B$ which will update $B$'s security level to be the context of the **goto**.

### 3.5 Manipulating Tags

One important advantage of Sapper compared to purely static mechanisms is that security labels can be read, reacted upon, and updated at runtime. As we have defined earlier, the security level of enforced tagged registers will not change until they are explicitly modified through the language provided interface. This feature can be used by system kernels to efficiently and securely share memory among different security levels (e.g., the kernel can allocate memory to a high process, then reclaim it, reset the memory's tag to low, and allocate it to a low process). Although we allow security tags to be modified explicitly, they cannot be modified arbitrarily, otherwise information can be leaked. Sapper provides a pre-defined command **setTag** to allow modification of the security tags of enforced tagged variables and states. Sapper language rules will ensure that no information can be leaked by using this command: (1) the security level of any data can only be changed under a context whose level is not higher than the data's (e.g., low data cannot be hoisted under a high context), thus no information can flow from high to low by manipulating tags; and (2) when data is downgraded (e.g., changed from high to low) the data is automatically *zeroed* instantly to avoid leakage. The logic for checking, changing the tag, and zeroing the data is generated by the Sapper compiler. The formal semantics of this instruction is provided in Figure 6(a) (SET-REG-TAG). Explicit declassification is not supported as Sapper is currently targeted to information-theoretic rather than cryptographic notions of security. Declassification can be added and is certainly useful in many cases (e.g. a crypto unit). It will be a simple relaxation of our existing mechanism for modifying security levels. Of course one must be careful how declassification is allowed; but these mechanisms have been extensively studied in the literature [21, 26].

### 3.6 Handling Security Violations

As previously described, the Sapper compiler will insert checking logic in the appropriate locations in the design to detect all security policy violations. The natural question, then, is how should the system react if the runtime check does not pass, i.e., the security policy is about to be violated. To handle this situation, the Sapper compiler inserts alternative actions that are executed instead of any violating operation. For each enforced operation, Sapper has a default replacement action that is guaranteed to be secure. These default actions are inserted into the generated Verilog code in the form of branches as shown in Figure 5(a). For example, a default secure action can turn a violating assignment into a noop, or turn a violating state transition into a different transition to a secure state.

To give hardware designers full flexibility to decide how to react to runtime security violations, Sapper provides a language interface for specifying the replacement behavior when violation is *about* to happen. The syntax is shown in Figure 5(b), which specifies that if there exists any security violation in *command, secure action* will be executed in replace of *command.* The above code will also be transformed into a branch by the Sapper compiler as shown in the figure.

Note that *command* will never be speculatively executed, instead, only one of *secure action* and *command* will be executed depending on the value of the generated condition. These *otherwise* rules can be defined recursively, meaning that the action in the otherwise branch can itself have potential violations or even another otherwise clause. These nested otherwise clauses are terminated by the default, guaranteed safe action; thus all commands in the program are guaranteed to be secure even if designers provide buggy otherwise clauses. figure 5(c) shows an example when the provided action is also a command that requires runtime enforcement.

### 3.7 Formal Semantics of Sapper

Figure 6(a) provides the formal semantics for Sapper. The semantic domains and evaluation context grammar used in these semantic rules are provided in Figure 6(d). The semantics in Figure 6(a) also makes use of big-step semantic relations for expressions (given by $\Downarrow_e$, which are standard and omitted) and big-step semantic rules for tag expressions provided in Figure 6(b). The definition of $\phi$, which is used in the semantic rules, is provided in Figure 6(c). The abstract machine configuration (provided in Figure 6(d)) for

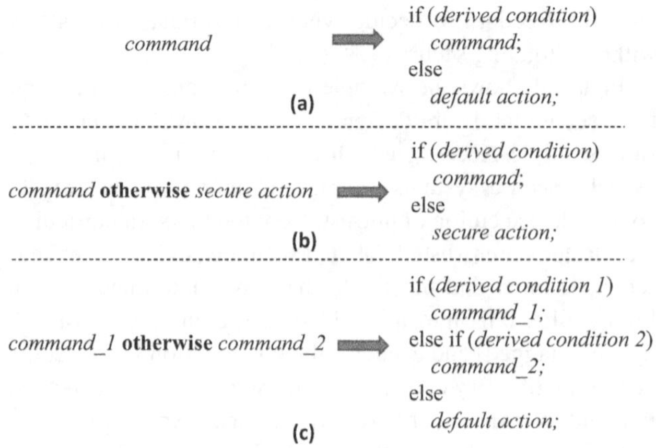


*Figure 5:* Violation handling logic generated by our Sapper compiler: (a) any command that requires enforcement will be guarded by conditions that enforce noninterference. These conditions are generated by static analysis on the context of the command. If the conditions fail, a secure default action (provided by the compiler) will be executed instead; (b) designers can also specify replacement actions of their own, using the *otherwise* clause; (c) When the designer-provided action also requires enforcement, our compiler will generate conditions and default secure actions recursively.

the semantic rules in Figure 6(a) consists of (1) the current program phrase $p$, (2) a fall map $\rho$, (3) a store $\sigma$, (4) a tag map $\theta$, (5) a security context stack $\mathcal{S}$, and (6) current time value $\delta$.

We define the following mappings for each $\ell \in$ *ProgramLabel* that are used in the semantic rules:

- if $\ell$ refers to a state name, $\mathcal{F}_{pnt}(\ell)$ maps to the label of state $\ell$'s parent state.
- if $\ell$ refers to a state name, $\mathcal{F}_{cmd}(\ell)$ maps to state $\ell$'s command.
- If $\ell$ is a label attached to an **if** statement, then $\mathcal{F}_{cd}(\ell)$ maps to the set of all the registers that are targets of assignments control-dependent on the **if** statement, union with the set of all dynamic states whose reachability (via **goto** or **fall**) is control dependent on the **if** statement.

In addition, $\mathcal{F}_{root}$ maps to the root command of the **prog** program phrase. Finally, we also define the following two helper functions:

- *ResetFallMap* takes a *FallMap* $\rho$ and a state label $\ell$ and returns a new *FallMap* $\rho'$ identical to $\rho$ except that label $\ell$ and the labels of all states that are descendents of $\ell$ in the state hierarchy are mapped to their default child states (the same as their initial values).
- *ResetTagMap* takes a *TagMap* $\theta$ and a state label $\ell$ and returns a new *TagMap* $\theta'$ identical to $\theta$ except that (1) labels of all dynamic states that are descendents of $\ell$ in the state hierarchy are mapped to $\bot$ (2) if *isDynamicState*$(\ell)$, $\ell$ is mapped to $\bot$.

A proof of non-interference is given in Appendix A.

$$\frac{\mathit{isEnforcedRegister}(r) \qquad \langle e,\sigma\rangle \Downarrow_e n \qquad \sigma' = \begin{cases} \sigma[r \mapsto n] & : \theta(r) \sqsupseteq \phi(e) \sqcup sc \\ \sigma & : \mathit{otherwise} \end{cases}}{\langle E[r := e], \rho, \sigma, \theta, \mathcal{S}, \delta\rangle \rightsquigarrow \langle E[\textbf{skip}], \rho, \sigma', \theta, \mathcal{S}, \delta\rangle} \text{(ASSIGN-ENF-REG)}$$

$$\frac{\langle te,\theta,\sigma\rangle \Downarrow_t t \qquad \theta' = \begin{cases} \theta[l \mapsto t] & : \theta(\ell) \sqsupseteq sc \wedge t \sqsupseteq sc \\ \theta & : \mathit{otherwise} \end{cases}}{\langle E[\textbf{setTag}(\ell, te)], \rho, \sigma, \theta, \mathcal{S}, \delta\rangle \rightsquigarrow \langle E[\textbf{skip}], \rho, \sigma, \theta', \mathcal{S}, \delta\rangle} \text{(SET-STATE-TAG)}$$

$$\frac{\neg\mathit{isEnforcedRegister}(r) \qquad \langle e,\sigma\rangle \Downarrow_e n}{\langle E[r := e], \rho, \sigma, \theta, \mathcal{S}, \delta\rangle \rightsquigarrow \langle E[\textbf{skip}], \rho, \sigma[r \mapsto n], \theta[r \mapsto \phi(e) \sqcup sc], \mathcal{S}, \delta\rangle} \text{(ASSIGN-DYN-REG)}$$

$$\frac{\begin{array}{c}\langle te,\theta,\sigma\rangle \Downarrow_t t \qquad \langle e,\sigma\rangle \Downarrow_e n \qquad a(n) = r \\ \theta' = \begin{cases} \theta[r \mapsto t] & : \theta(r) \sqsupseteq sc \wedge t \sqsupseteq sc \sqcup \phi(e) \\ \theta & : \mathit{otherwise} \end{cases} \\ \sigma' = \begin{cases} \sigma[r \mapsto 0] & : \theta(r) \sqsupset t \wedge t \sqsupseteq sc \sqcup \phi(e) \\ \sigma & : \mathit{otherwise} \end{cases}\end{array}}{\langle E[\textbf{setTag}(a[e], te)], \rho, \sigma, \theta, \mathcal{S}, \delta\rangle \rightsquigarrow \langle E[\textbf{skip}], \rho, \sigma', \theta', \mathcal{S}, \delta\rangle} \text{(SET-REG-ARR-TAG)}$$

$$\frac{\begin{array}{c}\langle e_1,\sigma\rangle \Downarrow_e n_1 \qquad \langle e_2,\sigma\rangle \Downarrow_e n_2 \\ a(n_1) = r \qquad \mathit{isEnforcedRegister}(r) \\ \sigma' = \begin{cases} \sigma[r \mapsto n_2] & : \theta(r) \sqsupseteq \phi(e_1) \sqcup \phi(e_2) \sqcup sc \\ \sigma & : \mathit{otherwise} \end{cases}\end{array}}{\langle E[a[e_1] := e_2], \rho, \sigma, \theta, \mathcal{S}, \delta\rangle \rightsquigarrow \langle E[\textbf{skip}], \rho, \sigma', \theta, \mathcal{S}, \delta\rangle} \text{(ASSIGN-ENF-REG-ARR)}$$

$$\langle E[\textbf{skip} \,;\, c], \rho, \sigma, \theta, \mathcal{S}, \delta\rangle \rightsquigarrow \langle E[c], \rho, \sigma, \theta, \mathcal{S}, \delta\rangle \text{ (SEQ)}$$

$$\frac{\begin{array}{c}\langle e_1,\sigma\rangle \Downarrow_e n_1 \qquad \langle e_2,\sigma\rangle \Downarrow_e n_2 \\ a(n_1) = r \qquad \neg\mathit{isEnforcedRegister}(r) \\ \theta_1 = \theta[r \mapsto \phi(e_1) \sqcup \phi(e_2) \sqcup sc]\end{array}}{\langle E[a[e_1] := e_2], \rho, \sigma, \theta, \mathcal{S}, \delta\rangle \rightsquigarrow \langle E[\textbf{skip}], \rho, \sigma[r \mapsto n_2], \theta_1, \mathcal{S}, \delta\rangle} \text{(ASSIGN-DYN-REG-ARR)}$$

$$\frac{\begin{array}{c}\mathit{isEnforcedState}(\ell) \qquad p' = \begin{cases} \mathcal{F}_{cmd}(\ell') & : \theta(\ell') \sqsupseteq sc \\ E[\textbf{goto}_\ell\ \ell] & : \mathit{otherwise} \end{cases} \\ \ell' = \rho(\ell) \qquad \mathcal{S}' = \begin{cases} \theta(\ell')::\mathit{Nil} & : \theta(\ell') \sqsupseteq sc \\ \mathcal{S} & : \mathit{otherwise} \end{cases}\end{array}}{\langle E[\textbf{fall}_\ell], \rho, \sigma, \theta, \mathcal{S}, \delta\rangle \rightsquigarrow \langle p', \rho, \sigma, \theta, \theta(\ell)::\mathit{Nil}, \delta\rangle} \text{(FALL-ENFORCED)}$$

$$\frac{\begin{array}{c}\langle e,\sigma\rangle \Downarrow_e n \qquad c' = \begin{cases} c_1 & : n = 0 \\ c_2 & : n \neq 0 \end{cases} \\ \theta' = \theta[\forall x. x \in \mathcal{F}_{cd}(\ell) : x \mapsto \theta(x) \sqcup \phi(e) \sqcup sc]\end{array}}{\langle E[\textbf{if}_\ell\ e\ \textbf{then}\ c_1\ \textbf{else}\ c_2\textbf{; endif}], \rho, \sigma, \theta, \mathcal{S}, \delta\rangle \rightsquigarrow \langle E[c'\textbf{; endif}], \rho, \sigma, \theta', (\phi(e) \sqcup sc)::\mathcal{S}, \delta\rangle} \text{(IF)}$$

$$\frac{\begin{array}{c}\mathit{isDynamicState}(\ell) \qquad \theta' = \theta[\ell' \mapsto sc \sqcup \theta(\ell')] \\ \mathcal{S}' = \theta'(\ell')::\mathit{Nil} \qquad \ell' = \rho(\ell)\end{array}}{\langle E[\textbf{fall}_\ell], \rho, \sigma, \theta, \mathcal{S}, \delta\rangle \rightsquigarrow \langle \mathcal{F}_{cmd}(\rho(\ell)), \rho, \sigma, \theta', \mathcal{S}', \delta\rangle} \text{(FALL-DYNAMIC)}$$

$$\langle E[\textbf{skip; endif}], \rho, \sigma, \theta, \mathcal{S}, \delta\rangle \rightsquigarrow \langle E[\textbf{skip}], \rho, \sigma, \theta, \Sigma, \delta\rangle \text{ (ENDIF)}$$

$$\frac{\begin{array}{c}\mathit{isEnforcedState}(\ell_2) \qquad \ell = \begin{cases} \ell_2 & : \theta(\ell_2) \sqsupseteq sc \\ \ell_1 & : \mathit{otherwise} \end{cases} \\ \rho_1 = \mathit{ResetFallMap}(\rho, \ell) \qquad \rho_2 = \rho_1[\mathcal{F}_{pnt}(\ell) \mapsto l] \\ \mathcal{S}' = \theta(\mathcal{F}_{root})::\mathit{Nil}\end{array}}{\langle E[\textbf{goto}_{\ell_1}\ \ell_2], \rho, \sigma, \theta, \mathcal{S}, \delta\rangle \rightsquigarrow \langle \mathcal{F}_{root}, \rho_2, \sigma, \theta, \mathcal{S}', \delta{+}1\rangle} \text{(GOTO-ENFORCED)}$$

$$\frac{\begin{array}{c}\langle te,\theta,\sigma\rangle \Downarrow_t t \\ \theta' = \begin{cases} \theta[r \mapsto t] & : \theta(r) \sqsupseteq sc \wedge t \sqsupseteq sc \\ \theta & : \mathit{otherwise} \end{cases} \\ \sigma' = \begin{cases} \sigma[r \mapsto 0] & : \theta(r) \sqsupset t \wedge t \sqsupseteq sc \\ \sigma & : \mathit{otherwise} \end{cases}\end{array}}{\langle E[\textbf{setTag}(r, te)], \rho, \sigma, \theta, \mathcal{S}, \delta\rangle \rightsquigarrow \langle E[\textbf{skip}], \rho, \sigma', \theta', \mathcal{S}, \delta\rangle} \text{(SET-REG-TAG)}$$

$$\frac{\begin{array}{c}\rho_1 = \mathit{ResetFallMap}(\rho, \ell_2) \qquad \rho_2 = \rho_1[\mathcal{F}_{pnt}(\ell_2) \mapsto \ell_2] \\ \mathit{isDynamicState}(\ell_2) \qquad \mathcal{S}' = \theta_2(\mathcal{F}_{root})::\mathit{Nil} \\ \theta_1 = \theta[\ell_2 \mapsto sc] \qquad \theta_2 = \mathit{ResetTagMap}(\theta_1, \ell_1)\end{array}}{\langle E[\textbf{goto}_{\ell_1}\ \ell_2], \rho, \sigma, \theta, \mathcal{S}, \delta\rangle \rightsquigarrow \langle \mathcal{F}_{root}, \rho_2, \sigma, \theta_2, \mathcal{S}', \delta{+}1\rangle} \text{(GOTO-DYNAMIC)}$$

(a) Semantic rules for Sapper. Throughout the rules, we assume $\mathcal{S} = sc :: \Sigma$. Various helper functions are used, which are described in the accompanying text.

$$\langle t,\theta,\sigma\rangle \Downarrow_t t \text{ (T-SEC-LBL)} \qquad \frac{\langle e,\sigma\rangle \Downarrow_e n \qquad a(n) = r}{\langle \textbf{tag}(a[e]),\theta,\sigma\rangle \Downarrow_t \theta(r) \sqcup \phi(e)} \text{(T-REG-ARR)}$$

$$\langle \textbf{tag}(r),\theta,\sigma\rangle \Downarrow_t \theta(r) \text{ (T-REG)} \qquad \langle \textbf{tag}(\ell),\theta,\sigma\rangle \Downarrow_t \theta(\ell) \text{ (T-STATE)}$$

(b) Big-step semantics for *TagExp*. $\Downarrow_t \subseteq \langle te,\theta,\sigma\rangle \times t$

$$\phi(n) = \bot \qquad \phi(e_1 \oplus e_2) = \phi(e_1) \sqcup \phi(e_2)$$

$$\phi(r) = \theta(r) \qquad \frac{\langle e,\sigma\rangle \Downarrow_e n \qquad a(n) = r}{\phi(a[e]) = \phi(e) \sqcup \theta(r)}$$

(c) Definition of $\phi : e \mapsto t$. $\Downarrow_e$ is the standard big step semantics relation.

$$\rho \in \mathit{FallMap} : \mathit{ProgramLabel} \rightarrow \mathit{ProgramLabel}$$
$$\theta \in \mathit{TagMap} : \mathit{TaggedEntity} \rightarrow \mathit{SecurityLevel}$$
$$\sigma \in \mathit{Store} : \mathit{Register} \rightarrow \mathbb{Z} \qquad \mathcal{S} \in \mathit{List} \qquad \delta \in \mathit{Time} : \mathbb{N}$$
$$\mathbb{C} \in \mathit{Config} : \langle p, \rho, \sigma, \theta, \mathcal{S}, \delta\rangle$$

$$\begin{array}{rl} E ::= & \square \mid x := E \mid E \,;\, c \mid \textbf{prog}\ \ell = \vec{r}, \vec{a}\ \textbf{in}\ E \\ & \mid \textbf{let}\ \vec{s}\ \textbf{in}\ E \mid \textbf{setTag}(\ell, E) \mid \textbf{setTag}(r, E) \\ & \mid \textbf{setTag}(a[E], te) \mid \textbf{setTag}(a[n], E) \end{array}$$

(d) Semantic domains and evaluation context grammar.

*Figure 6:* Sapper Semantics

| Instruction Type | Instruction List |
|---|---|
| Additive Arithmetic | add, addu, addiu, sub, subu |
| Binary Arithmetic | and, andi, or, ori, xor, xori, nor, sll, sllv, sra, srav, srl, srlv |
| Multiplicative Arithmetic | mult, multu, div |
| FPU instructions | add.s, sub.s, mul.s, div.s, neg.s, abs.s, mov.s cvt.s.w, cvt.w.s, le.s, lt.s, ge.s, gt.s |
| Branch | beq, bgt, ble, bne, bltz, bgez; beql, bnel, blel, bltzl; bc1t |
| Jump | j, jr, jal, jalr |
| Memory Operation | lb, lbu, lhu, lw, sb, sh, sw; lwl, lwr, swl, swr; swc1, lwc1 |
| Others | slti, sltiu, lui, mflo, mfhi, mtc1, mfc1 |
| Security Related | set-tag*, set-timer |

*Figure 7:* Complete ISA of our processor.

| Module Name | LOC |
|---|---|
| Fetch | 52 |
| Decode + Register File | 590 |
| Execute + ALU + FPU | 3981 |
| Memory + Cache | 442 |
| Write Back | 29 |
| Control Logic + Forwarding + Stalling | 303 |
| **Total** | **5397** |

*Figure 8:* Lines of Code (LOC) of each component in our processor.

# 4. Processor Design and Evaluation

Sapper is capable of building a wide variety of security critical hardware, e.g., an arbiter, a network-on-chip, or a secure co-processor. In this section, we evaluate Sapper's utility specifically on one of the most general purpose designs one might consider building: a pipelined microprocessor. Our microprocessor design is significantly more complex than any existing processor designs with strong security properties presented in the literature [18, 29, 30]. We describe in detail what kind of processor we have built, how we implement it in Sapper to enforce noninterference, and how we validate its functional correctness and security enforcement. Finally, we demonstrate the benefits of our technique through empirical evaluation of hardware overhead for two security policies: a simple two-level policy, and a more complicated "diamond" policy.

## 4.1 Processor Description

Our processor design is a 5-stage pipelined processor with a number of components that can be found in modern processors, including cache, a division/multiplication unit, and a floating point unit that alone accounts for 3000+ lines of code. Typical pipelining techniques, including hazard detection, stalling, and data forwarding, are all implemented. Figure 8 lists the components of the processor along with their lines of code (LOC). The total length of the implementation is over 5K LOC. A majority of the standard MIPS ISA is implemented as shown in Figure 7. The ability to design a practical processor with strict security properties that has logic similar to that found in modern CPUs has significant value—not only because more complex systems are simply harder to evaluate for security, but because it also demonstrates the expressiveness of our technique.

We implement an L1 cache, shared by both data and instructions. The main memory is modeled as a single large register array (64MB) that supports byte-level random access with one read port and one write port. This simplified memory system still allows us to exercise the basic functionality of the processor and cache in a non-trivial manner.

## 4.2 Security Enforcement

Along with the standard MIPS instructions, the processor supports two extra security related instructions called *set-tag* and *set-timer*. Neither instruction is part of the Sapper language syntax, rather, they are hardware-provided ISA instructions *implemented* in Sapper. It is worth noting that here *set-tag* is an ISA instruction of the processor, while **setTag** described in the previous section is a command in the Sapper syntax. The *set-tag* instruction allows software to explicitly modify the security tag of a word in memory (the memory is modeled as an array of enforced tagged words). This instruction is implemented through the **setTag** primitive in Sapper. Security checks to ensure the safety of the instruction are automatically generated as we have described in Section 3.5.

The *set-timer* instruction allows software to set the timing boundary of any untrusted program and allows for securely switching from a high to low security context under the control of software running on the processor. It is implemented in the hardware by taking advantage of the nested states feature in Sapper: the parent state controls the timer (an enforced tagged register) which is always labeled as low, and it checks whether the timer expires every cycle while running high code in child states. When the timer expires it always switches back to the low state. Calling the *set-timer* instruction from software will modify the value of the timer register. Because it is an enforced tagged register, the value change operation will always be checked to ensure that a high program can never change the value of timer. The state machine structure of our processor is similar to that shown in our previous example in Figure 4.

Without Sapper, one has to implement a cache very carefully, using sophisticated techniques in order to deliver strong security guarantees. However, even sophisticated designs can still be vulnerable to attacks due to unforeseen considerations [15]. In contrast, a cache implemented with Sapper is always guaranteed to enforce noninterference no matter how it is implemented. However, it is worth mentioning that an *insecure cache design if Sapper is not involved* will become a *buggy cache when Sapper is applied,* since the checking logic will change cache behavior when violations are about to occur. Designers must make certain that the resulting cache design is functionally correct, which fortunately is a requirement even when security is not a design goal—the processor can be tested without changing existing testing frameworks. In our processor design, we simply implement the cache as two partitions corresponding to the two security levels. We choose this scheme for its simplicity and effectiveness, however Sapper is not limited to this technique. For example, one could choose to flush the cache at every context switch from *low* to *high*. More advanced scheduling schemes can also be applied and their security guarantees can be easily tested.

The advantage of Sapper over previous techniques becomes clear when looking at the implementation of memory. Instead of being forced to partition the memory into independent sections with one per security level, as proposed by all previous approaches, Sapper allows sharing of the same memory among different security levels in a secure manner. The *set-tag* instruction allows the kernel to manage the memory and recall resources securely upon context switches.

### 4.3 Functional Validation

We implement our processor in Sapper and compile it to Verilog using the Sapper compiler. To demonstrate the complexity and functional completeness of our processor design, we use Mentor Graphics ModelSim to simulate our processor. We pick applications from various benchmark suites and load them into our processor. Since we have not developed a fully-featured operating system that supports I/O and dynamic memory allocation, we modify each application so that all I/O operations are in memory and memory resources are statically allocated. We pick benchmarks from two benchmark suites for evaluation, SPEC CPU 2006 [2] and MiBench [12], due to their popularity in evaluating architectural designs. We only choose a representative subset from each benchmark suite due to significant efforts required to modify each application to run on our processor without operating system support. Note that we do not modify the applications in any way that would change the functionality or behaviors that are not related to system calls. As such, we are able to validate our processor by cross-comparing the output of a benchmark on our processor with its output on a real machine.

The evaluated applications include three benchmarks (mcf, specrand and bzip2) from SPEC CPU2006, 2 security benchmarks (sha, rijndael), and one floating point benchmark (FFT) from MiBench. These applications are compiled with the GCC 3.4.4 cross-compiler targeting MIPS binaries, which are then loaded into a dedicated range of memory in our processor. We chose this GCC version due to its simplicity when used as a cross-compiler for generating well-formatted MIPS binaries. Being able to run realistic and diversified benchmark suites on the processor shows the potential and power of Sapper, that it is possible to design and implement a provably information flow secure processor that is comparable to commercial embedded processors. In fact, running real benchmarks forced us to debug all kinds of corner cases, some related to functional correctness and some captured by Sapper as security flaws. We spent roughly five times as long debugging the processor as we spent in its initial development.

### 4.4 Security Validation

We demonstrate that our processor enforces noninterference at runtime by running applications with different security levels on our processor. To do so, we implement a simplified micro-kernel in MIPS assembly. It contains a scheduler that can schedule among multiple processes with different security levels and be responsible for storing/restoring the registers during a context switch. A static memory allocation mechanism is also implemented to provide private stack space for each process. It is important to note that the micro-kernel is not providing any security enforcement: all security enforcement is achieved through Sapper in the processor. The major responsibility of the micro-kernel is to provide a useful interface to applications running on it.

To take advantage of the processor's capability to prevent *timing leaks*, the kernel issues a "set-timer" instruction before every switch to an untrusted application. The processor guarantees that when the timer expires, the control always jumps back to the kernel. The kernel will be responsible for storing all register values and restoring them before the next switch to the same application to ensure it continues from wherever it pauses. To make the system more efficient, the micro-kernel is responsible for reclaiming memory regions for reuse through *set-tag* instructions.

### 4.5 Quantitative Evaluation

For a quantitative analysis, we evaluate the overhead that Sapper imposes on the hardware by synthesizing our processor to a 90nm library provided by Synopsys [1] and compare this to an insecure base processor in terms of area (ASIC chip area), delay (estimates minimum clock period), and power (total power including both leakage power and dynamic power). We also compare Sapper with two existing secure hardware design mechanisms, namely GLIFT [31] and Caisson [18]. Since neither Caisson nor Sapper changes the number of cycles a program will execute, the clock delay determines performance.

We first implement our processor design without any security features using standard Verilog (designated the *Base Processor*). To collect overhead results for our processor design with GLIFT logic, the base processor is first synthesized using Synopsys' Design Compiler targeting its `and_or.db` library which contains only gate primitives (AND, OR, and Inverters) and flip-flops. At this stage, the processor is augmented with GLIFT logic by associating information flow tracking logic with each gate. Once the tracking logic has been added, the GLIFT processor is synthesized again, this time targeting the 90nm library to obtain area, delay and power results. Note that GLIFT only provides tracking logic without enforcement (which can be done through an architectural mechanism named Execution

| Processor | Chip Area ($\mu m^2$) | | Delay (ns) | | Power (mW) | | Memory |
|---|---|---|---|---|---|---|---|
| Base Processor | 560,687 | | 5.57 | | 2.79 | | |
| GLIFT | 4,277,412 | **7.6X** | 21.62 | **4X** | 13.4 | **5X** | **2X** |
| Caisson | 1,171,448 | **2X** | 6.36 | **1.14X** | 5.54 | **2X** | **2X** |
| Sapper | 582,333 | **1.04X** | 5.57 | **1X** | 2.93 | **1.05X** | **1.3X** |

*Figure 9:* Hardware overhead comparison of processors designed with different techniques: the original non-secure processor (Base Processor), processor designed under GLIFT, Caisson and Sapper, normalized to the Base Processor.

Lease [29]), however adding Execution Lease support would make the overhead even larger than GLIFT alone [29].

We then migrate our base processor (as a Verilog program) into both Caisson and Sapper, both enforcing the same noninterference guarantee. We also add the two new security-related instructions to the ISA in both processors to support an interface for software. Both designs are then compiled back into Verilog—the design in Caisson is type checked, while the design in Sapper is augmented with tracking and checking logic. Once both designs are in Verilog, the designs are synthesized using the same 90nm library to obtain results. Memory itself cannot be synthesized directly using this methodology, and depending on the technology, size, and type of memory, varying results would be obtained. As a result, we only synthesize the datapath and control logic of the processor. This does, however, include the logic associated with the memory subsystem, including cache control logic.

We now have four versions of the processor design, with almost identical functionality (because the GLIFT version does not provide enforcement). Figure 9 shows the overhead for the Base, GLIFT, Caisson, and Sapper processors. The GLIFT and Caisson processors incur a 7.6$\times$ and 2$\times$ area overhead, respectively. The Sapper processor, on the other hand, imposes an overhead of only 1.04$\times$. Similar observations also apply to delay and power. We also observe that Caisson's intensive use of multiplexers to select the right security level for each register/wire use leads to significant overhead when the processor design complexity increases. Elimination of those multiplexers is a big gain for Sapper. Furthermore, since both GLIFT and Caisson require duplication of resources, memory itself must be duplicated, while in Sapper no duplication is necessary (only extra tag store is required, taking 3% overhead). This provides further incentive for using Sapper in systems which are heavily memory dominated and have little space for extra functional logic.

### 4.6 Diamond Lattice

To demonstrate the scalability of Sapper, we further augment our processor with a more complex security lattice that contains four security levels ($L$, $H$, $M1$, and $M2$). This "diamond lattice" has $L$ as the lowest element, $H$ as the highest element, and $M1$ and $M2$ both being higher than $L$ and less than $H$ (and noncomparable with each other). This lattice can be used to demonstrate the enforcement of both secrecy and integrity in the same system, a big step towards implementing a practical provably secure system. We found that supporting a more complex lattice is as natural as implementing a two-level lattice, since all states will be traced and checked in similar ways. We did not need to modify the Sapper design except for the lattice specification. Major changes to the generated design (introduced by the Sapper compiler) include one more bit for each tag and relatively more complicated checking logic to compare among four different security levels. We do need to modify the micro-kernel to handle the scheduling among four different security levels, however this was straightforward. With the same evaluation method as used above, a secure processor enforcing noninterference on a diamond lattice using Sapper incurs only slightly more overhead (3% more) compared to a two-level lattice counterpart. While supporting such kind of lattice in Caisson would require duplicate all resource into four pieces.

## 5. Conclusions

This paper is a step towards a new class of tools that help inform hardware designers about the security ramifications of their design choices and that assist them in guarding against unforeseen exploits. We explore provable security properties in hardware designs through Sapper, an extension of the Verilog hardware description language that automatically augments a hardware design with appropriate security checks so that it is impossible to violate an information flow security policy. While there is still more work to do, we have proven the security of Sapper's constructions with respect to specified policies; we have shown Sapper's expressive power by designing a complex processor core that includes non-trivial microarchitectural features complete enough to execute a number of real-world programs; and we have performed a quantitative evaluation that shows we can provide security at a reasonably low cost while remaining expressive enough to describe complex and interesting designs.

## Acknowledgments

This work was supported by NSF grants CCF-1117165. The views and conclusions contained herein are those of the authors and should not be interpreted as necessarily representing the official policies or endorsements, either expressed or implied, of the sponsoring agencies.

## References

[1] 90nm generic CMOS library, Synopsys University program, Synopsys Inc.

[2] SPEC CPU 2006. http://www.spec.org/cpu2006/.

[3] What does CC EAL6+ mean? http://www.ok-labs.com/blog/entry/what-does-cc-eal6-mean/.

[4] O. Accigmez, J. pierre Seifert, and C. K. Koc. Predicting secret keys via branch prediction. In *The Cryptographers' Track at the RSA Conference*, 2007.

[5] D. Agrawal, S. Baktir, D. Karakoyunlu, P. Rohatgi, and B. Sunar. Trojan detection using IC fingerprinting. *Security and Privacy*, 2007.

[6] T. Alves. Trustzone: Integrated hardware and software security. *ARM white paper*, 3(4), 2004.

[7] R. Benadjila, O. Billet, S. Gueron, and M. J. Robshaw. The Intel AES instructions set and the SHA-3 candidates. In *Proceedings of the 15th International Conference on the Theory and Application of Cryptology and Information Security: Advances in Cryptology*, 2009.

[8] M. Dalton, H. Kannan, and C. Kozyrakis. Raksha: A flexible information flow architecture for software security. In *Proceedings of the 34th Annual International Symposium on Computer Architecture*, ISCA '07, pages 482–493, New York, NY, USA, 2007. ACM.

[9] J. Demme, R. Martin, A. Waksman, and S. Sethumadhavan. Side-channel vulnerability factor: A metric for measuring information leakage. In *Proceedings of the 39th Annual International Symposium on Computer Architecture*, ISCA '12, pages 106–117, Washington, DC, USA, 2012. IEEE Computer Society.

[10] D. E. Denning and P. J. Denning. Certification of programs for secure information flow. *Communications of the ACM*, 20(7):504–513, 1977.

[11] J. A. Goguen and J. Meseguer. Security policies and security models. In *Security and Privacy*, 1982.

[12] M. R. Guthaus, J. S. Ringenberg, D. Ernst, T. M. Austin, T. Mudge, and R. B. Brown. Mibench: A free, commercially representative embedded benchmark suite. In *WWC*, 2001.

[13] S. T. King, J. Tucek, A. Cozzie, C. Grier, W. Jiang, and Y. Zhou. Designing and implementing malicious hardware. In *Proceedings of the 1st Usenix Workshop on Large-Scale Exploits and Emergent Threats*, LEET'08, pages 5:1–5:8, Berkeley, CA, USA, 2008. USENIX Association.

[14] G. Klein, K. Elphinstone, G. Heiser, J. Andronick, D. Cock, P. Derrin, D. Elkaduwe, K. Engelhardt, R. Kolanski, M. Norrish, T. Sewell, H. Tuch, and S. Winwood. seL4: Formal verification of an os kernel. In *Proceedings of the ACM SIGOPS 22Nd Symposium on Operating Systems Principles*, SOSP '09, pages 207–220, New York, NY, USA, 2009. ACM.

[15] J. Kong, O. Aciiçmez, J.-P. Seifert, and H. Zhou. Deconstructing new cache designs for thwarting software cache-based side channel attacks. In *Proc. of the 2nd ACM workshop on Computer security architectures*, 2008.

[16] M. Krohn and E. Tromer. Noninterference for a practical difc-based operating system. In *Security and Privacy*, 2009.

[17] M. Krohn, A. Yip, M. Brodsky, N. Cliffer, M. F. Kaashoek, E. Kohler, and R. Morris. Information flow control for standard os abstractions. In *Proceedings of Twenty-first ACM SIGOPS Symposium on Operating Systems Principles*, SOSP '07, pages 321–334, New York, NY, USA, 2007. ACM.

[18] X. Li, M. Tiwari, J. K. Oberg, V. Kashyap, F. T. Chong, T. Sherwood, and B. Hardekopf. Caisson: A hardware description language for secure information flow. In *Proceedings of the 32Nd ACM SIGPLAN Conference on Programming Language Design and Implementation*, PLDI '11, pages 109–120, New York, NY, USA, 2011. ACM.

[19] R. Martin, J. Demme, and S. Sethumadhavan. Timewarp: Rethinking timekeeping and performance monitoring mechanisms to mitigate side-channel attacks. In *Proceedings of the 39th Annual International Symposium on Computer Architecture*, ISCA '12, pages 118–129, Washington, DC, USA, 2012. IEEE Computer Society.

[20] A. C. Myers, N. Nystrom, L. Zheng, and S. Zdancewic. Jif: Java information flow. Software release. http://www.cs.cornell.edu/jif, 2001.

[21] A. C. Myers, A. Sabelfeld, and S. Zdancewic. Enforcing robust declassification and qualified robustness. *J. Comput. Secur.*, 14(2):157–196, Apr. 2006.

[22] B. Parno, J. R. Lorch, J. R. Douceur, J. Mickens, and J. M. McCune. Memoir: Practical state continuity for protected modules. In *Proceedings of the IEEE Symposium on Security and Privacy*, 2011.

[23] C. Percival. Cache missing for fun and profit. In *Proc. of BSDCan*, 2005.

[24] I. Roy, D. E. Porter, M. D. Bond, K. S. McKinley, and E. Witchel. Laminar: Practical fine-grained decentralized information flow control. In *Proceedings of the 2009 ACM SIGPLAN Conference on Programming Language Design and Implementation*, PLDI '09, pages 63–74, New York, NY, USA, 2009. ACM.

[25] A. Sabelfeld and A. C. Myers. Language-based information-flow security. *IEEE Journal on Selected Areas in Communications*, 21(1), Jan. 2003.

[26] A. Sabelfeld and D. Sands. Dimensions and principles of declassification. In *Proceedings of the 18th IEEE workshop on Computer Security Foundations*, 2005.

[27] V. Simonet. Flow Caml in a nutshell. In *Proceedings of the first APPSEM-II workshop*, 2003.

[28] G. E. Suh, J. W. Lee, D. Zhang, and S. Devadas. Secure program execution via dynamic information flow tracking. In *Proceedings of the 11th International Conference on Architectural Support for Programming Languages and Operating Systems*, ASPLOS XI, pages 85–96, New York, NY, USA, 2004. ACM.

[29] M. Tiwari, X. Li, H. M. G. Wassel, F. T. Chong, and T. Sherwood. Execution leases: A hardware-supported mechanism for enforcing strong non-interference. In *Proceedings of the 42Nd Annual IEEE/ACM International Symposium on Microarchitecture*, MICRO 42, pages 493–504, New York, NY, USA, 2009. ACM.

[30] M. Tiwari, J. K. Oberg, X. Li, J. Valamehr, T. Levin, B. Hardekopf, R. Kastner, F. T. Chong, and T. Sherwood. Crafting a usable microkernel, processor, and i/o system with strict and provable information flow security. In *Proceedings of the 38th Annual International Symposium on Computer Architecture*, ISCA '11, pages 189–200, New York, NY, USA, 2011. ACM.

[31] M. Tiwari, H. M. Wassel, B. Mazloom, S. Mysore, F. T. Chong, and T. Sherwood. Complete information flow tracking from the gates up. In *Proceedings of the 14th International Conference on Architectural Support for Programming*

*Languages and Operating Systems*, ASPLOS XIV, pages 109–120, New York, NY, USA, 2009. ACM.

[32] J. Valamehr, M. Chase, S. Kamara, A. Putnam, D. Shumow, V. Vaikuntanathan, and T. Sherwood. Inspection resistant memory: Architectural support for security from physical examination. In *Proceedings of the 39th Annual International Symposium on Computer Architecture*, ISCA '12, pages 130–141, Washington, DC, USA, 2012. IEEE Computer Society.

[33] A. Vasudevan, J. McCune, J. Newsome, A. Perrig, and L. van Doorn. CARMA: A hardware tamper-resistant isolated execution environment on commodity x86 platforms. In *Proceedings of the ACM Symposium on Information, Computer and Communications Security (ASIACCS)*, 2012.

[34] D. Volpano, C. Irvine, and G. Smith. A sound type system for secure flow analysis. *J. Comput. Secur.*, 4, 1996.

[35] A. Waksman and S. Sethumadhavan. Tamper evident microprocessors. In *Security and Privacy*, 2010.

[36] A. Waksman and S. Sethumadhavan. Silencing hardware backdoors. In *Security and Privacy*, 2011.

[37] Z. Wang and R. B. Lee. New cache designs for thwarting software cache-based side channel attacks. In *Proceedings of the 34th Annual International Symposium on Computer Architecture*, ISCA '07, pages 494–505, New York, NY, USA, 2007. ACM.

[38] Z. Wang and R. B. Lee. A novel cache architecture with enhanced performance and security. In *Proceedings of the 41st Annual IEEE/ACM International Symposium on Microarchitecture*, MICRO 41, pages 83–93, Washington, DC, USA, 2008. IEEE Computer Society.

[39] N. Zeldovich, S. Boyd-Wickizer, E. Kohler, and D. Mazières. Making information flow explicit in HiStar. In *Proceedings of the 7th USENIX Symposium on Operating Systems Design and Implementation - Volume 7*, OSDI '06, pages 19–19, Berkeley, CA, USA, 2006. USENIX Association.

[40] D. Zhang, A. Askarov, and A. C. Myers. Language-based control and mitigation of timing channels. In *Proceedings of the 33rd ACM SIGPLAN Conference on Programming Language Design and Implementation*, PLDI '12, pages 99–110, New York, NY, USA, 2012. ACM.

[41] Z. Zhou, V. D. Gligor, J. Newsome, and J. M. McCune. Building verifiable trusted path on commodity x86 computers. In *Proceedings of the IEEE Symposium on Security and Privacy*, 2012.

# A. Proof of Noninterference

## A.1 Assumptions

We make the following assumptions on Sapper programs (each of these are easily enforced by a syntactic pass over the program):

- For each **fall**$_\ell$, the subscript $\ell$ must be the label of the state containing that **fall** command. A leaf state cannot contain a **fall**.
- For each **goto**$_{\ell_1}$ $\ell_2$, subscript $\ell_1$ must indicate the state containing that **goto** command, and $\ell_2$ must a state in the same group and at the same depth.
- Either both branches of an **if** command must execute a **goto** or **fall** or neither of them do. All paths through a state end in either a **goto** or a **fall**.
- Each **if** statement is given a unqiue label.
- The root state is fixed.

## A.2 L-equivalence

Our noninterference theorem uses the notion of *L-equivalence* between configurations, which we define in this section. For a given security level $t$, let $L = \{t' \mid t' \sqsubseteq t\}$ and $H = \{t' \mid t' \notin L\}$. We use this definition in the rest of the section. We then have the following L-equivalence definitions:

- **Store:** Two stores are L-equivalent if all L-tagged registers have the same value in both stores, i.e., $\sigma_1 \sim_L \sigma_2 \iff \forall x.\, x$ is a register $\wedge x \in dom(\sigma_{i=1,2}) \wedge \theta(x) \in L \Rightarrow \sigma_1(x) = \sigma_2(x)$
- **Stack:** Two stacks are L-equivalent, i.e.., $sc_1 :: \Sigma_1 \sim_L sc_2 :: \Sigma_2$, if both the following conditions hold: (1) $sc_1 \in L \vee sc_2 \in L \Rightarrow sc_1 = sc_2 \wedge \Sigma_1 = \Sigma_2$, (2) Let $\zeta_L(S)$ return a new stack obtained by popping out elements from $S$ until its top element $\in L$, then $sc_1 \in H \wedge sc_2 \in H \Rightarrow \zeta_L(\Sigma_1) = \zeta_L(\Sigma_2)$.
- **FallMap, TagMap:** Two pairs of *FallMap* and *TagMap* are L-equivalent, i.e.., $\langle \rho_1, \theta_1 \rangle \sim_L \langle \rho_2, \theta_2 \rangle$, if both the following conditions hold: (1) If one *FallMap* maps to a L-tagged state, then the other *FallMap* maps to the same state, i.e.., $\forall l.\, \theta_1(\rho_1(\ell)) \in L \vee \theta_2(\rho_2(\ell)) \in L \Rightarrow \rho_1(\ell) = \rho_2(\ell)$ (2) If in one *TagMap*, a *TaggedEntity* is tagged L, then it is tagged L in the other *TagMap* too, i.e.., $\forall u.\, \theta_1(u) \in L \iff \theta_2(u) \in L$.
- **Configuration:** Let $\mathbb{C}_1 = \langle p_1, \rho_1, \sigma_1, \theta_1, sc_1 :: \Sigma_1, \delta_1 \rangle$ and $\mathbb{C}_2 = \langle p_2, \rho_2, \sigma_2, \theta_2, sc_2 :: \Sigma_2, \delta_2 \rangle$. Two configurations $\mathbb{C}_1$ and $\mathbb{C}_2$ are L-equivalent, i.e.., $\mathbb{C}_1 \sim_L \mathbb{C}_2$, if the following conditions hold: (1) $p_1$ and $p_2$ are either syntactically equivalent or $sc_1 \in H \wedge sc_2 \in H$, (2) $\langle \rho_1, \theta_1 \rangle \sim_L \langle \rho_2, \theta_2 \rangle$, (3) $\sigma_1 \sim_L \sigma_2$, (4) $sc_1 :: \Sigma_1 \sim_L sc_2 :: \Sigma_2$, (5) $\delta_1 = \delta_2$

In effect, two L-equivalent configurations are indistinguishable to an observer at a security level in L.

## A.3 Lemmas

We provide two Lemmas in this subsection, which are used in the proof of noninterference in the next subsection. The Simple Security Lemma states that L-tagged expressions are made up of L-tagged subexpressions only. The Confinement Lemma states that program steps taken with security context in $H$ preserves L-equivalence.

**Lemma 1** (Simple Security). *$\phi(e) \in L \Rightarrow (\forall e'.\ e'$ is a subexpression of $e \Rightarrow \phi(e') \in L)$*

*Proof.* By induction on definition of $\phi$ in Figure 6(c). □

**Lemma 2** (Confinement). *Let $\mathbb{C}_1 = \langle p_1, \rho_1, \sigma_1, \theta_1, sc_1 :: \Sigma_1, \delta_1\rangle$ and $\mathbb{C}_2 = \langle p_2, \rho_2, \sigma_2, \theta_2, sc_2 :: \Sigma_2, \delta_2\rangle$. Then if $\mathbb{C}_1 \rightsquigarrow \mathbb{C}_2 \wedge sc_1 \in H \wedge sc_2 \in H \Rightarrow \sigma_1 \sim_L \sigma_2 \wedge \langle \rho_1, \theta_1\rangle \sim_L \langle \rho_2, \theta_2\rangle$.*

*Proof.* By induction on $p_1$ □

### A.4 Noninterference

The noninterference theorem states that if an L-observer cannot distinguish between two configurations at the beginning of a cycle, then she cannot distinguish between them at the beginning of the next cycle either. We assume that an L-observer can observe changes to L-tagged registers only at the beginning of each cycle, *not* during the cycle itself. This assumption is valid because we are designing synchronous hardware—changes to register values come into effect only at the end of a cycle. Two computations can take a different number of semantic steps within a single cycle, but the hardware is timed such that the two computations still complete at exactly the same time. We measure time in number of cycles and thus the theorem of noninterference we provide is timing-sensitive. The formal statement of noninterference is as follows:

**Theorem 1** (Noninterference). *Let*
$\mathbb{C}_1 = \langle \mathcal{F}_{root}, \rho_1, \sigma_1, \theta_1, \Sigma_1, \delta\rangle$, $\mathbb{C}_1' = \langle \mathcal{F}_{root}, \rho_1', \sigma_1', \theta_1', \Sigma_1', \delta{+}1\rangle$,
$\mathbb{C}_2 = \langle \mathcal{F}_{root}, \rho_2, \sigma_2, \theta_2, \Sigma_2, \delta\rangle$, $\mathbb{C}_2' = \langle \mathcal{F}_{root}, \rho_2', \sigma_2', \theta_2', \Sigma_2', \delta{+}1\rangle$
*and $\rightsquigarrow^*$ be the reflexive transitive closure of $\rightsquigarrow$.*
*Then $\mathbb{C}_1 \rightsquigarrow^* \mathbb{C}_1' \wedge \mathbb{C}_2 \rightsquigarrow^* \mathbb{C}_2' \wedge \mathbb{C}_1 \sim_L \mathbb{C}_2 \Rightarrow \mathbb{C}_1' \sim_L \mathbb{C}_2'$*

*Proof.* **Basis**: $\mathbb{C}_1 \sim_L \mathbb{C}_2$, because the $\rightsquigarrow^*$ is reflexive, the case holds trivially.
**Inductive Step**: Let

- $\mathbb{C}_a = \langle p_a, \rho_a, \sigma_a, \theta_a, sc_a :: \Sigma_a, \delta\rangle$
- $\mathbb{C}_b = \langle p_b, \rho_b, \sigma_b, \theta_b, sc_b :: \Sigma_b, \delta\rangle$
- $\mathbb{C}_a' = \langle p_a', \rho_a', \sigma_a', \theta_a', sc_a' :: \Sigma_a', \delta\rangle$
- $\mathbb{C}_b' = \langle p_b', \rho_b', \sigma_b', \theta_b', sc_b' :: \Sigma_b', \delta\rangle$

Also, let $\mathbb{C}_a \sim_L \mathbb{C}_b$, $\mathbb{C}_a \rightsquigarrow \mathbb{C}_a'$ and $\mathbb{C}_b \rightsquigarrow \mathbb{C}_b'$. Then we need to prove $\mathbb{C}_a' \sim_L \mathbb{C}_b'$. We divide this proof sketch into 2 cases:
(1) When $p_a = p_b$. We prove this by induction on $p_a$. Due to the lack of space, we only sketch the proof for a subset of what $p_a$ can stand for:

- When $p_a = r := e$ and $r$ is a enforced register (refer rule ASSIGN-ENF-REG): The register $r$ has the same tag in both $\theta_a$ and $\theta_b$. If the tag $\in L$, then the register $r$ is mapped to $n$ in both the stores (when the dynamic check, that the tag of the register is $\sqsupseteq$ tag of $e$ join the current security context, succeeds in both cases), or both the stores remain the same (if dynamic check in one fails, it fails in the other), using Lemma 1. If the tag $\in H$, then taking this step does not modify L-observable store. Hence this case holds.
- When $p_a =$ **if**$_\ell$ $e$ **then** $c$ **else** $c$; **endif** (refer rule IF): If $sc_a, sc_b \in L$, then executing the **if** statement will push the same tag onto the security context stack (hence $sc_a' = sc_b'$). Also, both $\theta_a, \theta_b$ are modified in the same way, because $\mathcal{F}_{cd}$ is a constant function (note that we update all registers that are control dependent on the **if** statement to handle implicit flows due to branches not taken). The tag of $e$ is $\ell$ in both cases (in which case $p_a' = p_b'$), or $H$ in both cases (in which case $sc_a', sc_b' \in H$). If $sc_a, sc_b \in H$, then from Lemma 2, L-equivalence is preserved by taking this step. Hence this case holds.
- When $p_a =$ **skip; endif** (refer rule ENDIF): This statement pops the top of the security context stack. Based on the definition of the L-equivalence of stacks, and our assumption that if one branch of an **if** does not have a **goto** or **fall**, the other branch does not either, this case holds.
- When $p_a =$ **goto**$_{\ell_1}$ $\ell_2$ and $\ell_2$ is a enforced state (refer rule GOTO-ENFORCED): In the step taken in both configurations, the security context stack is set to the tag of the root state. If $sc_a, sc_b \in L$, either the dynamic check (that tag of state $\ell_2 \sqsupseteq$ the current security context) succeeds in both cases or fails in both cases, modifying the fall map in the same way. If $sc_a, sc_b \in H$, then they do not modify the fall map for any states with tag $\in L$. Thus this case holds.

(2) When $sc_a, sc_b \in H$: for the cases where neither $p_a, p_b$ is **endif** or **goto**, proof follows from Confinement Lemma. Hence this case holds. Consider the case where one command is a **goto** and the other is not: since all program paths must end in **goto**, the other command will eventually be **goto**. Since the cycle length is enforced, both **goto**s are executed only at the end of each cycle. Hence even if they take different number of semantic steps to reach there, they take the same time. For the case where one command is a **endif** and other is not, because of the assumption that either both branches contain **fall** or **goto**, or neither of them do, the other command will eventually become **endif** (during which L-equivalence is preserved throughout, using Confinement Lemma)
This completes the proof sketch. □

# Finding Trojan Message Vulnerabilities in Distributed Systems

Radu Banabic
École Polytechnique Fédérale de Lausanne
radu.banabic@epfl.ch

George Candea
École Polytechnique Fédérale de Lausanne
george.candea@epfl.ch

Rachid Guerraoui
École Polytechnique Fédérale de Lausanne
rachid.guerraoui@epfl.ch

## Abstract

Trojan messages are messages that seem correct to the receiver but cannot be generated by any correct sender. Such messages constitute major vulnerability points of a distributed system—they constitute ideal targets for a malicious actor and facilitate failure propagation across nodes. We describe Achilles, a tool that searches for Trojan messages in a distributed system. Achilles uses dynamic white-box analysis on the distributed system binaries in order to infer the predicate that defines messages parsed by receiver nodes and generated by sender nodes, respectively, and then computes Trojan messages as the difference between the two.

We apply Achilles on implementations of real distributed systems: FSP, a file transfer application, and PBFT, a Byzantine-fault-tolerant state machine replication library. Achilles discovered a new bug in FSP and rediscovered a previously known vulnerability in PBFT. In our evaluation we demonstrate that our approach can perform orders of magnitude better than general approaches based on regular fuzzing and symbolic execution.

***Categories and Subject Descriptors*** D.2.5 [*SOFTWARE ENGINEERING*]: Testing and Debugging - Symbolic execution

***Keywords*** symbolic execution; distributed system; testing; Trojan

## 1. Introduction

Most reliability techniques in distributed systems are based on the assumption that failures are independent: if a node fails in some way, the impact on other nodes should be minimal, i.e., the failure should not propagate. But even if nodes are programmed independently and placed on geographically remote sites, nodes need to communicate, typically by exchanging messages. Such messages can propagate failures among nodes.

In this paper, we study what we call *Trojan messages*. These are messages that are intelligible to correct receiver nodes of a distributed system, but cannot be generated by any correct sender nodes in that system. Similar to divisions by zero or buffer overflows, Trojan messages result from absence of defensive programming and constitute a source of vulnerabilities. We know of no work that automatically discovers this type of messages.

Trojan messages often creep into the *implementation* of nodes, while being invisible in their high level *specification*. Such messages can have a major impact on the behavior of distributed systems. For example, the Amazon S3 storage system suffered several hours of downtime in 2008 [1]. The problem was caused by "a handful of messages [...] that had a single bit corrupted". Unfortunately for the system, "the message was still intelligible, but the system state information was incorrect". This allowed the initial corruption to propagate to other, correct nodes of the system, until most of the collective information in the system was corrupt. Such corner cases are difficult to identify. In order to prevent such downtime in the future, Amazon engineers added checks to "log any such messages and then reject them".

The core problem that caused the Amazon S3 downtime was the fact that nodes accepted the corrupt messages despite the fact that no correct node could have generated such messages in the respective context. We say that S3 nodes accepted Trojan messages. We argue that, if such messages exist in a system implementation, they represent an unnecessary vulnerability—servers should do what correct clients require them to do and not one bit more. Since, by definition, correct nodes cannot generate Trojan messages, it is likely that such messages will not be encountered during regular testing. Trojan messages are likely to exercise untested code paths and surface hidden, potentially undesired, behavior.

Current testing techniques face vast search spaces of possible inputs. This limits their ability to find the Trojan messages that could cause the system to fail at some point in the future. Recognizing the important distinction between specification and implementation, the most stringent operators of


*ASPLOS '14*, March 1–5, 2014, Salt Lake City, Utah, USA.

ACM 978-1-4503-2305-5/14/03...$15.00.
http://dx.doi.org/10.1145/2541940.2541984

distributed systems have started testing their live production systems with fault injection (e.g., Google organizes regular "fire drills" in which engineers intentionally cause failures in critical live systems [18]). Trojan messages are good candidates for such fault injection. However, guessing which messages are Trojan is still hard and mostly an elusive goal.

We propose Achilles, a system whose purpose is to identify Trojan messages that constitute the Achilles heel of any distributed system. Our approach is based on:

1. A new usage model for symbolic execution, aimed at discovering execution paths that accept Trojan messages.
2. A set of optimizations that enable efficient search for Trojan messages.

We applied Achilles to the File Service Protocol [12], a UDP-based file transfer protocol implementation that is distributed with some Debian versions, and to PBFT [6], an implementation of a Byzantine fault-tolerant replication protocol. We show that Achilles has high accuracy; it is orders of magnitude more efficient at finding Trojan messages than black-box fuzzing or classic symbolic execution. Achilles found in FSP a high-level semantic bug and also rediscovered a known vulnerability in PBFT—subtle bugs that would be difficult to discover using other techniques.

The rest of the paper is organized as follows: we first present the high-level idea of Achilles along with a working example of a system under test (§2). In §3 we describe the basic mechanism of Achilles and the optimizations that make it practical. We discuss the soundness and completeness of our approach in §4. Then, we describe our current prototype (§5) and evaluate Achilles on two real distributed systems (§6). Finally, we review related work (§7) and conclude (§8).

## 2. Achilles: A Primer

Achilles is a system designed to identify Trojan messages in a distributed system. For simplicity, we consider in our description of Achilles only client-server systems where the client generates requests and the server replies; it is straightforward to generalize the approach to peer-to-peer or other types of distributed systems.

We define Trojan messages as those that are accepted by correct server nodes in a distributed system but cannot be generated by any correct client node, as illustrated in Figure 1. By "correct" we mean nodes that execute the unaltered implementation of the distributed system, in contrast to incorrect nodes, which are nodes that have encountered a fault (e.g., memory bit flip), or are controlled by malicious users. Thus, in our definition, "correct" does not necessarily imply that nodes follow the high-level specification of the protocol, or do what the developers intended.

Achilles has two phases. In a first phase, it computes a predicate that defines all messages that can be generated by correct clients. We call this the *client predicate* $P_C$. The set

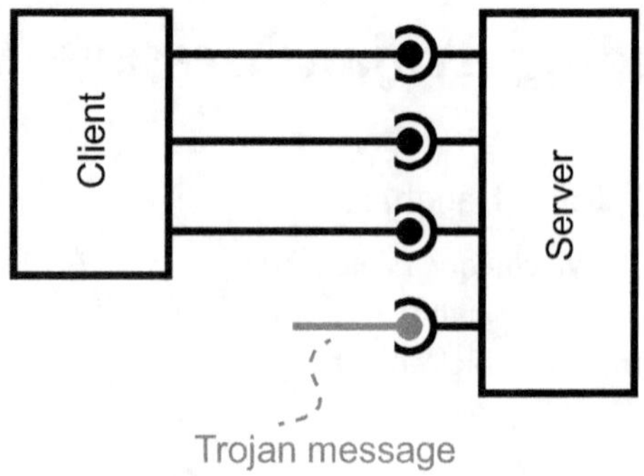


**Figure 1.** Trojan messages are messages that are accepted by a server but cannot be generated by any correct client.

of messages that can be generated by correct clients is $\mathcal{C} = \{msg \mid P_C(msg)\}$. In the second phase, Achilles computes a predicate that defines all messages that are accepted by the server, the *server predicate* $P_S$. The set of messages that are accepted as correct by correct servers is $\mathcal{S} = \{msg \mid P_S(msg)\}$. Then, the set of Trojan messages is defined as $\mathcal{T} = \mathcal{S} \setminus \mathcal{C}$, which can be expressed as $\mathcal{T} = \{msg \mid P_S(msg) \wedge \neg P_C(msg)\}$.

In essence, Achilles extracts the grammar of the communication protocol, as implemented in both the client and the server. It then operates on the two grammars, trying to determine the difference between the server's implementation of the grammar and the client's. As we describe later (§3), Achilles uses symbolic execution in order to analyze the implementation of clients and servers; it represents the extracted grammars using symbolic constraints.

### 2.1 Working Example

To illustrate the idea underlying our approach, consider the sample server implementation presented in Figure 2.

This is a simplified example, in which a server handles read or write requests from clients. The server first initializes its internal data structures (lines 2-3). Next, the server enters an event loop in which it handles client requests. The program receives a message and stores it in the local variable *msg* (line 5). Then, the server checks that the message sender is in a pre-configured group of known peers (line 6) and if the CRC error-detection code is correct.

If the message passes the general validation tests, the server reads the *request* field to get the message type—either a *READ* or a *WRITE* request. If the request is not one of the two, the message is discarded (line 29). For either of the request types, the server validates the address field and handles the respective request.

The client shown in Figure 3 follows the same protocol as the server. It reads user requests from standard input, validates the data (lines 5-7) and computes corresponding requests for the server.

The sample system has a Trojan message. The server validates that the requested address is below the maximum

```
#define DATASIZE 100
peers = initializePeers();
data = new int[DATASIZE];
while(TRUE) {
  msg = receiveMessage();
  if (!isInSet(msg.sender, peers))
    continue;
  if (!isValidCRC(msg, msg.CRC))
    continue;
  switch (msg.request) {
    case READ:
      if (msg.address >= DATASIZE)
        continue;
      //Security vulnerability: forgot to check
      //          address < 0
      sendMessage(msg.sender, REPLY,
                  data[msg.address]);
      continue;
    case WRITE:
      if (msg.address >= DATASIZE)
        continue;
      if (msg.address < 0)
        continue;
      data[msg.address] =
                msg.value;
      sendMessage(msg.sender, ACK);
      continue;
    default:
      continue};
  }
}
```

**Figure 2.** A simple server that handles requests from clients. The server accepts Trojan messages, as it does not correctly validate the address field of read requests.

*DATASIZE*, however, for *READ* requests it does not ensure that the address is greater than zero. The client, however, validates the input from the user before contacting the server. Therefore, no correct client can generate *READ* messages with negative offsets, although they are accepted by the server. Thus, any *READ* message with a negative address is a Trojan message.

In this example, the Trojan message can lead to a potential privacy leak, as attackers can read from negative offsets in the data array and discover, for instance, the list of peers that communicate with the server.

## 3. Design

At a high level, Achilles works as follows. In a first phase, it obtains the client predicate $P_C$. Then, it pre-processes $P_C$ to eliminate redundancy and to pre-compute structure information for the next phase (details follow in §3.3). In the second phase, Achilles computes the server predicate $P_S$, as well as incrementally discovering Trojan Messages. As an optimization, our implementation does not compute the entire formula of $P_S$ before computing Trojan messages, but rather searches for Trojan messages incrementally, as it builds $P_S$.

In this section, we first give an overview of how Achilles uses symbolic execution in order to extract the grammar

```
#define DATASIZE 100
peerID = getPeerID();
operationType = readFromKeyboard();
address = readFromKeyboard();
if (address >= DATASIZE)
  exit(1);
if (address < 0)
  exit(1);
//Client only sends addresses in [0,100)
if (operationType == READ) {
  msg = new ReadMessage();
  msg.sender = me;
  msg.request = READ;
  msg.address = address;
  msg.CRC = computeCRC(msg);
  sendMessage(server, msg);
}
if (operationType == WRITE) {
  value = readFromKeyboard();
  msg = new WriteMessage();
  msg.sender = me;
  msg.request = WRITE;
  msg.address = address;
  msg.value = value;
  msg.CRC = computeCRC(msg);
  sendMessage(server, msg);
}
```

**Figure 3.** A simple client that generates messages. Correct clients validate the address field, therefore cannot expose the bug in the server.

from both the client and the server (§3.1). We then describe how Achilles finds Trojan messages efficiently using off-the-shelf constraint solvers (§3.2). We present optimizations that enable Achilles to handle large client predicates (§3.3). Finally, we describe how Achilles handles local state in the client and in the server (§3.4).

### 3.1 Symbolic Execution and Message Grammars

Achilles uses symbolic execution [17] to extract the grammars of messages that can be sent/received by an implementation of a distributed system. Symbolic execution is a technique that systematically explores execution paths in a system. Rather than exercising a system with concrete inputs, a symbolic execution engine provides "symbolic" data, which can conceptually take any value. The symbolic execution engine then executes the system under test and interprets expressions symbolically. At each branching point that depends on symbolic data, the symbolic execution engine invokes a Satisfiability Modulo Theories (SMT) solver to assess the feasibility of each branch, based on the current state of the system. When a branch is deemed feasible, the execution engine follows the respective branch and also updates the symbolic data, keeping track of the constraints that need to be satisfied such that the branch is feasible. If both paths are feasible, the execution engine forks the exploration and follows both branches.

At every step of the symbolic execution, the engine keeps track of several possible execution states of the system, each

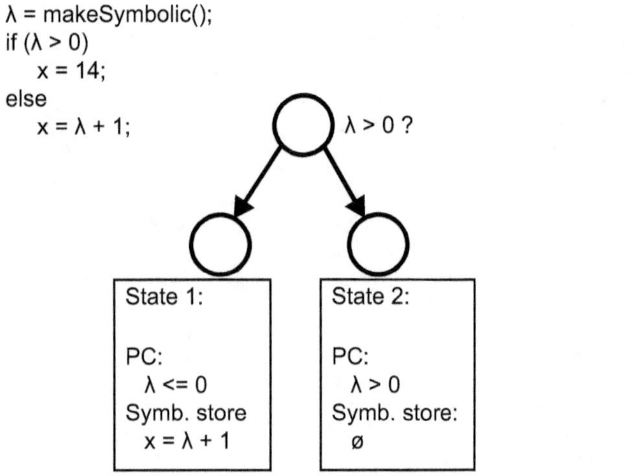


**Figure 4.** An example of symbolic execution for a small piece of code.

```
∃ symb_PeerID, symb_Address, symb_Value :

message.sender = symb_PeerID
⋀ message.request = READ
⋀ message.address = symb_Address
⋀ message.CRC = CRC(message)
⋀ symb_Address < 100
⋀ symb_Address >= 0
⋁
message.sender = symb_PeerID
⋀ message.request = WRITE
⋀ message.address = symb_Address
⋀ message.value = symb_Value
⋀ message.CRC = CRC(message)
⋀ symb_Address < 100
⋀ symb_Address >= 0
```

**Figure 5.** The client predicate $P_C(message)$ of the client in Figure 3, as discovered by the symbolic execution phase of Achilles.

corresponding to a possible execution path. Figure 4 shows a sample symbolic execution of a small piece of code. A symbolic execution state consists of a *symbolic store*, which maps variables from the system under test to expressions on symbolic inputs, and the set of *path constraints*, which represent the conditions on symbolic input that must hold for the respective execution path to be feasible.

In Achilles, we represent message grammars as sets of constraints obtained during symbolic execution. The server predicate $P_S$ is expressed by the set of path constraints that correspond to execution paths that handle accepted messages. The client predicate $P_C$ is expressed by the symbolic messages that the client sends over the network on different execution paths, along with their respective path constraints.

***Client Predicate.*** In a distributed system, clients receive "local" inputs, parse the inputs, generate corresponding messages conforming to the specification of the protocol (or, more precisely, to the client's implementation of that specification), and finally send the messages to the server. The client predicate is a representation of all valid messages that can be *sent*.

In order to obtain the set of all possible messages that can be generated by a client in a distributed system, we conceptually need to provide the client with all possible "local" inputs and then capture the messages it sends over the network. We start the client in a symbolic environment such that any local system call that the client emits in order to read input is intercepted, and the result is replaced with symbolic data. The symbolic execution engine keeps track of how the symbolic data flows through the client and, when the client attempts to send a message over the network, Achilles captures and stores the contents of the message and the corresponding path constraints. The message payload may contain concrete data, but also expressions on symbolic data.

Thus, the predicate $P_C$ is the disjunction of predicates $path_{C_1} \vee \cdots \vee path_{C_n}$, where each $path_{C_i}$ is a conjunction of path constraints and symbolic expressions for an execution path that sends a message. We call each such predicate $path_{C_i}$ a *client path predicate.*

For the example client in Figure 3, Achilles discovers the predicate presented in Figure 5. Names that begin with *symb_* indicate symbolic data automatically inserted by Achilles. There are two main execution paths in the client that lead to messages being sent. One path corresponds to a *READ* request, while the other corresponds to a *WRITE* request. In both cases, the *message.request* header contains concrete data. This is because there is no data flow dependency between the *message.request* header and any symbolic input; the values for the two paths only differ because of control flow dependencies.

All other headers except *message.request* contain symbolic data. The *message.value* and *message.sender* headers, for example, contain the respective unconstrained symbolic inputs. The *CRC* header contains an expression on all other symbolic inputs (in Figure 5, the expression is summarized by the CRC function, but in real deployments, the expression contains the full chain of operations that transform the symbolic inputs). Finally, the *address* header contains constrained symbolic data. There are no operations directly performed on *symb_Address*; however, the execution path that leads to the message imposes constraints on the possible values: *symb_Address* needs to have values between $[0, 100)$ in order for the message to be sent. This is reflected in the path constraints that are captured and stored by Achilles.

In distributed systems, messages usually have clearly differentiated fields. Developers might be interested to check only a subset of those fields for Trojan messages (e.g., only check the contents of the *address* field). We support this selective approach in Achilles (§5.2) and also refer to techniques that automatically avoid complex authentication or encryption functions (§7). Since the grammar extraction phase of Achilles is based on vanilla symbolic execution, Achilles can benefit from a variety of approaches that enhance symbolic execution.

***Server Predicate.*** In a distributed system, the server receives messages from a client, parses the message, and executes the operation requested by the client. The server should discard messages that do not follow the specification, and only execute operations corresponding to valid messages. The server predicate $P_S$ is a representation of all valid messages that can be *received*.

Each message received by the server triggers the execution of code to handle it. For simplicity, we refer to the sequence of executed instructions as the *execution path* triggered by the message. The execution path starts after the return of the *receive* instruction and ends when the message processing is complete—either the server exits, or it listens for new events.

After receiving a message, the server decodes it and parses its fields, checking if the message conforms to the specification of the protocol (or, more precisely, to the server node's implementation of that specification). In order to infer the set of valid messages, Achilles first classifies execution paths in the system under test as either *accepting* or *rejecting*. *Accepting* execution paths are those that are triggered by messages that pass the initial parsing stages of the system under test and cause the server to perform an action. Conversely, *rejecting* execution paths are those that are triggered by messages that are rejected by the server. Achilles automates the classification of paths, using some simple observations on the behavior of the server. Human operators of Achilles can also manually place tags in the code in order to speed up the analysis (details follow in §5.2).

In order to obtain the server predicate, Achilles executes the server node symbolically, feeding it an unconstrained symbolic message. The server analyzes the message and branches into different execution paths, one for each type of message in the protocol specification. Symbolic execution enumerates all these paths, keeping track of the constraints that make each path feasible.

We define the server predicate $P_S$ as the disjunction of all path constraints corresponding to *accepting* execution paths. Thus, $P_S$ represents all possible messages that can trigger *accepting* execution paths in the server.

Similarly to $P_C$, the server predicate $P_S$ is obtained using vanilla symbolic execution. Therefore, Achilles can benefit from any optimization that enhances the performance of symbolic execution engines.

In the example in Figure 2, we define *rejecting* execution paths as those that do not send a reply to the client (reach lines 7, 9, 13, 21, 23 or 29 of the server code), and *accepting* execution paths as those paths that send a reply (reach line 17 or 26). The server predicate, as discovered by our technique, is presented in Figure 6.

```
isInSet(message.sender, peers) = TRUE
∧ isValidCRC(message, message.CRC) = TRUE
∧ message.request = READ
∧ message.address < 100
∨
isInSet(message.sender, peers) = TRUE
∧ isValidCRC(message, message.CRC) = TRUE
∧ message.request = WRITE
∧ message.address < 100
∧ message.address ≥ 0
```

**Figure 6.** The server predicate $P_S(message)$ of the server in Figure 2, as discovered by the symbolic execution phase of Achilles.

### 3.2 Finding Trojan Messages

Trojan messages are, by definition, all messages in $\mathcal{S} \setminus \mathcal{C}$. This is equivalent to $\mathcal{T} = \{msg \mid P_S(msg) \wedge \neg P_C(msg)\}$. In Achilles, Trojan messages are computed incrementally, as it builds up the formula of $P_S$. This point is essential, as clients are usually less complex than servers. The extraction of the client predicate $P_C$ is easier than the extraction of the server predicate $P_S$.

For every explored execution path in the server, Achilles keeps track of a list of client path predicates that contain messages that can trigger the respective path, as shown in Figure 7. At every branch point encountered during the symbolic execution of the server, Achilles checks which of the client messages can still trigger each path, and whether the paths can be triggered by any Trojan messages. As soon as an execution path cannot be triggered by any Trojan messages, it is dropped from the exploration. Therefore, by construction, any execution path in the server that reaches an *accepting* marker has Trojan messages. For such execution paths, Achilles outputs a symbolic expression and a concrete example of the Trojan message.

Note that Trojan messages might be exclusive on execution paths (e.g., the accepting path on the right in Figure 7), or they might be bundled with other, non-Trojan messages (e.g., the accepting path on the left). The latter case means that classic symbolic execution by itself does not alleviate the problem of finding Trojan messages by much—it weeds out execution paths with dropped messages from those with accepted messages, but Trojan messages may be anywhere among the execution paths that handle accepted messages. In the example in Figure 2, the Trojan messages (those with $msg.address < 0$) are on the same execution path with valid messages (those that satisfy $msg.address >= 0$ and $msg.address < DATASIZE$); symbolic execution by itself would not point out the presence of a potential bug. This is also the case of the wildcard bug found by Achilles in FSP (§6.3) and the vulnerability found by Achilles in PBFT (§6.3).

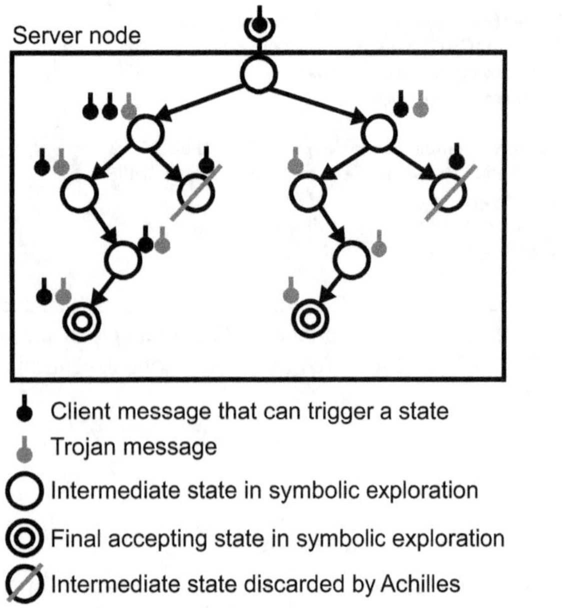


**Figure 7.** Symbolic execution of a server node in Achilles. Using the predicate collected from the client, Achilles restricts the server exploration to paths that can be triggered by Trojan messages.

We optimize the discovery of Trojan messages by adapting Achilles to the particularities of symbolic execution, as described in the following subsections.

***Constraint Solving.*** Predicates $P_C$ and $P_S$ are disjunctions of path predicates. Each path predicate $path \in P$ is a conjunction of constraints and assignments. A predicate defines a class of messages generated by a client, or accepted by a server. In order to compare two predicates $path_1$ and $path_2$, Achilles must combine the two in a single formula and then call an SMT solver in order to check satisfiability.

In order to combine a client and a server path predicate, Achilles adds a conjunction between their respective path constraints, and also adds an equality constraint between the value of the message generated in the client and the value of the message received in the server. In essence, the combination between a server and a client path predicate, $path_S$ and $path_C$, represents messages *msg* such that:

- $msg_S$ satisfies the server predicate
- $msg_C$ satisfies the client predicate
- $msg_S = msg_C = msg$

SMT solvers, such as STP [13] or Z3 [11], verify the satisfiability of a set of constraints and expressions on symbolic variables. Furthermore, SMT solvers can compute a concrete assignment of the symbolic variables that satisfies a set of expressions and constraints. For example, an SMT solver can determine that the set of constraints $\lambda > 0 \wedge \lambda < -5$ is unsatisfiable. However, $\lambda > 0 \wedge \lambda < 5$ is satisfiable and $\lambda = 3$ satisfies the constraints.

In terms of symbolic expressions, the definition of the set of Trojan messages $\mathcal{T}$ can be written as the set of messages that satisfy the server predicate, but not the client predicate:

$$\mathcal{T} = \{msg \mid P_S(msg) \wedge \neg P_C(msg)\}$$

$P_C$ contains an existential quantifier; negating it produces a universal quantifier. This makes solving the expression above difficult using current SMT solvers. Z3 has limited support for quantifiers, using heuristics and patterns to eliminate quantification. Achilles calls Z3, attempting to solve the predicate and check for the presence of Trojan messages. However, the heuristics may fail; in this case, Z3 cannot answer whether an expression is satisfiable or not. In the following subsection, we discuss how we under-approximate the negation of client path predicates and eliminate the universal quantifier.

***Negating Path Predicates.*** Recall that a client path predicate $path_C \in P_C$ represents all possible messages that can be generated on a particular execution path. Let $negate(path_C)$ be an operator that generates a predicate representing all possible messages that *cannot* be generated on that path.

Figure 8 shows the expression of READ messages generated by the sample client in Figure 3. There are three symbolic variables in the message, $\lambda_{PeerID}, \lambda_{Address}$ and $\lambda_{CRC}$, and one concrete variable, containing the value $READ$. $\lambda_{PeerID}$ is the unconstrained value of the *symb_PeerID* input. $\lambda_{Address}$ is the value of the *symb_Address* input, but it is subjected to the restrictions in the path constraint. Finally, $\lambda_{CRC}$ is a more complex operation on $\lambda_{PeerID}, \lambda_{Address}$ and $READ$.

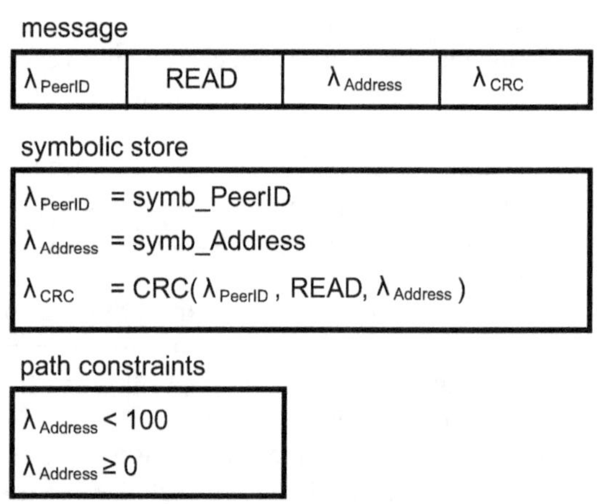


**Figure 8.** The expression of READ messages generated by the sample client.

Achilles under-approximates the true *negate* operator as follows. Achilles' custom operator computes the negation of a path predicate as a disjunction of the negation of each individual value in the message buffer. In order to negate a value, there are two cases:

1. If the value is a concrete value $C$, then replace the respective value with a new symbolic value $\lambda$ and add the constraint $\lambda \neq C$.
2. If the value is an expression on symbolic variables, then negate the set of constraints that influence the respective variables. If there are no constraints available, then abandon the negation of the current value.

For the example in Figure 8, the negation of the path predicate is a representation of the set of message where:

- the *request* field is different from *READ* or
- the *address* field is smaller than 0 or greater than 100 or
- the *CRC* field is the CRC function of a message where the *address* is smaller than 0 or greater than 100 or its *request* is different from READ.

In constraint form, this is written as:

$$(message.request = \lambda_{req}) \wedge \lambda_{req} \neq READ$$
$$\vee(message.address = \lambda_{Address}) \wedge(\lambda_{Address} \geq 100 \vee \lambda_{Address} < 0)$$
$$\vee(message.CRC = CRC(READ, \lambda_{Address}, \lambda_{PeerID})) \wedge(\lambda_{Address} \geq 100 \vee \lambda_{Address} < 0)$$

We discuss the soundness and completeness of the custom *negate* operator in a dedicated section (§4).

### 3.3 Handling Large Client Predicates.

The server analysis phase of Achilles is a search problem—find all possible execution paths that accept Trojan messages. Symbolic execution enumerates the possible execution paths in the server, with the added precondition that there exists at least one message that satisfies the path constraints in the server and the conjunction of all negated client path predicates. The negation operator allows checking for Trojan messages with a single query to the constraint solver; however, this query can be complex.

Achilles needs a strategy to efficiently handle the thousands of expressions that can appear in a client predicate. The key idea is to keep track of which path predicates can trigger an execution path explored in the server.

The $P_S$ extraction phase of Achilles incrementally adds constraints to each $path_S \in P_S$, as it explores execution paths. Rather than just checking whether there are Trojan messages on the current path (if $path_S \wedge negate(path_{C_1}) \wedge \cdots \wedge negate(path_{C_n})$ is satisfiable), Achilles also checks whether $path_S \wedge path_{C_i}$ is satisfiable, for each $path_{C_i} \in P_C$. Whenever the latter is not satisfiable, Achilles drops $negate(path_{C_i})$ from the solver query that checks for Trojan messages—if $path_S \wedge path_{C_i}$ is false, then $path_S \wedge negate(path_{C_i})$ is implicitly true (this is because $path_S$ and $path_{C_i}$ are both satisfiable, by construction). Once dropped, $path_{C_i}$ will never be checked again on the respective execution path; $path_{C_i}$ does not change, while $path_S$ only becomes more constrained, meaning that the conjunction can never become feasible in the future. As the symbolic execution engine explores longer execution paths, the number of client path predicates that can trigger the path decreases, and the size of the SMT query that checks for Trojan messages becomes smaller (we evaluate the effect of this optimization in our experiments §6.4).

In order to further optimize the search for Trojan messages, Achilles also exploits the process through which path predicates are generated. The intuition behind this optimization is that messages generated by the client are similar to each other. Two client path predicates can represent the same values for a certain field in a message, e.g., $path'_C = (msg.x = 1) \wedge (msg.y = 2)$ and $path''_C = (msg.x = 1) \wedge (msg.y = 7)$ have the same values for field $x$. In this case, if $path'_C$ is dropped due to a new server constraint on field $x$, then $path''_C$ can also be dropped without further checking.

Achilles pre-computes a data structure that stores information about relations between client path predicates. The data structure can be seen as a three-dimensional matrix *differentFrom*, where $differentFrom[i][j][field] = TRUE$ means that there exists at least one message $msg_i \in path_{C_i}$ such that there is no message $msg_j \in path_{C_j}$ with $msg_i.field = msg_j.field$. The data structure is computed by applying the *negate* operator for each field of messages, between each pair of client path predicates. The data structure is only computed for message fields that are independent, meaning that they do not appear in constraints with other fields. As can be seen in our evaluation (§6), this pre-computation is fast; moreover, it is trivially parallelizable.

While symbolically executing a server node, Achilles uses the information from *differentFrom* at every point where the exploration forks. If a branching point depends on field $a$ from the received message (and not on any other fields), and the new constraints of the branching point make $path_{C_i} \wedge path_S$ no longer satisfiable, then Achilles can drop $path_{C_i}$ from the current state, but also all path predicates $path_{C_j}$ such that $differentFrom[j][i][a] = FALSE$. In other words, if $path_{C_i}$ no longer holds, due to the additional checks on field $a$, then all path predicates $path_{C_j}$ can be dropped, because they cannot have any additional values for field $a$.

For the sample client predicates in Figure 5, $differentFrom[1][2][request] = TRUE$, because client predicate 1 is satisfied by an assignment $message.request = READ$, while predicate 2 is not. However, $differentFrom[1][2][address] = FALSE$, because the $message.address$ field of the $READ$ request is not satisfied by any other values than those that also satisfy the address of the *WRITE* request.

### 3.4 Local State

Distributed systems often keep local state across several rounds of messages and change their behavior based on the contents of the local state. For example, Paxos [19] uses three phases to achieve consensus. In each phase, Paxos nodes accept different types of messages—the predicate $P_S$ depends on the local state of the nodes. Thus, Achilles needs a mechanism to control the local state of the analyzed nodes. Achilles provides several alternatives to support local state.

***Concrete Local State.*** The analysis phase of Achilles can be started at any point in the execution of a distributed system. Achilles is implemented on top of S2E [8], a symbolic execution platform that can run whole systems: operating systems, libraries and user applications. This enables the possibility of running the distributed system concretely up to some point, implicitly building up concrete local state.

This mode of operation is useful when developers are interested in the behavior of their implementation in a specific scenario. For example, in the case of basic Paxos, developers might be interested in what happens when a Paxos Acceptor has just entered the second phase, with proposed value 7. It should only validate *Accept* messages for value 7—any other message is a Trojan message.

Another example where Concrete Local State is useful is the Amazon S3 bug [1], described in §1. The Trojan message that caused the outage incorrectly reported a high failure rate in the system. The message was not necessarily Trojan in all possible scenarios—there may be scenarios where there are indeed a lot of failures in the system. However, the message was Trojan in the concrete scenario in which it occurred. By building concrete state in a deployment with few failures, Achilles could discover that no correct client node can report high failure rates, yet the servers accept such messages.

***Constructed Symbolic Local State.*** As a generalization of the Concrete Local State mode, Achilles is able to pass symbolic messages between nodes of a distributed system, such that the nodes build up symbolic local state. The Constructed Symbolic Local State mode can capture entire sets of possible concrete execution scenarios. However, due to the additional symbolic variables and constraints, the Constructed Symbolic Local State mode can encounter difficulties with complex data structures, like any symbolic execution tool.

Consider again the example of Paxos. In order to be confident that there are no Trojan messages in the second phase of the protocol, developers need to re-use Achilles for every combination of concrete values in the local state. Using Concrete Local State, this entails re-running Paxos with different proposed values (1, 2, etc.) and then applying Achilles for each scenario. Alternatively, with Constructed Symbolic Local State, developers can run Paxos once, with a symbolic proposed value. Paxos nodes will store the symbolic value in their local state. Thus, Achilles can be applied a single time.

***Over-approximate Symbolic Local State.*** The third mode of operation allows distributed system developers to place annotations that describe the local state. Developers can insert annotations in the code of the distributed system nodes, or insert them directly in the binary at runtime, using S2E plugins that monitor execution. Essentially, developers can manually define memory as symbolic local state and specify constraints on the stored values.

In the Paxos example, developers can annotate the functions that deal with local state in order to directly return symbolic values. This approach is useful when the implementation uses complex data structures to store local state, as it makes it possible for developers to reduce the burden on SMT solvers.

# 4. Soundness and Completeness

The purpose of Achilles is to discover Trojan messages, i.e., messages that are accepted by a server but cannot be generated by any correct client. Achilles can have both false positives and false negatives and is therefore not guaranteed to be sound or complete. False positives, however, can be kept under control by the operator of Achilles, as described below. We believe this makes Achilles a useful testing tool for distributed system developers, who can incorporate the messages discovered by Achilles in fault injection testing.

## 4.1 False Positives

We say that Achilles has false positives when there exists a message $m$ that is falsely identified as Trojan. This can happen either when $m$ is rejected by the server, or when $m$ can be generated by a correct client.

Achilles relies on symbolic execution in order to extract predicates. Symbolic execution incrementally builds up an expression of an entire program by systematically exploring feasible execution paths. As long as symbolic execution does not completely explore all paths, the expression under-approximates the program. When the client is under-approximated, it might happen that a message $m$ can only be generated on the execution paths that were not yet explored — this leads to false positives in Achilles.

In our experiments in §6, we did not encounter any false positives of Achilles. We bounded the maximum messages size in both the client and server, allowing symbolic execution to complete. We also restricted symbolic execution to only some fields of a message. Essentially, we restrict symbolic execution to only a subset of the input space, as has also been proposed by Person et al. [21].

Achilles generates concrete values for the Trojan messages it discovers, as well as symbolic expressions, allowing testers to inject the concrete messages in a real deployment (such as in live fire drills) and check the effect of the messages, weeding out harmless messages. While this concretization does not disambiguate between Trojan and non-Trojan messages, it helps discover any adverse effects of the suspected Trojan messages.

As future work, we imagine using the expressions that define Trojan messages to guide a new symbolic execution of the client node; this approach is similar in spirit to the abstraction refinement in CEGAR [9]. As shown by ESD [23] or Demand-driven symbolic execution [2], this focused symbolic execution is significantly faster than "blind" exploration, and can help eliminate false positives in Achilles.

It is worth pointing out that Achilles does not also encounter false positives due to inaccuracy in Achilles' implementation of the *negate* operator. The implementation is strictly an under-approximation of the ideal *negate* operator. For each negated expression generated by the *negate*, we use the SMT solver to check if there is any common solution between the original expression and its negation; whenever there is such a solution, we discard the negated expression, eliminating any false positives that could have occurred.

### 4.2 False Negatives

We say that Achilles has false negatives when there exists a message $m$ that is not reported as a Trojan message, although it is actually accepted by the server and cannot be generated by any correct client.

False negatives can occur when the symbolic execution of the server does not exhaust all execution paths. If a message $m$ cannot be generated by any correct client, but is accepted by the server on an execution path not explored by Achilles, then $m$ is an undiscovered Trojan message.

False negatives can also occur due to the fact that our implementation of the *negate* operator under-approximates the real negate. As described in the Design section (§3.2), we use two alternative approaches to compute the negation: one approach relies on quantifier support in the Z3 SMT solver, while the other approach relies on tweaked constraints that are solved using the STP SMT solver. Z3 uses heuristics to eliminate quantifiers, and may fail to determine satisfiability. When this happens, Achilles falls back to customized constraints sent to STP. Achilles' customized *negate* is under-approximate; for example $negate((\lambda = 2 * x) \wedge (x > 0))$ produces $((\lambda = 2 * x) \wedge (x \leq 0))$, even though $-1$ and $1$ are also values for $\lambda$ that do not satisfy the initial expression. In our evaluation (§6), though, we found that although under-approximate, Achilles' customized implementation of *negate* can find Trojan messages in real distributed systems.

## 5. Implementation

In this section, we describe some implementation details of our Achilles prototype. We built Achilles on top of the S2E symbolic execution platform [8]. S2E can run whole systems; this means that S2E allows running the implementation of distributed system nodes in their real environment, enabling Achilles to also discover Trojan messages that are due to third party system components, such as libraries. S2E is also highly extensible through a rich plugin API, simplifying the development of Achilles.

### 5.1 Capturing System Calls

Achilles uses the *LD_PRELOAD* mechanism in Linux to intercept calls to the standard *libc* library. Thus, Achilles can insert symbolic data automatically by overwriting calls that read inputs, replacing concrete values with symbolic data.

Achilles also intercepts calls to network operations, in order to automatically mark server execution paths as *accepting* or *rejecting*. By default, we consider that any execution path that sends a reply to the user is *accepting*, while any execution path that waits for new messages is *rejecting*. The assumption behind this is that servers have a single event loop to listen for messages; restarting the loop means that the previous message was processed. This can be trivially extended to handle other common error signaling mechanisms (e.g., 4xx status codes in HTTP). Of course, human operators can also provide additional domain knowledge by manually placing *accept* or *reject* markers in the system under test. For example, if the target protocol uses encryption, it makes sense for the human operator to place an *accept* marker before the encryption of the reply.

Achilles uses system call interception in order to implement the Constructed Symbolic Local State mode. In order to avoid unnecessary forking in device drivers, Achilles intercepts network operations that send symbolic data and reroutes them through custom channels (currently, nodes are deployed within the same S2E instance and messages are rerouted through shared memory).

### 5.2 Annotations

Developers can use annotations to speed up Achilles. The annotations can be inserted in the code of the distributed system, or can be injected in the system at runtime, using S2E's plugin support.

*mark_accept* is a server-side annotation that marks an execution path as *accepting*, triggering the check for any Trojan messages.

*mark_reject* is a server-side annotation that marks an execution path as *rejecting*.

*function_start* and *function_end* are used in order to over-approximate the behavior of a function. The operator can add constraints between the two markers, in order to impose constraints on return values.

*drop_path* is used in conjunction with the *function_* markers in order to impose constraints on the return values.

*return_symbolic* is used in conjunction with the *function_* markers in order to set the return value of a function.

*make_symbolic* makes a system variable symbolic; it can be used in order to mark local state as symbolic.

For example, a developer can over-approximate the $getPeerID()$ function from the client code in Figure 3, as shown in Figure 9. The over-approximation bypasses the code of the function completely and returns a new symbolic value constrained to the interval $[0, 10]$. In our evaluation (§6) we used annotations to bypass cryptography and authentication code and speed up predicate extraction.

Achilles supports a mask to "hide" certain message fields from the analysis. The symbolic execution of the server still branches on the hidden values; however, Achilles does not check for Trojan messages involving those fields. The mask increases the signal-to-noise ratio of Achilles by hiding un-

```
int getPeerID() {
  function_start();
  int toRet = makeSymbolic();
  if ( toRet < 0 ) drop_path();
  if ( toRet > 10 ) drop_path();
  return_symbolic(toRet);
  function_end();
  ... //actual code of getPeerID
```

**Figure 9.** An example of using Achilles annotations in order to over-approximate a function to return values $[0, 10]$

interesting results, and also makes the analysis faster, since it reduces the workload of the SMT solver (Achilles applies the mask before calling the SMT solver).

## 6. Evaluation

In this section, we evaluate the ability of Achilles to analyze an implementation of a distributed system and extract Trojan messages. After a description of our experimental setup (6.1), we answer the following questions:

- How accurate is Achilles at finding Trojan messages in real distributed systems (§ 6.2)?
- What is the impact of Trojan messages discovered by Achilles on real distributed systems(§ 6.3)?
- How does Achilles manage large symbolic expressions (§ 6.4)?

### 6.1 Setup

We ran experiments on a 16-core (dual Intel E5-2690) machine with 256 GB of RAM running Ubuntu Linux 11.04.

Achilles gathered the client and server predicates by running individual system nodes in the S2E [7] platform. The S2E virtual machine ran 32-bit Ubuntu Linux 10.04.

We applied Achilles to FSP 2.8.1b26 [12], a UDP-based file transfer protocol, and to the latest version of PBFT [6], a Byzantine-fault-tolerant replication system.

***FSP*** is an implementation of a file transfer protocol. An FSP deployment consists of a server and several client utilities, which emulate well-known UNIX core utilities, such as *cp*, *mv*, *rm*, etc. The FSP implementation of these utilities parses command-line arguments (usually a target file path and a set of flags), tweaks the path to follow some protocol-specific rules (e.g., always start paths with '/'), and finally generates a corresponding command for the server. The server parses the command, performs the corresponding action on its local file system, and replies to the client.

An FSP command message has the following fields:

- *cmd* - 1-byte identifier of the requested action
- *sum* - 1-byte checksum
- *bb_key* - 2-byte message key
- *bb_seq* - 2-byte message sequence number
- *bb_len* - 2-byte length of file path
- *bb_pos* - 4-byte position of block in a file
- *buf* - arbitrary-length payload (file path + file data)

In our evaluation, we approximated the values of *sum*, *bb_key*, *bb_seq* and *bb_pos*: we added annotations in both the client and the server in order to bypass the checks on these fields, such that the client writes a predefined constant value and the server checks that value (in §7 we survey some approaches that can alleviate the problem of checksums, authentication or encryption). We focused our evaluation on how FSP parses file paths. We started the FSP clients with symbolic command line arguments (of fixed length) and inserted symbolic data in any system calls from the client. In the FSP server, we set *accept* markers at the point where it invokes system calls to make changes to its local file system, as requested by the command received from the client.

***PBFT*** is a Byzantine fault-tolerant replication protocol implementation. PBFT clients send requests to a set of replicas. The replicas ensure total order among requests from all clients, and forward them to an upper layer application.

A PBFT client request has the following fields:

- *tag* - 2-byte identifier of the message type
- *extra* - 2-byte flags field (1 bit per flag)
- *size* - 4-byte length of message
- *od* - 16-byte message digest
- *replier* - 2-byte identifier of responsible replica
- *command_size* - 2-byte length of command
- *cid* - 2-byte client id
- *rid* - 2-byte request id
- *command* - arbitrary-length command payload
- *MAC* - list of message authenticators, signed with a private key for each replica

In our evaluation, we approximated the values of the digest and authenticator fields: we used annotations in both the client and server in the same way as for FSP, replacing the digest and authenticators with predefined constant values. In the PBFT replica, we also over-approximated local state: the replicas keep an internal data structure to track previous requests from a given client, which we over-approximate with unconstrained symbolic values. We started a PBFT client and generated a request with symbolic *extra*, *replier*, *rid*, *cid*, and *command*. We set a fixed length for the *command*, list of authenticators, and for the overall message. We considered a message to be accepted when the replica generates a *Pre_prepare* message for the client request, initiating the agreement protocol.

### 6.2 Accuracy of Achilles

The purpose of this experiment is to quantify the accuracy of Achilles at finding Trojan messages. We compute the overlap between the expression of Trojan messages computed by

Achilles and a known set of Trojan messages in the protocol under test. Ideally, the overlap should be perfect—the representation generated by Achilles should cover all known Trojan messages, and no known non-Trojan messages.

We evaluated the accuracy of Achilles on real Trojan messages in FSP. Achilles discovered that the FSP server accepts messages where the file path length is less than the length reported in the message header (more details in §6.3).

To enable symbolic execution to complete, we restricted the FSP clients and servers to only handle file paths with length less than 5. For this scenario, we can mathematically compute how many different types of Trojan messages exist: there is one Trojan message for reported length 1 (the file path is empty), two Trojan messages for reported length 2 (file path is empty or has length 1), three Trojan messages for reported length 3 and four Trojan messages for reported length 4. We analyze eight FSP clients that have a single file path as argument. Therefore, there are in total $(1 + 2 + 3 + 4) * 8 = 80$ Trojan messages that differ in the reported length of the file path, request type or true length of the path.

The bounded path size enabled symbolic execution to run to completion. The total testing time for Achilles to find all Trojan messages was approximately 1 hour, which was split as follows:

- Gathering the client predicate took 3 minutes
- Preprocessing the client predicate took 15 minutes.
- Analyzing the server took 45 minutes.

Figure 10 shows the percentage of the known Trojan messages discovered by Achilles, as a function of server analysis time. Achilles produced the first Trojan message after 20 minutes of server analysis and discovered all Trojan messages in 43 minutes. Achilles did not produce any false positives. The figure shows how Achilles produces Trojan messages incrementally, as it analyzes the server; even if the analysis is interrupted before completion, Achilles produces valuable results.

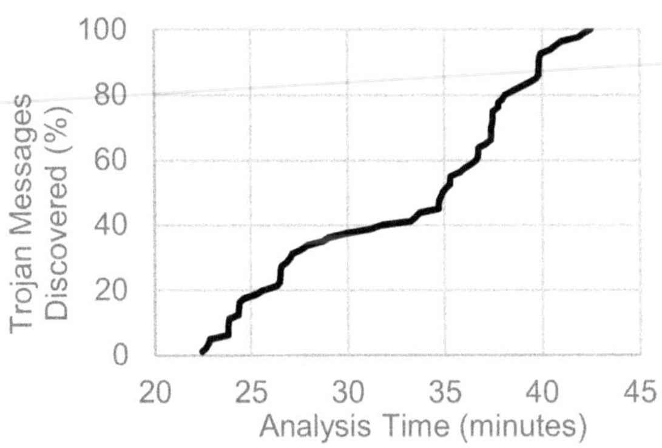


**Figure 10.** Percentage of real Trojan messages in FSP discovered by Achilles, as a function of time.

We compared Achilles to classic symbolic execution of a server node. We ran the FSP server in vanilla S2E, under the same conditions as Achilles (same bounds, annotations and approximation). Table 1 summarizes the results. Achilles discovers all Trojan messages and produces no false negatives. Classic symbolic execution also found all Trojan messages in 2 minutes, but with low signal-to-noise ratio. Trojan messages are "hidden" among valid messages, and it is left to the developer to sift among the results.

| | Achilles | Classic symbolic exec. |
|---|---|---|
| True Positives | 80 | 80 |
| False Positives | 0 | 7,520 |

**Table 1.** Results obtained by Achilles in 1 hour, compared to classic symbolic execution

As expected, classic symbolic execution of the server is faster than Achilles, since it performs fewer computations (it does not need to combine server and client constraints). However, classic symbolic execution cannot identify Trojan messages among other, valid messages. Even worse, in the case of FSP, all Trojan messages are on the same server execution paths as non-Trojan messages (as opposed to having execution paths that only contain Trojan messages and execution paths that only contain non-Trojan messages). This makes it difficult for the human operators to sift through results and discover Trojan messages—they need to investigate not only each execution path, but also each message on each execution path. This is a difficult task; as we also discuss in the Design section (§3.2), current SMT solvers are not designed to enumerate all values that satisfy a given constraint and are inefficient at doing so.

We ran the same experiment for PBFT. Achilles discovered a single type of Trojan message (more details in §6.3). Surprisingly, PBFT replicas make few checks on the data received from clients. They verify that request ids are recent and have not already been handled, verify that the client id is in a set of known clients and also check if the flags field marks the request as read-only.

Due to the simplicity of checks on the client request fields, Achilles completed the PBFT analysis in just a few seconds. The Trojan message discovered by Achilles appears on all execution paths in the server; however, just like for FSP, it is bundled on the same execution paths with valid messages. Thus, classic symbolic execution cannot easily identify the Trojan message among the valid messages, while Achilles identifies it accurately.

We also make a theoretical comparison between Achilles and a naive black-box fuzzing tool. There are other, more sophisticated fuzzers, which use various heuristics to improve performance. However, we are not aware of any fuzzer that optimizes towards anything similar to Trojan messages, so it would be difficult to obtain an unbiased comparison.

We first measured the maximum throughput that a fuzzing tool could achieve on FSP on our testbed: 75,000 tests per minute. Then, we compute the probability of discovering a Trojan message at random. In order to be fair, we only fuzz the same message fields that are analyzed by Achilles and by classic symbolic execution. There are 8 bytes relevant to the Trojan messages: *cmd*, *bb_len* and *buf*. There are 8 relevant possible values for the *command* field (corresponding to commands with a single file path argument). There are 4 relevant values for the *length* field. The FSP server only accepts printable characters in the file path (ASCII codes 33 to 126). Thus, there are $94 * 94 * 94 * 8 = 6.6$ million messages that exhibit a Trojan message for length 1 (first character in the message is '\0', second must be '\0' due to server checks, other three can be any ASCII character with code 33-126). In total, there are 66 million Trojan messages out of the $256^8 = 1.8 * 10^{19}$ possible bit combinations. This means that the expected number of Trojan messages found in 1 hour of fuzzing is 0.00001. Fuzzing also produces 4.5 million non-Trojan messages, which correspond to false positives.

Our experiments show that Achilles is significantly more efficient at discovering Trojan messages than fuzzing or classic symbolic execution. While classic symbolic can find all messages accepted by the server faster than Achilles, it cannot disambiguate between Trojan and non-Trojan messages. Black-box fuzzing is several orders of magnitude worse than symbolic execution.

### 6.3 The Impact of Trojan Messages

***FSP: The Wildcard Character.*** Achilles discovered a bug in FSP related to the handling of the '*' wildcard character. In essence, FSP clients always expand the '*' wildcard before sending a command to the server. There is no possibility of escaping the '*' character, thus correct clients cannot send a command with '*' in a source file path to the server. The server, however, accepts any printable character, including '*' in the file paths it receives. This leads to an interesting behavior where it is possible to create files containing '*' on the server, but not possible to delete them directly.

In UNIX environments, shells use a simple form of pattern matching in order to expand file paths using wildcard characters (this simple pattern matching is referred to as globbing). For example, the command *'rm file*'* will delete all files with name prefixed by *'file'* from the current directory. The '*' character is a wildcard that can be expanded to any sequence of characters. The expansion of the wildcard is handled directly by the shell, before invoking the *rm* utility. Suppose the current directory has files *'file1'*, *'file2'* and *'file3'* and that the user executes the command *'rm file*'*. The shell will initially parse the command and expand *'rm file*'* into *'rm file1 file2 file3'*. Then the shell invokes *'rm'* with the three command line arguments.

The FSP implementation emulates the regular UNIX globbing behavior. When parsing command-line arguments, the FSP client will first try to expand any *source* file path containing a wildcard. Unlike most shells, however, the FSP globbing does not allow the user to escape any wildcard character. *Destination* file paths, however, are not globbed; for example the *'mv file1* file2*'* will rename any file that matches the pattern *'file1*'* to the literal string *'file2*'*. The FSP server handles wildcards like any regular character.

Trojan messages in FSP can lead to an interesting scenario, where it is possible to create a file called *'file*'* on the server, but it is then difficult to actually remove the respective file. A file called *'file*'* can be created by a user of FSP (e.g., *'mv file file*'*), by a malicious third party that has access to the server, or even by a bit flip that appears on the client during a command execution (a single bit flip can convert the ASCII 'j' character into '*').

Once the file named *'file*'* appears on the server, it is difficult to remove. Calling *'rm file*'* would remove *'file*'*, but would also remove any other file prefixed by *'file'*, including a potentially valuable *'fileWithAllMyBankAccounts'*. Similarly, *'mv file* fileToDelete'* would rename all files prefixed by *'file'* to *'fileToDelete'*, removing all but one of the original files. Calling *'rm file*'* would delete all files prefixed by *'file\'*, since there is no escape character in the FSP globbing.

It is interesting to point out that this bug discovered using Achilles is a semantic bug, which makes it difficult to detect automatically using other approaches. While there are techniques to detect buffer overflows or divisions by zero automatically, the FSP bug cannot be found unless the developers write a complex (and potentially buggy) specification of correct behavior. This is one of the main benefits of finding Trojan messages.

***FSP: Mismatched String Lengths.*** Achilles also discovered that the FSP server does not check whether the file path lengths it receives in commands match the actual lengths. It accepts messages that have the actual file path length smaller than the value in the message's *length* field (i.e., there is a *'\0'* character in the file path). The bug allows malicious users to send an additional arbitrary payload to the server.

***PBFT: The MAC Attack.*** Achilles discovered that PBFT replicas (servers) accept client requests without checking their authentication code. This leads to a known vulnerability of the protocol, known as the MAC attack [10].

Clients can send messages with incorrect authenticators. The first replica to receive the client request does not verify any of the authenticators. If forwards the message to other replicas, which discover the incorrect authenticator, but cannot know whether the original client or the first replica have corrupted the message. In order to guarantee progress, they initiate an expensive recovery protocol, which impacts performance. This allows incorrect nodes to have a significant impact on the performance of the system. A node whose private key was corrupted due to a memory error will always produce incorrect MAC authenticators and will trigger recovery. Alternatively, a malicious client can also corrupt its own messages in order to trigger the expensive recovery mechanism and slow down the system, affecting the service of other, correct clients.

This vulnerability is an interesting example of the subtle effects that Trojan messages can have on a system.

### 6.4 Handling Large Client Predicates

In this section, we analyze internal details of Achilles. We look at how the optimizations described in §3.3 enable Achilles to handle large client predicates.

Figure 11 shows the number of client path predicates Achilles keeps for each execution path analyzed during the FSP server exploration, as a function of the length of the path. The figure shows results for the paths as they are incrementally generated—many of the points in the figure represent incomplete paths. A point at length 7 with 1,000 matching predicates means that there exists an execution path in the server which encountered 6 branching points that depend on symbolic data, and can be triggered by messages in 1,000 different path predicates. Recall from §3.2 that Achilles uses these path predicates to search for any existing Trojan messages—the more path predicates in a state, the more complex the check.

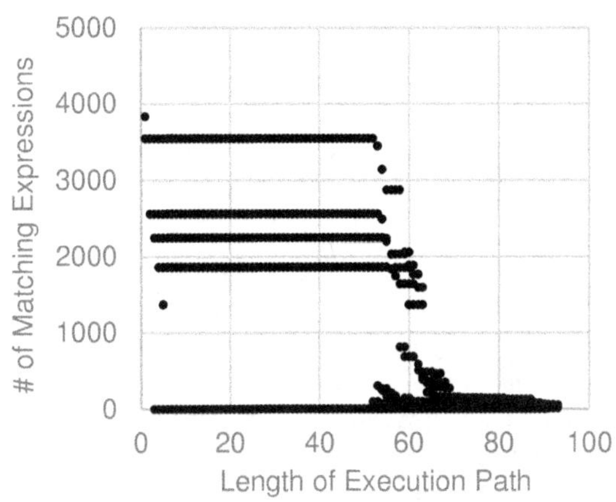


**Figure 11.** Number of client path predicates that can trigger each execution path in the FSP server, as a function of the length of the path.

The number of path predicates decreases as the length of paths increases—longer execution paths become more and more specialized, and can be triggered by a smaller group of messages. This makes the check for Trojan messages easier, as Achilles makes fewer calls to the solver.

To quantify the effect of optimizations, we compared Achilles to a non-optimized implementation of symbolic constraint differencing. We ran unmodified S2E on both the FSP client and server, and then computed Trojan messages a posteriori. The total execution time of the non-optimized implementation was 2 hours and 15 minutes, compared to the 1 hour and 3 minutes required by Achilles.

## 7. Related Work

To the extent of our knowledge, there is no previous work that directly targets Trojan messages.

Caballero and Song [5] use dynamic symbolic execution in order to reverse engineer the message format and semantics of an undocumented protocol. In this paper, we assume that Achilles is used by the distributed system developers, in order to detect corner cases in their implementation. Thus, the purpose is not to produce a documentation of the protocol, but concrete corner cases that trigger incorrect behavior.

Caballero et al. [4] used symbolic execution to find bugs in malware. They faced the challenge of handling encryption and obfuscation techniques used in the malware, and developed a technique that only solves subsets of path constraints and then restitches the individual solutions to obtain a complete input. Achilles is more targeted, focusing on a specific type of bugs that cannot be found with other techniques. The work by Caballero et al. can be integrated with Achilles to enable the predicate extraction to handle complex operations without human operator support.

Achilles analyzes distributed system nodes in isolation and then composes the results of the analyses. This is similar to the Compositional Dynamic Test Generation proposed by Patrice Godefroid [14]. The predicate $P_C$ of a client node can be seen as a functional summary, which is then integrated in the analysis of a server node. In the case of Achilles, though, we do not use the summary directly, as we are actually interested in the negation of the summary.

The idea of analyzing distributed nodes in isolation was also explored by Guerraoui and Yabandeh [15]. In their work, the authors proposed model checking individual nodes in isolation, separated from the complexity of network message interleaving. In Achilles, we do not analyze nodes in isolation for performance reasons, but in order to catch specific bugs.

Maurer and Brumley [20] use tandem symbolic execution of the pre- and post-patch versions of a given program. Their approach compares the behaviors of the two versions and checks that the patch only affects the buggy executions it was meant to fix. A similar approach is taken by Person et al. [21] to characterize code changes. This is similar in spirit to the way Achilles compares the predicate of the client and the predicate of the server in order to check for Trojan messages.

In Achilles, we currently ignore the order in which messages are received, focusing strictly on the effect of message contents. Achilles could be enhanced by techniques such as MODIST [22] to also consider alternative orderings. Alternatively, the distributed system under test can be deployed with DDOS [16], which ensures deterministic behavior.

Cloud9 [3] is a symbolic execution tool that can analyze distributed systems. Similar to Achilles' Constructed Local State, Cloud9 reroutes symbolic messages through alternative channels.

## 8. Conclusion

Trojan messages represent a type of bug specific to distributed systems—an artifact of different implementations of the same protocol specification. Trojan messages occur in real distributed systems and can cause unpredictable behavior: from low performance in the case of Amazon S3 and PBFT, to loss of data in the case of FSP.

We propose Achilles, a system designed to efficiently discover Trojan messages in distributed system implementations. Achilles uses dynamic white-box analysis in order to extract the grammar of messages accepted by servers, and the grammar of messages that can be generated by clients. Achilles then computes the set of Trojan messages as the difference between the two. We described the basic principles behind Achilles, as well as the optimizations that make it practical.

We applied Achilles to real distributed systems, discovering bugs that are difficult to find with alternative techniques. Our evaluation shows that Achilles is efficient at discovering Trojan messages; it discovered all instances of a Trojan message in FSP, while producing no false positives.

## Acknowledgments

We are indebted to the anonymous reviewers, and to Jonas Wagner and Volodymyr Kuznetsov for their insightful feedback and generous help in improving this paper. We are grateful to the SNF (Sinergia Project No. CRSII2_136318/1) and to IBM for supporting our work.

## References

[1] Amazon s3 availability event: July 20, 2008. Retrieved on 2013-07-20. http://status.aws.amazon.com/s3-20080720.html.

[2] S. Anand, P. Godefroid, and N. Tillmann. Demand-driven compositional symbolic execution. In *Intl. Conf. on Tools and Algorithms for the Construction and Analysis of Systems*, 2008.

[3] S. Bucur, V. Ureche, C. Zamfir, and G. Candea. Parallel symbolic execution for automated real-world software testing. In *ACM EuroSys European Conf. on Computer Systems*, 2011.

[4] J. Caballero, P. Poosankam, S. McCamant, D. Babic, and D. Song. Input Generation via Decomposition and Re-Stitching: Finding Bugs in Malware. In *Proceedings of the 17th ACM Conference on Computer and Communication Security*, Chicago, IL, October 2010.

[5] J. Caballero and D. Song. Automatic Protocol Reverse-Engineering: Message Format Extraction and Field Semantics. *Computer Networks*, 57(2):451 – 474, 2013.

[6] M. Castro and B. Liskov. Practical byzantine fault tolerance. In *Symp. on Operating Sys. Design and Implem.*, 1999.

[7] V. Chipounov, V. Kuznetsov, and G. Candea. S2E: A platform for in-vivo multi-path analysis of software systems. In *Intl. Conf. on Architectural Support for Programming Languages and Operating Systems*, 2011.

[8] V. Chipounov, V. Kuznetsov, and G. Candea. The S2E platform: Design, implementation, and applications. *ACM Transactions on Computer Systems*, 30(1), 2012. Special issue: Best papers of ASPLOS.

[9] E. Clarke, O. Grumberg, S. Jha, Y. Lu, and H. Veith. Counterexample-guided abstraction refinement for symbolic model checking. *JACM*, 50(5):752–794, 2003.

[10] A. Clement, E. Wong, L. Alvisi, M. Dahlin, and M. Marchetti. Making byzantine fault tolerant systems tolerate byzantine faults. In *Symp. on Networked Systems Design and Implem.*, 2009.

[11] L. M. de Moura and N. Bjørner. Z3: An efficient SMT solver. In *Intl. Conf. on Tools and Algorithms for the Construction and Analysis of Systems*, 2008.

[12] File service protocol. Retrieved on 24-Jul-2013. http://fsp.sourceforge.net/.

[13] V. Ganesh and D. L. Dill. A decision procedure for bit-vectors and arrays. In *Intl. Conf. on Computer Aided Verification*, 2007.

[14] P. Godefroid. Compositional dynamic test generation. In *Symp. on Principles of Programming Languages*, 2007.

[15] R. Guerraoui and M. Yabandeh. Model checking a networked system without the network. In *Symp. on Networked Systems Design and Implem.*, 2011.

[16] N. Hunt, T. Bergan, L. Ceze, and S. D. Gribble. Ddos: taming nondeterminism in distributed systems. In *Intl. Conf. on Architectural Support for Programming Languages and Operating Systems*, 2013.

[17] J. C. King. Symbolic execution and program testing. *Communications of the ACM*, 1976.

[18] K. Krishnan. Weathering the unexpected. *Queue*, 10(9):30:30–30:37.

[19] L. Lamport. The part-time parliament. *ACM Transactions on Computer Systems*, 16(2):133–169, 1998.

[20] M. Maurer and D. Brumley. Tachyon: tandem execution for efficient live patch testing. In *USENIX Security Symp.*, 2012.

[21] S. Person, M. B. Dwyer, S. Elbaum, and C. S. Păsăreanu. Differential symbolic execution. In *Symp. on the Foundations of Software Eng.*, 2008.

[22] J. Yang, T. Chen, M. Wu, Z. Xu, X. Liu, H. Lin, M. Yang, F. Long, L. Zhang, and L. Zhou. MoDist: Transparent model checking of unmodified distributed systems. In *Symp. on Networked Systems Design and Implem.*, 2009.

[23] C. Zamfir and G. Candea. Execution synthesis: A technique for automated debugging. In *ACM EuroSys European Conf. on Computer Systems*, 2010.

# Quasar: Resource-Efficient and QoS-Aware Cluster Management

Christina Delimitrou and Christos Kozyrakis
Stanford University
{cdel, kozyraki}@stanford.edu

## Abstract

Cloud computing promises flexibility and high performance for users and high cost-efficiency for operators. Nevertheless, most cloud facilities operate at very low utilization, hurting both cost effectiveness and future scalability.

We present Quasar, a cluster management system that increases resource utilization while providing consistently high application performance. Quasar employs three techniques. First, it does not rely on resource reservations, which lead to underutilization as users do not necessarily understand workload dynamics and physical resource requirements of complex codebases. Instead, users express performance constraints for each workload, letting Quasar determine the right amount of resources to meet these constraints at any point. Second, Quasar uses classification techniques to quickly and accurately determine the impact of the amount of resources (scale-out and scale-up), type of resources, and interference on performance for each workload and dataset. Third, it uses the classification results to jointly perform resource allocation and assignment, quickly exploring the large space of options for an efficient way to pack workloads on available resources. Quasar monitors workload performance and adjusts resource allocation and assignment when needed. We evaluate Quasar over a wide range of workload scenarios, including combinations of distributed analytics frameworks and low-latency, stateful services, both on a local cluster and a cluster of dedicated EC2 servers. At steady state, Quasar improves resource utilization by 47% in the 200-server EC2 cluster, while meeting performance constraints for workloads of all types.

***Categories and Subject Descriptors*** C.5.1 [Computer System Implementation]: Super (very large) computers; D.4.1 [Process Management]: Scheduling


*ASPLOS '14*, March 1–5, 2014, Salt Lake City, Utah, USA.

ACM 978-1-4503-2305-5/14/03... $15.00.
http://dx.doi.org/10.1145/http://dx.doi.org/10.1145/2541940.2541941

***Keywords*** Cloud computing, datacenters, resource efficiency, quality of service, cluster management, resource allocation and assignment.

## 1. Introduction

An increasing amount of computing is now hosted on public clouds, such as Amazon's EC2 [2], Windows Azure [65] and Google Compute Engine [25], or on private clouds managed by frameworks such as VMware vCloud [61], OpenStack [48], and Mesos [32]. Cloud platforms provide two major advantages for end-users and cloud operators: *flexibility* and *cost efficiency* [9, 10, 31]. Users can quickly launch jobs that range from short, single-process applications to large, multi-tier services, only paying for the resources used at each point. Cloud operators can achieve economies of scale by building large-scale datacenters (DCs) and by sharing their resources between multiple users and workloads.

Nevertheless, most cloud facilities operate at very low utilization which greatly adheres cost effectiveness [9, 51]. This is the case even for cloud facilities that use cluster management frameworks that enable cluster sharing across workloads. In Figure 1, we present a utilization analysis for a production cluster at Twitter with thousands of servers, managed by Mesos [32] over one month. The cluster mostly hosts user-facing services. The aggregate CPU utilization is consistently below 20%, even though reservations reach up to 80% of total capacity (Fig. 1.a). Even when looking at individual servers, their majority does not exceed 50% utilization on any week (Fig. 1.c). Typical memory use is higher (40-50%) but still differs from the reserved capacity. Figure 1.d shows that very few workloads reserve the right amount of resources (compute resources shown here, similar for memory); most workloads (70%) overestimate reservations by up to 10x, while many (20%) underestimate reservations by up to 5x. Similarly, Reiss et al. showed that a 12,000-server Google cluster managed with the more mature Borg system consistently achieves aggregate CPU utilization of 25-35% and aggregate memory utilization of 40% [51]. In contrast, reserved resources exceed 75% and 60% of available capacity for CPU and memory respectively.

Twitter and Google are in the high end of the utilization spectrum. Utilization estimates are even lower for cloud facilities that do not co-locate workloads the way Google and

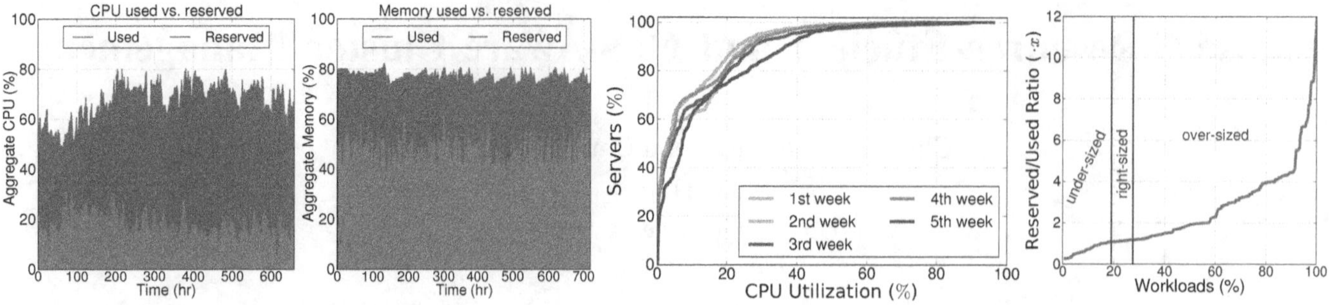


Figure 1: Resource utilization over 30 days for a large production cluster at Twitter managed with Mesos. (a) and (b): utilization vs reservation for the aggregate CPU and memory capacity of the cluster; (c) CDF of CPU utilization for individual servers for each week in the 30 day period; (d) ratio of reserved vs used CPU resources for each of the thousands of workloads that ran on the cluster during this period.

Twitter do with Borg and Mesos respectively. Various analyses estimate industry-wide utilization between 6% [15] and 12% [24, 59]. A recent study estimated server utilization on Amazon EC2 in the 3% to 17% range [38]. Overall, low utilization is a major challenge for cloud facilities. Underutilized servers contribute to capital expenses and, since they are not energy proportional [36, 42], to operational expenses as well. Even if a company can afford the cost, low utilization is still a scaling limitation. With many cloud DCs consuming 10s of megawatts, it is difficult to add more servers without running into the limits of what the nearby electricity facility can deliver.

In this work, we increase resource utilization in datacenters through better cluster management. The manager is responsible for providing resources to various workloads in a manner that achieves their performance goals, while maximizing the utilization of available resources. The manager must make two major decisions; first allocate the right amount of resources for each workload (*resource allocation*) and then select the specific servers that will satisfy a given allocation (*resource assignment*). While there has been significant progress in cluster management frameworks [21, 32, 54, 63], there are still major challenges that limit their effectiveness in concurrently meeting application performance and resource utilization goals. First, it is particularly difficult to determine the resources needed for each workload. The load of user-facing services varies widely within a day, while the load of analytics tasks depends on their complexity and their dataset size. Most existing cluster managers side-step allocation altogether, requiring users or workloads to express their requirements in the form of a reservation. Nevertheless, the workload developer does not necessarily understand the physical resource requirements of complex codebases or the variations in load and dataset size. As shown in Figure 1.d, only a small fraction of the workloads submitted to the Twitter cluster provided a right-sized reservation. Undersized reservations lead to poor application performance, while oversized reservations lead to low resource utilization.

Equally important, resource allocation and resource assignment are fundamentally linked. The first reason is heterogeneity of resources, which is quite high as servers get installed and replaced over the typical 15-year lifetime of a DC [9, 20]. A workload may be able to achieve its current performance goals with ten high-end or twenty low-end servers. Similarly, a workload may be able to use low-end CPUs if the memory allocation is high or vice versa. The second reason is interference between co-located workloads that can lead to severe performance losses [41, 69]. This is particularly problematic for user-facing services that must meet strict, tail-latency requirements (e.g., low $99^{th}$ percentile latency) under a wide range of traffic scenarios ranging from low load to unexpected spikes [16]. Naïvely co-locating these services with low-priority, batch tasks that consume any idling resources can lead to unacceptable latencies, even at low load [41]. This is the reason why cloud operators deploy low-latency services on dedicated servers that operate at low utilization most of the time. In facilities that share resources between workloads, users often exaggerate resource reservations to side-step performance unpredictability due to interference. Finally, most cloud facilities are large and involve thousands of servers and workloads, putting tight constraints on the complexity and time that can be spent making decisions [54]. As new, unknown workloads are submitted, old workloads get updated, new datasets arise, and new server configurations are installed, it is impractical for the cluster manager to analyze all possible combinations of resource allocations and assignments.

We present *Quasar*, a cluster manager that maximizes resource utilization while meeting performance and QoS constraints for each workload. Quasar includes three key features. First, it shifts from a *reservation-centric* to a *performance-centric* approach for cluster management. Instead of users expressing low-level resource requests to the manager, Quasar allows users to communicate the performance constraints of the application in terms of throughput and/or latency, depending on the application type. This high-level specification allows Quasar to determine the *least amount of the available resources* needed to meet performance constraints at any point, given the current state of the cluster in terms of available servers and active workloads. The allocation varies over time to adjust to changes in the workload or system state. The performance-centric approach simplifies both the user and cloud manager's roles as it removes the need for exaggerated reservations, allows transparent handling of unknown, evolving, or irregular workloads, and provides additional flexibility towards cost-efficient allocation.

Second, Quasar uses *fast classification techniques to determine the impact of different resource allocations and assignments on workload performance*. By combining a small amount of profiling information from the workload itself with the large amount of data from previously-scheduled workloads, Quasar can quickly and accurately generate the information needed for efficient resource assignment and allocation without the need for a priori analysis of the application and its dataset. Specifically, Quasar performs four parallel classifications on each application to evaluate the four main aspects of resource allocation and assignment: the impact of scale-up (amount of resources per server), the impact of scale-out (number of servers per workload), the impact of server configuration, and the impact of interference (which workloads can be co-located).

Third, Quasar *performs resource allocation and assignment jointly*. The classification results are used to determine the right amount and specific set of resources assigned to the workload. Hence, Quasar avoids overprovisioning workloads that are currently at low load and can compensate for increased interference or the unavailability of high-end servers by assigning fewer or lower-quality resources to them. Moreover, Quasar monitors performance throughout the workload's execution. If performance deviates from the expressed constraints, Quasar reclassifies the workload and adjusts the allocation and/or assignment decisions to meet the performance constraints or minimize the resources used.

We have implemented and evaluated a prototype for Quasar managing a local 40-server cluster and a 200-node cluster of dedicated EC2 servers. We use a wide range of workloads including analytics frameworks (Hadoop, Storm, Spark), latency-critical and stateful services (memcached, Cassandra), and batch workloads. We compare Quasar to reservation-based resource allocation coupled with resource assignment based on load or similar classification techniques. Quasar improves server utilization at steady state by 47% on average at high load in the 200-server cluster, while also improving performance of individual workloads compared to the alternative schemes. We show that Quasar can right-size the allocation of analytics and latency-critical workloads better than built-in schedulers of frameworks like Hadoop, or auto-scaling systems. It can also select assignments that take heterogeneity and interference into account so that throughput and latency constraints are closely met.

# 2. Motivation

## 2.1 Cluster Management Overview

A cluster management framework provides various services including security, fault tolerance, and monitoring. This paper focuses on the two tasks most relevant to resource efficiency: resource allocation and resource assignment of incoming workloads. Previous work has mostly treated the two separately.

**Resource allocation:** Allocation refers to determining the amount of resources used by a workload: number of servers, number of cores and amount of memory and bandwidth resources per server. Managers like Mesos [32], Torque [58], and Omega [54] expect workloads to make resource reservations. Mesos processes these requests and, based on availability and fairness issues [27], makes resource offers to individual frameworks (e.g., Hadoop) that the framework can accept or reject. Dejavu identifies a few workload classes and reuses previous resource allocations for each class to minimize reallocation overheads [60]. CloudScale [56], PRESS [29], AGILE [46] and the work by Gmach et al. [28] perform online prediction of resource needs, often without a priori workload knowledge. Finally, auto-scaling systems such as Rightscale [52] automatically scale the number of physical or virtual instances used by webserving workloads to react to observed changes in server load.

**Resource assignment:** Assignment refers to selecting the specific resources that satisfy an allocation. The two biggest challenges of assignment are server heterogeneity and interference between colocated workloads [41, 44, 69], when servers are shared to improve utilization. The most closely related work to this paper is Paragon [20]. Given a resource allocation for an unknown, incoming workload, Paragon uses classification techniques to quickly estimate the impact of heterogeneity and interference on performance. Paragon uses this information to assign each workload to server type(s) that provide the best performance and colocate workloads that do not interfere with each other. Nathuji et al. [45] developed a feedback-based scheme that tunes resource assignment to mitigate interference effects. Yang et al. developed an online scheme that detects memory pressure and finds colocations that avoid interference on latency-sensitive workloads [69]. Similarly, DeepDive detects and manages interference between co-scheduled applications in a VM system [47]. Finally, CPI2 [73] throttles low-priority workloads that induce interference to important services. In terms of managing heterogeneity, Nathuji et al. [44] and Mars et al. [40] quantified its impact on conventional benchmarks and Google services and designed schemes to predict the most appropriate server type for each workload.

## 2.2 The Case for Coordinated Cluster Management

Despite the progress in cluster management technology, resource utilization is quite low in most private and public clouds (see Figure 1 and [15, 24, 38, 51, 59]). There are two

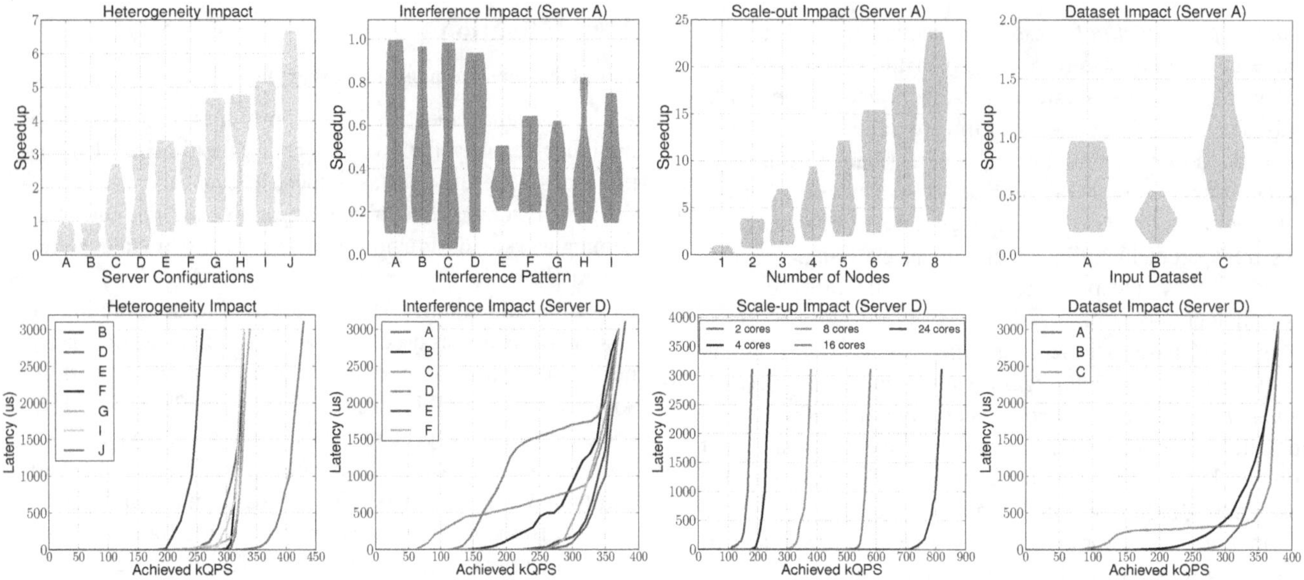


Figure 2: The impact of heterogeneity, interference, scale-out, scale-up, and dataset on the performance of Hadoop (top row) and memcached (bottom row). Server configurations, interference patterns, and datasets are summarized in Table 1. For Hadoop, the variability in the violin plots is due to scaling-up the resource allocations within a server (cores and/or memory).

| platforms | **A** | **B** | **C** | **D** | **E** | **F** | **G** | **H** | **I** | **J** |
|---|---|---|---|---|---|---|---|---|---|---|
| cores | 2 | 4 | 8 | 8 | 8 | 8 | 12 | 12 | 16 | 24 |
| memory(GB) | 4 | 8 | 12 | 16 | 20 | 24 | 16 | 24 | 48 | 48 |
| interference | **A** | **B** | **C** | **D** | **E** | **F** | **G** | **H** | **I** | |
| pattern | - | memory | L1I cache | LL cache | disk I/O | network | L2 cache | CPU | prefetch | |
| input dataset | | | **A** | | | **B** | | | **C** | |
| hadoop | | | netflix: 2.1GB | | | mahout: 10GB | | | wikipedia: 55GB | |
| memcached | | | 100B reads | | | 2KB reads | | | 100B reads-100B writes | |

Table 1: Server platforms (*A-J*), interference patterns (*A-I*) and input datasets (*A-C*) used for the analysis in Figure 2.

major shortcomings current cluster managers have. First, it is particularly difficult for a user or workload to understand its resource needs and express them as a reservation. Second, resource allocation and assignment are fundamentally linked. An efficient allocation depends on the amount and type of resources available and the behavior of other workloads running on the cluster.

Figure 2 illustrates these issues by analyzing the impact of various allocations, assignments, and workload aspects on two representative applications, one batch and one latency-critical: a large Hadoop job running a recommendation algorithm on the Netflix dataset [11] and a memcached service under a read-intensive load. For Hadoop, we report speedup over a single node of server configuration A using all available cores and memory. Server configurations, interference settings and datasets are summarized in Table 1. The variability in each violin plot is due to the different amounts of resources (cores and memory) allocated within each server. For memcached, we report the latency-throughput graphs. Real-world memcached deployments limit throughput to achieve 99th-percentile latencies between 0.2ms and 1ms.

The first row of Figure 2 illustrates the behavior of Hadoop. The heterogeneity graph shows that the choice of server configuration introduces performance variability of up to 7x, while the amount of resources allocated within each server introduces variability of up to 10x. The interference graph shows that for server A, depending on the amount of resources used, Hadoop may be insensitive to certain types of interference or slowdown by up to 10x. Similarly, the scale-out graph shows that depending on the amount of resources per server, scaling may be sublinear or superlinear. Finally, the dataset graph shows that the dataset complexity and size can have 3x impact on Hadoop's performance. Note that in addition to high variability, the violin plots show that the probability distributions change significantly across different allocations. The results are similar for memcached, as shown in the second row of Figure 2. The position of the knee of the throughput-latency curve depends heavily on the type of server used (3x variability), the interference patterns

(7x variability), the amount of resources used per server (8x variability), and workload characteristics such as data size and read/write mixes (3x variability).

It is clear from Figure 2 that it is quite difficult for a user or workload to translate a performance goal to a resource reservation. To right-size an allocation, we need to understand how scale-out, scale-up, heterogeneity in the currently available servers, and interference from the currently running jobs affect a workload with a specific dataset. Hence, separating resource allocation and assignment through reservations is bound to be suboptimal, either in terms of resource efficiency or in terms of workload performance (see Figure 1). Similarly, performing first allocation and then assignment in two separate steps is also suboptimal. Cluster management must handle both tasks in an integrated manner.

# 3. Quasar

## 3.1 Overview

Quasar differs from previous work in three ways. First, it shifts away from resource reservations and adopts a *performance-centric* approach. Quasar exports a high-level interface that allows users or the schedulers integrated in some frameworks (e.g., Hadoop or Spark) to express the performance constraint the workload should meet. The interface differentiates across workload types. For latency-critical workloads, constraints are expressed as a queries per second (QPS) target and a latency QoS constraint. For distributed frameworks like Hadoop, the constraint is execution time. For single node, single-threaded or multi-threaded workloads the constraint is a low-level metric of instructions-per-second (IPS). Once performance constraints are specified, it is up to Quasar to find a resource allocation and assignment that satisfies them.

Second, Quasar uses fast classification techniques to quickly and accurately estimate the impact different resource allocation and resource assignment decisions have on workload performance. Upon admission, an incoming workload and dataset is profiled on a few servers for a short period of time (a few seconds up to a few minutes - see Sec. 3.2). This limited profiling information is combined with information from the few workloads characterized offline and the many workloads that have been previously scheduled in the system using classification techniques. The result of classification is accurate estimates of application performance as we vary the type or number of servers, the amount of resources within a server, and the interference from other workloads. In other words, we estimate graphs similar to those shown in Figure 2. This classification-based approach eliminates the need for exhaustive online characterization and allows efficient scheduling of unknown or evolving workloads, or new datasets. Even with classification, exhaustively estimating performance for all allocation-assignment combinations would be infeasible. Instead, Quasar decomposes the problem to the four main components of allocation and assignment: resources per node and number of nodes for allocation, and server type and degree of interference for assignment. This dramatically reduces the complexity of the classification problem.

Third, Quasar uses the result of classification to jointly perform resource allocation and assignment, eliminating the inherent inefficiencies of performing allocation without knowing the assignment challenges. A greedy algorithm combines the result of the four independent classifications to select the number and specific set of resources that will meet (or get as close as possible to) the performance constraints. Quasar also monitors workload performance. If the constraint is not met at some point or resources are idling, either the workload changed (load or phase change), classification was incorrect, or the greedy scheme led to suboptimal results. In any case, Quasar adjusts the allocation and assignment if possible, or reclassifies and reschedules the workload from scratch.

Quasar uses similar classification techniques as those introduced in Paragon [20]. Paragon handles only resource assignment. Hence, its classification step can only characterize workloads with respect to heterogeneity (server type) and interference. In contrast, Quasar handles both resource allocation and assignment. Hence, its classification step also characterizes scale-out and scale-up issues for each workload. Moreover, the space of allocations and assignments that Quasar must explore is significantly larger than the space of assignments explored by Paragon. Finally, Quasar introduces an interface for performance constraints in order to decouple user goals from resource allocation and assignment. In Section 6, we compare Quasar to Paragon coupled with current resource allocation approaches to showcase the advantages of Quasar.

## 3.2 Fast and Accurate Classification

Collaborative filtering techniques are often used in recommendation systems with extremely sparse inputs [50]. One of their most publicized use was the Netflix Challenge [11], where techniques such as Singular Value Decomposition (SVD) and PQ-reconstruction [13, 35, 50, 66] were used to provide movie recommendations to users that had only rated a few movies themselves, by exploiting the large number of ratings from other users. The input to SVD in this case is a very sparse matrix $A$ with users as rows, movies as columns and ratings as elements. SVD decomposes $A$ to the product of the matrix of singular values $\Sigma$ that represents similarity concepts in $A$, the matrix of left singular vectors $U$ that represents correlation between rows of $A$ and similarity concepts, and the matrix of right singular vectors $V$ that represents the correlation between columns of $A$ and similarity concepts ($A = U \cdot \Sigma \cdot V^T$). A similarity concept can be that users that liked "Lord of the Rings 1" also liked "Lord of the Rings 2". PQ-reconstruction with Stochastic Gradient Descent (SGD), a simple latent-factor model [13, 66], uses $\Sigma$, $U$, and $V$ to reconstruct the missing entries in $A$. Starting with the SVD output, $P^T$ is initialized to $\Sigma V^T$ and $Q$ to $U$ which provides an initial reconstruction of $A$. Subsequently, SGD iterates over all elements of the reconstructed matrix $R$=$Q$·$P^T$ until convergence.

For each element $r_{ui}$ of $R$:

$$\epsilon_{ui} = r_{ui} - \mu - b_u - q_i \cdot p_u{}^T$$
$$q_i \leftarrow q_i + \eta(\epsilon_{ui} p_u - \lambda q_i)$$
$$p_u \leftarrow p_u + \eta(\epsilon_{ui} q_i - \lambda p_u)$$

until $|\epsilon|_{L_2} = \sqrt{\sum_{u,i} |\epsilon_{ui}|^2}$ becomes marginal. $\eta$ is the learning rate and $\lambda$ the regularization factor of SGD and their values are determined empirically. In the above model, we also include the average rating $\mu$ and a user bias $b_u$ that account for the divergence of specific users from the norm. Once the matrix is reconstructed, SVD is applied once again to generate movie recommendations by quantifying the correlation between new and existing users. The complexity of SVD is $O(min(N^2M, M^2N))$, where $M$, $N$ the dimensions of $A$, and the complexity of PQ-reconstruction with SGD is $O(N \cdot M)$.

In Paragon [20], collaborative filtering was used to quickly classify workloads with respect to interference and heterogeneity. A few applications are profiled exhaustively offline to derive their performance on different servers and with varying amounts of interference. An incoming application is profiled for one minute on two of the many server configurations, with and without interference in two shared resources. SVD and PQ-reconstruction are used to accurately estimate the performance of the workload on the remaining server configurations and with interference on the remaining types of resources. Paragon showed that collaborative filtering can quickly and accurately classify unknown applications with respect to tens of server configurations and tens of sources of interference.

The classification engine in Quasar extends the one in Paragon in two ways. First, it uses collaborative filtering to estimate the impact of resource scale-out (more servers) and scale-up (more resources per server) on application performance. These additional classifications are necessary for resource allocation. Second, it tailors classifications to different workload types. This is necessary because different types for workloads have different constraints and allocation knobs. For instance, in a webserver we can apply both scale-out and scale-up and we must monitor queries per second (QPS) and latency. For Hadoop, we can also configure workload parameters such as the number of mappers per node, heapsize, and compression. For a single-node workload, scaling up might be the only option while the metric of interest can be instructions per second. The performance constraints interface of Quasar allows users to specify the type of submitted applications.

Overall, Quasar classifies for scale-up, scale-out, heterogeneity, and interference. The four classifications are done independently and in parallel to reduce complexity and overheads. The greedy scheduler combines information from all four. Because of the decomposition of the problem the matrix dimensions decrease, and classification becomes fast enough that it can be applied on every workload submission, even if the same workload is submitted multiple times with different datasets. Hence there is no need to classify for dataset sensitivity.

**Scale-up classification:** This classification explores how performance varies with the amount of resources used within a server. We currently focus on compute cores, memory and storage capacity. We will address network bandwidth in future work. We perform scale-up classification on the highest-end platform, which offers the largest number of scale-up options. When a workload is submitted, we profile it briefly with two randomly-selected scale-up allocations. The parameters and duration of profiling depend on workload type. Latency-critical services, like memcached are profiled for 5-10 seconds under live traffic, with two different core/thread counts and memory allocations (see the validation section for a sensitivity analysis on the number of profiling runs). For workloads like Hadoop, we profile a small subset (2-6) of map tasks with two different allocations and configurations of the most important framework parameters (e.g., mappers per node, JVM heapsize, block size, memory per task, replication factor, and compression). Profiling lasts until the map tasks reach at least 20% of completion, which is typically sufficient to estimate the job's completion time using its progress rate [70] and assuming uniform task duration [32]. Section 4.3 addresses the issue of non-uniform task duration distribution and stragglers. Finally, for stateful services like Cassandra [14], Quasar waits until the service's setup is complete before profiling the input load with the different allocations. This takes at most 3-5 minutes, which is tolerable for long-running services. Section 4.2 discusses how Quasar guarantees side-effect free application copies for profiling runs.

Profiling collects performance measurements in the format of each application's performance goal (e.g., expected completion time or QPS) and inserts them into a matrix $A$ with workloads as rows and scale-up configurations as columns. A configuration includes compute, memory, and storage allocations or the values of the framework parameters for a workload like Hadoop. To constrain the number of columns, we quantize the vectors to integer multiples of cores and blocks of memory and storage. This may result into somewhat suboptimal decisions, but the deviations are small in practice. Classification using SVD and PQ-reconstruction then derive the workload's performance across all scale-up allocations.

**Scale-out classification:** This type of classification is only applicable to workloads that can use multiple servers, such as distributed frameworks (e.g., Hadoop or Spark), stateless (e.g., webserving) or stateful (e.g., memcached or Cassandra) distributed services, and distributed computations (e.g., MPI jobs). Scale-out classification requires one more run in

| | *Default density constraint: 2 entries per row, per classification* | | | | | | | | | | | | *8 entries per row* | | |
|---|---|---|---|---|---|---|---|---|---|---|---|---|---|---|---|
| | **scale-up** | | | **scale-out** | | | **heterogeneity** | | | **interference** | | | ***exhaustive*** | | |
| **Classification err.** | *avg* | *90 %ile* | *max* | *avg* | *90 %ile* | *max* | *avg* | *90 %ile* | *max* | *avg* | *90 %ile* | *max* | *avg* | *90 %ile* | *max* |
| **Hadoop (10 Jobs)** | 5.2% | 9.8% | 11% | 5.0% | 14.5% | 17% | 4.1% | 4.6% | 5.0% | 1.8% | 5.1% | 6% | 14.1% | 15.8% | 16% |
| **Memcached (10)** | 6.3% | 9.2% | 11% | 6.6% | 10.5% | 12% | 5.2% | 5.7% | 6.5% | 7.2% | 9.1% | 10% | 14.1% | 16.5% | 18% |
| **Webserver (10)** | 8.0% | 10.1% | 13% | 7.5% | 11.6% | 14% | 4.1% | 5.1% | 5.2% | 3.2% | 8.1% | 9% | 16.5% | 17.6% | 18% |
| **Single-node (413)** | 4.0% | 8.1% | 9% | - | - | - | 3.5% | 6.9% | 8.0% | 4.4% | 9.2% | 10% | 11.6% | 12.1% | 13% |

Table 2: Validation of Quasar's classification engine. We present average, $90^{th}$ percentile and maximum errors between estimated values and actual values obtained with detailed characterization. We also compare the classification errors of the four parallel classification to a single, exhaustive classification that accounts for all combinations of resource allocation and resource assignment jointly.

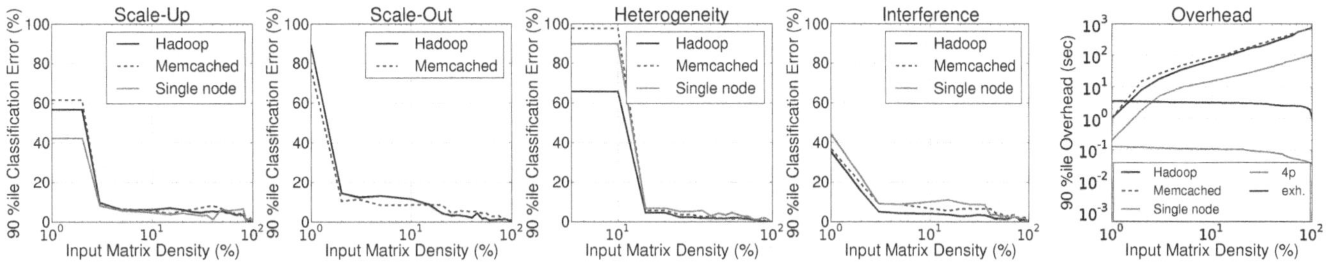


Figure 3: Sensitivity of classification accuracy to input matrix density constraints (Fig. 3(a-d)). Fig. 3e shows the profiling and decision overheads for different density constraints of the input matrices, assuming constant hardware resources for profiling.

addition to single-node runs done for scale-up classification. To get consistent results, profiling is done with the same parameters as one of the scale-up runs (e.g., JVM heapsize) and the same application load. This produces two entries for matrix $A$, where rows are again workloads and columns are scale-out allocations (numbers of servers). Collaborative filtering then recovers the missing entries of performance across all node counts. Scale-out classification requires additional servers for profiling. To avoid increasing the classification overheads when the system is online, applications are only profiled on one to four nodes for scale-out classification. To accurately estimate the performance of incoming workloads for larger node counts, in offline mode, we have exhaustively profiled a small number of different workload types (20-30) against node counts 1 to 100. These runs provide the classification engine with dense information on workload behavior for larger node counts. This step does not need to repeat unless there are major changes in the cluster's hardware or application structure.

**Heterogeneity classification:** This classification requires one more profiling run on a different and randomly-chosen server type using the same workload parameters and for the same duration as a scale-up run. Collaborative filtering estimates workload performance across all other server types.

**Interference classification:** This classification quantifies the sensitivity of the workload to interference caused and tolerated in various shared resources, including the CPU, cache hierarchy, memory capacity and bandwidth, and storage and network bandwidth. This classification does not require an extra profiling run. Instead, it leverages the first copy of the scale-up classification to inject, one at a time, two microbenchmarks that create contention in a specific shared resource [19]. Once the microbenchmark is injected, Quasar tunes up its intensity until the workload performance drops below an acceptable level of QoS (typically 5%). This point is recorded as the workload's sensitivity to this type of interference in a new row in the corresponding matrix $A$. The columns of the matrix are the different sources of interference. Classification is then applied to derive the sensitivities to the remaining sources of interference. Once the profiling runs are complete the different types of classification reconstruct the missing entries and provide recommendations on efficient allocations and assignments for each workload. Classification typically takes a few msec even for thousands of applications and servers.

**Multiple parallel versus single exhaustive classification:** Classification is decomposed to the four components previously described for both accuracy and efficiency reasons. The alternative design would consist of a single classification that examines all combinations of resource allocations and resource assignments at the same time. Each row in this case is an incoming workload, and each column is an allocation-assignment vector. Exhaustive classification addresses pathological cases that the four simpler classifications estimate poorly. For example, if TCP incast occurs for a specific allocation, *only* on a specific server platform that is not used for profiling, its performance impact will not be identified by classification. Although these cases are rare, they can result in unexpected performance results. On the other hand, the exponential increase in the column count in the exhaustive scheme increases the time required to perform classification [35, 50, 66] (note that this occurs at every application arrival). Moreover, because the number of columns now exceeds the number of rows, classification accuracy decreases, as SVD finds fewer similarities with high confidence [26, 49, 64].

To address this issue without resorting to exhaustive classification, we introduce a simple feedback loop that updates the matrix entries when the performance measured at runtime deviates from the one estimated through classification. This loop addresses such misclassifications, and additionally assists with scaling to server counts that exceed the capabilities of profiling, i.e., more than 100 nodes.

**Validation:** Table 2 summarizes a validation of the accuracy of the classification engine in Quasar. We use a 40-server cluster and applications from Hadoop (10 data-mining jobs), latency-critical services (10 memcached jobs, and 10 Apache webserver loads), and 413 single-node benchmarks from SPEC, PARSEC, SPLASH-2, BioParallel, Minebench and SpecJbb. The memcached and webserving jobs differ in their query distribution, input dataset and/or incoming load. Hadoop jobs additionally differ in terms of the application logic. Details on the applications and systems can be found in Section 5. We show average, $90^{th}$ percentile and maximum errors for each application and classification type. The errors show the deviation between estimated and measured performance or sensitivity to interference. On average, classification errors are less than 8% across all application types, while maximum errors are less than 17%, guaranteeing that the information that drives cluster management decisions is accurate. Table 2 also shows the corresponding errors for the exhaustive classification. In this case, average errors are slightly higher, especially for applications arriving early in the system [49], however, the deviation between average and maximum errors is now lower, as the exhaustive classification can accurately predict performance for the pathological cases that the four parallel classifications miss.

We also validate the selected number of profiling runs, i.e., how classification accuracy changes with the density of the input matrices. Figure 3(a-d) shows how the $90^{th}$ percentile of errors from classification changes as the density of the corresponding input matrix increases. For clarity, we omit the plots for Webserver, which has similar patterns to memcached. For all four classification types, a single profiling run per classification results in high errors. Two or more entries per input row result in decreased errors, although the benefits reach the point of diminishing returns after 4-5 entries. This behavior is consistent across application types, although the exact values of errors may differ. Unless otherwise specified, we use 2 entries per row in subsequent experiments. Figure 3e shows the overheads (profiling and classification) for the three application classes (Hadoop, memcached, single node) as input matrix density increases. We assume that the hardware resources used towards profiling and classification are kept constant. Obviously as the number of profiling runs increases the overheads increase significantly, without equally important accuracy improvements. The figure also shows the overheads from classification only (excluding profiling) for the four parallel classifications (*4p*) and the exhaustive scheme (*exh.*). As expected, the increase in column count corresponds in an increase in decision time, often by two orders of magnitude.

### 3.3 Greedy Allocation and Assignment

The classification output is given to a greedy scheduler that jointly determines the amount, type, and exact set of allocated resources. The scheduler's objective is to allocate the *least amount of resources needed to satisfy a workload's performance target*. This greatly reduces the space the scheduler traverses, allowing it to examine higher quality resources first, as smaller quantities of them will meet the performance constraint. This approach also scales well to many servers.

The scheduler uses the classification output, to first rank the available servers by decreasing resource quality, i.e., high performing platforms with minimal interference first. Next, it sizes the allocation based on available resources until the performance constraint is met. For example, if a webserver must meet a throughput of 100K QPS with 10msec $99^{th}$ percentile latency and the highest-ranked servers can achieve at most 20K QPS, the workload would need five servers to meet the constraints. If the number of highest-ranked servers available is not sufficient, the scheduler will also allocate lower-ranked servers and increase their number. The feedback between allocation and assignment ensures that the amount and quality of resources are accounted for jointly. When sizing the allocation, the algorithm first increases the per-node resources (scale-up) to better pack work in few servers, and then distributes the load across machines (scale-out). Nevertheless, alternative heuristics can be used based on the workload's locality properties or to address fault tolerance concerns.

The greedy algorithm has $O(M \cdot logM + S)$ complexity, where the first component accounts for the sorting overhead and the second for the examination of the top $S$ servers, and in practice takes a few msec to determine an allocation/assignment even for systems with thousands of servers. Despite its greedy nature, we show in Section 6 that the decision quality is quite high, leading to both high workload performance and high resource utilization. This is primarily due to the accuracy of the information available after classification. A potential source of inefficiency is that the scheduler allocates resources on a per-application basis in the order workloads arrive. Suboptimal assignments can be detected by sampling a few workloads (e.g., based on job priorities if they are available) and adjusting their assignment later on as resources become available when other workloads terminate. Finally, the scheduler employs admission control to prevent oversubscription when no resources are available.

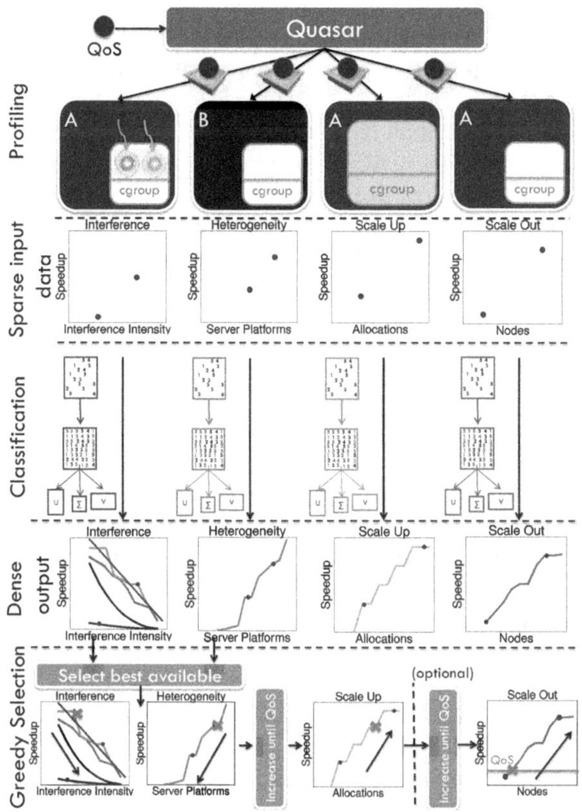


Figure 4: The steps for cluster management with Quasar. Starting from the top, short runs using sandboxed workload copies produce the initial profiling signal that classification techniques expand to information about relationship between performance and scale-up, scale-out, heterogeneity, and interference. Finally, the greedy scheduler uses the classification output to find the number and type of resources that maximize utilization and application performance.

### 3.4 Putting it All Together

Figure 4 shows the different steps of cluster management in Quasar. Upon arrival of a workload, Quasar collects profiling data for scale-out and scale-up allocations, heterogeneity, and interference. This requires up to four profiling runs that happen in parallel. All profiling copies are sandboxed (as explained in Section 4.2), the two platforms used are A and B (two nodes of A are used for the scale-out classification) and each profiling type produces two points in the corresponding speedup graph of the workload. The profiling runs happen with the actual dataset of the workload. The total profiling overhead depends on the workload type and is less than 5 min in all cases we examined. For non-stateful services, e.g., small batch workloads that are a large fraction of DC workloads [54], the complete profiling takes 10-15 seconds. Note that for stateful services, e.g., Cassandra, where setup is necessary, it only affects *one* of the profiling runs. Once the service is warmed-up, subsequent profiling only requires a few seconds to complete. Once the profiling results are available, classification provides the full workload characterization (speedup graph). Next, the greedy scheduler assigns specific servers to the workload. Overall, Quasar's overheads are quite low even for short-running applications (batch, analytics) or long running online services.

Quasar maintains per-workload and per-server state. Per-workload state includes the classification output. For a cluster with 10 server types and 10 sources of interference, we need roughly 256 bytes per workload. The per-server state includes information on scheduled applications and their cumulative resource interference, roughly 128B in total. The per-server state is updated on each workload assignment. Quasar also needs some storage for the intermediate classification results and for server ranking during assignment. Overall, state overheads are marginal and scale linearly with the number of workloads and servers. In our experiments, a single server was sufficient to handle the total state and computation of cluster management. Additional servers can be used for fault-tolerance.

## 4. Implementation

We implemented a prototype for Quasar in about 6KLOC of C, C++, and Python. It runs on Linux and OS X and currently supports applications written in C/C++, Java, and Python. The API includes functions to express the performance constraints and type of submitted workloads, and functions to check job status, revoke it, or update the constraints. We have used Quasar to manage analytics frameworks such as Hadoop, Storm, and Spark, latency-critical services such as NoSQL workloads, and conventional single-node workloads. There was no need to change any applications or frameworks. The framework-specific code in Quasar is 100-600 LOC per framework. In the future, we plan to merge the Quasar classification and scheduling algorithms in a cluster management framework like OpenStack or Mesos.

### 4.1 Dynamic Adaptation

Some workloads change behavior during their runtime, either due to phase changes or due to variation in user traffic. Quasar detects such changes and adjusts resource allocation and/or assignment to preserve the performance constraints.

**Phase detection:** Quasar continuously monitors the performance of all active workloads in the cluster. If a workload runs below its performance constraint, it either went through a phase change or was incorrectly classified or assigned. In any case, Quasar reclassifies the application at its current state and adjusts its resources as needed (see discussion below). We also proactively test for phase changes and misclassifications/misscheduling by periodically sampling a few active workloads and injecting interfering microbenchmarks to them. This enables partial interference classification in place. If there is a significant change compared to the original classification results, Quasar signals a phase change.

Proactive detection is particularly useful for long-running workloads that may affect co-located workloads when entering a phase change. We have validated the phase detection schemes with workloads from SPECCPU2006, PARSEC, Hadoop and memcached. With the reactive-only scheme, Quasar detects 94% of phase changes. By sampling 20% of active workloads every 10 minutes, we detect 78% of changes proactively with 8% probability of false positives.

**Allocation adjustment:** Once the phase has been detected or load increases significantly for a user-facing workload, Quasar changes the allocation to provide more resources or reclaim unused resources. Quasar adjusts allocations in a conservative manner. It first scales up or down the resources given to the workload in each of the servers it currently occupies. If needed, best-effort (low priority) workloads are evicted from these servers. If possible, a scale-up adjustment is the simplest option as it typically requires no state migration. If scale-up is not possible or cannot address the performance needs, scale-out and/or migration to other servers is used. For stateless services (e.g., adding/removing workers to Hadoop or scaling a webserver), scale-out is straightforward. For stateful workloads, migration and scale-out can be expensive. If the application is organized in microshards [16], Quasar will migrate a fraction of the load from each server to add capacity at minimum overhead. At the moment, Quasar does not employ load prediction for user-facing services [29, 46]. In future work, we will use such predictors as an additional signal to trigger adjustments for user-facing workloads.

### 4.2 Side Effect Free Profiling

To acquire the profiling data needed for classification, we must launch multiple copies of the incoming application. This may cause inconsistencies with intermediate results, duplicate entries in databases, or data corruption on file systems. To eliminate such issues, Quasar uses sandboxing for the training copies during profiling. We use *Linux containers* [8] with `chroot` to sandbox profiling runs and create a copy-on-write filesystem snapshot so that files (including framework libraries) can be read and written as usual [72]. Containers enable full control over how training runs interact with the rest of the system, including limiting resource usage through *cgroups*. Using virtual machines (VMs) for the same purpose is also possible [47, 62, 63, 68], but we chose containers as they incur lower overheads for launching.

### 4.3 Stragglers

In frameworks like Hadoop or Spark, individual tasks may take much longer to complete for reasons that range from poor work partitioning to network interference and machine instability [4]. These straggling tasks are typically identified and relaunched by the framework to ensure timely job completion [1, 3, 4, 17, 23, 37, 70]. We improve straggler detection in Hadoop in the following manner. Quasar calls the `TaskTracker` API in Hadoop and checks for under-performing tasks (at least 50% slower than the median). For such tasks, Quasar injects two contentious microbenchmarks in the corresponding servers and reclassifies them with respect to interference caused and tolerated. If the results of the in-place classification differ from the original by more than 20%, we signal the task as a straggler and notify the Hadoop JobTracker to relaunch it on a newly assigned server. This allows Quasar to detect stragglers 19% earlier than Hadoop, and 8% earlier than LATE [70] for the Hadoop applications described in the first scenario in Section 5.

### 4.4 Discussion

**Cost target:** Apart from a performance target, a user could also specify a cost constraint, priorities, and utility functions for a workload [55]. These can either serve as a limit for resource allocation or to prioritize allocations during very high load. We will consider these issues in future work.

**Resource partitioning:** Quasar does not explicitly partition hardware resources. Instead, it reduces interference by co-locating workloads that do not contend on the shared resources. Resource partitioning is orthogonal. If mechanisms like cache partitioning or rate limiting at the NIC are used, interference can be reduced and more workload colocations will be possible using Quasar. In that case, Quasar will have to determine the settings for partitioning mechanisms, in the same way it determines the number of cores to use for each workload. We will consider these issues in future work.

**Fault tolerance:** We use master-slave mirroring to provide fault-tolerance for the server that runs the Quasar scheduler. All system state (list of active applications, allocations, QoS guarantees) is continuously replicated and can be used by hot-standby masters. Quasar can also leverage frameworks like ZooKeeper [5] for more scalable schemes with multiple active schedulers. Quasar does not explicitly add to the fault tolerance of frameworks like MapReduce. In the event of a failure, the cluster manager relies on the individual frameworks to recover missing worker data. Our current resource assignment does not account for fault zones. However, this is a straight forward extension for the greedy algorithm.

## 5. Methodology

**Clusters:** We evaluated Quasar on a 40-server local cluster and a 200-server cluster on EC2. The ten platforms of the local cluster range from dual core Atom boards to dual socket 24 core Xeon servers with 48GB of RAM. The EC2 cluster has 14 server types ranging from small to x-large instances. All servers are dedicated and managed only by Quasar, i.e., there is no interference from external workloads.

The following paragraphs summarize the workload scenarios used to evaluate Quasar. Scenarios include batch and latency-critical workloads and progressively evaluate different aspects of allocation and assignment. Unless otherwise specified experiments are run 7 times for consistency and we report the average and standard deviation.

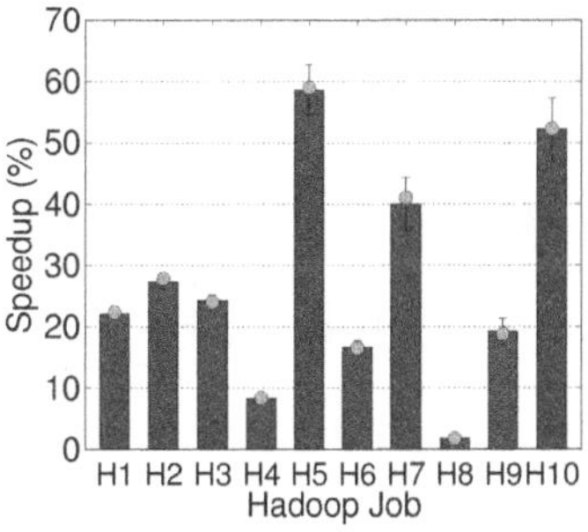


Figure 5: Performance of the ten Hadoop jobs.

| Parameter | Quasar | Hadoop |
|---|---|---|
| Block size | 64MB | 64MB |
| Compression rate | 7.6(gzip) | 5.1(lzo) |
| Heapsize | 0.75GB | 1GB |
| Replication | 2 | 2 |
| Mappers per node | 12 | 8 |
| Server type | E-F | A-E |

Table 3: Parameters setting for Hadoop job H8 by Quasar and the Hadoop scheduler.

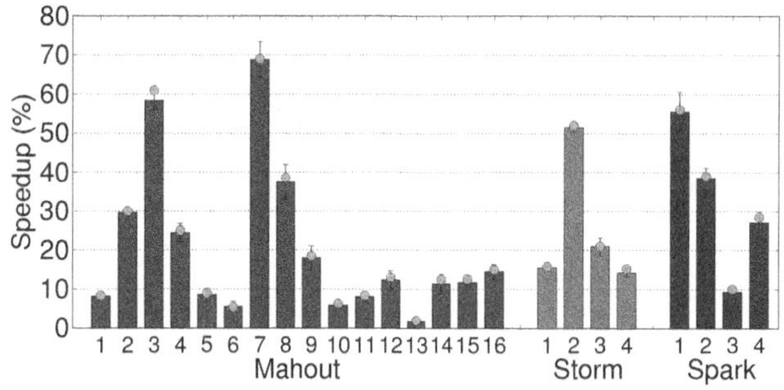


Figure 6: Performance speedup for the Hadoop, Storm and Spark jobs with Quasar.

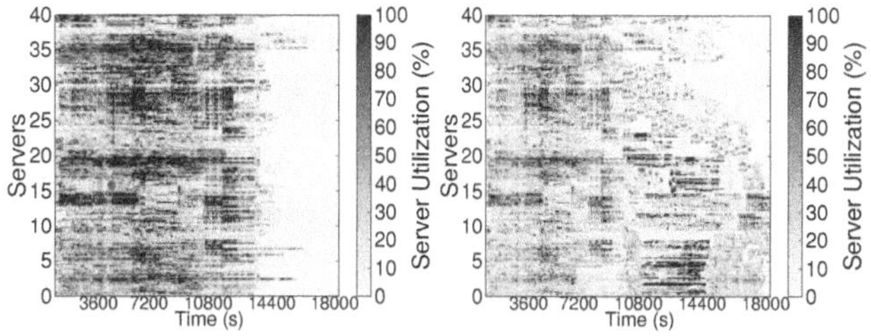


Figure 7: Cluster utilization with Quasar (left) and the framework schedulers (right).

**Single Batch Job:** Analytics frameworks like Hadoop [30], Storm [57], and Spark [71] are large consumers of resources on private and public clouds. Such frameworks have individual schedulers that set the various framework parameters (e.g., mappers per node and block size) and determine resource allocation (number of servers used). The allocations made by each scheduler are suboptimal for two reasons. First, the scheduler does not have full understanding of the complexity of the submitted job and dataset. Second, the scheduler is not aware of the details of available servers (e.g., heterogeneity), resulting in undersized or overprovisioned allocations. In this first scenario, a single Hadoop job is running at a time on the small cluster. This simple scenario allows us to compare the resource allocation selected by Hadoop to the allocation/assignment of Quasar on a single job basis. We use ten Hadoop jobs from the Mahout library [39] that represent data mining and machine learning analyses. The input datasets vary between 1 and 900GB. Note that there is no workload co-location in this scenario.

**Multiple Batch Jobs:** The second scenario represents a realistic setup for batch processing clusters. The cluster is shared between jobs from multiple analytics frameworks (Hadoop, Storm, and Spark). We use 16 Hadoop applications running on top of the Mahout library, four workloads for real-time text and image processing in Storm, and four workloads for logical regression, text processing and machine learning in Spark. These jobs arrive in the cluster with 5 sec inter-arrival times. Apart from the analytics jobs, a number of single-server jobs are submitted to the cluster. We use workloads from SPECCPU2006, PARSEC [12], SPLASH-2 [67], BioParallel [34], Minebench [43] and 350 multiprogrammed 4-app mixes from SPEC [53]. These single-server workloads arrive with 1 second inter-arrival times and are treated as best-effort (low priority) load that fills any cluster capacity unused by analytics jobs. There are not guarantees on performance of best-effort tasks, which may be migrated or killed at any point to provide resources for analytics tasks.

We compare Quasar to allocations done by the frameworks themselves (Hadoop, Spark, Storm schedulers) and assignments by a least-loaded scheduler that accounts for core and memory use but not heterogeneity or interference.

**Low-Latency Service:** Latency-critical services are also major tenants in cloud facilities. We constructed a webserving scenario using the HotCRP conference management system [33], which includes the Apache webserver, application logic in PHP, and data stored in MySQL. The front- and back-end run on the same machine, and the installation is replicated across several machines. The database is kept purposefully small (5GB) so that it is cached in memory and emphasis is placed on compute, cache, memory and networking issues, and not on disk performance. HotCRP traffic includes requests to fill in paper abstracts, update author information, and upload or read papers. Apart from throughput constraints, HotCRP requires a 100msec per-request latency.

We use three traffic scenarios: flat, fluctuating, and large spike. Apart from satisfying HotCRP constraints, we want to use any remaining cluster capacity for single-node, best-effort tasks (see description in previous scenario). We compare Quasar to a system that uses an auto-scaling approach to scale HotCRP between 1 and 8 servers based on the observed load of the servers used [6]. Auto-scale allocates an additional, least-loaded server for HotCRP when current load exceeds 70% [7] and redirects a fair share of the traffic to the new server instance. Load balancing happens on the workload generator side. Best-effort jobs are assigned by a least-loaded (LL) scheduler. Quasar deals with load changes in HotCRP by either scaling-up existing allocations or scaling-out (more servers) based on how the two affect performance.

**Stateful Latency-Critical Services:** This scenario extends the one above in two ways. First, there are multiple low-latency services. Second, these services involve significant volumes of state. Specifically, we examine the deployment

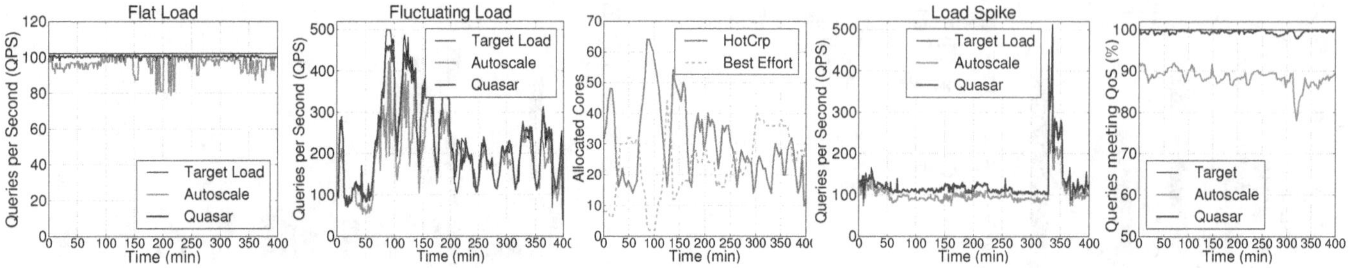


Figure 8: Throughput for HotCRP under (a) flat, (b) fluctuating and (d) spiking load. Fig. 8 (c) shows the core allocation in Quasar for the fluctuating load, and (e) shows the fraction of queries meeting the latency constraint for the load with spike.

of memory-based memcached [22] and disk-based Cassandra [14], two latency-critical NoSQL services. Memcached (1TB state) is presented with load that fluctuates following a diurnal pattern with maximum aggregate throughput target of 2.4M QPS and a 200usec latency constraint. The disk-bound Cassandra (4TB state) has a lower load of 60K QPS of maximum aggregate throughput and a 30 msec latency constraint. Any cluster capacity unused by the two services is utilized for best-effort workloads which are submitted with 10sec inter-arrival times. To show the fluctuation of utilization with load, and since scaling now involves state migration, this scenario runs over 24 hours and is repeated 3 times for consistency. Similarly to the previous scenario, we compare Quasar with the auto-scaling approach and measure performance (throughput and latency) for the two services and overall resource utilization. Scale-out in this case involves migrating one (64MB) or more microshards to a new instance, which typically takes a few msec.

**Large-Scale Cloud Provider:** Finally, we bring everything together in a general case where 1200 workloads of all types (analytics batch, latency-critical, and single-server jobs) are submitted in random order to a 200-node cluster of dedicated EC2 servers with 1 sec inter-arrival time. All applications have the same priority and no workload is considered best-effort (i.e., all paying customers have equal importance). The scenario is designed to use almost all system cores at steady-state, without causing oversubscription, under ideal resource allocation. We do, however, employ admission control to prevent machine oversubscription, when allocation is imperfect [18]. Wait time due to admission control counts towards scheduling overheads. Quasar handles allocation and assignment for all workloads. For comparison, we use an auto-scale approach for resource allocation of latency-critical workloads. For frameworks like Hadoop and Storm, the framework estimates its resource needs and we treat that as a reservation. For resource assignment, we use two schedulers: a least-loaded scheduler that simply accounts for core and memory availability and Paragon that, given a resource allocation, can do heterogeneity- and interference-aware assignment. The latter allows us to demonstrate the benefits of jointly solving allocation and assignment over separate (although optimized) treatment of the two.

# 6. Evaluation

## 6.1 Single Batch Job

**Performance:** Fig. 5 shows the reduction in execution time of ten Hadoop jobs when resources are allocated by Quasar instead of Hadoop itself. We account for all overheads, including classification and scheduling. Quasar improves performance for all jobs by an average of 29% and up to 58%. This is significant given that these Hadoop jobs take two to twenty hours to complete. The yellow dots show the execution time improvement needed to meet the performance target the job specified at submission. Targets are set to the best performance achieved after a parameter sweep on the different server platforms. Quasar achieves performance within 5.8% of the constraint on average, leveraging the information of how resource allocation and assignment impact performance. When resources are allocated by Hadoop, performance deviates from the target by 23% on average.

**Efficiency:** Table 3 shows the different parameter settings selected by Quasar and by Hadoop for the H8 Hadoop job, a recommendation system that uses Mahout with a 20GB dataset [39]. Apart from the block size and replication factor, the two frameworks set job parameters differently. Quasar detects that interference between mappers is low and increases the mappers per node to 12. Similarly, it detects that heap size is not critical for this job and reduces its size, freeing resources for other workloads. Moreover, Quasar allocates tasks to the two most suitable server types (E and F), while Hadoop chooses from all available server types.

## 6.2 Multiple Batch Frameworks

**Performance:** Fig. 6 shows the reduction in execution times for Hadoop, Storm, and Spark jobs when Quasar manages resource allocation and assignment. On average, performance improves by 27% and comes within 5.3% of the provided constraint, a significant improvement over the baseline. Apart from sizing and configuring jobs better, Quasar can aggressively co-locate them. For example, it can detect when two memory-intensive Storm and Spark jobs interfere and when they can efficiently share a system. Quasar allows the remaining cluster capacity to be used for best-effort jobs without disturbing the primary jobs because it is interference-aware. Best-effort jobs come within 7.8% on

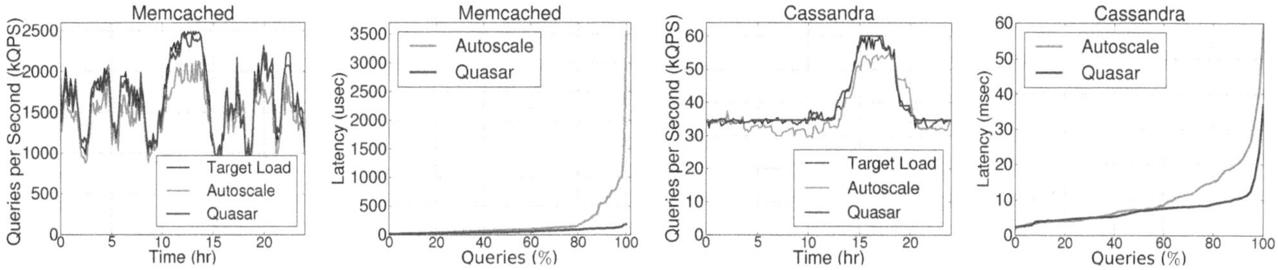


Figure 9: Throughput and latency for memcached and Cassandra in a cluster managed by Quasar or an auto-scaling system.

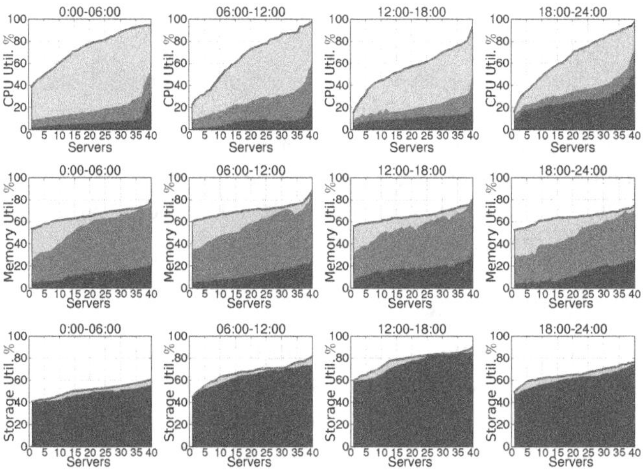


Figure 10: Average resource usage across all servers for four 6-hour snapshots. The cluster is running memcached (green), Cassandra (blue), and best-effort tasks (yellow) and is managed by Quasar.

average of the peak performance each job could achieve if it was running alone on the highest performing server type.

**Utilization:** Fig. 7 shows the per-server CPU utilization (average across all cores) over time in the form of a heatmap. Utilization is sampled every 5 sec. In addition to improving individual job performance, Quasar increases utilization, achieving 62% on average versus 34% with the individual framework schedulers (right heatmap). Because performance is now higher the whole experiment completes faster. Workloads after $t = 14400$ are mostly best-effort jobs that take longer than the main analytics workloads to complete.

### 6.3 Low-Latency Service

**Performance:** Fig. 8a shows the aggregate throughput for HotCRP achieved with Quasar and the auto-scaling system when the input traffic is flat. While the absolute differences are small, it is important to note that the auto-scaling manager causes frequent QPS drops due to interference from best-effort workloads using idling resources. With Quasar, HotCRP runs undisturbed and the best-effort jobs achieve runtimes within 5% of minimum, while with auto-scale, they achieve runtimes within 24% of minimum. When traffic varies (Fig. 8b), Quasar tracks target QPS closely, while autoscale provides 18% lower QPS on average, both due to interference and suboptimal scale-up configuration. Quasar's smooth behavior is due to the use of both scale-out and scale-up to best meet the new QPS target, leaving the highest number of cores possible for best-effort jobs (Fig. 8c). For the load with the sharp spike, Quasar tracks QPS within 4% on average (Fig. 8d) and meets the latency QoS for nearly all requests (Fig. 8e). When the spike arrives, Quasar first scales up each existing allocation, and then only uses two extra servers of suitable type to handle remaining traffic. The auto-scaling system observes the load increase when the spike arrives and allocates four more servers. Due to the higher latency of scale-out and the fact that auto-scaling is not aware of heterogeneity or interference, it fails to meet the latency guarantees for over 20% of requests around the spike arrival.

### 6.4 Stateful Latency-Critical Services

**Performance:** Fig. 9 shows the throughput of memcached and Cassandra over time and the distribution of query latencies. Quasar tracks throughput targets closely for both services, while the auto-scaling manager degrades throughput by 24% and 12% on average for memcached and Cassandra respectively. The differences in latency are larger between the two managers. Quasar meets latency QoS for memcached for 98.8% of requests, while auto-scaling only for 80% of requests. For Cassandra, Quasar meets the latency QoS for 98.6% of requests, while the auto-scaling for 93% of requests. Memcached is memory-based and has an aggressive latency QoS, making it more sensitive to suboptimal resource allocation and assignment on a shared cluster.

**Utilization:** Fig. 10 shows the utilization of CPU, memory capacity, and disk bandwidth across the cluster servers when managed by Quasar over 24h. Each column is a snapshot of average utilization over 6 hours. Since memcached and Cassandra have low CPU requirements, excluding the period 18:00-24:00 when Cassandra performs garbage collection, most of the CPU capacity is allocated to best-effort jobs. The number of best-effort jobs varies over time because the exact load of memcached and Cassandra changes. Most memory is used to satisfy the requirements of memcached, with small amounts needed for Cassandra and best-effort jobs. Cassandra is the nearly exclusive user of disk I/O. Some servers do not exceed 40-50% utilization for most of the experiment's

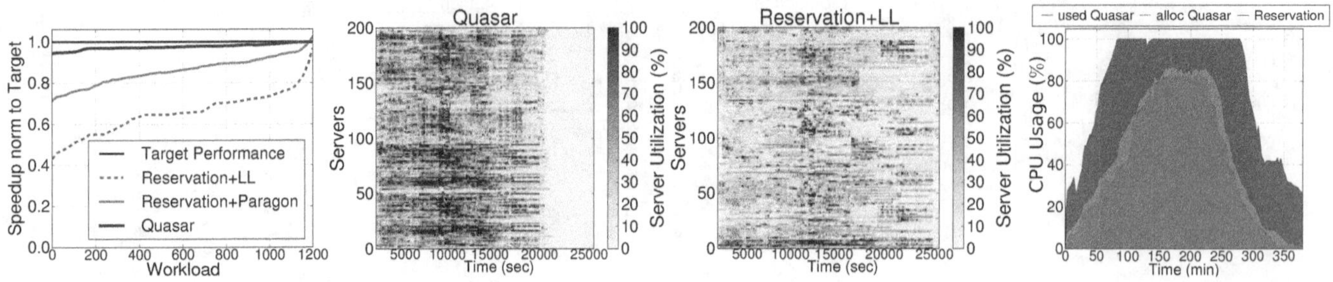


Figure 11: (a) Performance and cluster utilization for 1200 workloads on 200 EC2 servers with (b) Quasar and (c) the reservation+LL system. Fig. 11(d) shows the allocated versus used resources for Quasar and allocated for reservation+LL.

duration. These are low-end machines, for which higher utilization dramatically increases the probability of violating QoS constraints for latency-critical services. In general, the cluster utilization is significantly higher than if each service was running in dedicated machines.

### 6.5 Large-Scale Cloud Provider

**Performance:** Figure 11 presents the overall evaluation of Quasar managing a 200-node cluster running all previously-discussed types of workloads. We compare to resource allocation based on reservations (e.g., expressed by the Hadoop scheduler or an auto-scaling system) and resource assignment on least-loaded machines (LL) or based on the interference and heterogeneity-aware Paragon. Figure 11a shows the performance of the 1,200 workloads ordered from worst- to best-performing, normalized to their performance target. Quasar achieves 98% of the target on average, while the reservation-based system with Paragon achieves 83%. This shows the need to perform allocation and assignment together; the intelligent resource assignment by Paragon is not sufficient. Using reservations and LL assignment performs quite poorly, only achieving 62% of the target on average.

**Utilization:** Figures 11b-c show the per-server CPU utilization throughout the scenario's execution for Quasar and the reservation+LL system. Average utilization is 62% with Quasar, while meeting performance constraints for both batch and latency-critical workloads. The reservation+LL manager achieves average utilization of 15%, 47% lower than Quasar. Figure 11d shows the allocated and used resources for Quasar compared to the resources reserved by the reservation+LL manager over time. Overprovisioning with Quasar is low, with the difference between allocated and used being roughly 10%. This is significantly lower than the resources reserved by the reservation-based manager, which exceed the capacity of the cluster during most of the scenario. Because Quasar has detailed information on how different allocations/assignments affect performance, it can rightsize the allocations more aggressively, while meeting the performance constraints without QoS violations.

**Cluster management overheads:** For most applications the overheads of Quasar from profiling, classification, greedy selection and adaptation are low, 4.1% of execution time on average. For short-lived batch workloads, overheads are up to 9%. The overheads are negligible for any long-running service, and even for jobs lasting a few seconds, they only induce single-digit increases in execution time. In contrast with reservation+LL, Quasar does not introduce any wait time overheads due to oversubscription.

## 7. Conclusions

We have presented Quasar, a cluster management system that performs coordinated resource allocation and assignment. Quasar moves away from the reservation-based standard for cluster management. Instead of users requesting raw resources, they specify a performance target the application should meet and let the manager size resource allocations appropriately. Quasar leverages robust classification techniques to quickly analyze the impact of resource allocation (scale-up and scale-out), resource type (heterogeneity), and interference on performance. A greedy algorithm uses this information to allocate the least amount of resources necessary to meet performance constraints. Quasar currently supports distributed analytics frameworks, web-serving applications, NoSQL datastores, and single-node batch workloads. We evaluated Quasar over a variety of workload scenarios and compared it to reservation/auto-scaling-based resource allocation systems and schedulers that use similar classification techniques for resource assignment (but not resource allocation). We showed that Quasar improves aggregate cluster utilization and individual application performance.

## Acknowledgements

We sincerely thank Rob Benson, Jonathan Blandford, Chris Lambert, Brian Wickman, Ben Hindman and the entire Mesos and Aurora teams at Twitter for allowing us to include data from their production system and for helping with the collection of the measurements. We would also like to thank John Ousterhout, Mendel Rosenblum, Daniel Sanchez, Jacob Leverich, David Lo, and the anonymous reviewers for their feedback on earlier versions of this manuscript. This work was partially supported by a Google directed research grant on energy proportional computing. Christina Delimitrou was supported by a Stanford Graduate Fellowship.

## References


[1] Faraz Ahmad, Srimat T. Chakradhar, Anand Raghunathan, and T. N. Vijaykumar. Tarazu: optimizing mapreduce on heterogeneous clusters. In *Proc. of the International Conference on Architectural Support for Programming Languages and Operating Systems (ASPLOS)*. London, UK, 2012.

[2] Amazon ec2. `http://aws.amazon.com/ec2/`.

[3] Ganesh Ananthanarayanan, Ali Ghodsi, Scott Shenker, and Ion Stoica. Effective straggler mitigation: Attack of the clones. In *Proc. of the USENIX Symposium on Networked Systems Design and Implementation (NSDI)*. Lombard, IL, 2013.

[4] Ganesh Ananthanarayanan, Srikanth Kandula, Albert Greenberg, Ion Stoica, Yi Lu, Bikas Saha, and Edward Harris. Reining in the outliers in map-reduce clusters using mantri. In *Proc. of the 9th USENIX conference on Operating Systems Design and Implementation (OSDI)*. Vancouver, CA, 2010.

[5] Apache zookeeper. `http://zookeeper.apache.org/`.

[6] Autoscale. `https://cwiki.apache.org/CLOUDSTACK/autoscaling.html`.

[7] AWS Autoscaling. `http://aws.amazon.com/autoscaling/`.

[8] Gaurav Banga, Peter Druschel, and Jeffrey C. Mogul. Resource containers: a new facility for resource management in server systems. OSDI, 1999.

[9] L. Barroso. Warehouse-scale computing: Entering the teenage decade. *ISCA Keynote, SJ, June 2011.*

[10] Luiz Barroso and Urs Hoelzle. *The Datacenter as a Computer: An Introduction to the Design of Warehouse-Scale Machines.* Morgan and Claypool Publishers, 2009.

[11] R. Bell, M. Koren, and C. Volinsky. The BellKor 2008 Solution to the Netflix Prize. Technical report, AT&T Labs, 2008.

[12] Christian Bienia, Sanjeev Kumar, Jaswinder Pal Singh, and Kai Li. The parsec benchmark suite: Characterization and architectural implications. In *Proc. of the 17th International Conference on Parallel Architectures and Compilation Techniques (PACT)*. Toronto, CA, October, 2008.

[13] Leon Bottou. Large-scale machine learning with stochastic gradient descent. In *Proc. of the International Conference on Computational Statistics (COMPSTAT)*. Paris, France, 2010.

[14] Apache cassandra. `http://cassandra.apache.org/`.

[15] McKinsey & Company. Revolutionizing data center efficiency. In *Uptime Institute Symposium, 2008.*

[16] Jeffrey Dean and Luiz Andre Barroso. The tail at scale. In *Communications of the ACM, Vol. 56 No. 2, Pages 74-80.*

[17] Jeffrey Dean and Sanjay Ghemawat. Mapreduce: simplified data processing on large clusters. In *Proc. of OSDI*, pages 10–10, 2004.

[18] Christina Delimitrou, Nick Bambos, and Christos Kozyrakis. QoS-Aware Admission Control in Heterogeneous Datacenters. In *Proceedings of the International Conference on Autonomic Computing (ICAC)*. San Jose, June 2013.

[19] Christina Delimitrou and Christos Kozyrakis. iBench: Quantifying Interference for Datacenter Workloads. In *Proceedings of the 2013 IEEE International Symposium on Workload Characterization (IISWC)*. Portland, OR, September 2013.

[20] Christina Delimitrou and Christos Kozyrakis. Paragon: QoS-Aware Scheduling for Heterogeneous Datacenters. In *Proc. of the Eighteenth International Conference on Architectural Support for Programming Languages and Operating Systems (ASPLOS)*. Houston, TX, USA, 2013.

[21] Eucalyptus cloud services. `http://www.eucalyptus.com/`.

[22] Brad Fitzpatrick. Distributed caching with memcached. In *Linux Journal, Volume 2004, Issue 124, 2004.*

[23] R. Gandhi and A. Sabne. Finding stragglers in hadoop. In *Tech. Report.* 2011.

[24] Gartner says efficient data center design can lead to 300 percent capacity growth in 60 percent less space. `http://www.gartner.com/newsroom/id/1472714`.

[25] Google compute engine. `http://cloud.google.com/products/compute-engine.html`.

[26] Z. Ghahramani and M. Jordan. Learning from incomplete data. In *Lab Memo No. 1509, CBCL Paper No. 108, MIT AI Lab.*

[27] Ali Ghodsi, Matei Zaharia, Benjamin Hindman, Andy Konwinski, Scott Shenker, and Ion Stoica. Dominant resource fairness: fair allocation of multiple resource types. In *Proc. of the 8th USENIX conference on Networked systems design and implementation (NSDI)*. Boston, MA, 2011.

[28] Daniel Gmach, Jerry Rolia, Ludmila Cherkasova, and Alfons Kemper. Workload analysis and demand prediction of enterprise data center applications. In *Proc. of the 10th IEEE International Symposium on Workload Characterization.* Boston, 2007.

[29] Zhenhuan Gong, Xiaohui Gu, and John Wilkes. Press: Predictive elastic resource scaling for cloud systems. In *Proc. of the International Conference on Network and Service Management (CNSM)*. Niagara Falls, ON, 2010.

[30] Apache hadoop. `http://hadoop.apache.org/`.

[31] J Hamilton. Cost of power in large-scale data centers. `http://perspectives.mvdirona.com`.

[32] Ben Hindman, A. Konwinski, M. Zaharia, A. Ghodsi, A.D. Joseph, R. Katz, S. Shenker, and I. Stoica. Mesos: A platform for fine-grained resource sharing in the data center. In *Proc. of the 8th USENIX Symposium on Networked Systems Design and Implementation (NSDI)*. Boston, MA, 2011.

[33] Hotcrp conference management system. `http://read.seas.harvard.edu/~kohler/hotcrp/`.

[34] Aamer Jaleel, Matthew Mattina, and Bruce L. Jacob. Last level cache (llc) performance of data mining workloads on a cmp - a case study of parallel bioinformatics workloads. In *Proc. of the 12th International Symposium on High-Performance Computer Architecture (HPCA-12)*. Austin, Texas, 2006.

[35] K.C. Kiwiel. Convergence and efficiency of subgradient methods for quasiconvex minimization. In *Mathematical Programming (Series A) (Berlin, Heidelberg: Springer) 90 (1): pp. 1-25, 2001.*

[36] Jacob Leverich and Christos Kozyrakis. On the energy (in)efficiency of hadoop clusters. In *Proc. of HotPower*. Big Sky, MT, 2009.

[37] J. Lin. The curse of zipf and limits to parallelization: A look at the stragglers problem in mapreduce. In *Proc. of LSDS-IR Workshop*. Boston, MA, 2009.

[38] Host server cpu utilization in amazon ec2 cloud. `http://huanliu.wordpress.com/2012/02/17/host-server-cpu-utilization-in-amazon-\ec2-cloud/`.

[39] Mahout. `http://mahout.apache.org/`.

[40] Jason Mars and Lingjia Tang. Whare-map: heterogeneity in "homogeneous" warehouse-scale computers. In *Proc. of the 40th Annual International Symposium on Computer Architecture (ISCA)*. Tel-Aviv, Israel, 2013.

[41] Jason Mars, Lingjia Tang, Robert Hundt, Kevin Skadron, and Mary Lou Soffa. Bubble-up: increasing utilization in modern warehouse scale computers via sensible co-locations. In *Proc. of the 44th Annual IEEE/ACM International Symposium on Microarchitecture*, pages 248–259, 2011.

[42] David Meisner, Christopher M. Sadler, Luiz André Barroso, Wolf-Dietrich Weber, and Thomas F. Wenisch. Power management of online data-intensive services. In *Proceedings of the 38th annual international symposium on Computer architecture*, pages 319–330, 2011.

[43] Ramanathan Narayanan, Berkin Ozisikyilmaz, Joseph Zambreno, Gokhan Memik, and Alok N. Choudhary. Minebench: A benchmark suite for data mining workloads. In *Proceedings of the 9th IEEE International Symposium on Workload Characterization (IISWC)*. San Jose, California, 2006.

[44] R. Nathuji, C. Isci, and E. Gorbatov. Exploiting platform heterogeneity for power efficient data centers. In *Proc. of ICAC'07, FL, 2007*.

[45] R. Nathuji, A. Kansal, and A. Ghaffarkhah. Q-clouds: Managing performance interference effects for qos-aware clouds. In *Proc. of EuroSys France, 2010*, 2010.

[46] Hiep Nguyen, Zhiming Shen, Xiaohui Gu, Sethuraman Subbiah, and John Wilkes. Agile: Elastic distributed resource scaling for infrastructure-as-a-service. In *Proc. of the USENIX International Conference on Automated Computing (ICAC'13)*. San Jose, CA, 2013.

[47] Dejan Novakovic, Nedeljko Vasic, Novakovic, Stanko, Dejan Kostic, and Ricardo Bianchini. Deepdive: Transparently identifying and managing performance interference in virtualized environments. In *Proc. of the USENIX Annual Technical Conference (ATC'13)*. San Jose, CA, 2013.

[48] Openstack cloud software. `http://www.openstack.org/`.

[49] Nathan Parrish, Hyrum Anderson, Maya Gupta, and Dun Yu Hsaio. Classifying with confidence from incomplete information. In *Proc. of the Journal Machine Learning Research (JMLR)*. 2013.

[50] A. Rajaraman and J. Ullman. *Textbook on Mining of Massive Datasets*. 2011.

[51] Charles Reiss, Alexey Tumanov, Gregory Ganger, Randy Katz, and Michael Kozych. Heterogeneity and dynamicity of clouds at scale: Google trace analysis. In *Proc. of the Third ACM Symposium on Cloud Computing (SOCC)*. San Jose, CA, 2012.

[52] Rightscale. `https://aws.amazon.com/solution-providers/isv/rightscale`.

[53] Daniel Sanchez and Christos Kozyrakis. Vantage: Scalable and Efficient Fine-Grain Cache Partitioning. In *Proc. of the 38th annual International Symposium in Computer Architecture (ISCA-38)*. San Jose, CA, June, 2011.

[54] Malte Schwarzkopf, Andy Konwinski, Michael Abd-El-Malek, and John Wilkes. Omega: flexible, scalable schedulers for large compute clusters. In *Proc. of the 8th ACM European Conference on Computer Systems (EuroSys)*. Prague, Czech Republic, April 2013.

[55] Upendra Sharma, Prashant Shenoy, Sambit Sahu, and Anees Shaikh. A cost-aware elasticity provisioning system for the cloud. In *Proc. of the 2011 31st International Conference on Distributed Computing Systems (ICDCS)*. Minneapolis, MN, 2011.

[56] Zhiming Shen, Sethuraman Subbiah, Xiaohui Gu, and John Wilkes. Cloudscale: elastic resource scaling for multi-tenant cloud systems. In *Proc. of the 2nd ACM Symposium on Cloud Computing (SOCC)*. Cascais, Portugal, 2011.

[57] Storm. `https://github.com/nathanmarz/storm/`.

[58] Torque resource manager. `http://www.adaptivecomputing.com/products/open-source/torque/`.

[59] Arunchandar Vasan, Anand Sivasubramaniam, Vikrant Shimpi, T. Sivabalan, and Rajesh Subbiah. Worth their watts? an empirical study of datacenter servers. In *Proc. of the 16th International Symposium on High Performance Computer Architecture (HPCA)*. Bangalore, India, 2010.

[60] Nedeljko Vasić, Dejan Novaković, Svetozar Miučin, Dejan Kostić, and Ricardo Bianchini. Dejavu: accelerating resource allocation in virtualized environments. In *Proc. of the seventeenth international conference on Architectural Support for Programming Languages and Operating Systems (ASPLOS)*. London, UK, 2012.

[61] Vmware vcloud suite. `http://www.vmware.com/products/vcloud`.

[62] Virtualbox. `https://www.virtualbox.org/`.

[63] Vmware virtual machines. `http://www.vmware.com/`.

[64] C. Wang, X. Liao, L. Carin, and D. B. Dunson. Classification with incomplete data using dirichlet process priors. In *Journal of Machine Learning Research (JMLR), 2010*.

[65] Windows azure. `http://www.windowsazure.com/`.

[66] Ian H. Witten, Eibe Frank, and Geoffrey Holmes. *Data Mining: Practical Machine Learning Tools and Techniques*. 3rd Edition.

[67] Steven Cameron Woo, Moriyoshi Ohara, Evan Torrie, Jaswinder Pal Singh, and Anoop Gupta. The splash-2 programs: characterization and methodological considerations. In *Proc. of the 22nd International Symposium on Computer Architecture (ISCA)*. Santa Margherita Ligure, Italy, 1995.

[68] The xen project. `http://www.xen.org/`.

[69] Hailong Yang, Alex Breslow, Jason Mars, and Lingjia Tang. Bubble-flux: precise online qos management for increased utilization in warehouse scale computers. In *Proc. of the 40th Annual International Symposium on Computer Architecture (ISCA)*. Tel-Aviv, Israel, 2013.

[70] M Zaharia, A Konwinski, A.D Joseph, R Katz, and I Stoica. Improving mapreduce performance in heterogeneous environments. In *Proc. of the 8th USENIX Symposium on Operating Systems Design and Implementation (OSDI)*. San Diego, CA, 2008.

[71] Matei Zaharia, M Chowdhury, T Das, A Dave, J Ma, M McCauley, M.J Franklin, S Shenker, and I Stoica. Spark: Cluster computing with working sets. In *Proc. of the 9th USENIX Symposium on Networked Systems Design and Implementation (NSDI)*. San Jose, CA, 2012.

[72] Zfs. `http://www.freebsd.org/doc/handbook/filesystems-zfs.html`.

[73] Xiao Zhang, Eric Tune, Robert Hagmann, Rohit Jnagal, Vrigo Gokhale, and John Wilkes. Cpi2: Cpu performance isolation for shared compute clusters. In *Proc. of the 8th ACM European Conference on Computer Systems (EuroSys)*. Prague, Czech Republic, 2013.

# REF: Resource Elasticity Fairness with Sharing Incentives for Multiprocessors

Seyed Majid Zahedi
Duke University
seyedmajid.zahedi@duke.edu

Benjamin C. Lee
Duke University
benjamin.c.lee@duke.edu

## Abstract

With the democratization of cloud and datacenter computing, users increasingly share large hardware platforms. In this setting, architects encounter two challenges: sharing fairly and sharing multiple resources. Drawing on economic game-theory, we rethink fairness in computer architecture. A fair allocation must provide sharing incentives (SI), envy-freeness (EF), and Pareto efficiency (PE).

We show that Cobb-Douglas utility functions are well suited to modeling user preferences for cache capacity and memory bandwidth. And we present an allocation mechanism that uses Cobb-Douglas preferences to determine each user's fair share of the hardware. This mechanism provably guarantees SI, EF, and PE, as well as strategy-proofness in the large (SPL). And it does so with modest performance penalties, less than 10% throughput loss, relative to an unfair mechanism.

***Categories and Subject Descriptors*** B.3.2 [*Hardware*]: Memory Structures; C.1.2 [*Processor Architectures*]: Multiple Data Stream Architectures; F.2.2 [*Theory of Computation*]: Analysis of Algorithms and Problem Complexity

***Keywords*** Multiprocessor architectures, fair sharing, economic mechanisms, game theory

## 1. Introduction

Datacenter platforms are often poorly utilized, running at less than 30% of peak capability [1]. With poor utilization, server power is amortized over little computation. To address this inefficiency, software must share hardware. Mechanisms for fair resource allocation (or a lack thereof) determine whether users have incentives to participate in dynamic, shared hardware platforms. In this setting, architects encounter two challenges: sharing fairly and sharing multiple resources.

We rethink fairness in resource allocation for computer architecture. Adopting the game-theoretic definition, a fair hardware allocation is one in which

- *all users perform no worse than under an equal division,*
- *no user envies the allocation of another, and*
- *no other allocation improves utility without harming a user.*

Our resource allocation strategy relies on robust game theory, encouraging users to share hardware and ensuring equitable allocations when they do. Conventional wisdom, on the other hand, assumes that users have no choice but to share. In this setting, prior efforts devise mechanisms to equally distribute performance penalties from sharing, which is not equitable [14, 28].

Drawing on economic game theory, we present a fair, multi-resource allocation mechanism. This mechanism and its resulting allocations provide key game-theoretic properties. First, the mechanism provides sharing incentives (SI), ensuring that each agent is at least as happy as they would be under an equal division of shared resources. Without SI, agents would not participate in the proposed sharing mechanism. Instead, they would rather equally and inefficiently divide the hardware. Supposing agents share a system, they will desire a fair division of the hardware.

In economic game theory, a fair allocation is defined to be envy-free (EF) and Pareto efficient (PE) [37]. An allocation is EF if each agent prefers his own allocation to other agents' allocations. Equitable sharing is defined by EF for all agents. An allocation is PE if we cannot improve an agent's utility without harming another agent.

Finally, a mechanism to allocate hardware should be strategy-proof (SP), ensuring that agents cannot gain by misreporting their preferences. Without SP, strategic agents may manipulate the hardware allocation mechanism by lying. In practice, SP may be incompatible with SI, EF, and


*ASPLOS '14*, March 1–5, 2014, Salt Lake City, Utah, USA.

http://dx.doi.org/10.1145/2541940.2541962

PE [19]. But there exist allocation mechanisms that are approximately SP as long as many agents share a system. We refer to this weaker guarantee as strategy-proofness in the large (SPL).

Thus, we present a new framework for reasoning about fair resource allocation in computer architecture. Our contributions include the following:

- **Cobb-Douglas Utility in Computer Architecture.** We show that Cobb-Douglas utility functions are well suited to model user performance and preferences for multiple hardware resources. Given Cobb-Douglas utilities, we detail conditions for SI, EF, and PE. (§3)
- **Fair Allocation for Computer Architecture.** We present a new mechanism to fairly allocate multiple hardware resources to agents with Cobb-Douglas utilities. We prove its game-theoretic properties (SI, EF, PE, SPL) and describe its implementation. (§4)
- **Case Study for Cache Size and Memory Bandwidth.** We apply the mechanism to fairly allocate cache size and memory bandwidth. We evaluate with cycle-accurate processor and memory simulators for diverse application suites, including PARSEC, SPLASH-2x, and Phoenix MapReduce. (§5)
- **Performance Trade-offs.** We compare our mechanism against prior approaches that equalize slowdown, describing how the latter violates game-theoretic fairness. Our mechanism provides fairness with modest penalties ($< 10\%$ throughput loss) relative to a mechanism that does not provide SI, EF, PE, and SPL. (§5)

Without loss of generality, we evaluate our multi-resource allocation mechanism for cache size and memory bandwidth. In future, the mechanism can support additional resources, such as the number of processor cores. Collectively, our findings establish robust foundations for the fair division of multiple hardware resources.

## 2. Motivation and Background

We present a mechanism for allocating shared resources. This mechanism guarantees SI, EF, PE, and SPL. And we demonstrate its ability to allocate last-level cache capacity and off-chip memory bandwidth. Our mechanism design relies on two fundamental insights about utility functions for computer architecture.

First, we use Cobb-Douglas utility functions to accurately capture hardware performance. For example, $u = x^{\alpha_x} y^{\alpha_y}$ models performance $u$ as a function of resource allocations for cache capacity $x$ and memory bandwidth $y$. The exponents $\alpha$ capture non-linear trends and model performance elasticity (i.e., sensitivity) for each hardware resource. For example, if $\alpha_x > \alpha_y$, the agent prefers cache capacity to memory bandwidth.

Second, we design a mechanism that uses each agent's reported resource elasticity $\alpha$ to determine his fair share of hardware. Given Cobb-Douglas utilities, the fair share can be expressed in a closed-form equation. Thus, the mechanism is computationally trivial. Yet the resulting allocation provably guarantees each of the desired game-theoretic properties: SI, EF, PE, and SPL.

**Game-theoretic versus Heuristic Fairness.** Our approach addresses fundamental limitations in prior work. Prior mechanisms consider each user's performance penalty incurred from sharing [12, 13]. They then allocate a resource, such as memory bandwidth, trying to equalize slowdown [28]. While this approach produces equal outcomes, it is not fair in the economic sense. Our rigorous, game-theoretic analysis shows that equalizing slowdown provides neither SI nor EF.

Without these properties, strategic users would have no incentive to share. They would prefer an equal division of memory bandwidth rather than receive an equal slowdown guarantee from the allocation mechanism. Allocating multiple resources with heuristics, such as hill-climbing [4], is even more difficult and provides even fewer guarantees.

**Cobb-Douglas versus Leontief.** Cobb-Douglas allows us to guarantee fairness in computer architecture for the first time. Although Leontief [9, 15, 21] provides the same guarantees in distributed systems, they do not apply in a more fine-grained analysis of hardware behavior for two reasons.

First, unlike Leontief, Cobb-Douglas utilities capture diminishing returns and substitutability. Both of these effects are prevalent in architecture, whether in Amdahl's Law for multi-core parallelism [20], in data locality for cache sizing, or in communication intensity for bandwidth allocation. In these settings, linear Leontief preferences of the form $u = min(x_1/\alpha_1, x_2/\alpha_2)$ are ineffective.

Second, consider the complexity of Cobb-Douglas and Leontief. We use classical regression to fit log-linear Cobb-Douglas to architectural performance. In contrast, since Leontief is concave piecewise-linear, fitting it would require non-convex optimization, which is computationally expensive and possibly NP-hard [36]. Note that [9, 15, 21] did not encounter these difficulties because they assume that agents in a distributed system provide a demand vector (e.g., 2CPUs, 4GB-DRAM). Fitting architectural performance to Leontief is equivalent to finding the demand vector for substitutable microarchitectural resources (e.g., cache and memory bandwidth), which is conceptually challenging.

## 3. Fair Sharing and Cobb-Douglas

A mechanism for fair sharing should guarantee several game theoretic properties. First, the mechanism must provide sharing incentives (SI). Without such incentives, software agents would prefer equally divided resources to a sophisticated mechanism that shares hardware more efficiently.

If agents do intelligently share, they will want a fair division. In economic game theory, a fair allocation is envy-free (EF) and Pareto efficient (PE) [37]. We present an allocation mechanism that provides SI, EF, and PE for hardware resources given software agents with Cobb-Douglas utility.

**Cobb-Douglas Utility.** Suppose multiple agents share a system with several types of hardware resources $1, \ldots, R$. Let $x_i = (x_{i1}, \ldots, x_{iR})$ denote agent $i$'s hardware allocation. Further, let $u_i(x_i)$ denote agent $i$'s utility. Equation (1) defines utility within the Cobb-Douglas preference domain.

$$u_i(x_i) = \alpha_{i0} \prod_{r=1}^{R} x_{ir}^{\alpha_{ir}} \quad (1)$$

The exponents $\alpha$ introduce non-linearity, useful for capturing diminishing marginal returns in utility. The product models interactions and substitution effects between resources. The user requires both resources for progress because utility is zero when either resource is unavailable.

The parameters $\alpha_i = (\alpha_{i1}, \ldots, \alpha_{iR})$ quantify the elasticity with which an agent demands a resource. If $\alpha_{ir} > \alpha_{ir'}$, then agent $i$ benefits more from resource $r$ than from resource $r'$. These parameters are tailored to each agent and define her demand for resources.

With Cobb-Douglas utility functions, we reason about agents' preferences. Consider two allocations $x$ and $x'$ for agent $i$.

- If $u_i(x) > u_i(x')$, then $x \succ_i x'$ (strictly prefer $x$ to $x'$)
- If $u_i(x) = u_i(x')$, then $x \sim_i x'$ (indifferent to $x$ and $x'$)
- If $u_i(x) \geq u_i(x')$, then $x \succsim_i x'$ (weakly prefer $x$ to $x'$)

Cobb-Douglas preferences are a good fit for resources in computer architecture. They capture diminishing marginal returns and substitution effects in ways that linear Leontief preferences, which prior work uses [15], cannot.

**Example with Cache and Memory.** We use a recurring example to illustrate the allocation of multiple resources given Cobb-Douglas preferences. Consider processor cache size and memory bandwidth. Agents see diminishing marginal returns from larger caches since software tasks exhibit limited exploitable locality. Depending on its data access locality, software tasks can substitute cache size for memory bandwidth and vice versa.

Suppose a system has 24GB/s of memory bandwidth and 12MB cache. This setting is representative of a quad-core processor with two DDRx channels. The system is shared by two users or agents. Let $(x_1, y_1)$ denote the memory bandwidth and cache capacity allocated to the first user. Similarly, let $(x_2, y_2)$ denote the second user's allocation. Suppose users' utilities are described by Equation (2).

$$u_1 = x_1^{0.6} y_1^{0.4} \qquad u_2 = x_2^{0.2} y_2^{0.8} \quad (2)$$

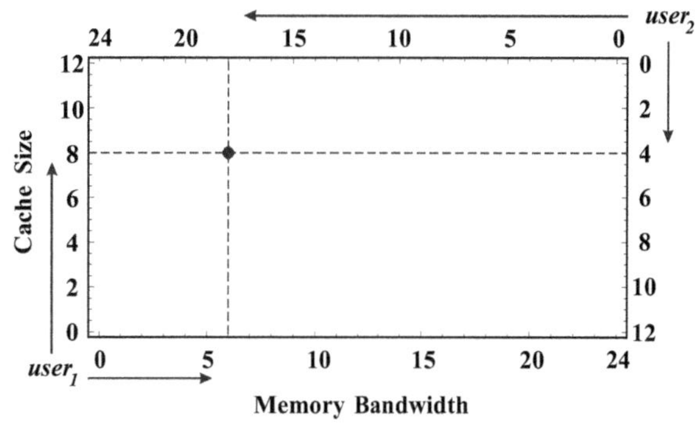


**Figure 1. Edgeworth Box Example.** Box height shows total cache size and box width shows total memory bandwidth. User 1's origin is at the lower left corner and User 2's origin is at the upper right corner. Each point in this box corresponds to a feasible resource allocation to users.

User 1 runs an application that exhibits bursty memory activity but little data re-use. For user 1, memory bandwidth $x_1$ is more useful than cache capacity $y_1$. In contrast, user 2 makes good use of its cache capacity $y_2$. We use profilers and regression to derive these utility functions (§4.4).

Software behavior translates into hardware demands, which in turn are reflected in the utility functions. These utility functions are representative of realistic applications. For example, $u_1$ and $u_2$ accurately model the relative cache and memory intensities for `canneal` and `freqmine` from the PARSEC benchmarks (§5).

**Visualization with Edgeworth Boxes.** To visualize feasible resource allocations, we use the Edgeworth box [11]. Figure 1 illustrates the allocation of two resources to two users. User 1's origin is at the lower left corner and User 2's origin is at the upper right corner. The total amount of cache is the height of the box and the total amount of memory bandwidth is the width. Therefore, each feasible allocation of resources can be represented as a point in the Edgeworth box. If user 1 gets 6GB/s memory bandwidth and 8MB cache, user 2 is left with 18GB/s memory bandwidth and 4MB cache.

The Edgeworth box includes all possible allocations. But only some of these allocations are fair. And only some of these provide sharing incentives. Thus, desired game-theoretic properties (sharing incentives, envy-freeness, and Pareto efficiency) define constraints on the allocation space. We use the Edgeworth box to visualize these constraints, beginning with sharing incentives.

## 3.1 Sharing Incentives (SI)

Sharing hardware is essential to increasing system utilization and throughput. An allocation mechanism should provide sharing incentives (SI) such that agents are at least as happy as they would be under an equal split of the resources. Without SI, users would prefer to partition hardware equally. But an equal partitioning would not reflect software diversity and heterogeneous hardware demands. Resources may be mis-allocated, leaving throughput unexploited.

Formally, let $C_r$ denote the total capacity of resource $r$ in the system. Suppose an allocation mechanism provides agent $i$ with resources $x_i = (x_{i1}, \ldots, x_{iR})$. For a system with $N$ users, this mechanism provides SI if

$$(x_{i1}, \ldots, x_{iR}) \succsim_i \left(\frac{C_1}{N}, \ldots, \frac{C_R}{N}\right) \tag{3}$$

for each agent $i \in [1, N]$. In other words, each agent weakly prefers its allocation of hardware to an equal partition.

Whether an allocation is preferred depends on the utility functions. Consider our example with cache size and memory bandwidth. User 1 compares its allocation $(x_1, y_1)$ against equally splitting 24GB/s of bandwidth and 12MB of cache. If user 1 always weakly prefers $(x_1, y_1)$, then the allocation mechanism provides user 1 an incentive to share.

$$x_1^{0.6} y_1^{0.4} \geq \left(\frac{24\text{GB/s}}{2}\right)^{0.6} \left(\frac{12\text{MB}}{2}\right)^{0.4} \tag{4}$$

$$x_2^{0.2} y_2^{0.8} \geq \left(\frac{24\text{GB/s}}{2}\right)^{0.2} \left(\frac{12\text{MB}}{2}\right)^{0.8} \tag{5}$$

In our example with two agents, Equations (4)–(5) must be satisfied. User 1 must receive allocations that satisfy Equation (4). Simultaneously, user 2 must receive allocations that satisfy Equation (5). A mechanism that provides SI will identify allocations that satisfy both constraints.

### 3.2 Envy-Freeness (EF)

Envy is the resentment of another agent's allocation combined with a desire to receive that same allocation. Allocations are envy-free (EF) if no agent envies another. Such allocations are considered equitable and equity is a game-theoretic requirement for fairness [37].

Specifically, suppose agent $i$ is allocated $x_i$. This allocation is EF if agent $i$ prefers its allocation to any other agent's allocation and has no desire to swap. That is, $x_i \succsim_i x_j, \forall j \neq i$. In this comparison, each agent considers herself in the place of other agents and evaluates their allocations in the same way she judges her own allocation.

In our cache and bandwidth example, the EF allocations for user 1 are those for which $u_1(x_1, y_1) \geq u_1(x_2, y_2)$. Note that $(x_2, y_2) = (24 - x_1, 12 - y_1)$. Thus, allocations that satisfy Equation (6) are EF for user 1. And Figure 2(a) illustrates regions in which these allocations are found. Similarly, Equation (7) and Figure 2(b) describe the set of EF allocations for user 2. A mechanism that satisfies EF will identify allocations that satisfy both constraints.

$$x_1^{0.6} y_1^{0.4} \geq (24 - x_1)^{0.6} (12 - y_1)^{0.4} \tag{6}$$

$$x_2^{0.2} y_2^{0.8} \geq (24 - x_2)^{0.2} (12 - y_2)^{0.8} \tag{7}$$

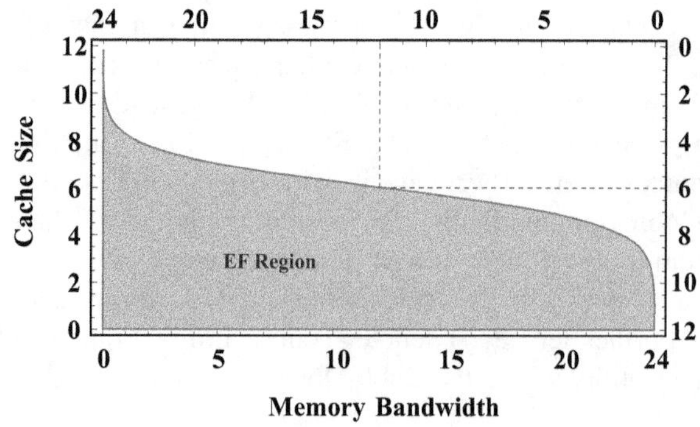


(a) Envy-free Allocations for User 1

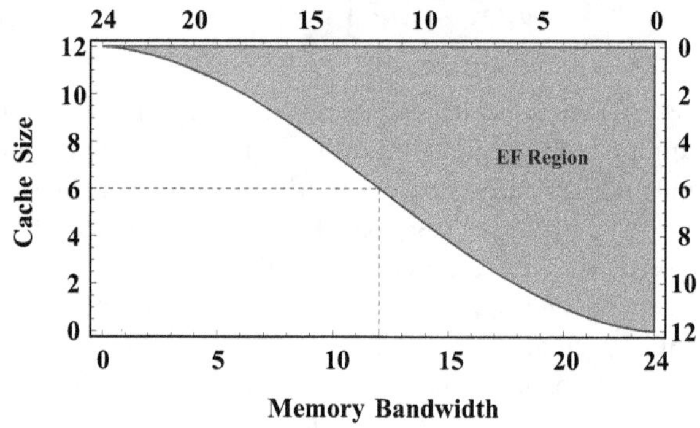


(b) Envy-free Allocations for User 2

**Figure 2. Visualizing Envy-freeness (EF).** EF allocations for user 1 satisfy $x_1^{0.6} y_1^{0.4} \geq (24 - x_1)^{0.6}(12 - y_1)^{0.4}$. Those for user 2 satisfy $x_2^{0.2} y_2^{0.8} \geq (24 - x_2)^{0.2}(12 - y_2)^{0.8}$. The mid-point (12GB/s, 6MB) and two corners (24GB/s, 0MB), and (0GB/s, 12MB) are always EF.

There are always at least three EF allocations, which are illustrated by the middle point and two corner points. The middle point corresponds to the situation in which all resources all equally divided between users. No user envies the other.

The corners correspond to situations in which all of one resource is given to one user and all of the other resource is given to the other. Both users derive zero utility and do not envy each other. In our example, the two corner allocations are (0GB/s, 12MB) and (24GB/s, 0MB). Users derive zero utility because both cache and memory are required for computation.

None of these obvious EF allocations is attractive. The middle point divides resources equally without accounting for differences in user utility. In this setting, system throughput could likely be improved. And corner points are clearly not useful. Thus, we need a mechanism to identify more effective EF allocations.

### 3.3 Pareto Efficiency (PE)

Pareto efficiency (PE) is another game-theoretic property that must be satisfied by a fair resource allocation [37]. An allocation is PE if increasing one user's utility necessarily

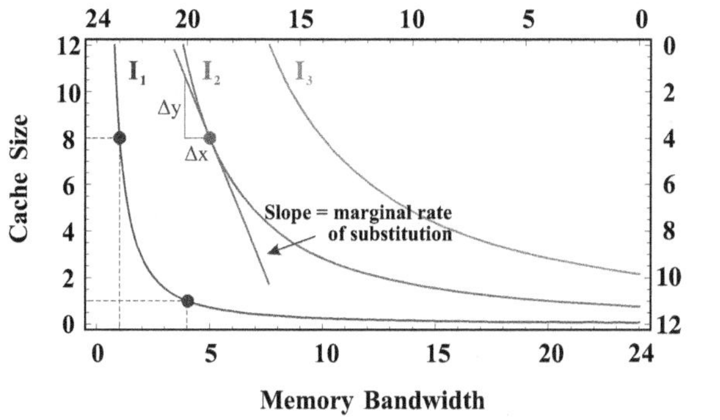


**Figure 3. Cobb-Douglas Indifference Curves.** On a given indifference curve, allocations provide the same utility. On different curves, utility of $I_3$ is greater than that of $I_1$. Slopes illustrate the marginal rate of substitution.

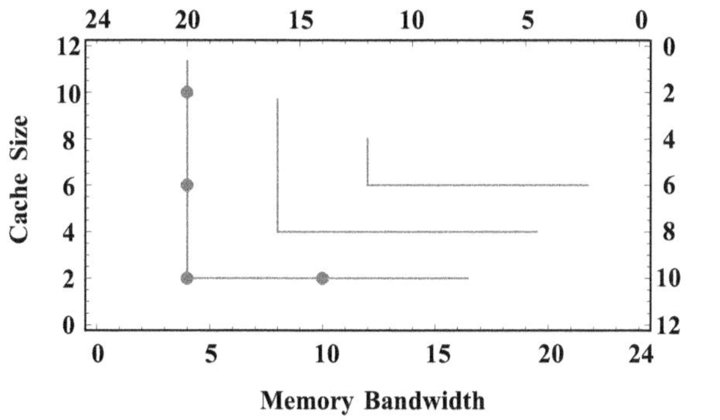


**Figure 4. Leontief Indifference Curves.** Resources are perfect complements and the marginal rate of substitution is either zero or infinity.

decreases another's utility. If an allocation is not PE, there exists another allocation that should have been chosen to improve total system utility.

More precisely, consider an allocation $x = (x_1, \ldots, x_N)$ for $N$ agents. Allocation $x$ is PE if there exists no other feasible allocation $x'$ that all agents $i$ weakly prefer ($x'_i \succsim_i x_i$) and at least one agent $j$ strictly prefers ($x'_j \succ_j x_j$). Finding PE allocations is inherently linked to navigating trade-offs between substitutable resources.

**Substitution Effects.** An indifference curve depicts the allocations that are substitutable for one another. Figure 3 shows three indifference curves for user 1. Allocations on the same curve provide the same utility. Allocations on different curves provide different utilities. The utility of $I_1$ is less than that of $I_2$, and the utility of $I_2$ is less than that of $I_3$. Therefore, all allocations on $I_2$ and $I_3$ are strictly preferred to those on $I_1$.

The Leontief preferences used in prior work do not permit substitution [15]. Suppose user 1 demands 2GB/s of memory bandwidth and 1MB of cache. With this demand vector, the user's Leontief utility function is shown in Equation (8).

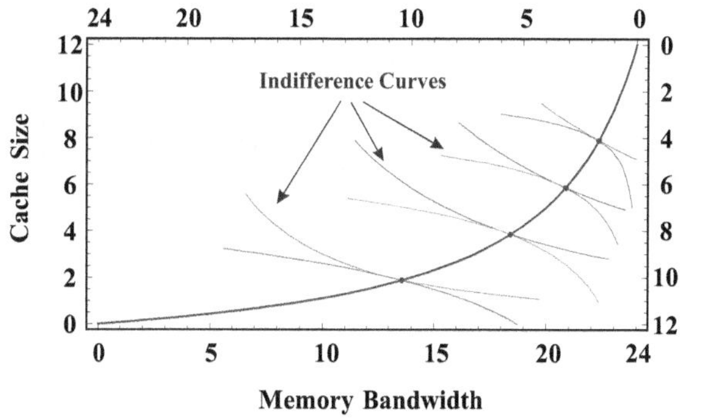


**Figure 5. Visualizing Pareto Efficiency (PE).** The contract curve includes all PE allocations for which the marginal rate of substitution (MRS) for both utility functions are equal.

Under Leontief, resources are perfect complements, leading to the L-shaped indifference curves in Figure 4.

$$u_1 = min\{x_1, 2y_1\} \tag{8}$$

User 1 demands bandwidth and cache in a 2:1 ratio. If the allocated ratio differs, then extra allocated resources are wasted. For example, user 1 derives the same utility from (4GB/s, 2MB) as it does from disproportional allocations such as (10GB/s, 2MB) or (4GB/s, 10MB). Leontief preferences do not account for marginal benefits from disproportional allocations. Nor do they allow for substitution in which more cache capacity compensates for less memory bandwidth.

In contrast, substitution is modeled by Cobb-Douglas preferences as illustrated by indifference curves' slopes in Figure 3. For instance, user 1 can substitute an allocation of (4GB/s, 1MB) for an allocation of (1GB/s, 8MB). Such flexibility provides the allocation mechanism with more ways to provide the same utility, which is particularly important as the set of feasible allocations are constrained by the conditions for SI, EF, and PE.

**Marginal Rates of Substitution.** The marginal rate of substitution (MRS), is the rate at which the user is willing to substitute one resource for the other. Visually, the MRS is the slope of the indifference curve. If MRS=2, the user will give up two units of $y$ for one unit of $x$. Under Leontief preferences, the MRS is either zero or infinity; the user has no incentive for substitution. But under Cobb-Douglas preferences, the MRS is more interesting. In our cache and bandwidth example, the marginal rate of substitution for user 1 is given by Equation (9).

$$MRS_{1,xy} = \frac{\partial u_1/\partial x_1}{\partial u_1/\partial y_1} = \left(\frac{0.6}{0.4}\right)\left(\frac{y_1}{x_1}\right) \tag{9}$$

For any PE allocation, the MRS for the two users must be equal. Visually, this means users' indifference curves are tangent for PE allocations. Suppose curves were not tangent

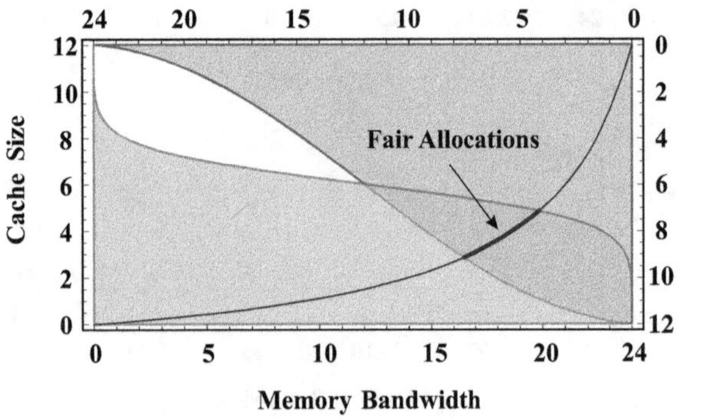


**Figure 6. Fair Allocation Set** All the points on the intersection of envy-free sets and the contract curve correspond to the fair allocations.

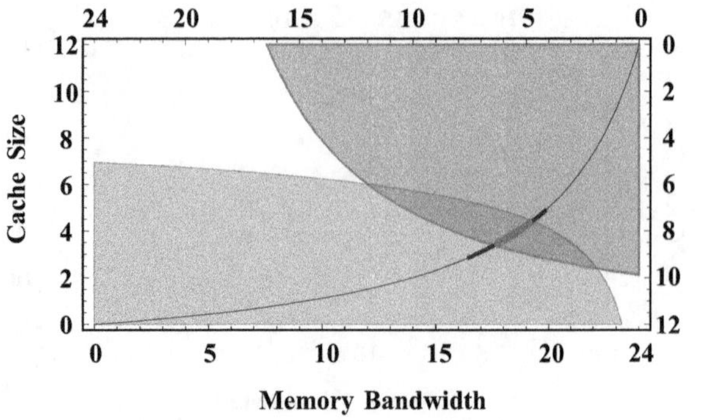


**Figure 7. Visualizing Sharing Incentives (SI).** Satisfying the sharing incentive property limits the set of feasible fair allocations.

for a particular allocation. Then a user $i$ could adjusts its allocation and travel along its indifference curve, substituting resources based on its MRS without affecting $u_i$. But the substitution would take the other user to a higher utility.

The MRS determines the contract curve, which shows all PE allocations. Figure 5 shows the contract curve and illustrates tangency for three allocations. With the tangency condition, formal conditions for PE is easily formulated. In our example, allocations $(x_1, y_1)$ and $(x_2, y_2)$ are PE if the users' marginal rates of substitution are equal; Equation (10) must be satisfied.

$$\left(\frac{0.6}{0.4}\right)\left(\frac{y_1}{x_1}\right) = \left(\frac{0.2}{0.8}\right)\left(\frac{y_2}{x_2}\right) \tag{10}$$

As seen in Figure 5, both origins are PE allocations. At these points, one user's utility is zero and the other's is maximized. Increasing a user's utility, starting from zero, necessarily decreases the other user's utility. While PE, these allocations are neither desirable nor fair. The user with zero utility envies the other user's allocation. Thus, we need a mechanism that identifies both PE and EF allocations.

## 4. Resource Elasticity Fairness (REF)

We present a fair allocation mechanism that satisfies three game-theoretic properties: sharing incentives (SI), envy-freeness (EF), and Pareto efficiency (PE). We begin with the space of possible allocations. We then add constraints to identify allocations with the desired properties.

Economic game theory defines a fair allocation as one that is equitable (EF) and efficient (PE) [37]. Figure 6 illustrates the effect of these constraints. Each user identifies its EF allocations. And the contract curve identifies PE allocations. The intersection of these three constraints define feasible, fair allocations. Figure 7 shows that SI further constrains the set of fair allocations.

Formally, finding fair multi-resource allocations given Cobb-Douglas preferences can be modeled as the following feasibility problem for $N$ agents and $R$ resources.

$$\begin{aligned} &\text{find} && x && && (11)\\ &\text{subject to} && u_i(x_i) \geq u_i(x_j) && i, j \in [1, N] \\ & && \frac{\alpha_{ir}}{\alpha_{is}}\frac{x_{is}}{x_{ir}} = \frac{\alpha_{jr}}{\alpha_{js}}\frac{x_{js}}{x_{jr}} && i, j \in [1, N]; r, s \in [1, R] \\ & && u_i(x_i) \geq u_i(C/N) && i \in [1, N] \\ & && \sum_{i=1}^{N} x_{ir} \leq C_r, && r \in [1, R] \end{aligned}$$

where $C/N$ is $(C_1/N, \ldots, C_R/N)$. In this formulation, the four constraints enforce EF, PE, SI, and capacity.

### 4.1 Procedure for Fair Allocation

To solve the multi-resource allocation problem, we present a mechanism to determine each agent's fair share of the hardware. $N$ agents share $R$ resources. For each agent $i$, we determine its allocation $x_i = (x_{i1}, \ldots, x_{iR})$ with the following procedure, which satisfies all constraints in Equation (11).

- **Fit Cobb-Douglas Utility.** Profile and characterize agent $i$'s performance for various resource allocations. Fit a Cobb-Douglas utility function $u_i(x_i) = \alpha_{i0} \prod_{r=1}^{R} x_{ir}^{\alpha_{ir}}$.
- **Re-scale Elasticities.** Parameters $\alpha$ in the Cobb-Douglas utility function are known as elasticities. For each agent $i$, re-scale its elasticities so that they sum to one.

$$\hat{\alpha}_{ir} = \frac{\alpha_{ir}}{\sum_{r=1}^{R} \alpha_{ir}} \tag{12}$$

- **Re-scale Utilities.** Redefine the Cobb-Douglas utility function with re-scaled elasticities $\hat{u}_i(x_i) = \prod_{r=1}^{R} x_{ir}^{\hat{\alpha}_{ir}}$.
- **Allocate in Proportion to Elasticity.** Examine re-scaled Cobb-Douglas utilities and use their elasticities to determine fair share for each agent $i$ and resource $r$.

$$x_{ir} = \frac{\hat{\alpha}_{ir}}{\sum_{j=1}^{N} \hat{\alpha}_{jr}} \times C_r \tag{13}$$

In effect, this allocation mechanism quantifies elasticity $\alpha$ to determine the extent each resource improves an agent's utility. Re-scaling elasticities allows us to compare values for different agents on the same scale. By allocating in proportion to elasticity, agents that benefit more from resource $r$ will receive a larger share of the total $C_r$.

In our cache and bandwidth example, two users provide Cobb-Douglas utility functions with elasticities. These elasticities are already scaled and sum to one (e.g., $u_1 = x_1^{0.6}y_1^{0.4}$). To determine the memory bandwidth allocation, we examine both user's bandwidth elasticity ($\alpha_{1x} = 0.6, \alpha_{2x} = 0.2$) and allocate proportionally.

$$x_1 = \left(\frac{0.6}{0.8}\right) \times 24 = 18\text{GB/s}, \quad y_1 = \left(\frac{0.4}{1.2}\right) \times 12 = 4\text{MB}$$

$$x_2 = \left(\frac{0.2}{0.8}\right) \times 24 = 6\text{GB/s}, \quad y_2 = \left(\frac{0.8}{1.2}\right) \times 12 = 8\text{MB}$$

### 4.2 Fairness and Sharing Incentives

The proportional elasticity mechanism has several attractive properties. The mechanism promotes sharing and guarantees fairness by satisfying conditions for SI, EF, and PE. We sketch the proofs for these properties.

First, we show that the allocation is a Nash bargaining solution. Observe that the allocation from Equation (13) is equivalent to finding an allocation that maximizes the product of re-scaled utilities $\hat{u}$. This equivalence can be shown by substituting re-scaled Cobb-Douglas utility functions into Equation (14) and using Lagrange multipliers for constrained optimization.

$$\max \prod_{i=1}^{N} \hat{u}_i(x_i) \quad \text{subject to} \quad \sum_{i=1}^{N} x_{ir} \leq C_r \tag{14}$$

In game theory, the bargaining problem asks how agents should cooperate to produce Pareto efficient outcomes. Nash's solution is to maximize the product of utilities [27, 30], which is equivalent to Equation (14) and our allocation mechanism. Thus, our mechanism produces an allocation that is also a Nash bargaining solution.

Next, we show that our allocation is also a Competitive Equilibrium from Equal Outcomes (CEEI), a well-known microeconomic concept for fair division. In CEEI, users are initially assigned equal resource allocations. Based on user preferences, prices are assigned to resources such that users trade and the market clears to produce an allocation.

The CEEI solution picks precisely the same allocation of resources as the Nash bargaining solution for homogeneous utility functions [26]. Let $x = (x_1, \ldots, x_R)$ be a vector of resources. Utility function $u$ is homogeneous if $u(kx) = ku(x)$ for some constant $k$. Our re-scaled Cobb-Douglas utilities are homogeneous because $\sum_{r=1}^{R} \hat{\alpha}_r = 1$. For this reason, our allocation is a solution to both the Nash bargaining problem and CEEI.

Finally, a CEEI allocation is known to be fair, satisfying both EF and PE [37]. CEEI solutions also satisfy SI because users start with an equal division of resources. Users would only deviate from this initial division if buying and selling resources in the CEEI market would increase utility. Thus, users can do no worse than an equal division and CEEI provides SI.

In summary, our allocation mechanism is equivalent to the Nash bargaining solution, which is equivalent to the CEEI solution. Because the CEEI solution provides SI, EF, and PE for re-scaled Cobb-Douglas utility functions, the proportional elasticity mechanism provides these properties as well.

### 4.3 Fairness and Strategy-Proofness in the Large

The proportional elasticity mechanism is strategy-proof in the large. An allocation mechanism is strategy-proof (SP) if a user cannot gain by mis-reporting its utility functions. Unfortunately, SP is too restrictive a property for Cobb-Douglas utility functions. For these preferences, no mechanism can provide both PE and SP [19]. However, our mechanism does satisfy a weaker property, strategy-proofness in the large (SPL). When there are many users in the system, users have no incentive to lie about their elasticities $\alpha$.

First, we define large. A large system has many users such that the sum of all agents' elasticities for any resource is much bigger than 1. In such a system, any one user's resource elasticity is small relative to the sum of all agents' elasticities for the resource. More formally, the system is large if $1 \ll \sum_j \alpha_{jr}$, for all resources $r$.

Next, suppose user $i$ decides to lie about her utility function, reporting $\alpha'_{ir}$ instead of the true value $\alpha_{ir}$ for resource $r$. Given other users' utilities, user $i$ would choose to report the $\alpha'_{ir}$ that maximizes her utility.

$$\frac{\partial}{\partial \alpha'_{ik}} \prod_{r=1}^{R} \left( \frac{\alpha'_{ir}}{\alpha'_{ir} + \sum_{j \neq i} \alpha_{jr}} C_r \right)^{\alpha_{ir}} = 0 \quad \forall k \in [1, R] \tag{15}$$

In her best scenario, user $i$ knows all other users' utilities and $\alpha_{jr}, \forall j \neq i$. Thus, by mis-reporting $\alpha'_{ir}$, user $i$ can precisely affect her proportional share of resource $r$. Yet, when user $i$ receives her allocation, she evaluates it with $\alpha_{ir}$, which reflects her true utility from resource $r$. Thus, the product in Equation (15) reflects user $i$'s utility from lying.

User $i$ attempts to maximize this utility from lying, taking partial derivatives with respect to $\alpha'_{ir}$. But it can be proven that this optimization produces $\alpha'_{ir} \approx \alpha_{ir}$ when $1 \ll \sum_j \alpha_{jr}$ for all resources $r$.[1] Thus, in a large system, our allocation mechanism is approximately strategy proof. A user cannot benefit by lying about her utility.

In theory, SPL holds when an individual agents elasticity is much smaller than the sum of all agents elasticities.

[1] See §A for the proof

In practice, we find that tens of agents are sufficient to provide SPL. In other words, a strategic agent performing the optimization of Equation (15) will not deviate from her true elasticity.

For example, consider 64 tasks sharing a large system. This is a realistic setting since modern servers can have four processor sockets (= 64 threads) that share eight-twelve memory channels (> 100 GB/s of bandwidth). Suppose each of the 64 tasks elasticities are uniformly random from (0,1). We analyze Equation (15) and find that SPL holds.

### 4.4 Implementing the Mechanism

To implement the proportional elasticity mechanism, we need Cobb-Douglas utilities. We describe the process for deriving these utilities based on performance profiles and statistical regression. We also describe how proportional shares can be enforced by leveraging known resource schedulers.

**Profiling Performance.** Suppose a user derives utility from performance. Without loss of generality, we measure performance as the number of instructions committed per cycle (IPC). Execution time, speed-ups over a baseline, and energy efficiency would all exhibit similar trends.

The user profiles its performance as a function of allocated resources. These profiles reveal the rate of diminishing returns and identify resource substitutability. For example, the user samples from the allocation space to determine sensitivity to cache size and memory bandwidth. These profiles provide the data needed to derive utilities.

Performance can be profiled in several ways. First, consider off-line profiling in which a user runs software while precisely varying the available hardware. For example, a user can co-locate its task with synthetic benchmarks that exert tunable pressure on the memory hierarchy [25]. Thus, profiles would quantify cache and bandwidth sensitivity.

Also off-line, the user might rely on cycle-accurate, full-system simulators. These simulators combine virtual machines, such as QEMU, with hardware timing models to accurately model processor and memory [33, 35]. Simulated and physical hardware may report different performance numbers. But simulators can accurately report trends and elasticities, identifying hardware resources that are more important for performance. We value relative accuracy over absolute accuracy when profiling hardware preferences.

Finally, consider on-line profiling. Without prior knowledge, a user assumes all resources contribute equally to performance. Such a naive user reports utility $u = x^{0.5}y^{0.5}$. As the system allocates for this utility, the user profiles software performance. And as profiles are accumulated for varied allocations, the user adapts its utility function.

**Fitting Cobb-Douglas Utility.** Given performance profiles for varied hardware allocations, each user fits her Cobb-Douglas utility function in the form of $u = \alpha_0 \prod_{r=1}^{R} x_r^{\alpha_r}$. For example, let $u$ be IPC, let $x_1$ be cache capacity, and let $x_2$ be memory bandwidth.

Fitting the utility function means identifying elasticities $\alpha = (\alpha_0, \ldots, \alpha_R)$ that best relate performance to the resources. We fit $\alpha$ with regression. Specifically, we apply a log transformation to linearize Cobb-Douglas. After this transformation, we have a standard linear model with parameters $\alpha$ as shown in Equation (16). Parameters are fit with least squares.

$$\log(u) \quad = \quad \log(\alpha_0) + \sum_{r=1}^{R} \alpha_r \log(x_r) \qquad (16)$$

**Allocating Proportional Shares.** We re-scale elasticities from each user's Cobb-Douglas utility function and compute proportional shares. The novelty of our mechanism is not in proportional sharing but in how we identify the proportions based on Cobb-Douglas elasticities to ensure SI, EF, and PE. After the procedure determines proportional shares for each user, we can enforce those shares with existing approaches, such as weighted fair queuing [8] or lottery scheduling [38].

### 4.5 Alternative Fair Mechanisms

There may exist multiple allocations $x$ that satisfy the fairness conditions in Equation (11). Our mechanism for proportional elasticity is only one possible mechanism for one possible solution. Alternative mechanisms may also produce fair allocations but increase computational complexity. Suppose we follow prior work in computer architecture and seek fair allocations that maximize system throughput.

To evaluate throughput for a multi-programmed system, architects define the notion of weighted progress, which divides each application's multi-programmed IPC by its single-threaded IPC [12]. Weighted system throughput is the sum of each user's weighted progress. This is the metric used to evaluate prior work on memory scheduling and multiprocessor resource management [4, 29].

$$\sum_{i=1}^{N} \frac{\text{IPC}(x_i)}{\text{IPC}(C)} \quad \approx \quad \sum_{i=1}^{N} \frac{u_i(x_i)}{u_i(C)} \quad = \quad \sum_{i=1}^{N} U(x_i) \qquad (17)$$

We adapt this notion of normalized throughput, expressing it in terms of our utility functions. This means dividing utility for an allocation in the shared machine $u_i(x_i)$ by utility when given all of the machine's capacity $u_i(C)$. Let $U(x_i) = u_i(x_i)/u_i(C)$ define the notion of weighted utility, which is equivalent to the notion of slowdown in prior work [4, 29].

**Fair Allocation for Utilitarian Welfare.** Rather than allocate in proportion to elasticities, we could allocate to maximize utilitarian welfare. Instead of finding $x$ subject to fairness conditions in Equation (11), we would optimize $\max \sum_i U_i(x_i)$ subject to the same conditions. While $\max \sum_i U_i(x_i)$ is computationally intractable, $\max \prod_i U_i(x_i)$

is similar but tractable with geometric programming.[2] But this mechanism would be more computationally demanding than our closed-form solution in Equation (13).

Yet a utilitarian mechanism is interesting. Overall system performance is an explicit optimization objective. A utilitarian mechanism likely provides the allocation that achieves the highest performance among all fair allocations. In effect, utilitarian allocations provides an empirical upper bound on fair performance.

**Fair Allocation for Egalitarian Welfare.** We could also find fair allocations to optimize egalitarian welfare. In Equation (11), we would optimize max-min $U_i(x_i)$ subject to fairness conditions. As before, geometric programming can perform this optimization but this mechanism would be more computationally demanding than our closed-form solution.

Egalitarian welfare is interesting because it optimizes for the least satisfied user. EF and PE define conditions for a fair allocation. But these conditions say nothing about equality in outcomes. An allocation could be fair but the difference between the most and least satisfied user in the system could be large. The max-min optimization objective mitigates inequality in outcomes, perhaps at the expense of system welfare. Egalitarian allocations might provide an empirical lower bound on fair performance.

**Unfair Allocation.** Finally, we could neglect game-theoretic fairness and ignore constraints imposed by SI, EF, and PE. In this setting, we would maximize welfare subject only to capacity constraints. Note that optimizing egalitarian welfare without fairness conditions is equivalent to the objective in prior work [29], which equalizes users' weighted progress such that $\max_i U_i(x_i) \;/\; \min_j U_j(x_j) \rightarrow 1$. The max-min objective for egalitarian welfare causes the denominator to approach the numerator. Assessing performance of unfair allocations reveals the penalty we must pay for SI, EF, and PE.

## 5. Evaluation

We evaluate the proportional elasticity mechanism when sharing the last-level cache and main memory bandwidth in a chip-multiprocessor. In this setting, we evaluate several aspects of the mechanism. First, we show that Cobb-Douglas utilities are a good fit for performance. Then, we interpret utility functions to identify applications that prefer cache capacity (C) and memory bandwidth (M).

Finally, we compare the proportional elasticity mechanism against an equal slowdown mechanism, which represents conventional wisdom. We find that equal slowdown fails to guarantee game-theoretic fairness. On the other hand, proportional elasticity guarantees SI, EF and PE with only modest performance penalties relative to an unfair approach.

[2] Cobb-Douglas is a monomial function (i.e., function with the form $f(x) = ax_1^{\alpha_1}x_2^{\alpha_2}, \ldots, x_m^{\alpha_m}$). And geometric programming can maximize monomials [5].

**Table 1.** Platform Parameters

| Component | Specification |
|---|---|
| Processor | 3 GHz OOO cores, 4-width issue and commit |
| L1 Cache | 32 KB, 4-way set associative, 64-byte block size, 2-cycle latency |
| L2 Cache | [128 KB, 256 KB, 512 KB, 1 MB, 2 MB], 8-way set associative, 64-byte block size, 20-cycle latency |
| DRAM Controller | Closed-page, Queue per rank, Rank then bank round-robin scheduling |
| DRAM Bandwidth | [0.8 GB/s, 1.6 GB/s, 3.2 GB/s, 6.4 GB/s, 12.8 GB], single channel |

### 5.1 Experimental Methodology

**Simulator.** We simulate the out-of-order cores using the MARSSx86 full system simulator [33]. We integrate the processor model with the DRAMSim2 simulator [35] to simulate main memory. To characterize application sensitivity to allocated cache size and memory bandwidth, we simulate 25 architectures spanning combinations of five cache sizes and five memory bandwidths. The platform parameters are described in Table 1.

Given simulator data, we use Matlab to fit Cobb-Douglas utility functions. Our mechanism includes a closed-form expression for each agent's fair allocation. But to evaluate other mechanisms that require geometric programming, we use CVX [16], a convex optimization solver.

**Workloads.** We evaluate our method on 24 benchmarks from PARSEC and SPLASH-2x suites [2]. We further evaluate applications from the Phoenix system for MapReduce programming [34], including histogram, linear regression, string match, and word count. For PARSEC 3.0 benchmarks, we simulate 100M instructions from the regions of interest (ROI), which are representative application phases identified by MARSSx86 developers. Phoenix applications we simulate 100M instructions from the beginning of the map phase.

### 5.2 Fitting Cobb-Douglas Utility

Each application is associated with a user. Application performance is measured as instructions per cycle (IPC). Using cycle-accurate simulations, we profile each benchmark's performance. Given these profiles for varied cache size and memory bandwidth allocations, we perform a linear regression to estimate utility functions.

For each application, we use a Cobb-Douglas utility function $u = \alpha_0 x^{\alpha_x} y^{\alpha_y}$ where $u$ is application performance measured with IPC, $x$ is memory bandwidth, and $y$ is cache size. Although a non-linear relationship exists between Cobb-Douglas utility and resource allocations, a logarithmic transformation produces a linear model (Equation (16)). Least squares regression estimates the resource elasticities $\alpha$ for each benchmark.

To evaluate this fit, we report the coefficient of determination (R-squared), which measures how much variance in the data set is captured by the model. R-squared $\rightarrow 1$ as fit improves. Figure 8(a) shows that most benchmarks are fitted with R-squared of 0.7-1.0, indicating good fits. Benchmarks with low R-squared, such as `radiosity`, have negligible variance and no trend for Cobb-Douglas to capture.

We consider representative workloads with high and low R-squared values in Figure 8, which plots simulated and fitted IPC. Cobb-Douglas utilities accurately track IPC and reflect preferences for cache and memory bandwidth. Even workloads with lower R-squared values, such as `radiosity`, do not deviate significantly from true values.

In practice, the proportional elasticity mechanism never uses the predicted value for $u$ to allocate hardware. It only uses the fitted parameters for $\alpha$ to determine fair shares. Thus, Cobb-Douglas fits need only be good enough to assess resource elasticities and preferences. But good predictions for $u$ give confidence in the accuracy of fitted $\alpha$.

We expect Cobb-Douglas utility functions to generalize beyond cache size and memory bandwidth. After applying log transformations to performance and each of the resource allocations, our approach to fitting the utility function is equivalent to prior work in statistically inferred microarchitectural models [23]. Prior work accurately inferred performance models with more than ten microarchitectural resources, which suggests our application of Cobb-Douglas utilities will scale as more resources are shared.

### 5.3 Interpreting Cobb-Douglas Utilities

After fitting Cobb-Douglas utilities, we re-scale elasticities as described in Equation (12). Resource elasticity quantifies the extent to which an agent demands a resource. In other words, in a multi-resource setting, elasticities quantify the relative importance of each resource to an agent.

Figure 9 depicts re-scaled elasticities for our workloads. If $\alpha_{cache} > \alpha_{mem}$, then the workload derives more utility from cache size than it does from memory bandwidth (e.g., `raytrace`). In contrast, if $\alpha_{mem} > \alpha_{cache}$, then the workload finds memory bandwidth more useful (e.g., `dedup`).

Given resource elasticities, we can classify workloads into two groups. Workloads in group M demand memory bandwidth and $\alpha_{mem} > 0.5$. Workloads in group C demand cache capacity and $\alpha_{cache} > 0.5$. This classification differentiates how workloads re-use data in their cache and whether they exhibit bursty memory behavior.

For example, `facesim`, `fluidanimate`, and `streamcluster` exhibit streaming behavior [3]. Increasing the cache size would only marginally increase performance. Streaming workloads clearly prefer memory bandwidth and this preference is reflected in their resource elasticities in Figure 9.

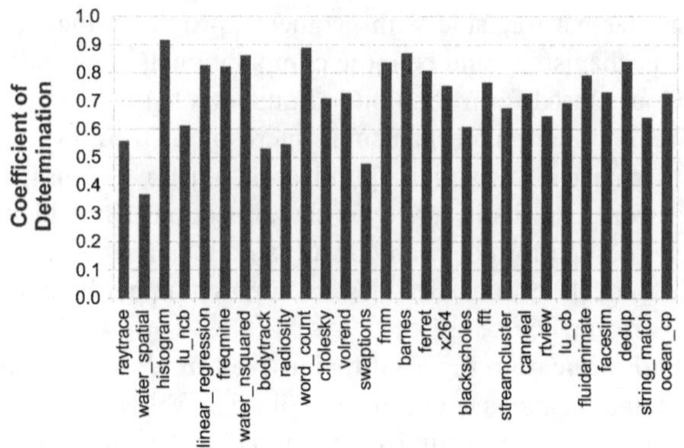


(a) Coefficient of determination (R-squared) measures goodness of fit for Cobb-Douglas utility functions. Larger values are better.

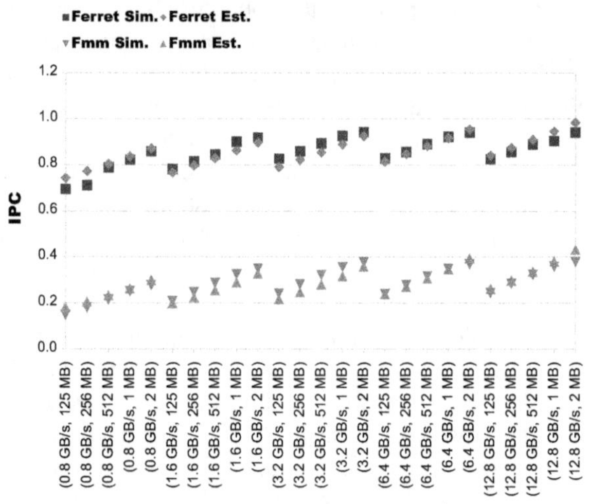


(b) Simulated versus fitted Cobb-Douglas performance for varied cache size, memory bandwidth allocations. Representative workloads with high R-squared.

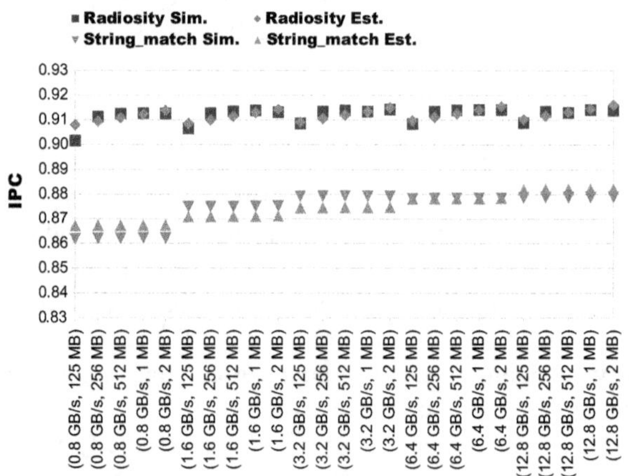


(c) Simulated versus fitted Cobb-Douglas performance for varied cache size, memory bandwidth allocations. Representative workloads with low R-squared.

**Figure 8.** Evaluating Cobb-Douglas utilities for cache size and memory bandwidth. $u = \alpha_0 x^{\alpha_x} y^{\alpha_y}$ where $u$ is IPC performance, $x$ is memory bandwidth, and $y$ is cache size. Cobb-Douglas is fit by finding $\alpha$ with method of least squares.

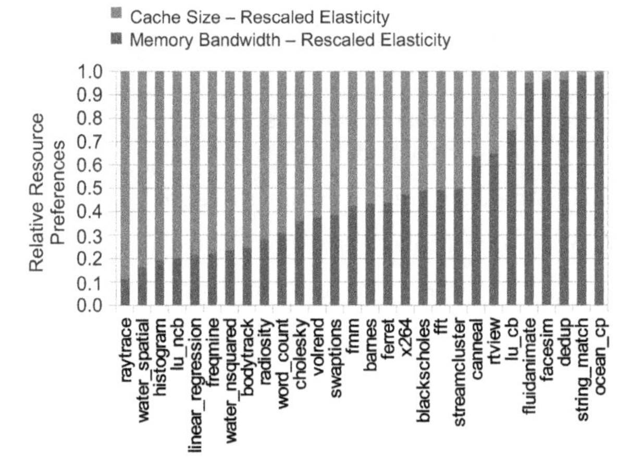


**Figure 9. Resource Preferences and Elasticities.** Rescaled elasticities from Equation (12) show relative importance of cache size and memory bandwidth for each workload. Workloads for which $\alpha_{mem} > 0.5$ are classified M. Otherwise, they are classified C.

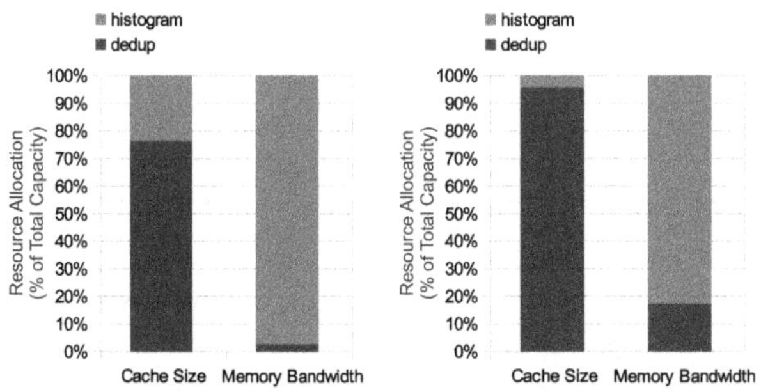


(a) Equal Slowdown

(b) Proportional Elasticity

**Figure 10.** Allocations for histogram (C) and dedup (M) show that equal slowdown can satisfy SI, EF, and PE in some scenarios.

## 5.4 Proportional Elasticity versus Equal Slowdown

Having demonstrated accurate Cobb-Douglas utility models, we now evaluate our mechanism that allocates in proportion to elasticity. We compare against a mechanism that allocates for equal slowdown, a commonly used approach in computer architecture that seeks to equally distribute the performance penalties from sharing [29], [4].

We compare proportional elasticity and equal slowdown with a series of representative examples. In the first example, all desirable properties (SI, EF, PE) are satisfied by both proportional elasticity and equal slowdown. But an equal slowdown mechanism cannot guarantee these properties. We present two other examples where both SI and EF are violated by an equal slowdown mechanism.

**Example 1: C-M satisfies SI, EF, PE.** Consider a system shared by `histogram` from group C and `dedup` from group M, which prefer cache capacity and memory bandwidth, respectively. Figure 10 illustrates allocations as a percentage

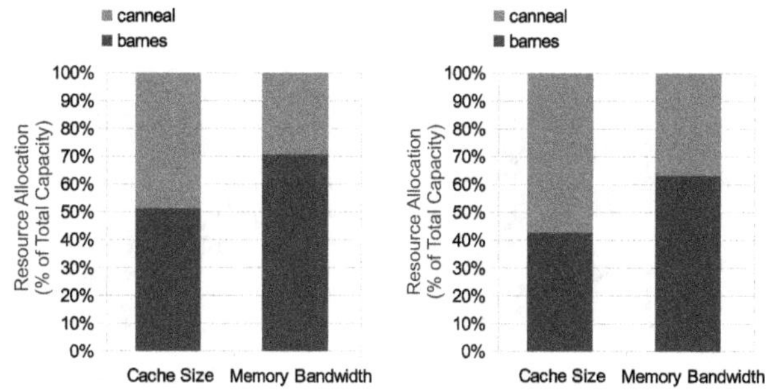


(a) Equal Slowdown

(b) Proportional Elasticity

**Figure 11.** Allocations for barnes (C) and canneal (M) show that equal slowdown can fail to satisfy SI and EF. Equal slowdown provides canneal less than half of both resources, which satisfies neither SI nor EF. Proportional elasticity satisfies SI, EF, and PE.

of total capacity for an equal slowdown mechanism and our proportional elasticity mechanism.

Both mechanisms allocate more cache capacity to `histogram` (C) and memory bandwidth to `dedup` (M). Consider a chip multiprocessor with 12MB cache and 24GB/s of memory bandwidth. We can compute the allocations and evaluate the conditions for SI, EF, and PE in Equation (11). In this particular case, the equal slowdown allocation satisfies all game-theoretic conditions for fairness. And, of course, we have proven that the proportional elasticity allocation is fair.

Unfortunately, while an equal slowdown mechanisms may provide SI and EF in this case, it cannot guarantee them. We cannot even generalize the properties of equal slowdown for broad classes of workloads. While equal slowdown happens to provide SI and EF for `histogram` (C) and `dedup` (M), it may not do so for other pairs of C and M workloads.

**Example 2: C-M violates SI and EF.** Figure 11 considers the allocations for `barnes` (C) and `canneal` (M). Barnes prefers cache size to memory bandwidth whereas cannel prefers bandwidth to cache. This example shows how an equal slowdown mechanism fails to satisfy SI and EF for `canneal`, which receives less than half of both resources in the system. In this setting, `cannel` would not be willing to participate in an equal slowdown mechanism and would rather statically receive half the hardware resources. Moreover, `canneal` envies `barnes`'s allocation. In contrast, our proportional elasticity mechanism allocates more than half of the memory bandwidth to `canneal`, giving it an incentive to share.

**Example 3: C-C violates SI and EF.** Finally, Figure 12 considers two workloads from the same group. In this, case `freqmine` (C) and `linear_regression` (C) both prefer cache capacity to memory bandwidth. But `freqmine` exhibits less memory activity than `linear`. To equalize slowdowns, `linear` must receive far more of both resources.

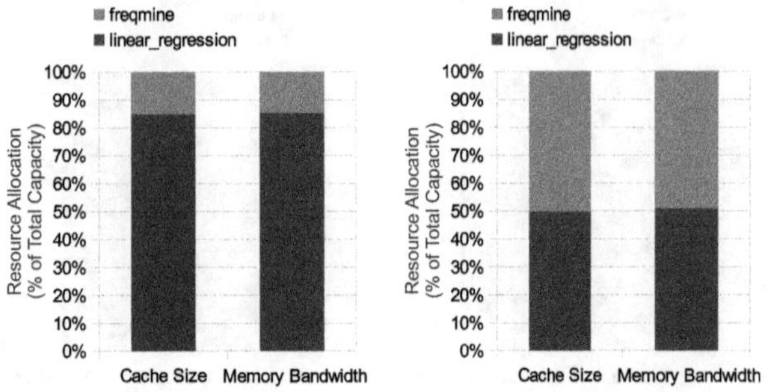


(a) Equal slowdown (b) Proportional elasticity

**Figure 12.** Allocations for freqmine (C) and linear_regression (C) show that equal slowdown can fail to satisfy SI and EF. Equal slowdown provides freqmine less than half of both resources, which satisfies neither SI nor EF. Proportional elasticity satisfies SI, EF, and PE.

In this setting, `freqmine` would not be willing to share the system, preferring an equal split of the resources rather than participate in an equal slowdown mechanism. Even if `freqmine` had been willing to share resources with `linear`, it would prefer `linear`'s allocation over its own. Thus, the allocation from equal slowdown is far from equitable. On the other hand, proportional elasticity divides resources almost equally between benchmarks to satisfy SI and EF.

However, proportional elasticity seems inefficient. It allocates resources equally when one user needs them more. Although the equal slowdown mechanism does not provide game-theoretic fairness, it likely provides higher system throughput in this example. Thus, in some cases, proportional elasticity pays a throughput penalty to provide game-theoretic fairness.

This trade-off between game-theoretic fairness and performance efficiency is fundamental to the mechanisms. The equal slowdown mechanism seeks to equalize normalized performance. If one more unit of a resource significantly improves `linear`'s performance and only modestly improve `freqmine`'s, the equal slowdown mechanism favors `linear`. And overall throughput should increase. In the next section, we quantify the performance penalty incurred by adding constraints for SI, EF, and PE.

### 5.5 Performance Penalty from Fairness

We investigate the performance lost due to game-theoretic fairness conditions. We define an agent's individual performance as $U_i(x_i) = u_i(x_i)/u_i(C)$, which divides utility when sharing by utility when not. $U_i$ is equivalent to the notion of weighted throughput [12] except that we use utility functions rather than IPC. For each allocation policy, we compare weighted system throughput in Equation (17) calculated from utility functions fitted to simulator data.

- **Max Welfare w/o Fairness.** Find an allocation that maximizes welfare subject only to capacity constraints. We use Nash social welfare ($\prod_i U_i(x_i)$), which is tractably maximized with geometric programming. This mechanism provides an empirical upper bound on performance.
- **Equal Slowdown w/o Fairness.** Find an allocation that maximizes the minimum $U_i(x_i)$. This max-min objective function is equivalent to equalizing slowdown by closing the gap between the best and worst performing agents.
- **Max Welfare w/ Fairness.** Find an allocation that maximizes welfare subject to SI, EF, and PE conditions. We use Nash social welfare ($\prod_i U_i(x_i)$), which is tractably maximized with geometric programming.
- **Proportional Elasticity w/ Fairness.** Allocate in proportions based on elasticities in Cobb-Douglas utility functions. Allocations are proven to provide SI, EF, and PE.

**Table 2.** Workload Characterization

| Name | Benchmarks | C/M |
|---|---|---|
| WD1 | histogram, linear_regression, water_nsquared, bodytrack | 4C |
| WD2 | radiosity, fmm, facesim, string_match | 2C-2M |
| WD3 | lu_cb, fluidanimate, facesim, dedup | 4M |
| WD4 | fft, streamcluster, canneal, word_count | 3C-1M |
| WD5 | streamcluster, facesim, dedup, string_match | 1C-3M |
| WD6 | histogram, linear_regression, water_nsquared, bodytrack, freqmine, word_count, x264, dedup | 7C-1M |
| WD7 | histogram, canneal, rtview, bodytrack, radiosity, word_count, linear_regression, water_nsquared | 6C-2M |
| WD8 | radiosity, word_count (2), canneal, rtview, freqmine, x264, dedup | 5C-3M |
| WD9 | radiosity (2), word_count, canneal, rtview, fmm, facesim, string_match | 4C-4M |
| WD10 | water_nsquared, barnes, ferret, lu_cb (2), fluidanimate, facesim, dedup | 3C-5M |

Thus, we compare two allocations with and without game-theoretic fairness. Note that our mechanism is computationally trivial based on the closed-form expression in Equation (13). In contrast, the other mechanisms require geometric programming and convex optimization.

Figure 13 presents weighted system throughput when four applications share cache and memory bandwidth. The workloads have different characteristics, as shown in Table 2. Performance penalties are larger when the allocation mechanism imposes more constraints. Least restricted, maximizing welfare without any fairness constraints provides an

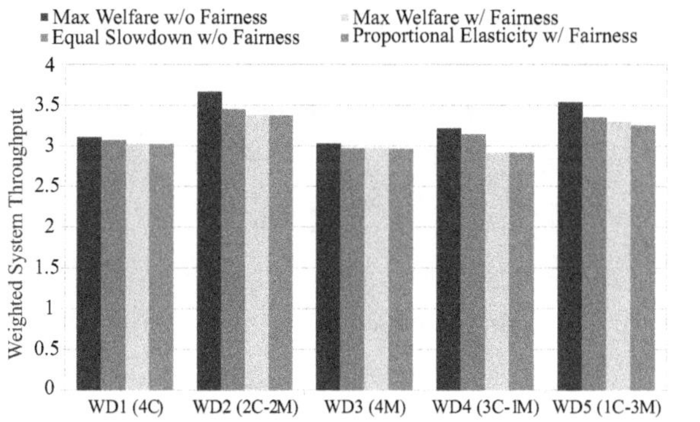


**Figure 13.** Performance Comparison for 4-core System. Penalties for game-theoretic fairness are less than 10%.

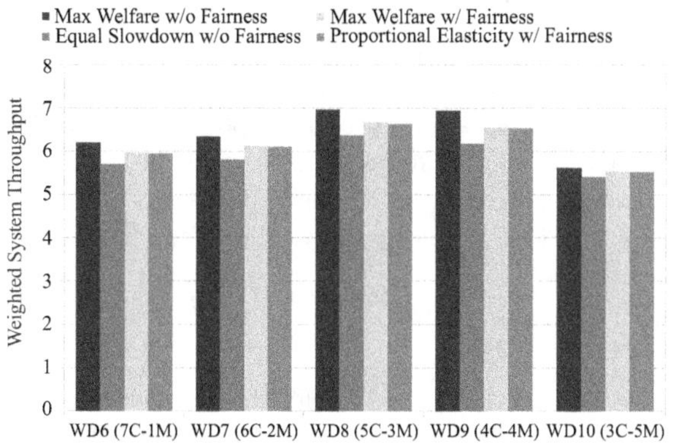


**Figure 14.** Performance Comparison for 8-core System. Penalties for game-theoretic fairness are less than 10%. Proportional elasticity out-performs equal slowdown.

empirical upper bound on throughput. Relative to this upper bound, equal slowdown optimizes worst-case performance, thereby lowering overall throughput. Yet, despite its lower performance, an equal slowdown mechanism does not guarantee game-theoretic fairness.

Among the two mechanisms that provide fairness with SI, EF and PE, we find no performance difference, which is a compelling result. First, our proportional elasticity mechanism is as good as explicitly optimizing throughput subject to fairness. Second, proportional elasticity provides fair performance in a complexity effective way. Our mechanism simply calculates fair shares whereas other mechanisms would require geometric programming.

The price for game-theoretic fairness is small. First, compare maximizing welfare with and without fairness. Constraints for SI, EF, and PE reduces throughput by less than 10%. Second, compare equal slowdown to proportional elasticity. With less than a 7% throughput penalty, proportional elasticity provides game-theoretic guarantees.

Figure 14 further presents throughput for an eight-core system in which eight applications share cache and memory bandwidth. We select five representative workloads to compare allocation mechanisms. In this setting, constraints for game-theoretic fairness reduce throughput by less than 10%.

More interesting, in an eight-core setting, equal slowdown may perform worse than proportional elasticity. Poor performance for an equal slowdown mechanism may be due to optimizing allocations to favor the least satisfied user (i.e., max-min $u_i$). As the number of users increases, the opportunity cost of favoring the least satisfied user also increases. Thus, not only does an equal slowdown mechanism fail to provide game-theoretic fairness, it may also perform worse than proportional elasticity in large systems with many agents.

## 6. Related Work

**Computer Science and Economics.** The fair resource allocation problem has been extensively studied in computer science and economics. While most prior studies focus on fairly allocating a single resource, Ghodsi et al. propose Dominant Resource Fairness (DRF) for fair, multi-resource allocation [15]. DRF satisfies SI, PE, EF and SP for Leontief preferences. Leveraging Leontief properties, Parkes et al. [32] and Joe-Wong et al. [21] extend DRF. Dolev et al. propose an alternative notion of multi-resource fairness [9]. Gutman et al. analyze fairness frameworks and present computational tractable algorithms [18].

While Leontief preferences might be appropriate for distributed systems [15], they cannot capture important trends in hardware architecture. Leontief utilities are linear and do not allow substitution between multiple resources. Moreover, specifying a demand vector for resources, which is required by DRF, is not always possible. In this paper, we consider fair, multi-resource allocation under Cobb-Douglas preferences, which are more realistic in computer architecture.

**Fairness in Computer Architecture.** Nesbit et al. [31] propose a memory scheduler to address fairness for a single memory resource. Other architects use an unfairness index [13, 28]. A variety of memory scheduling heuristics optimize this metric to fairly share memory bandwidth [4, 7, 10, 22, 29]. The unfairness index quantifies the ratio between the maximum and the minimum performance slowdown among workloads sharing the system. The allocation is considered fair if workloads experience equal slowdowns. However, we find that equal slowdowns cannot guarantee game-theoretic properties (e.g., SI, EF, PE).

We consider fairness in a multi-resource setting. Coordinating multi-resource allocation is more challenging due to substitution effects. Bitirgen et al. [4] consider multiple resources, relying on machine learning to predict performance for different allocations at run-time. Their objective is system throughput not fairness. Moreover, their learning technique is likely more computationally demanding than our equation for fair shares.

**Resource Allocation in Datacenters.** Within datacenters, market mechanisms allocate resources to maximize welfare, which is defined as user utility minus power cost [6], [24]. Guevara et. al. [17] apply market mechanisms for heterogeneous resources. Whereas these market mechanisms enhance welfare, we provide game-theoretic fairness.

## 7. Conclusions

Our results motivate new thinking in fairly allocating hardware resources. Rather than assume users must share hardware, we must provide allocation mechanisms to encourage sharing. We show that Cobb-Douglas utilities are well suited to modeling user preferences in computer architecture. For Cobb-Douglas utilities, we present an allocation mechanism that provides sharing incentives, envy-freeness, Pareto efficiency, and strategy-proofness in the large. By linking hardware resource management to robust, game-theoretic analysis, computer architects can qualitatively change the nature of performance guarantees in hardware platforms shared by strategic users.

## A. Strategy Proofness in the Large

Suppose user $i$ decides to lie about her utility function, reporting $\alpha'_{ir}$ instead of the true value $\alpha_{ir}$ for resource $r$. Given other users' utilities, user $i$ would choose to report the $\alpha'_{ir}$ that maximizes her utility. As mentioned in §4, in a large system $1 \ll \sum_j \alpha_{jr}$, for all resources $r$. Since $\alpha'_{ir} \leq 1$, we have $\alpha'_{ir} \ll \sum_j \alpha_{jr}$. Therefore:

$$u_i = \prod_{r=1}^{R} \left( \frac{\alpha'_{ir}}{\alpha'_{ir} + \sum_{j \neq i} \alpha_{jr}} C_r \right)^{\alpha_{ir}} \approx$$
$$\prod_{r=1}^{R} \left( \frac{\alpha'_{ir}}{\sum_{j \neq i} \alpha_{jr}} C_r \right)^{\alpha_{ir}} =$$
$$A_i \prod_{r=1}^{R} \alpha'^{\alpha_{ir}}_{ir},$$

where $A_i = \prod_{r=1}^{R} C_r / \sum_{j \neq i} \alpha_{jr}$ is a constant. Let us consider the following optimization problem:

$$\begin{aligned} \text{maximize} \quad & \prod_r \alpha'^{\alpha_{ir}}_{ir} \\ \text{subject to} \quad & \sum_r \alpha'_{ir} = 1. \end{aligned}$$

Now, consider the Lagrangian form:

$$L(\alpha', \lambda) = \prod_r \alpha'^{\alpha_{ir}}_{ir} - \lambda(1 - \sum_r \alpha'_{ir}),$$

where $\lambda$ is a Lagrange multiplier. Then, based on the KKT conditions:

$$\frac{\partial L}{\partial \alpha'_{ir}} = \alpha_{ir} \frac{\prod_r \alpha'^{\alpha_{ir}}_{ir}}{\alpha'_{ir}} - \lambda = 0 \quad \forall r$$
$$\frac{\partial L}{\partial \lambda} = 1 - \sum_r \alpha'_{ir} = 0$$

The solution to these equations is $\alpha'_{ir} = \alpha_{ir}$, for all resources $r$.


## Acknowledgments

We sincerely thank Vincent Conitzer for his feedback during various stages of this project. We also thank Marisabel Guevara, Blake Hechtman and the anonymous reviewers for their feedback. This work is supported by NSF grants CCF-1149252 (CAREER) and CCF-1337215 (XPS-CLCCA). This work is also supported by STARnet, a Semiconductor Research Corporation program, sponsored by MARCO and DARPA. Any opinions, findings, conclusions, or recommendations expressed in this material are those of the author(s) and do not necessarily reflect the views of these sponsors.


## References


[1] Luiz André Barroso and Urs Hölzle. The datacenter as a computer: An introduction to the design of warehouse-scale machines. *Synthesis Lectures on Computer Architecture*, 4(1):1–108, 2009.

[2] Christian Bienia. *Benchmarking Modern Multiprocessors*. PhD thesis, Princeton University, January 2011.

[3] Christian Bienia, Sanjeev Kumar, Jaswinder Pal Singh, and Kai Li. The parsec benchmark suite: Characterization and architectural implications. In *Proc. International Conference on Parallel Architectures and Compilation Techniques (PACT)*, pages 72–81, 2008.

[4] Ramazan Bitirgen, Engin Ipek, and Jose F Martinez. Coordinated management of multiple interacting resources in chip multiprocessors: A machine learning approach. In *Proc. International Symposium on Microarchitecture (MICRO)*, 2008.

[5] Stephen Boyd, Seung-Jean Kim, Lieven Vandenberghe, and Arash Hassibi. A tutorial on geometric programming. *Optimization and Engineering*, 8(1):67–127, 2007.

[6] Jeffrey S Chase, Darrell C Anderson, Prachi N Thakar, Amin M Vahdat, and Ronald P Doyle. Managing energy and server resources in hosting centers. In *Proc. Symposium on Operating System Principles (SOSP)*, 2001.

[7] Reetuparna Das, Onur Mutlu, Thomas Moscibroda, and Chita R Das. Application-aware prioritization mechanisms for on-chip networks. In *Proc. International Symposium on Microarchitecture (MICRO)*, pages 280–291. IEEE, 2009.

[8] Alan Demers, Srinivasan Keshav, and Scott Shenker. Analysis and simulation of a fair queueing algorithm. In *ACM SIGCOMM Computer Communication Review*, volume 19, pages 1–12. ACM, 1989.

[9] Danny Dolev, Dror G Feitelson, Joseph Y Halpern, Raz Kupferman, and Nathan Linial. No justified complaints: On fair sharing of multiple resources. In *Proc. Innovations in Theoretical Computer Science Conference*, pages 68–75. ACM, 2012.

[10] Eiman Ebrahimi, Chang Joo Lee, Onur Mutlu, and Yale N Patt. Fairness via source throttling: a configurable and high-performance fairness substrate for multi-core memory systems. In *Proc. International Conference on Architectural Support for Programming Languages and Operating Systems (ASPLOS)*, pages 335–346. ACM, 2010.

[11] Francis Ysidro Edgeworth. *Mathematical psychics: An essay on the application of mathematics to the moral sciences*. Number 10. C. Kegan Paul & Company, 1881.

[12] Stijn Eyerman and Lieven Eeckhout. System-level performance metrics for multiprogram workloads. *Micro, IEEE*, 28(3):42–53, 2008.

[13] Ron Gabor, Shlomo Weiss, and Avi Mendelson. Fairness and throughput in switch on event multithreading. In *Proc. International Symposium on Microarchitecture (MICRO)*, pages 149–160. IEEE, 2006.

[14] Ron Gabor, Shlomo Weiss, and Avi Mendelson. Fairness enforcement in switch on event multithreading. *ACM Transactions on Architecture and Code Optimization (TACO)*, 4(3):15, 2007.

[15] Ali Ghodsi, Matei Zaharia, Benjamin Hindman, Andy Konwinski, Scott Shenker, and Ion Stoica. Dominant resource fairness: fair allocation of multiple resource types. In *Proc. USENIX NSDI*, 2011.

[16] Michael Grant and Stephen Boyd. Cvx: Matlab software for disciplined convex programming, version 1.21, 2010.

[17] Marisabel Guevara, Benjamin Lubin, and Benjamin C Lee. Navigating heterogeneous processors with market mechanisms. In *Proc. International Symposium on High Performance Computer Architecture (HPCA)*, pages 95–106, 2013.

[18] Avital Gutman and Noam Nisan. Fair allocation without trade. In *Proc. International Conference on Autonomous Agents and Multiagent Systems (AAMAS)*, pages 719–728, 2012.

[19] Kazuhiko Hashimoto. Strategy-proofness versus efficiency on the cobb-douglas domain of exchange economies. *Social choice and welfare*, 31(3):457–473, 2008.

[20] Mark D Hill and Michael R Marty. Amdahl's law in the multicore era. *Computer*, 41(7):33–38, 2008.

[21] Carlee Joe-Wong, Soumya Sen, Tian Lan, and Mung Chiang. Multi-resource allocation: Fairness-efficiency tradeoffs in a unifying framework. In *Proc. INFOCOM*, pages 1206–1214. IEEE, 2012.

[22] Yoongu Kim, Dongsu Han, Onur Mutlu, and Mor Harchol-Balter. Atlas: A scalable and high-performance scheduling algorithm for multiple memory controllers. In *Proc. International Symposium on High Performance Computer Architecture (HPCA)*, pages 1–12. IEEE, 2010.

[23] Benjamin Lee and David Brooks. Accurate and efficient regression modeling for microarchitectural performance and power prediction. In *Proc. International Conference on Architectural Support for Programming Languages and Operating Systems (ASPLOS)*, 2006.

[24] Benjamin Lubin, Jeffrey O Kephart, Rajarshi Das, and David C Parkes. Expressive power-based resource allocation for data centers. In *Proc. International Joint Conferences on Artificial Intelligence (IJCAI)*, pages 1451–1456, 2009.

[25] Jason Mars, Lingjia Tang, Robert Hundt, Kevin Skadron, and Mary Lou Soffa. Bubble-up: Increasing utilization in modern warehouse scale computers via sensible co-locations. In *Proc. International Symposium on Microarchitecture (MICRO)*, pages 248–259. ACM, 2011.

[26] Hervé Moulin. *Fair division and collective welfare*. MIT press, 2004.

[27] Abhinay Muthoo. *Bargaining theory with applications*. Cambridge University Press, 1999.

[28] Onur Mutlu and Thomas Moscibroda. Stall-time fair memory access scheduling for chip multiprocessors. In *Proc. International Symposium on Microarchitecture (MICRO)*, pages 146–160. IEEE Computer Society, 2007.

[29] Onur Mutlu and Thomas Moscibroda. Parallelism-aware batch scheduling: Enhancing both performance and fairness of shared dram systems. In *Proc. International Symposium on Computer Architecture (ISCA)*, pages 63–74. IEEE Computer Society, 2008.

[30] John F Nash Jr. The bargaining problem. *Econometrica: Journal of the Econometric Society*, pages 155–162, 1950.

[31] Kyle J Nesbit, Nidhi Aggarwal, James Laudon, and James E Smith. Fair queuing memory systems. In *Proc. International Symposium on Microarchitecture (MICRO)*, pages 208–222. IEEE, 2006.

[32] David C Parkes, Ariel D Procaccia, and Nisarg Shah. Beyond dominant resource fairness: extensions, limitations, and indivisibilities. In *Proc. Conference on Electronic Commerce (EC)*, pages 808–825. ACM, 2012.

[33] Avadh Patel, Furat Afram, Shunfei Chen, and Kanad Ghose. MARSSx86: A Full System Simulator for x86 CPUs. In *Design Automation Conference 2011 (DAC'11)*, 2011.

[34] Colby Ranger, Ramanan Raghuraman, Arun Penmetsa, Gary Bradski, and Christos Kozyrakis. Evaluating MapReduce for multi-core and multiprocessor systems. In *Proc. International Symposium on High Performance Computer Architecture (HPCA)*, pages 13–24. IEEE, 2007.

[35] Paul Rosenfeld, Elliott Cooper-Balis, and Bruce Jacob. Dramsim2: A cycle accurate memory system simulator. *Computer Architecture Letters*, 10(1):16–19, 2011.

[36] Alejandro Toriello and Juan Pablo Vielma. Fitting piecewise linear continuous functions. *European Journal of Operational Research*, 219(1):86–95, 2012.

[37] Hal Varian. Equity, envy, and efficiency. *Journal of economic theory*, 9(1):63–91, 1974.

[38] Carl A Waldspurger and William E Weihl. Lottery scheduling: Flexible proportional-share resource management. In *Proc. USENIX Conference on Operating Systems Design and Implementation (OSDI)*, page 1. USENIX Association, 1994.

# Price Theory Based Power Management for Heterogeneous Multi-Cores

Thannirmalai Somu Muthukaruppan * Anuj Pathania * Tulika Mitra

School of Computing, National University of Singapore

{tsomu, pathania, tulika}@comp.nus.edu.sg

## Abstract

Heterogeneous multi-cores that integrate cores with different power-performance characteristics are promising alternatives to homogeneous systems in energy- and thermally constrained environments. However, the heterogeneity imposes significant challenges to power-aware scheduling. We present a price theory-based dynamic power management framework for heterogeneous multi-cores that co-ordinates various energy savings opportunities, such as dynamic voltage/frequency scaling, load balancing, and task migration in tandem, to achieve the best power-performance characteristics. Unlike existing centralized power management frameworks, ours is distributed and hence scalable with minimal runtime overhead. We design and implement the framework within Linux operating system on ARM big.LITTLE heterogeneous multi-core platform. Experimental evaluation confirms the advantages of our approach compared to the state-of-the-art techniques for power management in heterogeneous multi-cores.

***Categories and Subject Descriptors*** C.0 [*COMPUTER SYSTEMS ORGANIZATION*]: General; D.4.7 [*OPERATING SYSTEMS*]: Organization and Design

***Keywords*** Heterogeneous Multi-core, Power Management, Price Theory

## 1. Introduction

Relentless CMOS scaling at deep sub-micron level has resulted in increased power density in microprocessors, which forced computing systems to move in the direction of parallel architectures with homogeneous multi-cores. However, the emergence of dynamic and diverse workloads demand heterogeneous multi-cores, consisting of both *simple* and *complex* cores in the same chip, that can provide high performance at low energy consumption. Existing works show the potential of heterogenous computing in terms of energy efficiency and performance benefits [5, 8, 19, 20, 33]. There exist two different kinds of heterogeneity: *functional heterogeneity* and *performance heterogeneity*. Modern embedded systems exhibit functional heterogeneity by incorporating general-purpose processors, GPUs, and accelerators on a single chip. On the other hand, performance heterogeneity is demonstrated in asymmetric multi-cores, where the cores share the same instruction-set architecture but exhibit diverse power/performance characteristics. For example, ARM big.LITTLE (as shown in Figure 1) integrates high performing, complex, out-of-order ARM Cortex-A15 and energy-efficient, simple, in-order ARM Cortex-A7 cores in the same chip.

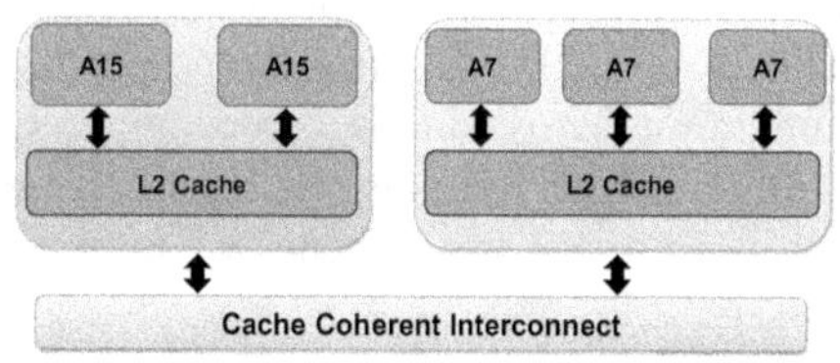


Figure 1: ARM big.LITTLE heterogeneous multi-core.

We propose a power management framework for asymmetric multi-cores exhibiting performance heterogeneity in mobile platforms. Our framework can satisfy the application demands expressed as Quality of Service (QoS) requirements with low energy consumption under a Thermal Design Power (TDP) constraint.

We first present the goals that our framework strives to achieve and then explain our design choices. Traditionally, centralized power management techniques [9, 18, 35] have been employed in embedded mobile platforms. However, centralized approaches suffer from scalability issues, especially in future many-core heterogeneous systems. The power management techniques for such platforms should have distributed decision making strategies.

* These authors contributed equally to this work.



*ASPLOS '14*, March 1–4, 2014, Salt Lake City, Utah, USA.

http://dx.doi.org/10.1145/2541940.2541974

Second, the power management in heterogeneous multi-cores involves coordinating multiple knobs. Dynamic Voltage and Frequency Scaling (DVFS) is the most common energy saving scheme [18, 23, 35]. A good power management approach should incorporate DVFS to provide satisfactory user experience at very low energy consumption. Apart from DVFS, load balancing and task migrations are two major techniques that have significant impact on power in multi-cores [28]. Load balancing and task migration challenges are further exacerbated in the presence of heterogeneity, where the right core should be selected for the right task due to differing power-performance characteristics.

Finally, mobile platforms are now facing strict thermal design power constraint that excludes the possibility of running all the cores at their maximum frequency levels. In such a peak power constrained environment, we have to judiciously select the appropriate voltage-frequency level for each core. Moreover, in an overloaded system exceeding the TDP constraint, all the applications may not be able to meet their QoS targets. In such situations, it is important to maximize the user experience by favoring tasks with higher priority. Therefore, power management schemes cannot be oblivious to the user-level task priorities. Finally, the power management approach should be incorporated in modern commodity operating systems with minimal modifications for easy acceptability.

Most of the existing works focus only on a subset of the aforementioned objectives. It is important to notice that employing multiple energy-saving features (DVFS, load balancing, and migration) requires a coordinated approach. For example, load balancing distributes the workload across the cores and DVFS takes advantage of the balanced workload to reduce the frequency of the cores. While load balancing is beneficial across the same core types, it may conflict with task migration across different core types. This is because task migration needs to ensure that the power hungry cores are used sparingly and switched on only when absolutely necessary. It is challenging to synergistically employ all the different power management techniques within a single framework. Moreover, in a dynamic system with large number of tasks/cores and time-varying workload, arriving at the appropriate decisions with low computational overheads introduces additional challenges.

The novelty of our power management approach is that it incorporates all the objectives outlined earlier within a unified and scalable framework based on the foundations of *price theory* [21] from economics. We implement our approach within the *Linux fair scheduler* with minimal modifications to the kernel. Moreover, our evaluations are performed on a real heterogenous multi-core chip *ARM big.LITTLE*. Our main contributions are:

- We propose *a comprehensive, unified, distributed, and scalable power management technique for heterogeneous multi-cores under thermal design power constraint.*
- The framework is based on price theory that unifies individual power management schemes like DVFS, load balancing, and task migration. Furthermore, our price theory-based approach strictly follows the supply-demand based market mechanisms [21], thereby ensuring stability and efficiency.
- We implement our framework within the commodity Linux operating system for a prototype version of the ARM big.LITTLE platform. All the results reported are from the real system as opposed to simulations. Experimental evaluations show that our technique outperforms existing techniques [3, 25] designed for heterogeneous multi-cores.

## 2. System Overview

**Architecture model.** We target single-ISA heterogeneous multi-core architectures, which exhibit power-performance heterogeneity as in big.LITTLE [15] and Tegra [26] platforms. The target system is comprised of a set of cores $\mathcal{C}$ grouped in a set of voltage-frequency clusters $\mathcal{V}$, with each cluster having a separate voltage and frequency regulator. Each cluster $v$ can operate at several discrete voltage-frequency (V-F) levels and consists of a set of cores $\mathcal{C}_v \subseteq \mathcal{C}$. All the cores within a cluster are symmetric in terms of micro-architecture and have to run at the same V-F level.

**Task model.** A task $t$ is a computational entity that can execute on a core. Each task $t$ is assigned a priority $r_t$ by the user, where higher value means higher priority. $\mathcal{T}$ represents the set of all tasks.

**Task to core mapping.** Our framework dynamically maps the tasks to the cores. A task $t$ is mapped to a core $c_t$. $\mathcal{T}_c \subseteq \mathcal{T}$ represents the set of tasks mapped to core $c$ and $\mathcal{T}_v = \cup_{c \in \mathcal{C}_v} \mathcal{T}_c$ denotes the set of tasks mapped to the cores in cluster $v$. The idle task $t_{idle}$ executes on a core without any active task. If there are no active tasks in an entire cluster, then we can power down that cluster. We define $R_c$, $R_v$, $R$ as the sum of the priorities of all the tasks mapped to core $c$, cluster $v$, and the entire system, respectively.

**Supply Model.** Each core $c$ can supply certain amount of computational resources $S_c$, which is constrained by the maximum supply $\hat{S}_c$. The computational resource is defined in terms of of *Processing Units* (PU), where one PU is equivalent to one million processor cycles per second. The higher the frequency of a core $c$, the more it can supply PUs (i.e., higher the value of $S_c$) and the maximum supply of PUs $\hat{S}_c$ is determined by the maximum possible frequency of the core. For example, a core running at 1000MHz (or 350MHz) produces a supply of 1000PUs (or 350PUs). Note that the amount of work (instruction processing) that can be achieved with one PU on a small core is generally less than the amount of work that can be done with one PU on a big core; that is, one PU on a big core is more valuable than one PU on a small core.

The supply of a cluster $S_v$ is the same as the supply of any of the constituent cores, which have identical $S_c$ values. The

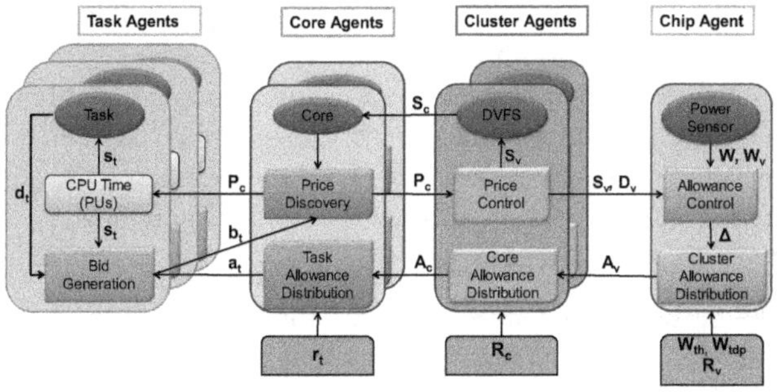


Figure 2: Agent Interaction Overview.

supply of the entire chip $S$ is the summation of the cluster supply values. The current supply of PUs to task $t$ on core $c_t$ is represented by $s_t$ ($\equiv s_t^{c_t}$). The supply of PUs to a task $t$ has to be less than the supply produced on the core $c_t$ it is mapped to, that is, $s_t \leq S_{c_t}$.

**Demand Model.** Each task $t$ demands a certain amount of computational resources (PUs), which can vary dynamically during the course of the execution. In heterogenous multi-cores, a task demands different amount of PUs across different core types. For example, a task would demand more PUs on a small core compared to a big core to achieve the same application-level performance. The differing demands for computational resources on different core types model the **heterogeneity** of the architecture. The current demand of task $t$ on core $c_t$ is represented by $d_t$ ($\equiv d_t^{c_t}$).

Let $D_c$ represent the sum of demands of all the tasks mapped to core $c$. The core with the highest demand in a cluster is called the constrained core of the cluster. Let $\tilde{c}_v \in \mathcal{C}_v$ represent the constrained core of the cluster $v$. Then the demand of the cluster $D_v = D_{\tilde{c}_v}$ is defined as the demand of its constrained core $\tilde{c}_v$ and the demand of the entire chip $D$ is the sum of the demands of the clusters.

**Power model.** The power consumption of a core $c$ represented by $W_c$ depends on the core type, its V-F level, and the workload. The power consumption of a cluster $v$ is represented by $W_v$, while the entire chip power consumption is represented by $W$. The quality of the cooling solution determines the value of the TDP constraint $W_{tdp}$. As mentioned before, our goal is to keep the total chip power consumption below the TDP ($W < W_{tdp}$) while meeting the task demands at minimal energy.

# 3. Power management Framework

Our power management framework is designed on the foundation of the *Price Theory* [21] and the *Quantity theory of money* [13]. The resource allocation, DVFS, task mapping and migration are all controlled through the virtual market place, where the commodity being traded is processing unit (PU) using virtual money.

The framework is realized as a collection of autonomous entities called *agents*. Each agent represents a transactional body in the market. An agent can perform various functionalities such as earning, bidding, purchasing, and distribution of computational resources. Furthermore, the actions of an agent are prompted by the goals of the client(s) it represents. For example, an agent representing a task is motivated to meet the demand imposed by the task. Similarly, the agent representing the entire chip ensures that the thermal design power constraint is not violated.

The efficient functioning of the market is ensured through the regulations imposed on the actions of the agents. The regulations introduced are reflections of the power management goals. Interested readers may refer to [13, 21] for more details on economic equilibrium, supply, demand, inflation and deflation concepts.

Our power management framework consists of two main components: *Supply-Demand module* and *Load-Balancing plus Task migration module (LBT)*. Given a task to core mapping, the supply-demand module attempts to satisfy the demands of all the tasks with minimal power consumption under the TDP constraint. It relies on the concept of regulating inflation-deflation. The LBT module aims to reach a power efficient task to core mapping through load balancing and task migrations and employs the concept of reduced spending. Both the modules work in tandem to achieve the final design goal of power management in heterogenous multi-cores.

## 3.1 Overview of Agents

Figure 2 shows the interaction among the agents.

**Task agent.** Each task is represented by an agent, who is a buyer in the market. A task agent can receive, spend, or save money to purchase the computational resources (PU). An agent corresponding to a task gets an allowance (virtual money) that it uses to bid for the resources according to the demands of the task.

**Core agent.** Each core is represented by an agent who determines the price of the computational resources produced by the core. The price for PUs in a core emerges from the bids submitted by the task agents and the current supply of the core. The core agent then distributes the available resources among the task agents according to the bids. A core agent also distributes the allowances received from the cluster agent to the task agents.

**Cluster agent.** A cluster agent controls the price of the resources by manipulating the supply of PUs in the cores under its purview. The increase (or decrease) of the supply is achieved by varying the V-F levels of the cluster. A cluster agent also distributes the allowance received from the chip agent to the core agents.

**Chip agent.** The chip agent controls the amount of money in circulation in the system by manipulating the allowances, thereby ensuring that the total chip power does not exceed the TDP constraint. It then distributes the allowances to the cluster agents.

### 3.2 Supply-Demand Module

In this section, we explain the mechanisms employed by the supply-demand module in manipulating the V-F levels to meet the task demands at minimal power consumption. The supply-demand module requires all the task, core, cluster, and chip agents to work in synergy. In terms of price theory, the demands of all the tasks are satisfied only in an economic market without inflation (or deflation). Thus, controlling inflation (or deflation) is equivalent to providing enough supply to satisfy the current demand in the market. This is the basic principle employed in the supply-demand module.

#### 3.2.1 Task and Core Dynamics

The main objective of the task agent is to sustain the demand of the task it represents. This objective is achieved through an iterative process consisting of three steps per round: bidding by the task agents, price discovery by the core agent, and purchase of the resources. The iterative process continues till the market stabilizes in an economic equilibrium.

The core agent gives an allowance $a_t$ (the virtual money) to each task agent according to the priority of the task. The task agent bids an amount $b_t$ to buy resources based on the current demand of the task $d_t$. If the bid is less than the allowance, then the difference $m_t = a_t - b_t$ is saved for future use. The bid cannot exceed the sum of allowance and savings. We also require the bid to be higher than a predefined minimum bid $b_{min}$. That is $b_{min} \leq b_t \leq a_t + m_t$.

For every round, each task agent submits a bid amount $b_t$ based on the experience in the previous round. The task agent increases (or decreases) the bid amount if the supply received was less (or more) than the demand in the previous round. The agents keep the bid unchanged when the demand is satisfied.

Given the bids from all the tasks mapped to core $c$, the core agent representing $c$ discovers the price per PU $P_c$ as follows $P_c = \frac{\sum_{t \in \mathcal{T}_c} b_t}{S_c}$. Each task agent now purchases the resources at the value determined by the core agent and obtains its current supply $s_t = \frac{b_t}{P_c}\big|_{t \in \mathcal{T}_c}$.

The bids in the $(N+1)^{th}$ round by the task agents depend on the supply, demand and prices observed in the $N^{th}$ round. As mentioned earlier, the bidding amount is capped by the summation of allowance $a_t$ and savings $m_t$ for the task.

$$b_t^{N+1} = \max\left(a_t + m_t,\ b_t^N + (d_t - s_t) \times P_c\right)\Bigg|_{t \in \mathcal{T}_c} \quad (1)$$

Table 1: Task and Core Level Dynamics Example

| Round | $b_{t_a}$ | $b_{t_b}$ | $P_c$ | $s_{t_a}$ | $s_{t_b}$ | $S_c$ |
|---|---|---|---|---|---|---|
| 1 | 1 | 1 | 0.0066 | 150 | 150 | 300 |
| 2 | 1.33 | 0.66 | 0.0066 | 200 | 100 | 300 |

**Running Example** Table 1 shows the working of the agents of two tasks $t_a$ and $t_b$ executing on core $c$ with supply $S_c = 300$ PUs. The current demands are $d_{t_a} = 200$ PUs and $d_{t_b} = 100$ PUs. Both the task agents begin with the initial bid of \$1. In round 1, the task $t_b$ is over-supplied, while $t_a$ is under-supplied. In round 2, by adjusting bids based on the supply-demand characteristics, the resources are effectively shared among the tasks according to their requirements.

#### 3.2.2 Cluster Dynamics

The cluster agents are responsible for controlling the price and preventing both price inflation and deflation in the cores. When a core is undersupplied (oversupplied), we observe price inflation (deflation). The cluster agent adjusts the supply using DVFS to avoid either over-supply or under-supply situations in the cores, which in turn is reflected in the stable price of the PU.

In our architecture, all the cores within a cluster have to run at the same V-F level. Thus the supply can be modified only at the cluster level and not at the core level. So the cluster agent observes and responds to price inflation (or deflation) of only the constrained core because the constrained core represents the highest demand among the cores within the cluster. Thus, the supply of the cluster is controlled by the most constrained core. Note that given a task mapping, a non-constrained core may suffer from deflation, while the constrained core suffers from inflation. The cluster agent takes care of the inflation in the constrained core, which can further magnify the deflation in the non-constrained core. The LBT module (discussed in Section 3.3) is responsible for fixing the deflation in the non-constrained core through load balancing.

In order to identify inflation/deflation, we need a base price from which the relative changes can be observed. Every time the V-F level changes, we reset the base price to the new price observed in the market. While the V-F level is changing, we do not allow the task agents to change their bids until they have observed the effect of the new supply on their existing bids.

A user supplied parameter called tolerance factor $\delta$ defines the rate of inflation (or deflation) that the cluster agent can tolerate before increasing (or decreasing) the supply, i.e., DVFS by one level. Let $P_c$ and $PBase_c$ represent the current and base price of the resources in a constrained core $c$, respectively. The cluster agent increases the supply when the current price $P_c \geq PBase_c + PBase_c * \delta$. Similarly, a decrease in supply is observed when $P_c \leq PBase_c - PBase_c * \delta$. The tolerance factor $\delta$ determines the response sensitivity of the cluster agents. The lower the value of $\delta$, the faster the response of the cluster agent. The faster response results in frequent V-F level transitions, and hence thermal cycling [29], which can be detrimental to both the performance and the reliability of the hardware. Thus, it is important to carefully select the value of $\delta$ by taking into consideration the underlying hardware.

**Running Example** We demonstrate the cluster level dynamics by extending the example from Table 1 to Table 2. In

Table 2: Cluster Level Dynamics Example

| Round | $b_{t_a}$ | $b_{t_b}$ | $P_c$ | $PBase_c$ | $s_{t_a}$ | $s_{t_b}$ | $S_c$ |
|---|---|---|---|---|---|---|---|
| 3 | 1.99 | 0.66 | 0.0088 | 0.0066 | 225 | 75 | 300 |
| 4 | 1.99 | 0.66 | 0.0066 | 0.0066 | 300 | 100 | 400 |

round 3, let us assume that the demand of $t_a$ increases from 200 PUs to 300 PUs. Let the tolerance factor $\delta$ be 0.2. In round 3, the price increases to \$0.0088, which is higher than the tolerable value of $\$0.00796 = \$(0.0066 + 0.0066 \times 0.2)$, thus causing inflation in the system. In round 3, the cluster agent responds by increasing the supply $S_c$ from 300 PUs to 400 PUs (highlighted in gray). At the new supply, both the tasks are satisfied and per unit price observed in fourth round is \$0.0066, which is set as new base price of $c$. Also, in round 4, the task agents do not change their bids as the new prices are determined only at the end of the round 4.

### 3.2.3 Chip Dynamics

While the cluster agent attempts to set the V-F level at the minimum value so as to meet the demand of the tasks, the chip level agent is responsible to ensure that the overall chip power does not exceed the TDP budget. The chip agent indirectly controls the power consumption of the chip by manipulating the allowance. It decides on the global allowance value $A$ for the current round. The allowance $A$ is distributed hierarchically throughout the system using the different cluster and core agents.

The global allowance is distributed as cluster allowances ($A_v$) to the cluster agents and the distribution is inversely proportional to power consumption. The cluster consuming more power is given less allowance, which is calculated as $A_v = A \cdot \frac{W - W_v}{W}$. The cluster allowance is distributed as core allowance ($A_c$) to the core agents of the cluster based on the priorities of task agents running on them, which is calculated as $A_c = A_v \cdot \frac{R_c}{R_v}$. Finally, the core allowance is further distributed as task allowances ($a_t$) to the task agents proportional to their priorities, which is calculated as $a_t = A_c \cdot \frac{r_t}{R_c}$.

When the chip agent increases the global allowance $A$, the task agents receive additional money to generate higher bids for the resources. The task agents with unsatisfied demands increase their bid with the additional money. This causes inflation in the under supplied clusters, triggering the respective cluster agents to control the inflation by increasing the supply (increase V-F level). This increased supply in the cluster results in increased power consumption.

On the other hand, when the chip agent decreases the global allowance $A$, all the task agents have less money at their disposal and hence are forced to bid lower values. This causes deflation in the clusters, which prompts the cluster agents to decrease the supply (decrease V-F level) to control the deflation, resulting in reduced power consumption.

When the chip agent decides to keep the allowance $A$ constant, all the cores will reach stable equilibrium prices. With stable prices, neither inflation or deflation will be observed by the cluster agents resulting in a *steady-state* with no changes in V-F levels.

The global allowance for the $(N+1)^{th}$ round is set as follows $A^{N+1} = A^N + \Delta$, where $A^{N+1}$ and $A^N$ are the current and previous round allowances, respectively and $\Delta$ is the change in the allowance. The key question is how to dynamically set the $\Delta$ value. The $\Delta$ value is set according to the current total power consumption of the chip.

When the chip power consumption $W$ is below the TDP, the primary goal of the chip agent is to meet the demands of the tasks. On the other hand, if the chip power exceeds TDP, then the chip agent is responsible to bring the power below TDP. In case the system has a demand that is unsatisfiable within the TDP, due to the discrete nature of the V-F levels the system will oscillate around the TDP. To stabilize the system near TDP when overloaded, we introduce a buffer zone near TDP where the system is ought to stabilize. The size of the buffer zone is decided by the parameter $W_{th}$. Thus, the spectrum of power consumption is divided into three regions:

**Normal State.** In the normal state, the power consumption of the entire chip is less than the pre-defined threshold $W < W_{th}$. In this state, the chip agent manipulates the $\Delta$ value based on the current total supply $S$ and total demand $D$ of the entire chip. When the demand is not satisfied in at least one of the clusters, the chip is under-utilized and the task agents need extra money to buy more resources. Therefore, the allowance is increased by an amount proportional to the difference between the supply and the demand. Therefore, the value of $\Delta$ is given by $\Delta = A^N \cdot \frac{D-S}{D}$.

**Threshold State.** In the threshold state, the power consumption of the chip is observed between $W_{th}$ and TDP $W_{tdp}$. Ideally, it is desirable for the power consumption of the chip to stabilize in threshold state when the system is overloaded. The stability is attained in the threshold state by keeping the allowance constant through $\Delta = 0$. With larger buffer zone ($W_{tdp} - W_{th}$), the number of oscillations around the TDP reduces and the stable state is reached quickly, but the chip might be severely under-utilized. On the contrary, a smaller buffer zone leads to frequent oscillations around the TDP, but achieves higher utilization. The idea of stability here is similar to the concept of hysteresis in control systems.

**Emergency State.** In the emergency state, the power consumption of the chip is above $W_{tdp}$ and must be brought down quickly. The allowances of the task agents have to be curbed to reduce the power consumption. In emergency state, the reduction in allowance is proportional to the deviation from the TDP. Hence, the value of $\Delta$ is given by $\Delta = A^N \cdot \frac{W_{tdp} - W}{W_{tdp}}$. Thus our system can achieve stability (stable equilibrium price) in either the normal state (supply

Table 3: Chip Level Dynamics Example

| Round | $A$ | $a_{t_a}$ | $a_{t_b}$ | $b_{t_a}$ | $b_{t_b}$ | $m_{t_a}$ | $m_{t_b}$ | $P_c$ | $PBase_c$ | $d_{t_a}$ | $d_{t_b}$ | $s_{t_a}$ | $s_{t_b}$ | $S_c$ | D | S | W |
|---|---|---|---|---|---|---|---|---|---|---|---|---|---|---|---|---|---|
| 4 | 4.5 | 3.0 | 1.5 | 1.99 | 0.66 | 1.01 | 0.84 | 0.0066 | 0.0066 | 300 | 100 | 300 | 100 | 400 | 400 | 400 | .8W |
| 5 | 4.5 | 3.0 | 1.5 | 1.99 | 0.66 | 1.01 | 0.84 | 0.0066 | 0.0066 | 300 | 300 | 300 | 100 | 400 | 600 | 400 | .8W |
| | 6.0 | 4.0 | 2.0 | 1.99 | 1.98 | 3.02 | 0.85 | 0.0099 | 0.0066 | 300 | 300 | 200 | 200 | 400 | 600 | 400 | .8W |
| | 6.0 | 4.0 | 2.0 | 1.99 | 1.98 | 3.02 | 0.85 | 0.0099 | 0.0066 | 300 | 300 | 200 | 200 | 500 | 600 | 500 | .8W |
| 6 | 6.0 | 4.0 | 2.0 | 1.99 | 1.98 | 5.03 | 0.86 | 0.0079 | 0.0079 | 300 | 300 | 250 | 250 | 500 | 600 | 500 | 2W |
| 7 | 6.0 | 4.0 | 2.0 | 2.38 | 2.38 | 6.64 | 0.47 | 0.0095 | 0.0079 | 300 | 300 | 250 | 250 | 500 | 600 | 500 | 2W |
| | 6.0 | 4.0 | 2.0 | 2.38 | 2.38 | 6.64 | 0.47 | 0.0095 | 0.0079 | 300 | 300 | 250 | 250 | 600 | 600 | 600 | 2W |
| 8 | 6.0 | 4.0 | 2.0 | 2.38 | 2.38 | 8.25 | 0.10 | 0.0079 | 0.0079 | 300 | 300 | 300 | 300 | 600 | 600 | 600 | 3W |
| 9 | 4.0 | 2.67 | 1.33 | 2.38 | 1.42 | 8.53 | 0 | 0.0063 | 0.0079 | 300 | 300 | 375 | 225 | 600 | 600 | 600 | 3W |
| | 4.0 | 2.67 | 1.33 | 2.38 | 1.42 | 8.53 | 0 | 0.0063 | 0.0079 | 300 | 300 | 375 | 225 | 500 | 600 | 500 | 3W |
| 10 | 4.0 | 2.67 | 1.33 | 2.38 | 1.33 | 8.81 | 0 | 0.0074 | 0.0074 | 300 | 300 | 320 | 180 | 500 | 600 | 500 | 2W |
| 11 | 4.0 | 2.67 | 1.33 | 2.23 | 1.33 | 9.25 | 0 | 0.0071 | 0.0074 | 300 | 300 | 313 | 187 | 500 | 600 | 500 | 2W |
| . | | | | | | | | | | | | | | | | | |
| . | | | | | | | | | | | | | | | | | |
| 16 | 4.0 | 2.67 | 1.33 | 2.01 | 1.33 | 12.26 | 0 | 0.0067 | 0.0074 | 300 | 300 | 300 | 200 | 500 | 600 | 500 | 2W |

meets demand), or the threshold state (when overloaded), but never in the emergency state.

**Savings** An important by-product of our price theory based power management scheme is the concept of allowance savings by the task agents in the form of non-zero $m_t$ values. How does a task end up with savings? The savings are incurred under two scenarios. First we note that the global allowance is increased by $\Delta$ when the demand is not satisfied in at least one of the clusters. Thus, the task agents belonging to the clusters in supply-demand equilibrium would have additional allowance that will be saved for future bidding. Second, the price per PU within a cluster is determined by the most constrained core. This leads to the savings of allowances by the task agents belonging to the non-constrained cores. The saved allowances would facilitate the task agents to outbid other task agents for more resources during the supply constrained situation in both the threshold state and the emergency state. The savings are especially beneficial for tasks with alternating high and low demand requirement. Such task agents save money during their dormant phase and use the saved allowance to outbid other tasks during their active phase.

We choose to cap the savings of a task agent at a fraction of its current allowance. This is because large amount of savings may allow the tasks to keep the system in an emergency state longer than permissible. The ideal factor for capping is determined by the designer with knowledge of the underlying hardware.

**Running Example** To illustrate the chip level dynamics, we further extend the example from Table 2 to Table 3. Let us set $W_{tdp}$ and $W_{th}$ to $2.25W$ and $1.75W$, respectively. Let us further assume that, for the given application, the system reaches the emergency state at 600 PUs supply ($3W$ power) and the threshold state at 500 PUs supply ($2W$).

The global allowance is $\$4.5$ in the beginning. Let the priorities of tasks $t_a$ and $t_b$ be 2 and 1 respectively. Thus task $t_a$ receives higher allowance relative to task $t_b$ due to the difference in priorities. In table 3, the change in values are highlighted in gray.

So far in round 4, we have met supply and demand of both the tasks by increasing the core supply to 400 PUs. Now the demand of task $t_b$ increases to 300 PUs in round 5. As the demand at the core level by the two tasks cannot be met with the current supply of 300 PUs, we observe an increase in allowance (from $\$4.5$ to $\$6.0$) as well as price inflation. This price inflation forces the cluster agent to increase the supply to 500 PUs, which brings the chip to threshold state consuming $2W$ power. In the threshold state, the allowance is kept constant (observed in rounds 6-7). Meanwhile, the savings ($m_{t_a}$ and $m_{t_b}$) are calculated based on the allowance allocated and bids by the tasks in each round.

In round 7, the price inflation again causes the supply to increase to 600 PUs, which pushes the system to the emergency state. Now we need to stabilize the system in the threshold state. This is achieved by decreasing the system-level allowance from $\$6.0$ to $\$4.0$. This decreased allowance percolates all the way to the tasks. By round 9, the task $t_b$ has also used up all its savings. This is because the allowance was held constant in the threshold state (rounds 6-7). So with decreased allowance and zero savings, the task $t_b$ is now forced to lower its bids. The lower bids cause price deflation, resulting in reduction of supply from 600 PUs to 500 PUs.

As the supply is brought down to 500 PUs, the system reaches the threshold state again. This time the allowances are constant; hence the tasks cannot increase their bids preventing price inflation and subsequent increased supply (higher frequency) that takes the system back to emergency state. So the system stabilizes (round 16) in the threshold state where the power consumption is close to the TDP and the higher priority task ($t_a$) meets its demand, while the lower priority task ($t_b$) suffers.

### 3.2.4 Stability of the Supply-Demand module

We show that given a fixed task-to-core mapping, the supply-demand module ensures that the system reaches a stable state. By stable state here, we imply that there are no changes in the V-F levels and the resources allocated to the tasks.

The principle of price theory states that the market is only stable at a price equilibrium, which is the price at which the supply is equal to the demand. Once the supply meets the demand, it automatically prevents further inflation or deflation within the market. Let us assume that we start off in a stable state. The stability is perturbed as tasks enter/exit the system, or the demand within a task changes due to phase behavior or change in the input conditions. We show that the system will reach a (possibly) different stable state assuming there is no task migration in between.

There are three possible scenarios when the demand changes. In the first scenario, the demand can be satisfied in the normal state. In this case, we observe price inflation/deflation till the supply is equal to the demand and the system reaches stability. We always round up the demand to the next supply value so as to prevent oscillation between two consecutive supply values. Note that the price equilibrium is reached in the constrained core, which determine the V-F level. For the non-constrained cores, the supply might be greater than the demand because all the cores have the same supply value (V-F level). In this case, the price in the core(s) with over-supply will fall till the bid price hits the minimal bid value $b_{min}$. The same situation happens when the demand on the constrained core is less than the minimum supply value (minimum frequency level) and the system stabilizes at the minimum frequency.

In the second scenario, the demand can be satisfied in the threshold state. Here, the allowance is kept constant, which eventually translates to fixed bid prices by the tasks (because bid price cannot exceed allowance), preventing further inflation/deflation. In the absence of inflation/deflation, the V-F levels are not modified and all the clusters in the system stabilize to fixed V-F levels.

The third scenario is the most interesting one where the system needs to be in the emergency state to meet the demand. But we clearly cannot keep the system in the emergency state for long and have to ensure that it quickly stabilizes in the threshold state. This is the scenario illustrated in the example in Table 3. The stability is ensured by defining a buffer zone near TDP (the difference between $W_{tdp}$ and $W_{th}$). The buffer zone should be designed such that the system cannot move from the normal state to the emergency state or vice versa without passing through the threshold state. Once the system reaches the emergency state, the allowances are reduced, which moves the system to the threshold state. Once in threshold state, the allowance is kept constant at reduced value, which leads to fixed bidding prices and hence price equilibrium.

### 3.3 Load Balancing and Task Migration (LBT) module

The supply-demand module achieves a steady-state with permissible power consumption for any given task mapping by manipulating the V-F levels. But the mapping itself may not be efficient in terms of performance and power leading to a sub-optimal solution. Thus, the goal of the LBT module is to find a task mapping that is superior in terms of both performance and/or power consumption relative to the current mapping. The LBT module first attempts to meet the task demands followed by improving power efficiency through load balancing within a cluster and task migration across the clusters. Load balancing within a cluster helps reduce the V-F level of the cluster, while task migration exploits the heterogeneity of the different clusters to potentially improve both the power and the performance behavior of the tasks. In the following, we first describe our task migration policy across heterogeneous clusters.

Give a fixed task-to-core mapping $\mathcal{M}$, let $s_t^{\mathcal{M}}$ and $b_t^{\mathcal{M}}$ be the steady-state supply and bid corresponding to the task $t$ on core $c_t^{\mathcal{M}}$. Also $d_t^{\mathcal{M}}$ be the demand of task $t$ on core $c_t^{\mathcal{M}}$. Recall that the demand of a task changes based on the core type; the demand is lower on a more powerful core compared to a simpler core for the same level of performance.

We define a metric $perf(\mathcal{M})$ to compare the performance of two different task mappings. Given two different mappings $\mathcal{M}$ and $\mathcal{M}'$, we define $perf(\mathcal{M}') > perf(\mathcal{M})$ if and only if

$$\left(\exists t \in \mathcal{T} : \frac{s_t^{\mathcal{M}'}}{d_t^{\mathcal{M}'}} > \frac{s_t^{\mathcal{M}}}{d_t^{\mathcal{M}}}\right) \text{AND} \left(\forall t' \in \mathcal{T} \text{ s.t. } r_{t'} > r_t : \frac{s_{t'}^{\mathcal{M}'}}{d_{t'}^{\mathcal{M}'}} \geq \frac{s_{t'}^{\mathcal{M}}}{d_{t'}^{\mathcal{M}}}\right)$$

Basically we sort all the tasks $\mathcal{T}$ in the system according to their priority $r_t$. For the mapping $\mathcal{M}'$ to be better than the mapping $\mathcal{M}$ in terms of performance, we need two conditions to be satisfied. The first condition is that there should exist a task $t$ for which the supply-demand ratio in the mapping $\mathcal{M}'$ denoted as $\frac{s_t^{\mathcal{M}'}}{d_t^{\mathcal{M}'}}$ is higher than the ratio in $\mathcal{M}$. The second condition requires all the tasks with higher priority than $t$ to have either better or equal supply-demand ratio in $\mathcal{M}'$ than $\mathcal{M}$.

We also define another metric $spend(\mathcal{M})$ to capture the aggregate spending by the tasks in the steady-state for the mapping $\mathcal{M}$. The value of $spend(\mathcal{M})$ is calculated as follows, $spend(\mathcal{M}) = \sum_{t \in \mathcal{T}} b_t^{\mathcal{M}}$. From the power perspective, it is desirable if a task movement brings down the aggregate spending without affecting the performance. The aggregate spending $spend(\mathcal{M})$ reduces only when the steady-state bids from all the tasks combined together is lower. This reduction in bid price is observed only when the steady-state demand lowers due to appropriate load balancing across the cores within a cluster and the migration of the tasks to the most efficient cluster in terms of heterogeneity. The reduced bids cause deflation by lowering the price, which in turn brings down the supply, i.e., V-F levels and hence the power consumption. Therefore, any reduction in aggregate spending will translate to reduction in the power consumption, provided that the performance remains unchanged. Thus mapping $\mathcal{M}'$ is more power efficient than mapping $\mathcal{M}$, that is, $power(\mathcal{M}') < power(\mathcal{M})$ if and only if

$$spend(\mathcal{M}') < spend(\mathcal{M}) \text{ AND } perf(\mathcal{M}') \geq perf(\mathcal{M})$$

In the LBT module, each task agent first estimates steady-state $perf(\mathcal{M})$ and $spend(\mathcal{M})$ for the current mapping $\mathcal{M}$. This is the baseline power-performance behavior that we want to improve upon. Next, each task agent estimates $perf(\mathcal{M}')$ and $spend(\mathcal{M}')$ for all possible mappings $\mathcal{M}'$ where only the task corresponding to this agent migrates to another cluster while the remaining tasks do not move.

Let us consider the potential migration of task $t$ from the cluster $v$ to the cluster $v'$. In order to estimate the performance and the spending of the current and the new mapping, we need the steady-state supply, demand, and bid price for the current cluster $v$ and the target cluster $v'$. This steady-state behavior is estimated as follows.

- *Demand*: In the current cluster $v$, the steady-state demand is assumed to be the currently observed demand. For the target cluster $v'$ (with different core type), the steady-state demand is estimated using off-line profiling, which is explained in detail in Section 5. We have recently developed a power-performance prediction model for single-ISA heterogeneous multi-core systems using a combination of program analysis, mechanistic modeling, and empirical modeling [27]. In future, we plan to include this estimation model within our price theory based power management framework to eliminate the off-line profiling step.
- *Supply*: The steady-state supply of a cluster is estimated to be the same as the steady-state demand, unless the supply is constrained by the TDP constraint. The steady-state supply per task can be estimated by distributing the total supply among the tasks in proportion to their priorities.
- *Bids*: The steady-state bids are calculated by estimating the price in the steady-state. The price at a higher V-F level *Z+1* can be estimated from the price observed in the current V-F level *Z* using the following equations,

$$P_{Z+1} = P_Z + (P_Z \times \delta) \quad (2)$$

where $\delta$ is the tolerance factor. Using recursion, the price at the steady-state supply can be estimated. For example, let $P_Z$ and $\delta$ be \$10 and 0.02 respectively. Let us also assume that the V-F level has to increase by 3 levels to achieve the steady-state supply. Then, by using Equation 2 recursively for each level, the price can estimated to be \$10.612.

Note that the task agents perform performance and savings estimations in parallel, which enables the computational overhead to be distributed across the entire chip, thus ensuring scalability. All the information required for the estimation is hierarchically disseminated from the cluster agents to the chip agents and subsequently to the task agents and is kept consistent with periodic message passing. The overhead of the computation and communication increases with increasing number of tasks, cores, and clusters.

To reduce this overhead, only the task agents in the constrained core of each cluster contemplate movement of the tasks. Furthermore, the overhead is high if the task agents consider migration possibility to all the other cores in the system. We only let the task agents consider the most over-supplied unconstrained core in the target cluster as a potential candidate for migration. Thus there exists a trade-off between the overhead and the quality of the solutions obtained. We demonstrate in Section 5 that this simple heuristic works quite well in practice.

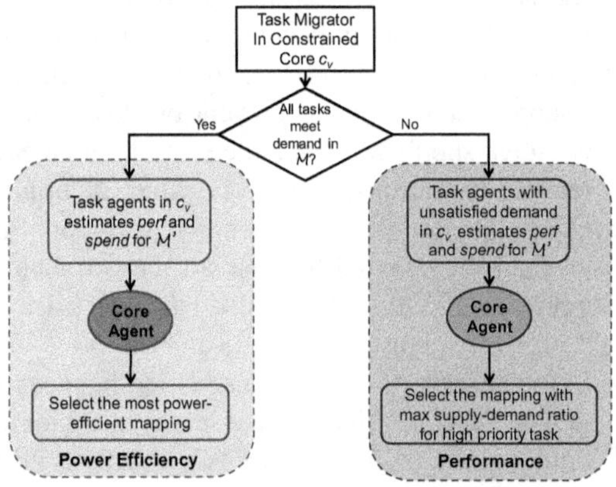


Figure 3: Task Migration in Constrained Core.

Figure 3 illustrates the flowchart of the task migration module in the constrained core $c$ of a cluster $v$. If the demands of all the tasks are expected to be satisfied in the steady-state of the current mapping $\mathcal{M}$, then the goal is to reduce the power consumption. In this case, all the task agents in $c$ estimate the performance and spending, if the task migrates to the most over-supplied unconstrained core in each of the other clusters, leading to a new mapping. Each task agent then sends the estimated $perf(\mathcal{M}')$ and $spend(\mathcal{M}')$ for the most power-efficient new mapping $\mathcal{M}'$ to the core agent. The core agent selects the most power-efficient mapping from the task agents and forwards this mapping to the chip agent through its cluster agent. The chip agent finally selects the most power-efficient mapping from all the clusters.

On the other hand, if some tasks are not expected to meet the demand in the steady-state in the constrained core, then only the clusters with unsatisfied demand consider possible task migration. For each such cluster, only the task agents with unsatisfied demand in the constrained core contemplate migration to the other clusters. In particular, at all levels (chip level, cluster level, and core level) we choose the highest priority task that improves its supply-demand ratio through migration without impacting the supply-demand ratio of the higher priority tasks. If two mappings have the same performance, then we select the one with better spending, i.e., better power consumption.

The load balancing process is very similar to the task migration. The only difference is that the target core is not in a different cluster but the most over-supplied unconstrained core within the same cluster. Thus only the cluster agent and the core agent are involved in this process. The chip or the cluster agent approves only one task movement at any given time. The movement of the other tasks, if any, will be performed in future LBT invocation.

### 3.3.1 Stability of the LBT module

The LBT module performs task migration either within the cluster or across clusters. It can introduce instability if and only if there exists cyclic movement of the tasks. However, our heuristic ensures that the number of task migrations is finite for the following reasons. If the demands of some tasks are not met in the current mapping, then we choose the mapping that improves the supply-demand ratio of the highest priority task with unsatisfied demand through migration. This, by definition, ensures that only the lower-priority tasks are impacted by this migration and the chain of task movements will end with the lowest priority tasks. Thus the number of migrations is bounded by $|\mathcal{T}|$.

On the other hand, if all the tasks meet their demands, then task migration reduces power consumption through reduced spending. This series of task migrations to reduce spending ends when the spending cannot be reduced further.

## 3.4 Invocation Frequency

The different modules involved in our framework have to be invoked at different rates to reduce the overhead in the system. As mentioned before, the bidding process by the task agents takes place in a series of rounds. The change in the supply level by the cluster agent occurs asynchronously based on inflation/deflation.

The load balancing within the cluster is invoked more frequently than the task migrator because task migration across clusters is expensive (2-4 ms) compared to migration within cluster (50-170 $\mu$s). The equations below summarize the periods for load balancing and task migration where linux scheduling epoch is 10ms.

$$task\_migration\_period = 2 \times load\_balancing\_period$$

$$load\_balancing\_period = 3 \times bid\_rounds\_period$$

$$bid\_rounds\_period = max\,(linux\_sched\_epoch,\ task\_period)$$

For workloads with periodic tasks, we set the bidding interval as the maximum of the linux scheduling epoch and the shortest period among the tasks. In our experiments, the shortest period for any task is 31.7ms; so we invoke the bidding round every 31.7ms, the load balancer every 95.1ms, and the task migrator every 190.2ms. The LBT module is disabled in the emergency state as the immediate goal is to bring the power below TDP through the supply-demand module.

# 4. Related Work

Increasing power consumption raises lot of challenges in modern embedded computing systems, where tablets, smart phones, PDAs are becoming widespread [24]. There exists a plethora of prior works on power management on homogeneous multi-core systems. Most of the works focus on power management using any combination of techniques like DVFS, load balancing and task migrations. Isci et al. [18] evaluate a DVFS based global power management policy with various objectives like prioritization, power balancing and throughput for different combinations of benchmarks. Rangan et al. [28] explore the use of thread migration in power management compared to the traditional DVFS scheme. In [35], the authors present a control theory based power management framework using per-core DVFS capability. Ma et al. [23] present a scalable power management solution for workloads that contain a mix of multi-threaded and single-threaded applications in homogeneous chip multiprocessor. However, these solutions are designed for homogeneous multi-core systems and require non-trivial modifications to adapt them to heterogeneous multi-cores.

Existing works [5, 8, 19, 20, 33] illustrate the potential of heterogeneous multi-cores to improve both the performance and power-efficiency. Craeynest et al. [33] propose a scheduling technique for asymmetric multi-cores using online performance estimation across different core types. Similarly, Koufaty et al. [19] propose a dynamic heterogeneity aware scheduler, which schedules tasks with very low memory stalls on complex cores for higher performance. Our approach handles both the performance and the power management in heterogeneous systems.

A study by Winter et al. [36] evaluates various scheduling and power management techniques for heterogenous multicores with special considerations to the scalability of the approaches. They propose a thread scheduling algorithm called Steepest Drop, which has little overhead but does not consider DVFS technique. The technique Pack & Cap proposed in [9] uses thread packing and DVFS to maximize performance under a TDP constraint. Schranzhofer et al. [31] introduce a static solution for task to core mapping problem in heterogeneous MPSoC. Our work dynamically incorporates all the three techniques (load balancing, task migration and DVFS) under a single price theory-based framework to meet performance demands at minimum energy consumption under a power budget. We have previously proposed [25] a hierarchical power management framework for heterogeneous multi-cores. The load balancing and task migration techniques proposed in [25] do not handle heterogeneity and task distribution efficiently.

Some existing works [4, 7, 10–12, 16, 22, 30] borrow economic theory ideas to develop power or thermal management schemes. Ebi et al. [10] propose an agent-based power distribution scheme for multi-cores, where the trading commodity is the power units. Agent based dynamic thermal management techniques are proposed in [4, 14], where negotiations are made in the market to make efficient task migration decisions. Roy et al. [30] propose an energy management technique for mobile devices based on abstractions such as isolation, delegation and subdivision. This technique requires building an offline energy model for a system, which consists of a multi-core that uses two different ISA (ARM11 and ARM9). In contrast, our technique targets single-ISA heterogeneous multi-core system that enables task migration.

Some prior works [7, 16, 22] employ welfare economics in datacenters to improve power efficiency. [16, 22] employ Mixed Integer Linear Programming (MILP) technique for determining the optimal allocation of resources. Lubin et al. [22] present power management in homogeneous multi-core datacenters. This approach is extended to heterogeneous systems in [16]. The solving time is quite high ($800ms$) for MILP formulation. This is only suitable for datacenter workloads exhibiting relatively stable phases so that allocation decisions can be made at long intervals (e.g., 10-minute interval). But such high overhead cannot be tolerated in a mobile platform with dynamic workloads where the allocation decisions need to be revised multiple times per second. Our dynamic price theory based power management mechanism is distributed in nature and thus accomplishes the optimization with minimal overhead.

## 5. Experimental Evaluation

We now proceed to evaluate our price-theory based power management framework, called *PPM*, for asymmetric multicores. First, we present the experimental setup and the workload selection. We compare PPM with a control-theory based power management framework for asymmetric multicores, called *HPM* [25] and the Linux asymmetry-aware scheduler [3]. Finally, we quantify the effects of savings and priorities followed by the overhead of PPM.

### 5.1 Experimental Setup

We use the Versatile Express development platform [2] for our experimental evaluation. It is a modular and flexible platform that allows for quick development of both hardware and software prototypes. The platform consists of a versatile express motherboard with a daughter board containing TC2 CoreTile test chip with ARM big.LITTLE heterogeneous multi-core at 45nm GP technology. The test chip consists of two core Cortex-A15 (big) cluster and three core Cortex-A7 (LITTLE) cluster as shown in Figure 1. Both big and LITTLE cores implement ARM v7A ISA and are connected together by CCI-400 cache coherent interconnect. The frequency can only be modified at the cluster level in the target platform. The architectural features of big and LITTLE core are detailed in [15, 27]. For heterogeneous multi-cores, it is important to discern the migration penalties across different clusters. As expected, we observe that the migration cost within a cluster is lower than the cost across the clusters. The migration cost within the big cluster is in the range of 54–105 $\mu s$ depending on the frequency level, while for the LITTLE cluster the observed cost is 71–167 $\mu s$. However, the migration cost across the clusters is much higher: 1.88–2.16 ms for the migration from LITTLE to big cluster at different frequency levels, and 3.54–3.83 ms for the migration from big to LITTLE cluster.

The firmware installed on the motherboard is responsible for booting the Linux kernel in the big.LITTLE chip. We use Ubuntu 12.10 Linaro release for Versatile Express [3] with Linux kernel release 3.8. The evaluation platform is equipped with sensors to measure frequency, voltage, power and energy consumption per cluster. The Linux 3.8 kernel release provides the hardware monitor (hwmon) communication interface to interact with all the sensors located in the test chip. The idle cluster (that did not boot the Linux kernel) can be powered down if necessary. We boot the Linux kernel in the LITTLE cluster. The powering down and modification of V-F levels are achieved using the drivers related to the oscillators.

In our framework, the agents are implemented in software as kernel modules. The core, cluster, and chip agents are instantiated during kernel boot process. The task agents are instantiated as and when the tasks are created. The communication between the tasks in user space and the agents in kernel space is performed using system calls. The cluster agent uses *cpufreq* utility to manipulate the frequency of the cluster. The voltage at each frequency level is automatically set by the hardware. The task migration is handled by the cluster and the chip agents using the task affinity through *sched_setaffinity* interface in the Linux scheduler.

The core agents are responsible for distributing the available resources among the tasks. This is achieved by manipulating the *nice* values of each task. In Linux kernel, *nice* values are the indirect indications of priorities for task management. For example, lower nice value manifests as higher priority and more resource consumption. As we use *nice* values for resource allocation, the user-level priorities of the tasks in our framework are set in the context of the Linux kernel by adding a new member *prio* in the structure *task_struct*. The *prio* value can be modified from the user space using system calls. For the sake of simplicity, we do not allow dynamic modification of the priorities (*prio*) of the tasks.

### 5.2 Workload Selection

We use benchmarks from PARSEC [6], Vision [34] and SPEC 2006 [1] suites. At present, our framework requires the tasks to express the performance demand. We employ the *Heart Rate Monitor* (HRM) [17] infrastructure to capture this information. HRM provides a simple and effective way to measure the performance of a task in terms of heartbeats per second (hb/s), which is defined as the throughput of the critical kernel in a task. For example, number of frames processed per second defines the heart rate of a video encoder.

Table 4: Illustration of conversion from heart rate to demand with min and max heart rate being 24 hb/s and 30 hb/s respectively.

| Prog. phase | Current hr (hb/s) | Frequency (Mhz) | Utilization (%) | s (PU) | d (PU) |
|---|---|---|---|---|---|
| 1 | 15 | 500 | 100 | 500 | 900 |
| 2 | 10 | 800 | 50 | 400 | 1080 |
| 3 | 40 | 1000 | 100 | 1000 | 675 |

For each application, the user can define the performance goal in terms of reference heart rate range and our goal is to maintain the heart rate within that range, while minimizing energy. Note that an application may have highly variable computation requirement due to phase behavior and hence may need different V-F levels or even migration to a different core type to keep the heart rate within the specified range. Table 4 illustrates the conversion of heart rate to demand for a particular task. Each row in Table 4 represents the different program phases of the same application. The user defines the performance goals in terms of minimum and maximum heart rate (24 hb/s – 30 hb/s). From the current observed heart rate, core frequency and task utilization, the demand of the task can be easily computed. For example, with the supply of 500 PUs, the current heart rate is 15 hb/s in program phase 1. It is clearly well below the reference range prescribed by the user. The required demand is estimated using the equation $d_t = \frac{target\ heart\ rate \times s_t}{current\ heart\ rate}$, where $target\ heart\ rate$ is the mean of the minimum and maximum heart rate range. In our example in Table 4, the $target\ heart\ rate = 27$. Similarly, in program phase 3, the current heart rate exceeds the predefined range and here the demand is lowered.

In the absence of HRM infrastructure, an approximate way to determine the demand in Linux operating system is to measure the time a task spends in the run-queue in a given epoch of scheduling. This per-entity load tracking proposed by Paul Turner [32] in kernels higher than 3.7 can be used in lieu of heartbeats. Table 5 summarizes the benchmarks along with inputs and the heartbeat insertion point.

We create 9 different multiprogrammed workload sets from the benchmarks based on the metric $intensity = \frac{\sum_{t \in T} d_t^{A7} - S_{A7}^{max\_freq}}{S_{A7}^{max\_freq}}$, where $\sum_{t \in T} d_t^{A7}$ is the total demand of all the tasks in the given workload and $S_{A7}^{max\_freq}$ is the supply at the maximum frequency in the A7 cluster. The metric $intensity$ shows whether the demand of the entire task set in a workload can be accommodated in the A7 cluster at the highest frequency. If $intensity \leq 0$, the supply exceeds the demand and hence the demand from all the tasks can be satisfied in A7 cluster at highest frequency. On the other hand, if $intensity > 0$, some tasks will not meet their demand on A7 cluster and need to move to the more powerful A15 cluster. Therefore, based on the $intensity$ metric, we classify the workload sets into three types: a) *light* ($metric \leq 0$), b) *medium* ($0 < metric \leq 0.30$) and c) *heavy* ($metric > 0.30$). Table 6 summarizes the workload sets and their classification based on the $intensity$ value.

Table 6: Workload Sets

| | | |
|---|---|---|
| *light* | l1 | texture_v, tracking_v, h264_s swaptions_l, x264_l, blackscholes_l |
| | l2 | texture_v, multicnt_v, h264_b swaptions_l, bodytrack_l, blackscholes_l |
| | l3 | tracking_v, multicnt_v, h264_s x264_l, bodytrack_l, blackscholes_l |
| *medium* | m1 | swaptions_l, bodytrack_l, blackscholes_l texture_v, tracking_v, h264_b |
| | m2 | texture_v, tracking_v, h262_s swaptions_n, bodytrack_n, x264_n |
| | m3 | tracking_v, multicnt_v, blackscholes_n bodytrack_n, texture_f, h264_fo |
| *heavy* | h1 | h264_fo, x264_n, blackscholes_n texture_f, swaptions_n, multicnt_f |
| | h2 | blackscholes_n, x264_n, tracking_f bodytrack_n, texture_f, h264_s |
| | h3 | h264_b, h264_fo, x264_n swaptions_n, bodytrack_n, tracking_f |
| * v-vga, f-fullhd, n-native, l-large * s-soccer, b-bluesky, fo-foreman | | |

The *LBT* module requires the average demand and power consumption of a task in different core types for speculation during load balancing and task migration. We obtain the average demand and power consumption of the tasks in both Cortex-A7 and Cortex-A15 through off-line profiling. The average metrics (demand and power consumption) do not capture the dynamic phases of a task. Nevertheless, it leads to better speculation than the absence of any knowledge whatsoever and the supply-demand module can handle wrong speculations by manipulating the V-F levels. Moreover, as mentioned before, we plan to include the power-performance estimation model for big.LITTLE [27] multi-core within our price theory based power management framework to eliminate the off-line profiling step in the future.

### 5.3 Comparative Study

We compare our price theory based power management framework *PPM* with Hierarchical Power Management (*HPM*) technique proposed in [25] and Heterogeneous aware scheduler in Linux kernel (*HL*) [3]. The HPM is a control-theory based power management framework that employs multiple PID controllers to meet the demand of tasks in asymmetric multi-cores under TDP constraint. However, the HPM scheduler uses naive load balancing and task migration strategy.

The HL scheduler released by Linaro in Linux kernel release 3.8 is aware of the heterogeneity in ARM big.LITTLE platform. The activeness of a task (the amount of time spent in the active task run-queue) is used as a proxy for migration decisions. For example, the HL scheduler migrates a task to A15 cluster (A7 cluster) once the time spent in the

Table 5: Benchmarks description

| Benchmark | Benchmarks suite | Description | Inputs | Heartbeat Location |
|---|---|---|---|---|
| swaptions | PARSEC | Monte Carlo (MC) simulation to compute the prices. | native and large | every "swaption" |
| bodytrack | PARSEC | Tracks a human body with multiple through a series of image sequence. | native and large | every frame |
| x264 | PARSEC | Video encoder. | native | every frame |
| blackscholes | PARSEC | Solves partial differential equation to calculate the prices for a portfolio. | native and and large | every 50000 option |
| h264 | SPEC2006 | Video encoder. | foreman, soccer and bluesky | every frame |
| texture | Vision | Motion, tracking and stereo vision | vga and fullhd | every frame |
| multicnt | Vision | Image Analysis | vga and fullhd | every frame |
| tracking | Vision | Motion, tracking and stereo vision | vga and fullhd | every frame |

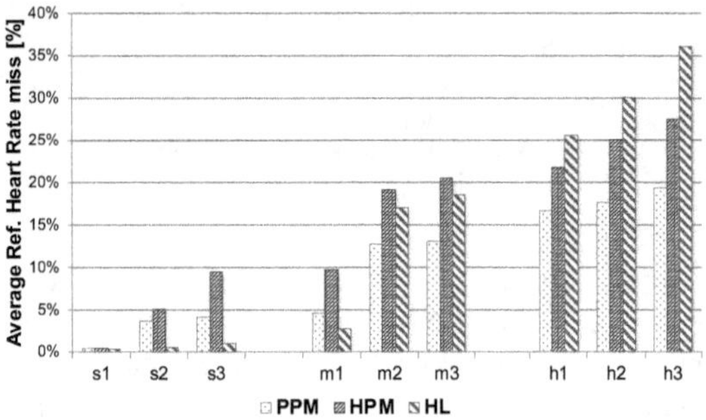


Figure 4: Comparison of the percentage of time the tasks do not meet the reference heart rate range (no TDP constraint).

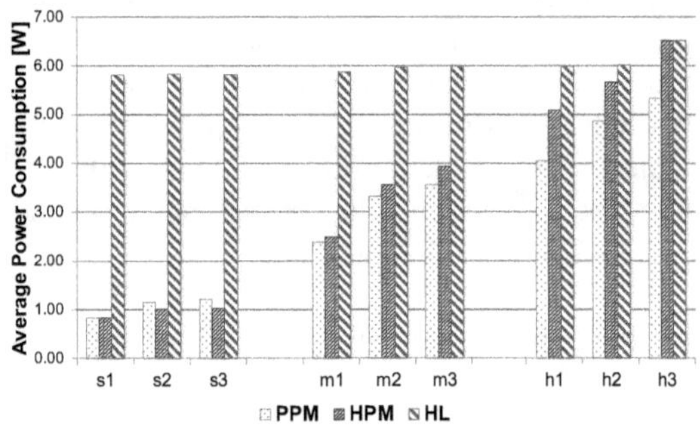


Figure 5: Comparison of power consumption (no TDP constraint).

active run-queue exceeds (falls below) certain predefined threshold. Furthermore, the HL scheduler does not react to the varying demands of the individual tasks. For the HL scheduler, we also employ *cpufreq on-demand* governor that changes the frequency value based on processor utilization. In all the experiments related to the comparative study, we set all the tasks to run at the same priority because HPM and HL do not take the priorities into consideration.

For the first comparative study, we assume that the system does not have any TDP constraint and hence can consume arbitrarily high power. Figure 4 plots the percentage of time the reference heart rate range of any task in the workload is not met, that is, the percentage of time the observed heart rate was smaller than the minimum prescribed heart rate for any of the task in the workload. It is evident that the HL performs better under light workloads (*l1, l2, l3*). This is expected as the HL scheduler migrates the tasks to the powerful A15 cluster at the first opportunity while HPM and PPM both take a more judicious approach. The impact is shown as significantly higher average power consumption for HL compared to HPM and PPM as shown in Figure 5.

On the contrary, the PPM scheduler outperforms both HPM and HL for medium (*m1, m2, m3*) and heavy (*h1, h2, h3*) workloads. The HPM scheduler implements a relatively simple and non-speculative load balancer and task migrator that is oblivious to the utilizations in the other clusters. As the HL scheduler migrates all the tasks to the A15 cluster, it results in inefficient usage of the resources for the more demanding workloads.

Figure 5 plots the average power consumption for the different techniques with no TDP constraint. HPM and PPM have comparable average power consumption across all types of workloads. The HL scheduler with on-demand governor results in an average power consumption of 5.99W, which is much higher than that of HPM (3.43W) and PPM (2.96W) across all the workloads.

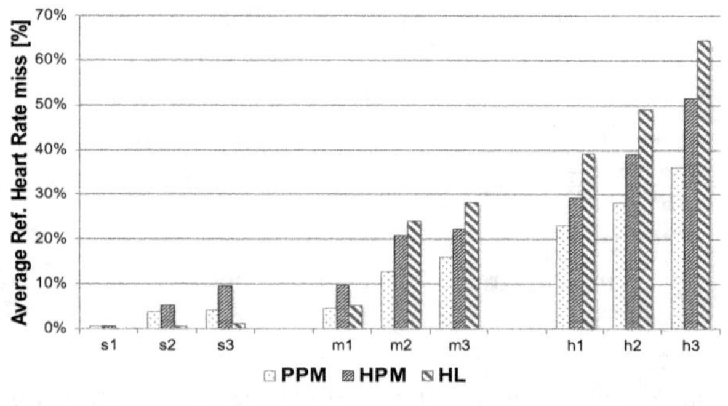


Figure 6: Comparison of the percentage of time the tasks do not meet the reference heart rate range under TDP constraint of 4W.

Next we study how the different techniques cope with strict TDP constraints. We observed through a series of ex-

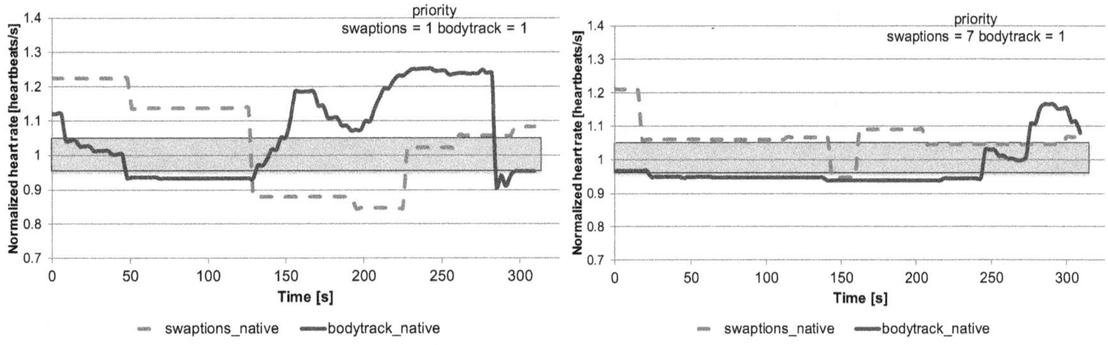


(a) (b)

Figure 7: Normalized performance of swaptions and bodytrack where [0.95,1.05] is the normalized performance goal.

periments that the TDP of our evaluation platform is 8W. To emulate a power-constrained environment, we artificially cap the power budget to 4W. For the HL scheduler, we switch off the A15 cluster once the power exceeds the TDP. This is because the observed maximum power in A7 cluster and A15 cluster are 2W and 6W, respectively. Thus powering down of the A15 cluster guarantees that the total power consumption will be well below the TDP constraint of 4W.

Figure 6 plots the percentage of time any task in the workload do not meet their reference heart rate range under TDP constraint of 4W. The tasks are able to meet their reference heart rate more often with PPM approach compared to HPM and HL. The improvements are 34% and 44% compared to HPM and HL, respectively under 4W TDP constraint.

## 5.4 Impact of priorities and savings

A unique aspect of our price theory-based solution is that we take into consideration the priorities of the tasks as well as their savings. To evaluate the effectiveness of these concepts, we schedule two demanding tasks on one core. We disable load balancing and task migration to study the behavior of the tasks with different priorities and phases of execution (where savings become useful).

Figure 7a shows the dynamically changing performance in terms of heartbeats per second for *swaptions* and *bodytrack* with the same priority. The black shaded region shows the expected performance range. In this case, *swaptions* and *bodytrack* spend 29.7% and 31.1% of time outside the expected performance range. In Figure 7b, we change the priority level of *swaptions* to 7. As can be observed from the figure, *swaptions* is now allocated more resources and hence spends 7.5% of time outside the performance range, while *bodytrack* now spends 57% of time outside the range.

To evaluate the advantage of savings, we choose *swaptions* and *x264*. Both the tasks are running at the same priority. In the initial phase (first 100s), *x264* exceeds the performance goals due to relatively less demand (dormant phase), while *swaptions* just about meets its demand. Thus *x264*

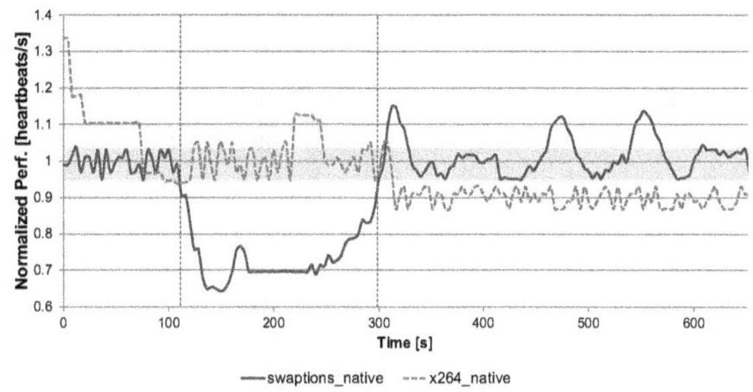


Figure 8: Normalized performance of swaptions and x264 when [0.95, 1.05] is the normalized performance goal.

manages to save a significant fraction of its allowance in this phase.

In the second phase (100 to 300 s), the performance demand of *x264* increases severely as it moves into its active phase. Now *x264* uses up its savings to buy more resources relative to *swaption*. At 300 s, the savings runs out and the high performance demand of *x264* cannot be sustained any further. This illustrate that the concept of savings offers transient benefits to the tasks that spend long time in the dormant phases with very few active phases.

## 5.5 Scalability

Our price theory based power management framework is scalable due to the distributed nature of the agents that work in parallel. We first provide a computational complexity analysis of our framework followed by quantitative results from the implementation.

The computational overhead arises from the calculations performed in the supply-demand module to decide on the bids, price, and supply level. It is evident that these computations are straightforward with negligible overhead. The primary overhead comes from the LBT module that needs to estimate the performance, spending of current and candidate future task mappings.

Let $V$ be the number of clusters on chip, $C$ be the number of cores per cluster, and $T$ be the average number of tasks per core. Let $M$ be the average computation performed to estimate $perf(\mathcal{M}')$ and $spend(\mathcal{M}')$ for each possible task mapping $\mathcal{M}'$. We estimate the cost and benefit of migrating a task to the most over-supplied unconstrained core in each cluster. Thus for each task in the constrained core, we consider $V$ task mappings. So the worst-case computational overhead in the constrained core is $T \times V \times M$. Clearly, the overhead increases with number of tasks and clusters.

Our evaluation platform has two clusters and five cores. To measure the overhead of our approach, we inject all the 8 benchmarks in the system. The supply-demand module is invoked every 31.7ms. As discussed in Section 3.4, the load balancing and task migration are invoked every 95.1ms and 190.2ms, respectively. The overhead per invocation of the LBT module in the ARM big.LITTLE platform is only 0.003ms.

In order to quantitatively evaluate the scalability of our approach, we *emulate* systems with large number of cores and clusters. We randomly generate tasks with varying demands and feed this information to the A7 core running at the lowest frequency level (350MHz), which is a highly pessimistic scenario. We assume that this core is the constrained core. We randomly generate the supply/demand information for the other clusters (up to 256) and the cores (up to 16), and provide this information to the constrained core. The supply and demands are randomly chosen between 10–50 PUs, while the maximum supply of the cores in different clusters are between 350–3000 PUs. We then measure the time spent in the supply-demand module and the LBT module by this constrained core when the task migration module is triggered every 190ms (see in Section 3.4). Table 7 summarizes the overhead in the constrained core for varying number of tasks, cores, and clusters. As we measure the overhead in the small core at the lowest frequency, the overhead will be much smaller on big cores. As recommended for Linux kernel, we also compile the supply-demand module and the LBT module with -O2 compiler optimization flag. For a system with 256 clusters (16 cores per cluster, 32 tasks per core for a total of 131,072 tasks), we observe that the overhead drastically reduces from 11.4ms to 1ms with -O3 optimization flag.

Some existing works [16, 22] provide mixed integer-linear programming (MILP) formulation of the power management problem, which can provide the optimal solution. The MILP-based approach has low overhead for small systems with fewer core types, clusters, and tasks. The complexity of the MILP approach increases exponentially with increasing number of clusters. The average overhead reported in [22] for solving the MILP formulation is 29 minutes, whereas a greedy approximation takes 5.16 minutes for 1000 homogeneous nodes, each node consisting of four cores. All the experiments in [22] were performed on

Table 7: Computational overhead for varying number of clusters $V$, cores per cluster $C$, and tasks per core $T$.

| $V$ | $C$ | $T$ | Total Tasks | Avg. overhead [%] | Avg. overhead [ms] |
|---|---|---|---|---|---|
| 4 | 2 | 8 | 64 | 0.02 | 0.038 |
| | | 32 | 256 | 0.11 | 0.21 |
| | 4 | 8 | 128 | 0.03 | 0.057 |
| | | 32 | 512 | 0.16 | 0.30 |
| 16 | 8 | 8 | 1024 | 0.75 | 1.42 |
| | | 32 | 4096 | 0.96 | 1.82 |
| | 16 | 8 | 2048 | 0.81 | 1.54 |
| | | 32 | 8192 | 1.37 | 2.67 |
| 256 | 8 | 8 | 16384 | 3.48 | 6.62 |
| | | 32 | 65536 | 5.12 | 9.74 |
| | 16 | 8 | 32768 | 4.16 | 7.90 |
| | | 32 | 131072 | 6.0 | 11.4 |

a 3.2GHz dual-processor dual-core platform with 8GB of memory. In [16], the authors report 800ms linear solver time per invocation at 10-minute interval in a datacenter environment consisting of 160 Xeon nodes or 225 Atom nodes or some combination of them. Clearly, the MILP based approaches are infeasible in a modern embedded platform with dynamically varying workloads requiring frequent invocation of the solver. In contrast, the estimated overhead of our price theory-based approach in a 256 cluster system (16 cores per cluster, 32 tasks per core for a total of 131,072 tasks) is only 11.4ms per invocation at 190ms interval on a Cortex-A7 running at 350 MHz.

## 6. Conclusion

In this paper, we propose a price theory-based power management framework for heterogeneous multi-cores to minimize the power consumption while satisfying the performance goals under a power budget constraint. We incorporate various power management techniques like DVFS, load balancing and task migrations in a single, unified and comprehensive framework, which is highly scalable and distributed in nature. Our solution is integrated within the Linux fair scheduler with minimal modifications to the kernel and implemented on a real heterogeneous multi-core platform. Empirical results confirm the superiority of our approach compared to the existing techniques.

## Acknowledgments

We would like to thank Mihai Pricopi and Vanchinathan Venkatramani from NUS for their help in setting up the evaluation platform, Sanjay Vishin from CSR for providing us the evaluation platform and the insightful discussions. We also thank the anonymous reviewers and our shepherd, Professor Margaret Martonosi, for their constructive feedback. This work was partially supported by CSR research funding and Singapore Ministry of Education Academic Research Fund Tier 2 MOE2012-T2-1-115.

## References


[1] SPEC CPU Benchmarks. http://www.spec.org/benchmarks.html.

[2] ARM Ltd., 2011. http://www.arm.com/products/tools/development-boards/versatile-express/index.php.

[3] Linaro Ubuntu release for Vexpress, November 2012. http://releases.linaro.org/13.02/ubuntu/vexpress/.

[4] M. A. Al Faruque, J. Jahn, T. Ebi, and J. Henkel. Run-time thermal management using software agents for multi-and many-core architectures. *Design & Test of Computers, IEEE*, 27(6):58–68, 2010.

[5] S. Balakrishnan, R. Rajwar, M. Upton, and K. Lai. The impact of performance asymmetry in emerging multicore architectures. In *ACM SIGARCH Computer Architecture News*, volume 33, pages 506–517. IEEE Computer Society, 2005.

[6] C. Bienia, S. Kumar, J. P. Singh, and K. Li. The PARSEC benchmark suite: characterization and architectural implications. In *Proceedings of the 17th international conference on Parallel architectures and compilation techniques*, pages 72–81. ACM, 2008.

[7] J. S. Chase, D. C. Anderson, P. N. Thakar, A. M. Vahdat, and R. P. Doyle. Managing energy and server resources in hosting centers. In *ACM SIGOPS Operating Systems Review*, volume 35, pages 103–116. ACM, 2001.

[8] J. Chen and L. K. John. Efficient program scheduling for heterogeneous multi-core processors. In *Proceedings of the 46th Annual Design Automation Conference*, pages 927–930. ACM, 2009.

[9] R. Cochran, C. Hankendi, A. K. Coskun, and S. Reda. Pack & Cap: adaptive DVFS and thread packing under power caps. In *Proceedings of the 44th annual IEEE/ACM international symposium on microarchitecture*, pages 175–185. ACM, 2011.

[10] T. Ebi, M. Faruque, and J. Henkel. Tape: Thermal-aware agent-based power economy multi/many-core architectures. In *Computer-Aided Design-Digest of Technical Papers, 2009. ICCAD 2009. IEEE/ACM International Conference on*, pages 302–309. IEEE, 2009.

[11] T. Ebi, J. Jahn, and J. Henkel. Agent-based thermal management for multi-core architectures. In *Organic ComputingA Paradigm Shift for Complex Systems*, pages 587–588. Springer, 2011.

[12] T. Ebi, D. Kramer, W. Karl, and J. Henkel. Economic learning for thermal-aware power budgeting in many-core architectures. In *Hardware/Software Codesign and System Synthesis (CODES+ ISSS), 2011 Proceedings of the 9th International Conference on*, pages 189–196. IEEE, 2011.

[13] M. Friedman. Quantity theory of money. *J. Eatwell et al*, pages 1–40, 1989.

[14] Y. Ge, Q. Qiu, and Q. Wu. A multi-agent framework for thermal aware task migration in many-core systems. *Very Large Scale Integration (VLSI) Systems, IEEE Transactions on*, 20(10):1758–1771, 2012.

[15] P. Greenhalgh. Big.LITTLE processing with ARM Cortex-A15 & Cortex-A7: Improving energy efficiency in high-performance mobile platforms. *white paper, ARM September*, 2011.

[16] M. Guevara, B. Lubin, and B. C. Lee. Navigating heterogeneous processors with market mechanisms. In *HPCA*, pages 95–106, 2013.

[17] H. Hoffmann, J. Eastep, M. D. Santambrogio, J. E. Miller, and A. Agarwal. Application heartbeats for software performance and health. In *ACM Sigplan Notices*, volume 45, pages 347–348. ACM, 2010.

[18] C. Isci, A. Buyuktosunoglu, C.-Y. Cher, P. Bose, and M. Martonosi. An analysis of efficient multi-core global power management policies: Maximizing performance for a given power budget. In *Microarchitecture, 2006. MICRO-39. 39th Annual IEEE/ACM International Symposium on*, pages 347–358. IEEE, 2006.

[19] D. Koufaty, D. Reddy, and S. Hahn. Bias scheduling in heterogeneous multi-core architectures. In *Proceedings of the 5th European conference on Computer systems*, pages 125–138. ACM, 2010.

[20] R. Kumar, K. I. Farkas, N. P. Jouppi, P. Ranganathan, and D. M. Tullsen. Single-ISA heterogeneous multi-core architectures: The potential for processor power reduction. In *MICRO*, pages 81–92, 2003.

[21] S. Landsburg. *Price theory and applications*. South-Western Pub, 2010.

[22] B. Lubin, J. O. Kephart, R. Das, and D. C. Parkes. Expressive power-based resource allocation for data centers. In *Proc. of the 21st International Joint Conference on Artificial Intelligence*, pages 1451–1456, 2009.

[23] K. Ma, X. Li, M. Chen, and X. Wang. Scalable power control for many-core architectures running multi-threaded applications. In *ACM SIGARCH Computer Architecture News*, volume 39, pages 449–460. ACM, 2011.

[24] T. Mudge. Power: A first class design constraint for future architectures. In *High Performance Computing–HiPC 2000*, pages 215–224. Springer, 2000.

[25] T. S. Muthukaruppan, M. Pricopi, V. Venkataramani, T. Mitra, and S. Vishin. Hierarchical power management for asymmetric multi-core in dark silicon era. In *Proceedings of the 50th Annual Design Automation Conference*, page 174. ACM, 2013.

[26] NVidia Corporation. The Benefits of Multiple CPU Cores in Mobile Devices., 2011.

[27] M. Pricopi, T. S. Muthukaruppan, V. Venkataramani, T. Mitra, and S. Vishin. Power-performance modeling on asymmetric multi-cores. In *Compilers, Architecture and Synthesis for Embedded Systems (CASES), 2013 International Conference on*, pages 1–10. IEEE, 2013.

[28] K. K. Rangan, G.-Y. Wei, and D. Brooks. Thread motion: fine-grained power management for multi-core systems. In *ACM SIGARCH Computer Architecture News*, volume 37, pages 302–313. ACM, 2009.

[29] T. S. Rosing, K. Mihic, and G. De Micheli. Power and reliability management of socs. *Very Large Scale Integration*

*(VLSI) Systems, IEEE Transactions on*, 15(4):391–403, 2007.

[30] A. Roy, S. M. Rumble, R. Stutsman, P. Levis, D. Mazières, and N. Zeldovich. Energy management in mobile devices with the cinder operating system. In *Proceedings of the sixth conference on Computer systems*, pages 139–152. ACM, 2011.

[31] A. Schranzhofer, J.-J. Chen, and L. Thiele. Dynamic power-aware mapping of applications onto heterogeneous MPSoC platforms. *Industrial Informatics, IEEE Transactions on*, 6 (4):692–707, 2010.

[32] P. Turner. Sched: Entity Load-tracking Re-work., 2011. `https://lkml.org/lkml/2012/2/1/763`.

[33] K. Van Craeynest, A. Jaleel, L. Eeckhout, P. Narvaez, and J. Emer. Scheduling heterogeneous multi-cores through performance impact estimation (PIE). In *Proceedings of the 39th International Symposium on Computer Architecture*, pages 213–224. IEEE Press, 2012.

[34] S. K. Venkata, I. Ahn, D. Jeon, A. Gupta, C. Louie, S. Garcia, S. Belongie, and M. B. Taylor. SD-VBS: The San Diego vision benchmark suite. In *Workload Characterization, 2009. IISWC 2009. IEEE International Symposium on*, pages 55–64. IEEE, 2009.

[35] X. Wang, K. Ma, and Y. Wang. Adaptive power control with online model estimation for chip multiprocessors. *Parallel and Distributed Systems, IEEE Transactions on*, 22(10):1681–1696, 2011.

[36] J. A. Winter, D. H. Albonesi, and C. A. Shoemaker. Scalable thread scheduling and global power management for heterogeneous many-core architectures. In *Proceedings of the 19th international conference on Parallel architectures and compilation techniques*, pages 29–40. ACM, 2010.

# Underprovisioning Backup Power Infrastructure for Datacenters

Di Wang* Sriram Govindan† Anand Sivasubramaniam* Aman Kansal†
Jie Liu † Badriddine Khessib†

*The Pennsylvania State University, †Microsoft Corporation
{diw5108, anand}@cse.psu.edu, {srgovin, kansal, jie.liu, bkhessib}@microsoft.com

## Abstract

While there has been prior work to underprovision the power distribution infrastructure for a datacenter to save costs, the ability to underprovision the backup power infrastructure, which contributes significantly to capital costs, is little explored. There are two main components in the backup infrastructure - Diesel Generators (DGs) and UPS units - which can both be underprovisioned (or even removed) in terms of their power and/or energy capacities. However, embarking on such underprovisioning mandates studying several ramifications - the resulting cost savings, the lower availability, and the performance and state loss consequences on individual applications - concurrently. This paper presents the first such study, considering cost, availability, performance and application consequences of underprovisioning the backup power infrastructure. We present a framework to quantify the cost of backup capacity that is provisioned, and implement techniques leveraging existing software and hardware mechanisms to provide as seamless an operation as possible for an application within the provisioned backup capacity during a power outage. We evaluate the cost-performance-availability trade-offs for different levels of backup underprovisioning for applications with diverse reliance on the backup infrastructure. Our results show that one may be able to completely do away with DGs, compensating for it with additional UPS energy capacities, to significantly cut costs and still be able to handle power outages lasting as high as 40 minutes (which constitute bulk of the outages). Further, we can push the limits of outage duration that can be handled in a cost-effective manner, if applications are willing to tolerate degraded performance during the outage. Our evaluations also show that different applications react differently to the outage handling mechanisms, and that the efficacy of the mechanisms is sensitive to the outage duration. The insights from this paper can spur new opportunities for future work on backup power infrastructure optimization.

***Categories and Subject Descriptors*** C.0 [*Computer Systems Organization*]: General

***Keywords*** Datacenters, Backup Power Infrastructure, Underprovision, UPS, Diesal Generator

## 1. Introduction

Considerable capital cost is spent on provisioning the power infrastructure for a datacenter. It can cost between \$10-\$25 for each watt of power provisioned [11, 29, 30, 34], even if that watt is not consumed, contributing to over a third of the amortized costs of a large datacenter. Consequently, recent works [22, 23, 29, 34, 63] have proposed to underprovision this infrastructure, sizing it to handle a high percentile of the power draw rather than the occasional high peaks. Power capping mechanisms are then employed to ensure safety when this limit is reached. Aside from the cost of equipment needed for power distribution, conversion and quality (e.g. switchgear, transformers, PDUs, etc.), a significant portion of this infrastructure's capital cost (over 20% [45]) goes into the backup power equipment - Diesel Generators (DGs) and Uninterrupted Power Supplies (UPS) - needed to sustain operation during utility power outages. To our knowledge, while much prior work has focused on underprovisioning the overall power distribution infrastructure in datacenters, the cost-benefit trade-offs of under-provisioning the backup capacity have not been considered. In this paper, we investigate the relatively unexplored area of underprovisioning, and perhaps even removing, parts of the backup power infrastructure.

Analogous to the distribution infrastructure which needs to handle occasional high peak draws, the backup infrastructure is called upon only when there is an occasional power outage. Figure 1 shows the distribution of power outages in a typical year for US businesses [50, 60]. In Figure 1(a), we observe that 6 or fewer outages are the overwhelming majority (in 87% of the businesses). Further, in Figure 1(b) we see that a large majority (over 58%) of these outages are


*ASPLOS '14*, March 1–4, 2014, Salt Lake City, Utah, USA.

http://dx.doi.org/10.1145/2541940.2541966

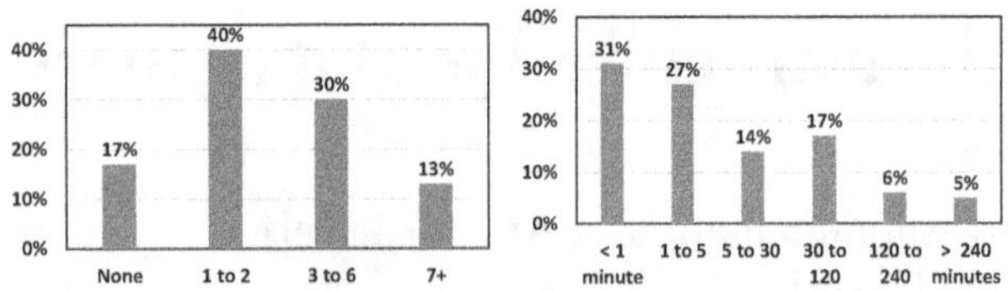


(a) Power Outage Frequency per Year (b) Power Outage Duration

**Figure 1.** Power Outages Distribution for U.S. Business (Source: [50, 60])

shorter than 5 minutes. While handling these rare and typically short outages is extremely important for a datacenter's availability, it is not clear whether the associated high costs for provisioning the backup infrastructure for every eventuality is justified. Provisioning a cost-effective backup infrastructure for datacenters based on these outage characteristics poses interesting research challenges. *Should we provide full backup capacity for the very long (> 4 hours) but extremely rare power outages?* With geo-replication often in use across large datacenters of an organization, a rare and prolonged outage may possibly be handled by load redirection/migration to other (power uncorrelated) sites, even if it is at a slight performance overhead in order to save backup infrastructure costs (e.g. as discussed in [32]). At the other end, *how should we provision a cost-effective backup to handle the load during periods of relatively shorter outages, which could be more frequent?* This paper investigates these questions, with more emphasis on the latter, while considering the consequences of cost-effective backup infrastructure choices on the resulting availability and performance of the datacenter.

**Underprovisioning Backup and Its Consequences:** Backup capacity costs can be expressed in two dimensions - power and energy, i.e. power load that needs to be sustained during the outage, and the energy (integral of power over time) in this period. These impact the cost of provisioning the two main components of the backup infrastructure, namely the Diesel Generators (DGs) and the UPS units. A DG's capital cost is mainly determined by its peak power load, much more than the energy (the cost of building fuel tanks whose capacity impacts the latter is much smaller than the DG itself). On the other hand, UPS cost is determined both by the power load as well as the duration (energy) over which its associated batteries have to be employed. In today's datacenters, UPSes are used mainly as a transition mechanism to switch over the load to Diesel Generators, which can take several seconds to a few minutes, to provide seamless operation for the computing load. However, there is no reason why one could not provision extra battery energy over and beyond this need, if it can offset some or all of the costs associated with DG provisioning. For instance, if we are to only handle outages lasting up to 10 minutes, it may be more cost-effective to eliminate DGs altogether and provision extra battery capacity to last 10 minutes.

When underprovisioning the backup infrastructure, we can have a spectrum of choices between (i) current practice of having full UPS power + energy capacity to hand over the load to DGs, which then can sustain the power need for the entire duration of the outage (assuming sufficient fuel reserve), to (ii) having no UPS or DGs, where the datacenter cannot operate during the outage. Between these extremes, one could opt for different operating points including (a) varying DG power capacity, (b) varying UPS power capacity, (c) varying UPS energy, or (d) combinations thereof. Based on such choices, compute availability and performance could be reduced during the power outage because some or all of the servers are powered off or operating in a lower power state. With reduced backup capacity, application state may be lost in case of an outage if the servers lose power abruptly, before the state is persisted on a stable medium. Within a provisioned backup power and energy capacity, there are different alternatives to improving such performance and availability, such as consolidation and shutting down servers, using low power working states, saving application state etc. In this paper, we use the term performability to loosely refer to both performance and availability of the datacenter during (and after) a power outage, though we quantify the two metrics (performance and availability) separately in our evaluation.

**Overview and Contributions:** This paper explores the design space trade-offs when building different backup capacity alternatives for a datacenter. Within the confines of a provisioned backup capacity, we leverage software and hardware techniques to enhance the performability of the datacenter during power outages of different duration. Some specific issues that we investigate include: Can we completely do away with DGs? Up to what outage duration? What is the minimum cost, and the resulting backup capacity, to handle different outage durations? What are the consequent ramifications on performability? How sensitive are different kinds of applications to these issues? What system mechanisms and online strategies are needed to improve the performability of these applications within the stipulated capacities?

The following are some of the insights from our evaluation of a spectrum of workloads with diverse dependence on the backup infrastructure:

- For outages up to 40 mins, DGs are not needed. It is cost effective to buy additional UPS energy capacity to support the availability and performance mandates. While a DG does translate long outages to smaller ones from the perspective of offered performability, it does so at a significant cost. Given that an overwhelming percentage of power outages are of the order of at most a few minutes, this warrants a re-thinking of current infrastructures which use DGs.
- UPSes play a crucial role in outages of short duration, and can be the sole backup for outages up to 100 minutes to offer similar performability at a similar cost as to-

day's infrastructures. If applications can tolerate a 40% performance degradation during such long power outages, we can get a 40% cost savings as well with just UPS as the backup source. Accommodating longer runtimes on a UPS battery is a more cost and performability effective alternative than using it for high power.

- Different applications react differently to the system mechanisms employed during an outage. In other words, the choice of the system mechanism for a given performability target can be different across multiple applications.
- In general, active power state modulation is better for short outages, sleep or hibernation along with power state modulation for medium outages, and migration and consolidation for long outages, for typical cost-performability tradeoffs.

## 2. Related Work

**Datacenter Power Reduction/Under-provisioning:** The high cost of power provisioning and consumption in datacenters has spurred several efforts to underprovision the power infrastructure [10, 14, 22, 23, 29, 34, 63, 65]. These efforts rely on system techniques for reducing demand and can be categorized in to (a) server-level power reduction using active processor power states [13, 20, 24, 36, 37, 49, 53, 54, 66, 67], inactive deep sleep states [1, 5, 6, 18, 41–43, 55], and power-aware workload scheduling techniques [17, 47], (b) consolidation via migration or load-distribution [4, 16, 39, 52, 59, 62], and the more recent (c) energy-storage/battery based peak shaving approaches [9, 27, 29, 34, 63].

Though related, *backup* power infrastructure underprovisioning and *normal* power under-provisioning are quite different: (a) Unlike normal distribution where only peak power capacity is under-provisioned, in the case of backup, both peak power as well as energy capacity could be underprovisioned. This is particularly true when we remove DGs, the potentially infinite energy source during an outage, creating several other considerations when operating within this limited capacity during an outage. (b) This limited energy capacity calls for additional system software mechanisms to handle the limited energy and the limited power capacity, as opposed to handling only limited power capacity (in normal under-provisioning). Prolonging operation becomes as important as capping peaks. (c) Backup needs to take over the entire load during outage, as opposed to complementing utility power in normal under-provisioning. This heightens the criticality of employed mechanisms to ensure seamless operation. (d) On the positive side, Backup is called upon only for occasional power outages, unlike peak suppression for normal power under-provisioning that could be more frequent. Consequently, issues such as battery wear due to rare outages are less important, and the need to ensure availability is more essential as explored in this paper.

**Backup Infrastructure Costs:** Specific solutions in this area have mainly studied varying the redundancy and placement configurations [28, 40] of the backup equipment, to derive different availability-cost options, popularized by the famous *Tier* [61] classification of datacenters.

**Application State Maintenance:** The loss of application state due to different kinds of faults such as server crashes, network failures, storage failures, and software bugs, has been extensively studied in prior work. Many of these solutions are relevant and applicable to power outages as well. In general, techniques such as state-machine replication, proactive check-pointing and logging can be used (e.g. [15, 19, 33, 51]) to save or replicate application state and resume from the saved state. Intermittently available power has been explicitly considered in [56], which uses proactive migration to save state on a remote server. Further, non-volatility in the memory hierarchy, whether it be through new memory technologies or with commercially available solutions such as NVDIMM [2], can maintain application state upon power failures without any backup power [48].

While we leverage many of the above solutions for reducing the peak power and energy requirement of the backup infrastructure, our contributions are in evaluating cost-performability trade-offs with different backup configurations, system mechanisms used during the outage, different outage durations, and diverse application characteristics.

## 3. Backup Infrastructure Cost Analysis

***Power Hierarchy and Backup Infrastructure:*** Power enters the datacenter from the utility substation (Figure 2). Datacenters typically use a backup secondary power source such as Diesel Generators (DG) to handle utility outages [1] [2]. An Automatic Transfer Switch (ATS) detects primary utility failures and subsequently switches the load over to DGs. This transfer is not instantaneous and can take several seconds. To ensure seamless operation despite such delays, datacenters employ Uninterrupted Power Supply (UPS) units with batteries as a ride-through mechanism to facilitate the transfer. DGs and UPSes, thus, constitute the backup infrastructure (cost of ATS is relatively small and we do not consider it in this paper).

Figure 2 shows UPS units placed at the rack-level which is popular in today's datacenters (as in Facebook [21] and Microsoft [46]) due to its efficiency and cost advantage over conventional centralized placement. The UPS units can either be configured as *online* (in series) or *offline* (in paral-

[1] Access to multiple independent, multi-megawatt utility lines in the same location is very rare and therefore we consider only single utility connection to a datacenter in this paper.

[2] DGs are also used for planned maintainence of the power distribution network without disrupting service. However, we only focus on its provisioning for handling power outages in this paper. One could possibly leverage mobile substations [12] with rapid on-demand deployment (with 12 to 24 hour advance notice) for maintenance purposes in case of non-/under-provisioned DGs.

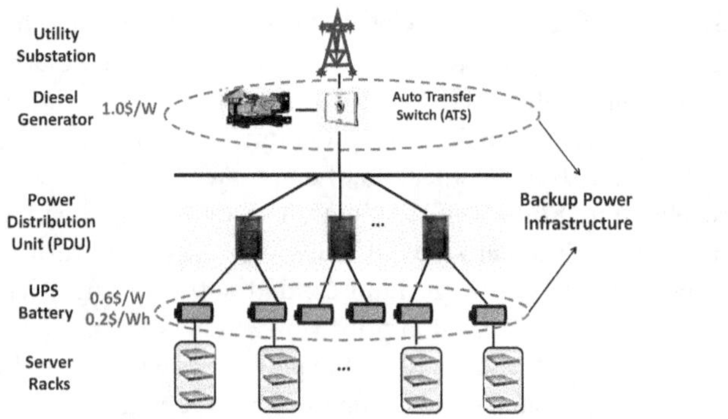


**Figure 2.** Datacenter Power Infrastructure

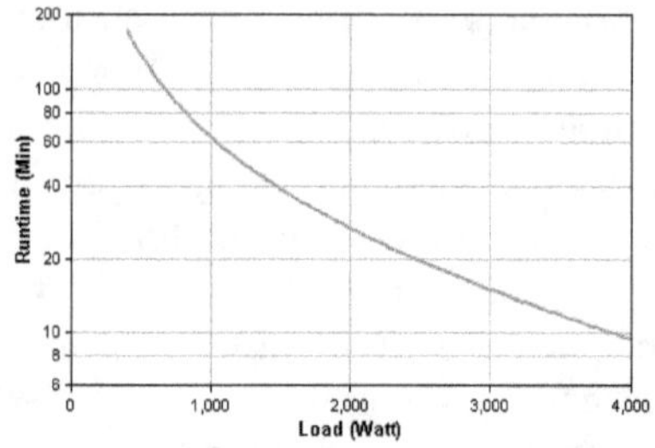


**Figure 3.** Runtime for a battery with max. power of 4KW.

lel), where the latter is preferred in today's datacenters to avoid double-conversion inefficiencies [38] associated with online UPSes. Unlike *online* UPSes which seamlessly transfer to sourcing from their batteries upon a utility failure, *offline* UPS design incurs a delay of about ~10ms to detect a utility failure event before switching over. Fortunately today's power supplies have inherent capacitance to power the server for over 30ms to ride-through this transfer delay after a power failure [48]. It is important to note that *offline* UPS units are exercised only during power outage duration [3] and therefore any under-provisioning in UPS capacity is unlikely to impact normal operation (when utility is active).

The peak power capacity of backup infrastructure including DG and UPS is generally provisioned for the peak capacity of the datacenter, since the entire datacenter load is transferred to them upon an outage. It takes about 20-30 seconds for the Diesel Generator to start and generate enough power to source the entire datacenter. In addition to this start-up delay, additional delay is incurred when transferring the load from UPS to DG, which is generally performed in gradual load-steps, making the overall transition delay to ~2-3 mins [8]. This translates in to a requirement of at least 2 minutes UPS battery runtime. It is important to note that even before starting to use the DG, the datacenter would have restored utility power for more than 30% of the power outages (see Figure 1).

UPS units come with certain base energy capacity whose exact quantity depends on the battery technology and the provisioned peak power capacity. For instance, 2-10 KW lead-acid batteries come with a base energy capacity of ~2-4 mins. This corresponds to where the certain energy storage technology (lead-acid batteries in this case) falls in the Ragone plot (a plot of power versus energy densities as discussed in [63]), wherein a required power from a given technology also determines its energy capacity (and vice-versa). Consequently, while composing the battery cells to achieve a certain amount of battery power, we would automatically get some amount of inherent base battery energy capacity for free. Additional battery modules can be added to this base capacity depending on the energy requirement.

The amount of time taken to drain the battery, i.e., runtime, is not a linear function of the load imposed on it. For illustration, we provide the runtime chart for an APC 4KW battery in Figure 3. Runtime is disproportionately higher at lower load levels. For instance, while the battery shown in the figure can last for 60 mins at 25% load (1000 W) effectively delivering 1kWh of energy, it lasts only for 10 mins at 100% load (4000 W) delivering 0.66kWh of energy. We exploit this crucial property to extend battery runtime during power outages.

***Cost Models:*** The capital expenditure (cap-ex) of the DG and UPSes includes the up-front procurement cost and the amortized future replacement cost. We express cap-ex as amortized $/year, using a linear depreciation model. The operational expenditure (op-ex) includes the cost related to using these devices, corresponding to the cost of diesel fuel and efficiency for the DG and the energy losses for the UPS. The op-ex cost is likely to be negligible since these are rarely called upon, compared to the cap-ex, and we consequently focus on the latter.

The DG cap-ex, *DGCost* (in $/year) is linear with respect to its provisioned peak power capacity, *DGPowerCapacity* (in KW), and can be expressed as:

$$DGCost = DGPowerCost \times DGPowerCapacity \quad (1)$$

where *DGPowerCost* (in $/KW/year) is the amortized cost of diesel generators per unit capacity.

The UPS cap-ex, *UPSCost* (in $/year) depends on (i) provisioned peak power capacity (*UPSPowerCapacity* in KW) and (ii) provisioned battery energy capacity, *UPSEnergyCapacity* (in KWh), both with corresponding per unit costs of *UPSPowerCost* and *UPSEnergyCost* in $/KW/year, respectively. Recall that we get a base energy capacity for free when provisioning the batteries for a given *UPSPowerCapacity*. Hence we subtract that cost, effectively implying that the energy related cost is only incurred for the extra energy capacity required in addition to the base capacity:

$$\begin{aligned} UPScost = {} & UPSPowerCost \times UPSPowerCapacity + \\ & UPSEnergyCost \times (UPSEnergyCapacity \\ & - (UPSPowerCapacity \times FreeRunTime)) \end{aligned} \quad (2)$$

[3] Although UPS units are also used to handle brief periods of brownouts and frequency/power sags and swells, in the context of this paper, we include these events as power outage events since there is no inherent difference in the way UPS is used for handling these events.

where *FreeRunTime* refers to the run time expected at base energy capacity at rated power.

The total backup infrastructure cost is simply the sum of DG and UPS costs. Table 1 lists the values of the parameters in these equations for current technology. The DG and UPS power/energy costs and the *FreeRunTime* values are obtained from [7]. The battery *FreeRunTime* assumes the rack-level battery placement and rated power capacity to supply a rack (in multiple of kilo-watts). We have also evaluated server-level battery configurations and conducted sensitivity analysis on *FreeRunTime*, and the corresponding results can be found in [64]. The cost values of DG power, UPS power and UPS energy are depreciated based on the lifetime of these components: 12 years for DG lifetime and UPS power electronics, and 4 years for lead-acid batteries [11].

| Parameter | Value |
|---|---|
| DGPowerCost | $83.3/KW/year |
| UPSPowerCost | $50/KW/year |
| UPSEnergyCost | $50/KWh/year |
| FreeRunTime | 2 min |

**Table 1.** DG and UPS cost estimation parameters [7, 11]. All cost values are depreciated based on a DG lifetime of 12 years and UPS battery lifetime of 4 years.

| Peak Power (MW) | DG cost (per year) | UPS runtime (minutes) | UPS cost (per year) | Total cost (per year) |
|---|---|---|---|---|
| 1 | 0.08 M$ | 2 | 0.05 M$ | 0.13 M$ |
| 10 | 0.83 M$ | 2 | 0.51 M$ | 1.34 M$ |
| 10 | 0.83 M$ | 42 | 0.83 M$ | 1.66 M$ |

**Table 2.** Estimated amortized cap-ex annual cost of backup infrastructure for different datacenter capacities. M$ indicates million dollars.

Table 2 shows the backup infrastructure cost at different peak power and UPS energy capacity (expressed as runtime) requirements. Three interesting observations are: (i) backup infrastructure costs amount to several million dollars of capital investment for multi-megawatt datacenters, (ii) while the backup infrastructure cost varies almost linearly with peak power, it rises very slowly with provisioned energy capacity (for instance, a 20 fold increase in UPS energy translated to just 24% increase in overall cost), and (iii) for less than 40 minutes of outage, the cost of using UPS batteries is lower than that of DG. Additionally, battery cost is continuing to drop due to its recent proliferation in commodity products (while DG cost has remained relatively stable), indicating that batteries will become more favorable in future.

## 4. Cost-Performance-Availability Tradeoffs

We now use the cost model to identify various underprovisioning options for the backup infrastructure and discuss their performance and availability implications. Recall that we use the term *performability* to loosely indicate both performance and availability during power outages.

| Configuration | DG Power | UPS Power | UPS Energy | Cost |
|---|---|---|---|---|
| MaxPerf | 1 | 1 | 2 mins | 1 |
| MinCost | 0 | 0 | 0 mins | 0 |
| NoDG | 0 | 1 | 2 min | 0.38 |
| NoUPS | 1 | 0 | 0 mins | 0.63 |
| DG-SmallPUPS | 1 | 0.5 | 2min | 0.81 |
| SmallDG-SmallPUPS | 0.5 | 0.5 | 2 mins | 0.5 |
| SmallPUPS | 0 | 0.5 | 2 min | 0.19 |
| LargeEUPS | 0 | 1 | 30 min | 0.55 |
| SmallP-LargeEUPS | 0 | 0.5 | 62 min | 0.38 |

**Table 3.** Different options for underprovisioning backup infrastructure. Cost is normalized to the current datacenter practice (*MaxPerf*). "P" in "SmallP-" stands for Power; "E" in "LargeE-" represents Energy.

Table 3 presents different backup infrastructure configurations with varying DG and UPS capacities, along with their cost estimates. *MaxPerf* indicates the current datacenter practice with both DG and UPS provisioned with full power capacity (equivalent to datacenter peak requirement) and offers seamless performance during power outages. *MaxPerf* uses UPS batteries merely as a transition mechanism to DG which amounts to ~2 mins of UPS battery runtime (refer Section 3). Since *MaxPerf* is popular with today's datacenters, we use it as a performability and cost baseline for comparison. The second configuration, *MinCost* in Table 3, points to the other extreme, where the datacenter is completely unavailable (offering no performance) during power outages. *MinCost* does not provision any backup infrastructure, and thereby not incurring any associated costs.

Datacenters may wish to operate in between these two performability-cost extremes. The ideal operating point would have the maximum performability as that of *MaxPerf* and the minimum cost as that of *MinCost*. There are different intermediary backup configurations with varying degrees of underprovisioning, that offer different trade-offs. Table 3 lists some of these, along with consequent cost benefits. Eliminating DG in *NoDG* results in 62% cost reduction compared to current practice (*MaxPerf*). Removing UPS in *NoUPS* translates to 37% savings. While underprovisioning UPS power capacity in *DG-SmallPUPS* saves 19%, underprovisioning both DG and UPS power capacity in *SmallDG-SmallPUPS* costs 50% less. *SmallPUPS* achieves 81% cost savings by eliminating DG and underprovisioning UPS power capacity. *LargeEUPS* shows an interesting configuration where even after increasing the UPS energy capacity to 30 minutes (a factor of 15 increase from MaxPerf), it still saves 45% of the cost by eliminating DG. More interestingly, *SmallP-LargeEUPS* achieves the same cost as *NoDG* (38% of *MaxPerf*) by trading power capacity for longer run time.

***Performability during Power Outages*** Underprovisioned backup infrastructure has multiple performance and availability ramifications: (i) degraded performance due to *re-*

*duced power capacity* of backup infrastructure, (ii) service or application unavailability (no performance) due to *insufficient backup energy capacity* to last for the duration of the outage, and (iii) impact to both performance and availability due to loss of application state.

Loss of application state, such as volatile application data in CPU registers, caches, and DRAM, can continue to impact application performance even after power is restored (either via utility or DG) . For instance, an outage in datacenters without UPS (e.g., *MinCost* and *NoUPS* in Table 3) will result in immediate loss of volatile application state (server/application crash). This loss continues to impact performance and availability due to several reasons including: (a) re-initialization of various server components such as CPU, disks and re-establishment of network sockets, external service authorizations etc; (b) consistency checks of various software components like file systems, networked systems etc., due to potential loss of partially committed state; (c) re-loading of the entire OS and application stack from disk to memory; (d) application specific warm-ups which includes pre-loading or pre-computing certain application state to improve performance, especially for applications that use significant memory such as Memcached, in-memory index search etc.; and, (e) re-computation of work that was earlier committed to memory but not persisted to disks. The above overheads may either manifest as extended unavailability beyond the power outage duration ((a), (b) and (c)) or as degraded performance upon resuming application execution after the power outage ((d) and (e)).

To summarize, performability of an application during power outages depends not just on the ability to sustain application execution but also on the ability to preserve application state. In the next section, we discuss the cost implications of various system techniques that allow us to either sustain application execution or preserve application state during outages.

## 5. Handling Outages With an Underprovisioned Backup Infrastructure

Given the above discussion, we classify system techniques to handle outages into two broad categories, *sustain-execution* and *save-state* as shown in Figure 4, and discuss them below.

| Technique | Time to take effect | Power after activation |
|---|---|---|
| Throttling | Tens of $\mu$secs | Throttled state |
| Migration | Few mins | Consolidated state |
| Proactive Migration | 100ms-few secs | Consolidated state |
| Sleep | ˜10 secs | 2-4W per DIMM |
| Hibernation | Few mins | 0 Watts |
| Proactive Hibernation. | Few mins | 0 Watts |

**Table 5.** Impact of system techniques on backup infrastructure capacity.

**Sustain-execution:** These techniques allow us to continue executing the application even after a power failure, possibly

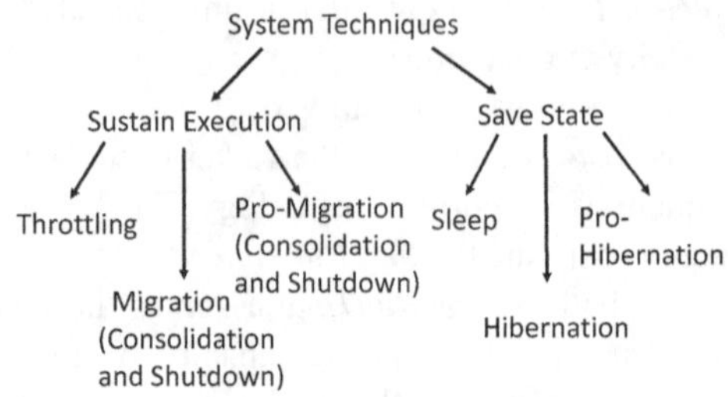


**Figure 4.** Techniques for realizing different application performability goals during power outages.

at a lower power draw to stay within the underprovisioned backup infrastructure capacity (power or energy).

*Throttling:* The application may be operated in a lower performance mode using active CPU power states (P/T states) [20, 24, 36, 54, 67]. Transitioning to these throttling states is almost instantaneous [4] (within tens of $\mu$secs) and therefore acts as an effective technique to reduce the peak power requirement from the backup infrastructure.

*Migration (Consolidation and Shutdown):* Throttling can reduce power but incurs the idle power penalty of keeping all servers active. An alternative is to consolidate applications on fewer servers, with each given a smaller fraction of the processor cycles, memory space and other resources [16, 26, 35, 52, 59, 69]. This can be more energy proportional for current technology. In this approach, immediately after a power failure, application state is migrated to a remote server while keeping the original server powered until migration is complete. Once all state is transferred, the originating server is powered down and the application is resumed at the remote server. In this approach, we assume the persistent state of the application is available in a shared storage server which continues to have power backup even when the power backup is under-provisioned. Hence, only the volatile state needs to be migrated. We use the existing implementation of live-migration in Xen for evaluating this technique [18].

*Proactive Migration (Consolidation and Shutdown):* The time required for migration depends primarily on the size of volatile application state. Datacenter applications may have huge in-memory application state (as high as the memory capacity - between ˜64 to 128GB for today's datacenter servers) which can result in large migration times (potentially exceeding the outage duration). This technique attempts to reduce the amount of state that needs to be moved after a power failure by periodically flushing application memory state to remote server memory [56] during normal operation (when utility power is active). Successive copying only needs to move the memory state that has been modified since the last migration (similar to how live migration

[4] Recall from section 3 that servers have ˜30ms of power supply capacitance which acts as a ride-through before transfer to backup infrastructure. This duration can be used to transition the server to the throttled state.

| Technique | Normal operation | Start of utility outage | During utility outage | After utility restored |
|---|---|---|---|---|
| Maxperf | Full service | Full service | Full service | Full service |
| Mincost | Full service | Server/App crash | No service | Server/App Restart |
| Throttling | Full service | Throttled Perf. | Throttled Perf. | Restore full service |
| Migration | Full service | Migrate to remote memory | Consolidated service | Migrate back |
| Proactive Migration | Periodic dirty-state flush to remote memory | Migrate remaining dirty state to remote memory | Consolidated service | Migrate back to full service |
| Sleep | Full service | Suspend to local memory | No service | Resume from memory |
| Hibernation | Full service | Persist to local storage | No service | Resume from disk |
| Proactive Hibernation | Periodic dirty-state flush to local storage | Persist remaining dirty state to local storage | No service | Resume from disk |

**Table 4.** Performance and Availability implications of underprovisioning techniques.

works). This reduces the amount of (volatile) state that needs to be transferred after a power failure and hence reduces the amount of backup energy capacity required for the migration. We leverage existing implementation of periodic virtual machine checkpointing in Remus [19] for evaluating this technique.

**Save-state** Immediately after a power failure event, the application state is preserved either by pushing the state to memory (while ensuring DRAM is supplied sufficient power to retain data) or to local persistent storage. The servers themselves stop continuing to execute application code.

*Sleep:* The application and the OS stack is suspended and the server enters the S3 (suspend to RAM) state where the volatile memory (DRAM) is operated in self-refresh mode and all other server components are turned off [1, 41–43, 55, 68]. Though this technique does not offer any application service during the power outage, the resume time is fast after power is restored (only the processor caches need to be loaded).

*Hibernation:* The application state is pushed to local persistent storage. Unlike *Sleep*, this allows completely powering down the servers once the state is pushed to the disk, but comes with a higher restore latency.

*Proactive Hibernation:* The modified volatile state of the application is periodically pushed to local persistent storage during normal operation (active utility). This may reduce the amount of state that needs to be pushed after a power failure compared to Hibernation and therefore may require less backup capacity for persisting the state.

Nearly all the hardware capabilities and APIs needed to implement these techniques are available in today's systems, though some may need to be tuned for our usage scenario, e.g., repeated copying of dirty state in live-migration can be tuned to reduce the overall migration time and hence the backup energy; the Remus technique takes a consistent snapshot by suspending the entire application whereas we are only interested in minimizing the amount of dirty state to be transferred after a power failure and do not care about the remote state being consistent at other times. In this paper, we use the available capabilities as-is and therefore present a conservative estimate of the efficacy of the techniques.

It is easier to visualize the contrasting performability implications of these system techniques during a power failure using four operational phases as identified in Table 4: (a) Normal operation – utility is active and powering the datacenter, (b) Start of Power Failure – activities performed immediately at the start of a power outage, (c) During Power Failure – activities performed during the power outage, and, (d) Power Restored – activity performed after power is restored. Along with the techniques discussed above, Table 4 also presents the performability offered by today's approach, *MaxPerf* and the zero cost baseline, *MinCost*. While the *sustain-execution* techniques continue to offer performance even during power failure, they may not have enough backup capacity to sustain the energy needs throughout the entire outage duration. On the other hand, the *save-state* techniques significantly reduce the energy capacity requirement from the backup infrastructure, but they do not offer any performance during power failure.

We also summarize the demand imposed by these techniques on the backup infrastructure capacity in Table 5. The amount of time required for the technique to take effect after a power failure, together with the power requirement after the technique is enforced, help quantify the required backup infrastructure energy and power capacity.

**Hybrid Techniques** The ability of the *sustain-execution* techniques to continue serving applications at low power during outages and the ability of *save-state* techniques to preserve application state at almost no power cost, suggest the possibility of combining them for better cost-performability tradeoffs.

The peak power capacity of the backup infrastructure is a crucial factor in determining the overall cost (for both UPS and DG as shown in Table 2). Among the basic techniques identified above, *Throttling* is the only technique that is guaranteed to reduce the peak power (refer Table 5) (even migration for subsequent shutdown can create a momentary spike). The other techniques are primarily geared towards reducing the energy requirement from the backup infrastructure and can be combined with *Throttling* to reduce the backup infrastructure cost. We use the '-L' notation (denoting low power) along with the name of the basic technique in Table 6 to refer to these hybrid combinations. The con-

| Hybrid technique | During power failure |
|---|---|
| Sleep-L | Throttle while going to sleep |
| Hibernate-L | Throttle while going to hibernate |
| Throttle+Sleep-L | Throttle + throttle while going to sleep |
| Throttle+Hibernate | Throttle + throttle while going to hibernate |
| Migration+Sleep-L | Migrate + throttle while going to sleep |

**Table 6.** Hybrid Sustain-Execution + Save-State techniques.

sequent reduction in peak power could possibly come at the cost of higher energy required from the UPS, but still reduce overall backup cost. For instance, hibernation may take a long time to complete when combined with throttling but the overall UPS cost may still be lower due to the asymmetry between UPS power and energy costs. We investigate these trade-offs and the efficacy of the hybrid combinations enumerated in Table 6 in our evaluations.

## 6. Experimental Evaluation

**Experimental Setup and Methodology:** We use identical dual socket servers with 6-core 3.4 GHz Intel processors (12 cores per server), 64 GB DRAM, and a 1 Gbps Ethernet interface and run our applications hosted on the Linux OS. The power consumption of each server is monitored using an external Yokogawa high-resolution power meter. The server idle power is around 80W and the peak power draw that we have measured is 250W. The dynamic power consumption can be modulated using 7 voltage/frequency P-states and 8 clock throttling T-states.

One would ideally like to carry out our experiments on a datacenter scale platform with all the backup infrastructure in place. However, a smaller setup can be used to glean nearly all the insights as that from a large scale platform, without explicit backup equipment such as UPSes or DGs, using the following methodology. We subject each application or server to the different system techniques described earlier and record the power consumption (both peak power and energy) using the external power meter. Along with power data, we also collect the application performance and down time, both when the application is subjected to the system techniques (during the assumed outage duration) and and when the application resumes normal operation (immediately after the assumed outage duration). The outage start and end times are noted. Power data collected at fine temporal resolution allow us to calculate the required DG and UPS power and energy capacities for each evaluation run.

**Implementation of System Techniques:** We build on existing functionality in current systems to implement these techniques as below. *Sleep* and *Hibernation*: standard OS commands in Linux; *Throttling: cpufreq* driver in Linux; *Migration (Consolidation):* We run applications on a Linux Virtual Machine (VM) with 28 GB of allocated physical memory. We leverage Xen live migration [18] and Remus implementations [19] for our migration related experiments. We use a relatively aggressive consolidation by powering down every alternative server, reducing the number of servers to half the original size; *Proactive Hibernation* and *Proactive Migration*: for each application, we profile the frequency at which its memory pages are being modified (analogous to the dirty bitmap used in live migration [18]) and estimate the amount of memory pages that need to be written to disk (in case of proactive hibernation) or copied to remote memory (in case of proactive migration). We limit the frequency of the periodic modified-page copying operation in order to avoid any perceivable performance impact during normal operation.

**Workloads:** We consider the following workloads (Table 7) that have different kinds of state, and consequently demands on the backup infrastructure for availability:

- Specjbb [58] emulates a supermarket retailer IT infrastructure using a three-tier architecture comprising web, application, and database tiers. We execute the benchmark and all its tiers on a single server. Specjbb uses an in-memory database, which has both read-only and modified data. Losing volatile state during a power failure may cause Specjbb to recompute lost computation and impacts its throughput.
- Web-search is an internally developed workload that emulates the index searching component of search engines. Web-search stores several hundred gigabytes of index data in persistent storage and uses volatile memory (DRAM) as a cache for frequently accessed index data – around ~40 GB index data in memory for our experiments. We use a real world query trace to generate client traffic. This workload measures performance as aggregate throughput (queries per second) that can be achieved by the server within a high-percentile latency constraint. The index data which occupies the major portion of server memory is read-only and can be read-back from persistent storage if volatile state is lost during a power failure with a consequent performance penalty.
- Memcached [44] is an in-memory key value store for small chunks of data. It primarily uses volatile memory to improve read performance. We use a read-only client workload to exercise the data and use throughput as its performance metric.
- SpecCPU benchmarks [57] represent High Performance Computing (HPC) applications. These applications may run for hours or even days. If volatile state is lost due to power outage, these applications will typically have to recompute the lost state (one can alleviate the performance impact by checkpointing partial results). We use *mcf* from SpecCPU2006 in our experiments as a representative for memory intensive scientific computation workloads. Since each *mcf* instance only consumes ~2GB memory, we instantiate multiple *mcf* instances to increase its memory usage to emulate large memory footprint HPC applications.

| Workload | Memory Usage | Performance Metric |
|---|---|---|
| Web-search | 40 GB | Latency-constrained, queries/sec |
| Specjbb | 18 GB | Latency-constrained, ops/sec |
| Memcached | 20GB | Queries/second |
| SpecCPU (mcf*8) | 16GB | Completion time |

**Table 7.** Workloads Description

**Evaluation Metrics:** We consider backup infrastructure cost, application performance and availability as metrics for evaluating the efficacy of our underprovisioning techniques.

- *Cost:* We use backup infrastructure (UPS and DG) capex based on the cost model in Section 3. We normalize the cost of the different under-provisioned configurations to that of today's datacenter configuration (*MaxPerf* in Table 3).
- *Down time:* We report the total time for which an application is unavailable (not performing computation or responding to users) during a power outage and immediately after power is restored.
- *Performance during power outage:* Table 7 lists the application specific performance metrics. For each application, we normalize its performance to that in *MaxPerf.* Since performance may continue to be impacted after power restoration for different lengths of time under different system techniques, we report performance impact over a common duration, the power outage duration. We report the impact beyond the outage as *down time* and distinguish between actual down time and performance induced down time.

## 6.1 Tradeoffs Between Backup Configurations

We first evaluate the cost and performability tradeoffs for different power backup configurations (i.e., different DG power capacities and UPS power and energy capacities) from Table 3. For each backup configuration, we choose the system technique (from Tables 4 and 6) that offers the highest performance and lowest down time.

Figure 5 presents the cost, performance and down time for *Specjbb* for various backup configurations. While today's approach, *MaxPerf,* offers the best performance and zero down time for all outage duration, the *MinCost* configuration offers no performance during an outage and suffers significant down time – as much as 400 seconds even for a short 30 seconds outage. The high down time suffered by *MinCost* is due to the server restart time, creation of Specjbb processes and time to catch up to the target throughput due to the loss of state.

The other configurations cover a large spectrum of offered performance and availability:

**Impact of DG:** For configurations with DG (*NoUPS* and *DG-SmallPUPS* in Table 3), long outages can be transformed into short outages from the perspective of performability since DG will supply power after the initial 2-minute start-up delay. In *NoUPS* (not shown for clarity), the down-time is same as that for *MinCost* in Figure 5(c). *DG-SmallPUPS* can ride-out the DG start-up delay with zero downtime but with a performance penalty since the smaller UPS implies reduced performance during DG start-up. Performance should not be compared across multiple outage duration since each one is normalized to the baseline for that duration, and different outage handling system techniques could have been selected depending on outage duration.

The smaller UPS capacity required is only 15s of runtime at 50% of *MaxPerf* power (using *sleep-L* as the outage handling technique for the DG start-up delay), but the minimum battery capacity dictated by the Ragone plot leads to higher battery runtime. The cost reduction of *DG-SmallPUPS* is hence only 20% compared to *MaxPerf.*

*SmallDG-SmallPUPS* (not shown for clarity) in Table 3 also has zero down time but at higher performance penalty. Configurations without DG cannot avoid down time during long outages.

**Impact of UPS:** UPS acts as a low-cost alternative to DG for handling short outages, that comprise the majority of outages. Consider configurations that completely eliminates the DG: *NoDG, LargeEUPS, SmallP-LargeEUPS* in Figure 5. While the *NoDG* configuration with limited UPS capacity suffers degradation in both performance (drops to 60% of *MaxPerf*) even for a 5 mins outage, one can significantly improve the performability by purchasing more UPS energy capacity. For instance, *LargeEUPS* with 30 minutes of UPS battery capacity achieves the same performance as *MaxPerf* upto 30 mins outage duration and sustains 60% of (degraded) performance for upto 1 hour outage duration, at only 55% of the cost of *MaxPerf.* Although *NoDG* and *SmallP-LargeEUPS* incur the same cost (38% of *MaxPerf*), the latter achieves better performability than *NoDG* (which do not sustain beyond 5 mins outage) for 30 mins or longer outages, by trading peak power (reduced by half) for higher energy (runtime of 62 mins).

**Summary of Insights:** (i) Though DG translates long outages into small ones from the perspective of offered performability, it does so at a significant cost. (ii) UPS plays a crucial role in improving performability for short outages irrespective of the presence of DG. (iii) UPS can eliminate DG for up to 100 mins of outage duration and offer the same performance as with today's approach at the same cost. (iv) UPS can result in 40% cost savings for outages as long as 1 hour for datacenter willing to tolerate 40% performance degradation during outages. (v) For the same cost, the performability offered by UPS with small power capacity and longer runtime may be better than that offered by UPS with high power capacity and shorter runtime for relatively long outages.

## 6.2 Effectiveness of Outage Handling Techniques

We now compare the performability-cost tradeoffs offered by different system techniques listed in Tables 4 and 6. In

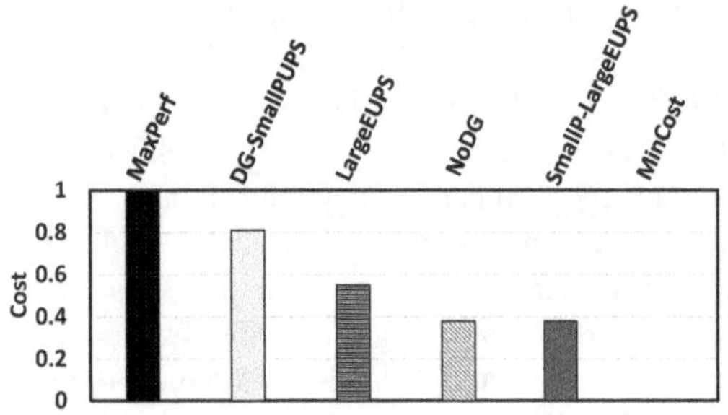


(a) Cost of configurations from Table 3.

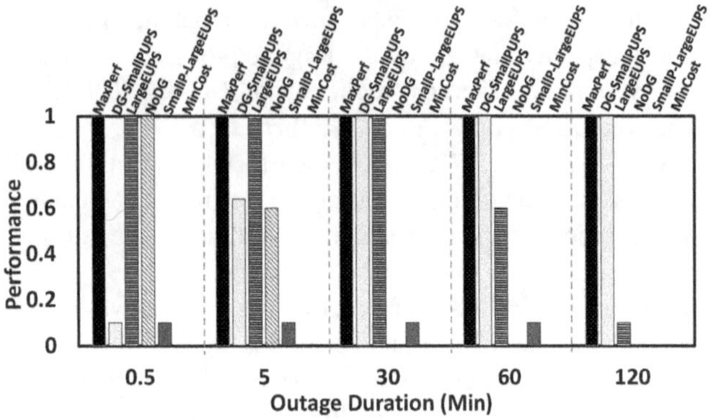


(b) Performance of configurations under different outage durations.

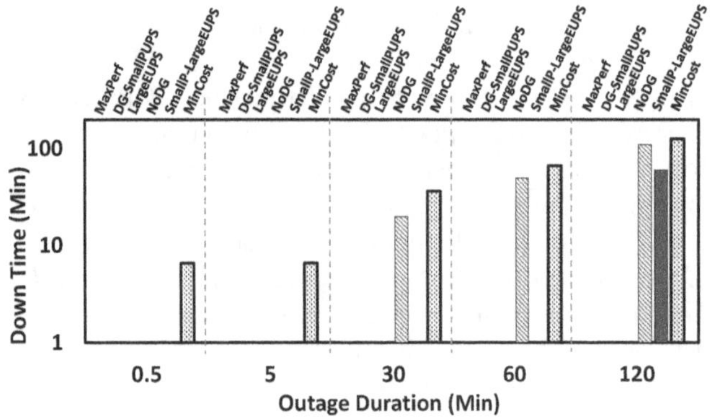


(c) Down time of configurations under different outage durations.

**Figure 5.** Cost and performability tradeoffs between the 6 configurations - *MaxPerf*, *DG-SmallPUPS*, *LargeEUPS*, *NoDG*, *SmallP-LargeEUPS* and *MinCost* - for Specjbb. In (a), we repeat the costs for these configurations from Table 3 for convenience. For each outage duration, in (b) and (c), we give the performance and downtime for these configurations. It is only for outages longer than 60 minutes that the *LargeEUPS* configurations become less attractive.

| Technique | Save time | Resume time | Peak power |
|---|---|---|---|
| Sleep | 6 secs | 8 secs | 1 |
| Hibernate | 230 secs | 157 secs | 1 |
| Proactive Hibernate | 179 secs | 157 secs | 1 |
| Sleep-L | 8 secs | 8 secs | 0.5 |
| Hibernate-L | 385 secs | 175 secs | 0.5 |

**Table 8.** Time to save and resume *Specjbb* memory state for different techniques. The save power draw (normalized to server peak) of these techniques is also presented.

the interest of clarity, we first show representative results for Specjbb, and then show specific results for the other applications. Recall from Section 6.1 that the presence of DG in the backup infrastructure is not only expensive but is also uninteresting in its performability implications for outages longer than the DG start-up time. Therefore, for the rest of the evaluation, we only consider backup configurations without DG and consider variations in the UPS peak power and energy capacity. For each system technique, we use the lowest cost backup configuration (combination of UPS peak and energy capacity) at each of the offered performance and availability operating points.

**Impact of Power Outage Duration:** Figure 6 shows the cost of backup infrastructure, application down time and application performance impact of the different system techniques for *Specjbb* application under different outage duration – from 30 seconds to 2 hours. In the case of techniques which employ DVFS throttling, we use two bars in the figure to show the minimum and maximum values (the range) offered based on the chosen voltage and frequency states.

*Sustain-execution Techniques:* These techniques offer high performance at low cost for short and medium outages, but incur high cost for long outages. For instance, *Throttling* can achieve the same performance as *MaxPerf* at less than 40% of its cost for outage duration up to 30 minutes. For long outages (> 1 hour), realizing similar cost reduction (60% of *MaxPerf*) results in degraded performance for *Throttling* (drops to 60% of *MaxPerf*) and even becomes infeasible to sustain the application beyond 4 hours outage duration. *Migration* techniques are better than throttling for medium to long outage duration since after migration the applications enjoy better performance under the same cost budget, due to lack of energy proportionality in today's servers [10]. However for short and even medium outages, throttling is preferred because migration overheads are high (*Specjbb* takes 10 minutes to migrate) and performance loss due to additional throttling required to suppress power spikes during migration [29]. *Proactive Migration (PM)* can reduce the application state that needs to be migrated after a power failure. For *Specjbb*, this resulted in a reduction from 18GB to 10GB, corresponding to a lower migration time of 5 minutes. This reduction in migration time translates into some cost savings (not visible in the figure).

*Save-state techniques:* These techniques do not offer any performance during the outage and are better suited to handle short outages where preserving state reduces the additional unavailability after power restoration. For instance, *Sleep-L*, which costs only 20% of *MaxPerf*, has a much lower down time of 38 seconds compared to *MinCost* which has over 400 seconds of down time for the 30 second power outage duration.

*Save-state* techniques may also incur a penalty to resume application state but this is generally much lower than that of *MinCost*. Table 8 shows the measured save and resume du-

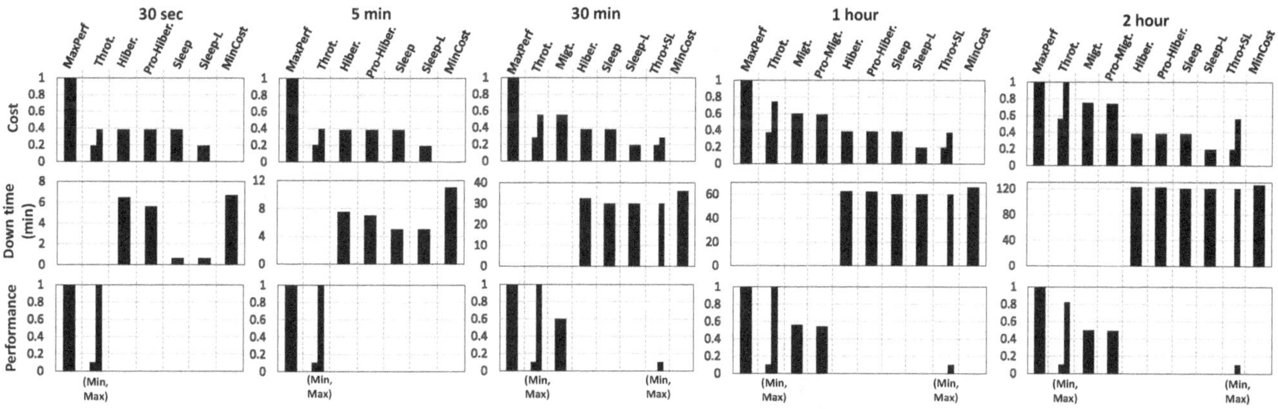

**Figure 6.** Power outage duration impact on different techniques for Specjbb. In techniques which use DVFS Throttling, the minimum and maximum values are shown to illustrate the range based on the chosen voltage-frequency states.

ration for the *Specjbb* application, along with its peak power draw when operating under these techniques. The low-power (*-L) techniques take a longer time to save the application state, especially for *Hibernate-L* (while *Sleep-L* save time remains unaffected) but reduces the peak power draw by half. While the resume time always manifests as additional down time for the application after power is restored, the save time impacts availability only when the outage duration is smaller than the save time. For instance, *Hibernation* may be a bad idea for a 30 second outage for *Specjbb* as shown in Figure 6. *Proactive Hibernate* can reduce the time required to save state (by 22%), but is still not well suited for short outages.

We find that the most effective technique is different for different outage duration. For short outages (0.5 min to 5 min), *Throttling* can achieve best performability and cost tradeoffs compared to other techniques. For medium outage duration (30 min to 1 hour), *Throttle+Sleep-L* is able to sustain and preserve state for the entire outage duration even with very limited battery capacity. This is primarily due to the extremely low power consumption of *sleep* technique which is around 5W per server and UPS runtimes stretch significant for lower load-levels (refer Section 3). And finally, for long outages (2 hours and beyond), *Throttling* and *Migration* become infeasible for cost less than 56% of *MaxPerf*, since they quickly drain the limited UPS battery capacity and are not able to sustain operation for the entire outage duration. On the other hand, *Throttle+Sleep-L* can sustain at as low as 20% cost. However, for long outages, preserving state may not buy much since the outage duration far outweighs the overheads of losing state. For handling such long outages, request or load redirection to geo-replicated datacenters would be a better solution [3, 32].

**Impact of Application Memory Usage:** The memory used by an appication impacts the time that it takes to save state, thereby also having a consequence on availability (whether the state can be saved before power runs out) as well as on performance (may need to employ more aggressive performance impacting power saving techniques). We have evaluated such performability-cost tradeoffs for varying memory state size of the *Specjbb* application, over different outage durations. We summarize the results here and the reader is referred to [64] for further details. As the state size reduces, the down time due to *Hibernation* and *Proactive Hibernation* techniques reduces, though the corresponding impact on cost is not perceivable (due to lower battery energy cost). Sleep based techniques (*Sleep* and *Sleep-L*) remain unaffected with application state size. Sustain-execution techniques achieve better performability and lower cost with smaller state size. For *Throttling*, this can be attributed to the lower injected load on *Specjbb* at lower memory footprint size, resulting in less power and energy draw from the UPS. For migration based techniques, smaller state size directly translates to shorter migration time. These insights could be exploited to develop an adaptive online strategy that tracks memory usage and dynamically employs the appropriately effective technique.

**Influence of Application Characteristics:** We now compare and contrast the effect of underprovisioning for applications with diverse performance and availability (state recovery time) characteristics. We mainly highlight the differences.

*Memcached (Figure 7):* Since Memcached loads the memory with the necessary data from disk before handling client requests, losing memory state will result in the reloading of the lost data. While the down time is 480 seconds for a 30 seconds outage with the *MinCost* configuration, somewhat surprisingly, the down time is even longer, 1140 seconds, for *Hibernation*. This implies that losing application state after a power failure (and re-loading the data after restoring power) may be more efficient compared to hibernation overheads for applications that directly uses data fetched from disk without any modification. We find that the performance offered by *Throttling* and *Migration* is much better than that for *Specjbb*. We suspect this is attributable to high memory-related CPU stalls for *Memcached* (due to its random memory access as opposed to *Specjbb*) which is better suited for throttling based techniques [67]. *Proactive Migration* combined with throttling achieves 20% more cost savings compared to *Migration* since proactive migration is able to significantly reduce the application state that needs to be migrated after the power outage. This implies that applications with lower frequency of page modifications may benefit more from the *Proactive Migration* technique.

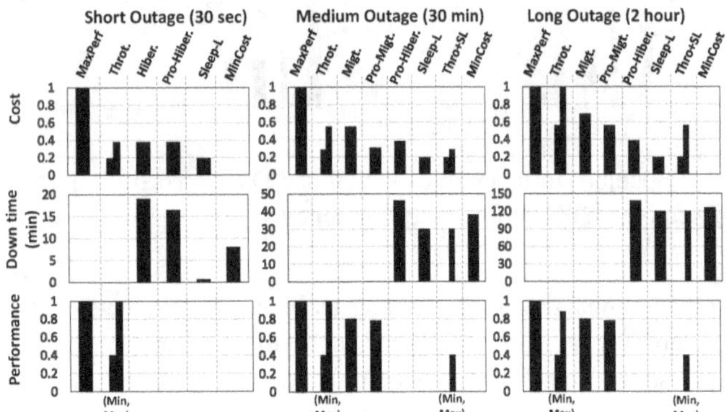


**Figure 7.** Tradeoffs for Memcached

*Web-search (Figure 8):* Web-search uses volatile memory as a cache for index data that are stored in persistent storage to improve query latency. Since the index data is read-only in memory, one might think its behavior will be similar to that of *Memcached* where we may afford to lose memory state (and re-load after restoring power) as opposed to persisting state to disk using hibernation. Instead, we find that losing memory state for *Web-search* can be extremely harmful to its performance and availability, especially for short outages as indicated using *MinCost* in Figure 8. For instance, *MinCost* results in a total application down time of 600 seconds as opposed to *Hibernation* which results only in 400 seconds down time for a 30-second outage. The 600 seconds down time for *MinCost* for this workload can be attributed to multiple factors including (i) server restart time ~2 mins, (ii) index data pre-population ~3.5 minutes and (iii) application warm-up duration ~4-5 minutes. Though the web-search workload is available after 5.5 minutes once power is restored, the queries suffer poor performance (almost 30-50% reduction in throughput) during the first 4-5 minutes (warmup duration) which we report as additional down time. Similar to other workloads, sleep when combined with throttling is an effective technique to achieve a good cost-performability tradeoff.

*SpecCPU (Figure 9):* These scientific applications may run for several hours before computing the end result and any loss of power during the execution may result in re-computation. We consider the amount of time required for re-computation after power is restored as part of down time and report performance only during the power outage duration. Depending on when the outage occurs during the application execution, the impact on down time can span a large

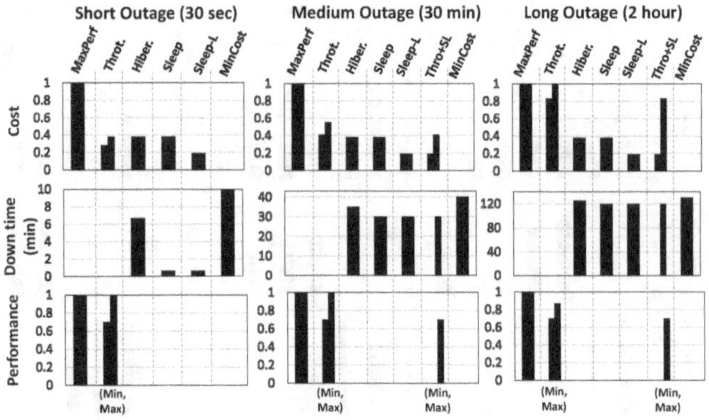


**Figure 8.** Tradeoffs for Web-search

range for *MinCost* as shown in Figure 9. We find the tradeoffs between other techniques very similar to that of Specjbb application.

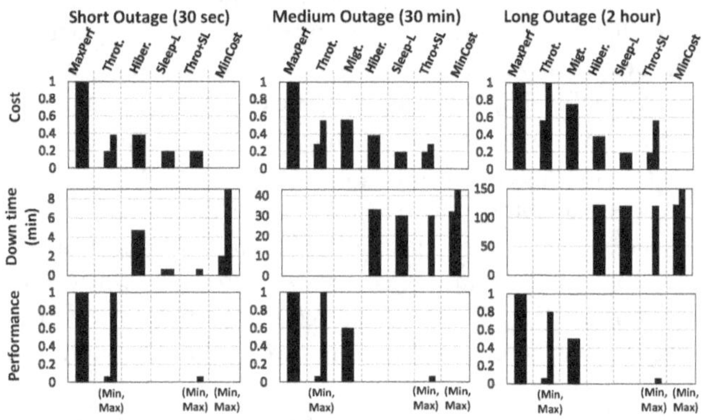


**Figure 9.** Tradeoffs for SpecCPU (mcf*8)

**Summary of Insights:** (i) Sleep is a low cost technique for achieving lower application down time for short to medium outages. (ii) Throttling can cover a large spectrum of cost-performability for short to medium outages, though it becomes infeasible at lower cost budgets. (iii) Migration/consolidation is preferred for longer outages due to better performability compared to throttling (owing to lack of energy proportionality in today's servers). (iv) Hybrid techniques allows us to traverse the entire cost-performability spectrum even for long outages. (v) For very long outages (> 4 hours), it is preferred to transfer load (request redirection) to geo-replicated datacenters if no DG is used. (vi) Application state size crucially impacts the performability-cost tradeoffs associated with techniques such as *Hibernation* and *Migration*.

## 7. Discussion and Future Enhancements

**TCO Considerations:** In addition to the power infrastructure related costs, an organization may need to base its decisions on a more holistic picture, including any revenue loss as a result of unavailability. Though such matters are very organization-centric, we illustrate how such an analysis could be done for an organization such as Google, where a large majority of its revenue comes from its datacenter operations. It has been reported that the power capacity across Google Datacenters was around 260 MW [31] in 2011, and Google's revenue in 2011 was about $38 billion [25]. Conservatively, assuming all of its revenue as coming from datacenter operations, we can calculate its revenue/kilowatt/minute as $0.28/KW/min. In addition to this revenue loss during an outage, the corresponding servers are also idle, and hence its capital expenditures (assumed cost of $2000 that is depreciated over a 4 year lifetime) should also be counted as a loss during the outage. This gives a number of $0.003/KW/min. Adding the revenue and capital losses, we can then capture the loss as a function of the minutes of unavailability as is shown in Figure 10. In the same Figure, we also plot the cost savings by not provisioning Diesel Generators (amortized over a lifetime of 12 years) as a horizontal line. All values to the left of the cross-over point (which turns out to be around 5 hours per year in this case) indicate profitable operations despite the corresponding revenue loss. An organization can use this to figure out whether to not provision DGs, or whether to provision additional UPS capacities while not provisioning DGs, or whether to provision full backup capacity. Such decisions would also depend on the organization's ability to seamlessly migrate operations to a different geo-separated datacenter (as discussed next). As mentioned, this is only to illustrate how different organizations may be able to make decisions based on the trade-offs associated with backup under-provisioning.

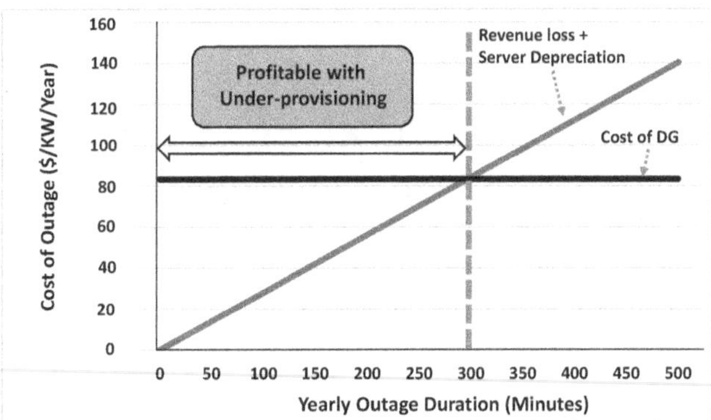


**Figure 10.** Revenue loss and server depreciation vs. savings from backup under-provisioning for Google 2011 data.

**Suitability for Different Datacenters and Organizations:** The results of such cost-performability analysis of backup infrastructure are relevant to a spectrum of datacenter sizes and types, since backup costs can be considerable across the spectrum. Further, many organizations today are inherently building multiple geo-distributed datacenters to handle different failures (not just power outages, but network failures, natural disasters, etc.). When geo-distribution/replication is inherent, our work suggests we could leverage these existing multi-datacenter operation capabilities to under-provision or even remove backup capacities in one or all these sites rather than build a highly outage-resilient single datacenter. At the other extreme, one could argue the need for any backup at all (whether DGs or UPS) with Geo-replication. In such cases, power outages can cause load increase at failed-over site, unless adequate spare capacity is set aside. Our solution of having some backup (UPS) capacity, can instead handle a bulk of these outages without requiring a fail-over, since a majority are of short duration. However, not all organizations may have geo-replicated datacenters. Such organizations could leverage cloud services from an external provider upon an outage (and when local backup runs out of energy capacity), to achieve the same functionality. Investigating the mechanisms, performance and costs for this, together with achieving this fail-over within the limited backup capacity, is part of future work.

**Challenges:** We pose two main challenges in translating the insights gained from our evaluation to an online solution and discuss possible directions.

*How do we deal with unknown outage duration?* We observed that the preferred system technique for an application with an under-provisioned backup depends on the duration of the outage. When a utility supply fails, it may not be possible (except for planned outages) to know the duration of the outage a priori. One option is for datacenters to use the historic utility outage data from their utility to construct an online predictor (e.g., an online Markov chain based transition matrix of different duration), and use the evolving outage to make dynamic decisions. For instance, with a outage distribution as in Figure 1, we may choose to start with the *throttling* at full performance mode (assuming outage will be short) and gradually transition to lower power modes and then finally (when outage exceeds 5 mins) use the *sleep* or *hibernate* techniques which are known to considerably reduce backup energy requirement.

*How do we provision for heterogeneous applications?* We found that application characteristics - state size, time for persisting state and restoring execution including subsequent warm-up, performance impact due to throttling, etc. - impact the performability, and hence the choice of the mechanisms and configurations when under-provisioning the backup. Given the diversity of such applications hosted in datacenters, understanding these characteristics, provisioning the infrastructure appropriately (which is done when datacenters are built), and adapting the techniques for these applications can pose interesting challenges. Multiple datacenters or sections in a datacenter could have different backup configurations, in the spectrum of cost-performability choices we outlined. Capacity planning could depend on historic data about multiple application requirements and cost preferences. With heterogeneity in the backup capacity, assigning and migrating workloads to the right infrastructure will help handle multiple types of outages.

**Promising Enhancements:** We discuss three technology advancements that can enhance the cost-performability tradeoffs for handling power outages.

*NVDIMM:* Recently, NVDIMMs [48] have been proposed as an alternative approach to persisting application state upon a power outage without the need for UPS. These NVDIMMs have a super-capacitor backed up DRAM+NAND Flash in the DIMM socket and a FPGA controller that transfers data from DRAM to Flash after a power outage without the need for any external backup power source. Though the NVDIMM does not offer any service during a power outage, it can be combined with other backup infrastructure options (similar to the options presented in Table 3). One crucial aspect of NVDIMMs is that the energy storage is localized to the volatile memory (and not the entire server) and it allows procrastinating the save/sustain operations – unlike today's UPS-based approach where the entire server load (even when throttled) is transferred to the UPS immediately after the power failure. This allows significant scope for underprovisioning the backup infrastructure since the load can be gradually shifted to the backup infrastructure (UPS unit) from these already persisted NVDIMM servers.

*RDMA over Sleep:* As high speed networks (dark fiber, infiniband, etc) become increasingly commonplace both within and across datacenters, RDMA techniques become more and more appealing for faster remote memory access. This will have a crucial bearing on how application state is transferred across machines (both within and across datacenters) during a power outage. For instance, the low cost *sleep* technique used in this paper does not offer any performance. But it can be combined with RDMA capability to access the memory state (on demand) from a remote server while keeping the server processors shutdown with only the memory controller active, similar to the recently proposed *barely-alive* memory servers [6]. NVDIMM can be combined with RDMA to effectively handle very long power outages.

*Newer Battery technologies:* Li-ion battery is gaining popularity due to its longer lifetime and higher power density. It offers different peak-power vs energy tradeoffs [63], compared to lead-acid (energy is more expensive for Li-ion than power). This may impact the cost-performability tradeoffs offered by the system techniques. For instance, the higher energy cost may prefer more energy saving techniques such as *proactive hibernation* and *proactive migration* compared to peak reduction techniques such as *Throttling*.

Evaluating these ideas opens interesting avenues for future work, and the insights from this paper would help drive such efforts.

## 8. Concluding Remarks

Towards realizing a low cost backup infrastructure, we have identified different underprovisioning configurations by varying the power and energy capacity of the Diesel Generator (DG) and UPSes, together with system techniques that offer an entire spectrum of cost, performance and availability operating points. We observed several interesting insights based on our evaluation using diverse datacenter applications, subjected to a variety of power outage duration. We found that the UPS plays a crucial role in ensuring high performance and availability for short (few seconds) to medium outages (tens of minutes), irrespective of the presence of DG. We also found that UPS provisioned with higher energy capacity (runtime) can realize significant cost savings by eliminating DG, while offering the same level of performance for outage duration up to 40 minutes. Further, we have shown that applications willing to tolerate performance impact during power outages can combine power reducing techniques such as workload throttling with state-preserving techniques like sleep or hibernation to sustain outages as long as 2 hours at a cost much lower than that of today's approach. We believe the insights gained from this paper can greatly influence the design of future under-provisioned backup infrastructure and development of techniques that allow applications to seamlessly operate during the power outages.

## Acknowledgments

We would like to thank our shepherd, Dr. Luiz Barroso, for his generous help and valuable inputs. We also thank the anonymous reviewers for their insightful comments and suggestions. This work has been supported in part by NSF grants 1302225, 1302557, 1205618, and 1213052.

## References

[1] Y. Agarwal, S. Hodges, R. Chandra, J. Scott, P. Bahl, and R. Gupta. Somniloquy: augmenting network interfaces to reduce pc energy usage. In *Proceedings of the 6th USENIX symposium on Networked systems design and implementation (NSDI)*, 2009.

[2] AGIGARAM: DDR3 Non-Volatile DIMM. `http://www.agigatech.com/pdf/pdf_ProductBrief_DDR3_12-0820.pdf`.

[3] M. K. Aguilera. Tutorial on geo-replication in data center applications. In *Proceedings of the ACM SIGMETRICS/international conference on Measurement and modeling of computer systems (SIGMETRICS)*, 2013.

[4] B. Aksanli, J. Venkatesh, L. Zhang, and T. Rosing. Utilizing green energy prediction to schedule mixed batch and service jobs in data centers. In *Proceedings of the 4th Workshop on Power-Aware Computing and Systems (HotPower)*, 2011.

[5] H. Amur, R. Nathuji, M. Ghosh, K. Schwan, and H.-H. S. Lee. Idlepower: Application-Aware Management of Processor Idle States. In *Proceedings of the Workshop on Managed Many-Core Systems (MMCS, in conjunction with HPDC)*, 2008.

[6] V. Anagnostopoulou, S. Biswas, H. Saadeldeen, A. Savage, R. Bianchini, T. Yang, D. Franklin, and F. T. Chong. Barely alive memory servers: Keeping data active in a low-power

state. *Journal on Emerging Technologies in Computing Systems*, 8(4), 2012.

[7] APC InfraStruxure Total Cost of Ownership, 2013. `http://www.apc.com/tools/isx/tco/index.cfm`.

[8] APC White paper: Comparing UPS System Design Configurations, 2008.

[9] A. Bar-Noy, M. P. Johnson, and O. Liu. Peak Shaving Through Resource Buffering. In *Workshop On Approximation and Online Algorithms (WAOA)*, 2008.

[10] L. A. Barroso and U. Holzle. The Case for Energy-Proportional Computing. *Computer*, 40(12), 2007.

[11] L. A. Barroso and U. Holzle. *The Datacenter as a Computer: An Introduction to the Design of Warehouse-Scale Machines*. Morgan and Claypool Publishers, 2009.

[12] Benefits OF Using Mobile Transformers and Mobile Substations for Rapidly Restoring Electrical Service, 2006. `http://energy.gov/sites/prod/files/oeprod/DocumentsandMedia/MTS_Report_to_Congress_FINAL_73106.pdf`.

[13] O. Bilgir, M. Martonosi, and Q. Wu. Exploring the Potential of CMP Core Count Management on Data Center Energy Savings. In *Workshop on Energy Efficient Design*, 2011.

[14] P. Bohrer, D. Cohn, E. Elnozahy, T. Keller, M. Kistler, C. Lefurgy, R. Rajamony, F. Rawson, and E. V. Hensbergen. Energy Conservation for Servers. In *Workshop on Power Management for Real-Time and Embedded Systems*, 2001.

[15] T. C. Bressoud and F. B. Schneider. Hypervisor-based fault tolerance. In *Proceedings of the fifteenth ACM symposium on Operating systems principles (SOSP)*, 1995.

[16] J. Chase, D. Anderson, P. Thakur, and A. Vahdat. Managing Energy and Server Resources in Hosting Centers. In *Proceedings of SOSP*, 2001.

[17] G. Chen, W. He, J. Liu, S. Nath, L. Rigas, L. Xiao, and F. Zhao. Energy-aware Server Provisioning and Load Dispatching for Connection-intensive Internet Services. In *Proceedings of NSDI*, 2008.

[18] C. Clark, K. Fraser, S. Hand, J. Hansen, E. Jul, C. Limpach, I. Pratt, and A. Warfield. Live Migration of Virtual Machines. In *Proceedings of the Symposium on Networked Systems Design and Implementation (NSDI)*, 2005.

[19] B. Cully, G. Lefebvre, D. Meyer, M. Feeley, N. Hutchinson, and A. Warfield. Remus: high availability via asynchronous virtual machine replication. In *Proceedings of the 5th USENIX Symposium on Networked Systems Design and Implementation (NSDI)*, 2008.

[20] Q. Deng, D. Meisner, A. Bhattacharjee, T. F. Wenisch, and R. Bianchini. Coscale: Coordinating cpu and memory system dvfs in server systems. In *Proceedings of the IEEE/ACM International Symposium on Microarchitecture*, 2012.

[21] Facebook Rack-level UPS for improved efficiency. Facebook Rack-level UPS for Improved Efficiency. `http://www.datacenterknowledge.com/archives/2011/04/07/`.

[22] X. Fan, W.-D. Weber, and L. A. Barroso. Power provisioning for a warehouse-sized computer. In *Proceedings of the International Symposium on Computer Architecture (ISCA)*, 2007.

[23] X. Fu, X. Wang, and C. Lefurgy. How Much Power Oversubscription Is Safe and Allowed in Data Centers. In *Proceedings of the ACM International Conference on Autonomic Computing (ICAC)*, 2011.

[24] A. Gandhi, M. Harchol-Balter, R. Das, and C. Lefurgy. Optimal Power Allocation in Server Farms. In *Proceedings of SIGMETRICS*, 2009.

[25] Google Revenue in 2011. `http://investor.google.com/earnings/2011/index.html`.

[26] S. Govindan, J. Choi, B. Urgaonkar, A. Sivasubramaniam, and A.Baldini. Statistical Profiling-based Techniques for Effective Power Provisioning in Data Centers. In *Proceedings of the ACM European Conference on Computer Systems (EuroSys)*, 2009.

[27] S. Govindan, A. Sivasubramaniam, and B. Urgaonkar. Benefits and Limitations of Tapping into Stored Energy For Datacenters. In *Proceedings of the International Symposium of Computer Architecture (ISCA)*, 2011.

[28] S. Govindan, D. Wang, L. Y. Chen, A. Sivasubramaniam, and B.Urgaonkar. Towards Realizing a Low Cost and Highly Available Datacenter Power Infrastructure. In *Workshop on HotPower*, 2011.

[29] S. Govindan, D. Wang, A. Sivasubramaniam, and B. Urgaonkar. Leveraging stored energy for handling power emergencies in aggressively provisioned datacenters. In *Proceedings of the international conference on Architectural Support for Programming Languages and Operating Systems*, 2012.

[30] J. Hamilton. Internet-scale Service Infrastructure Efficiency, ISCA Keynote, 2009.

[31] JAMES GLANZ. Google Details, and Defends, Its Use of Electricity. `http://www.nytimes.com/2011/09/09/technology/google-details-and-defends-its-use-of-electricity.html?_r=2&`.

[32] A. Kansal, B. Urgaonkar, and S. Govindan. Using dark fiber to displace diesel generators. In *Proceedings of the USENIX conference on Hot Topics in Operating Systems*, HotOS, 2013.

[33] S. T. King, G. W. Dunlap, and P. M. Chen. Debugging operating systems with time-traveling virtual machines. In *Proceedings of the annual conference on USENIX Annual Technical Conference*, 2005.

[34] V. Kontorinis, L. E. Zhang, B. Aksanli, J. Sampson, H. Homayoun, E. P. tis, D. M. Tullsen, and T. S. Rosing. Managing Distributed UPS Energy for Effective Power Capping in Data Centers. In *Proceedings of the International Symposium on Computer Architecture (ISCA)*, 2012.

[35] K. Le, R. Bianchini, M. Martonosi, and T. Nguyen. Cost- and Energy-Aware Load Distribution Across Data Centers. In *Workshop on Power-Aware Computing and Systems (HotPower)*, 2009.

[36] C. Lefurgy, X. Wang, and M. Ware. Server-Level Power Control. In *Proceedings of the International Conference on Autonomic Computing (ICAC)*, 2007.

[37] J. Leverich, M. Monchiero, V. Talwar, P. Ranganathan, and C. Kozyrakis. Power management of datacenter workloads

using per-core power gating. *IEEE Comput. Archit. Lett.*, 8 (2), 2009.

[38] D. Linden and T. B. Reddy. *Handbook of Batteries*. McGraw Hill Handbooks, 2002.

[39] M. R. Marty and M. D. Hill. Virtual Hierarchies to Support Server Consolidation. In *Proceedings of ISCA*, 2007.

[40] M. Marwah, P. Maciel, A. Shah, R. Sharma, T. Christian, V. Almeida, C. Araújo, E. Souza, G. Callou, B. Silva, S. Galdino, and J. Pires. Quantifying the Sustainability Impact of Data Center Availability. *SIGMETRICS Performance Evaluation Review*, 37(4), 2010.

[41] D. Meisner and T. F. Wenisch. Dreamweaver: architectural support for deep sleep. In *Proceedings of the seventeenth international conference on Architectural Support for Programming Languages and Operating Systems*, 2012.

[42] D. Meisner, B. T. Gold, and T. F. Wenisch. PowerNap: Eliminating Server Idle Power. In *Proceedings of ASPLOS*, 2009.

[43] D. Meisner, C. M. Sadler, L. A. Barroso, W. Weber, and T. F. Wenisch. Power Management of Online Data-intensive Services. In *Proceedings of the International Symposium on Computer Architecture (ISCA)*, 2011.

[44] MEMCACHED: Memory-object Caching System. `http://www.memcached.org`.

[45] Michael A. Bell. `http://www.it.northwestern.edu/bin/docs/DesignBestPractices_127434.pdf`.

[46] Microsoft Reveals its Specialty Servers, Racks, Apr. 2011. `http://www.datacenterknowledge.com/archives/2011/04/25/microsoft-reveals-its-specialty-servers-racks/`.

[47] J. Moore, J. Chase, P. Ranganathan, and R. Sharma. Making Scheduling Cool: Temperature-Aware Workload Placement in Data Centers. In *Proceedings of USENIX*, 2005.

[48] D. Narayanan and O. Hodson. Whole-system persistence. In *Proceedings of International Conference on Architectural Support for Programming Languages and Operating Systems (ASPLOS 2012)*, 2012.

[49] R. Nathuji and K. Schwan. VirtualPower: Coordinated Power Management in Virtualized Enterprise Systems. In *Proceedings of the Symposium on Operating Systems Principles (SOSP)*, 2007.

[50] National Survey of Datacenter Outages, 2010. `http://www.inquirere.com/wp-content/uploads/2010/11/National-Survey-on-Data-Center-Outages.pdf`.

[51] S. Osman, D. Subhraveti, G. Su, and J. Nieh. The design and implementation of zap: a system for migrating computing environments. *SIGOPS Oper. Syst. Rev.*, 36(SI), 2002.

[52] E. Pinheiro, R. Bianchini, E.Carrera, and T. Heath. Load Balancing and Unbalancing for Power and Performance in Cluster-Based Systems. In *Workshop on COLP*, 2001.

[53] R. Raghavendra, P. Ranganathan, V. Talwar, Z. Wang, and X. Zhu. No Power Struggles: Coordinated Multi-level Power Management for the Data Center. In *Proceedings of ASPLOS*, 2008.

[54] P. Ranganathan, P. Leech, D. Irwin, and J. Chase. Ensemble-level Power Management for Dense Blade Servers. In *Proceedings of the International Symposium on Computer Architecture (ISCA)*, 2006.

[55] N. Sharma, S. Barker, D. Irwin, and P. Shenoy. Blink: Managing Server Clusters on Intermittent Power. In *Proceedings of the International Conference on Architectural Support for Programming Languages and Operating Systems (ASPLOS)*, 2011.

[56] R. Singh, D. Irwin, P. Shenoy, and K. K. Ramakrishnan. Yank: Enabling green data centers to pull the plug. In *Proceedings of 10th USENIX Symposium on Networked Systems Design and Implementation (NSDI)*, 2013.

[57] SPEC CPU2006. http://www.spec.org/cpu2006/.

[58] SPEC JBB2005: Java Business Benchmark. `http://www.spec.org/jbb2005/`.

[59] J. Stoess, C. Lang, and F. Bellosa. Energy Management for Hypervisor-Based Virtual Machines. In *Usenix Technical Conference*, 2007.

[60] The Cost of Power Disturbances to U.S. Businesses, 2001. `http://www.onpower.com/pdf/EPRICostOfPowerProblems.pdf`.

[61] W. P. Turner, J. H. Seader, V. Renaud, and K. G. Brill. Tier classifications define site infrastructure performance. *Uptime Institute White Paper*, 2008.

[62] A. Verma, G. Dasgupta, T. Kumar, N. Pradipta, and R. Kothari. Server Workload Analysis for Power Minimization Using Consolidation. In *Proceedings of USENIX*, 2009.

[63] D. Wang, C. Ren, A. Sivasubramaniam, B. Urgaonkar, and H. Fathy. Energy storage in datacenters: what, where, and how much? In *Proceedings of the Conference on Measurement and Modeling of Computer Systems (SIGMETRICS)*, 2012.

[64] D. Wang, S. Govindan, A. Sivasubramaniam, A. Kansal, J. Liu, and B. Khessib. Underprovisioning backup power infrastructure for datacenters. Technical Report CSE-13-012, The Pennsylvania State University, 2013.

[65] D. Wang, C. Ren, and A. Sivasubramaniam. Virtualizing Power Distribution in Datacenters. In *Proceedings of the International Symposium on Computer Architecture (ISCA)*, 2013.

[66] X. Wang and M. Chen. Cluster-level Feedback Power Control for Performance Optimization. In *Proceedings of HPCA*, 2008.

[67] A. Weisel and F. Bellosa. Process Cruise Control-Event-Driven Clock Scaling for Dynamic Power Management. In *Proceedings of Compilers, Architecture and Synthesis for Embedded Systems (CASES)*, 2002.

[68] Windows Hybrid Low-power Sleep, 2009. `http://windows.microsoft.com/en-us/windows7/sleep-and-hibernation-frequently-asked-questions`.

[69] H. Zeng, C. S. Ellis, A. R. Lebeck, and A. Vahdat. Currentcy: A Unifying Abstraction for Expressing Energy Management Policies. In *Proceedings of the Usenix Annual Technical Conference (USENIX)*, 2003.

# Comprehending Performance from Real-World Execution Traces: A Device-Driver Case

Xiao Yu
North Carolina State University
xyu10@ncsu.edu

Shi Han Dongmei Zhang
Microsoft Research
{shihan, dongmeiz}@microsoft.com

Tao Xie
University of Illinois at Urbana-Champaign
taoxie@illinois.edu

## Abstract

Real-world execution traces record performance problems that are likely perceived at deployment sites. However, those problems can be rooted subtly and deeply into system layers or other components far from the place where delays are initially observed. To tackle challenges of identifying deeply rooted problems, we propose a new trace-based approach consisting of two steps: impact analysis and causality analysis. The impact analysis measures performance impacts on a component basis, and the causality analysis discovers patterns of runtime behaviors that are likely to cause the measured impacts. The discovered patterns can help performance analysts quickly identify root causes of perceived performance problems. We instantiate our approach to study the performance of device drivers on over 19,500 real-world execution traces. The impact analysis shows that device drivers constitute a non-trivial part ($\approx$ 38%) in the overall system performance, and a big part ($\approx$ 26%) is due to interactions between drivers. The causality analysis effectively discovers highly suspicious and high-impact behavioral patterns in device drivers, examined and confirmed by our automated evaluation, developers, and performance analysts.

***Categories and Subject Descriptors*** D.4.8 [*Operating Systems*]: Performance; D.2.5 [*Software Engineering*]: Testing and Debugging—Diagnostics, Tracing; D.2.8 [*Software Engineering*]: Metrics—Performance measures

***Keywords*** Device Drivers, Execution Traces, Performance Analysis, Bottlenecks, Contrast Data Mining


*ASPLOS '14*, March 1–4, 2014, Salt Lake City, Utah, USA.

http://dx.doi.org/10.1145/2541940.2541968

## 1. Introduction

Real-world execution traces collected by mature infrastructures, such as the Event Tracing for Windows (ETW) [1] and DTrace [2] for Unix-like systems, offer tracing events with timestampes and callstacks for both user-mode applications and system layers. Such traces can record performance problems that are likely perceived at deployment sites and usually triggered by complex runtime environments and real-world usage scenarios. By analyzing large-scale and diverse execution traces collected from deployment-site computers, performance analysts and developers can gain useful knowledge for system design and optimization.

However, finding performance problems from real-world traces is challenging. The problems can be rooted subtly and deeply into system layers or other components far from the place where delays are initially observed. Performance analysts have to spend great efforts to confirm the existence of subtle problems, and to figure out how they were caused and spread. Given many real-world execution traces where bad performance may be amortized over various underlying problems, such performance-analysis activities become harder or even infeasible.

Based on our observation in real-world traces, we identify and generalize the concept of *cost propagation* in systems consisting of interacting components as an important underlying mechanism that introduces the subtleness of performance problems. In particular, the term "cost propagation" refers to a phenomenon that the cost of executing a component is propagated and accumulated to the execution of another component through cross-component interactions.

There are different kinds of interactions causing cost propagation. Call dependency is a well-known kind, which accumulates costs from callees to callers. Lock contention is a subtle kind, which allows a delay to be propagated to all other components waiting for the same lock. In complex software ecosystems (e.g., Windows systems), different kinds of interactions can be combined together to create performance bottlenecks involving multiple victims. For example, there can be a very long propagation path or multiple propagation paths consisting of both call dependencies and contentions on different locks.

The cost propagation brings challenges to performance analysis of complex systems. Existing techniques, such as call-graph profiling [14] and lock-contention analysis [36], face two major limitations. First, these techniques cover a single aspect of underlying interactions only, which is either call dependency or lock contention. Their combinatorial effects are not generally considered or addressed. Second, these techniques usually work on a single program with a limited investigation scope, but cannot explain performance problems with complex cause-and-effect chains that are transparent to the program, but are grounded in the underlying system. To better reveal and explain these problems, a large number of system-level execution traces can be leveraged from real-world deployment sites. Handling these traces requires effective abstractions that can capture essential information, and classify similar and distinct runtime behaviors towards providing concise and actionable results.

To address these challenges, we propose a new approach consisting of two steps: impact analysis and causality analysis. The impact analysis extracts *Wait Graphs* [16] (Section 3.1) from execution traces, and measures performance impacts with respect to cost propagation on Wait Graphs. Performance analysts can narrow down the investigation scope by choosing highly suspicious components to measure, and decide whether the causality analysis is needed based on the significance of performance impacts.

The causality analysis discovers behavioral patterns of highly suspicious and high-impact components that are likely to cause perceived performance problems. To capture the essence of problematic behaviors with respect to cost propagation, we design the *Signature Set Tuple* (Section 4.1) as a pattern representation that presents abstracted and generalized behaviors to performance analysts. A Signature Set Tuple generalizes interacting behaviors among components in the form of signature sets (a set of function signatures extracted from callstacks). Such abstraction and generalization facilitate the comprehension of performance problems by narrowing down the investigation scope as well as preserving highly suspicious behaviors that may appear similarly in different traces.

The causality analysis is grounded in the technique of contrast data mining [7] to address challenges in discovering problematic behaviors. Such challenges are two-fold: bad performance can be amortized over multiple problematic behaviors, and there is no easy oracle for identifying problematic behaviors, especially for the expensive but necessary ones. Our technique exploits the fact that a large number of execution traces may contain various runtime behaviors with both good and bad performance. In particular, our technique defines two contrast classes over execution traces as a fast class and a slow class based on thresholds of execution time (usually specified by developers as the expectations on performance). The fast class contains expected runtime behaviors, whereas the slow class contains problems to be identified. Our technique applies two criteria to identify contrast patterns: (1) a pattern appears in the slow class but not in the fast class; (2) a pattern appears in both classes, but the pattern in the slow class shows a significant amount of execution time compared with the pattern in the fast class. The identified contrast patterns can reflect underlying key factors that discriminate the performance contrasts.

In this paper, we choose device drivers in Windows operating systems as a representative to demonstrate our approach and study performance problems. Device drivers constitute a majority part (about 70%) in the Linux code base [26], as well as in the Windows kernel [21]. Performance analysts in Microsoft product teams have noticed that a non-trivial number of response delays in user-mode applications were likely caused by device drivers. Therefore, it is interesting, as well as necessary, to study how device drivers affect overall system performance.

We notice that two key characteristics in device drivers can cause cost propagation. First, locks are widely used in device drivers to synchronize shared resources over the system kernel. Second, device drivers are organized in a hierarchical architecture (a.k.a driver stack) in which drivers can interact with each other via system services, e.g., the `IoCallDriver` routine in Windows. The form of hierarchical dependencies connecting multiple contention points of different locks can propagate a delay to all affected drivers and corresponding user-mode applications to create remarkable performance problems.

**Main Contributions.** In this paper, we make main contributions from two aspects. On performance analysis, we propose a practical two-step approach with effective data and pattern abstractions to measure performance impacts manifested through cost propagation, and discover behavioral patterns closely related to performance problems via contrast data mining. The effectiveness of the pattern discovery is examined and confirmed by our automated evaluation, driver developers, and performance analysts.

By applying the impact analysis on 19,500 real-world execution traces (339 hours of duration in total, collected from Windows machines), we show the empirical evidence of performance impacts posed by device drivers. Our findings show that device drivers constitute 36.4% on waiting time and 1.6% on running time in overall Windows performance, within which cost propagation causes 26.0% on waiting time. Moreover, by applying the causality analysis on some typical application scenarios, we show concrete examples of performance problems related to device drivers. These findings suggest that identifying and minimizing potential cost propagation in device drivers should be an important direction for designing a high-performance system, especially for the cases involving driver/driver interactions, which complement the discussion by Kadav *et al.* [21].

## 2. Background and Motivating Examples

In this section, we first briefly introduce the basic notions about execution traces, and then use a real-world performance problem to show cost propagation in device drivers, and how our approach helps analysts find such problem.

### 2.1 Execution Traces

Execution traces are the data source of our trace-based performance analysis. To simplify the data representation while preserving essential information, we use an abstracted schema called *trace stream*. The schema is compatible with existing popular tracing infrastructures, e.g., ETW [1] and DTrace [2].

**Trace Stream.** A trace stream $TS$ is a sequence of tracing events $e_0e_1e_2 \dots e_{L-1}$. Each event $e$ falls into one of the following four types: (1) a *running* event represents CPU usage sampled in a constant interval, e.g., 1 millisecond in ETW and DTrace; (2) a *wait* event occurs when a thread enters the waiting state due to blocking operations, e.g., a thread tries to acquire a lock being held by others; (3) an *unwait* event occurs when a running thread signals another thread in the waiting state to continue execution, e.g., a thread releases a lock or sends a message; (4) a *hardware service* event is recorded with a start timestamp and duration in the period of a hardware operation.

Each event $e$ is also related to a set of fields, which are callstack (denoted as $e.S$), timestamp ($e.T$), cost as time duration ($e.C$), the related thread ID ($e.TID$), and the ID of the other thread to be unwaited ($e.WTID$). These fields are sufficient for capturing and characterizing essential runtime behaviors under performance analysis from a cost-propagation perspective.

**Scenario.** Performance analysts usually start performance analysis with a scenario, e.g., *BrowserTabCreate* for creating a browser tab, to explore what run slow in that scenario. During a period of time, a system could have multiple ongoing scenarios simultaneously, since a user can browse websites while the system is performing other operations. Performance analysts have a set of predefined scenarios that are used to capture scenario-related execution traces.

**Scenario Instance.** A trace stream can contain events for multiple scenarios that were being performed by the system during the tracing period. Among these events, an event sequence representing the execution of a single scenario is called a *scenario instance*. A scenario instance typically starts and ends with the events from a single initiating thread, which initiates the execution of a particular scenario. For example, a browser UI thread that reacts to a user's request of creating a new browser tab is an initiating thread for *BrowserTabCreate*. Formally, a scenario instance *I* of a scenario *S* is a tuple $\langle TS, S, TID, t_0, t_1 \rangle$, indicating that the execution of the scenario *S* starting from a thread (with the identifier *TID*) within the time period between $t_0$ and $t_1$ is recorded in a trace stream *TS*.

Some events may overlap across multiple instances in the same trace stream. Such overlap indicates that other threads are suspended by the thread that triggers those overlapped events, so it is a typical manifestation of cost propagation. Such observation is the key to our approach to be effective in analyzing performance problems related to cost propagation.

### 2.2 A Real-World Case

We use a real-world case to show how cost propagation in device drivers is involved in producing a performance problem. Due to confidentiality, we anonymize the names of device drivers and relevant resources in this example.

An execution instance of the scenario *BrowserTabCreate* cost over 800 milliseconds to complete. From the user's perspective, the web browser fully displayed a new tab in over 800 milliseconds after the user had clicked "create a new tab". Such delay is perceivable on the user interface.

This problem involves three device drivers having lock contentions and hierarchical dependencies. First, File Virtualization filter driver *fv.sys* uses locks to synchronize queries on the entries of an internal *File Table* that maps some "virtual" files to their physical locations on the file system. Second, File System driver *fs.sys* acquires locks on *Meta Data Units* (*MDUs*) that contain file metadata when there are requests on reading or writing a file. Third, Storage Encryption driver *se.sys* performs computation-intensive encryption and decryption when data are being read and written on storage media. The three device drivers form a hierarchy in which the top-most driver *fv.sys* invokes *fs.sys*, whereas *fs.sys* invokes *se.sys*. To ease the illustration, we omit those less relevant drivers that may exist in the hierarchy on a real machine.

Figure 1 is a thread-level snapshot restructured from the trace stream to show the period of delay. The figure presents each thread by its corresponding callstack that contains ongoing operations. There were six threads executing the three device drivers during this period. We denote these threads by the notation $T_{X,Y}$, which means the thread $Y$ of the process $X$. The dotted arrows in the figure represent the directions of cost propagation among threads.

**Lock Contentions on the File Table.** When the user clicked "create a new tab" on the browser, the browser UI thread $T_{B,UI}$ started to access some "virtual" files. So $T_{B,UI}$ executed *fv.sys* to query the *File Table*. However, two other worker threads $T_{B,W0}$ and $T_{B,W1}$ were performing file operations in the background, and happened to execute *fv.sys* at the same time. As a consequence, the three threads were contending a lock on some entries in the *File Table*, thereby forming a region of lock contentions in *fv.sys* (shown as the upper dashed box in Figure 1). Among these three threads, $T_{B,W1}$ first got the lock, so the other two threads had to wait.

**Hierarchical Dependency between fv.sys and fs.sys.** $T_{B,W1}$ proceeded to execute *fs.sys* by a function call initiated from *fv.sys*, thereby creating a hierarchical dependency between the two device drivers (shown as the arrow (4)

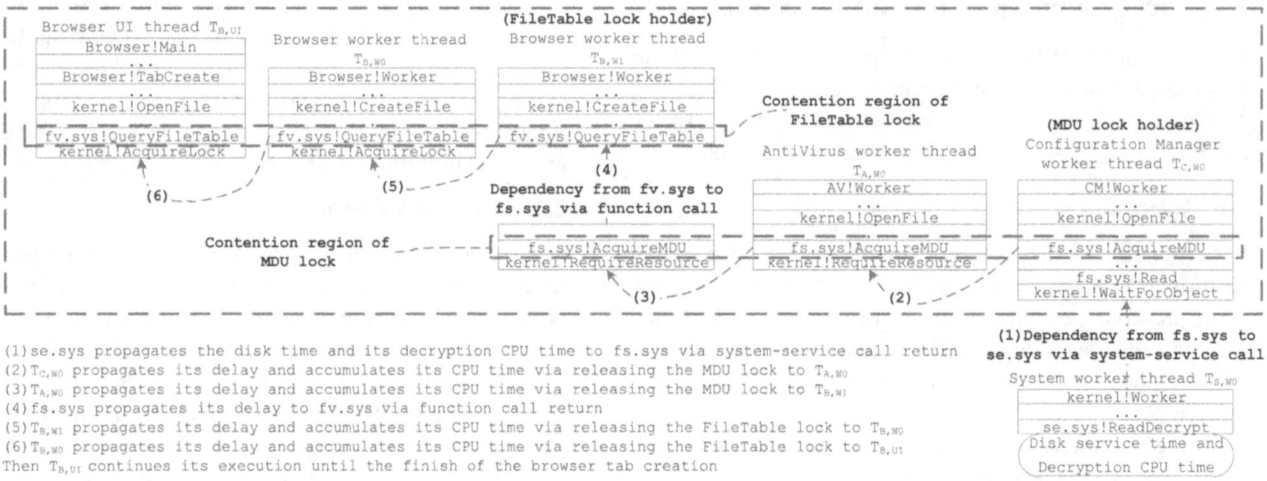


**Figure 1.** An illustration of cost propagation due to lock contentions and hierarchical dependencies among device drivers

in Figure 1). Thus, the continuation of executing *fv.sys* depended on the return of *fs.sys*.

**Lock Contentions on Meta Data Units (MDUs).** During the period that $T_{B,W1}$ was running, two threads $T_{A,W0}$ and $T_{C,W0}$ from two other applications (i.e., the AntiVirus and the Configuration Manager applications in Figure 1) were contending a lock on *MDU*s in *fs.sys*. Coincidentally, $T_{B,W1}$ joined to contend the same lock. Therefore, $T_{B,W1}$, $T_{A,W0}$, and $T_{C,W0}$ created another region of lock contentions in *fs.sys*, shown as the lower dashed box in Figure 1. $T_{C,W0}$ first got the lock, and proceeded.

**Hierarchical Dependency between fs.sys and se.sys.** $T_{C,W0}$ established a hierarchical dependency between *fs.sys* and *se.sys* by a system-service call that reads data from disk (shown as the arrow (1) in Figure 1). The system thread $T_{S,W0}$ was scheduled to serve the read request by fetching data from disk and executing *se.sys* to decrypt. To accomplish the task, $T_{S,W0}$ cost hundreds of milliseconds.

**Summary: Manifestation of Cost Propagation.** The three device drivers together created a bottleneck that consisted of two regions of lock contentions, and two hierarchical dependencies over the six threads (i.e., three browser threads, one AntiVirus thread, one Configuration-Manager thread, and one system thread). A delay occurring in $T_{S,W0}$ was propagated and accumulated through the path shown as the arrows from (1) to (6) in Figure 1 to the UI thread $T_{B,UI}$. Consequently, the user perceived an obvious delay when clicking a button on the browser to create a new tab. In addition, the other two applications in this case were also affected by such performance impact. Reducing the granularity of locks is a general principle to alleviate such problem.

## 2.3 How Our Approach Facilitates Performance Analysis

The preceding example shows the subtleness caused by cost propagation in real-world performance problems. In practice, a performance analyst has to start with the browser UI thread to examine many executed functions in many traces, since the costs may vary in different executions. Such work is usually tedious. Even if the analyst finds out that *fv.sys!QueryFileTable* could incur high execution cost in lock contentions among different browser threads under some circumstances, the analyst still needs to realize the relations across three drivers and many threads that constituted the whole performance. Realizing such relations is the key to future performance tuning.

By employing impact analysis, the analyst can first realize to which extent the performance of scenario *BrowserTabCreate* was affected by cost propagation. The analyst may conduct impact analysis on different scopes to realize performance impacts of different components. The results serve as the preliminary evidence pointing to some potentially hidden problems. Then the analyst can apply causality analysis on high-impact components, for instance, device drivers in this case. The causality analysis can suggest a list of contrast patterns sorted by their performance impacts. We pick the following one to explain in detail. The pattern is in the form of Signature Set Tuple, which is formally defined in Section 4.1.

$$wait\ signatures : \{fv.sys!QueryFileTable, fs.sys!AcquireMDU\}$$

$$unwait\ signatures : \{fv.sys!QueryFileTable, fs.sys!AcquireMDU\}$$

$$running\ signatures : \{se.sys!ReadDecrypt, DiskService\}$$

This pattern describes that the cost of the running signatures *se.sys!ReadDecrypt* and *Disk Service* can be propagated through the two unwait signatures *fv.sys!QueryFileTable* and *fs.sys!AcquireMDU* to the wait signatures, while functions represented by the wait signatures are invoked by the browser threads. The causality analysis can discover this pattern because in normal cases either such pattern does not appear, or it has much lower cost.

The discovered pattern can help an analyst from two aspects. First, it guides the analyst to realize the concrete performance incident by investigating a specific trace stream. The preceding example is actually restructured with the help of the discovered pattern. Second, the pattern as a generalized representation is a clue for similar cases. The analyst may prioritize the search of the three driver signatures in other cases to facilitate future analysis.

## 3. Impact Analysis

The goal of impact analysis is to scope and measure performance impacts for some chosen components, such as all device drivers. The impact analysis takes two inputs: (1) the instances of various scenarios over trace streams; (2) the component name(s) that are used to filter tracing events for the chosen components to be measured.

The impact analysis outputs three metric values: (1) the running percentage $IA_{run}$; (2) the wait percentage $IA_{wait}$; (3) $IA_{opt}$, the percentage of waiting time introduced by cost propagation.

The three metrics suggest three performance aspects of the chosen components. A large $IA_{wait}$ indicates that the execution of the components is frequently blocked by others, whereas a large $IA_{run}$ reflects a computation-intensive characteristic. $IA_{opt}$ suggests how much extra cost is introduced by waiting on others. It can also serve as an upper bound for the optimization potential.

### 3.1 Data Abstraction

The impact analysis measures the running time and the waiting time for the chosen components, respectively. To serve this purpose, we use the Wait Graph structure from StackMine [16] to model scenario instances. A Wait Graph encodes *wait* and *unwait* events into wait chains, with *running* events as well. So it enables an easy way to measure both running and waiting time for impact analysis; otherwise, we would need to simultaneously keep track of each *wait* event to its corresponding *unwait* event.

DEFINITION 1. *A Wait Graph is a graph* $WG = \langle V, E \rangle$. *V is a set of nodes* $V = \{e\}$, *where e is a tracing event. E is a set of directed edges* $E = \{e_i \rightarrow e_j\}$. *For each edge* $e_i \rightarrow e_j$, $e_i$ *must be a wait event, indicating that the thread triggering* $e_i$ *keeps suspended before* $e_j$ *occurs and completes, and* $e_j$ *is triggered by another thread during the wait interval of* $e_i$.

The Wait Graph of a scenario instance is basically constructed by (1) pairing each *wait* event with its corresponding *unwait* event to restore wait chains among threads, (2) edging events as graph nodes based on the restored wait chains, and (3) restoring the duration of *wait* events from the timestamps on paired *wait/unwait* events. StackMine [16] contains an algorithm description for constructing a Wait Graph. We construct Wait Graphs based on that algorithm for our impact analysis and causality analysis with characteristics of Windows systems.

### 3.2 Impact Measurement

**Basic Metrics.** For every scenario instance, the impact analysis constructs a corresponding Wait Graph. To evaluate the values for $IA_{run}$, $IA_{wait}$, and $IA_{opt}$, the impact analysis introduces the following metrics that are calculated from all constructed Wait Graphs.

**The total duration** $D_{scn}$ defines the aggregated execution time of all scenario instances in the input trace streams. Given the Wait Graph for each scenario instance, the impact analysis evaluates $D_{scn}$ by adding up the time periods of top-level tracing events in the Wait Graph instance by instance.

**The total wait duration** $D_{wait}$ defines the aggregated wait time cost by the chosen components in waiting for others. To determine which components should be counted, the impact analysis uses the names of the chosen components to filter the topmost signatures on the callstacks of tracing events. The impact analysis uses a breadth-first search on the Wait Graphs, and adds up the time periods of only top-level *wait* events of the chosen components to avoid counting child events that constitute the time cost already counted from their parent events.

**The total running duration** $D_{run}$ defines the aggregated running time cost by the chosen components. Similar to $D_{wait}$, the impact analysis evaluates $D_{run}$ by counting duration of the *running* events that contain signatures of the chosen components. Note that (1) some portions of periods in $D_{run}$ are overlapped with $D_{wait}$ because the *running* events are mostly the leaf nodes of some *wait* events; (2) $D_{run}$ is an approximate value since ETW samples *running* events every millisecond and thus those running costs are at the millisecond granularity.

**The total distinct-wait duration** $D_{waitdist}$ defines the aggregated duration of *distinct wait* events of the chosen components over all scenario instances. A *wait* event may be involved in multiple Wait Graphs for multiple scenario instances, indicating that (1) the enclosing instances are captured in a common or close period of time from the same deployment site, and (2) the event has performance impact on multiple instances. The impact analysis measures $D_{waitdist}$ by excluding the duration of duplicate events across different Wait Graphs from $D_{wait}$.

**Output-Metric Derivation.** The impact analysis derives the values of output metrics $IA_{run}$, $IA_{wait}$, and $IA_{opt}$ from the preceding metrics. In particular, $IA_{run} = D_{run}/D_{scn}$ represents the performance impact of running time, and $IA_{wait} = D_{wait}/D_{scn}$ represents the performance impact of wait time.

For deriving the severity of cost propagation across different scenario instances, there is $IA_{opt} = (D_{wait} - D_{waitdist})/D_{scn}$. $IA_{opt}$ comes from the observation that any performance impact involving the chosen components

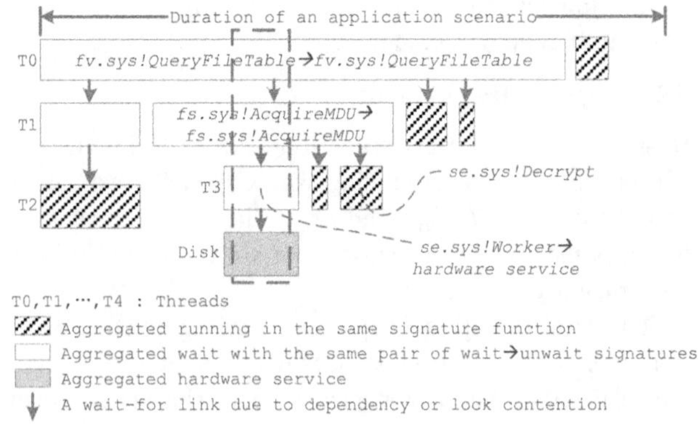


**Figure 2.** An illustration of an Aggregated Wait Graph for device drivers

can affect multiple different scenario instances. Namely, $D_{wait}/D_{waitdist} > 1$, which describes that the $D_{waitdist}$ of duration actually causes $D_{wait}$ long wait among multiple scenario instances. The cost propagation is the underlying reason causing such performance impact. For instance, in the motivating example (Section 2.2), the delay initiated by $T_{S,W0}$ actually affected not only *BrowserTabCreate*, but also other scenario instances corresponding to two other applications along the propagation path. If we suppose the optimal case $D_{scn}^{opt}$ as removing cost propagation between irrelevant scenarios, the extra percentage of cost introduced by cost propagation to the entire system would be $1 - D_{scn}^{opt}/D_{scn} = (D_{wait} - D_{waitdist})/D_{scn}$. This value is also an upper bound for the optimization of cost propagation. However, the actual optimization depends on the root causes of performance problems and other factors.

## 4. Causality Analysis

If the results from impact analysis indicate that the chosen components are of high impact, performance analysts can use causality analysis to discover runtime behaviors that may cause the observed performance impacts.

We adapt contrast data mining [7] to achieve causality analysis. Contrast data mining is the mining of patterns contrasting two or more classes for knowledge discovery [7]. In the setting of performance analysis, there are few specifications that can be used to distinguish between normal and problematic behaviors affecting performance, but we do know the difference on performance measurements. Contrast data mining can thus serve as a link from effect to cause. Namely, it allows us to discover behaviors that may cause the observed difference on measurements.

### 4.1 Data Abstraction and Pattern Representation

To adapt contrast data mining in performance analysis, we introduce the Signature Set Tuple as the pattern representation, and derive the Aggregated Wait Graph as the data abstraction from Wait Graphs. So the contrast data mining can discover contrast patterns in the form of Signature Set Tuple among different Aggregated Wait Graphs that are of distinguishable performance measurements.

**Aggregated Wait Graph.** An Aggregated Wait Graph is essentially the abstraction and aggregation of runtime behaviors in a set of Wait Graphs belonging to the same scenario, based on the fact that runtime behaviors in the same scenario represent the similar tasks under investigation. The definition of an Aggregated Wait Graph is as follows, in which the term *signature* specially denotes the topmost signature related to the chosen components on the callstack *e.S* of a tracing event *e*, if there exists such signature on the callstack.

DEFINITION 2. *An Aggregated Wait Graph is a graph AWG* $= \langle V, E \rangle$. *V is a set of nodes* $V = \{v\}$, *in which each node represents the aggregated execution of a function signature in one of the following statuses: running, waiting, or hardware service. E is a set of directed edges* $E = \{v_i \to v_j\}$, *in which each edge must start from a waiting node, indicating that the pointed node performs its operation within the waiting cost of the starting node.*

In addition, we attach some extra properties to the nodes in an Aggregated Wait Graph to ease our analysis.

DEFINITION 3. *In an Aggregated Wait Graph, each running node has a signature v.r; each hardware-service node has a dummy signature v.h; and each waiting node has two signatures: a wait signature v.w and its paired unwait signature v.u. Each node has a performance metric v.C as its duration of execution time, and has an occurrence counter v.N indicating the number of the same nodes from the source Wait Graphs.*

Figure 2 shows a partial Aggregated Wait Graph for the motivating example in Section 2.2. The region highlighted with a dashed box shows an aggregated path that represents a group of paths of similar cost propagation from multiple scenario instances. The aggregated path captures cost propagation from a hardware service via the *se.sys* driver and then the *fs.sys* driver, finally to *fv.sys*.

**Signature Set Tuple.** Causality analysis presents mined patterns in the form of Signature Set Tuple. A Signature Set Tuple generalizes runtime interactions related to cost propagation into three signature sets: a wait-signature set, an unwait-signature set, and a running-signature set. The wait-signature set contains signatures that reside in *wait* events; namely, such signatures can cause the caller thread to be suspended. The unwait-signature set contains signatures from *unwait* events, which signal suspended threads to continue. The running-signature set contains signatures recorded in *running* events, or a dummy signature representing *hardware service* events. We extract Signature Set Tuples from path segments on Aggregated Wait Graphs. The definitions of the path segment and Signature Set Tuple are as follows.

DEFINITION 4. *A path segment S of an Aggregated Wait Graph AWG is a sequence of nodes* $S := \langle v_i \rangle : v_0 v_1 \ldots v_{L-1}$, *where $v_i \in AWG.V$ and for $0 \leq i < L-1, v_i \rightarrow v_{i+1} \in AWG.E$. The performance metric of S is defined as the metric of its end node, i.e., $S.C := v_{L-1}.C$, as well as the occurrence counter $S.N := v_{L-1}.N$.*

DEFINITION 5. *A Signature Set Tuple P from a path segment S is in the form of $P(S) := \langle \bigcup v.w, \bigcup v.u, \bigcup v.r \rangle$, where $v \in S$. The performance metric of P(S) is defined as the metric of the path segment, i.e., $P(S).C := S.C$, as well as the occurrence counter $P(S).N := S.N$.*

We design such Signature Set Tuple based on two key rationales. First, the three signature sets appropriately generalize the phenomenon that the cost of some time-consuming operations (represented by the running-signature set) propagates to other parts in the system via interactions in the direction from functions represented by the unwait-signature set to those of the wait-signature set, regardless of the particular kinds of interactions. Second, signature sets can accommodate variations of the cost-propagation sequences. Consider a case of device drivers, in which two drivers contend a resource held by the third driver. Such case creates two possible execution sequences in reality, depending on which driver acquires the resource first. A pattern in the Signature Set Tuple can represent both possibilities.

### 4.2 Pattern Discovery

Given a set of instances of a particular scenario, and two performance thresholds $T_{fast}$ and $T_{slow}$ as inputs, the causality analysis adapts contrast data mining, and works in three steps: (1) classifying contrast classes, (2) constructing data abstractions, and (3) mining contrast patterns.

#### 4.2.1 Classifying Contrast Classes

The causality analysis first classifies these instances into two contrast classes $\{I\}_{fast}$ and $\{I\}_{slow}$ by comparing their recorded execution time against performance thresholds $T_{fast}$ and $T_{slow}$. In practice, developers need to explicitly specify the two thresholds for each application scenario as a part of performance specification. Specifically, $T_{fast}$ is the upper bound reflecting normal performance, and $T_{slow}$ is the lower bound of performance degradation. For example, the *BrowserTabCreate* scenario of a web browser should be completed within 300ms, and should not exceed 500ms, which typically makes users feel slow. In this case, $T_{fast} = 300ms$ and $T_{slow} = 500ms$, so the two classes would be *less-than-300ms* as the fast class and *more-than-500ms* as the slow class. The contrasts between the two classes are highly suspicious to be the constitution of performance problems. Typically we have $T_{slow} - T_{fast} \gg 0$, enabling little confusion between the two contrast classes.

#### 4.2.2 Constructing Data Abstractions

Given two contrast classes of instances $\{I\}_{fast}$ and $\{I\}_{slow}$, causality analysis constructs two Aggregated Wait Graphs $AWG_{fast}$ and $AWG_{slow}$ for the two classes. The corresponding Wait Graphs for the scenario instances to be aggregated come from the previous impact analysis. The aggregation uses the algorithm presented in Algorithm 1.

**Algorithm 1:** The algorithm to aggregate Wait Graphs

```
   Input: a set of Wait Graphs {WG}, a set of component names {C}
   Output: an Aggregated Wait Graph AWG
1  InitializeAWG(AWG);
2  foreach WG in {WG} do
3      repeat
4          rootNodes ← GetRootNodes(WG);
5          foreach e in rootNodes do
6              if e.S does not contain signature from {C} then
7                  RemoveNode(WG, e);
8      until ∀e ∈ rootNodes, e.S contains signature from {C};
9      foreach e in WG do
10         if e.Type is u then
11             e' ← GetSourceNode(WG, e);
12             MergeWaitUnwaitPair(WG, e, e');
13     foreach path ⟨e0, e1, ..., en⟩ from roots to sinks in WG do
14         MergeWithCommonSigPrefix(AWG, ⟨e0, e1, ..., en⟩);
15 ReduceAWG(AWG);
16 return AWG;
```

Algorithm 1 works in four steps. For each Wait Graph, it first eliminates nodes that are irrelevant to the components to be analyzed from Wait Graphs (Lines 3 to 8). Then it merges paired wait/unwait nodes (Lines 9 to 12). After that it aggregates the processed Wait Graph to the Aggregated Wait Graph (Lines 13 to 14). Finally, we introduce a heuristic to reduce the size of the graph in Line 15. We describe the key points for each step as follows.

**Eliminating Component-Irrelevant Nodes.** A node is component-irrelevant if none of the signatures on the callstack belongs to the specified components $\{C\}$. From roots of the graph, the algorithm removes each component-irrelevant node, and promotes its child nodes as new roots. The algorithm repeats until all root nodes are component-relevant. The processed Wait Graph contains only behaviors initiated by the components in $\{C\}$.

**Merging Wait/Unwait Nodes.** The algorithm merges *wait* events with corresponding *unwait* events as well as their edges to create waiting nodes (`MergeWaitUnwaitPair` in Line 12). The result structure represents that the child nodes perform operations within the cost of the parent node. In fact, the Aggregated Wait Graph is essentially a forest in which all inner nodes must represent *wait/unwait* event pairs, whereas all leaf nodes must be of *running* events or *hardware service* events.

**Aggregating Wait Graphs.** The algorithm aggregates the processed Wait Graphs based on common prefixes of paths (`MergeWithCommonSigPrefix` in Line 14). Paths having common prefix indicate that they have the identical sequence of signatures on nodes along their prefixes. Common prefixes indicate that there are common behaviors starting at the beginning of executions, and subsequent behaviors may be diverse due to external or internal reasons, such as various inputs from higher-level applications, or lock contentions and different dependencies.

**Non-Opimtizable Portions.** To help subsequent mining and eliminate data noises, the algorithm performs a reduction on Aggregated Wait Graphs (`ReduceAWG` in Line 15). Specifically, it prunes all structures in the pattern of a waiting node as a root pointing to a single hardware-service leaf. This pattern implies that the performance impact of hardware services is not propagated to other components. Developers usually do not have any chances to optimize such cases.

#### 4.2.3 Mining Contrast Patterns

The algorithm to discover contrast patterns between the two Aggregated Wait Graphs works in the following three steps. To address challenges from both data complexity and computational complexity, we particularly introduce a step of meta-pattern enumeration.

**Enumerating Meta-Patterns.** Given the two Aggregated Wait Graphs for the two contrast classes, the causality analysis first enumerates meta-patterns in the form of Signature Set Tuples from path segments in the two graphs. Specifically, we introduce a constant $k$ to bound the maximum length of path segments in order to improve efficiency. Given a certain value of $k$, the causality analysis iteratively enumerates all path segments that have the lengths from 1 to $k$, and collects meta-patterns from these segments. Given two path segments having a common meta-pattern $P$, the causality analysis aggregates their $P.C$ and $P.N$ values. After this step, we have two groups of meta-patterns for the fast and slow contrast classes.

We have three considerations of enumerating meta-patterns from a bounded number of path segments rather than from all possible path segments or full paths in the two Aggregated Wait Graphs. First, contrast mining on simple data abstractions such as sets is of high complexity [37]. For a complex data structure such as an Aggregated Wait Graph with a potentially large amount of data in it, the computation is challenging. Second, in fact meta-patterns collected from a bounded number of path segments are adequate without loss of patterns, compared with expensive all-segment enumeration. The causality analysis enumerates path segments from the smallest length; thereby, all other patterns could be the combinations of the smaller ones. Third, using patterns collected from complete paths is too specific for causality analysis. If a pattern of a complete path from one contrast class does not appear in another contrast class, we cannot claim that this path is a contrast, because its meta-patterns may appear frequently in both classes. So by conducting the segment enumeration, we can have these meta-patterns to exclude non-contrast paths.

**Discovering Meta-Pattern Contrasts.** The contrasts among meta-patterns in the two groups infer the behaviors having potential impacts to performance. There are two criteria to discover such contrasts. First, a meta-pattern appearing only in the slow class indicates that runtime behaviors represented by it may harm the whole performance to some extent, since such behaviors never happen in the cases of normal performance. The causality analysis selects such meta-pattern as a contrast. Second, a meta-pattern that is common in the two classes, but whose attached performance metrics are significantly higher in the slow class, also implies highly suspicious and high-impact runtime behaviors to the performance. In particular, for the common meta-pattern $P_s$ in the slow class, and $P_f$ in the fast class, whenever $\frac{P_s.C}{P_s.N} / \frac{P_f.C}{P_f.N} > \frac{T_{slow}}{T_{fast}}$, the causality analysis selects the meta-pattern as a contrast.

**Discovering Contrast Patterns.** Finally, the causality analysis discovers contrast patterns based on the contrast meta-patterns in two steps. First, the causality analysis uses contrast meta-patterns as clues to select contrast paths. It computes a pattern in the Signature Set Tuple for each full path in the Aggregated Wait Graph of the slow class. If the extracted pattern contains any contrast meta-patterns, the causality analysis selects it as a contrast pattern. Second, the causality analysis merges identical contrast patterns with their $P.C$ and $P.N$ counters. Recall that multiple paths representing the same kind of problem could share the same pattern, even when their cost-propagation sequences might be different.

These contrast patterns are the output of causality analysis. To further facilitate manual efforts on inspection, we rank these patterns by their performance impacts, with the highest impacts ranked the first. We define the impact of a contrast pattern by its average execution cost in performing its task, i.e., $P.C/P.N$.

## 5. Empirical Results and Evaluation on Device Drivers

We apply our approach to study the performance of device drivers in Windows. We first perform impact analysis on device drivers, and then present an evaluation of using causality analysis to reveal patterns of performance problems.

Our data set contains about 19,500 trace streams, consisting of about 505,500 scenario instances that fall into 1,364 usage scenarios of Windows and various applications. The total recorded execution time is approximately 339 hours. These trace streams are collected by the ETW infrastructure.

Our study and evaluation offer developers and performance analysts two main benefits. First, the study and evaluation uncover the impact and problems of device drivers in the real world. Second, the study and evaluation show that our approach can facilitate performance analysis by reducing manual efforts on the inspection of performance problems.

### 5.1 Results of Impact Analysis on Device Drivers

We set the impact analysis to analyze device drivers exclusively over all scenario instances in the data set, namely, by setting the names of components to include all device drivers (matching the wildcard pattern "*.sys" in all function signatures).

The impact analysis shows that the wait percentage $IA_{wait} \approx 36.4\%$, and running percentage $IA_{run} \approx 1.6\%$, which are compelling metrics to inform the performance impact. $IA_{wait}$ directly explains what percentage device drivers block application executions. We can consider it as the average percentage of performance impact introduced by device drivers in each instance. $IA_{run}$ indicates what percentage device drivers consume CPU time. The small percentage of $IA_{run}$ indicates that the running time of device drivers is not a dominating part in overall system performance.

The impact analysis also shows that the percentage of extra waiting time $IA_{opt} \approx 26\%$, indicating the severity of cost propagation in device drivers, and the fact that the total execution time $D_{scn}$ could be reducible by optimizing device drivers and/or relevant components. In addition, the ratio of the total wait duration to the total distinct-wait duration $D_{wait}/D_{waitdist} \approx 3.5$ shows that any cost involving device drivers in one scenario instance is propagated to the other 2.5 instances on average, indicating the severity of cost propagation from a high-level of view.

In summary, the results indicate that device drivers are worth being further investigated. In particular, the results disclose three aspects. First, device drivers constitute a non-trivial part ($\approx 36.4\%$) in OS and application performance. Second, the percentage of time likely wasted due to cost propagation would be 26%, which is also an upper bound for the optimization of cost propagation. Third, CPU consumption of device drivers has limited impact ($\approx 1.6\%$). It is consistent with the expectation that drivers do little computation [27], and thus their computation cost is not our focus of analysis.

### 5.2 Evaluation of Causality Analysis

Performance analysts can manually inspect output patterns to determine whether these patterns represent high-impact performance problems and need further actions towards optimization. To show the effectiveness of causality analysis, and how causality analysis can improve the efficiency of manual inspection, we address the following three research questions.

**RQ1:** To what extent would the discovered patterns explain the bad performance in device drivers?

**RQ2:** How does the ranking strategy applied on discovered patterns help improve efficiency of inspecting performance problems?

**RQ3:** What insights can the discovered patterns offer to performance analysts in identifying real performance problems?

#### 5.2.1 Evaluation Setup

We apply the causality analysis on 8 selected out of all 1,364 scenarios. There are 17,612 instances in the selected scenarios. Table 1 shows these scenarios. We choose these scenarios for two reasons: (1) the selected scenarios represent a set of typical applications (e.g., web browsers) that need to interact with multiple device drivers, and (2) the number of instances in the selected scenarios are relatively large to avoid data noises and biases affecting contrast data mining. There are 2,201 instances for each selected scenario on average, compared with the overall average of 370 instances per scenario in our data set.

| Scenario | #Instances | in $\{I\}_{fast}$ | in $\{I\}_{slow}$ |
|---|---|---|---|
| AppAccessControl | 1547 | 598 | 772 |
| AppNonResponsive | 631 | 164 | 392 |
| BrowserFrameCreate | 1304 | 437 | 707 |
| BrowserTabClose | 989 | 134 | 678 |
| BrowserTabCreate | 2491 | 597 | 1601 |
| BrowserTabSwitch | 2182 | 1122 | 914 |
| MenuDisplay | 743 | 171 | 499 |
| WebPageNavigation | 7725 | 4203 | 1175 |
| Total | 17612 | 7426 | 6738 |

**Table 1.** Selected Scenarios

Table 1 shows the selected scenarios, the number of scenario instances, and the numbers of instances in the two contrast classes. For confidentiality, we anonymize the real names of the selected scenarios, and use $T_{fast}$ and $T_{slow}$ to denote the two thresholds. These two thresholds are determined by application vendors, and may vary in different scenarios. We set the component names $\{C\}$ to be all device drivers, and the maximum length of segment enumeration to be 5 in all experiments to focus on the propagation of performance impact up to that length.

To address RQ1, we first use an automated rule to determine whether the discovered patterns represent high-impact driver behaviors. In particular, we determine that a contrast pattern is of high impact if at least one of its executions in trace streams exceeds $T_{slow}$. Such high-impact pattern indicates that the involved drivers must be able to constitute the bad performance as a significant factor. Otherwise, the pattern's impact to the bad performance is relatively low. After classifying the discovered patterns by the automated rule, we show two execution-time coverages for the classified patterns over the total time cost of device drivers in the slow class. In particular, the impactful-time coverage (ITC) is the sum of the time cost $P.C$ for the high-impact patterns over the total time cost of device drivers, and the total-time coverage (TTC) is the sum of the time cost $P.C$ for all patterns over the total time cost of device drivers. The ITC suggests the scope where there *must* be high-impact driver behaviors causing the bad performance, and the TTC suggests the scope where there *may* be such behaviors. The ITC and TTC can show the effectiveness of causality analysis, because high coverages indicate that the discovered patterns can interpret the bad performance to a great extent, which offers a higher chance for performance analysts to find high-impact performance problems.

For RQ2, we show an execution-time coverage of top $n\%$ patterns based on the ranking strategy. In practice, a perfor-

| Scenario ($T_{slow}$) | Driver Cost | ITC | TTC |
|---|---|---|---|
| AppAccessControl | 66.4% | 18.9% | 35.5% |
| AppNonResponsive | 64.6% | 41.0% | 48.7% |
| BrowserFrameCreate | 76.5% | 24.1% | 35.4% |
| BrowserTabClose | 21.9% | 27.1% | 38.0% |
| BrowserTabCreate | 51.3% | 23.1% | 35.3% |
| BrowserTabSwitch | 41.0% | 7.8% | 17.5% |
| MenuDisplay | 77.0% | 39.2% | 49.2% |
| WebPageNavigation | 34.7% | 18.4% | 28.5% |
| Average | 54.2% | 24.9% | 36.0% |

**Table 2.** Impactful-Time and Total-Time Coverages

| Scenario ($T_{slow}$) | #Patterns | 10% | 20% | 30% |
|---|---|---|---|---|
| AppAccessControl | 4875 | 55.3% | 91.1% | 98.3% |
| AppNonResponsive | 1158 | 29.6% | 39.2% | 95.1% |
| BrowserFrameCreate | 1933 | 51.6% | 92.0% | 96.8% |
| BrowserTabClose | 1075 | 55.1% | 90.0% | 93.5% |
| BrowserTabCreate | 5045 | 49.0% | 87.5% | 97.0% |
| BrowserTabSwitch | 1514 | 42.3% | 64.9% | 98.0% |
| MenuDisplay | 1855 | 64.5% | 86.5% | 91.9% |
| WebPageNavigation | 5122 | 35.6% | 89.3% | 96.5% |
| Average | 2822 | 47.9% | 80.1% | 95.9% |

**Table 3.** Coverages by Ranking

mance analyst needs to manually investigate the discovered patterns in trace streams to confirm the root causes, and prioritize the investigation efforts for high-impact patterns. So a relatively small $n\%$ with high coverage indicates that the ranking strategy prioritizes high-impact patterns properly, and can substantially improve the inspection efficiency.

For RQ3, we first present what kinds of drivers are involved in the top-10 patterns from each selected scenario (80 patterns in total). Then we describe three major observations that we can make from the relations between scenarios and drivers. We also use some representative cases to illustrate how causality analysis can help performance analysts identify real-world problems. Note that the analysis in this paper was conducted independently by the authors, but all cases described in detail have been reviewed and confirmed by performance analysts and developers at Microsoft. We are continuing the confirmation process for other cases.

### 5.2.2 RQ1: Effectiveness

We show the effectiveness of causality analysis by presenting the impactful-time and total-time coverages for the discovered patterns. Table 2 shows the results of the two coverages. The column "Driver Cost" presents total execution time of device drivers in each scenario. The columns "ITC" and "TTC" present the impactful-time and the total-time coverages on the total driver time.

Overall, the total driver cost in the slow class can be characterized by three portions. The first portion is represented by the driver behaviors that may account for the bad performance. The second one is represented by the driver behaviors that are likely of normal performance. The two portions do not have an easily distinguishable boundary. The causality analysis can help performance analysts identify the boundary. In particular, the contrast patterns that are counted in the ITC must fall into the first portion, whereas the rest of the contrast patterns may cross the boundary of the two portions, but still likely cause the bad performance. Let us take the *AppNonResponsive* scenario as an example. The total driver cost covers 64.6% of the total execution time. The ITC is 41.0%, and the difference between the ITC and the TTC is 7.7%. The contrast patterns counted in the ITC should be the first priority for performance analysts to inspect, and the rest of the patterns falling between the ITC and the TTC reflect a non-negligible amount of execution time that performance analysts should inspect to confirm potential problems.

On the other hand, the third portion is represented by the driver behaviors that directly interact with hardware without cost propagation. These behaviors are usually of high impact, but non-optimizable, since the real cost depends on external hardware. During the construction of an Aggregated Wait Graph, the reduction of non-optimizable portions would remove such behaviors, even though some of them could account for long-time executions. Since device drivers frequently interact with slow hardware, the non-optimizable portions are very common. For example, in the *BrowserTabSwitch* scenario, 66.6% of the total driver cost is manifested in direct hardware services without cost propagation, thus being removed from the Aggregated Driver Graph. The resulting graph represents the remaining 33.4%, and more than half of the remaining portions (17.5%) are represented by contrast patterns, and classified into the total-time coverage.

### 5.2.3 RQ2: Efficiency

We calculate another execution-time coverage to show the efficiency improvement brought by the causality analysis on manually confirming potential performance problems. Based on the ranking strategy used in the pattern discovery, we select the top 10%, 20%, and 30% contrast patterns, and measure their execution-time coverages over all discovered patterns. Table 3 shows the results, in which the column "#Patterns" presents the number of contrast patterns in each scenario, and the last three columns show the coverage for the top 10%, 20%, and 30% contrast patterns.

The numbers of the output patterns range from 1,075 to 5,122 across different scenarios. The thousand magnitude of patterns came from the scale of input traces and the high complexity of the OS ecosystem, especially the complexity of interactions and dependencies in device drivers. As shown in Table 3, the inspection of the top 10% patterns would involve 107 to 512 patterns and achieve 30% to 65% execution-time coverage. According to the evaluations provided for StackMine [16], a performance analyst could inspect the top 400 stack-trace patterns of an analysis within 8 hours to achieve 60% execution-time coverage in all analyzed regions of scenario instances, with over 90% inspection effort saved as an estimation. Such comparable experiences indicate the affordability and efficiency regarding inspection efforts required by the causality analysis as well.

### 5.2.4 RQ3: Real Cases

Table 4 shows that in each scenario what kinds of drivers are involved in top-10 patterns. Each cell shows the number of patterns containing the corresponding type of drivers. From Table 4, we have three major observations regarding the relations between scenarios and drivers. These observations can suggest proper starting points for the performance analysis on similar cases.

First, most patterns contain both file-system drivers and filter drivers, especially in the *AppAccessControl* scenario. In fact, most of those filter drivers belong to security software. Security software uses system-wide filter drivers to intercept various application requests, but usually uses a single process and database for security inspection. Such architecture makes the performance of security inspection very critical. Once the workload of the system increases, it is easy to form bottlenecks starting from those filter drivers. If the system also enables storage encryption, the situation could become worse, as the encryption drivers could induce extra overheads. The example described in Section 2.2 is a typical case of how filter drivers combined with encryption drivers slow down the system. Developers should estimate the granularity and potential contentions of locks in filter drivers to alleviate overheads.

Second, some scenarios are especially vulnerable to particular types of drivers. In addition to the *AppAccessControl* scenario, which suffers from file-system drivers and filter drivers, we can observe that network drivers take a big part in the scenario of *MenuDisplay* (7 out of 10). It is understandable that network drivers can be delayed by unstable bandwidth. So if a menu needs to display items from remote servers, developers should take into account such instability, and use an asynchronous mechanism or prefetched cache to prevent network delays from being propagated to user interfaces.

Third, hard faults can establish more subtler interactions between drivers, and cause severe performance degradation. In the *AppNonResponsive* scenario, an interesting pattern shows that a graphics driver *graphics.sys* appears with a file system driver *fs.sys* and a storage encryption driver *se.sys*. From driver signatures we can infer that *graphics.sys* should not have interactions with the other two in normal cases, because it does not need to access files on disk. Based on our knowledge, it is highly suspicious that this pattern hints a hard fault occurring in *graphics.sys*.

From trace streams, we find a corresponding instance that costs about 4.73 seconds to finish the execution. To simply describe this case, we next describe only three threads that are most relevant. The initiating one was a UI thread $T_{U,UI}$. $T_{U,UI}$ was executing *graphics.sys*, and the driver tried to acquire resources of a Graphics Processing Unit (GPU). At the same time, there was a system worker thread $T_{S,W0}$ in which *graphics.sys* was executing a routine in response to a system event. Since $T_{S,W0}$ had acquired GPU resources, $T_{U,UI}$ had to wait. At this point, a hard fault occurred in $T_{S,W0}$ when *graphics.sys* initialized an internal structure. To solve the hard fault, the system scheduled another worker thread $T_{S,W1}$ to perform a page read. $T_{S,W1}$ was actually executing *se.sys* because the system was storage-encrypted. Finally, the system spent about 4.7 seconds to complete the page read. This significant performance degradation was then spread to $T_{U,UI}$, and made the user interface unresponsive.

The preceding case indicates that solving hard faults could be very time-consuming, so device drivers should be developed to minimize the usage of paged memory in order to avoid expensive disk I/O and the consequence of potential cost propagation.

### 5.2.5 Validity and False Positives in Analysis Results

To validate the analysis supported by our approach, we sent the case described in Section 2.2, a representative case of security software, and the hard fault in *graphics.sys* as high-impact problems to relevant performance analysts and developers at Microsoft, and received their confirmations. The high impact was partially confirmed after their frequent observation of such problems, reflecting the limitations of the conventional performance analysis. One developer from a Windows product team for driver quality provided his enthusiastically positive feedback: "*...It is very impressive to see how performance issues of device drivers can be root caused in such a detail... yes, this is the technique we are interested in w.r.t. driver qualities...*".

Except those high-impact real cases, we can observe some false positives. In some special circumstances, our approach fails to distinguish between by-design behaviors and problematic behaviors. For instance, in Table 4 there is a type of drivers called "Disk Protection", which can halt hard drives to prevent damages when a computer is in motion. Drivers of this type are designed to block all disk reads and writes when necessary, and meanwhile performance can be compromised. The appearance of such driver patterns suggests that we need to incorporate such knowledge to filter out some known and exceptional cases.

## 6. Related Work

**Performance Analysis.** The high-level goal of our work is to help with the performance analysis of software ecosystems, particularly the evaluation of impacts and identification of root causes for performance degradation, by acquiring the knowledge from a large number of execution traces. We organize the discussion of related work by three major aspects, specifically, (1) handling cross-component interactions, (2) leveraging multiple executions, and (3) oracles for finding root causes.

Cross-component interactions may work concurrently and cause the effect of cost propagation. The potential transparency of these interactions to individual components

| Scenario | FileSystem, General Storage | FileSystem Filter | Network | Storage Encryption | Disk Protection | Graphics | Storage Backup | IO Cache | Mouse | ACPI |
|---|---|---|---|---|---|---|---|---|---|---|
| AppAccessControl | 9 | 9 | – | – | – | – | – | 1 | – | – |
| AppNonResponsive | 6 | 2 | 1 | 2 | 1 | 1 | – | – | – | 1 |
| BrowserFrameCreate | 7 | 4 | 2 | – | 1 | – | – | – | – | – |
| BrowserTabClose | 5 | 6 | – | 2 | – | – | 2 | – | – | – |
| BrowserTabCreate | 5 | 6 | 3 | 2 | – | 1 | – | – | 1 | – |
| BrowserTabSwitch | 6 | 5 | 3 | 1 | – | – | – | – | – | – |
| MenuDisplay | 2 | 3 | 7 | – | 2 | – | – | – | – | – |
| WebPageNavigation | 7 | 3 | 3 | 1 | 1 | – | – | – | – | – |

**Table 4.** Top-10 Patterns Categorized by Driver Types

makes the diagnosis of performance to be even harder. Some existing work [4, 35] identified the idleness as a performance characteristic of multithreaded and multi-component programs. Tallent *et al.* [35, 36] analyzed lock-based interactions as the source of such idleness. However, their work is limited to isolate the effect of a single lock only. In contrast, our work reveals the combinatorial effect of multiple locks connected by hierarchical dependencies, which commonly exist in large and complex systems.

Multiple executions of a system can provide diverse performance information. StackMine [16] and Magpie [10] also work on multiple ETW traces. Our previous StackMine work discovers callstack patterns via costly-pattern mining, resulting in patterns capturing within-thread behaviors. Our current work complements it with the mining of contrast patterns characterizing cross-thread behaviors. Magpie correlates workloads with events synthesized from traces to build performance models that support performance prediction and debugging. Our work can further help Magpie diagnose root causes by using workload-based scenarios. Jovic *et al.* [19] targeted at finding and prioritizing performance bugs in GUI applications from multiple profiles in the wild. However, this work relies on the manual selection of landmark methods to measure latency, and has the limitation of not being able to handle concurrency.

Using proper oracles is helpful to find performance problems and root causes effectively. Rule-based problem identification [4, 5, 18, 38] is limited due to finding only problems defined by existing rules. Some work performs thresholding and filtering on performance measurements [32] combined with frequencies of observed system behaviors [3]. However, in complex systems, no clear-cut criteria can be used to attribute bad performance to behaviors that may be expensive in nature and vary in different usage scenarios. Our work leverages information from the labeled normal executions as the criteria addressing such variations. Some work [6, 15, 30] proposed similar ideas exploiting contrasts between different executions to identify performance problems. Compared to such previous work, our work does not require concrete inputs of systems. These inputs are not always available especially when performance data are collected from client sites. Furthermore, our work provides useful data abstractions that group similar behaviors in a large volume of data, and provides a pattern representation to represent actionable patterns to further narrow down the scope of the root-cause localization.

**Quality Assurance for Device Drivers.** Quality of device drivers includes mainly reliability, security, and performance. Most existing research work is to improve driver reliability [8, 9, 12, 13, 20, 22, 24, 26–29, 31, 33, 34]. While certain kinds of reliability issues are handled, e.g., memory corruption, the security is also improved. In addition, isolation-based approaches [11, 31] were also introduced to improve driver security. In contrast, little work has been proposed on driver performance. In fact, there is a trade-off between reliability (together with security) and performance. Leslie *et al.* [23] and Ganapathy *et al.* [13] demonstrated that it is possible to build user-level drivers to improve reliability without significant performance overheads. Menon *et al.* [25] explored the opportunity to balance reliability, security, and performance with a framework allowing to create safe and efficient hypervisor drivers. Huang and Chen [17] developed an approach to find performance bottlenecks of TCP/IP protocol and the corresponding drivers. Such work usually addresses driver performance by a specific analysis or from a specific perspective, but not from a general perspective of real-world production ecosystems.

## 7. Conclusion

We have proposed a performance-analysis approach on real-world execution traces to address the challenges posed by cost propagation in complex systems. We have applied impact analysis to study the performance of device drivers on 19,500 execution traces. The results show that device drivers constitute approximately 38% of the overall system performance, and a big part ($\approx 26\%$) is introduced by cost propagation. To understand how device drivers affect system performance, we have conducted causality analysis to discover patterns of problematic behaviors. The discovered patterns can help identify high-impact performance problems.

## Acknowledgments

We would like to thank the conference reviewers and shepherds for their feedback in finalizing this paper. We would also like to thank the performance analysts and the developers at Microsoft who helped review and verify the studied cases.

## References


[1] http://msdn.microsoft.com/en-us/library/windows/desktop/bb968803(v=vs.85).aspx.

[2] http://en.wikipedia.org/wiki/DTrace.

[3] M. K. Aguilera, J. C. Mogul, J. L. Wiener, P. Reynolds, and A. Muthitacharoen. Performance Debugging for Distributed Systems of Black Boxes. In *Proceedings of the Nineteenth ACM Symposium on Operating Systems Principles*, SOSP '03, pages 74–89, New York, NY, USA, 2003. ACM.

[4] E. Altman, M. Arnold, S. Fink, and N. Mitchell. Performance Analysis of Idle Programs. In *Proceedings of the ACM International Conference on Object Oriented Programming Systems Languages and Applications*, OOPSLA'10, pages 739–753, New York, NY, USA, 2010. ACM.

[5] G. Ammons, J.-D. Choi, M. Gupta, and N. Swamy. Finding and Removing Performance Bottlenecks in Large Systems. In *Proceedings of ECOOP 2004 - Object-Oriented Programming*, volume 3086 of *Lecture Notes in Computer Science*, pages 172–196. Springer Berlin Heidelberg, 2004.

[6] M. Attariyan, M. Chow, and J. Flinn. X-ray: Automating Root-Cause Diagnosis of Performance Anomalies in Production Software. In *Proceedings of the 10th USENIX conference on Operating Systems Design and Implementation*, OSDI'12, pages 307–320, Berkeley, CA, USA, 2012. USENIX Association.

[7] J. Bailey and N. V. Laboratory. Contrast Data Mining: Methods and Applications. *Tutorial at ICDM*, 2007.

[8] G. Balakrishnan and T. Reps. Analyzing Stripped Device-Driver Executables. In *Proceedings of the 14th International Conference on Tools and Algorithms for the Construction and Analysis of Systems*, TACAS'08, pages 124–140, Berlin, Heidelberg, 2008. Springer-Verlag.

[9] T. Ball, E. Bounimova, B. Cook, V. Levin, J. Lichtenberg, C. McGarvey, B. Ondrusek, S. K. Rajamani, and A. Ustuner. Thorough Static Analysis of Device Drivers. *SIGOPS Oper. Syst. Rev.*, 40(4):73–85, Apr. 2006.

[10] P. Barham, A. Donnelly, R. Isaacs, and R. Mortier. Using Magpie for Request Extraction and Workload Modelling. In *Proceedings of the 6th Conference on Symposium on Opearting Systems Design & Implementation - Volume 6*, OSDI'04, pages 18–18, Berkeley, CA, USA, 2004. USENIX Association.

[11] S. Boyd-Wickizer and N. Zeldovich. Tolerating Malicious Device Drivers in Linux. In *Proceedings of the 2010 USENIX Conference on USENIX Annual Technical Conference*, USENIX ATC'10, pages 9–9, Berkeley, CA, USA, 2010. USENIX Association.

[12] V. Ganapathy, A. Balakrishnan, M. M. Swift, and S. Jha. Microdrivers: A New Architecture for Device Drivers. In *Proceedings of the 11th USENIX Workshop on Hot Topics in Operating Systems*, HOTOS'07, pages 15:1–15:6, Berkeley, CA, USA, 2007. USENIX Association.

[13] V. Ganapathy, M. J. Renzelmann, A. Balakrishnan, M. M. Swift, and S. Jha. The Design and Implementation of Microdrivers. In *Proceedings of the 13th International Conference on Architectural Support for Programming Languages and Operating Systems*, ASPLOS XIII, pages 168–178, New York, NY, USA, 2008. ACM.

[14] S. L. Graham, P. B. Kessler, and M. K. Mckusick. Gprof: A Call Graph Execution Profiler. In *Proceedings of the 1982 SIGPLAN Symposium on Compiler Construction*, CC'82, pages 120–126, New York, NY, USA, 1982. ACM.

[15] M. Grechanik, C. Fu, and Q. Xie. Automatically Finding Performance Problems with Feedback-Directed Learning Software Testing. In *Proceedings of the 2012 International Conference on Software Engineering*, ICSE'12, pages 156–166, Piscataway, NJ, USA, 2012. IEEE Press.

[16] S. Han, Y. Dang, S. Ge, D. Zhang, and T. Xie. Performance Debugging in the Large via Mining Millions of Stack Traces. In *Proceedings of the 2012 International Conference on Software Engineering*, ICSE'12, pages 145–155, Piscataway, NJ, USA, 2012. IEEE Press.

[17] J. H. Huang and C.-W. Chen. On Performance Measurements of TCP/IP and Its Device Driver. In *Proc. 17th Conference on Local Computer Networks*, pages 568–575, Sept. 1992.

[18] G. Jin, L. Song, X. Shi, J. Scherpelz, and S. Lu. Understanding and Detecting Real-World Performance Bugs. In *Proceedings of the 33rd ACM SIGPLAN conference on Programming Language Design and Implementation*, PLDI'12, pages 77–88, New York, NY, USA, 2012. ACM.

[19] M. Jovic, A. Adamoli, and M. Hauswirth. Catch Me If You Can: Performance Bug Detection in the Wild. In *Proceedings of the 2011 ACM International Conference on Object Oriented Programming Systems Languages and Applications*, OOPSLA'11, pages 155–170, New York, NY, USA, 2011. ACM.

[20] A. Kadav, M. J. Renzelmann, and M. M. Swift. Tolerating Hardware Device Failures in Software. In *Proceedings of the ACM SIGOPS 22nd Symposium on Operating Systems Principles*, SOSP'09, pages 59–72, New York, NY, USA, 2009. ACM.

[21] A. Kadav and M. M. Swift. Understanding Modern Device Drivers. In *Proceedings of the 17th International Conference on Architectural Support for Programming Languages and Operating Systems*, ASPLOS XVII, pages 87–98, New York, NY, USA, 2012. ACM.

[22] V. Kuznetsov, V. Chipounov, and G. Candea. Testing Closed-Source Binary Device Drivers with DDT. In *Proceedings of the 2010 USENIX Conference on USENIX Annual Technical Conference*, USENIXATC'10, pages 12–12, Berkeley, CA, USA, 2010. USENIX Association.

[23] B. Leslie, P. Chubb, N. Fitzroy-Dale, S. Gtz, C. Gray, L. Macpherson, D. Potts, Y.-T. Shen, K. Elphinstone, and G. Heiser. User-Level Device Drivers: Achieved Performance. *Journal of Computer Science and Technology*, 20(5):654–664, 2005.

[24] J. Li, F. Xie, T. Ball, V. Levin, and C. McGarvey. An Automata-Theoretic Approach to Hardware/Software Co-Verification. In *Proceedings of the 13th International Conference on Fundamental Approaches to Software Engineering*, FASE'10, pages 248–262, Berlin, Heidelberg, 2010. Springer-Verlag.

[25] A. Menon, S. Schubert, and W. Zwaenepoel. TwinDrivers: Semi-Automatic Derivation of Fast and Safe Hypervisor Network Drivers from Guest OS Drivers. In *Proceedings of the 14th International Conference on Architectural Support for Programming Languages and Operating Systems*, ASPLOS XIV, pages 301–312, New York, NY, USA, 2009. ACM.

[26] L. Ryzhyk, P. Chubb, I. Kuz, and G. Heiser. Dingo: Taming Device Drivers. In *Proceedings of the 4th ACM European Conference on Computer Systems*, EuroSys'09, pages 275–288, New York, NY, USA, 2009. ACM.

[27] L. Ryzhyk, P. Chubb, I. Kuz, E. Le Sueur, and G. Heiser. Automatic Device Driver Synthesis with Termite. In *Proceedings of the ACM SIGOPS 22nd Symposium on Operating Systems Principles*, SOSP'09, pages 73–86, New York, NY, USA, 2009. ACM.

[28] L. Ryzhyk, J. Keys, B. Mirla, A. Raghunath, M. Vij, and G. Heiser. Improved Device Driver Reliability through Hardware Verification Reuse. In *Proceedings of the 16th International Conference on Architectural Support for Programming Languages and Operating Systems*, ASPLOS XVI, pages 133–144, New York, NY, USA, 2011. ACM.

[29] L. Ryzhyk, Y. Zhu, and G. Heiser. The Case for Active Device Drivers. In *Proceedings of the 1st ACM Asia-Pacific Workshop on Systems*, APSys'10, pages 25–30, New York, NY, USA, 2010. ACM.

[30] K. Shen, C. Stewart, C. Li, and X. Li. Reference-Driven Performance Anomaly Identification. In *Proceedings of the 11th International Joint Conference on Measurement and Modeling of Computer Systems*, SIGMETRICS'09, pages 85–96, New York, NY, USA, 2009. ACM.

[31] M. F. Spear, T. Roeder, O. Hodson, G. C. Hunt, and S. Levi. Solving the Starting Problem: Device Drivers as Self-Describing Artifacts. *SIGOPS Oper. Syst. Rev.*, 40(4):45–57, Apr. 2006.

[32] K. Srinivas and H. Srinivasan. Summarizing Application Performance from a Components Perspective. In *Proceedings of the 10th European Software Engineering Conference Held Jointly with 13th ACM SIGSOFT International Symposium on Foundations of Software Engineering*, ESEC/FSE'13, pages 136–145, New York, NY, USA, 2005. ACM.

[33] M. M. Swift, M. Annamalai, B. N. Bershad, and H. M. Levy. Recovering Device Drivers. *ACM Trans. Comput. Syst.*, 24(4):333–360, Nov. 2006.

[34] M. M. Swift, B. N. Bershad, and H. M. Levy. Improving the Reliability of Commodity Operating Systems. In *Proceedings of the 19th ACM Symposium on Operating Systems Principles*, SOSP'03, pages 207–222, New York, NY, USA, 2003. ACM.

[35] N. R. Tallent and J. M. Mellor-Crummey. Effective Performance Measurement and Analysis of Multithreaded Applications. In *Proceedings of the 14th ACM SIGPLAN Symposium on Principles and Practice of Parallel Programming*, PPoPP'09, pages 229–240, New York, NY, USA, 2009. ACM.

[36] N. R. Tallent, J. M. Mellor-Crummey, and A. Porterfield. Analyzing Lock Contention in Multithreaded Applications. In *Proceedings of the 15th ACM SIGPLAN Symposium on Principles and Practice of Parallel Programming*, PPoPP'10, pages 269–280, New York, NY, USA, 2010. ACM.

[37] L. Wang, H. Zhao, G. Dong, and J. Li. On the Complexity of Finding Emerging Patterns. *Theor. Comput. Sci.*, 335(1):15–27, May 2005.

[38] A. Wert, J. Happe, and L. Happe. Supporting Swift Reaction: Automatically Uncovering Performance Problems by Systematic Experiments. In *Proceedings of the 2013 International Conference on Software Engineering*, ICSE'13, pages 552–561, Piscataway, NJ, USA, 2013. IEEE Press.

# Leveraging the Short-Term Memory of Hardware to Diagnose Production-Run Software Failures

Joy Arulraj Guoliang Jin Shan Lu

University of Wisconsin–Madison

{joy,aliang,shanlu@cs.wisc.edu}

## Abstract

Failures caused by software bugs are widespread in production runs, causing severe losses for end users. Unfortunately, diagnosing production-run failures is challenging. Existing work cannot satisfy privacy, run-time overhead, diagnosis capability, and diagnosis latency requirements all at once.

This paper designs a low overhead, low latency, privacy preserving production-run failure diagnosis system based on two observations. First, short-term memory of program execution is often sufficient for failure diagnosis, as many bugs have short propagation distances. Second, maintaining a short-term memory of execution is much cheaper than maintaining a record of the whole execution. Following these observations, we first identify an existing hardware unit, Last Branch Record (LBR), that records the last few taken branches to help diagnose sequential bugs. We then propose a simple hardware extension, Last Cache-coherence Record (LCR), to record the last few cache accesses with specified coherence states and hence help diagnose concurrency bugs. Finally, we design LBRA and LCRA to automatically locate failure root causes using LBR and LCR.

Our evaluation uses 31 real-world sequential and concurrency bug failures from 18 representative open-source software. The results show that with just 16 record entries, LBR and LCR enable our system to automatically locate the root causes for 27 out of 31 failures, with less than 3% run-time overhead. As our system does not rely on sampling, it also provides good diagnosis latency.

***Categories and Subject Descriptors*** B.8.1 [*Performance and Reliability*]: Reliability, Testing, and Fault-Tolerance; D.2.5 [*Software Engineering*]: Testing and Debugging; D.1.3 [*Programming Techniques*]: Concurrent Programming

***Keywords*** failure diagnosis; production runs; concurrency bugs; hardware performance monitoring unit



*ASPLOS '14*, March 1–5, 2014, Salt Lake City, Utah, USA.

http://dx.doi.org/10.1145/2541940.2541973

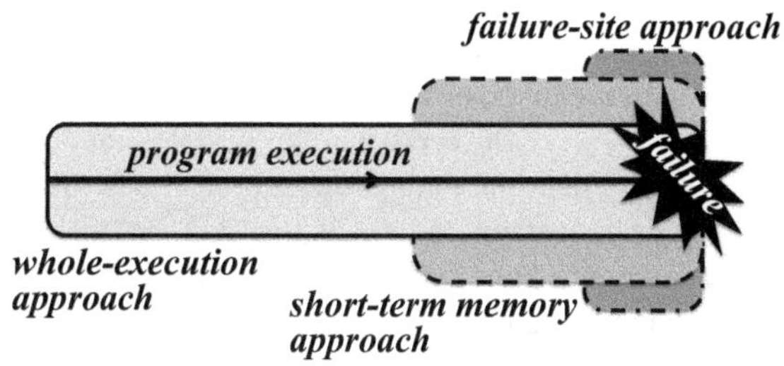


Figure 1: Approaches to diagnosing production-run failures (The rectangles illustrate program states directly collected by different approaches).

## 1. Introduction

### 1.1 Motivation

Software bugs are widespread. Although effective bug-detection tools have been proposed, many software bugs inevitably slip into production runs. They have led to many severe production-run failures, causing huge financial loss [8, 17, 30, 36] and threatening people's lives [21]. Consequently, diagnosing failures that occur on production machines is a critical task.

Unfortunately, diagnosing production-run failures is challenging. Different from in-house bug detection and testing, production-run failure diagnosis has to preserve privacy and minimize run-time overhead, which often leads to sacrifices in diagnosis latency (i.e. how long it takes to diagnose a failure after its first occurrence) or diagnosis capability (i.e., what types of failures can be diagnosed).

Many tools have been proposed for production-run failure diagnosis. Since the occurrence of failures is difficult to predict, previous work either collects program states at the failure site, referred to as *failure-site approach*, or collects program states throughout the execution, referred to as *whole-execution approach*, as illustrated in Figure 1. These two approaches make different tradeoffs among privacy, run-time overhead, diagnosis capability, and diagnosis latency.

The failure-site approach incurs negligible run-time overhead, but has difficulty in satisfying the other requirements. Fundamentally, inferring run-time information using the program states at failure sites is not only tedious but also often impossible. Making things even worse, sending a lot of program states, such as the whole coredump, back to developers could severely hurt end users' privacy. Some of these problems are alleviated by recent work that uses static analysis to automate log-variable selection and backward inference [43–45]. However, static analysis is not a panacea. It cannot help when software fails at unexpected locations (e.g., during a segmentation fault). Its help is limited for failures caused by concurrency bugs. Its analysis time also increases with the number of logging sites.

The whole-execution approach can achieve better diagnosis capability than the failure-site approach due to its access to the whole execution information. On the down side, it can easily lead to huge run-time overhead. Many dynamic bug detectors are suitable for in-house testing but not for production-run use, because they either lead to huge overhead or require complicated non-existing hardware support. Recent work [2, 18, 22, 23] uses random sampling to address the overhead problem. However, random sampling leads to long diagnosis latency. For example, with the default 1 out of 100 sampling rate used by previous work [22, 23], a failure often needs to occur for about 100 times before the developers obtain information useful for failure diagnosis. This is especially a concern for software that is not deployed on millions of machines and bugs that manifest infrequently, such as concurrency bugs.

In summary, more tools are needed to support production-run failure diagnosis.

### 1.2 Contribution

This paper presents a new approach to diagnosing a wide variety of production-run software failures with low run-time overhead and low diagnosis latency, while preserving end users' privacy. This new approach is based on the following two observations:

First, short-term memory is valuable and often sufficient for failure diagnosis. Previous empirical studies [12, 34, 48] have shown that most bugs have short propagation distances and hence have root causes located shortly before failures. Even for bugs with long propagation distances, information useful for failure diagnosis is generally not distributed evenly throughout the execution. Intuitively, information collected closer to a failure is more likely to be useful for diagnosis.

Second, short-term memory can be maintained with extremely low cost. In fact, existing hardware already maintains such short-term memory of software execution through facilities like Last Branch Record (LBR). With only 4–16 record entries maintained by LBR, the hardware cost is low and the run-time overhead is negligible.

In short, maintaining a short-term memory of program execution can achieve a nice balance in the design space:

- Comparing with the failure-site approach, it has access to more run-time information and hence can achieve better diagnosis capability.
- Comparing with the whole-execution approach, it only keeps the most recent execution history and can achieve better performance without sacrificing diagnosis latency.

Following these observations, we propose a new production-run failure diagnosis approach that leverages the short-term memory of program execution maintained by hardware[1]. Several questions need to be answered to design such an approach.

First, what to remember in the short-term memory? A lot of hardware events occur during every machine cycle. We need to select hardware events that are most useful for diagnosing software failures.

Second, how large is short-term memory? Are 4 – 16 record entries, the settings in existing hardware LBR, sufficient for real-world failure diagnosis? Can this short-term memory provide information that cannot be inferred by the program states at the failure site? How often can this short-term memory contain failure root-cause information? These questions have to be answered by thorough evaluation with real-world failures.

Third, how to use the short-term memory? We need to design a software system that accesses this hardware short-term memory and integrates it into an automated failure diagnosis algorithm. The detailed implementation also needs to be careful not to pollute the precious short-term memory with irrelevant events, such as those from library or code used to access the short-term memory.

This paper answers the above questions and makes the following contributions:

- We propose a short-term memory approach to diagnosing production-run failures, with a good balance among privacy, run-time overhead, failure-diagnosis capability, and failure-diagnosis latency (illustrated in Figure 1).
- We identify and design two hardware short-term memory facilities to support production-run failure diagnosis. Specifically, we identify an existing hardware performance monitoring unit, LBR, to help diagnose sequential-bug failures, and propose a simple hardware extension, Last Cache-coherence Record (LCR), to help diagnose concurrency-bug failures. The details are in Section 4.

[1] In this paper, we will refer to the hardware record of recent execution history as *short-term memory*. This short-term memory is composed of special machine registers, and has nothing to do with the main memory.

- We design and implement two ways to use the hardware short-term memory for production-run failure diagnosis. The basic way, referred to as LBRLOG and LCRLOG, is to use LBR and LCR as a generic mechanism to enhance failure logging. It provides developers a straightforward and generic mechanism to obtain the execution history right before a failure, which often contains hints of failure root causes. The advanced way, referred to as LBRA and LCRA, uses a statistical model to automatically locate failure root causes from LBR/LCR records. The details are presented in Section 5.
- A thorough evaluation based on 31 real-world failures from 18 open-source applications. Our evaluation based on 6945 failure-logging sites shows that more than 80% of LBR entries contain useful information that cannot be inferred by static control-flow analysis. LBRA can automatically locate branches that are closely related to failure root causes and bug patches for all the 20 evaluated sequential-bug failures, with less than 3% run-time overhead measured on commodity machines. In addition, LCRLOG and LCRA can help locate the root causes for 7 out of 11 tested concurrency-bug failures. Comparing with state-of-the-art systems that rely on sampling [2, 18, 22, 23], our failure-diagnosis system has tens to hundreds of times shorter diagnosis latency.

## 2. Background

### 2.1 Hardware branch-tracing facilities

There are two types of branch-tracing facilities in Intel processors. One is called *Last Branch Record* (LBR), which stores branch records in a circular ring of hardware registers. The other is called *Branch Trace Store* (BTS), which keeps branch records in cache or DRAM. BTS can store many more records than LBR. However, it incurs much larger overheads that is not suitable for production runs, ranging from 20% to 100% [31]. The following discussion will focus on LBR.

LBR is part of the hardware performance monitoring unit, originally designed for performance profiling. LBR branch recording uses special bus cycles on the system bus [14] and incurs negligible overhead. Its recording can be enabled and disabled through a special machine register, as shown in Table 1. Once enabled, LBR keeps recording newly retired branch instructions, with each new record evicting the oldest record. Each record contains the source and target addresses of a branch instruction. The total number of records in LBR varies in different microarchitectures, following an increasing trend over the years — it goes from 4 entries in Pentium 4 and Intel Xeon processors, to 8 in Pentium M processors, and to 16 in Nehalem processors [15]. All the experiments in this paper are conducted on an Intel Nehalem processor.

LBR can be configured to record different types of branch instructions, including conditional branches, unconditional jumps, calls, returns, and others, as shown in Table 1.

| IA32_DEBUGCTL | ID: 0x1d9 |
|---|---|
| 0x801 | Enable LBR |
| 0x0 | Disable LBR |
| **LBR_SELECT** | **ID: 0x1c8** |
| 0x1 | *Filter branches occurring in ring 0 |
| 0x2 | Filter branches occurring in other levels |
| 0x4 | Filter conditional branches |
| 0x8 | *Filter near relative calls |
| 0x10 | *Filter near indirect calls |
| 0x20 | *Filter near returns |
| 0x40 | *Filter near unconditional indirect jumps |
| 0x80 | Filter near unconditional relative branches |
| 0x100 | *Filter far branches |

Table 1: LBR related machine specific registers in Intel Nehalem (*: the masks used in this work).

```
if (a != 0)
  a++;
else
  a--;
```

(a)

```
1 cmpl $0x0,-0x4(%rbp)
2 je label<else>
3 ; jump of the false edge
4 addl $0x1,-0x4(%rbp)
5 jmp label<end>
6 ; jump of the true edge
7 label<else> :
8 subl $0x1,-0x4(%rbp)
9 label<end> :
```

(b)

Figure 2: Conditional branches in source and machine code.

A subtle yet important issue in using LBR is that a conditional branch in source code does not simply map to a conditional branch in machine code. Figure 2 shows a simple example. The conditional branch in Figure 2 (a) is translated into one conditional jump instruction on Line 2 and one unconditional jump instruction on Line 5 in Figure 2 (b). The former will be taken when the original conditional branch is evaluated `false`, and the latter will be taken if the original branch is evaluated `true`.

Previous work proposes inserting harmless unconditional branches along the fall-through edges [40] to make the mapping between machine-code branches and source-code branches easier. We reuse this technique and skip the details.

In general, no matter the `true` edge or the `false` edge of a conditional branch in the source code is taken, some corresponding machine-level branch will get recorded in LBR. Developers will be able to locate the source-level branch and know its outcome based on the LBR record.

### 2.2 Hardware performance counters

Many modern processors equip each core with a few hardware performance-counter registers. These registers can be configured to monitor and count a wide variety of hardware performance events. Different from the branch tracing facil-

| LOAD (STORE) | Event Code : 0x40 (0x41) |
|---|---|
| Unit mask | Description |
| 0x01 | Observe I state prior to a cache access |
| 0x02 | Observe S state prior to a cache access |
| 0x04 | Observe E state prior to a cache access |
| 0x08 | Observe M state prior to a cache access |

Table 2: L1 data-cache cache-coherence events in Intel Nehalem (The event code and mask IDs are used to configure which type(s) of events to monitor).

ity discussed above, each such register only contains a count, corresponding to a specific performance event.

One set of events that can be monitored on many Intel processors, including Core 2 and Nehalem, is L1 data-cache cache-coherence events [14]. As shown in Table 2, once enabled, every L1 data cache access that encounters specified coherence state(s) will trigger a counter increment in the corresponding register. There are also configurations that allow various types of filtering, such as filtering out user-level instructions or kernel-level instructions. The content of the register can be accessed through either polling or interrupts [2, 9]. We collectively refer to this set of L1 data-cache cache-coherence events as *cache-coherence events* or *coherence events* in this paper. Note that, counting coherence events through hardware performance counters incurs **no** perceivable overhead on commodity machines [2, 14].

## 3. Motivating Examples

### 3.1 Case 1: a sequential-bug failure

Figure 3 shows a memory bug in `sort` utility from Coreutils. When a user tries to merge already-sorted files such that the output file is one of the input files, the program crashes inside the `hash_lookup` function.

This segmentation fault is caused by a buffer overflow in `memmove` within `avoid_trashing_input` (marked as $B$ in Figure 3). This buffer overflow corrupts `files[i].pid`, which causes the control flow to deviate from the intended path at $C$. This eventually leads to a segmentation fault at $F$.

This buffer overflow is caused by the wrong while-loop condition at $A$. As we can see, the loop condition (`i+num_merged<nfiles`) is intended to avoid buffer overflow. However, since the value of `num_merged` is increased after this sanity check and before the access of `files` array, the buffer overflow occurs as long as this while-loop executes at least one iteration.

The *control-flow uncertainty* makes this failure very difficult to diagnose. First, the segmentation fault occurs in a function `hash_lookup` that has 9 different callers across 6 different files. Developers cannot even start their diagnosis without knowing the execution history. Second, even if the developers obtain the call-stack or even the core-dump from the end users' machines, they will likely ignore the

```
/* sort.c */
void merge (...) {
  avoid_trashing_input(...);
  for (...) {
    open_input_files(...);
  }
}
int avoid_trashing_input (...) {
  for (; i < nfiles; i++) {
    if (...)
      same = true;
    else if (...)
      break;
    ...
    if (same) {
      int num_merged = 0;
      while (i + num_merged < nfiles) { // A
        num_merged += mergefiles(...);
        memmove(&files[i], &files[i+num_merged], ...); // B
      ...
    }}}
  ...
}
int open_input_files (...) {
  if (files[i].pid != 0) // C
    open_temp(files[i].name, files[i].pid);
  else ...
}
/* lib/hash.c */
void *hash_lookup (Hash_table *table) {
  struct hash_entry *bucket = table->bucket; // F
} //called by wait_proc, which is called by open_temp
```

Figure 3: A sequential bug in `sort` utility in Coreutils-7.2.

`avoid_trashing_input` function, which is not on the call stack at the moment of failure. Third, even if developers pay attention to `avoid_trashing_input`, they do not know which basic blocks have executed, given the complicated control flow, not to mention discover the root cause at $A$.

In short, to effectively diagnose this failure, developers need to know the execution path leading to the failure. Otherwise, it is difficult to locate the root-cause code region and the root-cause branch. This path information often cannot be inferred by core-dumps, call-stacks, or log variables.

### 3.2 Case 2: a concurrency-bug failure

Figure 4 shows a concurrency bug in Mozilla JavaScript Engine. This bug is caused by unsynchronized accesses of the shared variable `st->table`. At runtime, the variable is initialized by `InitState` at $a_1$, and then checked at $a_2$. In most cases, this check will pass, as long as `New` has succeeded at $a_1$. Occasionally, `st->table` is set to `NULL` by another thread at $a_3$ right before the check is conducted. As a result, the software will fail with an "`out of memory`" message issued by `ReportOutOfMemory`.

Developers will encounter two major challenges in diagnosing this failure. First, control-flow uncertainties. The failure location in the source code is difficult to identify, because "`out of memory`" can be emitted by any one of the 55 locations where `ReportOutOfMemory` is invoked. Second, *interleaving uncertainties*. Even if the failure location

```
InitState(...){                          FreeState(...){
  // executed by Thread1                   //executed by Thread2
  st->table = New(st); // a1               ...
  ...                                      Destroy(st->table);
  if (!st->table) { // a2                  st->table = NULL; // a3
    ReportOutOfMemory(); // F              ...
    return JS_FALSE;                     }
  }
}

ReportOutOfMemory(){
  error("out of memory");
}
```

Figure 4: A concurrency bug in Mozilla JavaScript Engine.

is resolved, developers will probably mistakenly attribute the failure to memory-consumption problems in $a_1$, based on the control flow of `InitState`. Traditional log-enhancing techniques [44] provide little help here: developers cannot easily infer interleavings based on variable values logged at failure-logging site $F$, which is exactly why concurrency-bug failures are difficult to diagnose.

To successfully diagnose this failure, developers need at least two pieces of information: (1) "`out of memory`" is reported at $F$; (2) `st->table` is overwritten by another thread after the assignment at $a_1$ and before the checking at $a_2$. Both pieces can be collected from execution shortly before the failure. Unfortunately, existing production-run failure-diagnosis techniques cannot deterministically provide these two pieces of information with low overhead.

## 4. Maintaining Short-term Memory

In this section, we identify and design hardware facilities that maintain short-term memory of program execution to support production-run failure diagnosis.

Our main task is to identify the right types of information to keep in the short-term memory. There is a wide variety of runtime information accessible to the hardware, such as the program counter of every executed instruction and the value stored in every register. We cannot record all these hardware events due to hardware cost and performance concerns. Therefore, we need to identify events that are most useful for failure diagnosis to keep in the short-term memory.

### 4.1 LBR for sequential-bug failure diagnosis

The outcome of conditional branches in software is among the most useful information for failure diagnosis. It can address the control-flow uncertainties discussed in Section 3, explicitly presenting the execution path leading to the failure. In addition, previous work has shown that many sequential-bug failures are exactly caused by control-flow problems [23, 35].

Fortunately, the hardware facility that maintains the short-term memory of this information already exists in the form of Last Branch Record (LBR). There are different types of branches that could be recorded in LBR. Our system configures LBR to record three types of branches that can help resolve the outcomes of conditional branches in user-level programs, as shown in Table 1.

### 4.2 LCR for concurrency-bug failure diagnosis

#### 4.2.1 LCR design

Previous work [2] has found coherence events maintained by existing hardware performance counters, which are discussed in Section 2.2, useful in diagnosing concurrency-bug failures. Inspired by that, we propose a hardware extension that maintains the short-term memory of coherence events. We call it Last Cache-coherence Record, short as LCR.

Assuming a MESI cache-coherence protocol, LCR includes the following components on chip:

1. A special hardware register that configures which type of coherence events to record. The supported events are *exactly* those that can already be counted by existing hardware performance counters – load or store instructions that observe certain cache-coherence states right before the cache access, as discussed in Section 2.2. Detailed configuration options follow those that are provided by existing hardware for performance counter registers, as also discussed in Section 2.2. For example, the cache-coherence state can be any combination of modified state, exclusive state, shared state, and invalid state; this register can be configured to filter out kernel-level instructions or user-level instructions from LCR.
2. $K$ pairs of special hardware registers per core that record the latest $K$ LCR events. Each pair records the instruction counter and the specific cache-coherence state observed by that instruction[2]. By default, we set $K$ to be 16, resembling the setting of LBR on Nehalem processors.
3. Extra circuits that keep updating LCR on each core. After the retirement of L1 data-cache access instructions, the program counter of the instruction and the cache-coherence state observed by this instruction will be recorded in LCR, if the state matches the configuration.

We expect LCR to be a simple extension on machines that already support hardware cache-coherence performance events and LBR, such as Intel machines discussed in Section 2.2. LCR essentially requires extending these machines from being able to count cache-coherence events to being able to record while counting, just like building LBR in machines that can count branch-taken events.

It is difficult to accurately estimate the overhead incurred by LCR without building it in real hardware. We expect the overhead to be low for two reasons. (1) Counting cache-coherence events incurs no perceivable overhead on commodity machines [2, 14]. (2) Using LBR incurs negligible overhead on commodity machines, as shown in Section 8.

[2] Memory addresses are not recorded.

| Bug Type | FPE | Does FPE exist in failure thread? | Example | |
|---|---|---|---|---|
| RWR Atomicity Violation | Invalid Read | Almost Always | /*Thread 1*/<br>if(ptr) //$a_1$<br>puts(ptr); //$a_2$,F | /*Thread 2*/<br>ptr=NULL; //$a_3$ |
| RWW Atomicity Violation | Invalid Write | Often | /*Thread 1*/<br>tmp=cnt+deposit1; //$a_1$<br>cnt=tmp; //$a_2$<br>printf("Balance=%d",cnt); //F | /*Thread 2*/<br>tmp=cnt+deposit2;<br>cnt=tmp; //$a_3$ |
| WWR Atomicity Violation | Invalid Read | Almost Always | Figure 4 | |
| WRW Atomicity Violation | Invalid Read | Sometimes | /*Thread 1*/<br>log=CLOSE; //$a_1$<br>log=OPEN; //$a_2$ | /*Thread 2*/<br>if(log!=OPEN) //$a_3$<br>{//output failure} //F |
| Read-too-early Order Violation | Exclusive Read | Often | Figure 5 | |
| Read-too-late Order Violation | Invalid Read | Often | Figure 6 | |

Table 3: The failure predicting events (FPE) of concurrency bugs ( Invalid and Exclusive refer to the cache-coherence state observed by a load or store right before it accesses L1 data-cache; F denotes the location of failure.)

Since our LCR design is built upon existing hardware cache-coherence performance events, it will share some constraints of existing hardware performance counters. For example, the LCRs on different cores are separately maintained and accessed, just like how existing performance counters work. When we profile LCR from a particular thread in a multi-threaded program, only the LCR maintained by the core that is currently running this thread will be accessed. Extending LCR to access multiple cores' information simultaneously would require non-trivial change to existing hardware. As another example, on SMT machines, multiple hardware threads in one core currently share one LBR. We expect a similar design for LCR. This will shorten the execution history recorded for each thread.

### 4.2.2 How useful is LCR?

Is LCR helpful in diagnosing concurrency-bug failures? To some extent, the answer is always "yes", because LCR can help developers understand the thread interaction right before failures.

Can LCR directly point out the failure root cause? It depends on whether LCR contains a coherence event that is failure predicting and is from the failure thread. An event is considered *failure predicting*, if it mostly occurs during failure runs and is related to the failure root cause [2, 18, 23]. A *failure thread* is the thread where the failure first occurs, such as the thread that encounters a segmentation fault, violates an assertion, and so on. Coherence events that occur outside the failure thread cannot be obtained when we access LCR at the failure site.

The above question is partly answered by our previous work [2], which shows that failure predicting coherence events exist for all common types of concurrency bugs. The remaining question is whether such events occur in failure threads or not. In the following, we discuss this issue for two most common types of concurrency bugs: single-variable atomicity violations and order violations [25].

```
/* Thread1 (failure thread)*/              /*Thread2*/
printf("End at %f", Gend);//B1             //Gend uninitialized
printf("Takes %f",Gend - Init);//B2        //until here
                                           Gend=time();//A
```

Figure 5: A read-too-early order violation in FFT. Thread 2 should initialize `Gend` before thread 1 accesses it.

***Single-variable atomicity violations*** occur when two consecutive memory accesses from one thread, denoted as $a_1$ and $a_2$, are unserializably interleaved by an access, denoted as $a_3$, from another thread. All four types of single-variable atomicity violations are demonstrated in Table 3. Our previous work [2] discovered that failure predicting events exist at $a_2$ for all these atomicity violations[3]. Therefore, we will focus on discussing whether $a_2$ is in the failure thread below.

$a_2$ almost always exists in the failure thread for RWR and WWR atomicity violations, as the incorrect value read by $a_2$ will soon lead to failure in the same thread as $a_2$, such as a segmentation fault inside `puts` (the RWR example in Table 3) and the out-of-memory failure in Figure 4. Here, we leverage observations from previous empirical studies [47, 48], which show that concurrency-bug failures almost always occur in the thread that first reads an incorrect value from a shared variable.

$a_2$ often exists in the failure thread for RWW atomicity violations — after $a_2$ writes an incorrect value, the thread performing $a_2$ will very likely use this incorrect value which will lead to failure, as shown in the example in Table 3.

For WRW atomicity violations, failures usually occur in the thread containing $a_3$, instead of $a_2$, as shown in Table 3. Unfortunately, $a_3$ is not always a failure predicting event, unless it is preceded by another access to the same variable.

[3] The rationale is that $a_2$ would encounter different cache-coherence states during failure runs and success runs, due to the impact of $a_3$. For example, the invalid state of `st->table` encountered by `if(!st->table)` in Figure 4 is related to the failure root cause and can predict the failure.

```
/*Thread 1*/          /*Thread 2 (failure thread)*/
                      pthread_mutex_lock(mutex); // B1
mutex = NULL; // A    ...
                      pthread_mutex_unlock(mutex); // B2
                      ...
                      pthread_mutex_lock(mutex); // B3
```

Figure 6: A read-too-late order violation in PBZIP2. Thread 2 should use `mutex` before thread 1 destroys it.

***Order violations*** occur when the expected order between two operations from two threads is flipped. The two most common types of order violations occur either when a read instruction executes too early and hence accesses an uninitialized value (Figure 5) or when a read instruction executes too late and hence accesses a stale value (Figure 6). Previous work [2] has shown that the coherence event at the read instruction is often a failure predicting event. For the example shown in Figure 5, $B_2$ would encounter an exclusive state only during failure runs, when `Gend` is uninitialized. For the example shown in Figure 6, $B_3$ rarely encounters an invalid state during success runs, but always encounters an invalid state during failure runs when $B_3$ executes after the NULL-assignment from another thread.

The above failure predicting events do exist in failure threads, as the incorrect values returned by the read instructions quickly lead to failures, such as wrong outputs (Figure 5) and crashes (Figure 6).

In summary, LCR has a good chance of directly pointing out the root cause of almost all common types of concurrency-bug failures. Even if the root cause cannot be directly pointed out, the thread interaction information provided by LCR is still helpful.

***LCR configuration*** For extensibility and generality, we have designed LCR to record a wide variety of coherence events. Following the discussion in Table 3, the following two configurations are most useful for diagnosing user-level concurrency-bug failures.

The first configuration records invalid loads, invalid stores, and exclusive loads. These events cover all the different types of failure-predicting events for common concurrency bugs, as shown by Table 3. However, this configuration may waste the LCR space with stack accesses that are often exclusive loads.

A more space-saving configuration is to replace exclusive loads with shared loads, using the latter to replace the former in diagnosing read-too-early order violations. For instance, consider the bug shown in Figure 5. During success runs, $B_2$ will always encounter a shared state. Therefore, failures are highly correlated with $B_2$ not encountering a shared state. This configuration is more LCR space-saving than the first one, but it may not be as straightforward as the first configuration for developers to reason about.

```
fd = open("/dev/lbrdriver", O_RDWR);
ioctl(fd, DRIVER_CLEAN_LBR); // Reset LBR entries
ioctl(fd, DRIVER_CONFIG_LBR); // Configure filtering
ioctl(fd, DRIVER_ENABLE_LBR); // Enable LBR recording
...
ioctl(fd, DRIVER_DISABLE_LBR); // Disable LBR recording
ioctl(fd, DRIVER_PROFILE_LBR); // Profile LBR
error(); // Failure-logging function
```

Figure 7: Interface exported by our LBR kernel module.

### 4.3 Implementation details

***Accessing LBR*** This includes three steps. First, we configure which types of branches to record through the special register LBR_SELECT, as shown in Table 1. Second, we enable LBR through the IA32_DEBUGCTL register. Finally, the records in LBR can be accessed through registers BRANCH_0_FROM_IP through BRANCH_16_FROM_IP, where BRANCH_n_FROM_IP is the linear address of the $n^{th}$ branch instruction. Since the above registers cannot be accessed at user level, we implemented a Linux kernel module to support accesses from user level, mainly using kernel wrapper functions that execute `rdmsr` and `wrmsr` assembly instructions. The interface is shown in Figure 7.

***Minimizing LBR pollution*** As mentioned earlier, LBR has a limited capacity — 16 branch entries in Nehalem processors. To minimize the LBR pollution by branches that are irrelevant to user-level software failures, we use the following methods.

First, as discussed in Section 4.1, we configure LBR to filter out kernel level branches.

Second, we always disable LBR right before we read LBR. Our LBR-disabling code does not contain any user-level branches. Consequently, LBR will not be polluted by code executed to access it.

Finally, we remove pollution from common library functions through a collection of wrapper functions. Each wrapper function disables LBR on entry, invokes the original library function, and finally enables LBR on exit. We will refer to this method as LBR *toggling*. We wrote wrappers for glibc functions and application-specific error-reporting functions. For example, for MySQL, we wrote wrappers for three MySQL-specific functions: `_db_doprnt`, `my_error`, and `sql_print_error`. Each wrapper function contains fewer than 15 lines of code and follows the same routine.

***LCR simulation*** We expect that LCR will be added into the hardware performance monitoring unit in the future and will be accessed in a similar way as we access LBR. We expect that the pollution issue will be similarly solved by toggling around common library functions, filtering out kernel-level instructions, and disabling LCR before profiling.

We implement a LCR simulator using PIN binary-instrumentation infrastructure [27]. Our LCR simulator includes two parts. The first part is a simulated L1-cache with MESI coherence protocol, implemented by instrumenting every memory instruction in the user program and libraries. The second part simulates LCR configuration, disable, enable, and profiling functions. We implement LCR as a per-thread circular buffer with a configurable size. Once enabled, every thread's circular buffer gets filled by program counters and coherence states of instructions that are executed by the specific thread and satisfy the LCR configuration Once disabled, every thread's circular buffer is frozen. When a thread executes the profiling function, that thread's circular buffer content is retrieved. Finally, we simulate the pollution effect of these four functions by adding dummy entries into the corresponding circular buffer. Specifically, two user-level exclusive reads will be introduced by the `ioctl` call that enables LCR; two user-level exclusive reads and one user-level shared read will be introduced by the `ioctl` call that disables LCR.

Our simulation does not simulate OS events, such as exceptions and context switches. However, we believe it is accurate enough to provide a solid evaluation of LCR.

## 5. Using Short-term Memory

### 5.1 Log enhancement

The basic way of using LBR and LCR is to enhance failure logging, which we will refer to as LBRLOG and LCRLOG respectively. Developers can use the LBR/LCR record collected at a failure site to reconstruct the control flow and interleaving right before the failure. They may also find failure predicting events from the LBR/LCR record.

To ease the adoption and evaluation of LBRLOG and LCRLOG, we implemented a source-to-source code transformer to automatically enhance a program's failure logging. The transformation includes several steps:

(1) Changing the program compilation configuration to use our wrappers for common library functions (Section 4.3).

(2) Inserting LBR/LCR configuration and enabling code at the entry of `main` function, as shown in Figure 7.

(3) Inserting LBR/LCR profiling code right before every existing failure-logging function in the program, as shown in Figure 7. Currently, our implementation takes a developer configurable list of application-specific failure-logging functions, such as `ap_log_error` in Httpd and `error` in GNU core utilities software.

(4) Registering a custom segmentation-fault signal handler to profile LBR/LCR.

### 5.2 Automatic failure diagnosis

A more sophisticated way of using LBR/LCR is to automatically locate failure predicting events based on the LBR/LCR content collected from production runs. To achieve this goal, we have designed LBRA and LCRA.

LBRA/LCRA follows the existing statistical fault localization approach [22, 23]. It compares information collected from failure runs (i.e., failure-run profiles) with information

```
if (expr)
{
  error(...);
}
```

(a) Original code

```
tmp = expr;
LBR_LCR_PROFILE(); // success logging site
if (tmp)
{
  LBR_LCR_PROFILE(); // failure logging site
  error(...);
}
```

(b) Transformed code

Figure 8: The logging sites for success and failure profiles.

collected from success runs (i.e., success-run profiles) to figure out events that are most correlated with failure runs. We will go through the design of these three components below:

1. What is the failure-run profile and how to collect it?
2. What is the success-run profile and how to collect it?
3. How to make the comparison?

***Failure-run profile*** A good failure-run profile should have a high chance to contain failure-predicting events. In our system, we use the content of LBR and LCR collected by LBRLOG and LCRLOG as the failure-run profile. Clearly, the profile would contain exactly one LBR/LCR record for each run where a fail-stop failure occurs. For example, when the `sort` bug shown in Figure 3 manifests, a segmentation fault would occur at location $F$. The LBR/LCR record collected inside that segmentation fault handler would become the failure run profile.

***Success-run profile*** LBRLOG and LCRLOG do not profile LBR and LCR at all during success runs. Therefore, we need to design success-run profiling separately from LBRLOG and LCRLOG.

Intuitively, we expect success-run profiles to contain LBR/LCR record collected nearby the failure sites, so that success-run profiles and failure-run profiles are comparable.

Guided by this intuition, we define the following program locations as *success logging sites*: (1) If a segmentation fault can be triggered by instruction $i$, the program location right after $i$ is a success logging site; (2) If a failure logging function is located at $F$, a success logging site is right before where the program jumps to the basic block containing $F$, as shown in Figure 8.

Collecting LBR/LCR record at the success logging sites defined above will naturally provide success-run profiles that are comparable with failure-run profiles. In addition, it also naturally excludes irrelevant success runs from the failure diagnosis process — LBR/LCR will not be profiled during runs that do not execute the code around the failure site.

We have implemented two schemes to collect LBR/LCR at the success logging sites. The *proactive* scheme inserts LBR/LCR profiling code at every success logging site corresponding to every failure logging site before software release. The *reactive* scheme waits until a failure occurs at a particular location $F$, and then inserts LBR/LCR-profiling code at the success logging site corresponding to $F$. This change can be conducted either on the end users' machines through dynamic binary transformation [5] or at the development site. In the latter case, the changes will be propagated to the end users in the form of code patches.

These two schemes each have their own strengths. The proactive scheme does not require code redistribution, but incurs higher run-time overhead due to more frequent LBR/LCR profiling. In addition, it cannot help diagnose failures that manifest at unexpected locations, which is always the case for segmentation faults. The reactive scheme has better performance. However, it needs software updates to collect success-run profiles, which may take time. Of course, since failure runs are much rarer than success runs, delays in collecting success-run profiles rarely lead to longer diagnosis latency.

***How to compare?*** Each success/failure run profile is a set of events recorded in LBR and LCR. We want to identify the event whose occurrence can best predict the failure.

Similar to previous work on statistical debugging [2, 23], we identify the best failure-predicting event based on the expected prediction *precision* and *recall* of the events. Specifically, in our context, prediction *precision* measures how many runs indeed fail among those that are predicted to fail by the event. It can be calculated by $\frac{|F\&e|}{|e|}$, where $|e|$ denotes the number of runs where $e$ is recorded in the profile and $|F\&e|$ denotes the number of failure runs that contain $e$ in their profiles. Prediction *recall* measures how many runs are predicted to fail by the event among those that indeed fail. It can be calculated by $\frac{|F\&e|}{|F|}$, where $|F|$ denotes the number of failure runs. We rank all events based on the harmonic mean of the expected prediction precision and recall, and identify the highest ranked event as the best failure-predicting event.

### 5.3 Discussion

***Failure sites*** In our current implementation, LBRLOG and LCRLOG treat existing failure-logging functions and segmentation-fault handler as failure sites. Consequently, if software fails by silently corrupting data, LBR and LCR will not be collected in a timely manner and hence may not help the diagnosis. Fortunately, the problem of identifying the right places to insert log functions has been largely addressed by recent work [45].

***Multiple failures*** It is very natural for large software to encounter failures caused by different bugs during production runs. The existence of multiple failures will not affect our system. From each failure-run profile, we can identify the location of the failure site and hence separately handle failures that occur at different program locations. Very rarely, different root causes may lead to failures at the same location, such as the example shown in Figure 4. In this case, we will see that even the best failure predicting event does not appear in every failure run. Fortunately, this rarely affects the relative ranking among events, and our system can still identify the best failure predicting events.

***Log enhancement*** Traditional failure logging either dumps core images or call stacks, or records the values of selected program variables. LBR/LCR has its unique advantages and can well complement these traditional approaches.

In terms of preserving privacy, LBR/LCR is among the best, because it does not directly collect any variable values.

In terms of failure diagnosis capability, LCR provides interleaving related information that is difficult to obtain from traditional approaches. LBR can resolve uncertain control flows that cannot be inferred by traditional approaches. Note that, even the recently proposed LogEnhancer [44] can have difficulty in resolving control flows in sibling functions (i.e. functions that are not in the call-stack at the failure site). Of course, LBR and LCR content is limited to the execution shortly before the failure. In addition, coredumps and logging variables can provide concrete variable value information that may be unavailable from LBR/LCR.

In terms of logging latency, logging LBR/LCR is much faster than dumping cores and logging call-stacks. In our evaluation, logging LBR/LCR takes less than 20 $\mu s$; dumping core can easily take more than 200 ms; and recording the call stack takes about 200 $\mu s$. If developers want to conduct logging at locations beyond failure sites, logging LBR/LCR is more suitable than dumping cores or call-stacks.

In terms of run-time performance, LBR/LCR profiling incurs negligible overhead if toggling is disabled. Enabling toggling around library functions could cause perceivable overhead for applications that frequently invoke library functions, which will be evaluated in Section 7.

Finally, logging LBR/LCR is more generic than logging selected variables. At different program locations, different variables need to be selected to represent the most important program states for failure diagnosis. When software fails at an unexpected location, such as during a segmentation fault, variable logging usually cannot be applied.

***Automated failure diagnosis*** The cooperative bug isolation (CBI) approach, including CBI [22, 23], CCI [18], and PBI [2], are the state of the art production-run failure diagnosis techniques. This approach first evaluates certain predicates, such as whether a branch is taken, at randomly sampled locations. It then performs statistical analysis on the data collected from many success and failure runs to identify predicates that strongly correlate with failures. These predicates are referred to as *failure predictors*. To conduct random sampling, CBI and CCI use source-code instrumentation, while PBI leverages hardware performance counters.

LBRA/LCRA has much shorter diagnosis latency than the CBI approach. Suppose $e$ needs to occur in a couple of failure-run profiles to be identified as a high-confidence failure predictor. To identify $e$, LBRA/LCRA needs a failure to occur for a couple of times. The CBI approach needs a failure to occur for hundreds of times under their default sampling rate (1 out of 100). This difference, hundreds of failure occurrences, could mean a long time in practice, because bugs that slip into fields often manifest rarely.

In terms of run-time performance, LBRA/LCRA is better than CBI/CCI and is comparable with PBI. The advantage of LBRA/LCRA mainly comes from two sources. First, LBRA/LCRA collects failure-run profile only at one location, the failure-logging site. Instead, the CBI approach periodically evaluates predicates throughout the execution. Second, CBI and CCI pay extra cost to enable their random sampling. This overhead is often more than 30% for CPU-intensive applications for CBI [3] and more than 800% for CCI [2].

In terms of diagnosis capability, LBRA/LCRA is comparable with PBI and CCI when failures have reasonably short propagation distances, which is true for most failures [12, 29, 34, 48]. CBI is better than LBR-tools for sequential-bug failures whose root causes are not related to branches.

Finally, LBRA and LCRA have a much smaller impact on the executable-file size than CBI and CCI, leaving a much smaller footprint on cache and memory.

***Limitations*** The accuracy of our LBR/LCR based tools could be slightly affected by certain hardware issues. Hardware tracks the cache-coherence states at cache-line granularity, instead of variable granularity. This could lead to false sharing problems. Invalid cache states could be caused by both cache eviction and remote write accesses. This could cause one coherence event to appear in both success runs and failure runs. Of course, since the ranking model discussed in Section 5.2 naturally filters out random noises, we expect the diagnosis results to be rarely affected by these issues.

## 6. Methodology

We conduct all the experiments on an Intel Core i7 machine with 4 physical cores running Linux 3.5 kernel. We separately evaluate LBR and LCR related tools. LBR-related experiments are conducted directly on the real machine; LCR-related experiments are conducted on our PIN-based simulator.

We evaluate the failure-diagnosis capability and runtime performance of LBRLOG and LBRA using 20 real-world sequential-bug failures. We include in our benchmarks all the 10 failures from LogEnhancer [44] that we can reproduce. We also randomly pick 5 failures from 13 reproducible crash failures from Errlog [45]. Finally, since the above failures are all from C applications, we randomly selected 5 reproducible bugs from the bug database of open-source C++ applications Cppcheck and PBZIP.

To measure performance, we use workloads designed by the software developers that represent the common scenarios in production runs and do not lead to failures. The performance overheads reported are the mean of 10 measurements. To evaluate failure-diagnosis capability, we use the bug triggering inputs used by LogEnhancer, Errlog, and the original bug reports. For all these benchmarks, we conduct a head-to-head quantitative comparison between LBRA and CBI. Further, we evaluate how LBRLOG can help resolve control-flow uncertainties using all the 6945 logging points in 13 open-source applications. Detailed information about these benchmarks along with the main logging functions instrumented by LBRLOG is shown in Tables 4 and 5.

We evaluate the failure-diagnosis capability of our LCR proposal using all the 11 real-world concurrency-bug failures used in PBI [2] and CCI [18], following their experiment settings. Our LCR simulator simulates each core's L1 data-cache as a 2-way associative cache with a block size of 64 Bytes and a total size of 64 KB.

We evaluate different configurations of our LBR/LCR tools. By default, we enable toggling in all tools.

| Program | Version | KLOC | Root Cause | Failure Symptom | Log Points |
|---|---|---|---|---|---|
| Sequential-Bug Failures | | | | | |
| Apache 1 | 2.0.43 | 273 | config. | error message | 2534 |
| Apache 2 | 2.2.3 | 311 | semantic | error message | 2511 |
| Apache 3 | 2.2.9 | 333 | semantic | error message | 2515 |
| cp | 4.5.8 | 1.2 | semantic | error message | 108 |
| Cppcheck 1 | 1.58 | 138 | memory | crash | 304 |
| Cppcheck 2 | 1.56 | 131 | memory | crash | 284 |
| Cppcheck 3 | 1.52 | 118 | memory | crash | 225 |
| Lighttpd | 1.4.16 | 55 | config. | error message | 857 |
| ln | 4.5.1 | 0.7 | semantic | error message | 29 |
| mv | 6.8 | 4.1 | semantic | error message | 46 |
| paste | 6.10 | 0.5 | memory | hang | 23 |
| PBZIP1 | 1.1.5 | 5.7 | semantic | error message | 305 |
| PBZIP2 | 1.1.0 | 4.6 | memory | crash | 269 |
| rm | 4.5.4 | 1.3 | semantic | error message | 31 |
| sort | 7.2 | 3.6 | memory | crash | 36 |
| Squid1 | 2.5.S5 | 120 | semantic | error message | 2427 |
| Squid2 | 2.3.S4 | 102 | memory | crash | 2096 |
| tac | 6.11 | 0.7 | memory | crash | 21 |
| tar 1 | 1.22 | 82 | semantic | error message | 243 |
| tar 2 | 1.19 | 76 | semantic | error message | 188 |
| Concurrency-Bug Failures | | | | | |
| Apache 4 | 2.0.50 | 263 | A.V. | crash | 2412 |
| Apache 5 | 2.2.9 | 333 | A.V. | corrupted log | 2515 |
| Cherokee | 0.98.0 | 85 | A.V. | corrupted log | 184 |
| FFT | 2.0 | 1.3 | O.V. | wrong output | 59 |
| LU | 2.0 | 1.2 | O.V. | wrong output | 45 |
| Mozilla-JS1 | 1.5 | 107 | A.V. | crash | 343 |
| Mozilla-JS2 | 1.5 | 107 | A.V. | wrong output | 343 |
| Mozilla-JS3 | 1.5 | 107 | A.V. | error message | 343 |
| MySQL1 | 4.0.18 | 658 | A.V. | crash | 1585 |
| MySQL2 | 4.0.12 | 639 | A.V. | wrong output | 1523 |
| PBZIP3 | 0.9.4 | 2.1 | O.V. | crash | 163 |

Table 4: Features of real-world failures evaluated.

## 7. Experimental Results

### 7.1 LBRLOG evaluation

Our evaluation aims to answer the following questions:

1. Is the LBR record profiled by LBRLOG useful in resolving control-flow uncertainties?

| Application | Useful br. ratio | #LogSites | Main Log Fun. |
|---|---|---|---|
| Apache | 0.86 | 2515 | ap_log_error |
| cp | 0.77 | 108 | error |
| cppcheck | 0.98 | 304 | reportError |
| lighttpd | 0.84 | 857 | log_error_write |
| ln | 0.81 | 29 | error |
| mv | 0.74 | 46 | error |
| paste | 0.86 | 23 | error |
| pbzip | 0.81 | 305 | fprintf |
| rm | 0.79 | 31 | error |
| sort | 0.91 | 36 | error |
| Squid | 0.88 | 2427 | debug |
| tac | 0.89 | 21 | error |
| tar | 0.84 | 243 | open_fatal |

Table 5: Resolution of control-flow uncertainties by LBRLOG.

2. Is the LBR record profiled by LBRLOG useful in locating failure root causes?
3. Is the runtime performance of LBRLOG suitable for production-run deployment?

### 7.1.1 Resolving uncertain control flows

For each logging site $l$, a branch record in LBR is considered *useful* if the taken-ness of this branch cannot be inferred based on the execution of $l$ through static control flow analysis. We compute the ratio of useful branches in LBR record entries collected at every failure-logging site in an application. We refer to this ratio as *useful branch ratio*. Since it is impractical to design inputs to exercise all the logging sites, we implement an LLVM-based analyzer to calculate this ratio. Specifically, given a logging site, the analyzer explores backwards along all possible paths until each path contains 16 branches that could fill LBR and checks which branches are useful. The useful branch ratio shown in Table 5 is averaged across all logging sites in the application.

As shown in Table 5, the average useful branch ratio ranges from 0.74 to 0.98 for all the 6945 logging points across 13 applications. This shows that LBR provides a generic and useful mechanism to resolve control-flow uncertainties.

### 7.1.2 Failure diagnostic capability

To measure the failure-diagnosis capability of LBRLOG, we compare the branches captured by LBRLOG with the patches. We consider LBRLOG to be very helpful in locating the failure root cause, if the patch mainly changes one of the branches recorded by LBRLOG, denoted as ✓in Table 6. We will refer to this branch changed by the patch as *root-cause branch*. We consider LBRLOG to be helpful, if the patch mainly changes the computation or usage of a condition variable that is involved in one of the branches recorded by LBRLOG, denoted as ✓* in Table 6.

```
avoid_trashing_input (...)
- while (i + num_merged < nfiles) // A
+ do {
    ...
+ } while (i < nfiles);
```

(a) sort patch

```
int main (int argc, char **argv)
- if (n_files == 1)
+ if (!target_directory_specified && n_files == 1)
    ...
  if (target_directory_specified) // B
```

(b) ln patch

Figure 9: Branches captured by LBRLOG and patches.

As shown in Table 6, LBRLOG is very helpful for diagnosing 16 out of 20 failures. These 16 failures are caused by different types of software bugs: 8 by semantic bugs, 6 by memory bugs, and 2 by configuration errors. As an example, the simplified patch for the `sort` bug from Section 3.1 is shown in Figure 9a. The root cause branch $A$ is recorded as the $3^{rd}$ latest entry in LBR collected by LBRLOG.

LBRLOG fails to contain the root-cause branch, but is still helpful in diagnosing the remaining 4 failures. For example, the `ln` bug has a long error propagation distance. The root-cause branch would have been captured, if LBR had 4 more entries. LBRLOG captures the branch $B$ that is related to the root cause as shown in Figure 9b.

Table 6 also shows that most root-cause branches are located within the top 8 entries in LBR. This result validates the heuristic that most software bugs have short error propagation distances, and indicates that even on machines with smaller LBR, LBRLOG is still very useful.

Finally, we measure the distance between the LBR branches and the patch, comparing it with the distance between the failure site and the patch. In general, the former is much shorter than the latter. The patches are within 5 lines of code from some LBR branches in 14 out of 20 cases, while only 2 failure sites are within 5 lines of code from the patches. For 13 failures, some LBR branches are more than 30 lines of code closer to the patches than the failure sites, and all these branches are *useful* LBR records that cannot be inferred by static control-flow analysis. This further shows that LBRLOG can help diagnose failures and design patches.

### 7.1.3 Performance

As shown in Table 6, LBRLOG incurs at most 2.28% runtime overhead for all the benchmarks, which is suitable for production-run deployment.

The overhead mainly comes from toggling around library functions. Without toggling, the overhead is at most 0.23% across all benchmarks. This performance improvement comes at the expense of diagnosis capability. As shown

| App. | Locate Root Cause | | | | Patch distance (LoC) | | Overhead (%) | | | | |
|---|---|---|---|---|---|---|---|---|---|---|---|
| | LBRLOG w/ tog. | LBRLOG w/o tog. | LBRA | CBI | failure site | LBR | LBRLOG w/ tog. | LBRLOG w/o tog. | LBRA reactive | LBRA proactive | CBI |
| Apache1 | ✓ 3 | ✓ 3 | ✓ 1 | ✓ 2 | $\infty$ | **3** | 0.31 | 0.11 | 0.39 | 3.87 | 3.01 |
| Apache2 | ✓ 2* | ✓ 2* | ✓ 2* | - | $\infty$ | 475 | 0.42 | 0.09 | 0.43 | 4.61 | 5.48 |
| Apache3 | ✓ 2 | ✓ 2 | ✓ 1 | ✓ 1 | **1** | **1** | 0.33 | 0.17 | 0.52 | 3.43 | 2.70 |
| cp | ✓ 2 | - | ✓ 1 | ✓ 1 | 17 | 15 | 1.77 | 0.23 | 2.13 | 3.61 | 25.90 |
| Cppcheck1 | ✓ 5* | ✓ 5* | ✓ 1* | N/A | $\infty$ | $\infty$ | 2.04 | 0.04 | 2.73 | 5.61 | N/A |
| Cppcheck2 | ✓ 3 | ✓ 3 | ✓ 1 | N/A | $\infty$ | **2** | 0.24 | 0.02 | 0.29 | 2.09 | N/A |
| Cppcheck3 | ✓ 6 | ✓ 6 | ✓ 1 | N/A | $\infty$ | 10 | 1.16 | 0.06 | 1.39 | 4.68 | N/A |
| Lighttpd | ✓ 4 | ✓ 4 | ✓ 1 | - | **0** | **1** | 0.65 | 0.11 | 0.73 | 2.33 | 6.34 |
| ln | ✓ 13* | - | ✓ 1* | ✓ 1 | 254 | 33 | 1.88 | 0.18 | 1.95 | 4.69 | 22.48 |
| mv | ✓ 12 | ✓ 14 | ✓ 1 | ✓ 2 | 309 | **0** | 1.79 | 0.11 | 2.84 | 5.70 | 15.55 |
| paste | ✓ 6 | - | ✓ 1 | ✓ 1 | 35 | **3** | 1.31 | 0.08 | 1.78 | 2.50 | 14.32 |
| PBZIP1 | ✓ 4 | - | ✓ 1 | N/A | 41 | **1** | 0.29 | 0.07 | 0.34 | 5.73 | N/A |
| PBZIP2 | ✓ 1 | ✓ 1 | ✓ 1 | N/A | 12 | **1** | 0.79 | 0.04 | 0.91 | 4.62 | N/A |
| rm | ✓ 5 | ✓ 5 | ✓ 1 | ✓ 2 | 31 | **0** | 2.28 | 0.21 | 2.38 | 6.29 | 24.77 |
| sort | ✓ 3 | ✓ 5 | ✓ 1 | ✓ 1 | $\infty$ | **4** | 0.44 | 0.19 | 0.74 | 4.16 | 43.45 |
| Squid1 | ✓ 2 | ✓ 2 | ✓ 1 | - | 123 | **2** | 1.26 | 0.05 | 1.45 | 2.79 | 6.29 |
| Squid2 | ✓ 10 | ✓ 10 | ✓ 1 | ✓ 1 | 59 | **1** | 2.19 | 0.03 | 2.42 | 3.62 | 7.49 |
| tac | ✓ 3* | ✓ 3* | ✓ 1* | ✓ 3* | $\infty$ | $\infty$ | 2.13 | 0.06 | 2.57 | 2.82 | 26.43 |
| tar1 | ✓ 4 | ✓ 4 | ✓ 1 | ✓ 1 | $\infty$ | **2** | 0.52 | 0.09 | 0.73 | 3.10 | 14.30 |
| tar2 | ✓ 2 | - | ✓ 1 | ✓ 2 | 24 | **0** | 0.40 | 0.11 | 0.45 | 2.63 | 9.91 |

Table 6: Results of LBRLOG and LBRA. (The number $n$ after ✓ indicates the $n$-th latest LBR entry returned by LBRLOG or the $n$-th top predictor identified by LBRA/CBI; *: root-cause branch is missed, but a branch related to the root cause is identified; "-": no branches related to the root cause are identified; N/A: CBI does not work for C++ applications; $\infty$: in different files.)

in Table 6, without toggling, LBRLOG will fail to locate any branch that is related to the patch in 5 cases.

Overall, LBRLOG incurs small overheads across a wide range of applications and is suitable for production-run deployment. We can turn off toggling to satisfy even higher performance requirements.

### 7.2 LBRA evaluation

Our evaluation of LBRA targets the following questions:

1. Is LBRA able to automatically locate root-cause branches?
2. Is the performance of LBRA (reactive and proactive schemes) suitable for production-run deployment?
3. Can LBRA complement CBI, the state-of-the-art production-run failure diagnosis system?

Our experiments configure CBI using its default settings: 1/100 sampling rate; 1000 success runs and 1000 failure runs; with only branch predicates enabled. Our experiments for LBRA only use 10 success runs and 10 failure runs.

LBRA successfully and automatically locates *all* the 16 root-cause branches contained in LBR as the top 1 failure predictors. It identifies root-cause related branches as top predictors for all the 20 failures. In comparison, CBI identifies root-cause branches as top predictors for 11 out of 15 C-program failures. CBI fails to report any root-cause related branches in 3 cases, where its random sampling missed the relevant predicates too many times.

The above diagnosis results are achieved with LBRA analyzing much fewer failure runs than CBI (10 vs. 1000). When we applied CBI to 500, instead of 1000, failure-run profiles, CBI failed to identify any useful failure predictors for 10 out of 15 C-program failures. This difference would be crucial for software that is not deployed on millions of machines or failures that do not occur very frequently.

As shown in Table 6, the run-time overhead of LBRA (reactive mode) is always less than 3%, well suitable for production-run deployment. The overhead of LBRA in proactive mode is slightly larger, ranging between 2.09% and 6.29%. It is a good choice for software where updates are infrequent or very expensive. CBI incurs an average overhead of 15.23%, much larger than LBRA, mainly due to the instrumentation done by CBI to performs sampling.

The results show that LBRA well complements CBI.

### 7.3 LCR evaluation

Our evaluation tries to answer the following questions:

1. Can LCRLOG help diagnose concurrency-bug failures?
2. Can LCRA automatically locate the root causes of concurrency-bug failures?
3. Can LCR complement PBI and CCI, the state-of-the-art production-run concurrency-bug failure diagnosis tools?

**LCRLOG** We consider LCRLOG to directly locate the failure root cause, if the LCR profiled by it contains the failure-predicting coherence event (defined in Section 4.2.2).

As shown in Table 7, LCRLOG directly locates the root cause for 7 out of 11 concurrency-bug failures, which cover different types of root causes and symptoms.

LCRLOG does not directly locate the root cause for Apache5, Cherokee, and Mozilla-JS2 failures, because these bugs cause silent data corruption with no failure logging near the root cause. The MySQL1 failure is caused by a WRW atomicity violation. As shown in Table 3, since the failure-predicting event does not exist in the failure thread, it is not profiled by LCRLOG.

Further, as shown in Table 7, the capacity of LCR is not a problem for the failures we evaluated. Using the more space-saving configuration, the failure-predicting events are always contained in top 4 LCR entries. Even with the more space-consuming configuration, the failure-predicting events are still located within top 12 LCR entries.

| ID | LCRLOG (Conf1) | LCRLOG (Conf2) | LCRA |
|---|---|---|---|
| Apache4 | ✓ 3 | ✓ 5 | ✓ 1 |
| Apache5 | - | - | - |
| Cherokee | - | - | - |
| FFT | ✓ 4 | ✓ 6 | ✓ 1 |
| LU | ✓ 4 | ✓ 6 | ✓ 1 |
| Mozilla-JS1 | ✓ 3 | ✓ 8 | ✓ 1 |
| Mozilla-JS2 | - | - | - |
| Mozilla-JS3 | ✓ 3 | ✓ 11 | ✓ 1 |
| MySQL1 | - | - | - |
| MySQL2 | ✓ 3 | ✓ 9 | ✓ 1 |
| PBZIP3 | ✓ 3 | ✓ 7 | ✓ 1 |

Table 7: Failure diagnosis capability of LCR. (A number $n$ after the ✓ indicates the $n$-th latest entry returned by LCRLOG or the $n$-th best failure predictor returned by LCRA is the root-cause failure-predicting event; Conf1 is the space-saving configuration of LCR; Conf2 is the space-consuming configuration of LCR; LCRA uses Conf2.)

***LCRA*** We evaluate whether LCRA can automatically locate the failure-predicting event by applying LCRA to 10 failure runs and 10 success runs in each case.

LCRA successfully ranks the failure-predicting event at the top for all the 7 failures where the failure-predicting event is captured by LCRLOG. For example, for the failure discussed in Section 3.2 (Mozilla-JS3), LCRA automatically locates the invalid state observed by $a_2$ as the top failure predictor.

We expect LCRA to well complement PBI and CCI. In terms of performance, CCI incurs up to 10 times slow down, due to its software based sampling schemes. We expect LCRA to have similar performance as LBRA, which would be comparable to or slightly better than PBI. In terms of failure-diagnosis capability, LCRA is slightly worse than PBI, which can successfully diagnose all the 11 failures, and comparable with CCI, which can successfully diagnose 7 out of the 11 failures.

The biggest advantage of LCRA is its short failure-diagnosis latency. LCRA achieves the above diagnosis results using only 10 failure-run profiles, while PBI and CCI need the failures to occur hundreds to thousands of times [2, 18]. This is especially a problem for concurrency-bug failures that often occur non-deterministically and rarely.

## 8. Related Work

We briefly discuss related work that has not been discussed.

***Hardware performance monitoring unit*** The branch tracing facility has been used in several recent work, but has never been used for production-run failure diagnosis. THeME uses LBR for testing coverage analysis [40]. Recent work conducts vulnerability or malware analysis on branch traces generated by the branch tracing facility [41, 46]. Intel GNU* GDB tool [16] uses BTS to store all executed branches in an OS-provided ring buffer.

Our work uses the branch tracing facilities for different purposes from previous work, which leads to different designs. For example, all the above work collects the branch trace of the whole execution, while we focus on the LBR collected at the failure site. Our system aims to achieve very small run-time overhead for production-run deployment, while the above work does not share the same goal. Some of them [16, 46] intentionally use BTS which has higher overhead. THeME [40] uses LBR, but still incurs much larger overhead than our tools. The reason is that THeME's design goal, computing testing coverage, demands periodic LBR profiling throughout program execution. Instead, LBRLOG only profiles LBR when software fails.

General hardware performance counters have been used to identify malware [10] and detect data races [11, 37]. These tools all monitor and analyze the whole execution, instead of focusing on the execution leading to a failure. Race detectors [11, 37] focus on one specific type of software bugs, and cannot help diagnose general software failures. In addition, not being guided by a specific failure, race detectors would report a large number of false positives [18].

***Production-run failure diagnosis*** Record-and-replay techniques [1, 13, 19, 20] can help diagnose production-run failures. However, they could hurt the end users' privacy and incur large overhead for deterministic replay of multi-threaded software. Triage [38] diagnoses production-run failures by applying automated bug detection during on-site replay, which is supported by OS modifications. Overall, record-and-replay techniques and our system can complement each other in failure diagnosis.

An adaptive version of CBI was proposed based on dynamic binary rewriting [4]. CBI-adaptive iteratively changes sampling locations based on the failure location and the diagnosis results from earlier iterations. Without knowing the exact control-flow leading to failures, CBI-adaptive needs hundreds of iterations and evaluates about 40% of all program predicates before it finishes failure diagnosis.

***Hardware support for bug detection*** A lot of work has been done to speed up sequential-bug detection through hardware support [39, 49]. Different from LBRA and LBR-LOG, most of these proposals rely on non-existing hardware.

A lot of work has proposed detecting concurrency bugs through hardware support [6, 7, 24, 26, 32, 33, 42, 50]. LCR has drawn inspiration from these work. However, since previous work focuses on bug detection, it requires the hardware and software system to contiguously monitor and analyze program execution, while maintaining a long execution history. Many bug detectors need to report suspicious execution patterns even if they do no lead to failures. LCR leverages the unique need of failure diagnosis and designs a very simple hardware extension to maintain a short-term execution history.

Bugaboo [26] detects a wide variety of concurrency bugs by identifying rare communication patterns. The communication graph in Bugaboo associates with every memory instruction $m$ from thread $t$ a *context*, the sequence of communication events observed by $t$ immediately prior to $m$. A LCR record is similar to a context, as they both contain a short-term history of thread interaction. However, Bugaboo and our system have very different designs, because they have different goals — Bugaboo detects concurrency bugs even without failure information; our system helps diagnose production-run failures. Bugaboo maintains and checks the context of *every* memory instruction in *every* thread *throughout* the execution. Our system leverages the unique need of failure diagnosis and only uses LCR collected in the failure thread right before the failure. In addition, Bugaboo extends existing cache-coherence protocol to collect context events, while each LCR event is already supported by existing hardware performance monitoring unit.

ECMon [28] proposes a hardware extension that allows custom handlers to execute whenever certain type of cache (coherence) events happen. ECMon and LCR aim for different usage scenarios, and hence have different designs. Software uses ECMon to process cache events throughout the program execution; our system uses LCR to access the last few cache coherence events at the moment of failure. Also different from ECMon, the design of LCR is built upon existing hardware performance monitoring unit.

## 9. Conclusion

We design and implement a novel mechanism that leverages hardware's short-term memory to support production-run failure diagnosis. We identify an existing hardware performance monitoring unit, LBR, and design a simple hardware extension, LCR, to maintain a short-term memory of hardware events that are useful for failure diagnosis. Our evaluation of 31 sequential-bug and concurrency-bug failures from 18 open-source software shows that our LBR/LCR based tools can effectively enhance failure logging and automatically locate failure root causes with small run-time overhead. We believe that our LBR/LCR system provides a good balance between run-time performance, diagnosis latency, and diagnosis capability. Our experience demonstrates that short-term memory is sufficient for diagnosing a wide variety of real-world failures. It also shows that a very simple hardware-extension can provide significant help for production-run failure diagnosis.

## Acknowledgments

We thank the anonymous reviewers for their insightful feedback which has substantially improved the content and presentation of this paper; Ding Yuan and the Opera Group for their tremendous help in sharing the benchmarks; Ben Liblit, Piramanayagam Nainar and Peter Ohmann for their valuable guidance on using the CBI framework; Jason Mars and Asim Kadav for their insightful comments on designing the kernel interface to LBR. This work is supported in part by NSF grants CCF-1018180, CCF-1054616, and CCF-1217582; and a Clare Boothe Luce faculty fellowship.

## References

[1] G. Altekar and I. Stoica. ODR: Output-deterministic replay for multicore debugging. In *SOSP*, 2009.

[2] J. Arulraj, P.-C. Chang, G. Jin, and S. Lu. Production-run software failure diagnosis via hardware performance counters. In *ASPLOS*, 2013.

[3] P. Arumuga Nainar. *Applications of Static Analysis and Program Structure in Statistical Debugging*. PhD thesis, University of Wisconsin – Madison, 2012.

[4] P. Arumuga Nainar and B. Liblit. Adaptive bug isolation. In *ICSE*, 2010.

[5] B. Buck and J. K. Hollingsworth. An API for runtime code patching. *Int. J. High Perform. Comput. Appl.*, 2000.

[6] L. Ceze, P. Montesinos, C. von Praun, and J. Torrellas. Colorama: Architectural support for data-centric synchronization. In *HPCA*, 2007.

[7] L. Chew and D. Lie. Kivati: Fast detection and prevention of atomicity violations. In *EuroSys*, 2010.

[8] CNNMoneyTech. Is knight's $440 million glitch the costliest computer bug ever? http://money.cnn.com/2012/08/09/technology/knight-expensive-computer-bug/index.html.

[9] J. Demme and S. Sethumadhavan. Rapid identification of architectural bottlenecks via precise event counting. In *ISCA*, 2011.

[10] J. Demme, M. Maycock, J. Schmitz, A. Tang, A. Waksman, S. Sethumadhavan, and S. Stolfo. On the feasibility of online malware detection with performance counters. In *ISCA*, 2013.

[11] J. L. Greathouse, Z. Ma, M. I. Frank, R. Peri, and T. M. Austin. Demand-driven software race detection using hardware performance counters. In *ISCA*, 2011.

[12] W. Gu, Z. Kalbarczyk, R. K. Iyer, and Z. Yang. Characterization of Linux kernel behavior under errors. In *DSN*, 2003.

[13] D. R. Hower, P. Montesinos, L. Ceze, M. D. Hill, and J. Torrellas. Two hardware-based approaches for deterministic multiprocessor replay. *Commun. ACM*, 52(6), June 2009.

[14] Intel. Nehalem PMU programming guide. http://software.intel.com/sites/default/files/76/87/30320, 2010.

[15] Intel. Intel 64 and IA-32 architectures software developers manual. http://download.intel.com/products/processor/manual/325462.pdf, 2013.

[16] Intel. GDB - the GNU* project debugger for Intel architecture. http://software.intel.com/en-us/articles/intel-system-studio-gdb#Trace, March 2013.

[17] J. L. Lions et. al. ARIANE 5 Flight 501 Failure – report by the inquiry board. http://sunnyday.mit.edu/accidents/Ariane5accidentreport.html.

[18] G. Jin, A. Thakur, B. Liblit, and S. Lu. Instrumentation and sampling strategies for cooperative concurrency bug isolation. In *OOPSLA*, 2010.

[19] S. T. King, G. W. Dunlap, and P. M. Chen. Operating systems with time-traveling virtual machines. In *Usenix Annual Technical Conference*, 2005.

[20] D. Lee, B. Wester, K. Veeraraghavan, S. Narayanasamy, P. M. Chen, and J. Flinn. Respec: Efficient online multiprocessor replay via speculation and external determinism. In *ASPLOS*, 2010.

[21] N. Leveson and C. S. Turner. An investigation of the Therac-25 accidents. In *IEEE Computer*, 1993.

[22] B. Liblit, A. Aiken, A. X. Zheng, and M. I. Jordan. Bug isolation via remote program sampling. In *PLDI*, 2003.

[23] B. Liblit, M. Naik, A. X. Zheng, A. Aiken, and M. I. Jordan. Scalable statistical bug isolation. In *PLDI*, 2005.

[24] S. Lu, J. Tucek, F. Qin, and Y. Zhou. AVIO: Detecting atomicity violations via access interleaving invariants. In *ASPLOS*, 2006.

[25] S. Lu, S. Park, E. Seo, and Y. Zhou. Learning from mistakes – a comprehensive study of real world concurrency bug characteristics. In *ASPLOS*, 2008.

[26] B. Lucia and L. Ceze. Finding concurrency bugs with context-aware communication graphs. In *MICRO*, 2009.

[27] C.-K. Luk, R. Cohn, R. Muth, H. Patil, A. Klauser, G. Lowney, S. Wallace, V. J. Reddi, and K. Hazelwood. Pin: Building customized program analysis tools with dynamic instrumentation. In *PLDI*, 2005.

[28] V. Nagarajan and R. Gupta. ECMon: Exposing cache events for monitoring. In *ISCA*, 2009.

[29] S. Narayanasamy, G. Pokam, and B. Calder. BugNet: Continuously recording program execution for deterministic replay debugging. In *ISCA*, 2005.

[30] PCWorld. Nasdaq's Facebook Glitch Came From Race Conditions. http://www.pcworld.com/businesscenter/article/255911/nasdaqs_facebook_glitch_came_from_race_conditions.html.

[31] C. Pedersen and J. Acampora. Intel code execution trace resources. http://noggin.intel.com/content/intel-code-execution-trace-resources, 2012.

[32] M. Prvulovic. CORD: Cost-effective (and nearly overhead-free) order-reordering and data race detection. In *HPCA*, 2006.

[33] M. Prvulovic and J. Torrellas. ReEnact: Using thread-level speculation mechanisms to debug data races in multithreaded codes. In *ISCA*, 2003.

[34] F. Qin, J. Tucek, J. Sundaresan, and Y. Zhou. Rx: Treating bugs as allergies c a safe method to survive software failures. In *SOSP*, 2005.

[35] R. Santelices, J. A. Jones, Y. Yu, and M. J. Harrold. Lightweight fault-localization using multiple coverage types. In *ICSE*, 2009.

[36] SecurityFocus. Software bug contributed to blackout. http://www.securityfocus.com/news/8016.

[37] T. Sheng, N. Vachharajani, S. Eranian, R. Hundt, W. Chen, and W. Zheng. RACEZ: A lightweight and non-invasive race detection tool for production applications. In *ICSE*, 2011.

[38] J. Tucek, S. Lu, C. Huang, S. Xanthos, and Y. Zhou. Triage: Diagnosing production run failures at the user's site. In *SOSP*, 2007.

[39] G. Venkataramani, B. Roemer, Y. Solihin, and M. Prvulovic. MemTracker: Efficient and programmable support for memory access monitoring and debugging. In *HPCA*, 2007.

[40] K. Walcott-Justice, J. Mars, and M. L. Soffa. THeME: A system for testing by hardware monitoring events. In *ISSTA*, 2012.

[41] C. Willems, R. Hund, A. Fobian, D. Felsch, T. Holz, and A. Vasudevan. Down to the bare metal: Using processor features for binary analysis. In *ACSAC*, 2012.

[42] J. Yu and S. Narayanasamy. A case for an interleaving constrained shared-memory multi-processor. In *ISCA*, 2009.

[43] D. Yuan, H. Mai, W. Xiong, L. Tan, Y. Zhou, and S. Pasupathy. SherLog: Error diagnosis by connecting clues from run-time logs. In *ASPLOS*, 2010.

[44] D. Yuan, J. Zheng, S. Park, Y. Zhou, and S. Savage. Improving software diagnosability via log enhancement. In *ASPLOS*, 2011.

[45] D. Yuan, S. Park, P. Huang, Y. Liu, M. M. Lee, Y. Zhou, and S. Savage. Be conservative: Enhancing failure diagnosis with proactive logging. In *OSDI*, 2012.

[46] L. Yuan, W. Xing, H. Chen, and B. Zang. Security breaches as PMU deviation: Detecting and identifying security attacks using performance counters. In *APSys*, 2011.

[47] W. Zhang, C. Sun, and S. Lu. ConMem: Detecting severe concurrency bugs through an effect-oriented approach. In *ASPLOS*, 2010.

[48] W. Zhang, J. Lim, R. Olichandran, J. Scherpelz, G. Jin, S. Lu, and T. Reps. ConSeq: Detecting concurrency bugs through sequential errors. In *ASPLOS*, 2011.

[49] P. Zhou, F. Qin, W. Liu, Y. Zhou, and J. Torrellas. iWatcher: Efficient architecture support for software debugging. In *ISCA*, 2004.

[50] P. Zhou, R. Teodorescu, and Y. Zhou. Hard: Hardware-assisted lockset-based race detection. In *HPCA*, 2007.

# RelaxReplay: Record and Replay for Relaxed-Consistency Multiprocessors

Nima Honarmand and Josep Torrellas
University of Illinois at Urbana-Champaign
{honarma1,torrella}@illinois.edu
http://iacoma.cs.uiuc.edu

## Abstract

Record and Deterministic Replay (RnR) of multithreaded programs on relaxed-consistency multiprocessors has been a long-standing problem. While there are designs that work for Total Store Ordering (TSO), finding a general solution that is able to record the access reordering allowed by any relaxed-consistency model has proved challenging.

This paper presents the first complete solution for hardware-assisted memory race recording that works for any relaxed-consistency model of current processors. With the scheme, called *RelaxReplay*, we can build an RnR system for any relaxed-consistency model and coherence protocol. RelaxReplay's core innovation is a new way of capturing memory access reordering. Each memory instruction goes through a post-completion in-order counting step that detects any reordering, and efficiently records it. We evaluate RelaxReplay with simulations of an 8-core release-consistent multicore running SPLASH-2 programs. We observe that RelaxReplay induces negligible overhead during recording. In addition, the average size of the log produced is comparable to the log sizes reported for existing solutions, and still very small compared to the memory bandwidth of modern machines. Finally, deterministic replay is efficient and needs minimal hardware support.

***Categories and Subject Descriptors*** C.1.2 [**Processor Architectures**]: Multiple Data Stream Architectures (Multiprocessors) - MIMD Processors; D.1.3 [**Programming Techniques**]: Concurrent Programming - Parallel Programming

***Keywords*** Memory Race Recording, Record and Deterministic Replay, Relaxed Consistency

## 1. Introduction

Record and Deterministic Replay (RnR) of multithreaded programs in multiprocessors is a concept that involves logging enough of a parallel execution to be able to replay it later deterministically. RnR has broad uses in parallel program debugging [1, 13, 29], security analysis [8, 11, 12], and fault-tolerant, highly-available systems [5, 7]. RnR for a program typically requires logging two sources of non-determinism during execution, namely, external inputs to the program (e.g., results of system calls) and the interleaving of shared-memory accesses from different processors. The latter consists of capturing the relative order of conflicting memory accesses. Hence, it is called Memory Race Recording (MRR).

While input recording is done by the Operating System (OS), MRR typically requires special hardware. This is because inserting software instrumentation for MRR (*e.g.*, [16, 22, 32]) results in significant execution slow down or increases the number of processors required. In addition, all these schemes distort the timing of execution, which can be a drawback in concurrency debugging. Finally, they require modifying the binary of the program to be recorded. For these reasons, there are several proposals for hardware-assisted MRR (*e.g.*, [3, 6, 9, 10, 15, 17–21, 23–25, 27, 33, 35, 36]). These schemes typically identify conflicting accesses by leveraging cache coherence protocol transactions. Most recent proposals record a processor's execution as a series of *Chunks* (or Blocks or Episodes) of instructions executed between coherence actions with other processors. This approach results in low recording overhead and small logs.

The majority of current proposals for hardware-assisted MRR require that the recorded execution obeys Sequential Consistency (SC) [14]. Under SC, memory-access instructions execute in program order, which substantially simplifies what events need to be logged and when. Unfortunately, commercial machines almost universally use more relaxed memory consistency models, allowing loads and stores to reorder. Recording such execution is especially challenging.

There have been a few proposals for MRR under non-SC models. All but one of them require the Total Store Ordering (TSO) memory model [3, 6, 10, 17, 24, 25, 36], which only allows loads to bypass stores. Such proposals either log which stores are bypassed [24, 25], or log the values read by the bypassing loads [3, 6, 10, 36], or use off-line analysis to identify the actual order that occurred [17]. The other proposal, called Rainbow [27], focuses on detecting SC violations as they happen, and recording enough information


*ASPLOS '14*, March 1–5, 2014, Salt Lake City, Utah, USA.
Copyright © 2014 ACM 978-1-4503-2305-5/14/03...$15.00.
http://dx.doi.org/10.1145/2541940.2541979

to replay them. However, this scheme requires a coherence protocol that is centralized and that needs substantial hardware changes. Moreover, the operation of the scheme's major components is not clearly described in the paper. All these schemes are discussed in detail in Section 6. Overall, the long-standing problem of finding a general MRR solution that works for any relaxed-consistency model (such as that of ARM [2], Power [26] or Tile [30] processors) is still open.

This paper contributes with the first complete solution for hardware-assisted MRR that works for any relaxed-consistency model of current processors. With the scheme, called *RelaxReplay*, we can build an RnR system that works for any relaxed-consistency model and any cache coherence protocol. RelaxReplay's key innovation is a new approach to capture memory access reordering. Specifically, each memory instruction goes through a post-completion in-order counting step that detects any reordering, and efficiently records it in the log. We present two designs, called *RelaxReplay_Base* and *RelaxReplay_Opt*, with different emphases on hardware requirements, log size, and replay speed.

Several salient characteristics of the RelaxReplay mechanism to capture memory access reordering are:

• It only relies on the write atomicity property of coherence protocols, and not on knowing the detailed specifications of the particular relaxed-consistency model. Such specifications are often high-level and hard to map to implementation issues.
• It can be combined with the specific chunk-ordering algorithm of any existing chunk-based MRR proposal. As a result, that proposal, designed for a certain coherence protocol, can now record relaxed-consistency executions.
• It has modest hardware requirements. Its hardware is local to the processors and requires no change to the cache coherence protocol.
• It produces a compact log representation of a relaxed-consistency execution.
• The resulting log enables efficient deterministic replay with minimal hardware support.

We evaluate RelaxReplay with simulations of an 8-core Release-Consistent (RC) multicore running SPLASH-2 applications. The results show that RelaxReplay induces negligible overhead during recording. In addition, the average size of the log produced is 1–4x the log sizes reported by existing SC- or TSO-based MRR systems. Hence, the bandwidth required to save this log is still a small fraction of the bandwidth provided by current machines. Finally, deterministic replay using this log is efficient: the sequential replay of these 8-processor executions with minimal hardware support takes on average 6.7x as long as the parallel recording.

This paper is organized as follows: Section 2 provides a background; Sections 3 and 4 presents RelaxReplay's design and implementation, respectively; Section 5 evaluates RelaxReplay and Section 6 discusses related work.

## 2. Background on Chunk-Based Recording

State-of-the-art proposals for hardware-assisted MRR record each processor's execution as a series of *Chunks* (also called Blocks or Episodes) of instructions executed between communications with other processors [3, 9, 10, 18, 19, 23–25, 33]. The chunks of different processors are ordered in a graph based on inter-processor data dependences. A typical chunk-based recorder provides three main functionalities: (1) establishes chunk boundaries such that each chunk's execution appears atomic, (2) establishes a proper order between chunks that captures all data dependences (to ensure correct replay) and has no cycles (to avoid replay deadlocks), and (3) represents chunks in the log in an efficient format.

Chunk boundaries are set at points where the executing processor communicates with other processors. Chunk-based recorders usually keep track of the read and write operations performed by the instructions of the current chunk. Often, the addresses of these operations are hashed in Bloom filters [4] and stored as read and write signatures. At the same time, the hardware checks for cache-coherence transactions that conflict with the read or write set of the current chunk. When one does, we have detected an inter-processor data dependence. Then, in simple designs, the current chunk is terminated and a new chunk starts. There are optimizations that allow chunks to grow beyond the conflicts.

Chunk-based recorders must ensure that the chunk containing the source of a dependence is ordered before the chunk containing the destination of it. For this, some schemes piggyback ordering information on coherence messages (e.g., [10, 33]) or add new messages [23]. Specifically, when an incoming coherence request conflicts with the local chunk, the global order of the local chunk is sent to the requesting processor (or broadcasted to all processors in [23]), so that its chunk orders itself after the local one. Alternatively, other schemes rely on a globally-consistent clock (e.g., [9, 24, 25]) that is available to all processors to establish chunk ordering. In both cases, by replaying the chunks according to their global order, all data dependences will be enforced.

Chunk-based recorders log chunks in a very efficient format. Specifically, a chunk is represented as the number of instructions (or memory operations) performed in the chunk, together with the recorded global ordering of the chunk.

### 2.1 Advantages of Chunk-Based Recording

Chunk-based recorders have at least three advantages over non chunked-based ones that have made them popular. Firstly, their operation lends itself to a relatively simpler hardware implementation in the cache hierarchy, while still generating small log sizes. Secondly, they support application-level RnR especially well because their recording hardware can be easily virtualized [9, 19, 25] and shared by multiple independent applications.

A third advantage is that the resulting logs can be efficiently replayed with minimal hardware support [9]. Specifically, all that they need is a counter that counts the number of instructions (or memory-access instructions) executed, and then triggers a synchronous interrupt when the number of instructions in the chunk are exhausted. In this way, instructions can be replayed natively by the hardware rather than being simulated by an instruction simulator. At the same time, a simple software module can enforce the recorded chunk order [9]. This combined hardware/software solution enables efficient native replay. Moreover, with the appropriate design, the resulting logs can be replayed in parallel [3, 9], and deliver fast replay.

### 2.2 Main Limitation: Access Reordering

In its basic form, chunk-based recording (as well as non chunk-based one) relies on the assumption that processors expose their memory operations to the coherence subsystem in program order, providing a sequentially-consistent environment [14]. Hence, any execution that violates SC cannot be captured by these recorders.

Unfortunately, commercial machines almost universally use more relaxed memory models, allowing loads and stores to perform out of program order. For example, to show how aggressive modern processors are, Figure 1 shows the fraction of memory-access instructions that are performed out of program order — i.e., with some earlier memory instructions still pending. The details of the experiment are discussed in Section 5.1. Of all the memory instructions, on average, 59% are out-of-order loads and 3% are out-of-order stores.

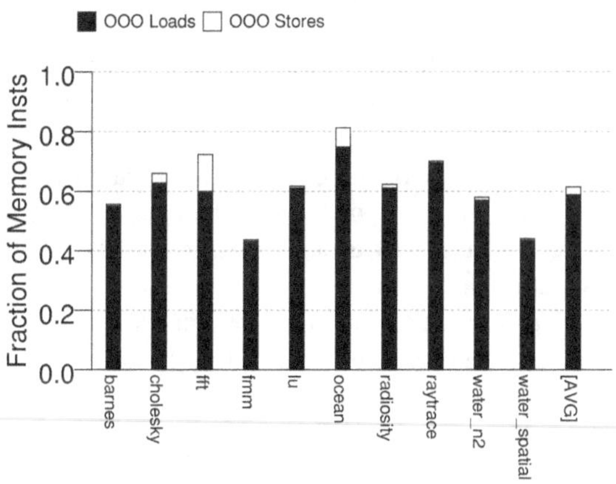


**Figure 1.** Fraction of all the memory-access instructions that are performed out of program order.

To begin to address this problem, there have been a few proposals for MRR under non-SC models. As indicated in Section 1 and discussed in Section 6, however, these proposals address only a conservative memory model (TSO), or are otherwise limited. To help popularize RnR, we need to find a general solution for MRR that works for any of the relaxed-consistency models used in current processors (such as ARM [2], Power [26] or Tile [30]). The rest of this paper presents a solution to this problem that is compatible with the use of chunk-based recording.

## 3. RelaxReplay Design

### 3.1 Concept of Interval

To understand RelaxReplay, we define the concepts of *performing* and *counting* a memory-access instruction, and the notion of an *Interval*. A load instruction *performs* when the data loaded returns from the memory system and is deposited into a register. Later, the load retires when it reaches the head of the Reorder Buffer (ROB) and has already performed. A store instruction retires when it reaches the head of the ROB and its address and data are available. At this point, the store is deposited into the write buffer. Depending on the memory consistency model, the store can be merged with the memory system right away, or has to wait to do so until all earlier stores have been removed from the write buffer. Merging may trigger a coherence transaction. When the coherence transaction terminates (i.e., when all the necessary replies and acknowledgments have been received), the store has *performed*. Finally, in RelaxReplay, each retired load and each performed store in the processor goes through an additional *logical* stage in program order that we call *Counting*. Counting records the completion of the instruction in program order. Hence, each memory-access instruction has a *Perform* event and a *Counting* event.

An *Interval* in the execution of a processor is the *period of time* between two consecutive communications of the processor with other processors. An interval has a *Perform Set* and a *Counting Set*. These are the sets of perform and counting events, respectively, that took place in the processor during the interval. The set of perform events in an interval may correspond to memory-access instructions that are *not* contiguous in program order. This is because, in a relaxed-consistency machine, accesses can perform out of order. This is in contrast to the instructions of a chunk in a conventional chunk-based recorder, which are required to be contiguous. However, the set of counting events in the interval do correspond to consecutive memory-access instructions, since counting is done in program order.

### 3.2 Main Idea in RelaxReplay

In an RnR environment that supports general relaxed consistency models, working with chunks of contiguous instructions, as in conventional chunk-based recorders, is inconvenient. Instead, we propose to use the interval abstraction, which directly corresponds to the work performed between communications. To show the usability of intervals, we make two observations.

**Observation 1: In memory-consistency models that support write atomicity, the perform event of a given access can only be placed in a single interval.**

The property of write atomicity means that a write operation by a processor can be observed by another processor only if it has been made visible to all other processors, and that writes to the same location are serialized [28]. This property, which is typically enforced by the coherence substrate, is provided by all the popular multiprocessor systems in use today. It implies that the execution of a memory access can be thought of as atomic, and can only be placed in a single interval, namely the one where the access *performs*. As a result, we can record the execution of a processor as a sequence of intervals, where each access is assigned to the interval where it performs.

Unfortunately, representing an interval as a set of perform events is inefficient. Indeed, since memory instructions are performed out of program order, we would have to record the complete list of such events. To reduce the state we need to log, it is better to record the interval as a set of counting events (which can be efficiently represented as a *range* of consecutive in-order memory instructions) plus some reorder information. A second observation allows us to keep this additional reorder information that we need to record to a minimum.

**Observation 2: For the large majority of memory-access instructions, we can logically move the perform event forward in time to coincide with its counting event.**

Given a memory-access instruction by a processor ($P_1$), we can logically move its perform event forward in time to coincide with its counting event if no other processor ($P_j$) has observed the access between the two points in time. $P_j$ observes the access if it issues a conflicting access to the same (line) address that causes a coherence transaction that reaches $P_1$ between the two points. By "moving", we mean that, as far as the other processors are concerned, the instruction can be assumed to have performed at the point of its counting. Since the access has not yet been observed by any other processor, this assumption will not affect any of the inter-processor dependences and, therefore, is correct. Fortunately, in practice, the large majority of accesses are not observed between the two events.

As an example, Figure 2(a) shows a store (ST) and a load instruction (LD) from a processor in program order, and their perform (P) and counting (C) event times. It also shows the time when an external communication occurs and, therefore, the interval terminates. In the figure, the perform events are in order. Figure 2(b) shows the case when the perform events are out of order. In both cases, each perform event happens in the same interval as its corresponding counting event and, thus, can be trivially moved to its counting time. Therefore, in both cases, we can concisely represent this interval as including the two accesses in program order.

In Figure 2(c), the load has its perform and counting events in two different intervals. In this paper, we present two version of RelaxReplay, depending on how we deal with this case. In a base design with simpler hardware, called *RelaxReplay_Base*, the perform event is never moved across intervals to its counting event; in an optimized design with more hardware, called *RelaxReplay_Opt*, the perform event is still moved across intervals to its counting event if none of the coherence transactions received between the two events conflicts with the (line) address of the access.

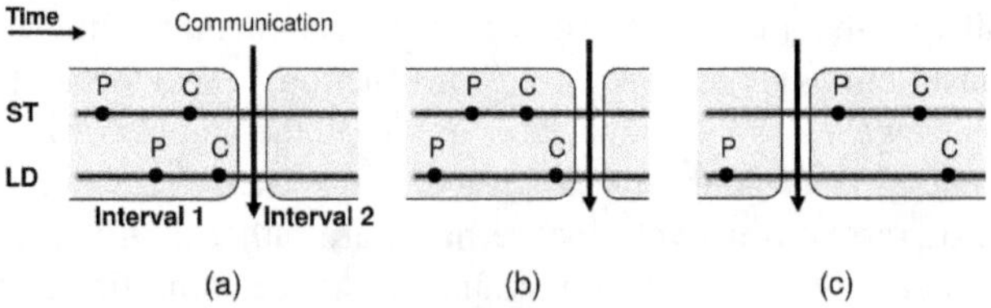


**Figure 2.** Examples of a two-instruction pattern with different timings for their perform (P) and counting (C) events.

If RelaxReplay is able to move all the perform events to their counting events, each interval is concisely logged as comprising a certain number of accesses in program order — irrespective of the *actual access reordering* that occurred during recording due to the relaxed consistency model. Otherwise, the log entry for an interval also includes additional information on what accesses were counted in the interval but were out of order. We will discuss the exact representation later. Since, for the large majority of accesses, RelaxReplay is able to move the perform events to the counting events, the RnR log of intervals is both *stored and replayed* efficiently.

Overall, RelaxReplay is able to record an execution under any memory consistency model with write atomicity, and store it in a log for efficient deterministic replay. RelaxReplay relies on hardware that tracks the perform and counting events of each memory access and, while watching for conflicting accesses from other processors, tries to combine them before storing a compact representation of intervals in the log.

Note that RelaxReplay's goal is to record intervals. For a full MRR solution, we also need a mechanism to establish a proper order between intervals of different processors. For this, we can use any of the existing chunk-based recording schemes. Such schemes now use coherence messages and read/write signatures to establish a proper order between intervals rather than chunks.

Next, we describe the architecture that processes perform and counting events, how it handles store-to-load forwarding, and how we replay a RelaxReplay log.

### 3.3 Tracking Instruction Events in RelaxReplay

Intuitively, the RelaxReplay architecture requires a longer ROB that keeps each memory-access instruction in the processor beyond retirement, and until it is ready to be counted. At that point, if the instruction's perform event can be moved to its counting event, the instruction is included in the current interval as an in-order access, and logged as such. Otherwise, the instruction is included in the current interval as a reordered access, with enough state added to the log so that it can be correctly replayed.

In practice, rather than enlarging the ROB, RelaxReplay adds a hardware structure to the processor that works in parallel with the ROB for memory-access instructions. The structure is a circular FIFO called *Tracking Queue* (TRAQ)

(Figure 3). As a memory-access instruction is inserted in the ROB, it is also inserted in the TRAQ. A memory-access instruction is removed from the TRAQ when it is at the head of the TRAQ and is ready to be counted — i.e., for a load, it is performed and retired, and for a store, it is retired and performed. At that point, the instruction is counted and added to the log record for the interval. Note that the TRAQ can contain both non-retired and retired accesses. The ROB-like structure of the TRAQ enables RelaxReplay to handle the squashing of speculative instructions easily, as we explain in Section 4.

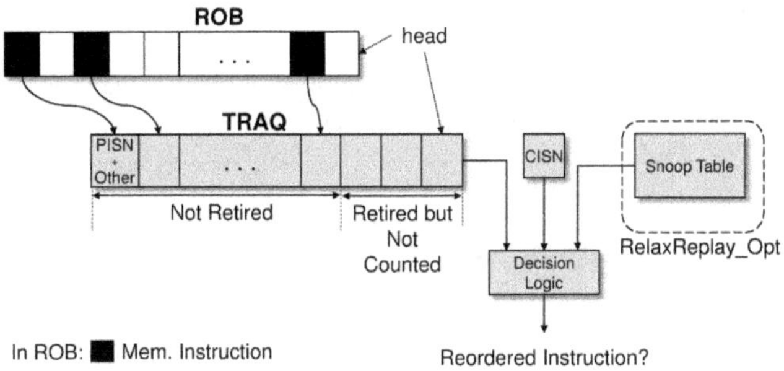


**Figure 3.** High-level architecture of RelaxReplay.

RelaxReplay keeps in a register the ID of the interval that is currently being processed at the head of the TRAQ. This ID is a counter called *Current Interval Sequence Number* (CISN) (Figure 3). Every time the processor communicates with another processor, the current interval is terminated, its information is stored in the memory log, the CISN is incremented, and a new interval starts.

The fundamental operation of the RelaxReplay hardware is simple. When a memory-access instruction is performed, the current value of the CISN is copied to the instruction's TRAQ entry. It is stored in a field called *Performance Interval Sequence Number* (PISN). When the instruction reaches the TRAQ head and is counted, its PISN is compared to the CISN. At this point, there are several possible outcomes.

First, if the two values are the same, the interval has not changed since the perform event. Hence, RelaxReplay logically assumes that the memory-access instruction performs at the point of counting. In this case, RelaxReplay simply increments the count of consecutive memory-access instructions that have executed in this interval. Such count will be included in the log record for the interval that will be stored to memory when the interval terminates. An example of this case is shown in Figure 4(a), which depicts a load that performs and is counted in interval 10, and whose perform point is logically moved by RelaxReplay to its counting point.

Second, if the PISN and CISN are different, the interval has changed because the processor has communicated between the perform and counting events. In RelaxReplay_Base, we process the access as reordered, as we will see later. In RelaxReplay_Opt, the hardware checks if the access is indeed reordered by comparing its (line) address to the (line) addresses of all the coherence transactions that the processor received since the PISN interval. Such addresses are collected in hardware in a structure called *Snoop Table* (Figure 3). This structure is only present in RelaxReplay_Opt, and is described in detail in Section 4.2.

If the comparison shows that no transaction conflicting with that address has been received, then RelaxReplay logically assumes that the memory-access instruction performs at this point, as in the first case. As before, RelaxReplay increments the count of consecutive memory-access instructions that have executed in this interval. An example is shown in Figure 4(b), which depicts a load that performs in interval 10 and is counted in 12. Since the processor has received no transaction that conflicts with this address in the meantime, the perform point is logically moved.

However, if the comparison finds that a conflicting transaction has been received, or the machine only supports RelaxReplay_Base, then the hardware records a reordered access. The following sections describe the cases of a reordered load and a reordered store separately.

### 3.3.1 Reordered Loads

To be able to record reordered loads, RelaxReplay needs to retain the values that loads obtain as they perform, until the loads' counting time. Such values are stored in the corresponding TRAQ entries, as part of what Figure 3 refers to as *Other*.

When RelaxReplay counts a load and finds that it is reordered, it does not increment the count of consecutive memory-access instructions executed in this interval. Instead, it adds a special type of entry in the log record for the interval. The entry contains the value that was returned by the load as it performed (and was retained in the TRAQ). Later, when the execution is deterministically replayed, the value is read from the log and supplied to the destination register of the load. In this way, the replay of the load in program order can correctly reproduce what happened in the recorded execution out of program order. If, instead, during the replay, the load tried to access the memory system as it replayed, it might read an incorrect value. Note that any consumers of the load, as they are replayed in program order, will obtain the correct value. Xu et al. [36] used this approach of recording the values returned by out-of-order loads in the log for TSO machines.

An example is shown in Figure 4(c). A load performs in interval 10, and the processor later receives a coherence event that conflicts with the loaded address. The load is counted in interval 12. RelaxReplay then takes the value read by the load and stores it in the log record for interval 12.

### 3.3.2 Reordered Stores

To be able to record reordered stores, RelaxReplay needs to retain the values they write and the addresses they write to, until the writes' counting time. Such values are saved in the TRAQ entries as part of the *Other* fields.

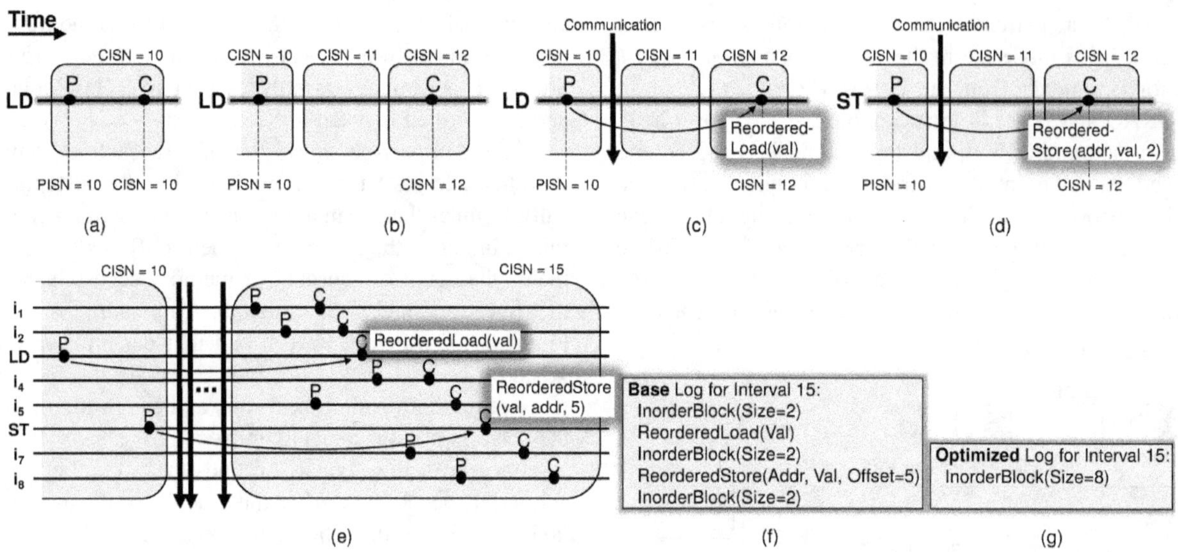


**Figure 4.** Examples of RelaxReplay operation with perform (P) and counting (C) events.

When RelaxReplay counts a store and declares it reordered, it does not increment the count of consecutive instructions executed in this interval. Instead, it adds another special type of entry in the log record for the interval. The entry contains the address written to, the value written, and the difference between CISN and the value of PISN in the store's TRAQ entry. We call this difference *Offset*; it denotes how many intervals ago the store performed.

Before this log can be used for deterministic replay, this entry needs to be extracted from this interval's record and inserted in the record of an earlier interval — specifically, at the end of the interval that is *Offset* positions earlier, which is the interval when the store performed. In the interval where the store is counted, we leave a dummy entry so that the store is not re-executed there. This "patching" step can be done as an off-line pass or on the fly as the log is read for replay.

After this change is made, the log is ready for replay. The store entry is found in the interval when it was performed, and the log contains the value to store and the address to store to. The store is thus executed, exactly reproducing the conditions in the recorded execution. In the interval where the store was counted, the store instruction is skipped (as indicated by the dummy entry mentioned above).

Figure 4(d) shows an example of a store that performs at interval 10, and the processor later receives a conflicting coherence event. The store is counted in interval 12. RelaxReplay then takes the value and address from the TRAQ and, together with an offset of 2, stores them in the log record for interval 12.

### 3.3.3 Example

To understand the format of the log record for an interval, Figure 4(e) shows the more extensive example of an interval that counts 8 memory-access instructions. Of these, $i_1$, $i_2$, $i_4$, $i_5$, $i_7$, and $i_8$ both perform and are counted in interval 15. However there is a load (*LD*) and a store (*ST*) that perform in interval 10 and are counted in interval 15. Assume that none of the communications between intervals 10 and 15 conflict with the addresses accessed by *LD* or *ST*.

If we use RelaxReplay_Base, the hardware does not know that there is no conflict and assumes that *LD* and *ST* are reordered. Hence, as shown in Figure 4(e), as it counts *LD*, it reads the value that *LD* loaded and saves it in the log record. As it counts *ST*, it reads the value that *ST* stored and the address it stored to, computes the offset of 5, and saves the three values in the log record.

Figure 4(f) shows the resulting log record for interval 15. It contains several entries, which are inserted in order as instructions are counted in order. As $i_1$ and $i_2$ are counted, they increment the counter of consecutive instructions that have executed in this interval. As RelaxReplay reaches *LD* and finds it reordered, it saves the counter in an entry of type *InorderBlock*, and resets the counter. This means that there is a group of 2 in-order instructions executed. Then, it records an entry of type *ReorderedLoad* with the value of the load. This means that the next instruction in program order is a reordered load. Then, for instructions $i_3$ and $i_4$, RelaxReplay records another entry of type *InorderBlock* with size 2. Then, RelaxReplay records an entry of type *ReorderedStore* for *ST*, with its address, value, and offset. This entry signifies that the next instruction in program order is a reordered store. Finally, RelaxReplay stores another entry of type *InorderBlock* with size 2 for $i_7$ and $i_8$. This information is enough for the deterministic replay of these instructions. As will be seen later, this log format enables efficient replay.

Figure 4(g) shows the log for the same interval using RelaxReplay_Opt. Since RelaxReplay_Opt discovers that none of the intervening coherence transactions conflicts with the addresses of *LD* or *ST*, it records *LD* and *ST* as in-order accesses. In general, since the number of truly reordered accesses is very small, this log format is often very compact.

More details of the hardware and logging are presented in Section 4. In particular, the *InorderBlock* entries count the number of total instructions in order, not just memory-access instructions. This design eases replay.

### 3.4 Handling Store-to-Load Forwarding

Modern superscalar processors typically allow store-to-load forwarding, whereby a load gets its value from an older store of the same processor that is pending in the write buffer. Such a load is not serviced off the coherent memory; it obtains its value from the non-coherent write buffer. In this section we show that RelaxReplay correctly records such loads.

Figure 5 shows the timing of a forwarding instance, where a load (*LD*) obtains its value from an older store (*ST*). Following RelaxReplay's operation, *LD* performs as soon as it gets the forwarded data, before *ST* merges with the memory system and performs. Later, *ST* is counted and *LD* is counted.

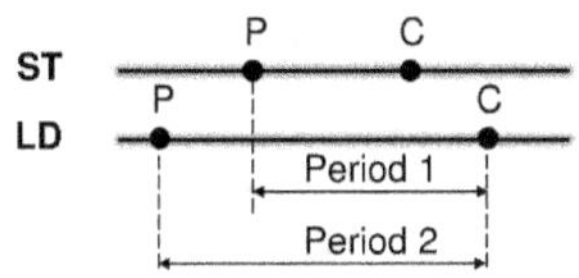


**Figure 5.** Timing of store-to-load forwarding.

RelaxReplay seamlessly supports this case. Since *LD* gets its value from *ST*, we can assume it *logically* performs at the same time as *ST*. Thus, in order to correctly record *LD*, we only need to monitor conflicting accesses between *ST*'s perform event and *LD*'s counting event (Period 1 in Figure 5). However, this period is properly contained between *LD*'s perform and counting events (Period 2 in Figure 5). Thus, if there is a change of interval (in RelaxReplay_Base) or reception of a conflicting coherence transaction (in RelaxReplay_Opt) in Period 2, we conservatively assume that it happened in Period 1. In this case, the hardware saves in the log the value obtained by *LD* at its perform point, and the replay system later uses it at the counting point. Otherwise, the hardware correctly moves *LD*'s perform point to its counting point. No change to RelaxReplay is needed.

### 3.5 Replaying a RelaxReplay Log

The log generated by RelaxReplay is very compact and enables efficient replay using only minimal hardware support. To replay an execution, we use a module in the OS as in the Cyrus system [9]. Specifically, during replay, the OS reads the log of intervals and enforces the order of the intervals. As the OS reads the record for an interval, before launching its execution, it waits until all intervals ordered before this interval finish executing. This can be accomplished using software synchronization through condition variables or semaphores. In addition, the OS also injects the application inputs that were recorded in the original execution.

The log record for an interval can have three types of relevant entries: *InorderBlock*, *ReorderedLoad*, and *ReorderedStore*. If an *InorderBlock* entry is found, the OS configures a hardware counter to generate an interrupt when the number of executed instructions equals the size of the block. This approach, proposed in the Cyrus system, requires a synchronous interrupt from the counter — *i.e.*, the interrupt should be triggered upon (and before) executing the first instruction after the block. When the block is complete, the interrupt transfers the control back to the OS. This instruction counting mechanism is similar to performance counters available in modern commercial microprocessors. It is the only hardware support needed to replay RelaxReplay logs.

If a *ReorderedLoad* entry is found, the OS reads the value from the log. It then saves it in the destination register of the load that is part of the architectural context of the application saved in the OS. Recall that the application context was saved upon entering the OS and will be restored before exiting the OS. The OS also advances the program counter, which is also stored as part of the architectural context.

If a *ReorderedStore* entry is found, the OS reads the address and value from the log and performs the memory update. Recall that we are now in the interval where this store *performed*, not where the store was counted. This is because this entry was processed earlier by a "patching step" (Section 3.3.2), which moved it from the store's counting interval to its perform interval. Hence, in the current interval, there is no corresponding store instruction. Therefore, the OS does not advance the program counter. Later, when the OS reaches the interval where the store was counted, the OS will find the corresponding dummy entry. At that point, the OS will take no action beyond advancing the program counter by one.

When all the entries of the interval are processed, the OS uses software synchronization to signal the completion of this interval to its successors. Then, it reads the next interval from the log. Note that the replay process is oblivious to whether the log comes from RelaxReplay_Base or RelaxReplay_Opt; both use the same log format.

### 3.6 Discussion

RelaxReplay can be used to convert any of the existing chunk-based MRR schemes [3, 9, 10, 23–25, 33] to an MRR solution for relaxed-consistency models. In this case, as shown in Figure 7, RelaxReplay uses the chunk-ordering mechanism of the specific MRR scheme to form and order intervals and, then, uses the techniques outlined in this paper to capture instruction reordering. In doing so, RelaxReplay retains the basic properties of the original chunk-based MRR scheme. For example, if the original scheme admits parallel replay of chunks [3, 9], then the resulting interval-based solution will admit parallel replay of intervals.

We designed RelaxReplay in a way that does not rely on knowing the detailed requirements of a particular relaxed-consistency memory model. RelaxReplay works for any relaxed-consistency model as long as the coherence substrate supports write atomicity. This is a well-established property of current memory subsystems that is likely to hold in future generations of processors. We chose this approach because

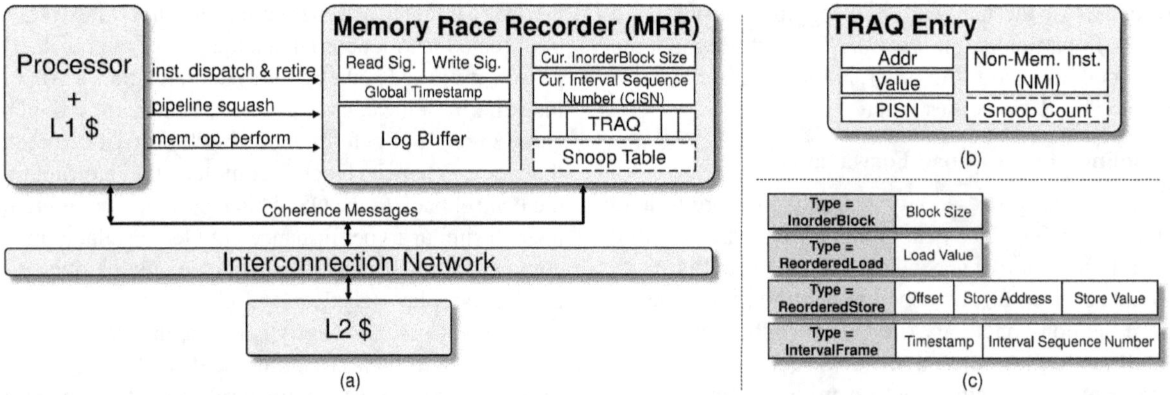


**Figure 6.** RelaxReplay architecture in detail: per-processor Memory Race Recorder (MRR) (a), TRAQ entry (b), and format of the different entry types in an interval's log record (c). The dashed boxes indicate the components specific to RelaxReplay_Opt.

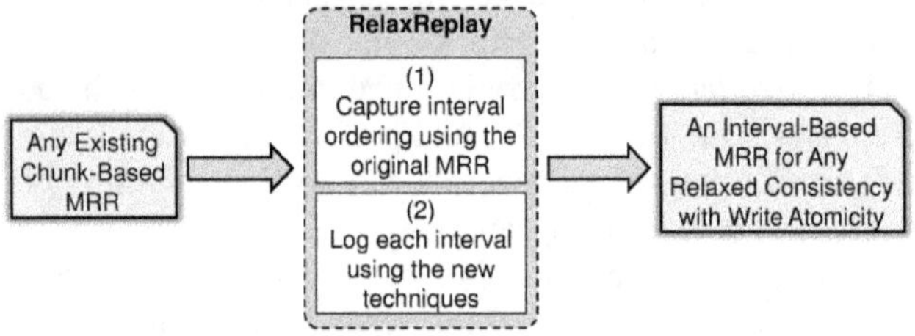


**Figure 7.** RelaxReplay can be paired with any chunk-based MRR scheme.

the memory models of most commercial processors are ill defined. In addition, new generations of processors may add new instructions to their ISAs that use different memory models than the older instructions. Finally, memory models are often defined in abstract, usually declarative, terms that do not provide much intuition about the implementation techniques used to support them.

## 4. Detailed Implementation Issues

### 4.1 Memory Race Recorder

Following previous RnR designs, we place the hardware for recording memory races in a per-processor Memory Race Recorder (MRR) module. This module is shown in the top right part of Figure 6(a). It comprises two parts. On the left side, there is the mechanism for creating and ordering intervals, which can reuse any of the designs proposed by existing chunk-based recorders. On the right side, there is the mechanism to track events within intervals, which is the proper RelaxReplay hardware. The inputs to the MRR module are processor signals (instruction dispatch into the ROB, instruction retirement, memory operation performed, and pipeline squash), and memory system signals (coherence transactions).

For the mechanism to create and order intervals, we show a design that follows the QuickRec [25] approach. This approach records a total order of intervals based on a globally-consistent scalar timestamp. The timestamp associated with each interval is the cycle count of a global clock when the interval was terminated. Intervals are ordered according to their timestamps. The scheme uses a snoopy coherence protocol.

As shown in the figure, the hardware needed is a pair of Bloom filters [4] as the read and write signatures of the current interval, a Global Timestamp counter that counts the number of cycles of a global clock, and a Log Buffer that automatically saves the log records. When memory operations are performed, their line addresses are inserted into the signatures. Snooped coherence transactions are checked against the signatures; if a conflict is detected, the current interval is terminated.

The proper RelaxReplay hardware is on the right side, and records the events within an interval. It comprises the TRAQ, the Current Interval Sequence Number (CISN), the Current InorderBlock Size count, and the Snoop Table. The latter is only needed in RelaxReplay_Opt and will be discussed later. The Current InorderBlock Size count is the number of in-order instructions that have so far been counted for the current block; this count is saved in the next *InorderBlock* entry logged.

Memory-access instructions are inserted into the TRAQ in program order when they are dispatched to the ROB. If the TRAQ is full, instruction dispatch stalls. The TRAQ also receives pipeline flush information from the processor, in order to keep its state consistent with the ROB's. Specifically, if the ROB is flushed, then the TRAQ is also flushed accordingly. This occurs, e.g., on a branch misprediction. If an individual instruction in the ROB is squashed and replayed, the TRAQ takes no action, since its entry in the TRAQ will be correctly overwritten upon the re-execution of the instruction. This occurs, e.g., when a speculative load is squashed and replayed due to memory consistency requirements.

Figure 6(b) shows a TRAQ entry. Each memory-access instruction allocates a TRAQ entry and stores the address accessed, the value read or written, and the PISN. The other two fields in a TRAQ entry are the Snoop Count and the Non-Memory Instruction (NMI) field. The former is only needed in RelaxReplay_Opt and will be discussed later. The NMI field enables RelaxReplay to log block sizes (in *InorderBlock* entries) in number of instructions rather than in number of memory-access instructions. This support may ease replay because processors are more likely to provide interrupt support for number of instructions executed than for number of memory-access instructions executed.

The NMI field works as follows. When a memory-access instruction (*M*) is dispatched and obtains a TRAQ entry, its NMI field is set to the number of instructions dispatched since the most recent memory-access instruction. Then, when *M* reaches the TRAQ's head and is counted, the Current InorderBlock Size count is incremented by the value in the NMI field (plus one if M is not reordered).

The NMI field has a limited number of bits, which is 4 in our implementation. It is possible that more than 15 instructions appear between two consecutive memory-access instructions. In this case, RelaxReplay allocates a TRAQ entry for each group of 15 such instructions. These TRAQ entries do not correspond to any memory-access instruction, and their NMI field is set to 15.

Figure 6(c) shows the format of the different types of entries in the log record of an interval. An *InorderBlock* entry is recorded for a group of consecutive instructions to be replayed in order. It includes the value of the Current InorderBlock Size count. A *ReorderedLoad* and *ReorderedStore* entry is recorded for each reordered load and store, respectively; their fields have been discussed before. An interval may log multiple instances of each of these three entry types. Finally, when an interval ends, an *IntervalFrame* entry is logged, with the value of CISN to identify the interval. In addition, an IntervalFrame must also contain some ordering information to establish its order among all the recorded intervals. The information required depends on the particular interval-ordering mechanism used. In our case, since we use the QuickRec interval ordering, it suffices to record the current value of the Global Timestamp.

### 4.2 Extension for RelaxReplay_Opt

RelaxReplay_Opt tracks the coherence transactions that a processor observes between the perform and counting events of a memory-access instruction. If the address of any of them conflicts with the address accessed by the instruction, the latter is declared reordered at counting time. To track transactions, RelaxReplay_Opt adds the *Snoop Table* in the MRR (Figure 6(a)) and the *Snoop Count* in each TRAQ entry (Figure 6(b)).

The Snoop Table consists of two arrays of counters (Figure 8). When the processor observes a coherence transaction, the transaction's line address is hashed, using a different function for each array, and the resulting two counters in the arrays are incremented. We use two arrays to reduce false positives caused by aliasing. When a memory-access instruction performs, its line address is hashed, and the corresponding two counters in the Snoop Table are read. The current values of these two counters are then stored in the Snoop Count field of the TRAQ entry. Later, when the instruction is counted, if its PISN is not equal to CISN, the two counters are read again from the Snoop Table. Their current values are compared to the values saved in the Snoop Count field. If none of the counters has changed or only one has (this case is due to aliasing), the instruction is declared in order; otherwise, it is declared reordered. If it is in order, since we are moving the perform event of the instruction to the current interval, we insert the address accessed by the instruction in the read or write signature (for a load or store, respectively), to ensure proper ordering of intervals.

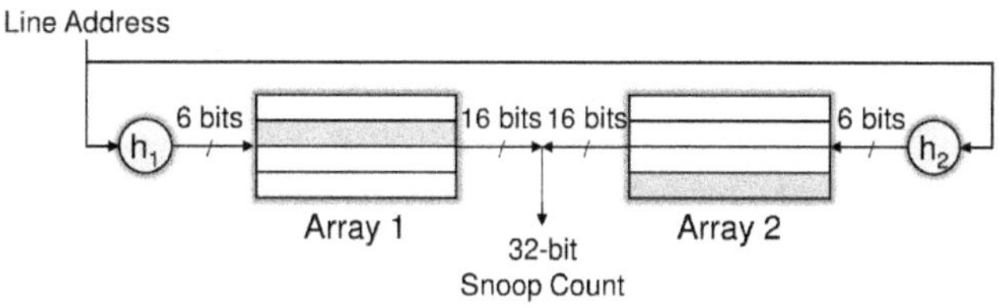


**Figure 8.** Snoop Table structure in RelaxReplay_Opt.

The counters are allowed to wrap around. Moreover, no action is taken when a line is evicted from the cache: there is no danger of missing a coherence transaction because, in a snoopy protocol, all caches see all the transactions.

Overall, although conservative, this design correctly detects all of the true conflicts. The only problem would be if the counter size was so small that between the perform and counting points, a counter could wrap around and reach exactly the same value. To prevent this case, we use sizable structures: two 64-entry arrays of 16-bit counters. This means that the overall Snoop Table size is 256 bytes. In addition, the Snoop Count field in each TRAQ entry is 4 bytes. For the 176-entry TRAQ that we evaluate, the combined size of all the Snoop Count fields is 704 bytes. These are minor costs for RelaxReplay_Opt's large reduction in log size and increase in replay speed (Section 5).

### 4.3 RelaxReplay for Directory Coherence

RelaxReplay's mechanism to track events within intervals remains unchanged for directory-based coherence, whether centralized or distributed, as long as write atomicity is guaranteed. The mechanism to order intervals may need to change, and we can use any of the proposed chunk-based MRR schemes that work for directories.

One issue that appears in directory-based protocols is that, after a dirty line is evicted from a cache, the cache is no longer able to observe coherence transactions on the line. In this case, the Snoop Table proposed in Section 4.2 for RelaxReplay_Opt would lose its ability to observe conflicting transactions. To solve this problem, when a dirty line is evicted, its address is hashed and the two corresponding counters in the Snoop Table are incremented. This ensures that any memory-access instruction that performed an access to that address but has not been counted yet, is conservatively declared reordered. Hence correctness is preserved.

### 4.4 Modest Hardware Complexity

RelaxReplay's hardware tracks events within intervals. Such hardware is local to the processors, rather than being distributed system-wide. Even within a processor, it leverages the well-understood general structure of the ROB. It does not require any changes to the cache coherence protocol of the machine. Moreover, its operation is independent of the scheme used to order intervals. Consequently, when RelaxReplay is paired with an interval ordering scheme that itself does not require modifications to the coherence protocol, such as QuickRec [25] or Cyrus [9], RelaxReplay provides a general MRR solution that works without coherence protocol modifications. This fact substantially lowers its hardware complexity. Finally, the resulting log can be replayed using minimal hardware support, which is very similar to existing performance counters.

## 5. Evaluation

### 5.1 Experimental Setup

We evaluate RelaxReplay with a cycle-level execution-driven simulator. We model a multicore with 4, 8 (default), or 16 cores. The cores are 4-issue out-of-order superscalars that use the RC memory model. Cores have a private L1 cache and a shared L2. The interconnection network is a ring that uses a MESI snoopy cache-coherence protocol. Table 1 shows the architectural parameters, including those of RelaxReplay. From the table, we can compute the overall size of the per-processor RelaxReplay structures. Specifically, for RelaxReplay_Base, the overall MRR module of Figure 6(a) is 2.3KB, of which the TRAQ uses 1.8KB; for RelaxReplay_Opt, the MRR is 3.3KB, of which the TRAQ uses 2.5KB. Since the processor has 2 Ld/St units, we design the TRAQ to be written twice (at perform events) and read twice (at counting events) per cycle. We design the Snoop Table to be read twice (typically at perform events) and written once (on a snoop) per cycle. We run SPLASH-2 codes [34].

The effectiveness of RelaxReplay's instruction tracking mechanism depends on the average size of the intervals. To a large extent, this size is determined by the maximum interval size chosen by the chunk-based recorder paired with RelaxReplay. Some recorders, such as Karma [3] and Cyrus [9] set the maximum interval size to a small value, in order to increase replay parallelism. Other schemes, such as CoreRacer [24] and QuickRec [25], use a very large maximum interval size because they replay sequentially, and large intervals have lower overheads. Thus, to assess the sensitivity of RelaxReplay to the maximum interval size, we evaluate RelaxReplay with two different maximum interval sizes: 4K instructions and infinitely large (INF).

To estimate replay performance, we have written a software module to control the replay according to the algorithm outlined in Section 3.5. In a real system, this module would be part of the OS. However, our execution-driven simulation setup does not run OS code. Thus, to measure the overhead

| Processor and Memory System Parameters | |
|---|---|
| Multicore | Ring-based with MESI snoopy protocol<br>4, 8 (default), or 16 cores |
| Core | 4-way out-of-order superscalar @ 2GHz<br>176-entry ROB, 2 Ld/St units<br>128-entry Ld/St queue |
| L1 Cache | Private, 64KB, 4-way assoc, 64-entry MSHR<br>32B line, write-back, 2-cycle round-trip |
| L2 Cache | Shared, 512KB per core, 16-way assoc<br>64-entry MSHR<br>32B line, write-back, 12-cycle avg. round-trip |
| Ring | 32B wide, 1-cycle hop delay |
| Memory | 32B bus, 150-cycle round-trip from L2 |
| **RelaxReplay Parameters** | |
| Read & Write Sigs. | Each: 4 × 256-bit Bloom filters with H3 hash |
| Glob time, Curr bl sz | 64bits, 32bits |
| CISN, Log buffer | 16bits, 8 cache lines |
| TRAQ | 176 entries, each is 14.5B (RelaxReplay_Opt) |
| Snoop Table | 2 arrays, 64 entries each, 16-bit entry |

**Table 1.** Architectural parameters.

of this control software, we link its code with the code of the application. With this setup, we can measure its performance cost. This control software uses the recorded total order of intervals to enforce interval ordering. For this, it uses condition variables. Then, for each interval, it follows the algorithm explained in Section 3.5: it executes the interval's *InorderBlock* blocks on the hardware, and emulates the execution of the reordered instructions.

In the following, we first characterize the logs. Then, we evaluate the recording and replay performance. Finally, we analyze RelaxReplay's scalability with the processor count.

### 5.2 Log Characterization

We start by analyzing how many memory-access instructions are found by RelaxReplay to be reordered. Figure 9 shows the number of such instructions as a fraction of all memory-access instructions, for 4K maximum intervals (Chart (a)) and INF maximum intervals (Chart (b)). Each chart shows bars for all the applications and the average. In each case, we have bars for RelaxReplay_Base and RelaxReplay_Opt.

On average, RelaxReplay_Base logs 1.7% and 0.17% of memory instructions as reordered for 4K and INF intervals, respectively. This number is much smaller than the 60% of memory-access instructions that are performed out of program order, as shown in Figure 1. This shows that most of the reorders are invisible to other processors. In fact, RelaxReplay_Opt reduces this fraction even more — to a minuscule 0.03% for both 4K and INF intervals. As we will see, this large reduction has a significant impact on the size of the generated logs and the replay speed.

In all cases, loads dominate the reordered instructions. Comparing the 4K and INF results, we see that larger intervals help RelaxReplay_Base reduce the fraction of reordered instructions. However, RelaxReplay_Opt's effectiveness is independent of the interval size. This is because RelaxReplay_Opt relies on the Snoop Table to detect reordered

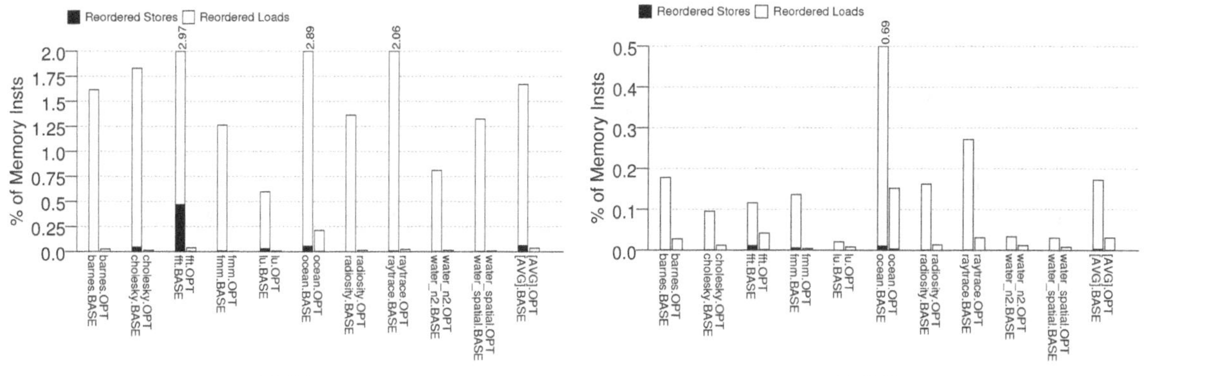


(a) 4K (b) INF

**Figure 9.** Fraction of memory-access instructions found by RelaxReplay to be reordered for 4K (a) and INF (b) intervals.

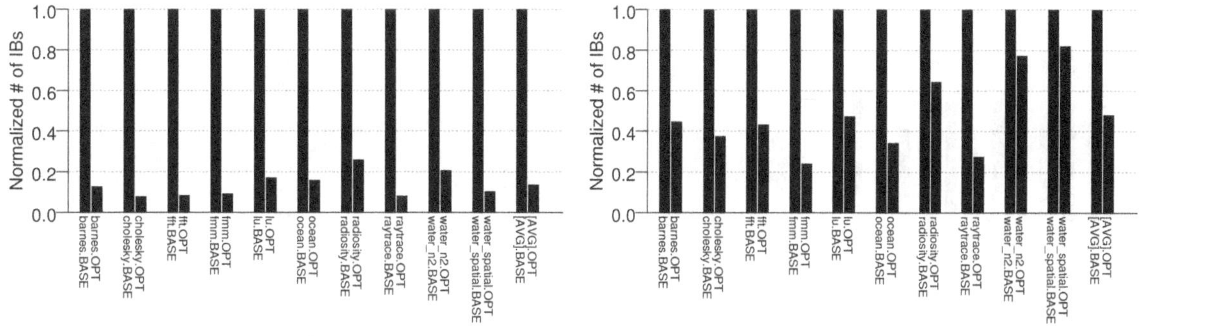


(a) 4K (b) INF

**Figure 10.** Number of *InorderBlock* entries (IBs), normalized to RelaxReplay_Base, for 4K (a) and INF (b) intervals.

instructions, rather than on whether perform and counting events are in the same interval.

The number of reordered instructions affects the number and size of the *InorderBlock* entries in the logs. Recall that an *InorderBlock* entry corresponds to a set of consecutive in-order instructions. An *InorderBlock* is terminated by either a reordered access or an interval termination. Hence, if an optimization such as RelaxReplay_Opt reduces the number of reordered accesses, the *InorderBlock* size increases and the number of *InorderBlock* entries goes down.

Figure 10 shows the number of *InorderBlock* entries in the logs for 4K (Chart (a)) and INF (Chart (b)) intervals. The figure is organized as the previous one except that, in each application, the bars are normalized to RelaxReplay_Base. The figure shows that RelaxReplay_Opt's ability to reduce the number of reordered access results in many fewer *InorderBlocks*. On average, it only logs 13% and 48% as many *InorderBlocks* as RelaxReplay_Base for 4K and INF intervals, respectively.

Finally, Figure 11 shows the *uncompressed* log size for the two designs, in bits per 1K instructions for 4K (Chart (a)) and INF (Chart (b)) intervals. We see that RelaxReplay_Opt reduces the log size over RelaxReplay_Base substantially — the result of its ability to reduce the number of reordered instructions. For 4K intervals, the average log size per 1K instructions goes down from 360 bits in RelaxReplay_Base to 22 bits in RelaxReplay_Opt; for INF intervals, it goes down from 42 bits to 12 bits. These are substantial reductions in logging needs.

The resulting RelaxReplay_Opt log sizes are 1–4x the log sizes reported for previous chunk-based recorders [6, 9, 10, 18, 23, 24] and are, therefore, comparable to them. This is despite the fact that the previous schemes required the strict SC or TSO models, while RelaxReplay_Opt handles the relaxed RC model. In fact, RelaxReplay_Opt's logs are quite small compared to the several GB/s of memory bandwidth available in modern machines. Indeed, in our experiments, RelaxReplay_Opt generates on average only 48 MB/s and 25 MB/s of logging state for 4K and INF intervals, respectively, which is a small rate. On the other hand, RelaxReplay_Base generates on average 840 MB/s and 90 MB/s. Although we consider the former excessive, the latter is small and shows that the simpler RelaxReplay_Base design is a viable solution if large intervals are acceptable — i.e., when replay parallelism is not required.

### 5.3 Characterization of Recording Performance

It can be shown that the execution overhead of recording under RelaxReplay_Opt, or under RelaxReplay_Base with INF intervals is negligible. This is consistent with past proposals for hardware-assisted RnR. To understand why recording overhead is negligible in these cases, consider the two main sources of overhead: memory bus contention as the log is being saved, and stalls due to lack of TRAQ entries. From the previous section, we deduce that the induced memory bus contention is negligible for RelaxReplay_Opt and for RelaxReplay_Base with INF intervals.

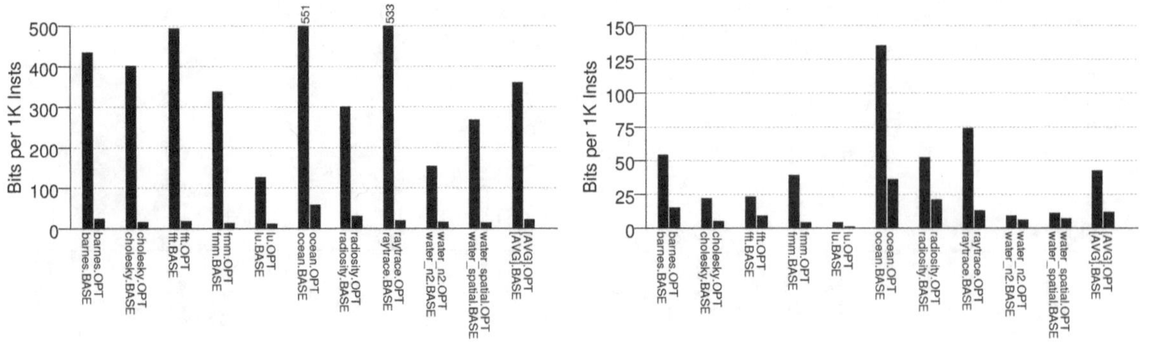


**Figure 11.** Uncompressed log size in bits per 1K instructions for 4K (a) and INF (b) intervals.

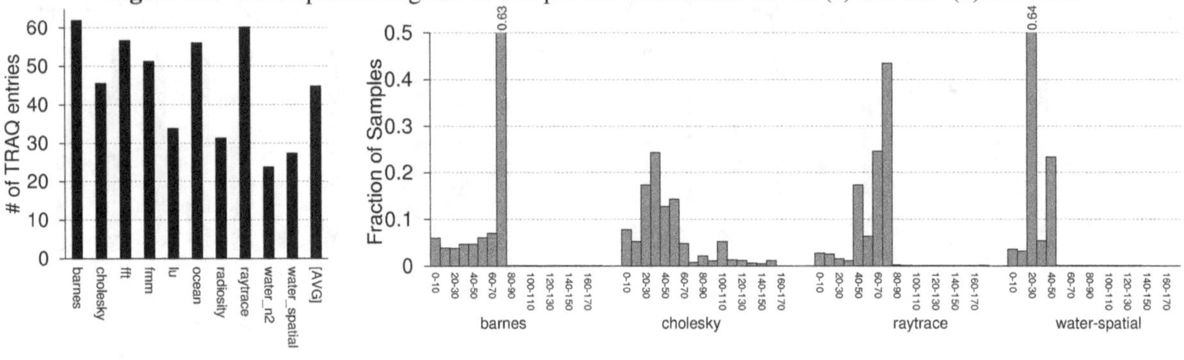


**Figure 12.** TRAQ utilization: average (a) and histograms for four representative applications (b).

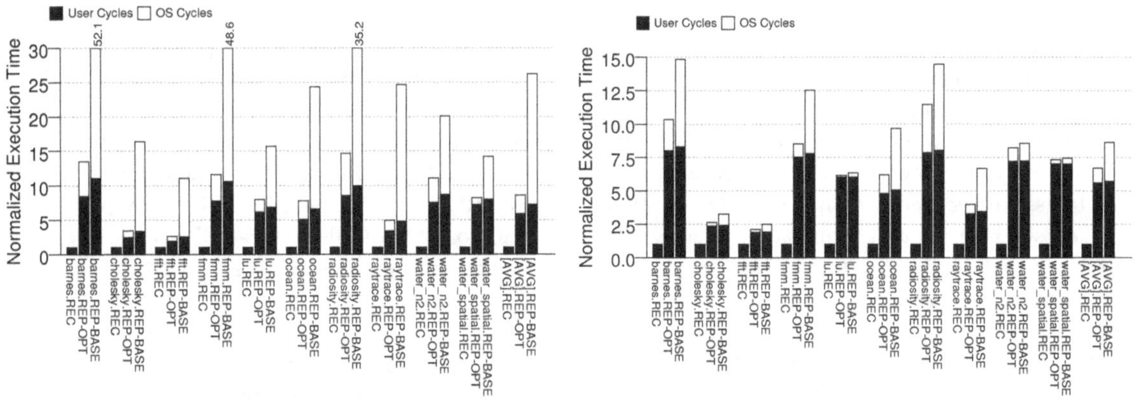


**Figure 13.** Replay time with Opt or Base logs, normalized to recording time, for 4K (a) and INF (b) intervals.

To assess the TRAQ stall, Figure 12 shows the TRAQ utilization. The figure applies to both RelaxReplay_Opt and RelaxReplay_Base. In Chart (a), we show the average number of TRAQ entries utilized by each application. We see that, in all cases, this number is less than 64. This is a small number compared to the TRAQ's 176 entries. In Chart (b), we show distributions of number of used TRAQ entries for four representative applications. In the figure, each bar corresponds to the fraction of samples where a certain number of entries (grouped in bins of 10) were used. As can be seen, although different applications have different overall shapes, in all cases, most of the time around 80 or fewer entries are used. Hence, TRAQ-induced stall is very rare. It can be shown that it accounts for less than 0.3% of the execution time for RelaxReplay_Opt and for RelaxReplay_Base with INF intervals.

### 5.4 Characterization of Replay Performance

Figure 13 shows the time it takes to replay the applications with RelaxReplay_Opt logs or RelaxReplay_Base logs, for 4K (Chart (a)) and INF (Chart (b)) intervals. For each application, the times are normalized to the time it takes to record the application, shown as the leftmost bar of each group. Note that, while recording was done in parallel with 8 processors, replay in these experiments is performed sequentially — because the interval-ordering mechanism records a total order of intervals. Moreover, the replay time is broken down into execution of the application (*User Cycles*) and execution of our control module that emulates the OS (*OS Cycles*). The latter orders intervals, reads log entries, and emulates reordered instructions.

From the figure, we see that replaying with the RelaxReplay_Opt log is fast. Although the replay is performed sequentially, it takes on average only 8.5x and 6.7x as long as the parallel recording for the 4K and INF intervals, respectively. OS time is about a third to a sixth of the replay time.

Replay with the RelaxReplay_Base log is a bit slower for INF intervals and substantially slower for 4K intervals. Specifically, sequential replay takes on average 8.6x and 26.2x as long as the parallel recording for the INF and 4K intervals, respectively. The slowdown is due to the larger fraction of reordered instructions. There is a substantial fraction of OS cycles, as the OS deals with reordered instructions. User cycles are sometimes higher than in the RelaxReplay_Opt bars because there are more pipeline flushes, as end-of-block interrupts transfer execution to the control module.

Overall, using the RelaxReplay_Opt log or the RelaxReplay_Base log with INF intervals ensures efficient replay. If we combine them with interval ordering schemes that admit parallel replay [3, 9], we expect substantially faster replay.

### 5.5 Scalability Analysis

To analyze RelaxReplay's scalability with the number of processors, we repeat the experiments with 4- and 16-core machine configurations. Figure 14 shows how the fraction of memory-access instructions that RelaxReplay perceives as reordered (Chart (a)) and the log generation rate (Chart (b)) change with 4, 8, and 16 processors (*P4*, *P8*, and *P16*) for RelaxReplay_Base and RelaxReplay_Opt. In each figure, the left- and right-hand sides present the results for the 4K and INF configurations, respectively. Each bar is the average of all the applications.

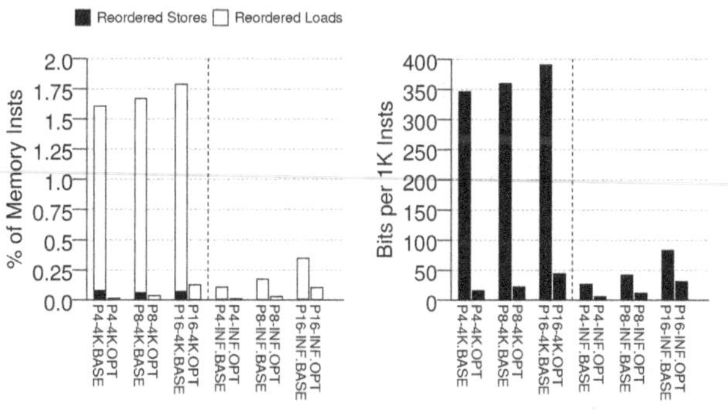


(a) Reordered instructions (b) Log size

**Figure 14.** The effect of processor count on recording.

The figures show that both the fraction of reordered instructions and the log size increase with the number of processors. Leaving aside the case of RelaxReplay_Base with 4K intervals, we see that both instruction reordering and log size are still small for up to 16 processors but increase noticeably, although not exponentially.

The reason for the increase is that, with more cores, we have more traffic and, in particular, more coherence traffic. Moreover, in our ring-based snoopy protocol, all processors observe all the traffic. As a result, there is more chance for false positives in the signatures and in the Snoop Table. The former causes additional terminations of intervals, which results in bigger logs and, in RelaxReplay_Base, more reordering; the latter causes RelaxReplay_Opt to count more reordered instructions. As a result, we see fast increases in both parameters. With directory coherence, we expect lower growth rates, as each core only sees coherence messages for the cache lines it accessed.

The case of RelaxReplay_Base with 4K intervals is less sensitive to the number of cores. The reason is that its behavior is largely determined by the small maximum interval size. Adding more coherence transactions only has a marginal impact in further reducing the interval sizes.

## 6. Related Work

Some of the proposals for RnR of multithreaded programs on multiprocessors do not require any special hardware and, instead, rely on the OS, compiler and/or runtime libraries for RnR (e.g., [16, 22, 32]). MRR with these techniques has a relatively-high performance overhead, perturbs the timing of parallel execution, and typically requires modified binaries. Due to space constraints, we do not discuss them.

Hardware-assisted MRR techniques use special hardware support for recording memory-access interleaving. FDR [35] and RTR [36] record dependences between pairs of communicating instructions. This can result in large log sizes or requires expensive hardware data structures to reduce the log size. Also, the resulting fine-grain ordering constraints can hurt replay efficiency. While FDR only supports SC, RTR supports TSO by recording the value of loads that may violate SC. Similar to our approach, it records a load's value if there is a conflicting access to its memory location between the time the load performs and all of its predecessors perform.

To remedy the large log size and fine-grain ordering constraints of earlier designs, chunk-based schemes were proposed. DeLorean [18] and Capo [19] use the speculative multithreading hardware of Bulk [31]. The underlying hardware enforces SC while allowing aggressive out-of-order execution of instructions. The execution is recorded by logging the order in which processors commit their chunks.

Rerun [10] and Karma [3] are chunk-based techniques for conventional multiprocessors with directory coherence. The papers also include proposals to integrate RTR's solution for TSO recording with their chunk-based schemes. As such, they can be considered as chunk-based recorders for TSO. However, they only provide high-level discussions about how the integration could be done without providing detailed designs or results. Timetraveler [33] builds on Rerun and reduces its log size. While Rerun terminates a chunk upon the first conflicting coherence transaction, Timetraveler allows the chunk to grow beyond that, to reduce the chunk count and, thus, the log size.

Intel MRR [23], Cyrus [9] and CoreRacer [24] are chunk-based recorders for snoopy protocols. While the first two assume SC, CoreRacer supports TSO by recording the number of stores pending in the processor's write buffer when a chunk terminates. CoreRacer can then correctly account for reordered and forwarded loads by simulating the write buffer's content during replay. However, replay efficiency may suffer because it requires write buffer simulation. Also, recording the pending stores for a chunk is often unnecessary, since the resulting reordering is rarely visible to other processors. QuickRec [25] is an FPGA implementation of a similar approach.

Some schemes have described parallel replay, such as DeLorean [18] and Capo [19] (both through speculative execution), Karma [3] and Cyrus [9].

LReplay [6] does not monitor coherence transactions; it includes a non-trivial centralized module that directly tracks the memory accesses performed by all cores. It relies on this module to detect inter-processor dependences. It supports TSO using RTR's approach. Due to its recording technique, its replay algorithm needs to simulate all instructions.

Strata [21] is designed for SC machines and records a stratum (i.e., one chunk for each processor in the system) when a dependence occurs between any two processors. A stratum is recorded only if the source and destination instructions are not already separated by a stratum. By replaying one stratum at a time, all data dependences can be enforced.

Lee et al. [15, 17] use off-line search to infer inter-thread dependences for SC [15] and TSO [17] executions. They do not record dependences. Instead, they log data fetched on a cache miss (when it is accessed for the first time). This allows independent replay of each thread. They also periodically record some Strata hints to speed-up the off-line search. Using the per-thread replays and the hints, inter-thread data dependences are determined off-line.

Rainbow [27] builds on the sequentially-consistent Strata and improves it in two ways. Firstly, it uses a centralized hardware structure, called Spectrum History, to reduce the number of recorded strata, and thus, improve the log size and replay speed. Secondly, it shows that the same data structure can aid in detecting potential SC violations in order to record non-SC executions. The idea is to record some information about delayed and pending instructions that allows it to replay the situation correctly when an SC violation happens. Although the paper discusses the hardware structures and algorithms required to implement the first improvement fairly extensively, the second part is only explained vaguely and at a very high level. In particular, detailed record and replay algorithms are only presented for the first contribution; the paper does not explain the mechanisms or hardware structures required to track and communicate the pending and delayed instructions that are central to its second contribution.

It is difficult to provide a detailed comparison between Rainbow and RelaxReplay, especially in terms of the hardware data structures, given Rainbow's lack of details and the complexity of its proposed SC-violation handling mechanism. However, it is clear that, similar to RelaxReplay, Rainbow requires write atomicity, since each instruction can only be recorded in a single spectrum. Unlike RelaxReplay, however, Rainbow cannot accommodate distributed directory protocols due to its centralized Spectrum History design. Also, unlike RelaxReplay, it needs to augment the coherence protocol messages and/or add new ones (if write-after-read dependences are to be explicitly recorded). In addition, it is unclear how the Spectrum History can be virtualized in order to accommodate application-level RnR (i.e., recording single applications instead of whole machines). Moreover, unlike RelaxReplay that can be applied to any chunk-based MRR scheme, the SC-violation handling mechanism of Rainbow is particular to its Strata-like design and cannot be directly used in conjunction with other MRR schemes.

## 7. Concluding Remarks

This paper proposed *RelaxReplay*, the first complete solution for hardware-assisted MRR that works for any relaxed-consistency model with write atomicity. With *RelaxReplay*, we can build an RnR system for any coherence protocol — whether snoopy, centralized directory or distributed directory. RelaxReplay's insight is a new way to capture memory-access reordering. Each memory instruction goes through a post-completion in-order counting step that detects any reordering, and efficiently records it. We presented two designs with different hardware needs, log sizes, and replay speeds.

RelaxReplay's mechanism to capture memory-access reordering does not rely on consistency model specifications. It can be combined with the chunk-ordering algorithm of any existing chunk-based MRR proposal — enabling that proposal to record relaxed-consistency executions. Its hardware is local to the cores and does not change the cache coherence protocol. Finally, it produces a log that is compact and efficient to use for replay with minimal hardware support.

We evaluated RelaxReplay with simulations of an 8-processor RC multicore running SPLASH-2 applications. The results showed that RelaxReplay induces negligible overhead during recording. In addition, the average size of its log was 1–4x the log sizes reported for existing SC- or TSO-based MRR systems, and still a small fraction of the bandwidth of current processors. Finally, deterministic replay is efficient, since the sequential replay of these 8 processors with minimal hardware support took on average only 6.7x as long as the parallel recording.

## Acknowledgments

This work was supported in part by NSF under grants CCF-1012759 and CNS-1116237, and Intel under the Illinois-Intel Parallelism Center (I2PC).

## References


[1] H. Agrawal, R. A. DeMillo, and E. H. Spafford. An Execution-Backtracking Approach to Debugging. *IEEE Software*, 8(3), May 1991.

[2] ARM. *ARM Architecture Reference Manual, ARMv7-A and ARMv7-R Edition Issue C*, July 2012.

[3] A. Basu, J. Bobba, and M. D. Hill. Karma: Scalable Deterministic Record-Replay. In *ICS*, June 2011.

[4] B. H. Bloom. Space/Time Trade-Offs in Hash Coding with Allowable Errors. *Comm. of the ACM*, 11(7), July 1970.

[5] T. Bressoud and F. Schneider. Hypervisor-Based Fault-Tolerance. *ACM TOCS*, 14(1), February 1996.

[6] Y. Chen, W. Hu, T. Chen, and R. Wu. LReplay: A Pending Period Based Deterministic Replay Scheme. In *ISCA*, June 2010.

[7] B. Cully, G. Lefebvre, D. Meyer, M. Feeley, N. Hutchinson, and A. Warfield. Remus: High Availability via Asynchronous Virtual Machine Replication. In *NSDI*, April 2008.

[8] G. W. Dunlap, S. T. King, S. Cinar, M. A. Basrai, and P. M. Chen. ReVirt: Enabling Intrusion Analysis through Virtual-Machine Logging and Replay. In *OSDI*, December 2002.

[9] N. Honarmand, N. Dautenhahn, J. Torrellas, S. T. King, G. Pokam, and C. Pereira. Cyrus: Unintrusive Application-Level Record-Replay for Replay Parallelism. In *ASPLOS*, March 2013.

[10] D. R. Hower and M. D. Hill. Rerun: Exploiting Episodes for Lightweight Memory Race Recording. In *ISCA*, June 2008.

[11] A. Joshi, S. T. King, G. W. Dunlap, and P. M. Chen. Detecting Past and Present Intrusions Through Vulnerability-Specific Predicates. In *SOSP*, October 2005.

[12] S. T. King and P. M. Chen. Backtracking Intrusions. In *SOSP*, October 2003.

[13] S. T. King, G. W. Dunlap, and P. M. Chen. Debugging Operating Systems with Time-Traveling Virtual Machines. In *USENIX Ann. Tech. Conf.*, April 2005.

[14] L. Lamport. How to Make a Multiprocessor Computer That Correctly Executes Multiprocess Programs. *IEEE Trans. Comput.*, 28(9), September 1979.

[15] D. Lee, M. Said, S. Narayanasamy, Z. Yang, and C. Pereira. Offline Symbolic Analysis for Multi-Processor Execution Replay. In *MICRO*, December 2009.

[16] D. Lee, B. Wester, K. Veeraraghavan, S. Narayanasamy, P. M. Chen, and J. Flinn. Respec: Efficient Online Multiprocessor Replay via Speculation and External Determinism. In *ASPLOS*, March 2010.

[17] D. Lee, M. Said, S. Narayanasamy, and Z. Yang. Offline Symbolic Analysis to Infer Total Store Order. In *HPCA*, February 2011.

[18] P. Montesinos, L. Ceze, and J. Torrellas. DeLorean: Recording and Deterministically Replaying Shared-Memory Multiprocessor Execution Efficiently. In *ISCA*, June 2008.

[19] P. Montesinos, M. Hicks, S. T. King, and J. Torrellas. Capo: A Software-Hardware Interface for Practical Deterministic Multiprocessor Replay. In *ASPLOS*, March 2009.

[20] S. Narayanasamy, G. Pokam, and B. Calder. BugNet: Continuously Recording Program Execution for Deterministic Replay Debugging. In *ISCA*, June 2005.

[21] S. Narayanasamy, C. Pereira, and B. Calder. Recording Shared Memory Dependencies Using Strata. In *ASPLOS*, Oct 2006.

[22] S. Park, Y. Zhou, W. Xiong, Z. Yin, R. Kaushik, K. H. Lee, and S. Lu. PRES: Probabilistic Replay with Execution Sketching on Multiprocessors. In *SOSP*, October 2009.

[23] G. Pokam, C. Pereira, K. Danne, R. Kassa, and A.-R. Adl-Tabatabai. Architecting a Chunk-Based Memory Race Recorder in Modern CMPs. In *MICRO*, December 2009.

[24] G. Pokam, C. Pereira, S. Hu, A.-R. Adl-Tabatabai, J. Gottschlich, H. Jungwoo, and Y. Wu. CoreRacer: A Practical Memory Race Recorder for Multicore x86 TSO Processors. In *MICRO*, December 2011.

[25] G. Pokam, K. Danne, C. Pereira, R. Kassa, T. Kranich, S. Hu, J. Gottschlich, N. Honarmand, N. Dautenhahn, S. T. King, and J. Torrellas. QuickRec: Prototyping an Intel Architecture Extension for Record and Replay of Multithreaded Programs. In *ISCA*, June 2013.

[26] Power.org. *Power ISA™ Version 2.06 Revision B*, July 2010.

[27] X. Qian, H. Huang, B. Sahelices, and D. Qian. Rainbow: Efficient Memory Dependence Recording with High Replay Parallelism for Relaxed Memory Model. In *HPCA*, Feb 2013.

[28] D. J. Sorin, M. D. Hill, and D. A. Wood. *A Primer on Memory Consistency and Cache Coherence*. Morgan & Claypool Publishers, 1st edition, 2011.

[29] S. M. Srinivasan, S. Kandula, C. R. Andrews, and Y. Zhou. Flashback: A Lightweight Extension for Rollback and Deterministic Replay for Software Debugging. In *USENIX Ann. Tech. Conf.*, June 2004.

[30] Tilera. *Tile Processor User Architecture Manual Rel. 2.4*, November 2011.

[31] J. Torrellas, L. Ceze, J. Tuck, C. Cascaval, P. Montesinos, W. Ahn, and M. Prvulovic. The Bulk Multicore Architecture for Improved Programmability. *Comm. of the ACM*, 52(12), 2009.

[32] K. Veeraraghavan, D. Lee, B. Wester, J. Ouyang, P. M. Chen, J. Flinn, and S. Narayanasamy. DoublePlay: Parallelizing Sequential Logging and Replay. In *ASPLOS*, March 2011.

[33] G. Voskuilen, F. Ahmad, and T. N. Vijaykumar. Timetraveler: Exploiting Acyclic Races for Optimizing Memory Race Recording. In *ISCA*, June 2010.

[34] S. C. Woo, M. Ohara, E. Torrie, J. P. Singh, and A. Gupta. The SPLASH-2 Programs: Characterization and Methodological Considerations. In *ISCA*, June 1995.

[35] M. Xu, R. Bodik, and M. D. Hill. A "Flight Data Recorder" for Enabling Full-System Multiprocessor Deterministic Replay. In *ISCA*, June 2003.

[36] M. Xu, R. Bodik, and M. D. Hill. A Regulated Transitive Reduction (RTR) for Longer Memory Race Recording. In *ASPLOS*, 2006.

# Prototyping Symbolic Execution Engines for Interpreted Languages


Stefan Bucur
École Polytechnique Fédérale de Lausanne
stefan.bucur@epfl.ch

Johannes Kinder
École Polytechnique Fédérale de Lausanne
Royal Holloway, University of London
johannes.kinder@rhul.ac.uk

George Candea
École Polytechnique Fédérale de Lausanne
george.candea@epfl.ch



## Abstract

Symbolic execution is being successfully used to automatically test statically compiled code [4, 7, 9, 15]. However, increasingly more systems and applications are written in dynamic interpreted languages like Python. Building a new symbolic execution engine is a monumental effort, and so is keeping it up-to-date as the target language evolves. Furthermore, ambiguous language specifications lead to their implementation in a symbolic execution engine potentially differing from the production interpreter in subtle ways.

We address these challenges by flipping the problem and using the interpreter itself as a specification of the language semantics. We present a recipe and tool (called CHEF) for turning a vanilla interpreter into a sound and complete symbolic execution engine. CHEF symbolically executes the target program by symbolically executing the interpreter's binary while exploiting inferred knowledge about the program's high-level structure.

Using CHEF, we developed a symbolic execution engine for Python in 5 person-days and one for Lua in 3 person-days. They offer complete and faithful coverage of language features in a way that keeps up with future language versions at near-zero cost. CHEF-produced engines are up to 1000× more performant than if directly executing the interpreter symbolically without CHEF.



***Categories and Subject Descriptors*** D.2.5 [*Software Engineering*]: Testing and Debugging—symbolic execution; D.3.4 [*Programming Languages*]: Processors—interpreters

***Keywords*** state selection strategies; software analysis optimizations; interpreter instrumentation





*ASPLOS '14*, March 1–4, 2014, Salt Lake City, Utah, USA.



ACM 978-1-4503-2305-5/14/03... $15.00.
http://dx.doi.org/10.1145/2541940.2541977


## 1. Introduction

Developers spend much of their time writing unit and performance tests and manually tracing hard-to-reproduce bugs; ideally, these tasks would be automated. Symbolic execution is a particularly successful technique for exploring multiple execution paths fully automatically. It has been used to find bugs and to generate high-coverage test suites for Windows media format parsers [16], Windows device drivers [19], and the Linux Coreutils [7], and it has helped to reproduce crashes for debugging [29]. Symbolic execution enumerates feasible execution paths by using a constraint solver to synthesize inputs that drive the program down paths that have not been covered before.

Most mature systems for symbolic execution target low-level code representations. The widely used symbolic execution engines KLEE [7], SAGE [16], Bitblaze [25], and S2E [9] all process either x86 machine code or LLVM [21] intermediate representation code. This makes them applicable to languages that are statically compiled to one of these representations.

However, an increasingly important class of software is never statically compiled: code in languages like Python, Perl, Lua, or Bash is directly executed by interpreters, and its dynamic features generally prevent static compilation. These languages are popular because they enable rapid prototyping and are easy to use; as a result, they are increasingly used in infrastructure and systems code [3, 18].

Consequently, there have been initial efforts to directly implement high-level symbolic execution engines for interpreted languages. For example, the NICE engine for Python [8] symbolically executes OpenFlow controller code, and the Kudzu engine for JavaScript [24] finds code injection vulnerabilities in web applications.

The implementation of a dedicated symbolic execution engine is a significant undertaking for each language. A symbolic execution engine is essentially a fully fledged interpreter for the language, operating on constraints and expressions instead of concrete memory objects. This is why existing dedicated engines usually do not support general programs in the full target language. They either support only a language subset that is relevant for a particular application domain [8, 24], or they require the developer to write their code to explicitly use custom types and libraries that provide symbolic execution functionality [11].

Even supporting just a portion of the language typically involves reading language specifications and carefully writing the engine to faithfully implement them. Unfortunately, language specifications are often imprecise or deliberately leave implementation choices to the developers of the interpreter, which gives rise to multiple dialects. Quoting the Python Language Reference: *"Consequently, if you were coming from Mars and tried to re-implement Python from this document alone, you might have to guess things and in fact you would probably end up implementing quite a different language."* [22, §1] Combined with the fact that languages like Ruby and Python are continuously evolving, this makes writing and maintaining language-specific symbolic execution engines a daunting task, thus excluding many languages from the benefits of symbolic execution-based analysis and automated testing.

In this paper, we propose and demonstrate the idea of building a symbolic execution engine for an interpreted language *from its interpreter*. The interpreter is the place where all subtleties of the language are precisely encoded, and it is the only specification that matters in practice.

We implement this idea in CHEF, a tool that takes a specially-packaged interpreter as input and becomes a fully functional symbolic execution engine for the interpreter's target language. CHEF's infrastructure for symbolic execution is language-agnostic and tailored for interpreters with a moderately-sized core (10s of KLOC), in the ballpark of Python, Ruby, and Lua. Languages as complex and large as Java are not yet a good target for CHEF. The interpreter has to be instrumented using a lightweight API to interact with CHEF.

Using CHEF, we developed symbolic execution engines for Python and Lua. In comparison to the cost of implementing a faithful new engine from scratch, adapting the language interpreters was orders of magnitude easier: for Python, 321 lines of code had to be added to the interpreter and took 5 person-days, while Lua required 277 lines of code written in 3 person-days.

We evaluated the two engines on 11 popular Python and Lua library packages, where they generated up to 1000× more test cases compared to applying plain symbolic execution on the interpreter executable. The generated tests obtained good coverage results and uncovered a number of bugs. We also compared the Python engine to dedicated implementations and found that its slower execution speed is balanced by more complete and accurate support of language features.

This paper makes two contributions:

- We show how to derive high-level symbolic execution of an interpreted language from low-level symbolic execution of the language's interpreter, while preserving full soundness and completeness.In addition, low-level symbolic execution allows to seamlessly support native library code.
- We introduce class-uniform path analysis (CUPA), a state selection heuristic that is crucial for a meaningful exploration of the interpreted program. CUPA partitions the set of symbolic execution states into classes based on their corresponding high-level program path. By adjusting the state selection probability of each class, CUPA ensures steady progress in the exploration of the interpreted program.

The remainder of the paper is organized as follows: we give background on symbolic execution and challenges related to interpreted languages (§2). We then describe CHEF and the CUPA heuristic (§3), followed by a recipe for preparing an interpreter for use with CHEF (§4). We describe how the symbolic execution engines for Python and Lua were produced (§5) and evaluate them (§6). Finally, we discuss related work (§7) and conclude (§8).

## 2. Symbolic Execution of Interpreted Code

We briefly describe symbolic execution and its use for test generation (§2.1). We then explain the problems in symbolically executing interpreted languages (§2.2). Finally, we present our idea of executing the target program through its interpreter and the challenges that arise from this (§2.3).

### 2.1 Symbolic Execution

The intuition behind symbolic execution is to execute target code with *symbolic* instead of concrete input values, to cover the entire input space and thus all possible paths. For instance, a function `foo(int x)` is executed with a symbolic variable $\lambda$ assigned to `x`. Statements using `x` manipulate it symbolically: `x := x * 3` updates the value of `x` to $3 \cdot \lambda$. The mappings from variables to expressions are kept in a *symbolic store* during symbolic execution.

***Path Condition*** Besides the symbolic store, the symbolic program state maintains a *path condition*. Whenever symbolic execution takes a conditional branch, the condition (or its negation, for `else` branches) is added to the path condition. Continuing our example, execution along the `true` branch of `if (x > 10)` would record $3 \cdot \lambda > 10$ in the path condition. Thus, each symbolic execution state represents a particular path through the program, and its path condition encodes the input constraints for taking this path.

***Dynamic Test Generation*** Dynamic test generation in the spirit of DART [15] (often referred to as *concolic* execution) executes the program symbolically along a single path that is given by a concrete input assignment. This has the benefit of reaching deeper program behaviors and reducing the number of constraint solver invocations. To this end, the symbolic execution state also contains a concrete store that keeps a

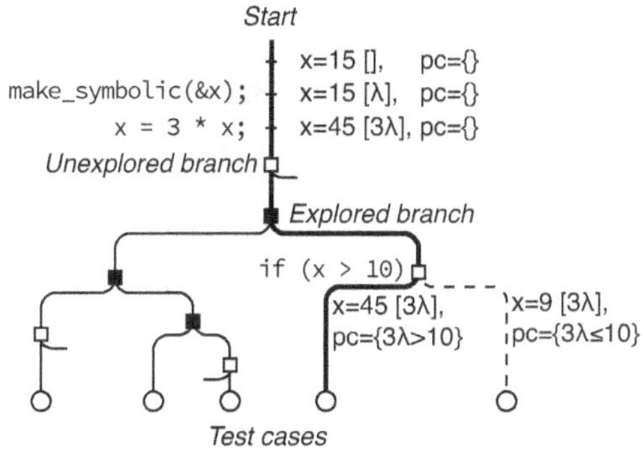


**Figure 1.** Symbolic execution tree for a simple example. States maintain concrete and symbolic values for `x` and carry a path condition (pc). The bold line represents the current concolic path, and boxes are branching points. When a candidate alternate branch (empty box) is selected, new input assignments are computed that satisfy the path condition of the new path (dashed line).

regular concrete value for each variable. We use a slight variation that avoids re-executing common path prefixes.

Consider the tree representation of program paths for the example in Figure 1. The current concrete path is the bold line. At each conditional branch, the symbolic execution engine forks the symbolic execution state. If the `then` branch is implied by the concrete value in the current state, the negated branch condition (for the `else` branch) is added to the path condition of the alternate state, and vice versa. The alternate state is tentatively added to the symbolic execution tree (empty boxes in Figure 1) for later exploration.

Once the concrete path reaches its end (the circle), the symbolic execution engine executes a new path (the dotted line) by picking an alternate state and asking a constraint solver whether the path condition of the alternate state is satisfiable. If it is, the satisfying assignment of input variables constitutes a test case that would take the program down this new path. Plugging the assignment into the expressions of the symbolic store yields a new concrete store for the alternate path. If the path condition is unsatisfiable, the path can never be taken at runtime—it is infeasible—and the corresponding state is discarded by the engine.

***Search Strategies*** The main scalability challenge for symbolic execution is *path explosion*: since each conditional branch can potentially fork the execution, the number of states (and thus paths) grows roughly exponentially in the size of the program. Several approaches exist for reducing path explosion to some extent [14, 20] but, in general, it cannot be completely avoided.

Due to path explosion, exhaustive exploration is unrealistic for most systems code, so symbolic execution can only cover a subset of the possible paths. Modern symbolic execution engines therefore use *search strategies* to reach exploration goals (e.g., line coverage) quickly [6, 7, 16, 28]. The search strategy prioritizes alternate paths it deems "interesting". Thus, the usage model for automated test generation by symbolic execution is to run for a fixed amount of time and generate as many test cases as possible, or run until a fixed coverage goal is reached (e.g., 80% line coverage).

Like all heuristics, search strategies are not universal, and their effectiveness depends on the code being explored. One of the challenges of effectively generating test cases by symbolic execution is thus to find the strategy that leads to the testing goal as fast as possible on the target code.

## 2.2 Supporting Interpreted Languages

Building a correct and complete symbolic execution engine for an interpreted language is generally harder than building one for a low-level language. Statements of interpreted languages can wrap complex operations that, in lower-level languages, would be implemented through libraries. For instance, Python strings are a built-in type offering more than 30 operations (such as `find`) as part of the language, implemented natively in the interpreter. Other language features that allow to inspect or even modify the code itself, i.e., runtime reflection, are even more tedious to implement and very hard to get right.

Finally, besides requiring an enormous initial effort to build a symbolic execution engine that fully supports them, dynamic languages also evolve fast. This implies constant, labor-intensive maintenance and co-evolution of the symbolic execution engine, if it is to keep up with the newest versions of the language.

## 2.3 Symbolically Executing the Interpreter

Considering the difficulty of directly supporting interpreted languages, we resort to symbolically executing the interpreter itself, since it completely defines the semantics of the target language as a function of the semantics of the language the interpreter is implemented in. After compiling the interpreter to a format supported by an existing symbolic execution engine, one can symbolically execute an interpreted program by symbolically executing the interpreter with the target program as argument. However, even though in principle this direct approach yields a symbolic execution engine for the target language, it is impractical, due to the engine not being aware of the control flow of the interpreted program.

***High- vs. Low-level Program Paths*** An interpreted program conceptually executes both on a high level—the level of the target language—and a low level—the level of the interpreter. A high-level program path is a sequence of values of the high-level program counter (HLPC). Each HLPC value corresponds to a program statement or bytecode instruction (both Python and Lua use intermediate bytecode). Branches can occur explicitly at control flow statements, or implicitly through exceptions. A low-level program path is a sequence of machine instructions from the interpreter binary, includ-

```
def validateEmail(email):
  at_sign_pos = email.find("@")
  ...
  if at_sign_pos < 3:
    raise InvalidEmailError()
  ...
```

```
def average(x, y):
  return (x + y) / 2
```

**Figure 2.** Two examples of Python code that lead to path explosion when the interpreter running it is symbolically executed.

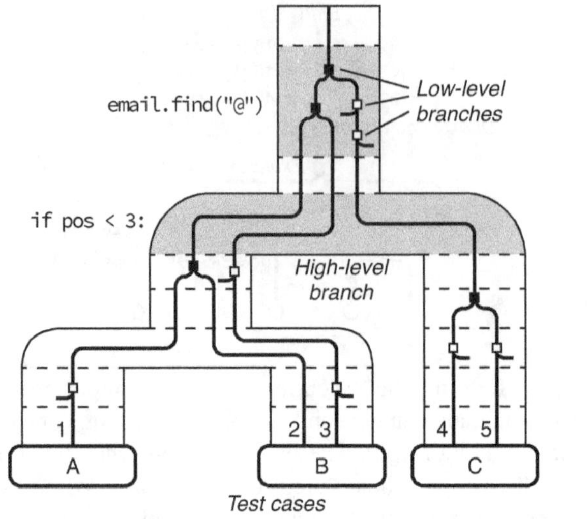


**Figure 3.** High-level execution tree (paths A, B, and C), as induced by its low-level execution paths (1–5) for the first running example in Figure 2. Dotted lines segment high-level execution paths into bytecode instructions. One high-level path may correspond to multiple low-level paths explored.

ing its code for internal bookkeeping (e.g., details of reference counting and garbage collection).

Due to the additional implementation details, a single high-level path can map to multiple low-level paths. Figure 2 shows two examples of Python code that have few high-level but many low-level paths. The **validateEmail** method has only two high-level paths, but its use of **string.find** leads to as many low-level paths as there can be characters in the **email** string. The second example **average** may come as more of a surprise: even though it has just a single high-level path, symbolic execution can end up enumerating many low-level paths: Python uses arbitrary-precision integers, so the interpreter may have to iterate over digit vectors of arbitrary length, which can in principle spawn arbitrarily many paths.

***Challenges for Search Strategies*** The search strategy of a low-level symbolic execution engine is oblivious to the high-level program structure of the target program, and it essentially just tries to cover the interpreter. This generally leads to covering the same high-level paths many times with multiple distinct low-level paths. For instance, a high-level statement like **find** can lead to hundreds of alternate states, whereas a primitive integer comparison might just create a single one. Therefore, the low-level search strategy is likely to explore multiple ways for **find** to succeed or fail, without increasing high-level coverage, before eventually exploring the alternate outcome of the comparison.

The key is to make the engine aware of the high-level interpreted program. By tracing the values of the HLPC, the engine can construct a high-level control flow graph (CFG) on the fly that can be be leveraged by the search strategy.

Alas, a strategy cannot straightforwardly determine future branching points in a high-level CFG: two low-level paths can fork from the same prefix *before* their corresponding high-level paths do. This can be due to having distinct bytecode instructions for comparisons and conditional jumps, or due to native library calls. In Figure 3, three low-level paths fork within the single HLPC location for **email.find**. The low-level paths remain on the same high-level path until reaching the branching HLPC, where they diverge into two distinct high-level paths. The relevant alternate low-level states for covering the distinct high-level paths thus were located away from the location of the code interpreting the high-level control flow statement. The issue of pre-determining branches is present also when exploring regular code, but it is ubiquitous when exploring code on interpreters.

## 3. The CHEF System

We now present the architecture of CHEF (§3.1) and introduce CUPA, our state selection mechanism (§3.2). We then describe CUPA optimized for exploring distinct high-level paths (§3.3) and optimized for high line coverage (§3.4).

### 3.1 System Overview

CHEF is a platform for language-specific symbolic execution. Provided with an interpreter environment, which acts as an executable language specification, it becomes a symbolic execution engine for the target language (see Figure 4). The resulting engine can be used like a hand-written one, in particular for test case generation. When fed with a target program and a symbolic test case (also called test driver or test specification in the literature), it outputs a set of concrete test cases, as shown in Figure 4.

CHEF is built on top of the S2E analysis platform [9]. S2E symbolically executes a virtual machine containing the interpreter and a testing library at the level of machine code, including the OS kernel, drivers, and user programs. S2E provides an API that guest code can use to declare memory buffers as symbolic. Comparisons on symbolic values cause S2E to fork new paths, which are enqueued and explored following a search strategy. CHEF extends the S2E guest API with a high-level instruction instrumentation call (§4.1), in-

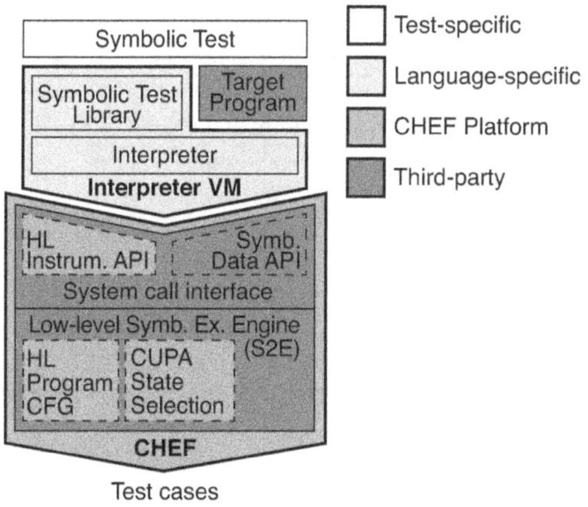


**Figure 4.** Schema of CHEF's architecture.

voked by interpreters to trace the currently executing high-level path. The explored high-level paths are used to construct a high-level execution tree and a low-level to high-level mapping (i.e., the data structure shown in Figure 3). CHEF uses a state selection strategy to maximize the ratio of high-level to low-level paths (§3.2).

The resulting engine is a correct symbolic execution engine for the target language *as defined by the interpreter*. It is fully precise and theoretically complete, i.e., it will not explore infeasible paths and will eventually explore all paths. The usual limitations of symbolic execution engines apply: completeness holds only under the assumption that the constraint solver can reason about all generated path conditions, and it is understood that exhaustive exploration is usually impossible in finite time.

### 3.2 Class-Uniform Path Analysis (CUPA)

Consider using symbolic execution for achieving statement coverage on a program containing a function with an input-dependent loop. At each iteration, the loop forks one additional state (or exponentially many, if there are branches in the loop). A strategy that selects states to explore uniformly is therefore biased toward selecting more states from this function, at the expense of states in other functions that fork less but contribute equally to the statement coverage goal.

We reduce this bias by introducing Class-Uniform Path Analysis (CUPA). The main idea is to group states into classes and then choose uniformly among classes instead of states. For instance, in the above example, the class of each state could be its current function. CUPA then first selects uniformly a function, then picks at random a state inside that function. This way, functions generating many states are still selected with equal probability to others.

In general, CUPA organizes the state queue into a hierarchy of state subsets rooted at the entire state queue (see Figure 5). The children of each subset partition the subset according to the *state classification scheme* at their level. A classification scheme is defined as a function $h : S \to C$,

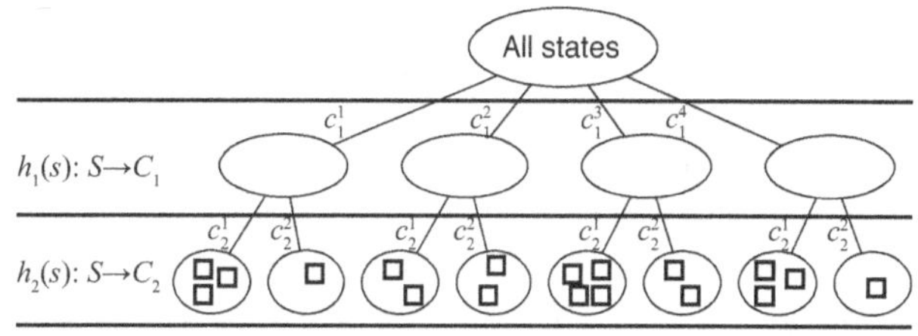


**Figure 5.** CUPA state partitioning. Each level corresponds to a state classification scheme. Child nodes partition the parent node according to the classification at their level.

where $h(s)$ maps each state $s$ into a class value $c$. States of the same parent with the same class value are sorted into the same child. CUPA selects a new state for exploration by performing a random descent in the classification tree, starting from the root. When reaching a leaf, the strategy takes out a random state from the state set and returns it to the symbolic execution engine for exploration. By default, all sibling classes on each level have equal probability of being picked, but they can be assigned weights if required.

A CUPA strategy is parameterized by the number $N$ of levels in the tree and a classification function $h_i$ for each level $i = 1 \ldots N$. CHEF uses two instantiations of CUPA: one optimized for covering high-level paths (§3.3) and one for covering the high-level CFG, i.e., statements (§3.4).

### 3.3 Path-Optimized CUPA

A low-level strategy unaware of the high-level program would be implicitly biased towards picking high-level instructions that fork more low-level states than others, such as string operations or native calls. To mitigate this, we instantiate a two-level CUPA strategy using the following classes:

1. The location of the state in the high-level symbolic execution tree. This is the occurrence of the state's high-level program counter (HLPC) in the unfolded high-level CFG, referred to as the dynamic HLPC. We choose the dynamic HLPC to give each high-level path reaching the HLPC the same chance to fork and subsequently diverge.
2. The low-level x86 program counter of the state. This classification reduces the selection bias of "hot spots" of path explosion within a single complex instruction, such as a native function call.

### 3.4 Coverage-Optimized CUPA

Based on a coverage-optimized strategy introduced by the KLEE symbolic execution engine [7], we developed a CUPA instance that partitions states according to their minimum distance to branches leading to uncovered code. Alas, dynamic language interpreters do not generally have a static CFG view of the program, so code that has not been covered yet is not accessible to the search strategy. The high-level CFG of the target program is dynamically discovered along each execution path. On this CFG, we employ heuristics that (1) identify the instruction opcodes that may branch, and (2) weigh the state selection toward states that are closer to these potential branching points.

First, CHEF identifies the branching opcodes by collecting all high-level instructions that terminate a basic block with an out-degree in the CFG of at least 2 (i.e., cause branching in the control flow). We then eliminate the 10% least frequent opcodes, which correspond to exceptions or other rare control-flow events. Second, CHEF identifies the potential branching points as those instructions in the CFG that have a branching opcode (as previously identified) but currently only one successor. Finally, CHEF computes for each execution state the distance in the CFG to the closest such potential branching point.

Having computed this information, we instantiate a two-level CUPA strategy with the following classes:

1. The static HLPC of the state in the high-level CFG. On this level, each class is weighted by $\frac{1}{d}$, where $d$ is the distance in the inferred high-level CFG to the closest potential branching point, making states at locations close to a target more likely to be selected.
2. The state itself (so each partition has a single element). On this level, the states are weighted by their *fork weight*.

Fork weight is computed by counting the number of consecutive forks at the same low-level program counter (i.e., at an input-dependent loop in machine code). States $1,\ldots,n$ forking from the same path at the same location get weights $p^n, p^{n-1},\ldots,1$, where $p < 1$ de-emphasizes states forked earlier ($p = 0.75$ in our implementation). The last state to fork at a certain location thus gets maximum weight, because alternating the last decision in a loop is often the quickest way to reach different program behavior (e.g., to satisfy a string equality check).

# 4. Preparing the Interpreter

We now explain how to prepare an interpreter for CHEF: the first and mandatory step is to instrument the main interpreter loop to report HLPCs (§4.1); the second and optional step is to optimize the interpreter for efficient symbolic execution (§4.2). CHEF provides an API (Table 1) that will be explained along with its use. Finally, we discuss the remaining work of building a language-specific testing API to the resulting engine (§4.3).

## 4.1 Exposing the High-Level Program Location

To reconstruct the high-level program paths and CFG, CHEF needs to identify the high-level instructions executed on each low-level path. CHEF provides the `log_pc(pc, opcode)` API call to the interpreter, which declares the current high-level program location and the type (opcode) of the next instruction. A high-level instruction is executed in between two consecutive `log_pc` calls. Interpreters typically contain a main interpretation loop that `switch`-es over the type of the current instruction and invokes specific handlers. The `log_pc` call can be added conveniently at the head of the interpreter loop.

| API Call | Description |
|---|---|
| `log_pc(pc, opcode)` | Log the interpreter PC and opcode |
| `start_symbolic()` | Start the symbolic execution |
| `end_symbolic()` | Terminate the symbolic state |
| `make_symbolic(buf)` | Make buffer symbolic |
| `concretize(buf)` | Concretize buffer of bytes |
| `upper_bound(value)` | Get maximum value for expression on current path |
| `is_symbolic(buf)` | Check if buffer is symbolic |
| `assume(expr)` | Assume constraint |

**Table 1.** The CHEF API used by the interpreters running inside the S2E VM.

In our design, we make minimal assumptions about the language structure, so the HLPC and opcode values are opaque; the CUPA strategies were designed accordingly. Nonetheless, more specific versions of the system could add structure to the two values, e.g. provide a pair of function name and offset as HLPC. The additional information can be used by CHEF to improve the exploration heuristics (e.g., by creating a CUPA class).

The granularity of `log_pc` calls depends on the language structure. CHEF's correctness does not depend on the specific instrumentation pattern, but the more closely the reported HLPC corresponds to statements in the target program, the more accurately CUPA can cluster states. In the extreme, if `log_pc` is never invoked, CHEF would see the entire program as a single high-level instruction and lose the advantage of CUPA clustering for HLPCs.

## 4.2 Optimizing for Symbolic Execution

In order to maximize performance, interpreters make heavy use of special cases and sophisticated data structures. Unfortunately, these features hurt the performance of symbolic execution by amplifying path explosion and increasing the complexity of symbolic formulas [27].

We identify a number of easy optimizations that preserve the interpretation semantics but significantly improve symbolic execution performance. The optimizations use the CHEF API in the last block of rows in Table 1.

***Neutralizing Hash Functions*** Hash functions are especially common in interpreters, due to the internal use of hash tables for associative data structures (e.g., Python dictionaries or Lua tables). However, they are generally a problem in symbolic execution: a symbolic value added to a hash table (a) creates constraints that essentially ask the constraint solver to reverse a hash function, which is often hard, and (b) causes the exploration to fork on each possible hash bucket the value could fall into. A simple and effective optimization is to *neutralize the hash function*, i.e., replace it with a degenerate one returning a single constant. This

```
void *malloc(size_t size) {
  if (is_symbolic(&size, sizeof(size))) {
    size_t upper_size = upper_bound(size);
    return old_malloc(upper_size);
  }
  return old_malloc(size);
}
```

**Figure 6.** Example of a symbolic execution-aware `malloc` function wrapper created using the CHEF API. If the allocation size is symbolic, the wrapper determines its upper bound and issues a concrete request to the underlying implementation.

change honors the usual contracts for hash functions (equal objects have equal hashes) and will turn hash lookups into list traversals.

***Avoiding Symbolic Pointers*** Input-dependent pointers (also referred to as symbolic pointers) may point to multiple locations in the program memory, so a pointer dereference operation would have to be resolved for each possible location. In practice, symbolic execution engines deal with this situation in one of two ways: (a) fork the execution state for each possible concrete value the symbolic pointer can take; or (b) represent the dereference symbolically as a read operation from memory at a symbolic offset and let the constraint solver "deal" with it. Both ways hurt symbolic execution, either by causing excessive path explosion or by burdening the constraint solver.

While there is no generic way to avoid symbolic pointers other than concretizing their values (the `concretize` API call) at the price of losing completeness, there are specific cases where they can be avoided.

First, *the size of a buffer can be concretized* before allocation. A symbolic size would most likely cause a symbolic pointer to be returned, since a memory allocator computes the location of a new block based on the requested size. To avoid losing completeness, a symbolic execution-aware memory allocator can determine a (concrete) upper bound on the requested size and use that value for reserving space, while leaving the original size variable symbolic. This way, memory accesses to the allocated block would not risk being out of bounds. Figure 6 shows how the CHEF API is used to wrap a call to the `malloc` function in the standard C library.

Second, *caching and "interning" can be eliminated.* Caching computed results and value interning (i.e., ensuring that a single copy of each possible value of a type is created) are common ways to improve the performance of interpreters. Alas, when a particular value is computed, its location in memory becomes dependent on its value. If the value was already in the cache or in the interned store, it is returned from there, otherwise a new value is computed. During symbolic execution, this logic becomes embedded in the value of the returned pointer, which becomes symbolic. Disabling caching and interning may hurt the native performance of the program, but it can give a significant boost when running inside a symbolic execution engine.

| Component | Python | Lua |
|---|---|---|
| Interpreter core size (C LoC) | 427,435 | 14,553 |
| HLPC instrumentation (C LoC) | 47 (0.01%) | 44 (0.30%) |
| Sym. optimizations (C LoC) | 274 (0.06%) | 233 (1.58%) |
| Native extensions (C LoC) | 1,320 (0.31%) | 154 (1.06%) |
| Test library (Python/Lua LoC) | 103 | 87 |
| Developer time (person-days) | 5 | 3 |

**Table 2.** Summary of the effort required to support Python and Lua in CHEF. The first row is the interpreter size without the standard language library. The next two rows are changes in the interpreter core, while the following two constitute the symbolic test library. The last item indicates total developer effort.

***Avoiding Fast Paths*** A common way to speed-up the native performance of a function is to handle different classes of inputs using faster specialized implementations ("fast paths"). For example, a string comparison automatically returns false if the two strings have different lengths, without resorting to byte-wise comparison.

Fast paths may hurt symbolic execution because they cause symbolic branches in the code checking for the special input conditions. *Eliminating short-circuited returns* can reduce path explosion. Instead of returning to the caller as soon as it produced an answer, the function continues running and stops on an input-independent condition. For example, when comparing two strings of concrete length, a byte-wise string comparison would then traverse the entire string buffers in a single execution path, instead of returning after the first difference found.

### 4.3 Testing API

Programs to be tested can be fed symbolic inputs by marking input buffers with `make_symbolic` and defining conditions over the input with the `assume` call, in accordance to the test specification. Note that the buffer is a memory region of concrete bounds. It is the job of the symbolic test library in the interpreter VM to convert from the language data structures (e.g., strings, integers) to the memory locations used to store the data in the interpreter implementation.

## 5. Case Studies

We used CHEF to generate symbolic execution engines for Python (§5.1) and Lua (§5.2). Table 2 summarizes the effort to set up the two interpreters for CHEF. The necessary changes to the interpreter amount to 321 lines of code for Python and 277 for Lua. The total developer time was 5 person-days for Python and 3 person-days for Lua, which is orders of magnitude smaller than the effort required for building a complete symbolic execution engine from scratch.

```
class ArgparseTest(SymbolicTest):
    def setUp(self):
        self.argparse = importlib.import_module("argparse")

    def runTest(self):
        parser = self.argparse.ArgumentParser()
        parser.add_argument(
            self.getString("arg1_name", '\x00'*3))
        parser.add_argument(
            self.getString("arg2_name", '\x00'*3))

        args = parser.parse_args([
           self.getString("arg1", '\x00'*3),
           self.getString("arg2", '\x00'*3)])
```

**Figure 7.** The symbolic test used to exercise the functionality of the Python **argparse** package.

### 5.1 Symbolic Execution Engine for Python

***Interpreter Instrumentation*** We instrumented the CPython interpreter 2.7.3 for use with CHEF, according to the guidelines presented in §4.

Python programs are composed of modules, corresponding to Python source files. Each source file is compiled into an interpreter-specific bytecode format, i.e., each source statement is translated into one or more lower-level primitive instructions. The instructions are grouped into blocks, corresponding to a single loop nesting, function, method, class, or global module definition. We define an HLPC as the concatenation of the unique block address of the top frame on the stack and the current instruction offset inside the block. We instrumented the Python interpreter to pass this program location to CHEF; this required adding less than 50 LoC to the main interpreter loop.

We performed several optimizations on the Python interpreter: we neutralized the hash functions of strings and integers, which are the most common objects; we concretized the memory sizes passed to the garbage-collected memory allocator; and we eliminated interning for small integers and strings. Most optimizations involved only adding preprocessor directives for conditional compilation of blocks of code. We gathered the optimizations under a new **-with-symbex** flag of the interpreter's **./configure** script.

***Symbolic Tests*** To validate the usefulness of the resulting symbolic execution engine, we use it as a test case generation tool. To this end, we implemented a symbolic test library as a separate Python package, used both inside the guest virtual machine, and outside, during test replay. Figure 7 is an example of a symbolic test class for the **argparse** command-line interface generator. It sets up a total of 12 symbolic characters of input: two 3-character symbolic arguments to configure the command-line parser plus another two to exercise the parsing functionality.

The test class derives from the library's **SymbolicTest** class, which provides two methods to be overridden: **setUp**, which is run once before the symbolic test starts, and **runTest**, which creates the symbolic input and can check properties. The symbolic inputs are created by calling the **getString** and **getInt** methods in the **SymbolicTest** API.

A symbolic test is executed by a symbolic test runner, which is also part of the library. The runner can work in either symbolic or replay mode. In *symbolic mode*, the runner executes inside the guest virtual machine. It creates a single instance of the test class, whose **getString** and **getInt** methods create corresponding Python objects and invoke the **make_symbolic** call to mark their memory buffers as symbolic. In *replay mode*, the runner creates one instance of the test class for each test case created by CHEF. The **getString** and **getInt** methods return the concrete input assignment of the test case.

### 5.2 Symbolic Execution Engine for Lua

Lua is a lightweight scripting language mainly used as an interpreter library to add scripting capabilities to software written in other languages. However, it also has a standalone interpreter and several Lua-only projects exist. We generated a symbolic execution engine for Lua based on version 5.2.2 of the Lua interpreter.

***Interpreter Instrumentation*** Similar to Python, Lua programs are composed of one or more Lua source files, compiled into a bytecode format. The code is compiled into a set of functions that operate on a global stack of values. Each function is composed of a sequence of bytecode instructions, where each instruction is defined by an offset, opcode, and parameters. We construct the HLPC as the concatenation of the unique address of the function in the top frame and the current instruction offset being executed. The instrumentation amounts to less than 50 LoC added to the interpreter loop.

We optimized the Lua interpreter for symbolic execution by eliminating string interning. In addition, we configured the interpreter to use integer numbers instead of the default floating point, for which S2E does not support symbolic expressions. This change was easy, because it was available as a macro definition in the interpreter's configuration header.

## 6. Evaluation

After presenting our testing targets and methodology (§6.1), we answer the following questions:

- Is a CHEF-based symbolic execution engine effective for automated test generation (§6.2)?
- How much do CUPA and interpreter optimizations contribute to the engine's effectiveness (§6.3)?
- How efficient is the test case generation (§6.4)?
- What is the impact of each optimization technique presented in §4.2 on effectiveness (§6.5)?
- How does a generated symbolic execution engine compare to a dedicated implementation (§6.6)?

All reported experiments were performed on a 48-core 2.3 GHz AMD Opteron 6176 machine with 512 GB of

RAM, running Ubuntu 12.04. Each CHEF invocation ran on 1 CPU core and used up to 8 GB of RAM on average.

### 6.1 Testing Targets and Methodology

***Testing Targets*** We evaluated the symbolic execution engines for Python and Lua on 6 Python and 5 Lua packages, respectively, including system, web, and office libraries. In total, the tested code in these packages amounts to about 12.8 KLOC. We chose the latest versions of widely used packages from the Python standard library, the Python Package Index, and the Luarocks repository. Whenever possible, we chose the pure interpreted implementation of the package over the native optimized one (e.g., the Python `simplejson` package). The first five columns of Table 3 summarize the package characteristics; LOC numbers were obtained with the `cloc` tool [1].

The reported package sizes exclude libraries, native extension modules, and the packages' own test suites. However, the packages ran in their unmodified form, using all the language features and libraries they were designed to use, including classes, built-in data structures (strings, lists, dictionaries), regular expressions, native extension modules, and reflection.

All testing targets have a significant amount of their functionality written in the interpreted language itself; we avoided targets that are just simple wrappers around native extension modules (written in C or C++) in order to focus on the effectiveness of CHEF at distilling high-level paths from low-level symbolic execution. Nevertheless, we also included libraries that depend on native extension modules. For instance, all the testing targets containing a lexing and parsing component use Python's standard regular expression library, which is implemented in C. To thoroughly test these parsers, it is important to also symbolically execute the native regular expression library. For this, the binary symbolic execution capabilities of CHEF are essential.

***Methodology: Symbolic Tests*** For each package, we wrote a symbolic test that invokes the package's entry points with one or more symbolic strings. Figure 7 in §5.1 is an example of such a symbolic test.

Each symbolic test ran for 30 minutes within CHEF, after which we replayed the collected high-level tests on the host machine, in a vanilla Python/Lua environment, to confirm test results and measure line coverage. To compensate for the randomness in the state selection strategies, we repeated each experiment 15 times. In each graph we present average values and error margins as +/- one standard deviation.

For our experiments, we did not use explicit specifications, but relied on generic checks for finding common programming mistakes. For both Python and Lua, we checked for interpreter crashes and potential hangs (infinite loops). For Python—which, unlike Lua, has an exception mechanism—we also flagged whenever a test case led to unspecified exceptions being thrown. In general, one could find application-specific types of bugs by adding specifications in the form of assertions, as in normal unit tests.

***Methodology: Coverage Measurement*** Line or statement coverage remains widely used, even though its meaningfulness as a metric for test quality is disputed. We measure and report line coverage to give a sense of what users can expect from a test suite generated fully automatically by a symbolic execution engine based on CHEF. For Python, we rely on the popular `coverage` package, and for Lua we use the `luacov` package.

Since our prototype only supports strings and integers as symbolic program inputs, we count only the lines of code that can be reached using such inputs. We report this number as "coverable LOC" in the fifth column of Table 3, and use it in our experiments as a baseline for what such a symbolic execution engine could theoretically cover directly. For example, for the `simplejson` library, this includes only code that decodes JSON-encoded strings, not code that takes a JSON object and encodes it into a string. Note that, in principle, such code could still be tested and covered by writing a more elaborate symbolic test that sets up a JSON object based on symbolic primitives [5].

### 6.2 Effectiveness for Automated Testing

We evaluate the effectiveness of the generated symbolic execution engines for bug detection and exception exploration.

***Bug Detection*** The specifications we used for our experiments are application-agnostic and only check for per-path termination within a given time bound and for the absence of unrecoverable crashes. The first specification checks whether a call into the runtime returns within 60 seconds. In this way, we discovered a bug in the Lua JSON package that causes the parser to hang in an infinite loop: if the JSON string contains the `/*` or `//` strings marking the start of a comment but no matching `*/` or line terminator, the parser reaches the end of the string and continues spinning waiting for another token. This bug is interesting for two reasons: First, comments are not part of the JSON standard, and the parser accepts them only for convenience, so this is a clear case of an interpreter-specific bug. Second, JSON encodings are normally automatically generated and transmitted over the network, so they are unlikely to contain comments; traditional testing is thus likely to miss this problem. However, an attacker could launch a denial of service attack by sending a JSON object with a malformed comment.

The second implicit specification checks that a program never terminates non-gracefully, i.e., the interpreter implementation or a native extension crashes without giving the program a chance to recover through the language exception mechanisms. In our experiments, our test cases did not expose any such behavior.

***Exception Exploration*** This scenario focuses on finding undocumented exceptions in Python code. Being memory-safe languages, crashes in Python and Lua code tend to be

| Package | LOC | Type | Description | Coverable LOC | Exceptions | Hangs |
|---|---|---|---|---|---|---|
| **Python** | | | | | | |
| argparse* | 1,466 | System | Command-line interface | 1,174 | 4 / 0 | — |
| ConfigParser* | 451 | System | Configuration file parser | 145 | 1 / 0 | — |
| HTMLParser* | 623 | Web | HTML parser | 582 | 1 / 0 | — |
| simplejson 3.10 | 1,087 | Web | JSON format parser | 315 | 2 / 0 | — |
| unicodecsv 0.9.4 | 126 | Office | CSV file parser | 95 | 1 / 0 | — |
| xlrd 0.9.2 | 7,241 | Office | Microsoft Excel reader | 4,914 | 5 / 4 | — |
| **Lua** | | | | | | |
| cliargs 2.1-2 | 370 | System | Command-line interface | 273 | — | — |
| haml 0.2.0-1 | 984 | Web | HTML description markup | 775 | — | — |
| sb-JSON v2007 | 454 | Web | JSON format parser | 329 | — | ✓ |
| markdown 0.32 | 1,057 | Web | Text-to-HTML conversion | 673 | — | — |
| moonscript 0.2.4-1 | 4,634 | System | Language that compiles to Lua | 3,577 | — | — |
| **TOTAL** | 18,493 | | | 12,852 | | |

**Table 3.** Summary of testing results for the Python and Lua packages used for evaluation. Items with (*) represent standard library packages. Exception numbers indicate total / undocumented exception types discovered.

due to *unhandled exceptions* rather than bad explicit pointers. When such exceptions are not caught by the program, they propagate to the top of the stack and cause the program to be terminated prematurely. In dynamic languages, it is difficult to determine all the possible exceptions that a function can throw to the callee, because there is no language-enforced type-based API contract. Users of an API can only rely on the documentation or an inspection of the implementation. Therefore, undocumented exceptions are unlikely to be checked for in `try-except` constructs and can erroneously propagate further. They can then hurt productivity (e.g., a script that crashes just as it was about to complete a multi-TB backup job) or disrupt service (e.g., result in an HTTP 500 Internal Server Error).

We looked at all the Python exceptions triggered by the test cases generated using CHEF and classified them into *documented* and *undocumented*. The documented exceptions are either exceptions explicitly mentioned in the package documentation or common Python exceptions that are part of the standard library (e.g., `KeyError`, `ValueError`, `TypeError`). Undocumented exceptions are all the rest.

The sixth column in Table 3 summarizes our findings. We found four undocumented exceptions in `xlrd`, the largest package. These exceptions occur when parsing a Microsoft Excel file, and they are `BadZipfile`, `IndexError`, `error`, and `AssertionError`. These errors occur inside the inner components of the Excel parser, and should have either been documented or, preferably, been caught by the parser and re-raised as the user-facing `XLRDError`.

### 6.3 Impact of CUPA Heuristics and Interpreter Optimizations

We now analyze the impact of the CUPA heuristics (described in §3.2) and the interpreter optimizations (described in §4.2) on test generation effectiveness. Specifically, we measure the number of paths (respectively source code lines) covered by the test suite generated in 30 minutes for the packages in Table 3.

We compare the results obtained in 4 different configurations: (1) the baseline, consisting of performing random state selection while executing the unmodified interpreter, and then either use (2) the path- or coverage-optimized CUPA only, (3) the optimized interpreter only, or (4) both CUPA and the optimized interpreter. This way we measure the individual contribution of each technique, as well as their aggregate behavior.

***Test Case Generation*** Figure 8 compares the number of test cases generated with each of the 4 CHEF configurations, using the path-optimized CUPA (§3.3). We only count the *relevant* high-level test cases, that is, each test case exercises a unique high-level path in the target Python program.

For all but one of the 11 packages (6 Python plus 5 Lua), the aggregate CUPA + interpreter optimizations performs the best, often by a significant margin over the baseline. This validates the design premises behind our techniques.

The CUPA strategy and the interpreter optimizations may interact non-linearly. In two cases (Python's `xlrd` and `simplejson`), the aggregate significantly outperforms either individual technique. These are cases where the result is better than the sum of its parts. In the other cases, the result is roughly the sum of each part, although the contribution of each part differs among targets. This is visually depicted on the log-scale graph: for each cluster, the heights of the middle bars measured from level 1× roughly add up to the height of the aggregate (left) bar.

In one case (Lua's `JSON`), the aggregate performs worse on average than using the interpreter optimizations alone. Moreover, the performance of each configuration is less predictable, as shown by the large error bars. This behavior is due to the generated tests that cause the interpreter to hang,

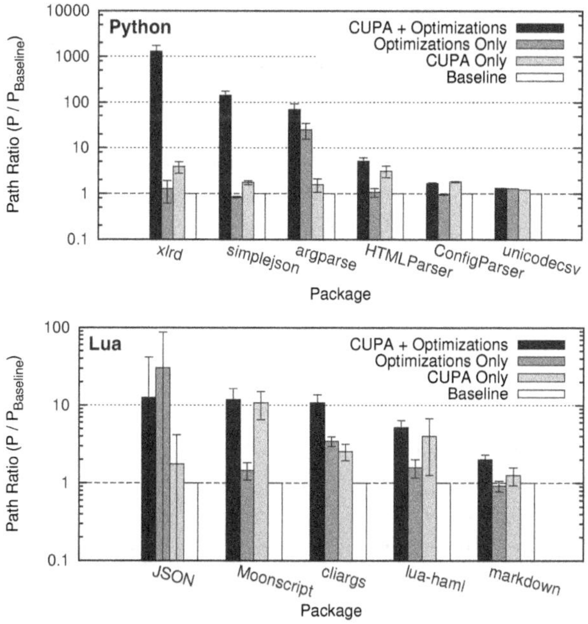


**Figure 8.** The number of Python and Lua test cases generated by coverage- and path-optimized CUPA relative to random state selection (logarithmic scale).

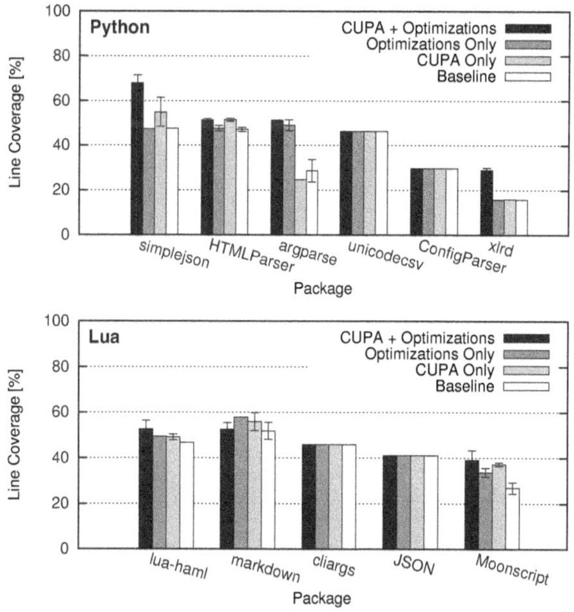


**Figure 9.** Line coverage for the experiments of Figure 8.

as explained in §6.2. To detect hangs, the test runs for 60 seconds before switching to another test case. This acts as a "penalty" for the configurations that find more paths leading to the hang and also skews the distribution of path execution times, since the hanging paths take significantly longer than the normal (terminating) paths.

***Line Coverage*** Figure 9 shows the line coverage achieved by each configuration, using CUPA optimized for line coverage (§3.4). In 6 out of 11 packages, the coverage improvement is noticeable, and for Python's **`simplejson`** and **`xlrd`**, the improvements are significant (80% and 40%).

Note that these coverage improvements are obtained using basic symbolic tests that do not make assumptions about the input format. We believe that tailoring the symbolic tests to the specifics of each package could improve these results significantly.

## 6.4 Efficiency of Test Case Generation

We now look at the efficiency of high level test case generation. Since some low-level paths do not contribute to high-level path coverage, we evaluate the ratio of high-level tests to the total number of low-level test cases produced. We again use the same four configurations as before.

Figure 10 shows what fraction of low-level paths cover new high-level paths over time; said differently, this shows the fraction of low-level tests that turn into high-level tests. A point $(t, \phi)$ on the graph represents the ratio $\phi$ between the number of high-level paths to low-level paths explored

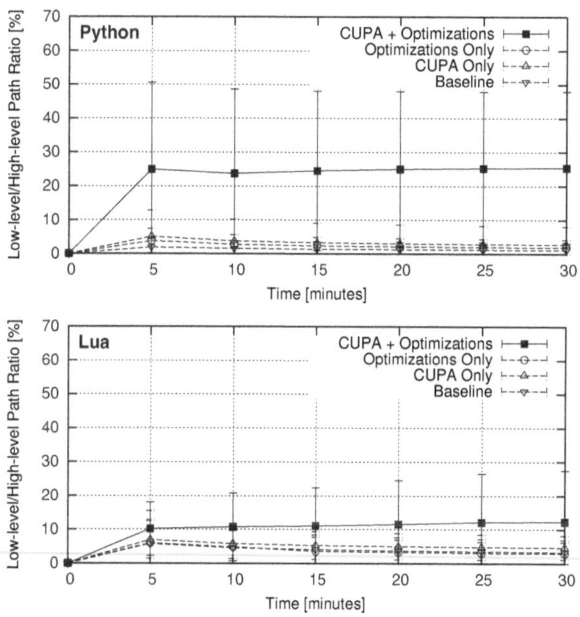


**Figure 10.** Average evolution in time of the fraction of low-level paths that contributed to high-level path coverage for Python and Lua.

in time $t$. Just like before, $\phi$ is averaged across all testing targets.

The aggregate configuration fares the best in the comparison, by a significant margin. Throughout the execution, the aggregate efficiency stays at about 25% for Python and 12% for Lua. This is about 10×, respectively 2.6× higher than the best performing among the other three configurations. This

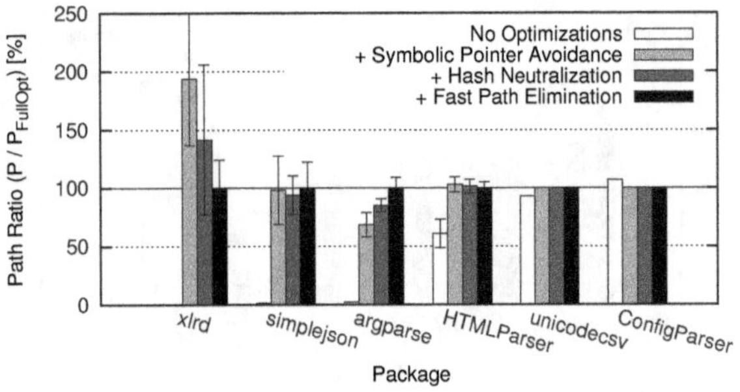


**Figure 11.** The contribution of interpreter optimizations for Python as number of high-level paths explored. Number of paths is relative to full optimizations (100%) for each package.

result justifies employing both CUPA and the interpreter optimizations during symbolic execution.

### 6.5 Breaking Down Interpreter Optimizations

We now analyze in more depth the impact of the interpreter optimizations by breaking them down into the three types mentioned in §4.2: avoiding symbolic pointers, hash neutralization, and fast-path elimination. We run again the symbolic tests for 30 minutes, using the path-optimized CUPA and four different interpreter builds, starting from the vanilla interpreter and adding the optimization types one by one. For each build and package, we count the number of high-level paths discovered by CHEF.

Figure 11 shows the results for Python. The data is normalized such that the number of high-level paths for each target reaches 100%. For 3 out of 6 packages (`simplejson`, `argparse`, and `HTMLParser`), CHEF's performance monotonically increases as more optimizations are introduced. For `unicodecsv` and `ConfigParser`, the optimizations do not bring any benefits or even hurt slightly.

However, in the case of `xlrd`, hash neutralization and fast path elimination seem to actually *hurt* symbolic execution, since the best performance is attained when only symbolic pointer avoidance is in effect. We explain this behavior by the fact that the different optimization levels cause the search strategy to explore different behaviors of the target package. `xlrd` is by far the largest Python package in our evaluation (7.2KLOC vs. the second largest of 1.4KLOC) and includes a diverse set of behaviors, each with its own performance properties.

This result suggests that, for large packages, a *portfolio* of interpreter builds with different optimizations enabled would help further increase the path coverage.

### 6.6 Comparison Against Hand-Made Engines

We now evaluate the trade-offs in using a symbolic execution engine generated with CHEF over building one "by hand".

***Hand-Made Engines*** To our knowledge, no symbolic execution engine for Lua exists. For Python, we found three research tools, which we compare CHEF to. (1) CutiePy [23] is a concolic engine based on a formal model of the Python language. It uses a custom CPython interpreter to drive a concrete execution, along with updating the symbolic state according to model semantics. (2) NICE-PySE [8] is part of the NICE framework for testing OpenFlow applications. We will refer to it as NICE, for brevity. It wraps supported data types into symbolic counterparts that carry the symbolic store, and uses Python's tracing mechanisms to implement the interpretation loop fully in Python. (3) The symbolic execution engine of the scalability testing tool Commuter [11] is also entirely built in Python. Its primary purpose is the construction of models that explicitly use an API of symbolic data types.

We perform our comparison along three aspects: language features supported, implementation faithfulness, and performance. The last two aspects are evaluated only against NICE, which, besides being open source, is most compatible with our symbolic data representation (based on STP [13]).

***Language Feature Support*** Table 4 summarizes the language feature support for CHEF, NICE, CutiePy, and Commuter, as implemented at the moment of writing. We relied on information from the respective papers in all cases and additionally on the implementation in the cases of NICE and Commuter, which are available as open source.

We distinguish engines designed to support arbitrary Python code (the "Vanilla" label) and those where the symbolic data types are an API used by model code (the "Model" label). Engines in the "Model" category essentially offer a "symbolic domain-specific language" on top of the interpreted language. CHEF, CutiePy, and NICE are "vanilla" engines, since their testing targets do not have to be aware that they are being symbolically executed. Commuter is a model-based engine, since its testing targets are bound to the symbolic API offered by the engine.

We grouped the supported language features into program state representation (the language data model and types) and manipulation (the operations on data). We divide data types into values (integers, strings and floating-point), collections (lists and dictionaries), and user-defined classes. The operations consist of data manipulation, basic control flow (e.g., branches, method calls), advanced control flow (e.g., exception handling, generators), and native method invocations (they are atomic operations at the high level). We also include in the comparison the ability to execute unsupported operations in concrete-only mode.

In a nutshell, CutiePy is able to complete correctly any execution in concrete mode by using the interpreter implementation directly. However, the symbolic semantics for each data type and native function must be explicitly provided by the developer, which makes CutiePy impractical to use with rich Python applications. NICE suffers from the additional limitation that it has to support each bytecode instruction explicitly, which makes the tool impossible to use

| | CHEF | CutiePy | NICE | Commuter |
|---|---|---|---|---|
| **Engine type** | Vanilla | Vanilla | Vanilla | Model |
| **Data types** | | | | |
| Integers | ● | ● | ● | ● |
| Strings | ● | ○ | ○ | ◐ |
| Floating point | ○ | ○ | ○ | ○ |
| Lists and maps | ●* | ◐ | ○ | ● |
| User-defined classes | ●* | ○ | ◐ | ◐ |
| **Operations** | | | | |
| Data manipulation | ● | ◐ | ◐ | ◐ |
| Basic control flow | ● | ● | ◐ | ● |
| Advanced control flow | ● | ● | ○ | ● |
| Native methods | ● | ◐ | ○ | ○ |

●Complete ◐Partial ○Not supported

**Table 4.** Language feature support comparison for CHEF and dedicated Python symbolic execution engines. Complete support with (*) refers to the internal program data flow and not to the initial symbolic variables.

beyond its target applications. Finally, Commuter provides a rich set of symbolic data types, including lists and maps, by taking advantage of Z3's extended support for arrays [12]. However, it supports only Python programs explicitly written against its API and does not handle native functions.

The engine generated by CHEF offers complete symbolic support for almost all language features. Floating point operations are supported only concretely, due to lack of support in STP, the constraint solver used by S2E. For the same reasons, the symbolic program inputs can only be integers and strings. However, all data structures are supported during the execution.

Each half or empty bullet in Table 4 implies that significant engineering effort would be required to complete a feature. While useful for their evaluation targets, NICE and CutiePy are unable to handle a complex software package that makes use of Python's many language features.

***Use as Reference Implementation*** When the need for performance justifies investing in a dedicated engine implementation, an engine created from CHEF can serve as a reference implementation during development. One can find bugs in a symbolic execution engine by comparing its test cases with those generated by CHEF. The process can be automated by tracking the test cases generated by the target engine along the high level paths generated by CHEF to determine duplicates and missed feasible paths.

In this mode, we found a bug in the NICE implementation, which was causing it to generate redundant test cases and miss feasible paths. The bug was in the way NICE handled `if not <expr>` statements in Python, causing the engine to select for exploration the wrong branch alternate and end up along an old path. We are assisting the NICE developers in identifying and fixing any other such bugs.

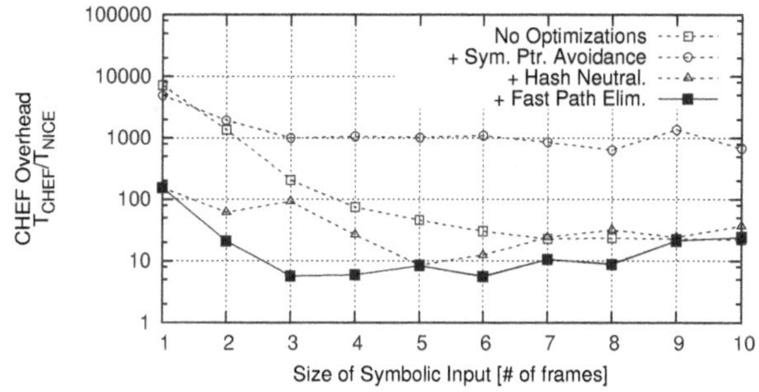


**Figure 12.** Average overhead of CHEF compared to NICE, computed as ratio of average per-path execution times. The average divides total tool execution time by number of high-level paths generated.

In conclusion, the experiment provides evidence that a system combining an established low-level symbolic execution engine (e.g., S2E) with a reference interpreter implementation is more robust than a symbolic execution engine built from scratch.

***Performance*** The downside of CHEF is that the symbolic execution engines produced are slower than their hand-written equivalents. We quantify this drawback by applying CHEF to the experimental setup of NICE, consisting of an OpenFlow switch controller program that implements a MAC learning algorithm. The controller receives as input a sequence of Ethernet frames and, in response, updates its forwarding table (stored as a Python dictionary). We use symbolic tests that supply sequences of between 1 and 10 Ethernet frames, each having the MAC address and frame types marked as symbolic.

Given the small size of the controller (less than 100 LOC), the number of execution paths is relatively small, and choosing low-level paths at random quickly discovers new high-level paths. Therefore, the search strategy has no impact (in the experiments we used path-optimized CUPA). However, the interpreter optimizations are crucial, since the controller code relies heavily on the dictionary. As in §6.5, we use several interpreter builds with optimizations introduced one-by-one.

Figure 12 illustrates the overhead for each optimization configuration, as a function of number of Ethernet frames supplied. The overhead is computed as the ratio between the average execution times per high-level path of NICE and CHEF. In turn, the execution time per high-level path is computed by dividing the entire execution time of each tool by the number of paths it produced.

The performance of each optimization configuration illustrates the sources of path explosion and slowdown in the vanilla interpreter. With no optimizations, symbolic keys in the MAC dictionary cause massive path explosion due to symbolic pointers. When avoiding symbolic pointers, performance drops even more due to symbolic hash computations. This penalty is reduced up to two orders of magnitude with hash neutralization. Finally, fast path elimination reduces the forking inside string key comparisons in the dictionary.

The shape of the final performance curve (the solid line) is convex. For 1 and 2 symbolic frames, the search space is quickly exhausted and the execution time is dominated by CHEF's initialization costs, i.e., setting up the symbolic VM and executing the interpreter initialization inside the guest. This results in an execution overhead as high as 120×. For more symbolic frames, the initialization cost is amortized, and the overhead goes below 5×. However, as the number of frames increases, so does the length of the execution paths and the size of the path constraints, which deepens the gap between CHEF's low-level reasoning and NICE's higher level abstractions. For 10 symbolic frames, the overhead is around 40×.

Despite CHEF's performance penalty, the alternative of writing an engine by hand is daunting. It involves developing explicit models that, for a language like Python, are expensive, error-prone, and require continuous adjustments as the language evolves. Where performance is crucial, a hand-written engine is superior; however, we believe that CHEF is a good match in many cases.

## 7. Related Work

To the best of our knowledge, we are the first to use symbolic execution on an interpreter to symbolically execute a program written in the target interpreted language. However, there has been work on writing dedicated symbolic execution engines for interpreted languages directly. Beside Python engines, the Kudzu [24] symbolic execution engine for JavaScript was used to detect code injection vulnerabilities. It relies on an intermediate representation of JavaScript that it directly executes symbolically. Apollo [2] is another engine targeting PHP code to detect runtime and HTML errors, while Ardilla [17] uses this system to discover SQL injection and cross-site scripting attacks in PHP.

The general area of automated software testing has a rich body of published literature. We highlight here only the closest concepts. Symbolic tests are closely related to the idea of parameterized unit tests [26]. These extend regular unit tests with parameters marked as symbolic inputs during symbolic execution. QuickCheck [10] allows writing specifications in Haskell, which again share their basic concept with symbolic tests, and tries to falsify them using random testing. Symbolic execution can offer an alternative to random testing in evaluating QuickCheck test specifications.

## 8. Conclusion

Implementing and maintaining a symbolic execution engine is a significant engineering effort. It is particularly hard for interpreted dynamic languages, due to their rich semantics, rapid evolution, and lack of precise specifications. Our system CHEF provides an engine platform that is instantiated with a language interpreter, which implicity defines the complete language semantics, and results in a correct and theoretically complete symbolic execution engine for the language. A language-agnostic strategy for selecting paths to explore in the interpreter allows the generated engine to systematically explore and test code in the target language (including possible native calls) effectively and efficiently. CHEF is available at `http://dslab.epfl.ch/proj/chef`.

## Acknowledgments

We thank the reviewers and Jonas Wagner for their valuable feedback on our paper. We thank Marco Canini, Peter Perešíni, and Daniele Venzano for their generous help with NICE. We are grateful to the European Research Council (StG #278656) and to Google for supporting our work.

## References

[1] Al Danial. Cloc. `http://cloc.sourceforge.net/`.

[2] S. Artzi, A. Kiezun, J. Dolby, F. Tip, D. Dig, A. Paradkar, and M. D. Ernst. Finding bugs in dynamic web applications. In *Intl. Symp. on Software Testing and Analysis*, 2008.

[3] T. F. Bissyandé, F. Thung, D. Lo, L. Jiang, and L. Réveillère. Popularity, interoperability, and impact of programming languages in 100,000 open source projects. In *Computer Software & Applications Conference*, 2013.

[4] E. Bounimova, P. Godefroid, and D. Molnar. Billions and billions of constraints: Whitebox fuzz testing in production. Technical Report MSR-TR-2012-55, Microsoft Research, 2012.

[5] S. Bucur, J. Kinder, and G. Candea. Making automated testing of cloud applications an integral component of PaaS. In *Proc. 4th Asia-Pacific Workshop on Systems (APSYS 2013)*. USENIX, 2013.

[6] J. Burnim and K. Sen. Heuristics for scalable dynamic test generation. In *Intl. Conf. on Automated Software Engineering*, 2008.

[7] C. Cadar, D. Dunbar, and D. R. Engler. KLEE: Unassisted and automatic generation of high-coverage tests for complex systems programs. In *Symp. on Operating Sys. Design and Implem.*, 2008.

[8] M. Canini, D. Venzano, P. Peresini, D. Kostic, and J. Rexford. A NICE way to test openflow applications. In *Symp. on Networked Systems Design and Implem.*, 2012.

[9] V. Chipounov, V. Kuznetsov, and G. Candea. S2E: A platform for in-vivo multi-path analysis of software systems. In *Intl. Conf. on Architectural Support for Programming Languages and Operating Systems*, 2011.

[10] K. Claessen and J. Hughes. QuickCheck: A lightweight tool for random testing of haskell programs. In *ACM SIGPLAN International Conference on Functional Programming*, 2000.

[11] A. T. Clements, M. F. Kaashoek, N. Zeldovich, R. T. Morris, and E. Kohler. The scalable commutativity rule: Designing scalable software for multicore processors. In *Symp. on Operating Systems Principles*, 2013.

[12] L. de Moura and N. Bjorner. Generalized, efficient array decision procedures. In *Intl. Conf. on Formal Methods in Computer-Aided Design*, 2009.

[13] V. Ganesh and D. L. Dill. A decision procedure for bit-vectors and arrays. In *Intl. Conf. on Computer Aided Verification*, 2007.

[14] P. Godefroid. Compositional dynamic test generation. In *Symp. on Principles of Programming Languages*, 2007.

[15] P. Godefroid, N. Klarlund, and K. Sen. DART: Directed automated random testing. In *Intl. Conf. on Programming Language Design and Implem.*, 2005.

[16] P. Godefroid, M. Y. Levin, and D. Molnar. Automated whitebox fuzz testing. In *Network and Distributed System Security Symp.*, 2008.

[17] A. Kiezun, P. J. Guo, K. Jayaraman, and M. D. Ernst. Automatic creation of SQL injection and cross-site scripting attacks. In *Intl. Conf. on Software Engineering*, 2009.

[18] R. S. King. The top 10 programming languages. *IEEE Spectrum*, 48 (10):84, 2011.

[19] V. Kuznetsov, V. Chipounov, and G. Candea. Testing closed-source binary device drivers with DDT. In *USENIX Annual Technical Conf.*, 2010.

[20] V. Kuznetsov, J. Kinder, S. Bucur, and G. Candea. Efficient state merging in symbolic execution. In *Intl. Conf. on Programming Language Design and Implem.*, 2012.

[21] C. Lattner and V. Adve. LLVM: A compilation framework for lifelong program analysis and transformation. In *Intl. Symp. on Code Generation and Optimization*, 2004.

[22] *The Python Language Reference*. Python Software Foundation. `http://docs.python.org/3/reference/`.

[23] S. Sapra, M. Minea, S. Chaki, A. Gurfinkel, and E. M. Clarke. Finding errors in python programs using dynamic symbolic execution. In *Intl. Conf. on Testing Software and Systems*, 2013.

[24] P. Saxena, D. Akhawe, S. Hanna, F. Mao, S. McCamant, and D. Song. A symbolic execution framework for JavaScript. In *IEEE Symp. on Security and Privacy*, 2010.

[25] D. Song, D. Brumley, H. Yin, J. Caballero, I. Jager, M. G. Kang, Z. Liang, J. Newsome, P. Poosankam, and P. Saxena. Bitblaze: A new approach to computer security via binary analysis. In *Intl. Conf. on Information Systems Security*, 2008.

[26] N. Tillmann and W. Schulte. Parameterized unit tests. In *Symp. on the Foundations of Software Eng.*, 2005.

[27] J. Wagner, V. Kuznetsov, and G. Candea. -OVERIFY: Optimizing programs for fast verification. In *Workshop on Hot Topics in Operating Systems*, 2013.

[28] T. Xie, N. Tillmann, J. de Halleux, and W. Schulte. Fitness-guided path exploration in dynamic symbolic execution. In *Intl. Conf. on Dependable Systems and Networks*, 2009.

[29] C. Zamfir and G. Candea. Execution synthesis: A technique for automated debugging. In *ACM EuroSys European Conf. on Computer Systems*, 2010.

# Q100: The Architecture and Design of a Database Processing Unit

Lisa Wu Andrea Lottarini Timothy K. Paine Martha A. Kim Kenneth A. Ross
Columbia University, New York, NY
{lisa,lottarini,martha,kar}@cs.columbia.edu/tkp2108@columbia.edu

## Abstract

In this paper, we propose Database Processing Units, or DPUs, a class of domain-specific database processors that can efficiently handle database applications. As a proof of concept, we present the instruction set architecture, microarchitecture, and hardware implementation of one DPU, called Q100. The Q100 has a collection of heterogeneous ASIC tiles that process relational tables and columns quickly and energy-efficiently. The architecture uses coarse grained instructions that manipulate streams of data, thereby maximizing pipeline and data parallelism, and minimizing the need to time multiplex the accelerator tiles and spill intermediate results to memory. This work explores a Q100 design space of 150 configurations, selecting three for further analysis: a small, power-conscious implementation, a high-performance implementation, and a balanced design that maximizes performance per Watt. We then demonstrate that the power-conscious Q100 handles the TPC-H queries with three orders of magnitude less energy than a state of the art software DBMS, while the performance-oriented design outperforms the same DBMS by 70X.

***Categories and Subject Descriptors*** C.3 [*Special-purpose and application-based systems*]: Microprocessor/microcomputer applications

***Keywords*** Accelerator; Specialized functional unit; Streaming data; Microarchitecture; Database; DPU

## 1. Introduction

Harvard Business Review recently published an article on Big Data that leads with a piece of artwork by Tamar Cohen titled "You can't manage what you don't measure" [28]. It goes on to describe big data analytics as not just important for business, but essential. The article emphasized that analyses must process large *volumes* of a wide *variety*, and at real-time or nearly real-time *velocity*. With the big data technology and services market forecast to grow from \$3.2B in 2010 to \$16.9B in 2015 [23], and 2.6 exabytes of data created each day [28], it is imperative for the research community to develop machines that can keep up with this data deluge.

For its part, the Database Management System (DBMS) software community has been exploring optimizations such as using column stores [1–3, 24, 27, 34], pipelining operations [4, 6], and vectorizing operations [40], to take advantage of commodity server hardware.

This work applies those same techniques, but in hardware, to construct a domain-specific processor for databases. Just as conventional DBMSs operate on data in logical entities of tables and columns, our processor manipulates these same data primitives. Like DBMSs use software pipelining between relational operators to reduce intermediate results, we too can exploit pipelining between relational operators implemented in hardware to increase throughput and reduce query completion time. In light of the SIMD instruction set advances in general purpose CPUs in the last decade, DBMSs also vectorize their implementations of many operators to exploit data parallelism. Our hardware does not use vectorized instructions, but exploits data parallelism by processing multiple streams of data, corresponding to tables and columns, at once.

Streams of data. Pipelines. Parallel functional units. All of these techniques have long been known to be excellent fits for hardware, creating what we believe to be an opportunity to address some very practical, real-world concerns regarding big data. Our vision is of a class of domain-specific processors called DPUs, that is analogous to GPUs. Whereas GPUs target graphics applications, DPUs target analytic database workloads. As GPUs operate on vertices, DPUs operate on tables and columns.

We design and evaluate a first DPU, called Q100. The Q100 is a performance and energy efficient data analysis accelerator. It contains a heterogeneous collection of


*ASPLOS '14*, March 1–5, 2014, Salt Lake City, Utah, USA.

http://dx.doi.org/10.1145/2541940.2541961

fixed-function ASIC tiles, each of which implements a well-known relational operator, such as a join or sort. The Q100 tiles operate on streams of data corresponding to tables and columns, over which the microarchitecture aggressively exploits pipeline and data parallelism.

This paper makes the following contributions:

- An energy-efficient instruction set architecture for processing data-analytic workloads, with instructions that both closely match standard relational primitives and are good fits for hardware acceleration.
- A high-performance, energy-efficient DPU, called Q100. Using custom processing tiles, all physically designed in 32nm standard cells, this chip provides orders of magnitude improvements in both TPC-H performance and energy consumption over state-of-the-art DBMS software.
- An in-depth tour of the Q100 design process, revealing the many opportunities, pitfalls, tradeoffs, and overheads one can expect to encounter when designing small accelerators to process big data.

In the following section, we present the design and specification of the Q100 ISA, the first DPU ISA. Then, in Section 3, we detail the step-by-step design process of the Q100, starting from physical design of the tiles and working up towards an exploration of resource scheduling algorithms. The results of this process are three Q100 designs, each optimized for a particular objective (e.g., low power, high performance, etc.). In Section 4 we compare the performance and energy consumption of TPC-H queries running on these Q100 designs to a state of the art, column store DBMS running on a Sandybridge server. Before concluding, we close with a survey of related work in Section 5.

## 2. Q100 Instruction Set Architecture

Q100 instructions implement standard relational operators that manipulate database primitives such as columns, tables, and constants. The producer and consumer relationship between operators are captured with dependencies specified by the instruction set architecture. Queries are represented as graphs of these instructions with the edges representing data dependencies between instructions. For execution, a query is mapped to a spatial array of specialized processing tiles, each of which carries out one of the primitive functions. When producer-consumer node pairs are mapped to the same temporal stage of the query, they operate as a pipeline with data streaming direction from producer to consumer.

The basic instruction is called a *spatial instruction* or *sinst*. These instructions implement standard SQL-esque operators, namely *select, join, aggregate, boolgen, colfilter, partition*, and *sort*. Figure 1 shows a simple query written in SQL to produce a summary sales quantity report per season for all items shipped as of a given date. Figure 1 bottom shows the query transformed into Q100 spatial instructions, retaining data dependencies. Together, *boolgen* and *colfil-*

```
▷ Sample query written in SQL
    SELECT     S_SEASON,
               SUM(S_QUANTITY) as SUM_QTY
    FROM       SALES
    WHERE      S_SHIPDATE <= '1998-12-01' - INTERVAL '90' DAY
    GROUP BY   S_SEASON,
    ORDER BY   S_SEASON,

▷ Sample query plan converted to proposed DPU spatial instructions
    Col1          ← ColSelect(S_SEASON from SALES);
    Col2          ← ColSelect(S_QUANTITY from SALES);
    Col3          ← ColSelect(S_SHIPDATE from SALES);
    Bool1         ← BoolGen(Col3, '1998-09-02', LTE);
    Col4          ← ColFilter(Col1 using Bool1);
    Col5          ← ColFilter(Col2 using Bool1);
    Table1        ← Stitch(Col4, Col5);
    Table2..Table5 ← Partition(Table1 using key column Col4);
    Col6..7       ← ColSelect(Col4..5 from Table2);
    Col8..9       ← ColSelect(Col4..5 from Table3);
    Col10..11     ← ColSelect(Col4..5 from Table4);
    Col12..13     ← ColSelect(Col4..5 from Table5);
    Table6 ← Append(Aggregate(SUM Col7 from Table2 group by Col6),
                    Aggregate(SUM Col9 from Table3 group by Col8));
    Table7 ← Append(Aggregate(SUM Col11 from Table4 group by Col10),
                    Aggregate(SUM Col13 from Table5 group by Col12));
    FinalAns ← Append(Table6, Table7);
```

**Figure 1.** An example query (top) is transformed into a *spatial instruction* plan (bottom) that map onto an array of heterogeneous specialized tiles for efficient execution.

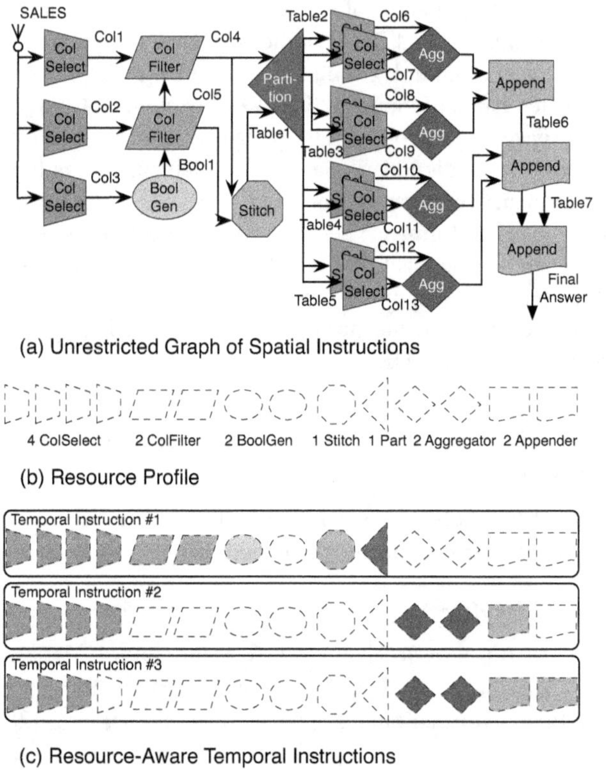


**Figure 2.** The example query from Figure 1 is mapped onto a directed graph with nodes as relational operators and edges as data dependencies. Given a set of Q100 resources, the graph is broken into three *temporal instructions* that are executed in sequence, one after another.

| | Tile | Area $mm^2$ | Area % Xeon [a] | Power mW | Power % Xeon | Critical Path ns | Design Width (bits) Record | Design Width (bits) Column | Design Width (bits) Comparator | Other Constraint |
|---|---|---|---|---|---|---|---|---|---|---|
| Functional | Aggregator | 0.029 | 0.07% | 7.1 | 0.14% | 1.95 | | 256 | 256 | |
| | ALU | 0.091 | 0.21% | 12.0 | 0.24% | 0.29 | | 64 | 64 | |
| | BoolGen | 0.003 | 0.01% | 0.2 | <0.01% | 0.41 | | 256 | 256 | |
| | ColFilter | 0.001 | <0.01% | 0.1 | <0.01% | 0.23 | | 256 | | |
| | Joiner | 0.016 | 0.04% | 2.6 | 0.05% | 0.51 | 1024 | 256 | 64 | |
| | Partitioner | 0.942 | 2.20% | 28.8 | 0.58% | ***3.17 | 1024 | 256 | 64 | |
| | Sorter | 0.188 | 0.44% | 39.4 | 0.79% | 2.48 | 1024 | 256 | 64 | 1024 entries at a time |
| Auxiliary | Append | 0.011 | 0.03% | 5.4 | 0.11% | 0.37 | 1024 | 256 | | |
| | ColSelect | 0.049 | 0.11% | 8.0 | 0.16% | 0.35 | 1024 | 256 | | |
| | Concat | 0.003 | 0.01% | 1.2 | 0.02% | 0.28 | | 256 | | |
| | Stitch | 0.188 | 0.44% | 5.4 | 0.11% | 0.37 | | 256 | | |

[a] Intel E5620 Xeon server with 2 chips. Each chip contains 4 cores 8 threads running at 2.4 $GHz$ with 12 $MB$ LLC, 3 channels of DDR3, providing 24 $GB$ RAM. Comparisons are done using estimated single core area and power consumption derived from published specification.

**Table 1.** The physical design characteristics of Q100 tiles post place and route, and compared to a Xeon core. ***The slowest tile, the partitioner, determines the frequency of Q100 at 315 $MHz$.

*ter* for example, support the `WHERE` clauses, while *partition* and *sort* are to support the `ORDER BY` clauses found in many query languages. Generating a column of booleans using a condition specified via a `WHERE` clause then filtering the projected columns is not a new concept, and is implemented by Vectorwise [40], a commercial DBMS, and other database software vendors that use column-stores.

Other helper spatial instructions perform a variety of auxiliary functions such as (1) tuple reconstruction (i.e. *stitch* individual columns of a row back into a row, or *append* smaller tables with the same attributes into bigger tables) to transform columns into intermediate or final table outputs, and (2) `GROUP BY` and `ORDER BY` clauses to perform aggregations and sorts (i.e. *concatenate* entries in a pair of columns to create one column in order to reduce the number of sorts performed when there are multiple `ORDER BY` columns).

In situations where a query does not fit on the array of available Q100 of tiles, it must be split into multiple temporal stages. These temporal stages are called *temporal instructions*, or *tinsts*, and are executed in order. Each tinst contains a set of spatial instructions, pulling input data from the memory subsystem and pushing completed partial query results back to the memory subsystem. Figure 2 walks through how a graph representation of spatial instructions, implementing the example query from Figure 1, is mapped onto available specialized processing tiles. Figure 2 (a) shows the entire query as one graph with each shape representing a different primitive and edges representing producer-consumer relationships (i.e., data dependencies). Figure 2 (b) shows an example array of specialized hardware tiles, or a *resource profile*, for a particular Q100 configuration. Figure 2 (c) depicts how the query must to be broken into three temporal instructions, because the resource profile does not have enough column selectors, column filters, aggregators, or appenders at each stage.

This instruction set architecture is energy efficient because it closely matches building blocks of our target domain, while simultaneously encapsulating operations that can be implemented very efficiently in hardware. Spatial instructions are executed in a dataflow-esque style seen in dataflow machines in the 80's [12, 17], in the 90's [19], and more recently [13, 31, 35], eliminating complex issue and control logic, exposing parallelism, and passing data dependencies directly from producer to consumer. All of these features provide performance benefit and energy savings.

## 3. Q100 Microarchitecture

In this section we walk through the Q100 design process. We start with descriptions of the hardware tiles that implement the Q100 ISA including their size and delays when implemented in 32nm physical design (Section 3.1). Then, using 19 TPC-H queries as benchmarks we perform a detailed Q100 design space exploration with which we explore the tradeoffs and select three interesting Q100 designs: minimal power, peak performance, and a balanced design that offers maximal performance per Watt (Section 3.2). We then explore the impact of communication – both intra tile and with memory – on these three designs (Section 3.3) as well as the instruction scheduling algorithm (Section 3.4).

### 3.1 Q100 Tile Implementation and Characterization

The Q100 contains eleven types of hardware tile corresponding to the eleven operators in the ISA. As in the ISA, we break the discussion into core functional tiles and auxiliary helper tiles. The facts and figures of this section are summarized in Table 1, while the text that follows focuses on the design choices and tradeoffs. The slowest tile determines the clock cycle of the Q100. As Table 1 indicates, the partitioner limits the Q100 frequency to 315 $MHz$.

**Methodology.** Each tile has been implemented in Verilog and synthesized, placed, and routed using Synopsys 32nm Generic Libraries[1] with the Synopsys [36] Design and IC Compilers to produce timing, area, and power numbers. We report the post-place-and-route critical path of each design as logic delay plus clock network delay, adhering to the industry standard of reporting critical paths with a margin.

**Q100 functional tiles.** The *sorter* sorts its input table using a designated key column and a bitonic sort [26]. In general, hardware sorters operate in batches, and require all items in the batch to be buffered at the ready prior to the start of the sort. As buffers and sorting networks are costly, this limits the number of items that can be sorted at once. For the Q100 tile, this is 1024 records, so to sort larger tables, they must first be partitioned with the partitioner.

The *partitioner* splits a large table into multiple smaller tables called partitions. Each row in the input table is assigned to exactly one partition based on the value of the key field. The Q100 implements range partitioner, which splits the space of keys into contiguous ranges. We chose this because it is tolerant of irregular data distributions [39] and produces ordered partitions, making it a suitable precursor to the sorter.

The *joiner* performs an inner-equijoin of two tables, one with a primary key and the other with a foreign key. To keep the design simple, the Q100 currently supports only inner-equijoins. It is by far the most common type of join, though extending the joiner to support other types (e.g., outer-joins) would not increase its area or power substantially.

The *ALU* tile performs arithmetic and logical operations on two input columns, producing one output column. It supports all arithmetic and logical operations found in SQL (i.e., ADD, SUB, MUL, DIV, AND, OR, and NOT) as well as constant multiplication and division. We use these latter operations to work around the current lack of a floating point unit in the Q100. In its place, we multiply any SQL *decimal* data type by a large constant, apply the integer arithmetic, finally divide the result by the original scaling factor, effectively using fixed point to support single precision floating point arithmetic, as most domain-specific accelerators have done. SQL does not specify precision requirements for floating point calculations and most commercial DBMS supports either single-precision floating point and/or double-precision floating point calculations.

The *boolean generator* compares an input column with either a constant or a second input column, producing a column of boolean values. Using just two hardware comparators, the tile provides all six comparisons used in SQL (i.e. EQ, NEQ, LTE, LT, GT, GTE). While this tile could have been combined with the ALU, offering two tiles à la carte leaves more flexibility when allocating tile resources. The boolean generator is often paired with the column filter (described next) with no need for an ALU. It is also often used in a chain or tree to form complex predicates, again not always in 1-to-1 correspondence with ALUs.

The *column filter* takes in a column of booleans (from a boolean generator) and a second data column. It outputs the same data column but dropping all rows where the corresponding bool is false.

Finally the *aggregator* takes in the column to be aggregated and a "group by" column whose values determine which entries in the first column to aggregate. For example, if the query sums purchases by zipcode, the data column are the purchase totals while the group-by is the zipcode. The tile requires that both input columns arrive sorted on the group-by column so that the tile can simply compare consecutive group-by values to determine where to close each aggregation. This decision has tradeoffs. A hash-based implementation might not require pre-sorting, but it would require a buffer of unknown size to maintain the partial aggregation results for each group. The Q100 aggregator supports all aggregation operations in the SQL spec, namely MAX, MIN, COUNT, SUM, and AVG.

**Q100 auxiliary tiles.** The *column selector* extracts a column from a table, and the *column stitcher* does the inverse, taking multiple input columns (up to a maximum total width) and producing a table. This operation often precedes partitions and sorts where queries frequently require column A sorted according to the values in column B. The *column concatenator* concatenates corresponding entries in two input columns to produce one output column. This can cut down on sorts and partitions when a query requires sorting or grouping on more than one attribute (i.e., column). Finally, the *table appender* appends two tables with the same schema. This is often used to combine the results of per-partition computations.

**Modifications to TPC-H due to tile limitations.** The design parameters such as record, column, key, and comparator widths are generally sized conservatively. However, we encountered a small number of situations where we had to modify the layout of an underlying table or adjust the operation, though never the semantics, of a query. When a column width exceeds the 32 byte maximum column width the Q100 can support, we divide the wide column vertically into smaller ones of no more than 32 bytes and process them in parallel. Out of 8 tables and 61 columns in TPC-H, just 10 were split in this fashion. Similarly, because the Q100 does not currently support regular expression matching, as with the SQL `LIKE` keyword, the query is converted to use as many `WHERE EQ` clauses as required. These are all minor side effects of the current Q100 design and may not be required in future implementations.

[1] Normal operating conditions (1.25V supply voltage at $25°C$) with high threshold voltage to minimize leakage.

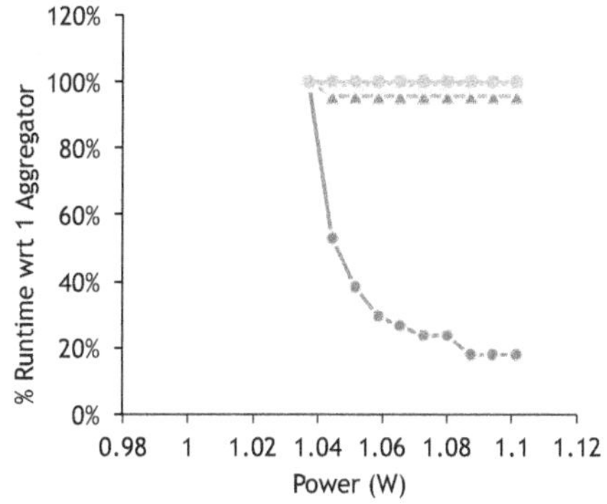


**Figure 3.** Aggregator sensitivity study shows that Q1 is the only query that is sensitive to number of aggregators, and its performance plateaus beyond 8 tiles.

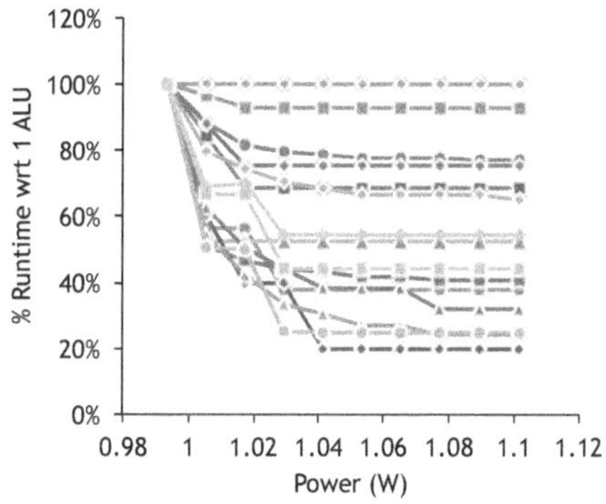


**Figure 4.** ALU tiles are more power hungry than aggregators, but adding more ALUs helps most query's performance. This tradeoff necessitates an exploration of the design space varying number of ALUs.

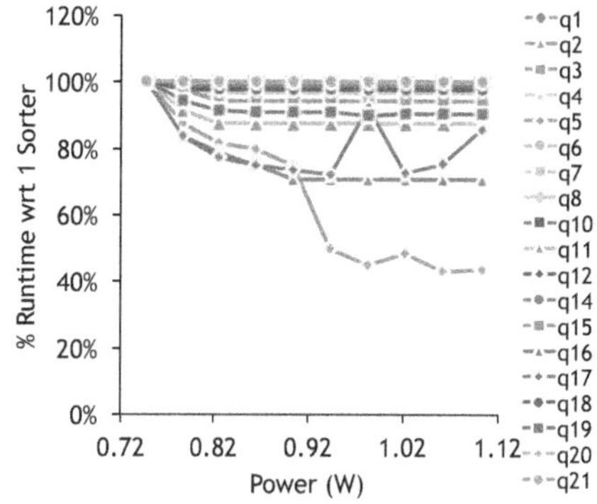


**Figure 5.** Sorter tiles are the most power hungry, dissipating almost 40 $mW$ per tile. Q17 exhibits a corner case where the scheduler makes bad decisions causing performance to degrade as number of sorters increase.

### 3.2 Q100 Tile Mix Design Space Exploration

To understand the relative utility of each type of tile, and the tradeoffs amongst them, we explore a wide design space of different sets of Q100 tiles. We start with a sensitivity analysis of TPC-H performance, evaluating each type of tile in isolation to bound the maximum number of useful tiles of each type. We then carry out a complete design space exploration considering multiple tiles at once, from which we understand the power performance shape of the Q100 space and select three configurations (i.e., tile mixtures) for further analysis.**Methodology.** We have developed a functional and timing Q100 simulator in C++. The function and throughput of each tile have been validated against simulations of the corresponding Verilog. As we do not yet have a compiler for the Q100, we have manually implemented each TPC-H query in the Q100 ISA. Using the simulator, we have confirmed that the Q100 query implementations produce the same results as the SQL versions running on MonetDB [8]. Given a query and a Q100 configuration, a scheduling algorithm described and evaluated later in Section 3.4 schedules each query into a sequence of temporal instructions. The simulator produces cycle counts, which we convert to wall clock time using a Q100 frequency of 315 $MHz$.

**Tile count sensitivity.** To understand how sensitive Q100 is to the number of each type of tile, say aggregators, we simulate a range of Q100 configurations, sweeping the number aggregators, while holding all other types of tiles at sufficiently high counts so as not to limit performance. Figure 3 shows how the runtime of each TPC-H varies with the number of aggregators in the design. Having run this experiment for each of the eleven types of tile, we highlight three sets of results here and in Figures 3-5. Just one query, Q1, is sensitive to the number of aggregators, while the performance of

| Tile | Maximum Useful Count | "Tiny" Tile | Tile Counts Explored |
|---|---|---|---|
| **Aggregator** | 4 | X | 4 |
| **ALU** | 5 | | 1 ... 5 |
| **BoolGen** | 6 | X | 6 |
| **ColFilter** | 6 | X | 6 |
| **Joiner** | 4 | X | 4 |
| **Partitioner** | 5 | | 1 ... 5 |
| **Sorter** | 6 | | 1 ... 6 |
| **Append** | 8 | X | 8 |
| **ColSelect** | 7 | X | 7 |
| **Concat** | 2 | X | 2 |
| **Stitch** | 3 | X | 3 |

**Table 2.** "Tiny" tiles are the ones that dissipate $<10$ $mW$ per tile as seen in Table 1. We eliminate configurations that will result in similar power or performance characteristics before running the design space exploration to cut down on the number of Q100 configurations under consideration.

the others is not affected. On the other hand, many queries benefit from more ALUs, with improvements flattening beyond 5 ALUs. Note that the aggregator and the ALU experiments are plotted with the same X-axis, while the sorter, at 39.4 $mW$ per tile, covers a much larger power range. Across the board, these sensitivity experiments reveal that for all queries and all tiles, performance plateaus by or before ten tiles of each type.

**Design space parameters.** A complete design space exploration, with 1 to 10 instances of each of 11 types of tile, would result in an overwhelmingly large design space. Using the tile sizes and the results of the sensitivity study above, we are able to prune the space substantially. First, we eliminate all of the "negligible" tiles from the design space. There are the tiles that are so tiny that the difference between one or two or ten will have a negligible impact on the results

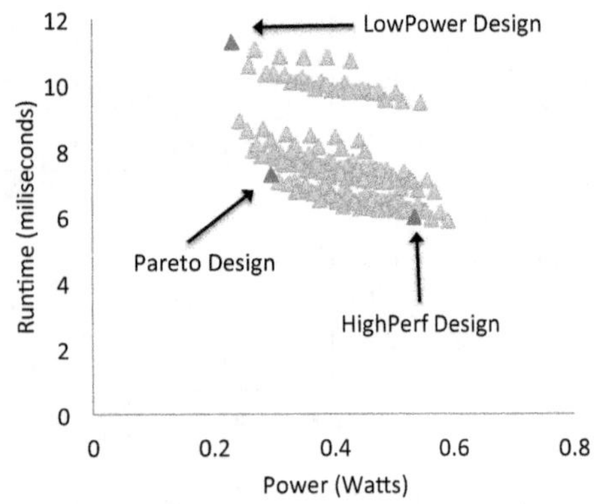


**Figure 6.** Out of 150 configurations, we selected three designs for further evaluation: LowPower for an energy-conscious configuration, HighPerf for a performance-conscious configuration, and Pareto for a design that maximizes performance per Watt.

of the exploration. For these tiny tiles, defined to be those eight tiles that consume less than 10 $mW$, we use the per-tile sensitivity analysis to identify the maximum number of useful tiles, and always allocate this many instances. For the remaining three non-tiny tiles (the ALU, partitioner, and sorter), we explore the design space only up to that count. Table 2 summarizes how the tile size and sensitivity reduce the design space from millions to 150 configurations.

**Power-performance design space.** Figure 6 plots the power-performance tradeoffs for 150 Q100 designs. Amongst these configurations we select the three designs indicated in the plot for further evaluation:

1. An energy-conscious design point (LowPower) that has just 1 partitioner, 1 sorter, and 1 ALU, and consumes the lowest power amongst all the configurations.
2. A balanced design on the Pareto-optimal frontier (Pareto), that, with 2 partitioners, 1 sorter, and 4 ALUs, provides the most performance per Watt amongst the designs.
3. A performance-optimized design (HighPerf), with 3 partitioners, 6 sorters, and 5 ALUs, that maximizes performance at the cost of a relatively higher power consumption.

### 3.3 Q100 Communication Needs

Having explored the Q100's computational needs, we now turn to its communication needs, both on-chip intra-tile communication and off-chip with memory. Because the target workload is large scale data, each of these channels will need to support substantial throughput.

**Communication topology.** In the experiments and simulations thus far, we have assumed all-to-all communication for all of the Q100 tiles and memory. However, analytic queries are not random, and we expect them to have certain tendencies. For example, one would expect that boolgen outputs are often fed into column selects. To test this hypothesis, we count the number of connections between each combination of tiles. For this analysis, we include memory as a "tile" as it is one of the communicating blocks in the system. Figures 7-9 indicate how many times a particular source (y-axis) feeds into a particular destination (x-axis) across all of TPC-H. Looking at this data we observe first that most tiles communicate to and from memory so often, that it will be important to properly understand and provision for the Q100 to/from memory bandwidth. Second, tiles do tend to communicate with a subset of each other, validating our hypothesis that the communication was not truly all-to-all. Thirdly, we note that these communication patterns do not vary across the three Q100 designs.

**On-chip bandwidth constraints.** We envision a NoC like the one implemented on Intel's TeraFlops chip [38]. It is a 2D mesh and can support 80 execution nodes[2]. While specific NoC design is outside the scope of this paper, we want to understand whether such a design can provide the bandwidth required by these queries. To make a conservative estimate, we scaled down TeraFlop's node-to-node 80 $GB/s$ at 4 $GHz$ to the frequency of the Q100, resulting in a conservative Q100 NoC bandwidth of 6.3 $GB/s$.

Figures 10-12 plot the peak bandwidth for each connection in the same fashion as the earlier connection counts. The cells marked with X are those for which the peak bandwidth at some point, during one or more of the TPC-H query executions, exceed our estimated limit of 6.3 $GB/s$. In those cases the NoC will slow down the overall query execution. We also note the following. First, that common connections (per Figures 7-9) do not require high bandwidth except for the Appender to Appender connection, which manipulates large volumes of data in a short amount of time. Second, there are a handful of very common, high-bandwidth connections that, if need be, can be fixed with point to point connections at some cost to instruction mapping flexibility, but at some potential energy and throughput savings.

To understand and quantify the performance impact of the Q100 NoC bandwidth, we perform a sensitivity study, sweeping the bandwidth from 5 $GB/s$ to 20 $GB/s$ as shown in Figure 13. The runtime of all queries in all three configurations are normalized to that of the HighPerf design with unlimited NoC bandwidth (IDEAL). We observe that only a handful of queries are sensitive to an imposed NoC bandwidth limit, however, the slowdown for those queries can be as much as 50X, making interconnect throughput a performance bottleneck when limited to 6.3 $GB/s$.

**Off-chip bandwidth constraints.** Memory, we have also seen, is a very frequent communicator, acting as a source or

[2] Though the more recent version of the Intel SCC [21] provides higher bandwidth and lower power, we chose TeraFlops because it connects execution units rather than CPU cores, and therefore better resembles the Q100.

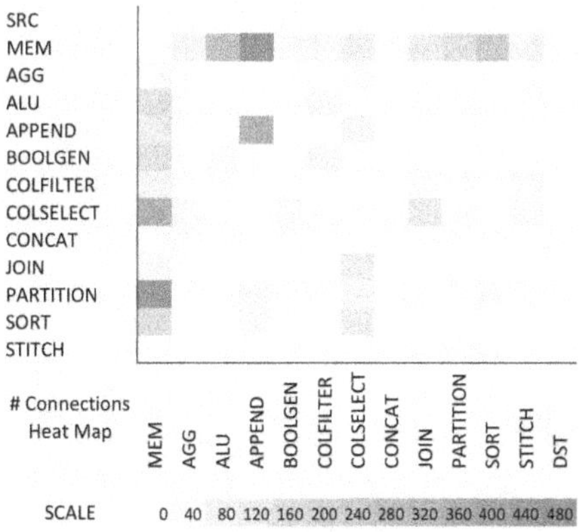


**Figure 7.** A heat map of tile-to-tile connection counts for the LowPower design shows that most intra-tile connections exist mostly when communicating to and from memory.

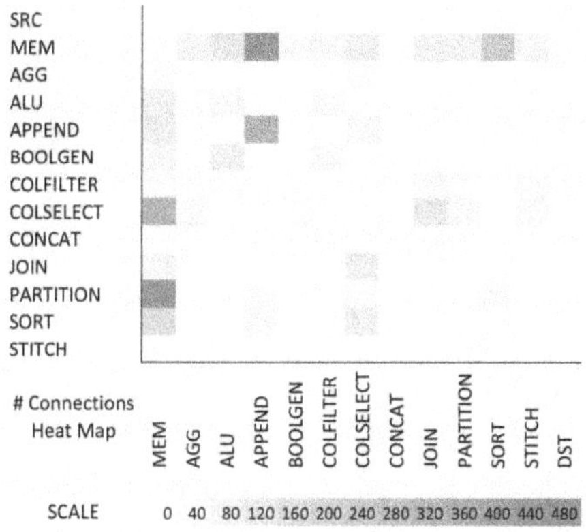


**Figure 8.** Our Pareto design uses slightly more connections than LowPower design when running the TPC-H suite, but memory is still the busiest communication tile.

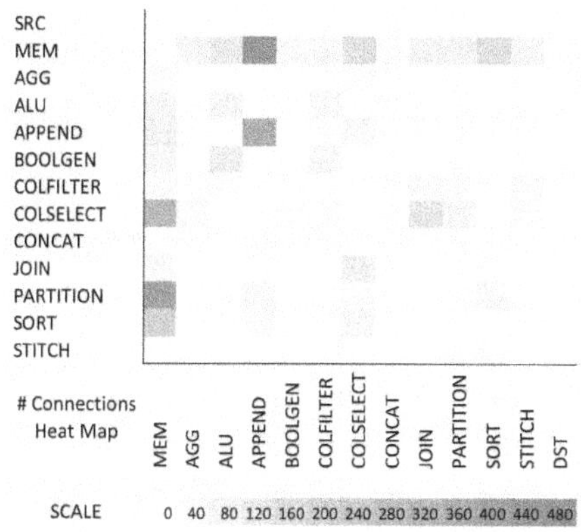


**Figure 9.** HighPerf design intra-tile heat map exhibits almost identical behavior as Pareto design.

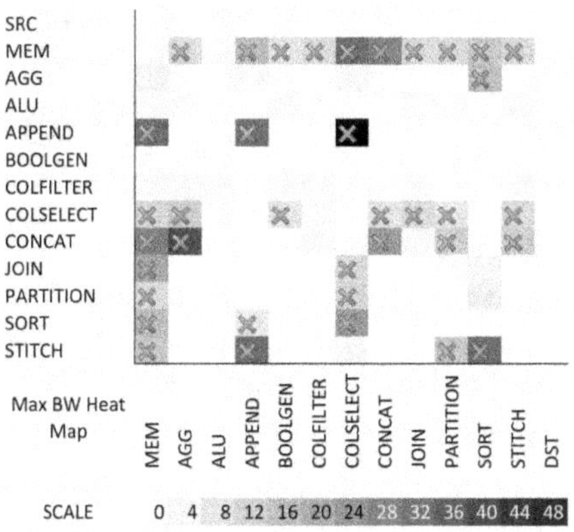


**Figure 10.** Even with a LowPower design, the communication bandwidth for most connections exceed the provisioned 6.3 $GB/s$ NoC bandwidth, marked as X's in the figures.

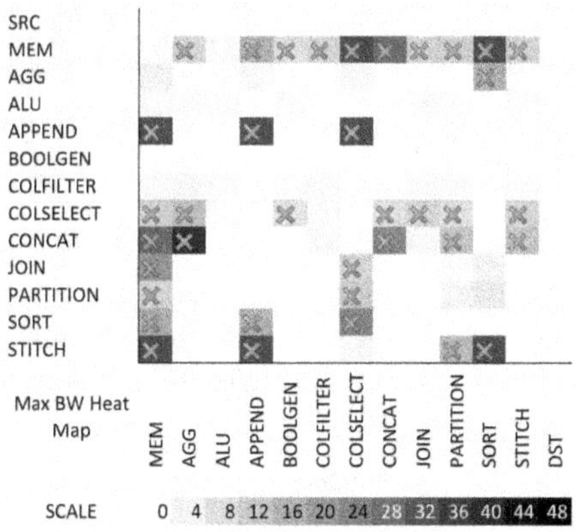


**Figure 11.** Similar to connection count heat map, Pareto design maximum intra-connection bandwidth exhibit almost identical behavior as HighPerf design.

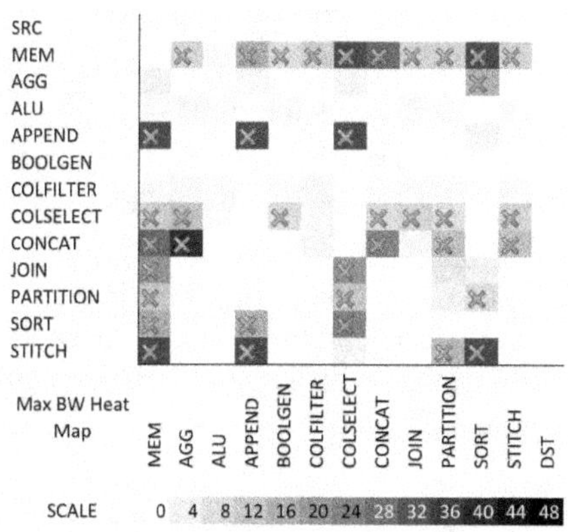


**Figure 12.** Heat map of HighPerf design max bandwidth per connection.

destination for all types of Q100 tiles. Half of those connections also require high throughput connections. In Figure 14 and Figure 15, we examine the high, low, and average read and write memory bandwidth for each query, sorted by average bandwidth. We first notice that queries vary substantially in their memory read bandwidths but relatively little in their write bandwidths. This is largely due to their being analytic queries, taking in large volumes of data and producing comparatively small results, matching the volcano style [16] of software relational database pipelined execution. Second, queries generally consume more bandwidth as the design becomes higher performance (i.e., going from LowPower to HighPerf), as the faster designs tend to process more data in a smaller period of time. Finally, in the same fashion that we expect the NoC will limit performance, realistic available bandwidth to and from memory is also likely to slow query processing.

Multiple instances of a streaming framework, such as the one described in recent work [39], could feed the Q100 assuming 5 $GB/s$ per stream. At that rate, the Q100 would require 4-6 inbound stream buffers depending on the configuration and 2 outbound stream buffers, reflecting the read/write imbalance noted earlier. The provided bandwidths from these stream buffers are shown in shaded rectangles in the figure.

To quantify the performance impact of memory bandwidth, we perform a sweep of memory read bandwidth from 10 $GB/s$ to 40 $GB/s$ and memory write bandwidth from 5

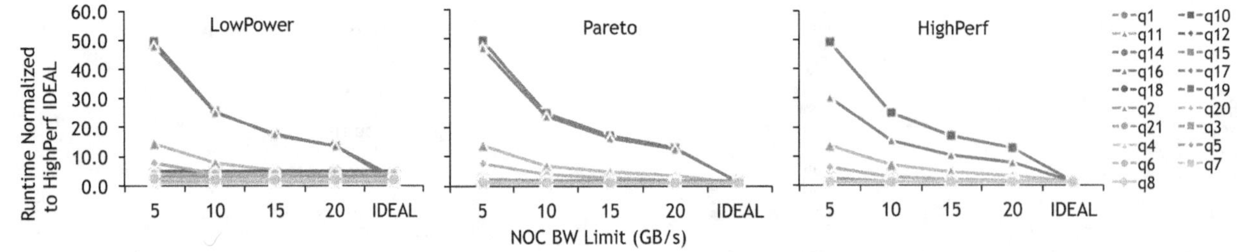


**Figure 13.** Most TPC-H queries are not sensitive to the Q100 intra-connection throughput, except for Q10, Q16, and Q11. These queries process large volumes of records throughout the query with little local selection conditions to "funnel" down the intermediate results. When NoC bandwidth is constrained, these queries could execute fifty times slower.

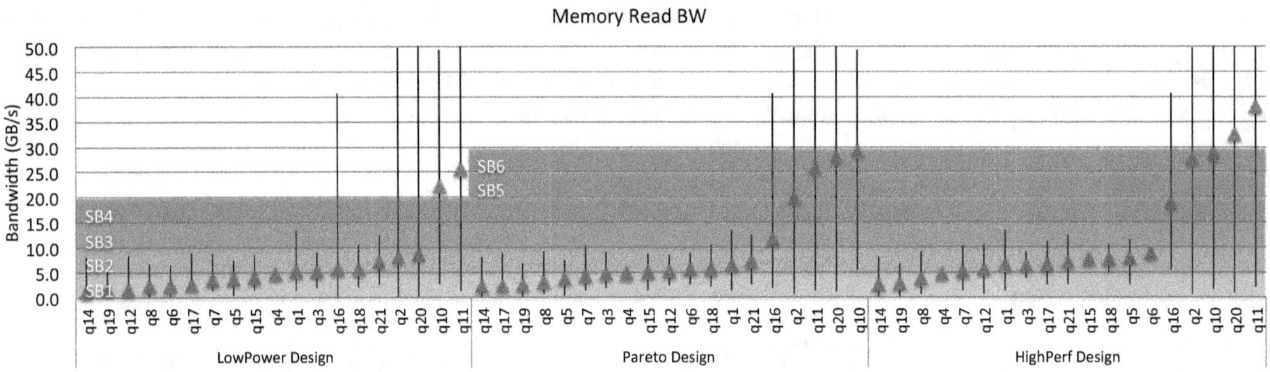


**Figure 14.** A plot of all TPC-H query read memory bandwidth demands (hi, lo, and avg) sorted by average. Read bandwidth varies quite a bit from query to query, having Q10 and Q11 being the most bandwidth starved. For Q100, LowPower design is provisioned with 4 stream buffers, and Pareto and HighPerf designs are provisioned with 6 stream buffers as shown in shaded gradations.

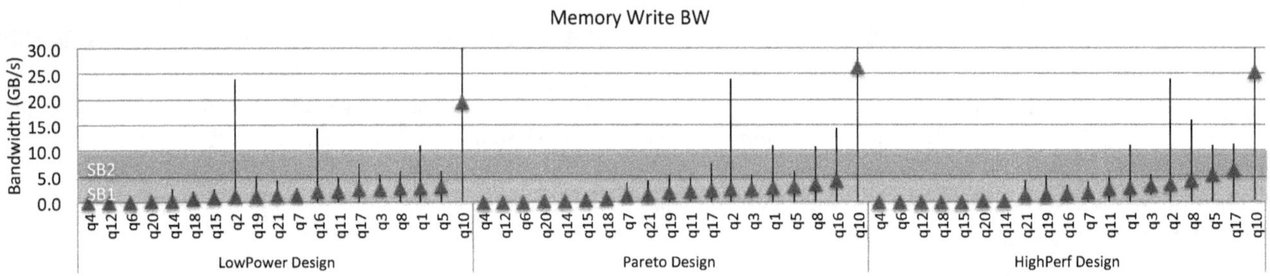


**Figure 15.** Write bandwidth demands are quite a bit lower than read bandwidth demands for most queries. We sized all three designs with 2 stream buffers, providing 10 $GB/s$ write bandwidth to memory.

$GB/s$ to 20 $GB/s$ as shown in Figure 16 and Figure 17. As with the NoC study, only 2 or 3 queries are sensitive to memory read and write bandwidth limits, but with much more modest slowdowns.

**Performance impact of communication resources.** Applying the NoC and memory bandwidth limits discussed above, we simulate a NoC bandwidth cap of 6.3 $GB/s$, memory read limit of 20 $GB/s$ for LowPower and 30 $GB/s$ for Pareto and HighPerf, and memory write limit of 10 $GB/s$. Figure 18 shows the impact as each of these limits is applied to an unlimited-bandwidth simulation. On account of on-chip communication, queries slow down 33-61%, with only a slight additional loss on account of memory to 34-62% slowdown overall. These effects are largely due to Q10 and Q11, the two most memory hungry queries, which suffer 1.4X-1.5X slowdown and 6X to 11X slowdown respectively compared to software.

Our simulator models a uniform memory access latency of 160ns, based on a 300 cycle memory access time from a 2 GHz CPU. When the imposed interconnect and memory throughput slow the execution of a spatial and a temporal

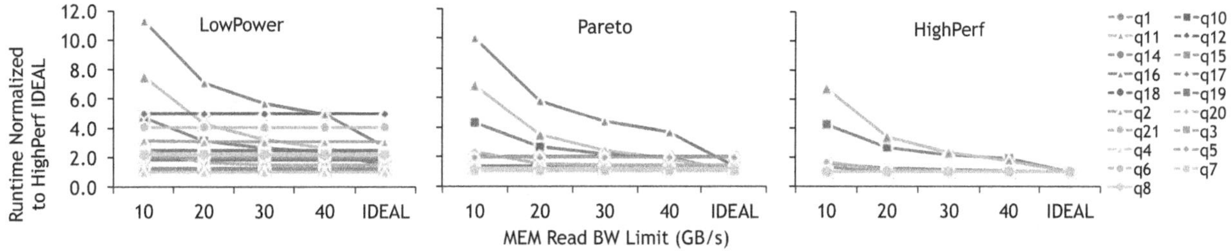


**Figure 16.** Similar to NoC bandwidth, most queries are not sensitive to memory read bandwidth. Q16 is particularly affected for the LowPower and Pareto designs suffering up to 12X slowdown. However, in the HighPerf design, more resources allow for a more efficient scheduling of temporal instructions, reducing high-volume communications to and from memory.

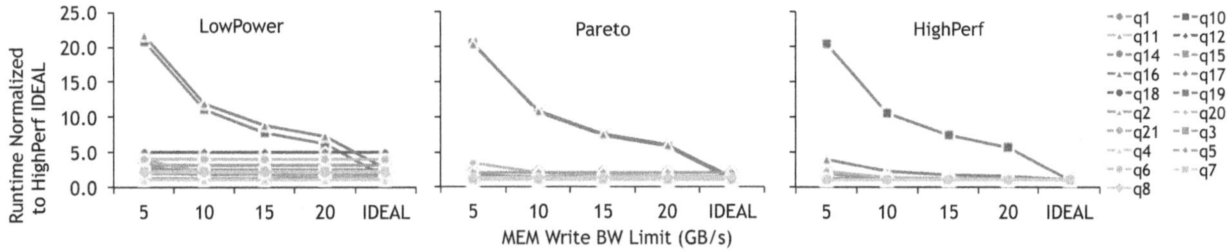


**Figure 17.** With 10 $GB/s$ of memory write bandwidth, only one (LowPower and Pareto) or two (HighPerf) queries are performance- limited by memory write bandwidth.

| | Area | | | | | Power | | | | |
|---|---|---|---|---|---|---|---|---|---|---|
| | Tiles $mm^2$ | NoC $mm^2$ | SBs $mm^2$ | Total $mm^2$ | Total % Xeon | Tiles $W$ | NoC $W$ | SBs $W$ | Total $W$ | Total % Xeon |
| **LowPower** | 1.890 | 0.567 | 0.520 | 2.978 | 7.0% | 0.238 | 0.071 | 0.400 | 0.710 | 14.2% |
| **Pareto** | 3.107 | 0.932 | 0.780 | 4.819 | 11.3% | 0.303 | 0.091 | 0.600 | 0.994 | 19.9% |
| **HighPerf** | 5.080 | 1.524 | 0.780 | 7.384 | 17.3% | 0.541 | 0.162 | 0.600 | 1.303 | 26.1% |

**Table 3.** Area and power of the three Q100 configurations, broken down by tile, on chip interconnect, and stream buffers.

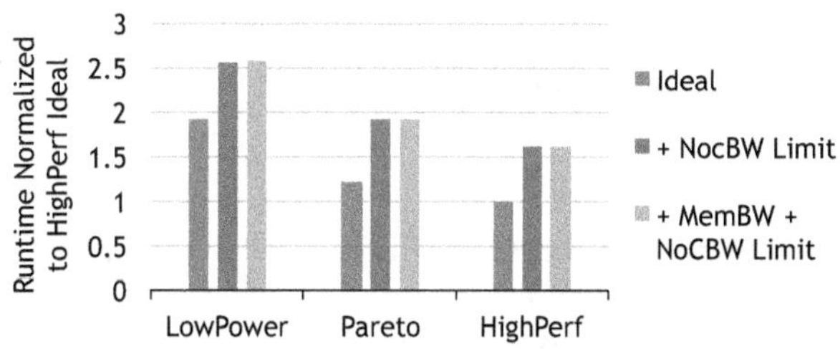


**Figure 18.** From the bandwidth heat maps plotted earlier, we see that Q100 was demanding a lot more NoC bandwidth than provisioned. Here, we plotted runtime with respect to no bandwidth limit penalties, and see a large slowdown at 30-60%, a caution for future implementations to design sufficient bandwidth for intra-tile connections.

instruction respectively, the simulator reflects that, although we found that throughput was primarily interconnect-limited and thus the visible slowdown beyond that due to memory was negligible. The Q100 reduces total memory accesses relative to software implementations by eliminating many reads and writes of intermediate results. For the remaining memory accesses, the Q100 is able to mask most stalls thanks to heavily parallelized computation that exploits both data and pipeline parallelism.

**Area and power impact of communication resources.** Starting with the area and power for the tiles in each Q100 design (based on Table 1), we add the additional area and power due to the NoC and stream buffers. Table 3 lists the area of the three design points broken down by tile, NoC, and stream buffers. We add an extra 30% area and power to the Q100 designs for the NoC, based on the characteristics of the TeraFlops implementation [38]. For the stream buffers, we add 0.13 $mm^2$ and 0.1 $Watts$ for each stream buffer [39]. In sum, the Q100 remains quite small, with the large, HighPerf configuration including NoC and stream buffers taking 17.3% area and 26.1% power of a single Xeon core.

## 3.4 Query Scheduling Algorithms

The final component of the Q100 design to explore is the scheduling algorithm, by which instructions are mapped to processing tiles.

**Problem formulation and experimental algorithms.** In the general case, the Q100 has fewer tiles than there are instructions in a query, so the algorithm must schedule them into multiple temporal instructions, subject to the following constraints. An instruction can be scheduled only (1) on a tile that performs its operation, and (2) if and only if all of

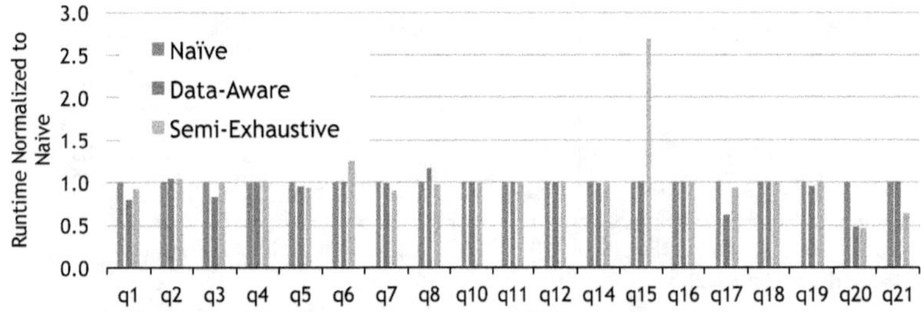


**Figure 19.** Completion time normalized to naive.

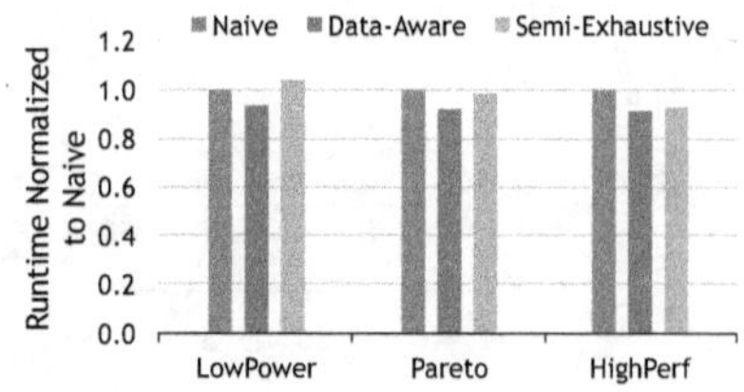


**Figure 20.** Average completion time normalized to completion time of naive.

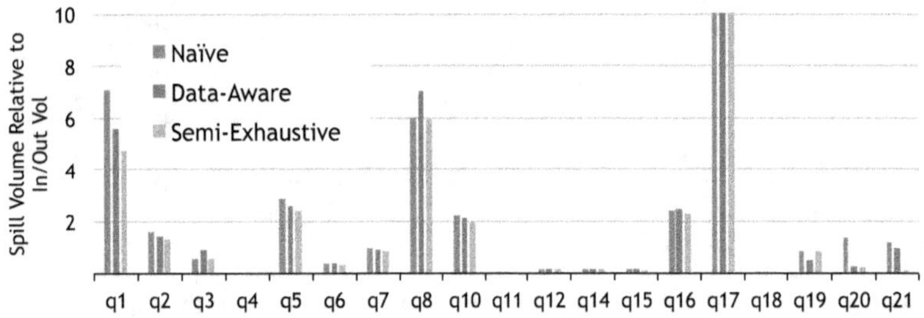


**Figure 21.** Data transfer size normalized to the volume of input and output data of the query.

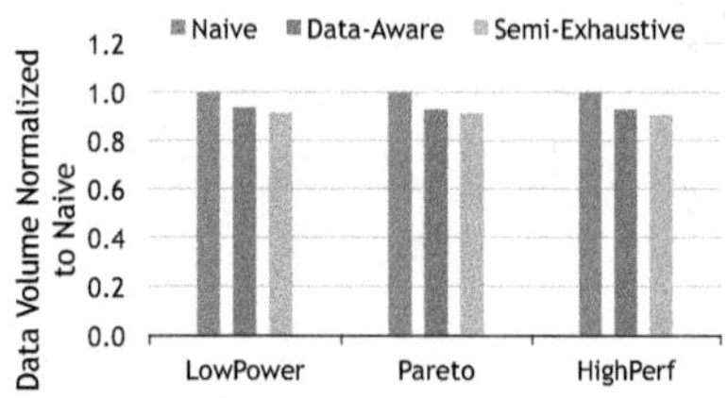


**Figure 22.** Average data transfer size normalized to size of naive.

its inputs producers have been scheduled in the same or in preceding temporal instructions.

We implemented and evaluated three scheduling algorithms:

- **Naive** greedily packs instructions into the Q100, subject to the constraints listed above, advancing to the next temporal instructions when no more instructions can fit, and stopping when all instructions have been scheduled. In doing this it presumes no knowledge of the volume of data flowing between instructions and therefore makes no effort to minimize data transfer between temporal instructions.
- In contrast, **data-aware** considers the volume of data passed between instructions, not as unrealistic as it may seem, as DBMSs estimate sample or otherwise estimate the rough size of various queries. The information we assume in this study is routinely available at query parse and planning time. It proceeds from largest to smallest data value, greedily attempting to pack all producers and consumers into the same temporal instruction to reduce spills to memory.
- Finally, because both naive and data-aware are greedy and subject to local minima, **semi-exhaustive** searches all legal schedules.[3] Because truly exhaustive search is infeasible – the longer runs are probably still going! – we use a heuristic to prune the search space, making it terminate, but only semi-exhaustive. While not feasible in practice, this algorithm gives us an approximate upper bound for schedule quality.

[3] Because the space of legal Q100 schedules is such a small portion of all Q100 schedules, algorithms that consider non-legal schedules, such as genetic algorithms, are not likely to be efficient for this use.

**Analysis of results.** We start our analysis on the LowPower Q100 configuration as it has the fewest tiles and is thus most likely to be sensitive to scheduling. We can see in Figures 19 and 21 that, relative to naive, data-aware usually succeeds in reducing the size of memory spills, and that this correlates with a decrease in the completion time.

We also see that, for most queries, semi-exhaustive succeeds in finding schedules with the smallest amount of data transferred amongst these algorithms. The exceptions are Q1, Q17, and Q19, which are so large that the semi-exhaustive approach can only cover a small portion of the search space. Most interestingly, we observe the following pattern. For queries that must spill large volumes of data during execution, the strategy of minimizing data spills is a good one. However, for queries with negligible spills in the first place, attempting to minimize these negligible transfers will cause the scheduler to sub-optimally allocate spatial instructions to temporal instructions. The specific problem we see in Q15, for instance, is the scheduler spreading multiple slow operations across several steps (in an attempt to minimize spills) which ends up increasing the overall completion time of the query. While the data-aware scheduler is sufficient for our current analyses, this indicates a multi-objective heuristic may produce higher quality schedules.

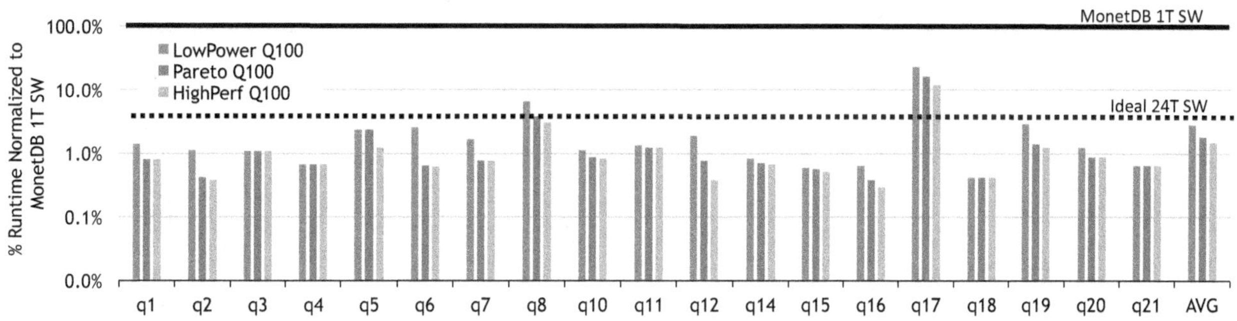


**Figure 23.** TPC-H query runtime normalized to MonetDB single-thread SW shows a 37X–70X performance improvement on average across all queries.

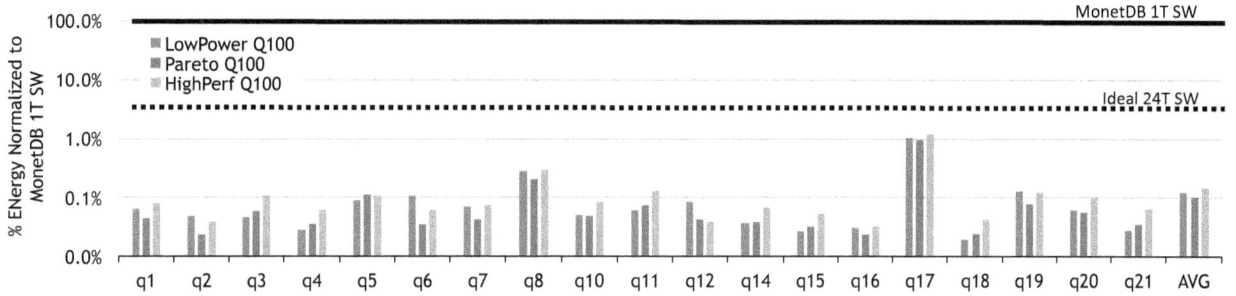


**Figure 24.** TPC-H query energy consumption normalized to MonetDB single-thread running on cores consuming non-idle power shows 691X–983X energy efficiency on average across all queries.

| System Configuration | |
|---|---|
| Chip | 2X Intel E5-2430<br>6C/12T, 2.2 $GHz$, 15 $MB$ LLC |
| Memory | 32 $GB$ per chip, 3 Channels, DDR3 |
| Max Memory BW | 32 $GB/sec$ per chip |
| Max TDP | 95 $Watts$ per chip |
| Lithography | 32 $nm$ |

**Table 4.** Hardware platform used in software measurements (Section 4. Source: Intel [25].)

## 4. Q100 Evaluation

Taking what we have learned about the Q100 system, its ISA, its implementation, and its communication both internal and external, we now compare our three configurations, LowPower, Pareto, and HighPerf, with a conventional software DBMS. This evaluation takes on three parts: initial power and performance benchmarking for the TPC-H queries as executed on a conventional DBMS+CPU system, comparison of Q100's execution of TPC-H to that system's, and finally an evaluation of how a Q100 designed for one scale of database handles the same queries over a database 100 times larger.

**Methodology.** We measure the performance and energy consumption of MonetDB 11.11.5 running on the Xeon server described in Table 4 and executing the set of TPC-H queries. Each reported result is the average of five runs during which we measured the elapsed time and the energy consumption. For the latter we used Intel's Running Average Power Limit (RAPL) energy meters [10, 20] which exposes energy usage estimates to software via model-specific registers. We sample the core energy counters at 10 $ms$ intervals throughout the execution of each TPC-H query. We further deduct any idle "background" power as measured by the same methods on a completely idle machine. The MonetDB energy measurements we report here include only the *additional energy consumption above idle*.

Although MonetDB supports multiple threads, our measurements of power and speedups indicate that individual TPC-H queries do not parallelize well, even for large databases (i.e., 40 $GB$). Here we will compare the Q100's performance and energy to the measured single threaded values, as well as to an optimistic estimate of a 24-way parallelized software query, one that runs 24 times faster than the single threaded at the same average power as a single software thread. In the upcoming comparisons, we will provide both the MonetDB single-thread SW and MonetDB 24-thread SW (Idealized) as reference points.

For the Q100, we use the full timing and power model, that incorporates the runtime, area, and energy of the on-chip NoC and off-chip memory communication as described in Section 3.3.

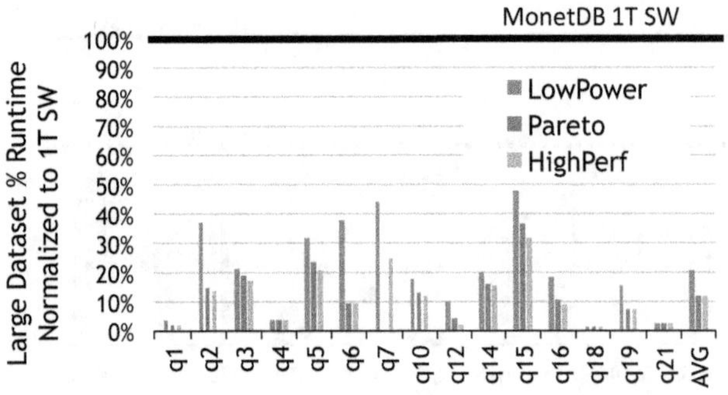


**Figure 25.** With a dataset that is 100X the size of our previous input tables, TPC-H still shows a 10X performance improvement relative to software on average.

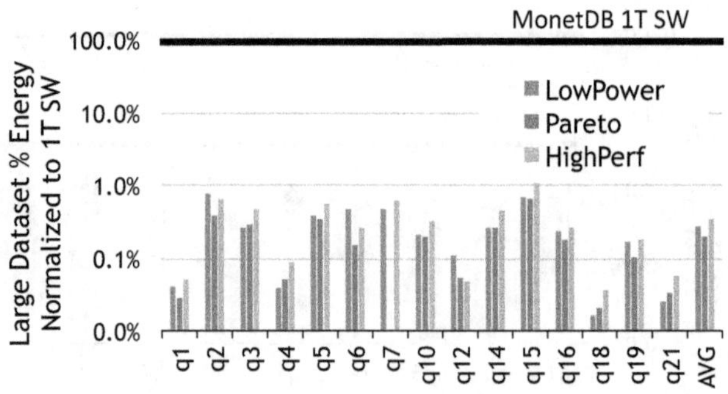


**Figure 26.** With a 100X larger dataset, the Q100 still consumes $1/100^{th}$ of the energy that software consumes.

**Q100 performance comparison.** Figure 23 plots the query execution time on the Q100 designs relative to the execution time on single threaded MonetDB. We see that Q100 performance exceeds a single software thread by 37X–70X, and exceeds a perfectly-scaled 24-thread software by 1.5X–2.9X. This is primarily due to Q100's reduced instruction control costs which are a byproduct of the large instruction granularity, where each Q100 instruction does the work of billions (or more, depending on the data size) software instructions. In addition, the Q100 processes many instructions at once, in pipelines and in parallel, generating further speedups. Finally the Q100, having brought some data onto the chip, exploits on-chip communication tile parallelism to perform multiple operations on the data before returning the results to memory, thereby maximizing the work per memory access and hiding the memory latency with computation.

**Q100 energy comparison.** Fixed function ASICs, which comprise the Q100, are inherently more energy efficient than general purpose processors. Both industry and academia, for example, state that GPUs are 10X-1000X more efficient than multi-core CPUs for well-suited graphics kernels; Similarly, the Q100 is 1400X-2300X more energy efficient than MonetDB when executing the analytic queries for which it was designed. We note that the energy efficiency of our Pareto design is 1.1X better than our LowPower design and 1.6X better than our HighPerf design.

**Scaling up data.** Finally, as big data continues to grow, we wish to evaluate how the Q100 handles databases that are orders of magnitude larger than the ones for which it was initially developed, we performed the same Q100-MonetDB comparison using 100X larger data. Figure 25 and Figure 26 show the results. With the input data having grown by 100X, Q100 speedup over software drops from 100X to 10X. The total energy remains 100X lower regardless of data size.

## 5. Related Work

**Hardware acceleration of databases.** Database machines were developed by the database community in the early 1980s as specialized hardware for database workloads. These efforts largely failed, primarily because commodity CPUs were improving so rapidly at the time, and hardware design was slow and expensive [7]. The architectures proposed at that time targeted a different set of challenges than those we face today, namely dark silicon, the utilization wall, the power wall, etc.

Much more recently, a flurry of projects accelerates queries by compiling them down to FPGAs, such as LINQits [9], Teradata [11], and [29]. Industry appliances using Xeon servers combined with FPGAs such as the IBM Netezza [22] also show promising performance and energy efficiency. Whereas we have designed a *domain specific circuit*, these projects produce *query-specific circuits*, a different point in the specialization space. Other have investigated using existing accelerators, such as network processors [14] or GPUs [15] to speed relational operators. Our work is similar in that we too accelerate database queries and relational operators, but differs in the overall strategy and specific hardware platform.

**Streaming computation.** StreamIt [37] is a programming language and a compilation infrastructure supporting parallel execution of stream-based applications. It relates to our work in as much as Q100 processes database queries in streams of data, forming direct communication between producing and consuming kernels. However, whereas we target database-specific, hardware kernels, StreamIt supports user-defined software kernels, from other domains including digital signal processing, multimedia, and cellular communications. It is worth noting that the Q100 does not process streams in the most general sense of the term. Our ISA and implementation operate on relational streams (i.e., where multiple streams have corresponding elements) which is a specific type of stream.

**Domain-specific accelerators.** The Q100 is a domain specific processor, of which there are many others targeting different domains. GPUs are perhaps the most visible and among the most successful such processors targeting graphics applications [5, 30]. There is a large body of research around other domain-specific acceleration: Convolution Engine [32] targets image processing kernels and stencil computations, [33] uses specialization to speed up regular expression matching in queries, and [18] accelerates H.264 video encoders. In spirit these projects share similarities with the Q100, but in their design and target particulars they are quite different.

## 6. Conclusion

As data quantities continue to explode, technology must keep pace. To mitigate commensurate increases in time and energy required to process this data with conventional DBMSs running on general purpose CPUs, this paper has presented the Q100, a DPU for analytic query workloads.

With the Q100, we have presented an instruction set architecture which closely resembles common SQL operators, together with a set of specialized hardware modules implementing these operators. The Q100 demonstrates a significant performance gain over optimistically scaled multithreaded software, and an order of magnitude gain over single threaded software, for less than 15% the area and power of a Xeon core at the evaluated configurations. Importantly, as inputs scale by 100X, the Q100 sees only a single order of magnitude drop in performance and negligible decrease in energy efficiency. Given the current gap between the Q100 and standard software query processing, as well as the growth rate in data volumes, it is clear that specialized hardware like the Q100 is the only way systems will be able to keep pace with increases in data without sacrificing energy efficiency.

## 7. Acknowledgements

This material is based upon work supported by the National Science Foundation under Grant No. 1065338. The infrastructure was partly supported by resources of Sethumadhavan's Comp Arch and Security Technology Lab (CASTL) which is funded through grants CNS/TC 1054844, FA 99500910389, FA 865011C7190, FA 87501020253 and gifts from Microsoft Research, WindRiver Corp, Xilinx Inc. and Synopsys Inc.. The authors also wish to thank Yunsung Kim, Stephen Edwards, and the anonymous reviewers for their time and feedback.

## References

[1] Kx systems. `http://kx.com/_papers/Kx_White_Paper-2013-02c.pdf`.

[2] Sybase IQ. `http://www.sybase.com/products/archivedproducts/sybaseiq`.

[3] D. J. Abadi, P. A. Boncz, and S. Harizopoulos. Column-oriented database systems. *VLDB*, August 2009.

[4] D. J. Abadi, D. S. Myers, D. J. DeWitt, and S. R. Madden. Materialization strategies in a column-oriented dbms. In *ICDE*, 2007.

[5] AMD/ATI. `http://www.amd.com`.

[6] P. A. Boncz, M. Zukowski, and N. Nes. Monetdb/x100: Hyper-pipelining query execution. In *CIDR*, 2005.

[7] Haran Boral and David J. DeWitt. Database machines: an idea whose time has passed? In *IWDM*, 1983.

[8] Centrum Wiskunde and Informatica. `http://www.monetdb.org`.

[9] E. S. Chung, J. D. Davis, and J. Lee. Linqits: Big data on little clients. In *ISCA*, 2013.

[10] Intel Corporation. Intel 64®and IA-32 architectures software developer's manual. `http://download.intel.com/products/processor/manual/253669.pdf`.

[11] Teradata Corporation. `http://www.teradata.com`.

[12] J. B. Dennis. *Advanced topics in data-flow computing*. Prentice-Hall, 1991.

[13] M. Gebhart, B. A. Maher, K. E. Coons, J. Diamond, P. Gratz, M. Marino, N. Ranganathan, B. Robatmili, A. Smith, J. Burrill, S. W. Keckler, D. Burger, and K. S. McKinley. An evaluation of the TRIPS computer system. In *ASPLOS*, 2009.

[14] B. Gold, A. Ailamaki, L. Huston, and B. Falsafi. Accelerating database operators using a network processor. In *DaMoN*, 2005.

[15] N. K. Govindaraju, B. Lloyd, W. Wang, M. Lin, and D. Manocha. Fast computation of database operations using graphics processors. In *SIGGRAPH*, 2005.

[16] G. Graefe and W. J. McKenna. The volcano optimizer generator: Extensivility and efficient search. In *ICDE*, 1993.

[17] J.R. Gurd, C. C. Kirkham, and I. Watson. The manchester prototype dataflow computer. *Communications of the ACM*, 1985.

[18] R. Hameed, W. Qadeer, M. Wachs, O. Azizi, A. Solomatnikov, B. C. Lee, S. Richardson, C. Kozyrakis, and M. Horowitz. Understanding sources of inefficiency in general-purpose chips. In *ISCA*, 2010.

[19] J. Hicks, D. Chiou, B. S. Ang, and Arvind. Performance studies of Id on the monsoon dataflow system. 1993.

[20] D. Howard, E. Gorbatov, U. R. Hanebutte, R. Khanna, and C. Le. Rapl: memory power estimateion and capping. In *ISLPED*, 2010.

[21] J. Howard, S. Dighe, Y. Hoskote, S. R. Vangal, D. Finan, G. Ruhl, D. Jenkins, H. Wilson, N. Borkar, G. Schrom, F. Pailet, S. Jain, T. Jacob, S. Yada, S. Marella, P. Salihundam, V. Erraguntla, M. Konow, M. Riepen, G. Droege, J. Lindemann, M. Gries, T. Apel, K. Henriss, T. Lund-Larsen, S. Steibl, S. Borkar, V. De, R. F. Van der Wijngaart, and T. G. Mattson. A 48-core IA-32 message-passing processor with DVFS in 45nm CMOS. In *ISSCC*, pages 108–109, 2010.

[22] IBM. IBM Netezza Data Warehouse Appliance. http://www-01.ibm.com/software/data/netezza/.

[23] IDC Research. IDC's most recent worldwide Big Data technology and services market forecast. http://www.idc.com/getdoc.jsp?containerId=prUS23355112.

[24] S. Idreos, F. Groffen, N. Nes, S. Manegold, K. S. Mullender, and M. L. Kersten. Monetdb: Two decades of research in column-oriented database architectures. *Data Engineering Bulletin*, 2012.

[25] Intel Corporation. Intel Xeon Processor E5-2430, 2012. http://ark.intel.com/products/64616/Intel-Xeon-Processor-E5-2430--(15M-Cache-2_20-GHz-7_20-GTs-Intel-QPI).

[26] M. F. Ionescu and K. E. Schauser. Optimizing parallel bitonic sort. In *IPDPS*, 1997.

[27] A. Lamb, M. Fuller, R. Varadarajan, N. Tran, B. Vandiver, L. Doshi, and C. Bear. The vertica analytic database: C-store 7 years later. In *VLDB*, 2012.

[28] A. McAfee and E. Brynjolfsson. Big Data: The management revolution. *Harvard Business Review*, October 2012.

[29] R. Muller and J. Teubner. FPGAs: A new point in the database design space, 2010. EDBT Tutorial.

[30] NVIDIA. http://www.nvidia.com.

[31] A. Parashar, M. Pellauer, M. Adler, B. Ahsan, N. Crago, D. Lustig, V. Pavlov, A. Zhai, M. Gambhir, A. Jaleel, R. Allmon, R. Rayess, and J. Emer. Triggered instructions: A control paradigm for spatially-programmed architectures. In *ISCA*, 2013.

[32] W. Qadeer, R. Hameed, O. Shacham, P. Venkatesan, C. Kozyrakis, and M. A. Horowitz. Convolution engine: Balancing efficiency and flexibility in specialized computing. In *ISCA*, 2013.

[33] V. Salapura, T. Karkhanis, P. Nagpurkar, and J. Moreira. Accelerating business analytics applications. In *HPCA*, 2012.

[34] M. Stonebraker, D. J. Abadi, A. Batkin, X. Chen, M. Cherniack, M. Ferreira, E. Lau, A. Lin, S. Madden, E. O'Neil, P. O'Neil, A. Rasin, N. Tran, and S. Zdonik. C-store: a column-oriented dbms. In *VLDB*, 2005.

[35] S. Swanson, A. Schwerin, M. Mercaldi, A. Petersen, A. Putnam, K. Michelson, M. Oskin, and S. J. Eggers. The wavescalar architecture. *ACM Trans. Comp. Syst.*, 2007.

[36] Synopsys, Inc. 32/28nm Generic Library for IC Design, Design Compiler, IC Compiler. http://www.synopsys.com.

[37] W. Thies and S. Amarasinghe. An empirical characterization of stream programs and its implications for language and compiler design. In *PACT*, 2010.

[38] S. Vangal, J. Howard, G. Ruhl, S. Dighe, H. Wilson, J. Tschanz, D. Finan, P. Iyer, A. Singh, T. Jacob, S. Jain, S. Venkataraman, Y. Hoskote, and N. Borkar. An 80-tile 1.28TFLOPS network-on-chip in 65nm CMOS. In *ISSCC*, February 2007.

[39] L. Wu, R. J. Barker, M. A. Kim, and K. A. Ross. Navigating big data with high-throughput, energy-efficient data partitioning. In *ISCA*, 2013.

[40] M. Zukowski and P. Boncz. Vectorwise: Beyond column stores. *Data Engineering Bulletin*, 2012.

# DianNao: A Small-Footprint High-Throughput Accelerator for Ubiquitous Machine-Learning

Tianshi Chen
SKLCA, ICT, China

Zidong Du
SKLCA, ICT, China

Ninghui Sun
SKLCA, ICT, China

Jia Wang
SKLCA, ICT, China

Chengyong Wu
SKLCA, ICT, China

Yunji Chen
SKLCA, ICT, China

Olivier Temam
Inria, France

## Abstract

Machine-Learning tasks are becoming pervasive in a broad range of domains, and in a broad range of systems (from embedded systems to data centers). At the same time, a small set of machine-learning algorithms (especially Convolutional and Deep Neural Networks, i.e., CNNs and DNNs) are proving to be state-of-the-art across many applications. As architectures evolve towards heterogeneous multi-cores composed of a mix of cores and accelerators, a machine-learning accelerator can achieve the rare combination of efficiency (due to the small number of target algorithms) and broad application scope.

Until now, most machine-learning accelerator designs have focused on efficiently implementing the computational part of the algorithms. However, recent state-of-the-art CNNs and DNNs are characterized by their large size. In this study, we design an accelerator for large-scale CNNs and DNNs, with a special emphasis on the impact of memory on accelerator design, performance and energy.

We show that it is possible to design an accelerator with a high throughput, capable of performing 452 GOP/s (key NN operations such as synaptic weight multiplications and neurons outputs additions) in a small footprint of 3.02 mm$^2$ and 485 mW; compared to a 128-bit 2GHz SIMD processor, the accelerator is 117.87x faster, and it can reduce the total energy by 21.08x. The accelerator characteristics are obtained after layout at 65nm. Such a high throughput in a small footprint can open up the usage of state-of-the-art machine-learning algorithms in a broad set of systems and for a broad set of applications.



*ASPLOS '14*, March 1–5, 2014, Salt Lake City, Utah, USA.

http://dx.doi.org/10.1145/http://dx.doi.org/10.1145/2541940.2541967

## 1. Introduction

As architectures evolve towards heterogeneous multi-cores composed of a mix of cores and accelerators, designing accelerators which realize the best possible tradeoff between flexibility and efficiency is becoming a prominent issue.

The first question is for which category of applications one should primarily design accelerators ? Together with the architecture trend towards accelerators, a second simultaneous and significant trend in high-performance and embedded applications is developing: many of the emerging high-performance and embedded applications, from image/video/audio recognition to automatic translation, business analytics, and all forms of robotics rely on *machine-learning techniques*. This trend even starts to percolate in our community where it turns out that about half of the benchmarks of PARSEC [2], a suite partly introduced to highlight the emergence of new types of applications, can be implemented using machine-learning algorithms [4]. This trend in application comes together with a third and equally remarkable trend in machine-learning where a small number of techniques, based on neural networks (especially Convolutional Neural Networks [27] and Deep Neural Networks

[16]), have been proved in the past few years to be state-of-the-art across a broad range of applications [25]. As a result, there is a unique opportunity to design accelerators which can realize the best of both worlds: significant application scope together with high performance and efficiency due to the limited number of target algorithms.

Currently, these workloads are mostly executed on multi-cores using SIMD [41], on GPUs [5], or on FPGAs [3]. However, the aforementioned trends have already been identified by a number of researchers who have proposed accelerators implementing Convolutional Neural Networks [3] or Multi-Layer Perceptrons [38]; accelerators focusing on other domains, such as image processing, also propose efficient implementations of some of the primitives used by machine-learning algorithms, such as convolutions [33]. Others have proposed ASIC implementations of Convolutional Neural Networks [13], or of other custom neural network algorithms [21]. However, all these works have first, and successfully, focused on efficiently implementing the computational primitives but they either voluntarily ignore memory transfers for the sake of simplicity [33, 38], or they directly plug their computational accelerator to memory via a more or less sophisticated DMA [3, 13, 21].

While efficient implementation of computational primitives is a first and important step with promising results, inefficient memory transfers can potentially void the throughput, energy or cost advantages of accelerators, i.e., an Amdahl's law effect, and thus, they should become a first-order concern, just like in processors, rather than an element factored in accelerator design on a second step. Unlike in processors though, one can factor in the specific nature of memory transfers in target algorithms, just like it is done for accelerating computations. This is especially important in the domain of machine-learning where there is a clear trend towards scaling up the size of neural networks in order to achieve better accuracy and more functionality [16, 26].

In this study, we investigate an accelerator design that can accommodate the most popular state-of-the-art algorithms, i.e., Convolutional Neural Networks (CNNs) and Deep Neural Networks (DNNs). We focus the design of the accelerator on memory usage, and we investigate an accelerator architecture and control both to minimize memory transfers and to perform them as efficiently as possible. We present a design at 65nm which can perform 496 16-bit fixed-point operations in parallel every 1.02ns, i.e., 452 GOP/s, in a 3.02mm$^2$, 485mW footprint (excluding main memory accesses). On 10 of the largest layers found in recent CNNs and DNNs, this accelerator is 117.87x faster and 21.08x more energy-efficient (including main memory accesses) on average than an 128-bit SIMD core clocked at 2GHz.

In summary, our main contributions are the following:

- A synthesized (place & route) accelerator design for large-scale CNNs and DNNs, the state-of-the-art machine-learning algorithms.
- The accelerator achieves high throughput in a small area, power and energy footprint.
- The accelerator design focuses on memory behavior, and measurements are not circumscribed to computational tasks, they factor in the performance and energy impact of memory transfers.

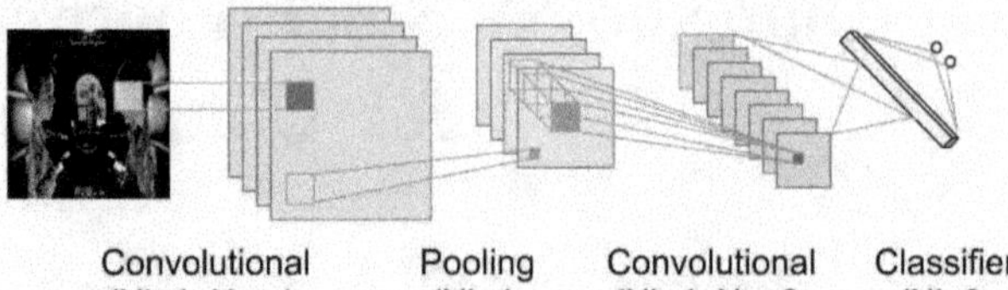


**Figure 1.** *Neural network hierarchy containing convolutional, pooling and classifier layers.*

The paper is organized as follows. In Section 2, we first provide a primer on recent machine-learning techniques and introduce the main layers composing CNNs and DNNs. In Section 3, we analyze and optimize the memory behavior of these layers, in preparation for both the baseline and the accelerator design. In section 4, we explain why an ASIC implementation of large-scale CNNs or DNNs cannot be the same as the straightforward ASIC implementation of small NNs. We introduce our accelerator design in Section 5. The methodology is presented in Section 6, the experimental results in Section 7, related work in Section 8.

## 2. Primer on Recent Machine-Learning Techniques

Even though the role of neural networks in the machine-learning domain has been rocky, i.e., initially hyped in the 1980s/1990s, then fading into oblivion with the advent of Support Vector Machines [6]. Since 2006, a subset of neural networks have emerged as achieving state-of-the-art machine-learning accuracy across a broad set of applications, partly inspired by progress in neuroscience models of computer vision, such as HMAX [37]. This subset of neural networks includes both Deep Neural Networks (DNNs) [25] and Convolutional Neural Networks (CNNs) [27]. DNNs and CNNs are strongly related, they especially differ in the presence and/or nature of convolutional layers, see later.

**Processing vs. training.** For now, we have implemented the fast processing of inputs (feed-forward) rather than training (backward path) on our accelerator. This derives from technical and market considerations. Technically, there is a frequent and important misconception that *on-line* learning is necessary for many applications. On the contrary, for many industrial applications *off-line* learning is sufficient, where the neural network is first trained on a set of data, and then shipped to the customer, e.g., trained on hand-

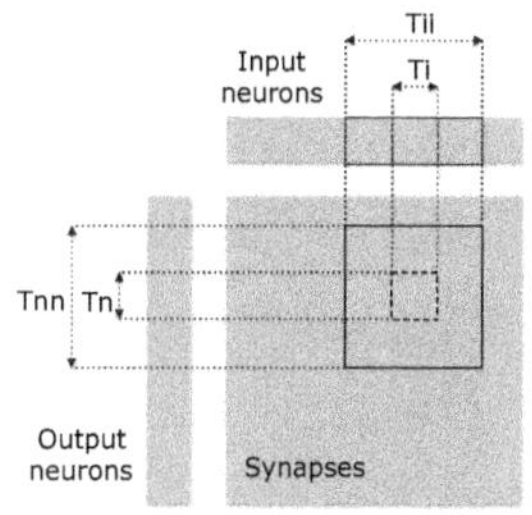


**Figure 2.** *Classifier layer tiling.*

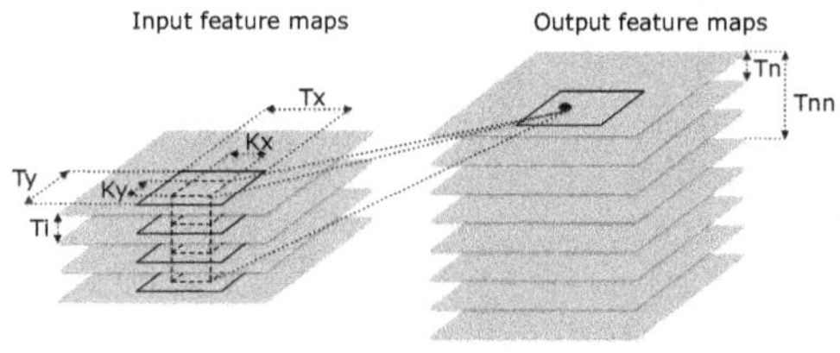


**Figure 3.** *Convolutional layer tiling.*

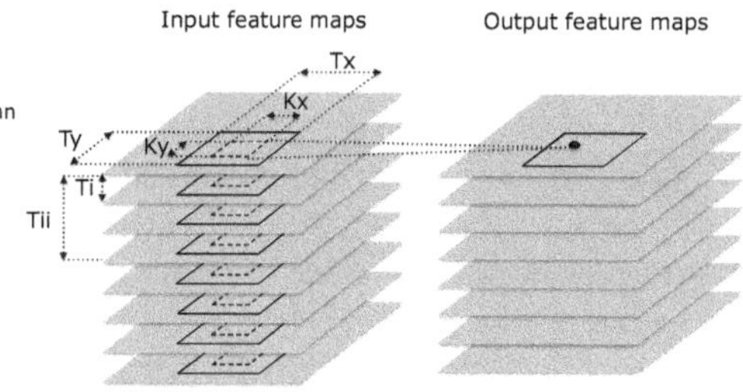


**Figure 4.** *Pooling layer tiling.*

written digits, license plate numbers, a number of faces or objects to recognize, etc; the network can be periodically taken off-line and retrained. While, today, machine-learning researchers and engineers would especially want an architecture that speeds up training, this represents a small market, and for now, we focus on the much larger market of *end users*, who need fast/efficient feed-forward networks. Interestingly, machine-learning researchers who have recently dipped into hardware accelerators [13] have made the same choice. Still, because the nature of computations and access patterns used in training (especially back-propagation) is fairly similar to that of the forward path, we plan to later augment the accelerator with the necessary features to support training.

**General structure.** Even though Deep and Convolutional Neural Networks come in various forms, they share enough properties that a generic formulation can be defined. In general, these algorithms are made of a (possibly large) number of *layers*; these layers are executed *in sequence* so they can be considered (and optimized) independently. Each layer usually contains several sub-layers called *feature maps*; we then use the terms *input feature maps* and *output feature maps*. Overall, there are three main kinds of layers: most of the hierarchy is composed of convolutional and pooling (also called sub-sampling) layers, and there is a classifier at the top of the network made of one or a few layers.

**Convolutional layers.** The role of convolutional layers is to apply one or several *local* filters to data from the input (previous) layer. Thus, the connectivity between the input and output feature map is local instead of full. Consider the case where the input is an image, the convolution is a 2D transform between a $K_x \times K_y$ subset (window) of the input layer and a kernel of the same dimensions, see Figure 1. The kernel values are the synaptic weights between an input layer and an output (convolutional) layer. Since an input layer usually contains several input feature maps, and since an output feature map point is usually obtained by applying a convolution to the same window of *all* input feature maps, see Figure 1, the kernel is 3D, i.e., $K_x \times K_y \times N_i$, where $N_i$ is the number of input feature maps. Note that in some cases, the connectivity is sparse, i.e., not all input feature maps are used for each output feature map. The typical code of a convolutional layer is shown in Figure 7, see *Original code*. A non-linear function is applied to the convolution output, for instance $f(x) = tanh(x)$. Convolutional layers are also characterized by the overlap between two consecutive windows (in one or two dimensions), see steps $s_x$, $s_y$ for loops $x, y$.

In some cases, the same kernel is applied to all $K_x \times K_y$ windows of the input layer, i.e., weights are implicitly *shared* across the whole input feature map. This is characteristic of CNNs, while kernels can be specific to each point of the output feature map in DNNs [26], we then use the term *private* kernels.

**Pooling layers.** The role of pooling layers is to aggregate information among a set of neighbor input data. In the case of images again, it serves to retain only the salient features of an image within a given window and/or to do so at different scales, see Figure 1. An important side effect of pooling layers is to reduce the feature map dimensions. An example code of a pooling layer is shown in Figure 8 (see *Original code*). Note that each feature map is pooled separately, i.e., 2D pooling, not 3D pooling. Pooling can be done in various ways, some of the preferred techniques are the *average* and *max* operations; pooling may or may not be followed by a non-linear function.

**Classifier layers.** Convolution and pooling layers are interleaved within deep hierarchies, and the top of the hierarchies is usually a *classifier*. This classifier can be linear or a multi-layer (often 2-layer) perceptron, see Figure 1. An example perceptron layer is shown in Figure 5, see *Original code*. Like convolutional layers, a non-linear function is applied to the neurons output, often a sigmoid, e.g., $f(x) = \frac{1}{1+e^{-x}}$; unlike convolutional or pooling layers, classifiers usually aggregate (flatten) all feature maps, so there is no notion of feature maps in classifier layers.

## 3. Processor-Based Implementation of (Large) Neural Networks

The distinctive aspect of accelerating large-scale neural networks is the potentially high memory traffic. In this section, we analyze in details the locality properties of the different layers mentioned in Section 2, we tune processor-based implementations of these layers in preparation for both our baseline, and the design and utilization of the accelerator. We apply the locality analysis/optimization to all layers, and we illustrate the bandwidth impact of these transformations with 4 of our benchmark layers (CLASS1, CONV3, CONV5, POOL3); their characteristics are later detailed in Section 6.

For the memory bandwidth measurements of this section, we use a cache simulator plugged to a virtual computational structure on which we make no assumption except that it is capable of processing $T_n$ neurons with $T_i$ synapses each every cycle. The cache hierarchy is inspired by Intel Core i7: L1 is 32KB, 64-byte line, 8-way; the optional L2 is 2MB, 64-byte, 8-way. Unlike the Core i7, we assume the caches have enough banks/ports to serve $T_n \times 4$ bytes for input neurons, and $T_n \times T_i \times 4$ bytes for synapses. For large $T_n, T_i$, the cost of such caches can be prohibitive, but it is only used for our limit study of locality and bandwidth; in our experiments, we use $T_n = T_i = 16$.

### 3.1 Classifier Layers

```
for (int nnn = 0; nnn ¡ Nn; nnn += Tnn) { // tiling for output neurons;
  for (int iii = 0; iii ¡ Ni; iii += Tii) { // tiling for input neurons;
    for (int nn = nnn; nn ¡ nnn + Tnn; nn += Tn) {
      for (int n = nn; n ¡ nn + Tn; n++)
        sum[n] = 0;
      for (int ii = iii; ii ¡ iii + Tii; ii += Ti)
        // — Original code —
        for (int n = nn; n < nn + Tn; n++)
          for (int i = ii; i < ii + Ti; i++)
            sum[n] += synapse[n][i] * neuron[i];
      for (int n = nn; n < nn + Tn; n++)
        neuron[n] = sigmoid(sum[n]);
}}}
```

**Figure 5.** *Pseudo-code for a classifier (here, perceptron) layer (original loop nest + locality optimization).*

We consider the perceptron classifier layer, see Figures 2 and 5; the tiling loops $ii$ and $nn$ simply reflect that the computational structure can process $T_n$ neurons with $T_i$ synapses simultaneously. The total number of memory transfers is (inputs loaded + synapses loaded + outputs written): $N_i \times N_n + N_i \times N_n + N_n$. For the example layer CLASS1, the corresponding memory bandwidth is high at 120 GB/s, see *CLASS1 - Original* in Figure 6. We explain below how it is possible to reduce this bandwidth, sometimes drastically.

**Input/Output neurons.** Consider Figure 2 and the code of Figure 5 again. Input neurons are reused for each output neuron, but since the number of input neurons can range anywhere between a few tens to hundreds of thousands, they will often not fit in an L1 cache. Therefore, we tile loop $ii$ (input neurons) with tile factor $T_{ii}$. A typical tradeoff of tiling is that improving one reference (here $neuron[i]$ for input neurons) increases the reuse distance of another reference ($sum[n]$ for partial sums of output neurons), so we need to tile for the second reference as well, hence loop $nnn$ and the tile factor $T_{nn}$ for output neurons partial sums. As expected, tiling drastically reduces the memory bandwidth requirements of input neurons, and those of output neurons increase, albeit marginally. The layer memory behavior is now dominated by synapses.

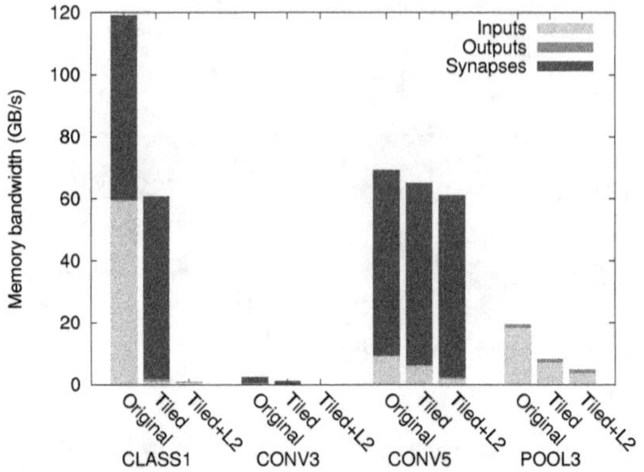


**Figure 6.** *Memory bandwidth requirements for each layer type (CONV3 has shared kernels, CONV5 has private kernels).*

**Synapses.** In a perceptron layer, all synapses are usually unique, and thus there is no reuse *within the layer*. On the other hand, the synapses are reused *across network invocations*, i.e., for each new input data (also called "input row") presented to the neural network. So a sufficiently large L2 could store all network synapses and take advantage of that locality. For DNNs with private kernels, this is not possible as the total number of synapses are in the tens or hundreds of millions (the largest network to date has a billion synapses [26]). However, for both CNNs and DNNs with shared kernels, the total number of synapses range in the millions, which is within the reach of an L2 cache. In Figure 6, see *CLASS1 - Tiled+L2*, we emulate the case where reuse across network invocations is possible by considering only the perceptron layer; as a result, the total bandwidth requirements are now drastically reduced.

### 3.2 Convolutional Layers

We consider two-dimensional convolutional layers, see Figures 3 and 7. The two distinctive features of convolutional layers with respect to classifier layers are the presence of input and output feature maps (loops $i$ and $n$) and kernels (loops $k_x, k_y$).

**Inputs/Outputs.** There are two types of reuse opportunities for inputs and outputs: the *sliding window* used to scan the (two-dimensional $(x, y)$) input layer, and the reuse across the $N_n$ output feature maps, see Figure 3. The former corresponds to $\frac{K_x \times K_y}{s_x \times s_y}$ reuses at most, and the latter to $N_n$ reuses. We tile for the former in Figure 7 (tiles $T_x, T_y$), but we often do not need to tile for the latter because the data to be reused, i.e., one kernel of $K_x \times K_y \times N_i$, fits in the L1 data cache since $K_x$, $K_y$ are usually of the order of 10 and $N_i$ can vary between less than 10 to a few hundreds; naturally, when this is not the case, we can tile input feature maps ($ii$) and introduce an second-level tiling loop $iii$ again.

**Synapses.** For convolutional layers with *shared* kernels (see Section 2), the same kernel parameters (synaptic weights) are reused across all $xout, yout$ output feature maps locations. As a result, the total bandwidth is already

```
for (int yy = 0; yy ¡ Nyin; yy += Ty) {
 for (int xx = 0; xx ¡ Nxin; xx += Tx) {
  for (int nnn = 0; nnn ¡ Nn; nnn += Tnn) {
   // — Original code — (excluding nn, ii loops)
   int yout = 0;
   for (int y = yy; y < yy + Ty; y += sy) { // tiling for y;
    int xout = 0;
    for (int x = xx; x < xx + Tx; x += sx) { // tiling for x;
     for (int nn = nnn; nn < nnn + Tnn; nn += Tn) {
      for (int n = nn; n < nn + Tn; n++)
       sum[n] = 0;
      // sliding window;
      for (int ky = 0; ky < Ky; ky++)
       for (int kx = 0; kx < Kx; kx++)
        for (int ii = 0; ii < Ni; ii += Ti)
         for (int n = nn; n < nn + Tn; n++)
          for (int i = ii; i < ii + Ti; i++)
           // version with shared kernels
           sum[n] += synapse[ky][kx][n][i]
                     * neuron[ky + y][kx + x][i];
           // version with private kernels
           sum[n] += synapse[yout][xout][ky][kx][n][i]}
                     * neuron[ky + y][kx + x][i];
      for (int n = nn; n < nn + Tn; n++)
       neuron[yout][xout][n] = non_linear_transform(sum[n]);
    } xout++; } yout++;
}}}}
```

**Figure 7.** *Pseudo-code for convolutional layer (original loop nest + locality optimization), both shared and private kernels versions.*

low, as shown for layer CONV3 in Figure 6. However, since the total shared kernels capacity is $K_x \times K_y \times N_i \times N_o$, it can exceed the L1 cache capacity, so we tile again output feature maps (tile $T_{nn}$) to bring it down to $K_x \times K_y \times N_i \times T_{nn}$. As a result, the overall memory bandwidth can be further reduced, as shown in Figure 6.

For convolutional layers with *private* kernels, the synapses are all unique and there is no reuse, as for classifier layers, hence the similar synapses bandwidth of CONV5 in Figure 6. As for classifier layers, reuse is still possible across network invocations if the L2 capacity is sufficient. Even though step coefficients $(s_x, s_y)$ and sparse input to output feature maps (see Section 2) can drastically reduce the number of private kernels synaptic weights, for very large layers such as CONV5, they still range in the hundreds of megabytes and thus will largely exceed L2 capacity, implying a high memory bandwidth, see Figure 6.

It is important to note that there is an on-going debate within the machine-learning community about shared vs. private kernels [26, 35], and the machine-learning importance of having private instead of shared kernels remains unclear. Since they can result in significantly different architecture performance, this may be a case where the architecture/performance community could weigh in on the machine-learning debate.

### 3.3 Pooling Layers

We now consider pooling layers, see Figures 4 and 8. Unlike convolutional layers, the number of input and output feature

```
for (int yy = 0; yy ¡ Nyin; yy += Ty) {
 for (int xx = 0; xx ¡ Nxin; xx += Tx) {
  for (int iii = 0; iii ¡ Ni; iii += Tii)
   // — Original code — (excluding ii loop)
   int yout = 0;
   for (int y = yy; y < yy + Ty; y += sy) {
    int xout = 0;
    for (int x = xx; x < xx + Tx; x += sx) {
     for (int ii = iii; ii < iii + Tii; ii += Ti)
      for (int i = ii; i < ii + Ti; i++)
       value[i] = 0;
      for (int ky = 0; ky < Ky; ky++)
       for (int kx = 0; kx < Kx; kx++)
        for (int i = ii; i < ii + Ti; i++)
         // version with average pooling;
         value[i] += neuron[ky + y][kx + x][i];
         // version with max pooling;
         value[i] = max(value[i], neuron[ky + y][kx + x][i]);
     }}}}
    // for average pooling;
    neuron[xout][yout][i] = value[i] / (Kx * Ky);
    xout++; } yout++;
}}}
```

**Figure 8.** *Pseudo-code for pooling layer (original loop nest + locality optimization).*

maps is the same, and more importantly, there is no kernel, i.e., no synaptic weight to store, and an output feature map element is determined only by $K_x \times K_y$ input feature map elements, i.e., a 2D window (instead of a 3D window for convolutional layers). As a result, the only source of reuse comes from the sliding window (instead of the combined effect of sliding window and output feature maps). Since there are less reuse opportunities, the memory bandwidth of input neurons are higher than for convolutional layers, and tiling $(T_x, T_y)$ brings less dramatic improvements, see Figure 6.

## 4. Accelerator for Small Neural Networks

In this section, we first evaluate a "naive" and greedy approach for implementing a hardware neural network accelerator where all neurons and synapses are laid out in hardware, memory is only used for input rows and storing results. While these neural networks can potentially achieve the best energy efficiency, we show that they are not scalable. Still, we use such networks to investigate the maximum number of neurons which can be reasonably implemented in hardware.

### 4.1 Hardware Neural Networks

The most natural way to map a neural network onto silicon is simply to fully lay out the neurons and synapses, so that the hardware implementation matches the conceptual representation of neural networks, see Figure 9. The neurons are each implemented as logic circuits, and the synapses are implemented as latches or RAMs. This approach has been recently used for perceptron or spike-based hardware neural networks [30, 38]. It is compatible with some embedded applications where the number of neurons and synapses can be small, and it can provide both high speed and low energy because the distance traveled by data is very small: from one

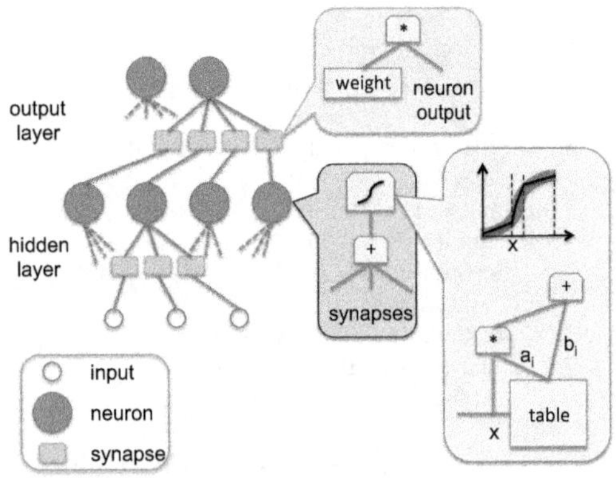


**Figure 9.** *Full hardware implementation of neural networks.*

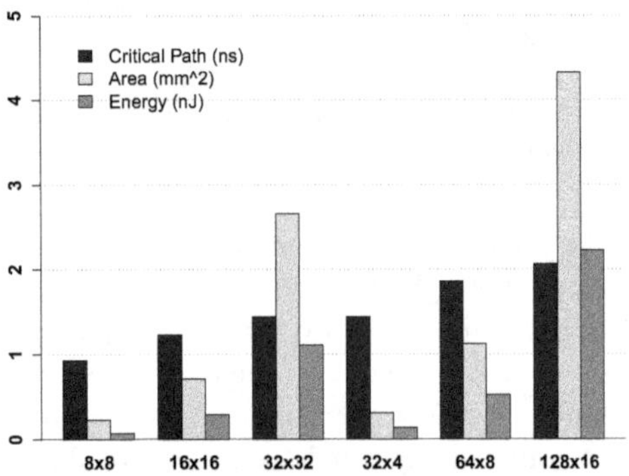


**Figure 10.** *Energy, critical path and area of full-hardware layers.*

neuron to a neuron of the next layer, and from one synaptic latch to the associated neuron. For instance, an execution time of 15ns and an energy reduction of 974x over a core has been reported for a 90-10-10 (90 inputs, 10 hidden, 10 outputs) perceptron [38].

### 4.2 Maximum Number of Hardware Neurons ?

However, the area, energy and delay grow quadratically with the number of neurons. We have synthesized the ASIC versions of neural network layers of various dimensions, and we report their area, critical path and energy in Figure 10. We have used Synopsys ICC for the place and route, and the TSMC 65nm GP library, standard VT. A hardware neuron performs the following operations: multiplication of inputs and synapses, addition of all such multiplications, followed by a sigmoid, see Figure 9. A $T_n \times T_i$ layer is a layer of $T_n$ neurons with $T_i$ synapses each. A 16x16 layer requires less than 0.71 mm$^2$, but a 32x32 layer already costs 2.66 mm$^2$. Considering the neurons are in the thousands for large-scale neural networks, a full hardware layout of just one layer would range in the hundreds or thousands of mm$^2$, and thus, this approach is not realistic for large-scale neural networks.

For such neural networks, only a fraction of neurons and synapses can be implemented in hardware. Paradoxically, this was already the case for old neural network designs

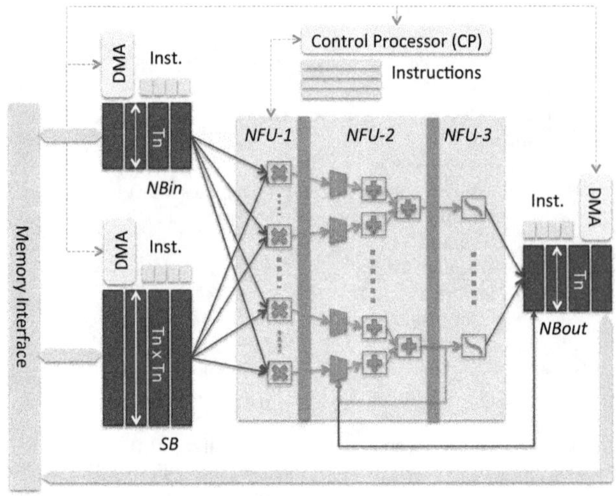


**Figure 11.** *Accelerator.*

such as the Intel ETANN [18] at the beginning of the 1990s, not because neural networks were already large at the time, but because hardware resources (number of transistors) were naturally much more scarce. The principle was to time-share the physical neurons and use the on-chip RAM to store synapses and intermediate neurons values of hidden layers. However, at that time, many neural networks were small enough that all synapses and intermediate neurons values could fit in the neural network RAM. Since this is no longer the case, one of the main challenges for large-scale neural network accelerator design has become the interplay between the computational and the memory hierarchy.

## 5. Accelerator for Large Neural Networks

In this section, we draw from the analysis of Sections 3 and 4 to design an accelerator for large-scale neural networks.

The main components of the accelerator are the following: an input buffer for input neurons (NBin), an output buffer for output neurons (NBout), and a third buffer for synaptic weights (SB), connected to a computational block (performing both synapses and neurons computations) which we call the Neural Functional Unit (NFU), and the control logic (CP), see Figure 11. We first describe the NFU below, and then we focus on and explain the rationale for the storage elements of the accelerator.

### 5.1 Computations: Neural Functional Unit (NFU)

The spirit of the NFU is to reflect the decomposition of a layer into computational blocks of $T_i$ inputs/synapses and $T_n$ output neurons. This corresponds to loops $i$ and $n$ for both classifier and convolutional layers, see Figures 5 and Figure 7, and loop $i$ for pooling layers, see Figure 8.

**Arithmetic operators.** The computations of each layer type can be decomposed in either 2 or 3 stages. For classifier layers: multiplication of synapses $\times$ inputs, additions of all

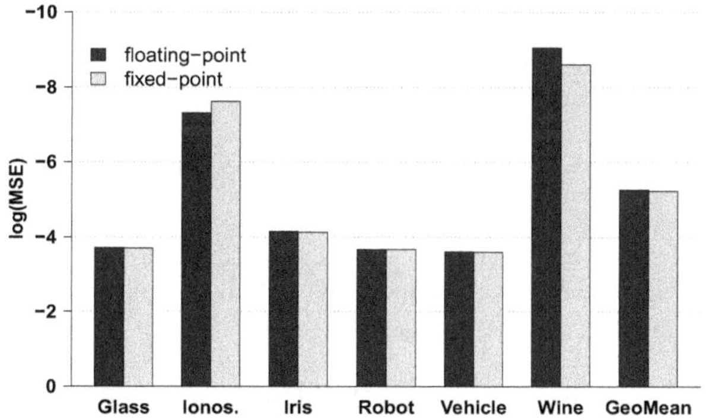


**Figure 12.** *32-bit floating-point vs. 16-bit fixed-point accuracy for UCI data sets (metric: log(*Mean Squared Error*)).*

| Type | Error Rate |
|---|---|
| 32-bit floating-point | 0.0311 |
| 16-bit fixed-point | 0.0337 |

**Table 1.** *32-bit floating-point vs. 16-bit fixed-point accuracy for MNIST (metric: error rate).*

multiplications, sigmoid. For convolutional layers, the stages are the same; the nature of the last stage (sigmoid or another non-linear function) can vary. For pooling layers, there is no multiplication (no synapse), and the pooling operations can be average or max. Note that the adders have multiple inputs, they are in fact *adder trees*, see Figure 11; the second stage also contains shifters and max operators for pooling layers.

**Staggered pipeline.** We can pipeline all 2 or 3 operations, but the pipeline must be staggered: the first or first two stages (respectively for pooling, and for classifier and convolutional layers) operate as normal pipeline stages, but the third stage is only active after all additions have been performed (for classifier and convolutional layers; for pooling layers, there is no operation in the third stage). From now on, we refer to stage $n$ of the NFU pipeline as NFU-$n$.

**NFU-3 function implementation.** As previously proposed in the literature [23, 38], the sigmoid of NFU-3 (for classifier and convolutional layers) can be efficiently implemented using piecewise linear interpolation ($f(x) = a_i \times x + b_i, x \in [x_i; x_{i+1}]$) with negligible loss of accuracy (16 segments are sufficient) [24], see Figure 9. In terms of operators, it corresponds to two 16x1 16-bit multiplexers (for segment boundaries selection, i.e., $x_i, x_{i+1}$), one 16-bit multiplier (16-bit output) and one 16-bit adder to perform the interpolation. The 16-segment coefficients ($a_i, b_i$) are stored in a small RAM; this allows to implement *any* function, not just a sigmoid (e.g., hyperbolic tangent, linear functions, etc) by just changing the RAM segment coefficients $a_i, b_i$; the segment boundaries ($x_i, x_{i+1}$) are hardwired.

**16-bit fixed-point arithmetic operators.** We use 16-bit fixed-point arithmetic operators instead of word-size (e.g., 32-bit) floating-point operators. While it may seem surprising, there is ample evidence in the literature that even smaller operators (e.g., 8 bits or even less) have almost no impact on the accuracy of neural networks [8, 17, 24]. To illustrate and further confirm that notion, we trained and tested multi-layer perceptrons on data sets from the UC Irvine Machine-Learning repository, see Figure 12, and on the standard MNIST machine-learning benchmark (handwritten digits) [27], see Table 1, using both 16-bit fixed-point and 32-bit floating-point operators; we used 10-fold cross-validation for testing. For the fixed-point operators, we use 6 bits for the integer part, 10 bits for the fractional part (we use this fixed-point configuration throughout the paper). The results are shown in Figure 12 and confirm the very small accuracy impact of that tradeoff. We conservatively use 16-bit fixed-point for now, but we will explore smaller, or variable-size, operators in the future. Note that the arithmetic operators are *truncated*, i.e., their output is 16 bits; we use a standard $n$-bit truncated multiplier with correction constant [22]. As shown in Table 2, its area is 6.10x smaller and its power 7.33x lower than a 32-bit floating-point multiplier at 65nm, see Section 6 for the CAD tools methodology.

| Type | Area ($\mu m^2$) | Power ($\mu W$) |
|---|---|---|
| 16-bit truncated fixed-point multiplier | 1309.32 | 576.90 |
| 32-bit floating-point multiplier | 7997.76 | 4229.60 |

**Table 2.** *Characteristics of multipliers.*

### 5.2 Storage: NBin, NBout, SB and NFU-2 Registers

The different storage structures of the accelerator can be construed as modified buffers of scratchpads. While a cache is an excellent storage structure for a general-purpose processor, it is a sub-optimal way to exploit reuse because of the cache access overhead (tag check, associativity, line size, speculative read, etc) and cache conflicts [39]. The efficient alternative, scratchpad, is used in VLIW processors but it is known to be very difficult to compile for. However a scratchpad in a dedicated accelerator realizes the best of both worlds: efficient storage, and both efficient and easy exploitation of locality because only a few algorithms have to be manually adapted. In this case, we can almost directly translate the locality transformations introduced in Section 3 into mapping commands for the buffers, mostly modulating the tile factors. A code mapping example is provided in Section 5.3.2

We explain below how the storage part of the accelerator is organized, and which limitations of cache architectures it overcomes.

#### 5.2.1 Split buffers.

As explained before, we have split storage into three structures: an input buffer (NBin), an output buffer (NBout) and a synapse buffer (SB).

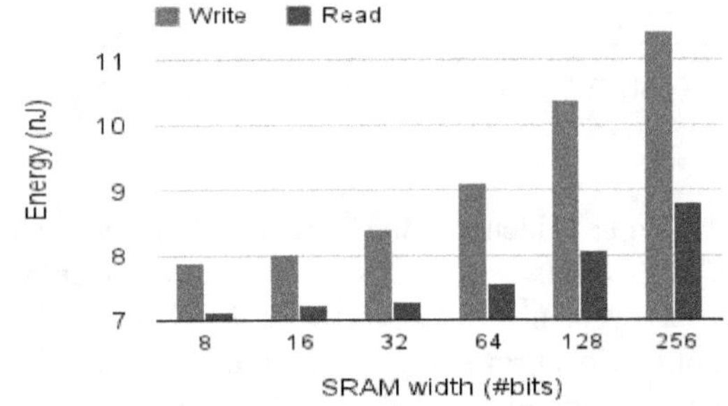


**Figure 13.** *Read energy vs. SRAM width.*

*Width.* The first benefit of splitting structures is to tailor the SRAMs to the appropriate read/write width. The width of both NBin and NBout is $T_n \times 2$ bytes, while the width of SB is $T_n \times T_n \times 2$ bytes. A single read width size, e.g., as with a cache line size, would be a poor tradeoff. If it's adjusted to synapses, i.e., if the line size is $T_n \times T_n \times 2$, then there is a significant energy penalty for reading $T_n \times 2$ bytes out of a $T_n \times T_n \times 2$-wide data bank, see Figure 13 which indicates the SRAM read energy as a function of bank width for the TSMC process at 65nm. If the line size is adjusted to neurons, i.e., if the line size is $T_n \times 2$, there is a significant time penalty for reading $T_n \times T_n \times 2$ bytes out. Splitting storage into dedicated structures allows to achieve the best time and energy for each read request.

*Conflicts.* The second benefit of splitting storage structures is to avoid conflicts, as would occur in a cache. It is especially important as we want to keep the size of the storage structures small for cost and energy (leakage) reasons. The alternative solution is to use a highly associative cache. Consider the constraints: the cache line (or the number of ports) needs to be large ($T_n \times T_n \times 2$) in order to serve the synapses at a high rate; since we would want to keep the cache size small, the only alternative to tolerate such a long cache line is high associativity. However, in an $n$-way cache, a fast read is implemented by speculatively reading all $n$ ways/banks in parallel; as a result, the energy cost of an associative cache increases quickly. Even a 64-byte read from an 8-way associative 32KB cache costs 3.15x more energy than a 32-byte read from a direct mapped cache, at 65nm; measurements done using CACTI [40]. And even with a 64-byte line only, the first-level 32KB data cache of Core i7 is already 8-way associative, so we need an even larger associativity with a very large line (for $T_n = 16$, the line size would be 512-byte long). In other words, a highly associative cache would be a costly energy solution in our case. Split storage and precise knowledge of locality behavior allows to entirely remove data conflicts.

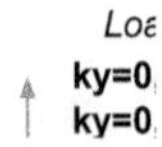


**Figure 14.** *Local transpose* ($K_y = 2, K_x = 1, N_i = 4$).

#### 5.2.2 Exploiting the locality of inputs and synapses.

**DMAs.** For spatial locality exploitation, we implement three DMAs, one for each buffer (two load DMAs, one store DMA for outputs). DMA requests are issued to NBin in the form of instructions, later described in Section 5.3.2. These requests are buffered in a separate FIFO associated with each buffer, see Figure 11, and they are issued as soon as the DMA has sent all the memory requests for the previous instruction. These DMA requests FIFOs enable to *decouple* the requests issued to all buffers and the NFU from the current buffer and NFU operations. As a result, DMA requests can be preloaded far in advance for tolerating long latencies, as long as there is enough buffer capacity; this *preloading* is akin to prefetching, albeit without speculation. Due to the combined role of NBin (and SB) as both scratchpads for reuse and preload buffers, we use a dual-port SRAM; the TSMC 65nm library rates the read energy overhead of dual port SRAMs for a 64-entry NB at 24%.

**Rotating NBin buffer for temporal reuse of input neurons.** The inputs of all layers are split into chunks which fit in NBin, and they are reused by implementing NBin as a *circular buffer*. In practice, the rotation is naturally implemented by changing a register index, much like in a software implementation, there is no physical (and costly) movement of buffer entries.

**Local transpose in NBin for pooling layers.** There is a tension between convolutional and pooling layers for the data structure organization of (input) neurons. As mentioned before, $K_x, K_y$ are usually small (often less than 10), and $N_i$ is about an order of magnitude larger. So memory fetches are more efficient (long stride-1 accesses) with the input feature maps as the innermost index of the three-dimensional neurons data structure. However, this is inconvenient for pooling layers because one output is computed *per input feature map*, i.e., using only $K_x \times K_y$ data (while in convolutional layers, all $K_x \times K_y \times N_i$ data are required to compute one output data). As a result, for pooling layers, the logical data structure organization is to have $k_x, k_y$ as the innermost dimensions so that all inputs required to compute one output are consecutively stored in the NBin buffer. We resolve this tension by introducing a mapping function in NBin which has the effect of *locally transposing* loops $k_y, k_x$ and loop $i$ so that data is loaded along loop $i$, but it is stored in NBin and thus sent to NFU along loops $k_y, k_x$ first; this is accomplished by interleaving the data in NBin as it is loaded, see Figure 14.

For synapses and SB, as mentioned in Section 3, there is either no reuse (classifier layers, convolutional layers with private kernels and pooling layers), or reuse of shared kernels in convolutional layers. For outputs and NBout, we need to reuse the partial sums, i.e., see reference $sum[n]$ in Figure 5. This reuse requires additional hardware modifications explained in the next section.

### 5.2.3 Exploiting the locality of outputs.

In both classifier and convolutional layers, the partial output sum of $T_n$ output neurons is computed for a chunk of input neurons contained in NBin. Then, the input neurons are used for another chunk of $T_n$ output neurons, etc. This creates two issues.

**Dedicated registers.** First, while the chunk of input neurons is loaded from NBin and used to compute the partial sums, it would be inefficient to let the partial sum exit the NFU pipeline and then re-load it into the pipeline for each entry of the NBin buffer, since data transfers are a major source of energy expense [14]. So we introduce *dedicated registers* in NFU-2, which store the partial sums.

**Circular buffer.** Second, a more complicated issue is what to do with the $T_n$ partial sums when the input neurons in NBin are reused for a new set of $T_n$ output neurons. Instead of sending these $T_n$ partial sums back to memory (and to later reload them when the next chunk of input neurons is loaded into NBin), we temporarily rotate them out to NBout. A priori, this is a conflicting role for NBout which is also used to store the final output neurons to be written back to memory (write buffer). In practice though, as long as all input neurons have not been integrated in the partial sums, NBout is idle. So we can use it as a temporary storage buffer by rotating the $T_n$ partial sums out to NBout, see Figure 11. Naturally, the loop iterating over output neurons must be tiled so that no more output neurons are computing their partial sums simultaneously than the capacity of NBout, but that is implemented through a second-level tiling similar to loop $nnn$ in Figure 5 and Figure 7. As a result, NBout is not only connected to NFU-3 and memory, but also to NFU-2: one entry of NBout can be loaded into the dedicated registers of NFU-2, and these registers can be stored in NBout.

## 5.3 Control and Code

### 5.3.1 CP.

In this section, we describe the control of the accelerator. One approach to control would be to hardwire the three target layers. While this remains an option for the future, for now, we have decided to use *control instructions* in order to explore different implementations (e.g., partitioning and scheduling) of layers, and to provide machine-learning researchers with the flexibility to try out different layer implementations.

| CP | SB | | | | NBin | | | | | | | NBout | | | | NFU | | | | | | |
|---|---|---|---|---|---|---|---|---|---|---|---|---|---|---|---|---|---|---|---|---|---|---|
| END | READ OP | REUSE | ADDRESS | SIZE | READ OP | REUSE | STRIDE | STRIDE BEGIN | STRIDE END | ADDRESS | SIZE | READ OP | WRITE OP | ADDRESS | SIZE | NFU-1 OP | NFU-2 OP | NFU-2 IN | NFU-2 OUT | NFU-3 OP | OUTPUT BEGIN | OUTPUT END |

**Table 3.** *Control instruction format.*

| CP | SB | | | | NBin | | | | | | | NBout | | | | NFU | | | | | | |
|---|---|---|---|---|---|---|---|---|---|---|---|---|---|---|---|---|---|---|---|---|---|---|
| NOP | LOAD | 0 | 0 | 32768 | LOAD | 1 | 0 | 0 | 0 | 4194304 | 2048 | NOP | WRITE | 0 | 0 | MULT | ADD | RESET | NBOUT | SIGMOID | 1 | 0 |
| NOP | LOAD | 0 | 32768 | 32768 | READ | 1 | 0 | 0 | 0 | 0 | 0 | NOP | WRITE | 0 | 0 | MULT | ADD | RESET | NBOUT | SIGMOID | 0 | 0 |
| ............................ | | | | | | | | | | | | | | | | | | | | | | |
| NOP | LOAD | 0 | 7864320 | 32768 | LOAD | 1 | 0 | 0 | 0 | 4225024 | 2048 | READ | STORE | 8388608 | 512 | MULT | ADD | NBOUT | NFU3 | SIGMOID | 1 | 0 |
| ............................ | | | | | | | | | | | | | | | | | | | | | | |

**Table 4.** *Subset of classifier/perceptron code ($N_i$ = 8192, $N_o = 256$, $T_n = 16$, 64-entry buffers).*

A layer execution is broken down into a set of instructions. Roughly, one instruction corresponds to the loops $ii, i, n$ for classifier and convolutional layers, see Figures 5 and 7, and to the loops $ii, i$ in pooling layers (using the interleaving mechanism described in Section 5.2.3), see Figure 8. The instructions are stored in an SRAM associated with the *Control Processor* (CP), see Figure 11. The CP drives the execution of the DMAs of the three buffers and the NFU. The term "processor" only relates to the aforementioned "instructions", later described in Section 5.3.2, but it has very few of the traditional features of a processor (mostly a PC and an adder for loop index and address computations); from a hardware perspective, it is more like a configurable FSM.

### 5.3.2 Layer Code.

Every instruction has five slots, corresponding to the CP itself, the three buffers and the NFU, see Table 3.

Because of the CP instructions, there is a need for code generation, but a compiler would be overkill in our case as only three main types of codes must be generated. So we have implemented three dedicated code generators for the three layers. In Table 4, we give an example of the code generated for a classifier/perceptron layer. Since $T_n = 16$ (16×16-bit data per buffer row) and NBin has 64 rows, its capacity is 2KB, so it cannot contain all the input neurons ($N_i = 8192$, so 16KB). As a result, the code is broken down to operate on chunks of 2KB; note that the first instruction of NBin is a LOAD (data fetched from memory), and that it is marked as *reused* (flag immediately after load); the next instruction is a *read*, because these input neurons are rotated in the buffer for the next chunk of $T_n$ neurons, and the read is also marked as *reused* because there are 8 such rotations ($\frac{16KB}{2KB}$); at the same time, notice that the output of NFU-2 for the first (and next) instruction is NBout, i.e., the partial output neurons sums are rotated to NBout, as explained in Section 5.2.3, which is why the NBout instruction is

WRITE; notice also that the input of NFU-2 is RESET (first chunk of input neurons, registers reset). Finally, when the last chunk of input neurons are sent (last instruction in table), the (store) DMA of NBout is set for writing 512 bytes (256 outputs), and the NBout instruction is STORE; the NBout write operation for the next instructions will be NOP (DMA set at first chunk and automatically storing data back to memory until DMA elapses).

Note that the architecture can implement either per-image or batch processing [41], only the generated layer control code would change.

## 6. Experimental Methodology

**Measurements.** We use three different tools for performance/energy measurements.

*Accelerator simulator.* We implemented a custom cycle-accurate, bit-accurate C++ simulator of the accelerator fabric, which was initially used for architecture exploration, and which later served as the specification for the Verilog implementation. This simulator is also used to measure time in number of cycles. It is plugged to a main memory model allowing a bandwidth of up to 250 GB/s.

*CAD tools.* For area, energy and critical path delay (cycle time) measurements, we implemented a Verilog version of the accelerator, which we first synthesized using the Synopsys Design Compiler using the TSMC 65nm GP standard VT library, and which we then placed and routed using the Synopsys ICC compiler. We then simulated the design using Synopsys VCS, and we estimated the power using PrimeTime PX.

*SIMD.* For the SIMD baseline, we use the GEM5+McPAT [28] combination. We use a 4-issue superscalar x86 core with a 128-bit (8×16-bit) SIMD unit (SSE/SSE2), clocked at 2GHz. The core has a 192-entry ROB, and a 64-entry load/store queue. The L1 data (and instruction) cache is 32KB and the L2 cache is 2MB; both caches are 8-way associative and use a 64-byte line; these cache characteristics correspond to those of the Intel Core i7. The L1 miss latency to the L2 is 10 cycles, and the L2 miss latency to memory is 250 cycles; the memory bus width is 256 bits. We have aligned the energy cost of main memory accesses of our accelerator and the simulator by using those provided by McPAT (e.g., 17.6nJ for a 256-bit read memory access).

We implemented a SIMD version of the different layer codes, which we manually tuned for locality as explained in Section 3 (for each layer, we perform a stochastic exploration to find good tile factors); we compiled these programs using the default -O optimization level but the inner loops were written in assembly to make the best possible use of the SIMD unit. In order to assess the performance of the SIMD core, we also implemented a standard C++ version of the different benchmark layers presented below, and on average (geometric mean), we observed that the SIMD core provides a 3.92x improvement in execution time and 3.74x in energy over the x86 core.

| Layer | $N_x$ | $N_y$ | $K_x$ | $K_y$ | $N_i$ | $N_o$ | Description |
|---|---|---|---|---|---|---|---|
| CONV1 | 500 | 375 | 9 | 9 | 32 | 48 | Street scene parsing (CNN) [13], (e.g., identifying "building", "vehicle", etc) |
| POOL1 | 492 | 367 | 2 | 2 | 12 | - | |
| CLASS1 | - | - | - | - | 960 | 20 | |
| CONV2* | 200 | 200 | 18 | 18 | 8 | 8 | Detection of faces in YouTube videos (DNN) [26], largest NN to date (Google) |
| CONV3 | 32 | 32 | 4 | 4 | 108 | 200 | Traffic sign identification for car navigation (CNN) [36] |
| POOL3 | 32 | 32 | 4 | 4 | 100 | - | |
| CLASS3 | - | - | - | - | 200 | 100 | |
| CONV4 | 32 | 32 | 7 | 7 | 16 | 512 | Google Street View house numbers (CNN) [35] |
| CONV5* | 256 | 256 | 11 | 11 | 256 | 384 | Multi-Object recognition in natural images (DNN) [16], winner 2012 ImageNet competition |
| POOL5 | 256 | 256 | 2 | 2 | 256 | - | |

**Table 5.** *Benchmark layers (CONV=convolutional, POOL=pooling, CLASS=classifier; CONVx* indicates private kernels).*

**Benchmarks.** For benchmarks, we have selected the largest convolutional, pooling and/or classifier layers of several recent and large neural network structures. The characteristics of these 10 layers plus a description of the associated neural network and task are shown in Table 5.

## 7. Experimental Results

### 7.1 Accelerator Characteristics after Layout

The current version uses $T_n = 16$ (16 hardware neurons with 16 synapses each), so that the design contains 256 16-bit truncated multipliers in NFU-1 (for classifier and convolutional layers), 16 adder trees of 15 adders each in NFU-2 (for the same layers, plus pooling layer if average is used), as well as a 16-input shifter and max in NFU-2 (for pooling layers), and 16 16-bit truncated multipliers plus 16 adders in NFU-3 (for classifier and convolutional layers, and optionally for pooling layers). For classifier and convolutional layers, NFU-1 and NFU-2 are active every cycle, achieving $256 + 16 \times 15 = 496$ fixed-point operations every cycle; at 0.98GHz, this amounts to 452 GOP/s (Giga fixed-point OPerations per second). At the end of a layer, NFU-3 would be active as well while NFU-1 and NFU-2 process the remaining data, reaching a peak activity of $496 + 2 \times 16 = 528$ operations per cycle (482 GOP/s) for a short period.

We have done the synthesis and layout of the accelerator with $T_n = 16$ and 64-entry buffers at 65nm using Synopsys tools, see Figure 15. The main characteristics and power/area breakdown by component type and functional block are shown in Table 6. We brought the critical path delay down to 1.02ns by introducing 3 pipeline stages in NFU-1 (multipliers), 2 stages in NFU-2 (adder trees), and 3 stages in NFU-3 (piecewise linear function approximation) for a total of 8 pipeline stages. Currently, the critical path is in the issue

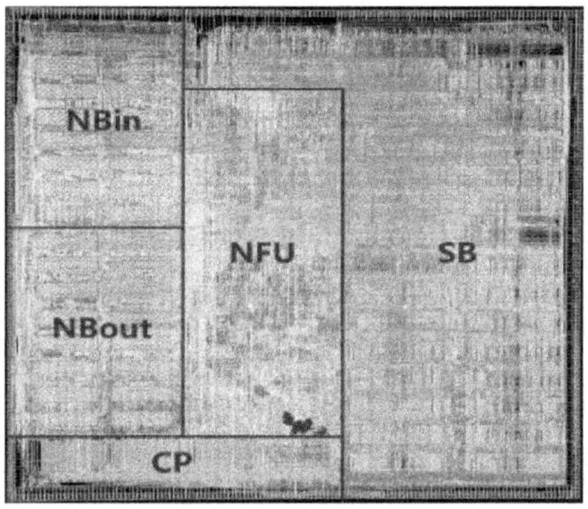


**Figure 15.** *Layout (65nm).*

| Component or Block | Area in $\mu m^2$ | (%) | Power in $mW$ | (%) | Critical path in $ns$ |
|---|---|---|---|---|---|
| ACCELERATOR | 3,023,077 | | 485 | | 1.02 |
| Combinational | 608,842 | (20.14%) | 89 | (18.41%) | |
| Memory | 1,158,000 | (38.31%) | 177 | (36.59%) | |
| Registers | 375,882 | (12.43%) | 86 | (17.84%) | |
| Clock network | 68,721 | (2.27%) | 132 | (27.16%) | |
| Filler cell | 811,632 | (26.85%) | | | |
| SB | 1,153,814 | (38.17%) | 105 | (22.65%) | |
| NBin | 427,992 | (14.16%) | 91 | (19.76%) | |
| NBout | 433,906 | (14.35%) | 92 | (19.97%) | |
| NFU | 846,563 | (28.00%) | 132 | (27.22%) | |
| CP | 141,809 | (5.69%) | 31 | (6.39%) | |
| AXIMUX | 9,767 | (0.32%) | 8 | (2.65%) | |
| Other | 9,226 | (0.31%) | 26 | (5.36%) | |

**Table 6.** *Characteristics of accelerator and breakdown by component type (first 5 lines), and functional block (last 7 lines).*

logic which is in charge of reading data out of NBin/NBout; next versions will focus on how to reduce or pipeline this critical path. The total RAM capacity (NBin + NBout + SB + CP instructions) is 44KB (8KB for the CP RAM). The area and power are dominated by the buffers (NBin/NBout/SB) at respectively 56% and 60%, with the NFU being a close second at 28% and 27%. The percentage of the total cell power is 59.47%, but the routing network (included in the different components of the table breakdown) accounts for a significant share of the total power at 38.77%. At 65nm, due to the high toggle rate of the accelerator, the leakage power is almost negligible at 1.73%.

Finally, we have also evaluated a design with $T_n = 8$, and thus 64 multipliers in NFU-1. The total area for that design is 0.85 $mm^2$, i.e., 3.59x smaller than for $T_n = 16$ due to the reduced buffer width and the fewer number of arithmetic operators. We plan to investigate larger designs with $T_n = 32$ or 64 in the near future.

### 7.2 Time and Throughput

In Figure 16, we report the speedup of the accelerator over SIMD, see *SIMD/Acc*. Recall that we use a 128-bit SIMD processor, so capable of performing up to 8 16-bit operations

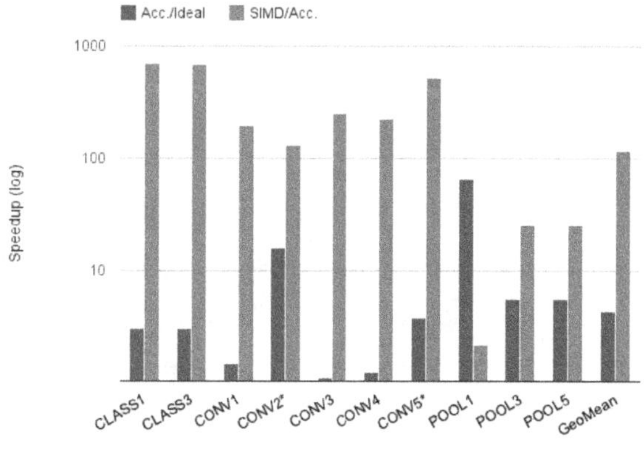


**Figure 16.** *Speedup of accelerator over SIMD, and of ideal accelerator over accelerator.*

every cycle (we naturally use 16-bit fixed-point operations in the SIMD as well). As mentioned in Section 7.1, the accelerator performs 496 16-bit operations every cycle for both classifier and convolutional layers, i.e., 62x more ($\frac{496}{8}$) than the SIMD core. We empirically observe that on these two types of layers, the accelerator is on average 117.87x faster than the SIMD core, so about 2x above the ratio of computational operators (62x). We measured that, for classifier and convolutional layers, the SIMD core performs 2.01 16-bit operations per cycle on average, instead of the upper bound of 8 operations per cycle. We traced this back to two major reasons.

First, better latency tolerance due to an appropriate combination of preloading and reuse in NBin and SB buffers; note that we did not implement a prefetcher in the SIMD core, which would partly bridge that gap. This explains the high performance gap for layers CLASS1, CLASS3 and CONV5 which have the largest feature maps sizes, thus the most spatial locality, and which then benefit most from preloading, giving them a performance boost, i.e., 629.92x on average, about 3x more than other convolutional layers; we expect that a prefetcher in the SIMD core would cancel that performance boost. The spatial locality in NBin is exploited along the input feature map dimension by the DMA, and with a small $N_i$, the DMA has to issue many short memory requests, which is less efficient. The rest of the convolutional layers (CONV1 to CONV4) have an average speedup of 195.15x; CONV2 has a lesser performance (130.64x) due to private kernels and less spatial locality. Pooling layers have less performance overall because only the adder tree in NFU-2 is used (240 operators out of 496 operators), 25.73x for POOL3 and 25.52x for POOL5.

In order to further analyze the relatively poor behavior of POOL1 (only 2.17x over SIMD), we have tested a configuration of the accelerator where all operands (inputs and synapses) are ready for the NFU, i.e., ideal behavior

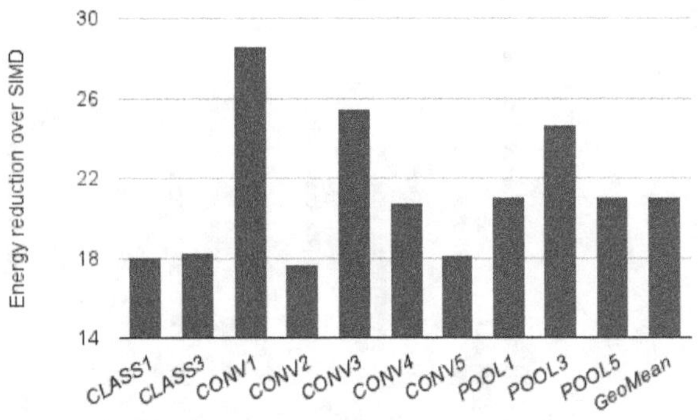


**Figure 17.** *Energy reduction of accelerator over SIMD.*

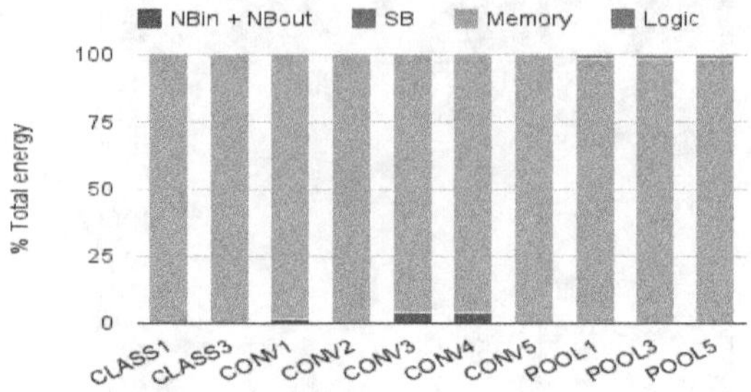


**Figure 18.** *Breakdown of accelerator energy.*

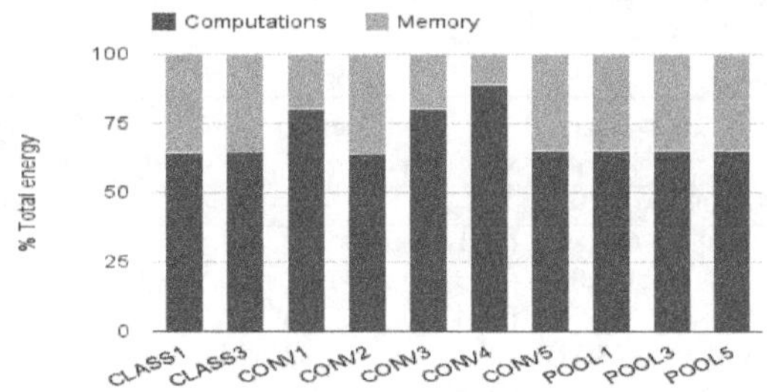


**Figure 19.** *Breakdown of SIMD energy.*

of NBin, SB and NBout; we call this version "Ideal", see Figure 16. We see that the accelerator is significantly slower on POOL1 and CONV2 than the ideal configuration (respectively 66.00x and 16.14x). This is due to the small size of their input/output feature maps (e.g., $N_i = 12$ for for POOL1), combined with the fewer operators used for POOL1. So far, the accelerator has been geared towards large layers, but we can address this weakness by implementing a 2D or 3D DMA (DMA requests over $i, k_x, k_y$ loops); we leave this optimization for future work.

The second reason for the speedup over SIMD beyond 62x lays in control and scheduling overhead. In the accelerator, we have tried to minimize lost cycles. For instance, when output neurons partial sums are rotated to NBout (before being sent back to NFU-2), the oldest buffer row ($T_n$ partial sums) is eagerly rotated out to the NBout/NFU-2 input latch, and a multiplexer in NFU-2 ensures that either this latch or the NFU-2 registers are used as input for the NFU-2 stage computations; this allows a rotation without any pipeline stall. Several such design optimizations help achieve a slowdown of only 4.36x over the ideal accelerator, see Figure 16, and in fact, 2.64x only if we exclude CONV2 and POOL1.

### 7.3 Energy

In Figure 17, we provide the energy ratio between the SIMD core and the accelerator. While high at 21.08x, the average energy ratio is actually more than an order of magnitude smaller than previously reported energy ratios between processors and accelerators; for instance Hameed et al. [14] report an energy ratio of about 500x, and 974x has been reported for a small Multi-Layer Perceptron [38]. The smaller ratio is largely due to the energy spent in memory accesses, which was voluntarily not factored in the two aforementioned studies. Like in these two accelerators and others, the energy cost of computations has been considerably reduced by a combination of more efficient computational operators (especially a massive number of small 16-bit fixed-point truncated multipliers in our case), and small custom storage located close to the operators (64-entry NBin, NBout, SB and the NFU-2 registers). As a result, there is now an Amdahl's law effect for energy, where any further improvement can only be achieved by bringing down the energy cost of main memory accesses. We tried to artificially set the energy cost of the main memory accesses in both the SIMD and accelerator to 0, and we observed that the average energy reduction of the accelerator increases by more than one order of magnitude, in line with previous results.

This is further illustrated by the breakdown of the energy consumed by the accelerator in Figure 18 where the energy of main memory accesses obviously dominates. A distant second is the energy of NBin/NBout for the convolutional layers with shared kernels (CONV1, CONV3, CONV4). In this case, a set of shared kernels are kept in SB so the memory traffic due to synapses becomes very low, as explained in Section 3 (shared kernels + tiling), but the input neurons must still be reloaded for each new set of shared kernels, hence the still noticeable energy expense. The energy of the computational logic in pooling layers (POOL1, POOL3, POOL5) is similarly a distant second expense, this time because there is no synapse to load. The slightly higher energy reduction of pooling layers (22.17x on average), see Figure 17, is due to the fact the SB buffer is not used (no synapse), and the accesses to NBin alone are relatively cheap due to its small width, see Figure 13.

The SIMD energy breakdown is in sharp contrast, as shown in Figure 19, with about two thirds of the energy spent in computations, and only one third in memory accesses.

While finding a computationally more efficient approach to SIMD made sense, future work for the accelerator should focus on reducing the energy spent in memory accesses.

## 8. Related Work

Due to stringent energy constraints, such as Dark Silicon [10, 32], there is a growing consensus that future high-performance micro-architectures will take the form of heterogeneous multi-cores, i.e., combinations of cores and accelerators. Accelerators can range from processors tuned for certain tasks, to ASIC-like circuits such as H264 [14], or more flexible accelerators capable of targeting a broad range of, but not all, tasks [12, 44] such as QsCores [42], or accelerators for image processing [33].

The accelerator proposed in this article follows this spirit of targeting a specific, but broad, domain, i.e., machine-learning tasks here. Due to recent progress in machine-learning, certain types of neural networks, especially Deep Neural Networks [25] and Convolutional Neural Networks [27] have become state-of-the-art machine-learning techniques [26] across a broad range of applications such as web search [19], image analysis [31] or speech recognition [7].

While many implementations of hardware neurons and neural networks have been investigated in the past two decades [18], the main purpose of hardware neural networks has been fast modeling of biological neural networks [20, 34] for implementing neurons with thousands of connections. While several of these neuromorphic architectures have been applied to computational tasks [30, 43], the specific bio-inspired information representation (spiking neural networks) they rely on may not be competitive with state-of-the-art neural networks, though this remains an open debate at the threshold between neuroscience and machine-learning.

However, recently, due to simultaneous trends in applications, machine-learning and technology constraints, hardware neural networks have been increasingly considered as potential accelerators, either for very dedicated functionalities within a processor, such as branch prediction [1], or for their fault-tolerance properties [15, 38]. The latter property has also been leveraged to trade application accuracy for energy efficiency through hardware neural processing units [9, 11].

The focus of our accelerator is on large-scale machine-learning tasks, with layers of thousands of neurons and millions of synapses, and for that reason, there is a special emphasis on interactions with memory. Our study not only confirms previous observations that dedicated storage is key for achieving good performance and power [14], but it also highlights that, beyond exploiting locality at the level of registers located close to computational operators [33, 38], considering memory as a prime-order concern can profoundly affect accelerator design.

Many of the aforementioned studies stem from the architecture community. A symmetric effort has started in the machine-learning community where a few researchers have been investigating hardware designs for speeding up neural network processing, especially for real-time applications. Neuflow [13] is an accelerator for fast and low-power implementation of the feed-forward paths of CNNs for vision systems. It organizes computations and register-level storage according to the sliding window property of convolutional and pooling layers; but in that respect, it also ignores much of the first-order locality coming from input and output feature maps. Its interplay with memory remains limited to a DMA, there is no significant on-chip storage, though the DMA is capable of performing complex access patterns. A more complex architecture, albeit with similar performance as Neuflow, has been proposed by Kim et al. [21] and consists of 128 SIMD processors of 16 PEs each; the architecture is significantly larger and implements a specific neural vision model (neither CNNs nor DNNs), but it can achieve 60 frame/sec (real-time) multi-object recognition for up to 10 different objects. Maashri et al. [29] have also investigated the implementation of another neural network model, the bio-inspired HMAX for vision processing, using a set of custom accelerators arranged around a switch fabric; in the article, the authors allude to locality optimizations across different orientations, which are roughly the HMAX equivalent of feature maps. Closer to our community again, but solely focusing on CNNs, Chakradhar et al. [3] have also investigated the implementation of CNNs on reconfigurable circuits; though there is little emphasis on locality exploitation, they pay special attention to properly mapping a CNN in order to improve bandwidth utilization.

## 9. Conclusions

In this article we focus on accelerators for machine-learning because of the broad set of applications and the few key state-of-the-art algorithms offer the rare opportunity to combine high efficiency and broad application scope. Since state-of-the-art CNNs and DNNs mean very large networks, we specifically focus on the implementation of large-scale layers. By carefully exploiting the locality properties of such layers, and by introducing storage structures custom designed to take advantage of these properties, we show that it is possible to design a machine-learning accelerator capable of high performance in a very small area footprint. Our measurements are not circumscribed to the accelerator fabric, they factor in the performance and energy overhead of main memory transfers; still, we show that it is possible to achieve a speedup of 117.87x and an energy reduction of 21.08x over a 128-bit 2GHz SIMD core with a normal cache hierarchy. We have obtained a layout of the design at 65nm.

Besides a planned tape-out, future work includes improving the accelerator behavior for short layers, slightly altering the NFU to include some of the latest algorithmic improvements such as Local Response Normalization, further reducing the impact of main memory transfers, investigating scalability (especially increasing $T_n$), and implementing training in hardware.

## Acknowledgments

This work is supported by a Google Faculty Research Award, the Intel Collaborative Research Institute for Computational Intelligence (ICRI-CI), the French ANR MHANN and NEMESIS grants, the NSF of China (under Grants 61003064, 61100163, 61133004, 61222204, 61221062, 61303158), the 863 Program of China (under Grant 2012AA012202), the Strategic Priority Research Program of the CAS (under Grant XDA06010403), the 10,000 and 1,000 talent programs.

## References

[1] R. S. Amant, D. A. Jimenez, and D. Burger. Low-power, high-performance analog neural branch prediction. In *International Symposium on Microarchitecture*, Como, 2008.

[2] C. Bienia, S. Kumar, J. P. Singh, and K. Li. The PARSEC benchmark suite: Characterization and architectural implications. In *International Conference on Parallel Architectures and Compilation Techniques*, New York, New York, USA, 2008. ACM Press.

[3] S. Chakradhar, M. Sankaradas, V. Jakkula, and S. Cadambi. A dynamically configurable coprocessor for convolutional neural networks. In *International symposium on Computer Architecture*, page 247, Saint Malo, France, June 2010. ACM Press.

[4] T. Chen, Y. Chen, M. Duranton, Q. Guo, A. Hashmi, M. Lipasti, A. Nere, S. Qiu, M. Sebag, and O. Temam. BenchNN: On the Broad Potential Application Scope of Hardware Neural Network Accelerators. In *International Symposium on Workload Characterization*, 2012.

[5] A. Coates, B. Huval, T. Wang, D. J. Wu, and A. Y. Ng. Deep learning with cots hpc systems. In *International Conference on Machine Learning*, 2013.

[6] C. Cortes and V. Vapnik. Support-Vector Networks. In *Machine Learning*, pages 273–297, 1995.

[7] G. Dahl, T. Sainath, and G. Hinton. Improving Deep Neural Networks for LVCSR using Rectified Linear Units and Dropout. In *International Conference on Acoustics, Speech and Signal Processing*, 2013.

[8] S. Draghici. On the capabilities of neural networks using limited precision weights. *Neural Netw.*, 15(3):395–414, 2002.

[9] Z. Du, A. Lingamneni, Y. Chen, K. V. Palem, O. Temam, and C. Wu. Leveraging the Error Resilience of Machine-Learning Applications for Designing Highly Energy Efficient Accelerators. In *Asia and South Pacific Design Automation Conference*, 2014.

[10] H. Esmaeilzadeh, E. Blem, R. S. Amant, K. Sankaralingam, and D. Burger. Dark Silicon and the End of Multicore Scaling. In *Proceedings of the 38th International Symposium on Computer Architecture (ISCA)*, June 2011.

[11] H. Esmaeilzadeh, A. Sampson, L. Ceze, and D. Burger. Neural Acceleration for General-Purpose Approximate Programs. In *International Symposium on Microarchitecture*, number 3, pages 1–6, 2012.

[12] K. Fan, M. Kudlur, G. S. Dasika, and S. A. Mahlke. Bridging the computation gap between programmable processors and hardwired accelerators. In *HPCA*, pages 313–322. IEEE Computer Society, 2009.

[13] C. Farabet, B. Martini, B. Corda, P. Akselrod, E. Culurciello, and Y. LeCun. NeuFlow: A runtime reconfigurable dataflow processor for vision. In *CVPR Workshop*, pages 109–116. Ieee, June 2011.

[14] R. Hameed, W. Qadeer, M. Wachs, O. Azizi, A. Solomatnikov, B. C. Lee, S. Richardson, C. Kozyrakis, and M. Horowitz. Understanding sources of inefficiency in general-purpose chips. In *International Symposium on Computer Architecture*, page 37, New York, New York, USA, 2010. ACM Press.

[15] A. Hashmi, A. Nere, J. J. Thomas, and M. Lipasti. A case for neuromorphic ISAs. In *International Conference on Architectural Support for Programming Languages and Operating Systems*, New York, NY, 2011. ACM.

[16] G. Hinton and N. Srivastava. Improving neural networks by preventing co-adaptation of feature detectors. *arXiv preprint arXiv: ...*, pages 1–18, 2012.

[17] J. L. Holi and J.-N. Hwang. Finite Precision Error Analysis of Neural Network Hardware Implementations. *IEEE Transactions on Computers*, 42(3):281–290, 1993.

[18] M. Holler, S. Tam, H. Castro, and R. Benson. An electrically trainable artificial neural network (ETANN) with 10240 floating gate synapses. In *Artificial neural networks*, pages 50–55, Piscataway, NJ, USA, 1990. IEEE Press.

[19] P. Huang, X. He, J. Gao, and L. Deng. Learning deep structured semantic models for web search using clickthrough data. In *International Conference on Information and Knowledge Management*, 2013.

[20] M. M. Khan, D. R. Lester, L. A. Plana, A. Rast, X. Jin, E. Painkras, and S. B. Furber. SpiNNaker: Mapping neural networks onto a massively-parallel chip multiprocessor. In *IEEE International Joint Conference on Neural Networks (IJCNN)*, pages 2849–2856. Ieee, 2008.

[21] J.-y. Kim, S. Member, M. Kim, S. Lee, J. Oh, K. Kim, and H.-j. Yoo. A 201.4 GOPS 496 mW Real-Time Multi-Object Recognition Processor With Bio-Inspired Neural Perception Engine. *IEEE Journal of Solid-State Circuits*, 45(1):32–45, Jan. 2010.

[22] E. J. King and E. E. Swartzlander Jr. Data-dependent truncation scheme for parallel multipliers. In *Signals, Systems & Computers, 1997. Conference Record of the Thirty-First Asilomar Conference on*, volume 2, pages 1178–1182. IEEE, 1997.

[23] D. Larkin, A. Kinane, V. Muresan, and N. E. O'Connor. An Efficient Hardware Architecture for a Neural Network Activation Function Generator. In J. Wang, Z. Yi, J. M. Zurada, B.-L. Lu, and H. Yin, editors, *ISNN (2)*, volume 3973 of *Lecture Notes in Computer Science*, pages 1319–1327. Springer, 2006.

[24] D. Larkin, A. Kinane, and N. E. O'Connor. Towards Hardware Acceleration of Neuroevolution for Multimedia Processing Applications on Mobile Devices. In *ICONIP (3)*, pages 1178–1188, 2006.

[25] H. Larochelle, D. Erhan, A. Courville, J. Bergstra, and Y. Bengio. An empirical evaluation of deep architectures on problems with many factors of variation. In *International Conference on Machine Learning*, pages 473–480, New York, New York, USA, 2007. ACM Press.

[26] Q. V. Le, M. A. Ranzato, R. Monga, M. Devin, K. Chen, G. S. Corrado, J. Dean, and A. Y. Ng. Building High-level Features Using Large Scale Unsupervised Learning. In *International Conference on Machine Learning*, June 2012.

[27] Y. Lecun, L. Bottou, Y. Bengio, and P. Haffner. Gradient-based learning applied to document recognition. *Proceedings of the IEEE*, 86, 1998.

[28] S. Li, J. H. Ahn, R. D. Strong, J. B. Brockman, D. M. Tullsen, and N. P. Jouppi. McPAT: an integrated power, area, and timing modeling framework for multicore and manycore architectures. In *Proceedings of the 42nd Annual IEEE/ACM International Symposium on Microarchitecture*, MICRO 42, pages 469–480, New York, NY, USA, 2009. ACM.

[29] A. A. Maashri, M. Debole, M. Cotter, N. Chandramoorthy, Y. Xiao, V. Narayanan, and C. Chakrabarti. Accelerating neuromorphic vision algorithms for recognition. *Proceedings of the 49th Annual Design Automation Conference on - DAC '12*, page 579, 2012.

[30] P. Merolla, J. Arthur, F. Akopyan, N. Imam, R. Manohar, and D. Modha. A digital neurosynaptic core using embedded crossbar memory with 45pJ per spike in 45nm. In *IEEE Custom Integrated Circuits Conference*, pages 1–4. IEEE, Sept. 2011.

[31] V. Mnih and G. Hinton. Learning to Label Aerial Images from Noisy Data. In *Proceedings of the 29th International Conference on Machine Learning (ICML-12)*, pages 567–574, 2012.

[32] M. Muller. Dark Silicon and the Internet. In *EE Times "Designing with ARM" virtual conference*, 2010.

[33] W. Qadeer, R. Hameed, O. Shacham, P. Venkatesan, C. Kozyrakis, and M. A. Horowitz. Convolution engine: balancing efficiency & flexibility in specialized computing. In *International Symposium on Computer Architecture*, 2013.

[34] J. Schemmel, J. Fieres, and K. Meier. Wafer-scale integration of analog neural networks. In *International Joint Conference on Neural Networks*, pages 431–438. Ieee, June 2008.

[35] P. Sermanet, S. Chintala, and Y. LeCun. Convolutional Neural Networks Applied to House Numbers Digit Classification. In *Pattern Recognition (ICPR), . . .*, 2012.

[36] P. Sermanet and Y. LeCun. Traffic sign recognition with multi-scale Convolutional Networks. In *International Joint Conference on Neural Networks*, pages 2809–2813. Ieee, July 2011.

[37] T. Serre, L. Wolf, S. Bileschi, M. Riesenhuber, and T. Poggio. Robust object recognition with cortex-like mechanisms. *IEEE transactions on pattern analysis and machine intelligence*, 29(3):411–26, Mar. 2007.

[38] O. Temam. A Defect-Tolerant Accelerator for Emerging High-Performance Applications. In *International Symposium on Computer Architecture*, Portland, Oregon, 2012.

[39] O. Temam and N. Drach. Software assistance for data caches. *Future Generation Computer Systems*, 11(6):519–536, 1995.

[40] S. Thoziyoor, N. Muralimanohar, and J. Ahn. CACTI 5.1. *HP Labs, Palo Alto, Tech*, 2008.

[41] V. Vanhoucke, A. Senior, and M. Z. Mao. Improving the speed of neural networks on CPUs. In *Deep Learning and Unsupervised Feature Learning Workshop, NIPS 2011*, 2011.

[42] G. Venkatesh, J. Sampson, N. Goulding-hotta, S. K. Venkata, M. B. Taylor, and S. Swanson. QsCORES : Trading Dark Silicon for Scalable Energy Efficiency with Quasi-Specific Cores Categories and Subject Descriptors. In *International Symposium on Microarchitecture*, 2011.

[43] R. J. Vogelstein, U. Mallik, J. T. Vogelstein, and G. Cauwenberghs. Dynamically reconfigurable silicon array of spiking neurons with conductance-based synapses. *IEEE Transactions on Neural Networks*, 18(1):253–265, 2007.

[44] S. Yehia, S. Girbal, H. Berry, and O. Temam. Reconciling specialization and flexibility through compound circuits. In *International Symposium on High Performance Computer Architecture*, pages 277–288, Raleigh, North Carolina, Feb. 2009. Ieee.

# K2: A Mobile Operating System for Heterogeneous Coherence Domains

Felix Xiaozhu Lin, Zhen Wang, and Lin Zhong
Rice University, Houston, TX
{xzl, zhen.wang, lzhong}@rice.edu

## Abstract

Mobile System-on-Chips (SoC) that incorporate heterogeneous coherence domains promise high energy efficiency to a wide range of mobile applications, yet are difficult to program. To exploit the architecture, a desirable, yet missing capability is to replicate operating system (OS) services over multiple coherence domains with minimum inter-domain communication. In designing such an OS, we set three goals: to ease application development, to simplify OS engineering, and to preserve the current OS performance. To this end, we identify a shared-most OS model for multiple coherence domains: creating per-domain instances of core OS services with no shared state, while enabling other extended OS services to share state across domains. To test the model, we build K2, a prototype OS on the TI OMAP4 SoC, by reusing most of the Linux 3.4 source. K2 presents a single system image to applications with its two kernels running on top of the two coherence domains of OMAP4. The two kernels have independent instances of core OS services, such as page allocator and interrupt management, as coordinated by K2; the two kernels share most extended OS services, such as device drivers, whose state is kept coherent transparently by K2. Despite platform constraints and unoptimized code, K2 improves energy efficiency for light OS workloads by 8x-10x, while incurring less than 6% performance overhead for a device driver shared between kernels. Our experiences with K2 show that the shared-most model is promising.

***Categories and Subject Descriptors*** D.4.7 [*Operating Systems*]: Organization and Design

***General Terms*** Design, Experimentation, Performance


*ASPLOS '14*, March 1–4, 2014, Salt Lake City, Utah, USA.

ACM 978-1-4503-2305-5/14/03...$15.00.
http://dx.doi.org/10.1145/2541940.2541975

***Keywords*** Energy efficiency; heterogeneous architecture; mobile; coherence domains

## 1. Introduction

Today's mobile devices face a wide range of workloads, from demanding tasks such as interactive applications with rich graphics to light tasks running in the background such as cloud synchronization and context awareness. A recognized, effective approach to achieve high energy efficiency for such diverse workloads is to exploit hardware heterogeneity, i.e., to execute a workload with the hardware component offering the best performance-power tradeoff.

Today, cutting-edge mobile SoCs have already embraced hardware heterogeneity. For instance, the ARM big.LITTLE architecture has cores of different strengths in one cache coherence domain, or *coherence domain*. Cores in the same coherence domain have the same memory view backed by hardware-supported cache coherence. The coherence allows a process to move between big and little cores at the cost close to context switch. Because hardware coherence forbids the little core from being much weaker than the big ones, many mobile SoCs have gone one step further to include multiple coherence domains, where hardware coherence only exists within each domain but not among them. One coherence domain can host high-performance cores for demanding tasks; another domain can host low-power cores for light tasks. In this work, we call them *strong domain* and *weak domain*, respectively. We purposefully use *strong* and *weak* in order to distinguish them from heterogeneous cores in the same domain that are already known as *big* and *little*. The absence of hardware coherence allows cores in the weak domain to be orders of magnitude weaker and lower-power than those in the strong domains, providing much better energy efficiency for light tasks than the big.LITTLE architecture.

In tapping into the energy efficiency benefit of multiple coherence domains, the biggest challenge is *programmability*. Processors from multiple coherence domains essentially constitute a distributed system; programming them is known to be difficult to mass programmers, who must maintain consistency of partitioned program components with messages.

Many have recognized this challenge and proposed a handful of systems solutions [17, 26], which, however, mainly focus on user workloads. They usually implement a small set of OS services from scratch for a weak domain, e.g., sensor reading, and assume that all other OS services are provided by a fixed strong domain. The resulting OS services are limited in functionality, complicate application development because of a fragmented system image, and incur heavy burdens in OS engineering. More importantly, with this design, only light tasks without a need for OS services beyond those crafted for weak domains can benefit from the efficiency of weak domains.

In this paper, we seek to answer the following question: *is it possible to span an OS across multiple coherence domains?* In doing so, we seek to achieve three important goals. (*i*) The resulting OS should preserve the established programming models for mobile applications, as the models have been used in over a million mobile application by a similar number of developers, many of whom do not have sophisticated programming skills. (*ii*) The resulting OS itself shall leverage mature OSes in wide use without reinventing many wheels. An overhaul of existing mobile OSes is increasingly difficult and even undesirable nowadays: they consist of huge codebases and keep receiving contributions from many parties including device vendors. (*iii*) The OS should deliver the same peak performance for demanding tasks.

We show that we can span an OS across coherence domains by properly refactoring, but not overhauling, an existing OS. We identify a *shared-most* OS model where most OS services are replicated in all domains under question with transparent state coherence, while a small, selective set of services operates independently in each domain. We call these services *shadowed services* and *independent services*, respectively. The shared-most model resides midway of two well-studied extremes, *shared-nothing* and *shared-everything*. While the shared-most model promises both benefits of simplified OS engineering and performance for multi-domain mobile SoCs, the other two models, however, provide only one of the two benefits.

By applying the shared-most model, we build K2, an OS that runs multiple kernels on a multi-domain SoC. As an early research prototype, K2 has unoptimized code and is constrained by the limitations of the test platform. Yet, K2 has met the three goals above, showing that the shared-most model is promising. (*i*) K2 presents a coherent, single Linux image to applications, and therefore preserves the widely used programming model; it also provides a familiar abstraction, called NightWatch threads, for distributing user workloads over heterogeneous domains. (*ii*) K2 replicates existing extended OS services, e.g., device drivers, across multiple domains and transparently maintains coherence for them. As a result, K2 is able to reuse most of the kernel source. (*iii*) K2 preserves the current level of OS performance by alleviating inter-domain contention: it creates independent instances of core OS services and properly coordinates them; it avoids multi-domain parallelism within individual processes through scheduling. Throughout its design, K2 adopts asymmetric principles that greatly favor the performance of the strong domain.

In summary, we have made three contributions in this work:

- First, we identify a shared-most OS model for exploiting the energy efficiency potential of multi-domain mobile SoCs, without complicating programming or hurting performance.
- Second, in applying the shared-most OS model, we present a set of guidelines and experiences of refactoring a mature OS, Linux. We classify its OS services as private, independent, and shadowed, in order to replicate them across coherence domains.
- Third, we describe K2, the outcome of refactoring and a working OS prototype for multi-domain mobile SoCs. With the shared-most model applied, K2 reuses most of the Linux kernel source and presents a single system image. The resulting energy efficiency and performance show that our model is promising.

## 2. Background

To provide a background, we first discuss the characteristics of light tasks in mobile systems, and then review the mobile architectural trend that is moving towards heterogeneity and incoherence.

### 2.1 Light tasks in mobile systems

Serving as the personal information hub, today's mobile devices execute a rich set of 'background' tasks, or *light tasks*, e.g., sensing user physical activities, monitoring surrounding environment [27], and keeping users connected with social networks and the cloud [41]. Light tasks usually have the following characteristics:

- *Not performance demanding:* Without an awaiting user, light tasks do not directly affect the user experience and thus do not require high processor MIPS.
- *Mostly IO-bound:* Light tasks perform extensive IO operations for exchanging information with the external world. During IO operations, core idle periods are many, however not long enough for a core to become inactive.
- *Requiring both user and OS execution:* Light tasks not only run user code for application logic, but also invoke diverse OS services such as device drivers [18] and page allocator.
- *Scheduled to execute throughout daily usage:* Light tasks are executed not only when a user is interacting with the device, but also during user's think periods between interactions and when a user pays no attention. Since

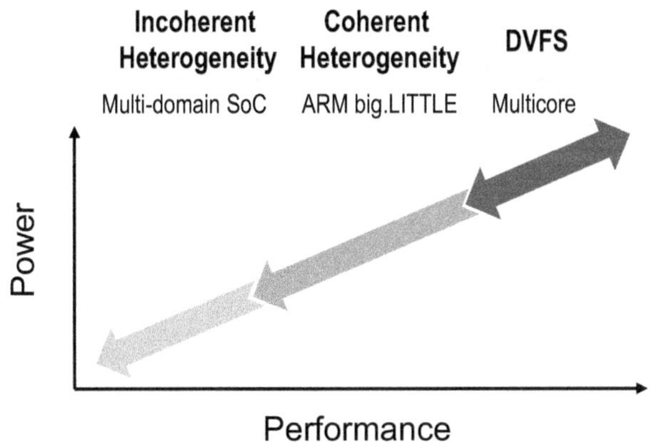


**Figure 1.** Trend in mobile SoC architectures. Both axes are logarithmic.

user interaction periods are sparse and usually short, most executions of light tasks happen when the entire system is lightly loaded.

- *High impact on battery life:* The nature of frequent executions has a high impact on battery life. For instance, a recent study [41] shows that each run of background email downloading reduces device standby time by 10 minutes.

### 2.2 Trend in architectures

To meet the compute demand of modern applications, mobile devices are equipped with powerful cores that have gigahertz frequency and rich architectural features. These powerful cores, however, offer poor energy efficiency for light tasks, due to three sources of inefficiency:

- *High penalty in entering/exiting active power state.* Since strong cores are inactive for most of the time, periodic executions of light tasks will inevitably wake them up from time to time.
- *High idle power.* In executing IO-bound light tasks, powerful cores will spend a large number of short periods (of milliseconds) in idle, which are known to consume a large portion of energy in mobile systems [42].
- *Over-provisioned performance.* Although a strong core may increase its energy efficiency by lowering its frequency, shown as 'DVFS' in Figure 1, the lowest possible frequency and active power are limited by its architecture and fabrication process, which still over-provision performance to light tasks with a low performance demand.

***Coherent heterogeneous SoC*** To offer a remedy, today's SoCs incorporate heterogeneous cores with different tradeoffs between performance and power, by placing them in a single or multiple coherence domains.

A handful of heterogeneous SoCs host all heterogeneous cores with a single coherence domain [15, 24]. As shown as 'coherent heterogeneity' in Figure 1, although the introduced heterogeneity indeed widens dynamic power range, the global cache coherence becomes the bottleneck for more aggressive energy efficiency, for a few reasons: *i)* a unified hardware coherence mechanism restricts architectural asymmetry, *ii)* the coherent interconnect itself consumes significant power, and *iii)* cores co-located in the same coherence domain are likely to suffer from similar thermal constraints.

***Incoherent heterogeneous SoC*** For aggressive energy efficiency, several newer SoCs remove chip-level hardware coherence. They embrace multiple coherence domains, each of which can host multiple cores; hardware coherence exists within a domain but not across domains. Examples include OMAP4 [36], OMAP5 [37], and Samsung Exynos [29]. As shown in Figure 1, the absence of hardware coherence enables high asymmetry among cores belonging to different domains. For instance, while the lowest power of different cores in the same domain can differ by 6x [32], that of different domains can differ by up to 20x. This allows using weak cores to greatly reduce the three inefficiencies mentioned above.

## 3. The case for replicating OS services

To fully exploit multi-domain SoCs for energy efficiency, the key is to enable OS to serve a request from the domain that is able to deliver the needed performance with the lowest power possible. This requires *replicating* OS services on all the candidate domains.

As shown by a recent study of mobile workloads [18], the same OS services are usually invoked with disparate performance and power expectations. For instance, light tasks often access IO regularly, thus sharing the OS services with demanding tasks such as UI rendering. Neither pinning OS services on a single domain nor partitioning them among domains [22] will work here: on one hand, light tasks invoking OS services provided on a strong domain will suffer from all inefficiencies described in §2.1; on the other, demanding tasks invoking OS services provided on a weak domain are likely to fail their performance expectations. Targeting exploiting incoherent heterogeneity for energy efficiency, most prior systems are focused on supporting user workloads and usually adopt ad-hoc solutions for OS services on weak domains [17, 26, 34]. Without systematically replicated OS services, light tasks can only implement a limited set of functionalities.

When running replicated OS services over multiple coherence domains, the OS state is essentially distributed among domains. Inter-domain state synchronization must be done in software explicitly, and is much slower than hardware coherence. This challenges application development, OS engineering, and system performance, as discussed below.

***Applications assume a single system image*** Mobile applications expect the OS to present a single system image, including a unified OS namespace and a global resource management. The single system image has served as the substrate of one million mobile applications and has been accepted by the similar number of application developers.

***OS Software assume coherent state*** All layers of a mainstream mobile OS, from top down, assume hardware coherence. Significant changes to core services, e.g., interrupt and memory management, for coping with incoherent state are difficult and undesirable: their mechanisms and policies have been heavily tuned and proved to work over years. Rewriting extended services, such as device drivers, is costly. For instance, they constitute 70% of the Linux source code [28], and are developed by various software and hardware vendors, such as Google and Samsung.

***Performance impact*** The absence of hardware coherence necessitates explicit inter-domain communication in coordinating OS replicas or keeping their state consistent – a much slower mechanism than hardware coherence. For example, flushing a L1 cache line takes tens of cycles, while sending an IPI usually takes a few thousand cycles. Such communication overheads will be magnified by inter-domain contention for the same shared state.

## 4. Design

In this section, we sketch our design. We state the design goals, describe the architectural assumptions, and then derive the shared-most OS model.

### 4.1 Design goals

We seek to design an OS that is capable of replicating its services over multiple coherence domains of a mobile SoC, in order to exploit hardware heterogeneity for energy efficiency. The OS design should meet the following goals:

1. Facilitate application development by relieving app developers from dealing with incoherent program state and fragmented system images.
2. Simplify OS engineering and avoid disruptive changes by maximizing reuse of legacy OS code.
3. Maintain the current performance level of demanding tasks.

### 4.2 Architectural assumptions

We design our system under the assumption of the following architectural features of a mobile SoC:

- **Heterogeneous cores.** The SoC has multiple types of cores that provide disparate performance-power tradeoffs. Cores may have different ISAs. Process migration is difficult and, if possible, requires sophisticated software [11, 33]. Cores have hardware MMUs.
- **Multiple coherence domains.** All cores on the SoC are isolated into a few (2-3) coherence domains, for the sake of high heterogeneity, decoupled power management and reduced thermal constraints. Within a coherence domain, multiple cores (2-8) function as a traditional multicore. There is no hardware cache coherence among domains.
- **Shared platform resources.** Coherence domains are connected to a chip-level interconnect and thus share all platform resources, including RAM and IO peripherals. Interrupts generated by IO peripherals are physically wired to all domains.
- **Aggressive power management.** Cores are taken online (active) and then offline (inactive) from time to time. The system energy efficiency is highly dependent on core power state, i.e., how long cores remain inactive and how often they are woken up.

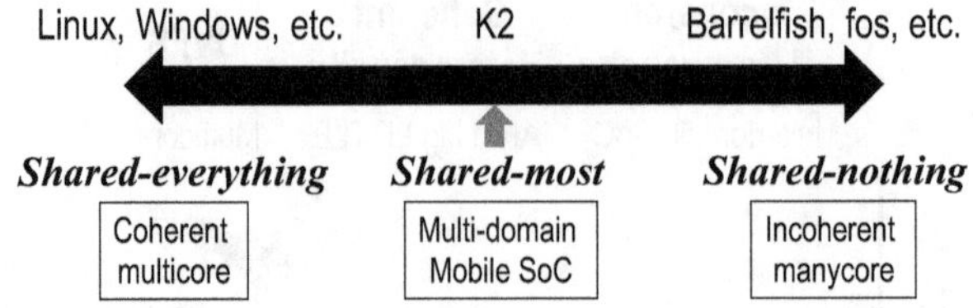


**Figure 2.** K2 in the spectrum of OS structures

### 4.3 The shared-most OS model

In order to meet the design goals stated in §4.1, we identify a shared-most OS model: *i)* to transparently maintain state coherence for extended services, or *shadowed services*, *ii)* to coordinate separated instances of core services, or *independent services*, and *iii)* to avoid multi-domain parallelism within individual process. We view our model as an outcome of considering both the underlying incoherent architecture and the programming challenges mentioned in §3. In the spectrum of OS structures shown in Figure 2, the shared-most model sits in the middle, with two extremes being 'shared-everything' monolithic OS and 'shared-nothing' OS. The two extremes, while suiting their respective target architectures well, either incur high performance overheads or heavy programming burdens for multi-domain mobile SoCs. We next discuss the three aspects of the shared-most model in detail, explaining how each of them is connected to the design goals.

***Transparent shared state for extended services*** We argue that the OS should transparently maintain state coherence for replicas of extended services, including device drivers and file systems, for the goal of simplified OS engineering. First, as mentioned in §3, as extended services constitute the majority of an OS codebase and evolve rapidly, it is difficult to manually transform them for multiple coherence domains. Second, extended OS services are less likely to suffer from inter-domain contention, and are more tolerant of the performance overheads of software coherence, such as the inter-domain communication latency.

***Independent instances of core services*** For a core service, the OS creates independent, per-domain instances that share no internal state. As mentioned in §3, core services such as memory management are invoked frequently and are performance-critical. In replicating such services over multiple domains, contention must be carefully avoided for performance.

Creating independent instances of core service raises two design problems: (*i*) How and when the OS should coordinate independent instances of the same service: the coordination is key to maintain a single system image, and has to be efficient as inter-domain communication can be expensive. (*ii*) How to minimize modifications to the mature implementations of core services, as a way to meet the goal of simplified OS engineering. The two problems have to be addressed on a per-service basis. In §6 and §7, we will describe our solutions for two important core services, physical page allocator and interrupt management.

***Avoid multi-domain parallelism within individual process*** Threads belonging to the same process share an extensive set of OS state, e.g., opened files. Running them simultaneously on multiple domains may lead to expensive contention. Since an application would gain little benefit from such parallelism, we argue that such contention should be prevented by always deferring light task execution if the same process has more demanding tasks to run. The extra delay introduced to light tasks is acceptable. First, the delay is unlikely to be long: in principle, mobile demanding tasks should not saturate strong cores for more than a few hundred milliseconds for avoiding sluggish GUI. Second, the deferral only applies to light tasks belonging to the same process.

Multi-domain parallelism, however, should be supported among processes, for fairness in scheduling and encouraging applications to use the weak domain. If strong and weak domains were restricted to run alternately, all light tasks in the system, which likely belong to different processes, will block if any normal task is running, according to our model discussed above. This essentially makes light task execution dependent on other applications' behaviors, discouraging developers from placing code on the weak domain.

## 5. The K2 OS

In order to test the shared-most model, we build K2, an OS prototype for multi-domain mobile SoC. In this section, we give an overview of K2: we describe the hardware platform, sketch the structure of K2, present our heuristics in refactoring Linux, and discuss how K2 is built from source.

### 5.1 Hardware platform

We experimentally test our OS model with TI OMAP4, one of the many emerging multi-domain mobile SoCs [23, 29] that has the best public information. OMAP4 has been powering popular mobile devices of various form factors, including Amazon Kindle Fire, Samsung Galaxy S2, and Google Glass.

| | Cortex-A9 (strong) | Cortex-M3 (weak) |
|---|---|---|
| ISA | ARM | Thumb-2 |
| Freq. | 350-1200MHz | 100-200MHz |
| Cache | L1 64KB, L2 1MB | 32KB |
| MMU | One ARM v7-A | Two connected in series |

**Table 1.** Heterogeneous cores in the two coherence domains of OMAP4

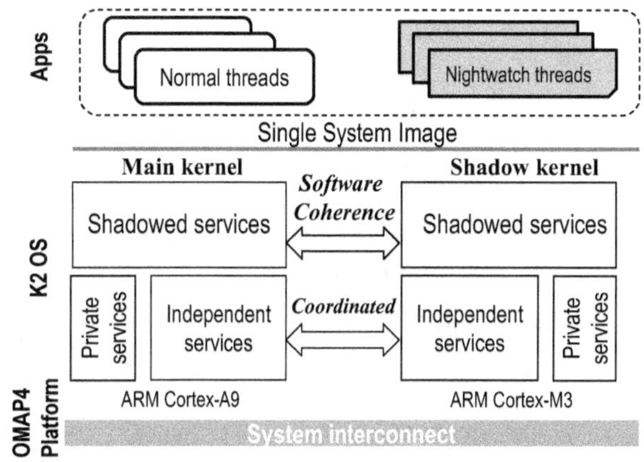


**Figure 3.** The structure of K2

OMAP4 has two coherence domains, each of which hosts one type of 32-bit ARM core: the performance-oriented Cortex-A9 and the efficiency-oriented Cortex-M3. Their specifications are listed in Table 1. The Cortex-M3 on OMAP4 has a non-standard MMU in which two levels are connected in series, which affects the design of K2 software coherence as will be discussed in §6.3. Each domain has dual cores and a private interrupt controller. Both domains are connected to the system interconnect, which further connects the shared RAM and all IO peripherals.

To support multiple coherence domains, OMAP4 provides two facilities. The hardware spinlocks are for inter-domain synchronization, which are a set of memory-mapped bits that support atomic test-and-set. The hardware mailboxes are for inter-domain communication: cores can pass 32-bit messages across domains with interrupting each other. We measured the message round-trip time as around 5 $\mu$s.

While K2 is geared towards OMAP4 with many platform-specific optimizations and workarounds, its design is driven by our OS model and based on the architectural assumptions in §4.2. We expect the design to be applicable to other multi-domain SoCs.

### 5.2 OS structure

Figure 3 depicts the structure of K2. As shown on the top of the figure, K2 carefully exposes hardware heterogeneity to application developers, by requiring them to statically partition their applications in coarse grains for heterogeneous domains. From an application developer's perspective, they develop the performance-critical parts of their applications as normal threads for execution on the strong domain; they wrap their light tasks in special *NightWatch* threads which will be pinned on the weak domain. We will discuss the details of NightWatch threads in §8.

Under the single system image, K2 runs two kernels on OMAP4: the full-fledged *main kernel* in `ARM` ISA running on the strong Cortex-A9 cores, and the lean *shadow kernel*[1] in `Thumb-2` ISA running on a weak Cortex-M3 core. The two kernels share the same virtual address space (§6.1), the same pool of physical memory (§6.2), and cooperate to handle IO interrupts (§7). As shown in Figure 3, most OS services, including device drivers and file systems, are shadowed between both kernels: they are built from the same source code and K2 transparently keeps their state coherent at run time. A few 'hotspot' core services are independent in both kernels and K2 coordinates them on the meta level. Each kernel has its private services.

### 5.3 Refactoring Linux

As a key step in applying the shared-most OS model, we refactor a recent Linux kernel 3.4 into both the main and shadow kernels of K2. In particular, in bringing up Linux on the Cortex-M3 of OMAP4, we adopt code from the linux-panda project [21]. The central job of refactoring is to decide how should individual Linux OS services be adopted by K2. We tackle the problem based on their dependence on processor cores, their functionalities, and the performance impact, with the following steps:

1. First, services that are specific to one type of core or that manage domain-local resources are kept private, implemented differently in each kernel, and with different state. Examples include core power management.
2. In the rest of the services, those performing complicated, rarely-used global operations will be kept private only in the main kernel. Examples include platform-level initializations.
3. In the rest of the services, those having high performance impact are replicated as independent instances in each kernel, with K2 coordinating the instances.
4. The remaining services, which manage platform resources and have low to moderate performance impact, are made as shadowed service in both kernels, with K2 automatically keeping their state coherent. In refactoring, we augment their locks by using the hardware spinlocks for inter-domain synchronization. This is the largest category which includes device drivers, file systems, and network service.

### 5.4 Build K2 from source

We implement both kernels of K2 in a unified source tree. To build K2, we run two passes of compilations, for the main kernel and for the shadow kernel respectively. In compilation, we apply a suite of techniques to bridge the heterogeneity gap between cores, with the help of automated scripts.

First, the compilation process makes sure each shared memory object has identical load addresses in both kernels. For both kernels, it pads data structures, enforces the same output order of memory objects in each object file, and enforces the same link order of object files. Second, the compilation process treats function pointers, which are prevalent in the Linux data structures and thus shared among two kernels. According to its ISA [4], when Cortex-M3 attempts to execute a Cortex-A9 instruction, it falls into an *unrecoverable* core state. To prevent such a situation, the compilation process statically rewrites `blx` instruction – the long jump instruction emitted by GCC for implementing function pointer dereference – with `Undef` instruction. At run time, when Cortex-M3 attempts to dereference a function pointer and thus hits `Undef`, it triggers an exception that is *recoverable*; K2 handles the exception and dispatches the control flow to the Cortex-M3 version of the function. `blx` is sparse in kernel code, constituting 0.1% of all instructions and 6% of all jump instructions.

## 6. Memory management

In the next three sections, we describe the core components of K2: memory management in §6, interrupt management in §7, and scheduling in §8. Among them, we will focus on memory management, which is the core mechanism in providing state coherence and unified resource management. In this section, we describe the major building blocks of the K2 memory management: the layout of kernel virtual addresses, the physical memory management, and the software coherence.

### 6.1 Unified kernel address space

K2 creates a unified address space for both kernels, while preserving the key assumption made by the Linux kernel virtual memory. In this section, we briefly recap the background of the Linux kernel virtual memory, describe the design constraints faced by K2, and then present our design.

Linux maps a large portion (sometimes all) of physical memory into kernel space directly. The mapping is linear and permanent: any virtual address is mapped to a physical address that only differs by a constant offset. Such direct-mapping greatly simplifies kernel virtual memory design: accessing direct-mapped memory will never trigger a page fault and conversions between kernel virtual and physical addresses are fast. As a result, direct-mapped memory usually hosts all important kernel data structures. [2]

In managing virtual memory for multiple kernels, K2 has to satisfy the following constraints:

[1] "Shadow" reflects the fact that the two kernels are kept coherent in their extended OS services.

[2] We are aware of the SPARSEMEM feature for servers, which, however, is rarely enabled for mobile devices.

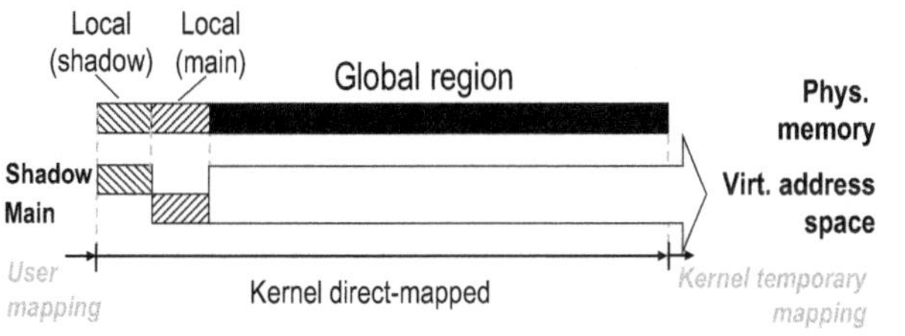


**Figure 4.** The unified kernel virtual address space of K2

1. Memory objects shared between kernels must have identical virtual addresses in both kernels. In addition, private memory objects should reside in non-overlapping address ranges to help catch software bugs.
2. For each kernel, the assumption of linear mapping holds for the entire direct-mapped memory.
3. Contiguous physical memory should be maximized, in particular for the main kernel which usually needs large physical memory blocks for multimedia applications.

K2 arranges its kernel address space as shown in Figure 4. From each kernel's view, its available physical memory consists of two regions, both direct-mapped. *(i)* A small *local* region hosts executable code (in local ISA) and the memory objects statically allocated for private or independent OS services (e.g., those in `bss` and `data` sections). *(ii)* All the rest of the physical memory belongs to the *global* region, which hosts the memory objects for shared OS services and all free physical pages for dynamic allocation. The global region is typically from several hundred MB to one GB.

From the start of physical memory (the left side of Figure 4), K2 populates all local regions: first for the shadow kernel and then for the main kernel. From the end of the last local region, the global region spans to the end of physical memory. By putting the main kernel's local region right before the global region, K2 avoids memory holes in the main kernel. With this memory layout, K2 keeps both kernels' virtual-to-physical offsets identical, thus essentially creating a unified virtual address space.

***Temporary mapping*** In addition to the direct-mapped memory discussed above, the OS may need to establish temporary mapping and thus make changes to the unified kernel address space. In supporting so, K2 treats two major types of temporary mappings differently. First, the OS may need temporary mappings for accessing IO memory. As creations and destructions of such mappings are infrequent, K2 adopts a simple protocol between two kernels for propagating page table updates from one to the other. Second, on platforms with abundant memory resources, the amount of physical pages may exceed that can be directly mapped into kernel space. Thus, temporary mappings are needed on-demand in accessing the extra pages (i.e., `highmem` in Linux's term). In the current implementation for the 32-bit ARM, K2 does not support `highmem`; as a workaround, it increases the size of kernel virtual space from the default 1GB to 2GB, which is large enough for directly mapping physical memory available on today's mainstream mobile devices. We do not expect this to be a fundamental limitation, as the emerging 64-bit ARM allows kernel to directly map a much larger amount of physical memory.

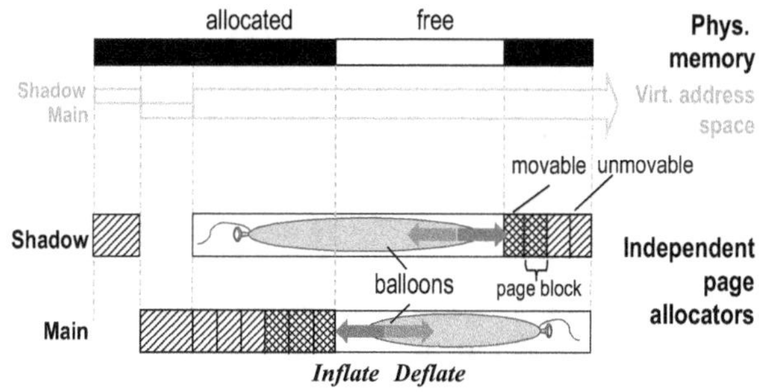


**Figure 5.** The physical memory management of K2

### 6.2 Physical memory management

Physical memory, as managed by OS page allocator, is one of the most important resources. The page allocator is frequently invoked, performance-critical, with its state among the hottest data structures in the OS. In managing physical memory for multiple coherence domains, K2 should:

1. Require minimum inter-domain communication in memory allocation and free.
2. Enable both kernels to dynamically share the entire pool of free pages.
3. Avoid disruptive changes to the existing Linux page allocator, which is already a mature design with sophisticated mechanisms and policies.
4. Minimize physical memory fragmentation.

An overview of the K2 memory management is shown in Figure 5. To achieve the first objective above, K2 applies the shared-most model and creates instances of page allocator in both the main and the shadow kernel, with separated state. Allocation requests are always served by the local instance on the same coherence domain; free requests are redirected asynchronously to the instance which allocated the pages, based on a simple address range check implemented as a thin wrapper over the existing free interface.

We next describe how K2 coordinates multiple page allocator instances to achieve objective 2-4 above, by first discussing the mechanism (balloon drivers) and then the policy (the meta-level manager).

***Balloon drivers*** K2 retrofits the idea of balloon driver from virtual machines [39] for controlling the amount of contiguous physical memory available to individual kernels. To individual kernels, balloon driver creates the key illusion of on-demand resizable physical memory.

A balloon driver is a pseudo device driver and each kernel has its own private instance. Controlled by K2, the driver's job is to occupy contiguous physical memory to keep the memory from the local page allocator. As shown in Figure 5, to K2, a balloon driver provides two primitives that operate on physically contiguous blocks of pages, or page blocks: *deflate*, i.e., the driver frees a page block to the local page allocator, which essentially transfers the ownership of the page block from K2 to the local kernel; *inflate*, i.e., the driver allocates a page block from the kernel, by forcing the kernel to evacuate pages from that page block, which essentially transfers the ownership of the page block from the local kernel back to K2. In the early stage of kernel boot, balloon drivers of both kernel are initialized to occupy the entire shared region so that K2 owns all physical pages in that region.

We implement K2 balloon drivers based on Linux's contiguous memory allocation framework. Balloon drivers require no change to the Linux page allocator: from each kernel's perspective, a balloon behaves like a common device driver that reserves a large contiguous memory region at boot time and later allocates and frees page blocks within that region autonomously.

***Meta-level manager*** On top of the balloon drivers, K2 provides a meta-level manager to decide when to take and give page blocks from and to kernels. The meta-level manager is implemented as a set of distributed probes, one in each kernel. Each probe monitors local memory pressure with hooks inserted into the local kernel page allocator; the probes coordinate through hardware messages, and take actions by invoking local balloon drivers. Generally, when memory pressure increases and before the local kernel reacts to the pressure (e.g., activating the Android low-memory killer), the meta-level manager instructs the balloon driver to free page blocks to alleviate the pressure; when free pages run low in the entire system, the meta-level manager instructs a balloon driver to inflate for reclaiming pages. Like the Linux kernel swap daemon, the meta-level manager performs operations in the background when OS is idle in order to minimize performance impact on individual allocations.

***Optimizations*** K2 has applied a few optimizations in physical memory management, as shown in Figure 5. First, to reduce inter-domain communication, the meta-level manager operates on large-grain page blocks, which are 16MB in the current implementation. Second, to maximize the size of physically contiguous area available to the main kernel, the meta-level manager instructs balloons to deflate from the two ends of the free portion in the shared region, and inflates in the reverse directions. Thus, blocks allocated to the main kernel grow from right after its private region. Third, to maximize the chance of successfully reclaiming page blocks from kernels, K2 commands local page allocators to place *movable* pages (e.g., those containing user data) close to the 'frontier' of the balloon with best efforts. The efforts are likely to succeed, as movable pages usually constitute 70%-80% of total pages based on our experiments with mobile systems. As a result, when the balloon inflates, those movable pages can be evacuated from the requested page block to elsewhere.

### 6.3 Software coherence

As mentioned in §5.2, K2 provides transparent coherence for shadowed services. This is implemented with software Distributed Shared Memory (DSM), a classic approach to hide distributed program state from programmers [16], which also has been applied to recent incoherent architectures such as CPU-GPU systems [14] and smartphones [17]. Like most DSM designs, the K2 DSM maintains the key one-writer invariant [16], by automatically translating memory accesses to inter-domain communication for coherence. While most software DSMs are designed to back user applications [16, 30], the K2 DSM backs OS services. Thus, we carefully construct fault handlers and coherence communication to avoid interference or lockup with other OS components.

***Basic design*** The K2 DSM implements sequential consistency. Although many DSMs [14, 17] implement relaxed consistency which relies on applications' correct locking behaviors, K2 neither relaxes the consistency model assumed by the existing OS, nor makes any assumption of OS locking behaviors which may be complicated. In implementing sequential consistency, the K2 DSM performs coherence operations upon each access fault and keeps the order of coherence messages. The K2 DSM adopts a page-based granularity, using 4KB page as the smallest memory unit that is kept coherent. This is for leveraging MMU to trap accesses to shared memory, as page is the unit used by the MMU for enforcing protection.

The K2 DSM has adopted a simple, standard two-state protocol. For each shared page, every kernel keeps track of its state, being `Valid` or `Invalid`. Kernels communicate with two types of coherence messages: *GetExclusive* and *PutExclusive*. When a page is `Valid`, a kernel can perform read or write of the page. Before performing read or write of a `Invalid` page, a kernel must send *GetExclusive* to the other kernel who currently owns the page; upon receiving *GetExclusive*, the latter kernel flushes and invalidates the requested page from its local cache, and acknowledges with a *PutExclusive* message. After that, the former kernel can proceed to access the memory.

The K2 DSM detects accesses to shared memory as follows: when a page transits from `Valid` to `Invalid` state, the DSM modifies the corresponding page table entry to be ineffective and handles the resulting page fault triggered by the subsequent access to the page. The fault handling is transparent to the OS code that made the memory access.

***Coherence communication*** For performance, the coherence communication directly leverages the OMAP4 hardware mailboxes. Each message is 32-bit, the size of a hardware mail, with 20 bits for page frame number, 3 bits for message type, and the rest for message sequence number. The mailbox will guarantee that messages are delivered in order.

We carefully construct coherence communication to avoid lockup. The communication must be synchronous to the requester: this is because interrupt handlers, which cannot sleep, may access shared state and thus initiates communication. Thus, when a requester kernel sends out a *GetExclusive* message, it spins waiting until the destination kernel sends back a *PutExclusive* message. For the same reason, handling *GetExclusive* must avoid sleeping as well, e.g., it must use atomic memory allocation. More importantly, handling *GetExclusive* must avoid accessing shared state which may trigger new page faults, resulting in an infinite request loop between kernels.

We optimize the communication latency in favor of the main kernel, by setting their priorities of handling coherence messages differently. The main kernel handles *GetExclusive* in bottom halves, and will further defer the handling if under high workloads; in contrast, the shadow kernel handles the request before any other pending interrupt. Through this, K2 reduces the impact of weak cores on system performance.

***Optimize memory footprint*** The K2 DSM incurs a low overhead in storing protocol information, asking for three bits per page. Furthermore, although shared memory areas have to be mapped in 4KB granularity, the K2 DSM allows non-shared areas to be mapped in larger grains (1 MB or 16 MB) as supported by the ARM hardware, thus reducing the size of page tables and alleviating TLB pressure. To achieve this, the K2 DSM turns on software coherence for memory addresses and replaces the existing large-grain mapping on-demand, only when an address (or its neighbouring area) has been accessed by both kernels.

***An alternative design*** While we are aware of a more common three-state protocol [35] that supports read-only sharing, our choice of the two-state protocol is based on the hardware limitation of the Cortex-M3 MMU on OMAP4.

In general, supporting read-only sharing requires DSM to use MMU for differentiating memory reads from writes in order to handle them separately. However, this is expensive on the OMAP4 Cortex-M3, which relies on the first level of its two cascading MMUs for read/write permissions. The first-level MMU has no page table but just a software-loaded TLB which only contains ten entries for 4KB pages. According to our experiment, using the MMU for read access detection puts a high pressure on its TLB and leads to severe thrashing. In contrast, without supporting read-only sharing, the K2 DSM detects both read and write accesses solely with the second-level MMU, which has a larger TLB and a hardware page table walker.

## 7. Interrupt management

Multiple coherence domains share interrupts generated by IO peripherals. Although any interrupt signal is physically delivered to all domains, K2 must ensure that it is only handled by exactly one kernel. If multiple kernels compete for the same interrupt signal, peripherals may enter incorrect states or cores may have spurious wakeups. The choice of kernel in handling interrupts does not affect OS correctness, thanks to the K2 software coherence; however, it does affect performance and efficiency.

K2 coordinates its two kernels in handling shared interrupts, by following two simple rules. First, for energy efficiency, K2 does not allow shared interrupts to wake up the strong domain from an inactive power state, in which case the shadow kernel should handle the interrupts. Second, for performance, when the strong domain is awake, K2 lets the main kernel handle all shared interrupts.

K2 has implemented the rules on the OMAP4 platform, where coherence domains have private interrupt controllers. K2 inserts a few hooks into the Linux power management code to configure interrupt controllers. When the shadow kernel boots on a weak domain, it masks all shared interrupt locally. When a strong domain transits to an inactive state, K2 unmasks all shared interrupts on the weak domain and masks them on the strong domain; when the strong domain is woken up from the inactive state, K2 reverses such operations, by masking shared interrupts on the weak domain and unmasking them on the strong domain.

## 8. Nightwatch threads

As mentioned in §5.2, K2 provides an abstraction called *NightWatch* thread for application developers to implement light tasks. NightWatch threads are pinned on a weak domain; after being created, a NightWatch thread enters the shadow kernel runqueue for execution. From a developer's view, a NightWatch thread is identical to a normal thread: for instance, they share a unified process address space and a single system image. The only exception is that in order to limit multi-domain parallelism (the third aspect of the shared-most model in §4.3), K2 enforces that:

*A NightWatch thread will only be considered for scheduling when all normal threads of the same process are suspended.*

The scheduling strategy, together with the single system image, distinguishes NightWatch threads from other abstractions that also encapsulate code for targeting heterogeneous hardware [17]. It is worth noting that K2 does not change the mechanism or policy of the Linux scheduler; all normal threads are scheduled as they are in Linux.

***Preempt NightWatch threads*** K2 preempts the execution of all NightWatch threads in a process when any normal thread of the same process is about to execute. After the main kernel decides to schedule-in a normal thread, it examines if any NightWatch threads belong to the same pro-

| Existing Implementations | Changed SLoC | Original SLoC |
|---|---|---|
| Exception handling | 1151 | 395 |
| Page allocator, interrupt, scheduler | 205 | 12119 |
| **New Implementations** | | **SLoC** |
| DSM | | 883 |
| Memory management | | 468 |
| Bootstrap | | 1306 |
| OMAP4-specific Cortex-M3 | | 772 |
| Debugging, etc. | | 1362 |
| Total | | 4791 |

**Table 2.** Source code changes and additions to the Linux kernel 3.4, which contains around 10 million SLoC. Much of the OMAP4-specific Cortex-M3 code is adopted from the linux-panda project [21].

| | Active | Idle |
|---|---|---|
| Cortex-M3 (200MHz)* | 21.1 | 3.8 |
| Cortex-A9 (350MHz)* | 79.8 | 25.2 |
| Cortex-A9 (1200MHz) | 672 | 25.2 |

**Table 3.** Power consumptions of the heterogeneous OMAP4 cores, in mW. Both cores consumes less than 0.1 mW when inactive. The frequencies with asterisks are used in the benchmarks for testing energy efficiency.

cess. If so, the kernel sends a `SuspendNW` hardware message to the shadow kernel. Interrupted by the `SuspendNW` message, the shadow kernel immediately responds with an `AckSuspendNW` message and then removes all NightWatch threads of the same process from the local runqueue by flagging them. On receiving the `AckSuspendNW`, the main kernel lands the normal thread on a core for execution.

To reduce latency, the main kernel overlaps the wait for `AckSuspendNW` with the context switch to the schedule-in thread: after sending `SuspendNW`, the main kernel proceeds to context switch, and only waits for `AckSuspendNW` after the context switch is done, before returning to user space. Given that a message round trip takes around 5 $\mu$s and a context switch usually takes 3-4 $\mu$s, the extra overhead for the main kernel is 1-2 $\mu$s for every context switch.

***Resume NightWatch threads*** When the main kernel finds that all normal threads of a process blocked, e.g., waiting for IO, it sends a `ResumeNW` message to the shadow kernel. On receiving the message, the shadow kernel removes flags from all NightWatch threads of the given process and will consider them in future scheduling.

## 9. Evaluation

We evaluate how well K2 meets the design goals we set in §4.1 by reporting our efforts in refactoring Linux and testing the energy efficiency harvested by K2. We then evaluate the benefits and overheads of the shared-most model by benchmarking the physical page allocator and the DMA device driver.

### 9.1 Efforts in refactoring

In building K2, we have achieved the goal of reusing mature OS source at the refactoring cost shown in Table 2. K2 introduces small changes to the Linux source. The biggest portion of changes is exception handling, where K2 handles page faults for DSM operations and dispatches function pointers. To core OS components such as the page allocator, K2 only adds a small portion of source lines. Device drivers, such as the one for DMA, can be reused by K2 with few modifications. K2 introduces a set of new software modules to implement its core components like DSM and memory management. It also includes extensive debugging support to help ourselves understand Linux.

### 9.2 Energy efficiency benefits

We show that K2 greatly improves energy efficiency for light tasks, by running a series of OS benchmarks to exercise K2 and the original Linux 3.4. In the benchmarks, we measure power consumption of coherence domains by sampling current on their separate power rails [12]. We measure elapsed time using hardware performance counters when cores are active, and using a 32KHz platform timer when idle.

In the benchmarks, K2 is able to use the weak core for OS execution, while Linux can only use the strong core. As summarized in Table 3, we configure the platform to favor the energy efficiency of Linux: we fix the strong core at its *most* efficient operating point while the weak core has to run at its *least* efficient operating point. This is because the OMAP4 implementation limits DVFS on the weak core, by coupling its voltage with that of the system interconnect and RAM. There is no way to scale down the voltage without crashing the entire SoC, to the best of our knowledge.

Our benchmarks test energy efficiency of three representative OS services: device driver, file system, and network stack. The benchmarks mimic mobile light tasks: in each run of a benchmark, cores are woken up, execute the workloads as fast as possible, and then stay idle until becoming inactive. We set the core inactive timeout as 5 sec, as reported in a recent study of mobile device power [41].

***DMA driver*** We choose the DMA driver as a representative device driver for testing, which is used in almost all bulk IO transfers, e.g., for flash and WiFi. The driver executes DMA transfers by operating the OMAP4 DMA engine. As shown in Figure 6(a), we pick a set of DMA transfer sizes typical to light tasks. Each run of the benchmark repeatedly invokes the DMA driver to execute multiple memory-to-memory transfers, where each transfer copies *BatchSize* bytes and for a total of *TotalSize* bytes copied. In each transfer, the DMA driver clears the destination memory region, looks for empty resources, programs the DMA engine and initiates the transfer. When the transfer is done, the DMA

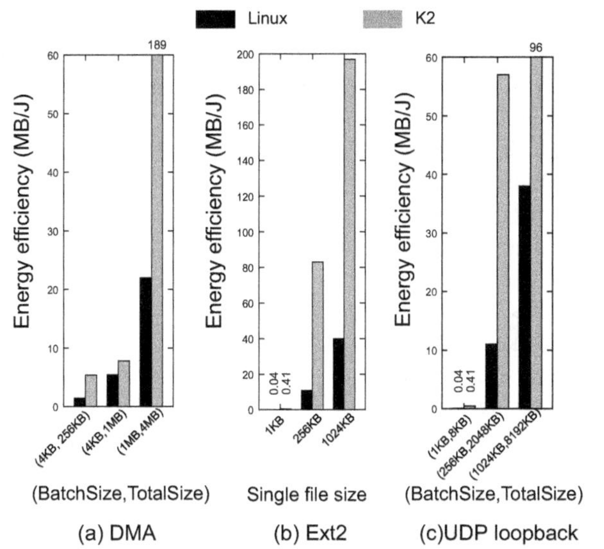


**Figure 6.** OS benchmarks for testing energy efficiency

driver is interrupted to free resources and complete the transfer. We calculate the energy efficiency as the amount of transferred bytes per Joule.

***ext2 file system*** We choose ext2, a file system widely used for flash storage, to test the energy efficiency of file system workloads. We use ramdisk as the underlying block device, as the SD card driver of K2 is not yet fully functional. This favors the energy efficiency of Linux: ramdisk is a much faster block device than real flash storages; using it shortens idle periods that are more expensive to strong cores. We design the benchmark to mimic a light task synchronizing contents from the cloud. As shown in Figure 6(b), for each run, a NightWatch thread operates on eight files sequentially: it creates a file, writes to it and closes it. We vary the write size to represent different content types: 1KB (emails), 256KB (pictures), and 1MB (short videos). We calculate the energy efficiency as the number of bytes written per Joule.

***UDP loopback*** To test network workloads efficiency, we design a UDP loopback benchmark to mimic the networking activities when light tasks fetch contents from the cloud. In the benchmark, a NightWatch thread creates two UDP sockets; it writes to one and reads from the other one for a total number of *TotalSize* bytes at full speed. Once every *BatchSize* bytes transferred, the thread destroys both sockets and recreates new ones. As shown in Figure 6(c), we choose sizes to represent typical contents as done for the ext2 benchmark. We calculate the energy efficiency as the amount of bytes sent per Joule.

***Results analysis*** In all three benchmarks, K2 shows significant advantages of energy efficiency over Linux, by improving the energy efficiency by up to 9x, 8x, and 10x, respectively. Based such results and the mobile device usage reported in recent literature [41], we estimate that K2 will

| Allocation Size | Main | Shadow |
|---|---|---|
| 4KB | 1 | 12 |
| 256KB | 5 | 45 |
| 1024KB | 13 | 146 |
| **Balloon** | | |
| deflate | 10,429 | 12,813 |
| inflate | 11,612 | 20,408 |

**Table 4.** Latencies of physical memory allocations in K2, in $\mu s$. The performance of K2's main kernel allocator has no noticeable difference from the Linux page allocator.

extend the reported device standby time by 59%, from 5.9 days to 9.4 days.

Overall, K2 gains the advantages mainly by exploiting the much lower-power idle periods of the weak core, which exist within each OS invocation (such as file operations in the ext2 benchmark) as well as in the inactive timeout periods. This is shown by the fact that when workloads are more IO-bound (e.g., the batch size of DMA transfers increases) or when the total task size of each run is smaller (e.g., in UDP loopback with fewer total sent bytes), the advantages of K2 are even more significant. In addition, over all benchmarks, K2 is able to use the weak core to deliver peak performance that is 20%-70% of the strong core performance at 350MHz, which can accommodate a wide range of light tasks that have low to moderate performance expectations.

### 9.3 Benefits of independent service

In order to evaluate our model of independent core services, we study the performance of the K2 physical memory management, with a microbenchmark to exercise the independent page allocators as well as the meta-level manager. In the benchmark, we measure the latency in allocating memory of different sizes, and in balloon deflating and inflating.

As shown in Table 4, K2 preserves the memory allocation performance of Linux. In comparing the memory allocation latency of the K2 main kernel with that of Linux, we find no noticeable difference: with separate state, the allocators of two kernels can operate independently without communication for most of the time. For each allocation, the pressure-monitoring probes inserted by the K2 meta-level manager incur less than twenty instructions, which is negligible compared to the allocation time. A balloon operation is more expensive: it intensively updates the page allocator state and moves pages, introducing around ten milliseconds latency that may be perceivable to users. This validates our design of triggering them asynchronously in the background. With allocation and free operations interleaved in practice and K2's large-grain page blocks, we expect that balloon operations are triggered infrequently and thus have their overheads amortized over a large number of memory allocations.

To contrast with K2's independent page allocators, we attempted but found it infeasible to implement the page allocator as a shadowed service. The contention between

| Operations | *GetExclusive* sender Main | Shadow |
|---|---|---|
| Local fault handling | 3 | 17 |
| Protocol Execution | 2 | 13 |
| Inter-domain communication | 5 | 9 |
| Servicing request | 24 | 7 |
| Exit fault, cache miss | 18 | 2 |
| Total | 52 | 48 |

**Table 5.** A breakdown of the latency in a DSM page fault, in $\mu s$.

| | DMA BatchSize 4K | 128K | 256K | 1M |
|---|---|---|---|---|
| Linux | 37.8 | 40.3 | 40.3 | 40.5 |
| K2 | 35.7 | 39.9 | 40.5 | 43.1 |
| | (-5.5%) | (-1.0%) | (+0.5%) | (+%6.4) |
| *K2:Main* | 35.6 | 28.4 | 28.6 | 28.8 |
| *K2:Shadow* | 0.1 | 11.5 | 11.9 | 14.3 |

**Table 6.** DMA throughputs of K2 when the DMA driver is invoked in both kernels concurrently, in MB/Sec. The throughput differences as compared to the original Linux are also shown.

coherence domains is very high, incurring four to five DSM page faults in every allocation, leading to a 200x slowdown. What is even worse, OS lockups happen frequently and are difficult to debug.

### 9.4 Performance of shadowed service

With transparent coherence provided by the DSM, K2's shadowed OS services are able to achieve performance very close to Linux. We show the latency of a single DSM page fault and its breakdown in Table 5. Although further optimizations are possible (e.g., local fault handling and protocol execution contribute more than 30% of the latency), the DSM provides acceptable performance to most extended OS services where sharing usually happens at a time scale of milliseconds or seconds.

We examine the performance of shadowed services by running a DMA driver benchmark on the main and the shadow kernel concurrently. In each run of the benchmark, both kernels repeatedly invoke the DMA driver to execute transfers at full speed with a given batch size. The run is repeated for multiple times with different batch sizes. As a comparison, we also run the same benchmark using the original Linux kernel that uses the strong domain only. The DMA throughputs of the Linux and the K2 kernels, together with their differences, are summarized in Table 6.

As shown in the results, in backing the DMA shadowed service with software coherence, K2 incurs low overhead, reducing the throughput by up to 5.5%. Since K2 runs two kernels from two domains simultaneously, the throughput reduction seen by the main kernel is contributed by two factors: software coherence overhead incurred by K2 and the DMA engine bandwidth allocated to the shadow kernel. With small batch sizes such as 4KB, the benchmark is CPU-bound: the contention for shared kernel state is relatively high and the DMA engine is not fully utilized. Due to the asymmetry in processor performance and in K2's design, the coherence overhead is low – a 50 $\mu$s DSM page fault happens around every 10 transfers, or 1200 $\mu$s. As batch size increases, the benchmark is becoming more IO-bound; the shadow kernel starts to get better chances in competing for the bandwidth of DMA engine. In this situation, as the rate of accessing shared state decreases, the coherence overhead is even lower – one DSM page fault in every 18 ms. Thus, the DMA engine serving two domains has a higher utilization, leading to a small increase in throughput (by up to 6%) as compared to the Linux case.

## 10. Related Work

K2 is related to a few areas in systems research. Hardware heterogeneity is a recognized way to improve energy efficiency. Driven by the pursuit of heterogeneity, mobile architectures with multiple coherence domains that can operate independently are popular in both industry [23, 36] and academia [1, 17, 26, 34]. However, existing system support has focused on user policies [26] and programming models as in our prior work Reflex [17]; none offers OS support as K2 does. The lack of OS support will defeat the goal of energy efficiency: as shown by a recent study of smartphone workloads [18], demanding and non-demanding tasks share an extensive set of OS services, which must be executed on each coherence domain. In particular, our prior work Reflex [17] features a DSM that transparently maintains state consistency for applications. The user-level DSM of Reflex is complementary to the OS-level DSM of K2; unlike in Reflex, the K2 DSM targets generic OS workloads, and thus has performance as one of the major goals, e.g., by leveraging hardware MMUs.

Programming on top of multiple kernels can be made a lot easier with a single system image. Many systems provide single system images by forwarding service requests among kernels. For example, the V distributed system [10] distributes microkernels over workstations and forwards requests to OS servers via network. Multicelluar OSes such as Hive [9] and Cellular IRIX [31] provide single system images over multiple cells by running independent kernels which cooperate using explicit communication, e.g., RPC. Since kernels are independent, an IO request must be served in the only cell where the IO device is located. Disco [8], which runs different unmodified OSes on a single machine, does coordination at user-level with standard network protocols, thus providing a partial single system image. fos [40], Helios [22], and NIX [5] dedicate a set of cores or hardware accelerators to specific OS services, and send them the corresponding services requests with explicit messages. Unlike all of them, K2 must realize a single system image by replicating OS services, in order to execute the same OS services on each domain for energy efficiency.

To improve resource utilization, unified resource management is relevant when multiple kernels share the same resource pool. Statically partitioning resources is wasteful and thus undesirable. Many research OSes [6, 40] redesign their local resource managers to cooperate at fine grains, which is effective yet difficult to apply to mature mobile OSes. Similarly, Libra [2] enables a general-purpose OS and multiple specialized library OSes to share physical memory dynamically; it also employs redesigned memory managers in the specialized OSes. Virtual machines [39] enable resource sharing among multiple OSes while minimizing modifications to them. For memory management, K2 retrofits the balloon driver idea from virtual machines, and additionally moves physically contiguous regions around individual kernels, without assuming virtualization hardware.

Reducing sharing in OS has been extensively studied for shared memory machines, mostly for scalability. Many argue for structural overhauls. Hurricane [38] organizes OS in a hierarchical way to improve scalability. Barrelfish [6] takes an extreme design point to make all OS state non-shared by default. fos [40] argues to replicate given OS services to a subset of processors and coordinate them with messages. New programming abstractions have been proposed, too. Tornado [13] and K42 [3] argue for object-oriented OS designs, enabling each OS service to have its internal mechanism to distribute over SMP. Inspired by them, K2 treats OS services differently in how to replicate them over coherence domains; unlike them, K2 targets reusing legacy OS code rather than a clean-slate implementation. For manycore machines, Corey [7] enables applications to control sharing within processes. Inspired by it, K2 employs NightWatch thread as a hint of performance expectation.

In reusing mature OSes for new architectures, virtualization and refactoring are two major approaches. While K2 borrows idea from virtual machines for memory management, the latter usually sets out to enforce isolation among OS instances, rather than providing a single system image over them. Refactoring, as done in DrawBridge [25] and Unikernels [19] recently, restructures OS while keeping individual OS components. Their approaches are inspiring, but solve a different problem – rearranging OS services vertically across layers. In comparison, for K2 we refactor Linux by replicating OS services horizontally across coherence domains.

## 11. Concluding Remarks

***Discussion*** K2 is designed for a typical mobile SoC which consists of a few heterogeneous domains. As compute resources keep increasing, we next discuss how K2 should be adapted for the following architecture trends.

First, individual domains will accommodate more cache-coherent cores. Since individual kernels of K2 already have the Linux SMP support, K2 can (almost) transparently scale with these additional cores.

Second, one system may embrace *more*, but not *many*, types of heterogeneous domains, as determined by the current spectrum of mobile workloads. For $N$ domains ($N$ being moderate), K2 can be extended without structural changes: the DSM (§6.3) will track page ownership among $N$ domains as in [17]; the unified kernel address space (§6.1) will host the additional $N$-2 local virtual regions; the global physical region will still be managed by balloon drivers (§6.2), yet the relative locations of $N$ local physical regions depend on the intended use of the added domains. Overall, the asymmetric aspects of K2 (e.g., page allocation favoring strong domains) will remain.

Another possibility is that a system incorporates *many* coherence domains of the same type, as seen on some scalability-oriented systems including the 48-domain Intel SCC [20]. Our shared-most model (§4.3) will be useful, while new OS implementations should be engineered for scalability. However, we do not expect to see so many domains on a mobile device in the foreseeable future.

In developing K2, we find that the following architectural features will greatly benefit system performance and efficiency, yet are still missing in today's multi-domain SoCs: direct channels for inter-domain communication that bypass the system interconnect, efficient MMUs for weak domains with permission support, and finer-grained power domains.

***Conclusion*** Multi-domain SoCs promise high energy efficiency to a wide range of mobile applications, yet are difficult to program. To address this challenge, we identify a shared-most OS model for the architecture, and argue for transparently maintaining state coherence for extended OS services while creating per-domain, shared-nothing instances of core OS services. By applying the model, we build K2, a prototype OS on the TI OMAP4 SoC. K2 presents a single system image and reuses most of the Linux kernel source. Although still in an early stage under development, K2 improves energy efficiency for light OS workloads by up to 10x and provides almost the same performance as Linux, showing that the shared-most model is promising. The source of K2 is available from `http://www.k2os.org`.

## Acknowledgments

This work was supported in part by NSF CAREER Award #1054693. The authors thank NICTA researchers for publishing their `linux-panda` source code, and the anonymous reviewers for their useful comments.

## References

[1] Y. Agarwal, S. Hodges, R. Chandra, J. Scott, P. Bahl, and R. Gupta. Somniloquy: Augmenting network interfaces to reduce PC energy usage. In *Proc. USENIX Symp. Networked*

*Systems Design and Implementation (NSDI)*, pages 365–380, 2009.

[2] G. Ammons, J. Appavoo, M. Butrico, D. Da Silva, D. Grove, K. Kawachiya, O. Krieger, B. Rosenburg, E. Van Hensbergen, and R. W. Wisniewski. Libra: a library operating system for a jvm in a virtualized execution environment. In *Proc. Int. Conf. Virtual Execution Environments (VEE)*, pages 44–54. 2007.

[3] J. Appavoo, D. D. Silva, O. Krieger, M. Auslander, M. Ostrowski, B. Rosenburg, A. Waterland, R. W. Wisniewski, J. Xenidis, M. Stumm, et al. Experience distributing objects in an SMMP OS. *ACM Transactions on Computer Systems (TOCS)*, 25(3):6, 2007.

[4] ARM. ARM v7-M architecture reference manual, 2010.

[5] F. J. Ballesteros, N. Evans, C. Forsyth, G. Guardiola, J. McKie, R. Minnich, and E. Soriano. Nix: An operating system for high performance manycore computing. *Bell Labs Technical Journal*, 2012.

[6] A. Baumann, P. Barham, P.-E. Dagand, T. Harris, R. Isaacs, S. Peter, T. Roscoe, A. Schüpbach, and A. Singhania. The multikernel: a new os architecture for scalable multicore systems. In *Proc. ACM Symp. Operating Systems Principles (SOSP)*, pages 29–44. 2009.

[7] S. Boyd-Wickizer, H. Chen, R. Chen, Y. Mao, M. F. Kaashoek, R. Morris, A. Pesterev, L. Stein, M. Wu, Y.-h. Dai, Y. Zhang, and Z. Zhang. Corey: An operating system for many cores. In *Proc. USENIX Conf. Operating Systems Design and Implementation (OSDI)*, pages 43–57, 2008.

[8] E. Bugnion, S. Devine, K. Govil, and M. Rosenblum. Disco: Running commodity operating systems on scalable multiprocessors. *ACM Transactions on Computer Systems (TOCS)*, 15(4):412–447, 1997.

[9] J. Chapin, M. Rosenblum, S. Devine, T. Lahiri, D. Teodosiu, and A. Gupta. Hive: Fault containment for shared-memory multiprocessors. In *Proc. ACM Symp. Operating Systems Principles (SOSP)*, pages 12–25, 1995.

[10] D. Cheriton. The V distributed system. *Communications of the ACM*, 31(3):314–333, 1988.

[11] M. DeVuyst, A. Venkat, and D. M. Tullsen. Execution migration in a heterogeneous-isa chip multiprocessor. In *Proc. ACM Int. Conf. Architectural Support for Programming Languages & Operating Systems (ASPLOS)*, pages 261–272, 2012.

[12] eLinux.org. PandaBoard Power Measurements. `http://elinux.org/PandaBoard_Power_Measurements`.

[13] B. Gamsa, O. Krieger, J. Appavoo, and M. Stumm. Tornado: Maximizing locality and concurrency in a shared memory multiprocessor operating system. In *Proc. USENIX Conf. Operating Systems Design and Implementation (OSDI)*, pages 87–100, 1999.

[14] I. Gelado, J. E. Stone, J. Cabezas, S. Patel, N. Navarro, and W.-m. W. Hwu. An asymmetric distributed shared memory model for heterogeneous parallel systems. In *Proc. ACM Int. Conf. Architectural Support for Programming Languages & Operating Systems (ASPLOS)*, pages 347–358, 2010.

[15] P. Greenhalgh. Big.LITTLE processing with ARM Cortex-A15 and Cortex-A7. Technical report, 2011.

[16] K. Li and P. Hudak. Memory coherence in shared virtual memory systems. *ACM Trans. Comput. Syst.*, 7(4):321–359, Nov. 1989.

[17] F. X. Lin, Z. Wang, R. LiKamWa, and L. Zhong. Reflex: using low-power processors in smartphones without knowing them. In *Proc. ACM Int. Conf. Architectural Support for Programming Languages & Operating Systems (ASPLOS)*, pages 13–24, 2012.

[18] F. X. Lin, Z. Wang, and L. Zhong. Supporting distributed execution of smartphone workloads on loosely coupled heterogeneous processors. In *Proc. Workshp. Power-Aware Computing and Systems (HotPower)*, pages 2–2, 2012.

[19] A. Madhavapeddy, R. Mortier, C. Rotsos, D. Scott, B. Singh, T. Gazagnaire, S. Smith, S. Hand, and J. Crowcroft. Unikernels: Library operating systems for the cloud. In *Proc. ACM Int. Conf. Architectural Support for Programming Languages & Operating Systems (ASPLOS)*, pages 461–472. 2013.

[20] T. G. Mattson, M. Riepen, T. Lehnig, P. Brett, W. Haas, P. Kennedy, J. Howard, S. Vangal, N. Borkar, G. Ruhl, and S. Dighe. The 48-core SCC processor: the programmer's view. In *Proc. ACM/IEEE Int. Conf. High Performance Computing, Networking, Storage and Analysis (SC)*, pages 1–11. 2010.

[21] NICTA. Linux-panda project. `http://www.ertos.nicta.com.au/downloads/linux-panda-m3.tbz2`, 2012.

[22] E. B. Nightingale, O. Hodson, R. McIlroy, C. Hawblitzel, and G. Hunt. Helios: heterogeneous multiprocessing with satellite kernels. In *Proc. ACM Symp. Operating Systems Principles (SOSP)*, pages 221–234, 2009.

[23] NVIDIA. Tegra2 Family: Technical reference manual, 2011.

[24] NVIDIA. Tegra3 HD mobile processors: Technical reference manual, 2012.

[25] D. E. Porter, S. Boyd-Wickizer, J. Howell, R. Olinsky, and G. C. Hunt. Rethinking the library os from the top down. In *Proc. ACM Int. Conf. Architectural Support for Programming Languages & Operating Systems (ASPLOS)*, pages 291–304, 2011.

[26] B. Priyantha, D. Lymberopoulos, and J. Liu. Littlerock: Enabling energy-efficient continuous sensing on mobile phones. *Pervasive Computing, IEEE*, 10(2):12–15, 2011.

[27] M.-R. Ra, B. Priyantha, A. Kansal, and J. Liu. Improving energy efficiency of personal sensing applications with heterogeneous multi-processors. In *Proc. Int. Conf. Ubiquitous Computing (UbiComp)*, pages 1–10. 2012.

[28] L. Ryzhyk, P. Chubb, I. Kuz, and G. Heiser. Dingo: Taming device drivers. In *Proc. The European Conf. Computer Systems (EuroSys)*, pages 275–288. 2009.

[29] Samsung. Exynos 4210 application processor. `http://www.samsung.com/global/business/semiconductor/productInfo.do?fmly_id=844&partnum=Exynos%204210`.

[30] D. Scales, K. Gharachorloo, and C. Thekkath. Shasta: A low overhead, software-only approach for supporting fine-grain shared memory. *ACM SIGOPS Operating Systems Review*, 30(5):174–185, 1996.

[31] SGI. Cellular IRIX 6.4 technical report. `http://www.sgistuff.net/software/irixintro/documents/irix6.4TR.html`.

[32] Y. Shin, K. Shin, P. Kenkare, R. Kashyap, H.-J. Lee, D. Seo, B. Millar, Y. Kwon, R. Iyengar, M.-S. Kim, A. Chowdhury, S.-I. Bae, I. Hong, W. Jeong, A. Lindner, U. Cho, K. Hawkins, J. C. Son, and S. H. Hwang. 28nm high-metal-gate heterogeneous quad-core CPUs for high-performance and energy-efficient mobile application processor. In *Proc. IEEE Int. Solid-State Circuits Conf. (ISSCC)*, pages 154–155. 2013.

[33] P. Smith and N. C. Hutchinson. Heterogeneous process migration: The Tui system. *Software-Practice and Experience*, 28(6):611–640, 1998.

[34] J. Sorber, N. Banerjee, M. D. Corner, and S. Rollins. Turducken: hierarchical power management for mobile devices. In *Proc. USENIX/ACM Int. Conf. Mobile Systems, Applications, & Services (MobiSys)*, pages 261–274. 2005.

[35] D. J. Sorin, M. D. Hill, and D. A. Wood. A primer on memory consistency and cache coherence. *Synthesis Lectures on Computer Architecture*, 6(3):1–212, 2011.

[36] Texas Instruments. OMAP4 applications processor: Technical reference manual. `http://www.ti.com/product/OMAP4470`, 2010.

[37] Texas Instruments. OMAP543x: Technical reference manual. `http://www.ti.com/litv/pdf/swpu249v`, 2010.

[38] R. C. Unrau, O. Krieger, B. Gamsa, and M. Stumm. Hierarchical clustering: A structure for scalable multiprocessor operating system design. *The Journal of Supercomputing*, 9(1-2):105–134, 1995.

[39] C. A. Waldspurger. Memory resource management in VMware ESX server. *SIGOPS Oper. Syst. Rev.*, 36(SI):181–194, Dec. 2002.

[40] D. Wentzlaff and A. Agarwal. Factored operating systems (fos): the case for a scalable operating system for multicores. *SIGOPS Oper. Syst. Rev.*, 43(2):76–85, 2009.

[41] F. Xu, Y. Liu, T. Moscibroda, R. Chandra, L. Jin, Y. Zhang, and Q. Li. Optimizing background email sync on smartphones. In *Proc. USENIX/ACM Int. Conf. Mobile Systems, Applications, & Services (MobiSys)*, 2013.

[42] L. Zhong and N. K. Jha. Dynamic power optimization targeting user delays in interactive systems. *IEEE Trans. Mobile Computing*, 5(11):1473–1488, 2006.

# Disengaged Scheduling for Fair, Protected Access to Fast Computational Accelerators

Konstantinos Menychtas Kai Shen Michael L. Scott
University of Rochester
{kmenycht,kshen,scott}@cs.rochester.edu

## Abstract

Today's operating systems treat GPUs and other computational accelerators as if they were simple devices, with bounded and predictable response times. With accelerators assuming an increasing share of the workload on modern machines, this strategy is already problematic, and likely to become untenable soon. If the operating system is to enforce fair sharing of the machine, it must assume responsibility for accelerator scheduling and resource management.

Fair, safe scheduling is a particular challenge on fast accelerators, which allow applications to avoid kernel-crossing overhead by interacting directly with the device. We propose a *disengaged* scheduling strategy in which the kernel intercedes between applications and the accelerator on an infrequent basis, to monitor their use of accelerator cycles and to determine which applications should be granted access over the next time interval.

Our strategy assumes a well defined, narrow interface exported by the accelerator. We build upon such an interface, systematically inferred for the latest Nvidia GPUs. We construct several example schedulers, including *Disengaged Timeslice* with overuse control that guarantees fairness and *Disengaged Fair Queueing* that is effective in limiting resource idleness, but probabilistic. Both schedulers ensure fair sharing of the GPU, even among uncooperative or adversarial applications; Disengaged Fair Queueing incurs a 4% overhead on average (max 18%) compared to direct device access across our evaluation scenarios.

***Categories and Subject Descriptors*** C.1.3 [*Processor Architectures*]: Other Architecture Styles; D.4.1 [*Operating Systems*]: Process Management—Scheduling; D.4.8 [*Operating Systems*]: Performance

***Keywords*** Operating system protection; scheduling; fairness; hardware accelerators; GPUs


*ASPLOS '14*, March 1–5, 2014, Salt Lake City, Utah, USA.

http://dx.doi.org/10.1145/2541940.2541963

## 1. Introduction

Future microprocessors seem increasingly likely to be highly heterogeneous, with large numbers of specialized computational accelerators. General-purpose GPUs are the canonical accelerator on current machines; other current or near-future examples include compression, encryption, XML parsing, and media transcoding engines, as well as reconfigurable (FPGA) substrates.

Current OS strategies, which treat accelerators as if they were simple devices, are ill suited to operations of unpredictable, potentially unbounded length. Consider, for example, a work-conserving GPU that alternates between requests (compute "kernels," rendering calls) from two concurrent applications. The application with larger requests will tend to receive more time. A greedy application may intentionally "batch" its work into larger requests to hog resources. A malicious application may launch a denial-of-service attack by submitting a request with an infinite loop.

Modern accelerator system architectures (Figure 1) pose at least two major challenges to fair, safe management. First, microsecond-level request latencies strongly motivate designers to avoid the overhead of user/kernel domain switching (up to 40% for small requests according to experiments later in this paper) by granting applications direct device access from user space. In bypassing the operating system, this direct access undermines the OS's traditional responsibility for protected resource management. Second, the application-hardware interface for accelerators is usually hidden within a stack of black-box modules (libraries, run-time systems, drivers, hardware), making it inaccessible to programmers outside the vendor company. To enable resource management in the protected domain of the OS kernel, but outside such black-box stacks, certain aspects of the interface must be disclosed and documented.

To increase fairness among applications, several research projects have suggested changes or additions to the application-library interface [12, 15, 19, 20, 32], relying primarily on open-source stacks for this purpose. Unfortunately, as discussed in Section 2, such changes invariably serve either to replace the direct-access interface, adding a per-request syscall overhead that can be significant, or to impose a voluntary level of cooperation in front of that interface. In this latter case, nothing prevents an application

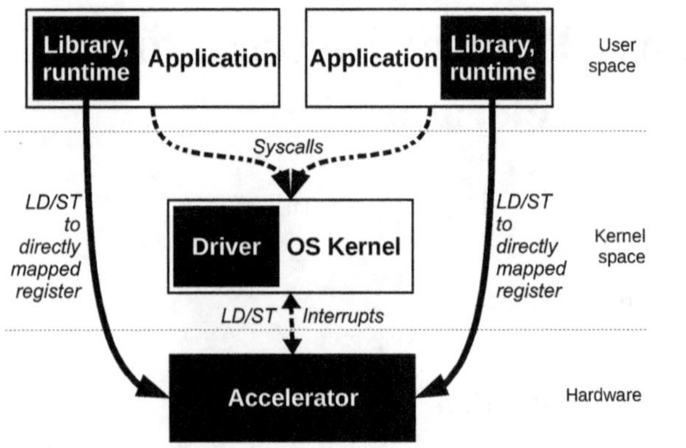


**Figure 1.** For efficiency, accelerators (like Nvidia GPUs) receive requests directly from user space, through a memory-mapped interface. The syscall-based OS path is only used for occasional maintenance such as the initialization setup. Commonly, much of the involved software (libraries, drivers) and hardware is unpublished (black boxes).

from ignoring the new interface and accessing the device directly. Simply put, the current state of the art with respect to accelerator management says "you can have at most two of protection, efficiency, and fairness—not all three."

While we are not the first to bemoan this state of affairs [29], we are, we believe, the first to suggest a viable solution, and to build a prototype system in which accelerator access is simultaneously protected, efficient, and fair. Our key idea, called *disengagement*, allows an OS resource scheduler to maintain fairness by interceding on a small number of acceleration requests (by disabling the direct-mapped interface and intercepting resulting faults) while granting the majority of requests unhindered direct access. To demonstrate the versatility and efficiency of this idea, we build a prototype: a Linux kernel module that enables disengaged scheduling on three generations of Nvidia GPUs. We construct our prototype for the proprietary, unmodified software stack. We leverage our previously proposed state machine inferencing approach to uncover the black-box GPU interface [25] necessary for scheduling.

We have built and evaluated schedulers that illustrate the richness of the design space. Our *Disengaged Timeslice* scheduler ensures fully protected fair sharing among applications, but can lead to underutilization when applications contain substantial "off" periods between GPU requests. Our *Disengaged Fair Queueing* scheduler limits idleness and maintains high efficiency with a strong probabilistic guarantee of fairness. We describe how we build upon the uncovered GPU interface; how we enable protection, efficiency, and fairness; and how hardware trends may influence—and be influenced by—our scheduling techniques.

## 2. Related Work

Some GPU management systems—e.g., PTask [32] and Pegasus [15]—provide a replacement user-level library that arranges to make a system or hypervisor call on each GPU request. In addition to the problem of per-request overhead, this approach provides safety from erroneous or malicious applications only if the vendor's direct-mapped interface is disabled—a step that may compromise compatibility with pre-existing applications. Elliott and Anderson [12] require an application to acquire a kernel mutex before using the GPU, but this convention, like the use of a replacement library, cannot be enforced. Though such approaches benefit from the clear semantics of the libraries' documented APIs, they can be imprecise in their accounting: API calls to start acceleration requests at this level are translated asynchronously to actual resource usage by the driver. We build our solution at the GPU software / hardware interface, where the system software cannot be circumvented and resource utilization accounting can be timely and precise.

Other systems, including GERM [11], TimeGraph/Gdev [19, 20] and LoGV [13] in a virtualized setting, replace the vendor black-box software stack with custom open-source drivers and libraries (e.g., Nouveau [27] and PathScale [31]). These enable easy operating system integration, and can enforce an OS scheduling policy if configured to be notified of all requests made to the GPU. For small, frequent acceleration requests, the overhead of trapping to the kernel can make this approach problematic. The use of a custom, modified stack also necessitates integration with user-level GPU libraries; for several important packages (e.g., OpenCL, currently available only as closed source), this is not always an option. Our approach is independent of the rest of the GPU stack: it intercedes at the level of the hardware-software interface. (For prototyping purposes, this interface is uncovered through systematic reverse engineering [25]; for production systems it will require that vendors provide a modest amount of additional documentation.)

Several projects have addressed the issue of fairness in GPU scheduling. GERM [11] enables fair-share resource allocation using a deficit round-robin scheduler [34]. TimeGraph [19] supports fairness by penalizing overuse beyond a reservation. Gdev [20] employs a non-preemptive variant of Xen's Credit scheduler to realize fairness. Beyond the realm of GPUs, fair scheduling techniques (particularly the classic fair queueing schedulers [10, 14, 18, 30, 33]) have been adopted successfully in network and I/O resource management. Significantly, all these schedulers track and/or control each individual device request, imposing the added cost of OS kernel-level management on fast accelerators that could otherwise process requests in microseconds. Disengaged scheduling enables us to redesign existing scheduling policies to meet fast accelerator requirements, striking a better balance between protection and efficiency while maintaining good fairness guarantees.

Beyond the GPU, additional computational accelerators are rapidly emerging for power-efficient computing through increased specialization [8]. The IBM PowerEN processor [23] contains accelerators for tasks (cryptography, compression, XML parsing) of importance for web services. Altera [1] provides custom FPGA circuitry for OpenCL. The faster the accelerator, and the more frequent its use, the greater the need for direct, low-latency access from user applications. To the extent that such access bypasses the OS kernel, protected resource management becomes a significant challenge. The ongoing trend toward deeper CPU/accelerator integration (e.g., AMD's APUs [7, 9] or HSA architecture [24], ARM's Mali GPUs [4], and Intel's QuickAssist [17] accelerator interface) and low-overhead accelerator APIs (e.g. AMD's Mantle [3] for GPUs), leads us to believe that disengaged scheduling can be an attractive strategy for future system design.

Managing fast devices for which per-request engagement is too expensive is reminiscent of the Soft Timers work [5]. Specifically, Aron and Druschel argued that per-packet interrupts are too expensive for fast networks and that batched processing through rate-based clocking and network polling is necessary for high efficiency [5]. Exceptionless system calls [35] are another mechanism to avoid the overhead of frequent kernel traps by batching requests. Our proposal also avoids per-request manipulation overheads to achieve high efficiency, but our specific techniques are entirely different. Rather than promote batched and/or delayed processing of system interactions, which co-designed user-level libraries already do for GPUs [21, 22, 28], we aim for synchronous involvement of the OS kernel in resource management, at times and conditions of its choosing.

Recent projects have proposed that accelerator resources be managed in coordination with conventional CPU scheduling to meet overall performance goals [15, 29]. Helios advocated the support of affinity scheduling on heterogeneous machines [26]. We recognize the value of coordinated resource management—in fact we see our work as enabling it: for accelerators that implement low-latency requests, coordinated management will require OS-level accelerator scheduling that is not only fair but also safe and fast.

## 3. Protected Scheduling with Efficiency

From the kernel's perspective, and for the purpose of scheduling, accelerators can be thought of as processing resources with an event-based interface. A "task" (the resource principal to which we wish to provide fair service—e.g., a process or virtual machine) can be charged for the resources occupied by its "acceleration request" (e.g., compute, graphics). To schedule such requests, we need to know when they are submitted for processing and when they complete.

Submission and completion are easy to track if the former employs the syscall interface and the latter employs interrupts. However, and primarily for reasons of efficiency, vendors like Nvidia avoid both, and build an interface that is directly mapped to user space instead. A request can be submitted by initializing buffers and a descriptor object in shared memory and then writing the address of the descriptor into a queue that is watched by the device. Likewise, completion can be detected by polling a flag or counter that is set by the device.

Leveraging our previous work on state-machine inferencing of the black-box GPU interface [25], we observe that the kernel can, when desired, learn of requests passed through the direct-mapped interface by means of *interception*—by (temporarily) unmapping device registers and catching the resulting page faults. The page fault handler can then pass control to an OS resource manager that may dispatch or queue/delay the request according to a desired policy. Request completion can likewise be realized through independent polling. In comparison to relying on a modified user-level library, interception has the significant advantage of enforcing policy even on unmodified, buggy, or selfish / malicious applications. All it requires of the accelerator architecture is a well-defined interface based on scheduling events—an interface that is largely independent of the internal details of black or white-box GPU stacks.

***Cost of OS management*** Unfortunately, trapping to the OS—whether via syscalls or faults—carries nontrivial costs. The cost of a user / kernel mode switch, including the effects of cache pollution and lost user-mode IPC, can be thousands of CPU cycles [35, 36]. Such cost is a substantial addition to the base time (305 cycles on our Nvidia GTX670-based system) required to submit a request directly with a write to I/O space. In applications with small, frequent requests, high OS protection costs can induce significant slowdown. Figure 2 plots statistics for three realistic applications, selected for their small, frequent requests: glxgears (standard OpenGL [22] demo), Particles (OpenCL / GL from CUDA SDK [28]), and Simple 3D Texture (OpenCL / GL from CUDA SDK [28]). More than half of all GPU requests from these applications are submitted and serviced in less than 10 $\mu$s. With a deeply integrated CPU-GPU microarchitecture, request latency could be lowered even more—to the level of a simple memory/cache write/read, further increasing the relative burden of interception.

To put the above in perspective, we compared the throughput that can be achieved with an accelerator software / hardware stack employing a direct-access interface (Nvidia Linux binary driver v310.14) and with one that relies on traps to the kernel for every acceleration request (AMD Catalyst v13.8 Linux binary driver). The comparison uses the same machine hardware, and we hand-tune the OpenCL requests to our Nvidia (GTX670) or AMD (Radeon HD 7470) PCIe GPU such that the requests are equal-sized. We discover that, for requests in the order of 10–100 $\mu$s, a throughput increase of 8–35% can be expected by simply accessing the device directly, without trapping to the kernel for every request. These throughput gains are even higher (48–170%) if the traps to the kernel actually entail nontrivial processing in GPU driver routines.

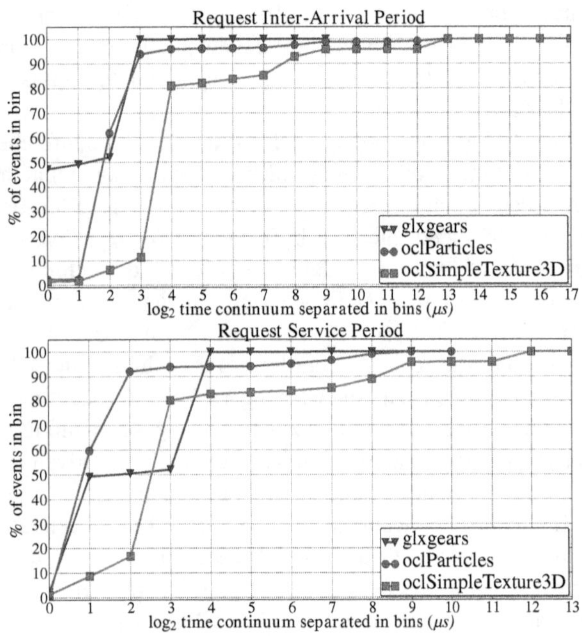


**Figure 2.** CDFs of request frequency and average service times for several applications on an Nvidia GTX670 GPU. A large percentage of arriving requests are short and submitted in short intervals ("back-to-back").

***Overview of schedulers*** Sections 3.1, 3.2, and 3.3 present new request schedulers for fast accelerators that leverage interception to explicitly balance protection, fairness, and efficiency. The *Timeslice* scheduler retains the overhead of per-request kernel intervention, but arranges to share the GPU fairly among unmodified applications. The *Disengaged Timeslice* scheduler extends this design by eliminating kernel intervention in most cases. Both variants allow only one application at a time to use the accelerator. The *Disengaged Fair Queueing* scheduler eliminates this limitation, but provides only statistical guarantees of fairness.

Our disengaged schedulers maintain the high performance of the direct-mapped accelerator interface by limiting kernel involvement to a small number of interactions. In so doing, they rely on information about aspects of the accelerator design that can affect resource usage and accounting accuracy. For the purposes of the current description, we assume the characteristics of an Nvidia GPU, as revealed by reverse engineering and public documentation. We describe how device features affect our prototype design as we encounter them in the algorithm descriptions; we revisit and discuss how future software / hardware developments can influence and be influenced by our design in Section 6.

### 3.1 Timeslice with Overuse Control

To achieve fairness in as simple a manner as possible, we start with a standard token-based timeslice policy. Specifically, a token that indicates permission to access the shared accelerator is passed among the active tasks. Only the current token holder is permitted to submit requests, and all request events (submission, completion) are trapped and communicated to the scheduler. For the sake of throughput, we permit overlapping nonblocking requests from the task that holds the token.

Simply preventing a task from submitting requests outside its timeslice does not suffice for fairness. Imagine, for example, a task that issues a long series of requests, each of which requires 0.9 timeslice to complete. A naive scheduler might allow such a task to issue two requests in each timeslice, and to steal 80% of each subsequent timeslice that belongs to some other task. To avoid this overuse problem, we must, upon the completion of requests that overrun the end of a timeslice, deduct their excess execution time from future timeslices of the submitting task. We account for overuse by waiting at the end of a timeslice for all outstanding requests to complete, and charging the token holder for any excess. When a task's accrued overuse exceeds a full timeslice, we skip the task's next turn to hold the token, and subtract a timeslice from its accrued overuse.

We also need to address the problem that a single long request may monopolize the accelerator for an excessive amount of time, compromising overall system responsiveness. In fact, Turing-complete accelerators, like GPUs, may have to deal with malicious (or poorly written) applications that submit requests that never complete. In a timeslice scheduler, it is trivial to identify the task responsible for an over-long request: it must be the last token holder. Subsequent options for restoring responsiveness then depend on accelerator features.

***From model to prototype*** Ideally, we would like to preempt over-long requests, or define them as errors, kill them on the accelerator, and prevent the source task from sending more. Lacking vendor support for preemption or a documented method to kill a request, we can still protect against over-long requests by killing the offending task, provided this leaves the accelerator in a clean state. Specifically, upon detecting that overuse has exceeded a predefined threshold, we terminate the associated OS process and let the existing accelerator stack follow its normal exit protocol, returning occupied resources back to the available pool. While the involved cleanup depends on (undocumented) accelerator features, it appears to work correctly on modern GPUs.

***Limitations*** Our Timeslice scheduler can guarantee fair resource use in the face of unpredictable (and even unbounded) request run times. It suffers, however, from two efficiency drawbacks. First, its fault-based capture of each submitted request incurs significant overhead on fast accelerators. Second, it is not *work-conserving*: the accelerator may be idled during the timeslice of a task that temporarily has no requests to submit—even if other tasks are waiting for accelerator access. Our *Disengaged Timeslice* scheduler successfully tackles the overhead problem. Our *Disengaged Fair Queueing* scheduler also tackles the problem of involuntary resource idleness.

### 3.2 Disengaged Timeslice

Fortunately, the interception of every request is not required for timeslice scheduling. During a timeslice, direct, unmonitored access from the token holder task can safely be allowed. The OS will trap and delay accesses from all other tasks. When passing the token between tasks, the OS will update page tables to enable or disable direct access. We say such a scheduler is largely *disengaged*; it allows fast, direct access to accelerators most of the time, interceding (and incurring cost) on an infrequent basis only. Note that while requests from all tasks other than the token holder will be trapped and delayed, such tasks will typically stop running as soon as they wait for a blocking request. Large numbers of traps are thus unlikely.

When the scheduler re-engages at the start of a new timeslice, requests from the token holder of the last timeslice may still be pending. To account for overuse, we must again wait for these requests to finish.

***From model to prototype*** Ideally, the accelerator would expose information about the status of request(s) on which it is currently working, in a location accessible to the scheduler. While we strongly suspect that current hardware has the capability to do this, it is not documented, and we have been unable to deduce it via reverse engineering. We have, however, been able to discover the semantics of data structures shared between the user and the GPU [2, 16, 19, 25, 27]. These structures include a reference counter that is written by the hardware upon the completion of each request. Upon re-engaging, we can traverse in-memory structures to find the reference number of the last submitted request, and then poll the reference counter for an indication of its completion. While it is at least conceivable that a malicious application could spoof this mechanism, it suffices for performance testing; we assume that a production-quality scheduler would query the status of the GPU directly.

***Limitations*** Our Disengaged Timeslice scheduler does not suffer from high per-request management costs, but it may still lead to poor utilization when the token holder is unable to keep the accelerator busy. This problem is addressed by the third of our example schedulers.

### 3.3 Disengaged Fair Queueing

Disengaged resource scheduling is a general concept—allow fast, direct device access in the common case; intercede only when necessary to efficiently realize resource management objectives. Beyond Disengaged Timeslice, we also develop a disengaged variant of the classic fair queueing algorithm, which achieves fairness while maintaining work-conserving properties—i.e., it avoids idling the resource when there is pending work to do.

A standard fair queueing scheduler assigns a *start tag* and a *finish tag* to each resource request. These tags serve as surrogates for the request-issuing task's cumulative resource usage before and after the request's execution. Specifically, the start tag is the larger of the current system virtual time (as of request submission) and the finish tag of the most recent previous request by the same task. The finish tag is the start tag plus the expected resource usage of the request. Request dispatch is ordered by each pending request's finish tag [10, 30] or start tag [14, 18, 33]. Multiple requests (potentially from different tasks) may be dispatched to the device at the same time [18, 33]. While giving proportional resource uses to active tasks, a fair queueing scheduler addresses the concern that an inactive task—one that currently has no work to do—might build up its resource credit without bound and then reclaim it in a sudden burst, causing prolonged unresponsiveness to others. To avoid such a scenario, the scheduler advances the system virtual time to reflect only the progress of active tasks. Since the start tag of each submitted request is brought forward to at least the system virtual time, any claim to resources from a task's idle period is forfeited.

***Design*** For the sake of efficiency, our disengaged scheduler avoids intercepting and manipulating most requests. Like other fair queueing schedulers, however, it does track cumulative per-task resource usage and system-wide virtual time. In the absence of per-request control, we replace the request start/finish tags in standard fair queueing with a probabilistically-updated per-task virtual time that closely approximates the task's cumulative resource usage. Time values are updated using statistics obtained through periodic engagement. Control is similarly coarse grain: the interfaces of tasks that are running ahead in resource usage may be disabled for the interval between consecutive engagements, to allow their peers to catch up. Requests from all other tasks are allowed to run freely in the disengaged time interval.

Conceptually, our design assumes that at each engagement we can acquire knowledge of each task's active/idle status and its resource usage in the previous time interval. Actions then taken at each engagement are as follows:

1. We advance each active task's virtual time by adding its resource use in the last interval. We then advance the system-wide virtual time to be the oldest virtual time among the active tasks.
2. If an inactive task's virtual time is behind the system virtual time, we move it forward to the system virtual time. As in standard fair queueing, this prevents an inactive task from hoarding unused resources.
3. For the subsequent time interval, up to the next engagement, we deny access to any tasks whose virtual time is ahead of the system virtual time by at least the length of the interval. That is, even if the slowest active task acquires exclusive resource use in the upcoming interval, it will at best catch up with the tasks whose access is being denied.

Compared to standard fair queueing, which captures and controls each request, our statistics maintenance and control are both coarse grained. Imbalance will be remedied only

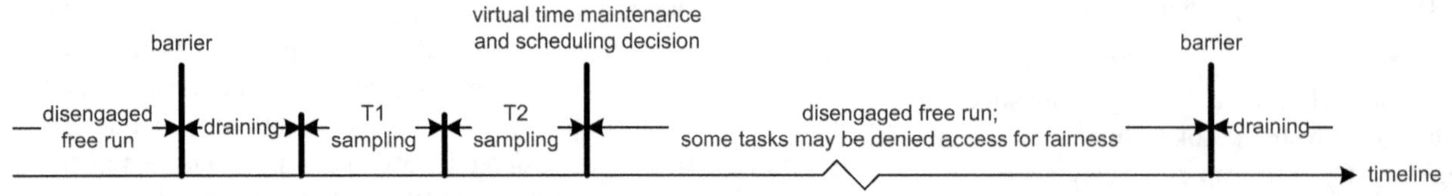


**Figure 3.** An illustration of periodic activities in Disengaged Fair Queueing. An engagement episode starts with a barrier and the draining of outstanding requests on the GPU, which is followed by the short sampling runs of active tasks (two tasks $T_1$ and $T_2$ in the case), virtual time maintenance and scheduling decision, and finally a longer disengaged free-run period.

when it exceeds the size of the inter-engagement interval. Furthermore, the correctness of our approach depends on accurate statistics gathering, which can be challenging in the absence of hardware assistance. We discuss this issue next.

***From model to prototype*** Ideally, an accelerator would maintain and export the statistics needed for Disengaged Fair Queueing, in a location accessible to the scheduler. It could, for example, maintain cumulative resource usage for each task, together with an indication of which task(s) have requests pending and active. Lacking such hardware assistance, we have developed a software mechanism to estimate the required statistics. In general, accelerators (like our GPU) accept processing requests through independent queues mapped in each task's address space, cycling round-robin among queues with pending requests and processing each request separately, one after the other. Most times, there is (or can be assumed) a one-to-one mapping between tasks and queues, so the resource share attributed to each task in a given time interval is proportional to the average request run-time experienced from its requests queue. The design of our software mechanism relies on this observation. To obtain the necessary estimates, we cycle among tasks during a period of re-engagement, providing each with exclusive access to the accelerator for a brief interval of time and actively monitoring all of its requests. This interval is not necessarily of fixed duration: we collect either a predefined number of requests deemed sufficient for average estimation, or as many requests as can be observed in a predefined maximum interval length—whichever occurs first. As in the timeslice schedulers, we place a (documented) limit on the maximum time that any request is permitted to run, and kill any task that exceeds this limit.

Figure 3 illustrates key activities in Disengaged Fair Queueing. Prior to sampling, a barrier stops new request submission in every task, and then allows the accelerator to drain active requests. (For this we employ the same reference-counter-based mechanism used to detect overuse at the end of a timeslice in Section 3.2.) After sampling, we disengage for another free-run period. Blocking new requests while draining is free, since the device is known to be busy. Draining completes immediately if the device is found not to be working on queued requests at the barrier.

Because an engagement period includes a sampling run for every active task, its aggregate duration can be non-negligible. The disengaged free-run period has to be substantially longer to limit the draining and sampling cost. To ensure this, we set the free-run period to be several times the duration of the last engagement period.

***Limitations*** The request-size estimate developed during the sampling period of Disengaged Fair Queueing acts as a resource-utilization proxy for the whole task's free-run period. In the common case, this heuristic is accurate, as accelerated applications tend to employ a single request queue and the GPU appears to schedule among queues with outstanding requests in a round-robin fashion. It is possible, however, to have applications that not only maintain multiple queues (e.g. separate compute and graphics rendering queues), but also keep only some of them active (i.e. holding outstanding requests) at certain times. When at least one task among co-runners behaves this way, estimating the average request size on every queue might not be enough for accurate task scheduling. In principle, better estimates might be based on more detailed reverse engineering of the GPU's internal scheduling algorithm. For now, we are content to assume that each task employs a single queue, in the hope that production systems will have access to statistics that eliminate the need for estimation.

Our estimation mechanism also assumes that observed task behavior during an engagement interval reflects behavior in the previous disengaged free-run. However, this estimate can be imprecise, resulting in imperfect fairness. One potential problem is that periodic behavior patterns—rather than overall task behavior—might be sampled. The non-fixed sampling period run time introduces a degree of randomness in the sampling frequency and duration, but further randomizing these parameters would increase confidence in our ability to thwart any attempt by a malicious application to subvert the scheduling policy. If the disengaged free-run period is considered to be too long (e.g., because it dilates the potential time required to identify and kill an infinite-loop request), we could shorten it by sampling only a subset of the active tasks in each engagement-disengagement cycle.

Our implementation of the Disengaged Fair Queueing scheduler comes very close to the work-conserving goal of not idling the resource when there is pending work to do. Specifically, it allows multiple tasks to issue requests in the dominant free-run periods. While exclusive access is enforced during sampling intervals, these intervals are bounded, and apply only to tasks that have issued requests in the preceding free-run period; we do not waste sampling time on idle tasks. Moreover, sampling is only required in the absence of true hardware statistics, which we have already argued that vendors could provide.

The more serious obstacle to true work conservation is the possibility that all tasks that are granted access during a disengaged period will, by sheer coincidence, become simultaneously idle, while tasks that were not granted access (because they had been using more than their share of accumulated time) still have work to do. Since our algorithm can be effective in limiting idleness, even in the presence of "selfish," if not outright malicious applications, and on the assumption that troublesome scenarios will be rare and difficult to exploit, the degree to which our Disengaged Fair Queueing scheduler falls short of being fully work conserving seems likely to be small.

## 4. Prototype Implementation

Our prototype of interception-based OS-level GPU scheduling, which we call NEON, is built on the Linux 3.4.7 kernel. It comprises an autonomous kernel module supporting our request management and scheduling mechanisms (about 8000 lines of code); the necessary Linux kernel hooks (to `ioctl`, `mmap`, `munmap`, `copy_task`, `exit_task`, and `do_page_fault`—less than 100 lines); kernel-resident control structs (about 500 lines); and a few hooks to the Nvidia driver's binary interface (initialization, `ioctl`, `mmap` requests). Some of the latter hooks reside in the driver's binary-wrapper code (less than 100 lines); others, for licensing reasons, are inside the Linux kernel (about 500 lines).

Our request management code embodies a state-machine model of interaction among the user application, driver, and device [25], together with a detailed understanding of the structure and semantics of buffers shared between the application and device. Needed information was obtained through a combination of publicly available documentation and reverse engineering [2, 16, 19, 25, 27].

From a functional perspective, NEON comprises three principal components: an initialization phase, used to identify the virtual memory areas of all memory-mapped device registers and buffers associated with a given *channel* (a GPU request queue and its associated software infrastructure); a page-fault–handling mechanism, used to catch the device register writes that constitute request submission; and a polling-thread service, used within the kernel to detect reference-counter updates that indicate completion of previously submitted requests. The page-fault–handling mechanism and polling-thread service together define a kernel-internal interface through which any event-based scheduler can be coupled to our system.

The goal of the initialization phase is to identify the device, task, and GPU *context* (address space) associated with every channel, together with the location of three key virtual memory areas (VMAs). The GPU context encapsulates channels whose requests may be causally related (e.g., issued by the same process); NEON avoids deadlocks by avoiding re-ordering of requests that belong to the same context. The three VMAs contain the *command buffer*, in which requests are constructed; the *ring buffer*, in which pointers to consecutive requests are enqueued; and the *channel register*, the device register through which user-level libraries notify the GPU of ring buffer updates, which represent new requests. As soon as the NEON state machine has identified all three of these VMAs, it marks the channel as "active"—ready to access the channel registers and issue requests to the GPU.

During engagement periods, the page-fault–handling mechanism catches the submission of requests. Having identified the page in which the channel register is mapped, we protect its page by marking it as non-present. At the time of a fault, we scan through the buffers associated with the channel to find the location of the reference counter that will be used for the request, and the value that will indicate its completion. We then map the location into kernel space, making it available to the polling-thread service. The page-fault handler runs in process context, so it can pass control to the GPU scheduler, which then decides whether the current process should sleep or be allowed to continue and access the GPU. After the application is allowed to proceed, we single-step through the faulting instruction and mark the page again as "non-present."

Periodically, or at the scheduler's prompt, the polling-thread service iterates over the kernel-resident structures associated with active GPU requests, looking for the address/value pairs that indicate request completion. When an appropriate value is found—i.e., when the last submitted command's target reference value is read at the respective polled address—the scheduler is invoked to update accounting information and to block or unblock application threads as appropriate.

The page-fault–handling mechanism allows us to capture and, if desired, delay request submission. The polling-thread service allows us to detect request completion and, if desired, resume threads that were previously delayed. These request interception and completion notification mechanisms support the implementation of all our schedulers.

Disengagement is implemented by letting the scheduling policy choose if and when it should restore protection on channel register VMAs. A barrier requires that all the channel registers in use on the GPU be actively tracked for new requests—thus their respective pages must be marked "non-present." It is not possible to miss out on newly established channel mappings while disengaged: all requests to establish such a mapping are captured as syscalls or invocations of kernel-exposed functions that we monitor.

Though higher level API calls may be processed out of order, requests arriving at the same channel are always processed in order by the GPU. We rely on this fact in our post–re-engagement status update mechanism, to identify the current status of the last submitted request. Specifically, we inspect the values of reference counters and the reference number values for the last submitted request in every active channel. Kernel mappings have been created upon first encounter for the former, but the latter do not lie at fixed addresses in the application's address space. To access them safely, we scan through the command queue to identify their locations and build temporary memory mappings in the kernel's address space. Then, by walking the page table, we can find and read the last submitted commands' reference values.

## 5. Experimental Evaluation

NEON is modularized to accommodate different devices; we have deployed it on several Nvidia GPUs. The most recent is a GTX670, with a "Kepler" microarchitecture (GK104 chip core) and 2 GB RAM. Older tested systems include the GTX275 and NVS295, with the "Tesla" microarchitecture (200b and G98 chip cores, respectively), and the GTX460, with the "Fermi" microarchitecture (F104 chip core). We limit our presentation here to the Kepler GPU, as its modern software / hardware interface (faster context switching among channels, faster memory subsystem) lets us focus on the cost of scheduling small, frequent requests. Our host machine has a 2.27 GHz Intel Xeon E5520 CPU (Nehalem microarchitecture) and triple-channel 1.066 GHz DDR3 RAM.

### 5.1 Experimental Workload

NEON is agnostic with respect to the type of workload: it can schedule compute or graphics requests, or even DMA requests. The performance evaluation in this paper includes compute, graphics, and combined (CUDA or OpenCL plus OpenGL) applications, but is primarily focused on compute requests—they are easy to understand, are a good proxy for broad accelerator workloads, and can capture generic, possibly unbounded requests. Our experiments employ the Nvidia 310.14 driver and CUDA 5.0 libraries, which support acceleration for OpenCL 1.1 and OpenGL 4.2.

Our intent is to focus on behavior appropriate to emerging platforms with on-chip GPUs [7, 9, 24]. Whereas the criss-crossing delays of discrete systems encourage programmers to create massive compute requests, and to pipeline smaller graphics requests asynchronously, systems with on-chip accelerators can be expected to accommodate applications with smaller, more interactive requests, yielding significant improvements in flexibility, programmability, and resource utilization. Of course, CPU-GPU integration also increases the importance of direct device access from user space [3], and thus of disengaged scheduling. In an attempt to capture these trends, we have deliberately chosen benchmarks with relatively small requests.

Our OpenCL applications are from the AMD APP SDK v2.6, with no modifications except for the use of high-resolution x86 timers to collect performance results. In addition to GPU computation, most of these applications also contain some setup and data transfer time. They generally make repetitive (looping) requests to the GPU of roughly similar size. We select inputs that are meaningful and non-trivial (hundreds or thousands of elements in arrays, matrices or lists) but do not lead to executions dominated by data transfer.

| Application | Area | $\mu s$ per round | $\mu s$ per request |
|---|---|---|---|
| BinarySearch | Searching | 161 | 57 |
| BitonicSort | Sorting | 1292 | 202 |
| DCT | Compression | 197 | 66 |
| EigenValue | Algebra | 163 | 56 |
| FastWalshTransform | Encryption | 310 | 119 |
| FFT | Signal Processing | 268 | 48 |
| FloydWarshall | Graph Analysis | 5631 | 141 |
| LUDecomposition | Algebra | 1490 | 308 |
| MatrixMulDouble | Algebra | 12628 | 637 |
| MatrixMultiplication | Algebra | 3788 | 436 |
| MatrixTranspose | Algebra | 1153 | 284 |
| PrefixSum | Data Processing | 157 | 55 |
| RadixSort | Sorting | 8082 | 210 |
| Reduction | Data Processing | 1147 | 282 |
| ScanLargeArrays | Data Processing | 197 | 72 |
| glxgears | Graphics | 72 | 37 |
| oclParticles | Physics/Graphics | 2006 | 12/302 |
| simpleTexture3D | Texturing/Graphics | 2472 | 108/171 |

**Table 1.** Benchmarks used in our evaluation. A "round" is the performance unit of interest to the user: the run time of compute "kernel(s)" for OpenCL applications, or that of a frame rendering for graphics or combined applications. A round can require multiple GPU acceleration requests.

Our OpenGL application (glxgears) is a standard graphics microbenchmark, chosen for its simplicity and its frequent short acceleration requests. We also chose a combined compute/graphics (OpenCL plus OpenGL) microbenchmark from Nvidia's SDK v4.0.8: oclParticles, a particles collision physics simulation. Synchronization to the monitor refresh rates is disabled for our experiments, both at the driver and the application level, and the performance metric used is the raw, average frame rate: our intent is to stress the system interface more than the GPU processing capabilities.

Table 1 summarizes our benchmarks and their characteristics. The last two columns list how long an execution of a "round" of computations or rendering takes for each application, and the average acceleration request size realized when the application runs alone using our Kepler GPU. A "round" in the OpenCL applications is generally the execution of one iteration of the main loop of the algorithm, including one or more "compute kernel(s)." For OpenGL applications, it is the work to render one frame. The run time of a round indicates performance from the user's perspective; we use it to quantify speedup or slowdown from the perspective of a given application across different workloads (job mixes) or using different schedulers. A "request" is the basic unit of work that is submitted to the GPU at the device interface. We capture the average request size for each application through our request interception mechanism (but without applying any scheduling policy). We have verified that our GPU request size estimation agrees, within of 5% or less, to the time reported by standard profiling tools. Combined compute/graphics applications report two average request sizes, one per request type. Note that requests are not necessarily meaningful to the application or user, but they are the focal point of our OS-level GPU schedulers. There is no necessary correlation between the API calls and GPU requests in a compute/rendering round. Many GPU-library API calls do not translate to GPU requests, while other calls could translate to more than one. Moreover, as revealed in the course of reverse engineering, there also exist trivial requests, perhaps to change mode/state, that arrive at the GPU and are never checked for completion. NEON schedules requests without regard to their higher-level purpose.

To enable flexible adjustment of workload parameters, we also developed a "Throttle" microbenchmark. Throttle serves as a controlled means of measuring basic system overheads, and as a well-understood competitive sharer in multiprogrammed scenarios. It makes repetitive, blocking compute requests, which occupy the GPU for a user-specified amount of time. We can also control idle (sleep/think) time between requests, to simulate nonsaturating workloads. No data transfers between the host and the device occur during throttle execution; with the exception of a small amount of initial setup, only compute requests are sent to the device.

### 5.2 Overhead of Standalone Execution

NEON routines are invoked during context creation, to mark the memory areas to be protected; upon every tracked request (depending on scheduling policy), to handle the induced page fault; and at context exit, to safely return allocated system resources. In addition, we arrange for timer interrupts to trigger execution of the polling service thread, schedule the next task on the GPU (and perhaps dis/re-engage) for the Timeslice algorithm, and sample the next task or begin a free-run period for the Disengaged Fair Queueing scheduler.

We measure the overhead of each scheduler by comparing standalone application performance under that scheduler against the performance of direct device access. Results appear in Figure 4. For this experiment, and the rest of the evaluation, we chose the following configuration parameters: For all algorithms, the polling service thread is woken up when the scheduler decides, or at 1 ms intervals. The (engaged) Timeslice and Disengaged Timeslice use a 30 ms timeslice. For Disengaged Fair Queueing, a task's sampling period lasts either 5 ms or as much as is required to intercept a fixed number of requests, whichever is smaller. The follow-up free-run period is set to be 5× as long, so in the

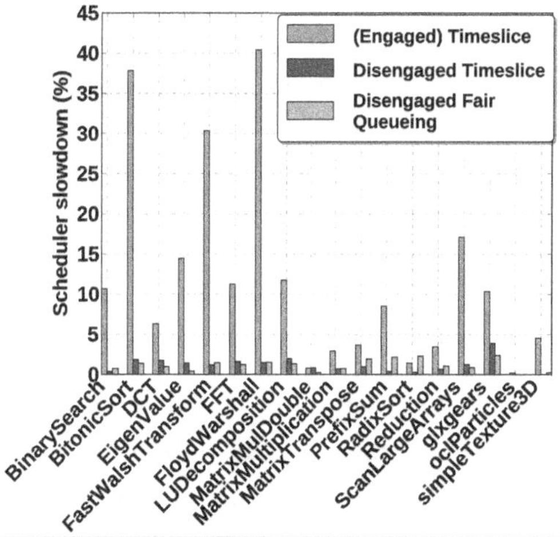


**Figure 4.** Standalone application execution slowdown under our scheduling policies compared to direct device access.

standalone application case it should be 25 ms (even if the fixed request number mark was hit before the end of 5 ms).

NEON is not particularly sensitive to configuration parameters. We tested different settings, but found the above to be sufficient. The polling thread frequency is fast enough for the average request size, but not enough to impose a noticeable load even for single-CPU systems. A 30 ms timeslice is long enough to minimize the cost of token passing, but not long enough to immediately introduce jitter in more interactive applications, which follow the "100 ms human perception" rule. For most of the workloads we tested, including applications with a graphics rendering component, 5 ms or 32 requests is enough to capture variability in request size and frequency during sampling. We increase this number to 96 requests for combined compute/graphics applications, to capture the full variability in request sizes. Though real-time rendering quality is not our goal, testing is easier when graphics applications remain responsive as designed; in our experience, the chosen configuration parameters preserved fluid behavior and stable measurements across all tested inputs.

As shown in Figure 4, the (engaged) Timeslice scheduler incurs low cost for applications with large requests—most notably MatrixMulDouble and oclParticles. Note, however, that in the latter application, the performance metric is frame rendering times, which are generally the result of longer non-blocking graphics requests. The cost of (engaged) Timeslice is significant for small-request applications (in particular, 38% slowdown for BitonicSort, 30% for FastWalshTransform, and 40% FloydWarshall). This is due to the large request interception and manipulation overhead imposed on all requests. Disengaged Timeslice suffers only the post re-engagement status update costs and the infrequent trapping to the kernel at the edges of the timeslice, which is generally no more than 2%. Similarly, Disengaged Fair Queueing incurs costs only on a small subset of GPU requests; its overhead is no more than 5% for all our appli-

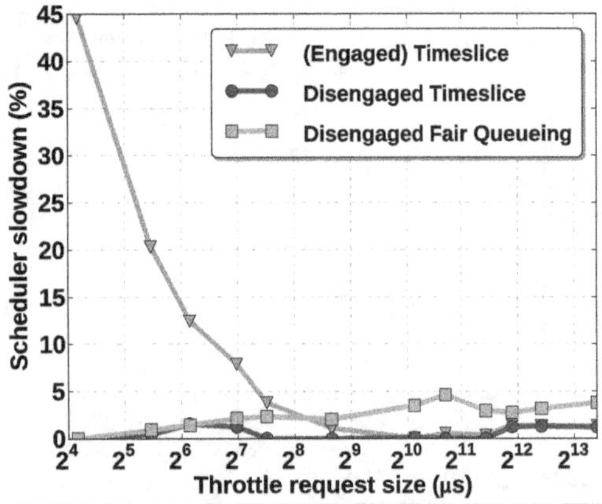


**Figure 5.** Standalone Throttle execution (at a range of request sizes) slowdown under our scheduling policies compared to direct device access.

cations. The principal source of extra overhead is idleness during draining, due to the granularity of polling.

Using the controlled Throttle microbenchmark, Figure 5 reports the scheduling overhead variation at different request sizes. It confirms that the (engaged) Timeslice scheduler incurs high costs for small-request applications, while Disengaged Timeslice incurs no more than 2% and Disengaged Fair Queueing no more than 5% overhead in all cases.

### 5.3 Evaluation on Concurrent Executions

To evaluate scheduling fairness and efficiency, we measure the slowdown exhibited in multiprogrammed scenarios, relative to the performance attained when applications have full, unobstructed access to the device. We first evaluate concurrent execution between two co-running applications—one of our benchmarks together with the Throttle microbenchmark at a controlled request size. The configuration parameters in this experiment are the same as for the overheads test, resulting in 50 ms "free-run" periods.

***Fairness*** Figure 6 shows the fairness of our concurrent executions under different schedulers. The normalized run time in the direct device access scenario shows significantly unfair access to the GPU. The effect can be seen on both co-runners: a large-request-size Throttle workload leads to large slowdown of some applications (more than 10× for DCT, 7× for FFT, 12× for glxgears), while a smaller request size Throttle can suffer significant slowdown against other applications (more than 3× for DCT and 7× for FFT). The high-level explanation is simple—on accelerators that issue requests round-robin from different channels, the one with larger requests will receive a proportionally larger share of device time. In comparison, our schedulers achieve much more even results—in general, each co-scheduled task experiences the expected 2× slowdown. More detailed discussion of variations appears in the paragraphs below.

There appears to be a slightly uneven slowdown exhibited by the (engaged) Timeslice scheduler for smaller Throttle request sizes. For example, for DCT or FFT, the slowdown of Throttle appears to range from 2× to almost 3×. This variation is due to per-request management costs. Throttle, being our streamlined control microbenchmark, makes back-to-back compute requests to the GPU, with little to no CPU processing time between the calls. At a given request size, most of its co-runners generate fewer requests per timeslice. Since (engaged) Timeslice imposes overhead on every request, the aggressive Throttle microbenchmark tends to suffer more. By contrast, Disengaged Timeslice does not apply this overhead and thus maintains an almost uniform 2× slowdown for each co-runner and for every Throttle request size.

A significant anomaly appears when we run the OpenGL glxgears graphics application vs. Throttle (19 μs) under Disengaged Fair Queueing, where glxgears suffers a significantly higher slowdown than Throttle does. A closer inspection shows that glxgears requests complete at almost one third the rate that Throttle (19 μs) requests do during the free-run period. This behavior appears to contradict our (simplistic) assumption of round-robin channel cycling during the Disengaged Fair Queueing free-run period. Interestingly, the disparity in completion rates goes down with larger Throttle requests: Disengaged Fair Queueing appears to produce fair resource utilization between glxgears and Throttle with larger requests. In general, the internal scheduling of our Nvidia device appears to be more uniform for OpenCL than for graphics applications. As noted in the "Limitations" paragraph of Section 3.3, a production-quality implementation of our Disengaged Fair Queueing scheduler should ideally be based on vendor documentation of device-internal scheduling or resource usage statistics.

Finally, we note that combined compute/graphics applications, such as oclParticles and simpleTexture3D, tend to create separate channels for their different types of requests. For multiprogrammed workloads with multiple channels per task, the limitations of imprecise understanding of internal GPU scheduling are even more evident than they were for glxgears: not only do requests arrive on two channels, but also for some duration of time requests may be outstanding in one channel but not on the other. As a result, even if the GPU did cycle round-robin among active channels, the resource distribution among competitors might not follow their active channel ratio, but could change over time. In a workload with compute/graphics applications, our request-size estimate across the two (or more) channels of every task becomes an invalid proxy of resource usage during free-run periods and unfairness arises: in the final row of Figure 6, Throttle suffers a 2.3× to 2.7× slowdown, while oclParticles sees 1.3× to 1.5×. Completely fair scheduling with Disengaged Fair Queueing would again require accurate, vendor-provided information that our reverse-engineering effort in building this prototype was unable to provide.

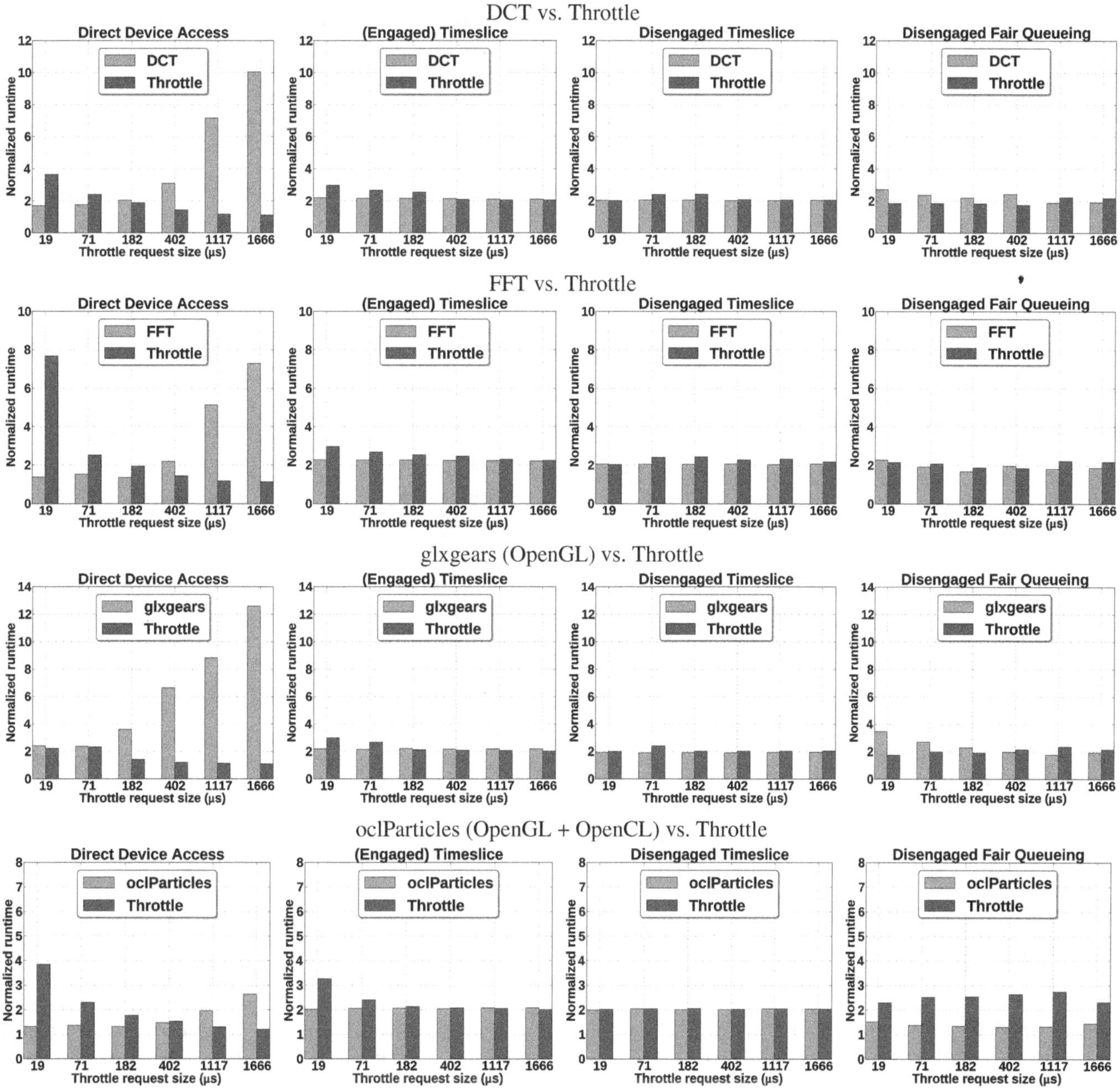


**Figure 6.** Performance and fairness of concurrent executions. Results cover four application-pair executions (one per row) and four schedulers (one per column). We use several variations of Throttle with different request sizes (from 19 $\mu$s to 1.7 ms). The application runtime is normalized to that when it runs alone with direct device access.

***Efficiency*** In addition to fairness, we also assess the overall system efficiency of multiprogrammed workloads. Here we utilize a *concurrency efficiency* metric that measures the performance of the concurrent execution relative to that of the applications running alone. We assign a base efficiency of 1.0 to each application's running-alone performance (in the absence of resource competition). We then assess the performance of a concurrent execution relative to this base. Given $N$ concurrent OpenCL applications whose per-round run times are $t_1, t_2, ..., t_N$ respectively when running alone on the GPU, and $t_1^c, t_2^c, ..., t_N^c$ when running together, the concurrency efficiency is defined as $\Sigma_{i=1}^{N}(t_i/t_i^c)$. The intent of the formula is to sum the resource shares allotted to each application. A sum of less than one indicates that resources have been lost; a sum of more than one indicates mutual synergy (e.g., due to overlapped computation).

Figure 7 reports the concurrency efficiency of direct device access and our three fair schedulers. It might at first be surprising that the concurrency efficiency of direct device access deviates from 1.0. For small requests, the GPU may fre-

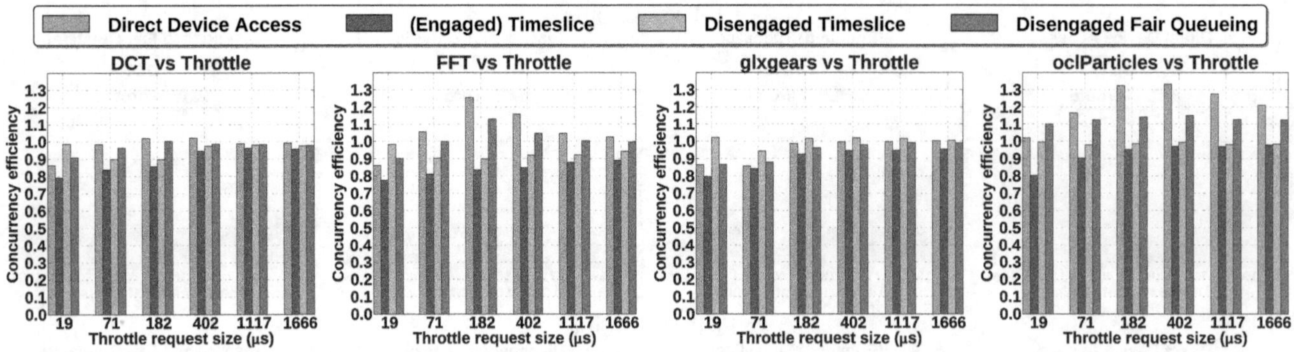


**Figure 7.** Efficiency of concurrent executions. The metric of concurrency efficiency is defined in the text.

quently switch between multiple application contexts, leading to substantial context switch costs and <1.0 concurrency efficiency. Conversely, the efficiency of direct device access may also be larger than 1.0, due to overlap between DMA and compute requests.

For its part, the (engaged) Timeslice scheduler incurs high request management costs. Its efficiency losses with respect to direct device access can be on average 19% or as high as 42%; specifically, average/max efficiency losses are 10%/16% (DCT vs. Throttle), 27/42% (FFT vs. Throttle), 5%/6% (glxgears vs. Throttle) and 35/37% (oclParticles vs. Throttle).

Disengaged Timeslice adds little per-request overhead while also limiting channel switching on the GPU, so it enjoys some efficiency advantage over (engaged) Timeslice: average/max losses with respect to direct device access are 10%/35% (3%/12%, 16%/35%, −5%/0%, and 27%/33% per respective test).

Overall, Disengaged Fair Queueing does a better job at allowing "background concurrency": its average/max losses with respect to direct device access are only 4%/18% (0%/3%, 6%/12%, 0%/2% and 11%/18% per respective test). Unfortunately, our incomplete understanding of GPU internal scheduling limits our achievable efficiency, as the imprecise slowdown applied for applications with multiple channels results in wasted opportunities for Disengaged Fair Queueing. This is why oclParticles exhibits the worst efficiency loss among the tested cases.

***Scalability*** The performance, fairness, and efficiency characteristics of our schedulers are maintained under higher concurrency. Figure 8 shows that for four concurrent applications, including one making large requests (Throttle) and three making smaller ones (BinarySearch, DCT, FFT), the average slowdown remains at 4–5×. Following the pattern we have observed before, the efficiency of concurrent runs drops more when the scheduler is fully engaged (13% over direct device access), but less so when we use disengaged scheduling: 8% for Disengaged Timeslice and 7% for Disengaged Fair Queueing.

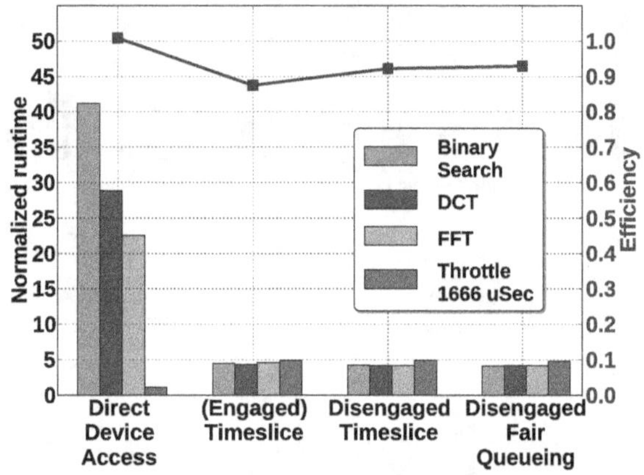


**Figure 8.** Fairness (bars, left Y axis) and efficiency (line, right Y axis) when running four concurrent applications.

### 5.4 Evaluation on Nonsaturating Workloads

Next we assess our scheduler performance under nonsaturating workloads—those that interleave GPU requests with "off" periods of CPU-only work. Nonsaturating workloads lead to GPU under-utilization with non-work-conserving schedulers. In timeslice scheduling, for instance, resources are wasted if a timeslice is only used partially. As explained in Section 3.3, Disengaged Fair Queueing maintains work-conserving properties, and therefore wastes less time on nonsaturating workloads. Direct device access, of course, is fully work-conserving.

To create nonsaturating workloads, we interleave sleep time in our Throttle microbenchmark to reach a specified ratio (the proportion of "off" time under standalone execution). Figure 9 illustrates the results for DCT and the nonsaturating Throttle workload. Note that fairness does not necessarily require co-runners to suffer equally: execution is fair as long as no task slows down significantly more than 2×. The results for Disengaged Fair Queueing should thus be regarded as better than those for the timeslice schedulers, because Throttle does not suffer, while DCT actually benefits from its co-runner's partial idleness. Figure 10 further shows the efficiency losses for our three schedulers and direct device access. At an 80% Throttle sleep ratio, the losses

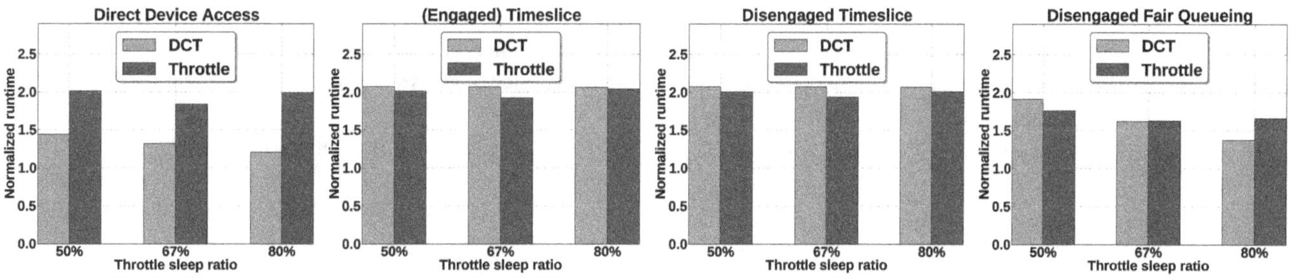


**Figure 9.** Performance and fairness of concurrent executions for nonsaturating workloads, demonstrated for DCT vs. Throttle with GPU "off" periods.

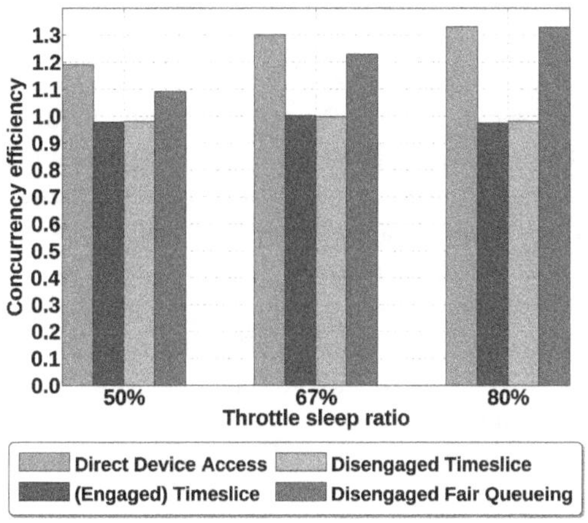


**Figure 10.** Efficiency of concurrent executions for nonsaturating workloads.

relative to direct access are 36%, 34%, and essentially 0% for (engaged) Timeslice, Disengaged Timeslice, and Disengaged Fair Queueing, respectively.

## 6. Future System Considerations

### 6.1 Interface Specification

Protected OS-level accelerator management requires relatively little information: an event-based scheduling interface that allows us to identify when acceleration requests have been made or completed, utilization information that allows us to account for per-channel resource usage, and sufficient semantic understanding of requests to avoid deadlocks and any unnecessary resource idleness.

Both standard interfaces (system calls) and alternative approaches (virtual memory) can capture request submission and completion. We believe that the increasing integration of CPUs and accelerators will only increase the need for fast, memory-based interfaces. By documenting basic information regarding the layout of accelerator request queues and core component interactions, and by exposing necessary performance counters to obtain accurate utilization statistics, vendors could enable OS kernel involvement in accelerator scheduling without high overheads, enabling full protection and efficiency through disengaged scheduling. Vendor assistance at this level is necessary, as systems like NEON, relying on reverse engineering and inference techniques, cannot reach production-level quality.

A "partial opening" of interface specifications, as envisioned here, would still allow vendors to retain proprietary control over much of the accelerator software / hardware system. For instance, while a request submission event needs to be identifiable for manipulation, much of the data layout and semantics within a request data structure can remain unpublished. On the other hand, in order to enable deep scheduling optimizations, vendors would have to reveal request-ordering semantics and synchronization models. For our work with NEON we assumed no request reordering within GPU contexts, an assumption that flows naturally from the semantics of the context concept. For a higher degree of optimizations (e.g., reordering of requests across CUDA streams [28]), vendors could tag requests to indicate the requirements to be met.

A hardware accelerator may accept multiple requests simultaneously to exploit internal parallelism or to optimize for data affinity. The OS desires additional information to manage such parallelism. Most obviously, completion events need to carry labels that link them to the corresponding requests. For NEON, the task, context, channel, and request reference number have served as surrogate labels. More subtly, under concurrent submission, an outstanding request may be queued in the device, so that the time between submission and completion does not accurately reflect its resource usage. The hardware can facilitate OS accounting by including resource usage information in each completion event.

Direct accelerator access from other (e.g., I/O) devices is currently limited to DMA (e.g., RDMA for GPUDirect in the CUDA SDK [28]). Applications and services using the GPU and I/O devices will still initiate DMA and compute requests through the same memory-mapped interface, and thus be amenable to scheduling. Appropriate specifications for any alternative, peer-to-peer communication path to the accelerator would be necessary if devices other than the CPU were to enjoy rich, direct accelerator interactions.

### 6.2 Hardware Preemption Support

The reverse-engineering efforts of the open-source community [27, 31] suggest that some type of request arbitration is possible for current GPUs, but true hardware preemption is officially still among the list of upcoming GPU features (e.g., in the roadmap of AMD HSA [24]). In its absence, tricks, like cutting longer requests into smaller pieces, have been shown to enhance GPU interactivity, at least for mutually cooperative applications [6]. True hardware preemption support would save state and safely context-switch from an ongoing request to the next in the GPU queue. If the preemption decision were left to a hardware scheduler, it would be fast but oblivious to system scheduling objectives. Disengaged scheduling can help make context-switching decisions appropriately coarse grain, so they can be deferred to the OS. Simple documentation of existing mechanisms to identify and kill the currently running context would enable full protection for schedulers like Disengaged Fair Queueing. True hardware preemption would allow us to tolerate requests of arbitrary length, without sacrificing interactivity or becoming vulnerable to infinite loops.

### 6.3 Protection of Other Resources

Beyond the scheduling of cycles, OS-level protection can enforce the safe use of other GPU resources, such as channels and memory, to prevent unfair or abusive behavior. Channels establish a user-mapped address range through which commands are submitted to the hardware. Existing GPUs do not multiplex requests from different tasks on a channel; instead, an established channel is held by the task that created it (and its associated context) for as long as the application deems necessary. It is thus possible to devise a simple denial-of-service attack by creating many contexts and occupying all available GPU channels, thus denying subsequent requests from other applications; on our Nvidia GTX670 GPU, after 48 contexts had been created (with one compute and one DMA channel each), no other application could use the GPU.

An OS-level resource manager may enable protected allocation of GPU channels to avoid such DoS attacks. We describe a possible policy below. First, we limit the number of channels in any one application to a small constant $C$, chosen to match the characteristics of anticipated applications. Attempts to allocate more than $C$ channels return an "out of resources" error. Second, with a total of $D$ channels available on the GPU, we permit no more than $D/C$ applications to use the GPU at any given time. More elaborate policies, involving prioritization, preemption, etc., could be added when appropriate.

Our GTX670 GPU has 2 GB of onboard RAM that is shared by active tasks. This memory is managed with the help of the system's virtual memory manager and the IOMMU, providing already sufficient isolation among tasks. It is conceivable that an erroneous or malicious application might exhaust the GPU memory and prevent normal use by others. In theory, our OS-level protection framework could prevent such abuses by accounting for application uses of GPU memory and blocking excessive consumption. This, however, requires uncovering additional GPU semantics on memory buffer management that we have not yet explored.

## 7. Conclusion

This paper has presented a framework for fair, safe, and efficient OS-level management of GPU resources—and, by extension, of other fast computational accelerators. We believe our request interception mechanism, combined with disengagement, to be the first resource management technique capable of approaching the performance of direct device access from user space. Our Timeslice scheduler with overuse control can guarantee fairness during multiprogrammed executions. Its disengaged variant improves performance without sacrificing either fairness or protection, by intercepting only a small subset of requests, allowing most to reach the device directly. Our Disengaged Fair Queueing scheduler is effective at limiting idleness, and incurs only 4% average overhead (max 18%) relative to direct device access across our evaluation cases.

While our prototype Disengaged Fair Queueing scheduler ensures fairness between multiple compute (OpenCL) applications, its fairness support is less than ideal for graphics (OpenGL)-related applications. This is due to our insufficient understanding of the device-internal scheduling of concurrent graphics/compute requests during free-run periods; a production-quality implementation based on vendor-supplied information would not suffer from this limitation. Even in our prototype, the limitation does not affect the fairness of our Disengaged Timeslice scheduler, which grants GPU access to no more than one application at a time.

We have identified necessary and/or desirable hardware features to support disengaged resource management, including the ability to identify the currently running GPU request, to account for per-context resource usage during disengaged execution, to cleanly terminate an aberrant context, and (ideally) to suspend and resume requests. For the purposes of prototype construction, we have identified surrogates for some of these features via reverse engineering. We encourage device vendors to embrace a limited "opening" of the hardware-software interface specification sufficient for production use.

## Acknowledgments

This work was supported in part by the National Science Foundation under grants CCF-0937571, CCR-0963759, CCF-1116055, CNS-1116109, CNS-1217372, CNS-1239423, CCF-1255729, and CNS-1319417. Our thanks as well to Shinpei Kato and the anonymous reviewers, for comments that helped to improve this paper.

## References


[1] Altera. www.altera.com.

[2] AMD. Radeon R5xx Acceleration: v1.2, Feb. 2008.

[3] AMD's revolutionary Mantle. http://www.amd.com/us/products/technologies/mantle.

[4] ARM graphics plus GPU compute. www.arm.com/products/multimedia/mali-graphics-plus-gpu-compute.

[5] M. Aron and P. Druschel. Soft timers: Efficient microsecond software timer support for network processing. *ACM Trans. on Computer Systems*, 18(3):197–228, Aug. 2000.

[6] C. Basaran and K.-D. Kang. Supporting preemptive task executions and memory copies in gpgpus. In *Real-Time Systems (ECRTS), 2012 24th Euromicro Conference on*, pages 287–296. IEEE, 2012.

[7] N. Brookwood. AMD Fusion™ family of APUs. AMD White Paper, Mar. 2010.

[8] C. Cascaval, S. Chatterjee, H. Franke, K. Gildea, and P. Pattnaik. A taxonomy of accelerator architectures and their programming models. *IBM Journal of Research and Development*, 54(5):5–1, 2010.

[9] M. Daga, A. M. Aji, and W.-C. Feng. On the efficacy of a fused CPU+GPU processor (or APU) for parallel computing. In *Proc. of the 2011 Symp. on Application Accelerators in High-Performance Computing*, Knoxville, TN, July 2011.

[10] A. Demers, S. Keshav, and S. Shenker. Analysis and simulation of a fair queueing algorithm. In *Proc. of the ACM SIGCOMM Conf.*, Austin, TX, Sept. 1989.

[11] A. Dwarakinath. A fair-share scheduler for the graphics processing unit. Master's thesis, Stony Brook University, Aug. 2008.

[12] G. A. Elliott and J. H. Anderson. Globally scheduled real-time multiprocessor systems with GPUs. *Real-Time Systems*, 48(1):34–74, Jan. 2012.

[13] M. Gottschlag, M. Hillenbrand, J. Kehne, J. Stoess, and F. Bellosa. LoGV: Low-overhead GPGPU virtualization. In *Proceedings of the 4th Intl. Workshop on Frontiers of Heterogeneous Computing*. IEEE, 2013.

[14] A. G. Greenberg and N. Madras. How fair is fair queuing. *Journal of the ACM*, 39(3):568–598, July 1992.

[15] V. Gupta, K. Schwan, N. Tolia, V. Talwar, and P. Ranganathan. Pegasus: Coordinated scheduling for virtualized accelerator-based systems. In *Proc. of the USENIX Annual Technical Conf.*, Portland, OR, June 2011.

[16] Intel. OpenSource HD Graphics Programmer's Reference Manual: vol. 1, part 2, May 2012.

[17] Intel Corporation. Enabling consistent platform-level services for tightly coupled accelerators. White Paper, 2008.

[18] W. Jin, J. S. Chase, and J. Kaur. Interposed proportional sharing for a storage service utility. In *Proc. of the ACM SIGMETRICS Conf.*, New York, NY, June 2004.

[19] S. Kato, K. Lakshmanan, R. Rajkumar, and Y. Ishikawa. TimeGraph: GPU scheduling for real-time multi-tasking environments. In *Proc. of the USENIX Annual Technical Conf.*, Portland, OR, June 2011.

[20] S. Kato, M. McThrow, C. Maltzahn, and S. Brandt. Gdev: First-class GPU resource management in the operating system. In *Proc. of the USENIX Annual Technical Conf.*, Boston, MA, June 2012.

[21] Khronos OpenCL Working Group and others. The OpenCL specification, v1.2, 2011. A. Munshi, Ed.

[22] Khronos OpenCL Working Group and others. The OpenGL graphics system: A specification, v4.2, 2012. Mark Segal and Kurt Aekeley, Eds.

[23] A. Krishna, T. Heil, N. Lindberg, F. Toussi, and S. VanderWiel. Hardware acceleration in the IBM PowerEN processor: Architecture and performance. In *Proc. of the 21st Intl. Conf. on Parallel Architectures and Compilation Techniques (PACT)*, Minneapolis, MN, Sept. 2012.

[24] G. Kyriazis. Heterogeneous system architecture: A technical review. Technical report, AMD, Aug. 2012. Rev. 1.0.

[25] K. Menychtas, K. Shen, and M. L. Scott. Enabling OS research by inferring interactions in the black-box GPU stack. In *Proc. of the USENIX Annual Technical Conf.*, San Jose, CA, June 2013.

[26] E. B. Nightingale, O. Hodson, R. McIlroy, C. Hawblitzel, and G. Hunt. Helios: Heterogeneous multiprocessing with satellite kernels. In *Proc. of the 22nd ACM Symp. on Operating Systems Principles (SOSP)*, Big Sky, MT, Oct. 2009.

[27] Nouveau: Accelerated open source driver for Nvidia cards. nouveau.freedesktop.org.

[28] NVIDIA Corp. CUDA SDK, v5.0. http://docs.nvidia.com/cuda/.

[29] S. Panneerselvam and M. M. Swift. Operating systems should manage accelerators. In *Proc. of the Second USENIX Workshop on Hot Topics in Parallelism*, Berkeley, CA, June 2012.

[30] A. K. Parekh and R. G. Gallager. A generalized processor sharing approach to flow control in integrated services networks: The single-node case. *IEEE/ACM Trans. on Networking*, 1(3), June 1993.

[31] Nouveau, by PathScaleInc. github.com/pathscale/pscnv.

[32] C. J. Rossbach, J. Currey, M. Silberstein, B. Ray, and E. Witchel. PTask: Operating system abstractions to manage GPUs as compute devices. In *Proc. of the 23rd ACM Symp. on Operating Systems Principles (SOSP)*, Cascais, Portugal, Oct. 2011.

[33] K. Shen and S. Park. FlashFQ: A fair queueing I/O scheduler for Flash-based SSDs. In *Proc. of the USENIX Annual Technical Conf.*, San Jose, CA, June 2013.

[34] M. Shreedhar and G. Varghese. Efficient fair queueing using deficit round robin. In *Proc. of the ACM SIGCOMM Conf.*, Cambridge, MA, Aug. 1995.

[35] L. Soares and M. Stumm. FlexSC: Flexible system call scheduling with exception-less system calls. In *Proc. of the 9th USENIX Conf. on Operating Systems Design and Implementation (OSDI)*, Vancouver, BC, Canada, Oct. 2010.

[36] P. M. Stillwell, V. Chadha, O. Tickoo, S. Zhang, R. Illikkal, R. Iyer, and D. Newell. HiPPAI: High performance portable accelerator interface for SoCs. In *Proc. of the 16th IEEE Conf. on High Performance Computing (HiPC)*, Kochi, India, Dec. 2009.

# Neuromorphic Processing: A New Frontier in Scaling Computer Architecture

Jeff Gehlhaar

Vice President, Technology
Qualcomm Research San Diego
Qualcomm Technologies, Inc.

jbg@qti.qualcomm.com

## Abstract

The desire to build a computer that operates in the same manner as our brains is as old as the computer itself. Although computer engineering has made great strides in hardware performance as a result of Dennard scaling, and even great advances in "brain like" computation, the field still struggles to move beyond sequential, analytical computing architectures. Neuromorphic systems are being developed to transcend the barriers imposed by silicon power consumption, develop new algorithms that help machines achieve cognitive behaviors, and both exploit and enable further research in neuroscience. In this talk I will discuss a system implementing spiking neural networks. These systems hold the promise of an architecture that is event based, broad and shallow, and thus more power efficient than conventional computing solutions.

This new approach to computation based on modeling the brain and its simple but highly connected units presents a host of new challenges. Hardware faces tradeoffs such as density or lower power at the cost of high interconnection overhead. Consequently, software systems must face choices about new language design. Highly distributed hardware systems require complex place and route algorithms to distribute the execution of the neural network across a large number of highly interconnected processing units. Finally, the overall design, simulation and testing process has to be entirely reimagined. We discuss these issues in the context of the Zeroth processor and how this approach compares to other neuromorphic systems that are becoming available.


*ASPLOS'14,* March 1–5, 2014, Salt Lake City, Utah, USA.
ACM 978-1-4503-2305-5/14/03.
http://dx.doi.org/10.1145/2541940.2564710.

***Categories and Subject Descriptors*** C.1.3 Neural nets, C.1.4, D.1.m Miscellaneous

***Keywords*** neuromorphic; low power; spiking neural network, neural network; parallel computing; Zeroth

## Speaker Bio

Jeff Gehlhaar is Vice President of Technology for Qualcomm Research and currently leads the engineering team developing Qualcomm's Zeroth neuromorphic processor, pursuing fundamental research into spiking neural networks, spiking sensors and hardware and software architectures for neuromorphic computing. During his 23 years at Qualcomm, led a variety of projects encompassing software for networking and embedded system, hardware bring up, and software engineering. Jeff lead the software research team developing LTE and LTE-Advanced networking protocols, and has worked across a broad range of technologies and programs: from the integration of an on-board microprocessor into Qualcomm's first fully integrated CDMA mobile modem (early SoC), to large-scale network management software for cellular systems. From 1999-2003 he was Vice President of Engineering and COO for Mohomine, an In-Q-Tel backed knowledge mining startup applying machine learning algorithms to text classification and information extraction applications for both government and commercial customers. He is a graduate of the Jacobs School of Engineering, UC San Diego.

# I/O Paravirtualization at the Device File Boundary

Ardalan Amiri Sani Kevin Boos Shaopu Qin Lin Zhong

Rice University

## Abstract

Paravirtualization is an important I/O virtualization technology since it uniquely provides all of the following benefits: the ability to share the device between multiple VMs, support for legacy devices without virtualization hardware, and high performance. However, existing paravirtualization solutions have one main limitation: they only support one I/O device class, and would require significant engineering effort to support new device classes and features. In this paper, we present Paradice, a solution that vastly simplifies I/O paravirtualization by using a common paravirtualization boundary for various I/O device classes: Unix device files. Using this boundary, the paravirtual drivers simply act as a class-agnostic indirection layer between the application and the actual device driver.

We address two fundamental challenges: supporting cross-VM driver memory operations without changes to applications or device drivers and providing fault and device data isolation between guest VMs despite device driver bugs. We implement Paradice for x86, the Xen hypervisor, and the Linux and FreeBSD OSes. Our implementation paravirtualizes various GPUs, input devices, cameras, an audio device, and an Ethernet card for the netmap framework with ~7700 LoC, of which only ~900 are device class-specific. Our measurements show that Paradice achieves performance close to native for different devices and applications including netmap, 3D HD games, and OpenCL applications.

***Categories and Subject Descriptors*** C.0 [*Computer Systems Organization*]: General—System architectures; D.4.6 [*Operating Systems*]: Security and Protection; D.4.8 [*Operating Systems*]: Performance; I.3.4 [*Computer Graphics*]: Graphics Utilities—Virtual device interfaces

***Keywords*** I/O; Virtualization; Paravirtualization; Isolation



*ASPLOS '14*, March 1–5, 2014, Salt Lake City, Utah, USA.

http://dx.doi.org/10.1145/2541940.2541943

## 1. Introduction

Virtualization has become an important technology for computers of various form factors, from servers to mobile devices, because it enables hardware consolidation and secure co-existence of multiple operating systems in one physical machine. I/O virtualization enables virtual machines (VMs) to use I/O devices in the physical machine, and is increasingly important because modern computers have embraced a diverse set of I/O devices, including GPU, DSP, sensors, GPS, touchscreen, camera, video encoders and decoders, and face detection accelerator [4].

Paravirtualization is a popular I/O virtualization technology because it uniquely provides three important benefits: the ability to share the device between multiple VMs, support for legacy devices without virtualization hardware, and high performance. Existing paravirtualization solutions have one main drawback: they only support one I/O device class, and would require significant engineering effort to support new device classes and features. As a result of the required engineering effort, only network and block devices have enjoyed good paravirtualization solutions so far [28, 31, 33, 44]. Limited attempts have been made to paravirtualize other device classes, such as GPUs [27], but they provide low performance and do not support new class features, such as GPGPU. Significant engineering effort is an increasingly important problem to paravirtualization in light of the ever-increasing diversity in I/O devices.

We present Paradice (*Para*virtual *Dev*ice), a solution that greatly simplifies I/O paravirtualization by using a common, class-agnostic I/O paravirtualization boundary, *device files*. Unix-like OSes employ device files to abstract most I/O devices [9], including GPU, camera, input devices, and audio devices. To leverage this boundary, Paradice creates a virtual device file in the guest OS corresponding to the device file of the I/O device. Guest applications issue file operations to this virtual device file as if it were the real one. The paravirtual drivers act as a thin indirection layer and forward the file operations to be executed by the actual device driver. Since device files are common to many I/O devices, Paradice reduces the engineering effort to support various I/O devices. Moreover, as we will demonstrate, Paradice maintains the three aforementioned advantages of I/O paravirtualization.

We address two fundamental challenges: (*i*) the guest process and the device drivers reside in different virtualization domains, creating a memory barrier for executing the driver memory operations on the guest process. Our solution to this problem is to redirect and execute the memory operations efficiently in the hypervisor without any changes to the device drivers or applications. (*ii*) malicious applications can exploit device driver bugs [25, 29] through the device file interface to compromise the machine that hosts the device driver [1, 2]. Our solution to this problem is a suite of techniques that provide fault and device data isolation between the VMs that share a device. Paradice guarantees fault isolation even with unmodified device drivers. However, it requires modest changes to the device driver for device data isolation (i.e., ~400 LoC for the Linux Radeon GPU driver).

We present a prototype implementation of Paradice for the x86 architecture, the Xen hypervisor, and the Linux and FreeBSD OSes. Our prototype currently supports five important classes of I/O devices with about 7700 LoC, of which about 900 are specific to device classes: GPU, input device, camera, audio device, and Ethernet for the netmap framework [43]. Approximately 400 lines of this class-specific code are for device data isolation for GPU. We note that GPU has not previously been amenable to virtualization due to its functional and implementation complexity. Yet, Paradice easily virtualizes GPUs of various makes and models with full functionality and close-to-native performance.

Paradice supports cross-OS I/O paravirtualization. For example, our current implementation virtualizes I/O devices for a FreeBSD guest VM using Linux device drivers. Hence, Paradice is useful for driver reuse between these OSes too, for example, to reuse Linux GPU drivers on FreeBSD, which typically does not support the latest GPU drivers.

We report a comprehensive evaluation of Paradice and show that it: (*i*) requires low development effort to support various I/O devices, shares the device between multiple guest VMs, and supports legacy devices; (*ii*) achieves close-to-native performance for various devices and applications, both for Linux and FreeBSD VMs; and (*iii*) provides fault and device data isolation without incurring noticeable performance degradation.

## 2. Background

### 2.1 I/O Stack

Figure 1(a) shows a simplified I/O stack in a Unix-like OS. The kernel exports device files to the user space through a special filesystem, `devfs` (the `/dev` directory). A process thread issues file operations by calling the right system calls on the device file. These system calls are handled by the kernel, which invokes the *file operation handlers* implemented by the device driver. The commonly used file operations are `read`, `write`, `poll`, `ioctl`, and `mmap`.

When servicing a file operation, the device driver often needs to perform memory operations on the process memory. There are two types of memory operations: copying a kernel buffer to/from the process memory, which are mainly used by the `read`, `write`, and `ioctl` file operations, and mapping a system or device memory page into the process address space, which is mainly used by the `mmap` file operation and its supporting `page_fault` handler.

Instead of using the `poll` file operation, a process can request to be notified when events happen, e.g., where there is a mouse movement. Linux employs the `fasync` file operation for setting up the asynchronous notification. When there is an event, the process is notified with a signal.

To correctly access an I/O device, an application may need to know the exact make, model or functional capabilities of the device. For example, the X Server needs to know the GPU make in order to load the correct libraries. As such, the kernel collects this information and exports it to the user space, e.g., through the `/sys` directory in Linux, and through the `/dev/pci` file in FreeBSD.

The I/O stack explained here is used for most I/O devices in Unix-like OSes. Famous exceptions are network and block devices, which have their own class-specific I/O stacks. See §8 for more details.

### 2.2 I/O Paravirtualization

An I/O paravirtualization solution uses a pair of drivers: a frontend driver in the guest VM and a backend driver in the same domain as the main device driver, e.g., the Xen driver domain [28]. The frontend and backend drivers cooperate to enable guest VM applications to use the I/O device. For example, the paravirtual network drivers exchanges packets that the applications need to send or receive [28, 44]. We refer to the boundary in the I/O stack that the paravirtual drivers are located at as the *paravirtualization boundary*.

### 2.3 Memory Virtualization

The hypervisor virtualizes the physical memory for the VMs. While memory virtualization was traditionally implemented entirely in software, i.e., the shadow page table technique [35], recent generations of micro-architecture provide hardware support for memory virtualization, e.g., the Intel Extended Page Table (EPT). In this case, the hardware Memory Management Unit (MMU) performs two levels of address translation from guest virtual addresses to guest physical addresses and then to system physical addresses. The guest page tables store the first translation and are maintained by the guest OS. The EPTs store the second translation and are maintained by the hypervisor.

## 3. Paradice Design

### 3.1 Architectural Design Choices

**Design choice 1: device files as the paravirtualization boundary.** Our key observation in this work is that Unix-like OSes abstract most I/O devices with device files, which can be used as a common paravirtulization boundary. With this

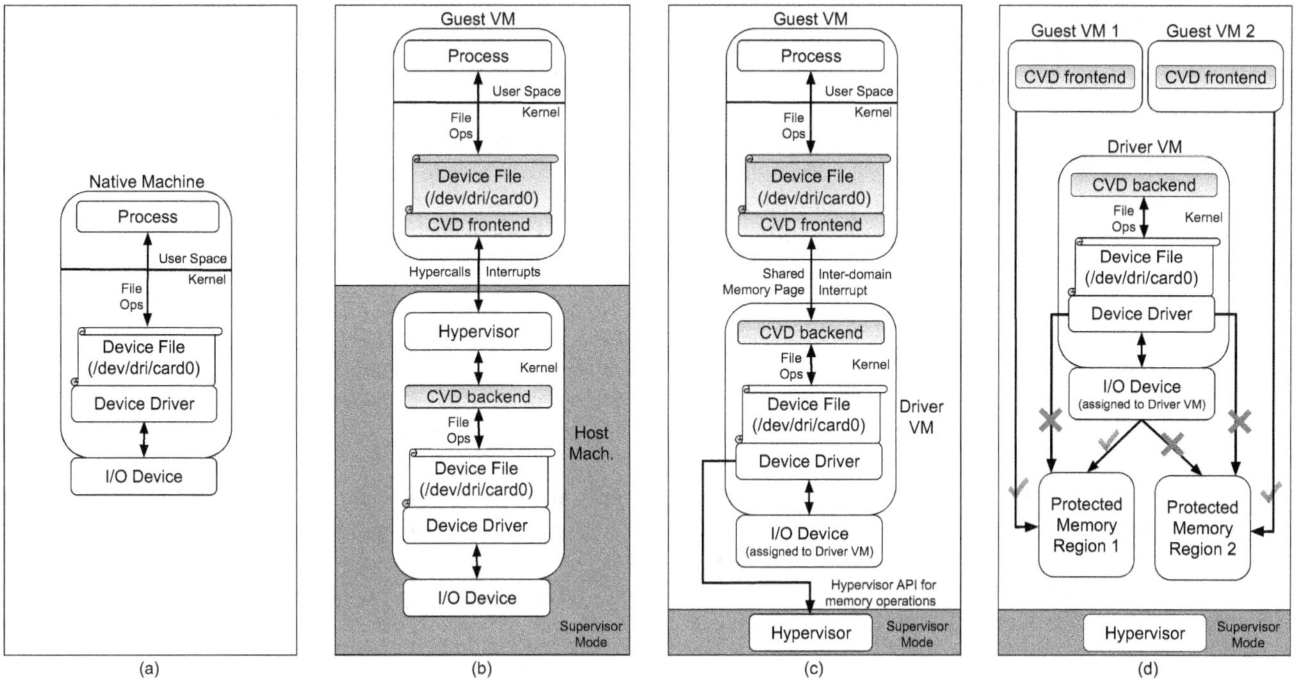


**Figure 1.** (a) The simplified I/O stack in a Unix-like OS. (b) Devirtualization's design, our previous work that also paravirtualizes I/O devices at the device file boundary. This design can be abused by a malicious guest VM to compromise the host machine, and hence the hypervisor and other guest VMs. (c) Paradice's design, which sandboxes the device and its driver in a driver VM and performs strict runtime checks on requested memory operations for fault isolation. (d) Device data isolation, enforced by the hypervisor, which creates non-overlapping protected memory regions for each guest VM's data and enforces appropriate access permissions to these regions. Each protected region includes part of driver VM system memory and device memory.

boundary, the paravirtual drivers simply act as an indirection layer between the application and the actual device driver.

In order to paravirtualize I/O devices at the device file boundary, we create a virtual device file inside the guest VM that mirrors the actual device file. Applications in the guest VM issue file operations to this virtual device file as if it were the real one. The paravirtual drivers, i.e., the *Common Virtual Driver* (*CVD*) frontend and backend, deliver these operations to the actual device file to be executed by the device driver.

Figure 1(b) shows a simple design for using the device file boundary for paravirtualization with a Type II (i.e., hosted) hypervisor. In this design, the device driver, device file, and also the hypervisor reside in supervisor mode. The CVD frontend and backend are in the guest VM and in the host OS, respectively. We used this design in our previous work, called devirtualization [20]. However, devirtualization's design does not provide isolation between guest VMs. As device drivers run in the host OS, which executes in supervisor mode, a malicious guest VM application can use the driver bugs to compromise (i.e., crash, gain root access in, or execute malicious code in) the whole system including the hypervisor and other guest VMs. This important flaw led us to the design of Paradice, described below.

**Design choice 2: device and driver sandboxing and strict runtime checks of driver memory operations for fault isolation.** Paradice solves the flaw in devirtualization's design by sandboxing the device and its driver in a separate VM, called the *driver VM*, using device assignment [19, 24, 30, 39]. This design uses a Type I (i.e., bare-metal) hypervisor, as shown in Figure 1(c). For device assignment, the hypervisor maps the device registers and memory to the driver VM and restricts the device DMA addresses to the driver VM memory using the hardware I/O Memory Management Unit (IOMMU). The CVD frontend and backend use shared memory pages and inter-VM interrupts to communicate, e.g., for forwarding the file operations.

Executing driver memory operations (§2.1) in Paradice introduces new challenges since the device driver and the guest process reside in different VMs with isolated memory. As a solution, we implement the two types of memory operations efficiently in the hypervisor and provide an API for the driver VM to request them. Further, to support unmodified drivers, we provide wrapper stubs in the driver VM kernel that intercept the driver's kernel function invocations for memory operations and redirect them to the hypervisor through the aforementioned API.

In Paradice's design, a malicious guest VM can still compromise the driver VM through the device file interface. Therefore, we perform strict runtime checks on the memory operations requested by the driver VM in order to guarantee that the compromised driver VM cannot be abused to pollute other guest VMs. For the checks, the CVD frontend in the guest VM identifies and declares the legitimate memory operations to the hypervisor before forwarding a file operation to the backend. §4.1 explains this issue in more detail.

**Design choice 3: hypervisor-enforced access permissions for device data isolation.** Applications exchange data with I/O devices. Device data isolation requires such data to be accessible only to the guest VM that owns the data but not to any other guest VMs. We enforce device data isolation in the hypervisor by allocating non-overlapping protected memory regions on the driver VM memory and on the device memory for each guest VM's data and assigning appropriate access permissions to these regions (Figure 1(d)). §4.2 elaborates on this technique.

Unmodified device drivers cannot normally function correctly in the presence of the hypervisor-enforced device data isolation. In §5.3, we explain how we added only ~400 LoC to the complex Linux Radeon GPU driver for this purpose. Unlike all other Paradice components, device data isolation is not generic. However, many of the techniques we developed for the Radeon GPU driver apply to other device drivers as well.

### 3.2 Key Benefits of Paradice Design

#### 3.2.1 One Paravirtual Driver, Many I/O Devices

The key benefit of Paradice is that it requires a single pair of paravirtual drivers, i.e., the CVD frontend and backend, and very small class-specific code to support many different device classes. In contrast, prior solutions employ class-specific paravirtual drivers. Moreover, Paradice supports all features of an I/O device class since it simply adds an indirection layer between applications and device drivers. In contrast, prior solutions only support a limited set of features and require more engineering effort to support new ones.

#### 3.2.2 Compatibility between Different OSes

The device file interface is compatible across various Unix-like OSes; therefore Paradice can support guest VMs running different versions of Unix-like OSes in one physical machine, all sharing the same driver VM. We investigated the file operations interface in FreeBSD and many versions of Linux and observed the following: (*i*) the file operations that are mainly used by device drivers (§2.1) exist in both Linux and FreeBSD and have similar semantics; (*ii*) these file operations have been part of Linux since the early days and have seen almost no changes in the past couple of years, i.e., from Linux 2.6.35 (2010) to 3.2.0 (2012). §5.1 discusses our deployment of a Linux driver VM, a FreeBSD guest VM, and a Linux guest VM running a different major version of Linux. In order to use a device driver, applications might require appropriate libraries, e.g., the Direct Rendering Manager (DRM) libraries for graphics. These libraries are usually available for different Unix-like OSes. If not, porting the library from another OS is possible since Unix-like OSes are mostly source code compatible.

#### 3.2.3 Concurrent Device Access by Multiple Guests

If supported by the device driver, Paradice allows for multiple guest VMs to concurrently use the device because the device file interface allows multiple processes to issue file operations simultaneously. In this case, the same CVD backend supports requests from CVD frontends of all guest VMs. Some device drivers, e.g., the Linux GPU drivers, can handle concurrency, but some others, e.g., the Linux camera drivers, only allow one process at a time. §5.1 discusses the issue of concurrency for different classes of devices.

## 4. Isolation between Guest VMs

Device drivers are buggy [25, 29], and these bugs can be used by malicious applications to compromise the machine, either virtual or physical, that hosts the driver [1, 2]. Compromising a machine refers to crashing, gaining root access in, or executing malicious code inside the machine. This section elaborates on how we provide fault and device data isolation between guest VMs despite such driver bugs.

### 4.1 Fault Isolation

Fault isolation requires that a malicious guest VM cannot compromise other guest VMs. To provide fault isolation, we must prevent guest VMs from access to unauthorized and sensitive parts of the system memory, e.g., the hypervisor's memory or other guest VMs' memory. We employ two techniques to achieve this. First, to protect the hypervisor, we sandbox the device driver and the device inside the driver VM, resulting in the design of Paradice as was explained in §3.1. With this design, a malicious guest VM can compromise the driver VM, but not the hypervisor. Therefore, in the rest of the discussion, we assume that the driver VM is controlled by a malicious guest VM and cannot be trusted. This leads us to the second technique. To protect other guest VMs, we employ strict runtime checks in the hypervisor to validate the memory operations requested by the driver VM, making sure that they cannot be abused by the compromised driver VM to compromise other guest VMs, e.g., by asking the hypervisor to copy data to some sensitive memory location inside a guest VM kernel.

For validation, the CVD frontend identifies the legitimate memory operations of each file operation and declares them to the hypervisor using a grant table before forwarding the file operation to the backend. The legitimate memory operations can be easily identified in the CVD frontend by using the file operation's input arguments. For example, the `read` file operation requires the driver to copy some data to the process memory, and the `read` input arguments include the start address and size of the user space buffer that the driver needs to write to. However, the input arguments are not always enough for `ioctl`.

To identify the memory operations of an `ioctl`, we use two techniques. First, we use the `ioctl` input arguments, if possible. The arguments of an `ioctl` include a command number and an untyped pointer. The device driver may execute different memory operations based on the value of these two arguments. The most common `ioctl` memory operations are to copy a command-specific data structure from the process memory to the kernel memory and vice-versa. Fortunately, device drivers often use OS-provided macros to generate `ioctl` command numbers, which embed the size of these data structures and the direction of the copy into it. Moreover, the `ioctl` untyped pointer holds the address of this data structure in the process memory. Therefore in these cases, the CVD frontend simply parses the command number and uses it along with the value of the untyped pointer to determine the arguments of the memory operations. We have successfully tested this approach with the UVC camera driver and the majority of `ioctl` commands in Radeon GPU driver.

However, this approach is not applicable if the driver performs memory operations other than simple copying of a data structure, or if the driver does not use the OS-provided macros. For example, for some Radeon driver `ioctl` commands, the driver performs nested copies, in which the data from one copy operation is used as the input arguments for the next one. Therefore, we provide a second solution that can identify such memory operations. For this solution, we develop a static analysis tool that analyzes the unmodified driver and extracts a simplified part of its `ioctl` handler. This code extract has no external dependencies and can even be executed without the presence of the actual device. We then execute this code offline and generate the arguments of legitimate memory operations in the form of static entries in a source file that is included in the CVD frontend. Given an `ioctl` command, the CVD frontend can look up these entries to find the legitimate operations. However, offline execution is impossible for some memory operations, such as the nested copies mentioned above. In this case, the CVD frontend identifies the memory operation arguments just-in-time by executing the extracted code at runtime. Our tool correctly analyzes the Radeon GPU driver. It detects instances of nested copies in 14 `ioctl` commands in the Radeon driver. For these commands, it automatically generates about 760 lines of extracted code from the driver that are added to the source file used by the CVD frontend.

The memory operations executed by the driver for each `ioctl` command rarely change across driver updates because any such changes can break application compatibility. Therefore, the existing code and entries in the source file generated by our tool do not need to be updated with every driver update. However, newer `ioctl` commands might be added to a driver, which then need to be analyzed by our tool. Our investigation of Radeon drivers of Linux kernel 2.6.35 and 3.2.0 confirms this arguments as the memory operations of common `ioctl` commands are identical in both drivers, while the latter has four new `ioctl` commands.

### 4.2 Device Data Isolation

Guest VM processes exchange data with the I/O device. Device data isolation requires such data to be isolated and not accessible to other guest VMs. Processes' data may either be on the device memory, or on the driver VM system memory, which can be accessed by the device through DMA. Isolating these data is challenging since the driver VM is compromised, and hence the malicious VM has full access to driver VM system memory and to the device memory. We enforce device data isolation in the hypervisor by protecting the device memory and part of the driver VM system memory from the driver VM for hosting the guest VMs' data. We then split the protected memory into non-overlapping memory regions for each guest VM's data, and then assign appropriate access permissions to these regions, as illustrated in Figure 1(d). The CPU code in the driver VM, including the device driver, does not have permission to read these memory regions. Each guest VM has access to its own memory region only (through the memory operations executed by the hypervisor), and the device has access permission to one memory region at a time.

This set of access permissions prevents a malicious guest VM from stealing the data of another guest VM because it stops the following attacks: first, the malicious VM cannot use the hypervisor API to access the data buffers allocated for other VMs because the hypervisor prohibits that. Second, the malicious VM cannot use the compromised driver VM to read the data buffer, because the driver VM does not have read permission to the memory regions. Finally, the malicious VM cannot program the device to copy the buffer outside a memory region because the device can only access one memory regions at a time.

When adding device data isolation support to a driver, we need to determine which guest VM's data buffers are sensitive and need to be protected. For example for GPU, we protected all the raw data that guest VMs share with the GPU including the graphics textures and GPGPU input data. Some data that are moved from the guest applications to driver VM are not sensitive and do not need to be protected. For example, most `ioctl` data structures are mainly instructions for the driver and do not contain raw application data. After determining the sensitive data, we use the hypervisor to protect them. It is then important to make sure that the driver does not try to read the data, otherwise the driver VM crashes. Indeed, we observed that all the sensitive data that we determined for the GPU were never read by the driver. They were only accessed by the device itself or by the process, making it easy to add device data isolation. In case a driver normally reads the sensitive data, it needs to be modified to avoid that access in order to be compatible with device data isolation in Paradice. Finally, we need a policy to tell the hypervisor which data buffers to protect. We observed that most applications typically use `mmap` to move sensitive data buffers to/from the device mainly because it provides better performance compared to copying. For example with the Radeon driver, applications only use `mmap` to move graphics textures and GPGPU input data to the device. As a result, we currently use a simple policy in the hypervisor to enforce isolation for mapped buffers only. More sophisticated policies that enforce isolation for other sensitive data, that are for example copied from the guest VM to the driver VM, are also possible.

Next, we explain how the hypervisor enforces the access permissions. Access permissions for the driver VM are enforced by removing the EPT read permission for the protected memory regions. This technique is adequate since both the system and the device memory need to be mapped by EPTs in order to be accessible to the driver VM.

System memory access permissions for the device are enforced using the IOMMU. Normally with device assignment, the hypervisor programs the IOMMU to allow the device to DMA to all physical addresses in the driver VM. For device data isolation, the hypervisor does not initially create any mappings in the IOMMU. The IOMMU mappings are added per request from the device driver. When asking to add a page to the IOMMU, the driver needs to attach the corresponding memory region ID. The hypervisor maintains a list of which pages have been mapped in IOMMU for each region. Whenever the device needs to work with the data of one guest VM, the driver asks the hypervisor to switch to the corresponding memory region. When switching the region, the hypervisor unmaps all the pages of the previous region from the IOMMU and maps the pages of the new region.

Enforcing device memory access permissions for the device requires device-specific solutions. For the Radeon Evergreen series (including the HD 6450), we leveraged the GPU memory controller, which has two registers that set the lower and upper bounds of device memory accessible to the GPU cores. The hypervisor takes full control of the GPU memory controller registers and does not map them into the driver VM, so that it can enforce the accessible device memory for the GPU at any time. If the GPU tries to access memory outside these bounds, it will not succeed. Note that this solution partitions and shares the GPU memory between guest VMs and can affect the performance of guest applications that require more memory than their share.

## 5. Implementation

We implement Paradice for the Xen hypervisor, 32-bit x86 architecture with Physical Address Extension (PAE), and Linux and FreeBSD OSes. The implementation is modular and can be revised to support other hypervisors, architectures, and Unix-like OSes. It virtualizes various GPUs, input devices (such as keyboard and mouse), cameras, a speaker, and an Ethernet card for netmap, all with about 7700 LoC, of which only about 900 LoC are specific to device classes. Moreover, around 400 lines of this class-specific code are for device data isolation for GPU. Table 1 shows the list of devices that we have paravirtualized with Paradice. Table 2 breaks down the Paradice code structure. We use CLOC [3] (v1.56) for counting code. We do not count comments or debugging code.

| Class | Class-spec. code (LoC) | Device Name | Driver Name |
|---|---|---|---|
| GPU | 92 | Disc. ATI Radeon HD 6450 | DRM/Radeon |
| | | Disc. ATI Radeon HD 4650 | DRM/Radeon |
| | | Int. ATI Mobility Radeon X1300(*) | DRM/Radeon |
| | | Int. Intel Mobile GM965/GL960(*) | DRM/i915 |
| Input | 58 | Dell USB Mouse | evdev/usbmouse |
| | | Dell USB Keyboard | evdev/usbkbd |
| Camera | 43 | Logitech HD Pro Webcam C920 | V4L2/UVC |
| | | Logitech QuickCam Pro 9000 | V4L2/UVC |
| Audio | 37 | Intel Panther Point HD Audio Cont. | PCM/snd-hda-intel |
| Ethernet | 21 | Intel Gigabit Adapter | netmap/e1000e |

**Table 1.** I/O devices paravirtualized by our Paradice prototype with very small class-specific code. For correct comparison, we do not include the code for device data isolation and graphics sharing. Those can be found in Table 2. (*) marks the devices that we have tested only with our previous system design, devirtualization (§3.1). We include them here to show that the device file boundary is applicable to various device makes and models.

### 5.1 Paradice Architecture Details

**Common Virtual Driver (CVD):** The CVD frontend and backend constitute a large portion of the implementation consist of two parts each. The first part implements the interface to the hypervisor, e.g., invoking the hypervisor API in the backend, or sharing a grant table with the hypervisor in the frontend. The second part interacts with the OS kernel only, e.g., by invoking the device driver's file operation handlers in the backend, or by handling (and forwarding) the file operations in the frontend.

The CVD frontend and backend use shared memory pages and inter-VM interrupts to communicate. The frontend puts the file operation arguments in a shared page, and uses an interrupt to inform the backend to read them. The backend communicates the return values of the file operation in a similar way. Because interrupts have noticeable latency (§6.1.1), CVD supports a polling mode for high-performance applications such as netmap. In this mode, the frontend and backend both poll the shared page for 200$\mu s$ before they go to sleep to wait for interrupts. The polling period is chosen empirically and is not currently optimized. Moreover, for asynchronous notifications (§2.1), the CVD backend uses similar techniques to send a message to the frontend, e.g., when the keyboard is pressed.

| Type | Total LoC | Platform | Component | LoC |
|---|---|---|---|---|
| Generic | 6833 | Linux | CVD: | |
| | | | - frontend | 1553 |
| | | | - backend | 1950 |
| | | | - shared | 378 |
| | | | Linux kernel wrapper stubs | 198 |
| | | | Virtual PCI module | 285 |
| | | | - Supporting kernel code | 50 |
| | | FreeBSD | FreeBSD CVD frontend: | |
| | | | - New code (approx.) | 451 |
| | | | - From Linux CVD (approx.) (not calculated in the total) | 758 |
| | | | - Supporting kernel code | 15 |
| | | | Virtual PCI module | 74 |
| | | | - Supporting kernel code | 29 |
| | | Xen | Paradice API | 1349 |
| | | Clang | Driver `ioctl` analyzer | 501 |
| Class-specific | 825 | Linux | Device info modules: | |
| | | | - GPU | 92 |
| | | | - input device | 58 |
| | | | - camera | 43 |
| | | | - audio device | 37 |
| | | | - Ethernet (netmap) | 21 |
| | | | Graphics sharing code | 145 |
| | | | - Supporting DRM driver code | 15 |
| | | | Data isol. for Radeon driver | 382 |
| | | FreeBSD | Device info modules: | |
| | | | - Ethernet (netmap) | 32 |

**Table 2.** Paradice code breakdown.

The CVD frontend uses a grant table to declare the legitimate memory operations to the hypervisor (§4.1). The grant table is a single memory page shared between the frontend VM and the hypervisor. After storing the operations in the table, the CVD frontend generates a grant reference number and forwards it to the backend along with the file operation. The backend then needs to attach the reference to every request for the memory operations of that file operation. The reference number acts as an index and helps the hypervisor validate the operation with minimal overhead.

The CVD backend puts new file operations on a wait-queue to be executed. We use separate wait-queues for each guest VM. We also set the maximum number of queued operations for each wait-queue to 100 to prevent malicious guest VMs from causing denial-of-service problems by issuing too many file operations. We can modify this cap for different queues for better load balancing or enforcing priorities between guest VMs.

**Device Info Modules:** As mentioned in §2.1, applications may need some information about the device before they can use it. In Paradice, we extract device information and export it to the guest VM by providing a small kernel module for the guest OS to load. Developing these modules is easy because they are small, simple, and not performance-sensitive. For example, the device info module for GPU has about 100 LoC, and mainly provides the device PCI configuration information, such as the manufacturer and device ID. We also developed modules to create or reuse a virtual PCI bus in the guest for Paradice devices.

**Device File Interface Compatibility:** Paradice supports guest VMs using different versions of Unix-like OSes in one physical machine. For example, we have successfully deployed Paradice with a Linux driver VM, a FreeBSD guest VM and a Linux guest VM running a different major version of Linux (versions 2.6.35 and 3.2.0). To support a different version of Linux, we added only 14 LoC to the CVD to update the list of all possible file operations based on the new kernel (although none of the new file operations are used by the device drivers we tested). To support FreeBSD, we redeveloped the CVD frontend with about 450 new LoC and about 760 LoC from the Linux CVD frontend implementation. To support `mmap` and its `page_fault` handler, we added about 12 LoC to the FreeBSD kernel to pass the virtual address range to the CVD frontend, since these addresses are needed by the Linux device driver and by the Paradice hypervisor API.

**Concurrency Support:** As mentioned in §3.2.3, the device file interface allows for concurrent access from multiple processes if the driver supports it. We define the policies for how each device is shared. For GPU for graphics, we adopt a foreground-background model. That is, only the foreground guest VM renders to the GPU, while others pause. We assign each guest VM to one of the virtual terminals of the driver VM, and the user can easily navigate between them using simple key combinations. For input devices, we only send notifications to the foreground guest VM. For GPU for computation (GPGPU), we allow concurrent access from multiple guest VMs. For camera and Ethernet card for netmap, we only allow access from one guest VM at a time because their drivers do not support concurrent access. Note that Paradice will automatically support sharing of these devices too if concurrency support is added to their drivers, as is the plan for netmap (see [43]).

### 5.2 Hypervisor-Assisted Memory Operations

Hypervisor supports the two types of memory operations needed by the device drivers. For copying to/from the process memory, the hypervisor first translates the virtual addresses of the source and destination buffers (which belong to different VMs) into system physical addresses and then performs the copy. If the source or destination buffers span more than one page, the address translation needs to be performed per page since contiguous pages in the VM address spaces are not necessarily contiguous in the system physical address space. To perform the translation, the hypervisor first translates the VM virtual address to the VM physical address by walking the VM's own page tables in software. It then translates the VM physical address to the system physical address by walking the EPTs.

For mapping a page into the process address space, the hypervisor fixes the EPTs to map the page to an (arbitrary) physical page in the guest physical address space, and then fixes the guest page tables to map the guest physical page to the requested virtual address in the guest process address space. We can use any guest physical page address in the mappings as long as it is not used by the guest OS. The hypervisor finds unused page addresses in the guest and uses them for this purpose. Moreover, before forwarding the `mmap` operation to the backend, the CVD frontend checks the guest page tables for the mapping address range, and creates all missing levels except for the last one, which is later fixed by the hypervisor. This approach provides better compatibility with the guest kernel than fixing all the levels of the guest page tables in the hypervisor. Upon unmapping a previously mapped page, the hypervisor only needs to destroy the mappings in the EPTs since the guest kernel destroys the mappings in its own page tables before informing the device driver of the unmap.

As mentioned in §3.1, we employ wrapper stubs in the driver VM kernel to support unmodified device drivers. For this purpose, we modified 13 Linux kernel functions, e.g., the `insert_pfn` function, which maps a page to a process address space. When the CVD backend invokes a thread to execute the file operation of a guest VM, it marks the thread by setting a flag in the thread-specific `task_struct` data structure. The wrapper stubs will invoke the appropriate hypervisor API when executed in the context of a marked thread.

### 5.3 Isolation between Guest VMs

**Fault Isolation:** As described in §4.1, we have developed a static analysis tool to identify the legitimate memory operations of driver `ioctl` commands. We implemented this tool as a standalone C++ application built upon the LLVM compiler infrastructure [37] and its C language frontend, Clang [12]. Using Clang, our tool parses the driver source code into an Abstract Syntax Tree (AST) and then analyzes the AST to extract memory operations of interest. Our Clang tool uses classic program slicing techniques [51] to shrink the source code by selecting the subset of functions and statements that affect the input arguments of a given memory operation. This analysis is almost fully automated, requiring manual annotation only when human knowledge of the code is necessary to resolve function pointers or other external dependencies.

**Device Data Isolation:** As mentioned earlier, we added ~400 LoC to the Radeon driver to support the device data isolation enforced by the hypervisor. Currently, our changes only support the Radeon Evergreen series (including the Radeon HD 6450 in our setup), but the code can be easily refactored to support other Radeon series as well. Moreover, our current implementation has minimal support for switching between memory regions; improving the switching is part of our future work.

We made four sets of changes to the driver. (*i*) In the driver, we explicitly ask the hypervisor to map pages in or unmap pages from IOMMU for different memory regions. For better efficiency, we allocate a pool of pages for each memory region and map them in IOMMU in the initialization phase. The hypervisor zeros out the pages before unmapping. (*ii*) The driver normally creates some data buffers on the device memory that are used by the GPU, such as the GPU address translations buffer. We create these buffers on all memory regions so that the GPU has access to them regardless of the active memory region. (*iii*) We unmap from the driver VM the MMIO page that contains the GPU memory controller registers used for determining the device memory accessible by the GPU (§4.2). If the driver needs to read/write to other registers in the same MMIO page, it issues a hypercall. (*iv*) While removing the read permissions from EPTs of protected memory regions are enough for device data isolation, we had to remove both read and write permissions since x86 does not support write-only permissions. In rare cases, the driver needs write permissions to some memory buffers such as the GPU address translation buffer. If the buffer is on the system memory, we emulate write-only permissions by making the buffer read-only to the device through the IOMMU and giving read/write permissions to the driver VM. If the buffer is on the device memory, we require the driver VM to issue a hypercall.

For device data isolation, we need to make sure that the driver VM cannot access the GPU memory content through any other channels. For this purpose, we studies the register programming interface of the Evergreen series, and confirmed that the driver cannot program the device to copy the content of memory buffers to registers that are readable by the device driver.

We faced one problem with interrupts. Some Radeon series, including the Evergreen series, use system memory instead of registers to convey the interrupt reason from the device to the driver. That is, the device writes the reason for the interrupt to this pre-allocated system buffer and then interrupts the driver. However, to enforce device data isolation, we cannot give the driver read permission to any system memory buffer that can be written by the device. Therefore, we currently disable all interrupts, except for the fence interrupt needed to monitor the GPU execution, and then interpret all interrupts as fences. The main drawback of this approach is that we cannot support the VSync interrupts, which can be used to cap the GPU graphics performance to a fixed number of frames per second. As a possible solution, we are thinking of emulating the VSync interrupts in software. We do not expect high overhead since VSync happens relatively rarely, e.g., every 16ms for rendering 60 frames per second.

As a guideline for our implementation, we did not add device-specific code to the hypervisor and implemented the hypervisor functions in the form of a generic API. In the few cases that device-specific information was needed, we leveraged the *driver initialization phase* to call generic hypervisor API to achieve the required function, such as unmapping the memory controller MMIO page from the driver VM. Since no guest VM can communicate with the driver before the initialization phase is over, we assume that the driver is not malicious in this phase. We believe this approach is superior to implementing such device-specific functions in the hypervisor because it minimizes the new code in the hypervisor and improves the system reliability as a whole.

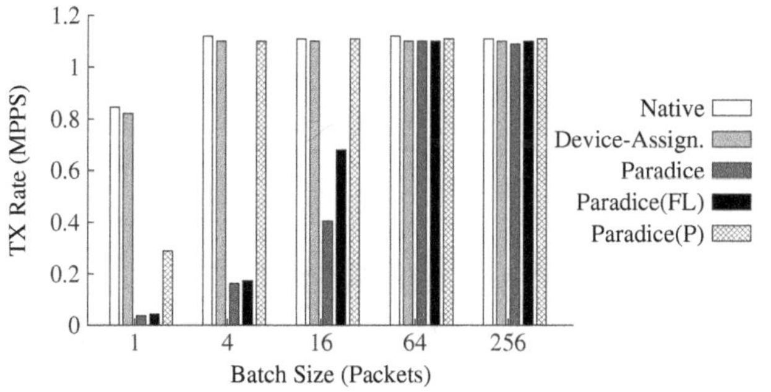


**Figure 2.** netmap transmit rate with 64 byte packets. (FL) indicates FreeBSD guest VM using a Linux driver VM. (P) indicates the use of polling mode in Paradice.

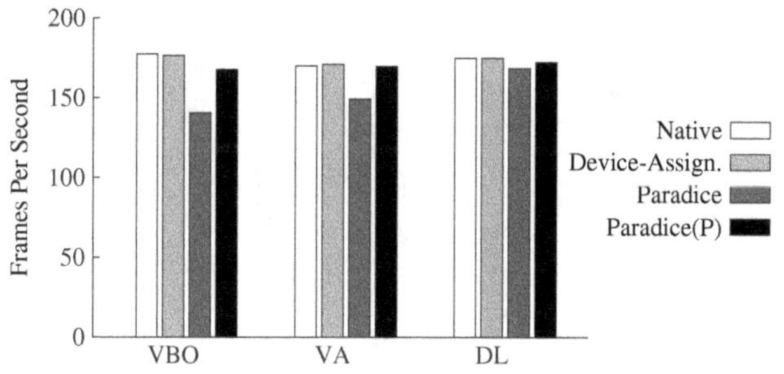


**Figure 3.** OpenGL benchmarks FPS. VBO, VA, and DL stand for Vertex Buffer Objects, Vertex Arrays, and Display Lists. (P) indicates the use of polling mode in Paradice.

## 6. Evaluation

Using the implementation described above, we evaluate Paradice and show that it: (*i*) requires low development effort to support various I/O devices, shares the device between multiple guest VMs, and supports legacy devices; (*ii*) achieves close-to-native performance for various devices and applications, both for Linux and FreeBSD guest VMs; and (*iii*) provides fault and device data isolation without incurring noticeable performance degradation.

Before we evaluate the performance of Paradice, we demonstrate that Paradice achieves the desired properties mentioned in §1. First, supporting new I/O devices with Paradice is easy and only requires developing small device info modules for new device classes (Table 2). These modules typically took us only a few person-hours each to implement. It took us a few person-weeks to add device data isolation support to the Radeon driver, a very complex drivers with ~111000 LoC in Linux 3.2. A big portion of this time was spent on implementing the supporting hypervisor code, therefore, we anticipate less development effort to add device data isolation to other drivers.

Second, Paradice effectively shares I/O devices between guest VMs (§3.2.3). For example in one experiment, we ran two guest VMs, one executing a 3D HD game and the other one running an OpenGL application, both sharing the GPU based on our foreground-background model (§5.1). In the next section, we show the performance of GPU when used by more than one VM for GPGPU computations.

Third, Paradice supports legacy devices. None of the devices that we have successfully virtualized so far have hardware support for virtualization.

### 6.1 Performance

In this section, we quantify the overhead and performance of Paradice. We compare the performance of Paradice with the native performance (when an application is executed natively on the same hardware), as well as with the performance of direct device assignment (when an application is executed in a VM with direct access to the I/O device). The performance of direct device assignment is the upper-bound on the performance of Paradice due to our use of device assignment to sandbox the device and its driver.

For our experiment setup, we use a desktop with a quad-core Intel Core i7-3770 CPU, 8GB of DDR3 memory, and an ASRock Z77 Extreme6 motherboard. For I/O devices, we use a Radeon HD 6450 GPU connected to a 24" Dell LCD for both graphics and GPGPU benchmarks, Intel Gigabit Network Adapter for netmap, Dell mouse, Logitech HD Pro Webcam C920, and the on-board Intel Panther Point HD Audio Controller for speaker. We configure the VMs with one virtual CPU and 1GB of memory. For device data isolation between two guest VMs, we split the 1GB GPU memory between two memory regions, therefore, all the benchmarks with data isolation can use a maximum of 512MB of GPU memory. As the default configuration for Paradice, we use the interrupts for communication, Linux guest VM and Linux driver VM, and do not employ device data isolation. Other configurations will be explicitly mentioned.

#### 6.1.1 Overhead Characterization

There are two potential sources of overhead that can degrade Paradice's performance compared to native: the added latency to forward a file operation from the application to the driver and isolation.

We first measure the added latency using a simple no-op file operation, where the CVD backend immediately returns to the frontend upon receiving the operation. The average of 1 million consecutive no-op operations shows that the added latency is around 35$\mu$s, most of which comes from two inter-VM interrupts. With the polling mode, this latency is reduced to 2$\mu$s.

The overhead of isolation comes from both fault and device data isolation. The main overhead of fault isolation is sandboxing the device and the driver. Therefore, this overhead is equal to the performance difference between native and direct device assignment. In all the benchmarks below, we report the performance of direct device assignment as well and show that it is almost identical to native; hence,

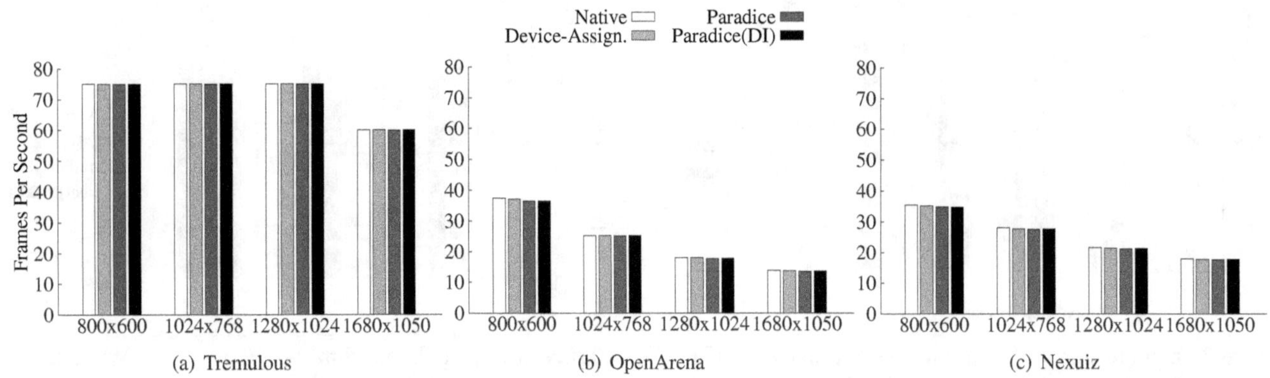


**Figure 4.** 3D HD games FPS at different resolutions. (DI) indicates the use device data isolation in Paradice.

fault isolation has no noticeable overhead on our benchmarks. The overhead of data isolation is mainly due to additional hypercalls issued by the driver. However, we show that this overhead does not noticeably impact the GPU's performance either, both for graphics and computation. We have not, however, quantified the impact of partitioning the GPU memory for device data isolation on applications requiring high amounts of GPU memory.

### 6.1.2 Ethernet Card for netmap

We evaluate the performance of netmap, a framework that can send and receive packets at the line rate on 1 and 10 gigabit Ethernet cards [43]. We use the netmap packet generator application that transmits fixed-size packets as fast as possible. In each experiment, we transmit 10 million packets and report the transmit rate. We run two sets of experiments for Paradice: one with Linux guest VM and Linux driver VM, and another with FreeBSD guest VM and Linux driver VM.

Figure 2 shows that Paradice can achieve a transmit rate close to that of native and device assignment. The figure shows the netmap transmit rate for 64-byte packets and for different packet batch sizes. The packet generator issues one `poll` file operation per batch, therefore, increasing the batch size improves the transmit rate as it amortizes the cost of the `poll` system call and, more importantly, the cost of forwarding the `poll` file operation in Paradice. When using the polling mode, a minimum batch size of 4 allows Paradice to achieve similar performance to native. However, with interrupts, a minimum batch size of around 30 is required. The figures also shows that both Linux and FreeBSD guest VMs achieve similarly high performance. Moreover, our experiments, not shown here, show that Paradice can maintain a transmit rate close to native for different packet sizes.

### 6.1.3 GPU for Graphics

We evaluate the performance of 3D HD games and OpenGL applications. In all evaluations, we report the standard Frames Per Second (FPS) metric. We also disable the GPU VSync feature, which would otherwise cap the GPU FPS to 60 (display refresh rate).

We use three 3D first-person shooter games: *Tremulous* [8], *OpenArena* [15], and *Nexuiz* [7], which are all widely used for GPU performance evaluation [14]. For all games, we use the Phoronix Test Suite engine [16] (v3.6.1), a famous test engine that automatically runs a demo of the game for a few minutes, while stressing the GPU as much as possible. We test the games at all possible resolutions.

We also use some OpenGL benchmarks in our experiments. The benchmarks use different OpenGL API including Vertex Buffer Objects, Vertex Arrays, and Display Lists [13, 18] to draw a full-screen teapot that consists of about 6000 polygons. In each experiment, we run the benchmark for 3 minutes and measure the average FPS.

Figures 3 and 4 show the results. There are four important observations. First, Paradice achieves close performance to native and device assignment for various benchmarks, including OpenGL benchmarks and 3D HD games. Second, Paradice (with interrupts) achieves relatively better performance for more demanding 3D games that it does for simpler OpenGL benchmarks. This is because Paradice adds a constant overhead to the file operations regardless of the benchmark load on the GPU. Therefore, for 3D games that require more GPU time to render each frame, it incurs a lower percentage drop in performance. Third, Paradice with polling can close this gap and achieve close-to-native performance for all the benchmarks. Finally, data isolation has no noticeable impact on performance.

### 6.1.4 GPU for Computation

We evaluate the performance of OpenCL applications. We use the Gallium Compute implementation of OpenCL [5] and use an OpenCL program that multiplies two square matrices of varying orders. We run the benchmark for different matrix orders and measure the experiment time, i.e., the time from when the OpenCL host code sets up the GPU to execute the program until when it receives the resulting matrix.

Figure 5 shows the results. It shows that Paradice performance is almost identical to native and device assignment. Moreover, the figure shows that device data isolation has no

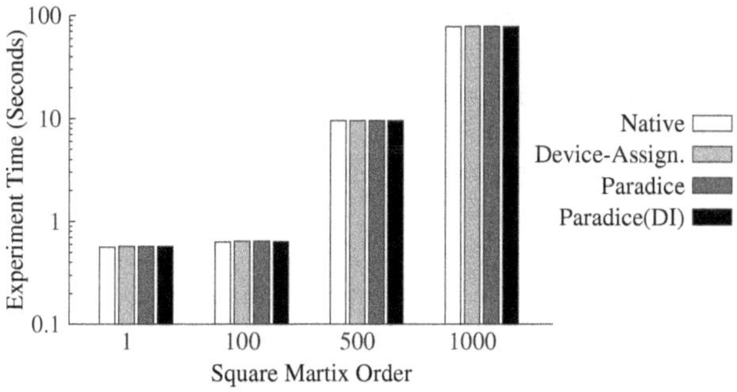


**Figure 5.** OpenCL matrix multiplication benchmark results. The x-axis shows the order of the input square matrices. (DI) indicates the use device data isolation in Paradice.

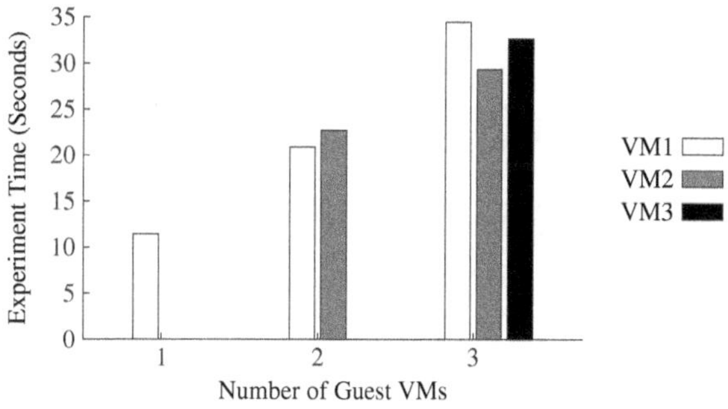


**Figure 6.** Guest VMs concurrently running the OpenCL matrix multiplication benchmark on a GPU shared through Paradice. The matrix order in this experiment is 500.

noticeable impact on performance. The reason for the high Paradice performance is that OpenCL benchmarks issue few file operations, and most of the experiment time is spent by the GPU itself.

We also measure the performance of the same OpenCL benchmark when executed from more than one guest VM concurrently on the same GPU. For this experiment, we use a matrix order of 500 and execute the benchmark 5 times in a row from each guest VM simultaneously and report the average experiment time for each guest VM. Figure 6 shows that the experiment time increases almost linearly with the number of guest VMs. This is because the GPU processing time is shared between the guest VMs.

#### 6.1.5 Mouse

We measure the latency of the mouse. Our results show that native, direct assignment, Paradice using interrupts, and Paradice using polling achieve about 39$\mu$s, 55$\mu$s, 296$\mu$s, and 179$\mu$s of latency, respectively, no matter how fast the mouse moves. The extra latency of Paradice does not result in a human-perceivable difference since the latency is well below the 1ms latency required for input devices [17]. Much of the latency in Paradice comes from the communication between the CVD frontend and backend, and therefore, the polling mode reduces the latency significantly. We note that the most accurate way of measuring the latency of input devices is to measure the elapsed time between when the user interacts with the device, e.g., moves the mouse, and when this event shows up on the screen. However, such measurement is very difficult, especially for the mouse, which generates many events in a short time period. Instead, we measure the time from when the mouse event is reported to the device driver to when the `read` operation issued by the application reaches the driver.

#### 6.1.6 Camera & Speaker

We run the GUVCview [6] camera applications in the three highest video resolutions supported by our test camera for MJPG output: 1280×720, 1600×896, and 1920×1080. For all the resolutions, native, device assignment, and Paradice achieve about 29.5 FPS.

We play the same audio file on our test speaker. Native, device assignment, and Paradice all take the same amount of time to finish playing the file, showing that they all achieve similar audio rates.

## 7. Related Work

### 7.1 I/O Virtualization

Paradice is an I/O paravirtualization solution. Existing paravirtualization solutions [22, 27, 28, 44] only support one device class, and require significant development effort to support new device classes and features. In addition to paravirtualization, there are three main solutions for I/O virtualization in whole system virtualization. *Emulation* [23, 47] is known to have poor performance. *Direct Device Assignment* [19, 24, 30, 39] provides high performance by allowing the VM to directly own and access the physical devices; however, it can only support a single VM. Paradice, in fact, leverages device assignment in its design by assigning the I/O device to the driver VM (§3.1), but it allows multiple guest VMs to share the device, which is not possible with device assignment alone. *Self-virtualization* [26, 42, 52] requires virtualization support in the I/O device hardware, e.g., [10, 11], and therefore does not apply to legacy devices. Table 3 compares different I/O virtualization solutions.

Cells [21] employs user space virtualization and virtualizes I/O devices in the Android OS. A virtual phone in Cells has its own user space, but shares the kernel with other virtual phones hence resulting in weaker isolation compared to whole system virtualization targeted by Paradice.

Some solutions provide GPU framework virtualization by remoting OpenGL [32, 36, 46] or CUDA [45] APIs. These solutions are more limited than Paradice because they are only applicable to those particular frameworks.

### 7.2 Other Related Work

Paradice allows the guest to reuse the device drivers with a common indirection layer. It therefore provides a useful

| | High Performance | Low Develop. Effort | Device Sharing | Legacy Device |
|---|---|---|---|---|
| **Emulation** | *No* | *No* | Yes | Yes |
| **Direct I/O** | Yes | Yes | *No* | Yes |
| **Self Virt.** | Yes | Yes | Yes *(limited)* | *No* |
| **Paravirt.** | Yes | *No* | Yes | Yes |
| **Paradice** | Yes | Yes | Yes | Yes |

**Table 3.** Comparing I/O virtualization solutions. "Paravirt." indicates paravirtualization solutions other than Paradice.

way to leverage device drivers since driver development is complicated and bug-prone [25, 48]. There have been related efforts in reusing device drivers. LeVasseur et al. [38] execute the device driver in a separate virtual machine and allow other guests to communicate with this VM for driver support. They demonstrate support for network and block devices and use device class-specific interfaces, i.e., the translation modules, for the guest to communicate with the driver. In contrast, Paradice supports a different set of I/O devices, while building the virtualization boundary on device files, a common interface for many I/O devices, thus significantly reducing the development effort.

iKernel [50] and VirtuOS [40] run device drivers in VMs to improve system reliability. They are therefore different from Paradice that is designed for I/O paravirtualization. iKernel forwards the file operations from the host to a driver VM. It demonstrates support for a simple LED device, unlike Paradice that supports sophisticated I/O devices such as GPU. Moreover, iKernel authors do not report support for the `mmap` file operation, which is used by many device drivers.

Willman et al. [53] propose different strategies to use the IOMMU to provide protection when VMs are given direct access to devices with DMA capability. However, Paradice's use of the IOMMU to isolate the data of guest VMs shared with I/O devices is not addressed in [53].

Plan 9 distributed system [41] uses files to share resources, including I/O devices, between machines. In contrast, Paradice uses device files for I/O paravirtualization for Unix-like OSes. Moreover, Plan 9 files do not support `mmap` and `ioctl` file operations, making it difficult to support modern I/O devices such as GPUs.

## 8. Limitations of Current Design

Virtualization at the device file boundary is not possible if the driver does not employ the device file interface to interact with applications. Important examples include network device drivers that employ sockets and sit below the kernel network stack, block device drivers that sit below the kernel file systems, and the device drivers that are implemented completely in the user space. However, as we demonstrated with netmap, Paradice can still be useful for other frameworks using these devices.

Paradice does not currently support performance isolation between the guest VMs that share a device. This has two implications: first, Paradice does not guarantee fair and efficient scheduling of the device between guest VMs. The solution is to add better scheduling support to the device driver, such as in [34]. Second, a malicious guest VM can break the device by corrupting the device driver and writing unexpected values into the device registers. One possible solution to this problem is to detect the broken device and restart it by simply restarting the driver VM or by using techniques such as shadow drivers [49].

Paradice cannot currently guarantee the correct behavior of the I/O device. Malicious guest VMs can use carefully-designed attacks to cause incorrect performance by the device, e.g., rendering unwanted content on the screen. One possible solution is to protect certain parts of the device programming interface that allows us to achieve either *correct performance or no performance at all*. Taking GPU as an example, we can consider protecting the command streamer interface to ensure that an application's GPU commands either execute as expected or do not execute at all.

While we demonstrated Paradice for a bare-metal hypervisor, it is also applicable to hosted hypervisors as long as the driver and device can be sandboxed in a VM using the device assignment technique.

Paradice currently requires the guest VM and the I/O device to reside in the same physical machine as it uses the physical shared memory to execute the driver memory operations. We are currently working on a DSM-based solution that allows the guest and driver VM to reside in separate physical machines, which will then support the migration of the guest VM while maintaining its access to the I/O device.

Finally, Paradice uses the Unix device file as the paravirtualization boundary and hence cannot support non-Unix-like OSes, most notably, the Windows OS.

## 9. Conclusions

We have presented Paradice, an I/O paravirtualization solution that uses a novel boundary, device files, to support many I/O devices with low engineering effort. We are able to virtualize various GPUs, input devices, cameras, an audio device, and an Ethernet card (for netmap). Our measurements show that Paradice achieves close-to-native performance for various benchmarks such as interactive 3D HD games. We believe that Paradice opens a new door for I/O virtualization across computing platforms of various form factors.

## Acknowledgments

The work was supported in part by NSF Awards #0923479, #1054693, and #1218041. The authors would like to thank Jon Howell from Microsoft Research and Dan Wallach from Rice University for their feedback on isolation. The authors would also like to thank Sreekumar Nair, then at Nokia Research, who first suggested the use of the device file boundary and contributed significantly to the devirtualization project [20].

## References


[1] Privilege escalation using NVIDIA GPU driver bug. http://www.securelist.com/en/advisories/50085,.

[2] Privilege escalation using DRM/Radeon GPU driver bug. https://lkml.org/lkml/2010/1/18/106,.

[3] CLOC. http://cloc.sourceforge.net/.

[4] OMAP4 Face Detection Module, Chapter 9 of the TRM. http://focus.ti.com/pdfs/wtbu/OMAP4460_ES1.0_PUBLIC_TRM_vF.zip.

[5] GalliumCompute. http://dri.freedesktop.org/wiki/GalliumCompute/.

[6] Guvcview. http://guvcview.sourceforge.net/.

[7] Nexuiz. http://www.alientrap.org/games/nexuiz.

[8] Tremulous. http://www.tremulous.net/.

[9] Everything is a file in Unix. http://ph7spot.com/musings/in-unix-everything-is-a-file.

[10] VGX. http://www.nvidia.com/object/vgx-hypervisor.html.

[11] VMDq. http://www.intel.com/content/www/us/en/network-adapters/gigabit-network-adapters/io-acceleration-technology-vmdq.html.

[12] Clang: a C Language Family Frontend for LLVM. http://clang.llvm.org/.

[13] OpenGL Microbenchmarks: Display List. http://www.songho.ca/opengl/gl_displaylist.html.

[14] GPU Benchmarking. http://www.phoronix.com/scan.php?page=article&item=virtualbox_4_opengl&num=2.

[15] OpenArena. http://openarena.ws/smfnews.php.

[16] Phoronix Test Suite. http://www.phoronix-test-suite.com/.

[17] Touchscreen Latency. http://www.engadget.com/2012/03/10/microsoft-cuts-touchscreen-lag-to-1ms/.

[18] OpenGL Microbenchmarks: Vertex Buffer Object and Vertex Array. http://www.songho.ca/opengl/gl_vbo.html.

[19] D. Abramson. Intel Virtualization Technology for Directed I/O. *Intel Technology Journal*, 10(3):179–192, 2006.

[20] A. Amiri Sani, S. Nair, L. Zhong, and Q. Jacobson. Making I/O Virtualization Easy with Device Files. *Technical Report 2013-04-13, Rice University*, 2013.

[21] J. Andrus, C. Dall, A. V. Hof, O. Laadan, and J. Nieh. Cells: a Virtual Mobile Smartphone Architecture. In *Proc. ACM SOSP*, 2011.

[22] P. Barham, B. Dragovic, K. Fraser, S. Hand, T. Harris, A. Ho, R. Neugebauer, I. Pratt, and A. Warfield. Xen and the Art of Virtualization. In *Proc. ACM SOSP*, 2003.

[23] F. Bellard. QEMU, a Fast and Portable Dynamic Translator. In *USENIX ATC, FREENIX Track*, 2005.

[24] M. Ben-Yehuda, M. D. Day, Z. Dubitzky, M. Factor, N. Har'El, A. Gordon, A. Liguori, O. Wasserman, and B. A. Yassour. The Turtles Project: Design and Implementation of Nested Virtualization. In *Proc. USENIX OSDI*, 2010.

[25] A. Chou, J. Yang, B. Chelf, S. Hallem, and D. Engler. An Empirical Study of Operating Systems Errors. In *Proc. ACM SOSP*, 2001.

[26] Y. Dong, Z. Yu, and G. Rose. SR-IOV Networking in Xen: Architecture, Design and Implementation. In *Proc. USENIX Workshop on I/O Virtualization (WIOV)*, 2008.

[27] M. Dowty and J. Sugerman. GPU Virtualization on VMware's Hosted I/O Architecture. *ACM SIGOPS Operating Systems Review*, 2009.

[28] K. Fraser, S. Hand, R. Neugebauer, I. Pratt, A. Warfield, and M. Williamson. Safe Hardware Access with the Xen Virtual Machine Monitor. In *Proc. Wrkshp. Operating System and Architectural Support for the On demand IT InfraStructure (OASIS)*, 2004.

[29] A. Ganapathi, V. Ganapathi, and D. Patterson. Windows XP Kernel Crash Analysis. In *Proc. USENIX LISA*, 2006.

[30] A. Gordon, N. Amit, N. Har'El, M. Ben-Yehuda, A. Landau, D. Tsafrir, and A. Schuster. ELI: Bare-Metal Performance for I/O Virtualization. In *Proc. ACM ASPLOS*, 2012.

[31] A. Gordon, N. Har'El, A. Landau, M. Ben-Yehuda, and A. Traeger. Towards Exitless and Efficient Paravirtual I/O. In *Proc. SYSTOR*, 2012.

[32] J. G. Hansen. Blink: Advanced Display Multiplexing for Virtualized Applications. In *Proc. ACM Network and Operating System Support for Digital Audio and Video (NOSSDAV)*, 2007.

[33] N. HarEl, A. Gordon, A. Landau, M. Ben-Yehuda, A. Traeger, and R. Ladelsky. Efficient and Scalable Paravirtual I/O System. In *Proc. USENIX ATC*, 2013.

[34] S. Kato, K. Lakshmanan, R. R. Rajkumar, and Y. Ishikawa. TimeGraph: GPU Scheduling for Real-time Multi-tasking Environments. In *Proc. USENIX ATC*, 2011.

[35] A. Kivity, Y. Kamay, D. Laor, U. Lublin, and A. Liguori. kvm: the Linux Virtual Machine Monitor. In *Proc. Linux Symposium*, 2007.

[36] H. A. Lagar-Cavilla, N. Tolia, M. Satyanarayanan, and E. D. Lara. VMM-Independent Graphics Acceleration. In *Proc. ACM VEE*, 2007.

[37] C. Lattner and V. Adve. LLVM: A Compilation Framework for Lifelong Program Analysis & Transformation. In *Proc. IEEE Int. Conf. on Code Generation and Optimization*, 2004.

[38] J. LeVasseur, V. Uhlig, J. Stoess, and S. Götz. Unmodified Device Driver Reuse and Improved System Dependability via Virtual Machines. In *Proc. USENIX OSDI*, 2004.

[39] J. Liu, W. Huang, B. Abali, and D. K. Panda. High Performance VMM-Bypass I/O in Virtual Machines. In *Proc. USENIX ATC*, 2006.

[40] R. Nikolaev and G. Back. VirtuOS: An Operating System with Kernel Virtualization. In *Proc. ACM SOSP*, 2013.

[41] D. Presotto, R. Pike, K. Thompson, and H. Trickey. Plan 9, a Distributed System. In *Proc. of the Spring 1991 EurOpen Conf.*, 1991.

[42] H. Raj and K. Schwan. High Performance and Scalable I/O Virtualization via Self-Virtualized Devices. In *Proc. ACM HPDC*, 2007.

[43] L. Rizzo. netmap: a Novel Framework for Fast Packet I/O. In *Proc. USENIX ATC*, 2012.

[44] R. Russel. virtio: Towards a De-Facto Standard for Virtual I/O Devices. *ACM SIGOPS Operating Systems Review*, 2008.

[45] L. Shi, H. Chen, and J. Sun. vCUDA: GPU Accelerated High Performance Computing in Virtual Machines. In *IEEE Int. Symp. Parallel & Distributed Processing*, 2009.

[46] C. Smowton. Secure 3D Graphics for Virtual Machines. In *Proc. ACM European Wrkshp. System Security*, 2009.

[47] J. Sugerman, G. Venkitachalam, and B. H. Lim. Virtualizing I/O Devices on VMware Workstation's Hosted Virtual Machine Monitor. In *Proc. USENIX ATC*, 2001.

[48] M. M. Swift, B. N. Bershad, and H. M. Levy. Improving the Reliability of Commodity Operating Systems. In *Proc. ACM SOSP*, 2003.

[49] M. M. Swift, M. Annamalai, B. N. Bershad, and H. M. Levy. Recovering Device Drivers. In *Proc. USENIX OSDI*, 2004.

[50] L. Tan, E. M. Chan, R. Farivar, N. Mallick, J. C. Carlyle, F. M. David, and R. H. Campbell. iKernel: Isolating buggy and malicious device drivers using hardware virtualization support. In *Proc. IEEE Int. Symp. Dependable, Autonomic and Secure Computing (DASC)*, 2007.

[51] M. Weiser. Program slicing. In *Proc. IEEE Int. Conf. on Software engineering*.

[52] P. Willmann, J. Shafer, D. Carr, A. Menon, S. Rixner, A. L. Cox, and W. Zwaenepoel. Concurrent Direct Network Access for Virtual Machine Monitors. In *Proc. IEEE High Performance Computer Architecture (HPCA)*, 2007.

[53] P. Willmann, S. Rixner, and A. L. Cox. Protection Strategies for Direct Access to Virtualized I/O Devices. In *Proc. USENIX ATC*, 2008.

# KVM/ARM: The Design and Implementation of the Linux ARM Hypervisor

Christoffer Dall
Department of Computer Science
Columbia University
cdall@cs.columbia.edu

Jason Nieh
Department of Compouter Science
Columbia University
nieh@cs.columbia.edu

**Abstract**

As ARM CPUs become increasingly common in mobile devices and servers, there is a growing demand for providing the benefits of virtualization for ARM-based devices. We present our experiences building the Linux ARM hypervisor, KVM/ARM, the first full system ARM virtualization solution that can run unmodified guest operating systems on ARM multicore hardware. KVM/ARM introduces split-mode virtualization, allowing a hypervisor to split its execution across CPU modes and be integrated into the Linux kernel. This allows KVM/ARM to leverage existing Linux hardware support and functionality to simplify hypervisor development and maintainability while utilizing recent ARM hardware virtualization extensions to run virtual machines with comparable performance to native execution. KVM/ARM has been successfully merged into the mainline Linux kernel, ensuring that it will gain wide adoption as the virtualization platform of choice for ARM. We provide the first measurements on real hardware of a complete hypervisor using ARM hardware virtualization support. Our results demonstrate that KVM/ARM has modest virtualization performance and power costs, and can achieve lower performance and power costs compared to x86-based Linux virtualization on multicore hardware.

***Categories and Subject Descriptors*** C.0 [*Computer Systems Organization*]: General–Hardware/software interface, System architectures; D.4.7 [*Operating Systems*]: Organization and Design; D.4.8 [*Operating Systems*]: Performance

***Keywords*** Virtualization, Hypervisors, Operating Systems, Multicore, ARM, Linux


*ASPLOS '14*, March 1–4, 2014, Salt Lake City, Utah, USA.

ACM 978-1-4503-2305-5/14/03. . . $15.00.
http://dx.doi.org/10.1145/2541940.2541946

## 1. Introduction

ARM-based devices are seeing tremendous growth across smartphones, netbooks, and embedded computers. While ARM CPUs have benefited from their advantages in power efficiency in these markets, ARM CPUs also continue to increase in performance such that they are now within the range of x86 CPUs for many classes of applications. This is spurring the development of new ARM-based microservers and an upward push of ARM CPUs into traditional server, PC, and network systems.

To help bring the benefits of virtualization to ARM-based devices, ARM CPUs now include hardware support for virtualization. Although virtualization is commonly used on x86-based systems, there are key differences between ARM and x86 virtualization. First, ARM and x86 virtualization extensions have important differences such that x86 hypervisor designs are not directly amenable to ARM. These differences impact hypervisor performance and design, especially for multicore systems, but have not been evaluated with real hardware. Second, unlike x86-based systems, there is no PC-standard hardware equivalent for ARM. The ARM market is fragmented with many different vertically integrated ARM platforms with non-standard hardware. Virtualizing ARM in a manner that works across the diversity of ARM hardware in the absence of any real hardware standard is a key challenge.

We describe our experiences building KVM/ARM [13, 23], the ARM hypervisor in the mainline Linux kernel. KVM/ARM is the first hypervisor to leverage ARM hardware virtualization support to run unmodified guest operating systems (OSes) on ARM multicore hardware. Our work makes four main contributions. First, we introduce split-mode virtualization, a new approach to hypervisor design that splits the core hypervisor so that it runs across different privileged CPU modes to take advantage of the specific benefits and functionality offered by each CPU mode. This approach provides key benefits in the context of ARM virtualization. ARM introduced a new CPU mode for running hypervisors called Hyp mode, but Hyp mode has its own set of features distinct from existing kernel modes. Hyp mode targets running a standalone hypervisor underneath the OS kernel, and was not designed to work well with a hosted hypervisor design, where the hypervisor is integrated with a host kernel. For example, standard OS mechanisms in Linux would have to be significantly redesigned to run in Hyp mode. Split-mode virtualization makes it possible to take advantage of the benefits of a hosted hypervisor design by running the hypervisor in normal privileged CPU modes to leverage existing OS mechanisms without modification while at the same time still using Hyp mode to leverage ARM hardware virtualization features.

Second, we designed and implemented KVM/ARM from the ground up as an open source project that would be easy to maintain and integrate into the Linux kernel. This is especially important in the context of ARM systems which lack standard ways to integrate hardware components, features for hardware discovery such as a standard BIOS or PCI bus, and standard mechanisms for installing low-level software. A standalone bare metal hypervisor would need to be ported to each and every supported hardware platform, a huge maintenance and development burden. Linux, however, is supported across almost all ARM platforms and by integrating KVM/ARM with Linux, KVM/ARM is automatically available on any device running a recent version of the Linux kernel. By using split-mode virtualization, we can leverage the existing Kernel-based Virtual Machine (KVM) [22] hypervisor interface in Linux and can reuse substantial pieces of existing kernel code and interfaces to reduce implementation complexity. KVM/ARM requires adding less than 6,000 lines of ARM code to Linux, a much smaller code base to maintain than standalone hypervisors. KVM/ARM was accepted as the ARM hypervisor of the mainline Linux kernel as of the Linux 3.9 kernel, ensuring its wide adoption and use given the dominance of Linux on ARM platforms. Based on our open source experiences, we offer some useful hints on transferring research ideas into implementations likely to be adopted by the open source community.

Third, we demonstrate the effectiveness of KVM/ARM on real multicore ARM hardware. Our results are the first measurements of a hypervisor using ARM virtualization support on real hardware. We compare against the standard widely-used Linux KVM x86 hypervisor and evaluate its performance overhead for running application workloads in virtual machines (VMs) versus native non-virtualized execution. Our results show that KVM/ARM achieves comparable performance overhead in most cases, and significantly lower performance overhead for two important applications, Apache and MySQL, on multicore platforms. These results provide the first comparison of ARM and x86 virtualization extensions on real hardware to quantitatively demonstrate how the different design choices affect virtualization performance. We show that KVM/ARM also provides power efficiency benefits over Linux KVM x86.

Finally, we make several recommendations regarding future hardware support for virtualization based on our experiences building and evaluating a complete ARM hypervisor. We identify features that are important and helpful to reduce the software complexity of hypervisor implementations, and discuss mechanisms useful to maximize hypervisor performance, especially in the context of multicore systems.

This paper describes the design and implementation of KVM/ARM. Section 2 presents an overview of the ARM virtualization extensions and a comparison with x86. Section 3 describes the design of the KVM/ARM hypervisor. Section 4 discusses the implementation of KVM/ARM and our experiences releasing it to the Linux community and having it adopted into the mainline Linux kernel. Section 5 presents experimental results quantifying the performance and energy efficiency of KVM/ARM, as well as a quantitative comparison of real ARM and x86 virtualization hardware. Section 6 makes recommendations for designing future hardware virtualization support. Section 7 discusses related work. Finally, we present some concluding remarks.

## 2. ARM Virtualization Extensions

Because the ARM architecture is not classically virtualizable [27], ARM introduced hardware virtualization support as an optional extension in the latest ARMv7 [6] and ARMv8 [7] architectures. For example, the Cortex-A15 [4] is a current ARMv7 CPU with hardware virtualization support. We present a brief overview of the ARM virtualization extensions.

***CPU Virtualization*** Figure 1 shows the CPU modes on the ARMv7 architecture, including TrustZone (Security Extensions) and a new CPU mode called Hyp mode. TrustZone splits the modes into two worlds, secure and non-secure, which are orthogonal to the CPU modes. A special mode, monitor mode, is provided to switch between the secure and non-secure worlds. Although ARM CPUs always power up starting in the secure world, ARM bootloaders typically transition to the non-secure world at an early stage. The secure world is only used for specialized use cases such as digital rights management. TrustZone may appear useful for virtualization by using the secure world for hypervisor execution, but this does not work because trap-and-emulate is not supported. There is no means to trap operations executed in the non-secure world to the secure world. Non-secure software can therefore freely configure, for example, virtual memory. Any software running at the highest non-secure privilege level therefore has access to all non-secure physical memory, making it impossible to isolate multiple VMs running in the non-secure world.

Hyp mode was introduced as a trap-and-emulate mechanism to support virtualization in the non-secure world. Hyp mode is a

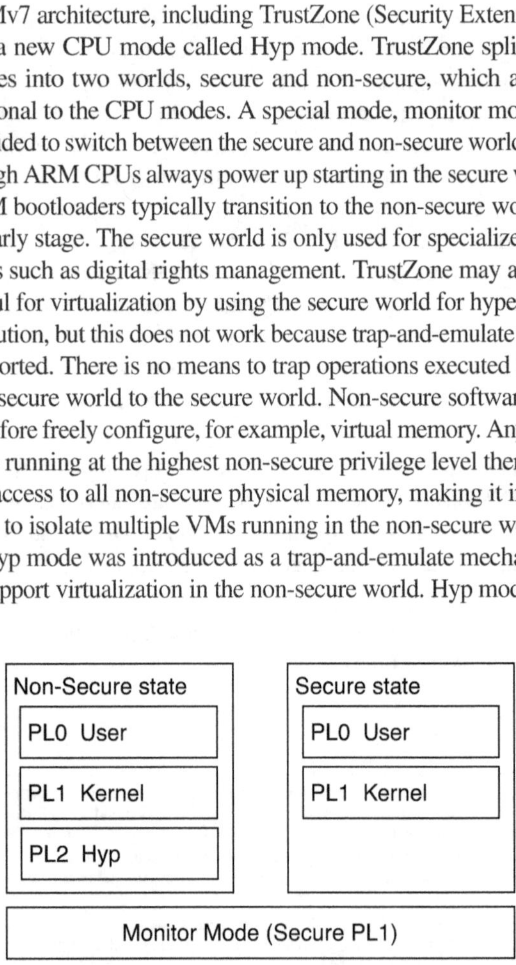


Figure 1: ARMv7 Processor Modes

CPU mode that is strictly more privileged than other CPU modes, user and kernel modes. Software running in Hyp mode can configure the hardware to trap from kernel mode into Hyp mode on various sensitive instructions and hardware interrupts. To run VMs, the hypervisor must at least partially reside in Hyp mode. The VM will execute normally in user and kernel mode until some condition is reached that requires intervention of the hypervisor. At this point, the hardware traps into Hyp mode giving control to the hypervisor, which can then manage the hardware and provide the required isolation across VMs. Once the condition is processed by the hypervisor, the CPU can be switched back into user or kernel mode and the VM can continue executing.

The ARM architecture allows each trap to be configured to trap directly into a VM's kernel mode instead of going through Hyp mode. For example, traps caused by system calls or page faults from user mode can be configured to trap to a VM's kernel mode directly so that they are handled by the guest OS without intervention of the hypervisor. This avoids going to Hyp mode on each system call or page fault, reducing virtualization overhead. Additionally, all traps into Hyp mode can be disabled and a single non-virtualized kernel can run in kernel mode and have complete control of the system.

ARM designed the virtualization support around a separate CPU mode distinct from existing kernel mode, because they envisioned a standalone hypervisor underneath a more complex rich OS kernel [14]. They wanted to make it simpler for hypervisor developers to implement the hypervisors, and therefore reduced the number of control registers available in Hyp mode compared to kernel mode. Similarly, they mandated certain bits to be set in the page table entries, because they did not envision a hypervisor sharing page tables with software running in user space, which is for example what the Linux kernel does with kernel mode.

***Memory Virtualization*** ARM also provides hardware support to virtualize physical memory. When running a VM, the physical addresses managed by the VM are actually *Intermediate Physical Addresses* (IPAs), also known as *guest physical addresses*, and need to be translated into *physical addresses* (PAs), also known as *host physical addresses*. Similarly to nested page tables on x86, ARM provides a second set of page tables, Stage-2 page tables, which translate from IPAs to PAs corresponding to guest and host physical addresses, respectively. Stage-2 translation can be completely disabled and enabled from Hyp mode. Stage-2 page tables use ARM's new LPAE page table format, with subtle differences from the page tables used by kernel mode.

***Interrupt Virtualization*** ARM defines the Generic Interrupt Controller (GIC) architecture [5]. The GIC routes interrupts from devices to CPUs and CPUs query the GIC to discover the source of an interrupt. The GIC is especially important in multicore configurations, because it is used to generate Inter-Processor Interrupts (IPIs) from one CPU core to another. The GIC is split in two parts, the distributor and the CPU interfaces. There is only one distributor in a system, but each CPU core has a GIC CPU interface. Both the CPU interfaces and the distributor are accessed over a Memory-Mapped interface (MMIO). The distributor is used to configure the GIC, for example, to configure the CPU core affinity of an interrupt, to completely enable or disable interrupts on a system, or to send an IPI to another CPU core. The CPU interface is used to acknowledge (ACK) and to signal End-Of-Interrupt (EOI). For example, when a CPU core receives an interrupt, it will read a special register on the GIC CPU interface, which ACKs the interrupt and returns the number of the interrupt. The interrupt will not be raised to the CPU again before the CPU writes to the EOI register of the CPU interface with the value retrieved from the ACK register.

Interrupts can be configured to trap to either Hyp or kernel mode. Trapping all interrupts to kernel mode and letting OS software running in kernel mode handle them directly is efficient, but does not work in the context of VMs, because the hypervisor loses control over the hardware. Trapping all interrupts to Hyp mode ensures that the hypervisor retains control, but requires emulating virtual interrupts in software to signal events to VMs. This is cumbersome to manage and expensive because each step of interrupt and virtual interrupt processing, such as ACKing and EOIing, must go through the hypervisor.

The GIC v2.0 includes hardware virtualization support in the form of a virtual GIC (VGIC) so that receiving virtual interrupts does not need to be emulated in software by the hypervisor. The VGIC introduces a VGIC CPU interface for each CPU and a corresponding hypervisor control interface for each CPU. VMs are configured to see the VGIC CPU interface instead of the GIC CPU interface. Virtual interrupts are generated by writing to special registers, the *list registers*, in the VGIC hypervisor control interface, and the VGIC CPU interface raises the virtual interrupts directly to a VM's kernel mode. Because the VGIC CPU interface includes support for ACK and EOI, these operations no longer need to trap to the hypervisor to be emulated in software, reducing overhead for receiving interrupts on a CPU. For example, emulated virtual devices typically raise virtual interrupts through a software API to the hypervisor, which can leverage the VGIC by writing the virtual interrupt number for the emulated device into the list registers. This causes the VGIC to interrupt the VM directly to kernel mode and lets the guest OS ACK and EOI the virtual interrupt without trapping to the hypervisor. Note that the distributor must still be emulated in software and all accesses to the distributor by a VM must still trap to the hypervisor. For example, when a virtual CPU sends a virtual IPI to another virtual CPU, this will cause a trap to the hypervisor, which emulates the distributor access in software and programs the list registers on the receiving CPU's GIC hypervisor control interface.

***Timer Virtualization*** ARM defines the Generic Timer Architecture which includes support for timer virtualization. Generic timers provide a *counter* that measures passing of time in real-time, and a *timer* for each CPU, which is programmed to raise an interrupt to the CPU after a certain amount of time has passed. Timers are likely to be used by both hypervisors and guest OSes, but to provide isolation and retain control, the timers used by the hypervisor cannot be directly configured and manipulated by guest OSes. Such timer accesses from a guest OS would need to trap to Hyp mode, incurring additional overhead for a relatively frequent operation for some workloads. Hypervisors may also wish to virtualize VM time, which is problematic if VMs have direct access to counter hardware.

ARM provides virtualization support for the timers by introducing a new counter, the *virtual counter* and a new timer, the *virtual timer*. A hypervisor can be configured to use physical timers while VMs are configured to use virtual timers. VMs can then access, program, and cancel virtual timers without causing traps to Hyp mode. Access to the physical timer and counter from kernel mode is controlled from Hyp mode, but software running in kernel mode always has access to the virtual timers and counters.

***Comparison with x86*** There are a number of similarities and differences between the ARM virtualization extensions and hardware virtualization support for x86 from Intel and AMD. Intel and AMD extensions are very similar, so we limit our comparison to ARM and Intel. ARM supports virtualization through a separate CPU mode, Hyp mode, which is a separate and strictly more privileged CPU mode than previous user and kernel modes. In contrast, Intel has root and non-root mode [20], which are orthogonal to the CPU protection modes. While sensitive operations on ARM trap to Hyp mode, sensitive operations can trap from non-root mode to root mode while staying in the same protection level on Intel. A crucial difference between the two hardware designs is that Intel's root mode supports the same full range of user and kernel mode functionality as its non-root mode, whereas ARM's Hyp mode is a strictly different CPU mode with its own set of features. A hypervisor using ARM's Hyp mode has an arguably simpler set of features to use than the more complex options available with Intel's root mode.

Both ARM and Intel trap into their respective Hyp and root modes, but Intel provides specific hardware support for a VM control block which is automatically saved and restored when switching to and from root mode using only a single instruction. This is used to automatically save and restore guest state when switching between guest and hypervisor execution. In contrast, ARM provides no such hardware support and any state that needs to be saved and restored must be done explicitly in software. This provides some flexibility in what is saved and restored in switching to and from Hyp mode. For example, trapping to ARM's Hyp mode is potentially faster than trapping to Intel's root mode if there is no additional state to save.

ARM and Intel are quite similar in their support for virtualizing physical memory. Both introduce an additional set of page tables to translate guest to host physical addresses. ARM benefited from hindsight in including Stage-2 translation whereas Intel did not include its equivalent Extended Page Table (EPT) support until its second generation virtualization hardware.

ARM's support for virtual timers have no real x86 counterpart, and until the recent introduction of Intel's virtual APIC support [20], ARM's support for virtual interrupts also had no x86 counterpart. Without virtual APIC support, EOIing interrupts in an x86 VM requires traps to root mode, whereas ARM's virtual GIC avoids the cost of trapping to Hyp mode for those interrupt handling mechanisms. Executing similar timer functionality by a guest OS on x86 will incur additional traps to root mode compared to the number of traps to Hyp mode required for ARM. Reading a counter, however, is not a privileged operation on x86 and does not trap, even without virtualization support in the counter hardware.

## 3. Hypervisor Architecture

Instead of reinventing and reimplementing complex core functionality in the hypervisor, and potentially introducing tricky and fatal bugs along the way, KVM/ARM builds on KVM and leverages existing infrastructure in the Linux kernel. While a standalone bare metal hypervisor design approach has the potential for better performance and a smaller Trusted Computing Base (TCB), this approach is less practical on ARM. ARM hardware is in many ways much more diverse than x86. Hardware components are often tightly integrated in ARM devices in non-standard ways by different device manufacturers. ARM hardware lacks features for hardware discovery such as a standard BIOS or a PCI bus, and there is no established mechanism for installing low-level software on a wide variety of ARM platforms. Linux, however, is supported across almost all ARM platforms and by integrating KVM/ARM with Linux, KVM/ARM is automatically available on any device running a recent version of the Linux kernel. This is in contrast to bare metal approaches such as Xen [32], which must actively support every platform on which they wish to install the Xen hypervisor. For example, for every new SoC that Xen needs to support, the developers must implement a new serial device driver in the core Xen hypervisor.

While KVM/ARM benefits from its integration with Linux in terms of portability and hardware support, a key problem we had to address was that the ARM hardware virtualization extensions were designed to support a standalone hypervisor design where the hypervisor is completely separate from any standard kernel functionality, as discussed in Section 2. In the following, we describe how KVM/ARM's novel design makes it possible to benefit from integration with an existing kernel and at the same time take advantage of the hardware virtualization features.

### 3.1 Split-mode Virtualization

Simply running a hypervisor entirely in ARM's Hyp mode is attractive since it is the most privileged level. However, since KVM/ARM leverages existing kernel infrastructure such as the scheduler, running KVM/ARM in Hyp mode implies running the Linux kernel in Hyp mode. This is problematic for at least two reasons. First, low-level architecture dependent code in Linux is written to work in kernel mode, and would not run unmodified in Hyp mode, because Hyp mode is a completely different CPU mode from normal kernel mode. The significant changes that would be required to run the kernel in Hyp mode would be very unlikely to be accepted by the Linux kernel community. More importantly, to preserve compatibility with hardware without Hyp mode and to run Linux as a guest OS, low-level code would have to be written to work in both modes, potentially resulting in slow and convoluted code paths. As a simple example, a page fault handler needs to obtain the virtual address causing the page fault. In Hyp mode this address is stored in a different register than in kernel mode.

Second, running the entire kernel in Hyp mode would adversely affect native performance. For example, Hyp mode has its own separate address space. Whereas kernel mode uses two page table base registers to provide the familiar 3GB/1GB split between user address space and kernel address space, Hyp mode uses a single page table register and therefore cannot have direct access to the user space portion of the address space. Frequently used functions to access user memory would require the kernel to explicitly map user space data into kernel address space and subsequently perform necessary teardown and TLB maintenance operations, resulting in poor native performance on ARM.

These problems with running a Linux hypervisor using ARM Hyp mode do not occur for x86 hardware virtualization. x86 root mode is orthogonal to its CPU privilege modes. The entire Linux kernel can run in root mode as a hypervisor because the same set of CPU modes available in non-root mode are available in root mode. Nevertheless, given the widespread use of ARM and the advantages of Linux on ARM, finding an efficient virtualization solution for ARM that can leverage Linux and take advantage of the hardware virtualization support is of crucial importance.

KVM/ARM introduces split-mode virtualization, a new approach to hypervisor design that splits the core hypervisor so that it runs across different privileged CPU modes to take advantage of the specific benefits and functionality offered by each CPU mode. KVM/ARM uses split-mode virtualization to leverage the ARM hardware virtualization support enabled by Hyp mode, while at the same time leveraging existing Linux kernel services running in kernel mode. Split-mode virtualization allows KVM/ARM to be integrated with the Linux kernel without intrusive modifications to the existing code base.

This is done by splitting the hypervisor into two components, the lowvisor and the highvisor, as shown in Figure 2. The lowvisor is designed to take advantage of the hardware virtualization support available in Hyp mode to provide three key functions. First, the lowvisor sets up the correct execution context by appropriate configuration of the hardware, and enforces protection and isolation between different execution contexts. The lowvisor directly interacts with hardware protection features and is therefore highly critical and the code base is kept to an absolute minimum. Second, the lowvisor switches from a VM execution context to the host execution context and vice-versa. The host execution context is used to run the hypervisor and the host Linux kernel. We refer to an execution context as a world, and switching from one world to another as a *world switch*, because the entire state of the system is changed. Since the lowvisor is the only component that runs in Hyp mode, only it can be responsible for the hardware reconfiguration necessary to perform a world switch. Third, the lowvisor provides a virtualization trap handler, which handles interrupts and exceptions that must trap to the hypervisor. The lowvisor performs only the minimal amount of

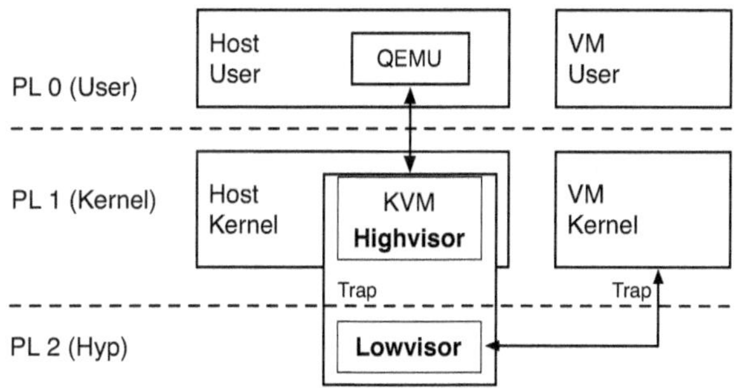


Figure 2: KVM/ARM System Architecture

processing required and defers the bulk of the work to be done to the highvisor after a world switch to the highvisor is complete.

The highvisor runs in kernel mode as part of the host Linux kernel. It can therefore directly leverage existing Linux functionality such as the scheduler, and can make use of standard kernel software data structures and mechanisms to implement its functionality, such as locking mechanisms and memory allocation functions. This makes higher-level functionality easier to implement in the highvisor. For example, while the lowvisor provides a low-level trap-handler and the low-level mechanism to switch from one world to another, the highvisor handles Stage-2 page faults from the VM and performs instruction emulation. Note that parts of the VM run in kernel mode, just like the highvisor, but with Stage-2 translation and trapping to Hyp mode enabled.

Because the hypervisor is split across kernel mode and Hyp mode, switching between a VM and the highvisor involves multiple mode transitions. A trap to the highvisor while running the VM will first trap to the lowvisor running in Hyp mode. The lowvisor will then cause another trap to run the highvisor. Similarly, going from the highvisor to a VM requires trapping from kernel mode to Hyp mode, and then switching to the VM. As a result, split-mode virtualization incurs a double trap cost in switching to and from the highvisor. On ARM, the only way to perform these mode transitions to and from Hyp mode is by trapping. However, as shown in Section 5, this extra trap is not a significant performance cost on ARM.

KVM/ARM uses a memory mapped interface to share data between the highvisor and lowvisor as necessary. Because memory management can be complex, we leverage the highvisor's ability to use the existing memory management subsystem in Linux to manage memory for both the highvisor and lowvisor. Managing the lowvisor's memory involves additional challenges though, because it requires managing Hyp mode's separate address space. One simplistic approach would be to reuse the host kernel's page tables and also use them in Hyp mode to make the address spaces identical. This unfortunately does not work, because Hyp mode uses a different page table format from kernel mode. Therefore, the highvisor explicitly manages the Hyp mode page tables to map any code executed in Hyp mode and any data structures shared between the highvisor and the lowvisor to the same virtual addresses in Hyp mode and in kernel mode.

| Action | Nr. | State |
|---|---|---|
| Context Switch | 38 | General Purpose (GP) Registers |
| | 26 | Control Registers |
| | 16 | VGIC Control Registers |
| | 4 | VGIC List Registers |
| | 2 | Arch. Timer Control Registers |
| | 32 | 64-bit VFP registers |
| | 4 | 32-bit VFP Control Registers |
| Trap-and-Emulate | - | CP14 Trace Registers |
| | - | WFI Instructions |
| | - | SMC Instructions |
| | - | ACTLR Access |
| | - | Cache ops. by Set/Way |
| | - | L2CTLR / L2ECTLR Registers |

Table 1: VM and Host State on a Cortex-A15

### 3.2 CPU Virtualization

To virtualize the CPU, KVM/ARM must present an interface to the VM which is essentially identical to the underlying real hardware CPU, while ensuring that the hypervisor remains in control of the hardware. This involves ensuring that software running in the VM must have persistent access to the same register state as software running on the physical CPU, as well as ensuring that physical hardware state associated with the hypervisor and its host kernel is persistent across running VMs. Register state not affecting VM isolation can simply be context switched by saving the VM state and restoring the host state from memory when switching from a VM to the host and vice versa. KVM/ARM configures access to all other sensitive state to trap to Hyp mode, so it can be emulated by the hypervisor.

Table 1 shows the CPU register state visible to software running in kernel and user mode, and KVM/ARM's virtualization method for each register group. The lowvisor has its own dedicated configuration registers only for use in Hyp mode, and is not shown in Table 1. KVM/ARM context switches registers during world-switches whenever the hardware supports it, because it allows the VM direct access to the hardware. For example, the VM can directly program the Stage-1 page table base register without trapping to the hypervisor, a fairly common operation in most guest OSes. KVM/ARM performs trap and emulate on sensitive instructions and when accessing hardware state that could affect the hypervisor or would leak information about the hardware to the VM that violates its virtualized abstraction. For example, KVM/ARM traps if a VM executes the WFI instruction, which causes the CPU to power down, because such an operation should only be performed by the hypervisor to maintain control of the hardware. KVM/ARM defers switching certain register state until absolutely necessary, which slightly improves performance under certain workloads.

The difference between running inside a VM in kernel or user mode and running the hypervisor in kernel or user mode is determined by how the virtualization extensions have been configured by Hyp mode during the world switch. A world switch from the host to a VM performs the following actions: (1) store all host GP registers on the Hyp stack, (2) configure the VGIC for the VM, (3) configure the timers for the VM, (4) save all host-specific configuration registers onto the Hyp stack, (5) load the VM's configuration registers onto the hardware, which can be done without affecting current execution, because Hyp mode uses its own configuration registers, separate from the host state, (6) configure Hyp mode to trap floating-point operations for lazy context switching, trap interrupts, trap CPU halt instructions (WFI/WFE), trap SMC instructions, trap specific configuration register accesses, and trap debug register accesses, (7) write VM-specific IDs into shadow ID registers, (8) set the Stage-2 page table base register (VTTBR) and enable Stage-2 address translation, (9) restore all guest GP registers, and (10) trap into either user or kernel mode.

The CPU will stay in the VM world until an event occurs, which triggers a trap into Hyp mode. Such an event can be caused by any of the traps mentioned above, a Stage-2 page fault, or a hardware interrupt. Since the event requires services from the highvisor, either to emulate the expected hardware behavior for the VM or to service a device interrupt, KVM/ARM must perform another world switch back into the highvisor and its host. The world switch back to the host from a VM performs the following actions: (1) store all VM GP registers, (2) disable Stage-2 translation, (3) configure Hyp mode to not trap any register access or instructions, (4) save all VM-specific configuration registers, (5) load the host's configuration registers onto the hardware, (6) configure the timers for the host, (7) save VM-specific VGIC state, (8) restore all host GP registers, and (9) trap into kernel mode.

### 3.3 Memory Virtualization

KVM/ARM provides memory virtualization by enabling Stage-2 translation for all memory accesses when running in a VM. Stage-2 translation can only be configured in Hyp mode, and its use is completely transparent to the VM. The highvisor manages the Stage-2 translation page tables to only allow access to memory specifically allocated for a VM; other accesses will cause Stage-2 page faults which trap to the hypervisor. This mechanism ensures that a VM cannot access memory belonging to the hypervisor or other VMs, including any sensitive data. Stage-2 translation is disabled when running in the highvisor and lowviser because the highvisor has full control of the complete system and directly manages the host physical addresses. When the hypervisor performs a world switch to a VM, it enables Stage-2 translation and configures the Stage-2 page table base register accordingly. Although both the highvisor and VMs share the same CPU modes, Stage-2 translations ensure that the highvisor is protected from any access by the VMs.

KVM/ARM uses split-mode virtualization to leverage existing kernel memory allocation, page reference counting, and page table manipulation code. KVM/ARM handles Stage-2 page faults by considering the IPA of the fault, and if that address belongs to normal memory in the VM memory map, KVM/ARM allocates a page for the VM by simply calling an existing kernel function, such as `get_user_pages`, and maps the allocated page to the VM in the Stage-2 page tables. In comparison, a bare metal hypervisor would be forced to either statically allocate memory to VMs or write an entire new memory allocation subsystem.

### 3.4 I/O Virtualization

KVM/ARM leverages existing QEMU and Virtio [29] user space device emulation to provide I/O virtualization. At a hardware level, all I/O mechanisms on the ARM architecture are based on load/store operations to MMIO device regions. With the exception of devices directly assigned to VMs, all hardware MMIO regions are inaccessible from VMs. KVM/ARM uses Stage-2 translations to ensure that physical devices cannot be accessed directly from VMs. Any access outside of RAM regions allocated for the VM will trap to the hypervisor, which can route the access to a specific emulated device in QEMU based on the fault address. This is somewhat different from x86, which uses x86-specific hardware instructions such as `inl` and `outl` for port I/O operations in addition to MMIO. As we show in Section 5, KVM/ARM achieves low I/O performance overhead with very little implementation effort.

### 3.5 Interrupt Virtualization

KVM/ARM leverages its tight integration with Linux to reuse existing device drivers and related functionality, including handling interrupts. When running in a VM, KVM/ARM configures the CPU to trap all hardware interrupts to Hyp mode. On each interrupt, it performs a world switch to the highvisor and the host handles the interrupt, so that the hypervisor remains in complete control of hardware resources. When running in the host and the highvisor, interrupts trap directly to kernel mode, avoiding the overhead of going through Hyp mode. In both cases, all hardware interrupt processing is done in the host by reusing Linux's existing interrupt handling functionality.

However, VMs must receive notifications in the form of virtual interrupts from emulated devices and multicore guest OSes must be able to send virtual IPIs from one virtual core to another. KVM/ARM uses the VGIC to inject virtual interrupts into VMs to reduce the number of traps to Hyp mode. As described in Section 2, virtual interrupts are raised to virtual CPUs by programming the list registers in the VGIC hypervisor CPU control interface. KVM/ARM configures the Stage-2 page tables to prevent VMs from accessing the control interface and to allow access only to the VGIC virtual CPU interface, ensuring that only the hypervisor can program the control interface and that the VM can access the VGIC virtual CPU interface directly. However, guest OSes will still attempt to access a GIC distributor to configure the GIC and to send IPIs from one virtual core to another. Such accesses will trap to the hypervisor and the hypervisor must emulate the distributor.

KVM/ARM introduces the virtual distributor, a software model of the GIC distributor as part of the highvisor. The virtual distributor exposes an interface to user space, so emulated devices in user space can raise virtual interrupts to the virtual distributor and exposes an MMIO interface to the VM identical to that of the physical GIC distributor. The virtual distributor keeps internal software state about the state of each interrupt and uses this state whenever a VM is scheduled, to program the list registers to inject virtual interrupts. For example, if virtual CPU0 sends an IPI to virtual CPU1, the distributor will program the list registers for virtual CPU1 to raise a virtual IPI interrupt the next time virtual CPU1 runs.

Ideally, the virtual distributor only accesses the hardware list registers when necessary, since device MMIO operations are typically significantly slower than cached memory accesses. A complete context switch of the list registers is required when scheduling a different VM to run on a physical core, but not necessarily required when simply switching between a VM and the hypervisor. For example, if there are no pending virtual interrupts, it is not necessary to access any of the list registers. Note that once the hypervisor writes a virtual interrupt to a list register when switching to a VM, it must also read the list register back when switching back to the hypervisor, because the list register describes the state of the virtual interrupt and indicates, for example, if the VM has ACKed the virtual interrupt. The initial unoptimized version of KVM/ARM uses a simplified approach which completely context switches all VGIC state including the list registers on each world switch.

### 3.6 Timer Virtualization

Reading counters and programming timers are frequent operations in many OSes for process scheduling and to regularly poll device state. For example, Linux reads a counter to determine if a process has expired its time slice, and programs timers to ensure that processes don't exceed their allowed time slices. Application workloads also often leverage timers for various reasons. Trapping to the hypervisor for each such operation is likely to incur noticeable performance overheads, and allowing a VM direct access to the time-keeping hardware typically implies giving up timing control of the hardware resources as VMs can disable timers and control the CPU for extended periods of time.

KVM/ARM leverages ARM's hardware virtualization features of the generic timers to allow VMs direct access to reading counters and programming timers without trapping to Hyp mode while at the same time ensuring the hypervisor remains in control of the hardware. Since access to the physical timers is controlled using Hyp mode, any software controlling Hyp mode has access to the physical timers. KVM/ARM maintains hardware control by using the physical timers in the hypervisor and disallowing access to physical timers from the VM. The Linux kernel running as a guest OS only accesses the virtual timer and can therefore directly access timer hardware without trapping to the hypervisor.

Unfortunately, due to architectural limitations, the virtual timers cannot directly raise virtual interrupts, but always raise hardware interrupts, which trap to the hypervisor. KVM/ARM detects when a VM virtual timer expires, and injects a corresponding virtual interrupt to the VM, performing all hardware ACK and EOI operations in the highvisor. The hardware only provides a single virtual timer per physical CPU, and multiple virtual CPUs may be multiplexed across this single hardware instance. To support virtual timers in this scenario, KVM/ARM detects unexpired timers when a VM traps to the hypervisor and leverages existing OS functionality to program a software timer at the time when the virtual timer would have otherwise fired, had the VM been left running. When such a software timer fires, a callback function is executed, which raises a virtual timer interrupt to the VM using the virtual distributor described above.

## 4. Implementation and Adoption

We have successfully integrated our work into the Linux kernel and KVM/ARM is now the standard ARM hypervisor on Linux platforms, as it is included in every kernel beginning with version 3.9. Its relative simplicity and rapid completion was faciliated by specific design choices that allow it to leverage substantial existing infrastructure despite differences in the underlying hardware. We share some lessons we learned from our experiences in hopes that they may be helpful to others in getting research ideas widely adopted by the open source community.

***Code maintainability is key.*** It is a common misconception that a research software implementation providing potential improvements or interesting new features can simply be open sourced and thereby quickly integrated by the open source community. An important point that is often not taken into account is that any implementation must be maintained. If an implementation requires many people and much effort to be maintained, it is much less likely to integrated into existing open source code bases. Because maintainability is so crucial, reusing code and interfaces is important. For example, KVM/ARM builds on existing infrastructure such as KVM and QEMU, and from the very start we prioritized addressing code review comments to make our code suitable for integration into existing systems. An unexpected but important benefit of this decision was that we could leverage the community for help to solve hard bugs or understand intricate parts of the ARM architecture.

***Be a known contributor.*** Convincing maintainers to integrate code is not just about the code itself, but also about who submits it. It is not unusual for researchers to complain about kernel maintainers not accepting their code into Linux only to have some known kernel developer submit the same idea and have it accepted. The reason is an issue of trust. Establishing trust is a catch-22: one must be well-known to submit code, yet one cannot become known without submitting code. One way to do this is to start small. As part of our work, we also made various small changes to KVM to prepare support for ARM, which included cleaning up existing code to be more generic and improving cross platform support. The KVM maintainers were glad to accept these small improvements, which generated goodwill and helped us become known to the KVM community.

***Make friends and involve the community.*** Open source development turns out to be quite a social enterprise. Networking with the community helps tremendously, not just online, but in person at conferences and other venues. For example, at an early stage in the development of KVM/ARM, we traveled to ARM headquarters in Cambridge, UK to establish contact with both ARM management and the ARM kernel engineering team, who both contributed to our efforts.

As another example, an important issue in integrating KVM/ARM into the kernel was agreeing on various interfaces for ARM virtualization, such as reading and writing control registers. Since it is an established policy to never break released interfaces and compatibility with user space applications, existing interfaces cannot be changed, and the community puts great effort into designing extensible and reusable interfaces. Deciding on the appropriateness of an interface is a judgment call and not an exact science. We were fortunate enough to receive help from well-known kernel developers such as Rusty Russell, who helped us drive both the implementation and communication about our interfaces, specifically for user space save and restore of registers, a feature useful for both debugging and VM migration. Working with an established developer like Rusty was a tremendous help because we benefited from both his experience and strong voice in the kernel community.

***Involve the community early.*** An important issue in developing KVM/ARM was how to get access to Hyp mode across the plethora of available ARM SoC platforms supported by Linux. One approach would be to initialize and configure Hyp mode when KVM is initialized, which would isolate the code changes to the KVM subsystem. However, because getting into Hyp mode from the kernel involves a trap, early stage bootloader must have already installed code in Hyp mode to handle the trap and allow KVM to run. If no such trap handler was installed, trapping to Hyp mode could end up crashing the kernel. We worked with the kernel community to define the right ABI between KVM and the bootloader, but soon learned that agreeing on ABIs with SoC vendors had historically been difficult.

In collaboration with ARM and the open source community, we reached the conclusion that if we simply required the kernel to be booted in Hyp mode, we would not have to rely on fragile ABIs. The kernel then simply tests when it starts up whether it is in Hyp mode, in which case it installs a trap handler to provide a hook to re-enter Hyp mode at a later stage. A small amount of code must be added to the kernel boot procedure, but the result is a much cleaner and robust mechanism. If the bootloader is Hyp mode unaware and the kernel does not boot up in Hyp mode, KVM/ARM will detect this and will simply remain disabled. This solution avoids the need to design a new ABI and it turned out that legacy kernels would still work, because they always make an explicit switch into kernel mode as their first instruction. These changes were merged into the mainline Linux 3.6 kernel, and official ARM kernel boot recommendations were modified to recommend that all bootloaders boot the kernel in Hyp mode to take advantage of the new architecture features.

***Know the chain of command.*** There were multiple possible upstream paths for KVM/ARM. Historically, other architectures supported by KVM such as x86 and PowerPC were merged through the KVM tree directly into Linus Torvalds' tree with the appropriate approval of the respective architecture maintainers. KVM/ARM, however, required a few minor changes to

ARM-specific header files and the idmap subsystem, and it was therefore not clear whether the code would be integrated via the KVM tree with approval from the ARM kernel maintainer or via the ARM kernel tree. Russell King is the ARM kernel maintainer, and Linus pulls directly from his ARM kernel tree for ARM-related code. The situation was particularly interesting, because Russell King did not want to merge virtualization support in the mainline kernel [24] and he did not review our code. At the same time, the KVM community was quite interested in integrating our code, but could not do so without approval from the ARM maintainers, and Russell King refused to engage in a discussion about this procedure.

***Be persistent.*** While we were trying to merge our code into Linux, a lot of changes were happening around Linux ARM support in general. The amount of churn in SoC support code was becoming an increasingly big problem for maintainers, and much work was underway to reduce board specific code and support a single ARM kernel binary bootable across multiple SoCs. In light of these ongoing changes, getting enough time from ARM kernel maintainers to review the code was challenging, and there was extra pressure on the maintainers to be highly critical of any new code merged into the ARM tree. We had no choice but to keep maintaining and improving the code, and regularly send out updated patch series that followed upstream kernel changes. Eventually Will Deacon, one of the ARM maintainers, made time for several comprehensive and helpful reviews, and after addressing his concerns, he gave us his approval of the code. After all this, when we thought we were done, we finally received some feedback from Russell King.

When MMIO operations trap to the hypervisor, the virtualization extensions populate a register which contains information useful to emulate the instruction (whether it was a load or a store, source/target registers, and the length of MMIO accesses). A certain class of instructions used by older Linux kernels do not populate such a register. KVM/ARM therefore loads the instruction from memory and decodes it in software. Even though the decoding implementation was well tested and reviewed by a large group of people, Russell King objected to including this feature. He had already implemented multiple forms of instruction decoding in other subsystems and demanded that we either rewrite significant parts of the ARM kernel to unify all instruction decoding to improve code reuse, or drop the MMIO instruction decoding support from our implementation. Rather than pursue a rewriting effort that could drag on for months, we abandoned the otherwise well-liked and useful code base. We can only speculate about the true motives behind this decision, as the ARM maintainer would not engage in a discussion about the subject.

After 15 main patch revisions and more than 18 months, the KVM/ARM code was successfully merged into Linus's tree via Russell King's ARM tree in February 2013. In getting all these things to come together in the end before the 3.9 merge window, the key was having a good relationship with many of the kernel developers to get their help, and being persistent in continuing to push to have the code merged in the face of various challenges.

## 5. Experimental Results

We present some experimental results that quantify the performance of KVM/ARM on multicore ARM hardware. We evaluate the virtualization overhead of KVM/ARM compared to native execution by running both microbenchmarks and real application workloads within VMs and directly on the hardware. We measure and compare the performance, energy, and implementation costs of KVM/ARM versus KVM x86 to demonstrate the effectiveness of KVM/ARM against a more mature hardware virtualization platform. These results provide the first real hardware measurements of the performance of ARM hardware virtualization support as well as the first comparison between ARM and x86.

### 5.1 Methodology

ARM measurements were obtained using an Insignal Arndale board [19] with a dual core 1.7GHz Cortex A-15 CPU on a Samsung Exynos 5250 SoC. This is the first and most widely used commercially available development board based on the Cortex A-15, the first ARM CPU with hardware virtualization support. Onboard 100Mb Ethernet is provided via the USB bus and an external 120GB Samsung 840 series SSD drive was connected to the Arndale board via eSATA. x86 measurements were obtained using both a low-power mobile laptop platform and an industry standard server platform. The laptop platform was a 2011 MacBook Air with a dual core 1.8GHz Core i7-2677M CPU, an internal Samsung SM256C 256GB SSD drive, and an Apple 100Mb USB Ethernet adapter. The server platform was a dedicated OVH SP 3 server with a dual core 3.4GHz Intel Xeon E3 1245v2 CPU, two physical SSD drives of which only one was used, and 1GB Ethernet connected to a 100Mb network infrastructure. x86 hardware with virtual APIC support was not yet available at the time of our experiments.

Given the differences in hardware platforms, our focus was not on measuring absolute performance, but rather the relative performance differences between virtualized and native execution on each platform. Since our goal is to evaluate hypervisors, not raw hardware performance, this relative measure provides a useful cross-platform basis for comparing the virtualization performance and power costs of KVM/ARM versus KVM x86.

To provide comparable measurements, we kept the software environments across all hardware platforms the same as much as possible. Both the host and guest VMs on all platforms were Ubuntu version 12.10. We used the mainline Linux 3.10 kernel for our experiments, with patches for huge page support applied on top of the source tree. Since the experiments were performed on a number of different platforms, the kernel configurations had to be slightly different, but all common features were configured similarly across all platforms. In particular, Virtio drivers were used in the guest VMs on both ARM and x86. We used QEMU version v1.5.0 for our measurements. All systems were configured with a maximum of 1.5GB of RAM available to the respective guest VM or host being tested. Furthermore, all multicore measurements were done using two physical cores and guest VMs with two virtual CPUs, and single-core measurements were configured with SMP disabled in the kernel configuration of both the guest and host system; hyperthreading was disabled on the x86 platforms. CPU frequency scaling was disabled to ensure that native and virtualized performance was measured at the same clock rate on each platform.

For measurements involving the network and another server, 100Mb Ethernet was used on all systems. The ARM and x86 laptop platforms were connected using a Netgear GS608v3 switch, and a 2010 iMac with a 3.2GHz Core i3 CPU with 12GB of RAM running Mac OS X Mountain Lion was used as a server. The x86 server platform was connected to a 100Mb port in the OVH network infrastructure, and another identical server in the same data center was used as the server. While there are some differences in the network infrastructure used for the x86 server platform because it is controlled by someone else, we do not expect these differences to have any significant impact on the relative performance between virtualized and native execution.

We present results for four sets of experiments. First, we measured the cost of various micro architectural characteristics of the hypervisors on multicore hardware using custom small guest OSes [11, 21] with some bugfix patches applied. We further instrumented the code on both KVM/ARM and KVM x86 to read the cycle counter at specific points along critical paths to more accurately determine where overhead time was spent.

Second, we measured the cost of a number of common low-level OS operations using lmbench [25] v3.0 on both single-core and multicore hardware. When running lmbench on multicore configurations, we pinned each benchmark process to a separate CPU to measure the true overhead of interprocessor communication in VMs on multicore systems.

Third, we measured real application performance using a variety of workloads on both single-core and multicore hardware. Table 2 describes the eight application workloads we used.

Fourth, we measured energy efficiency using the same eight application workloads used for measuring application performance. ARM power measurements were performed using an ARM Energy Probe [3] which measures power consumption over a shunt attached to the power supply of the Arndale board. Power to the external SSD was delivered by attaching a USB power cable to the USB ports on the Arndale board thereby factoring storage power into the total SoC power measured at the power supply. x86 power measurements were performed using the `powerstat` tool, which reads ACPI information. `powerstat` measures total system power draw from the battery, so power measurements on the x86 system were run from battery power and could only be run on the x86 laptop platform. Although we did not measure the power efficiency of the x86 server platform, it is expected to be much less efficient that the x86 laptop platform, so using the x86 laptop platform provides a conservative comparison of energy efficiency against ARM. The display and wireless features of the x86 laptop platform were turned off to ensure a fair comparison. Both tools reported instantaneous power draw in watts with a 10Hz interval. These measurements were averaged and multiplied by the duration of the test to obtain an energy measure.

| | |
|---|---|
| apache | Apache v2.2.22 Web server running ApacheBench v2.3 on the local server, which measures number of handled requests per seconds serving the index file of the GCC 4.4 manual using 100 concurrent requests |
| mysql | MySQL v14.14 (distrib 5.5.27) running the SysBench OLTP benchmark using the default configuration |
| memcached | memcached v1.4.14 using the `memslap` benchmark with a concurrency parameter of 100 |
| kernel compile | kernel compilation by compiling the Linux 3.6.0 kernel using the vexpress_defconfig for ARM using GCC 4.7.2 on ARM and the GCC 4.7.2 `arm-linux-gnueabi-` cross compilation toolchain on x86 |
| untar | `untar` extracting the 3.6.0 Linux kernel image compressed with bz2 compression using the standard `tar` utility |
| curl 1K | `curl` v7.27.0 downloading a 1KB randomly generated file 1,000 times from the respective iMac or OVH server and saving the result to `/dev/null` with output disabled, which provides a measure of network latency |
| curl 1G | `curl` v7.27.0 downloading a 1GB randomly generated file from the respective iMac or OVH server and saving the result to `/dev/null` with output disabled, which provides a measure of network throughput |
| hackbench | `hackbench` [26] using unix domain sockets and 100 process groups running with 500 loops |

Table 2: Benchmark Applications

### 5.2 Performance and Power Measurements

Table 3 presents various micro-architectural costs of virtualization using KVM/ARM on ARM and KVM x86 on x86. Measurements are shown in cycles instead of time to provide a useful comparison across platforms with different CPU frequencies. We show two numbers for the ARM platform where possible, with and without VGIC and virtual timers support.

Hypercall is the cost of two world switches, going from the VM to the host and immediately back again without doing any work in the host. KVM/ARM takes three to four times as many cycles for this operation versus KVM x86 due to two main factors. First, saving and restoring VGIC state to use virtual interrupts is quite expensive on ARM; available x86 hardware does not yet provide such mechanism. The ARM no VGIC/vtimers measurement does not include the cost of saving and restoring VGIC state, showing that this accounts for over half of the cost of a world switch on ARM. Second, x86 provides hardware support to save and restore state on the world switch, which is much faster. ARM requires software to explicitly save and restore state, which provides greater flexibility, but higher costs. Nevertheless, without the VGIC state, the hypercall costs are only about 600 cycles more than the hardware accelerated hypercall cost on the x86 server platform. The ARM world switch costs have not been optimized and can be reduced further. For example, a small patch eliminating unnecessary atomic operations reduces the hypercall cost by roughly 300 cycles, but did not make it into the mainline kernel until after v3.10 was released. As another example, if parts of the VGIC state were lazily context switched instead of

| Micro Test | ARM | ARM no VGIC/vtimers | x86 laptop | x86 server |
|---|---|---|---|---|
| Hypercall | 5,326 | 2,270 | 1,336 | 1,638 |
| Trap | 27 | 27 | 632 | 821 |
| I/O Kernel | 5,990 | 2,850 | 3,190 | 3,291 |
| I/O User | 10,119 | 6,704 | 10,985 | 12,218 |
| IPI | 14,366 | 32,951 | 17,138 | 21,177 |
| EOI+ACK | 427 | 13,726 | 2,043 | 2,305 |

Table 3: Micro-Architectural Cycle Counts

being saved and restored on each world switch, this may also reduce the world switch costs.

Trap is the cost of switching the hardware mode from the VM into the respective CPU mode for running the hypervisor, Hyp mode on ARM and root mode on x86. ARM is much faster than x86 because it only needs to manipulate two registers to perform this trap, whereas the cost of a trap on x86 is roughly the same as the cost of a world switch because the same amount of state is saved by the hardware in both cases. The trap cost on ARM is a very small part of the world switch costs, indicating that the double trap incurred by split-mode virtualization on ARM does not add much overhead.

I/O Kernel is the cost of an I/O operation from the VM to a device, which is emulated inside the kernel. I/O User shows the cost of issuing an I/O operation to a device emulated in user space, adding to I/O Kernel the cost of transitioning from the kernel to a user space process and doing a small amount of work in user space on the host for I/O. This is representative of the cost of using QEMU. Since these operations involve world switches, saving and restoring VGIC state is again a significant cost on ARM. KVM x86 is faster than KVM/ARM on I/O Kernel, but slightly slower on I/O User. This is because the hardware optimized world switch on x86 constitutes the majority of the cost of performing I/O in the kernel, but transitioning from kernel to a user space process on the host side is more expensive on x86 because x86 KVM saves and restores additional state lazily when going to user space. Note that the added cost of going to user space includes saving additional state, doing some work in user space, and returning to the kernel and processing the `KVM_RUN` ioctl call for KVM.

IPI is the cost of issuing an IPI to another virtual CPU core when both virtual cores are running on separate physical cores and both are actively running inside the VM. IPI measures time starting from sending an IPI until the other virtual core responds and completes the IPI. It involves multiple world switches and sending and receiving a hardware IPI. Despite its higher world switch cost, ARM is faster than x86 because the underlying hardware IPI on x86 is expensive, x86 APIC MMIO operations require KVM x86 to perform instruction decoding not needed on ARM, and completing an interrupt on x86 is more expensive. ARM without VGIC/vtimers is significantly slower than with VGIC/vtimers even though it has lower world switch costs because sending, EOIing and ACKing interrupts trap to the hypervisor and are handled by QEMU in user space.

EOI+ACK is the cost of completing a virtual interrupt on both platforms. It includes both interrupt acknowledgment and completion on ARM, but only completion on the x86 platform. ARM requires an additional operation, the acknowledgment, to the interrupt controller to determine the source of the interrupt. x86 does not because the source is directly indicated by the interrupt descriptor table entry at the time when the interrupt is raised. However, the operation is roughly 5 times faster on ARM than x86 because there is no need to trap to the hypervisor on ARM because of VGIC support for both operations. On x86, the EOI operation must be emulated and therefore causes a trap to the hypervisor. This operation is required for every virtual interrupt including both virtual IPIs and interrupts from virtual devices.

Figures 3 to 7 show virtualized execution measurements normalized relative to their respective native execution measurements, with lower being less overhead. Figures 3 and 4 show normalized performance for running lmbench in a VM versus running directly on the host. Figure 3 shows that KVM/ARM and KVM x86 have similar virtualization overhead in a single core configuration. For comparison, we also show KVM/ARM performance without VGIC/vtimers. Overall, using VGIC/vtimers provides slightly better performance except for the pipe and ctxsw workloads where the difference is substantial. The reason for the high overhead in this case is caused by updating the runqueue clock in the Linux scheduler every time a process blocks, since reading a counter traps to user space without vtimers on the ARM platform. We verified this by running the workload with VGIC support, but without vtimers, and we counted the number of timer read exits when running without vtimers support.

Figure 4 shows more substantial differences in virtualization overhead between KVM/ARM and KVM x86 in a multicore configuration. KVM/ARM has less overhead than KVM x86 fork and exec, but more for protection faults. Both systems have the worst overhead for the pipe and ctxsw workloads, though KVM x86 is more than two times worse for pipe. This is due to the cost of repeatedly sending an IPI from the sender of the data in the pipe to the receiver for each message and the cost of sending an IPI when scheduling a new process. x86 not only has higher IPI overhead than ARM, but it must also EOI each IPI, which is much more expensive on x86 than on ARM because this requires trapping to the hypervisor on x86 but not on ARM. Without using VGIC/vtimers, KVM/ARM also incurs high overhead comparable to KVM x86 because it then also traps to the hypervisor to ACK and EOI the IPIs.

Figures 5 and 6 show normalized performance for running application workloads in a VM versus running directly on the host. Figure 5 shows that KVM/ARM and KVM x86 have similar virtualization overhead across all workloads in a single core configuration except for the MySQL workloads, but Figure 6 shows that there are more substantial differences in performance on multicore. On multicore, KVM/ARM has significantly less virtualization overhead than KVM x86 on Apache and MySQL. Overall on multicore, KVM/ARM performs within 10% of running directly on the hardware for all application workloads,

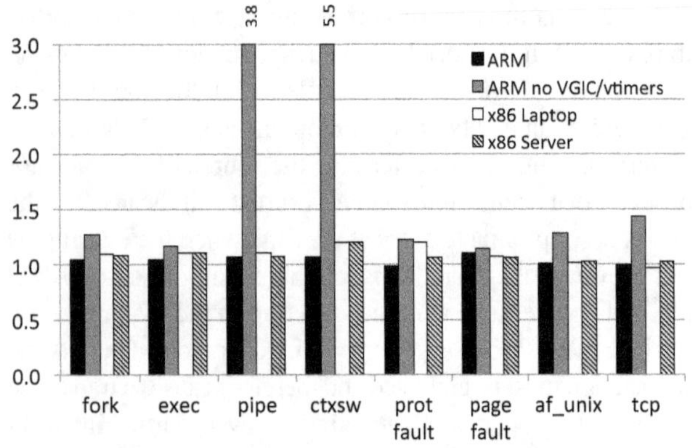


Figure 3: UP VM Normalized lmbench Performance

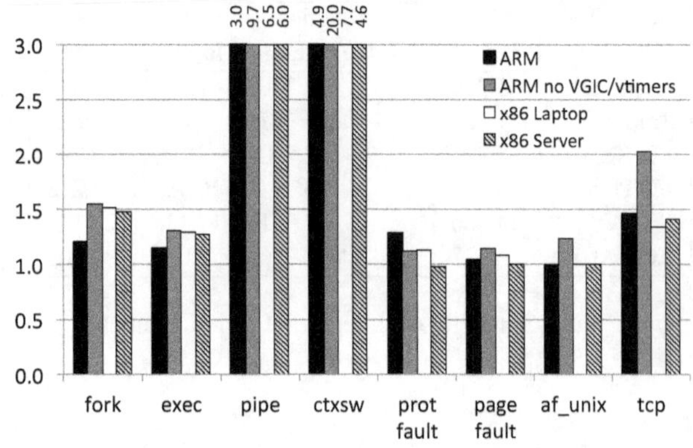


Figure 4: SMP VM Normalized lmbench Performance

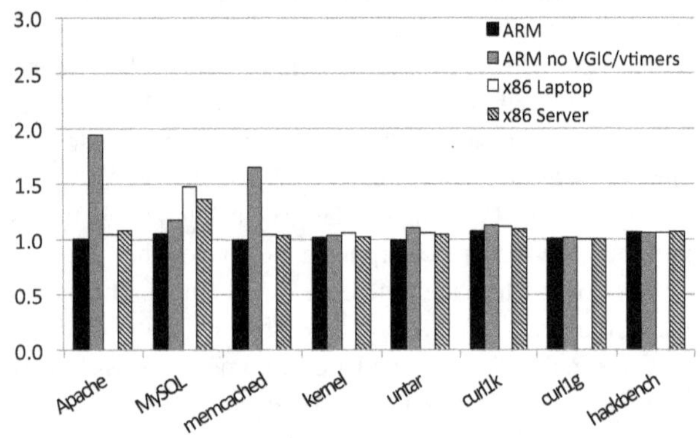


Figure 5: UP VM Normalized Application Performance

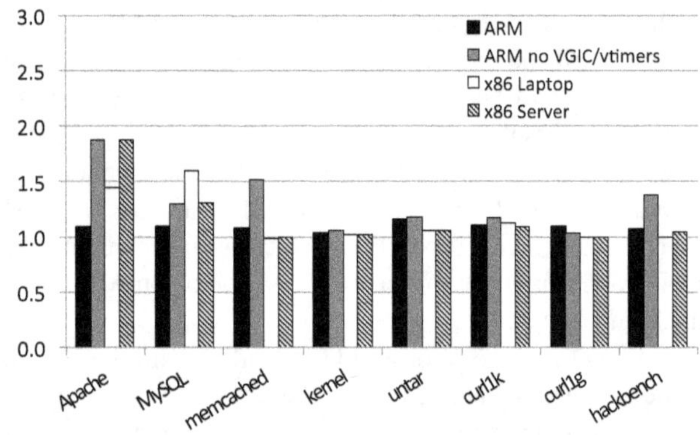


Figure 6: SMP VM Normalized Application Performance

while the more mature KVM x86 system has significantly higher virtualization overheads for Apache and MySQL. KVM/ARM's split-mode virtualization design allows it to leverage ARM hardware support with comparable performance to a traditional hypervisor using x86 hardware support. The measurements also show that KVM/ARM performs better overall with ARM VGIC/vtimers support than without.

Figure 7 shows normalized power consumption of using virtualization versus direct execution for various application workloads on multicore. We only compared KVM/ARM on ARM against KVM x86 on x86 laptop. The Intel Core i7 CPU used in these experiments is one of Intel's more power optimized processors, and we expect that server power consumption would be even higher. The measurements show that KVM/ARM using VGIC/vtimers is more power efficient than KVM x86 virtualization in all cases except memcached and untar. Both workloads are not CPU bound on both platforms and the power consumption is not significantly affected by the virtualization layer. However, due to ARM's slightly higher virtualization overhead for these workloads, the energy virtualization overhead is slightly higher on ARM for the two workloads. While a more detailed study of energy aspects of virtualization is beyond the scope of this paper, these measurements nevertheless provide useful data comparing ARM and x86 virtualization energy costs.

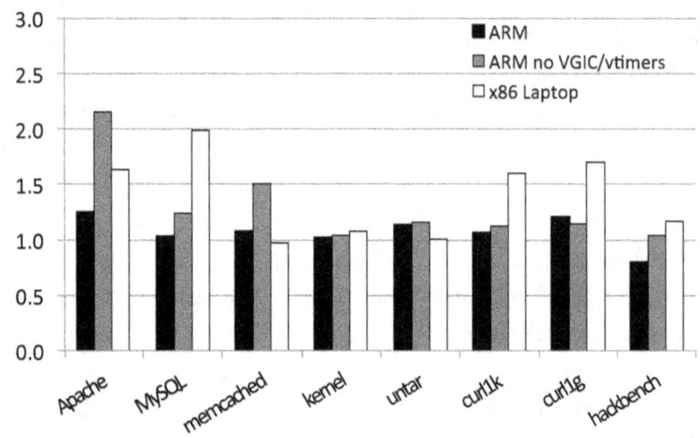


Figure 7: SMP VM Normalized Energy Consumption

### 5.3 Implementation Complexity

We compare the code complexity of KVM/ARM to its KVM x86 counterpart in Linux 3.10. KVM/ARM is 5,812 lines of code (LOC), counting just the architecture-specific code added to Linux to implement it, of which the lowvisor is a mere 718 LOC. As a conservative comparison, KVM x86 is 25,367 LOC, excluding guest performance monitoring support, not yet supported by KVM/ARM, and 3,311 LOC required for AMD support. These numbers do not include KVM's architecture-generic code, 7,071 LOC, which is shared by all systems. Table 4 shows a

| Component | KVM/ARM | KVM x86 (Intel) |
|---|---|---|
| Core CPU | 2,493 | 16,177 |
| Page Fault Handling | 738 | 3,410 |
| Interrupts | 1,057 | 1,978 |
| Timers | 180 | 573 |
| Other | 1,344 | 1,288 |
| Architecture-specific | 5,812 | 25,367 |

Table 4: Code Complexity in Lines of Code (LOC)

breakdown of the total hypervisor architecture-specific code into its major components.

By inspecting the code we notice that the striking additional complexity in the x86 implementation is mainly due to the five following reasons: (1) Since EPT was not supported in earlier hardware versions, KVM x86 must support shadow page tables. (2) The hardware virtualization support have evolved over time, requiring software to conditionally check for support for a large number of features such as EPT. (3) A number of operations require software decoding of instructions on the x86 platform. KVM/ARM's out-of-tree MMIO instruction decode implementation was much simpler, only 462 LOC. (4) The various paging mode on x86 requires more software logic to handle page faults. (5) x86 requires more software logic to support interrupts and timers than ARM, which provides VGIC/vtimers hardware support that reduces software complexity.

KVM/ARM's LOC is less than partially complete bare-metal microvisors written for Hyp mode [31], with the lowvisor LOC almost an order of magnitude smaller. Unlike standalone hypervisors, KVM/ARM's code complexity is so small because lots of functionality simply does not have to be implemented because it is already provided by Linux. Table 4 does not include other non-hypervisor architecture-specific Linux code, such as basic bootstrapping, which is significantly more code. Porting a standalone hypervisor such as Xen from x86 to ARM is much more complicated because all of that ARM code for basic system functionality needs to be written from scratch. In contrast, since Linux is dominant on ARM, KVM/ARM just leverages existing Linux ARM support to run on every platform supported by Linux.

## 6. Recommendations

From our experiences building KVM/ARM, we offer a few recommendations for hardware designers to simplify and optimize future hypervisor implementations.

***Share kernel mode memory model.*** The hardware mode to run a hypervisor should use the same memory model as the hardware mode to run OS kernels. Software designers then have greater flexibility in deciding how tightly to integrate a hypervisor with existing OS kernels. ARM Hyp mode unfortunately did not do this, preventing KVM/ARM from simply reusing the kernel's page tables in Hyp mode. This reuse would have simplified the implementation and allowed for performance critical emulation code to run in Hyp mode, avoiding a complete world switch in some cases. Some might argue that this recommendation makes for more complicated standalone hypervisor implementations, but this is not really true. For example, ARM kernel mode already has a simple option to use one or two page table base registers to unify or split the address space. Our recommendation is different from the x86 virtualization approach, which does not have a separate and more privileged, hypervisor CPU mode. Having a separate CPU mode potentially improves stand-alone hypervisor performance and implementation, but not sharing the kernel memory model complicates the design of hypervisors integrated with host kernels.

***Make VGIC state access fast, or at least infrequent.*** While VGIC support can improve performance especially on multicore systems, our measurements also show that access to VGIC state adds substantial overhead to world switches. This is caused by slow MMIO access to the VGIC control interface in the critical path. Improving the MMIO access time is likely to improve VM performance, but if this is not possible or cost-effective, MMIO accesses to the VGIC could at least be made less frequent. For example, a summary register could be introduced describing the state of each virtual interrupt. This could be read when performing a world switch from the VM to the hypervisor to get information which can currently only be obtained by reading all the list registers (see Section 3.5) on each world switch.

***Completely avoid IPI traps.*** Hardware support to send virtual IPIs directly from VMs without the need to trap to the hypervisor would improve performance. Hardware designers may underestimate how frequent IPIs are on modern multicore OSes, and our measurements reveal that sending IPIs adds significant overhead for some workloads. The current VGIC design requires a trap to the hypervisor to emulate access to the IPI register in the distributor, and this emulated access must be synchronized between virtual cores using a software locking mechanism, which adds significant overhead for IPIs. Current ARM hardware supports receiving the virtual IPIs, which can be ACKed and EOIed without traps, but unfortunately does not address the also important issue of sending virtual IPIs.

## 7. Related Work

Virtualization has a long history [27], but has enjoyed a resurgence starting in the late 1990s. Most efforts have almost exclusively focused on virtualizing the x86 architecture. While systems such as VMware [1, 10] and Xen [8] were originally based on software-only approaches before the introduction of x86 hardware virtualization support, all x86 virtualization platforms, VMware [2], Xen, and KVM [22], now leverage x86 hardware virtualization support. Because x86 hardware virtualization support differs substantially from ARM in the ability to completely run the hypervisor in the same mode as the kernel, x86 virtualization approaches do not lend themselves directly to take advantage of ARM hardware virtualization support.

Some x86 approaches also leverage the host kernel to provide functionality for the hypervisor. VMware Workstation's hypervisor creates a VMM separate from the host kernel, but this approach is different from KVM/ARM in a number of important ways. First, the VMware VMM is not integrated into the host kernel source code and therefore cannot reuse existing host kernel code, for example, for populating page tables relating to the VM. Second, since the VMware VMM is specific to x86 it does not run across different privileged CPU modes, and therefore does not use a design similar to KVM/ARM. Third, most of the emulation and fault-handling code required to run a VM executes at the most privileged level inside the VMM. KVM/ARM executes this code in the less privileged kernel mode, and only executes a minimal amount of code in the most privileged mode. In contrast, KVM benefits from being integrated with the Linux kernel like KVM/ARM, but the x86 design relies on being able to run the kernel and the hypervisor together in the same hardware hypervisor mode, which is problematic on ARM.

Full-system virtualization of the ARM architecture is a relatively unexplored research area. Most approaches are software only. A number of standalone bare metal hypervisors have been developed [16, 17, 28], but these are not widespread, are developed specifically for the embedded market, and must be modified and ported to every single host hardware platform, limiting their adoption. An abandoned port of Xen for ARM [18] requires comprehensive modifications to the guest kernel, and was never fully developed. An earlier prototype for KVM on ARM [12, 15] used an automated lightweight paravirtualization approach to automatically patch kernel source code to run as a guest kernel, but had poor performance. VMware Horizon Mobile [9] uses hosted virtualization to leverage Linux's support for a wide range of hardware platforms, but requires modifications to guest OSes and its performance is unproven. None of these paravirtualization approaches could run unmodified guest OSes.

An earlier study attempted to estimate the performance of ARM hardware virtualization support using a software simulator and a simple hypervisor lacking important features like SMP support and use of storage and network devices by multiple VMs [31]. Because of the lack of hardware or a cycle-accurate simulator, no real performance evaluation was possible. In contrast, we present the first evaluation of ARM virtualization extensions using real hardware, provide a direct comparison with x86, and present the design and implementation of a complete hypervisor using ARM virtualization extensions, including SMP support.

A newer version of Xen exclusively targeting servers [32] is being developed using ARM hardware virtualization support. Because Xen is a bare metal hypervisor that does not leverage kernel functionality, it can be architected to run entirely in Hyp mode rather than using split-mode virtualization. At the same time, this requires a substantial commercial engineering effort. Since Xen is a standalone hypervisor, porting Xen from x86 to ARM is difficult in part because all ARM-related code must be written from scratch. Even after getting Xen to work on one ARM platform, it must be manually ported to each different ARM device that Xen wants to support. Because of Xen's custom I/O model using hypercalls from VMs for device emulation on ARM, Xen unfortunately cannot run guest OSes unless they have been configured to include Xen's hypercall layer and include support for XenBus paravirtualized drivers. In contrast, KVM/ARM uses standard Linux components to enable faster development, full SMP support, and the ability to run unmodified OSes. KVM/ARM is easily supported on new devices with Linux support, and we spent almost no effort to support KVM/ARM on ARM's Versatile Express boards, the Arndale board, and hardware emulators. While Xen can potentially reduce world switch times for operations that can be handled inside the Xen hypervisor, switching to Dom0 for I/O support or switching to other VMs would involve context switching the same state as KVM/ARM.

Microkernel approaches for hypervisors [16, 30] have been used to reduce the hypervisor TCB and run other hypervisor services in user mode. These approaches differ both in design and rationale from split-mode virtualization, which splits hypervisor functionality across privileged modes to leverage virtualization hardware support. Split-mode virtualization also provides a different split of hypervisor functionality. KVM/ARM's lowvisor is a much smaller code base that implements only the lowest level hypervisor mechanisms. It does not include higher-level functionality present in the hypervisor TCB used in these other approaches.

## 8. Conclusions

KVM/ARM is the mainline Linux ARM hypervisor and the first system that can run unmodified guest operating systems on ARM multicore hardware. KVM/ARM's split-mode virtualization makes it possible to use ARM hardware virtualization extensions while leveraging Linux kernel mechanisms and hardware support. Our experimental results show that KVM/ARM (1) incurs minimal performance impact from the extra traps incurred by split-mode virtualization, (2) has modest virtualization overhead and power costs, within 10% of direct native execution on multicore hardware for real application workloads, and (3) achieves comparable or lower virtualization overhead and power costs on multicore hardware compared to widely-used KVM x86 virtualization. Based on our experiences integrating KVM/ARM into the mainline Linux kernel, we provide some hints on getting research ideas and code adopted by the open source community, and recommendations for hardware designers to improve future hypervisor implementations.

## 9. Acknowledgments

Marc Zyngier helped with development, implemented VGIC and vtimers support, and assisted us with hardware bring up. Rusty Russell worked on the coprocessor user space interface and assisted with upstreaming. Will Deacon and Avi Kivity provided numerous helpful code reviews. Peter Maydell helped with QEMU support and debugging. Gleb Natapov helped us better understand KVM x86 performance. Marcelo Tosatti and Nicolas Viennot helped with resolving what became known as the voodoo bug. Keith Adams, Hani Jamjoom, and Emmett Witchel provided helpful comments on earlier drafts of this paper. This work was supported in part by ARM and NSF grants CNS-1162447, CCF-1162021, and CNS-1018355.

## References


[1] K. Adams and O. Agesen. A Comparison of Software and Hardware Techniques for x86 Virtualization. In *Proceedings of the 12th International Conference on Architectural Support for Programming Languages and Operating Systems*, pages 2–13, Oct. 2006.

[2] O. Agesen, J. Mattson, R. Rugina, and J. Sheldon. Software Techniques for Avoiding Hardware Virtualization Exits. In *Proceedings of the 2012 USENIX Annual Technical Conference*, pages 373–385, June 2012.

[3] ARM Ltd. ARM Energy Probe. `http://www.arm.com/products/tools/arm-energy-probe.php`.

[4] ARM Ltd. ARM Cortex-A15 Technical Reference Manual ARM DDI 0438C, Sept. 2011.

[5] ARM Ltd. ARM Generic Interrupt Controller Architecture version 2.0 ARM IHI 0048B, June 2011.

[6] ARM Ltd. ARM Architecture Reference Manual ARMv7-A DDI0406C.b, July 2012.

[7] ARM Ltd. ARM Architecture Reference Manual ARMv8-A DDI0487A.a, Sept. 2013.

[8] P. Barham, B. Dragovic, K. Fraser, S. Hand, T. Harris, A. Ho, R. Neugebauer, I. Pratt, and A. Warfield. Xen and the Art of Virtualization. In *Proceedings of the 19th ACM Symposium on Operating Systems Principles*, pages 164–177, Oct. 2003.

[9] K. Barr, P. Bungale, S. Deasy, V. Gyuris, P. Hung, C. Newell, H. Tuch, and B. Zoppis. The VMware Mobile Virtualization Platform: is that a hypervisor in your pocket? *SIGOPS Operating Systems Review*, 44(4):124–135, Dec. 2010.

[10] E. Bugnion, S. Devine, M. Rosenblum, J. Sugerman, and E. Y. Wang. Bringing Virtualization to the x86 Architecture with the Original VMware Workstation. *ACM Transactions on Computer Systems*, 30(4):12:1–12:51, Nov. 2012.

[11] C. Dall and A. Jones. KVM/ARM Unit Tests. `https://github.com/columbia/kvm-unit-tests`.

[12] C. Dall and J. Nieh. KVM for ARM. In *Proceedings of the Ottawa Linux Symposium*, pages 45–56, July 2010.

[13] C. Dall and J. Nieh. Supporting KVM on the ARM architecture. LWN.net, July 2013. `http://lwn.net/Articles/557132/`.

[14] David Brash, Architecture Program Manager, ARM Ltd. Personal communication, Nov. 2012.

[15] J.-H. Ding, C.-J. Lin, P.-H. Chang, C.-H. Tsang, W.-C. Hsu, and Y.-C. Chung. ARMvisor: System Virtualization for ARM. In *Proceedings of the Ottawa Linux Symposium (OLS)*, pages 93–107, July 2012.

[16] General Dynamics. OKL4 Microvisor. `http://www.ok-labs.com/products/okl4-microvisor`.

[17] Green Hills Software. INTEGRITY Secure Virtualization. `http://www.ghs.com/products/rtos/integrity_virtualization.html`.

[18] J. Hwang, S. Suh, S. Heo, C. Park, J. Ryu, S. Park, and C. Kim. Xen on ARM: System Virtualization using Xen Hypervisor for ARM-based Secure Mobile Phones. In *Proceedings of the 5th Consumer Communications and Newtork Conference*, Jan. 2008.

[19] InSignal Co. ArndaleBoard.org. `http://arndaleboard.org`.

[20] Intel Corporation. Intel 64 and IA-32 Architectures Software Developers Manual, 325462-044US, Aug. 2012.

[21] A. Kivity. KVM Unit Tests. `https://git.kernel.org/cgit/virt/kvm/kvm-unit-tests.git`.

[22] A. Kivity, Y. Kamay, D. Laor, U. Lublin, and A. Liguori. **kvm**: The Linux Virtual Machine Monitor. In *Proceedings of the Ottawa Linux Symposium (OLS)*, volume 1, pages 225–230, June 2007.

[23] KVM/ARM Mailing List. `https://lists.cs.columbia.edu/cucslists/listinfo/kvmarm`.

[24] Linux ARM Kernel Mailing List. A15 H/W Virtualization Support, Apr. 2011. `http://archive.arm.linux.org.uk/lurker/message/20110412.204714.a36702d9.en.html`.

[25] L. McVoy and C. Staelin. lmbench: Portable Tools for Performance Analysis. In *Proceedings of the 1996 USENIX Annual Technical Conference*, pages 279–294, Jan. 1996.

[26] I. Molnar. Hackbench. `http://people.redhat.com/mingo/cfs-scheduler/tools/hackbench.c`.

[27] G. J. Popek and R. P. Goldberg. Formal Requirements for Virtualizable Third Generation Architectures. *Communications of the ACM*, 17(7):412–421, July 1974.

[28] Red Bend Software. vLogix Mobile. `http://www.redbend.com/en/mobile-virtualization`.

[29] R. Russell. virtio: Towards a De-Facto Standard for Virtual I/O Devices. *SIGOPS Operating Systems Review*, 42(5):95–103, July 2008.

[30] U. Steinberg and B. Kauer. Nova: A Microhypervisor-Based Secure Virtualization Architecture. In *Proceedings of the 5th European Conference on Computer Systems*, pages 209–222, Apr. 2010.

[31] P. Varanasi and G. Heiser. Hardware-Supported Virtualization on ARM. In *Proceedings of the Second Asia-Pacific Workshop on Systems*, pages 11:1–11:5, July 2011.

[32] Xen.org. Xen ARM. `http://xen.org/products/xen_arm.html`.

# VSWAPPER: A Memory Swapper for Virtualized Environments

Nadav Amit Dan Tsafrir Assaf Schuster

Technion – Israel Institute of Technology

{namit,dan,assaf}@cs.technion.ac.il

## Abstract

The number of guest virtual machines that can be consolidated on one physical host is typically limited by the memory size, motivating memory overcommitment. Guests are given a choice to either install a "balloon" driver to coordinate the overcommitment activity, or to experience degraded performance due to uncooperative swapping. Ballooning, however, is not a complete solution, as hosts must still fall back on uncooperative swapping in various circumstances. Additionally, ballooning takes time to accommodate change, and so guests might experience degraded performance under changing conditions.

Our goal is to improve the performance of hosts when they fall back on uncooperative swapping and/or operate under changing load conditions. We carefully isolate and characterize the causes for the associated poor performance, which include various types of superfluous swap operations, decayed swap file sequentiality, and ineffective prefetch decisions upon page faults. We address these problems by implementing VSWAPPER, a guest-agnostic memory swapper for virtual environments that allows efficient, uncooperative overcommitment. With inactive ballooning, VSWAPPER yields up to an order of magnitude performance improvement. Combined with ballooning, VSWAPPER can achieve up to double the performance under changing load conditions.

***Categories and Subject Descriptors*** D.4.2 [*Operating Systems*]: Storage Management—Virtual memory, Main memory, Allocation/deallocation strategies, Storage hierarchies

***General Terms*** Design, Experimentation, Measurement, Performance

***Keywords*** Virtualization; memory overcommitment; memory balloon; swapping; paging; page faults; emulation; virtual machines; hypervisor



*ASPLOS '14*, March 1–4, 2014, Salt Lake City, UT, USA.

ACM 978-1-4503-2305-5/14/03. . . $15.00.
http://dx.doi.org/10.1145/2541940.2541969

## 1. Introduction

The main enabling technology for cloud computing is machine virtualization, which abstracts the rigid physical infrastructure and turns it into soft components easily managed and used. Clouds and virtualization are driven by strong economic incentives, notably the ability to consolidate multiple guest servers on one physical host. The number of guests that one host can support is typically limited by the physical memory size [6, 25, 27, 87]. So hosts overcommit their memory to increase their capacity.

Memory of guest virtual machines is commonly overcommitment via a special "balloon" driver installed in the guest [84]. Balloons allocate pinned memory pages at the host's request, thereby ensuring that guests will not use them; the pages can then be used by the host for some other purpose. When a balloon is "inflated," it prompts the guest operating system to reclaim memory on its own, which often results in the guest swapping out some of its less frequently used pages to disk.

Ballooning is a common-case optimization for memory reclamation and overcommitment, but, inherently, it is not a complete solution [28, 68, 84, 88]. Hosts cannot rely on guest cooperation, because: (1) clients may have disabled or opted not to install the balloon [10, 53, 74]; (2) clients may have failed to install the balloon due to technical difficulties [77, 78, 79, 80, 81, 82, 83]; (3) balloons could reach their upper bound, set by the hypervisor (and optionally adjusted by clients) to enhance stability and to accommodate various guest limitations [14, 19, 59, 69, 75, 84]; (4) balloons might be unable to reclaim memory fast enough to accommodate the demand that the host must satisfy, notably since guest memory swapping involves slow disk activity [31, 46, 84]; and (5) balloons could be temporarily unavailable due to inner guest activity such as booting [84] or running high priority processes that starve guest kernel services. In all these cases, the host must resort to uncooperative swapping, which is notorious for its poor performance (and which has motivated ballooning in the first place).

While operational, ballooning is a highly effective optimization. But estimating the memory working set size of guests is a hard problem, especially under changing conditions [27, 35, 45], and the transfer of memory pages between guests is slow when the memory is overcommitted [17, 31,

36, 46]. Thus, upon change, it takes time for the balloon manager to adjust the balloon sizes and to achieve good results. Hosts might therefore rely on uncooperative swapping during this period, and so guests might experience degraded performance until the balloon sizes stabilize.

We note in passing that the use of ballooning constitutes a tradeoff that embodies both a benefit and a price. The benefit is the improved performance achieved through curbing the uncooperative swapping activity. Conversely, the price for clients is that they need to modify their guest operating systems by installing host-specific software, which has various undesirable consequences such as burdening the clients, being nonportable across different hypervisors, and entailing a small risk of causing undesirable interactions between new and existing software [39]. The price for vendors is that they need to put in the effort to support different drivers for every guest operating system kernel and version. (We speculate that, due to this effort, for example, there is no balloon driver available for OS X under KVM and VirtualBox, and the latter supports ballooning for only 64-bit guests [16].) Therefore, arguably, reducing the overheads of uncooperative swapping could sway the decision of whether to employ ballooning or not.

Our goal in this paper is twofold. To provide a superior alternative to baseline uncooperative host swapping, to be used by hosts as a performant fall back for when balloons cannot be used. And to enhance guests' performance while ballooning is utilized under changing load conditions. We motivate this goal in detail in Section 2.

We investigate why uncooperative swapping degrades performance in practice and find that it is largely because of: (1) "silent swap writes" that copy unchanged blocks of data from the guest disk image to the host swap area; (2) "stale swap reads" triggered when guests perform explicit disk reads whose destination buffers are pages swapped out by the host; (3) "false swap reads" triggered when guests overwrite whole pages previously swapped out by the host while disregarding their old content (e.g., when copying-on-write); (4) "decayed swap sequentiality" that causes unchanged guest file blocks to gradually lose their contiguity while being kept in the host swap area and thereby hindering swap prefetching; and (5) "false page anonymity" that occurs when mislabeling guest pages backed by files as anonymous and thereby confusing the page reclamation algorithm. We characterize and exemplify these problems in Section 3.

To address the problems, we design VSWAPPER, a guest-agnostic memory swapper to be used by hypervisors. VSWAPPER is implemented as a KVM extension and is comprised of two components. The first is the Swap Mapper, which monitors the disk I/O performed by a guest while maintaining a mapping between its unmodified memory pages and their corresponding origin disk blocks. When such mapped memory pages are reclaimed, they need not be written to the host swap file; instead the Mapper records their location in the guest's virtual disk for future reference and discards them, thereby eliminating the root cause of silent writes, stale reads, decayed sequentiality, and false page anonymity. The second component is the False Reads Preventer, which eliminates false reads by emulating faulting write instructions directed at swapped out pages. Instead of immediately faulting-in the latter, the Preventer saves the written data in a memory buffer for a short while, in the hope that the entire buffer would fill up soon, obviating the need to read. We describe VSWAPPER in detail in Section 4.

We evaluate VSWAPPER in Section 5 and find that when memory is tight, VSWAPPER is typically much better than baseline swapping and is oftentimes competitive with ballooning. At its worst, VSWAPPER is respectively 1.035x and 2.1x slower than baseline and ballooning. At its best, VSWAPPER is respectively 10x and 2x faster than baseline and ballooning, under changing load conditions. In all cases, combining VSWAPPER and ballooning yields performance comparable to the optimum.

We discuss the related work in Section 6, outline possible future work in Section 7, and conclude in Section 8.

## 2. Motivation

### 2.1 The Benefit of Ballooning

Current architectural support for machine virtualization allows the host operating system (OS) to manage the memory of its guest virtual machines (VMs) as if they were processes, and it additionally allows the guest OSes to do their own memory management for their internal processes, without host involvement.

Hardware provides this capability by supporting a two-level address translation mechanism (Figure 1). The upper level is controlled by the guest and is comprised of page tables translating "guest virtual addresses" (GVAs) to "guest physical addresses" (GPAs). The lower level is controlled by the host and is comprised of tables translating guest physical addresses to "host physical addresses" (HPAs). A guest physical address is of course not real in any sense. The host can (1) map it to some real memory page or (2) mark it as non-present, which ensures the host will get a page fault if/when the guest attempts to access the non-present page. Consequently, when memory is tight, the host can temporarily store page content on disk and read it back into memory only when handling the corresponding page faults [62]. We denote the latter activity as *uncooperative swapping*, because the host can conduct it without guest awareness or participation .

The problem with uncooperative swapping is that it might lead to substantially degraded performance due to unintended interactions with the memory management subsystem of the guest OS. A canonical example used to highlight the problematic nature of uncooperative swapping is that of *double paging* [22, 24, 84], whereby the guest kernel attempts to reclaim a page that has already been swapped out

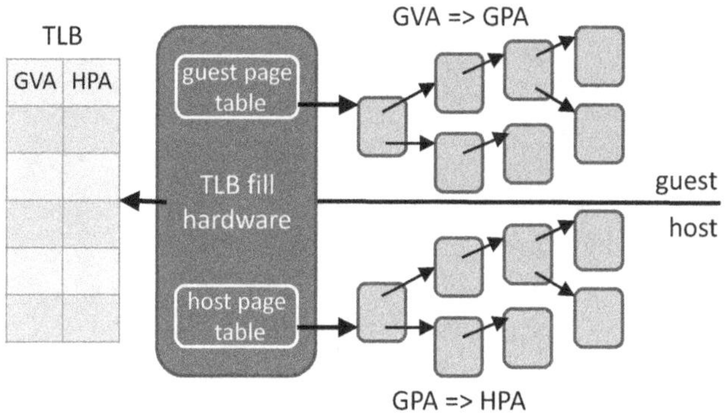


**Figure 1.** *The Translation Lookaside Buffer (TLB) translates guest virtual addresses (GVAs) to host physical addresses (HPAs), disregarding guest physical addresses (GPAs). Upon a miss, the TLB fill hardware adds the missing entry by walking the guest and host page tables to translate GVAs to GPAs and GPAs to HPAs, respectively. The hardware delivers a page fault to the host if it encounters a non-present GPA⇒HPA, allowing the host to fault-in the missing guest page, on demand. (Figure reproduced from [18].)*

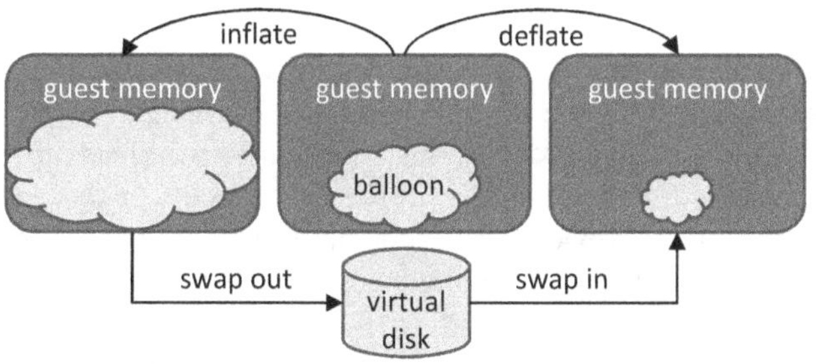


**Figure 2.** *Inflating the balloon increases memory pressure and prompts the guest to reclaim memory, typically by swapping out some of its pages to its virtual disk. Deflating relieves the memory pressure. (Figure reproduced from [84].)*

by the host, a fact unknown to the guest since it is uncooperative. When such an event occurs, it causes the page contents to be faulted-in from the host swap area, only to be immediately written to the guest swap area, generating wasteful I/O activity that host/guest cooperation would have obviated.

To circumvent difficulties of this sort, Waldspurger proposed to delegate to the guest the decision of which pages to reclaim, by utilizing *memory ballooning* [84]. A memory balloon is a paravirtual pseudo-driver installed in the guest. The balloon communicates with, and gets instructions from, the host through a private channel. It is capable of performing two operations: *inflating* and *deflating*, that is, allocating and freeing pages pinned to the guest memory. Inflating increases memory demand, thereby prompting the guest to run its page reclamation procedure and swap memory on its own (Figure 2). The pinned pages can then be used by the host for other purposes. Ballooning is the prevailing mechanism for managing memory of guest virtual machines.

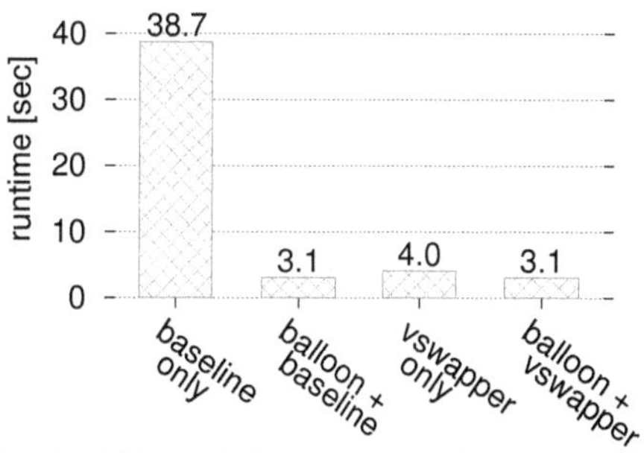


**Figure 3.** *Time it takes a guest to sequentially read a 200MB file, believing it has 512MB of physical memory whereas in fact it only has 100MB. (This setup is analyzed in detail later on.) The results shown are the best we have observed in favor of ballooning.*

## 2.2 Ballooning is Not a Complete Solution

Memory ballooning typically provides substantial performance improvements over the baseline uncooperative swapping. Ballooning likewise often outperforms the VSWAPPER system that we propose in this paper. An extreme example is given in Figure 3. The baseline is 12.5x slower than ballooning. And while VSWAPPER improves the baseline by 9.7x, it is still 1.3x slower than the ballooning configurations. One might therefore perceive swapping as irrelevant in virtualized setups that employ balloons. But that would be misguided, because ballooning and swapping are complementary activities.

Since its inception, ballooning has been positioned as a common-case optimization for memory reclamation, *not* as a complete solution [84]. Ballooning cannot be a complete solution, because, inherently, hypervisors cannot exclusively rely on any mechanism that requires guest cooperation, which cannot be ensured in any way. Thus, for correctness, host-level swapping must be available to forcibly reclaim guest memory when necessary. Indeed, when introducing ballooning, Waldspurger noted that "[d]espite its advantages, ballooning does have limitations. The balloon driver may be uninstalled, disabled explicitly, unavailable while a guest OS is booting, or temporarily unable to reclaim memory quickly enough to satisfy current system demands. Also, upper bounds on reasonable balloon sizes may be imposed by various guest OS limitations" [84]. The balloon size is limited, for example, to 65% of the guest memory in the case of VMware ESX [14, 85].

Guests might also lack a balloon due to installation and configuration problems [77, 78, 79, 80, 81, 82, 83], as installing hypervisor tools and making them work appropriately is not always easy. For example, Googling the quoted string "problem with vmware tools" returns 118,000 hits, describing many related difficulties that users experience. Balloon configuration becomes more complex if/when clients need to experiment with their software so as to configure memory reservations for their VMs [19, 59, 69, 75].

Virtualization professionals attest to repeatedly encountering clients who disable ballooning or do not install hypervisor tools for misguided reasons. Brambley reports that "[i]t happens more frequently than I would ever imagine, but from time to time I find clients [that] have not installed the VMware tools in their virtual machine [...] Some times the tools install is overlooked or forgotten, but every once in a while I am told something like: Does Linux need VMware tools? or What do the VMware tools do for me anyways?" [10]. Ozar reports that "There's plenty of bad advice out on the web saying things like: just disable the balloon driver" [53]. van Zanten concludes that the "Misconceptions on memory overcommit [amongst clients include believing that] overcommit is always a performance hit; real world workloads don't benefit; the gain by overcommitment is negligible; [and] overcommitment is dangerous" [74].

Regardless of the reason, balloons are sometimes unavailable or unusable. In such cases, the hypervisor falls back on uncooperative swapping for memory reclamation and overcommitment. We submit that it is far more preferable to fall back on VSWAPPER than on baseline swapping.

### 2.3 Ballooning Takes Time

So far, we have considered VSWAPPER as a more performant alternative to baseline swapping, to only be used as a fallback for when a balloon is not available or cannot be utilized due to, e.g., reaching its size limit. We have noted that VSWAPPER yields better performance than the baseline, but we have seen that this performance is still inferior relative to when ballooning is employed (Figure 3). Ballooning, however, is superior to VSWAPPER under steady-state conditions only. Steady-state occurs when (1) the balloon manager has had enough time to reasonably approximate the memory needs of the VMs and to inflate/deflate their balloons accordingly, and (2) the VMs have had enough time to react to decisions of the balloon manager by swapping data in or out as depicted in Figure 2.

Alas, the process of transferring memory pages from one VM to another is slow [31], and estimating the size of guests' working sets is hard, especially under changing conditions [27, 35, 45]. Ballooning performance is hence suboptimal under changing load conditions, during which the balloon manager is approximating and adjusting the balloon sizes and prompting the VMs to engage in swapping activity. Ballooning is consequently recognized as "useful for shaping memory over time, but inadequately responsive enough to ensure that, for example, the rapidly growing working set of one or more VMs can be instantly satisfied" [17]. Kim et al. observe that "ballooning is useful to effectively reclaim idle memory, but there may be latency, especially when inflating a large balloon; more importantly, when an idle domain that donates its memory becomes active, reclaimed memory must be reallocated to it via balloon deflating [and] this process could be inefficient when an idle domain has a varying working set, since prediction of the active working set size is difficult" [36]. Likewise, Magenheimer et al. observe that "if the light load is transient and the memory requirements of the workload on the VM suddenly exceed the reduced RAM available, ballooning is insufficiently responsive to instantaneously increase RAM to the needed level" [46].

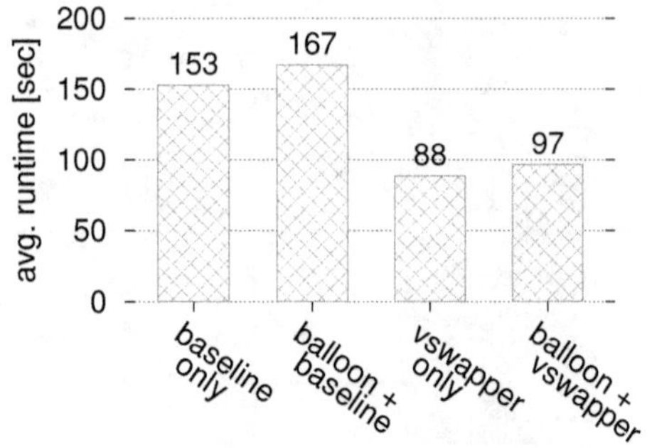


**Figure 4.** *Average completion time of ten guests running map-reduce workloads in a dynamic setup that starts them 10 seconds apart. (This setup is described in detail later on.)* VSWAPPER *configuration are up to twice as fast as baseline ballooning.*

VSWAPPER proves to be a highly effective optimization that can greatly enhance the performance under dynamic, changing memory load conditions. Its effectiveness is exemplified in Figure 4, which shows the average completion time of ten VMs running map-reduce workloads that are started 10 seconds apart. (The exact details of this experiment are provided in Section 5.2.) In this dynamic scenario, non-VSWAPPER ballooning worsens performance over baseline swapping by nearly 10%, and it yields an average runtime that is up to 2x slower than the VSWAPPER configurations. Ballooning is about 10% worse in the VSWAPPER configurations as well. It is counterproductive in this setup, because the balloon sizes are inadequate, and there is not enough time for the balloon manager to adjust them.

We thus conclude that not only is VSWAPPER an attractive fallback alternative for when ballooning is nonoperational, it is also an effective optimization on top of ballooning that significantly enhances the performance under dynamic conditions.

### 2.4 The Case for Unmodified Guests

Earlier, we provided evidence that clients sometimes have trouble installing and correctly configuring hypervisor tools, and that there are those who refrain from installing the tools because they wrongfully believe the tools degrade or do not affect the performance. Arguably, such problems would become irrelevant if hypervisors were implemented in a way that provides fully-virtualized (unmodified) guests with performance comparable to that of modified guests. We do not argue that such a goal is attainable, but VSWAPPER takes a step in this direction by improving the performance of unmodified guests and being agnostic to the specific kernel/version that the guest is running.

A guest OS is *paravirtual* if it is modified in a manner that makes it aware that it is being virtualized, e.g., by installing hypervisor tools. Paravirtualization has well-known merits, but also well-known drawbacks, notably the effort to continuously provide per-OS support for different kernels and versions. In particular, it is the responsibility of the hypervisor vendor to make sure that a balloon driver is available for every guest OS. Thus, from the vendor's perspective, it could be easier to maintain only one mechanism (the likes of VSWAPPER), as it works the same for all OSes.

Avoiding paravirtualization could similarly be advantageous for clients in terms of portability. Note that the balloon drivers of KVM, vSphere, XenServer, and Hyper-V, for example, are incompatible, such that the per-guest driver of one will not work with another. In the era of IaaS clouds, it is in the interest of clients to be able to move their VMs from one cloud provider to another without much difficulty, on the basis of the technical and economical merits of the cloud systems, optimally in a transparent manner [11, 44, 48]. Having paravirtualization interfaces negates this interest, as they are hypervisor specific. For example, installing the tools of the hypervisor used by Amazon EC2 will not serve VMs in Microsoft Azure and vice versa. Also, every additional installation and removal of hypervisor tools risks triggering problems, compatibility issues, and undesirable interactions between new and existing software [39]. Anecdotal evidence based on interaction with enterprise cloud clients indeed suggests that they tend to prefer not to install hypervisor tools as long as their workloads performance remains reasonable [20].

A final benefit of refraining from installing a balloon in a guest is that it prevents *over-ballooning*, whereby the guest OS experiences a sudden spike in memory demand that it cannot satisfy, causing it to terminate some of its running applications before the balloon manager deflates its balloon. We have conducted some limited experiments with the VMware hypervisor, vSphere 5.1, and learned that in this environment over-ballooning seems to be a rare corner case.[1] Conversely, in the KVM/QEMU-based experimental setup we utilize in this paper, over-ballooning was more frequent, prompting our Ubuntu guests to terminate running applications with their out-of-memory (OOM) or low-memory killers under memory pressure. Using VSWAPPER without ballooning eliminated this problem, as depicted in Figure 5.

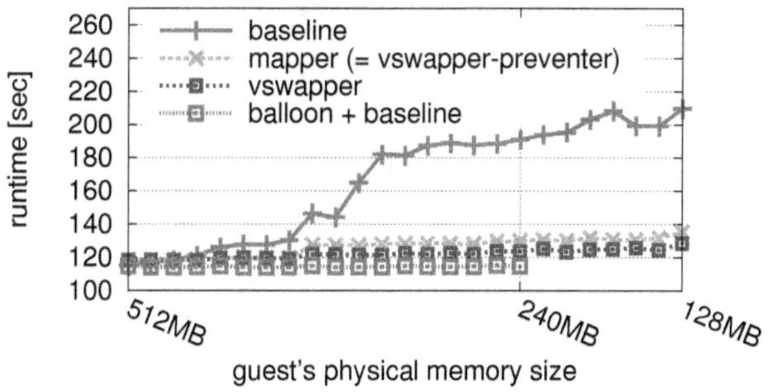


**Figure 5.** *Over-ballooning in our KVM/QEMU experimental setup, when compressing the Linux kernel code with pbzip2 from within a 512MB guest whose actual physical memory size is displayed along the X axis. Ballooning delivers better performance, but the guest kills bzip2 when its memory drops below 240MB.*

## 3. Problems in Baseline Swapping

If we are to improve the performance of virtual systems that employ uncooperative swapping, we need to have a thorough understanding of why it really hinders performance. We have characterized the root causes of the degraded performance through careful experimentation. The aforementioned double paging problem did not turn out to have a dominant effect or notable volume in our experiments, probably because bare metal (non-virtualized) swapping activity is typically curbed so long as the system is not thrashing [6], and because the uncooperative guest believes it operates in an environment where memory is sufficient.[2] The problems that did turn out to have a meaningful effect and that we were able to address are listed next.

***Silent Swap Writes:*** So long as memory is plentiful, much of the memory of general purpose OSes is dedicated to caching file content long after the content is used, in the hope that it will get re-used in the future [6]. When memory gets tight, unused content is discarded and the corresponding memory frames are freed by the OS.

In a virtual setup with uncooperative swapping, it is the host that decides which pages to swap, whereas the guest OS remains unaware. The host can nonetheless make an informed decision, as it too maintains per-frame usage statistics, allowing it to victimize unused pages. If a victim page is dirty, the host writes it to its swap area so as to later be able to recover the correct data.

The question is what to do if the page being reclaimed is clean. One alternative is to just discard it. But then the host would need: (1) to track and maintain correspondence between guest memory pages and the original file blocks from which they were read; (2) to handle subtle consistency issues (to be addressed later on); and (3) to treat clean and dirty reclaimed pages differently, mapping the former to the original file and the latter to its swap area. The easier alternative—that hypervisors like KVM and VMware's vSphere favor [76, p. 20]—is to keep all reclaimed guest pages in the host swap area, saving them there even if they are clean and identical to their origin file blocks. Worse, current x86 server hardware does not yet support dirty bits for

[1] Triggered, for example, when two guests allocate (what they perceive to be) pinned memory that collectively amounts to 1.5x of the physical memory available to the hypervisor.

[2] Conversely, when a guest is cooperative, the explicit purpose of inflating the balloon is to prompt the guest to swap out pages, in which case double paging is probably more likely.

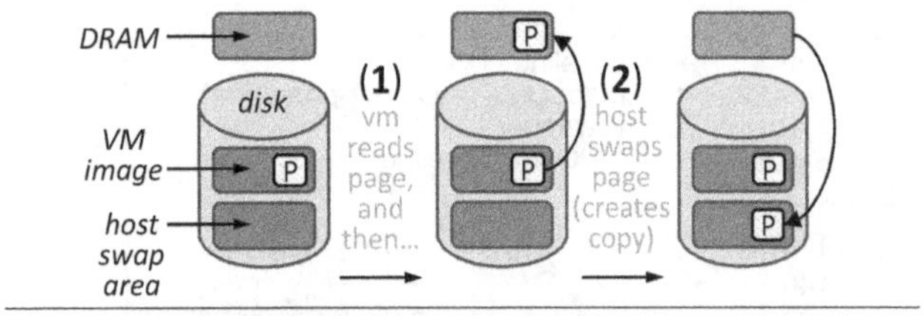


**Figure 6.** *Silent swap writes.*

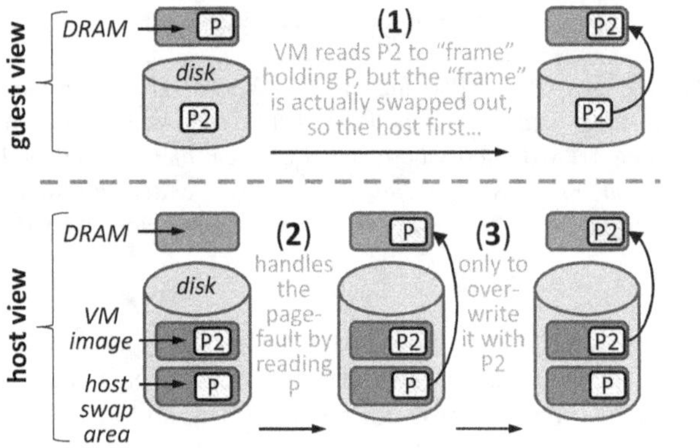


**Figure 7.** *Stale swap reads.*

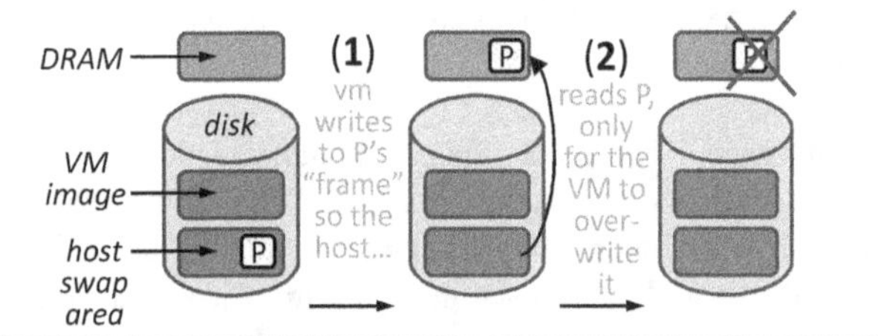


**Figure 8.** *False swap reads.*

guest pages,[3] so hosts assume that reclaimed pages are *always* dirty. Since hosts write to disk data that is already there, we denote this activity as *silent swap writes* (see Figure 6).[4]

***Stale Swap Reads:*** Suppose a guest generates an explicit I/O request to read some block from its (virtual) disk into one of its memory pages, denoted *P*. The virtual I/O operation generated by the guest triggers an exit to the host that generates a corresponding physical I/O request directed at the physical disk. Page *P* is hence designated to be the destination of the physical I/O operation as well.

Consider what happens if *P* was previously reclaimed by the host. In such a case, the host would experience a page fault as part of the processing of the virtual I/O request, before the corresponding physical request is issued. *P*'s old content would thus be faulted-in, only to be overwritten shortly after by the physical I/O operation and the newly read block. We denote such host reads, whose outcome is never read and is instantly superseded by subsequent reads, as *stale swap reads* (see Figure 7).

Note that after a file block is read, so long as the uncooperative guest keeps it in its file cache, it will never again be accompanied by a stale read, because, by definition, stale reads only occur due to explicit guest I/O requests.

***False Swap Reads:*** Memory management performed by guests includes activities like zeroing pages before they are (re)allocated [57], copying memory pages on write (COW) [34], and migrating pages from one DRAM location to another due to memory compaction [15], e.g., for super paging [23, 51]. Whether by copying memory or zeroing it, guests often overwrite full pages without regard to their old content. Such activity has no undesirable side effects in bare metal setups. But in virtual setups with uncooperative swapping, the target page being overwritten might be swapped out, generating an outcome similar to that of stale reads. Namely, the old content would be read and immediately overwritten. We denote such useless reads as *false swap reads* (see Figure 8).

The difference between stale and false reads is the computational entity that does the overwriting. It is the disk device that overwrites the stale reads via direct memory access (DMA). And it is the (guest) CPU that overwrites the false reads by copying or zeroing content. Clearly, it will be harder to identify and eliminate false reads, because the host has no a priori knowledge about whether the CPU is going to overwrite an entire target page or only part of it; in the latter case, the reads are necessary and hence are not false.

***Decayed Swap Sequentiality:*** OSes perform file prefetching to alleviate the long latencies that programs endure when forced to wait for disk reads. The most rewarding and straightforward read pattern to anticipate is sequential access. It is easy for the OS to notice. And it is easy to issue reads for subsequent parts of the file beforehand. Additionally, contiguous file pages tend to be contiguous on disk, minimizing the movement of the head of the hard drive and thus making prefetching relatively inexpensive.

Being an OS, the guest does its own prefetching from its virtual disk. The host merely acts as proxy by issuing the I/O operations generated by the guest. But things change when memory becomes scarcer under uncooperative swapping. When the host reclaims pages, it swaps their content out. And from this point onward, any prefetch activity related to those pages is inevitably performed only by the host, as the uncooperative guest is not even aware that the pages are not there. Importantly, the swap prefetch activity is *exclusively* initiated by the host page fault handler when it must swap in previously swapped out content. Namely, (swap) file prefetching is in fact a memory management issue.

The problem that consequently arises is the outcome of a detrimental guest-host interaction. Unaware that memory is scarce, the guest too aggressively prefetches/caches file content from its virtual disk. So the host swaps out some other

[3] The expected features of Intel's next generation "Haswell" server architecture (to be released not before the end of 2014 [86]) include support for access and dirty bits for guest pages [72].

[4] The chosen term is analogous to "silent stores," which characterize cases whereby a value being written by the store machine operation matches the exact value already stored at that corresponding memory location [42].

guest pages to accommodate the excessive memory demand. It therefore happens that cached file content from the guest virtual disk ends up in host swap area. But whereas the content blocks are contiguous on the virtual disk, they become scattered and uncoupled in the swap area, because spatial locality is secondary when victimizing pages for reclamation (as opposed to usage, which is primary). Host swap prefetching therefore becomes ineffective, such that the longer the execution, the more pronounced the effect. We call this phenomenon *decayed swap sequentiality*.

***False Page Anonymity:*** Memory pages backed by files are called *named pages*. Such are the pages of loaded executables and of files mapped to memory [52]. Conversely, memory pages not backed by files are called *anonymous pages*. Such are the pages of heaps and stacks of processes. Note that any page that could be moved to the swap area is anonymous, or else it would have been backed by some other (non-swap) file. As explained above, all the guest disk image pages are classified by the host as anonymous. This (mis)classification turns out to have negative consequences.

OSes are generally configured to have some preference to evict named pages when the need arises, because they can be reclaimed faster without write-back to swap, and because file access patterns typically exhibit more spatial locality than access to pages residing in the swap [55], making named pages easier to prefetch. Alas, guests are unable to enjoy such a preferential reclamation with uncooperative swapping, as the host (mis)classifies all their pages as anonymous. Worse, when the hypervisor is hosted (as is the case with QEMU/KVM), the hypervisor executable code within the otherwise-anonymous guest address space is classified as named, making the host OS inclined to occasionally reclaim these vital pages, thereby hindering performance further. We characterize this deficiency as *false page anonymity*.

### 3.1 Demonstration

Having enumerated the problems in uncooperative swapping that we have identified, we now experimentally demonstrate the manifestation of each individual problem in isolation. We use a simple experiment whereby one guest iteratively runs a Sysbench benchmark configured to sequentially read a 200MB file. The guest believes it has 512MB, whereas in fact it is allocated only 100MB and all the rest has been reclaimed by the host. The results are depicted in Figure 9.

The performance of baseline uncooperative swapping is roughly U-shaped (Figure 9a), taking about 40 seconds in the first iteration, which are halved in the second iteration, only to gradually work their way back to 40 seconds in the final iteration. The first iteration performance is largely dominated by stale swap reads. Those occur when the guest performs explicit I/O reads from its virtual disk, bringing content into memory that has been reclaimed by the host. The counterproductive activity is evident when examining the number of page faults experienced by the host while executing its own code in service of the guest (Figure 9b; first iteration). From the second iteration onward, no stale reads occur because the guest stops generating explicit I/O requests, believing it caches the entire file in memory and servicing all subsequent reads from its file cache. Thus, it is the absence of stale reads from all iterations but the first that accounts for the left side of the aforementioned U-shape.

With the exception of the first iteration, all page faults shown in Figure 9b are due to the hosted hypervisor code faulted-in while it is running. The code was swapped out because it was the only named part of the guest's address space, a problem we have denoted as false page anonymity. The problem becomes more pronounced over time as evident by the gradual increase in the baseline curve in Figure 9b.

Contributing to the gradually worsened performance (second half of U-shape) is the increasingly decayed sequentially of the host swap area. The file content is read to memory and then swapped out to disk, over and over again. As the content moves back and forth between disk and memory, it gradually loses its contiguity. Special locality is diminished, and host swap prefetching becomes ineffective. This negative dynamic is evident when plotting the number of page faults that fire when the guest accesses its memory in Figure 9c. Such faults occur due to non-present GPA⇒HPA mappings[5] while the *guest* is running (as opposed to Figure 9b, which depicts faults that occur while the *host* is running, servicing explicit virtual I/O requests generated by the guest). Every such page fault immediately translates into a disk read from the host swap area, which may or may not succeed to prefetch additional adjacent blocks. Importantly, only if the prefetch is successful in bringing the next file block(s) to be accessed will the next memory access(es) avoid triggering another page fault. Thus, amplified sequentiality decay implies greater page fault frequency, which is what we see in Figure 9c for the baseline curve. (Conversely, the VSWAPPER curve implies no decay, as it is horizontal.)

Baseline uncooperative swapping copies unchanged blocks of data to the swap area, although the corresponding source blocks are identical and stored within the guest disk image. We have denoted this phenomenon as silent swap writes. We find that the volume of this activity is significant, but that it contributes equally to the degraded performance exhibited by all iterations (Figure 9d).

The remaining problem we have not yet demonstrated is that of false reads, which occur when the guest attempts to overwrite memory pages that have been reclaimed by the host, e.g., when reallocating and initializing a page that previously held some information the guest no longer needs. We did not encounter false reads in the above Sysbench benchmark because it reads, rather than writes. We therefore extend the benchmark such that after it finishes all the read activity, it forks off a process that allocates and sequentially accesses 200MB. The simplest way to get a sense of the

[5] See Figure 1 for the meaning of GPA and HPA.

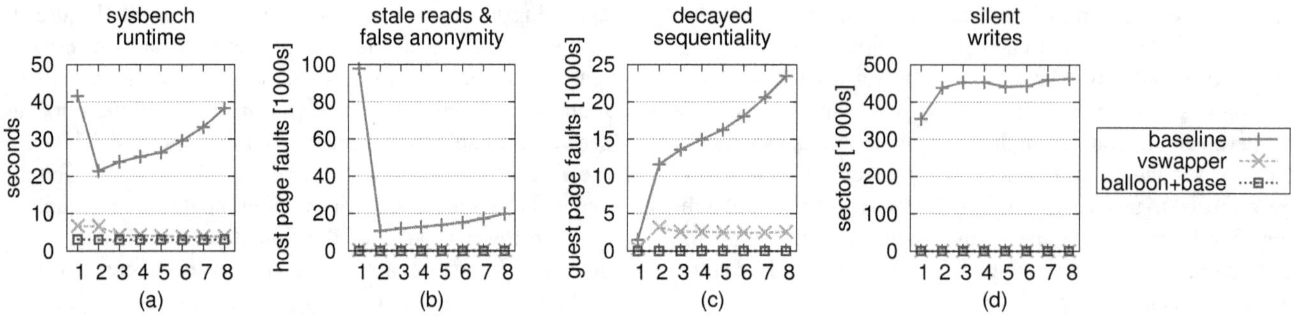


**Figure 9.** *Sysbench iteratively reads a 200MB file within a 100MB guest that believes it has 512MB. The x-axis shows the iteration number. The y-axis shows: (a) the benchmark's runtime; (b) the number of page faults triggered while the host code is running (first iteration faults are caused by stale reads, and the rest are due to false page anonymity); (c) number of page faults triggered while the guest code is running (a result of decayed sequentially); and (d) the number of sectors written to the host swap area (a result of silent writes).*

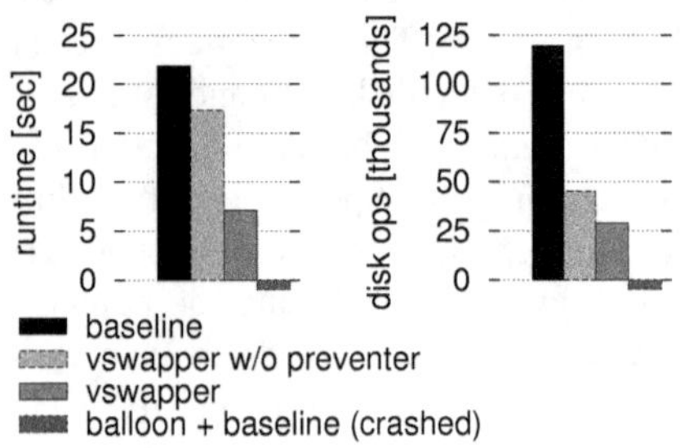


**Figure 10.** *Effect of false reads on a guest process that allocates and accesses 200MB.*

effect of false reads on this newly added microbenchmark is to measure its performance when using VSwapper without and with its False Reads Preventer component. Figure 10 shows the results. (The balloon performance is missing since it crashed the workload due to over-ballooning.) Comparing the two VSwapper configurations, we see that enabling the Preventer more than doubles the performance and that the performance is tightly correlated to the disk activity.

## 4. VSwapper Design and Implementation

We mitigate the problems of uncooperative swapping by introducing two new mechanisms. The first is the Swap Mapper (§4.1), which tracks the correspondence between disk blocks and guest memory pages, thereby addressing the problems of silent writes, stale writes, decayed sequentially, and false page anonymity. The second mechanism is the False Reads Preventer (§4.2), which temporarily buffers data written by unaware guests to swapped out pages, thereby addressing the problem of false reads.

### 4.1 The Swap Mapper

The poor performance of uncooperative swapping is tightly related to how guests utilize page caches, storing in memory large volumes of currently unused disk content because they (wrongfully) believe that memory is plentiful. Hypervisors need to learn to cope with this pathology if they are to efficiently exercise uncooperative swapping. The Swap Mapper achieves this goal by tracking guest I/O operations and by maintaining a mapping between corresponding disk and memory locations. When used carefully (so as to avoid subtle consistency issues), the mapping equips the hypervisor with the much-needed ability to treat relevant guest pages as file-backed. This ability counteracts the harmful effect of large page caches within unaware guests, because it allows the hypervisor to reasonably identify the pages that populate the cache and to efficiently discard them when the need arises, without undesirable consequences.

The Mapper's goal is to bridge a semantic gap. It needs to teach the hypervisor which guest pages are backed by which disk blocks. This goal could in principle be achieved through intrusive modifications applied to the guest [61] or through exhaustive memory/disk scans. But we favor a much simpler approach. Our Mapper leverages the fact that guest disk I/O is overwhelmingly implemented via emulation [67] or paravirtualization [5, 56], whereby the hypervisor serves all I/O request directed at the virtual disk. The Mapper can thus interpose on this activity and maintain the required association between disk blocks and memory pages.

The core of our Mapper implementation is simple. In the KVM/QEMU environment, each guest VM resides within (and is served by) a regular user-level QEMU process. The guest I/O requests are trapped by QEMU, which uses standard read and write system calls to satisfy the requests. Our Mapper replaces these reads/writes with mmap system calls [52], which provide the basic functionality of mapping guest pages to disk blocks, out of the box. The pages thus become named and are treated by the host Linux kernel accordingly. We establish "private" mappings (via standard mmap flags), which preserve the per-page disk association only so long as the page remains unchanged. A subsequent write instruction directed at the page will prompt the host kernel to copy-on-write the page and to make it anonymous. Thus, the disk-to-memory association is correctly maintained only as long as the content of the memory page is identical to the corresponding disk blocks. Future memory store operations by the unaware guest will *not* alter the disk.

As a result of this change, native uncooperative swapping done by the host Linux kernel automagically becomes more effective. Since the pages are named, they are evicted more frequently than anonymous pages, as their reclamation and retrieval is more efficient [55] (no false page anonymity). Specifically, when the kernel's page frame reclaiming mechanism selects a guest page for eviction, it knows the page is backed by a file, so it discards the page by discarding the mapping, instead of by swapping the page out (no silent swap writes). Later on, if/when the reclaimed page is accessed, the kernel knows from where to retrieve it using the information associated with the faulting non-present page table entry. Realizing the page is backed by a file, the kernel re-maps it instead of swapping it in, disregarding the specific target memory frame (no stale swap reads). At that point, host prefetch mechanisms perform disk read-ahead, benefiting from the sequential structure of the original guest disk image (no decayed swap sequentiality).

***Data Consistency:*** While the core idea is simple, we need to resolve several problems to make the Mapper correct, as the mmap mechanism was not designed to be used in such a way. The first problem stems from the fact that a memory mapped file region can, in parallel, be written to through ordinary I/O channels. To better understand this difficulty, suppose that (1) a named page $P$ with content $C_0$ is mapped to memory, that (2) $P$ previously resided in DRAM because the guest accessed it via the memory, that (3) $C_0$ currently resides on disk because $P$'s frame was reclaimed by the host, and that (4) the guest has now issued an explicit disk I/O write directed at the blocks holding $C_0$ in order to write to them new content $C_1$. In this situation, it would be an error to naively process the latter I/O write, because, later, if the guest reads $P$ via memory, it will rightfully expect to get $C_0$, but it will instead erroneously get $C_1$ (after $P$ is faulted in).

To solve the problem, we modify the host open system call to support a new flag, used by QEMU when opening the guest virtual disk file. The flag instructs the kernel to invalidate page mappings when associated disk blocks are being written to through the corresponding file descriptor. Invalidation involves reading $C_0$ and delaying the processing of $C_1$ until $C_0$ is fetched. Then, the mapping is destroyed and $C_1$ is finally written to disk. The host kernel (not QEMU) is the natural place to implement this semantic extension, as the kernel maintains the page mappings.

***Host Caching & Prefetching:*** It is generally recommended to turn off host caching and prefetching for guest disk images [30, 41, 63, 64]. The reasoning is that guest OSes do their own caching/prefetching, and that they are inherently better at it because the hypervisor suffers from a semantic gap. (For example, a guest knows about files within its virtual disk, whereas, for the hypervisor, the disk is just one long sequence.) For this reason, all non-VSWAPPER configurations in the evaluation section (§5) have host caching disabled. Conversely, VSWAPPER must utilize the host "caching" for the prosaic reason that mmaped pages reside in the host page cache. Our implementation, however, carefully makes sure that, beyond this technicality, the host page cache never truly functions as a cache; namely, it holds virtual disk blocks only if they are currently residing in guest memory. Thus, when a guest writes to a host filed-backed page, the page is COWed (due to being privately mapped), and then VSWAPPER removes the source page from the host page cache.

In all configurations, host prefetching activity is prompted by page faults. It is limited to reading content that is already cached by the guest and has been reclaimed due to uncooperative swapping. But whereas non-VSWAPPER configurations only prefetch from their host swap area, the VSWAPPER design allows it to prefetch these pages from the disk image.

Using the host page cache does not break crash consistency guarantees of guest filesystems. QEMU supports crash consistency by default with its "writethrough" disk caching mode, which synchronizes writes to the disk image upon guest flush commands [32]. Guests are notified that their flushes succeed only after the synchronization, thereby ensuring the Mapper does not deny crash consistency.

***Guest I/O Flow:*** Explicit disk read requests issued by the guest are translated by QEMU to a preadv system call invocation, which reads/scatters a contiguous block sequence to/within a given vector of guest pages. There is no mmapv equivalent. So, instead, the Mapper code within QEMU initiates reading the blocks to the page cache by invoking readahead (an asynchronous operation). It then iteratively applies mmap to the pages, using the "populate" mmap flag. The latter ensures that the readahead completes and that the pages are mapped in QEMU's page tables, thereby respectively preventing future major and minor page faults from occurring when QEMU accesses the pages. Alas, an undesirable side-effect of using "populate" is that the pages will be COWed when they are first accessed. We therefore patch the host's mmap to support a "no_COW" flag and thus avoid this overhead. Lastly, the Mapper iteratively invokes ioctl, requesting KVM to map the pages in the appropriate GPA⇒HPA table so as to prevent (minor) page faults from occurring when the guest (not QEMU) accesses the pages.

A second problem that immediately follows is how to correctly mmap a guest page $P$ that is being written to a disk block $B$ via a write request that has just been issued by the guest. Due to our newly added open flag (see "Data Consistency" above), $B$ is not mmaped right before the request is processed, even if $B$ was accessed in the past. Conversely, we want $B$ to be mmaped right after the request is processed, such that, later, if $P$ is reclaimed, we will not need to swap it out. The Mapper therefore: (1) writes $P$ into $B$ using the write system call, (2) mmaps $P$ to $B$, and (3) only then notifies the guest that its request is completed.

***Page Alignment:*** An inherent constraint of file-backed memory is that it mandates working in whole page granularity. The standard mmap API indeed dictates that both the file offset and the mapped memory address should be 4KB-aligned. The Mapper therefore must arrange things such that virtual disk requests coming from guests will comply with this requirement. Our Mapper imposes compliance by informing the guest that its virtual disk uses a 4KB logical sector size upon the creation of the virtual disk image. This approach will not work for preexisting guest disk images that utilize a smaller block size. Such preexisting images will require a reformat. (We remark that disks are expected to gradually shift to employing a 4KB *physical* block size [13].)

### 4.2 The False Reads Preventer

A dominant contributor to the poor performance of uncooperative swapping is the host's inability to know a-priori when guests overwrite entire pages and discard their old content. Such events routinely happen, e.g, when guests allocate pages to new processes. Unaware, the hypervisor needlessly reads the old content if it happens to be swapped out, a costly operation paid only because the host does not understand the guest semantics. The False Reads Preventer alleviates this problem by trapping guest write instructions directed at a swapped out pages, emulating them, and storing their result in page-sized, page-aligned buffers. If a buffer fills up, the Preventer maps it to the guest, thereby eliminating the extraneous disk accesses, which we have denoted as "false reads."

The Preventer does not utilize any knowledge about guest OS internals, nor does it resort to paravirtual guest/host collaboration that others deem necessary [61]. Instead, it optimistically intercepts and emulates guest write instructions directed at swapped out pages, hoping that all bytes comprising the page will soon be overwritten, obviating the need to read the old content from disk. When that happens, the Preventer stops emulating and repurposes its write buffer to be the guest's page.

The Preventer can sustain the emulation of all writes and all reads directed at already-buffered data. But emulation is slow, so we stop emulating a page when a predetermined interval has elapsed since the page's first emulated write (1ms), or if the write pattern is not sequential. We further avoid emulating a newly accessed page if too many pages are already being emulated (32). (The two values—1ms and 32—were empirically set.) In both cases, the corresponding missing page is read asynchronously. The guest is allowed to continue to execute so long as it does not read unavailable data; if it does, then the Preventer suspends it. When the disk content finally arrives, the Preventer merges the buffered and read information, and it resumes regular execution.

The Preventer design is architected to avoid a data hazard created by the fact that, in addition to the guest, the guest's memory pages can also be directly accessed by QEMU, which is the user-level part of the hypervisor that resides in an ordinary (non-virtualized) process. To preserve correctness and consistency, QEMU must observe exactly the same data as its guest, motivating the following design.

| *component* | *user (QEMU)* | *kernel* | *sum* |
|---|---|---|---|
| Mapper | 174 | 235 | 409 |
| Preventer | 10 | 1,964 | 1,974 |
| sum | 184 | 2,199 | 2,383 |

**Table 1.** *Lines of code of* VSWAPPER.

Let $P$ be a reclaimed page frame that is being emulated. The data we maintain for $P$ includes the time of $P$'s first emulated write, a page-sized buffer that stores emulated writes at the same offset as that of the real writes, the number of buffered bytes, and a bitmap marking all the buffered bytes, utilized to decide if reads can be emulated and to determine how to merge with the original disk content. The data structure also contains a reference to the original memory mapping of the reclaimed page (a vm_area_struct denoted here as $M_{old}$), to be used for reading the preexisting data in case a merge is required. Upon the first emulated write to $P$, we break the association between $P$ and $M_{old}$, and we associate $P$ with a new vm_area_struct (denoted $M_{new}$).

Note that $P$ is respectively accessed by QEMU and the guest via HVAs and GVAs (see Figure 1), such that the two types of accesses trigger different page fault handlers. Faulting HVAs trigger a "regular" handler (denoted $h$), whereas faulting GVAs trigger a special virtualization handler (denoted $g$).[6] The Preventer associates $M_{new}$ with an $h$ handler that, when invoked, terminates the emulation by merging the buffer with the old content, reading the latter via $M_{old}$ if it is needed; QEMU is suspended until $h$ finishes, ensuring it will always get up-to-date data when it faults. In contrast, the Preventer patches $g$ to sustain the emulation by buffering writes and serving reads if their data has been previously buffered. When $g$ decides to terminate the emulation (e.g., because 1ms has elapsed since the first write), it initiates the termination by invoking $h$.

We have identified a number of emulated instructions that allow the Preventer to recognize outright that the entire page is going to be rewritten, when the x86 REP prefix is used [33]. The Preventer short-circuits the above mechanism when such instructions are encountered. We expect that advanced binary translation techniques [1] could do better.

The number of lines of code of VSWAPPER is detailed in Table 1. The VSWAPPER source code is publicly available [3].

## 5. Evaluation

We implement VSWAPPER within QEMU [65] and KVM, the Linux kernel-based hypervisor [37]. We run our experiments on a Dell PowerEdge R420 server equipped with two 6-core 1.90GHz Intel Xeon E5-2420 CPUs, 16GB of memory,

[6] This handler serves "extended page table (EPT) violations," which occur when the hardware traverses GPA⇒HPA page table entries (bottom of Figure 1) that are marked non-present, e.g., due to uncooperative swapping.

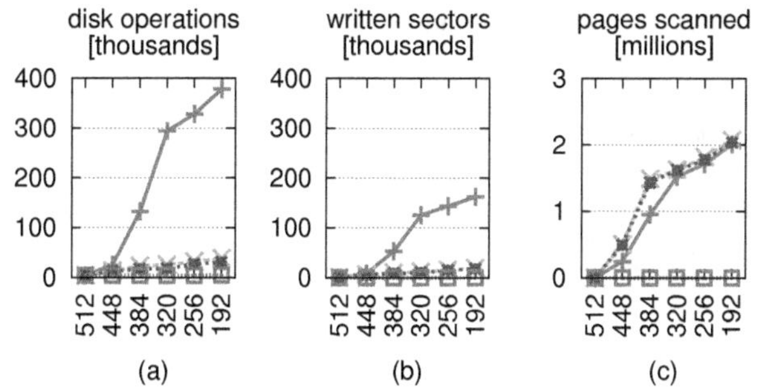


**Figure 11.** *Pbzip's 8 threads compressing Linux within a guest whose actual memory size is displayed along the X axis (in MB).*

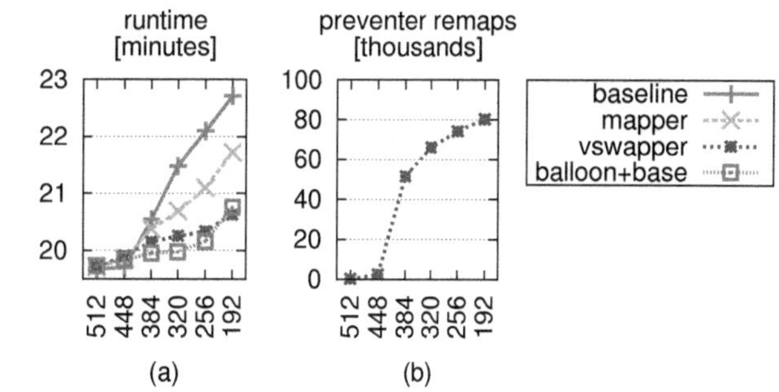


**Figure 12.** *Compiling the Linux kernel source code with Kernbench. (The X axis is the same as in Figure 11.)*

and a 2TB Seagate Constellation 7200 enterprise hard drive. Host and Linux guests run Ubuntu 12.04, Linux 3.7, and QEMU 1.2 with their default settings. The Windows guest runs Windows Server 2012. Guests have 20GB raw image disk drives, paravirtual disk controllers, and 1–2 VCPUs as indicated. We disable host kernel memory deduplication (KSM) and compression (zRAM) to focus on ballooning. We constrain guest memory size using container groups ("cgroups") as recommended [40]. The host caching policy is as specified in §4.1.

We evaluate five configurations: (1) "baseline," which relies solely on uncooperative swapping; (2) "balloon," which employs ballooning and falls back on uncooperative swapping; (3) "mapper," which denotes VSWAPPER without the Preventer; (4) "vswapper," which consists of both Mapper and Preventer; and (5) "balloon + vswapper," which combines ballooning and VSWAPPER. We typically run each experiment 5 times and present the average. When balloon values are missing it is because the workload crashed due to over-ballooning (§2.4).

### 5.1 Controlled Memory Assignment

We begin by executing a set of experiments whereby we systematically reduce and fix the size of the memory assigned to a 1-VCPU Linux guest, such that the guest believes it has 512MB of memory but it may actually have less. Balloon configurations communicate this information to the guest by appropriately inflating the balloon driver, whereas baseline and VSWAPPER configurations leave the guest unaware. The exact memory size allocated to the guest is displayed along the X-axis of the respective figures.

In this subsection, the results of the two balloon configurations (with and without VSWAPPER) were similar, so the respective figures display the balloon + baseline configuration only, to avoid clutter.

***Pbzip2:*** In our first set of experiments, the guest runs pbzip2, which is a parallel implementation of the bzip2 block-sorting file compressor [21]. We choose this multi-threaded benchmark to allow the baseline configuration to minimize uncooperative swapping overheads by leveraging the "asynchronous page faults" mechanism employed by Linux guests [50]. This mechanism exploits intra-guest parallelism to allow guests to continue to run despite experiencing page faults caused by host swapping (the host delivers a special page fault exception advising the guest to context switch or else it would block). We evaluate the performance by applying pbzip2 to the Linux kernel source code.

The execution time is shown in Figure 5, indicating that despite the asynchronous faults, the baseline performance rapidly worsens with memory pressure, yielding an execution time up to 1.66x slower than ballooning. VSWAPPER and its mapper-only configuration improve upon the baseline, respectively yielding performance within 1.03–1.08x and 1.03–1.13x of ballooning, since they greatly reduce the number of disk operations (Figure 11a). Baseline disk operations include a notable component of writes, which is largely eliminated by VSWAPPER (Figure 11b), thus making it beneficial for systems that employ solid state drives (SSDs).

***Kernbench:*** For our second benchmark evaluation, we reproduce an experiment reported in a VMware white paper [76] in which the authors executed Kernbench—a standard benchmark measuring the time it takes to build the Linux kernel [38]—inside a 512MB guest whose actual memory allocation was 192MB. Relative to the runtime measured when the guest was allocated the entire 512MB, the authors reported 15% and 4% slowdowns with baseline uncooperative swapping and ballooning, respectively. Although our experimental environment is different, we observe remarkably similar overheads of 15% and 5%, respectively (Figure 12a).

The performance of the baseline, mapper, and VSWAPPER configurations relative to ballooning is 0.99–1.10x, 1.00–1.05x, and 0.99–1.01x faster/slower, respectively. The Preventer eliminates up 80K false reads (Figure 12b), reducing guest major page faults by up to 30%.

***Eclipse:*** Our final set of controlled memory experiments executes Eclipse workloads that are part of the DaCapo Java benchmark suite [7]. (Eclipse is a popular integrated development environment.) Java presents a challenge for virtual environments, as its garbage collector subsystem causes an LRU-related pathological case of degraded performance

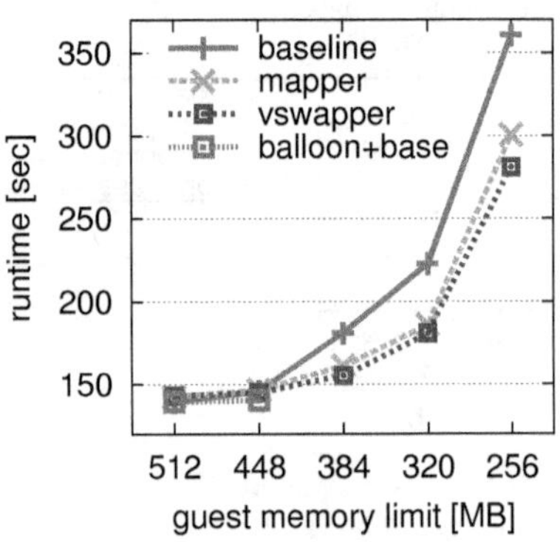


**Figure 13.** *Eclipse IDE workload from the DaCapo benchmark suite.*

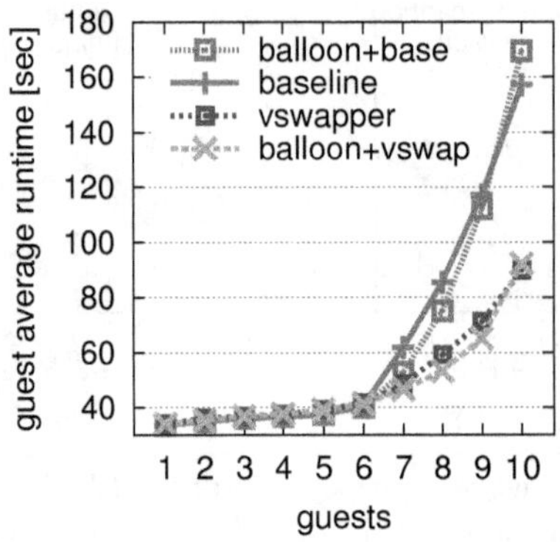


**Figure 14.** *Phased execution of multiple guests running the MapReduce runtime.*

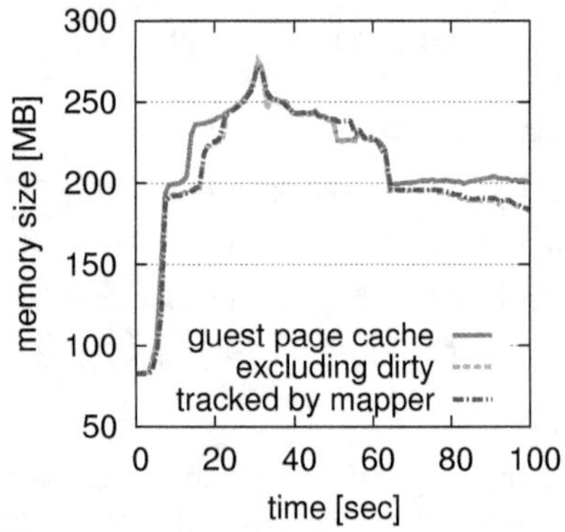


**Figure 15.** *Size of page cache as time progresses. (From the Eclipse benchmark.)*

when the physical memory allocated to the guest is smaller than the Java virtual machine (JVM) working set [76].

Figure 13 depicts the benchmark results, executed using OpenJDK and a 128MB heap. While it manages to run, ballooning is 1–4% faster than the other configurations, but Eclipse is occasionally killed by the ballooning guest when its allocated memory is smaller than 448MB. Relative to VSWAPPER, the baseline and mapper configurations are 0.97–1.28x and 1.00–1.08x faster/slower, respectively.

### 5.2 Dynamic Memory Assignment

So far, we have utilized benchmarks whereby the amount of memory allocated to guests is fixed. Virtualization setups, however, commonly run multiple guests with memory demands that dynamically change over time. To evaluate the performance in this scenario, we execute a workload whose dispatch is phased so that guests start the benchmark execution one after the other ten seconds apart. Handling such workloads is challenging for balloon managers, yet similar resource consumption spikes in virtualization environments are common [66].

In our dynamic experiment set, we vary the number of guests from one to ten. Each guest runs the Metis Mapreduce runtime for multicores [9, 47, 54], which comes with a benchmark suite comprised of 8 applications. The results we present here are of the word-count application, which uses a 300MB file holding 1M keys. The memory consumption of Metis is large, as it holds large tables in memory, amounting to roughly 1GB in this experiment. We assign each guest with 2 VCPUs and 2GB of memory, and we limit the host memory to 8GB so that it will eventually overcommit. (We note that each guest virtual disk is private, and so VSWAPPER does not exploit file caching to improve performance by saving fewer data copies.)

We employ MOM, the Memory Overcommitment Manager [43], to manage and adapt the balloon sizes. MOM is a host daemon which collects host and guest OS statistics and dynamically inflates and deflates the guest memory balloons accordingly. MOM requires that we use libvirt [8], a virtualization API for controlling virtual machines.

Figure 14 presents the average runtime as a function of the number of guests comprising the experiment. Running seven or more guests creates memory pressure. From that point on we observe a cascading effect, as guest execution is prolonged due to host swap activity and therefore further increases memory pressure. Clearly, the slowdown is lowest when using VSWAPPER, whereas memory ballooning responds to guest memory needs belatedly. Relative to the combination of ballooning and VSWAPPER, we get that: ballooning only, baseline, and VSWAPPER are 0.96–1.84x, 0.96–1.79x, and 0.97–1.11x faster/slower, respectively, suggesting that the combination is the preferable configuration.

### 5.3 Overheads and Limitations

***Slowdown:*** VSWAPPER introduces slowdowns which might degrade the performance by up to 3.5% when memory is plentiful and host swapping is not required. The slowdowns are mostly caused by our use of Linux mmap, which was advantageous for simplifying our prototype but results in some added overheads. Firstly, because using mmap is slower than regular reading [29]. And secondly, because a COW (which induces an exit) is required when a named page is modified, even if there are no additional references to that page. The latter overhead could be alleviated on hardware that supports dirty bits for virtualization page tables, which would allow VSWAPPER to know that pages have changed only when it needs to, instead of immediately when it happens.

We uncovered another source of overhead introduced by the page frame reclamation mechanism, which scans the pages in search for eviction candidates when the need arises. Due to subtleties related to how this mechanism works in Linux, the impact of VSWAPPER is such that it up to doubles the length of the mechanism traversals when memory pressure is low (Figure 11c).

The aforementioned 3.5% overhead can be compared to the overhead of "Geiger," a guest page cache monitoring mechanism by Jones et al., which introduced overheads of up to 2% [35]. Part of the 1.5% difference is probably accounted for by the fact that Geiger was evaluated on a system that did not support guest memory virtualization in hardware, forcing the hypervisor to write-protect newly mapped pages in the baseline setup and thereby creating exits that Geiger leveraged for tracking.

***Memory Consumption:*** The Mapper's use of the native Linux memory area data structures (vm_area_struct and i_mmap) increases memory consumption and might fragment the hypervisor address space. These structures consume 200 bytes, so theoretically, in the worst case, the overhead might be 5% of the guest memory size, if every 4KB page requires its own structure. Underlying this upper bound is our decision to use the already existing mmap mechanism. A dedicated mechanism for tracking guest page caches can achieve a similar goal with only 20 bytes per page [35]. Empirically, the Mapper consumed not more than 14MB across all of our experiments.

The Mapper is quite successful in tracking only the memory pages that reside in the guest page cache. The Mapper's effectiveness is illustrated in Figure 15, which shows that the memory size it tracks coincides with the size of the guest page cache excluding dirty pages. The Mapper correctly avoids tracking dirty pages, as they do not correspond to disk blocks. The Mapper occasionally tracks more pages than found in the page cache (time≈50 in Figure 15), because guests sometimes repurpose pages holding disk content for other uses. The Mapper will break the disk association of these pages when they are subsequently modified.

The Mapper will lose track of disk-backed pages if guests perform memory migration, e.g., for superpages [23, 51] or due to NUMA considerations. This drawback can be eliminated in a straightforward manner via paravirtual interfaces [73]; the question of whether it could be efficiently done for fully virtualized guests remains open, but the wealth of efficient memory deduplication techniques [25] suggests the answer is yes.

### 5.4 Non-Linux Guests and Hosts

***Windows:*** We validate the applicability of VSWAPPER to non-Linux guests using a VM running Windows 2012 Server. Windows does not align its disk accesses to 4KB boundaries by default. The hypervisor should therefore report that the disk uses 4KB physical *and* logical sectors to enforce the desired behavior. Our patched QEMU reports a 4KB physical sector size. But alas, QEMU virtual BIOS does not support 4KB logical sectors. We therefore formatted the Windows guest disk before installation as if the BIOS reported 4KB logical sectors by: creating aligned partitions, setting the cluster size to be 4KB, and using large file record segments (FRS). We remark that despite this configuration we still observed sporadic 512 byte disk accesses.

Our first experiment consists of Sysbench reading a 2GB file from within a single VCPU 2GB guest that is allocated only 1GB of physical memory. The resulting average runtime without VSWAPPER is 302 seconds, reduced to 79 seconds with VSWAPPER. Our second experiment consists of bzip2 running within the same guest with 512 MB of physical memory. The average runtime without and with VSWAPPER is 306 and 149 seconds, respectively.

| | balloon enabled | balloon disabled |
|---|---|---|
| runtime (sec) | 25 | 78 |
| swap read sectors | 258,912 | 1,046,344 |
| swap write sectors | 292,760 | 1,042,920 |
| major page faults | 3,659 | 16,488 |

**Table 2.** *Runtime and swap activity of executing a 1GB sequential file read from within a Linux VM on VMware Workstation.*

***VMware:*** In our last experiment we attempt to demonstrate that the benefit of using a VSWAPPER-like system is not limited to just KVM. We use the VMware Workstation 9.0.2 hypervisor as an example, running the Sysbench benchmark to execute a sequential 1GB file read from within a Linux guest. We set the host and guest memory to 512MB and 440MB, and we reserve a minimum of 350MB for the latter. The results (Table 2) indicate that disabling the balloon more than triples the execution time and creates substantial additional swap activity, coinciding with VMware's observation that "guest buffer pages are unnecessarily swapped out to the host swap device" [76]. (It is interesting to note that a similar benchmark on KVM using VSWAPPER completed in just 12 seconds.)

## 6. Related Work

Many paravirtual memory overcommitment techniques were introduced in recent years. Memory ballooning is probably the most common [5, 84]. CMM2 is a collaborative memory management mechanism for Linux guests that makes informed paging decisions on the basis of page usage and residency information [61]. CMM2 can discard free and file-backed guest page frames and thereby eliminate undesirable swap writes, yet it requires substantial and intrusive guest modifications. Transcendent memory [46] uses a pool of underutilized memory to allow the hypervisor to quickly respond to changing guest memory needs. This approach does not suit situations in which multiple guests require more memory all at once [4]. Application-level ballooning [58] can mitigate negative side effects of ballooning on applications that manage their own memory. Like OS-level ballooning, this approach does not render host swapping unnecessary. In contrast to all these paravirtual approaches, VSWAPPER does not require guest modifications.

Memory overcommitment can also be performed by emulating memory hotplug. The hypervisor can inform the guest about "physical" removal/addition of DRAM by emulating the corresponding architectural mechanisms. This approach is fully-virtual, but it has several shortcomings: it takes a long time to hot-unplug memory due to memory migration, the operation might fail [60], and it is unsupported by popular OSes, such as Windows. Like memory ballooning, memory hotplug cannot cope with memory consumption spikes of guests, and therefore requires host-swapping fallback for good performance under high memory pressures [28].

Regardless of how memory is overcommitted, improved memory utilization can lead to greater server consolidation. Unrelated mechanisms that help to achieve this goal include transparent page sharing [12], cooperative page sharing [49], memory deduplication [70], and sub-page level sharing [25]. All are complementary to VSWAPPER (and to ballooning).

Improving uncooperative host swapping performance was discussed before in Cellular Disco [24], in which two cases of undesirable disk traffic in virtualization environments were presented and addressed: writes of unallocated guest pages to the host swap, and double paging (explained in §2.1). Neither of these cases are addressed by VSWAPPER. Cellular Disco requires guest OS annotations to avoid writing unallocated guest pages to the host swap. VSWAPPER requires no such cooperation.

Our Mapper monitoring techniques resemble those used by Jones et al. for guest buffer cache monitoring [35]. That work used the monitoring techniques to estimate the guest working set size. Lu and Shen used similar techniques for guest memory access tracing [45]. Disco, by Bugnion et al., used "COW disks" for efficient disk sharing across multiple guests in order to eliminate memory redundancy [12]. To this end, they used memory mappings of a single shared disk. The Mapper uses similar techniques for monitoring, but it leverages them for a different purpose: improving host swapping reclamation and prefetching decisions by "teaching" the host memory management subsystem about guest memory to disk image mappings.

Useche used asynchronous page faults and write buffering in OSes to allow non-blocking writes to swapped-out pages [71]. His work implied that such methods have limited potential, as the additional overhead often surpasses the benefits obtained by reducing I/O wait time. Conversely, our work shows that write buffering is beneficial when deployed by hypervisors to enhance uncooperative swapping performance. The opposing conclusions are due to the different nature and purpose of the systems. Useche strives to handle page faults asynchronously in bare metal OSes, whereas VSWAPPER reduces the faults for hypervisors.

## 7. Future Work

OSes gather knowledge about their pages and use it for paging decisions. Although such information is located in intrinsic OS data structures, the hypervisor may be able to infer some of it and base its paging decisions on common OS paradigms. For instance, since OSes tend not to page out the OS kernel, page tables, and executables, the hypervisor may be able to improve guest performance by adapting a similar policy. The hypervisor can acquire the information by write-protecting and monitoring the guest state upon guest page faults. Alternatively, the hardware could be enhanced to perform such tracking more efficiently, by supporting additional usage flags beyond "accessed" and "dirty." The hardware could, for example, indicate if a page was used: in user mode (which means it is not a kernel page); for page walks while resolving a TLB miss (which means it is a page table); and for fetching instructions (which means it is part of an executable).

VSWAPPER techniques may be used to enhance live migration of guests and reduce the migration time and network traffic by avoiding the transfer of free and clean guest pages. Previous research suggested to achieve this goal via guest cooperation by inflating the balloon prior to live migration [26], or by migrating non-page-cache pages first [2]. The Mapper and the Preventer techniques can achieve the same goal without guest cooperation. Hypervisors that migrate guests can migrate memory mappings instead of (named) memory pages; and hypervisors to which a guest is migrated can avoid requesting memory pages that are wholly overwritten by guests.

## 8. Conclusions

To this day, uncooperative host swapping is considered a necessary evil in virtual setups, because it is commonly unavoidable but induces high overheads. We isolate, characterize, name, and experimentally demonstrate the major causes for the poor performance. We propose VSWAPPER to address these causes, and we show that VSWAPPER is highly effective in reducing the overheads without or in addition to memory ballooning.

## Availability

The source code of VSWAPPER is publicly available [3].

## Acknowledgments

We thank Ilya Kravets for his technical help. We thank the reviewers and especially Carl Waldspurger, our shepherd, for their insightful feedback, which has helped to improve this paper greatly. This research was partially supported by The Israel Science Foundation (grant No. 605/12) and by the Hasso Plattner Institute.

## References

[1] Ole Agesen, Jim Mattson, Radu Rugina, and Jeffrey Sheldon. Software techniques for avoiding hardware virtualization exits. In *USENIX Annual Technical Conference (ATC)*, volume 12, 2011.

[2] S. Akiyama, T. Hirofuchi, R. Takano, and S. Honiden. Fast wide area live migration with a low overhead through page cache teleportation. In *IEEE/ACM International Symposium on Cluster, Cloud and Grid Computing (CCGrid)*, pages 78–82, 2013.

[3] Nadav Amit. VSwpapper code. http://nadav.amit.to/vswapper, 2014.

[4] Ishan Banerjee, Fei Guo, Kiran Tati, and Rajesh Venkatasubramanian. Memory overcommitment in the ESX server. *VMware technical journal (VMTJ)*, Summer, 2013.

[5] Paul Barham, Boris Dragovic, Keir Fraser, Steven Hand, Tim Harris, Alex Ho, Rolf Neugebauer, Ian Pratt, and Andrew Warfield. Xen and the art of virtualization. In *ACM Symposium on Operating Systems Principles (SOSP)*, 2003.

[6] Robert Birke, Lydia Y Chen, and Evgenia Smirni. Data centers in the wild: A large performance study. Technical Report RZ3820, IBM Research, 2012. http://tinyurl.com/data-centers-in-the-wild.

[7] Stephen M Blackburn, Robin Garner, Chris Hoffmann, Asjad M Khang, Kathryn S McKinley, Rotem Bentzur, Amer Diwan, Daniel Feinberg, Daniel Frampton, Samuel Z Guyer, et al. The DaCapo benchmarks: Java benchmarking development and analysis. In *ACM SIGPLAN Conference on Object-Oriented Programing, Systems, Languages, and Applications (OOPSLA)*, pages 169–190, 2006.

[8] Matthias Bolte, Michael Sievers, Georg Birkenheuer, Oliver Niehörster, and André Brinkmann. Non-intrusive virtualization management using libvirt. In *Conference on Design, Automation and Test in Europe*, pages 574–579, 2010.

[9] Silas Boyd-Wickizer, Austin T Clements, Yandong Mao, Aleksey Pesterev, M Frans Kaashoek, Robert Morris, and Nickolai Zeldovich. An analysis of Linux scalability to many cores. In *USENIX Symposium on Operating Systems Design & Implementation (OSDI)*, 2010.

[10] Rich Brambley. Why do I need to install VMware tools? http://vmetc.com/2008/08/30/why-do-i-need-to-install-vmware-tools/, 2008.

[11] Mary Brandel. The trouble with cloud: Vendor lock-in. http://www.cio.com/article/488478/The_Trouble_with_Cloud_Vendor_Lock_in, 2009.

[12] Edouard Bugnion, Scott Devine, Kinshuk Govil, and Mendel Rosenblum. Disco: running commodity operating systems on scalable multiprocessors. *ACM Transactions on Computer Systems (TOCS)*, 15(4):412–447, November 1997.

[13] P. Chicoine, M. Hassner, E. Grochowski, S. Jenness, M. Noblitt, G. Silvus, C. Stevens, and B. Weber. Hard disk drive long data sector white paper. Technical report, IDEMA, 2007.

[14] YP Chien. The yin and yang of memory overcommitment in virtualization: The VMware vSphere 4.0 edition. Technical Report MKP-339, Kingston Technology Corporation, Fountain Valley, CA, 2010. http://media.kingston.com/images/branded/MKP_339_VMware_vSphere4.0_whitepaper.pdf.

[15] Jonathan Corbet. Memory compaction. http://lwn.net/Articles/368869/, 2010.

[16] Oracle Corporation. Virtual box manual. https://www.virtualbox.org/manual/, 2013.

[17] Orcale Corporation. Project: Transcendent memory – new approach to managing physical memory in a virtualized system. https://oss.oracle.com/projects/tmem/, 2010. Visited: Dec 2013.

[18] Johan De Gelas. Hardware virtualization: the nuts and bolts. AnandTech, 2008. http://www.anandtech.com/show/2480/10.

[19] Frank Denneman. Impact of memory reservation. http://frankdenneman.nl/2009/12/08/impact-of-memory-reservation/, 2009.

[20] Michael Factor. Enterprise cloud clients tend to prefer unmodified guest virtual machines. Private communication, 2013.

[21] Jeff Gilchrist. Parallel data compression with bzip2. In *IASTED International Conference on Parallel and Distributed Computing and Systems (ICPDCS)*, volume 16, pages 559–564, 2004.

[22] Robert P. Goldberg and Robert Hassinger. The double paging anomaly. In *ACM National Computer Conference and Exposition*, pages 195–199, 1974.

[23] Mel Gorman and Andy Whitcroft. Supporting the allocation of large contiguous regions of memory. In *Ottawa Linux Symposium (OLS)*, pages 141–152, 2007.

[24] Kinshuk Govil, Dan Teodosiu, Yongqiang Huang, and Mendel Rosenblum. Cellular Disco: resource management using virtual clusters on shared-memory multiprocessors. In *ACM Symposium on Operating Systems Principles (SOSP)*, pages 154–169, 1999.

[25] Diwaker Gupta, Sangmin Lee, Michael Vrable, Stefan Savage, Alex C. Snoeren, George Varghese, Geoffrey M. Voelker, and Amin Vahdat. Difference engine: harnessing memory redundancy in virtual machines. *Communications of the ACM (CACM)*, 53(10):85–93, 2010.

[26] Michael R Hines and Kartik Gopalan. Post-copy based live virtual machine migration using adaptive pre-paging and dynamic self-ballooning. In *ACM/USENIX International Conference on Virtual Execution Environments (VEE)*, pages 51–60, 2009.

[27] Michael R Hines, Abel Gordon, Marcio Silva, Dilma Da Silva, Kyung Dong Ryu, and Muli Ben-Yehuda. Applications know best: Performance-driven memory overcommit with Ginkgo. In *IEEE Cloud Computing Technology and Science (CloudCom)*, pages 130–137, 2011.

[28] Eric Horschman. Hypervisor memory management done right. http://blogs.vmware.com/virtualreality/2011/02/hypervisor-memory-management-done-right.html, 2011.

[29] Yiming Hu, Ashwini Nanda, and Qing Yang. Measurement, analysis and performance improvement of the Apache web server. In *IEEE International Performance Computing & Communications Conference (IPCCC)*, pages 261–267, 1999.

[30] Khoa Huynh and Stefan Hajnoczi. KVM / QEMU storage stack performance discussion. In *Linux Plumbers Conference*, 2010.

[31] Woomin Hwang, Yangwoo Roh, Youngwoo Park, Ki-Woong Park, and Kyu Ho Park. HyperDealer: Reference pattern

aware instant memory balancing for consolidated virtual machines. In *IEEE International Conference on Cloud Computing (CLOUD)*, pages 426–434, 2014.

[32] IBM documentation. Best practice: KVM guest caching modes. `http://pic.dhe.ibm.com/infocenter/lnxinfo/v3r0m0/topic/liaat/liaatbpkvmguestcache.htm`. Visited: Dec 2013.

[33] Intel Corporation. Intel 64 and IA-32 Architectures Software Developer's Manual, 2013.

[34] Francisco Javier, Thayer Fábrega, Francisco, and Joshua D. Guttman. Copy on write. `http://citeseerx.ist.psu.edu/viewdoc/summary?doi=10.1.1.33.3144`, 1995.

[35] Stephen T. Jones, Andrea C. Arpaci-Dusseau, and Remzi H. Arpaci-Dusseau. Geiger: Monitoring the buffer cache in a virtual machine environment. In *ACM Architectural Support for Programming Languages & Operating Systems (ASPLOS)*, pages 14–24, 2006.

[36] Hwanju Kim, Heeseung Jo, and Joonwon Lee. XHive: Efficient cooperative caching for virtual machines. *IEEE Transactions on Computers*, 50(1):106–119, Jan 2011.

[37] Avi Kivity, Yaniv Kamay, Dor Laor, Uri Lublin, and Anthony Liguori. KVM: the Linux virtual machine monitor. In *Ottawa Linux Symposium (OLS)*, 2007.

[38] Con Kolivas. KernBench project. `freecode.com/projects/kernbench`.

[39] Ilia Kravets and Dan Tsafrir. Feasibility of mutable replay for automated regression testing of security updates. In *Runtime Environments/Systems, Layering, & Virtualized Environments workshop (RESoLVE)*, 2012.

[40] KVM. Tuning kernel for KVM. `http://www.linux-kvm.org/page/Tuning_Kernel`.

[41] KVM. Tuning KVM. `http://www.linux-kvm.org/page/Tuning_KVM`.

[42] Kevin M. Lepak and Mikko H. Lipasti. On the value locality of store instructions. In *ACM/IEEE International Symposium on Computer Architecture (ISCA)*, pages 182–191, 2000.

[43] Adam Litke. Automatic memory ballooning with MOM. `http://www.ibm.com/developerworks/library/l-overcommit-kvm-resources/`, 2011. Visited: Dec 2013.

[44] Pengcheng Liu, Ziye Yang, Xiang Song, Yixun Zhou, Haibo Chen, and Binyu Zang. Heterogeneous live migration of virtual machines. In *International Workshop on Virtualization Technology (IWVT)*, 2008.

[45] Pin Lu and Kai Shen. Virtual machine memory access tracing with hypervisor exclusive cache. In *USENIX Annual Technical Conference (ATC)*, pages 3:1–3:15, 2007.

[46] Dan Magen heimer, Chris Mason, Dave McCracken, and Kurt Hackel. Transcendent memory and Linux. In *Ottawa Linux Symposium (OLS)*, pages 191–200, 2009.

[47] Yandong Mao, Robert Morris, and Frans Kaashoek. Optimizing MapReduce for multicore architectures. Technical Report MIT-CSAIL-TR-2010-020, Massachusetts Institute of Technology, 2010. URL http://pdos.csail.mit.edu/metis/.

[48] Cade Metz. The meta cloud—flying data centers enter fourth dimension. `http://www.theregister.co.uk/2009/02/24/the_meta_cloud/`, 2009.

[49] Grzegorz Miłós, Derek G Murray, Steven Hand, and Michael A Fetterman. Satori: Enlightened page sharing. In *USENIX Annual Technical Conference (ATC)*, 2009.

[50] Gleb Natapov. Asynchronous page faults - AIX did it. KVM Forum `www.linux-kvm.org/wiki/images/a/ac/2010-forum-Async-page-faults.pdf`.

[51] Juan Navarro, Sitaram Iyer, Peter Druschel, and Alan Cox. Practical, transparent operating system support for superpages. In *USENIX Symposium on Operating Systems Design & Implementation (OSDI)*, 2002.

[52] The Open Group. *mmap - map pages of memory*, 2004. The Open Group Base Specifications Issue 6. IEEE Std 1003.1. `http://pubs.opengroup.org/onlinepubs/009695399/functions/mmap.html`.

[53] Brent Ozar. Top 10 keys to deploying SQL server on VMware. `http://www.brentozar.com/archive/2011/05/keys-deploying-sql-server-on-vmware/`, 2011.

[54] Colby Ranger, Ramanan Raghuraman, Arun Penmetsa, Gary Bradski, and Christos Kozyrakis. Evaluating MapReduce for multi-core and multiprocessor systems. In *IEEE International Symposium on High Performance Computer Architecture (HPCA)*, pages 13–24, 2007.

[55] Rikvan Riel. Linux page replacement design. `http://linux-mm.org/PageReplacementDesign`, 2010.

[56] Rusty Russell. virtio: towards a de-facto standard for virtual I/O devices. *ACM SIGOPS Operating Systems Review (OSR)*, 42(5):95–103, 2008.

[57] Mark E. Russinovich and David A. Solomon. *Microsoft Windows Internals, Fourth Edition*. Microsoft Press, 2004.

[58] Tudor-Ioan Salomie, Gustavo Alonso, Timothy Roscoe, and Kevin Elphinstone. Application level ballooning for efficient server consolidation. In *ACM SIGOPS European Conference on Computer Systems (EuroSys)*, pages 337–350, 2013.

[59] Vinay Sastry. Virtualizing tier 1 applications - MS SQL server. `http://blogs.totalcaos.com/virtualizing-tier-1-sql-workloads`, 2012.

[60] Joel H Schopp, Keir Fraser, and Martine J Silbermann. Resizing memory with balloons and hotplug. In *Ottawa Linux Symposium (OLS)*, volume 2, pages 313–319, 2006.

[61] Martin Schwidefsky, Hubertus Franke, Ray Mansell, Himanshu Raj, Damian Osisek, and JongHyuk Choi. Collaborative memory management in hosted Linux environments. In *Ottawa Linux Symposium (OLS)*, volume 2, 2006.

[62] L. H. Seawright and R. A. MacKinnon. VM/370—a study of multiplicity and usefulness. *IBM Systems Journal*, 18(1):4–17, Mar 1979.

[63] Prateek Sharma and Purushottam Kulkarni. Singleton: system-wide page deduplication in virtual environments. In *International Symposium on High Performance Distributed Computer (HPDC)*, pages 15–26, 2012.

[64] Balbir Singh. Page/slab cache control in a virtualized environment. In *Ottawa Linux Symposium (OLS)*, volume 1, pages 252–262, 2010.

[65] Balbir Singh and Vaidyanathan Srinivasan. Containers: Challenges with the memory resource controller and its performance. In *Ottawa Linux Symposium (OLS)*, page 209, 2007.

[66] Vijayaraghavan Soundararajan and Jennifer M. Anderson. The impact of management operations on the virtualized datacente. In *ACM/IEEE International Symposium on Computer Architecture (ISCA)*, pages 326–337, 2010.

[67] Jeremy Sugerman, Ganesh Venkitachalam, and Beng-Hong Lim. Virtualizing I/O devices on VMware workstation's hosted virtual machine monitor. In *USENIX Annual Technical Conference (ATC)*, pages 1–14, 2001.

[68] Taneja Group. Hypervisor shootout: Maximizing workload density in the virtualization platform. `http://www.vmware.com/files/pdf/vmware-maximize-workload-density-tg.pdf`, 2010.

[69] Ryan Troy and Matthew Helmke. *VMware Cookbook*. O'Reilly Media, Inc., 2009. Section 4.1: Understanding Virtual Machine Memory Use Through Reservations, Shares, and Limits.

[70] Irina Chihaia Tuduce and Thomas R Gross. Adaptive main memory compression. In *USENIX Annual Technical Conference (ATC)*, pages 237–250, 2005.

[71] Luis Useche. *Optimizing Storage and Memory Systems for Energy and Performance*. PhD thesis, Florida International University, 2012.

[72] Bob Valentine. Intel next generation microarchitecture codename Haswell: New processor innovations. In *6th Annual Intel Software Developer Conference & User Group*, June 2013. `http://ftp.software-sources.co.il/Processor_Architecture_Update-Bob_Valentine.pdf`. Visited: Dec 2013.

[73] Rik van Riel. KVM and memory managment updates. KVM Forum`http://www.linux-kvm.org/wiki/images/1/19/2012-forum-memory-mgmt.pdf`, 2012.

[74] Gabrie van Zanten. Memory overcommit in production? YES YES YES. `http://www.gabesvirtualworld.com/memory-overcommit-in-production-yes-yes-yes/`, 2010.

[75] VMware, Inc. *vSphere 4.1 - ESX and VCenter*. VMware, Inc., 2010. Section: "VMware HA Admission Control". `http://tinyurl.com/vmware-admission-control`.

[76] VMware, Inc. Understanding memory management in VMware vSphere 5, 2011. Technical white paper. `http://www.vmware.com/files/pdf/mem_mgmt_perf_vsphere5.pdf`.

[77] VMware Knowledge Base (KB). Problems installing VMware tools when the guest CD-ROM drive is locked. `http://kb.vmware.com/kb/2107`, 2011. Visited: Dec 2013.

[78] VMware Knowledge Base (KB). Troubleshooting a failed VMware tools installation in a guest operating system. `http://kb.vmware.com/kb/1003908`, 2012. Visited: Dec 2013.

[79] VMware Knowledge Base (KB). Unable to upgrade existing VMware tools. `http://kb.vmware.com/kb/1001354`, 2012. Visited: Dec 2013.

[80] VMware Knowledge Base (KB). VMware tools may not install on a windows guest operating system after upgrading to a newer version of ESX/ESXi. `http://kb.vmware.com/kb/1012693`, 2012. Visited: Dec 2013.

[81] VMware Knowledge Base (KB). Troubleshooting a failed VMware tools installation in Fusion. `http://kb.vmware.com/kb/1027797`, 2013. Visited: Dec 2013.

[82] VMware Knowledge Base (KB). Updating VMware tools fails with the error. `http://kb.vmware.com/kb/2007298`, 2013. Visited: Dec 2013.

[83] VMware Knowledge Base (KB). Updating VMware tools operating system specific package fails with dependency errors and driver issues on RHEL 6 and CentOS 6. `http://kb.vmware.com/kb/2051322`, 2013. Visited: Dec 2013.

[84] Carl A. Waldspurger. Memory resource management in VMware ESX server. In *USENIX Symposium on Operating Systems Design & Implementation (OSDI)*, volume 36, pages 181–194, 2002.

[85] Carl A. Waldspurger. Default ESX configuration for balloon size limit. Personal communication, 2013.

[86] Wikipedia. Haswell microarchitecture – expected server features. `http://en.wikipedia.org/wiki/Haswell_(microarchitecture)#Expected_Server_features`, 2013. Visited: Dec 2013.

[87] Timothy Wood, Gabriel Tarasuk-Levin, Prashant Shenoy, Peter Desnoyers, Emmanuel Cecchet, and Mark D. Corner. Memory buddies: exploiting page sharing for smart colocation in virtualized data centers. *ACM SIGOPS Operating Systems Review (OSR)*, 43:27–36, 2009.

[88] Xiaowei Yang. Evaluation and enhancement to memory sharing and swapping in Xen 4.1. In *Xen Summit*, 2011. `http://www-archive.xenproject.org/xensummit/xensummit_summer_2011.html`.

# Cider: Native Execution of iOS Apps on Android

Jeremy Andrus, Alexander Van't Hof, Naser AlDuaij,
Christoffer Dall, Nicolas Viennot, and Jason Nieh

Department of Computer Science
Columbia University
{jeremya, alexvh, alduaij, cdall, nviennot, nieh}@cs.columbia.edu

## Abstract

We present Cider, an operating system compatibility architecture that can run applications built for different mobile ecosystems, iOS or Android, together on the same smartphone or tablet. Cider enhances the domestic operating system, Android, of a device with kernel-managed, per-thread personas to mimic the application binary interface of a foreign operating system, iOS, enabling it to run unmodified foreign binaries. This is accomplished using a novel combination of binary compatibility techniques including two new mechanisms: compile-time code adaptation, and diplomatic functions. Compile-time code adaptation enables existing unmodified foreign source code to be reused in the domestic kernel, reducing implementation effort required to support multiple binary interfaces for executing domestic and foreign applications. Diplomatic functions leverage per-thread personas, and allow foreign applications to use domestic libraries to access proprietary software and hardware interfaces. We have built a Cider prototype, and demonstrate that it imposes modest performance overhead and runs unmodified iOS and Android applications together on a Google Nexus tablet running the latest version of Android.

***Categories and Subject Descriptors*** C.0 [*Computer Systems Organization*]: General–System architectures; D.2.7 [*Software Engineering*]: Distribution, Maintenance, and Enhancement; D.2.11 [*Software Engineering*]: Software Architectures; D.3.4 [*Programming Languages*]: Processors–Run-time environments; D.4.7 [*Operating Systems*]: Organization and Design; D.4.9 [*Operating Systems*]: Systems Programs and Utilities



*ASPLOS '14,* March 1–4, 2014, Salt Lake City, Utah, USA.

ACM 978-1-4503-2305-5/14/03... $15.00.
http://dx.doi.org/10.1145/2541940.2541972

***Keywords*** Android, iOS, Mobile Computing, Binary Compatibility, Operating System Compatibility

## 1. Introduction

Mobile devices such as tablets and smartphones are changing the way that computing platforms are designed, from the separation of hardware and software concerns in the traditional PC world, to vertically integrated platforms. Hardware components are integrated together in compact devices using non-standard interfaces. Software is customized for the hardware, often using proprietary libraries to interface with specialized hardware. Applications (apps) are tightly integrated with libraries and frameworks, and often only available on particular hardware devices.

These design decisions and the maturity of the mobile market can limit user choice and stifle innovation. Users who want to run iOS gaming apps on their smartphones are stuck with the smaller screen sizes of those devices. Users who prefer the larger selection of hardware form factors available for Android are stuck with the poorer quality and selection of Android games available compared to the well populated Apple App Store [21]. Android users cannot access the rich multimedia content available in Apple iTunes, and iOS users cannot easily access Flash-based Web content. Some companies release cross-platform variants of their software, but this requires developers to master many different graphical, system, and library APIs, and creates additional support and maintenance burden on the company. Many developers who lack such resources choose one platform over another, limiting user choice. Companies or researchers that want to build innovative new devices or mobile software platforms are limited in the functionality they can provide because they lack access to the huge app base of existing platforms. New platforms without an enormous pool of user apps face the difficult, if not impossible, task of end user adoption, creating huge barriers to entry into the mobile device market.

While virtual machines (VMs) are useful for desktop and server computers to run apps intended for one platform on a different platform [36, 44], using them for smartphones and tablets is problematic for at least two reasons. First, mobile devices are more resource constrained, and running an entire additional operating system (OS) and user space environment in a VM just to run one app imposes high overhead. High overhead and slow system responsiveness are much less acceptable on a smartphone than on a desktop computer because smartphones are often used for just a few minutes or even seconds at a time. Second, mobile devices are tightly integrated hardware platforms that incorporate a plethora of devices, such as GPUs, that use non-standardized interfaces. VMs provide no effective mechanism to enable apps to directly leverage these hardware device features, severely limiting performance and making existing VM-based approaches unusable on smartphones and tablets.

To address these problems, we created *Cider*, an OS compatibility architecture that can simultaneously run apps written and compiled for different mobile ecosystems, iOS or Android, simultaneously on the same smartphone or tablet. Cider runs *domestic* binaries, those developed for a given device's OS, the domestic OS, and *foreign* binaries, those developed for a different OS, the foreign OS, together on the same device. In our prototype, Android is the domestic OS, running domestic Android apps, and iOS is the foreign OS. We use the terms foreign and iOS, and domestic and Android interchangeably. Cider defines a *persona* as an execution mode assigned to each *thread* in the system, identifying the thread as executing either foreign or domestic code, using a foreign persona or domestic persona, respectively. Cider supports multiple personas within a single process by extending the domestic kernel's application binary interface (ABI) to be aware of both foreign and domestic threads.

Cider provides OS compatibility by augmenting the domestic Android kernel with the ability to simultaneously present both a domestic kernel ABI as well as a foreign kernel ABI. Foreign user space code interacts with a Cider-enabled kernel in exactly the same way as a foreign kernel, i.e., iOS apps trap into the Linux kernel exactly as if they were trapping into a kernel running on an iPhone or iPad. Modifying the domestic kernel in this way allows Cider both to avoid the traditional VM overhead of running a complete instance of a foreign kernel, and reuse and run unmodified foreign user space library code. The latter is essential since mobile ecosystem libraries and frameworks are often complex, closed-source, and proprietary.

To run unmodified foreign libraries and apps on a domestic OS, we had to overcome two key challenges: the difficulty of porting and reimplementing complex functionality of one OS in another, and the use of proprietary and opaque kernel interfaces to access custom hardware. In particular, tightly integrated libraries on mobile devices will often directly access proprietary hardware resources of a particular device through opaque kernel interfaces such as the `ioctl` system call. Proprietary and opaque foreign kernel interfaces cannot easily be implemented in the domestic kernel, and custom foreign hardware is often missing from the domestic device. Our solution takes advantage of two aspects of mobile ecosystems. First, although user space libraries and frameworks are often proprietary and closed, even closed mobile ecosystems increasingly build on open source kernel code through well-defined interfaces; iOS builds on the open source XNU kernel [6]. Second, although libraries on mobile devices will access custom hardware through opaque kernel interfaces, the actual functionality provided is often cross platform as companies mimic the best features of their competitors' devices such as the use of touchscreens for input and OpenGL ES for graphics on mobile ecosystems.

Based on these observations, Cider supports running unmodified foreign apps on a domestic OS through a novel combination of binary compatibility techniques, including two new OS compatibility mechanisms. Cider introduces *duct tape*, a novel compile-time code adaptation layer, that allows unmodified foreign kernel code to be directly compiled into the domestic kernel. Foreign binaries can then use these new kernel services not otherwise present in the domestic kernel. Brute force implementation of these services and functionality can be error-prone and tedious. Duct tape maximizes reuse of available foreign open source OS code to substantially reduce implementation effort and coding errors. Cider introduces *diplomatic functions* to allow foreign apps to use domestic libraries to access proprietary software and hardware interfaces on the device. A diplomatic function is a function which temporarily switches the persona of a calling thread to execute domestic code from within a foreign app, or vice-versa. Using diplomatic functions, Cider replaces calls into foreign hardware-managing libraries, such as OpenGL ES, with calls into domestic libraries that manage domestic hardware, such as a GPU. Diplomatic functions make it possible to deliver the same library functionality required by foreign apps without the need to reverse engineer and reimplement the opaque foreign kernel interfaces used by proprietary foreign libraries.

Using these OS compatibility mechanisms, we built a Cider prototype that can run unmodified iOS and Android apps on Android devices. We leverage existing software infrastructure as much as possible, including unmodified frameworks across both iOS and Android ecosystems. We demonstrate the effectiveness of our prototype by running various iOS apps from the Apple App Store together with Android apps from Google Play on a Nexus 7 tablet running the latest version of Android. Users can interact with iOS apps using multi-touch input, and iOS apps can leverage GPU hardware to display smooth, accelerated graphics. Our microbenchmark and app measurements show that Cider imposes modest performance overhead, and can deliver faster performance for iOS apps than corresponding Android counterparts on Android hardware. The faster performance is due to the greater efficiencies of running native iOS code instead of interpreted bytecode as used by Android.

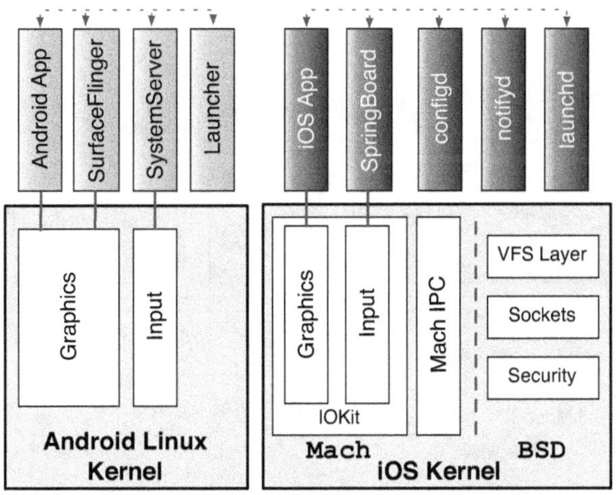


**Figure 1: Android and iOS architectures**

## 2. Overview of Android and iOS

To understand how Cider runs iOS apps on Android, we first provide a brief overview of the operation of Android and iOS. We limit our discussion to central components providing app startup, graphics, and input on both systems.

Figure 1 shows an overview of these two systems. Android is built on the Linux kernel and runs on ARM CPUs. The Android framework consists of a number of system services and libraries used to provide app services, graphics, input, and more. For example, SystemServer starts Launcher, the home screen app on Android, and SurfaceFlinger, the rendering engine which uses the GPU to compose all the graphics surfaces for different apps and display the final composed surface to the screen.

Each Android app is compiled into Dalvik bytecode (dex) format, and runs in a separate Dalvik VM instance. When a user interacts with an Android app, input events are delivered from the Linux kernel device driver through the Android framework to the app. The app displays content by obtaining window memory (a graphics surface) from SurfaceFlinger and draws directly into the window memory. An app can attach an OpenGL context to the window memory and use the OpenGL ES framework to render hardware-accelerated graphics into the window memory using the GPU.

iOS runs on ARM CPUs like Android, but has a very different software ecosystem. iOS is built on the XNU kernel [6], a hybrid combination of a monolithic BSD kernel and a Mach microkernel running in a single kernel address space. XNU leverages the BSD socket and VFS subsystems, but also benefits from the virtual memory management [42] and IPC mechanisms [47] provided by Mach. iOS makes extensive use of both BSD and Mach XNU services. The iOS user space framework consists of a number of user space daemons. `launchd` is responsible for booting the system, and starting, stopping, and maintaining services and apps. `launchd` starts Mach IPC services such as `configd`, the system configuration daemon, `notifyd`, the asynchronous notification server, and `mediaserverd`, the audio/video server. `launchd` also starts the SpringBoard app, which displays the iOS home screen, handles and routes user input to apps, and uses the GPU to compose app display surfaces onto the screen. SpringBoard is analogous to an amalgamation of SurfaceFlinger, Launcher, and SystemServer in Android.[1]

iOS apps are written in Objective-C, and compiled and run as native binaries in an extended Mach-O [4] format. In contrast, the Java archives used by Android apps are interpreted by the Dalvik VM, not loaded as native binaries. On iOS, apps are loaded directly by a kernel-level Mach-O loader which interprets the binary, loads its text and data segments, and jumps to the app entry point. Dynamically linked libraries are loaded by `dyld`, a user space binary, which is invoked from the Mach-O loader. Examples of frequently used libraries in iOS apps include UIKit, the user interface framework; QuartzCore and OpenGL ES, the core graphics frameworks; and WebKit, the web browser engine.

## 3. System Integration

Cider provides a familiar user experience when running iOS apps on Android. Apps are launched from the Android home screen, just like any other Android app, and users can switch seamlessly between domestic Android apps and foreign iOS apps. Cider accomplishes this without running the iOS XNU kernel or the SpringBoard app. Cider overlays a file system (FS) hierarchy on the existing Android FS, and provides several background user-level services required by iOS apps. The overlaid FS hierarchy allows iOS apps to access familiar iOS paths, such as `/Documents`, and the background services establish key microkernel-style functionality in user space necessary to run iOS apps. Figure 2 shows an overview of the integration of iOS functionality into our Android-based Cider prototype.

iOS apps running on Cider need access to a number of framework components including iOS libraries and user-level Mach IPC services. Instead of reimplementing these components, a task which would require substantial engineering and reverse-engineering efforts, we simply copy the existing binaries from iOS and run them on the domestic system, leveraging Cider's OS compatibility architecture. Background user-level services such as `launchd`, `configd`, and `notifyd` were copied from an iOS device, and core framework libraries were copied from the Xcode SDK, Apple's development environment.

To provide seamless system integration, and minimize Android user space changes, Cider introduces a proxy service, *CiderPress*. The launch procedure and binary format of iOS and Android apps are completely different, so iOS app startup and management cannot be directly performed by the Android framework. *CiderPress* is a standard Android app that integrates launch and execution of an iOS app with Android's Launcher and system services. It is directly started by

[1] In newer versions of iOS, graphics rendering and input event pumping have been offloaded to `backboardd`.

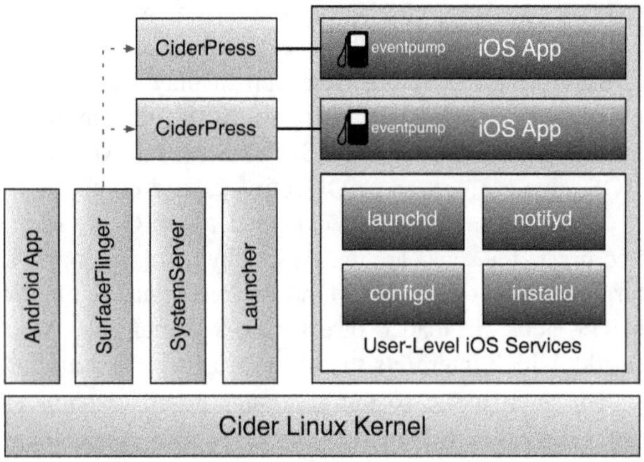


**Figure 2: System integration overview**

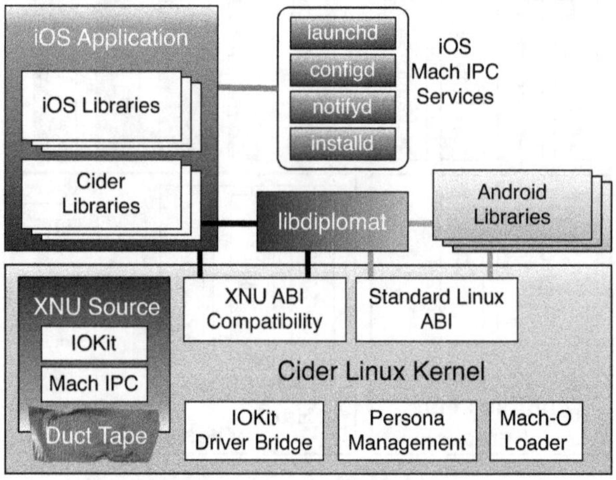


**Figure 3: Overview of Cider architecture**

Android's Launcher, receives input such as touch events and accelerometer data from the Android input subsystem, and its life cycle is managed like any other Android app. *CiderPress* launches the foreign binary, and proxies its own display memory, incoming input events, and app state changes to the iOS app. An Android Launcher short cut pointing to *CiderPress* allows a user to click an icon on the Android home screen to start an iOS app, and the proxied display surface allows screen shots of the iOS app to appear in Android's recent activity list. Proxied app state changes allow the iOS app to be started, stopped, and paused (put into the background) like a standard Android app.

## 4. Architecture

The primary goal of Cider is to run unmodified iOS binaries on Android, including iOS apps, frameworks, and services. This is challenging because iOS binaries are built to run on iOS and XNU, not Android and Linux. The XNU kernel provides a different system call (syscall) interface from Linux, and iOS apps make extensive use of OS services not available on Linux, such as Mach IPC [5]. Clearly, more than just binary compatibility is necessary: Cider must make Android compatible with iOS. Cider's multi-persona OS compatibility architecture solves this problem.

Figure 3 provides an overview of the Cider OS compatibility architecture which can be divided into three key components. First, Cider provides XNU kernel compatibility by implementing a Mach-O loader for the Linux kernel, supporting the XNU syscall interface, and facilitating proper signal delivery – together referred to as the kernel application binary interface (ABI). Second, Cider provides a *duct tape* layer to import foreign kernel code that supports syscalls and subsystems not available in Linux. Third, Cider introduces diplomatic functions, implemented in the `libdiplomat` iOS library, to support apps that use closed iOS libraries which issue device-specific calls such as opaque Mach IPC messages or `ioctl`s. We describe these components in further detail in the following sections.

### 4.1 Kernel ABI

At a high-level, providing an OS compatibility solution is straightforward. The interaction between apps and an OS is defined by the kernel application binary interface (ABI). The ABI defines all possible interactions between apps and the kernel. The ABI consists of a binary loader which interprets the physical contents of the application binary and associated libraries, asynchronous signal delivery, and the syscall interface. To run iOS apps in Android, we need to implement these three components of the XNU ABI in the Linux kernel.

Cider provides a Mach-O binary loader built into the Linux kernel to handle the binary format used by iOS apps. When a Mach-O binary is loaded, the kernel tags the current thread with an iOS *persona*, used in all interactions with user space. Personas are tracked on a per-thread basis, inherited on `fork` or `clone`, and enable processes with multiple threads to simultaneously support multiple personas. Multi-persona processes play a key role in supporting hardware-accelerated graphics as discussed in Section 5.3.

Cider provides a translation layer for asynchronous signal delivery that converts signals from the Linux kernel (generated from events such as an illegal instruction, or a segmentation fault) into signals which would have been generated by the XNU kernel. The XNU signals are then delivered to iOS applications, as appropriate, where they can be properly handled. Cider also converts XNU signals generated programmatically from iOS applications into corresponding Linux signals, so they can be delivered to non-iOS applications or threads. Cider uses the persona of a given thread to deliver the correct signal. Android apps (or threads) can deliver signals to iOS apps (or threads) and vice-versa.

Since an app's primary interface to the kernel is through syscalls, Cider provides multiple syscall interfaces to support different kernel ABIs. Cider maintains one or more syscall dispatch tables for each persona, and switches among them based on the persona of the calling thread and the syscall number. Cider is aware of XNU's low-level syscall interface, and translates things such as function parameters and CPU flags into the Linux calling convention, making it possible to directly invoke existing Linux syscall implementations. Different kernels have different syscall entry and exit code paths. For example, iOS apps can trap into the kernel in four different ways depending on the system call being executed, and many XNU syscalls return an error indication through CPU flags where Linux would return a negative integer. Cider manages these syscall entry and exit path differences through persona-tagged support functions.

Because the iOS kernel, XNU, is based on POSIX-compliant BSD, most syscalls overlap with functionality already provided by the Linux kernel. For these syscalls, Cider provides a simple wrapper that maps arguments from XNU structures to Linux structures and then calls the Linux implementation. To implement XNU syscalls that have no corresponding Linux syscall, but for which similar Linux functionality exists, the wrapper reuses one or more existing Linux functions. For example, Cider implements the `posix_spawn` syscall, which is a flexible method of starting a thread or new application, by leveraging the Linux `clone` and `exec` syscall implementations.

### 4.2 Duct Tape

Simple wrappers and combinations of existing syscall implementations are not enough to implement the entire XNU ABI. Many XNU syscalls require a core subsystem that does not exist in the Linux kernel. Reimplementing these mechanisms would be a difficult and error-prone process. Mach IPC is a prime example of a subsystem missing from the Linux kernel, but used extensively by iOS apps. It is a rich and complicated API providing inter-process communication and memory sharing. Implementing such a subsystem from scratch in the Linux kernel would be a daunting task. Given the availability of XNU source code, one approach would be to try to port such code to the Linux kernel. This approach is common among driver developers, but is time consuming and error-prone given that different kernels have completely different APIs and data structures. For example, the Linux kernel offers a completely different set of synchronization primitives from the XNU kernel.

To address this problem, Cider introduces *duct tape*, a novel compile-time code adaptation layer that supports *cross-kernel compilation*: direct compilation of unmodified foreign kernel source code into a domestic kernel. Duct tape translates foreign kernel APIs such as synchronization, memory allocation, process control, and list management, into domestic kernel APIs. The resulting module or subsystem is a first-class member of the domestic kernel and can be accessed by both foreign and domestic apps.

To duct tape foreign code into a domestic kernel, there are three steps. First, three distinct coding *zones* are created within the domestic kernel: the domestic, foreign, and duct tape zones. Code in the domestic zone cannot access symbols in foreign zone, and code in the foreign zone cannot access symbols in the domestic zone. Both foreign and domestic zones can access symbols in the duct tape zone, and the duct tape zone can access symbols in both the foreign and domestic zones. Second, all external symbols and symbol conflicts with domestic code are automatically identified in the foreign code. Third, conflicts are remapped to unique symbols, and all external foreign symbols are mapped to appropriate domestic kernel symbols. Simple symbol mapping occurs through preprocessor tokens or small static inline functions in the duct tape zone. More complicated external foreign dependencies require some implementation effort within the duct tape or domestic zone.

Duct tape provides two important advantages. First, foreign code is easier to maintain and upgrade. Because the original foreign code is not modified, bug fixes, security patches, and feature upgrades can be applied directly from the original maintainer's source repository. Second, the code adaptation layer created for one subsystem is directly reusable for other subsystems. For example, most kernel code will use locking and synchronization primitives, and an adaptation layer translating these APIs and structures for one foreign subsystem into the domestic kernel will work for all subsystems from the same foreign kernel. As more foreign code is added, the duct tape process becomes simpler.

Cider successfully uses duct tape to add three different subsystems from the XNU kernel into Android's Linux kernel: pthread support, Mach IPC, and Apple's I/O Kit device driver framework, the latter is discussed in Section 5.1. iOS pthread support differs substantially from Android in functional separation between the pthread library and the kernel. The iOS user space pthread library makes extensive use of kernel-level support for mutexes, semaphores, and condition variables, none of which are present in the Linux kernel. This support is found in the `bsd/kern/pthread_support.c` file in the XNU source provided by Apple. Cider uses duct tape to directly compile this file without modification.

The Mach IPC subsystem is significantly more complicated than pthread support. Cider uses duct tape to directly compile the majority of Mach IPC into the Linux kernel. However, code relying on the assumption of a deeper stack depth in XNU required reimplementation. In particular, XNU's Mach IPC code uses recursive queuing structures, something disallowed in the Linux kernel. This queuing was rewritten to better fit within Linux.

Note that the BSD kqueue and kevent notification mechanisms were easier to support in Cider as user space libraries because of the availability of existing open source user-level implementations [25]. Because they did not need to be incorporated into the kernel, they did not need to be incorporated using duct tape, but simply via API interposition [27].

### 4.3 Diplomatic Functions

XNU kernel ABI support coupled with duct tape allows Cider to successfully handle most kernel interactions from iOS apps, however, the behavior of several key syscalls is not well-defined. For example, the `ioctl` syscall passes a driver-specific request code and a pointer to memory, and its behavior is driver-specific. Without any understanding of how `ioctls` are used, simply implementing the syscall itself is of little benefit to apps.

Additionally, Mobile apps often make use of closed and proprietary hardware and software stacks. Compressed consumer production time lines and tight vertical integration of hardware and software lead developers to discard cumbersome abstractions present on Desktop PCs in favor of custom, direct hardware communication. For example, the OpenGL ES libraries on both Android and iOS directly communicate with graphics hardware (GPU) through proprietary software and hardware interfaces using device-specific ioctls (Android), or opaque IPC messages (iOS).

Cider cannot simply implement kernel-level support for foreign, closed libraries which directly manipulate hardware through proprietary interfaces. Not only are the semantics of the closed library unknown, but they are likely closely tied to foreign hardware not present on the domestic device.

Cider solves the problem of direct access to proprietary hardware through the novel concept of *diplomatic functions*. A diplomatic function temporarily switches the persona of a calling thread to execute domestic functions from within a foreign app. A thread's persona, or execution mode, selects the kernel ABI personality and thread local storage (TLS) information used during execution. The TLS area contains per-thread state such as `errno` and a thread's ID.

Cider's diplomatic function support comprises three key components: **(1)** The ability to load and interpret domestic binaries and libraries within a foreign app. This involves the use of a domestic loader compiled as a foreign library. For example, Cider incorporates an Android ELF loader cross-compiled as an iOS library. **(2)** Kernel-level persona management at a thread level including both kernel ABI and TLS data management. The Cider kernel maintains kernel ABI and TLS area pointers for every persona in which a given thread executes. A new syscall (available from all personas) named `set_persona`, switches a thread's persona. Different personas use different TLS organizations, e.g., the `errno` pointer is at a different location in the iOS TLS than in the Android TLS. After a persona switch, any kernel traps or accesses to the TLS area will use the new persona's pointers. This allows the thread to invoke functions from libraries compiled for a different persona. For example, in Section 5.3 we describe how, using diplomatic functions, an iOS app can load and execute code in the Android OpenGL ES library and thereby directly interact with the underlying GPU hardware **(3)** The ability to mediate foreign function calls into domestic libraries, appropriately loading, switching, and managing the domestic persona; this is done through *diplomats*. A diplomat is a function stub that uses an arbitration process to switch the current thread's persona, invoke a function in the new persona, switch back to the calling function's persona, and return any results.

The Cider arbitration process for calling a domestic function from foreign code through a diplomat is as follows: **(1)** Upon first invocation, a diplomat loads the appropriate domestic library and locates the required entry point, storing a pointer to the function in a locally-scoped static variable for efficient reuse. **(2)** The arguments to the domestic function call are stored on the stack. **(3)** The `set_persona` syscall is invoked from the foreign persona to switch the calling thread's kernel ABI, and TLS area pointer to their domestic values. **(4)** The arguments to the domestic function call are restored from the stack. **(5)** The domestic function call is directly invoked through the symbol stored in step 1. **(6)** Upon return from the domestic function, the return value is saved on the stack. **(7)** The `set_persona` syscall is invoked from the domestic persona to switch the kernel ABI and TLS area pointer back to the foreign code's values. **(8)** Any domestic TLS values, such as `errno`, are appropriately converted and updated in the foreign TLS area. **(9)** The domestic function's return value is restored from the stack, and control is returned to the calling foreign function.

Because Cider maintains kernel ABI and TLS information on a per-thread basis, a single app can simultaneously execute both foreign and domestic code in multiple threads. For example, while one thread executes complicated OpenGL ES rendering algorithms using the domestic persona, another thread in the same app can simultaneously process input data using the foreign persona. Unlike previous binary compatibility work [13, 19, 20, 23], which only allowed an app to use a single persona, Cider allows an app to switch among personas and use multiple personas simultaneously. Cider can replace an entire foreign library with diplomats, or it can define a single diplomat to use targeted functionality in a domestic library such as popping up a system notification. Section 5.3 describes how Cider replaces the iOS OpenGL ES library with diplomats that use Android's OpenGL ES libraries.

## 5. iOS Subsystems on Android

We highlight three examples of key iOS subsystems to show how Cider's OS compatibility architecture supports each subsystem on an Android device. Due to space constraints, we only provide an overview of the XNU I/O Kit subsystem, multi-touch input, and graphics support. A full discussion of all supported subsystems is beyond the scope of this paper.

### 5.1 Devices

Cider uses duct tape to make Android hardware devices available to iOS apps via Apple's I/O Kit. I/O Kit is Apple's open source driver framework based on NeXTSTEP's DriverKit. It is written primarily in a restricted subset of C++, and is accessed via Mach IPC. iOS Apps and libraries access Android devices via I/O Kit drivers in Cider exactly as they would access Apple devices on iOS.

To directly compile the I/O Kit framework, Cider added a basic C++ runtime to the Linux kernel based on Android's Bionic. Linux kernel Makefile support was added such that compilation of C++ files from within the kernel required nothing more than assigning an object name to the `obj-y` Makefile variable. Cider uses duct tape and its Linux kernel C++ runtime to directly compile the majority of the I/O Kit code, found in the XNU `iokit` source directory, without modification.[2] In fact, we initially compiled Cider with the I/O Kit framework found in XNU v1699.24.8, but later directly applied source code patches upgrading to the I/O Kit framework found in XNU v2050.18.24.

Cider makes devices available via both the Linux device driver framework and I/O Kit. Using a small hook in the Linux `device_add` function, Cider creates a Linux device node I/O Kit registry entry (a device class instance) for every registered Linux device. Cider also provides an I/O Kit driver class for each device that interfaces with the corresponding Linux device driver. This allows iOS apps to access devices as well as query the I/O Kit registry to locate devices or properties.

For example, iOS apps expect to interact with the device framebuffer through a C++ class named `AppleM2CLCD` which derives from the `IOMobileFramebuffer` C++ class interface. Using the C++ runtime support added to the Linux kernel, the Cider prototype added a single C++ file in the Nexus 7 display driver's source tree that defines a class named `AppleM2CLCD`. This C++ class acts as a thin wrapper around the Linux device driver's functionality. The class is instantiated and registered as a driver class instance with I/O Kit through a small interface function called on Linux kernel boot. The duct taped I/O Kit code matches the C++ driver class instance with the Linux device node (previously added from the Linux `device_add` function). After the driver class instance is matched to the device class instance, iOS user space can query and use the device as a standard iOS device. We believe that a similar process can be done for most devices found on a tablet or smartphone.

### 5.2 Input

No user-facing app would be complete without input from both the user and devices such as the accelerometer. In iOS, every app monitors a Mach IPC port for incoming low-level event notifications and passes these events up the user space stack through gesture recognizers and event handlers. The events sent to this port include mouse, button, accelerometer, proximity and touch screen events. A system service, SpringBoard, is responsible for communicating with the lower-level iOS input system, determining which app should receive the input, and then sending corresponding input events to the app via its respective Mach IPC port.

[2] Portions of the I/O Kit codebase such as `IODMAController.cpp` and `IOInterruptController.cpp` were not necessary as they are primarily used by I/O Kit drivers communicating directly with hardware.

Replicating the interactions between SpringBoard and the lower-level input system on Android would potentially involve reverse engineering complex device driver interactions with input hardware that is not present in Android devices.

Cider takes a simpler approach to provide complete, interactive, multi-touch input support for iOS. Cider does not attempt to replicate the lower-level iOS input system. Instead, it simply reads events from the Android input system, translates them as necessary into a format understood by iOS apps, and sends them to the Mach IPC port used by apps to receive events. In particular, Cider creates a new thread in each iOS app to act as a bridge between the Android input system and the Mach IPC port expecting input events. This thread, the *eventpump* seen in Figure 2, listens for events from the Android *CiderPress* app on a BSD socket. It then pumps those events into the iOS app via Mach IPC. In the future, this intermediary thread could be avoided with a minimal Linux Mach IPC wrapper ABI. Using this approach, Cider is able to provide complete, interactive, multi-touch input support in a straightforward manner. Panning, pinch-to-zoom, iOS on-screen keyboards and keypads, and other input gestures are also all completely supported.

### 5.3 Graphics

Cider leverages kernel-level personas through diplomatic functions to provide 2D and 3D graphics support in iOS apps. User space libraries such as WebKit, UIKit, and Core-Animation render content, such as buttons, text, web pages, and images, using the OpenGL ES and IOSurface iOS libraries. These libraries communicate directly to the iOS kernel via Mach IPC. They use I/O Kit drivers to allocate and share graphics memory, control hardware facilities such as frame rates and subsystem power, and perform more complex rendering tasks such as those required for 3D graphics.

Supporting the iOS graphics subsystem is a huge OS compatibility challenge; highly optimized user space libraries are tightly integrated with mobile hardware. Libraries such as OpenGL ES, call into a set of proprietary, closed source, helper libraries which, in turn, use opaque Mach IPC messages to closed source kernel drivers that control black-box pieces of hardware. Opaque Mach IPC calls to kernel drivers are essentially used as device-specific syscalls. Unlike the modern desktop OS, there are no well-defined mobile interfaces to graphics acceleration hardware, such as the Direct Rendering Infrastructure used by the X Window system. Neither implementing kernel-level emulation code nor duct taping a piece GPU driver code, if it were even available, will solve this problem.

Cider enables 2D and 3D graphics in iOS apps through a novel combination of I/O Kit Linux driver wrappers, and diplomatic IOSurface and OpenGL ES libraries. The IOSurface iOS library provides a zero-copy abstraction for all graphics memory in iOS. An IOSurface object can be used to render 2D graphics via CPU-bound drawing routines, efficiently passed to other processes or apps via Mach IPC, and even used as the backing memory for OpenGL ES textures in 3D rendering. Cider interposes diplomatic functions on key IOSurface API entry points such as `IOSurfaceCreate`. These diplomats call into Android-specific graphics memory allocation libraries such as `libgralloc`. Well-known API interposition techniques are used to force iOS apps to link against the Cider version of a particular entry point.

To support more complicated 2D and 3D graphics, Cider replaces the entire iOS OpenGL ES library with diplomats. We leverage the fact that while the implementation of proprietary libraries, such as OpenGL ES, and their interface to kernel drivers is closed, the app-facing API is well-known, and is typically similar across platforms such as iOS and Android.[3] The iOS OpenGL ES library consists of two parts: the standardized OpenGL ES API [29, 31] and the Apple-specific *EAGL* [7] extensions. Cider provides a replacement iOS OpenGL ES library with a diplomat for every exported symbol in both of these categories.

For standard OpenGL ES API entry points, Cider provides a set of diplomats that use the arbitration process, described in Section 4.3, to load, initialize, and call into the Android OpenGL ES libraries. Because each of these entry points has a well-defined, standardized function prototype, the process of creating diplomats was automated by a script. This script analyzed exported symbols in the iOS OpenGL ES Mach-O library, searched through a directory of Android ELF shared objects for a matching export, and automatically generated diplomats for each matching function.

Cider provides diplomats for Apple's EAGL extensions that call into a custom Android library to implement the required functionality. Apple-specific EAGL extensions, used to control window memory and graphics contexts, do not exist on Android. Fortunately, the EAGL extensions are Apple's replacement for the Native Platform Graphics Interface Layer (EGL) standard [30], and this is implemented in an Android EGL library. To support Apple's EAGL extensions, Cider uses a custom domestic Android library, called `libEGLbridge`, that utilizes Android's `libEGL` library and SurfaceFlinger service to provide functionality corresponding to the missing EAGL functions. Diplomatic EAGL functions in the Cider OpenGL ES library call into the custom Android `libEGLbridge` library to fully support Apple's EAGL APIs in iOS apps. Allocating window memory via the standard Android SurfaceFlinger service also allows Cider to manage the iOS display in the same manner that all Android app windows are managed.

## 6. Experimental Results

We have implemented a Cider prototype for running both iOS and Android apps on an Android device, and present some experimental results to measure its performance. We compared three different Android system configurations to measure the performance of Cider: (1) Linux binaries and Android apps running on unmodified (vanilla) Android, (2) Linux binaries and Android apps running on Cider, and (3) iOS binaries and apps running on Cider. For our experiments, we used a Nexus 7 tablet with a 1.3 GHz quad-core NVIDIA Tegra 3 CPU, 1 GB RAM, 16 GB of flash storage, and a 7" 1280x800 display running Android 4.2 (Jelly Bean). We also ran iOS binaries and apps on a jailbroken iPad mini with a 1 GHz dual-core A5 CPU, 512 MB RAM, 16 GB of flash storage, and a 7.9" 1024x768 display running iOS 6.1.2. Since the iPad mini was released around the same time as the Nexus 7 and has a similar form factor, it provides a useful point of comparison even though it costs 50% more.

We used both microbenchmarks and real apps to evaluate the performance of Cider. To measure the latency of common low-level OS operations, we used microbenchmarks from `lmbench` 3.0 and compiled two versions: an ELF Linux binary version, and a Mach-O iOS binary version, using the standard Linux GCC 4.4.1 and Xcode 4.2.1 compilers, respectively. We used four categories of `lmbench` tests: basic operations, syscalls and signals, process creation, and local communication and file operations. To measure real app performance, we used comparable iOS and Android PassMark apps available from the Apple App Store [37] and Google Play [38], respectively. PassMark conducts a wide range of resource intensive tests to evaluate CPU, memory, I/O, and graphics performance. We used PassMark because it is a widely used, commercially-supported app available on both iOS and Android, and provides a conservative measure of various aspects of app performance. We normalize all results using vanilla Android performance as the baseline to compare across systems. This is useful to measure Cider performance overhead, and also provides some key observations regarding the characteristics of Android and iOS apps.

### 6.1 Obtaining iOS Apps

The iOS apps used in our evaluation were downloaded from the Apple App Store. In the future, we envision that developers and app distributors would be incentivized to provide alternative distribution methods. For example, Google Play might be incentivized to take advantage of Cider to make a greater number and higher quality of apps available for Android devices. However, using the App Store required a few more steps to install the applications on an Android device because of various security measures used by Apple.

App Store apps, unlike iOS system apps such as Stocks, are encrypted and must be decrypted using keys stored in encrypted, non-volatile memory found in an Apple device. We modified a widely used script [43] to decrypt apps on any jailbroken iOS device using gdb [22]. To illustrate this point, we used an old iPhone 3GS with iOS 5.0.1 for this purpose. The script decrypts the app, and then re-packages the decrypted binary, along with any associated data files, into a single `.ipa` file (iOS App Store Package). Each `.ipa` file

[3] Cider could also leverage a Direct3D to OpenGL translation layer from the Wine project to support Windows Mobile devices.

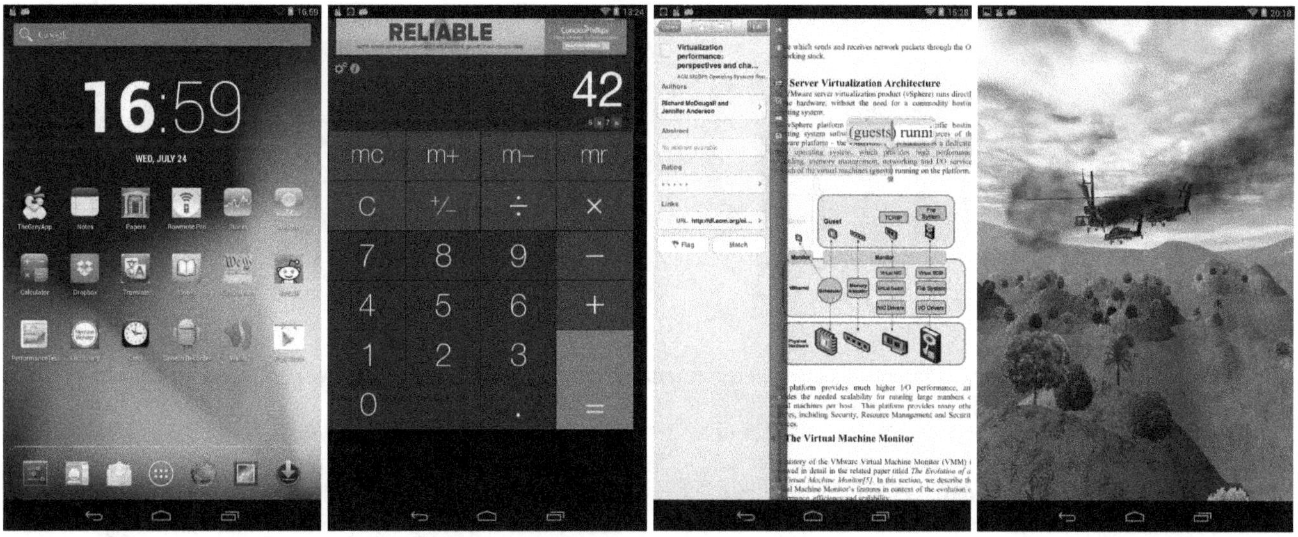


(a) Cider home screen (b) Calculator Pro for iPad Free (c) Papers for iOS by Mekentosj B.V. (d) PassMark 3D Benchmark

**Figure 4: Cider displaying and running iOS apps**

was copied to the Cider prototype, and a small background process automatically unpacked each `.ipa` and created Android shortcuts on the Launcher home screen, pointing each one to the *CiderPress* Android app. The iOS app icon was used for the Android shortcut. Decrypted iOS apps work on Cider exactly as they would on an iPhone or iPad, including displaying ads using Apple's iAd framework.

Figure 4 shows screenshots of the Nexus 7 tablet with various iOS apps that we installed and ran on the device (from left to right): the Nexus 7 home screen with iOS and Android apps, the *Calculator Pro for iPad Free* [3], one of the top three free utilities for iPad, displaying a banner ad via the iAd framework, the highly-rated *Papers* [11] app highlighting text in a PDF, and the *PassMark* [37] app running the 3D performance test.

## 6.2 Microbenchmark Measurements

Figure 5 shows the results of running `lmbench` microbenchmarks on the four system configurations. Vanilla Android performance is normalized to one in all cases, and the results are not explicitly shown. Measurements are latencies, so smaller numbers are better. Measurements are shown at two scales to provide a clear comparison despite the wide range of results. Results are analyzed in four groups.

First, Figure 5 shows basic CPU operation measurements for integer multiply, integer divide, double precision floating point add, double precision floating point multiply, and double precision bogomflop tests. They provide a comparison that reflects differences in the Android and iOS hardware and compilers used. The basic CPU operation measurements were essentially the same for all three system configurations using the Android device, except for the integer divide test, which showed that the Linux compiler generated more optimized code than the iOS compiler. In all cases, the measurements for the iOS device were worse than the Android device, confirming that the iPad mini's CPU is not as fast as the Nexus 7's CPU for basic math operations.

Second, Figure 5 shows syscall and signal handler measurements including null syscall, `read`, `write`, `open/close`, and signal handler tests. The null syscall measurement shows the overhead incurred by Cider on a syscall that does no work, providing a conservative measure of the cost of Cider. The overhead is 8.5% over vanilla Android running the same Linux binary. This is due to extra persona checking and handling code run on every syscall entry. The overhead is 40% when running the iOS binary over vanilla Android running the Linux binary. This demonstrates the additional cost of using the iOS persona, and translating the syscall into the corresponding Linux syscall. These overheads fall into the noise for syscalls that perform some useful function, as shown by the other syscall measurements. Running the iOS binary on the Nexus 7 using Cider is much faster in these syscall measurements than running the same binary on the iPad mini, illustrating a benefit of using Cider to leverage the faster performance characteristics of Android hardware.

The signal handler measurement shows Cider's signal delivery overhead when the signal is generated and delivered within the same process. This is a conservative measurement because no work is done by the process as a result of signal delivery. The overhead is small: 3% over vanilla Android running the same Linux binary. This is due to the added cost of determining the persona of the target thread. The overhead is 25% when running the iOS binary over vanilla Android running the Linux binary. This shows the overhead of the iOS persona which includes translation of the signal information and delivery of a larger signal delivery structure expected by iOS binaries. Running the iOS binary on the iPad mini takes 175% longer than running the same binary on the Nexus 7 using Cider for the signal handler test.

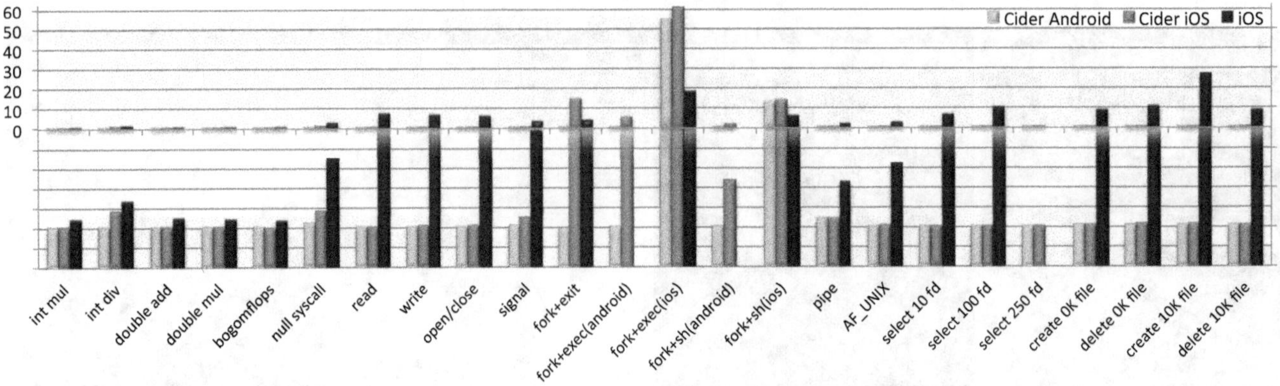


**Figure 5: Microbenchmark latency measurements normalized to vanilla Android; lower is better performance.**

Third, Figure 5 shows five sets of process creation measurements, `fork+exit`, `fork+exec`, and `fork+sh` tests. The `fork+exit` measurement shows that Cider incurs negligible overhead versus vanilla Android running a Linux binary despite the fact that it must do some extra work in Mach IPC initialization. However, Cider takes almost 14 times longer to run the iOS binary version of the test compared to the Linux binary. The absolute difference in time is roughly 3.5 ms, the Linux binary takes 245 $\mu$s while the iOS binary takes 3.75 ms. There are two reasons for this difference. First, the process running the iOS binary consumes significantly more memory than the Linux binary because the iOS dynamic linker, `dyld`, maps 90 MB of extra memory from 115 different libraries, irrespective of whether or not those libraries are used by the binary. The `fork` syscall must then duplicate the page table entries corresponding to all the extra memory, incurring almost 1 ms of extra overhead. Second, an iOS process does a lot more work in user space when it forks because iOS libraries use a large number of `pthread_atfork` callbacks that are called before and after `fork`. Similarly, for each library, `dyld` registers a callback that is called on `exit`, resulting in the execution of 115 handlers on exit. These user space callbacks account for 2.5 ms of extra overhead. Note that the `fork+exit` measurement on the iPad mini is significantly faster than using Cider on the Android device due to a shared library cache optimization that is not yet supported in the Cider prototype. To save time on library loading, iOS's `dyld` stores common libraries prelinked on disk in a shared cache in lieu of storing the libraries separately. iOS treats the shared cache in a special way and optimizes how it is handled.

The `fork+exec` measurement is done in several unique variations on Cider. This test spawns a child process which executes a simple hello world program. We compile two versions of the program: a Linux binary and an iOS binary. The test itself is also compiled as both a Linux binary and an iOS binary. A vanilla Android system can only run a Linux binary that spawns a child to run a Linux binary. Similarly, the iPad mini can only run an iOS binary that spawns a child to run an iOS binary. Using Cider, the test can be run four different ways: a Linux binary can spawn a child to run either a Linux or an iOS binary, and an iOS binary can spawn a child to run either a Linux or an iOS binary. To compare the different `fork+exec` measurements, we normalize performance against the vanilla Android system running a Linux binary that spawns a child running a Linux binary. Figure 5 shows all four `fork+exec` measurements using Cider.

The `fork+exec(android)` test forks a child that execs a Linux binary. The Cider Android bar shows results of a Linux test program while the Cider iOS bar shows results of an iOS test program. Cider incurs negligible overhead in the Cider Android case. The actual test run time is roughly 590 $\mu$s, a little more than twice the time it takes to run the `fork+exit` measurement, reflecting the fact that executing the hello world program is more expensive than simply exiting. Cider takes 4.8 times longer to run the test in the Cider iOS case. The extra overhead is due to the cost of an iOS binary calling `fork`, as discussed previously in the `fork+exit` measurement. Interestingly, the `fork+exec(android)` Cider iOS measurement is 3.42 ms, less than the `fork+exit` measurement because the child process replaces its iOS binary with the hello world Linux binary. This is less expensive than having the original iOS binary exit because of all the exit handlers that must execute.

The `fork+exec(ios)` test forks a child that execs an iOS binary. The Cider Android bar shows results of a Linux test program. The Cider iOS and iOS bars show results of an iOS test program. This test is not possible on vanilla Android, thus the comparison is intentionally unfair and skews the results against this test. Nevertheless, using this comparison, Figure 5 shows that spawning a child to run an iOS binary is much more expensive. This is because the Cider prototype uses non-prelinked libraries, and `dyld` must walk the filesystem to load each library on every `exec`. The extra overhead of starting with an iOS binary versus a Linux binary is due to the cost of the iOS binary calling `fork`, as discussed previously in the `fork+exit` measurement. Running the `fork+exec` test on the iPad mini is faster than using Cider on the Android device because of its shared cache optimization which avoids the need to walk the filesystem to load each library.

Similar to the `fork+exec` measurement, the `fork+sh` measurement is done in four variations on Cider. The `fork+sh(android)` test launches a shell that runs a Linux binary. Cider incurs negligible overhead versus vanilla Android when the test program is a Linux binary, but takes 110% longer when the test program is an iOS binary. The extra overhead is due to the cost of an iOS binary calling `fork`, as discussed previously in the `fork+exec` measurement. Because the `fork+sh(android)` measurement takes longer, 6.8 ms using the iOS binary, the relative overhead is less than the `fork+exec(android)` measurement.

The `fork+sh(ios)` test launches a shell that runs an iOS binary. This is not possible on vanilla Android, so we normalize to the `fork+sh(android)` test, skewing the results against this test. Using this comparison, Figure 5 shows that spawning a child to run an iOS binary is much more expensive for the same reasons as the `fork+exec` measurements. Because the `fork+sh(ios)` test takes longer, the relative overhead is less than the `fork+exec(ios)` measurement.

Finally, Figure 5 shows local communication and filesystem measurements including `pipe`, `AF_UNIX`, `select` on 10 to 250 file descriptors, and creating and deleting 0 KB and 10 KB files. Measurements were quite similar for all three system configurations using the Android device. However, measurements on the iPad mini were significantly worse than the Android device in a number of cases. Perhaps the worst offender was the `select` test whose overhead increased linearly with the number of file descriptors to more than 10 times the cost of running the test on vanilla Android. The test simply failed to complete for 250 file descriptors. In contrast, the same iOS binary runs using Cider on Android with performance comparable to running a Linux binary on vanilla Android across all measurement variations.

### 6.3 Application Measurements

Figure 6 shows the results of the iOS and Android PassMark benchmark apps [37, 38] on the four different system configurations. Vanilla Android performance is normalized to one in all cases, and not explicitly shown. Measurements are in operations per second, so larger numbers are better. In all tests, Cider adds negligible overhead to the Android PassMark app. Test results are analyzed in five groups.

First, Figure 6 shows CPU operation measurements for integer, floating point, find primes, random string sort, data encryption, and data compression tests. Unlike the basic `lmbench` CPU measurements, the PassMark measurements show that Cider delivers significantly faster performance when running the iOS PassMark app on Android. This is because the Android version is written in Java and interpreted through the Dalvik VM while the iOS version is written in Objective-C and compiled and run as a native binary. Because the Android device contains a faster CPU than the iPad mini, Cider outperforms iOS when running the CPU tests from the same iOS PassMark application binary.

Second, Figure 6 shows storage operation measurements for write and read tests. Cider has similar storage read performance to the iPad mini when running the iOS app. However, the iPad mini has much better storage write performance than either the iOS or Android app running on Cider. Because storage performance can depend heavily on the OS, these results may reflect differences in both the underlying hardware and the OS.

Third, Figure 6 shows memory operation measurements for write and read tests. Cider delivers significantly faster performance when running the iOS PassMark app on Android. This is, again, because Cider runs the iOS app natively while Android interprets the app through the Dalvik VM. Cider outperforms the iPad mini running the memory tests from the same iOS PassMark app binary, again reflecting the benefit of using faster Android hardware.

Fourth, Figure 6 shows graphics measurements for a variety of 2D graphics operations including solid vectors, transparent vectors, complex vectors, image rendering, and image filters. With the exception of complex vectors, the Android app performs much better than the iOS binary on both Cider and the iPad mini. This is most likely due to more efficient/optimized 2D drawing libraries in Android. Additionally, since these tests are CPU bound, Cider generally outperforms iOS due to the Nexus 7's faster CPU. However, bugs in the Cider OpenGL ES library related to "fence" synchronization primitives caused under-performance in the image rendering tests.

Finally, Figure 6 shows graphics measurements for simple and complex 3D tests, the latter shown in Figure 4d. Because the iPad mini has a faster GPU than the Nexus 7, it has better 3D graphics performance. The iOS binary running on Cider performs 20-37% worse than the Android PassMark app due to the extra cost of diplomatic function calls. Each function call into the OpenGL ES library is mediated into the Android OpenGL ES library through diplomats. As the complexity of a given frame increases, the number of OpenGL ES calls increases, which correspondingly increases the overhead. This can potentially be optimized by aggregating OpenGL ES calls into a single diplomat, or by reducing the overhead of a diplomatic function call. Both optimizations are left to future work.

### 6.4 Limitations

We have not encountered any fundamental limitations regarding the feasibility of the Cider approach, such as any unbridgeable compatibility issues between iOS and Android. However, while we have implemented an initial Cider prototype that successfully runs many iOS apps on Android devices, the implementation is incomplete. In particular, smartphones and tablets incorporate a plethora of devices that apps expect to be able to use, such as GPS, cameras, cell phone radio, Bluetooth, and others. Support for the full range of devices available on smartphones and tablets is beyond the scope of this paper. Cider will not currently run iOS apps that depend on such devices. For example, an app such as Facetime that requires use of the camera does not currently work with Cider. If the iOS app has a fall-back code path, it can still partially function. For example, the iOS Yelp [46]

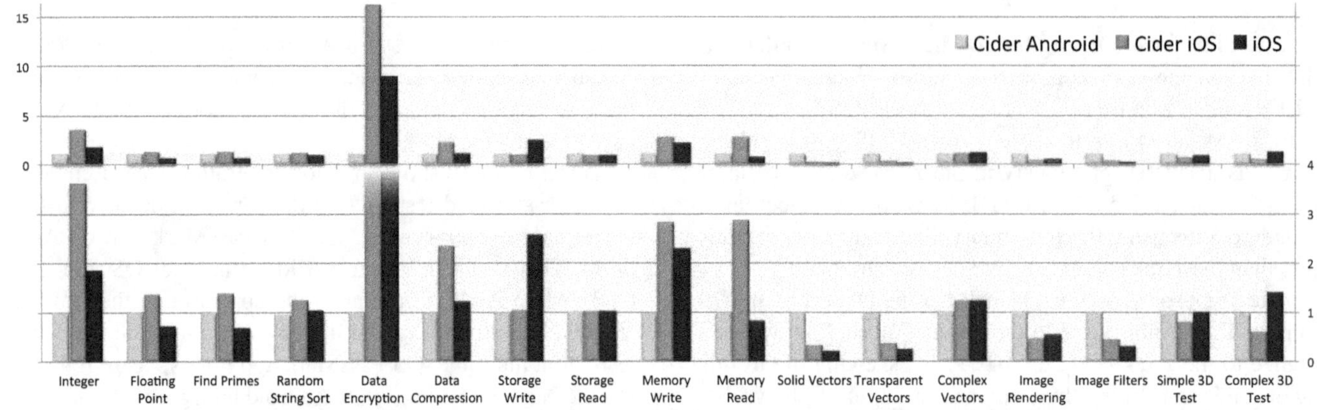


**Figure 6: App throughput measurements normalized to vanilla Android; higher is better performance.**

app runs on Cider even though GPS and location services are currently unsupported. Yelp simply assumes the user's current location is unavailable, and continues to function as it would on an Apple device with location services disabled.

Implementation of Cider device support varies with device and interface complexity. Devices with a simple interface, such as GPS, can be supported with I/O Kit drivers, discussed in Section 5.1, and diplomatic functions. Devices that use more standardized interfaces can be supported either through duct tape given an open source implementation, or diplomatic functions given a well-defined API. More complicated devices such as the camera and cell radio were not investigated as part of this research, but we believe that techniques similar to those used in Section 5.3 could be used to support these devices. For example, iOS exposes a camera API to apps. By replacing these API entry points with diplomatic functions that interact with native Android hardware, it may be possible to provide camera support for iOS apps.

The current prototype also has some other implementation limitations. Incorrect "fence" synchronization primitive support in the Cider OpenGL ES library, discussed in Section 6.3, degraded our graphics performance, and the iOS WebKit framework is only partially supported due to its multi-threaded use of the OpenGL ES API. We expect these limitations to be removed with additional engineering effort.

Finally, Cider does not map iOS security to Android security. Android's permission-based security model differs significantly from the more dynamic iOS security, which is enforced at runtime. A complete mapping of the two models is left to future work.

## 7. Related Work

Many approaches have tried to run apps from multiple OSes on the same hardware, though primarily in the context of desktop computers, not mobile devices. Several BSD variants maintain binary compatibility layers for other OSes [18, 19, 23] at the kernel level. BSD reimplements foreign syscalls in the OS, using a different syscall dispatch table for each OS to glue the calls into the BSD kernel. It works for foreign OSes that are close enough to BSD such as Linux, but attempts to extend this approach to Mac OS X apps only provide limited support for command-line tools, not GUI apps [20]. Similarly, Solaris 10 Zones [33, 34] provided an lx brand mechanism that emulates outdated Linux 2.4 kernel system call interfaces to run some Linux binaries on Solaris, though this feature is no longer available as of Solaris 11 [35]. Cider goes beyond these approaches by introducing duct tape to make it easier to add foreign kernel code to an OS and diplomatic functions to support the use of opaque foreign kernel interfaces, providing a richer OS compatibility layer that supports GUI apps with accelerated graphical interfaces.

Operating at user instead of kernel level, Wine [1] runs Windows apps on x86 computers running Linux. It achieves this by attempting to reimplement the entire foreign user space library API, such as Win32, using native APIs. This is tedious and overwhelmingly complex. Wine has been under development for over 20 years, but continues to chase Windows as every new release contains new APIs that need to be implemented. Darling [17] takes a similar approach to try to run Mac OS X apps on Linux, though it remains a work in progress unable to run anything other than simple command-line apps. In contrast, Cider provides kernel-level persona management that leverages existing unmodified libraries and frameworks to avoid rewriting huge amounts of user space code. Cider's duct tape layer and diplomatic function calls facilitate this by incorporating existing foreign kernel code without tedious reimplementation, and allowing foreign apps to directly leverage existing domestic libraries.

Wabi [26] from Sun Microsystems ran Windows apps on Solaris. It supported apps developed for Windows 3.1, but did not support later versions of Windows and was discontinued. Unlike Wine, it required Windows 3.1 and leveraged existing Windows libraries except for the lowest layers of the Windows environment, for which it replaced low-level Windows API libraries with versions that translated from Windows to Solaris calls. It also provided CPU emulation to allow x86 Windows apps to run on Sparc, similar to binary translation systems such as DEC's FX!32 [13]. Wabi ran on top of Solaris and provided all of its functionality outside of the OS, limiting its ability to support apps that require kernel-level services not available in Solaris. In contrast, Cider provides binary personality support in the OS to support foreign kernel services, uses diplomatic functions to make custom domestic hardware accessible to foreign apps, and does not need to perform any binary translation since both iOS and Android run on ARM CPUs.

While most previous approaches have not considered mobile software ecosystems, AppPlayer from BlueStacks [10] allows users to run Android apps on a Windows PC or Apple OS X computer by utilizing a cross-compiled Dalvik VM and ported Android services such as `SurfaceFlinger`. This is possible because Android is open source, and the whole system can be easily cross-compiled. Since many Android apps are entirely Java-based and consist of bytecodes run in a VM, it is relatively easy to run them anywhere. However, many popular Android apps increasingly incorporate native libraries for performance reasons – these apps will not work. Similarly, this approach will not work for iOS apps which are native binaries running on a proprietary system for which source code is not available. In contrast, Cider utilizes kernel-level persona management and diplomatic function calls to support unmodified iOS binaries which link against unmodified iOS libraries and communicate with unmodified iOS support services such as `notifyd` and `syslogd`.

Some developer frameworks [14, 39, 45] allow mobile app developers to target multiple OSes from a single code base. This requires apps to be written using these frameworks. Because such frameworks are often more limited than those provided by the respective mobile software ecosystems, the vast majority of apps are not written in this manner, and are thus tied to a particular platform. Cider does not require developers to rewrite or recompile their apps to use specific non-standard frameworks, but instead runs unmodified iOS binaries on an Android device.

Other partial solutions to OS compatibility have been explored for desktop systems. Shinichiro Hamaji's Mach-O loader for Linux [24] can load and run some desktop OS X command-line binaries in Linux. This project supports binaries using the "misc" binary format, and dynamically overwrites C entry points to syscalls. NDISWrapper [32] allows the Linux kernel to load and use Windows NDIS driver DLLs. The project's kernel driver implements the Network Driver Interface Specification (NDIS) [41], and dynamically links the Windows DLL to this implementation. It is narrowly focused on a single driver specification, does not support incorporation of general foreign kernel subsystems, and does not support app code. In contrast, Cider makes it possible to incorporate general kernel subsystems, such as Mach IPC, without substantial implementation effort and provides a complete environment for foreign binaries including graphics libraries and device access.

VMs are commonly used to run apps requiring different OS instances on desktop computers. Various approaches [8, 15, 28] have attempted to bring VMs to mobile devices, but they cannot run unmodified OSes, incur higher overhead than their desktop counterparts, and provide at best poor, if any, graphics performance within VMs. Some of these limitations are being addressed by ongoing work on KVM/ARM using ARM hardware virtualization support [16]. Lightweight OS virtualization [2, 12] claims lower performance overhead, but does not support different OS instances and therefore cannot run foreign apps at all. Unlike Cider, none of these previous approaches can run iOS and Android apps on the same device.

Drawbridge [40] and Bascule [9] provide user mode OS personalities for desktop apps by refactoring traditional OSes into library OSes that call down into a host OS. Refactoring is a complex and tedious process, and there is no evidence that these systems would work for mobile devices. For example, Bascule has no support for general inter-process sharing, and relies on an external X11 server using network-based graphics, running on the host OS, to support GUI apps. It is unclear how these systems might support vertically integrated libraries that require direct communication to hardware, or multi-process services based on inter-process communication. In contrast, Cider provides duct tape to easily incorporate kernel subsystems that facilitate the multi-process communication required by iOS apps, and leverages diplomatic function calls to support direct communication with closed or proprietary hardware – a feature crucial for vertically integrated mobile devices.

## 8. Conclusions

Cider is the first system that can run unmodified iOS apps on non-Apple devices. It accomplishes this through a novel combination of binary compatibility techniques including two new operating system compatibility mechanisms: duct tape and diplomatic functions. Duct tape allows source code from a foreign kernel to be compiled, without modification, into the domestic kernel. This avoids the difficult, tedious, and error prone process of porting or implementing new foreign subsystems. Diplomatic functions leverage per-thread personas and mediate foreign function calls into domestic libraries. This enables Cider to support foreign libraries that are closely tied to foreign hardware by replacing library function calls with diplomats that utilize domestic libraries and hardware. We built a Cider prototype that reuses existing unmodified frameworks across both iOS and Android ecosystems. Our results demonstrate that Cider has modest performance overhead and runs popular iOS and Android apps together seamlessly on the same Android device.

## 9. Acknowledgments

Yan Zou helped with running benchmarks to obtain many of the measurements in this paper. Lin Zhong provided helpful comments on earlier drafts of this paper. This work was supported in part by a Facebook Graduate Fellowship and NSF grants CNS-1162447, CNS-1018355, and CNS-0905246.

## References


[1] B. Amstadt and M. K. Johnson. Wine. *Linux Journal*, 1994 (4es), Aug. 1994. ISSN 1075-3583.

[2] J. Andrus, C. Dall, A. Van't Hof, O. Laadan, and J. Nieh. Cells: A Virtual Mobile Smartphone Architecture. In *Proceedings of the* $23^{rd}$ *ACM Symposium on Operating Systems Principles*, pages 173–187, Cascais, Portugal, Oct. 2011.

[3] Apalon Apps. Calculator Pro for iPad Free on the App Store on iTunes. `https://itunes.apple.com/us/app/calculator-pro-for-ipad-free/id749118884`, Dec. 2013. Accessed: 12/20/2013.

[4] Apple, Inc. OS X ABI Mach-O File Format Reference. `https://developer.apple.com/library/mac/#documentation/DeveloperTools/Conceptual/MachORuntime/Reference/reference.html`, Feb. 2009. Accessed: 3/20/2013.

[5] Apple, Inc. Porting UNIX/Linux Applications to OS X. `https://developer.apple.com/library/mac/#documentation/Porting/Conceptual/PortingUnix/background/background.html`, June 2012. Accessed: 3/27/2013.

[6] Apple, Inc. Source Browser. `http://www.opensource.apple.com/source/xnu/xnu-2050.18.24/`, Aug. 2012. Accessed: 3/21/2013.

[7] Apple, Inc. OpenGL ES Programming Guide for iOS: Configuring OpenGL ES Contexts. `https://developer.apple.com/library/ios/documentation/3DDrawing/Conceptual/OpenGLES_ProgrammingGuide/WorkingwithOpenGLESContexts/WorkingwithOpenGLESContexts.html`, Sept. 2013. Accessed: 12/4/2013.

[8] K. Barr, P. Bungale, S. Deasy, V. Gyuris, P. Hung, C. Newell, H. Tuch, and B. Zoppis. The VMware Mobile Virtualization Platform: Is That a Hypervisor in Your Pocket? *ACM SIGOPS Operating Systems Review*, 44(4):124–135, Dec. 2010. ISSN 0163-5980.

[9] A. Baumann, D. Lee, P. Fonesca, L. Glendenning, J. R. Lorch, B. Bond, R. Olinsky, and G. C. Hunt. Composing OS Extensions Safely and Efficiently with Bascule. In *Proceedings of the 8th ACM European Conference on Computer Systems*, pages 239–252, Prague, Czech Republic, Apr. 2013.

[10] BlueStacks. Run Mobile Apps on Window PC or Mac With BlueStacks — Android App Player. `http://www.bluestacks.com/`. Accessed: 7/23/2013.

[11] M. B.V. Papers on the App Store on iTunes. `https://itunes.apple.com/us/app/papers/id304655618`, Oct. 2013. Accessed: 12/10/2013.

[12] Cellrox. Cellrox ThinVisor Technology. `http://www.cellrox.com/how-it-works/`, Feb. 2013. Accessed: 4/5/2013.

[13] A. Chernoff, M. Herdeg, R. Hookway, C. Reeve, N. Rubin, T. Tye, S. B. Yadavalli, and J. Yates. FX!32: A Profile-Directed Binary Translator. *IEEE Micro*, 18(2):56–64, Mar. 1998. ISSN 0272-1732. .

[14] D. Connelly, T. Ball, and K. Stanger. j2objc - A Java to iOS Objective-C translation tool and runtime. - Google Project Hosting. `https://code.google.com/p/j2objc/`. Accessed: 7/23/2013.

[15] C. Dall and J. Nieh. KVM for ARM. In *Proceedings of the Ottawa Linux Symposium*, Ottawa, Canada, June 2010.

[16] C. Dall and J. Nieh. KVM/ARM: The Design and Implementation of the Linux ARM Hypervisor. In *Proceedings of the 19th International Conference on Architectural Support for Programming Languages and Operating Systems*, Salt Lake City, UT, Mar. 2014.

[17] L. Doleel. The Darling Project. `http://darling.dolezel.info/en/Darling`, Aug. 2012. Accessed: 4/5/2013.

[18] E. Dreyfus. Linux Compatibility on BSD for the PPC Platform. `http://onlamp.com/lpt/a/833`, May 2001. Accessed: 5/11/2012.

[19] E. Dreyfus. IRIX Binary Compatibility, Parts 1–6. `http://onlamp.com/lpt/a/2623`, Aug. 2002. Accessed: 5/11/2012.

[20] E. Dreyfus. Mac OS X binary compatibility on NetBSD: challenges and implementation. In *Proceedings of the 2004 EuroBSDCon*, Karlsruhe, Germany, Oct. 2004.

[21] Faraday, Owen. Android is a desolate wasteland when it comes to games (Wired UK). `http://www.wired.co.uk/news/archive/2012-10/31/android-games`, Oct. 2012. Accessed: 3/21/2013.

[22] Free Software Foundation. GDB: The GNU Project Debugger. `https://www.gnu.org/software/gdb/`, Dec. 2013. Accessed: 12/10/2013.

[23] FreeBSD Documentation Project. Linux Binary Compatibility. In B. N. Handy, R. Murphey, and J. Mock, editors, *The FreeBSD Handbook 3rd Edition, Vol.1: User Guide*, chapter 11. Mar. 2004.

[24] S. Hamaji. Mach-O Loader for Linux. `https://github.com/shinh/maloader`, Mar. 2011. Accessed: 3/15/2013.

[25] M. Heily. libkqueue. `http://www.heily.com/~mheily/proj/libkqueue/`, Mar. 2011. Accessed: 1/3/2014.

[26] P. Hohensee, M. Myszewski, and D. Reese. Wabi CPU Emulation. In *Hot Chips 8*, Palo Alto, CA, Aug. 1996.

[27] G. C. Hunt and D. Brubacher. Detours: Binary Interception of Win32 Functions. In *Proceedings of the 3rd USENIX Windows NT Symposium*, Seattle, WA, July 1999.

[28] J. Hwang, S. Suh, S. Heo, C. Park, J. Ryu, S. Park, and C. Kim. Xen on ARM: System Virtualization using Xen Hypervisor for ARM-based Secure Mobile Phones. In *Proceedings of the* $5^{th}$ *Consumer Communications and Network Conference*, pages 257–261, Las Vegas, NV, Jan. 2008.

[29] Khronos Group. OpenGL ES Common Profile Specification Version 2.0.25 (Full Specification). `http://www.khronos.org/registry/gles/specs/2.0/es_full_spec_2.0.25.pdf`, Nov. 2010. Accessed: 4/8/2013.

[30] Khronos Group. Khronos Native Platform Graphics Interface (EGL Version 1.4). `http://www.khronos.org/registry/egl/specs/eglspec.1.4.20130211.pdf`, Feb. 2013. Accessed: 12/4/2013.

[31] Khronos Group. OpenGL ES – The Standard for Embedded Accelerated 3D Graphics. http://www.khronos.org/opengles/, Jan. 2013. Accessed: 3/22/2013.

[32] J. Kiszka, G. Pemmasani, and P. Fuchs. SourceForge.net: ndiswrapper. http://ndiswrapper.sourceforge.net/. Accessed: 7/23/2013.

[33] N. Nieuwejaar, E. Schrock, W. Kucharski, R. Blaine, E. Pilatowicz, and A. Leventhal. Method for Defining Non-Native Operating Environments. US 7689566, Filed Dec. 12, 2006, Issued Mar. 30, 2010. http://www.patentlens.net/patentlens/patent/US_7689566/.

[34] Oracle Corporation. System Administration Guide: Oracle Solaris Containers-Resource Management and Oracle Solaris Zones. http://docs.oracle.com/cd/E19253-01/817-1592/817-1592.pdf, Sept. 2010. Accessed: 1/3/2014.

[35] Oracle Corporation. Transitioning From Oracle Solaris 10 to Oracle Solaris 11. http://docs.oracle.com/cd/E23824_01/pdf/E24456.pdf, Mar. 2012. Accessed: 1/3/2014.

[36] Parallels IP Holdings GmbH. Parallels Desktop. http://www.parallels.com/products/desktop/. Accessed: 3/22/2013.

[37] PassMark Software, Inc. PerformanceTest Mobile on the App Store on iTunes. https://itunes.apple.com/us/app/performancetest-mobile/id494438360, June 2012. Accessed: 12/10/2013.

[38] PassMark Software, Inc. PassMark PerformanceTest – Android Apps on Google Play. https://play.google.com/store/apps/details?id=com.passmark.pt_mobile, Jan. 2013. Accessed: 3/14/2013.

[39] PhoneGap. PhoneGap — Home. http://phonegap.com/. Accessed: 7/23/2013.

[40] D. E. Porter, S. Boyd-Wickizer, J. Howell, R. Olinsky, and G. C. Hunt. Rethinking the Library OS from the Top Down. In *Proceedings of the 16th International Conference on Architectural Support for Programming Languages and Operating Systems*, pages 291–304, Newport Beach, CA, Mar. 2011.

[41] I. Printing Communications Assoc. NDIS Developer's Reference. http://www.ndis.com/. Accessed: 7/24/2013.

[42] R. Rashid, A. Tevanian, M. Young, D. Golub, R. Baron, D. Black, W. Bolosky, and J. Chew. Machine-independent Virtual Memory Management for Paged Uniprocessor and Multiprocessor Architectures. *ACM SIGOPS Operating Systems Review*, 21(4):31–39, Oct. 1987. ISSN 0163-5980.

[43] C. K. Tung. CK's IT blog: How To Decrypt iPhone IPA file. http://tungchingkai.blogspot.com/2009/02/how-to-decrypt-iphone-ipa-file.html, Feb. 2009. Accessed: 3/14/2013.

[44] VMware, Inc. VMware Workstation. http://www.vmware.com/products/workstation/. Accessed: 3/22/2013.

[45] Yeecco, Ltd. www.yeeccoo.com. http://http://www.yeecco.com/stella. Accessed: 6/27/2013.

[46] Yelp. Yelp on the App Store on iTunes. https://itunes.apple.com/us/app/yelp/id284910350, Dec. 2013. Accessed: 1/8/2014.

[47] M. Young, A. Tevanian, R. Rashid, D. Golub, J. Eppinger, J. J. Chew, W. J. Bolosky, D. Black, and R. Baron. The Duality of Memory and Communication in the Implementation of a Multiprocessor Operating System. In *Proceedings of the 11th ACM Symposium on Operating Systems Principles*, pages 63–76, Austin, TX, Nov. 1987. ACM.

# SI-TM: Reducing Transactional Memory Abort Rates through Snapshot Isolation


Heiner Litz
Stanford University
heiner.litz@stanford.edu

David Cheriton
Stanford University
david.cheriton@stanford.edu

Amin Firoozshahian
HICAMP Systems
aminf13@hicampsystems.com

Omid Azizi
HICAMP Systems
oazizi@hicampsystems.com

John P. Stevenson
Stanford University
jpete@stanford.edu



## Abstract

Transactional memory represents an attractive conceptual model for programming concurrent applications. Unfortunately, high transaction abort rates can cause significant performance degradation. Conventional transactional memory realizations not only pessimistically abort transactions on every read-write conflict but also because of false sharing, cache evictions, TLB misses, page faults and interrupts. Consequently, the use of transactions needs to be restricted to a very small number of operations to achieve predictable performance, thereby, limiting its benefit to programming simplification. In this paper, we investigate snapshot isolation transactional memory in which transactions operate on memory snapshots that always guarantee consistent reads. By exploiting snapshots, an established database model of transactions, transactions can ignore read-write conflicts and only need to abort on write-write conflicts. Our implementation utilizes a memory controller that supports multiversion memory, to efficiently support snapshotting in hardware. We show that snapshot isolation can reduce the number of aborts in some cases by three orders of magnitude and improve performance by up to 20$x$.



***Categories and Subject Descriptors*** B.3.1 [*Memory Structures*]: Semiconductor Memories

***Keywords*** Transactional Memory; Snapshot Isolation; Multiversion Concurrency; Abort Rate




*ASPLOS '14*, March 1–4, 2014, Salt Lake City, Utah, USA.



ACM 978-1-4503-2305-5/14/03...$15.00.
http://dx.doi.org/10.1145/2541940.2541952


## 1. Introduction

Twenty years after Herlihy and Moss [26] introduced the architectural concept of *transactional memory (TM)*, IBM [12] and Intel [58] have finally released processors that provide a restricted form of hardware TM (HTM). These products are reflective of a substantial body of prior research [19, 21, 25, 31, 40, 45, 50, 52] which all share the property of implementing a consistency mechanism that is equivalent to *2-phase locking (2PL)*. 2PL restricts performance in that it pessimistically aborts transactions on every read-write and write-write conflict. Contemporary HTM realizations are also restricted in the size of transactions they can support. The isolation principle enforced by 2PL semantics requires storing uncommitted writes in a version buffer realized as the L1 cache. Consequently, if this version buffer overflows, the associated transaction is forced to abort. The transaction then needs to be re-executed, leading to unpredictable performance and reduced concurrency.

In this paper, we investigate an HTM that utilizes *snapshot isolation (SI)* [6] that we refer to as SI-TM. The snapshot isolation model has been successfully deployed by transactional databases as a means of improving concur-

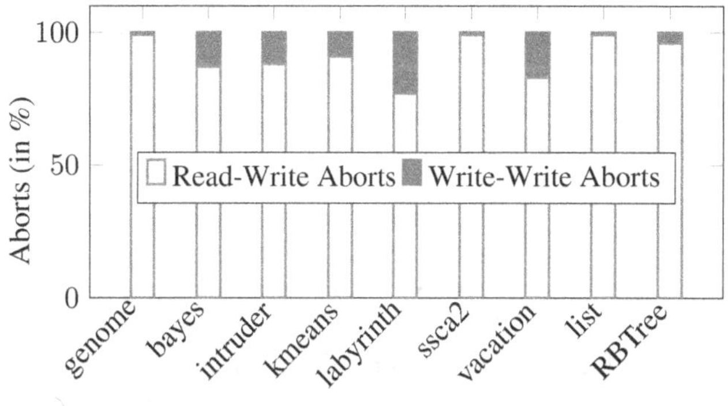


Figure 1: Read-Write and Write-Write Aborts in 2PL

| TX0 | TX1 | TX2 | TX3 |
|---|---|---|---|
| Start | Start | Start | Start |
| Read(A) | - | - | Read(A) |
| Write(A) | - | Read(B) | - |
| Write(B) | Read(A) | Write(C) | Write(A) |
| Commit | - | - | - |
| | Commit | Read(A) | Commit |
| | | Commit | |

(time ↓)

Figure 2: Example Transaction Schedule

rency and is used in most systems including PostgreSQL, Oracle, and SAP HANA. SI provides some attractive features by allowing *concurrent* reads and writes to the same data item and by always, even in the presence of a conflict, presenting a transaction-consistent state of shared memory to the application. Reducing transaction aborts to write-write conflicts holds the potential of significantly improving performance, because, as illustrated in Figure 1, 75%-99% of all transaction aborts in applications as the STAMP [39] benchmark suite are caused by read-write conflicts.

SI has received little attention in TM research despite its prospect of eliminating read-write conflicts. Implementing a TM mechanism based on SI is challenging as it requires a cheap and efficient mechanism for creating snapshots of main memory state. Therefore, we introduce a new memory subsystem that incorporates the notion of time to store multiple versions of the same data item. By utilizing a copy-on-write mechanism, our memory system supports generation of new data versions on the fly, minimizing the cost of snapshot generation. Enabling multiple versions of the same datum to coexist in the same memory space solves the issue of version buffer overflows and avoids aborts otherwise inflicted by interrupts and context switches.

SI suffers from the well-known write skew anomaly which increases programming complexity. Under certain situations, SI permits transaction schedules that are impossible in a serializable TM system and that can lead to unexpected program behavior. Although write skew anomalies are rare, programmers need to be aware of the relaxed SI consistency model or rely on programming language and tool support. Recent advancements [11] made by the database community yielded a methodology that can detect and resolve those consistency anomalies. In this paper, we analyze how these techniques can be applied to transactional memory and furthermore present a tool that helps to remove write skew anomalies from transactional memory programs.

The remainder of this paper is structured as follows. Section 2 discusses snapshot isolation and compares it to other concurrency mechanisms. Section 3 introduces our multiversioned memory system. Section 4 introduces SI-TM, a novel TM proposal that aborts transactions only on write-write conflicts. Section 5 addresses the write skew anomaly. Section 6 evaluates our technique. Section 7 provides an overview of related work, before we conclude in Section 8.

## 2. Concurrency in TM systems

In TM applications, concurrency is reduced by threads that either stall or abort due to conflicting accesses. In both cases the threads do not perform useful work. *2PL* implementations provide linearizability but limit performance by aborting transactions on every read-write or write-write conflict. As shown in Figure 2, in 2PL systems the commit of transaction TX0 forces all other three transactions to abort which is unnecessarily pessimistic, as committing TX1 after TX0 does not violate serializability.

*Conflict serializability (CS)* relaxes 2PL by allowing conflicting accesses as long as a valid ordering of the transactions can be found that matches the order of conflicting accesses. Therefore, CS implementations as SONTM [4] do not abort on every conflict but rather track dependencies between the involved transactions whose direction depends on the order of the conflicting actions. In the example, under CS TX0 and TX1 commit, however, TX2 and TX3 need to abort as there exists a cyclic dependency between T0 and T2 involving the accesses to variables A and B.

In *SI*, transactions always read data from a snapshot of committed data valid as of the time the transaction started. Updates of other transactions that started at a later point in time are not visible to the transaction. If a transaction commits, for each item in its write set, it checks that no overlapping transaction that previously committed has written the same data item. Serving reads from a transaction-specific snapshot isolates the updates of TX0. Therefore, TX2 and TX1 can safely commit under SI. Only TX3 has to abort under SI, because of the write-write conflict.

SI-TM utilizes *lazy conflict detection*, performing validation at commit time in contrast to *eager conflict detection* schemes that check for conflicts on every transactional memory access. Lazy conflict detection is preferable as it guarantees forward progress and mitigates the impact of certain conflicts [10], whereas eager conflict detection is prone to livelock due to repeating mutual aborts. Previous works including TCC [25], Bulk [13] and FlexTM [54] have shown that lazy implementations are able to outperform eager systems. SI-TM further improves on existing lazy systems by introducing a new validation technique based on timestamps. Our technique enables local commits, as transactions can validate their write set by comparing it against the state of main memory instead of broadcasting it to the other cores in the system.

## 3. Multiversioned Memory Architecture

SI-TM requires a mechanism to generate snapshots of main memory to serve transactional read operations. This is challenging as, in general, the read set of a transaction is unknown at transaction begin. To avoid creating a copy of the process's entire memory space to form a snapshot, our memory system generates new data versions on the fly using copy-on-write. Each time a data item, in our implementation

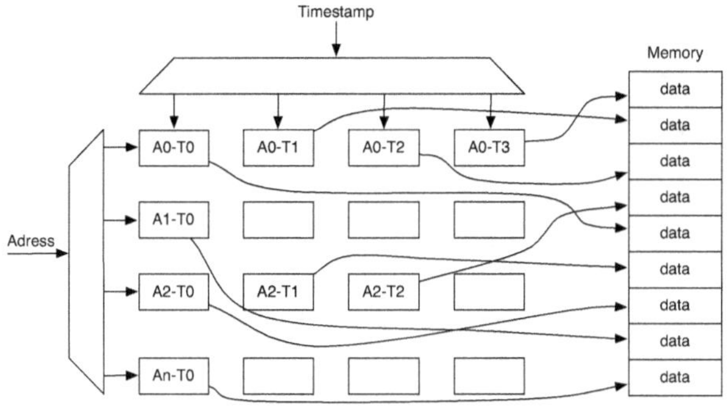


Figure 3: Multiversioned Memory Architecture

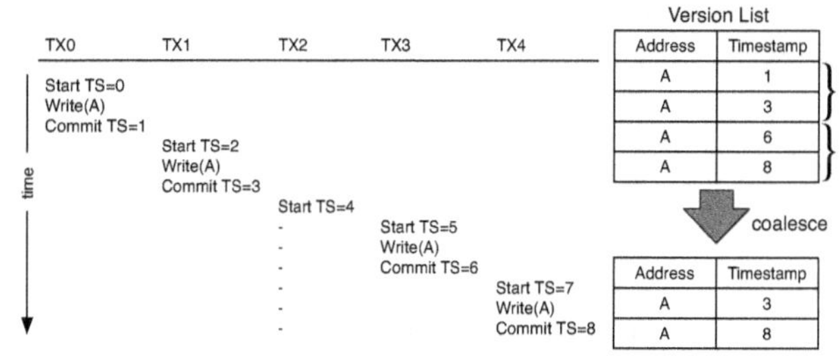


Figure 4: Version Coalescing

a cache line, is transactionally written, instead of modifying it in-place, a copy is created incorporating the modifications. This makes shared data *immutable* which guarantees that every read operation accessing shared data always returns a consistent value. To support multiple versions of a cache line, our memory system introduces an indirection layer called version list. Lines in memory are accessed by retrieving a pointer from the version list using both an address and timestamp. The pointer is then dereferenced to access the data in memory. Figure 3 shows how memory is accessed using the indirection layer. Timestamps are transparent to software and hence do not require changes to the ISA or load/-store API. In SI-TM, every transaction obtains unique start and end timestamps which are used by the MVM to locate the correct version. On a non-transactional read access, the MVM returns the newest version. Non-transactional writes modify the most current version in place. SI-TM provides architectural support for version management and allocation of shared data. Therefore, main memory is partitioned into conventional memory and multiversion memory. Multiversion memory exposes the same interface as conventional memory to the OS, however, on allocation e.g. through `malloc()`, only the mapping between physical address and version list entry is installed. Physical memory on the other hand is allocated on the first write. Both the version list as well as multiversioned data is stored in the MVM partition.

### 3.1 Garbage Collection

There exists a variable number of versions for each address in the MVM depending on the number of transactional writes to the address as well as on the age of the active transactions. Thus, the oldest active transaction determines the number of versions that need to be retained. SI-TM, therefore, stores all start timestamps in a priority queue whose head represents the oldest in flight transaction. Instead of searching the entire indirection matrix for obsolete versions on every commit, we delete unneeded versions of an address on every write to that address by analyzing the timestamp of the oldest existing version. While this maintains obsolete versions longer than required, it significantly reduces garbage collection overhead.

In principle, the number of versions is unlimited as one thread might commit an arbitrary number of modifications while another thread is executing a long running transaction. To limit the number of existing versions we implement version coalescing. The key idea is that only the most current state older than the start timestamp of a particular transaction needs to be provided. The number of active transactions, respectively hardware threads, therefore, bounds the number of versions. We implement coalescing by checking every time a new version is generated whether a start timestamp exists that is older than the version to be created and newer than the previous version. Only in this case a new version is created, otherwise the previous version is overwritten. Figure 4 shows an example schedule of five transactions that update a shared datum in memory. Each time a transaction commits, it generates a new version of **A** tagged with its end timestamp (TS). As no new transaction starts in between the commit points of TX0 and TX1 as well as in between TX3 and TX4, versions 1 and 3 as well as versions 6 and 8 can be coalesced into single versions. After applying coalescing, the number of existing versions is in fact much smaller than the number of hardware threads. As an example, when using 32 threads running the STAMP applications, in less than 1% of the cases there exist more than 4 versions of the same address (see Appendix A). While this might not apply to all applications, there exist three reasons why the number of versions in general is limited. (1) the number of concurrent transactions is usually less than the number of threads, (2) consecutive writes to the same cache line in a short period of time are rare and (3) if there exists write contention on a cache line, transactions have to abort due to write-write conflicts anyway. We, therefore, decided to restrict the number of versions to 4 and simply abort a transaction if it tries to create a fifth version. An alternative approach is to discard the oldest version on each write and to keep a limited history. In this case, transactions abort on reads, if they cannot find a version older than their timestamp. Both implementations affect the abort rates and performance by less than 1%. Yet another alternative is to revert to using the conventional virtual memory page-level copy-on-write at this point.

### 3.2 Overheads

The indirection layer of the MVM architecture consumes extra memory capacity. Our current implementation utilizes 32 bit pointers to support a maximum of $2^{32}$ cache lines, or 256 GByte of shared multiversioned memory. For each cache line address, the version list needs to store four 32 bit references as well as four 32 bit timestamps. Hence, if there exist four versions per address, the overhead is $2 \cdot 32/512 = 12.5\%$ per line. In the worst case there exists only one active line resulting in an overhead of $50\%$ per allocated MVM line. These overheads can be addressed by increasing the version granularity, e.g. by combining 8 lines into a bundle, the worst case overhead is reduced by a factor of 8 to 6%. This solution trades memory capacity for write overheads as the copy-on-write operation now requires copying an entire bundle on the first write. However, writes are usually not on the latency critical path and the cost is amortized in the existence of writes that exhibit spatial locality. It can be further reduced by techniques such as Rowclone [30]. Finally, HICAMP [15] introduced a deduplication technique for increasing memory capacity which can be implemented utilizing MVM's indirection layer.

Writing to the MVM does not simply update data in place but requires allocating a new line in memory, storing the cache line at this location and modifying the version list accordingly. Providing dedicated hardware support to compare timestamps in parallel, allocate a cache line from the free list and install the reference to the indirection layer addresses these overheads. Furthermore, writes are not on the critical path and usually less latency sensitive than reads.

Memory reads incur a latency penalty, as on a load the entry needs to be obtained from the indirection layer before the correct data version determined by the timestamp can be retrieved from main memory. In our architecture we assume per core private L1 and L2 data caches and hence, multiple versions of the same data only exist in shared memory, respectively the L3 cache and DRAM. Placing the MVM controller at the L3 level leaves L1 and L2 latency unaffected. Version list entries can be cached in the L3 and by providing hardware support, we expect read access of multiversion data to be less costly than two full round trip times. As indirection level entries are much smaller than the referenced data cache lines, a small translation cache accessed in parallel to L2 can compensate for most of the extra latency. The bandwidth overhead introduced by the MVM depends on data locality and access patterns. As a single cache line contains eight version references, a single cache line access fetches multiple indirection references, resulting in a best case bandwidth increase of 12.5%.

### 3.3 Indirection Layer

The indirection layer introduced by the MVM represents a powerful mechanism that can be exploited for other purposes. While a detailed analysis of the following techniques is out of the scope of this paper they provide further motivation for our multiversioned memory system. As described in HICAMP [15] an indirection layer can be used for memory deduplication by mapping multiple addresses to the same data cache line, if their content is identical. The mechanism works particularly well for common cases like the zero cache line that only consists of zeros. Snapshots can be applied not only to multiversion concurrency control but also to provide an efficient checkpointing mechanism that can be utilized by speculation techniques or for resiliency by allowing rollback to a consistent state in response to an error. Furthermore, the indirection layer provides bit steering capability to redirect traffic in heterogeneous memory systems transparently to software and it enables fine grain chipkill to deactivate defect memory cells on a per line basis to improve reliability and yield. Finally, the indirection layer can reduce fragmentation due to fine-grained memory line mapping.

## 4. SI-TM

SI-TM increases concurrency in multithreaded applications by reducing transaction aborts in four ways: (1) Transactions can commit in the presence of read-write conflicts, SI-TM only aborts on write-write conflicts. (2) Read-only transactions are guaranteed to commit. (3) SI-TM enables a unique lazy conflict detection mechanism which reduces aborts over eager conflict detection and (4) SI-TM supports unbounded transactions and hence transactions do not need to abort in the case of a versions buffer (L1 cache) overflow. SI-TM achieves these properties by presenting the software process with the illusion of a snapshot of memory taken at transaction begin. Concurrent writes are isolated to the transaction that issued the writes, guaranteeing that reads always return consistent data.

SI-TM is based on multiversion concurrency control which guarantees that writes are not only isolated from other transactions until a transaction commits, but even beyond if the other transactions started beforehand. Adding multiversion awareness to the memory hierarchy not only allows maintaining older versions for a virtually unlimited time but also enables transactions to exceed the size of the L1 cache by just spilling over to memory. SI-TM does not require tracking read sets as on commit SI-TM only checks for write-write conflicts.

### 4.1 Hardware Components

To implement SI-TM we extend a typical processor architecture with the components shown in Figure 5. Write sets are added to the cores to track the memory addresses that are transactionally written. One additional tag bit per cache line is added to the L1 and L2 cache to denote whether the cache line has been accessed transactionally. An optional translation cache can be added to the core that holds recently used translation lines. It can be accessed in parallel to the L2 cache to mitigate the access penalty of the indirection layer

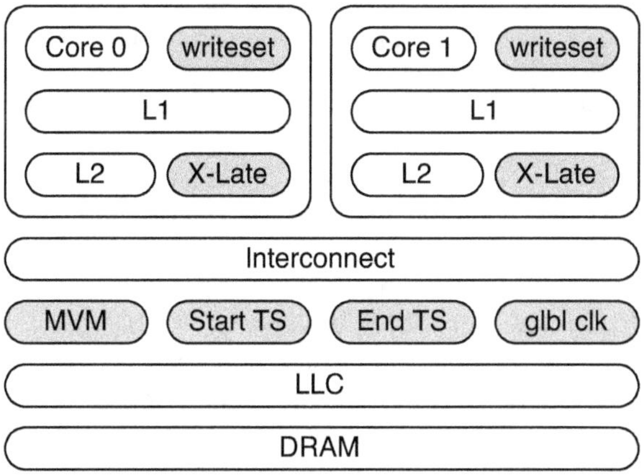


Figure 5: SI-TM Hardware Components

in the case of a L2 miss. The multiversion memory controller is located within the uncore part of the system. On a transactional memory access, it reads the corresponding entry from the version list and compares the versions to the start timestamp of the calling transaction. It then issues the data cache line read. It furthermore manages allocation of shared memory lines and garbage collection of obsolete entries from the version list. Additional components in the uncore part of the system are the vectors for start and end timestamps as well as the global timestamp counter. In the rare case of a timestamp counter overflow, all active transactions are aborted and an interrupt is thrown to handle the overflow in software.

### 4.2 Transactional Actions

Transactional actions are implemented in SI-TM as follows.

`TM_BEGIN`: A logical snapshot for the transaction is generated by obtaining a unique timestamp using an atomic increment to the global timestamp counter.

`TM_WRITE`: The affected memory address is inserted into the write set, the data is written into the L1 cache and the cache line is marked as transactionally written. As we implement lazy conflict detection no coherency messages are emitted. If the cache line is evicted to the shared L3 cache, the MVM creates a new version for this cache line, allocates a memory line and updates the version list. Modified lines which are not yet committed can be evicted as they do not overwrite data in place. For uncommitted lines, the commit timestamp is yet unknown, hence a temporary ID is used in place of a timestamp to mark the line as *transient*, making it only visible to the owning transaction. Therefore, the N largest timestamps are reserved for temporary IDs, where N represents the number of threads.

`TM_READ`: Transactional reads need to be served by the corresponding snapshot. Therefore, on an L3 read access, the MVM compares the start timestamp of the calling thread's transaction and compares it to the timestamps in the version list. If the version list entry is not contained in the L3, it needs to be fetched from main memory. The most current version older than the start timestamp of the calling transaction is then returned to the processor either from L3 or in the case of a miss from main memory. No read-set validation is necessary for loads (e.g. by broadcasting via the cache coherency protocol) as the isolation provided by SI supports invisible readers.

`TM_COMMIT`: Read-only transactions commit with zero overhead. They neither obtain an end timestamp, nor perform any checks. All other transactions start the commit phase by obtaining an end timestamp from the global timestamp counter. The transaction then traverses its write set and writes back the corresponding lines which might still be buffered in the private caches to the MVM. For each line, the MVM creates a new version assigned with the obtained end timestamp. It also determines for each line whether the timestamp of the most recent corresponding entry in the version list is greater than the begin timestamp of the committing transaction. If a newer version exists for one of the written elements a write-write conflict exists and the transaction needs to abort. As an optimization, in the case of a write-write conflict, the two lines can be compared to the snapshot version on a word granularity to eliminate false sharing [56] and silent store [34] conflicts. This approach combines the performance of a fine grain (word based) conflict detection scheme with low overhead, as all meta data including timestamps and write set entries are tracked per cache line only. In the case of a true conflict, the transaction iterates over its write set again, removes all written lines from the MVM, empties its write set and performs rollback in software. In the absence of write-write conflicts, the transaction can now safely commit.

We refer to our commit technique as *timestamp-based* conflict detection. Timestamping of transactions has been applied in TinySTM [23] among others, whereas HTMs have primarily used it for guaranteeing fairness and forward progress [2, 40, 47]. The benefits of timestamp-based conflict detection over write/read set validation based techniques are twofold: (1) No nested loop is required to compare the two read/write sets or alternatively no false positives occur as in bloom filter [7] based approaches. In fact, due to SI, read sets do not have to be analyzed at all. (2) It enables lazy conflict detection by comparing against a history of committed writes at once using a single operation. For example, in the presence of a long running transaction and many concurrent short update transactions we do not perform conflict detection against all short update transactions but only against the committed state at the end of the long running transaction. In timestamp-based conflict detection a new version of the accessed data is created on every write while in value-based conflict detection as used in JudoSTM [41], NOrec [18] and KILO-TM [24], a copy of the original data version needs to be generated on each read. As writes are generally less common than reads, timestamp-based conflict detection introduces less overheads.

Lazy conflict detection schemes reduce overheads of transactional memory accesses, by coalescing the operations and performing bulk validation at commit time. However, serializing bulk commits can become a performance bottleneck [44]. Commit generally needs to be performed atomically, as otherwise races can occur between transaction validation and actual commit, leaving existing conflicts undetected and overwriting data in-place. To address this problem, BulkSC [13, 44], Scalable TCC [14] and SRC [43] use a variant of partitioning the shared memory space and allowing concurrent validation to independent regions. The mechanisms usually obtain a lock for each line in their write set, then perform conflict detection and then update those lines. In the case of disjoint write sets the validation process can be performed in parallel. All those techniques require modifications of the cache coherency protocol, directory structure and need to apply complex mechanisms to guarantee forward progress and fairness.

SI-TM avoids the problem altogether by never overwriting data in-place. As a result, to perform conflict detection a transaction does not need to acquire locks for each line in its write set. Instead, it optimistically creates a new version and only in the case of a conflict rolls back its newly created versions, making the validation process itself transactional. There exists a possible race condition in the case new transactions start while a commit is performed. Consider a write set of values A and B that is being committed. It is possible that a newly started transaction reads A and B whereas only A has been made visible by the committing transaction. We address this issue by obtaining an end timestamp that is equal to $current\ global\ timestamp + \Delta$, in addition we increment the current value by one. New transactions, therefore, obtain start timestamps smaller than the end timestamp of the commit being processed and hence cannot see the new values. In the case $\Delta + 1$ transactions start during a commit, the starting transaction needs to stall until the commit is processed. This case is rare as the commit process is usually of short duration. On a commit the global timestamp is set to the end timestamp of the committing transaction.

### 4.3 Unbounded Transactional Memory

Ideally, HTM systems should support transactions of arbitrary size and duration with predictable performance. SI-TM provides unbounded transactions in hardware as it does not rely on the processor caches to act as version buffers. Multiversioned memory effectively enables transactions to eagerly update data in memory without overwriting the original state. On abort, no time-consuming undo needs to be performed as the previous version still exists. Readers never wait or stall on a conflicting access by accessing their consistent snapshot. Deleting aborted versions is off the critical path and can be performed as a background process. Therefore, SI-TM represents a more feasible and easier to verify implementation as there exist no complex interactions and races between hardware and software.

In contrast, conventional TM approaches that utilize the L1 cache as a version buffer only support bounded transactions. For example, Intel's Haswell may abort transactions that contain only 9 write operations because of associativity conflicts and it aborts every transaction that accesses more than 16KByte of data due to version buffer overflows [33]. LogTM [40] addresses this problem by performing eager version management and updating memory in place. To enable rollback on abort, LogTM creates an undo log in thread local virtual memory. While this approach enables fast commits, transaction abort is complex and needs to be handled by software. Also, while abort is handled in software the requesting transaction has to wait. VTM [46], PTM [16] and UTM [2] apply similar techniques by storing state for small transactions in hardware and by overflowing into virtualized per thread memory. Relying on software and virtualized memory introduces significant overheads and impairs predictability.

### 4.4 System Implications

Many contemporary HTM implementations utilize the cache coherency protocol to perform eager conflict detection. SI-TM does not require emitting coherency messages on transactional loads and stores due to lazy conflict detection. A written cache line is simply marked as transactionally accessed and remains unversioned in the private caches until it reaches the shared LLC, either due to eviction or because of transaction commit. On a transactional read, the appropriate version is fetched from the MVM, stored into the cache and marked as transactional. Snapshots need to be invalidated during commit to force update to the current state in subsequent transactions.

Multiversioned memory is allocated as a new memory region next to the heap and thread local data as the stack. It can be administered by a conventional heap manager with the only difference that it spans a different memory region. Usually physical memory is allocated in page sized chunks, the allocator then hands out smaller portion to the application. In SI-TM, on page allocation, a consecutive range of physical addresses is mapped to the page. For each address an entry in the version list is created, however, only on the first write to a cache line, the entry is populated and a data line is allocated. This process is transparent to the allocator and to the virtual memory system, as the MVM exposes a consecutive range of physical memory to software.

Our prototype implementation supports dynamically allocated multiversioned memory utilizing a `mvmalloc()` API. Applications can either replace their `malloc()` calls with our version or link against our library to replace all `malloc()` calls within the application. The STAMP [39] benchmark suite which we use in our evaluation already contains macros for allocating shared memory and hence required minimal code changes to support MVM. We assume that upcoming TM APIs [1, 53] and compilers support means to manage transactionally accessed memory.

Listing 1: Withdraw code exhibiting write skew.

```
void Withdraw(bool account, int value){
  if(checking+saving>value)
    if(account)
      checking-=value;
    else
      saving-=value;
}
```

Listing 2: Linked list code exhibiting write skew

```
1  void remove(int value){
2    Node prev = head;
3    Node next = prev.getNext();
4    while(next.getValue()<value){
5      prev = next;
6      next = prev.getNext();
7    }
8    if(next.getValue()==value){
9      prev.setNext(next.getNext());
10     //next.setNext(null);
11     free(next);
12   }
13 }
```

## 5. Write Skew Anomaly

Snapshot isolation is non-serializable as it permits the write skew anomaly. Write skew occurs if there exists an invariant whose component variables span multiple concurrent transactions and the transactions have disjoint write sets. One example write skew is shown in Listing 1 describing the withdraw function of a banking application. If one thread transactionally withdraws money from the credit account while a concurrent thread withdraws money from the savings account using snapshot transactions, the resulting sum of the accounts can be smaller than zero which is impossible in a serializable TM system. In the example, both writes require that the invariant $checking + saving > value$ holds, however, one transaction can invalidate the invariant without notifying the other transaction thereof.

A study of the STAMP benchmark's source code showed that none of the applications comprises a single write skew anomaly, however, there exist anomalies in the data structure library utilized by said applications.

One example is the linked-list container, shown in Listing 2. If two concurrent threads remove adjacent elements from the list using snapshot transactions, elements might be dropped from the list turning it into an inconsistent state. The anomaly can be avoided by setting the next pointer to `Null` when removing an element, as shown in line 10 of Listing 2, enforcing a write-write conflict in the respective scenario. While data structure anomalies can be resolved by the library developer and application anomalies appear to be rare, programmers need to assure application correctness. Data races within parallel programs are notoriously hard to detect. However, as shown above, write skew anomalies only occur under certain well known conditions. Based on this knowledge we developed a methodology for detecting and resolving write skew in transactional memory programs.

### 5.1 Write Skew Detection and Prevention

Cahill et al. have proposed a technique [11] to reliably detect write skew using dependency graph analysis. A write skew dependency graph is a directed graph whose vertices represent transactions and whose edges define read-write dependencies between those transactions. A cycle within the dependency graph represents the necessary condition for a write skew. Determining write skews based on dangerous situations is safe but might introduce false positives. Applications that suffer from write skew can be corrected by determining all read operations that are part of a dependency cycle and by including them in the transaction's validation process. We refer to this technique as *read promotion* as it selectively promotes read operations to be treated as writes for conflict detection.

Read promotion can be applied by the programmer to resolve write skew comparable as to adding fences and locks to avoid data races. However, because reasoning about dependency cycles is difficult, Dias et al. [20] proposed to automatically generate the dependency graph of transactional memory programs using static code analysis, based on separation logic. While the approach is sound, it is compute intensive and hence can only be applied to small kernels.

To address this issue, we developed a best-effort technique based on dynamic code analysis which resulted in a tool that is able to handle large applications. The tool is implemented using PIN [36] and instruments transactional memory applications at runtime. In particular, it intercepts transactional operations and generates a trace of globally ordered `TM_BEGIN`, `TM_READ`, `TM_WRITE` and `TM_COMMIT` operations. In addition, for each read and write operation it backtraces the callstack to determine the line in the source code which called the transactional memory access. When the application terminates, the trace is post-processed, building a dependency graph for determining write skews and their location in the source code. We chose to defer the main work into the post-processing phase to minimize the effect of our tool on the application's execution behavior and concurrency.

The tool works with all applications that either support the C++ STM [1] or RSTM [37] APIs and only requires the applications to disable inlining of the `TM_*` calls and to be compiled with symbol information. Subsequently, write skews found by the tool can be either resolved by the programmer or fully automatically by our tool. The tool applies read promotion for every transactional read that is part of a write skew. Promoted reads are inserted into the write set to trigger an abort in the case of a write skew. However, a promoted read is not treated as a write in that they do not create new data versions in the MVM.

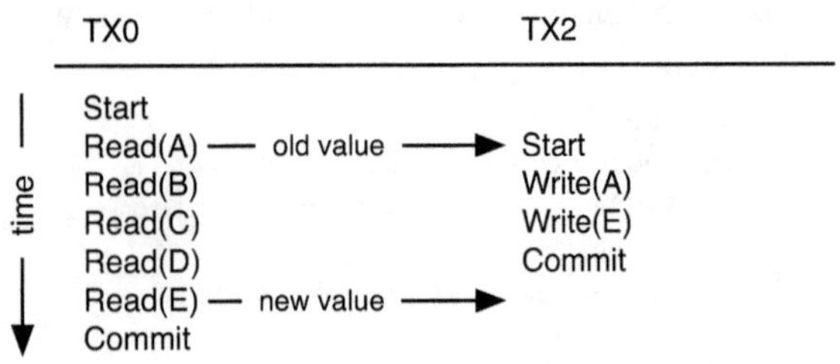


Figure 6: Schedule with Temporal Cyclic Dependency

We applied our tool to all applications of STAMP and to several microbenchmarks. The results are consistent with our previous study, showing anomalies exclusively in transactional data structures including the aforementioned linked list, a doubly-linked list as well as multiple write skews in a Red-Black Tree implementation.

The tool represents a best-efforts approach because it utilizes dynamic analysis to detect write skew. In particular, it does not provide full soundness in the sense of guaranteeing the detection of all write skews. The quality of the results, thereby, depends on the number of tested transaction schedules and input vector combinations. Only a sufficiently large test coverage leads to meaningful results while the required execution time of the tool increases proportionally with the size of the analyzed source code or more precisely with the number of critical sections defined in the source code.

From a practical perspective, the tool has proven successful. The tool detected anomalies within minutes of runtime and corrected applications never showed inconsistent behavior even after extensive testing. We are currently extending our methodology to provide information on test coverage which is particularly interesting in cases where the tool achieves coverage of all schedules for a given input vector. In addition, programmers can always enforce serializability by enforcing read-write conflict detection for all or a subset of transactions. In this case SI-TM still provides the benefit of committing all read-only transactions safely even in the case of a read-write conflict. Finally, SI-TM can be extended to incorporate dependency checking in hardware to provide full serializability, as described next.

### 5.2 Serializable Snapshot Isolation

A simplified version of the graph based write skew detection scheme can be implemented in hardware and performed at runtime to make SI-TM fully serializable. We sketch a possible implementation, leaving the details to future work.

As dynamic dependency graphs are unbounded in size, their analysis in hardware is unfeasible. We, therefore, define a *dangerous situation* as the case where a transaction exhibits an incoming as well as an outgoing read-write dependency because this represents the minimum requirement to form a cycle and respectively a write skew. Aborting transactions in the presence of dangerous situations is safe. It only introduces false positives. To implement serializable snapshot isolation (SSI-TM) it is sufficient to track read sets in addition to the write sets and to perform conflict detection for those as well. On the first read-write conflict we record either an incoming or outgoing dependency by setting a flag bit. If another conflict arises that has the opposite direction, we abort the transaction.

It is important to note that cyclic dependencies in SI-TM are different from cyclic dependencies in conflict serializable approaches. In particular, SI-TM defines type based dependencies, whereas CS uses temporal dependencies. This difference is depicted in Figure 6. In this schedule TX0 accesses A before TX1 modifies A and commits, while D is accessed after its committed modification by TX1. This results in a cyclic dependency for CS and subsequently leads to an abort. SSI-TM on the other hand records two incoming dependencies as in both cases TX0 reads and TX1 writes but no outgoing dependencies. A common example for the described schedule is the concurrent execution of a long running transaction that iterates over a vector or linked list and short update transactions to the same data structure.

## 6. Evaluation

We evaluated our SI-TM implementation using the ZSim [51] x86 simulator, a fast, multithreaded and cycle accurate simulator built on PIN [36]. We chose ZSim for its performance and ability to accurately model load-store operations, a multilevel memory hierarchy with pipelined caches, contention and precise DDR3 memory controller timings.

To implement SI-TM and our two TM baselines, we extended the memory subsystem of ZSim, in particular the L3 shared cache, the cache coherency protocol and the memory controller. We added new instructions to offer allocation of version controlled memory, snapshot generation as well as transaction commit. In addition to timing models we implement functional models for the different TM algorithms for example by instrumenting load and store instructions within PIN to redirect memory accesses to the version controlled memory.

The additional, non x86 instructions provided by the simulator are made accessible to software through a lightweight API integrated into the Rochester Software Transactional Memory (RSTM) framework [37]. Integrating our architecture into the RSTM framework enables SI-TM to utilize the entire STM ecosystem including tests, benchmarks as well as Intel's proposed Transactional Language Constructs for C++ [1] which are supported by both GCC and the Intel C++ STM Compiler. The latter allows execution of all specification compliant TM applications with our simulator.

The platform we have chosen to simulate SI-TM is shown in Table 1. Most parameters resemble a state-of-the-art Intel Nehalem-like processor. We use an increased core count of 32 to evaluate the scalability of the different TM mechanisms.

| CPU Cores | 32 |
|---|---|
| CPU Type | 4-way Out-of-Order |
| CPU Clock | 3 GHz |
| L1D cache size | 32KByte |
| L1I cache size | 32KByte |
| L1 cache associativity | 4-way |
| L1 cache latency | 4 cycles |
| L2 cache size | 256KByte |
| L2 cache associativity | 8-way |
| L2 cache latency | 8 cycles |
| L3 cache size | 32MByte |
| L3 cache MVM partition | 8MByte |
| L3 cache associativity | 16-way |
| L3 cache latency | 30 cycles |
| Memory controllers | 4 |
| Aggregate memory bandwidth | 10 GByte/s |
| Memory latency | 100 cycles |

Table 1: Simulated Architecture

### 6.1 Baseline

We compare SI-TM against two transactional memory baselines. The 2-phase locking baseline resembles a state of the art TM system similar to that described in [10]. It implements eager conflict detection with a "requester wins" policy and lazy version management. Conflicts are detected by broadcasting the address of a transactional access using the cache coherency mechanism. On a transactional read, cores receive a get-shared message which is handled by comparing the corresponding address to the entries in their write set and abort on a conflict. Consequently, on a write, cores receive a get-exclusive message handled by checking the associated address against their read and write set. Conflicts are detected on a cache line granularity and read and write sets are modeled using perfect bloom filters [7] with no false positives. On transaction abort, read and write logs are discarded and the transaction is restarted in software. Implementing compiler supported rollback in software significantly simplifies the functional model of the simulator and in our experience does not introduce perceptible overheads which would justify providing hardware support for saving and restoring processor state. On commit, the corresponding thread obtains a commit token, iterates over its write log and commits the speculative writes to main memory.

We also compare against a conflict serializable consistency mechanism by implementing the SONTM architecture as described in [4]. SONTM determines the transactions that may commit in presence of conflicting accesses by using serializability order numbers (SONs). Each transaction maintains a SON range defined by an upper and a lower bound. If at the end of a transaction the range is not empty, it may commit. Part of a successful commit is the broadcast of the transaction's SON to all other concurrent transactions allowing them to adjust their own SON range.

SONTM needs to tag all committed transactional writes with their corresponding SON. Hence, SONTM maintains a global write numbers hashtable in main memory with an entry per transactionally written cache line. Transferring speculative writes to main memory on commit, therefore, introduces overheads in terms of hashing and additional memory write operations. To serialize writer transactions after committed readers each core maintains a local read-history table. Each entry in the read-history table holds the readset of a committed transaction. Every time a transaction tries to commit, it broadcasts its write set to each core to compare it against *every* readset in the read-history table. We model an optimisitic but non-practical read-history with infinite size. This, in fact, represents a weak point of SONTM as the overheads of maintaining and checking conflicts against this table are high. Lastly, each core in SONTM maintains a set of conflict flags which are set on an conflicting access and evaluated during commit.

Note that although SI-TM supports word based conflict detection, in the following evaluation, we perform conflict detection on a per cache line granularity for both SI-TM and the two baselines approaches to exclude the effects of false sharing. The performance results we present for SI-TM can, therefore, be regarded as a lower bound.

### 6.2 Benchmarks

We evaluated SI-TM against the two baseline approaches using three microbenchmarks from the RSTM framework as well as seven applications from STAMP [39]. The microbenchmarks simulate concurrent access to transactional data structures which are commonly used in many parallel applications. *Array* implements an array structure with fixed size of 30K entries and allows concurrent conflict free access to disjoint cells. For the benchmark we utilize two types of transactions. Long running read transactions that iterate over the entire array as well as short update transactions that update two random elements within the array. We execute 1000 transactions per thread using a ratio of 20% long running read and 80% update transactions. *List* implements a single linked list initialized to a size of 1000 elements. We execute 1000 transactions per thread using a ratio of 40% insert, 40% remove and 20% lookup operations. We chose a small ratio of lookup transactions to show that SI-TM not only performs well in the presence of read-only transactions but also for transactions that show many reads and few writes. The *Red Black Tree* data structure is initialized with 100 elements and the benchmark executes a ratio of 50:25:25 lookup, insert, delete operations.

In addition, we evaluated seven applications from the STAMP benchmark suite: *Bayes* an algorithm for learning the structure of Bayesian networks from observed data, *Genome* a genome sequencing and segment matching application, *Intruder* which performs signature based network in-

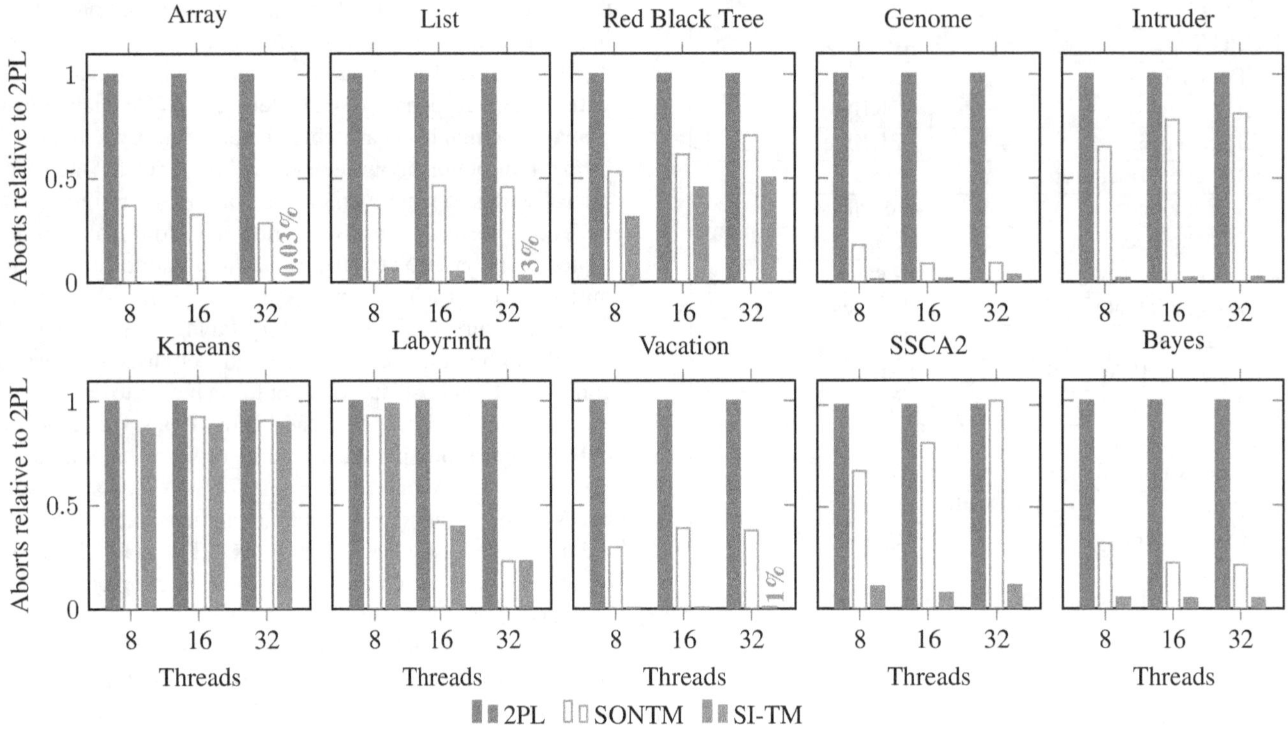


Figure 7: Abort rates

trusion detection, *Kmeans* a clustering algorithm, *Labyrinth* which performs path routing in a 3D grid used in CAD applications, *Scalable Synthetic Compact Applications (ssca2)* which contains four kernels that operate on a large, directed, weighted multi-graph and finally *Vacation*, an online transaction processing system. For all applications we utilized the standard configuration as suggested by the STAMP authors for simulated systems. Each benchmark we run using 1, 2, 4, 8, 16 and 32 threads and we average each run over 5 measurements which we obtain using different random seeds. We note that the standard deviation for all measurements is below 5%. We measure the abort rate and application speedup of every benchmark for 2PL, CS, and SI-TM.

### 6.3 Abort Rate

The abort rate of the evaluated applications is presented in Figure 7. *Array* utilizes transactions that iterate over the entire array in the presence of many update transactions. Hence for 2PL, a sufficiently long running iteration transaction contains many values in its read set, such that any concurrent update transaction causes its abort. In fact, 2PL aborts every long running transaction as long as update transactions are present which essentially leads to livelock. The CS policy reduces the probability of abort as it requires at least two conflicting writes (a transaction with a single write conflict and no read dependencies can always be serialized before or after the long running transaction) and one read-write conflict needs to occur before the commit point and another one thereafter. SI-TM in contrast, allows multiple concurrent read and write accesses to the same elements enabling all long running read-only transactions to commit. Write-write conflicts are rare due to the large size of the array. In this microbenchmark SI-TM reduces the aborts by $3000x$ over 2PL and by $1000x$ over CS. *List* represents another well suited benchmark for SI-TM due to its read heaviness. Each insert, delete and lookup operation requires iteration over the list starting from the first element until the seeked element is found, but at most modifies a single element. The probability for write-write conflicts is, therefore, significantly smaller than for read-write conflicts which reduces aborts in the case of SI-TM for 32 threads by over $30x$ over 2PL and $10x$ over CS. In *Red Black Tree* implementations a single update operation can lead to many transactional writes due to rebalancing. SI-TM benefits from the fact that lookup operations are read-only and hence do not conflict, however, for insert and delete operations only, the three TM implementations perform similar. For all STAMP transactions, SI-TM shows the least number of aborts, although the characteristics differ significantly for each benchmark. In *Genome*, both CS and SI-TM significantly reduce aborts over 2 PL and perform almost on par, whereas in Intruder SI-TM reduces aborts over CS significantly. *Intruder* only utilizes transactions to perform concurrent access to data structures including a list and a tree which as we have seen perform well under SI. In intruder, for 32 threads, SI-TM reduces aborts by $50x$ over 2PL and by $40x$ over CS. *Kmeans* performs a series of read-

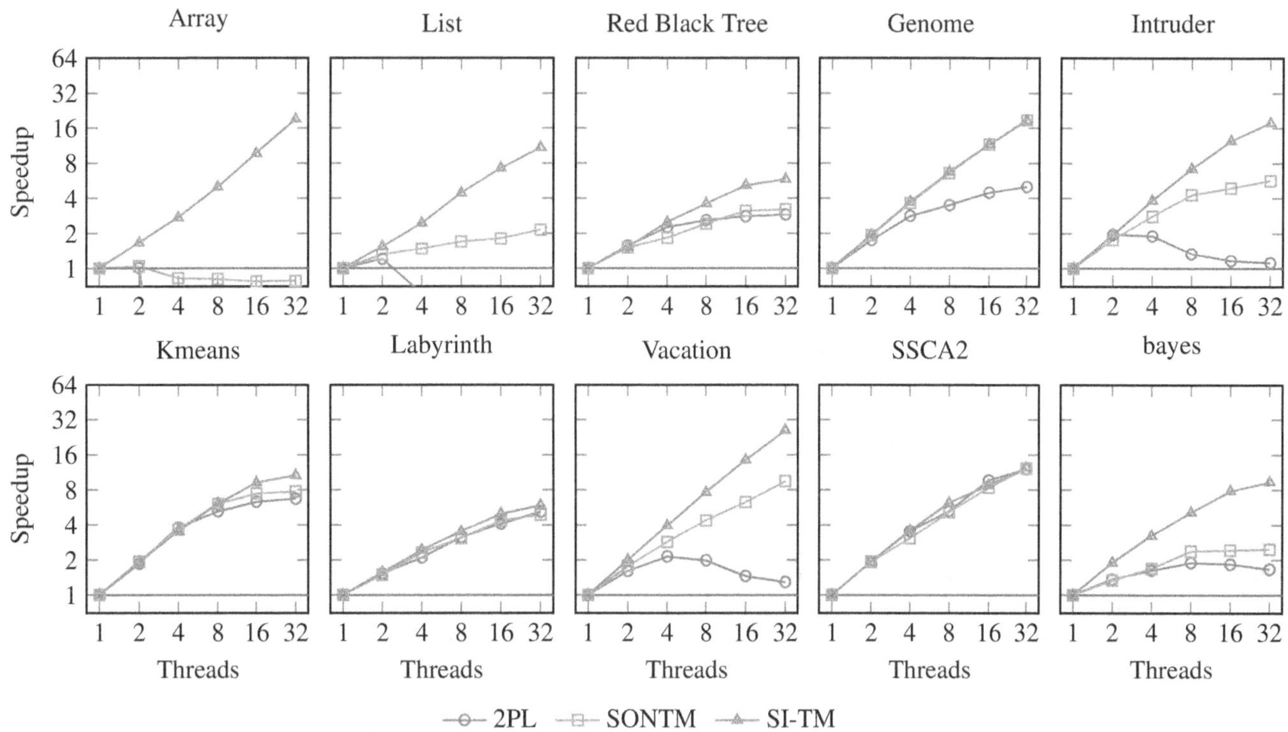


Figure 8: Application Speedup

modify-write operations within each transaction and therefore, each accessed value is both contained in the read as well as in the write set. Both CS and SI-TM cannot significantly reduce aborts over 2PL in this case. *Labyrinth* shows improvements for CS and SI-TM. However, *Labyrinth* in general has very low abort rates such that the absolute improvement is less significant. *Vacation* exhibits long running transactions with a high read ratio, which makes it an ideal candidate for SI-TM. In fact, SI-TM shows less than 1% of the aborts of 2PL in this benchmark. *SSCA2* represents another read heavy kernel, however, the absolute abort rates are already low under 2PL (less than 5%), so we do not expect high performance improvements for SI-TM. *Bayes* exhibits few, but long and costly transactions with a read-only transaction ratio of 25% enabling SI-TM to reduce aborts by $20x$ over 2PL.

In summary, SI-TM performs well in all benchmarks that exhibit a high read:write ratio. Being able to avoid aborts on read-write conflicts is particularly compelling for applications that utilize long running transactions as these transactions increase the probability of conflicts and are also more costly to reexecute. In these cases SI-TM can reduce aborts by multiple orders of magnitude over existing approaches.

### 6.4 Speedup

Reducing the abort rate leads to improved performance, as shown in Figure 8. SI-TM shows a linear scaling, $20x$ for 32 threads in the Array and $14x$ in the List benchmarks whereas 2PL shows a negative speedup for both in the case more than two threads access the data structure concurrently. For the Red Black Tree, performance improvements are not as significant with SI-TM showing a $2x$ increase over the two baselines. In Genome, both CS and SI-TM reduced the abort rate which translates to a speedup of $3.8x$ for both techniques over 2PL. In Kmeans, all three systems show similar abort rates and performance characteristics. In Labyrinth and SSCA2, the obtained speedups are similar for all three implementations which is explained by the fact that 2PL already shows low abort rates and hence scalability is not limited by the transactional memory policy. Vacation benefits significantly from the low abort rate of SI-TM and scales linearly to 32 threads and possibly beyond. CS also shows nice scalability for low thread count but drops off for more than 8 threads. Finally, bayes shows improved scalability for SI-TM leading to a speedup of $10x$ for 32 threads, whereas CS and 2PL do not scale beyond 8 threads. It is worth noticing that the two eager mechanisms utilize exponential backoff to avoid livelock in situations where transactions consecutively abort each other which particularly occurs in Genome. As the impact of this technique can be significant, we profiled the applications and tuned the mechanism such that performance and not the abort rate is optimized. Without exponential backoff 2PL and CS show even higher abort rates and consequently lower performance.

## 7. Related Work

The importance of reducing aborts in transactional memory systems has been emphasized before and addressed using different approaches. Bobba et al. [10] determine certain pathologies that can lead to high abort rates. Blundell et al. [8] propose to commit transactions even in the case of read-write conflicts by repairing (re-executing reads to obtain the current version) transactions instead of replaying transactions entirely. Their approach does not apply to arbitrary conflicts but only to "non critical conflicts" occurring on auxiliary or bookkeeping data. Waliullah et al. [56] propose to detect and ignore non critical conflicts including false sharing, silent stores and write-write conflicts without intermittent reads. Improving TM performance by reducing the number of aborts has been addressed by Ansari et al. using transaction reordering [3]. Finally, Ramadan et al. [48] and Aydonat et al. [4, 5] propose conflict serializability to reduce aborts by relaxing concurrency control. While all approaches reduce abort rates in certain cases, none provides the capability of tolerating read-write conflicts entirely.

Reducing transactional overheads while maintaining unbounded transactions has been the goal of Tokentm [9], LiteTM [28] and EazyHTM [55]. While reducing overheads, the approaches are complex and introduce a significant amount of state that needs to be kept in main memory. In contrast, our multi-version memory controller provides all properties using a simple hardware indirection structure.

Yan et al. [57] propose a TM system that manages multiple data versions in main memory concurrently and decides during commit which version should be made visible to the other threads. The approach enables isolation similar to SI-TM, however, it does not avoid read-write conflicts.

Exploiting snapshot isolation as a means of concurrent programming has been extensively used in the database domain [22], in distributed systems including Google's Spanner [17], as a Middleware for clusters [35] as well as in high level programming languages like Clojure [27]. Riegel et al. propose to utilize snapshot isolation [49] for STM systems, however, the system is unable to support efficient snapshot generation in software and hence only supports Lazy-SI, a consistency model that is relaxed over SI. Write skew has been addressed in the scope of SI based database systems including the works for InnoDB [11], PostgreSQL [42], MySQL [29] and Hekaton [32]. Cheriton et al. propose HICAMP [15], a segment-based memory system that also supports multiversion concurrency control. However, the described architecture appears to require a significantly different processor architecture, while our approach only requires changes to the memory system. Merrifield et al. present Conversion, a multiversion concurrency control mechanism [38] based on the virtual memory system. Conversion supports creation of snapshots. However, it uses a repository-like commit-update API without being able to handle conflicts and hence does not provide transactional semantics.

## 8. Conclusions

Snapshot isolation transactional memory (SI-TM) provides significant benefit in reducing the abort rate of transactions. This allows applications to use larger-scale transactions and provides higher degrees of concurrency without the concern of poor and unpredictable performance that arises with conventional TM approaches.

We showed that SI-TM reduces aborts significantly except for applications with already low abort rates, in particular, by up to $1000x$ for microbenchmarks and by up to $100x$ for applications of the STAMP benchmark suite. We also show that SI-TM can provide speedups of up to $20x$ with higher degrees of concurrency over conventional two phase locking based TM approaches. Thus, the performance benefits appear to be significant on top of the fact that read-only transactions never need to abort in SI-TM.

Our implementation efficiently supports snapshots by leveraging a multi-version memory controller at the hardware level. Writes are implemented by creating a new version of the modified data item using copy-on-write which enables threads to operate in isolation and to concurrently access shared data without interfering on read operations. To reduce the cost of copy-on-write, we present a feasible hardware implementation of a multi-version memory controller. We evaluate our design using detailed microarchitectural analysis and show that a small number of versions, i.e. 4, are adequate for highly concurrent transactional environments. We plan to further evaluate the benefits of our hardware implementation versus a software multi-version virtual memory system as part of future work.

Overall, we believe that the SI-TM model with its significantly lower abort rates and better scalability has the potential to deliver on the original promise and hope for TM, namely to provide a simple concurrent programming model that offers good performance at a low implementation cost.

## 9. Acknowledgements

We are thankful to Pascal Marlier for the support on RSTM. We are thankful to Daniel Sanchez for his support on ZSim. We are grateful to Timothy Harris, Michael Chan, Ricardo Dias, Tor Aamodt, Stephan Diestelhorst and the anonymous reviewers for their useful feedback on earlier versions of this manuscript.

## References


[1] A.R. Adl-Tabatabai and T. Shpeisman. Draft specification of transactional language constructs for c++. In *Specification Draft*, 2009.

[2] C.S. Ananian, K. Asanovic, B.C. Kuszmaul, C.E. Leiserson, and S. Lie. Unbounded transactional memory. In *11th International Symposium on High-Performance Computer Architecture, (HPCA-11)*. IEEE, 2005.

[3] M. Ansari, M. Luján, C. Kotselidis, K. Jarvis, C. Kirkham, and I. Watson. Steal-on-abort: Improving transactional memory performance through dynamic transaction reordering. *High Performance Embedded Architectures and Compilers*, 2009.

[4] U. Aydonat and T.S. Abdelrahman. Hardware support for relaxed concurrency control in transactional memory. In *Microarchitecture (MICRO), 2010 43rd Annual IEEE/ACM International Symposium on*. IEEE, 2010.

[5] Utku Aydonat and Tarek Abdelrahman. Serializability of transactions in software transactional memory. In *Second ACM SIGPLAN Workshop on Transactional Computing*, 2008.

[6] H. Berenson, P. Bernstein, J. Gray, J. Melton, E. O'Neil, and P. O'Neil. A critique of ansi sql isolation levels. *ACM SIGMOD Record*, 1995.

[7] B.H. Bloom. Space/time trade-offs in hash coding with allowable errors. *Communications of the ACM*, 1970.

[8] Colin Blundell, Arun Raghavan, and Milo M.K. Martin. Retcon: transactional repair without replay. In *Proceedings of the 37th annual international symposium on Computer architecture*, ISCA '10, New York, NY, USA, 2010. ACM.

[9] J. Bobba, N. Goyal, M.D. Hill, M.M. Swift, and D.A. Wood. Tokentm: Efficient execution of large transactions with hardware transactional memory. In *ACM SIGARCH Computer Architecture News*. IEEE Computer Society, 2008.

[10] J. Bobba, K.E. Moore, H. Volos, L. Yen, M.D. Hill, M.M. Swift, and D.A. Wood. Performance pathologies in hardware transactional memory. In *ACM SIGARCH Computer Architecture News*, pages 81–91. ACM, 2007.

[11] M.J. Cahill, U. Röhm, and A.D. Fekete. Serializable isolation for snapshot databases. *ACM Transactions on Database Systems (TODS)*, 2009.

[12] Harold W. Cain, Maged M. Michael, Brad Frey, Cathy May, Derek Williams, and Hung Le. Robust architectural support for transactional memory in the power architecture. In *Proceedings of the 40th Annual International Symposium on Computer Architecture*, ISCA '13, pages 225–236, New York, NY, USA, 2013. ACM.

[13] Luis Ceze, James Tuck, Pablo Montesinos, and Josep Torrellas. Bulksc: bulk enforcement of sequential consistency. In *ACM SIGARCH Computer Architecture News*, pages 278–289. ACM, 2007.

[14] Hassan Chafi, Jared Casper, Brian D Carlstrom, Austen McDonald, Chi Cao Minh, Woongki Baek, Christos Kozyrakis, and Kunle Olukotun. A scalable, non-blocking approach to transactional memory. In *High Performance Computer Architecture, 2007. HPCA 2007. IEEE 13th International Symposium on*, pages 97–108. IEEE, 2007.

[15] D. Cheriton, A. Firoozshahian, A. Solomatnikov, J.P. Stevenson, and O. Azizi. Hicamp: architectural support for efficient concurrency-safe shared structured data access. In *Proceedings of the seventeenth international conference on Architectural Support for Programming Languages and Operating Systems*. ACM, 2012.

[16] Weihaw Chuang, Satish Narayanasamy, Ganesh Venkatesh, Jack Sampson, Michael Van Biesbrouck, Gilles Pokam, Brad Calder, and Osvaldo Colavin. Unbounded page-based transactional memory. In *ACM Sigplan Notices*. ACM, 2006.

[17] J.C. Corbett, J. Dean, M. Epstein, A. Fikes, C. Frost, JJ Furman, S. Ghemawat, A. Gubarev, C. Heiser, and P. Hochschild. Spanner: Googles globally-distributed database. In *Proceedings of the tenth Symposium on Operating System Design and Implementation (OSDI'12), Hollywood, CA, October, 2012*. IEEE Computer Society, 2012.

[18] L. Dalessandro, M.F. Spear, and M.L. Scott. Norec: streamlining stm by abolishing ownership records. In *ACM Sigplan Notices*. ACM, 2010.

[19] P. Damron, A. Fedorova, Y. Lev, V. Luchangco, M. Moir, and D. Nussbaum. Hybrid transactional memory. In *ACM Sigplan Notices*. ACM, 2006.

[20] R.J. Dias, J.M. Lourenço, and N.M. Preguiça. Efficient and correct transactional memory programs combining snapshot isolation and static analysis. In *Proceedings of the 3rd USENIX conference on Hot topics in parallelism (HotPar'11), HotPar*, volume 11, 2011.

[21] Dave Dice, Ori Shalev, and Nir Shavit. Transactional locking ii. In *Proceedings of the 20th international conference on Distributed Computing*, DISC'06, pages 194–208, Berlin, Heidelberg, 2006. Springer-Verlag.

[22] S. Elnikety, F. Pedone, and W. Zwaenepoel. Database replication using generalized snapshot isolation. In *Reliable Distributed Systems, 2005. SRDS 2005. 24th IEEE Symposium on*. IEEE, 2005.

[23] Pascal Felber, Christof Fetzer, Patrick Marlier, and Torvald Riegel. Time-based software transactional memory. *IEEE Transactions on Parallel and Distributed Systems*, 21(12):1793–1807, 2010.

[24] W.W.L. Fung, I. Singh, A. Brownsword, and T. Aamodt. Kilo tm: Hardware transactional memory for gpu architectures. *Micro, IEEE*, 2012.

[25] Lance Hammond, Vicky Wong, Mike Chen, Brian D. Carlstrom, John D. Davis, Ben Hertzberg, Manohar K. Prabhu, Honggo Wijaya, Christos Kozyrakis, and Kunle Olukotun. Transactional memory coherence and consistency. In *Proceedings of the 31st annual international symposium on Computer architecture*, ISCA '04, pages 102–, Washington, DC, USA, 2004. IEEE Computer Society.

[26] Maurice Herlihy and J. Eliot B. Moss. Transactional memory: architectural support for lock-free data structures. In *Proceedings of the 20th annual international symposium on computer architecture*, ISCA '93, pages 289–300, New York, NY, USA, 1993. ACM.

[27] R. Hickey. The clojure programming language. In *Proceedings of the 2008 symposium on Dynamic languages*. ACM, 2008.

[28] S.A.R. Jafri, M. Thottethodi, and TN Vijaykumar. Litetm: Reducing transactional state overhead. In *High Performance Computer Architecture (HPCA), 2010 IEEE 16th International Symposium on*. IEEE, 2010.

[29] Hyungsoo Jung, Hyuck Han, Alan Fekete, Uwe Röhm, and Heon Young Yeom. Performance of serializable snapshot isolation on multicore servers. In *DASFAA (2)*, pages 416–430. IEEE Computer Society, 2013.

[30] Vivek Seshadri Yoongu Kim, Chris Fallin, Donghyuk Lee, Rachata Ausavarungnirun, Gennady Pekhimenko Yixin Luo, Onur Mutlu, Phillip B Gibbons, Michael A Kozuch, and Todd C Mowry. Rowclone: Fast and efficient in-dram copy and initialization of bulk data. In *Microarchitecture, 2013. MICRO-46. 46th Annual IEEE/ACM International Symposium on*, 2013.

[31] S. Kumar, M. Chu, C.J. Hughes, P. Kundu, and A. Nguyen. Hybrid transactional memory. In *Proceedings of the eleventh ACM SIGPLAN symposium on Principles and practice of parallel programming*. ACM, 2006.

[32] Per-Åke Larson, Spyros Blanas, Cristian Diaconu, Craig Freedman, Jignesh M Patel, and Mike Zwilling. High-performance concurrency control mechanisms for main-memory databases. *Proceedings of the VLDB Endowment*, 5(4):298–309, 2011.

[33] Viktor Leis, Alfons Kemper, and Thomas Neumann. Exploiting hardware transactional memory in main-memory databases. In *Proc. of ICDE*, 2014.

[34] Kevin M. Lepak, Gordon B. Bell, and Mikko H. Lipasti. Silent stores and store value locality. *IEEE Trans. Comput.*, pages 1174–1190, November 2001.

[35] Y. Lin, B. Kemme, M. Patiño-Martínez, and R. Jiménez-Peris. Middleware based data replication providing snapshot isolation. In *Proceedings of the 2005 ACM SIGMOD international conference on Management of data*. ACM, 2005.

[36] C.K. Luk, R. Cohn, R. Muth, H. Patil, A. Klauser, G. Lowney, S. Wallace, V.J. Reddi, and K. Hazelwood. Pin: building customized program analysis tools with dynamic instrumentation. In *ACM SIGPLAN Notices*. ACM, 2005.

[37] V.J. Marathe, M.F. Spear, C. Heriot, A. Acharya, D. Eisenstat, W.N. Scherer III, and M.L. Scott. Lowering the overhead of nonblocking software transactional memory. In *Workshop on Languages, Compilers, and Hardware Support for Transactional Computing (TRANSACT)*, 2006.

[38] Timothy Merrifield and Jakob Eriksson. Conversion: multi-version concurrency control for main memory segments. In *Proceedings of the 8th ACM European Conference on Computer Systems*, pages 127–139. ACM, 2013.

[39] C.C. Minh, J.W. Chung, C. Kozyrakis, and K. Olukotun. Stamp: Stanford transactional applications for multi-processing. In *Workload Characterization, 2008. IISWC 2008. IEEE International Symposium on*. IEEE, 2008.

[40] K.E. Moore, J. Bobba, M.J. Moravan, M.D. Hill, and D.A. Wood. Logtm: Log-based transactional memory. In *Proceedings of the 12th International Symposium on High-Performance Computer Architecture (HPCA-12)*. Austin: IEEE Computer Society, 2006.

[41] M. Olszewski, J. Cutler, and J.G. Steffan. Judostm: A dynamic binary-rewriting approach to software transactional memory. In *Parallel Architecture and Compilation Techniques, 2007. PACT 2007. 16th International Conference on*. IEEE, 2007.

[42] D.R.K. Ports and K. Grittner. Serializable snapshot isolation in postgresql. *Proceedings of the VLDB Endowment*, 2012.

[43] Seth H Pugsley, Manu Awasthi, Niti Madan, Naveen Muralimanohar, and Rajeev Balasubramonian. Scalable and reliable communication for hardware transactional memory. In *Proceedings of the 17th international conference on Parallel architectures and compilation techniques*, pages 144–154. ACM, 2008.

[44] Xuehai Qian, Wonsun Ahn, and Josep Torrellas. Scalablebulk: Scalable cache coherence for atomic blocks in a lazy environment. In *Proceedings of the 2010 43rd Annual IEEE/ACM International Symposium on Microarchitecture*, pages 447–458. IEEE Computer Society, 2010.

[45] R. Rajwar and J.R. Goodman. Speculative lock elision: Enabling highly concurrent multithreaded execution. In *Proceedings of the 34th annual ACM/IEEE international symposium on Microarchitecture*, pages 294–305. IEEE Computer Society, 2001.

[46] R. Rajwar, M. Herlihy, and K. Lai. Virtualizing transactional memory. In *Computer Architecture, 2005. ISCA'05. Proceedings. 32nd International Symposium on*. IEEE, 2005.

[47] Ravi Rajwar and James R. Goodman. Transactional lock-free execution of lock-based programs. In *Proceedings of the 10th international conference on Architectural support for programming languages and operating systems (ASPLOS)*. IEEE Computer Society, 2002.

[48] Hany E Ramadan, Christopher J Rossbach, and Emmett Witchel. Dependence-aware transactional memory for increased concurrency. In *Proceedings of the 41st annual IEEE/ACM International Symposium on Microarchitecture*, pages 246–257. IEEE Computer Society, 2008.

[49] T. Riegel, C. Fetzer, and P. Felber. Snapshot isolation for software transactional memory. In *TRANSACT06*, volume 298, 2006.

[50] B. Saha, A.R. Adl-Tabatabai, and Q. Jacobson. Architectural support for software transactional memory. In *Microarchitecture, 2006. MICRO-39. 39th Annual IEEE/ACM International Symposium on*. IEEE, 2006.

[51] Daniel Sanchez and Christos Kozyrakis. ZSim: Fast and Accurate Microarchitectural Simulation of Thousand-Core Systems. In *Proceedings of the 40th annual International Symposium in Computer Architecture (ISCA-40)*, June 2013.

[52] Nir Shavit and Dan Touitou. Software transactional memory. *Distributed Computing*, pages 99–116, 1997.

[53] Tatiana Shpeisman, Ali-Reza Adl-Tabatabai, Robert Geva, Yang Ni, and Adam Welc. Towards transactional memory semantics for c++. In *Proceedings of the twenty-first annual symposium on Parallelism in algorithms and architectures*,

SPAA '09, pages 49–58, New York, NY, USA, 2009. IEEE Computer Society, ACM.

[54] Arrvindh Shriraman, Sandhya Dwarkadas, and Michael L Scott. Flexible decoupled transactional memory support. In *ACM SIGARCH Computer Architecture News*, pages 139–150. IEEE Computer Society, 2008.

[55] S. Tomić, C. Perfumo, C. Kulkarni, A. Armejach, A. Cristal, O. Unsal, T. Harris, and M. Valero. Eazyhtm: eager-lazy hardware transactional memory. In *Proceedings of the 42nd Annual IEEE/ACM International Symposium on Microarchitecture*, pages 145–155. ACM, 2009.

[56] Mridha-Mohammad Waliullah and Per Stenstrom. Classification and elimination of conflicts in hardware transactional memory systems. In *SBAC-PAD*. IEEE Computer Society, 2011.

[57] Zhichao Yan, Hong Jiang, Dan Feng, Lei Tian, and Yujuan Tan. Suv: A novel single-update version-management scheme for hardware transactional memory systems. In *Proceedings of the 2012 IEEE 26th International Parallel and Distributed Processing Symposium*, IPDPS '12, Washington, DC, USA, 2012. IEEE Computer Society.

[58] Richard M. Yoo, Christopher J. Hughes, Konrad Lai, and Ravi Rajwar. Performance evaluation of intel® transactional synchronization extensions for high-performance computing. In *Proceedings of SC13: International Conference for High Performance Computing, Networking, Storage and Analysis*, SC '13, pages 19:1–19:11, New York, NY, USA, 2013. ACM.

# Appendices

## A. Active Versions

To investigate the number of data versions that are actually needed within the MVM, we configured the SI-TM system to support an unbounded number of versions. We then ran the benchmarks using 32 threads and counted the number of transactional accesses to each version. We do not include non transactional accesses which always target the most current snapshot. Table 2 lists the number of accesses to the five most recent versions. Accesses to older versions are summed up and shown as tail. As it can be seen, most accesses target the most current version and less than 1% of the accesses target versions older than the 4th. Thus, an MVM supporting up to 4 versions would be adequate to avoid aborts due to excessive versions with this level of concurrency.

| Ver. | Array | List | RBTree | Genome |
|---|---|---|---|---|
| 1st | 20410450 | 6909 | 44187 | 964624 |
| 2nd | 1152514 | 10 | 30198 | 8256 |
| 3rd | 30659 | 1 | 12231 | 553 |
| 4th | 1344 | 1 | 3188 | 96 |
| 5th | 0 | 1 | 562 | 36 |
| tail | 0 | 1 | 300 | 20 |
| Ver. | Kmeans | Bayes | SSCA2 | Labyrinth |
| 1st | 382768 | 6944 | 46018 | 3922 |
| 2nd | 143171 | 107 | 400 | 2413 |
| 3rd | 9121 | 12 | 1 | 306 |
| 4th | 1553 | 9 | 1 | 27 |
| 5th | 1465 | 1 | 0 | 2 |
| tail | 3000 | 0 | 9 | 0 |
| Ver. | Vacation | Intruder | | |
| 1st | 61962 | 26369635 | | |
| 2nd | 614 | 481590 | | |
| 3rd | 4 | 348473 | | |
| 4th | 2 | 26142 | | |
| 5th | 0 | 31169 | | |
| tail | 0 | 7000 | | |

Table 2: Number of accesses to specific MVM Versions

# Transactionalizing Legacy Code: an Experience Report Using GCC and Memcached *

Wenjia Ruan, Trilok Vyas, Yujie Liu, and Michael Spear
Lehigh University
{wer210, trv211, yul510, spear}@cse.lehigh.edu

## Abstract

The addition of transactional memory (TM) support to existing languages provides the opportunity to create new software from scratch using transactions, and also to simplify or extend legacy code by replacing existing synchronization with language-level transactions. In this paper, we describe our experiences transactionalizing the memcached application through the use of the GCC implementation of the Draft C++ TM Specification. We present experiences and recommendations that we hope will guide the effort to integrate TM into languages, and that may also contribute to the growing collective knowledge about how programmers can begin to exploit TM in existing production-quality software.

***Categories and Subject Descriptors*** D.1.3 [*Programming Techniques*]: Concurrent Programming—Parallel Programming

***Keywords*** Transactional Memory; memcached; GCC; C++

## 1. Introduction

For over a decade, Transactional Memory (TM) [13, 31] has been promoted as an efficient programming idiom for simplifying the creation of concurrent software. In recent years, the C/C++ community has made great strides toward integrating TM into mainstream products, and today there is both a draft specification [1] and a set of reference compiler implementations (GCC, Intel CC, LLVM, and xlC).

The integration of TM into C++ enables its use in two directions. First, it allows programmers to create new software from scratch that is designed around transactional constructs. Second, it enables existing software to be retrofitted with transactions, either to simplify the creation of new features, or to improve (from a performance or maintenance perspective) existing code. In the former category, studies by Rossbach et al. [28] and Pankratius and Adl-Tabatabai [24] have shown that TM can simplify the creation of new software. Similarly, there are several microbenchmark and benchmark suites that demonstrate the use of TM, most notably STAMP [23], EigenBench [15], Atomic Quake [37], Lee-TM [2], SynQuake [20], and RMS-TM [16].

While these benchmarks and studies collectively provide a good platform for evaluating TM implementations, they treat the STM interface as a constant. Our effort in this paper is complementary: we are interested in evaluating the proposed C++ TM interface. Our approach is to transactionalize a real-world application using the Draft C++ TM Specification, with an eye towards identifying (a) what common programming patterns and idioms are not well supported, (b) what features are cumbersome or difficult to use, and (c) what performance implications the specification carries.

For the purpose of this study, we used the open-source GCC compiler to replace locks with transactions in the popular memcached in-memory web cache. We used the developmental GCC version 4.9.0, which implements the Draft C++ TM Specification, for two reasons. First, it is widely available and easy to modify, which suggested that if we encountered bugs, we would be able to remedy them quickly. Second, its relatively transparent TM library enabled us to investigate the behavior of different TM algorithms and low-level design decisions.

Similarly, we chose memcached for two reasons. First, it is a popular and realistic application, but one that is still of a tractable size. It was not unreasonable to analyze all language-level locks within the application, or to conduct whole-program reasoning about the correctness of code transformations. Second, it is sufficiently complex to represent a challenge for TM: locks and condition variables are intertwined; there is a statically defined order in which locks must be acquired; there is a reference counting mechanism that employs in-line assembly and volatile variables (i.e.,

* This work was supported in part by the National Science Foundation through grants CNS-1016828 and CCF-1218530.


*ASPLOS '14*, March 1–5, 2014, Salt Lake City, Utah, USA.

http://dx.doi.org/10.1145/2541940.2541960

C++11 `atomics`); and it uses high-performance external libraries, such as a worklist implemented via libevent [21]. Furthermore, memcached uses some of these primitives in unconventional ways. For example, while there is a strict locking order (item, cache, slab, and then stats locks), this order is sometimes violated by using `trylock` to acquire an item lock while holding the cache lock. Similarly, in some cases a pthread lock is used as a spinlock, by acquiring it using a trylock inside of a while loop.

In our study, we used memcached version 1.4.15, which contains recent scalability enhancements. While our work is similar to a recent effort by Pohlack and Diestelhorst [26], it differs in that we are using memcached to analyze the Draft C++ TM Specification, rather than to assess the utility of a particular hardware TM mechanism.

The remainder of this paper is organized as follows. Section 2 describes the key features of the Draft C++ TM Specification that we evaluate in this paper. Section 3 then chronicles the steps we took to transactionalize memcached, and reports the performance impact of our efforts. In Section 4, we explore changes to GCC that would affect our results. Section 5 presents recommendations for designers and implementors of TM libraries, and Section 6 makes recommendations for programmers intending to use the Draft C++ TM Specification. Section 7 concludes.

## 2. The Draft C++ TM Specification

The Draft C++ TM Specification [1] integrates transactional memory support into C++ through the addition of several new keywords and annotations. The extensions can be roughly broken down into three categories.

***Transaction Declarations:*** Most substantially, the specification introduces the `__transaction_atomic` and `__transaction_relaxed` keywords. These keywords are used to indicate that the following statement or lexically scoped block of code is intended to execute as a transaction. There are numerous interpretations of the difference between these two keywords. For our purposes, *atomic* transactions can be thought of as being statically checked to ensure that they contain no unsafe operations. While the specification does not guarantee that the meaning of *unsafe* will not evolve over time, a reasonable approximation is to assume that atomic transactions cannot perform I/O, access volatile variables (i.e., C++ `atomics`), or call any function (to include inline assembly) that the compiler cannot prove will be safely rolled back by the TM library if the calling transaction aborts.

Relaxed transactions do not carry the same restrictions as atomic transactions; they are allowed to perform I/O and other unsafe operations. This is achieved by enabling a relaxed transaction to become irrevocable [34, 36], or perhaps to run in isolation, starting at the point where it attempts an instruction that the compiler is not certain can be undone. Such transitions are invisible, though they may present a scalability bottleneck and can introduce the possibility of deadlock (e.g., if two relaxed transactions attempt to communicate with each other through `atomic` variables, then since both must become serial and irrevocable, they cannot run concurrently). However, in the absence of such unsafe code, the two types of transactions are indistinguishable; both should scale equally well.

In addition, the specification supports *transaction expressions*. Transaction expressions are syntactic sugar to simplify code such as using a transaction to initialize a variable, or using a transaction to evaluate a conditional.

***Function Annotations:*** The specification supports two function annotations, `transaction_safe` and `transaction_callable`. A *safe* function is one that contains no *unsafe* operations. That is, it can be called from an atomic transaction. The compiler statically checks that safe functions only call safe functions, and that atomic transactions only call safe functions. In addition, the compiler must generate two versions of any safe function: the first is intended for use outside of transactions; the second contains instrumentation on every load and store, so that the function can be called from within a transaction and safely unwound upon abort. The compiler generates an error if it encounters a function that is marked *safe* but contains unsafe operations.

The *callable* annotation indicates to the compiler that a function will be called from a transactional context, but is not safe. We interpreted this as indicating that it is possible, but not guaranteed, that the function will call unsafe code. This, in turn, means the function can only be called from relaxed transactions. In contrast to the `transaction_safe` annotation, `transaction_callable` is strictly a performance optimization. An implementation is free to execute all relaxed transactions serially, or to try to execute them concurrently as long as no running transaction requires irrevocability in order to perform an unsafe operation. If a relaxed transaction attempts to call a function that the programmer has not annotated as `callable` or `safe`, then unless the compiler has inferred the safety of that function, the transaction must become serial and irrevocable.

Based on this interpretation, we concluded that if a function cannot be marked `safe`, on account of possibly performing I/O or some other unsafe operation, then it should be marked `callable` to ensure that calls to that function from a relaxed transaction do not cause serialization in those instances where the function does not perform an unsafe operation. As an example, consider the following code segment:

```
__transaction_relaxed {
  ...
  if (verbose)
    fprintf(stderr, message);
  ...
}
```

When `verbose` is false, this transaction need not become irrevocable. When it is true, the inability of the TM system to undo writes to stderr necessitates that it become irrevocable before calling fprintf. Regardless of the value of verbose, it must be relaxed: the compiler cannot guarantee that it will never require irrevocability.

***Exception Support:*** The third category of extensions in the Draft C++ TM Specification pertain to exceptions. When a transaction encounters a throw statement, failure atomicity may require the transaction to undo all of its effects; in other cases it may be desirable for the transaction to commit its partial state. To express this difference, the specification provides the __transaction_cancel statement.

Clearly, an irrevocable relaxed transaction cannot undo its effects, and indeed it is not correct in the current specification for any relaxed transaction to cancel itself. Atomic transactions may explicitly cancel themselves, and may even do so in the absence of exceptions. This, however, creates a challenge: with separate compilation, the compiler may not be able to determine whether a transaction_safe function called by a relaxed transaction will attempt to cancel. To remedy the problem, an additional may_cancel_outer annotation is required on some safe functions.

***Extensions*** For the purposes of our work, it is useful to consider two extensions to the Draft C++ TM Specification, both of which are supported in GCC. The first is the transaction_pure annotation, which allows programmers to indicate that certain functions are transaction safe without their memory accesses being instrumented. While this is intended as a performance optimization, its implementation is not checked: for example, one could annotate printf as being transaction_pure, and then the compiler would allow calls to printf from within a transaction.

The second extension allows registration of functions to run after a transaction commits or aborts. Functions registered as onCommit handlers run after a transaction commits. Functions registered via onAbort handlers run after an aborted transaction had undone any memory effects, but before it retries. Both take a single untyped parameter.

## 3. Transactionalizing Memcached

The Draft C++ TM Specification appears to offer a simple route to transactionalizing legacy code: one need only replace all lock-based critical sections with relaxed transactions. Since the existing lock-based code does not require compiler support to undo effects, there is no need for __transaction_cancel. Consequently, it would seem that atomic transactions are unnecessary, and transaction_callable annotations optional.

There are two flaws in this line of thinking. First, many programs contain condition variables, which require the use of an associated mutex. Dealing with condition synchronization currently requires ad-hoc solutions, and we discuss our solution for memcached below. Secondly, relaxed transactions are prone to serialization when they encounter an unsafe operation. Currently, there are no tools for easily identifying serialization points in relaxed transactions. Thus we claim that programmers should think of relaxed and atomic transactions as differing in terms of the performance model they carry: relaxed transactions have no performance guarantees, but atomic transactions guarantee that serialization will be avoided wherever possible.

Given this performance model, programmers can replace relaxed transactions with atomic transactions to gain a static guarantee that those transactions will not cause unnecessary serialization. To guide this effort, the programmer can use error messages from incorrect uses of atomic transactions and transaction_safe attributes as a tool for identifying unsafe operations.

We eliminated all contended locks in memcached, without requiring relaxed transactions in the final code. We first identified the locks that should be replaced, and then modified any condition synchronization built atop those locks. Next, we applied the Draft C++ TM Specification to the fullest extent possible to replace locks with atomic or relaxed transactions. We then developed transaction-safe alternatives to unsafe standard libraries. Finally, we applied onCommit handlers to eliminate all remaining relaxed transactions, resulting in a program in which no transaction required serialization to complete.

### 3.1 Identifying Locks

Our first step was to identify those locks that indeed were worthy of removal. There are four categories of locks in memcached, which are acquired in the following order:

1. item locks: These locks protect individual elements in the hash table that serves as the central data structure in the application.
2. cache_lock: This lock prevents concurrent modifications to the structure of the hash table (i.e., resizing).
3. slabs_lock: This lock protects the slab allocator. Slabs are memory blocks that store sets of objects of the same maximum size.
4. stats_lock: This lock protects a set of counters for program-wide statistics. While much effort has gone into moving these counters into per-thread structures, some remain as global variables.

We profiled the contention on locks by using mutrace [25]. This revealed that the cache_lock and stats_lock were the only locks that threads frequently failed to acquire on their first attempt. Thus it was necessary to replace at least these two locks with transactions. However, several more locks ultimately required replacing:

There were three instances in which the first operation of a cache_lock-protected critical section was to acquire the slabs_lock. When cache_lock was replaced with a transaction, the transaction immediately would serialize on account of the call to pthread_mutex_lock. Since the two locks are also released together at the end of the critical section, in these cases it is correct to change the lock order,

```
1  void func1a() {
2    __transaction_atomic {
3      if (tm_trylock(i.lock))
4        use_item(i);
5        tm_unlock(i.lock);
6      else
7        save_for_later(i);
8    }
9  }
10
11 void func2a() {
12   tm_lock(i.lock);
13   use_item(i);
14   tm_unlock(i.lock);
15 }
```

(a) `func2` privatizes `i`.

```
1  void func1b() {
2    __transaction_atomic {
3      // save_for_later isn't needed, since
4      // func2 no longer accesses i via
5      // privatization.  Instead, this
6      // transaction and line 11 might conflict
7      use_item(i);
8    }
9  }
10
11 void func2b() {
12   __transaction_atomic {
13     use_item(i);
14   }
15 }
```

(b) `func2` does not privatize `i`.

Figure 1: Example of privatization that may arise under less aggressive approaches to transactionalization.

i.e., acquire the `slabs_lock` and then begin a transaction in place of acquiring the `cache_lock`. However, in other cases the `slabs_lock` was only acquired well after the `cache_lock`, and the only way to prevent `cache_lock` transactions from becoming serial and irrevocable was to also replace the `slabs_lock` with transactions.

Another challenge related to per-thread statistics. Over the past few years, many of the statistics counters in memcached have been transformed from global counts to per-thread counters, which are protected by per-thread locks. Unfortunately, *any* operation on a mutex lock is unsafe to perform in an atomic transaction, and thus, we had to replace these locks with transactions. This highlights a flaw with relaxed transactions: when an unsafe operation is performed in a context where conflicts are exceedingly rare, it still necessitates the serialization of all transactions. One solution to this problem would be to make lock operations transaction-safe. Barring such an option, we were forced to replace uncontended per-thread locks with transactions.

Indeed, "transaction-safe" locks were required when replacing the lock governing slab re-balancing. In memcached, a "slab rebalance" lock is used by the cache and slab maintenance threads to prevent concurrent maintenance of the cache and slab data structures. While holding other locks, these threads might use `trylock` calls to determine whether a concurrent maintenance operation is in-flight. To remedy this, we replaced the rebalance lock with a boolean that was modified via transactions. This allowed concurrent transactions to check the state of the lock. While the lock was primarily acquired via a spin loop and `trylock`, in one case it was acquired via a blocking call. Lacking any better alternative, we followed any failed blocking acquire with a call to `pthread_yield`.

Finally, and most unfortunately, we had to replace the item locks, even though they were never contended. While the locking order in memcached is item, cache, slabs, and then stats locks, there are cases in which a maintenance thread attempts to lock an item while holding other locks that come later in the locking order. In these cases, either a spin loop wraps a call to `trylock`, or else a `trylock` is used and failure to acquire results in a handler being registered so that missed items can be processed at a later time (see Line 7 of Figure 1a). While all `item_locks` are acquired using spin loops and `trylock`, we were still faced with an uncomfortable decision: as with the rebalance lock, we could make the lock acquire and release into mini-transactions on a boolean variable, or we could replace every item lock critical section with a transaction. The former choice immediately led to explicit *privatization* [22, 33]: some data protected by item locks would be accessed within transactions, and also outside of transactions (but with the item lock held). We ultimately chose both routes, and developed two branches of the code, one with privatization and the other without.

An illustration of the difference is provided in Figure 1. In branch 'b', where item lock critical sections are replaced with transactions, func1 and func2 may run concurrently and cause conflicts, but `i` is only accessed from within transactions. In branch 'a', where item locks were acquired and released with transactions, func1a is able to inspect the lock, and to use `i` within a transaction as long when the lock is not held, but `i` itself might be accessed outside of a transaction in func2a. Furthermore, the small transaction to acquire the lock in func2a will implicitly take priority over the larger transaction that reads the item's lock in func1a. Note that while branch 'b' is more aggressive with respect to replacing locks with transactions, both branches are correct, since the default TM algorithm in GCC is privatization safe, and this level of safety is a requirement of the Draft C++ TM Specification. Note too that neither option is clearly simpler: branch 'a' required fewer net lines of code to change, but branch 'b' enabled the removal of several corner cases (e.g., the `save_for_later` code path).

```
/* initially mx_can_run = true */

void worker() {
  lock(L);
  do_work();
  if (mx_needed())
    if (!mx_running)
      mx_running = true;
      cond_signal(C); //replace with sem_post(S);
  do_cleanup();
  unlock(L);
}

void halt_maintainer() {
  lock(L);
  mx_can_run = false;
  cond_signal(C);       //replace with sem_post(S);
  unlock(L);
}

void maintainer() {
  while(mx_can_run);
    lock(L);
    do_maintenance();
    unlock(L);
    lock(L);
    mx_running = false;
    cond_wait(L, C);  //replace with unlock(L);
    unlock(L);        //replace with sem_wait(S);
}
```

Figure 2: Comments depict a transformation for removing condition variables used to wake maintenance threads.

```
    lock(stats_lock);
    increment(counter1);
    unlock(stats_lock);
    if (unlikely_condition) {
      lock(stats_lock);
      increment(counter2);
      unlock(stats_lock);
    }
```

Figure 3: Rapid re-locking in memcached.

### 3.2 Refactoring Condition Synchronization

The `slabs_lock` and `cache_lock` are used by memcached both to protect critical sections and as the lock object for condition synchronization using `pthread_cond_t` variables. The current Draft C++ TM Specification does not support condition variables, and thus we were required to manually transform all condition synchronization.

A simplifying factor is that condition synchronization in memcached follows two simple patterns. First, there are condition variables for notifying threads when work arrives on a network connection. These are not associated with contended locks, and we did not consider them. The second pattern is for coordinating data structure maintenance. In this pattern, many worker threads can attempt to wake a maintenance thread, which will then modify a data structure. A simplified version of this pattern is depicted in Figure 2. This pattern appears twice, for re-balancing the hash table (via `cache_lock`) and maintaining slabs (via `slabs_lock`).

One flag exists for thread shutdown, and another for determining if the maintainer is currently active. Every attempt to wait on a condition is immediately followed by a lock release, a back edge in the control flow graph, and a lock re-acquire. Furthermore, the code already ensures that there are no spurious wake-ups. Consequently, one can replace the condition variables with semaphores. The changes are trivial, and appear as comments in Figure 2. Rather than call `cond_wait` within a lock-based critical section, maintenance threads call `sem_wait` immediately after completing the critical section. At this stage of the transactionalization, worker threads called `sem_post` from within a lock-based critical section. In stage 3, these critical sections became relaxed transactions, and in stage 5, these calls were moved to `onCommit` handlers within atomic transactions.

This transformation resulted in changes to 10 lines of code, not counting comments, and had no impact on performance. While the transformation suffices for memcached, it may still be beneficial for TM to explicitly support condition synchronization (possibilities include conditional critical regions/retry[3, 12], punctuated transactions [32], communicators [19], and transactional condvars [8]). In particular, when `pthread_cond_wait` is not the last instruction in a critical section, and is in a deeper lexical scope, compiler support will be needed to transform the two "halves" of the critical section into separate transactions.

### 3.3 Maximally Applying the Specification

Having identified the locks requiring replacement, and having developed alternative condition synchronization mechanisms for those locks also associated with condition variables, we were at last able to begin using transactions. We replaced all targeted critical sections with relaxed transactions, maximally applied the callable attribute, and then systematically replaced unsafe operations with safe operations, so that transactions could be marked atomic. Recall that in the absence of transaction cancellation, it would have been correct to leave transactions relaxed after making their operations safe, but that the absence of relaxed transactions guarantees the absence of mandatory serialization.

***Replacing Locks, Adding Annotations*** We began by developing two branches, corresponding to the two approaches to item locks discussed above, in which the `cache_lock`, `slabs_lock`, and `stats_lock` were also transactionalized. This resulted in 51 relaxed transactions in each branch. We then traced all function calls from within relaxed transactions, and marked all functions for which we had the source as callable. This led to 38 annotations in the privatizing itemlocks (IP) branch, and 49 annotations in the transactional itemlocks (IT) branch.

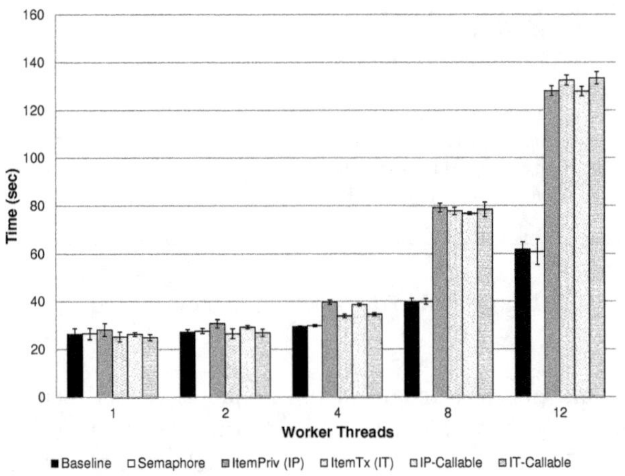


Figure 4: Performance of baseline transactional memcached.

Note that on a few occasions, a function would acquire a lock multiple times within a short region of code (see Figure 3). This pattern does not match with a mental model in which lock acquisitions are expensive. Furthermore, when this entire code region appears within an atomic transaction, transforming each critical section into a nested transaction seems unnecessary. This, in turn, implies that under some circumstances, using TM will encourage programmers to enlarge critical sections.

Figure 4 presents the performance of memcached with semaphores in place of condition variables, and then for each branch with (a) relaxed transactions but no callable annotations, and (b) relaxed transactions and callable annotations. Experiments were performed on a dual-chip Intel Xeon 5650 system with 12 GB of RAM. The Xeon 5650 presents 6 cores/12 threads, giving our system a total of 12 cores/24 hardware threads. The underlying software stack included Ubuntu Linux 13.04, kernel version 3.8.0-21, and an experimental GCC version 4.9.0. All code was compiled for 64-bit execution, and results are the average of 5 trials. Error bars depict a range of +/- one standard deviation.

We generated a workload for memcached using memslap v1.0, downloaded as part of the Ubuntu libmemcached-0.31_1 source package. To ensure that network overheads were not hiding the higher latency of transactions, we ran the memcached server and memslap on the same machine. We ran memslap with parameters `--concurrency=x --execute-number=625000 --binary`. We varied the memslap concurrency parameter (x)from 1 to 12 and matched memcached runs with the same number of worker threads plus an additional two maintenance threads. Note that perfect scaling corresponds to an execution time that remains constant at higher thread counts, since each thread executes 625K operations.

In Figure 4, we see that the switch from condition variables to semaphores is negligible, and that privatization (IP) appears to scale better than using transactions in place of

| Branch | Trans-actions | In-Flight Switch | Start Serial | Abort Serial |
|---|---|---|---|---|
| ItemPriv (IP) | 11201538 | 625K (5.6%) | 625K (5.6%) | 10 |
| ItemTx (IT) | 3462735 | 625K (18.0%) | 1.25M (36.1%) | 0 |
| IP-Callable | 10511717 | 625K (5.9%) | 625K (5.9%) | 10 |
| IT-Callable | 3467927 | 625K (18.0%) | 1.25M (36.0%) | 0 |

Table 1: Frequency and cause of serialized transactions for a 4-thread execution.

item lock critical sections (IT). However, there is no evidence to suggest that the callable attribute (IP-Callable / IT-Callable) improves performance.

Table 1 presents the serialization rates for each branch. Naturally, there are fewer total transactions when transactions replace item locks, since each item lock acquire and release is a separate transaction in the IP branch. However, IP and IT have practically the same number of relaxed transactions that encounter unsafe code on a branch, and must become serial (In-Flight Switch), and that encounter unsafe code on every code path, and must begin in serial mode (Start Serial). A trivial number of transactions abort 100 times in a row, and serialize for the sake of progress.

***Handling Volatiles and Reference Counts*** Many critical sections in memcached access volatile variables as part of periodic maintenance operations or condition synchronization. Strictly speaking, the semantics of such accesses are not defined, though in practice one can expect these volatile variable accesses to be an approximation of C++11's `atomic` types. Accesses to `volatile` and `atomic` variables are both considered unsafe, can not be performed in an atomic transaction, and force transactions to serialize. Therefore, our only hope of achieving scalability was to replace all volatile variable accesses with transactional accesses to non-volatile variables.

This transformation was straightforward. We renamed volatile variables, traced all compilation bugs, and resolved all errors by adding transactions that accessed the new non-volatile variables. In all, we only changed three variables, and the availability of transaction expressions meant that the total lines-of-code count did not change.

However, this transformation raises many questions. First, this transformation was only correct because we manually inspected the code to ensure that concurrent critical sections never interact via volatile variables. Second, memcached only consists of 7400 lines of code, and it is not clear that such a change would be realistic to push through a larger program. Third, GCC currently does not optimize single-location transactions, and thus this change could have a significant impact on performance. Finally, the specification must guarantee that the semantics of transactions are no weaker than the semantics of C++ atomic variable accesses. That is, a transaction expression for reading a variable must have the same ordering guarantees as a read of an atomic variable, and a transaction that sets a variable's

```
if (volatile_var == 1)
   block 1;
else if (volatile_var == 2)
   block 2;
else
   block 3;
```

Figure 5: Re-reading a volatile within a conditional.

value must have at least the same ordering guarantees as a store to a C++ atomic, where in both cases the access uses `std::memory_order_seq_cst`. This is already the case in the Draft C++ TM Specification.

Surprisingly, we found that in some places within memcached, nested `if` statements will re-read the same volatile variable (Figure 5). Based on the assumption that memcached is correct, we did not rewrite these codes.

Memcached uses atomic read-modify-write operations (e.g., `lock incr` on the x86) for reference counting. As with volatile variables, replacing these accesses with transactions was straightforward: we replaced every increment and decrement with a transaction, and replaced every read of these variables with a transaction expression. There was no change to the total lines of code. The main concern with such a transformation is that these assembly operations have memory fence semantics, which must then be guaranteed at transaction boundaries. There is also a question of optimality, since many critical sections increment the reference count, access a datum, and then decrement the reference count. With transactions, it might be possible to replace the modifications of the reference count with a simple read [7].

Performance for this "maximal" transactionalization is presented in Figure 6 and Table 2. For reference, the baseline memcached and "Callable" results are reproduced. At all thread counts, performance degrades, with significant slowdown at high thread counts. Even worse, serialization increased for both branches. In the IP branch, our transformation reduced the number of transactions that started in serial mode, but virtually all of these transactions still ultimately serialized. Such an outcome will consistently hurt performance, since code executes in an instrumented slow path up until the point where serialization is necessary, at which point GCC aborts the transaction and restarts it serially but with less instrumentation. By delaying the point of serialization, we actually hurt performance.

In the IT-Max branch, the transformation was less profitable, and the slowdown more pronounced. Two contributing factors are the increased number of transactions (each of which has higher latency than the code it replaced), and the dramatic increase in transactions that fall back to serial mode due to high abort rates. Since GCC's TM uses direct update [9, 29], the cost of aborts is expected to be high.

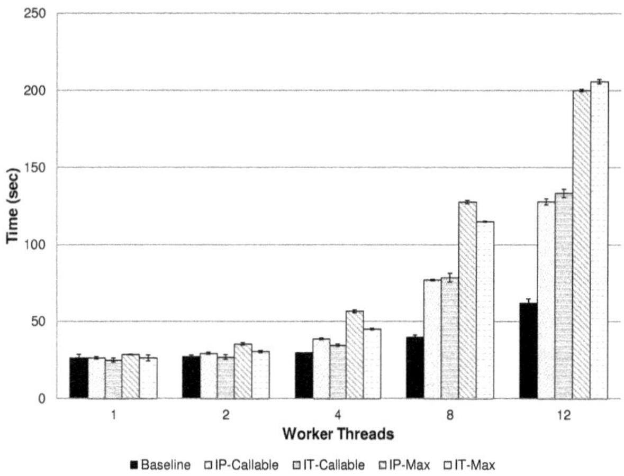


Figure 6: Performance of maximally transactionalized memcached.

| Branch | Transactions | In-Flight Switch | Start Serial | Abort Serial |
|---|---|---|---|---|
| IP-Callable | 10511717 | 625K (5.9%) | 625K (5.9%) | 10 |
| IT-Callable | 3467927 | 625K (18.0%) | 1.25M (36.0%) | 0 |
| IP-Max | 24085893 | 1162K (4.8%) | 0 | 87K |
| IT-Max | 6370739 | 559K (8.8%) | 1.25M (19.6%) | 66K |

Table 2: Frequency and cause of serialized transactions for a 4-thread execution.

### 3.4 Making Libraries Safe

The most prominent remaining cause of serialization was calls to unsafe standard library functions. These calls fell into a few categories. First, there were operations on untyped memory: `memcmp`, `memcpy`, and `realloc`. Second, there were basic string functions: `strlen`, `strncmp`, `strchr`, `strncpy`, `isspace`, `strtol`, `strtoull`, `atoi`, and `snprintf`. Third, there were calls related to variable arguments: `vsnprintf`, `va_start`, and `va_end`. Lastly, there was a single call to `htons`.

***Safety via Reimplementation*** Most of these functions are simple to transactionalize: we re-implemented the function and marked it transaction safe. This addressed calls to `memcmp`, `memcpy`, `strlen`, `strncmp`, `strncpy`, and `strchr`. Similarly, we re-implemented `realloc` in the naive way, by always allocating a new buffer and using `memcpy`.[1] Unfortunately, the Draft C++ TM Specification requires the transactional and nontransactional versions of a function to be generated from the same source. Thus to make our functions safe, we could not use custom assembly (e.g., vector instructions in memcpy), and thus we had to slow down the non-transactional code path by replacing calls to optimized standard library functions with calls to our naive implementations.

[1] We were able to optimize this slightly, since the initial size of the input is always known in memcached.

```
//wrap library function foo inside a
//pure function
[[transaction_pure]]
int pure_foo(char *in, char *out) {
  return foo(in, out);
}

...
//assume that max sizes of input and output
//strings are known otherwise, use malloc
//since alloca is not transaction-safe
int size = tm_strlen(shared_in_string);
char in[size1];
char out[size2];
//marshall data onto stack
for (int i = 0; i < size; ++i)
  in[i] = shared_in_string[i];
//invoke function with non-shared parameters
size = pure_foo(in, out);
//marshall data off of stack
for (int i = 0; i < size; ++i)
  shared_out_string[i] = out[i];
```

Figure 7: Example of marshaling shared memory onto the stack to invoke an unsafe library function `foo()`.

***Safety via Marshaling*** To make the remaining functions safe, we relied on a novel but unsafe technique. GCC is aggressive about avoiding instrumentation, in particular by noticing when reads and writes are performed to the stack [27] and/or captured memory [6]. By combining this observation with the `transaction_pure` extension, we were able to implement a pattern in which data was marshaled from shared memory onto the stack, so that an unsafe library function could then be invoked using only thread-local parameters. As needed, the result would then be marshaled back into shared memory. A generic example of this approach appears in Figure 7.

Using this technique could be dangerous in buffered update STM algorithms [5], unless the programmer can be sure that the first marshaling operation does not buffer its writes. Although the GCC TM implementation does not use buffered update, we still verified that GCC does not instrument the writes to `in`, or the reads from `out`.

The `isspace`, `strtol`, `strtoull`, and `atoi` functions could all be made safe in this manner, by marshaling the input string onto the stack, calling a wrapped version of the function, and then using the scalar return value without any further marshaling. `htons` did not require any marshaling, since its input and return values are both integers. Similarly, `snprintf` required all its parameters to be marshaled onto the stack, and its output parameter to be marshaled back to shared memory.

***Variable Arguments*** GCC does not yet support variable arguments within transaction-safe functions. Our solution was to manually clone and replace every variable-argument function with a unique version for every combination of parameters that appeared in the program. While this approach is tedious and does not generalize, we believe the effort is valid for a study such as this: there are no performance or correctness reasons why variable arguments will not eventually be transaction safe.

| Branch | Trans-actions | In-Flight Switch | Start Serial | Abort Serial |
|---|---|---|---|---|
| IP-Callable | 10511717 | 625K (5.9%) | 625K (5.9%) | 10 |
| IT-Callable | 3467927 | 625K (18.0%) | 1.25M (36.0%) | 0 |
| IP-Max | 24085893 | 1162K (4.8%) | 0 | 87K |
| IT-Max | 6370739 | 559K (8.8%) | 1.25M (19.6%) | 66K |
| IP-Lib | 25658618 | 625K (2.4%) | 0 | 15K |
| IT-Lib | 8211858 | 0 | 625K (7.6%) | 10K |

Table 3: Frequency and cause of serialized transactions for a 4-thread execution.

Unfortunately, the techniques discussed in this subsection are not general. For example, while one might argue that even after standard libraries become transaction-safe, marshaling would still be useful for third-party libraries, there are many dangers. Chief among them are that a third-party library might at some point begin using transactions internally, resulting in erroneous behavior (especially with buffered update STM), and that marshaling requires, in all cases, that the assembly code be inspected to guarantee that on-stack buffers are being updated appropriately. Another concern is that one must predict the sizes of buffers. In memcached, maximum buffer sizes were easy to discern in all but one location, for which we used a generous 4KB buffer for the input, and 8KB for the output. Furthermore, when a transaction employs the marshaling technique multiple times within a single transaction, the illusion of atomicity may be violated. For example, `snprintf` relies on locale information when handling floating-point values. In a pathological case, the locale could be changed by an administrator between two of these marshaled calls by the same transaction. The output would clearly not appear to be *atomic*. Finally, the absence of side effects in a library is not always certain. A function's implementation might change, introducing static variables or logging that is invisible to the caller.

Figure 8 and Table 3 present the performance when standard library functions were made transaction safe. We see a notable improvement in performance, especially at higher thread counts, though still not as good as the earlier IP-Callable effort. Analyzing the frequency of serialization, we see a marked improvement in all areas: fewer transactions require serialization when they start, fewer become serialized during execution, and fewer abort at a high enough rate to require serialization to ensure progress.

### 3.5 Moving Code Out of Transactions

Only 6 unsafe functions remained in transactions: `event_get_version`, `assert`, `sem_post`, `fprintf`, `perror`, and `abort`. We began by handling `assert` and

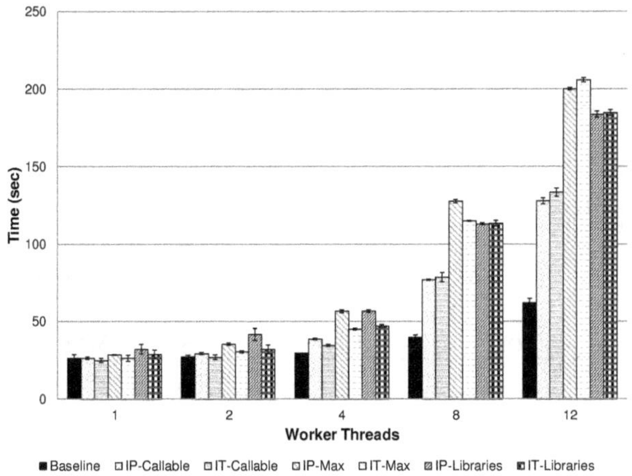


Figure 8: Performance with safe library functions.

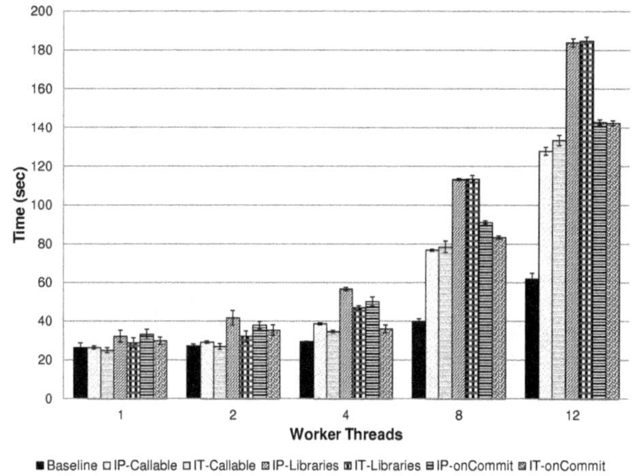


Figure 9: Performance with onCommit handlers.

| Branch | Transactions | In-Flight Switch | Start Serial | Abort Serial |
|---|---|---|---|---|
| IP-Callable | 10511717 | 625K (5.9%) | 625K (5.9%) | 10 |
| IT-Callable | 3467927 | 625K (18.0%) | 1.25M (36.0%) | 0 |
| IP-Lib | 25658618 | 625K (2.4%) | 0 | 15K |
| IT-Lib | 8211858 | 0 | 625K (7.6%) | 10K |
| IP-onCommit | 40305505 | 0 | 0 | 48K |
| IT-onCommit | 8130896 | 0 | 0 | 8K |

Table 4: Frequency and cause of serialized transactions for a 4-thread execution.

abort, which can immediately terminate a program, without calling any atexit functions. If the underlying TM is opaque [11], then at the point where the assertion evaluates to false or the abort is encountered, there exists an equivalent lock-based execution in which termination would be justified. Furthermore, since atexit functions are not called, other threads should not be able to observe the intermediate state of the transaction calling assert or abort. Consequently, it is safe to simply terminate the program at these points. To achieve this effect, we wrapped the assert/abort code and accompanying I/O in a pure function. Note that the I/O only involved string literals. Note, too, that while this change allowed many relaxed transactions to be marked as atomic, there was no impact on the frequency of serialization, since the relevant code never runs in a correct execution of memcached.

To handle event_get_version, we assumed that the version of libevent would not change during program execution. We then called the function outside of a transaction, and used the stored value in place of a function call.

Finally, we removed remaining fprintf (which log certain events to stderr when a program-wide flag is set), perror, and sem_post calls by registering onCommit handlers. In GCC, these handlers all run after the respective transaction commits *and releases all locks*. That being the case, our use of onCommit handlers has the potential to produce output in a different order than a lock-based program, since I/O performed by the handler does not complete atomically with the associated critical section. Furthermore, in the case of perror, we could not simply delay the function, but instead saved the errno and then called strerror_r in the commit handler. Unlike I/O, there are no concerns about ordering when delaying sem_post via an onCommit handler, since the only uses of condition synchronization are to wake up maintenance threads.

The only other challenge when using commit handlers was that some code could be called from both transactional and nontransactional contexts. GCC's TM does not expose the function for checking if a thread is in a transaction. We made this function visible to the program, in order to check for cases when the onCommit handler should be registered, versus those times when the handler should run immediately.

The performance following these changes took a remarkable turn. As shown in Figure 9, running times dropped to almost as low as the previous best, the simple IP-Callable branch. More importantly, when there is no mandatory serialization, transactionalization of item locks performs better than the use of privatization. Table 4 verifies that transactions no longer serialize at begin time, or due to an unsafe call during their execution. With all unsafe operations removed, the impact of serialization due to aborts becomes the dominant factor distinguishing the two approaches to item locks. The transactional version, which does not prioritize the small lock acquire/release transactions of the IP branches, has fewer serializations, leading to lower execution times.

## 4. Modifying GCC-TM

In the previous section, we eliminated *all* relaxed transactions, to include those that performed logging (via fprintf and perror) and those that ultimately would terminate the program (via assert and abort). Throughout this paper, we have claimed that atomic transactions provide a perfor-

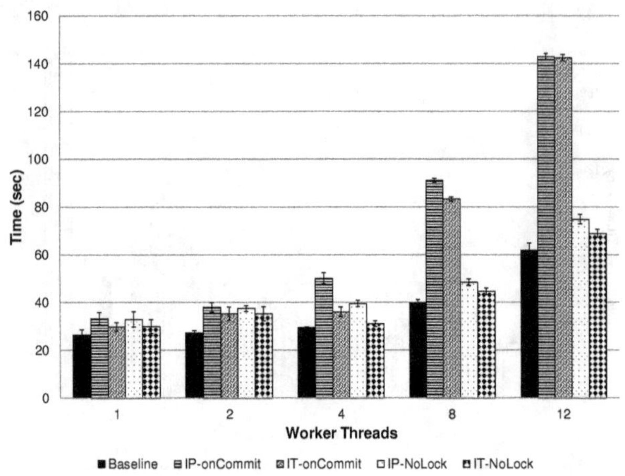


Figure 10: Performance without the readers/writer lock.

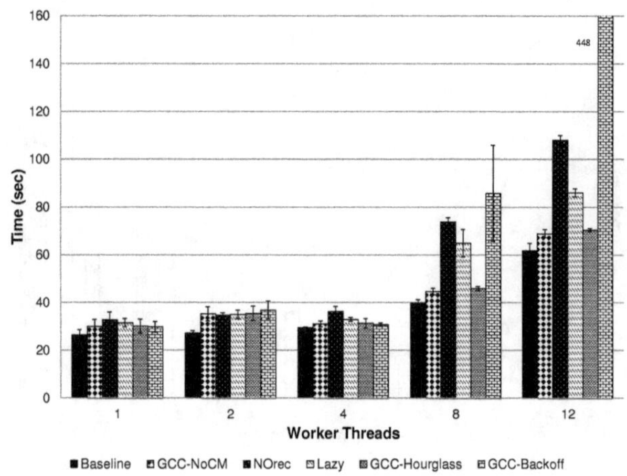


Figure 11: Comparison to other TM algorithms and contention managers.

mance model to the programmer. To illustrate the significance of this model, we made two further changes.

The GCC implementation of TM assumes that serialization is a common occurrence. To make serialization cheap, all transactions acquire a single global readers/writer lock in read mode when beginning a transaction, and release it on commit or abort. Transactions that require serialization acquire the lock in write mode. The availability of this lock makes switching to serial mode cheap, simplifies corner cases related to thread creation and joining, and enables a simple contention management policy, wherein a transaction becomes serial after 100 consecutive aborts.

The single readers/writer lock is an obvious bottleneck, but for programs with even a single relaxed transaction, serialization may be required for correctness. This holds true even with other contention managers [30]. Once we removed the last relaxed transaction, we removed the readers/writer lock from the GCC TM library, and added a separate lock exclusively for thread creation/joining. We then added a variety of simple contention managers (exponential backoff [14], a modified form of serialization called "hourglass" [10, 18], or simply no contention management), as well as a "lazy" STM algorithm[2] and the NOrec STM algorithm [4].

Figure 10 repeats the IT and IP results with onCommit handlers, and adds two new curves for GCC without the readers/writer lock. In these curves, there is no contention management: transactions immediately retry until they succeed. At high thread counts, we now can see that contention on the readers/writer lock is the primary source of overhead. Furthermore, performance is within 30% of the baseline memcached. This is despite expensive instrumentation (every read and write of shared data involves a function call, and every transaction boundary involves the creation of a checkpoint), and is in comparison to a highly optimized lock-based baseline.

[2] This algorithm uses the same lock table as the default GCC algorithm, but buffers updates and acquires locks at commit time

In Figure 11, we consider only the best-performing of these algorithms, IP-NoLock, which we now call "GCC-NoCM". We compare it to the Lazy and NOrec STM algorithms, also configured without contention management, as well as versions of the GCC STM algorithm using backoff or the hourglass contention manager (configured to prevent new transactions after 128 consecutive aborts).

With regard to contention managers, we see that the hourglass performance best matches performance without any contention management, making it an interesting candidate for cases where livelock is not expected, but programmers desire some guarantee of forward progress. At high thread counts, backoff performs poorly due to preemption. Furthermore, since the workload is heterogeneous, with dozens of source-code transactions of varying sizes and access patterns, backoff is not an optimal choice even at lower thread counts.

Similarly, we found that the GCC algorithm, which does not have buffered update, had the lowest latency and the best scalability. This is despite extremely high abort rates: at 12 threads, NOrec worker threads aborted once per 5 commits, Lazy worker threads aborted 14 times per 1 commit, and GCC worker threads aborted 12.6 times per 1 commit. In the case of NOrec, the frequency of small writer transactions induced a bottleneck on internal NOrec metadata; for both NOrec and the Lazy algorithm, the need to buffer byte-by-byte stores in `memcpy` and then read them later as words necessitated an expensive logging mechanism. Additionally, the variance in abort rate among threads was an order of magnitude lower for GCC than for Lazy, suggesting that Lazy was more prone to bouts of starvation.

These results suggest that real workloads do exhibit sensitivity to contention management and STM algorithm decisions, that real workloads place stresses on TM algorithms that research prototypes often ignore, and that expert programmers should be able to tune these parameters.

## 5. Recommendations for System Designers

We believe that the most viable path forward is for programmers to strive to avoid serialization, and system developers to both (a) optimize for the serialization-free case, and (b) facilitate the creation of programs that do not require serialization. To this end, we offer the following recommendations to designers of transactional runtime libraries, and to the authors of future TM language specifications.

***Implementors Should Assume Serialization is Rare*** The ultimate success or failure of transactional programming will depend on performance. Serialization of relaxed transactions is a dangerous obstacle. The GCC TM library assumes serialized relaxed transactions are common, and optimizes that case at the expense of workloads in which non-serializing atomic transactions abound.

To be clear, relaxed transactions are necessary: they are the only way to perform I/O using transactional data, and in the absence of I/O, relaxed transactions should perform on par with atomic transactions. When transactionalizing legacy C programs, the only justification for atomic transactions is the static guarantee that they will not force serialization. While it ought to be possible to approach the performance in Figure 10 with a different lock implementation [17], even a scalable lock will be a bottleneck: if many transactions must serialize, then the serial fraction of the program will be too high to achieve good performance. It is probably better to increase overhead for the serial transaction to avoid bottlenecks [35, 36]. Note, too, that the latest version of GCC requires every *hardware* transaction to use this lock, suggesting that hardware TM will not achieve its full potential as long as serialized transactions are the common case.

***The Specification Must Address Condition Synchronization*** The C++ Draft TM Specification does not allow a lock to be replaced with a transaction if that lock is also used in conjunction with a condition variable. In this work, we were able to leverage the specific communication pattern between threads, and replace condition variables with semaphores. Our technique does not generalize, and relies on the availability of `onCommit` handlers. Given the widespread use of condition variables in real-world programs, it is essential that the specification provide a solution. Otherwise, TM adoption will remain limited.

***Specify More Transaction-Safe Libraries*** Serialized relaxed transactions are currently the only mechanism by which calls to standard library functions are possible. Our ad-hoc work-arounds, while necessary for evaluating the specification, do not generalize, and are not safe in the common case. Programmers should not develop ad-hoc approaches, marshal parameters into private memory, or use `transaction_pure`. The programming environment should also provide support for managing terminating exceptions (e.g., asserts), so that programmers can continue to develop robust, self-diagnosing code while using transactions.

Furthermore, transaction safety should not inhibit nontransactional performance. In the current specification, a single function body is used to produce two code "clones" appropriate for transactional and nontransactional uses, and thus transaction-safe code cannot include inline assembly. In the long term, application programmers and system developers alike will benefit from the ability to provide different implementations of a function depending on the calling context.

***OnCommit Handlers Should Be Part of the Specification*** Our experience greatly benefited from `onCommit` handlers, which were removed from the 1.1 Draft Specification. Their return to the specification will allow programmers to avoid serialization, and to move non-critical code (i.e., logging) out of critical sections. We are less convinced that `onAbort` handlers are needed: the only role we envisioned for them in memcached was to employ backoff after a failed transaction. Specifying a simple contention manager interface is likely more appropriate.

***Ignore Further Ease of Use Concerns*** Finally, we believe that the developers of transactional environments should not worry too much about ease-of-use. In particular, we found that manual annotation of safe and callable functions, while tedious, was not difficult. Furthermore, it was not error-prone, since incorrect `transaction_safe` annotations immediately generated compiler errors. Similarly, being forced to re-implement volatile variables, locks, and condition synchronization was unpleasant, but ultimately rewarding. We discovered, for example, that replacing item locks with transactions removed corner cases, and indeed there are several optimizations to memcached that are now possible on account of transactional reference counts and the elimination of delayed maintenance code paths. If locks and volatiles were transaction-safe, we would not have identified these opportunities.

## 6. Recommendations for Programmers

The success of transactional programming will depend on cooperation between the programmer and system developer, where both work together to avoid serialization. Our recommendations to application developers appear below:

***Performance Model*** While there are semantic differences between relaxed and atomic transactions, for legacy code the key difference relates to the performance model exposed to the programmer. When a transaction is atomic, the programmer can be sure that there is no artificial obstacle to concurrency, whereas a relaxed transaction might contain some operation (to include a seemingly benign call to a variable argument function) that forces serialization. For this reason, we believe that programmers should rewrite code to avoid relaxed transactions whenever possible.

Our study entailed only one application, written in C, and did not use any of the exception-related features of the Draft C++ TM Specification, which apply only to atomic transactions. While it would be premature to draw any conclusions about the need for both atomic and relaxed transactions, we nonetheless feel that both play an important role. In our view, atomic transactions carry a performance model that is statically checked, and about which the programmer can reason. Even when performance does not match the model, the fact that atomic transactions were used guides the programmer's analysis: some potential problems, such as mandatory serialization, simply are not possible.

On the other hand, relaxed transactions provide a safety guarantee for operations that cannot be atomic, at the expense of a performance model. The best case performance for relaxed transactions should match atomic transactions, but without the compiler's guidance, we would not have been able to achieve any confidence that our use of transactions would avoid serialization. Relaxed transactions play a necessary role in allowing I/O with transactional data, calling libraries that are not yet instrumented for transactions, and allowing transactions to interact with nontransactional threads. Programmers must be savvy enough to know when a relaxed transaction is the right choice.

***Incremental Transactionalization is a Myth*** Our initial goal was to replace `cache_lock`. However, we had no choice but to expand our scope to include an array of item locks, as well as every major lock in the program, whether it was contended or not. When transactionalizing legacy code, we expect this experience to be the norm: if the last lock in a lock hierarchy is the only contended lock, then either the program lacks concurrency, or there is a trivial technique for splitting that lock into a set of low-contention locks. It is far more likely that some intermediate lock in the hierarchy will be contended, requiring the programmer to replace many locks with transactions.

While any transactionalization will entail considerable effort, it resembles a refactor more closely than a redesign. While we may be overly optimistic, we found that the tedious process of annotating functions and replacing locks and volatile variables provided an opportunity to identify optimizations in a number of areas (reference counting, interaction with the maintenance threads, statistics reporting), which we intend to improve as future work.

***Expect Limited Tool Support*** Manually diagnosing the causes of aborts and serialization in our program was challenging, and we eventually extended the GCC TM library to use the Linux `execinfo.h` infrastructure to provide more meaningful profiling data. While static information about serialization could be generated at compile time, and dynamic information about aborts at run time, we did not see the absence as unreasonable. These tools will arrive eventually, but system developers' effort should first be placed on making standard libraries safe, and condition synchronization possible.

Similarly, tools for automatically annotating functions do not seem particularly valuable. To achieve good performance, we had to modify most source files in memcached. That being the case, the additional task of annotating functions was not overly burdensome. We expect tools to eventually make this task easier, but in our opinion it is not urgent.

***Expect to Fork the Code*** Ultimately, we believe that the annotations and transformations we made to memcached are too complex and widespread to hide behind macros. Currently, memcached compiles on many operating systems and platforms, to include those that lack compiler support for atomic operations (e.g., `lock inc`), with macros hiding platform-specific implementation differences. The need for cross-platform support can be an obstacle to progress: it is even unlikely that memcached `volatiles` will be replaced with C++ `atomic` data types any time soon, and if such a conversion occurs, it will likely be handled via even more macros. Preserving multi-platform support while performing the modifications discussed in this paper would create inscrutable, un-maintainable code.

## 7. Conclusions

In this paper, we presented our experiences transactionalizing the memcached in-memory web cache using GCC. Our focus was analyzing the Draft C++ TM Specification, not on evaluating a particular TM mechanism or tool. Nonetheless, our version of memcached is a valuable benchmark, which we will release as open source code.

Our main findings related to the cost of unintended serialization, the effort required to avoid serialization, and the contract between system developer and programmer that is most likely to result in a viable transactional programming environment. Throughout the paper we identified areas where the specification could be changed to improve programmability, transformations and analyses that programmers will need to perform, opportunities for tool creators, and maintenance and performance challenges that will arise during the piecemeal transactionalization of multi-platform programs.

We hope that this study will assist standardization efforts by providing further insight into the challenges that will be faced when transactionalizing legacy code, and that our source code will provide TM algorithm designers with a new workload for evaluating implementations.

## Acknowledgments

We thank our anonymous reviewers, whose detailed suggestions greatly improved this paper. We also thank Justin Gottschlich, Victor Luchangco, Jens Maurer, and Torvald Riegel for many helpful conversations about the Draft C++ TM Specification.

## References


[1] A.-R. Adl-Tabatabai, T. Shpeisman, and J. Gottschlich. Draft Specification of Transactional Language Constructs for C++, Feb. 2012. Version 1.1, `http://justingottschlich.com/tm-specification-for-c-v-1-1/`.

[2] M. Ansari, C. Kotselidis, K. Jarvis, M. Lujan, C. Kirkham, and I. Watson. Lee-TM: A Non-trivial Benchmark for Transactional Memory. In *Proceedings of the International Conference on Algorithms and Architectures for Parallel Processing*, June 2008.

[3] P. Charles, C. Donawa, K. Ebcioglu, C. Grothoff, A. Kielstra, C. von Praun, V. Saraswat, and V. Sarkar. X10: An Object-Oriented Approach to Non-Uniform Cluster Computing. In *Proceedings of the 20th ACM Conference on Object-Oriented Programming, Systems, Languages, and Applications*, San Diego, CA, Oct. 2005.

[4] L. Dalessandro, M. Spear, and M. L. Scott. NOrec: Streamlining STM by Abolishing Ownership Records. In *Proceedings of the 15th ACM Symposium on Principles and Practice of Parallel Programming*, Bangalore, India, Jan. 2010.

[5] D. Dice, O. Shalev, and N. Shavit. Transactional Locking II. In *Proceedings of the 20th International Symposium on Distributed Computing*, Stockholm, Sweden, Sept. 2006.

[6] A. Dragojevic, Y. Ni, and A.-R. Adl-Tabatabai. Optimizing Transactions for Captured Memory. In *Proceedings of the 21st ACM Symposium on Parallelism in Algorithms and Architectures*, Calgary, AB, Canada, Aug. 2009.

[7] A. Dragojevic, M. Herlihy, Y. Lev, and M. Moir. On The Power of Hardware Transactional Memory to Simplify Memory Management. In *Proceedings of the 30th ACM Symposium on Principles of Distributed Computing*, San Jose, CA, June 2011.

[8] P. Dudnik and M. M. Swift. Condition Variables and Transactional Memory: Problem or Opportunity? In *Proceedings of the 4th ACM SIGPLAN Workshop on Transactional Computing*, Raleigh, NC, Feb. 2009.

[9] P. Felber, C. Fetzer, and T. Riegel. Dynamic Performance Tuning of Word-Based Software Transactional Memory. In *Proceedings of the 13th ACM Symposium on Principles and Practice of Parallel Programming*, Salt Lake City, UT, Feb. 2008.

[10] F. E. Fich, V. Luchangco, M. Moir, and N. Shavit. Obstruction-free Algorithms Can Be Practically Wait-free. In *Proceedings of the 19th International Symposium on Distributed Computing*, Cracow, Poland, Sept. 2005.

[11] R. Guerraoui and M. Kapalka. On the Correctness of Transactional Memory. In *Proceedings of the 13th ACM Symposium on Principles and Practice of Parallel Programming*, Salt Lake City, UT, Feb. 2008.

[12] T. Harris, S. Marlow, S. Peyton Jones, and M. Herlihy. Composable Memory Transactions. In *Proceedings of the 10th ACM Symposium on Principles and Practice of Parallel Programming*, Chicago, IL, June 2005.

[13] M. P. Herlihy and J. E. B. Moss. Transactional Memory: Architectural Support for Lock-Free Data Structures. In *Proceedings of the 20th International Symposium on Computer Architecture*, San Diego, CA, May 1993.

[14] M. P. Herlihy, V. Luchangco, M. Moir, and W. N. Scherer III. Software Transactional Memory for Dynamic-sized Data Structures. In *Proceedings of the 22nd ACM Symposium on Principles of Distributed Computing*, Boston, MA, July 2003.

[15] S. Hong, T. Oguntebi, J. Casper, N. Bronson, C. Kozyrakis, and K. Olukotun. Eigenbench: A Simple Exploration Tool for Orthogonal TM Characteristics. In *Proceedings of the IEEE International Symposium on Workload Characterization*, Atlanta, GA, Dec. 2010.

[16] G. Kestor, S. Stipic, O. Unsal, A. Cristal, and M. Valero. RMS-TM: A Transactional Memory Benchmark for Recognition, Mining and Synthesis Applications. In *Proceedings of the 4th ACM SIGPLAN Workshop on Transactional Computing*, Raleigh, NC, Feb. 2009.

[17] Y. Lev, V. Luchangco, and M. Olszewsk. Scalable Reader-Writer Locks. In *Proceedings of the 21st ACM Symposium on Parallelism in Algorithms and Architectures*, Calgary, AB, Canada, Aug. 2009.

[18] Y. Liu and M. Spear. Toxic Transactions. In *Proceedings of the 6th ACM SIGPLAN Workshop on Transactional Computing*, San Jose, CA, June 2011.

[19] V. Luchangco and V. Marathe. Transaction Communicators: Enabling Cooperation Among Concurrent Transactions. In *Proceedings of the 16th ACM Symposium on Principles and Practice of Parallel Programming*, San Antonio, TX, Feb. 2011.

[20] D. Lupei, B. Simion, D. Pinto, M. Misler, M. Burcea, W. Krick, and C. Amza. Transactional Memory Support for Scalable and Transparent Parallelization of Multiplayer Games. In *Proceedings of the EuroSys2010 Conference*, Paris, France, Apr. 2010.

[21] N. Mathewson and N. Provos. Libevent – An Event Notification Library, 2011–2013. http://libevent.org/.

[22] V. Menon, S. Balensiefer, T. Shpeisman, A.-R. Adl-Tabatabai, R. Hudson, B. Saha, and A. Welc. Practical Weak-Atomicity Semantics for Java STM. In *Proceedings of the 20th ACM Symposium on Parallelism in Algorithms and Architectures*, Munich, Germany, June 2008.

[23] C. C. Minh, J. Chung, C. Kozyrakis, and K. Olukotun. STAMP: Stanford Transactional Applications for Multi-processing. In *Proceedings of the IEEE International Symposium on Workload Characterization*, Seattle, WA, Sept. 2008.

[24] V. Pankratius and A.-R. Adl-Tabatabai. A Study of Transactional Memory vs. Locks in Practice. In *Proceedings of the 23rd ACM Symposium on Parallelism in Algorithms and Architectures*, San Jose, CA, June 2011.

[25] L. Poettering. Measuring Lock Contention, 2009–2013. http://0pointer.de/blog/projects/mutrace.html.

[26] M. Pohlack and S. Diestelhorst. From Lightweight Hardware Transactional Memory to Lightweight Lock Elision. In *Proceedings of the 6th ACM SIGPLAN Workshop on Transactional Computing*, San Jose, CA, June 2011.

[27] T. Riegel, C. Fetzer, and P. Felber. Automatic Data Partitioning in Software Transactional Memories. In *Proceedings of*

*the 20th ACM Symposium on Parallelism in Algorithms and Architectures*, Munich, Germany, June 2008.

[28] C. Rossbach, O. Hofmann, and E. Witchel. Is Transactional Programming Really Easier? In *Proceedings of the 15th ACM Symposium on Principles and Practice of Parallel Programming*, Bangalore, India, Jan. 2010.

[29] B. Saha, A.-R. Adl-Tabatabai, R. L. Hudson, C. C. Minh, and B. Hertzberg. McRT-STM: A High Performance Software Transactional Memory System For A Multi-Core Runtime. In *Proceedings of the 11th ACM Symposium on Principles and Practice of Parallel Programming*, New York, NY, Mar. 2006.

[30] W. N. Scherer III and M. L. Scott. Advanced Contention Management for Dynamic Software Transactional Memory. In *Proceedings of the 24th ACM Symposium on Principles of Distributed Computing*, Las Vegas, NV, July 2005.

[31] N. Shavit and D. Touitou. Software Transactional Memory. In *Proceedings of the 14th ACM Symposium on Principles of Distributed Computing*, Ottawa, ON, Canada, Aug. 1995.

[32] Y. Smaragdakis, A. Kay, R. Behrends, and M. Young. Transactions with Isolation and Cooperation. In *Proceedings of the 22nd ACM Conference on Object Oriented Programming, Systems, Languages, and Applications*, Montreal, Quebec, Canada, Oct. 2007.

[33] M. Spear, V. Marathe, L. Dalessandro, and M. Scott. Privatization Techniques for Software Transactional Memory (POSTER). In *Proceedings of the 26th ACM Symposium on Principles of Distributed Computing*, Portland, OR, Aug. 2007.

[34] M. Spear, M. M. Michael, and M. L. Scott. Inevitability Mechanisms for Software Transactional Memory. In *Proceedings of the 3rd ACM SIGPLAN Workshop on Transactional Computing*, Salt Lake City, UT, Feb. 2008.

[35] M. Spear, M. Silverman, L. Dalessandro, M. M. Michael, and M. L. Scott. Implementing and Exploiting Inevitability in Software Transactional Memory. In *Proceedings of the 37th International Conference on Parallel Processing*, Portland, OR, Sept. 2008.

[36] A. Welc, B. Saha, and A.-R. Adl-Tabatabai. Irrevocable Transactions and their Applications. In *Proceedings of the 20th ACM Symposium on Parallelism in Algorithms and Architectures*, Munich, Germany, June 2008.

[37] F. Zyulkyarov, V. Gajinov, O. Unsal, A. Cristal, E. Ayguade, T. Harris, and M. Valero. Atomic Quake: Using Transactional Memory in an Interactive Multiplayer Game Server. In *Proceedings of the 14th ACM Symposium on Principles and Practice of Parallel Programming*, Raleigh, NC, Feb. 2009.

# Fence-Free Work Stealing on Bounded TSO Processors

Adam Morrison *

Computer Science Department
Technion – Israel Institute of Technology

Yehuda Afek

Blavatnik School of Computer Science
Tel Aviv University

## Abstract

Work stealing is the method of choice for load balancing in task parallel programming languages and frameworks. Yet despite considerable effort invested in optimizing work stealing task queues, existing algorithms issue a costly *memory fence* when removing a task, and these fences are believed to be necessary for correctness.

This paper refutes this belief, demonstrating work stealing algorithms in which *a worker does not issue a memory fence* for microarchitectures with a *bounded* total store ordering (TSO) memory model. Bounded TSO is a novel restriction of TSO – capturing mainstream x86 and SPARC TSO processors – that bounds the number of stores a load can be reordered with.

Our algorithms eliminate the memory fence penalty, improving the running time of a suite of parallel benchmarks on modern x86 multicore processors by 7% – 11% on average (and up to 23%), compared to the Cilk and Chase-Lev work stealing queues.

***Categories and Subject Descriptors*** D.1.3 [*Programming Techniques*]: Concurrent Programming

***Keywords*** work stealing; memory fences; TSO

## 1. Introduction

The *task-based* parallel programming model – which exposes parallelism by expressing a computation as a set of tasks that can be scheduled in parallel – is used in many programming languages and frameworks, as well as in (multicore) MapReduce. These implementations of task-based parallelism dominantly employ *work stealing* for dynamic load balancing of the executed tasks [3, 11, 13, 20, 27, 32, 33].

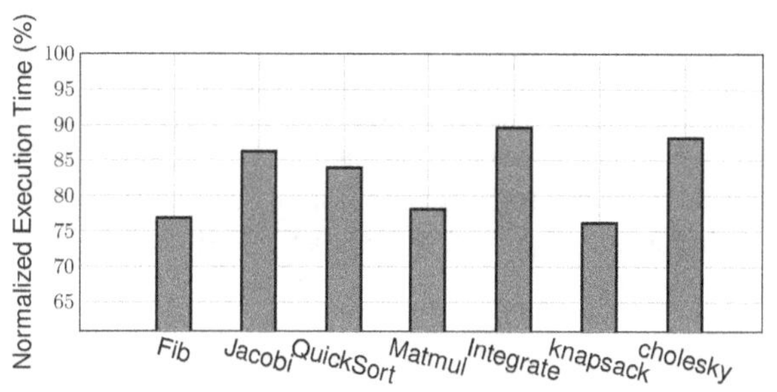


Figure 1: Single threaded execution time of several widely used CilkPlus benchmarks when not issuing a memory fence on task removal, normalized to the standard CilkPlus runtime on an Intel Haswell (Core i7-4770) 3.4 GHz processor.

In work stealing, each *worker* thread has a queue of tasks from which it continuously removes the next task to execute. While executing a task the worker might create and add new tasks to its queue. If a worker's queue empties, the worker becomes a *thief* and tries to steal a task from another worker.

Today's work stealing synchronization protocols [4, 9, 14, 20] are based on the *flag principle* [23]. The worker publishes the task it is about to take, and then checks whether a thief intends to steal the same task. If not, the worker can safely take the task because any future thief will observe its publication and avoid stealing the task. But for this reasoning to hold, the worker must issue a costly *memory fence* instruction to prevent the checking load from being *reordered* before the publishing store. As Figure 1 shows, this fence can account for up to $\approx 25\%$ of execution time.

It would thus seem that the worker's memory fence is unavoidable. In fact, Attiya et al.'s "laws of order" [10] are sometimes interpreted as saying just this [8]. In truth, however, the "laws of order" rely on certain assumptions [10] and may not hold when these underlying assumptions are invalidated – as they are in this work.

This paper demonstrates that *linearizable fence-free work stealing is possible* on mainstream multicore architectures with a total store ordering (TSO [1, 34]) memory model,



*ASPLOS '14*, March 1–4, 2014, Salt Lake City, Utah, USA.

ACM 978-1-4503-2305-5/14/03...$15.00.
http://dx.doi.org/10.1145/2541940.2541987

*Work done while a PhD student at Tel Aviv University.

such as x86 and SPARC. Our insight is that these processors' TSO implementation only allows *bounded* store/load reordering (i.e., a load can be reordered with at most $S$ prior stores), and that this bound can be used by a thief *instead of relying on the worker's fence* to verify that the worker could not have already removed the task it is stealing.

### 1.1 Bounded TSO

This paper introduces the *bounded* TSO memory model, which places a fixed bound on the size of the abstract *store buffer* [34] that models store/load reordering in TSO. This is the only type of reordering possible in TSO: a stored value gets buffered in the store buffer before reaching memory, allowing a later load from a different address to be satisfied from memory before the earlier store is written to memory.

We show that the mainstream TSO architectures – x86 and SPARC – implement bounded TSO (except for a corner case when there are consecutive stores to the same location, which can be prevented in software), and describe how to determine the reordering bound in practice.

### 1.2 Fence-free work stealing using bounded reordering

In a typical work stealing task queue, the worker works its way from the tail of the queue to its head and the thief works from the head towards the tail. The worker's fence removes uncertainty about the worker's position in the task queue by draining its store buffer.

Our insight is that if the worker does not issue a memory fence, a thief can use knowledge of the store buffer's capacity to detect when it can safely steal a task by bounding the number of task removals hidden in the worker's store buffer. To see this, consider the system's state after a worker works its way through tasks #10, #9 and #8 – without issuing any fences – on a processor with a 4-entry store buffer:

| | **stores by worker** | |
|---|---|---|
| in memory: | about to take task #10 | (earliest store) |
| buffered stores: | about to take task #9 | |
| | some store | |
| | about to take task #8 | |
| | another store | (latest store) |

If a thief now reads from memory it will only see that the worker is about to take task #10. But the thief knows it is missing at most 4 worker announcements due to store buffering, implying that the furthest store the worker could have issued is "about to take task #6." Therefore, if the thief intends to steal task $i <$ #6, it is assured that the worker has not taken this task yet.

Based on this idea, we describe the FF-THE and FF-CL algorithms, fence-free variants of Cilk's THE algorithm [20] and of the Chase-Lev algorithm [14]. In FF-THE and FF-CL, if a thief remains *uncertain* about whether it can safely steal – say, if it intends to steal task #6 above – it refuses to steal and returns a special ABORT value instead. In doing so we are *relaxing* the work stealing semantics, but unlike previous semantic relaxations [31], our relaxation maintains the queue's *safety* and does not allow a task to be removed twice – an intolerable behavior for many applications.

We further show that work stealing can be implemented fence-free *without* relaxing its semantics. We describe the THEP algorithm, which resolves the uncertainty in FF-THE using an *echo* mechanism. When a thief cannot steal due to uncertainty, it writes a value to memory and *waits* for the worker to *echo* it back, at which point the thief is guaranteed that the worker has observed its presence and will correctly synchronize with it if necessary. The thief does not risk waiting indefinitely because in programs using work stealing the worker keeps taking tasks until the queue empties, so it will eventually notice and echo the thief's value.

***Evaluation*** Modifying Intel's Cilk Plus [3] runtime (which is used by the C/C++ parallel extensions in Intel's compilers) to use FF-THE and THEP instead of THE improves the running time of the benchmarks from Figure 1 by 11% – 15% on average (and by up to 23%) on Intel Westmere-EX and Haswell processors. In addition, FF-CL outperforms the Chase-Lev algorithm by 17% on average on common graph problems, achieving performance comparable to that of Michael et al.'s idempotent work stealing queues [31], which are fence-free but can dequeue a task more than once.

***Sidestepping the laws of order*** Our algorithms violate a *tightness* assumption of the "laws of order" impossibility result [10], namely that every legal sequential execution can actually occur in the algorithm. In our algorithms, the execution in which a thief running alone steals from a queue containing one item cannot occur. FF-THE and FF-CL avoid this execution by refusing to steal in such a state, whereas in THEP the thief would wait for the worker and never complete. (We discuss this in detail in § 6.)

In showing how the use of bounded reordering enables circumventing the "laws of order" theorem by violating its tightness assumption, we hope to open the door for removing memory fences in other concurrent algorithms.

### 1.3 Contributions

To summarize, our contributions are:

- Introducing the bounded TSO memory model, showing that it captures mainstream TSO processors, and describing how to measure reordering bounds in practice.
- The FF-THE, FF-CL and THEP work stealing algorithms, which achieve fence-freedom by exploiting the reordering bound.
- Describing how the use of bounded reordering enables violating the "laws of order" tightness assumption.
- Implementation and evaluation of our fence-free work stealing algorithms, showing they eliminate the overhead of fences and outperform existing algorithms.

## 2. TSO[$S$]: Bounded TSO memory model

This section defines TSO[$S$], a bounded TSO memory model in which a load can be reordered with at most $S$ prior stores. The model is defined via an abstract machine whose execution provides an operational explanation for observable program behaviors under TSO[$S$]. In other words, any execution on a real TSO[$S$] machine should produce the same read values and final memory state as some execution of the abstract TSO[$S$] machine.

The abstract TSO[$S$] machine is essentially Sewell et al.'s x86-TSO abstract machine [34] in which the store buffers are bounded. We therefore describe the TSO[$S$] machine informally, and refer the reader to Sewell et al.'s work [34] for the full formal definitions.

***Abstract TSO[S] machine*** The machine consists of a set of threads that interact through a memory subsystem. Each thread corresponds to an in-order stream of instructions. The memory subsystem contains one FIFO store buffer per thread, whose *capacity* – the number of stores it can hold – is $S$. The memory subsystem is protected by a global fair lock, which is used to model atomic read-modify-write instructions (e.g., `compare-and-swap`) as being performed while holding the lock. (Elsewhere in this paper we simply use atomic operations directly.) The execution of the machine is a sequence of events describing actions performed by the memory subsystem and the threads, under the following rules.

The following actions are possible only when the memory subsystem lock is unlocked or held by thread $T$:

1. The memory subsystem can dequeue $T$'s oldest entry from $T$'s store buffer and propagate it to memory. We assume that each memory write is eventually propagated from the relevant store buffer to the shared memory [34].
2. $T$ can read. If $T$ reads from an address for which a matching store exists in its store buffer, the read returns the newest corresponding value in the store buffer. Otherwise, the read returns the value from memory.
3. $T$ can acquire the lock if it does not already hold it.
4. $T$ can release the lock if it holds the lock and its store buffer is empty (if $T$ wishes to release the lock while its store buffer is not empty, the memory subsystem must take steps propagating $T$'s writes to memory until $T$'s store buffer empties).

The following are allowed at any time:

5. $T$ can execute a `fence` if its store buffer is empty (similarly to #4, the memory subsystem must take enough steps to empty $T$'s store buffer first).
6. $T$ can write, enqueuing an entry to its store buffer, provided the store buffer is not full (if the store buffer is full, the memory subsystem must first dequeue and propagate at least one entry to memory, similarly to #4 and #5).

## 3. Work stealing

### 3.1 Work stealing sequential specification

A *work stealing queue* is a double-ended queue that supports three methods: `put()`, `take()` and `steal()`. A `put(`$y$`)` enqueues $y$ to the tail of the queue. A `take()` applied to a non-empty queue dequeues from its tail. A `steal()` applied to a non-empty queue dequeues from its head. A `take()` or `steal()` applied to an empty queue return EMPTY.

### 3.2 Background: work stealing synchronization

Modern work stealing algorithms [4, 9, 14, 20] strive to reduce the overhead experienced by workers performing the computation [20], even at the cost of making steal operations more expensive. As a result, these algorithms have converged on a similar design in which the worker uses a protocol based on the *flag principle* [23] to detect if a conflict with a thief might exist. If so, the worker switches to a heavier synchronization protocol to decide whether the worker or thief gets the task.

Figure 2a shows the general design. The queue consists of a (cyclic) array of $W$ tasks with non-wrapping head and tail indices, i.e., an index with value $i$ points to element $i$ mod $W$ of the tasks array. The head, $H$, points to the oldest task in the queue. The tail, $T$, points to the first unused array element. If $T = H$ the queue is *empty*. (For simplicity, we omit details of resizing the array if it becomes full.)

A worker performs a `put()` by storing the task at the tail of the queue, and then incrementing $T$. The TSO model guarantees that the store of the task and the subsequent store incrementing $T$ are not reordered.

To `take()` a task, the worker "raises its flag" by decrementing $T$ from $t+1$ to $t$, thereby publishing its intent to take task $t$ (i.e., the task pointed to by index $t$). It then *reads* the head index $H$ after issuing a memory fence to ensure that reading $H$ is not reordered before decrementing $T$.

If the worker observes that $t > H$, it can safely remove task $t$ from the queue, as it has verified there can be no conflict for task $t$: when the tail update became globally visible, thieves have announced intent to steal only tasks up to $H < t$, which means that a new steal operation will observe a queue that does not contain task $t$.

However, if the worker observes that $t \leq H$ there may be a conflict with a thief. The algorithms differ in the synchronization protocol used to handle such a conflict. In the following we continue with the description of each algorithm's protocol:

***Cilk's THE algorithm (Figure 2b)*** Cilk's THE algorithm uses a per-queue lock to synchronize between a worker and a thief, and also to enforce mutual exclusion among thieves. In case of a conflict on a task, the protocol picks the worker as the winner.

A thief acquires the queue lock and then "raises its flag" by incrementing the head index $H$ from $h$ to $h+1$, thereby

```
// shared variables
H : 64-bit int , initially 0
T : 64-bit int , initially 0
tasks : array of W work items

put(task) {
  t := T
  tasks[t mod W] := task
  T := t+1
}

take() {
  t := T - 1
  T := t
  fence()
  h := H
  if (t > h) {
    // Thief will observe t and will not try
    // to steal task t.
    return tasks[t mod W]
  }
  [Synchronization protocol (worker side)]
}

steal () {
  [Synchronization protocol (thief side)]
}
```

(a) Algorithm outline.

```
1  take() {
2    [Initial code (Figure 2a take()) goes here]
3    if (t < h) {
4      lock()
5      if (H ≥ t + 1) {
6        T := t + 1
7        unlock()
8        return EMPTY
9      }
10     unlock()
11   }
12   return tasks[t mod W]
13 }

15 steal () {
16   lock()
17   h := H
18   H := h + 1
19   fence()
20   if (h + 1 ≤ T) { // H ≤ T
21     ret := tasks[h mod W]
22   } else { // H > T
23     H := h
24     ret := EMPTY
25   }
26   unlock()
27   return ret
28 }
```

(b) Cilk THE [20].

```
29 take() {
30   [Initial code (Figure 2a take()) goes here]
31   if (t < h) {
32     T := h
33     return EMPTY
34   }
35   // t = h
36   T := h + 1
37   if (!CAS(&H, h, h+1))
38     return EMPTY
39   else
40     return tasks[t mod W]
41 }

44 steal () {
45   while (true) {
46     h := H
47     t := T
48     if (h ≥ t)
49       return EMPTY
50     task := tasks[h mod W]
51     if (!CAS(&H, h, h+1)) // goto Line 45
52       continue
53     return task
54   }
55 }
```

(c) Chase-Lev [14].

Figure 2: Design of modern work stealing task queues. Both the Cilk THE and Chase-Lev algorithms use the flag principle to detect when the worker and thief might contend for a task. They differ in the synchronization used to manage such a conflict.

publishing its intent to steal task $h$. It then issues a memory fence before checking if $H \leq T$. If so, the thief knows its increment of $H$ will be observed by any future worker and thus the thief can safely steal task $h$. Otherwise ($H > T$), there are two possible cases: either the queue was empty ($T = H$) when the thief arrived, or a worker has just published its intent to take the same task (e.g., initially $T = 1$ and $H = 0$, then the worker's decrement and the thief's increment cross, leading to a state in which $T = 0$ and $H = 1$). Either way, the thief restores $H$ to its original value and aborts the steal attempt.

This behavior makes it safe for a worker which (following its decrement of $T$) finds that $T = H$ to take the task. The remaining case, in which a worker observes $T < H$ after its decrement, is again caused either by an initially empty queue or because of a concurrent steal attempt (which will abort). The worker therefore acquires the queue lock and returns the task or restores the queue to a consistent state if it was empty.

***Chase-Lev algorithm (Figure 2c)*** The Chase-Lev non-blocking [21] algorithm uses an atomic `compare-and-swap` (CAS) operation to pick the winner in a conflict on a task. A thief reads the queue's head and tail, and if the queue is not empty (i.e., $T > H$) the thief tries to atomically increment $H$ from $h$ to $h+1$ using a CAS. If the CAS succeeds, the thief has stolen the task.

To support this simple stealing protocol (and in contrast to the THE algorithm) a worker must always increment $H$ to remove the last task. After decrementing $T$, if the worker finds that $T = H$, it restores $T$ to its original value and attempts to take this last task by incrementing $H$ with a CAS. Otherwise ($T < H$) then the queue was initially empty or a thief has concurrently incremented $H$. In either case, the worker returns `EMPTY` after fixing the queue's state by setting $T$ to $H$.

### 3.3 Linearizability of work stealing algorithms

The standard correctness condition for concurrent algorithms is *linearizability* [24], which requires that a method appears to take effect at some point in time during its execution. However, the Cilk THE and Chase-Lev work stealing algorithms are not linearizable under TSO [30]. For example, a `put()` may be delayed in the worker's store buffer and missed by a thief, causing a linearizability violation as the following Chase-Lev execution shows:

initially, $T = 0$ and $H = 0$

| | **worker** | **thief** |
|---|---|---|
| | `put()` invoked | |
| buffered stores: | $tasks[0] := item$<br>$T := 1$ | |
| | `put()` completes | |
| | | `steal()` invoked |
| | | read $H = 0, T = 0$ |
| | | return EMPTY |
| | | `steal()` completes |

In practice, such linearizability violations do not affect work stealing clients: The worker keeps dequeuing tasks until the queue empties, and so either it or a `steal()` invoked after the `put()`'s stores flush to memory will remove the task. Therefore, while adding a fence before the `put()` completes fixes these violations [30], deployed work stealing implementations do not do so.

Our fence-free algorithms have similar linearizability violations (and fix). We point this out to emphasize that these fixable linearizability violations are shared by existing work stealing algorithms, and are *not* the reason we circumvent the "laws of order" theorem and obtain fence-freedom.

# 4. Fence-freedom by reasoning about bounded reordering

This section derives our first technique for (worker) fence-free work stealing. We use Cilk's THE algorithm as a concrete running example, developing the FF-THE algorithm. We apply the same principles to develop FF-CL, a fence-free version of the Chase-Lev algorithm, in § 4.1.

The task queue we obtain does not comply with the original (deterministic) work stealing specification (§ 3.1), but with a *relaxed non-deterministic* specification in which a `steal()` operation can non-deterministically return `ABORT` without changing the state of the queue. We use non-determinism because the condition under which a `steal()` operation returns `ABORT` will be internal to the implementation and not part of the specification. Importantly, this relaxation does not impact the correctness of the work stealing's client (program), as it still maintains the task queue's *safety* and does not allow a task to be removed twice.

***Task queue safety*** Once a thief makes its intent to steal task $h$ globally visible (by incrementing $H$ and issuing a fence), it needs *to verify that the worker is not concurrently trying to take the same task*, i.e., that $T > h$. Knowing this makes stealing task $h$ safe: any subsequent `take()` attempt will observe the updated queue head and not try to remove task $h$ without acquiring the lock. The standard THE protocol ensures that the thief observes $T$'s exact value, so it can compare $T$ to $h$. But the point is that *any method* for answering the question "is $T > h$?" will do.

***Bounding worker position*** The technique we propose is to leverage the bounded store buffer capacity in the bounded TSO model to deduce how far off the worker's real position is from the position read from memory by the thief.

Let $S$ be the store buffer's capacity. (We discuss how to determine $S$ in practice in § 7.) A worker `take()` does one store to $T$ which decrements it by 1. Therefore, at the time at which a thief observes that $T = t$, the last value stored by the worker must be at least $t - S$. So if $t - S > h$, the thief can safely steal the task. Otherwise, it must return the new `ABORT` value. More generally, a thief can safely steal task $h$ whenever it observes $T > h + \delta$, where $\delta \geq 1$ is

```
steal () {
  lock()
  h := H
  H := h + 1
  fence()
  if (T − δ> h) {
    ret := tasks[h mod W]
  } else {
    H := h
    ret := ABORT
  }
  unlock()
  return ret
}
```

Figure 3: FF-THE: fence-free THE algorithm. The code of `put()` and `take()` remains the same, but for the removal of the memory fence in `take()`. The parameter $\delta$ is the maximum number of stores to $T$ by `take()` operations that can exist in the store buffer.

the maximum number of stores to $T$ by `take()` operations that can exist in the store buffer – which can also contain stores executed by the client program in between task queue operations. Thus, if we know that the client always does at least $x$ stores between consecutive `take()` operations, we have

$$\delta = \left\lceil \frac{S}{x+1} \right\rceil .$$

Figure 3 shows the modifications required to implement reasoning about the worker's store buffer in the THE algorithm. Notice that now the thief never knows for certain whether the queue is empty, because there is always uncertainty about the final store performed by the worker (i.e., $\delta \geq 1$). Thus, the condition for returning `ABORT` subsumes the condition for returning `EMPTY` in the original algorithm.

***Determining $\delta$*** To determine $\delta$, we need to obtain a lower bound on $x$, the number of stores between `take()`s. We can easily get a bound by inspecting the runtime's code. For example, the CilkPlus runtime [3] updates a field in the dequeued task after removing it from the queue. Thus, we trivially have that $x \geq 1$ for any CilkPlus program.

To obtain a better bound, we can run a static analysis on the basic block control-flow graph of the program and search for a weighted shortest path from `take()` to itself, where we assign the number of stores performed in a basic block $B$ as the weight of each edge going out of $B$.

***Context switches*** The discussion thus far assumes the worker always uses the same store buffer. This does not hold if the operating system reschedules the worker thread, moving it from one core to another. However, it is easy to see that an operating system moving a thread from core $C_1$ to core $C_2$ must drain $C_1$'s store buffer. For example, if the thread loads from a location stored to on $C_1$ while it runs on $C_2$, it must observe the value previously stored. Indeed, vendor manuals document this requirement [6]. The discussion in this section thus rightfully considers only the last core a worker runs on.

### 4.1 FF-CL: Fence-free version of the Chase-Lev queue

The technique of bounding the worker's position applies to the Chase-Lev algorithm, but with a somewhat different correctness argument. In the Chase-Lev algorithm a worker about to remove the last task undoes its update of $T$ and uses CAS to advance the queue's head. Thus, a thief about to remove task $h$ needs to verify that the worker's store writing $T := h$ cannot be in the store buffer. If this is the case, the thief is guaranteed that if the worker tries to remove task $h$, it will synchronize with the thief using a CAS. As before, checking that $T > h + \delta$ establishes this. Figure 4 shows the pseudo code of the modified algorithm.

```
70 steal () {
71   while (true) {
72     h := H
73     t := T
74     if (h ≥ t)
75       return EMPTY
76     if (t − δ ≤ h)
77       return ABORT
78     task := tasks[h mod W]
79     if (!CAS(&H, h, h+1)) // goto Line 71
80       continue
81     return task
82   }
83 }
```

Figure 4: FF-CL: fence-free Chase-Lev algorithm. The code of `put()` and `take()` remains the same, but for the removal of the memory fence in `take()`.

## 5. Fence-free work stealing without relaxed semantics

This section shows that work stealing can be implemented fence-free *without* relaxing its semantics. We achieve this by adding *worker echoes* to the FF-THE algorithm (§ 4) to obtain the THEP algorithm, a fence-free implementation of the standard work stealing specification. THEP also avoids a potential problem in FF-THE, in which a thief misses a stealing opportunity if it reads a true value of the queue's tail that happens to be within $\delta$ from the head. (Though in some cases this may not be a real problem, since it means the queue is almost empty and the worker can empty it soon.)

***Echoes*** To safely steal, the thief needs to verify that the worker has observed its update of $H$. To establish this, the thief maintains a "heartbeat" counter which it increments on each `steal()`. In turn, the worker writes the value it reads from this counter to a new variable, $P$, allowing the thief to wait for $P$ to reflect its counter. (Hence, the name THEP of the new algorithm.) TSO guarantees that any value the thief subsequently reads from $T$ was written by the worker after it observed the thief's update of $H$. The thief thus listens for the worker's "echo," reflected in $P$, until it knows the worker has observed its update of $H$.

```
84  // shared variables
85  H : struct { s:32 bits , h:32 bits }
86  P : initially ⊥
87  // T and tasks remain unchanged
88
89  take() {
90    t := T − 1
91    T := t
92    <s, h> := H
93    if (t < h) {
94      lock ()
95      P := ⊥
96      <s, h> := H
97      if (h ≥ t + 1) {
98        T := t + 1
99        unlock()
100       return EMPTY
101     }
102     unlock()
103   } else {
104     P := s
105   }
106   return tasks[t mod W]
107 }
```

```
108 steal () {
109   lock()
110   <s, h> := H
111   H := <s + 1, h + 1>
112   fence()
113   if (T − δ ≤ h) {
114     while (P ≠ s+1) {
115       if (h+1 > T))
116         goto Line 122
117     }
118     t := T
119     if (h + 1 ≤ t) {
120       ret := tasks[h mod W]
121     } else {
122       H := <s + 1, h>
123       ret := EMPTY
124     }
125   } else {
126     ret := tasks[h mod W]
127   }
128   unlock()
129   return ret
130 }
131
```

Figure 5: The fence-free THEP algorithm. As before, $\delta \geq 1$ is the maximum number of stores to $T$ by `take()` operations that can exist in the store buffer.

Using this approach yields an algorithm that meets the original deterministic specification of work stealing (§ 3.1) and never needs to abort a steal attempt. The price we pay is that occasionally a thief must block and cannot make progress until the worker arrives and updates $P$. Fortunately, in clients using work stealing the worker keeps taking tasks until the queue is empty, because it cannot rely on the work being stolen. Thus, if the queue is not empty, the worker eventually arrives and the thief can proceed.

However, we must make certain that the thief does not have to wait when the queue is empty, because in that case the worker may never arrive to respond. Therefore, if while waiting the thief notices that $T = H$ (the queue is empty) it stops and returns EMPTY. (The thief can miss a buffered `put()` and wrongly return EMPTY, resulting in a non-linearizable execution of the same kind that already exists in the THE algorithm, as described in § 3.3.)

***The THEP algorithm (Figure 5)*** The thief maintains its counter in the top bits of $H$. (The counter can also be maintained in a separate variable, at the cost of an extra load in the `take()` path.) On each `steal()` attempt, the thief increments the counter when it updates $H$. Then, if it is uncertain about the worker's position, it spins, reading $T$ and $P$ until one of the following occurs: (1) If the queue becomes empty (i.e., $T < H$ which means $T$ was equal to $H$ before the thief incremented $H$), the thief returns EMPTY (Lines 115-116). (2) If $P$ echoes back the updated counter value, the thief reads $T$ and proceeds as in the original THE algorithm (Lines 118- 127).

***THEP algorithm correctness*** The safety of the THEP algorithm follows from the safety of the FF-THE variant (§ 4). The remaining issue is whether waiting for a worker to arrive while holding the queue lock can introduce deadlock. To see why this cannot happen, notice that the worker tries to acquire the queue's lock if $T < H$. A waiting thief eventually notices this and returns EMPTY, releasing the lock.

***Why not use only echoes?*** We could still obtain a fence-free algorithm by *always* blocking the thief until it sees the worker's echo. However, this would harm the load balancing properties of the THE algorithm. For example, suppose there is one worker whose queue contains $W$ tasks of unit length, and $W-1$ thieves. Then if thieves always block, completing all tasks would take $\approx W/2$ time units whereas the original THE takes one time unit. In contrast, reasoning about the worker's buffered stores allows a thief to steal without blocking when the queue contains $> \delta$ tasks, enabling completion of all tasks in $\approx \delta/2$ time units.

***Chase-Lev algorithm*** Unlike the THE algorithm, the Chase-Lev algorithm is *nonblocking* [21]. In particular, a thief running alone always completes its operation. The echo method is inherently blocking as it may prevent a thief from completing until the worker takes steps. It is thus not applicable to the Chase-Lev algorithm since it would destroy its non-blocking progress property.

## 6. Sidestepping the laws of order

Having described our fence-free algorithms, we now pinpoint how they get around Attiya et al.'s "laws of order" impossibility result [10].

***Impossibility result*** The "laws of order" theorem states that any linearizable [24] implementation of a *strongly non-commutative* (SNC) method must use an atomic operation or memory fence [1] in some execution. The sequential specification of the implemented data structure determines whether a method is SNC. Method $M$ is SNC if there is another method $M'$ (possibly the same method as $M$) such that applying $M$ followed by $M'$ from some initial state $\rho$ yields different outputs for both $M$ and $M'$ than applying $M'$ followed by $M$.

`take()` ***and*** `steal()` ***are SNC*** Consider the state $\rho$ in which the work stealing task queue contains one task, $x$. When applying `take()` first it returns $x$ and a subsequent `steal()` returns EMPTY. Similarly, if `steal()` is applied first it returns $x$ and then `take()` returns EMPTY when applied. It is easy to see that $\rho$ is the only state from which `take()` and `steal()` can influence each other in this way.

[1]The actual theorem statement does not mention memory fences, as it uses a sequentially consistent system model. Instead, the theorem states that either an atomic operation or a read-after-write (RAW) pattern must be used, where a RAW means a write to shared variable $X$ is followed by a read to another shared variable $Y$ without a write to $Y$ in between. However, TSO requires issuing a memory fence after the write to $X$ to prevent the read of $Y$ from being reordered before it.

***Tightness assumption*** The "laws of order" proof assumes that the concurrent implementation is *tight* – that any sequential execution which complies with the specification can occur in a sequential execution of the implementation. (This is referred to as "Assumption 1" in the paper [10].) The proof needs this assumption to argue that an execution exhibiting the strong non-commutativity of a method actually occurs in the implementation. Our algorithms break the tightness assumption.

***Violating tightness by relaxing semantics*** The FF-THE and FF-CL algorithms refuse to steal when the queue contains one task, because there might be a `take()` of this task hidden in worker's store buffer. Instead, they return `ABORT` without changing the state of the queue – which the standard work stealing specification does not allow. Thus, reasoning about the store buffer enables implementing a relaxed specification that allows `steal()` to run first from the $\rho$ state without affecting the return value of a later `take()`.

***Violating tightness by blocking*** In the THEP algorithm a `steal()` invoked when the queue contains one task blocks and does not return until `take()` is invoked. This prevents the SNC execution in which `steal()` affects the return value of `take()` from occurring without relaxing the work stealing semantics, as the `steal()` would simply not terminate when running alone. THEP sidesteps the impossibility result by leveraging a property of work stealing clients (programs): that the worker *keeps taking tasks until the queue empties*. Therefore, in actual work stealing clients, indefinite blocking of a thief does not occur.

## 7. Bounded TSO in mainstream processors

Here we show that the mainstream TSO architectures – x86 and SPARC – implement bounded TSO, except for a corner case in which there are consecutive stores to the same location, which can be prevented in software.

We use Intel's Xeon E7-4870 (Westmere-EX) processor as a running example, since it is representative of mainstream out-of-order TSO processors. (Similar but simpler reasoning applies to in-order processors.) First, we explain how the processor's implementation of TSO leads to bounded reordering except when consecutive stores to the same location are *coalesced* (§ 7.1). Then we derive the exact bound on the amount of reordering, and show how to adjust the work stealing runtime to avoid store coalescing (§ 7.2-7.3).

### 7.1 Cause of bounded store/load reordering

To hide the latency of writing to the memory subsystem (which may include resolving a cache miss) the processor retires a store instruction from the reorder buffer without waiting for its value to reach the memory subsystem (henceforth simply "memory"). Instead, the processor holds the instruction's target address and data in a *store buffer entry*, from

```
for S = 1,2,...
  T0 = get_cycle_count()
  repeat K times
    store to location #1
    store to location #2
      ...
    store to location #S
    long latency instruction sequence
  T1 = get_cycle_count()
  output ⟨S, (T1 − T0)/K⟩
```

Figure 6: Code for determining store buffer's capacity.

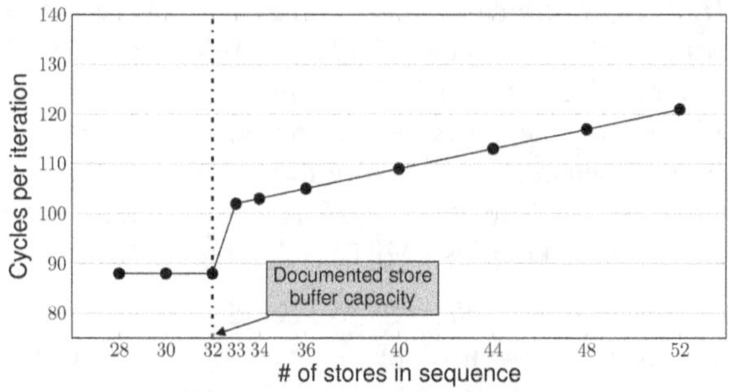


Figure 7: Measuring store buffer capacity on a Westmere-EX processor which has a documented 32-entry store buffer.

which it moves the data to memory as a background task once the store retires [2, 5, 6].

Store buffering makes store/load reordering possible because a load can retire, having read from memory, before the value of an earlier store to a different location gets written to memory. In fact, this is the only way reordering may happen. Out-of-order execution does not lead to further store/load reordering because, to maintain TSO, the processor retires a load only if the value it read remains valid at retirement time [5, 25].

The processor has a fixed number, $S$, of store buffer entries. However, this does *not* automatically imply that it implements a TSO[$S$] memory model, because the processor's store buffer is not equivalent to the store buffer of the abstract TSO[$S$] machine. To show that the processor implements TSO[$S$], we need to show that a load instruction cannot be reordered with more than $S$ prior stores.

The reason for such bounded reordering is the *implementation* of store buffering, which assigns a store buffer entry to a store when it *enters* the pipeline and *prevents* it from entering the pipeline if the store buffer is full (i.e., all $S$ entries have not been written to memory) [2, 5, 6]. In such a case, the entire execution stalls since later instructions also cannot enter the pipeline as pipeline entry occurs in program order.

It thus appears that a load cannot be reordered past more than $S$ prior stores, conforming to the TSO[$S$] model. However, if the processor *coalesces* multiple stores to the same location into one store buffer entry, then the $S$ store buffer entries will represent more than $S$ stores and violate this reasoning. We ignore this issue for now and address it in § 7.3.

### 7.2 Measuring store buffer capacity

This section shows how to empirically determine the capacity of the processor's store buffer. The idea is to measure the time it takes to complete sequences of stores of increasing length, and find the spot at which execution starts to stall.

***Measurement algorithm (Figure 6)*** We alternate between issuing a sequence of stores and a sequence of non-memory instructions whose execution latency is long enough to drain the store buffer. As long as the length of the store sequence does not exceed the store buffer capacity, both the execution of the stores and the flushing of their store buffer entries occur in parallel to the execution of the non-memory instructions, due to out-of-order execution. Consequently, the latency of the non-memory instruction sequence dominates the entire execution time.

However, when the length of the store sequence exceeds the store buffer capacity, the resulting stalls delay the subsequent instruction sequences from entering the pipeline and increase execution time. Importantly, stalls in the $k+1$-th iteration do not overlap the execution of the non-memory instructions in the $k$-th iteration, and so the stalls are not absorbed by the latency of the non-memory instructions and affect every iteration. The reason is that stores in the $k+1$-th sequence can start draining to memory only after all non-memory instructions in the $k$-th sequence retire, since store buffer entries are flushed post-retirement and instructions retire in program order.

Figure 7 shows the results of running the measurement algorithm on the Westmere-EX processor. Our measurement results match Intel' documented store buffer capacity for this processor [5, 6]. Measurement results on a Haswell processor are similarly accurate, correctly identifying the documented capacity of 42 [5, 6].

### 7.3 From store buffer capacity to a reordering bound

Knowing the capacity of the processor's store buffer does not necessarily provide a bound on store/load reordering. For example, if the processor coalesces multiple stores to the same location into a single store buffer entry, the $S$ store buffer entries can represent more than $S$ stores and thus allow reordering beyond $S$ prior stores. There may also be other implementation issues that affect the reordering bound.

Therefore, we develop a *litmus test* that, given a presumed bound $S$ on the reordering, can be used to prove that the processor *violates* the TSO[$S$] model. We can then gain confidence that a processor implements TSO[$S$] if extensive testing does not show a violation of the model, although testing will never *prove* that the processor implements TSO[$S$].

The test program (Figure 9) runs a worker and thief who concurrently try to empty an FF-THE queue (Figure 3) that initially contains 512 tasks. The queue uses a user-supplied

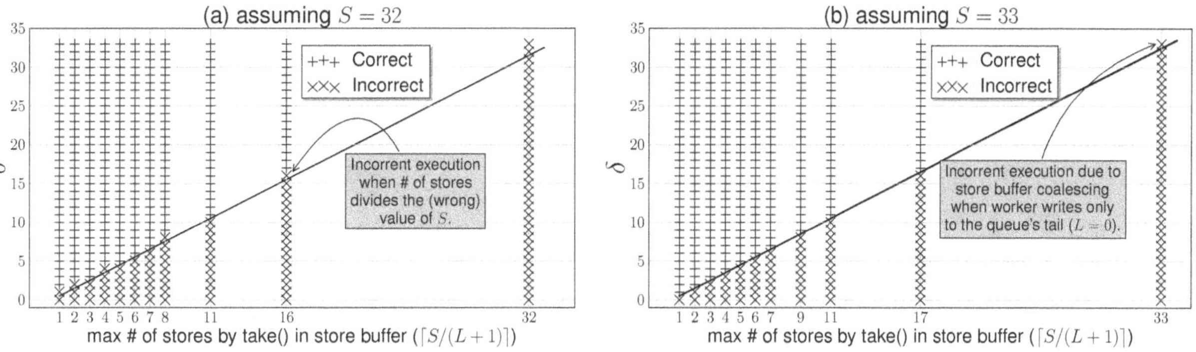


Figure 8: Testing if the processor implements TSO[$S$]. If $S$ is the correct bound, executions on or above the line $y = x$ should be correct.

```
Initially:  initialize work stealing queue with 512 items.

            worker                              thief
  taken := 0                            stolen := 0
  while (take() ≠ EMPTY) {              while ( steal () ≠ ABORT) {
    taken := taken + 1                    stolen := stolen + 1
    store to location #1                }
    ...
    store to location #L
  }

Finally:  if (taken + stolen = 512) output CORRECT, else output INCORRECT
```

Figure 9: Program for finding executions not valid under a bounded TSO model. We vary the $\delta$ parameter of our work stealing algorithm and $L$, the number of stores performed by the worker.

value for $\delta$ (the maximum number of `take()`s not visible in memory due to store buffering). The worker performs a sequence of $L$ stores to distinct locations between each invocation of `take()`, where $L$ is a program parameter. The worker performs no other stores except for these and the single store in `take()`. Therefore, if the processor implements TSO[$S$], an execution with $\delta \geq \lceil \frac{S}{L+1} \rceil$ should always be *correct* – the total number of tasks removed by the worker and the thief equals the initial size of the queue.

We run the litmus test using various values of $L$ and $\delta$. For each pair $(L, \delta)$, we perform $10^7$ runs with each of the following assignments of threads to cores: (1) default OS placement, (2) both threads placed on hyperthreads of the same core, and (3) each thread placed on a different core.

We interpret the litmus test results in light of a supposed ordering bound $S$. For each $\alpha \in \{1, \ldots, S\}$ we consider all pairs $(L, \delta)$ such that $\lceil \frac{S}{L+1} \rceil = \alpha$. If any run of such a pair is incorrect, we consider the point $(\alpha, \delta)$ *incorrect*; otherwise, we consider it *correct*. Figure 8a depicts the results when $S = 32$, the processor's store buffer capacity. Interestingly, the processor fails to implement TSO[32], as demonstrated by the incorrect executions when the maximum number of stores between `take()` operations divides 32.

We instrumented the litmus test to understand these failures, and observed that when they occur there always appear to be 33 worker stores in flight and never more. Therefore, we analyzed the litmus test data using $S = 33$ (Figure 8b). This time there is an almost perfect match with the model, with one exception: when $L = 0$. In this case the only stores the worker performs are to the tail of the work stealing queue, $T$. The $T$ variable is then always at the tail of the store buffer, and in fact is the *only* store pending in the store buffer. In such a case, the processor apparently coalesces stores.

***Store buffer coalescing*** Coalescing under TSO can take place only for consecutive stores, otherwise – as the following example shows – the TSO guarantees may be violated:

| | initially $A = B = 0$ | |
|---|---|---|
| buffered stores: | $A := 1$ | (earliest store) |
| | $B := 1$ | |
| | $A := 2$ | (latest store, entering buffer) |

If next $A := 2$ is coalesced with $A := 1$ and this entry is then written to memory, another processor can now observe $A = 2$ while $B = 0$ which is illegal under TSO.

To understand the processor's coalescing implementation, we repeat the store buffer capacity benchmark (Figure 6) using sequences of stores to the *same* location – and still obtain the *same results*. This shows that coalesced stores still get assigned distinct store buffer entries, so coalescing is done at a later execution stage. We hypothesize that the oldest store gets written to memory by first moving its address and data into an additional buffer $B$, which frees its store buffer entry, and then writing $B$ to the memory subsystem. If the oldest store is to the same address that $B$ holds, $B$ is overwritten with its data, resulting in coalescing. Otherwise, $B$ is overwritten only after its data is written to memory.

***Deriving the reordering bound of 33*** Because $B$ holds a retired store's data, it *observably behaves as an additional store buffer entry*. Therefore, if we avoid store buffer coalescing, we can assume we are running on a TSO[33] machine (since our concern is the observable store buffer capacity, i.e., the bound on the reordering). To avoid coalescing of stores by `take()` in work stealing, we need to prevent consecutive invocations of `take()` *with no store in between*. This is easy to do in practice: The CilkPlus `take()` already writes to the structure of a removed task before returning it, and thus avoids coalescing. Other runtimes can similarly perform an extra store before returning from `take()`. Performing an additional store generalizes to processors with coarser coalescing granularity: for example, if a processor coalesces stores to the same cache line, we need to write to another cache line before returning from `take()`.

## 8. Evaluation

This section evaluates the performance impact of applying our techniques in the THE and Chase-Lev work stealing algorithms. In addition, we compare our techniques to the idempotent work stealing queues of Michael et al. [31], which avoid the worker's memory fence at the cost of relaxing the queue's safety by allowing a task to be removed more than once. Thus, we seek to understand whether comparable performance can be obtained without compromising safety.

***Platform*** We run our experiments on Intel Haswell and Westmere-EX processors. The Westmere-EX (Xeon E7-4870) processor has 10 2.4 GHz cores, each multiplexing 2 hyperthreads. The Haswell (Core i7-4770) processor has 4 3.4 GHz cores, each with 2 hyperthreads. We measure a reordering bound of $S = 33$ on the Westmere-EX and $S = 43$ on the Haswell (ignoring coalescing, which we avoid in software; see § 7.3).

### 8.1 The FF-THE and THEP algorithms

We implement our techniques in Intel's CilkPlus runtime library (Build 3365, released on May 2013) which uses the THE algorithm.

To understand the individual contribution of our methods, we evaluate both THEP and the FF-THE variant (§ 4) which refuses to steal in case of uncertainty. By default, both versions use a value of $\delta = \lceil \frac{S}{2} \rceil$ derived from the fact that the CilkPlus runtime performs an additional store after each `take()`. To measure the impact of $\delta$, we also test $\delta = 4$, which we determine to be safe by accounting for the program stores and compiler register spills between `take()`s in the benchmark binaries. Finally, we benchmark THEP with $\delta = \infty$, i.e., with thieves always waiting for the worker.

***Methodology*** We measure the running time of a set of 11 CilkPlus programs (Table 1), which have by now become standard benchmarks in the literature on work stealing and task parallel runtimes [7, 19, 20, 26, 28]. We use the `jemalloc` [18] memory allocator to prevent program memory allocation from being a bottleneck (the runtime uses its own memory allocator). Both runtime and programs are compiled version 13.1.1 of Intel's `icc` compiler. We run

| **Benchmark** | **Description** | **Input size** |
|---|---|---|
| Fib | Recursive Fibonacci | 42 |
| Jacobi | Iterative mesh relaxation | $1024 \times 1024$ |
| QuickSort | Recursive QuickSort | $10^8$ |
| Matmul | Matrix multiply | $1024 \times 1024$ |
| Integrate | Recursively calculate area under a curve | 10000 |
| knapsack | Recursive branch-and-bound knapsack solver | 32 items |
| cholesky | Cholesky factorization | $4000 \times 4000$, 40000 nonzeros |
| Heat | Heat diffusion simulation | $4096 \times 1024$ |
| LUD | LU decomposition | $1024 \times 1024$ |
| strassen | Strassen matrix multiply | $4096 \times 4096$ |
| fft | Fast Fourier transform | $2^{26}$ |

Table 1: CilkPlus benchmark applications.

each program 10 times (except for `knapsack`, which we run 50 times) and report the median run time, normalized to the default CilkPlus run time, as well as 10-th and 90-th percentiles.

***Results*** Figure 10 shows the results using the maximum level of parallelism on each platform without hyperthreading (i.e., 10 threads on the Westmere-EX, one assigned to each core, and 4 threads on the Haswell). Due to space constraints we omit the figures depicting results with hyperthreading enabled, but we summarize the findings below.

On the Westmere-EX (Figure 10a) the THEP algorithm improves the run time on 8 of the benchmarks by up to 23% and by 11% on (geometric) average, and degrades the remaining 3 programs by 3%. The average improvement across the entire suite is by 7%. On the Haswell (Figure 10b), the run time of 9 programs improves by up to 23% (13% on average) and is not affected on the rest. The average improvement over the entire suite is by 11%.

Varying $\delta$ does not significantly impact the performance of the THEP variants on most programs, as stealing is infrequent enough that waiting for the worker does not make much of a difference. However, for `Heat` on the Westmere-EX introducing more stealing opportunities resolves the run time degradation caused by THEP.

In contrast, FF-THE is very sensitive to $\delta$. On 6 programs the default $\delta$ prevents FF-THE from stealing altogether and makes the programs run at single threaded speed. Decreasing $\delta$ to a more precise value resolves the problem in all programs but `LUD`, showing that the ability to resolve a thief's uncertainty can be important.

When using hyperthreading the processor can schedule one hyperthread when its sibling stalls due to a memory fence. Consequently, the improvements from avoiding fences are reduced. On the Westmere-EX, the average improvement of programs that improve drops to 4% and is at most 12%, while the degradation increases to 5%, yielding an average improvement of 3.6% across the whole suite. The

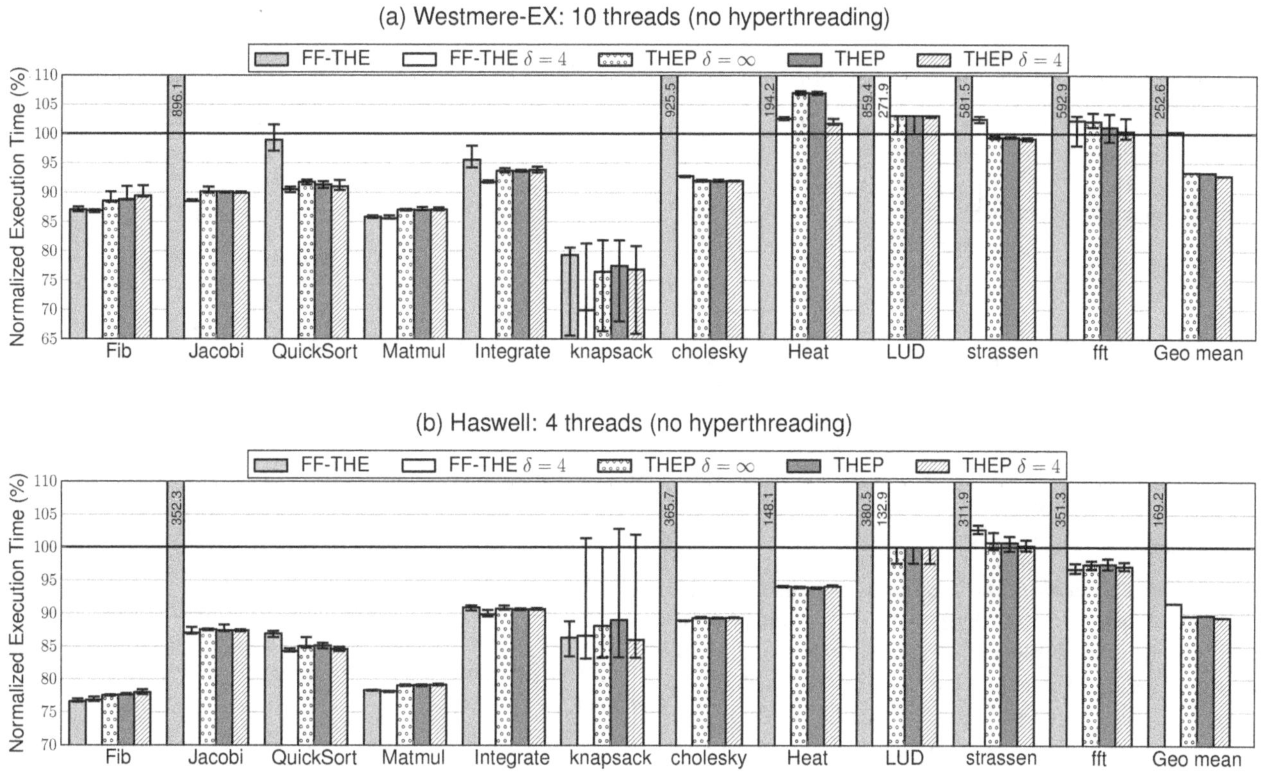


Figure 10: CilkPlus programs run time, normalized to the default CilkPlus runtime.

effect on the Haswell is similar, with overall improvement dropping to 7% (and at most 12%).

### 8.2 FF-CL vs. idempotent work stealing queues

Here we compare FF-CL to Michael et al.'s idempotent work stealing queues [31]. (Since our goal is not to evaluate how well Chase-Lev does compared to THE, we do not test the THE variants in these experiments.) We test the LIFO and double-ended FIFO idempotent queues. The LIFO queue is a stack in which both worker and thieves remove (possibly the same) tasks from the top of the stack. In the double-ended FIFO queue, the last task can be removed concurrently by both the worker and a thief.

We use Michael et al.'s benchmark programs and inputs, but we implement the idempotent task queues ourselves as their code is not publicly available. (However, our performance results match those of Michael et al. [31].) There are two benchmarks, computing the transitive closure and the spanning tree of a graph. The parallel algorithms used [15] manage synchronization internally, because the same task (e.g., "visit node $u$") can inherently be *repeated* by different threads (e.g., who are working on different neighbors of $u$). We report results only for the transitive closure; spanning tree results are similar.

The input graphs consists of: (1) a $K$-graph, which is a $K$-regular graph in which each node is connected to $K$ nodes, (2) a random graph of $n$ nodes and $m$ edges, and (3) a two-dimensional torus (grid).

We run the transitive closure program 10 times on each input, using the maximum level of parallelism usable by the workload, both with and without hyperthreading. For the $K$-graph and random graph, this is the maximum parallelism in the machine, but on the torus graph the programs do not scale past 2 threads, so we report results from 2 threads.

Figure 11a depicts the Haswell results for the transitive closure application with large inputs without hyperthreading. (Due to space constraints, we omit hyperthreading and Westmere-EX results, which are similar.) We show median, 10-th and 90-th percentile run times, normalized to the standard Chase-Lev algorithm.

All the fence-free work stealing queues obtain comparable performance. The torus input enjoys the greatest improvement in running time, $\approx 33\%$ for both our FF-CL and the LIFO idempotent queue.

In contrast to the CilkPlus experiments (Figure 10), here the default $\delta$ value does not prevent a thread from stealing. This can be seen by observing the non-zero percent of stolen work for our variant in Figure 11b.

Also apparent in Figure 11b is that the vast majority of work is performed by the worker and not by thieves, thus emphasizing the importance of removing overhead – e.g., the memory fence – from the worker's code path.

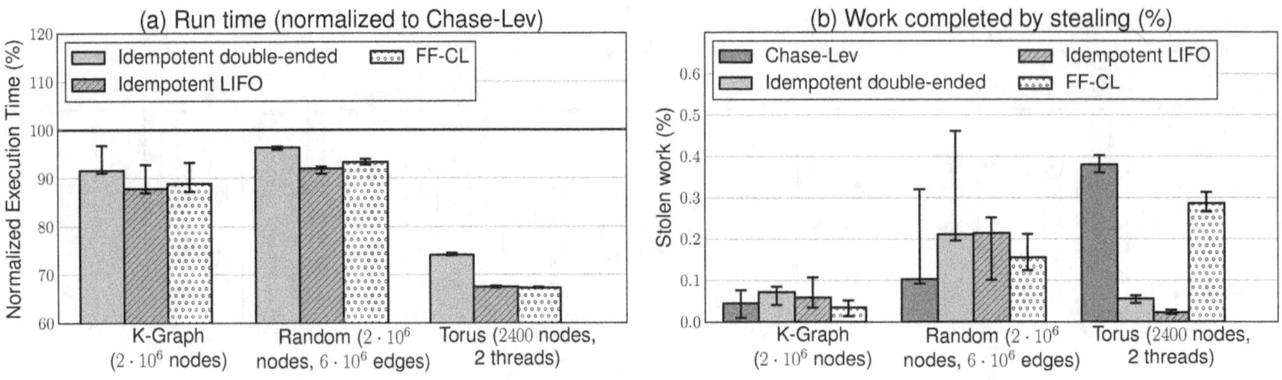


Figure 11: Transitive closure at maximum parallelism on Haswell (no hyperthreading).

# 9. Related work

***Fence-free work stealing task queues*** Michael et al.'s idempotent work stealing algorithms [31] avoid worker fences, but are only applicable to applications that can tolerate a task being executed twice, whereas our techniques are relevant to any application on a bounded TSO processor. Kumar et al. [26] use yieldpoint mechanisms to stop the worker at a known-safe location before stealing. Such mechanisms are not available in unmanaged environments such as C/C++, whereas our technique applies there. Dice et al.'s asymmetric synchronization [16] can be used to eliminate memory fences in work stealing. However, this requires heavyweight actions by the thief (e.g., suspending the worker thread) whereas our approach is lightweight.

***Eliminating fence penalty in hardware*** Below we describe microarchitectural designs that eliminate the penalty of fences, thereby obviating the need for our fence-free techniques. In contrast to all these proposals, our algorithms offer an *immediately usable software-only solution* for mainstream multicore architectures available today.

***Speculative memory fences*** Store-wait-free processing [36] and Invisifence [12] use speculation to eliminate the penalty of memory fences. Instead of a fence stalling the processor until all prior stores are written to memory, these designs initiate transactional memory [22] style speculative execution which commits when all prior stores have been drained to memory. However, this speculation may interact badly with work stealing, as each time a thief reads the queue's tail it might abort the worker's speculative execution, which can contain several `take()`s.

***Stalling fences only when needed*** In WeeFence [17] and address-aware fences [29] a fence stalls the processor only if a post-fence access is about to violate the memory model. Thus, a steal attempt can stall the worker, whereas with our techniques – which appear to be applicable to these designs when fences are not used – steals do not affect the worker.

***Multiple store buffers*** Singh et al. [35] propose to use different store buffers for shared and private memory locations. Fences then only need to drain the shared-location store buffer. However, the processor needs to distinguish between private and shared accesses, which requires compiler and instruction set changes, or extending the hardware memory management unit and page table structures [35].

# 10. Conclusion and future work

This paper shows that mainstream TSO processors only allow *bounded* store/load reordering and that this can be exploited to derive fence-free work stealing algorithms. The idea is that we can compensate for reading stale values from memory by reasoning about the number of stores that are hidden in the store buffer.

More generally, because our approach enables circumventing the recent "laws of order" impossibility result [10] by violating its *tightness* assumption, we hope it opens the door for removing memory fences in other concurrent algorithms.

The notion of a memory model with bounded reordering raises several questions for future research. How does bounded reordering extend to weaker memory models which admit other forms of reordering beyond store/load? Do mainstream implementations of weak memory models such as PowerPC and ARM also exhibit forms of bounded reordering? Finally, it will be interesting to explore microarchitectures that *explicitly* provide bounds on reordering.


# Acknowledgments

We thank our shepherd, Martin Vechev, and the ASPLOS reviewers for their insightful comments which helped to considerably improve the presentation of this paper.

This work was supported by the Israel Science Foundation (grants 1386/11 and 1227/10) and by Yad-HaNadiv foundation. Adam Morrison is supported in part at the Technion by an Aly Kaufman Fellowship.

## References


[1] *The SPARC Architecture Manual Version 8*. Prentice Hall, 1992.

[2] UltraSPARC T1 Supplement to the UltraSPARC Architecture 2005. `http://www.oracle.com/technetwork/systems/opensparc/t1-08-ust1-uasuppl-draft-p-ext-1537736.html`, March 2006.

[3] Intel CilkPlus Language Specification. Technical report, Intel Corporation, 2011.

[4] Intel Threading Building Blocks. `http://threadingbuildingblocks.org/`, June 2012.

[5] Intel 64 and IA-32 Architectures Optimization Reference Manual. `https://www-ssl.intel.com/content/www/us/en/architecture-and-technology/64-ia-32-architectures-optimization-manual.html`, July 2013.

[6] Intel 64 and IA-32 Architectures Software Developers Manual, Volume 3: System Programming Guide. `http://download.intel.com/products/processor/manual/325384.pdf`, June 2013.

[7] Umut A. Acar, Arthur Chargueraud, and Mike Rainey. Scheduling parallel programs by work stealing with private deques. In *Proceedings of the 18th ACM SIGPLAN Symposium on Principles and Practice of Parallel Programming*, PPoPP '13, pages 219–228, New York, NY, USA, 2013. ACM.

[8] Samy Al Bahra. Nonblocking algorithms and scalable multicore programming. *Communications of the ACM*, 56(7):50–61, July 2013.

[9] Nimar S. Arora, Robert D. Blumofe, and C. Greg Plaxton. Thread scheduling for multiprogrammed multiprocessors. *Theory of Computing Systems*, 34:115–144, 2001.

[10] Hagit Attiya, Rachid Guerraoui, Danny Hendler, Petr Kuznetsov, Maged M. Michael, and Martin Vechev. Laws of order: expensive synchronization in concurrent algorithms cannot be eliminated. In *Proceedings of the 38th Annual ACM SIGPLAN-SIGACT Symposium on Principles of Programming Languages*, POPL '11, pages 487–498, New York, NY, USA, 2011. ACM.

[11] Eduard Ayguadé, Nawal Copty, Alejandro Duran, Jay Hoeflinger, Yuan Lin, Federico Massaioli, Xavier Teruel, Priya Unnikrishnan, and Guansong Zhang. The Design of OpenMP Tasks. *IEEE Transactions on Parallel and Distributed Systems*, 20(3):404–418, March 2009.

[12] Colin Blundell, Milo M.K. Martin, and Thomas F. Wenisch. Invisifence: Performance-transparent memory ordering in conventional multiprocessors. In *Proceedings of the 36th Annual International Symposium on Computer Architecture*, ISCA '09, pages 233–244, New York, NY, USA, 2009. ACM.

[13] Philippe Charles, Christian Grothoff, Vijay Saraswat, Christopher Donawa, Allan Kielstra, Kemal Ebcioglu, Christoph von Praun, and Vivek Sarkar. X10: an object-oriented approach to non-uniform cluster computing. In *Proceedings of the 20th Annual ACM SIGPLAN Conference on Object-Oriented Programming, Systems, Languages, and Applications*, OOPSLA '05, pages 519–538, New York, NY, USA, 2005. ACM.

[14] David Chase and Yossi Lev. Dynamic circular work-stealing deque. In *Proceedings of the 17th Annual ACM Symposium on Parallelism in Algorithms and Architectures*, SPAA '05, pages 21–28, New York, NY, USA, 2005. ACM.

[15] Guojing Cong David A. Bader. A fast, parallel spanning tree algorithm for symmetric multiprocessors (SMPs). *Journal of Parallel and Distributed Computing*, 65(9):994–1006, 2005.

[16] Dave Dice, Hui Huang, and Mingyao Yang. Asymmetric Dekker Synchronization. `http://home.comcast.net/~pjbishop/Dave/Asymmetric-Dekker-Synchronization.txt`, 2001.

[17] Yuelu Duan, Abdullah Muzahid, and Josep Torrellas. WeeFence: toward making fences free in TSO. In *Proceedings of the 40th Annual International Symposium on Computer Architecture*, ISCA '13, pages 213–224, New York, NY, USA, 2013. ACM.

[18] Jason Evans. Scalable memory allocation using jemalloc. `http://www.facebook.com/notes/facebook-engineering/scalable-memory-allocation-using-jemalloc/480222803919`, 2011.

[19] Karl-Filip Faxen. Efficient work stealing for fine grained parallelism. In *Proceedings of the 2010 39th International Conference on Parallel Processing*, ICPP '10, pages 313–322, Washington, DC, USA, 2010. IEEE Computer Society.

[20] Matteo Frigo, Charles E. Leiserson, and Keith H. Randall. The implementation of the Cilk-5 multithreaded language. In *Proceedings of the 19th ACM SIGPLAN Conference on Programming Language Design and Implementation*, PLDI '98, pages 212–223, New York, NY, USA, 1998. ACM.

[21] Maurice Herlihy. Wait-free synchronization. *ACM Transactions on Programming Languages and Systems (TOPLAS)*, 13:124–149, January 1991.

[22] Maurice Herlihy and J. Eliot B. Moss. Transactional memory: architectural support for lock-free data structures. In *Proceedings of the 20th Annual International Symposium on Computer architecture*, ISCA '93, pages 289–300, New York, NY, USA, 1993. ACM.

[23] Maurice Herlihy and Nir Shavit. *The Art of Multiprocessor Programming*. Morgan Kaufmann Publishers Inc., San Francisco, CA, USA, 2008.

[24] Maurice P. Herlihy and Jeannette M. Wing. Linearizability: a correctness condition for concurrent objects. *ACM Transactions on Programming Languages and Systems (TOPLAS)*, 12:463–492, July 1990.

[25] David Kanter. Haswell Transactional Memory Alternatives. `http://www.realworldtech.com/haswell-tm-alt/`, August 2012.

[26] Vivek Kumar, Daniel Frampton, Stephen M. Blackburn, David Grove, and Olivier Tardieu. Work-stealing without the baggage. In *Proceedings of the ACM International Conference on Object Oriented Programming Systems Languages and Applications*, OOPSLA '12, pages 297–314, New York, NY, USA, 2012. ACM.

[27] Doug Lea. A Java fork/join framework. In *Proceedings of the ACM 2000 Conference on Java Grande*, JAVA '00, pages 36–43, New York, NY, USA, 2000. ACM.

[28] I-Ting Angelina Lee, Silas Boyd-Wickizer, Zhiyi Huang, and Charles E. Leiserson. Using memory mapping to support cactus stacks in work-stealing runtime systems. In *Proceedings of the 19th International Conference on Parallel Architectures and Compilation Techniques*, PACT '10, pages 411–420, New York, NY, USA, 2010. ACM.

[29] Changhui Lin, Vijay Nagarajan, and Rajiv Gupta. Address-aware fences. In *Proceedings of the 27th International Conference on Supercomputing*, ICS '13, pages 313–324, New York, NY, USA, 2013. ACM.

[30] Feng Liu, Nayden Nedev, Nedyalko Prisadnikov, Martin Vechev, and Eran Yahav. Dynamic synthesis for relaxed memory models. In *Proceedings of the 33rd ACM SIGPLAN Conference on Programming Language Design and Implementation*, PLDI '12, pages 429–440, New York, NY, USA, 2012. ACM.

[31] Maged M. Michael, Martin T. Vechev, and Vijay A. Saraswat. Idempotent work stealing. In *Proceedings of the 14th ACM SIGPLAN Symposium on Principles and Practice of Parallel Programming*, PPoPP '09, pages 45–54, New York, NY, USA, 2009. ACM.

[32] Colby Ranger, Ramanan Raghuraman, Arun Penmetsa, Gary Bradski, and Christos Kozyrakis. Evaluating MapReduce for Multi-core and Multiprocessor Systems. In *Proceedings of the 2007 IEEE 13th International Symposium on High Performance Computer Architecture*, HPCA '07, pages 13–24, Washington, DC, USA, 2007. IEEE Computer Society.

[33] James Reinders. *Intel Threading Building Blocks*. O'Reilly Media, July 2007.

[34] Peter Sewell, Susmit Sarkar, Scott Owens, Francesco Zappa Nardelli, and Magnus O. Myreen. x86-TSO: a rigorous and usable programmer's model for x86 multiprocessors. *Communications of the ACM*, 53(7):89–97, July 2010.

[35] Abhayendra Singh, Satish Narayanasamy, Daniel Marino, Todd Millstein, and Madanlal Musuvathi. End-to-end sequential consistency. In *Proceedings of the 39th Annual International Symposium on Computer Architecture*, ISCA '12, pages 524–535, Washington, DC, USA, 2012. IEEE Computer Society.

[36] Thomas F. Wenisch, Anastasia Ailamaki, Babak Falsafi, and Andreas Moshovos. Mechanisms for store-wait-free multiprocessors. In *Proceedings of the 34th Annual International Symposium on Computer Architecture*, ISCA '07, pages 266–277, New York, NY, USA, 2007. ACM.

# Heterogeneous-race-free Memory Models

Derek R. Hower[†], Blake A. Hechtman[†§], Bradford M. Beckmann[†], Benedict R. Gaster[†], Mark D. Hill[‡†], Steven K. Reinhardt[†], David A. Wood[‡†]

[†]AMD Research
{derek.hower, brad.beckmann, benedict.gaster,steve.reinhardt}@amd.com

[§]Duke University
Electrical and Computer Engineering
blake.hechtman@duke.edu

[‡]University of Wisconsin-Madison
Computer Sciences
{markhill, david}@cs.wisc.edu

## Abstract

Commodity heterogeneous systems (e.g., integrated CPUs and GPUs), now support a unified, shared memory address space for all components. Because the latency of global communication in a heterogeneous system can be prohibitively high, heterogeneous systems (unlike homogeneous CPU systems) provide synchronization mechanisms that only guarantee ordering among a subset of threads, which we call a scope. Unfortunately, the consequences and semantics of these scoped operations are not yet well understood. Without a formal and approachable model to reason about the behavior of these operations, we risk an array of portability and performance issues.

In this paper, we embrace scoped synchronization with a new class of memory consistency models that add scoped synchronization to data-race-free models like those of C++ and Java. Called sequential consistency for heterogeneous-race-free (SC for HRF), the new models guarantee SC for programs with "sufficient" synchronization (no data races) of "sufficient" scope. We discuss two such models. The first, HRF-direct, works well for programs with highly regular parallelism. The second, HRF-indirect, builds on HRF-direct by allowing synchronization using different scopes in some cases involving transitive communication. We quantitatively show that HRF-indirect encourages forward-looking programs with irregular parallelism by showing up to a 10% performance increase in a task runtime for GPUs.

***Categories and Subject Descriptors*** C.0 [**Computer Systems Organization**]: Hardware/software interfaces, systems specifications methodology

***Keywords***: memory consistency model; heterogeneous systems; data-race-free; task runtime

## 1 Introduction

Though it took nearly 30 years, languages for CPU systems like C++ [7] and Java [26] have started to adopt a class of memory models called sequential consistency for data-race-free (SC for DRF) [3]. These models are formal and precise definitions that allow many low-level optimizations. SC for DRF models are also accessible to most programmers because they guarantee sequential consistency to any program that is synchronized correctly – meaning that most programmers need not concern themselves with the gory details. A goal of this work is to achieve the same benefits for heterogeneous systems in significantly less time.

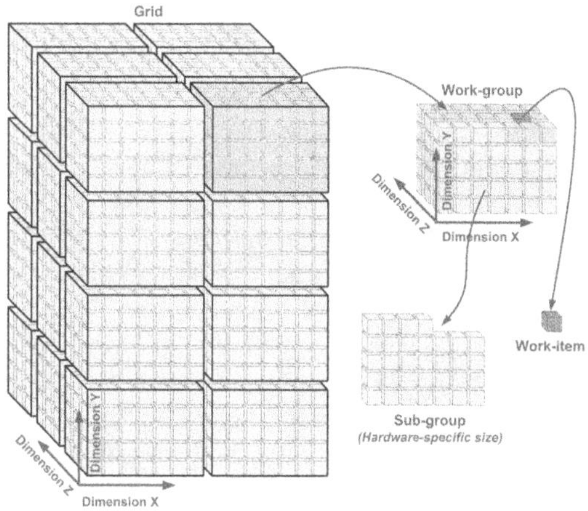


**Figure 1. The OpenCL execution hierarchy.**

Unfortunately, it is not straightforward to apply SC for DRF models in heterogeneous systems because current heterogeneous systems support synchronization operations with non-global side effects. For performance reasons, languages like OpenCL™ [29] and CUDA [12] decompose a problem into execution groups. Figure 1 shows the OpenCL execution model, in which a work-item (like a CPU thread) belongs to four different groups (which we call scopes): sub-group[1], work-group, device, and system[2]. Starting with OpenCL 2.0 [28], programmers can synchronize a work-item through shared memory[3] with respect to any one of these groups using what we call *scoped synchronization* operations. For example, OpenCL provides a fence opera-

[1] Sub-groups are optional in OpenCL, but will usually be defined on an SIMT GPU, and correspond to vector units.

[2] We use OpenCL terminology in this paper. In Section 6 we discuss the CUDA equivalents.

[3] As in CPU shared memory, not the CUDA "shared memory" scratchpad.


*ASPLOS'14*, March 1–5, 2014, Salt Lake City, Utah, USA.

http://dx.doi.org/10.1145/2541940.2541981

tion that synchronizes a work-item with other work-items in its own work-group but not with work-items in a different work-group.

Scoped synchronization breaks some fundamental tenets of SC for DRF models. For example, in OpenCL 2.0 it is possible to write a racey program that is composed entirely of atomics if those atomics do not use scopes correctly. It may also be possible to write a program in which all ordinary accesses are protected with atomics such that there can be no concurrent conflicting accesses, yet that program may still contain a race if those atomics are not scoped correctly. We find that many of the consequences of these differences are not yet well understood.

In this paper, we propose a new class of memory models for platforms that use scoped synchronization called sequential consistency for heterogeneous-race-free (SC for HRF). SC for HRF models define correctness in terms of a sequentially consistent execution and rules for what is considered "enough" synchronization to avoid races. The SC for HRF models achieve two fundamental goals: they provide a precise definition of memory behavior in a heterogeneous execution and they provide a framework to describe that behavior in a way that typical programmers can understand. While we focus on GPUs in this paper due to their prevalence, we expect the SC-for-HRF concepts and insights to apply to other heterogeneous parts (e.g., DSPs).

We describe two possible SC for HRF variants:

- **HRF-direct** requires communicating work-items to synchronize using the exact same scope.
- **HRF-indirect** extends HRF-direct to support transitive communication using different scopes.

In *HRF-direct*, if a producer wants to synchronize with a consumer, the producer must execute a release to scope S and the consumer must later execute an acquire to that exact same scope S. Even though it is (relatively) simple, we find that HRF-direct is a perfectly adequate model to use with highly regular data-parallel algorithms like the ones that currently exist in most general-purpose GPU (GPGPU) applications. In these workloads, it is easy to precisely determine the work-items involved in a communication, thereby making it easy to choose the correct minimal scope for synchronization (Section 3.1). HRF-direct can also be used to understand the OpenCL 2.0 (and likely CUDA; see Section 5.1.3) memory model, thereby giving programmers a more intuitive description of the memory behavior of existing languages.

While HRF-direct is good for today's workloads, it may not be sufficient for emerging heterogeneous applications. First, it makes it difficult to optimize applications with irregular parallelism in which the producer and consumer may not be known *a priori*. For this same reason it can be difficult to write composable library functions in HRF-direct. Second, HRF-direct is overly conservative for current GPU memory systems; some actual hardware will support a more permissive model (from the software perspective). For these reasons, we define an alternative model that relaxes HRF-direct's strict scoping requirements and may enable a wider range of parallel software on heterogeneous accelerators.

In the forward-looking *HRF-indirect* model, two threads can synchronize indirectly through a third party even if the two threads interact with that third party using different scopes. For example, threads A and C can communicate if A synchronizes with another thread B using scope S1 and then B synchronizes with C using scope S2. This type of transitive interaction can enable more irregular parallelism in future heterogeneous applications (e.g., in an algorithm in which A does not know who C is or where C is located). HRF-indirect better supports programmability features like composability and is currently supported by existing GPU hardware. However, HRF-indrect may be harder to support if heterogeneous memories are non-hierarchical and it can prevent some future low-level optimizations allowed by HRF-direct (Section 6).

To explore the practical differences between HRF-direct and HRF-indirect, we have developed a task-parallel runtime for GPUs that performs automatic load balancing as an example of irregular parallelism. We describe the runtime in Section 7 focusing on the design differences between HRF-direct and HRF-indirect implementations of the runtime. In Section 8 we evaluate the performance consequences of those differences, showing that the HRF-indirect version can outperform the HRF-direct version by 3-10% in a system resembling modern hardware. However, we also point out the caveats to this result, including considerations about system optimizations prohibited by HRF-indirect that could be used in HRF-direct systems.

HRF-direct and HRF-indirect are two of many possible formulations of an SC for HRF model. In Section 5.2 we discuss some other properties that SC for HRF models could adopt in the future, notably including a property called *scope inclusion* that exploits the hierarchical nature of most scope definitions. In summary, in this paper we make the following contributions to the state of the art:

***Define with Scoped Synchronization:*** We identify the need to more formally define and better describe the semantics of scoped synchronization operations, especially when work-items interact through different scopes.

***SC for HRF Models:*** We propose a class of programmer-centric memory models called sequential consistency for heterogeneous-race-free to describe systems with scoped synchronization support.

***HRF-direct:*** We define the HRF-direct model for today's highly regular GPGPU programs with current standards (e.g., OpenCL 2.0).

***HRF-indirect:*** We define the forward-looking HRF-indirect model for future irregular GPGPU programs with runtime-determined data flow from producers to consumers.

```
  atomic<int> A = {0};
  atomic<int> B = {0};
  int X;

Thread t1

X = 1;
A.store(1, memory_order_seq_cst);      // release

Thread t2

  while(!A.load(memory_order_seq_cst)); // acquire
  int R2 = X; // R2 will receive X=1 from t1
  B.store(1, memory_order_seq_cst);      // release

Thread t3

    while(!B.load(memory_order_seq_cst)); // acquire
    int R3 = X;  // R3 will receive X=1 from t1
```

**Figure 2. An example of a data-race-free execution in C++11. t1 and t3 do not race on location X because of a transitive interaction through t2.**

# 2 Background and Setup

In this section, we first provide a history of memory consistency models for CPUs, focusing particularly on the data-race-free models that we build on in this paper. Then we describe the features of modern GPU hardware that necessitate scoped synchronization for good performance.

## 2.1 Memory Consistency Models

A *memory (consistency) model* specifies the semantics of shared memory, so that both users and implementers can push limits using precise correctness definitions [2, 36]. *Low-level models* interface low-level software (e.g., compilers, JITs, and runtime) to hardware, while *high-level models* interface high-level languages (e.g., C++ and Java) to the "system" that includes low-level software and hardware.

For microprocessors and multi-core chips, low- and high-level memory models have arguably taken (at least) *three decades to mature*. Microprocessors emerged in 1971 for uniprocessors and were also put in multiprocessors in the early 1980's (e.g., Sequent Balance [37]). Even though Lamport [24] specified sequential consistency (SC) in 1979, most multiprocessors do not implement SC due to their use of write buffers. In 1991, Sindhu et al. [35] formalized total store order (TSO) as a low-level memory consistency model that captured what microprocessors often do in the presence of a write buffer. Meanwhile, to increase flexibility, academics investigated more relaxed low-level memory models, such as weak ordering [14], release consistency [15], and data-race-free (DRF) [3]. Notably, providing sequential consistency to data-race-free programs (SC for DRF) [3], became a cornerstone of the Java [26] and C++ [7] models in 2005 and 2008, respectively. In 2008, a full 15 years after the first multiprocessor x86 architecture came to market, Intel released a formalization of x86-TSO (summarized by Owen, et al. [33]).

A goal of this work is to accelerate the process of defining high- and low-level memory models for heterogeneous systems so that it takes much less than three decades.

## 2.2 Sequential Consistency for Data-race-free

Sequentially consistency guarantees that the observed order of all memory operations is consistent with a theoretical execution in which each instruction is performed one at a time by a single processor [24]. SC preserves programmer sanity by allowing them to think about their parallel algorithms in sequential steps. Unfortunately, true SC can be difficult to implement effectively without sacrificing performance or requiring deeply speculative execution [17]. As a result, most commercially relevant architectures, runtimes, and languages use a model weaker than SC that allows certain operations to appear out of program order at the cost of increased programmer effort.

To bridge the gap between the programming simplicity of SC and the high performance of weaker models, a class of models, called SC for DRF, was created that guarantees an SC execution if the program has no data races (i.e., is protected by control synchronization and memory fences). In the absence of data races, the system is free to perform any reordering as long as it does not cause an observable violation of SC. SC for DRF models differ on the defined behavior in the presence of race, and vary from providing no guarantees [3, 7] to providing weak guarantees like write causality [26].

In Figure 2 we give a concrete example of a sequentially consistent data-race-free program in C++.[4] In this program, the load into R2 does not race with the store X=1 because they are separated by paired synchronization accesses on atomic variable A. The later load into R3 also does not cause a race because in SC for DRF models, synchronization has a transitive effect (a property that will be important in our subsequent discussion of HRF models). In the example, the load into R3 does not form a race with the store X=1 by thread t1 even though t1 and t3 do not use the same synchronization variable. In this case, the threads are synchronized indirectly through the causal chain involving atomics A and B.

## 2.3 Modern GPU Hardware

Because current GPU hardware is optimized to stream through data (as is common for graphics), GPU caches are managed differently than CPU caches. CPU memory systems optimize for reads and writes with high locality via read-for-ownership (RFO) cache coherence protocols. RFO protocols obtain exclusive permission for a line before writing it. Fortunately, good locality makes it likely that this initial cost gets amortized over many subsequent low-cost cache hits.

[4] Those familiar with C++ will notice that the explicit memory order syntax is unnecessary. We use the verbose form to match with OpenCL examples later.

RFO protocols make less sense for GPUs whose data streams afford little opportunity to amortize the latency of obtaining exclusive coherence permission because subsequent caches hits are less common. Current GPU caches behave less like conventional CPU caches and more like streaming write-combining buffers that complete writes without obtaining exclusive coherence permission (Section 3.2).

With GPU write-combining (non-RFO) caches, when two work-items in a GPU synchronize, hardware must ensure both work-items read/write from a mutually shared cache or memory level. To implement this correctly, current hardware may make potentially shared data uncachable, disable private caches for all potentially shared data, or flush/invalidate caches at synchronization points [4, 30]. In the final approach, the particular caches that need to be flushed/invalidated depend on which work-items are synchronizing (i.e., what the scope of synchronization is), and *therefore some synchronizations are more costly than others*. This is in stark contrast to a CPU using RFO coherence, in which the hardware actions necessary at synchronization events (e.g., handling probes or flushing a store buffer) are the same regardless of which threads are involved in the communication.

### 2.4 Data-race-free is Not Enough

There are two ways to achieve the benefits of SC for DRF models in heterogeneous systems. First, we could use an existing SC for DRF model as-is by forcing all synchronization to use global scope. However, this would eschew the benefits of scoped operations, likely resulting in inefficient and poorly performing software.

Second, we could adapt the SC for DRF models to deal with the behavior of scoped operations. In our view, this approach fundamentally changes the understanding of race-free. Informally, many understand data-race-free to mean "conflicting accesses do not occur at the same time" [1]. As we will show in the next section, that informal understanding is not strong enough with scoped synchronization. With scoped synchronization, control flow (with synchronization semantics) can ensure that the conflicting data accesses will not be concurrent, but because of scope there is no guarantee that the result will be sequentially consistent. Also, as we will show, certain properties of an SC for HRF model are quite foreign to SC for DRF models – for example, in the models presented in this paper, it is possible for two atomic accesses to race with each other.

That is why we next extend the understanding of race-free to include what we call heterogeneous races involving synchronization of insufficient scope.

## 3 HRF-direct: Basic Scope Synchronization

In the HRF-direct synchronization model, if two threads communicate, they must synchronize using operations of the ***exact same*** scope. If – in some sequentially consistent execution of a program – two conflicting data accesses are

**Formal Definition of HRF-direct**

We formally define the HRF-direct model using set relational notation, using the style adopted by Adve and Hill [3].

*Conflict Definitions*

**Ordinary Conflict:** Two operations op1 and op2 conflict iff both are to the same address, at least one is a write, and at least one is an ordinary data operation.

**Synchronization Conflict:** Two synchronization operations op1 and op2 conflict iff both are to the same location, at least one is a write (or a read-modify-write), and are performed with respect to different scopes.

*Definitions for a Sequentially Consistent Candidate Execution*

**Program Order ($\overrightarrow{po}$):** op1 $\overrightarrow{po}$ op2 iff both are from the same work-item or thread and op1 completes before op2.

**Scoped Synchronization Order ($\overrightarrow{so_S}$):** Release rel1 appears before acquire acq2 in $\overrightarrow{so_S}$ iff both are performed with respect to scope S, and rel1 completes before acq2.

**Heterogeneous-happens-before-direct ($\overrightarrow{hhb.d}$):** The union of the irreflexive transitive closures of all scope synchronization orders with program order:

$$\bigcup_{\forall S \in \mathbb{S}} (\overrightarrow{po} \cup \overrightarrow{so_S})^+$$

where $\mathbb{S}$ is the set of all scopes in an execution. Note that in the above equation, the closure applies only to the inner union and is not applied to the outer union.

**Heterogeneous Race:** A heterogeneous race occurs iff a pair of operations op1 and op2 that are either an ordinary or a synchronization conflict are unordered in $\overrightarrow{hhb.d}$.

**Heterogeneous-race-free Execution:** An execution is heterogeneous-race-free iff there are no heterogeneous races.

*Program and Model Definitions*

**Heterogeneous-Race-Free Program:** A program is heterogeneous-race-free iff all possible sequentially consistent executions of the program are heterogeneous-race-free.

**Sequential Consistency for Heterogeneous-race-free-direct (HRF-direct):** A system obeys the HRF-direct memory model iff all actual executions of a heterogeneous-race-free program are sequentially consistent.

*Corollary*

**Other Total Orders:** Because any heterogeneous-race-free program is sequentially consistent in HRF-direct, implementations must ensure an apparent total order of all heterogeneous-race-free operations, including these notable subsets:

- *A total order of all synchronization operations with respect to the same scope.*
- *A total order of all the heterogeneous-race-free synchronization operations that could be observed by any single work-item or thread.*

```
For t=0; t < nsteps; t+= group_step_size:
    group_step_size times do:
        <stencil calculation on shared grid>
        BarrierSync(work-group scope)
    BarrierSync(device scope)
    <exchange work-group boundary conditions>
```

**Figure 3. An example race-free HRF-direct algorithm**

performed without being separated by paired synchronization of identical scope, then those accesses form a *heterogeneous race* and the result on an HRF-direct system is undefined. Otherwise, a conforming implementation will guarantee that the execution is sequentially consistent. HRF-direct is a good match for *existing*, highly regular GPGPU workloads and provides considerable hardware implementation flexibility (Section 6).

If a memory model is effective, programmers should be able to easily determine the minimal amount of synchronization that must be performed for correctness. In a system with scoped synchronization, this includes selecting the smallest (i.e., fastest) scope operation possible. In HRF-direct, programmers can follow a simple rule to achieve a correct and fast execution: *use the smallest scope that includes all producers and all consumers of the data being shared.* If, for example, work-items in a work-group are coordinating to share data only within the work-group, then a work-group scope should be used. If, on the other hand, some of that data may be shared beyond that work-group in the future, a larger (e.g., device) scope must be used *by all of the work-items*.

In the sidebar on page 2 we provide a formal definition of HRF-direct that can be used to reason rigorously about program behavior or system optimizations in terms of a well-defined happens-before relation. There are two key differences in HRF-direct compared to a traditional DRF model. First, HRF-direct considers synchronization operations performed at different scopes to be conflicting operations. Second, HRF-direct creates a separate happens-before order relative to each scope. For each scope S1, the S1 happens-before order is the conventional notion of DRF happens-before but where all synchronization with respect to a different scope $S2 \neq S1$ is treated as an ordinary operation. An execution contains a race in HRF-direct if any two conflicting operations are unordered in *all* the scope-relative happens-before orders.

For now, we focus on the high-level concepts behind HRF-direct by applying it to an example to show how it can be used to reason about a high-performance heterogeneous application. We will discuss more in-depth details of the model in Section 3.3.

### 3.1 Race-free Example

In Figure 3 we show the skeleton of a simple GPGPU kernel that is synchronized correctly under HRF-direct. The algorithm, loosely modeled after the HotSpot application in the Rodinia benchmark suite [11], performs a stencil computation over a series of timesteps. The application uses a small amount of data and computation replication to reduce global synchronization. Rather than globally synchronize between each timestep, the program instead computes several timesteps locally within a work-group before having to exchange boundary conditions with neighboring work- groups. Notably, within the inner loop of Figure 3, work-items communicate only with other work-items inside their work-group and in the outer loop work-items communicate only with other work-items outside their work-group.

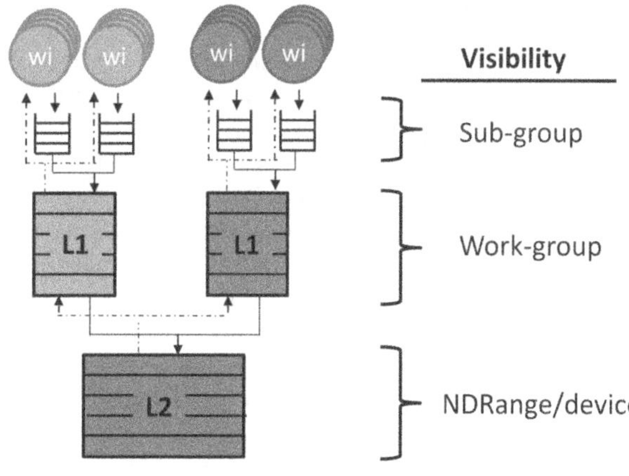


**Figure 4. Example hardware implementation for HRF-direct that closely approximates a GPU architecture.**

Because the communication pattern in the application is highly regular and predictable, it is easy to choose minimal scope for the synchronization points that will be race-free in HRF-direct. The timestep barrier in the inner loop should use work-group scope and the timestep barrier in the outer loop should use device (assuming the CPU is not involved) scope. The programmer can be sure this is race-free because between any work-item communication there is (a) synchronization using (b) scope to which both work-items belong.

While this example may seem simple, this pattern of communication is common in today's GPGPU applications. However, readers familiar with Rodinia or OpenCL / CUDA programming in general will notice two notable simplifications in the pseudocode. First, in the actual applications, the inner loop uses the GPU scratchpad memory ("local memory" in OpenCL and "shared memory" in CUDA) for all work-item communication. Second, the outer "barrier" is actually a series of distinct kernel launches. We believe that both of these characteristics will be less common in future GPGPU applications as global memory caches increase in size and inter-work-group communication becomes more possible. Models like HRF-direct will help ease that transition and ultimately make GPUs more programmable.

### 3.2 Implementation

In Figure 4, we show a baseline memory architecture similar to a modern GPU. It has a two-level cache hierarchy in which each compute unit (which runs a work-group) has a private L1 cache and the device as a whole shares an L2 cache. We assume that all caches use a write-combining strategy, and notably do not use a read-for-ownership coherence protocol. Because the caches write without exclusive permission, they keep track of partial cache block writes to avoid data corruption in the presence of false sharing. For each block, the caches maintain a bitmask of dirty bytes. When a block is evicted to the next level of cache/memory, only those dirty bytes are written back.

In general, we make this example implementation compatible with HRF-direct by (1) on a release event, flushing dirty data from any cache/memory that are not visible to all threads in the scope of synchronization, (2) on an acquire event, invalidating the now-stale data from caches/memories that are not visible to all threads in the scope of synchronization, and (3) completing all atomic operations in the cache/memory corresponding to the scope of the atomic. For example, on a work-group-scope release, the sub-group (i.e., SIMT vector)-private write buffers will be flushed to the L1 because the write buffers are not visible to all work-items in the work-group. On a device-scope acquire, the system would invalidate the acquiring work-item's L1 cache because it is not visible to all work-items on the device. On a device-scope atomic increment, the system would perform the read-modify-write entirely in the L2 cache controller.

This policy results in an SC execution of race-free HRF-direct programs. To see why, recall that HRF-direct requires conflicting accesses (same location, at least one is a write) to be separated by synchronization of the same scope. In the example implementation, that means the conflicting accesses both will have reached (at least) the same level in the memory hierarchy, and the location's most recent update will be returned. The location could not see some other value because that would constitute a race.

While this example implementation is simple, it is also representative of current hardware. Qualitatively, it also clearly shows the performance benefit of scoped synchronization; there is an obvious difference in the cost of a work-group-scope release (flush write buffers, if any) compared to a system-scope release (flush dirty data from L1 and L2 caches). When combined with the previous observation that HRF-direct is easy to use in regular heterogeneous applications, we conclude that HRF-direct is a reasonable and useful model for heterogeneous systems.

### 3.3 Subtleties of Synchronization

In HRF-direct, a program composed entirely of atomic synchronization operations could contain a race – and therefore the execution would be undefined. This is a major divergence from SC for DRF models in which any program composed entirely of synchronizing atomics is race-free. In Figure 5 we show an example all-atomic program that is racey in HRF-direct when the work-items are in different work-groups.

```
__global atomic<int> A = {0};
__global atomic<int> B = {0};
// __global means "not in a scratchpad" in OpenCL

Work-item wi1

  A.store(1, memory_order_seq_cst,
          memory_scope_work_group);
  B.load(memory_order_seq_cst,
         memory_scope_device);

Work-item wi2

     B.store(1, memory_order_seq_cst,
             memory_scope_device);

     // A.load forms a race when
     // workgroup of wi1 ≠ workgroup of wi2
     A.load(memory_order_seq_cst,
            memory_scope_work_group);
```

**Figure 5. Subtleties of synchronization order.**
**This is race-free if work-group of wi1 = work-group of wi2.**
**This is racey if work-group of wi1 ≠ work-group of wi2.**

In general, to avoid confusion about racing synchronization, a best practice when using HRF-direct is to associate a single scope with each atomic or synchronization variable. For example, software could be constructed so that variable A is always used with work-group-scope, variable B with device-scope, etc. If this practice is followed, atomic or synchronization operations will never race with each other (though other types of heterogeneous races can certainly still occur). Future languages may want to provide first-class support for mapping synchronization variables to scopes in this way.

#### 3.3.1 Digging Deep: The Order of Atomics

An HRF-direct implementation must ensure an observable total order among some atomics but not others. In a hierarchical scope layout (like OpenCL's in Figure 1), an HRF-direct implementation is free to reorder two atomics if they are performed with respect to disjoint scopes. If the scopes are disjoint, no work-item or thread in the system could observe the atomic operations without forming a race[5]. Because all attempts to observe an order directly would form a race, an implementation is not bound to produce any reliable order or even ensure atomicity. In the racey version of Figure 5, in which the two work-items belong to different work-groups, an implementation does not need to ensure the two accesses to A are ordered or atomic because the two accesses use disjoint scopes.

However, an implementation must still produce an observable total order (1) among all race-free atomics per-

[5] Unless the atomic operations are ordered as ordinary loads/stores through other, race-free, synchronization

> **Formal Definition of HRF-indirect**
>
> The structure of HRF-indirect is identical to the HRF-direct definition but with a different happens-before relation:
>
> **Heterogeneous-happens-before-indirect ($\overrightarrow{hhb.i}$):** The irreflexive transitive closure of all scope synchronization orders and program order:
>
> $$\left(\overrightarrow{po} \cup \bigcup_{\forall S \in \mathbb{S}} \overrightarrow{so_S}\right)^+$$
>
> where $\mathbb{S}$ represents the set of all scopes in an execution.

formed with respect to the same scope and (2) among all race-free atomics performed with respect to overlapping scopes. We illustrate this point in the race-free version of Figure 5, in which both work-items belong to the same work-group. Because the example is race-free, an implementation must ensure a total order between the four accesses to A and B (i.e., A = B = 0 not allowed) even though the accesses to A and B are performed with respect to different (but overlapping) scopes.

Our example implementation in Section 3.2 seeks high performance by exploiting the weaker order of atomics relative to an SC for DRF-compliant system. In that implementation, atomics are completed in the cache or memory associated with target scope (e.g., a work-group scope atomic increment is completed in the L1 cache without obtaining exclusive global permission). This implementation meets the requirements of an HRF-direct system: all race-free atomic accesses will use the same physical resource, ensuring that all work-items will observe race-free accesses in the same order.

### 3.3.2 Function Composition

Scopes complicate generic library functions that synchronize. In HRF-direct, because producers and consumers must use the same scope, it is not good enough for a generic library function to assume the worst and always synchronize with global scope. A future consumer of the data produced by that function may synchronize with a different scope, forming a race. To get around this problem, libraries may need to accept a scope as a parameter. For example, a library might provide a `lock(memory_scope s)` routine that guarantees the caller is synchronized with respect to scope `s` after the lock is acquired.

## 3.4 Limitations

While we have shown HRF-direct is a sufficient and (relatively) easy-to-understand model for programs with highly regular parallelism, it does have limitations that may impede the adoption of forward-looking software. Most notably, the HRF-direct requirement that all threads use the exact same scope could make it difficult to write high-performance synchronization in software with irregular parallelism. In situations when the producer and consumer are not known *a priori*, HRF-direct software will likely be forced to conservatively use the largest scope that includes any work-item that could be a consumer. Often, this will be the much slower device or system scope (see Section 7 for a more in-depth analysis).

```
   __global atomic<int> A = {0};
   __global atomic<int> B = {0};
   __global int X;
// __global means "not in a scratchpad" in OpenCL

Work-item wi1 -- in work-group wgX

  11: X = 1;
  12: A.store(1, memory_order_seq_cst,        // release
                 memory_scope_work_group);

Work-item wi2 -- in work-group wgX

   21: while(!A.load(memory_order_seq_cst,   // acquire
                     memory_scope_work_group));
   22: int R2 = X; // R2 will get value 1
   23: B.store(1, memory_order_seq_cst,       // release
                  memory_scope_device);

Work-item wi3 -- in work-group wgY (Note! not wgX)

   31: while(!B.load(memory_order_seq_cst,   // acquire
                     memory_scope_device));
   32: int R3 = X;  // R3 will get value 1
```

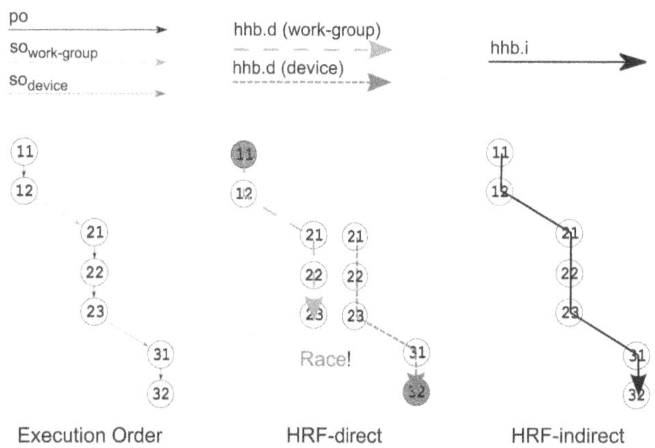


**Figure 6. An example of a racey execution in HRF-direct that is data-race-free in HRF-indirect.**

**In the diagram below the code, we show the orders established in both HRF models (left) and the happens-before order in HRF-direct (middle) and HRF-indirect (right).**

# 4 HRF-indirect: Adding Transitivity

HRF-indirect builds on the HRF-direct model by permitting communication that involves a transitive chain of synchronization that uses different scopes. We show an example of HRF-indirect's scope transitivity in Figure 6 in which work-item wi1 synchronizes with wi2 in their shared work-group scope and then wi2 synchronizes with wi3 with a different device scope. Note that this is the same execution as the DRF example in Figure 2, but altered so that the two synchronization pairs use different scopes. Notably, each pair of *direct* synchronization (e.g., between wi1 and wi2 using A) must still use the same scope (we discuss relaxing this requirement in Section 5.2).

From the programming standpoint, HRF-indirect has several advantages relative to HRF-direct. First, as Figure 6 shows, in HRF-indirect producers and consumers do not have to be aware of each other, which can expand the types of algorithms practically possible on accelerator architectures. In Section 7 we show how this situation may arise in practice. Second, it gives programmers more flexibility in the choice of scope and could lead to improved performance. If, for example, a producer knows that a work-item outside its work-group will eventually consume its data, but also knows that several steps must first occur within the work-group, then the producer may choose to perform a smaller work-group-scope synchronization and rely on work-group peers to synchronize with the more distant work-items later.

HRF-direct is compatible with HRF-indirect: all programs that are race-free in HRF-direct are also race-free in HRF-indirect. This property opens the possibility of extending existing models to support HRF-indirect in the future; such a change will not break the compatibility of existing well-behaved software.

We provide a formal definition of HRF-indirect in the sidebar on page 2. In HRF-indirect, operations are ordered in the happens-before relation if they can be linked by any transitive combination of synchronization and program order. Figure 6 visually shows the difference between the happens-before relations of HRF-direct and HRF-indirect, and emphasizes the fact that in HRF-direct, order can only be established with respect to a single scope. In Figure 6, we break the happens-before relation of HRF-direct into components attributable to the work-group and device scopes, respectively.

Like HRF-direct, in HRF-indirect synchronization release and acquire operations are only paired if they are from the same scope. As such, it is still possible to write a racey program consisting entirely of atomics. In fact, the same subtleties of synchronization mentioned in Section 3.3 for HRF-direct also apply to HRF-indirect.

### 4.1 Example Implementation

As a testament to practicality of HRF-indirect, the example implementation described in Section 3.2 for HRF-direct works as-is. That simple system, which is a good approximation of existing hardware, is a conservative implementation of HRF-direct. With HRF-indirect, software can better exploit the capabilities of existing hardware. Though, as we discuss in Section 6, HRF-indirect does not allow as many potential optimizations in the future as HRF-direct.

To see why the example implementation is compatible with HRF-indirect, consider Figure 4. When the system performs a release to device scope by flushing the L1 cache, it is not just flushing prior writes performed by that work-item – it is also flushing any prior write in the L1 performed by a different work-item in the same work-group. Therefore, in the implementation, the release actions effectively perform on behalf of the entire scope associated with that cache/memory. That is why the example in Figure 6 works. When wi2 performs the device-scope release and flushes the L1, it is also flushing the prior store to X by wi1 that must be in (at least) the L1 cache because of the prior work-group-scope release.

## 5 Exploring HRF Properties

In this section, we compare the properties of HRF-direct and HRF-indirect to existing academic and commercial memory models. Then we discuss another property that is not present in either HRF variant that future models may consider.

### 5.1 Memory Model Comparisons

#### 5.1.1 DRF

Both HRF-direct and HRF-indirect are compatible with a DRF model. In other words, any program that exclusively uses system-scope synchronization and is free of ordinary data races will be sequentially consistent with either model. Notably, this means that programmers have the option of writing data-race-free programs to begin with for functional correctness, and then adjusting scope later for performance.

#### 5.1.2 OpenCL

The first OpenCL specifications (1.x) have very restrictive memory models that do not support *any* communication outside of a work-group between kernel invocations. OpenCL 2.0 solves this particular issue with a broader definition of atomic operations.

OpenCL 2.0's execution model [28] is extended to support, among other things, fine-grain shared virtual memory (SVM), a single flat address space, and an extended subset of the recently introduced C11-style atomics [7]. The specification also contains a rigorously defined memory model that brings each of these disjoint features together into a single framework.

```
__global atomic<int> A = {0};
__global atomic<int> B = {0};
// __global means "not in a scratchpad" in OpenCL

Work-item wi1 - in workgroup wgX

  A.store(1, memory_order_seq_cst,
          memory_scope_device);
  B.load(memory_order_seq_cst,
         memory_scope_device);

Work-item wi2 - in same workgroup wgX

      B.store(1, memory_order_seq_cst,
              memory_scope_work_group);
      A.load(memory_order_seq_cst,
             memory_scope_work_group);
```

**Figure 7. An example of scope inclusion.**

The OpenCL 2.0 memory model is an SC for HRF model when the sequentially consistent ordering (`memory_order_seq_cst`) is used. OpenCL 2.0 is more restrictive than either HRF-direct or HRF-indirect– for example, in OpenCL 2.0, a program can use either device scope or system scope for atomics but not both within the same kernel. This intermix of different scoped atomics is disallowed even if individual locations are consistently accessed using atomics of the same scope. Should the designers want to relax the model in the future to allow intermixing atomics with different scope, they will need to consider the issues discussed above.

#### 5.1.3 CUDA

Recent versions of CUDA (compute capability $\geq 2.0$) support global shared memory and scoped synchronization. More specifically, CUDA supports a `__threadfence` instruction that acts as a memory fence with block (work-group), device (GPU), or system (GPU + CPU) scope. Other instructions with control-flow effects like `__syncthreads` also have scoped synchronization semantics.

Because CUDA uses a different framework to define its memory model, it is hard to make a direct comparison to the HRF models. CUDA does support a form of scope transitivity (e.g., example in Section B.5 of the CUDA Programming Guide [12]). However, because CUDA is not defined axiomatically, it is difficult to say if it has the same properties of scope transitivity defined for HRF-indirect.

#### 5.1.4 Heterogenous System Architecture and Parallel Thread Execution

HRF models are not limited to high-level languages. Low-level intermediate languages like HSAIL [21] and PTX [30] also use synchronization scopes and could benefit from a formal HRF definition. HSAIL is particularly well-suited for the HRF models in this paper because it uses a variant of scoped acquire/release synchronization.

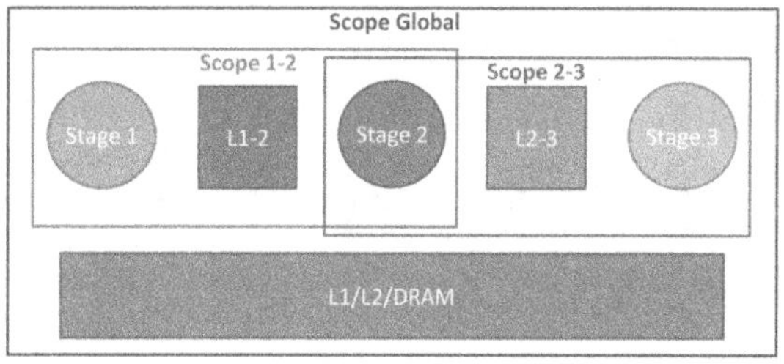


**Figure 8. Architecture and scope layout of a possible programmable pipeline.**

#### 5.1.5 Non-global Memory Types

In our discussion we have disregarded the scratchpad memories that exist in GPUs and that are exposed by both the OpenCL and CUDA programming models. While our models could be extended to include these software-controlled memories, we assume they will be less relevant in the future as heterogeneous software becomes more portable. As evidence for this trend, the more recent OpenACC programming model [32] does not include scratchpads.

### 5.2 Future HRF Models -- Scope Inclusion

Other HRF models are possible that support properties beyond those in HRF-direct/indirect. One such property is what we call *scope inclusion*[6], in which two work-items are allowed to synchronize directly (e.g., non-transitively) with each other using operations of different scope. Informally, scope inclusion would support race-free paired synchronization when the scope of the first is a subset of the scope of the second (i.e., one includes the other). We show an example in Figure 7.

Scope inclusion would require an implementation to ensure that synchronization operations with respect to inclusive scopes are ordered. This requirement is very similar to the requirement already present both in HRF-direct and HRF-indirect (and discussed in Section 3.3.1) – that atomics from overlapping scopes must be ordered. Therefore, we expect any conceivable implementation of HRF-direct or HRF-indirect would also support scope inclusion.

We did not define scope inclusion as part of the model because precisely defining when scope inclusion does and does not apply can be nuanced (as demonstrated by the complexity of Section 3.3.1 describing a similar property). However, given a concise and understandable definition, scope inclusion could be added to either HRF model by altering the definition of a synchronization conflict.

[6] OpenCL 2.0 uses the term "scope inclusion" to mean "the exact same scope." However, the term is defined in such a way that extending to the notion of inclusion described here would be straightforward in the future.

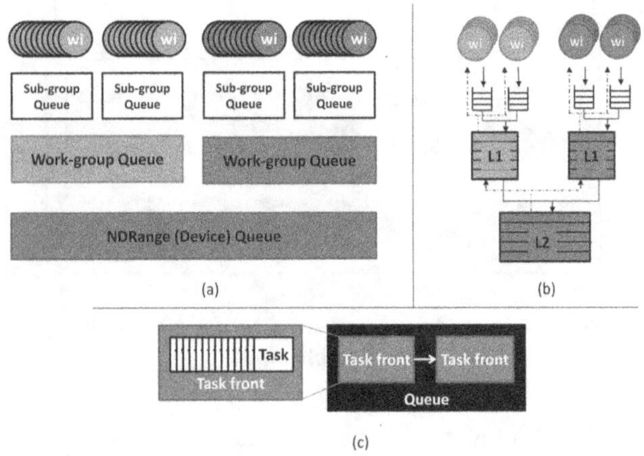


**Figure 9. (a) Task queue hierarchy, (b) the heterogeneous hardware it maps to (same as Figure 4), and (c) queue contents.**

## 6 System Optimizations

While the more permissive HRF-indirect model enables higher performance on current hardware, it may limit some hardware optimizations in the future compared to HRF-direct. To support HRF-direct in a system like the one in Figure 4, on a release, an implementation only needs to flush locations that have been written by the releasing work-item. Other blocks in the cache could remain untouched, potentially reducing the negative effect synchronization has on other work-items sharing those resources.

The same targeted flush optimization would be incorrect on an HRF-indirect-compatible system. Because of the transitivity property, a release in HRF-indirect does not just guarantee visibility of locations touched by the releasing work-item. Rather, it also guarantees visibility of any location touched by another work-item that previously synchronized with the releasing work-item. Thus, while an implementation with more targeted flush operations is possible, it would take considerable design effort to determine which blocks are safe to ignore.

An efficient implementation of HRF-indirect in a non-RFO system relies on a hierarchical memory layout and scopes that do not partially overlap. This is likely to be a feature of foreseeable GPU architectures but could be an issue with future non-hierarchical memory systems. For example, the architecture of the recently proposed Convolution Engine by Qadeer, et al. [34] resembles a programmable pipeline. To reduce the latency of communicating between neighboring pipeline stages, a designer might want to build a cache between the stages that can be controlled with an HRF scope, as shown in Figure 8. While possible, it would likely take considerable engineering effort to avoid flushing the inter-stage caches on all synchronization events, even when an inter-stage scope is used.

## 7 Case Study: Work-sharing Task Runtime

We have previously argued that HRF-direct is suitable for current regular GPGPU programs and that both HRF-direct and HRF-indirect are supported by some current hardware.

Here we seek to show that programmers who confront HRF-indirect's complexity can be rewarded with higher performance than with HRF-direct. To this end, we have developed a work-sharing, task-parallel runtime for GPUs that serves as an example of a workload with irregular parallelism and unpredictable synchronization. This section describes the design of that runtime and discusses how HRF-direct and HRF-indirect affect software design decisions. In Section 8, we will show how those decisions affect performance on a system resembling modern GPU hardware.

We have built a work-sharing runtime whose internal task queue is split into a hierarchy resembling the entities in the OpenCL execution model and, by extension, physical components in GPU hardware. For now, the runtime only supports GPU work-item workers and does not support CPU (host) thread workers. In the future the runtime could be extended to support participation from the CPU. The work-sharing task queue is broken into three levels, namely the device queue, multiple work-group queues, and multiple sub-group queues, as shown in Figure 9(a).

### 7.1 Runtime Description

Applications use the runtime by defining tasks from the perspective of a single, independent worker. Notably, the programmer does not need to consider the OpenCL execution hierarchy, because the runtime scheduler effectively hides those details. The runtime itself is built using the persistent threads [18] execution model, and takes complete control of task scheduling and load balancing by bypassing the hardware scheduler (by monopolizing all execution units).

To map the task-parallel execution model exposed by the runtime onto the OpenCL hierarchy, the runtime collects tasks created by workers into sub-group-sized (e.g., 64) groups called *task-fronts*. As shown in Figure 9c, task-fronts are the objects held in the task queues, and are assigned to ready sub-groups. Each task in a task front will run on a different work-item in the sub-group. To reduce control divergence that could decrease performance, the runtime ensures that all tasks in a task front call the same function. A sub-group will generally wait until a task front is full before dequeueing work except in some corner cases where it may be beneficial to grab a partial task-front and tolerate idle work-items (e.g., at the beginning of execution).

The runtime implements a work-sharing, as opposed to a work-stealing, load-balancing policy. When a sub-group has produced enough tasks to fill a task front, it will first enqueue it onto its own private sub-group queue. Then, the sub-group may decide to donate one or more task fronts from its private queue if the occupancy of either the work-group or device queues is below a minimum threshold. A

Table 1. Configuration Parameters

| Parameter | Value |
|---|---|
| # Compute Units | 8 |
| # SIMD Units / Compute Unit | 4 |
| L1 cache | 32Kb, 16-way |
| L2 cache | 2MB, 16-way |

sub-group always donates the oldest task in the queue under the assumption that the oldest task will create the most new work and thus avoid future donations.

### 7.2 HRF-direct/HRF-indirect Runtimes

In the runtime, inter-worker communication occurs at task enqueue/dequeue points. At those points, the runtime must decide which scope to use for synchronization. The decision is complicated by the fact that the worker does not know at enqueue time who the eventual consumer will be. For example, if a worker makes a donation to the work-group queue, it must assume that another worker could later donate the work to the device queue. Thus, the eventual consumer could be anywhere in the system.

This unknown-consumer aspect makes it difficult to efficiently synchronize with the HRF-direct model. Recall that HRF-direct mandates that both producer and consumer use identical scope to synchronize. In a straightforward HRF-direct implementation, all synchronization must use device (NDRange) scope since neither producer nor consumer know each other. There may be ways to avoid an always-global scope policy, but it would complicate the runtime and could require invasive policies such as a restriction on which tasks can be donated from a queue (potentially impacting performance since "oldest first" donation, which has been shown to have optimal performance in some task runtimes [6], would not be straightforward).

In contrast, the transitive property of HRF-indirect makes it possible to perform smaller scope synchronization even when the exact producer/consumer pair is not known *a priori*. Consider the problematic (for HRF-direct) case above in which a task front is donated by a different worker than the one that originally performed the enqueue. When the donation occurs, the donating worker will perform a larger scope synchronization operation and will form a transitive link between the original producer and the eventual consumer, much like the interaction shown in Figure 6. Thus, the execution will be race-free and workers can use smaller scope in the common (non-donating) case.

# 8 Evaluation

In this section, we seek to qualitatively show that there are practical differences between the HRF-direct and HRF-indirect models in current heterogeneous hardware. We do so by evaluating the performance of HRF-direct and HRF-indirect versions of the task runtime previously discussed.

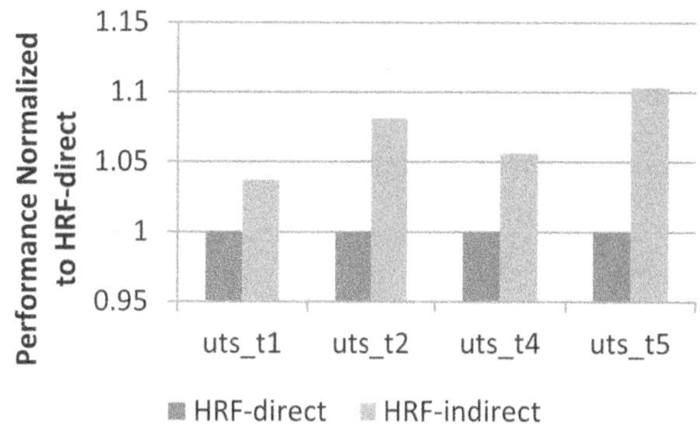


Figure 10. Performance normalized to HRF-direct.

### 8.1 Methodology

We wrote the task runtime in OpenCL 2.0, extended to support HRF-indirect in addition to HRF-direct. On top of that, we ported the Unbalanced Tree Search (`uts`) synthetic workload [31]. `uts` represents the traversal of an unbalanced graph whose topology is determined dynamically as the program runs. On visiting a node, the program computes how many children to create using (deterministic) SHA-1 hash computation. Thus, the tasks themselves are short and the number of children varies widely, making the workload a good test of task-parallel runtimes.

We evaluate the runtime using four different input sets to `uts`. The four represent scaled-down versions of the T1, T2, T4, and T5 graphs suggested in the source code release [38], and contain approximately 125K nodes each. We do not include results from the T3 graph because it does not have enough parallelism for GPU execution.

To calculate the performance of the workload, we run it in a version of the gem5 simulator [5] that has been extended with a GPU execution and memory model. We configured the GPU to resemble a modern mid-sized device with eight compute units, with the precise options shown in Table 1. The memory system for the GPU operates like the example system in Section 3.2, in which caches are write-combining and are flushed/invalidated based on the scope of synchronization. We do not implement the potential future hardware optimizations discussed in Section 6.

### 8.2 Results

Figure 10 shows the performance of each input set for the HRF-direct and HRF-indirect versions of the task runtime. In all cases, the HRF-indirect version has higher performance due to the reduction in the number of expensive L1 flush/invalidate operations. The exact speed-ups vary between 3% and 10%, and correlate with the number of donations that occur during the traversal of a particular graph. Generally, more donations (caused by a more unbalanced tree) lead to better relative performance with the HRF-indirect implementation.

#### 8.2.1 Limitations and Caveats

We have not implemented the HRF-direct hardware optimizations discussed in Section 6 nor the HRF-direct software improvements discussed in Section 7.2. Doing any one or a combination of these optimizations may alter the results and conclusions discussed above. However, for reasons discussed in Section 7.2, including a sub-optimal task ordering, our intuition tells us it is unlikely to surpass the performance of HRF-indirect in this workload.

## 9 Related Work

Hechtman and Sorin recently argued that GPU systems should implement SC, in part, by showing that the performance of an SC GPU is comparable to one implementing a weaker model [20]. Their analysis, however, assumes a GPU that implements read-for-ownership coherence and does not take interaction with a CPU core into account. In this paper, we assume hardware that better represents current GPUs (e.g., write combining buffers, scoped synchronization, and no read-for-ownership coherence), and propose SC for HRF as a class of models to reason about consistency in similar current and future GPUs.

Other implementations of an HRF-direct/indirect compatible system are also possible. Hechtman et al. proposed a compatible cache hierarchy that will perform better that our basic example implementation in Section 3.2 for programs that make use of fine-grain synchronization [19].

Scoped synchronization is not limited to GPU systems. The Power7 CPU system uses scoped broadcasts in its coherence protocol [22]. Though this scoping is not ex-posed to the programmers, it nonetheless represents the trend toward scoped synchronization in modern hardware.

One could argue that message-passing models like MPI provide scoped consistency by allowing threads to specify senders and receivers explictly [16]. Of course, message-passing models do not use shared memory, and as a result are difficult to use with algorithms involving pointer-based data structures like linked lists. In addition, shared memory programs are easier for compilers to optimize because in MPI compilers must have semantic knowledge of the API to perform effective operation reordering [13].

Recently, there has been an effort in the high-performance community to push programming models that make use of a partitioned global address space (PGAS). These include languages like X10 [10], UPC [8], and Chapel [9]. Like SC for HRF models, these PGAS languages present a single shared address space to all threads. However, not all addresses in that space are treated equally. Some addresses can be accessed only locally while others can be accessed globally but have an affinity or home node. As a result, PGAS programs still explicitly copy data between memory regions for high performance. In contrast, in an SC for HRF model, a particular address is not bound to a home node and there is no need for application threads to copy data explicitly between memory regions. Instead, an SC for HRF model uses scoped synchronization operations to limit the communication overhead between a subset of threads.

There has been recent work on coherence alternatives for shared memory in GPU architectures. Cohesion is a system for distinguishing coherent and incoherent data on GPU accelerators [23]. The incoherent data has to be managed by software with explicit hardware actions like cache flushes. SC for HRF models, on the other hand, abstract away hardware details for programmers and rely on an implementation to manage memory resources.

One downside of both the SC for DRF and SC for HRF models is that racey software has undefined behavior. This can be especially problematic in codes that use intentional (benign) data races or in codes containing unintentional bugs. To address this, Marino, et al. proposed the DRFx model that, in addition to guaranteeing sequential consistency for data-race-free programs, will raise a memory model exception when a racey execution violates sequential consistency [27]. To do so, the authors propose adding SC violation detection hardware similar to conflict detection mechanisms in hardware transactional memory proposals. Either of the HRF variants discussed in this paper could benefit from a similar memory model exception should designers wish to support it. Lucia et al. concurrently proposed conflict exceptions that, like DRFx, raise a memory model exception on a race [25]. However, conflict exceptions are more precise and mandate that the exception be raised at the point of conflicting address.

## 10 Conclusions

We have introduced sequential consistency for heterogeneous-race-free (SC for HRF), a class of memory models to intuitively and robustly define the behavior of scoped synchronization operations in heterogeneous systems. We motivated the need for SC for HRF by showing why the existing understanding of race freedom in homogeneous CPU systems is insufficient when applied to systems using synchronization scopes. We proposed two initial SC for HRF models. HRF-direct represents the capabilities of existing heterogeneous languages and requires synchronizing threads to use the exact same scope. In the forward-looking HRF-indirect model, threads can synchronize transitively using different scopes. Our results show that HRF-indirect may have performance advantages for software with irregular parallelism, but may also restrict some future hardware optimizations.


## Acknowledgements

We thank the anonymous reviewers and Hans Boehm for their insightful comments and feedback. We also thank Marc Orr and Shuai Che for their participation in many constructive discussions.


## References


[1] Adve, S.V. and Boehm, H.-J. 2010. Semantics of shared variables & synchronization a.k.a. memory models.

[2] Adve, S.V. and Gharachorloo, K. 1996. Shared memory consistency models: A tutorial. *Computer*. 29, 12 (1996), 66–76.

[3] Adve, S.V. and Hill, M.D. 1990. Weak ordering—a new definition. *Proceedings of the International Symposium on Computer Architecture* (New York, NY, USA, 1990), 2–14.

[4] AMD, Inc. 2012. Southern Islands series instruction set architecture. Advanced Micro Devices.

[5] Binkert, N., Beckmann, B., Black, G., Reinhardt, S.K., Saidi, A., Basu, A., Hestness, J., Hower, D.R., Krishna, T. and Sardashti, S. 2011. The gem5 simulator. *ACM SIGARCH Computer Architecture News*. 39, 2 (2011), 1–7.

[6] Blumofe, R.D., Joerg, C.F., Kuszmaul, B.C., Leiserson, C.E., Randall, K.H. and Zhou, Y. 1995. *Cilk: An efficient multithreaded runtime system*. ACM.

[7] Boehm, H.-J. and Adve, S.V. 2008. Foundations of the C++ concurrency memory model. *International Symposium on Programming Language Design and Implementation (PLDI)* (Tuscon, AZ, Jun. 2008), 68–78.

[8] Carlson, W.W., Draper, J.M., Culler, D.E., Yelick, K., Brooks, E. and Warren, K. 1999. *Introduction to UPC and language specification*. Center for Computing Sciences, Institute for Defense Analyses.

[9] Chamberlain, B.L., Callahan, D. and Zima, H.P. 2007. Parallel programmability and the chapel language. *International Journal of High Performance Computing Applications*. 21, 3 (2007), 291–312.

[10] Charles, P., Grothoff, C., Saraswat, V., Donawa, C., Kielstra, A., Ebcioglu, K., Von Praun, C. and Sarkar, V. 2005. X10: an object-oriented approach to non-uniform cluster computing. *ACM SIGPLAN Notices* (2005), 519–538.

[11] Che, S., Boyer, M., Meng, J., Tarjan, D., Sheaffer, J.W., Lee, S.-H. and Skadron, K. 2009. Rodinia: a benchmark suite for heterogeneous computing. *IEEE International Symposium on Workload Characterization, 2009. IISWC 2009* (Oct. 2009), 44 –54.

[12] CUDA 5.5 C programming guide: 2013. *http://docs.nvidia.com/cuda/cuda-c-programming-guide/*. Accessed: 2013-12-19.

[13] Danalis, A., Pollock, L., Swany, M. and Cavazos, J. 2009. MPI-aware compiler optimizations for improving communication-computation overlap. *Proceedings of the 23rd international conference on Supercomputing* (2009), 316–325.

[14] Dubois, M., Scheurich, C. and Briggs, F. 1986. Memory access buffering in multiprocessors. *ISCA '86 Proceedings of the 13th annual international symposium on Computer architecture* (1986), 434–442.

[15] Gharachorloo, K., Lenoski, D., Laudon, J., Gibbons, P., Gupta, A. and Hennessy, J. 1990. Memory consistency and event ordering in scalable shared-memory multiprocessors. *Proceedings of the 17th annual International Symposium on Computer Architecture* (1990), 376–387.

[16] Gropp, W., Lusk, E. and Skjellum, A. 1999. *Using MPI: portable parallel programming with the message passing interface*. MIT press.

[17] Guiady, C., Falsafi, B. and Vijaykumar, T.N. 1999. Is SC+ILP=RC? *Proceedings of the 26th International Symposium on Computer Architecture, 1999* (1999), 162 –171.

[18] Gupta, K., Stuart, J. and Owens, J.D. 2012. A study of persistent threads style GPU programming for GPGPU workloads. *Proceedings of Innovative Parallel Computing (InPar '12)* (May 2012).

[19] Hechtman, B.A., Che, S., Hower, D.R., Tian, Y., Beckmann, B.M., Hill, M.D., Reinhardt, S.K. and Wood, D.A. 2014. QuickRelease: a throughput oriented approach to release consistency on GPUs. *Proceedings of the 20th International Symposium on High Performance Computer Architecture (HPCA)* (Orland, FL, Feb. 2014).

[20] Hechtman, B.A. and Sorin, D.J. 2013. Exploring memory consistency for massively-threaded throughput-oriented processors. *Proceedings of the 40th International Symposium on Computer Architecture (ISCA)* (Tel Aviv, Israel, Jun. 2013).

[21] HSA Foundation 2012. *Heterogeneous System Architecture: A Technical Review*.

[22] Kalla, R., Sinharoy, B., Starke, W.J. and Floyd, M. 2010. Power7: IBM's next-generation server processor. *IEEE Micro*. 30, 2 (2010), 7–15.

[23] Kelm, J.H., Johnson, D.R., Tuohy, W., Lumetta, S.S. and Patel, S.J. 2010. Cohesion: a hybrid memory model for accelerators. *Proceedings of the 37th annual international symposium on Computer architecture* (New York, NY, USA, 2010), 429–440.

[24] Lamport, L. 1979. How to make a multiprocessor computer that correctly executes multiprocess programs. *IEEE Transactions on Computers*. C-28, 9 (Sep. 1979), 690 –691.

[25] Lucia, B., Ceze, L., Strauss, K., Qadeer, S. and Boehm, H.J. 2010. Conflict exceptions: providing simple concurrent language semantics with precise hardware exceptions. *International Symposium on Computer Architecture (ISCA)* (2010).

[26] Manson, J., Pugh, W. and Adve, S.V. 2005. The Java memory model. *Proceedings of the 32nd ACM SIGPLAN-SIGACT symposium on Principles of programming languages* (New York, NY, USA, 2005), 378–391.

[27] Marino, D., Singh, A., Millstein, T., Musuvathi, M. and Narayanasamy, S. 2010. DRFX: a simple and efficient memory model for concurrent programming languages. *Proceedings of the 2010 ACM SIGPLAN conference on Programming language design and implementation* (New York, NY, USA, 2010), 351–362.

[28] Munshi, A. ed. 2013. The OpenCL Specification, Version 2.0 (Provisional). Khronos Group.

[29] Munshi, A., Gaster, B. and Mattson, T.G. 2011. *OpenCL programming guide*. Addison-Wesley Professional.

[30] NVIDIA Corporation 2012. *Parallel Thread Execution ISA Version 3.1*.

[31] Olivier, S., Huan, J., Liu, J., Prins, J., Dinan, J., Sadayappan, P. and Tseng, C.-W. 2007. UTS: An unbalanced tree search benchmark. *Languages and Compilers for Parallel Computing*. Springer. 235–250.

[32] OpenACC, Inc 2011. The OpenACC™ Application Programming Interface, Version 1.0.

[33] Owens, S., Sarkar, S. and Sewell, P. 2009. A better x86 memory model: x86-TSO. *Proceedings of the 22nd International Conference on Theorem Proving in Higher Order Logics* (Berlin, Heidelberg, 2009), 391–407.

[34] Qadeer, W., Hameed, R., Shacham, O., Venkatesan, P., Kozyrakis, C. and Horowitz, M.A. 2013. Convolution engine: balancing efficiency & flexibility in specialized computing.

*Proceedings of the 40th Annual International Symposium on Computer Architecture* (2013), 24–35.

[35] Sindhu, P.S., Frailong, J.-M. and Cekleov, M. 1992. Formal specification of memory models. *Scalable Shared Memory Multiprocessors: Proceedings*. (1992), 25.

[36] Sorin, D.J., Hill, M.D. and Wood, D.A. 2011. A Primer on Memory Consistency and Cache Coherence. *Synthesis Lectures on Computer Architecture*. 6, 3 (2011), 1–212.

[37] Thakkar, S., Gifford, P. and Fielland, G. 1988. The balance multiprocessor system. *IEEE Micro*. 8, 1 (Jan. 1988), 57–69.

[38] UTS source distribution: *http://sourceforge.net/p/uts-benchmark/wiki/Home/*.

# Triple-A: A Non-SSD Based Autonomic All-Flash Array for High Performance Storage Systems


Myoungsoo Jung[1], Wonil Choi[1], John Shalf[3], and Mahmut Taylan Kandemir[2]

[1] Department of EE, The University of Texas at Dallas, Computer Architecture and Memory Systems Laboratory
[2] Department of CSE, The Pennsylvania State University, Microsystems Design Laboratory
[3] National Energy Research Scientif c Computing Center, Lawrence Berkeley National Laboratory
{jung, wonil.choi}@utdallas.edu, jshalf@lbl.gov, kandemir@cse.psu.edu



## Abstract

Solid State Disk (SSD) arrays are in a position to (as least partially) replace spinning disk arrays in high performance computing (HPC) systems due to their better performance and lower power consumption. However, these emerging SSD arrays are facing enormous challenges, which are not observed in disk-based arrays. Specif cally, we observe that the performance of SSD arrays can signif cantly degrade due to various array-level resource contentions. In addition, their maintenance costs exponentially increase over time, which renders them diff cult to deploy widely in HPC systems. To address these challenges, we propose Triple-A, a non-SSD based Autonomic All-Flash Array, which is a self-optimizing, from-scratch NAND f ash cluster. Triple-A can detect two different types of resource contentions and autonomically alleviate them by reshaping the physical data-layout on its f ash array network. Our experimental evaluation using both real workloads and a micro-benchmark show that Triple-A can offer a 53% higher sustained throughput and a 80% lower I/O latency than non-autonomic SSD arrays.



***Categories and Subject Descriptors*** B.3.1 [*Memory Structures*]: Semiconductor Memories; D.4.2 [*Operating Systems*]: Storage Management; C.4 [*Computer System Organization*]: Performance of Systems

***General Terms*** Solid State Disk; NAND Flash; High Performance Computing; Flash Array Network; Resource Contention; Self Optimizing.


## 1. Introduction

Over past years, High Performance Computing (HPC) storage systems have increased storage capacity by adding expansion enclosures with low-cost spinning disks. While such a scale-up HPC storage system achieves high aggregate storage processing capacity, its data processing capacity does not increase linearly. In addition, the bandwidth improvements brought by this traditional HPC storage system started to stagnate since a large fraction of spinning disks are underutilized most of the time. For instance, [10] observed that IBM Blue Gene/P system, called Intrepid, achieves only one-third bandwidth of its full capacity in 99% of the time. As the computational power and degree of parallelism of HPC increase, this underutilization becomes a more problematic challenge in meeting HPC users' high bandwidth and low latency demands [10, 30].




*ASPLOS '14*, March 1–5, 2014, Salt Lake City, Utah, USA.





http://dx.doi.org/10.1145/2541940.2541953


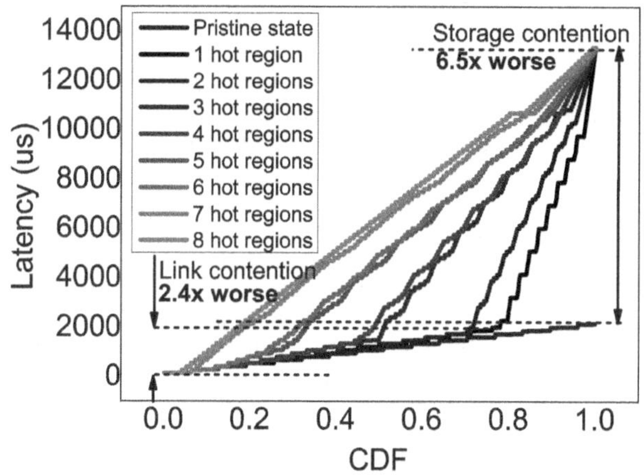


Figure 1: Cumulative distribution function with varying hot regions, which refer to a group of SSDs having at least 10% of the total data in a f ash array. Note that, as we increase the number of hot regions (i.e., put more pressure on the f ash array), resulting link- and storage-contentions degrade performance by 2.4x and 6.5x, respectively.

To address this problem, several HPC systems employ Solid State Disks (SSDs) [9, 13, 20, 31, 39]. For example, Carver [36], an IBM iDataPlex cluster, of NERSC at Lawrence Berkley National Laboratory employs two high-performance SSDs for each storage server node (known as Lustre Router Node) [7, 33]. These sever nodes are connected to thousands of compute nodes over 4x QDR Inf niBand, and their SSDs are connected to the RAID couplets for the Lustre storage on the back-end as a storage cache. These multiple SSD caches are mainly used for very data-intensive applications such as out-of-core computations [53] that primarily exhibit read-intensive access patterns [9, 27, 31, 53].

In contrast, Argonne National Laboratory and Los Alamos National Laboratory employ multiple SSDs as a burst buffer in I/O nodes at the compute node side [30, 40]. The main purpose of this SSD server is to absorb the heavy write traff c exhibited by check-pointing and some other I/O-intensive HPC applications before storing actual data into back-end f le servers and enterprise storage servers over Ethernet and Inf niBand.

One of main challenges behind these HPC SSD use-cases is that they are *not* designed for scalability. Specif cally, the SSDs are directly connected to individual HPC compute nodes or server storage nodes and optimized for specif c applications. Recently, industry have announced SSD-based, all-f ash storage systems, composed of hundreds or thousands enterprise-scale SSDs in the form of one-large-pool storage server. For example, NetApp announced that an all-SSD server for transactional, database-driven applications will be available sometime in 2014 [37]. Pure Storage and EMC proposed a 100% f ash storage array composed of multiple SAS-based SSDs [18, 46]. While these SSD arrays offer better performance and scalability as one-large-pool storage systems, *the cost of an SSD is still too high to replace a conventional disk*, and *the maintenance costs of these SSD arrays are unacceptable compared to current main memory technologies* (the costs exponentially increase). In addition, architectural and implementation details of these emerging all-SSD arrays are not known; to our knowledge, there are no publicly available specif cations for all-f ash arrays.

More importantly, we observe that these SSD arrays face enormous challenges, which are not normally observed in disk-based arrays. Figure 1 plots the cumulative distribution function of an *all-f ash* array consisting of 256GB 80 SSDs with varying data localities. One can see from this graph that the performance of the SSD array degrades as the number of hot regions increases – a hot region in this context corresponds to a group of SSDs having at least 10% of the total data in a f ash array. There are two main reasons behind this performance degradation: 1) *link contention* and 2) *storage contention*. Even though the target SSD associated with incoming I/O requests may be ready to serve them immediately, if there already exists another SSD delivering data over the I/O bus shared by the target device, the incoming I/O requests have to be stalled until the I/O bus is released. This is referred to as link contention. On the other hand, the incoming I/O requests could also be stalled at a system-level (even though the data path is available), if the target SSD is busy in serving other I/O requests submitted in a previous stage, referred to as storage contention in this paper.

In this paper, we propose *Triple-A*, a *non-SSD based Autonomic All-Flash Array*, which is a self-optimizing, from-scratch NAND f ash cluster. Triple-A enables autonomic resource management, which can in turn alleviate both link-contention and storage-contention. Our experimental study shows that the proposed Triple-A offers about 53% and 80% higher sustained bandwidth and lower latency than non-autonomic SSD arrays, respectively. Our main **contributions** in this paper can be summarized as follows:

- *Autonomic link contention management.* Triple-A is able to detect the straggler I/O requests caused by link contention and migrate the corresponding data from the destination f ash module(s) of the stragglers to new locations where the local shared bus is almost underutilized. Even though our autonomic link contention management is performed online, the required data migration can be overlapped with the data movement involved in serving the straggler I/O requests.
- *Autonomic storage contention management.* Triple-A autonomically reshapes the physical data-layout for the specif c f ash module suffering from storage contention, referred to as *Laggard*. In this reshaping, data on different physical blocks are moved from the laggard to adjacent f ash modules in the background. As a result, Triple-A can address the storage contention problem and hide the data/storage processing time on reshaping the physical data-layout on its f ash array network.
- *A from-scratch, all-f ash array architecture.* A unique characteristic of Triple-A is that it employs f ash modules rather than SSDs, by taking the bare NAND f ash memory out from an SSD box. This *unboxing* the f ash modules can deduct the costs of auxiliary internal counterparts from the cost of SSD, which can in turn lead to 50% cost reduction when building and managing hot-swappable and scalable all-f ash arrays.

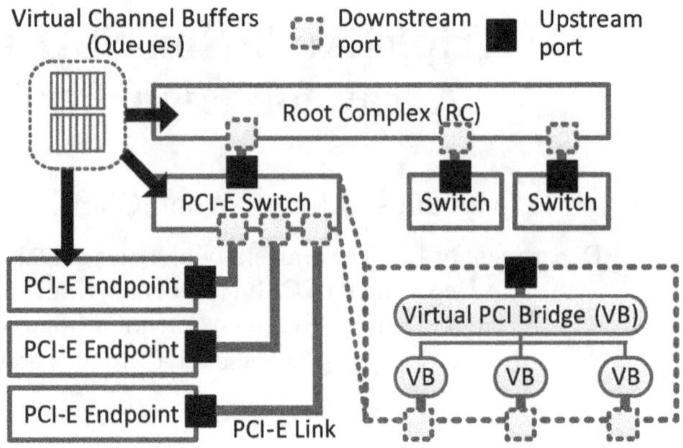


Figure 2: PCI Express topology and corresponding devices.

## 2. Background

Before presenting the details of our proposed system, we discuss background on f ash arrays. We f rst introduce PCI-E devices and their network topology, which is used for interconnecting NAND f ash modules in our all-f ash array, and then explain the modern NAND f ash technology that we leverage in this work. We conclude this section with an explanation of the fundamental functionality of f ash software modules and the software stack.

### 2.1 PCI Express

Unlike a conventional I/O bus that handles data from multiple resources, PCI Express (PCI-E) implements a point-to-point serial connection, which is dual-simplex, high speed and high performance. As shown in Figure 2, this network-like connection makes PCI-E a promising interface to build large-scale high-speed storage mediums. Below, we explain the main PCI-E components employed in building our all-f ash array.

**Root Complex (RC).** PCI-E RC supports one or more PCI ports, each of which is connected to a PCI-E switch device or underlying endpoint devices. PCI-E RC generates I/O transaction requests on behalf of host processor(s) and can route requests from one port to another. In practice, RC implements central computing resources including hot-plug, power management and interrupt controllers. In a f ash array

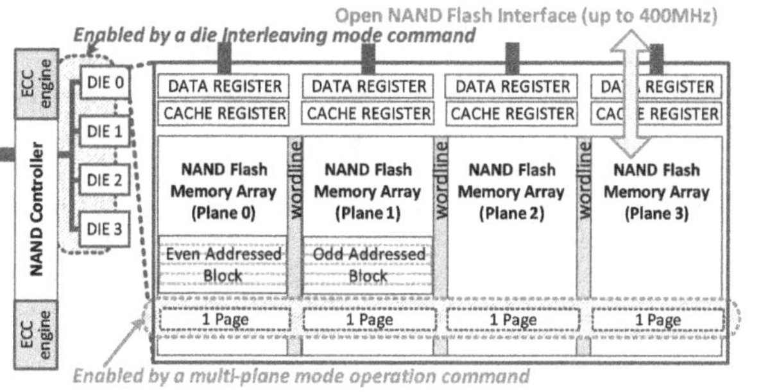


Figure 3: Bare NAND f ash memory package.

architecture, root complex can also implement f ash software and def ne the corresponding f ash storage stack.

**Switch Device.** PCI-E switch consists of two or more virtual PCI-E to PCI-E bridges, which can in turn create multiple PCI-E endpoints (peripheral device). Considering Figure 2 as an example, a four-port switch is composed of four virtual bridges internally connected by an undef ned bus; the upstream port is the port in the direction of PCI-E RC, and, all other ports are referred to as downstream ports, away from the RC. This switch can forward *packets* encoding the request transactions to the next device or destination based on address routing or device-ID routing through these upstream and downstream ports. It should be noted that this switch device can form a sub-hierarchy underneath RC, which in turn makes PCI-E systems highly scalable.

**Flow Control.** Each PCI-E device, including RC, switch and endpoints, implements its own *virtual channel buffer*. Therefore, a transmitted PCI-E packet is received into the virtual channel buffer of the target PCI-E device, called receiver. In practice, receivers periodically update transmitters on how much buffer/queue space they have available to serve incoming requests, and the transmitters send new packets only when the receivers have enough queue entries or buffer space to hold them. Clearly, if the destination is unavailable to serve or link associated with the target is occupied by other receivers or transmitters, the packet should be stalled in the virtual channel queue, which normally causes performance degradation.

### 2.2 Bare NAND Flash Package

**Internals.** As shown in Figure 3, NAND f ash packages usually employ multiple f ash dies which can operate in parallel to serve incoming memory requests. Each die is formed by putting multiple planes together over shared wordline(s). Different planes are identif ed by even or odd block addresses and can also concurrently service multiple requests. In addition, f ash packages employ internal cache and data registers to mitigate the latency gap between the I/O interface and the memory array.

**Parallelism and Commands.** The different internal storage components shown in the f gure can be activated in different fashions based on which NAND f ash command is received at runtime. For example, the die-interleaving mode f ash command can interleave memory requests among multiple dies, whereas the multi-plane mode f ash command activates multiple planes in one or more dies in a f ash package. Note also that, the cache mode f ash command is required to take advantage of the internal cache registers.

**Embedded Controller and ECC Engines.** The NAND f ash controller within f ash packages is connected to the NAND internal buses via the ONFi interface. This embedded controller parses the f ash commands and handles the protocols associated them. In addition, the controller of a modern f ash package typically implements an ECC engine, which implements a 128 bit (or more) error correction capability. This controller decouples reliability management from f ash software and simplif es the design of a f ash array.

### 2.3 Flash Software Modules

**Hardware Abstract Layer (HAL).** To extract the true performance of a bare NAND f ash, it is essential to compose f ash commands which can take advantage of high degree of internal parallelism. HAL creates f ash commands and handles the corresponding NAND f ash protocols. Specif cally, HAL commits a series of commands to the underlying f ash packages, handles data movements, and oversees transaction completions. Thanks to HAL, other f ash software modules are free from hardware specif c operations and treat multiple f ash packages over block device APIs (e.g., they read and write on physical address space that HAL abstracts).

**Flash Translation Layer (FTL).** FTL is a key component of any f ash software stack, which hides the complexities and constraints of the underlying f ash medium like the erase-before-write requirement and endurance limits. Generally speaking, FTL translates/remaps addresses between the virtual and physical spaces in order to offer block-level storage interface compatibility with spinning disks. It also performs wear-leveling, garbage collection, and data access parallelization across multiple f ash packages.

**Flash Software Stack.** The f ash software modules discussed above are usually implemented within solid state disks (SSDs) in the form of f rmware or embedded system software. However, as NAND f ash memories are widely deployed across diverse computing domains and become increasingly popular, SSD vendors are increasingly motivated to take out these f ash software modules from their devices and place them into the host-side. This software stack reorganization can improve the management of the underlying devices by being aware of the host-level information and by taking advantage of abundant host-level resources (e.g., multicores). In a similar manner, these f ash modules can be also implemented in one or more PCI-E devices within a PCI-E network.

## 3. Non-SSD based All-Flash Array

In this section, we f rst provide the motivation behind our proposed *non-SSD* f ash module approach, and then explain a f ash array architecture that can be used to build a highly scalable storage server. Lastly, we describe how such non-SSD f ash modules can be organized and discuss how they can be incarnated as a storage cluster beneath the f ash array topology.

### 3.1 Motivation

SSD-based all-f ash arrays [18, 37, 46] are expandable by adding more SSD storage shelves, and maintained by replacing the worn-out SSDs with new ones. Clearly, the price of an individual SSD is key to enabling these SSD arrays in HPC or major enterprise-scale systems with high scalability and serviceability. Unfortunately, SSDs are com-

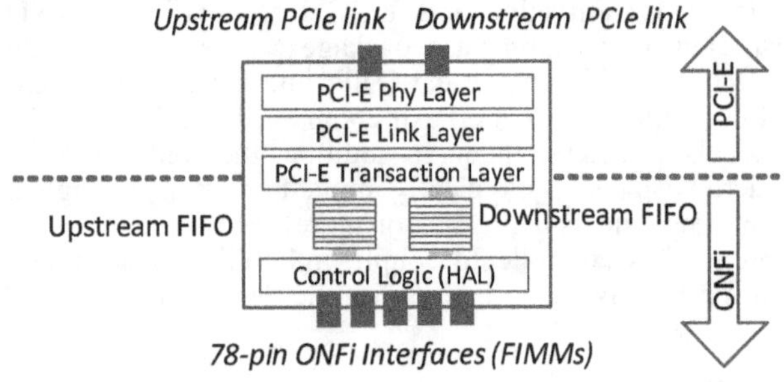


Figure 4: An endpoint device that can be used to build a cluster.

plex systems, which makes them expensive (even though NAND f ash costs are expected to continue going down). Specif cally, bare NAND f ash packages in an SSD only account for 50% $\sim$ 65% of the total SSD cost (in comparison, DRAMs on Dual Inline Memory Module (DIMM) are 98% of the DIMM's cost [1]). This is because SSDs include costly f rmware and controllers such as host interface controllers, f ash controllers, microprocessors, and internal DRAM buffer modules (256MB $\sim$ 2GB) in addition to the NAND f ash storage itself, whereas most of the control logic in DRAM is implemented in outside of DIMM. Consequently, SSD-based all-f ash arrays needs to pay more than required for these extra software/hardware modules every time a worn-out SSD need to be replaced, and this cost penalty makes the large-scale deployment of SSD-based arrays diff cult in HPC systems.

Motivated by this, we introduce a novel *non-SSD based* all-f ash array architecture, which is a highly-scalable storage system built from scratch by *unboxing SSDs and interconnecting them over a PCI-E network*. This from-scratch (i.e., non-SSD based) array architecture can remove about 35% $\sim$ 50% extra hardware/software costs, making it a very promising storage solution for HPC.

### 3.2 Flash Array Architecture

Figure 5 illustrates the high-level view of our Triple-A. At a high-level, Triple-A treats each unboxed f ash module as a "passive memory device" like DIMMs. It manages the underlying f ash modules by employing an *autonomic* f ash array management module implemented in external multi-cores and DRAM buffer, which needs no replacement over time. This enables the bare NAND f ash packages to form a *Flash Inline Memory Module* (FIMM) with minimum physical-level protocol logic. One or more of these passive memory modules can be connected via a small PCI-E device called endpoint (EP) [8] over ONFI 3.x [38], which is a standard f ash interface offering a 400MHz bus clock speed. In this work, the set of FIMMs connected to a PCI-E EP as a hot-swappable device is referred to as *cluster*. While each FIMM within a cluster can expose the true NAND f ash performance over ONFI 3.x, the cluster offers an aggregated performance of them to host(s) over the external link of its PCI-E EP – the technical details of the FIMM and cluster are later given in Sections 3.3 and 3.4, respectively. From a system-level viewpoint, a set of clusters help us incarnate a f ash array by interconnecting the autonomic f ash array management module through multiple PCI-E links and ports on a PCI-E switch [44]. Further, a PCI-E network is formed from multiple switches to root complex's (RC) multi-ports. Finally, multiple compute nodes or hosts can access each FIMM over the RC's multi-ports managed by the autonomic f ash array management module.

### 3.3 Flash Inline Memory Module (FIMM)

Even though unboxing SSDs can help us reduce the costs involved in building and maintaining storage blocks of all-f ash arrays, *it is important to design the f ash module to be easily connected to one of the conventional SSD interfaces.* Fortunately, ONFi industry workgroup specif es a DDR2-like standard physical connector for NAND f ash modules in their 78-pin vertical NV-DDR2 interface design [52]. This NV-DDR2 describes not only the mechanical interface but also the signal groups and pin assignments, which can be used for forming a non-SSD f ash module by integrating multiple NAND f ash packages into a printed circuit board. Based on this specif cation, we def ne a standard NAND f ash memory module, referred to as *Flash Inline Memory Module* (FIMM). FIMM minimizes the number of hardware components and simplif es the SSDs' internal complexities. Consequently, a FIMM can be easily replaced (like DIMM) by a new one when it is worn out. The FIMM internal organization is illustrated in Figure 6. Specif cally, FIMM has been designed from the ground-up to work with eight NAND f ash packages wired with a 16 data-pin channel and connected to the NV-DDR2 interface as depicted in Figure 6a. From a control signal conf guration perspective, all the f ash packages have separate chip enable control pins so that an external PCI-E device can activate an individual NAND f ash package appropriately. However, their ready/busy pins used for checking up the f ash chip status are connected using a single control wire as shown in Figure 6b. In this manner, FIMMs can exclude internal resources not related to storage mediums such as microprocessors, control units and extra DRAM buffers, unlike traditional SSDs over the NV-DDR2 interface.

### 3.4 Endpoint Design for a Cluster

To integrate multiple FIMMs into a cluster as a hot-swappable device of our Triple-A's PCI-E topology, we need to understand two different protocols between the front-end PCI-E and back-end ONFi NV-DDR2 interfaces. To this end, A PCI-E endpoint is implemented at the forefront of the cluster by employing three main components: 1) PCI-E device layers, 2) upstream and downstream buffers, and 3) a control logic including HAL, as shown in Figure 4. While device layers handle the PCI-E interface, HAL in the control logic is responsible for managing the underlying FIMMs over the multiple ONFi 78-pin NV-DDR2 slots. Specif cally, PCI-E device layers disassemble a PCI-E packet by striping the header, sequence number and CRC f eld of each layer (e.g., phy, link, transaction). The disassembled packet is enqueued into the downstream buffer and waits to get serviced if the underlying control logic is busy. HAL dequeues the disassembled packet from the downstream buffer and constructs a NAND f ash command based on the core section of the packet. Once the service is performed, a new packet is assembled in a similar manner to what we described above.

## 4. Autonomic Flash Array Management

In Triple-A, the f ash control logic is moved from the inside of conventional SSDs to the autonomic f ash array management module that resides in the external multicores (as

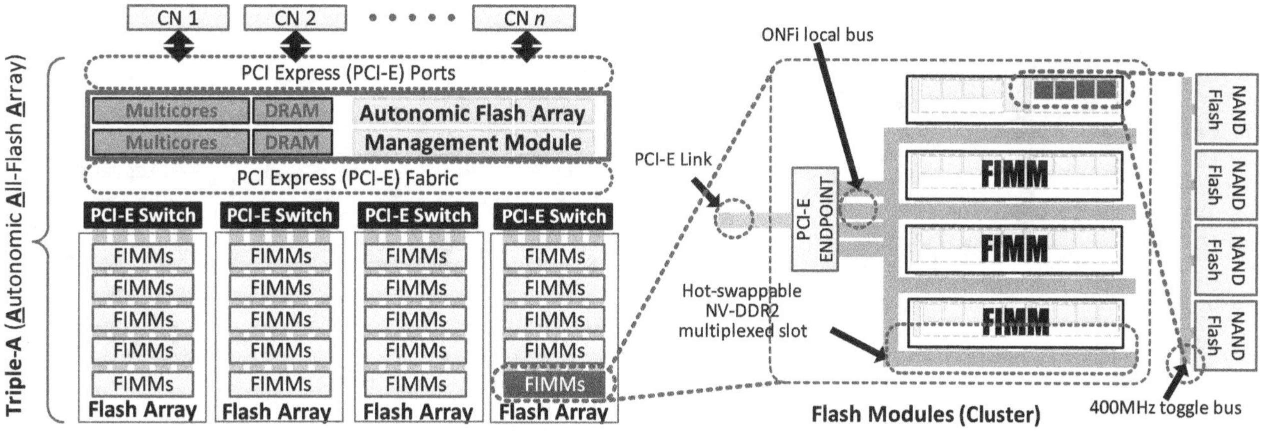


Figure 5: High-level view of our Autonomic All-Flash Array (Triple-A) architecture.

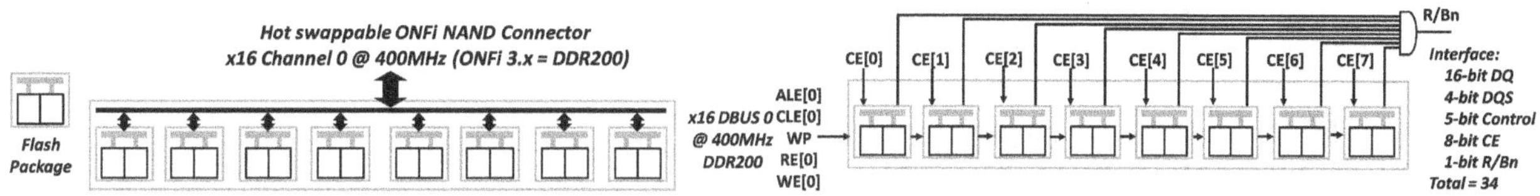


(a) Data Bus Connections (b) Control Signal Connections

Figure 6: Internal organization of FIMM.

shown on the left part of Figure 5). This f ash control logic (e.g., address translation [19, 29, 41], garbage collection [16, 23, 24], IO scheduler [25, 35], and page allocation [21, 22, 42]) can be implemented in many different ways, which we postpone to investigate in a future work. Instead, in this paper, we focus on presenting the details of the autonomic f ash array management in the context of addressing the internal resource contention. To address the link contention problem, Triple-A identif es *hot-clusters* whose shared local bus is busy at any given time and excuses them (temporarily) from serving incoming I/O requests. Also, to solve the storage contention problem, Triple-A detects *laggard*, which is a specif c FIMM that introduces a high number of stalled I/O requests in a cluster, and redistributes the data originally in the laggard to other FIMMs.

It should be noted that these types of contentions *cannot* simply be addressed by using a static or dynamic network routing methods. This is because, even though a intelligent data path could be selected using a different routing method, the destination would not be changed, and this would still introduce the same link- and storage-contention.

### 4.1 Link Contention Management

**Hot-cluster detection.** A cluster is classif ed as "hot", if the following condition is satisf ed when the target FIMM device is available to serve I/O requests:

$$t_{Latnecy} \geq t_{DMA} * (n_{page} + n_{FIMM} - 1) + t_{exe} * n_{page}, \quad (1)$$

where $t_{latency}$ is the device-level latency of an I/O request monitored by the autonomic f ash-array module, $t_{DMA}$ is the data movement latency per underlying physical f ash page, $n_{page}$ is the number of pages associated with the I/O request, $n_{FIMM}$ is the number of FIMMs in the cluster, and f nally $t_{exe}$ is the I/O latency for loading data (or storing data) into a specif c location. Note that this expression can capture the cases where 1) the local shared bus is always busy to move data from the underlying FIMMs to the PCI-E EP, and 2) all the FIMMs in the cluster contend to acquire the local shared bus most of the time.

**Autonomic data migration.** Once the hot-cluster is detected, Triple-A clones the corresponding data from the hot-cluster to a cold-cluster, the local shared bus of which is currently a non-critical resource (as far as serving the I/O requests is concerned), and unlinks its original data location. This process is termed as *autonomic data migration*, and its details are illustrated in Figure 7. The target cold-cluster can be identif ed with the help of the following expression:

$$u_{Bus} < \frac{n_{size}/t_{DMA}}{n_{Pins} * 1/f_{inf}}, \quad (2)$$

where $u_{Bus}$ is the bus utilization of a cluster, $n_{Pins}$ is the number of I/O pins of a single f ash package, $n_{size}$ is the physical NAND f ash page size, and $f_{inf}$ is the shared bus clock frequency. This expression implies that $u_{Bus}$ is lower than the case where on average only a single FIMM in the cluster uses the local shared bus.

Consequently, the request that causes a cluster to be hot will be served by a different location from the next I/O access; this in turn shortens the device-level latency and improves throughput by removing the stalled I/O requests heading to the hot cluster in the switch-level queue. Further, the stalled I/O requests targeting the hot-cluster can also deduct the cycles imposed by $t_{DMA} * n_{page}$ from their $t_{Latency}$, which can eventually turn a hot-cluster into a cold one.

**Shadow cloning.** Triple-A needs to check $t_{Latency}$ in order to detect a hot-cluster. In other words, the corresponding data is already available in the PCI-E EP of the hot-cluster when it is detected (no need to additionally access the underlying

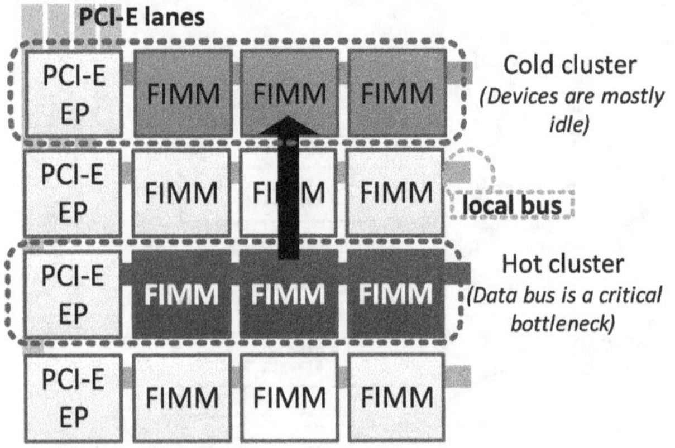


Figure 7: Autonomic hot cluster management. Once the hot-cluster is detected, Triple-A clones the corresponding data from the hot-cluster to a cold-cluster, the local shared bus of which is currently a non-critical resource.

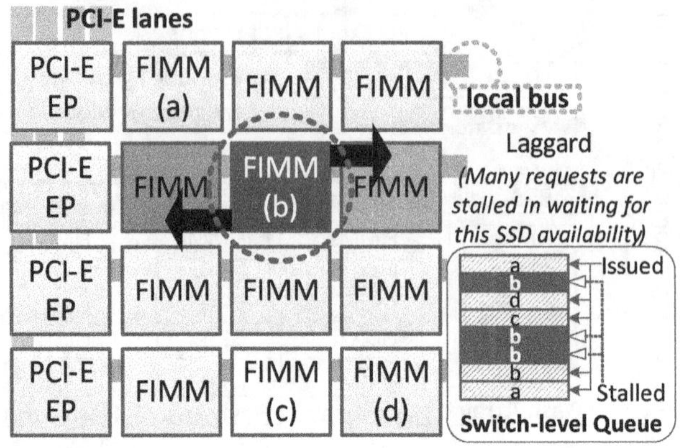


Figure 8: Laggard handling. FIMM marked using 'b' introduces most of the stalled I/O requests, which in turn makes it a laggard.

FIMMs). Since the I/O service routine employed by the f ash array is moving the data from PCI-E EP to a host over the internal PCI-E fabric (to serve the current I/O request), there is a room to *overlap* this data movement with the autonomic data migration. Thus, Triple-A can migrate data from the hot-cluster to the cold-cluster, while the data is on its way to the host over the network. This *shadow cloning* can reduce the potential overheads brought by the autonomic data migration.

### 4.2 Storage Contention Management

Reads can be stalled at a switch-level queue while the target FIMM (i.e., laggard) is busy in serving the previous I/O requests. This can lead to higher latencies on the cluster associated with the target device. In contrast, writes might be buffered and return immediately even though a laggard exists, which allows the corresponding cluster to be temporarily available. However, during an I/O congestion period, the writes could also be stalled if the buffer needs to evict an I/O request to the underlying FIMM(s) in order to secure available room. Consequently, for both reads and writes, the longer latency imposed by storage-contention can potentially violate quality-of-service (QoS) requirements or service-level-agreements (SLAs). From a f ash array perspective, if the queue is fully-occupied by a number of stalled I/O requests targeting the laggard, this can degrade the performance until all the stalled requests are f ushed. Our autonomic storage contention management addresses these challenges by reshaping the physical data-layout.

**Laggard detection.** Triple-A can detect laggards based on two different strategies: 1) *latency-monitoring* and 2) *queue-examination.* While the latency-monitoring strategy can detect laggard(s) based on a QoS/SLA violation, the queue-examination strategy can detect them based on the f ash array level serviceability. Let $t_{SLA}$ be the time target aimed by SLA (or QoS), which Triple-A has to meet. *Stalled* I/O requests correspond to the requests at a switch-level queue that are not issued to an underlying FIMM yet. In contrast, issued I/O requests correspond to the requests that the target FIMM is currently processing, but not completed yet. Thus, a laggard can be detected by monitoring latency through the following expression:

$$t_{SLA} < \sum_{i=0}^{n_{stalled}} (t_{DMA} + t_{exe}) * n^{i}_{page}, \qquad (3)$$

where $n_{stalled}$ is the number of stalled I/O requests targeting the same FIMM and $n^{i}_{page}$ is the number of pages associated with the $i^{th}$ stalled request. On the other hand, with the queue-examination strategy, Triple-A counts the number of stalled requests for each FIMM when the queue has no more room for accepting incoming I/O requests. It thus identif es the FIMM that has the most stalled I/O requests as the laggard. Considering the queue shown on the right side of Figure 8 as an example, FIMM marked using 'b' introduces most of the stalled I/O requests (occupies 37% of the total queue entries), which in turn makes it a laggard. Note that in cases where all the target FIMMs have similar number of stalled I/O requests, Triple-A classif es all of them as laggards; normally this should not happen very frequently, but if it happens, the cluster will be managed by the autonomic data-layout reshaping scheme described next.

**Autonomic data-layout reshaping.** Unlike data migration on link contention, Triple-A reshapes the physical data-layout within the cluster by moving the data associated with all the stalled I/O requests from the laggard to other FIMMs, as shown in Figure 8. This is because the link is not the performance bottleneck in such cases and the contention solely stems from the actual data location. As mentioned earlier, in cases where all the FIMMs are laggards, the data will be migrated to another cluster across their PCI-E EPs, similar to what the autonomic data migration would do in the hot-cluster management. The data movement to reshape the physical data-layout can be performed by leveraging the shadow copying method if the laggard detection is invoked on reads. On the other hand, for writes, since the data is partially in its PCI-E EP or will arrive at the PCI-E EP from a host, Triple-A can redirect the stalled I/O requests to adjacent FIMMs *within the same cluster*. It then updates the address mapping information managed by the f ash control logic, which is an essential functionality of any NAND f ash memory storage system, for all incoming I/O requests.

It should be noted that if the bus-utilization keeps increasing after reshaping the physical data-layout (which may in turn introduce link contention), it will be handled by the autonomic link contention module again. Consequently, the loads between link contention and storage contention would be naturally balanced.

## 5. Experimental Setup

To evaluate our proposed autonomic f ash array management strategies, we need a large f ash memory array server, which can offer a high-f delity evaluation environment and generate reproducible results. To the best of our knowledge, currently, there is no publicly-available all-f ash array system. Therefore, in this work, we perform a simulation-based study with real workloads collected at thousand nodes on an IBM iDataPlex machine [36, 51] and published by SNIA [2] and UMASS [6]. In this section, we discuss the details of our simulation framework, the conf gurations we tested, and our workloads.

### 5.1 Flash Array

**Flash Array Network Simulation Model.** We modeled a PCI-E based mesh network for the all-f ash array I/O simulation. Our simulation framework[1] can capture all the PCI-E specif c characteristics on an all-f ash array, including PCI-E data movement delay, switching and routing latencies, and I/O request contention cycles. In addition, it employs a reconf gurable network simulation based on numerous architecture/system parameters such as network size, link width, and routing strategy.
**All-Flash Array Conf guration.** To collect our results, we conf gured 16TB *non-autonomic* and *autonomic* all-f ash arrays. In our default f ash-array conf guration, the cluster is composed of four 64GB FIMMs connected to a single PCI-E EP. Our *baseline* network consists of four PLX technology PCI-E switches, each composed of sixteen EP clusters (e.g., 4x16 conf guration). In this conf guration, a single RC (root complex) has four ports, each connected to an individual switch over the PCI-E fabric. We used 3.3 $\mu$sec as our SLA value, and employed 650 $\sim$ 1000 queue entries for RC. For our sensitivity experiments presented later, we also evaluated diverse network sizes with varying number of clusters ranging from 4x8 (32 clusters, 8TB) to 4x20 (80 clusters, 20TB).

### 5.2 Workloads

Important characteristics of the real workloads we tested are given in Table 1. This table gives, for each workload, the read/write ratio, the percentage of randomness for both reads and writes, the number of hot-clusters, and the ratio between I/O requests heading to the hot-clusters and the total number of I/O requests. It should be pointed out that the most real workloads have 20% $\sim$ 60% of their I/O requests destined for the hot-clusters in our all-f ash array, except for *cfs* and *web* workloads. For presentation purposes, we categorize these workloads into three different groups as explained below.
**Enterprise Workload.** We evaluate our all-f ash array using a set of enterprise-scale workloads. Read and write ratios vary based on the application characteristics. For example, *proj* and *usr* exhibit write-intensive patterns (write ratio is around 70%) whereas *prn* and *web* are read-intensive workloads (read ratio is almost 100%). In these workloads, we allocated all-f ash array as one large pool storage server that offers a single global address space to multiple worker threads.

[1] This simulation framework will be available in http://pcienetsim.camelab.org.

| Workload | Read ratio (%) | Read randomness (%) | Write randomness (%) | # of hot clusters | I/O ratio on hot clusters (%) |
|---|---|---|---|---|---|
| cfs | 76.5 | 94.1 | 73.8 | 0 | 0 |
| fn | 50.2 | 90.4 | 99.1 | 5 | 55.7 |
| hm | 55.1 | 93.3 | 99.2 | 5 | 43.7 |
| mds | 25.9 | 80.2 | 94.8 | 4 | 54.1 |
| msnfs | 52.8 | 90.9 | 84.9 | 4 | 28.8 |
| prn | 97.1 | 94.8 | 46.6 | 2 | 50.9 |
| proj | 29.1 | 80.7 | 8.5 | 6 | 61.3 |
| prxy | 61.1 | 97.3 | 59.4 | 3 | 39.3 |
| usr | 28.9 | 90.3 | 96.9 | 5 | 40.1 |
| web | 100 | 95 | 0 | 0 | 0 |
| websql | 54.3 | 73.9 | 67.6 | 4 | 50.6 |
| g-eigen | 100 | 17.1 | 0 | 6 | 70.6 |
| l-eigen | 100 | 17.1 | 0 | 11 | 48.1 |

Table 1: Important characteristics of our workloads.

**HPC Workload.** We used an HPC workload generated by Eigensolver application [53] that simulates many-fermion dynamics in nuclear physics on one thousand IBM iDataPlex compute nodes [51]. Specif cally, the workload was collected under Global Parallel File System (GPFS) [47], which is installed in ten Luster Router Nodes of Carver cluster at National Energy Research Scientif c Computing Center [36]. Based on our observations, a majority of the I/O requests in this application (named *g-eigen*) are read, and many of them tend to head to a specif c set of clusters (hot) in our all-f ash array. We also evaluated this Eigensolver application in a different conf guration, referred to as *l-eigen*. This version allocates a separate PCI-E switch to each router node, which can in turn expose multiple local address spaces of f ash array.
**Micro-benchmark.** We also used a micro-benchmark for our specif c evaluations, including sensitivity analysis and execution breakdown analysis. In our micro-benchmark, a workload composed of only random read I/O requests is called as *read*, whereas *write* indicates a workload that includes only random writes. Most I/O request sizes are 4KB, which is the maximum payload size in PCI-E 3.0 [43].

## 6. Experimental Results

We f rst evaluate our real workloads with both non-autonomic all-f ash array and Triple-A in order to show the performance impact brought by our proposal. We then dig deeper into detailed analyses using our micro-benchmark, which include execution breakdown study and sensitivity tests with varying number of hot clusters and network sizes.

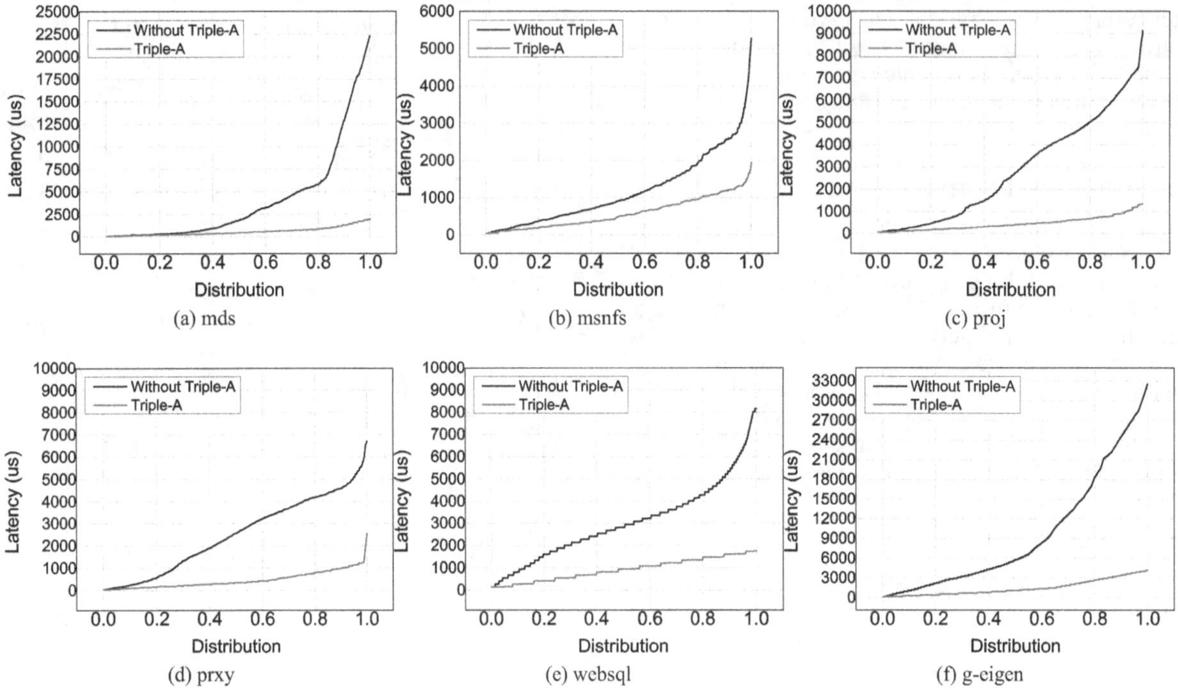


Figure 11: Cumulative distribution function of the real workload latency on a non-autonomic all-f ash array and Triple-A. Triple-A shortens a large portion of latencies, particularly, the long tail is signif cantly improved.

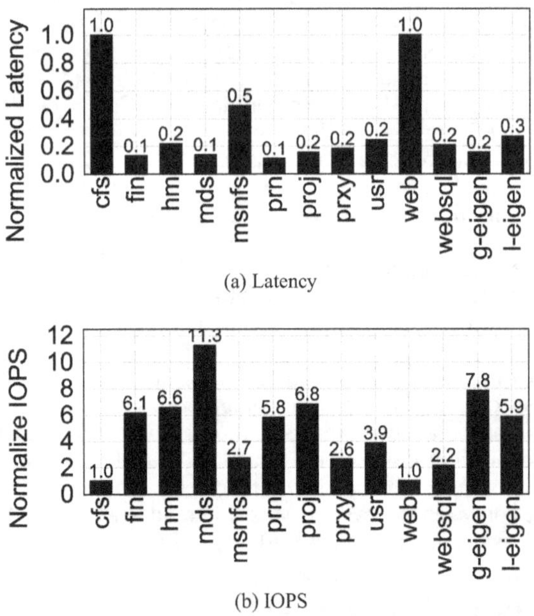


Figure 9: Latency and IOPS values normalized with respect to a non-autonomic all-f ash array.

| Workload | Avg. Latency (us) | IOPS | Avg. link-cont. time (us) | Avg. storage-cont. time (us) | Avg. queue stall time (us) |
|---|---|---|---|---|---|
| cfs | 940 | 229K | 173 | 637 | 811 |
| f n | 5,457 | 39K | 4,814 | 550 | 5,365 |
| hm | 1,806 | 112K | 1,270 | 461 | 1,731 |
| mds | 4,064 | 35K | 3,573 | 419 | 3,992 |
| msnfs | 1,172 | 152K | 742 | 341 | 1,084 |
| prn | 6,733 | 42K | 6,115 | 532 | 6,648 |
| proj | 2,860 | 87K | 2,384 | 411 | 2,796 |
| prxy | 2,521 | 119K | 2,021 | 422 | 2,444 |
| usr | 1,772 | 134K | 1,364 | 338 | 1,702 |
| web | 1,148 | 181K | 239 | 768 | 1,008 |
| websql | 4,737 | 57K | 4,242 | 431 | 4,674 |

Table 2: Absolute values for our major performance metrics on a 4x16 non-autonomic all-f ash array.

### 6.1 Results with Real Workloads

We use IOPS and average I/O latency as our main metrics. In the view of the overall performance of an all-f ash array, IOPS is an appropriate system-level metric. However, since our all-f ash array is essentially a networked system where a request moves around, the latency of each I/O request is also a big concern, irrespective of the entire system performance.

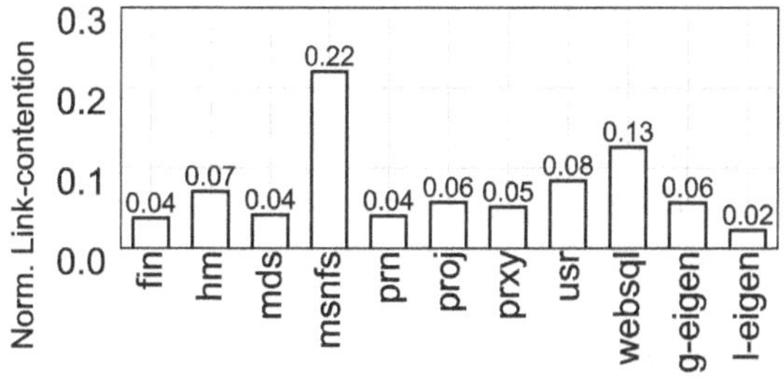


(a) Link-contention

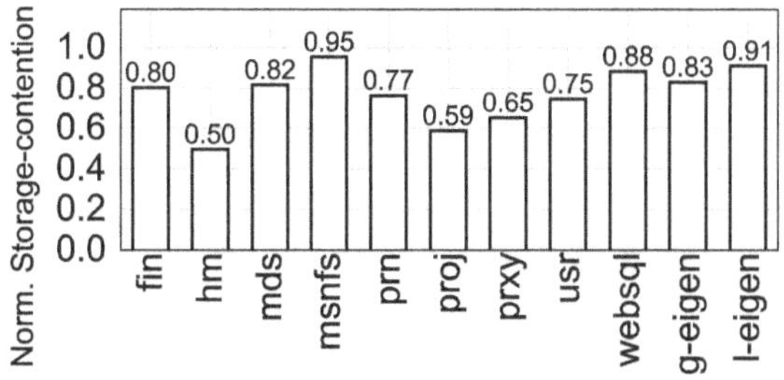


(b) Storage-contention

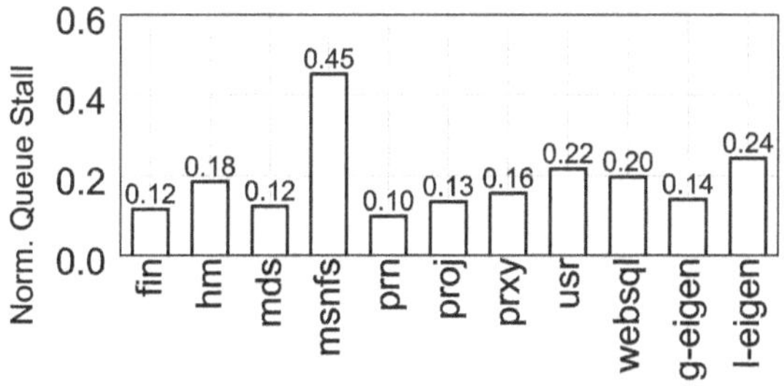


(c) Queue stall time

Figure 10: Contention and queue stall time comparison between a non-autonomic all-flash array and our Triple-A.

To better understand the performance differences between non-autonomic and autonomic all-flash arrays, we *normalized* both IOPS and latency value observed with Triple-A to the corresponding values of the non-autonomic all-flash array. The absolute values of our performance metrics under the non-autonomic all-flash array are given in Table 2.

Figures 9a and 9b plot the normalized latency and IOPS, respectively, under the enterprise and HPC workloads. One can see from these figures that Triple-A achieves significant performance improvements, thanks to its autonomic data migration and data-layout reshaping. Specifically, Triple-A offers 5 times shorter latency, on average, compared to the non-autonomic flash array, and improves IOPS by about 2 times. The performance gains achieved by Triple-A are more pronounced when there is a small number of hot-clusters with high I/O rates. For example, Triple-A cuts the average latency by 98% and improves throughput by 7.8 times under *g-eigen* workload. This is because the performance degradations in a flash array network are mainly caused by resource contentions, not SSDs themselves. In contrast, there is no performance gain in the case where the all-flash array has no significant resource contention induced by the hot-clusters (e.g., *cfs* and *web* workloads). Interestingly, even though *websql* results in four hot-clusters with a high I/O request rate (see Table 1), the IOPS improvement brought by Triple-A is limited to around 2x. One of the reasons why the performance improvements under *websql* are not as high as other applications is that all the hot clusters (four) caused by *websql* belong to the same PCI-E switch. As a result, the storage space that Triple-A targets to move (for data migration) is limited. Recall that Triple-A does not migrate data across clusters located in different PCI-E switches in an attempt to avoid extra contentions. However, we want to emphasize that the latency (and also throughput) values even in this worst-case are still much better than the non-autonomic flash array (see Section 6.3).

## 6.2 Quantifying Contention Handling

Figures 10a, 10b, and 10c present the normalized latency related to link contention, storage contention, and queue stall, respectively. The queue stall time indicates the amount of time an I/O request in a queue should wait until the I/O request submitted in the previous step is completed. These latencies are measured by the same evaluation scenario used in the previous section. Note that the average contention values and the average queue stall times resulting from the non-autonomic all-flash array are given in Table 2. It can be observed from Figures 10a and 10b that most of the overheads caused by the link contention can be dramatically reduced by Triple-A. In comparison, Triple-A reduces storage contention by only 15%. This is because Triple-A tries to reshape data-layout within a cluster first, and moves them to other clusters *only if* all the FIMM in clusters are classified as laggards. As one can see from Figure 10c, Triple-A can shorten the queue stall time by about 85% by using these minimum data movement strategy – we further analyze the stall times in our execution time breakdown study in Section 6.4.

## 6.3 The Details of Latency Improvements

The cumulative distribution functions for six workloads on the non-autonomic all-flash array and Triple-A given in Figure 11 indicate Triple-A's great capability to improve the I/O request latency originating from the resource contentions. The long-tailed distribution of these real workload latencies on the non-autonomic all-flash array illustrates the seriousness of the resource contention that takes place in all-flash arrays. The latency gap between the non-autonomic all-flash array and Triple-A indicates that our proposed approach copes well with the contentions and brings significant performance benefits. In addition to slight variations in the overall performance improvement, there are some interesting observations to remark. Compared to other workloads, the degree of improvement in *msnfs* is relatively low even though four hot clusters are caused by its access patterns. We see from Table 1 that the ratio of I/O requests heading to the hot clusters in *msnfs* is not very high. This means the clusters are detected as hot, but less hot than the (hot) clusters found in other workloads. In *msnfs*, we note that Triple-A's data migration and physical data-layout reshaping are less effective in the workloads with these less-hot clusters. In contrast, *proj* shows great performance improvement based on a number of relatively hotter clusters. In addition to the degree of hotness, the distribution of hot clusters is a crucial element in determining Triple-A's effectiveness on a given workload. The four hot clusters of *websql* are hot enough to shorten the latency more, while there is little improvement in IOPS. Since all the hot clusters are located in the same

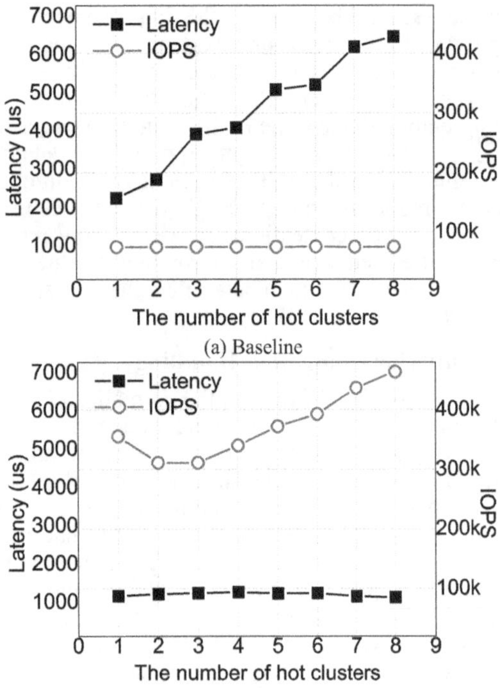


(a) Baseline

(b) Triple-A

Figure 12: Hot cluster sensitivity: IOPS and latency of *read* micro-benchmark with varying number of hot clusters on a non-autonomic all-f ash array (a) and Triple-A (b). Note that, as the number of hot clusters increases, Triple-A tends to show stable latency and improved IOPS.

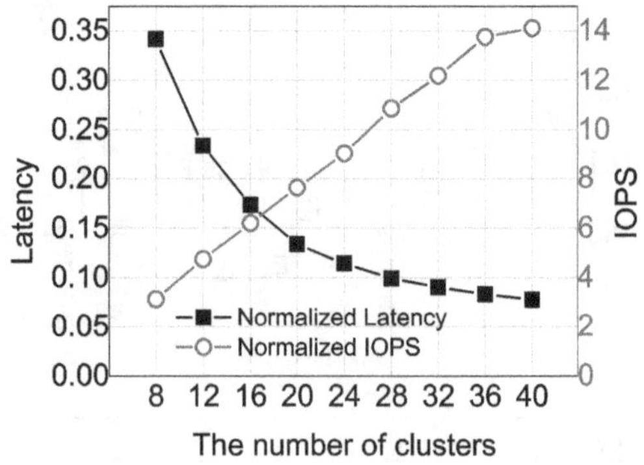


Figure 13: Network size sensitivity: IOPS and latency of *read* micro-benchmark normalized to a non-autonomic all-f ash array under varing network sizes. As the network size increases, Triple-A shows better performance.

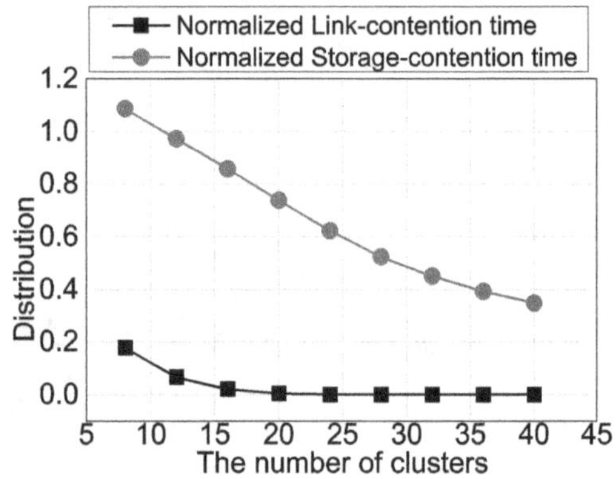


Figure 14: Two types of contention time of *read* micro-benchmark normalized to a non-autonomic all-f ash array under varying network sizes. The big decrease in both contention times proves the effectiveness of Triple-A.

switch, the imbalance of the number of I/O requests among PCI-E switches dictates the total execution time, resulting in low IOPS. Therefore, both the hotness and the distribution of hot clusters characterized by each workload affect Triple-A's performance.

Emerging HPC environments are likely to employ all-f ash arrays as their main storage system. In this context, we pay attention to Triple-A's effectiveness on *g-eigen*, which is a version of the Eigensolver scientif c application widely-used in HPC. This read-intensive workload results in many hot clusters, which in turn creates opportunities for Triple-A. As shown in Figure 11f, the magnitude of latency improvement brought by our approach is signif cant in this workload.

### 6.4 Sensitivity Analysis

**Hot-cluster Size.** Figure 12 plots the aggregate performance variation of the non-autonomic all-f ash array and Triple-A under varying number of hot clusters. One can see from Figure 12a that increasing the number of hot clusters in the non-autonomic all-f ash array worsens the average latency of the workload. Since I/O requests heading to the hot clusters compete with one another for the shared resources, more hot clusters we have, higher the ratio of I/O requests that suffer from the resource contention. In other words, the number of I/O requests benef ting from Triple-A increases as the number of hot clusters increases. As can be seen in Figure 12b, Triple-A achieves a stable latency with better IOPS under the increasing number of hot clusters. Therefore, we can expect that our technique would work well and improve performance more in cases where the target application has an access pattern that results in a high number of hot clusters.

**Network Size.** Figure 13 shows that the performance (both IOPS and latency) of Triple-A gets better as the size of the all-f ash network increases (the x-axis indicates the number of clusters under each PCI-E switch). Because Triple-A tries to redistribute the excessive I/O requests on the hot clusters to other (cold) clusters under the same switch, increasing the network size means employing more neighboring clusters in sharing the heavy load on the hot clusters. Theoretically speaking, the degree of the latency improvement would saturate when the cumulative I/O load is evenly distributed across a large number of clusters under the same switch.

To analyze the behavior of Triple-A better, we quantif ed the link contention time and storage contention time in the non-autonomic all-f ash array. As shown in Figure 14, Triple-A successfully reduces both kinds of contentions by distributing the extra load of the hot clusters through data migration and physical data-layout mapping, as the number of clusters increases. In particular, the link contention time is almost completely eliminated while the storage contention time is steadily reduced as the number of clusters increases. This is because the storage contention time is bounded by

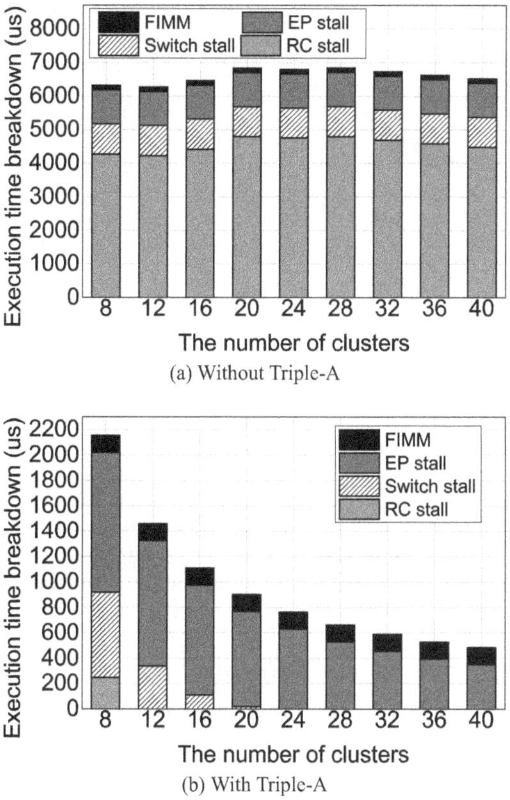


Figure 15: Breakdown of the average execution time of *read* micro-benchmark on a nonautonomic all-f ash array (a) and Triple-A (b) under varying network sizes. Various queue stall times representing the resource contentions are largely decreased by Triple-A.

the number of I/O requests to the target clusters, but the link contention time is not.

**Execution Time Breakdown.** The average execution time breakdown can show us how Triple-A actually optimizes I/O latency. Figures 15a and 15b plot the breakdown of the execution time on the non-autonomic all-f ash array and Triple-A. respectively. We see that the signif cant reductions in both the link and storage contention times are the main contributors for improved latency. Excluding the FIMM throughput, which is not Triple-A's concern, stall times at the three different queues are gradually reduced as the network gets bigger. For instance, when using Triple-A, switch stalls and RC stalls are completely eliminated beyond a cluster size of 20.

### 6.5 Data Migration Overheads

**Latency.** Figure 16a gives the series of latency of *read* traces on the non-autonomic all-f ash array while Figure 16d gives the same with Triple-A. As can be observed from these plots, Triple-A improves the performance by employing autonomic data migration, which migrates data from hot-clusters to cold-clusters. However, since the data migration activity shares the resources of the all-f ash array with the normal I/O requests, it has an impact on overall performance. Therefore, it is worthwhile to consider the overheads our data migration strategy may bring.

Note that a single data migration involves reading the data from the hot-cluster, transmitting the data towards the switch, transmitting the data towards the target EP, and writing the data into the cluster. This overhead, particularly the data read from hot-clusters, can seriously hurt Triple-A's performance. Figure 16b shows the increased latency of I/O requests suffering from the interferece by data migrations. In order to reduce this overhead, shadow cloning described in Section 4.1 overlaps the original read I/O request and the data read as a part of data migration. The minimized latency overhead by shadow cloning is shown in Figure 16c.

**Wear-out.** Data migraion for high-performance f ash arrays incurs extra writes, which reduces the lifetime of f ashes by accelerating wear-out speed. According to our quantitative approximation, in the worst case, the data migration generates 34% additional writes, which leads to 23% decrease in lifetime and, in turn, makes the f ash replacement earlier. However, the 50% cost reduction of our all-f ash array architecture can offset the increased f ash replacement frequency caused by the data migration. It should be noted that our Triple-A's architecture focuses on improving the system performance by sacrif cing the f ash lifetime. This a worthwhile trade-off since all-f ash array signif cantly cut the cost by unboxing f ash modules.

### 6.6 Effectiveness of DRAM Relocation

In Triple-A's architecture, all on-board DRAMs are removed; instead, large DRAMs are placed with the management module on top of all-f ash arrays as described in Figure 5. The purpose of DRAM relocation is the cost reduction of f ash arrays. Note that DRAM needs no replacement over time, whereas f ash cells have limited lifetime due to the wear-out characteristic. We expect that this DRAM relocation does not degrade the system performance due to two reasons. Firstly, on-board DRAMs cannot resolve the link and storage contentions. Regardless of on-board DRAM's data caching, multiple successive I/O requests destined to the same SSD should share I/O bus and system-level data path, which is the main cause for contentions. (Instead, f ash read/write latency can be eliminated when the requests make DRAM hit). In addition, the relocated and aggregated large DRAMs in Triple-A has the potential of reducing the number of I/O requests which can cause two types of contentions before they travel over the f ash array network. We want to emphasize that the basic functionality of DRAMs like caching and alignment and its effects can be preserved since they are only relocated.

### 6.7 Wear Leveling

As shown in Figure 5, FTL functions including wear leveling are moved from individual SSDs to the central management module on top of the f ash array network. Compared to conventional SSDs where FTL functions target only inside f ashes, FTL functions of Triple-A can manage the f ash arrays in a global fashion. Since the management module is able to centrally know both hotness information and erase counts of each cluster, there is certainly a chance to overlap garbage collection and data migration by considering wear leveling, which is left as a future work.

## 7. Related Work

Recently, all-f ash arrays have been an active area of development in industry. Even though shipping all-f ash arrays is

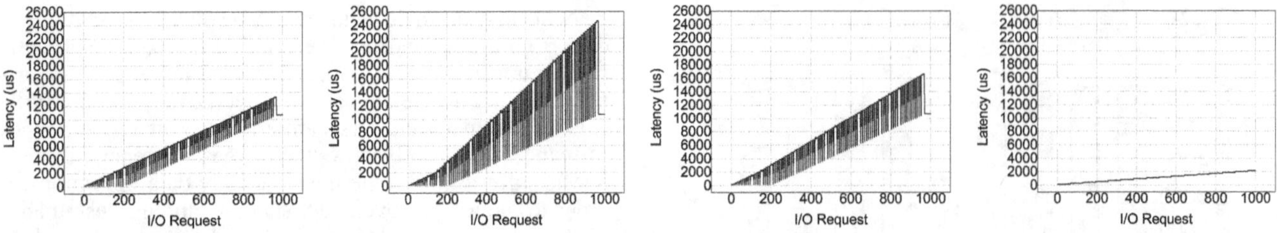


(a) Latency of non-autonomic all-f ash array.

(b) Effectiveness of naive data migration.

(c) Effectiveness of data migration using shadow cloning.

(d) Improved latency of Triple-A.

Figure 16: Latency series of I/O requests under the non-autonomic array (a), the data migrations (b) and (c), and Triple-A (d). The difference between (b) and (c) is that latter employs shadow cloning to minimize migration overheads.

in an early-stage, some vendors (e.g., Pure Storage) already have their one-large pool storage system composed by 100% NAND f ash based SSDs. One of the challenges that render the all-f ash array diff cult to widely deploy is the high price per GB of individual SSDs. To make the f ash array more competitive compared to conventional disk arrays, many in-line deduction techniques are being applied, which include deduplication [17, 54], compression [45, 45], and thin provisioning [32, 48], among others. These inline deduction techniques are expected to reduce the amount of data by 5x to 10x, which can in turn drive $/GB down.

In the meantime, academia also begins to explore the ways in which eff cient SSD arrays can be built. [11] proposed QuickSAN, which is an SSD-based storage area network. In this approach, SSDs can communicate with one another to serve I/O requests as quickly as possible, which can in turn reduce system intervention and array-level software costs. Since QuickSAN integrates a network adopter into SSDs, it will increase the costs of individual storage components in an all-f ash array approach. [4, 15] proposed a high performance SSD architecture built from emerging non-volatile memories. [12, 14] studied the benef ts brought by NVM on high performance I/O intensive computing. In comparison, [5] proposed an SSD-optimized RAID system, which offers better reliability for individual SSDs than RAID-4 and RAID-5 by creating age disparities within arrays. [34] investigated the effectiveness of SSD-based RAID and discussed the potential benef ts and drawbacks in terms of reliability. We believe that these SSD-RAID techniques (designed for an SSD appliance composed by small number of SSDs) could be extended to all-f ash arrays as well.

Even though all these prior studies and industry efforts greatly contribute to bring all-f ash array to the real world, there exists plenty of room for improvement. The inline deduction schemes are general techniques and can be applied to any storage devices (not just for all-f ash array). Therefore, it is desirable to develop an approach that fundamentally reduces $/GB of all-f ash arrays, which can employ all the inline modules as well. The architectural concept behind Triple-A can signif cantly reduce the maintenance costs in terms of hardware and software and drive down the prices of individual SSDs by building f ash modules from scratch.

Very recently, a few vendors have already started to announce commercial products employing f ash array similar to Triple-A's architecture. Texas Memory Systems's [49] is 2D f ash-RAID with high availability, which is suitable for database, HPC, and cloud infrastructures. Violin Memory [50] also has a f ash memory array architecture on the market. The cluster of 1000s of f ash cells with multiple controllers provides high throughput, which is suitable for transactional business applications and big data analytics environments. Compared to these systems, however, our Triple-A brings further improvements on the performance of this architecture by dealing with I/O congestion problems caused by resource sharing in all-f ash arrays.

## 8. Conclusions and Future Work

The primary goal of this paper was to address the link and storage contentions in emerging all-f ash arrays. Our results showed that Triple-A can offer 53% higher sustained throughput and 80% lower latency with 50% less cost than non-autonomic SSD arrays. Our ongoing efforts include 1) developing different large-scale f ash modules such as array-level garbage collection schedulers, wear-levelers, queuing mechanisms and f ash translation algorithms, 2) expanding Triple-A to a reconf gurable network-based all-f ash array, and 3) developing different dynamic I/O routing mechanisms for all-f ash arrays. We also plan integrate our PCI-E I/O simulation framework into other f ash simulation models such as DiskSim+SSD extension [3], NANDFlashSim [26] and FlashSim [28].

## Acknowledgments

This research is supported in part by University of Texas at Dallas Start-up Grants, NSF grants 1302557, 1017882, 0937949, and 0833126 as well as DOE grant DE-SC0002156, and DESC0002156. It also used resources of the National Energy Research Scientif c Computing Center supported by the Off ce of Science of the U.S. Department of Energy under Contract No. DE-AC02-05CH11231.

## References

[1] http://www.dramexchange.com/.

[2] SNIA IOTTA repository. URL `http://iotta.snia.org/tracetypes/3`.

[3] N. Agrawal, V. Prabhakaran, T. Wobber, J. D. Davis, M. Manasse, and R. Panigrahy. Design tradeoffs for SSD performance. In *USENIX ATC*, 2008.

[4] A. Akel, A. M. Caulf eld, T. I. Mollov, R. K. Gupta, and S. Swanson. Onyx: a protoype phase change memory storage array. *HotStorage*, 2011.

[5] M. Balakrishnan, A. Kadav, V. Prabhakaran, and D. Malkhi. Differential RAID: Rethinking RAID for SSD reliability. *Trans. Storage*, 2010.

[6] K. Bates and B. McNutt. Umass Trace Repository. URL `traces.cs.umass.edu/index.php/Main/Traces`.

[7] J. Borrill, L. Oliker, J. Shalf, and H. Shan. Investigation of leading hpc i/o performance using a scientif c-application derived benchmark. In *Proceedings of the 2007 ACM/IEEE conference on Supercomputing*, 2007.

[8] R. Budruk, D. Anderson, and E. Solari. *PCI Express System Architecture*. Pearson Education, 2003. ISBN 0321156307.

[9] M. Canim, G. A. Mihaila, B. Bhattacharjee, K. A. Ross, and C. A. Lang. SSD bufferpool extensions for database systems. *Proc. VLDB Endow.*, 2010.

[10] P. Carns, K. Harms, W. Allcock, C. Bacon, S. Lang, R. Latham, and R. Ross. Understanding and improving computational science storage access through continuous characterization. *Mass Storage Systems and Technologies, IEEE / NASA Goddard Conference on*, 2011.

[11] A. M. Caulf eld and S. Swanson. Annual international symposium on computer architecture (isca). In *QuickSAN: A Storage Area Network for Fast, Distributed, Solid State Disks*, 2013.

[12] A. M. Caulf eld, L. M. Grupp, and S. Swanson. Gordon: using f ash memory to build fast, power-eff cient clusters for data-intensive applications. In *ASPLOS*, 2009.

[13] A. M. Caulf eld, L. M. Grupp, and S. Swanson. Gordon: Using f ash memory to build fast, power-eff cient clusters for data-intensive applications. In *Proceedings of Architectural Support for Programming Languages and Operating Systems (ASPLOS)*, 2009.

[14] A. M. Caulf eld, J. Coburn, T. Mollov, A. De, A. Akel, J. He, A. Jagatheesan, R. K. Gupta, A. Snavely, and S. Swanson. Understanding the impact of emerging non-volatile memories on high-performance, IO-intensive computing. In *Proceedings of SC*, 2010.

[15] A. M. Caulf eld, A. De, J. Coburn, T. I. Mollow, R. K. Gupta, and S. Swanson. Moneta: A high-performance storage array architecture for next-generation, non-volatile memories. In *MICRO*, 2010.

[16] S. Choudhuri and T. Givargis. Deterministic service guarantees for NAND f ash using partial block cleaning. In *Proceedings of the International Conference on Hardware-Software Codesign and System Synthesis*, 2008.

[17] B. Debnath, S. Sengupta, and J. Li. Chunkstash: speeding up inline storage deduplication using f ash memory. In *USENIX ATC*, 2010.

[18] EMC. Vnx5500-f unif ed storage f ash array.

[19] A. Gupta, Y. Kim, and B. Urgaonkar. DFTL: A f ash translation layer employing demand-based selective caching of page-level address mappings. In *ASPLOS*, 2009.

[20] J. He, J. Bennett, and A. Snavely. DASH-IO: An empirical study of f ash-based IO for HPC. *TeraGrid' 10*, August 2010.

[21] Y. Hu, H. Jiang, D. Feng, L. Tian, H. Luo, and S. Zhang. Performance impact and interplay of ssd parallelism through advanced commands, allocation strategy and data granularity. In *ISC*, 2011.

[22] M. Jung and M. Kandemir. An evaluation of different page allocation strategies on high-speed SSDs. In *USENIX HotStorage*, 2012.

[23] M. Jung and J. Yoo. Scheduling garbage collection opportunistically to reduce worst-case I/O performance in solid state disks. In *Proceedings of the International Workshop on Software Support for Portable Storage*, 2009.

[24] M. Jung, R. Prabhakar, and M. Kandemir. Taking garbage collection overheads off the critical path in ssds. In *Middleware*, 2012.

[25] M. Jung, E. Willson, and M. Kandemir. Physically addressed queueing (PAQ): Improving parallelism in solid state disks. In *ISCA*, 2012.

[26] M. Jung, E. H. Wilson, D. Donofrio, J. Shalf, and M. Kandemir. NANDFlashSim: Intrinsic latency variation aware NAND f ash memory system modeling and simulation at microarchitecture level. In *IEEE Conference on Massive Data Storage*, 2012.

[27] T. Kgil, D. Roberts, and T. Mudge. Improving NAND f ash based disk caches. In *International Symposium on Computer Architecture*, 2008.

[28] Y. Kim, B. Tauras, A. Gupta, and B. Urgaonkar. Flashsim: A simulator for NAND f ash-based solid-state drives. In *SIMUL*, 2009.

[29] S. W. Lee, W. K. Choi, and D. J. Park. FAST: An eff cient f ash translation layer for f ash memory. In *EUC Workshops Lecture Notes in Computer Science*, 2006.

[30] N. Liu, J. Cope, P. Carns, C. Carothers, R. Ross, G. Grider, A. Crume, and C. Maltzahn. On the role of burst buffers in leadership-class storage systems. In *IEEE Conference on Massive Data Storage*, 2012.

[31] Y. Liu, J. Huang, C. Xie, and Q. Cao. Raf: A random access f rst cache management to improve SSD-based disk cache. *NAS*, 2010.

[32] H. V. Madhyastha, J. C. McCullough, G. Porter, R. Kapoor, S. Savage, A. C. Snoeren, and A. Vahdat. scc: cluster storage provisioning informed by application characteristics and slas. *FAST'12*, 2012.

[33] N. Master, M. Andrews, J. Hick, S. Canon, and N. Wright. Performance analysis of commodity and enterprise class f ash devices. In *PDSW*, 2010.

[34] S. Moon and A. L. N. Reddy. Hotstorage). In *Dont Let RAID Raid the Lifetime of Your SSD Array*, 2013.

[35] E. H. Nam, B. Kim, H. Eom, and S.-L. Min. Ozone (O3): An out-of-order f ash memory controller architecture. *Computers, IEEE Transactions on*, 2011.

[36] NERSC. In *http://www.nersc.gov/users/computational-systems/carver/*.

[37] NetApp. Netapp EF540 f ash array.

[38] ONFI Working Group. Open nand f ash interface 3.0. In *http://onf.org/*, 2012.

[39] Y. Ou, T. Härder, and P. Jin. Cfdc: a f ash-aware replacement policy for database buffer management. In *the Fifth International Workshop on Data Management on New Hardware*, 2009.

[40] X. Ouyang, S. Marcarelli, and D. K. Panda. Enhancing checkpoint performance with staging I/O and SSD. In *International Workshop on Storage Network Architecture and Parallel I/O*, 2010.

[41] C. Park, W. Cheon, Y. Lee, W. C. Myoung-Soo Jung, and H. Yoon. A re-conf gurable FTL architecture for NAND f ash based applications. In *IEEE/IFIP International Workshop on Rapid Prototyping*, 2007.

[42] C. Park, E. Seo, J.-Y. Shin, S. Maeng, and J. Lee. Exploiting internal parallelism of f ash-based ssds. In *Computer Architecture Letters*, page 9, January 2010.

[43] PCI-SIG. PCI express base 3.0 specif cation. 2012.

[44] PLX Technology. PLX 8796 PLX expresslane gen 3 PCI Express compliant switches.

[45] C. Policroniades and I. Pratt. Alternatives for detecting redundancy in storage systems data. In *USENIX Annual Technical Conference*, 2004.

[46] Pure Storage. Fa-300 series technical specif cations.

[47] F. B. Schmuck and R. L. Haskin. GPFS: A shared-disk f le system for large computing clusters. In *FAST*, 2002.

[48] P. Shivam, A. Demberel, P. Gunda, D. Irwin, L. Grit, A. Yumerefendi, S. Babu, and J. Chase. Automated and on-demand provisioning of virtual machines for database applications. In *ACM SIGMOD international conference on Management of data*, 2007.

[49] Texas Memory Systems. Texas memory systems RamSan-820.

[50] Violin Memory. Violin memory 6000 Series Flash Memory Arrays.

[51] D. Watts and M. Bachmaier. *Implementing an IBM System x iDataPlex Solution*. Redbooks, 2012.

[52] O. C. Workgroup". Open nand f ash interface specif cation: NAND connector.

[53] Z. Zhou, E. Saule, H. Aktulga, C. Yang, E. Ng, P. Maris, J. Vary, and U. Catalyurek. An out-of-core dataf ow middleware to reduce the cost of large scale iterative solvers. In *Parallel Processing Workshops (ICPPW), 2012 41st International Conference on*, 2012.

[54] B. Zhu, K. Li, and R. H. Patterson. Avoiding the disk bottleneck in the data domain deduplication f le system. In *FAST*, 2008.

# NVM Duet: Unified Working Memory and Persistent Store Architecture

Ren-Shuo Liu*, De-Yu Shen*, Chia-Lin Yang*†‡, Shun-Chih Yu*, Cheng-Yuan Michael Wang§

* Department of Computer Science and Information Engineering, National Taiwan University, Taipei, Taiwan
† Graduate Institute of Networking and Multimedia, National Taiwan University, Taipei, Taiwan
‡ Graduate Institute of Electronics Engineering, National Taiwan University, Taipei, Taiwan
§ Macronix International Co., Ltd., Hsinchu, Taiwan

renshuo@ntu.edu.tw; {r99922118, yangc, r01922008}@csie.ntu.edu.tw; michaelwang@mxic.com.tw

## Abstract

Emerging non-volatile memory (NVM) technologies have gained a lot of attention recently. The byte-addressability and high density of NVM enable computer architects to build large-scale main memory systems. NVM has also been shown to be a promising alternative to conventional persistent store. With NVM, programmers can persistently retain in-memory data structures without writing them to disk. Therefore, one can envision that in the future, NVM will play the role of both working memory and persistent store at the same time.

Persistent store demands consistency and durability guarantees, thereby imposing new design constraints on the memory system. Consistency is achieved at the expense of serializing multiple write operations. Durability requires memory cells to guarantee non-volatility and thus reduces the write speed. Therefore, a unified architecture oblivious to these two use cases would lead to suboptimal design. In this paper, we propose a novel unified working memory and persistent store architecture, NVM Duet, which provides the required consistency and durability guarantees for persistent store while relaxing these constraints if accesses to NVM are for working memory. A cross-layer design approach is adopted to achieve the design goal. Overall, simulation results demonstrate that NVM Duet achieves up to 1.68× (1.32× on average) speedup compared with the baseline design.



*ASPLOS '14*, March 1–4, 2014, Salt Lake City, Utah, USA.

ACM 978-1-4503-2305-5/14/03...$15.00.
http://dx.doi.org/10.1145/2541940.2541957

***Categories and Subject Descriptors*** C.0 [***Computer Systems Organization***]: General—System architectures; Hardware/software interfaces; D.4.2 [***Operating Systems***]: Storage Management—Main memory; Secondary storage; B.8 [***Hardware***]: Performance and Reliability

***Keywords*** Non-volatile memory; storage-class memory; phase-change memory; consistency; durability; memory management; memory scheduler; resistance drift, resistance distribution; refresh

## 1. Introduction

Recently, several non-volatile memory (NVM) technologies, including phase-change memory (PCM), spin-transfer torque RAM (STT-RAM), and memristors, have emerged in the field of memory hierarchy design. These technologies are collectively referred to as storage-class memory (SCM) because they are non-volatile like NAND flash and byte-addressable like DRAM and SRAM. SCM blurs the line between working memory and persistent store. Many current studies place SCM (e.g., PCM) on the memory bus to serve as working memory [31, 32, 50, 74]. PCM has the advantages of superior density and scalability compared with DRAM. Currently, 20-nm PCM prototypes have been demonstrated [16, 55], and devices as small as 8 nm are projected [3]. Furthermore, two to four bits of data can be stored in a PCM cell using the multi-level cell (MLC) technique [8, 9, 29, 43]. All of these advantages enable the construction of large-scale working memory for future multi-core computer needs. SCM has also been demonstrated to be a promising alternative to conventional persistent store, i.e., NAND flash and hard disk drives. SCM-based persistent store can be connected to CPUs via a direct memory access path, which offers the advantage of fast and fine-grained access. Several studies [18, 19, 65] have presented frameworks that allow data structures (e.g., arrays, linked lists, trees, and files) to be persistent in SCM rather than in traditional storage. With SCM, persistent data can be easily manipulated using ordinary load and store instructions without the need to resort to time-consuming and block-based disk I/O.

Therefore, one can envision that in the future, SCM will be used for working memory and persistent store simultaneously [7, 14, 54]. This projection is also in agreement with the vision shared by the NVM Programming Technical Work Group [1]. The goal of this work is to architect an SCM-based memory to play the dual roles at the same time. In particular, we target PCM-based memory systems. Given the newly proposed software architecture for using SCM as persistent store (i.e., NV-heaps [18] and Mnemosyne [65]), persistent store and working memory are accessed by applications in the same manner, via load and store instructions. Therefore, current memory architecture can easily support the two different use cases simultaneously. However, this situation leads to suboptimal design. Persistent store demands *consistency* and *durability* guarantees, which impose several design constraints on the memory system. Consistency is achieved at the expense of serializing multiple write operations. Durability requires memory cells to guarantee non-volatility, thereby reducing the write speed. If the memory system is oblivious to these two use cases, we lose many optimization opportunities and are not able to take advantage of the best characteristics of PCM.

In this paper, we propose NVM Duet, a unified working memory and persistent store architecture that provides the required *consistency* and *durability* guarantees for persistent store while relaxing these constraints if access to PCM is for working memory. The proposed system does not require advance partitioning of PCM resources between persistent store and working memory, and all the management is transparent to applications. Therefore, the architecture provides flexibility and adaptability for different usage scenarios, which may demand different capacity combinations for working memory and persistent store. The NVM Duet framework includes the following:

- A new hardware/software (HW/SW) interface that enables the memory controller to differentiate between the two types of PCM usage, working memory and persistent store. The proposed HW/SW interface is built around the memory management module in the operating system (OS) and is transparent to applications.
- A new memory scheduler is proposed to fully exploit the bank-level parallelism present in the address stream while respecting the write order specified by programmers to guarantee the consistency of persistent store.
- A new PCM architecture that provides dual retention guarantees to meet the durability requirement of persistent store while relaxing the retention requirement of working memory in return for write-latency reduction. To reduce refresh overhead, we propose a smart refreshing scheme that eliminates unnecessary refresh operations. Unlike DRAM, which requires complicated methods to minimize refresh operations (e.g., additional counters and off-line profiling for cells' retention capability), we demonstrate that with PCM, we can easily detect whether a memory cell needs to be refreshed by checking its resistance level. This process makes the proposed dual-retention design appealing for practical adoption.

We conduct experiments based on full-system simulations with workload mixes of persistent workloads and conventional workloads. The results demonstrate that the proposed scheduling strategy can improve instructions per cycle (IPC) by up to 1.53× (1.23× on average). The proposed dual-retention strategy can improve IPC by up to 1.22× (1.11× on average). Our proposed NVM Duet design combines the two strategies simultaneously and achieves an IPC speedup of up to 1.68× (1.32× on average) the baseline.

The remainder of this paper is organized as follows. Section 2 elaborates the performance implications of supporting persistent store on PCM, and in particular, the performance cost of guaranteeing consistency and durability. Section 3 describes our proposed NVM Duet design for optimizing system performance. Section 4 evaluates the proposed performance optimization strategies. Section 5 describes related works, and Section 6 presents our conclusions.

## 2. Performance Implications of Supporting Persistent Store on PCM

Persistent store demands *consistency* and *durability* guarantees that impose several design constraints on the memory system. In this section, we discuss how these design constraints limit the write performance of a PCM memory system in contrast with the design in which PCM is adopted as working memory. PCM is widely known to have poor write performance, which can affect system performance in the following two manners. First, memory controllers have size-limited queues to serve the read and write requests issued by the cores and caches. If the write queue is nearly full, the memory controllers prioritize the write requests over the read requests. Write requests thus delay read requests, which are critical for system performance [26, 51]. Second, once the write queue is full, the queue can no longer accept writes and evictions from cores and caches. This process can result in last-level cache stalls and degrade the system performance [23].

### 2.1 Data Consistency vs. Bank-Level Parallelism

Consistency refers to the property that any write to persistent store brings the persistent store from one valid state to another valid state. Consistency is vital for persistent store to guard against data corruption due to system crashes or power failures. The primary technique used to achieve consistency is adoption of *persistent update* mechanisms at the software level, such as journaling and shadow updates, and enforcing *ordering writes* at the hardware level [19, 65]; i.e., when manipulating a persistent data structure, programmers explicitly specify the order (more specifically, the partial or-

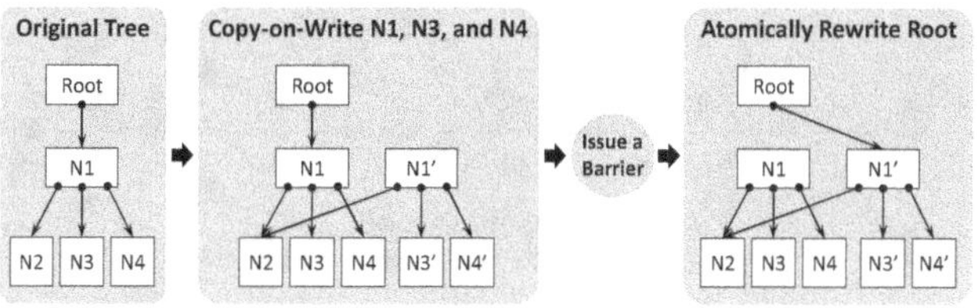


Figure 1: Consistent updating of a tree using shadow updates and ordering writes

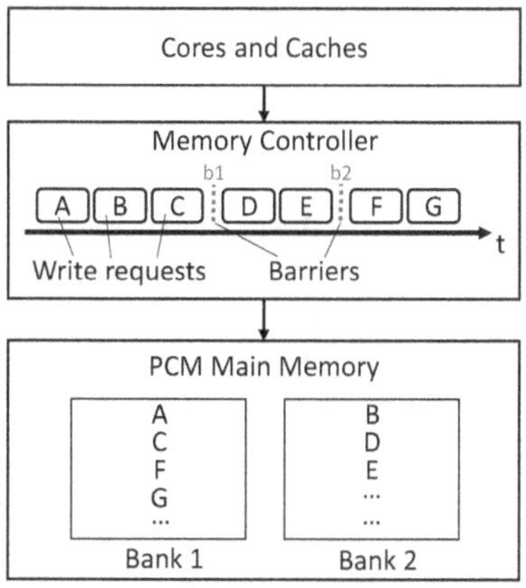


Figure 2: Example of write requests and barriers queued in the memory controller and their corresponding PCM banks

der) in which multiple writes can be reflected to the persistent store.

Let's take updating the contents of a tree structure in the NVM-based main memory using the shadow update mechanism for example. As shown in Figure 1, the tree originally consists of a *Root* node, an intermediate node (*N1*), and three leaf nodes (*N2*, *N3*, and *N4*). Supposing that both *N3* and *N4* must be updated, the program can adopt the following steps. First, the program issues write requests to create *N3'* and *N4'* that update *N3* and *N4* in a copy-on-write manner. Similarly, *N1* is updated by issuing write requests to create *N1'*, which points to *N2*, *N3'*, and *N4'*. Next, before issuing the write request to make *Root* point to *N1'* to complete the update of the tree, the program issues a barrier[1]. The barrier is explicitly coded by the programmer in the program to notify the hardware that all of the following write requests (including the one that updates *Root*) cannot be reflected to the persistent store until all of the preceding write requests (including those that create *N1'*, *N3'*, and *N4'*) are finished [19, 65]. Using the above steps, the tree data structure is guaranteed to always be in a valid state even if a failure occurs when the tree is being updated. More specifically, the tree either remains in its original state (*N1'*, *N3'*, and *N4'* are not visible through the *Root* node) or

[1] Barriers are also referred to as write barriers or epoch barriers. Barriers are special primitives that allow software to delimit write requests into epochs and declare ordering of the epochs [19].

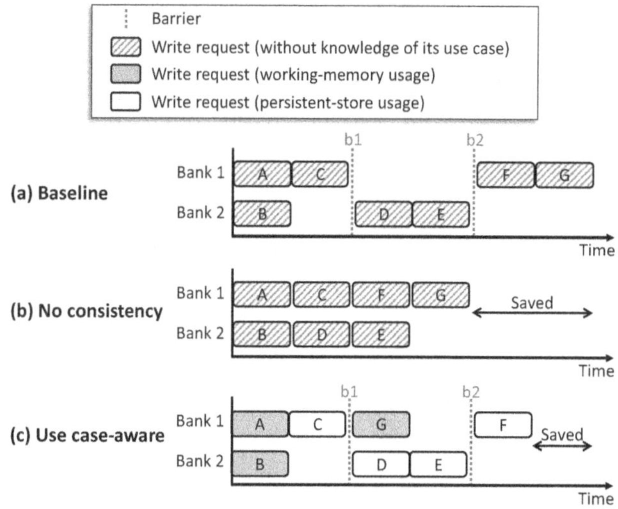


Figure 3: Schedule with mixing requests for persistent store and working memory

presents the new valid state (all of the updates are completed and no dangling pointers exist).

To guarantee consistency of the NVM-based main memory, at the hardware level, the cache controller, write buffer, memory controller, and other components must respect the barriers when performing write requests. In this work, we focus on analyzing the performance implications at the memory controller level. We take Figure 2 as an example. Seven write requests (*A*, *B*, ..., and *G*) and two barriers (*b1* and *b2*) are sent to the memory controller; *A*, *C*, *F*, and *G* go to the first bank[2] of the memory, and *B*, *D*, and *E* go to the second bank of the memory. Figure 3(a) displays a schedule that respects the barriers. In this schedule, *D* and *E* cannot be issued until *C* is finished because of the *b1* barrier. Similarly, *F* and *G* are pending until *D* and *E* complete.

From the example shown in Figure 3(a), we observe that consistency prohibits the scheduler from fully exploiting the available bank-level parallelism in the address stream, which is a critical performance factor in current memory architectures [30]. Figure 3(b) shows a schedule that we could use if the barriers were not present. This phenomenon causes a sub-optimal design if the PCM system needs to serve the dual roles of working memory and persistent store simultaneously. For example, suppose that among the seven write requests, *A*, *B*, and *G* belong to working memory, and the others belong to persistent store. As shown in Figure 3(c), we can observe that *G* can actually be served concurrently with *D* because *G* belongs to working memory. However, without knowledge of the use case for each write, we cannot schedule *G* ahead of the *b2* barrier.

[2] Unless otherwise specified, "row" and "bank" refer to logical units that cross all of the chips in a rank

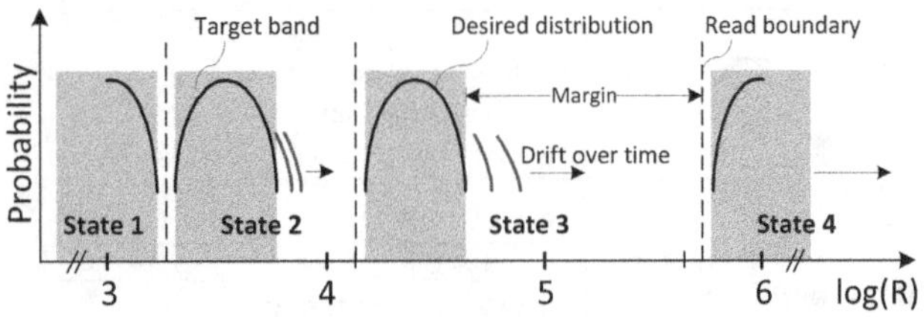


Figure 4: Target band allocation for tolerating resistance drift

## 2.2 Data Durability vs. Write Speed

Durability refers to the guarantee that committed data are retained even if the power is shut off or the system is restarted. To ensure durability, the storage medium must be non-volatile. However, maintaining a retention guarantee in non-volatile memory (e.g., of at least three months [2]) often comes at the cost of a slower write speed. Previous works have proposed volatile STT-RAM-based caches [27, 42, 62, 63] and Retention Relaxation for NAND flash-based solid-state drives (SSDs) [36, 45] to improve the NVM write speed. In this section, we target PCM and quantify how PCM's non-volatility correlates with its write speed by modeling 2-bit MLC PCM.

PCM's limited non-volatility (also known as retention capability) is determined by a phenomenon known as *resistance drift*, i.e., the resistance of PCM cells drifts upward over time. Resistance drift results in data losses at a certain point because PCM represents different data using different resistances. Resistance drift can be modeled using the following equation [5, 68, 73]:

$$R(t) = R_0 \times (\frac{t}{t_0})^{\nu} \quad (1)$$

where $R_0$ is the initial resistance of a PCM cell, $R(t)$ is the resistance at time $t$, $t_0$ is a time constant, and $\nu$ is a drift coefficient. This equation suggests that the amount of resistance drift (on a logarithmic scale) is proportional to the logarithm of the time elapsed after a cell is written, as captured by the following equation:

$$log(R(t)) - log(R_0) = \nu \times log(\frac{t}{t_0}) \quad (2)$$

To avoid data losses due to resistance drift, margins that tolerate drift for a required period of time are necessary. Thus, the resistance of PCM cells must lie within specified ranges known as *target band*s when the cells are written. As illustrated in Figure 4, the available resistance range of PCM ($10^3$ to $10^6\Omega$) is partitioned into four regions, with each region representing one data state. The dashed lines indicate the read boundaries, and the shaded regions denote the so-called target bands. The margins are the spaces between a target band and a read boundary.

Figure 5 compares the target band allocation with different non-volatility guarantees. Table 1 shows the drift coefficients for deriving the allocation, which are also adopted in previous studies [5, 68]. Figure 5(a) is the baseline that guar-

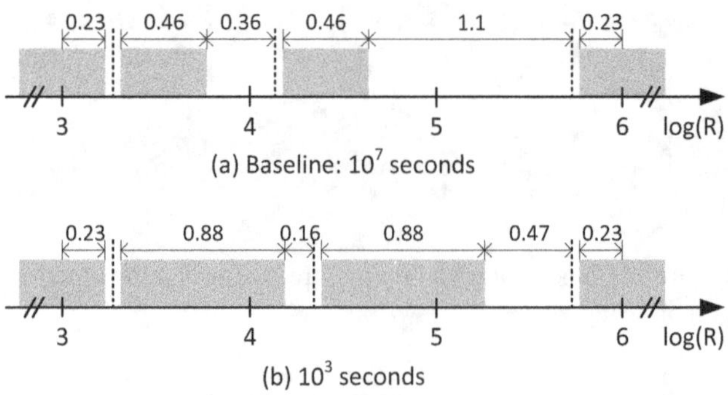


Figure 5: Target band allocation for $10^7$-s and $10^3$-s retention capability

antees three-month (i.e., $10^7$-s) non-volatility[3]. In comparison, Figure 5(b) shows an allocation that guarantees 1000-s non-volatility. The drift margins of the 1000-s allocation are $\frac{3}{7}$ narrower than those of the $10^7$-s version because the required drift margins are proportional to the logarithm of the required periods of non-volatility, according to Equation (2).

Table 1: Drift factors for 2-bit MLC PCM; $t_0 = 1$s. SDMR stands for the standard-deviation-to-mean ratio

| State | Data | ν | |
|---|---|---|---|
| | | Mean | SDMR |
| 1 | '00' | 0.001 | 40% |
| 2 | '01' | 0.02 | |
| 3 | '10' | 0.06 | |
| 4 | '11' | 0.10 | |

The write speed can be estimated based on the target band allocation and the PCM write scheme. PCM adopts the *iterative write* scheme that requires multiple iterations to write a cell. Each iteration involves a write pulse that alters the cell's resistance by a small amount $\Delta R$. At the end of each pulse, the cell resistance is compared with the target band to determine whether the write has finished. The value of $\Delta R$ is determined according to the width of the target band. A small $\Delta R$ is used for a narrow target band to prevent the iterative write from completely missing the target band. Therefore, the average number of required iterations (write latency) is approximately inversely proportional to both $\Delta R$ and the width of the target band [5]:

$$\textit{Write Latency} \propto \frac{1}{\Delta R} \propto \frac{1}{\textit{Target Band Width}} \quad (3)$$

[3] To achieve three months (i.e., $10^7$-s) of non-volatility, the target band width of the baseline is set to 0.46 in our analysis. Such a width conforms well to the PCM prototype shown in [43], which is the referenced work of recent PCM studies [26, 51]. We consider that the available resistance range of PCM is divided non-uniformly (i.e., non-uniform banding) such that the non-volatility of the two intermediate states is balanced. A recent paper about PCM [5] considers a similar width (0.46) but only reports 500 seconds of non-volatility because the non-volatility is not balanced (the second state is 10 years and the third state is just 500 seconds), and the PCM is limited by the worst case.

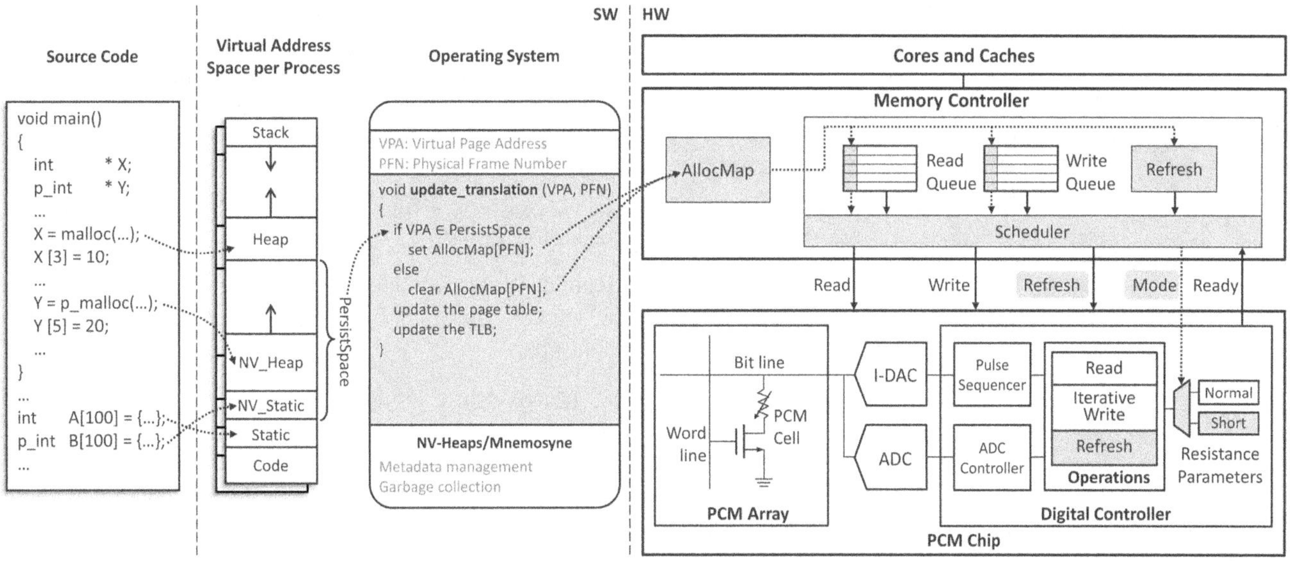


Figure 6: HW/SW interface design (the modified components are shaded). The figure is not drawn to scale.

Based on this model, Table 2 summarizes the relative write speed of the PCM given various non-volatility guarantees. We observe that by lowering the retention guarantee, we can obtain a significant write latency reduction. For example, compared with the baseline, the write latency is reduced by 1.9× for a PCM with 1000-s retention capability. This observation suggests that if a write to PCM is needed for working memory, relaxing the retention guarantee has great potential for improving the write speedup. However, in unified working memory and persistent store architectures, without differentiating the sources of write requests, the PCM system must be designed in such a way that non-volatility is guaranteed at all times.

Table 2: Write speedup factors with different retention guarantees

| Non-Volatility (s) | Target Band log(R) | Write Speedup |
|---|---|---|
| $10^7$ | 0.46 | **Baseline** |
| $10^6$ | 0.56 | **1.2 ×** |
| $10^5$ | 0.67 | **1.5 ×** |
| $10^4$ | 0.77 | **1.7 ×** |
| $10^3$ | 0.88 | **1.9 ×** |
| $10^2$ | 0.98 | **2.1 ×** |

# 3. NVM Duet

The proposed NVM Duet system is a PCM-based memory system that simultaneously serves as working memory and persistent store. The design goal of NVM Duet is to provide the required *consistency* and *durability* guarantees for persistent store while relaxing these constraints if PCM is used for working memory. NVM Duet contains a HW/SW interface that enables the memory controller to differentiate the use case of each access, a novel memory scheduler that seeks to fully exploit the bank-level parallelism present in the address stream while respecting the write order specified by programmers to guarantee the consistency of persistent store, and a dual-retention PCM architecture that meets the durability requirement for persistent store while relaxing the retention requirement of working memory in return for write-latency reduction.

## 3.1 HW/SW Interface

The proposed HW/SW interface is built on recently proposed software frameworks that enable programmers to declare persistent data in the PCM main memory, e.g., NV-heaps [18] and Mnemosyne [65]. These frameworks consist of language, compiler, and runtime system supports to facilitate persistent data management. As shown in Figure 6, at the program level, special keywords and library calls such as "p_int" (a persistent version of int) and "p_malloc()" (a persistent version of malloc()) are available to programmers. Programmers are obligated to handle data that demand persistence using the keywords and library calls. The compiler and runtime library link persistent data to a reserved virtual address space (*PersistSpace*). When the reserved space is accessed, the OS maps PCM frames to the virtual address space to serve the request. Persistent store is self-contained. Once a frame stores persistent data, the OS also retains the required metadata for indexing and garbage collection in the PCM main memory.

To convey to the memory controller the OS's knowledge of the use case of each piece of data, a component named as *AllocMap* is added to the memory controller, as shown in Figure 6. *AllocMap* consists of a bit map, one bit for

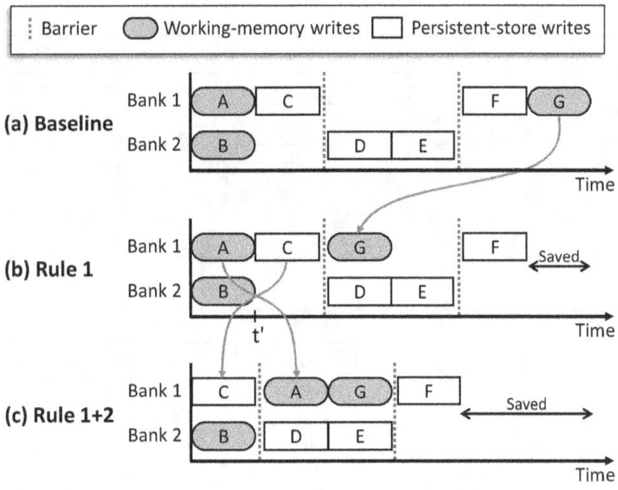


Figure 7: Benefits of applying the proposed scheduling rules

each PCM frame, and is indexed by the physical address of the PCM frames. These bits indicate whether a PCM frame serves as working memory or persistent store. A bit is set if the associated PCM frame is working memory; otherwise, the bit is reset. The size of *AllocMap* is 256KB for a system with 8 GB of PCM (8 GB/4 KB $\times$ 1 bit/8 = 256 KB). Upon power-on, all of the bits are reset, i.e., the memory controller presumes that all frames by default are persistent store.

*AllocMap* is updated by the OS at run time. We take Figure 6 as an example. When the OS updates the virtual-to-physical translations (i.e., page tables), the OS can compare the virtual address with *PersistSpace* to determine the use case of the allocated physical memory frame. This information is transmitted to the memory controller by updating *AllocMap*. Because *AllocMap* is volatile, one may worry that bits in *AllocMap* might be lost upon power failure. In fact, data losses in *AllocMap* are not an issue. After a power failure, *AllocMap* is reset at power-on, and the OS reboots and updates *AllocMap* as usual.

### 3.2 Duet Scheduler

The design goal of Duet Scheduler is to fully exploit the bank-level parallelism present in the address stream while respecting the write order specified by programmers to guarantee the consistency of persistent store. With the new HW/SW interface in the NVM Duet framework, the memory controller now has the knowledge of whether a write request is intended for persistent store or working memory. The Duet scheduler adopts two scheduling rules:

**Rule 1:** Writes to working memory can be scheduled regardless of barriers.

Because barriers are only intended to restrict the order of the write requests to persistent store, with the proposed HW/SW interface, the memory controller can schedule working-memory writes free from the barrier constraints. Figure 7(a) and Figure 7(b) compare the schedule before and after adoption of Rule 1 using the same address stream example as in Figure 3. Figure 7(a) shows the baseline schedule, and Figure 7(b) shows the resulting schedule if Rule 1 is adopted. In this schedule, request *G* is performed immediately after request *C* because Bank 1 is available and request *G* is a working-memory request, which can be performed regardless of barriers.

**Rule 2:** Writes to persistent store are prioritized over writes to working memory if a barrier is pending in the memory controller.

The concept behind Rule 2 is to prioritize write requests on dependency chains. A barrier delimits multiple writes into two epochs and creates dependency between the two epochs, i.e., the following epoch cannot begin execution until the preceding epoch completes. Therefore, by scheduling writes to persistent store first in the presence of barriers, we can make subsequent persistent writes available to the memory scheduler earlier, thereby exposing additional opportunities for exploiting bank-level parallelism. As indicated in Figure 7(b), at time *t'*, bank 2 is idle because request *D* and *E* cannot be issued until request *C* completes. By scheduling request *C* before *A*, request *D* and *E* can be freed from the barrier constraint earlier, as is request F. We can observe that the resulting schedule shown in Figure 7(c) fully exploits the available bank-level parallelism in the address stream.

To support Duet Scheduler, as shown in Figure 6, each request in the write queue has an additional bit that indicates whether the request belongs to working memory or persistent store. These bits are determined by checking *AllocMap* when write requests are enqueued. The scheduler applies the aforementioned scheduling rules based on this information. Please note that Duet Scheduler does not violate any existing write-ordering constraint for working memory. For example, the write-after-write, read-after-write, and write-after-read dependencies are maintained.

### 3.3 Dual-Retention PCM Architecture

The NVM Duet framework provides two-level retention guarantees to meet the durability requirement for persistent store while relaxing the retention requirement of working memory in return for write latency reduction. There are two key features in the proposed dual-retention PCM architecture. First, the PCM chips provide two access modes with different retention guarantees such that a memory cell can be programmed differently at run time according to its use case, i.e., working memory or persistent store. Second, to fully exploit the performance gain from retention relaxation, we avoid unnecessary refreshing by exploiting a PCM-specific property: the remaining retention capability of a cell can be inferred according to the resistance of the cell. In the following section, we elaborate on these two features.

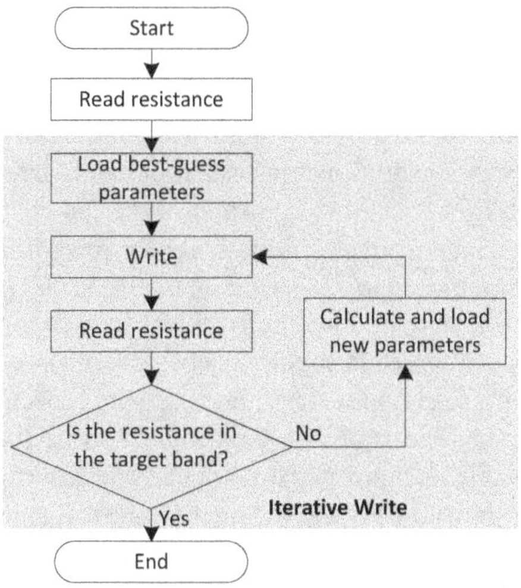


Figure 8: Basic refresh procedure

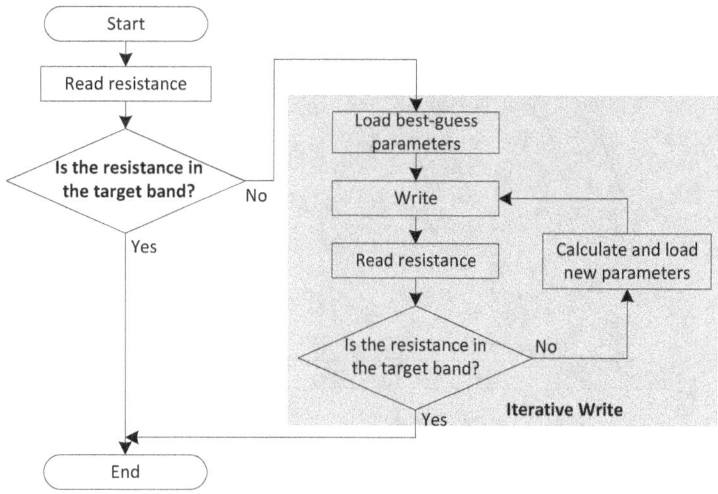


Figure 9: Smart Refresh

**Dual-Retention PCM Chips**

As mentioned in Section 2, PCM's retention capability is related to the width of the target bands. Therefore, to provide two write modes with different retention guarantees to the memory controller, as shown in Figure 6, a PCM chip includes two sets of resistance parameters (i.e., target bands and read boundaries), which correspond to the two retention levels for working memory and persistent store. These parameters are indicated as "normal" and "short" in the figure. For example, Figure 5 shows the target-band and read-boundary settings for $10^7$-s and 1000-s retention capabilities.

To allow the memory controller to invoke different types of access, as shown in Figure 6, the command interface between the memory controller and the PCM chips is extended with an additional *mode* signal to select one of the two sets of resistance parameters. Each request in the read/write queue has an additional bit to indicate its use case, either working memory or persistent store. Its value is determined by checking *AllocMap* when the request is enqueued.

When performing reads, the PCM chips [17] employ I-DACs (current-output digital-to-analog converters) and ADCs (analog-to-digital converters) to determine the stored data by comparing PCM cells' resistance with the read boundaries selected by the memory controller. When performing writes, the PCM chips [17] employ I-DACs and ADCs to heat the selected cells and verify whether the resulting resistance falls into the target bands selected by the memory controller.

**Smart Refresh**

To avoid data losses for working memory, a DRAM-like periodic refresh (*basic refresh* for short) is employed. Refreshing contributes to the major overhead of the proposed dual-retention PCM design. To minimize the impact from refreshing, we propose Smart Refresh to avoid unnecessary refreshing operations.

The sources of unnecessary refreshing operations are twofold. First, for those memory cells that are frequently written, their retention capability is also frequently renewed even if they are not refreshed. The other major source stems from the fact that PCM cells' retention capability varies because the initial resistance and drift factor of PCM cells form distributions. The concept of avoiding unnecessary refreshing has been used in DRAM. However, detecting whether a DRAM cell has the capability to retain data until the next retention interval is challenging. DRAM's smart refresh scheme [21] requires a counter for each row to track the row's remaining retention capability. When a row is accessed, the associated counter is reset. Exploiting the retention capability variation among DRAM cells is even more difficult. Certain works [33, 34] demand off-line profiling of DRAM cells to understand the required refreshing frequency of each cell. However, as indicated in [35], retention profiling is not reliable because DRAM's retention can change randomly over time (i.e., the variable retention time phenomenon). Unlike DRAM, which requires complicated methods to avoid unnecessary refresh operations, we show that with PCM, we can easily detect whether a memory cell needs to be refreshed, which makes the proposed dual-retention design appealing for practical adoption.

To avoid unnecessary refresh operations, our proposed Smart Refresh exploits a PCM-specific property: the remaining retention capability of a cell can be inferred according to the resistance of the cell. More specifically, if the resistance of a cell remains in the target band, the cell can retain data until the next refreshing interval because the rate of resistance drift (i.e., resistance changes in logarithm per unit of time) is time decreasing according to Equation (2). Therefore, the refresh of this type of cell can be deferred.

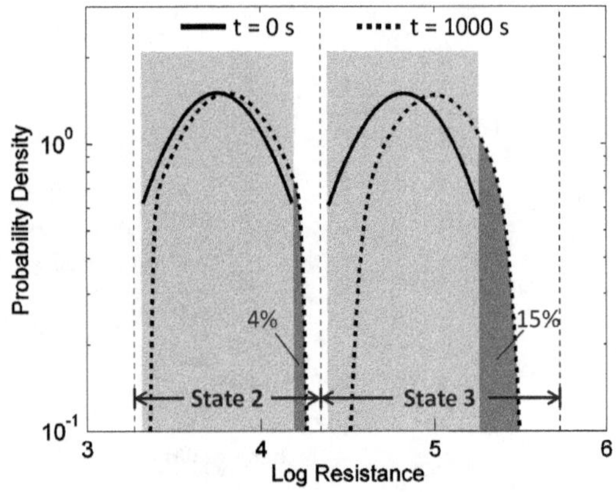


Figure 10: Resistance distribution before and after 1000-s drift

Smart Refresh can reduce the number of refreshed cells quite significantly. We take a PCM with a 1000-s retention capability as an example to quantify the effectiveness of Smart Refresh. Figure 10 shows the simulation results of the resistance distributions of PCM cells. In this analysis, we only show the second and third data states. We do not show the first and fourth states because the drift coefficient of the first state is negligibly small, and the fourth state is the state with the highest resistance, whose stored data are not affected by the upward drift. Therefore, cells in these two states do not need refreshing and can be omitted in this analysis. Light-gray shading indicates the target bands with a 1000-s retention guarantee. The dashed vertical lines denote the read boundaries, and the solid and dashed bell-shaped lines indicate the resistance distributions of a cell at $t = 0$ and $t = 1000$ s, respectively. First, we observe that a cell does contain valid data at $t = 1000$ s because the two resistance distributions have not yet drifted across the read boundaries. We can further observe that a cell's resistance actually has a high probability of remaining in the target bands, a 96% and 85% chance for the second and third states, respectively. Therefore, assuming that data exist in one of the four states with equal probability, Smart Refresh can reduce the number of refreshed cells to 5% of the basic refresh ($\frac{(4\%+15\%)}{4} = 5\%$).

Smart Refresh reduces energy consumption and wearout caused by refreshing. Furthermore, Smart Refresh decreases the required power for each individual refresh and thus can increase the parallelism of refreshing. For example, the basic refresh scheme rewrites all 256 cells for a 64-byte row. Therefore, at most two rows from two banks in a rank (i.e., a total of 512 cells) can be refreshed simultaneously because of the power limitation of PCM chips [23]. In comparison, because Smart Refresh involves only 5% of the cells in a row, eight rows from eight banks in a rank can be refreshed simultaneously without violating the power limitation, i.e., Smart Refresh has $4\times$ higher parallelism.

To support Smart Refresh, as shown in Figure 6, the command interface between the memory controller and the PCM chip is extended with an additional refresh command. A refresh unit is added to the memory controller to periodically send refresh commands to the working-memory rows in a staggered manner according to *AllocMap*. In the PCM chips, in addition to read and write operations, the chips support refresh operations. As shown in Figure 8, a basic refresh operation consists of a read and a write, both of which occur in the volatile mode. The refresh interval is set to be the same as the achievable retention capability of a volatile write (e.g., 1000 s). As shown in Figure 9, Smart Refresh is similar to basic refresh except for the additional step that detects whether a cell's resistance is within the target bands and bypasses the on-going refresh accordingly. This additional detection step can be seamlessly integrated into the refresh procedure because the same step is also employed in the iterative write procedure.

# 4. Evaluation

## 4.1 Experimental Setup

We conducted simulation using the Micro-Architectural and System Simulator (MARSS) [47] and DRAMSim2 [56]. MARSS is a cycle-accurate full-system simulator that uses PTLsim [71] for CPU simulation on top of the QEMU emulator [10]. DRAMSim2 is a cycle-accurate simulator of main-memory systems. Table 3 presents the configurations of the simulated four-core CMP system. We extend DRAMSim2 to model a PCM-based main-memory system. The PCM main memory consists of 8 GB in total arranged in two ranks, and each rank contains eight banks. Each bank has an eight-entry read queue and a 32-entry write queue in the memory controller to buffer pending requests [26, 51]. The read requests are prioritized over write requests unless the write queue is $> 80\%$ full [26, 51]. The proposed refreshing and scheduling policies are also simulated. The baseline guarantees a $10^7$-s retention and respects all barriers for all writes.

Table 3: System configurations

| | |
|---|---|
| CPU | 4-core, 2 GHz, 4 issue, out-of-order |
| L1 I/D | 32KB/32KB, 4-way, private, 64B line |
| L2 | 2 MB, 4-way, private, 64B line |
| L3 | 8 MB, 8-way, private, 64B line, 50 ns |
| Memory Controller | 32-entry write queue and 8-entry read queue per bank<br>Read-first scheduling unless the write queue is >80% full |
| PCM Main Memory | 8 GB, 2-bit MLC, 4 ranks of 8 banks each, 64 B row<br>Read latency: 250 ns<br>Write latency: 250 ns per iteration |

Table 4 presents the average iterations of writes and refreshes adopted in the simulation. We consider that a write involves changing 32 cells (one-eighth of a 256-cell line) because of the differential write scheme, and eight writes to eight banks in a rank can be performed in parallel. According to the iterative write model of PCM [51], we estimate that each write takes 5.7 iterations on average with the specified baseline retention capability ($10^7$ s). For the basic refresh scheme, refreshing involves all cells in a row. Thus, two rows from two banks in a rank are refreshed simultaneously with an average latency of 8.5 iterations. For Smart Refresh, due to the reduced number of refreshed cells, eight rows from eight banks in a rank can be refreshed simultaneously with the same latency as the basic refresh, as explained in Section 3.3. For 1000-s and 100-s operations, the average latency is adjusted according to the speedup factor listed in Table 2.

Table 4: Average iterations for write and refresh operations

| | Write (one 64B row) | Basic Refresh (two 64B rows) | Smart Refresh (eight 64B rows) |
|---|---|---|---|
| $10^7$-s | 5.7 | 8.5 | |
| 1000-s | 5.7/1.9 | 8.5/1.9 | |
| 100-s | 5.7/2.1 | 8.5/2.1 | |

Table 5 summarizes the workload mixes that we use. To evaluate the NVM Duet system, each workload mix combines one persistent workload and three SPEC CPU2006 workloads. The persistent workload (SPS), which performs random swaps within a 1-GB array of integers, is similar to the one in [18]. For SPS, we simulate write-through stores, and on average, one barrier is issued per 20 stores. The SPEC CPU2006 workloads are executed in a rate mode (i.e., three cores execute the same benchmarks). The RPKI and WPKI (i.e., main-memory reads/writes per kilo instructions) of the workloads are given in the table. Furthermore, we list the percentage of working-memory writes among all of the main-memory writes (referred to as *WM%*). The workload mixes are sorted in ascending order of *WM%*. For the workload mixes that we use, *WM%* ranges from 22% to 76%.

Table 5: Workload mixes

| Name | Description | RPKI | WPKI | WM% |
|---|---|---|---|---|
| zeus | 1 SPS + 3 copies of 434.zeusmp | 4.6 | 2.2 | 22% |
| libq | 1 SPS + 3 copies of 462.libquantum | 43 | 17 | 31% |
| mcf | 1 SPS + 3 copies of 429.mcf | 41 | 16 | 31% |
| sopl | 1 SPS + 3 copies of 450.soplex | 2.5 | 1.9 | 31% |
| gcc | 1 SPS + 3 copies of 403.gcc | 3.0 | 1.9 | 41% |
| lesl | 1 SPS + 3 copies of 437.leslie3d | 18 | 9.6 | 42% |
| milc | 1 SPS + 3 copies of 433.milc | 1.8 | 1.4 | 44% |
| asta | 1 SPS + 3 copies of 473.astar | 1.1 | 1.0 | 51% |
| lbm | 1 SPS + 3 copies of 470.lbm | 22 | 15 | 63% |
| cact | 1 SPS + 3 copies of 436.cactusADM | 24 | 16 | 63% |
| bwav | 1 SPS + 3 copies of 410.bwaves | 14 | 9.0 | 65% |
| perl | 1 SPS + 3 copies of 400.perlbench | 6.4 | 5.5 | 70% |
| gems | 1 SPS + 3 copies of 459.GemsFDTD | 2.5 | 2.2 | 71% |
| bzip | 1 SPS + 3 copies of 401.bzip2 | 47 | 32 | 76% |

The metrics that we evaluate are IPC and load latency. The load latency is defined as follows:

$$Load\ latency = \frac{\sum_{All\ loads} (t_{finish} - t_{issue})}{Number\ of\ loads} \quad (4)$$

where $t_{issue}$ is the time of a load request issued to the L1 data cache and $t_{finish}$ is the time at which the load finishes and data are retrieved. This metric quantifies the responsiveness of the memory system, including the caches and main memory.

### 4.2 Experimental Results

The semantics and correctness of persistent data handling were described in Section3.1. Our evaluation thus focuses on the performance gain achieved by NVM Duet.

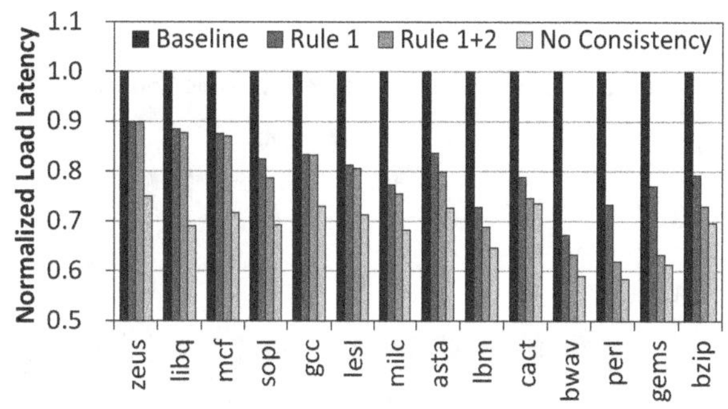


Figure 11: Benefits of Duet Scheduler for load latency

#### 4.2.1 Duet Scheduler

We first focus on evaluating the benefits of Duet Scheduler only (i.e., Dual-Retention PCM is not adopted). Figure 11 shows the average load latency in the simulated system. We compare the **baseline** with a system that adopts **Rule 1** and a system that adopts both **Rule 1 + 2**. We also evaluate a system in which the memory scheduler ignores all barriers and offers **no consistency** guarantee. The no-consistency system represents the ideal case that fully exploits the bank-level parallelism of write requests. The results are normalized to the baseline. We can observe that the load latency of the no-consistency system is reduced by up to 42% (30% on average) compared with the baseline. The proposed Duet Scheduler can effectively reduce the load latency. With Rule 1, the load latency is reduced by up to 33% (19% on average). If Rule 1 and Rule 2 are both adopted, the load latency is reduced by up to 38% (24% on average).

Figure 12 plots the IPC speedup achieved by Duet Scheduler. With Rule 1, IPC is improved by up to 1.44× (1.2× on average). Combining Rule 1 and Rule 2 improves IPC by up to 1.53× (1.23× on average). We observe that Duet Scheduler achieves an IPC speedup that is close to that of the no-consistency case. The difference is within 7% on average, which means that the proposed scheduling rules successfully maximize the utilization of the available bank-level parallelism.

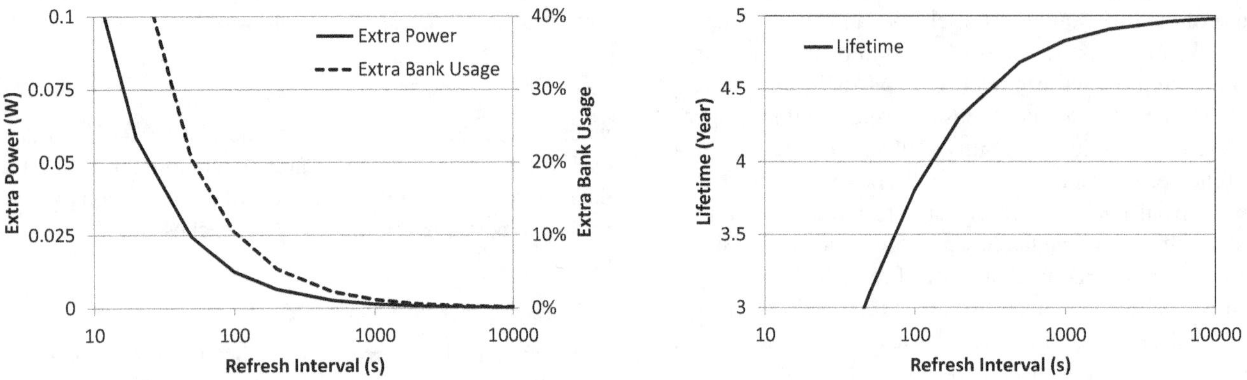


Figure 13: Overhead analysis vs. refresh interval

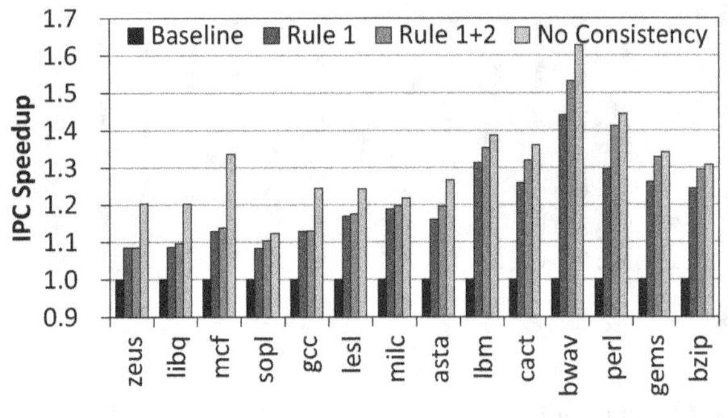


Figure 12: Benefits of Duet Scheduler for IPC

Note that in Figure 12, the speedup increases along the horizontal axis, reaches a peak, and then gradually decreases. This is due to the fact that we arrange the workload mixes in ascending order of *WM*% (the percentage of working-memory writes among all writes). Duet Scheduler is beneficial to write streams containing a mix of working-memory and persistent-store accesses. Duet Scheduler neither helps nor hurts workloads with only working-memory or persistent-store writes. Therefore, the speedup increases when *WM*% increases and reaches a peak for *bwav*, which consists of a mix of 35% persistent-store writes and 65% working-memory writes. Subsequently, the speedup gradually drops when *WM*% further increases to 76% for *bzip*.

### 4.2.2 Deciding on the Appropriate Refresh Interval

Before we analyze Dual-Retention PCM, we must decide on the appropriate refresh interval (which is the same as the retention capability of the working memory). A shorter retention time requires more-frequent refreshes. Therefore, the refresh interval is a key design parameter in NVM Duet. The refresh interval can range by several orders of magnitude, from $10^7$ seconds down to a few seconds or even shorter. Thus, it would be time-consuming to perform a full exploration in such a large design space using a detailed simulation. Therefore, in this section, we first present analytical models that enable quick evaluation of the refresh overhead in terms of power, lifetime, and performance. We identify two refresh-interval candidates of 1000 s and 100 s. Full-system simulations are subsequently performed to evaluate the overall performance of the proposed architecture.

Refreshing PCM not only causes power and performance overhead but also degrades the PCM lifetime because of extra writes. Estimating the extra power incurred by refreshing is straightforward. Given that each cell must be refreshed every $T_{refresh}$ interval, during the $T_{refresh}$ interval, the energy consumption of refresh operations is $(N \cdot E)$, where $N$ is the total number of PCM cells and $E$ is the average energy consumption required to refresh a cell. Therefore, the extra power $P$ is the total energy consumed by refreshing all PCM cells divided by the refresh interval:

$$P = \frac{N \cdot E}{T_{refresh}} \tag{5}$$

Compared with power, it is more challenging to estimate the impact of refreshes on a memory system without resorting to a detailed simulation. To perform a first-order estimation, we use a simple metric known as bank usage, i.e., the average percentage of time that a PCM bank spends in accessing its array. The extra bank usage, $U\%$, due to refreshes can be modeled as follows:

$$U\% = \frac{N \cdot R}{B \cdot C} \cdot \frac{1}{T_{refresh}} \tag{6}$$

where $N$ is the total number of PCM cells, $R$ is the latency of each refresh, $B$ is the number of memory banks, and $C$ is the number of cells that are refreshed at a time (per bank). Then, $\frac{N \cdot R}{B \cdot C}$ is the total time that a bank spends in refresh operations during a $T_{refresh}$ interval.

The lifetime aspect can be estimated by dividing the endurance of a cell (denoted as $D$) by the worn-out rate, assuming that perfect wear leveling is adopted. The worn-out rate is composed of two components: those due to normal writes and those due to refreshes. The former is $\frac{D}{5 \times 365 \times 24 \times 60 \times 60}$, assuming that the original lifetime is five years. The latter is $\frac{Y}{T_{refresh}}$, where $Y$ is the average number of iterations for refreshing a cell and $T_{refresh}$ is the refresh interval. Therefore,

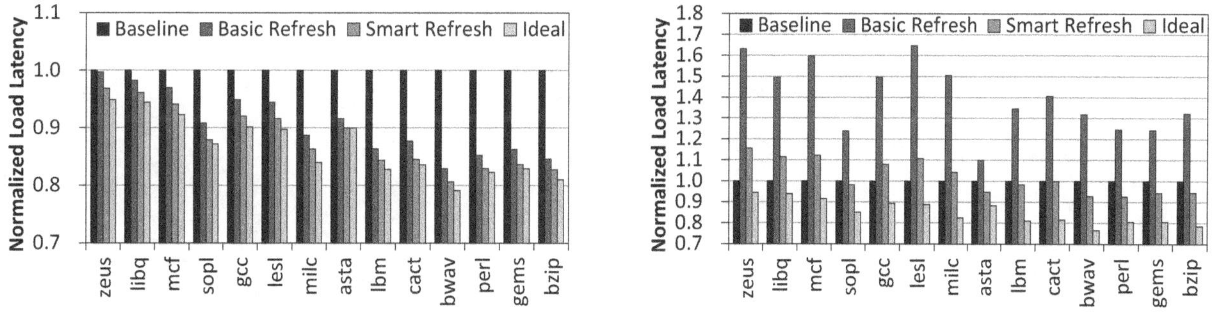


(a) 1000-s retention guarantee

(b) 100-s retention guarantee

Figure 14: Benefits of Dual-Retention PCM for load latency

the resulting lifetime with refresh (denoted as $L$) can be evaluated as follows:

$$L = \frac{D}{\underbrace{(\frac{D}{5 \times 365 \times 24 \times 60 \times 60})}_{\text{due to normal writes}} + \underbrace{(\frac{Y}{T_{refresh}})}_{\text{due to refreshes}}} \quad (7)$$

Figure 13 shows the estimated extra power, extra bank usage, and resulting lifetime for a system with 8 GB of PCM. The setting of each parameter is detailed in Table 6 (the read and write energy is from [32]). We can observe that for power overhead, refreshes incur at most an extra 0.013 W if the refresh interval is no shorter than 100 s. For the performance aspect, with a 1000-s refresh interval, the bank usage is increased by 1.1%, and the overhead increases to 10% if the refresh interval is shortened to 100 s. For the lifetime analysis, the resulting lifetime is 4.8 years with 1000-s refreshes and decreases to 3.8 years with 100-s refreshes.

Table 6: Parameters for deciding on the appropriate refresh interval

| | Value | Unit | Notes |
|---|---|---|---|
| N | $(8 \times 2^{30} \times 8)/2$ | Cell | 8GB, 2 bits per cell |
| B | 8x2 | Bank | 2 ranks of 8 banks |
| C | (64x8)/2 | Cell | 64B line, 2 bits per cells |
| D | $10^7$ | Cycle | |
| S | Please see Table 2 | | Speedup factor due to wider target bands |
| R | 250 + (8.5/S)x250 | ns | Read: 250 ns<br>Write: (8.5/S) iterations of 250 ns |
| E | 2.5 + 17x(8.5/S)x50% | pJ | Read: 2.5 pJ/cell (peripheral is included)<br>Write: 17 pJ/cell (peripheral is included)<br>Assume a 50% chance a cell is refreshed |
| Y | (8.5/S)x50% | Cycle | Write iterations for refreshing: (8.5/S)<br>Assume a 50% chance a cell is refreshed |

From the above analysis, we can note that a 1000-s refresh interval leads to small overheads: 0.0014 W of extra power, 1.1% of extra bank usage, and a small degradation in lifetime from 5 to 4.8 years. In contrast, the overhead caused by 100-s refreshes begins to increase dramatically. Therefore, a refresh interval shorter than 100 s should not be considered any further. Although a 100-s refresh interval causes significantly higher overhead than the 1000-s interval in terms of performance and lifetime in the preliminary analysis, a 100-s refresh also offers additional benefits from relaxing the retention guarantee for the PCM. To evaluate the overall effects, these two intervals are both considered in the detailed simulation. Below, we present the results from full-system simulations in terms of performance. Because the lifetime impact and extra power due to refresh have been estimated using the analytical models, further analysis of the lifetime and power is omitted in this paper.

### 4.2.3 Dual-Retention PCM

In this section, we evaluate the benefits of Dual-Retention PCM alone (i.e., Duet Scheduler is not adopted). Figure 14 shows the load latency of the **baseline** and Dual-Retention PCM. We compare two candidates of Dual-Retention PCM, one candidate whose working memory adopts a 1000-s retention capability and the other whose working memory adopts a 100-s retention capability. We also compare different refresh schemes: the **basic refresh** scheme, the proposed **Smart Refresh** scheme, and a hypothetical **ideal** case that relaxes the working memory's retention requirement but requires no refreshes. We first observe that for the ideal case, lowering the PCM's non-volatility to 1000 s and 100 s can reduce the load latency by up to 21% and 23% (14% and 16% on average), respectively. If the overheads of basic refresh are considered, load latency is reduced by up to 17% (10% on average) for the 1000-s configuration. However, the 100-s configuration even performs worse than the baseline. The load latency increases by up to 65% (41% on average). The proposed Smart Refresh reduces the refreshing overhead. With Smart Refresh, the load latency for the 1000-s configuration is within 1% of the ideal case on average, but the 1000-s configuration still performs worse than the baseline. We can observe that the 1000-s configuration consistently outperforms the 100-s version, and therefore, we only evaluate the 1000-s case from now on.

Figure 15 shows the IPC speedup achieved by Dual-Retention PCM. There is potential for a speedup of up to 1.26× (1.14× on average) for the ideal case. With the

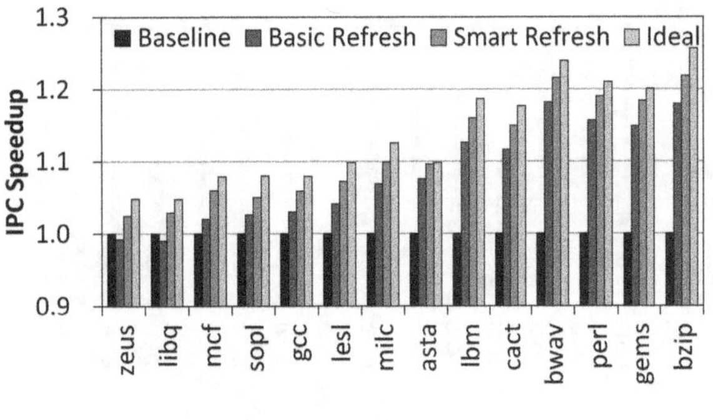


Figure 15: Benefits of Dual-Retention PCM for IPC

refreshing overheads considered, the basic refresh design achieves a speedup of up to 1.18× (1.08× on average). With the proposed Smart Refresh optimization, the speedup reaches up to 1.22× (1.11× on average), which is within 3% of the ideal case. This result implies the proposed optimization can effectively reduce and hide the refresh overhead. We can observe that in Figure 15, the speedup trend increases as *WM%* increases because the performance gain of Dual-Retention PCM comes from relaxing the retention capability of working-memory writes. Higher *WM%* thus implies that a larger portion of the workloads is optimized.

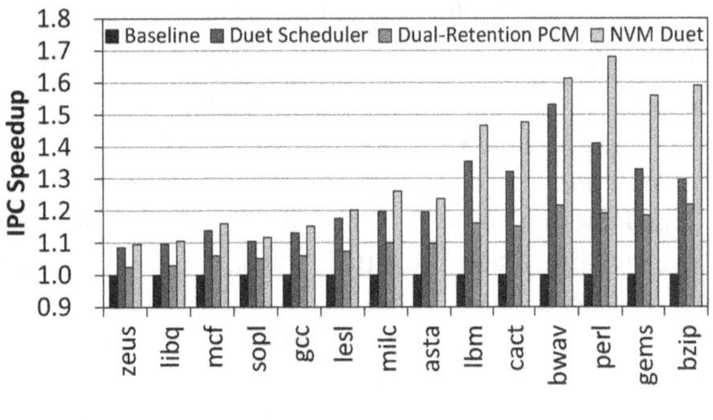


Figure 16: Benefits of NVM Duet for IPC

### 4.2.4 NVM Duet — Putting It All Together

Duet Scheduler and Dual-Retention PCM improve the unified architecture from different aspects. The former exploits bank-level parallelism, and the latter reduces the average write latency. Therefore, combining the two mechanisms can lead to greater performance gains. Figure 16 compares the IPC speedup achieved by Duet Scheduler, Dual-Retention PCM, and NVM Duet, in which all of the proposed techniques are simultaneously adopted. The results demonstrate that NVM Duet significantly improves performance by up to 1.68× (1.32× on average). The IPC speedup of NVM Duet is within 5% of the product of the IPC speedup numbers of the two individual mechanisms. This result suggests that the two mechanisms can cooperate well with each other. We also observe that NVM Duet is especially effective for write-intensive workloads, such as *bwav* and *bzip*, with *WM%* ranging from 65% to 76%.

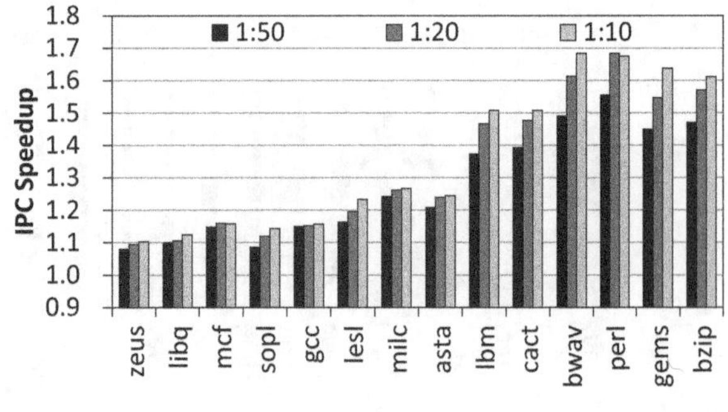


Figure 17: Benefits of NVM Duet for IPC with different ratios of barriers to persistent-store writes

Figure 17 shows the IPC speedup achieved by NVM Duet with different ratios of barriers to persistent-store writes. With a higher ratio of barriers, NVM Duet is a bit more effective. The performance speedup reaches 1.68× (1.34× on average) when the ratio is 1:10. The speedup is close to 1.55× (1.27× on average) when the ratio is 1:50.

## 5. Related Work

Several previous studies have proposed using PCM as working memory [32, 50, 74]. Limited write endurance and relatively poor write performance are the two major concerns for PCM-based working memory. To address the write-endurance issue, differential write [32, 50, 74] eliminates unnecessary writes to PCM. Wear leveling [49, 52, 59, 74] spreads the writes across the entire PCM space to avoid concentrated memory wear. Error correction schemes [6, 20, 24, 48, 58, 60, 70] keep the PCM functional even if certain cells wear out. To address PCM's write-performance issue, write cancellation and write pausing [51] allow critical reads to abort or pause on-going writes. Write truncation [26] exploits the error-correcting code's ability to curtail a write operation before all of the bits are written correctly. In [53, 72], PCM asymmetries are exploited to improve write performance. In [15, 23, 25], bit flipping and power budgeting are used to maximize PCM's write parallelism, given a limited chip power supply.

PCM is also considered to be a promising solution for building high-performance persistent store. Because of the differences between PCM and traditional block-based storage in terms of access speed and access granularities, significant efforts in innovative programming models and system architecture design are ongoing [12, 13, 18, 19, 40, 41, 64–67]. For example, BPFS [19] incorporates a new file system and hardware architecture. NV-heaps [18] and Mnemosyne [65] propose languages and libraries that enable in-memory persistence. In [40, 41], memory allocation, memory protection, and cache architecture tailored to NVM-based persistent store are proposed.

Unification of working memory and persistent store in NVM was envisioned in [7, 14, 54]. Based on a unified architecture, [44] integrates the space management of working memory and persistent store. This approach maximizes the available working memory and reduces page swapping. Memorage [28] performs global wear leveling between working memory and persistent store to maximize the achievable lifetime.

Prior studies have presented Retention Relaxation for NVM to optimize the write performance or write endurance of NVM systems. In particular, these studies target STT-RAM caches [27, 42, 62, 63] and NAND flash SSDs [11, 36, 37, 39, 45], and refreshing is adopted. For PCM, selected patent applications [22, 38, 46] also present refreshing the PCM but do not focus on trading off retention capability and write performance in the manner emphasized by Retention Relaxation. Several papers [4, 5, 61, 69] also analyze PCM's retention capability and refreshing overhead, but they assume a pure working memory architecture instead of a unified structure, as in this work, and their analyses are based on PCM with a uniform target-band allocation. The work in [61] proposes lowering the PCM's information density in return for enlarging the target bands and improving the write speed. Concurrent with our work, Approximate Storage [57] relaxes the error rate guarantee for data that are error-tolerable. Similar to the Dual-Retention PCM portion of our work, Approximate Storage manipulates PCM's target bands for improved write speed.

## 6. Conclusions

In this paper we present a novel unified working memory and persistent store architecture, NVM Duet. We observe that naively making NVM serve as both working memory and persistent store is a suboptimal approach because of the intrinsic differences between the two use cases. This problem occurs because without knowledge of the use case of an individual request, a unified memory architecture must serve all requests under the highest design constraints in terms of consistency and durability.

NVM Duet adopts a cross-layer approach to provide the required consistency and durability guarantees for persistent store while relaxing these constraints if accesses to NVM are for working memory, thereby improving system performance. Specifically, a new HW/SW interface allows the OS to convey the use case of data declared by the programmer (working memory or persistent store) to the memory controller. The memory controller is then enhanced with a new scheduler, Duet Scheduler, which seeks to fully exploit the parallelism present in the address stream while respecting the write order to guarantee the consistency of persistent store. Furthermore, a new PCM architecture, Dual-Retention PCM, is proposed to provide two retention levels and relax the durability constraint for working memory. To make Dual-Retention PCM appealing for practical adoption, NVM Duet employs Smart Refresh that exploits PCM devices' property to eliminate unnecessary refresh overhead. Experiments based on full-system simulations and workload mixes of persistent and conventional workloads demonstrate that our NVM Duet design achieves up to a $1.68\times$ ($1.32\times$ on average) speedup over the baseline.

## Acknowledgments

We thank the program committee and anonymous reviewers for their insightful feedback. We also thank Hsiang-Pang Li, Ming-Hsiu Lee, Jau-Yi Wu, and Yen-Hao Shih at Macronix for their helpful suggestions. This work is supported in part by research grants from Macronix International Co., Ltd. (101-S-C54), the National Science Council of Taiwan (NSC-102-2220-E-002-005-, NSC-102-2220-E-002-001-, and NSC-100-2221-E-002-248-MY3), the Excellent Research Projects of National Taiwan University (103R890822), Etron Technology Inc. (102R7150), and the Industrial Technology Research Institute of Taiwan (B5-10210-2F-1).

## References

[1] SNIA non volatile memory (NVM) programming technical work group (TWG). http://snia.org/forums/sssi/nvmp.

[2] JESD218A: Solid-state drive (SSD) requirements and endurance test method, Feb. 2011.

[3] Process integration, devices, and structures (PIDS). Technical report, ITRS, 2012.

[4] M. Awasthi, M. Shevgoor, K. Sudan, R. Balasubramonian, B. Rajendran, and V. Srinivasan. Handling PCM resistance drift with device, circuit, architecture, and system solutions. In *NVMW*, 2011.

[5] M. Awasthi, M. Shevgoor, K. Sudan, B. Rajendran, R. Balasubramonian, and V. Srinivasan. Efficient scrub mechanisms for error-prone emerging memories. In *HPCA*, 2012.

[6] R. Azevedo, J. D. Davis, K. Strauss, P. Gopalan, M. Manasse, and S. Yekhanin. Zombie memory: Extending memory lifetime by reviving dead blocks. In *ISCA*, 2013.

[7] K. Bailey, L. Ceze, S. D. Gribble, and H. M. Levy. Operating system implications of fast, cheap, non-volatile memory. In *HotOS*, 2011.

[8] F. Bedeschi, R. Fackenthal, C. Resta, E. Donze, M. Jagasivamani, E. Buda F. Pellizzer, D. Chow, A. Cabrini, G. Calvi, R. Faravelli, A. Fantini, G. Torelli, D. Mills, R. Gastaldi, and G. Casagrande. A multi-level-cell bipolar-selected phase-change memory. In *ISSCC*, 2008.

[9] F. Bedeschi, R. Fackenthal, C. Resta, E. Donze, M. Jagasivamani, E. Buda, F. Pellizzer, D. Chow, A. Cabrini, G. Calvi, R. Faravelli, A. Fantini, G. Torelli, D. Mills, R. Gastaldi, and G. Casagrande. A bipolar-selected phase change memory featuring multi-level cell storage. *IEEE J. Solid-St. Circ.*, 44(1):217–227, 2009.

[10] F. Bellard. QEMU, a fast and portable dynamic translator. In *USENIX ATC*, 2005.

[11] Y. Cai, G. Yalcin, O. Mutlu, E. F. Haratsch, A. Cristal, O. S. Unsal, and K. Mai. Flash correct-and-refresh: Retention-aware error management for increased flash memory lifetime. In *ICCD*, 2012.

[12] A. M. Caulfield, A. De, J. Coburn, T. I. Mollow, R. K. Gupta, and S. Swanson. Moneta: A high-performance storage array architecture for next-generation, non-volatile memories. In *MICRO*, 2010.

[13] A. M. Caulfield, T. I. Mollov, L. A. Eisner, A. De, J. Coburn, and S. Swanson. Providing safe, user space access to fast, solid state disks. In *ASPLOS*, 2012.

[14] J. Chang, P. Ranganathan, T. Mudge, D. Roberts, M. A. Shah, and K. T. Lim. A limits study of benefits from nanostore-based future data-centric system architectures. In *CF*, 2012.

[15] S. Cho and H. Lee. Flip-N-Write: A simple deterministic technique to improve PRAM write performance, energy and endurance. In *MICRO*, 2009.

[16] Y. Choi, I. Song, M.-H. Park, H. Chung, S. Chang, B. Cho, J. Kim, Y. Oh, D. Kwon, J. Sunwoo, J. Shin, Y. Rho, C. Lee, M. G. Kang, J. Lee, Y. Kwon, S. Kim, J. Kim, Y.-J. Lee, Q. Wang, S. Cha, S. Ahn, H. Horii, J. Lee, K. Kim, H. Joo, K. Lee, Y.-T. Lee, J. Yoo, and G. Jeong. A 20nm 1.8V 8Gb PRAM with 40MB/s program bandwidth. In *ISSCC*, 2012.

[17] G. F. Close, U. Frey, J. Morrish, R. Jordan, S. Lewis, T. Maffitt, M. Breitwisch, C. Hagleitner, C. Lam, and E. Eleftheriou. A 512Mb phase-change memory (PCM) in 90nm CMOS achieving 2b/cell. In *VLSIC*, 2011.

[18] J. Coburn, A. M. Caulfield, A. Akel, L. M. Grupp, R. K. Gupta, R. Jhala, and S. Swanson. NV-heaps: Making persistent objects fast and safe with next-generation, non-volatile memories. In *ASPLOS*, 2011.

[19] J. Condit, E. B. Nightingale, C. Frost, E. Ipek, B. Lee, D. Burger, and D. Coetzee. Better I/O through byte-addressable, persistent memory. In *SOSP*, 2009.

[20] J. Fan, S. Jiang, J. Shu, Y. Zhang, and W. Zhen. Aegis: Partitioning data block for efficient recovery of stuck-at-faults in phase change memory. In *MICRO*, 2013.

[21] M. Ghosh and H.-H. S. Lee. Smart refresh: An enhanced memory controller design for reducing energy in conventional and 3D die-stacked DRAMs. In *MICRO*, 2007. .

[22] T. Happ and J. B. Philipp. Resistive memory including selective refresh operation. U.S. Patent Application No. 2008/0117704 A1, 2008.

[23] A. Hay, K. Strauss, T. Sherwood, G. H. Loh, and D. Burger. Preventing PCM banks from seizing too much power. In *MICRO*, 2011.

[24] E. Ipek, J. Condit, E. B. Nightingale, D. Burger, and T. Moscibroda. Dynamically replicated memory: Building reliable systems from nanoscale resistive memories. In *ASPLOS*, 2010.

[25] L. Jiang, Y. Zhang, B. R. Childers, and J. Yang. FPB: Fine-grained power budgeting to improve write throughput of multi-level cell phase change memory. In *MICRO*, 2012.

[26] L. Jiang, B. Zhao, Y. Zhang, J. Yang, and B. R. Childers. Improving write operations in MLC phase change memory. In *HPCA*, 2012.

[27] A. Jog, A. K. Mishra, C. Xu, Y. Xie, V. Narayanan, R. Iyer, and C. R. Das. Cache revive: Architecting volatile STT-RAM caches for enhanced performance in CMPs. In *DAC*, 2012.

[28] J.-Y. Jung and S. Cho. Memorage: Emerging persistent RAM based malleable main memory and storage architecture. In *ICS*, 2013.

[29] D.-H. Kang, J.-H. Lee, J. Kong, D. Ha, J. Yu, C. Um, J. Park, F. Yeung, J. Kim, W. Park, Y. Jeon, M. Lee, Y. Song, J. Oh, G. Jeong, and H. Jeong. Two-bit cell operation in diode-switch phase change memory cells with 90nm technology. In *2008 Symposium on VLSI Technology*, 2008. .

[30] Y. Kim, V. Seshadri, D. Lee, J. Liu, and O. Mutlu. A case for exploiting subarray-level parallelism (SALP) in DRAM. In *ISCA*, 2012.

[31] E. Kultursay, M. Kandemir, A. Sivasubramaniam, and O. Mutlu. Evaluating STT-RAM as an energy-efficient main memory alternative. In *ISPASS*, 2013.

[32] B. C. Lee, E. Ipek, O. Mutlu, and D. Burger. Architecting phase change memory as a scalable DRAM alternative. In *ISCA*, 2009.

[33] C.-H. Lin, D.-Y. Shen, Y.-J. Chen, C.-L. Yang, and M. Wang. SECRET: Selective error correction for refresh energy reduction in DRAMs. In *ICCD*, 2012.

[34] J. Liu, B. Jaiyen, R. Veras, and O. Mutlu. RAIDR: Retention-aware intelligent DRAM refresh. In *ISCA*, 2012.

[35] J. Liu, B. Jaiyen, Y. Kim, C. Wilkerson, and O. Mutlu. An experimental study of data retention behavior in modern DRAM devices: Implications for retention time profiling mechanisms. In *ISCA*, 2013.

[36] R.-S. Liu, C.-L. Yang, and W. Wu. Optimizing NAND flash-based SSDs via retention relaxation. In *FAST*, 2012.

[37] R.-S. Liu, C.-L. Yang, C.-H. Li, and G.-Y. Chen. DuraCache: A durable SSD cache using MLC NAND flash. In *DAC*, 2013.

[38] H.-L. Lung. Refresh circuitry for phase change memory. U.S. Patent Application No. 2011/0013446 A1, 2011.

[39] V. Mohan, S. Sankar, and S. Gurumurthi. reFresh SSDs: Enabling high endurance, low cost flash in datacenters. Technical Report CS-2012-05, University of Virginia, 2012. Presented at FMS '12.

[40] I. Moraru, D. Andersen, M. Kaminsky, P. Ranganathan, N. Tolia, and N. Binkert. From filesystem designer to persistent data structure designer: Enabling safe memory management for byte-addressable NVRAM. In *NVMW*, 2013.

[41] I. Moraru, D. G. Andersen, M. Kaminsky, N. Tolia, P. Ranganathan, and N. Binkert. Consistent, durable, and safe memory management for byte-addressable non volatile main memory. In *TRIOS*, 2013.

[42] A. Nigam, C. W. Smullen, V. Mohan, E. Chen, S. Gurumurthi, and M. R. Stan. Delivering on the promise of universal memory for spin-transfer torque RAM (STT-RAM). In *ISLPED*, 2011.

[43] T. Nirschl, J. B. Philipp, T. D. Happ, G. W. Burr, B. Rajendran, M.-H. Lee, A. Schrott, M. Yang, M. Breitwisch, C.-F. Chen, E. Joseph, M. Lamorey, R. Cheek, S.-H. Chen, S. Zaidi, S. Raoux, Y. Chen, Y. Zhu, R. Bergmann, H.-L. Lung, and C. Lam. Write strategies for 2 and 4-bit multi-level phase-change memory. In *IEDM*, 2007.

[44] S. Oikawa. Integrating memory management with a file system on a non-volatile main memory system. In *SAC*, 2013.

[45] Y. Pan, G. Dong, Q. Wu, and T. Zhang. Quasi-nonvolatile SSD: Trading flash memory nonvolatility to improve storage system performance for enterprise applications. In *HPCA*, 2012.

[46] W. D. Parkinson and T. A. Lowrey. Refreshing memory cells of a phase change material memory device. U.S. Patent Application No. 2004/0022085 A1, 2004.

[47] A. Patel, F. Afram, S. Chen, and K. Ghose. MARSS: A full system simulator for multicore x86 CPUs. In *DAC*, 2011.

[48] M. K. Qureshi. Pay-as-you-go: Low-overhead hard-error correction for phase change memories. In *MICRO*, 2011.

[49] M. K. Qureshi, J. Karidis, and M. Franceschini. Enhancing lifetime and security of PCM-based main memory with start-gap wear leveling. In *MICRO*, 2009.

[50] M. K. Qureshi, V. Srinivasan, and J. A. Rivers. Scalable high performance main memory system using phase-change memory technology. In *ISCA*, 2009.

[51] M. K. Qureshi, M. M. Franceschini, and L. A. Lastras-Montano. Improving read performance of phase change memories via write cancellation and write pausing. In *HPCA*, 2010.

[52] M. K. Qureshi, A. Seznec, L. A. Lastras, and M. M. Franceschini. Practical and secure PCM systems by online detection of malicious write streams. In *HPCA*, 2011.

[53] M. K. Qureshi, M. M. Franceschini, A. Jagmohan, and L. A. Lastras. PreSET: Improving performance of phase change memories by exploiting asymmetry in write times. In *ISCA*, 2012.

[54] P. Ranganathan. From microprocessors to nanostores: Rethinking data-centric systems. *Computer*, 44(1):39–48, 2011.

[55] S. Raoux, G. W. Burr, M. J. Breitwisch, C. T. Rettner, Y.-C. Chen, R. M. Shelby, M. Salinga, D. Krebs, S.-H. Chen, H.-L. Lung, and C. H. Lam. Phase-change random access memory: A scalable technology. *IBM J. Res. Dev.*, 52(4):465–479, July 2008.

[56] P. Rosenfeld, E. Cooper-Balis, and B. Jacob. DRAMSim2: A cycle accurate memory system simulator. *IEEE Comput. Archit. Lett.*, 10 (1):16 –19, 2011.

[57] A. Sampson, J. Nelson, K. Strauss, and L. Ceze. Approximate storage in solid-state memories. In *MICRO*, 2013.

[58] S. Schechter, G. H. Loh, K. Straus, and D. Burger. Use ECP, not ECC, for hard failures in resistive memories. In *ISCA*, 2010.

[59] N. H. Seong, D. H. Woo, and H.-H. S. Lee. Security Refresh: Prevent malicious wear-out and increase durability for phase-change memory with dynamically randomized address mapping. In *ISCA*, 2010. .

[60] N. H. Seong, D. H. Woo, V. Srinivasan, J. A. Rivers, and H.-H. S. Lee. SAFER: Stuck-at-fault error recovery for memories. In *MICRO*, 2010.

[61] N. H. Seong, S. Yeo, and H.-H. S. Lee. Tri-level-cell phase change memory: Toward an efficient and reliable memory system. In *ISCA*, 2013.

[62] C. W. Smullen, V. Mohan, A. Nigam, S. Gurumurthi, and M. R. Stan. Relaxing non-volatility for fast and energy-efficient STT-RAM caches. In *HPCA*, 2011.

[63] Z. Sun, X. Bi, H. H. Li, W.-F. Wong, Z.-L. Ong, X. Zhu, and W. Wu. Multi retention level STT-RAM cache designs with a dynamic refresh scheme. In *MICRO*, 2011.

[64] S. Venkataraman, N. Tolia, P. Ranganathan, and R. H. Campbell. Consistent and durable data structures for non-volatile byte-addressable memory. In *FAST*, 2011.

[65] H. Volos, A. J. Tack, and M. M. Swift. Mnemosyne: Lightweight persistent memory. In *ASPLOS*, 2011.

[66] H. Volos, S. Panneerselvam, S. Nalli, and M. M. Swift. Storage-class memory needs flexible interfaces. In *APSys*, 2013.

[67] X. Wu and A. L. N. Reddy. SCMFS: A file system for storage class memory. In *SC*, 2011.

[68] W. Xu and T. Zhang. Using time-aware memory sensing to address resistance drift issue in multi-level phase change memory. In *ISQED*, 2010.

[69] S. Yeo, N. H. Seong, and H.-H. S. Lee. Can multi-level cell PCM be reliable and usable? Analyzing the impact of resistance drift. In *WDDD*, 2012.

[70] D. H. Yoon, N. Muralimanohar, J. Chang, P. Ranganathan, N. P. Jouppi, and M. Erez. FREE-p: Protecting non-volatile memory against both hard and soft errorss. In *HPCA*, 2011.

[71] M. T. Yourst. PTLsim: A cycle accurate full system x86-64 microarchitectural simulator. In *ISPASS*, 2007.

[72] J. Yue and Y. Zhu. Accelerating write by exploiting PCM asymmetries. In *HPCA*, 2013.

[73] W. Zhang and T. Li. Helmet: A resistance drift resilient architecture for multi-level cell phase change memory system. In *DSN*, 2011.

[74] P. Zhou, B. Zhao, J. Yang, and Y. Zhang. A durable and energy efficient main memory using phase change memory technology. In *ISCA*, 2009.

# SDF: Software-Defined Flash for Web-Scale Internet Storage Systems

Jian Ouyang  Shiding Lin
Baidu, Inc.
{ouyangjian, linshiding}@baidu.com

Song Jiang *
Peking University and Wayne State University
sjiang@wayne.edu

Zhenyu Hou  Yong Wang  Yuanzheng Wang
Baidu, Inc.
{houzhenyu, wangyong03, wangyuanzheng}@baidu.com

## Abstract

In the last several years hundreds of thousands of SSDs have been deployed in the data centers of Baidu, China's largest Internet search company. Currently only 40% or less of the raw bandwidth of the flash memory in the SSDs is delivered by the storage system to the applications. Moreover, because of space over-provisioning in the SSD to accommodate non-sequential or random writes, and additionally, parity coding across flash channels, typically only 50-70% of the raw capacity of a commodity SSD can be used for user data. Given the large scale of Baidu's data center, making the most effective use of its SSDs is of great importance. Specifically, we seek to maximize both bandwidth and usable capacity.

To achieve this goal we propose *software-defined flash* (SDF), a hardware/software co-designed storage system to maximally exploit the performance characteristics of flash memory in the context of our workloads. SDF exposes individual flash channels to the host software and eliminates space over-provisioning. The host software, given direct access to the raw flash channels of the SSD, can effectively organize its data and schedule its data access to better realize the SSD's raw performance potential.

Currently more than 3000 SDFs have been deployed in Baidu's storage system that supports its web page and image repository services. Our measurements show that SDF can deliver approximately 95% of the raw flash bandwidth and provide 99% of the flash capacity for user data. SDF increases I/O bandwidth by 300% and reduces per-GB hardware cost by 50% on average compared with the commodity-SSD-based system used at Baidu.

* This work was performed during his visiting professorship at Peking University.



*ASPLOS '14*, March 01 - 05 2014, Salt Lake City, UT, USA.

http://dx.doi.org/10.1145/2541940.2541959

***Categories and Subject Descriptors*** B.3.2 [*Memory Structures*]: Design Styles - mass storage (e.g., magnetic, optical, RAID)

***Keywords*** Solid-State Drive (SSD), Flash Memory, Data Center.

## 1. Introduction

To accommodate ever-increasing demand on I/O performance in Internet data centers, flash-memory-based solid-state drives (SSDs) have been widely deployed for their high throughput and low latency. Baidu was one of the first large-scale Internet companies to widely adopt SSDs in their storage infrastructures and has installed more than 300,000 SSDs in its production system over the last seven years to support I/O requests from various sources including indexing services, online/offline key-value storage, table storage, an advertisement system, mySQL databases, and a content delivery network. Today SSDs are widely used in data centers, delivering one order of magnitude greater throughput, and two orders of magnitude greater input/output operations per second (IOPS), than conventional hard disks. Given SSD's much higher acquisition cost per unit capacity, achieving its full performance and storage potential is of particular importance, but we have determined that both raw bandwidth and raw storage capacity of commodity SSDs, in a range of performance categories, are substantially underutilized.

In the investigation of bandwidth utilization we chose three commodity SSDs—Intel 320, Huawei Gen3, and Memblaze Q520—as representative low-end, mid-range, and high-end SSD products currently on the market. The raw bandwidth of an SSD is obtained by multiplying its channel count, number of flash planes in each channel, and each plane's bandwidth. The raw bandwidth of each plane is mainly determined by the flash feature size and was dis-

| SSD Type | Interface | NAND Type | Channels | Planes/ channel | NAND speed | Raw R/W Bandwidths (MB/s) | Measured R/W Bandwidths (MB/s) |
|---|---|---|---|---|---|---|---|
| Low-end | SATA 2.0 | 25nm MLC | 10 | 4 | ONFI 2.x | 300/300 | 219/153 |
| Mid-range | PCIe 1.1 x8 | 25nm MLC | 44 | 4 | 40MHz async | 1600/950 | 1200/460 |
| High-end | PCIe 1.1 x8 | 34nm MLC | 32 | 16 | ONFI1.x async | 1600/1500 | 1300/620 |

**Table 1.** Specifications and bandwidths of different types of SSDs. "NAND speed" specifies the NAND flash interface, which indicates the flash speed.

closed to us by the respective vendors. To obtain a device's peak read and write bandwidths we read or write data sequentially in erase-block units. Table 1 lists specifications and read/write bandwidths of the SSDs with 20% over-provisioning. As shown, the measured bandwidths range from 73% to 81% for read, and 41% to 51% for write, of the corresponding raw bandwidths. Interestingly, these ratios are relatively constant ranging from the low-end drive with the SATA 2.0 interface with maximum transfer rate of 300 MB/s, to the mid-range and high-end drives that cost 4-8 times more per unit capacity and use the PCIe 1.1 x8 interface with maximum transfer rate of 1.6GB/s. In practice the effective bandwidth received at the storage system serving real-world workloads can be much lower because I/O requests from upper-level software, such as file systems, databases, and key-value stores, are usually not optimized to generate SSD-friendly access patterns. The consequence is that the realized I/O bandwidth of Baidu's storage system is only 50% of the raw bandwidth of the flash hardware.

Another challenge in Baidu's web-scale storage system is the large amount of reserved flash space unavailable for storing user data. Space is reserved for two purposes: storing parity coding across channels for data loss protection, which accounts for approximately 10% of the flash space, and over-provisioning for accommodating random writes. In the conventional SSD architecture the amount of over-provisioned space can be critical to performance. Figure 1 shows random write throughput as a function of the over-provisioning ratio for the low-end SSD that has been widely deployed in Baidu's data centers. Though 50% over-provisioning seems to be excessive, 25% over-provisioning may be justified in this SSD architecture because it can improve throughput by 21% relative to 7% over-provisioning and by more than 400% relative to 0% over-provisioning. In our production system the over-provisioning is usually configured between 10% and 40% depending on the workload characteristics and performance requirements. For a workload with mixed random writes and sequential reads, raising the ratio from 22% to 30% can result in an increase of sustained throughput from less than 100MB/s to 400MB/s (more than 400%) because the read throughput can be greatly degraded by random writes triggering more frequent garbage collection when there is less over-provisioning.

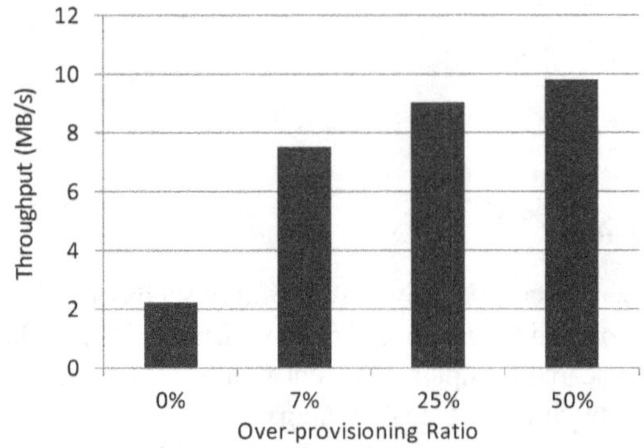


**Figure 1.** Throughput of the low-end SSD (Intel 320) with random writes of 4KB pages when various fractions of its raw capacity are allocated as over-provisioned space.

Significant under-utilization of resources in a large data center with hundreds of thousands of servers can have severe implications in terms of both initial and recurring costs. First, the hardware cost increases substantially because additional device acquisition is required to make up for unexploited performance and capacity potential. Second, the energy cost associated with additional hardware, such as servers and cooling equipment, increases. Third, physical space requirement increases. Finally, all of these contribute to increased maintenance costs.

In building a large-scale data center on a limited budget the common practice at major Internet companies such as Google, Facebook, and Baidu has been to use a large number of inexpensive commodity parts and servers that collectively meet the performance and storage requirements. With increasing performance requirements the system is expanded by adding more parts and servers and consequently pushing hardware, energy, and maintenance costs ever higher. A more economical strategy is to better exploit existing (and future) resources wherever possible. This is especially effective for devices that are relatively expensive and whose potential is significantly under-exploited, such as the SSD. However, current software, including system software, usually has been extensively optimized for managing the devices and extracting their maximum potentials as far as their standard interfaces allow. To unlock their full potential the devices need to be modified to provide an interface such that the software can more directly access the devices' internal operations, and interact with the devices in a manner more friendly to their performance characteristics. This customization has a cost barrier because new design and manufacturing are needed. However, if the device is deployed in large numbers (100,000+), the additional cost could be easily recouped. Accordingly, we should rethink the design and implementation of SSDs used in a data center with its particular workload characteristics as opposed to general-purpose use in, e.g., desktop and portable devices.

Baidu's *Software Defined Flash* (SDF) project is such an effort. By exposing the channels in commodity SSD hardware to software and requiring the write unit to be of the flash erase-block size, we can match the workload concurrency with the hardware parallelism provided by the multiple channels and minimize the interference in a flash channel serving requests from different threads, thereby exploiting individual flash's raw bandwidth. SDF requires the software to explicitly initiate block erasure operations, and requires the software erasure of a block before writing into it so that the drive does not need to reserve space for internal garbage collection. At the same time the system software can schedule the erasures during a flash's idle period to minimize their effect on the service quality of regular requests. In addition, we remove the parity coding across channels and, to minimize the possibility of data loss, rely on the system-level data replication that is already in place for data persistence. Together these make almost all raw flash space available for storing user data.

In addition to the concerns about the performance and cost of SSD, the SDF project is also motivated and enabled by a significant workload characteristic in data centers supporting Internet-wide services. Specifically, most write requests are sequential and are issued in a unit much larger than what conventional block devices assume (e.g., 4KB). At one extreme, write requests by some major services can be naturally sequential. For example, there are over 10,000 servers at Baidu for generating a large volume of index data that is not subject to later modification, and sequentially writing it to storage. At the other extreme, because serving small write requests can be unacceptably slow and subsequent reads can be expensive due to an unmanageably large body of metadata in a conventional file system, a common practice is to direct small-write traffic to a storage system managed as a log-structured merge (LSM) tree [16] such as Google's BigTable or Baidu's CCDB. In such systems writes are served in a unit as large as several megabytes. As a consequence, imposing a write unit of erase-block size in SDF does not demand significant software changes to accommodate the device's new interface.

In summary, in this paper we make three major contributions:

- We propose SDF (Software Defined Flash), an SSD device with a customized architecture and interface supported by an FPGA-based controller, to allow the software to realize its raw bandwidth and storage capacity. This represents an effort to customize hardware to specifically meet the requirements of the data center with respect to system performance, cost, and maintenance, and is distinct from today's common practice of relying only on the large number of commodity devices for system capability.
- To ensure that the raw bandwidth and space are fully delivered to the applications, we deploy SDF mainly to serve a major class of workloads involving large writes, including dumping sequential index files into storage and accessing storage for LSM-tree-style data management. We demonstrate that for these major applications the potential I/O performance can be attained with unsophisticated request scheduling strategies. Because of the high concurrency exhibited by the workloads the exposed multiple channels in SDF can be effectively exploited for much higher bandwidth. In this sense SDF is motivated by, and receives its name from, the software-shaped workloads.
- We have implemented the SDF controller using the Xilinx Spartan-6 FPGA in place of the commodity SSD flash translation layer (FTL), and using the Xilinx virtex-5 to implement its PCIe interface. SDF is installed in more than 3000 servers now running in Baidu's data center and supporting the web page and image repository services. Measurements on the production system show that the SDF can deliver up to 95% of the raw bandwidth while the commodity SSDs with a similar configuration can only deliver less than 50% on these real-world workloads, and that the bandwidth is comparable to that of the high-end PCIe-interfaced SSDs. In addition, SDF provides 99% of the raw flash capacity for user data, and its per-GB cost is about 50% less than that of high-end commodity SSDs used at Baidu.

The remainder of this paper is organized as follows. Section 2 describes the SDF design, including the hardware and interface designs. Section 3 presents and analyzes experimental results. Related work is presented in Section 4 and Section 5 concludes.

## 2. Design of SDF

Each SDF consists of a customized flash device wrapped with a layer of software providing a symmetric block access interface (8 MB write/erase unit and 8 KB read unit). While the device provides multiple independent channels for parallel access, it is the software layer that makes this functionality accessible to applications and translates the hardware parallelism into significantly improved throughput delivered to the applications. Next we describe SDF's hardware structure including its FPGA-based controller design, design choices to reduce hardware cost, the design of the SDF interface, and the use of SDF in Baidu's storage system.

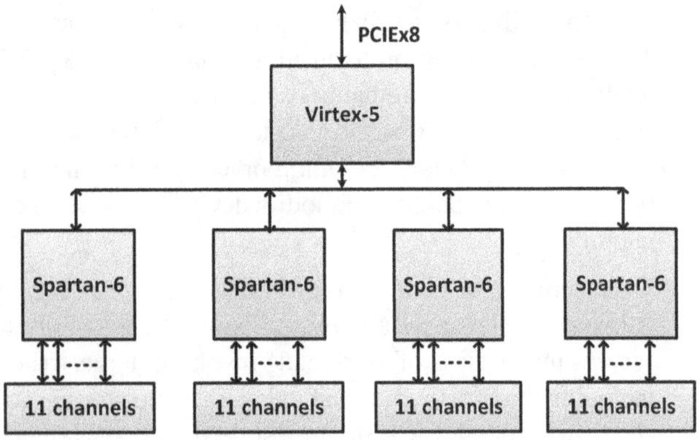


**Figure 2.** The hardware architecture of SDF.

**Figure 3.** Photograph of the SDF board.

### 2.1 SDF Hardware Structure

The SDF controller is composed of five FPGAs. A Xilinx Virtex-5 FPGA is used as a data path controller to implement PCIe DMA and chip-to-chip bridging as shown in Figure 2. It connects to four Xilinx Spartan-6 FPGAs. Each Spartan-6 FPGA implements an independent flash translation layer (FTL) for each of its 11 channels. Each of the 44 channels controls two Micron 25nm MLC flash chips—mainstream NAND chips currently used in a wide range of commodity SSDs. Each flash chip has two planes supporting parallel access, and each chip has 8 GB capacity giving the SDF device a raw capacity of 704GB.

To expose individual flash channels as independent devices to applications, each flash channel has a dedicated channel engine providing FTL functionality including block-level address mapping, dynamic wear leveling, and bad block management, as well as logic for the flash data path. The block mapping table and erase count table for dynamic wear leveling are stored in an on-chip SRAM exclusively accessed by the FPGA. A lookup into the block mapping table requires only one clock cycle. The SRAM memory consists of four SRAM banks that can be independently accessed. Because the operation on the erase-count table is a time-consuming search for the smallest count value, we distribute the table across the banks to allow a parallel search. Figure 3 is a photograph of an SDF hardware board.

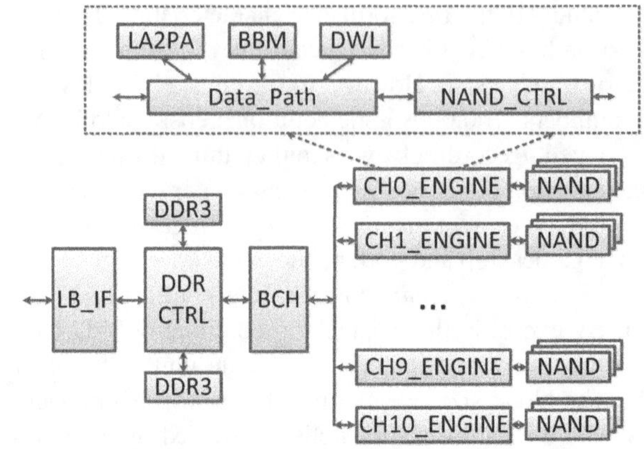


**Figure 4.** Logic diagram of a Spartan-6 FPGA for accessing a group of 11 channels in an SDF.

Figure 4 shows the logic diagram of the Spartan-6 FPGA that manages the data path between the NAND flash and the SDF interface. As shown, the local bus interface ("LB_IF") is a chip-to-chip bus connecting to the Virtex-5 FPGA chip-to-chip bridge. The bandwidth of the chip-to-chip bus is 16 times that available from each of the 11 channel engines. To fully utilize the chip-to-chip bandwidth all the channel engines share the same high-bandwidth data path, and data into and out of each channel is buffered in a DRAM to give more leeway in data transmission scheduling. Specifically, we have two 512 MB DDR3 16-bit DRAMs running at 533 MHz under the management of a DDR memory controller between the LB_IF and the channel engine. In each channel's dedicated controller ("CH_ENGINE") there are modules for translating logical addresses to physical addresses ("LA2PA"), bad block management ("BBM"), and dynamic wear leveling ("DWL"). To support applications demanding high IOPS, SDF adopts an interrupt reduction technique to reduce CPU load and thereby improve IOPS. SDF merges interrupts for channel engines in the same Spartan-6 and then merges interrupts from all of the Spartan-6s in the Virtex-5. With this merging, the rate of interrupts is only 1/5 to 1/4 of the maximum IOPS.

In the SDF, 59% of the logic area of each Spartan-6 is used to implement its functionalities, of which 42% (25% of total) is used for BCH codec for individual flash chips. The Huawei Gen3 is a conventional SSD whose structure is the same as that of SDF as described in Figure 2 and so can be considered the predecessor of SDF. In comparison, the Huawei Gen3 uses 70% of the logic area of the Spartan-6. By removing logic for garbage collection, inter-chip parity coding, and static wear leveling, SDF reduces the use of logic space on the Spartan-6 FPGAs by 16%. The remaining FPGA logic capacity in our design can be used for "computing in storage" as demonstrated elsewhere [17].

## 2.2 Reducing Hardware Cost

We have expended significant effort to reduce the hardware cost of the SDF device by including features and functionalities only when they are proven truly necessary in the environment for which they were designed. This is in contrast with the design of commodity SSD intended for serving various workloads covering a large spectrum of characteristics in terms of request operation (read or write), request size, and request locality. In particular, because of flash's out-of-place data update, in the design of commodity SSD substantial attention has been paid to the optimization of logic for effectively serving small writes, which are associated with expensive garbage collection operations and carry a significant performance implication. In favor of reduced cost, streamlined design, and much improved performance over versatility, we omit a number of features implemented by conventional SSDs from the SDF design. This simplification also enabled a complete production-quality design in only seven months by two engineers. These simplifications and their motivation are detailed following.

The capacity provided by the SDFs is small relative to the total storage requirement, so the SDFs are mainly used as cache for hard disks. For this reason, data that is rarely accessed is not expected to reside in the cache for a long period of time, so the SDF does not conduct static wear leveling wherein blocks that have experienced relatively few writes have their data migrated elsewhere within the device to free them for future writes. This not only simplifies the hardware design but also reduces the performance variation caused by the associated sporadic data movement.

The SDF hardware does not include a DRAM cache. Conventional SSDs usually include a large DRAM cache for reducing access latency. However, with DRAM cache data consistency can be compromised by a power failure so a battery or capacitor must be employed to prevent data loss. The cache and the battery (or capacitor) add to the hardware cost. In Baidu's storage infrastructure, recently accessed data have been cached in the host memory, and the access patterns experienced by a storage device are not expected to have such strong temporal locality that reused data is likely to be retained in an SSD's internal DRAM cache. Therefore SDF does not provide such a cache at all to save cost. Write requests are acknowledged only after the data is actually stored on the flash so all writes in SDF are effectively atomic operations.

SSDs consist of multiple NAND flash chips, and conventional SSDs provide data protection by using RAID 5 parity coding across the flash chips in addition to powerful BCH ECC protection within individual flash chips for fault detection and correction with attendant cost, complexity, and reduced flash space available for user data. However, in our large-scale Internet service infrastructure, data reliability is provided by data replication across multiple racks. Therefore SDF excludes the parity-based data protection and relies on BCH ECC and software-managed data replication. Our experience has shown that even without the parity-based protection, failures reported by SDF are rare in our system: during the six months since over 2000 704GB SDFs were deployed in Baidu's storage system there has been only one data error that could not be corrected by BCH ECC on the flash chips and had to be reported to the software for data recovery. Besides the benefits of smaller controller logic and removed performance penalty, elimination of the parity code also saves substantial space. For example, assuming that every 10 flash channels are protected by one flash channel storing parity in a conventional SSD, SDF increases the usable flash capacity by 10% relative to conventional practice. In Baidu's previous SSD-based storage system, over-provisioning was usually about 25% to maintain sustained throughput for the regular workloads. However, when the SSD was almost full and served very intensive writes, it was sometimes necessary to raise over-provisioning to 40%. By removing the over-provisioned space and other hardware costs, SDF achieves 20% to 50% cost reduction per unit capacity, mainly as a function of the amount of over-provisioning in systems used for comparison. In Baidu's CCDB storage systems, where most SDFs are currently employed to support performance-critical services such as on-line construction of inverted indices for hot webpages, the cost reduction is around 50% after eliminating the need of having 40% over-provisioning space in its SSD devices.

## 2.3 SDF Interface Design

A major concern in the effort to tap the raw performance of SSD is the cost of write amplification and its associated cost for garbage collection operations. In flash data cannot be over-written in place. Instead, logically over-written data is first invalidated and the space later reclaimed by garbage collection. Then the data needs to be erased before the space can be re-used for writing new data. There is an asymmetry in the flash's read/write/erase operations, where read and write are in the unit of page size, usually 8 KB, and erase is in the unit of block size, usually 2 MB, i.e., 256 times larger. To reclaim a block, the FTL must copy all of the valid data in a block to an erased block before the erase operation can be carried out, resulting in amplified write operations. It is well known that amplified writes, though necessary with the asymmetry between write and erase units, can significantly degrade the device's performance and demand a substantial portion of the device's raw space to accommodate out-of-place writes to achieve acceptable performance, as well as reduce the life of the flash by the amplification factor. This effect is more strongly exhibited when a workload contains a large number of small random writes. To alleviate these negative effects on SSD's performance and longevity we make three optimizations in the SDF interface, as follows.

First, we expose the asymmetry in the read/write/erase operations to the software. Current SSDs provide a symmetric interface, where both read and write use the same unit

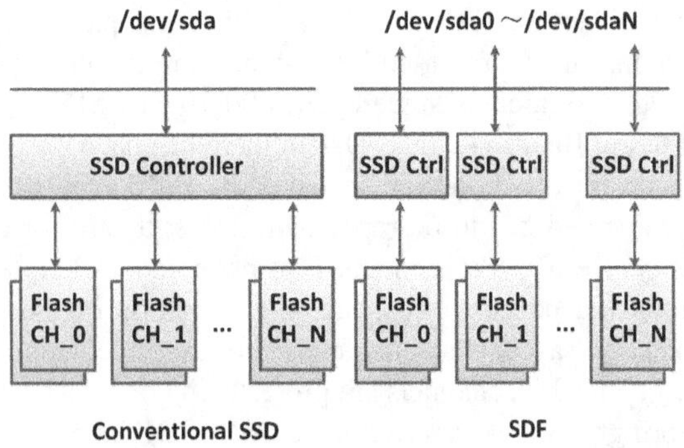


**Figure 5.** Comparison of (a) conventional SSD's structure (b) and SDF's structure.

size, which is one or a few flash pages (usually 4 KB). We keep the small read unit but greatly increase the write unit size to be a multiple of the flash erase block size and require write addresses to be block-aligned. Thus write amplification is eliminated because no flash block can contain both valid and invalided data pages at the time of garbage collection.

Second, we expose the device's internal parallelism to the workloads. As mentioned, each of the 44 channels of an SDF has its own controller or FTL engine. As shown in Figure 5, unlike a conventional SSD where there is only one controller for the entire device, and the device is software mounted as a single logical device (such as */dev/sda*—partitioning a conventional SSD is only notional), SDF presents each channel to the applications as an independent device, such as */dev/sda0* through */dev/sda43*. This exposure of parallelism is an innovation in maintaining high service concurrency to exploit the device's raw bandwidth without losing the benefit of writing in the erase-block unit in individual flash chips for minimal garbage collection overhead. In a conventional SSD service concurrency is maintained by striping data across the channels so that one request can be served by multiple channels. However, using this approach to achieving high bandwidth is in conflict with the goal of eliminating write amplification, which requires writes into individual flash chips to be in the unit of erase block units. There are two flash chips, or four planes, in a channel, and each channel needs an 8 MB write in service of one request to exploit the in-channel parallelism. To have high service concurrency in the whole device, a request would have to be excessively long (tens of MB). This requirement on workloads would be too demanding and unlikely to be met in a data center environment. By exposing SDF's 44 channels individually to the software we can leave the task of exploiting the parallelism on the channels to the software, which can employ multiple threads to concurrently issue requests to different channels. To exploit the parallelism (four flash planes) within one channel, we set SDF's write unit at 8 MB and data are striped over the flash chips in a channel with a stripe size of 2 MB, the per-chip erase unit size.

Third, we expose the erase operation as a new command to the device that is invoked by the software. The erase operation is much more expensive than read or write: for example, erasing a 2 MB block takes approximately 3 ms. When an erase operation is in process in a channel the servicing of regular requests to the channel can be significantly delayed. Erase operations scheduled by an SSD's internal logic at times unknown to the applications can cause unpredictable service quality variation, which is especially problematic for performance-critical workloads. Furthermore, if the erase operation were not exposed, SDF would still need to over-provision space to accommodate out-of-place overwriting of data. To be ready to quickly serve bursts of writes, SDF would have to provision a high percentage of raw space for this purpose. By providing applications the erase command, SDF does not need to reserve any space for out-of-place writes and garbage collection. Instead, SDF exposes all of its raw space to the software and moves the responsibility for garbage collection to the software. Either programs or an I/O scheduler are required to conduct an erase operation on a block before it can write data into it. With the software in control of the garbage collection operation it can schedule these operations in the background, or at lower priority than the servicing of high-priority requests.

### 2.4 SDF in Baidu's Storage System

Baidu's data centers store hundreds of petabytes of data with a daily data processing volume reaching dozens of petabytes. With an ever-increasing performance requirement on the storage system, hard disks, and even conventional SSDs, are becoming inadequate. SDF represents Baidu's latest effort to increase performance. There are different types of data in Baidu's storage systems, including web pages and their indices, images, data in cloud storage, and various system log data. For operational convenience and efficiency, applications prefer to present and access different data to the storage system in a variety of formats including database tables, files in a file system, or simple key-value pairs. Accordingly, the storage system includes three data management subsystems, namely *Table*, *FS*, and *KV*, to serve the aforementioned data formats. Internally all three are treated as key-value pairs. In the *Table* system, the key is the index of a table row, and the value is the remaining fields of the row. In the *FS* system, the path name of a file is the key and the data or a segment of data of the file is the value.

Each of the subsystems is hosted on a cluster of storage servers. According to their keys, requests from clients are hashed into different hash buckets called *slices* in our system. A slice uses Baidu's CCDB system to manage its KV pairs using a log-structured merge (LSM) tree [16]. Similarly to Google's BigTable [5], CCDB uses a container for receiving KV items arriving in write requests. The container has a maximum capacity of 8 MB. Data that are being accu-

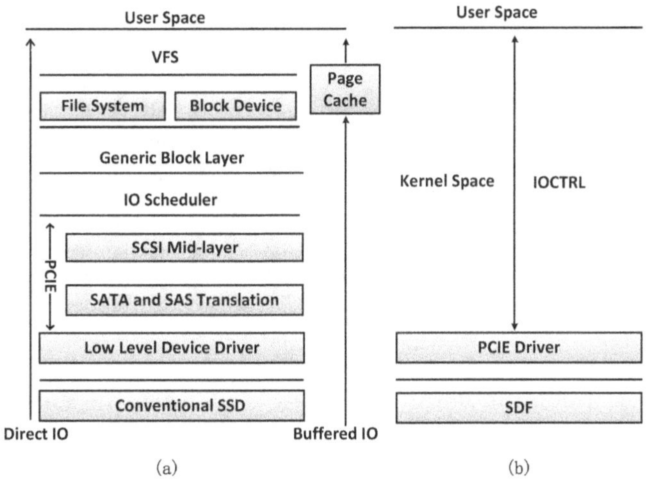


**Figure 6.** Comparison of (a) conventional SSD's I/O stack and (b) SDF's I/O stack supporting its block interfaces.

mulated in the in-memory container are immediately saved in a log in an SSD or a hard disk to prevent data loss. When a container is full, a *patch* is formed, and the patch is written into the SDF device on the server. Patches on the storage experience multiple merge-sorts, or multiple reads and writes before they are placed in the final large log. All write requests in CCDB are to store patches to the SDF and match the 8 MB SDF write unit. By managing data in the LSM tree, all metadata of the KV pairs can be accommodated in DRAM memory, and a read request from clients can be served with only one SDF read.

Underneath the slice abstraction is a unified user-space block layer for processing and passing I/O requests from the slices to the SDF device. Currently this layer dictates a fixed 8 MB write size and requires that each write request arrive with a 128-bit ID. At this time only the low 64 bits of an ID is used to uniquely identify a write or the block of data involved in a write. A client requests the 64-bit part of an ID, to serve as a key, from a server that maintains a counter for generating unique IDs. The block layer uniformly hashes the ID to determine a channel to serve the write. Specifically, blocks with consecutive IDs are written to the 44 channels in a round-robin fashion. This arrangement abstracts the tasks of managing storage space, such as determining which channels to write, what physical spaces have been erased and are ready for receiving new data, and what spaces are not. In future work we will introduce more intelligent scheduling policies to balance the load across the channels should a skewed workload occur, and coordinate timings for the SDF to serve different types of requests so that on-demand reads take priority over writes and erasures.

For Google's BigTable, a distributed file system (GFS [9]) is responsible for its I/O requests as well as data replication for reliability. For Baidu's CCDB, data is replicated over slices. Since slices reside on individual server nodes, a question arises of whether we should retain the local file system between the slices and the SDF. A general-purpose operating system such as Linux, as well as the file system part of it, performs functionalities such as access authorization, name parsing, address space protection between different users, and data caching and prefetching. On our servers operations in this software layer impose as much as 12 $\mu$s additional time spent on a single I/O request. This overhead can be substantial relative to the high-speed flash data access. Currently SDF is used exclusively by the CCDB data management software on a local server, so most of the file system's functionalities are unnecessary. For efficiency, we open the device as a raw device file and use the IOCTRL interface to largely bypass the kernel and directly access its low-level PCIE driver. Some basic file system functionalities, such as block allocation and logical-to-physical address translation, are implemented in the block layer. A comparison of the I/O stacks of SDF and a conventional SSD is depicted in Figure 6. The resulting latency of SDF's software stack is only about 2-4 $\mu$s, which is mostly used for handling message signaled interrupts (MSIs) from the PCIe interface.

| CPU | Intel E5620x2 2.4 GHz |
|---|---|
| Memory | 32 GB |
| OS | Linux 2.6.32 kernel |
| NIC | Intel 82599 |

**Table 2.** Client and server node configuration.

## 3. Performance Evaluation

In this section we evaluate SDF's performance in Baidu's storage infrastructure. Currently there are more than 3000 SDFs deployed in the production system. The SDFs have been in use for over six months and a large amount of performance data has been collected from the monitoring and profiling system. We first describe the experimental setup, then the evaluation results for both microbenchmarks and Baidu's production workloads.

### 3.1 Experimental Setup

For the experiments we set up a number of client nodes to send KV read and write requests to a server node. The client and server nodes have the same configuration as described in Table 2, and are in the same cluster. The server is connected to a switch by two 10 Gbps NICs, and the clients each use one 10 Gbps NIC. The SDF is installed on the server, and its specification is given in Table 3. The specification of the Huawei Gen3, the predecessor of SDF, is the same. In the evaluation we use the Huawei Gen3 and the SATA-based Intel 320 for comparison. We will focus our comparison primarily on the Huawei Gen3 to examine the performance implications of SDF's architectural changes. In the experiment we leave 25% of the raw capacity of the Huawei Gen3 as over-provisioned space for internal use such as garbage col-

| Host Interface | PCIe 1.1x8 |
|---|---|
| Channel Count | 44 |
| Flash Chips per Channel | 2 |
| Planes per Flash Chip | 2 |
| Channel Interface | Asynchronous 40 MHz |
| Flash Capacity per Channel | 16 GB |
| NAND Type | 25 nm MLC |
| Page Size | 8 KB |
| Block Size | 2 MB |

**Table 3.** Device configuration for both the Baidu SDF and the Huawei Gen3.

lection. In the Huawei Gen3 data is striped over its 44 channels with a striping unit size of 8 KB. The Intel 320 uses 25 nm MLC NAND flash and the SATA 2.0 interface. The Intel 320 has 10 channels, and 20 GB (12.5%) of its raw capacity of 160 GB is reserved for internal use including garbage collection.

### 3.2 Experiments with Microbenchmarks

SDF is designed to deliver I/O service with high throughput and low latency to applications with high concurrency. To reveal the storage devices' performance, in the evaluation we first generate synthetic workloads on the server. For SDF we send requests to the SDF as a raw device, bypassing the kernel I/O stack. For the Intel and Huawei SSDs the requests are sent to the respective devices via the Linux I/O stack.

In the experiments we first run microbenchmarks that issue random read requests of different sizes (8 KB, 16 KB, and 64 KB) and 8 MB write requests to each of the three devices. For SDF we use 44 threads—one for each channel—to exploit its hardware parallelism. For the other two devices only one thread is used because they expose only one channel, and the thread issues asynchronous requests. For SDF all requests are synchronously issued and the benchmarks issue requests as rapidly as possible to keep all channels busy. The results are reported in Table 4. Because SDF does not allow writes smaller than 8 MB we use only 8 MB writes in the test.

To put SDF's performance in perspective we need to know the throughout limits imposed by the PCIe interface and the flash itself. The maximum PCIe throughputs when it is used for data read and write are 1.61 GB/s and 1.40 GB/s, respectively, and SDF's aggregate flash raw read/write bandwidths are 1.67 GB/s and 1.01 GB/s, respectively. From the table we can see that SDF enables throughput close to the architectural limits: for read its 8 MB-request throughout of 1.59 GB/s is 99% of the bandwidth limit imposed by the PCIe interface, and for write, 0.96 GB/s throughout is 94% of the flash's raw bandwidth. Even for reads with requests as small as 8 KB the throughout is 76% or more of the PCIe bandwidth limit. The expensive erasure operation can reach a 40 GB/s throughput in SDF (not shown in the table).

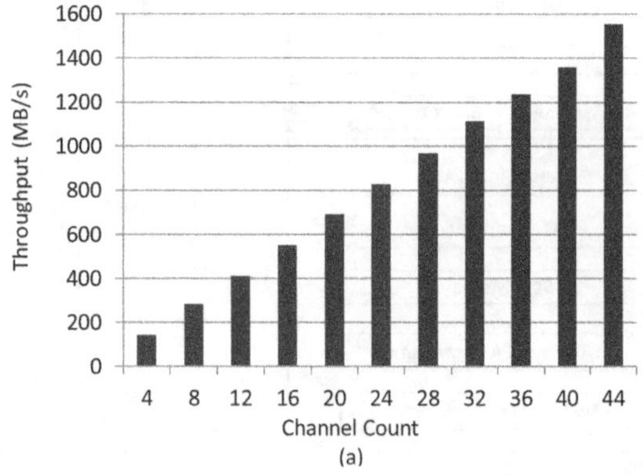


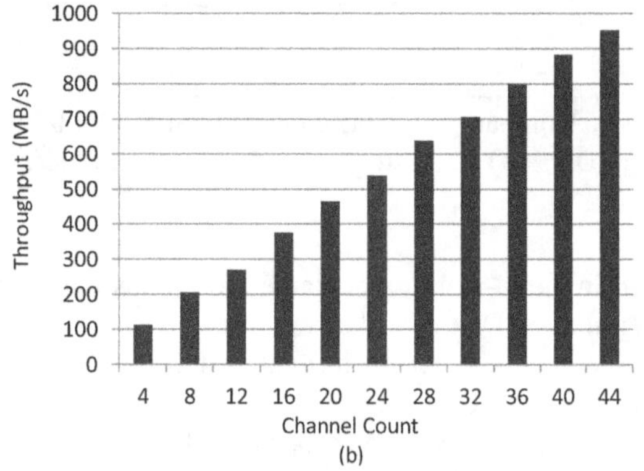


**Figure 7.** Throughputs of SDF with sequential reads (a) and writes (b) when different numbers of channels are used.

Though the Huawei Gen3 has the same number of channels, type and count of flash chips, and FPGA controller hardware, its throughput is consistently lower than that of SDF. In particular, with a request size of 64 KB or smaller its throughput is substantially lower. In SDF, as long as a request is not larger than 8 MB it is serviced by one channel. In contrast, in the Huawei Gen3 the logical address space is striped over 44 channels with an 8 KB striping unit. A large request is split into multiple sub-requests, which are serviced in different channels. Accordingly, requested data has to be split (for write) or merged (for read) in the request service, and each channel serves a larger number of smaller requests. This adds to the overhead and reduces throughput.

We also experimented with the SDF when only limited numbers of channels are concurrently accessed, still with each channel receiving requests from a dedicated thread. Figures 7(a) and 7(b) show the throughput of the SDF with sequential 8 MB read and write requests when different numbers of channels are employed. As shown, the throughput increases almost linearly with the number of channels before the PCIe's bandwidth limit is reached, demonstrating that the SDF architecture scales well.

Because performance predictability can be important in a data center, especially for on-line service, we evaluate latency variation for write requests on the Huawei Gen3 and the Baidu SDF. Note that for SDF an erase operation is ex-

| Operations | 8 KB Read | 16 KB Read | 64 KB Read | 8 MB Read | 8 MB Write |
|---|---|---|---|---|---|
| Baidu SDF (GB/s) | 1.23 | 1.42 | 1.51 | 1.59 | 0.96 |
| Huawei Gen3 (GB/s) | 0.92 | 1.02 | 1.15 | 1.20 | 0.67 |
| Intel 320 (GB/s) | 0.17 | 0.20 | 0.22 | 0.22 | 0.13 |

**Table 4.** Throughputs of the Baidu SDF, Huawei Gen3, and Intel 320 devices with different request sizes for read and write operations. Because the SDF's write unit is 8 MB, only write throughputs for 8 MB are reported.

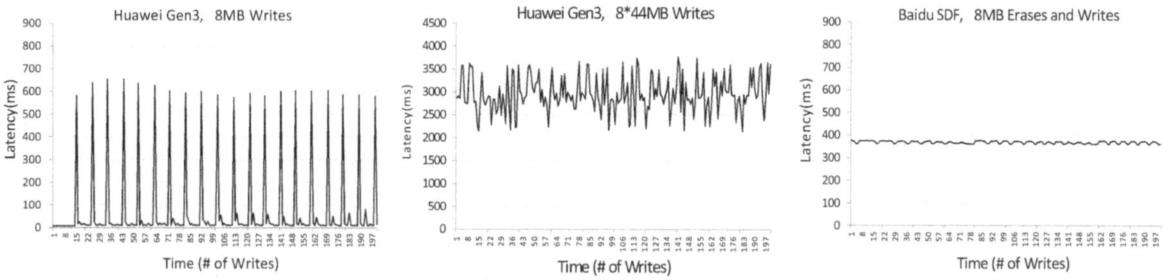


**Figure 8.** Latencies of write requests on the Huawei Gen3 and the Baidu SDF when writes with an aggregate total of 28 GB data are in progress. The Huawei Gen3 serves write requests of either 8 MB or 352 MB. The Baidu SDF serves write requests of 8 MB. By design these devices were almost full at the beginning of the experiments.

plicitly performed immediately before a write, so we include the erase time in its write latency as reported in Figure 8. We first send 8 MB write requests to the Huawei Gen3 and the SDF. As shown in Figure 8 the latency of the Huawei Gen3 varies widely—between 7 ms and 650 ms—with an average of 73 ms. In contrast, SDF's latency is 383 ms with little variation. The Huawei Gen3 has a 1GB on-board DRAM buffer and a hit in the buffer produces very low latencies. However, this buffer has been removed in SDF. By performing erase operations explicitly before individual writes rather than conducting bursty garbage collection, SDF provides consistent write performance. This makes SDF a competitive device for application demanding high performance predictability. If we increase the size of requests to the Huawei Gen3 to 352 MB so that each of its 44 channels accesses 8 MB data, the latency variance is reduced to 25% of average request latency (2.94 seconds). However, the requirement of such large requests is impractical for most applications.

### 3.3 Experiments on the Production System

Currently the deployed SDFs are supporting web page services on the production system. The crawler collects web pages from the Internet and stores them in the web page repository on a storage system. Web pages in the repository will undergo various processing steps including extraction of their abstracts, analysis of the link relationship among pages, and construction of a reverse index to feed into index servers. As showed in Figure 9, the web page repository is the central component of the search engine. We use the CCDB's Table system to process the web page repository.

In the system each storage server hosts one or multiple slices. A slice provides storage and access service in a LSM-tree fashion for KV pairs whose keys fall into a specific range. So that each slice is always loaded with requests from a single client, each client continuously sends synchronous read/write KV requests to one slice by setting its request keys within the slice's designated key range. A client sends a request immediately after it receives the response to its previous request. To improve network and server efficiency requests can be batched, that is, one request may contain multiple read/write sub-requests, each reading or writing one KV pair. The number of sub-requests contained in a request is called the request's *batch size*.

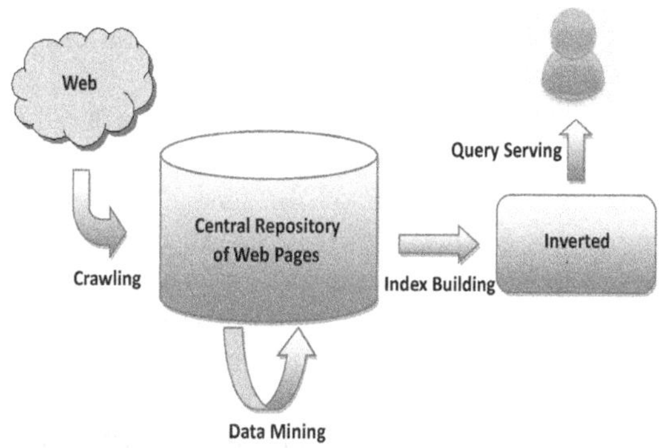


**Figure 9.** Building and indexing in a Web page repository.

#### 3.3.1 Random Reads

We first let the clients issue 512 KB random read requests to one or a number of slices. That is, each requested value is of 512 KB and the key is randomly and uniformly selected from a slice's key range. Figure 10 shows the throughputs with different batch sizes when only one slice is used with

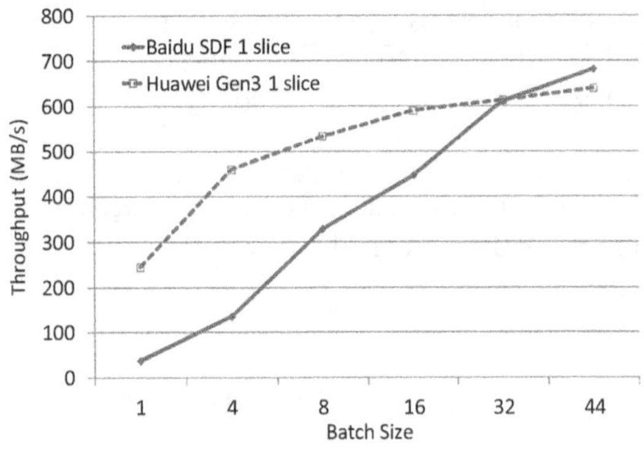


**Figure 10.** Throughputs of one storage node with Baidu SDF and Huawei Gen3 with one slice with varying batch size. Random 512 KB read requests are used in this experiment.

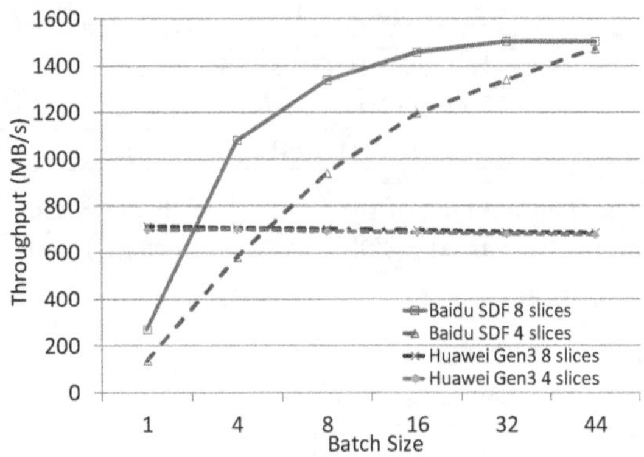


**Figure 11.** Throughputs of one storage node with the Baidu SDF and the Huawei Gen3 when running four or eight slices with various batch sizes. Random 512 KB read requests were used in the experiment.

the Baidu SDF and the Huawei Gen3. As shown, SDF's throughput lags behind the Huawei Gen3 until the batch size reaches 32. SDF's performance advantage with high channel concurrency cannot be realized with synchronous requests and only one slice. For example, when the batch size is one, requests are served at one channel at a time in SDF, delivering only 38 MB/s throughput. With increasing batch size, different sub-requests are more likely to be served at different channels in parallel and the throughput steadily increases. However, for the Huawei Gen3 throughput with a batch size of only one is 245 MB/s, much greater than its counterpart for SDF. The FTL of the Huawei Gen3 maps contiguous logical addresses across the channels in a round-robin manner with a striping unit of only 8 KB. The requested 512 KB data are well distributed over all 44 channels and service of even one request can be fully parallelized. In contrast, in SDF with only one slice the service parallelism is limited by requests' batch sizes because each request is served by only one channel.

Another interesting observation from Figure 10 is that the Huawei Gen3 still has higher throughput than SDF when the batch size is substantially large (up to 32). SDF exploits the parallelism among sub-requests in a synchronous request, while the Huawei Gen3 exploits parallelism within one sub-request, so the Huawei Gen3 can service one sub-request faster than SDF. Once it is done with a sub-request, it can send the data back to the client at the same time that it is serving the next sub-request. In this scenario the SDF does not have the efficiency achieved by the Huawei Gen3 with its pipelined data access because SDF completes the service of all sub-requests in a request at almost the same time.

If multiple slices are used in a server the concurrency of requests from different slices would increase SDF's throughput by keeping more channels busy at the same time. Figure 11 shows the throughput for four and eight slices. As shown, when the batch size is one, for SDF only a few of its 44 channels are in parallel service (at most 4 or 8 channels when 4 or 8 slices are used, respectively). In contrast, with 8 KB striping these numbers of slices are sufficient to keep all of the channels in the Huawei Gen3 fully occupied. Accordingly, it's no surprise that the Huawei Gen3 has greater throughput than SDF. However, with increasing batch size SDF's throughput correspondingly increases. For example, with a batch size of 4, the 8-slice throughput increases by almost four times, from 270 MB/s to 1081 MB/s. When the batch size is sufficiently large the increase in throughput of SDF seems to flatten as all channels become busy. Interestingly, the increase does not stop when the product of slice count and batch size reaches the channel count (44). With round-robin address mapping the random requests cannot be evenly distributed over the channels when the request count is only slightly larger than the channel count. That is, more concurrent requests are needed to have a better balanced load. In future work a load-balance-aware scheduler will be employed to help SDF reach its peak throughput (approximately 1.5 GB/s) with a smaller number of concurrent requests. Though with a small number of concurrent requests the Huawei Gen3 can achieve high throughput (approximately 700 MB/s), further increasing the concurrency does not further increase the throughput. To the contrary, the throughput actually decreases slightly with higher concurrency. With 512 KB requests and an 8 KB data striping unit on 44 channels, each channel is accessed for only 8 KB or 16 KB data in the service of one request, leading to very high access concurrency. Accordingly, the scheduling overhead may increase and the service time of unsynchronized requests at different channels may increase some requests' service time. In addition, the curves for the 4-slice and 8-slice throughputs of the Huawei Gen3 are nearly coincident, indicating that the increased concurrency cannot be taken advantage of.

To see how request size affects throughput, in Figure 12 we plot the throughput with different request sizes (32 KB, 128 KB, and 512 KB) and different slice counts (1, 4, and 8) when the batch size is fixed at 44. These request sizes are representative for web pages, thumbnails, and images,

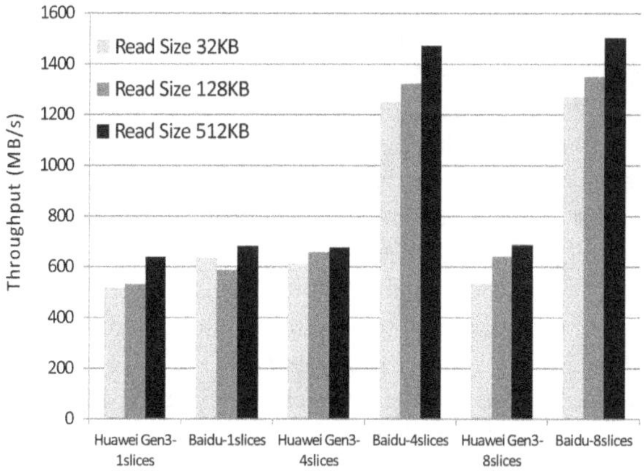


**Figure 12.** Throughputs of one storage node with the Baidu SDF and the Huawei Gen3 when running one, four, or eight slices with batch size of 44. Random read requests of 32 KB, 128 KB, and 512 KB were used in this experiment.

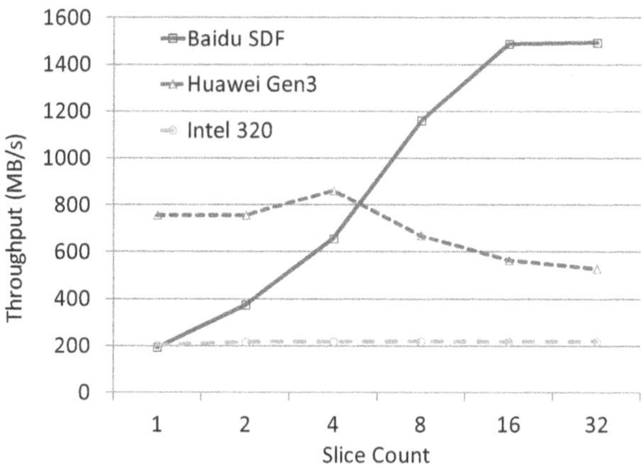


**Figure 13.** Throughputs of one storage node with sequential reads on the Baidu SDF, the Huawei Gen3, and the Intel 320 with various numbers of slices.

respectively, in the system's workloads. As shown in the figure, as long as requests are served in parallel at different channels in SDF, both small and large requests can lead to high I/O throughput, though large requests have moderately greater throughput ("Baidu-4slices" and "Baidu-8slices" in the figure). Only when the concurrency in the workload is very limited is SDF's throughput as low as that of the Huawei Gen3 ("Baidu-1slice"). By exposing all 44 channels to the software, with highly concurrent workloads we expect the software to be able to fully exploit the exposed parallelism.

### 3.3.2 Sequential Reads

At Baidu, an important I/O-intensive operation is to build inverted index tables from web page tables. As shown in Figure 9, the inverted index servers send a request for building the inverted index table to the 'Central Repository of Web Pages' servers, where the web page data is stored on SDFs.

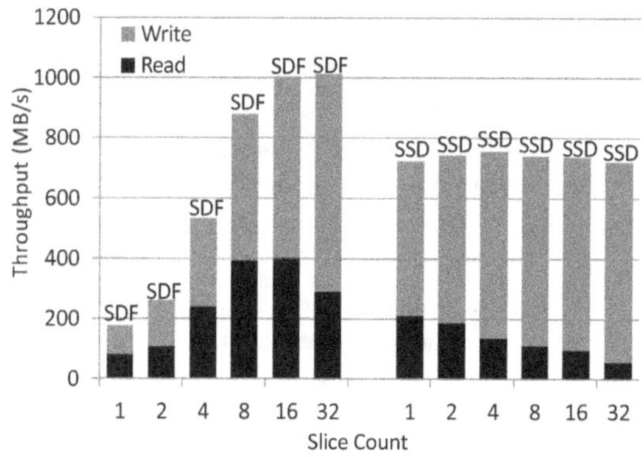


**Figure 14.** Throughputs of one storage node with the Baidu SDF and the Huawei Gen3 SSD running various numbers of slices with write requests whose sizes are primarily in the range between 100 KB and 1 MB. The requests are not batched (equivalently, the batch size is 1) in the experiment.

On each of the web page servers one or multiple slices can be started. As previously stated, each slice is responsible for storing and accessing keys in a specific range. Because keys for different tables are created in different ranges, each table is managed by a different slice. According to their needs the inverted index servers may ask for a varying number of inverted index tables to be built at a given time. Accordingly, the number of busy slices can vary. The I/O operation in an index-building slice is to scan, or sequentially read, all the KV pairs in the designated key range. To limit the I/O demand of a slice, each slice uses six threads issuing synchronous requests to the storage in the production system. Figure 13 shows the throughput when different numbers of slices are requested in the service. The throughput of SDF scales well with the increase in slice count up to 16 slices where SDF's peak throughput is reached. In contrast, the throughput of the Huawei Gen3 does not scale at all. Even worse, it can become lower when a large number of slices are requested. In this experiment we included the Intel 320 which shows almost constant throughput. This experiment clearly demonstrates the advantage of exposing internal channels to the software.

### 3.3.3 Writes

In CCDB, Baidu's KV store system, all writes are accumulated into 8 MB patches, which are equivalent to SSTable in Google's BigTable, before being written into storage. Because write requests from the clients cause compaction operations, which entail reading patches from storage, merge-sorting the patches, and writing them back to the storage, a storage device services I/O requests originating from both the clients' write requests and CCDB's internal read and write requests, all with 8 MB request size.

In the experiment each client continuously sends synchronous write requests to a slice. Figure 14 shows the read and write throughput of the Baidu SDF and the Huawei

Gen3. Because only the compaction operation incurs reads, the read throughput shown in Figure 14 represents the intensity of the internal data cleanup operation. At the beginning of the experiment, all patches on the storage have been sorted. Therefore, the volume of new written data is correlated to the demand on the compaction operation. Requests from the clients take priority over compaction-incurred requests.

As shown, SDF's throughput continues to increase until the slice count reaches 16 where the throughput peaks at around 1 GB/s. When the slice count is small, the limited concurrency leads to SDF's low throughout in serving client write requests. Accordingly, the compaction intensity, indicated by the read throughput, is also low. However, SDF can take good advantage of high concurrency where its peak throughput reaches a value between the device's peak write throughput (approximately 0.95 GB/s) and its peak read throughput (approximately 1.50 GB/s). Considering the presence of erasure operations, SDF achieves excellent peak throughput. When the slice count increases from 16 to 32 the percentage of the throughput attributable to reads is reduced because the increased demand from the clients' write requests pushes the compaction load lower. In contrast, the Huawei Gen3 exploits channel parallelism for individual 8 MB-patch accesses so it can achieve much higher throughout when the slice count is small, but its throughput does not increase with increasing slice count. Furthermore, because of its limited throughput, the Huawei Gen3 compaction throughput decreases with increasing slice count. With 32 slices the throughput is less than 15% of the aggregate throughput, indicating that most of new written data is left unsorted. This would significantly compromise performance of subsequent read requests from clients.

## 4. Related Work

We organize our discussion of related work as addressing the reduction of the overhead of random writes, the support of high I/O concurrency, and the reduction of access latency.

### 4.1 Reducing the Overhead of Random Writes

Though SSD's random-write throughput is higher than that of hard disks, it is much less than its sequential-write throughput [15]. Even for modern high-end SSDs the throughput of random write is only about 1/10 to 1/7 of sequential writes [15]. Further, random writes can cause internal fragmentation and lead to performance degradation by an order of magnitude and can significantly reduce lifetime of the device because write amplification is much greater than for sequential write [15]. To address these issues researchers have tried to transform random writes to sequential writes at either the file system level or at the FTL level.

At the file system level, Min proposed a log-structured file system (SFS) to transform random writes in the file system into sequential writes at the SSD [15]. Other log-based file systems, such as JFFS2 [19], YAFFS2 [4], and UBIFS [3], are designed by considering NAND flash characteristics and are used widely, especially in mobile and embedded domains. The log-based file system can eliminate random writes to the flash memory. By requiring a large write unit, SDF essentially forces the software to batch write data as a log. On top of SDF, at Baidu a user-space distributed log-based storage system is implemented. It knows the data types and how actively particular data is accessed, so it can implement a more intelligent block cleaning scheme compared to a log-based file system.

At the FTL level some researchers have used a log buffer at the FTL level to reduce the overhead of random writes. Kawaguchi et al. proposed a flash memory driver that uses a log-based FTL and provides a block interface to the flash that sequentially writes data to the flash memory in a way similar to log-structured file system [11]. Kim et al. proposed BAST, a hybrid FTL scheme [12]. It uses page-level mapping for random writes and block-level mapping for sequential writes [13]. The FAST FTL improves on BAST with a flexible address mapping in the log buffer to improve space utilization. Some FTLs reduce the overhead caused by random writes by considering data access characteristics. LAST reduces the garbage collection overhead by exploiting data locality [14]. CAFTL reduces write traffic to the flash memory by eliminating duplicate writes and redundant data [7]. Both the file-system-level and the FTL-level efforts cannot completely eliminate the garbage collection overhead caused by random writes. SDF eliminates random writes by setting the write size to a multiple of the size of NAND physical erase block. Thus SDF's FTL does not need to conduct garbage collection, and write amplification ratio is kept at one.

### 4.2 Supporting High I/O Concurrency

SSDs may be deployed in an environment with a large number of applications or threads simultaneously issuing requests to them, that is, with workloads of high concurrency, and it is necessary to exploit parallelism at multiple layers of the I/O stack to achieve high throughput. Here there are three layers that are most relevant. The first is the Linux I/O subsystem, which includes VFS, the file system, the generic block layer, the scheduler layer, the SCSI mid-layer, and the SATA/SAS translation layer. The second is the device driver, which includes command queues, interrupt handlers, and a hardware register interface. The third is in the SSD itself, including the host interface, on-device DRAM, internal data paths, and multiple NAND channels. Many previous works have investigated parallelism at each of these three layers. Seppanen et al. suggest exploiting the parallelism of the Linux I/O subsystem with multiple AIO requests or by using multiple threads issuing synchronous I/O requests [18]. To take advantage of this parallelism applications need to use AIO or be multi-threaded, necessitating modification of legacy programs. SDF uses multiple threads with synchronous I/O requests to exploit Linux I/O subsystem parallelism because synchronous I/O is easier to implement and is compatible with many legacy applications.

Modern drivers support multiple deep command queues such as NCQ [18] for SATA II, and NVM Express [2] which is designed to address the challenges of system scalability. NVM Express provides optimized command issuance mechanisms and multiple deep queues. Using multiple queues can support concurrent operations and help to improve scalability. Moreover, when the queues are operated on multiple CPU cores, interrupt handling can be more efficient. Following the same principle, SDF creates a queue for each channel. Hahn et al. consider issues with the request scheduling when SSD channels are exposed [10]. We leave studies on intelligent request scheduling on SDF as future work.

Chen et al. investigated the performance implications of SSD's internal parallelism [6]. As we have demonstrated, the aggregate channel-level bandwidth of a commodity SSD can be greater than that made available at the host interface by a significant factor, implying that the internal parallelism in an SSD is far from fully exploited. By exposing flash channels to applications, SDF can effectively increase available channel-level parallelism, and applications can manage data layout among channels or among planes in a channel.

### 4.3 Reducing Access latency

Foong et al. break down the latency overhead for a request at the granularity of the layers of the I/O stack [8]. As reported, the Linux I/O subsystem takes about 9100 CPU cycles to issue a request to the device and about 21900 CPU cycles to process I/O completion. The total time spent in the Linux I/O subsystem for one I/O request is about 12.9 $\mu$s on a 2.4GHz mainstream server processor. In contrast, reading a NAND page from the cell to the host interface takes only about 75 $\mu$s for 25nm MLC flash [1], so the software I/O stack is responsible for about 17% of the total request service time for a page read request, which we regards as substantial. Our solution is to simply bypass the Linux I/O subsystem and traditional driver layer, using instead an ultra-light-weight user-space interface and thin driver. The SDF driver provides a register interface and a message signaled interrupt handler. Thus the software layer of SDF is able to significantly reduce the software overhead compared with conventional systems.

## 5. Conclusions and Future Work

In the paper we present SDF, a software-defined SSD, for web-scale Internet storage infrastructures. SDF is a high-performance and low-cost SSD architecture with high utilization of raw bandwidth and storage space and with predictable performance. It has successfully replaced traditional SSDs at Baidu's Internet storage infrastructure with 3000 SDFs deployed and more scheduled. SDF's success derives from its hardware-software co-design. In SDF, the hardware exposes the internal channels to the applications through customized FTL controllers. Dovetailing with the hardware design, the software layer enforces large-granularity writes and provides primitive and light-weight functionalities through kernel bypass. Our experimental measurements show that SDF can deliver about 95% of the raw flash bandwidth and provide 99% of the flash capacity for user data. SDF increases the I/O bandwidth by 3 times and reduces per-GB hardware cost by 50% on average compared with Baidu's commodity-SSD-based system.

The success of the SDF at Baidu is highly dependent on two key workload characteristics that we believe are also prevalent in most data centers supporting Internet services. One is large sequential writes. Because write requests have been mostly served in log-structured storage systems, such as Google's LevelDB and Facebook's Haystack, SDF's performance advantage on write can be realized without re-writing or re-structuring existing software. The other is high concurrency for exploiting SDF's exposed channels. Because Internet service is mostly multi-threaded and transaction-based for supporting millions of users, high concurrency in the I/O workload is expected and is the reality in most cases.

The Baidu SDF research is ongoing on multiple fronts. First, as previously described we will implement a load-balance-aware scheduler to help SDF reach its peak throughput with a smaller number of concurrent requests. Also, to further pursue our hardware/software co-design approach, we intend to further investigate the possibility of "moving compute to the storage," that is, integrating specialized computational functionality into the storage devices themselves to minimize I/O traffic; an initial success has already been reported [17]. Finally, recognizing that flash memory has finite write endurance, we believe that that it would be both possible and useful to incorporate, and expose, a data reliability model for flash memory in our infrastructure.

## Acknowledgments

The SDF project has benefited greatly from constructive input from many engineers and interns at Baidu, in particular Guangjun Xie, Wei Qi, Hao Tang, and Bo Peng. We would like to thank Kei Davis for constructive input on the final composition of this paper. We are also thankful to Jason Cong for his support and suggestions on the paper.

## References

[1] "Micron 25nm MLC Product Datasheet." *http://www.micron.com.*

[2] "NVMe: Non-volatile Memory Express." *http://www.nvmexpress.org/.*

[3] "UBIFS: Unsorted Block Image File System." *http://www.linux-mtd.infradead.org/doc/ubifs.html/.*

[4] "YFFS: Yet Another Flash File System." *http://www.yaffs.net/.*

[5] F. Chang, J. Dean, S. Ghemawat, W. C. Hsieh, D. A. Wallach, M. Burrows, T. Chandra, A. Fikes, and R. E. Gruber. "Bigtable: A Distributed Storage System for Structured Data." In *Seventh Symposium on Operating System Design and Implementation*, 2006.

[6] F. Chen, R. Lee, and X. Zhang. "Essential Roles of Exploiting Internal Parallelism of Flash Memory based Solid State Drives in High-speed Data Processing." In *IEEE 17th International Symposium on High Performance Computer Architecture*, 2011.

[7] F. Chen, T. Luo, and X. Zhang, "CAFTL: A Content-Aware Flash Translation Layer Enhancing the Lifespan of Flash Memory based Solid State Drives." In *9th USENIX Conference on File and Storage Technologies*, 2011.

[8] A. Foong, B. Veal, and F. Hady. "Towards SSD-ready Enterprise Platforms." In *1st International Workshop on Accelerating Data Management Systems Using Modern Processor and Storage Architectures*, 2010.

[9] S. Ghemawat, H. Gobioff, and S.-T. Leung. "The Google File System" In *19th ACM Symposium on Operating Systems Principles*, 2003.

[10] S. S. Hahn, S. Lee, and J. Kim. "SOS: Software-based Out-of-order Scheduling for High-performance NAND Flash-based SSDs." In *IEEE 29th Symposium on Mass Storage Systems and Technologies*, 2013.

[11] A. Kawaguchi, S. Nishioka, and H. Motoda. "A Flash-memory based File System." In *Winter USENIX Technical Conference*, 1995.

[12] J. Kim, J. M. Kim, S. H. Noh, S. L. Min, and Y. Cho. "A Space-efficient Flash Translation Layer for Compact-flash Systems." In *IEEE Transactions on Consumer Electronics*, 2002.

[13] S. W. Lee, D. J. Park, T. S. Chung, D. H. Lee, S. Park, and H. J. Song. "A Log Buffer-based Flash Translation Layer Using Fully-associative Sector Translation." In *Trans. on Embedded Computing Systems*, 2007.

[14] S. Lee, D. Shin, Y. J. Kim, and J. Kim. "LAST: Locality-aware Sector Translation for NAND Flash Memory-based Storage Systems." In *SIGOPS Operating Systems Review*, 2008.

[15] C. Min, K. Kim, H. Cho, S. Lee, and Y. Eom. "SFS: Random Write Considered Harmful in Solid State Drives," In *10th USENIX Conference on File and Storage Technologies*, 2012.

[16] P. O'Neil, E. Cheng, D. Gawlick, and E. O'Neil. "The Log-structured Merge-tree (LSM-tree)." In *Acta Informatica* 33(4):351-385, 1996.

[17] J. Ouyang, S. Lin, Z. Hou, P. Wang, Y. Wang, and G. Sun. "Active SSD Design for Energy-efficiency Improvement of Web-scale Data Analysis." In *International Symposium on Low Power Electronics and Design*, 2013.

[18] E. Seppanen, M. T. O'Keefe, and D. J. Lilja. "High Performance Solid State Storage under Linux." In *IEEE 26th Symposium on Mass Storage Systems and Technologies*, 2010.

[19] D. Woodhouse. "JFFS: The Journaling Flash File System." In *Ottowa Linux symposium*, 2012.

# Integrated 3D-Stacked Server Designs for Increasing Physical Density of Key-Value Stores

Anthony Gutierrez Michael Cieslak Bharan Giridhar
Ronald G. Dreslinski Luis Ceze[†] Trevor Mudge

Advanced Computer Architecture Laboratory
University of Michigan - Ann Arbor, MI
{atgutier, mrciesla, bharan, rdreslin, tnm}@umich.edu

[†]Computer Science and Engineering Department
University of Washington - Seattle, WA
luisceze@cs.washington.edu

## Abstract

*Key-value stores, such as Memcached, have been used to scale web services since the beginning of the Web 2.0 era. Data center real estate is expensive, and several industry experts we have spoken to have suggested that a significant portion of their data center space is devoted to key-value stores. Despite its wide-spread use, there is little in the way of hardware specialization for increasing the efficiency and density of Memcached; it is currently deployed on commodity servers that contain high-end CPUs designed to extract as much instruction-level parallelism as possible. Out-of-order CPUs, however have been shown to be inefficient when running Memcached.*

*To address Memcached efficiency issues, we propose two architectures using 3D stacking to increase data storage efficiency. Our first 3D architecture, Mercury, consists of stacks of ARM Cortex-A7 cores with 4GB of DRAM, as well as NICs. Our second architecture, Iridium, replaces DRAM with NAND Flash to improve density. We explore, through simulation, the potential efficiency benefits of running Memcached on servers that use 3D-stacking to closely integrate low-power CPUs with NICs and memory. With Mercury we demonstrate that density may be improved by 2.9×, power efficiency by 4.9×, throughput by 10×, and throughput per GB by 3.5× over a state-of-the-art server running optimized Memcached. With Iridium we show that density may be increased by 14×, power efficiency by 2.4×, and throughput by 5.2×, while still meeting latency requirements for a majority of requests.*



*ASPLOS '14*, March 1–4, 2014, Salt Lake City, Utah, USA.

http://dx.doi.org/10.1145/2541940.2541951

***Categories and Subject Descriptors*** C.5.5 [*Computer System Implementation*]: Servers

***General Terms*** Design, Performance

***Keywords*** 3D Integration, Data Centers, Key-Value Stores, Physical Density, Scale-Out Systems

## 1. Introduction

Since the emergence of the Web 2.0 era, scaling web services to meet the requirements of dynamic content generation has been a challenge—engineers quickly discovered that creating content for each visitor to a web site generated a high load on the back-end databases. While it is easy to scale the number of servers generating HTML and responding to client requests, it is harder to scale the data stores. This two-tier infrastructure becomes increasingly difficult to scale and requires many redundant systems to prevent a single point of failure. In order to meet the performance and reliability requirements of handling such a massive volume of data, highly distributed scale-out architectures are required.

*Memcached* is one example of a distributed, in-memory key-value store caching system. Memcached is used as the primary piece of scaling infrastructure for many of today's most widely-used web services, such as Facebook, Twitter, and YouTube; although not prepared to go on the record, several industry experts we've spoken with have estimated that approximately 25% of their data center is dedicated to key-value stores. Due to its wide-spread use, and the high cost of data center real estate, it is important that Memcached be run as efficiently as possible. Today, however, Memcached is deployed on commodity hardware consisting of aggressive out-of-order cores, whose performance and efficiency are measured with respect to how well they are able to run CPU benchmarks, such as SPEC [17].

Realizing that aggressive out-of-order cores are not an efficient choice for many classes of server applications, several studies have advocated the use of low-power embedded CPUs in data centers: [2, 23, 28, 38]. There are challenges with this approach as well—embedded cores are un-

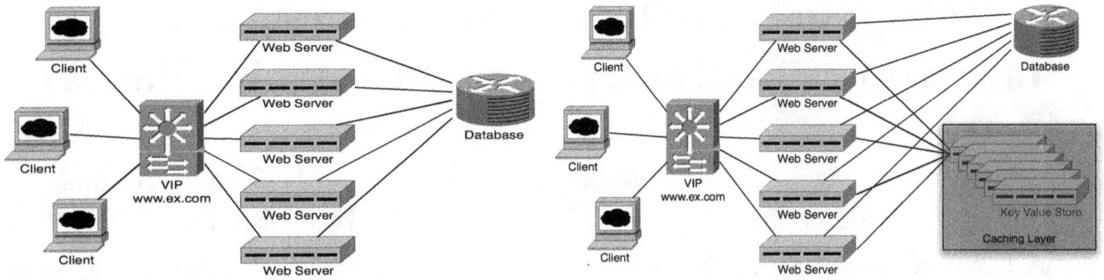


(a) **The database handles all reads and writes.**

(b) **The database only handles writes and reads that miss in the cache.**

Figure 1: **Configurations with 2 and 3 layers behind a vip to service web requests.**

able to provide the throughput and latency guarantees that are required to supply responsive dynamic content. More recently, Lim et al. [29] have shown that mobile cores alone are not enough to improve the efficiency of distributed key-value store caching systems. Instead, they create a custom Memcached accelerator, and rely on recent technology scaling trends to closely integrate their accelerator into a system-on-chip (SoC) design they call *Thin Servers with Smart Pipes* (TSSP). These approaches may improve overall energy and performance, however they do not address density. Dense servers, on the other hand, have been shown to provide greater efficiency for CPU-bound electronic commerce workloads in the past [10], however for workloads that required large amounts of memory, traditional servers were found to be a better solution.

We take the notion of an efficient, integrated system one step further to include density as a primary design constraint. We propose two integrated 3D-stacked architectures called Mercury and Iridium[1]. With Mercury we are able to tightly couple low-power ARM Cortex-A7 cores with NICs and DRAM, while maintaining high bandwidth and low latency. Recently, Facebook introduced McDipper [13], a Flash-based Memcached server using the observation that some Memcached servers require higher density with similar latency targets, but are accessed at much lower rates. To address these types of Memcached servers we introduce Iridium, a Flash based version of Mercury that further increases density at the expense of throughput while still meeting latency requirements. These two architectures allow density to be significantly increased, resulting in more effective use of costly data center space.

In summary we make the following contributions:

- Given data center costs, we contend that server density should be considered a first-class design constraint.
- We propose Mercury, an integrated, 3D-stacked DRAM server architecture which has the potential to improve density by 2.9×, making more efficient use of costly data center space.
- By closely coupling DRAM and NICs with low-power Cortex-A7 cores, we show that it is possible to improve power efficiency by 4.9×.
- By increasing density, and closely coupling DRAM, NICs, and CPUs, it is possible to increase *transactions per second* (TPS) by 10× and TPS/GB by 3.5×.
- Finally, we propose Iridium for McDipper [13] style Memcached servers, which replaces the DRAM with NAND Flash to improve density by 14×, TPS by 5.2×, and power efficiency by 2.4×, while still maintaining latency requirements for a bulk of requests. This comes at the expense of 2.8× less TPS/GB due to the much higher density.

The rest of this paper is organized as follows: in Section 2 we motivate the need for efficient Memcached servers; related work is presented in Section 3; our proposed architectures, Mercury and Iridium, are described in Section 4; in Section 5 we outline our experimental methodology; results are presented in Section 6; finally, we provide concluding remarks in Section 7.

## 2. Background and Motivation

### 2.1 Cloud Computing Design

Figure 1a shows the design of a standard web server setup. A load balancer typically has one or more virtual-IPs (VIP) configured. Each domain is routed by a DNS to a particular load balancer, where requests are then forwarded to a free server. After the load balancer a fleet of front-end servers service the web request. If needed, these web servers will contact a back-end data store to retrieve custom content that pertains to the user, which means that all servers could connect to the back-end data store.

In Figure 1b a caching layer is added, which can service any read request that hits in the cache. A request will first be forwarded to the caching layer on any read. If the requested data is present, the caching layer returns its copy to the

[1] Mercury, the Roman god, is extremely fast, while the element of the same name is very dense. Iridium, while not a god, is more dense than mercury.

client. If the data is not present, a query will be sent to the back-end data store. After the data returns, the server handling the request will issue a write to the caching layer along with the data. Future requests for that data can then be serviced by the caching layer. All write requests are sent directly to the back-end data store. Updating values in the caching layer depends on how it is configured. The two most common cases are that writes are duplicated to the caching layer or a time-to-live is placed on data in the caching layer.

### 2.2 Scaling in the Cloud

In general, the traffic to a website varies by the time of day and time of year. Data published by Netflix [35] demonstrates how traffic to their site varies over a three day period. As their data shows, traffic peaks during midday, and is at its lowest point around midnight. They also quantify the corresponding number of front-end servers needed to maintain equal load throughout the day, which tracks closely with the traffic. While this is easy to do for front-end servers, because they maintain little state, back-end data stores are not easily scaled up and down. Netflix overcomes this problem by the extensive use of caching, which is a cheaper solution than scaling back-end data stores.

While turning on and off servers helps save power, it does not help reduce space because the servers must still be physically present in order to meet peak demand. To cope with the physical demands of scaling, new data centers must be built when a given data center is either over its power budget, or out of space. A recent report states Google is spending 390 million USD to expand their Belgium data center [37]. Facebook also has plans to build a new 1.5 billion USD center in Iowa[32]. Because of this high cost, it is critical to avoid scaling by means of simply building new data centers or increasing the size of existing ones. This paper focuses on increasing physical density within a fixed power budget in order to reduce the data center footprint of key-value stores.

### 2.3 Memcached

In this paper we use Memcached 1.4 as our key-value store. We choose Memcached as our key-value store because of its widespread use in cloud computing. Memcached does not provide data persistence and servers do not need to communicate with each other, because of this it achieves linear scaling with respect to nodes. To date, the largest Memcached cluster with published data was Facebook's, which contained over 800 servers and had 28TB of DRAM in 2008 [45].

The ubiquity of Memcached stems from the fact that it is easy to use, because of its simple set of verbs. Only three details about Memcached need to be understood: first, it is distributed, which means that not every key will be on every server. In fact, a key should only be on one server, which allows the cluster to cache a large amount of data because the cache is the aggregate size of all servers. Second, the cache does not fill itself. While this may seem intuitive, the software using Memcached needs to ensure that after a read from the database, the data is stored in the cache for later retrieval. Entering data in the cache uses a *PUT*, and retrieving data from the cache uses a *GET*. Lastly, there are several options to denote when data expires from the cache. Data can either have a time-to-live, or be present in the cache indefinitely. A caveat to using Memcached is that data will be removed from your cache if a server goes down as Memcached does not have persistent storage.

#### 2.3.1 Versions and Scaling

There are several versions of Memcached: the current stable release is 1.4, and 1.6 is under development. Version 1.6 aims to fix scaling issues caused by running Memcached with a large number of threads. A detailed analysis is presented in [43]. Prior research has shown that Memcached saturates neither the network bandwidth, nor the memory bandwidth [29], due to inefficiencies in the TCP/IP stack. In this work, we distribute the work of the TCP/IP stack among many small cores to provide greater aggregate bandwidth while increasing the storage density. This is possible because 3D stacking provides higher bandwidth and a faster memory interface.

## 3. Related Work

Prior work has focused on increasing the efficiency or performance with respect to the *transactions per second (TPS)* of Memcached systems, rather than density. As previously mentioned, we believe that density should be studied as a first class design constraint due to the high cost of scaling out data centers.

### 3.1 Characterizing Cloud Workloads

Ferdman et al. have demonstrated the mismatch between cloud workloads and modern out-of-order cores [11, 12]. Through their detailed analysis of scale-out workloads on modern cores, they discovered several important characteristics of these workloads: 1) Scale-out workloads suffer from high instruction cache miss rates, and large instruction caches and pre-fetchers, are inadequate; 2) instruction and memory-level parallelism are low, thus leaving the advanced out-of-order core underutilized; 3) the working set sizes exceed the capacity of the on-chip caches; 4) bandwidth utilization of scale-out workloads is low.

### 3.2 Efficient 3D-Stacked Servers

Prior work has shown that 3D stacking may be used for efficient server design. PicoServer [23] proposes using 3D stacking technology to design compact and efficient multicore processors for use in tier 1 servers. The focus of the PicoServer is on energy efficiency—they show that by closely stacking low-power cores on top of DRAM they can remove complex cache hierarchies, and instead, add more low-power

| Component | Power (mW) | Area (mm$^2$) |
|---|---|---|
| A7@1GHz | 100 | 0.58 |
| A15@1GHz | 600 | 2.82 |
| A15@1.5GHz | 1,000 | 2.82 |
| 3D DRAM (4GB) | 210 (per GB/s) | 279.00 |
| 3D NAND Flash (19.8GB) | 6 (per GB/s) | 279.00 |
| 3D Stack NIC (MAC) | 120 | 0.43 |
| Physical NIC (PHY) | 300 | 220.00 |

Table 1: **Power and area for the components of a 3D stack.**

| DRAM | BW (GB/s) | Capacity |
|---|---|---|
| DDR3-1333 [36] | 10.7 | 2GB |
| DDR4-2667 [36] | 21.3 | 2GB |
| LPDDR3 (30nm) [4] | 6.4 | 512MB |
| HMC I (3D-Stack) [36] | 128.0 | 512MB |
| Wide I/O (3D-stack, 50nm) [25] | 12.8 | 512MB |
| Tezzaron Octopus (3D-Stack)[1] | 50.0 | 512MB |
| Future Tezzaron (3D-stack)[14] | 100.0 | 4GB |

Table 2: **Comparison of 3D-stacked DRAM to DIMM packages.**

cores. The improved memory bandwidth and latency allow for adequate throughput and performance at a significant power savings. Nanostores [9] build on the PicoServer design and integrate Flash or Memristors into the stack. Both PicoServer and Nanostores could be used in a scale-out fashion to improve density, although this was not addressed in the work. This paper builds on their designs to address density, particularly in the context of Memcached.

More recently, Scale-Out Processors [30] were proposed as a processor for cloud computing workloads. The Scale-Out Processor design uses 3D stacked DRAM as a cache for external DRAM and implements a clever prefetching technique[19]. Our designs differ in that we only use the on-chip DRAM or Flash for storage with no external backing memory. This is possible because we share the Memcached data over several independent stacks in the same 1.5U box.

### 3.3 Non-Volatile Memory File Caching in Servers

In addition to Nanostores, several prior studies have proposed using non-volatile memory for energy-efficiency in servers [22, 24, 39]. They propose using non-volatile memory (NAND Flash and phase-change memory) for file caching in servers. The use of a programmable Flash memory controller, along with a sophisticated wear-leveling algorithm, allow for the effective use of non-volatile memory for file caching, while reducing idle power by an order of magnitude.

### 3.4 Super Dense Servers

Super Dense Servers (SDS) [10] have been shown to provide greater performance and efficiency for CPU-bound electronic commerce workloads. However, for workloads that require a large amount of physical memory—such as Memcached—traditional servers provided a better solution. By utilizing state-of-the-art 3D-stacked memory technology, we overcome the limitation of SDS by providing a very high level of memory density in our proposed server designs.

### 3.5 McDipper

Memcached has been used at Facebook for a wide range of applications, including MySQL look-aside buffers and photo serving. Using DRAM for these applications is relatively expensive, and for working sets that have very large footprints but moderate to low request rates, more efficient solutions are possible. Compared with DRAM, Flash solid-state drives provide up to 20$\times$ the capacity per server and still supports tens of thousands of operations per second. This prompted the creation of McDipper, a Flash-based cache server that is compatible with Memcached. McDipper has been in active use in production at Facebook for nearly a year to serve photos [13]. Our Iridium architecture targets these very large footprint workloads which have moderate to low request rates. We further extend their solution by using Toshiba's emerging 16-layer pipe-shaped bit cost scalable (p-BiCS) NAND Flash [21], which allows for density increases on the order of 5$\times$ compared to 3D-DRAM.

### 3.6 Enhancing the Scalability of Memcached

Wiggins and Langston [43] propose changes in Memcached 1.6 to remove bottlenecks that hinder performance when running on many core systems. They find that the locking structure used to control access to the hash table and to maintain LRU replacement for keys hinders Memcached when running with many threads. To mitigate the lock contention they use fine grain locks instead of a global lock. In addition, they modify the replacement algorithm to use a pseudo LRU algorithm, which they call Bags. Their proposed changes increase the bandwidth to greater than 3.1 MTPS, which is over 6$\times$ higher than an unmodified Memcached implementation.

### 3.7 TSSP

Lim et al. propose TSSP [29], which is an SoC including a Memcached accelerator to overcome the need for a large core in Memcached clusters. They find that, due to the network stack, Intel Atom cores would not be able to replace Intel Xeons in a standard cluster configuration. TSSP is able to offload all GET requests from the processor to the accelerator. The offload is accomplished by having a hash table stored in hardware and having a smart NIC that is able to forward GET requests to the accelerator. After data for a key is found, the hardware generates a response. Because little work needs to be done by software, an ARM Cortex-A9 is a suitable processor. The TSSP architecture achieves 17.63 KTPS/Watt.

### 3.8 Resource Contention in Distributed Hash Tables

Distributed hash tables (DHT) can suffer from issues that arise because there is not a uniform distribution of requests across resources. Keys in a key value store are assigned a

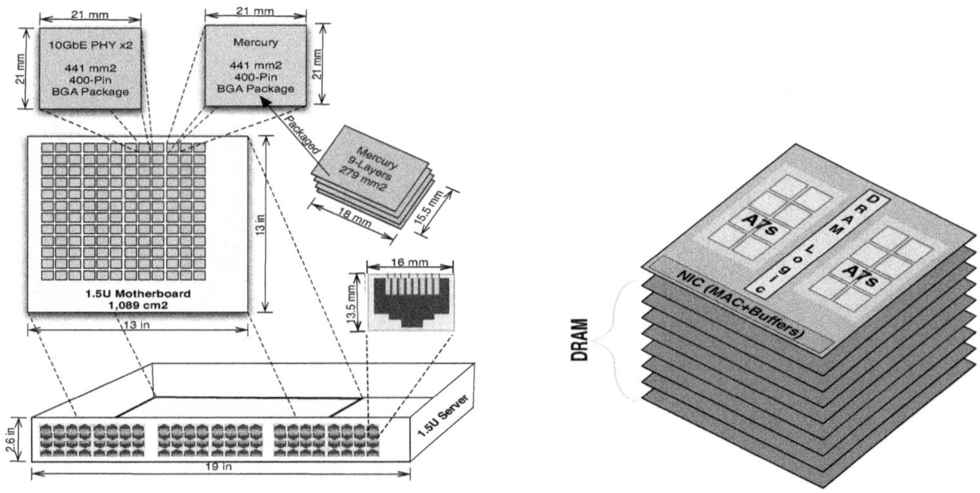


(a) **1.5U server with 96 Mercury stacks**

(b) **The 3D-stacked Mercury architecture**

Figure 2: **A Mercury server and a single stack.** A Mercury stack is made up of 8 DRAM layers, each 15.5mm×18mm, stacked with a logic layer containing the processing elements, DRAM peripheral logic, and NIC MAC & buffers. These stacks are then placed in a 400-pin BGA package. The 1.5U enclosure is limited to 96 Ethernet ports, each of which will be connected to a Mercury stack. Therefore, 96 Mercury stacks and 48 Dual NIC PHY chips are placed in the 1.5U enclosure. Due to space limitations a separate diagram of Iridium is omitted, however the high-level design is similar—the only difference being that we use a single layer of 3D-stacked Flash for the Iridium design.

resource by mapping a key onto a point in a circle. From this circle each node is assigned a portion of the circle, or arc. A server is responsible to store all data for keys that map onto their arc. Prior work dealing with resource contention in DHTs shows that increasing the number of nodes in the DHT reduces the probability of resource contention, because each node is responsible for a smaller arc [20, 41]. Typically, increasing the number of nodes has been accomplished by assigning one physical node to several virtual nodes. These virtual nodes are then distributed around the circle, which results in a more uniform utilization of resources. Because we increase the number of physical cores with Mercury and Iridium, resource contention should be minimized.

### 3.9 TILEPro64

Berezecki et al. [6] focus on adapting Memcached to run on the *TILEPro64*. In this work they cite power consumption of data centers as an important component for the success of a web service. With this in mind, they aim to improve the efficiency of Memcached by running it on a TILEPro64. They compare their implementation to both Opteron and Xeon processors running Memcached, and report an TPS/W of 5.75KTPS/W, which is an improvement of 2.85× and 2.43× respectively.

### 3.10 FAWN

Andersen et al. design a new cluster architecture, called FAWN, for efficient, and massively parallel access to data [2]. They develop FAWN-KV—an implementation of their FAWN architecture for key-value stores that uses low-power embedded cores, a log-structured datastore, and Flash memory. With FAWN-KV they improve the efficiency of queries by two orders of magnitude over traditional disk-based systems. The FAWN system focuses on the key-value and filesystem design, whereas our work focuses on designing very dense servers.

## 4. Mercury and Iridium

The Mercury and Iridium architectures are constructed by stacking ARM Cortex-A7s, a 10GbE NIC, and either 4GB of DRAM or 19.8GB of Flash into a single 3D stack. The MAC unit of the NIC, which is located on the 3D stack, is capable of routing requests to the A7 cores. A conceptual representation is presented in Figure 2a. To evaluate the use of 3D stacks with key-value stores, we vary the number of cores per stack and measure the throughput and power efficiency for each server configuration. We designate the different architectures as Mercury-$n$ or Iridium-$n$, where $n$ is the number of cores per stack. We estimate power and area requirements based off of the components listed in Table 1.

### 4.1 Mercury

While the primary goal of Mercury and Iridium is to increase data storage density, this cannot be done at the expense of latency and bandwidth—the architecture would not be able to meet the *service-level agreement* (SLA) requirements that are typical of Memcached clusters. Thus we utilize low-power, in-order ARM Cortex-A7 cores in our 3D-stacked architecture, and as we will show in section 6, we are able to service a majority of requests within the sub-millisecond range.

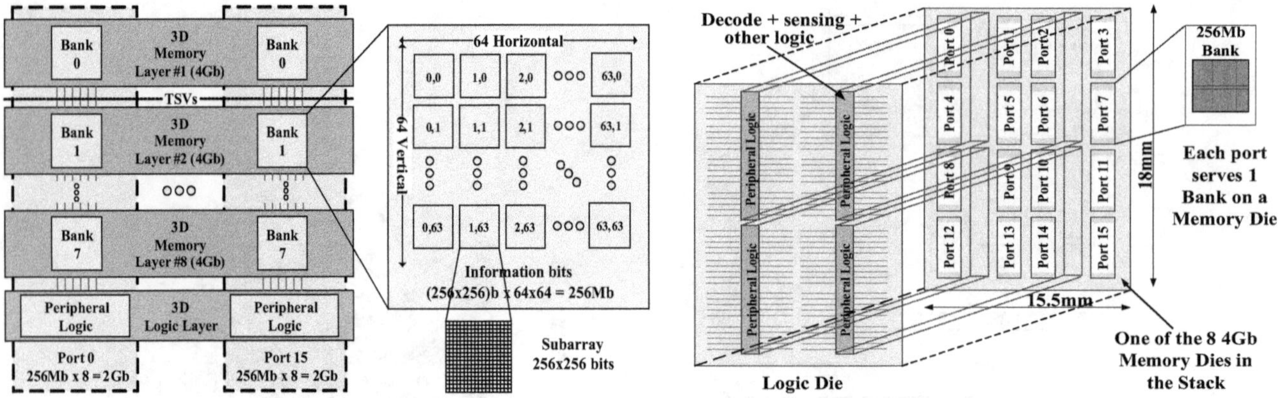


(a) **Logical organization of the 4GB 3D-stacked DRAM.**

(b) **Physical floor plan of the logical die and a 512MB memory die in the 3D stack.** The top-down view of the stack shows that DRAM banks are arranged around spines of peripheral logic.

Figure 3: **Logical organization and physical floorplan of the 3D DRAM.**

#### 4.1.1 3D Stack

The proposed Mercury architecture relies on devices from Tezzeron's 3D-stacking process [40]. This process allows us to stack 8 memory layers on a logic die through finely-spaced (1.75μm pitch), low-power through silicon vias (TSV). The TSVs have a feedthrough capacitance of 2-3fF and a series resistance of $< 3\Omega$. This allows as much as 4GB of data in each individual stack.

The 4GB stack's logical organization is shown in Figure 3a. Each 4GB 3D chip consists of eight 512MB DRAM memory dies stacked on top of a logic die. The organization of the DRAM die is an extension [14] of Tezzaron's existing Octopus DRAM solution [1]. Each 3D stack has 16 128-bit data ports, with each port accessing an independent 256MB address space. Each address space is further subdivided into eight 32MB banks. Each bank, in turn, is physically organized as a 64×64 matrix of subarrays. Each subarray is a 256×256 arrangement of bit cells, and is 60μm×35μm.

Figure 3b shows the physical floor plan of each DRAM memory die and the logic die. The logic die is fabricated in a 28nm CMOS process and consists of address-decoding logic, global word line drivers, sense amplifiers, row buffers, error correction logic, and low-swing I/O logic with pads. Each memory die is partitioned into 16 ports with each port serving 1 of the 16 banks on a die. The memory die is fabricated in a 50nm DRAM process and consists of the DRAM subarrays along with some logic, such as local wordline drivers and pass-gate multiplexers.

While there are more advanced DRAM processes (e.g. 20nm), TSV yield in existing 3D-stacked prototypes has only been proven up to the 50nm DRAM process node [25, 36]. All subarrays in a vertical stack share the same row buffer using TSVs, and at most one row of subarrays in a vertical stack can have its contents in the row buffer, which corresponds to a physical page. Assuming an 8kb page, a maximum of 2,048 pages can be simultaneously open per stack (128 8kb pages per bank × 16 banks per physical layer). The device provides a sustained bandwidth of 6.25GB/s per port (100GB/s total).

#### 4.1.2 Address Space

The 3D stack DRAM has 16 ports for memory access, this segments the 4GB stack into 256MB chunks. Each core is allocated one or more ports for memory access, which prevents Memcached processes from overwriting each other's address range. If the Mercury or Iridium architectures increase past 16 cores, additional ports would need to be added, or cores would need to share ports.

#### 4.1.3 Memory Access

Other studies have shown that small cores alone are not able to provide the needed bandwidth to be useful in key-value stores [29]. Mercury differs from this research because it is coupled with a memory interface that provides higher bandwidth at a lower latency through 3D integration. For comparison, Table 2 shows the bandwidth and capacity of several current and emerging memory technologies. Coupling cores on the 3D stack allows Mercury to forego using an L2 cache, which prior research has shown to be inefficient [29], and issue requests directly to memory. The 3D DRAM has a closed page latency of 11 cycles at 1GHz. By having a faster connection to memory we mitigate the cache thrashing by the networking stack reported in [29].

#### 4.1.4 Request Routing

To simplify design and save power we do not use a router at the server level. Instead, the physical network port is tied directly to a 3D stack. This allows for each stack to act as a single node, or multiple nodes, without having contention from other stacks. At the stack, we base our design off of the integrated NIC on the Niagra-2 chip [5, 26]. The integrated NIC is capable of buffering a packet and then forwarding it to the correct core. Cores on the same stack will need to run Memcached on different TCP/IP ports. This simplifies request routing on the stack. The physical port (PHY) portion of the 10GbE is based on the Broadcom design [8] and is not located on the stack.

### 4.2 Iridium

Due to the high cost of server real estate, physical density is first-class design constraint for key-value stores. Facebook has developed McDipper [13], which utilizes Flash memory to service low-request-rate transactions while improving density by up to 20×. McDipper has been in use for over a year to service photos at Facebook. With Iridium we target these low-request-rate applications and explore the tradeoff between physical density and throughput by replacing the DRAM in a Mercury stack with NAND Flash memory. This comes at the expense of throughput per GB of storage, but is still applicable to low-request-rate high-density Memcached clusters, such as Facebook's photo server.

#### 4.2.1 3D Stacked Flash

McDipper reported an increase in density by 20× when moving from DRAM DIMMs to Solid-State drives. Because the Mercury design already improved density through 3D-DRAM we will not see as significant a gain. To quantify the improvement in the density of the stack we estimate our Flash density using the cell sizes of Toshiba's emerging pipe-shaped bit cost scalable (p-BiCS) NAND Flash [21]. Flash cells are smaller than DRAM cells, offering a 2.5× increase in density. Because p-BiCS has 16 layers of 3D Flash[2], as opposed to 8 layers for 3D-stacked DRAM, this leads to an overall 4.9× increase in density for Iridium stacks. For our access organization we maintain Mercury's 16 separate ports to DRAM by including 16 independent Flash controllers. The read/write latency values and energy numbers used for simulation are drawn from [15], which are conservative for 3D-stacked Flash. The power and area numbers for Flash are shown in table 1. In addition, because the Flash latency is much longer, an L2 cache is needed to hold the entire instruction footprint. Our results in Section 6.2 will confirm this assumption.

## 5. Methodology

The following sections describe our Memcached setup, as well as our simulation framework and power models.

### 5.1 Memcached

For our experiments we utilize the latest stable version of Memcached cross-compiled for the ARM ISA. We modify our simulation infrastructure, which will be described in the next section, to collect timing information. We do this, as opposed to using library timing functions such as *gettimeofday()*, because they do not perturb the system under test. All experiments are run with a single Memcached thread.

For our client we use an in-house Java client that is based on the work by Whalin [42]. Because we measure performance from the server-side, the overhead of running Java is not included with the measurements.

### 5.2 Simulation Infrastructure

To calculate the request rates that Mercury and Iridium are able to achieve, we used the gem5 full-system simulator [7]. With gem5, we are able to model multiple networked systems with a full operating system, TCP/IP stack, and Ethernet devices. We use Ubuntu 11.04 along with version *2.6.38.8* of the Linux kernel for both the server and client systems. For our client-side Java VM, we use *Java SE 1.7.0_04-ea* from Oracle.

While Mercury and Iridium both utilize ARM Cortex-A7 cores, we also explore the possibility of using the more aggressive, out-of-order Cortex-A15 core by modelling both cores in our simulation infrastructure. Simulations use a memory model with a memory latency varied from 10-100ns for DRAM and 10-20$\mu$s for Flash Reads. Our memory model represents a worst-case estimate as it assumes a closed-page latency for all requests. To measure the TPS we vary request size from 64B to 1MB, doubling request size at each iteration. We do not consider values greater than 1MB for the following reasons: 1) Memcached workloads tend to favor smaller size data; 2) prior work [3, 29, 43], against which we compare, present bandwidth per watt at data sizes of 64B and 128B; and, 3) requests that are 64KB or larger have to be split up into multiple TCP packets.

### 5.3 TPS calculation

To calculate the TPS we collect the round-trip time (RTT) for a request, i.e., the total time it takes for a request to go from the client to the server, then back to the client. Because we use only a single thread for Memcached, the TPS is equal to the inverse of the RTT. The RTT for each request is obtained by dumping TCP/IP packet information from gem5's Ethernet device models. The packet trace is run through TShark [44] to parse out timing information. After timing information is obtained from gem5 for a single core, we apply linear scaling to calculate TPS at the stack and server level. Linear scaling is a reasonable approach in this context because each core on a stack is running a separate instance of Memcached. Running separate instances avoids the contention issue raised by the work of Wiggins and Langston[43]. For the Mercury-32 and Iridium-32 configurations we use the same approach, however we assume two cores per memory port (as mentioned previously we can fit a maximum of 16 memory ports on a stack), because Memcached has been shown to scale well for two threads [43].

[2] The 16 Flash layers are contained in a single monolithic layer of 3D Flash, and are not 3D die-stacked.

| | | 1.5U Mercury Server | | | | | | 1.5U Iridium Server | | | | | |
|---|---|---|---|---|---|---|---|---|---|---|---|---|---|
| | Number of Cores per Stack | 1 | 2 | 4 | 8 | 16 | 32 | 1 | 2 | 4 | 8 | 16 | 32 |
| A15 1.5GHz | Area($cm^2$) | 635 | 635 | 576 | 331 | 179 | 86 | 635 | 635 | 635 | 363 | 185 | 93 |
| | Power(W) | 449 | 569 | 749 | 750 | 750 | 720 | 328 | 449 | 690 | 740 | 737 | 730 |
| | Density(GB) | 384 | 384 | 348 | 200 | 108 | 52 | 1,901 | 1,901 | 1,901 | 1,089 | 554 | 277 |
| | Max BW(GB/s) | 27 | 55 | 99 | 114 | 123 | 118 | 1 | 3 | 6 | 7 | 7 | 7 |
| A15 1GHz | Area($cm^2$) | 635 | 635 | 635 | 496 | 278 | 139 | 635 | 635 | 635 | 595 | 304 | 152 |
| | Power(W) | 401 | 473 | 618 | 745 | 742 | 728 | 281 | 353 | 498 | 750 | 740 | 728 |
| | Density(GB) | 384 | 384 | 384 | 300 | 168 | 84 | 1,901 | 1,901 | 1,901 | 1,782 | 911 | 455 |
| | Max BW(GB/s) | 27 | 54 | 108 | 169 | 189 | 189 | 2 | 3 | 6 | 11 | 11 | 11 |
| A7 1GHz | Area($cm^2$) | 635 | 635 | 635 | 635 | 635 | 616 | 635 | 635 | 635 | 635 | 635 | 635 |
| | Power(W) | 341 | 353 | 378 | 429 | 529 | 749 | 221 | 233 | 258 | 309 | 410 | 612 |
| | Density(GB) | 384 | 384 | 384 | 384 | 384 | 371 | 1,901 | 1,901 | 1,901 | 1,901 | 1,901 | 1,901 |
| | Max BW(GB/s) | 19 | 37 | 75 | 149 | 299 | 578 | 1 | 3 | 6 | 12 | 22 | 44 |

Table 3: **Power and area comparison for 1.5U maximum configurations.** For each configuration we utilize the maximum number of stacks we can fit into a 1.5U server, which is 96, or until we reach our power budget of 750W. The power and bandwidth numbers are the maximum values we observed when servicing requests from 64B up to 1MB.

### 5.4 Power Modeling

Table 1 has a breakdown of power per component, and Table 3 has the cumulative power totals for each configuration of Mercury and Iridium at their maximum sustainable bandwidths. To calculate the power of an individual stack we add together the power of the NIC, cores, and memory. The integrated 10GbE NIC is comprised of a MAC and buffers. The MAC power estimates come from the Niagra-2 design [5, 26], and the buffers are estimated from CACTI [34]. The ARM Cortex-A7 and Cortex-A15 power numbers are drawn from [16], and the 3D DRAM is calculated from a technical specification obtained from Tezzaron [14]. Because DRAM active power depends on the memory bandwidth being used, we must calculate the stack power for the maximum bandwidth that a given number of cores can produce. Similar calculations are used to obtain NAND Flash power, which use read and write energy values drawn from [15]. Finally, each stack requires an off-stack physical Ethernet port. Power numbers for the PHY are based on a Broadcom part [8].

#### 5.4.1 Power Budget for 1.5U Mercury System

In calculating the power for the 1.5U server system we multiply the per stack power by the number of stacks. To determine how many stacks can fit in a 1.5U power budget, we start with a 750W power supply from HP [18]. First 160W is allotted for other components (disk, motherboard, etc.), after this we assume a conservative 20% margin for miscellaneous power and delivery losses in the server. This results in a maximum power of $(750 - 160) \times 0.8 = 472$W for Mercury or Iridium components.

#### 5.4.2 TPS/Watt calculation

When calculating the maximum number of 3D stacks that fit in a system, we used the maximum memory bandwidth that Mercury and Iridium can produce. However, for proper TPS/Watt calculation, we estimate power by using the GB/s power consumption of DRAM and Flash at the request size we are testing.

### 5.5 Area

Area estimates for the 10GbE NIC were obtained by scaling the Niagra-2 MAC to 28nm and the buffers were obtained from CACTI. The area for an ARM Cortex-A7 chip in 28nm technology is taken from [16]. DRAM design estimates for the next generation Tezzaron Octopus DRAM were obtained from Tezzaron [14]. Given the available area on the logic die of the Tezzaron 3D-stack, we are able to fit >400 cores on a stack. However, the memory interface becomes saturated if there are $\geq 64$ cores in a stack. We are further limited, by the number of DRAM ports in a stack, to 16 cores per stack unless cores share the memory controller. In each 1.5U server, multiple 3D stacks are used to increase the bandwidth and density. Once packaged into a 400-pin 21mm×21mm ball grid array (BGA) package, each stack consumes 441mm$^2$. Each NIC PHY chip is also 441mm$^2$ and contains 2 10GbE PHYs/chip. If 77% of a 1.5U, 13in×13in motherboard [27] is used for Mercury or Iridium stacks and associated PHYs, then the server can fit 128 Mercury or Iridium stacks. However, only 96 Ethernet ports can fit on the back of a 1.5U server [31]. Therefore, we cap the maximum number of stacks at 96.

### 5.6 Density

We define density to be the amount of DRAM that we can fit in the system. We then maximize density within three constraining factors: power, area, and network connections. As more cores are added to the system, the power requirement for both core power and DRAM bandwidth will increase, because of this there is a tradeoff between throughput and density. Each stack can fit 4GB of DRAM or 19.8GB of Flash and each server can fit up to 128 3D stacks, which gives a maximum density of 512GB of DRAM for Mercury or 2.4TB of Flash for Iridium. Each server can fit a maximum of 96 network connections, capping the number of stacks to 96 and density to 384GB of DRAM for Mercury or 1.9TB of Flash for Iridium.

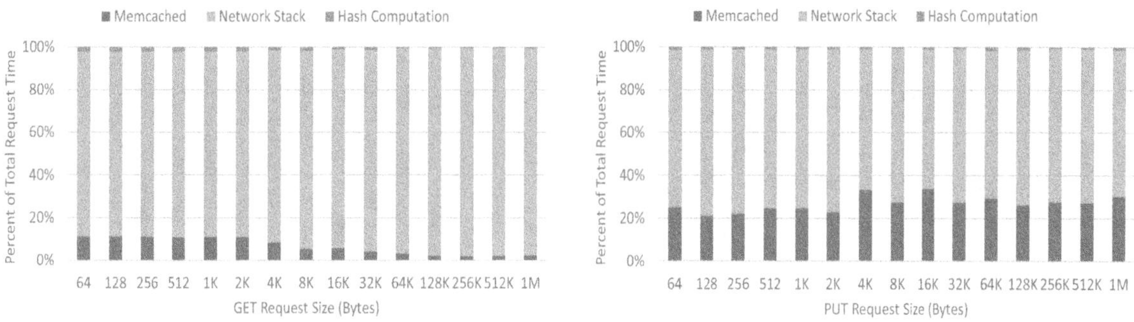


(a) **GET execution time** (b) **PUT execution time**

Figure 4: **Components of GET and PUT requests.**

# 6. Results

We evaluate several different 3D-stacked server configurations, which are differentiated based on the number (and type) of cores per stack, and on the type of memory used. DRAM-based configurations we call Mercury, while Flash-based configurations are called Iridium (because Iridium is more dense).

## 6.1 Request Breakdown

We first explore the different components of GET and PUT requests. Figure 4 shows a breakdown of execution time for both GET and PUT requests; execution is broken down into three components: hash computation time (*Hash Computation*), the time in metadata processing to find the memory location of the data (*Memcached*), and time spent in the network stack and data transfer (*Network Stack*). These experiments were run using a single A15 @1GHz, with a 2MB L2 cache, and DRAM with a latency of 10ns. We ran these experiments for various configurations, however the results were similar.

### 6.1.1 GET and PUT requests

Figure 4a shows the breakdown of execution during a GET request. For requests up to 4KB roughly 10% of time is spent in Memcached, 2-3% is spend in hash computation, and a vast majority of the time (87%) is spent in the network stack. At higher request sizes nearly all of the time is spent in the network stack, which is in agreement with prior research [29].

Figure 4b shows the breakdown of execution during a PUT request. As expected, hash computation takes up the same amount of time for a PUT request as it does for a GET request, however it represents a much smaller portion of the time: only around 1%. Also as expected, Memcached metadata manipulation takes up more computation for a PUT request: up to 30% in some cases. Network processing is still the largest component at nearly 70% for some request sizes.

Because the network stack takes up a significant portion of the time, utilizing aggressive out-of-order cores is inefficient. As we will demonstrate, by closely integrating memory with many low-power cores, we can achieve a high-level of throughput much more efficiently than traditional servers.

## 6.2 3D-Stack Memory Access Latency Sensitivity

While the focus of this work is on improving density for Memcached servers, this cannot be provided at the expense of latencies that would violate the SLA. To explore the effect memory latency and CPU performance have on overall request RTT we measure the average TPS, which is the inverse of the average RTT for single-core Mercury and Iridium stacks. The lower the RTT the higher the TPS, thus a higher TPS indicates better overall performance for individual requests.

Figure 5 shows the TPS sensitivity to memory latency, with respect to GET/PUT request size, for a Mercury-1 stack. We evaluate a Mercury-1 stack for an A15 and an A7, both with and without an L2 cache. We also explored using an A15 @1.5GHz, which is the current frequency limit of the A15, however we do not report these results because they are nearly identical to an A15 @1GHz. For each configuration we sweep across memory latencies of 10, 30, 50, and 100ns. Similarly, figure 6 demonstrates the throughput sensitivity to memory latency for an Iridium-1 stack. For Iridium-1 we sweep across Flash read latencies of 10 and 20$\mu$s; write latency is kept at 200 $\mu$s.

Figures 5a and 5b show the average TPS for an A15-based Mercury-1 stack with and without an L2 cache respectively. As can be seen, at a latency of 10ns the L2 provides no benefit, and may hinder performance. Because the DRAM is much faster than the core, the additional latency of a cache lookup, which typically has poor hit rates, degrades the average TPS. However, at the higher DRAM latencies the L2 cache significantly improves performance; while the stored values are typically not resident in the L2 cache, instructions and other metadata benefit from an L2 cache.

Similarly, figures 5c and 5d report average TPS for an A7-based Mercury-1 stack with and without and L2 cache.

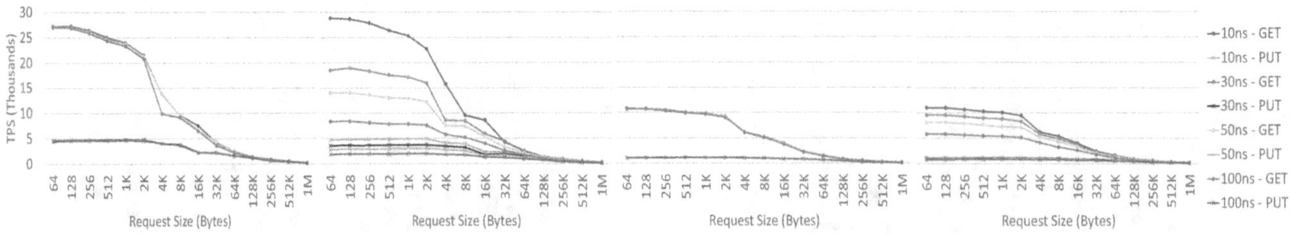


(a) **A15 @1GHz with a 2MB L2** (b) **A15 @1GHz with no L2** (c) **A7 with a 2MB L2** (d) **A7 with no L2**

Figure 5: **Transactions per second for a Mercury-1 stack for the different CPU configurations and DRAM latency.**

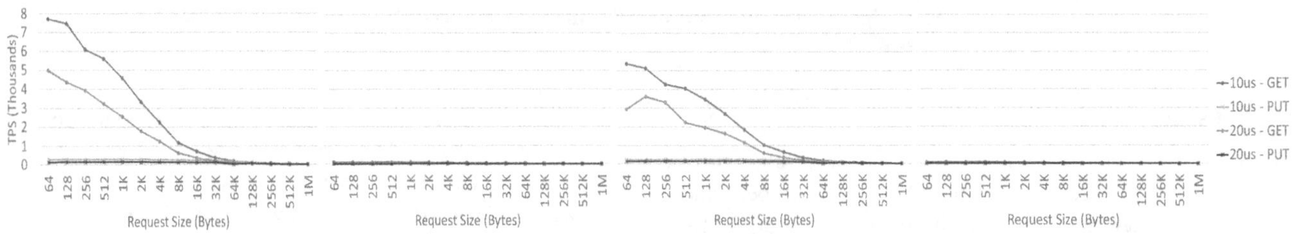


(a) **A15 @1GHz with a 2MB L2** (b) **A15 @1GHz with no L2** (c) **A7 with a 2MB L2** (d) **A7 with no L2**

Figure 6: **Transactions per second for a Iridium-1 stack for the different CPU configurations and Flash latency.**

Because of the less aggressive core, the L2 cache makes less of a difference for an A7-based Mercury-1 stack. The A15-based Mercury-1 stack significantly outperforms an A7-based Mercury-1 stack by about 3× at the lower request sizes. If the L2 cache is removed, the A15 only outperforms the A7 by 1-2× at the lower request sizes.

Finally, figure 6 reports the average TPS for an Iridium-1 stack. Because of the relatively slow read and write latencies of Flash, an L2 cache is crucial for performance; removing the L2 cache yields average an average TPS below 100 for both the A7 and A15, which is not acceptable. However, with an L2 cache both the A15 and A7 can sustain an average of several thousand TPS for GET requests, with a bulk of the requests being serviced under 1ms. For PUT requests the average TPS is below 1,000, however GET requests have been shown to make up a bulk of the requests for typical Memcached applications [3]. Because of Flash's relatively slow speed, the A15 outperforms an A7 by around 25% on average.

These results demonstrate the tradeoff between core and memory speed and performance. If very low response time is required for individual requests, faster memory and cores are desired. If, however, throughput and density are first-class constraints, then less aggressive cores and memory may be used without violating the SLA; as we will show in the next sections, density and efficiency may be vastly improved.

### 6.3 Density and Throughput

We define the density of a stack to be the total amount of memory it contains. Figure 7 illustrates the tradeoff between density and total throughput for different Mercury and Iridium configurations. Throughput is measured as the average TPS for 64B GET requests; prior works have shown that small GET requests are the most frequent requests in Memcached applications, and base their evaluations on such requests [3, 43]. Each configuration is labelled Mercury-$n$ or Iridium-$n$, where $n$ is the number of cores per stack. For all Mercury configurations we use a DRAM latency of 10ns, and for all Iridium configurations we use Flash read and write latencies of 10 and 200$\mu$s respectively. In each configuration the core contains a 2MB L2 cache. Table 3 lists the details of each separate Mercury and Iridium configuration.

The core power (listed in table 1) is the limiting factor when determining how many total stacks our server architecture can support. As figure 7 shows, the A15's higher power consumption severely limits the number of stacks that can fit into our power budget. At 8 cores per stack we see a sharp decline in density, while performance levels off. The A15's peak efficiency comes at 1GHz for both Mercury-8 and Iridium-8 stacks, where we are able to fit 75 stacks (600 cores) and 90 stacks (720 cores) respectively; Mercury-8 can sustain an average of 17.29 million TPS with 300GB of memory, while Iridium-8 can sustain an average of 5.45 million TPS with approximately 2TB of memory.

The A7's relatively low power allows us to fit nearly the maximum number of stacks into our server, even at 32 cores per stack. Because of this, the A7-based Mercury and Iridium designs are able to provide significantly higher performance and density than their A15-based counterparts. Mercury-32 can sustain an average TPS of 32.7 million with

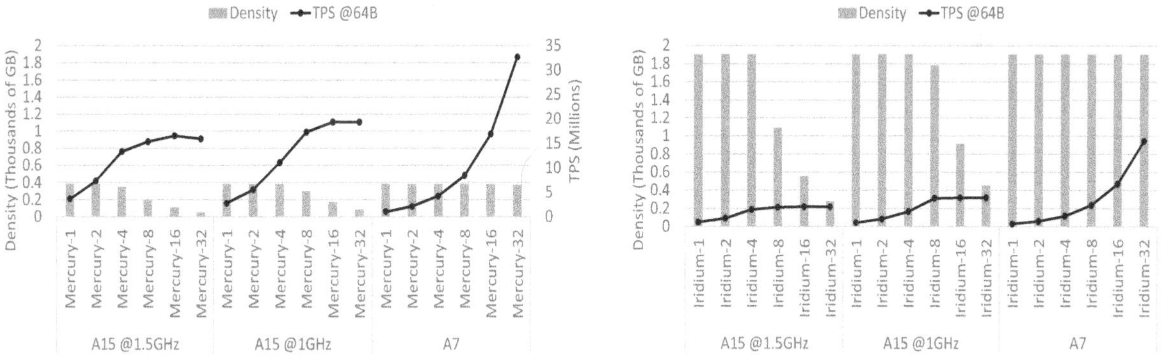


(a) **Mercury density vs. TPS** (b) **Iridium density vs. TPS**

Figure 7: **Density and throughput for Mercury and Iridium stacks servicing 64B GET requests.**

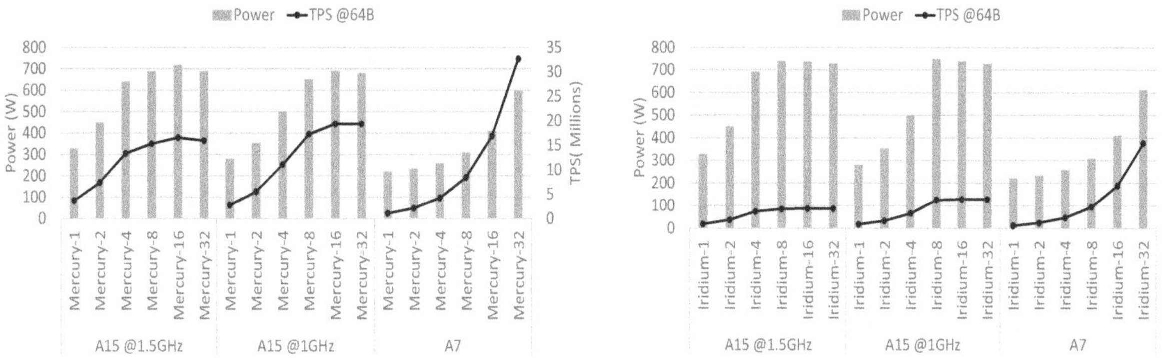


(a) **Mercury power vs. TPS** (b) **Iridium power vs. TPS**

Figure 8: **Power and throughput for Mercury and Iridium stacks servicing 64B GET requests.**

372GB of memory, while Iridium-32 can sustain an average TPS of 16.48 with approximately 2TB of memory.

The A7 provides the most efficient implementation for both Mercury and Iridium stacks, however Mercury-32 provides around 2× more throughput when compared to Iridium-32; Iridium-32, on the other hand, provides nearly 5× more density. If performance is a primary concern Mercury-32 is the best choice. If high density is needed, Iridium-32 provides the most memory and is still able to satisfy the SLA requirements.

### 6.4 Power and Throughput

The power and throughput tradeoff is shown in figure 8. Again, we measure the throughput of our system while servicing 64B GET requests. Because we are limited to a maximum of 96 stacks for a single server, the configurations that contain 1, 2, or 4 cores are well under our maximum power budget of 750W, however as we add more cores per stack we come close to saturating our power budget. As power becomes a constraint, the number of stacks we are able to fit into our power budget is reduced. Thus, there is a tradeoff between total throughput and overall power. We seek to maximize throughput while staying within our power budget, therefore we always opt for a system with the maximum number of stacks if possible.

Figure 8a shows that, for Mercury, the A15's power quickly becomes prohibitive, limiting the number of cores we can fit into a server given our 750W power budget. The best A15 configuration is a Mercury-16 system that uses A15s @1GHz. An average of 19.36 million TPS can be sustained at a power of 678W. The max throughput for a Mercury-32 system using A15s @1GHz uses slightly less power than the Mercury-16 system, while delivering nearly the same throughput, because less stacks are used. Using A7s we are able to fit nearly the maximum number of stacks, while staying well below our power budget. A Mercury-32 system using A7s is the most efficient design, delivering 32.7 million TPS at a power of 597W.

For Iridium, the A15 is even less efficient, as seen in figure 8b—the A15's extra power does not help performance because it often waits on memory. The throughput for an A7-based Iridium-32 system is half that of an A7-based Mercury-32 system at roughly the same power budget. However, as noted above the Iridium-32 system provides 5× more density. The power of Iridium is slightly higher than Mercury because the relatively low power of Flash allows for more stacks.

| | | Mercury | | | Iridium | | | Memcached | | | TSSP |
|---|---|---|---|---|---|---|---|---|---|---|---|
| | Version | n=8 | n=16 | n=32 | n=8 | n=16 | n=32 | 1.4 | 1.6 | Bags | — |
| 1.5U Server @64B Request | Stacks | 96 | 96 | 93 | 96 | 96 | 96 | 1 | 1 | 1 | 1 |
| | Cores | 768 | 1,536 | 2,976 | 768 | 1,536 | 3,072 | 6 | 4 | 16 | 1 |
| | Memory(GB) | 384 | 384 | 372 | **1,901** | **1,901** | **1,901** | 12 | 128 | 128 | 8 |
| | Power(W) | 309 | 410 | 597 | 309 | 410 | 611 | 143 | 159 | 285 | 16 |
| | TPS(millions) | 8.44 | 16.88 | 32.70 | 4.12 | 8.24 | 16.49 | 0.41 | 0.52 | 3.15 | 0.28 |
| | TPS(thousands)/Watt | 27.33 | 41.21 | **54.77** | 13.35 | 20.13 | 26.98 | 2.9 | 3.29 | 11.1 | 17.6 |
| | TPS(thousands)/GB | 21.98 | 43.96 | **87.91** | 2.17 | 4.34 | 8.67 | 34.2 | 4.1 | 24.6 | 35.3 |
| | Bandwidth(GB/s) | 0.54 | 1.08 | 2.09 | 0.26 | 0.53 | 1.06 | 0.03 | 0.03 | 0.20 | 0.04 |

Table 4: **Comparison of A7-based Mercury and Iridium to prior art.** We compare several versions of Mercury and Iridium (recall $n$ is the number of cores per stack) to different versions of Memcached running on a state-of-the-art server, as well as TSSP. The bold values represent the highest density (GB), efficiency (TPS/W), and accessibility (TPS/GB).

### 6.5 Cooling

The TDP of a Mercury-32 server is 597W (the same as today's 1.5U systems) and is spread across all 96 stacks; in contrast to a conventional server design where all the power is concentrated on a few chips. This yields a TDP for an individual stack of 6.2W. Thus, we expect the power of each Mercury chip to be within the capabilities of passive cooling, and an active fan in the 1.5U box can be used to extract the heat. Prior work on the thermal characterization of cloud workloads also supports this notion [33].

### 6.6 Comparison to Prior Work

To gauge the performance of Mercury and Iridium we compare their efficiency, density, and performance to modern versions of Memcached running on a state-of-the-art server. Table 4 lists the pertinent metrics for the best performing Mercury and Iridium configurations, and compares them to prior art. As can be seen in this table both Mercury and Iridium provide more throughput, 10× and 5.2× more than Bags respectively, primarily due to the massive number of cores they can support. At the same time, the use of low-power cores and integrated memory provides greater efficiency: 4.9× higher TPS/W for Mercury and 2.4× more for Iridium. Because of the speed of memory used in Mercury systems, it can even make better use of its density yielding an average TPS/GB that is 3.4× higher than Bags. Iridium has 2.8× less TPS/GB on average due to its much higher density. Overall, Mercury and Iridium provide 2.9 × and 14.8× more density on average, while still servicing a majority of requests within the sub-millisecond range.

The table also reports the same metrics for TSSP, which is an accelerator for Memcached. While this work aims to improve the efficiency of Memcached by using specialized hardware, the 3D-stacked Mercury and Iridium architectures are able to provide 3× and 1.5× more TPS/W respectively.

## 7. Conclusion

Distributed, in-memory key-value stores, such as Memcached, are so widely used by many large web companies that approximately 25% of their servers are devoted solely to key-value stores. Data centers are expensive, a fact which requires that each unit be used as efficiently as possible. While previous works have recognized the importance of key-value stores, and the fact that they are inefficient when run on commodity hardware, the approach has typically been to try to improve the performance and efficiency of existing server systems.

In this work we propose using state-of-the-art 3D stacking techniques to develop two highly-integrated server architectures that are not only able to allow low-power, embedded CPUs to be used without sacrificing bandwidth and performance, but are also able to drastically improve density. This is a crucial component to keeping the cost of ownership for data centers down. Through our detailed simulations, we show that, by using 3D stacked DRAM (Mercury), density may be improved by 2.9×, efficiency by 4.9×, TPS by 10×, and TPS/GB by 3.5× over a current state-of-the-art server running an optimized version of Memcached. By replacing the DRAM with Flash our Iridium architecture can service moderate to low request rate servers with even better density while maintaining SLA requirements for the bulk of requests. Iridium improves density by 14×, efficiency by 2.4×, TPS by 5.2×, with only a 2.8× reduction in TPS/GB compared to current Memcached servers.

## Acknowledgments

We would like to than the anonymous reviewers for their feedback. This work was supported by a grant from ARM Ltd.

## References

[1] Octopus 8-Port DRAM for Die-Stack Applications . Technical report, Tezzaron, 2012. Accessed: May 29, 2013.

[2] D. G. Andersen, J. Franklin, M. Kaminsky, A. Phanishayee, L. Tan, and V. Vasudevan. FAWN: A Fast Array of Wimpy Nodes. In *the Proceedings of the ACM SIGOPS 22nd Symposium on Operating Systems Principles (SOSP)*, pages 1–14, 2009.

[3] B. Atikoglu, Y. Xu, E. Frachtenberg, S. Jiang, and M. Paleczny. Workload Analysis of a Large-Scale Key-Value Store. In *Proceedings of the*

*12th ACM SIGMETRICS/PERFORMANCE Joint International Conference on Measurement and Modeling of Computer Systems*, pages 53–64, 2012.

[4] Y.-C. Bae, J.-Y. Park, S. J. Rhee, S. B. Ko, Y. Jeong, K.-S. Noh, Y. Son, J. Youn, Y. Chu, H. Cho, M. Kim, D. Yim, H.-C. Kim, S.-H. Jung, H.-I. Choi, S. Yim, J.-B. Lee, J.-S. Choi, and K. Oh. A 1.2V 30nm 1.6Gb/s/pin 4Gb LPDDR3 SDRAM with Input Skew Calibration and Enhanced Control Scheme. In *Proceedings of the 2012 IEEE International Solid-State Circuits Conference Digest of Technical Papers (ISSCC)*, pages 44–46, 2012.

[5] J. Barreh, J. Brooks, R. Golla, G. Grohoski, R. Hetherington, P. Jordan, M. Luttrell, C. Olson, and M. Shah. Niagara-2: A Highly Threaded Server-on-a-Chip. In *Proceedings of the 18th Hot Chips Symposium*, 2006.

[6] M. Berezecki, E. Frachtenberg, M. Paleczny, and K. Steele. Many-Core Key-Value Store. In *Proceedings of the 2011 International Green Computing Conference and Workshops (IGCC)*, pages 1–8, 2011.

[7] N. Binkert, B. Beckmann, G. Black, S. K. Reinhardt, A. Saidi, A. Basu, J. Hestness, D. R. Hower, T. Krishna, S. Sardashti, R. Sen, K. Sewell, M. Shoaib, N. Vaish, M. D. Hill, and D. A. Wood. The gem5 Simulator. *SIGARCH Computer Architecture News*, 39(2):1–7, 2011.

[8] Broadcom. Broadcom Introduces Industry's Lowest Power Octal 10GbE PHY. `http://www.broadcom.com/press/release.php?id=s706156`, 2012. Accessed: May 29, 2013.

[9] J. Chang, P. Ranganathan, T. Mudge, D. Roberts, M. A. Shah, and K. T. Lim. A Limits Study of Benefits from Nanostore-Based Future Data-Centric System Architectures. In *Proceedings of the 9th Conference on Computing Frontiers (CF)*, pages 33–42, 2012.

[10] W. Felter, T. Keller, M. Kistler, C. Lefurgy, K. Rajamani, R. Rajamony, F. Rawson, B. A. Smith, and E. Van Hensbergen. On the Performance and Use of Dense Servers. *IBM Journal of Research and Development*, 47(5.6):671–688, 2003.

[11] M. Ferdman, A. Adileh, O. Kocberber, S. Volos, M. Alisafaee, D. Jevdjic, C. Kaynak, A. D. Popescu, A. Ailamaki, and B. Falsafi. Clearing the Clouds: A Study of Emerging Scale-out Workloads on Modern Hardware. In *Proceedings of the Seventeenth International Conference on Architectural Support for Programming Languages and Operating Systems (ASPLOS)*, pages 37–48, 2012.

[12] M. Ferdman, A. Adileh, O. Kocberber, S. Volos, M. Alisafaee, D. Jevdjic, C. Kaynak, A. D. Popescu, A. Ailamaki, and B. Falsafi. Quantifying the Mismatch Between Emerging Scale-Out Applications and Modern Processors. *ACM Transactions on Computing Systems*, 30 (4):15:1–15:24, 2012.

[13] A. Gartrell, M. Srinivasan, B. Alger, and K. Sundararajan. McDipper: A Key-Value Cache for Flash Storage. `http://www.facebook.com/notes/facebook-engineering/mcdipper-a-key-value-for-flash-storage/10151347090423920`, 2013. Accessed: July 1, 2013.

[14] B. Giridhar, M. Cieslak, D. Duggal, R. G. Dreslinski, R. Patti, B. Hold, C. Chakrabarti, T. Mudge, and D. Blaauw. Exploring DRAM Organizations for Engery-Efficient and Resilient Exascale Memories. In *Proceedings of the 2013 International Conference for High Performance Computing, Networking, Storage and Analysis (SC)*, pages 23:1–23:12, 2013.

[15] L. M. Grupp, A. M. Caulfield, J. Coburn, S. Swanson, E. Yaakobi, P. H. Siegel, and J. K. Wolf. Characterizing Flash Memory: Anomalies, Obervations, and Applications. In *Proceedings of the 42nd Annual IEEE/ACM International Symposium on Microarchitecture (MICRO)*, pages 24–33, 2009.

[16] L. Gwennap. How Cortex-A15 Measures Up. *Microprocessor Report*, May 2013.

[17] J. L. Henning. SPEC CPU2006 Benchmark Descriptions. *SIGARCH Computer Architecture News*, 34(4):1–17, 2006.

[18] *HP Common Slot Platinum Power Supplies*. HP, 2010.

[19] D. Jevdjic, S. Volos, and B. Falsafi. Die-Stacked DRAM Caches for Servers: Hit Ratio, Latency, or Bandwidth? Have It All with Footprint Cache. In *Proceedings of the 40th Annual International Symposium on Computer Architecture (ISCA)*, 2013.

[20] D. Karger, E. Lehman, T. Leighton, R. Panigrahy, M. Levine, and D. Lewin. Consistent Hashing and Random Trees: Distributed Caching Protocols for Relieving Hot Spots on the World Wide Web. In *Proceedings of the Twenty-Ninth Annual ACM Symposium on Theory of Computing (STOC)*, pages 654–663, 1997.

[21] R. Katsumata, M. Kito, Y. Fukuzumi, M. Kido, H. Tanaka, Y. Komori, M. Ishiduki, J. Matsunami, T. Fujiwara, Y. Nagata, L. Zhang, Y. Iwata, R. Kirisawa, H. Aochi, and A. Nitayama. Pipe-Shaped BiCS Flash Memory with 16 Stacked Layers and Multi-Level-Cell Operation for Ultra High Density Storage Devices. In *Proceedings of the 2009 Symposium on VLSI Technology*, pages 136–137, 2009.

[22] T. Kgil and T. Mudge. FlashCache: A NAND Flash Memory File Cache for Low Power Web Servers. In *Proceedings of the 2006 International Conference on Compilers, Architecture and Synthesis for Embedded Systems (CASES)*, pages 103–112, 2006.

[23] T. Kgil, S. D'Souza, A. Saidi, N. Binkert, R. Dreslinski, T. Mudge, S. Reinhardt, and K. Flautner. PicoServer: Using 3D Stacking Technology To Enable A Compact Energy Efficient Chip Multiprocessor. In *Proceedings of the 12th International Conference on Architectural Support for Programming Languages and Operating Systems (ASPLOS)*, pages 117–128, 2006.

[24] T. Kgil, D. Roberts, and T. Mudge. Improving NAND Flash Based Disk Caches. In *Proceedings of the 35th Annual International Symposium on Computer Architecture (ISCA)*, pages 327–338, 2008.

[25] J.-S. Kim, C. S. Oh, H. Lee, D. Lee, H.-R. Hwang, S. Hwang, B. Na, J. Moon, J.-G. Kim, H. Park, J.-W. Ryu, K. Park, S.-K. Kang, S.-Y. Kim, H. Kim, J.-M. Bang, H. Cho, M. Jang, C. Han, J.-B. Lee, K. Kyung, J.-S. Choi, and Y.-H. Jun. A 1.2V 12.8GB/s 2Gb Mobile Wide-I/O DRAM with 4x128 I/Os Using TSV-Based Stacking. In *Proceedings of the 2011 IEEE International Solid-State Circuits Conference Digest of Technical Papers (ISSCC)*, pages 496–498, 2011.

[26] P. Kongetira, K. Aingaran, and K. Olukotun. Niagara: A 32-way multithreaded sparc processor. *IEEE Micro*, 25(2):21–29, 2005.

[27] H. Li and A. Michael. *Intel Motherboard Hardware v1.0*. Open Compute Project, 2013.

[28] K. Lim, P. Ranganathan, J. Chang, C. Patel, T. Mudge, and S. Reinhardt. Understanding and Designing New Server Architectures for Emerging Warehouse-Computing Environments. In *Proceedings of the 35th Annual International Symposium on Computer Architecture (ISCA)*, pages 315–326, 2008.

[29] K. Lim, D. Meisner, A. Saidi, P. Ranganathan, and T. Wenisch. Thin Servers with Smart Pipes: Designing SoC Accelerators for Memcached. In *Proceedings of the 40th Annual International Symposium on Computer Architecture (ISCA)*, 2013.

[30] P. Lotfi-Kamran, B. Grot, M. Ferdman, S. Volos, O. Kocberber, J. Picorel, A. Adileh, D. Jevdjic, S. Idgunji, E. Ozer, and B. Falsafi. Scale-Out Processors. In *Proceedings of the 39th Annual International Symposium on Computer Architecture (ISCA)*, pages 500–511, 2012.

[31] *SX1016 64-Port 10GbE SDN Switch System*. Mellanox Technologies, 2013.

[32] C. Metz. Facebook Data Center Empire to Conquer Heartland in 2014. `http://www.wired.com/wiredenterprise/2013/04/facebook-iowa-2014/`, 2013. Accessed: May 31, 2013.

[33] D. Milojevic, S. Idgunji, D. Jevdjic, E. Ozer, P. Lotfi-Kamran, A. Panteli, A. Prodromou, C. Nicopoulos, D. Hardy, B. Falsari, and Y. Sazeides. Thermal Characterization of Cloud Workloads on a Power-Efficient Server-on-Chip. In *Proceedings of the IEEE 30th International Conference on Computer Design (ICCD)*, pages 175–182, 2012.

[34] N. Muralimanohar, R. Balasubramonian, and N. Jouppi. Optimizing NUCA Organizations and Wiring Alternatives for Large Caches with CACTI 6.0. In *Proceedings of the 40th Annual IEEE/ACM International Symposium on Microarchitecture (MICRO)*, pages 3–14, 2007.

[35] G. Orzell and J. Becker. Auto Scaling in the Amazon Cloud. `http://techblog.netflix.com/2012/01/auto-scaling-in-amazon-cloud.html`, 2012. Accessed: May 29, 2013.

[36] J. Pawlowski. Hybrid Memory Cube: Breakthrough DRAM Performance with a Fundamentally Re-Architected DRAM Subsystem. In *Proceedings of the 23rd Hot Chips Symposium*, 2011.

[37] A. Press. Google to invest $300m in data center in Belgium. `http://finance.yahoo.com/news/google-invest-390m-data-center-081818916.html`, 2013. Accessed: May 31, 2013.

[38] V. J. Reddi, B. C. Lee, T. Chilimbi, and K. Vaid. Web Search Using Mobile Cores: Quantifying and Mitigating the Price of Efficiency. In *Proceedings of the 37th Annual International Symposium on Computer Architecture (ISCA)*, pages 314–325, 2010.

[39] D. Roberts, T. Kgil, and T. Mudge. Using Non-Volatile Memory to Save Energy in Servers. In *Proceedings of the 2009 Design, Automation Test in Europe Conference Exhibition (DATE)*, pages 743–748, 2009.

[40] T. Semiconductor. `http://www.tezzaron.com`. Accessed: May 29, 2013.

[41] I. Stoica, R. Morris, D. Karger, M. F. Kaashoek, and H. Balakrishnan. Chord: A Scalable Peer-to-peer Lookup Service for Internet Applications. In *Proceedings of the 2001 Conference on Applications, Technologies, Architectures, and Protocols for Computer Communications (SIGCOMM)*, pages 149–160, 2001.

[42] G. Whalin. Memcached Java Client. `http://github.com/gwhalin/Memcached-Java-Client`. Accessed: May 29, 2013.

[43] A. Wiggins and J. Langston. Enhancing the Scalability of Memcached. Technical report, Intel, 2012.

[44] Wireshark. `http://wireshark.org`. Accessed: July 1, 2013.

[45] M. Zuckerberg. Facebook and memcached. `http://www.facebook.com/video/video.php?v=631826881803`, 2008. Accessed: May 29, 2013.

# Deterministic Galois: On-demand, Portable and Parameterless *

Donald Nguyen Andrew Lenharth Keshav Pingali

The University of Texas at Austin, Texas, USA

{ddn@cs, lenharth@ices, pingali@cs}.utexas.edu

## Abstract

Non-determinism in program execution can make program development and debugging difficult. In this paper, we argue that solutions to this problem should be *on-demand, portable* and *parameterless*. On-demand means that the programming model should permit the writing of non-deterministic programs since these programs often perform better than deterministic ones for the same problem. Portable means that the program should produce the same answer even if it is run on different machines. Parameterless means that if there are machine-dependent scheduling parameters that must be tuned for good performance, they must not affect the output.

Although many solutions for deterministic program execution have been proposed in the literature, they fall short along one or more of these dimensions. To remedy this, we propose a new approach, based on the Galois programming model, in which (i) the programming model permits the writing of non-deterministic programs and (ii) the runtime system executes these programs deterministically if needed. Evaluation of this approach on a collection of benchmarks from the PARSEC, PBBS, and Lonestar suites shows that it delivers deterministic execution with substantially less overhead than other systems in the literature.

***Categories and Subject Descriptors*** D.3.3 [*Programming Languages*]: Concurrent programming structures

***Keywords*** Deterministic scheduling; Irregular programs; Multicore processors

* The work presented in this paper has been supported by NSF grants CCF 1337281, CCF 1218568, ACI 1216701, and CNS 1064956. Donald Nguyen was supported by a DOE Sandia Fellowship.



*ASPLOS '14*, March 1–4, 2014, Salt Lake City, Utah, USA.

ACM 978-1-4503-2305-5/14/03...$15.00.
http://dx.doi.org/10.1145/2541940.2541964

## 1. Introduction

Non-determinism in program execution can make program development and debugging difficult. A number of systems for executing parallel programs deterministically have been proposed recently.

Some solutions make programs deterministic by *construction* by restricting the programming model to prevent application developers from writing non-deterministic programs; data-parallel, stream and functional programming models are well-known examples [7, 9, 11, 27].

Other solutions provide determinism by *scheduling*: they permit developers to write non-deterministic programs but restrict the possible schedules of operations in these programs to ensure deterministic execution. These restrictions can be enforced at different levels of the execution stack including hardware [16, 17, 21], OS [2, 4], compiler [3], and software runtime [24, 25].

Ideally, a deterministic parallel system would provide the following three features.

- **On-demand determinism.** It should be possible to turn deterministic execution on and off without much effort. As we show in Section 5, deterministic execution often imposes a substantial runtime overhead, particularly for parallel programs with fine-grain tasks. This overhead may be acceptable in some cases, but it should be possible to turn off determinism when desired.
- **Portability.** The output of a deterministic program should be the same regardless of the machine that it runs on. At the very least, this means that the output should not depend on the number of executing threads. Portability ensures that programs enjoy the benefits of determinism even when moving between machines.
- **Parameter-freedom.** If there are scheduling parameters that must be tuned to achieve good performance, they should not affect the output state. Since optimal values for such parameters vary by machine, such scheduling parameters hinder portability by providing an incentive for producing different results on different machines.

No existing system for deterministic parallel execution currently provides on-demand determinism, portability and parameter-freedom.

Programming models such as DPJ [9], revisions with deterministic merges [11], StreamIt [27], and nested data-parallel programs [8] are deterministic by construction, but they are incompatible with on-demand determinism. Other programming models like Grace [5] are not deterministic by construction, but the output of a program may depend on the number of threads used to execute the program. There are deterministic programming models that have "escapes" that allow non-deterministic programs to be written, such as DPJ with non-determinism [10] and PBBS [7], but there is no convenient method for producing deterministic executions on demand from such programs.

When determinism is provided by scheduling, it is usually not portable. In hardware systems like RCDC [17] and Calvin [21], the number of threads is a fundamental part of program representation, and any deterministic execution is always with respect to a particular number of threads. At the OS and compiler level, it is possible to virtualize the concept of threads to achieve portability, but current systems such as Determinator [2], CoreDet [3] and dOS [4] do not do this. Runtime approaches are replacements for non-deterministic program libraries. Both DThreads [24] and Kendo [25] model the behavior of pthreads, an explicitly threaded library, and are not portable.

Finally, some of the above systems have user-tunable scheduling parameters that affect execution performance *and* output: examples are RCDC, CoreDet, Kendo, and PBBS.

In this paper, we present a deterministic parallel system that is on-demand, portable and parameter-free. It takes high-level, non-deterministic programs written in the Galois programming model [26] as input. These programs can be executed non-deterministically with the Galois runtime, or they can be executed deterministically using a technique that we call *deterministic interference graph (DIG) scheduling*. The application program does not have to change when switching between non-deterministic and deterministic scheduling since the desired scheduler is specified through a command-line parameter.

To evaluate the quality of our deterministic programs, we compare their performance with handwritten deterministic parallel programs from the PBBS benchmark suite [7]. Our results show a median performance of 0.62X compared to the handwritten PBBS implementations. To highlight the importance of on-demand determinism, we compare the performance of non-deterministic Galois programs with that of deterministic PBBS programs. The non-deterministic programs achieve a median improvement of 2.4X over the PBBS implementations.

In addition, we compare our DIG scheduling approach with a prior deterministic system, CoreDet [3], on non-deterministic PBBS programs. CoreDet can make any threaded program deterministic. The CoreDet execution achieves scaling for only one out of the four applications. This is because unlike the PARSEC benchmarks [6] commonly used to evaluate deterministic parallel systems, our benchmarks have much more synchronization and smaller task sizes, which severely taxes systems with high scheduling overheads.

```
foreach Task t in P:
  atomic:
    t() // execute task
    enqueue(S(t)) // enqueue new tasks, if any
```

**(a) Non-deterministic program.**

```
foreach Task t in P:
  if writeMarks(0, id(t), L(t)):
    // all writes successful
    t()
    enqueue(S(t))
  else:
    enqueue(t)
  writeMarks(id(t), 0, L(t))
```

**(b) Scheduling non-deterministic programs.**

**Figure 1: Non-deterministic program and scheduling (see Figure 3 for auxiliary function definitions).**

The rest of this paper is organized as follows. In Section 2, we describe the non-deterministic Galois programming model and provide a high-level overview of scheduling with interference graphs. In Section 3, we discuss the implementation of this approach in the Galois system. Section 4 summarizes the benchmarks used in the evaluation. In Section 5, we measure the performance of various deterministic and non-deterministic programs, as well as the performance of the programs with CoreDet. Section 6 summarizes related work, and Section 7 concludes the paper.

## 2. Galois programming model

The programming model used is an abstract version of the Galois programming model for unordered algorithms [26]. There are no explicitly parallel constructs like threads and locks; instead, parallelism is specified implicitly through the use of the iterator shown in Figure 1a. Key features are the following.

- $P$ is a pool of tasks that can be performed in *any* order. The program terminates when all tasks have been executed.
- When task $t$ is completed, it may create a set of new tasks $S(t)$, which are added to the task pool. Task $t$ is the *parent* of the tasks it creates; the transitive closure of the parent relation is called the *ancestor* relation.
- Each task performs computation and reads and writes shared-memory locations. The set of locations read $R(t)$ and written $W(t)$ by a task $t$ is said to constitute its *neighborhood*, which is denoted by $L(t) = R(t) \cup W(t)$.

Tasks are required to be *cautious*: that is, a task must read all of the locations in its neighborhood before it can write to any of them.

- A *conflict* occurs between tasks $t_1$ and $t_2$ if (i) neither task is an ancestor of the other, and (ii) one of them writes to the neighborhood of the other ($W(t_1) \cap L(t_2) \neq \emptyset$). If there can be no conflicts between tasks, parallel execution is straightforward since the program is a generalized data-parallel loop in which the iteration range can grow dynamically. In the presence of conflicts, a correct parallel schedule for the program should be serializable: it must appear as if all tasks were performed atomically in some order that respects the ancestor relation.

Although neighborhoods can be defined as sets of concrete memory locations, it is better to define them as sets of *abstract* memory locations; for example, for a graph algorithm, these abstract locations might correspond to graph elements such as nodes and edges of the graph, rather than to the concrete memory locations implementing this abstract data type. The Galois runtime system implements synchronization by associating abstract locks or marks with abstract locations (§2.1).

### 2.1 Non-deterministic scheduling

In most programs, neighborhoods of tasks are not known statically. One parallelization strategy is to use speculative execution: a free thread selects an arbitrary task from the task pool $P$ and executes it, rolling back the task if a conflict with another concurrently executing task is detected. Tracking of neighborhoods can be done using a transactional-memory-like approach over abstract memory locations [19, 20].

For programming models with cautious tasks, conflict detection and correction can be done using much lighter weight mechanisms because the synchronization problem reduces to the well-known dining philosopher's problem [12]. Conceptually, each abstract location can be *acquired* by an owner. The execution of a task can be divided into two phases: in the first phase, a task reads locations but does not write to any of them, acquiring ownership of these locations, and in the second phase, the task writes to some locations, but it does not write to any location that it did not read in the first phase. The point between the first and second phase is called the *failsafe point*. For cautious tasks, conflicts are detected in the first phase, and rollback is implemented simply by releasing ownership of all locations. Once the failsafe point has been crossed, global data structures can be updated in place without the need for backup copies of modified data.

Figure 1b implements this idea for non-deterministic task scheduling. For each abstract memory location $l$, we maintain a mark location Mark($l$). Each task $t$ has a unique id id($t$), and there is an id 0 that is distinct from all other ids. For this implementation, ids need only be unique. For the deterministic scheduler below (§3), ids must also have a total order, and 0 must be less than any other id. Mark locations initially contain the value 0. The scheduler chooses a task $t$ and tries to acquire ownership of all the locations in the neighborhood of that task, using compare-and-set instructions for example. If successful, the task executes and adds new tasks $S(t)$ to the pool. If unsuccessful, there is a conflict, and the scheduler adds $t$ back to the pool for re-execution. In either case, any marks acquired are reset back to 0.

## 3. Deterministic scheduling

In this section, we describe our implementation of deterministic scheduling. It is based on finding independent sets in an implicitly constructed *interference graph* of tasks. We first describe the high-level idea (§3.1), then its implementation (§3.2), and finally some important optimizations (§3.3).

### 3.1 DIG scheduling

**Definition 1.** *Given a set of tasks $P$, an* interference graph *for $P$ is an undirected graph $G_P = (V_P, E_P)$ in which there is a distinct node in $V_P$ representing each task in $P$, and there is an undirected edge $(v_1, v_2) \in E_P$ if the tasks represented by $v_1$ and $v_2$ have a conflict.*

The interference graph for a set of tasks can be built by executing each task up to its failsafe point while tracking its neighborhood and putting a conflict edge between two tasks if their neighborhoods overlap. This is a conservative approach since it puts a conflict edge between two tasks even if they both read a location that neither of them writes to. Program analysis can be used to determine conflicts more accurately; for the purposes of this paper, any conservative interference graph is adequate.

Interference graphs can be used to schedule tasks as follows. The tasks in the task pool $P$ are executed in *rounds*. In each round, the scheduler performs the following activities:

- *inspect:* build an interference graph $G_P$ for the tasks in $P$,
- *select:* find an *independent set* $\mathcal{I}$ of nodes in $G_P$ and remove the corresponding tasks from $P$, and
- *execute:* execute the tasks in $\mathcal{I}$ in parallel, adding any newly created tasks to $P$.

Scheduling is completed when all tasks have been executed. During the *select* phase, it is desirable but not necessary to find a maximal independent set of nodes in the graph.

A subtle point is that the interference graph must in general be rebuilt from scratch each round since the neighborhood of a task is relative to the global state, which is modified by tasks in the *execute* phase.

There is one enhancement to this basic scheme that is useful for reducing the overhead of interference graph construction. Note that the scheduling strategy works correctly even if, in each round, the interference graph is constructed only for a subset of tasks in the pool; the remaining tasks are simply delayed to later rounds. This *windowing* scheme can reduce the overhead of interference graph construction

```
1  Tasks cur, next, todo
2  todo = P;
3  while ||todo|| > 0:
4    // order tasks in todo deterministically
5    next = sort(todo)
6    todo = {}
7    // execute sorted tasks
8    while ||next|| > 0: // for each round...
9      calculateWindow()
10     barrier
11     // get prefix of size window from next
12     cur,next = getWindowOfTasks(next)
13     // compute neighborhoods of tasks in cur
14     inspect(cur)
15     barrier
16     // execute successful tasks, move
17     // failed tasks to next, and add any
18     // newly created tasks to todo set
19     todo = todo ∪ selectAndExec(cur, next)
20     barrier
```

**Figure 2: Deterministic scheduler.**

when the number of tasks is much larger than the number of threads. For the windowed scheduler to be deterministic, we must also ensure the following in each round: (i) tasks for the current window are chosen deterministically from the task pool, and (ii) during the select phase, the independent set of nodes is chosen deterministically.

### 3.2 Implementation of DIG scheduling

Figure 2 shows the pseudocode for the implementation of deterministic scheduling; auxiliary functions are shown in Figure 3. In the pseudocode, **doall** indicates a loop whose iterations are run in parallel. Instead of explicitly building an interference graph, this code directly finds an independent set of tasks by using marks on locations.

A summary of what the scheduler does is the following. The task set *todo* is initialized to the initial set of tasks *P*. These tasks are ordered deterministically to form a sequence *next*. This sequence of tasks is executed over several rounds; in each round, a prefix *cur* of tasks in *next* is tried for execution. Some of these will succeed and others may fail. Tasks created by successful tasks are added to *todo*; these are executed after *next* becomes empty. Failed tasks are added back to *next* and retried in later rounds. Execution terminates when *todo* and *next* become empty.

Some important implementation details are the following.

The *inspect* operation uses *writeMarksMax* to mark the neighborhood of a task, stealing ownership of neighborhood locations from tasks with lower ids. While the mark on a given location may be updated non-deterministically depending on how the tasks in *cur* are scheduled, the final mark will be the same regardless of the order in which tasks were processed in the inspect phase. This is because computing the maximum (or minimum) element of a set with a total order is deterministic (the set in question is the set of

```
Tasks sort(Tasks todo):
  // sort tasks in set todo

void inspect(Tasks cur):
  doall t in cur:
    writeMarksMax(id(t), L(t))

Tasks selectAndExec(Tasks cur, Tasks next):
  Tasks newWork = {}
  doall t in cur:
    if readMarks(L(t)) = {id(t)}:
      // all reads equal id, so execute task t
      t()
      // add new work if any to newWork
      newWork = newWork ∪ S(t)
    else:
      next = next ∪ t
    writeMarks(id(t), 0, L(t))
  return newWork


bool writeMarks(Id expected, Id id, Set<Loc> locs):
  for loc in locs:
    atomic:
      if Mark(loc) == expected:
        Mark(loc) = id
      else: return false
  return true

void writeMarksMax(Id id, Set<Loc> locs):
  for loc in locs:
    atomic:
      if Mark(loc) < id:
        Mark(loc) = id

Set<Id> readMarks(Set<Loc> locs):
  // return set of ids in mark locations
```

**Figure 3: Auxiliary functions for deterministic scheduler.**

ids of the tasks that read or wrote to a particular location in the current round). The cumulative effect of the writeMarkMax operations implicitly creates an interference graph. An edge in the interference graph exists between tasks $t_1$ and $t_2$ if id$(t_2) \in$ readMarks$(L(t_1))$.

One important difference between writeMarks and writeMarksMax is that writeMarks can fail early if it cannot update a mark location, but in order to be deterministic, writeMarksMax must attempt to update all mark locations even if it failed to update some of them. If a task skips some mark locations, it changes the set that writeMarksMax is computing the maximum of, and if the mark locations skipped depend on a scheduling choice, then the resulting maximums are non-deterministic.

In the second phase, the scheduler selects and executes an independent set of tasks (line 19 in Figure 2 and function selectAndExec in Figure 3). A task is selected if all of its neighborhood locations are still marked with its id at the end of the inspection phase. Tasks selected this way form an independent set in the interference graph. This set is unique because of the total order on ids. If any of the neighborhood locations of a task does not contain its id, the task is not part of the independent set, and it is placed in the *next* set to be executed in a future round. In either case, the marks written by a task are cleared in preparation for the next round.

Execution continues in rounds until there are no tasks left in *next*. If there are no tasks in the *todo* set, the scheduler terminates; otherwise these tasks are moved to *next*, and execution continues. Note that in each round, the task in *cur* with maximum id is guaranteed to execute, so each round executes at least one task.

Before enqueued tasks can be scheduled, they must be assigned a unique id. The assignment of ids must also be deterministic. Ids are assigned as follows. The initial tasks are given ids based on the iteration order of the C++ iterator that contains the tasks. When task $t$ creates task $u$, the scheduler stores with task $u$ the id of the task that created it id($t$) and a number $k$ indicating whether it was the first, second, third, etc. task created by $t$. In the sort function, tasks are sorted lexicographically based on the pair $(\text{id}(t), k)$, and the scheduler uses the position in the total order defined by the sort as the id for the new tasks.

The performance of this scheduler depends critically on the window size, so we implemented an adaptive algorithm that grows and shrinks the window size each round depending on the number of tasks that successfully committed in the previous round. The getWindowOfTasks and calculateWindow functions in Figure 2 implement this functionality. The calculateWindow function computes the window size for the current round based on the fraction of tasks that committed in the previous round. If the commit ratio is less than some target threshold, the next window size is scaled down proportionally. If the commit ratio is above the threshold, the window size is doubled. The getWindowOfTasks function simply returns this prefix of tasks in *cur* and postpones the remainder to *next*. Since the number of tasks that commit in a round is independent of the number of executing threads, this heuristic is portable across machines.

To implement the deterministic marking scheme in the Galois system, we make two changes to the existing system.

First, the default mark values in the Galois system are not ordered. We modify the marking code to keep track of the id of a task and to use that value appropriately when writing mark values.

Second, neighborhoods are not explicitly maintained by the Galois system. Marks are acquired incrementally during execution via user code calls to a data structure library. The only way to get the neighborhood of a task is to execute the task and observe which marks are acquired. To implement the inspect phase, we simply execute a task, which, by its normal execution, marks locations in its neighborhood. When the task reaches its failsafe point (the first write to a global location), it immediately returns. To implement the selectAndExec phase, we re-execute the task from the beginning, and instead of writing marks, we check whether the marks that we would have written match the values that have been written. This implements line 11 of Figure 3. If a task reads a mark value that is not its id, we go to line 17.

This baseline implementation is sufficient to deterministically schedule any program written in the programming model of Figure 1a.

### 3.3 Optimizations

The baseline deterministic scheduler described in Section 3.2 contains several inefficiencies, which we now address.

First, it redundantly executes the prefix of a task up to its failsafe point when a task is selected and executed. A more efficient method would be to suspend execution of a task at the failsafe point during the inspect phase and to resume execution in the commit phase. On resumption, the task must check that all the mark values still match its id (Figure 3 line 11). The capability to pause and resume execution can be achieved generally using additional threads or creating continuations. In our optimized implementation, we use a more ad-hoc approach, which simulates the effect of forming a continuation without implementing a full compiler transform. We provide a library function that allows users to allocate objects in the inspect phase which can be recalled during the commit phase. Programmers can use this functionality to manually achieve the same effect as task suspend and resume.

To make sure that resumed tasks are valid to commit, we make a small change to the protocol in the inspect phase. Instead of just writing the maximum mark value, a task $t$ checks if the previous value of the mark location is not 0 and not id($t$); if so, by writing its mark, task $t$ will prevent the task $u$ that corresponds to the current mark value from committing. Normally, task $u$ detects this case when the scheduler executes line 11, or in the case of the baseline scheduler, when task $u$ is executed a second time. When using the continuation optimization, $t$ is now responsible for preventing $u$ from executing. It does this by writing to a flag variable that $u$ checks before resuming execution.

Second, the performance of the scheduler is very sensitive to initial task order. Applications that exploit temporal locality execute tasks with overlapping neighborhoods close in time. This typically translates to those tasks being close together in iteration order, which, in the baseline scheduler implementation, means that they typically will be executed in the same round, where they will certainly conflict with each other. This leads to the perverse situation where the scheduler needs to reduce locality to improve performance. We address this issue by assuming that tasks placed close together in iteration order have high locality and place those tasks in separate rounds if possible.

Third, the cost of sorting enqueued tasks can be large relative to the application time. There is a common special case where a task enqueues tasks, but those tasks are drawn from a fixed set of tasks. In this case, tasks can be assigned unique ids before parallel execution, and the programmer can pass these ids to the scheduler, which uses them directly instead of generating new ids via the sort function.

### 3.4 Comparison of non-deterministic and deterministic schedulers

Compared to the non-deterministic scheduling in Section 2.1, DIG scheduling adds several overheads, whose performance impact we evaluate in Section 5.

- As seen in Figures 1b and 2, the deterministic scheduler executes many more instructions.
- The deterministic scheduler introduces a concept of rounds that is not present in the original program. These rounds are implemented using global synchronization. Rounds extend the critical path length of a program because the scheduler cannot proceed to the next round until all of the tasks are processed for the current round.
- The scheduler executes tasks according to a particular schedule, but that schedule may not be the best performing one among possible program schedules.
- The execution of a task is broken into two parts, the inspect phase and the execution phase, separated by a barrier. The memory locations accessed during the inspect phase of a task are very likely to be accessed by the execution phase of the same task, but under DIG scheduling, these two phases are temporally separated by a factor that is a function of number of tasks attempted during a round, which is typically very large. Conversely, increasing locality by reducing the number tasks attempted in a round, increases the number of rounds executed, which increases the critical path length of the program.

## 4. Experimental setup

### 4.1 Applications

The benchmarks in our study are drawn from three different sources: the PARSEC (v2.1) benchmark suite [6], the problem based benchmark suite (PBBS) (v0.1) [7], and the Lonestar (v2.1.5) benchmark suite [22].

***PARSEC*** The PARSEC benchmark suite has been used in previous evaluations of deterministic scheduling [3, 17, 24]. It contains twelve applications or kernels. Most are parallelized using the pthreads library. We chose the three benchmarks that have OpenMP implementations: **blackscholes**, **bodytrack** and **freqmine**.

***PBBS*** The PBBS programs [7] are organized by problem, and each problem has one or more solution programs, at least one of which is deterministic. There are a total of sixteen problems, but many of these programs are data-parallel or nested data-parallel, and their performance depends largely on factors like good load balancing, which is not the subject of this paper. We therefore excluded them from our study. We chose deterministic programs that solved the four remaining problems: breadth-first search (**bfs**), Delaunay triangulation (**dt**), Delaunay mesh refinement (**dmr**), and maximal independent set (**mis**). We exclude maximal matching because of its similarity to maximal independent set. In these codes, determinism is ensured by application-specific techniques customized to each application, and they typically involve bulk-synchronous execution in rounds. The PBBS maximal independent set program is data-parallel, but we have included it in our study for comparison with a non-deterministic maximal independent set program that exists in the Lonestar suite.

***Lonestar*** From the Lonestar benchmark suite, we selected four programs that solve the same problems as those we included from PBBS, using the same algorithms, and an implementation of the preflow-push algorithm (**pfp**) that uses the global relabeling heuristic to improve convergence [13]. We automatically generate deterministic implementations of all Lonestar programs by applying the DIG scheduling of Section 3, including the optimizations of Section 3.3.

There is one small difference between the PBBS and Lonestar implementations of Delaunay triangulation (dt). The algorithmic complexity of Delaunay triangulation depends on the order in which points are inserted, and random insertion order has been shown to be optimal [14]. In the PBBS implementation, points are randomized offline. In the Lonestar implementation, points are reordered online using the biased randomized insertion order algorithm [1]. For comparison purposes, we do not include the reordering time in either implementation.

As mentioned above, the Lonestar maximal independent set program is non-deterministic while the PBBS version is data-parallel.

***Application variants*** In the experimental results, the variant **g-n** denotes the original non-deterministic Lonestar application, and the deterministic variant generated from DIG scheduling is called **g-d**. The variant **PBBS** denotes the PBBS version of the application.

### 4.2 Data-sets

For the PARSEC benchmarks, we use the simlarge inputs for blackscholes and freqmine and the native input for bodytrack.

The performance of the PBBS and Lonestar benchmarks can vary significantly with the type of input. In our experience, the behavior across random inputs for an application is largely similar, so we choose a single representative input for each application. These inputs are largely drawn from the evaluation of Blelloch et al. [7]. For bfs, we use a random graph of 10 million nodes where each node is connected to five randomly selected nodes. For dmr, we use a Delaunay triangulated mesh of 2.5 million randomly selected points from the unit square. For dt, we use 10 million points randomly selected from a unit square. For mis, we use the same input as bfs. For pfp, we use a random graph of $2^{23}$ nodes with each node connected to 4 random neighbors.

### 4.3 Platforms

We use three machines in our evaluations and take the average of at least three runs for each application/machine/thread-count combination. The three machines are (i) **m4x10**, a machine running Ubuntu Linux 10.04 LTS 64-bit (Linux 2.6.32) with four ten-core Intel Xeon E7-4860 (2.27 GHz) processors; (ii) **m4x6**, a machine running Ubuntu Linux 10.04 LTS 64-bit (Linux 2.6.32) with four six-core Intel Xeon E7540 (2.0 GHz) processors; and (iii) **numa8x4**, an SGI UV machine (ccNUMA) running SuSE Enterprise 11 SP1 64-bit (Linux 2.6.32.24) with eight four-core Intel E7520 (1.87 GHz) processors. The processors of numa8x4 are divided into blades of two processors each and enclosures of two blades each. Inter-blade communication uses SGI NUMALink 5.

We compile the PBBS and Lonestar programs with icc version 12.1 with the -O3 optimization flag. For the PBBS programs, we use the Cilk runtime to manage and load balance threads. For the Lonestar programs, we use the Galois runtime system.

## 5. Evaluation

In Section 5.1, we describe applications characteristics useful for understanding the performance results.

In Section 5.2, we compare the performance of non-deterministic programs with their performance when executed with CoreDet [3], a system that provides determinism by scheduling. Because the C++ language primitives used in the Lonestar programs are not supported by CoreDet, we used non-deterministic versions of the PBBS programs as our representative non-deterministic benchmarks. We show that with CoreDet, the non-deterministic PBBS programs do not perform well and have a median slowdown of 3.7X (min: 1.3X, max: 55X) compared to running without CoreDet. These experiments show that systems like CoreDet that provide determinism through deterministic thread scheduling are not suitable for irregular applications, which have relatively fine-grain tasks.

In Section 5.3, we compare the performance of non-deterministic Galois programs (g-n), generated deterministic implementations of these Galois programs (g-d), and handwritten deterministic PBBS programs for the same problems. Overall, our results show that at the maximum number of threads on each machine, (i) g-n variants achieve a median improvement of 4.2X compared to g-d, (ii) g-n variants are 2.4X faster than the PBBS variants, and (iii) g-d variants are only 0.62X slower than the PBBS variants.

These results show that the automatically generated deterministic Galois programs are comparable in performance to the handwritten PBBS programs and that there is a significant performance penalty for deterministic execution. A study with performance counters in Section 5.4 reveals that, for the most part, non-deterministic programs perform better than deterministic ones because they exploit more locality.

| | | | $p=1$ | | $p=40$ | |
|---|---|---|---|---|---|---|
| | Variant | Rounds | Abort Ratio | Tasks per $\mu s$ | Abort Ratio | Tasks per $\mu s$ |
| bfs | g-d | 1700 | 0.08 | 0.45 | 0.08 | 9.76 |
| bfs | g-n | 0 | 0 | 1.32 | 0 | 39.92 |
| bfs | pbbs | 11 | 0 | 1.24 | 0 | 24.27 |
| dmr | g-d | 1287 | 0.11 | 0.13 | 0.11 | 2.53 |
| dmr | g-n | 0 | 0 | 0.26 | $<0.01$ | 8.98 |
| dmr | pbbs | 1165 | 0.03 | 0.18 | 0.03 | 2.90 |
| dt | g-d | 35213 | 0.27 | 0.12 | 0.27 | 1.78 |
| dt | g-n | 0 | 0 | 0.24 | $<0.01$ | 7.47 |
| dt | pbbs | 1330 | 0.10 | 0.11 | 0.10 | 2.48 |
| mis | g-d | 100 | 0.08 | 0.77 | 0.08 | 21.05 |
| mis | g-n | 0 | 0 | 3.98 | $<0.01$ | 79.69 |
| mis | pbbs | 29 | 0.05 | 14.59 | 0.05 | 143.12 |
| pfp | g-d | 21047 | 0.04 | 0.26 | 0.04 | 2.58 |
| pfp | g-n | 0 | 0 | 0.67 | $<0.01$ | 14.99 |

**Figure 4: Abort ratio and task execution rates on machine m4x10.**

| | | $p=1$ | | $p=40$ | |
|---|---|---|---|---|---|
| | Variant | Count | Rate | Count | Rate |
| mis | pbbs | $<1$ | $<0.01$ | $<1$ | $<0.01$ |
| freqmine | | $<1$ | $<0.01$ | $<1$ | $<0.01$ |
| bodytrack | | $<1$ | $<0.01$ | 15 | 0.07 |
| dt | pbbs | 1445 | 0.55 | 1522 | 0.66 |
| blackscholes | | $<1$ | $<0.01$ | 48 | 0.77 |
| bfs | pbbs | 7191 | 1.24 | 7162 | 1.36 |
| dmr | pbbs | 2360 | 1.00 | 2634 | 1.37 |
| pfp | g-n | 4622 | 2.24 | 1519 | 27.57 |
| dmr | g-n | 707 | 1.59 | 583 | 36.21 |
| dt | g-n | 1376 | 3.10 | 920 | 79.94 |
| mis | g-n | 19292 | 10.27 | 4628 | 100.17 |

**Figure 5: Atomic updates by application measured by binary instrumentation on machine m4x10. Variant g-d omitted. Count is atomic updates per million instructions executed. Rate is atomic updates per microsecond.**

### 5.1 Application characteristics

The first set of measurements is concerned with the parallel behavior of applications, such as task granularity, frequency of synchronization, and how often inter-task conflicts occur during execution. These metrics are of interest for the following reasons.

Previous evaluations of deterministic scheduling have focused mostly on applications with coarse-grain tasks that communicate relatively infrequently. Deterministic scheduling for these kinds of applications can be supported using relatively heavyweight mechanisms since the overhead of the system is a small fraction of the overall execution time. However, these mechanisms may not be useful for applications with very lightweight tasks that communicate frequently. On a shared-memory system, the concept of communication is less well-defined compared to a distributed system, but one approximation is the number of atomic updates an application performs. Figures 4 and 5 show task execution rates, abort ratios, and atomic update rates for our applications on 1 thread and 40 threads on machine m4x10. For the deterministic variants, the number of rounds is also shown. For PBBS variants, this is the number of bulk-synchronous rounds of the handwritten deterministic scheduling.

First, we see that the PBBS and Lonestar benchmarks have very fine-grain tasks. For example, the g-n version of dmr, running on one thread, commits 0.26 tasks per microsecond (see Figure 4), which translates to 3.8 microseconds per task (this is the parallel version of the code with synchronization, running on one thread), which is on the order of a thousand cycles. On 40 threads, this parallel program commits roughly 9 tasks per microsecond, which translates to a throughput of roughly 0.11 microseconds per task.

Second, we see that the abort ratios of the g-n variants of all applications are essentially zero even at 40 threads. Conflicts between tasks in the non-deterministic variants are very rare: this is because there are a large number of tasks compared to the number of threads. The deterministic variants g-d and PBBS have larger abort ratios because in each round, the number of tasks whose neighborhoods are inspected is typically larger than the number of threads. Conflicts can also happen with only one thread when two tasks with overlapping neighborhoods are inspected in the same round.

Third, the PARSEC benchmarks—blackscholes, bodytrack and freqmine, which are frequently used to evaluate deterministic schedulers—have orders of magnitude fewer atomic updates than the irregular algorithms of the PBBS and Lonestar suites (see Figure 5). For example, blackscholes at 40 threads performs atomic updates at a rate of about 1 update per microsecond, while the mis g-n variant performs atomic updates at the rate of 100 updates per microsecond.

These qualitative differences in application characteristics significantly impact the design of deterministic schedulers, as we show in the following sections.

### 5.2 Deterministic thread scheduling

In this section, we present performance results from using CoreDet, a deterministic thread scheduler, on our benchmark applications. Unlike DIG scheduling, CoreDet runs on unmodified pthread programs.

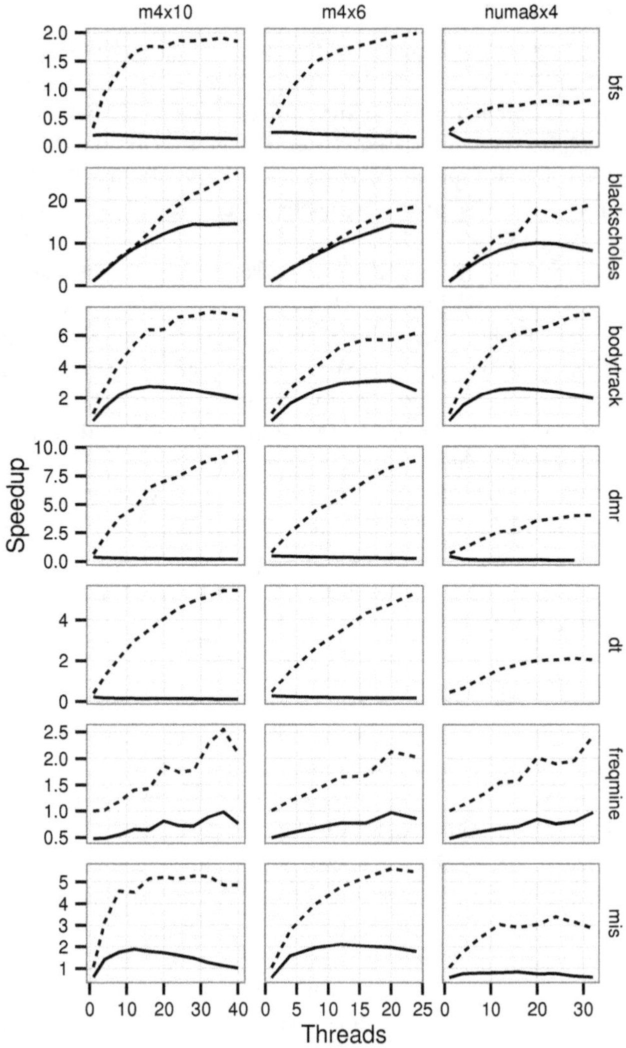


**Figure 6: Speedup with (solid lines) and without (dotted lines) CoreDet system on non-deterministic programs. Speedup baselines are in Figure 8. Some dmr and dt runs on numa8x4 timed out after 10 minutes.**

Ideally, we would like to run the PARSEC and g-n non-deterministic programs with CoreDet to make them deterministic. Unfortunately, the CoreDet compiler is based on the older LLVM 2.6 compiler, and it is unable to compile any of the g-n programs. To get around this problem, we exploit the fact that bfs, dmr and dt in PBBS are deterministic implementations of non-deterministic algorithms. To make them non-deterministic, we transform the programs by hand to match the non-deterministic program pattern shown in Figure 1 and run these with CoreDet. We leave the mis benchmark as a data-parallel program.

We use the CoreDet system in low-overhead, synchronization-only mode, which reduces the system to an implementation of the Kendo algorithm [25] and requires all synchronization between threads to use the pthread library.

For all our CoreDet comparisons, we replace calls to the OpenMP or Cilk runtimes with calls to a simple pthread-only runtime. The simple pthread-only runtime likely introduces minor inefficiencies compared to the more optimized Cilk and OpenMP runtimes, but they are dwarfed by the overheads of CoreDet. We used the LLVM 2.6 compiler with the -O3 optimization flag to compile programs.

Figure 6 summarizes our results using the CoreDet system to make PARSEC and modified PBBS programs deterministic. CoreDet works well for blackscholes: the performance with CoreDet is almost the same as without CoreDet for a small number of threads. As the number of threads increases, the gap between using CoreDet and not using CoreDet increases, hinting at a serialization bottleneck in the deterministic scheduler. The bodytrack and freqmine applications show more limited speedups. For the modified PBBS programs, the performance with CoreDet is poor except for mis, the data-parallel code. The bfs, dmr and dt applications perform substantially more synchronization than the PARSEC applications and the mis code (§5.1). Overall, at the maximum number of threads on each machine, the benchmarks in this suite experience a median slowdown of 3.7X (min: 1.3X, max: 55X) compared to non-CoreDet runs.

Although this evaluation uses CoreDet, the other deterministic thread schedulers that we are familiar with such as Kendo and DThreads have similar scheduling algorithms and differ mainly in how they deal with racy data accesses, which none of the modified PBBS programs have.

*These results make the case that a different approach than deterministic thread scheduling is needed to handle applications that perform orders of magnitude more synchronization than more conventional programs like the PARSEC benchmarks.*

### 5.3 End-to-end performance of g-n, g-d and PBBS

Figure 7 shows the speedups of g-n, g-d and PBBS relative to the best performing serial implementations shown in Figure 8. For bfs, the baseline is the highly optimized code of Schardl and Leiserson that uses data structures customized to the bfs problem [23]. For preflow-push, we use the highly optimized hi_pr implementation from Goldberg and Tarjan [18]. For the other benchmarks, the best performing versions that we were able to find were from the benchmark suites considered in this paper.

Figure 7 shows that the best performing variant overall is g-n with a median improvement of 2.4X over corresponding PBBS programs at the maximum number of threads on each machine. The benefit is largest on the numa8x4 machine where the scalability of the PBBS variant is particularly poor, but there are positive benefits for almost all non-deterministic variants. Figure 7 suggests that there are also significant scalability advantages to the non-deterministic variants compared to the deterministic ones. The g-n variants are able to achieve at least a 15X speedup on m4x10 for four of the five applications.

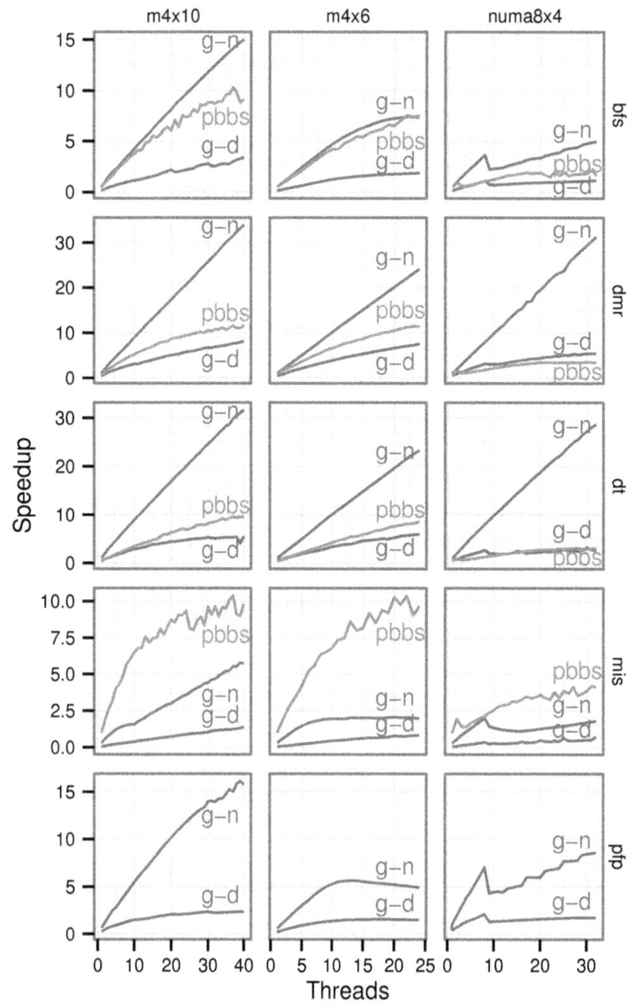


**Figure 7: Speedup for selected deterministic and non-deterministic variants. Speedup baselines are in Figure 8.**

| | Machine | Var. | Time (s) | | Machine | Var. | Time (s) |
|---|---|---|---|---|---|---|---|
| bfs | m4x10 | cilk | 3.76 | dt | m4x10 | g-nd | 42.35 |
| bfs | m4x6 | cilk | 4.36 | dt | m4x6 | g-nd | 56.37 |
| bfs | numa8x4 | cilk | 4.85 | dt | numa8x4 | g-nd | 61.15 |
| bs | m4x10 | | 8.42 | fm | m4x10 | | 7.95 |
| bs | m4x6 | | 11.27 | fm | m4x6 | | 10.57 |
| bs | numa8x4 | | 12.01 | fm | numa8x4 | | 11.33 |
| bt | m4x10 | | 164.84 | mis | m4x10 | pbbs | 0.72 |
| bt | m4x6 | | 216.31 | mis | m4x6 | pbbs | 0.90 |
| bt | numa8x4 | | 249.07 | mis | numa8x4 | pbbs | 0.91 |
| dmr | m4x10 | g-nd | 44.48 | pfp | m4x10 | hi_pr | 13.64 |
| dmr | m4x6 | g-nd | 60.04 | pfp | m4x6 | hi_pr | 14.64 |
| dmr | numa8x4 | g-nd | 63.29 | pfp | numa8x4 | g-nd | 26.17 |

**Figure 8: Baseline times in seconds for speedup calculations (bs: blackscholes, bt: bodytrack, fm: freqmine). These are the best times for any variant with one thread. Cilk is a parallel bfs code [23]. hi_pr is a sequential implementation of pfp [18].**

The main outlier in these results is the behavior of mis. As mentioned above, the PBBS variant of mis is a data-parallel program, and its execution characteristics are significantly different than the g-n or g-d variants. The main conclusion from this benchmark is that if one has a deterministic algorithm for some problem, it may be better to use that algorithm rather than deterministically schedule a non-deterministic algorithm for the same problem. However, as we will see in Section 5.4, the PBBS variant is more sensitive to input ordering than g-n.

The sharp drop in performance at eight threads in some of the numa8x4 runs is caused by inter-NUMA node communication. Runs of eight threads or less are scheduled to run on a single NUMA node. Runs with more than eight threads use more than one NUMA node, and remote memory accesses are significantly more expensive than local memory accesses. The g-n variants for dmr and dt are able to tolerate the transition to inter-node communication due to locality optimizations in the Galois runtime system. Exploiting locality may be difficult in deterministically scheduled programs, as we describe in Section 5.4.

*We conclude that for irregular applications, determinism comes at a significant price in performance, even if the determinism is obtained through hand-optimized, application-specific code.*

We note that a previous study by Blelloch et al. [7] reached the opposite conclusion; for example, they found that the deterministic PBBS version of dt was substantially faster than the non-deterministic dt program in the Lonestar suite. Unfortunately, their study did not ensure that the same algorithm was used for a given problem; in particular, the dt algorithm in the PBBS suite is different (and more efficient) than the one that was used in the Lonestar suite at the time their study was performed. For the study in this paper, we reimplemented in the Lonestar suite the dt algorithm used in PBBS, so in our measurements, the performance differences between non-deterministic and deterministic programs for a given problem are not entangled with algorithmic differences.

***DIG scheduling vs. determinism by construction*** How good is the general-purpose deterministic scheduler described in Figure 2 compared to the application-specific, hand-optimized deterministic code in the PBBS programs? Figure 9 shows the performance for different variants relative to the same baseline, the PBBS variant.

Across all machines and benchmarks and at the maximum number of threads ($I_{max}$), the median performance of the g-d variant relative to PBBS is 0.62X. If we drop mis from the set of benchmarks, the median performance is 0.70X.

*We conclude that the general-purpose deterministic scheduler described in Figure 2 provides reasonable performance compared to application-specific, hand-optimized determinism by construction code, although there is room for improvement.*

For dmr and dt, the PBBS variants correspond to a handwritten version of DIG scheduling of the g-nd variants. We believe the performance difference between the g-d and PBBS variants is largely due to the application-specific implementation of resuming tasks and the handtuned window selection policy used in PBBS. It would be interesting to study whether a compiler could optimize the generic code of Figure 2 and provide tuned implementations for each application.

***Impact of continuation optimization*** The g-d variants use the continuation optimization described in Section 3.3, which requires some user input to form proper continuations (this transformation could be done by a compiler, but we have not implemented this yet). To weigh the effect of this optimization, we measure the performance of programs without this optimization. Overall, the continuation optimization provides a median improvement of 1.14X for our deterministic programs. As seen in Figure 10, the continuation optimization provides a significant improvement only for the relatively more complicated dmr and dt programs.

### 5.4 Determinism and locality

In Section 3.4, we describe how DIG scheduling can decrease the performance of an application relative to its non-deterministic implementation. In this section, we quantify two of those costs. First, DIG scheduling can make it more difficult to exploit locality, and second, DIG scheduling can reduce existing locality.

***Performance counter measurements for locality*** As mentioned in Section 3.4, DIG scheduling decreases locality by splitting a task, which might have significant intra-task locality, into two phases well-separated in time. We can quantify the impact of this transformation by measuring performance counter information about memory-level events.

Figure 11 gives the number of data requests satisfied from DRAM for the g-n, g-d, and PBBS versions of our applications. The non-deterministic variants typically have far fewer samples than the deterministic ones, but is the change in samples enough to explain the difference in performance?

One way to answer this question is to see how the observed data fits a simple model of performance. Let efficiency be speedup normalized by the number of threads. One simple model is that there is a linear relationship between the change in efficiency and the change of some performance counter. Symbolically, let $\text{eff}_{\text{var}}$ and $\text{PC}_{\text{var}}$ be the efficiency and performance counter value, respectively, of some application variant with some number of threads on a machine, and let $\text{eff}_{\text{ref}}$ and $\text{PC}_{\text{ref}}$ be the likewise for a particular reference variant of the same application with the same number of threads. We would like to know how well the following linear model fits the observed data

$$\text{eff}_{\text{var}} = B_0 + B_1(\text{PC}_{\text{ref}}/\text{PC}_{\text{var}})\text{eff}_{\text{ref}}.$$

|  |  | m4x10 |  |  |  | m4x6 |  |  |  | numa8x4 |  |  |  |
|---|---|---|---|---|---|---|---|---|---|---|---|---|---|
|  | Variant | Mean | Max | $I_1$ | $I_{max}$ | Mean | Max | $I_1$ | $I_{max}$ | Mean | Max | $I_1$ | $I_{max}$ |
| bfs | g-n | 1.28 | 1.68 | 1.07 | 1.64 | 1.10 | 1.20 | 1.00 | 0.98 | 2.23 | 3.48 | 1.00 | 3.09 |
| bfs | g-d | 0.31 | 0.37 | 0.33 | 0.37 | 0.29 | 0.32 | 0.28 | 0.25 | 0.61 | 1.03 | 0.30 | 0.71 |
| bfs | pbbs | 1.00 | 1.00 | 1.00 | 1.00 | 1.00 | 1.00 | 1.00 | 1.00 | 1.00 | 1.00 | 1.00 | 1.00 |
| dmr | g-n | 2.12 | 2.99 | 1.39 | 2.90 | 1.63 | 2.11 | 1.11 | 2.11 | 5.45 | 9.12 | 1.18 | 9.12 |
| dmr | g-d | 0.62 | 0.71 | 0.57 | 0.70 | 0.60 | 0.66 | 0.52 | 0.66 | 1.38 | 1.75 | 0.55 | 1.59 |
| dmr | pbbs | 1.00 | 1.00 | 1.00 | 1.00 | 1.00 | 1.00 | 1.00 | 1.00 | 1.00 | 1.00 | 1.00 | 1.00 |
| dt | g-n | 2.81 | 3.34 | 2.34 | 3.34 | 2.43 | 2.76 | 1.92 | 2.73 | 6.70 | 9.30 | 2.07 | 9.26 |
| dt | g-d | 0.72 | 0.95 | 0.87 | 0.58 | 0.77 | 0.89 | 0.79 | 0.70 | 1.15 | 2.08 | 1.11 | 0.86 |
| dt | pbbs | 1.00 | 1.00 | 1.00 | 1.00 | 1.00 | 1.00 | 1.00 | 1.00 | 1.00 | 1.00 | 1.00 | 1.00 |
| mis | g-n | 0.40 | 0.64 | 0.29 | 0.59 | 0.27 | 0.35 | 0.31 | 0.21 | 0.48 | 0.94 | 0.28 | 0.44 |
| mis | g-d | 0.09 | 0.15 | 0.05 | 0.14 | 0.07 | 0.09 | 0.05 | 0.08 | 0.12 | 0.18 | 0.05 | 0.18 |
| mis | pbbs | 1.00 | 1.00 | 1.00 | 1.00 | 1.00 | 1.00 | 1.00 | 1.00 | 1.00 | 1.00 | 1.00 | 1.00 |

**Figure 9: Performance of variants relative to PBBS variant. Let $\text{time}_{\text{PBBS}}(p)$ and $\text{time}_{\text{var}}(p)$ be the times for variant PBBS and var respectively with $p$ threads. The performance number shown is $\text{time}_{\text{PBBS}}(p)/\text{time}_{\text{var}}(p)$. $I_1$ and $I_{max}$ show performance at 1 and the maximum number of threads respectively.**

|  |  | m4x10 |  |  |  |
|---|---|---|---|---|---|
|  | Variant | Mean | Max | $I_1$ | $I_{max}$ |
| bfs | g-d | 0.31 | 0.37 | 0.33 | 0.37 |
| bfs | without | 0.27 | 0.32 | 0.30 | 0.32 |
| dmr | g-d | 0.62 | 0.71 | 0.57 | 0.70 |
| dmr | without | 0.48 | 0.54 | 0.43 | 0.52 |
| dt | g-d | 0.72 | 0.95 | 0.87 | 0.58 |
| dt | without | 0.56 | 0.71 | 0.68 | 0.49 |
| mis | g-d | 0.09 | 0.15 | 0.05 | 0.14 |
| mis | without | 0.08 | 0.13 | 0.05 | 0.12 |

**Figure 10: Performance without continuation optimization relative to PBBS variant on machine m4x10. $I_1$ and $I_{max}$ show performance at 1 and the maximum number of threads respectively.**

Fitting the above linear model to our observed data on machine m4x10 reveals that the change in DRAM accesses significantly predicts the change in performance, $\beta = 0.35$, $t(108) = 16.8$, $p < 0.001$. The change in this performance counter also explained a significant portion of the variance in change of performance, $R^2 = 0.72$, $F(1, 108) = 282$, $p < 0.001$. There are performance counters that are more highly correlated ($R^2 \geq 0.75$), clock cycles for instance, but that relationship is trivial.

***Inter-task locality*** Figure 12 shows how the performance of mis can vary on the same input, depending on whether the input is randomized or sorted. The input graph is a 2D mesh which is ordered by sorting nodes according to a space-filling curve. Figure 12(ordered) shows that the g-n variant is able to effectively exploit the locality in the input data and obtains far better performance than the g-d or PBBS variants. When the input graph is randomized, there is no locality to be exploited, and the PBBS version performs slightly better than the g-n version.

*Non-deterministic programs can more readily exploit both intra-task and inter-task locality. The execution of a single task is not divided into phases separated in time, so they can exploit intra-task locality better. Furthermore, locality in the input data, which leads to inter-task locality, is easier to exploit.*

## 6. Related work

The majority of deterministic parallel systems work by executing tasks in rounds and deterministically resolving conflicts when two tasks access the same resource in a round. A common way to resolve conflicts is to buffer updates privately and then deterministically merge updates to form the new state for the next round. Hardware systems like RCDC [17] and Calvin [21] work this way, as well as runtime replacements like DThreads [24] and Kendo [25], compiler-based systems like CoreDet [3], OS systems like dOS [4] and Determinator [2], and some parallel programming models like Grace [5].

In systems that are deterministic by construction such as DPJ [9], nested data-parallel programs [8], stream programs [27] and commutativity-based techniques [7, 11], tasks have no conflicts. However, it is not possible to write non-deterministic programs in these approaches. Bocchino et al. have shown how to extend DPJ to compose safely with non-deterministic programs [10], but there is as yet no system to make the resulting program deterministic on demand.

For round-based systems, an important characteristic of the system is how tasks are determined. The hardware systems and Kendo use the number of instructions executed (or a similar proxy) to divide sequences of instructions into tasks. Depending on how conflicts are detected, task boundaries may also have to be formed at every memory fence, synchronization instruction, store buffer completion, etc. RCDC and the bounded mode of Calvin form tasks based on when the store buffer is full, which is a micro-architectural event. This means that programs may not be deterministic across different processor implementations. CoreDet, Kendo and the unbounded mode of Calvin form tasks based on the number of executed instructions, so their results should be the same between processors.

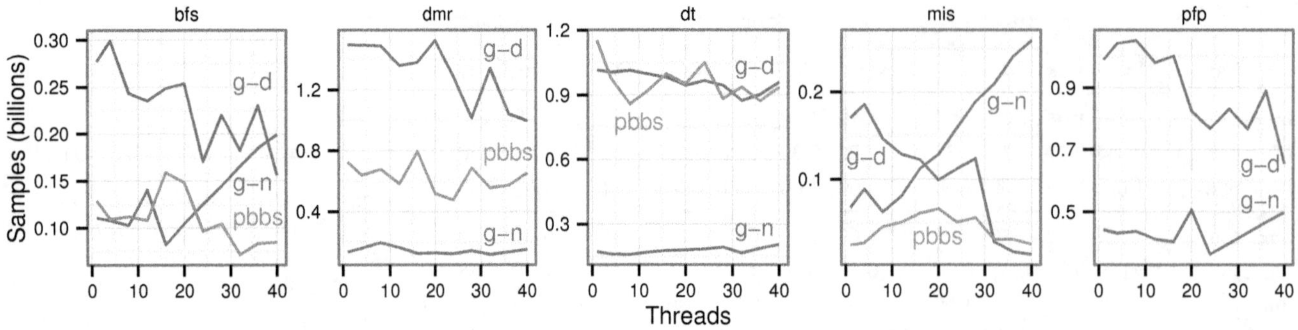


**Figure 11: Samples of DRAM access performance counter on machine m4x10.**

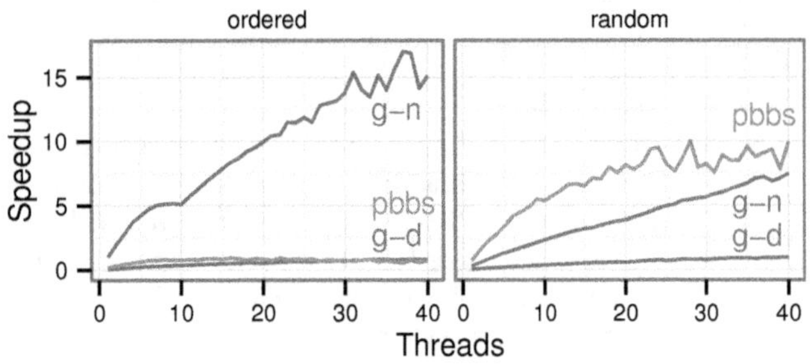


**Figure 12: Effect of ordering input for mis. Speedup is relative to the best variant with one thread among the two inputs (g-n, 4.3 seconds). The ordered input is a graph of a 2D mesh. The nodes are sorted according to a space-filling curve.**

The determinism guarantee of these systems is still quite fragile, because the insertion of a single instruction will produce a program that generates different outputs. Also, performance is sensitive to the task length. Devietti et al. show that system overheads can vary between 160%–250% depending on the task size parameter [17].

In contrast, systems like Grace and DThreads form their tasks based on synchronization instructions, which means that adding non-synchronization instructions will not change the decomposition of the program into tasks. However, this flexibility comes at a cost as tasks are now quite long, and load balancing becomes an issue. DThreads uses a sequential token passing algorithm to deterministically process synchronization events, so the entire sequence of instructions bounded by synchronization instructions is blocked waiting for the token. Kendo, which breaks tasks up into smaller pieces, can extract more parallelism by executing a prefix of instructions before the synchronization instruction. More recently, Cui et al. have proposed that users add performance hints akin to thread barriers to improve the load balancing of a deterministic scheduler [15].

Kendo, CoreDet, Determinator and some PBBS programs [7] have a tunable parameter that controls the task or round size, but no method to adaptively set that parameter based on observed execution. dOS uses instruction-based task formation, but it uses an adaptive algorithm like the one described in Section 3.2 to deterministically adjust the task size based on observed parallelism. Calvin uses a standard hardware two-bit predictor to dynamically increase task size when there is no synchronization in a task.

## 7. Conclusion

Deterministic execution of parallel programs has certain advantages such as reproducibility of results, which makes debugging easier. There is a substantial body of recent work on enforcing determinism at the programming language and programming model level, and at the system level through deterministic scheduling. We believe that any such system should provide three features: on-demand determinism, portability and parameter-freedom across platforms, which no existing system currently does.

In this paper, we considered the problem of ensuring deterministic execution for irregular programs, which are particularly challenging because task sizes are smaller and tasks communicate more frequently than in conventional parallel programs like the PARSEC benchmarks. Irregular programs have not been studied much in this context, and we showed that these programs do not scale when executed on a current determinism by scheduling system.

Our solution takes high-level non-deterministic programs written in the Galois model and implements determinism automatically by runtime scheduling. In many instances, the resulting programs have performance comparable to handwritten deterministic programs.

However, we showed on three different platforms that non-deterministic programs perform substantially better than their handwritten deterministic counterparts, demonstrating that there is a performance penalty for enforcing deterministic execution. This performance difference arises because the deterministic versions have less intra-task and inter-task locality. Therefore, we believe that determinism on demand, which leaves the choice between performance and determinism to the application user, is a reasonable design point.

## References


[1] N. Amenta, S. Choi, and G. Rote. Incremental constructions con brio. In *Proc. Symp. on Computational Geometry (SCG)*, 2003.

[2] A. Aviram, S.-C. Weng, S. Hu, and B. Ford. Efficient system-enforced deterministic parallelism. In *Proc. USENIX Conf. Operating Systems Design and Implementation*, OSDI, pages 1–16, 2010.

[3] T. Bergan, O. Anderson, J. Devietti, L. Ceze, and D. Grossman. CoreDet: a compiler and runtime system for deterministic multithreaded execution. In *Proc. Intl Conf. Architectural Support for Programming Languages and Operating Systems*, ASPLOS, pages 53–64, 2010.

[4] T. Bergan, N. Hunt, L. Ceze, and S. D. Gribble. Deterministic process groups in dOS. In *Proc. USENIX Conf. Operating Systems Design and Implementation*, OSDI, pages 1–16, 2010.

[5] E. D. Berger, T. Yang, T. Liu, and G. Novark. Grace: safe multithreaded programming for C/C++. In *Proc. ACM SIGPLAN Conf. Object Oriented Programming Systems Languages and Applications*, OOPSLA, pages 81–96, 2009.

[6] C. Bienia, S. Kumar, J. P. Singh, and K. Li. The PARSEC benchmark suite: characterization and architectural implications. In *Proc. Intl Conf. Parallel Architectures and Compilation Techniques*, PACT, pages 72–81, 2008.

[7] G. E. Blelloch, J. T. Fineman, P. B. Gibbons, and J. Shun. Internally deterministic parallel algorithms can be fast. In *Proc. ACM SIGPLAN Symp. Principles and Practice of Parallel Programming*, PPoPP, pages 135–146, 2012.

[8] R. D. Blumofe, C. F. Joerg, B. C. Kuszmaul, C. E. Leiserson, K. H. Randall, and Y. Zhou. Cilk: An efficient multithreaded runtime system. In *Proc. ACM SIGPLAN Symp. Principles and Practice of Parallel Programming*, PPoPP, 1995.

[9] R. L. Bocchino, Jr., V. S. Adve, S. V. Adve, and M. Snir. Parallel programming must be deterministic by default. In *Proc. USENIX Conf. Hot Topics in Parallelism*, HotPar, pages 4–4, 2009.

[10] R. L. Bocchino, Jr., S. Heumann, N. Honarmand, S. V. Adve, V. S. Adve, A. Welc, and T. Shpeisman. Safe nondeterminism in a deterministic-by-default parallel language. In *Proc. ACM SIGPLAN-SIGACT Symp. Principles of Programming Languages*, POPL, pages 535–548, 2011.

[11] S. Burckhardt, A. Baldassin, and D. Leijen. Concurrent programming with revisions and isolation types. In *Proc. ACM SIGPLAN Conf. Object Oriented Programming Systems Languages and Applications*, OOPSLA, 2010.

[12] K. M. Chandy and J. Misra. The drinking philosophers problem. *ACM Trans. Program. Lang. Syst.*, 6(4), Oct. 1984.

[13] B. V. Cherkassy and A. V. Goldberg. On implementing push-relabel method for the maximum flow problem. In *Proc. Intl Conf. Integer Programming and Combinatorial Optimization*, IPCO, pages 157–171, 1995.

[14] K. L. Clarkson and P. W. Shor. Applications of random sampling in computational geometry, II. *Discrete Comput. Geom.*, 4(5):287–421, 1989.

[15] H. Cui, J. Simsa, Y.-H. Lin, H. Li, B. Blum, X. Xu, J. Yang, G. A. Gibson, and R. E. Bryant. Parrot: A practical runtime for deterministic, stable, and reliable threads. In *Proc. ACM Symp. Operating Systems Principles*, SOSP, pages 388–405, 2013.

[16] J. Devietti, B. Lucia, L. Ceze, and M. Oskin. DMP: deterministic shared memory multiprocessing. In *Proc. Intl Conf. Architectural Support for Programming Languages and Operating Systems*, ASPLOS, pages 85–96, 2009.

[17] J. Devietti, J. Nelson, T. Bergan, L. Ceze, and D. Grossman. RCDC: a relaxed consistency deterministic computer. In *Proc. Intl Conf. Architectural Support for Programming Languages and Operating Systems*, ASPLOS, 2011.

[18] A. V. Goldberg and R. E. Tarjan. A new approach to the maximum-flow problem. *J. ACM*, 35(4):921–940, 1988.

[19] T. Harris and K. Fraser. Language support for lightweight transactions. In *Proc. ACM SIGPLAN Conf. Object Oriented Programming Systems Languages and Applications*, OOPSLA, pages 388–402, 2003.

[20] M. Herlihy and E. Koskinen. Transactional boosting: a methodology for highly-concurrent transactional objects. In *Proc. ACM SIGPLAN Symp. Principles and Practice of Parallel Programming*, PPoPP, pages 207–216, 2008.

[21] D. Hower, P. Dudnik, M. D. Hill, and D. A. Wood. Calvin: Deterministic or not? free will to choose. In *IEEE Intl Symp. High Performance Computer Architecture*, HPCA, pages 333–334, 2011.

[22] M. Kulkarni, M. Burtscher, C. Casçaval, and K. Pingali. Lonestar: A suite of parallel irregular programs. In *IEEE Intl Symp. Performance Analysis of Systems and Software*, ISPASS, pages 65–76, 2009.

[23] C. E. Leiserson and T. B. Schardl. A work-efficient parallel breadth-first search algorithm (or how to cope with the nondeterminism of reducers). In *Proc. ACM Symp. Parallelism in Algorithms and Architectures*, SPAA, pages 303–314, 2010.

[24] T. Liu, C. Curtsinger, and E. D. Berger. Dthreads: Efficient deterministic multithreading. In *Proc. ACM Symp. Operating Systems Principles*, SOSP, pages 327–336, New York, NY, USA, 2011.

[25] M. Olszewski, J. Ansel, and S. Amarasinghe. Kendo: efficient deterministic multithreading in software. In *Proc. Intl Conf. Architectural Support for Programming Languages and Operating Systems*, ASPLOS, 2009.

[26] K. Pingali, D. Nguyen, M. Kulkarni, M. Burtscher, M. A. Hassaan, R. Kaleem, T.-H. Lee, A. Lenharth, R. Manevich, M. Méndez-Lojo, D. Prountzos, and X. Sui. The tao of parallelism in algorithms. In *Proc. ACM SIGPLAN Conf. Programming Language Design and Implementation*, PLDI, pages 12–25, 2011.

[27] W. Thies, M. Karczmarek, and S. P. Amarasinghe. StreamIt: A language for streaming applications. In *Proc. Intl Conf. Compiler Construction*, CC, pages 179–196, 2002.

# Energy-Efficient Work-Stealing Language Runtimes

Haris Ribic and Yu David Liu

SUNY Binghamton
Binghamton NY 13902, USA
{hribic1,davidL}@binghamton.edu

## Abstract

Work stealing is a promising approach to constructing multi-threaded program runtimes of parallel programming languages. This paper presents HERMES, an energy-efficient work-stealing language runtime. The key insight is that threads in a work-stealing environment – thieves and victims – have varying impacts on the overall program running time, and a coordination of their execution "tempo" can lead to energy efficiency with minimal performance loss. The centerpiece of HERMES is two complementary algorithms to coordinate thread tempo: the *workpath-sensitive* algorithm determines tempo for each thread based on thief-victim relationships on the execution path, whereas the *workload-sensitive* algorithm selects appropriate tempo based on the size of work-stealing deques. We construct HERMES on top of Intel Cilk Plus's runtime, and implement tempo adjustment through standard Dynamic Voltage and Frequency Scaling (DVFS). Benchmarks running on HERMES demonstrate an average of 11-12% energy savings with an average of 3-4% performance loss through meter-based measurements over commercial CPUs.

***Categories and Subject Descriptors*** D.3.4 [*Programming Languages*]: Processors— Run-Time Environments; D.3.3 [*Programming Languages*]: Language Constructs and Features

***Keywords*** work stealing; energy efficiency; language runtimes; thread management; DVFS

## 1. Introduction

Work stealing is a thread management strategy effective for maintaining multi-threaded language runtimes, with parallel architectures as specific target and with a primary goal of load balancing. In the multi-core era, work stealing received considerable interest in language runtime design. With its root in Cilk [6, 16], work stealing is widely available in industry-strength C/C++/C#-based language frameworks such as Intel TBB [20], Intel Cilk Plus [21], and Microsoft .NET framework [25]. The core idea of work stealing has also made its way into mainstream languages such as Java [24], X10 [10, 23, 30], Haskell [28], and Scala [32]. There is an active interest in research improving its performance-critical properties, such as adaptiveness [2, 18], scalability [13], and fairness [14].

In comparison, energy efficiency in work-stealing systems has received little attention. At a time where power-hungry data centers and cloud computing servers are the norm of computing infrastructure, energy efficiency is a first-class design goal with direct consequences on operational cost, reliability, usability, maintainability, and environmental sustainability. The lack of energy-efficient solutions for work-stealing systems is particularly unfortunate, because the platforms on which work stealing is most promising to make impact – systems with a large number of parallel units – happen to be large power consumers and require more sophisticated techniques to achieve energy efficiency [8, 12, 17, 22, 27, 33, 38].

HERMES is a first step toward energy efficiency for work-stealing runtimes. Program execution under HERMES is *tempo-enabled*[1]: different threads may execute at different speeds (*tempo*), achieved by adjusting the frequencies of host CPU cores through standard DVFS. The effect of DVFS on energy management is widely known. The real challenge lies upon balancing the trade-off between energy and performance, as lower frequencies may also slow down program execution. The primary design goal of HERMES is to tap inherent and unique features of the work-stealing runtime to help make judicious DVFS decisions, ultimately maximizing energy savings while minimizing performance loss. Specifically, HERMES is endowed with two algorithms:



*ASPLOS '14*, March 1–4, 2014, Salt Lake City, Utah, USA.

http://dx.doi.org/10.1145/2541940.2541971

[1] The term is inspired by music composition, where each movement of a musical piece is often marked with a different tempo – *e.g.*, *allegro* ("fast") and *lento* ("slow") – to indicate the speed of execution.

- **workpath-sensitive tempo control**: thread tempo is set based on control flow, with threads tackling "immediate work" [7] executing at a faster tempo. This design approach corresponds to a key design principle in work-stealing algorithms: the work-first principle.
- **workload-sensitive tempo control**: thread tempo is set based on the number of work items a thread needs to tackle, as indicated by the size of the deque in work-stealing runtimes. Threads with a longer deque execute at a faster tempo.

HERMES unifies the two tempo control strategies in one. Our experiments show that the two strategies are highly *complementary*. For instance, on a 32-core machine, each strategy can contribute to 6% and 7% energy savings respectively, whereas the unified algorithm can yield 11% energy savings. In the same setting, each strategy incurs 6% and 5% performance loss respectively, whereas the unified algorithm incurs 3% loss.

This paper makes the following contributions:

1. The first framework, to the best of our knowledge, addressing energy efficiency in work-stealing systems. The framework achieves energy efficiency through thread tempo control.
2. Two novel, complementary tempo control strategies: one workpath-sensitive and one workload-sensitive.
3. A prototyped implementation and experimental evaluation demonstrating an average of 11-12% energy savings with 3-4% performance loss over work-stealing benchmarks. The results are stable throughout comprehensive design space exploration.

## 2. Background: Work Stealing

Work stealing was originally developed in Cilk [6, 16], a C-like language designed for parallel programming. The main appeal of work stealing is its synergic solution spanning the compute stack, bridging the gap between abstraction layers such as architectures, operating systems, compilers, program runtimes, and programming models.

Work stealing is a load balancing scheduler for multi-threaded programs over parallel architectures. The program runtime consists of multiple threads called *workers*, each executing on a host CPU core (or hardware parallel unit in general). Each worker maintains a queue-like data structure – called a *double-ended queue* or *deque* – each item of which is a *task* to be processed by the worker. When a worker finishes processing a task, it picks up next one from its deque and continues the execution of that task. When the deque is empty (we say the worker or its host core is *idle*), the worker *steals* a task from the deque of another worker. In this case we call the stealing worker a *thief* whereas the worker whose task was stolen a *victim*. The selection of victims follows the principles observed by load balancing and may vary in different implementations of work stealing.

What sets work stealing apart from standard load balancing techniques is how the runtime structure described above corresponds to program structures and compilation units. Each task on the deque is a block of executable code – or more strictly, a program counter pointing to the executable code – demarcated by the programmer and optimized by the compiler. In that sense, to have a worker "pick up a task" is indeed to have the worker continue its execution over the executable code embodied in the task. To describe the process in more detail, let us use the following Cilk example:

```
 L1 cilk int f()
 L2 {    int n1 = spawn f1();
 L3        ...  // other statements
 L4 }
 L5 cilk int f1() {
 L6      int n2 = spawn f2();
 L7      ... // other statements
 L8 }
 L9 cilk int f2() {
L10      ... // other statements
L11 }
```

Logically, each `spawn` can be viewed as a thread creation. On the implementation level however, a work-stealing runtime adopts Lazy Task Creation [31], where for each `spawn`, the executing worker simply puts a task onto its own deque, either to pick it up later or to be stolen by some other worker. This strategy aligns thread management with the underlying parallel architecture: a program that invokes `f` above 20 times but runs on a dual-core CPU can operate only with 2 threads (workers) instead of 40.

***Work-First Principle*** The question here is what the item placed on the deque should embody. For instance, when L2 is executed, one tempting design would be to consider `f1` as the task placed on the deque. The Cilk-like work-stealing algorithm takes the opposite approach: it places the *continuation* of the current `spawn` statement onto the deque. In the example above, it is the program counter pointing to L3. The current worker continues to invoke `f1` as if `spawn` were elided.

This design reflects a fundamental principle well articulated in Cilk: the *work-first principle*. The principle concerns the relationship between the parallel execution of a program and its corresponding serial execution. (A logically equivalent view for the latter would be to have the parallel program execute on a single-core machine.) Let us revisit the example above. If it is executed on a single-core machine, `f1` is the "immediate" work when L2 is reached, and hence carries more urgency. For that reason, `f1` should be immediately executed by the current worker, whereas the continuation is not as urgent and is hence placed on the deque.

Work-first principle plays a pivotal role in the design of work-stealing systems. In Cilk, it further leads to a compila-

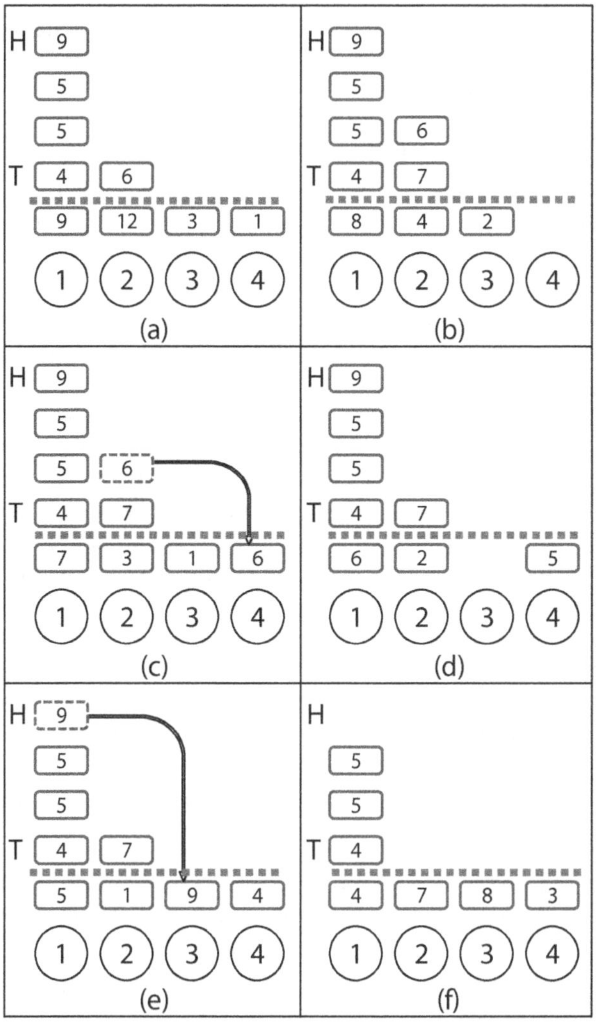

**Figure 1.** Work Stealing: An Illustration

tion strategy known as fast/slow clones, and a distinct solution for locking [16]. Both are out of the scope of this paper.

***Deque Management*** One natural consequence of placing continuations onto the deque is that the order of tasks on the deque reflects the immediacy of processing these items as defined by the work-first principle: the earlier the item is placed, the less immediate it is. For example, if the control flow of a worker reaches L10, two tasks are placed on the deque, the program counter for L3 (when the `spawn` in L2 is executed) and the program counter for L7 (when the `spawn` in L6 is executed). In a serial execution, L3 will only be encountered after L7.

With this observation, deque is designed as a data structure that can be manipulated on both ends. Let us call the *head* of the deque as the earliest item placed on the deque by the worker, whereas the *tail* of the deque as the latest. When a worker becomes idle, it always retrieves from the tail of its own deque, *i.e.*, the most immediate task. On the other hand, when a thief attempts to steal from a worker, it always retrieves from the head of that worker's deque, *i.e.*, the least immediate task. From now on, we call the worker placing a task to its own deque a *push*, while removing a task from its own deque a *pop*. We continue to use term *steal* to refer to a worker removing a task from another worker's deque.

**Algorithm 2.1** Worker

```
w : WORKER
procedure SCHEDULE(w)
  loop
    t ← POP(w)
    if t==null then
      v = SELECT()
      t ← STEAL(v)
      if t==null then
        YIELD(w)
      else
        WORK(w, t)
      end if
    else
      WORK(w, t)
    end if
  end loop
end procedure
```

**Structures**

```
structure WORKER
  DQ // deque (array)
  H // head index
  T // tail index
end structure

structure TASK
  ... // program counter, etc
end structure
```

**Other Definitions**

```
procedure WORK(w, t)
// worker w runs task t
procedure SELECT()
// select and return a victim
procedure YIELD(w)
// yield worker w
procedure LOCK(w)
procedure UNLOCK(w)
// lock/unlock w
```

**Algorithm 2.2** Push

```
w : WORKER
t : TASK
procedure PUSH(w,t)
  w.T++
  w.DQ[w.T] ← t
end procedure
```

**Algorithm 2.3** Pop

```
w : WORKER
procedure POP(w)
  w.T– –
  if w.H > w.T then
    w.T++
    LOCK(w)
    w.T– –
    if w.H > w.T then
      w.T++
      UNLOCK(w)
      return null
    end if
  end if
  UNLOCK(w)
  return w.DQ[w.T]
end procedure
```

**Algorithm 2.4** Steal

```
v : WORKER // victim
procedure STEAL(v)
  LOCK(v)
  v.H++
  if v.H > v.T then
    v.H– –
    UNLOCK(v)
    return null
  end if
  UNLOCK(v)
  return v.DQ[v.H]
end procedure
```

**Figure 2.** Work Stealing Algorithm

Figure 1 illustrates the time sequence of a typical program execution on a 4-core CPU (numbered as 1-4 at the bottom of each sub-figure). For each pair of adjacent figures, the elapsed time is one time unit. The rectangle below the dotted line is the currently executed task, and the rectangles above form the deque for the worker on that core, with the top rectangle representing the "head" task (H) and the bottom representing the "tail" task (T). The number inside the rectangle represents the number of time units needed to complete that task if the task were to run serially. In the first elapsed time unit – from Figure 1(a) to Figure 1(b) – core 2 spawn's another task with 2 time units. Its continuation, with 12-1-4 = 7 time units left, is pushed onto the tail of its deque. In the same elapsed time, core 4 completes its executing task. Since its deque is empty, core 4 steals from the head of the deque of core 2, as shown in Figure 1(c). Another stealing happens in Figure 1(e), after core 3 becomes idle in Figure 1(d). In Figure 1(f), core 2 completes its current task, but since its deque is not empty, it pops a task from the tail of its deque.

***Work-Stealing Scheduler*** Figure 2 provides a simplified specification of the classic work-stealing algorithm. The state of each worker thread is maintained by data structure WORKER, which consists of a deque DQ and two indices for its head (H) and (T) respectively. As shown in Algorithm 2.1, a worker either attempts to POP a task from its deque – or if not available – SELECT a victim and STEAL a task from it. Once a task is obtained, the worker WORK's on it, during which (we elide the WORK specification here) it may spawn new tasks and PUSH them onto its deque. If no task is available either through POP or STEAL, the worker thread YIELD's its host core. We leave out the definition of SELECT: a typical implementation (such as Cilk) is a randomized algorithm.

The definitions of PUSH, POP, and STEAL are predictable. PUSH increments the tail index, POP decrements the tail index, and STEAL increments the head index. The scheduler maintains one invariant to check if the head index is less than or equal to the tail index. When head index and tail index are equal, possibility exists that a thief and a victim attempt to work on the same task. To resolve potential contention, LOCK and UNLOCK are introduced. The locking strategy adopted by most work-stealing runtimes are reminiscent of optimistic locking. This somewhat stylistic protocol is known as THE [16], orthogonal to the rest of the paper.

## 3. Energy-Efficient Work Stealing

In this section, we describe how HERMES improves energy efficiency of work-stealing runtimes. The overall technique of HERMES is DVFS-guided tempo control: different workers execute at different speeds – workers tackling more urgent tasks run at the faster tempos to retain high performance, whereas others run at the slower tempos to save energy. The main design challenges were the determination of the appropriate tempo for each worker thread and the timing for tempo adjustment. To achieve these goals, we developed two novel algorithms.

### 3.1 Workpath-Sensitive Tempo Control

Our *workpath-sensitive* tempo control strategy is fundamentally aligned with the work-first principle of classic work-stealing algorithms: tasks encountered earlier – if the program were to be executed serially – carry more immediacy and will be executed at the faster tempos. Recall that in work-stealing systems, the order of tasks on the deque reflects the immediacy, with the head being the least immediate. Further, recall that a thief always steals from the head of a victim's deque. Hence, every worker executing a stolen task carries less immediacy than its victim worker.

The workpath-sensitve tempo control strategy says that the victim worker takes precedence over the thief worker in a thief-victim relationship, or in other words, the thief worker should be executing at a slower tempo than the victim worker. It is important to realize that the thief-victim relationship between workers has a dynamic lifespan: it is formed at steal time, and terminates when either the thief or the victim completes its current set of tasks and becomes idle again.

Specifically, workpath-sensitive tempo control entails two important design ideas:

- **Thief Procrastination**: At the begin of the thief-victim relationship, the tempo of the thief worker should be set to be slower than the victim worker.
- **Immediacy Relay**: If the thief-victim relationship terminates because the victim runs out of work, the tempo of the thief should be raised. In this case, the previous victim worker simply becomes an idle thread, and the immediacy should be "relayed" to the thief.

Intuitively, the design of **Immediacy Relay** can be analogously viewed as a relay race. When a worker finishes the tasks that carry immediacy, it needs to pass on the immediacy "baton" to the next worker.

Figure 3 demonstrates the key ideas of workpath sensitivity, with the 6 subfigures representing (not necessarily consecutive) "snapshots" of a program execution sequence. We use different gray-scales to represent different tempos. The darker the shade of the circle is, the slower tempo the hosted worker is executed at. Worker 1 starts in Figure 3(a) with a task of 100 time units. In Figure 3(b), a task with 94 time units is pushed to the deque and subsequently stolen by worker 2. According to **Thief Procrastination**, worker 2 executes at a tempo one level slower than worker 1. In Figure 3(c), worker 3 steals from worker 2 (*i.e.*, "a thief's thief") executing at a tempo further slower than worker 2. At Figure 3(d), worker 1 finishes all its tasks. According to **Immediacy Relay**, its thief (worker 2 in this case) needs to

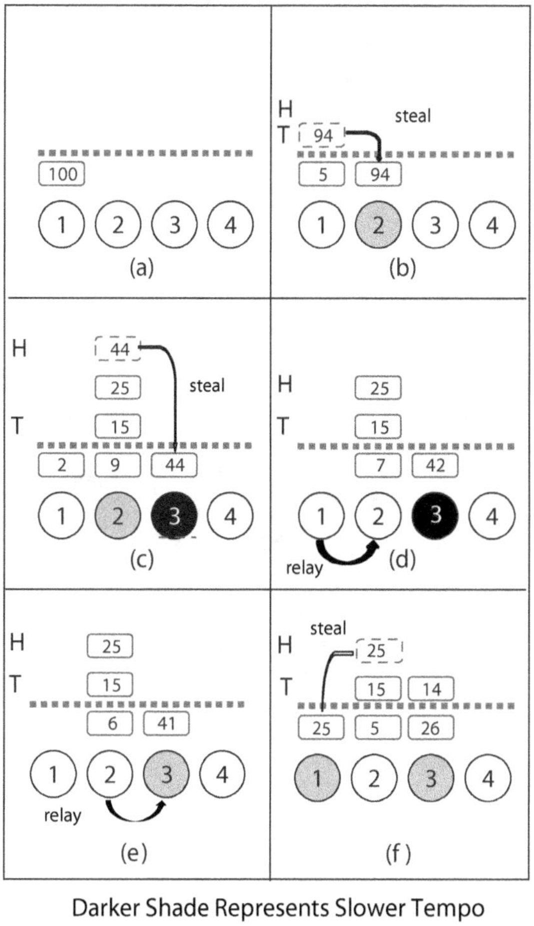


**Figure 3.** Example: Workpath-Sensitive Tempo Control

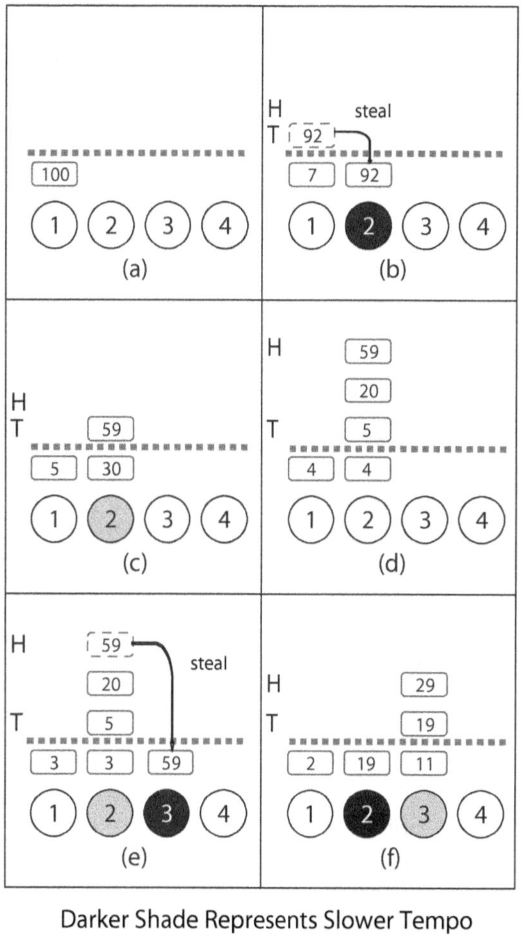


**Figure 4.** Example: Workload-Sensitive Tempo Control

raise its tempo. Intuitively, what worker 2 currently works on is the "unfinished business" when the 100 time units started on worker 1. When worker 2 raises its tempo by one level, HERMES transitively raises the tempo of worker 2's thief. This is demonstrated in Figure 3(e). In Figure 3(f), worker 1 steals again, starting a new thief-victim relationship with worker 2, except that worker 1 this time is the thief.

### 3.2 Workload-Sensitive Tempo Control

HERMES is further equipped with a *workload-sensitive* strategy for tempo control. The intuition is simple: a worker needs to work faster when there are more tasks to handle. In the case of work stealing, a natural indicator of the workload is the deque size: the number of tasks waiting to be processed by a worker.

We demonstrate the ideas of workload-sensitivity through Figure 4. Let us assume we have three tempo levels, set based on the deque size with two thresholds: 1 and 3. As a convention, HERMES always bootstraps the program execution with the fastest tempo, as in Figure 4(a). At snapshot Figure 4(b), core 2 steals one task. Since its deque is of size 0, lower than the first threshold, the tempo for worker 2 is set at the lowest one. As worker 2 progresses such as PUSH more tasks to its deque, its tempo rises to the medium level in Figure 4(c), and then fastest level in Figure 4(d). The tempo is slow downed again when worker 2 is stolen, dropping its deque size below the second threshold in Figure 4(e), and even slower when it pops more items from its own deque in Figure 4(f).

HERMES determines the thresholds through a lightweight form of online profiling. Our runtime periodically samples deque sizes, and computes the average of the last fixed number of samples. Let that average be $L$. In an execution with $K$ thresholds, the thresholds for the next period are set at

$$thld_i = (\frac{2 \times L}{K+1}) \times i$$

where $1 \leq i \leq K$. For example, if the average deque size is 15 and there are 2 thresholds, we apply the fastest tempo if the deque size is no less than 20, the medium tempo for a deque size between 10 and 20, and the slowest tempo otherwise.

**Algorithm 3.1** Worker

```
w : WORKER
procedure SCHEDULE(w)
  loop
    t ← POP(w)
    if t==null then
      w0 = w.next
      for w0 != null do
        UP(w0)
        w0 ← w0.next
      end for
      w.prev.next ← w.next
      w.next.prev ← w.prev
      w.next ← null
      w.prev ← null
      v = SELECT()
      t ← STEAL(v)
      if t==null then
        YIELD(w)
      else
        DOWN(w, v)
        if v.next != null then
          w.next ← v.next
          v.prev ← w.prev
        end if
        v.next ← w
        w.prev ← v
        WORK(w, t)
      end if
    else
      WORK(w, t)
    end if
  end loop
end procedure
```

**Algorithm 3.2** Tempo Adjustment

```
procedure DOWN(w, v)
// set w to one tempo lower than v
procedure DOWN(w)
// set w to one tempo lower
procedure UP(w)
// set w to one tempo higher
```

**Algorithm 3.3** Push

```
w : WORKER
K: number of thresholds
t: TASK
procedure PUSH(w, t)
  w.T++
  w.DQ[w.T] ← t
  if w.T - w.H > w.thld[w.S] then
    if w.S < K-1 then
      w.S++
      UP(w)
    end if
  end if
end procedure
```

**Algorithm 3.4** Pop

```
w : WORKER
procedure POP(w)
  w.T−−
  if w.H > w.T then
    w.T++
    LOCK(w)
    w.T−−
    if w.H > w.T then
      w.T++
      UNLOCK(w)
      return null
    end if
  end if
  UNLOCK(w)
  if w.T - w.H < w.thld[w.S] then
    if w.S > 0 then
      if w.prev ! = null then
        w.S−−
        DOWN(w)
      end if
    end if
  end if
  return w.DQ[w.T]
end procedure
```

**Algorithm 3.5** Steal

```
v : WORKER // victim
procedure STEAL(v)
  LOCK(v)
  v.H++
  if v.H > v.T then
    v.H−−
    UNLOCK(v)
    return null
  end if
  UNLOCK(v)
  if v.T - v.H < v.thld[v.S] then
    if v.S > 0 then
      if v.prev ! = null then
        v.S −−
        DOWN(v)
      end if
    end if
  end if
  return v.DQ[v.H]
end procedure
```

**Structures**

```
structure WORKER
  DQ // deque (array)
  H // head index
  T // tail index
  next // next immediate work
  prev // prev immediate work
  thld // size thresholds (array)
  S // size threshold index
end structure
```

**Figure 5.** Core HERMES Algorithm ( X for Workpath Sensitivity and X for Workload Sensitivity)

### 3.3 Unified Algorithm Specification

The two tempo control strategies are designed to complement each other. In workpath-alone executions, a major "anti-pattern" is that a non-immediate worker may have many deque items to work on. With a slower tempo, the worker may be left with a large number of work items when it becomes immediate. In other words, a slower tempo increases the workpath length. A second opinion based on workload-sensitive control helps speed up such workers early on. Similarly, in workload-alone executions, an immediate worker with fewer deque items is set to a lower tempo, increasing the workpath length. A second opinion based on workload-sensitive control can differentiate such workers from others. In both cases, an increased workpath length means increased execution time, which potentially leads to additional energy consumption. In this section, we specify the unified algorithm.

Figure 5 presents the pseudocode of the core HERMES algorithm. The modifications on top of the classic work-stealing algorithm are highlighted, with two colors indicating workpath-sensitive and workload-sensitive support respectively.

The key data structure to support workpath sensitivity is a double-linked list across workers, connected by the `next` and `prev` pointers. The list maintains the order of immediacy: when worker `w1`'s `next` worker is `w2`, it means `w2` is processing a task immediately following the tasks processed by worker `w1`, where immediacy is defined according to the work-first principle.

When stealing succeeds (lines 20-27), the thief worker becomes the immediate `next` worker of the victim. The tempo of the thief is set to be one level slower than the victim (line 20), and the `prev` and `next` references are properly set (lines 25-26). We will detail the implementation of tempo adjustment in the next subsection. One issue to address is that the victim might already be stolen by another thief before. In that case, the algorithm inserts the current thief ahead of the previous thief on the linked list (lines 21-24). In other words, the current thief is more immediate than the previous thief. This corresponds to how the order of tasks on the victim's deque reflects immediacy: the tasks stolen earlier are not as immediate as the tasks stolen later (recall Section 2).

When a worker becomes idle again and out of work (line 6), it effectively terminates the thief-victim relationship previously developed since it became out of work last time. If the current worker is a victim, then according to the design of **Immediacy Relay**, the tempos of its thieves are raised, passing on the immediacy (lines 7-10). Note that UP(`w`) is defined to raise the tempo of `w` one level up from its current level, so in a scenario where a thief worker `w1` is further stolen by another thief `w2`, both workers will have their tempo raised by one level, and `w2` can still maintain a slower tempo than `w1`. Finally, the current worker is removed from the linked list (lines 11-14).

Workload sensitivity is relatively simple to support. Each worker maintains an array `thld` to record its thresholds, with the number of thresholds defined by constant $K$. The computation of the `thld` was described in Section 3.2. The algorithm increases the tempo when PUSH makes the deque size reach the next threshold up, or decreases the tempo when either POP or STEAL reduces the deque size to the next threshold down.

One interesting aspect of our algorithm is that workpath sensitivity and workload sensitivity work largely independently – workpath-sensitive tempo control is applied when the deque is empty whereas workload-sensitive tempo control is applied when the deque is not – so the unification of the two is a simple matter. The only intersection of the two lies in one fact: when a worker is at the beginning of the immediacy list, we choose not to reduce its tempo even if workload sensitivity advises so. This can be seen in the `w.prev!= null` condition in POP and the similar `v.prev!= null` condition in STEAL. In other words, if the task a worker processes is immediate, we still execute it with a fast tempo regardless of deque size.

### 3.4 Lower-Level Design Considerations

***Tempo-Frequency Mapping*** HERMES achieves tempo adjustment through DVFS and modern CPUs usually support a limited, discrete number of frequencies. We now define tempo adjustment in the presence of a fixed number of frequencies. Let $\{f_1, f_2, \ldots, f_n\}$ be frequencies supported by a CPU core, where $f_i > f_{i+1}$ for any $1 <= i <= n-1$. For simplicity, let us assume all cores of a CPU support the same frequencies. The algorithm in the previous section stays the same, except UP and DOWN procedures should be refined. For instance,

**procedure** DOWN(w, v)
  $f \leftarrow$ frequency of core hosting v
  **if** $f == f_i$ and $i < N$ **then**
    ... // scale core hosting w to $f_{i+1}$
  **end if**
**end procedure**

where $N <= n$ is a constant to further restrict the range of frequencies used for the runtime. In other words, a CPU may support $n$ frequencies, but a runtime may only choose to use the highest $N$-number. In practice, a subset of frequencies often strikes a better trade-off between energy and performance: they are sufficient to yield energy savings, yet without incurring significant performance penalties due to low operating CPU frequencies. We call this design $N$-frequency tempo control.

***Worker-Core Mapping*** HERMES relies on the knowledge of the relationship between workers (threads) and their hosting CPU cores, information readily available in work-stealing runtimes. To maintain this mapping, we allow for two scheduling strategies in our experiments: (a) static scheduling: each worker thread is pre-assigned to a CPU core; (b) dynamic scheduling: each worker thread may migrate from one core to another during program execution. The only requirement for dynamic scheduling is that during the processing of a task (*i.e.* an invocation of the WORK procedure), a worker stays on its host core. With this, OS cannot re-assign a worker to a different core if preempted, invalidating frequency settings at context switch time. We think this is a reasonable design because (1) work stealing by design is a load balancing strategy, overlapping with the goal of OS-level load balancing; (2) work-stealing tasks usually take a short amount of time to complete.

We achieve the goal of binding workers to cores through affinity setting. For dynamic scheduling, affinity is set right before each WORK invocation (line 27 and line 30) and reset at the completion of each invocation.

One scenario common in standard multi-threaded program runtimes is the support of multiple threads executing concurrently on the same core. This is a non-issue for work-stealing runtimes. Lazy task creation fundamental in work stealing entails that the number of workers can be statically bound by CPU resources, not program logic.

***Tempo Setting of Idle Workers/Cores*** HERMES does not adjust CPU frequencies when a worker becomes idle but fails to steal. This corresponds to lines 17-18 in the algorithm where YIELD happens. In work-stealing systems, there are usually more tasks to keep all workers busy, either through POP or STEAL, with YIELD relatively uncommon. When a YIELD does happen, the core is often reallocated to another worker, which sets its CPU frequency based on its own workpath-sensitive and workload-sensitive rules.

***Overhead*** The overhead of our approach comes in 3 aspects: (1) DVFS switching cost. DVFS switching time is usually in the tens of microseconds, magnitudes smaller than the execution time of tasks. Our use of DVFS is relatively coarse-grained: tempo control is not applied during the execution of a task; (2) online profiling of workload threshold; (3) affinity setting in dynamic scheduling.

## 4. Implementation and Evaluation

HERMES is implemented on top of Intel Cilk Plus (build 2546). In this section, we present the experimental results.

### 4.1 Experiment Setup

We selected benchmarks from the Problem-Based Benchmark Suite (PBBS) [5]. The benchmarks support parallel programming, and our selection of the benchmarks support Cilk-like syntax such as `spawn`.

K-Nearest Neighbors (`KNN`) uses pattern recognition methods to classify objects based on closest training examples in the feature space. Sparse-Triangle Intersection (`Ray`) benchmark calculates for each ray the first triangle it intersects given a set of triangles contained inside a 3D bounding box and a set of rays that penetrate the box. Integer Sort (`Sort`) is an implementation of parallel radix sort. Comparison Sort (`Compare`) is similar to `Sort` but uses sample sort. Convex Hull (`Hull`) is a computational geometry benchmark.

To measure the effectiveness of our approach across platforms, we constructed our experiments on two systems:

- System A: a machine with 2×16-core AMD Opteron 6378 processors (Piledriver microarchitecture) running Debian 3.2.46-1 x86-64 Linux (kernel 3.2.0-4-amd64) and 64GB of DDR3 1600 memory. Each processor supports 5 frequencies: 1.4GHz, 1.6GHz, 1.9GHz, 2.2GHz and 2.4GHz.
- System B: a machine with an 8-core AMD FX-8150 processor (Bulldozer microarchitecture) running Debian 3.2.46-1 Linux (kernel 3.2.0-4-amd64) and 16GB of DDR3 1600 memory. The processor supports 5 frequencies: 1.4GHz, 2.1GHz, 2.7GHz, 3.3GHz and 3.6GHz.

Piledriver/Bulldozer microarchitectures are among the latest commercial CPUs that support *multiple clock-domains*, *i.e.*, CPUs whose individual cores can have their frequencies adjusted independently. Specifically, in both architectures, every two cores share one clock domain. In other words, System A has 16 independent clock domains, whereas System B has 4. To avoid the undesirable DVFS interference, all our experiments are performed over cores with distinct clock domains. For example, our experiments on System A consider as many as 16 workers, and no two workers may share the same clock domain.

Energy consumption is measured through current meters over power supply lines to the CPU module. Data is converted through an NI DAQ and collected by NI LabVIEW SignalExpress with 100 samples per second. Since the supply voltage is stable at 12V, energy consumption is computed as the sum of current samples multiplied by $12 \times 0.01$. We executed each benchmark using our HERMES scheduler. The results reported below are often normalized to a control, defined as executing the same benchmark with the unmodified Intel Cilk Plus scheduler running at the maximum CPU frequency. For each benchmark, we run 20 trials and calculate the average of the trials, disregarding the first 2 trials.

### 4.2 Experimental Results

***Overall Results*** Figure 6 and Figure 7 summarize the energy/performance results of HERMES on System A and System B respectively. All data are normalized against the baseline execution over unmodified Intel Cilk Plus. The blue columns are the percentage of energy savings of HERMES, while the red columns are the percentages of performance (time) loss. The results are grouped by benchmarks, and within each group, the columns show different numbers of workers. On System A, we conducted experiments using 2, 4, 8, and 16 workers (hence each group in Figure 6 has 4 columns, in that order). On System B, we conducted experiments using with 2, 3, and 4 workers (hence each group in Figure 7 has 3 columns, in that order). The last columns in both Figures show the average.

In both systems, HERMES averages 11-12% energy savings over 3-4% performance loss. We have further computed the Energy-Delay Product (EDP) of the benchmarking results, and the normalized results are shown in Figure 8 and

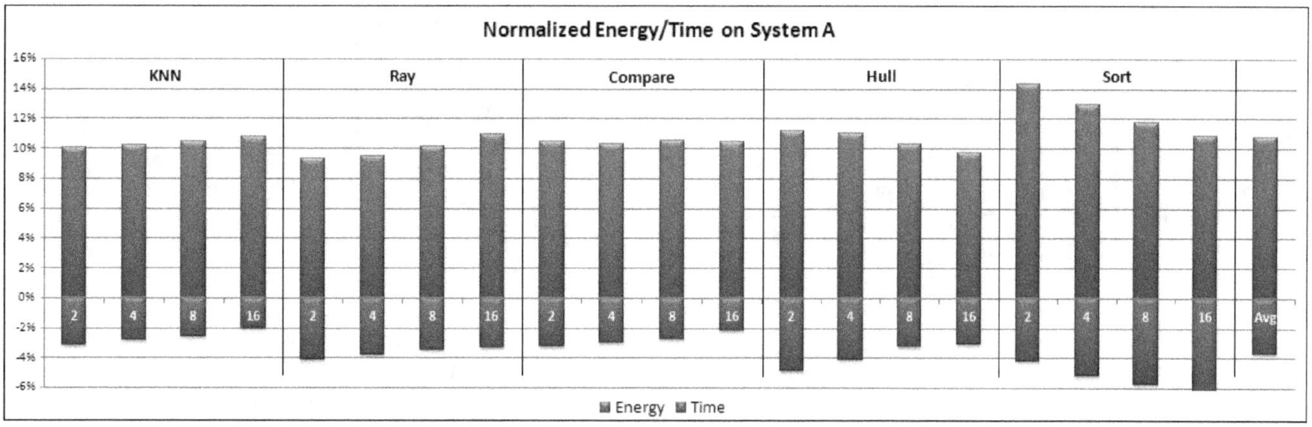


**Figure 6.** Normalized Energy Savings (Blue) and Time Loss (Red) of HERMES w.r.t. Intel Cilk Plus on System A

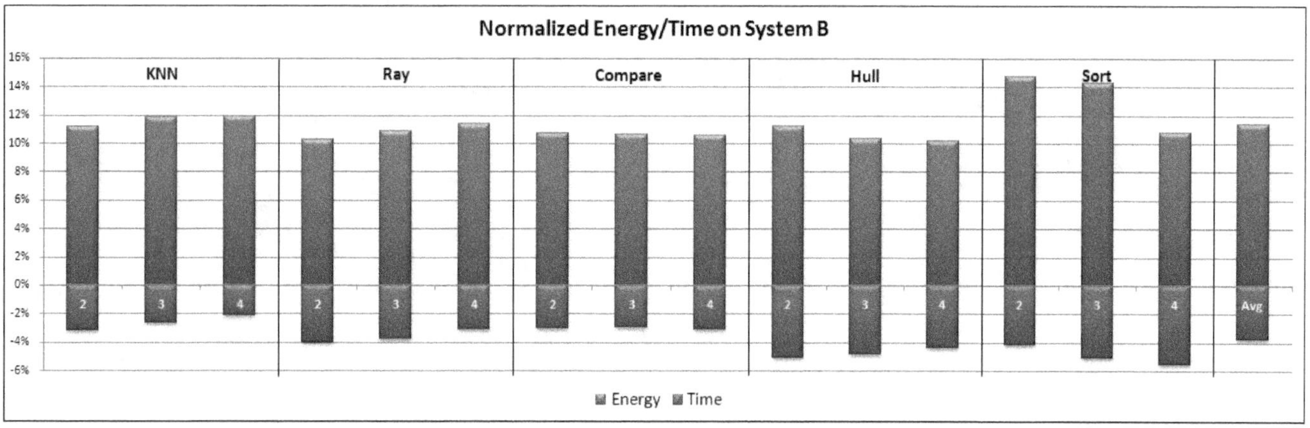


**Figure 7.** Normalized Energy Savings (Blue) and Time Loss (Red) of HERMES w.r.t. Intel Cilk Plus on System B

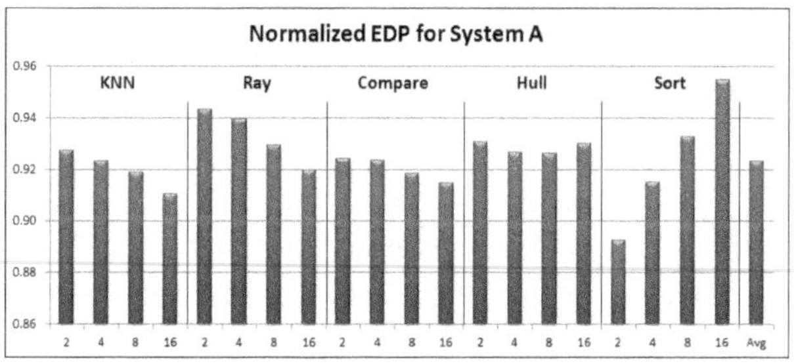


**Figure 8.** Normalized EDP for System A

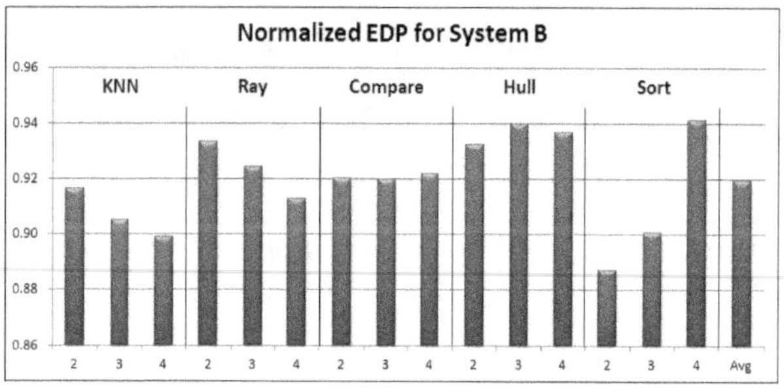


**Figure 9.** Normalized EDP for System B

Figure 9 respectively. Often used as an indicator for demonstrating the energy/performance trade-off, EDP is the product of energy consumption and execution time. A smaller value in EDP is aligned with our intuition of improved energy efficiency. In both System A and System B, the average normalized EDP is about 0.92. HERMES shows remarkable stability across benchmarks, worker counts, and underlying systems. EDP is improved without exception. This is an unexpected feature while experimenting in a highly dynamic setting.

***Relative Effectiveness of Workpath vs. Workload Sensitivity*** To determine how much workpath sensitivity and workload sensitivity contribute to HERMES, we also run benchmarks with only one of the two strategies enabled. Figure 10 and Figure 11 shows the energy/time effects on System A, while Figure 12 and Figure 13 shows the energy/time ef-

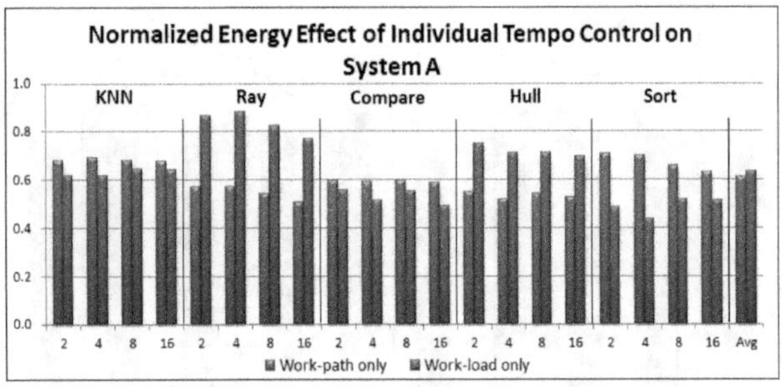


**Figure 10.** Energy: Workpath vs. Workload on System A

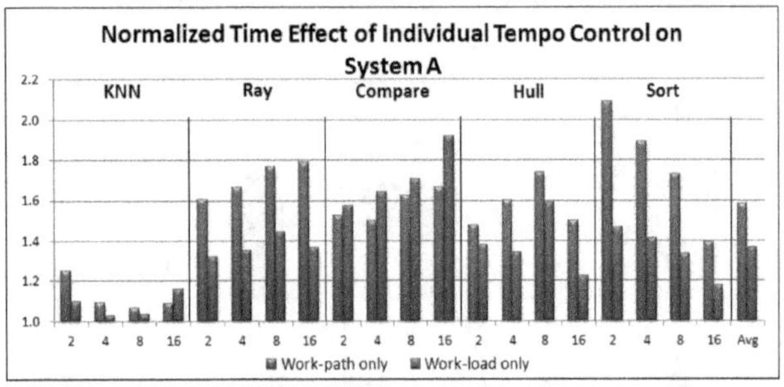


**Figure 11.** Time: Workpath vs. Workload on System A

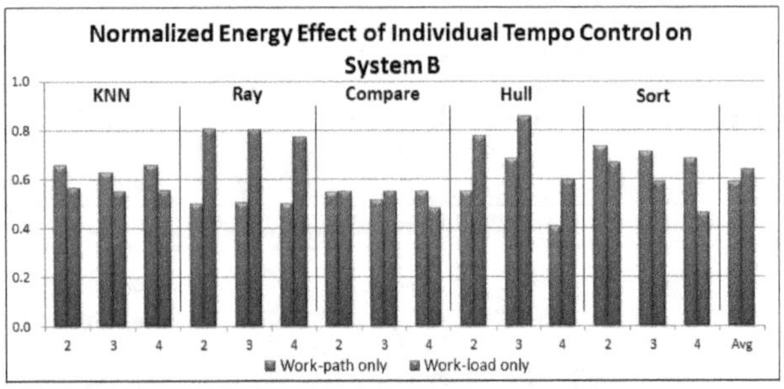


**Figure 12.** Energy: Workpath vs. Workload on System B

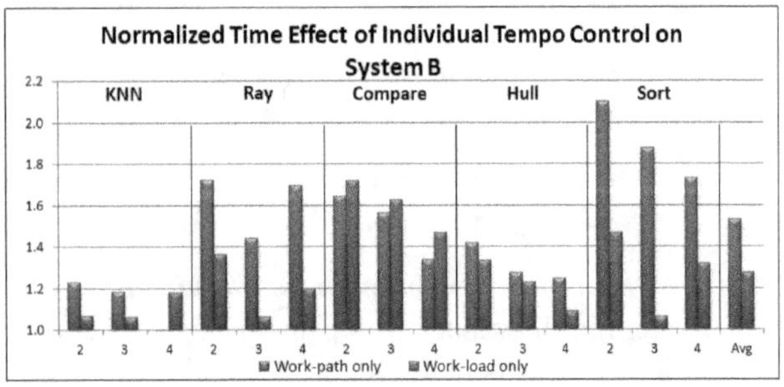


**Figure 13.** Time: Workpath vs. Workload on System B

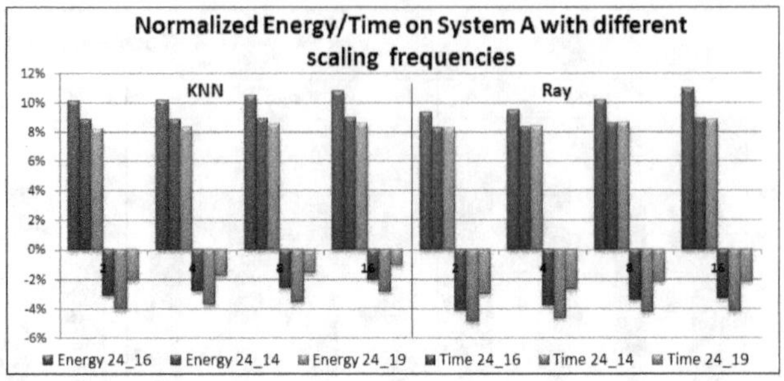


**Figure 14.** The Effect of Frequency Selections on System A (For each benchmark, the 4 groups are for 2, 4, 8, 16 workers respectively. Within each group, columns 1 and 4 are energy saving and time loss for frequency pair 2.4/1.6GHz; columns 2 and 5 are energy saving and time loss for frequency pair 2.4/1.4Ghz; columns 3 and 6 are energy saving and time loss for frequency pair 2.4/1.9Ghz)

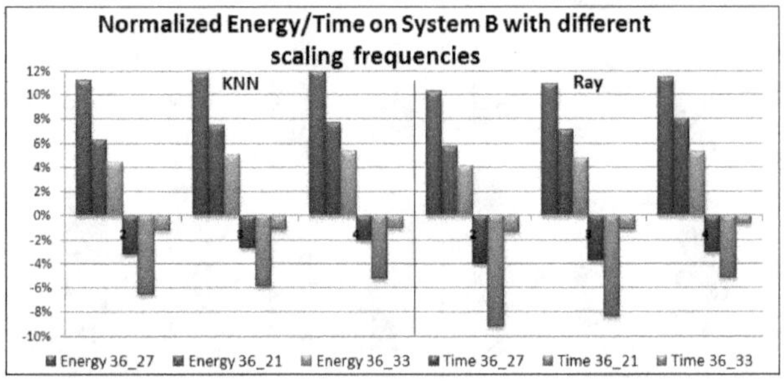


**Figure 15.** The Effect of Frequency Selection on System B (For each benchmark, the 3 groups are for 2, 3, 4 workers respectively. Within each group, columns 1 and 4 are energy saving and time loss for frequency pair 3.6/2.7GHz; columns 2 and 5 are energy saving and time loss for frequency pair 3.6/2.1Ghz; columns 3 and 6 are energy saving and time loss for frequency pair 3.6/3.3Ghz)

fects on System B. To highlight the individual contributions of the two tempo control strategies to the unified HERMES algorithm, we normalize the percentage of savings/loss. For instance, if a tempo control strategy alone can lead to 6% energy savings whereas the HERMES algorithm (unified with both strategies) can lead to 12% energy savings, we record $6/12 = 0.5$ in Figure 10 and Figure 12. For another instance, if a tempo control strategy alone can lead to 6% performance loss whereas the HERMES algorithm (unified with both strategies) can lead to 3% performance loss, we record $6/3 = 2$ in Figure 11 and Figure 13. In all figures, the blue columns are the workpath-only results and the red columns are the workload-only results.

This set of figures show the complementary nature of workpath sensitivity and workload sensitivity. Take the 8-core execution of `Compare` on System A for example. In Figure 10, workpath sensitivity alone leads to around 60%

energy savings relative to the unified HERMES algorithm, and workload sensitivity alone leads to around 55% energy savings relative to the unified HERMES algorithm. The overall energy saving is nearly the sum of saving from the two strategies alone. In Figure 11, again for the 8-core execution of `Compare`, the time loss of workpath-alone strategy is about 1.6 time of the time loss of the unified algorithm, and the time loss of workload-alone strategy is about 1.7 time of the time loss of the unified algorithm. In other words, the unified algorithm obtains the best of the two worlds: the unified strategy leads to more energy savings (almost the sum of the strategies alone), but incurs less performance loss (almost half of the strategies alone).

***The Effect of Frequency Selection*** We conceptually explored the design space of tempo-frequency mapping in Section 3.4, and now experimentally evaluate the effects of different frequency mapping strategies. Figure 14 and Figure 15 are results for mapping tempos to different CPU frequencies. For simplicity, we only consider 2-frequency tempo control, where the fastest tempo is mapped to the first frequency, and all other tempos are mapped to the second frequency. In all experiments, we fix the frequency for the fast tempo – 2.4Ghz for System A and 3.6GHz for System B – and experiment with different settings for the slow tempo.

As predicted, selecting a higher frequency for the slow tempo is likely to yield less performance loss, but also fewer energy savings. This is demonstrated by columns 3 and 6 in each benchmark for both Figures, and the effect is particularly evident in System B. Selecting a very low frequency for the slow tempo (columns 2 and 5 in each benchmark for both Figures) will lead to significant performance loss. In fact, such a selection is not wise for energy savings either: significant increase in the execution time may increase energy consumption, because the latter also holds a linear relationship with time. Heuristically, our experiments seem to suggest the optimal combination often comes with the golden ratio: the frequency for the slow tempo is about 60% percent of the one for the fast tempo.

***N-Frequency Tempo Control*** In the next set of experiments, we study how the number of frequencies impact the results, demonstrated in Figure 16 and Figure 17. Overall, the results between 2-frequency tempo control and 3-frequency tempo control are similar. A 3-frequency tempo control can sometimes incur less loss on performance, as demonstrated by column 6 for each group in Figure 16 and column 4 for each group in Figure 17, but the 2-frequency tempo control has a slight edge on energy savings. We surmise the small advantage of 2-frequency tempo control on energy savings might be due to its lesser overhead on DVFS. In this context, tempo adjustment occurs less frequently.

***Static Scheduling vs. Dynamic Scheduling*** In Section 3.4, we discussed the design choices between static scheduling and dynamic scheduling of workers. Figure 18 demonstrates

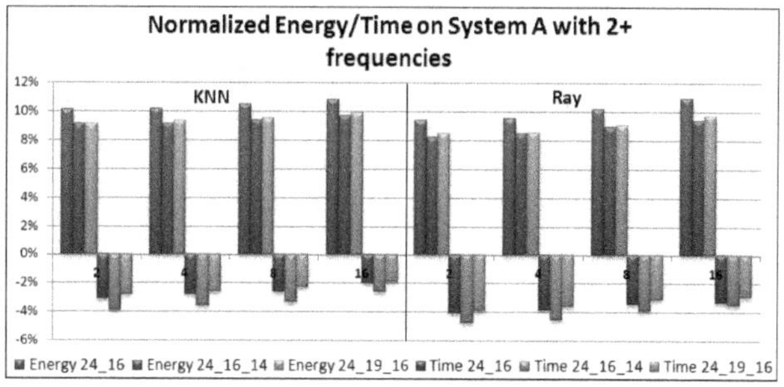


**Figure 16.** N-Frequency Tempo Control on System A (For each benchmark, the 4 groups are for 2, 4, 8, 16 workers respectively. Within each group, columns 1 and 4 are energy saving and time loss for 2-frequency combination 2.4/1.6GHz; columns 2 and 5 are energy saving and time loss for 3-frequency combination 2.4/1.6/1.4Ghz; columns 3 and 6 are energy saving and time loss for 3-frequency combination 2.4/1.9/1.6Ghz)

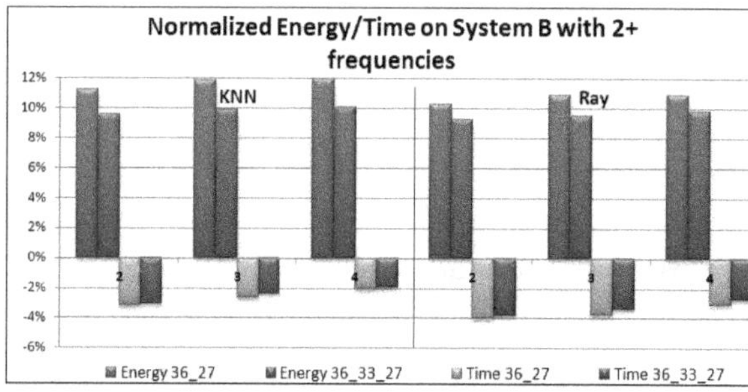


**Figure 17.** N-Frequency Tempo Control on System B (For each benchmark, the 3 groups are for 2, 3, 4 workers respectively. Within each group, columns 1 and 3 are energy saving and time loss for 2-frequency combination 3.6/2.7GHz; columns 2 and 4 are energy saving and time loss for 3-frequency combination 3.6/3.3/2.7Ghz)

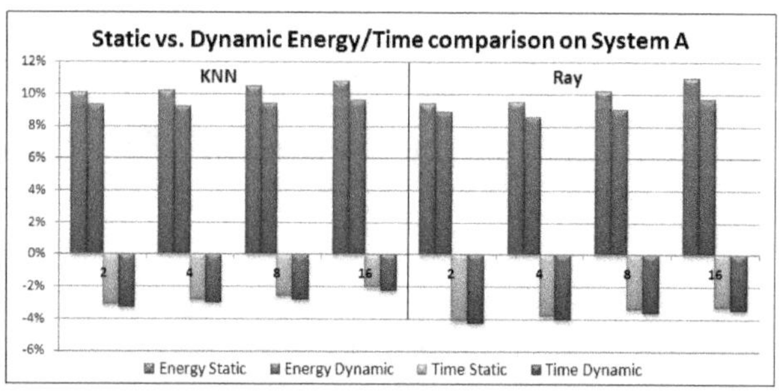


**Figure 18.** Static vs. Dynamic Scheduling

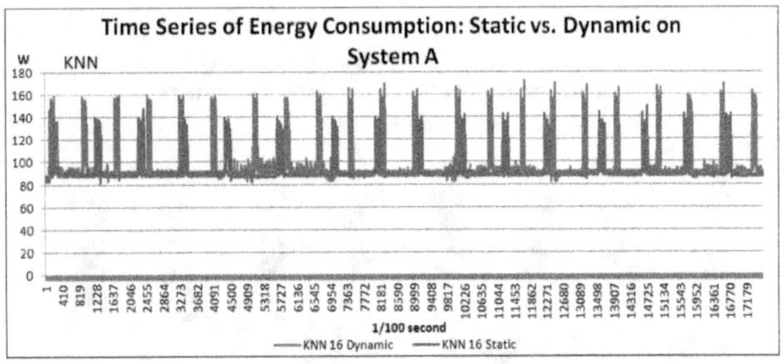


**Figure 19.** Static vs. Dynamic Scheduling (time series, KNN, 16 workers, System A)

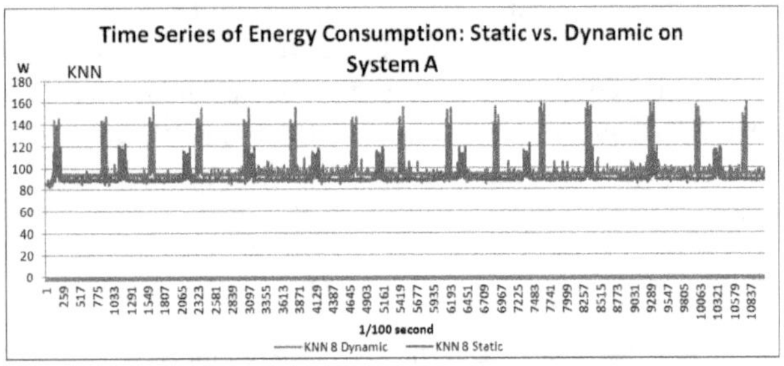


**Figure 20.** Static vs. Dynamic Scheduling (time series, KNN, 8 workers, System A)

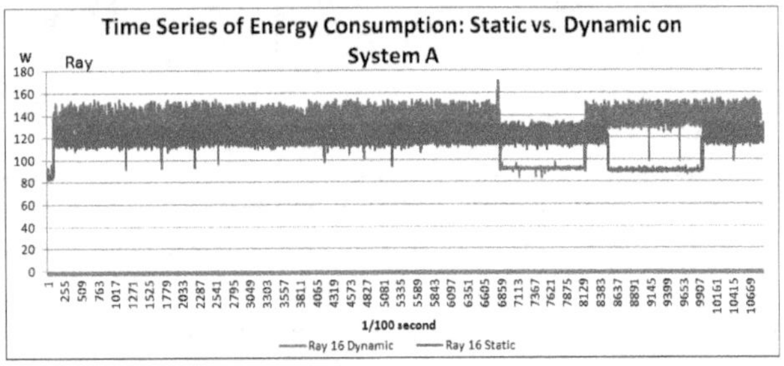


**Figure 21.** Static vs. Dynamic Scheduling (time series, Ray, 16 workers, System A)

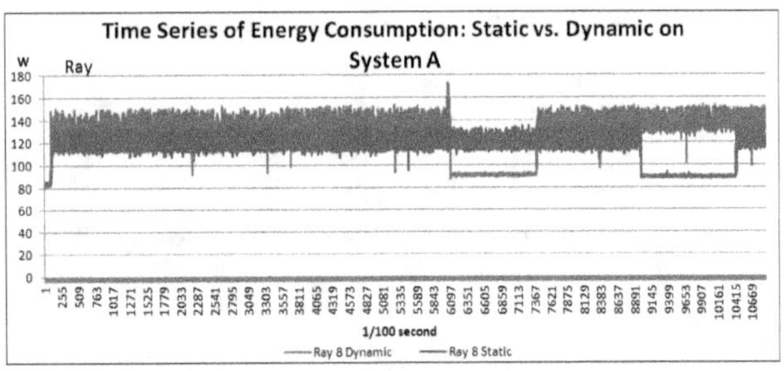


**Figure 22.** Static vs. Dynamic Scheduling (time series, Ray, 8 workers, System A)

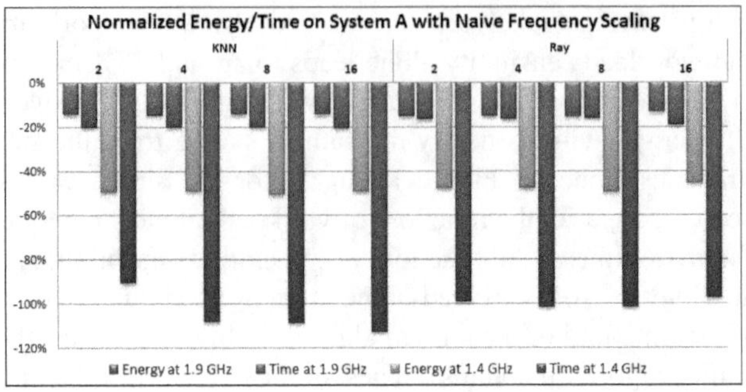


**Figure 23.** Naive Frequency Scheduling (System A)

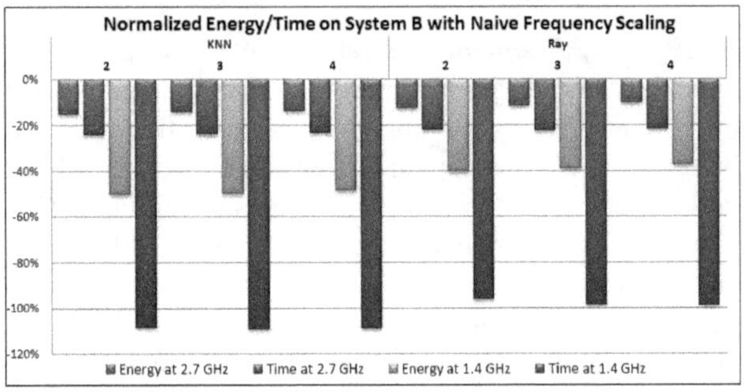


**Figure 24.** Naive Frequency Scheduling (System B)

the effectiveness of HERMES under static scheduling and dynamic scheduling respectively. Figures 19-22 are a more detailed analysis, demonstrating the time series of power consumption. The "shape" of the time series are clearly dependent on the nature of the benchmarks and their settings (such as worker numbers). For each benchmark with the same number of workers, the executions of static scheduling vs. dynamic scheduling display similar patterns. Note that in each figure, the two time series are from different executions. For parallel programs with significant non-determinism, it should come as no surprise that two executions of the same program do not "spike" at the same time.

As demonstrated in the figures, dynamic scheduling incurs a slightly higher level of energy consumption. We believe this is due to the overhead needed for setting/resetting affinity to workers for each WORK invocation, a topic discussed in Sec. 3.4. We investigated into a large number of time series, but found no evidence static scheduling led to significant imbalance (*e.g.* times series with drastically different patterns from their dynamic scheduling counterparts).

***Naive Frequency Scaling*** Finally, we investigate the impact of naively applying frequency scaling, *i.e.*, without the tempo control algorithm of HERMES. Figures 23-24 show the impact of performance and energy if CPU frequencies are naively scaled down at a fixed frequency throughout the program execution. We select two benchmarks, `KNN` and `Ray`. For System A, the CPU frequencies of all cores are fixed at 1.9GHz and 1.4GHz respectively (Figures 23). For

System B, the CPU frequencies are fixed at 2.7GHz and 1.4Ghz respectively (Figures 24). In both figures, a negative value on the Y-axis indicates performance loss or energy over-consumption, normalized against the same control defined in Section 4.1. The figures show that the naive approach not only yields performance loss, but also energy waste.

## 5. Related Work

Energy efficiency in work-stealing run-times is an emerging problem that has received little attention. The only prior work we know of is a short essay [26] that called for the coordination between the thief and the victim to improve energy efficiency. We now summarize related work in two more established areas: optimization of work-stealing runtimes and energy efficiency of multi-threaded programs.

Improving various aspects of work-stealing system efficiency has been a central issue throughout the development of work-stealing systems. Indeed, the original work-stealing algorithm [16] was designed for load balancing, with direct impact on the performance of multi-threaded systems. A-Steal [2] is an adaptive thread scheduler to take parallelism feedback into account at scheduling time. Dinan et. al [13] improved the scalability of work-stealing runtimes through optimizations ranging from lock reduction to work splitting. SLAW [18] is a work-stealing scheduler with adaptive scheduling policies based on locality information. AdaptiveTC [36] improves system performance through adaptive thread management at thread creation time. BWS [14] improves system throughput and fairness in time-sharing multicore systems. Kumar *et. al.* [23] applies run-time techniques such as dynamic compilation and speculative optimization to further reduce the overhead in the context of managed X10. Acar *et. al.* [1] designed a non-shared-memory model to replace the locking model based on shared memory. Performance characterization of Intel TBB with work stealing was systematically conducted by Wu *et. al.* [11]. Bender and Rabin [4] formally analyzed the performance of work-stealing systems on top of a heterogeneous platform, where parallel units may operate on different, yet fixed, frequencies.

There is a large body of work studying the energy efficiency of multi-threaded programs on parallel architectures. On the architecture level, Iyer and Marcelescu [22] studied the impact of DVFS on multi-clock-domain architectures. Wu *et. al.* [38] designed a DVFS-based strategy where the interval of DVFS use is adaptive to recent instance issue queue occupancy. Magklis *et. al.* [27] designed a profiling-based DVFS algorithm on CPUs with multiple clock domains. On the OS level, numerous efforts exist to apply DVFS for energy management, starting with the seminal work by Weiser *et. al.* [37]. Recent examples include CPU Miser [17] (DVFS based on job workload in clusters) and Dhiman *et. al.* [12] (DVFS based on online learning). Beyond DVFS, approaches for energy management of multi-threaded programs include thread migration [33], a combination of thread migration and DVFS [8], and software/hardware approximation [15, 34]. The boundary between architecture and OS for energy efficiency is often blurred. For example, Merkel *et. al.* [29] designed an energy-aware scheduling policy for thermal management, with inputs from hardware performance counters. Further afield, energy efficiency can be achieved via compiler optimization (*e.g.*,[19, 39]) and language designs (*e.g.*, [3, 9, 34, 35]).

## 6. Conclusion

This paper introduced HERMES, a novel and practical solution for improving energy efficiency of work-stealing applications. HERMES addresses the problem through judicious tempo control over workers, guided by a unified workpath-sensitive and workload-sensitive algorithm. HERMES only requires minor changes to the work-stealing runtime. With no changes necessary for the underlying architectures, OS, or higher-level programming models, this minimalistic approach can still yield significant energy savings with little performance overhead.

HERMES illustrates the mutually beneficial relationship between architecture features and language runtime features, and offers a "sweet spot" unifying the strength of the two. With DVFS, the language runtime becomes tempo-enabled, leading to improved energy efficiency. With unique features of the work-stealing language runtime design — specifically, the relationship between tasks as defined by the work-first principle, and the meta-level structure of deques — HERMES is able to answer challenging questions every DVFS-based energy management system must answer: "when to scale frequencies?" and "what frequency to scale to?" The latter point is particularly relevant in the context of multi-threaded language design: compared with more established programming/runtime models (such as Pthreads), work-stealing language runtimes are intrinsically endowed with features friendly for energy management, which HERMES takes advantage of. As a result, HERMES is a *language*-level solution without the need of characterizing program executions on a *per-application* basis.

The workpath-sensitive and workload-sensitive tempo control strategies of HERMES are experimentally effective. In the future, we plan to theoretically analyze the two heuristics through work-span analysis [16], formally establishing their impact on the performance/energy trade-off.

***Acknowledgments*** We thank anonymous reviewers for their constructive comments. We thank Thomas Bartenstein and Tyler Stachecki for system configurations, Guy Blelloch and Charles Leiserson for pointers on benchmarks, Doug Lea, Barry Tannenbaum and Jim Sukha for their comments. The project is partially supported by a Google award, and NSF CCF-1054515. Any opinions expressed here are from the authors and do not necessarily reflect the views of the sponsors.

## References


[1] ACAR, U. A., CHARGUERAUD, A., AND RAINEY, M. Scheduling parallel programs by work stealing with private deques. In *PPoPP '13* (2013), pp. 219–228.

[2] AGRAWAL, K., HE, Y., AND LEISERSON, C. E. Adaptive work stealing with parallelism feedback. In *PPoPP '07* (2007), pp. 112–120.

[3] BAEK, W., AND CHILIMBI, T. M. Green: a framework for supporting energy-conscious programming using controlled approximation. In *PLDI'10* (2010), pp. 198–209.

[4] BENDER, M. A., AND RABIN, M. O. Scheduling cilk multithreaded parallel programs on processors of different speeds. In *SPAA '00* (2000), pp. 13–21.

[5] BLELLOCH, G., FINEMAN, J., GIBBONS, P., KYROLA, A., SHUN, J., TANGWONSAN, K., AND SIMHADRI, H. V. Problem based benchmark suite, 2012.

[6] BLUMOFE, R. D. *Executing Multithreaded Programs Efficiently*. PhD thesis, Massachusetts Institute of Technology, Department of Electrical Engineering and Computer Science, Cambridge, MA 02139, 1995.

[7] BLUMOFE, R. D., AND LEISERSON, C. E. Scheduling multithreaded computations by work stealing. *J. ACM 46*, 5 (Sept. 1999), 720–748.

[8] CAI, Q., GONZÁLEZ, J., MAGKLIS, G., CHAPARRO, P., AND GONZÁLEZ, A. Thread shuffling: combining dvfs and thread migration toreduce energy consumptions for multi-core systems. In *ISLPED '11* (2011), pp. 379–384.

[9] COHEN, M., ZHU, H. S., EMGIN, S. E., AND LIU, Y. D. Energy types. In *OOPSLA'12* (October 2012).

[10] CONG, G., KODALI, S., KRISHNAMOORTHY, S., LEA, D., SARASWAT, V., AND WEN, T. Solving large, irregular graph problems using adaptive work-stealing. In *ICPP'08* (2008), pp. 536–545.

[11] CONTRERAS, G., AND MARTONOSI, M. Characterizing and improving the performance of intel threading building blocks. In *IEEE International Symposium on Workload Characterization (2008)* (2008), pp. 57–66.

[12] DHIMAN, G., AND ROSING, T. S. Dynamic voltage frequency scaling for multi-tasking systems using online learning. In *ISLPED '07* (2007), pp. 207–212.

[13] DINAN, J., LARKINS, D. B., SADAYAPPAN, P., KRISHNAMOORTHY, S., AND NIEPLOCHA, J. Scalable work stealing. In *SC '09* (2009).

[14] DING, X., WANG, K., GIBBONS, P. B., AND ZHANG, X. Bws: balanced work stealing for time-sharing multicores. In *EuroSys '12* (2012), pp. 365–378.

[15] ESMAEILZADEH, H., SAMPSON, A., CEZE, L., AND BURGER, D. Architecture support for disciplined approximate programming. In *ASPLOS'12* (2012), pp. 301–312.

[16] FRIGO, M., LEISERSON, C. E., AND RANDALL, K. H. The implementation of the cilk-5 multithreaded language. In *PLDI '98* (1998), pp. 212–223.

[17] GE, R., FENG, X., CHUN FENG, W., AND CAMERON, K. Cpu miser: A performance-directed, run-time system for power-aware clusters. In *ICPP'07* (2007), pp. 18–18.

[18] GUO, Y., ZHAO, J., CAVÉ, V., AND SARKAR, V. Slaw: A scalable locality-aware adaptive work-stealing scheduler. In *IPDPS* (2010), pp. 1–12.

[19] HSU, C.-H., KREMER, U., AND HSIAO, M. Compiler-directed dynamic voltage/frequency scheduling for energy reduction in microprocessors. In *ISLPED'01* (2001), pp. 275–278.

[20] INTEL. Threading Building Blocks, `http://threadingbuildingblocks.org/`.

[21] INTEL. Intel cilk plus, 2013.

[22] IYER, A., AND MARCULESCU, D. Power efficiency of voltage scaling in multiple clock, multiple voltage cores. In *ICCAD '02* (2002), pp. 379–386.

[23] KUMAR, V., FRAMPTON, D., BLACKBURN, S. M., GROVE, D., AND TARDIEU, O. Work-stealing without the baggage. In *OOPSLA '12* (2012), pp. 297–314.

[24] LEA, D. A java fork/join framework. In *Proceedings of the ACM 2000 conference on Java Grande* (2000), JAVA '00, pp. 36–43.

[25] LEIJEN, D., SCHULTE, W., AND BURCKHARDT, S. The design of a task parallel library. In *OOPSLA '09* (2009), pp. 227–242.

[26] LIU, Y. D. Green thieves in work stealing. In *ASPLOS'12 (Provactive Ideas session)* (2012).

[27] MAGKLIS, G., SCOTT, M. L., SEMERARO, G., ALBONESI, D. H., AND DROPSHO, S. Profile-based dynamic voltage and frequency scaling for a multiple clock domain microprocessor. In *ISCA '03* (2003), pp. 14–27.

[28] MARLOW, S., PEYTON JONES, S., AND SINGH, S. Runtime support for multicore haskell. In *ICFP '09* (2009), pp. 65–78.

[29] MERKEL, A., AND BELLOSA, F. Balancing power consumption in multiprocessor systems. In *EuroSys '06* (2006), pp. 403–414.

[30] MICHAEL, M. M., VECHEV, M. T., AND SARASWAT, V. A. Idempotent work stealing. In *PPoPP '09* (2009), pp. 45–54.

[31] MOHR, E., KRANZ, D. A., AND HALSTEAD, JR., R. H. Lazy task creation: a technique for increasing the granularity of parallel programs. In *Proceedings of the 1990 ACM conference on LISP and functional programming* (1990), LFP '90, pp. 185–197.

[32] PROKOPEC, A., BAGWELL, P., ROMPF, T., AND ODERSKY, M. A generic parallel collection framework. In *Euro-Par'11* (2011), pp. 136–147.

[33] RANGAN, K. K., WEI, G.-Y., AND BROOKS, D. Thread motion: fine-grained power management for multi-core systems. In *ISCA '09* (2009), pp. 302–313.

[34] SAMPSON, A., DIETL, W., FORTUNA, E., GNANAPRAGASAM, D., CEZE, L., AND GROSSMAN, D. EnerJ: Approximate Data Types for Safe and General Low-Power Computation. In *PLDI'11* (June 2011).

[35] SORBER, J., KOSTADINOV, A., GARBER, M., BRENNAN, M., CORNER, M. D., AND BERGER, E. D. Eon: a language and runtime system for perpetual systems. In *SenSys'07* (2007), pp. 161–174.

[36] WANG, L., CUI, H., DUAN, Y., LU, F., FENG, X., AND YEW, P.-C. An adaptive task creation strategy for work-stealing scheduling. In *CGO '10* (2010), pp. 266–277.

[37] WEISER, M., WELCH, B., DEMERS, A., AND SHENKER, S. Scheduling for reduced cpu energy. In *OSDI '94* (1994).

[38] WU, Q., JUANG, P., MARTONOSI, M., AND CLARK, D. W. Voltage and frequency control with adaptive reaction time in multiple-clock-domain processors. In *HPCA* (2005), pp. 178–189.

[39] XIE, F., MARTONOSI, M., AND MALIK, S. Compile-time dynamic voltage scaling settings: opportunities and limits. In *PLDI '03* (2003), pp. 49–62.

# Data-Parallel Finite-State Machines


Todd Mytkowicz
Microsoft Research
toddm@microsoft.com

Madanlal Musuvathi
Microsoft Research
madanm@microsoft.com

Wolfram Schulte
Microsoft
schulte@microsoft.com



## Abstract

A finite-state machine (FSM) is an important abstraction for solving several problems, including regular-expression matching, tokenizing text, and Huffman decoding. FSM computations typically involve data-dependent iterations with unpredictable memory-access patterns making them difficult to parallelize. This paper describes a parallel algorithm for FSMs that breaks dependences across iterations by efficiently enumerating transitions from all possible states on each input symbol. This allows the algorithm to utilize various sources of data parallelism available on modern hardware, including vector instructions and multiple processors/cores. For instance, on benchmarks from three FSM applications: regular expressions, Huffman decoding, and HTML tokenization, the parallel algorithm achieves up to a 3× speedup over optimized sequential baselines on a single core, and linear speedups up to 21× on 8 cores.



***Categories and Subject Descriptors*** D.1.3 [*Concurrent Programming*]: Parallel programming; F.1.2 [*Modes of Computation*]: Parallelism and concurrency

***Keywords*** Parallelism, Finite State Machines, Regular Expression Matching, Huffman Decoding


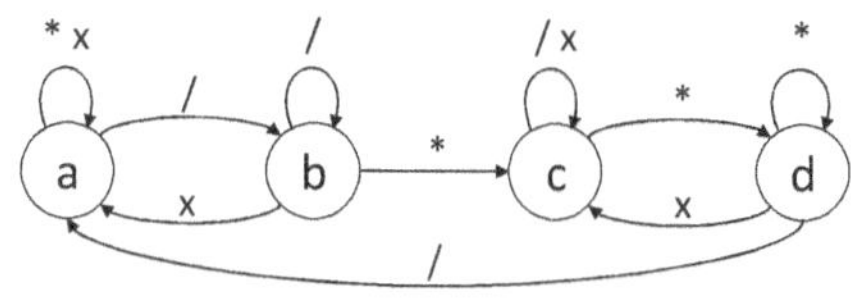


(a)

| T: | / | * | x |
|---|---|---|---|
| a | b | a | a |
| b | b | c | a |
| c | c | d | c |
| d | a | d | c |

(b)

```
state = a;
foreach (input in)
  state = T[in][state];
```

(c)

**Figure 1.** An FSM containing four states that accepts C-style comments in source code delineated by /* and */. The input x represents all characters other than / and *.

## 1. Introduction

Hardware is parallel. While desktops, tablets, and even phones have vector instructions, multiple cores, and GPUs, many important algorithms are unable to exploit all of this parallelism. This paper focuses on finite-state machines, a class of applications that has previously been hard to parallelize.

A finite-state machine (FSM) is a fundamental model of computation [10] that is at the core of many practical applications ranging from regular-expression matching, tokenizing text, dictionary-based decoding, network intrusion detection, and feature extraction from web pages. Figure 1(a) shows an example FSM that identifies C-style comments. The table in Figure 1(b) determines how the FSM states transition on each input symbol, and Figure 1(c) is a straightforward implementation of this FSM that iteratively accesses the transition table to obtain the state after each input symbol.

FSMs are difficult to parallelize for two reasons. First, there is a tight dependence between successive loop-iterations making it nontrivial to distribute loops across multiple processors. Second, FSMs perform little computation in each iteration with memory-access patterns that are input-dependent and unpredictable.[1] This makes it difficult for FSM implementations to use parallelism *within* a processor, namely instruction-level parallelism, vector (SIMD) capabilities and memory-level parallelism.

This paper presents an efficient parallel algorithm for FSM computations that is able to utilize various kinds of data parallelism available on modern hardware, both paral-




*ASPLOS '14*, March 1–5, 2014, Salt Lake City, Utah, USA.



http://dx.doi.org/10.1145/2541940.2541988


[1] Alternately, FSM implementations can encode transition tables using a large `switch` statement — trading unpredictable data accesses for unpredictable control flow.

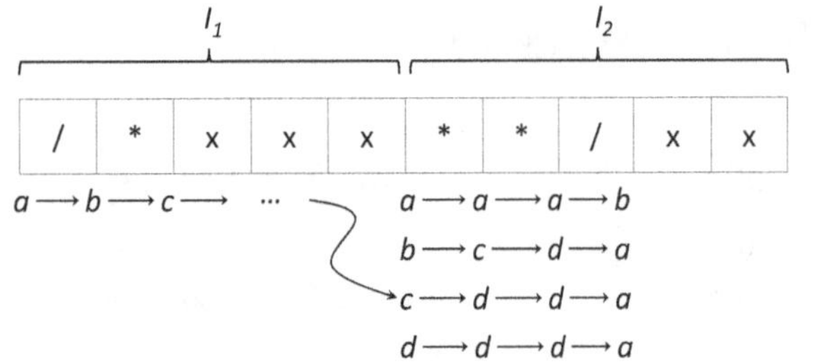


**Figure 2.** Enumerative computation for parallelizing FSMs.

lelism across multiple processors and parallelism within a single processor. The algorithm is up to 3× faster than optimized sequential implementations on a single processor and achieves subsequent multiplicative speedups with multiple processors.

Figure 2 shows the key idea behind our parallel algorithm. Consider a run of the FSM in Figure 1(a) on the input shown in Figure 2. We can parallelize this computation by splitting the input into two chunks $I_1$ and $I_2$ and performing the two subcomputations in parallel. Obviously, this is not possible unless we know the start state for the second subcomputation, which is the final state of the first subcomputation.

One way to break this dependency is to fork a version of the second subcomputation starting from *every* state of the FSM as shown in Figure 2. We call this an *enumerative* computation as it enumerates all possible start states. Once the first subcomputation has finished, we pick the version of the enumerative computation that started from the correct state, which in this case is state $c$. It is possible to generalize this approach by splitting the input many times where all but the first computation is done enumeratively in parallel (Section 3).

The obvious disadvantage of this approach is the overhead of the enumerative computation. For an FSM with $n$ states, an enumerative computation performs $n$ times more work than the sequential version. In other words, a naïve implementation requires a linear number of processors to achieve constant speedups and does not scale for all but small FSMs.

The main contributions of this paper are optimizations that make this enumerative computation efficient. The first optimization relies on the observation that different enumerations perform redundant work when multiple states *converge* to the same state on some input symbol (Section 5.2). For instance, after reading a *, both states $c$ and $d$ transition to state $d$ in Figure 1(a). This causes the three of the four enumerations to converge after reading the first two input symbols in Figure 2. We call the states of such non-redundant computations *active* states. By dynamically utilizing convergence, the overhead of the enumerative computation is proportional to the number of active states and not to the total number of state in the FSM.

Using realistic examples, this paper demonstrates that most FSMs, even those with many states, often converge to 16 or less active states for *any* input. This makes the convergence optimization worthwhile. Our experiments also show that while convergence is common, convergence to a single state is rare. As a result, the enumerative computation is still more expensive than the sequential computation.

A major component of this overhead is the transition-table lookup required for each active state. To optimize this cost, we use a *range-coalesced* representation of the transition table (Section 5.3). In this representation, states get different identifiers based on the most recently seen input. By appropriately assigning these identifiers, we ensure that accesses made by active states are coalesced into a smaller range of memory, reducing memory pressure.

Finally, we observe that different enumerations are *independent* and thus can be performed simultaneously using different lanes of a single-instruction multiple-data (SIMD) processor. One challenge in using SIMD instructions is the need for a *gather* operation that accesses the transition table at different offsets from each lane. Unfortunately, current desktop processors do not *yet* support generic gather operations. We use an existing SIMD primitive, `shuffle`, to implement this operation.

Our benchmarks consist of thousands of FSMs from three case studies: regular-expression matching, Huffman decoding, and HTML tokenization (Section 6). For more than 80% of these FSMs, our implementation performs one or two `shuffle` operations per input symbol. The associativity of these operations [26] allows the hardware to process multiple input symbols simultaneously, increasing instruction-level parallelism. As a result, our parallel implementation is up to 3× faster than optimized sequential implementations on a single processor core. We further demonstrate multiplicative speedups on multiple processor cores, up to 21× on 8 cores.

## 2. Background

This section provides a brief primer on FSMs and introduces terminology used in the rest of the paper. It then describes a general approach for parallelizing FSM computations.

### 2.1 Primer on Finite-State Machines

We assume that the reader is familiar with classic automata theory, as described in Hopcroft and Ullmann [10]. A deterministic *finite-state machine* $D$ is a tuple $(Q, \Sigma, q_0, \delta, F)$, where $Q$ is a finite set of states, $\Sigma$ is a fixed alphabet, $q_0 \in Q$ is the initial state, $F \subseteq Q$ is the set of final states, and $\delta$ is the transition function with type $Q \times \Sigma \rightarrow Q$. This paper focuses on deterministic FSMs. A nondeterministic FSM can be converted to a deterministic FSM using standard techniques [10], albeit with a worst-case exponential blowup in the number of states. Applying the techniques discussed in this paper to parallelize nondeterministic FSMs is left for future work.

To determine if a string $s = s_1, s_2, \ldots, s_m$ is accepted by an FSM $D$, the FSM starts in state $q_0$ and iteratively applies the transition function to determine the state $q_i$ on reading $s_i$ using the recurrence $q_i = \delta(q_{i-1}, s_i)$. If the final state $q_m$ is in $F$, then the string $s$ is *accepted* by the FSM $D$. When discussing our algorithm, we will also refer to a *transition function* $T_a$ that maps states to states such that $T_a(q) = r$ iff $r = \delta(q, a)$. In implementations, the transition function is implemented as an array or arrays, in which case, we will refer to $T_a$ simply as `T[a]`.

Applications sometimes perform actions on each state transition (e.g. tokenization or decoding) apart from accepting or rejecting the input string. This paper uses the Mealy formalism [20] and assumes the existence of a $\phi$ function that is invoked with the current input symbol $s_i$ and the state $q_i$ reached after reading that symbol. In the context of parallelizing FSMs, we will make a simplistic assumption that the $\phi$ function can be invoked out of order. Modifying sequential clients of FSMs to satisfy this assumption is not discussed in this paper.

### 2.2 Identifying Associative Operations in FSM

The relationship between FSM computations and semirings is well known [2]. A semiring is an algebraic structure with a generalized additive and multiplicative operations defined on a domain. The properties of these operations ensure that the generalized matrix multiplication in semirings is associative. In theory, this allows one to parallelize problems that can be cast as matrix multiplications in semirings.

Consider the semiring on the Boolean domain with disjunction as the additive operation and conjunction as the multiplicative operation. For an FSM with $n$ states, let $M_s$ be the $n \times n$ Boolean matrix, such that $M_s[i, j] = true$ iff state $i$ transitions to state $j$ on symbol $s$. For a given input string $s = s_1, s_2, \ldots s_m$, the matrix product

$$M = M_{s_m} \cdot \ldots \cdot M_{s_2} \cdot M_{s_1}$$

has the property that $M[i, j]$ is true iff the FSM reaches state $q_j$ on reading the input $s$ starting from state $q_i$. Thus, the FSM accepts the input iff $M[0, j]$ is true for some state $q_j \in F$.

Ladner and Fischer [15] exploit this formulation to parallelize FSM computation using parallel prefix-sums. Their algorithm generalizes to nondeterministic FSMs and executes in $O(log(m) \times n^3)$ time with $m$ processors, using the standard cubic algorithm for matrix multiplication.

Hillis and Steele [8] describe an improved parallel prefix computation for evaluating deterministic FSMs that reduces the overhead to $O(log(m) \times n)$. The basic idea, which forms the basis for the enumerative computation described in Section 1, is to succinctly encode FSM computations as *composition* of transition functions. If $T_{s_i}$ represents the transition function on input $s_i$ and $\otimes$ represents function composition, then the function

$$T = T_{s_m} \otimes \ldots \otimes T_{s_2} \otimes T_{s_1}$$

determines the final state of the FSM starting from some state on input $s_1, s_2, \ldots, s_m$. Parallelization follows from the fact that function composition is associative.

This paper builds on these theoretical insights. The key contribution of this paper is in optimizing away the dependence on $n$, the number of states in the FSM, using properties of FSMs seen in practice, and on demonstrating a scalable implementation that exploits both fine-grained and coarse-grained parallelism available in modern hardware.

## 3. Parallel Algorithm

This section describes the data-parallel FSM algorithm but first introduces a primitive used to describe the algorithm.

### 3.1 Gather Primitive

Let $S$ and $T$ be arrays of length $m$ and $n$ respectively. A gather operation, represented by $S \otimes_{m,n} T$, is an array of length $m$ such that

$$(S \otimes_{m,n} T)[i] = T[S[i]]$$

In essence, the array $S$ contains indices (or addresses) that are used to lookup the array $T$. Obviously, the lookup is well-formed only when the indices are within the bounds of $T$. For convenience, we will assume that the index modulo $n$ is used for such out-of-bound indices. Unless when necessary, we will drop the subscripts and simply refer to the gather of $S$ and $T$ as $S \otimes T$. Gather is associative.

$$((S \otimes T) \otimes U)[i] = U[(S \otimes T)[i]] = U[T[S[i]]]$$

$$(S \otimes (T \otimes U))[i] = (T \otimes U)[S[i]] = U[T[S[i]]]$$

When $S$ is a set of FSM states and $T$ is the transition function for some input symbol, the elements of $S \otimes T$ are the respective successor states for the states in $S$. In other words, gather implements the functional composition of the transition functions.

There is a trivial sequential implementation of $\otimes_{m,n}$ that performs $m$ memory lookups, assuming the contents of $S$ are already available in registers. More efficient implementations are possible with appropriate hardware support. For instance, Intel SSE3 architectures provide a `shuffle` instruction that performs $\otimes_{16,16}$ for byte arrays. Section 4 describes a way to implement a general $\otimes_{m,n}$ using $m/16 * n/16$ invocations of $\otimes_{16,16}$.

### 3.2 Base Enumerative Algorithm

Figure 3 provides the base enumerative algorithm for a given start state `st` and an input sequence `in`. When compared to the sequential algorithm in Figure 1(c), the enumerative

```
Base(State st, Input in){
  States S = Id;
  for (i=0; i<in.len; i++) {
    a = in[i];
    S = S ⊗ T[a];
    φ(a, S[st]);                }}
```

**Figure 3.** Base Enumerative Algorithm.

```
Base_ILP(State st, Input in){
  States S = Id;
  for (i=0; i<in.len/3; i+=3) {
    (a,b,c) = (in[i], in[i+1], in[i+2]);
    Sa = S ⊗ T[a];  Tbc = T[b] ⊗ T[c];
    Sb = Sa ⊗ T[b]; S = Sa ⊗ Tbc;
    φ(a, Sa[st]); φ(b, Sb[st]); φ(c, S[st]); }}
```

**Figure 4.** Unrolling the loop in Figure 3 exposes ILP. Instructions in the same line can be executed in parallel.

algorithm maintains an array of states, S, at each step rather than a single state. At each step, element $i$ of S is the state reached at that step if the FSM had started from state $i$. S is initialized to the identity array Id whose element $i$ is $i$.

On an input symbol a, the algorithm obtains the transition function T[a]. The gather operation provides S for the next iteration. In addition, the algorithm calls the output $\phi$ function on the actual FSM state S[st]. Of course, invoking the $\phi$ function at each step is unnecessary when the FSM is only determining an accept/reject decision on the input (say, when performing regular-expression matching). In such cases, we will assume that invoking the $\phi$ function after processing all of the input provides the accept or reject decision.

### 3.3 Using Fine-Grained Parallelism

When compared to the sequential algorithm in Figure 1(c), the base enumerative algorithm performs more work. However, the associativity of gather alleviates this overhead by exposing instruction-level parallelism (ILP). For instance, Figure 4 unrolls the loop three times (and assumes that the input length is divisible by three). The instructions on the same line do not depend on each other and thus can execute in parallel. Assuming an efficient implementation of gather, this additional ILP can make the base enumerative algorithm run faster than the sequential version, despite performing more work. Optimizations described in Section 5 enable this possibility.

### 3.4 Using Coarse-Grained Parallelism

Figure 5 shows the parallelization of the base enumerative algorithm on multiple cores/machines, using an implementation of parallel-prefix sum [1, 15]. The parallel algorithm distributes the input equally among available processors and each processor processes its chunk in three phases. In the first phase, each processor runs the base enumerative algo-

```
Base_Multicore(State st, Input in){
  chunk = in.len/NumProc;

  // Run chunks in parallel
  States S[NumProc];
  parallel.for (proc p in [0...NumProc-1]){
    my_in = in[p*chunk .. (p+1)*chunk-1];
    S[p] = T[my_in[0]];
    for (i = 1; i<chunk; i++){
      S[p] = S[p] ⊗ T[my_in[i]];          }}

  // Compute start states for each chunk
  State st[NumProc];
  st[0] = st;
  for (p in [1..NumProc-1]){
    st[p] = S[p-1][st[p-1]];}

  // Compute output in parallel
  parallel.for (proc p in [0...NumProc-1]){
    my_in = in[p*chunk .. (p+1)*chunk-1];
    Base(st[p], my_in);                   }}
```

**Figure 5.** Using multiple cores to parallelize the base enumerative algorithm.

rithm on its chunk of the input in parallel. The end goal of the first phase is to compute for each processor S[p], an array that determines the final state of the FSM when processing the input chunk from every starting state.

The sequential second phase (which can be parallelized, if necessary), computes the start states for each processor using these arrays. With the correct start states known, the third phase simply invokes the base enumerative algorithm for each input chunk in parallel. Note, the $\phi$ function is only called in the third phase, making the first two phases extremely fast. The implementations of the first and the third phase can additionally benefit from fine-grained parallelism as shown in Figure 4.

There are a variety of ways to implement a parallel-prefix sum on modern parallel hardware. For example, prior work has implemented these primitives on GPUs [4, 7, 29], on a cluster [6, 36], or using threads [31]. In contrast, the algorithm in Figure 5 is designed to minimize communication when the number processors is much smaller than the amount of parallelism available (proportional to the size of the input), which is the case for our applications.

## 4. Implementation of Gather

The performance of the parallel algorithms in Section 3 depend on an efficient gather. This sections provides such an implementation.

### 4.1 Non-SIMD Gather

The straightforward implementation of $S \otimes_{m,n} T$ is with $m$ memory lookups. Figure 6 illustrates the performance of this implementation on a *gather microkernel*. The microkernel emulates the inner-loop of the base algorithm in Figure 3 on random inputs and random transition funtions. In particular,

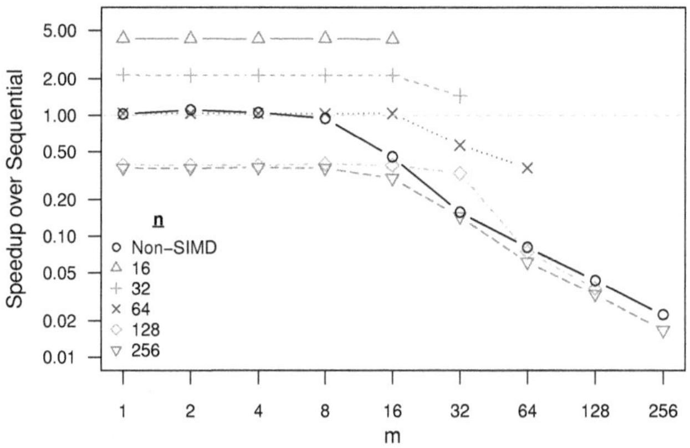


**Figure 6.** Performance of $\otimes_{m,n}$ on a machine with SIMD width $W = 16$.

the microkernel allocates 1024 arrays of size $n = 1024$, each initialized with random values between 0 and $n - 1$. Then for different values of $m$, it enters a tight loop that computes $S = S \otimes_{m,n} T_r$ for a table $T_r$ randomly picked from the allocated arrays. Figure 6 compares the performance of the microkernel with a sequential baseline of Figure 1(c).

The "Non-SIMD" line in Figure 6 shows that the compiler and the hardware are able to hide the cost of multiple lookups (i.e., performance is at 1.0) for $m$ up to 8. This suggests that for small FSMs with less than or equal to 8 states, the enumerative algorithm incurs no additional overhead. However, the performance degrades for larger values of $m$.

### 4.2 SIMD Gather

Modern microprocessors are equipped with Single Instruction Multiply Data (SIMD) registers that apply an operation on $W$ data items in one instruction. In particular, `x86` has support for *byte* level `shuffle` of an array of $W = 16$ characters that essentially implements $\otimes_{16,16}$ for two SIMD registers. Future architectures are expected to increase the width up to 1024 bytes along with a support for general purpose gather [12].

Now, we will describe how to implement a general $\otimes_{m,n}$ using multiple invocations of $\otimes_{16,16}$. In this paper, we will only need instances where $m \leq n$. The implementation is best understood through an example. Suppose the SIMD width is $W = 4$ and we desire to implement $S \otimes_{m,n} T$ when $n = m = 8$ for the following arrays

$$S = [3, 5, 0, 1, 5, 4, 6, 2], T = [A, B, C, D, E, F, G, H]$$

The desired answer is $[D, F, A, B, F, E, G, C]$. Let us store S and T into two SIMD registers $S_{03}$ and $S_{47}$, and $T_{03}$ and $T_{47}$ respectively. Current implementations of `shuffle` use the index modulo $W$ when an index exceeds $W$. The first four values of $S \otimes T$ can be obtained by performing

$$S_{03} \otimes T_{03} = [D, B, A, B], \quad S_{03} \otimes T_{47} = [H, F, E, F]$$

and blending the results based on whether the index exceeds $W$ or not. In fact, `x86` supports a `blend` instruction for this purpose. Thus,

$$(S \otimes T)_{03} = \texttt{blend}(S_{03} \otimes T_{03}, S_{03} \otimes T_{47}, S_{03} < 4)$$

$$(S \otimes T)_{47} = \texttt{blend}(S_{47} \otimes T_{03}, S_{47} \otimes T_{47}, S_{47} < 4)$$

Generalizing this example, $\otimes_{m,n}$ can be implemented using $(m * n)/W$ invocations of $\otimes_{W,W}$.

SIMD gather provides two benefits. First, it utilizes the entire memory bandwidth between the processor and its L1 data cache. A single SIMD load fetches 128 bits while a non-SIMD load can only fetch 64 bits. Second, SIMD gather exploits the fact that FSMs are memory bound computations with underutilized functional units. The `shuffle` and `blend` instructions use the functional units that would have otherwise been idle.

Figure 6 illustrates the performance of SIMD gather for various values of $m$ and $n$ for the gather microkernel running on a machine with $W = 16$. When $n = W$, the SIMD gather is 4.4× faster than the sequential baseline. The optimizations discussed in Section 5 enable many of the FSMs from our benchmarks to exploit this performance. For $n$ up to 64, the SIMD gather still outperforms the non-SIMD version. For larger values of $m$, the overhead of performing $(m * n)/16$ `shuffle` operations becomes a bottleneck. However, this overhead can be hidden by parallelizing the enumerative computation on multiple processor cores.

### 4.3 Implementation Details

The implementation uses C++ template specialization to instantiate gather for appropriate values of $m$ and $n$. We hand-coded specialized implementations for all pairs of $m$ and $n$ that are multiples of 16 in the range $[16, 256]$. Peculiarities of `x86` make the implementation nontrivial. For instance, the `shuffle` instruction in SSE 4.2 (`_mm_shuffle_epi8`) treats indices as signed bytes and treats negative indices as index 0. Supporting FSMs with greater than 127 states requires additional bit manipulation to handle the sign bit correctly. Similarly, byte level `shuffle` is not implemented on $AVX$ and so our current implementation cannot utilize 256 bit wide registers despite running on $AVX$ hardware.

## 5. Optimizations

As discussed in the previous section, the cost of $\otimes_{m,n}$ depends both on $m$ and $n$. This section describes two optimizations for the parallel FSM algorithm, namely *convergence* that reduces $m$ and *range coalescing* that reduces $n$. We start with a primitive necessary to explain these optimizations.

### 5.1 Factor Primitive

Given an array $S$, $Factor(S)$ is a pair $(L, U)$ such that $S = L \otimes U$ and $U$ contains only the unique elements of $S$. (Here $L$ stands for "lookup" and $U$ stands for "unique".)

```
1  Convergence( State st, Input in ){
2    States S = Id;
3    States Acc = Id;
4
5    for (i=0; i<in.len; i++){
6      S = S ⊗ T[in[i]];
7      if (conv_check()){
8        (L, U) = Factor(S);
9        S = U;
10       Acc = Acc ⊗ L; }
11     S_base = Acc ⊗ S;
12     φ(i, S_base[st]);          }}
```

**Figure 7.** Convergence Algorithm

An example is given below:

$$[s,t,u,t,t,u,s] = [0,1,2,1,1,2,0] \otimes [s,t,u]$$

Note, $|U| \leq |S|$. When performing $S \otimes T$, identical elements in $S$ result in redundant lookups of $T$. We can eliminate this redundancy by factoring $S$ into $(L, U)$ and only performing $U \otimes T$. This is particularly useful if the result of the gather is used to perform subsequent gathers as in the base enumerative algorithm in Figure 3.

Unfortunately, there is no direct support for the factor operation in architectures today. Therefore, we implement the straightforward sequential algorithm for this operation that takes linear time. Accordingly, it is important to use the factor operation sparingly.

### 5.2 Convergence Optimization

The key observation behind the convergence optimization is that transition functions in most FSMs are not permutations—many states transition to the same state on a symbol. In Figure 1(a) for instance, both states $c$ and $d$ transition to $d$ on reading a $*$. Accordingly, many elements of the array S in the base algorithm in Figure 3 are likely to be the same. The convergence optimization eliminates this redundancy by factoring.

***Convergence Algorithm.*** Figure 7 shows the algorithm with the convergence optimization. Periodically at line 8, the algorithm factors S into L and U, uses U for subsequent iterations. It also accumulates L into Acc (line 10). The correctness of the algorithm follows from the loop invariant that $S_{base}$ at line 11 is the same as S at line 5 in Figure 3. This invariant follows from the fact that S = L $\otimes$ U and the associativity of $\otimes$.

We define *active* states as the states in S at the end of a particular iteration. The number of active states is non-increasing during the execution of this algorithm. As the number of active states become smaller, gathers in subsequent loop iterations are faster. In essence, convergence allows us to move left toward smaller values of $m$ (number of active states) along a performance curve in Figure 6 determined by $n$ (the number of states in the FSM).

The algorithm in Figure 7 can be implemented to use both the fine-grained parallelism within a core and the coarse-grained parallelism across cores by appropriately modifying the respective algorithms in Figure 4 and Figure 5. Also, it is not necessary to compute all elements $S_{base}$ in an implementation as only the entry corresponding to the start state `st` is required for the output $\phi$ function. We chose to present the algorithm this way to make its correctness evident.

***Frequency of Convergence Checks*** The `conv_check()` predicate at line 7 determines how often the algorithm checks for convergence. Since factoring is not natively supported in the hardware, it is important to only check for convergence when we expect the number of active states to dramatically decrease since the last convergence check. For our SIMD-based implementation, this decrease has to be larger than the number of states that fit in a SIMD register (which in many cases is 16) to reduce the cost of subsequent gathers

We use two heuristics in our implementation. First, we statically analyze the convergence characteristics (Section 5.2 below) of the given FSM to determine the frequency of convergence checks. Second, for every input symbol, we pre-calculate the size of the range of the transition function for that symbol. For instance, if the FSM can only go to one of three states on an input symbol, then we know that the number of active states after reading that symbol is less than or equal to three.

***Convergence in Practice*** Convergence arises when multiple states transition to the same state on an input symbol—that is, the transition function is many-to-one. There are $n^n$ possible functions from $n$ states to $n$ states, but there are only $n!$ permutations. From Stirling's approximation for the factorial, it follows that there are exponentially more ($e^n$) many-to-one functions than permutations. Thus, randomly chosen FSMs are not likely to have transition functions that are permutations, for reasonably large $n$.

FSMs, in practice, have more structure than randomly generated FSMs and are likely to converge faster. For instance, the transition function for a symbol might only be defined for some of the states with the rest transitioning to an error state or a reset state. To evaluate the rate convergence in practice, we performed two experiments on FSMs generated from 2711 regular expressions in the Snort suite [27]. The number of states in these FSMs range from 1 to 4020, with a median of 25.

***Adversarial Inputs*** The first experiment studies convergence under *adversarial* worst-case inputs. We emulated the enumerative computation for *all* inputs of length $k$, and picked the input that resulted in the most number of active states. For these FSMs, the inputs are arbitrary character strings, and thus there are $256^k$ possible inputs of length $k$. To perform the emulation efficiently, we systematically explore the state space of all configurations reached during an

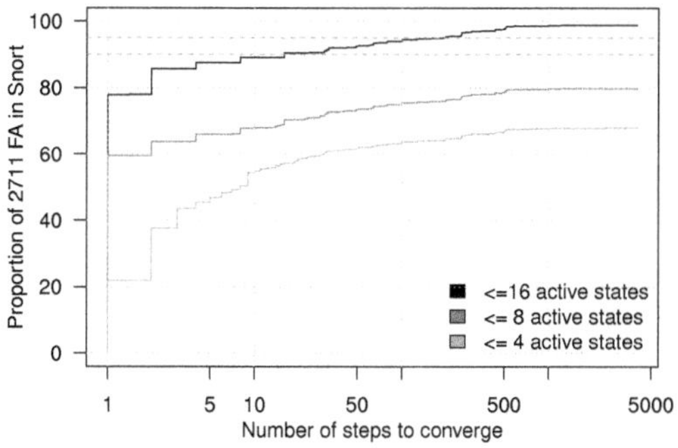


**Figure 8.** Almost all FSMs converge to 16 active states or less for adversarial inputs.

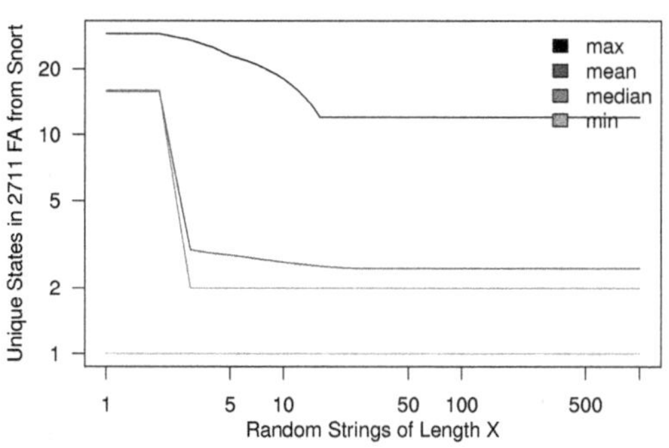


**Figure 9.** FSMs converge on randomly chosen inputs. All FSMs converge to less than 16 active states after 20 steps.

enumerative computation, where a configuration is the set of active states. There are $2^n$ possible configurations. The very fact that we are able to explore such a large state space is a testament to convergence — many of the possible configurations are not reachable from the initial configuration that contains the set of all states.

Figure 8 shows the worst-case convergence for inputs of length $k$ shown on the logarithmic x-axis. The y-axis shows the proportion of FSMs for which the number of active states is respectively less than or equal to 16, 8, and 4 for a given $k$. The figure shows that around 90% of FSMs converge to 16 active states or less after a mere 10 steps, and 95% converge after 200 steps. For inputs longer than this, the convergence algorithm is guaranteed to use the fastest SIMD-gather possible for a given $n$, the number of FSM states, as shown in Figure 6.

Figure 8 also shows that only 80% ever converge to 8 active states, and less than 70% converge to 4 active states. This has two important implications. First, an adversary can always make the enumerative computation asymptotically more expensive than the sequential computation. Second, speculative approaches [13, 14, 24] that rely on predicting the likely state of an FSM after reading some input will fail on carefully designed inputs.

***Random Inputs*** Our second experiment studies convergence on non-adversarial inputs. Unfortunately, the Snort regular expressions are designed for matching against (adversarial) network traffic, and obtaining expected input distribution for these FSMs is not possible. We approximated this by using inputs at *random offsets* in a large dump of Wikipedia pages. Figure 9 shows the average number of active states (y-axis) after running an FSM on 10 randomly chosen inputs of a particular length (x-axis). The various lines show respectively, the max, min, median, and the mean number of active states for the 2711 Snort regular expressions. As expected, we see better convergence than for adversarial inputs. All of the FSMs converged to 16 active states or less. But, more than half of the FSMs did not converge to one active state.

## 5.3 Range Coalescing

Like convergence, range coalescing relies on the observation that transition functions of FSMs are likely to be many-to-one. In particular, the range of a transition function is likely to be smaller than the number of states in the FSM. Range coalescing uses this observation to reduce the range of memory addresses accessed by an enumerative computation for each input symbol.

***Running Example*** Consider the FSM in Figure 10 with five states, $p$ through $t$, and two input symbols $a$ and $b$. The range of $a$ is $\{p, q, t\}$ and the FSM is guaranteed to be in one of these three states after reading $a$. This means that in the next step, the FSM will only access three of the five rows of the transition table $T$. The goal of range coalescing is to ensure that these three rows are contiguous in memory. Similarly, the range of $b$ is $\{p, r, s\}$ and we desire to make these three rows contiguous after reading a $b$.

To achieve this, range coalescing maintains different *names* for each state, one for each input symbol whose range the state belongs to. In Figure 10, $p_a$ and $p_b$ are the two names for $p$ corresponding to $a$ and $b$ respectively. All other states, get one name as they belong to the range of only one symbol. We will refer to state names corresponding to a symbol $a$ simply as *names of* $a$.

Range coalescing generates a transition table for each input symbol indexed by the names of that symbol. For instance, the table $T_a$ is indexed by $p_a, q_a, t_a$. The FSM will use $T_a$ (instead of $T$) for the lookup after reading an $a$ and $T_b$ after reading a $b$. To ensure correct lookups, range coalescing maintains the invariant that the current name always corresponds to the last input symbol read by the FSM. This requires that the transition tables use the names of a particular symbol when representing the destination of a transition on that symbol. For instance, the columns of the transitions tables $T_a$ and $T_b$ for $a$ use the names of $a$.

***Generation of Transition Tables*** The generation of range-coalesced transition tables can be elegantly described using the factor primitive. Let $(L_a, U_a) = Factor(T[a])$ be the factorization of $T[a] = [q, t, t, q, p]$, the transition function

| T | a | b |
|---|---|---|
| p | q | r |
| q | t | s |
| r | t | p |
| s | q | r |
| t | p | s |

⇒

| $T_a$ | a | b |
|---|---|---|
| $p_a$ | $q_a$ | $r_b$ |
| $q_a$ | $t_a$ | $s_b$ |
| $t_a$ | $p_a$ | $s_b$ |

| $T_b$ | a | b |
|---|---|---|
| $p_b$ | $q_a$ | $r_b$ |
| $r_b$ | $t_a$ | $p_b$ |
| $s_b$ | $q_a$ | $r_b$ |

**Figure 10.** Range-Coalescing Example.

```
1  RangeCoalescing( State st, Input in ){
2    a = in[0];
3    S = La;
4    T = Ta;
5    for (i=1; i<in.len; i++){
6      b = in[i];
7      S = S ⊗ T[b];
8      T = Tb;
9      Sbase = S ⊗ Ub;
10     φ (i, Sbase[st]);          }}
```

**Figure 11.** Range-Coalescing Algorithm.

of $a$ in Figure 10. We have

$$T[a] = (L_a = [1, 2, 2, 1, 0]) \otimes (U_a = [p, q, t])$$

We will use the indices of states in $U_a$ as its names of $a$: $p_a = 0, q_a = 1, t_a = 2$. Then, $L_a$ maps how states transition on $a$ when using the names of $a$ for the destination states. $U_a$ provides a map from names of $a$ to states. Similarly, we will use $L_b = [1, 2, 0, 1, 2]$ and $U_b = [p, r, s]$ to describe corresponding maps for $b$.

The transition function $T_a[b]$ describes how names of $a$ transition to names of $b$ on reading $b$. This is given by

$$T_a[b] = U_a \otimes L_b$$

where $U_a$ maps from names of $a$ to states and $L_b$ performs the lookup but uses the names of $b$ for the destination states. Similarly, $T_a[a] = U_a \otimes L_a$. Such pairwise combination of two symbols generates all the entries in the range-coalesced transition tables, as shown in Figure 10.

***Range-Coalescing Algorithm*** Figure 11 describes the range-coalescing algorithm. The algorithm precomputes the transition tables for every input symbol as described above. The algorithm initializes the set of states $S$ with $L_a$ for the first symbol $a$ at line 3. $S$ now represents the states, represented as names of $a$, reached after reading $a$ for all initial states. Then, the algorithm sets $T$ to $T_a$ to be used for the lookup in the next iteration.

For each input symbol $b$, the algorithm performs a gather with the transition function $T[b]$ at line 7. If the previous symbol was $a$, then $T$ points to $T_a$ and $T_a[b]$ performs the transition lookup from names of $a$ to names of $b$. The algorithm then switches $T$ to $T_b$ to be used in the next step.

The correctness of the algorithm follows from the invariant that $S_{base}$ at line 9 is the the same as $S$ at line 5 in Figure 3. This invariant holds because $T_a[b] = U_a \otimes L_b$ and gather is associative. This algorithm can be parallelized using both fine-grained and coarse-grained parallelism by appropriately modifying the algorithms in Figure 4 and Figure 5.

***Performance Discussion*** The key performance gain comes from using smaller transition tables at each step. Range-coalescing allows the use of $\otimes_{m,n}$ operations where $n$ is reduced from the number of states in the FSM to the range size of the last seen input symbol. In effect, range coalescing allows us to move to a higher performance curve in Figure 6. In contrast, the convergence optimization discussed in Section 5.2 allows us to move left along a performance curve (by reducing $m$). In practice, however, we avoid dynamically switching between code that uses $\otimes_{m,n}$ for different values of $n$. Thus, we set $n$ to the maximum of the range size for all input symbols.

Another benefit of range-coalescing is that the algorithm only requires state names when processing input. Mapping back to states is only required when calling the output $\phi$ function. This can lead to efficient state encodings. For instance, if an FSM has more than 256 states but the maximum range size is less than 256, then the range-coalescing algorithm can encode state names with a byte and use byte-level SIMD gathers. In contrast, encoding states directly will otherwise require the use of much-slower word-level gathers.

On the downside, a state gets as many names as its incoming edges in the FSM. For an FSM with $n$ states, $e$ edges, and $k$ symbols in its input language, the original transition table will have $n \times k$ entries (one for each state and input symbol), while the range-coalesced tables will together have $e \times k$ entries. In the worst case, the FSM is total and a transition is defined for every symbol and every state. In this case, the range tables can have as many as $n \times k^2$ entries. An implementation should ensure that this blow up does not impact the runtime performance, say when the working set of the range-coalesced tables no longer fit in the first-level cache.

Finally, in addition to the static overhead above, the algorithm requires an additional memory access at line 8 when compared to the base enumerative algorithm in Figure 3. As discussed in Section 6, this additional lookup in the tight-loop can deteriorate performance.

## 6. Case Studies

This section demonstrates the efficacy of our approach by instantiating three real-world implementations: Snort regular expressions, Huffman decoding, and HTML Tokenization.

***Platform*** We conducted all experiments on an unloaded Intel 2.67GHz Xeon (X5650) workstation with 16 cores and 16GB RAM, running Windows 8. We use the Intel C++ compiler, version 12.1. For generality, we also repeated our

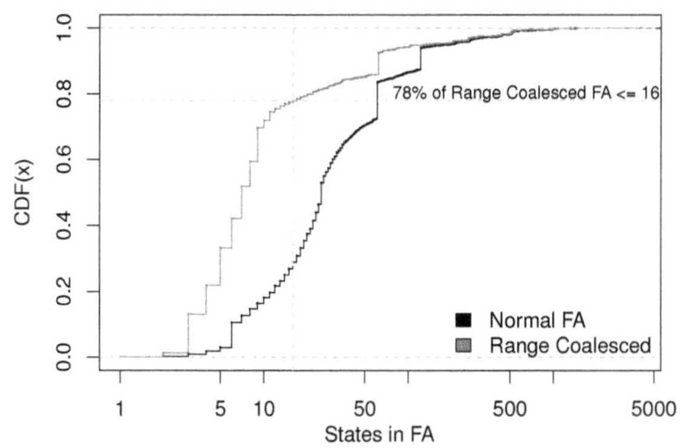


**Figure 12.** Distribution of the number of states and the maximum range sizes for 2711 Snort regular expressions.

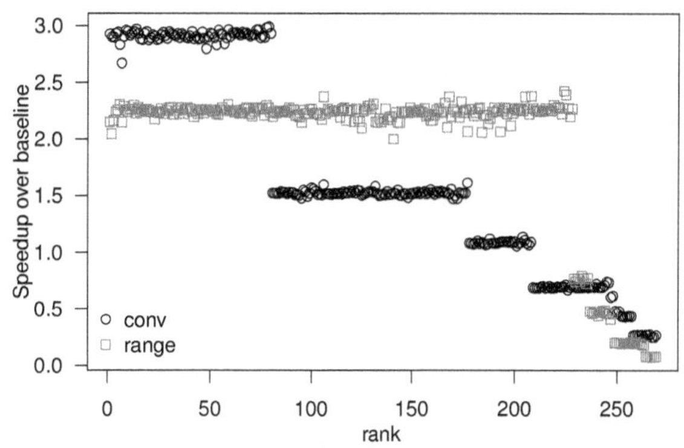


**Figure 13.** Single-core performance for Snort regular expressions.

experiments (not shown) on an older 8-core Intel 2GHz (L5420) workstation and found slightly slower (e.g. due to fewer cores and slower clock) but qualitatively similar results.

***Measurement*** We measure *time* from within each process using `clock_t` to record ticks. The experiments do not measure setup costs—only the time taken for one invocation of each program. When we compare against a baseline, we modify that code to provide comparable measurements. Our benchmarks read all data into memory and then operate on that data. The speed of commodity disks are in the order of 100 MByte/Sec and many of our implementations are an order of magnitude faster.

Finally, to get statistically significant results, we run each experiment 30 times and report the mean. We do not report the 95% confidence interval of the mean when there is no significant variation from the mean. We found that our performance numbers are usually predictable as gather, our key primitive, is dominated by regular computations.

### 6.1 Snort Regular Expressions

Snort [27] is a network intrusion prevention and detection system. Snort comes with a large body of rules and signatures that are used to match against network packets to detect suspicious activity or attacks.

***Benchmarks*** Regular expressions studied in this paper are obtained from version 2.9.4.0 snapshot of the Snort rules. We extracted the `pcre:` attribute from the rules and obtained 2711 regular expressions that our Perl-regular-expression compatible front-end could parse. The remaining 2828 regular expressions contain Snort-specific extensions that our front-end is not able to parse.

Figure 12 shows the distribution of the number of states in the FSMs for the parsed regular expressions. More than 95% of these regular expressions have less than 256 states, but the maximum number of states is 4020. The median state size is 25. Figure 12 also shows the opportunity for range coalescing and reports the maximum range size of the transition functions for these FSMs. 78% of these FSMs have a maximum range less than or equal to 16. The convergence properties of these FSMs are already discussed in Section 5.2.

***Single-Core Performance*** Figure 13 shows the performance of enumerative computation on a single processor core using the SIMD-gather (Section 4.2). To reduce experiment times, we randomly sampled 269 regular expressions and the figure shows the speedup for both optimizations, over the sequential baseline of Figure 1(c) with optimal loop unrolling. For our convergence experiments (conv), we sort along the $x$ axis by the number of states in the FSM while for our range-coalescing experiments (range), we sort by the maximum range size of the transition functions. The graph shows a series of plateaus. For convergence, each plateau denotes $16 * \lceil n/16 \rceil$, where $n$ is the number of states in the FSM. For range coalescing each plateau is for $16 * \lceil m/16 \rceil$, where $m$ is the maximum range size of the transition function across all input symbols.

For FSMs with a maximum of 16 states, our implementation with either of the two optimization performs one `shuffle` operation per input character. We observe up to a 3× speedup with convergence (first plateau of figure). Due to the increase in the size of the range-coalesced transition tables and the additional memory lookup required to chose the transition table at line 8 in Figure 11, we only see a 2.2× speedup. However, many of the FSMs with more than 16 states, have a maximum range size that is less than 16. Range coalescing benefits these FSMs. Since the maximum range of the transition function is statically known, it is possible for an FSM compiler to predetermine if the range coalescing optimization will perform well or not.

***Multi-Core Performance*** The benefit of an enumerative computation with good single-core performance implies multiplicative multi-core performance. Figure 14 demonstrates the speedup obtained with multiple cores for both convergence and range coalescing, where the baseline is the respective single-core performance for each FSM. Both implementations achieve near linear strong-scaling up to 8

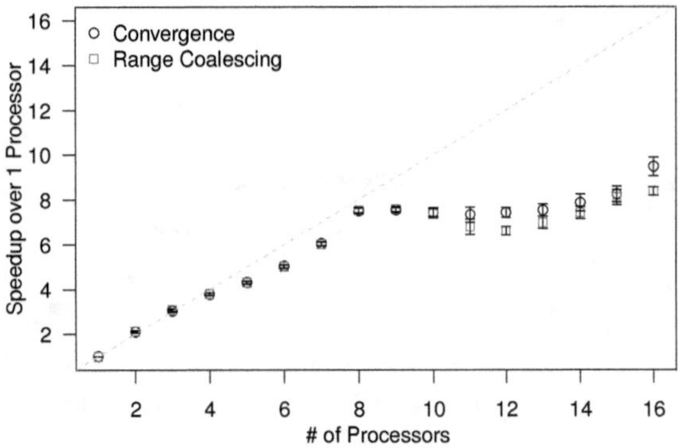


**Figure 14.** Multi-core performance for Snort regular expressions.

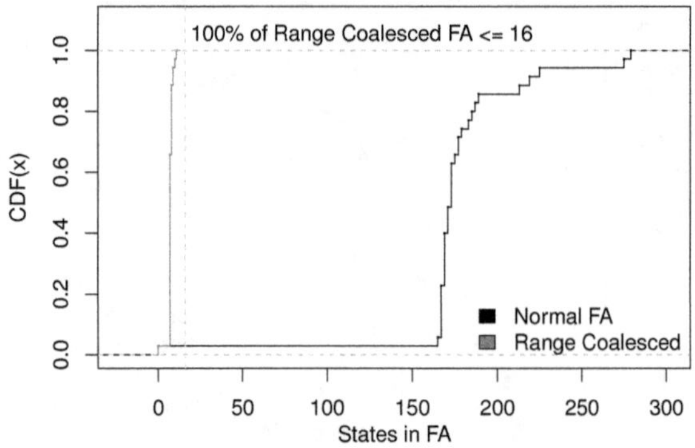


**Figure 15.** Distribution of states in Huffman trees, before and after range coalescing.

cores, after which the size of the input chunks per core is not sufficient to justify the cost invoking more threads. Also, the multi-core performance is mostly independent of the technique used to achieve single-core performance.

***Larger FSMs*** Our goal in using Snort benchmark is to obtain a large class of useful regular expressions. While we generated FSMs from individual regular expressions, the typical use of these Snort rules is to match an incoming packet with *all* of the regular expressions at once. One way to obtain much larger FSM ([19], for instance), is to create a disjunction of all these expressions into a single regular expression. The resulting orders-of-magnitude blowup up in the number is well known [35]. It is unclear if our enumerative approach scales to such large FSM. On the other hand, creating a disjunction of regular expressions sequentializes a problem that is originally embarrassingly parallel — matching an input against many independent regular expressions.

### 6.2 Huffman Decoding

Another interesting application of FSMs is Huffman decoding. Huffman coding is a variable length encoding/decoding scheme, where each input character is encoded by a binary string whose length is inversely proportional to its occurrence probability. These encodings are represented as paths in a binary Huffman tree. Since the tree is finite, one can consider Huffman decoding as an FSM that traverses the Huffman tree on each input bit and emits the decoded character whenever it reaches a leaf. Huffman encoding is an embarrassingly parallel problem [11]. Instead, this paper focuses on the decoding phase.

***Baseline*** We initially used `libhuffman` [16], an open source `C` library for Huffman encoding/decoding, which is used in PHP, as the baseline. We soon realized that `libhuffman` sequentially walks through each bit of an input and updates the position of a pointer in a Huffman binary tree. It spends most of its time performing bit operations and pointer chasing and can decode at most 5 MB/s.

We implemented a sequential baseline that is two orders of magnitude faster. Our baseline processes bytes rather than bits. The idea is to *unroll* the FSM such that each transition is a composition of 8 original transitions. Such an unrolling increases the number of edges in the FSM but not in the number of states. The resulting sequential baseline can decode at speeds greater than 300 MB/s.

Due to unrolling, each transition can potentially output more than one character. This complicates the output $\phi$ function. We encode the output as a sequence of (statically predetermined) strings, rather than a sequence of characters. This allows the $\phi$ function to be performed out of order. This requires an additional pass to process the output into appropriate form. We account for this pass in our evaluation.

***Benchmarks*** We obtained 34 Huffman trees, each from the 34 most downloaded books (as of July 4th, 2013) from Project Gutenberg [25]. Each tree is slightly different based on the distribution of characters in these texts. Similar to the sequential baseline, we use an unrolled FSM whose inputs are 8-bit characters.

Figure 15 shows the distribution of number of states and the maximum range sizes of these FSM. The interesting observation is that while these Huffman trees can have as many as 300 states, the maximum range size is at most 16 states. Range coalescing provides two crucial advantages. First, we can encode state names with bytes allowing us to use Intel's byte-level `shuffle` instruction. Second, since the lookup tables are not more than 16, the implementation requires a single `shuffle` instruction for every input character. With such efficient encoding, there is no advantage to use the convergence optimization. The downside is that we create 256 range tables each of size 16*256. Accessing the 1MB of range tables reduces the performance due to L1-cache limits.

***Single-Core Performance*** Figure 16 shows the single-core performance of our implementation using the SIMD-gather (Section 4.2). A bar on this plot provides the (i) sequential baseline and (ii) the range-coalesced FSM for the 34 Huffman trees when decoding a 1GB file. We observe a 2×

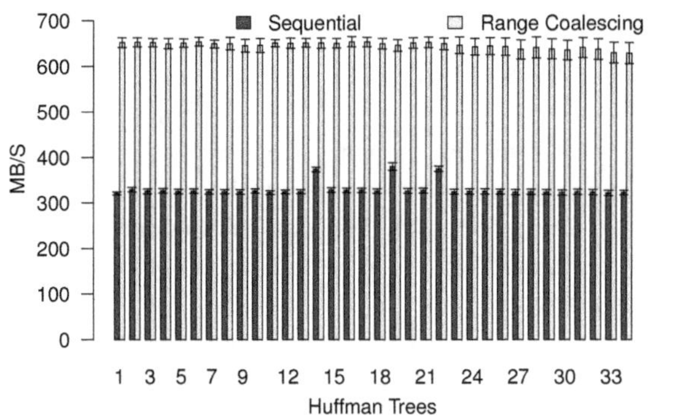


**Figure 16.** Single-core performance for Huffman decoding

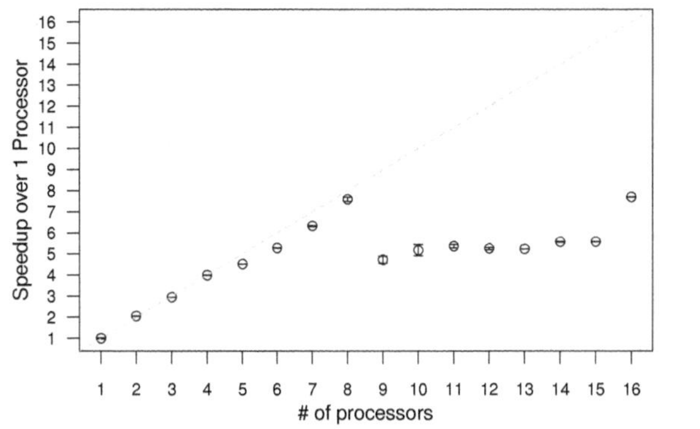


**Figure 17.** Multi-core performance for Huffman decoding

speedup over the sequential baseline for almost all Huffman trees (three give 1.75×).

***Multi-Core Performance*** Figure 17 demonstrates the strong scaling of our approach with multiple cores. A point on this graph $(x,y)$ gives the runtime in seconds $(y)$ as a function of the number of processor cores used $(x)$. We see near linear speedups until 8 processors after which the scaling stops. We expect our approach to scale for more processors with larger inputs.

### 6.3 HTML Tokenization

The third case study uses another important application of FSMs — lexing or tokenizing text. A tokenizer reads a sequence of bytes, character by character, and categorizes subsequences of those characters into *tokens*. In this section, we implement a data-parallel tokenizer for HTML that is a binary drop-in replacement for the one used in the crawler of the web-search engine `bing` .

***Baseline*** `bing` uses an optimized hand-written tokenizer that uses switch statements to encode the FSM. For our experiments, we tokenize a 6MB dump of HTML from Wikipedia.

***Benchmark*** We reverse engineered the `bing` implementation manually into an FSM with 27 states. The output $\phi$ function produces exactly the same output as `bing` allowing our

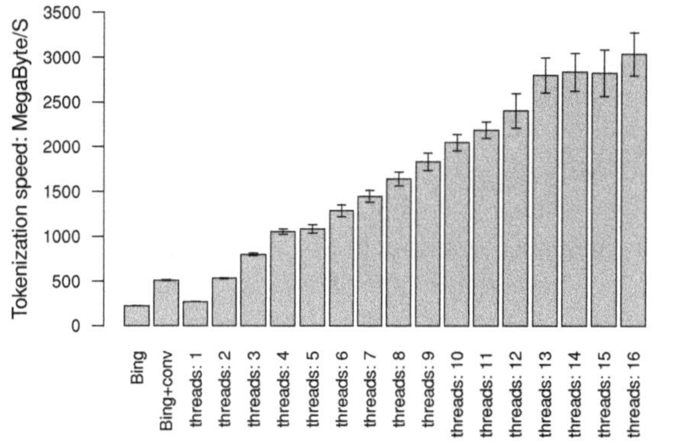


**Figure 18.** Multi-core performance of HTML tokenization.

implementation to be integrated with existing clients. Additionally, this enables us to verify that our manually generated FSM provides the same functionality as the hand-optimized version in `bing` . As the FSM has less than 32 total states, range-coalescing did not provide performance beyond what the convergence optimization provided. We only report numbers with the convergence optimization.

The manual effort of extracting an FSM prevents us from evaluating other tokenizers as part of this case study. To the best of our knowledge, modern compilers use similar hand-optimized lexers. Currently, we are not able to extract FSMs from automatic lexer generators, such as flex [23], that account for the complex acceptance and backtracking semantics implemented in these lexers.

***HTML-Tokenization Performance*** Figure 18 compares the throughput of our baseline (`Bing`) to our implementation with a single-core implementation of convergence (`Bing+conv`) and our multi-core implementations (from `threads:1` to `threads:16`). The y-axis is the tokenization throughput in megabytes per second.

Our single-core implementation is 2.3× faster than the baseline. Our multi-core implementations require two passes over the input (Figure 5), once to determine the start state for each processor core and a second time to invoke the $\phi$ function. This explains the loss in performance between `Bing+conv` and `threads:1`. With 16-cores, our implementation tokenizes at 3025 MByte/Sec; faster than the line-rate of many networks (1000 MByte/Sec). This is 14× faster than the baseline.

## 7. Related Work

Due to its importance, optimizing FSM computations has received considerable attention in prior literature. This section describes closely related work.

***Parallel FSMs*** As described in Section 2, parallel algorithms for FSMs have long been known [8, 15]. This paper builds on these ideas and demonstrates an efficient implementation that uses both fine-grained and coarse-grained parallelism. The most related prior works are optimized implementations [9, 22] of the Hillis and Steele algorithm [8]. Holub et al. [9] rely on the input FSM being *k-local*, which requires that any two states converge to the same state on any input of length $k$. As our experiments show (Figure 8), most FSMs seen in practice are not k-local. Pan et al. [22] use a powerset construction, similar to the one used to determinize nondeterministic FSMs, to build an FSM that emulates the enumerative computation of the input FSM. This construction indirectly captures the convergence properties observed in this paper. However, the power set construction can result in exponential blow up in the number of states. Our algorithm can be considered as a dynamic variant of theirs which performs enumerative computation only on the given input, thereby avoiding this exponential blowup.

***Speculative Parallelization*** One way to parallelize across dependencies is to speculate [13, 14, 19, 24]. When applied to FSMs, this amounts to guessing, rather than enumerating, the start state for all but the first chunk of the input (See Figure 2). The key observation behind these approaches is that two distinct states, the guessed state and the true start state, are likely to converge to the same state after reading some input. There are two major issues with a speculative approach. First, the efficacy of a speculative approach is difficult to predict. As seen in our convergence studies (Figure 8 and Figure 9), convergence is not always guaranteed. Further, if a processor does not converge on its chunk, then the next processor is forced to restart from a new state. The probability of such cascading misspeculations increases with the number of processors, thereby limiting scalability. Second, a speculative approach is still limited by the sequential implementation on a single core. In contrast, enumerative computation can use the fine-grained parallelism of a single processor.

***Bit-Parallel FSMs*** Another closely related approach uses vector instructions to speed up single-core FSM performance. In contrast, our goal is to achieve multi-core parallelism through enumerative computation and use vector instructions to optimize the enumerative computation.

Parabix [18] converts an FSM computation into a sequence of bit operations where a bit is assigned for each input symbol. This allows Parabix to process $W$ characters simultaneously on a SIMD machine of width $W$. Parabix uses bitstream addition [3] to preserve dependences across characters that occur in common text processing applications, such as XML parsing. While providing significant single-core speedups, Parabix achieves limited parallelization across multiple processors/cores. Moreover, their approach requires nontrivial processing to transform the input string into a sequence of bitstreams. For tasks such as XML processing, the resulting FSM is small enough that our implementation requires a single `shuffle` instruction per input symbol and we expect the single-core performance of our implementation to be competitive with Parabix. However, Parabix will provide better performance as future hardware architectures support larger SIMD widths. In contrast, our approach can scale the enumerative computation to larger FSMs with larger SIMD widths.

NR-grep [21] uses bit-parallelism to simulate a nondeterministic FSM for the purpose of pattern matching. By appropriately assigning the bits of a machine word (or a SIMD register), it transforms the FSM computation into a sequence of bit operations. While this technique can be optimized for special classes of patterns, matching regular expression in their generality requires an input-dependent memory lookup similar to the sequential algorithm in Figure 1(c).

***Regular Expression Engines*** There is a large body of work on parallel regular expression matching on FPGAs [30, 34], GPUs [32], and CELL [28]. These approaches all parallelize regular expression matching by running multiple inputs in parallel on each hardware context. For example, Scarpazza et al. uses builds a $Flex$ like tokenizer to tokenize SGML. In contrast, our approach is data parallel *within* a single input and is complementary to these approaches.

***Parallelizing Huffman Decoding*** Like the speculative approaches mentioned above, researchers have used speculation to speed up Huffman decoding in software [14] and in hardware [17, 33]. Klein et al. [14] parallelize Huffman decoding using the observation that decoding at different offsets are likely to *synchronize* after reading a few symbols. Such synchronization is not always guaranteed for certain codes—fixed length encodings, for instance. Convergence of finite state machines strictly generalizes synchronization and uniformly works for all codes. Others [5] have observed that if the compression algorithm is modified to generate independent compressed blocks, each of these blocks can be decompressed in parallel.

## 8. Conclusion

This paper demonstrates an efficient parallel algorithm finite state machines that uses enumerative computations. While an enumerative computation strictly performs more work than a sequential one, we demonstrate optimizations and implementation strategies, which in concert allow many of the FSMs we evaluate in this paper to take advantage of fine-grained parallelism (e.g., ILP/SIMD) and coarse-grained parallelism (e.g., multi-core).

We show significant multi-factor performance improvements on three real world problems, regular expressions from Snort, Huffman decoding, and HTML tokenization. This paper mainly focuses on parallelism found in a modern workstation; however, we believe our approach is suitable for *any* modern data parallel architecture, from GPUs to large clusters running MapReduce like frameworks. We also believe that future FSM compilers will be able to automatically explore the various tradeoffs described in the paper to obtain fast implementations for a given hardware architecture.

## References


[1] G. E. Blelloch. Prefix sums and their applications. Technical Report CMU-CS-90-190, School of Computer Science, Carnegie Mellon University, Nov. 1990.

[2] J. A. Brzozowski. Canonical regular expressions and minimal state graphs for definite events. *Mathematical Theory of Automata*, 12:529–561, 1962.

[3] R. D. Cameron, E. Amiri, K. S. Herdy, D. Lin, T. C. Shermer, and F. Popowich. Parallel scanning with bitstream addition: An XML case study. In *European Conference on Parallel and Distributed Computing, Part II*, pages 2–13, 2011.

[4] B. Catanzaro, N. Sundaram, and K. Keutzer. A map reduce framework for programming graphics processors. In *In Workshop on Software Tools for MultiCore Systems*, 2008.

[5] R. L. Cloud, M. L. Curry, H. L. Ward, A. Skjellum, and P. Bangalore. Accelerating lossless data compression with GPUs. *Computing Research Repository (CoRR)*, abs/1107.1525, 2011.

[6] J. Dean and S. Ghemawat. MapReduce: Simplified data processing on large clusters. *Commun. ACM*, 51(1):107–113, Jan. 2008.

[7] B. He, W. Fang, Q. Luo, N. K. Govindaraju, and T. Wang. Mars: A MapReduce framework on graphics processors. In *International Conference on Parallel Architectures and Compilation Techniques*, PACT '08, pages 260–269, 2008.

[8] W. D. Hillis and G. L. Steele. Data parallel algorithms. In *Commun. ACM*, volume 29, pages 1170–1183, Dec 1986.

[9] J. Holub and S. Štekr. On parallel implementations of deterministic finite automata. In *Implementation and Application of Automata*, CIAA '09, pages 54–64, 2009.

[10] J. E. Hopcroft and J. D. Ullman. *Formal languages and their relation to automata*. Addison-Wesley Longman Publishing Co., Inc., Boston, MA, USA, 1969.

[11] P. Howard and J. Vitter. Parallel lossless image compression using Huffman and arithmetic coding. In *Data Compression Conference, 1992. DCC '92.*, pages 299 –308, March 1992.

[12] Intel Haswell Microarchitecture, 2013. URL `http://software.intel.com/en-us/haswell`.

[13] C. G. Jones, R. Liu, L. Meyerovich, K. Asanović, and R. Bodík. Parallelizing the web browser. In *Hot Topics in Parallelism (HotPar)*, pages 7–7, 2009.

[14] S. T. Klein, Y. Wiseman, S. T. Klein, and Y. Wiseman. Parallel Huffman decoding with applications to JPEG files. *The Computer Journal*, 46:487–497, 2003.

[15] R. E. Ladner and M. J. Fischer. Parallel prefix computation. *Journal of the ACM*, 27(4):831–838, 1980.

[16] libhuffman. URL `http://huffman.sourceforge.net/`.

[17] C.-H. Lin and C.-W. Jen. Low power parallel Huffman decoding. *Electronics Letters*, 34(3):240 –241, Feb 1998.

[18] D. Lin, N. Medforth, K. S. Herdy, A. Shriraman, and R. D. Cameron. Parabix: Boosting the efficiency of text processing on commodity processors. In *High Performance Computer Architecture (HPCA)*, pages 373–384, 2012.

[19] D. Luchaup, R. Smith, C. Estan, and S. Jha. Speculative parallel pattern matching. *IEEE Transactions on Information Forensics and Security*, 6(2):438–451, June 2011.

[20] G. H. Mealy. A method for synthesizing sequential circuits. *Bell System Technical Journal*, 34(5):1045–1079, 1955.

[21] G. Navarro. NR-grep: A fast and flexible pattern matching tool. *Software: Practice and Experience*, 31(13):1265–1312, 2001.

[22] Y. Pan, Y. Zhang, and K. Chiu. Simultaneous transducers for data-parallel XML parsing. *International Symposium on Parallel and Distributed Processing*, pages 1–12, 2008.

[23] V. Paxson. flex - fast lexical analyzer generator, 1988.

[24] G. R. Prakash Prabhu and K. Vaswani. Safe programmable speculative parallelism. In *Programming Languages Design and Implementation (PLDI)*, June 2010.

[25] Project Gutenberg. URL `http://www.gutenberg.org/`.

[26] G. Ren, P. Wu, and D. Padua. Optimizing data permutations for SIMD devices. In *Programming Languages Design and Implementation (PLDI)*, pages 118–131, 2006.

[27] M. Roesch. Snort - Lightweight intrusion detection for networks. In *Proceedings of the 13th USENIX conference on System administration*, LISA '99, pages 229–238, 1999.

[28] D. P. Scarpazza and G. F. Russell. High-performance regular expression scanning on the Cell/B.E. processor. In *International Conf. on Supercomputing*, ICS '09, pages 14–25, 2009.

[29] S. Sengupta, M. Harris, Y. Zhang, and J. Owens. Scan primitives for GPU computing. In *SIGGRAPH/EUROGRAPHICS Symposium on Graphics Hardware*, pages 97–106. Eurographics Association, 2007.

[30] P. Sutton. Partial character decoding for improved regular expression matching in FPGAs. In *Field-Programmable Technology*, pages 25 – 32, Dec. 2004.

[31] J. Talbot, R. M. Yoo, and C. Kozyrakis. Phoenix++: Modular MapReduce for shared-memory systems. In *Workshop on MapReduce and its Applications*, pages 9–16, 2011.

[32] G. Vasiliadis, M. Polychronakis, S. Antonatos, E. Markatos, and S. Ioannidis. Regular expression matching on graphics hardware for intrusion detection. In *Recent Advances in Intrusion Detection*, volume 5758, pages 265–283. 2009.

[33] B. Wei and T. Meng. A parallel decoder of programmable Huffman codes. *Circuits and Systems for Video Technology*, 5 (2):175 –178, Apr 1995.

[34] Y.-H. E. Yang, W. Jiang, and V. K. Prasanna. Compact architecture for high-throughput regular expression matching on FPGA. In *Architectures for Networking and Communications Systems*, ANCS '08, pages 30–39, 2008.

[35] F. Yu, Z. Chen, Y. Diao, T. V. Lakshman, and R. H. Katz. Fast and memory-efficient regular expression matching for deep packet inspection. In *Architecture for Networking and Communications Systems*, ANCS '06, pages 93–102, 2006.

[36] Y. Yu, M. Isard, D. Fetterly, M. Budiu, U. Erlingsson, P. K. Gunda, and J. Currey. DryadLINQ: A system for general-purpose distributed data-parallel computing using a high-level language. In *Operating Systems Design and Implementation*, OSDI'08, pages 1–14, 2008.

# Challenging the "Embarrassingly Sequential": Parallelizing Finite State Machine-Based Computations through Principled Speculation

Zhijia Zhao Bo Wu Xipeng Shen

College of William and Mary, Williamsburg, VA, USA

{zzhao,bwu,xshen}@cs.wm.edu

## Abstract

Finite-State Machine (FSM) applications are important for many domains. But FSM computation is inherently sequential, making such applications notoriously difficult to parallelize. Most prior methods address the problem through speculations on simple heuristics, offering limited applicability and inconsistent speedups.

This paper provides some principled understanding of FSM parallelization, and offers the first disciplined way to exploit application-specific information to inform speculations for parallelization. Through a series of rigorous analysis, it presents a probabilistic model that captures the relations between speculative executions and the properties of the target FSM and its inputs. With the formulation, it proposes two model-based speculation schemes that automatically customize themselves with the suitable configurations to maximize the parallelization benefits. This rigorous treatment yields near-linear speedup on applications that state-of-the-art techniques can barely accelerate.

***Categories and Subject Descriptors*** D3.4 [*Programming Languages*]: Processors

***General Terms*** Languages, Performance

***Keywords*** FSM, Speculative Parallelization, Lookback, DFA, Multicore, Partial Commit

## 1. Introduction

Parallelization is key to the computing efficiency and scalability of modern applications. In the spectrum of parallelism, at the most challenging end lies the category of Finite-State Machine (FSM) applications, which are also known as "embarrassingly sequential" applications [6].

In these applications, the core computation can be formulated as an abstract machine with a finite number of possible states. Transitions among the states follow some predefined mechanism that can be represented with a state-transition graph. Each node in the graph stands for a state and each transition edge is labeled with the symbol that triggers that transition. Figure 1 (a) shows the state-transition graph for a pattern-matching FSM, along with an example input to it.

To check whether a string matches the pattern, the FSM starts with the initial state (state A) and processes the input character one after one. At each input character, the FSM moves to a state specified by the state-transition graph. Its arrival at state D indicates the recognition of a string that matches the pattern; such states are called *acceptance states*.

The special difficulty for parallelizing FSM applications is as suggested by its nickname: They are inherently sequential. Dependences exist between every two steps of their computations. Consider the string matching example in Figure 1 (a). On a machine with two computing units, a natural way to parallelize the pattern matching is to evenly divide the input string, $S$, into two segments as illustrated by the broken vertical line in Figure 1 (a), and let the threads process the segments concurrently, one segment per thread. The difficulty is in determining the correct state for the second thread to start with. It should equal the state at which the FSM ends when the first thread finishes processing the first segment. Such dependences connect all threads into a dependence chain, preventing concurrent executions of any two threads.

For the extreme difficulty, parallelizing general FSM applications has been lying beyond the reach of existing techniques. The problem, however, is hard to circumvent any longer, partially thanks to the increasing importance of handheld applications; FSM is the backbone of many of them. Take web browsers as an example. FSM-like computations form the core of many activities inside a browser, ranging from lexing, to parsing, syntax-directed translation, image



*ASPLOS '14,* March 1–5, 2014, Salt Lake City, Utah, USA.
Copyright © 2014 ACM 978-1-4503-2305-5/14/03...$15.00.
http://dx.doi.org/10.1145/2541940.2541989

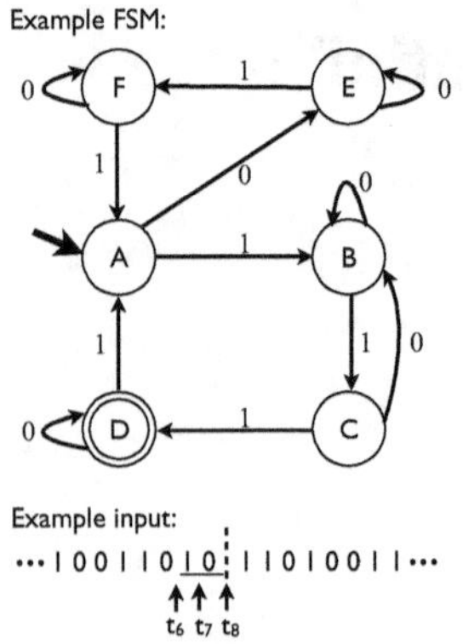


(a) Example FSM

| State $s$ | | A | B | C | D | E | F |
|---|---|---|---|---|---|---|---|
| $P(s)(\%)$ | | 14.2 | 28.9 | 13.9 | 13.9 | 14.7 | 14.4 |
| Expected | A | 0 | 101.00 | 89.61 | 59.71 | 39.12 | 59.71 |
| Merging | B | 101.00 | 0 | 16.45 | 81.99 | 66.94 | 81.99 |
| Length | C | 89.61 | 16.45 | 0 | 70.60 | 51.99 | 70.60 |
| $L_M(x, y)$ | D | 59.71 | 81.99 | 70.60 | 0 | 69.91 | 1.79 |
| | E | 39.12 | 66.94 | 51.99 | 69.91 | 0 | 69.91 |
| | F | 59.71 | 81.99 | 70.60 | 1.79 | 69.91 | 0 |
| $p(R = 0\|s)$ (%) | | 51.69 | 51.85 | 50.72 | 50.65 | 50.10 | 49.10 |
| $p(R = 1\|s)$ (%) | | 48.31 | 48.15 | 49.28 | 49.35 | 49.903 | 50.90 |

(b) Attributes of the FSM

**Figure 1.** An FSM for pattern matching and its attributes. In graph (a), each circle represents an FSM state. State A is the initial state (marked by the extra incoming edge), and state D is an acceptance state. The symbols on the edges indicate conditions for state transitions.

decoding. As prior research shows, even without counting image decoding, such computations could take about 40% of the loading time of many web pages [1]. Besides browsers, most applications on handheld devices use visual or audio media and hence involve media encoding and decoding—which both are typical FSM computations. For its appearance on the critical path of the many applications, improving FSM performance is vital for the response time and hence users experience on handheld devices. At the same time, FSM is essential to many other domains. It consumes most time in pattern matching [6], XML validation [26], front end of a compiler [4], compression and decompression [20], model checking, network intrusion detection [17], and many other important applications. According to Amdahl's Law, without parallelizing FSM operations, it is infeasible for these applications to achieve sustained performance improvement on modern machines, no matter how well other parts of these applications are parallelized.

## 2. Overview

This section describes the state of the art in parallelizing FSM computations, with an important concept, *lookback*, explained. It then points out their limitations and gives an overview of this work.

***State of the Art*** Among various forms of FSM, Deterministic Finite Automaton (DFA) has been the focus in prior studies, thanks to its broad usage and its capability to approximate other forms of state machines (e.g., Context-Free Grammars with a limited levels of self-embedding recursions [9].) We hence focus our discussion on such FSMs.

A classic approach to parallelizing FSM computations is through variations of the parallel prefix sum algorithm [22]. The idea is to treat each character in the vocabulary of an FSM as a function. FSM computations can then become a series of associative operations of these functions, which can be done in the manner of parallel prefix sum. The method increases the total computation by a factor of $\log N$ and incurs $O(N * |S|)$ space overhead, where $N$ is the length of the input, and $|S|$ is the size of the FSM state set. So the method is beneficial only when the number of processors is greater than $\log N$ and the FSM has a small state set[1].

Recent studies [18, 26] have attempted to address the problem through speculation. As aforementioned, the key difficulty for parallelizing FSM applications is to determine the start state for a thread. The basic idea of these studies is to guess that state. Letting a thread, say $T_7$, guess the correct FSM state for it to start processing segment $S_7$ is equivalent to guessing at which state the FSM stops when thread $T_6$ finishes processing the preceding segment $S_6$. A random guess is subject to large errors. Previous studies [18, 26] have found it helpful to do a **lookback**—that is, thread $T_7$ runs the FSM on a number of ending symbols (called a *suffix*) of the preceding segment $S_6$, and uses the ending state as its speculated start state.

For instance, in Figure 1, a lookback (from state A) by the second thread on the suffix "1 0" stops at state B; the thread will then start processing its segment from state B. Lookback helps speculation by offering some context. The context may not completely determine the actual start state, but is often helpful to avoid some impossible states. In our example, the lookback can safely avoid picking state A as the start state because the FSM structure determines that no state can transit to state A on the end of the suffix, "0".

Lookback-based speculative parallelization has been the central technique of all state-of-the-art FSM parallelizations [18, 26]. As Figure 2 shows, on an 8-core Intel Xeon E5620 system, the approach [18, 26] yields almost ideal speedups on the Huffman decoding "huff" and XML lexing programs "lexing". However, its performance is inconsistent. On the other five programs in Figure 2, it produces

[1] The original paper [22] proposes to represent each function with a boolean matrix, which incurs even a higher time and space complexity.

speedups less than two. One of the programs, *div*, even runs slower than its sequential execution.

The primary reason for the inconsistent performance is the lack of rigor in existing designs of speculation, reflected in multiple aspects. For instance, the length of the suffix to examine by a lookback directly affects the parallelization benefits. A longer suffix exposes more context, but at the same time incurs more overhead. Previous studies [18, 26] select it by simply trying several lengths in profiling runs, while leaving the vast remaining space unexplored. Another example is the state used for starting a lookback. Previous studies always use the initial state of the FSM (state A in Figure 1 (a)) for lookbacks. It could seriously limit lookback benefits. For the example in Figure 1 (a), if the lookback starts from state D rather than A, it would end at the correct state, state E. A further example is that all prior studies have used the ending state of a lookback as the speculated start state for processing the next segment. Although seeming an intuitive decision, does it always maximize the parallelization benefits? If not, is it ever possible to efficiently find a state that does?

Answering these open questions, or more generally, creating a rigorous design requires some comprehensive understanding of the relationship between speculative parallelization and the target FSM and its inputs. It demands models that are able to capture the effects of various speculative parallelizations. Without them, it is hard to determine the design that best fits a given FSM problem.

Meeting these demands involves many challenges. Both FSMs and their inputs are of various size, structure, and complexity. How to characterize them and capture their features that are critical for speculative parallelization? How to formulate the effects of lookback? How to quantify the likelihood for a state to be the true state? How to select the best state after a lookback? And how to formulate the overall benefits of a speculative parallelization with the effects of its different components integrated together? All these questions are important for achieving a principled understanding of speculative parallelization, but they all remain open.

***Overview of This Work*** The goal of this work is to present a rigorous approach to parallelization of FSM computations. Our solution comes from the observation that the likelihoods for a state to be the actual start state at a speculation point are usually non-uniform: Some states in an FSM may be more often to be visited than others, and more importantly, the likelihoods vary from one FSM to another and from one context (or input suffix) to another. *The principle of our approach is to match the design of a speculation scheme with the properties of the target FSM and input.*

To that end, we propose a set of techniques, organized into five boxes in Figure 3. Specifically, we introduce three novel abstractions (Box ①) to effectively characterize the stochastic properties of an FSM. With the abstractions, we build up a probabilistic performance model to quantify the expected performance of a speculatively parallel execution (Box ②.) The model unifies the considerations of lookback overhead, misspeculation penalty, and parallelization benefits into a single formulae. Based on the probabilistic performance formulation, we develop two model-based speculation schemes (Box ③), which automatically customize themselves to suit the probabilistic properties of an FSM and its inputs. For practical deployment, we integrate the models into a library named *OptSpec* with a simple API. An important challenge in characterizing an FSM is to capture how its structure influences the effects of a lookback on a speculation, for which, through a formal analysis, we uncover the connections between state transitions and the probability for a speculation to succeed (Box ④.) In addition, as part of the *OptSpec* library construction, we explore the attainment of the FSM properties through both online and offline profiling (Box ⑤.)

The benefits brought by the rigorous treatment are significant. It boosts the parallelization speedups by more than a factor of four over the state of the art for most programs as shown in Figure 2. It yields near optimum performance on five programs, and reverses the slowdown on *div* to a 31%

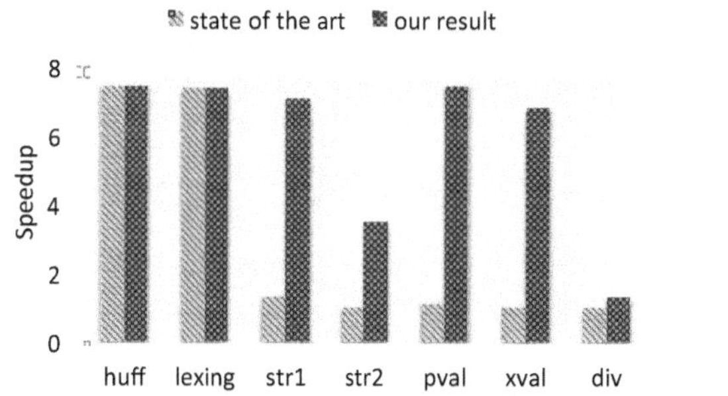


**Figure 2.** The speedups brought by the state-of-the-art speculation scheme [26] are limited on some complex FSM applications. The results are for 8 threads running on an 8-core machine. Details are shown in Section 7.

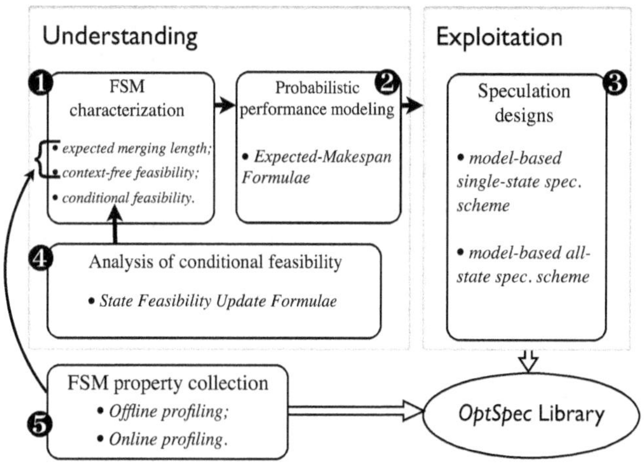


**Figure 3.** Overview of this work.

speedup. The unprecedented level of speedup challenges the common perception of FSM being "embarrassingly sequential", showing that they are inherently sequential *but very parallelizable*.

***Contributions*** This work makes several contributions:

- To the best of our knowledge, this work provides the first principled understanding of speculative parallelization of FSM computations, and gives the first rigorous analysis of it.
- It offers the first probabilistic model of lookback and its influence on speculative parallelization, and produces the first probabilistic performance model for speculative FSM parallelization.
- The two stochastic model-based speculation schemes, for the first time, enable an automatic match between speculative parallelization and the properties of FSM and its inputs.
- It yields near optimal speedups on FSMs that the state-of-the-art techniques can barely accelerate.
- It sheds insights on the importance of adding rigor into heuristic-based speculative parallelizations, and gives new understanding to the potential of parallelizing "embarrassingly sequential" applications.

***A Running Example*** As most of our explanations will draw on the example in Figure 1, we provide some more information about it. The FSM was deliberately made simple for illustration purpose. The table in Figure 1 (b) presents some statistical attributes of the FSM, obtained by running the FSM on a typical input consisting of a string of 0 and 1. The second row ($P(s)$) shows the frequency of each of the states reached in the FSM execution. The second section of the table shows the expected merging length of the states. For instance, the second number in the third row of the table shows that if the FSM processes an input segment in two ways—one starts from state A and the other starts from state B—on average (across various input segments), the two runs don't reach the same state until finishing processing 101 characters. This length section in the table is symmetric because the expected merging length is apparently a symmetric metric. (Section 6 will describe how the lengths can be measured efficiently in practice.) The bottom two rows in the table show the frequencies in which 0 or 1 follows a particular state of the FSM. For instance, the first number in the bottom row shows that during the execution, in 48.31% of time when the FSM is at state A, the next input character is 1. These attributes will be used in our following discussions.

***Paper Organizations*** In the following, we explain each component in Figure 3. We first present the components for enhancing the understanding of FSM properties and their connections with speculative executions (Sections 3 and 4), and then describe the two speculative schemes and the OptSpec library (Sections 5 and 6.) For the nature of rigorous analysis, some formalism and mathematical inferences are hard to avoid in the following description, for which, we create some figures and examples to assist understanding. To make the presentation especially easy to follow, we also include all the important notations in Table 1.

**Table 1.** Notations

| Notation | Description |
|---|---|
| $N$ | FSM input length |
| $T$ | number of threads |
| $S, V$ | the state set and vocabulary of an FSM |
| $s \xrightarrow{c} r$ | state $s$ transits to state $r$ after reading $c$ |
| $P(s)$ | initial feasibility of $s$ |
| $P^v(s)$ | state feasibility of $s$ after a lookback on suffix $v$ |
| $S_k$ | the feasible state set after a $k$-long lookback |
| $C_t$ | cost of a state transition |
| $C_p, C_w$ | cost of a probability update, and workload |
| $\lambda$ | $C_p/C_t$ |
| $\beta$ | workload parameter, ie., $C_w/C_t$ |
| $\omega(l)$ | $l$-long lookback overhead |
| $\chi(v, s)$ | reexecution time when $s$ is speculation state after a lookback on suffix $v$ |
| $L_M(s, r)$ | expected merging length between states $s$ and $r$ |
| $L_M^v(s)$ | expected merging length between $s$ and all possible real states after a lookback on suffix $v$ |
| $ES$ | the expectation make-span |
| $ES(l)$ | ES when looking back length is $l$ |
| $r_i$ | the real state at the $i$th time point |
| $L_i, R_i$ | the contexts before and after the $i$th time point |

## 3. Probabilistic Analysis of FSM Speculation

When analyzing the benefits of an FSM speculation scheme, it is important to take a probabilistic perspective: A speculative execution is inherently stochastic. The result of a speculation may be a success or failure, depending on what will happen in the future.

This section presents a probabilistic formulation for modeling the expected benefits of a speculative parallelization of FSM. The formulation is fundamental as it enables a systematic assessment of various designs of speculation, and hence paves the path for creating an effective design.

### 3.1 Essence of Lookback

As lookback is a key operation in FSM speculation, to build up the performance model, we have to understand the essence of lookback. To that end, we introduce a term *feasibility*:

**Definition 1.** *For a speculation point, the* feasibility *of a state $s$ is the probability for $s$ to be the correct state at that point.*

Without consideration of contexts, statistically, the feasibility of a state $s$ is the same at every speculation point (although the feasibilities of different states may differ), approximately equaling the frequency for the FSM to visit that state in its executions. We call these probabilities *initial feasibilities* or *context-free feasibilities*, denoted with $P(s)$, as the second row of Figure 1 (b) illustrates. We call the feasibilities after an input string $v$ *conditional feasibilities*, denoted with $P^v(s)$.

A straightforward way to estimate the conditional feasibility, $P^v(s)$ or equivalently $P(\text{real state}{=}s \mid \text{left string}{=}v)$, is to count the frequency for $s$ to appear after a string $v$ in profiling runs. But because the value space of $v$ grows exponentially with its length, the approach is generally infeasible.

A key insight exploited in this study is that lookback is essentially a process that tries to use context (i.e., a suffix, $v$) to improve the knowledge about feasibilities. It implicitly exploits the property that the conditional state feasibilities, to a certain degree, are dictated by the inter-state relations specified by the FSM. For instance, processing a suffix ending with "0" cannot stop at states A or C in Figure 1 (a). By running the FSM on the suffix, lookback essentially employs the state transitions specified by the FSM to help focus the estimation of the conditional probabilities, and prune impossible states for speculation.

### 3.2 Formulation of Performance Expectation

With the essence of lookback understood, we are ready to build up a performance model for lookback-based speculative parallelization of FSM. We use make-span for performance. The make-span of an execution (either sequential or parallel) is the time elapsed from the start to the end of the execution. The *expected make-span* is the statistical mean of the make-spans of all executions of an application on various inputs of a given length, denoted as $ES$.

Specifically, our goal in this section is to come up with a set of formulae that can answer the following question: Given an FSM and a speculation scheme to use, what is the expected make-span of the speculative execution on an arbitrary input of a given length? Here, we use $\mathbb{S}$ to represent a speculation scheme, which indicates the lookback length $l$ to use and the state to take as the speculation at each speculation point.

Having such a formulae is fundamental as it allows a systematic examination of the design space of FSM speculations.

The make-span of a thread in a lookback-based speculative execution is the sum of three components: its lookback overhead, the time for processing its own workload, and the reprocessing time if the speculation fails, as shown in Figure 4. We discuss the calculation of each as follows.

***1) Lookback Overhead*** Lookback overhead depends on lookback length $L$. We denote the overhead with $\omega(L)$. The basic operations during a lookback are the transitions (and associated probability update) from one state to another on the suffix.

***2) Workload Processing Time*** One step in the workload processing by an FSM includes a state transition, and often

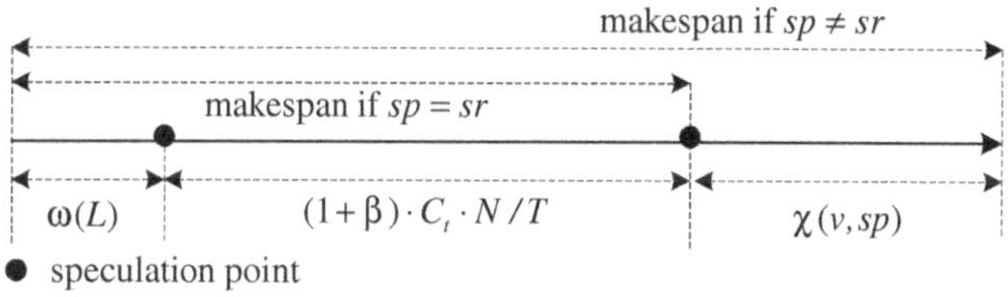


**Figure 4.** The make-spans of a thread, in cases of correct speculation ($s_p = s_r$) and wrong speculation ($s_p \neq s_r$), where, $s_p$ and $s_r$ are the speculation and real states respectively.

some additional operations to consume the results produced by the FSM state transition. In an XML-based database constructor, for example, once an object is recognized by its FSM, it is stored into a relational database. We use $C_w$ to represent the average time consumed by such an operation. Sometimes, the operations are buffered until the end of the FSM processing, in which case, $C_w$ equals the time to do the buffering. If we use $C_t$ to represent the time consumed by one state transition, the time taken by one step of the processing is $(C_t + C_w)$. Let $N$ be the length of the entire input, $T$ be the number of threads. An input segment is hence $N/T$ long. The processing time for an input segment is $(C_t + C_w) \cdot N/T$. Both $C_t$ and $C_w$ can be easily measured through profiling. Let $\beta$ equal $C_w/C_t$. The processing time for an input segment is $(1+\beta) \cdot C_t \cdot N/T$. We call $\beta$ the *workload parameter*.

***3) Reexecution Time*** Upon a failed speculation, the data segment needs to be reprocessed from the real state, $sr$. However, often not the entire data segment needs to be reprocessed because even though the speculation state $sp$ differs from $sr$, state transitions starting from them tend to converge gradually. For example, when the FSM in Figure 1 sees string "0 0 1 1 0", no matter it starts with state B or C, after processing the first three characters "0 0 1", it always reaches state C. We call the number of state transitions needed before two states converge *the merging length* of the two states, illustrated by the second section in Figure 1 (b).

Typically, reexecution is needed only for the data processed before $sp$ and $sr$ converge. Apparently the merging length depends on input strings and what the real state $sr$ is. Recall that our goal is to compute the statistical expectation of make-span. So it is natural to use the statistical expectation of the merging length across all inputs and all possible true states, denoted as $L_M(sp)$.

Suppose after a lookback on a suffix $v$, the feasible states set (i.e., the set of states whose feasibilities are positive) is $S_v$ and feasibilities are $\{P^v(s) | s \in S_v\}$. The expected merging length, $L_M^v(sp)$ is computed as follows:

$$L_M^v(sp) = \sum_{s_i \in S_v} L_M(sp, s_i) \cdot P^v(s_i), \qquad (1)$$

where, $L_M(sp, s_i)$ is the statistical expectation of the merging length of $sp$ and $s_i$ on all possible inputs. To understand the formula, one only needs to notice that $L_M(sp, s_i)$ is the reexecution time needed if $s_i$ turns out to be the real state, while $P^v(s_i)$ is the probability for that case to happen.

As the actual reexecution length cannot exceed the length of the segment $(N/T)$, $min\{L^v_M(sp), N/T\}$ is the expected reexecution length for a given speculation $sp$. Because a reexecution needs to reprocess the workload besides conducting state transitions, the expected reexecution time for a thread is

$$\chi(v, sp) = min\{L^v_M(sp), N/T\} \cdot (1+\beta) \cdot C_t. \quad (2)$$

***Putting All Together*** The sum of the three components gives the make-span of a thread. Without loss of generality, assume that all threads start at the same time. For the make-span of the entire execution, it may be tempting to think that it equals the maximum of the make-spans of all threads. It is incorrect because all reexecutions have to happen in serial: A thread does not know the real state until all the prior threads have completed their needed reexecutions[2] The correct way to compute the expected make-span of the execution, for a given $\mathbb{S}$, is as follows:

$$ES(\mathbb{S}) = \omega(l) + N/T \cdot (1+\beta) \cdot C_t + \sum_{i=2}^{T} \chi(v, sp(i)). \quad (3)$$

where, $l$ is the length of the suffix $v$, and $sp(i)$ is the speculated state of thread $i$, specified in $\mathbb{S}$. The three components on the right side of the formula respectively correspond to the overhead of one lookback, the time to process one input segment, and the reexecution time of all threads (other than the first as it needs no reexecution). We call this formulae, along with its assistant formulas 1 and 2, the *ES Formula*.

***Example*** We now show how the ES Formula applies to the example DFA in Figure 1. Suppose that our goal here is to compute the expected make-span in the following case: The second thread looks back at 2 characters. If by the end of the lookback, the thread picks state A as its speculated start state, some part of the second chunk of input may have to be reprocessed as A may not be the real start state $r$. The length of that part is the expected merging length between $A$ and $r$, denoted as $L_M(r, A)$. The third row of the table in Figure 1 (b) gives all the lengths. The real state $r$ could be any of the seven states, but the examination of the suffix "1 0" helps refine the probabilities. As explained earlier, the refined probabilities are denoted as $P^v(s)$, meaning the probabilities for the real state to equal state $s$ ($s = A, B, \cdots, F$) following suffix $v$ (i.e., $p(r = s|v =$"1 0")). So if we use $L^v_M(A)$ to represent the statistical expectation of the merging length between $A$ and all possible real start states after $v$, according to Equation 1, $L^v_M(A)$ can be computed as follows:

$L^v_M(A)=\sum_{s\in S} P^v(s) L_M(s, A)$

The computation of $P^v(s)$ (i.e., $p(r = s|v =$"1 0")) will be explained in the next section. Here, we list their values: $P^v(s)$=0, 0.42, 0, 0.14, 0.29, 0.15 ($s = A, B, \cdots, F$). The third row of the table in Figure 1(b) gives all the values of $L_M(s, A)$. Together, they give us the follows:

$L^v_M(A)$=0.42*101+0.14*59.71+0.29*39.12+0.15*59.71 =71.

From Formula 2, we know that in this case, the expected reexecution time is

$\chi$("1 0", A) $= min\{L^{\text{"10"}}_M(A), N/T\} \cdot (1+\beta) \cdot C_t$.

Assuming $N = 400$, $T = 2$, $\beta = 1$, $C_t = 1$, we get $\chi$("1 0", $A$) = 142. The look-back overhead is $2 \cdot C_t = 2$. The time to process the second chunk of input is $N/T \cdot (1+\beta) \cdot C_t = 200 \cdot 2 \cdot 1 = 400$. So the expected make-span in this case (i.e., when the second thread looks back by two characters and picks $A$ as the speculated start state) is $ES(A) = 2 + 400 + 142 = 544$. In the same way, we can compute the expected make-span of the second thread when it picks any other state as the start state: $ES(s) = 488, 487, 512, 499, 512$ ($s = B, \cdots, F$). State C is hence the best to pick as it minimizes the make-span. In the same vein, we can compute the minimum make-span when some other length of lookback is used. The results can help select the best lookback length (further elaborated in Section 5).

***Discussion*** The ES Formula allows us to compute the expected performance of an arbitrary speculation scheme. It is fundamental for finding a suitable speculation scheme for an FSM. All parameters in the formula—$l$, $sp(i)$, N, T, $\beta$, $C_t$, $L_M(sp, s_i)$—are given by the FSM or $\mathbb{S}$ or can be measured easily (shown in Section 6) from the FSM, except for the conditional feasibilities $P^v(s_i)$ that appears in Formula 1. We next show how to compute $P^v(s_i)$ from state transitions.

## 4. Computing Conditional Feasibilities

Recall that conditional feasibility $P^v(s_i)$ is the probability for $s_i$ to be the correct state following a lookback on suffix $v$. A key insight used in our design is that $P^v(s_i)$ is essentially a refinement of the context-free feasibility, $P(s_i)$, with the influence of the suffix considered. Given that suffixes cast their influence by dictating the FSM state transitions in an execution, the key to computing $P^v(s_i)$ is hence to find out the connections between state transitions and conditional feasibilities.

For convenience, we introduce several notations:

$r_i$: the real state of the FSM at time point $t_i$.
$L_i$: the string processed before the time point $t_i$.
$R_i$: the string processed after the time point $t_i$.
$S$: the entire set of states in an FSM.

[2] Theoretically speaking, reexecutions can be speculatively parallelized as well. But it adds more complexity.

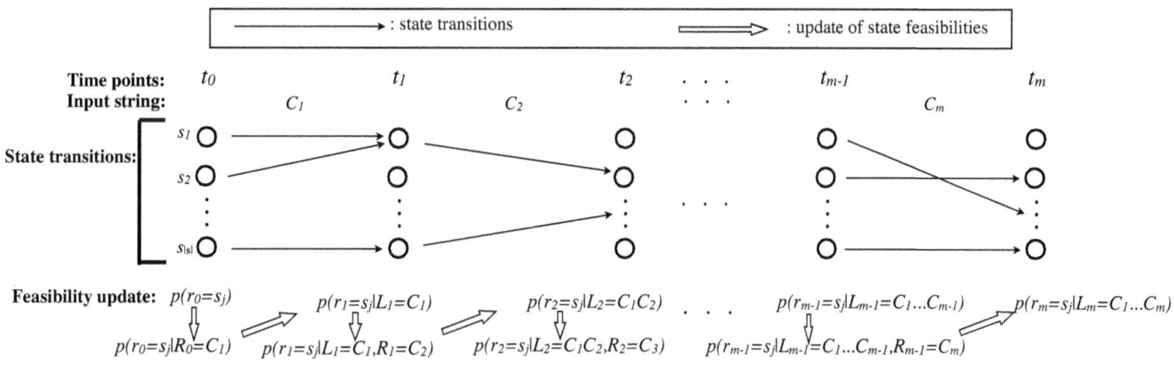

**Figure 5.** Gradual refinement of conditional feasibilities along with state transitions. The state transitions graph in the middle shows all possible transitions allowed by the FSM on the input characters.

Our analysis centers on the following observation: State transitions essentially lead to an incremental propagation of conditional feasibilities, with the conditions enriched gradually.

We will use Figure 5 to assist the explanation. The graph in the middle of the figure illustrates all possible state transitions upon a string $v = C_1C_2 \cdots C_m$. Our goal is to compute the conditional feasibility of each state after the $m$ stages of state transitions on the string. It is essentially the conditional probability $p(r_m = s_j | L_m = C_1C_2 \cdots C_m)$—that is, the probability for $s_j$ to be the true state at time $t_m$ given that the segment processed before that point equals $C_1C_2 \cdots C_m$ $(j = 1, 2, \cdots, |S|)$.

The calculation starts with the context-free feasibilities of all the states, $P(s_j)$, which is the $p(r_0 = s_j)$ shown in the leftmost column in Figure 5. Context-free feasibilities are easily obtainable through profiling (Section 6); they are considered as given. As the input characters are added to the condition of the feasibilities one after one, initial probabilities $p(r_0 = s_j)$ $(j = 1, 2, \cdots, |S|)$ are gradually enriched to the conditional feasibilities $p(r_m = s_j | L_m = C_1C_2 \cdots C_m)$.

***Intuition*** Let us examine the first stage of state transitions to gain some intuition. At this stage, we aim at putting the first input character $C_1$ into the condition of the feasibilities. In another word, we try to compute $p(r_1 = s_j | L_1 = C_1)$ $(j = 1, 2, \cdots, |S|.)$ We solve it by decomposing the computation into two steps. The first step uses $p(r_0 = s_j)$ to compute $p(r_0 = s_j | R_0 = C_1)$—that is, the state feasibilities when the upcoming character is $C_1$ at time $t_0$. The second step computes $p(r_1 = s_j | L_1 = C_1)$ from $p(r_0 = s_j | R_0 = C_1)$. The first step is a simple application of the standard Bayes' Theorem. It is easy to understand. We describe it later in this section.

We explain the second step here. This step exploits state transitions encoded in the FSM. In the transition graph in the middle of Figure 5, both and only states $s_1$ and $s_2$ transit to $s_1$ from $t_0$ to $t_1$ upon the input character $C_1$. Therefore, for $s_1$ to be the real state at time $t_1$, either $s_1$ or $s_2$ must be the real state at time $t_0$. Hence, the feasibility of $s_1$ at time $t_1$ with $L_1 = C_1$ as the condition equals the sum of the feasibilities of $s_1$ and $s_2$ at time $t_0$ with $C_1$ as the upcoming character, that is, $p(r_1 = s_1 | L_1 = C_1) = p(r_0 = s_1 | R_0 = C_1) + p(r_0 = s_2 | R_0 = C_1)$.

These two steps of context enrichment are called *inner-stage update* and *inter-stage update* respectively, corresponding to the downward arrow and right upward arrow from time $t_0$ to $t_1$ in the bottom graph of Figure 5. With all $P(r_1 = s_j | L_1 = C_1)$ $(s_j \in S)$ computed, we can add the second character $C_2$ into the condition in the same manner. Continuously doing this leads to the ultimate goal, $p(r_m = s_j | L_m = C_1C_2 \cdots C_m)$.

***General Form*** The formulae in Figure 6 express the two types of feasibility update. We call them *Feasibility Formulae*. The inner-stage formula captures the feasibility changes when the upcoming character $C_i$ is considered, given that all the conditional feasibilities at time $t_{i-1}$, $p(r_{i-1} = s_j | L_{i-1} = C_{1 \cdots (i-1)})$, have been computed. The first line of the inner-stage formula comes directly from the Bayes' Theorem. The second line comes from a simple inference on the fact that $\sum_{s_j \in S} p(r_{i-1} = s_j | L_{i-1} = C_{1 \cdots (i-1)}, R_{i-1} = C_i) = 1$. The inter-stage formula computes the conditional feasibilities at time $t_i$ based on the results of the inner-stage update. Its rationale is the same as the intuition given by the example in the previous paragraph. The computation results of the inter-stage update are then used by the inner-stage update (as they appear on the righthand side of the inner-stage formula) of the next stage. In this manner, these two kinds of update go hand in hand, leading to the final conditional feasibilities.

As the righthand side of the inner-stage update equation shows, using the formulae needs context-free feasibilities and conditional probabilities $p(R_{i-1} = C_i | r_{i-1} = s_j, L_{i-1} = C_{1 \cdots (i-1)})$ $(s_j \in S.)$ Context-free feasibilities are easy to obtain through profiling, but conditional ones are hard: There are too many variations of the condition to profile. However, notice that even though the string before $t_{i-1}$, $L_{i-1}$, has influence on the probabilities of which

Inner-stage update of feasibilities:

$$p(r_{i-1}=s_j|L_{i-1}=C_{1\cdots(i-1)},R_{i-1}=C_i) = \frac{p(R_{i-1}=C_i|r_{i-1}=s_j,L_{i-1}=C_{1\cdots(i-1)})\cdot p(r_{i-1}=s_j|L_{i-1}=C_{1\cdots(i-1)})\cdot p(L_{i-1}=C_{1\cdots(i-}}{p(L_{i-1}=C_{1\cdots(i-1)},R_{i-1}=C_i)}$$

$$= \frac{p(R_{i-1}=C_i|r_{i-1}=s_j,L_{i-1}=C_{1\cdots(i-1)})\cdot p(r_{i-1}=s_j|L_{i-1}=C_{1\cdots(i-1)})}{\sum_{s\in S}p(R_{i-1}=C_i|r_{i-1}=s,L_{i-1}=C_{1\cdots(i-1)})\cdot p(r_{i-1}=s|L_{i-1}=C_{1\cdots(i-1)})}$$

Inter-stage update of feasibilities:

$$p(r_i=s_j|L_i=L_{i-1}C_i) = \sum_{\substack{s\in S\\ s\xrightarrow{C_i}s_j}} p(r_{i-1}=s|L_{i-1}=C_{1\cdots(i-1)},R_{i-1}=C_i).$$

**Figure 6.** Formulae for inner-stage and inter-stage update of state feasibilities, where, $C_{1\cdots(i-1)}$ stands for $C_1C_2\cdots C_{i-1}$, and $\{s|s\in S; s\xrightarrow{C_i}s_j\}$ contains all the states that can transit to $s_j$ on input character $C_i$ from time $t_{i-1}$ to $t_i$.

character to appear next, the influence is largely throttled when the real state at $t_{i-1}$, $r_{i-1}$, is given: As a result of $L_{i-1}$, $r_{i-1}$ already captures most of its influence. Therefore, $p(R_{i-1}=C_i|r_{i-1}=s_j)$ is used as a replacement of $p(R_{i-1}=C_i|r_{i-1}=s_j,L_{i-1}=C_{1\cdots(i-1)})$. The probability $p(R_i=C|r_{i-1}=s_j)$ ($C\in V$; $V$ is the FSM vocabulary) can be obtained through profiling as Section 6 will show. With that replacement, the inner-stage update of $p(r_{i-1}=s_j|L_{i-1}=C_{1\cdots(i-1)},R_{i-1}=C_i)$ becomes

$$\frac{p(R_{i-1}=C_i|r_{i-1}=s_j)\cdot p(r_{i-1}=s_j|L_{i-1}=C_{1\cdots(i-1)})}{\sum_{s\in S}p(R_{i-1}=C_i|r_{i-1}=s)\cdot p(r_{i-1}=s|L_{i-1}=C_{1\cdots(i-1)})}. \quad (4)$$

***Example*** We now show how the formulae can be used to compute the conditional feasibility of $p(r=B|v=$"1 0") for the example FSM in Figure 1. We decompose the computation into four steps so that the inner-stage and inter-stage updates of the probabilities can be seen clearly.

*Step 1:* The calculation starts with using initial probabilities $p(r=s)$ ($s=A,B,\cdots,F$) to compute the conditional probabilities when the upcoming character is "1"—that is, $p(r=s|R=$"1"). This step corresponds to the point $t_6$ in Figure 1 (a). When s=A, for instance, the conditional probability is computed as follows:

$$p(r=A|R=\text{"1"}) = \frac{p(R=\text{"1"}|r=A)\cdot p(r=A)}{p(R=\text{"1"})}.$$

The components of the numerator are attributes of the DFA given in the table in Figure 1. The denominator equals $\sum_{s\in S}p(R=\text{"1"}|s)\cdot p(s)$ and hence can also be computed from the table. The results of this step are as follows:

$p(r=s|R=\text{"1"}) = 0.14, 0.28, 0.14, 0.14, 0.15, 0.15$ $(s=A,B,\cdots,F)$.

*Step 2:* We are now ready to compute the conditional probability when the left character is "1": $p(r=s|L=\text{"1"})$, which corresponds to the point $t_7$ in Figure 1 (a). When s=A, for instance, it is computed as follows:

$$\begin{aligned} p(r=A|L=\text{"1"}) &= \sum_{s\in S,s\xrightarrow{1}A} p(r=s|R=\text{"1"}) \\ &= p(r=D|R=\text{"1"})+p(r=F|R=\text{"1"}) \\ &= 0.29. \end{aligned}$$

The results from this step are as follows:

$p(r=s|L=\text{"1"}) = 0.29, 0.14, 0.28, 0.14, 0, 0.15$ $(s=A,B,\cdots,F)$.

*Step 3:* We now add the second lookback character into the condition to compute the probabilities $p(r=s|L=\text{"1"},R=\text{"0"})$. This step still corresponds to the point $t_7$ in Figure 1 (a). When s=A, for instance, the probability is computed as follows based on Formula 4:

$$p(r=A|L=\text{"1"},R=\text{"0"}) = \frac{p(R=\text{"0"}|r=A)\cdot p(r=A|L=\text{"1"})}{\sum_{s\in S}p(R=\text{"0"}|r=s)\cdot p(r=s|L=\text{"1"})}$$

The results from this step are as follows:

$p(r=s|L=\text{"1"},R=\text{"0"}) = 0.295$, $0.143$, $0.279$, $0.139$, $0$, $0.145$ $(s=A,B,\cdots,F)$.

*Step 4:* We are now ready to compute the conditional feasibilities, $p(r=s|L=\text{"1 0"})$. When s=A, for instance, it is computed as follows:

$$p(r=A|L=\text{"1 0"}) = \sum_{s\in S,s\xrightarrow{0}A} p(r=s|L=\text{"1"},R=\text{"0"}).$$

As there are no state transiting to $A$ through "0", the probability is 0. When s=B, the conditional feasibility, $p(r=B|L=\text{"1 0"})$ equals $p(r=B|L=\text{"1"},R=\text{"0"})+p(r=C|L=\text{"1"},R=\text{"0"})=0.422$.

***Discussion*** With the Feasibility Formulae computing the conditional feasibilities, the ES Formulae is finally complete for modeling the expected performance of an FSM on a speculation scheme. It paves the way for a rigorous design of FSM parallelization. With it, some intuitive designs manifest their problems immediately. For instance, at a speculation point, choosing the state that is most likely to be the true state (i.e., with the largest $P^v(.)$) may not be the best strategy. As Equation 1 shows, the reexecution length, when $sp$ is used for speculation, is a weighted sum of all feasibilities $P^v(s_i)$, with weights equaling the expected merging length, $L_M(sp, s_i)$ ($s_i \in S_l$). Hence, the most plausible state may result in a long reexecution for certain values of $L_M(sp, s_i)$. We next describe how the performance model helps find the best configurations for some speculation schemes.

## 5. Towards Optimal Designs

In this section, we first discuss the major dimensions in designing speculative parallelization of FSM. We then demonstrate how the described formulations help appropriately configure speculation schemes.

### 5.1 Design Dimensions

There are three main dimensions in configuring a lookback-based speculation scheme for FSM computations. The first is lookback length, which has some mixed effects: A long lookback may help reduce misspeculation by exploiting more context, but it meanwhile increases lookback overhead.

The second dimension is the set of states for starting a lookback. All previous speculation schemes use the default initial state of the FSM as the start state for lookback, which restraints the lookback benefit. As we will show, a larger start state set tends to yield a better speculation result. The main design questions in this dimension are how large the set should be, and which states the set should contain.

The third design dimension is the selection of lookback results for speculation. When the start state set of a lookback includes more than one state, the FSM executions from each of them will reach a state by the end of the lookback. For example, if we use states C and E as the start states for lookback for the FSM in Figure 1, on a suffix "1 0", the two lookbacks will end up at states D and F respectively. Choosing the best lookback ending state for speculation is the core question in this dimension.

These three dimensions interrelate with one another. For instance, optimal lookback lengths depend on what start states the lookback uses. Designs in all these dimensions together determine the quality of a speculation scheme. But it is difficult to compute the optimal values for all three dimensions at the same time.

In this section, we take the following strategy. We fix the configuration of the second dimension (i.e., the set of start states for lookback), and try to find the appropriate configurations for all other dimensions. In particular, we concentrate on two configurations of the second dimension. One uses the complete state set $S$ as the lookback start state set, the other uses a single state (adaptively determined) as the lookback start state set. Our analysis will demonstrate how the formalization described in the previous sections makes it possible to configure the two speculation schemes effectively. After that, we briefly discuss some other possible configurations of the second dimension.

### 5.2 Speculation through All-State Lookback

In this scheme, the lookback uses the complete state set as the start state set—that is, during the lookback, each thread other than the first processes a suffix for $|S|$ times, each time starting with a different state. The key design questions are how to determine suitable lookback lengths and how to select a state for speculation. To minimize make-span, the first step in the design is to instantiate the form of make-span given by the ES Formulae (Equations 1,2,3). To do so, we need to calculate lookback overhead $\omega(l)$ and expected reexecution time. We start with $\omega(l)$.

***Lookback Overhead*** $\omega(l)$ Because of the use of all states when a lookback starts, it is easy to see that the total number of state transitions throughout a lookback is $\sum_{k=0}^{l} |S_k|$, where, $S_k$ is the set of feasible states after $k$ stages of state transitions since the start of a lookback. In all-state lookback, there is an update to the feasibility of a state after every state transition in a lookback. Suppose the cost of a state transition is $C_t$, and the cost of a feasibility update is $C_p$. Then the overhead of an $l$-long lookback is

$$\omega(l) = (\sum_{k=0}^{l} |S_k|) \cdot (C_t + C_p). \tag{5}$$

Suppose $C_p = \lambda \cdot C_t$, then we have

$$\omega(l) = (\sum_{k=0}^{l} |S_k|) \cdot (1 + \lambda) \cdot C_t. \tag{6}$$

Both $C_t$ and $\lambda$ can be easily measured (Section 6.)

***Selecting the Speculation State*** In this all-state lookback scheme, after a lookback, there are typically multiple ending states. Which is selected for speculation determines the expected reexecution time. Our selection algorithm is as follows. With state feasibilities computed using the technique given in Section 4, for a given $l$, it is easy to use Equation 1 to compute the expected merging length, $L_M^v(sp)$, between every $sp$ and the real state—that is, the expected reexecution length when $sp$ is selected for speculation. The best speculation state can then be selected: It is the one that minimizes $L_M^v(sp)$ (hence the make-span.) We use $s^*$ to represent such a state. Based on Equation 2, the minimal reexecution cost can be computed as follows:

$$\chi(v, s^*) = min\{L_M^v(s^*), N/T\} \cdot (C_t + C_w). \tag{7}$$

***Determining Lookback Length*** The selection of the appropriate lookback length is based on the expectation of make-span (i.e., Equation 3.) The first two components of the make-span are easy to compute. The third component is the sum of all threads' reexecution overhead, which is unavailable before the execution finishes. It can be approximated by running $l$-long lookback on a number of typical suffixes and then using Equation 7 to compute the reexecution overhead of each. Let $\overline{\chi(l, s^*)}$ be the average. The expectation of make-span using $l$-long lookback can be calculated as follows:

$$ES(l) = \omega(l) + N/T \cdot (C_t + C_w) + (T-1) \cdot \overline{\chi(l, s^*)}. \quad (8)$$

A brute-force way to obtain the best lookback length is to use equation 8 to compute the $ES(l)$ for all values of $l$ and then find the minimum. It is unappealing because of the need for collecting $P^l(s)$ for all $l$ and the corresponding overhead.

We use curve fitting to circumvent the problem. Curve fitting is applied to the first and third components of Equation 8 individually. These two are the only components relevant to $l$ in the formula. Fitting them individually is easier than fitting their summation because their summation is often not monotonic while the two components are individually: The lookback overhead $\omega(l)$ increases as $l$ increases, and the expected reexecution cost $(T-1) \cdot \overline{\chi(l, s^*)}$ decreases as $l$ increases. The monotonicity simplifies curve fitting.

The implementation of the curve fitting is in a standard way. Using many suffixes, it first obtains a number of samples of $\omega(l)$ and $(T-1) \cdot \overline{\chi(l, s^*)}$ at some sample values of $l$ ($l = 2^i, i = 0, 1, \cdots, K$). It then uses a set of functions of $i$ to fit the points, and finds the functions producing the least mean square errors for $\omega(l)$ and $(T-1) \cdot \overline{\chi(l, s^*)}$ respectively. The best value of $l$ is then directly computed as the value that minimizes the sum of the two functions. Please refer to our technical report [35] for details.

With the techniques described in this sub-section, we can configure an all-state lookback-based speculation scheme to best meet the probabilistic properties of the FSM and inputs. The implementation, including the needed profiling, is detailed in Section 6.

### 5.3 Speculation through Single-State Lookback

All prior FSM speculation methods use a single state to start lookback. We show that the probabilistic analysis can also help such single-state schemes.

In the prior schemes [18, 26], the execution by a thread (except the first) starts with a lookback using the default initial state as the start state. After that, it uses the ending state of the lookback as the start state to process the input segment assigned to it. Reprocessing is done upon a misspeculation.

We now show how the scheme can be enhanced through probabilistic models. We start with its make-span. If we use $l_b$ and $l_x$ to represent the lookback length and expected reexecution length respectively, we can rewrite the ES Formula (Equation 3) to

$$ES(l_b) = l_b \cdot (1+\lambda) \cdot C_t + N/T \cdot (1+\beta) \cdot C_t + (T-1) \cdot l_x \cdot (1+\beta) \cdot C_t. \quad (9)$$

Let $s'_d$ represent the start state of a lookback. The ES Formula can be simplified with the following lemma:

**Lemma 1.** *For single-state speculative executions, if $L^0_M(s'_d) > l_b$, then $l_x = L^0_M(s'_d) - l_b$, otherwise, $l_x = 0$.*

In the lemma, $L^0_M(s'_d)$ is the expected merging length between state $s'_d$ and all other states without looking back. The lemma is proved in our technical report [35].

Putting $l_x$ values from Lemma 1 into Equation 9, the make-span equation is simplified, from which, we get the following theorem:

**Theorem 1.** *For single-state speculative execution ($T \geq 2$ and $\beta \geq \lambda$), the best lookback length equals $L^0_M(s'_d)$, and the expected make-span equals $L^0_M(s'_d) \cdot (1+\lambda) \cdot C_t + N/T \cdot (1+\beta) \cdot C_t$, where $s'_d$ is the lookback start state.*

The theorem is proved in our technical report [35].

All parameters in the theorem, including $L^0_M(s)$ ($s \in S$), can be obtained through profiling (Section 6.) Based on this theorem, one can easily compute the minimum expected make-span $min\_em(s)$ for each $s$. The suitable state to use for lookback is just the one whose $min\_em(s)$ is the smallest; its corresponding best lookback length is the overall best choice of lookback length. This gives the configuration that minimizes the expectation of make-span. The theorem has two conditions: $T \geq 2$ and $\beta \geq \lambda$. The first says that there are more than one thread in the FSM computation, and the second says that the time overhead of a probability update is no greater than the average time overhead in workload processing upon a FSM state transition. Both hold in a typical parallel FSM execution.

### 5.4 Other Configurations

Besides the all-state and single-state lookback schemes, the configurations can also use a subset of $S$ for lookback. The appropriate designs can be obtained in a manner similar to the all-state case. One complexity is that the use of a subset of all states leaves some state transitions unexamined during the lookback. Some approximations may have to be used as remedy when computing conditional state feasibilities. Details are out of the scope of this paper.

## 6. Implementation and Library Development

The implementations of the two speculation schemes both consist of a profiler and a controller. The controller runs online. By feeding information collected by the profilers to the analytic models described in the previous section, it configures the speculation schemes (e.g., lookback length, start states, selection of speculation states) on the fly to suite the properties of the FSM and inputs.

The profiler collects data needed by the analytic models. The single-state scheme requires the following data: context-free state feasibilities $P(s)$ ($s \in S$), expected merging length between every pair of states $L_M(s, r)$ ($s, r \in S$) (for computing $L^0_M(s)$), overhead parameters $\lambda$ and $\beta$, the number of threads $T$, and the length of the input string $N$. The actual values of all these parameters may vary across FSM as well as input strings. The all-state scheme needs the following additional data: $p(R_i = C|r_{i-1} = s_j)$ $(C \in V)$ for inner-stage probabilities update, and the values of $L_M^l(s^*)$ and $\omega(l)$ at 17 sampled values of $l$ $(2^k, k = 0, 1, \cdots, 16)$ for finding the suitable lookback length through curve fitting.

The profiler can run either online or offline. We explain the online case first. The online profiler has an adaptive switch. It first collects the values of $T$, $N$, $S$, $\lambda$, and $\beta$, with negligible overhead. It then uses these values to estimate the time needed to collect the remaining parameters, based on their computational complexities. If the overhead is larger than 10% of the single-thread workload processing time, it falls back to the default simple heuristic-based parallelization. Otherwise, it collects the other parameters as follows.

The collection of all $P(s)$ and $p(R_i = C|r_{i-1} = s_j)$ is through a sequential execution of the FSM on the first 2% input. As the execution is normal rather than speculated, the results are used as part of the final output of the FSM. As side products of the execution, the two kinds of probabilities are estimated based on their occurring frequencies in the execution. The overhead of this step is small.

The step to collect all the expected state merging length, $L_M(s,r)$, is quadratic to $|S|$. It is the most likely cause of the shutdown of the online profiling. The collection runs the FSM on an $l$-long segment of the input string $|S|$ times, with a different state in $S$ used as the start state each time. Meanwhile, during each process of the string segment, the FSM is reset to the start state after processing every $l$/5 input symbols. It ensures that the start state is visited by at least 5 times during the process. The state sequence in each run is recorded. After all the $|S|$ runs finish, the comparison between every two sequences gives at least 5 merging lengths of the two corresponding states (say $s$ and $r$.) The average is used for $L_M(s,r)$. The whole collection process runs in parallel across different states. In our experiments, $l$ is set to 1.6 million or the length of the training input if it is less than 1.6 million. Choosing 1.6 million is because it is greater than 5 times of largest merging length in our measurements. Such a length also ensures that with 99% confidence, the distribution of the characters in the training input is no more than 0.0011 off (in terms of the proportion of each character) that in the testing input [30]. If two states have not merged by 100,000 state transitions, their $L_M$ is set to $\infty$.

When online profiling is not affordable, offline profiling is always an option. A shortcoming of offline profiling is the input sensitivity issue. But in many uses of FSM applications, the same FSM runs on many similar inputs again and again, for example, an XML validator that deals with a large collection of XML files from similar sources. Furthermore, most input-sensitive parameters (e.g., $T$, $N$, $|S|$, $P(s)$, $p(R_i = C|r_{i-1} = s_j)$) can still be collected during runtime as they consume little overhead.

**Table 2.** Benchmarks

| Name | Description | $\lvert S\rvert$ | $L_M(s,r)$ | $P(s)$ | $L^*$ | Input |
|---|---|---|---|---|---|---|
| huff | Huffman Decoding | 46 | 4∼25 | 0∼0.21 | 23 | 209MB |
| lexing | XML Lexing | 3 | 1.0∼6.8 | 0.06∼0.5 | 2 | 76MB |
| str1 | String Pattern Search | 496 | 10∼41K | 0∼0.037 | 362 | 70MB |
| str2 | String Pattern Search | 131 | 2.98∼∞ | 0∼0.063 | 724 | 70MB |
| pval | Pattern Validation | 28 | 0∼∞ | 0∼0.50 | 0 | 96MB |
| xval | XML Validation | 742 | ∞ | 0∼0.054 | 229 | 57MB |
| div | Unary Divisibility | 7 | ∞ | 0.143 | 0 | 97MB |

The space overhead of data collection is $max(|S|^2, |S| \cdot |V|)$, negligible for all the tested FSM executions ($V$ for vocabulary.)

To make the model-based speculative schemes easy to use, we develop a library named *OptSpec* which integrates the all-state and single-state speculative schemes and the online and offline profiling procedures together. It is implemented in C and POSIX Threads, detailed in our technical report [35].

## 7. Evaluation

We evaluate the proposed techniques on seven FSMs listed in Table 2. They are developed based on the literatures in the web XML processing community (e.g., *lexing* and *xval* [34]), mathematics (e.g., *div* [5]), classical Huffman decoding (*huff* [20]), and string pattern matchings (*str1*, *pval*, and *str2* [2].) FSM computations take majority (mostly over 90%) of their execution time. They are selected for their wide usage in practice, and the spectrum of statistic features and complexities they exhibit as the right columns in Table 2 show. The features shown are those mostly related with the difficulty for speculative parallelization. The third column shows the ranges of state merging lengths (averaged over 100 runs.) The infinities ($\infty$) indicate that some pairs of states in that FSM never converge. The $P(s)$ column shows the ranges of context-free state feasibilities. An FSM with flat distribution of state feasibilities, such as *div* and *xval*, is usually hard to speculate. The $L^*$ column shows the lookback length that our approach finds for the all-state scheme ($\beta = 50$.) The rightmost column shows the size of the testing inputs. We collected inputs mostly from some public sources. For example, the input to pval, str1 and str2 are some novels; the input to huff is a 209MB pre-encoded text file; the input to lexing is a large XML file containing the information on the students in some college. We used the first about 2% of the collected data set as the training input.

Our experiments run on a dual-socket quad-core machine equipped with Intel Xeon E5620 processors. The machine runs Linux 2.6.22 and has GCC 4.4.1 as the compiler with "-O3" optimization flag. All timing results reported are the average of 10 repetitive runs with all runtime cost included.

For each benchmark, we compare the results from the following speculative executions:

**heuris:** Previous scheme [26].

**heuris+:** Our simple extension to previous scheme [26].

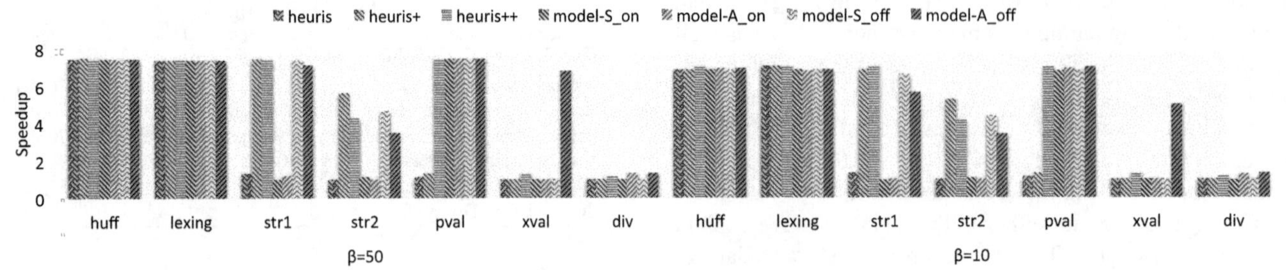


**Figure 7.** The overall speedup when 8 threads used.

**heuris++:** Our further extension to previous scheme [26].
**model-S_on:** Our single-state scheme with online profiling.
**model-A_on:** Our all-state scheme with online profiling.
**model-S_off:** Our single-state scheme with offline profiling.
**model-A_off:** Our all-state scheme with offline profiling.

The *heuris* shows the performance from the state-of-the-art scheme described in recent work [26]. It has lookback and other recent techniques incorporated, but relies on simple heuristics and is not adaptive to FSM properties or input strings. As the previous work offers no systematic solutions for finding the suitable lookback length, we implement the scheme with three lookback lengths, 32, 128, 512, that are used by the previous study [26] and use the best performance for *heuris*.

To examine the value of the insights and techniques described in this work, we develop six extra versions of speculative parallelization, which exhibit a spectrum of complexity and generality.

The *heuris+* version is our simplest extension to *heuris*. It leverages one of the insights in Section 3.2: Upon a failed speculation, often only the first part of the data segment needs to be reprocessed as state transitions starting from the wrong speculation state and the real state may converge. At a failed speculation, the reprocessing of this version stops at the convergence. This partial reprocessing has been used before, but only for some special DFA [20].

The *heuris++* version extends the *heuris+* version by using the state with the largest initial feasibility $P(s)$ as the start state for lookback. Similar to *heuris*, for these two extended versions, we try the three lookback lengths and report the best results.

The other four versions are based on the full model presented in this paper, with either online or offline profiling.

Figure 7 reports the overall speedups compared with the sequential performance when 8 threads are used. Results on 4 threads are similar.

As executions of an FSM may have different workload parameters ($\beta$) in different uses of the FSM, we report the results upon two different $\beta$ values, 10 and 50. Figure 8 reports the influence of input size on the performance of model-A_off with $\beta$=10, where, the "medium" size is the same as the testing input in Table 2, and the "small" and "large" sizes are five times smaller and larger than the "medium".

***Results*** The speedups differ between FSMs. The following two properties of an FSM are especially critical:

(1) *Probability distribution*: How biased the state probabilities are determines the difficulty for speculating the right state. If there is an extremely popular state, simple speculations would suffice as long as it picks that popular state. But if the distribution is flat, finding the right state would rely more on effective exploitations of contexts and probabilistic analysis.

(2) *Merging length*: How fast two states merge determines the cost of a misspeculation. If all states merge quickly, a misspeculation causes only a small segment of input to be reprocessed, and hence, a simple method may work fine even if it makes lots of wrong speculations.

In our experiments, *huff* and *lexing* have much skewed probability distributions and short merging lengths. All methods work well on them. As the FSM gets more challenging, those versions start showing disparity in the speedups. The *heuris* shows less than 20% speedups on all remaining five benchmarks, partial reexecution helps *heuris+* achieve 5-7X speedups on *str1* and *str2*, and *heuris++* gives more than 7X speedup on one more FSM, *pval* by exploiting the unconditional feasibilities in lookback. The *model-A_off* version gives significant speedups on all FSMs except for the most challenging one, *div*, demonstrating the generality brought by the principled speculation on the full model. The online model-based methods are beneficial to small FSMs only; the overhead of online profiling prevents them from taking effect on large FSMs.

Overall, the results show that simple capitalization of partial reexecution and state unconditional feasibilities can significantly improve the effectiveness of speculative speculations, making it suffice for most FSMs. But the full model-based method has the greatest generality, and may serve for very complex FSMs.

We further examine each individual program to provide a more detailed analysis.

*a) huff and lexing.* The program, *huff*, is a Huffman decoding tool. The input is a 209MB pre-encoded text file. The program, *lexing*, is an XML lexing tool, whose FSM contains only three states. Its testing input is a 76MB XML file. We include the two programs because they are used in prior studies [20, 26]. They turn out to be the only programs, on which, the previous technique shows speedups comparable to the other extended methods. The observed speedups agree with the results reported previously [26]. An examination of the two FSM shows that they have one or two very popular states. As a result, all lookbacks lead to those states, yielding 100% speculation accuracy, and large speedups.

*b) str1, str2.* These two programs are both for string pattern searching. The pattern for *str1* is $(.^*l.^*i.^*k.^*e)^6)|(.^*a.^*p.^*p.^*l.^*e)^5$; the pattern for *str2* is $((.^+,.^+ \setminus .)^4|(.^+,)^4|(.^+ \setminus .)^4)^3$. The "." in the patterns is for any character, "\." for the period, and superscripts for repetitions. They are selected to represent some complex cases in string pattern matching. The FSM of *str2* has some states that never converge, but most do. The ad hoc lookback in the *heuris* version gives almost entirely wrong speculation states. However, because most states in the FSMs have a short merging length, partial reexecution is sufficient to exploit the parallelism. The online model-based versions are shut down automatically for the required large profiling overhead. The offline model-based versions provide comparable speedups with *heuris+*.

*c) pval.* The program, *pval*, validates a binary string pattern, $111([01]^*00[01]^*)^{10}111$, where the superscript "10" means that the pattern in the parentheses repeats for 10 times. The speculation accuracy of the *heuris* method drops to 0–27%. In contrast, the all-state methods keep most prediction accuracies higher than 70%. Coupled with the minimization of reexecution time, they give the near linear speedups shown in Figure 7. Similar speedups are obtained by *heuris++*, indicating that exploiting unconditional feasibility and partial reexecution is sufficient for this FSM.

*d) xval.* The program, *xval*, checks the validity of an XML file. It has a more complex FSM than the previous five, including 742 states to implement an simplified Schema validation algorithm [34]. It does both lexical and syntactic validations for XML files containing up to five levels of nested tags on college personnel dataset. For this complex FSM, our online methods automatically fall back to the basic speculative scheme. Our *method-A_off* method produces 5.7 times of speedup, while none of the other methods gives any noticeable speedup.

On *str1*, *str2*, *pval* and *xval*, the *heuris* method is subject to near zero speculation accuracy, while the probabilistic models boost the accuracy to about 50%. Moreover, as the time breakdown shows (Figure 9), the model-based speculation selects the state that has a small penalty of misspeculation. The majority of the speculative execution is hence still valid (except *div*), yielding the much larger speedups.

*e) div.* This program checks whether an input binary string is 7 divisible. The FSM is a classical solution to the problem from the mathematic community [5]. Structure-

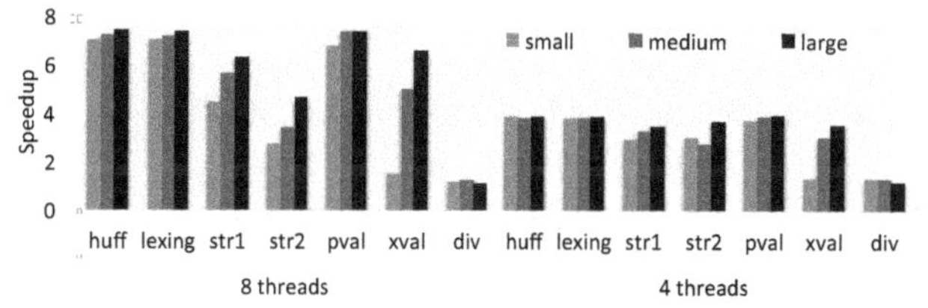


**Figure 8.** "Model-A off" on different input sizes.

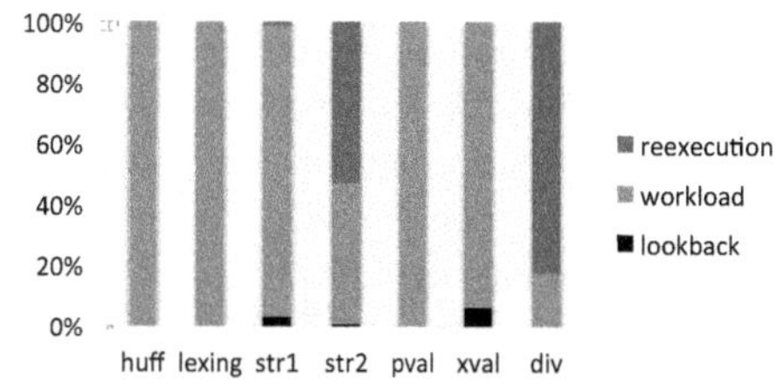


**Figure 9.** Time breakdown of model-A_off with $\beta$=50. Notations: "lookback" for lookback overhead, "workload" for workload processing time, "reexecution" for reexecution time.

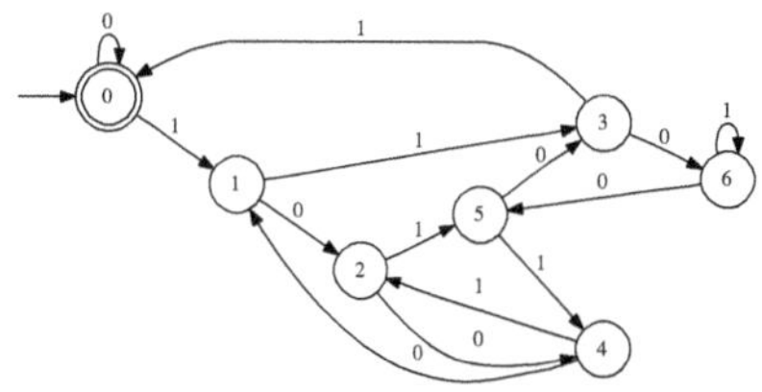

**Figure 10.** The FSM of *div*.

wise, it is simple, containing only seven states, shown in Figure 10.

However, it is extremely challenging for speculation. The seven states have exactly the same state feasibilities, and any two states never merge regardless of input. Consequently, making speculation is both difficult and risky—a wrong speculation leads to completely useless execution by a thread. All of the four model-based approaches select 0 as the lookback length, achieving 14.4% and 28.8% speculation accuracies and 1.06-1.31X speedups. The heuristic method yields 0 speculation accuracy but pays 1–5% overhead.

The offline profiling of the FSMs took less than a minute for most programs and about 10 minutes for *xval* for its many states. The cost could be further reduced through a more efficient implementation. But as these programs often serve as frequently used utilities for many inputs, the one-time training process is acceptable in many practical scenarios.

***Summary of Results*** The results lead to the following conclusions:

(1) State probability distribution and merging length primarily decide the difficulty for speculative parallelization.

(2) The basic heuristic method works only on FSMs with a highly skewed state distribution. Extending it with partial reexecution and unconditional feasibilities improves it significantly for FSMs with short merging lengths.

(3) The all-state model-based speculation, when used with offline profiling, has the greatest generality, leading to near linear speedups for most FSMs.

(4) The online version of model-based speculations is effective when the FSM is not large. Compared to other methods, it is the only method that can be applied on the fly with no need for offline profiling, which makes it potentially more resilient to input sensitivity issues.

(5) FSMs with uniform state probabilities and infinite merging lengths have little potential for speculative parallelization. However, if such an FSM contains only a few states, each input segment could be processed from all states in parallel. This method however, increases the amount of computation by a factor of $|S|$, and is hence not scalable nor energy efficient.

## 8. Related Work

Program parallelization has drawn explorations from language design (e.g. Cilk [15], X10 [11]), to hardware support (e.g., TLS [16, 29]) and programming models (e.g., STM [3, 10]). For lack of space, we concentrate on work closely related with FSM and software speculation.

Some studies try to parallelize some specific FSM applications. Jones and others, for instance, focus on a browser's front-end [18]. They introduce lookback (called overlap) for enhancing speculation accuracy, but did not study how to design the scheme to maximize the benefits. Klein and Wiseman [20] have designed a parallel JPEG decoder, which explores parallel Huffman decoding. Luchaup and others [25] have used hot state prediction in a pattern matching FSM to identify intrusions. Other examples include speculative parsing [19] and speculative simulated annealing [32]. These studies shed important insights into parallelizing FSM applications. But they all rely on simple heuristics rather than a systematic exploration of the design space.

There have been some studies in implementing parallel Non-deterministic Finite Automata (NFA) [36]. Unlike other types of FSM, the non-determinism in NFA inherently exposes a large amount of parallelism. There have been many efforts in parallel parsing. They can be roughly classified into two categories. The first tries to decompose the grammar among threads [7, 8] by exploiting some special properties of the target language or parsing algorithm (e.g., LR parsing in Fischer's seminal work [14]). The second tries to decompose the input [24], and can often leverage more parallelism than the first approach. They typically use a sequential prescan to partition data at appropriate places. Prescan is sequential and can benefit from the parallelization proposed in this work. The prescan-based data decomposition is often subject to load imbalance because the cutting points can only be the boundaries of certain constructs. Some work tries to allow even data partition by leveraging speculation for parallel parsing [33]. Similar to many prior speculative parallelizations, they are also based on heuristics and can potentially benefit from the rigorous analysis proposed in this work.

There are some efforts on speculatively parallelizing applications beyond a specific domain. Prabhu and others [26] proposed two new language constructs to simplify programmers' job in using speculation schemes to parallelize applications. Some other work has used software speculation to selectively parallelize programs with dynamic, uncertain parallelism, either at the level of processes [12] or threads [13, 28, 31]. They are mainly based on simple heuristics exposed in program runtime behaviors (e.g., speculation success rate). Llanos and others use probabilities of a dependence violation to guide loop scheduling of randomized incremental algorithms in the context of speculative parallelization [23]. Kulkarni and others have showed the usage of abstraction to find parallelism in some irregular applications [21]. The pre-computation used by Quinones and others for speculative threading [27] shares the spirit with lookback in exploiting some part of the program execution for speculation. They construct no rigorous speculation models, but relies on subset of instructions to resolve dependences.

## 9. Conclusion

This paper introduces formal analysis into speculative parallelization by formulating FSM speculative executions and the connections between the design of speculation schemes and the characteristics of FSM and their inputs. It deepens the understanding to speculative execution of FSM computations with a series of theoretical findings, including the essence and effects of lookback for speculation, the connections between state transitions and conditional feasibilities, and the relationship between partial committing and overall running times. It provides a set of model-based speculation schemes, with suitable configurations automatically determined. Experiments demonstrate that the new techniques outperform the state of the art by a factor of four on most programs, showing that "embarrassingly sequential" applications are in fact quite parallelizable. The insights, especially the importance of rigor and how to achieve it, could potentially benefit speculative parallelization of programs beyond FSM.

## Acknowledgment

We thank Ras Bodik, Thomas Dillig, Isil Dillig, and Weizhen Mao for their feedback. This material is based upon work supported by DOE Early Career Award, IBM CAS Fellowship, and the National Science Foundation under Grant No. 0811791, 1320796, and CAREER Award. Any opinions, findings, and conclusions or recommendations expressed in this material are those of the authors and do not necessarily reflect the views of the National Science Foundation or DOE or IBM.

## References


[1] R. Bodik. Browsing web 3.0 on 3.0 watts: Why browsers will be parallel and implications for education. Invited talk at The 3rd Workshop on Software Tools for MultiCore Systems, April, 2008.

[2] Regular expression. http://www.regular-expressions.info.

[3] M. Abadi, A. Birrell, T. Harris, and M. Isard. Semantics of transactional memory and automatic mutual exclusion. In *Proceedings of ACM Symposium on Principles of Programming Languages*, 2008.

[4] A. V. Aho, M. S. Lam, R. Sethi, and J. D. Ullman. *Compilers: Principles, Techniques, and Tools*. Addison Wesley, 2nd edition, August 2006.

[5] B. Alexeev. Minimal DFA for testing divisibility. *Journal of Computer and System Sciences*, 69(2), 2004.

[6] K. Asanovic, R. Bodik, B. Catanzaro, J. Gebis, P. Husbands, K. Keutzer, D. Patterson, W. Plishker, J. Shalf, S. Williams, and K. Yelick. The landscape of parallel computing research: A view from berkeley. Technical Report UCB/EECS-2006-18, University of California at Berkele, 2006.

[7] Franois Baccelli and Thierry Fleury. On parsing arithmetic expressions in a multiprocessing environment. *Acta Inf.*, 17:287–310, 1982.

[8] Franois Baccelli and Philippe Mussi. An asynchronous parallel interpreter for arithmetic expressions and its evaluation. *IEEE Trans. Computers*, 35(3):245–256, 1986.

[9] H.C. Bunt and A. Nijholt. *Advances in probabilistic and other parsing technologies*. Kluwer Academic Publishers, 2000. Chapter 12.

[10] B. Carlstrom, A. McDonald, H. Chafi, J. Chung, C. Minh, C. Kozyrakis, and K. Olukotun. The atomos transactional programming langauges. In *Proceedings of ACM SIGPLAN Conference on Programming Language Design and Implementation*, 2006.

[11] P. Charles, C. Grothoff, V. Saraswat, C. Donawa, A. Kielstra, K. Ebcioglu, C. von Praun, and V. Sarkar. X10: an object-oriented approach to non-uniform cluster computing. In *OOPSLA*, 2005.

[12] C. Ding, X. Shen, K. Kelsey, C. Tice, R. Huang, and C. Zhang. Software behavior-oriented parallelization. In *Proceedings of ACM SIGPLAN Conference on Programming Language Design and Implementation*, 2007.

[13] M. Feng, R. Gupta, and Y. Hu. Spicec: Scalable parallelism via implicit copying and explicit commit. In *Proceedings of the ACM SIGPLAN Symposium on Principles Practice of Parallel Programming*, 2011.

[14] Charles N. Fischer. *On Parsing Context Free Languages in Parallel Environments*. PhD thesis, Cornell University, 1975.

[15] M. Frigo, C. E. Leiserson, and K. H. Randall. The implementation of the Cilk-5 multithreaded language. In *Proceedings of ACM SIGPLAN Conference on Programming Language Design and Implementation*, 1998.

[16] M. Herlihy and J. E. Moss. Transactional memory: Architectural support for lock-free data structures. In *Proceedings of the International Symposium on High Performance Computer Architecture (HPCA)*, 1993.

[17] K. Ingham, A. Somayaji, J. Burge, and S. Forrest. Learning DFA representations of HTTP for protecting web applications. *Computer Networks*, 51(5):1239–1255, April 2007.

[18] C. Jones, R. Liu, L. Meyerovich, K. Asanovic, and R. Bodik. Parallelizing the web browser. In *HotPar*, 2009.

[19] B. Kaplan. Speculative parsing patch. In bugzilla.mozilla.org, 2009.

[20] S. Klein and Y. Wiseman. Parallel Huffman decoding with applications to JPEG files. *Jounal of Computing*, 46(5), 2003.

[21] M. Kulkarni, K. Pingali, B. Walter, G. Ramanarayanan, K. Bala, and L.P. Chew. Optimistic parallelism requires abstractions. In *Proceedings of ACM SIGPLAN Conference on Programming Language Design and Implementation*, 2007.

[22] Richard E. Ladner and Michael J. Fischer. Parallel prefix computation. *J. ACM*, 27(4):831–838, October 1980.

[23] D.R. Llanos, D. Orden, and B. Palop. New scheduling strategies for randomized incremental algorithms in the context of speculative parallelization. *IEEE Transactions on Computers*, 2007.

[24] Wei Lu, Kenneth Chiu, and Yinfei Pan. A parallel approach to XML parsing. In *Proceedings of the 7th IEEE/ACM International Conference on Grid Computing*, GRID '06, pages 223–230, 2006.

[25] D. Luchaup, R. Smith, C. Estan, and S. Jha. Multi-byte regular expression matching with speculation. In *RAID*, 2009.

[26] P. Prabhu, G. Ramalingam, and K. Vaswani. Safe programmable speculative parallelism. In *Proceedings of ACM SIGPLAN Conference on Programming Languages Design and Implementation*, 2010.

[27] C.G. Quinones, C. Madriles, J. Sanchez, P. Marcuello, A. Gonzalez, and D. M. Tullsen. Mitosis compiler: an infrastructure for speculative threading based on pre-computation slices. In *Proceedings of ACM SIGPLAN Conference on Programming Languages Design and Implementation*, 2005.

[28] A. Raman, H. Kim, T. R. Mason, T. B. Jablin, and D. I. August. Speculative parallelization using software multi-threaded transactions. In *Proceedings of the international conference on Architectural support for programming languages and operating systems*, 2010.

[29] J. G. Steffan, C. Colohan, A. Zhai, and T. C. Mowry. The STAMPede approach to thread-level speculation. *ACM Transactions on Computer Systems*, 23(3):253–300, 2005.

[30] Steven K. Thompson. Sample size for estimating multinomial proportions. *The American Statistician*, 1987.

[31] C. Tian, M. Feng, V. Nagarajan, and R. Gupta. Copy or discard execution model for speculative parallelization on multicores. In *Proceedings of the International Symposium on Microarchitecture*, 2008.

[32] E. Witte, R. Chamberlain, and M. Franklin. Parallel simulated annealing using speculative computation. *IEEE Transactions on Parallel and Distributed Systems*, 2(4):483–494, 1991.

[33] Zhiqiang Yu, Yu Wu, Qi Zhang and Jianhui Li. A hybrid parallel processing for XML parsing and schema validation. In *Balisage: The Markup Conference 2008*.

[34] Y. Zhang, Y. Pan, and K. Chiu. Speculative p-DFAs for parallel XML parsing. In *Proceedings of the International Conference on High Performance Computing*, 2009.

[35] Z. Zhao, B. Wu, and X. Shen. Probabilistic analysis for optimal speculation of finite-state machine applications. Technical Report WM-CS-2014-01, College of William and Mary, 2014.

[36] Y. Zu, M. Yang, Z. Xu, L. Wang, X. Tian, K. Peng, and Q. Dong. GPU-based NFA implementation for memory efficient high speed regular expression matching. In *PPoPP '12: Proceedings of the ACM SIGPLAN symposium on Principles and practice of parallel programming*, pages 129–140, 2009.

# The Sharing Architecture:

## Sub-Core Configurability for IaaS Clouds

Yanqi Zhou
Princeton University
F210 E2 Engineering Quadrangle, Olden St.
Princeton, NJ 08544
yanqiz@princeton.edu

David Wentzlaff
Princeton University
B228 Engineering Quandrangle, Olden St.
Princeton, NJ 08544
wentzlaf@princeton.edu

## Abstract

Businesses and Academics are increasingly turning to Infrastructure as a Service (IaaS) Clouds such as Amazon's Elastic Compute Cloud (EC2) to fulfill their computing needs. Unfortunately, current IaaS systems provide a severely restricted pallet of rentable computing options which do not optimally fit the workloads that they are executing. We address this challenge by proposing and evaluating a manycore architecture, called the Sharing Architecture, specifically optimized for IaaS systems by being reconfigurable on a sub-core basis. The Sharing Architecture enables better matching of workload to micro-architecture resources by replacing static cores with Virtual Cores which can be dynamically reconfigured to have different numbers of ALUs and amount of Cache. This reconfigurability enables many of the same benefits of heterogeneous multicores, but in a homogeneous fabric, and enables the reuse and resale of resources on a per ALU or per KB of cache basis. The Sharing Architecture leverages Distributed ILP techniques, but is designed in a way to be independent of recompilation. In addition, we introduce an economic model which is enabled by the Sharing Architecture and show how different users who have varying needs can be better served by such a flexible architecture. We evaluate the Sharing Architecture across a benchmark suite of Apache, SPECint, and parts of PARSEC, and find that it can achieve up to a 5x more economically efficient market when compared to static architecture multicores. We implemented the Sharing Architecture in Verilog and present area overhead results.



*ASPLOS '14*, March 1–5, 2014, Salt Lake City, Utah, USA.

ACM 978-1-4503-2305-5/14/03... $15.00.
http://dx.doi.org/10.1145/2541940.2541950

***Categories and Subject Descriptors*** C.1.3 [*Processor Architectures*]: Other Architecture Styles–Adaptable architectures; C.5.5 [*Computer System Implementation*]: Servers

***Keywords*** Infrastructure as a Service (IaaS); Slice; Cache; Cache Banks; Virtual Core (VCore); Virtual Machine (VM); utility; market efficiency.

## 1. Introduction

Cloud computing and Infrastructure as a Service (IaaS) Clouds have enabled convenient, on-demand, self-service, access to vast quantities of computing that can be provisioned with minimal effort. Current IaaS systems utilize commodity multicore processors as the computational substrate to service this diverse computational need. Unfortunately, the individual core, the foundation of commodity multicore processors, is optimized across a set of applications, but by definition it is not optimized for any particular application. **In this work, we propose a new architecture, we call the Sharing Architecture, which is specifically inspired by the needs of IaaS Cloud providers.** Namely, that Cloud providers require an architecture which enables efficient markets to match customer's needs with computational resources, enables the customization of micro-architecture hardware to a customer's application, and enables the reuse of idle hardware resources thereby maximizing profit. The Sharing Architecture addresses these needs by providing a manycore architecture where the core can be reconfigured, customized, and leased on a sub-core basis.

The movement of computation and storage into the Cloud and into large data centers has been at an explosive rate [7, 12]. For example, the number of objects stored in Amazon's S3 storage service [3] has more than doubled every year since its inception [9]. Likewise, the number of Virtual Machine (VM) instances active in Amazon's Elastic Compute Cloud (EC2) [1, 35] has been estimated to be growing at a similar rate [62]. Many diverse applications which have traditionally been desktop applications have successfully been transitioned into the Cloud, including word processing (eg. Google Apps [2]), spreadsheets (eg. Google Apps), data backup clients (eg. Box.net, Dropbox, Mozy, Backblaze ), email clients (Gmail, Hotmail, Yahoo Mail), and even gaming (eg. OnLive). The growth in data center computing has not only been fueled by desktop applications moving to the Cloud, but also startups and established companies moving computationally intensive [38, 46] and data serving tasks into the Cloud.

In this work, we focus specifically on IaaS Cloud systems. An IaaS Cloud provider typically leases managed computational, storage, or network resources to customers. We focus on the computational facet which usually comes in the form of leasing Virtual Machine (VM) instances. For a fee, an IaaS Cloud provider agrees to run a client's VM on the Cloud provider's computing infrastructure. Examples of computational IaaS Public Cloud providers include: Amazon's EC2[1], Microsoft's Azure Virtual Machines [4], Terremark, Linode, Rackspace Cloud, Joynet, and Google's Compute Engine. IaaS infrastructure is also gaining traction within an enterprise setting by leveraging many of the same technologies of Public Clouds, but in a Private Cloud setting [15, 43, 61].

IaaS Cloud providers typically provide a very limited pallet of Virtual Machine configurations. For example, Amazon's EC2 currently supports only eighteen machine configurations. The configurations presented by Amazon do not allow the customer to choose different intra-core parameters, such as cache size, but rather only allow the customer to choose fixed combinations of core count, the amount of DRAM, and the amount of disk in a VM instance. The lack of intra-core, micro-architecture VM configuration options leaves the Cloud customer utilizing a VM configuration which does not match their workload's needs. This disconnect leads to Cloud customers overpaying for resources or experiencing sub-optimal application performance. The inability for the Cloud provider to customize a VM instance to a customer's needs also harms the provider. This leads to a less efficient marketplace, where the Cloud provider is unable to price fine-grain resources according to their marginal cost thereby contributing to wasted resources and wasted revenue opportunities. A Cloud provider's inability to provide fine-grain micro-architecture choices is directly due to the failing of current commodity multicores not being divisible below the core level.

To address this challenge, we propose the IaaS-influenced Sharing Architecture along with a modification to how IaaS markets are priced to enable the fine-grain assignment of processor resources to Virtual Cores. The Sharing Architecture enables the assignment of fine-grain processor resources to a configurable Virtual Core all the way down to the individual ALU, fetch unit, and KB of cache. One or more Virtual Cores are then composed into Virtual Machine instances. Figure 1 shows a conceptual view of the Sharing Architecture. The Sharing Architecture is designed to allow a nearly arbitrary set of sub-core resources to be composed into a single Virtual Core. These different fine-grain resources are connected together by multiple, pipelined, switched interconnection networks providing connectivity for the sea-of-ALUs and sea-of-cache banks. While the Sharing Architecture enables nearly arbitrary configurations of resources into Virtual Cores, due to the added communication latency when sharing distant resources, we do not expect all combinations to provide performance benefit. By enabling a fluid assignment of ALUs and cache to Virtual Cores, the Sharing Architecture enables the Cloud user to choose whether to optimize for single-stream performance at the expense of area, for throughput, or complex mixes.

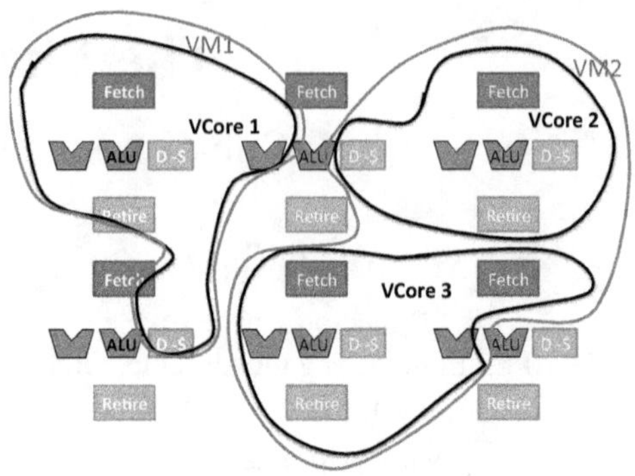


**Figure 1.** High Level View of Sharing Architecture showing two Virtual Machines. VM1 has two VCores, VM2 has one VCore.

The Sharing Architecture has much of the same motivation and performance benefit of heterogeneous multicore systems [33, 34], but is built out of a large homogeneous fabric. Applications can be more area efficient, energy efficient, and perform better if they run on properly sized cores. **Unlike heterogeneous multicore systems, the Sharing Architecture does not require the mix of core sizes to be determined at chip design time.** This is even more important in IaaS Cloud systems where the mixture of applications is determined by dynamic external customers. The Sharing Architecture is inspired by Core Fusion [24], WiDGET [64], the Distributed ILP mechanisms in the TRIPS architecture [11, 17, 49, 50, 53], and how ILP is mapped across multiple cores in the Raw [63] and Tilera [65] architectures.

An important aspect of the Sharing Architecture is that it enables more efficient markets by enabling the Cloud provider to price different portions of a core on a sub-core basis. For instance, instead of simply charging $0.065 per CPU-hour, the Cloud provider is able to charge per ALU-hour, per cache KB-hour, etc. This capability empowers a more dynamic Cloud pricing market and ultimately leads to a more economically efficient marketplace. In this paper, we explore how different IaaS Cloud users (customers) garner different utility as a function of sub-core (ALUs, Cache, etc) and beyond-core (Number of cores, VMs, DRAM, etc.) resources. Different Cloud customers can have different utility curves due to technical, price, and policy needs. Unlike fixed architectures, the Sharing Architecture does not judge which utility function is superior, but rather simply allows the Cloud user to express their preferences and have the market meet these preferences.

The Sharing Architecture is designed to enable dynamic reconfiguration of Virtual Cores and to run the same binary independent of Virtual Core configurations (no recompilation). This dynamic nature enables the Cloud provider to price sub-core resources dynamically and based on instantaneous market demand. The programmer or IaaS Cloud user must determine, based on the market rates for sub-core resources, how many resources to utilize to best fit their demand and utility needs. While this work focuses on the hardware aspects of the Sharing Architecture and the market it can create, we also outline software implications. For instance, the IaaS Cloud user could provide a meta-program along with their Virtual Machine which decides the desired machine configuration based off the market prices for resources. Alternatively, an auto-tuner could be used if the customer lacks a detailed application performance model.

## 2. Economic Model

Optimizing computer architecture for IaaS cloud systems has different criteria than traditional computer architecture. In traditional computer architecture, systems are typically optimized for performance, cost, energy, or some combination of these constraints. In contrast, when computer architecture is optimized for IaaS Clouds, the ability to enable more efficient markets dominates traditional computer architecture constraints. This is amplified by the fact that different IaaS customers can have conflicting optimization criteria such that it is impossible to satisfy all customers with a fixed design. Economists have shown that by having economically efficient markets, both the seller and buyer can be enriched, or in our case, **the Cloud provider can make additional revenue and simultaneously the Cloud user (customer) can pay less.** In this section, we describe the current IaaS marketplace, the diversity of customer needs, and how the Sharing Architecture facilitates a more economically efficient market.

### 2.1 Current IaaS Pricing Model

IaaS Public Cloud providers such as Amazon's Elastic Compute Cloud (EC2) and Microsoft's Azure Virtual Machines use an instance-based pricing model. In these models, customers are able to choose from a relatively limited number of VM instance types and they pay on a per-VM instance-hour basis. For example, in EC2, for \$0.065/h, a VM instance with 1.7GB of RAM, a single core, and 160GB local disk can be leased. In addition to these fixed cost models, EC2 has a market, named Spot Pricing, which provides an auction for VM instances. Cloud customers use IaaS Cloud systems as a way to reduce the risk of over-provisioning or under-provisioning purchased computational resources by turning capital purchases into operational expenditures. In contrast to instance-based pricing, private IaaS Cloud systems such as VMWare's VCloud [31] system provide a richer ability to configure a VM instance, but the parameters are still limited to resources outside of the core such as core count, amount of DRAM, and disk size.

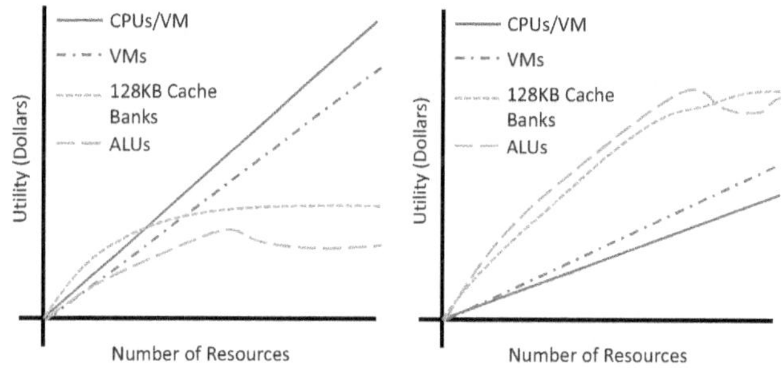


(a) Throughput Applications (b) Single Stream Applications

**Figure 2.** Resource Utility Functions for Different Applications

### 2.2 Diversity of Needs

Consumers have diverse desires. Economists use *utility* to measure how well a particular resource satisfies an individual's wants. Economists measure total utility to determine how economically efficient a market is. A more economically efficient market will have higher global utility than a less efficient market for a fixed number of resources. In effect, an efficient market will enable better matching of resources to consumers who are willing to pay more for those resources (assuming consumers are willing to pay commensurate with the utility they gain). One way to make a market more efficient is to disentangle, disaggregate, or sub-divide resources, thereby enabling consumers to more accurately express their desires and allowing sellers to more accurately express their costs. Given these assumptions, by maximizing global utility, cloud providers maximize profit.

In an IaaS Cloud market, different customers can have different utility functions. In this paper, we do not try to make any judgment or assumption about customers' utility functions, but rather we provide hardware that enables different utility functions to be well served. Figure 2a shows a set of utility functions for a *hypothetical* throughput oriented application (ex. web serving). In this application, the computation scales linearly with VMs and CPUs/VM, but the customer favors having more CPUs per VM to reduce administrative overhead. As more Cache per core is added, the marginal utility gained by the customer diminishes. Last, as can be seen, as more ALUs are added per core, the utility goes up at first, but then this customer's application begins to slow down due to the added communication cost between ALUs. It should be noted that these utility functions are simply 2D approximations of the true multi-dimensional utility space as one resource may affect the utility gained from a second resource. A savvy customer will profile their application and use policy decisions to determine what their utility functions are. Hence the same customer with the same policy may have different utility functions when running a

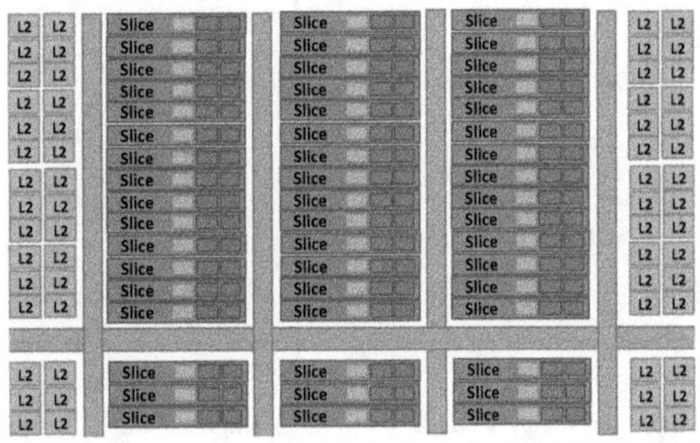


**Figure 3.** Slices, Cache Banks and Interconnection Network

different application due to how the application responds to different resources.

In contrast to the throughput example, a second customer running an application (potentially the same application) may favor single-stream performance. This may be because they know that their application does not parallelize well across cores or may simply be a policy decision. Figure 2b shows an example customer's utility functions where they favor $(sequential\ performance)^2$ as a metric. $Performance^2$ or $Performance^3$ may be very reasonable metrics if a customer favors sequential time to completion and these metrics have much similarity to $Energy * Delay^2$ and $Energy * Delay^3$ used in energy efficient computing research. Finally, a single customer and a single application may have different utility functions as a function of time of day or program phase [34]. Programs commonly have different phases and if properly expressed, a per-phase machine-application fit can be made.

### 2.3 New Model

To create a more efficient market, we propose changing the typical IaaS market and software APIs from one which has a limited pallet of VM instance types that have differences at the core level and above into a market where the cloud provider auctions off all resources down to the ALU, KB of cache, fetch unit, retire unit, and even on-chip or off-chip memory bandwidth. To realize this change, a hardware fabric that is more flexible than multicore processors is needed. The Sharing Architecture is the first step in building such an architecture.

## 3. Architecture

The Sharing Architecture is a fine-grain composable architecture which provides the flexibility to dynamically "synthesize" a flexible core out of the correct amount of ALUs, fetch bandwidth, and cache, based on an application's demand and the need to optimize cost. Unlike multicore and manycore architectures where the processor core is statically fixed at design and fabrication time, the Sharing Architecture enables the core to be reconfigured and use resources from a wide array of resources across a single chip. This level of reconfigurability is especially useful in a competitive

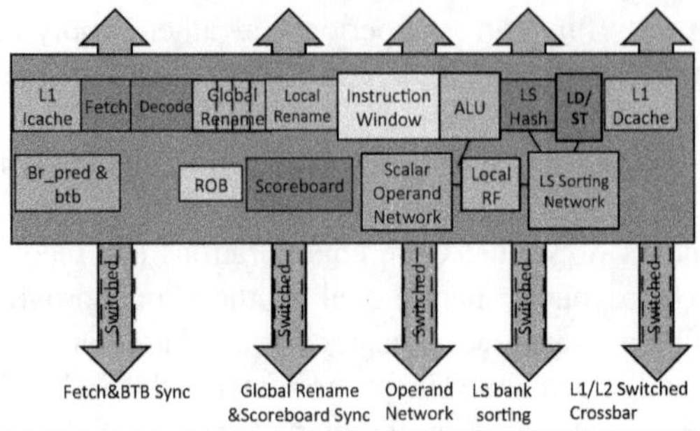


**Figure 4.** Slice Overview and Inter-Slice Network

IaaS data center setting where many applications and different customers' codes and Virtual Machines will all share a single multicore processor.

At the top level, like current day multicore chips used for IaaS applications, the Sharing Architecture has multiple cores that can be grouped together to create multicore *Virtual Machines* (VMs). Unlike fixed architecture multicore processors, the VMs in the Sharing Architecture are composed of cores which themselves are composed of a variable number of ALUs, fetch bandwidth, and cache. We call this flexible core a *Virtual Core* (VCore). A VCore is composed out of one or more *Slices* and zero or more *L2 Cache Banks*. Figure 3 shows an example array of Slices and Cache Banks. A full chip will have 100's of Slices and Cache Banks.

The basic unit of computation in the Sharing Architecture is a *Slice* as shown in Figure 4. A Slice is effectively a simple out-of-order processor with one ALU, one Load-Store Unit, the ability to fetch two instructions per cycle, and a small Level 1 Cache. Multiple Slices can be grouped together to increase the performance of sequential programs thereby empowering users to make decisions about trading off ILP vs. TLP vs. Process level parallelism vs. VM level parallelism while all utilizing the same resources.

In order to reduce fragmentation, the Sharing Architecture is designed to enable very flexible sharing of resources and does not impose hierarchical grouping of Slices or Cache Banks. In order to achieve this, we use general purpose switched interconnects wherever possible. Neither Slices or Cache Banks need to be contiguous in a VCore for functionality. But we do impose a few limited restrictions for the purpose of performance. For instance, when Slices are joined into a single VCore, those Slices need to be contiguous to reduce operand communication cost, but Cache Banks do not need to be contiguous or near by and we model the latency as such. We do not see the need for contiguous Slices to be a limitation as all Slices are interchangeable and equally connected therefore fixing fragmentation problems is as simple as rescheduling Slices to VCores.

The ability to group multiple Slices into a single VCore adds not only logical complexity, but also a small area and performance overhead which we study in detail in Section 5.1. In this work, we leverage many of the ideas from Distributed ILP architectures such as TRIPS, Raw,

| Component | Branch Predictor | BTB | Scoreboard | Issue Window | Load Queue | Store Queue | ROB | Local RAT | Global RAT | Physical RF |
|---|---|---|---|---|---|---|---|---|---|---|
| Replicated | | ✓ | ✓ | | | | | | ✓ | |
| Partitioned | ✓ | | | ✓ | ✓ | ✓ | ✓ | ✓ | | ✓ |

**Table 1.** Replicated vs. Partitioned Structures

and Tilera as well as fusible core ideas from Core Fusion and WiDGET to address the challenge of partitioning one VCore across multiple Slices. The approach we take is designed for wider sharing of resources than the fusible core approach and hence the Sharing Architecture tries to enable more decoupling between Slices.

When grouping multiple Slices to work together to execute a single sequential program, each intra-core component (e.g. Reorder Buffer (ROB), Scoreboard, etc) has to be considered to see if the component needs to be logically replicated, partitioned, or centralized. These decisions are made based off how tolerant a structure is to increased latency when accessing different elements in the structure. The advantage of partitioning a structure over replicating a structure is that when partitioned, the number of logical resources scales with the number of Slices. Conversely, replicated resources need to be sized for the largest number of Slices in a VCore configuration (8) and waste area for smaller configurations. Table 1 presents a table of which structures are replicated or partitioned in the Sharing Architecture. The rest of this section steps through the design decisions of the Sharing Architecture.

### 3.1 Front-End

Each Slice has its own copy of the program counter. The replication of the program counter enables each Slice in a VCore to fetch two instructions per cycle. The fetching of instructions is interleaved such that each Slice fetches two contiguous instructions in one cycle and instructions $2*number\_of\_slices$ and $(2*number\_of\_slices)+1$ later in the program on a subsequent cycle. Whenever there is a stall that ripples back to the fetch stage of the pipeline, it stalls all of the Slices in a VCore.

Similar to Core Fusion [24], a distributed branch predictor is used, thus the effective branch predictor capacity grows with number of Slices. Because instructions are fetched in an interleaved fashion, the same PC is always fetched by the same Slice. Therefore branch instructions are always mapped to the same Slice and the same predictor. Unlike Core Fusion, each Slice replicates Branch Target Buffer (BTB) entries in order to enable Slices which do not execute a given branch to fetch the appropriate next instruction. These fake BTB entries are added into the BTBs of Slices in the same fetch group as a branch and are tagged by the appropriate offset and point to the correct Slice-interleaved target address, not the actual branch target. Branch misprediction and Branch Target Buffer (BTB) training information is transmitted over the switched interconnect. When a branch mispredicts, all speculative instructions in the branching Slice are flushed and misprediction messages are sent to

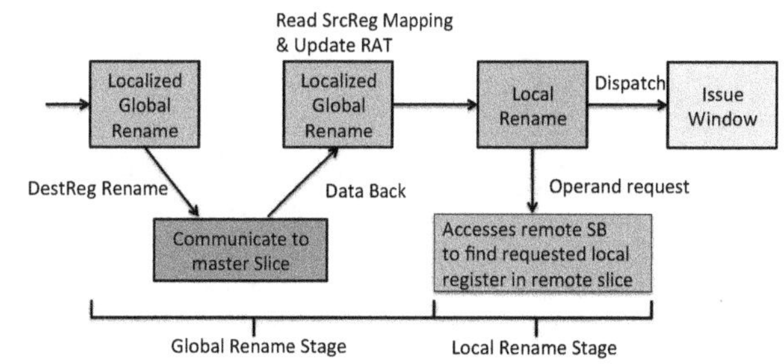


**Figure 5.** Flow Chart of Rename Stage. Multi-stage global rename and local rename.

Slices which contain newer speculative instructions to cause those instructions to be flushed.

The Sharing Architecture uses a local bimodal branch predictor [40], which indexes the prediction table by the program counter value. In order to utilize a global prediction scheme, such as gshare, gselect, etc., a Global History Register needs to be composed across Slices. This could be achieved with appropriate delay across the switched interconnect.

### 3.2 Register Renaming

Renaming registers on the Sharing Architecture occurs in a two step process as shown in Figure 5. At a high-level, architectural registers are first renamed into a global logical register space which is shared across Slices. After inter-Slice dependencies are determined, a second renaming step renames from the global logical register space into a Slice-local physical register number. Each Slice contains a Local Register File (LRF) [52] and enables the number of physical registers to increase as Slices are added. The global logical register space is sized for the maximum number of Slices in a VCore.

#### 3.2.1 Global Rename: Local Decision with Global Help

Instructions are decoded in parallel and renaming is first done from the architectural register space to a large, global logical register space, which eliminates false dependencies. The free-list of global logical registers is distributed across Slices in a VCore removing the need for a centralized free-list. Each Slice contains a global Register Alias Table (RAT) which tracks the mapping from architectural register to global logical register. Global renaming of destination registers takes place in several steps as shown in Figure 6b. First, all destination operands are renamed in their local Slice. Second, this rename mapping (both architectural register and global logical register) is sent to a master Slice within the VCore. The master Slice broadcasts this rename information to the other Slices which then correct their own rename operations based off of instruction ordering. This correction step is done locally, but uses global information in order to handle the case where two instructions that are fetched across different Slices write the same destination or there is an inter-Slice read-after-write (RAW) dependency

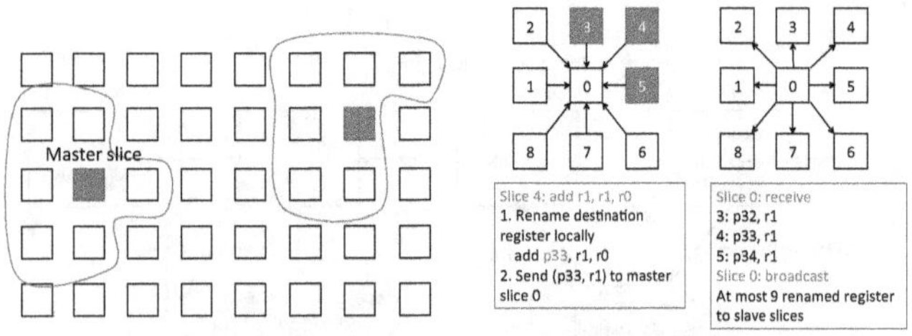


(a) Master Slice (b) Multi-stage Rename

**Figure 6.** Global Rename

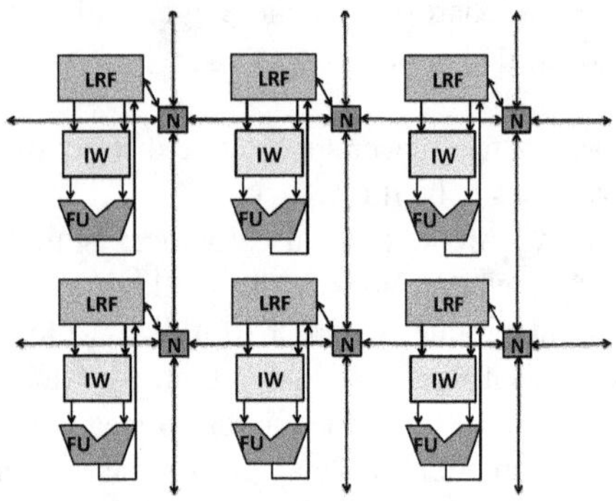


**Figure 7.** Local Register Files (LRF) and Scalar Operand Networks (N). IW: Issue Window; FU: Functional Unit.

between instructions in a fetch group. This information updates each Slice's copy of the global RAT and scoreboard which tracks which Slice contains the most up-to-date value for a given register. Finally, source operands are renamed using the global RAT's old and new values dependent on instruction order.

Figure 6a shows how Slices can be grouped around a master Slice for global renaming and Figure 6b shows an example of multi-stage rename. Alternatives include centralizing the rename information and then broadcasting this information using a multicast network or choosing different Slices to handle global rename based on architectural register number.

#### 3.2.2 Local Rename and Remote Operand Request

After global rename occurs, each global logical register operand is locally renamed into the physical register LRF namespace. By using distributed LRFs as shown in Figure 7, the number of physical registers in a VCore scales with the number of Slices in a core. Using the information from the global rename step, the scoreboard contains a mapping from global logical register to Slice number. Destination registers are always renamed into the LRF space, allocating entries from the LRF. Source operands read a local RAT which keeps a mapping from global register number to LRF physical register number. If a global logical source register is found from the scoreboard to be in a remote Slice, an *operand request* message is generated and sent to the remote Slice. When the operand request is sent, the destination is allocated into the LRF and marked as pending until an *operand reply* message is received. By renaming and allocating remote operands into the LRF, subsequent reads from a global logical register which has been previously read and renamed by that Slice do not generate remote operand requests, but rather simply read the LRF.

Operand request and operand reply messages transit a 2-Dimensional, switched, Scalar Operand Network (SON) [59, 65] to move operand requests and operand responses between different Slices. Section 3.4, below, describes how the Scalar Operand Network is integrated with each Slice's execution units. When an operand request message is received by a remote Slice, the local RAT is used to determine the physical LRF number that either stores the value or will store the value. If the remote Slice's LRF already contains the operand value, the SON is used to send back the value. If the operation which generates the operand value is pending, the request is enqueued to a *wait list*, and the reply will be generated once the value is ready. After renaming and operand request messages are sent, but responses not necessarily received, instructions enter an instruction window.

### 3.3 Instruction Window and Dispatch

Each Slice has a separate issue window for ALU instructions and loads/stores. Instructions wait in the issue window until their dependent operands are going to be available the next cycle. At that point, the instructions leave the issue window, possibly out-of-order, and execute. Special attention must be paid to operands that come from remote Slices. In order to wake up an instruction waiting for a remote operand, the issue window not only is matched against local finishing instructions, but also matched against wake-up signals that indicate that a operand reply will be returning on the next cycle. It is possible to have this one-cycle head start because a wake-up signal is sent when the instruction in the remote Slice issues, which is in the cycle before it executes.

### 3.4 Execution Units

Once an instruction is issued, it executes on the ALU or Load-Store unit. An important aspect of the Sharing Architecture is that it uses a switched, dynamically scheduled, 2D Scalar Operand Network (SON) to move operand values between different Slices. The SON is directly tied into the bypass network and where results are generated in the ALUs. This enables operand values to be sent right after they are generated and enables values to be forwarded to a destination instruction and the LRF in a remote Slice with low latency. This design is similar to how the on-chip networks are integrated into the pipelines of the Raw and Tilera processors and reduces latency between ALUs in different Slices. We model a two-cycle communication cost between nearest neighbor Slices and an additional cycle for each additional network hop, the same latency as on a Tilera processor. The LRF has an additional read port and an additional write port to process operand request messages and operand reply messages.

### 3.5 Cache

Each Slice contains an L1 I-Cache and an L1 D-Cache. The L1 I-Cache cache line size is reduced to accommodate two instructions, and a next line predictor is used to prefetch the next instruction according to the number of Slices in a virtual core. The L1 D-Cache is private to each Slice. Beyond the L1 D-Cache is a configurable L2 cache. Any L2 Cache Bank in the system can be used by any VCore. This is achieved by connecting L2 Cache Banks to a 2D switched dynamic network interconnect. In our results section, we assume each L2 Cache Bank is 64KB. On a L1 cache miss, a message is sent across the switched interconnect to retrieve data and response data is sent via that same network. Addresses are low-order interleaved by cache line across L2 Cache Banks, thereby simplifying the mapping of address to Cache Banks. Latency increases as L2 banks are further away from the cache miss issuing Slice.

In order to prevent the processor cores from stalling due to long memory latencies, the Sharing cache subsystem uses non-blocking caches and a small store buffer in each Slice. Loads and stores are sorted to Slices after issue and address generation as shown in Figure 8. A hashing function low-order interleaves accesses by cache line. Because addresses to the same cache line are always sorted to the same Slice, there is no need to keep the caches coherent between Slices in a VCore.

In a multi-VCore VM, caches need to be keep coherent between VCores when you step beyond the VCore such as in a multi-threaded program or inter-program shared memory. The coherence point can be between the L1 and L2 or after the L2s. If the coherence point is before the L2, the L2 can be shared by multiple VCores. If it is after the L2, the L2s are private to a VCore. Both of these solutions enable a manner of flexible L2 cache sizing. In our presented results, we put the coherence point between the L1 and L2 caches therefore having a shared L2 cache per VM. We modeled this with a detailed model which has a directory in the L2. Our modeled cache coherence protocol includes switched network cost based on distance and L1 invalidations. An important portion of this design is that each Slice maintains a table which maps a portion of the VM's physical address space to a particular L2 Cache Bank (IE a home-node mapping table). We do not currently allow inter-VM physical memory sharing so there are currently no coherence challenges beyond the VM (L2 cache). The implication of this is that the reallocation of an L2 Cache Bank requires flushing that bank to main memory. In terms of inter-VM coherence, the L2s themselves could be kept coherent with the addition of a directory-based cache coherence system beyond the L2 caches therefore enabling VM-level page sharing. Such a solution could leverage the Virtual Hierarchy work [39]. Last, if we only have per-VCore private L2 caches, much of this complexity goes away as the L2 caches could simply be kept coherent with a flat directory-based cache coherence protocol.

### 3.6 Distributed LSQ and LS Instruction Sorting

Conventional load/store queues (LSQs) are challenging to build in wide-issue processors. The Sharing Architecture

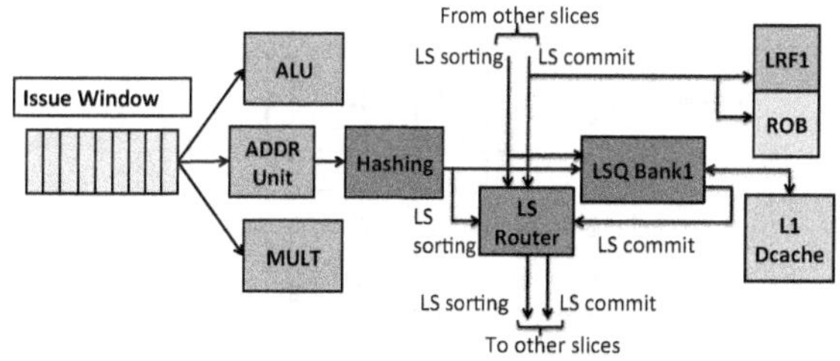


**Figure 8.** Distributed LSQ and LS Sorting

sorts loads and stores to a given Slice based on its address, therefore allowing the LSQ to operate local to a Slice as shown in Figure 8. Unlike the Sharing Architecture, most banked-by-address LSQs, such as those in clustered processors [8] and Core Fusion [24] require LSQ bank prediction because a memory operation's effective address is unknown until the execution stage. Clustered processors and Core Fusion use this approach because they allocate into the LSQ when entering the issue window. In contrast, the Sharing Architecture uses an unordered LSQ such as those in prior work [54] in order to reduce LSQ occupancy and power consumption. Our work is the first to utilize a general-purpose switched network to sort load/store instructions mixed with an unordered LSQ.

The LSQ bank is unordered with respect to age, and an extra age-tag field is added to maintain the load/store order. The LSQ buffers all stores and only allows stores to be written out when they are non-speculative. In the Sharing Architecture, a store is determined to be non-speculative if it is the head instruction in the ROB. A search is necessary in the LSQ to match the ROB tag with the LSQ entry tag on store commit.

Loads access memory speculatively after the address is resolved. Load data values are returned to the issuing Slice and are marked as speculative until all earlier stores have committed. The LSQ reports a violation when it detects that a younger load in program order to the same address executes before a store to the same address. In order to achieve this, each committing store searches the LSQ bank for any issued loads younger than it to the same address as the store. Figure 9 shows a committing store checking all younger loads in a local LSQ. Each store needs to check against all of the loads in a particular LSQ bank when it commits, but loads do not need to check against stores in this design. The address banked nature of the LSQ across Slices enables more memory bandwidth and a large aggregate LSQ capacity as more Slices are added to a VCore and it eliminates the need for inter-Slice LSQ alias checking.

### 3.7 Distributed Reorder Buffer

We partition and distribute Reorder Buffer (ROB) entries across Slices. We leverage the approach used by Core Fusion[24] which uses a pre-commit pointer to guarantee that all ROBs are up to date several cycles before true commit.

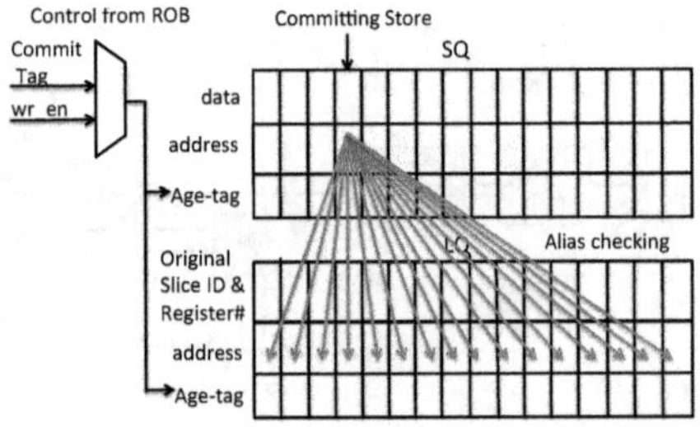


**Figure 9.** LSQ Bank

### 3.8 Reconfiguration

In order to reconfigure VCores, we rely on the Hypervisor to control the connections of the Slice and Cache interconnect. We propose having the hypervisor be time sliced on the same resources as the client VMs. But, unlike client VMs which run on reconfigurable cores, we propose having the hypervisor execute only on single-Slice VCores. By having the Hypervisor execute on single Slices only, the hypervisor can then locally reconfigure protection registers and interconnection state to setup and tear-down client VCores. The hypervisor is designed to bypass use of the reconfigurable cache system or use hypervisor dedicated L2 banks in order to prevent having to flush the L2 Caches on every time slice.

When a VCore is reduced in the number of Slices, there is potentially register state which needs to be transmitted to the surviving Slices within the VCore. In order to carry this out, we use a Register Flush instruction which pushes all of the dirty architectural register state to other Slices in the same VCore using operand reply messages. This can be done quickly because there are only 64 local physical registers per Slice and the Scalar Operand Network is fast for transferring register data. When VCore L2 Cache configurations change, we propose that all dirty state in L2 Cache Banks be flushed to main memory before reconfiguration.

## 4. Software Implications

While this paper focuses on a new IaaS optimized architecture, we wanted to address some of the software implications of using such a system in an IaaS Cloud. The first question which comes up is how does the IaaS user determine their utility functions and how might they react to variable pricing? A basic solution would be for the IaaS user to provide a meta-program along with the VM workload that they want to execute. The meta-program can express the user's multi-dimensional utility function as a function of different resources and can understand how to react to changing pricing. The user can profile their application on different architectures to build performance models which will allow them to back-compute their utility functions.

Alternatively, they could utilize an auto-tuner [5, 6, 44, 51, 55]. The auto-tuner would slowly search the configuration space by varying the VM instance configuration and number of VMs. The auto-tuner can then pick good configurations provided a high-level goal from the user. Such an auto-tuning system would likely require the use of a heartbeat [22] or performance feedback to evaluate the success criteria. An example of this can be seen in current day IaaS auto-scaling systems such as Amazon's Auto Scaling and RightScale. Other options include having a human-in-the-loop to make decisions or employing a decision system to make configuration changes.

We could use a sophisticated control theory based or machine learning based software adaptation engine, such as PTRADE [23]. This software engine asks application developers to specify objective functions and asks system developlers to specify components that affect their objective functions. The software runtime system takes these specifications and tunes component usage to meet goals while reducing the cost (power consumption, computation and storage cost).

The Sharing Architecture is designed to minimize changes to the software stack, but some changes will be needed. From the IaaS client's perspective, they will still create VM instances like before, but now will have to provide a meta-program as described above, rely on auto-tuners, or fall back on the previous market solution of fixed instance types. Because all of the different micro-architecture configurations of the Sharing Architecture are binary compatible, the user **does not need to recompile** to use different Slice and Cache configurations. The user could further optimize by using multi-architecture (FAT) binaries optimized for different micro-architectures. Our presented results do not recompile or use this optimization.

Next we analyze the changes to the system stack. The OS should not need to change for the Sharing Architecture. The Hypervisor will likely need modification in order to manage resources on a sub-core basis. Finally, the Cloud management software (scheduler) will have to change in order to schedule new resources. Changing the Cloud scheduler is a challenging problem, but the Sharing Architecture opens up many opportunities for interesting research in this space that can leverage prior work in large scale scheduling [14, 19, 21, 25, 48, 56]. These Cloud provider changes can enable improvements in economic efficiency and revenue.

## 5. Evaluation

### 5.1 Design Area

In order to assess the feasibility of the Sharing Architecture, we have implemented the Sharing Architecture Slice in synthesizable Verilog. We use this to measure the added area overhead that the Sharing Architecture adds to an out-of-order superscalar. We synthesized the design utilizing the Synopsys tool flow and took the design through Design Compiler and IC compiler to a fully place-and-routed netlist. We use Synopsys's TSMC 45nm cell library as the implementation technology. Cache sizes, timing, and power are generated utilizing CACTI [42] at the 45nm node. Figure 10 and Figure 11 present the area breakdown of the Sharing Ar-

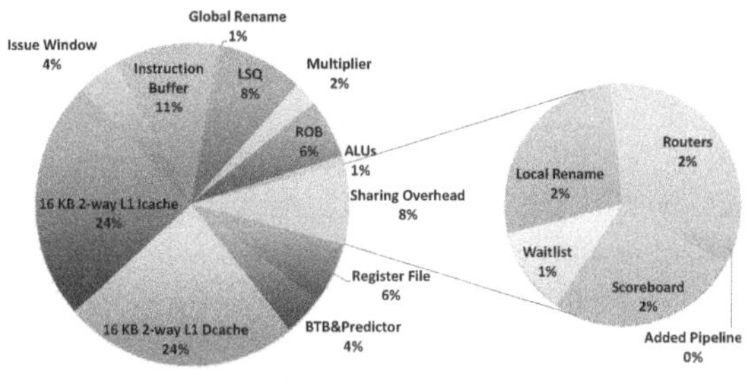


**Figure 10.** Area Decomposition without L2 cache

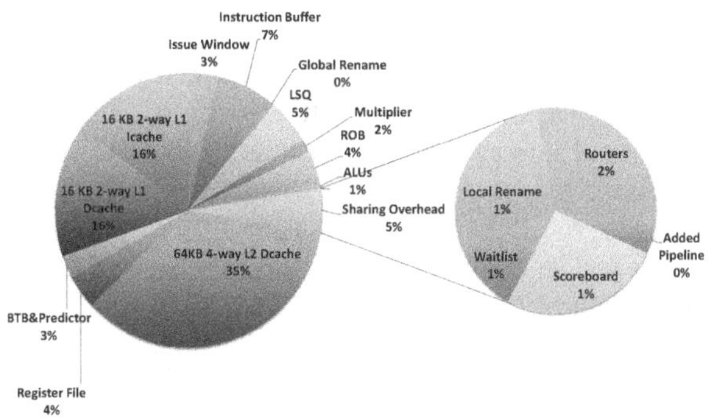


**Figure 11.** Area Decomposition including 64KB L2 cache

chitecture. We call out the area overhead of the Sharing Architecture as the right sub-pie-charts. The total area of one Slice is $1.8mm^2$ (not including L2) at 1GHz. The Sharing Architecture area overhead is 8% without L2 cache and 5% with 64KB L2 cache area included.

We found that the area overhead of the inter-Slice on-chip Networks to be significant as there are three dedicated networks modeled for different purposes (operand network, load/store sorting, and global renaming). A single operand network is used for both operand request and operand reply messages as we found that the operand network provides sufficient bandwidth. By conducting a sensitivity study on operand communication bandwidth, we discovered that by adding a second operand network, performance would improve by only 1% across our applications. The overhead of the Sharing Architecture as a percentage of the total area is also affected by our choice of modestly sized structures such as the ROB, Load/Store queue, etc. If a more complex base design were to be chosen, the area overhead of the Sharing Architecture as a percentage of the total would be smaller. In addition, we do not model the area of the floating-point unit in our design, but this structure does not change due to the Sharing Architecture, therefore our area estimations are conservative.

## 5.2 Experimental Setup

We have created a trace-based simulator, *SSim*, to model the Sharing Architecture and measure its effectiveness. This

| Number of Functional Units/Slice | 2 | ROB size | 64 |
|---|---|---|---|
| Number of Physical Registers | 128 | Store Buffer Size | 8 |
| Number of Local Registers/Slice | 64 | Maximum In-flight Loads | 8 |
| Issue Window Size | 32 | Memory Delay | 100 |
| Load/Store Queue Size | 32 | | |

**Table 2.** Base Slice Configuration

| Level | Size(KB) | Block Size(Byte) | Associativity | Hit Delay |
|---|---|---|---|---|
| L1D | 16 | 64 | 2 | 3 |
| L1I | 16 | 64 | 2 | 3 |
| L2 | 64*2 | 64 | 4 | distance*2+4 |

**Table 3.** Base Cache Configurations: L2 cache hit delays depends on the distance to the cache bank

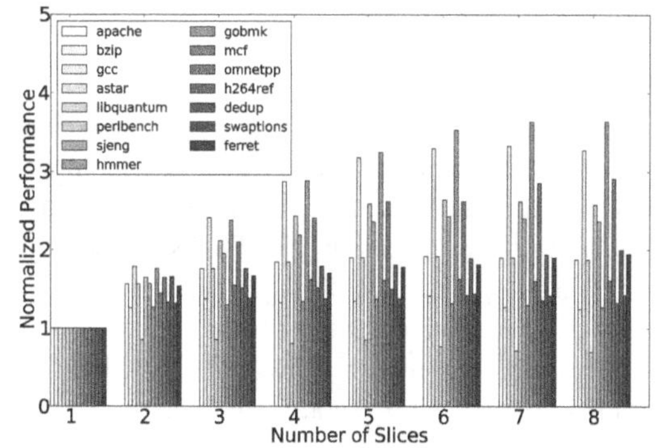


**Figure 12.** Scalability of VCore Performance. Includes One Cycle Insertion Delay Plus One Cycle per Hop. Normalized to One Slice with 128KB L2 Cache VCore

cycle-level simulator models each subsystem of the Sharing Architecture (fetch, rename, issue, execution, memory, commit, and on-chip network) along with accurately modeling the Out-of-Order execution and inter-Slice and Slice-to-memory latency. SSim is driven by full system traces generated by the Alpha version of GEM5[10]. We use the complete SPEC CINT2006 benchmark suite, a static web-serving workload of Apache driven by ApacheBench, and a subset of PARSEC benchmarks to explore the Sharing Architecture. SSim is very flexible, allowing all critical micro-architecture parameters and latencies to be set from a XML configuration file. When a simulation completes, SSim reports the cycles executed for a given workload along with cache miss rates and stage-based micro-architecture stalls and statistics. In the following sections, when aggregate results are shown, we use the geometric mean (GME) of different benchmark results following how SPEC creates aggregate results. Throughout these results, we use an area model derived from our results in Section 5.1.

## 5.3 Scalability

We begin by evaluating the Sharing Architecture's ability to increase both single-stream performance and multithreaded performance by adding Slices to a VCore. Table 2 contains the base configuration of a single Slice which we will use throughout this section. The base cache configuration is shown in Table 3. Figure 12 presents these scalability results.

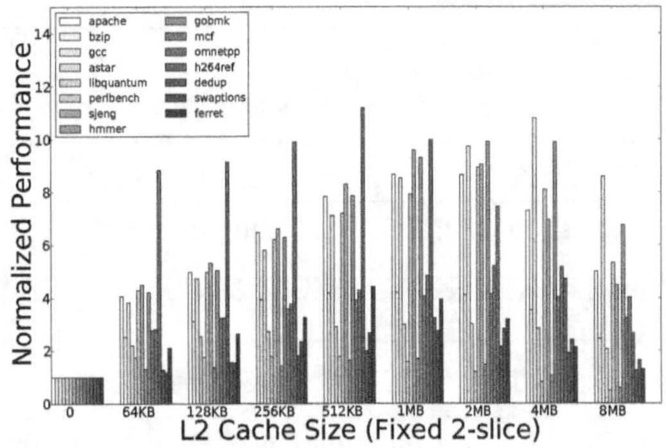


**Figure 13.** Performance Scaling with Cache Size. Normalized to No L2 2-Slice VCore.

Since the default Sharing Architecture requires two base cycles to transport operands between Slices and another cycle network delay for additional hops, performance can degrade for larger VCore configurations. For PARSEC, benchmarks use four threads on four equally configured VCores which share an L2 Cache. The number of Slices per VCore is varied in unison. Compared with SPEC, PARSEC benchmarks have less ILP; the speedup is bounded by 2.

### 5.4 Cache Sensitivity

We study the sensitivity of performance to cache size by varying the L2 cache size from 0KB up to 8MB. As can be seen in Figure 13, some applications such as omnetpp are extremely sensitive to cache size while benchmarks such as astar, libquantum, and gobmk are insensitive to cache size. This variable sensitivity motivates the Sharing Architecture which can take advantage of the variable micro-architecture requirements of applications. Performance can actually decrease as more cache is added because we model an additional 2-cycles of communication delay for each additional 256KB of cache, thereby making the latency of the large cache significant.

### 5.5 Performance-Area Efficiency

This section studies VCore performance-area efficiency as a function of Slice count and L2 Cache size. We use the area model described in Section 5.1 along with an exhaustive search of performance for different Slice count and Cache configurations. Table 4 presents the optimal configurations for three different metrics across 15 benchmarks (apache, SPEC, and PARSEC). The non-uniformity of optimal configurations, even for the performance per area metric, shows that benefits can be achieved even before we take into account Cloud user utility functions.

We next turn our attention to the $performance^2/area$ metric to mimic users whose applications do not scale across processors well, or who favor single-thread performance. As can be seen in Table 4, gobmk favors 5 Slices and 1MB of cache while under the same criteria, hmmer prefers 64KB cache and a single Slice. For sequential performance-oriented applications, some customers will pay significantly more for higher performance. We use $performance^3/area$ to model these needs. Under this constraint the optimal VCore configurations vary significantly across different benchmarks. What is even more interesting is that within a single benchmark, the optimal configuration varies greatly dependent on the efficiency metric. For instance, gcc in a throughput computation favors 128KB L2 cache and two Slices, while under a performance metric favors 4 Slices and a 1MB cache. gcc has over a factor of two in performance gain between optimal configurations for different metrics.

### 5.6 Utility Optimization

As developed in Section 2.2, IaaS Cloud customers have varied needs for resources based on the characteristics of the workloads that they execute (how it reacts to different resources) and internal policy decisions. In the Sharing Architecture, customers decide which and how many resources to purchase in order to maximize their utility while staying within a budget constraint. In the Sharing Architecture, resources include: Slices, L2 Cache banks, VCores, and VMs. For the balance of the paper, we define a Cloud user's utility function as: $U_{b_i}(c, s, vc, vm)$,

where $U_{b_i}$ is the utility for benchmark $b_i$ as a function of $c$, the amount of L2 cache per VCore, $s$, the number of Slices per VCore, $vc$, the number of VCores per VM, and $vm$, the number of VMs purchased. We simplify this by combining $vc$ and $vm$ into one value $v$ which is the number of cores a customer uses. We can do this without losing generality as we assume that benchmarks can be replicated within a VM or between VMs providing a new utility of: $U_{b_i}(c, s, v)$.

We define an application's single-thread performance as $P(c, s)$, a function of Cache size and Slice count. For example, one Cloud customer may run Online Data-Intensive (OLDI) workloads driven by queries that interact with massive data sets and require responsiveness at a sub-second time scale[41]. Such a workload may give substantial weight to single-stream performance to reduce latency. This can lead the OLDI customer to use a utility function such as Equation 1 where utility is proportional to the cube of single-stream performance. A utility function is not enough to drive the Cloud customer's decision making, instead, the cost of resources becomes an important consideration. We define $C_c$ as the cost of one cache bank, $C_s$ as the cost of one Slice, and $B$ as the overall budget that a user can spend. Combining these costs with a budget, we find the constraints in Equation 2 as well as constraints which are derived from valid VCore configurations in Equation 3. A Cloud customer would then maximize their utility given these constraints.

$$U_{OLDI} = \sqrt[3]{v} * P^3(c, s) \qquad (1)$$

$$v = \frac{B}{C_c * c + C_s * s} \qquad (2)$$

$$0KB \leq c \leq 8MB, 1 \leq s \leq 8 \qquad (3)$$

| Area Efficiency Metric | VCore Config | apache | astar | bzip | gcc | h264ref | libq | hmmer | sjeng | perlb | mcf | omnetpp | gobmk | dedup | swaptions | ferret | optimal GME | Dyn/Static Gain |
|---|---|---|---|---|---|---|---|---|---|---|---|---|---|---|---|---|---|---|
| $performance/area$ | L2 cache size (KB) | 256 | 64 | 128 | 128 | 64 | 64 | 0 | 64 | 64 | 64 | 64 | 256 | 1024 | 256 | 512 | 64 | 5.2% |
| | Slice Number | 2 | 1 | 1 | 2 | 1 | 1 | 1 | 1 | 1 | 1 | 1 | 3 | 2 | 1 | 1 | 1 | |
| $performance^2/area$ | L2 cache size (KB) | 512 | 128 | 256 | 512 | 64 | 64 | 64 | 512 | 256 | 128 | 256 | 1024 | 1024 | 512 | 512 | 512 | 36.6% |
| | Slice Number | 3 | 2 | 1 | 4 | 2 | 1 | 1 | 3 | 3 | 2 | 4 | 5 | 3 | 3 | 2 | 3 | |
| $performance^3/area$ | L2 cache size (KB) | 512 | 1024 | 256 | 1024 | 512 | 64 | 128 | 1024 | 512 | 256 | 1024 | 1024 | 1024 | 512 | 512 | 1024 | 56.2% |
| | Slice Number | 3 | 5 | 2 | 4 | 3 | 1 | 2 | 4 | 4 | 2 | 5 | 6 | 3 | 3 | 2 | 3 | |

**Table 4.** Optimal VCore Configurations for Performance-Area Efficiency on Apache Server, CINT SPEC2006 and PARSEC

| Three Utility Functions | | Analogy | Representative Workloads |
|---|---|---|---|
| Utility1 | $v * P(c, s)$ | $Energy * Delay$ [13] | Media Streaming, MapReduce, Database[16] |
| Utility2 | $\sqrt[2]{v} * P^2(c, s)$ | $Energy * Delay^2$ [36] | Web Search, Web Fronted, Data serving [16] |
| Utility3 | $\sqrt[3]{v} * P^3(c, s)$ | $Energy * Delay^3$ | Mobile Interactive, Business Analytics[7] |

**Table 5.** Three Different User Utility Functions

In contrast to the OLDI workload, some cloud workloads are completely throughput oriented and insensitive to additional latency. Examples of this include a data backup service which has to encrypt and compress large amounts of bulk data, bulk image resizing photo sharing sites such as Picassa or SmugMug, and many MapReduce applications which are not directly connected to a user. For these latency tolerant applications, we define the utility function in Equation 4. In the balance of the paper, we will use three utility functions as example Cloud user utility functions as shown in Table 5. We will refer to these as Utility1, Utility2, and Utility3, sorted from favoring throughput computing to favoring increasing amounts of single-thread performance.

$$U_{LT} = v * P(c, s) \tag{4}$$

To provide some intuition about what a utility function looks like, we plot in Figure 14 the utility function Utility1 and Utility2 for gcc and bzip. In Figure 14, the x-axis represents the number of Slices $[0, 8]$ and the y-axis represents the number of 64 KB L2 cache banks on a binary log scale $[0, 8]$ $(64KB * 2^{(y\_axis)} - 64KB)$. As can be seen, when comparing Figure 14a (gcc Utility1) versus Figure 14b (gcc Utility2), simply changing the utility function can drastically change which configuration provides peak utility. Likewise when we compare Figure 14d (bzip Utility2) versus Figure 14b (gcc Utility2), we can see that when holding the utility function constant but changing the workload, the configurations with peak utility substantially change. For instance, bzip favors both a 256KB L2 cache and a single Slice to obtain peak utility for Utility2 while gcc favors a 512KB L2 cache and 4 Slices per VCore to maximize Utility2.

### 5.7 Market Efficiency

We simulated the performance of all of our benchmarks at different Slice and L2 Cache configurations and computed the peak utility for the three different utility functions (Utility1, Utility2, Utility3 in Table 5) and in three different market scenarios and present configurations that exhibit the highest utility for each in Table 6. Market2 is the market which sets the cost of resources equal to their area (1 Slice

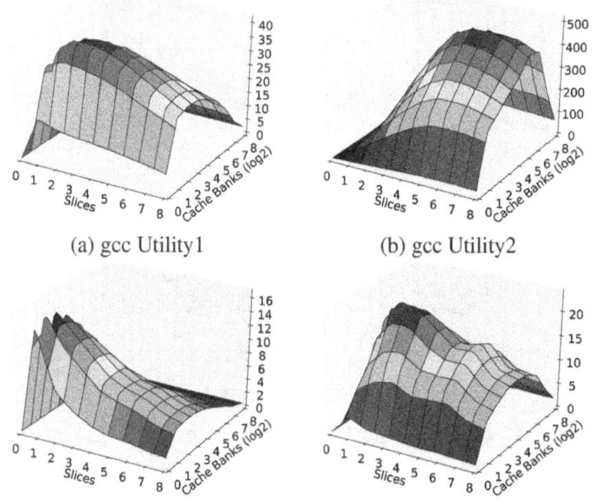


(a) gcc Utility1 (b) gcc Utility2

(c) bzip Utility1 (d) bzip Utility2

**Figure 14.** Two Utility Functions for bzip and gcc as a Function of Slice count and L2 Cache Size: x-axis is number of Slices, y-axis is number of 64 KB L2 banks in binary log scale

costs the same as 128KB Cache). In Market1, we set Slices to be four times the equal area cost of Cache and in Market3, we set Cache to be four times the equal area cost of a Slice. We use these different markets to show how optimal configurations change when market demand for resources does not track area costs.

### 5.8 Efficiency Comparisons with Static Fixed Architecture and Heterogeneous Architecture

We turn our attention to how much market efficiency gain (profit gain) can be achieved when compared to a fixed multicore architecture or heterogeneous multicore architecture when used in an IaaS Cloud provider setting. For this, we restrict our study to Market2 where resource cost is commensurate with the area used. In order to study the market efficiency gain, we pairwise choose two benchmarks and two utility functions from Table 6 and compare the utility of running those benchmarks on a fixed resource architecture versus running those benchmarks on the Sharing Architecture with configurable Slice count and Cache size.

We first compare the Sharing Architecture with the best static fixed architecture as determined across all benchmarks and the three utility functions such that it minimizes the geometric mean of the utility gained in Figure 15. **This shows how much market efficiency gain can be had when compared with the current IaaS commodity multicore**

| Markets | Utilities | apache | astar | bzip | gcc | h264ref | libquantum | hmmer | sjeng | perlbench | mcf | omnetpp | gobmk | dedup | swaptions | ferret |
|---|---|---|---|---|---|---|---|---|---|---|---|---|---|---|---|---|
| Market1: Higher Slice Price | Utility1 | 256, 1 | 128, 1 | 256, 1 | 512, 2 | 64, 1 | 64, 1 | 128, 1 | 512, 1 | 256, 1 | 128, 1 | 256, 1 | 512, 2 | 1024, 1 | 512, 1 | 512, 1 |
| | Utility2 | 1024, 3 | 2048, 6 | 512, 2 | 2048, 5 | 512, 3 | 256, 1 | 512, 2 | 1024, 4 | 2048, 4 | 512, 2 | 1024, 5 | 1024, 6 | 1024, 3 | 512, 3 | 512, 2 |
| | Utility3 | 1024, 4 | 2048, 7 | 512, 2 | 2048, 6 | 512, 3 | 256, 1 | 1024, 4 | 1024, 5 | 2048, 5 | 2048, 4 | 2048, 8 | 2048, 6 | 1024, 3 | 512, 3 | 512, 3 |
| Market2: Equal Area Price | Utility1 | 256, 2 | 64, 1 | 128, 1 | 128, 2 | 64, 1 | 64, 1 | 0, 1 | 64, 1 | 64, 1 | 64, 1 | 64, 1 | 256, 3 | 1024, 2 | 256, 1 | 512, 1 |
| | Utility2 | 1024, 4 | 1024, 6 | 256, 2 | 1024, 5 | 512, 3 | 128, 1 | 512, 2 | 1024, 5 | 1024, 5 | 512, 4 | 1024, 7 | 1024, 6 | 1024, 3 | 512, 3 | 512, 3 |
| | Utility3 | 1024, 4 | 2048, 8 | 512, 3 | 2048, 7 | 512, 3 | 256, 1 | 1024, 4 | 1024, 5 | 1024, 5 | 1024, 4 | 2048, 8 | 1024, 6 | 1024, 3 | 512, 3 | 512, 3 |
| Market3: Higher Cache Price | Utility1 | 64, 2 | 0, 1 | 0, 1 | 64, 3 | 64, 1 | 0, 1 | 0, 1 | 64, 2 | 64, 3 | 64, 2 | 64, 2 | 64, 3 | 0, 1 | 256, 1 | 64, 1 |
| | Utility2 | 512, 4 | 1024, 6 | 256, 2 | 1024, 6 | 64, 3 | 64, 1 | 64, 2 | 1024, 5 | 256, 5 | 128, 4 | 256, 7 | 1024, 6 | 1024, 3 | 512, 3 | 512, 3 |
| | Utility3 | 1024, 5 | 2048, 8 | 512, 3 | 2048, 7 | 512, 3 | 128, 1 | 1024, 4 | 1024, 5 | 1024, 5 | 512, 4 | 1024, 8 | 1024, 6 | 1024, 3 | 512, 3 | 512, 3 |

**Table 6.** Optimal VCore Configurations in Different Markets (L2 Cache Size in KB, Slice Number)

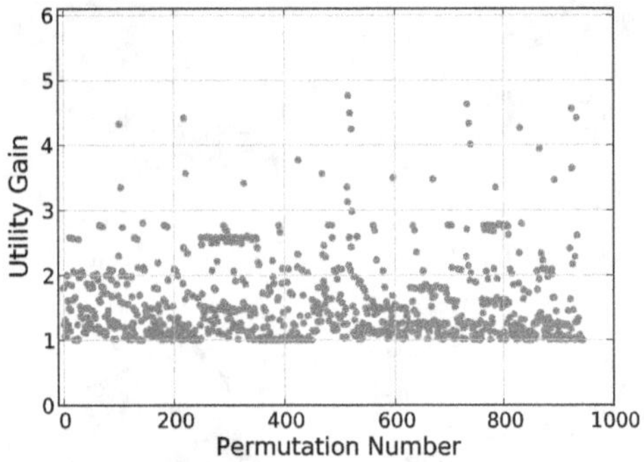


**Figure 15.** Utility Gain Compared with Static Fixed Architecture (Optimal Configuration Across Benchmark Suite and the Three Utility Functions). Points represent utility gain of one benchmark and utility mixed with another benchmark and utility.

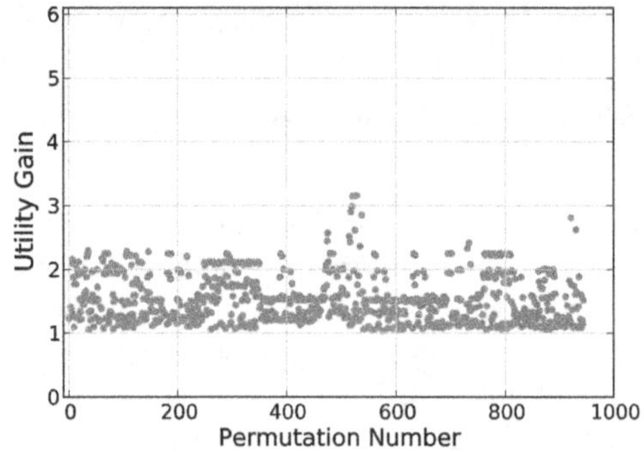


**Figure 16.** Utility Gain Compared with Heterogenerous Architecture (Optimal Configurations Across Benchmark Suite for the Particular Utility Functions).

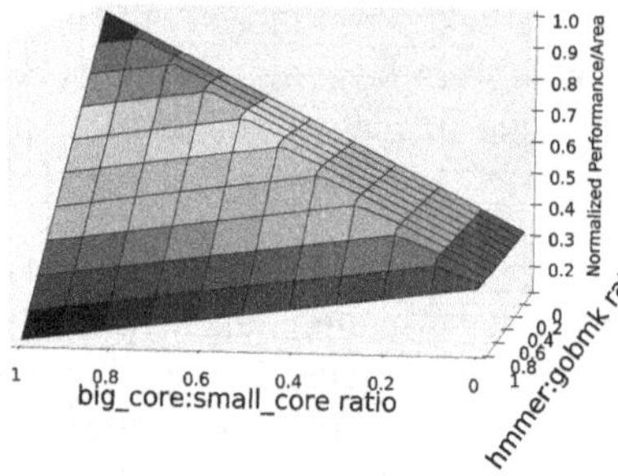


**Figure 17.** Normalized performance/area of hmmer and gobmk vs. big core to small core ratio and application mix ratio.

**processors.** For example, point 1 in Figure 15 represents astar using Utility1 combined with bzip using Utility1. As can be seen, there are significant gains, up to 5x, in market efficiency by using the Sharing Architecture over an optimal fixed architecture.

We also compare the sum of the two benchmarks' utility running on the Sharing Architecture to the sum of those benchmarks' utility running on configurations that are optimal across all benchmarks for the particular utility function: $(U_{b_1}(sharing) + U_{b_2}(sharing))/(U_{b_1}(fixed_c) + U_{b_2}(fixed_d))$. This mimics what a heterogenous multicore proposed in previous reseach [18] could achieve when optimized across a suite of applications. Figure 16 shows the utility gained when mixing one benchmark and utility with another benchmark and utility for all benchmarks and three utility functions. Over 3x market efficiency gains can be achieved.

### 5.9 Datacenter Heterogeneity Comparison

Heterogeneous architectures allow a datacenter to combine benefits of specialization with the performance guarantees of traditional high-performance servers [18]. However a static mix of high-end and low-end processors falls short for certain applications. While computationally intensive workloads favor large server-class processors, throughput workloads, such as web search, have better power efficiency running on mobile-class processors [27]. Utilizing Table 6's optimal configuations, hmmer favors having a small core configuration with one Slice and zero L2 cache, while gobmk achieves peak Utility1 using a large core with three Slices and 256KB L2 cache. We vary the ratio of big cores (with 3 Slices and 256KB L2 cache) and small cores (with 1 Slice and 0 L2 cache), and the application ratio, and then measure the utility of hmmer and gobmk under different ratios. In Figure 17, we can see depending on application mix, different ratios of big and small cores are required for optimal $performance/area$ efficiency. **A fixed mixture of big and small cores therefore cannot always optimally service heterogeneous workloads in the cloud.**

### 5.10 Dynamic Phases

The Sharing Architecture provides flexibility to reconfigure VCores and VMs as a workload changes. It is well known that different program phases can require different resources to perform optimally. For instance, some program phases

| Metric | Core Configurations | phase1 | phase2 | phase3 | phase4 | phase5 | phase6 | phase7 | phase8 | phase9 | phase10 | optimal GME | Dyn/Static Gain |
|---|---|---|---|---|---|---|---|---|---|---|---|---|---|
| $performance/area$ | L2 cache size (KB) | 256 | 256 | 128 | 256 | 128 | 128 | 256 | 128 | 64 | 64 | 128 | 9.1% |
| | Slice Number | 2 | 2 | 2 | 2 | 2 | 2 | 2 | 1 | 1 | 1 | 2 | |
| $performance^2/area$ | L2 cache size (KB) | 512 | 256 | 256 | 512 | 512 | 256 | 256 | 128 | 128 | 512 | 512 | 15.1% |
| | Slice Number | 4 | 4 | 4 | 3 | 3 | 3 | 2 | 2 | 2 | 2 | 3 | |
| $performance^3/area$ | L2 cache size (KB) | 1024 | 1024 | 1024 | 512 | 1024 | 256 | 1024 | 128 | 128 | 512 | 1024 | 19.4% |
| | Slice Number | 5 | 4 | 4 | 3 | 4 | 3 | 4 | 2 | 2 | 3 | 4 | |

**Table 7.** Optimal VCore Configurations for 10 Phases in "gcc "Benchmark: The dynamic average is compared with the static best average, Dyn/Static gain takes into account 10000 cycles reconfiguration cost after each phase that reconfigures L2 cache, and 500 cycles reconfiguration cost after each phase that reconfigures only Slices.

may be more CPU intensive while other phases are memory intensive. We study program phases for gcc by evenly dividing gcc into 10 segments. We run these on SSim independently and find the optimal VCore configuration for different performance-area metrics as shown in Table 7. We account for reconfiguration overhead by adding 10,000 cycles when the cache configuration changes, but only 500 cycles when only the Slice count changes as the L2 Cache does not need to be flushed. Even within a single program and a single metric, optimal VCore configurations change with phase. We compare to the optimal static configuration for gcc (more stringent than the optimal across benchmarks) and find that significant gain can be achieved with up to a 19.4% gain for the $performance^3/area$ metric.

## 6. Related Work

The Sharing Architecture leverages many ideas from Distributed ILP work and fused-core architectures as compared in Table 8. Distributed ILP work tries to remove large centralized structures by replacing them with distributed structures and functional units and has been explored in Raw [59], Tilera [65], TRIPS [17, 49, 50], and Wavescalar [58]. Tiled architectures distribute portions of the register file, cache, and functional units across a switched interconnect. We adopt a similar network topology for communicating instruction operands between function units in different Slices, but unlike Raw and Tilera, we do not expose all of the hardware to software, do not require recompilation, and use dynamic assignment of resources, dynamic transport of operands, and dynamic instruction ordering. TRIPS [11, 49] has an array of ALUs connected by a Scalar Operand Network and uses dynamic operand transport similar to the Sharing Architecture. Unlike the Sharing Architecture, TRIPS requires compiler support, and a new EDGE ISA which encodes data dependencies directly. In contrast, the Sharing architecture uses a dynamic request-and-reply message based distributed local register file to exploit ILP across Slices without the need of a compiler.

The TFlex CLP micro-architecture [30] allows dynamic aggregation of any number of cores up to 32 for each thread, to target an optimal goal: performance, area efficiency, or energy efficiency, with the support of an EDGE ISA. The Sharing Architecture does not rely on compiler level support, but provides sub-core composability for different customer util-

| Features | Distributed ILP | TRIPS/ CLP | Core Fusion | WiDGET | Conjoined | Clustered | Heterogeneous | SMT/ Morph | **Sharing Architecture** |
|---|---|---|---|---|---|---|---|---|---|
| Scale up/down | Y | Y | N | Y | N | N | N | N | Y |
| Distributed | Y | Y | N | N | N | N | N | N | Y |
| Switched | Y | Y | N | N | N | N | N | N | Y |
| Symmetric | Y | Y | Y | Y | Y | Y | N | Y | Y |
| Dynamic OoO | N | N | Y | N | Y | Y | Y/N | Y/N | Y |
| ISA Compatible | Y | N | Y | Y | Y | Y | Y | Y | Y |
| Partition L2 | Y | Y | N | N | N | N | N | N | Y |
| Multi-Metric | N | Y | N | N | N | N | N | N | Y |

**Table 8.** Taxonomy of Differences with Related Work. Dynamic OoO stands for dynamic instruction assignment, transport, and ordering.

ity functions in a dynamic manner. The dynamic assignment of instructions to ALUs and operands to interconnect can potentially make the Sharing Architecture more flexible than TFlex, but possibly with less potential to exploit high ILP.

The Sharing Architecture leverages many ideas from Core Fusion [24] on how to distribute resources across cores, but unlike Core Fusion, the Sharing Architecture is designed to scale to larger numbers of Slices (cores). Core Fusion requires centralized structures for coordnating fetch, steering, and commit across fused cores, while we distributed the structures. Also, we take a more Distributed ILP approach to operand communication and other inter-Slice communication by using a switched interconnect between Slices instead of Core Fusion's operand crossbar. Also, the Sharing Architecture is designed as a 2D fabric which is created across a large manycore with 100's of cores which can avoid some of the fragmentation challenges that smaller configurations like Core Fusion can have. The interconnect of Slices to Cache is also designed to be flexible across the entire machine unlike Core Fusion which has a shared cache. This can lead to better efficiency and provides a way to partition cache traffic and working sets.

WiDGET [64] decouples computation resources to enable flexibility in provisioning execution units to optimize power-performance. WiDGET only studies trading off single-stream performance for power, while the Sharing Architecture trades ILP for TLP and enables an IaaS Cloud user to use their own utility function. WiDGET uses a sea-of-resources design with a hierarchical operand interconnect with local broadcast while the Sharing Architecture uses a point-to-point switched interconnect. WiDGET's hierarchical design restricts what resources can be shared while the Sharing Architecture enables wider sharing. Unlike WiDGET's in-order design, the Sharing Architecture is Out-of-Order including its memory system.

Conjoined-cores [32] allows resource sharing between adjacent cores of a chip multiprocessor. The degree of sharing depends on the topology, and the shared resources are allocated to different processors in a time-partitioned manner. The Sharing Architecture tears down the rigid boundary of cores, allowing more flexible sub-core configurations. Conjoined-cores has high wiring overhead and therefore only large structures are shared while we aim at finer grain sharing.

Clustered Architectures [45] and dynamically configurable clustered architectures [8] exploit ILP when there is latency between functional units. While dynamic clustered architectures trade off parallelism for latency, they do not enable wide spread sharing and the reconfigurability of Cache resources.

SMT [37, 60] enables trade-offs of ILP and TLP. Like the Sharing Architecture, SMT does not require recompilation, but SMT does not enable fine grain resource sharing between cores and has rigid core boundaries. The Sharing Architecture does not time multiplex resources, unlike SMT. MorphCore [29] transforms a high-performance OoO core into a highly-threaded in-order SMT core. Unlike the Sharing Architecture, MorphCore is unable to scale up and down flexibly.

A heterogeneous CMP [33] can combine superscalar cores for ILP with simple cores for TLP. Unlike the Sharing Architecture, heterogeneous architectures only allow selection out of a few fixed architectures. Also, if a heterogeneous architecture has the incorrect mixture of core types to match the application mix, efficiency is lost. Last, the Sharing architecture requires the design of one replicated architecture while a heterogeneous CMP can have higher design effort.

Building datacenters out of a heterogeneous mix of server and mobile cores can improve welfare and energy efficiency [18]. Unfortunately statically choosing a mix of big-cores and small-cores in the datacenter can lead to a poor processor match when the workload deviates from the expected. For instance, if the workload favors a single type of core. Also, unlike the Sharing Architecture, this approach cannot adapt the core to a customer's utility function dynamically.

Application interference is prevalent in datacenters due to contention over shared hardware resources [28]. Sharing last-level cache (LLC) and DRAM bandwidth degrades responsiveness of workloads. Paritioning a shared LLC potentially mitigates the negative performance effects of co-scheduling [20, 26, 47, 57]. The Sharing Architecture builds upon this work by providing a flexible LLC along with the additive benefits of ALU configuration.

## Acknowledgments

We acknowledge Yaosheng Fu for developing PriME cache simulator, Sharad Malik for the suggestions of comparison with heterogeneous data center, Princeton Research Computing for providing computation support. This work is supported by NSF Grant No CCF-1217553.

## References

[1] Amazon elastic compute cloud. http://aws.amazon.com/ec2/.

[2] Google Apps. http://www.google.com/apps/business/index.html.

[3] Amazon simple storage service. `http://aws.amazon.com/s3/`.

[4] Windows Azure Platform, 2009. http://www.microsoft.com/azure/.

[5] A. Ali-Eldin, J. Tordsson, and E. Elmroth. An adaptive hybrid elasticity controller for cloud infrastructures. In *Network Operations and Management Symposium (NOMS), 2012 IEEE*, pages 204–212, 2012.

[6] J. Ansel, M. Pacula, Y. L. Wong, C. Chan, M. Olszewski, U.-M. O'Reilly, and S. Amarasinghe. Siblingrivalry: online autotuning through local competitions. In *Proceedings of the 2012 international conference on Compilers, architectures and synthesis for embedded systems*, CASES '12, pages 91–100, 2012.

[7] M. Armbrust, A. Fox, R. Griffith, A. D. Joseph, R. H. Katz, A. Konwinski, G. Lee, D. A. Patterson, A. Rabkin, and M. Zaharia. Above the Clouds: A Berkeley View of Cloud Computing. Technical Report UCB/EECS-2009-28, EECS Department, University of California, Berkeley, Feb 2009.

[8] R. Balasubramonian, S. Dwarkadas, and D. Albonesi. Dynamically managing the communication-parallelism trade-off in future clustered processors. In *Computer Architecture, 2003. Proceedings. 30th Annual International Symposium on*, pages 275 – 286, june 2003.

[9] J. Barr. Amazon Web Services Blog, January 28, 201, January 28, 20111. http://aws.typepad.com/aws/2011/01/amazon-s3-bigger-and-busier-than-ever.html.

[10] N. Binkert, B. Beckmann, G. Black, S. K. Reinhardt, A. Saidi, A. Basu, J. Hestness, D. R. Hower, T. Krishna, S. Sardashti, R. Sen, K. Sewell, M. Shoaib, N. Vaish, M. D. Hill, and D. A. Wood. The GEM5 simulator. *SIGARCH Comput. Archit. News*, 39(2):1–7, Aug. 2011. ISSN 0163-5964.

[11] D. Burger, S. Keckler, K. McKinley, M. Dahlin, L. John, C. Lin, C. Moore, J. Burrill, R. McDonald, and W. Yoder. Scaling to the end of silicon with EDGE architectures. *Computer*, 37(7):44–55, july 2004.

[12] R. Buyya, C. S. Yeo, and S. Venugopal. Market-oriented cloud computing: Vision, hype, and reality for delivering it services as computing utilities. In *Proceedings of the 10th IEEE International Conference on High Performance Computing and Communications 2008*.

[13] J. Cong, A. Jagannathan, G. Reinman, and Y. Tamir. Understanding the energy efficiency of smt and cmp with multiclustering. In *Low Power Electronics and Design, 2005. ISLPED '05. Proceedings of the 2005 International Symposium on*, pages 48–53, 2005.

[14] C. Delimitrou and C. Kozyrakis. Paragon: Qos-aware scheduling for heterogeneous datacenters. In *Proceedings of the eighteenth international conference on Architectural support*

*for programming languages and operating systems*, ASPLOS '13, pages 77–88, New York, NY, USA, 2013.

[15] Eucalyptus. Eucalyptus. http://www.eucalyptus.com/.

[16] M. Ferdman, A. Adileh, O. Kocberber, S. Volos, M. Alisafaee, D. Jevdjic, C. Kaynak, A. D. Popescu, A. Ailamaki, and B. Falsafi. Clearing the Clouds: A Study of Emerging Scale-out Workloads on Modern Hardware. In *17th International Conference on Architectural Support for Programming Languages and Operating Systems (ASPLOS)*, 2012.

[17] P. Gratz, C. Kim, R. McDonald, S. Keckler, and D. Burger. Implementation and evaluation of on-chip network architectures. In *Computer Design, 2006. ICCD 2006. International Conference on*, pages 477–484, oct. 2006.

[18] M. Guevara, B. Lubin, and B. C. Lee. Navigating heterogeneous processors with market mechanisms. In *High Performance Computer Architecture (HPCA2013), 2013 IEEE 19th International Symposium on*, pages 95–106, 2013.

[19] A. Gulati, G. Shanmuganathan, A. Holler, and I. Ahmad. Cloud-scale resource management: challenges and techniques. In *Proceedings of the 3rd USENIX conference on Hot topics in cloud computing*, HotCloud'11, pages 3–3, Berkeley, CA, USA, 2011.

[20] F. Guo, Y. Solihin, L. Zhao, and R. Iyer. A framework for providing quality of service in chip multi-processors. In *Proceedings of the 40th Annual IEEE/ACM International Symposium on Microarchitecture*, MICRO 40, pages 343–355, Washington, DC, USA, 2007.

[21] B. Hindman, A. Konwinski, M. Zaharia, A. Ghodsi, A. D. Joseph, R. Katz, S. Shenker, and I. Stoica. Mesos: a platform for fine-grained resource sharing in the data center. In *Proceedings of the 8th USENIX conference on Networked systems design and implementation*, NSDI'11, pages 22–22, 2011.

[22] H. Hoffmann, J. Eastep, M. D. Santambrogio, J. E. Miller, and A. Agarwal. Application heartbeats for software performance and health. In *Proceedings of the ACM SIGPLAN Symposium on Principles and Practice of Parallel Programming*, pages 347–348, 2010.

[23] H. Hoffmann, M. Maggio, M. D. Santambrogio, A. Leva, and A. Agarwal. A generalized software framework for accurate and efficient managment of performance goals. In *EMSOFT*, 2013.

[24] E. Ipek, M. Kirman, N. Kirman, and J. F. Martinez. Core Fusion: accommodating software diversity in chip multiprocessors. In *Proceedings of the 34th annual international symposium on Computer architecture*, pages 186–197, 2007.

[25] M. Isard, V. Prabhakaran, J. Currey, U. Wieder, K. Talwar, and A. Goldberg. Quincy: fair scheduling for distributed computing clusters. In *Proceedings of the ACM SIGOPS 22nd symposium on Operating systems principles*, SOSP '09, pages 261–276, 2009.

[26] R. Iyer, L. Zhao, F. Guo, R. Illikkal, S. Makineni, D. Newell, Y. Solihin, L. Hsu, and S. Reinhardt. Qos policies and architecture for cache/memory in cmp platforms. In *Proceedings of the 2007 ACM SIGMETRICS international conference on Measurement and modeling of computer systems*, SIGMETRICS '07, pages 25–36, 2007.

[27] V. Janapa Reddi, B. C. Lee, T. Chilimbi, and K. Vaid. Web search using mobile cores: quantifying and mitigating the price of efficiency. In *Proceedings of the 37th annual international symposium on Computer architecture*, ISCA '10, pages 314–325, 2010.

[28] M. Kambadur, T. Moseley, R. Hank, and M. A. Kim. Measuring interference between live datacenter applications. In *Proceedings of the International Conference on High Performance Computing, Networking, Storage and Analysis*, SC '12, pages 51:1–51:12, 2012.

[29] K. Khubaib, M. Suleman, M. Hashemi, C. Wilkerson, and Y. Patt. Morphcore: An energy-efficient microarchitecture for high performance ilp and high throughput tlp. In *Microarchitecture (MICRO), 2012 45th Annual IEEE/ACM International Symposium on*, pages 305–316, 2012.

[30] C. Kim, S. Sethumadhavan, M. S. Govindan, N. Ranganathan, D. Gulati, D. Burger, and S. W. Keckler. Composable lightweight processors. In *Proceedings of the 40th Annual IEEE/ACM International Symposium on Microarchitecture*, MICRO 40, pages 381–394, 2007. ISBN 0-7695-3047-8.

[31] O. Krieger, P. McGachey, and A. Kanevsky. Enabling a marketplace of clouds: Vmware's vcloud director. *SIGOPS Oper. Syst. Rev.*, 44(4):103–114, Dec. 2010. ISSN 0163-5980.

[32] R. Kumar, N. P. Jouppi, and D. M. Tullsen. Conjoined-core chip multiprocessing. In *Proceedings of the 37th annual IEEE/ACM International Symposium on Microarchitecture*, MICRO 37, pages 195–206, 2004. ISBN 0-7695-2126-6.

[33] R. Kumar, D. M. Tullsen, P. Ranganathan, N. P. Jouppi, and K. I. Farkas. Single-ISA heterogeneous multi-core architectures for multithreaded workload performance. In *Computer Architecture, Proceedings. International Symposium on*, pages 64 – 75, june 2004.

[34] R. Kumar, D. Tullsen, N. Jouppi, and P. Ranganathan. Heterogeneous Chip Multiprocessors. *Computer*, 38(11):32 – 38, nov. 2005. ISSN 0018-9162. .

[35] R. M. Lerner. At the forge: Amazon web services. *Linux J.*, 2006(143):12, 2006. ISSN 1075-3583.

[36] Y. Li, D. Brooks, Z. Hu, K. Skadron, and P. Bose. Understanding the energy efficiency of simultaneous multithreading. In *Low Power Electronics and Design, 2004. ISLPED '04. Proceedings of the 2004 International Symposium on*, pages 44–49, 2004.

[37] J. L. Lo, S. J. Eggers, J. S. Emer, H. M. Levy, R. L. Stamm, and D. M. Tullsen. Converting thread-level parallelism to instruction-level parallelism via simultaneous multithreading. *ACM Trans. Comput. Syst.*, 15(3):322–354, Aug. 1997.

[38] D. MacAskill. SkyNet Lives! (aka EC2 at SmugMug). http://don.blogs.smugmug.com/2008/06/03/skynet-lives-aka-ec2-smugmug/.

[39] M. R. Marty and M. D. Hill. Virtual hierarchies to support server consolidation. In *Proceedings of the 34th Annual International Symposium on Computer Architecture*, ISCA '07, pages 46–56, 2007. ISBN 978-1-59593-706-3.

[40] S. McFarling. Combining branch predictors. Technical Report TN-36, WRL Technical Note, 1993.

[41] D. Meisner, C. M. Sadler, L. A. Barroso, W.-D. Weber, and T. F. Wenisch. Power management of online data-intensive services. In *Proceedings of the 38th annual international symposium on Computer architecture*, ISCA '11, pages 319–330, 2011.

[42] Muralimanohar, Naveen, Balasubramonian, Rajeev, Jouppi, and N. P. Cacti 6.0: A tool to model large caches. Technical Report HPL-2009-85, HP Laboratories, 2009.

[43] Openstack. Openstack Cloud Software. http://www.openstack.org/.

[44] P. Padala, K.-Y. Hou, K. G. Shin, X. Zhu, M. Uysal, Z. Wang, S. Singhal, and A. Merchant. Automated control of multiple virtualized resources. In *Proceedings of the 4th ACM European conference on Computer systems*, EuroSys '09, pages 13–26, 2009.

[45] S. Palacharla, N. P. Jouppi, and J. E. Smith. Complexity-effective superscalar processors. In *Proceedings of the International Symposium on Computer Architecture*, pages 206–218, June 1997.

[46] M. R. Palankar, A. Iamnitchi, M. Ripeanu, and S. Garfinkel. Amazon S3 for science grids: a viable solution? In *DADC '08: Proceedings of the 2008 international workshop on Data-aware distributed computing*, pages 55–64, New York, NY, USA, 2008. ACM. ISBN 978-1-60558-154-5. .

[47] M. K. Qureshi and Y. N. Patt. Utility-based cache partitioning: A low-overhead, high-performance, runtime mechanism to partition shared caches. In *Proceedings of the 39th Annual IEEE/ACM International Symposium on Microarchitecture*, MICRO 39, pages 423–432, 2006.

[48] A. Ranadive, A. Gavrilovska, and K. Schwan. Resource-exchange: Latency-aware scheduling in virtualized environments with high performance fabrics. In *Cluster Computing (CLUSTER), 2011 IEEE International Conference on*, pages 45–53, 2011.

[49] K. Sankaralingam, R. Nagarajan, H. Liu, C. Kim, J. Huh, D. Burger, S. Keckler, and C. Moore. Exploiting ILP, TLP, and DLP with the polymorphous TRIPS architecture. In *Proceedings of the International Symposium on Computer Architecture*, pages 422–433, 2003.

[50] K. Sankaralingam, R. Nagarajan, R. McDonald, R. Desikan, S. Drolia, M. S. Govindan, P. Gratzf, D. Gulati, H. Hanson, C. Kim, H. Liu, N. Ranganathan, S. Sethumadhavan, S. Shariff, P. Shivakumar, S. Keckler, and D. Burger. Distributed microarchitectural protocols in the TRIPS prototype processor. In *Microarchitecture, 2006. MICRO-39. 39th Annual IEEE/ACM International Symposium on*, pages 480 –491, dec. 2006.

[51] M. Santambrogio, H. Hoffmann, J. Eastep, and A. Agarwal. Enabling technologies for self-aware adaptive systems. In *Adaptive Hardware and Systems (AHS), 2010 NASA/ESA Conference on*, pages 149–156, 2010.

[52] B. Santithorn. *Fully Distributed Register Files for Heterogeneous Clustered Mircroarchitectures.* PhD thesis, Georgia Institute of Technology, 2005.

[53] S. Sethumadhavan, R. McDonald, D. Burger, S. Keckler, and R. Desikan. Design and implementation of the TRIPS primary memory system. In *Computer Design, 2006. ICCD 2006. International Conference on*, pages 470 –476, oct. 2006.

[54] S. Sethumadhavan, F. Roesner, J. S. Emer, D. Burger, and S. W. Keckler. Late-binding: Enabling unordered load-store queues. In *In Proceedings of the 34th Annual International symposium on Computer Architecture*, pages 347–357, 2007.

[55] Z. Shen, S. Subbiah, X. Gu, and J. Wilkes. Cloudscale: elastic resource scaling for multi-tenant cloud systems. In *Proceedings of the 2nd ACM Symposium on Cloud Computing*, SOCC '11, pages 5:1–5:14, 2011.

[56] Y. Song, H. Wang, Y. Li, B. Feng, and Y. Sun. Multi-tiered on-demand resource scheduling for vm-based data center. In *Proceedings of the 2009 9th IEEE/ACM International Symposium on Cluster Computing and the Grid*, CCGRID '09, pages 148–155, Washington, DC, USA, 2009.

[57] G. Suh, S. Devadas, and L. Rudolph. A new memory monitoring scheme for memory-aware scheduling and partitioning. In *High-Performance Computer Architecture, 2002. Proceedings. Eighth International Symposium on*, pages 117–128, 2002.

[58] S. Swanson, K. Michelson, A. Schwerin, and M. Oskin. Wavescalar. In *Proceedings of the 36th annual IEEE/ACM International Symposium on Microarchitecture*, MICRO 36, pages 291–, 2003. ISBN 0-7695-2043-X.

[59] M. Taylor, M. B. Taylor, W. Lee, S. Amarasinghe, and A. Agarwal. Scalar operand networks: on-chip interconnect for ilp in partitioned architectures. In *High-Performance Computer Architecture, 2003. HPCA-9 2003. Proceedings. The Ninth International Symposium on*, pages 341 – 353, feb. 2003.

[60] D. Tullsen, S. Eggers, and H. Levy. Simultaneous multithreading: maximizing on-chip parallelism. In *Proceedings of the international symposium on Computer architecture*, ISCA '95, pages 392–403, 1995.

[61] VMWare. VMware Virtual Appliance Marketplace: Virtual Applications for the Cloud. http://www.vmware.com/appliances/.

[62] T. von Eicken. Amazon Usage Estimates, RightScale Blog. http://blog.rightscale.com/2009/10/05/amazon-usage-estimates/.

[63] E. Waingold, M. Taylor, D. Srikrishna, V. Sarkar, W. Lee, V. Lee, J. Kim, M. Frank, P. Finch, R. Barua, J. Babb, S. Amarasinghe, and A. Agarwal. Baring it all to software: Raw machines. *Computer*, 30(9):86 –93, sep 1997.

[64] Y. Watanabe, J. D. Davis, and D. A. Wood. WiDGET: Wisconsin decoupled grid execution tiles. *SIGARCH Comput. Archit. News*, 38(3):2–13, June 2010.

[65] D. Wentzlaff, P. Griffin, H. Hoffmann, L. Bao, B. Edwards, C. Ramey, M. Mattina, C.-C. Miao, J. F. Brown III, and A. Agarwal. On-chip interconnection architecture of the Tile Processor. *IEEE Micro*, 27(5):15–31, Sept. 2007.

# ASC: Automatically Scalable Computation

Amos Waterland
Elaine Angelino
Ryan P. Adams
Harvard University
apw@seas.harvard.edu
elaine@eecs.harvard.edu
rpa@seas.harvard.edu

Jonathan Appavoo
Boston University
jappavoo@bu.edu

Margo Seltzer
Harvard University
margo@eecs.harvard.edu

## Abstract

We present an architecture designed to transparently and automatically scale the performance of sequential programs as a function of the hardware resources available. The architecture is predicated on a model of computation that views program execution as a walk through the enormous state space composed of the memory and registers of a single-threaded processor. Each instruction execution in this model moves the system from its current point in state space to a deterministic subsequent point. We can parallelize such execution by predictively partitioning the complete path and speculatively executing each partition in parallel. Accurately partitioning the path is a challenging prediction problem. We have implemented our system using a functional simulator that emulates the *x*86 instruction set, including a collection of state predictors and a mechanism for speculatively executing threads that explore potential states along the execution path. While the overhead of our simulation makes it impractical to measure speedup relative to native *x*86 execution, experiments on three benchmarks show scalability of up to a factor of 256 on a 1024 core machine when executing unmodified sequential programs.

***Categories and Subject Descriptors*** I.2.6 [*Artificial Intelligence*]: Learning—Connectionism and neural nets; C.5.1 [*Large and Medium ("Mainframe") Computers*]: Super (very large) computers

***Keywords*** Machine learning, Automatic parallelization

## 1. Introduction

The Automatically Scalable Computation (ASC) architecture is designed to meet two goals: it is straightforward to program and it automatically scales up execution according to available physical resources. For the first goal, we define "straightforward to program" as requiring only that the programmer write sequential code that compiles into a single-threaded binary program. The second goal requires that performance improves as a function of the number of cores and amount of memory available.

We begin with a computational model that views the data and hardware available to a program as comprising an exponentially large state space. This space is composed of all possible states of the registers and memory of a single-threaded processor. In this model, execution of a single instruction corresponds to a transition between two states in this space, and an entire program execution corresponds to a path or trajectory through this space. Given this model and a system with $N$ processors we would ideally be able to automatically reduce the time to execute a trajectory by a factor of $N$. In theory, this could be achieved by dividing the trajectory into $N$ equal partitions and executing each of them in parallel. Of course, we do not know the precise trajectory a program will follow, so we do not know, *a priori*, the precise points on the trajectory that will equally partition it. Nevertheless, if we attempt to predict $N-1$ points on the trajectory and speculatively execute the trajectory segments starting at those points, we will produce a speedup if even a small subset of our predictions are accurate. From this vantage point, accurately predicting points on the future trajectory of the system suggests a methodology for automatically scaling sequential execution.

The primary design challenge in realizing this architecture is accurately predicting points that partition a trajectory. We break this challenge into two parts: (1) recognizing states from which accurate prediction is possible and will result in useful speedup, and (2) predicting future states of the system when the current state of execution is recognized as one from which prediction is possible.

Given solutions for these two challenges, a basic ASC architecture works as follows. While sequentially executing on one core, ASC allocates additional cores for predictive execution. Each predictive execution core begins executing at a different predicted state and continues executing for a given length of time. We then store the results of predictive execution in a state cache: for example, as compressed pairs of start and end states. At appropriate times, the sequential execution core consults the state cache. If its current state matches a cached start state on all relevant coordinates, it achieves speedup by "fast-forwarding" to the associated cached end state and then resumes execution. If the predicted states correctly and evenly partition the execution trajectory and the ASC components operate efficiently, we will achieve per-


*ASPLOS '14*, March 01 - 05 2014, Salt Lake City, UT, USA.

ACM 978-1-4503-2305-5/14/03...$15.00.
http://dx.doi.org/10.1145/2541940.2541985

fect and automatic linear speedup of the sequential execution. Thus, our architecture has the potential to produce arbitrary scalability, but its true efficacy will be a function of an implementation's ability to (1) recognize good points from which to make predictions, (2) make accurate predictions, (3) efficiently query the cache, (4) efficiently allocate cores to the various parts of the architecture, and (5) execute trajectory-based computation efficiently.

The primary challenges to efficiently implementing ASC are (1) manipulating the potentially enormous state space and (2) managing the cache of state pairs. Although the entire state space of a program is sufficiently large (e.g., $10^7$ bits for one of our benchmark programs) that efficient manipulation seems intractable, we exploit the fact that predictable units of computation (think "functions or loops") often touch only a tiny fraction of that space (e.g., $10^3$ bits). Thus, we encode cache entries using a sparse representation that is itself compressible. In addition, a single cache entry can be used at multiple points in a program's execution, effecting a generalized form of memoization.

We present an implementation of ASC, the Learning-based Automatically Scalable Computation (LASC) system. It is a trajectory-based functional simulator (TBFS) that emulates the $x86$ instruction set with a fast, adaptive algorithm for recognizing predictable states, a set of on-line learning algorithms that use observed states to learn predictors for future states, a resource allocator that selects optimal combinations of predictors in an on-line setting, and a cache that stores compressed representations of speculative executions.

We evaluate the performance of our system on a set of sequential benchmark programs with surprisingly good results. LASC achieves near-linear scaling up to a few hundred cores and continues non-negative scaling up to a few thousand cores. Our benchmark programs are purely computational (i.e., they do not perform I/O after loading their initial input), and they have obvious parallel structure that makes them amenable to manual parallelization. However, they differ in the kinds of parallelism they exhibit and how amenable they are to traditional automatic parallelization approaches. Our goal is to demonstrate the potential of the ASC architecture to automatically identify and exploit statistical patterns that arise during program execution.

The contributions of this paper are: (1) a system architecture that automatically scales performance as a function of the number of cores or size of memory available, (2) a fast and adaptive method for automatically identifying states from which predictions are tractable, (3) a set of general-purpose predictors that learn from observed states, (4) a theoretically sound method to adaptively combine predictions, and (5) a prototype that demonstrates significant scaling on certain classes of unmodified $x86$ sequential binary programs on systems of up to 4096 cores.

The rest of this paper is organized as follows. We begin with a discussion of prior work, showing how conventional techniques can be cast into the ASC architecture in §2. We then present the ASC architecture in §3 and our learning-based implementation of the ASC architecture (LASC) in §4. In §5, we present both theoretical and analytical results that demonstrate the potential of the architecture and the strengths and weaknesses of our prototype. In §6, we discuss the implications of this work and avenues for future research.

## 2. Related work

There are three broad categories of work that share our goal of automatically scaling program execution: parallelizing compilers, software systems that parallelize binary programs, and hardware parallelization. Although each category of work arises from conceptual models rather different from ours, notions of statistical prediction and speculative execution have independently arisen in all three.

### 2.1 Compiler parallelization

Traditional compiler parallelization based on static analysis [1] has produced sophisticated research compilers [3, 9]. Although these compilers can automatically parallelize most loops that have regular, well-defined data access patterns [32], the limitations of static analysis have become apparent [27]. When dealing with less regular loops, parallelizing compilers either give up or generate both sequential and parallel code that must use runtime failsafe checking [55]. The ASC architecture is able to speed up irregular loops by using on-line probabilistic inference to predict likely future states, as we show in §5. However, it can also import the sophisticated static analyses of traditional parallelizing compilers in the form of probability priors on loops that the compiler was almost but not quite able to prove independent.

Thread-Level Speculation (TLS) [14, 60, 61] arose in response to the limits of compile-time static analysis. TLS hardware applies speculative execution to code that was not fully parallelized by the compiler. This hardware backstop allows automatic speculative parallelization by TLS compilers [31, 40, 41, 48, 51, 62, 70] without fully proving the absence of dependences across the threaded code they generate. However, TLS performance sensitively depends upon the compiler making good choices for speculative thread code generation and spawning. The ASC architecture can exploit TLS hardware or transactional memory [26, 34] if it is available and makes it easy to experiment with decompositions of execution flow. Compiler choices that yield good decompositions for TLS are also likely to produce recognizable and predictable patterns for ASC, and vice versa.

Clusters of computers have been targets of recent speculative parallelizing compilers demonstrating scaling on up to hundreds of nodes for loops without loop-carried dependencies [33]. Our LASC prototype implementation currently runs on clusters and would benefit from importing hints produced by these compilers in the form of probability distributions.

### 2.2 Binary parallelization

Software systems that automatically parallelize binary programs also have a long research history. They share with ASC the properties of not requiring the program source code, of having perfect visibility into patterns that arise at runtime, and of inducing some runtime overhead.

Binary rewriter parallelization systems [35, 64, 68] take as input a sequential binary executable program and produce as output a parallel binary executable. Dynamic code generating binary parallelization systems [13, 27] assume the existence of TLS hardware and apply the same control flow graph analyses used by conventional TLS compilers to sequential binary programs not originally compiled for TLS. Dynamic binary parallelization systems [67], inspired by dynamic binary optimization systems [6], transparently parallelize sequential binary programs by identifying hot traces of instructions that can sometimes be replaced with a shorter, speculatively executed instruction sequence whose semantics are equivalent on the current input dependencies.

The ASC architecture contrasts with these systems in that it does not itself attempt any analysis of instruction control flow semantics or basic block optimizations. It simply models execution as the time evolution of a stochastic process through a state space. This means that it will exploit *any* method that can produce probabilistic predictions of future state vectors. Most instruction control flow analysis and optimization techniques can be transformed into probabilistic predictors by using appropriately rich feature representations. While engineering such representations may be challenging, "kernelized" machine learning algorithms can efficiently perform predictive computation in potentially large or infinite feature spaces with minimal overhead. Such savings is possible because many important machine learning tools interact with the data via the inner products of feature vectors. By replacing these inner products with positive definite Mercer kernels (the so-called "kernel trick" [7, 19]), we can give the algorithm implicit access to large and rich feature spaces. This means that ASC can import existing work in binary parallelization as "run ahead" approximators [71] that take a completely consistent probabilistic form.

### 2.3 Hardware parallelization

Hardware that transparently speeds up sequential binary programs as a function of transistor count is the subject of intense research and has resulted in many successful commercial implementations. Superscalar processors [49] execute individual instructions in parallel, speculatively executing around dependencies using powerful branch prediction [30, 57, 58] and load value prediction [38] strategies and can use trace caches [54] to implicitly enable multiple simultaneous branch predictions. Other approaches make multiple cores appear as one fast out-of-order core [10, 28], shorten execution time by speculatively removing nonessential instructions in parallel [47], and speculatively parallelize programs at the thread [2, 14, 18, 24, 60, 69] or SIMD [16] level, many of which rely on some degree of compiler or runtime [17] assistance.

ASC makes the same contract to the programmer as a superscalar or dynamic multithreading processor: transparent, automatic scaling of sequential binary programs as a function of transistor count. ASC prediction is more general than branch, load value, and return value prediction because it models the time evolution of the *complete* state vector and exploits the fact that correlations between bits can give rise to a low-entropy joint distribution over points in state space.

Although LASC presently exists only as a software implementation of the ASC architecture, our goal is that every component be amenable to an efficient hardware implementation. For example, probabilistic computing hardware [22, 63] can greatly accelerate our learning algorithms, trace caches could be extended to store our results from executing a trace of instructions, and circuitry similar to transactional memory implementations can expedite dependency tracking.

## 3. The ASC architecture

We begin our description of the ASC architecture by discussing the trajectory-based model of computation. We then discuss each main component of our architecture.

### 3.1 Trajectory-based computation

We base our model of computation on the *trajectory-based computation* framework of Waterland et al. [65, 66]. Consider the memory and registers of a single-threaded processor as comprising an exponentially large state space. Program execution then traces out a *trajectory* through this state space. If all input data is loaded up front, this execution is memoryless in that it produces a deterministic sequence of states, where each state depends only on the previous state.

In order to parallelize a program using $N$ cores, we can in principle achieve a speedup of $N$ by partitioning its trajectory into $N$ equal segments that we execute in parallel. Unfortunately, such partitioning requires that we are able to accurately predict $N-1$ specific future states of the machine. If we were able to perfectly predict states, we would simply predict the end state and ignore the computation entirely. If trajectories were random sequences of states through this state space then prediction would be intractable. However, trajectories are not random, and many programs have regularly structured trajectories. Our experience is that many real-world programs exhibit regular structure, suggesting that prediction may often be feasible.

Three features of real-world program execution make the prediction problem significantly easier in practice: (1) each transition depends on and modifies only a small part of the state, (2) large portions of the state are constant, such as the program's machine instructions, or nearly constant, such as data that is written once, and (3) real programs tend to be built from modular and repeating structures, such as functions and loops. Many aspects of execution have been empirically shown to have repetitive or predictable patterns [56]. These include branch directions [30, 58], branch targets [37], memory data addresses [5], memory data values [21], and dependencies [43], while values produced by instructions tend to repeat from a small set [38], and instructions often have the same input and output values [59].

These repetitive or predictable aspects of execution are particularly amenable to the modeling approach of trajectory-based computation [65], which illuminates unexpected geometric and probabilistic structure in computer systems by focusing attention on their *state vectors*, each of which contain all information necessary to deterministically transition to the next state vector. The ASC architecture is designed to amplify predictable patterns in execution into automatic scaling.

### 3.2 Architecture components

We present our architecture by walking through Figure 1, along the way illustrating some possible design decisions that map existing work into this architecture.

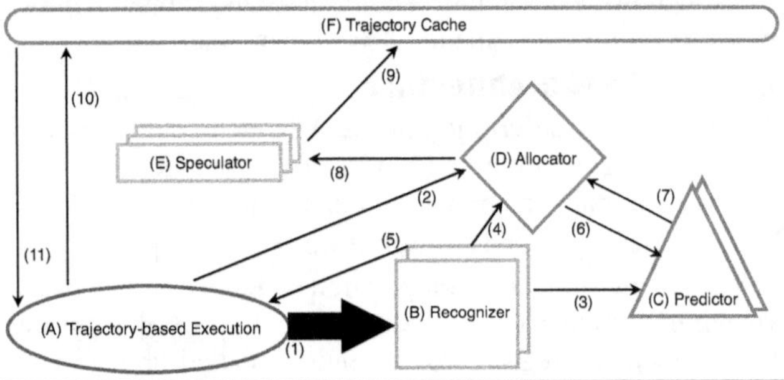


**Figure 1.** ASC Architecture. The trajectory-based execution engine sends its current state to the recognizers (1) and to the allocator (2). The collection of recognizers selects particular states that appear to be good input to the predictors and sends them to the predictors (3), the allocator (4), and back to the trajectory-based execution engine (5). Using the filtered stream of states obtained from the recognizers, the predictors build models of execution from which they will predict future states. The allocator's job is to assign predictors, recognizers and speculative threads to cores. Based on the states obtained from the recognizer, the allocator sends the current state to the predictors (6), requesting that they use that state to generate a predicted future state (7). Given those predictions, the allocator dispatches speculative threads, each with a different predicted state and number of instructions to execute (8). Each speculative thread executes its specified number of instructions and inserts its start-state/end-state pair into the trajectory cache (9). Finally, at intervals suggested by the recognizer (5), the trajectory-based execution engine consults the state cache to determine if its current state matches any start-states in the cache (10). If there are any matches, the cache returns the end-state farthest in the future (11).

A single thread, called the main thread, begins program execution (A). While the program runs, recognizers (B) strategically identify states along a program's trajectory that are amenable to prediction. Intuitively, states are easier to predict when they follow a recognizable pattern or are drawn from a recognizable distribution. For example, a recognizer could use static analysis to determine a condition that, when satisfied by a state, indicates that the program is at the top of a loop or is entering a function that is called repeatedly. A different recognizer could use metric learning to dynamically identify states that are similar to previously seen states. As we will explain in §4.3, the default recognizer in our prototype identifies regular, widely-spaced points that form a sequence of 'supersteps' for which our predictors make accurate predictions.

A set of on-line learning algorithms train predictors (C), which build models for strategic points along the trajectory. Individual models may predict the whole state, single bits or larger features such as bytes, words, or combinations of words. Different predictors may produce competing models of any flavor: deterministic, stochastic, probabilistic or heuristic. Regardless of the type of model, each predictor must accept an input state and generate a prediction for a future state. It is reasonable, but optional, for the recognizer to use feedback from the predictors to identify characteristics of 'predictable' states.

The allocator (D) is responsible for allocating and scheduling hardware resources for the predictors, recognizers and speculative execution threads (E). It determines how many threads to schedule for each component and how long to spend on each task. Using information from the recognizer, the allocator decides when to ask the predictors for their estimates for future states along with their uncertainty. The allocator then attempts to maximize its expected utility as it decides which predicted states to dispatch to speculative execution threads and how long each thread should execute for each prediction.

The speculative execution threads then enter their results into the trajectory cache (F), which maintains pairs of start/end states that correspond to execution of a specific number of instructions. The main thread can query the cache, and if it ever matches a start state in the cache, it fast-forwards to the farthest corresponding end state, thus speeding up execution by jumping forward in state space and execution time. Like the allocator, the main thread uses information from the recognizer to decide when to query the cache.

Any implementation of the ASC architecture must maintain correctness of program execution. Speeding up execution only when there is a strict match on the entire state would lead to a conceptually straightforward but suboptimal cache design in which cached trajectories are simply represented as key-value pairs that map complete start states to complete end states. A much better cache design is possible, as we explain in §4.2, by keeping track of the bits read from and written to each state vector during execution, which allows for speeding up execution any time there is a match on the subset of the state upon which that execution depends.

### 3.3 Discussion

There are several different ways to think about the ASC architecture. For example, when the strategic points picked by the recognizer correspond to function boundaries and the speculative execution threads cache the results of function call execution, ASC is "speculatively memoizing" function calls. ASC memoization is more general than conventional memoization [42], because it can memoize any repeated section of computation, not just function calls.

ASC exploits the same patterns as a parallelizing compiler when it identifies states corresponding to the top of a loop, speculatively executes many iterations of the loop in parallel, then stores the resulting state pairs in its cache. ASC parallelization of loop execution is more general than conventional compiler loop parallelization, because it can speculatively execute in parallel the iterations of any loop whose dependencies have a learnable pattern, including loops with significant data and control dependencies, rather than just loops that static analysis can prove to have no dependencies.

The ASC architecture is a general model that scales unmodified sequential programs compiled with a standard toolchain. It can scale in two ways: (1) by adding more memory so that more cache entries can be stored, and (2) by adding more cores for prediction, speculation and cache lookup. In §4, we present details of our prototype implementation of the ASC architecture.

# 4. Implementation

LASC, the learning-based ASC, is an implementation of our architecture that turns the problem of automatically scaling sequential computation into a set of machine learning problems. We begin with an overview of our implementation and then discuss the details of each component.

In LASC, the cache, recognizer, predictors, and allocator are all built into the trajectory-based functional simulator (TBFS) that we discuss in §4.1. At the heart of the TBFS is a transition function that interprets its input as an $x86$ state vector, simulates one instruction, and outputs a new state vector. The main and speculative threads execute by repeated calls to this transition function.

Each time the TBFS executes an instruction on the main thread, it invokes the recognizer to rapidly decide whether the resultant state matches a pattern that the recognizer has identified. If the current state matches the recognizer's pattern, it sends the current state to the predictors and queries the distributed cache – fast-forwarding on a cache hit. Meanwhile, the predictors update their models and predict future states based on the current state. The allocator then combines the predictions and selects a set of predicted states on which to launch speculative threads.

By factoring the problem of predicting a complete state vector into the problems of predicting smaller, conditionally independent portions of a state vector, we parallelize both training, the task of learning a predictive model for future states, and prediction itself, the task of using a learned model to materialize a predicted state.

## 4.1 Trajectory-based functional simulator

Our simulator's key data structure is the *state vector*, which represents the complete state of computation. Our system executes an instruction by calling the *transition function*: `transition(uint8_t *x, uint8_t *g, int n)`, where `x` is the state vector of length $n$ bits passed as a byte array of dimension $\frac{n}{8}$, and `g` is the *dependency vector* also of dimension $\frac{n}{8}$. The transition function has no hidden state and refers to no global variables. The transition function simply fetches the 32 bits that contain the instruction pointer of the location in state space represented by `x`, fetches the referenced instruction, simulates the instruction according to the $x86$ architecture, and writes the resultant state changes back to the appropriate bits in the state vector. It may seem a poor choice to represent state as a bit array, but this gives us the mathematical structure of a vector space, and allows us to learn and make predictions using massively bit-parallel binary classifiers.

The transition function accumulates dependency information in `g` at the byte—rather than bit—granularity. For each byte in the state vector `x`, the corresponding byte in `g` maintains one of four statuses: `read`, `written_after_read`, `written` or `null`, with the remaining $256 - 4$ codes reserved. When a speculative execution worker starts, it first sets all bytes in `g` to `null`, then calls the transition function in a loop. The transition function automatically uses a simple finite state machine to update the dependency vector on every call. When the transition function reads a byte whose status is `null`, it updates the corresponding status to `read`. If it later writes to that same byte, it updates the corresponding status to `written_after_read`. If it writes to a byte that has never been read, it updates the corresponding status to `written`.

Without this dependency tracking, we could exploit speculative trajectories only when the current state of execution matched a cached start state in its entirety. However, the dependency state lets us match significantly more frequently. When we stop a speculative thread, the set of bytes with dependency state `read` or `written_after_read` (but *not* `written` or `null`) identifies precisely those bytes on which the speculative computation depends. Therefore, we can match a cache entry when the current state matches the start state of the cache entry merely on bytes having statuses of `read` or `written_after_read`. Not only does this improve the cache hit rate, but it makes the predictors' jobs easier too: they need to correctly predict only those same bytes. When we find a cache hit, the main thread fast-forwards to the end state of the cache entry by updating only those bytes with statuses `written` or `written_after_read`; this has an interpretation as a translation symmetry in state space.

## 4.2 Cache

We exploit dependencies to efficiently represent cache entries. Each cache entry is a representation of a start state and an end state. The start state represents only those bytes with `read` or `written_after_read` statuses and the end state represents only those bytes with `write` or `written_after_read` statuses. We store a sparse representation of the relevant byte indices and their corresponding values.

A portion of the cache exists on each core participating in a computation, because we implement the cache directly in the TBFS. Each core that generates a speculative execution stores that execution in its portion of the cache. The main thread queries this parallel distributed cache at intervals indicated by the recognizer by broadcasting its current state vector, either as a binary delta against its last query or as the full state vector, depending on the computation/communication tradeoff. Each node responds with an integer value indicating the length of its longest matching trajectory – zero for a cache miss. Finding the largest integer, and thus the most useful matching trajectory in the whole cache, is a reduction, so we use MPI's parallel binary tree `max` operator to limit bandwidth consumption. On our Blue Gene/P system, each pairwise `max` comparison is implemented in an ASIC, further speeding up the reduction. The main thread then does a point-to-point communication with the node that sent the largest integer to obtain the corresponding end state to which it will fast-forward, while all other nodes go back to running learning algorithms and doing speculative execution.

## 4.3 Recognizer

The recognizer's job is to identify states in the trajectory from which prediction is both tractable and useful. This requires finding states for which the speculative execution from predicted states will produce few non-`null` bytes in the dependency vector and the values of the corresponding bytes in the state vector are predictable. In other words, states for which resultant speculative computation depends on a small number of predictable values.

We find these states by exploiting the geometric and probabilistic structure of our state space. In particular, we find a hyperplane that cuts the execution trajectory at regular, widely-spaced intervals, as depicted in Figure 2. Our default recognizer induces such a hyperplane by picking only states that share a particular instruction pointer (IP) value. Thus, given a sequence of state vectors corresponding to the same IP, the predictors try to learn the relevant parts of the state vector that will occur at future instances of this IP value. Fortunately, long-running programs tend to be composed of loop structures and functions that correspond to repeated sequences of instructions [45].

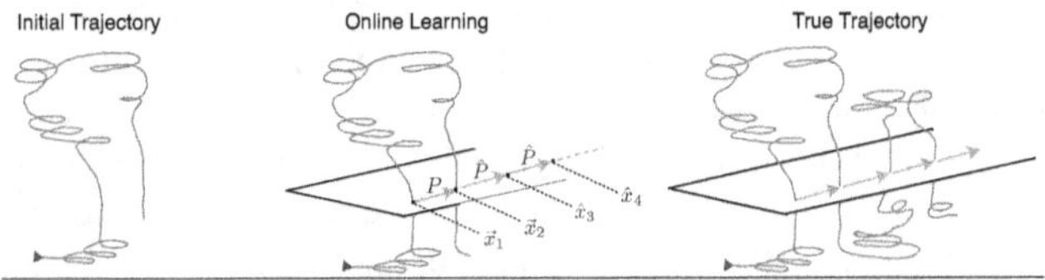


**Figure 2.** From the initial trajectory, we recognize a hyperplane that cuts the true trajectory at regular, widely-spaced points $\{\vec{x}_1, \vec{x}_2, \ldots\}$, all sharing the same IP value. Our online learning problem is then to learn an approximation $\hat{P}$ to the true function $P$ that maps $\vec{x}_i$ to $\vec{x}_{i+1}$. Once we have learned $\hat{P}$, we make predictions as $\hat{x}_{i+1} = \hat{P}(\vec{x}_i)$.

We use the following parallel algorithm to find a good IP value. The allocator dispatches all the available cores to particular IP values that have been observed but not yet rejected. Each core initializes a private copy of our learning algorithms and executes the program from its current state. When it encounters a state with its assigned IP value, it sends that state vector to the predictors. The (local) allocator integrates all the predictions to produce a predicted state, which it caches (locally). As the core continues execution, it checks for matches against its growing local cache of predictions. When it finds a match, it records the number of instructions between the state from which a prediction was made and the predicted state, which is a proxy for the utility of the speculative execution that would result if the prediction had been used.

Some IP values are easily predicted but are so closely spaced on the trajectory that speculative execution from them is not worth the communication and lookup costs. Other IP values are widely spaced on the trajectory but very hard to predict. The recognizers select the set of IPs whose resulting states were the best predicted relative to the other IP values considered. We call these the set of *recognized IPs* (RIP) and the lengths of the corresponding trajectories *supersteps*. After selecting one or more RIPs, workers are allocated to the various RIPs, and their predictors begin making predictions for future states with that same RIP. For the purposes of exposition, we will assume only a single RIP, but everything applies when we have multiple RIPs on which we are speculating.

We investigated many heuristics for finding good IP values before settling on this method. In retrospect, this method should have been obvious as it is biased towards the precise criterion of interest: how well the predictors can predict future states. In our prototype, speculative executions need to be at least $10^4$ instructions for their benefit to outweigh their cost, so we ignore predictions, regardless of accuracy, if they are not sufficiently far in the future.

### 4.4 Predictors

Our default implementation invokes the predictors only when the current state has the recognized IP. Thus, given an example sequence of state vectors all having the same IP, our predictors try to predict future state vectors that will also have that IP. This is an *on-line learning* problem [8], in which we wish to learn from the sequence of examples a probability distribution $p(\hat{\mathbf{x}}' \mid \mathbf{x})$ that represents our belief that $\hat{\mathbf{x}}'$ will be the next state vector that will have the same IP as the current state vector $\mathbf{x}$.

By definition, each state vector contains all the information necessary to compute future states. We decompose the prediction problem into a set of conditionally independent predictors, where each predictor conditions on the state vector $\mathbf{x}$ to model a particular bit, a 32-bit quantity, or other feature of the next observation $\mathbf{x}'$. The case of bits is particularly interesting, because it reduces to the binary classification problem, one of the best developed areas of machine learning [52].

We exploit the bit-level conditional independence decomposition to formulate our prediction problem probabilistically, in light of this viewpoint's practical [7, 52] and theoretical [29] advantages. When the current state $\mathbf{x}$ has the RIP value, $p(\hat{\mathbf{x}}' \mid \mathbf{x}, \boldsymbol{\theta})$ expresses our belief that $\hat{\mathbf{x}}'$ is the next state with that IP value according to our model with parameters $\boldsymbol{\theta}$. Since each state is simply a binary vector of $n$ bits, we factor the joint predictive distribution for $\hat{\mathbf{x}}' \mid \mathbf{x}$ into a product of per-bit predictive distributions

$$p(\hat{\mathbf{x}}' \mid \mathbf{x}, \boldsymbol{\theta}) = \prod_{j=1}^{n} p(\hat{x}'_j \mid \mathbf{x}, \boldsymbol{\theta}) \tag{1}$$

$$= \prod_{j=1}^{n} \text{Bernoulli}(\hat{x}'_j \mid \theta_j(\mathbf{x})) \tag{2}$$

where $\hat{x}'_j$ is the $j$-th bit of the predicted state $\hat{\mathbf{x}}'$. This factoring is a convenient computational choice that means we learn $n$ separate binary classifiers $\theta_j(\cdot)$, which is straightforward to parallelize. The $j$-th term in Eq. 2 is the probability that $\hat{x}'_j = 1$, conditioned on a model $\theta_j(\cdot)$ that takes a state $\mathbf{x}$ as input. Under this model, the probability of a predicted state $\hat{\mathbf{x}}'$ is the product of these $n$ terms.

We use Eq. 2 to make allocation decisions, as at any moment it encapsulates everything our learning algorithms have currently discovered, even when the learners themselves are not probabilistic. One of the allocator's jobs is to generate a pool of predictions and then decide which ones to send to speculative threads. Given a state $\mathbf{x}$ and model $\boldsymbol{\theta}$, there are two straightforward methods for generating predictions from Eq. 2. The most probable prediction, $\hat{\mathbf{x}}'_{\text{ML}}$, is produced by maximizing each term, i.e., setting each bit to its most probable value. Alternate predictions for $\hat{\mathbf{x}}'$ can be generated, for example, by strategically flipping the most uncertain bits of $\hat{\mathbf{x}}'_{\mathrm{ML}}$ to give the second and third most likely predictions, and so on. These predictions can be used as input to Eq. 2 to recursively generate predictions farther along the trajectory. Eq. 2 gives the probability of each of these predictions under the model, providing a direct way to compare them. As we describe in §4.5, this allows us to use expected utility maximization to decide which predictions to use for speculation.

In practice, we learn binary classifiers only for the *excitations* of program execution, defined as those bits that have been observed to change more than some threshold number of times (once, by default) from one instance of the RIP value to the next. One of the recognizer's key responsibilities is to find RIP values that exploit our observation that many temporary and even some global variables change but then reset to their starting values during execution between state vectors sharing certain RIP values. The program's excitations induce a strong form of sparsity, as we need learn only those bits that change across states with the same IP value rather than all bits that ever change. Some of the programs we evaluate in §5 have a state space dimensionality of $n > 10^7$, of which $> 10^5$ bits change over the lifetime of the program, but of which $< 300$ change between observations of a certain RIP value.

#### 4.4.1 Interfaces

Each predictor must at minimum implement three interfaces: `update(x,j)`, `predict(x,j)` and `reset()`. For each bit $j$ known to be non-constant between occurrences of the RIP, the main thread calls `update(x,j)`. Each predictor then uses the difference between its previous prediction $\hat{x}_j$ for the $j$-th bit of $\mathbf{x}$ and the newly observed actual value $x_j$ of that bit to update its internal model parameters [25].

After the predictors have updated their models, the main thread asks for predictions by calling `predict(x,j)` for each non-constant bit $j$. The predictors then issue predictions for bit $j$ at the next instance of the recognized IP value. These per-bit predictions are mixed and matched, as will be described in §4.5.1, weighted by each predictor's past performance on each bit, into the single distribution in Eq. 2. Predictors are free to extract whatever features from $\mathbf{x}$ they wish, but must express predictions at the bit level. Predictors at the feature level share state between related bits to make this efficient.

Our system invokes predictors in multiple contexts, so each must supply a `reset()` routine that causes them to discard their current models and start building new ones. For example, the recognizer calls `reset` when searching for an initial RIP or when a change in program behavior renders the current RIP useless.

#### 4.4.2 Prediction algorithms

LASC is extensible, so it can support any number of predictors that implement the interfaces described in §4.4.1. The results in this paper use only four discrete learning algorithms – two trivial ones, *mean* and *weatherman*, and two interesting ones, *logistic regression* and *linear regression*. The mean predictor simply learns the mean value of each bit and issues predictions by rounding. The weatherman predictor predicts that the next value of each bit will be its current value.

Logistic regression is a widely-used learning algorithm for binary classification [7], in which one is given a vector $\mathbf{x}$ that one must classify as either 1 or 0. It assumes that one has a stream of labeled examples $\{(\mathbf{x}, y), (\mathbf{x}', y'), \dots\}$, where each label $y$ is a 1 or 0. The goal is to correctly predict a new vector $\mathbf{x}''$ as 1 or 0 before seeing its true label $y''$. In our setup, the labels $y$ are the $j$-th bit of the next state vector $\mathbf{x}'$ given the current state vector $\mathbf{x}$. Logistic regression defines a family of functions, each parameterized by a weight vector $\mathbf{w}$ of dimension $n + 1$. We do on-line learning for logistic regression via one fast stochastic gradient descent weight vector update per new observation, where $\mathbf{w}$ is updated to $\mathbf{w}'$ based on the difference between the true label $x'_j$ and the label predicted by $\mathbf{w}$ when evaluated as $\hat{x}'_j = (1+e^{-\mathbf{w}\cdot\mathbf{x}})^{-1}$, where $\mathbf{w}\cdot\mathbf{x} = w_0 + w_1x_1 + \dots + w_nx_n$. Although strictly speaking logistic regression can be thought of as treating each input bit as independent, it is not by any means naive or inappropriate, as many seemingly difficult learning problems boil down to linear separability in a high dimensional space [15], which is precisely what its weight vector $\mathbf{w}$ models.

Linear regression is a widely-used learning algorithm used to fit a curve to real-valued data [7]. The word "linear" refers to the fact that the predicted curve is a *linear combination* of the input data, and does not imply that the predicted curve will be a straight line. It takes as input a stream of examples $\{(\mathbf{x}, y), (\mathbf{x}', y'), \dots\}$, where each label $y$ is a real number. The goal is to correctly predict the $y''$ associated with each new vector $\mathbf{x}''$ before seeing the true answer. In our setup, the labels $y = \phi_i(\mathbf{x}')$ are produced by interpreting the $i$-th 32-bit word of the state vector $\mathbf{x}'$ as an integer. Like logistic regression, linear regression defines a family of functions, each parameterized by a weight vector $\mathbf{w}$ of dimension $K + 1$, and on-line learning involves updating the current weights $\mathbf{w}$ to $\mathbf{w}'$ based on the difference between the true label $\phi_i(\mathbf{x}')$ and the label predicted by $\mathbf{w}$ when evaluated as the polynomial $\widehat{\phi_i(\mathbf{x}')} = w_0 + \sum_{k=1}^{K} w_k\phi_i(\mathbf{x})^k$.

Linear regression is most useful when our system needs to predict integer-valued features such as loop induction variables, while logistic regression is more general and attempts to predict any bit whatsoever. We run multiple instances of each predictor with different learning rates, and then unify their predictions using the Randomized Weighted Majority Algorithm discussed in the next section. Learning, like speculative execution, occurs in parallel and out of band with execution on the main thread. We use the fast, on-line forms of the gradient descent learning algorithms for both linear and logistic regression.

### 4.5 Allocator

The allocator is responsible for unifying multiple predictions into state vectors from which it schedules speculative execution.

#### 4.5.1 Combining multiple predictions

We use an approach known as "prediction from expert advice" [8]. This approach makes no assumptions about the quality or independence of individual predictors or 'experts'.

Some predictors are better at predicting certain bits of our state vectors than others, so we want to mix and match predictors at the bit level, even if some of the predictors internally operate at a higher semantic level. Prediction from expert advice gives us a theoretically sound way to combine wildly-different predictors. In this approach, the goal is to minimize *regret*: the amount by which the predictive accuracy of an ensemble of predictors falls below that of the single best predictor in hindsight [8, 11, 12, 39].

The allocator uses the Randomized Weighted Majority Algorithm (RWMA) [39] because it comes with strong theoretical guarantees that bound regret. These regret bounds say, intuitively, that for each bit of the current program, if there exists in our ensemble a good predictor for that particular bit, then after a short time the error incurred by the weighted majority votes for that bit will be nearly as low as if we had clairvoyantly only used that best predictor from the start. We get this guarantee at the cost of having to keep track of the per-bit error rate of each learning algorithm, since the RWMA algorithm uses these error rates to adjust the weights it assigns to each predictor.

#### 4.5.2 Scheduling speculative threads

The allocator is responsible for combining predictions and then scheduling speculative executions. It picks the states from which to speculate and for how long to run each speculative computation by balancing the payoff of each state against its uncertainty about that state. For each potential speculative execution, the allocator uses Eq. 2 to calculate the *expected utility*: the length of the cached trajectory times the probability that it will be used by the main thread.

By combining per-bit predictions, the allocator produces a single distribution with the form of Eq. 2. Thus, the allocator combines the results of multiple on-line learning algorithms using a regret minimization framework to form a single unified conditional probability distribution. This distribution is general in the sense that it can take any state as input. This includes unobserved states, and in particular, predicted states. It allows us to both generate predictions and assign them probabilities that represent our belief that they will be correct. The allocator then uses this equation to 'roll out' predictions for $k$ supersteps in the future by using predicted states as input to recursively generate later predictions. Out of the total set of generated predictions, the allocator selects the subset that maximizes the expected utility of speculating from these predictions.

## 5. Evaluation

ASC is a new architecture strongly motivated by current trends in hardware and, in the case of LASC, demonstrates a way to leverage machine learning techniques for transparent scaling of execution. As such, we have no expectation for our implementation to *immediately* outperform decades of research on parallelizing compilers and hardware-based speculation. ASC is a promising long-term approach for which we have two goals in our evaluation. First, we want to demonstrate the potential of ASC by showing that we are able to make accurate predictions and that it is possible to use these predictions to produce significant scalability of sequential binary programs. Second, we want to demonstrate that our prototype system achieves some of these benefits in practice, limited only by implementation details that require further engineering and tuning.

We first introduce the three benchmark programs we use and then present data that demonstrates the efficacy of our predictors and method for combining their predictions. Next, we describe the hardware platforms on which we evaluate our software implementation of the ASC architecture and present micro-benchmark results to quantify critical aspects of its implementation. Then we present scaling results for both idealized and actual realizations of our implementation.

### 5.1 Benchmarks

We evaluate three benchmark programs to illustrate different weaknesses and strengths in our system. While each of the three benchmarks is an unmodified $x86$ binary program, their opcode use is fairly standard and simple. Our fine-grained dependency-tracking simulator is undergoing active improvement, but it does not yet fully support executing benchmark programs with the complexity of SPECINT.

Each of our three benchmark programs can be manually parallelized; this choice allows us to compare ASC's performance to manual parallelization and is also motivated by the widespread existence of diverse programs that could be manually parallelized but are not. In our collaborations with computational scientists, we repeatedly encounter situations where the scientific team either lacks the expertise to manually parallelize their programs or have invested significant time in parallelizing an application for one piece of hardware only to discover that porting to a new machine requires essentially rewriting their parallel implementation from scratch. To escape this treadmill, our work demonstrates the exciting possibility of simply running *one* sequential binary program on a laptop, a commodity multicore system, and a massively parallel supercomputer, obtaining attractive scalability on all three.

Our first benchmark is the `Ising` kernel, a pointer-based condensed matter physics program. It came to our attention because our colleagues in applied physics found that existing parallelizing compilers were unable to parallelize it. The program walks a linked list of spin configurations, looking for the element in the list producing the lowest energy state. Computing the energy for each configuration is computationally intensive. Programs that use dynamic data structures are notoriously difficult to automatically parallelize because of the difficulties of alias analysis in pointer-based code [50]. We demonstrate that by predicting the addresses of linked list elements, LASC parallelizes this kernel.

The second benchmark is the `2mm` multiple matrix multiply kernel in Polybench/C, the Polyhedral Benchmark suite [46]. It computes $D = \alpha ABC + \beta D$, where $A, B, C, D$ are square integer matrices and $\alpha, \beta$ are integers. This benchmark is, in principle, highly amenable to conventional parallelizing compiler techniques, at least on a shared memory multiprocessor if not on a supercomputer. We tried every setting of loop parallelization that we could find for GCC 4.7.3, but in the best case the resultant OPENMP parallel binary still ran *slower* than the sequential binary. In any case, we use this benchmark to demonstrate that the on-line learning algorithms in LASC automatically identify the same structure that a static compiler identifies, but without requiring language-level semantic analysis. By identifying the dependencies of repeating patterns in execution—e.g., dot products between rows of $A$ and columns of $B$—neither LASC nor conventional compilers do value prediction for the entries of $D$.

The third benchmark is the `Collatz` kernel. This program iterates over the positive integers in its outer loop, and in its inner loop performs a notoriously chaotic property test [36]. The property being tested is the conjecture that, starting from a positive integer $n$, then repeatedly dividing by 2 if $n$ is even and multiplying by 3 and adding 1 if $n$ is odd, this sequence will eventually converge to 1. This program is easily parallelized by spawning separate threads to test different values of $n$. LASC identifies the latter parallelization opportunity in the outer loop, but importantly also automatically memoizes parts of the inner loop, since in practice the sequence does converge for all integers being tested.

### 5.2 Predictor accuracy

As our prediction accuracy relies in part on the recognizer's ability to find IP values that induce a predictable sequence of hyperplane intersections, we first examine our superstep statistics. Then, we examine the accuracy of our individual predictors, the regret-minimized error rate of the predictor ensemble, and the resulting trajectory cache hit rates.

One of the recognizer's responsibilities is to find a value of the recognized instruction pointer (RIP) that occurs often enough to be useful but not so often as to make the speculative execution stored in each resultant cache entry too short to be worth the lookup cost. In Table 1 we show the recognizer's performance on our three benchmarks in terms of the number of instructions in the full program execution (total time), how long it took to identify a useful RIP (converge time), and the number of speculatively executed instructions encapsulated in a typical cache entry (average jump).

| | Ising | 2mm | Collatz |
|---|---|---|---|
| Total time (cycles) | $2.3 \times 10^{10}$ | $7.5 \times 10^{9}$ | $2.0 \times 10^{11}$ |
| Converge time (cycles) | $2.3 \times 10^{7}$ | $2.5 \times 10^{7}$ | $1.0 \times 10^{5}$ |
| Average jump (cycles) | $1.2 \times 10^{7}$ | $1.3 \times 10^{7}$ | $3.8 \times 10^{6}$ |
| State vector size (bits) | $2.0 \times 10^{5}$ | $5 \times 10^{7}$ | $3 \times 10^{3}$ |
| Cache query size (bits) | 640 | 808 | 160 |
| Lines of C code | 75 | 154 | 15 |
| Unique IP values | 206 | 162 | 40 |

**Table 1.** Recognizer statistics for each benchmark.

Since our cache is distributed over parallel machines, queries to and responses from the cache are compressed using the Meyers binary differencing algorithm [44]. Table 1 shows that the average cache query message size for our three benchmark programs is 3200 parts per million (ppm), 16 ppm, and 53331 ppm, respectively, of the full state vector size (cache response messages are even smaller).

Since the recognizer is effecting an optimization over the set of IP values, Table 1 also shows the number of lines of C code and the number of instruction addresses for each benchmark. Since speculative execution begins and ends at RIPs, the average jump is identical to the average interval between RIP occurrences. The ratio between total time and average jump approximates the program's available scalability (in our system), while the converge time is a lower bound on its sequential portion (in our system). As Table 1 shows, our system converges to a useful RIP and begins speculative execution in less than $10^8$ instructions, and fast-forwards execution by about $10^7$ instructions per jump, so we can in principle automatically scale these benchmarks to thousands of cores.

In Table 2 we examine the error rates of our learning algorithm ensemble in terms of the percentage of incorrect state vector predictions. The data demonstrate that we derive benefit from combining multiple predictors and that it is important to weight the various predictors correctly. The first row of Table 2 gives the default error rate that occurs when we weight each predictor on each bit equally. The second row gives the optimal achievable error rate for our set of predictors if we were able to clairvoyantly use the best predictor for each bit. The third row shows that our on-line regret minimization is able to mix and match the best predictor per bit to achieve an actual error rate within 0.3% of optimal.

| | Ising | 2mm | Collatz |
|---|---|---|---|
| Equal-weight error rate (1 core) | 99.1% | 92.6% | 99.9% |
| Hindsight-optimal error rate (1 core) | 1.1% | 10.2% | 1.7% |
| Actual error rate (1 core) | 1.2% | 3.2% | 1.9% |
| Total predictions (1 core) | 2003 | 599 | 25000 |
| Incorrect predictions (1 core) | 25 | 19 | 475 |
| Cache miss rate (32 cores) | 0.5% | 2.9% | 0.3% |

**Table 2.** Prediction error rates and cache miss rates.

The error rates reported in Table 2 are lower than one might expect for high-dimensional spaces. Since state vectors need only match cache entries on the latter's dependencies, our predictor ensemble need only correctly predict a subset of all bits in order to get credit for a correct overall prediction. The cache miss rates on 32 cores reported in Table 2 are even lower than the error rates in Table 2, since with more available parallelism a wider variety of learning algorithm hyperparameters are explored, resulting in more than one prediction per future state of interest. For example, although `Ising` shows an ensemble error rate of 1.2%, we observe that with 32 cores its cache miss rate is just 0.5%.

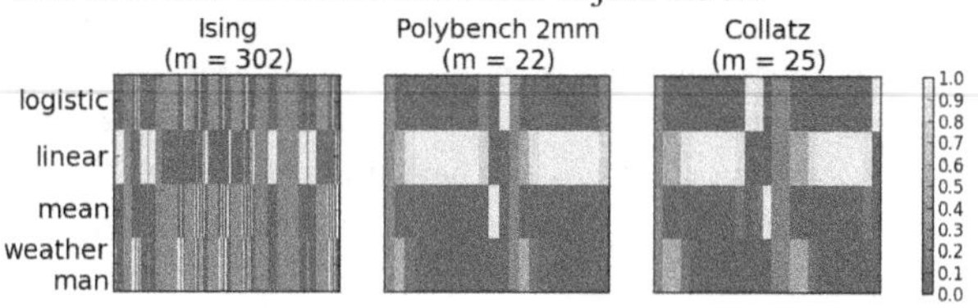


**Figure 3.** Weight matrices for the benchmarks; rows are the four predictors; columns are the $m$ excited bits (bits that have changed from one instance of the RIP to the next).

To evaluate our system's regret minimization, Figure 3 shows the final weight matrices for each benchmark. The columns are the program excitations; i.e., bits that changed at least once between occurrences of the RIP. The rows are the four learning algorithms we described in §4.4.2, and the cells of the matrix are shaded by the magnitude of the weight assigned to each predictor for each bit. Both `Collatz` and `2mm` show a strong preference for the linear regressor, although there are several bits in the flags register for which the logistic regressor is absolutely crucial. We almost removed the mean and weatherman predictors, assuming they would be too simple to provide additional value, but the `Ising` weight matrix clearly shows that all four algorithms contribute significantly.

### 5.3 Software implementation of the ASC architecture

The instruction execution component of TBFS implements 79 opcodes of the 32-bit $x86$ instruction set. It executes free-standing static binary programs compiled with GCC. This produces a simple implementation about which we can easily reason and manually verify, while permitting us to run C programs. The restricted functionality is due to the simplified nature of our prototype and is not fundamental to LASC.

We used three experimental testbeds: an $x86$ server with 32 cores clocked at 1.4 GHz with 6.4 GB of RAM total, an IBM Blue Gene/P supercomputer of which we used up to 16384 cores clocked at 850 MHz each with 512 MB of RAM, and a single-core laptop clocked at 2.4 GHz. The 32-core server runs Linux, while the Blue Gene/P runs the lightweight CNK operating system, and the laptop runs MacOS. All three systems provide an MPI communication infrastructure, but the Blue Gene/P has ASIC hardware acceleration for reduces.

Our software implementation of the ASC architecture has a baseline instruction simulation rate of 2.6 million instructions per second (MIPS) and a dependency tracking instruction simulation rate of 2.3 MIPS. The baseline instruction rate is the number of instructions per second executed when dependency tracking and cache lookups are disabled. The dependency instruction rate shows that dependency tracking has an overhead of approximately 13% above pure architecture simulation. At 2.3 MIPS, our execution overhead is less than that of cycle-accurate simulators, which are usually at around 100 KIPS [20], but more than that of conventional functional simulators, which are usually at around 500 MIPS [20]. There is nothing inherent in either ASC or LASC that necessitates our current execution overhead. Rather, the goal of this paper is to demonstrate the potential of ASC, so we use a testbed that prioritizes ease of experimentation over performance.

Our simple implementation of speculative threads also incurs a significant overhead. Workers make predictions for some $k$-th future instance of the RIP by making recursive predictions. Currently, each worker does this independently to avoid communication costs. The worker with rank $k$ predicts $k$ supersteps in the future, which means that prediction time is currently a linear function of rank, with a prediction wall-clock time of about $103 \cdot k$ $\mu$s on Blue Gene/P.

### 5.4 Scaling results

In this section we show *scaling* results, measured by dividing the single-threaded wall clock time of each benchmark by its parallel execution wall clock time. This ratio normalizes for fixed cost overheads in our system, almost all of which arise from our relatively slow functional simulator, but we do *not* subtract the cost of learning, lookup or any other cost from the wall clock times.

Figure 4 shows scaling results on the `Ising` benchmark for both the 32-core server and the Blue Gene/P supercomputer.

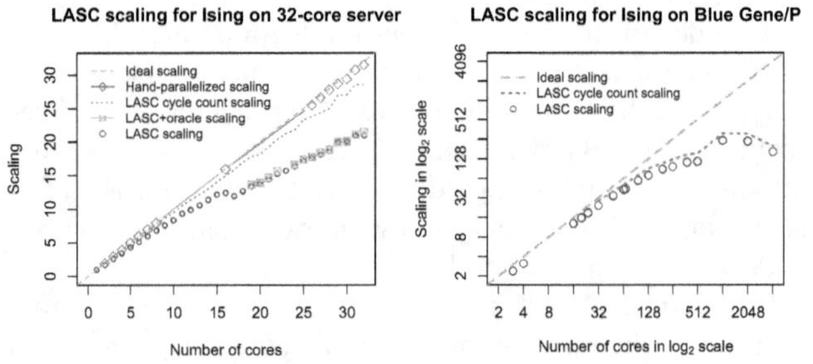


**Figure 4.** Scaling results for `Ising` benchmark.

We show several parallelization results to tease apart the inherent scalability of the program, the limits of our predictors, and the bottlenecks in our implementation. On the 32-core server, the hand-parallelized results show that it is possible to achieve perfect scaling by first iterating over the list, partitioning it into up to 32 separate lists and then computing on each list in parallel. In LASC, potential scaling is limited by the cache hit rate. With infinitely fast cache lookups, we would obtain the performance illustrated by the "cycle count scaling" line. However, our cache lookup is not infinitely fast and produces the results shown in the LASC lines. The "oracle scaling" illustrates the performance our system could achieve with perfect predictions; this measurement holds everything else constant—including the recognizer and allocator policies as well as the times to compute predictions, speculative trajectories and cache queries—while ensuring that the prediction for any particular state is correct. The fact that the actual and oracle scaling lines overlap demonstrates that we are limited only by inefficiencies in our prototype, rather than by prediction accuracy.

There are two different forces at work in the scaling curves of Figure 4. The first arises from the inherent parallelism of the `Ising` benchmark, and the second arises from the artifacts of our prototype. Although the potential energy calculation of `Ising` involves many deeply nested loops, the outermost pattern is just a linked list walk, which enables the recognizer to quickly find a good IP value for speculation; namely, one a few instructions into the prologue of the energy function.

As shown in Table 1, `Ising`'s superstep accounts for approximately 0.05% of its total instruction count, so the best scaling we can expect is approximately 2000. Unsurprisingly, code inspection reveals that its internal linked list has exactly 2000 nodes, which explains the drop-off we see on Blue Gene/P at 2000 cores. However, our scaling peaks at roughly 1024 cores, due to the cost of our current implementation of recursive prediction. When LASC has many cores at its disposal, cores are dispatched to make predictions at increasingly distant instances of the RIP. As explained in §5.3, workers make predictions from predictions for future instances of the RIP, but do not currently share this 'rollout' computation across cores, so prediction time grows linearly in the number of cores. Our next release will use a parallel transitive closure to greatly improve this.

Figure 5 shows scaling results for Polybench/C `2mm` on the 32-core server. Although `2mm` (matrix multiply) also has

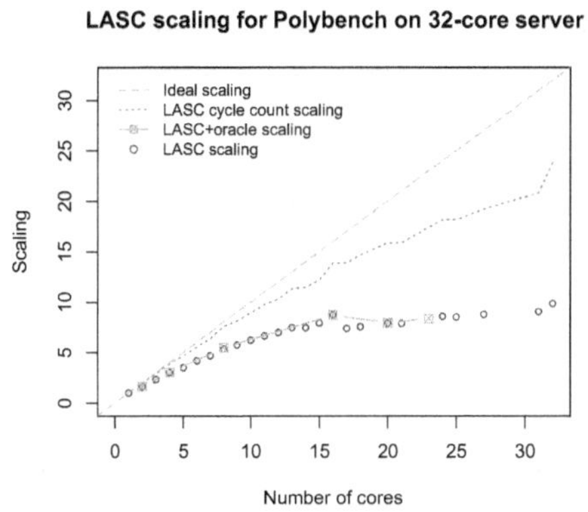


**Figure 5.** Scaling results for Polybench 2mm.

somewhat regular structure arising from its dot product loops, its scaling is less impressive than that of `Ising` in that it asymptotes at about 10×, which makes it not worth benchmarking on Blue Gene/P. Again, there are two different forces at work. For 2mm, the superstep accounts for slightly less than 0.2% of the total execution, which limits its potential scalability to 600. The cycle count line for 2mm in Figure 5 shows encouraging potential scaling possible with our predictors. The oracle line in Figure 5 indicates that LASC is not limited by prediction accuracy for 2mm, but, as with `Ising`, it is limited by the fact that it does not currently parallelize recursive prediction. The effect is more pronounced here, because we have more bits to predict. As discussed in §5.2, we track two orders of magnitude more bits for 2mm than for `Ising`, so predictions take two orders of magnitude longer. Given the relatively small message sizes our prototype achieved for transmitting predicted state vectors, we are optimistic that once we parallelize recursive prediction, our prototype will demonstrate greatly improved overall scalability.

Figure 6 shows scaling results for the `Collatz` benchmark on all three of our platforms. Tables 1 and 2 indicate that our system finds `Collatz` to be easily predicted (98.1% accuracy) with an available parallelism of about 25000 ×. However, the relatively small number of instructions between each of the $10^8$ iterations of the outer loop forces our recognizer to adapt and consider only every 4000 instances of the RIP, which limits the overall parallelism. Our scaling results for `Collatz` on the 32-core and Blue Gene/P platforms are encouraging but somewhat expected, given that the outer loop of the benchmark is effecting an exhaustive search. What is more interesting is the structure that LASC automatically discovered in the inner loop of the benchmark. Recall that testing the Collatz conjecture is an iterative process of computing $n/2$ or $3n+1$. As the conjecture is never disproven, ultimately, every integer tested eventually converges to 1 through shared final subsequences that end in 1. For example, for all but very small integers, the final five elements must be 16, 8, 4, 2, 1. As the inner loop tests the conjecture, even though the process is chaotic, it produces patterns exploited by LASC. We demonstrate this by running `Collatz` on our single-core laptop, on which parallel speculation is not possible, but on which the recognizer still detects frequently occurring IP values and uses the intervening computation to effect generalized memoization. LASC scales up execution on a single core by using cache entries from the program's own past, which results in the scaling shown in the rightmost graph of Figure 6. As the outer loop tests increasingly large integers, memoized subsequences comprise smaller relative fractions of execution, so scaling eventually asymptotes. Note that we disabled this pure memoization capability for the 32-core server and Blue Gene/P experiments to highlight the scaling available exclusively from prediction and speculation.

### 5.5 Limitations

While we find these early results exciting, there are obvious limitations to our current implementation as well as limitations inherent in ASC. The results in §5.4 all showed relative scaling, rather than absolute speedup, because our prototype is several orders of magnitude slower than a native core at sequential execution. We are exploring the following directions for improving its performance. There are four components required to implement our architecture: (1) an execution engine used for both ground truth and speculative execution, (2) a mechanism for dependency tracking during execution, (3) a lookup mechanism for large, sparse bit vectors, and (4) a recursive prediction mechanism. For the first component, we are exploring dynamic compilation and process tracing. For the second component, we are exploring compiler static analysis that proves or probabilistically bounds which regions of state space are immutable, as well as transactional memory hardware that tracks dependencies and modifications in state space, reporting them in a representation efficient for transmitting state vector differences between processors. Current measurements of Intel's Haswell transactional memory report less than a factor of two slowdown for large read transactions and almost no slowdown for writes [53]. For the third component, we are exploring a binary decision trie that maximizes the expected utility of our cache by balancing the payoff of each cache entry against the probability of its use. For the fourth component, we are implementing a parallel transitive closure for recursive prediction.

A second limitation is that we have chosen benchmarks that programmers find trivial to parallelize. This was by design. While humans are capable of manually parallelizing programs, ensuring that the resultant parallel program runs well on a machine of any size remains challenging. Further, most computation is invoked by people whose interests lie in the results of the computation and not in the creation of the program. For such users with whom we've interacted, manual parallelization feels like wasted work that gets redone every time they change to a new machine. Our goal is to provide a mechanism that relieves programmers of this burden.

The class of programs for which our architecture is appropriate is, in principle, any program that has "information bottlenecks" in its state space; i.e., segments of execution whose results, when transmitted forward in time as dependencies of later segments of execution, can be significantly compressed. In practice, the limitations of our architecture arise from our system's ability to automatically identify and

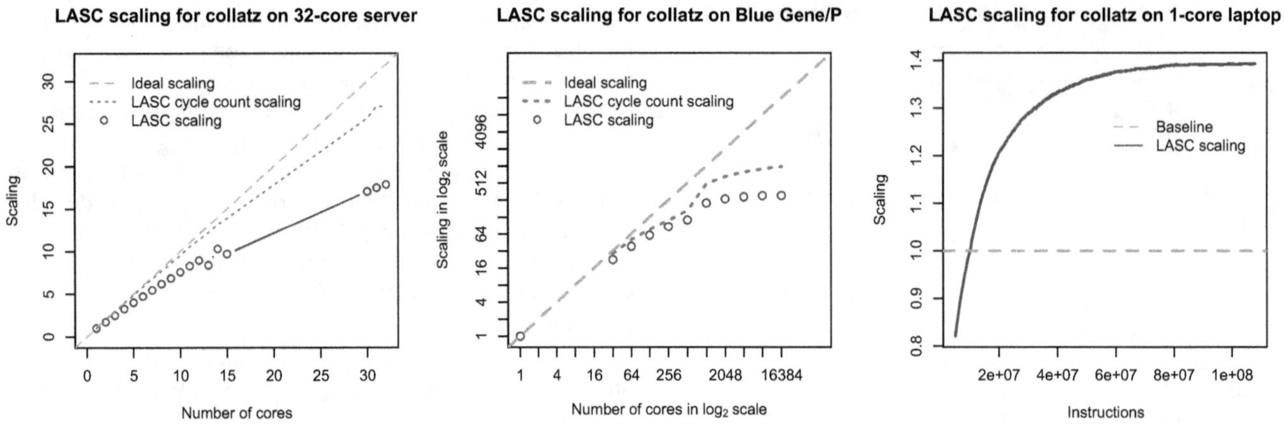


**Figure 6.** Scaling results for `Collatz` benchmark. The left and center plots are the same measurements as in Figure 4, illustrating scaling resulting from prediction and speculative trajectory evaluation. In contrast, the rightmost plot illustrates scaling by simply caching the program's past trajectory – a form of generalized memoization with no predictions involved.

approximate these information-flow structures in state space. Like other architectures that have tried to exploit parallelism over large windows of execution, we are also limited by our ability to store and look up large speculative state vectors. While these identification, prediction, and lookup problems are difficult in general, taken together they are a promising reduction from the overall automatic parallelization problem, as they are themselves inherently highly scalable. Since it is relatively straightforward for our architecture to incorporate the results of static analysis, the class of programs for which our architecture is appropriate has a large overlap with the set of programs targeted by conventional parallelizing compilers.

Lastly, the theory of P-completeness tells us that there are fundamental limits to parallelism [4, 23]. Some problems simply do not admit any parallel solution that runs significantly faster than their sequential solution, e.g., it is extremely unlikely that any system, human or automatic, will ever significantly parallelize an iterated cryptographic hash. Our goal is to design an architecture capable of pushing up against these information-theoretic limits of parallelism; our regret minimization framework (§4.5.1) is explicitly designed with this in mind, as it allows us to coherently incorporate predictive hints from a wide breadth of tools.

## 6. Conclusion

We have presented an architecture and implementation that extracts parallelism automatically from structured programs. Although `Collatz` and `2mm` have easily parallelized structure, `Ising` uses dynamically allocated structures, which are frequently not amenable to automatic parallelization. Our learning-based implementation is currently limited by its recursive prediction time, but is still able to scale to hundreds of cores. It is particularly encouraging that we are able to achieve high predictive accuracy, and that we obtain cache hit rates even higher than our predictive accuracy by tracking dependencies during speculative execution. There are a number of avenues for extending this work. A few straightforward improvements to our implementation will bring actual performance much closer to possible performance. Developing and evaluating different predictors and recognizers is an obvious next step. Hybrid approaches that use the compiler to identify structure have the potential to alleviate the bottleneck due to training time – we could begin speculative execution immediately based upon compiler input and simultaneously begin training models to identify additional opportunities for speculation. We have only just begun exploring reusing the trajectory cache across different invocations of the same program as well as slightly modified versions of the program. Incorporating persistent storage into this model is also a challenging avenue of future work. On one hand, persistent storage simply makes the state bigger; on the other, it makes the state sufficiently large that the approach could prove ineffective. The ASC architecture can be extended naturally to encompass I/O. Like the contents of memory and registers, output data is computed from existing state. Input data will be handled by naturally extending LASC's prediction framework to modeling the input distribution, e.g., learning a probabilistic model consistent with the histogram of observed inputs. There are obvious parallels between our dependency tracking and transactional memory. It would be interesting to explore hybrid hardware/software approaches to ASC. While we have realized ASC in a learning-based framework, there are radically different approaches one might take. We hope to explore such alternatives with other researchers.

## Acknowledgments

The authors would like to thank Gerald Jay Sussman, Miguel Aljacen, Jeremy McEntire, Ekin Dogus Cubuk, Liz Bradley, Eddie Kohler, Benjamin Good and Scott Aaronson for their contributions. This work was supported by the National Science Foundation with a Graduate Research Fellowship under Fellow ID 2012116808 and a CAREER award under ID CNS-1254029 and CNS-1012798, and by the National Institutes of Health under Award Number 1R01LM010213-01. This research was awarded resources at the Argonne Leadership Computing Facility under the INCITE program, which is supported by the Office of Science of the U.S. Department of Energy under contract DE-AC02-06CH11357.

## References


[1] Vikram S. Adve, John Mellor-Crummey, Mark Anderson, Jhy-Chun Wang, Daniel A. Reed, and Ken Kennedy. An integrated compilation and performance analysis environment for data parallel programs. In *Proceedings of the 1995 ACM/IEEE conference on Supercomputing (CDROM)*, Supercomputing '95, New York, NY, USA, 1995. ACM.

[2] Haitham Akkary and Michael A. Driscoll. A dynamic multithreading processor. In *Proceedings of the 31st annual ACM/IEEE international symposium on Microarchitecture*, MICRO 31, pages 226–236, Los Alamitos, CA, USA, 1998. IEEE Computer Society Press.

[3] Saman P. Amarasinghe and Monica S. Lam. Communication optimization and code generation for distributed memory machines. In *Proceedings of the ACM SIGPLAN 1993 conference on Programming language design and implementation*, PLDI '93, pages 126–138, New York, NY, USA, 1993. ACM.

[4] Sanjeev Arora and Boaz Barak. *Computational complexity: a modern approach*. Cambridge University Press, 2009.

[5] Jean-Loup Baer and Tien-Fu Chen. An effective on-chip preloading scheme to reduce data access penalty. In *Proceedings of the 1991 ACM/IEEE conference on Supercomputing*, Supercomputing '91, pages 176–186, New York, NY, USA, 1991. ACM.

[6] Vasanth Bala, Evelyn Duesterwald, and Sanjeev Banerjia. Dynamo: a transparent dynamic optimization system. *ACM SIGPLAN Notices*, 35(5):1–12, 2000.

[7] Christopher M. Bishop. *Pattern Recognition and Machine Learning (Information Science and Statistics)*. Springer-Verlag New York, Inc., Secaucus, NJ, USA, 2006.

[8] Avrim Blum. On-line algorithms in machine learning. In Amos Fiat and Gerhard J. Woeginger, editors, *Online Algorithms*, volume 1442 of *Lecture Notes in Computer Science*, pages 306–325. Springer, 1996.

[9] Bill Blume, Rudolf Eigenmann, Keith Faigin, John Grout, Jay Hoeflinger, David Padua, Paul Petersen, Bill Pottenger, Lawrence Rauchwerger, Peng Tu, and Stephen Weatherford. Polaris: The next generation in parallelizing compilers. In *Proceedings Of The Workshop On Languages And Compilers For Parallel Computing*, pages 10–1. Springer-Verlag, Berlin/Heidelberg, 1994.

[10] Michael Boyer, David Tarjan, and Kevin Skadron. Federation: Boosting per-thread performance of throughput-oriented manycore architectures. *ACM Trans. Archit. Code Optim.*, 7(4):19:1–19:38, December 2010.

[11] Nicolò Cesa-Bianchi, Yoav Freund, David Haussler, David P. Helmbold, Robert E. Schapire, and Manfred K. Warmuth. How to use expert advice. *J. ACM*, 44(3):427–485, May 1997.

[12] Nicolo Cesa-Bianchi and Gabor Lugosi. *Prediction, Learning, and Games*. Cambridge University Press, New York, NY, USA, 2006.

[13] Michael K. Chen and Kunle Olukotun. The jrpm system for dynamically parallelizing java programs. In *Proceedings of the 30th annual international symposium on Computer architecture*, ISCA '03, pages 434–446, New York, NY, USA, 2003. ACM.

[14] Marcelo Cintra, José F. Martínez, and Josep Torrellas. Architectural support for scalable speculative parallelization in shared-memory multiprocessors. In *Proceedings of the 27th annual international symposium on Computer architecture*, ISCA '00, pages 13–24, New York, NY, USA, 2000. ACM.

[15] Adam Coates, Andrew Y Ng, and Honglak Lee. An analysis of single-layer networks in unsupervised feature learning. In *International Conference on Artificial Intelligence and Statistics*, pages 215–223, 2011.

[16] A Dasgupta. Vizer: A framework to analyze and vectorize intel x86 binaries. Master's thesis, Rice University, 2002.

[17] James C. Dehnert, Brian K. Grant, John P. Banning, Richard Johnson, Thomas Kistler, Alexander Klaiber, and Jim Mattson. The transmeta code morphing software: using speculation, recovery, and adaptive retranslation to address real-life challenges. In *Proceedings of the international symposium on Code generation and optimization: feedback-directed and runtime optimization*, CGO '03, pages 15–24, Washington, DC, USA, 2003. IEEE Computer Society.

[18] Pradeep K. Dubey, Kevin O'Brien, Kathryn M. O'Brien, and Charles Barton. Single-program speculative multithreading (spsm) architecture: compiler-assisted fine-grained multithreading. In *Proceedings of the IFIP WG10.3 working conference on Parallel architectures and compilation techniques*, PACT '95, pages 109–121, Manchester, UK, UK, 1995. IFIP Working Group on Algol.

[19] Maria florina Balcan, Manuel Blum, Yishay Mansour, Tom Mitchell, and Santosh Vempala. New theoretical frameworks for machine learning, 2008.

[20] Björn Franke. Fast cycle-approximate instruction set simulation. In *Proceedings of the 11th international workshop on Software & compilers for embedded systems*, pages 69–78. ACM, 2008.

[21] Freddy Gabbay and Freddy Gabbay. Speculative execution based on value prediction. Technical report, EE Department TR 1080, Technion - Israel Institue of Technology, 1996.

[22] Noah D. Goodman, Vikash K. Mansinghka, Daniel M. Roy, Keith Bonawitz, and Daniel Tarlow. Church: a language for generative models. *CoRR*, abs/1206.3255, 2012.

[23] Raymond Greenlaw, H. James Hoover, and Walter L. Ruzzo. *Limits to parallel computation: P-completeness theory*. Oxford University Press, Inc., New York, NY, USA, 1995.

[24] Lance Hammond, Mark Willey, and Kunle Olukotun. Data speculation support for a chip multiprocessor. In *Proceedings of the eighth international conference on Architectural support for programming languages and operating systems*, ASPLOS VIII, pages 58–69, New York, NY, USA, 1998. ACM.

[25] Milos Hauskrecht. Linear and logistic regression. Class lecture, 2005.

[26] Maurice Herlihy and J. Eliot B. Moss. Transactional memory: architectural support for lock-free data structures. In *Proceedings of the 20th annual international symposium on computer architecture*, ISCA '93, pages 289–300, New York, NY, USA, 1993. ACM.

[27] Ben Hertzberg. *Runtime Automatic Speculative Parallelization of Sequential Programs*. PhD thesis, Stanford University, 2009.

[28] Engin Ipek, Meyrem Kirman, Nevin Kirman, and Jose F. Martinez. Core fusion: accommodating software diversity in chip multiprocessors. In *Proceedings of the 34th annual international symposium on Computer architecture*, ISCA '07, pages 186–197, New York, NY, USA, 2007. ACM.

[29] E.T. Jaynes. *Probability Theory: The Logic of Science.* Cambridge University Press, 2003.

[30] Daniel A. Jiménez and Calvin Lin. Dynamic branch prediction with perceptrons. In *Proceedings of the 7th International Symposium on High-Performance Computer Architecture*, HPCA '01, pages 197–, Washington, DC, USA, 2001. IEEE Computer Society.

[31] Troy A. Johnson, Rudolf Eigenmann, and T. N. Vijaykumar. Speculative thread decomposition through empirical optimization. In *Proceedings of the 12th ACM SIGPLAN symposium on Principles and practice of parallel programming*, PPoPP '07, pages 205–214, New York, NY, USA, 2007. ACM.

[32] Ken Kennedy and John R. Allen. *Optimizing compilers for modern architectures: a dependence-based approach.* Morgan Kaufmann Publishers Inc., San Francisco, CA, USA, 2002.

[33] Hanjun Kim, Nick P. Johnson, Jae W. Lee, Scott A. Mahlke, and David I. August. Automatic speculative DOALL for clusters. In *Proceedings of the Tenth International Symposium on Code Generation and Optimization*, CGO '12, pages 94–103, New York, NY, USA, 2012. ACM.

[34] Tom Knight. An architecture for mostly functional languages. In *Proceedings of the 1986 ACM conference on LISP and functional programming*, LFP '86, pages 105–112, New York, NY, USA, 1986. ACM.

[35] Aparna Kotha, Kapil Anand, Matthew Smithson, Greeshma Yellareddy, and Rajeev Barua. Automatic parallelization in a binary rewriter. In *Proceedings of the 2010 43rd Annual IEEE/ACM International Symposium on Microarchitecture*, MICRO '43, pages 547–557, Washington, DC, USA, 2010. IEEE Computer Society.

[36] Jeffrey C. Lagarias. The 3x+1 Problem: An Annotated Bibliography, II (2000-2009). *Arxiv*, August 2009.

[37] J. K. F. Lee and A. J. Smith. Branch prediction strategies and branch target buffer design. *Computer*, 17(1):6–22, January 1984.

[38] Mikko H. Lipasti, Christopher B. Wilkerson, and John Paul Shen. Value locality and load value prediction. In *ASPLOS*, pages 138–147, 1996.

[39] Nick Littlestone and Manfred K. Warmuth. The weighted majority algorithm. *Inf. Comput.*, 108(2):212–261, February 1994.

[40] Wei Liu, James Tuck, Luis Ceze, Wonsun Ahn, Karin Strauss, Jose Renau, and Josep Torrellas. POSH: A TLS compiler that exploits program structure. In *Proceedings of the eleventh ACM SIGPLAN symposium on Principles and practice of parallel programming*, PPoPP '06, pages 158–167, New York, NY, USA, 2006. ACM.

[41] Mojtaba Mehrara, Jeff Hao, Po-Chun Hsu, and Scott Mahlke. Parallelizing sequential applications on commodity hardware using a low-cost software transactional memory. In *Proceedings of the 2009 ACM SIGPLAN conference on Programming language design and implementation*, PLDI '09, pages 166–176, New York, NY, USA, 2009. ACM.

[42] Donald Michie. "Memo" Functions and Machine Learning. *Nature*, 218(5136):19–22, April 1968.

[43] Andreas Moshovos, Scott E. Breach, T. N. Vijaykumar, and Gurindar S. Sohi. Dynamic speculation and synchronization of data dependences. In *Proceedings of the 24th annual international symposium on Computer architecture*, ISCA '97, pages 181–193, New York, NY, USA, 1997. ACM.

[44] Eugene W. Myers. An o(nd) difference algorithm and its variations. *Algorithmica*, 1:251–266, 1986.

[45] Todd Mytkowicz, Amer Diwan, and Elizabeth Bradley. Computer systems are dynamical systems. *Chaos: An Interdisciplinary Journal of Nonlinear Science*, 19(3):033124, 2009.

[46] Louis-Noel Pouchet. Polybench/c: the polyhedral benchmark suite.

[47] Zach Purser, Karthik Sundaramoorthy, and Eric Rotenberg. A study of slipstream processors. In *Proceedings of the 33rd annual ACM/IEEE international symposium on Microarchitecture*, MICRO 33, pages 269–280, New York, NY, USA, 2000. ACM.

[48] Carlos García Quiñones, Carlos Madriles, Jesús Sánchez, Pedro Marcuello, Antonio González, and Dean M. Tullsen. Mitosis compiler: an infrastructure for speculative threading based on pre-computation slices. In *Proceedings of the 2005 ACM SIGPLAN conference on Programming language design and implementation*, PLDI '05, pages 269–279, New York, NY, USA, 2005. ACM.

[49] George Radin. The 801 minicomputer. In *Proceedings of the first international symposium on Architectural support for programming languages and operating systems*, ASPLOS I, pages 39–47, New York, NY, USA, 1982. ACM.

[50] Easwaran Raman, Neil Vachharajani, Ram Rangan, and David I. August. Spice: speculative parallel iteration chunk execution. In *Proceedings of the 6th annual IEEE/ACM international symposium on Code generation and optimization*, CGO '08, pages 175–184, New York, NY, USA, 2008. ACM.

[51] Ram Rangan, Neil Vachharajani, Manish Vachharajani, and David I. August. Decoupled software pipelining with the synchronization array. In *Proceedings of the 13th International Conference on Parallel Architectures and Compilation Techniques*, PACT '04, pages 177–188, Washington, DC, USA, 2004. IEEE Computer Society.

[52] David Stork Richard Duda, Peter Hart. *Pattern Classification (Second Edition).* John Wiley & Sons, Inc., 2001.

[53] C. G. Ritson and F. R. M. Barnes. Evaluating intel rtm for cpas. In P. H. Welch et al, editor, *Proceedings of Communicating Process Architectures 2013.* Open Channel Publishing Limited, 2013.

[54] Eric Rotenberg, Steve Bennett, and James E. Smith. Trace cache: a low latency approach to high bandwidth instruction fetching. In *Proceedings of the 29th annual ACM/IEEE international symposium on Microarchitecture*, MICRO 29, pages 24–35, Washington, DC, USA, 1996. IEEE Computer Society.

[55] Silvius Rus, Lawrence Rauchwerger, and Jay Hoeflinger. Hybrid analysis: static & dynamic memory reference analysis. *Int. J. Parallel Program.*, 31(4):251–283, August 2003.

[56] Yiannakis Sazeides. Instruction-isomorphism in program execution. In *In Proceedings of the Value Prediction Workshop*, pages 47–54, 2003.

[57] Jeremy Singer, Gavin Brown, and Ian Watson. Deriving limits of branch prediction with the fano inequality, 2006.

[58] James E. Smith. A study of branch prediction strategies. In *Proceedings of the 8th annual symposium on Computer Architecture*, ISCA '81, pages 135–148, Los Alamitos, CA, USA, 1981. IEEE Computer Society Press.

[59] Avinash Sodani and Gurindar S. Sohi. An empirical analysis of instruction repetition. In *Proceedings of the eighth international conference on Architectural support for programming languages and operating systems*, ASPLOS VIII, pages 35–45, New York, NY, USA, 1998. ACM.

[60] Gurindar S. Sohi, Scott E. Breach, and T. N. Vijaykumar. Multiscalar processors. In *Proceedings of the 22nd annual international symposium on Computer architecture*, ISCA '95, pages 414–425, New York, NY, USA, 1995. ACM.

[61] J. Greggory Steffan, Christopher B. Colohan, Antonia Zhai, and Todd C. Mowry. A scalable approach to thread-level speculation. In *Proceedings of the 27th annual international symposium on Computer architecture*, ISCA '00, pages 1–12, New York, NY, USA, 2000. ACM.

[62] J. Gregory Steffan, Christopher Colohan, Antonia Zhai, and Todd C. Mowry. The stampede approach to thread-level speculation. *ACM Trans. Comput. Syst.*, 23(3):253–300, August 2005.

[63] Benjamin Vigoda. *Analog logic: Continuous-Time analog circuits for statistical signal processing*. PhD thesis, Massachusetts Institute of Technology, 2003.

[64] Cheng Wang, Youfeng Wu, Edson Borin, Shiliang Hu, Wei Liu, Dave Sager, Tin-fook Ngai, and Jesse Fang. Dynamic parallelization of single-threaded binary programs using speculative slicing. In *Proceedings of the 23rd international conference on Supercomputing*, ICS '09, pages 158–168, New York, NY, USA, 2009. ACM.

[65] Amos Waterland, Jonathan Appavoo, and Margo Seltzer. Parallelization by simulated tunneling. In *Proceedings of the 4th USENIX conference on Hot Topics in Parallelism*, HotPar'12, pages 9–14, Berkeley, CA, USA, 2012. USENIX Association.

[66] Amos Waterland, Elaine Angelino, Ekin D. Cubuk, Efthimios Kaxiras, Ryan P. Adams, Jonathan Appavoo, and Margo Seltzer, *Computational caches*, Proceedings of the 6th International Systems and Storage Conference (New York, NY, USA), SYSTOR '13, ACM, 2013, pp. 8:1–8:7.

[67] J. Yang, K. Skadron, M. Soffa, and K. Whitehouse. Feasibility of dynamic binary parallelization. In *Proceedings of the 4th USENIX conference on Hot Topics in Parallelism*, 2011.

[68] Efe Yardimci and Michael Franz. Dynamic parallelization and mapping of binary executables on hierarchical platforms. In *Proceedings of the 3rd conference on Computing frontiers*, CF '06, pages 127–138, New York, NY, USA, 2006. ACM.

[69] Jenn yuan Tsai and Pen-Chung Yew. The superthreaded architecture: Thread pipelining with run-time data dependence checking and control speculation. In *Proceedings of the conference on Parallel architectures and compilation techniques*, PACT '96, pages 35–46, 1996.

[70] Hongtao Zhong, M. Mehrara, S. Lieberman, and S. Mahlke. Uncovering hidden loop level parallelism in sequential applications. In *High Performance Computer Architecture, 2008. HPCA 2008. IEEE 14th International Symposium on*, pages 290–301, Feb.

[71] Craig Zilles and Gurindar Sohi. Master/slave speculative parallelization. In *Proceedings of the 35th annual ACM/IEEE international symposium on Microarchitecture*, MICRO 35, pages 85–96, Los Alamitos, CA, USA, 2002. IEEE Computer Society Press.

# The Benefit of SMT in the Multi-Core Era: Flexibility towards Degrees of Thread-Level Parallelism

Stijn Eyerman Lieven Eeckhout
Ghent University, Belgium
Stijn.Eyerman@elis.UGent.be, Lieven.Eeckhout@elis.UGent.be

## Abstract

The number of active threads in a multi-core processor varies over time and is often much smaller than the number of supported hardware threads. This requires multi-core chip designs to balance core count and per-core performance. Low active thread counts benefit from a few big, high-performance cores, while high active thread counts benefit more from a sea of small, energy-efficient cores.

This paper comprehensively studies the trade-offs in multi-core design given dynamically varying active thread counts. We find that, under these workload conditions, a homogeneous multi-core processor, consisting of a few high-performance SMT cores, typically outperforms heterogeneous multi-cores consisting of a mix of big and small cores (without SMT), within the same power budget. We also show that a homogeneous multi-core performs almost as well as a heterogeneous multi-core that also implements SMT, as well as a dynamic multi-core, while being less complex to design and verify. Further, heterogeneous multi-cores that power-gate idle cores yield (only) slightly better energy-efficiency compared to homogeneous multi-cores.

The overall conclusion is that the benefit of SMT in the multi-core era is to provide flexibility with respect to the available thread-level parallelism. Consequently, homogeneous multi-cores with big SMT cores are competitive high-performance, energy-efficient design points for workloads with dynamically varying active thread counts.

***Categories and Subject Descriptors*** C.1.4 [*Processor Architectures*]: Parallel Architectures

***Keywords*** Chip Multi-Core Processor; SMT; Single-ISA Heterogeneous Multi-Core; Thread-Level Parallelism


*ASPLOS '14*, March 1–5, 2014, Salt Lake City, Utah, USA.

http://dx.doi.org/10.1145/2541940.2541954

## 1. Introduction

The number of active threads in a processor varies over time, and is often (much) smaller than the number of available hardware thread contexts. This observation has been made across different application domains. Desktop applications exhibit a limited amount of thread-level parallelism, with typically only 2 to 3 active threads [4]. Datacenter servers are often underutilized and seldomly operate near their maximum utilization; they operate most of the time between 10 to 50 percent of their maximum utilization level [2]. Even parallel, multi-threaded applications do not utilize all cores all the time. Threads may be waiting because of synchronization primitives (locks, barriers, etc.) and may yield the processor to avoid active spinning [6]. Finally, in a multi-programmed environment, jobs come and go, and hence, the amount of available thread-level parallelism varies over time.

Workloads with dynamically varying active thread counts imply that multi-core chip designs should balance core count and per-core performance. Few high-performance cores are beneficial at low active thread counts, while a sea of energy-efficient cores are preferred at high active thread counts. The key question is what processor architecture is best able to deal with dynamically varying degrees of thread-level parallelism. A heterogeneous single-ISA multi-core with a few big cores and many small cores [19], might schedule threads onto the big cores in case there are few active threads, and only schedule threads on the small cores when the number of active threads exceeds the number of big cores. A conventional homogeneous multi-core with Simultaneous Multi-Threading (SMT) cores [31] might schedule threads across the various cores if there are fewer active threads than cores. Each thread would then have an entire core to its disposal, and only when the number of active threads exceeds total core count, could one engage SMT to improve chip throughput. Ideally, core count and size should be dynamically changed depending on the number of active threads, and people have proposed to fuse small cores to bigger cores as a function of the number of active threads [11, 17]. Determining the appropriate processor architecture is not only important in the context of delivering high performance under various workload conditions, it also involves other design concerns such as power/energy as well as cost to design and verify the design, i.e., a heterogeneous and core fusion processor architecture is likely more costly to design and verify than a homogeneous multi-core.

This paper studies major multi-core design trade-offs in the face of dynamically varying degrees of available thread-level parallelism. Through a set of comprehensive experiments, we find that a homogeneous multi-core with big SMT cores outperforms heterogeneous designs, under the same power envelope, when there is a varying degree of thread-level parallelism, for both multi-program and multi-threaded workloads. The intuition is that when there are few active threads, they can be scheduled across the available big cores with a few, or even a single, SMT hardware thread contexts active, and hence achieve good single-thread performance. We also find that a homogeneous multi-core with SMT performs almost as well as a heterogeneous design that also exploits SMT, and that its performance is also close to that of a dynamic multi-core design, in which the configuration (number of big and small cores) can change dynamically depending on the number of active threads.

The result that the performance of a homogeneous multi-core with big SMT cores is comparable to a heterogeneous multi-core design, we believe, is counter-intuitive. It is well-known, and confirmed by our experimental results, that a number of small cores achieve better aggregate performance (throughput) than a high-performance SMT core under the same power budget. Hence, it is to be expected that overall performance will be higher for a homogeneous multi-core with many small cores as well as for a heterogeneous multi-core with a few big cores and many small cores, when there are many active threads in the system. However, under variable active thread workload conditions, a homogeneous design with big SMT cores is a competitive design point because it can more easily adapt to software diversity, and deliver both best possible chip throughput when there are few active threads, and comparable performance when there are many active threads.

While we show that a homogeneous multi-core consisting of all big cores with SMT is competitive to a heterogeneous multi-core in terms of performance, the latter has more opportunities to save power by power-gating idle cores. Cores can only be switched off when there are fewer active threads than cores, resulting in fewer power-gating opportunities for configurations with fewer cores. We find however, that a heterogeneous multi-core has only a slightly better energy-efficiency compared to a homogeneous all-big-core configuration under variable thread-level parallelism.

The overall conclusion from this paper is that, although SMT was designed to improve single-core throughput [31], the real benefit of SMT in the multi-core era is to provide flexibility with respect to the available thread-level parallelism. Consequently, we find that a homogeneous multi-core with big SMT cores is a competitive high-performance, energy- and cost-efficient design point when the active thread count varies dynamically in the workload.

## 2. Motivation

### 2.1 Varying thread-level parallelism

We identify at least four application domains that exhibit varying degrees of available thread-level parallelism during runtime.

**Multi-programmed workloads.** The most obvious reason for having a varying degree of active threads is due to multi-programming. Jobs come and go, and hence the amount of thread-level parallelism varies over time. Jobs are also scheduled out when performing I/O (disk and network activity).

**Desktop applications.** A recent study by Blake et al. [4] quantifies the amount of thread-level parallelism in contemporary desktop applications. They find the amount of thread-level parallelism to be small, with typically only 2 to 3 active threads on average, even after ten years of multi-core processing.

**Server workloads.** Servers in datacenters operate between 10 to 50 percent of their maximum utilization level most of the time according to Barroso and Hölzle [2]. They found the distribution of utilization at a typical server within Google to have a peak around zero utilization and 30 percent utilization. A multi-core server that is underutilized implies that there are only few active threads.

**Multi-threaded applications.** Even multi-threaded applications may not have as many active threads as there are software threads at all times during the execution. Threads may be waiting because of synchronization due to locks, barriers, etc., and may yield to the operating system to avoid active spinning. Figure 1 quantifies the number of active threads when running the PARSEC benchmarks [3] on a twenty-core processor. (We refer to Section 3 for details on the experimental setup.) Some benchmarks have 20 active threads most of the time (blackscholes, canneal and raytrace), whereas others have 20 active threads only a small fraction of the time (e.g., ferret, freqmine and swaptions). Some benchmarks have either one or twenty active threads (e.g., bodytrack and swaptions), others have a larger variation in the number of active threads (e.g., dedup, ferret and freqmine). On average across all PARSEC benchmarks running on 20 cores, we find that there are 20 active threads only half of the time, and 31% of the time, only 4 or fewer threads are active. Note that these numbers are generated for the parallel part of the application — the so-called region of interest (ROI) as it is defined for the PARSEC benchmarks — so the limited number of active threads only stems from inter-thread synchronization during parallel execution, and is not due to other sequential code such as initialization.

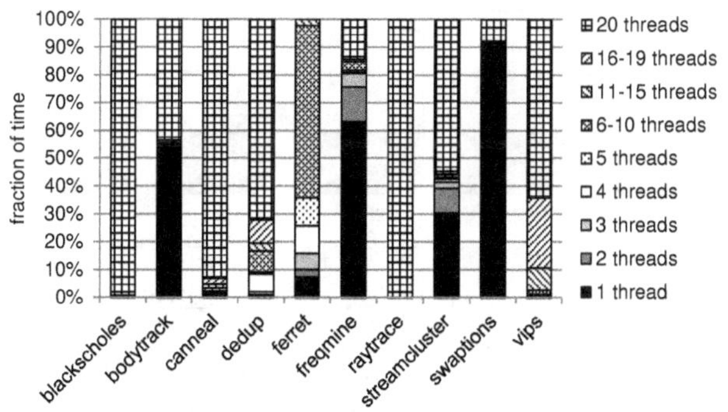


**Figure 1.** Distribution of the number of active threads for the PARSEC benchmarks on a twenty-core processor.

### 2.2 Multi-core design choices

There exist three major multi-core architectures: symmetric or homogeneous, asymmetric or heterogeneous, and dynamic [10]. All cores in a homogeneous multi-core have the same organization; examples are the Intel Sandy Bridge CPU [25], AMD Opteron [15], IBM POWER7 [14], etc. Each core typically implements Simultaneous Multi-Threading (SMT), effectively providing a many-thread architecture, e.g., an 8-core processor with 4 SMT threads per core effectively yields a 32-threaded processor.

A heterogeneous (or asymmetric) multi-core features one or more cores that are more powerful than others. In case of a single-ISA heterogeneous multi-core, there are so-called big, high-performance cores and small, energy-efficient cores. NVidia's Kal-El [22] integrates four performance-tuned cores along with one energy-tuned core, and ARM's big.LITTLE [8] combines a high-performance core with a low-energy core.

A dynamic multi-core is able to combine a number of cores to boost performance of sequential code sections. Core fusion [11, 17] dynamically morphs cores to form a bigger, more powerful core. Thread-level speculation and helper threads [9, 28], in which assist-threads running on other cores help speeding up another thread, could also be viewed as a form of dynamic multi-core. Recently, Khubaib et al. [16] propose MorphCore, which is a high-performance out-of-order core that can morph into a many-threaded in-order core when the demand for parallelism is high.

### 2.3 Goal of this paper

Given the background in workloads and the multi-core design space as just described, the following key question arises: ***How to best design a single-ISA multi-core processor in light of varying degrees of thread-level parallelism in contemporary workloads?*** As mentioned in the introduction, all three design options can deal with varying numbers of active threads, one way or the other. A homogeneous multi-core can distribute the active threads across the various cores and only activate SMT when there are more active threads than cores. A heterogeneous multi-core can schedule the active threads on the big cores and only schedule threads on the small cores when there are more active threads than big cores. A dynamic multi-core can form as many cores as there are active threads. However, without a detailed and comprehensive study, it is unclear which multi-core architecture paradigm yields best performance under varying active thread counts. This paper, to the best of our knowledge, is the first to explore this multi-core design space and comprehensively compare multi-core paradigms in light of variable active thread count. Note that specialized accelerators are not in this paper's scope, as we focus on single-ISA multi-cores.

| | Big core | Medium core | Small core |
|---|---|---|---|
| Frequency | 2.66GHz | 2.66GHz | 2.66GHz |
| Type | Out-of-Order | Out-of-Order | In-Order |
| Width | 4 | 2 | 2 |
| ROB size | 128 | 32 | N/A |
| Func. units | 3 int, 2 ld/st<br>1 mul/div<br>1 FP | 2 int, 1 ld/st<br>1 mul/div<br>1 FP | 2 int, 1 ld/st<br>1 mul/div<br>1 FP |
| SMT contexts | up to 6 | up to 3 | up to 2 |
| L1 I-cache | 32KB<br>4-way assoc | 16KB<br>2-way assoc | 6KB<br>2-way assoc |
| L1 D-cache | 32KB<br>4-way assoc | 16KB<br>2-way assoc | 6KB<br>2-way assoc |
| L2 cache | 256KB<br>8-way assoc | 128KB<br>4-way assoc | 48KB<br>4-way assoc |
| Last-level cache | 8MB, 16-way assoc | | |
| On-chip interconn. | 2.66GHz, full cross-bar | | |
| DRAM | 8 banks, 45ns access time | | |
| Off-chip bus | 8GB/s | | |

**Table 1.** Big, medium and small core configurations.

## 3. Experimental Setup

### 3.1 Multi-core design space

To evaluate the various multi-core paradigms in the context of varying thread counts, we use the following experimental setup. We consider three types of cores: a four-wide out-of-order core (big core), a two-wide out-of-order core (medium core), and a two-wide in-order core (small core), see also Table 1 for more details about these microarchitectures.

We compare all multi-core architectures under the (approximate) same power envelope. We therefore estimate power consumption using McPAT [20] (assuming 45 nm technology and aggressive clock gating). The big core consumes approximately 1.8 times the power of the medium two-wide OoO core on average, and 4.4 times the power of the small two-wide in-order core. We conservatively assume that one big core is power-equivalent to two medium cores and five small cores. We validate later in this section that these scaling factors result in an approximately equal power consumption, even when the big cores execute six threads through SMT (which leads to higher utilization and therefore higher dynamic power consumption). When evaluating energy efficiency in Section 7, we assume idle cores are power gated.

We keep total on-chip cache capacity constant when exploring the multi-core design space, in order to focus on the impact of core types and organization, and not cache capacity. This implies that we have to set the private cache size of the medium core two times smaller compared to the big core, and five times for the small core, see also Table 1. (We pick numbers that are powers of two or just in between two powers of two). The last-level cache (LLC) is shared across all cores, and has the same size for all multi-core configurations (8MB). The on-chip network is a full crossbar between all cores and the shared LLC. Although not realistic, a full crossbar ensures that the results are not skewed in favor of the few large cores configuration, which would experience less contention in the on-chip network compared to a many small cores configuration. We use the multi-core simulator Sniper [5] enhanced with cycle-level out-of-order and in-order core models, as well as SMT support.

Total chip power budget is equivalent to 4 big cores or 8 medium cores or 20 small cores, plus a shared LLC. This allows for 9 possible designs, see Figure 2. (For the heterogeneous designs, we only consider mixes of big cores and medium cores or small cores; we do not consider mixes of medium and small cores). In the remainder of the paper, these designs are referred to as 4B, 3B2m, 3B5s, 2B4m, 2B10s, 1B6m, 1B15s, 8m and 20s, as indicated in the figure. 4B, 8m and 20s are homogeneous multi-cores (all cores of the same type), while the others are heterogeneous. With SMT enabled, we assume that a big core is able to execute up to six threads; a medium core can execute up to three threads; and a small in-order core can execute up to two threads (using fine-grained multithreading), so that all configurations can run up to 24 threads. The SMT core that we simulate implements static ROB partitioning and a round-robin fetch policy [24].

The average total (static plus dynamic) power consumption of the three homogeneous configurations running 24 threads is 46 Watt for 4B, 50 Watt for 8m, and 45 Watt for 20s (averaged across all homogeneous multi-program workloads, see later). The power consumption of the heterogeneous configurations varies between 46 and 50 Watt. This justifies our claim that all configurations operate more or less under the same power envelope.

### 3.2 Workloads

***Multi-program workloads.*** We consider multi-program workloads using the SPEC CPU 2006 benchmarks with their reference inputs. In order to limit the number of simulations, we select 12 representative benchmark-input combinations. The selection is based on the relative performance of the benchmarks on the three core types. We evaluated all 55 SPEC CPU 2006 benchmark-input combinations on the three core designs (big, medium and small) and calculated relative performance with respect to the big core. We then picked 12 benchmarks that cover the full performance range, i.e., the benchmarks that have the highest and lowest relative performance, along with in-between benchmarks picked such as to provide good coverage.

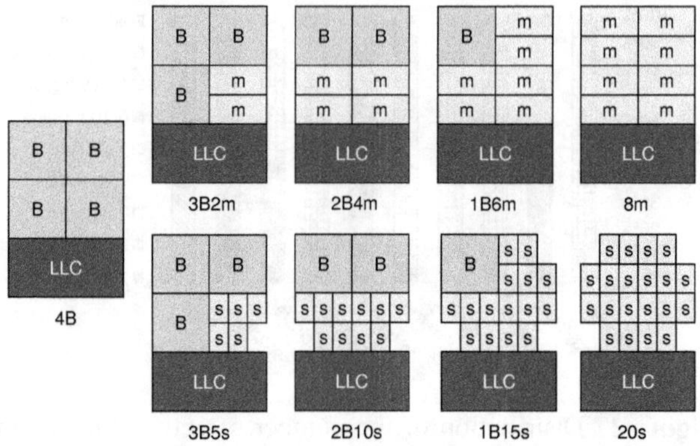


**Figure 2.** The nine power-equivalent multi-core designs considered in this study (B=big core, m=medium core, s=small core).

For each benchmark, we take a 750 million instruction single simulation point to reduce simulation time [26]. When running a multi-program workload, we stop the simulation when all of the programs have executed at least 750 million instructions, thereby restarting programs that reached the end of the 750 million instruction simulation point. We summarize multi-program performance using the system throughput (STP) metric [7] or weighted speedup [27], which is a measure for the number of jobs completed per unit of time. For computing STP, we normalize against isolated execution on the big core. When reporting STP numbers averaged across a set of workloads, we use the harmonic mean because STP is a rate metric (inversely proportional to time). We also calculate average normalize turnaround time (ANTT [7]) to show the impact of the multi-core design on per-program performance.

We evaluate homogeneous multi-program workloads (multiple copies of the same benchmark) as well as heterogeneous multi-program workloads (different benchmarks co-run). We vary the number of programs from 1 to 24. For the heterogeneous multi-program workloads, we randomly construct 12 two-, 12 three-, 12 four-, etc., up to 12 twenty-four-thread combinations, while making sure that every benchmark is included an equal number of times for all thread counts. Velasquez et al. [32] show that this balanced random sampling technique is more representative compared to fully random sampling.

We intentionally limit the number of active threads to 24 to reflect a (realistic) situation with a modest and variable thread count. Given the hardware budget of 4 big cores, this is already a considerable number of threads (6 threads per core). Our results confirm that at a (constantly) large thread count, a design with many small cores is optimal, but in this study we specifically target those workloads that exhibit a variable active thread count. Furthermore, we believe our results are general enough to be projected to larger hardware budgets and thread counts (e.g., 8 large cores and up to 48 threads).

Scheduling also plays an important role in multi-program workload performance. A general principle that we maintain is to first schedule threads on the big core(s) in a heterogeneous design before scheduling on the small cores. Likewise for SMT, we first distribute threads across cores before engaging SMT, e.g., when there are fewer active threads than cores, we run each thread on a separate core, but when there are more active threads than cores, we need to co-run threads on a single core through SMT. A heterogeneous design also implies deciding which thread to execute on which core. Similarly, in the case of SMT, we need to decide which threads to co-run on a core, since different co-runner schedules may have significant impact on performance [27]. As exploring all possible combinations of program schedules is infeasible because of simulation time considerations, we use offline analysis for determining the best possible schedule. We run each benchmark on each of the different core types in isolation, and use this analysis to steer application-to-core mapping for the heterogeneous design points for best performance. Likewise for SMT, we run all possible two-, three-, etc., up to six-program combinations on the big core (up to four for the medium and two for the small cores), and select the best possible co-schedule. This approach ignores the impact of resource sharing among cores to steer scheduling, however, we do account for resource sharing (shared cache, memory bandwidth, etc.) during detailed simulation for the selected schedules.

***Multi-threaded workloads.*** We also evaluate multi-threaded workloads, using the PARSEC benchmarks [3]. We vary the number of threads from 4 to 24 in steps of 4. We only included the benchmarks that allow for a number of threads that is not fixed to a power of 2. We use the medium size input set for all benchmarks, and evaluate the execution time for the parallel part only (the so-called region of interest or ROI) and for the whole program (including the sequential initialization and finalization code). We report speedups versus a four-threaded execution on the 4B configuration.

## 4. Multi-Program Workloads

We now evaluate the performance of the nine multi-core designs for multi-program workloads, i.e., workloads consisting of multiple single-threaded programs. (We will discuss multi-threaded workloads in the next section.) We first discuss performance as a function of thread count, and subsequently compute aggregate performance under the assumption of various active thread count distributions.

### 4.1 Performance as function of thread count

Figure 3 shows average performance for the nine multi-core configurations as a function of the number of threads from 1 to 24. All designs have SMT enabled in all cores, the non-SMT curves can be reconstructed by leveling off performance as soon as thread count equals core count. The interesting observation is that the homogeneous 4B configuration performs well compared to the other homogeneous and heterogeneous designs. Although the heterogeneous designs outperform the 4B configuration for some thread counts, 4B performs well over the full range of thread counts. When thread count is low, 4B yields the highest performance, and when thread count is high, 4B yields only slightly lower performance compared to the many medium and small core designs (8m and 20s).

It is not surprising that multi-core configuration 4B performs well for low thread counts: for 4 or fewer threads, each powerful big core has only one thread running. What is more remarkable is that the SMT multi-core performs also relatively well when thread count is high: for example, when there are 24 threads, each core executes six threads concurrently, but performance is close to that of running 24 threads on 8 medium cores (each three-way SMT) or 24 threads on 20 small cores (4 cores use 2-way SMT, the others execute only one thread).

To explain this behavior, Figure 4 shows the same graphs for two homogeneous workloads, which were picked to illustrate the interesting diversity observed across the various benchmarks; we found the benchmarks to roughly classify into these two categories. Tonto (left graph) shows the intuitively expected behavior: up to 8 threads, performance of the SMT multi-core is better than or similar to the performance of the heterogeneous architectures, but beyond 8 threads, its performance is inferior. Tonto clearly benefits from the higher aggregate execution resources available in the heterogeneous design points as well as in the homogeneous multi-core with all medium or small cores at high active thread counts. For libquantum (right graph) on the other hand, the multi-core with SMT performs approximately as well as the other design points for high thread counts. What happens here is that as the number of threads increases, more and more pressure is put onto the shared resources (shared last-level cache, memory bandwidth, DRAM banks, etc.), upto the point that performance gets largely dominated by shared resource contention and less by individual core performance. In particular, we observe that, for libquantum, memory access time is 4 times higher for 24 threads than for one isolated thread for both the 20s and 4B configurations due to contention on the memory bus. This tightens the gap and flattens out the performance differences between the various multi-core configurations.

It is interesting to note that, at high thread counts, the performance of 4B versus the other design points is slightly smaller for the homogeneous workloads than for the heterogeneous workloads, compare graphs (a) versus (b) in Figure 3. In fact, for heterogeneous workloads and 24 threads, we notice that the performance of 4B is only 7.1% lower than the maximum (2B10s), while for homogeneous workloads, 4B's performance is 11.6% lower than

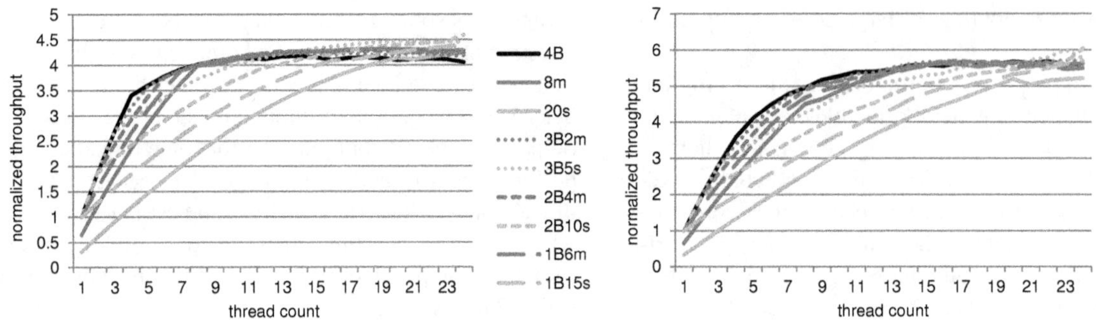


(a) Homogeneous workloads (b) Heterogeneous workloads

**Figure 3.** Comparing the performance for the nine multi-core design points with homogeneous and heterogeneous multi-program workloads.

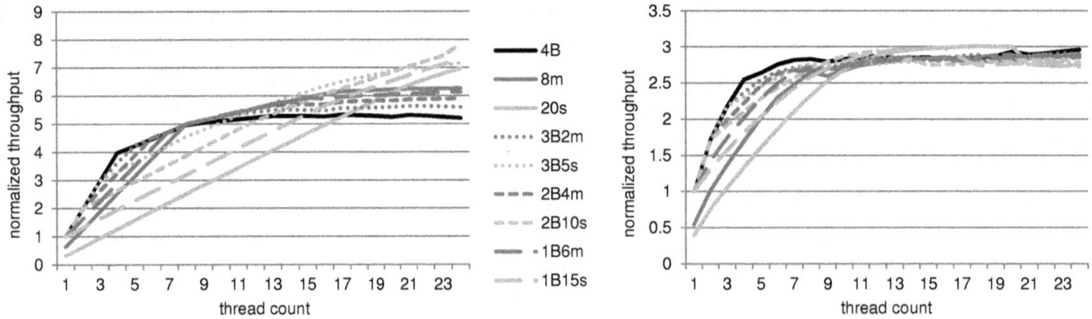


(a) tonto (b) libquantum

**Figure 4.** Performance of the nine multi-core design points for two representative benchmarks (both homogeneous multi-program workloads): (a) tonto and (b) libquantum.

the maximum (2B10s). This is due to the fact that heterogeneous workloads consist of mixes of both memory-intensive and compute-intensive benchmarks. Scheduling a memory-intensive benchmark with compute-intensive benchmarks on one core using SMT enables the memory-intensive benchmark to occupy a larger fraction of the core's private cache (256KB in our study), as the compute-intensive benchmarks are less demanding for cache space. In case of a multi-core with many small cores (20s), each core has a small private cache (48KB in our setup), hence, a memory-intensive benchmark would not get as much cache space. By intelligently scheduling benchmarks to cores and SMT thread contexts, the 4B multi-core is better capable of utilizing cache space than a multi-core with many small cores and relatively smaller private caches.

For completeness, Figure 5 shows the average normalized turnaround time (ANTT) for the homogeneous workloads as a function of thread count (the results for heterogeneous workloads are similar). At small thread counts, the 4B design results in the lowest per-program execution time (highest per-program performance), because all threads can run on a big core. Per-program execution time increases as thread count goes up, because more threads share a core through SMT, reducing per-program performance. For the other extreme configuration 20s, the turnaround time is larger for low thread counts, because of the poorly performing cores, but it remains more stable as thread count increases, due to a smaller degree of sharing. The conclusions are similar to that of the througput results: at low thread counts, 4B has the highest throughput and the lowest per-program execution time, and at high thread counts, the configurations with more and smaller cores have the highest throughput and the lowest per-program execution time, but the 4B configuration remains close.

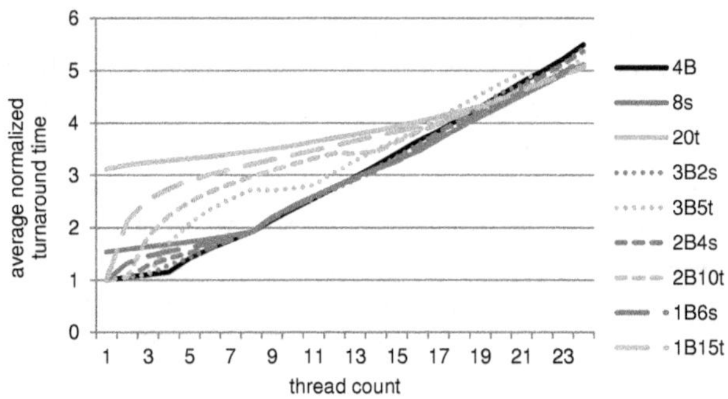


**Figure 5.** Comparing the ANTT for the nine multi-core design points with homogeneous multi-program workloads.

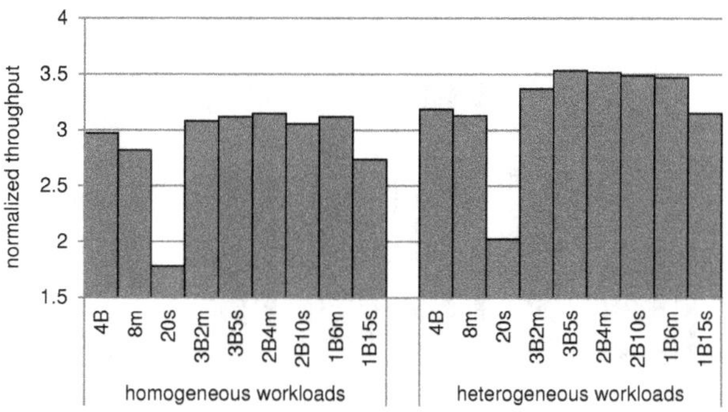


**Figure 6.** Average performance assuming a uniform thread count distribution and no SMT.

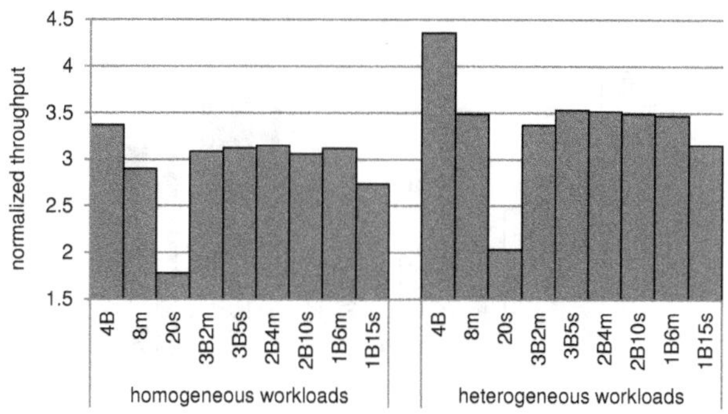


**Figure 7.** Average performance assuming a uniform thread count distribution and SMT in the homogeneous configurations.

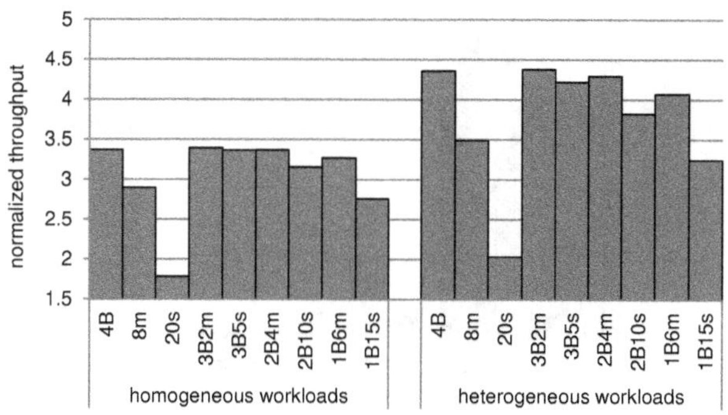


**Figure 8.** Average performance assuming a uniform thread count distribution and SMT in all configurations.

We conclude this section with our first finding:

**Finding #1:** *A homogeneous multi-core consisting of all big SMT cores yields better performance than a heterogeneous multi-core for a small number of threads* (due to the bigger cores) *and only slightly worse for a large number of threads* (because shared resource contention largely dominates performance for workload mixes of memory-intensive applications, and cache capacity can be used more efficiently through intelligent scheduling).

## 4.2 Thread count distributions

We now compare the multi-core designs under various active thread distributions, assuming uniform distributions as well as distributions observed in datacenter operations.

### 4.2.1 Uniform distribution.

We begin with assuming a uniform distribution over 24 threads, i.e., each thread count (1 to 24 threads) has equal probability.

*No SMT.* We first assume that none of the cores implement SMT. Figure 6 shows the average performance for all of the multi-core designs *without* SMT. Each core can execute only one thread at a time, and when there are more threads than cores, multiple threads run on one core sequentially through time-sharing.

Clearly, the 4B configuration outperforms the other *homogeneous* configurations (8m, 20s). Being able to execute faster at low thread counts is more important than achieving a high throughput at high thread counts. This is in line with Amdahl's law: as parallelism increases, the performance of the sequential part (low thread count) dominates the performance of the program as a whole.

The most important conclusion is that the optimal design without SMT is 2B4m for homogeneous workloads and 3B5s for heterogeneous workloads — both heterogeneous multi-core designs. Hence our second finding:

**Finding #2:** *In the absence of SMT, heterogeneous multi-cores outperform homogeneous multi-cores across varying thread counts.* At low thread counts, the big cores in a heterogeneous multi-core can be used to get high performance, while at high thread counts, the larger amount of small cores can be used to exploit thread-level parallelism. This is in line with recent work that advocates single-ISA heterogeneous multi-core processors [10, 19].

***SMT in homogeneous designs.*** We now assume SMT is implemented in the homogeneous designs (4B, 8m and 20s), but not the heterogeneous designs. Figure 7 shows average performance for the various designs. It is interesting to compare this graph against the one in Figure 6, which showed that heterogeneous multi-cores yield higher performance than homogeneous multi-cores when the number of threads varies. Now, through Figure 7, we observe that by adding SMT to the homogeneous multi-cores, the 4B design outperforms the other designs. This leads to:

**Finding #3:** *A homogeneous multi-core with big SMT cores outperforms a heterogeneous multi-core (without SMT) under the same power budget. Put differently, SMT outperforms heterogeneity as a means to cope with varying thread counts.* The intuition is that, at low thread counts, the 4B design with SMT is able to use all 4 big cores, while the number of big cores in the heterogeneous designs is always smaller. At high thread counts, a homogeneous multi-core with big SMT cores allows for more concurrent threads (24 in total) compared to heterogeneous multi-cores (at most 20 in the

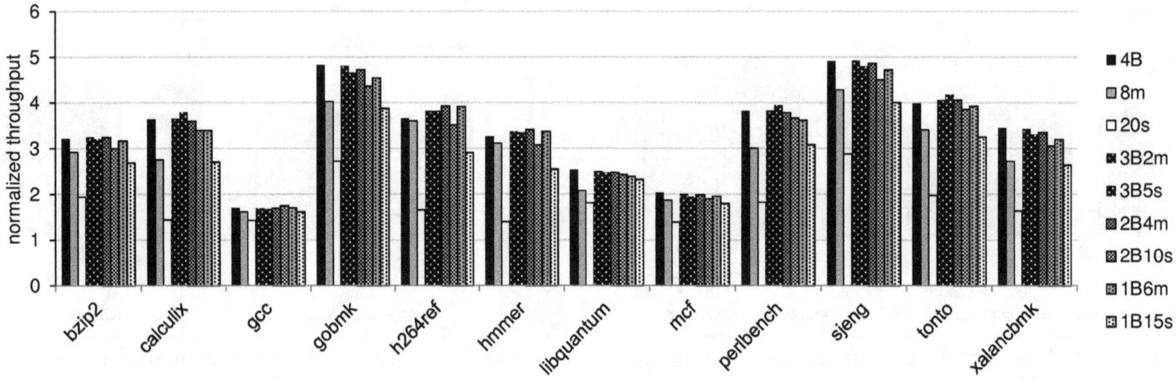


**Figure 9.** Average performance per benchmark assuming a uniform thread count distribution.

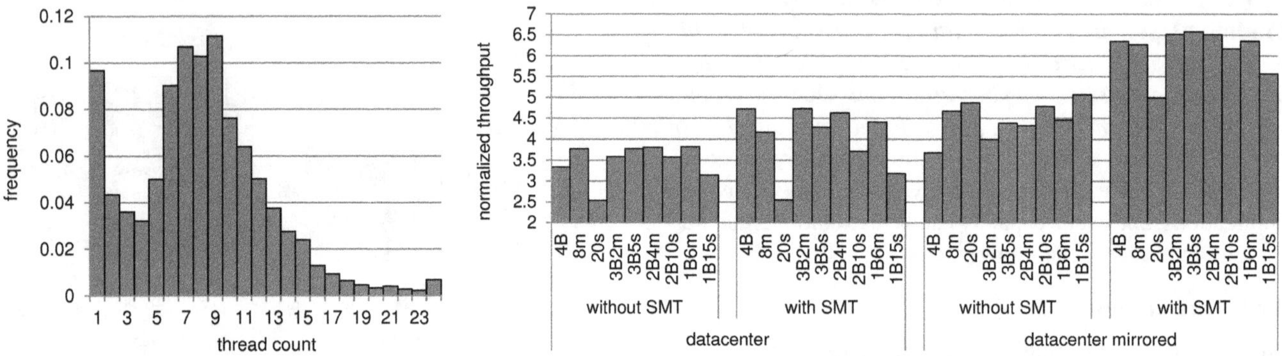


(a) Datacenter distribution

(b) Average throughput

**Figure 10.** Datacenter distribution and average performance using the datacenter distribution and the mirrored datacenter distribution.

20s design point), yielding higher overall throughput within the same power budget.

***SMT in all designs.*** Finally, Figure 8 shows average performance when SMT is enabled in all cores of all designs. For homogeneous workloads, the performance for the best heterogeneous configuration is 5.6% higher than that of 4B *without* SMT in all configurations (Figure 6), but only 0.6% higher than *with* SMT in all designs (Figure 8). For heterogeneous workloads, the homogeneous 4B design even outperforms the best heterogeneous design by 0.5%. Thus, in other words:

**Finding #4:** *The added benefit of combining heterogeneity and SMT is limited.*

It is also interesting to observe that the optimal heterogeneous design shifts from 2B4m without SMT to 3B2m with SMT for the homogeneous workloads, and from 3B5s to 3B2m for the heterogeneous workloads. Hence:

**Finding #5:** *Adding SMT to the heterogeneous designs makes the optimum shift towards fewer and larger cores.* This is in line with the general observation that SMT in larger cores enables flexibility as a function of active thread count.

***Per-benchmark results.*** Figure 9 shows average performance for the various multi-core configurations (SMT enabled in all cores) for each benchmark, assuming a uniform distribution. The results vary across benchmarks: for some benchmarks (calculix, h264ref, hmmer and tonto), 4B performs worse than the best heterogeneous multi-core, while for others it performs similarly, or even slightly better (libquantum and mcf). Detailed analysis of the results revealed that the latter category of benchmarks have high memory bandwidth demands, resulting in bandwidth-bound performance numbers for high thread counts. Section 8.2 contains results with a higher memory bandwidth setting.

### 4.2.2 Datacenter distributions.

Figure 10(b) shows average performance across two different thread count distributions, assuming heterogeneous workload mixes. "Datacenter" is the distribution taken from [2] for CPU utilization in a datacenter, adapted to a workload of at most 24 threads; Figure 10(a) shows the distribution: there is a peak at 1 thread (low utilization) and one at 7 to 9 threads (30%-40% utilization). "Mirrored datacenter" is the same distribution, mirrored around the center. This means that there now is a peak at 24 threads, and one around 16 to 18 threads. We use this distribution to model a more heavily

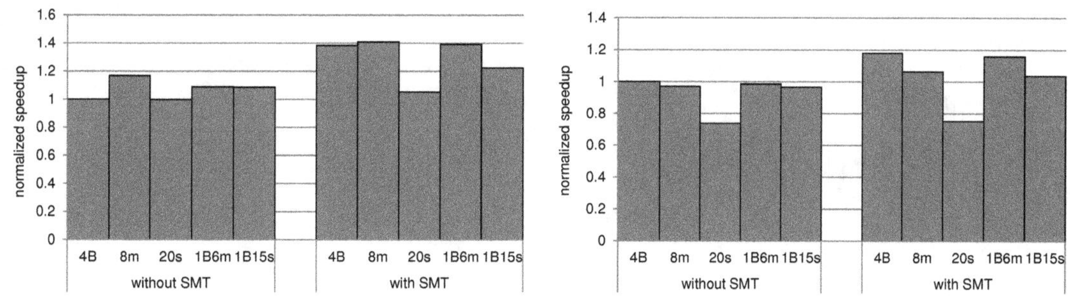


(a) ROI only (b) Whole program

**Figure 11.** Average normalized speedup for all PARSEC benchmarks.

loaded server park, with a distribution skewed to the higher thread counts.

For the datacenter distribution, 1B6m is the best performing configuration without SMT, see Figure 10(b). This is as expected: we have 1 big core for the peak at 1 thread, and 7 cores in total to cover the peak around 7 threads. Adding SMT again makes the fewer but bigger cores configurations more optimal, with the best performance for the 4B configuration. For the mirrored datacenter distribution, the optimum without SMT is 1B15s, because there is a peak at 16 threads. For the configurations with SMT, 3B2m is optimal, with 4B performing only 0.6% worse.

**Finding #6:** *For distributions that are skewed to fewer threads, the 4B configuration with SMT is optimal. For distributions that are skewed towards more active threads, 4B with SMT becomes less optimal, but its performance is very close to the optimum.*

## 5. Multi-Threaded Workloads

As discussed in Section 2, multi-threaded programs can also have a variable number of active threads. When threads have to wait due to synchronization (e.g., a barrier), they can be scheduled out by the operating system to free resources for other runnable threads. Periods with low active thread count are critical to performance, since they exhibit little parallelism and are therefore more difficult to speed up [6]. Achieving high performance at low thread counts is therefore likely to be even more crucial for multi-threaded workloads than for multi-programmed workloads.

We use the PARSEC benchmarks in this section, and always report the maximum speedup across all possible thread counts. Note this does not necessarily equal total core count because of interference between threads in shared resources. We further assume pinned scheduling which pins threads to cores to improve data locality (as done in modern multi-core schedulers [13]); and we execute serial phases on the big core when reporting whole program performance results. We limit the discussion in this section to heterogeneous designs with a single big core as we assume pinned scheduling which does not enable benefiting from multiple big cores. (We verified that none of the other heterogeneous designs have larger speedups than the ones reported here.)

The results, averaged across all benchmarks, are shown in Figure 11. We split up the results for the ROI-only and the whole program, and show the speedups without SMT (i.e., number of threads equal to number of cores) and with SMT. For the ROI-only results without SMT, 8m is the optimal design. This is because most of the applications scale well up to 8 threads, but not beyond. Adding SMT boosts the speedup for the 4B design, and makes its speedup very close to that of 8m. Overall, the 4B design with SMT performs well for benchmarks that have poor parallelism, and performs only slightly worse for programs that scale well.

For the whole-program results, the 4B design performs best both without and with SMT. The 4B design performs best for applications with limited parallelism, and close to optimal for applications that scale better, but that have a large initialization and finalization serial phase. Without SMT, the heterogeneous designs perform close to the 4B configuration: they speed up the serial phases, but on average, the poorly scaling benchmarks achieve better performance on the 4B configuration and this dominates the average. With SMT enabled, the difference between the 4B configuration and the heterogeneous configurations is larger, because 4B with SMT speeds up well-scaling benchmarks more.

Figure 12 shows per-benchmark speedups. For the ROI-only results (top graph), it clearly shows the difference across benchmarks: 20s is optimal for well-scaling benchmarks, while 4B or a heterogeneous design are optimal for poorly scaling benchmarks. For the whole program results (bottom), the optimal configuration is 4B or a heterogeneous design for most of the benchmarks.

**Finding #7:** *SMT is also beneficial for multi-threaded workloads. As for the multi-program workloads, adding SMT lets the optimal design shift to fewer but larger cores. A homogeneous design with big SMT cores outperforms the best heterogeneous design without SMT, and performs close to, and sometimes even slightly better than, the best heterogeneous design with SMT.*

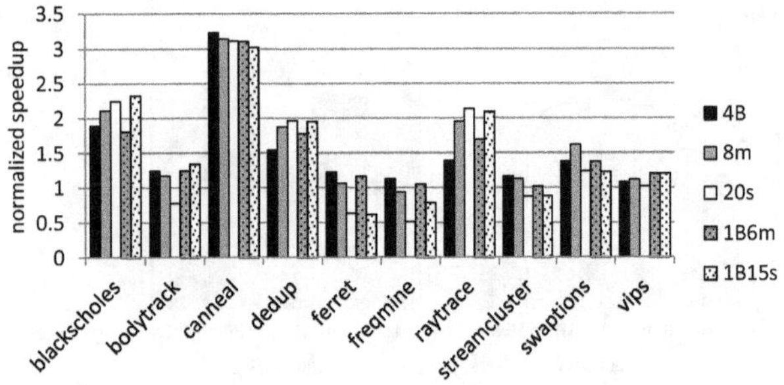


(a) ROI-only

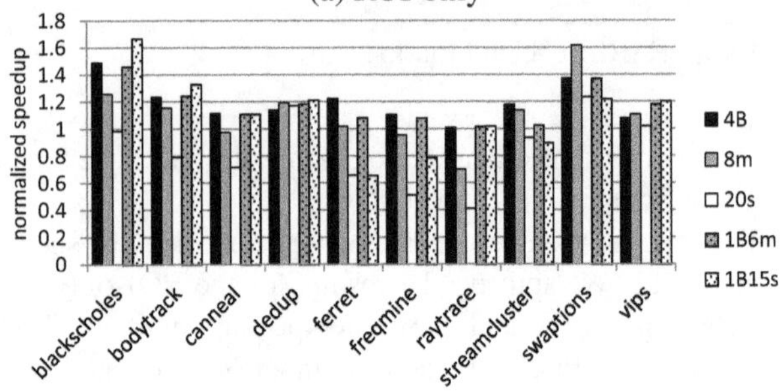


(b) Whole program

**Figure 12.** Normalized speedup for the individual PARSEC benchmarks.

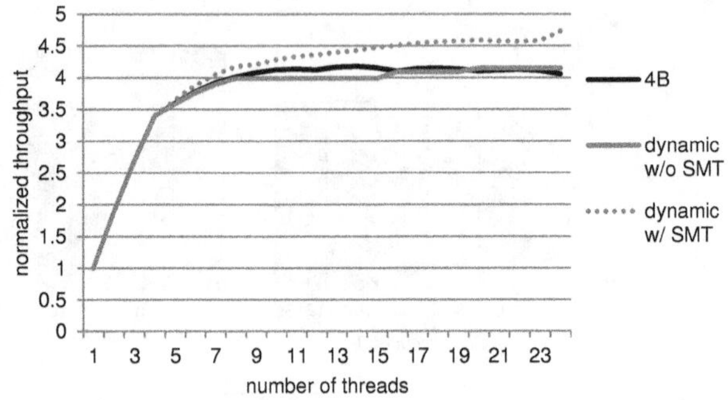


(a) Homogeneous multi-program workloads

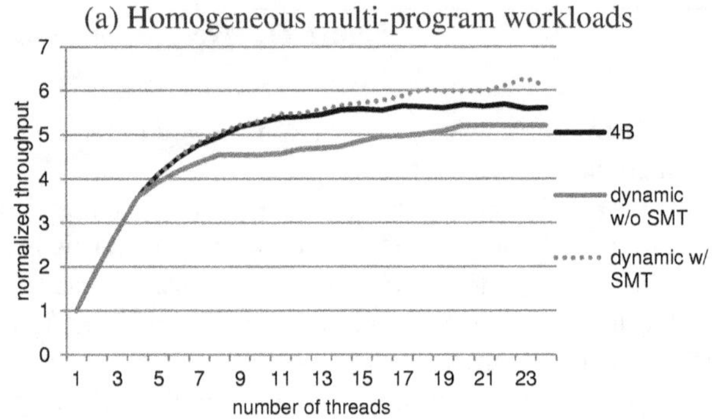


(b) Heterogeneous multi-program workloads

**Figure 13.** Throughput as a function of the number of threads for the 4B configuration with SMT and the dynamic core fusion configuration with and without SMT.

## 6. Dynamic Multi-Cores

Dynamic multi-cores are multi-core processors with a dynamic configuration [11, 17]: core configuration and the number of cores can dynamically vary between many small cores and a few large cores, and in-between heterogeneous configurations. Theoretical studies, such as the one of Hill and Marty [10], show that this type of multi-core is optimal in the context of varying parallelism and varying thread count. Through dynamic adaptation, one or a few big cores can be formed when there is low parallelism, while the configuration is changed to many small cores when there are a lot of active threads. This technique is essentially the inverse of SMT: an SMT core executes a single thread but can execute multiple threads at higher active thread counts; a dynamic multi-core executes threads on independent cores, which can be fused to bigger cores at low active thread counts.

To compare the abilities of a homogeneous multi-core with big SMT cores (4B) versus a dynamic multi-core to cope with varying active thread counts, we assume an ideal dynamic multi-core that can be morphed without overhead into any of the 9 multi-core configurations in Figure 2. This ideal dynamic multi-core chooses the best performing configuration (out of the 9 possible configurations) at each thread count for each workload. This is an optimistic assumption in favor of dynamic multi-cores, since fusing cores is likely to involve a non-negligible time, area and power overhead. Figure 13 compares dynamic multi-cores (both with and without SMT) against the 4B configuration (with SMT) for the homogeneous and heterogeneous multi-program workloads. This figure shows that dynamic multi-cores without SMT yield similar or even worse overall performance. Especially for heterogeneous workloads, SMT seems to perform better than a dynamic multi-core design. The reason is that SMT enables better utilization and higher throughput within the same power budget, especially when the programs are complementary in their resource demands. SMT also allows for more fine-grained parallelism: for the dynamic multi-core, a big core can be split up into 2 medium cores or 5 small cores, but an SMT core can also execute 3 and 4 threads concurrently, while fully utilizing all resources. As a result, the 4B line in Figure 13(b) smoothly increases, while the dynamic line (without SMT) shows multiple plateaus with jumps when the configuration changes. A dynamic multi-core that also supports SMT performs the best, but this will probably result in a very complex design and an even more complex scheduling and reconfiguration policy. We thus conclude:

**Finding #8:** *Homogeneous multi-cores with big SMT cores outperform (or are at least competitive to) dynamic multi-cores as a way to cope with variable active thread counts. A combination of both is optimal, but is also the most complex, both with respect to design and run-time scheduling.*

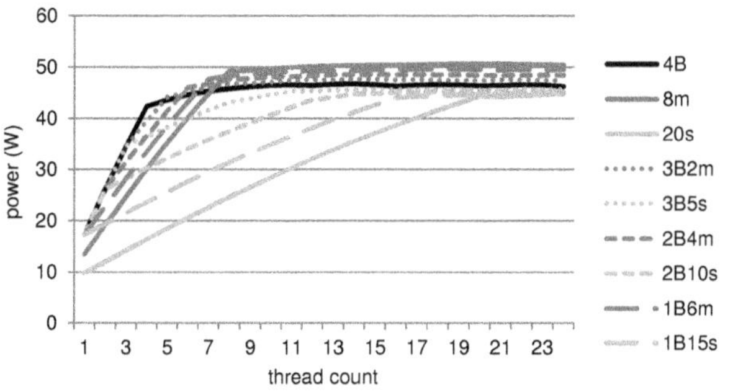


**Figure 14.** Power consumption as a function of thread count for all configurations assuming power gating.

## 7. Energy Efficiency

In the previous sections, we focused on performance under an equal total power budget. However, power-gating can be used to turn off idle cores, resulting in lower power consumption at low active thread counts. Especially for the configurations with many medium or small cores, this may result in improved power/energy-efficiency compared to the homogeneous configuration with a few big SMT cores.

***Power consumption as a function of thread count.*** Figure 14 shows average power consumption for all configurations (all configurations have SMT enabled in all cores) as a function of thread count when power-gating unused cores (averaged across all homogeneous multi-program workloads). It is interesting to study power consumption along with performance as shown in Figure 3: the 4B configuration consumes most power at low active thread counts while delivering highest performance; the 20s configuration consumes least power while delivering poorest performance; on the other hand, at high thread counts, all configurations perform nearly as well while consuming similar levels of power.

Figure 14 also shows that activating SMT contexts increases power consumption, due to the increase in resource utilization, but not as much as the increase in power consumption from activating cores (see for example the 4B configuration: power consumption increases from 42 Watt for 4 threads to 46 Watt for 24 threads). Note that the numbers for one thread (leftmost points) do not show the 1/2/5 relative power difference for the big, medium and small cores (the power consumption for one active core is 17.3, 13.5 and 9.8 Watt, for B, m and s, respectively). This is because the shared L3 cache and the main memory (DRAM) are active all the time, irrespective of active thread count — these resources consume approximately 7 Watt. The relative difference in power consumption for the three core types is reflected in the slopes of the 4B, 8m and 20s configurations (part of the curves that do not use SMT, i.e., with thread count lower than or equal to core count).

***Pareto-optimal designs.*** Figure 15 shows the power and energy consumption as a function of performance for the heterogeneous multi-program workloads (assuming a uniform thread count distribution). There are several interesting observations to be made. First, the 20s configuration consumes the least power, but results in high energy consumption due to its poor performance. In other words, a configuration with many small cores is not energy-optimal. Second, the 4B configuration is the best performing, but also has higher power and energy consumption. Third, the Pareto-optimal frontier is populated with heterogeneous design points, along with the best-performance 4B and lowest-power 20s configurations: the Pareto-optimal frontier consists of the following design points, 4B, 3B2m, 2B4m, 3B5s, 2B10s, 1B15s and 20s, for power versus performance (top graph in Figure 15), and 4B, 3B2m and 3B5s, for energy versus performance (bottom graph). In other words, heterogeneity trades off performance for power and energy consumption. The design point with the minimum energy-delay product (EDP) across all the designs considered is the 3B5s configuration, yet this heterogeneous design point improves EDP by as little as 4.1% and 1.8% over the 4B design point for the homogeneous and heterogeneous workloads, respectively. This leads to the following finding:

**Finding #9:** *Heterogeneous multi-core designs, when power gating idle cores, yield an (only) slightly better energy-efficiency compared to homogeneous multi-cores with big SMT cores under variable active thread count conditions.*

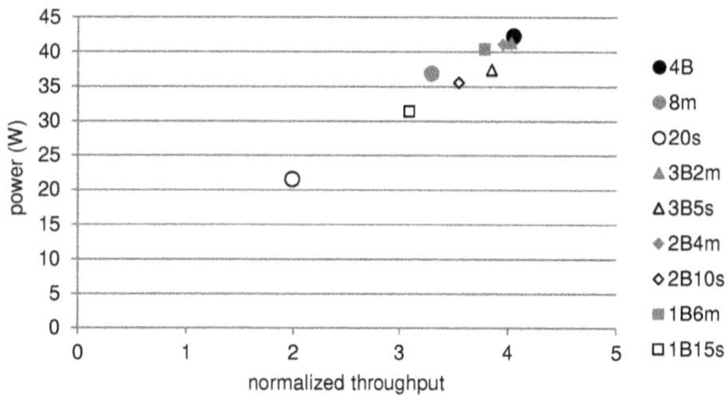


(a) Power versus performance

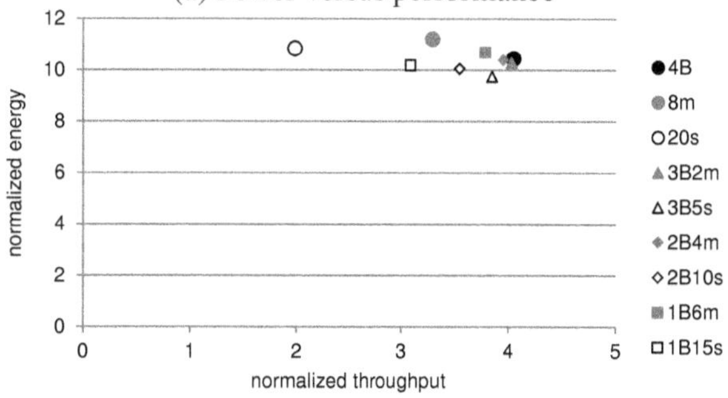


(b) Energy versus performance

**Figure 15.** Throughput versus power (top) and energy (bottom) consumption for heterogeneous multi-program workloads (assuming a uniform thread count distribution).

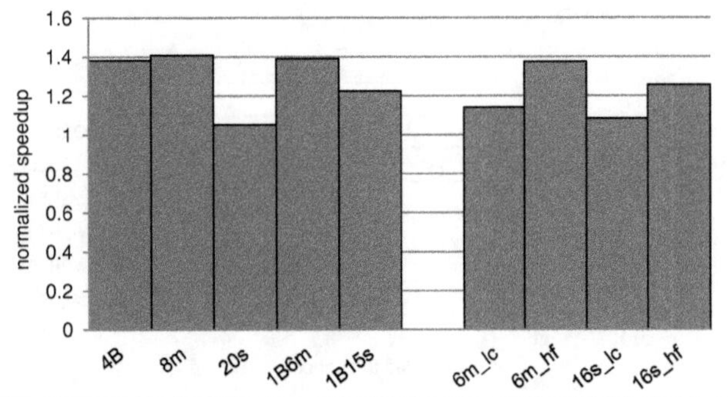


**Figure 16.** Average multi-threaded benchmark performance with alternative large-cache and high-frequency configurations.

## 8. Alternative Multi-Core Designs

### 8.1 Larger caches or higher frequency for the small cores

In Section 3, we assumed particular design decisions that may impact the final results. One decision was to keep total cache capacity constant across all designs. The motivation was to evaluate the impact of core type and organization, not cache capacity. Nevertheless, we noticed that sharing a cache between multiple programs co-executing on an SMT core can lead to better cache usage. We therefore now evaluate the effect of keeping private cache sizes constant across core types. We also evaluate the impact of increasing frequency of the small cores to improve its performance.

Figure 16 shows average speedup for the multi-threaded benchmarks (ROI-only). 6m_lc and 16s_lc (lc stands for larger cache) are configurations where the private L1 and L2 cache sizes for the medium and small cores are equal to that of the big core. Larger caches consume more power, leading to a different power-equivalence among core types: a big core is now power-equivalent to 1.5 medium cores and 4 small cores, which explains the decreased core count for the configurations with a larger cache. Further, the 6m_hf and 16s_hf configurations contain 6 medium cores or 16 small cores with clock frequency increased from 2.66 GHz to 3.33 GHz. This increase in frequency also results in a 1 to 1.5, and a 1 to 4 power-equivalence between the big and medium cores, and the big and small cores, respectively.

The results in Figure 16 show that a larger cache and, more distinctly, higher frequency leads to a higher speedup for the small-core configuration (compare 16s_lc and 16s_hf versus 20s). This is because many benchmarks do not scale well up to 20 threads, and reducing core count in exchange for more cache capacity or a higher frequency results in higher speedup. For the medium-core configuration (8m) on the other hand, enlarging the cache or increasing the frequency has a negative impact on performance: the benefits of a large cache or a higher frequency do not compensate for the reduction in core count. Overall, we observe that a homogeneous multi-core with big SMT cores achieves best performance for the given power budget. Hence, we conclude that:

**Finding #10:** *Enlarging the caches or increasing the frequency of the medium and small cores does not affect the general observation that a homogeneous multi-core with big SMT cores is close to optimal.*

### 8.2 Higher memory bandwidth

Another decision made in our initial setup was to set the memory bandwidth to 8 GB/s. However, as mentioned before, for some benchmarks, memory bandwidth turns out to be a bottleneck. We therefore now double memory bandwidth to 16 GB/s, see Figure 17. Comparing this Figure to Figures 8 and 11, we observe that performance increases for all configurations, albeit by a small margin. For the homogeneous multi-program workloads, 4B now achieves a 0.8% lower throughput than the optimum (which was 0.6% for 8 GB/s), and a 0.4% lower throughput for the heterogeneous multi-program workloads (used to be 0.5% *higher*). For the multi-threaded programs, considering ROI only, we observe a speedup for 4B that is 2.9% lower than the optimum (which was 1.8% before), and a 1.8% higher speedup when considering the whole program (1.9% before). The programs that were bandwidth-bound in the 8 GB/s setup now achieve better performance across all configurations. These memory-bound benchmarks especially benefit from SMT, more so than compute-bound programs [21]. Hence, our conclusion:

**Finding #11:** *Even under high available memory bandwidths does the performance of a homogeneous design with big SMT cores remain close to the heterogeneous configurations.*

## 9. Related Work

Olukotun et al. [23] make the case for multi-core processing. By comparing an aggressive single-core processor (6-wide out-of-order) and a dual-core processor consisting of 2-wide out-of-order cores, they found that parallelized applications with limited parallelism achieve comparable performance on both architectures, and that applications with large amount of coarse-grained parallelism achieve significantly better performance on the dual-core.

Kumar et al. [19] argue that a single-ISA heterogeneous multi-core processor covers a spectrum of workloads better than a conventional multi-core processor, providing good single-thread performance when thread-level parallelism is low, and high throughput when thread-level parallelism is high. Our results confirm this finding: the heterogeneous multi-core configurations achieve better overall performance compared to 4B across the broad range of active thread counts when SMT is not enabled. However, Kumar et al. did not consider and compare against a homogeneous multi-core with big SMT cores, which we find to achieve a level of performance that is competitive to a heterogeneous design

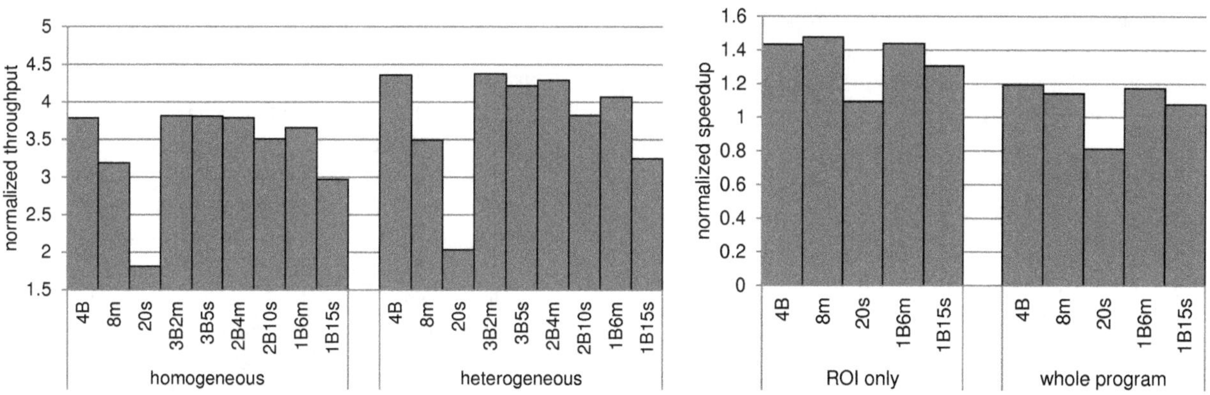


(a) multi-program (b) multi-threaded

**Figure 17.** Performance numbers assuming 16 GB/s memory bandwidth.

under varying degrees of thread-level parallelism, while being less costly to design and verify.

Ipek et al. [11] and Kim et al. [17] propose to fuse small cores to form bigger cores when there are few active threads. By doing so, the multi-core processor becomes more dynamic and can more easily adapt to software diversity. Our results indicate that similar performance benefits can be achieved through the opposite mechanism: instead of fusing small cores to form a big core when there are few active threads, one could schedule threads across big SMT cores (and have few active SMT threads per core) in a homogeneous multi-core. Khubaib et al. [16] build on a similar insight when proposing MorphCore, an aggressive out-of-order core with 2-way SMT that can morph into an energy-efficient 8-way SMT in-order core. The idea is to switch between the two modes of operation depending on the amount of available thread-level parallelism: with few (one or two) active threads, the core runs in out-of-order mode, and switches to in-order SMT with more active threads. Whereas Khubaib et al. focus on the proposal of an energy-efficient core design that can switch between out-of-order and wide-SMT in-order operation, the focus of our work is to study the impact of variable thread-level parallelism in the workload, and how this affects multi-core design decisions. More specifically, we consider distributions of active thread counts in multi-program workloads next to multi-threaded workloads to compare homogeneous multi-cores with SMT against heterogeneous and dynamic multi-cores. MorphCore is complementary to our work and can be leveraged to further improve energy-efficiency of the big SMT cores when running multiple SMT threads.

Hill and Marty [10] evaluate the three major multi-core processor architecture paradigms — homogeneous, heterogeneous and dynamic multi-core — and derive high-level insights from Amdahl's Law. Their model did not consider SMT and assumed that software is either sequential or infinitely parallel. One of the results that they obtain is that heterogeneous multi-cores can achieve better performance than homogeneous multi-cores; also, they find that dynamic processors achieve better performance than heterogeneous multi-cores with identical functions of performance per unit area. While this is true considering the assumptions made, our results show that this is not necessarily the case when the number of available threads varies over time.

A number of papers have explored how to take advantage from heterogeneity to improve multi-threaded application performance. Annavaram et al. [1] propose running sequential portions of a multi-threaded application at a higher power budget, thereby significantly improving performance while remaining within a given power budget. Intel's TurboBoost [25] offers similar functionality by boosting clock frequency. Suleman et al. [29] accelerate the execution of critical sections by exploiting high-performance cores in a heterogeneous multi-core, i.e., a thread that executes a critical section is migrated to a big core in order to reduce serialization time — a technique called Accelerating Critical Sections (ACS). Joao et al. [12] generalize this principle to other types of synchronization bottlenecks, including critical sections, barriers and pipes. All of these approaches exploit the fact that the number of active threads varies over time and leverage heterogeneity to improve performance. This paper suggests that similar performance benefits might potentially be achieved through SMT on a homogeneous multi-core. More specifically, when a thread is executing sequential code (e.g., initialization, critical section, etc.), scheduling it on a single core with the other SMT threads throttled, might achieve similar performance benefits, and does not require migrating (or marshaling [30]) data when a thread is migrated from a small to a big core in ACS.

Li et al. [21] compare the energy-efficiency and thermal characteristics of SMT versus multi-core. They report that, assuming an equal area budget, SMT is more energy-efficient than multi-core for memory-intensive workloads; the inverse is true for compute-intensive workloads. Kumar et al. [18] exploit dynamic time-varying application behavior to schedule applications on the most energy-efficient core in a heterogeneous multi-core, and they report substantial energy savings compared to a homogeneous multi-core. In contrast to this prior work, we explore multi-core configurations under variable thread-level parallelism conditions.

## 10. Conclusion

The number of active threads varies over time in today's computer systems. This has been observed across many application domains, ranging from multi-program systems, desktop applications, datacenter servers, and even multi-threaded applications. This paper studied how varying degrees of thread-level parallelism in the workload affect multi-core design decisions. We considered homogeneous, heterogeneous and dynamic multi-cores under an equal power budget, and conclude that a homogeneous multi-core consisting of big SMT cores achieves comparable or slightly better performance compared to heterogeneous multi-cores (both with and without SMT) and dynamic multi-cores. The reason is that a homogeneous multi-core with big SMT cores can better adapt to varying degrees of thread-level parallelism in the workload, and achieves higher per-thread performance at low active thread counts and competitive throughput at high active thread counts. Finally, we also find that heterogeneous multi-cores are (only) slightly more energy-efficient compared to a homogeneous all-big-core configuration with SMT, when power gating idle cores.

The overall conclusion is that, while multi-cores with many small cores, be it homogeneous or heterogeneous architectures, outperform homogeneous multi-cores with big SMT cores at full utilization, the inverse is typically true under variable active thread workload conditions, which makes homogeneous multi-cores with big SMT cores an appealing, cost-effective design point for the variable active threads workloads commonly observed in modern-day systems.

## Acknowledgments

We thank the anonymous reviewers for their valuable and constructive feedback. Stijn Eyerman is a postdoctoral fellow of the Research Foundation–Flanders. Additional support is provided by the European Research Council under the European Community's Seventh Framework Programme (FP7/2007-2013) / ERC Grant agreement no. 259295. Experiments were run at the VSC Flemish Supercomputer Center.

## References

[1] M. Annavaram, E. Grochowski, and J. Shen. Mitigating Amdahl's law through EPI throttling. In *Proceedings of the International Symposium on Computer Architecture (ISCA)*, pages 298–309, June 2005.

[2] L. A. Barroso and U. Hölzle. The case for energy-proportional systems. *IEEE Computer*, 40:33–37, Dec. 2007.

[3] C. Bienia, S. Kumar, J. P. Singh, and K. Li. The PARSEC benchmark suite: Characterization and architectural implications. In *Proceedings of the International Conference on Parallel Architectures and Compilation Techniques (PACT)*, pages 72–81, Oct. 2008.

[4] G. Blake, R. G. Dreslinski, T. N. Mudge, and K. Flautner. Evolution of thread-level parallelism in desktop applications. In *Proceedings of the International Symposium on Computer Architecture (ISCA)*, pages 302–313, June 2010.

[5] T. E. Carlson, W. Heirman, and L. Eeckhout. Sniper: Exploring the level of abstraction for scalable and accurate parallel multi-core simulation. In *Proceedings of 2011 International Conference for High Performance Computing, Networking, Storage and Analysis (SC)*, pages 52:1–52:12, Nov. 2011.

[6] K. Du Bois, S. Eyerman, J. Sartor, and L. Eeckhout. Criticality stacks: Identifying critical threads in parallel programs using synchronization behavior. In *Proceedings of the International Symposium on Computer Architecture (ISCA)*, pages 511–522, June 2013.

[7] S. Eyerman and L. Eeckhout. System-level performance metrics for multi-program workloads. *IEEE Micro*, 28(3):42–53, May/June 2008.

[8] P. Greenhalgh. Big.LITTLE processing with ARM Cortex-A15 & Cortex-A7: Improving energy efficiency in high-performance mobile platforms. http://www.arm.com/files/downloads/big_LITTLE_Final_Final.pdf, Sept. 2011.

[9] L. Hammond, M. Willey, and K. Olukotun. Data speculation support for a chip multiprocessor. In *Proceedings of the International Conference on Architectural Support for Programming Languages and Operating Systems (ASPLOS)*, pages 58–69, Oct. 1998.

[10] M. D. Hill and M. R. Marty. Amdahl's law in the multicore era. *IEEE Computer*, 41(7):33–38, July 2008.

[11] E. Ipek, M. Kirman, N. Kirman, and J. F. Martinez. Core fusion: Accommodating software diversity in chip multiprocessors. In *Proceedings of the International Symposium on Computer Architecture (ISCA)*, pages 186–197, June 2007.

[12] J. A. Joao, M. A. Suleman, O. Mutlu, and Y. N. Patt. Bottleneck identification and scheduling in multithreaded applications. In *Proceedings of the International Conference on Architectural Support for Programming Languages and Operating Systems (ASPLOS)*, pages 223–234, Mar. 2012.

[13] M. T. Jones. Inside the Linux scheduler: The latest version of this all-important kernel component improves scalability. http://www.ibm.com/developerworks/linux/library/l-scheduler/index.html, June 2006.

[14] R. Kalla, B. Sinharoy, W. J. Starke, and M. Floyd. Power7: IBM's next-generation server processor. *IEEE Micro*, 30:7–15, March/April 2010.

[15] C. N. Keltcher, K. J. McGrath, A. Ahmed, and P. Conway. The AMD Opteron processor for multiprocessor servers. *IEEE Micro*, 23(2):66–76, Mar. 2007.

[16] K. Khubaib, M. Suleman, M. Hashemi, C. Wilkerson, and Y. Patt. MorphCore: An energy-efficient microarchitecture for high performance ILP and high throughput TLP. In *45th Annual IEEE/ACM International Symposium on Microarchitecture (MICRO)*, pages 305–316, Dec. 2012.

[17] C. Kim, S. Sethumadhavan, M. S. Govindan, N. Ranganathan, D. Gulati, D. Burger, and S. Keckler. Composable lightweight processors. In *Proceedings of the International Symposium on Microarchitecture (MICRO)*, pages 381–394, Dec. 2007.

[18] R. Kumar, K. I. Farkas, N. P. Jouppi, P. Ranganathan, and D. M. Tullsen. Single-ISA heterogeneous multi-core architectures: The potential for processor power reduction. In *Proceedings of the ACM/IEEE Annual International Symposium on Microarchitecture (MICRO)*, pages 81–92, Dec. 2003.

[19] R. Kumar, D. M. Tullsen, P. Ranganathan, N. P. Jouppi, and K. I. Farkas. Single-ISA heterogeneous multi-core architectures for multithreaded workload performance. In *Proceedings of the International Symposium on Computer Architecture (ISCA)*, pages 64–75, June 2004.

[20] S. Li, J. H. Ahn, R. D. Strong, J. B. Brockman, D. M. Tullsen, and N. P. Jouppi. McPAT: An integrated power, area, and timing modeling framework for multicore and manycore architectures. In *Proceedings of the IEEE/ACM International Symposium on Microarchitecture (MICRO)*, pages 469–480, Dec. 2009.

[21] Y. Li, D. Brooks, Z. Hu, and K. Skadron. Performance, energy, and thermal considerations for SMT and CMP architectures. In *Proceedings of the International Symposium on High-Performance Computer Architecture (HPCA)*, pages 71–82, Feb. 2005.

[22] NVidia. Variable SMP – a multi-core CPU architecture for low power and high performance. http://www.nvidia.com/content/PDF/tegra_white_papers/Variable-SMP-A-Multi-Core-CPU-Architecture-for-Low-Power-and-High-Performance-v1.1.pdf, 2011.

[23] K. Olukotun, B. A. Nayfeh, L. Hammond, K. Wilson, and K.-Y. Chang. The case for a single-chip multiprocessor. In *Proceedings of the International Conference on Architectural Support for Programming Languages and Operating Systems (ASPLOS)*, pages 2–11, Oct. 1996.

[24] S. E. Raasch and S. K. Reinhardt. The impact of resource partitioning on SMT processors. In *Proceedings of the 12th International Conference on Parallel Architectures and Compilation Techniques (PACT)*, pages 15–26, Sept. 2003.

[25] E. Rotem, A. Naveh, D. Rajwan, A. Ananthakrishnan, and E. Weissmann. Power-management architecture of the intel microarchitecture code-named sandy bridge. *IEEE Micro*, 32: 20–27, March/April 2012.

[26] T. Sherwood, E. Perelman, G. Hamerly, and B. Calder. Automatically characterizing large scale program behavior. In *Proceedings of the International Conference on Architectural Support for Programming Languages and Operating Systems (ASPLOS)*, pages 45–57, Oct. 2002.

[27] A. Snavely and D. M. Tullsen. Symbiotic jobscheduling for simultaneous multithreading processor. In *Proceedings of the International Conference on Architectural Support for Programming Languages and Operating Systems (ASPLOS)*, pages 234–244, Nov. 2000.

[28] G. S. Sohi, S. E. Breach, and T. N. Vijaykumar. Multiscalar processors. In *Proceedings of the 22nd Annual International Symposium on Computer Architecture (ISCA)*, pages 414–425, June 1995.

[29] M. A. Suleman, O. Mutlu, M. K. Qureshi, and Y. N. Patt. Accelerating critical section execution with asymmetric multicore architectures. In *Proceedings of the International Conference on Architectural Support for Programming Languages and Operating Systems (ASPLOS)*, pages 253–264, Mar. 2009.

[30] M. A. Suleman, O. Mutlu, J. A. Joao, Khubaib, and Y. N. Patt. Data marshaling for multi-core architectures. In *Proceedings of the International Symposium on Computer Architecture (ISCA)*, pages 441–450, June 2010.

[31] D. M. Tullsen, S. J. Eggers, J. S. Emer, H. M. Levy, J. L. Lo, and R. L. Stamm. Exploiting choice: Instruction fetch and issue on an implementable simultaneous multithreading processor. In *Proceedings of the 23rd Annual International Symposium on Computer Architecture (ISCA)*, pages 191–202, May 1996.

[32] R. Velasquez, P. Michaud, and A. Seznec. Selecting benchmark combinations for the evaluation of multicore throughput. In *The IEEE International Symposium on Performance Analysis of Systems and Software (ISPASS)*, pages 173–182, Apr. 2013.

# Finding the Limit: Examining the Potential and Complexity of Compilation Scheduling for JIT-Based Runtime Systems

Yufei Ding, Mingzhou Zhou, Zhijia Zhao, Sarah Eisenstat*, Xipeng Shen

Computer Science Department, The College of William and Mary

*Computer Science and Artificial Intelligence Lab, Massachusetts Institute of Technology

{yding,mzhou,zzhao,xshen}@cs.wm.edu

*seisenst@csail.mit.edu

## Abstract

This work aims to find out the full potential of compilation scheduling for JIT-based runtime systems. Compilation scheduling determines the order in which the compilation units (e.g., functions) in a program are to be compiled or recompiled. It decides when what versions of the units are ready to run, and hence affects performance. But it has been a largely overlooked direction in JIT-related research, with some fundamental questions left open: How significant compilation scheduling is for performance, how good the scheduling schemes employed by existing runtime systems are, and whether a great potential exists for improvement. This study proves the strong NP-completeness of the problem, proposes a heuristic algorithm that yields near optimal schedules, examines the potential of two current scheduling schemes empirically, and explores the relations with JIT designs. It provides the first principled understanding to the complexity and potential of compilation scheduling, shedding some insights for JIT-based runtime system improvement.

***Categories and Subject Descriptors*** D3.4 [*Programming Languages*]: Processors

***General Terms*** Performance

***Keywords*** JIT, Compilation Scheduling, Compilation Order, NP-completeness, Heuristic Algorithm, Runtime System



*ASPLOS '14*, March 1–5, 2014, Salt Lake City, Utah, USA.



ACM 978-1-4503-2305-5/14/03...$15.00.

http://dx.doi.org/10.1145/2541940.2541945

## 1. Introduction

Just-In-Time (JIT) has been the major code translation paradigm in Java runtime, binary translation, and other settings. Enhancing the performance of programs compiled by JIT has received steady attentions in the last decade. The attentions have been reinforced recently as the runtime engines of some popular web scripting languages (e.g., Javascript) starts to embrace JIT as a replacement or complement of interpreters for better performance.

Enhancing the performance of JIT-based runtime systems is a multi-dimensional problem. So far, research efforts have been largely focused on the various facets of the internal design of JIT [9, 10, 13, 16], and the determination of suitable optimization levels for a function [5, 27, 32]. Few have been devoted to the compilation scheduling of JIT. It has remained preliminarily understood when a JIT should be invoked to compile which function, or in other words, how compilation order affects the performance of JIT-based runtime systems.

Formally, *a compilation order* refers to an order in which the compilation units in a program (e.g., functions or traces) are being compiled or recompiled[1]. Compilation order determines what is the earliest time the executable of a function (or trace) becomes available, which in turn affects the performance of the program. For instance, consider a call sequence "a b g g g g e g". Let $C_i(x)$ represent the compilation of function $x$ at level $i$—a higher level means deeper optimizations and also larger compilation time overhead. A compilation order, $(C_1(a), C_1(b), C_1(g), C_1(e), C_2(g))$, dictates that the better optimized version of function $g$ is not available before $C_1(e)$ finishes. If we switch $C_1(e)$ with $C_2(g)$, the better version of $g$ can become available earlier, benefit more invocations of $g$, and hence possibly produce better performance. For mobile applications, better performance translates to shorter response time and often higher energy efficiency, which are key variables for user satisfaction in handheld systems [25, 30].

[1] It should not be confused with the order of the various optimization phases in a compilation, which is related with internal design rather than usage of a compiler.

Despite the natural connection between compilation orders and JIT performance, there has been little work concentrated on it. Some fundamental questions have never been systematically explored, such as how significant the connection is, how good the orders employed by existing runtime systems are, whether there is a great potential for improvement. Answers to these questions are directional. They will indicate whether enhancing compilation orders is valuable and promising, and guide research in this preliminarily understood direction.

This paper aims to answer those fundamental questions, and provide a principled understanding to the problem of compilation ordering in JIT-based runtime systems.

Specifically, we concentrate on two aspects. The first is on optimal compilation orders: For a given execution, are optimal orders feasible to compute? If so, how to compute them efficiently? If not, how to approximate them effectively? Answers to these open questions are essential for revealing the full impact of compilation orders on a runtime system.

Through a series of rigorous analysis, we provide a threefold answer to the questions (Sections 3 to 5.) First, we prove that a simple, linear algorithm can give optimal compilation orders when compilation and execution have to happen on the same core. Second, through a reduction from PARTITION and 3-SAT, we prove that in other settings, the problem becomes strongly NP-complete—that is, no polynomial algorithms exist for computing optimal compilation orders unless NP=P, even if the compilation and execution times of the functions are all bounded to a polynomial in the length of the call sequence. Prompted by the NP-completeness, we develop the Init-Append-Replace (IAR) algorithm, a polynomial-time approximation algorithm that is able to produce near optimal compilation sequences efficiently in general settings. These findings make the examination of the full potential of compilation orders possible. More fundamentally, they add the first deep understanding to the compilation ordering problem.

Based on the theoretical findings, the second part of this work (Section 6) empirically evaluates the quality of the compilation order given by existing JIT-based runtime systems, and measures the potential of better compilation orders in enhancing the system performance. Specifically, we use a modern Java Virtual Machine (JVM) named Jikes RVM [4] as the basic framework, and strive to include some of the most relevant factors into our measurement. These factors include concurrency in a JIT, machine parallelism, the cost-benefit models a JIT may use to determine the suitable compilation levels for a function, and so on. We evaluate the compilation scheduling scheme used in Jikes RVM, as well as the one used in V8, the runtime Engine behind Google Chrome. Experiments on call sequences collected on a set of Dacapo benchmarks [6] conclude that a good compilation order can lead to an average speedup of as much as a factor of two over existing runtime systems, clearly demonstrating the importance and potential of compilation ordering. Meanwhile, the results unveil some insights in the relations among compilation order, machine concurrency, and parallel JIT, and provide a discussion on enhancing compilation orders in practice.

Overall, this work makes the following major contributions.

- It provides the first systematic exploration to the impact of compilation ordering for the performance of JIT-based runtime systems in various settings.
- It reveals that the compilation scheduling schemes used by existing runtime systems are far from optimal, pointing out the importance of research efforts in enhancing compilation schedules—a direction largely overlooked by previous studies.
- It, for the first time, unveils the inherent complexity of the compilation scheduling problem, proving the NP-completeness of getting optimal compilation schedules in a general setting. It further shows that intelligent searching algorithms like $A^*$-search, although offering some alleviation, are not feasible in practice. The result is significant as it will help the community avoid wasting time in finding algorithms to compute the optimal orders and instead devote the efforts into the more promising direction of designing effective approximation algorithms.
- It proves the optimality of a simple algorithm for computing optimal compilation schedules for single-core settings, and contributes an efficient approximation algorithm, the IAR algorithm, for getting near optimal schedules in general settings. These findings are crucial for assessing the room left for improvement of practical runtime systems, and meanwhile, shed insights for designing better compilation scheduling modules in practice.

This work may benefit the JIT community in several ways. (1) It points out an important research direction for enhancing JIT-based runtime systems. (2) Its complexity findings will help avoid efforts in searching for algorithms to compute optimal JIT schedules. (3) It offers the first practical way to assess the JIT scheduling of runtime systems, from which, virtual machine developers can easily see the room left for improvement and allocate their efforts appropriately. (4) It provides an effective scheduling algorithm (IAR) that is efficient for possible online uses (although some other conditions are needed for its integration in an actual runtime system.)

The rest of the paper is organized as follows. We start with some background on JIT in Section 2, provide a definition of the optimal compilation scheduling problem in Section 3, then present the algorithms and complexity analysis in Sections 4 and 5, and finally report the experimental results, discuss related work, and conclude with a summary.

## 2. Background

This section takes Jikes RVM as an example to provide some brief background on how JIT compilation is currently being used in many runtime systems. Jikes RVM [4] is an open-source JVM originated from IBM. It uses method-level JIT compilation[2]. Its employment of JIT is typical. A function can be compiled at four levels by the JIT; the higher the level is, the deeper the optimizations are, and also the larger compilation overhead it incurs. In an execution of a program, Jikes RVM maintains a queue for compilation requests. When it encounters a Java method for the first time, it enqueues a request to compile the method at the lowest level. During the execution of the program, it observes the behaviors of the application through sampling, whereby, it determines the importance of each Java method in the application. When it realizes that a Java method is important enough to deserve some deeper optimizations, it enqueues a request to recompile the method at a higher level. The level is determined by a cost-benefit model prebuilt inside Jikes RVM, the information which draws on includes the hotness of the method and its code size.

Jikes RVM has a number of threads, including a compilation thread. The compilation thread dequeues the compilation tasks and conducts the corresponding compilation work. As a result, the order in which the compilation tasks are enqueued and the time when they are enqueued determines the compilation sequence of the program in that execution.

## 3. Problem Definition and Scope

This section provides a formal definition of the optimal compilation scheduling problem, and then discusses the assumptions and scope of the problem.

**Definition 1. Optimal Compilation Scheduling Problem (OCSP)**

Given: *A sequence of function invocations, where, each element (say $m_i$) represents an invocation of a function $m_i$. A function can appear once or multiple times in the invocation sequence. For each function, there are multiple possible compilation levels. Let $c_{i,j}$ represent the length of the time needed to compile function $m_i$ at level $j$, $e_{i,j}$ represent the length of the corresponding execution time of the produced code. Assuming all $c_{i,j}$ and $e_{i,j}$ are known and independent of compilation orders, and $\forall$ $i$ and $j_1 < j_2$, we have $c_{i,j_1} \leq c_{i,j_2}$, $e_{i,j_1} \geq e_{i,j_2}$. A function cannot run unless it has been compiled at least once (no matter at which level) in an execution of the invocation sequence. A function can be compiled once or multiple times in a run. The code produced by the latest compilation is used for execution.*

Goal: *To find a sequence of compilation events that minimizes the make-span of the program execution. Here, make-span is the time spanning from the start of the first compilation event to the end of the program execution.*

The definition contains several assumptions. We explain them as follows.

- *Assumption 1:* The compilation and execution time of a function is all known. In actual runtime systems, such as Jikes RVM [4], there are often some kind of cost-benefit models. They estimate the compilation and execution time from function size and hotness (to determine the suitable compilation levels for a function.) How to accurately estimate the time is not the focus of this work; we use measured time in our experiments. In addition, in the definition of OCSP, both $c_{i,j}$ and $e_{i,j}$ through a program execution are assumed to be constant for some given $i$ and $j$. In reality, the compilation time of a function $c_{i,j}$ is largely stable, but the execution time $e_{i,j}$ may differ from one call of function $m_i$ to another, thanks to the differences in calling parameters and contexts. The variations however do not affect the major conclusions our analysis produces, as Section 8 will discuss. In our experiments, we set $e_{i,j}$ with the average length of all calls to function $m_i$ that is compiled at level $j$.
- *Assumption 2:* A function can be compiled at multiple levels. This assumption is consistent with most runtime systems (e.g., V8, Jikes RVM, J9, Hotspot.) A higher level usually means deeper optimizations, and hence a longer compilation time and shorter execution time of the function.
- *Assumption 3:* The sequence of function invocations is known. This assumption is necessary for revealing the full potential impact of compilation scheduling. In our experiment, the sequence is collected through profiling. How to estimate such a sequence in an actual deployment of a runtime system is a problem relevant to the construction of a practical scheduler, but orthogonal to the investigation of optimal compilation scheduling problem.

In addition, besides function compilation, function inlining may also affect the overall performance. We discuss its effects in Section 8.

## 4. Algorithms and Complexities for Finding the Optimal

In this section, we investigate the feasibility in finding solutions to the OCSP. The motivation for this investigation is multifold. First, an optimal solution, if it is feasible to obtain, exposes the limit of the scheduling benefit, which is essential for examining the full potential of compilation scheduling. Second, understanding the computational complexity of the problem is important for guiding the direction of efforts: If the problem is strongly NP-hard, efforts may be more worthwhile to be spent on finding effective heuristic algorithms

[2] In this paper, "function" and "method" are inter-changable terms.

than designing optimal algorithms. We describe our findings by classifying the scenarios into two categories.

### 4.1 Optimality in the Case of Single Core

When there is only one CPU core available, both compilation and execution have to happen on that core. In this case, determining the best compilation order is straightforward. For each function (say $m_i$), we find the *most cost-effective compilation level* for that function, denoted as $l_i$, such that $\forall k, n_i * e_{i,l_i} + c_{i,l_i} \le n_i * e_{i,k} + c_{i,k}$, where, $n_i$ is the number of invocations of function $m_i$ in the execution sequence. We have the following theorem:

**Theorem 1.** *An arbitrary compilation sequence of the methods, as long as every method appears once in it and is compiled at its most cost-effective compilation level, yields the minimum make-span for the program.*

The correctness of the theorem is easy to see. As there is only one core, the machine is always running, doing either the compilation or execution jobs. The make-span is hence the sum of the compilation and execution times. The most cost-effective level ensures that the total time taken by each method is minimum. Hence the conclusion. The optimality is subject to the assumptions listed in the previous section, which will be discussed in Section 8.

The implication of this result is that on single-core machines, research efforts should be put on the prediction of the most cost-effective compilation levels. The reason is that if those levels are predicted accurately, using on-demand compilation—that is, compiling a function when it gets invoked for the first time, as what most existing runtime systems are using—can already give us an optimal compilation order. This insight has its practical values: Despite that most machines are equipped with multicores, lots of times, an application is using only one core when multiple applications are running. It is especially common on smartphone-like portable devides that contain only several cores.

### 4.2 Complexity in the Case of Multiple Cores

In the case of multiple cores, the compilation and execution can happen largely in parallel. The determination of a best compilation order becomes complicated.

***An Example*** To illustrate the complexity, consider the example showing in Figure 1. The call sequence is simple, containing just four calls to three functions. For simplicity, we assume that compilation and execution happen on two different cores, and only one level of compilation is worthwhile for functions $f_0$ and $f_2$ and two levels for function $f_1$. Just based on the execution times, it may be tempting to think that the best way to compile the functions is to pick the highest compilation levels for all the functions—as they provide the shortest running times for the functions—and then schedule the compilations in the order of the first-time appearance of those functions. The middle bottom box in Figure 1 shows

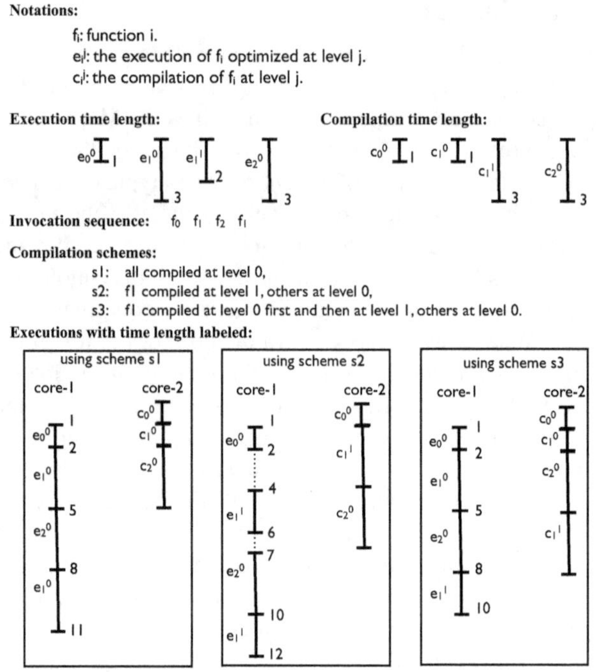


**Figure 1.** An example illustrating the complexity of compilation scheduling. Assuming execution happens on core-1 and compilation happens on core-2.

this schedule. It turns out to result in the longest make-span among all the three schedules shown in Figure 1. The reason is that the highest level of compilation of $f_1$ causes delays to the start of the second and third function calls—we call such delays *bubbles* from now on. The best schedule of the three is the third schedule, in which, function $f_1$ is compiled twice: The first time is at the lowest level to avoid causing delays, and the second time is at the highest level to speedup its second invocation. From this result, one may think that a schedule that compiles all functions at the lowest level first and then recompiles them would work well.

But a simple extension of the example can immediately prove the hypothesis incorrect. As Figure 2 shows, we add another call to function $f_2$. It also shows that the compilation of $f_2$ at level 1 takes 5 time units and execution at that level takes 1 time unit. The bottom three boxes in Figure 2 show how the three schedules in Figure 1 would perform in this case when we consider the possibility of appending a recompilation of $f_2$ at level 1 to the schedule. This appending turns the previously best schedule (schedule 3) to the worst. (The third box in Figure 2 does not have that recompilation appended because appending it is apparently not beneficial.) The first schedule with such an appending becomes the best of the three. This schedule has function $f_2$ but not others recompiled, despite that $f_2$ takes the longest time to recompile.

These two examples are simple, involving only three functions and five invocations. They reflect the high complexity OCSP can have on real program executions. Which

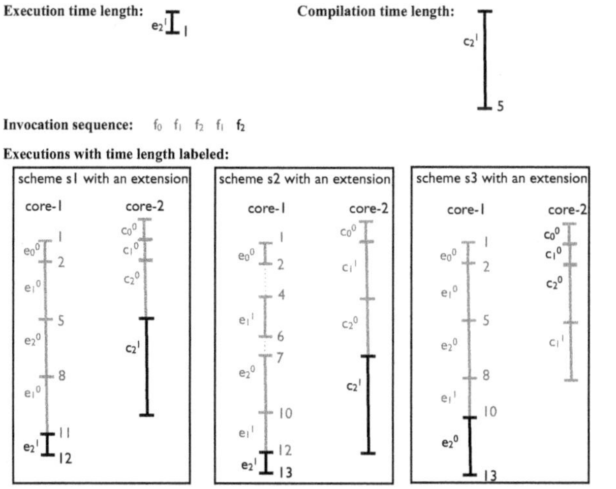


**Figure 2.** Continuing the example in Figure 1 with a call to $f_2$ appended to the invocation sequence.

functions need to be recompiled and when each (re)compilation should happen depend on how frequently the functions are each invoked, when they are invoked, how long the execution and compilation of each take, and so on.

Prompted by the observed complexities, we conduct a theoretical analysis of the computational complexity of the OCSP. Findings are shown next.

***Strong NP-Completeness*** Our analysis produces the following conclusion:

**Theorem 2.** *When compilation and execution can happen in parallel, the OCSP problem is NP-complete.*

We prove the NP-completeness through a reduction from the classic NP-complete problem, PARTITION, to a simple case of OCSP, where there are only two machines, both compilation and execution are single threaded, and there are only two optimization levels.

*Proof.* Suppose we are given a set of non-negative integers $S = s_1, s_2, \cdots, s_n$. Let $t = (1/2) \times \sum_{i=1}^{n} s_i$. The goal of the PARTITION problem is to find a subset $X$ whose sum is $t$. (By the definition of $t$, this ensures that $S - X$ also sums to $t$.)

For each $s_i$, we construct one function with $c_{i1} = 1$, $c_{i2} = s_i + 1$, $e_{i1} = s_i + 1$, $e_{i2} = 1$. Pick an arbitrary order to execute these functions. We then construct two additional functions, which have the same compilation time and execution time for both levels. One of these functions, which we require to execute first, has compilation time 1 and execution time $t+n$. The other function, which we require to execute last, has compilation time $t + n$ and execution time 1.

Suppose that we have a set $X$ satisfying the PARTITION constraints. Then we can construct the corresponding compilation sequence by compiling all of the functions in the set $X$ at level 1, and compiling all other functions at level 2. The long execution time of the initial function guarantees that we have lots of time to compile all of the functions in the middle before we have to execute them. So if we let one machine (named E) conduct only executions and the other (named C) compilations, both machines can work constantly (with the exception of the first time unit for Machine E and the last time unit for Machine C).

Because the numbers in $X$ sum to $t$, the total execution time for functions in $X$ is $|X| + t$, and the total compilation time for functions in $X$ is $|X|$. Similarly, the total execution time for functions not in $X$ is $n - |X|$, while the total compilation time for functions not in $X$ is $n - |X| + t$. Hence, the total compilation time for all but the first and last functions is $t + n$. The execution time is also $t + n$. When combined with the time for the first and last functions, as well as the slack time, the total make-span is $2(1 + t + n)$.

It is easy to see that $2(1 + t + n)$ must be the minimum make-span. Machine E cannot work in the first timestep (before anything is compiled) while Machine C can't work in the last timestep (while the last function is executing). So with make-span less than $2 + 2t + 2n$, the total processing time that we get out of Machines C and E is less than $2 \times (2 + 2t + 2n - 1) = 2(2t + 2n + 1)$. However, the total amount of work to be done (execution and compilation combined) is at least $2(2n+2t+1)$ regardless of which level the functions are compiled at, so we cannot have make-span less than $2 + 2t + 2n$.

We can also show the converse: that a schedule with that make-span must imply the existence of a partition. The total run time of all functions (execution plus compilation) is fixed at $(2n+2t)+2(n+t)+2 = 2(2n+2t+1)$. To finish that work within time $2(1+t+n)$, Machine C has to work constantly (aside from the last time-step, which is unavoidable), and Machine E also has to work constantly (aside from the first time-step, which is unavoidable). This means that the total compilation time must sum to exactly $t+n$, and so the set of functions compiled at level 2 must correspond to a set that sums to exactly $t$. □

We further prove that the 3-SAT problem can be also reduced to the OCSP problem in polynomial time and hence prove that the OCSP is not only NP-complete, but also strongly NP-complete. It means that even if the compilation and execution times of the functions are all bounded to a polynomial in the length of the call sequence (which could be true in practice), the problem remains NP-complete. The implication to practice is that the OCSP is unlikely to admit efficient solutions in practice. We put the proof into a technical report [12].

## 5. Challenging the NP-Completeness

The strong NP-completeness proved in the previous section has some significant implications. It enhances the fundamental understanding to the compilation scheduling problem of JIT, suggesting that polynomial-time solutions are unlikely to exist for OCSP as soon as the number of cores goes beyond one. This result entails difficult challenges for studying the full potential of compilation scheduling for JIT as the optimal schedules are probably infeasible to obtain for a real program execution.

This section presents several options we have pursued to overcome the NP-completeness to reveal the potential of compilation scheduling. The first option explores heuristic algorithms for approximating the optimal; the algorithms include a single-level scheme and a several-round algorithm. The objective of this option is to obtain some schedules that are both valid and close to the optimal in performance so that they can provide a tight upper bound for the minimum make-span. The second option computes the lower bound of the make-span. Together, these two options lead to a range covering the minimum make-span. The rationale is that if that range is small, it would be sufficient to substitute the optimal in the examination of the potential of compilation scheduling. At the end of this section, we describe the third option, which tries heuristic search to directly find the optimal.

### 5.1 Approximating the Limit

The goal of this option is to obtain some legal schedule with a performance close to the optimal.

***Single-Level Approximation*** Following Occam's razor, before designing sophisticated algorithms, we start with a simple way to do the approximation. It limits the compilations of all methods to only one level. In this case, as there are no recompilations, it is easy to prove that the best schedule is just to order the compilations of all the functions based on the order of their first-time appearance in the call sequence. We call this simple approach single-level approximation.

***IAR Algorithm*** The single-level approximations are simple but ignores recompilation, an operation that can be beneficial as Figure 1 illustrates. To better approximate the optimal schedules, we design an algorithm that consists of an initialization step and several rounds of refinement with each round enhancing the schedule produced by earlier rounds. We call this algorithm the *IAR algorithm* in short for it centers around *initialization*, *appending*, and *replacement* operations.

Figure 3 outlines the algorithm. For simplicity of explanation, the description of the algorithm assumes that there is one execution thread and one compilation thread only and they run on two cores respectively. Additionally, it assumes that the JIT has only two levels of compilation. We will discuss the case with more than two levels at the end of this section and the case with more threads in Section 6.2.3.

The first step of the IAR algorithm creates an initial compilation schedule, which consists of the lowest-level compilations of all functions in the program, arranged in the order of the first-time appearances of the functions in the call sequence. Such a schedule tries to prevent bubbles (i.e. waiting time) from occurring in the execution that the long compilation time at the higher compilation level could cause.

It then classifies the functions into three categories: $A(ppend)$, $R(place)$, $O(ther)$. The categorization examines the benefits of doing a higher-level compilation for each function. The examination employs the collected compilation and execution time at all compilation levels. If a higher-level compilation appears to be not beneficial for a function (Formula 1 in Figure 3), it is put into $O$. Otherwise, it should be compiled at the higher level either at its first-time compilation (i.e., to replace its low-level compilation in the initial compilation sequence with a high-level compilation of it) or after the initial compilation stage is done (i.e., to append its high-level compilation to the end of the current compilation sequence.) These two cases correspond to adding the function to $R$ and $A$ respectively. The Formula 2 in Figure 3 shows the criterion for classifying these two cases. The rationale is that when the high-level compilation overhead is much larger than the attainable benefits at the beginning part of the run, putting the high-level compilation into the initial schedule may cause bubbles into the execution, and it is hence better to be appended to the end of the initial schedule. In our experiment, we tried different values of "K" in Formula 2 and found that as long as it falls into a range between 3 and 10, the results are quite similar (in our reported results, K=5.)

Based on the classification, the second step of the IAR algorithm simply replaces the low-level compilations of all functions in $R$ with high-level compilations in the initial compilation sequence. To append functions in $A$ to the sequence, however, we need to decide the order of appending. The heuristics we use is the compilation overhead. The rationale is that putting a costly recompilation early would cause large delays to the attainment of high-quality code for other functions.

The third step is a fine adjustment to the compilation sequence. It tries to find the slacks in the initial part of the schedule and exploit the slacks by replacing a low-level compilation with a high-level compilation as long as the replacement does not add bubbles into the execution. A slack is defined as the time between the finish of the first-time compilation of a function and its first invocation in the execution. The selective replacement accelerates the execution of the function without causing a negative effect. At a replacement, the following high level compilation of that function is deleted if there is one.

The final step is another fine adjustment. It tries to append more high-level compilations as long as there is time between the finish of all compilations and the finish of all executions. This filling does not cause any negative effect to the execution but could accelerate the execution of some functions that are not yet compiled at the high level. We tried various ways to prioritize these additional appending opera-

```
// Eseq: the call sequence;
// F: the set of functions;
// K: a constant (5 in our experiment);
// f.cl, f.ch: the compilation time of function f at low and high levels;
// f.el, f.eh: the execution time of function f at low and high levels;
// f.n: the number of calls to function f in Eseq;

step1 (init):
  Cseq = {};
  // get the sequence of first-time calls of all the functions
  Eseq1 = getSeq1stCalls (Eseq);
  Cseq = Eseq1;

  // categorize functions into sets A(ppend), R(eplace), O(thers).
  O={}; A={}; R={};
  foreach f in F
    if (f.ch+f.n*f.eh > f.cl+f.n*f.el)   // Formula 1
      O.append (f);
    else {
      f.n1 = numbers of calls to f during the compilation of current Cseq;
      if (f.ch - f.cl > K * f.n1 * (f.el - f.eh))   // Formula 2
        A.append (f);
      else
        R.append (f);
    }

step2 (append & replace):
  // ascending sort on the compilation time at the high level
  A = ascendingSortOnCh (A);
  Cseq.append (A); // append ch of members of A
  Cseq = replace (Cseq, R); // replace cl with ch for members of R

step3 (fill slack through replacement):
  Tc1 = computeTheEnd1stCompile (Cseq);
  Te1 = computeTheStart1stCall (Eseq, Cseq);
  slacks = findSlacks (Tc1, Te1);
  // replace some cl with ch to fill slacks
  Cseq = fillSlacksWithReplacement (Cseq, slacks);

step4 (append more to fill ending gap):
  L  = functions that are compiled at low level only in Cseq;
  M =  numbers of calls to functions in L in Eseq after Cseq finishes;
  L  = desendingSort (L, M);
  Tgap = time between end of compilations and end of executions;
  Append as many ch of functions in L as possible until filling up Tgap.
```

**Figure 3.** IAR algorithm.

tions by considering factors ranging from optimization overhead, to benefits, and positions of the calls in the sequence. But they do not outperform the simple heuristics Figure 3 shows. As Section 6 will show, the reason is that there is only a marginal room left for improvement by this fine adjustment.

This IAR algorithm offers a more sophisticated way to approximate the optimal schedules than the single-level approximation. It capitalizes on both the order of first-time appearances of the functions and their invocation frequencies, considers both the compilation overhead and overall benefits, and exploits each individual level of compilation and their combinations. Section 6 will show that the design enables a much better approximation than other methods do.

The time and space complexity of the IAR algorithm is $O(N+MlogM)$, where $N$ is the length of the call sequence, and $M$ is the number of unique functions in the sequence. Typically $N >> M$ and the complexity is linear to $N$ in practice.

The description of the IAR algorithm has assumed that the JIT has only two candidate compilation levels. That assumption is only for explanation simplicity. The algorithm itself works as long as a function has two levels of optimizations to choose; the two levels can differ for different functions. For a JIT with more than two levels, our design is to take the most responsive level and the most cost-effective level of a function as the two candidate levels for that function when applying the IAR algorithm. The most responsive level is the one taking the least time to compile, usually corresponding to the lowest level. The most cost-effective level is the level at which the compilation time plus the total execution time of all invocations to the function is minimum. The cost-effective level can be determined by the default **cost-benefit model** in most virtual machines. The cost-benefit model takes the hotness of a function, its size, and other information as inputs and estimates the most cost effective compilation level for that function [4]. An alternative way is offline profiling that measures the performance at every compilation level.

Our experiments in Section 6 will confirm that IAR on the two levels is enough to get a schedule close to the optimal.

### 5.2 Bounding the Limit

The algorithms in the previous subsection produce schedules that are attainable, the results of which may be regarded as the upper bounds of the minimum make-span of the program execution. Getting a lower bound of the minimum make-span is relatively simple. It is clear that the make-span cannot be smaller than the sum of the shortest execution time of each function call in the call sequence. Therefore, the lower bound is computed as $\sum_{i=1}^{N} {e_{f_i}}^K$, where $K$ is the highest compilation level, $e_{f_i}^K$ is the execution time of the $i$th function call in the invocation sequence at level $K$. The upper bound and lower bound reveal the limits of the value range of the minimum make-span. If the range is tight, it may serve as an alternative to minimum make-span for examining the potential of compilation scheduling.

### 5.3 Searching for the Limit

In addition to approximation, another way to solve the OCSP is to use some search algorithms to cleverly search through the design space for an optimal schedule. These search algorithms may substantially outperform naive search by avoiding some subspaces that are impossible to contain the optimal solution. However, they do not lower the computational complexity of the problem and may still consume too much time, space or both for large problems.

For completeness of the exploration, we examine the feasibility by applying A*-search, an algorithm that is optimally efficient for any given heuristic function—that is, for a given heuristic function, no other search-tree–based optimal algo-

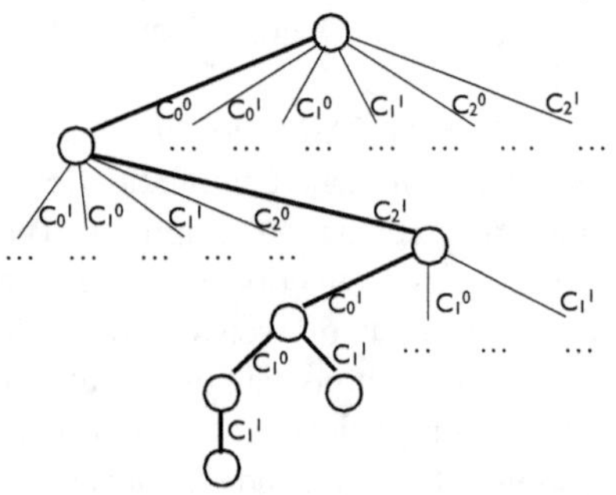

**Figure 4.** An example for modeling the compilation scheduling of three functions as a tree search problem. Notation: $C_i^j$ for the compilation of method $i$ at the $j$th level. The two highlighted paths denote two complete compilation sequences.

rithm is guaranteed to expand fewer nodes than A* search does [31].

***A*-Search*** For a tree search, where the goal is to find a path from the root to an arbitrary leaf with the total cost minimized, A* search defines a function $f(v)$ to estimate the lowest cost of all the paths passing through the node $v$. A* search maintains a priority list, initially containing only the root node. Each time, A* search removes the top element—that is, the node with the highest priority—from the priority list, and expands that node. After the expansion, it computes the $f(v)$ values of all the newly generated nodes, and puts them into the priority list. The priority is proportional to $1/f(v)$. This expansion process continues until the top of the list is a leaf node, indicating that no other nodes in the list need to be expanded any more as their lowest cost exceeds the cost of the path that is already discovered.

The definition of function $f(v)$ is the key for the solution's optimality and the algorithm's efficiency. There are two properties related to $f(v)$:

- A* search is optimal if $f(v)$ never overestimates the cost.
- The closer $f(v)$ is from the real lowest cost, the more effective A*-search is in pruning the search space.

***Problem Modeling*** A typical way to apply A*-search is to model the target problem as a tree-search problem. Figure 4 illustrates how we model the compilation scheduling problem. The tree contains all possible schedules for compiling three functions at two compilation levels. Every path from the root to a leaf represents one feasible compilation sequence. Each node on the path represents the compilation of a function at a level. The construction of the tree ensures that a lower-level compilation of a function does not appear after a higher-level compilation of the function in any path, as it is impossible to be an optimal schedule under the assumptions on execution times in Section 3. For instance, in Figure 4, $C_2^0$ never appears in a path below $C_2^1$.

To explain the search heuristic function $f(v)$, we use the following notations: $s(v)$ for the compilation schedule represented by the path segment from the root to node $v$, $t(v)$ for the time period from the start to the end of compilations in $s(v)$. In our exploration, the most effective definition of $f(v)$ we find is $f(v) = b(v) + e(v)$, where, $b(v)$ is the sum of the lengths of all the execution bubbles in $t(v)$ when $s(v)$ is used, and $e(v)$ is the sum of the extra execution time in $t(v)$ because the functions are not compiled at the highest level in $s(v)$.

## 6. Experiments

We design our experiments to answer the following questions:

- **Limit Estimation or Computation** Can the algorithms in Sections 5.1 and 5.2 provide a tight range for the minimum make-span? How effective and scalable is the A*-search algorithm in searching for optimal compilation schedules?
- **Potential of Existing Systems** Is there a substantial room left for improving the compilation scheduling used in modern runtime systems?
- **Influence of Other Factors** How do other factors, such as the concurrency and cost-benefit model in a JIT, influence answers to the questions above?

### 6.1 Methodology

***Experimental Framework*** To validate whether the proposed algorithms can provide a good estimation of the optimal compilation schedules, one just needs to apply the algorithms to a set of data that include a call sequence of a number functions and the compilation and execution times of those functions at various optimization levels. For collecting some realistic data, we develop a data collection framework for collecting the required data from real Java programs.

The collection framework is based on Jikes RVM [4] v3.1.2. As an open-source JVM that has gone through many years of enhancement by the community, Jikes RVM now shows competitive performance with top commercial systems [1]. It contains a basic compiler and an optimizing compiler, both single-threaded. The optimizing compiler supports three compilation levels. So counting them together means that a function can be compiled at any of the four levels. Jikes RVM has a replay mode, in which, it takes some *advice files* that indicate how each Java method should be compiled, and runs the program with the JIT following those instructions. By manipulating the advice files, we stimulate the compilation of each function (i.e. Java method) at each of the four levels in 20 repetitive runs, during which we collect the execution times of every function at each level, the average of which is taken as the execution time of that function at that level. By adding a timer into the JIT, we also collect the compilation time of each function at every level [3]. The runs for measuring compilation time are separate from the runs for measuring execution times to avoid possible perturbations by each other.

Also through the Jikes RVM, we collect the call sequence for every run of the programs. For a multithreaded application, we still get a single sequence; the calls by different threads are put into the sequence in order of the profiler's output. This order roughly corresponds to the invocation timing order by those threads. An alternative is to separate calls by different threads into different call sequences. But given that the threads typically share the same native code base generated by the same JIT, we find it more reasonable to put them together when considering compilation scheduling.

These collected data together form the data set we use for assessing the quality of the various schedules. Examination of the data shows that for most functions, the condition in Definition 1 holds—that is, $\forall\ i$ and $j_1 < j_2$, we have $c_{i,j_1} \leq c_{i,j_2}$, $e_{i,j_1} \geq e_{i,j_2}$.

The harness in the Dacapo suite, when running a benchmark, starts the JVM and runs the benchmark for a number of times (without restarting the JVM.) So in the late runs, the program enters a steady-state without many compilations happening. In the reported performance results, we concentrate on the first-time run (or called warmup run), for two reasons. First, compilation scheduling is mostly relevant to warmup runs as that is when most compilations happen. Second, despite that steady-state performance is critical for server applications, for most utility programs and smartphone applications, warmup run performance is often more crucial. These programs usually do not have a long execution time, but their response time is essential for user satisfaction.

In addition to data collection, the experimental framework includes a component that, for a given compilation schedule, computes the make-span of a call sequence based on the compilation and execution times of the involved functions, along with the number of cores used for compilation and execution.

Comparing the make-spans reported by such a framework provides a clear, direct evaluation of the scheduling algorithms. An alternative method is to deploy the compilation schedules in real executions of JVMs and measure the program finish time. That method, unfortunately, cannot provide a direct measurement of the quality of the scheduling algorithms, as we will discuss in Section 8.

***Benchmarks and Machines*** Our experiment uses the Dacapo [6] 2006 benchmark suite (default input)[4]. Two programs are not used: *chart* fails to run on Jikes RVM (3.1.2), and *xalan* cannot run in the replay mode of Jikes RVM. Table 1 reports the basic information of the benchmarks. Two of the programs, *hsqldb* and *lusearch*, are multithreading. The lengths of the call sequences range from 467K calls to 43M calls, and the numbers of unique functions in sequences range from 543 to 2128. All experiments happen on a machine equipped with X5570 with totally 16 cores. It has Linux 3.1.10 installed.

**Table 1.** Benchmarks

| Program | parallelism | #functions | call seq length | default time(s) |
|---|---|---|---|---|
| antlr | seq | 1187 | 2403584 | 1.6 |
| bloat | seq | 1581 | 9423445 | 5.0 |
| eclipse | seq | 2194 | 467372 | 28.4 |
| fop | seq | 1927 | 1323119 | 1.5 |
| hsqldb | parallel | 1006 | 8022794 | 2.9 |
| jython | seq | 2128 | 23655473 | 6.7 |
| luindex | seq | 641 | 20582610 | 6.1 |
| lusearch | parallel | 543 | 43573214 | 3.2 |
| pmd | seq | 1876 | 12543579 | 3.5 |

### 6.2 Results

We report the experimental results in three parts. The first part examines the full potential of compilation scheduling compared to the default scheduling scheme in Jikes RVM. The second and third parts investigate how an oracle cost-benefit model and concurrent JIT influence the observed potential. Then we examine the potential when the scheduling scheme in V8 is applied to those Java programs, the feasibility of finding optimal schedules through A*-search, and the potential of the IAR algorithm for online usage.

#### 6.2.1 Comparison with the Jikes RVM Scheme

In this part, we compare various schedules to reveal the potential in enhancing the scheduling algorithm in the default Jikes RVM. We first describe the default scheduling algorithm briefly. At the first invocation of a function, it always compiles the function at the lowest level. During the execution of a Java program, after every sampling period, the runtime checks whether any function could benefit from a recompilation. The cost of a compilation at level $j$ is computed as $e_j * k + c_j$, where $e_j$ and $c_j$ are the execution and compilation times of the function at level $j$, and $k$ is the number of times the sampler has seen the function on the call stack since the start of the program. Let $l$ be the level of the last compilation of the function, and $m$ be the level with the minimal cost among all levels higher than $l$. If $e_m * k + c_m < e_l * k$, the JIT recompiles the function at level $m$.

We implement the scheduling algorithm in our experimental framework. Figure 5 shows the normalized make-span (i.e., end-to-end running time) of the benchmarks under the default scheduling scheme and other compilation schedules. The IAR algorithm considers only two compilation levels for a function: the lowest level, and the most cost-effective level that is determined by the default cost-benefit

[3] To minimize measurement errors, we insert a loop into the JIT so that we can time 100 compilations of a function and get the average time.

[4] We didn't use the latest version of Dacapo as it cannot fully work on Jikes RVM [20].

model in the Jikes RVM. These two levels are respectively used for the two single-level compilation scheme. The baseline used for the normalization is the lower bound computed with the algorithm in Section 5.2. So the lower a bar is in the figure, the better the corresponding schedule is.

The results lead to several observations. First, there is a large gap between the make-span by the default schedule and the lower bound. More than half of the programs show a gap greater than 50%. The average gap is over 70%. However, just from that gap, it is hard to tell whether there is a large room for improvement as the minimum make-span may exist anywhere between the lower bound and the default. So besides the lower bound, we still need a decent estimation of the minimum make-span.

Following descriptions in Section 5.1, we experiment with the single-level approximation, with the base level ("base-level") and the suitable highest compilation level ("optimizing-level") used respectively. Both of them show even longer make-spans than the default on most programs. The base-level scheme saves compilation time but results in a longer execution time for less efficient code it generates. The optimizing-level scheme, on the other hand, saves execution time, but results in a longer compilation time and execution bubbles. A more sophisticated approximation is necessary.

The IAR algorithm meets the needs. Using the schedules from IAR, none of the programs shows a gap wider than 17% from the lower bound. On average, the gap is only 8.5% wide. It indicates that to examine the full potential, it is sufficient to compare to either the lower bound or the make-span from the IAR algorithm, as the minimum make-span is close to both of them. Compared to the IAR results, the default compilation scheduling scheme in Jikes RVM is largely behind in performance, with a gap from the lower bound as wide as eight times of the IAR gap, suggesting that significant potential exists in enhancing the performance of Jikes RVM by optimizing its compilation scheduling. It is worth mentioning that the time savings by the IAR schedule is not only due to the reduction of compilation-incurred bubbles on the critical path, but also to the reduction of execution time as some highly optimized code become available earlier than in the default run.

As a side note, the results also confirm that using only two levels of optimizations for each function is enough for the IAR algorithm to work sufficiently well, despite more than two levels are supported by the JIT.

### 6.2.2 With an Oracle Cost-Benefit Model

In the study so far, we rely on the default cost-benefit model in Jikes RVM to determine the suitable optimizing levels for each method. This subsection examines whether the large impact of the scheduling diminishes if the cost-benefit model is improved. A positive answer would mean that enhancing the cost-benefit model could be sufficient.

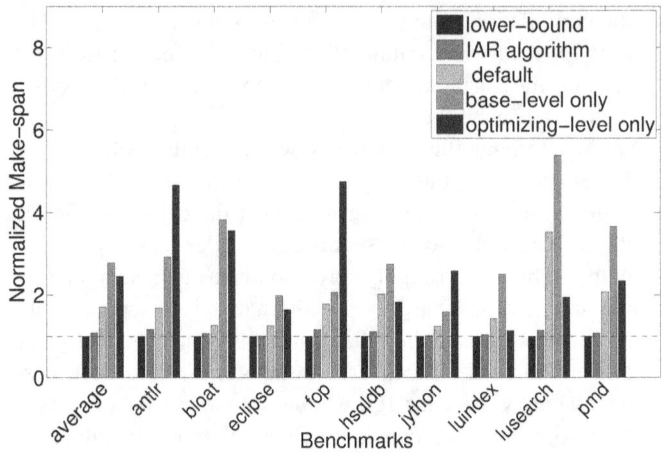


**Figure 5.** Normalized running time based on the JIT in the default Jikes RVM.

To answer the question, we repeat the experiments while replacing the cost-benefit model in Jikes RVM with an oracle model. The default cost-benefit model tries to estimate the compilation time and execution time of a function at various optimization levels, and pick the level that if it is used, the sum of the estimated compilation time of that function and the estimated execution time of all invocations to that function is minimized. In our oracle cost-benefit model, we simply replace the estimated time with the actual time. The model is not necessarily the optimal model, but it is the best the default cost-benefit model can do.

Figure 6 reports the result. Compared to the result in Figure 5, there are several differences. First, the gap between the IAR schedules and the lower-bound increases, but by no more than 6% on average. The range of the make-span defined by the IAR and lower-bound remains tight. Second, the average gap between the default and the lower-bound doubles in size. Using the optimizing level only results in a similar gap. The reason for the gap expansion is two-fold. The lower-bound becomes lower as the pure execution of the program gets faster with a better optimizing level determined, and meanwhile, the longer time in the higher-level compilation causes more bubbles into the execution in the default and optimizing-level only cases. Many of these bubbles however can be avoided by a better compilation schedule as the IAR results demonstrate.

Overall, the results suggest that the importance of compilation scheduling actually increases as the cost-benefit model gets enhanced, further reinforcing the importance of the compilation scheduling dimension in improving modern runtime systems.

### 6.2.3 With a Concurrent JIT

The JIT in the default Jikes RVM is single-threaded. There are some JVMs (e.g., Hotspot) that support concurrent compilation of multiple functions on a multicore system. The concurrency offers an alternative way to reduce compilation

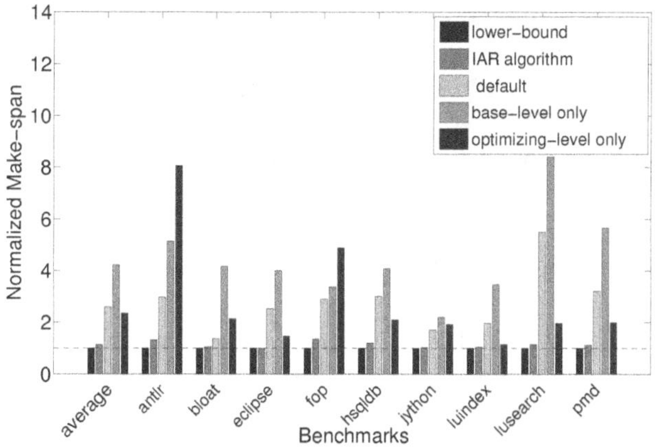


**Figure 6.** Normalized running time when an oracle cost-benefit model is used in the JIT.

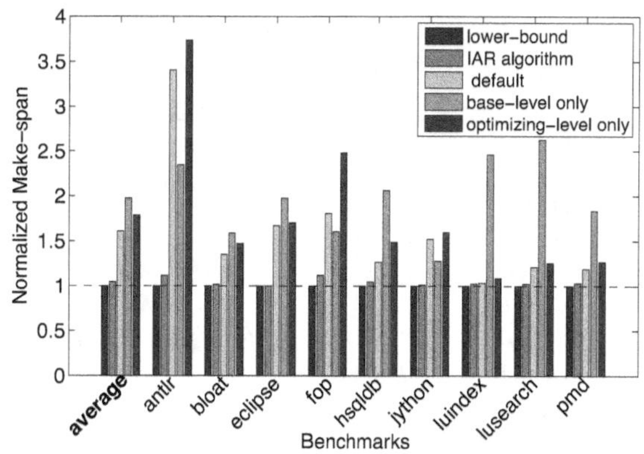


**Figure 8.** Normalized make-span, compared with the results by the compilation scheduling scheme in Google V8.

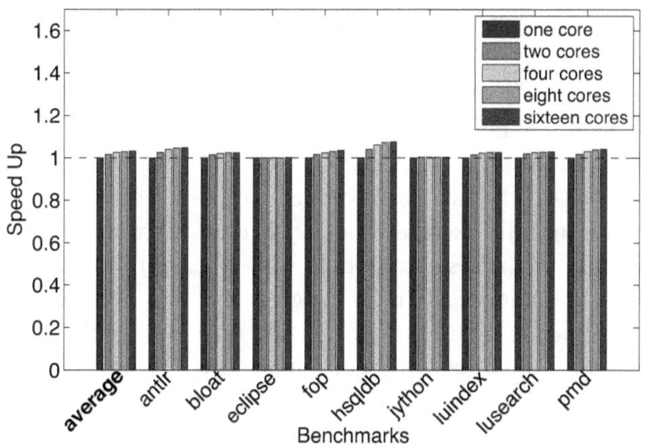


**Figure 7.** Speedups brought by concurrency JIT when the IAR schedule is used. The legend shows the number of cores used for compilation.

overhead and the delays to executions. We apply the idea to the IAR schedules by allowing multiple compilation tasks to be processed in parallel (the tasks are ordered in a queue based on the IAR schedules.) The graph in Figure 7 reports the speedups (in terms of make-span) brought by the concurrency, when the default cost-benefit model is used. As the number of cores increases, the speedup increases but slightly and always remains quite minor. The largest speedup is 13% when 16 cores and the oracle cost-benefit model are used. The average speedups are no greater than 7% in all the cases. Similar results are seen when the oracle cost-benefit model is used.

The reason for the speedups being minor is that most compilation time is already hided when the IAR schedules are used. In another word, when a good compilation schedule is used, there is a small room left for performance improvement by concurrent JIT. Given that concurrent JIT may compete for computing resources with worker threads, the results indicate that compilation scheduling is a more cost-effective way for enhancing modern runtime systems than concurrent JIT[5].

### 6.2.4 Comparison with the V8 Scheme

In addition to Jikes RVM, we also compare with the compilation scheduling algorithm used in V8, the primary Javascript runtime engine from Google, and also one of the most efficient Javascript runtime engines on the market. We apply its scheduling scheme to the Java programs we use. The purpose is to examine the inherent quality of the scheduling scheme, rather than the actual performance of the engine on Javascript applications.

In V8, there are only two optimization levels: *low* and *high*. By default, it compiles a function at the *low* level at the first encounter of it and then recompiles it at the *high* level at its second invocation.

We apply that algorithm to the call sequences we obtained from the Jikes RVM on the Java benchmarks, with the lowest two levels in Jikes RVM JIT as the *low* and *high* in this experiment. Figure 8 shows the make-spans. The gap between the IAR schedule and the lower bound remains small, only 4% on average. The schedule from the V8 scheme results in a smaller gap from the lower bound than the Jikes RVM results, 61% on average. The gaps between the two single-level compilation schedules and the lower bound also become smaller than in the Jikes RVM case. The main reason is not that the V8 scheme is better than the Jikes RVM one, but that as the *highest* optimizing level is lower than that in the Jikes RVM, the lower bound in this V8 experiment is higher than in the Jikes RVM experiment. But the high-level observation is consistent: The IAR algorithm still produces near optimal results while the default scheduling has a large room for improvement.

[5] Note that this point does not rule out the value of concurrent JIT. It could be quite valuable when an inferior compilation scheduling is used.

**Table 2.** IAR Algorithm Time

| Program | IAR time (sec) | percentage over whole program time (%) |
|---|---|---|
| antlr | 0.006 | 0.37 |
| bloat | 0.023 | 0.47 |
| eclipse | 0.001 | 0.004 |
| fop | 0.003 | 0.21 |
| hsqldb | 0.020 | 0.67 |
| jython | 0.059 | 0.87 |
| luindex | 0.051 | 0.84 |
| lusearch | 0.108 | 3.38 |
| pmd | 0.031 | 0.89 |

#### 6.2.5 Effectiveness of Heuristic Search

For the nature of strongly NP-completeness, it is unlikely to find a search algorithm that can produce the optimal compilation schedule efficiently. Our experiments on the A*-search algorithm offers a confirmation. For tiny problems, the algorithm can find the optimal schedules by searching through a fraction of all possible paths. For instance, for a call sequence with six unique functions called for 50 times in total and two levels of compilations, the A*-search algorithm finds an optimal compilation schedule by searching through 96 out of 4 billion (12!) paths. However, due to the heuristics A*-search uses for space pruning, it stores all incompletely examined paths in memory. As the search tree grows exponentially with the problem size, the space requirement increases rapidly. In our experiments, when the number of unique methods is larger than 6, the A*-search program (written in Java) aborts for out of memory (2GB is used for the heap size.)

#### 6.2.6 IAR Overhead

Table 2 reports the time overhead of the IAR algorithm. For most programs, the overhead is less than 1% of the whole program execution time. The low overhead makes it affordable for online usage. But to achieve a good scheduling result, many other factors have to be considered as Section 8 will discuss.

### 6.3 Summary of Results

Overall, the experiments show that the IAR algorithm is effective for approximating the optimal compilation schedules. It produces schedules efficiently with a near optimal performance on most programs; its linear time and space complexity grants it high efficiency and scalability. On the other hand, the experiments show that neither simple heuristic algorithms (e.g. the single-level approximation) nor heuristic search (e.g., A*-search) can provide scalable, satisfying results.

By comparing the scheduling used in Jikes RVM with the IAR algorithm and lower bounds, we see that a better compilation schedule can bring speedup by as much as 1.6X on average. And the potential increases to a factor of 2.3 when the perfect cost-benefit model is used. These results suggest that enhancing the compilation scheduling is an important direction to explore, and improvement in the cost-benefit model in a JIT compiler only highlights its importance further. Meanwhile, it shows that concurrent JIT adds minor improvement when a good compilation schedule is used.

## 7. Potential Impact

The primary goal of this work is to enhance understanding of how compilation ordering affects the performance of JIT-based runtime systems. This study produces some major findings towards that goal: It reveals the inherent computational complexity of the scheduling problem, offers methods for effectively approximating the optimal schedules, and shows the large room left for improvement in existing systems.

The potential impact of this work is multifold. It points out that compilation scheduling is an important direction for enhancing JIT-based runtime systems. Its complexity findings will help avoid efforts in searching for algorithms to compute optimal JIT schedules. It offers the first practical way to assess the JIT scheduling of runtime systems, from which, virtual machine developers can easily see the room left for improvement and allocate their efforts appropriately. In addition, the insights from this work may offer some immediate guidance for enhancing current virtual machines. For instance, it shows that the first-time compilation of a method should generally get a higher priority than recompilations of other methods.

## 8. Complexities from Actual Runtime Systems

The findings in this work shed some insights into enhancing compilation schedules in virtual machines, but producing a ready-to-use virtual machine with much enhanced compilation schedules is a goal beyond the scope of this paper. This section discusses some complexities for achieving that goal in an actual runtime system.

The first barrier is in getting or estimating the call sequence of a production run. It could be tackled through some recently developed techniques, such as cross-run learning and prediction. Some studies (e.g., [5, 33]) have shown the feasibility to learn various types of behavior patterns of a program (e.g., loop trip-counts, function call relations) by accumulating the data transparently sampled across *production runs* of the program. There have been a lot of studies in small-scope program behavior prediction [8, 18, 28, 35, 36]. And recent years have seen some development towards large-scope program behavior sequence prediction [34]. Extending these techniques into call sequence prediction could help remove this barrier.

The second barrier is in obtaining the accurate compilation and execution times of a function at various optimization levels. In some virtual machines, there are already some kind of models for estimating those times. In Jikes RVM, for instance, the times are estimated through some simple linear functions of the size of the function. The parameters of those functions are obtained through some offline training during the installation of Jikes RVM on a machine. However, such static estimations are often quite rough. For example, different invocations of a function, even if they use the same executable, may have different running lengths due to differences in their calling parameters and contexts. Moreover, function inlining that happens in a run may substantially change the length and execution time of the caller function. Furthermore, the time when a compilation happens may also affect the execution time of a function. A later compilation in a run may produce better code as the online profiler collects more information about the program execution. All these factors suggest that existing static estimations of the execution times of a function are unlikely to provide an accurate estimation. Development of the aforementioned cross-run learning methods may help enhance the estimation quality. On the other hand, finding out the relations between estimation errors and the quality of an advanced scheduling algorithm will also help: If the scheduling can tolerate a good degree of estimation errors, building up an estimation model to meet the requirement may be still feasible.

It is worth mentioning that due to the variations in execution times as mentioned in the previous paragraph, desirable results often cannot get produced when one directly applies the results of the IAR algorithm—obtained on offline collected average times—to a real program execution. Some ways to extend the IAR algorithm to accommodate the variations in execution times will help its practical usage.

Unlike Jikes RVM, some runtime environments have interpreters as part of their code translators for quick code generation. In fact, the lowest level of compilation in Jikes RVM is designed in that spirit for the same purpose. It does not build an intermediate representation nor perform register allocation. In another word, that lowest-level compilation can be regarded as a method-level interpreter. Similar schemes are taken in other runtimes (e.g., V8). If we treat interpretation as the lowest level compilation in the optimal compilation schedule problem, the analysis and algorithms discussed in this paper can still be applied. Some extra care may be needed for the interpreters that operate at the level of a single statement.

We note that although these complexities complicate the enhancement of compilation scheduling in real systems, they do not alter the major conclusions from this study. For instance, recall that we have used the average value of $e_{i,j}$, for each given $i$ and $j$, when computing the lower bounds of program execution times. Because the total time a function takes in a run equals the sum of the time it takes in all its invocations, using the average does not skew the computed lower bound of the execution time of the whole program run. For the same reason, the variation does not affect the optimality of the scheduling algorithm in the single-core case in Section 4.1.

## 9. Related Work

The ParcPlace Smalltalk VM [11] and the Self-93 VM [17] pioneer adaptive optimization techniques employed in current virtual machines. Recent years have seen increasing attentions payed to enhancing the performance of JIT-based runtime systems. These efforts can be largely classified into two categories, based on the main target of their optimizations.

The first category focuses on the internal design of the JIT in runtime systems. Examples include the work on using machine learning to help JIT better decide the optimizations suitable for a Java method [10, 24]. Several recent studies on Javascript JIT have explored static and dynamic inferences of dynamic types to enable better code specialization [2, 16, 19, 23]. In addition, a number of recent studies have tried to refine trace detection, management, and optimizations in trace JIT for modern scripting languages [9, 13]. As Section 6 shows, enhancing the design of JIT does not replace but reinforce the need for compilation scheduling by exposing an even higher potential benefit of scheduling.

The second category concentrates on JIT compilation policies, especially on the determination of the appropriate optimization level to use for compiling a function (or trace). Most adaptive virtual machines use selective compilation, which tries to find hot functions and optimize them more than other functions [3, 27]. They typically contain a cost-benefit model that decides the suitable optimization level for a function based on its hotness, size, and other information. Predicting the hotness of a function is critical for these systems. Most of them have relied on online profiling with the assumption that a hot method in the past will remain hot in the future [4, 21]. Some studies try to predict hotness based on loop trip-counts [26] or phases [14]. All these studies use information within a run to make the predictions. The scheduling of the compilation events in the those studies is mostly on-demand, just as the default scheme in Jikes RVM: When a function is loaded or is selected by the online profiling to be recompiled, the compilation event is inserted into a compilation queue and is processed in the order of their arrival. Their general guideline is to use a low level to compile a function when it is loaded to get a good startup time and later recompile it at a higher level when it appears to be hot. This current study shows that the intuition-based scheme leads to schedules that are far from being optimal in practice.

Several studies try to exploit cross-run observations [5, 32]. They make it possible to predict the suitable optimizing levels for a set of methods as program starts running. Such predictions allow more flexibility in scheduling (re)compilations beyond the on-demand scheduling. However, these studies did not exploit the flexibility and used similar scheduling schemes as the default system uses.

All these studies on compilation policies have aimed at answering the questions on what functions are hot and what levels to compile them, rather than when to (re)compile them or in what order to (re)compile them.

There have been explorations on using concurrent JIT to enhance the performance of virtual machines [7, 15, 22]. They have not systematically explored the influence of the order of compilation events. Concurrent JIT may give some performance boost to the default JVM, but introduce contentions for computing resources with the application threads. As Section 6 shows, when a good compilation order is used, the gain from concurrent JIT over sequential JIT becomes marginal. How to combine these two complementary approaches in practice is a problem for the future.

Another body of related work is ahead-of-time (AOT) compilation for Java and other managed code. The idea of AOT is to compile a program into native machine code before executions of the program. Another technique that shares a similar spirit of reusing native code cross runs is persistent code caching [29], which stores the native code produced in a run into some persistent storage for reuses by later runs. Both techniques have shown some benefits in performance enhancement. However, in practice, they have been used in just some limited settings. Most programs in managed languages are still JIT compiled at runtime, plausibly for the portability and seamless handling of dynamic types by JIT, and the maturity of modern runtime environments.

## 10. Conclusion

This paper describes the first principled study on unveiling the full potential of compilation scheduling for JIT-based runtime systems. Through some rigorous analysis, it reveals the inherent computational complexity of finding optimal compilation orders, proving the strong NP-completeness of the problem. It empirically demonstrates the difficulty in searching for an optimal schedule with the A*-search algorithm. Prompted by the challenges, it proposes a heuristic algorithm named the *IAR algorithm*, which yields near optimal schedules for a set of benchmarks. The results enable a systematic examination of the full potential of compilation scheduling in modern runtime systems. This paper reports experiments on two scheduling schemes, respectively corresponding to those used in Jikes RVM and V8, concluding that significant potential (1.6X on average) exists in adjusting compilation schedules. It further shows that the potential is even larger as the JIT internal design gets better. It also reveals that concurrent JIT gives only marginal gain in performance when the compilation order is near optimal, suggesting that enhancing compilation orders may be a more cost-effective option than concurrent JIT in enhancing the performance of JIT-based runtime systems. Overall, this study concludes that improving compilation scheduling in modern runtime systems is an important direction (although being largely overlooked so far) for future runtime system designs. The theoretical results, the IAR algorithms, and multi-fold insights produced in this work lay the foundation for this direction of research.

## Acknowledgment

We thank the anonymous reviewers of the earlier versions of this paper for their helpful feedback. This material is based upon work supported by DOE Early Career Award, and the National Science Foundation under Grant No. 0811791, 1320796, and CAREER Award. Any opinions, findings, and conclusions or recommendations expressed in this material are those of the authors and do not necessarily reflect the views of the National Science Foundation or DOE.

## References

[1] Jikes rvm. `http://jikesrvm.org`.

[2] C. Anderson, S. Drossopoulou, and P. Giannini. Towards type inference for javascript. In *ECOOP*, 2005.

[3] M. Arnold, S. Fink, D. Grove, M. Hind, and P. F. Sweeney. A survey of adaptive optimization in virtual machines. *Proceedings of the IEEE*, 92(2), 2005.

[4] M. Arnold, M. Hind, and B. G. Ryder. Online feedback-directed optimization of Java. In *Proceedings of ACM Conference on Object-Oriented Programming Systems, Languages and Applications*, pages 111–129, 2002.

[5] M. Arnold, A. Welc, and V.T. Rajan. Improving virtual machine performance using a cross-run profile repository. In *the Conference on Object-Oriented Programming, Systems, Languages, and Applications*, pages 297–311, 2005.

[6] S. M. Blackburn et al. The DaCapo benchmarks: Java benchmarking development and analysis. In *Proceedings of ACM SIGPLAN Conference on Object-Oriented Programming Systems, Languages and Applications*, October 2006.

[7] I. Bohm, T. Koch, S. Kyle, B. Franke, and N. Topham. Generalized just-in-time trace compilation using a parallel task farm in a dynamic binary translator. In *Proceedings of ACM SIGPLAN Conference on Programming Languages Design and Implementation*, 2011.

[8] M. Burtscher and B. G. Zorn. Hybrid load-value predictors. *IEEE Transactions on Computers*, 2002.

[9] J. Castanos, D. Edelsohn, K. Ishizaki, P. Nagpurkar, T. Nakatani, T. Ogasawara, and P. Wu. On the benefits and pitfalls of extending a statically typed language jit compiler for dynamic scripting languages. In *OOPSLA*, 2012.

[10] J. Cavazos and M. O'Boyle. Method-specific dynamic compilation using logistic regression. In *Proceedings of ACM SIGPLAN Conference on Object-Oriented Programming Systems, Languages and Applications*, 2006.

[11] L. P. Deutsch and A. M. Schiffman. Efficient implementation of the smalltalk-80 system. In *POPL*, 1984.

[12] Y. Ding, M. Zhou, Z. Zhao, S. Eisenstat, and X. Shen. The potential and complexity of compilation scheduling in jit-

based runtime systems. Technical Report WM-CS-2014-02, College of William and Mary, 2014.

[13] A. Gal, B. Eich, M. Shaver, D. Anderson, et al. Trace-based just-in-time type specialization for dynamic languages. In *Proceedings of the ACM SIGPLAN Conference On Programming Language Design and Implementation*, 2009.

[14] D. Gu and C. Verbrugge. Phase-based adaptive recompilation in a JVM. In *Proceedings of the International Symposium on Code Generation and Optimization*, pages 24–34, 2008.

[15] J. Ha, M. Haghighat, S. Cong, and K. S. McKinley. A concurrent trace-based just-in-time compiler for single-threaded javascript. In *Workshop on Parallel Execution of Sequential Programs on Multicore Architectures*, 2009.

[16] B. Hacket and S. Guo. Fast and precise hybrid type inference for javascript. In *PLDI*, 2012.

[17] U. Holzle and D. Ungar. Reconciling responsiveness with performance in pure object-oriented languages. *ACM Transactions on Programming Language Systems*, 18(4), 1996.

[18] S. Hu, R. Bhargava, and L. K. John. The role of return value prediction in exploiting speculative method-level parallelism. *Journal of Instruction-Level Parallelism*, 2003.

[19] S. H. Jensen, A. Mller, and P. Thiemann. Type analysis for javascript. In *SAS*, 2009.

[20] Jikes rvm project and status. http://http://jikesrvm.org/Project+Status.

[21] T. Kotzmann, C. Wimmer, H. Mossenbock, T. Rodriguez, K. Russell, and D. Cox. Design of the java hotspot client compiler for java 6. *Transactions on Architecture and Code Optimization*, 5(1), 2008.

[22] P.A. Kulkarni. Jit compilation policy for modern machines. In *Proceedings of the annual ACM SIGPLAN conference on Object-oriented programming, systems, languages, and applications*, 2011.

[23] F. Logozzo and H. Venter. Rata: Rapid atomic type analysis by abstract interpretation. In *CC*, 2010.

[24] R. Nabinger-Sanchez, J. Amaral, D. Szafron, M. Pirvu, and M. Stoodley. Using machines to learn method-specific compilation strategies. In *CGO*, 2011.

[25] F. Nah. Study on tolerable waiting time: How long are web users willing to wait? *Behavior and Information Technology*, 23(3):153–163, 2004.

[26] M. A. Namjoshi and P. A. Kulkarni. Novel online profiling for virtual machines. In *Proceedings of the International Conference on Virtual Execution Environments (VEE)*, pages 133–144, 2010.

[27] M. Paleczny, C. Vick, and C. Click. The java hotspot server compiler. In *Symposium on JavaTM Virtual Machine Research and Technology*, 2001.

[28] C. J. Pickett, C. Verbrugge, and A. Kielstra. Adaptive software return value prediction. Technical Report 1, McGill University, 2009.

[29] V. Reddi, D. Connors, R. Cohn, and M. Smith. Persistent code caching: Exploiting code reuse across executions and applications. In *CGO*, 2007.

[30] A. Rushinek and S. Rushinek. What makes users happy? *Communications of the ACM*, 29(7):594–598, 1986.

[31] S. Russell and P. Norvig. *Artificial Intelligence*. Prentice Hall, 2002.

[32] K. Tian, Y. Jiang, E. Zhang, and X. Shen. An input-centric paradigm for program dynamic optimizations. In *the Conference on Object-Oriented Programming, Systems, Languages, and Applications (OOPSLA)*, 2010.

[33] K. Tian, E. Zhang, and X. Shen. A step towards transparent integration of input-consciousness into dynamic program optimizations. In *the Conference on Object-Oriented Programming, Systems, Languages, and Applications (OOPSLA)*, 2011.

[34] B. Wu, Z. Zhao, X. Shen, Y. Jiang, Y. Gao, and R. Silvera. Exploiting inter-sequence correlations for program behavior prediction. In *Proceedings of the annual ACM SIGPLAN conference on Object-oriented programming, systems, languages, and applications*, 2012.

[35] T. Yeh and Y. N. Patt. A comparison of dynamic branch predictors that use two levels of branch history. In *Proceedings of the 20th Annual International Symposium on Computer Architecture*, pages 257–266, May 1993.

[36] Y. Zhong, X. Shen, and C. Ding. Program locality analysis using reuse distance. *ACM Transactions on Programming Languages and Systems*, 31(6), 2009.

# Speculative Hardware/Software Co-Designed Floating-Point Multiply-Add Fusion

Marc Lupon[1] Enric Gibert[1] Grigorios Magklis[1] Sridhar Samudrala[2] Raúl Martínez[1]
Kyriakos Stavrou[1] David R. Ditzel[3]

[1] Intel Barcelona Research Center, Intel Labs

[1]{marc.lupon,enric.gibert.codina,grigorios.magklis,raul.martinez,kyriakos.stavrou}@intel.com
[2]samudrala_yh@yahoo.com [3]dave.ditzel@gmail.com

## Abstract

A Fused Multiply-Add (FMA) instruction is currently available in many general-purpose processors. It increases performance by reducing latency of dependent operations and increases precision by computing the result as an indivisible operation with no intermediate rounding. However, since the arithmetic behavior of a single-rounding FMA operation is different than independent FP multiply followed by FP add instructions, some algorithms require significant revalidation and rewriting efforts to work as expected when they are compiled to operate with FMA—a cost that developers may not be willing to pay. Because of that, abundant legacy applications are not able to utilize FMA instructions. In this paper we propose a novel HW/SW collaborative technique that is able to efficiently execute workloads with increased utilization of FMA, by adding the option to get the same numerical result as separate FP multiply and FP add pairs. In particular, we extended the host ISA of a HW/SW co-designed processor with a new Combined Multiply-Add (CMA) instruction that performs an FMA operation with an intermediate rounding. This new instruction is used by a transparent dynamic translation software layer that uses a speculative instruction-fusion optimization to transform FP multiply and FP add sequences into CMA instructions. The FMA unit has been slightly modified to support both single-rounding and double-rounding fused instructions without increasing their latency and to provide a conservative fall-back path in case of mispeculation. Evaluation on a cycle-accurate timing simulator showed that CMA improved SPECfp performance by 6.3% and reduced executed instructions by 4.7%.



*ASPLOS '14*, March 1–5, 2014, Salt Lake City, Utah, USA.

http://dx.doi.org/10.1145/2541940.2541978

***Categories and Subject Descriptors*** D.3.4 [*Programming Languages*]: Processors - optimization, run-time environments, translator writing systems and compiler generators

***General Terms*** Algorithms, Performance, Design

***Keywords*** Binary translator, HW/SW co-designed processors, Instruction fusion, FMA, Combined Multiply-Add

## 1. Introduction

The Fused Multiply-Add (FMA) operation has recently been added in the revised IEEE 754-2008 standard [1] as a floating-point (FP) arithmetic instruction that computes A*B±C with a single rounding of the final result. FMA-capable execution units have been available in high-end processors since the early 90's [32, 43], and have recently been introduced in many popular general-purpose processors [8, 22, 28, 34, 36]. The usage of FMA has the potential to increase the arithmetic precision of algorithms because the rounding steps on the intermediate results are reduced [3, 6]; and to improve the performance because implementation of FMA instructions have shorter latencies than their equivalent FP multiply (from now on, FPMul) and FP add (from now on, FPAdd) sequences [5, 16].

Unfortunately, there are some issues that can hinder the wide adoption of FMA in present-day applications. Although more accurate, the results generated by an FMA instruction are not the same as those produced by the traditional FPMul followed by FPAdd sequence because they perform different rounding [18, 24]. As a consequence, a straightforward FMA-enabled recompilation of a program may produce a different output than a robust and trusted legacy binary. Moreover, certain mathematical expressions behave differently than expected when indiscriminately using FMA instructions [19], which may introduce difficult-to-identify bugs and unpredictability [24]. Real-life experiences have demonstrated how sensitive FP workloads are to imprecisions in the arithmetic behavior [10, 31, 45]. Because

[2,3] work performed while at Intel Corporation

backward compatibility is a must, software developers have to spend time, energy and money to revalidate the code and adapt it through non-trivial changes if they want to take full advantage of the FMA capability.

FMA extensions can be very useful on FP applications that require higher precision results where the compiler is able to fuse FPMul and FPAdd pairs and that do not require such a strict validation procedure. Hence, it is important to provide fast execution for applications that contain *either* fused (FMA) and unfused (FPMul and FPAdd) instructions. Binaries with unfused instructions can be problematic since many processors do not include specialized FPMul and FPAdd units anymore in order to simplify design, save area and reduce leakage [8, 32, 34, 36]. Instead, these processors execute those operations in the FMA hardware. The cost of this design decision is an increased latency on unfused instructions, which penalizes those applications that have not been adapted to include FMA instructions.

Hardware/Software (HW/SW) co-designed architectures provide a way to obtain the benefits of an enhanced machine-specific instruction set without the need to alter the visible instruction-set architecture nor to recompile the program from source code. In such systems, an internal entity called a Dynamic Binary Translator (DBT) that is transparent to the entire SW stack transforms the binaries at runtime to use machine-specific instructions, and optimizes the code to take maximum benefit of the underlying HW. These architectures have been proposed to improve performance, power consumption and energy efficiency, to lower design complexity, for backward and forward ISA compatibility, and/or for better design customization; and they have been studied both in academia and in industry [4, 9, 11, 12, 14, 20, 26, 27, 30, 35, 37, 38, 42, 46, 47].

In this paper, we present **a novel HW/SW technique that allows a natural adoption of FMA capability** on existing software—all of this, **without requiring changes in original programs or in compilers**. As a result, legacy binaries as well as new applications that contain separate FPMul and FPAdd instructions can run faster using in-place FMA hardware without requiring software rewriting or revalidation.

The core of the technique consists of a new Combined Multiply-Add (CMA) instruction that is exposed only to the internal ISA and that performs an extra rounding between the FPMul and the FPAdd to reproduce the same result as executing the two instructions separately. We have extended a conventional FMA unit with an intermediate rounding logic that is not complete in order not to increase the latency for *any* FMA operation—including the new CMA instruction—and to minimize the area impact in the FP cluster. This means that the unit generates non-compatible results on few infrequent situations. When this happens, an intermediate rounding fault is raised and control is passed to the software DBT layer that is responsible to maintain full compatibility for these corner case scenarios in a totally transparent manner. In fact, **the ability to execute the common case in the simplified HW while supporting rare scenarios by SW is one of the key elements for the success of the technique.**

The transparent DBT layer implements an instruction-fusion algorithm that converts FPMul and FPAdd pairs into a single CMA instruction *speculatively* when optimizing hot code regions. This new optimization applies smart heuristics to fuse instructions only when expected to be beneficial and it is speculative because it assumes that the CMA outcome will be valid. The algorithm is extended with a reactive mechanism in which fusion is selectively disabled when intermediate rounding faults (mispeculations) affect performance. Unlike other fusion mechanisms, our algorithm is able to fuse FPMul and FPAdd pairs that are not consecutive in program order (even if they are separated by hundreds of instructions) and identify which is the most valuable option in case of finding multiple candidates to fuse with.

We have modified the source code of a product-quality and highly-tuned DBT to integrate the entire proposed technique and we have evaluated it using a cycle-accurate performance and power simulator. Our evaluation shows that this HW/SW collaborative technique improves SPECfp execution time by 6.3% while only increasing power consumption by 1.5%. The main contributions of the paper are three-fold:

- We present a **non-invasive and direct solution that allows any FP program to obtain maximum profit of the FMA hardware.** The proposed technique includes a new hardware design and a set of novel software-managed mechanisms to deal with it. Although the solution envisioned targets a HW/SW co-designed processor, it can easily be incorporated in a more conventional framework.
- We corroborate that a holistic HW/SW co-designed implementation can simplify the hardware design without losing potential performance. This confirms that a **tight collaboration between the different layers of the HW/SW stack can bring noticeable synergies in HW/SW designs**. As a result, these processors can introduce new features much faster than pure HW solutions.
- We show that HW/SW co-designed processors offer effective mechanisms to rapidly assimilate new hardware capabilities without exposing them to the user. **HW/SW co-designed processors can help in closing the gap between the time a new feature is available** (in this particular case, the FMA operation) **and when it is broadly used in the community.**

The rest of the paper is organized as follows. Section 2 details the background on HW/SW co-designed processors and describes the problems associated with FMA instructions. Section 3 explains the internal HW and SW modifications introduced to support CMA instructions. Section 4 presents the experimental methodology, while Section 5 evaluates the feature. Section 6 compares the technique with other proposals, and Section 7 concludes the work.

## 2. Background

The following paragraphs describe the compatibility issues that surround FMA operations and give an overview of the Code Morphing Software (CMS), a mature and high performance DBT that is used as our transparent software layer.

### 2.1 Fused Multiply-Add Extensions

Fused Multiply-Add (FMA) extensions enable evaluation of the $\pm$(A*B)$\pm$C expression [1] with a single instruction. As FMA operations only perform a single rounding at the end of the operation, the result that they produce has higher precision than the original FPMul followed by FPAdd sequence. This makes the usage of FMA very attractive for implementing algorithms that require greater accuracy, as it reduces the numbers of arithmetic errors approximately by half.

The IBM RS/6000 processor [32] introduced FMA hardware to support single-rounding $\pm$(A*B)$\pm$C in just one instruction. To simplify the design, the FMA unit replaced separate FPMul and FPAdd units, reproducing the results by forcing A*1.0$\pm$C for additions and A*B$\pm$0.0 for multiplications. Other succeeding commercial processors like Intel® Itanium® [43] or AMD Bulldozer [8] followed this approach. In such environments, an FMA operation has the same latency as an FPMul or FPAdd, making it appealing for performance purposes too. Although in other FMA designs the latency of FPMul and FPAdd can be substantially reduced [5, 16, 39, 40], in all schemes the number of cycles required by an FMA is shorter than the time spent in the two instruction sequence. This makes FMA one of the most promising features on recently launched general-purpose processors [22, 28], which support FMA through ARM VFP4, AMD FMA4, or Intel® AVX2 extensions.

### 2.2 Need for FP Multiply and FP Add Compatibility

There are several challenges that may prevent FMA instructions from becoming ubiquitous. First, legacy applications must be recompiled using compilers augmented to generate binaries with FMA instructions [17, 23, 29]. This makes the new hardware underutilized for inherited binaries that do not support it. Second, an FMA operation performs one single rounding after the addition, while the traditional FPMul and FPAdd sequences round twice—after the multiplication and after the addition [3, 6]. As a result, the outcome of any particular FMA instruction may not match what is expected from an already validated and trusted program that uses the two-instruction sequence, potentially making the program buggy and/or non-deterministic. For instance, FMA can generate non-real results when evaluating quadratic expressions, while IEEE arithmetic assumes the opposite [19]. Third, there are situations where a compiler may not succeed disambiguating memory references or may operate with FMA-related optimizations disabled because they introduced unpredictability in the final result [24], thus missing instruction fusion opportunities.

For the above reasons, software tested with legacy FPMul and FPAdd sequences may not work as expected if directly replaced with FMA instructions. Past incidents have shown how sensitive critical military, aerospace or industrial applications can lead to disasters caused by rounding miscalculations [10, 31, 45]. Similar tragedies may happen when using FMA carelessly. To avoid the aforementioned problems, software vendors must adapt and validate legacy FP code, a tedious and expensive task both in time and man power. This fact may discourage software developers to utilize FMA capabilities, at least in the short term [18]. Our proposal reproduces identical FPMul and FPAdd results in the FMA hardware without the need of revalidating the code and/or rewriting legacy software, enabling a smooth and instantaneous utilization of the FMA capability.

### 2.3 Code Morphing Software Overview

Code Morphing Software (CMS [12]) is a product-quality and highly-tuned piece of SW that dynamically interprets, translates and optimizes x86 instructions (guest ISA) into internal host instructions (host ISA). Such a software layer sits below the OS and is totally transparent to the entire software stack [25, 26]. CMS is designed as a staged dynamic compiler. It first interprets individual x86 instructions one at a time to provide a low-latency cold start and collect enough profiling information to build complex code regions in later stages. Once it detects that a particular x86 instruction has been interpreted a specific amount of times, CMS promotes the code to a second compilation stage (second gear) and it decides to build a lightweight-optimized code region for the host code starting at that particular address. Optimized code regions or *translations* may have complex control flow such as hammocks, subroutine calls and returns, and inner and outer loops and they are stored in a reserved memory region called the translation cache. If a translation in second gear is executed enough times, it is promoted to a third and even a fourth gear, in which translations are collapsed into successively larger translations and sophisticated code transformations (such as loop unrolling, constant folding or if-conversion) and aggressive speculative optimizations (such as data and control speculation or critical path instruction scheduling) are performed. Once a particular piece of code is detected as hot, the CMS translation/optimization process is divided into the steps shown in Figure 1. Note that the optimizations applied in each step and/or their heuristics depend on whether the translation has been promoted to second, third or fourth gear. The instruction-fusion optimizations presented in this paper co-exist easily with all CMS optimizations—in fact, fusion opportunities may be increased when all other optimizations are applied, loops are unrolled, and redundant or dead computations are removed, although the particular interactions between the other optimizations and instruction fusion are left for future work.

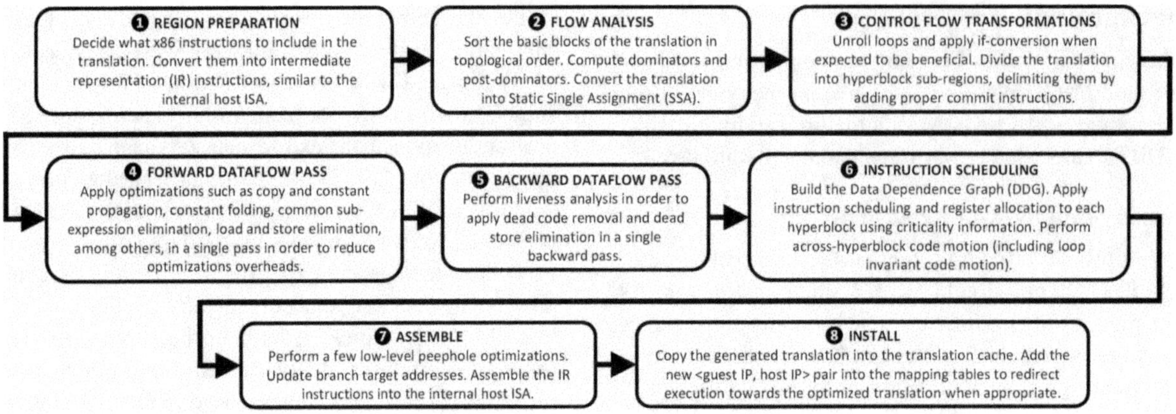


**Figure 1.** Pipeline overview of the Code Morphing Software (CMS)

### 2.4 Precise Exception Handling

Most aggressive CMS transformations rely on the hardware ability to provide isolated and atomic execution of instruction blocks through low overhead commit and rollback instructions controlled via the host ISA. This fast speculative execution support allows the CMS to perform data and control speculative transformations when it believes it is beneficial [35]. In particular, a commit instruction is used to specify the successful execution of the previous speculative translation and the beginning of a new one. This implies: (1) promoting previous memory and register speculative accesses to committed host architectural state (including copying the contents of the register file into a shadowed register file), thus creating a valid architectural checkpoint, and (2) marking all future host register and memory updates as speculative. An exception while executing a speculative translation diverts the control flow to the CMS runtime, which is in charge of detecting whether the exception is an internal host ISA exception or it is a guest exception that requires OS handling. If the exception is a host ISA exception (e.g. due to an overly aggressive optimization), the CMS runtime executes a rollback instruction, which discards the memory and register speculative state and restores the architectural state from the previous checkpoint. CMS then decides whether to execute a less aggressive version of the translation or perform forward progress through the interpreter or other means.

The technique proposed in this paper relies on the support to perform speculative optimizations on FP code. In particular, the HW uses a few speculative copies of the control and status register (MXCSR [33] in x86 architecture) to accumulate the IEEE-754 floating point arithmetic flags so FP instructions are able to delay raising exceptions [1]. The internal host ISA provides instructions to merge the contents of these speculative MXCSR registers, to promote them to an architectural state and to inspect them in order to raise exceptions properly. This allows, for example, moving a long latency FP instruction above a conditional branch. In order to perform such optimization, the system has to accumulate the instruction's FP flags into an internal MXCSR and schedule a check instruction in the home basic block of the instruction (corresponding to the original basic block where the instruction resided). This mechanism allows the hardware to raise an exception only if the instruction would have been executed in the original flow of the guest code.

## 3. A Co-Designed Implementation of Combined FP Multiply-Add Instructions

In this paper we propose a HW/SW collaborative approach in which dependent FPMul and FPAdd instructions can be executed as a single Combined FP Multiply-Add (CMA) operation that is analogous to the original pair of instructions. Central to the proposed technique is an algorithm accommodated in the SW layer that optimizes native x86 code by merging FPMul and FPAdd instructions into a single CMA instruction—only when it identifies that there is a potential benefit from a performance or power perspective (Section 3.3). The proposed CMA instruction is executed in an extended FMA unit that introduces intermediate rounding logic for this particular instruction between the multiplier and the adder, although it may generate incorrect values in few corner cases to simplify the HW and to not impact the FMA latency (Section 3.2). Whenever this happens, a fault has to be notified to the runtime system, which guarantees the expected behavior of the program with minimal performance impact (Section 3.4). This novel FMA design also supports the more common single-rounding FMA operations as well as individual FPMul and FPAdd instructions. Combining an FPMul and an FPAdd into a double-rounding CMA instruction is applied speculatively in the sense that the algorithm assumes that neither the CMA instruction generates an incorrect result nor any instruction placed between the two fused pair faults or causes incorrect behavior.

We assume the proposed feature runs on top of a HW/SW co-designed processor that has support for speculative execution such as that found in the Transmeta Efficeon [26]. We have chosen an enhanced CMS [12] as our DBT reference

| Instruction Syntax | Arithmetic Expression |
|---|---|
| cmadd dst = src1,src2,src3 | dst = src1*src2 + src3 |
| cmaddr dst = src1,src2,src3 | dst = src3 + src1*src2 |
| cmsub dst = src1,src2,src3 | dst = src1*src2 - src3 |
| cmsubr dst = src1,src2,src3 | dst = src3 - src1*src2 |

**Table 1.** CMA definition in host ISA

system and the IBM RS/6000 architecture as our FMA unit baseline [32], and we have designed the proposed components to be compatible with them. Although the proposed technique is evaluated in such environment, it can be easily adapted to embrace other platforms (Section 3.5).

### 3.1 Internal ISA Extensions

To support CMA we extend the host ISA with four different instructions to be able to execute any ±(A*B)±C computation with two roundings in a single host instruction, such that it gets the same numerical answer as the FPMul and FPAdd would otherwise compute. We refer to the first rounding of the FPMul as the *intermediate rounding*, which is normally not present in an FMA operation. Note that, in contrast to single-rounding FMA instructions, the new CMA instructions do not alter the guest ISA, as they are handled internally in the host ISA. In other words, only the CMS can inject CMA instructions into a translated binary when creating optimized versions of the hot code regions. Although single-rounding FMA instructions are also available in the host ISA, only double-rounding CMA instructions generate the analogous result to an FPMul and FPAdd sequence.

Table 1 summarizes the definition of the new instructions and their arithmetic expression. These instructions multiply the FP value(s) in *src1* with the FP value(s) in *src2*, round the product(s), add/subtract the FP value(s) in *src3* to the intermediate result(s), perform a second rounding and store the resulting FP value(s) to the *dst* register. These instructions can be performed in single- or double-precision, either in the scalar or packed flavor, and support all IEEE rounding modes. Note that CMA can only be performed if the data type and rounding mode of both FPMul and FPAdd instructions are identical. In the case of "cmaddr/cmsubr" the order of the operands is reversed, so the product is added to *src3*, guarantying the ordering if one of the sources is Not-a-Number (NaN [1]). FP numeric exception flags are accumulated into one of the speculative MXCSR registers. Specifically, if an intermediate rounding fault occurs, a dedicated field in the speculative MXCSR register specified by the instruction is set to true.

### 3.2 An FMA Unit with Intermediate Rounding

**FMA Execution:** We assume an FMA design similar to the one present in IBM RS/6000 [32] as our reference architecture, which executes double-precision FMA instructions as follows. The 53-bit mantissa of the first operand *A* is multiplied with the 53-bit mantissa of the second operand *B* to produce a product presented in the 106-bit carry-save format. The third operand *C* is aligned in the bit range of the product, and may be inverted before sending it to a 3:2 Carry Save Adder (CSA), together with all the output bits coming from the product. The CSA generates a sum in a redundant form that goes through a 108-bit Wide Adder and a Leading Zero Anticipatory (LZA) circuit. Later on, the outcome of the Wide Adder is complemented, normalized (using the value generated by LZA) and rounded. Logic required for executing FMA instructions is depicted in white in Figure 2—input and output paths are highlighted in bold.

**CMA Overview:** We slightly extended this unit to perform intermediate rounding in the product generated on the multiplier—specific blocks for CMA operations are shown in grey in Figure 2. Note that we wanted to keep the latency unaltered for all its instructions, including CMA. At the same time, we wanted to minimize the hardware cost and keep the design simple. To overcome HW constraints, our implementation handles corner cases in the CMS software layer, which allows the scheme to meet the required timing while saving area and power in the unit. From the high-level perspective, CMA operations round the result produced by the multiplier in two different bit positions—assuming overflow or not—and sum the addend afterwards. An overflow detector implemented as product carry chain determines which computation has to be delivered to the complement and normalization logic, previous to the final rounding. The following paragraphs describe the purpose of each block and provide a more accurate description of the intermediate rounding process.

**CMA Execution:** Like in the FMA operation, operands *A* and *B* are injected in the Multiplier to generate the product mantissa. The product mantissa consists of a 106-bit result: 104 bits used to represent the fractional part and 2 for the integer part. In parallel, operands *A* and *B* are sent to a Trailing Zero Detector (TRZ) to generate the *sticky* bit, which represents bits 53 to 103 in the product mantissa. Contrary to FMA, only the most significant bits from the product mantissa are needed while adding operand *C* in the CSA. Nonetheless, we need to include a *Round* bit as an extra input in the CSA in order to perform rounding of the intermediate result, increasing its inputs from three to four. The *Round* bit is computed using the rounding mode stored in the MXCSR register together with discarded bits in the product mantissa—including the sticky bit produced in the TRZ. Let's name the Least Significant Bit (*LSB* bit) of the product mantissa the one that will be the right-most in the final CMA result (i.e. bit 51 in the product mantissa), and the guard bit (*G* bit) the first one that is discarded (i.e. bit 52). The *Round* bit has to be aligned with the *G* bit position, although that position has to be shifted to the right if the product mantissa overflows. As there is no time slack to perform such shift, we decided to compute the two cases (overflow and no overflow) separately, and then select the right value based on the

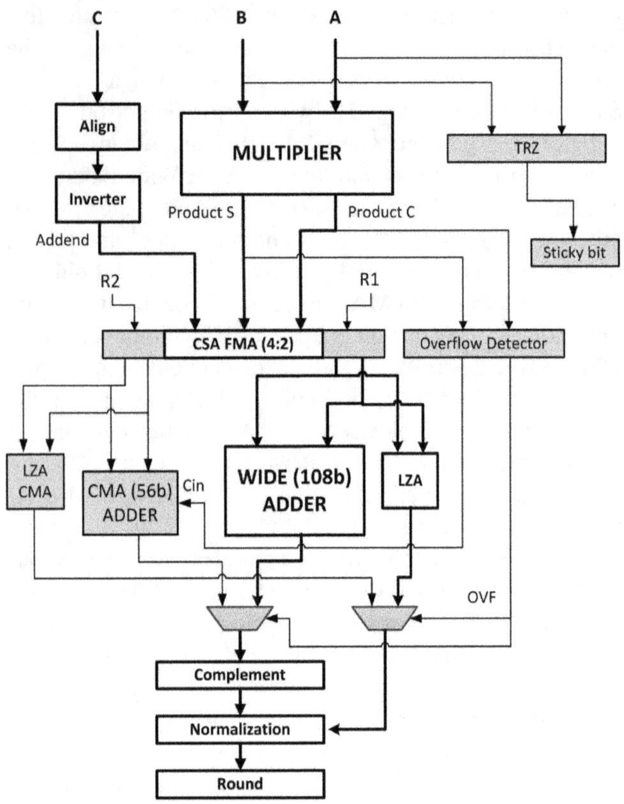


**Figure 2.** An FMA design with single and double rounding

overflow detector. The overflow detector reads the product mantissa in its carry-save form and inserts it in a carry-chain adder to calculate whether the product mantissa overflows or not (this information is in the most significant bit of the output, named *OVF*). It also generates the carry-in (*Cin*) bit which represents the carry chain to the G bit position from the 51 less significant bits of the product. This allows us to limit the size of the second adder to 56 bits, which is considerably smaller than the Wide Adder. Overflow detection and intermediate rounding/addition (both with and without overflow) are done in parallel. Note that the *Round* bit in the case of overflow (from now on, *R2* bit) may hold a different value than in the opposite case (from now on, *R1* bit), as *R2* bit is computed assuming the shifted product mantissa. In the case of no overflow, the *R1* bit is aligned with the *G* bit of the product mantissa, and after going through the CSA it is passed to the Wide Adder. Nonetheless, in the case of overflow, the *R2* bit is aligned with the *LSB*, and after crossing the CSA it delivers the output to a smaller 56-bit adder (around half the size of the Wide Adder), which only adds the most significant bits from the product mantissa. This adder also requires the *Cin* as an input, which is produced approximately in the middle of the Wide Adder execution. Practically, the outputs of both adders are available at the same time. Similarly, the LZA logic has to be modified to generate two results based on whether there is overflow or

| FMA logic block | FMA Area (%) |
|---|---|
| TRZ | 5% |
| Product carry chain | 3% |
| CMA adder (56b) | 4% |
| Additional latches and muxes | 1% |
| Changes in CSA + LZA | 2% |
| **Total** | **15%** |

**Table 2.** Area estimations of the additional hardware support to execute CMA instructions

not. The results from the adders/LZA are delivered to the complement/normalization hardware based on the *OVF* bit.

**Area, Power and Timing Analysis:** We implemented the proposed design in RTL and computed the additional area using the blocks already implemented in the FMA unit. We also estimated the power in the unit required to support CMA instructions. Table 2 shows that the total unit area increases around 15%, expecting similar increment in *idle* and *leakage* power. Although some pieces of logic appear as different blocks in Figure 2, most of the logic in the CSA and in the LZA can be reused, so it does not need to be replicated. The unit critical path only increases by a delay of a 2:1 mux, which does not impact the cycle time.

**Intermediate Rounding Problems:** The FMA is also extended to identify situations where the hardware is unable to deliver the correct result for CMA instructions. This happens when the unit has to manipulate the product mantissa before performing the intermediate rounding, which would require additional time in the FMA hardware—unacceptably increasing the latency of the CMA operation. As we want to simplify the design and maintain the original FMA latency for CMA instructions, our design does not produce the valid computation on those situations. Instead, the system sets a specific field in the corresponding speculative version of the MXCSR register before completion, which is accessed later to raise intermediate rounding faults (more on this in Section 3.4). This Intermediate Rounding Flag (IRF) is only used to report CMA rounding problems, and no other instruction modifies its value. Corner case situations that cause an intermediate rounding fault are: (1) one of the product inputs is denormal (need to normalize the product mantissa before rounding it), (2) the product exponent underflows (need to right shift the product mantissa before rounding it), and (3) intermediate product mantissa overflow results in a FP overflow (special operands must substitute the product).

### 3.3 The Instruction-Fusion Optimization Pass

**Algorithm Overview**: The instruction-fusion optimization pass introduces a lightweight software algorithm in the CMS execution flow. Instruction fusion is in charge of finding pairs of FPMul and FPAdd instructions and replacing them with a single CMA instruction—only if fusion is expected to be valuable. There are situations where fusion may incur in additional overheads respect to the original sequence,

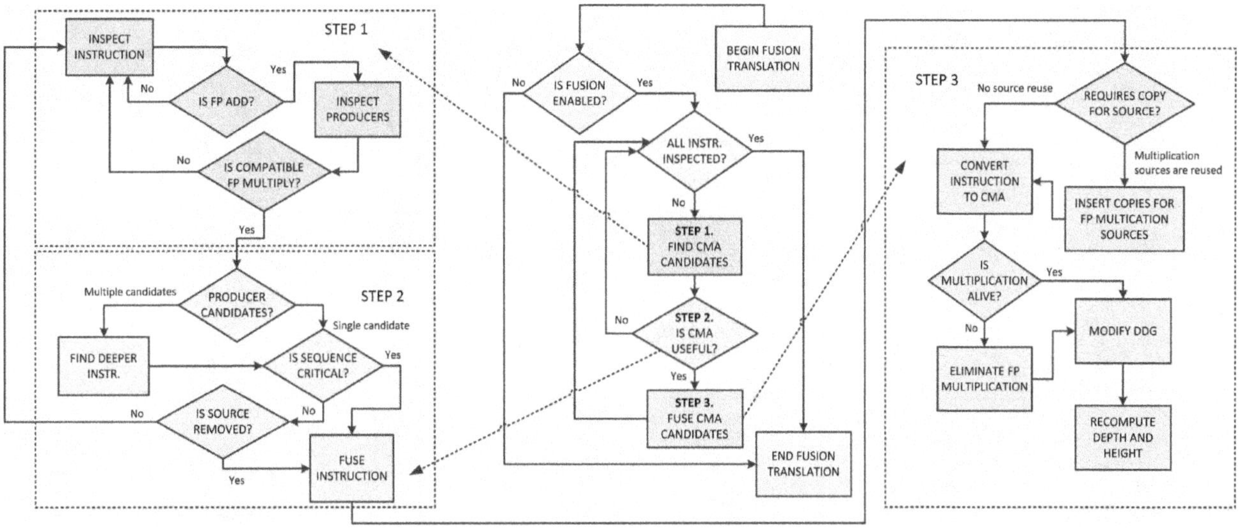


**Figure 3.** Flow diagram of the CMA instruction-fusion optimization pass

for example when fusing instructions increases the size of the code or the execution generates more activity in the FMA unit. Also, when an instruction can be fused with multiple choices, the algorithm has to pick which of them is the most attractive. To this end, the algorithm implements a set of heuristics that use data flow information to take informed decisions about whether it is profitable or not on each fusion opportunity. The process is analogous for FPMul and FPSub pairs, although we do not refer to the latter in the following paragraphs to avoid redundancy. Instruction fusion, like other software optimizations, is applied at the granularity of a translation, and it can be easily generalized to exploit other fusion proposals not explored in this paper.

**Algorithm Location**: The fusion optimization pass is placed just before instruction scheduling (step 6 in Figure 1) and after the Data Dependence Graph (DDG) is built because the algorithm uses the criticality of the sequence as one of the metrics for measuring the benefits of fusing instructions. Moreover, being placed in one of the last CMS steps allows the instruction-fusion pass to run on top of traditional code transformations such as data versioning or code elimination that are performed earlier in the CMS optimization flow. As a result, the instruction-fusion pass kicks in after specialized code is generated, which helps the engine to take confident decisions about which sequences are critical or not.

**DDG and Critical Sequences of Instructions**: The DDG consists of a graph where each instruction executed in a program is represented as a node, and any dependence between instructions is depicted as a single-direction edge that links instructions that produce a value with instructions that consume it. The weight of each edge corresponds to the time the producer starts executing the operations until its result is available to a consumer. We refer to an instruction as critical if it is placed in the static critical path of a translation. This means that the depth of the instruction—the longest distance from the translation entry node to the instruction in the DDG—plus the height of the instruction—the longest distance from the instruction to the translation exit node in the DDG—is equal to the length of the longest dependence chain in the translation. Height and depth are computed adding the latencies of the producer-consumer chains of the instruction following dependencies in the DDG. Critical sequences are those formed by chains of dependent critical instructions. In order to provide some flexibility, instructions that are close to the critical path are treated as pseudo-critical, so the algorithm takes them into account for fusion purposes too.

**Implementation in CMS**: Figure 3 presents a diagram that shows the three main steps required for the instruction-fusion optimization pass. For this initial discussion, let us pay attention to the central block diagram of the figure. First, the algorithm checks whether fusion is enabled—as we will see in Section 3.4, CMS may decide to disallow fusion on certain translations—and, if so, it walks the instructions of the translation in program order. For each CMA fusion candidate (in this case, an FPAdd instruction), the CMS builds a list of CMA candidate pairs consisting on the aforementioned instruction and corresponding FPMul instruction producers (step 1). Then CMS inspects the pairs in order to attest if any is a candidate for a profitable fusion (step 2). In such case, the algorithm performs some transformations in the DDG and modifications in the instruction structure in order to complete the CMA conversion (step 3). This inspect-select-fuse process is repeated until all instructions from a translation are examined. These steps are explained in more detail in the forthcoming paragraphs.

**Finding Fusion Candidates (Step 1):** The algorithm starts iterating among all the instructions of the translation. Each time that it finds an FPAdd or FPSub, it analyzes its producers in order to confirm if they have compatible types for

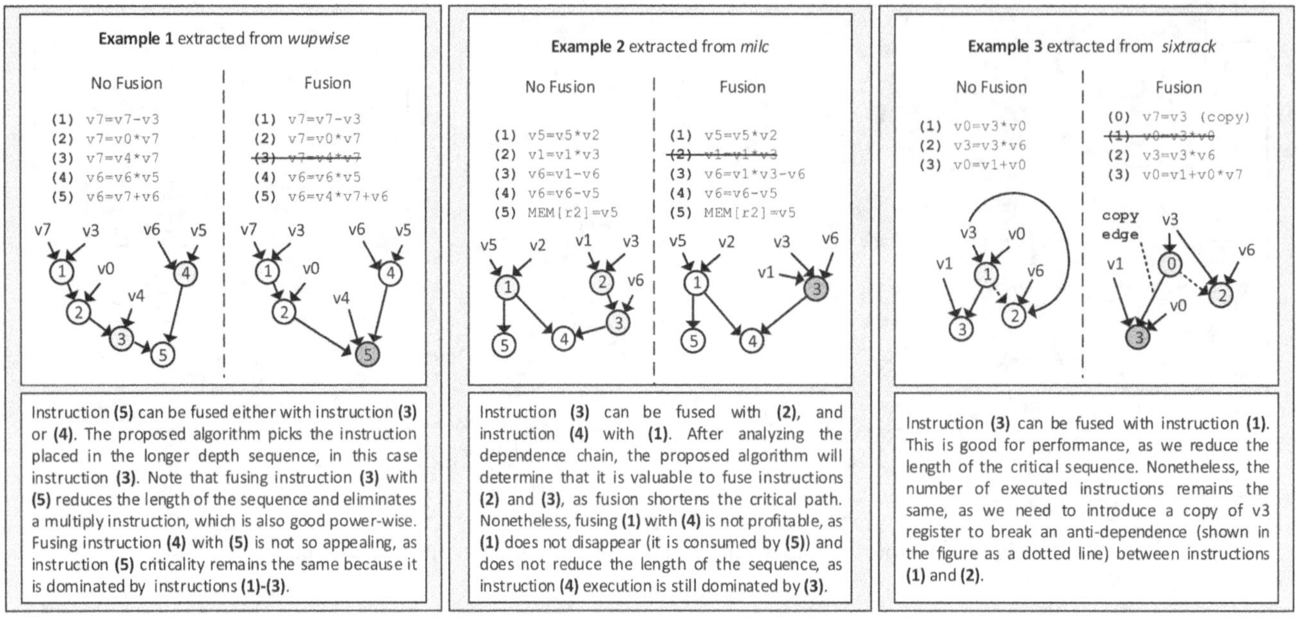


**Figure 4.** SPECfp scenarios for CMA instruction-fusion. Code appears in arithmetic expression to ease comprehension. A DDG version of the code is also presented to show how fusion impacts the length of the dependent sequences. Eligible instruction pairs for fusion are highlighted in light grey, while fused CMA instructions appear in dark grey.

fusion—i.e. producer has to be an FPMul with the same vector element size, scalar/packed type, rounding mode and exception mask as the candidate. A list of eligible pairs of instructions for fusion is then created.

**Selecting Fusion Candidates using Heuristics (Step 2)**: Once the algorithm constructs a list of fusion candidate pairs for a given consumer operation, it inspects the DDG to take an informed decision to select one of the candidate pairs and to assess whether the chosen candidate should be fused or not. In particular, the algorithm selects the pair that contains the FPMul producer with the longer depth in the DDG in case of multiple possible candidates. This is so because the algorithm is able to shorten the length of the sequence by fusing with the deeper instruction, as shown in Example 1 from Figure 4. Otherwise (both operands have the same length), the algorithm chooses the pair affecting the first operand of the consumer. After choosing a candidate pair, the algorithm inspects the criticality of both instructions to determine if CMA conversion will potentially reduce the length of the translation. If so, fusion is marked as profitable, given that it is good for performance (shorter critical path). However, non-critical pairs of instruction candidates can also be profitable from power perspective if they favor instruction reduction. Hence, the algorithm checks if the FPMul has no other consumers besides the FPAdd candidate and it is not a live-out. If this is the case, the FPMul instruction can be eliminated after fusion and the algorithm estimates fusion to be profitable (fewer instructions executed and less activity in the cluster). For example, a single CMA instruction only requires three register file operand reads and a unique write, while a complete FPMul followed by an FPAdd sequence requires four register file operand reads and two writes. If fusion is not expected to shorten the critical path or reduce the amount of instructions, the algorithm decides to keep the original two-instruction sequence because CMA would increase power (more instructions executed or more activity in the cluster). Example 2 from Figure 4 shows a case where fusion is only profitable for the first pair of eligible instructions, while it is not for the second pair.

**Converting Candidates to CMA Instructions (Step 3):** The fusion pass modifies the internal structure of the FPAdd and converts it into a CMA instruction. The first action is to propagate the source operands from the FPMul instruction to the FPAdd. Note that this means lengthening the live range of the source operands. However, it may potentially happen that another instruction rewrites one of the FPMul sources. If so, the algorithm saves the value of the operand in an available register by adding a new copy instruction in the DDG. If no register is available, fusion is discarded for this particular pair. One anti-dependency edge is inserted in the DDG between the copy and the overwriting instruction to ensure that the copy is executed first. A new edge is also added between the copy and the CMA instruction, which can be removed if it is not required (more on this later). Once copies are in-place, the fusion engine converts the FPAdd into a CMA instruction by changing its opcode and operands. The DDG is also modified to add proper dependences between the CMA instruction and the FPMul producers. Anti-dependencies between CMA and younger instructions may need to be modified as well, and edges from/to the new CMA instruction are

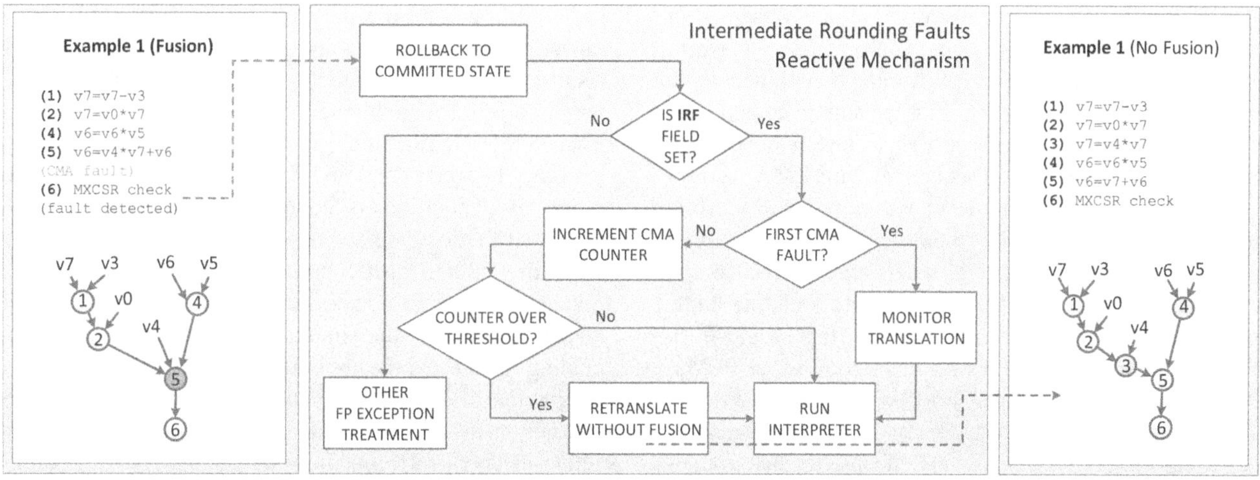


**Figure 5.** Instruction **(5)** in Example 1 (Fusion) fails to reproduce the intermediate rounding, setting the IRF field in the MXCSR. When this register is tested in **(6)**, the fault is detected and the exception handler gives control to the runtime system, which rolls back to the previously committed state and starts monitoring the translation. If this code region has faulted multiple times, the CMS runtime decides to retranslate it by disabling fusion as shown in Example 1 (No Fusion).

updated with the real cost. After completing all the modifications in the data flow, the algorithm re-computes the DDG height and depth of each instruction belonging to the translation. Finally, if the FPMul has no consumers and is not a live-out, it is eliminated from the DDG, so it is never scheduled. The instruction scheduler is also extended with a forward pass that identifies those copies introduced in the fusion pass that are no longer needed—this happens when the CMA is scheduled before the instruction that overwrites its sources—and to eliminate them. Example 3 from Figure 4 shows how the proposed algorithm modifies a DDG when fusion is performed.

### 3.4 Handling Intermediate Rounding Faults

Speculative MXCSRs are merged and examined before exiting an optimized translation or after executing several FP instructions through an internal host ISA operation. Having any fault bit set in the MXCSR means that there has been corruption in an optimized translation, so the system traps to the corresponding exception handler in the CMS runtime system as explained in Section 2.4. The runtime handler rolls-back the processor to the previous committed (non-speculative) state and passes control to the interpreter.

The interpreter executes the same guest code by emulating one x86 instruction at a time, without applying any kind of code optimization. As the instruction-fusion optimization pass does not engage while interpreting, CMA instructions are not generated and the program progresses normally. Nonetheless, trapping to the exception handler and interpreting the code carries significant overheads that reduce the appeal of the technique. In order to create efficient code in the presence of CMA faults, we propose a reactive mechanism that prevents fusion in the presence of frequent exceptions. To achieve this goal, the exception handler distinguishes CMA rounding faults from the rest of FP faults by testing the content of the triggering MXCSR register. Masking the result and extracting the IRF field is enough to identify those exceptions generated by CMA instructions.

The first time that an optimized translation reports a CMA rounding fault, the system starts monitoring its behavior. In particular, each optimized translation has an individual software counter for tracking CMA faults in its associated translation descriptor area in memory. Hence, each time that a CMA rounding fault occurs, the runtime increments the corresponding dedicated counter. Once the counter is over a certain threshold, the system forces a re-optimization of the offending translation by setting the instruction-fusion optimization pass to inoperative. Thus, the generated code becomes non-faulty as it does not contain CMA instructions, being more efficient than the fused counterpart. Note that, in a common scenario, only a small set of CMA instructions are defused, given that we disable the instruction-fusion optimization pass in a few selected offending translations. Figure 5 describes the main steps of the proposed reactive mechanism from the time a fault is generated until the end of the retranslation process. In order to avoid overcounting CMA faults for long periods of time that would make all counters to overpass the threshold at some point in time, the counters are reset to zero periodically. In particular, we empirically reset the counters every 10M host instructions.

### 3.5 Applicability in Traditional Architectures

Although previous sections present the mechanisms to implement the CMA instruction-fusion proposal under a HW/SW co-designed processor, the technique can be easily applicable to more conventional designs. To achieve that, the CMA instruction has to be exposed to the ISA, and the compiler must be adapted to perform instruction fusion and emit

CMA instructions in order to exercise the unit presented in Section 3.2. Dynamic/Just-in-Time compilers may perform the optimization for legacy applications at runtime, while static compilers require recompiling the source code. Compilers must modify the in-place FMA conversion pass to substitute FPMul and FPAdd sequences with CMA instructions in order to retain full bit-level data compatibility, while using FMA instructions only when the programmer explicitly requests or enables it (e.g. when higher precision in the rounding is needed). CMA intermediate rounding faults could be handled by micro-code routines, that would flush the pipeline and replay the CMA instruction as an FPMul and FPAdd sequence, similar to other internal micro-code faults in the machine. On processors with Hardware Transactional Memory (HTM) support [21], the intermediate rounding fault could be exposed to the ISA as a transaction-abort reason. The HTM abort handler could be used to undo the changes introduced by the faulty FMA instruction and all other instructions belonging to the same optimized region. The main disadvantage of moving CMA into a traditional processor design is that all the required changes have to be visible to the architecture, while HW/SW co-design can do it smoothly and without requiring modifications to the ISA. Moreover, unique HW/SW features based on runtime information, like code specialization or memory disambiguation, may enable the instruction-fusion DBT optimization to find more fusion opportunities compared to other implementations on traditional compilers.

## 4. Simulation Methodology

We have evaluated the proposed technique using SPECfp 2000 (SPECfp00) and SPECfp 2006 (SPECfp06). Benchmarks were compiled using the "-xSSE3 -O3 ipo" flags with the Intel® C++ Compiler (ICC) version 11 and with ICC version 12 using the smart heap library [2]. We have selected the binary that performs best in the baseline configuration (described later) as it has been shown that particular benchmarks benefit significantly by the use of such a library [7]. For each benchmark, we have generated a checkpoint every 10B x86 instructions for a total of 3500 checkpoints. Each checkpoint has been executed for 4B x86 instructions to warm-up the CMS (1B in case of SPECfp00), for a following 5M x86 instructions to warm-up the micro-architectural structures and then for 25M x86 instructions to gather accurate timing and power statistics. In order to reduce simulation time, we have applied k-means clustering [44] concentrating on several micro-architectural and CMS statistics and we have weighted each selected checkpoint properly. This allowed us to reduce the amount of checkpoints to 109 and 127 for SPECfp00 and SPECfp06 respectively with a negligible impact on accuracy. The reported results use this weighted subset of checkpoints for all configurations.

The different micro-architectural configurations have been evaluated using an internal, industry-validated and cycle-accurate timing simulator complemented by a precise power model. The timing simulation has been developed by a substantial team of architects and designers using the same methodology as commercial products. The timing simulator runs on top of a functional simulator that validates the compatibility between guest and host executed code. The power model uses thousands of counters to feed energy formulas to extract the idle and active power consumed on each unit assuming a 22nm CMOS process, and then adds leakage to obtain overall core power. Performance and power results are extracted from the simulation of the entire system, including all the overheads introduced by the CMS like the interpreter, the optimizer (including the time executing the instruction-fusion pass) and the runtime (including the reactive mechanism to handle intermediate rounding faults). Note that all the evaluated configurations include the different CMS optimizations described in Section 2.3.

For our baseline architecture we assume an in-order, low-power and single-threaded HW/SW co-designed processor similar to an enhanced version of the Transmeta Efficeon processor [26]. The architecture is compatible with modern 64-bit x86 ISA extensions—for instance, the vector unit can support Intel® AVX2 extensions. The processor is organized as a VLIW, where non-dependent instructions are wrapped in a seven-wide structure called molecule. Instructions in the same molecule are fetched, executed and committed in parallel. CMS is responsible for packing independent instructions into molecules, guaranteeing that there are no resource conflicts within a molecule and all fixed latency dependencies are satisfied. For instructions depending on variable-latency producers (i.e. memory loads), the CMS schedules them assuming the best case (e.g. L1 hit latency) and the HW stalls the pipeline and restarts it once the data is ready in case of miss.

The core has separate 32KB 8-way Instruction and Data L1 caches, a gshare-like 5KB branch predictor, a 256KB 8-way L2 cache and an 8MB 16-way L3 cache, a 128-entry TLB and state-of-the-art HW stream and stride pre-fetchers. L1 hit is 4 cycles, while L2 hit latency is 18 cycles and L3 hit latency is 50 cycles. Average main memory latency is around 140 cycles. The VPU is pipelined and contains different units to execute SIMD and FP instructions, including four 64-bit FP units (FPU). Each FPU contains an FMA unit to execute FP packed and scalar instructions with single and double precision. We compare the proposed technique with different FPU configuration alternatives. Table 3 shows the main characteristics of each configuration, pointing out the latency of main instructions and area increase in the FPU over the Classic FMA configuration, based on data in [39]. The paragraphs below describe each configuration in more detail. Only the *Classic+CMA* configuration is compatible with the instruction-fusion technique proposed in this paper.
**Classic FMA [32]:** the FPU contains a single FMA unit that performs all the FP computation. All FP instructions

| FPU config. | FPMul latency | FPAdd latency | FMA/CMA latency | Area increase |
|---|---|---|---|---|
| Classic [32] | 5 | 5 | 5/- | 0% |
| Classic+CMA | 5 | 5 | 5/5 | 15% |
| Three-Path [39] | 3 | 5 | 5/- | 38% |
| Bridge [40] | 3 | 4 | 6/- | 53% |
| Replication | 3 | 3 | 5/- | 101% |

**Table 3.** FPU configurations considered in the evaluation

require the same latency to execute, needing less HW than the approaches described below. The IBM RS/6000 [32] and the Intel® Itanium® [43] among others implement such architecture, which we use as a reference system.

**CMA (Classic+CMA in Table 3):** this is our proposal where a *Classic FMA* design is extended to execute CMA instructions. This configuration also implies modifications to the CMS to fuse FPMul and FPAdd pairs into CMA instructions, and incorporates a reactive mechanism to handle intermediate faults as described in Section 3.

**Three-Path FMA [39]:** this FPU provides a fast path for an accelerated FP multiplication, while maintaining longer latencies for FMA and FP addition operations.

**Bridge FMA [40]:** this FPU is extended with a set of bypasses and replicated blocks (e.g. rounding unit) to provide fast path for FP addition and FP multiplication. This penalizes the FMA latency, which requires one more cycle.

**Replication:** this FPU includes one FPMul unit, one FPAdd unit and one *Classic FMA* unit. Although having separate units provides peak performance for all FP instructions, it also has a substantial increase in area [39].

## 5. Evaluation

Figure 6 shows the x86 Instructions per Cycle (xIPC) improvement obtained by four different FPU configurations over the Classic FMA approach, which we use as a reference. The CMA bar shows the normalized xIPC gains of the CMA fusion technique implemented on the FMA unit described in Section 3.2. Note that, although CMA reduces the amount of executed host ISA instructions, the same binaries are run in all configurations, and the number of executed x86 instructions (translated and optimized or interpreted) in each is identical. Because the number of x86 instructions does not change and cycle time does not vary among different configurations, xIPC gains can be directly converted to improvements in execution time. The rest of the bars (from left to right) show how Three-Path FMA, Bridge FMA and Replication configurations improve the performance of SPECfp workloads by adding complexity to the FPU.

### 5.1 Comparison with Alternative FPU Designs

CMA instruction fusion provides 6.7% and 5.9% IPC increment for SPECfp00 and SPECfp06 respectively over Classic FMA, with performance gains up to 18% in *sixtrack* or 13% in *lbm*. This performance improvement includes the additional CMS overheads associated with the technique. In particular, we have observed a minor increase in the time spent in the interpreter, runtime and translator that is overcome by the improvements in code executed from optimized translations. Only 7 over 236 analyzed checkpoints show (minimal) slow-downs due to CMS collateral effects.

The proposed CMA configuration also outperforms two of the three FPU configurations analyzed in the study, even requiring much less hardware. This is the case for Three-Path FMA (-2.4% IPC with respect to CMA) and Bridge FMA (-1.1% IPC with respect to CMA), which offer reduced latency for FPMul and FPAdd instructions, but present longer latencies for unfused sequences (7-8 cycles) over CMA (5 cycles). Only the Replication approach, which needs almost twice the hardware in the FPU, delivers better performance than the proposed CMA.

Figure 7 shows a breakdown of the executed instructions in Classic **FMA** (labeled as ***.F**) and **CMA** (labeled ***.C**) proposals including the CMS overheads. Instructions are distributed in four categories: FP MUL for FP multiplications, FP ADD for FP additions and subtractions, FP FMA for fused instructions (including CMA instructions) and OTHER for the rest of instructions. As it can be seen, the evaluated technique does a good job at fusing instructions, as CMA exercises FMA on 6.2% of the instructions, over seven times more than in the reference system. Around half of the multiplications are removed, and almost two thirds of the FP additions are converted to CMA. Overall, 4.9% (SPECfp00) and 4.5% (SPECfp06) of the instructions are eliminated on average, with positive outliers such as *sixtrack* or *milc*, which are able to eliminate more than 10% of the executed instructions.

Figure 8 shows that the increment on dynamic (idle and active) capacitance (Cdyn) between CMA and Classic FMA units is only a 1.5% overall, reporting a 1:4 power:performance ratio—numbers account for the new logic in the FPU, which increases idle and active power in the cluster, and adds more leakage in the core. This 1:4 ratio indicates that the proposed CMA configuration is an energy efficient technique. In particular, Table 4 shows how Cdyn is affected in each cluster by the proposed technique compared to the Classic baseline, where FE, EXE, VPU, L1 and L2 refer to the frontend (including the instruction L1), the integer ALUs, the FPU and SIMD units, the data L1 cache (including the TLB) and the L2 cache clusters respectively. As it can be observed, the VPU cluster—which includes the FPUs—reduces its activity because CMA eliminates some instructions during the fusion process, and the VPU physical register file is exercised less. Power in the rest of the clusters is slightly increased due to the increment in overall xIPC.

### 5.2 Alternative SW Fusion Algorithms

Figure 9 presents the xIPC increment obtained by distinct software alternatives that manage CMA instruction-fusion in different ways compared to the algorithm we have described

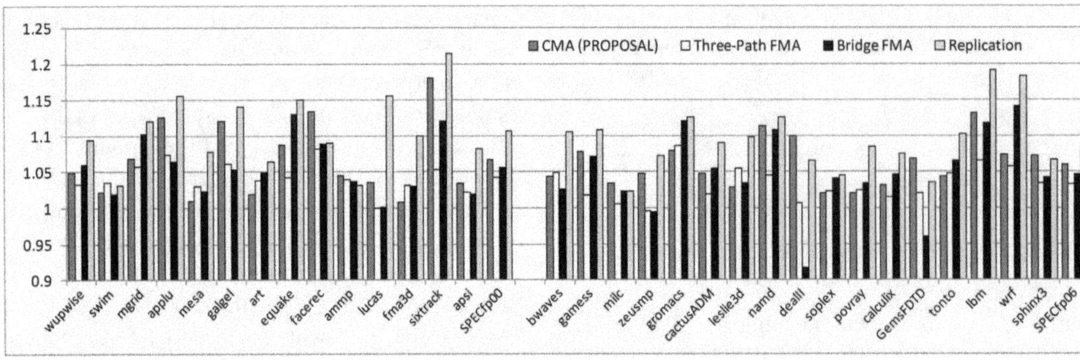

**Figure 6.** Relative xIPCs using distinct FPU config over a Classic FMA unit. Only CMA bar supports CMA instructions

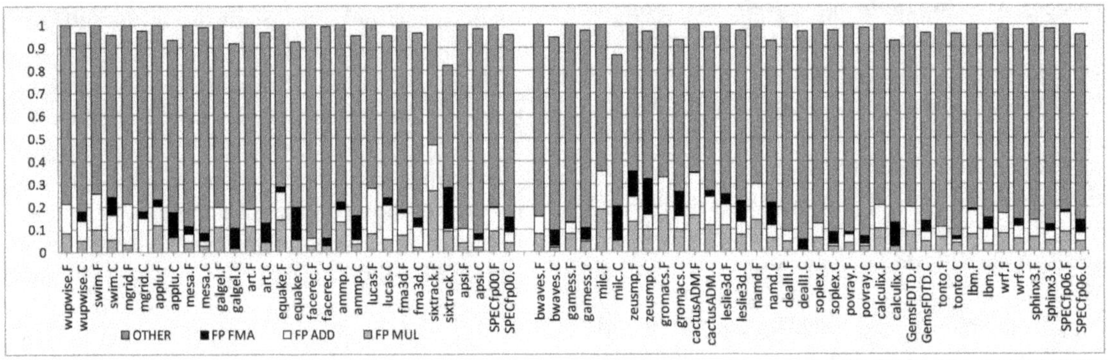

**Figure 7.** Instruction breakdown distribution from Classic (baseline) and CMA configurations

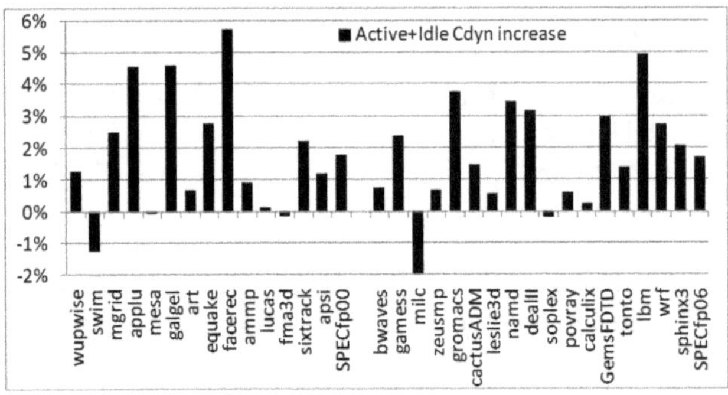

**Figure 8.** Active+idle CMA Cdyn over Classic FMA Cdyn

in Section 3.3. All the alternatives have been evaluated in the CMA FPU configuration. Software alternatives are constructed by enabling/disabling three different parameters of the proposed algorithm. First, we evaluate approaches that integrate the reactive mechanism (labeled REACT) with those that do not (labeled NO REACT). Second, we analyze the importance of placing the fusion optimization pass close to the instruction scheduler (labeled LATE) over placing it earlier in the CMS pipeline (labeled EARLY). More precisely, the EARLY configuration places the fusion algorithm in the forward pass of the CMS optimization flow where no information about the instruction criticality is available (step 4 in Figure 1). Third, we show the importance of having

| suite/cluster | L1 | VPU | EXE | FE | L2 |
|---|---|---|---|---|---|
| SPECfp00 | +3.8% | -1.6% | +2.7% | +2.2% | +1.9% |
| SPECfp06 | +3.4% | -1.5% | +2.6% | +2.0% | +1.7% |

**Table 4.** CMA vs Classic FMA active Cdyn distribution

astute heuristics to determine when fusion is profitable (labeled HEUR) versus not having them (labeled NO HEUR). In this case, fusion is always performed when a candidate is found and, if multiple candidates, it is performed with the first source operand. Note that the described heuristics (HEUR) can only be applied when fusion is performed close to instruction scheduling (LATE approach). The REACT+LATE+HEUR bar corresponds to the approach described and evaluated across this paper, as we found it to be the most efficient.

As can be seen in Figure 9, having the reactive mechanism on intermediate rounding faults is important for performance, as it provides a 0.9% (SPECfp00) and 1.6% (SPECfp06) xIPC benefits. This is because frequent exceptions that pass control to the interpreter have a non-negligible cost. Instead, reacting to intermediate faults by selectively disabling CMA fusion mitigates the problem on conflicting hot translations, allowing benchmarks with frequent faults like *fma3d* (+8.5% xIPC) and *cactusADM* (+15% xIPC) to perform much better than the NO REACT baseline.

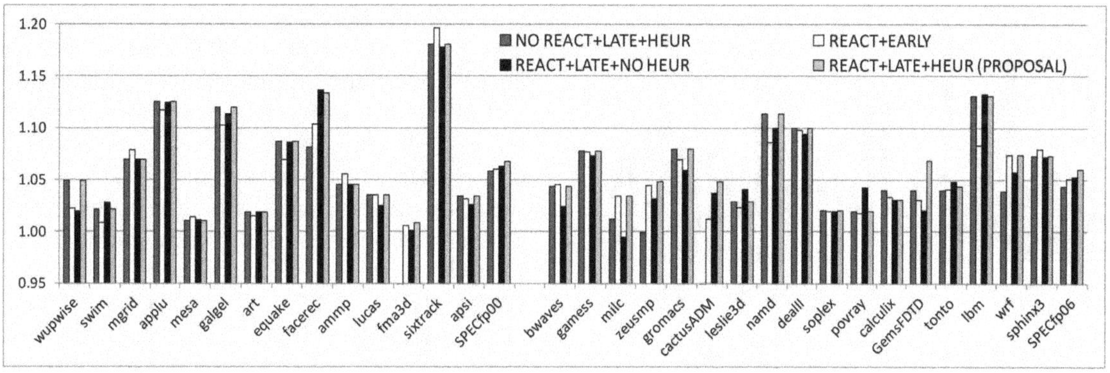


**Figure 9.** xIPC improvement of different software alternatives for CMA instruction-fusion in the SW layer

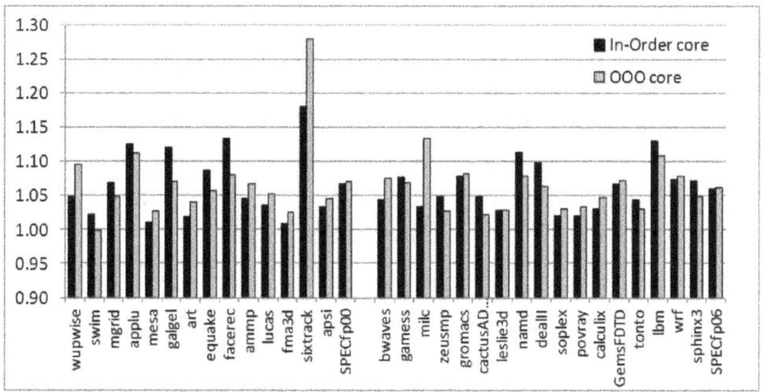


**Figure 10.** CMA instruction-fusion xIPC improvement over same core configuration with Classic FMA

Figure 9 also shows the importance of having an intelligent instruction-fusion optimization pass in order to extract maximum advantage of the feature. First, placing the algorithm in a prior stage (i.e. EARLY) is productive in simple benchmarks like *sixtrack* or *mgrid*, as eliminating instructions early in the CMS pipeline simplifies the scheduling pass and reduces translator overheads. Nonetheless, applications with complex data paths like *facerec* or *lbm* can get more profit if they perform fusion as close to instruction scheduling as possible (i.e. LATE) because fusion heuristics become more precise. In addition, checking for CMA conversion once most of the optimizations have taken place increases the fusion opportunity. This is translated into an average 0.8% xIPC gain. And second, Figure 9 shows the benefits produced by the aforementioned heuristics (i.e. HEUR). Benchmarks with instructions that have multiple fusion candidates, like *wupswise* or *GemsFDTD*, can choose the right instruction to fuse with, achieving up to 4% xIPC improvement. Applying heuristics improves the behavior of CMA by 0.6% overall, although on some occasions like in *povray*, we can miss some fusion opportunities that would result in a better scheduling.

### 5.3 Results for an Out-of-Order Processor Design

In order to quantify the impact of the technique in more aggressive core designs, we have also extended our baseline processor with a simple Out-of-Order (OOO) engine, which provides +32 extra physical registers for renaming purposes and implements a 64-entry ROB. To simplify allocation and retirement logic, we restrict the number of instructions that can fit in a molecule to four. The rest of micro-architectural components remain the same as in the in-order design.

Figure 10 shows the relative xIPC performance achieved by CMA instruction-fusion for in-order and OOO cores, where baseline is the same core configuration without CMA fusion. Evaluation shows the importance of the technique in both approaches. While CMA for the in-order configuration shows an average 6.3% xIPC improvement, it shows 6.6% xIPC gains for an OOO design. CMA is more effective in OOO cores in applications like *sixtrack* or *milc*, where OOO execution can hide memory misses that directly impact in-order performance. The reasons why the proposed technique achieves good results in an out-of-order execution pipeline are two-fold. First, instruction windows in the order of tens of instructions are effective at hiding some long latency operations (5-10 cycles), but they suffer when these operations are predominant and dependent, as it is the case in the evaluated benchmarks (due to FPMul and FPAdd sequences, for example). And second, removing a significant number of instructions from the program increases the effective capacity of the micro-architectural structures. As shown in Figure 11, allocation stalls are diminished by around 4% when CMA is enabled in an OOO core, reducing the pressure on specific hardware components. These results show that the proposed technique is not only helpful for simple in-order designs but that it can also be applied very efficiently to more aggressive designs with an OOO back-end.

Note that CMA does not behave equally when it is implemented on in-order and OOO configurations. In-order performance is dominated by dynamic events like cache misses, while OOO performance is dominated by the number of in-flight instructions the underlying hardware can handle. Since CMS optimizations are tuned for the best performance in both scenarios independently (pursuing the best possible configuration on each), code executed in both experiments is different (so is the way CMA is exercised).

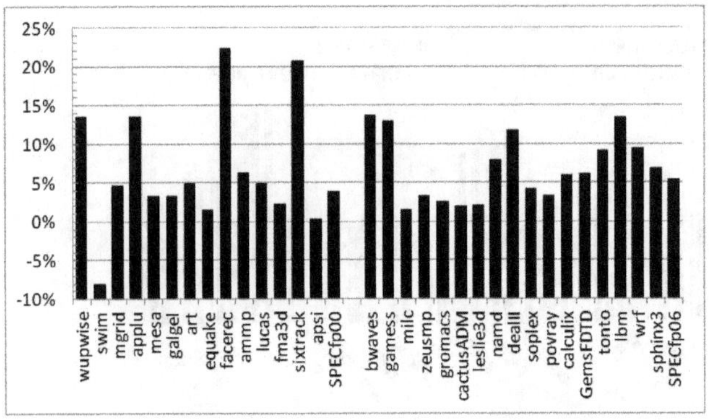


**Figure 11.** Allocation stalls reduction in OOO core when using CMA configuration over Classic FMA

## 6. Related Work

FP multiplication followed by an FP addition is one of the most common arithmetic expressions on compute-intensive workloads [18], and most modern processors already include an FMA unit [8, 22, 28, 34, 36, 43]. Several architectures have been proposed to speed up FP instructions executed in the FMA hardware. Lang and Bruguera combined addition and rounding together with FPAdd bypass to reduce the delay of single FP instructions [5]. The Bridge FMA architecture [40] includes specialized components to reuse the functionality of the multiplier and adder, creating fast paths to shorten the latency of single FP operations. None of the previously proposed designs conceived an FMA unit with intermediate rounding.

Combining multiple instructions into a single fused instruction has been studied from different perspectives. Current general-purpose processors perform micro fusion (at the uop level) and/or macro fusion (at the x86 level) by hardware in the front-end pipeline of the processor [8, 13]. However, the scope is extremely limited, as the hardware is only able to inspect one or two consecutive x86 instructions. From our experiments, we have observed that in most cases the fused instructions are several instructions apart. In addition, we have shown that properly choosing the best fuse-able pair is important, something the HW cannot do.

Others have proposed to include an optimizer functional unit in the processor in charge of building optimized instruction traces [15, 41, 48]. In this case, either the optimization scope is still limited (on the order of 64 straight line instructions) or it requires extremely big buffers to hold long straight line code sequences. In contrast, CMS is able to optimize code regions with complex control-flows containing hundreds of instructions and it does not require extra hardware to transform and optimize the code. Furthermore, a hardware only implementation of an optimizer has less flexibility than a software implementation. For example, it would likely have severe limitations at using critical path information to fuse instructions and at providing a smart reactive mechanism.

Instruction fusion can also be performed in software through a static compiler, a JIT compiler or a binary optimizer. This implies, though, that the fused opcode becomes part of the ISA, changing the architecture and thus future processor designs. This is why adding fused opcodes to the ISA has been limited to very specific and general opcodes such as FMA. In addition, fusion is implemented in a non-speculative manner as most modern processors do not have support for speculative execution. For instance, ICC [23], LLVM [29] and GCC [17] compilers combine dependent FPMul and FPAdd instructions into an FMA instruction when they expect the latter to be faster than the original sequence and the programmer has specified non strict optimizations.

Performing instruction fusion using a HW/SW co-design strategy solves the ISA issue. In fact, in the closest work to ours, authors propose extremely specialized functional units able to perform fused computations as a unit very efficiently [9, 11, 20] . Our work, on the other hand, takes a less risky approach by extending functional units that are currently available in modern processors.

## 7. Conclusions

Although FMA hardware is already available in most commercial processors, we believe that its widespread adoption will be slow because it requires modifications to the program source code and sometimes compilers fail while attempting to fuse. In this paper, we propose a HW/SW collaborative technique to benefit from FMA hardware transparently on existing binaries. Our proposal consists of minimal modifications in the FMA unit to support both single-rounding and double-rounding fused instructions, exposing the latter functionality to the host ISA through the Combined Multiply-Add (CMA) family of instructions. Also, we propose an instruction-fusion algorithm, as part of the Code Morphing Software (CMS), capable of dynamically fusing FP multiply and FP add pairs into CMA instructions. We have shown that the proposed design speeds up execution time by 6.3% for FP workloads and reduces the amount of executed instructions by 4.7% compared to a conventional FMA design. In addition, the proposed strategy outperforms other FMA designs that incur in higher hardware complexity. With these results we also show how HW/SW co-designed processors are an effective paradigm to rapidly assimilate and take advantage of new hardware capabilities.

## Acknowledgments

We would like to thank team members in Intel Barcelona Research Center and Hybrid Computer Architecture Lab for their feedback, comments and help in the development of this work. We would also like to thank Neil Campbell for his technical advice on how to integrate the proposed optimizations in the CMS toolchain.

## References


[1] IEEE Standard for Floating-Point Arithmetic. IEEE Std 754, 2008.

[2] http://www.microquill.com/smartheap/.

[3] S. Boldo and J. Muller. Exact and Approximated Error of the FMA. *IEEE Transactions on Computers*, 60(2):157–164, 2011.

[4] A. Brankovic, K. Stavrou, E. Gibert, and A. Gonzalez. Warm-up Simulation Methodology for HW/SW Co-Designed Processors. In *International Symposium on Code Generation and Optimization*, 2014.

[5] J. Bruguera and T. Lang. Floating-Point Fused Multiply-Add: Reduced Latency for Floating-Point Addition. In *17th Symposium on Computer Arithmetic*, 2005.

[6] N. Brunie, F. de Dinechin, and B. de Dinechin. A Mixed-Precision Fused Multiply and Add. In *45th Asilomar Conference on Signals, Systems and Computers*, 2011.

[7] B. Buros, E. Stahl, P. Wong, C. Skawratananond, and D. Jones. An Assessment of Leadership Performance with POWER6 Processors and Red Hat Enterprise Linux 5.1. In *White paper*, 2008.

[8] M. Butler, L. Barnes, D. Sarma, and B. Gelinas. Bulldozer: An Approach to Multithreaded Compute Performance. *IEEE Micro*, 31(2):6–15, 2011.

[9] N. Clark, A. Hormati, and S. Mahlke. VEAL: Virtualized Execution Accelerator for Loops. In *35th International Symposium on Computer Architecture*, 2008.

[10] M. Collins, F. J. Vecchio, R. G. Selby, and P. R. Gupta. The Failure of an Offshore Platform. *Concrete Internationa Detroit*, 19(8):28–35, 1997.

[11] A. Deb, J. Codina, and A. Gonzalez. A HW/SW Co-designed Programmable Functional Unit. *IEEE Computer Architecture Letters, 11*, 2012.

[12] J. Dehnert, B. Grant, J. Banning, R. Johnson, T. Kistler, A. Klaiber, and J. Mattson. The Transmeta Code Morphing Software: Using Speculation, Recovery, and Adaptive Retranslation to Address Real-life challenges. In *International Symposium on Code Generation and Optimization*, 2003.

[13] J. Doweck. Inside the Core™ Microarchitecture. *Hot Chips: A Symposium on High Performance Chips, 18*, 2006.

[14] K. Ebcioglu, E. Altman, M. Gschwind, and S. Sathaye. Dynamic binary translation and optimization. *IEEE Transactions on Computers*, 50(6):529–548, 2001.

[15] B. Fahs, S. Bose, M. Crum, B. Slechta, F. Spadini, T. Tung, S. Patel, and S. Lumetta. Performance Characterization of a Hardware Mechanism for Dynamic Optimization. In *34th International Symposium on Microarchitecture*, 2001.

[16] S. Galal and M. Horowitz. Latency Sensitive FMA Design. In *20th Symposium on Computer Arithmetic*, 2011.

[17] GNU project, http://gcc.gnu.org/gcc-4.7/.

[18] A. Heinecke, T. Auckenthaler, and C. Trinitis. Exploiting State-of-the-Art x86 Architectures in Scientific Computing. In *11th International Symposium on Parallel and Distributed Computing*, 2012.

[19] N. Higham. *Accuracy and Stability of Numerical Algorithms*. Society for Industrial and Applied Mathematics, 2002.

[20] S. Hu, I. Kim, M. Lipasti, and J. Smith. An Approach for Implementing Efficient Superscalar CISC Processors. In *12th Symposium on High-Performance Computer Architecture*, 2012.

[21] Intel Corporation, Intel® Architecture Instruction Set Extensions Programming Reference. Chapter 8: Intel Transactional Synchronization Extensions.

[22] Intel Corporation. Intel® Advanced Vector Extensions 2 Programming Reference. www.intel.com, 2013.

[23] Intel Corporation, http://software.intel.com/en-us/intel-compilers/.

[24] W. Kahan. IEEE Standard 754 for Binary Floating-Point Arithmetic. *Lecture Notes on the Status of IEEE 754*, 1996.

[25] A. Klaiber. The Technology Behind Crusoe Processors. *Transmeta Whitepaper*, 2000.

[26] K. Krewell. Transmeta Gets More Efficeon. *Microprocessor Report*, 17(10), 2003.

[27] R. Kumar, A. Martinez, and A. Gonzalez. Speculative Dynamic Vectorization to Assist Static Vectorization in a HW/SW Co-designed Environment. In *19th International Conference on High Performance Computing*, 2013.

[28] T. Lanier. Exploring the Design of the Cortex-A15 Processor. In *ARM, Tech. Rep*, 2011.

[29] LLVM Project, http://llvm.org/docs/LangRef.html/.

[30] J. Mars and N. Kumar. Blockchop: Dynamic squash elimination for hybrid processor architecture. In *International Symposium on Computer Architecture*, 2012.

[31] B. D. McCullough and H. D. Vinod. The Numerical Reliability of Econometric Software. *Journal of Economic Literature, 37.6:633-665*, 1999.

[32] R. Montoye, E. Hokenek, and S. Runyon. Design of the IBM RISC System/6000 Floating-Point Execution Unit. *IBM Journal of Research and Development*, 1990.

[33] J. Muller, N. Brisebarre, F. de Dinechin, C. Jeannerod, V. Lefevre, G. Melquiond, N. Revol, D. Stehle, and S. Torres. *Handbook of Floating-Point Arithmetic*. Birkhauser, 2009.

[34] A. Naini, A. Dhablania, W. James, and D. D. Sarma. 1 GHz HAL SPARC64 Dual Floating Point Unit with RAS features. In *Symposium on Computer Arithmetic*, 2001.

[35] N. Neelakantam, D. Ditzel, and C. Zilles. A Real System Evaluation of Hardware Atomicity for Software Speculation. In *15th International Conference on Architectural Support for Programming Languages and Operating Systems*, 2010.

[36] F. P. O'Connell and S. W. White. POWER3: The Next Generation of PowerPC Processors. *IBM Journal of Research and Development*, 2000.

[37] G. Ottoni, G. Chinya, G. Hoflehner, J. Collins, A. Kumar, E. Schuchman, D. Ditzel, R. Singhal, and H. Wang. AstroLIT: Enabling Simulation-Based Microarchitecture Comparison Between Intel and Transmeta Designs. In *8th International Conference on Computing Frontiers*, 2011.

[38] D. Pavlou, E. Gibert, F. Latorre, and A. Gonzalez. DDGacc: Boosting Dynamic DDG-based Binary Optimizations through Specialized Hardware Support. In *8th International Conference on Virtual Execution Environments*, 2012.

[39] E. Quinnell, E. Swartzlander, and C. Lemonds. Floating-Point Fused Multiply-Add Architectures. In *41st Asilomar Conference on Signals, Systems and Computers*, 2007.

[40] E. Quinnell, E. Swartzlander, and C. Lemonds. Bridge Floating-Point Fused Multiply-Add Design. In *IEEE Transactions on Very Large Scale Integration Systems*, 2008.

[41] R. Rosner, Y. Almog, M. Moffie, N. Schwartz, and A. Mendelson. Power Awareness through Selective Dynamically Optimized Traces. In *31st International Symposium on Computer Architecture*, 2004.

[42] S. Sathaye, J. L. P. Ledak, M. G. S. Kosonocky, J. Fritts, A. Bright, E. Altman, and C. Agricola. Boa: Targeting multi-gigahertz with binary translation. In *Workshop on Binary Translation*, 1999.

[43] H. Sharangpani and H. Arora. Itanium processor microarchitecture. *IEEE Micro*, 20(5):24–43, 2000.

[44] T. Sherwood, E. Perelman, G. Hamerly, and B. Calder. Automatically Characterizing Large Scale Program Behavior. In *10th International Conference on Architectural Support for Programming Languages and Operating Systems*, 2002.

[45] R. Skeel. Roundoff error and the Patriot missile. *SIAM News*, 25(4):11, 1992.

[46] C. Wang, Y. Wu, and M. Cintra. Acceldroid: Co-Designed Acceleration of Android Bytecode. In *International Symposium on Code Generation and Optimization*, 2012.

[47] Y. Wu, S. Hu, E. Borin, and C. Wang. A HW/SW Co-Designed Heterogeneous Multi-Core Virtual Machine for Energy-Efficient General Purpose Computing. In *International Symposium on Code Generation and Optimization*, 2011.

[48] S. Yehia and O. Temam. From Sequences of Dependent Instructions to Functions: an Approach for Improving Performance without ILP or Speculation. In *31st International Symposium on Computer Architecture*, 2004.

# Post-compiler Software Optimization for Reducing Energy

Eric Schulte* Jonathan Dorn† Stephen Harding* Stephanie Forrest* Westley Weimer†

*Department of Computer Science
University of New Mexico
Albuquerque, NM 87131-0001
{eschulte,stharding,forrest}@cs.unm.edu

†Department of Computer Science
University of Virginia
Charlottesville, VA 22904-4740
{dorn,weimer}@cs.virginia.edu

## Abstract

Modern compilers typically optimize for executable size and speed, rarely exploring non-functional properties such as power efficiency. These properties are often hardware-specific, time-intensive to optimize, and may not be amenable to standard dataflow optimizations. We present a general post-compilation approach called Genetic Optimization Algorithm (GOA), which targets measurable non-functional aspects of software execution in programs that compile to x86 assembly. GOA combines insights from profile-guided optimization, superoptimization, evolutionary computation and mutational robustness. GOA searches for program variants that retain required functional behavior while improving non-functional behavior, using characteristic workloads and predictive modeling to guide the search. The resulting optimizations are validated using physical performance measurements and a larger held-out test suite. Our experimental results on PARSEC benchmark programs show average energy reductions of 20%, both for a large AMD system and a small Intel system, while maintaining program functionality on target workloads.

***Categories and Subject Descriptors*** D.3.4 [*Processors*]: Optimization; D.1.2 [*Programming Techniques*]: Automatic Programming; D.2.5 [*Software Engineering*]: Testing and Debugging; I.2.8 [*Artificial Intelligence*]: Heuristic methods

***Keywords*** Evolutionary Computation; Power Modeling; Assembly Code; Compilation; Profile-guided Optimization; Superoptimization; Mutational Robustness



*ASPLOS '14*, March 1–5, 2014, Salt Lake City, Utah, USA.

ACM 978-1-4503-2305-5/14/03...$15.00.
http://dx.doi.org/10.1145/2541940.2541980

## 1. Introduction

From embedded systems to large datacenters, extreme scales of computation are increasingly popular. At such extremes, properties such as energy consumption [10] and memory utilization can be as important as runtime. For example, data centers are estimated to have consumed over 1% of total global electricity usage in 2010 [28]. However, there are few program optimizations targeting these *non-functional* [19] performance requirements. The few existing methods must cope with complex architectures and workload interactions [62]. Although techniques such as voltage scaling and resource hibernation can be applied at the hardware level to reduce energy consumption [43], software optimizations tend to focus on cycle counts and instruction scheduling [35] for consecutive instructions to lower the switching activity [47, § 4.3.3].

Software engineers are studying methods that trade the guarantee of semantic preservation [11, 15, 22, 27, 65] for greater reliability and robustness [2, 8, 49, 58], availability and security [50], compile-time algorithmic flexibility [5], or performance and quality of service [6, 39, 40]. Interest in such tradeoffs spans domains as diverse as computer graphics [59] and networked servers [50].

Stochastic search methods are increasingly successful at evolving and repairing off-the-shelf software [14, 26, 33, 42, 65]. Similar to profile-guided optimizations, such techniques leverage existing test suites or annotations [64] to ensure that proposed modifications preserve required functionality. Analysis of the test-based stochastic searches suggests that software is *mutationally robust*, i.e., simple randomized program transformations often produce semantically distinct program implementations that still meet functional requirements [54]. This surprising result suggests an approach to optimizing non-functional properties of programs.

We propose a post-compilation, software-based "Genetic Optimization Algorithm" (GOA) for discovering optimizations and managing tradeoffs among non-functional software properties. We illustrate the approach by focusing on the example of energy usage, which combines runtime and other more difficult-to-measure properties. GOA maintains a population of randomly mutated program *variants*, first selecting those that retain required functionality, and second looking for those that improve a non-functional property (encoded in an objective function). Our approach leverages ideas from evolutionary computation (population-based stochastic search), mutational robustness (random mutations yield independent implementations of the same specification), profile-guided optimization (performance measured on workloads) and relaxed notions of program semantics (customizing software to particular runtime goals and environments provided by a software engineer). Evolutionary algorithms such as GOA are well-suited for exploring difficult search spaces [29]. As input, GOA requires only the assembly code of the program to be optimized, a regression test suite that captures required functionality, and a measurable optimization target.

We demonstrate GOA on the problem of reducing energy consumption for the PARSEC [9] benchmark programs running on both desktop-class Intel and server-class AMD hardware. We define an efficient and accurate architecture-specific linear power model, which is parameterized by hardware counters. This model provides the objective function used by GOA; we validate results found by the model using physical wall-socket measurements. Experimentally, GOA discovers both hardware- and workload-specific optimizations, and reduces energy consumption of the PARSEC benchmarks by 20% on average compared to the best available compiler optimizations.

The main contributions of this paper are as follows:

- GOA, a post-compiler method for optimizing non-functional properties of assembly programs.
- A specialization of GOA that incorporates efficient predictive models to optimize energy consumption in assembly programs.
- An empirical evaluation using PARSEC benchmarks across two microarchitectures. We find that GOA reduces energy consumption by 20% as compared to the best available compiler optimizations, generates optimizations that generalize across different size workloads, and in most cases fully retains program functionality even against held-out test cases.

The next section provides three examples of optimizations found using GOA. We then describe the GOA algorithm more formally (Section 3), report experimental results (Section 4) discuss the relevant background material and related work (Section 5), and discuss the significance of our results and conclude (Sections 6 and 7).

## 2. Motivating Examples

This section describes three illustrative examples of energy optimizations found by GOA in the PARSEC benchmark suite.

`blackscholes` implements a partial differential-equation model of a financial market. Because the model runs so quickly, the benchmark artificially adds an outer loop that executes the model multiple times. These redundant calculations are not detected by standard static compiler analyses. GOA has discovered multiple ways to avoid this redundancy by making slight random variations on the original assembly code. For example, some variations can change the number of floating point operations or cache accesses. Each candidate is validated dynamically on the regression test suite, and if it passes all tests, retaining required functionality, it is then evaluated for energy efficiency using a linear combination of hardware performance counters. Over time, the best variants are subject to further modifications, until a stopping criterion is reached, and the most energy-efficient variant found is validated using physical energy measurements.

The validated `blackscholes` optimization returned by GOA discovered and removed the redundant calculation on both AMD and Intel hardware. However, the optimization strategy differed between the two architectures. In the Intel case, a "subl" instruction was removed, preventing multiple executions of a loop, while in the AMD case a similar effect was obtained by inserting a literal address which (due to the density of valid x86 instructions in random data [7]) is interpreted as valid x86 code to jump out of the loop, skipping redundant calculations.

GOA also finds hardware-specific optimizations in the `swaptions` benchmark, which prices portfolios. On AMD systems, GOA reduces the total `swaptions` energy consumption by 42% from the value produced by the least-energy combination of flags to `gcc` (Section 4.1). We believe this improvement is mostly due to the reduction of the rate of branch miss-prediction. Although it is not practical for general compilers to reason about branch prediction strategies for every possible hardware target, GOA can find these environment-specific specialized adaptations.

We found that no single edit (or small subset of edits) accounted for this improvement. Rather, many edits distributed throughout the `swaptions` program collectively reduced mispredictions. Typical edits included insertions and deletions of `.quad`, `.long`, `.byte`, etc., all of which change the absolute position of the executing code. Absolute position affects branch prediction when the value of the instruction pointer is used to index into the appropriate predictor. For example, AMD [25, § 6.2] advocates inserting `REP` before returns in certain scenarios.

Finally, GOA finds unintuitive optimizations. In the `vips` image processing program, it found an optimization that reduced the total energy used by 20.3% on the Intel system. The optimization actually increased cache misses by 20× but decreased the number of executed instructions by 30%, in effect trading increased off-chip communication for decreased computation.

In each example, neither the PARSEC-provided compiler flags nor the usual `gcc` "–O$x$" flags produced these optimizations. These examples show that beneficial energy optimizations exist that are not exploited by common compilers, suggesting the need for a technique to automatically find them.

## 3. Genetic Optimization Algorithm (GOA)

This section describes the Genetic Optimization Algorithm (GOA) for optimizing non-functional behavior of off-the-shelf assembly programs. The main components of GOA are depicted in Figure 1. GOA takes as input the original program source, a regression test suite capable of exercising program executables, and a scalar-valued objective (or *fitness*) function. The objective function takes as input any program variant that passes the regression test suite and assesses its non-functional behavior.

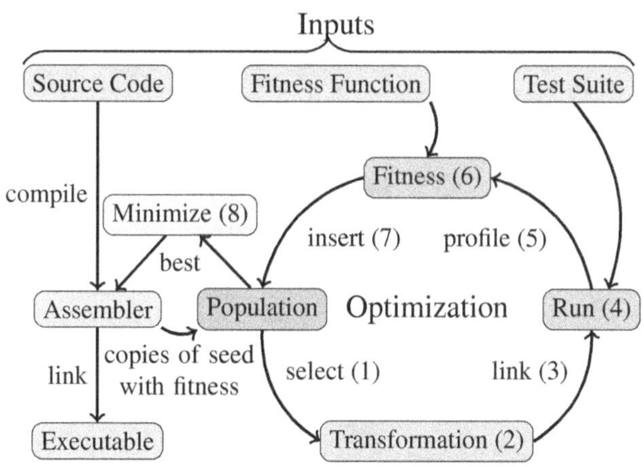


**Figure 1.** Overview of the program optimization process.

During compilation and linking, the intermediate assembly code representation of the program is extracted from the build process (Section 3.1) assigned a fitness as in steps 4, 5, 6 below and used to seed a population of mutated copies of the program (Section 3.3). An evolutionary computation (EC) algorithm (Section 3.2) then searches for optimized versions of the original program. Every iteration of the main search loop: (1) selects a candidate optimization from the population, (2) transforms it (Section 3.3), (3) links the result into an executable, (4) runs the resulting executable against the supplied test suite, (5) collects performance information for programs that pass all tests, (6) combines the profiling information into a scalar fitness score using the fitness function (Section 3.4), and (7) reinserts the optimization and its fitness score into the population. The process continues until either a desired optimization target is reached or a predetermined time budget is exceeded. When the algorithm completes, a post-processing step (8) takes the best individual found in the search and minimizes it with respect to the original program (Section 3.5). Finally, the result is linked into an executable and returned as the result.

The remainder of this section details the particulars of this process.

### 3.1 GOA Inputs

The program to be optimized is presented as a single assembly file, which can either be extracted from the build process, or provided directly, for example, using gcc's "–combine" flag for C. For C++, manual concatenation may be required. In practice this was straightforward for the PARSEC programs used as benchmarks in this work. Any performance-critical library functions must be included in the assembly file, because GOA optimizes only visible assembly code and not the contents of external libraries.

The algorithm also takes as input a test suite or indicative workload that serves as an implicit specification of correct behavior; a program variant that passes the test suite is assumed to retain all required functionality [65]. There are two well-known costs associated with adequate test suites—the cost of creating the test suite, and the cost of running it. Both are costs that GOA shares with profile-guided optimization [45], and we view the task of efficient testing as orthogonal to this work. For test suite construction, we note that many techniques for automated test input and test suite generation are available (e.g., [16]). Our scenario allows us to use the original program as an oracle, comparing the output of the original to that of the modified variant, which dramatically reduces costs. For the cost of running the test suite, we note that our approach is amenable to test suite reduction and prioritization (e.g., [60]).

The final input is the fitness function, detailed in Section 3.4, which evaluates behavior on the non-functional properties of interest.

### 3.2 Genetic Optimization Algorithm

Unlike recent applications of evolutionary computation to software engineering (e.g,. [33]), we use a *steady state* EC algorithm [36]. This means that the population is not completely replaced in discrete steps (generations). Instead, individual program variants (candidate optimizations) are selected from the population for additional transformations, and then reinserted. The steady state method simplifies the algorithm, reduces the maximum memory overhead, and is more readily parallelized.

The pseudocode for GOA is shown in Figure 2. The main evolutionary loop can be run in parallel across multiple threads of execution. Threads require synchronized access to the population $Pop$ and evaluation counter $EvalCounter$.

The population is initialized with a number of copies of the original program (line 1). In every iteration of the main loop (lines 3–15) the search space of possible optimizations is explored by transforming the program using random mutation and crossover operations (described in the next subsection). The probability $CrossRate$ controls the application of the crossover operator (lines 6–8). If a crossover is to be performed, two high-fitness parents are chosen from the population via *tournament selection* [46, § 2.3] and combined to form one new optimization (line 8). Otherwise, a

```
Input: Original Program, P : Program
Input: Workload, Run : Program → ExecutionMetrics
Input: Fitness Function, Fitness : ExecutionMetrics → ℝ
Parameters: PopSize, CrossRate, TournamentSize, MaxEvals

Output: Program that optimizes Fitness
 1: let Pop ← PopSize copies of ⟨P, Fitness(Run(P))⟩
 2: let EvalCounter ← 0
 3: repeat in every thread
 4:    let p ← null
 5:    if Random() < CrossRate then
 6:       let p1 ← Tournament(Pop, TournamentSize, +)
 7:       let p2 ← Tournament(Pop, TournamentSize, +)
 8:       p ← Crossover(p1, p2)
 9:    else
10:       p ← Tournament(Pop, TournamentSize, +)
11:    end if
12:    let p' ← Mutate(p)
13:    AddTo(Pop, ⟨p', Fitness(Run(p'))⟩)
14:    EvictFrom(Pop, Tournament(Pop, TournamentSize, −))
15: until EvalCounter ≥ MaxEvals
16: return Minimize(Best(Pop))
```

**Figure 2.** High-level pseudocode for the main loop of GOA.

single high-fitness optimization is selected. In either case, the candidate optimization is mutated (line 12), its fitness is calculated (by linking it and running it on the test suite, see Section 3.4), and it is reinserted into the population (line 13). The steady state algorithm then selects a member of the population for eviction using a "negative" tournament to remove a low-fitness candidate and keep the population size constant (line 14). Fitness penalizes variants heavily if they fail any test case and they are quickly purged from the population. Eventually, the fittest candidate optimization is identified, minimized to remove unnecessary or redundant changes (Section 3.5), and is returned as the result.

We report results using a population of size $MaxPop = 2^9$, a crossover probability of $CrossRate = \frac{2}{3}$, a tournament size of $TournamentSize = 2$ for both selection and eviction, and a total of $MaxEvals = 2^{18}$ fitness evaluations. In preliminary runs these parameters proved sufficient to find significant optimizations for most programs with runtimes of 16 hours or less (using 12 threads on a server-class AMD machine), meeting our goal of "overnight" optimization.

### 3.3 Program Representation and Operations

Each individual program in the population is represented as a linear array of assembly statements, with one array position allocated for each line in the assembly program [52]. Programs are transformed by mutation and crossover operators defined over the arrays of instructions. Argumented instructions are treated as atomic in the sense that arguments to individual instructions are never changed directly. This potentially limits the search, but in practice most useful instructions are available to be copied from elsewhere in the program. This decision avoids the "problem of argumented instructions" (cf. [61]) when modifying assembly code.

The mutation step selects one of the three mutation operations (*Copy*, *Delete* or *Swap*) at random and applies it to locations in the program, selected uniformly at random, with replacement. When crossover is performed, two program locations are selected from within the length of the shorter program to be crossed. Two-point crossover is then applied at these points to generate a single output program variant from the two input program variants, as shown in Figure 3.

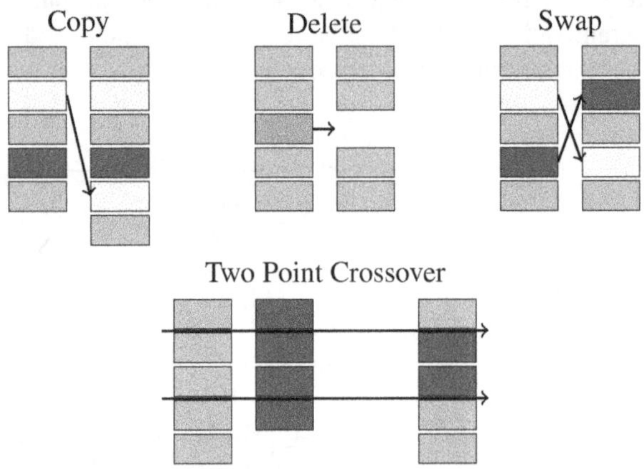


**Figure 3.** Mutation and Crossover operations on programs represented as linear arrays of argumented assembly instructions.

The mutation operations are not language or domain specific, and they never create entirely new code. Instead, they produce new arrangements of the argumented assembly instructions present in the original program. Our operators are reasonable extensions of the standard EC mutation and crossover operations, which are typically defined over bitstrings. Mutation operators explore the search space through small local changes, while crossover can escape local optima, either by combining the best aspects of partial solutions or by taking long jumps in the search space.

### 3.4 Evaluation and Fitness

The goal of GOA is to optimize a given fitness function. In our energy-optimizing implementation, the fitness function uses hardware performance counters [18] captured during test suite execution and combines them into a single scalar using a linear energy model (Section 4.3) defined over the values of those counters. Although we demonstrate GOA using this complex fitness function, it could also be applied to simpler fitness functions such as reducing runtime or cache accesses.

Test input data were selected to fulfill two requirements: (1) minimize the runtime of each evaluation, and (2) return sufficiently stable hardware performance counter values to allow reliable fitness assessment. The full test suite, which validates that candidate optimizations retain required functionality, need not be the same as the abbreviated test data used to measure non-functional fitness.

### 3.5 Minimization

The randomized nature of EC algorithms sometimes produces irrelevant or redundant transformations. We prefer optimizations that attain the largest fitness improvement with the fewest changes to the original program. To accomplish this, we include a final minimization step to remove changes that do not improve the fitness. Minimization allows us both to focus on mutations that produce a measurable improvement (Section 4.4) and to avoid altering functionality that is not exercised during the fitness evaluation.

Our minimization algorithm is based on Delta Debugging [67]. Here, Delta Debugging takes a set of deltas (edit operations) between two versions of a program and determines a 1-minimal subset of those deltas that cause the first program to act identically to the second. We reduce the best optimization found by the evolutionary search to a set of single-line insertions and deletions against the original (e.g., as generated with the `diff` Unix utility). We then use Delta Debugging to minimize that set with respect to the fitness function. If the application of a particular delta has no measurable effect on the fitness function, we do not consider it to be a part of the optimization. Experimentally, we find that eliminating such superfluous deltas reduces problems with untested program functionality. We apply the minimal set of changes identified by Delta Debugging to the original program to produce the final optimized program.

### 3.6 Algorithm Summary

GOA maintains a population of linear arrays of assembly instructions, mutating and combining them with the goal of optimizing a given objective function while retaining all required functionality as indicated by a test suite. In the next section we evaluate the effectiveness of GOA by applying it to the problem of reducing energy consumption.

## 4. Experimental Evaluation

Our experiments address three research questions:

- Does GOA reduce energy consumption? (RQ1)
- Do our results generalize to multiple architectures and held-out workloads? (RQ2)
- Do GOA optimizations retain required functionality? (RQ3)

Recall that GOA requires three inputs: a program to be optimized, a fitness function, and a workload or test suite. We evaluate effectiveness and usability against the PARSEC benchmark suite (Section 4.1). For a fitness function, we develop an efficient energy consumption model, based on hardware counter values (Section 4.3). The test suite was chosen by selecting from the PARSEC suite the smallest inputs that generate a runtime of at least one second on each hardware platform. After running GOA, we evaluate the optimized program using physical wall-plug measurements of energy. All software tools described in this work, including installation and usage instructions, are publicly available at `https://github.com/eschulte/goa/tree/asplos2014`.

| Program | C/C++ Lines of Code | ASM Lines of Code | Description |
|---|---|---|---|
| blackscholes | 510 | 7,932 | Finance modeling |
| bodytrack | 14,513 | 955,888 | Human video tracking |
| ferret | 15,188 | 288,981 | Image search engine |
| fluidanimate | 11,424 | 44,681 | Fluid dynamics animation |
| freqmine | 2,710 | 104,722 | Frequent itemset mining |
| swaptions | 1,649 | 61,134 | Portfolio pricing |
| vips | 142,019 | 132,012 | Image transformation |
| x264 | 37,454 | 111,718 | MPEG-4 video encoder |
| total | 225,467 | 1,707,068 | |

**Table 1.** Selected PARSEC benchmark applications.

### 4.1 Benchmark Programs and Systems

We use the popular PARSEC [9] benchmark suite of programs representing "emerging workloads." We evaluate GOA on all of the PARSEC applications that produce testable output and include more than one input set. Testable output is required to ensure that the optimizations retain required functionality. Multiple input sets are required because we use one (training) input set during the GOA optimization and separate held-out ("testing") inputs to test after GOA completes (Section 4.2). The eight applications satisfying these requirements are shown with sizes and brief descriptions in Table 1. Two PARSEC applications were excluded: `raytrace` which does not produce any testable output, and `facesim` which does not provide multiple input sets.

We evaluate on an Intel Core i7 and an AMD Opteron. The Intel system has 4 physical cores, Hyper-Threading, and 8 GB of memory, and it is indicative of desktop or personal developer hardware. The AMD system has 48 cores and 128 GB of memory, and is representative of more powerful server-class machines.

We compare the performance of GOA's optimized executables to the original executable compiled using the PARSEC tool with its built-in optimization flags or the `gcc` "–O$x$" flag that has the least energy consumption.[1]

### 4.2 Held-Out Test Suite

We use a large held-out test suite to evaluate the degree to which the optimizations found by GOA customize the program semantics to the training workload. For each benchmark besides `blackscholes`, we randomly generated 100 sets of command-line arguments (and argument values, as

[1] PARSEC includes a version of `x264` with non-portable hand-written assembly. To compare fairly against both Intel and AMD, we report `x264` numbers using the portable C implementation.

appropriate) from the valid flags accepted by the program. `blackscholes` accepts no flags, but instead requires a fixed sequence of arguments, one of which indicates an input file containing a number of independent records. We generated 100 test input files for `blackscholes` by randomly sampling between $2^{14}$ and $2^{20}$ records from the set of all records in any of the available PARSEC tests.

Each test was run using the original program and its output as an oracle to validate the output of the optimized program. If the original program rejected the input or arguments (e.g., because some flags cannot be used together), we rejected that test and generated a new one. We also rejected tests for which the original program did not generate the same output when run a second time, or for which the original program took more than 30 seconds to run.

The optimized programs were evaluated by running them with the same inputs and test data, comparing the output against the oracle. In most cases, we used a binary comparison between the output files. However, for `x264` tests producing video output, we used manual visual comparison to determine output correctness.

### 4.3 Energy Model

Our fitness function uses a linear energy model based on process-specific hardware counters similar to that developed by Shen *et al.* [57]. We simplify their model in two ways:

- We do not build workload-specific power models. Instead, we develop one power model per machine trained to fit multiple workloads and use this single model for every benchmark on that machine.
- We do not consider shared resources.

Incorporating these simplifications gives the following model:

$$\begin{aligned} power = C_{const} + C_{ins}\frac{ins}{cycle} + C_{flops}\frac{flops}{cycle} \\ + C_{tca}\frac{tca}{cycle} + C_{mem}\frac{mem}{cycle} \end{aligned} \quad (1)$$

$$energy = seconds \times power \quad (2)$$

Total energy (Equation 2) is given by the predicted power (Equation 1) multiplied by the runtime. The values for the constant coefficients are given in Table 2. They were obtained empirically for each target architecture, using data collected for each PARSEC benchmark, the SPEC CPU benchmark suite, and the `sleep` UNIX utility. For each program, we collected the performance counters as well as the average Watts consumed, measured by a Watts up? PRO meter. We combined these data in a linear regression to determine the coefficients shown in Table 2.

The disparity between the AMD and Intel coefficients is likely explained by significant differences in the size and class of the two machines. For example, the 13× increase in idle power of the AMD machine as compared to the Intel machine is reasonable given the presence of 12 times as many cores, and 15 times as much memory.

| Coefficient | Description | Intel (4-core) | AMD (48-core) |
|---|---|---|---|
| $C_{const}$ | constant power draw | 31.530 | 394.74 |
| $C_{ins}$ | instructions | 20.490 | -83.68 |
| $C_{flops}$ | floating point ops. | 9.838 | 60.23 |
| $C_{tca}$ | cache accesses | -4.102 | -16.38 |
| $C_{mem}$ | cache misses | 2962.678 | -4209.09 |

**Table 2.** Power model coefficients.

Even without our simplifications, the predictive power of linear models is rarely perfect. McCullough *et al.* note that on a simple multi-core system, CPU-prediction error is often 10–14% with 150% worst case error prediction [38]. We checked for the presence of overfitting using 10-fold cross-validation and found a 4–6% difference in the average absolute error, which is adequate for our application. Since we ultimately evaluate energy reduction using physical wall-socket measurements, our energy model is required only to be accurate and efficient enough to guide the evolutionary search.

We find that our models have an average of 7% absolute error relative to the wall-socket measurements. Collecting the counter values and computing the total power increases the test suite runtime by a negligible amount. Thus, our power model is both sufficiently efficient and accurate to serve as our fitness function.

The Intel Performance Counter Monitor (PCM) counter can also be used to estimate energy consumption. We did not use this counter because the model used to estimate energy is not public, and because it estimates energy consumption for an entire socket and does not provide per-process energy consumption. Relying on the PCM would reduce the parallelism available to our GOA implementation.

### 4.4 RQ1 — Reduce Energy Consumption

Table 3 reports our experimental results. The "Energy Reduction" columns report energy reduction while executing the tests by the GOA-optimized program, as measured physically and compared to the original. For example, if the original program requires 100 units and the optimized version requires 20, that corresponds to an 80% reduction.

GOA found optimizations that reduced energy consumption in many cases, with the overall reduction on the supplied workloads averaging 20%. Although in some cases—such as in `bodytrack` on AMD or `bodytrack`, `ferret`, `fluidanimate`, `freqmine` and `x264` on Intel—GOA failed to find optimizations that reduced energy consumption, it found optimizations that reduce energy consumption by an order of magnitude for `blackscholes` and over one-third for `swaptions` on both systems. We find that CPU-bound programs are more amenable to improvement than those that perform large amounts of disk IO. This result suggests that

| | Program Changes | | | | Energy Reduction | | | | Runtime Reduction | | Functionality | |
|---|---|---|---|---|---|---|---|---|---|---|---|---|
| | Code Edits | | Binary Size | | Training | | Held-Out | | Held-Out | | Held-Out | |
| Program | AMD | Intel | AMD | Intel | AMD | Intel | AMD | Intel | AMD | Intel | AMD | Intel |
| blackscholes | 120 | 3 | -8.2% | 0% | 92.1% | 85.5% | 91.7% | 83.3% | 91.7% | 81.3% | 100% | 100% |
| bodytrack | 19656 | 3 | -38.7% | 0% | 0% | 0% | 0.6% | 0% | 0.3% | 0.2% | 92% | 100% |
| ferret | 11 | 1 | 84.8% | 0% | 1.6% | 0% | 5.9% | 0% | -7.9% | -0.1% | 100% | 100% |
| fluidanimate | 27 | 51 | -3.3% | 11.4% | 10.2% | 0% | — | — | — | — | 6% | 31% |
| freqmine | 14 | 54 | 18.7% | 34.9% | 3.2% | 0% | 3.3% | -1.6% | 3.2% | 0.1% | 100% | 100% |
| swaptions | 141 | 6 | 27.0% | 18.5% | 42.5% | 34.4% | 41.6% | 36.9% | 42.0% | 36.6% | 100% | 100% |
| vips | 57 | 66 | -52.8% | 0% | 21.7% | 20.3% | 21.3% | — | 29.8% | — | 100% | 100% |
| x264 | 34 | 2 | 0% | 0% | 8.3% | 0% | 9.2% | 0% | 9.8% | 0% | 27% | 100% |
| average | 2507.5 | 23.3 | 3.4% | 8.1% | 22.5% | 17.5% | 24.8% | 19.8% | 24.1% | 19.7% | 78.1% | 91.4% |

**Table 3.** GOA energy-optimization results on PARSEC applications. The "Code Edits" column shows the number of unified diffs between the original and optimized versions of the assembly program. "Binary Size" indicates the change in size of the compiled executable. The "Energy Reduction" columns report the physically measured energy reduction compared to the original required to run the tests in the fitness function ("Training Workload") or to run all other PARSEC workloads for that benchmark ("Held-Out Workloads"). The "Runtime Reduction" columns report the decrease in runtime compared to the original. In some cases, the measured energy reduction is statistically indistinguishable from zero ($p > 0.05$). Note that for some benchmarks (e.g., `bodytrack`), although there is no measured improvement, the minimization algorithm maintains modeled improvement, resulting in a new binary. We do not report energy reduction on workloads for which the optimized variant did not pass the associated tests (indicated by dashes). The "Functionality" columns report accuracy on the held-out test suite.

GOA is likely better at generating efficient sequences of executing assembly instructions than at improving patterns of memory access. Overall, when considering only those programs with non-zero improvement, average energy reduction was 39%. The increased improvement on held-out workloads compared to training workloads was expected given the increased comparative size and runtime of most held-out workloads.

In most benchmark programs energy reduction is very similar to runtime reduction (see Columns "Energy Reduction" and "Runtime Reduction", Table 3). This is not surprising given the important role of time in our energy model. However, in some cases (e.g., `ferret`) energy was reduced despite an increase in runtime.

Although some optimizations are easily analyzed through inspection of assembly patches (e.g., the deletion of "`call im_region_black`" from `vips` skipping unnecessary zeroing of a region of data), many optimizations produce unintuitive assembly changes that are most easily analyzed using profiling tools. Such inspection reveals optimizations (Section 2) that run the gamut from removing explicit semantic inefficiencies in `blackscholes` to re-organizing assembly instructions in `swaptions` and `vips` in such a way as to decrease the rate of branch mispredictions. The AMD versions of `fluidanimate` and `x264` seem to improve performance by reducing idle cycles spent waiting for off-chip resources.

### 4.5 RQ2 — Generality

We evaluate the generality of our results on the two architectures and using the held-out test cases described earlier.

The "AMD" and "Intel" columns in Table 3 show results for the two architectures (described in Section 4.1). On both architectures, optimizations fix branch mispredictions in `swaptions` and `vips`; rely on relaxed notions of program semantics, such as by eliminating unnecessary loops in `blackscholes`; or remove redundant zeroing behavior in `vips`.

The GOA technique appears to find more optimizations on AMD than Intel. We hypothesize that the higher overall energy usage of the larger server-class AMD system affords more opportunity for improvement. It is also notable that the two programs with better results on AMD than Intel (`fluidanimate` and `x264`) are also the only two programs for which we find significant failures on held-out test data. This suggests that workload-specific improvements or customizations are more easily accomplished (or more readily rewarded) on the AMD than the Intel system. Despite these differences, GOA substantially reduces energy consumption on both AMD-based server-class and Intel-based workstation-class systems.

We also evaluate generality in terms of held-out workloads. GOA only has access to the supplied workload (Section 3.2). The PARSEC benchmark includes multiple workloads of varying size for each of our benchmark applications. The "Energy Reduction on Held-Out Workloads" columns in Table 3 show how optimizations learned on the smaller workloads apply to the larger held-out workloads.

Overall, we find that performance gains on the training workload generalize well to workloads of other sizes. The energy reduction of 20% on the training workloads is similar to the 22% observed for held-out workloads. However, when the optimizations customized to the training workload change the semantics on the held-out workload and produce different answers, the energy consumption varies dramatically. On Intel, `fluidanimate` and `vips` consume significantly more energy, while on AMD `fluidanimate` consumes significantly less. We attribute this improvement on held-out workloads to their increased size, which leads to a larger fraction of runtime spent in the inner loops where most optimizations are located. This generalization is important for the practical application of GOA. The training workload must execute quickly, because it is run as part of the inner loop of the GOA algorithm.

Although high-quality training data remains an essential input to our approach, the energy reductions found by GOA in this experiment generalized beyond the particular training data, and no special care was required in selecting training workloads. The defaults supplied as part of the PARSEC benchmark proved sufficient.

### 4.6 RQ3 — Functionality and Relaxed Semantics

A strength of our approach is its ability to tailor optimizations to the workload and architecture available [17, 45]. In many situations (e.g., if the deployment scenario is controlled, as in a datacenter, or if the available test suite is extensive) this is advantageous, and "relaxed semantics" may be an acceptable tradeoff for improvements to important non-functional properties. However, in some situations it may be more important to replicate original program behavior even in untested scenarios. We constructed a set of held-out test cases (see 4.2) and evaluated untested behavior by measuring the accuracy of the optimizations on these tests (the final columns in Table 3).

Recall that the optimizations are required to pass all available held-in test cases. The "Functionality on" columns show that GOA generally finds optimizations that behave just as the original, even on held-out tests not seen during the optimization process. The exceptions are `x264` (in which the AMD optimization works across every held-out input, but does not appear to work at all with some option flags) and `fluidanimate` (where the optimizations appeared to be brittle to many changes to the input, including workloads of different sizes). Notably, the minimization step (Section 3.5) ensures that changes to parts of the program not exercised by the training set are likely to be dropped (because removing those changes does not influence the energy consumption on the training set). Anecdotally we note that the unminimized optimizations typically showed worse performance on held-out tests than did the minimized optimizations. Although not a proof, this gives confidence that the technique produces optimizations that retain, or only slightly relax, the original program semantics.

Developers concerned with retaining the exact behavior of the original program have several available off-the-shelf random testing techniques (e.g., [16, 20, 32, 56]) that could be used by interpreting the original program's behavior as the oracle. This would restrict the search to considering only optimizations that are even more similar to the original. It would also increase the time cost for running GOA, but does not limit its applicability. As mentioned earlier, there is increasing willingness to trade guarantees of exact semantic preservation for other desired system properties [1, 2, 5, 6, 8, 39, 40, 50, 58, 59]. Taken together, the growing popularity of acceptability-oriented computing [48–50] and the difficulty of manually optimizing for energy [17, 35, 47], suggest that automatically reducing energy and manually focusing on semantics is a profitable tradeoff compared to the traditional converse.

### 4.7 Threats to Validity

Although the experimental results suggest that GOA can optimize energy, the results may not generalize to other non-functional properties or to other programs. One threat to generality is that energy consumption and our modeling are machine- or architecture-specific, and our optimizations are only individually valid for a particular target architecture. We attempt to mitigate this threat by considering two distinct architectures. We note that this is a general issue for performance optimization [41] and not specific to our approach. A second threat is that energy consumption can differ dramatically by workload—optimizations developed for training test cases may not be as effective when deployed. We mitigate this threat by physically measuring energy reduction on held-out workloads. A third threat is that our approach requires high-quality test cases (or specifications, etc.). If the test suite does not ensure that the implementation adheres to its specification, the resulting optimizations may over-customize the program to the environment and specific workload.

The performance of this post-compiler optimization technique may depend on the compiler used to generate the assembly code. Our evaluation considered only GCC, and it is possible that our results will not generalize to assembler produced by other compilers (e.g., the improvements in branch prediction might not be achieved in code generated by a compiler with better branch prediction capability).

Finally, by embracing relaxed program semantics we acknowledge that our optimizations may change the behavior of the program. Section 4.6 on held-out test suites provides one way to assess this threat in cases where relaxed semantics are undesirable. Earlier studies of a similar approach used for program repair suggest that our minimization step mitigates this threat significantly [34, 55].

## 5. Background and Related Work

Our approach combines (1) fundamental software engineering tools such as compilers and profilers, (2) mutation operations and algorithms from evolutionary computation, (3) relaxed notions of program semantics to customize software to a specified environment, and (4) software mutational robustness and neutral spaces.

## 5.1 Compilers and Profilers

***Compilers.*** Optimizing compilers are well-established in both research and industrial practice [3]. Our work provides *post*-compilation optimizations that refine compiler-generated assembly code.

Traditional compiler optimizations consider only transformations that are provably semantics-preserving (e.g., dataflow analysis). In practice, the C language includes undefined behavior which may lead to compiler- and architecture-dependent runtime behavior, often with surprising effects, such as compilers eliding null checks in programs that rely on undefined behavior [63, §3.3.4].

The difficulty of proving transformations to be semantics-preserving, combined with large differences in energy consumption across machines, means that semantics-preserving compiler optimizations to reduce energy consumption remain unlikely in the near future. For example, a feature request that the popular `llvm` compiler add an "–Oe" flag to optimize for energy was rejected with the counter-suggestion to use the established optimizations for speed instead.[2]

***Profiling.*** Profiling techniques are an established method for guiding both automated and manual optimizations [21]. We use hardware counters, allowing for fine-grained measurements of hardware events without requiring virtualization or instrumentation overheads. This allows test programs to operate at native speeds, which is critical in a search that explores hundreds of thousands of program variants. Our prototype implementation uses the Linux Perf [18] framework to collect hardware counters on a per-process basis.

***Profile Guided Optimization.*** Profile guided optimization (PGO) techniques combine test runs with instrumented programs (or, more recently, with hardware counters) to profile program runtime behavior. These profiles then guide the application of standard compiler optimizations to improve runtime performance, especially to reposition code to reduce instruction loads [45].

PGO can be used to tailor optimizations to a particular workload and architecture. However, the actual transformations provide the same guarantees and limitations of traditional compiler passes. That is, PGO typically narrows its search space by focusing on particular parts of the program (e.g., hot paths). By contrast, our work broadens the scope of possible optimizations through randomized operators and relaxed semantics.

***Auto-tuning.*** Auto-tuning extends PGO, providing additional performance enhancements and the ability to aggressively customize an application to specific hardware. It often requires that applications be written in a distinct modular style. For example, the exceptional performance gains found by the popular FFTW [17] required that the fast Fourier transform (FFT) source code be written in "codelets" (small optimized sub-steps) which were then combined into hardware dependent "plans."

Auto-tuning addresses the same problem as this work, namely that "computer architectures have become so complex that manually optimizing software is difficult to the point of impracticality." [17, § 5] Unlike auto-tuning, however, our method does not require that software be written in any special manner.

***Superoptimization.*** Massalin's classic work introducing superoptimization [37] exhaustively tested all possible combinations of instructions in Motorola's 68020 assembly language to find the fastest possible implementation of simple programs up to 14 instructions in length. The more recent MCMC project [51] leverages increased computing power and heuristic search to find optimizations on the same scale of ~10 instructions in the much larger x86 instruction set.

Despite its impressive results, the MCMC technique is not directly comparable to this work. They focus on very short sequences of assembly instructions while we operate on entire programs (hundreds of thousands of lines of assembly on average). Because of the extremely small size and simple functionality of their benchmark code, they initialize their heuristic search using a *random* sequence of x86 assembly instructions (using all instructions, including vector operations), and work back from these random sequences to functional code. Such an approach is not feasible for larger programs such as the PARSEC benchmarks.

Both approaches to superoptimization use simple tests of random sequences of assembly instructions to find faster assembly sequences than those accessible through traditional compiler optimizations. Although GOA addresses an entirely different scale in terms of functional and size complexity of the programs analyzed, we exploit the same insights that optimal instruction sequences are often not directly accessible through semantics-preserving operations and that tests can restrict attention to desired modifications. Ultimately, we see superoptimization as complementary, possibly being used in conjunction with our technique (e.g., as an alternating phase targeting the hottest profiled paths).

## 5.2 Evolutionary Computation

***Program Repair.*** Evolutionary computation is one of several techniques for automatically repairing program defects by searching for patches (sequences of edits) [14, 26, 33, 42, 65], including at the assembly level [52, 53]. GOA differs from this earlier work by addressing a different problem with a continuous complex objective function (reducing power consumption), rather than a discrete single-dimensional objective (passing all test cases).

***Evolutionary Improvement.*** Previous work on the evolutionary improvement of software was limited to modifying abstract syntax trees of simple ~10-line C functions [66].

[2] `http://llvm.org/bugs/show_bug.cgi?id=6210`

While optimizations were found that are not possible using standard compiler transformations, the small program size and simplified build environment suggest that results may not generalize to legacy software.

***Exploring Tradeoffs.*** EC techniques have recently been used to explore tradeoffs between execution time and visual fidelity in graphics shader programs [59]. This work is similar in spirit to ours but lacks an implicit specification through test cases. Instead, all mutants are valid and a Pareto-optimal frontier of non-dominated options with respect to execution time and visual fidelity is produced.

### 5.3 Relaxed Program Semantics

As mentioned earlier (Section 1), there is increasing interest in the tradeoff between exact semantics-preserving transformations and improving non-functional properties of programs. "Loop perforation" removes loop iterations to reduce program resource requirements while maintaining an acceptable Quality of Service (QoS) [39, 40]. Other systems change program behavior by switching function implementations [5] at runtime in response to QoS monitoring [23]. A formal system has even been developed to prove "acceptability properties" of some applications of the "relaxed" program transformations [11].

We view our work as partially customizing software to particular runtime goals and environments provided by a software engineer. While we do change explicitly programmed behavior (e.g., removing loop iterations, dropping calculations, etc.), we do not rely on QoS, but always give the *exact* right answer on tested inputs.

### 5.4 Mutational Robustness and Neutral Spaces

Recent work [54] showed that software functionality is surprisingly robust to random mutations similar to those used in this work, with over 30% of mutations producing *neutral* program variants that still pass an original test suite. These results were obtained over a wide variety of software (including both large open source projects and extensively tested benchmarks from the software testing community [24]). Many of these neutral mutations introduced nontrivial algorithmic changes to the program, yielding new implementations of the program's implicit specification.

These results help explain how random mutations can modify programs without "breaking" them, and it provides a rationale for why GOA succeeds in building "smart" optimizations from "dumb" program transformations.

## 6. Discussion

The experimental results support the claim that GOA can significantly reduce energy consumption on PARSEC benchmark programs in a way that generalizes to multiple architectures and to held-out workloads and tests. We next discuss the relationship between our work and traditional biological notions of trait selection (optimization), and we outline promising directions for future work.

### 6.1 Mathematical models of evolution

GOA's evolutionary computation algorithm is inspired by widely accepted theories of biological evolution, a field with a mature literature of mathematical results. Insights from the *Breeders Equation* guided our design of the linear power model fitness function, and analyses of Darwinian selection suggested larger population sizes and higher recombination rates than those used in similar applications to software engineering [33, 59].

Predating Darwin's Origin of Species [13], breeders used the *Breeder's Equation* to measure the effectiveness with which they could select for particular traits. The modern formulation of this classic model helped us analyze heritability and dependencies between traits. In our work, fitness is directly measurable in kilowatt hours, and hardware counters measure *phenotypic traits*. Analysis using biological theory pointed directly to the choice of a simple energy model based on hardware counters (Section 4.3). We used the fitness function to create a selection gradient analogous to $\beta$ in Equation 3 and derived in the same way. This equation decomposes the effect of natural selection into measurable phenotypic traits by regressing phenotypic traits $\beta$ against fitness [12, Chpt. 4].

The *Multivariate Breeder's Equation* is shown in Equation 3, where $\Delta\hat{Z}$ is a vector representing the change in phenotypic means, $G$ is a matrix of the additive variance-covariance between traits and $\beta$ is a vector representing the strength of selection. This equation quantifies the notion of heritability and the likely side effects of optimizing a given phenotypic trait in terms of other uncontrolled traits. The mathematical foundation provided by the Breeders Equation will provide a starting point for designing fitness functions for other GOA applications, for example, as outlined in Section 6.3.

$$\Delta\hat{Z} = G\beta \tag{3}$$

### 6.2 Fault Localization

Previous applications of EC to software engineering have relied on fault localization techniques as a way to limit the space of possible code modifications to the execution paths of the given test suite [33, 34]. In this paper we did not impose that restriction, and we discovered that minimized optimizations often did not modify the instructions executed by the test cases. We speculate that these optimizations may operate through changes to program offset and alignment, or by modifying non-executable data portions of program memory.

### 6.3 Future Work

***Other Architectures.*** To date, we have applied GOA only to x86 assembly code. Our program representations and mutation operations are quite general, and we believe that GOA would apply equally well to other instruction sets, such as ARM [52] or Java bytecode [44]. We note, however, that the high density of x86 instructions in random data [7] may have played a role in our results (Section 2),

***Co-evolutionary Model Improvement.*** GOA could be extended to iteratively refine the models that predict measurable values from hardware performance counters (such as the energy model used in this work). At a high level, the approach would be as follows:

1. Build an initial model from hardware counters and empirical measurements across multiple benchmark programs.
2. Evolve benchmark variants that maximize the difference between the model and reality.
3. Re-train the model using the evolved versions of benchmark programs.

Assuming that the measurable quantity predicted by the model (e.g., energy) can be changed only a limited amount, the evolutionary process would likely find and exploit errors in the initial model. Adding individuals to the training data that exploit these errors would improve subsequent versions of the model. Over multiple iterations, this *competitive co-evolution* [4] between the model and the candidate optimizations could improve both the model and the final optimizations.

***Mathematical Analysis.*** Our energy reduction optimizations of `vips` on both systems produce optimized versions that (despite running for fewer cycles) generate significantly more page faults than the original. It would be desirable to predict unintuitive results of optimization such as these, i.e. program features that are not included in the fitness function or energy model.

The concept of *Indirect selection* [12, Chpt. 6] suggests an approach for predicting some side effects of the search. Indirect selection is defined as the impact of selection on properties (traits) that are not themselves targets of selection but are strongly correlated with the selected traits. Variance-covariance matrices ($G$ in Equation 3) could be used to predict the effects of optimization on program characteristics that are not included directly in the fitness function but likely affected by the optimization process. This would require constructing and analyzing the program's variance-covariance matrix of traits of neutral mutations before the optimization run.

***Compiler Flags.*** Finding effective combinations and orderings of compiler passes is an open research question, and it is known that no single sequence of compiler passes is optimal for all programs [30] or even for all methods in a single program [31]. GOA could be extended to include multiple populations, each generated using unique combinations of compiler optimizations. By allowing each population to search independently for optimizations and occasionally exchanging high-fitness individuals among the populations, it may be possible to mitigate this problem.

## 7. Conclusion

We present an automated post-compilation technique for optimizing non-functional properties of software, such as energy consumption. Our Genetic Optimization Algorithm (GOA) combines insights from profile-guided optimization, superoptimization, evolutionary computation and mutational robustness. GOA is a steady-state evolutionary algorithm, which maintains a population of candidate optimizations (assembly programs), using randomized operators to generate variations, and selecting those that improve an objective function (the power model) while retaining all required functionality expressed in a test suite.

We describe experiments that optimize the PARSEC benchmarks to reduce energy consumption, evaluated via physical wall-socket power measurements. The use case is an embedded deployment or datacenter where the program will be run multiple times. Our technique successfully reduces energy consumption by 20% on average. Our results show that GOA is effective on multiple architectures, is able to find hardware-specific optimizations and to correct inefficient program semantics, that the optimizations found generalize across held-out workloads, and that in most cases the optimizations retain correctness on held-out test cases.

To summarize, GOA is: *powerful*, significantly reducing energy consumption beyond the best available compiler optimizations and capable of customizing software to a target execution environment; *simple*, leveraging widely available tools such as compilers and profilers and requiring no code annotation or technical expertise; and *general*, using general program transformations from the EC community, able to target multiple measurable objective functions, and applicable to any program that compiles to x86 assembly code.

## 8. Acknowledgments

The authors gratefully acknowledge the support of the National Science Foundation (SHF-0905236, CCF-1116289, CCF-0954024), Air Force Office of Scientific Research (FA9550-07-1-0532,FA9550-10-1-0277), DARPA (P-1070-113237), and the Santa Fe Institute.

## References

[1] Harold Abelson, Don Allen, Daniel Coore, Chris Hanson, George Homsy, Thomas F Knight Jr, Radhika Nagpal, Erik Rauch, Gerald Jay Sussman, and Ron Weiss. Amorphous computing. *Communications of the ACM*, 43(5):74–82, 2000.

[2] David H. Ackley and Daniel C. Cannon. Pursue robust indefinite scalability. *Proc. HotOS XIII, USA*, 2011.

[3] Alfred Aho, Ravi Sethi, and Jeffrey Ullman. *Compilers: Principles, Techniques and Tools*. Addison Wesley, 1986.

[4] Peter J Angeline and Jordan B Pollack. Competitive environments evolve better solutions for complex tasks. In *ICGA*, pages 264–270, 1993.

[5] J. Ansel, C. Chan, Y.L. Wong, M. Olszewski, Q. Zhao, A. Edelman, and S. Amarasinghe. *PetaBricks: a language and compiler for algorithmic choice*, volume 44. ACM, 2009.

[6] Woongki Baek and Trishul M Chilimbi. Green: a framework for supporting energy-conscious programming using controlled approximation. In *ACM Sigplan Notices*, volume 45, pages 198–209. ACM, 2010.

[7] E.G. Barrantes, D.H. Ackley, S. Forrest, and D. Stefanović. Randomized instruction set emulation. *ACM Transactions on Information and System Security (TISSEC)*, 8(1):3–40, 2005.

[8] J. Beal and Gerald Jay Sussman. Engineered robustness by controlled hallucination. In *AAAI 2008 Fall Symposium "Naturally-Inspired Artificial Intelligence"*, November 2008.

[9] C. Bienia, S. Kumar, J.P. Singh, and K. Li. The parsec benchmark suite: Characterization and architectural implications. In *Proceedings of the 17th international conference on Parallel architectures and compilation techniques*, pages 72–81. ACM, 2008.

[10] D. Brooks, V. Tiwari, and M. Martonosi. Wattch: a framework for architectural-level power analysis and optimizations. In *Computer Architecture, 2000. Proceedings of the 27th International Symposium on*, pages 83–94, 2000.

[11] Michael Carbin, Deokhwan Kim, Sasa Misailovic, and Martin C Rinard. Proving acceptability properties of relaxed nondeterministic approximate programs. In *Programming Language Design and Implementation*, pages 169–180, 2012.

[12] Jeffrey K Conner and Daniel L Hartl. *A primer of ecological genetics*. Sinauer Associates Incorporated, 2004.

[13] Charles Darwin. *On the origin of species*, volume 484. John Murray, London, 1859.

[14] Vidroha Debroy and W. Eric Wong. Using mutation to automatically suggest fixes for faulty programs. In *International Conference on Software Testing, Verification, and Validation*, pages 65–74, 2010.

[15] Hadi Esmaeilzadeh, Adrian Sampson, Luis Ceze, and Doug Burger. Neural acceleration for general-purpose approximate programs. In *International Symposium on Microarchitecture*, pages 449–460, 2012. DOI=10.1109/MICRO.2012.48.

[16] Gordon Fraser and Andreas Zeller. Mutation-driven generation of unit tests and oracles. *Transactions on Software Engineering*, 38(2):278–292, 2012.

[17] M. Frigo and S.G. Johnson. FFTW: An adaptive software architecture for the FFT. In *Acoustics, Speech and Signal Processing*, volume 3, pages 1381–1384, 1998.

[18] Thomas Gleixner. Performance counters for Linux, 2008. `http://lwn.net/Articles/310176/`.

[19] Martin Glinz. On non-functional requirements. In *Requirements Engineering Conference, 2007. RE'07. 15th IEEE International*, pages 21–26. IEEE, 2007.

[20] Patrice Godefroid, Nils Klarlund, and Koushik Sen. Dart: directed automated random testing. In *Programming Language Design and Implementation*, pages 213–223, 2005.

[21] Susan L. Graham, Peter B. Kessler, and Marshall K. McKusick. gprof: a call graph execution profiler (with retrospective). In *Programming Languages Design and Implementation*, pages 49–57, 1982.

[22] Mark Harman, William B. Langdon, Yue Jia, David R. White, and Andrea Arcuriand John A. Clark. The gismoe challenge: constructing the pareto program surface using genetic programming to find better programs (keynote paper). In *Automated Software Engineering*, pages 1–14, 2012.

[23] H. Hoffmann, J. Eastep, M.D. Santambrogio, J.E. Miller, and A. Agarwal. Application heartbeats for software performance and health. In *ACM SIGPLAN Notices*, volume 45, pages 347–348. ACM, 2010.

[24] Monica Hutchins, Herb Foster, Tarak Goradia, and Thomas Ostrand. Experiments of the effectiveness of dataflow-and control flow-based test adequacy criteria. In *International Conference on Software Engineering*, pages 191–200, 1994.

[25] Advanced Micro Devices Incorporated. Software optimization guide for amd64 processors. Technical report, Advanced Micro Devices Incorporated, September 2005. `http://support.amd.com/TechDocs/25112.PDF`.

[26] Dongsun Kim, Jaechang Nam, Jaewoo Song, and Sunghun Kim. Automatic patch generation learned from human-written patches. In *International Conference on Sofware Engineering*, 2013.

[27] Christoph M. Kirsch and Hannes Payer. Incorrect systems: it's not the problem, it's the solution. In *Design Automation Conference*, pages 913–917, 2012. DOI=10.1145/2228360.2228523.

[28] Jonathan Koomey. Growth in data center electricity use 2005 to 2010. *Oakland, CA: Analytics Press. August*, 1:2010, 2011.

[29] John R. Koza, Forrest H. Bennett III, David Andrew, and Martin A. Keane. *Genetic Programming III: Darwinian Invention and Problem Solving*. Morgan Kaufmann, 1999.

[30] Prasad Kulkarni, Wankang Zhao, Hwashin Moon, Kyunghwan Cho, David Whalley, Jack Davidson, Mark Bailey, Yunheung Paek, and Kyle Gallivan. Finding effective optimization phase sequences. In *ACM SIGPLAN Notices*, volume 38, pages 12–23. ACM, 2003.

[31] Prasad A Kulkarni, David B Whalley, Gary S Tyson, and Jack W Davidson. Exhaustive optimization phase order space exploration. In *Code Generation and Optimization 2006. International Symposium on*, pages 13–pp. IEEE, 2006.

[32] K. Lakhotia, M. Harman, and P. McMinn. A multi-objective approach to search-based test data generation. In *Genetic and Evolutionary Computation Conference*, 2007.

[33] Claire Le Goues, Michael Dewey-Vogt, Stephanie Forrest, and Westley Weimer. A systematic study of automated program repair: Fixing 55 out of 105 bugs for $8 each. In *International Conference on Software Engineering*, 2012.

[34] Claire Le Goues, ThanhVu Nguyen, Stephanie Forrest, and Westley Weimer. GenProg: A generic method for automated software repair. *Transactions on Software Engineering*, 38(1):54–72, 2012.

[35] M.T.-C. Lee, V. Tiwari, S. Malik, and M. Fujita. Power analysis and minimization techniques for embedded dsp software.

*Very Large Scale Integration Systems*, 5(1):123–135, 1997.

[36] Sean Luke. *Essentials of Metaheuristics*. Lulu, second edition, 2013. `http://cs.gmu.edu/~sean/book/metaheuristics/`.

[37] H. Massalin. Superoptimizer: a look at the smallest program. *ACM SIGARCH Computer Architecture News*, 15(5):122–126, 1987.

[38] John C McCullough, Yuvraj Agarwal, Jaideep Chandrashekar, Sathyanarayan Kuppuswamy, Alex C Snoeren, and Rajesh K Gupta. Evaluating the effectiveness of model-based power characterization. In *USENIX Annual Technical Conf*, 2011.

[39] S. Misailovic, D.M. Roy, and Martin Rinard. Probabilistically accurate program transformations. *Static Analysis*, 2011.

[40] S. Misailovic, S. Sidiroglou, H. Hoffmann, and Martin Rinard. Quality of service profiling. In *International Conference on Software Engineering*, pages 25–34, 2010.

[41] Todd Mytkowicz, Amer Diwan, Matthias Hauswirth, and Peter F. Sweeney. Producing wrong data without doing anything obviously wrong! In *Architectural support for programming languages and operating systems*, pages 265–276, 2009.

[42] Hoang Duong Thien Nguyen, Dawei Qi, Abhik Roychoudhury, and Satish Chandra. SemFix: Program repair via semantic analysis. In *International Conference on Sofware Engineering*, pages 772–781, 2013.

[43] Kevin J Nowka, Gary D Carpenter, Eric W MacDonald, Hung C Ngo, Bishop C Brock, Koji I Ishii, Tuyet Y Nguyen, and Jeffrey L Burns. A 32-bit powerpc system-on-a-chip with support for dynamic voltage scaling and dynamic frequency scaling. *Solid-State Circuits, IEEE Journal of*, 37(11):1441–1447, 2002.

[44] Michael Orlov and Moshe Sipper. Flight of the FINCH through the Java wilderness. *Transactions on Evolutionary Computation*, 15(2):166–192, 2011.

[45] Karl Pettis and Robert C Hansen. Profile guided code positioning. In *ACM SIGPLAN Notices*, volume 25. ACM, 1990.

[46] R. Poli, W.B. Langdon, and N.F. McPhee. *A field guide to genetic programming*. Lulu Enterprises Uk Ltd, 2008.

[47] Sherief Reda and Abdullah N. Nowroz. Power modeling and characterization of computing devices: a survey. *Electronic Design Automation*, 6(2):121–216, 2012.

[48] Martin Rinard. Acceptability-oriented computing. In *Object-oriented programming, systems, languages, and applications*, pages 221–239, 2003.

[49] Martin Rinard. Survival strategies for synthesized hardware systems. In *Formal Methods and Models for Co-Design*, pages 116–120, 2009.

[50] Martin Rinard, Cristian Cadar, Daniel Dumitran, Daniel M. Roy, Tudor Leu, and Jr. William S. Beebee. Enhancing server availability and security through failure-oblivious computing. In *Operating Systems Design and Implementation*, 2004.

[51] Eric Schkufza, Rahul Sharma, and Alex Aiken. Stochastic superoptimization. In *Architectural Support for Programming Languages and Operating Systems*, 2013.

[52] Eric Schulte, Jonathan DiLorenzo, Stephanie Forrest, and Westley Weimer. Automated repair of binary and assembly programs for cooperating embedded devices. In *Architectural Support for Programming Languages and Operating Systems (ASPLOS)*, 2013.

[53] Eric Schulte, Stephanie Forrest, and Westley Weimer. Automatic program repair through the evolution of assembly code. In *Automated Software Engineering*, pages 33–36, 2010.

[54] Eric Schulte, ZacharyP. Fry, Ethan Fast, Westley Weimer, and Stephanie Forrest. Software mutational robustness. *Genetic Programming and Evolvable Machines*, pages 1–32, 2013.

[55] Eric Schulte, Westley Weimer, and Stephanie Forrest. Repairing security vulnerabilities in the netgear router binary. *Computer Communications Review*, (submitted).

[56] Koushik Sen, Darko Marinov, and Gul Agha. CUTE: a concolic unit testing engine for C. In *Foundations of Software Engineering*, pages 263–272, 2005.

[57] Kai Shen, Arrvindh Shriraman, Sandhya Dwarkadas, Xiao Zhang, and Zhuan Chen. Power containers: An OS facility for fine-grained power and energy management on multicore servers. In *Architectural support for programming languages and operating systems*, pages 65–76, 2013.

[58] Stelios Sidiroglou, Oren Laadan, Carlos Perez, Nicolas Viennot, Jason Nieh, and Angelos D. Keromytis. Assure: automatic software self-healing using rescue points. In *Architectural Support for Programming Languages and Operating Systems*, pages 37–48, 2009.

[59] Pitchaya Sitthi-Amorn, Nicholas Modly, Westley Weimer, and Jason Lawrence. Genetic programming for shader simplification. *ACM Transactions on Graphics*, 30(5), 2011.

[60] Adam M. Smith and Gregory M. Kapfhammer. An empirical study of incorporating cost into test suite reduction and prioritization. In *Symposium on Applied Computing*, 2009.

[61] Thomas Sperl. Taking the redpill: Artificial evolution in native x86 systems. *CoRR*, abs/1105.1534, 2011.

[62] Lingjia Tang, Jason Mars, Xiao Zhang, Robert Hagmann, Robert Hundt, and Eric Tune. Optimizing Google's warehouse scale computers: The NUMA experience. In *High Performance Computer Architecture*, pages 188–197, 2013.

[63] Xi Wang, Haogang Chen, Zhihao Jia, Nickolai Zeldovich, and M Frans Kaashoek. Improving integer security for systems with kint. In *Operating Systems Design and Implementation*, pages 163–177, 2012.

[64] Yi Wei, Yu Pei, Carlo A. Furia, Lucas S. Silva, Stefan Buchholz, Bertrand Meyer, and Andreas Zeller. Automated fixing of programs with contracts. In *International Symposium on Software Testing and Analysis*, pages 61–72, 2010.

[65] Westley Weimer, ThanhVu Nguyen, Claire Le Goues, and Stephanie Forrest. Automatically finding patches using genetic programming. In *International Conference on Software Engineering*, pages 364–367, 2009.

[66] David R. White, Andrea Arcuri, and John A. Clark. Evolutionary improvement of programs. *Transactions on Evolutionary Computation*, 15(4):515–538, 2011.

[67] Andreas Zeller. Yesterday, my program worked. Today, it does not. Why? In *Foundations of Software Engineering*, pages 253–267, 1999.

# Resolved: Specialized Architectures, Languages, and System Software Should Largely Supplant General-purpose Alternatives within the Next Decade

Moderator: David A. Wood
University of Wisconsin-Madison
david@cs.wisc.edu

## Abstract

The field of computing has struggled since its inception with the tension between specialization and generalization. Specialized architectures, programming languages, and system software promise better performance (across many metrics, including efficiency, productivity, etc.) for workloads that match their specialization objective. General-purpose architectures, languages, and system software sacrifice extremes of performance for specific workloads, seeking acceptable performance across a much wider range. While specialized alternatives have always had their place, general-purpose architectures, languages, and system software have dominated main-stream computing systems for the past several decades. But with Dennard scaling already gone and the end of Moore's Law looming, some have argued that general-purpose computing platforms must naturally give way to specialization.

In this debate, two teams of highly-opinionated experts will debate the proposition that specialized architectures, languages, and system software should largely supplant general-purpose alternatives within the next decade. Arguments in favor of specialization include energy efficiency in the post-Dennard scaling era, performance scaling in the post-Moore's law era, and improvements in programmer productivity. Arguments against include the large investment needed to create specialized hardware and software components, lack of tools and interfaces to create reusable components, the semantic gap from overspecialization, and security vulnerabilities and general correctness issues due to interoperation of specialized components.

***Categories and Subject Descriptors*** C.0 [*GENERAL*]: System architectures; Hardware/software interfaces; C.3 [*SPECIAL-PURPOSE AND APPLICATION-BASED SYSTEMS*]; D.3.0 [*PROGRAMMING LANGUAGES*]: General; D.4.0 [*OPERATING SYSTEMS*]: General

***General Terms*** Design, Languages, Performance, Reliability, Security

***Keywords*** general-purpose, special-purpose, domain-specific



*ASPLOS '14*, March 1-5, 2014, Salt Lake City, Utah, USA.

ACM 978-1-4503-2305-5/14/03.
http://dx.doi.org/10.1145/2541940.2563369

# Guardrail: A High Fidelity Approach to Protecting Hardware Devices from Buggy Drivers

Olatunji Ruwase[1] * Michael A. Kozuch[2] Phillip B. Gibbons[2] Todd C. Mowry[3]

[1]Microsoft Research [2]Intel Labs Pittsburgh [3]Carnegie Mellon University

olruwase@microsoft.com, {michael.a.kozuch, phillip.b.gibbons}@intel.com, tcm@cs.cmu.edu

## Abstract

Device drivers are an Achilles' heel of modern commodity operating systems, accounting for far too many system failures. Previous work on *driver reliability* has focused on protecting the kernel from unsafe driver side-effects by interposing an invariant-checking layer at the driver interface, but otherwise treating the driver as a black box. In this paper, we propose and evaluate Guardrail, which is a more powerful framework for run-time driver analysis that performs *decoupled, instruction-grain* dynamic correctness checking on arbitrary kernel-mode drivers as they execute, thereby enabling the system to detect and mitigate more challenging correctness bugs (e.g., data races, uninitialized memory accesses) that cannot be detected by today's fault isolation techniques. Our evaluation of Guardrail shows that it can find serious data races, memory faults, and DMA faults in native Linux drivers that required fixes, including previously unknown bugs. Also, with hardware logging support, Guardrail can be used for online protection of persistent device state from driver bugs with at most 10% overhead on the end-to-end performance of most standard I/O workloads.

***Categories and Subject Descriptors*** C.4 [*Performance of Systems*]: Reliability, availability, and serviceability; D.2.5 [*Software Engineering*]: Testing and Debugging—Monitors, Tracing

***Keywords*** Device Drivers; Dynamic Analysis

* Work done at Carnegie Mellon University



*ASPLOS '14,* March 1–5, 2014, Salt Lake City, Utah, USA.

http://dx.doi.org/10.1145/2541940.2541970

## 1. Introduction

Because device drivers have been identified as a critical weak link in overall systems reliability [8, 17, 31, 39, 46], researchers have attempted to improve their robustness through strategies such as *static analysis* [1, 8, 21, 31], *specification* [26, 40, 50], *type safety* [35, 44, 54], *user-level drivers* [4, 18, 25, 50], and *run-time analysis* [4, 5, 14, 18, 45, 50]. While each of these approaches has its merits, we focus on *run-time analysis* in this paper because it is complementary to the other approaches and can potentially catch problems that the other techniques may miss due to practical limitations.

The main focus of run-time driver analysis to date has been on *fault isolation* [4, 5, 14, 18, 45, 50], where the goal is to augment the driver interfaces to prevent a buggy driver from corrupting the OS kernel. The basic idea behind fault isolation is to interpose a run-time checking layer at the driver interface that performs a sanity check before the driver is allowed to proceed with performing any side effects outside of the driver (e.g., writing to kernel memory [45]).

### 1.1 Limitations of Existing Fault Isolation Techniques

While existing fault isolation techniques are useful, they suffer from two key limitations. First, they *only check invariants at the driver's interface*, treating the bulk of the driver's execution as a *black box*. For example, most fault isolation techniques ignore driver *reads* (since normal reads do not have side-effects), which means that they are unable to recognize problems such as *data races* within drivers. In other words, existing fault isolation techniques do not focus on whether the driver software is executing correctly (at a fundamental level), but rather on whether the driver has obviously harmful side-effects beyond its interface.

Second, while fault isolation research has focused on the driver's interface with the kernel, arguably the driver's interface to its *hardware device* is equally important (if not more important) since rebooting the kernel may do little good once persistent device state has been corrupted. In contrast with the driver/kernel interface, which tends to be relatively uniform across drivers, the driver/device interfaces are far more diverse and device-specific, which makes it

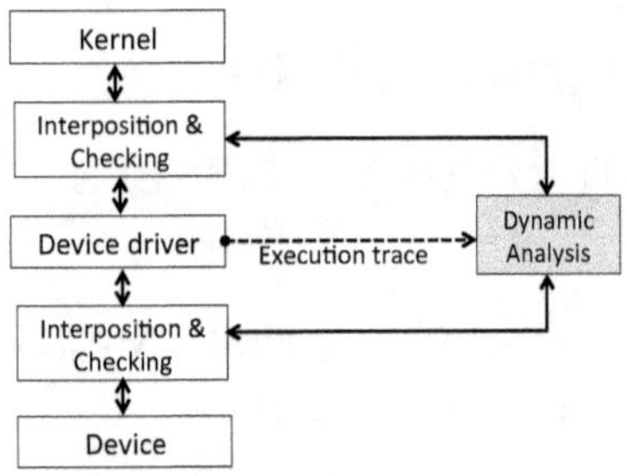


Figure 1: Incorporating decoupled dynamic analysis to protect the system from driver faults.

far more challenging to interpose and successfully check invariants across this latter interface [50].

### 1.2 Our Approach: Protecting Devices through Decoupled, Instruction-Grain Dynamic Driver Analysis

In this paper, we present a new framework (called *Guardrail*) that focuses on preventing buggy device drivers from corrupting hardware device state. Rather than treating the bulk of the driver execution as a black box, Guardrail's decision of whether to allow the driver to proceed with a side-effect-causing operation is driven not simply by invariant checks at the driver's interface, but rather by instruction-grain dynamic analysis of the driver software as it executes, as illustrated in Figure 1. Indeed, Guardrail typically identifies correctness problems within the driver before they even reach the driver's interface. Hence Guardrail enables a more comprehensive analysis of whether or not the driver software is behaving *correctly* than what is practical today; for example, handling the case where a buggy driver stores the wrong value in a valid target location (in either kernel memory or its device).

To achieve this higher fidelity of dynamic correctness checking without sacrificing driver performance, we propose a *decoupled* approach to performing the dynamic instruction-by-instruction analysis of the driver as it executes. In our decoupled approach, an execution trace of the driver software is captured (e.g., via a hardware-assisted logging mechanism [6, 47] or through binary instrumentation [15, 32]) and stored in a buffer that is consumed asynchronously by a dynamic analysis tool running concurrently in a separate virtual machine. Because the dynamic analysis tool can lag behind the driver in our decoupled approach, the interposition layer stalls any side-effect-causing operations at the driver interface until the dynamic analysis is able to catch up. Guardrail effectively achieves a "sweet spot" between *synchronous* instruction-grain analysis (which results in too large of a performance overhead for latency-critical driver operations such as interrupt handling) and *offline* (or post-mortem) instruction-grain analysis (which avoids run-time overhead but occurs too late to prevent faulty drivers from corrupting persistent state). Although the dynamic analysis enabled by Guardrail does increase overall computational load on the system, our decoupled approach allows the bulk of this overhead to be offloaded onto idle CPUs (unless the system is already saturated on CPU throughput). Hence Guardrail is suitable for either a fast debug/testing environment or a production environment that is not already throughput limited.

### 1.3 Related Work

As described above, our work complements earlier research on *fault isolation* [4, 5, 14, 18, 45, 50] by not only using interpositioning to prevent harmful side effects from escaping from the driver, but also by "opening the black box": i.e., using instruction-by-instruction dynamic analysis of the driver software to hopefully identify problems that are not obvious to interface invariant checks. In contrast with the previous proposal for isolating *devices* from driver faults [50], which required modifying the driver and moving it into user-space, our approach is transparent to both the driver and the device, therefore enabling Guardrail to work with arbitrary driver binaries and devices.

Regarding dynamic checking for faults *within* drivers, SafeDrive [54] and KAddrcheck [15] perform run-time checks to detect memory addressability issues in kernel code, including drivers. In contrast with SafeDrive [54], which instruments drivers at compile-time, our approach works directly on binaries and does not require access to driver source code. In contrast with KAddrcheck [15], our approach uses *decoupled* analysis to reduce the impact on driver performance and can detect problems with memory *initialization* (in addition to addressability). Moreover, within the same Guardrail framework, a wide variety of tools are readily supported. For example, our *DMACheck* tool dynamically detects DMA bugs in drivers; this runtime approach is complimentary to a static analysis approach [3] detecting similar bugs using separation logic with permissions.

Finally, DataCollider [13] detects data races through a sampling-based approach by stalling kernel threads in critical sections and using data breakpoints to detect conflicting accesses in other threads. There are three fundamental differences between DataCollider and our Guardrail-enabled data race detection tool (*DRCheck*, which we describe in detail later in this paper). First, DataCollider can only detect whether a data race occurred in a specific observed interleaving, whereas *DRCheck* can detect race conditions that might occur in other interleavings (because *DRCheck* models synchronization protocols used in the driver). Second, DataCollider uses *sampling* to reduce run-time overheads, whereas *DRCheck* uses decoupled analysis to reduce overhead while still checking all driver invocations for potentially harmful behavior. Third, DataCollider's stalling approach is not suited for threads servicing time-critical interrupts, making it less effective for drivers (which are frequently in interrupt contexts) than *DRCheck*.

### 1.4 Contributions

This paper makes the following contributions:

- We propose and implement a novel framework, *Guardrail*, for detecting incorrect driver behavior at run-time and preventing the faulty driver from corrupting the rest of the system (including persistent state on hardware devices). In contrast to previous proposals, Guardrail performs instruction-grain correctness checking as the driver executes, and uses a decoupled VM-based approach to provide isolation and minimize the impact on driver performance. Guardrail supports arbitrary kernel-mode driver binaries and devices for commodity operating systems.
- Within Guardrail, we demonstrate three new instruction-grain correctness checking tools that detect data races (*DRCheck*), DMA faults (*DMACheck*), and unsafe uses of uninitialized data (*DMCheck*), none of which are supported by existing driver fault isolation techniques. *DRCheck* improves upon prior approaches by minimizing false positives and avoiding false negatives, while handling the complexities of kernel-mode drivers.
- Our experimental results show that Guardrail is more effective at catching driver bugs than previous tools, e.g., by finding a bug in the popular *qla2xxx* SCSI driver that was undetected for years. Moreover, with hardware logging support, Guardrail modestly impacts the end-to-end performance of standard I/O workloads in most cases.

## 2. System Design

To foster a principled approach while designing Guardrail, we developed a set of high-level design goals. In particular, Guardrail should:

**(generality)** support the monitoring of unmodified driver binaries running in common computing environments (e.g., stock multithreaded OS, arbitrary applications and run-time environments, etc.);

**(detection fidelity)** enable fine-grain correctness-checking and identification of errors, while supporting a wide variety of monitoring tools;

**(containment)** provide mechanisms for preventing detected driver errors from erroneously affecting external state;

**(response flexibility)** allow users to control what Guardrail does on detecting an error (e.g., disable I/O operations from the driver, or simply record information for post-mortem analysis); and

**(trustworthiness)** rely on a minimal trusted computing base for containment.

The system architecture that resulted from these goals is shown in Figure 2. To simultaneously satisfy the *containment* and *generality* goals, we adopted a virtual machine-based system. The driver(s) of interest, along with the stock

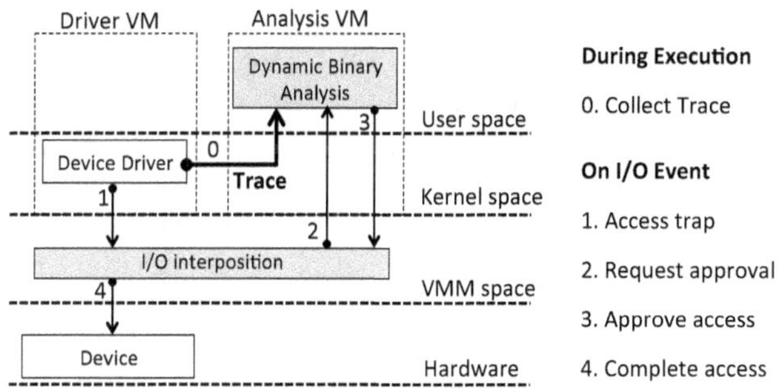


Figure 2: System architecture of Guardrail.

OS (Linux, in our prototype) and related applications, execute in one virtual machine (VM), labeled the "Driver VM" in the figure. The virtual machine monitor (VMM) provides the interposition mechanism. I/O operations are intercepted in this layer, and should an error be detected, the VMM prevents the error from propagating outside the Driver VM by simply not delivering it to the physical hardware.

While the driver executes, a trace of its operations is collected and delivered to a second virtual machine, the "Analysis VM." An instruction-level trace supporting high *detection fidelity* can be captured through one of several mechanisms: binary translation [15, 32] in the Driver VM, VMM-based monitoring [9, 52], or monitoring hardware [6, 47, 48]. Because driver code is potentially executed by an unbounded number of kernel threads, logical logs are maintained per virtual processor in the Driver VM, rather than per kernel thread, to avoid scalability issues.

The execution trace is streamed, possibly with some buffering delay, to the Dynamic Binary Analysis tool, which runs in user space in the Analysis VM. This tool consumes the execution trace and checks for driver errors, such as data races or memory access violations, to help the VMM determine when (or if) an intercepted I/O operation can be safely dispatched to the device (see Section 2.2 for details). If a fault is identified in the driver's execution then it is potentially unsafe to dispatch the intercepted I/O operation to the device. However, the appropriate course of action in this situation often depends on the particular requirements of the user (e.g., willingness to sacrifice system availability to ensure persistent data integrity). Therefore, to accommodate the variety of constraints in production sites, end users have the *response flexibility* of configuring Guardrail to operate in one of 3 modes: (i) *stringent*, (ii) *permissive*, and (iii) *triage*. In *stringent* mode, Guardrail blocks the intercepted and subsequent I/O operations from the driver, effectively disabling the I/O device. *Permissive* mode is the other extreme, where after performing user specified actions (e.g., alerting the user, recording event information for additional off-line post-mortem analysis, taking a system checkpoint, enabling additional online analysis, etc.) Guardrail dispatches the offending I/O operation to the device and resumes normal execution. *Triage* mode represents a middle ground between these two extremes, where Guardrail performs a best-effort estimation of the safety of completing the I/O operation by automatically triaging the fault [22, 27, 34]. If the I/O operation is deemed safe, Guardrail behaves like *permissive* mode, otherwise it behaves like *stringent* mode. Although this flexibility allows Guardrail to be configured in interesting ways for different real-world deployment scenarios, this paper is however focused on *stringent* Guardrail.[1]

Note that in this design, the *trustworthiness* of the containment mechanism is maintained because any complexity associated with tracking the driver state, emulating device-specific logic, or correctness checking is managed in the dynamic analysis tool. Consequently, device-independent I/O interpositioning may be implemented through a simple addition to the VMM layer; less than 500 lines of C code were required to retrofit a commodity VMM (Xen [2]) with I/O interpositioning. The complexity of the checking tool may be non-trivial, however, primarily because the system was designed to accommodate arbitrary correctness-checking to cope with the wide variety of bug types that plague drivers [8, 17, 31]. Fortunately, these tools run in user space of the Analysis VM, easing their development and deployment.

## 2.1 Analysis Scope

An important question that arises in our design is: which events should be captured in the execution trace? For example, the trace could capture all instructions events in the Driver VM, all kernel-level events only, or solely events associated with the driver. Naturally, capturing a larger set of events than necessary incurs a performance overhead, so ideally, the driver analysis tool would only need to process events generated by the driver. In our case, this would mean instructions whose addresses belong to the loaded driver module.

However, we soon observed that many operations critical to determining whether a driver is behaving correctly are in fact performed outside the driver. In particular, the I/O subsystem (or protocol stack) (e.g., network, SCSI, sound), which manages the driver, provides certain invariants upon which the driver writer may rely. For example, the network stack will acquire certain locks prior to driver execution to protect shared data accesses within the driver, as illustrated by the code snippet from Linux 2.6.18 in Figure 3. Here, the network stack serializes packet transmission by locking the execution of the driver's `hard_start_xmit()` callback. A race detector focused solely on the driver's execution would not observe the lock acquire, which happens outside the driver context, and hence would incorrectly flag as data races

[1] Permissive and Triage modes only affect Guardrail's response to suspected driver correctness issues *within* the context of the Driver VM. The interposition layer always enforces the virtual machine definition. For example, an attempt to read/write past the end of a virtual disk will be strictly enforced under all modes.

```
HARD_TX_LOCK(dev, cpu);
 . . .
 rc = dev->hard_start_xmit(nskb, dev);
 . . .
HARD_TX_UNLOCK(dev);
```

Figure 3: The Linux interface to network drivers serializes packet transmission by locking `hard_start_xmit()`.

all pairs of accesses in `hard_start_xmit()` by different threads with at least one writer.

To address this issue, Guardrail monitors and analyzes operations occurring in the relevant portions of the I/O subsystem (e.g., the *scsi_mod* module in the Linux SCSI subsystem) as well as those originating in the driver, itself. Extending the scope to include this interface captured all such "critical" operations that we observed. Our goal is not to determine whether there are errors in the interface, but rather to detect operations that are critical to driver correctness, and this extension was useful for both our memory fault and data race detectors. A possible drawback of our approach is that interface changes across kernel versions will require corresponding modifications to our checking tools—fortunately, such changes are likely infrequent because they require corresponding modifications to the entire driver code base.

## 2.2 I/O Interposition Details

Because devices are controlled by reading/writing device registers, the interposition layer prevents driver errors from propagating beyond the VM boundary by: (i) intercepting all[2] device register accesses, (ii) coordinating with a decoupled correctness checker to determine the safety of the accesses, and (iii) ensuring their timely completion as soon as they are deemed safe. Because the Driver VM has direct access to the device [51], the interposition layer is transparent to both the driver and device, and therefore supports arbitrary drivers and devices. Figure 2 depicts the steps associated with the transparent handling of a device register access.

***Intercepting device register access*** Device register accesses from the driver are intercepted by ensuring that device register accesses from the Driver VM fault to the VMM. In virtualized x86 environments, the I/O port address space is typically considered to be privileged by default and accesses to this space will fault. Many modern devices, however, are managed through memory-mapped I/O registers that are accessed through regular load and store instructions. Because these operations are subject to the usual address translation mechanisms, Guardrail intercepts accesses to the device registers by configuring the page tables of the Driver VM such that these accesses fault to the VMM. The page faults resulting from this interposition can be distinguished from normal memory management page faults based on the faulting ad-

[2] Some performance improvements could be obtained by not intercepting I/O operations that do not affect externally-visible state, such as side-effect free reads, but such optimizations would require scrutiny of the operations and were not pursued in this work.

dress. Note that interposition only affects communication originating from the Driver VM; interrupts *to* the Driver VM may be delivered normally.

***Coordinating with decoupled correctness checking*** To limit the performance penalty of I/O interposition, intercepted device accesses should be verified and re-issued as soon as possible. If correctness checking is coupled with I/O interposition [50], this can be relatively straightforward; however, in our decoupled checking approach, additional coordination is required between the interposition and checking components. After intercepting a device register access, the interposition layer uses a memory-based communication channel to request approval from the checker to complete the access. Details of the faulting instruction (e.g., thread id, faulting address) are included in the request. If the checker verifies that no errors occurred in the execution trace up to the point where the access was encountered, the access will be approved. Otherwise, if the access is disapproved because of a driver fault, the interposition layer can initiate recovery using appropriate techniques [5, 24, 46].

Because the checker's response will typically incur some latency, the interposition layer has at least two options regarding what to do while waiting for the checker's response. The first is to hold the request in the hypervisor until the response arrives, effectively freezing the virtual CPU. To maintain the responsiveness of the guest OS, if interrupts are generated during this period, they should be delivered to the virtual CPU at the point just before the faulting instruction.[3] For development expediency, we selected a different option: the interposition layer simply returns control to the faulting instruction periodically. In other words, a guest OS thread that accesses a device register will continue executing the access and trapping into the interposition layer, until either the checker verifies the safety of the access or the thread is preempted.

***Completing device register access*** After the checking tool has verified that the intercepted register access is safe, there are two ways of issuing the operation: (i) retrying the faulting instruction after temporarily making the device register available to the guest OS [10], or (ii) emulating the faulting instruction in the hypervisor. Because the concurrently executing kernel threads of commodity OSes share a single kernel address space, the first option requires great care in attempting to ensure that the temporarily accessible page is only accessed by the verified operation in the intended thread at an appropriate time. Consequently, in our current implementation, we chose the emulation option in order to avoid potential containment errors, especially in SMP environments.

[3] We assume that the faulting instruction will eventually be re-executed, and the matching approval from the checker can then be applied. The VMM may need to monitor the guest to ensure it doesn't make an adjustment to prevent such re-execution (e.g. re-writing the stack). Such adjustments were not encountered in our experiments.

## 3. Driver Correctness Tools

Guardrail enables a wide range of driver correctness checking tools. In this work, we focus on tools for memory safety and concurrency, and OS protocol issues, because studies have shown that these account for a significant fraction of production driver faults [8, 17, 31, 39]. This section describes the three instruction-grain dynamic analysis tools that we developed for finding (i) data races, (ii) violations of OS rules for using DMA, and (iii) memory faults in unmodified Linux driver binaries.

### 3.1 DRCheck: Detecting Data Races

Our first dynamic analysis tool, *DRCheck*, detects data races in kernel-mode drivers. A *data race condition* occurs whenever there are two unserialized accesses to the same shared data with at least one being a write. Race conditions are difficult to avoid during driver development because of the complex concurrency setting in which drivers operate, and difficult to find during pre-release testing because of their non-deterministic nature. Moreover, most drivers are developed by third parties who are unlikely to be kernel experts [17, 31]. As modern OS kernels and their drivers increasingly exploit parallelism to improve performance, avoiding race conditions becomes all the more challenging, posing a serious threat to system stability.

#### 3.1.1 Complexity of concurrency issues in drivers

While there have been many studies on user-mode data race detection [16, 41, 42, 53], existing tools cannot be easily adapted for drivers, because the concurrency issues of kernel-mode execution are more complex than user-mode execution. For example, the LockSet algorithm [41], which associates a *lockset* state with each memory location, assumes that all synchronization occurs through well-defined library primitives. To integrate the LockSet techniques into *DRCheck*, any kernel synchronization mechanisms that do not use library primitives would need to be adapted to the framework. We identified the following four sources of additional complexity that must be addressed in kernel-mode driver execution:

1. a form of concurrency that makes it possible for a *single* thread to make racy accesses to shared data (i.e., to race itself);
2. synchronization invariants based on the context of the device state;
3. synchronization based on deferred execution using softirqs and kernel timers; and
4. *ad hoc* mutual exclusion techniques that avoid lock overheads, such as disabling interrupts and preemption.

These issues can lead to excessive false positives and false negatives for user-mode race detectors, as shown by our experimental study in Section 4. We discuss these concurrency issues in more details below, and then describe how

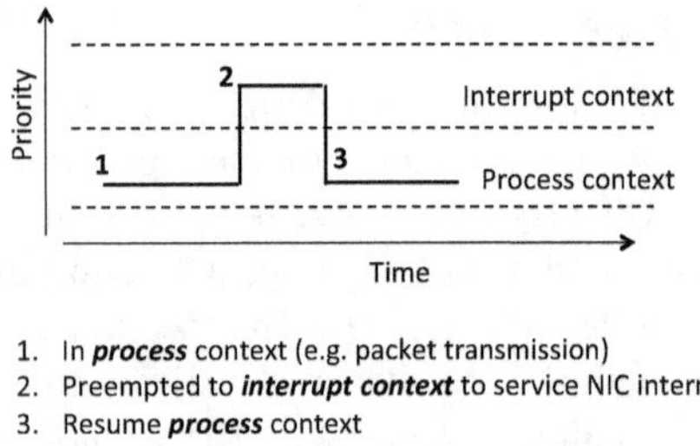


Figure 4: A kernel thread executing network driver code in different Linux kernel contexts.

*DRCheck* addresses them to reduce false positives and avoid false negatives.

***Sources of concurrency in drivers*** The most basic source of driver concurrency is multi-threaded execution of driver code that accesses shared data. In addition, a subtle form of concurrency is introduced by the multiple execution contexts of varying priority levels that are provided by commodity preemptive OS kernels, in order to enable scheduling flexibility for time-constrained, privileged work. For example, Linux kernel threads execute either in *process* context (lowest priority) or in *interrupt* context—further divided into *bottom half* and *top half* (highest priority). Kernel-mode execution contexts are critical to driver performance—they enable the prompt completion of higher priority tasks (e.g., interrupt handling) by hijacking a thread that is performing a lower priority task and using it for the higher priority task. As an example, Figure 4 illustrates the time line of a kernel thread executing network driver code in *process* and *interrupt* contexts of the Linux kernel. The thread is initially executing the packet transmission routine of the driver in *process* context, next it is switched to *top half* context to service a network card interrupt using the interrupt handling routine, and afterwards it resumes the packet transmission routine. However, execution contexts complicate concurrency in drivers in the sense that if the high priority code shares data with the suspended low priority code then the kernel thread could race itself.[4] For example, a race would occur in Figure 4 if on resumption of *process* context the thread reads data that was updated in *top half* context. Such a race will be missed by existing race detection tools because only one thread is involved.

***Device state-based synchronization*** Many peripheral devices (ethernet, scsi, usb, etc.) behave like finite state machines (FSM), and drivers often use their states to protect critical sections. The set of valid operations for a device depends on the state of the device, and so the kernel, in order to prevent device failures, invokes only driver callbacks that are valid for the current device state. In other words, device states act as the invariants that guard the invocation

[4] A restricted form of this issue arises in user-space due to signal handling (i.e., reentrancy), and to our knowledge has been ignored by prior work on user-space data race detection.

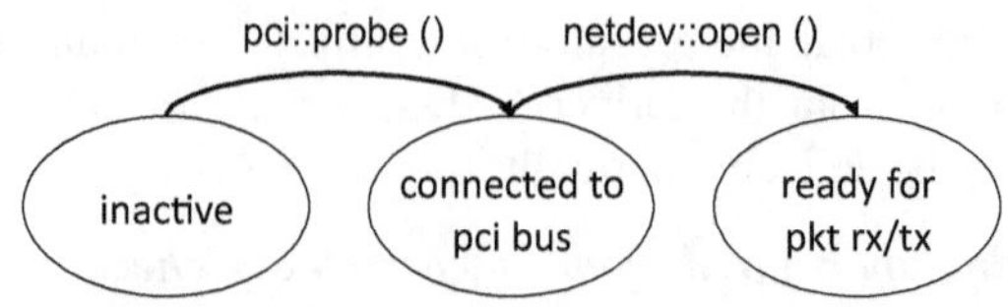


Figure 5: State transitions for a Linux PCI network device, showing that the `probe()` and `open()` functions of the driver are serialized.

of certain driver callbacks by the kernel. Thus, any pair of driver callbacks that are never concurrently valid (i.e., they have conflicting invariants) will not execute concurrently, and their critical sections are mutually serialized as a result. For example, consider the FSM snippet in Figure 5 for a Linux network device. It shows that the `pci::probe` and `netdev::open` callbacks of a network driver are valid in different device states, and hence cannot race with each other. Existing race detection tools are oblivious to the invariants (or states) in which driver callbacks are executed, and hence they can incorrectly report races between callbacks with conflicting invariants. Indeed, our experimental study in Section 4 shows that ignoring state-based synchronization results in a high false positive rate.

***Deferred execution*** Kernel threads that execute under tight deadlines (e.g., interrupt service routines) often have important tasks (e.g., copying received packets from the network card) that cannot be completed in a timely manner. Thus, most OS kernels provide mechanisms for postponing work until a more convenient time, such as *softirqs* in Linux, *deferred procedure calls (DPCs)* in Windows, and *software interrupts* in Solaris. *Kernel timers* are also provided for deferring the execution of functions, such as checking that tasks are completed on schedule or that a device is still functional, until at least a specified time in future.

Softirqs are commonly used by interrupt handlers of high performance drivers to defer work to a future context, e.g., to the *bottom half* context. However, the way the interrupt thread deferring work synchronizes with the polling thread that will do the work poses a challenge for data race analysis because these threads do not share any locks. Kernel timers also pose some challenges to data race detection. For example, although a delay is specified when registering a timer, only the operations that were performed by the thread prior to timer registration are guaranteed to be serialized with execution (possibly by a different thread) of the deferred function. This is because the thread could be preempted for a period longer than the timer delay. Also, successive executions of the function of a timer are serialized, even though synchronization primitives (e.g., locks) are not used in the function. On the other hand, executions of functions with different timers are not serialized.

***Kernel-mode mutual exclusion primitives*** The kernel provides a variety of synchronization primitives for mutual exclusion: (i) locking primitives such as spinlocks and mutexes, (ii) operations that disable interrupts and preemption, and (iii) hardware atomic instructions such as test_and_set. Detecting (and tracking) locking primitives such as spinlocks and mutexes is easy because of their modularized interface (e.g., spin_lock()/spin_unlock()). However, other primitives, such as interrupt enabling/disabling and hardware atomic instructions (e.g., test_and_set) require more effort to detect because they are not accessed through modularized interfaces.

### 3.1.2 Addressing driver concurrency issues

Before describing how *DRCheck* addresses the concurrency issues of kernel-mode drivers, we first discuss how DataCollider [13] (discussed in Section 1.3) addresses these issues.

DataCollider purposely stalls kernel threads and detects synchronization errors by observing "collisions" between the stalled thread and improperly synchronized threads. A thread "collides" with a purposely stalled thread only if there is nothing preventing them from colliding—the tool need not reason about the particular mechanisms used to serialize threads. However, because such stalling is not suited for threads servicing time-critical interrupts, DataCollider provides only limited coverage of interrupt contexts. This makes DataCollider less effective for drivers, because interrupt contexts represent significant portions of driver executions.

*DRCheck*, in contrast, covers interrupt contexts as well as all other contexts. Furthermore, *DRCheck* can detect not just realized race conditions but also some potential race conditions that may occur in thread execution interleavings other than the one(s) observed.

***Detecting driver concurrency*** *DRCheck* uses thread identifier information to detect and disambiguate the concurrency associated with multi-threaded execution of driver code, similar to user-mode tools. To detect concurrency due to interleaved execution of different execution contexts by a single kernel thread, *DRCheck* also tracks the execution context of each kernel thread. Basically, just as memory operations of a user-mode thread are considered serialized, *DRCheck* considers the memory accesses of a kernel thread *in a particular context* to be serialized. In other words, except when explicitly synchronized by any of the methods discussed in this section, a kernel thread's memory access in one context is considered to be concurrent with its memory accesses from other contexts.

***Detecting synchronization based on device state*** As discussed in Section 3.1.1, devices can be in certain disjoint states known to the kernel, and the kernel may (implicitly or explicitly) guarantee that certain driver entry points are only invoked in particular device states. Figure 6, for example, shows how the Linux kernel networking stack uses device states to guard the execution of the open() callback of a network driver. Consequently, driver code need not include explicit synchronization between two access if those accesses are known to only occur in particular states.

```
int dev_open (dev) {
  ...

if (! test_bit(__LINK_STATE_PRESENT, &dev->state))
     return -ENODEV;

  ...
 dev->open (dev)
  ...
```

Figure 6: Snippet of Linux network code that uses device state to guard the open() callback of a network driver.

*DRCheck* detects the use of device state for synchronization by drivers by exploiting the fact that the kernel already leverages device state information to guard driver execution. For each driver callback, *DRCheck* dynamically maintains the set of all the device states in which the callback has been invoked. With this information, *DRCheck* can identify callbacks that are invoked under disjoint sets of device states. Because such callbacks cannot execute concurrently with one another, their accesses to shared data are implicitly serialized and therefore not races. An alternative to dynamically building the set of device states for each callback would be to obtain such information from kernel experts [12, 19], perhaps reducing runtime overhead. However, we adopted our dynamic discovery approach because it does not rely on the availability of correct specifications.

Because drivers routinely change device states, the basic approach of tracking states at driver entry points is not sufficient: other regions of a callback might execute under a different set of states. As a refinement, *DRCheck* also tracks device states at code points that follow device state changes. So far, we have focused on device states that are used by the kernel to control driver execution. Some examples include status of the PCI connection, interrupt request line (IRQL), polling/interrupt handling, etc. However, it is possible for a driver to use other state information internally to manage critical sections. Nevertheless, our focus is on kernel-aware device states, because most OS kernels organize devices into classes (e.g., network, scsi, graphics, usb) and export a standard interface to the drivers of a given class. It is therefore more scalable to design for the kernel interface rather than for individual drivers.

***Handling deferred execution*** Although Linux interrupt threads that defer work using *softirqs* do not share locks with the polling threads that will eventually do the work, they do invoke the polling threads using the raise_softirq call. Further, the Linux softirq infrastructure guarantees that only one polling thread, on the same processor as the interrupt thread, will respond to a given call and complete the deferred work. Hence, *DRCheck* recognizes the raise_softirq call as the serializing operation between threads.

For kernel timers, *DRCheck* associates a virtual state with each timer. A timer is *inactive* before its registration, and *active* until it executes, after which it becomes *inactive* again.

This serializes the execution of the timer to operations preceding its registration. Additionally, *DRCheck* associates a virtual lock with each timer that is held throughout the execution of the timer function. This serializes successive execution of the timer's function.

***Detecting non-lock based mutual exclusion*** Interrupt enabling/disabling can be detected (and tracked) by observing the specific instructions (e.g., `STI`, `CLI`, `POPF`, `IRET`, etc. in x86) in the execution trace. Hardware atomic instructions like `test_and_set` are more challenging because of the need to determine whether the instruction guards a critical section and, if so, whether or not it succeeded in entering. *DRCheck* uses pattern matching over a small window of the trace starting with the `test_and_set` instruction (`btsl` in x86) in order to determine whether the sequence matches a known critical section preamble for the specific kernel. If so, it checks the value returned by the `test_and_set` to determine whether it succeeded.

#### 3.1.3 DRCheck implementation

*DRCheck* is an extension of the *Lockset* algorithm in Eraser [41]. *Lockset* detects races in multithreaded applications by checking that shared data access is protected by a consistent locking discipline. *Lockset* maintains metadata for each word of shared memory indicating whether the location has been accessed by multiple threads, and if so, the set of locks consistently held by all threads accessing the location from that point on. If there is no such common lock, *Lockset* reports a potential data race.

*DRCheck* extends *Lockset* as follows. First, adapting *Lockset* for kernel-mode locking primitives was straightforward for the ones that behave similarly to user-mode primitives (e.g., kernel spinlocks). However, some kernel-mode locking primitives, such as `spin_lock_irq`, also disable interrupts. Based on previous *Lockset* proposals for supporting interrupts, per-CPU virtual locks are associated with *interrupt* contexts, and are acquired by threads that disable preemption or interrupts. Logical locks are maintained for virtual and real locks, e.g. spinlocks, including *bitlocks* of atomic `test_and_set` instructions. In the evaluation, we call this variant *KLockset*.

Second, we add the mechanisms for handling deferred execution discussed in Section 3.1.2. Finally, we further include state-based synchronization tracking, as follows. For each shared data, in addition to tracking the set of locks held by threads on each access, the set of device states is also tracked. The state variable field in the device class data structure of each driver is used to track device states. When a shared data's set of locks becomes empty at an access, a race is not reported only if the current device state is disjoint with the state set of the data. Instead, the location's metadata is reset to the "exclusive" (i.e., no longer accessed by multiple threads) state.

Note that, as in all our tools (recall Section 2.1), *DRCheck* tracks synchronization in both the driver and kernel-driver interface execution, while reporting races only in the driver execution.

### 3.2 Direct Memory Access (DMA) Faults

Direct Memory Access (DMA) is a common technique for transferring data to and from devices without consuming CPU cycles. To detect incorrect DMA operations that might harm the system, we created a new tool within our Guardrail framework called *DMACheck*, which performs instruction-grain dynamic analysis of drivers to ensure that they correctly address the following issues related to *DMA buffers* (i.e. regions of system memory used in DMA transfers):

**Sharing**: Because DMA buffers are shared between the driver and the device, there is the potential for data races (e.g., writes by the driver into source DMA buffers could corrupt outgoing I/O data). Hence the driver should assume that the device has exclusive access during a transfer in order to avoid data corruption.

**Management**: DMA buffers are system resources, and should be carefully managed by drivers. Drivers should avoid leaking (i.e., failing to unmap) DMA buffers, or redundantly mapping or unmapping them.

**Coherence**: Because devices access DMA buffers directly (bypassing any caches) on non-coherent systems while drivers' accesses to DMA buffers can be cached, cache lines should never mix DMA buffer data with other types of data (including other DMA buffers). Proper alignment and padding of data can prevent this problem.

*DMACheck* detects DMA buffer bugs in Linux drivers by monitoring how they manipulate DMA buffers. Because Linux drivers operate on DMA buffers through both *virtual and physical* addresses (e.g., a driver reads or writes a DMA buffer using the virtual address, but synchronizes the cache and memory copies of the buffer using the physical address), *DMACheck* tracks the mapping of a DMA buffer in both the virtual and physical address spaces; this makes it unusual compared with other tools. (*DRCheck* and *DMCheck* (Section 3.3), for example, need to track only virtual addresses.) Although some DMA buffer bugs (e.g., misaligned DMA buffers) can be detected simply by inspecting the arguments that drivers use to make DMA function calls (e.g., `dma_map_single()`), *data races* require instruction-grain dynamic analysis to identify when driver accesses to a DMA buffer overlap with those from the device.

*DMACheck* detects races on DMA buffers by checking for unserialized accesses by the driver and device to a DMA buffer. One challenge is that device access to DMA buffers cannot be directly observed by *DMACheck*. To overcome this, *DMACheck* defines a time interval that includes the period during which a DMA buffer could be accessed by the device, and checks that no driver accesses are made to the buffer during that interval. We identified two pairs of driver operations for defining this interval: (i) between mapping the buffer into the I/O address space and the corresponding unmapping, and (ii) between specifying the buffer as part of a DMA transfer to the device and the corresponding servicing of the completion interrupt. While the latter option may appear to provide a smaller correct interval, *DMACheck* uses the former, more conservative, option for two practical reasons. First, some coherence issues of DMA are addressed when DMA buffer(s) are mapped/unmapped into/from the I/O address space. For example, the cache lines of a source DMA buffer are flushed when it is mapped for the device to read, and thus, later driver updates may be lost in the transfer. In fact, Linux kernel documentation recommends that drivers should not touch DMA buffers that are accessible to the device without unmapping the buffer or synchronizing the cache and memory copies. Second, the latter option requires understanding the device-specific way that drivers setup DMA transfer—an unscalable undertaking, given the large number of available devices.

### 3.3 DMCheck: Detecting Memory Faults

Kernel-mode drivers for commodity OSes are prone to type safety issues because they are written in unsafe languages (C and C++). Common memory faults in drivers include accesses to unallocated memory, unsafe use of uninitialized data, and memory leaks. The objective of our analysis is to detect such faults in driver executions. To this end, we adapt the analysis in *Memcheck* [28], a popular tool for finding memory faults in *application* binaries, to kernel-mode drivers. Specifically, we use *Memcheck*'s algorithm for finding memory faults by maintaining *metadata* for each byte of memory indicating whether the byte is currently allocated and, if so, whether it has been initialized. The metadata is updated in response to instructions that initialize data or system calls that allocate or free memory. An error is reported if an instruction accesses unallocated memory or uses uninitialized data in an unsafe way, or a memory leak is detected.

Our tool, *DMCheck*, adapts *Memcheck* to kernel-mode drivers by addressing two issues: (i) recognizing kernel functions for (de)allocating memory, and (ii) dealing with memory objects that are (de)allocated outside the driver. The first issue is trivially handled by recognizing that kernel memory management functions such as `kmalloc()` and `kfree()` are analogous to user-space functions such as `malloc()` and `free()`.

The second issue arises because of the need for drivers to communicate with the kernel in an efficient manner. Sometimes, this means the driver will manipulate memory objects that are allocated by other parts of the kernel. An example can be found in how socket buffers, for storing network packets, are handled in the network stack. The packet transmission path of a network driver receives socket buffers from the network stack and deallocates them after transmission. Conversely, the packet reception path allocates socket buffers, for received packets, and expects the network stack to deallocate them. *DMCheck* addresses this issue by incorporating the kernel-driver interface module into our analysis, as described in Section 2.1, so that the address range for each such memory object can be captured by the analysis.[5]

### 3.4 Discussion

As we demonstrate through evaluation with production Linux drivers (Section 4.2), our checking tools can detect errors that are missed by current techniques. This suggests that our techniques can be used to improve driver debugging and testing, and to make production systems more resilient to defective drivers. However, in evaluating how to deploy our techniques in these scenarios, it is worth considering the practical implications of false positives and false negatives that certain analysis tools may incur.

*DRCheck* is a tool that may incur false positives. The underlying *Lockset* algorithm of *DRCheck* leads to false data race reports for code that while properly synchronized, deviates from the expected locking discipline. This is a serious limitation for production deployments, because halting a system for a false alarm is simply unacceptable. Moreover, the fact that 76%–90% of true races are actually *benign* [27] means that simply avoiding false alarms (e.g., by incorporating a *Happens-Before* approach [53]) is insufficient. However, rather than foregoing race detection entirely on production systems, we believe that Guardrail's *triage* mode (Section 2) can help, when armed with techniques seeking to automatically classify the alarms raised by *DRCheck* into harmless and harmful races. Furthermore, *DRCheck* could be extended to recognize the synchronization patterns and *benign* data sharing patterns that it had incorrectly flagged in the past, to improves its classifier and reduce the number of spurious alarms.

The dynamic nature of our techniques creates the possibility of false negatives—run-time analysis cannot guarantee driver correctness. Rather, our tools can determine only whether or not the observed driver executions (i.e., code paths, thread interleavings, and input) are fault-free. For production deployments, this is not a problem because the goal is to keep the system running (i.e., *availability*), until there is a compelling reason to do otherwise (i.e., driver misbehaving). In contrast, for driver debugging or testing, false negatives make it difficult to reproduce bugs or guarantee their absence. Thus, our tools will be more effective for prerelease purposes when combined with techniques for achieving high coverage driver execution [7, 36].

[5] As in prior work, we trust the kernel-driver interface module. E.g., we assume that pointer and size arguments passed to the driver correspond to a properly allocated memory object for the given address range. The design can be readily extended to correctness check the kernel, but this is beyond the paper's driver-checking scope.

| I/O type | Benchmark | Description | Workload |
|---|---|---|---|
| Audio & Video | Mplayer | Multimedia player | Full HD movie trailer (i.e., 1920 x 1080*p* resolution, 24 fps) |
| Network | Apache | Webserver | $16K$ requests for 40KB static page using 16 concurrent requests |
| | Memcache | In-memory key value store | 256 client threads each making 100K *get* requests |
| | Netperf | Network perf. meter | 20 secs run with 16KB msg for stream and 32B for request/response |
| Storage | GNU Make | Compilation utility | 4-way parallel build of Linux 2.6.18 kernel with default configuration |
| | Postmark | Filesystem benchmark | 100K transactions on 20K files of size range 10KB–20KB |

Table 1: I/O intensive benchmarks and workload settings for evaluating Guardrail.

## 4. Evaluation

We evaluated our Guardrail prototype to answer two questions:

1. How effectively do our techniques detect driver faults, particularly when compared with existing techniques?
2. What is the impact on the system end-to-end performance, particularly if the monitored device is heavily used?

### 4.1 Methodology

The I/O interposition layer of our Guardrail prototype was implemented by extending paravirtualized Xen-3.3.1 VMM with our techniques for containing potential driver faults. The guest OS in the Driver and Analysis VMs was a 32 bit Fedora Core 6 OS, based on the Linux 2.6.18 kernel. We used a variety of audio, video, network and storage devices in our evaluation, along with the corresponding stock, unmodified Linux driver binaries. In all experiments, the device is directly assigned [51] to the Driver VM to minimize I/O virtualization overheads [11].

***Benchmarks*** We generated driver workloads using a set of popular I/O benchmarks, listed in Table 1. We used the open source media player, *Mplayer*, to evaluate the audio and video drivers. We evaluated the network drivers using the *Apache* web server, the *Memcache* in-memory key-value store, and the *Netperf* network performance measurement tool. Network load for *Apache* and *Memcache* were generated using their respective benchmarking tools: *ApacheBench* and *Memslap*, while *Netperf* load was generated using its *stream* tests (TCP_STREAM & UDP_STREAM) and *request/response* tests (TCP_RR & UDP_RR). The storage drivers were evaluated using the *Postmark* filesystem benchmark and a kernel compilation workload. Table 1 shows the workload settings for the results in this paper.

| Class | Driver | Device |
|---|---|---|
| Audio | snd_hda_intel | High Definition Audio (ICH7) |
| Network | tg3 | Broadcom 5754 1Gpbs NIC |
| Storage | ahci | ICH7 SATA disk (200GB) |
| Video | nvidia | Quadro NVS 285 |

Table 2: Drivers and devices evaluated in real hardware.

***Experimental setup*** We conducted experiments on both real and simulated multicore x86 hardware, but used the same software stack in both environments.

Our evaluation of Guardrail on real hardware focused on the performance of virtualization-based I/O interpositioning and software-based instruction tracing of kernel-mode drivers. The devices and corresponding drivers that were used in these experiments are presented in Table 2. The test system for these experiments was a Dell Precision 390 workstation that had Dual-Core Intel Core 2 Duo processors running at 2.66 GHZ and with 2GB of physical memory. For the network experiments, the server ran on the test system while the client ran on a Dell Precision T3400 workstation with Quad-Core Intel Core 2 Extreme processors running at 3 GHz and with a 4GB physical memory. The client system was running 32-bit Ubuntu 10 (2.6.32 kernel) Linux OS. The client and server systems were in the same local area network so that network latency was negligible in our results.

For our Guardrail evaluation on simulated hardware, we used the Simics [43] full system simulator (academic package, version 4.0.63) to model hardware-assisted instruction-level streaming of a driver's execution from the Driver VM to the Analysis VM. We used these experiments to study the bug detection effectiveness of Guardrail and the end-to-end performance of online protection of I/O operations from buggy drivers. Our kernel-mode instruction tracing hardware is based on previous hardware proposals [6, 48] for tracing user-mode execution. We carefully chose the simulation parameters illustrated in Table 3a to derive a similar environment to the real hardware platform. The lack of audio and video device models in our simulation package restricted our evaluation to the network and storage drivers and devices shown in Table 3b.

### 4.2 Fault Detection

We evaluated how Guardrail improves driver bug detection by using the framework to implement our proposed dynamic binary analysis tools: (i) *DRCheck*, for detecting data races (Section 3.1), (ii) *DMACheck*, for detecting DMA faults (Section 3.2), and (iii) *DMCheck*, for detecting memory faults (Section 3.3). The results show that Guardrail enables better detection of driver bugs than previous approaches.

| Parameter | Values used |
|---|---|
| Processors | Dual-Core, Intel Pentium 4, 2.6Ghz, 2GB RAM |
| Private L1I | 16KB, 64B line, 2-way assoc, 1-cycle access lat. |
| Private L1D | 16KB, 64B line, 2-way assoc, 1-cycle access lat. |
| Shared L2 | 2MB, 64B line, 8-way assoc, 10-cycle access lat, 4 banks |
| Main Memory | 200-cycle access latency |
| Tracing | 512KB log buffer |
| Driver VM | 2 VCPU, 1GB RAM |
| Analysis VM | 1 VCPU, 512MB RAM |

(a)

| Class | Driver | Device |
|---|---|---|
| Network | e100 | I82559 100Mbps NIC |
| | e1000 | I82543gc 1Gbps NIC |
| | pcnet32 | AM79C973 100Mbps NIC |
| | tg3 | BCM5703C 1Gbps NIC |
| | tulip | DEC21143 100Mbps NIC |
| Storage | qla1280 | ISP1040 SCSI disk |
| | qla2xxx | ISP2200 SCSI disk |
| | sym53c8xx | SYM53C875 SCSI disk |

(b)

Table 3: The simulation parameters, and the drivers and devices used for simulation based evaluation.

| Tool | Count |
|---|---|
| DRCheck | 9 |
| Det-DataCollider | 2 |
| Ideal-DataCollider | 6 |

(a) Data races detected

| Tool | Count |
|---|---|
| DataCollider | 0 |
| DRCheck | 11 |
| DeferExec | 67 |
| KLockset | 111 |

(b) False data race alarms

Table 4: Races and false alarms reported by Guardrail.

| Bug type | Count |
|---|---|
| Data race | 7 |
| Leak | 4 |
| Repeat map/unmap | 4 |
| Misaligned buffer | 10 |

(a) DMA buffer bugs

| Tool | Count |
|---|---|
| DMCheck | 2 |
| DDT | 1 |
| KAddrcheck | 1 |
| KMemcheck | 2 |

(b) Memory bugs

Table 5: DMA buffer bugs detected by Guardrail by type, and memory bugs detected by different tools.

### 4.2.1 Data races

As shown in Table 4a, *DRCheck* found nine serious data races in five Linux drivers (six of which have either been confirmed or fixed). Also, using this table, we compare *DRCheck* with DataCollider based on the details in [13]. We made two assumptions in our analysis to increase the chances that DataCollider's sampling will detect the races. First, we assume that the racy accesses, outside of interrupt contexts, are deterministically sampled (*Det-DataCollider*). DataCollider does not sample interrupt context accesses for robustness reasons. Second, for races involving interrupt and non-interrupt contexts, we assume that the non-interrupt context access occurred earlier (*Ideal-DataCollider*). With these assumptions, two races will be detected by *Det-DataCollider*, and six races by *Ideal-DataCollider*.

However, unlike *DataCollider* which has no false positives, *DRCheck* generated a small number of false alarms while detecting these driver races, as shown in Table 4b. The number of false alarms, though, is an order of magnitude fewer than *KLockset*. *DeferExec*, which is *DRCheck* without state-based synchronizations (Section 3.1.2), falls in between. We were not able to compare with *DDT* [23], an existing data race detector for the Windows kernel, because it was not described in sufficient detail to enable comparisons.

### 4.2.2 DMA faults

The different DMA buffer faults found by *DMACheck* in six drivers are summarized in Table 5a. Races on DMA buffers, which are the most serious of these bugs, affected only the *tulip* network driver. *DMACheck* found seven unique driver writes (i.e., static instruction addresses) that could potentially corrupt I/O data being read by the network card. DMA buffers with unaligned virtual addresses (assuming 32 byte cache lines) are the most common fault type—affecting five drivers (i.e., *e100*, *e1000*, *pcnet32*, *tg3*, *tulip*). As discussed earlier, this bug is a serious issue in non-coherent systems. The *sym5c8xx* driver was the only one that leaked DMA buffers (i.e., failed to unmap DMA buffers before unloading), whereas *tulip* and *tg3* were the only drivers to map previously mapped DMA buffers, or unmap previously unmapped DMA buffers. Although these faults reflect programmer error in managing DMA operations, and should be avoided, we did not observe any resulting system failures during our experiments.

### 4.2.3 Memory faults

As shown in Table 5b, *DMCheck* found two serious memory faults, which have been fixed. In particular, the *qla2xxx* memory bug was previously unknown until reported by our tool. Based on our report, the bug was eventually fixed in the 3.2 release of the Linux kernel six years after the 2.6.18 version we used for our study. Because these bugs involve memory that is exclusively used by the driver, they cannot be detected using fault isolation techniques that only check driver interaction with the kernel [5, 18, 45, 49, 50, 54]. For example, the *e1000* memory bug is an unsafe use of uninitialized stack data, while the *qla2xxx* memory bug is an out-of-bounds read of memory-mapped device registers.

Furthermore, we use Table 5b to compare *DMCheck* against existing kernel-mode memory fault detectors for the Windows kernel (*DDT* [23]) and the Linux kernel (*KAddrcheck* [15], *KMemcheck* [30]). *DDT* and *KAddrcheck* track memory addressability, and therefore can only detect the out-of-bounds bug. *KMemcheck*, on the other hand, tracks both memory addressability and initialization, and therefore detected both the memory faults.

### 4.2.4 Fault detection summary

In summary, our evaluation validated our thesis that instruction-grained dynamic analysis can be used to improve the reliability of device drivers by detecting bugs in their execution. Guardrail's instruction-grained dynamic analysis enables detection of a significant number of hard-to-find bugs in production Linux drivers (i.e., data races, DMA buffer faults, and memory faults) that are missed by other tools, including a previously unknown buffer overflow in the *qla2xxx* storage driver. Guardrail sometimes incurs a small number of false positives, e.g., for data race detection. Guardrail's support for a variety of sophisticated checking tools demonstrates its value as a general-purpose framework, in contrast to fault-specific tools such as *DataCollider*.

## 4.3 Instruction-Grained Tracing Performance

Guardrail's instruction-grained tracing of driver execution can be implemented using software or hardware techniques. To evaluate the performance of a purely software approach, we obtained an early version of the *Granary* binary instrumentation framework for OS kernels [20] from the authors. *Granary* can instrument individual kernel modules rather than the entire kernel. In the version we used, *Granary* employs a trap-based mechanism to toggle instrumentation as execution switches between the kernel and the instrumented module. We modified *Granary* to stream the execution trace of a module, containing program counter values, instruction opcodes, and effective addresses, into a 256KB per-CPU circular buffer[6]. We refer to our *Granary* modifications as *Granary-Trace*.

We used the *tg3* driver to measure the impact of *Granary-Trace* on server throughput and CPU utilization. We compared against running the server on a native Linux system (i.e., *Linux*), and on a *Granary* system with no instrumentation (i.e., *Granary-Null*). For this experiment, the server system was running a 64 bit Linux 3.8.2 kernel version because *Granary* was implemented in that OS. The results, normalized to *Linux*, are presented in Figure 7. We observed that *Granary-Trace* noticeably impacts both throughput and CPU utilization in most cases. Even *Apache*, which suffers no throughput loss, more than doubles its CPU consumption. Other benchmarks were impacted more significantly. For example, *Memcache*[7] suffered a 60% reduction in throughput, while the *Netperf* consumed 4.6x and over 10x more CPU cycles for TCP and UDP streaming, respectively. Although, *Granary-Null* outperforms *Granary-Trace*, it still performs poorly in some cases, such as a 23% reduction in *Memcache* throughput and a 4.4x increase in CPU utilization for TCP streaming. The results show that while the overheads of a software-based implementation of Guardrail instruction tracing are acceptable in test environments, hardware-assisted instruction tracing is needed for practical deployment of Guardrail in production environments.

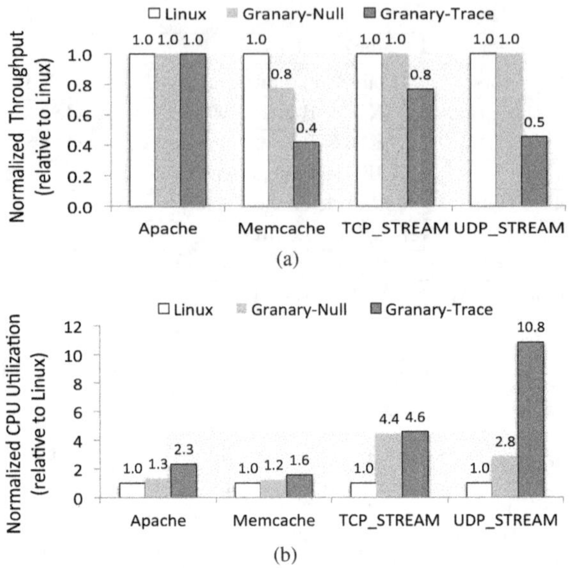


Figure 7: Impact of software-based instruction tracing on (a) server throughput and (b) CPU utilization.

## 4.4 I/O Interposition Performance

We studied the impact of Guardrail's I/O interposition on audio, video, network and storage I/O performance. For convenience, we use the following naming convention to report the results. *Linux* means a non-virtualized Linux system and is the baseline in all experiments. *Xen* means *Linux* as a guest OS on Xen VMM with directly assigned physical devices (i.e., only CPU and memory are virtualized). *IO-Interpose* is *Xen* with Guardrail's I/O interposition enhancements. Unless stated otherwise, the reported results are the median of 10 runs.

### 4.4.1 Audio and video performance

We used *Mplayer* to measure the impact of *IO-Interpose* on the audio and video quality of multimedia movie playback using the workload shown in Table 1. *Mplayer* was configured to use the *ALSA* audio output and the *X11* video output modes. The results are summarized in Table 6, and show that the playback was of similar audio and video quality on

| | Time (s) | Frame Rate | CPU (%) |
|---|---|---|---|
| Linux | 150.51 | 23.94 | 33 |
| Xen | 150.52 | 23.93 | 35 |
| IO-Interpose | 150.52 | 23.91 | 36 |

Table 6: Impact of I/O interposition on movie playback.

[6] Trace records were overwritten when the buffer filled up.

[7] 16 client threads were used because of robustness issues in *Granary*.

*Linux*, *Xen*, and *IO-Interpose*, with virtually the same frame rates achieved on all 3 systems. The CPU utilization of *IO-Interpose* was 3% higher than *Linux* and 1% higher than *Xen*. Overall, these results suggest that I/O interpositioning is unlikely to degrade the user experience of modern multimedia playback in any noticeable way.

### 4.4.2 Network performance

We used *Apache*, *Memcache*, and *Netperf*, and the workload settings in Table 1 to study the impact of *IO-Interpose* on server throughput or transaction rate (for *request/response*). Figure 8 reports server performance normalized to *Linux*. In most cases, *IO-Interpose* imposes at most 8% overhead on server performance. Since *Xen* performs similarly in these situations, most of the overheads could be attributed to it. The exception is *Memcache*, which loses 38% of its throughput on *IO-Interpose*. *Xen* appears to be responsible for over half of this degradation. CPU utilization for *Apache* (*Memcache*) was 35% (85%) on *Linux*, 52% (89%) on *Xen*, and 58% (92%) on *IO-Interpose*.

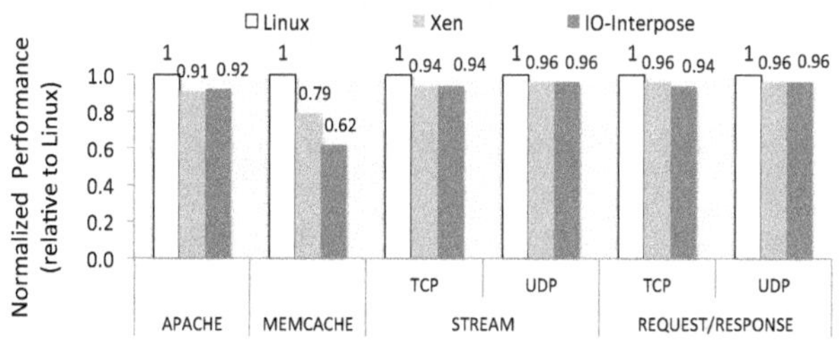


Figure 8: Impact of I/O interposition on network performace.

*Memcache*'s exceptionally poor performance can be attributed to (i) frequent device register accesses and (ii) high CPU utilization in *Linux*. *Memcache*'s device register access rate (184K/sec) is at least an order of magnitude higher than the other benchmarks, which means "trap-and-emulate" overheads are incurred more frequently. Furthermore, high CPU utilization means there are fewer idle CPU cycles available to handle the frequent "trap-and-emulate" operations.

### 4.4.3 Storage performance

We used the GNU *Make* compilation utility and the *Postmark* benchmark with the workload settings in Table 1 to evaluate how I/O interpositioning affects disk storage performance. The results, in terms of normalized performance relative to *Linux*, are reported in Figure 9. Compilation is 32% slower on *IO-Interpose* compared to *Linux*. Also, *IO-Interpose* consumes about 93% of the CPU, which is about 8% higher than *Linux*. On the other hand, *Xen*'s performance is identical to *IO-Interpose*, which suggests that in this case most of *IO-Interpose* overheads are due to *Xen* (i.e., CPU and memory virtualization). For *Postmark*, the read, write, and transaction rates of *IO-Interpose* are 9–10% lower than *Linux*. Again, the performance of *Xen* is similar to *IO-Interpose*. The CPU utilization of *Linux*, *Xen*, and *IO-Interpose* were 7%, 11%, and 8% respectively.

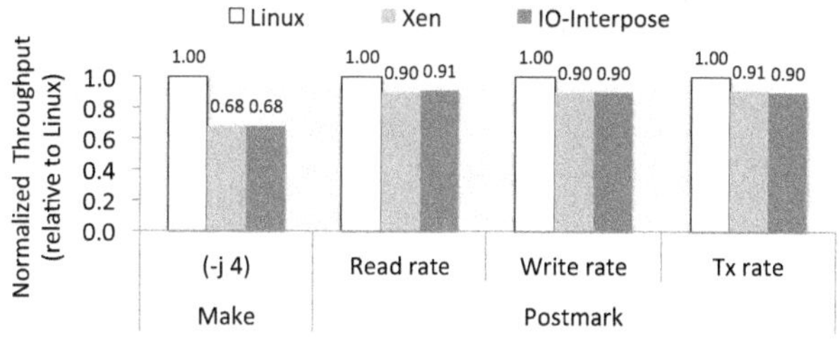


Figure 9: Impact of I/O interposition on storage performance.

### 4.4.4 I/O interposition performance summary

Our evaluation shows that Guardrail's I/O interposition layer imposed at most 10% overheads on common I/O workloads in most cases, and that code compilation (32%) and *Memcache* (40%) were the exceptions. All of the code compilation overheads and over half of the *Memcache* overheads could be attributed to CPU and memory virtualization. Finally, the combination of *Memcache*'s frequent device register accesses and high CPU utilization in Linux is a worst-case scenario for Guardrail.

## 4.5 End-to-End Performance

We evaluated the end-to-end performance impact on common I/O workloads of using Guardrail for online protection of persistent device state from defective drivers. We ran Guardrail in *permissive* mode (Section 2) to ensure that the experiments ran to completion without being abruptly halted for detected driver faults. We conducted this experiment in simulation so as to study the benefits of hardware logging support. We specifically measured the performance of I/O workloads while the corresponding driver is being monitored by the Guardrail checking tools—*DRCheck*, *DMACheck*, and *DMCheck*—normalized to the workload's performance without driver monitoring in a non-virtualized Linux system. Robustness issues of the device models forced us to reduce the workload size and study only the *tg3* and *sym53c8xx* drivers.

### 4.5.1 Network performance

*Apache* received a total of 1600 requests, *Memcache* was loaded by 16 client threads issuing 1K *get* requests each, and *Netperf* runs for 5 seconds. The results are presented in Figure 10. With the exception of network streaming using TCP and UDP, Guardrail imposed modest overheads on the workloads ($\leq$ 6%). However, the throughput reduction for TCP streaming was up to 60% (*DMCheck*) and for UDP streaming, up to 53% (*DMCheck*). The high rate of device register accesses (up to 300K/sec) of network streaming caused these high overheads, because the driver had to be stalled for the checking tool to catch up.

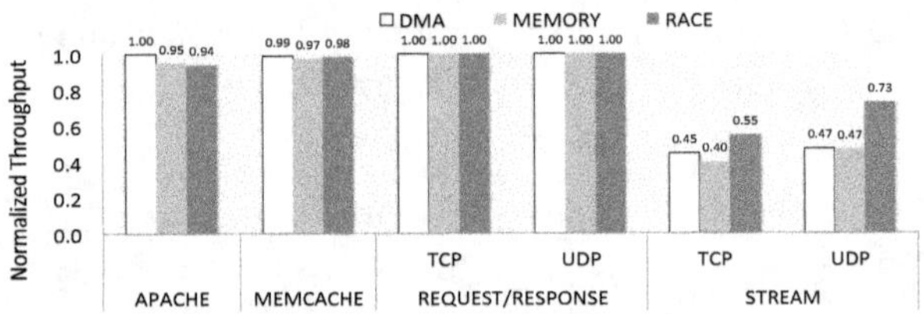


Figure 10: Network performance with Guardrail protection.

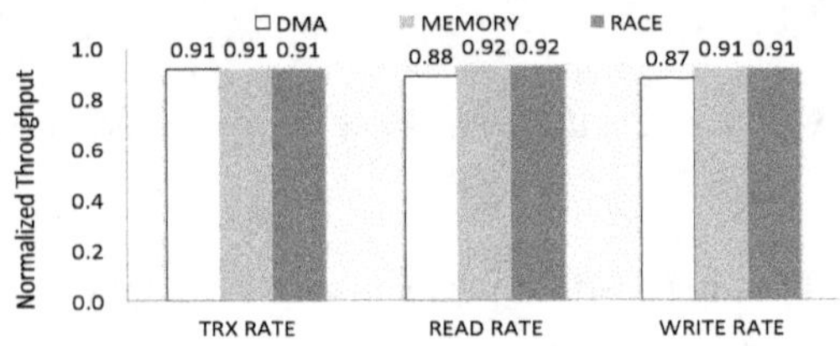


Figure 11: *Postmark* performance with Guardrail protection.

### 4.5.2 Storage performance

*Postmark*'s workload setting was configured as in Table 1, except with 1K input files. The normalized transaction, read, and write rates of the benchmark with Guardrail monitoring are reported in Figure 11. The overheads were less than 10% in most cases. The sole exceptions were a 12–13% reduction in read and write rates for *DMACheck*. The relatively better performance compared to network streaming is because the device register access rate of *Postmark* is orders of magnitude lower (i.e., 3K/sec.).

### 4.5.3 End-to-end performance summary

Our experiments showed that online protection of the persistent state of I/O devices from subtle driver bugs (e.g., memory faults, data races) can be achieved with minimal impact on the end-to-end performance of most I/O intensive benchmarks. Network streaming was the exception to this, and we observed up to 60% drop in throughput. However, we expect that these overheads can be significantly reduced through software [29, 33, 37, 38] and hardware [6, 48] techniques for accelerating dynamic analysis.

## 5. Conclusion

While device driver code is both (i) critical to proper system operation and (ii) more susceptible to bugs than other system software, relatively little work has been done in the area of online driver correctness monitoring (perhaps due to the performance-sensitive nature of driver software). The results of this paper demonstrate that decoupled correctness-checking together with VM-based I/O interpositioning can provide a high performance driver monitoring framework that achieves each of our system goals: generality, detection fidelity, containment, response flexibility, and trustworthiness. Guardrail represents a promising direction in driver correctness-checking that provides better safety not only for system devices, but also for the user data entrusted to those devices.

**Acknowledgments.** We are grateful to Peter Goodman, Angela Demke Brown and Ashvin Goel from the University of Toronto for providing us an early copy of Granary for our evaluation. We also thank Michael Swift (University of Wisconsin-Madison) and Brad Chen (Google) for their valuable input on this research. This work is supported in part by a grant from the National Science Foundation and by the Intel Science and Technology Center for Cloud Computing.

## References

[1] T. Ball, E. Buonimova, B. Cook, V. Levin, J. Lichtenberg, C. McGarvey, B. Ondrusek, S. K. Rajamani, and A. Ustunner. Thorough Static Analysis of Device Drivers. In *EuroSys*, 2006.

[2] P. Barham, B. Dragovic, K. Fraser, S. Hand, T. Harris, A. Ho, R. Neugebauer, I. Pratt, and A. Warfield. Xen and The Art of Virtualization. In *SOSP*, 2003.

[3] M. Botincan, M. Dodds, A. F. Donaldson, and M. J. Parkinson. Safe Asynchronous Multicore Memory Operations. In *ASE*, 2011.

[4] S. Boyd-Wickizer and N. Zeldovich. Tolerating Malicious Device Drivers in Linux. In *USENIX*, 2010.

[5] M. Castro, M. Costa, J.-P. Martin, M. Peinado, P. Akritidis, A. Donelly, P. Barham, and R. Black. Fast Byte-Granularity Software Fault Isolation. In *SOSP*, 2009.

[6] S. Chen, M. Kozuch, T. Strigkos, B. Falsafi, P. B. Gibbons, T. C. Mowry, V. Ramachandran, O. Ruwase, M. Ryan, and E. Vlachos. Flexible Hardware Acceleration for Instruction-grain Program Monitoring. In *ISCA*, 2008.

[7] V. Chipounov, V. Kuznetsov, and G. Candea. S2E: A Platform for In-Vivo Multi-Path Analysis of Software Systems. In *ASPLOS*, 2011.

[8] A. Chou, J. Yang, B. Chelf, S. Hallem, and D. Engler. An Empirical Study of Operating Systems Errors. In *SOSP*, 2001.

[9] J. Chow, T. Garfinkel, and P. M. Chen. Decoupling Dynamic Program Analysis from Execution in Virtual Environments. In *USENIX*, 2008.

[10] A. Dinaburg, P. Royal, M. Sharif, and W. Lee. Ether: Malware Analysis via Hardware Virtualization Extensions. In *CCS*, 2008.

[11] Y. Dong, X. Yang, X. Li, J. Li, K. Tian, and H. Guan. High Performance Network Virtualization with SR-IOV. In *HPCA*, 2010.

[12] D. Engler, B. Chelf, A. Chou, and S. Hallem. Checking System Rules using System-specific, Programmer-written Compiler Extensions. In *OSDI*, 2000.

[13] J. Erickson, M. Musuvathi, S. Burckhardt, and K. Olynyk. Effective Data-Race Detection for the Kernel. In *OSDI*, 2010.

[14] U. Erlingsson, M. Abadi, M. Vrable, M. Budiu, and G. C. Necula. XFI: Software Guards for System Address Spaces. In *OSDI*, 2006.

[15] P. Feiner, A. D. Brown, and A. Goel. Comprehensive Kernel Instrumentation via Dynamic Binary Translation. In *ASPLOS*, 2012.

[16] C. Flanagan and S. N. Freund. FastTrack: Efficient and Precise Dynamic Race Detection. In *PLDI*, 2009.

[17] A. Ganapathi, V. Ganapathi, and D. Patterson. Windows XP Kernel Crash Analysis. In *LISA*, 2006.

[18] V. Ganapathy, M. Renzelmann, A. Balakrishnan, M. Swift, and S. Jha. The Design and Implementation of Microdrivers. In *ASPLOS*, 2008.

[19] Q. Gao, W. Zhang, Z. Chen, M. Zheng, and F. Qin. 2ndStrike: Toward Manifesting Hidden Concurrency Typestate Bugs. In *ASPLOS*, 2011.

[20] P. Goodman, A. Kumar, A. D. Brown, and A. Goel. Granary: A Sane Framework for Instrumenting an Insane Environment. Manuscript, 2013.

[21] A. Kadav, M. J. Renzelmann, and M. M. Swift. Tolerating Hardware Device Failures in Software. In *SOSP*, 2009.

[22] B. Kasikci, C. Zamfir, and G. Candea. Data Races vs. Data Race Bugs: Telling the Difference with Portend. In *ASPLOS*, 2012.

[23] V. Kuznetsov, V. Chipounov, and G. Candea. Testing Closed-Source Binary Device Drivers with DDT. In *USENIX*, 2010.

[24] A. Lenharth, V. S. Adve, and S. T. King. Recovery Domains: An Organizing Principle for Recoverable Operating Systems. In *ASPLOS*, 2009.

[25] B. Leslie, P. Chubb, N. Fitzroy-dale, S. Gtz, C. Gray, L. Macpherson, D. Potts, Y. Shen, K. Elphinstone, and G. Heiser. User-level Device Drivers: Achieved Performance. *J. Computer Science and Technology*, 20, 2005.

[26] F. Mérillon, L. Réveillère, C. Consel, R. Marlet, and G. Muller. Devil: An IDL for Hardware Programming. In *OSDI*, 2000.

[27] S. Narayanasamy, Z. Wang, J. Tigani, A. Edwards, and B. Calder. Automatically Classifying Benign and Harmful Data Races Using Replay Analysis. In *PLDI*, 2007.

[28] N. Nethercote and J. Seward. Valgrind: A Framework for Heavyweight Dynamic Binary Instrumentation. In *PLDI*, 2007.

[29] E. B. Nightingale, D. Peek, P. M. Chen, and J. Flinn. Parallelizing Security Checks on Commodity Hardware. In *ASPLOS*, 2008.

[30] V. Nossum. Getting started with KMemcheck. *http://www.mjmwired.net/kernel/Documentation/kmemcheck.txt*, 2012.

[31] N. Palix, G. Thomas, S. Saha, C. Calvès, J. Lawall, and G. Muller. Faults in Linux: Ten Years Later. In *ASPLOS*, 2011.

[32] H. Patil, C. Pereira, M. Stallcup, G. Lueck, and J. Cownie. PinPlay: A Framework for Deterministic Replay and Reproducible Analysis of Parallel Programs. In *CGO*, 2010.

[33] F. Qin, C.Wang, Z. Li, H. Kim, Y. Zhou, and Y. Wu. LIFT: A Low-Overhead Practical Information Flow Tracking System for Detecting Security Attacks. In *MICRO-39*, 2006.

[34] V. Raychev, M. Vechev, and M. Sridharan. Effective Race Detection for Event-driven Programs. In *OOPSLA*, 2013.

[35] M. Renzelmann and M. Swift. Decaf: Moving Device Drivers to a Modern Language. In *USENIX*, 2009.

[36] M. J. Renzelmann, A. Kadav, and M. M. Swift. SymDrive: Testing Drivers without Devices. In *OSDI*, 2012.

[37] O. Ruwase, P. B. Gibbons, T. C. Mowry, V. Ramachandran, S. Chen, M. Kozuch, and M. Ryan. Parallelizing Dynamic Information Flow Tracking. In *SPAA*, 2008.

[38] O. Ruwase, S. Chen, P. B. Gibbons, and T. C. Mowry. Decoupled Lifeguards: Enabling Path Optimizations for Dynamic Correctness Checking Tools. In *PLDI*, 2010.

[39] L. Ryzhyk, P. Chubb, I. Kuz, and G. Heiser. Dingo: Taming Device Drivers. In *EuroSys*, 2009.

[40] L. Ryzhyk, P. Chubb, I. Kuz, E. L. Sueur, and G. Heiser. Automatic Device Driver Synthesis with Termite. In *SOSP*, 2009.

[41] S. Savage, M. Burrows, G. Nelson, P. Sobalvarro, and T. Anderson. Eraser: A Dynamic Race Detector for Multithreaded Programs. *ACM TOCS*, 15(4), 1997.

[42] K. Serebryany and T. Iskhodzhanov. ThreadSanitzer - Data Race Detection in Practice. In *WBIA*, 2009.

[43] Simics. Wind River Simics Full System Simulator. http://www.simics.net/, 2010.

[44] M. F. Spear, T. Roeder, O. Hodson, G. C. Hunt, and S. Levi. Solving the Starting Problem: Device Drivers as Self-describing Artifacts. In *Eurosys*, 2006.

[45] M. M. Swift, B. N. Bershad, and H. M. Levy. Improving the Reliability of Commodity Operating Systems. In *SOSP*, 2003.

[46] M. M. Swift, M. Annamalai, B. N. Bershad, and H. M. Levy. Recovering Device Drivers. *ACM TOCS*, 24(4), 2006.

[47] M. Tiwari, S. Mysore, and T. Sherwood. Quantifying the Potential of Program Analysis Peripherals. In *PACT*, 2009.

[48] E. Vlachos, M. L. Goodstein, M. A. Kozuch, S. Chen, B. Falsafi, P. B. Gibbons, and T. C. Mowry. ParaLog: Enabling and Accelerating Online Parallel Monitoring of Multithreaded Applications. In *ASPLOS*, 2010.

[49] R. Wahbe, S. Lucco, T. E. Anderson, and S. L. Graham. Efficient Software-based Fault Isolation. In *SOSP*, 1993.

[50] D. Williams, P. Reynolds, K. Walsh, E. G. Sirer, and F. B. Schneider. Device Driver Safety through a Reference Validation Mechanism. In *OSDI*, 2008.

[51] Xen. Xen PCI Passthrough. http://wiki.xen.org/wiki/XenPCIpassthrough, 2012.

[52] M. Xu, V. Malyugin, J. Sheldon, G. Venkitachalam, and B. Weissman. ReTrace: Collecting Execution Trace with Virtual Machine Determinstic Replay. In *MoBS*, 2007.

[53] Y. Yu, T. Rodeheffer, and W. Chen. RaceTrack: Efficient Detection of Data Race Conditions via Adapative Tracking. In *SOSP*, 2005.

[54] F. Zhou, J. Condit, Z. Anderson, I. Bagrak, R. Ennals, M. Harren, G. Necula, and E. Brewer. SafeDrive: Safe and Recoverable Extensions Using Language-Based Techniques. In *OSDI*, 2006.

# Low-Level Detection of Language-Level Data Races with LARD

Benjamin P. Wood Luis Ceze Dan Grossman
University of Washington
{bpw,luisceze,djg}@cs.washington.edu

## Abstract

Researchers have proposed always-on *data-race exceptions* as a way to avoid the ill effects of data races, but slow performance of accurate dynamic data-race detection remains a barrier to the adoption of always-on data-race exceptions. Proposals for accurate low-level (*e.g.*, hardware) data-race detection have the potential to reduce this performance barrier. This paper explains why low-level data-race detectors are *wrong* for programs written in high-level languages (*e.g.*, Java): they miss true data races and report false data races in these programs. To bring the benefits of low-level data-race detection to high-level languages, we design *low-level abstractable race detection* (LARD), an extension of the interface between low-level data-race detectors and run-time systems that enables accurate language-level data-race detection using low-level detection mechanisms. We implement accurate LARD data-race exception support for Java, coupling a modified Jikes RVM Java virtual machine and a simulated hardware race detector. We evaluate our detector's accuracy against an accurate dynamic Java data-race detector and other low-level race detectors without LARD, showing that naïve accurate low-level data-race detectors suffer from many missed and false language-level races in practice, and that LARD prevents this inaccuracy.

***Categories and Subject Descriptors*** D.1.3 [*Programming Techniques*]: Concurrent Programming; D.2.4 [*Software Engineering*]: Software/Program Verification—reliability; C.1.4 [*Processor Architectures*]: Parallel Architectures; D.3.4 [*Programming Languages*]: Processors—Run-time environments.

***Keywords*** data-race detection; data-race exceptions; dynamic analysis; run-time systems



*ASPLOS '14*, March 1–5, 2014, Salt Lake City, Utah, USA.

ACM 978-1-4503-2305-5/14/03...$15.00.
http://dx.doi.org/10.1145/10.1145/2541940.2541955

## 1. Introduction

A *data race* is a pair of accesses to the same memory location by different threads where at least one access is a write and no synchronization orders the two accesses. Data races in shared-memory multithreaded programs notoriously result in problematic and confusing bugs. Data races also play a part in other multithreading errors such as atomicity violations or determinism violations and permit violations of sequential consistency due to reordering of memory operations by the compiler and hardware.

Some researchers have proposed *data-race exceptions* to mitigate the ill effects of data races by making *every* data race explicit at run-time [1, 10, 13, 24, 28]: on the second in a pair of accesses that race, raise an exception instead of doing the access. Data races become obvious at run-time like null pointer dereferences. Implementing *accurate* dynamic data-race detection, reporting a data race if and only if a true data race occurs, is challenging. Most techniques miss true races, report false races, or incur heavy performance overhead. We use *accurate* to mean sound *and* complete: an accurate dynamic data-race detector misses no true data races and reports no false data races in the execution it observes.

Recent proposals for low-level dynamic data-race detection have full accuracy and improved performance. RADISH [12] uses a mix of software and hardware support for data-race detection fast enough for many deployment situations. Aikido [34] uses hypervisor support and page-protection to accelerate software analyses. These are *low-level data-race detectors*: they analyze virtual memory accesses in the instruction set architecture (ISA) and store access history for virtual memory locations. Low-level implementation allows for (1) hardware acceleration and (2) reuse of fast data-race detection mechanisms by many systems.

Naïvely, one might run an unmodified low-level dynamic data-race detector "underneath" a high-level language implementation like a Java virtual machine (JVM) to detect *language-level data races* in the Java program. By *language-level data race*, we mean a data race between accesses in the high-level language memory abstraction. This paper focuses on detecting these (and only these) data races.

We present the first full treatment of why an unmodified low-level data-race detector *does not work* to detect language-level data races. We then develop extensions to low-level race detection and high-level language implementations to remove all sources of missed races and false races. Finally, we implement and evaluate a prototype hardware-based dynamic data-race detector for Java, showing that our extensions enable accurate data-race detection for high-level languages using general low-level hardware support.

### 1.1 Low-Level Races ≠ Language-Level Races

*Neither low-level data races nor language-level data races subsumes the other.* Some low-level (*e.g.* x86) data races are not language-level (*e.g.*, Java) data races and some language-level data races are not low-level data races. Thus *a low-level race detector reports false data races and misses true data races for programs written in high-level languages.*

Consider a Java program running on a JVM on a multicore processor with data-race detection that analyzes all memory loads and stores for races. The Java abstraction of execution, with field accesses and lock operations, is fundamentally different from the low-level abstraction of instructions accessing virtual memory, as analyzed by the race detector. Two broad features of the translation cause false and missed language-level data races for low-level race detectors.

First, low-level executions contain instructions not derived from equivalent – or *any* – operations of the language-level execution. Memory accesses and synchronization in implicit JVM services like garbage collection are not derived from explicit operations of a Java program. Some low-level memory accesses implement language-level synchronization operations.

Second, language-level semantics of low-level resources change during execution. The allocator or garbage collector reuses memory or moves objects in memory. By analyzing accesses to a single virtual memory location reused by the JVM to store distinct Java objects, a race detector can report false races. By analyzing distinct virtual memory locations when a single Java object has moved, the detector can miss true races. If a threading implementation multiplexes language-level threads on low-level threads, two operations of the same low-level thread do not necessarily belong to the same language-level thread, and vice versa, leading to false or missed races subject to thread placement.

### 1.2 Low-Level Detection of Language-Level Races

This paper's main contribution is *low-level abstractable race detection* (LARD), an extended low-level race detector interface that lets run-time systems and compilers communicate a language-level view of execution in sufficient detail. The extensions are minimal: they let run-time systems and compilers (1) mark language-level memory accesses and synchronization operations explicitly for analysis, leaving system operations unanalyzed, (2) report changes in the language-level/low-level memory mapping due to memory reuse and movement, and (3) report language-level thread identity. The low-level race detector then analyzes only the memory accesses and synchronization operations of the language-level program and updates its state according to changes in memory allocation to reflect the language-level memory abstraction.

LARD allows data-race detectors for high-level languages to harness the performance and generality of low-level detection mechanisms while maintaining accuracy. The focus of this paper is a simple execution stack consisting of a language run-time running on hardware, but the design may generalize to a range of dual-level execution environments, including operating systems, hypervisors, and interpreters.

To the best of our knowledge, this paper presents the first design for *virtualizing data-race detection.* Earlier exclusively low-level or language-level data-race detectors (*e.g.*, [12, 16, 44]) have support for marking custom synchronization routines to avoid false races on these accesses and track their synchronization effects. Low-level detection of language-level data races requires similar support, but may also need to distinguish the semantics of such operations based on context.

Some C race detectors (*e.g.*, [40, 44]) treat allocation specially to help reduce false races and some JVM race detectors work around object movement to avoid missed races (*e.g.*, [11, 37]), but these previous efforts have focused mainly on ad hoc *reduction* of imprecision in fundamentally imprecise data-race detection algorithms implemented at a single level of abstraction. In this paper, we characterize the effects of the language-level/low-level translation on race detection in depth and develop a unified approach to *eliminate all* missed and *all* false races, achieving accurate language-level data-race detection in high-level programs using low-level race detectors.

### 1.3 LARD Implementation and Evaluation

To evaluate the feasibility of low-level abstractable race detection, we implemented an accurate data-race detector for Java using LARD. Our implementation includes two independent systems, communicating only via LARDx86, an extension of the x86 ISA with flags to mark memory access instructions explicitly to be checked for races and instructions to report synchronization, memory reuse, movement, and thread identity. We simulated an accurate, low-level, mostly-hardware, dynamic data-race detector based on RADISH [12], and extended to support LARDx86. We modified Jikes RVM [2] to emit race-checked accesses for application code and unchecked accesses for JVM code, report synchronization events in application code, and report memory reuse and movement events in the JVM. Our results show that our extensions are necessary and sufficient to avoid false and missed races in practice.

### 1.4 Contributions and Outline

We discuss background on data races, data-race exceptions, and data-race detection in §2. Our main contributions follow:

- We explain why low-level race detectors are incorrect for high-level programs (§3), synthesizing disparate issues encountered in prior contexts [11, 37, 40, 46].

- We design *low-level abstractable race detection* (LARD), a simple interface for low-level race detectors and language implementations that enables accurate language-level data-race detection using a low-level data-race detector, and compare our approach to some prior systems (§3).
- We implement our approach for Java, coupling a simulated hardware-supported ISA-level dynamic data-race detector and a modified Jikes RVM through a version of the x86 ISA extended with LARD primitives (§4).
- We evaluate our implementation's accuracy, comparing against FastTrack [16], a naïve low-level data-race detector similar to RADISH [12], and various partial implementations of LARD, finding that, *in practice*, naïve ISA-level race detectors suffer from false and missed races for Java programs, but LARD does not (§5).

Finally, we discuss more related work (§6) and conclude (§7).

## 2. Background

### 2.1 Data Races and Data-Race Exceptions

A *data race* is defined formally as a pair of *concurrent, conflicting* memory accesses [32]. Two accesses *conflict* if they are executed by different threads and at least one access is a write. Operations are *concurrent* if they are not ordered by the *happens-before* relation [22], a partial order over operations, composed of *program order*, the order of operations within each thread, and *synchronization order*, the ordering between synchronization operations in different threads (*e.g.*, lock acquire and release or thread fork and join).

In the presence of memory access reorderings by the compiler or hardware, data races may let programs observe states of memory that correspond to no simple sequential interleaving of threads, violating *sequential consistency*. The Java [26] and C/C++ [7] memory models both guarantee sequential consistency given data-race freedom, but if a data race occurs, a much weaker – or undefined – semantics applies [1, 6]. Even if sequential consistency is preserved [24, 28], data races play a part in other concurrency errors such as atomicity violations or determinism violations.

***Data-Race Exceptions*** Some researchers have proposed *data-race exceptions* (*DREs*) to mitigate the ill effects of data races by making every data race explicit at run-time [1, 10, 13]. A memory model with accurate DREs is stronger than the Java and C/C++ memory models, guaranteeing data-race freedom or an exception on each memory access. Data-race freedom still guarantees sequential consistency, and data-race-free programs never generate DREs. DREs ensure an execution forbids a data race before any ill effects can occur.

### 2.2 Dynamic Data-Race Detection

An accurate dynamic data-race detector misses no true data races and reports no false data races *in the execution it observes*. Races possible in other executions are irrelevant. We consider dynamic data-race detection with respect to the execution semantics and memory abstractions of the *source language*. A ***language-level data-race detector*** analyzes execution at the same level of abstraction provided by the source language. We typically mean a race detector for a language like Java, analyzing field accesses, etc. A ***low-level data-race detector*** analyzes execution at a machine abstraction below that of the source language. We typically mean hardware analyzing virtual memory accesses at the ISA level, but the same principles apply to a binary-instrumenting software implementation, for example.

The literature is flush with methods for dynamically detecting or avoiding data races; each is limited by accuracy or performance and designed for a specific programming language or execution abstraction. Some dynamic analyses allow false races or missed races in exchange for speed. Detection of data races that violate sequential consistency is fast [24, 28, 41], but does not detect *all* data races, which remain important. Atomicity violation detection, determinism enforcement, and other analyses often rely on accurate data-race detection [18] or assume data-race freedom [33]. Accurate software dynamic data-race detectors such as FastTrack [16, 17] and Goldilocks [13] miss no races and report no false races, but are too slow for always-on deployment, even after elimination of provably redundant checks [17].

### 2.3 Benefits of Low-Level Race Detection

Advances in accurate dynamic data-race detection have used low-level support to **improve performance** and accelerate checking in common cases where no data-sharing occurs. Mechanisms include page protections and hypervisor support in Aikido [34] or cache coherence tricks and specialized hardware in RADISH [12]. These systems exploit the fact that memory accesses can be tracked efficiently with hardware or hypervisor support and are much more frequent than synchronization operations. Implementing the critical core of race detection logic once in a **general**, reusable, low-level mechanism is appealing. Although a low-level mechanism *alone* is insufficient for language-level race detection, it can *reduce* the complexity of high-performance race detection in a language implementation. Our implementation (§4) shows that the engineering required is feasible for a system as complex as a JVM. For unmanaged targets like C programs, it is simpler.

### 2.4 Vector-Clock Race Detectors

This paper considers data-race detectors derived from a canonical algorithm using vector clocks [14, 29] to track the happens-before order induced by synchronization and determine if pairs of conflicting memory accesses are concurrent. *Vector clocks* track the most recent operation in each thread that happens before a given event. A vector clock for each thread represents all operations that happen before that thread's next operation. A vector clock for each lock represents all operations that happen before that lock's last release.

| Operation | Prevents | Translation Issue |
|---|---|---|
| (un)tracked access | false races | program vs. system |
| (un)tracked sync. | missed races | program vs. system |
| clear history | false races | memory reuse |
| move history | missed races | memory movement |
| set thread identity | false and missed races | thread scheduling |

**Table 1.** The LARD interface.

Thread and lock vector clocks are updated on synchronization. An *access history* for each shared memory location records the last write to the location by any thread and the last read from the location by each thread. When a thread accesses a location, it compares the access history with its own vector clock to check if earlier conflicting accesses happen before or race with its current access, then records its own access in the history. Writes must be totally ordered with respect to conflicting reads and writes, but reads are allowed to execute concurrently with other reads. We refer the reader to Appendix A for more detail.

## 3. Low-Level Abstractable Race Detection

*Low-level abstractable race detection* (LARD) extends the interface and functionality of low-level data-race detectors to abstract (*i.e.*, virtualize) data-race detection to high-level execution environments. The key idea is to preserve relevant information from language-level operations in the low-level execution. LARD requires cooperation from the high-level language implementation and the low-level race detector to implement two types of extensions: (1) distinguish between source operations and run-time system operations; and (2) maintain the mutable mappings from language-level memory to low-level memory and from language-level threads to low-level threads.

We explain LARD by examining the five fundamental operations where relevant differences arise between language-level and low-level views of execution: memory access (§3.1), synchronization (§3.2), memory allocation (§3.3), memory movement (§3.4), and thread mapping (§3.5). For each operation, we show how information lost in translation can cause missed or false data races. Then we extend the low-level race detector interface to retain sufficient language-level information. Table 1 summarizes the five interface extensions. Finally, we argue that LARD's five extensions are sufficient to virtualize general low-level data-race detection for use by language implementations (§3.6).

We focus on Java programs executed by a modern JVM on hardware that detects ISA-level data races, although we believe that these five issues arise in any setting where data-race detection is implemented at a significantly different abstraction level than the source program. Others have previously identified or mitigated some of these issues. (We discuss related work inline and in §6.) However, we believe our research is the first to consider the full set of techniques needed to virtualize data-race detection.

### 3.1 Memory Access

JVM execution contains both memory accesses compiled from explicit field and array accesses in Java programs and accesses in the JVM itself. Observing the latter may cause the detector to report data races involving at least one JVM access. These are false Java data races because they involve access outside the Java program and its execution abstraction.

RULE 1. *The race detector should check only accesses explicit in the source program for races.*

***Examples*** The implementation of locks, for example, is necessarily lock-free, using memory reads and writes plus hardware synchronization primitives like fences and atomic compare-and-swap. These memory operations may race, but are chosen carefully with respect to the hardware memory model to ensure correct behavior regardless. The need to ignore these *synchronization races* is well-understood.

Consider JVM accesses to the Java heap. A concurrent mark-sweep garbage collector, for example, traverses the heap while Java threads continue to mutate it, compensating in a safe, algorithm-specific way, for the races that are bound to result. Figure 1 shows an example: A GC thread reads `o.x` (stored in memory at address `0x8c+4`) at `A` during a concurrent heap traversal. A low-level race detector will report a race with this read on Thread 1's later write at `B`.

Since data-race detector access histories typically store only the *last* write by any thread and *last* read by each thread, a false data race can overwrite history necessary in the future to detect a true data race with a previous program access.

***Extension*** It is natural to distinguish source-program and run-time system accesses with explicit *tracked* and *untracked* access instructions. Both have the conventional functionality of memory accesses. The low-level race detector analyzes tracked accesses only.

### 3.2 Synchronization

Witnessing implicit JVM synchronization where no Java synchronization exists can cause the race detector to miss true data races in the Java program: the racing accesses appear well-ordered to the low-level race detector. A race detector that observes *all* synchronization never misses a data race that may cause a sequential consistency violation, because it only misses races due to *extra* synchronization, but it can miss other problematic data races.

RULE 2. *The race detector should analyze only synchronization explicit in the source program.*

***Example*** Consider the upper left example in Figure 1, which shows views of the same multithreaded execution at the Java, JVM implementation, and low-level race detector levels of abstraction. In the Java view, Threads 1 and 2 both increment the `n` field of the same object at `C` and `D`, respectively. Neither thread synchronizes, so the accesses race. A low-level race detector misses this data race if a

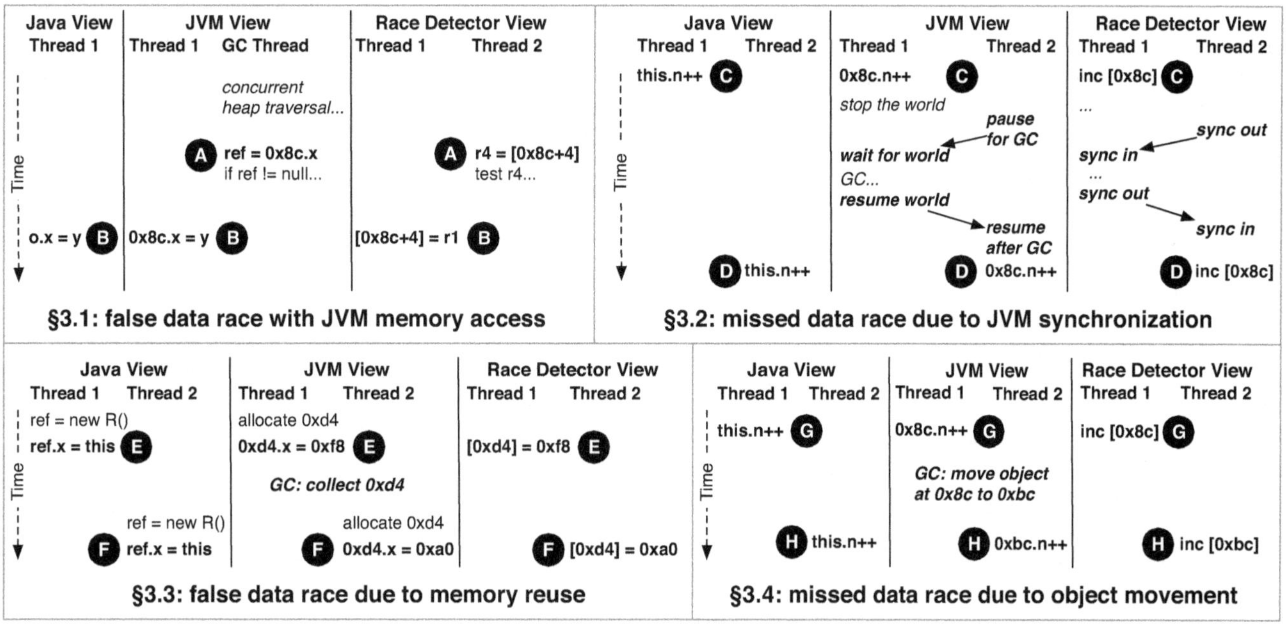


**Figure 1.** A naïve low-level data-race detector reports false data races and misses true data races in Java programs. Solid arrows are happens-before edges observed by the race detector. Each example contains three views of the same execution.

stop-the-world garbage collection occurs between the two accesses. If the race detector witnesses the global barrier synchronization, accesses C and D appear well-ordered. This Java data race is not a low-level data race in this execution, due to this JVM synchronization, but it could be in another execution depending on the timing of garbage collection.

***Extension*** Accurate ISA-level dynamic data-race detectors such as RADISH [12] provide primitives for synchronization libraries to report happens-before effects of synchronization to the race detector. This approach is easily adaptable for LARD: synchronization reports should be issued only for synchronization operations explicit in the source program.

### 3.3 Memory Allocation

Without knowledge that a low-level memory location has been reused to store a new, distinct language-level memory object, a low-level race detector may report false races between accesses to the new and old language-level occupants.

RULE 3. *The race detector should clear access histories of low-level memory locations atomically with collection or freeing of their language-level occupants.*

***Example*** Consider the example in the lower left of Figure 1. In the Java view, Thread 1 allocates an R object then writes to its x field at E. Later, Thread 2 allocates a distinct R object then writes to its x field at F. Clearly these Java accesses to fields of distinct objects cannot race, but a low-level race detector may report a data race between the writes at E and F if the memory manager reuses the same memory to store these two objects and threads accessing these objects do not synchronize, as shown in Figure 1. The race detector ignores memory accesses and synchronization in the garbage collector, per Rules 1 and 2, and reports a data race on the concurrent, conflicting writes to address 0xd4.

***Extension*** Synchronization in the memory manager that makes reuse of memory across threads must not be observed by the race detector, since it could also hide true data races in the Java program (§3.2). In the C/C++ memory model [9], freeing a location *happens before* a later allocation of the same memory location, but the ordering applies only to accesses to that memory location.

We choose to clear low-level race detector access histories on deallocation. Thus newly allocated low-level memory locations appear fresh to the race detector whether or not they have been accessed before. This approach matches the language-level memory abstraction and is safe given memory safety, making it valid for managed environments and well-behaved C/C++ programs. It is the responsibility of the race detector to clear access histories when requested. The run-time system must use this support to ensure it clears access histories of a memory location before reallocating it. Helgrind [44] and RACEZ [40], two race detectors for C programs, take a similar approach, treating malloc/free specially. Helgrind additionally provides C preprocessor macros to mark custom allocation routines to help reduce false race reports.

### 3.4 Memory Movement

Some garbage collectors move language-level memory objects in low-level memory during collection to defragment the heap. Movement is not part of the language-level memory abstraction. Collectors update all references to moved objects to maintain a consistent heap. Without knowing a language-level memory object has moved, a low-level race detector may miss true data races between accesses at the object's old and new low-level memory locations. Choi, *et al.*, briefly identified (but did not solve) one aspect of this problem in [11], §3.3. Similar issues arise for an operating system or hypervisor running above a physical-memory race detector when remapping virtual-memory pages.

RULE 4. *The race detector should move access histories of low-level memory locations to follow atomically with language-level memory objects moved by the run-time system.*

***Example*** Consider the example execution in the lower right of Figure 1, in which two Java threads increment the n field of the same Java object, with no synchronization. Clearly, this is a Java data race. However, garbage collection is triggered after Thread 1 increments n at G but before Thread 2 does at H and the garbage collector moves shared object at address 0x8c to address 0xbc. The low-level race detector ignores accesses and synchronization by the collector, as it should. Because the object moves, the two threads access different low-level memory locations and the race detector misses a true Java data race.

***Extension*** Moving a language-level object in low-level memory may be a non-atomic operation, requiring copying the contents of several low-level memory locations. Some concurrent copying collectors (*e.g.*, [35]) may begin movement operations optimistically, abort midway, or copy a single low-level memory location multiple times to support continued non-blocking access by program threads during object movement. Since object movement is rarely implemented by a single, atomic, low-level operation and clearing access history is already required to support memory allocation, it is natural to add a primitive to *copy* the access history for one low-level memory location to another. Once the language-level object is fully copied, the old copy can be deallocated, at which point its access history is cleared. Garbage collectors already ensure that the movement of data appears atomic; it is also their responsibility to ensure that they request access history movement from the low-level race detector in a way that ensures access history is moved atomically with program data. Neither the run-time system nor the race detector can accomplish this alone.

An alternative is to use logical addresses for race detection analysis so it is resilient to movement [37], but this adds a logical address lookup indirection to the critical path of memory accesses, along with the cost of managing available unique identifiers. For low-level race detectors, each tracked memory instruction in the ISA would need to take an extra logical address argument. TLB-like hardware support to cache the low-level to logical address mapping could speed the lookup at the cost of lengthening the critical path for cache accesses, which is unmodified in hardware race detectors such as RADISH [12], and would require shootdown on object movement anyway. While reporting movement has overheads to copy access histories, race-checked memory accesses occur *far* more frequently than object movement. We choose reporting movement (copying) as a less invasive and higher-performance option.

### 3.5 Thread Identity

Some threading implementations (*e.g.*, user-level threads or work-stealing schedulers) multiplex a set of language-level threads on a fixed set of low-level (kernel or hardware) threads. Without knowledge of this mapping, a low-level race detector may report false data races between accesses in a single language-level thread or miss true data races between accesses in distinct language-level threads.

RULE 5. *The race detector should use language-level thread identities in its analysis.*

***Example*** When two language threads execute conflicting accesses without synchronization, they clearly race. However, if they execute their accesses while scheduled on the same kernel thread (at different times), the low-level race detector observes two accesses by the same kernel thread and misses a true data race. When a single language thread executes multiple accesses to the same location, it cannot race with itself, but if these accesses are executed while it is scheduled on distinct kernel threads (at different times), the low-level race detector observes conflicting accesses between distinct kernel threads and may report a false data race.[1]

***Extension*** We take an approach similar to object movement, reporting a new thread identity whenever a threading system schedules a language-level thread onto a low-level thread. The low-level race detector uses this thread identity for all operations of the low-level thread until the next such report.

### 3.6 Sufficiency

Data races – and accurate algorithms for their detection – are defined in terms of memory, synchronization, and threads. Program translation must affect one of these features to affect post-translation data-race detection. To derive the set of translation issues affecting data-race detection, we enumerated all differences introduced in the language-to-ISA translation that interact with these features, to the best of our knowledge, finding that only the issues in §3.1-3.5 affect data-race detection. The five extensions described above ensure data-race detection is performed only on language-level memory and synchronization operations (§3.1, §3.2) and on the language's abstractions of memory (§3.3, §3.4) and thread identity (§3.5). While each issue and extension is fairly simple, it is their composition that allows data-race detection to virtualize. We believe our research is the first to consider the full set of techniques needed to virtualize data-

[1] We assume the race detector ignores synchronization involved in the context-switching of language threads, as it should.

race detection. This perspective was essential for guiding our implementation and evaluation.

LARD's effectiveness depends on the contract between the low-level race detector and the language implementation; it does *not* free the language implementation from reasoning about all details of race detection. It is up to the language implementation to ensure that its use of the LARD primitives meets its particular semantics. For example, garbage collectors are responsible for ensuring that primitives like access history clearing and copying appear atomic with respect to memory accesses by program threads. The language implementation is also responsible for compilation choices. For example, some compiler optimizations allowed by the Java [26] and C/C++ [7] memory models may remove races from the original program, but none introduce races where races did not exist. *Roach-motel reordering* allows the movement of memory operations into – but not out of – critical sections [45]. As a result, the access may now be well-ordered when it would have raced if the transformation was not applied. We do not consider this a missed race. It is explicitly allowable behavior in the language memory model and, unlike with the issues above, the program can never manifest this race as compiled. If the language implementers *do* consider this a missed race, they must choose compiler optimizations appropriately. Regardless, this is the language implementer's choice and is an issue common to dynamic race detectors implemented at *all* levels of abstraction, not just low-level race detection for high-level languages.

## 4. Implementation

To validate the efficacy and feasibility of low-level detection of language-level data races, we implemented a data-race detector for Java using a low-level data-race detector and a Java virtual machine that communicate through the LARD interface. This section describes four parts of our implementation (bold items in Figure 2): LARDx86 (§4.1) is an extension of the x86 ISA with LARD primitives. LARDISH (§4.2) is a simulated hardware implementation of LARDx86 that performs accurate, LARD-aware, data-race detection derived from the RADISH [12] hardware-based race detector. Jikes LARDVM (§4.3) is a Java virtual machine that runs on LARDx86 and implements accurate Java data-race detection using the LARDx86 primitives. We also extended these three parts for fine-grained accuracy evaluation of LARD and naïve low-level data-race detectors (§4.4).

### 4.1 The LARDx86 ISA

LARDx86 extends the x86 ISA to provide a LARD interface between software run-time systems and low-level vector-clock race detectors. To support the tasks described in §3, LARDx86 extends the x86 ISA with Tracked accesses, a Thread instruction to report thread identity, WriteVC and ReadVC instructions to report synchronization, and ClearHistory and CopyHistory to manipulate access histories.

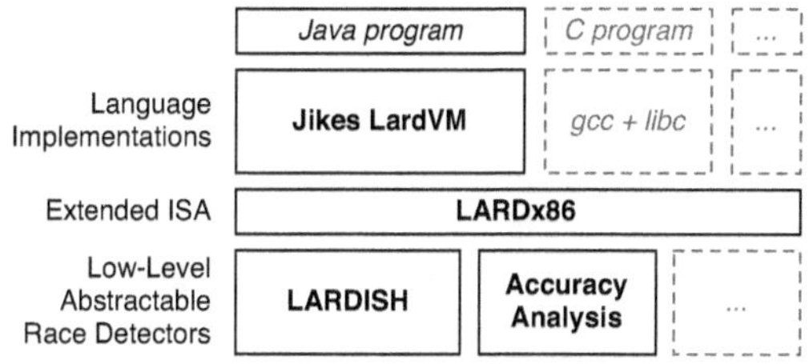


**Figure 2.** The LARD environment.

***ISA Extensions for Memory Access and Synchronization*** Explicit Tracked memory access instructions, distinguished by separate opcodes or a prefix, have the usual semantics of memory accesses, but are additionally checked for races by the low-level race detector. Untracked accesses are never checked. The low-level race detector must store a vector clock for each thread internally, representing the most recent event from each thread that happens before the current event of this thread. It is used when checking Tracked accesses for races. The run-time system must track ordering effects of synchronization using vector clocks, using the ReadVC and WriteVC instructions to read and write entries in the low-level race detector's per-thread vector clocks.

Alternatively, the run-time system could report synchronization on a particular memory object (*e.g.*, lock), leaving storage and tracking of all vector clocks to the low-level race detector. This hides vector clocks from the run-time system, but is best suited for locks or barriers. Additional purpose-built instructions would be necessary to support synchronization operations that also atomically manipulate data, such as language-level atomic CAS operations or Java's volatile field accesses (§4.3). Since the semantics of synchronization is best understood in its implementation (*i.e.*, above the ISA), exposing vector clocks is more flexible and ultimately has lower complexity.

***ISA Extensions for Mapping Memory Management*** The ClearHistory and CopyHistory instructions clear and copy low-level race detector access histories of given memory locations. They are intended for use by a memory manager when it frees or moves language-level memory objects. ClearHistory takes two arguments, the address and size of a memory region whose access histories should be discarded. CopyHistory takes three arguments, the address of a source region of memory, the address of a destination region of memory, and the size of the two regions. (They must be the same size.) In response to a CopyHistory instruction, a low-level race detector copies the access history for each memory location in the source region to use as the access history for the corresponding memory location in the destination region. Specifying regions of memory rather than individual locations allows the race detector to optimize bulk updates internally, but regions are restricted to a single virtual memory page to simplify support in hardware-based race detectors.

***Encapsulated vs. Exposed Access Histories*** LARDx86 assumes that the low-level race detector is solely responsible for managing access histories. Exposing control of access history storage to a language implementation may be more natural and efficient if access histories can be colocated with the data they shadow and automatically moved and deallocated by the garbage collector. This is not feasible with our implementation because the hardware race detector manages access histories based on physical – not virtual – addresses (§4.2). Reverse address translation or virtually addressed caches would be necessary to support efficient external software management of access histories.

### 4.2 The LARDISH Hardware Race Detector

To evaluate the performance potential of a hardware-based LARD system, we designed LARDISH, an extension of RADISH [12], a hardware-supported race detector. This section outlines our extensions to RADISH to support low-level abstractable race detection with LARDx86.

RADISH [12] is a hybrid hardware-software race detector that is accurate for low-level programs. It optimizes the canonical vector clock race detection algorithm by caching access histories in the hardware data cache, allowing most accesses to be checked for races purely in hardware. Several optimizations ensure that the common case race check has little or no latency. A software system handles storage of race detector access histories after cache evictions and context switches and support for occasional race checks that require access history information not cached in hardware. The software stores access histories in a format independent from the in-cache hardware representation.

***LARD Extensions*** Supporting LARD requires minor adjustments to RADISH's access and synchronization tracking and modest hardware extensions to support LARD's memory management. RADISH checks for races on all memory accesses except stack accesses and accesses in its software manager. We generalize this to use LARDx86's explicit Tracked memory access instructions. We implement the WriteVC and ReadVC instructions with RADISH's existing support for tracking and reporting synchronization in libraries.[2] The Thread instruction is identical a to context switch in RADISH, swapping the thread's vector clock and requiring eager or lazy flushing of the old thread's cached access histories to the software manager, which maintains the mapping between processor cores, kernel threads, and language threads. ClearHistory and CopyHistory instructions must perform tasks similar to context switches or virtual memory paging in RADISH. Manipulating access histories in RADISH's software manager is straightforward when they are not cached in hardware, but hardware support is need to invalidate or move cached access histories.

[2] The original RADISH simulator hard-codes pthreads support; we implement true vector-clock instructions.

***Manipulating Cached Access Histories*** The RADISH software manager identifies access histories by physical addresses, since it receives physically addressed access history cache lines on eviction. We use the existing address translation mechanism to map the virtual addresses specified by ClearHistory and CopyHistory instructions to physical addresses that the extended RADISH software manager can use to manipulate the relevant access histories.

When a hardware cached access history is not available to perform a check, the RADISH hardware requests it from software. When dirty cached access history is evicted, RADISH calls its software manager manager to persist it instead of storing it to memory. The software manager keeps track of what access histories may be in-cache (on calls for fills and evictions). If an access history to be cleared or copied is not cached, it can be handled by the software manager alone. If an access history is cached, ClearHistory and CopyHistory must explicitly invalidate or copy hardware-cached access histories to ensure they stay consistent with the software-managed copies and the new mapping of language-level to low-level memory. For ClearHistory, we instead invalidate the cached access history without calling the software handler.

CopyHistory must persist hardware-cached histories for its source location. In this case, hardware first forces eviction of the source locations' cached access histories via the normal RADISH eviction handler. We assume that the destination of an object movement has no preexisting access histories. If it does, the memory manager must use ClearHistory to explicitly invalidate any cached version before copying. Once the software manager has persisted any cached access histories for the source region, it copies all access histories for the source region to become access histories for the destination region. On the first access to a location in the destination region after copying, hardware will request the software-managed access history as usual.

If the language implementation allows program threads to access objects concurrently with copying, the software manager must ensure the atomicity of the copy operation by disallowing hardware requests for access histories of the affected regions for the duration of the copy, effectively blocking access to the region during access history copying. To allow finer-grained access, concurrent copying collectors may issue smaller CopyHistory operations, ensuring atomicity of the full copy themselves.

An alternative is to copy cached access histories directly in cache, moving stale software-managed access histories "underneath" them. This approach must consider whether it is profitable to keep the history in cache, but evict another cache line at its destination. We implement a simpler evict-and-copy policy. Additionally, a MoveHistory instruction could enable optimizations when the intent is to copy an access history and immediately clear the original, as in stop-the-world copying collectors. We have not explored this.

### 4.3 The Jikes LARDVM Java Virtual Machine

Jikes LARDVM is a modified version of Jikes RVM [2] 3.1.1 that implements accurate data-race detection for Java using LARDx86. Jikes LARDVM marks source program accesses for race checks (§4.3.1), tracks source program thread identity and synchronization (§4.3.2), and reports garbage collector operations (§4.3.3). Our implementation was designed for detailed accuracy analysis and is only lightly optimized for performance.

#### 4.3.1 Memory Tracking

The Jikes LARDVM JIT compiler emits Tracked accesses for potentially racing field and array accesses in Java programs. All other accesses in the system are unmarked, to be ignored by the low-level race detector. This includes JVM code like garbage collector write barriers that are inlined into compiled code. In write barriers, the memory write on behalf of the source program is marked Tracked, but all other accesses are untracked. The compiler may decide not to mark some source program accesses Tracked if it can prove their data-race-freedom, such as for read-only final fields. We have not yet enabled thread-escape analysis.

Since Jikes RVM is a self-hosted JVM written in Java and compiled to machine code by its own compiler, the compiler must distinguish Jikes RVM Java code from source program Java code, emitting Tracked accesses and synchronization reporting only for the source program. Compilers in conventional JVMs written in lower-level languages can emit Tracked accesses everywhere except inlined VM code.

#### 4.3.2 Thread Identity and Synchronization

Jikes RVM uses kernel threads directly, so we issue a Thread instruction only once per thread. Every Java object may be used as a lock. To track lock synchronization, we shadow each lock with a vector clock indicating the last logical time it was released. A word in the object header stores a pointer to a lazily allocated vector clock. We also augment each Jikes RVM thread with a thread vector clock tracking its logical time and synchronization with other threads. We instrument lock operations and thread fork/join to track happens-before ordering with vector clocks in the JVM, reporting updates to the race detector's per-thread vector-clock using WriteVC/ReadVC. Jikes RVM and source programs share synchronization implementations. We added an instrumentation-wrapped version of each for program synchronization.

Under the Java Memory Model [26], volatile field accesses never race; they induce synchronization instead. There is a happens-before edge from a volatile write to each volatile read observing the write, enforced by hardware memory fences and restrictions on compiler reorderings. Jikes LARDVM never marks volatile accesses Tracked. Each volatile field is shadowed by a vector clock representing the last logical time a volatile write occurred on that field. The field contents and the vector clock must be updated and observed atomically. Volatile reads have the same type of happens-before effects as lock acquires (volatile writes are like lock releases), but provide no mutual exclusion. The vector clock to store on a volatile write operation depends on the field's vector clock at the time of the write, which requires allocating one new vector clock per volatile write operation. To avoid introducing a lock into the source program's lock-free code, we align volatile fields with an adjacent vector clock pointer and use a wide CAS to operate atomically over the two, optimistically computing the vector clock to store and retrying under contention in a standard lock-free manner.

#### 4.3.3 Memory Management and Mapping

We modified the classical mark-sweep and semispace collectors in Jikes RVM and MMTk [4] to issue a CopyHistory instruction when moving an object and a ClearHistory instruction when reclaiming an object, including after movement. The garbage collector handles source program objects and objects representing Jikes RVM internals (including vector clocks). We issue ClearHistory and CopyHistory conservatively for all objects whose contents *may* have been used by race-checked source program accesses and thus may have access histories in the race detector. Unlike synchronization and access, conservative reporting of memory-management events cannot cause missed or false races.

Other more advanced garbage collectors do not introduce other issues beyond the reuse and movement exhibited by mark-sweep or semispace. For example, accesses to metadata in generational write barriers are properly left untracked, as they are not explicit in the program.

#### 4.3.4 Extent of Changes to Jikes RVM

Our modifications to Jikes RVM add or change 8229 lines of code. The core LARD additions account for well under half those lines, with the rest devoted to extensions for accuracy analysis (§4.4), extensive debugging/profiling, and significant code duplication for garbage collector access barriers.

The core LARD additions mainly track synchronization events mark tracked accesses in the compiler. Other significant additions involved object layout for volatile fields with adjacent vector clocks and proper garbage collector tracing of vector clock references. Those aspects of the race detector that are shared in common with software implementations (*i.e.*, synchronization tracking) were the most complicated to implement. Memory reuse and movement reporting was relatively simple once we understood the memory management architecture in Jikes RVM and MMTk.

### 4.4 Extensions for Accuracy Analysis

For the accuracy analysis in §5.2, we built an analysis tool that runs multiple race detection algorithms on the same LARDx86 execution, comparing their results at each memory access. Specifically, we support several detectors that each ignore one of the LARD extensions in their analysis. It is simple to analyze all accesses instead of Tracked accesses only.

To ignore memory reuse or movement, a detector ignores the ClearHistory or CopyHistory instructions, respectively. To analyze all synchronization instead of language-level synchronization only, we must explicitly report all synchronization. Tracking all synchronization in Jikes LARDVM on the same execution where we track language-level synchronization requires a separate vector clock for each lock, volatile field, and thread. This addition is needed only for the accuracy evaluation (§5.2) and not in real deployments.

## 5. Evaluation

We evaluate the efficacy of LARD and multiple naïve low-level data-race detectors for implementing accurate dynamic data-race detection for Java. We validate LARD's capacity to eliminate missed races and false races by comparing the results of our LARD-based Java data-race detector with the accurate FastTrack Java data-race detector [16] and a naïve low-level vector-clock data-race detector (§5.1) and quantify the effects of individual LARD extensions in terms of the missed races and false races they eliminate (§5.2). Although the accuracy analysis is the main contribution of our evaluation, we include initial evaluation of the performance of a LARD implementation composed of Jikes LARDVM executing on LARDISH via simulation (§5.3). Additionally, we evaluate the performance of Jikes LARDVM alone on conventional x86 hardware (§5.4).

***Experimental Configuration*** We ran experiments with multithreaded benchmarks from Java Grande [43] and DaCapo 9.12 [3].[3] The Java Grande benchmarks are mostly small scientific applications with relatively static memory footprints.We replace Java Grande's custom racy spin-waiting barriers with data-race-free versions to verify LARD's accuracy for data-race-free programs. We report their results as one unit. DaCapo is composed of larger applications with varied concurrency patterns. Where applicable, benchmarks were configured to use 4 threads. To make heavyweight accuracy analyses and simulations feasible, we used small inputs. For performance experiments on real hardware, we used the largest inputs. We ran two configurations each of Jikes RVM and Jikes LARDVM, using the mark-sweep (MS) and semispace (SS) garbage collectors. All experiments were run on quad-core 64-bit 2.8GHz Intel Xeon Pentium 4 machines with 4GB of RAM and a Linux 2.6.32 kernel.

### 5.1 False Races and Missed Races

To validate the accuracy of our LARD implementation and illustrate the degree to which naïve low-level race detectors can suffer from false and missed races, we compare the race reports from three data-race detectors. **FastTrack** [16] is an accurate data-race detector for Java implemented via bytecode instrumentation. We compared FastTrack race reports

[3] We omit DaCapo benchmarks that crash on unmodified Jikes RVM or take too long to complete under simulation.

| Benchmark | FastTrack | | GC | LARD | | Naïve | |
|---|---|---|---|---|---|---|---|
| | DRE | PC | | DRE | PC | DRE | PC |
| Java Grande | 0 | 0 | MS | 0 | 0 | 28211 | 124 |
| | | | SS | 0 | 0 | 7899 | 175 |
| avrora | 83315 | 6 | MS | 106405 | 8 | 1997242 | 129 |
| | | | SS | 104579 | 8 | 139131 | 194 |
| luindex | 0 | 0 | MS | 0 | 0 | 2841482 | 745 |
| | | | SS | 0 | 0 | 539216 | 528 |
| lusearch | 0 | 0 | MS | 0 | 0 | 2823974 | 2395 |
| | | | SS | 0 | 0 | 26469692 | 2865 |
| pmd | 3 | 3 | MS | 9 | 9 | 827934 | 87 |
| | | | SS | 9 | 9 | 17378 | 189 |
| sunflow | 32 | 7 | MS | 84 | 16 | 3224426 | 123 |
| | | | SS | 64 | 16 | 65075 | 203 |
| xalan | 588 | 8 | MS | 703 | 34 | 4152344 | 149 |
| | | | SS | 704 | 36 | 203473 | 237 |

**Table 2.** Numbers of dynamic accesses on which data-race reports occur (DRE) and distinct PCs of these reports.

with those of our **LARD** implementation (described in §4) and a **Naïve** low-level vector-clock race detector equivalent to RADISH [12]. LARD and Naïve are run over the same exact execution of the benchmarks, but FastTrack uses separate executions. We have not reimplemented FastTrack within Jikes LARDVM due to the complexity of co-hosting the two. FastTrack ignores accesses and synchronization in the JDK standard libraries. LARD instruments all Java code by default.

Table 2 contains results from running these data-race detectors on the Java Grande benchmarks and selected DaCapo benchmarks. Exact numbers can vary across executions; we show the highest number of races reported by each detector on any *single* execution. Column **DRE** shows the number of dynamic accesses on which races were reported. Column **PC** shows the number of distinct program counters of these reports. Each racy access (DRE) races with one *or more* previous accesses, hence counting DREs is slightly different than counting distinct *races*. We report data races on the second of a racing pair of accesses and only report those racing pairs where the previous access has happened since (or is) the last write to an address. Due to this optimization, FastTrack and LARD are accurate (sound and complete) through the first data race. In practice, accuracy is not often compromised thereafter, so we report total data race reports in each execution as is conventional in the literature.

***FastTrack vs. LARD*** We compared data-race reports from FastTrack and LARD to validate LARD's accuracy. LARD consistently reported at least as many data races and at least as many racy accesses as FastTrack, though generally in the same order of magnitude. We examined the differing reports and found three sources. None is inaccuracy in LARD.

First, LARD instruments all Java code in the source program, including the JDK. It therefore reports some races involving JDK code, where applications misused unsynchronized JDK data structures. FastTrack misses these since it does not instrument the JDK. In pmd, LARD reports the same 3 data races on 3 accesses as reported by FastTrack and LARD, as well as 6 data races on unsynchronized ArrayLists from the JDK. Data races on the contents of java.util.Properties objects in xalan cause similar disparities.

Second, for each benchmark, FastTrack and LARD analyzed separate executions on entirely different JVMs, so some dynamic race-count variance is expected. Some benchmarks, such as sunflow, had wide variance even between runs on the same detector and JVM. There is large overlap in the races reported. We carefully examined races reported by only one detector. All appear possible in some executions and hidden in others, accounting for differences in sunflow and avrora. LARD reports more DREs, but at related program points.

Third, Jikes RVM is implemented for IA32 and emits two 32-bit accesses to implement accesses for Java's 64-bit long and double types. The Java Memory Model allows non-atomic long/double accesses, so we report races individually. These duplicated reports inflate LARD's race counts compared to those of FastTrack, though they report the same races, and account for the remaining disparities between LARD and FastTrack. We plan to remove this duplication in future implementations.

***Comparison with a Naïve Low-Level Race Detector*** The Naïve configuration reports up to several orders of magnitude more races than LARD or FastTrack, as shown in Table 2. The majority of these are false races involving system accesses; some are false races between language-level accesses. The Naïve detector also misses some races reported by LARD or FastTrack, as discussed in §5.2, and reports races on a large number of PCs, including many outside the source program.

### 5.2 Impacts of LARD Extensions

To understand the practical impact of each LARD extension on missed and false races, we compared the accurate LARD detector to variants with one or all of the LARD extensions disabled. The detectors are as follows, labeled as in Table 3:

- **LARD** is accurate, with all LARD extensions enabled.
- **AllMem** tracks *all* non-stack memory accesses in the JVM and the source program.
- **AllSync** tracks *all* synchronization in the JVM and the source program (§4.4).
- **NoClear** ignores reports of memory deallocation.
- **NoCopy** ignores reports of memory movement.
- **Naïve** tracks all non-stack memory accesses and all synchronization and ignores all memory management.

Jikes RVM uses a one-to-one mapping between kernel threads and Java threads, so we do not evaluate a detector that ignores thread identity. For each benchmark and garbage collector (mark-sweep (MS) or semispace (SS)), we ran all six detectors *over the same execution*, comparing their results on each dynamic memory access, with LARD as ground truth (by proxy to FastTrack). Table 3 shows the results.

The LARD column repeats the count of racy accesses and distinct PCs for LARD from Table 2. For the other detectors, we report: (1) the number of false DREs (**F DRE**) – those accesses on which LARD does not report a race but the other detector does, (2) the number of distinct PCs of false DREs (**F PC**), (3) the number of missed DREs (**M DRE**) – those accesses on which LARD reports a race but the other detector does not, and (4) the number of distinct PCs of missed DREs (**M PC**). All four of these are reported for Naïve. For the remaining four detectors, only one of missed or false is reported. The omitted columns contain only zeroes.

The most notable feature of these results is that disabling any one extension in our experiments results in false or missed races in at least one benchmark. *All of these LARD extensions are necessary for accuracy in practice.*

***Program vs. System*** All benchmarks in our experiments have false data races under **AllMem**, with tracking of program *and* system accesses. The majority of false data races are reported on accesses outside the source program, but false data races are also reported on program accesses. *Filtering out race reports on PCs in system code does not eliminate false data races.* Conversely, **AllSync** misses data races on all benchmarks, often (*e.g.*, pmd, sunflow, xalan) missing all or nearly all the data races reported by LARD.

***Memory Management*** Empirically, most benchmarks do not lead to false races when memory reuse is ignored (**NoClear**), but avrora and sunflow do suffer false races under semispace collection. Short executions and low garbage collection pressure make problematic reuse of memory rare in these experiments. In particular, the Java Grande benchmarks generally use large, long-lived arrays, rather than short-lived shared objects. Nonetheless, false races occurred under these relatively favorable conditions.

Ignoring memory movement in the **NoCopy** detector has no effect on the accuracy of data-race detection when using mark-sweep garbage collection, since mark-sweep never moves objects. Ignoring movement never leads to missed races in data-race-free executions such as the Java Grande benchmarks, but missed races do occur under semispace collection in pmd and sunflow.

### 5.3 Jikes LARDVM Performance on LARDISH

We have begun evaluation of the performance potential of hardware-based LARD data-race detection for Java by running benchmarks from DaCapo Jikes LARDVM on simulated LARDISH hardware. We model the same baseline configuration as in [12], extended with mechanisms described in §4.2. A PIN [25] binary instrumentation tool emulates LARDx86 to drive the simulator, an extension of the simulator used in [12]. Our main addition is to model the costs of ClearHistory and CopyHistory. For each, we charge 100 cycles to transition to the software manager. Next we simulate memory accesses for

| Bench | GC | LARD | | AllMem | | AllSync | | NoClear | | NoCopy | | Naïve | | | |
|---|---|---|---|---|---|---|---|---|---|---|---|---|---|---|---|
| | | DRE | PC | F DRE | F PC | M DRE | M PC | F DRE | F PC | M DRE | M PC | F DRE | F PC | M DRE | M PC |
| Java Grande | MS | 0 | 0 | 762969 | 222 | 0 | 0 | 0 | 0 | 0 | 0 | 28211 | 124 | 0 | 0 |
| | SS | 0 | 0 | 753437 | 226 | 0 | 0 | 0 | 0 | 0 | 0 | 7899 | 175 | 0 | 0 |
| avrora | MS | 106405 | 8 | 95644 | 276 | 3374 | 7 | 0 | 0 | 0 | 0 | 1894211 | 121 | 3374 | 7 |
| | SS | 104579 | 8 | 68010 | 174 | 1236 | 7 | 2 | 1 | 0 | 0 | 35788 | 186 | 1236 | 7 |
| luindex | MS | 0 | 0 | 42670 | 157 | 0 | 0 | 0 | 0 | 0 | 0 | 2841482 | 745 | 0 | 0 |
| | SS | 0 | 0 | 43460 | 159 | 0 | 0 | 0 | 0 | 0 | 0 | 539216 | 528 | 0 | 0 |
| lusearch | MS | 0 | 0 | 17079935 | 839 | 0 | 0 | 2823974 | 370 | 0 | 0 | 41760642 | 2395 | 0 | 0 |
| | SS | 0 | 0 | 16690434 | 873 | 0 | 0 | 3770587 | 264 | 0 | 0 | 26469692 | 2865 | 0 | 0 |
| pmd | MS | 9 | 9 | 43123 | 613 | 9 | 9 | 0 | 0 | 0 | 0 | 827934 | 87 | 9 | 9 |
| | SS | 9 | 9 | 17899 | 236 | 9 | 9 | 0 | 0 | 6 | 6 | 17378 | 189 | 9 | 9 |
| sunflow | MS | 84 | 16 | 99250 | 481 | 81 | 15 | 0 | 0 | 0 | 0 | 3224423 | 121 | 81 | 15 |
| | SS | 64 | 16 | 104457 | 255 | 61 | 15 | 17 | 10 | 9 | 6 | 65072 | 201 | 61 | 15 |
| xalan | MS | 703 | 34 | 837451 | 723 | 699 | 34 | 0 | 0 | 0 | 0 | 4152340 | 147 | 699 | 34 |
| | SS | 704 | 36 | 596556 | 649 | 700 | 36 | 0 | 0 | 0 | 0 | 203469 | 235 | 700 | 36 |

**Table 3.** False/missed races with individual LARD extensions disabled.

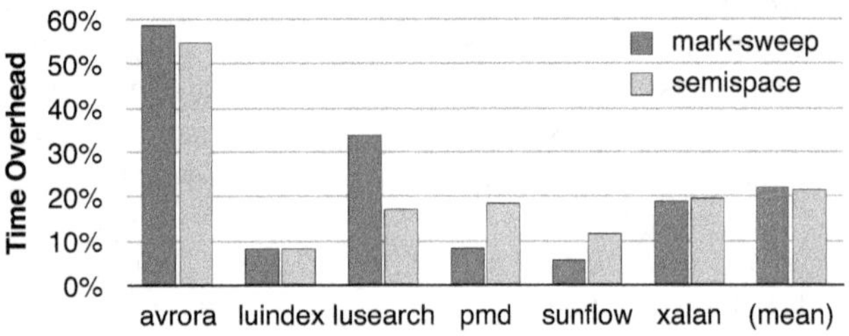


**Figure 3.** Execution time overhead of Jikes LARDVM normalized to unmodified Jikes RVM, both run on native x86.

software manager lookups of what access histories may need to be invalidated in the cache, issuing invalidations (the same cost as a cache hit for the cache where the access history lives in the cache hierarchy). For CopyHistory, we simulate the accesses of the software handler for eviction; in ClearHistory there is no handler for eviction since the data is discarded. Finally, we simulate each memory access required in the software manager to clear or copy software access histories.

Results from these initial simulations suggest Jikes LARDVM on LARDISH has overheads under 50% in most cases, comparable to those reported for C programs in [12], while lower on average. JVM accesses are not race-checked, so LARDISH can introduce less overhead than RADISH does for C programs in which all accesses are checked.

### 5.4 Jikes LARDVM Performance on x86

We evaluated the performance overhead of our JVM modifications alone on real x86 hardware (with compilers emitting no LARDx86 instructions) to measure the costs of tracking synchronization and memory management in software. We ran benchmarks from DaCapo with their largest input 10 times each with Jikes LARDVM and with an unmodified Jikes RVM, and with the mark-sweep and semispace collectors. Figure 3 shows the additional overheads of Jikes LARDVM normalized to unmodified Jikes RVM using the same garbage collector. Overheads average 22% for mark-sweep and 21% for semispace. All overheads are under 60% and most are under 20%. These results show that synchronization and memory management events can be tracked in software with relatively low overhead, even in our relatively unoptimized prototype.

## 6. Related Work

We believe LARD is the first approach for accurate dynamic data-race detection in high-level languages using hardware support or other low-level implementations.

### 6.1 General Data-Race Detection

Static data-race detectors, such as Chord [31] and RccJava [15], are imprecise, employing conservative analyses to avoid missing races at the cost of reporting false races. Race-free programming models such as Cyclone [19] and Deterministic Parallel Java [5] use conservative language restrictions to ensure race-freedom and other properties. Model checking approaches, as in Java RaceFinder [21], can use precise happens-before race detection to avoid reporting false races, but they remain subject to the limits of model checking, potentially missing races beyond the state-space they explore. This paper focuses on dynamic data-race detection, which can avoid precision problems for general programs.

This paper focuses on accurate dynamic data-race detection (§2). *Imprecise* dynamic data-race detectors use heuristics such as the *single protecting lock* pattern checked by the lockset algorithm in Eraser [38] to approximate data-race detection. While Eraser misses no races, it reports many false races since it does not reason about synchronization patterns beyond simple locking. Industrial-strength tools such as Helgrind [44], Google's ThreadSanitizer [39], and Intel's Inspector [20] also have limited precision and may impose high performance overheads. Other low-level data-race detectors have been proposed (CORD [36], HARD [48], SigRace [30], etc.), but they do not guarantee accuracy. Other data-race detectors, such as LiteRace [27], Pacer [8], and SOS [23], start from accurate algorithms and use sampling or other methods to trade full accuracy for performance. While the inaccuracy of all of these techniques renders them unsuitable for our goal of accurate data-race exceptions, our approach nonetheless could be applied to fundamentally inaccurate detectors. LARD could also bring hardware support to dynamic data-race detectors that generalize the current execution to detect data races possible in other executions [42, 47].

### 6.2 Sequential Consistency Violation Exceptions

DRFx [28, 41] and Conflict Exceptions [24] are proposals for precise low-level detection of data races that may violate sequential consistency. While LARD addresses full data-race detection, some of the same translation problems arise when using low-level support to check language-level sequential consistency. For example, ensuring sequential consistency for Java may not require sequential consistency of the full low-level execution, if run-time systems use careful lock-free techniques. Regardless, the stronger property of data-race freedom remains desirable in many contexts. Full data-race detection is a part of many other concurrency analyses.

### 6.3 Memory Management and Synchronization Issues

Others have previously identified memory management or custom synchronization as potential sources of inaccuracy, but have provided only partial solutions in general.

Helgrind [44] offers C preprocessor macros to annotate custom synchronization and allocation in C/C++ programs to reduce false race reports, but there is no way to turn off analysis of synchronization instrumented by default (*e.g.*, pthreads) or to specify memory movement in a way that preserves data-race detection access history. LARD provides a general interface to communicate the salient details of language-level synchronization and memory abstractions to the low-level race detector for accurate data-race detection.

Choi, *et al.*, mention that memory reuse and movement in garbage collection could break their JVM-level race detector, since it stores addresses of objects in its analysis state [11]. Their solution, a large enough heap size that garbage collection never occurs, is not feasible for production systems. Qi, *et al.*, address this problem in their MulticoreSDK [37] JVM race detector implementation with logical addresses for race-checked locations. As discussed in §3.4, this approach adds overhead to the memory access critical path and is poorly suited for low-level race detectors. LARD uses explicit movement of analysis state to follow the movement of objects, which occurs much less frequently than memory accesses.

RACEZ [40] is an offline, dynamic data-race detector for C/C++ that uses the imprecise lockset algorithm [38], sampling of memory accesses via hardware performance monitoring, and offline log analysis to improve run-time performance at the cost of missing some true races and reporting some false races. RACEZ uses memory allocation events as a *heuristic* to filter false positives, but the authors give no discussion of why tracking memory allocation is important – nor to what extent it is effective – in reducing false positives. Memory movement is not considered.

This prior work indicates that memory management affects the accuracy of data-race detection, but our work is the first to provide a single clear interface for managing all aspects of the gap between language-level and low-level memory abstractions and to make low-level data-race detection implementations accurate for language-level data-race detection.

## 7. Conclusions

LARD is a set of extensions to low-level data-race detectors and run-time systems. LARD's five extensions – distinguishing program vs. system memory accesses, distinguishing program vs. system synchronization, reporting memory reuse, reporting memory movement, and reporting thread identity – are sufficient for low-level detection of language-level data races. We have implemented a prototype system to detect data races in Java programs using a low-level data-race detector and modifications to a JVM. Our results demonstrate that basic low-level detection mechanisms alone do not provide accurate detection of language-level data races, but a LARD implementation does. LARD admits general hardware implementations of performance-critical race-checking logic, while allowing language implementations to customize the semantics of memory, synchronization, and thread identity. This result is a step toward feasible data-race exceptions for high-level languages.

## Acknowledgments

This work was supported in part by NSF grants CCF-1016495 and CCF-0811405; and C-FAR, one of six centers of STARnet, a Semiconductor Research Corporation program sponsored by MARCO and DARPA. Several colleagues contributed insights to this project: Joe Devietti assisted with the RADISH simulator; Laura Effinger-Dean discussed the C/C++ memory model semantics for allocation; Sebastian Burckhardt confirmed that thread identity can be an issue in analyses at the kernel level; Hadi Esmailzadeh, Jacob Nelson, and Adrian Sampson provided insights on hardware design; Tom Bergan, Joe Devietti, and Brandon Lucia gave helpful feedback on the manuscript. Finally, our anonymous reviewers gave insightful and constructive feedback that improved the presentation of our work.

## References

[1] Sarita V. Adve and Hans-J. Boehm. Memory Models: A Case for Rethinking Parallel Languages and Hardware. *CACM*, 53, August 2010.

[2] Bowen Alpern, C. Richard Attanasio, John J. Barton, Anthony Cocchi, Susan Flynn Hummel, Derek Lieber, Ton Ngo, Mark F. Mergen, Janice C. Shepherd, and Stephen E.

Smith. Implementing Jalapeño in Java. In *OOPSLA*, 1999. http://www.jikesrvm.org.

[3] S. M. Blackburn, R. Garner, C. Hoffman, A. M. Khan, K. S. McKinley, R. Bentzur, A. Diwan, D. Feinberg, D. Frampton, S. Z. Guyer, M. Hirzel, A. Hosking, M. Jump, H. Lee, J. E. B. Moss, A. Phansalkar, D. Stefanović, T. VanDrunen, D. von Dincklage, and B. Wiedermann. The DaCapo Benchmarks: Java Benchmarking Development and Analysis. In *OOPSLA*, 2006.

[4] Stephen M. Blackburn, Perry Cheng, and Kathryn S. McKinley. Oil and Water? High Performance Garbage Collection in Java with MMTk. In *ICSE*, 2004.

[5] Robert L. Bocchino, Jr., Vikram Adve, Danny Dig, Sarita V. Adve, Stephen Heumann, Rakesh Komuravelli, Jeffrey Overbey, Patrick Simmons, Hyojin Sung, and Mohsen Vakilian. A Type and Effect System for Deterministic Parallel Java. In *OOPSLA*, 2009.

[6] Hans-J. Boehm and Sarita V. Adve. You Don't Know Jack About Shared Variables or Memory Models. *CACM*, 55(2):48–54, February 2012.

[7] Hans-Juergen Boehm and Sarita V. Adve. Foundations of the C++ Concurrency Memory Model. In *PLDI*, 2008.

[8] Michael D. Bond, Katherine E. Coons, and Kathryn S. McKinley. PACER: Proportional Detection of Data Races. In *PLDI*, 2010.

[9] C++ Standards Comittee, Stefanus Du Toit, *ed.* Working Draft, Standard for Programming Language C++. 2012. http://www.open-std.org/jtc1/sc22/wg21/docs/papers/2012/n3376.pdf.

[10] Luis Ceze, Joseph Devietti, Brandon Lucia, and Shaz Qadeer. A Case for System Support for Concurrency Exceptions. In *HotPar*, 2009.

[11] Jong-Deok Choi, Keunwoo Lee, Alexey Loginov, Robert O'Callahan, Vivek Sarkar, and Manu Sridharan. Efficient and Precise Datarace Detection for Multithreaded Object-Oriented Programs. In *PLDI*, 2002.

[12] Joseph Devietti, Benjamin P. Wood, Karin Strauss, Luis Ceze, Dan Grossman, and Shaz Qadeer. RADISH: Always-On Sound and Complete Race Detection in Software and Hardware. In *ISCA*, 2012.

[13] Tayfun Elmas, Shaz Qadeer, and Serdar Tasiran. Goldilocks: A Race and Transaction-Aware Java Runtime. In *PLDI*, 2007.

[14] Colin Fidge. Logical Time in Distributed Computing Systems. *Computer*, 24, August 1991.

[15] Cormac Flanagan and Stephen N. Freund. Type-Based Race Detection for Java. In *PLDI*, 2000.

[16] Cormac Flanagan and Stephen N. Freund. FastTrack: Efficient and Precise Dynamic Race Detection. In *PLDI*, 2009.

[17] Cormac Flanagan and Stephen N. Freund. RedCard: Redundant Check Elimination For Dynamic Race Detectors. In *ECOOP*, 2013.

[18] Cormac Flanagan, Stephen N. Freund, and Jaeheon Yi. Velodrome: A Sound And Complete Dynamic Atomicity Checker for Multithreaded Programs. In *PLDI*, 2008.

[19] Dan Grossman. Type-Safe Multithreading in Cyclone. In *TLDI*, 2003.

[20] Intel. Inpector XE. http://software.intel.com/en-us/intel-inspector-xe, 2013.

[21] Huafeng Jin, Tuba Yavuz-Kahveci, and Beverly A. Sanders. Java Memory Model-Aware Model Checking. *TACAS*, 7214, 2012.

[22] Leslie Lamport. Time, Clocks, and the Ordering of Events in a Distributed System. *CACM*, 21, July 1978.

[23] Du Li, Witawas Srisa-an, and Matthew B. Dwyer. SOS: Saving Time in Dynamic Race Detection with Stationary Analysis. In *OOPSLA*, 2011.

[24] Brandon Lucia, Luis Ceze, Karin Strauss, Shaz Qadeer, and Hans-Juergen Boehm. Conflict Exceptions: Simplifying Concurrent Language Semantics with Precise Hardware Exceptions for Data-Races. In *ISCA*, 2010.

[25] Chi-Keung Luk, Robert Cohn, Robert Muth, Harish Patil, Artur Klauser, Geoff Lowney, Steven Wallace, Vijay Janapa Reddi, and Kim Hazelwood. PIN: Building Customized Program Analysis Tools With Dynamic Instrumentation. In *PLDI*, 2005. http://www.pintool.org.

[26] Jeremy Manson, William Pugh, and Sarita V. Adve. The Java Memory Model. In *POPL*, 2005.

[27] Daniel Marino, Madanlal Musuvathi, and Satish Narayanasamy. LiteRace: Effective Sampling for Lightweight Data-race Detection. In *PLDI*, 2009.

[28] Daniel Marino, Abhayendra Singh, Todd D. Millstein, Madanlal Musuvathi, and Satish Narayanasamy. DRFx: A Simple and Efficient Memory Model for Concurrent Programming Languages. In *PLDI*, 2010.

[29] Friedemann Mattern. Virtual Time and Global States of Distributed Systems. In *International Workshop on Parallel and Distributed Algorithms*, pages 215–226, 1989.

[30] Abdullah Muzahid, Dario Suárez, Shanxiang Qi, and Josep Torrellas. SigRace: Signature-Based Data Race Detection. In *ISCA*, 2009.

[31] Mayur Naik, Alex Aiken, and John Whaley. Effective Static Race Detection for Java. In *PLDI*, 2006.

[32] Robert H. B. Netzer and Barton P. Miller. What Are Race Conditions?: Some Issues and Formalizations. *ACM Letters on Programming Languages and Systems*, 1(1):7488, March 1992.

[33] Marek Olszewski, Jason Ansel, and Saman Amarasinghe. Kendo: Efficient Deterministic Multithreading in Software. In *ASPLOS*, 2009.

[34] Marek Olszewski, Qin Zhao, David Koh, Jason Ansel, and Saman Amarasinghe. Aikido: Accelerating Shared Data Dynamic Analyses. In *ASPLOS*, 2012.

[35] Filip Pizlo, Erez Petrank, and Bjarne Steensgaard. A Study of Concurrent Real-Time Garbage Collectors. In *PLDI*, 2008.

[36] Milos Prvulovic. CORD: Cost-effective (and nearly overhead-free) Order-Recording and Data race detection. In *HPCA*, 2006.

[37] Yao Qi, Raja Das, Zhi Da Luo, and Martin Trotter. MulticoreSDK: A Practical and Efficient Data Race Detector for Real-World Applications. In *PADTAD*, 2009.

[38] Stefan Savage, Michael Burrows, Greg Nelson, Patrick Sobalvarro, and Thomas Anderson. Eraser: A Dynamic Data Race Detector for Multithreaded Programs. *TOCS*, 15(4), 1997.

[39] Konstantin Serebryany and Timur Iskhodzhanov. ThreadSanitizer: Data Race Detection in Practice. In *Workshop on Binary Instrumentation and Applications*, 2009.

[40] Tianwei Sheng, Neil Vachharajani, Stephane Eranian, Robert Hundt, Wenguang Chen, and Weimin Zheng. RACEZ: a Lightweight and Non-Invasive Race Detection Tool for Production Applications. In *ICSE*, 2011.

[41] Abhayendra Singh, Daniel Marino, Satish Narayanasamy, Todd D. Millstein, and Madanlal Musuvathi. Efficient Processor Support for DRFx, a Memory Model with Exceptions. In *ASPLOS*, 2011.

[42] Yannis Smaragdakis, Jacob Evans, Caitlin Sadowski, Jaeheon Yi, and Cormac Flanagan. Sound Predictive Race Detection in Polynomial Time. In *POPL*, 2012.

[43] L. A. Smith, J. M. Bull, and J. Obdrzálek. A Parallel Java Grande Benchmark Suite. In *Supercomputing*, 2001.

[44] Valgrind Project. Helgrind: a thread error detector. http://valgrind.org/docs/manual/hg-manual.html, 2013.

[45] Jaroslav Ševčík. Safe optimisations for shared-memory concurrent programs. In *PLDI*, 2011.

[46] Benjamin P. Wood, Luis Ceze, and Dan Grossman. Data-Race Exceptions Have Benefits Beyond the Memory Model. In *MSPC*, 2011.

[47] Xinwei Xie and Jingling Xue. Acculock: Accurate and Efficient Detection of Data Races. In *CGO*, 2011.

[48] P. Zhou, R. Teodorescu, and Y. Zhou. HARD: Hardware-Assisted Lockset-based Race Detection. In *HPCA*, 2007.

## A. A Canonical Race Detector

The algorithm optimized by the state-of-the-art accurate software [16] and hardware [12] race detectors uses *vector clocks* [14, 29] to represent the happens-before graph. Each thread maintains its own local integer logical time, starting at zero. A *vector clock* contains an integer logical clock for each thread, indexed by thread ID. Each thread maintains a vector clock representing the last logical time in each thread that happened before the current logical time in this thread. (The $i$th entry in thread $i$'s vector clock is its local logical time.) Each lock in the program also has an associated vector clock representing the last logical time in each thread that happened before the last release of the lock.

Synchronization updates the vector clocks of threads and locks as follows: When thread $t$ forks thread $u$, thread $u$'s vector clock is initialized with a copy of thread $t$'s current vector clock. Afterwards, both threads' local clocks are incremented. When thread $t$ joins thread $u$, thread $t$'s vector clock is updated to be the pairwise maximum of the current vector clocks of threads $t$ and $u$. When thread $t$ acquires lock $l$, thread $t$'s vector clock is updated to be the pairwise maximum of the current vector clocks of thread $t$ and lock $l$. When thread $t$ releases lock $l$, lock $l$'s vector clock is updated to the pairwise maximum of the vector clocks of thread $t$ and lock $l$. (Note this maximum is always equivalent to thread $t$'s vector clock, since lock $l$'s vector clock was merged into thread $t$'s vector clock on the preceding acquire, and no other thread may have released the lock since.) Other types of synchronization are handled similarly: incoming synchronization merges into the thread's vector clock and outgoing synchronization merges from the thread's vector clock and then advances the thread's local time.

Each memory location has an access history storing the thread that performed the last write to the location and the local time at which it performed that write, as well as, for each thread, the last local time at which that thread read from the location. When a memory access is executed, it is first checked against the access history. On any access to $x$, we check that the current thread's vector clock entry for the thread $t$ that last wrote $x$ is greater than or equal to the time at which $t$ last wrote to $x$. On a write to $x$, we check, for each thread $t$, that the current thread's vector clock entry for $t$ is greater than or equal to the time at which $t$ last read from $x$. If any of these checks fails, a data race is reported, otherwise the access is safe and it must be recorded in the access history. For a write, we set the last writer of $x$ to the current thread and the last write clock to be the current thread's current local time. As an optimization, we typically zero all the last reads as well. On a write, we set the last read of $x$ by the current thread to the current thread's current local time.

# EnCore: Exploiting System Environment and Correlation Information for Misconfiguration Detection

Jiaqi Zhang[†], Lakshminarayanan Renganarayana[§], Xiaolan Zhang[§], Niyu Ge[§], Vasanth Bala[§], Tianyin Xu[†], Yuanyuan Zhou[†]

[†]University of California San Diego
{jiz013, tixu, yyzhou}@cs.ucsd.edu

[§]IBM Watson Research Center
{lrengan, cxzhang, niyuge, vbala}@us.ibm.com

## Abstract

As software systems become more complex and configurable, failures due to misconfigurations are becoming a critical problem. Such failures often have serious functionality, security and financial consequences. Further, diagnosis and remediation for such failures require reasoning across the software stack and its operating environment, making it difficult and costly.

We present a framework and tool called EnCore to automatically detect software misconfigurations. EnCore takes into account two important factors that are unexploited before: the interaction between the configuration settings and the executing environment, as well as the rich correlations between configuration entries. We embrace the emerging trend of viewing systems as data, and exploit this to extract information about the execution environment in which a configuration setting is used. EnCore learns configuration rules from a given set of sample configurations. With training data enriched with the execution context of configurations, EnCore is able to learn a broad set of configuration anomalies that spans the entire system. EnCore is effective in detecting both injected errors and known real-world problems – it finds 37 new misconfigurations in Amazon EC2 public images and 24 new configuration problems in a commercial private cloud. By systematically exploiting environment information and by learning correlation rules across multiple configuration settings, *EnCore* detects $1.6x$ to $3.5x$ more misconfiguration anomalies than previous approaches.

***Categories and Subject Descriptors*** D.4.5 [*Operating Systems*]: Reliability

***Keywords*** Configuration, Data Mining, Inference



*ASPLOS '14,* March 1–5, 2014, Salt Lake City, Utah, USA.
Copyright © 2014 ACM 978-1-4503-2305-5/14/03...$15.00.
http://dx.doi.org/10.1145/2541940.2541983

## 1 Introduction

As software systems become more flexible and feature-rich, their configurations have become highly complicated. For example, MySQL and Apache httpd server, individually, has more than 200 configuration entries. As a result, correctly configuring software systems has become a highly complex task that renders manual effort difficult and error-prone [21, 41, 43, 44]. Studies show that configuration errors are both common and highly detrimental to businesses [29, 30, 41, 46]. Not only do misconfigurations lead to lost business due to system unavailability [1, 19, 24], they also demand substantial resources be devoted to troubleshooting [43, 44]. In one particular case of a large commercial corporation, misconfiguration has contributed to as many as 27% of the trouble tickets in the customer support database [46]. The situation is exacerbated by the fact that many organizations impose security and performance policies for best practices. Configuration settings that are otherwise valid from a functional perspective may not conform to these policies, leading to security flaws or performance anomalies. Detecting such sub-optimal configurations is also highly desireable.

A promising approach for taming the configuration problem (or the configuration hell [43]) is to automatically check a set of configuration settings for potential errors before deployment, just as one would normally do with application source code. However, most configuration files used today lack the rich structural and semantic information available in programming languages which enable sophisticated analysis for errors [40, 41]. To overcome the limitation, researchers have attacked the problem of misconfiguration detection by learning, for each configuration entry, the common values used in a large collection of configurations (i.e. the training set), and flagging those values that deviate from the common ones as potential misconfigurations [34, 41, 42].

While proven useful in some scenarios, the potential of these tools [34, 41, 42] is greatly limited due to the simplistic treatment of each configuration setting as a string literal in isolation. Configuration settings bridge applications to their operating environment. Therefore the diagno-

**Related Config:** *extension_dir*= "C:\Program Files\...\php\php_mysqli.dll"
**Root Cause:** *extension_dir* should be a directory, not regular file
*PHP*

(a) Wrong value causes modules not loaded. Environment information needs to be considered to detect the problem.

**Related Config:** *datadir*=/var/lib/mysql
*user* = mysql — ***should be owner***
**Root Cause:** *user* is not owner of *datadir*, causing permission denial error
*MySQL*

(b) Wrong file owner causes permission problem. The correlation between different configuration entries needs to be examined.

Figure 1: **Real-world system problems caused by misconfigurations.** The root causes of these problem are hidden in (a) environment factors, and (b) the correlation between two configuration entries. Neither of these configuration errors can be detected by analyzing configuration values because (a) the value varies widely in the training set, and (b) the values are common in the training set and no correlation is considered.

sis and remediation of misconfigurations requires reasoning across both sides. Figure 1 shows two real-world misconfigurations, neither of which can be detected with existing approaches. In Figure 1(a), `extension_dir` specifies the location of the extension libraries. While it should be a directory, the user incorrectly supplied a regular file. Existing approaches that detect errors by relying on anomalies in the configuration values cannot detect this error because the value of `extension_dir` often varies across a set of samples and hence cannot be meaningfully considered as an anomaly [41]. However, by analyzing a set of sample values for this setting in the context of the executing system, one can detect that the value should be a directory and not a file.

In the example shown in Figure 1(b), `datadir` points to the directory where MySQL stores the table data, and `user` specifies the system user id with which MySQL operates on the data. MySQL requires that the user `mysql` should own the `datadir`, while in this example this is not the case in this example. Existing methods that compare the values of these configuration settings across a set of samples cannot detect this error because detecting this error requires reasoning along two dimensions: (i) correlation between multiple configuration settings – correlating `user` and `datadir`, and (ii) validation of the configuration settings in the context of the system (environment) they are used – checking in the system if `datadir` is owned by user `mysql`.

In order to detect the misconfigurations that are not explicitly reflected in their text values, we need to broaden the scope of the analysis and look beyond single configuration settings. Based on our observations (described in Section 2) we propose to widen the analysis to include two important factors: (i) multiple configuration settings and (ii) the execution context or environment.

Cloud computing and related technologies such as virtual machine images have made it possible to easily capture and analyze the execution environment of systems. This ability has enabled researchers to view systems as structured data [11]. Our approach embraces this view of *systems as data* and exploits it to extract the environment information relevant to configuration settings in a system.

### 1.1 Contributions

Our contributions include (i) a general framework for systematic inclusion of the properties of execution environment, (ii) a tool, called *EnCore*, for efficient learning and effective checking of misconfigurations and (iii) a set of findings from experimental evaluation of the limitations of using off-the-shelf data mining techniques for misconfiguration detection.

Our tool *EnCore* provides a generic configuration data analysis framework that can be readily used for learning misconfiguration rules based on correlation among multiple configuration entries. It also provides features to capture domain knowledge and best practices. The framework has a novel type inference scheme that exploits environment information to derive semantic types for each configuration setting. It also includes an annotator which augments each configuration entry with all its environment related properties. The type information significantly speeds up the rule inference process, and reduces the number of false positives.

We demonstrate the effectiveness of *EnCore* in rules learning and misconfiguration detection from three widely used server applications: Apache, MySQL, and PHP. By systematically exploiting environment information and learning correlation rules across multiple configuration settings, *EnCore* detects 1.6 to 3.5 times more misconfigurations than previous approaches.

To the best of our knowledge, our work is the first one to combine environment information and correlations among multiple configuration settings to automatically generate an effective configuration anomaly detector.

## 2 Design Principle

In this section, we elaborate the findings that motivate and influence the design choices of *EnCore* . Our design principles derive from observations made in two exercises: the study of configuration entries, and our experience in applying off-the-shelf data mining techniques for misconfiguration detection.

### 2.1 Characteristics of Configuration Parameters

To understand the use and importance of the environment information and correlations between configuration entries, we manually studied the configuration entries in 4 representative server applications – Apache, MySQL, PHP, and sshd. In this section, we describe our key observations on the correlation characteristics, which validate the prevalence of the phenomena, and motivates *EnCore*. Together with the examples in Figure 1, they show the benefits of exploiting the environment and correlation in misconfiguration detection.

**Finding 1: Configuration entries are not isolated, but have relation to the execution environment.**

| Apps | Total Studied | Env-Related | Correlated |
|---|---|---|---|
| Apache | 94 | 29 (31%) | 42 (46%) |
| MySQL | 113 | 19 (17%) | 31 (27%) |
| PHP | 53 | 16 (30%) | 20 (38%) |
| sshd | 57 | 12 (21%) | 29 (51%) |

Table 1: **Number (percentage) of configuration parameters that are associated with environment and correlations.** "Total" is the number of entries we examined. "Env-Related" is the number of entries related to the environment. "Correlated" is the number of entries correlated with the others. Apache includes the entries of two main modules: core and mpm; PHP includes the core entries; MySQL's entries are randomly sampled.

In our study, many configuration entries connect the application functionalities to its execution environment, and the values of these configuration entries are associated with the properties of the environment. In other words, these configuration values should not be seen as arbitrary strings. Rather, they reflects the system properties, and have rich semantic information. *This is the key characteristic that distinguishes them from other program variables.*

Although neglected by most existing work, the environment information is critical for detecting a range of configuration errors. Taking the example in Figure 1(a), if a misconfiguration detector catches the fact that *extension_dir* should be a directory in the file system, it can easily identify the one in Figure 1(a) as an anomaly since it is not a directory.

Table 1 shows the statistics of configuration entries whose values refer to system environment objects in the studied applications, where a significant portion, more than 20% of the configuration entries, point to environment objects. With the abundant environment information we can extract from systems, there is great potential for exploiting them in misconfiguration detection.

**Finding 2: Many configuration entries are correlated.**

From Figure 1(b), we have seen that the setting of one configuration entry depends on the setting of the other entries, or the environment objects. Thus, the correlation information is essential for correctly setting these configuration entries and for detecting errors. Though some types of correlations (e.g., the equality and inequality) can be observed in the textual values, many correlations are often indirect or even implicit. For example, in Figure 1(b), the correlation between `datadir` and `user` goes beyond the textual values and requires one to understand the semantics of the two entries.

As shown in Table 1, around one third to half of the configuration entries have correlation with each other. This indicates that the correlation among configuration entries should be an important component in a misconfiguration detection tool. Unfortunately, impaired by treating configuration values as textual strings, the state-of-the-art detection tools are limited and unable to leverage these correlation information.

| | Apache | MySQL | PHP |
|---|---|---|---|
| Original | 5773 | 175 | 1672 |
| Augmented | 9853 | 555 | 1942 |
| Binominal | 12921 | 859 | 2374 |

Table 2: **The number of attributes generated using data mining methods in the studied software.** "Original" is the number of attributes originated from the configuration files. "Augmented" is the number after environment infomation integration. "Binomial" is the number after conversion from nominal data to binomial.

## 2.2 Challenges in Applying Data Mining

Since our goal is to extract the configuration correlations, either with the executing environment or between different configuration entries, the straightforward idea is to apply data mining methods to learn the association rules, as proposed in [34] and shown to be effective in other works [45, 47]. We started out by trying to use off-the-shelf data mining methods (association rule mining) on our configuration data set. We tried standard association rule mining algorithms including Apriori [33] and FP-Growth [20] provided by two widely used data mining tool sets – Weka [10] and RapidMiner [8]. In this section, we describe our experience and findings of applying these data mining methods on the configuration data and motivate the design choices of *EnCore*. In the discussion, we mainly use the results from FP-Growth as Apriori does not scale to large data sets [23, 35]).

**Finding 3: The state-of-the-art mining algorithms are not scalable to handle the scale of configuration settings.**

Configuration files (especially after augmented with system information) usually contain a large number of settings, which are turned into *attributes* in data mining algorithms. Table 2 shows the number of configuration settings (in terms of columns) in the studied software. While the number of unique configuration entries are limited, the mining algorithms treat each occurrence of an entry as a different attribute. Further, the addition of environment information as additional attributes (described in Section 4) increases the total number of attributes. At the same time, Apriori and FP-Growth suffer from the boolean discretization problem [38] – before the mining process, the nominal attributes need to be discretized into boolean values, which causes a dramatic growth in the number of attributes. Table 3 shows the execution time and size of the intermediate frequent item set for Apache, MySQL and PHP, where the number of settings range from 100 to 200+. The experiments were carried on a server with 8 processors and 16GB of memory. Note that when the number of settings increase, both the execution time and the size of frequent item set increase exponentially, making it impossible to reason about the results or even finish the experiments.

Feature selection (and reduction) is a common technique used to attack the scalability problems of data mining methods. There are two approaches: (i) scheme-independent selection and (ii) wrapper methods that involve the machine

| entries | Apache | | | MySQL | | | PHP | | |
|---|---|---|---|---|---|---|---|---|---|
| | attrs | time(s) | freq. | attrs | time(s) | freq. | attrs | time(s) | freq. |
| 100 | 219 | 0.15 | 6K | 217 | 0.13 | 13.9K | 150 | 0.52 | 6K |
| 150 | 436 | 1.6 | 173K | 286 | 62 | 3.8M | 235 | 3.8 | 542K |
| 175 | 503 | 170 | 14M | 315 | 358 | 10M | 279 | 106 | 4.9M |
| 200+ | 554 | OOM | - | 343+ | OOM | - | 336+ | OOM | - |

Table 3: **Time cost (in seconds) and size of frequent item set with different number of attributes.** With more than 200 attributes, some experiments are terminated with Out Of Memory (OOM) exception. The entries are randomly selected. The number of attributes refer to the scale involved in the mining after adding enviornment attributes and discretization.

learning methods themselves to decide the useful attributes. Neither of these two schemes can directly help reduce the number of attributes in our case. The first method requires the users to select attributes based on domain knowledge [12]. Although both Weka and RapidMiner provide interface for such selection, it is not possible for the users to choose from hundreds to thousands of configuration attributes without any clue on what might be a better combination. The second method, data mining techniques developed to wrap themselves in the attribute eliminating process [16, 37], are mostly useful for classification purposes and are not suited for the correlation learning.

In summary, off-the-shelf data mining techniques do not scale well to the large number of attributes in the configuration data enriched with environment information. We attack this scalability challenge in *EnCore* by using a type-based and template-guided approach to learning. As described in Section 5.1, *EnCore* effectively addresses the scalability problem by restricting the types of the involved attributes and limiting the rule types; it also expresses the various correlations by providing different learning templates.

**Finding 4: Frequent-item-sets style relations are not expressive enough to describe domain-specific correlations.**

In the data mining community, correlations among different objects are usually described using frequent item sets or linear regression models. While they are sufficient in describing co-occurrence (things likely appearing together) and linear relationship of objects, they cannot capture the complex relations between configurations. For example, a "directory" configuration entry could be concatenated with another "file name" entry to form a "file path" entry; the file specified by the "file path" entry can be owned by the user specified by a "user name" entry. Clearly, these complex domain-specific correlations cannot be expressed by frequent item sets. This motivates the need for new techniques to learn the correlations among configuration settings. As described in Section 5.1, *EnCore* addresses this challenge via rule templates that capture the complex correlation patterns (not actual correlations, but patterns of correlations).

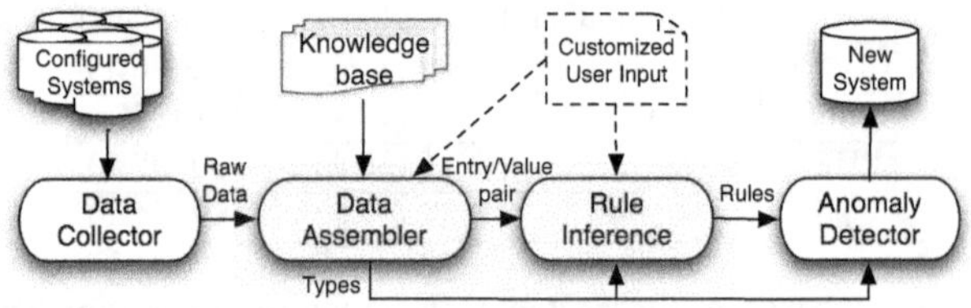


Figure 2: **The architecture of *EnCore*.** Both of the data assembler and the rule inference can be customized by users optionally.

## 3 System Architecture

Based on the above observations, we propose a framework and tool, called *EnCore*, which incorporates both system environment information and the correlations among multiple configuration entries to effectively and efficiently infer the best-practice rules from the the configured systems. These inferred rules are further applied by a configuration checker to detect configuration anomalies.

As depicted in Figure 2, *EnCore* has four major steps: data collecting, data assembling, rule inferencing, and anomaly detection. This section briefly describes each component.

**Data Collector.** The data collector gathers the necessary information from the training set (a set of configured systems). Its output is the raw data including all files relevant for analysis, as well as additional environment information in text format. Since we assume that the users have access to the images, privacy is not of concern. But if needed, techniques such as FTN [22] can be used to alleviate the issue.

**Data Assembler.** The data assembler first parses the collector's output and converts them (both configuration files and environment data) to uniform key-value pairs. It then infers the type of each configuration entry, which forms the foundation of the *EnCore* analysis framework, as all subsequent analyses incorporate the type information. Each configuration entry is then augmented with the additional environment information collected from the system. The assembler relies on a set of heuristics to infer the predefined types, but it also accepts an optional user input file that specifies heuristics to infer new types. The details are described in Section 4.

After data assembly, the environment data and the original configuration entries are integrated together, and treated equally in the following components. Therefore we use "attribute" to refer to both of them in the following sections.

**Rule Generator.** *EnCore* learns the best-practice configuration rules deployed in the training set. In order to address the challenges discussed in Section 2.2 and cater the learning process for the characteristics of configuration files, *EnCore* utilizes the rule templates, either predefined or user specified, to guide the learning process. The templates specify the possible relationships (e.g. association rules or file ownership) among configuration entry types, not entry values. Thus, a small set of templates can cover a wide range of concrete rules. Section 7 shows that a total of 79 concrete rules are generated from the 11 predefined templates in 3 applications. The template concept is shown to be also effective in other works [18].

Templates are formalized with a concise grammar to facilitate the creation of new templates by users of *EnCore*. For example, the following template

[A<FilePath>]=>[B<UserName>] *T1*

specifies that 'an entry of type *UserName* is the owner of another entry of type *FilePath*', where the types are inferred in the previous step. Based on the given templates and input key-value pairs, the rule generator iterates over all the possible combinations of attributes and selects concrete rules that best fit the templates. A concrete rule has the placeholders (e.g. A and B in *T1*) filled with concrete attribute names. For example, after learning from the training set that contains images of MySQL, a concrete rule *datadir→user* is instantiated from the template *T1*. This rule dictates that the user specified by the *user* entry should be the owner of the directory specified by the *datadir* entry, and helps detect misconfigurations such as the one shown in Figure 1(b). This step also prunes possible false rules with multiple filters. The output of the inferences are the rules that can be utilized by the anomaly detector. More details are in Section 5.

**Anomaly Detector.** The anomaly detector detects the rule violations in the configurations of the target systems. Its input is the rules, the type information, and the target systems. It outputs warnings whenever it finds an anomaly, such as a violation of a correlation rule, a wrong type, or a suspicious value. The results are ranked based on the type of the violation and the underlying independent statistical model. Since the checking and the learning are cleanly separated, the learned rules can be reused to check different systems. More details are in Section 6.

*EnCore* can be used either after a new system is configured, or after a failure happens. The user inputs the training set to *EnCore* together with the system to be checked. *EnCore* reports warnings that pinpoint to the potential problematic configuration entries. The usage scenario is similar to that of other misconfiguration detection tools [41, 42], except that the user can also optionally provide *EnCore* with additional types and templates that are specific to the user's environment.

# 4 Data Assembler

The data assembler takes the raw system files including the target configuration files, as well as the system environment information such as metadata of files in the file system, system configurations, and hardware specifications. It parses these files, infers the types of configuration entries, and augments each configuration entry with the environment information according to its type. The output is a set of well formed key-value pairs. Figure 3 summarizes the process.

## 4.1 Parsing Configuration Files

The data assembler first converts the configuration files from application-specific format to uniform key-value pairs. We

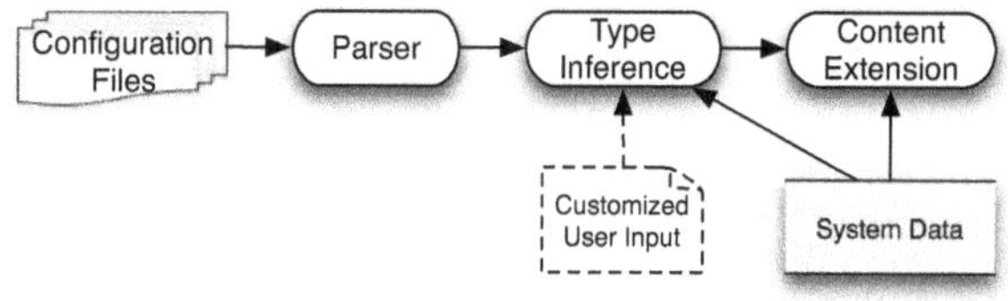


Figure 3: **Data assembling.** In addition to the configuration files, the assembler also takes the system environment data and users' input for type inference and augmenting the configuration entries.

build the parser on top of Augeas [27], a general configuration file parser supporting various software configuration formats. Augeas provides an extensible interface to import other parsers, enabling users to easily import their own configuration parser into *EnCore*. After parsing the configuration files, the assembler stores and organizes all the data in a *.csv* file. Each column represents a structured configuration entry generated by the parser, and each row represents the values of all the entries in a system.

## 4.2 Inferring Configuration Entry Types

*EnCore* relies on the type information of each configuration entry for further environment data integration and correlation detection. Similar to previous work on type inferring [31], *EnCore* needs to have the domain knowledge of what the types are and how to determine them.

Without the source code information which is required in [31], the type inference employed in *EnCore* is a novel two-step process that leverages both syntactic patterns of data values as well as the environment information of the system. The first step performs *syntactic matching*, making a crude *guess* at the type of the entry using a predefined syntactic pattern. For example, any string that contains a slash is a potential `FilePath` type. This step is followed by a heavy-weight *semantic verification* that validates the type by checking the corresponding external resources (such as the file system). For example, if an entry value is classified as a `FilePath` type by the first step, the verification searches the full file system meta-data to validate the existence of the path in the file system. The first step prunes away most of the improbable types , making the inference efficient; the second step guarantees the inference accuracy. The combination of the syntactic matching and heavy-weight semantic verification proves to be both effective and accurate (see Section 7.2). Table 4 shows the details of each step and default types *EnCore* infers.

*EnCore* is able to infer most configuration entry types in the taxonomy of [31]. Certain types such as `TimeInterval` and `Count`, however, are not easily distinguishable, due to the identical syntactic patterns and lack of verification methods. Since our purpose of type inference is to detect type violations and to provide a better foundation for correlation detection instead of precise type analysis, we consider this limitation acceptable – missing this information means possible lower rule detection efficiency as it affects the effec-

| Types | Syntactic | Semantic |
|---|---|---|
| FilePath | /.+(/.+)* | File System |
| UserName | [a-zA-Z][a-zA-Z0-9_]* | /etc/passwd |
| GroupName | [a-zA-Z][a-zA-Z0-9_]* | /etc/group |
| IPAdress | [\d]{1,3}(.[\d]{1,3}){3} | N/A |
| PortNumber | [\d]+ | /etc/services |
| FileName | [\w _-]+.[\w _-]+ | File System |
| Number | [0-9]+[.0-9]* | N/A |
| URL | [a-z]+://.* | N/A |
| PartialFilePath | /?.+/(.+)* | File System |
| MIME Types | [\w/-. ]+ | IANA [3] |
| Charset | [ \w]+ | IANA |
| Language | [a-zA-Z]{2} | ISO 639-1 |
| Size | [\d]+[KMGT] | N/A |
| Boolean | Values Set | N/A |
| String | N/A | N/A |

Table 4: **Predefined type and inference methods.** Due to space limit, we show here simplified regular expressions used in syntactic matching. More complicated expressions are used for other values, e.g., IPv6 address, which is not shown in the table.

| AttrType/Example/Ref. | Augmented Attributes | Type | Value |
|---|---|---|---|
| FilePath datadir=/usr/data File System | datadir.owner | UserName | mysql |
| | datadir.group | GroupName | mysql |
| | datadir.type | Enum | dir |
| | datadir.permission | Permission | 664 |
| | datadir.contents | String | dirDes |
| | datadir.hasDir | Boolean | True |
| | datadir.hasSymLink | Boolean | True |
| IPAddress AllowFrom=10.0.1.1 RFC 1918, RFC 4193 | AllowFrom.Local | Boolean | True |
| | AllowFrom.IPv6 | Boolean | False |
| | AllowFrom.AnyAddr | Boolean | False |
| UserName user=mysql /etc/group | user.isRootGroup | Boolean | False |
| | user.isAdmin | Boolean | False |
| | user.isGroup | GroupName | mysql |

(a) **Augmented attributes for eligible types by default.** For each configuration entry type, *EnCore* augments it with attributes that reflect system context. Each augmented type is shown with an example entry, the information source in the system (we call it reference) used to compute the augmented values, and the values of the example augmented attributes. Each augmented attribute is assigned with a type.

| Env Type | Augmented Attributes |
|---|---|
| Sys Config | Sys.IPAddress, Sys.HostName, Sys.FSType, Sys.Users |
| OS Related | OS.DistName, OS.Version, OS.SEStatus |
| Hw Spec | CPU.Threads, CPU.Freq, MemSize, HDD.AvailSpace |

(b) **Augmented attributes for environment info by default.** The attributes are gathered from corresponding files or commands. *EnCore* can be easily customized to consider more data.

Table 5: **Default augmented environment information.**

tiveness of type-based attribute selection (see Section 5), but does not affect the effectiveness. As described in Section 5, we use other ways to accelerate the detection process.

### 4.3 Environment Information Integration

One of the essential ideas of *EnCore* is to enrich the original data with additional environment information, and take them into consideration in the analysis. *EnCore* selects types inferred in Section 4.2 that carry system semantics, and augments them by attaching new attributes that represent the properties of each type. For example, an entry type of `FilePath` can be augmented with a new attribute that tells whether it is a directory or a regular file. We call these attributes *augmented attributes*. Certain environment data that is independent of the configuration entries are also collected, such as the system hardware specification.

Table 5a shows the types that *EnCore* augments by default. For example, for each entry of type `FilePath`, we attach seven attributes: the owner and group information, whether it's a directory or file, the permission associated with the object, and if it is a directory, the contents of the directory, whether it contains sub directories, and whether it contains symbolic links. This information is retrieved from the file system meta-data collected by the collector. Different types have different attributes, whose values are determined using different sources of information (see Table 5a.)

As shown in the examples in Table 5a, the augmented attributes are directly appended to the original entry names with a dot separator. Table 5b shows the environment information that is independent of the configuration files. These attributes are appended to the existing csv file as additional columns, and are treated equally as other attributes in the rule inference process.

*EnCore* is designed to be highly customizable. Section 5.3 details how *EnCore* can be customized to infer new types and to include new attributes.

## 5 Rules Inference

With the extended configuration data as the training set, *EnCore* infers rules using a template-based method. The inferred rules are then written to a file with detailed description of the attributes involved and the relation type, so that they can be used to perform the checking against the target systems.

### 5.1 Template-Guided Inference Based on Types

To overcome the challenges faced by directly applying data mining techniques (Section 2.2), the rule inference in *EnCore* adopts a template-guided approach. A template aims at capturing the common correlations among the configuration entries and system information, such as the association rules or the file ownership relations in Figure 1(b). Unlike Lint-like checkers [2, 4, 7] which require hand-written rules, *EnCore* only needs a guidance on the type of rules that the users are interested in. It infers concrete rules automatically from the training set.

Figure 4 shows three example templates, their meanings, and the concrete rules inferred from them in different softwares. For instance, the template in Figure 4(a) defines the possible ownership relationship between two entries. Learning from the system images with MySQL, *EnCore* infers the concrete rule that describes the ownership relation between

**Template**: [A<FilePath>] => [B<UserName>]
**Rule:** DataDir => user //MySQL

(a) Rule Template: an entry B of type UserName should be the owner of an entry A of type FilePath

**Template**: [A<FilePath>]+[B<FilePath>] => <FilePath>
**Rule:** ServerRoot + LoadModule/arg2 => <FilePath> //Apache

(b) Rule Template: the concatenation of two entries (A of type FilePath and B of type FilePath) forms a file path

**Template**: [A<Size>] < [B<Size>]
**Rule:** upload_max_filesize < post_max_size //PHP

(c) Rule Template: an entry A of type Size should be smaller than an entry B of type Size

Figure 4: **Examples of templates and the concrete rules generated from them.**

entries *DataDir* and *User*, which is used to identify the misconfiguration described in Figure 1(b).

**Why use templates?** The use of templates brings three benefits to address the challenges faced by direct data mining. 1) It effectively describes the possible types of correlations beyond frequent item set relation; 2) It avoids wasting the computation and resource on patterns that are not likely to exist in the configuration entries; and 3) It makes the learning process "*extensible*": the more templates are used, the larger coverage of possible rules is achieved. Note that the templates can be easily customized, as discussed in Section 5.3.

The template specification uses data type information to restrict the eligible configuration entries. For example, in Figure 4(a), *B* needs to be of type `UserName`, which means when the learning process tries to instantiate the template, it only fills in *B* with the attributes of type `UserName`.

The type information provides an intuitive and effective way of attribute selection, which is critical to solve the scalability problem in the learning phase. In addition, it is a natural base for associating environment information. For example, as described in Section 4, the file permission data are only meaningful to a configuration entry of type `FilePath`.

*EnCore* provides several predefined templates that make it readily usable. They are shown in Table 6 with their descriptions. Our evaluations are based on these templates.

**Rule Inference Process.** With the type-based templates, *EnCore* learns rules from the training set. Figure 5 summarizes the workflow of the learning process. In *EnCore*, each correlation is associated with a validation method that determines whether the correlation holds or not. The validation methods are identified by the relation operators(such as < and ==) together with the types of the participating attribute placeholders (such as `A` and `B` in Figure 4; we discuss the correlation interface in detail in Section 5.3 when introducing how to customize correlations).

For each template, *EnCore* tries to instantiate the template by replacing the placeholders with eligible attributes that match the data type specified in the template. *EnCore* iter-

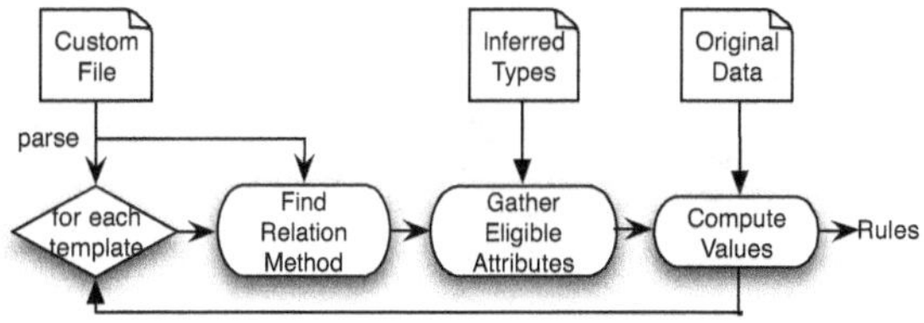


Figure 5: **Workflow of rule inference.**

ates over every possible instance of the template and checks whether it is valid using the validation method. If the correlation is valid, *EnCore* regards it as a rule candidate, which would further go into the filtering(Section 5.2). Note that this process is highly parallelizable because there is zero state sharing between each instance computation. As a result, we implement *EnCore* as a multi-process program to achieve high performance.

## 5.2 Rule Filtering

As accurately as the templates may be defined, like any data-driven method, there are false positives in the resulting rules. *EnCore* use three metrics to filter them. The first two metrics are *support* and *confidence*, which are typical metrics used in association rule detection. *Support* means how many times the frequent item set (in our context, the attributes involved in the rules) occurrs in the data set, and *confidence* means the percentage that the rule is valid.

Configuration entries have a unique characteristic: values of certain attributes are stable in many systems. For example, the warning level in PHP has consistently been set to 10 in our training set. If an entry seldomly changes, the values it carries are not interesting, and the rules involving this entry are likely to be noise. To take this into account, we use a third metric: *entropy* [36]. It measures the diversity of the dataset: its value increases when more diverse values are seen for a given entry. The value of entropy is defined as

$$H = -\sum_{i=1}^{n} p_i \ln p_i, \qquad p_i = N_i/N,$$

where $n$ is the number of different values, $p_i$ is the probability of taking the $i$th value, $N$ is the times this entry appears in the training set, and $N_i$ is the times it is assigned with $i$th value. We set a threshold value for each of the three metrics. The threshold for the entropy is denoted by $H_t$. When there are two values, each having a probablility of of 90% and 10% respectively, it is set to $H_t = 0.325$. For an attribute to be included, it needs to have $H > H_t$, meaning it is more diverse than the minimum threshold. For a rule to be included, all the involved attributes need to be included.

## 5.3 Customization

*EnCore* is a fully customizable framework. Users can extend it with different levels of customization using different interfaces. Specifically, users can 1) specify new templates to infer new types of rules; 2) define new types in addition to the default types; and 3) tag new environment information for the environment data integration.

| Template | Description |
|---|---|
| [A<AnyTypeA>] == [B<AnyTypeA>] | An entry should be equal to another entry of same type |
| [A<AnyTypeA>] = [B<AnyTypeA>] | One instance of an entry should equal to at least one instance of another entry of same type |
| [A<ExtBoolean>] → [B<Boolean>] | An extended boolean indicates a boolean entry whose extended attribute has boolean value |
| [A<IPAddress>] < [B<IPAddress>] | An entry of IPAddress is a subnet of another entry |
| [A<FilePath>]+[B<FileName>]=><FilePath> | Concatenation of a file path entry with a partial file path entry forms a full file path |
| [A<String>] < [B<String>] | An entry is substring of another entry |
| [A<UserName>]<[B<GroupName>] | The user name belongs to the group name |
| [A<FilePath>] ! = [B<UserName>] | The file path is not accessible by the user specified in the entry |
| [A<FilePath>] => [B<UserName>] | The entry of UserName is the owner of the file path specified in the entry A |
| [A<Number>] < [B<Number>] | The number in one entry is less then that of the other entry |
| [A<Size>] < [B<Size>] | The size in one entry is smaller then that of the other entry |

Table 6: **Predefined templates with description.** The templates are created based on the common correlations of configuration settings. The operators carry different meanings for different types, and can be overridden by users' customization.

#### 5.3.1 The Customization Interface

A user customizes *EnCore* using a customization file. It has seven sections, each specifying a customizable aspect of the system. Figure 6 shows its format and some sample input. Note that *EnCore* provides predefined types, operators, and templates so that *the customization file is optional.*

As illustrated in Figure 6, each section's name is specified and is prefixed with the "$$" symbol. New type information is specified in the top 3 sections including its name declaration, how to infer it, and how to verify it. To define a new data type, users need to implement the syntactic matching and an optional semantic verification method. The method takes the values to be inferred as input, and returns a boolean value to indicate whether the value is of this type. When an attribute can be inferred for multiple types, customized types have priority over predefined ones, and priority of the customized types is determined by the order they appear in the customization file. The other sections define additional augmented attributes besides predefined ones in Table 5. The augmented attributes are first declared, followed by the methods to compute their values.

The type operator section defines the operators used in the templates, including both aggregation and comparison (see Section 5.3.2). The template section specifies the types of rules to be attempted in the learning.

#### 5.3.2 Customizing Rule Templates

Specifying new rule templates allows users to customize *EnCore*'s rule inference. As discussed in Section 3, a template is a general relation specification, composed of two major parts: the *slots* (the capitalized letter and the type in square brackets in Figure 4) and the *relations* (the plus and arrow symbols in Figure 4). A slot is to be filled in the learning process. It has a name and a data type. The name will be filled with the concrete entry name after a rule is found, while the data type is specified by the user. The data type is used by the rule inference to select eligible attributes.

There are two types of relations. The first defines how different attributes can be aggregated, e.g. string concatenation, arithmetic addition, or any other aggregation methods

```
$$TypeDeclaration
    <NewType>
$$TypeInference
    <NewType> (value): { return True }
$$TypeValidation
    <NewType> (value):{ return True }
$$TypeAugmentDeclaration
    <NewType>.Group
$$TypeAugment
    <NewType>.Group (value):{ return '' }
$$TypeOperator
    <NewType>:<NewType> Operator '<' (v1,v2): { return True }
$$Template
    [A<Types.NewType>] < [B<Types.NewType>] -- 90%
```

Figure 6: **Format of the customization file and a sample input.**

specified by the users. The second type is for comparison, which defines how values are compared, e.g. "greater than" or "equal to."

The templates aim at capturing the general correlations among configuration entries and are not specific to any particular software or system. We envision that with more usage of *EnCore*, more templates would be created and shared among users, increasing coverage of rule inference.

#### 5.3.3 Accessible Environment Information

When users are specifying their methods for customization, they may need to access system information. *EnCore* provides users access to all the environment information collected in the data collecting phase, in the form of global variables. They are accessible in any place in the customization file. Table 7 shows the data structures accessible to the users, as well as the sources from which the system gets the information. They are organized in both array lists and maps. For example, with FS.FileList, the user can iterate all the file names (including their paths) in the system. With FS.FileMetaMap, users can retrieve the metadata of the file using the file path as the key.

The programming complexity of each new type inference or template depends on its semantics. Given the easily accessible data provided by *EnCore*, the programs are usually short and straightforward. The predefined type inference methods have 7 to 12 lines of Python code, and the LOC of the predefined template methods range from 4 to 20.

| Category | Data Structure | Sources |
|---|---|---|
| Files Data | FS.FileList | File System |
| | FS.FileMetaMap | |
| Account Info | Acct.UserList | /etc/passwd<br>/etc/group |
| | Acct.GroupList | |
| | Acct.UserGroupMap | |
| Service | Service.Ports | /etc/services |
| | Service.PortServMap | |
| Env Variables* | Env.VarValueMap | env |
| Security | Sec.SELinux | /selinux/* |
| Hardware** | HW.Cores | /proc/* |
| | HW.Memory | |
| | HW.DiskSize | |

Table 7: **Data structures for accessing environment information.** *Only available when collecting data from running instances; **The hardware specifications are not available for newly instantiated virtual machine images such as those from Amazon EC2.

# 6 Anomaly Detector

With the learned rules, *EnCore* looks for potential anomalies in the target systems. It goes through the same data assembling process for the new system as in the learning phase, including parsing, type inferencing, and environment information integration. Then, it checks the following aspects of the target configuration and produces a ranked list of errors.

**1. Entry Name Violation.** Previous studies show that misspelling is an important source of misconfigurations [31]. If the new system includes entries not seen before, it is likely a misspelled one.

**2. Correlation Violation.** *EnCore* checks if the target system follows the correlation rules learned from the training set. Since each rule is an expression, the detector of *EnCore* evaluates the expression with the values from the target configuration and reports warnings when violation is found. The rule is ignored if the involved entries are absent in the target configuration file.

**3. Data Type Violation.** For each entry to be checked, the checker reads its type information inferred from the training set, and gets the corresponding syntactic matching function and semantic verification function. The two functions are used to match and verify the target configuration value. A type violation is reported if the verification or matching fails.

**4. Suspicious Values.** The detector compares the values of configuration entries from the new system with the values in the training set. It reports a warning if the new value is different from all the previous ones. When multiple entries have unseen values, we adopt the *Inverse Change Frequency* method [42] that gives higher ranks to entries with less diverse values in the training set. Note that the statistical method used here is orthogonal to how rules are learned in *EnCore*: other methods (e.g., those in PeerPressure) can also be adopted here. We chose this simple design and found it satisfy our need. In fact, *with more environment information integrated, more aspects of the configuration entries can be checked against suspicious values.* For example, the detection of the error in Figure 1(a) is directly attributed to the extended attribute of *extension_dir.type* – all the values in the training set have type *directory*, but the value in the target system has type *regular file*. This warning is ranked much higher than other possible suspicious values since its value set in the training set has a cardinality of only 1.

| App | Total | Baseline | Baseline+Env | EnCore |
|---|---|---|---|---|
| Apache | 15 | 4 | 9 | 14 |
| MySQL | 15 | 5 | 14 | 15 |
| PHP | 15 | 9 | 12 | 15 |

Table 8: **The number of injected misconfigurations detected by *EnCore* in the injection experiment.** "Baseline" is the non-correlation and environment-unawared approach, adopted in most existing work. "Baseline+Env" is non-correlation but environment-aware, i.e., only using the type-based environment infomation integrated by *EnCore*.

# 7 Evaluation

We evaluate the effectiveness of *EnCore* with the rules learned from public images crawled from Amazon EC2. The experiments are carried out with 3 softwares: Apache Web server, MySQL, and PHP. For each software, we have different number of training data according to the availability of the software on EC2 images: 127 images for Apache, 187 images for MySQL, and 123 images for PHP.

## 7.1 Effectiveness of Misconfiguration Detection

We perform three experiments to evaluate *EnCore*'s capability of misconfiguration detection. In the first experiment, we inject random errors into correctly configured systems and use *EnCore* to detect the injected errors. In the second experiment, we apply *EnCore* to check against real-world misconfiguration problems. In the last experiment, to see whether *EnCore* is able to detect new configuration errors, we directly apply the anomaly detector to the public images from Amazon EC2 and the virtual machine images from a commercial company's private cloud.

### 7.1.1 Injected Misconfigurations

For each software, we randomly pick an image that is not in the training set and inject 15 errors with ConfErr [25] into the configuration file. We compare the detection results with the following two approaches: 1) The baseline that does not consider environment information nor correlation information. It resembles the state-of-the-art detection approaches based on value comparison such as PeerPressure [41]. 2) Baseline+Env that enhances the baseline approach with the type-based environment information integration. It takes into account both the configuration values and the environment information, without correlation information.

Table 8 shows the detection results of the three approaches. Compared with *Baseline* and *Baseline+Env*, *EnCore* achieves a significantly higher coverage of errors. The result also shows that the environment information integra-

| ID | Software | Problem Description | Info | Rank |
|---|---|---|---|---|
| 1 | Apache | Website not granted desired protection because DocumentRoot does not have related Directory | Corr | 1(5) |
| 2 | PHP | Does not connect to database due to extension_dir pointing to a file instead of the directory | Env | 1(1) |
| 3 | MySQL | File creation error due to datadir's wrong owner | Env + Corr | 1(1) |
| 4 | MySQL | Data writing error due to undesired protection from AppArmor | Env | 1(2) |
| 5 | PHP | Modules not loaded because extension_dir is set to a wrong location | Env | 1(1) |
| 6 | Apache | Website unavailability because directory contains symbolic links when FollowSymLinks is off | Env + Corr | 1(3) |
| 7 | Apache | Website visitors are unable to upload files due to the wrong permission set to Apache user. | Env + Corr | 1(1) |
| 8 | MySQL | Out of memory error due to too large table size allowed in configuration | Env + Corr | - |
| 9 | MySQL | Logging is not performed even with relevant entry set correctly due to wrong permission | Env + Corr | 1(1) |
| 10 | PHP | Failure when uploading large file due to the wrong setting of file size limit | Corr | 2(2) |

Table 9: **Detection of real world misconfigurations.** The "Info" column describes the information needed to detect the misconfigurations: "Corr" refers to correlation, and "Env" refers to environment infomation. The "Rank" column shows the rank of the real misconfiguration in the warning report, with the total number of warnings shown in "()". "-" means the misconfiguration is missed by *EnCore*. Note that the majority of them require both environment and correlation information.

tion and type detection can greatly enhance existing value comparison based approaches in terms of misconfiguration detection. For example, *Baseline* does not detect wrong file paths, as they usually vary substantially across the training set, but they are captured by *Baseline+Env* and *EnCore*.

Notice that the error injection of ConfErr is within the scope of configuration files and does not touch other system locations. For example, it does not change permissions or ownerships of files specified in the configurations. Thus, the results in this section only reflect *EnCore*'s capability in detecting misconfigurations residing in configuration files.

#### 7.1.2 Real-World Misconfigurations

To evaluate *EnCore*'s ability of detecting real-world misconfigurations, we use the real-world cases described in [46] that are collected from ServerFault (an online user forum focusing on system administration). We randomly sampled 15 problems that are easily reproducible, and reproduced the misconfiguration-induced failures on a new testing image. Table 9 describes these cases, the information required, and the detection results. Among the 15 problems, 8 of them require the environment information and/or the correlation to be detected. The remaining 7 problems depend on either pure configuration entry value checking or unseen configuration name detection and can be detected by both *EnCore* and existing works. In addition, we show two failure cases caused by misconfigurations detected by *EnCore* in EC2 image (details in Section 7.1.3), which are verified to have already caused real world problems.

Table 9 shows that the only misconfiguration missed by *EnCore* is Problem #8. The misconfiguration is that the value of *max_heap_table_size* equals the system memory size, but the system cannot allocate all the space to MySQL. The reason is the lack of hardware information in the training set. The hardware information is intentionally skipped when we crawl the EC2 images, since the images can be instantiated with different hardware configuration at instantiation time. If the data were crawled on a running instance instead of a dormant image, *EnCore* can incorporate such hardware information.

*EnCore* generates other warnings in addition to the real configuration errors. In the case of Apache, the false warnings are generated mostly from configuration entry name checking. Apache allows nested configuration entries at arbitrary levels. If the combination of the section and entries has not been seen before, a warning will be reported. In Problem #10, the error was ranked No.2 due to another true misconfiguration in the file, which violates a rule with higher confidence.

#### 7.1.3 New Detected Misconfigurations

We collect 120 new images from EC2 which are excluded from the training set and then apply *EnCore* directly on the new images with the rules learned from the training images. It is quite surprising that *EnCore* finds a total of 37 misconfiguration in 25 images. This was not expected because the public images are mostly used as system templates for producing other images and are considered to be correct.

We also apply *EnCore* to 300 images from a commercial private cloud of an IT company using the rules learned from EC2 training images. *EnCore* finds 24 misconfigurations in 22 images. Table 10 summarizes the categories of these misconfigurations. All of them are manually verified to be configuration *errors* that can either cause security holes inside the systems or lead to unexpected behaviors. It is noticeable that the fraction of problematic images in the commercial private cloud is lower than that of EC2. This is expected because they have been deployed in real usage for a long time and should have most problems discovered already.

We also find that many of these new misconfigurations cannot be detected by the software itself because the related rules are not enforced in the source code. This is true even when the undesirable behaviors or security problems caused by the same misconfiguration have already been encountered by the other users [5, 6]. In one case, the log file in MySQL should not be accessible to other users, because it may con-

| Source | FilePath | Permission | ValueCompare | Total |
|---|---|---|---|---|
| EC2 | 3 | 10 | 24 | 37 |
| PrivateCloud | 10 | 3 | 11 | 24 |

Table 10: **Categories of new detected misconfigurations.** "FilePath" means that file path configuration is missing or set wrongly. "Permission" means the permission configuration is wrong. "ValueCompare" shows the misoncifugraions that violate value comparison rules.

tain sensitive data [5]. Despite the significance of the security vulnerability, MySQL does not report any warning or error, and as a result such misconfiguration remains undetected. Another case is in PHP configuration. The size of the uploaded file is limited by two entries: *post_max_size* and *upload_max_filesize* with the former one having higher priority. Thus, for the latter one to take effect, it needs to be smaller than the former one; otherwise the upload of a file larger than *post_max_size* fails even if the file size is smaller than *upload_max_filesize*.

It is interesting to notice that none of these misconfigurations can be detected without the use of environment and correlation information. For example, the permission violation is detected by the rule found from the 8th template in Table 6, where file path permission is correlated with user names. In this case, it checks the accessibility of the Linux system user "nobody." In summary, the experiments validate the effectiveness and neccessity of these two important factors when dealing with misconfiguration issues.

### 7.2 Type Inference Accuracy

Table 11 shows the results of type inference (described in Section 4.2). For the entries that do not match any hint or do not pass verification, we assign them with the type String or Number (trivial). It may include the configurations that specify a regular expression or a numerical number.

To verify the results, we manually check the semantics of all the entries and compare them with the inference output. A major source for the false inference is the use of regular expression and wildcards in the configuration files to specify the file names or paths. Also, sometimes the specified file names or paths may not necessarily exist in the system. For example, in Apache users could specify the index file to serve a directory. But the file may actually not exist, and the software handles its absence automatically. Another example is the log files of MySQL that will be created when the software is running. For PHP, the wrong inferences mostly come from the integer values mistakenly determined as Boolean, where all the training images use the values of 0 or 1. Note however, that these happen because we are using the data set from template images of Amazon EC2, which represent pristine, uninitialized states of systems. We believe that the results will be significantly improved if we crawled running production systems that are properly initialized, and have more customized configuration values.

| Apps | Entries | NonTrivial | FalseTypes | Undetected |
|---|---|---|---|---|
| Apache | 371 | 207 | 14 | 20 |
| MySQL | 131 | 86 | 3 | 11 |
| PHP | 249 | 164 | 13 | 8 |

Table 11: **Data type detection results.** The "Entries" column is the total number of configuration entries. The "NonTrivial" column refers to the types with semantic meanings that are not regarded as "string" or "number." "FalseTypes" / "Undetected" show the number of entries with wrongly detected or undetected types.

| Apps | Detected Rules | False Positives |
|---|---|---|
| Apache | 42 | 9 |
| MySQL | 29 | 4 |
| PHP | 31 | 10 |

Table 12: **Detected correlation rules with the filters.**

### 7.3 Correlation Rule Inference

Table 12 shows the total number of rules inferred from the predefined templates (shown in Table 6). We use the confidence of 90%, support number of 10% of the total number of images in the training set, and the entropy ($H_t$) of 0.325 (Section 5.2). The threshold values are selected based on the nature of our training set – EC2 images are often used as general template images for the users to customize them for their own needs. Therefore, many of the images' configurations are set as default. In this case, the entropy is usually small. For the same reason, the occurrence of certain optional configuration entries (especially those not appearing in the sample configuration files) is small. As a result, we use a small support number for the purpose of filtering.

A significant source of false rules is undetected types, which causes the comparison of unrelated entries. For example, in Apache, both *MinSpareServers* and *Timeout* are inferred as Numeric type. They do not have correlation, but they are compared in *EnCore*. Since the value of *MinSpareServers* is usually numerically smaller than *Timeout*, it is reported as a rule that "*MinSpareServers* is smaller than *Timeout*".

As described in Section 5.2, besides the standard filters of confidence and support number, we use the entropy threshold. To evaluate its effectiveness in our data set, Table 13 shows the number of false rules filtered in each software.

In our experiments, entropy is mostly effective against the false positives in the correlations related to numeric rules, as well as binomial association rules. The reason is that some of these values are directly derived from the sample configuration files and not changed by the image developers. For example, the *HostnameLookups* directive in Apache is always set to *Off*, and the *min_server_severity* directive in PHP is always set to *10*. The high number of originally reported rules in PHP is mostly caused by the comparison of numeric entries. Since many of these settings are not changed much, the filter would effectively rule them out.

| Apps | Original | FP Reduced | FN Introduced |
|---|---|---|---|
| Apache | 113 | 71 | 7 |
| MySQL | 52 | 23 | 1 |
| PHP | 567 | 536 | 1 |

Table 13: **Effectiveness of the entropy filter.** "Original" shows the number of rules after applying the confidence and support filters. FP (False Positive) Reduced is the number of false rules filtered by entropy filter. FN (False Negative) Introduced is the number of true rules that are filtered.

For the same reason, entropy also filters some true correlations. For example, while *net_buffer_length* should be smaller than *max_allowed_packet* in MySQL, the rule is filtered because all the values of *net_buffer_length* is set as *8K*. Although some may argue that exposing more correlations is more important than suppressing false reports when detecting misconfigurations, given the false positives and false negatives data shown in Table 13, we consider the trade-off worthwhile and beneficial to the end users.

## 8 Related Work

**Misconfiguration Detection.** There are generally two types of approaches for misconfigurations detection and troubleshooting: black-box approaches [13, 22, 39, 41, 42, 47] and white-box approaches [14, 15, 31, 32]. The former learns configuration rules from large-scale configuration settings, while the latter infer rules by analyzing source code. Compared with white-box approaches, black-box approaches require no source code or heavy-weight program analysis and can go across the software boundary (which is hard for white-box approaches). Since *EnCore* is a black-box approach, we mainly discuss the related black-box detection approaches in this section.

Strider [42], PeerPressure [41], and [34] detect misconfigurations by comparing configuration values of one system with those of peer systems. Strider uses manually labeled working/failing configuration cases, as well as changing frequency to filter the suspicious entries. PeerPressure enhances Strider with a statistical model and eliminates the need of manual labeling. Ramachandran et al. [34] use both frequency and Google results as ranking heuristics to discover the string dependencies between configuration entries across different components. None of them exploit the environment information, nor the various correlations between configuration entries. The evaluation shows that by examining the whole system software stack and its internal correlations, *EnCore* goes beyond the existing approaches in terms of the capability of misconfiguration detection.

Other works address different aspects of the black-box approaches. FTN [22] focuses on the integrity and privacy issues of the peer contents. AutoBash [39] learns from the peers' problem solution. CODE [47] targets on the configuration access pattern anomaly. *EnCore* complements these work with both environment and correlation information as the new information source.

**Configuration Languages.** In order to make the configurations more expressive, some software use programming languages in configuration files, including Emacs Lisp, Google's GCL (General Configuration Language) used internally for configuring software, and the Click language that configures Click routers [26]. The results are mixed – while use of programming languages provides stronger expressive power and allows configurations to be analyzed like programs, the added complexity makes it more difficult for end users [9, 28]. The use of programming language does not preclude the need for *EnCore*. Though the type checking of the language may mitigate the burden of type inference of *EnCore*, the need for integrated environment information and configuration rule learning is still desired.

**Configuration Testing.** Configuration testing tools, such as SPEX [44], ConfErr [25], and KLEE [17], can be used to generate realistic, high-coverage test cases to defend the systems against misconfigurations. Those tools can benefit from *EnCore* since it provides new error injection opportunities such as erroneous environment settings and violations of correlation rules.

## 9 Conclusion and Future Work

Configuration settings serve as a bridge between applications and their executing environment. Therefore detecting misconfiguration requires reasoning on both sides. We have presented *EnCore*, a misconfiguration detection tool that enriches the plain configuration values with the environment information and unveils their implicit rules and correlations. Based on the configuration rules learned from the enriched data, *EnCore* is able to detect misconfigurations that are beyond the capability of existing tools.

Our future work includes several appealing applications of *EnCore*. First, the idea of integrating environment information can be naturally extended to deal with cross-component misconfigurations: the configuration of other components can be seen as one kind of environment factors. Also, the information integrated by *EnCore* (including both the assembled values and inferred rules) can be used to enhance configuration testing and assist the process of auto-configuration.

## Acknowledgments

We thank the anonymous reviewers for their insightful comments and suggestions. We also thank Mona Attariyan for providing us with misconfiguration examples from her research work. This research is supported by NSF CNS-1017784, NSF CNS-1321006, and IBM Graduate Fellowship.

## References


[1] Misconfiguration brings down entire .se domain in Sweden. http://www.circleid.com.

[2] Google Code Style Guide. http://google-styleguide.googlecode.com.

[3] Internet Assigned Numbers Authority. http://www.iana.org.

[4] Lint, a C program Verifier. http://www.unix.com/man-page/FreeBSD/1/lint.

[5] Mysql log security. http://www.securityfocus.com /advisories/3803.

[6] PHP configuration error. http://stackoverflow.com/ questions/7754133.

[7] PyLint. http://www.logilab.org/project/pylint/.

[8] RapidMiner. http://www.rapid-i.com.

[9] At what point does a config file become a programming language? http://stackoverflow.com/questions/648246/at-what-point-does-a-config-file-become-a-programming-language.

[10] Weka. http://www.cs.waikato.ac.nz/ml/weka.

[11] G. Ammons, V. Bala, T. Mummert, D. Reimer, and X. Zhang. Virtual machine images as structured data: the Mirage image library. In *HotCloud*, 2011.

[12] S. Anand, D. Bell, and J. Hughes. The Role of Domain Knowledge in Data Mining. In *Proceedings of 4th International Conference on Information and Knowledge Management (CIKM'95)*, December 1995.

[13] M. Attariyan and J. Flinn. Using Causality to Diagnose Configuration Bugs. In *Proceedings of 2008 USENIX Annual Technical Conference*, June 2008.

[14] M. Attariyan and J. Flinn. Automating Configuration Troubleshooting with Dynamic Information Flow Analysis. In *Proceedings of the 9th USENIX Conference on Operating Systems Design and Implementation (OSDI'10)*, October 2010.

[15] M. Attariyan, M. Chow, and J. Flinn. X-ray: Diagnosing Performance Misconfigurations in Production Software. In *Proceedings of the 10th USENIX Conference on Operating Systems Design and Implementation (OSDI'12)*, October 2012.

[16] P. S. Bradley and O. L. Mangasarian. Feature Selection via Concave Minimiation and Support Vector Machiens. In *Proceedings of the 5th International Conference on Machine Learning (ICML'98)*, July 1998.

[17] C. Cadar, D. Dunbar, and D. Engler. KLEE: Unassisted and Automatic Generation of High-Coverage Tests for Complex Systems Programs. In *Proceeedings of the 8th USENIX conference on Operating Systems Design and Implementation (OSDI'08)*, December 2008.

[18] D. Engler, D. Y. Chen, S. Hallem, A. Chou, and B. Chelf. Bugs as Deviant Behavior: A General Approach to Inferring Errors in Systems Code. In *Proceedings of the 18th ACM Symposium on Operating Systems Principles (SOSP'01)*, October 2001.

[19] J. Gray. Dependability in the Internet Era, 2001. Keynote presentation at the 2nd HDCC Workshop.

[20] J. Han, J. Pei, and Y. Yin. Mining Frequent Pattern without Candidate Generation. In *Proceedings of the 2000 ACM International conference on Management of Data (SIGMOD'00)*, May 2000.

[21] M. Hong, Z. Lu, and Y. Fuqing. A Component-based software configuration management model and its supporting system. In *Proceedings of the 24th International Conference on Software Engineering (ICSE'02)*, May 2002.

[22] Q. Huang, H. J. Wang, and N. Borisov. Privacy-Preserving Friends Troubleshooting Network. In *Proceedings of the 12th Network and Distributed System Security Symposium (NDSS'05)*, February 2005.

[23] R. J. and B. Jr. Efficiently Mining Long Patterns from Database. In *Proceedings ACM SIGMOD International Conference on Management of Data (SIGMOD'98)*, June 1998.

[24] R. Johnson. More details on today's outage. http://www.facebook.com/notes /facebook-engineering/more-details-on-todays-outage/431441338919.

[25] L. Keller, P. Upadhyaya, and G. Candea. ConfErr: A Tool for Assessing Resilience to Human Configuration Errors. In *Proceedings of the 38th Annual IEEE/IFIP International Conference on Dependable Systems and Networks (DSN'08)*, June 2008.

[26] E. Kohler, B. Chen, M. F. Kaashoek, R. Morris, and M. Poletto. Programming language techniques for modular router configurations. Technical Report MIT-LCS-TR-812, MIT Laboratory for Computer Science, August 2000.

[27] D. Lutterkort. Augeas - a Configuration API. In *2008 Linux Symposium*, 2008.

[28] J. Mason. Against The Use Of Programming Languages in Configuration Files. http://taint.org/2011/02/18/001527a.html.

[29] K. Nagaraja, F. Oliveria, R. Bianchini, R. P. Martin, and T. D. Nguyen. Understanding and Dealing with Operator Mistakes in Internet Services. In *Proceedings of the 6th USENIX Conference on Operating Systems Design and Implementation (OSDI'04)*, December 2004.

[30] D. Oppenheimer, A. Ganapathi, and D. A. Patterson. Why Do Internet Services Fail, and What Can Be Done About It? In *Proceedings of the 4th USENIX Symposium on Internet Technologies and Systems (USITS'03)*, March 2003.

[31] A. Rabkin and R. Katz. Static Extraction of Program Configuration Options. In *Proceedings of the 33th International Conference on Software Engineering (ICSE'11)*, May 2011.

[32] A. Rabkin and R. Katz. Precomputing Possible Configuration Error Diagnoses. In *Proceedings of the 26th IEEE/ACM International Conference on Automated Software Engineering (ICSE'11)*, May 2011.

[33] A. Rakesh and S. Ramakrishnan. In *Proceedings of the 20th International Conference on Very Large Data Bases (VLDB'94)*, September 1994.

[34] V. Ramachandran, M. Gupta, M. Sethi, and S. R. Chowdhury. Determining Configuration Parameter Dependencies via Analysis of Configuration Data from Multi-tiered Enterprise Applications. In *Proceedings of the 6th International Conference on Autonomic Computing and Communications (ICAC'09)*, June 2009.

[35] B. S., M. R., U. J., and T. S. Dynamic Itemset Counting and Implication Rules for Market Basket Data. In *Proceedings ACM SIGMOD International Conference on Management of Data (SIGMOD'97)*, May 1997.

[36] C. Shannon. A Mathematical Theory of Communication. *The Bell System Technical Journal*, 27:379–423, July 1984.

[37] K. Smets and J. Vreeken. SLIM: Directly Mining Descriptive Patterns. In *Proceedings of 2012 SIAM International Conference on Data Mining (SDM'12)*, April 2012.

[38] R. Srikant and R. Agrawl. Mining Quantative Association Rules in Large Relational Tables. In *Proceedings ACM SIGMOD International Conference on Management of Data (SIGMOD'96)*, June 1996.

[39] Y.-Y. Su, M. Attariyan, and J. Flinn. AutoBash: Improving Configuration Management with Operating System Causality Analysis. In *Proceedings of the 21st ACM Symposium on Operating Sytems Principles (SOSP'07)*, October 2007.

[40] S. Traugott and J. Huddleston. Bootstrapping an Infrastructure. In *Proceedings of the 13th Systems Administration Conference (LISA'99)*, November 1999.

[41] H. J. Wang, J. C. Platt, Y. Chen, R. Zhang, and Y.-M. Wang. Automatic Misconfiguration Troubleshooting with PeerPressure. In *Proceedings of the 6th USENIX Conference on Operating Systems Design and Implementation (OSDI'04)*, December 2004.

[42] Y.-M. Wang, C. Verbowski, J. Dunagan, Y. Chen, H. Wang, C. Yuan, and Z. Zhang. STRIDER: A Black-box, State-based Approach to Change and Configuration Management and Support. In *Proceedings of the 17th Large Installation Systems Admistration Conference (LISA'03)*, October 2003.

[43] M. Welsh. What I wish systems researchers would work on. http://http://matt-welsh.blogspot.com/2013/05.

[44] T. Xu, J. Zhang, P. Huang, J. Zheng, T. Sheng, D. Yuan, Y. Zhou, and S. Pasupathy. Do not Blame Users for Misconfigurations. In *Proceedings of the 24th ACM Symposium on Operating Systems Principles (SOSP'13)*.

[45] W. Xu, L. Huang, A. Fox, D. Patterson, and M. Jordan. Detecting Large-Scale System Problems by Mining Console Logs. In *Proceedings of the 2009 Symposium on Operating Systems Principles*, 2009.

[46] Z. Yin, X. Ma, J. Zheng, Y. Zhou, L. N. Bairavasundaram, and S. Pasupathy. An Empirical Study on Configuration Errors in Commercial and Open Source Systems. In *Proceedings of the 23rd ACM Symposium on Operating Systems Principles (SOSP'11)*, October 2011.

[47] D. Yuan, Y. Xie, R. Panigrahy, J. Yang, C. Verbowsky, and A. Kumar. Context-based Online Configuration-Error Detection. In *Proceedings of 2011 USENIX Anuual Technical Conference*, June 2011.

# High-Performance Fractal Coherence

Gwendolyn Voskuilen and T. N. Vijaykumar

School of Electrical and Computer Engineering, Purdue University
{geinfeld,vijay}@ecn.purdue.edu

## Abstract

Bugs in cache coherence protocols can cause system failures. Despite many advances, verification runs into state explosion for even moderately-sized systems. As multicores' core counts increase, coherence verifiability continues to be a key problem. A recent proposal, called *fractal coherence*, avoids the state explosion problem by applying the idea of observational equivalence between a larger system and its smaller sub-systems. A fractal protocol for a larger system is verified by design if a minimal sub-system is verified completely. While fractal coherence is a significant step forward, there are two shortcomings: (1) Architectural limitation: To achieve fractal coherence's logical hierarchy, *TreeFractal*, the specific fractal protocol, employs a tree architecture where each miss traverses many levels up and down the tree and each level redundantly holds its sub-trees' coherence tags. (2) Protocol restrictions: TreeFractal imposes a restriction on responses to read requests that forces read requests to obtain clean blocks from the nearest sharer even if the shared L2 or L3 is faster. These limitations impose significant performance and coherence tag state overheads. In this paper, we propose architectural support for coherence protocols to achieve scalable performance and verifiability. To address the architectural limitation, we propose *FlatFractal*, a directory-based architecture which decouples fractal coherence's logical hierarchy from the architecture and eliminates redundant tag state. To address the protocol restriction, we propose a simple change to the protocol that, while preserving observational equivalence, allows read requests to obtain the blocks from the shared L2 or L3. Our simulations show that for 16 cores, FlatFractal performs, on average, 57% better than TreeFractal and within 3% of a conventional directory.

***Categories*** B.3.2 [**Memory Structures**]: Design Styles – cache memories, shared memory; C.1.4 [**Processor Architectures**]: Parallel Architectures

***Keywords*** cache coherence; verification; multicore


*ASPLOS '14*, March 1–5, 2014, Salt Lake City, Utah, USA

http://dx.doi.org/10.1145/2541940.2541982

## 1. Introduction

Cache coherence protocols support shared-memory functionality in multicore and multiprocessor systems. Unfortunately, protocol bugs can cause the system to fail. Verifying that a protocol is correct and deadlock- and livelock-free entails checking that all reachable system states are valid (e.g., only a single writing core at a time). Consequently, as the number of system components (e.g., caches) and the complexity of the protocols increase, both the number of reachable system states and the number of interleavings among protocol actions increase exponentially (i.e., the state space explosion problem).

As a result, the straightforward state-exploration approach to verification, even when combined with state-pruning techniques (e.g., [15]), incurs unreasonable time and memory requirements at moderate system scales (e.g., more than eight cores). Further, because state-exploration relies on system states (the set of all valid combinations of the individual components' states), a protocol verified for a smaller system is not necessarily guaranteed to be correct for a larger system. More powerful verification approaches [23, 25, 29] exploit inherent symmetries in some protocols to enable more scalable verification. Such approaches have been applied successfully to a few protocols (e.g., S3.mp [26]). However, because these approaches are protocol-specific and often require significant human effort, they do not guarantee scalable verification in general. For this reason, commercial coherence protocols are commonly verified only partially (e.g., SCI [10, 12, 13, 27], Nehalem despite using a 1000-node cluster running for a year [7], and HyperTransport [34]) and bugs do occur [5, 14]. As multicores scale, verification effort will only increase. Consequently, scalable cache coherence verifiability is, and will continue to be, a key problem in multicore design.

Rather than reduce the state space explosion or identify symmetries in existing protocols, a recent break-through proposal, called *fractal coherence* [35], avoids the problem by constructing coherence protocols that facilitate scalable verification. Fractal coherence applies the property of observational equivalence [21] between a larger system and its smaller sub-systems. That is, the larger system's observable interactions with entities *outside* the system are identical to those of the sub-system with entities outside the sub-system. The larger system is verified by design if the sub-system has been verified completely using conventional verification.

Fractal coherence naturally imposes a *logical* hierarchy on the system due to the inductive construction of self-similar systems from smaller sub-systems. The specific previous fractal coherence protocol in [35], TreeFractal, adopts a *real* tree architecture to achieve fractal coherence's *logical* hierarchy. Cores form the leaves of the tree and each internal node is a *coherence interface* for the node's two sub-trees. We clarify that while both fractal protocols and conventional hierarchical coherence protocols [17, 20, 32], which target scalability, have hierarchical structures, the two are fundamentally different. Fractal protocols maintain observational equivalence and therefore are hierarchical and verifiable, but hierarchical protocols are not constrained so and therefore are not necessarily fractal or verifiable. For example, reply forwarding, a common optimization employed in hierarchical protocols, is not fractal.

While fractal coherence is a significant step forward, TreeFractal has two key shortcomings: (1) an architectural limitation and (2) protocol restrictions, both of which significantly degrade performance compared to a conventional directory protocol. The first limitation stems from TreeFractal's hierarchical architecture which degrades performance and incurs space overhead. Because the smallest sub-system in a fractal protocol must be small enough to be verified fully, TreeFractal's hierarchy is fine-grained and its tree is deep. As a result, most cache misses traverse many levels up and down the TreeFractal tree, from the requestor to the sender and back (e.g., 1-4 levels in a 16-core system), incurring latency for a coherence-interface (internal node) lookup at each level and multiple network hops between the levels. In contrast, cache misses in conventional directory schemes perform only one lookup at the directory and incur a few network hops for the request and response. Conventional hierarchical protocols employ shallow hierarchies (e.g., two levels) precisely to balance latency and scalability. We show that TreeFractal's higher cache miss latency results in 61% worse performance than a directory protocol for a 16-core system. Additionally, each of TreeFractal's coherence interfaces holds a redundant summary of the coherence tags of the interface's sub-tree, resulting in a 47% tag state overhead compared to a directory scheme which holds a single copy of the tags.

The second limitation is that TreeFractal's protocol imposes a restriction on responses to read requests. For read requests to clean blocks in the protocol, the response comes from the nearest sharer (if one exists) instead of the shared L2 or L3, exploiting sub-tree locality in TreeFractal's architecture. While sub-tree locality makes sense in TreeFractal's architecture, this protocol choice incurs unnecessary performance overheads in our architecture.

The performance and tag state overheads worsen with system size, degrading TreeFractal's performance scalability. Unfortunately, large systems are precisely where fractal coherence's verifiability excels. Given multicores' increasing core counts over technology generations, addressing these shortcomings is vital. In this paper, we propose architectural support to retain fractal coherence's verifiability while achieving directory-like scalability and good performance.

To address TreeFractal's architectural limitation, we decouple fractal coherence's logical hierarchy from the protocol architecture and propose a directory-based architecture, called *FlatFractal*, for fractal protocols. Such decoupling is not straightforward; even if all of TreeFractal's coherence interfaces (internal nodes) are co-located at the directory, the interface lookups would still be strictly sequential in tree traversal order and incur performance degradation (our results show 35%). Instead, FlatFractal flattens the hierarchical protocol actions — interface lookups and state transitions.

The key challenge addressed by FlatFractal is that blindly eliminating the logical hierarchy would introduce non-fractal interactions among sub-systems To retain the fractal nature, we make the key observation that though FlatFractal's interface lookups are not hierarchical, its coherence interactions can remain fractal if they occur through the same interfaces and in the same manner as they do in the fractal protocol. To ensure this condition, we derive FlatFractal's protocol from TreeFractal's protocol via a simple mapping. To address TreeFractal's tag state overhead, we observe that our mapping ensures that the states of FlatFractal's interfaces are strictly redundant. Therefore, the states can be summarized in a single set of tags, similar to that in a directory scheme, without the need for separate tags for each interface.

TreeFractal's second limitation of protocol restrictions on responses to read requests still applies to the FlatFractal architecture, which has to implement a fractal protocol. While a read response for a clean block in the protocol comes from the nearest sharer, FlatFractal's directory, like a conventional multicore directory, is located at the shared L2 or L3 which has the block. Therefore, obtaining the block from any sharer, even the nearest one, would add unnecessary network hops. Accordingly, we propose a simple change to the protocol that, while preserving observational equivalence, allows read requests to obtain the blocks from the shared L2 or L3.

We present a straightforward proof that FlatFractal, including the above mapping and protocol change, is observationally equivalent to TreeFractal, and hence retains the fractal property.

To summarize, our contributions are:

- To address the TreeFractal architecture's performance and tag overheads, we propose the directory-based *FlatFractal* architecture which decouples fractal coherence's logical hierarchy from the architecture and eliminates redundant coherence tag state;

- To address the TreeFractal protocol's restriction on responses to read requests, we propose a simple change to the protocol to eliminate the restriction while preserving observational equivalence; and
- Our simulations show that for a 16-core system, FlatFractal performs, on average, 57% better than TreeFractal, and within 3% of a conventional directory.

The rest of the paper is organized as follows. We provide background on fractal coherence in Section 2. We describe the FlatFractal architecture and protocol in Section 3. Section 4 describes our experimental methodology. We present our results in Section 5. We discuss some related work in Section 6 and conclude in Section 7.

# 2. Fractal Coherence: Background

As described in Section 1, fractal coherence [35] avoids the state explosion problem of conventional verification by enforcing observational equivalence between a larger system and its smaller sub-systems (i.e., equivalence in their observable interactions with *external* entities). Intuitively, sub-systems *A* and *B* are *observationally equivalent* [21] if an external entity *C* that interacts with the sub-systems by sending and receiving messages cannot differentiate between *A* and *B*. Once the smallest sub-system is verified completely, observational equivalence implies that the larger system needs no verification. Due to the inductive construction of self-similar systems from smaller sub-systems, fractal coherence naturally imposes a logical hierarchy on the system.

## 2.1 Fractal coherence protocols

Figure 1 shows an example of a tree hierarchy where two two-core systems are composed to form a four-core system such that the interactions between each cache and its parent (an external entity) in the two-core system are identical to the interactions of each two-core system with its parent (an external entity) in the four-core system. Thus, sub-systems *1*, *2*, and *3* in Figure 1 are observationally equivalent to each other and to the entire system. We explain the rest of the figure as we go. Because a cache is observationally equivalent to a sub-system, the hierarchy can grow to include arbitrarily more caches without changing the protocol behavior and without introducing new interactions that would need to be verified.

As an example of how observational equivalence may be enforced in a protocol, consider Figure 1 where caches form the leaves and each internal node is a *coherence interface* for the two sub-trees below it and holds a summary of the sub-trees' coherence tags. Assume that child *A* issues a read request to its parent $P_1$ for a block that child *B* has in *shared* state (left sub-tree in Figure 1). $P_1$ forwards the request to $P_2$. Because *B* has the block in *shared*, $P_2$'s summary does as well. But, because a cache normally would not make an external read request for a block already in the cache in

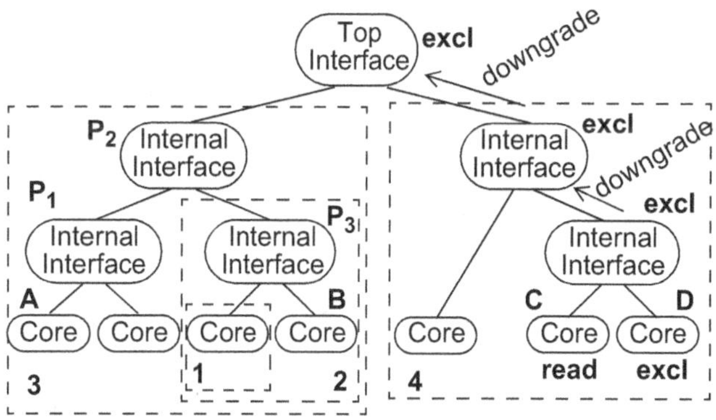

**Figure 1. Fractal coherence**

*shared* state, $P_2$ cannot externally forward *A*'s request to its own parent without violating observational equivalence between *B* and $P_2$'s sub-tree. Instead, the request is handled internally within $P_2$'s sub-tree where $P_2$ forwards the request to *B* via $P_3$. *B* sends the data to *A* via $P_3$, $P_2$, and $P_1$. Similar care must be taken with other coherence transitions to ensure observational equivalence between each set of interfaces. For example, in the right sub-tree (sub-system *4*) in Figure 1, upon a read request from cache *C* to an *exclusive* block in cache *D* (all upper interfaces are in *exclusive*), an interface issues an external *exclusive*-to-*owned* downgrade to its parent interface because the block is no longer *exclusive*. However, a cache performing a local read to an *exclusive* block normally would not issue such an external downgrade to its parent interface. To remove this dissimilarity, the caches' coherence interface includes "dummy" transitions that issue spontaneous downgrades from *exclusive* without any processor request. These dummy transitions are formally verified and are present in the cache's interface but are not triggered in real execution (removing these transitions from the interface would mean that the implemented protocol is different from the verified protocol). A key point is that observational equivalence constrains only the external interactions of sub-systems but not the details within the sub-systems. Also, though there may be protocol design choices that are different from our examples, such choices would still need to ensure observational equivalence.

## 2.2 TreeFractal

The specific fractal protocol proposed in [35], *TreeFractal*, uses a binary tree architecture with caches at the leaves, *internal* interfaces within the tree, and a *top* interface at the root of the tree. TreeFractal's architecture mimics fractal coherence's logical hierarchy shown in Figure 1.

As discussed in Section 1, because the smallest sub-system in a fractal protocol must be small enough to be verified fully, TreeFractal's hierarchy is fine-grained and its tree is deep. Thus, most cache misses traverse many levels in the tree, incurring both lookup latencies to access each interface and network latency between the interfaces. In contrast, cache misses in conventional directory schemes perform

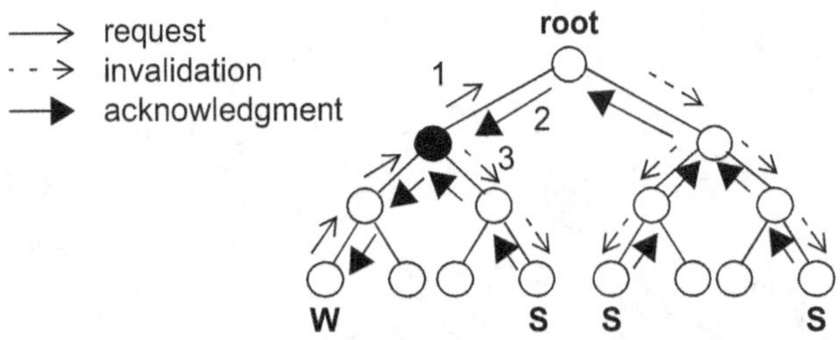

**Figure 2. Writes in the TreeFractal protocol**

only one lookup at the directory and incur a few network hops for the request and response. Conventional hierarchical protocols employ shallow hierarchies (e.g., two levels) to avoid this problem. Further, because each upper interface in TreeFractal holds summaries of its sub-trees' coherence tags, there is significant redundancy, and hence overhead, in the tag state. As the tree scales to more cores, these latency and tag state overheads increase. Our first contribution, *FlatFractal*, addresses these overheads.

TreeFractal's protocol imposes a restriction on responses to read requests. While conventional coherence allows a shared L2 or L3 cache to respond to requests if the block is clean, TreeFractal's protocol requires that the response come from the sharer closest to the requestor, instead of the shared L2 or L3. This requirement exists for the same observational-equivalence reason that requires *B* to respond to *A*'s request in our example above. Thus, read requests traverse up to the root of the smallest sub-tree containing the requestor's nearest sharer and then down to that sharer (e.g., *A*'s request goes up to $P_2$ and then down to *B*). The response is sent back through the hierarchy to the requestor. This nearest-sharer choice exploits sub-tree locality in the TreeFractal architecture but imposes unnecessary network hops in our FlatFractal architecture. Our second contribution, a simple change to the FlatFractal protocol, addresses this restriction of the TreeFractal protocol.

Write requests in the TreeFractal protocol traverse up to either a shared (internal) parent if a sibling already has write permissions or to the root of the tree, ensuring that all copies of the requested block are invalidated. In the former case, the shared parent serializes the writes, while in the latter, the root serializes the writes. In Figure 2, cache *W* sends a write request up to the tree root, for a shared block present in the leaves marked *S*. Upon receiving the request from its left child, the root sends invalidations to its right child which then forwards the invalidations down to its nodes that have a copy of the block, all the way to the leaves, as shown in Figure 2. The leaves send the acknowledgments back up the tree and each internal node waits to obtain acknowledgments from one child or both children, as appropriate, before sending an acknowledgment up. Finally, the root sends an acknowledgment to the left sub-tree where each internal node waits for the acknowledgment from its parent *before* sending an invalidation down to the appropriate child, as shown by the req-ack-inv numbering at the solid internal node in Figure 2. This ordering ensures that the write has been serialized properly in external sub-systems before the internal node's sub-system is invalidated. Once all sub-systems are invalidated, *W* receives an acknowledgment for its write request. If the request is for a write miss as opposed to an upgrade, then the nearest sharer sends the block with its invalidation acknowledgment, analogous to read responses.

Despite our optimizations, there are some conventional protocol optimizations that are not fractal and therefore cannot be included in a fractal protocol. One key example is reply forwarding where the responder *directly* forwards its responses to the requestor. This optimization violates observational equivalence because (1) caches and sub-systems would appear to handle responses differently (i.e., requestors receive response messages while upper interfaces do not) and (2) adding new cores to the system would increase the set of possible interactions at each core. Because multicore on-chip latencies are shorter than traditional distributed shared-memory system latencies, reply forwarding's hop count reduction may have a lower performance impact in the former case than the latter. Nevertheless, the impact is seen even in multicores, as our results show.

### 2.3 Verifying fractal protocols

Verifying fractal protocols is a two-step process. The first step uses conventional state exploration (e.g., *Murphi* [9]) to verify formally a minimal *complete* system consisting of at least one of each type of coherence interface (e.g., sub-system *4* in Figure 1 with a top interface instead of an internal interface at the sub-system's root). The second step uses a formal verification tool (e.g., *CADP* [11]) to check for observational equivalence of the interactions between the interfaces in the minimal system (e.g., the *core-to-internal*, *internal-to-internal*, *internal-to-top*, and *core-to-top* interactions in Figure 1 are *all* equivalent).

## 3. FlatFractal Architecture & Protocol

To address TreeFractal's overheads, we decouple fractal coherence's logical hierarchy from the protocol architecture, as described in Section 1. We propose *FlatFractal*, a directory-based architecture that retains fractal coherence's logical hierarchy while eliminating TreeFractal's network and sequential tree-order lookup latencies. FlatFractal avoids the former by co-locating the upper interfaces (i.e., *internal* and *top* in Figure 1) at the directory; and the latter by flattening the hierarchical protocol actions — interface lookups and coherence state transitions. Because FlatFractal's directory holds only one copy of the coherence tags, FlatFractal eliminates TreeFractal's tag state overhead. FlatFractal's architecture resembles that of a typical multicore with directory coherence, as shown in Figure 3.

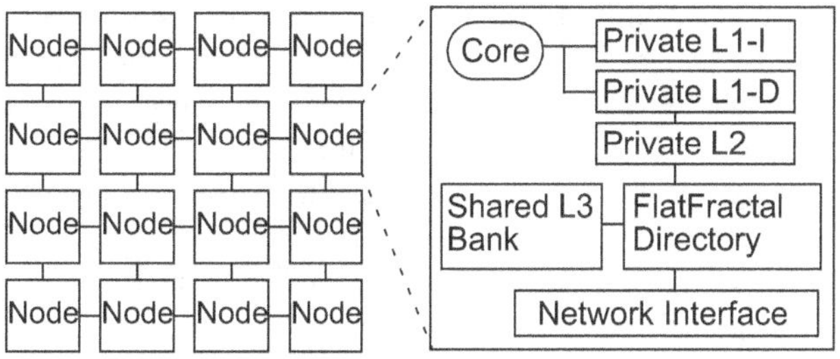

**Figure 3. FlatFractal architecture**

### 3.1 Interface co-location

The first step, co-locating the interfaces, is straightforward: we simply place all of the tree's non-leaf interfaces at the directory. The leaf interfaces are the private caches which are located with their cores. As in a conventional directory scheme, there is only one network hop from a requestor to all the interfaces at the directory as opposed to TreeFractal's traversal of multiple tree levels. Unlike in a directory, however, each request must still sequentially lookup the interfaces in tree order to conform to fractal coherence's logical hierarchy. The sum of these lookup latencies would significantly exceed the latency for a directory lookup, degrading performance relative to a directory scheme (our results show 35%).

### 3.2 Flattening the logical hierarchy

The second step, flattening the logical hierarchy poses the following challenge: to achieve a flat lookup for all the interfaces together, the protocol must merge the interfaces' state machines into a single state machine such that the merged protocol conforms to fractal coherence's logical hierarchy.

#### 3.2.1 Conforming to fractal's logical hierarchy

One may think to merge the co-located interfaces' state machines by simply collapsing them into a single, directory-like interface. However, any naive collapsing would allow the interfaces to interact arbitrarily as in a conventional directory protocol and thereby destroy the protocol's logical hierarchy and fractal structure. Instead, to preserve verifiability, the merged coherence interface must obey the logical hierarchy, although the architecture is no longer hierarchical. For example, consider the scenario described in Section 2.1 and Figure 1: child *A* issues a read request for a block that child *B* has in *shared*. In the original (sequential) fractal protocol, *A*'s request is forwarded to *B* which responds with the block. In the merged FlatFractal protocol the same actions should occur even though there may be other sharers (or a shared L2) that could supply the block.

To ensure that the merging maintains the fractal protocol's logical hierarchy, we derive the FlatFractal protocol from TreeFractal's protocol via a simple mapping, as mentioned in Section 1. Recall from Section 2.2 that a request from a cache interface is passed up the tree and then down to the responder. Similarly, responses are passed up the tree and then down to the requestor. Figure 4(a) shows this sequence of actions ($Q_1$, $I_1$, $I_2$, $Q_2$) at each upper interface when

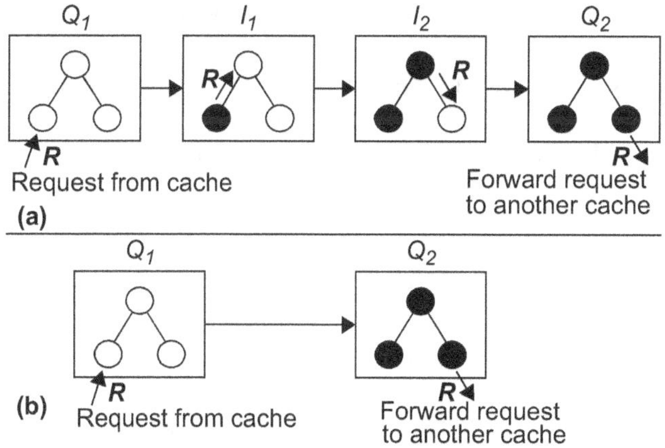

**Figure 4. Mapping (a) TreeFractal to (b) FlatFractal**

request *R* is handled. Each circle represents an upper interface (caches are not shown) where the request has looked up black interfaces but has yet to reach white interfaces. Instead of sequential lookups and transitions, FlatFractal simultaneously transitions *all* the relevant interfaces and performs the necessary actions (e.g., forward a request to an exclusive cache). Figure 4(b) shows FlatFractal's tree transitioning directly from $Q_1$ to $Q_2$ on receiving request *R*. As suggested by this example, our TreeFractal-FlatFractal mapping has three attributes. First, each of FlatFractal's state transitions corresponds to a series of transitions across TreeFractal's multiple interfaces. Second, the externally observable actions taken upon a FlatFractal transition (e.g., send a forward request or invalidation to the cache) are the same actions taken by TreeFractal's series of transitions. Thus, in Figure 4, both TreeFractal and FlatFractal send a forwarded request from state $Q_2$. Finally, FlatFractal's states are the same as or a strict subset of TreeFractal's states with some transitions modified according to the first attribute (i.e., FlatFractal's states have a one-to-one correspondence with a subset of TreeFractal's states). In Figure 4, the states $Q_1$ and $Q_2$ are the same in FlatFractal and TreeFractal.

We derive the FlatFractal protocol using the above mapping. We first consider the case where the protocol handles a single request at a time followed by the case of multiple simultaneous requests. Because of this single-request assumption, the state of each interface in TreeFractal is stable (e.g., shared, exclusive, not-present, etc.) when a request is handled. In this case, each interface holds a precise summary of its children's states. We refer to such a state of TreeFractal's tree as *quiescent* whereas an *inquiescent* tree state occurs when a message, currently traveling between interfaces, has caused some interfaces to change state but has not yet reached all the interfaces in its path. The not-yet-reached interfaces do not yet hold precise summaries of their children. Assume that the tree is in a stable, quiescent state, $Q_1$, when a request arrives. The request's arrival may cause interfaces along the request's path through the tree to transition to new (intermediate or stable) states. Similarly, one or more interfaces may issue messages to caches (e.g., an invalidation or forwarded request). In Figure 4(a), for example, $R$ causes the TreeFractal tree to pass through inquiescent states $I_1$ and $I_2$, and eventually issue a forwarded request. In general, let the set of inquiescent states that the tree passes through as it handles a request be $I_1, I_2, ..., I_n$. Eventually, the request reaches all interfaces along its path, putting the tree in a quiescent (intermediate or stable) state $Q_2$. Any messages sent by the tree in state $Q_2$ may cause caches to respond with new messages (e.g., forwarded data). Each new message goes through the tree and updates any interfaces along its way, possibly sending further new messages to caches as necessary. The result is a new (stable or intermediate) quiescent state $Q_3$. Because TreeFractal's verification shows that eventually a request will complete (e.g., no livelock or deadlock), the tree will eventually reach a quiescent stable state $Q_n$. In contrast to TreeFractal, a FlatFractal protocol consists *only* of these quiescent states $Q_1, Q_2, Q_3,...,Q_n$. Thus, FlatFractal's states and transitions are identical to the corresponding quiescent states and transitions in TreeFractal for requests occurring one at a time. Each transition between states $Q_i$ and $Q_{i+1}$ in FlatFractal occurs in response to a single message sent by a cache and may result in some actions taken by the upper tree (e.g., messages sent to the caches). As required by our mapping, these actions are the same as the externally observable actions taken by TreeFractal during the transitions $Q_i, I_1,..., I_n, Q_{i+1}$.

Next we address allowing multiple requests simultaneously. Recall that because the interfaces are distributed in TreeFractal, multiple requests can access different interfaces in the tree at the same time. Such concurrent requests may be non-conflicting (i.e., multiple read requests to the same block) or conflicting (i.e., read-write or write-write requests to the same block). Concurrent, non-conflicting requests are allowed by TreeFractal as well as some directory protocols (e.g., SGI Origin [8, 16]). For such requests, TreeFractal's tree transitions from a subset $X$ of quiescent states to another subset $Y$ by going through a series of subsets of inquiescent states (the subset size depends on the number of concurrent requests). FlatFractal also allows such requests by transitioning directly from $X$ to $Y$. Thus, for serial requests (described above) and for non-conflicting concurrent requests there is a one-to-one correspondence between TreeFractal's quiescent states and FlatFractal's states.

If the concurrent requests are conflicting, TreeFractal will serialize the requests at the root of a sub-tree, similar to conventional directory schemes which serialize at the directory (i.e., one request proceeds while the rest wait). FlatFractal also similarly serializes such requests. A minor difference between TreeFractal and FlatFractal is that while TreeFractal serializes at a sub-tree root, FlatFractal serializes at its directory which is equivalent to serializing requests at the entry to TreeFractal's upper tree. In TreeFractal, conflicting requests may concurrently traverse different paths of the tree and be serialized at a sub-tree root, causing the interfaces in the paths to enter some intermediate states. Because FlatFractal serializes such requests before they reach the interfaces (essentially at the upper tree entry), FlatFractal disallows such intermediate state combinations. However, FlatFractal's serialized combinations can occur in TreeFractal simply by the requests occurring non-concurrently, one after another. Therefore, FlatFractal's interactions are not only a strict subset of TreeFractal's but are identical to the interactions of a conflict-free TreeFractal protocol. Further, because FlatFractal performs one directory look-up while TreeFractal looks up many interfaces as a request traverses up and down the sub-tree, FlatFractal's serialization delays are shorter than TreeFractal's and similar to a conventional directory's.

Before formally proving that FlatFractal's mapping preserves TreeFractal's logical hierarchy, we present some informal, intuitive arguments that FlatFractal maintains the fractal property (i.e., does not introduce new interactions) and correctness (i.e., does not lead to deadlock or livelock). Because (1) a conflict-free TreeFractal protocol is itself fractal (we confirm this claim using CADP), (2) TreeFractal's inquiescent states are not externally visible to caches (also confirmed using CADP), and (3) there is a one-to-one correspondence between TreeFractal's conflict-free quiescent states and FlatFractal's states, FlatFractal is observationally equivalent to a conflict-free TreeFractal protocol and therefore maintains the fractal property (i.e., verifiability). This implication guarantees that FlatFractal is deadlock- and livelock-free. The waiting for conflict serialization cannot cause deadlock as such waiting also exists in TreeFractal which avoids deadlock by ensuring that a waiting request cannot block another request's responses or forwarded requests and responses (a standard deadlock-avoidance strategy).

### 3.2.2 Verifying FlatFractal's mapping

In this section, we present a straightforward proof that FlatFractal retains the fractal property. We denote a TreeFractal system (protocol and architecture) by $T(i)$, a conflict-free TreeFractal system by $T'(i)$, and a FlatFractal system by $F(i)$, where $i$ indicates the number of caches in the system. Further, we denote observational equivalence by the $\approx$ relation. We first verify that $T'(i)$ is a correct, fractal protocol and then show that $T'(i) \approx F(i)$ for $i \geq 3$ so that $F(i)$ is fractal because $T'(i)$ is fractal.

To verify $T'(i)$, we follow Section 2.3: (1) we use Murphi to verify a minimal three-cache system, $T'(3)$; and (2) we use CADP to verify that observational equivalence holds among the sub-systems in $T'$. Recall from the previous section that $T'(i)$ serializes all concurrent conflicting requests and is derived from $T(i)$ by eliminating protocol states and transitions that correspond to the upper levels of the tree (i.e., internal and top interfaces) handling conflicting requests concurrently. While $T'(i)$ is implicitly conflict-free, this conflict freedom needs to be modeled in each of the above verification steps. To that end, we employ a different method in each verification tool. In the Murphi step, we serialize conflicting requests by employing a single queue between all cores and the upper tree. In the CADP step, we ensure that the serialization does not affect observational equivalence by using a hidden process that conflicting requests use to lock the upper tree (CADP allows the use of such hidden processes). Note that these serialization methods allow us to easily model conflict freedom in the tools, but both $T'(i)$ and the FlatFractal architecture implicitly implement conflict freedom and do not require any such serialization method.

To show that $T'(i) \approx F(i)$, we recall from the previous section that FlatFractal employs a one-to-one mapping from the quiescent states, together with their transitions, in $T'(i)$ to quiescent states and transitions in $F(i)$. The remaining, inquiescent states in $T'(i)$ do not exist in $F(i)$. Because inquiescent states do not lead to any externally observable behavior (i.e., do not send or receive messages from caches), which we confirm using CADP, eliminating the inquiescent states does not violate observational equivalence. Thus, $T'(i) \approx F(i)$ for $i \geq 3$.

In general, we can apply this proof to any TreeFractal protocol by first verifying that the TreeFractal protocol maintains coherence and is fractal, and then by deriving a one-to-one mapping between the TreeFractal and FlatFractal protocols, as described above. Importantly, because the mapping is not specific to a particular protocol (e.g., MSI, MOESI, MOSI, MESI), any new mapping is likely to be similar to the one described above.

### 3.2.3 Eliminating tag overhead

FlatFractal's mapping eliminates much of the coherence tag overhead found in TreeFractal. Recall that TreeFractal stores redundant coherence tags at each level in its tree (Section 2.2). By construction, FlatFractal's states include only the quiescent states; in the presence of inquiescent states, the higher interfaces in the tree may not reflect the states of the lower interfaces, a condition that cannot occur with quiescent states. Consequently, the states of the interfaces above the lowest-level internal interfaces (i.e., the level above the leaves in Figure 1) are strictly redundant with respect to the lowest-level internal interfaces. Therefore, we can eliminate all but the lowest-level internal interfaces' states from FlatFractal, eliminating much of TreeFractal's tag overhead. However, comparing FlatFractal to a conventional directory, we observe that two dissimilarities arise. First, unlike a directory, fractal protocols forward read requests to the nearest sharer and therefore the protocols have a distinct read-shared state for each combination of sharers. In contrast, directory protocols use a single read-shared state combined with a sharer list. Second, fractal protocols order write-invalidations (Section 2.2), giving rise to many intermediate states to track the ordering. In contrast, directory protocols' use a few intermediate invalidation states to track only whether some or all acknowledgments have been received. To address these issues, we propose an efficient state representation that approaches a conventional directory's representation but is compatible with the FlatFractal architecture. While FlatFractal's read-shared states can be represented similarly to a conventional directory, the write-invalidation states cannot be as easily represented. Unfortunately, left as they are, the invalidation states would result in significant tag overhead compared to a directory.

We begin with the read-shared states which can be represented in FlatFractal similarly to a conventional directory. We separate fractal coherence's logical hierarchy, which identifies the cache(s) that should be involved in a coherence action (e.g., given a requestor, which cache should receive the forwarded request), from FlatFractal's state machine, which determines the actions that should be taken (e.g., forward a request to another cache). This separation allows us to use a conventional directory's compact state representation in FlatFractal.

To attain the separation, we observe that observational equivalence among TreeFractal' interfaces implies that the tree as a whole responds to a cache's request with the same observable actions as another cache would for the same request. For example, upon receiving a read request when some caches are in *shared*, the tree transitions the requestor to an intermediate state; and forwards the request to the sharer nearest to the requestor which provides the block to the requestor (Section 2.2). These actions occur regardless of which cache is the requestor and which combination of caches are in *shared* state. Therefore, we can represent these states as a single *shared* state with a list of sharers, like a conventional directory. The sharer list ensures that FlatFractal's actions for a particular request are the same as those taken by TreeFractal's tree as a whole. Because the sharer list retains the identity of the sharers, the logical hierarchy can be reconstructed on-the-fly to determine which cache, in this example, should receive the forwarded request. While this state representation mimics a conventional directory, FlatFractal's directory (*A'*, on the right in Figure 5) conceptually plays the roles of the top and all the relevant internal interfaces (*A*, on the left in Figure 5) for a given request. Recall from Section 2.1 that for observational equivalence we need ensure only that sub-systems' external interactions, and not internal details, are identical. By forcing FlatFractal to take the same actions as TreeFractal, we ensure that FlatFractal's sub-systems inherit observational equivalence from TreeFractal's sub-systems. Specifically, though the state with the sharer list contains complete global information, FlatFractal cannot use the global information (as a conventional directory might) to deviate in its actions from TreeFractal's logical hierarchy's actions. Instead, FlatFractal must use the information to mimic TreeFractal's logical hierarchy. In the case of read requests, FlatFractal determines the nearest

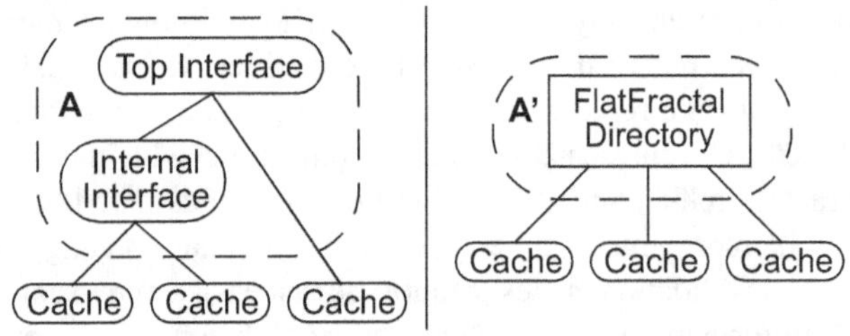


**Figure 5. TreeFractal (left) and FlatFractal (right)**

sharer from the sharer list using a simple nearest-bit-set computation and obtains the block from that sharer.

Handling write-requests as done in TreeFractal however, exposes a larger difference between FlatFractal and a directory. For write requests, FlatFractal cannot issue invalidations to all sharers in one shot, like a conventional directory. Instead, the invalidations and waiting for acknowledgments must proceed in the same fractal order among the sub-trees as in TreeFractal (Section 2.2 and Figure 2). As a result, FlatFractal contains a number of intermediate states to ensure that write invalidations occur in this order. While write-invalidations are sent to multiple sharers in multiple steps, the read requests discussed previously contact the single nearest-sharer in one step, and therefore do not incur such extra states for ordering. Conventional directories do not order invalidations and so do not have these intermediate invalidation states. As a result, fractal protocols incur a coherence tag overhead relative to directories. Fortunately, we observe that the invalidation order is fixed for a given requestor regardless of which block is being invalidated, leading to redundancy across blocks in FlatFractal. To eliminate this redundancy, we propose to pre-compute at *design time* this order for every requestor and store that in a *read-only* table in FlatFractal's directory. Assuming *n* cores, each core's list has *n* items each of $lg(n)$ bits for a total of $n^2 * lg(n)$ bits in the table (this table is for the entire directory, *not* per block). For a 64-core system, the table size is 3 KB. For a write request, FlatFractal looks up the invalidation order for the requestor and uses the sharer list to send invalidations to the sharers in that order. Though this somewhat restrictive ordering curtails overlap among invalidations to multiple sharers, we saw modest performance loss in one benchmark.

By representing most of FlatFractal's states compactly, and by eliminating cross-block redundancy for write-invalidations, FlatFractal's tag size is close to that of a conventional directory. Finally, because our optimization affects only the state representation, and not the protocol itself, the optimization does not affect our correctness proof.

### 3.3 FlatFractal protocol change

While the FlatFractal architecture is similar to a conventional directory architecture, the fractal protocol implemented by the architecture still imposes the fractal constraints of observational equivalence. As such, blindly using the TreeFractal protocol would inherit its restrictions on the responses to read requests. Recall from Section 2.2 that in the protocol, a response to a read request for a clean block comes from the nearest sharer, instead of the shared L2 or L3. This nearest-sharer choice exploits sub-tree locality in TreeFractal. However, FlatFractal's directory, like a conventional multicore directory, is located at the shared L2 or L3 which has the block and therefore obtaining the block from any sharer, even the nearest one, would add unnecessary network hops. To address this problem, we propose a simple change to the FlatFractal protocol that, while preserving observational equivalence, allows read requests to obtain the blocks from the shared L2 or L3.

Recall from Section 2.2 that the key reason for the nearest-sharer choice is to achieve observational equivalence between the cache's coherence interface and the internal interface. Specifically, because a cache interface would not make a read request for a block already present in *shared*, the internal interface should not make a read request for a block already present in its sub-tree and rather should require that the nearest sharer in its sub-tree provide the block. Instead, to have the shared L2 or L3 provide the block, we introduce a dummy transition in FlatFractal's cache interface to make read requests for already-present blocks. Then, even if their sub-trees have the block, FlatFractal's internal interfaces can forward a read request for the block all the way up to the root of the whole tree to obtain the block from the shared L2 or L3. Recall from Section 2.1 that dummy transitions are necessary only for preserving observational equivalence. The transitions are therefore fully verified and present in the cache interfaces but are not triggered in real execution.

In the FlatFractal architecture, this protocol implies that a read request to a clean block goes to the directory and obtains the block directly from the shared L2 or L3 (without needing to find the closest sharer). Thus, TreeFractal's extra network hops are eliminated.

#### 3.3.1 Verifying the protocol change

To verify our protocol change we integrate the new transitions (both real and dummy) into the original TreeFractal protocol and verify the new TreeFractal protocol using the method described in Section 2.3.

## 4. Methodology

We simulate FlatFractal using Wisconsin GEMS-2.1 [19] built on top of Simics, a full-system simulator [18]. We simulate a SPARC-based multicore system running Solaris 10. The hardware parameters are given in Table 1. We simulate TreeFractal using interface lookup latencies obtained from CACTI [28], as shown in Table 1. FlatFractal's directory lookup latency adds one cycle to that of the conventional directory for looking up the 128-byte (16 cores) or 640-byte (32 cores) invalidation-order table (Section 3.2.3). Though the table lookup is needed only for writes, we conservatively charge all accesses. We use three commercial workloads and

**Table 1. Hardware parameters**

| | |
|---|---|
| Cores | 16, in-order |
| L1+L2 Caches | Split I&D, Private, 32KB 4-way set associative + 256KB 8-way set associative, write-back, 64B block, LRU replacement, 3 cycles |
| L3 Cache | Unified, Shared, 32 MB 16-way set associative, write-back, 16 banks, LRU replacement, 10 cycles |
| Network | Mesh, 5 cycles for router+link |
| Coherence | MOSI full bit-vector directory at L3, 10 cycles/ 256 KB *16 banks = 4 MB for base and 11 cycles/ 256 KB *16 banks = 4 MB for FlatFractal |
| Memory | 16 GB, 250 cycles |
| TreeFractal | Interfaces bottom to top: 6, 7, 8, and 10 cycles and 80*8, 160*4, 320*2, and 640 KB = 1.875 MB + 4 MB (root+L3) |

five scientific applications from Splash-2 suite [33], as described in Table 2. We do not use Splash-2's kernels due to simulation constraints. To account for statistical variations, we use randomly-perturbed runs to achieve 95% confidence [4] for at most a 2% variation on the mean.

# 5. Experimental Results

We start by verifying the FlatFractal architecture and protocol change (Section 5.1). We then compare the performance of TreeFractal and FlatFractal against that of a conventional directory (Section 5.2), followed by a breakdown analysis of the execution time showing network and interface lookup components (Section 5.3). Next, we isolate the contributions of the FlatFractal architecture and FlatFractal protocol change (Section 5.4). We then present FlatFractal's sensitivity to the network latency and scalability with the number of cores (Section 5.5 and Section 5.6). Finally, we identify FlatFractal's overheads and analyze their effect on FlatFractal's scalability (Section 5.7).

**Table 2. Benchmarks**

| Commercial (com) |
|---|
| **Apache** 2.2.11 [30] and SURGE v1.3 [6] with http 1.1 capability; repository of 20,000 files (~500MB); 3200 clients; 25ms think time between requests; warm up for ~1,500,000 transactions; measure 2000 transactions. |
| **Online Transaction Processing (OLTP)** PostgreSQL v9.2.0 [2] and Open Source Development Labs Test Suite DBT-2 v0.40[1] modeling TPC-C-like specifications; 2GB database; 10 warehouses; 256 users with 0 think time; warm up for 20,000 transactions; measure 200 transactions. |
| **SPECjbb2005** v1.07[3] with Sun J2SE v1.5.0 JVM; 1.5 warehouses per processor with 0 think time; warm up for 350,000 transactions; measure for 10,000 transactions. |
| **Scientific (sci)** |
| **SPLASH-2:** We use *raytrace, ocean, water-spatial, volrend,* and *water-$n^2$* from SPLASH-2 [33]. We run these applications using default parameters. For *raytrace*, we render the "car" object as provided by the SPLASH-2 suite. |

### 5.1 Verification

As per Section 3.2.2, Section 3.3.1 and Section 2.3, we use (1) Murphi to confirm that a conflict-free TreeFractal protocol (Section 3.2.2), including our changes to allow read responses from the L3 (Section 3.3) and to use an out-of-order network, maintains coherence; and (2) CADP to verify that the protocol is fractal. Recall that our mapping in Section 3.2 preserves observational equivalence between a conflict-free TreeFractal protocol and FlatFractal.

### 5.2 Performance

In Figure 6, we compare the execution times of FlatFractal and TreeFractal normalized to those of a conventional directory. We also include *Co-locate* which is TreeFractal with all the internal interfaces and top interface co-located together at each L3 bank, similar to a directory (Section 3.1). While such co-location is straightforward and removes network hops between interfaces, the architecture still incurs the latency of sequential interface lookups. Figure 6 shows the normalized execution time (Y-axis, lower is better) for each benchmark (X-axis). The three right-most clusters show the mean for the commercial benchmarks (*mean-com*), scientific benchmarks (*mean-sci*), and all benchmarks (*mean-all*). Because the commercial and scientific benchmarks behave quite differently, we separate their means.

Because TreeFractal traverses many tree levels each of which adds network hops and interface lookup latency, TreeFractal's execution time is significantly longer, on average 61%, than the base directory. While Co-locate removes the network hops, there is still a significant gap of 35% due to the interface lookups. FlatFractal eliminates almost all of these overheads and performs close to the base directory. In *raytrace* and *ocean,* FlatFractal lags a little because of ordering write invalidations to match TreeFractal (Section 3.2.3) and because fractal protocols in general disallow reply forwarding. Section 5.7 discusses these issues further.

We note that our performance numbers for TreeFractal are different from those in the TreeFractal paper [35] which does

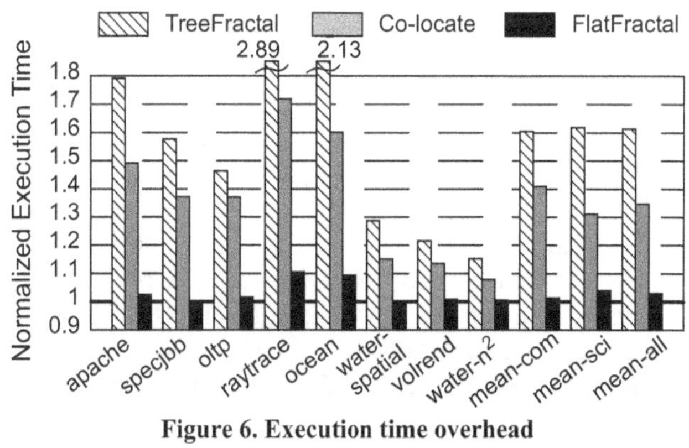


**Figure 6. Execution time overhead**

**Table 3. Per-L2-miss latency and bandwidth (relative to base directory)**

| Benchmarks | | Total Miss Latency | | | | Network Latency / Miss | | | | Lookup Latency / Miss | | | | Bytes*Links / Miss | | | |
|---|---|---|---|---|---|---|---|---|---|---|---|---|---|---|---|---|---|
| | (A) MPKI | (B) Directory | (C) TreeFractal | (D) Co-locate | (E) FlatFractal | (F) Directory | (G) TreeFractal | (H) Co-locate | (I) FlatFractal | (J) Directory | (K) TreeFractal | (L) Co-locate | (M) FlatFractal | (N) Directory | (O) TreeFractal | (P) Co-locate | (Q) FlatFractal |
| **apache** | 36 | 1 | 2.0 | 1.6 | 1.0 | 0.4 | 1.0 | 0.6 | 0.4 | 0.1 | 0.5 | 0.5 | 0.1 | 1 | 1.8 | 1.3 | 1.1 |
| **specjbb** | 10 | 1 | 2.2 | 1.7 | 1.1 | 0.4 | 1.0 | 0.7 | 0.4 | 0.1 | 0.6 | 0.6 | 0.1 | 1 | 1.9 | 1.4 | 1.0 |
| **oltp** | 7.2 | 1 | 2.7 | 2.2 | 1.1 | 0.6 | 1.5 | 1.1 | 0.6 | 0.1 | 0.8 | 0.8 | 0.1 | 1 | 2.0 | 1.7 | 1.0 |
| **raytrace** | 7.4 | 1 | 4.5 | 2.8 | 1.4 | 0.5 | 1.1 | 1.0 | 0.7 | 0.4 | 3.2 | 1.6 | 0.5 | 1 | 2.2 | 1.9 | 1.1 |
| **ocean** | 3.9 | 1 | 3.3 | 2.4 | 1.2 | 0.7 | 1.9 | 1.2 | 0.8 | 0.1 | 1.2 | 1.1 | 0.1 | 1 | 2.4 | 1.6 | 1.2 |
| **water-spat** | 2.6 | 1 | 3.2 | 2.4 | 1.0 | 0.6 | 1.4 | 1.0 | 0.6 | 0.3 | 1.6 | 1.0 | 0.3 | 1 | 1.8 | 2.0 | 1.1 |
| **volrend** | 1.2 | 1 | 3.2 | 2.4 | 1.1 | 0.6 | 1.7 | 1.1 | 0.8 | 0.1 | 1.3 | 1.0 | 0.2 | 1 | 2.4 | 1.9 | 1.1 |
| **water-n$^2$** | 0.7 | 1 | 3.0 | 2.4 | 1.1 | 0.8 | 1.7 | 1.2 | 0.8 | 0.1 | 1.1 | 0.9 | 0.1 | 1 | 2.2 | 1.8 | 1.2 |
| **mean - com** | | 1 | 2.3 | 1.8 | 1.1 | 0.5 | 1.2 | 0.8 | 0.5 | 0.1 | 0.6 | 0.6 | 0.1 | 1 | 1.9 | 1.4 | 1.0 |
| **mean - sci** | | 1 | 3.4 | 2.5 | 1.2 | 0.6 | 1.6 | 1.1 | 0.7 | 0.2 | 1.7 | 1.1 | 0.2 | 1 | 2.2 | 1.8 | 1.1 |

not compare TreeFractal to a realistic on-chip directory, as done here. Instead, the paper finds that (1) TreeFractal with on-chip interfaces is better than an off-chip directory and (2) when both TreeFractal and an on-chip directory have an ideal, 1-cycle latency, the two perform similarly. Though the paper proposes the breakthrough idea of fractal coherence, these comparisons are inconclusive. The first comparison's base case is too weak and the second comparison removes all differences between the two schemes.

Table 1 shows the tag space for the base directory, FlatFractal, and TreeFractal (rows "Coherence" and "TreeFractal"). TreeFractal's total tag space is 47% larger than the base directory while FlatFractal incurs virtually no overhead (128-640 bytes over 4 MB to order write invalidations as described in Section 3.2.3).

We now analyze the reasons behind our above performance results. In Table 3, we compare the per-L2-miss latency and bandwidth cost of the various schemes. The table shows the total per-L2-miss latency and the per-L2-miss network and interface lookup components for TreeFractal, Co-locate, and FlatFractal normalized to the total per-L2-miss latency for the base directory. All latencies and components are normalized to the base directory's total miss latency and the network and lookup components do *not* add up to the total miss latency which includes L3 + memory access latencies. The lookup component includes queuing at the interfaces or directory, as appropriate. We also include the L2 miss rate — expressed in misses per 1000 instructions (MPKI) — to gauge the importance of these latencies (low miss rate implies less importance as is the case for *volrend* and *water-n*$^2$). We see that TreeFractal's total miss latency (column *C*) is more than double that of the base directory (column *B*), explaining TreeFractal's longer execution times in Figure 6. This extra latency is from the network (column *G*) and lookup (column *K*) components; TreeFractal's component latencies are larger than the corresponding base directory's components (columns *F* and *J*). Co-locate's total miss latency (column *D*) is lower than TreeFractal's (column *C*) but still worse than the base directory's. Because of interface co-location, Co-locate's network component (column *H*) is closer to the base directory's (column *F*) than TreeFractal's (column *G*). Still, Co-locate's network latency component is worse than the base directory's for two reasons: (1) the read response restriction and (2) the lack of reply forwarding (Section 2.2). These two issues also contribute to queuing at the directory, which causes Co-locate's lookup component (column *L*) to exceed the base directory's (column *J*). As expected from FlatFractal's and the base directory's similar execution times in Figure 6, FlatFractal's total miss latency, network component, and lookup component (columns *E*, *I*, and *M*) are close to those of the base directory (columns *B*, *F*, and *J*). FlatFractal incurs some extra total latency (column *E*) in the scientific benchmarks due to write-invalidation ordering and the lack of reply forwarding, as mentioned above. However, only *ocean* and *raytrace* worsen in execution time (Figure 6) due to their higher miss rates among the scientific benchmarks (column *A*).

Table 3 also shows the per-miss bandwidth in terms of the product of bytes and network links (columns *N* through *Q*). As expected, TreeFractal (column *O*) incurs significantly higher bandwidth overhead than the base directory (column *N*). Co-locate (column *P*) is better than TreeFractal but still incurs overhead due to the reasons explained above. *Water-spatial* is an exception; Co-locate's bandwidth is greater than

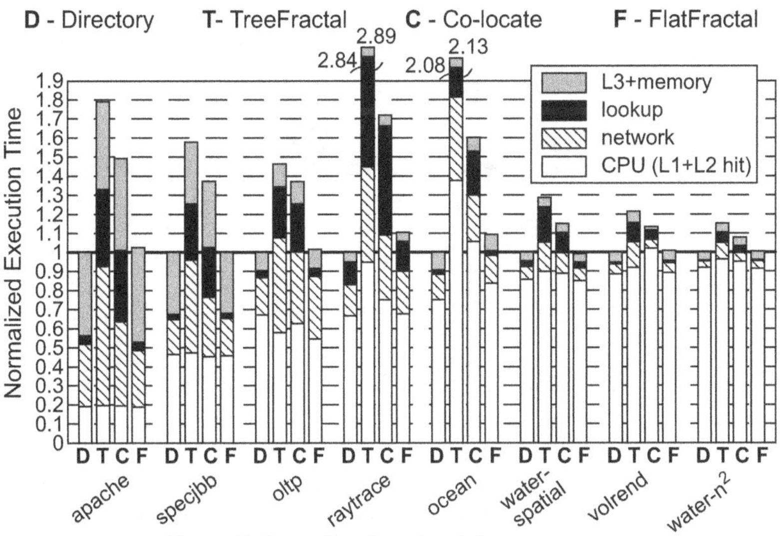


**Figure 7. Execution time breakdown**

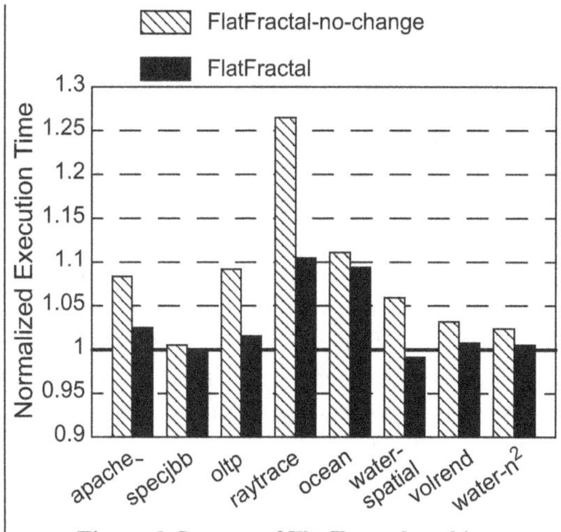


**Figure 8. Impact of FlatFractal architecture and protocol**

TreeFractal's because co-location changes the timing which happens to result in more forwarding. FlatFractal (column *Q*) is close to the base directory but still incurs some overhead due to the lack of reply forwarding. The considerable difference between Co-locate and FlatFractal (columns *P* and *Q*) is due to FlatFractal's protocol change for read responses.

### 5.3 Execution time breakdown

While the previous section presents the per-miss latency and bandwidth costs, this section shows a breakdown of execution time to connect the per-miss costs to overall performance. Figure 7 shows execution time normalized to that of the base directory for TreeFractal, Co-locate, and FlatFractal broken down into four components: CPU (including L1+L2 hits), network, directory lookup, and memory hierarchy (L3 + memory latencies). In general, the commercial workloads (*apache*, *specjbb*, and *OLTP*) have much lower CPU (L1+L2 hit) components than the scientific benchmarks, highlighting the commercial workloads' memory-hierarchy-intense nature. The figure confirms that TreeFractal's and Co-locate's longer execution times come from the much larger network and interface lookup components than those of the base directory. *Raytrace*, running on TreeFractal, incurs significant queuing at the directory which enlarges *raytrace*'s lookup component. In contrast to TreeFractal and Co-locate, FlatFractal's network and lookup components are similar to those of the base directory, which explains the similarity in their execution times. *Ocean*'s CPU component is larger for TreeFractal and Co-locate due to higher load imbalance (longer spinning at barriers) exacerbated by the network and interface lookup overheads.

### 5.4 Impact of FlatFractal architecture & protocol

In this section, we isolate the benefits of the FlatFractal architecture and protocol (read response change in Section 3.3). Figure 8 shows execution time normalized to that of the base directory for the FlatFractal architecture without the protocol change (*FlatFractal-no-change*) and with the change (*FlatFractal*). The protocol change brings modest improvements commensurate with the simplicity of the change. This result also implies that most of FlatFractal's improvement over TreeFractal is due to the architecture.

### 5.5 Sensitivity to network latency

Because TreeFractal exercises the network much more than the base directory, we study TreeFractal's sensitivity to network router+link latency, Figure 9 shows the sensitivity of TreeFractal and FlatFractal as we decrease the network router+link latency from five cycles (default) to an optimistic one cycle. The Y-axis shows execution time normalized to that of the base directory with the corresponding network latency. As we decrease its latency, the network becomes less significant to overall execution time. Accordingly, TreeFractal improves with the optimistic one-cycle latency, especially for *raytrace* and *OLTP* due to their significant network components (Figure 7). Even with the optimistic latency setting, there is still a substantial gap between TreeFractal and the base directory, especially for the memory-hierarchy-intensive commercial workloads (Figure 7). Because FlatFractal's

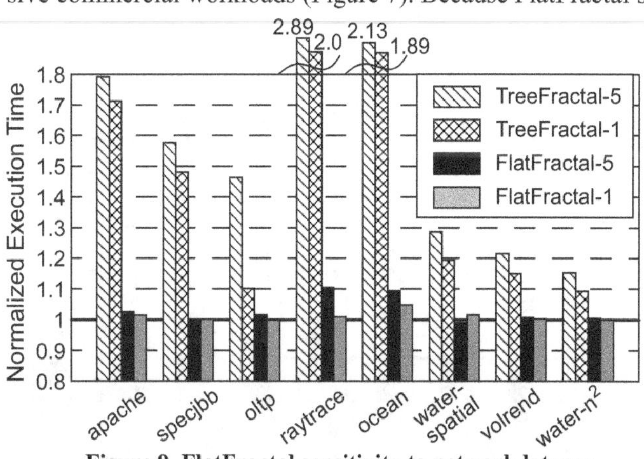


**Figure 9. FlatFractal sensitivity to network latency**

performance degradation is low even with the five-cycle latency, FlatFractal is not affected appreciably by the change in network latency.

### 5.6 Scaling the number of cores

In Figure 10, we show how TreeFractal and FlatFractal scale as we increase the number of cores from 16 (default) to 32. The Y-axis shows execution time normalized to that of the base directory with the corresponding number of cores. TreeFractal's performance degrades with more cores due to the deepening of the tree which adds more network hops and interface lookups to misses. This lack of performance scaling is problematic especially because fractal coherence's verifiability is more important for larger systems. In contrast, FlatFractal tracks the base directory closely, highlighting FlatFractal's performance scalability while preserving verifiability. *Raytrace* running on 32-core FlatFractal incurs some performance loss relative to the base directory, which we discuss next.

### 5.7 FlatFractal's performance overhead

As mentioned above and in Section 5.2, *raytrace*, and to a lesser degree, *ocean* and *OLTP*, incur some execution time overhead due the lack of reply forwarding and ordered write-invalidations. Figure 11 shows along the Y-axis the execution time for a 32-core FlatFractal normalized to that of the base directory (16-core FlatFractal behaves similarly). The normalized execution time is divided into three components: overhead due to no reply forwarding, overhead due to write-invalidation ordering, and the remaining execution time. The third component matches the base directory's execution time (line at Y = 1), indicating that the first two components are the only sources of overhead in FlatFractal. Reply forwarding contributes more to the overhead than ordered write invalidations because the former affects both read requests and write-invalidation acknowledgments whereas the latter affects only write invalidations. Finally, these sources of overhead have a moderate effect on just a few benchmarks (i.e., *OLTP*, *raytrace,* and *ocean*), even for 32 cores. However, reducing the overhead may be useful as the system scales beyond 32 cores.

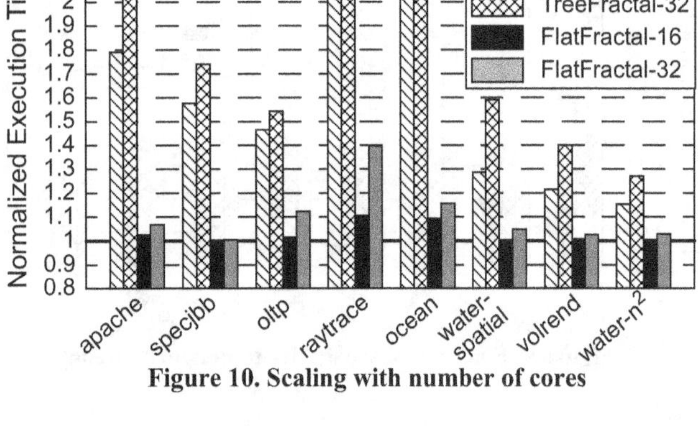


**Figure 10. Scaling with number of cores**

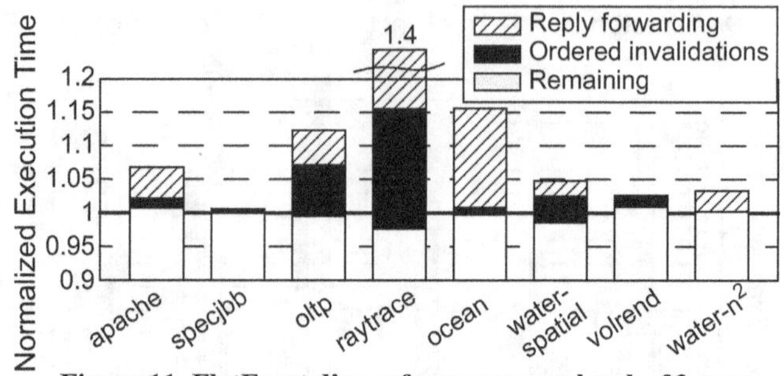


**Figure 11. FlatFractal's performance overheads, 32 cores**

# 6. Related Work

As mentioned in Section 1, state exploration, one approach to coherence protocol verification, suffers from the state explosion problem. Verification optimizations, such as exploiting inherent symmetry (i.e., caches' states are symmetric), have been proposed to alleviate the problem [15], however, the optimizations generally delay rather than eliminate state explosion. In addition to brute-force state exploration, many other approaches exist, most of which fall into two classes. One class is model-checking (including symbolic model checking), which uses a formal description to express a protocol and then verifies various properties about the protocol [23, 25, 29], using state exploration on the smaller formal description. Notably, model-checking has been used to verify a few existing protocols, such as the Futurebus protocol [31] and S3.mp [26]. While model-checking is powerful, the approach still relies on the underlying protocol's states and interactions and therefore is also susceptible to state explosion [24]. To avoid such explosion, parameterized model-checking [29] uses scale-independent abstractions. However, all model-checking approaches generally require significant human effort to identify appropriate abstractions for a given protocol. Further, using abstractions creates the possibility that the verified abstraction and implementation are different. The second class is semi-automated theorem proving [22], which, by relying on proofs can be independent of system scale. However, because the approach often requires significant effort from the designer to prove theorems, this approach is less commonly used.

Fractal coherence [35] is the first architectural approach to apply the idea of observational equivalence for designing coherence protocols that are verifiable by design (i.e., protocols with a property that facilitates verification). We extensively cover fractal coherence in the previous sections. As mentioned in Section 1, while fractal protocols are hierarchical, conventional hierarchical protocols [17, 20, 32], which target scalability, are not necessarily fractal.

# 7. Conclusion

Fractal coherence is a breakthrough solution for scalable verification of cache coherence protocols. By applying the idea of observational equivalence between a larger system and its smaller sub-systems, the fractal approach ensures that a protocol for a larger system is verified by design if a minimal sub-system is verified completely. Thus, fractal coherence naturally imposes a *logical* hierarchy on the system due to the inductive construction of self-similar systems from smaller sub-systems. However, the specific fractal protocol, TreeFractal, incurs significant performance and coherence tag state overheads due to two limitations: (1) In TreeFractal's tree architecture, each miss traverses many levels up and down the tree and each level redundantly holds its subtrees' coherence tags. (2) TreeFractal imposes a restriction on responses to read requests that forces read requests to obtain clean blocks from the nearest sharer even if accessing the shared L2 or L3 is faster.

To address these limitations, we proposed architectural support to retain fractal coherence's verifiability while achieving directory-like scalability and good performance. Our first idea, *FlatFractal,* is a directory-based architecture which decouples fractal coherence's logical hierarchy from the architecture and eliminates redundant tag state. Our second idea is a simple change to the protocol that, while preserving observational equivalence, allows read requests to obtain the blocks from the shared L2 or L3. Using a combination of verification tools and a straightforward proof, we verified our FlatFractal protocol and architecture. Using simulations, we showed that for 16 cores, FlatFractal performs, on average, 57% better than TreeFractal, and within 3% of a conventional directory.

Given multicores' increasing core counts over technology generations and the scale-out trends in systems for handling the ever-increasing data, FlatFractal's approach for achieving both performance and verification scalability will be important. In our future work, we will improve FlatFractal's scalability by addressing some of the key protocol performance optimizations that violate observational equivalence.

# References


[1] Open source development labs database test suite 2 v0.40 http://osdldbt.sourceforge.net/.

[2] Postgresql. v9.2.0. http://www.postgresql.org/.

[3] The standard performance evaluation corporation. SPECjbb2005 suite. http://www.spec.org/jbb2005/.

[4] A. R. Alameldeen and D. A. Wood. Variability in architectural simulations of multi-threaded workloads. In *Proceedings of the 9th International Symposium on High-Performance Computer Architecture*, 2003.

[5] AMD. Revision Guide for AMD Family 14H Models 00h-0Fh Processors, revision 3.,18. February 2013.

[6] P. Barford and M. Crovella. Generating representative web workloads for network and server performance evaluation. In *Proceedings of the 1998 ACM SIGMETRICS Joint International Conference on Measurement and Modeling of Computer Systems*, pages 151-160, 1998. ACM.

[7] B. Bentley. Simulation Driven Verification. Presentation at *Design Automation Summer School.* 2009.

[8] D. Culler, J. Singh, and A. Gupta. *Parallel Computer Architecture: A Hardware/Software Approach.* Morgan Kaufmann, 1st edition, 1998. The Morgan Kaufmann Series in Computer Architecture and Design.

[9] D. Dill, A. Drexler, A. Hu, and C. Yang. Protocol verification as a hardware design aid. In *Proceedings of the IEEE 1992 International Conference on Computer Design: VLSI in Computers and Processors,* pages 522 –525, 1992.

[10] A. Felty and F. Stomp. A correctness proof of a cache coherence protocol. In *Proceedings of the 11th Annual Conference on Computer Assurance*, pages 128-141, Oct 1992.

[11] H. Garavel, F. Lang, R. Mateescu, and W. Serwe. CADP 2010: A toolbox for the construction and analysis of distributed processes. In P. Abdulla and K. Leino, editors, *Tools and Algorithms for the Construction and Analysis of Systems*, volume 6605 of *Lecture Notes in Computer Science*, pages 372–387. Springer Berlin / Heidelberg, 2011. 10.1007/978-3-642-19835-9_33.

[12] S. Gjessing, S. Krogdahl, and E. Munthe-Kaas. A linked list cache coherence protocol: verifying the bottom layer. In *Proceedings of the 5th International Parallel Processing Symposium*, pages 324-329, 1991.

[13] S. Gjessing, S. Krogdahl, and E. Munthe-Kaas. A top down approach to the formal specification of SCI cache coherence. In *Computer Aided Verification, 3rd International Workshop*, pages 83-91. Springer, 1991.

[14] Intel. Intel Xeon Processor E7-800/4800/2800 Product Families Specification Update. August 2013.

[15] C. N. Ip and D. L. Dill. Better verification through symmetry. *Formal Methods in System Design*, 9(1-2):41–75, Aug. 1996.

[16] J. Laudon and D. Lenoski. The SGI Origin: a ccNUMA highly scalable server. In *Proceedings of the 24th Annual International Symposium on Computer Architecture*, pages 241–251, 1997. ACM.

[17] D. Lenoski, J. Laudon, K. Gharachorloo, A. Gupta, and J. Hennessy. The directory-based cache coherence protocol for the DASH multiprocessor. In *Proceedings of the 17th Annual International Symposium on Computer Architecture*, pages 148–159, 1990. ACM.

[18] P. S. Magnusson, M. Christensson, J. Eskilson, D. Forsgren, G. Hållberg, J. Högberg, F. Larsson, A. Moestedt, and B. Werner. Simics: A full system simulation platform. *Computer*, 35(2):50–58, Feb. 2002.

[19] M. M. K. Martin, D. J. Sorin, B. M. Beckmann, M. R. Marty, M. Xu, A. R. Alameldeen, K. E. Moore, M. D. Hill, and D. A. Wood. Multifacet's general execution-driven multiprocessor simulator (GEMS) toolset. *SIGARCH Computer Architecture News*, 33(4):92–99, Nov. 2005.

[20] M. R. Marty and M. D. Hill. Virtual hierarchies to support server consolidation. In *Proceedings of the 34th Annual International Symposium on Computer Architecture*, pages 46–56, New York, NY, USA, 2007. ACM.

[21] R. Milner. *A Calculus of Communicating Systems.* Springer-Verlag New York, Inc., Secaucus, NJ, USA, 1982.

[22] S. Park and D. L. Dill. Verification of FLASH cache coherence protocol by aggregation of distributed transactions. In *Proceedings of the 8th Annual ACM Symposium on Parallel Algorithms and Architectures*, pages 288–296, 1996. ACM.

[23] F. Pong and M. Dubois. The verification of cache coherence protocols. In *Proceedings of the 5th Annual ACM Symposium on Parallel Algorithms and Architectures*, pages 11–20, 1993. ACM.

[24] F. Pong and M. Dubois. Verification techniques for cache coherence protocols. *ACM Computing Surveys*, 29(1):82–126, Mar. 1997.

[25] F. Pong and M. Dubois. Formal verification of complex coherence protocols using symbolic state models. *Journal of the ACM*, 45(4):557–587, July 1998.

[26] F. Pong, A. Nowatzyk, G. Aybay, and M. Dubois. Verifying distributed directory-based cache coherence protocols: S3.mp, a case study. In *Euro-Par '95: Parallel Processing*, volume 966 of *Lecture Notes in Computer Science*, pages 287-300, Springer Berlin/Heidelberg, 1995.

[27] U. Stern and D. Dill. Automatic verification of the SCI cache coherence protocol. In *Correct Hardware Design and Verification Methods: IFIP WG10.5 Advanced Research Working Conference Proceedings*, 21-34, 1995.

[28] S. Thoziyoor, N. Muralimanohar, J. H. Ahn, and N. P. Jouppi. Cacti 5.1. Technical report, HP Technical Report, 2008.

[29] C. tsun Chou, P. K. Mannava, and S. Park. A simple method for parameterized verification of cache coherence protocols. In *Formal Methods in Computer Aided Design*, pages 382–398. Springer, 2004.

[30] Apache HTTP Server v2.2.11. The apache software foundation. http://httpd.apache.org/.

[31] K. Williams and R. Esser. Verification of the Futurebus+ cache coherence protocol: a case study in model checking. In *Proceedings of the 27th Australasian Conference on Computer Science - Volume 26*, pages 65–71, Darlinghurst, Australia, Australia, 2004. Australian Computer Society, Inc.

[32] A. W. Wilson, Jr. Hierarchical cache/bus architecture for shared memory multiprocessors. In *Proceedings of the 14th Annual International Symposium on Computer Architecture*, pages 244–252, 1987. ACM.

[33] S. C. Woo, M. Ohara, E. Torrie, J. P. Singh, and A. Gupta. The SPLASH-2 programs: characterization and methodological considerations. In *Proceedings of the 22nd Annual International Symposium on Computer Architecture*, pages 24–36, 1995. ACM.

[34] P. Yeung and K. Larsen. Practical assertion-based formal verification for SoC designs. In *Proceedings of the 2005 International Symposium on System-on-Chip*, pages 58-61, 2005.

[35] M. Zhang, A. R. Lebeck, and D. J. Sorin. Fractal coherence: Scalably verifiable cache coherence. In *Proceedings of the 2010 43rd Annual IEEE/ACM International Symposium on Microarchitecture*, pages 471–482, Washington, DC, USA, 2010. IEEE Computer Society.

# Locality-Oblivious Cache Organization leveraging Single-Cycle Multi-Hop NoCs

Woo-Cheol Kwon
Department of EECS, MIT
Cambridge, MA 02139
wckwon@csail.mit.edu

Tushar Krishna *
Intel Corporation, VSSAD
Hudson, MA 01749
tushar.krishna@intel.com

Li-Shiuan Peh
Department of EECS, MIT
Cambridge, MA 02139
peh@csail.mit.edu

## Abstract

Locality has always been a critical factor in on-chip data placement on CMPs as accessing further-away caches has in the past been more costly than accessing nearby ones. Substantial research on locality-aware designs have thus focused on keeping a copy of the data private. However, this complicates the problem of data tracking and search/invalidation; tracking the state of a line at all on-chip caches at a directory or performing full-chip broadcasts are both non-scalable and extremely expensive solutions. In this paper, we make the case for Locality-Oblivious Cache Organization (LOCO), a CMP cache organization that leverages the on-chip network to create virtual single-cycle paths between distant caches, thus redefining the notion of locality. LOCO is a clustered cache organization, supporting both homogeneous and heterogeneous cluster sizes, and provides near single-cycle accesses to data anywhere within the cluster, just like a private cache. Globally, LOCO dynamically creates a virtual mesh connecting all the clusters, and performs an efficient global data search and migration over this virtual mesh, without having to resort to full-chip broadcasts or perform expensive directory lookups. Trace-driven and full system simulations running SPLASH-2 and PARSEC benchmarks show that LOCO improves application run time by up to 44.5% over baseline private and shared cache.

***Categories and Subject Descriptors*** C.1.2 [*PROCESSOR ARCHITECTURES*]: Multiple Data Stream Architectures (Multiprocessors)

* This work was carried out while Tushar Krishna was a graduate student at MIT



*ASPLOS '14*, March 1–5, 2014, Salt Lake City, Utah, USA.

ACM 978-1-4503-2305-5/14/03... $15.00.
http://dx.doi.org/10.1145/2541940.2541976

***Keywords*** Multiprocessor; CMP Cache Design; Cache Coherence; Locality; Network-On-Chip

## 1. Introduction

Chip Multi-Processors (CMPs) have become mainstream in recent years, providing increased parallelism as core counts scale. While a tiled CMP with a mesh Network-on-Chip (NoC) is widely accepted to be a scalable architecture for the many-core era [21, 22, 39, 43], on-chip cache organization and coherence are far from solved problems.

Private and shared LLCs (Last Level Caches) form two extremes of the design spectrum for cache organization. Private caches offer the fastest access to data ($\sim$10-20 cycles for L2) but lead to overall reduction in cache capacity due to replication, and make invalidations expensive (via broadcasts or precise multicasts if all sharers are tracked). Shared caches offer the best utilization of cache capacity, but every access becomes remote, bringing in on-chip network delay which conventionally increases as hop count scales with core count. Almost all works on scalable cache organization try to mimic the capacity of a shared cache and the performance of a private cache. Prior approaches fundamentally boil down to keeping data as close as possible to the requesting core, like a private cache, but minimizing unnecessary replication. These Locality-*Aware* approaches include optimized page placement [3, 10, 14, 15, 19], line placement [12], intelligent replication [7, 13, 46] and clustering [9, 18, 31, 35].

However, we believe that the locality-aware approach is not just hard (ask any software/OS developer!), but also fighting a losing battle since private cache capacity is not expected to increase much while applications are continuously becoming more heavily multi-threaded with lots of sharing and larger data sets. Current commercial designs, such as Intel's latest Xeon 5500 Series use a single homogeneous chunk of 8MB L3 cache shared by 4-8 cores which takes 40-75 cycles to access. Having a large many-ported central LLC will lead to high delay, area and power penalties, and hence the approach has been to physically distribute LLC banks across tiles [7, 13, 30, 46]. At 256 cores, distributing a 16MB LLC will lead to only 64kB chunks per tile. Moreover, com-

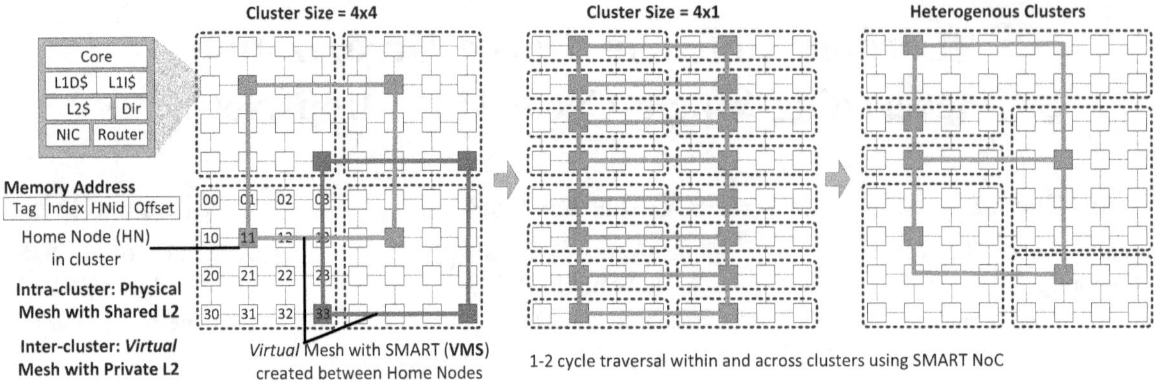


Figure 1: Overview of LOCO

plex locality-aware approaches tend to complicate the cache coherence protocol by adding more states and indirection to the already non-scalable directory [17, 30, 32, 42] to track these "intelligently" placed lines on-chip. Global data search via full-state directories, or full-chip broadcasts are both non-scalable and expensive. Hierarchical (clustered) cache designs mitigate the tracking problem since the directory can track lines at the cluster rather than core granularity. However, data search now requires multiple indirections (search within local cluster → indirection to directory → forward to remote cluster → search within remote cluster → response).

The underlying premise behind all locality-aware approaches is the conventional wisdom that accessing a remote cache is expensive. Thus these designs actively optimize both the cache allocation and replacement algorithms to keep copies of data being used by the core in the local (private) cache, and to minimize useless replicas that hog up precious cache space. In this paper, we challenge this assumption, and show that on-chip networks can be designed in today's (and future) technology to realize a single-cycle access to a remote L2, essentially killing the motivation for keeping data private in the first place.

We introduce Locality-*Oblivious* Cache Organization (LOCO). LOCO is a co-design of the on-chip network and cache-coherence protocol to support a hierarchical, flexible private-shared cache organization. An overview is shown in Figure 1. LOCO groups cores into virtual clusters of any size, sharing a (distributed) chunk of the LLC. Within each cluster, there can be only one copy of data. We leverage a recently proposed network-on-chip (NoC) design called SMART(Single-cycle Multi-hop Asynchronous Repeated Traversal), that dynamically creates multi-hop paths in the network and traverses messages within a single-cycle by using clockless drivers at each router. SMART enables near single-cycle access to the home node within each cluster. LOCO creates a Virtual Mesh with SMART(VMS) between the home nodes of each cluster, and allows data replication across the home nodes. Efficient global searches are performed across the chip by multicasting over the VMS, instead of full-chip broadcasts or expensive full-bit directories. Creating virtual topologies rather than using fixed, physical ones provides immense flexibility in choosing the cluster size at running applications, rather than at design time. To increase effective on-chip capacity, LOCO allows evicted data from one cluster to migrate to another, without adding any complexity to the coherence protocol since there is no directory tracking the lines across clusters that needs to be updated. This is in contrast to prior work which has looked at cache line migration [16] which tends to complicate the coherence protocol and directory to support migration.

Evaluation results show that LOCO provides much superior performance over private and shared cache. For 64 cores, full system simulation shows that LOCO reduces application run time by 44.5% on average. In trace-driven simulation conducted for both 64 and 256 cores, LOCO shows scalability to higher core counts, giving 17.9% improvement for 256 cores, while the run time reduction for 64 cores is 13.9%. Further, we show that LOCO can give higher performance by providing adaptive cluster size according to application characteristics.

The rest of this paper is organized as follows. Section 2 presents relevant background on SMART NoCs and the underlying technology. Section 3 presents our LOCO design. Section 4 reports experimental results. Section 5 reviews related work, and Section 6 concludes this paper.

## 2. Background: SMART NoC

A key enabler for LOCO is a network that allows single-cycle traversals, thereby making an access to a remote L2 no worse than an access to the local (in tile) L2 within a cluster. What limits us from designing such single-cycle networks today? It turns out that it is not the wires themselves. Global wires (i.e. wires connecting two tiles) with repeaters have been shown to traverse 10-16mm within 1ns [11, 20, 25, 29] at technologies today. Assuming a tile-size of 1mm, this translates to 10 to 16 hops at a GHz clock. As technology scales, this delay is expected to remain similar[1] [29]. This trend of wires not becoming faster with scaling has often

[1] Intuitively, as the feature size goes down, wires become thinner so their resistance goes up, while their capacitance goes down (assuming wires are kept at 2.5-3 times the minimum pitch in that technology to mitigate effects of coupling capacitance), keeping wire delay approximately the same.

been considered a thorn in the flesh, and has been the motivation for most locality-aware designs. But we argue that this trend does not hurt us since chip dimensions are expected to remain similar as well (~20mm×20mm) due to yield, and clock frequencies are going to remain constant due to the power wall. If we couple these two observations with the trend of same wire delay and smaller tile sizes (with scaling), we can conclude that future technologies will allow wires to traverse even more *hops* within a cycle, making a compelling case for locality-oblivious designs.

But wire delay is not the end of the story. Even if wires can allow cross-chip traversals at a GHz, the limiter is the on-chip network, which multiplexes multiple flows over the same wire segments, forcing a hop-by-hop traversal via routers. The best router designs today [38] have been able to reduce arbitration delay for the crossbar and wire segment to a single-cycle, leading to 2 cycles per hop (one in the router, and one on the link). But this still does not help if the data to be fetched is many hops away on the chip. Adding 1-cycle dedicated wires [25] across distant routers [28] has been one approach for reducing network delay, but this comes with the exorbitant cost of multi-stage arbiters and crossbars at each multi-port router, thus forcing practical designs to make do with few physical express links which then pay off only if the traffic maps well to the topology.

SMART (Single-cycle Multi-hop Asynchronous Repeated Traversal) [29] is a recent NoC architecture that builds *virtual* single-cycle multi-hop paths within the network. SMART can be overlaid on any topology, but throughout this paper, we will assume a mesh topology. The reason why we use SMART, and not a physical express topology like Flattened Butterfly [28] with LOCO is to enable us to create virtual meshes over varying cluster sizes. Here, we briefly explain how SMART NoCs work. We will discuss how we extend SMART for efficient broadcasts over LOCO's VMS in Section 3.2.

SMART replaces conventional clocked drivers on each router-to-router link by *clockless* repeaters[2]. This is shown in Figure 2a. Now, flits can traverse multiple hops within a cycle, latched only at the final hop. Whether a flit is buffered at intermediate routers is controlled by the buffer enable and crossbar select signals, which are preset one cycle before the flit arrives. The maximum number of hops that can be traversed within a cycle is a design time parameter called $HPC_{max}$ (Hops Per Cycle) which will be described later.

A typical network traversal is shown in Figure 2b. At every router, the winner of the arbitration for the switch's output port broadcasts a SMART Setup Request (SSR) up to $HPC_{max}$ hops via dedicated SMART links. The SSR carries the length (in hops) up to which the flit wishes to go. For instance, in Figure 2b, $SSR_A = 3$ indicates a 3-hop path request from Flit A. Each router arbitrates among the SSRs that it receives, giving higher priority to local/nearer flits over farther flits, and sets up the buffer enable, and crossbar select signals appropriately. In the next cycle, the actual flits traverse the switches and links, bypassing intermediate nodes, potentially going all the way through $HPC_{max}$ hops before stopping and being buffered. This process of sending SSRs that pre-set routers a cycle before flits arrive continues until the flit arrives at its destination.

We define *SMART-hop* to be $\lceil hops\_to\_dest/HPC_{max} \rceil$, i.e. the minimum number of multi-hop single-cycle traversals required to reach the destination. The best case latency for a SMART-hop is 2 cycles (SSR followed by ST-LT)[3]. But it could be more depending upon contention because a flit could be stopped prematurely, before it completes its SMART-hop, and/or because it could take multiple cycles within the router before it wins the switch. Figure 2c illustrates an example of contention, where Router 31 arbitrates between the SSRs of Flit A and Flit B, prioritizing the latter to use the output link, and prematurely buffering the former. In the next cycle, Flit A will arbitrate for the local switch, and should it win, continue its traversal by sending a fresh SSR.

In this work, we use the simpler SMART_1D design [29] which does not allow bypassing at turns, i.e. turning flits have to stop at the turning router, and send fresh SSRs for the other dimension[4]. Thus an X-only and Y-only traversal takes at least one SMART-hop, while an X+Y traversal takes at least two SMART-hops as shown in Figure 2b. Each SMART-hop takes 2-cycles in the best case. Going from one corner of a $8 \times 8$ mesh to the opposite corner (i.e. 14 hops), with $HPC_{max}$=4, takes 4 SMART-hops, i.e. 8 cycles in the best case. In a conventional NoC, it would take 28 cycles in the best case.

**Derivation of HPC$_{max}$.** A test chip at 45nm recently demonstrated that clockless repeated links can go up to 13mm with 1.0V full-swing (16mm with 300mV low-swing) within 1ns [11]. Post-layout simulations of the synthesized SMART control and data paths in 45nm indicate that SSR traversal followed by arbitration limits the speed to 9-11mm/ns [29]. In this work we choose 8mm/ns-sized repeaters (to allow us to size our clusters as a power of 2 (Section 3.1). At 2GHz, for 1mm×1mm tiles, this gives us a $HPC_{max}$ of 4.

[2] As for the energy consumption, clockless repeaters require 14.3% lower energy than clocked drivers, but there is additional overhead due to multi-hop data-path and SSR signaling, leading to similar overall energy to conventional NoC [29].

[3] The best case latency for a conventional state-of-the-art NoC router is also 2 cycles per hop [38] as described earlier. Thus a conventional NoC will take $2\times HPC_{max}$-cycles to cover a SMART-hop in the best case.

[4] This is because SMART_1D was shown to be good enough to achieve most of the performance benefits of SMART for LOCO, without the complexity of incorporating bypass at turns.

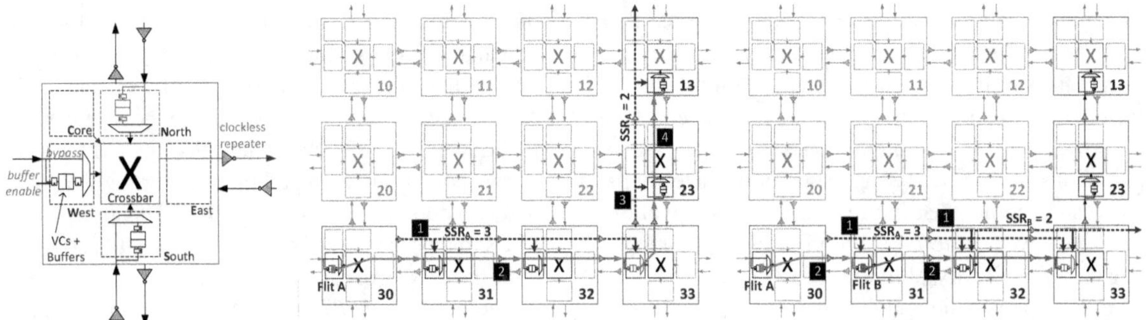


(a) SMART Router Microarchitecture (b) XY Traversal for Flit A with no contention. (c) Flit A prematurely stopped at Router 31 due to contention with Flit B.

Figure 2: SMART: Single-cycle Multi-hop Asynchronous Repeated Traversal [29]

# 3. Locality-Oblivious Cache Organization

## 3.1 Local Cache Clustering

LOCO proposes a two-level hierarchical approach for L2 cache organization. At the local level, it first partitions the CMP into multiple cache clusters. The clusters can be 1D or 2D meshes of any size, as shown in Figure 1. The size of the cluster depends on the applications' working sets and/or aggregate cache requirement [18, 23, 31, 35], and is not the focus of this work. However, we do believe that $HPC_{max}$ should drive the cluster sizes, since any cache within $HPC_{max}$ hops can typically be accessed in 1 (X-only or Y-only) to 2 (X+Y) SMART-hops (which corresponds to 2 to 4 cycles low-load latency), as explained in Section 2. Cluster sizes less than $HPC_{max}$ do not buy us much since they only result in more replication without lowering access delay.

Within a cluster, the organization of L2 cache slices is like that of a distributed shared cache [4] where the mapping of data to L2 cache slice is statically determined given the address. As shown in Figure 1, the least significant bits of a block address (HNid) are used to identify the home node for fair load balancing as is usually done in shared caches.

Several prior works have proposed fully flexible data mapping to L2 slices, so that the first requestor of data becomes the home node of the data [14, 19, 45]. These approaches aim at minimizing L2 access latency by placing data into the local L2 cache in the same tile as the requesting core, which is especially beneficial when the majority of data is local (accessed by only one core). In contrast, LOCO employs static data mapping by address. The rationale behind this is that, via SMART links, properly sized local clusters provide low latency to any L2 slice inside the cluster. With the width and height of the cluster set within $HPC_{max}$, accessing any L2 slice and back mostly takes only 4-8 cycles in the network, which is of the same order as typical private L2 access latencies. Fixed data mapping also allows only one data copy inside a cluster, which leads to higher cache hit rate by increasing effective cache capacity. Hence, LOCO leverages SMART NoC to ensure fast L2 cache access within a cluster, while delivering a larger shared cache that overcomes the lower cache hit rate of small individual private caches.

Static data mapping within a cluster has an additional advantage over flexible mapping - when searching for data in the other clusters, it suffices to check only one candidate L2 per cluster. Moreover the locations are known *a priori* by the address. As a result, static data mapping significantly reduces the search space, and thus facilitates an efficient global data search strategy over the entire chip. We will present this strategy in the next section.

In a distributed shared cache with inclusive L2, any cache request should first access the L2 cache slice at the home node. As a result, a directory-based protocol is a natural choice for maintaining cache coherence within LOCO clusters. Directories at each home node keep track of sharers only from the local cluster, not across the entire chip. This, in turn, ensures that the storage overhead for directory is manageable.

## 3.2 Global Data Search

At the global level, LOCO operates each cluster like a large private cache. When the first requesting core receives data from off-chip memory, the data is stored in its local cluster. Subsequent requestors search for the data on-chip and replicate them in their own local clusters for fast future look-up.

To realize fast access to data in other clusters, LOCO adopts a broadcast protocol to maintain cache coherence between clusters. Unlike a directory-based counterpart, a broadcast protocol sends requests directly to all possible sharers, thereby saving indirection latency in looking up a tag directory.

However, broadcasting over the entire chip does not scale to high core counts, as power consumption and bandwidth demand grow prohibitively costly with increasing number of cores. To tackle this scalability problem, we take advantage of the nice topological property that LOCO's cluster organization offers. As already mentioned, the home node location within a cluster is fixed by the address. We can create a Virtual Mesh with SMART links(VMS) between these home nodes. Since SMART creates virtual multi-hop bypass paths, different cluster sizes/shapes can result in different VMS sizes/shapes. Figure 1 shows two 4x4 VMSs, for HNid=11 and HNid=33, in a 64-core system. The highlighted routers on each VMS are called home routers, while all other routers along the route are called intermediate routers. Flits only stop at the home routers, and try to bypass all intermediate routers by creating single-cycle multi-hop paths between home routers.

LOCO broadcasts a global cache requests only on a specific VMS (based on the address), avoiding costly broadcasts to the entire chip. While the original SMART design only supported unicasts, we extend it to support broadcasts over VMSs. We modify two components in each router: route computation and switch arbitration. Each broadcast uses an XY-tree multicast routing algorithm, connecting all nodes in the VMS into a tree, as shown in Figure 3 for the VMS with HNid=11. At each home router, including the starting home router, the flit requests for one or more output ports depending on its location on the tree (which can be identified by its input port). For example, in the highlighted router in Figure 3, the flit enters the home router at the East input port, and places a request for the West, North, South and Ejection output ports. Each output port arbitrates independently, and the flit can be granted one or more output ports depending on contention. Each output port winner then sends out SSRs, just like in the baseline SMART, except that a broadcast triggers simultaneously SSRs across multiple directions, with the SSR always set to $HPC_{max}$ (4 in this design), indicating a request to stop at the next home router on the VMS. In the next cycle, the flit performs ST-LT across multiple hops along one or more directions. Forking of flits does not stretch timing because select lines of the crossbar muxes automatically fork the flit, and each output link has its own repeater. In Figure 3, the flit completes the broadcast in 4 SMART-hops, i.e., 8 cycles in the best case[5]. Without this broadcast extension to SMART, 15 copies of the flit would have to be created and sent from the source as unicasts, increasing contention at routers, adding to network delay.

### 3.3 Inter-Cluster Victim Replacement (IVR)

To maximize usage of precious on-chip cache capacity, LOCO leverages other clusters for victim caching. On any L2 eviction at the cluster home node, a *replacement request* is sent to the corresponding home node in a randomly chosen cluster, with the timestamp of its last access. Timestamps are approximations, implemented by incrementing a counter every $T$ cycles to reduce area overhead. On receiving this

[5] The best case occurs when there is no contention in establishing SMART paths in the network. In the worst case, the flit might stop at every intermediate router, which results in 32 cycles, the delay of a conventional network with a single-cycle router pipeline. Network contention can further aggravate the delay, forcing the flit to waste more cycles at each router waiting to win arbitration. This downside of virtual SMART paths (compared to physical express links) is modeled in our simulations.

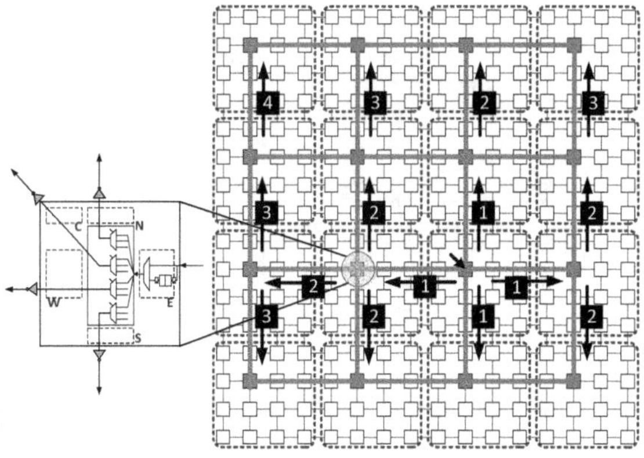

Figure 3: Example broadcast over a VMS

replacement request, the remote home node selects a local victim, and compares the timestamp of its victim to that of the migrating data. The cache line with the older timestamp is chosen to be the final victim, and is evicted to other clusters for another replacement attempt. Choosing target clusters randomly ensures balanced utilization of L2 cache resource across the chip.

IVR effectively extends the reach of one cluster into others. A cluster can retrieve its data stored in other clusters in very few cycles, owing to the fast global data search explained in the previous section. IVR enables cores that heavily use caches to offload to relatively underutilized clusters, since evicted cache data from more cache demanding cores are likely to have more recent timestamps.

We avoid deadlock by prohibiting the L2 cache from waiting for the outgoing queue to the network during IVR. If the L2 cache finds that the outgoing queue is full, it sends the victim date directly to the off-chip memory via the write-back virtual network. There is also a potential livelock scenario in which the evicted data with the oldest timestamp loops in the on-chip system endlessly. To prevent this, we add a *replacement counter* in the header flit of the migrating victim data. When this counter hits a certain threshold (4 is assumed in this design), the data is sent back to off-chip memory.

### 3.4 Walkthrough Examples

The example system is a 64-core CMP employing a $8 \times 8$ mesh network, which is partitioned into 4 fixed-size local clusters, each comprising $4 \times 4$ tiles; the entire system consists of $2 \times 2$ local clusters. For our example, we assume hierarchical L1/L2 cache organization with inclusive L2 cache. L1 cache has MSI states for cache coherence, while L2 cache has MOESI states. We will indicate the specific coherence state for L1 or L2 caches by State:L1 or L2 respectively.

Figure 4a shows the steps involved in a cache hit. (1) Node C, initially in I:L1 state, sends a READ request to local home node H. (2) H, in S:L2 state, returns the data to the requestor. When a cache hit occurs, the request is handled within the cluster by a directory-based protocol, tracking the 16 potential sharers of the cluster. Hence, with no network

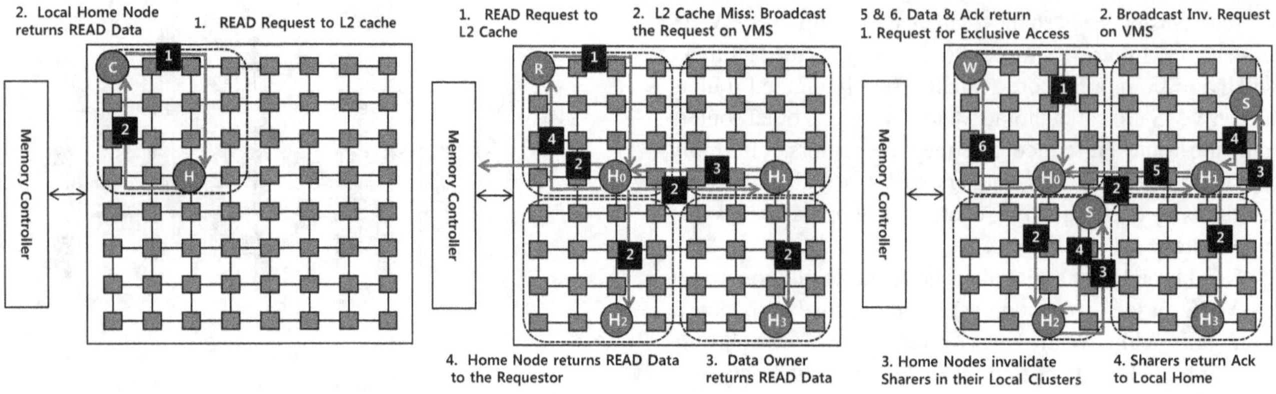


(a) Cache Hit Example (b) READ Miss Example (c) WRITE Example

Figure 4: Walkthrough Examples

contention, a SMART path enables L2 cache hits to take only 4 cycles at most. Figure 4b shows a case where the READ request results in a cache miss. (1) The request sent from R arrives at its local home node $H_0$. (2) $H_0$, in I:L2 state, finds no matching tag entry at its L2 cache. Now it invokes the second level protocol by broadcasting the request to other clusters on the VMS for the address. The request is delivered to $H_1$, $H_2$, and $H_3$ along SMART links. The request is sent to off-chip memory as well. (3) To ensure only one sharer returns the data among multiple shares, the one with ownership, i.e. in O state ($H_1$ in our example) responds to the request. For simplicity, this example only shows the case where the data is cached on-chip. If there is no cached data on-chip, the memory controller assumes the ownership and returns the data from off-chip memory. (4) Finally, $H_0$ stores the data into its L2 cache and transits to S:L2 state. Now it goes back to the first level protocol, and returns the data to the requestor, $R$.

Next, we turn to WRITE operations in Figure 4c. (1) Node $W$, in I:L1 state, issues the request for exclusive access to its local home node $H_0$. (2) To get exclusive access right, $H_0$ broadcasts *invalidation* requests on the VMS. (3) Home nodes in each cluster invalidate their local sharers by the first level protocol. Each home node checks a tag directory to retrieve the local sharer list and invalidates them. (4) Local sharers in S:L1 state transit to I:L1 state, and send acknowledgements to local home nodes. (5) After invalidating local sharers, home nodes also transit to I:L2 state. In this example, $H_1$ was in O:L2 state. It sends the data back to the home node of the requesting cluster, $H_0$. On receiving the data, $H_0$ changes its state to M:L2 state. (6) $W$ finally receives the data, and transits to M:L1 state.

Next we will walk through inter-cluster victim replacement in Figure 5. (1) A new READ request causes cache replacement at the local home node $H_0$. (2) $H_0$ selects a victim cache line and sends it to a random destination $H_1$ (3) $H_1$ receives the replacement request, and selects a local victim cache line via timestamp comparison. If the timestamp of the migrated data is newer, $H_1$ stores the migrated

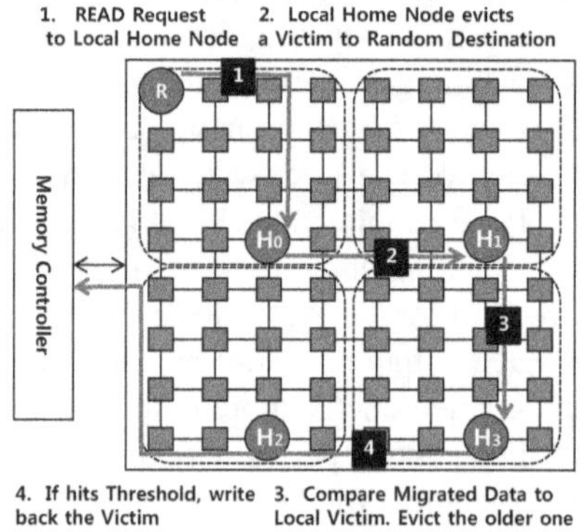


Figure 5: Inter-Cluster Victim Replacement Example

data in its L2 cache and evicts its local victim, migrating it to a random destination, repeating the entire process. Otherwise, replacement is denied, and instead the data is steered to another random node. (4) $H_3$ receives the victim data and finds that the replacement counter has hit the threshold. It sends the data as write-back to the off-chip memory.

# 4. Evaluation

We implemented LOCO and the underlying SMART NoC (extended for efficient VMS broadcasts) in the C++-based multi-core simulation tool GEMS [34], which incorporates the cycle-accurate network model GARNET [1].

We perform trace-driven simulations for both 64-core and 256-core CMPs by feeding traces generated by Graphite [37][6] into GEMS. We also verify LOCO with full-system simulations to provide more realistic evaluation results. As full-system simulations on GEMS lead to unfeasibly long simulation time beyond 64 cores, full-system simulations were conducted only for 64-core CMP to maintain the simulation time within a week.

We ran SPLASH-2 [44] and PARSEC [8] benchmark suites. Statistics are gathered at the end of the parallel por-

[6] While Graphite provides fast, scalable full-system simulation up to 1000 cores, it does not at the moment provide a cycle-accurate network model yet, which is crucial for correct evaluation of LOCO.

tion of each benchmark. Simulations run to completion for the 64-core full-system simulations. However, due to simulation time limitation, our trace-driven simulations simulate up to 2 billion memory instructions including cache warm-up sequences.

Table 1: Target System Configuration

| Processing Tile | |
|---|---|
| Processing cores | 2-way in-order SPARC |
| Cache line size | 32 Bytes |
| L1 cache | Split 16KB I&D, 4-way, 1-cycle access latency |
| L2 cache | Inclusive unified 64KB per each tile<br>8-way, 4-cycle access latency |
| Cache coherence | MSI for L1 Cache, MOESI for L2 Cache |
| **On-Chip Network** | |
| Topology | 8x8 mesh for 64-core, 16x16 mesh for 256-core |
| Routing | XY dimension-ordered |
| Virtual Networks (VNs) | 5 |
| Virtual Channels per VN | 4 |
| Link channel width | 16 Bytes |
| $HPC_{max}$ for SMART | 4 |
| **Memory Interface** | |
| Directory | 10-cycle access latency |
| Memory | 4 memory controllers (one on each edge)<br>200-cycle access latency |

### 4.1 Target CMP System

Our target system consists of strictly hierarchical L1/L2 caches. L1 cache is allowed to communicate only with L2 caches, not directly with other L1 caches. We compare LOCO with two baseline cache organizations: distributed private and shared caches. Both baseline cache organizations and LOCO naturally get performance benefits from SMART NoCs, since all multi-hop traversals can now take just a single cycle. By running all cache organizations over SMART NoCs, we seek to highlight that the performance improvement over the baselines is strictly due to LOCO.

**Cache Coherence.** The baseline configurations operate on a directory-based protocol. When a L1 cache miss occurs, the request is delivered to the local L2 or the static home node in the shared and private L2 respectively. Then, the L2 cache communicates with other L2 caches or memory controllers to retrieve data from the sharers or to invalidate all shared data copies. The sharer information of each cache line is stored in a directory at the home node (shared cache) or at the memory controller (private cache).

LOCO uses 4x4 clusters (Figure 1), unless specified. We use directory-based coherence within clusters, and a broadcast protocol between clusters. Broadcast protocols assume an ordered interconnect, but LOCO's virtual meshes (VMS) do not provide ordering. As there have been recent proposals such as Token coherence [33] and INSO [2] for maintaining global ordering on a mesh topology, we can apply either one to LOCO. For our evaluations, we used Token Coherence, where a reader is required to have at least one token, while a writer must collect all tokens to obtain exclusive access right. With a L2 cache miss, the request is broadcast to all relevant L2 caches for the cache line address. On receiving cache requests, L2 caches respond to the request by returning tokens or data.

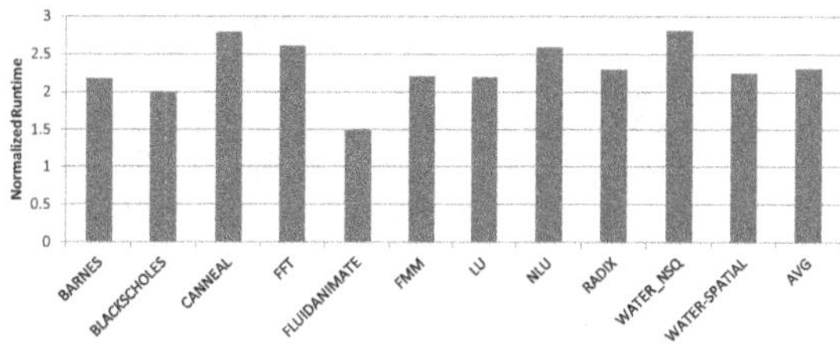

Figure 6: Normalized runtime of distributed private caches vs. distributed shared caches (64-core).

**Directory Storage and Latency Overhead.** One important parameter impacting evaluation results is directory access latency. For baseline caches, the directory should cover sharers across the entire chip. A naive implementation based on a bit-vector, for instance, will require additional 256 bits per each cache line to keep track of sharers for a 256-core system, which is the same amount of storage needed for our 32-byte cache line. In contrast, a cluster-based approach like LOCO requires just a 16-bit vector for tracking sharers within the cluster. Directory storage overhead is one of key problems in maintaining scalability of directory-based protocols. There have been a plethora of suggestions such as sparse directory [17] or hierarchical directory [42] to mitigate directory storage overhead with a trade-off between performance and scalability. Addressing the scalability issues of a directory-based protocol is beyond the scope of this paper. Instead, we assume that the home node can access its directory in parallel with an L2 cache access without additional latency. Further we do not consider any adverse effect of directory storage overhead, which otherwise can be traded off for larger L2 cache capacity. This is a generous assumption for the baseline distributed shared cache organization. LOCO's inter-cluster broadcast protocol also needs a directory to record the ownership and related state bits, but it requires less storage overhead thanks to clustering.

### 4.2 Evaluation Results: Trace-Driven Simulation

To evaluate the performance of LOCO, we simulated three cache configurations: **LOCO CC** represents LOCO with just local cache clusters managed by a directory-based protocol providing global coherence. In LOCO CC, when a L2 cache miss occurs, the request is sent to the directory at the memory controller to obtain the sharer list. Next, it either receives a data copy from one of the sharers, or invalidates all sharers upon writes. It should be noted that the traversals to/from the directory are expedited through the SMART NoC as well. **LOCO CC+VMS** adds broadcasting on VMS between LOCO clusters. Finally, **LOCO CC+VMS+IVR** incorporates inter-cluster victim replacement as well.

**Private vs Shared Cache.** Figure 6 plots the runtimes of private caches , normalized to that of shared caches, both running atop SMART NoCs. It should be pointed out that baseline shared caches stand to gain more benefit from SMART

NoCs as there is more global, cross-chip traffic compared to private caches. We observe that the performance of private caches is severely degraded due to high cache miss, on average 2.3 times slower than shared cache. This is due to small L2 cache slice (64KB),[7] assumed, which is arrived at given our assumption of small 1mm×1mm tiles in a many-core chip. From here onwards, we thus assume distributed shared caches as the baseline for comparison, unless stated otherwise.

**L2 Cache Hit Latency.** LOCO's clustering is designed to provide fast L2 cache access within a cluster, mimicking a large private L2 cache. Figure 7 shows the additional cache access latency of each cache configuration over that of a distributed private cache, i.e. the average latency of the baseline private cache is deducted from the other configurations.

For the 64-core CMP, as shown in Figure 7a, LOCO adds 2.9 cycle-latency on average for L2 cache access than private cache, while shared cache adds 11.5 cycles on average. Since each SMART-hop takes 2 cycles without network contention, LOCO requires just 1.5 more SMART-hop-delay than private cache, while the baseline shared cache needs additional 3.7-SMART-hop delay. In other words, since a baseline private caches takes 1-hop to send a request, and 1-hop to receive a response, LOCO takes just 3.5-SMART-hop delay on average.

As core counts increase, the benefit of LOCO also increases in comparison with shared cache. For 256-core CMP, as shown in Figure 7b, L2 access latency of shared cache increases by 4.5 cycles over 64-core CMP, while the latency of LOCO remains relatively unchanged with a marginal increase of 0.08 cycles.

**L2 Cache Miss Rate.** High cache hit rate is another goal of LOCO's clustering, enabled by the larger cache capacity of an entire cluster. Figure 8 shows L2 cache misses per a thousand instructions of various benchmarks, averaged across the entire simulation time. For 64-core CMP, LOCO increases L2 cache miss moderately over shared cache, by 0.33% for 64-core CMP and by 0.43% for 256-core CMP. Combined with L2 hit latency results above, this shows that LOCO comes reasonably close to our goal of offering low latency benefits of private cache while delivering the high cache hit rate of shared cache at the same time.

**Impact of LOCO's Broadcast over Virtual Meshes.** Figure 9 shows the cost involved in searching on-chip cached data with and without VMS, i.e. the average delay needed to find on-chip data stored in other clusters. This delay includes L2 cache access latency, directory latency, and network delay. In LOCO without VMS, the search is based on a directory protocol, which incurs indirection latency for directory look-up. As shown in the figures, VMS provide 34.8% reduction in search cost for 64-core, and 39.9% for 256-core, respectively. This reduction is achieved via fast hardware broadcast support for VMS within SMART NoC routers, and by avoiding directory look-up latency. We note that VMS gives higher benefit for 256-core CMP with increased network delay.

**Impact of LOCO's inter-cluster victim replacement.** Another goal of LOCO is to effectively utilize on-chip cache capacity to reduce expensive off-chip memory access. LOCO CC+VMS+IVR is designed to address this. Figure 10 compares the number of off-chip memory accesses of different cache configurations, normalized against the baseline shared cache. IVR shows 15.6% reduction of off-chip memory access over LOCO CC for 64-core, and 17.9% for 256-core. Overall, LOCO CC+VMS+IVR almost matches that of shared cache on average.

It is interesting to note that although shared cache has the largest effective cache capacity, in disallowing any redundancy across L2 cache slices, LOCO CC+VMS+IVR sometimes outperforms shared cache in reducing off-chip memory access, for example, *barnes* and *swaptions* for 64-core CMP. This is because LOCO CC+VMS+IVR extends the limited 8-way set-associativity of shared cache by migrating victims to other clusters. In a 64-core CMP, for instance, LOCO effectively creates a 8x4=32-way cache distributed across 4 distant clusters.

**Overall Performance.** Figure 11a shows normalized runtimes of each feature of LOCO progressively, against the baseline shared cache for 64-core CMP with trace-driven simulations. On average, LOCO CC delivers 5.5 % reduction in application runtime, LOCO CC+VMS results in further 4.8% reduction, and LOCO CC+VMS+IVR gives an additional 3.7% reduction. Overall, LOCO improves runtime by 13.9%, on average, across all benchmarks. For 256-core CMP, as shown in Figure 11b, LOCO gives higher runtime reduction of 17.9%, which shows scalability of LOCO to higher core counts.

**Comparison to LOCO with Alternative NoC Architectures.** So far, all simulations for both the baselines and LOCO run on top of SMART NoC. To demonstrate that LOCO's performance is hinged upon SMART NoC's capability to instantly establish a virtual, single-cycle multi-hop path, we turn to evaluation of LOCO with an alternative NoC architectures: conventional NoC and high-radix routers. When LOCO runs on top of conventional NoC and thus without VMS broadcasting, it is essentially reduced to the baseline clustered cache with increased network latency by stopping at every intermediate router.

High-Radix routers use the same clockless repeated wire technology as SMART, to go up to 4 hops within 1 cycle, and represent an alternate way of leveraging low wire delay. We implement a Flattened Butterfly topology [28] which adds dedicated physical links from every router to its 1-hop, 2-hop, 3-hop and 4-hop neighbors to enable LOCO to run with 4x4 cluster sizes. Each home node is now always

[7] We note that we used very small-scale working sets in our simulations for tractability. In a real system, larger L2 caches will not result in significantly lower cache miss rates with realistic working sets.

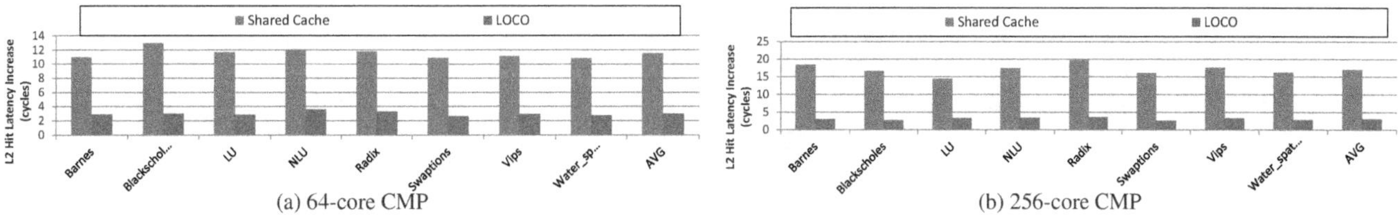


(a) 64-core CMP (b) 256-core CMP

Figure 7: Increase of L2 access latency over Private Cache

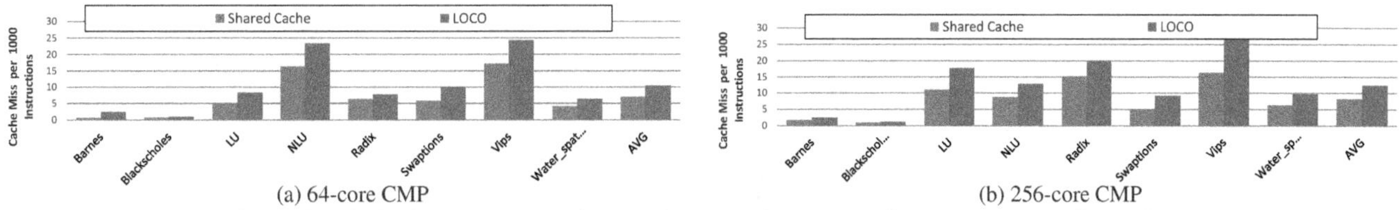


(a) 64-core CMP (b) 256-core CMP

Figure 8: L2 Cache miss per a thousand instructions according to cache configurations

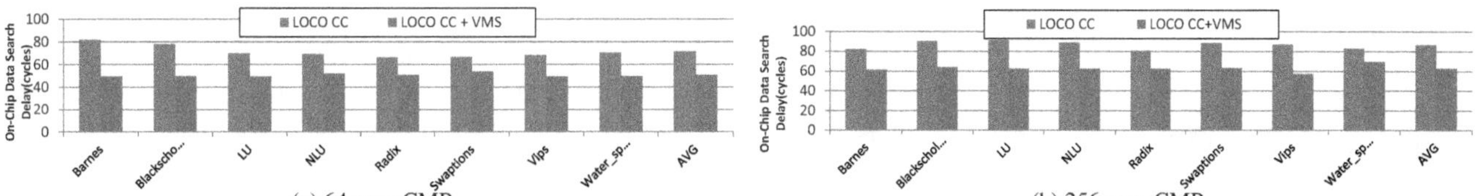


(a) 64-core CMP (b) 256-core CMP

Figure 9: Global search delay for data cached on-chip

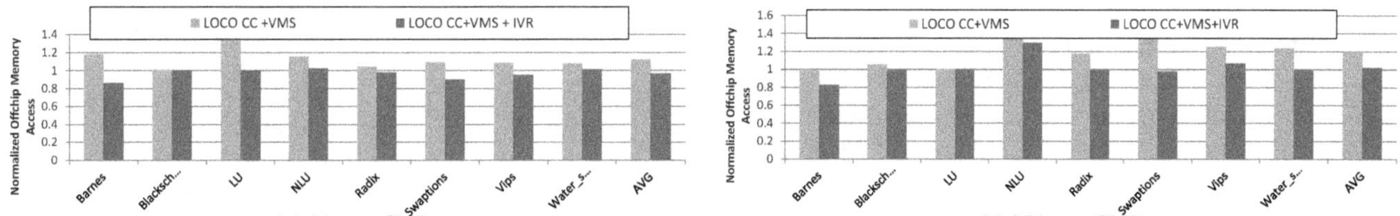


(a) 64-core CMP (b) 256-core CMP

Figure 10: Normalized off-chip memory access against baseline Shared Cache

1-cycle away unlike SMART where 1-cycle is opportunistic, and the network has 4x higher bisection throughput because of the additional wires. However, each router is now 20-ported instead of the 5-ported SMART/baseline router, which requires multi-stage arbiters and crossbars, increasing the router pipeline to at least 4-stages [27, 28, 40] unlike the 2-stage SMART router. There is also a 6.7X area and 2.3X power overhead as compared to SMART by modeling both designs in DSENT [41].

Figure 12 shows that conventional NoC and high-radix routers increase both L2 access latency and global on-chip data search delay. For 256-core, the overhead by conventional NoC is 2.01x for L2 hit latency, and 1.99x for global on-chip data search delay, while the overhead by high-radix routers is 3.10x for L2 hit latency, and 1.59x for global on-chip data search delay. Figure 13 shows the runtimes normalized against shared cache running atop SMART NoC. LOCO with SMART NoC reduces the runtime by 18.9% for 64-core, and by 24.6% for 256-core , compared to LOCO with conventional NoC. The increased router latencies of high-radix routers result in 22.7% runtime increase for 64-core, and 24.4% increase for 256-core, compared to LOCO with SMART. We note that LOCO with high-radix routers underperform even LOCO with conventional NoC. This is because high-radix routers increases L2 access latency significantly within a cluster, since the request always go through 4-stage pipelined routers both at the source and at the destination.

**Cluster Size and Topology.** Till now we presented results with 4x4 clusters. Now, for 64-core CMP, we explore the impact of alternative cluster sizes and topology: 4x1 and 8x1. Cluster sizes of 4x1 allow a SMART-hop distance of 1 for every pair of two nodes within the cluster, while cluster sizes of 8x1 and 4x4 have up to 2 SMART-hops. As shown Figure 14a, smaller cluster sizes lead to reduced L2 cache hit latencies; 1.17 and 0.45 cycles are reduced for cluster size 4x1 and 8x1, respectively. However, smaller cluster sizes lead to 35% and 20% higher L2 cache miss rates on average, as shown in Figure 14b. Cluster size should be chosen considering trade-off between L2 cache hit latency and miss rate. Figure 14d compares the runtimes of LOCO with different cluster sizes. The optimal cluster size and topology is dependent on application, since these trade-offs

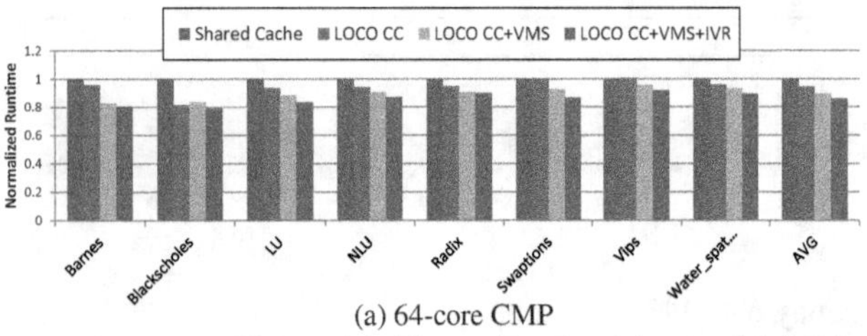

(a) 64-core CMP

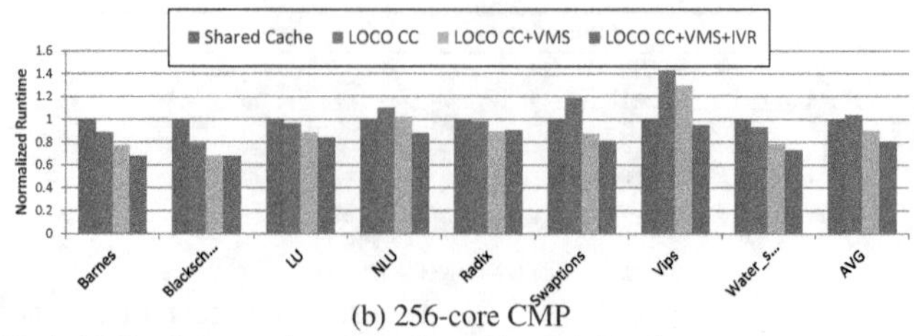

(b) 256-core CMP

Figure 11: Normalized runtimes of LOCO and Hybrid Caches against baseline Shared Cache

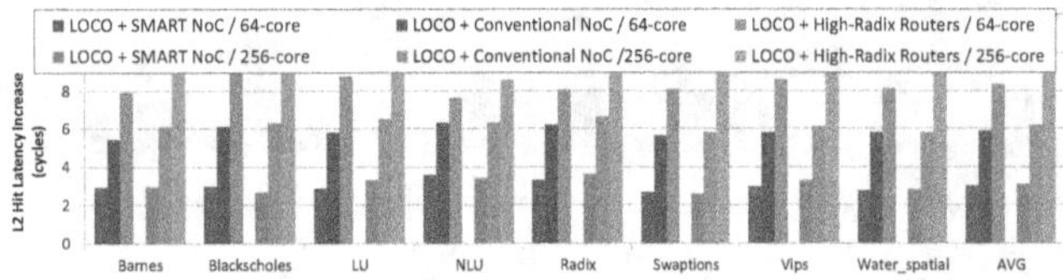

(a) L2 Hit Latency

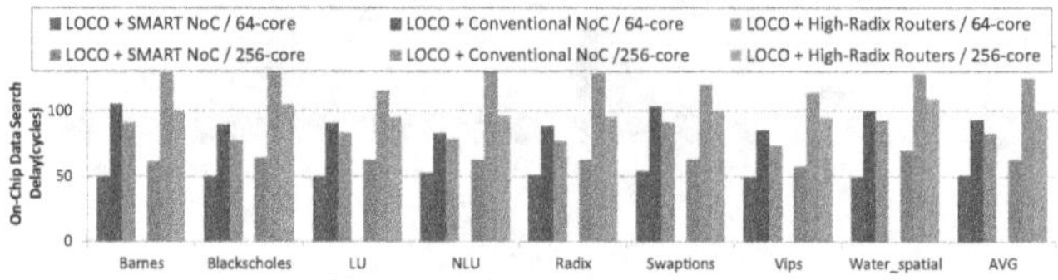

(b) Global on-chip Data Search Delay

Figure 12: Comparison to LOCO with Conventional NoC and with High-Radix routers: Memory Latency

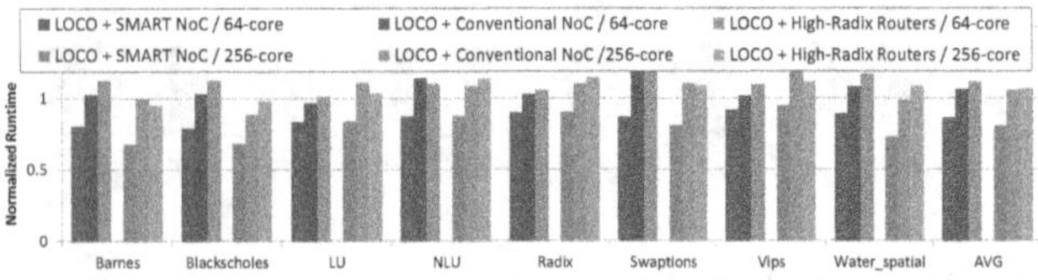

Figure 13: Comparison to LOCO with Conventional NoC and with High-Radix routers: Normalized Runtime

can have different impact on the performance according to application characteristic. For example, cluster size 4x1 has 89.9% higher cache miss rate for *swaptions* than cluster size 4x4, while the increase is mere 15.6% for *water_spatial*. As a result, cluster size 4x1 has the worst runtime for *swaptions*, while it is the best for *water_spatial*.

Table 2: Multi-program workloads for 64-core CMP

| Work-load | Description<br>Number of instances x Benchmark( Number of Threads ) |
|---|---|
| W0 | 4xBlackscholes(4), 4xFerret(4), 4xFmm(4), 4xLu(4) |
| W1 | 4xNlu(4), 4xSwaptions(4), 4xWater_Nsq(4), 4xWater_Spatial(4) |
| W2 | 4xBlackscholes(4), 4xFerret(4), 4xWater_Nsq(4), 4xWater_Spatial(4) |
| W3 | 4xFmm(4), 4xLu(4), 4xNlu(4), 4xSwaptions(4) |
| W4 | 4xBlackscholes(4), 4xFerret(4), 4xNlu(4), 4xSwaptions(4) |
| W5 | 2xBlackscholes(8), 2xFerret(8), 2xFmm(8), 2xLu(8) |
| W6 | 2xNlu(8), 2xSwaptions(8), 2xWater_Nsq(8), 2xWater_Spatial(8) |
| W7 | 2xBlackscholes(8), 2xFerret(8), 2xWater_Nsq(8), 2xWater_Spatial(8) |
| W8 | 1xBlackscholes(16), 1xFerret(16), 1xFmm(16), 1xLu(16) |
| W9 | 1xNlu(16), 1xSwaptions(16), 1xWater_Nsq(16), 1xWater_Spatial(16) |

**Multi-program Workloads.** The need for clustering in cache organization naturally occurs with mapping of heterogeneous tasks onto CMP, where the memory is shared mostly within the same task. Thus, local L2 caches of cores running the same task can be clustered into a shared cache to provide reduced L2 hit latency within the cluster, while it operates as private cache globally [18, 31, 35]. The resulting clustered cache is similar to LOCO CC, where the cluster size is determined by the number of threads(cores) required for individual task. One of important design goals in clustered cache is to allocate the cache resource among different tasks for high utilization of on-chip cache, and thus to reduce costly off-line memory access. Several previous works have proposed dynamic reallocation of cache resources adapted by memory demand of each task [18, 31], which, in turn, poses intriguing problem of managing the increased cost of global data search. LOCO can address this problem by inter-cluster victim replacement, which allows one cluster to utilize less utilized cache resource in other clusters across the chip.

In the evaluation, both the baseline clustered cache and LOCO provide shared cache within clusters. On the other hand, each task in the workloads is assumed to have exclusive address space with each other, thus the second level cache coherence is not required. The baseline clustered cache is modelled only to provide shared cache and cache coherence within the cluster. Atop the baseline clustered cache, LOCO performs inter-cluster victim replication with faster retrieval of migrated data on VMS in global scale. Table 2 summarizes the workloads used for the evaluation. While LOCO supports flexible heterogeneous clusters in which each cluster can have any size and can be changed at any time as depicted in Figure 1, we assume that all clusters are of the same size while running each workload for the ease of simulation; clustered cache and LOCO have cluster size 4x1 for W0 through W4, cluster size 8x1 for W5 through W8, and cluster size 4x4 for the rest. Each individual task is mapped onto a single cluster. For example, with the workload W0, every instance of tasks requires 4 threads, thus 64-core CMP is divided into 16 clusters of size 4x1. As there are 4 instances of *barnes*, 4 clusters run their own instance of *barnes* independently, another 4 clusters run *blackscholes*, and so on. For all cache organizations, the same SMART NoC with $HPC_{max} = 4$ is applied as usual. Figure 15a shows off-chip memory access normalized against shared cache. On average, clustered cache increases off-line memory access by 26.6%, while LOCO reduces off-

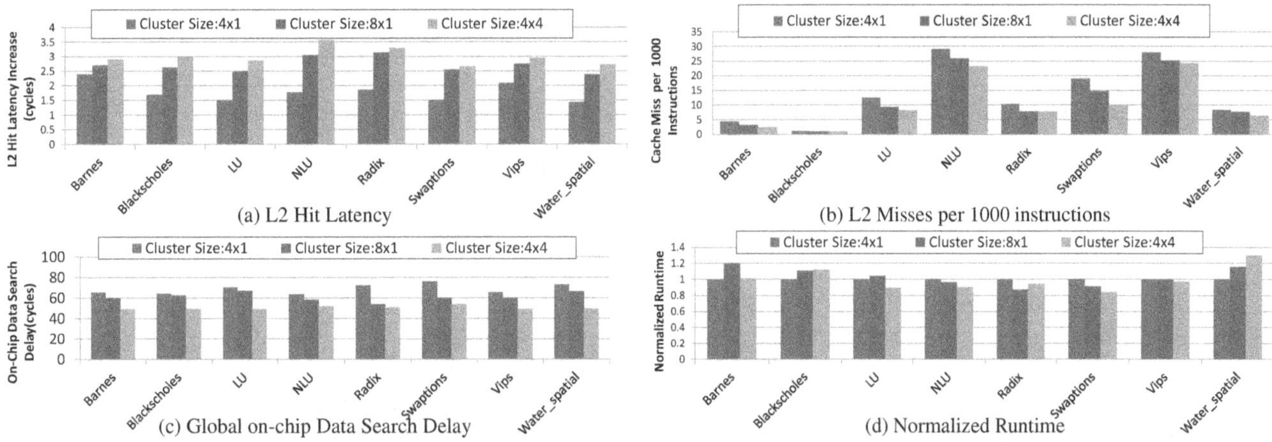


(a) L2 Hit Latency (b) L2 Misses per 1000 instructions

(c) Global on-chip Data Search Delay (d) Normalized Runtime

Figure 14: Performance of LOCO according to different cluster sizes

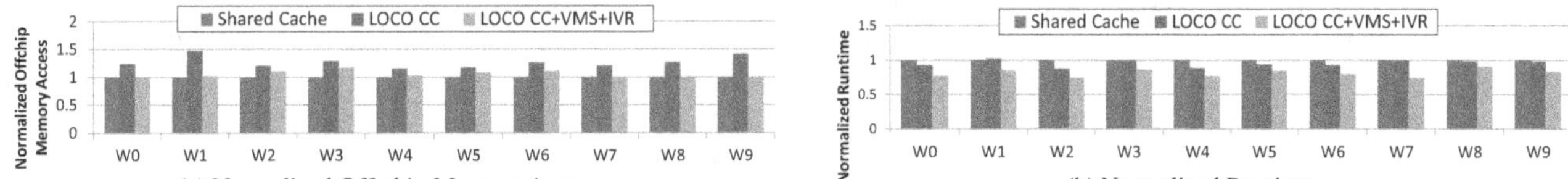


(a) Normalized Off-chip Memory Access (b) Normalized Runtime

Figure 15: LOCO with multi-program workloads

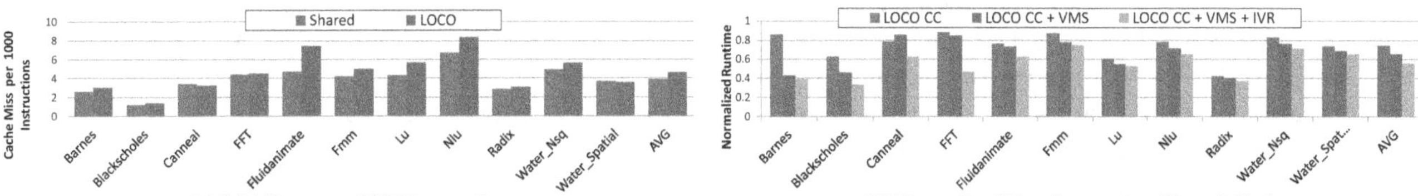


(a) L2 Misses per 1000 instructions (b) Normalized Runtime against Shared Cache

Figure 16: Full system simulation of LOCO for 64-core CMP

line memory access to almost the same level as shared cache, just 5.1% higher than shared cache. As a result, Figure 15b shows that LOCO reduces the runtime of clustered cache by 13.8%, which is 20% improvement over shared cache.

### 4.3 Full System Simulations

Trace-driven simulations do not properly capture dependencies between instructions that cause busy-waiting or spinning, which can have high performance impact. In this section, we present full system simulation results to evaluate the performance of LOCO more realistically. Due to tool limitation, we conducted full system simulations only for 64-core CMP. We leave verifying LOCO with full system simulations at high core counts as future work.

Figure 16b shows normalized runtimes for PARSEC and SPLASH-2 benchmarks[8] against shared cache. On average, LOCO CC delivers 26% reduction in application runtime, LOCO CC+VMS further results in 8% reduction, and LOCO CC+VMS+IVR gives an additional 10% reduction. Overall, LOCO improves runtime by 44.5% on average. We note that benchmarks such as *blackscholes*, *lu*, and *radix*, show significantly reduced runtime with just clustering. In contrast, *barnes* and *fft* are not improved much by only clustering. This is because the communication pattern in the first group is highly concentrated between neighboring cores, while the latter group exhibits widely distributed communication patterns across the die [5]. Although the latter benchmarks lack locality by nature, LOCO successfully reduces the runtimes of *barnes* with VMS, or *fft* with IVR, giving consistent performance improvement across the benchmarks.

[8] For full system simulations, we were unable to obtain results of *swaptions* and *vips* due to long simulation time. Instead, we added results of *canneal*, *fft*, *fmm fluidanimate*, and *water_nsq*, which in turn, failed in trace-driven simulations due to out-of-memory errors.

## 5. Related Work

For the first time, SMART NoC provides a practical mechanism by which any core within $H_{max}$ hops away can be reached in a single cycle, at any time. LOCO leverages this unique mechanism with adaptive cluster sizes, virtual meshes for inter-cluster broadcasts, and using remote nodes for storing victims. None of these make sense without SMART, and as we will next discuss, many prior cache organizations will work better with SMART, but none leverages SMART as well as LOCO.

**Locality-optimized data placement.** There has been a plethora of recent studies that optimizes locality for higher performance. One such approach is the dynamic mapping of pages to L2 cache slices in a shared cache, often with the aid of the OS [3, 10, 14, 15, 19]. There has been significant work on improving data locality at the cache line granularity as well. Cache line is relocated closer to the core [12, 26], or replicated into the local L2 cache [45, 46], which can be further improved by selective replication [7, 13].

All these works will have to be reformulated to leverage SMART NoCs. For instance, with SMART, locality-aware mapping or replication need no longer be limited to a local L2 cache slice, but instead, can be expanded to all L2 caches within $H_{max}$. Similarly, we can remove unnecessary redundancy by retaining only a single copy of data within a radius of $H_{max}$. In fact, these are exactly the observations that motivated LOCO's clustering. However, unlike these previous approaches, LOCO is not only concerned with data locality, but also leverages SMART NoC to maximize cache utilization by way of inter-cluster broadcasts and victim replacement.

**Clustered cache organizations.** Hierarchical or clustered caches have been proposed as a scalable cache solution by many researchers. In [32, 42], the communication bottleneck to a central directory is mitigated by distributing hierarchical directories across the chip. More recent studies have focused on providing flexible sized clusters to best serve application demands [9, 18, 23, 31, 35]. LOCO provides an efficient mechanism for supporting flexible clusters while maintaining coherence and balancing cache utilization across clusters with IVR, unlike the complex hardware monitoring and remapping mechanisms required by prior techniques.

In this paper, we did not focus on the policies for determining the most appropriate cluster size, as this depends on the applications' working sets and/or aggregate cache requirement [18, 23, 31, 35]. To find optimal cluster size, LOCO can leverage previous works which flexibly adjust cluster sizes according to the cache performance [18, 23, 31].

**Cache search and coherence.** Substantial research has proposed flexible data location in L2 cache slices, which leads to the additional overhead of searching for the current data location. Here, we focus on search techniques that manages at the granularity of cache lines. One approach is to use a central tag to keep track of dynamic locations of each cache line [9, 12]. As a central tag directory might be a communication bottleneck, several researchers employed local tag directories instead [13, 24, 35]. A local tag directory can only function as a backup, since it is impossible to assign to every core its own tag directory covering the entire on-chip cached memory. The most common strategy is to maintain the tag directory at static home node locations [19, 24, 31, 45, 46], while actual data can be stored at other places. This leads to an indirection cost to access the home node whenever accessing data.

To avoid this indirection cost, broadcast can be used [7, 12, 13, 18, 26, 35, 36]. However broadcasting over large-scale CMPs is simply unacceptable in terms of latency and energy consumption. The broadcasting cost is mitigated by using local tag directories as caches [13, 35], or by broadcasting only to relevant destinations [18, 36], which is similar to our approach. In this paper, we further optimize broadcast latency with our virtual meshes (VMS) leveraging SMART NoC (Section 3.2), which offers a scalable solution to many-core CMPs.

**Co-design of cache organization with novel interconnects.** There have been prior studies that investigate alternative cache designs driven by emerging interconnect technologies as well. Transmission line caches [6] enable area and energy-efficient cache organization by exploiting on-chip transmission lines which can substantially reduce wire delay at the cost of wire bandwidth density. ATAC [30] leverages on-chip optical links as a high-bandwidth, low-energy broadcast bus for scalable broadcast-based coherence. Like these prior works, LOCO is motivated by novel interconnects, SMART. However, LOCO is not limited to a specific topology of custom-designed links determined at the design time, due to the flexible nature of SMART NoC. LOCO can adapt to applications or programmers' needs, and thus tailor a cache organization to SMART characteristics so as to truly be locality-oblivious.

## 6. Conclusion

This work presents LOCO, a locality-oblivious cache organization scheme that leverages recent innovations in low-latency NoC architectures to redefine the notion of locality. SMART NoCs enable flits to traverse up to $HPC_{max}$-hops (4 in this design) within one cycle at 2GHz. LOCO is a hybrid private-shared cache organization that partitions the chip into virtual clusters of varying sizes. It provides increased hit rate within each cluster with fast access latencies, and fast global data search across chip over virtual meshes. It also enables data migration across clusters to reduce off-chip accesses. LOCO demonstrates better performance than both private and shared caches, and provides a scalable cache organization and management solution as we move towards 1000-core chips.

## Acknowledgments

The authers acknowledge the support of Semiconductor Research Corporation (SRC) and the Defense Advanced Research Projects Agency (DARPA) through the Semiconductor Technology Advanced Research network (STARnet), under the Center for Future Architectures (C-FAR) research center.

## References


[1] N. Agarwal, T. Krishna, L.-S. Peh, and N. K. Jha. Garnet: A detailed on-chip network model inside a full-system simulator. In *ISPASS*, 2009.

[2] N. Agarwal, L.-S. Peh, and N. K. Jha. In-network snoop ordering (inso): Snoopy coherence on unordered interconnects. In *HPCA*, 2009.

[3] M. Awasthi, K. Sudan, R. Balasubramonian, and J. B. Carter. Dynamic hardware-assisted software-controlled page placement to manage capacity allocation and sharing within large caches. In *HPCA*, 2009.

[4] R. Balasubramonian, N. P. Jouppi, and N. Muralimanohar. *Multi-Core Cache Hierarchies*. Synthesis Lectures on Computer Architecture. Morgan & Claypool Publishers, 2011.

[5] N. Barrow-Williams, C. Fensch, and S. W. Moore. A communication characterisation of splash-2 and parsec. In *IISWC*, 2009.

[6] B. M. Beckmann and D. A. Wood. TLC: Transmission Line Caches. In *MICRO*, 2003.

[7] B. M. Beckmann, M. R. Marty, and D. A. Wood. Asr: Adaptive selective replication for cmp caches. In *MICRO*, 2006.

[8] C. Bienia, S. Kumar, J. P. Singh, and K. Li. The parsec benchmark suite: characterization and architectural implications. In *PACT*, 2008.

[9] J. Chang and G. S. Sohi. Cooperative caching for chip multiprocessors. In *ISCA*, 2006.

[10] M. Chaudhuri. Pagenuca: Selected policies for page-grain locality management in large shared chip-multiprocessor caches. In *HPCA*, 2009.

[11] C.-H. O. Chen, S. Park, T. Krishna, S. Subramanian, A. P. Chandrakasan, and L.-S. Peh. SMART: A Single-Cycle Reconfigurable NoC for SoC Applications. In *DATE*, 2013.

[12] Z. Chishti, M. D. Powell, and T. N. Vijaykumar. Distance associativity for high-performance energy-efficient non-uniform cache architectures. In *MICRO*, 2003.

[13] Z. Chishti, M. D. Powell, and T. N. Vijaykumar. Optimizing replication, communication, and capacity allocation in cmps. In *ISCA*, 2005.

[14] S. Cho and L. Jin. Managing distributed, shared l2 caches through os-level page allocation. In *MICRO*, 2006.

[15] B. Cuesta, A. Ros, M. E. Gómez, A. Robles, and J. Duato. Increasing the effectiveness of directory caches by deactivating coherence for private memory blocks. In *ISCA*, 2011.

[16] N. Eisley, L.-S. Peh, and L. Shang. Leveraging on-chip networks for data cache migration in chip multiprocessors. In *PACT*, 2008.

[17] A. Gupta, W.-D. Weber, and T. C. Mowry. Reducing memory and traffic requirements for scalable directory-based cache coherence schemes. In *ICPP (1)*, 1990.

[18] M. Hammoud, S. Cho, and R. G. Melhem. Dynamic cache clustering for chip multiprocessors. In *ICS*, 2009.

[19] N. Hardavellas, M. Ferdman, B. Falsafi, and A. Ailamaki. Reactive nuca: near-optimal block placement and replication in distributed caches. In *ISCA*, 2009.

[20] R. Ho. *On-Chip Wires: Scaling and Efficiency*. PhD thesis, Stanford University, 2003.

[21] Y. Hoskote, S. R. Vangal, A. Singh, N. Borkar, and S. Borkar. A 5-ghz mesh interconnect for a teraflops processor. *IEEE Micro*, 27(5):51–61, 2007.

[22] J. Howard, S. Dighe, S. R. Vangal, G. Ruhl, N. Borkar, S. Jain, V. Erraguntla, M. Konow, M. Riepen, M. Gries, G. Droege, T. Lund-Larsen, S. Steibl, S. Borkar, V. K. De, and R. F. V. der Wijngaart. A 48-Core IA-32 Message-Passing Processor with DVFS in 45nm CMOS. In *ISSCC*, 2010.

[23] J. Huh, C. Kim, H. Shafi, L. Zhang, D. Burger, and S. W. Keckler. A nuca substrate for flexible cmp cache sharing. In *ICS*, 2005.

[24] N. D. E. Jerger, L.-S. Peh, and M. H. Lipasti. Virtual tree coherence: Leveraging regions and in-network multicast trees for scalable cache coherence. In *MICRO*, 2008.

[25] B. Kim and V. Stojanovic. Characterization of equalized and repeated interconnects for noc applications. *IEEE Design and Test of Computers*, 25:430–439, 2008.

[26] C. Kim, D. Burger, and S. W. Keckler. An adaptive, non-uniform cache structure for wire-delay dominated on-chip caches. In *ASPLOS*, 2002.

[27] J. Kim, W. J. Dally, B. Towles, and A. K. Gupta. Microarchitecture of a high-radix router. In *ISCA*, 2005.

[28] J. Kim, W. J. Dally, and D. Abts. Flattened butterfly: a cost-efficient topology for high-radix networks. In *ISCA*, 2007.

[29] T. Krishna, C.-H. O. Chen, W. C. Kwon, and L.-S. Peh. Breaking the on-chip latency barrier using SMART. In *HPCA*, 2013.

[30] G. Kurian, J. E. Miller, J. Psota, J. Eastep, J. Liu, J. Michel, L. C. Kimerling, and A. Agarwal. ATAC: All-to-All Computing Using On-Chip Optical Interconnects. In *BARC*, 2007.

[31] H. Lee, S. Cho, and B. R. Childers. Cloudcache: Expanding and shrinking private caches. In *HPCA*, 2011.

[32] Y.-C. Maa, D. K. Pradhan, and D. Thiébaut. A hierarchical directory scheme for large-scale cache-coherent multipmcessors. In *IPPS*, 1992.

[33] M. M. K. Martin, M. D. Hill, and D. A. Wood. Token coherence: Decoupling performance and correctness. In *ISCA*, 2003.

[34] M. M. K. Martin, D. J. Sorin, B. M. Beckmann, M. R. Marty, M. Xu, A. R. Alameldeen, K. E. Moore, M. D. Hill, and D. A. Wood. Multifacet's general execution-driven multiprocessor simulator (gems) toolset. *SIGARCH Computer Architecture News*, 33(4):92–99, 2005.

[35] M. R. Marty and M. D. Hill. Virtual hierarchies to support server consolidation. In *ISCA*, 2007.

[36] M. R. Marty, J. D. Bingham, M. D. Hill, A. J. Hu, M. M. K. Martin, and D. A. Wood. Improving multiple-cmp systems using token coherence. In *HPCA*, 2005.

[37] J. E. Miller, H. Kasture, G. Kurian, C. G. III, N. Beckmann, C. Celio, J. Eastep, and A. Agarwal. Graphite: A distributed parallel simulator for multicores. In *HPCA*, 2010.

[38] S. Park, T. Krishna, C.-H. Chen, B. Daya, A. Chandrakasan, and L.-S. Peh. Approaching the theoretical limits of a mesh

NoC with a 16-node chip prototype in 45nm SOI. In *DAC*, 2012.

[39] K. Sankaralingam, R. Nagarajan, H. Liu, C. Kim, J. Huh, D. Burger, S. W. Keckler, and C. R. Moore. Exploiting ilp, tlp, and dlp with the polymorphous trips architecture. *IEEE Micro*, 23(6):46–51, 2003.

[40] S. Scott, D. Abts, J. Kim, and W. J. Dally. The BlackWidow high-radix clos network. In *ISCA*, 2006.

[41] C. Sun, C.-H. O. Chen, G. Kurian, L. Wei, J. Miller, A. Agarwal, L.-S. Peh, and V. Stojanovic. DSENT - a tool connecting emerging photonics with electronics for opto-electronic networks-on-chip modeling. In *NoCS*, 2010.

[42] D. A. Wallach. *PHD: A Hierarchical Cache Coherent Protocol.* MS Thesis. MIT, 1992.

[43] D. Wentzlaff, P. Griffin, H. Hoffmann, L. Bao, B. Edwards, C. Ramey, M. Mattina, C.-C. Miao, J. F. B. III, and A. Agarwal. On-chip interconnection architecture of the tile processor. *IEEE Micro*, 27(5):15–31, 2007.

[44] S. C. Woo, M. Ohara, E. Torrie, J. P. Singh, and A. Gupta. The splash-2 programs: Characterization and methodological considerations. In *ISCA*, 1995.

[45] M. Zhang and K. Asanovic. Victim migration: Dynamically adapting between private and shared cmp caches. Technical report, MIT, 2005.

[46] M. Zhang and K. Asanovic. Victim replication: Maximizing capacity while hiding wire delay in tiled chip multiprocessors. In *ISCA*, 2005.

# Ubik: Efficient Cache Sharing with Strict QoS for Latency-Critical Workloads

Harshad Kasture Daniel Sanchez

Computer Science and Artificial Intelligence Laboratory
Massachusetts Institute of Technology
{harshad, sanchez}@csail.mit.edu

## Abstract

Chip-multiprocessors (CMPs) must often execute workload mixes with different performance requirements. On one hand, user-facing, latency-critical applications (e.g., web search) need low tail (i.e., worst-case) latencies, often in the millisecond range, and have inherently low utilization. On the other hand, compute-intensive batch applications (e.g., MapReduce) only need high long-term average performance. In current CMPs, latency-critical and batch applications cannot run concurrently due to interference on shared resources. Unfortunately, prior work on quality of service (QoS) in CMPs has focused on guaranteeing average performance, not tail latency.

In this work, we analyze several latency-critical workloads, and show that guaranteeing average performance is insufficient to maintain low tail latency, because microarchitectural resources with state, such as caches or cores, exert *inertia* on instantaneous workload performance. Last-level caches impart the highest inertia, as workloads take tens of milliseconds to warm them up. When left unmanaged, or when managed with conventional QoS frameworks, shared last-level caches degrade tail latency significantly. Instead, we propose Ubik, a dynamic partitioning technique that predicts and exploits the transient behavior of latency-critical workloads to maintain their tail latency while maximizing the cache space available to batch applications. Using extensive simulations, we show that, while conventional QoS frameworks degrade tail latency by up to 2.3×, Ubik simultaneously maintains the tail latency of latency-critical workloads and significantly improves the performance of batch applications.

**Categories and Subject Descriptors** B.3.2 [*Memory structures*]: Design styles—Cache memories; C.1.4 [*Processor architectures*]: Parallel architectures

**Keywords** multicore, interference, isolation, quality of service, tail latency, resource management, cache partitioning



*ASPLOS '14*, March 1–4, 2014, Salt Lake City, Utah, USA.

ACM 978-1-4503-2305-5/14/03...$15.00.
http://dx.doi.org/10.1145/2541940.2541944

## 1. Introduction

General-purpose systems are designed to maximize *long-term average performance*. They focus on optimizing the common case and rely on best-effort techniques. While this is a good match to batch applications, many applications are latency-critical, and *short-term worst-case response times* determine their performance. This disconnect between how systems are designed and used causes large inefficiencies.

While latency-critical workloads are common in embedded, mobile, and datacenter computing, in this work we focus on datacenters. Datacenter servers often execute user-facing applications that need low tail latencies. For example, web search nodes need to provide $99^{th}$ percentile latencies of a few milliseconds at worst [11, 43]. Moreover, to avoid being dominated by queuing delays, latency-critical workloads are typically executed at low loads. These stringent requirements limit the utilization of servers dedicated to a single application. For example, Meisner et al. report average server utilization of 14% for applications with medium QoS needs, and 7% for real-time services [35]. Barroso and Hölzle report an average utilization below 30% on the Google fleet [3], which includes both real-time services (e.g., search), and batch applications (e.g., MapReduce). This poor utilization wastes billions of dollars in equipment and terawatt-hours of energy yearly [3].

Fortunately, datacenters also support a large amount of batch applications that only require high average performance. Ideally, systems should be designed to execute mixes of latency-critical and batch applications, providing strict performance guarantees to latency-critical applications and achieving high utilization at the same time. However, this is not possible in current chip-multiprocessors (CMPs), because concurrent applications contend on shared resources, such as cache capacity, on-chip network bandwidth, and memory bandwidth, causing unpredictable interference.

To sidestep this issue, prior work has proposed several techniques to provide quality of service (QoS) in CMPs and datacenters. On one hand, several software-only solutions [12, 33, 54, 60] rely on empirically detecting interference, and throttling, migrating, or avoiding to run applications that induce too much degradation. These schemes often avoid interference, but do not prevent it. On the other hand, prior work has introduced hardware to explicitly partition shared resources [9, 16, 21, 25, 38, 45], and frameworks that manage these resources dynamically to provide QoS [5, 13, 17, 29, 31, 37, 42, 49, 61]. However, all these techniques only provide guarantees on long-term average performance (e.g., IPC or queries per second over billions of instructions), instead of on worst-case, short-term behavior.

The fundamental issue with conventional QoS frameworks is that, despite having hardware that enforces explicit partitioning, they reconfigure at coarse-grained intervals and assume instant transitions between steady states, *ignoring transient behavior*. For example, cache partitioning policies [39, 42, 52] periodically reallocate space across applications. When an application gets additional space, it can take tens of milliseconds to fill it with its own cache lines and reap the benefits of a larger allocation. We call this effect *performance inertia*. Conventional QoS schemes avoid the effects of inertia by reconfiguring at long enough intervals (making transients rare), and adapt across intervals (e.g., giving more resources to an application that is below its target performance [60]). This long-term adaptation works for batch workloads, but not for latency-critical workloads, as long low-performance periods dominate tail latency. Alternatively, we can implement fixed, conservative resource allocations. For example, if a latency-critical application needs 2 MB of cache to meet its target tail latency, we can statically assign it 2 MB of cache. This eliminates transients, but it is too conservative. Instead, we advocate a more efficient approach: by understanding and leveraging transient behavior, we can still perform dynamic, aggressive resource sharing without sacrificing short-term performance.

In this paper, we develop adaptive techniques that provide *strict QoS guarantees on tail latency* for latency-critical applications. We focus on last-level caches as they have the largest amount of microarchitectural, hardware-managed state and therefore induce significant inertia. Although we expect our findings to apply to other resources with inertia, we leave such evaluation to future work. Specifically, our contributions are:

- We develop a suite of representative latency-critical workloads, and define a methodology to accurately measure the interaction between tail latency and microarchitecture using simulation. We then show that most workloads exhibit significant inertia, which impacts tail latency considerably.
- We extend conventional partitioning policies that achieve a single objective (e.g., maximizing cache utilization) to achieve the dual objectives of maximizing cache utilization while providing strict QoS guarantees for latency-critical workloads (Section 4). We show that, without accounting for inertia, these solutions either preserve tail latency but are too inefficient, or degrade tail latency significantly.
- We propose *Ubik*, a cache partitioning policy that characterizes and leverages inertia to share space dynamically while maintaining tail latency (Section 5). Ubik safely takes space away from latency-critical applications when they are idle, and, if needed, temporarily boosts their space when they are active to maintain their target tail latency. In designing Ubik, we show that transient behavior can be accurately predicted and bounded. Ubik is mostly implemented in software and needs simple hardware extensions beyond partitioning.
- We evaluate Ubik against conventional and proposed management schemes (Section 7). While conventional adaptive partitioning policies [42] degrade tail latency by up to 2.3×, Ubik strictly maintains tail latency and simultaneously achieves high cache space utilization, improving batch application performance significantly. Moreover, by enabling latency-critical and batch applications to coexist efficiently, Ubik considerably improves server utilization.

## 2. Background and Related Work

Lack of quality of service fundamentally limits datacenter utilization, due to the combination of three factors. First, low-latency datacenter-wide networks [22] and faster storage (e.g., Flash) have turned many I/O-bound workloads into compute-bound, often making compute the major source of latency [40, 43]. Second, single-node latencies must be small and tightly distributed, since servicing each user request involves hundreds to thousands of nodes, and the slowest nodes often determine end-to-end latency. As a result, responsive online services (100-1000 ms) often require single-node tail latencies in the millisecond range [11]. Third, frequency scaling, which drove compute latency down for free, has stopped. Instead, we now rely on CMPs with more cores and shared resources, which suffer from interference and degrade performance. Therefore, in this work we focus on QoS on CMPs.

### 2.1. Quality of Service in CMPs

Prior work has proposed two main approaches to provide QoS in CMPs: software-only schemes that detect and disallow colocations that cause excessive interference, and software-hardware schemes where software explicitly manages shared hardware resources. Both approaches only guarantee average long-term performance, instead of worst-case, short-term performance, and ignore transients and performance inertia.

**Software-only QoS management:** Prior work has proposed profiling, coscheduling, and admission control techniques to perform QoS-aware scheduling in datacenters [12, 33, 60] (e.g., coscheduling latency-sensitive applications only with workloads that are not memory-intensive). When used across the datacenter, these techniques are complementary with hardware QoS schemes, since they can select workloads that use resources in a complementary way, improving system utilization. However, while usable in current best-effort hardware, these schemes do not disallow short-term interference, and must be conservative, only colocating workloads that have low memory utilization, which leaves shared memory resources underutilized. With QoS-enforcing hardware, these techniques could coschedule workloads much more aggressively, relying on hardware to prevent interference.

**Hardware-based QoS enforcement:** Prior work has proposed hardware schemes to partition shared resources [9, 16, 21, 25, 38, 45], as well as software QoS frameworks that leverage these mechanisms to implement fairness, maximize throughput, or provide differentiated service [5, 13, 17, 20, 29, 31, 37, 42, 49, 61]. However, these techniques have been developed with the goal of meeting *long-term performance goals* (e.g., IPC or queries per second over billions of instructions), instead of providing strict guarantees on worst-case, short-term behavior (e.g., bounding the performance degradation of a 1 ms request). These systems reconfigure at coarse-grained intervals and assume instant transitions between steady states. However, for many resources, reconfigurations cause relatively long transients, inducing *performance inertia.* While inertia can be safely ignored for batch workloads by reconfiguring at long enough intervals, it *cannot be ignored for latency-critical workloads.*

Different microarchitectural resources induce different degrees of performance inertia. On one hand, bandwidth has minimal inertia: reallocating it can be done in tens of cycles [21], and applications instantly start benefiting from it. On the other hand, components with significant state (such as cores or caches) take time to warm up, causing significant transients. While core state is relatively small, the memory wall keeps driving the amount of cache per core up [7, 58], making cache-induced inertia a growing concern. Therefore, we focus on shared cache management.

### 2.2. Cache Partitioning in CMPs

We first discuss hardware schemes to enforce partition sizes, then review relevant policies to manage them.

**Partitioning schemes:** A partitioning scheme should support a large number of partitions with fine-grained sizes, disallow interference among partitions, avoid hurting cache associativity or replacement policy performance, support changing partition sizes efficiently, and require small overheads. For our purposes (Section 4), fine-grained partition sizes, strict isolation, and fast resizing are especially important. Achieving all these properties simultaneously is not trivial. For example, way-partitioning [9], the most common technique, restricts insertions from each partition to its assigned subset of ways. It is simple, but it supports a small number of coarsely-sized partitions (in multiples of way size); partition associativity is proportional to its way count, so partitioning degrades performance; and more importantly, reconfigurations are slow and unpredictable (Section 7). Alternatively, Vantage [45] leverages the statistical properties of skew-associative caches [48] and zcaches [44] to implement partitioning efficiently. Vantage supports fine-grained partitions (defined in cache lines), provides strict guarantees on partition sizes and isolation, can resize partitions without moves or invalidations, reconfiguration transients are much faster than in way-partitioning [45], and it is cheap to implement (requiring $\approx$1% extra state and negligible logic). For these reasons, we use Vantage to enforce partition sizes, although the policies we develop are not strictly tied to Vantage.

**Partitioning policies:** Partitioning policies consist of a monitoring mechanism, typically in hardware, that profiles partitions, and a controller, in software or hardware, that uses this information to set partition sizes.

Utility-based cache partitioning (UCP) is a frequently used policy [42]. UCP introduces a *utility monitor* (UMON) per core, which samples the address stream and measures the partition's *miss curve*, i.e., the number of misses that the partition would have incurred with each possible number of allocated ways. System software periodically reads these miss curves and repartitions the cache to maximize cache utility (i.e., the expected number of cache hits). Although UCP was designed to work with way-partitioning, it can be used with other schemes [45, 59]. Ubik uses UMONs to capture miss curves, and extends them to enable quick adaptation for latency-critical workloads.

Partitioning policies can have goals other than maximizing utility. In particular, CoQoS [29] and METE [49] combine cache and bandwidth partitioning mechanisms to provide end-to-end performance guarantees. As discussed before, these guarantees are only on long-term performance. For example, METE uses robust control theory to efficiently meet target IPCs for each application, but adding new applications and dynamic application behavior cause variability on short-term IPCs [49, Figure 10]. Prior work has proposed policies that optimize for responsiveness. PACORA [5] uses convex optimization to find resource partitionings that minimize penalty functions. These functions can encode both average performance and latency requirements. Cook et al. [10] propose a software-only gradient descent algorithm that limits the average degradation that one or more background applications exert on a foreground application. While both techniques can be used to reduce latency and responsiveness, they still use periodic reconfiguration and ignore transients, so they only work when the desired latency is much larger than the transient length, which makes them inapplicable to latency-critical applications (Section 3).

### 2.3. Cache Management in Real-Time Systems

Latency-critical datacenter workloads are one instance of an application with soft real-time requirements running on commodity systems. Prior work on soft real-time systems has used static cache partitioning to provide strict QoS [8, 28]. In contrast, Ubik manages partition sizes dynamically and at fine granularity to provide QoS to latency-critical workloads, and, at the same time, maximize the space available to batch applications. Ubik should be directly applicable to other domains with mixes of soft real-time and batch applications (e.g., mobile and embedded computing).

Caches are problematic for hard-real time applications, which must not violate deadlines [47]. As a result, hard real-time systems often favor scratchpads or locked caches [41, 57]. We do not target hard-real time workloads in this work.

## 3. Understanding Latency-Critical Applications

Latency-critical applications are significantly different from the batch workloads typically used in architectural studies. In

| Workload | Configuration | Requests |
|---|---|---|
| xapian | English Wikipedia, zipfian query popularity | 6000 |
| masstree | mycsb-a (50% GETs, 50% PUTs), 1.1GB table | 9000 |
| moses | opensubtitles.org corpora, phrase-based mode | 900 |
| shore | TPC-C, 10 warehouses | 7500 |
| specjbb | 1 warehouse | 37500 |

Table 1: Parameters of the latency-critical workloads studied.

this section, we analyze several representative latency-critical workloads, with a focus on understanding these differences.

### 3.1. Applications

We have selected five latency-critical workloads, intended to capture a broad variety of domains and behaviors:

- `xapian`, a web search engine, typically a latency-critical, compute-intensive workload [11, 43], configured to represent a leaf node, executing search queries over Wikipedia.
- `masstree`, a high-performance in-memory key-value store that achieves speeds similar to memcached [32].
- `moses`, a statistical machine translation system [26], represents a real-time translation service (e.g., Google Translate).
- `shore-mt`, a modern DBMS, running TPC-C, an OLTP workload [23].
- `specjbb`, representative of the middle-tier portion of 3-tier business logic systems. We run it using the HotSpot JVM v1.5, and configure the warmup period and garbage collector to ensure that the measured portion is not dominated by JIT overheads and is free of garbage collection periods. This avoids having the JVM dominate tail latencies; commercial real-time JVMs [55] achieve a similar effect.

Table 1 details their input sets and simulated requests.

### 3.2. Methodology

Prior architectural studies consider similar workloads [6, 15, 18], but they execute them at full load and measure their average throughput. Instead, we are interested in their *tail latency* characteristics, which requires a different methodology.

**Simulation:** We simulate these workloads using zsim [46], and model a CMP with six OOO cores validated against a real Westmere system (Section 6 details the simulated system). We focus on application-level characteristics, not including OS and I/O overheads. We have verified that this is reasonable by profiling OS time, I/O time, and request distributions in a real system. For `shore-mt`, this is only accurate if the database and log are stored in a ramdisk (0.8 ms $95^{th}$ pct service time in real system vs 0.9 ms simulated), or on an SSD (1.4 ms $95^{th}$ pct service time in real). `shore-mt` becomes I/O-bound on a conventional HDD (86 ms $95^{th}$ pct service time in real). For the other workloads, these simplifications are accurate.

**Client-server setup:** We integrate client and server under a single process, and measure the server running the realistic stream of requests generated by the client. A common harness throttles these requests to achieve exponential interarrival times at a configurable rate (i.e., a Markov input process, common in datacenter workloads [34]). This harness adds negligible server work (155 ns/request). Finally, this approach does not include network stack overheads. These can be relatively high and unpredictable in conventional architectures, but recent work has shown that user-level networking can reduce them to microseconds even in network-intensive workloads [24]. However, the networking stack introduces delays due to interrupt coalescing. Therefore, we model interrupt coalescing with a 50 µs timeout [36].

For the characterization experiments, we pin the application to one core, and simulate a 2 MB LLC except when noted (in line with the per-core LLC capacity of current CMPs [27]). All applications run a single server worker thread, although some applications have additional threads (e.g., `shore-mt` uses log writer threads to reduce I/O stalls). Section 3.3 qualitatively discusses multithreaded latency-critical workloads.

**Metrics:** While percentiles are often used to quantify tail latency [11] (e.g., $95^{th}$ percentile latency), we report tail latency as the *mean latency of all requests beyond a certain percentile*. Our goal is to design adaptive systems, so it would be easy to design schemes that game percentile metrics by degrading requests beyond the percentile being measured. Instead, tail means include the whole tail, avoiding this problem. Additionally, while $99^{th}$ percentile latencies are commonly used [11], we use $95^{th}$ tail metrics, as gathering statistically significant $99^{th}$ tail metrics would require much longer runs. Our analysis is equally applicable to higher-percentile metrics.

**Statistical significance:** Despite using $95^{th}$ instead of $99^{th}$ tail metrics, measuring tail latency accurately is much more expensive than measuring average performance. Intuitively, only 5% of the work influences tail latency, requiring many repeated simulations to reduce measurement error. Indeed, together, the results we present in this paper required simulating over one quadrillion ($10^{15}$) instructions, several orders of magnitude higher than typical architectural studies.

Each sample run executes the same requests (fixed work), but interarrival times are randomized, introducing variability and ensuring that we model a representative distribution instead of just one instance. We run enough simulations to obtain tight confidence intervals for the results we present (e.g., mean and tail latencies). However, some tail latencies are so variable that making their confidence intervals negligible would require an unreasonable number of simulations. Therefore, we omit the 95% confidence intervals when they are within $\pm 1\%$, and plot them (as error bars) otherwise.

### 3.3. Load-Latency Analysis

Figure 1a shows the load-latency plots for each application. Each graph shows the mean latency (blue) and tail latency (red) as a function of offered load ($\rho = \lambda/\mu$, which matches processor utilization). We make three observations that have significant implications for adaptive systems:

**Observation 1: Tail $\neq$ mean.** Tail latencies are significantly higher than mean latencies, and the difference between both is highly dependent on the application and load. In general, tail latencies are caused by the complex interplay of arrival

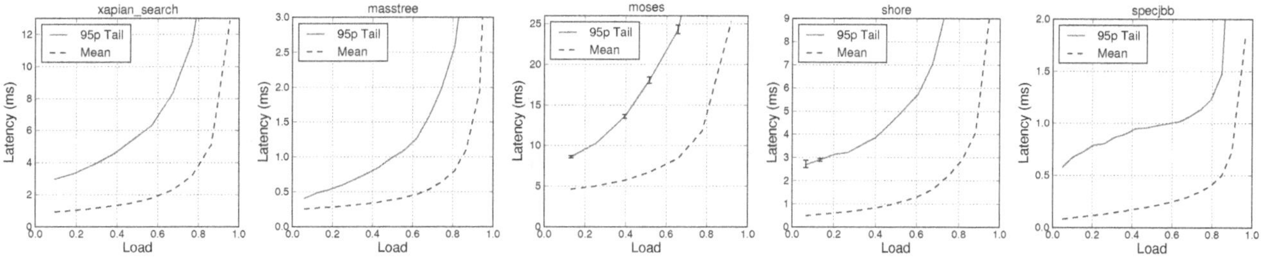


(a) Load-latency diagrams for mean (dashed blue) and $95^{th}$ percentile tail (solid red) latencies.

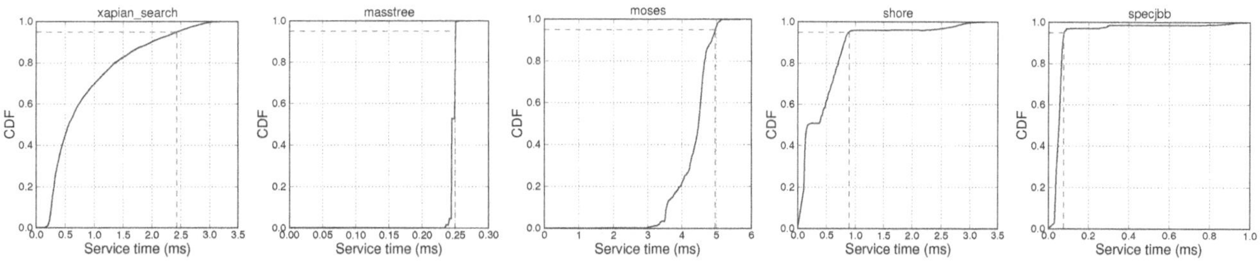


(b) Cumulative distribution functions (CDFs) of request service time (no queueing delay). Dashed lines indicate the $95^{th}$ percentile service times.

Figure 1: Load-latency and service time distributions of the latency-critical applications studied.

and service times for each request. Figure 1b shows the cumulative distribution functions (CDFs) of request service times for each workload. Some workloads (e.g., `masstree`, `moses`) have near-constant service times, but others (e.g., `xapian`, `shore-mt`, `specjbb`) are multi-modal or long-tailed. While applications with more variable service times have a larger difference between tail and mean latencies, there is no general way to determine the relationship between both. Therefore, QoS guarantees on mean performance are insufficient to guarantee tail latency efficiently. Instead, adaptive systems should be designed to guarantee tail latency directly.

**Observation 2: Latency-critical workloads have limited utilization.** Figure 1a shows that tail latency quickly increases with load, even in applications with regular service times. Most applications must run at 10-20% utilization if reducing latency is crucial, and cannot run beyond 60-70% load. Even if tail latency is secondary, traffic spikes and interference impose large guardbands that reduce utilization [11]. Due to this inherently low utilization, dedicating systems to latency-critical applications is fundamentally inefficient. This motivates building systems that achieve high utilization by colocating mixes of latency-critical and batch workloads.

**Observation 3: Tail latency degrades superlinearly.** When processor performance degrades, tail latency suffers from two compounding effects. First, requests take longer (in Figure 1a, all the curves scale up). Second, load increases (in Figure 1a, the operating point moves right). For example, `masstree` has a 1.2 ms tail latency at 60% load. If processor performance drops 25%, at the same absolute request rate (queries per second), load increases to $1.25 \cdot 60 = 75\%$, and tail latency grows to $1.25 \cdot TailLat(75\%) = 2.9$ ms, 2.3× higher. In adaptive systems, this places very stringent requirements on performance variability.

Note that, as configured, these applications service one request at a time in FIFO order. Servers with multiple worker threads have more nuanced tradeoffs. On one hand, being able to service multiple requests simultaneously reduces queuing delay, especially at high load. On the other hand, we have observed that server threads often interfere among themselves, block on critical sections, and in some workloads (e.g., OLTP) concurrent requests cause occasional aborts, degrading tail latency. Since providing QoS for multithreaded workloads is far more complex, and single-threaded latency-critical workloads are common in datacenters [11, 34], we defer studying multi-threaded latency-critical workloads to future work.

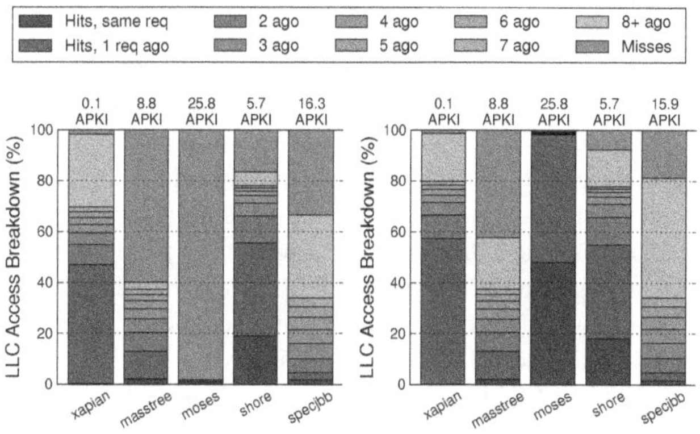


(a) 2 MB LLC (b) 8 MB LLC

Figure 2: Breakdown of LLC accesses for the applications studied, with 2 and 8 MB LLCs. To quantify inertia, hits are classified by how many requests ago they were last accessed.

### 3.4. Performance Inertia

In latency-critical applications, the performance of each request largely depends on the microarchitectural state at the start of the request (e.g., caches, TLBs, branch predictors, etc). On long requests, ignoring this dependence may be a good

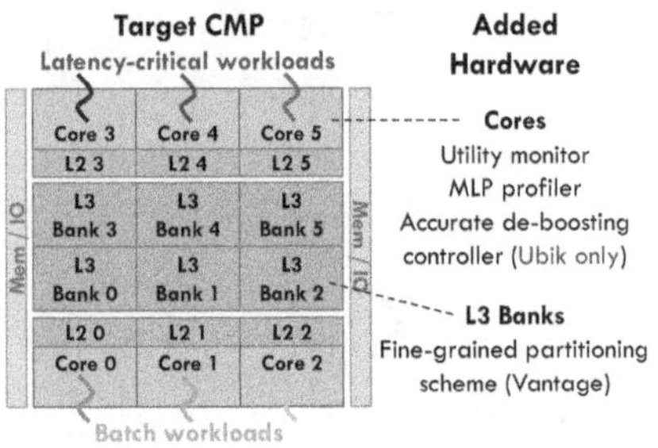


Figure 3: Target CMP and added hardware structures.

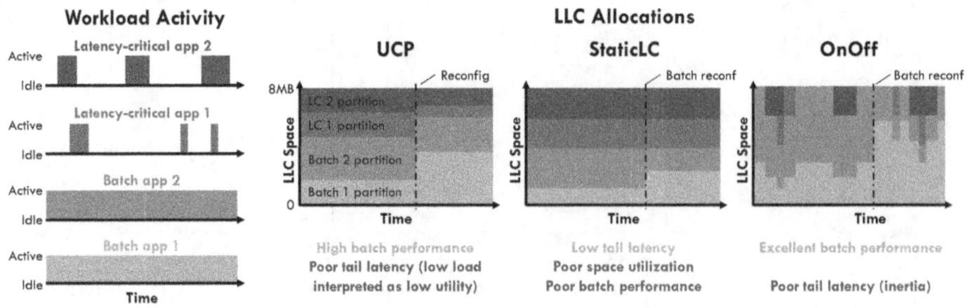


Figure 4: Example operation of UCP, StaticLC, and OnOff on a mix of two latency-critical and two batch workloads, and main properties of each partitioning policy.

approximation, but this is not the case for short requests. We call this dependence *performance inertia*. We focus on the last-level cache, the microarchitectural component with the most state. Figure 2a classifies LLC accesses into hits and misses for each application, using a 2 MB LLC. Furthermore, hits are classified according to how many requests ago they were last accessed, and shown in different shades of red (with the lowest one being during the current request, and the highest one being 8 or more requests ago). Classifying hits this way is sensible because, in these workloads, most gains can be achieved by taking space away between servicing requests, when the application is idle. To quantify intensity, each bar also shows the LLC accesses per thousand instructions (APKI).

As we can see, all applications, and especially those with shorter response times, have significant reuse across requests. In all cases, more than half of the hits come from lines that were brought in or last touched by previous requests. Moreover, this inertia largely depends on cache size. Figure 2b shows LLC access distributions for an 8 MB LLC. Compared to the 2 MB LLC, all workloads exhibit (a) significantly lower miss rates, and (b) higher cross-request reuse, often going back many requests. Thus, larger eDRAM and 3D-stacked caches are making performance inertia a growing issue for latency-critical workloads (e.g., POWER7+ has 10MB of LLC per core [58], and Haswell has up to 32 MB of L4 per core [7]).

# 4. Simple Cache Partitioning Policies for Mixes of Latency-Critical and Batch Workloads

Although latency-critical workloads have limited utilization, we can achieve high utilization by coscheduling mixes of latency-critical and batch applications in the same machine. Figure 3 illustrates this scenario, showing a six-core CMP with a three-level cache hierarchy (private L2s and a shared, banked L3), where three cores are executing latency-critical applications, while the other three execute batch applications.

Achieving safe operation and efficient utilization with latency-critical and batch mixes requires a *dual-goal* partitioning policy. First, it must not degrade the tail latency of latency-critical applications beyond a given bound. Second, it should maximize the average performance of batch workloads. With this approach, each latency-critical application must be given a target tail latency. In this work, we set this target to the tail latency achieved when running the workload alone with a smaller, fixed-size LLC, as in Figure 1a. This ensures that the target tail latency is achievable, and is a reasonable strategy for multi-machine deployments: operators can easily find the achievable tail latency bound, and the system will guarantee that it is not violated. In contrast, to allow high utilization, we do not set performance targets for batch workloads: since they are not latency-sensitive, they can be migrated to another machine if they are not meeting their performance target [12, 60].

Previously proposed policies focus on improving or guaranteeing long-term performance only, so they are not directly applicable to our purposes. In this section, we develop simple extensions to these policies, and show that they have serious shortcomings because they ignore transient behavior and performance inertia. Figure 4 illustrates these schemes through a simple example, and summarizes their characteristics.

**UCP baseline:** Figure 3 shows our baseline system and the hardware structures added to support cache partitioning. Cores can be in-order or out-of-order. As discussed in Section 2, we use Vantage [45] to perform fine-grained partitioning. We also add some monitoring structures to the core: UMONs [42] to gather miss curves efficiently (Section 2), and the simple long-miss memory-level parallelism (MLP) profiling scheme from Eyerman et al. [14].

We choose utility-based cache partitioning (UCP) enhanced with MLP information to illustrate the behavior of conventional partitioning policies. UCP maximizes overall throughput, and improves fairness as well [42]. UCP repartitions periodically (e.g., every 50 ms) by reading the per-core UMONs and MLP profilers; using the UMON data to construct miss curves, combining them with the MLP information to construct *miss-per-cycle* curves (i.e., misses per cycle the core would incur for each possible partition size) and using the Lookahead algorithm (Section 2) to find the partition sizes that minimize the expected misses per cycle in the next interval[1]. Figure 4 shows the behavior of UCP in a mix of two latency-critical and two batch workloads. UCP suffers from two problems. First, UCP maximizes cache utilization with no concern for performance bounds, and will happily degrade tail latency if doing so improves overall throughput. Second,

[1] Using MLP instead of miss curves as in UCP has been shown to provide modest performance improvements [30, 37], because UCP already accounts for miss intensity indirectly. We include this mechanism in fairness to Ubik, which uses MLP profiling to derive transient behavior.

UCP interprets the low average utilization of latency-critical workloads as low utility, and assigns them smaller partitions. Other partitioning techniques, even those that strive to maintain average IPCs, also suffer from this issue [37, 42, 49, 61].

**StaticLC — Safe but inefficient:** An easy solution to these problems is to give a fixed-size partition to each latency-critical application, and perform UCP on the batch applications' partitions only. We call this policy *StaticLC*. Figure 4 shows its behavior when both latency-critical applications have target sizes of 2 MB (25% of the cache) each. Unlike prior policies (Section 2), StaticLC safely maintains tail latencies and improves batch application performance somewhat, but it wastes a lot of space, as latency-critical applications hold half of the cache even when they are not active (i.e., most of the time).

**OnOff — Efficient but unsafe:** To improve space utilization, we develop the *OnOff* policy, which operates as follows: whenever a latency-critical application is active (i.e., *on*), it gets its full target allocation; when it goes idle (i.e., *off*), its space is reassigned to the batch partitions, which share the space using UCP. Using UCP's reconfiguration algorithm every time a latency-critical application shifts between idle and active would be expensive, so at periodic intervals (as in the UCP baseline), we precompute the batch partition sizes for all possible allocations ($N + 1$ cases with $N$ latency-critical workloads). Figure 4 shows OnOff's behavior. Note how the latency-critical applications only get allocated space when active, as shown on the left. OnOff gives space to batch apps aggressively, solving StaticLC's shortcoming. Unfortunately, Section 3 showed that latency-critical apps have significant *cross-request reuse*, so taking away their allocations when they are idle degrades their tail latency.

In summary, both StaticLC and OnOff have significant drawbacks, which Section 7 quantifies. As we will see now, we can do much better by understanding and leveraging transients instead of avoiding or ignoring them.

## 5. Ubik: Inertia-Based Cache Management

Ubik leverages the insight that the transient behavior caused by resizing a partition can be derived analytically, and uses it to manage the partition sizes of latency-critical apps more aggressively than StaticLC. When a latency-critical app goes idle, Ubik downsizes its partition below its *target size* while providing a high-level guarantee: when the app goes from idle to active, after a configurable time, which we call the *deadline*, both its overall progress and performance will be the same as if the partition size had been kept at the target instead of downsized. By setting the deadline to the $95^{th}$ percentile latency at the target size, Ubik does not degrade tail behavior (it can, however, make short requests slower, which reduces variability). Ubik achieves this by determining how much to downsize safely, and by temporarily boosting the partition beyond its target size when the app is active to make up for the lost performance. Idle periods are common, so Ubik frees a significant fraction of cache space, and uses it to improve batch app throughput. We have developed two variants of Ubik: *strict Ubik*, which makes conservative assumptions to provide strict guarantees, and *Ubik with slack*, which relaxes these assumptions to manage space more aggressively with a graceful, controllable degradation in tail latency.

### 5.1. Strict Ubik

**Transient behavior:** When we increase a partition's target size, its application takes some time to fill the extra space. During this time, the partition's hit rate is lower than when it reaches its target size. Ubik relies on this transient behavior being analyzable. In general, this is not true for all partitioning schemes. For example, in way-partitioning, when an application is given an extra way, it has to have misses in all the sets to claim the way. This heavily depends on the application's access pattern, and although prior work in analytical modeling of set-associativity has approximated them [1, 53], transients cannot be accurately derived online.

To avoid these issues, Ubik uses Vantage [45]. In Vantage, transients happen *as fast as possible* and are *independent of the application's access pattern*: when a partition is upsized, nothing is evicted from that partition until it reaches its target size. Every miss in that partition grows its size by one line, evicting lines from partitions that are being downsized (through Vantage's two-stage demotion-eviction process [45]). Vantage leverages the statistical properties of zcaches [44] to guarantee that a growing partition has a negligible probability of suffering an eviction (about once in a million accesses) independently of the access pattern, so we can safely assume that no line is evicted until the partition reaches its target[2].

Under these conditions, transients are easy to predict. Specifically, assume that we upsize a partition from $s_1$ to $s_2$ cache lines ($s_2 > s_1$). Figure 5 illustrates this process. We are interested in two quantities: how long does the transient last ($T_{transient}$), and how many cycles do we lose compared to not having the transient, i.e., if we started at $s_2$ lines ($L$).

First, consider what happens at a specific size $s$. If the probability of experiencing a miss is $p_s$, the average time between accesses is $T_{access} = c + p_s \cdot M$, where $M$ is the average number of cycles that the processor stalls due to a cache miss, and $c$ would be the cycles between cache accesses if all accesses were hits. We can find all these quantities from basic performance counters and the MLP profiler. For example, suppose the core has $IPC = 1.5$, issues 5 L3 accesses per thousand instructions, and 10% of them miss. The MLP profiler computes $M$ directly [14] (e.g., $M = 100$ cycles); $p_s = 0.1$, and $T_{access} = c + 0.1 \cdot 100 = 1000/(5 \cdot 1.5) = 133$ cycles, so $c = 123$ cycles. Moreover, the UMON produces a miss curve, which we can express as a *miss probability curve*, getting $p_s$ for all sizes. Using these, we can find the transient's length.

Since only a fraction $p_s$ of accesses miss, the average time between two consecutive misses is $T_{miss,s} = T_{access,s}/p_s = c/p_s + M$. To find the duration of a transient, we simply need

[2] In general, Ubik can be used with any analyzable partitioning scheme; Section 7 evaluates Ubik under different partitioning schemes and arrays.

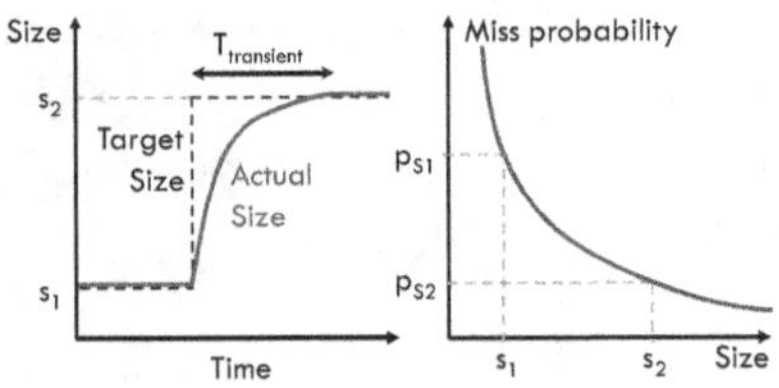


Figure 5: Transient length can be lower-bounded using miss curves and simple performance counters.

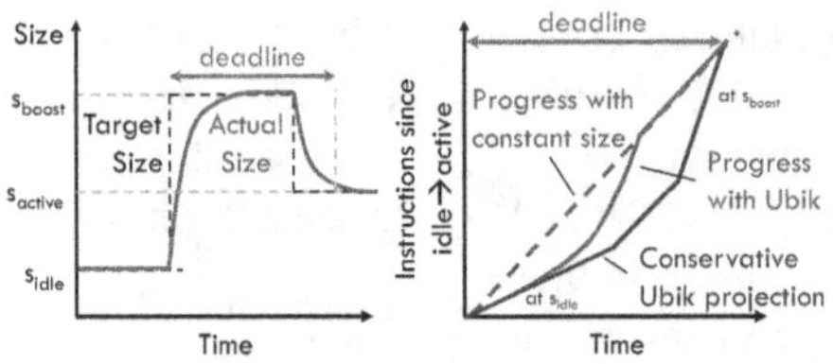


Figure 6: Example transient in Ubik: target and actual sizes, and execution progress compared to a constant partition size.

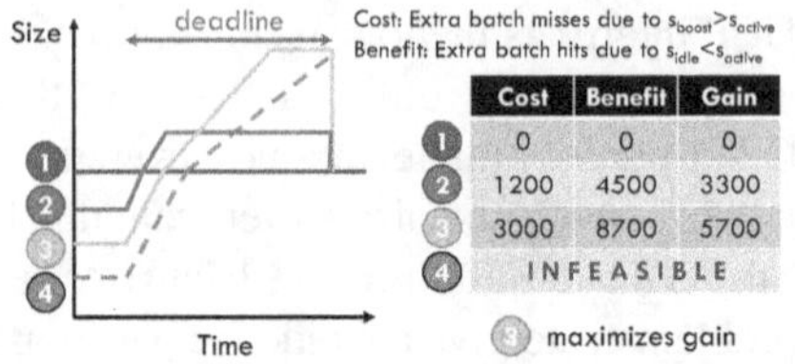


Figure 7: Sizing a latency-critical partition: determining $s_{boost}$ for feasible values of $s_{idle}$, and cost-benefit analysis.

to add these intervals up:

$$T_{transient} = \sum_{s=s_1}^{s_2-1} T_{miss,s} = \sum_{s=s_1}^{s_2-1} \frac{c}{p_s} + M$$

Note that $p_s$ is a variable: it decreases as the partition grows, as shown in Figure 5. Though this summation is complex, we can easily compute a conservative upper bound:

$$T_{transient} \leq \sum_{s=s_1}^{s_2-1} \frac{c}{p_{s_2}} + M = (s_2 - s_1)\left(\frac{c}{p_{s_2}} + M\right)$$

For the example above, if a transient starts at $s_1 = 1\,\text{MB}$ and ends at $s_2 = 2\,\text{MB}$ ($s_2 - s_1 = 16384$ 64-byte cache lines), $p_{s_1} = 0.2$, and $p_{s_2} = 0.1$, then the transient will take at most $16384 \cdot (123/0.1 + 100) = 21.8$ million cycles.

During this transient, we incur $\sum_{s=s_1}^{s_2-1}(1 - p_{s_2}/p_s)$ more misses than if we started at size $s_2$, and each miss costs $M$ cycles on average. Therefore, we can compute the number of lost cycles, $L$, as well as a conservative upper bound:

$$L = M \sum_{s=s_1}^{s_2-1} 1 - \frac{p_{s_2}}{p_s} \leq M\,(s_2 - s_1)\left(1 - \frac{p_{s_2}}{p_{s_1}}\right)$$

This upper bound assumes that the application does not enjoy the extra reuse from a larger partition until it finishes the transient. For the example above, we lose at most $100 \cdot 16384 \cdot (1 - 0.5) = 819$ thousand cycles.

As we can see, the transient duration mainly depends on the miss rate, while the cycles lost depend on the difference between miss rates. Thus, Ubik works best with cache-intensive workloads that are mildly sensitive to partition size.

#### 5.1.1. Managing latency-critical applications

**Boosting:** Ubik's goal is to give the same performance as having a constant partition size, which we call the *active* size, $s_{active}$. In strict Ubik, $s_{active}$ is the desired target size. When the app goes idle, Ubik downsizes its partition to its *idle* size, $s_{idle}$. When the app becomes active, to make up for the lost performance, Ubik upsizes its partition to the *boost* size, $s_{boost} > s_{active}$. Once the application has recovered the cycles it lost in the transient, Ubik downsizes it to $s_{active}$ until the app goes idle again. Figure 6 shows this behavior.

Ubik periodically computes the best $s_{idle}$ and $s_{boost}$ for each partition. Figure 7 illustrates this process. Ubik evaluates $N$ options for the idle size: $s_{idle} = s_{active}$, $s_{idle} = s_{active}(N-1)/N$, ..., $s_{idle} = 0$ (we set $N = 16$ in our experiments; Figure 7 shows $N = 4$). For each option, Ubik computes the $s_{boost}$ needed so that, by the deadline, the number of cycles gained by being at $s_{boost}$ instead of at $s_{active}$ equals the upper bound on lost cycles at the transient. We limit $s_{boost}$ to $s_{boost,max}$ = total lines/latency-critical apps. This way, latency-critical apps never interfere with each other (even when all are boosted). The lower $s_{idle}$ is, the higher $s_{boost}$. Ubik stops evaluating options when either the transient is too long, or the needed $s_{boost}$ is too high. For example, in Figure 7 Ubik stops at option 4, which is too aggressive. Then, among the feasible options, Ubik performs a simple cost-benefit analysis to determine the best one. The benefit is the extra hits that batch apps would gain by having $s_{active} - s_{idle}$ more lines available when the app is idle, and the cost is the extra misses they incur by having $s_{boost} - s_{active}$ fewer lines for *deadline* cycles. These are computed using the batch apps' miss curves. For example, in Figure 7 Ubik chooses option 3 ($s_{idle} = s_{active}/2$), which yields the maximum gain.

**Accurate de-boosting:** By using upper bounds on both the transient length and the lost cycles, Ubik downsizes conservatively. Therefore, most requests have faster transients, and regain the performance lost by downsizing much earlier than the deadline. Waiting until the deadline to downsize from $s_{boost}$ to $s_{active}$ would improve the latency-critical application's performance unnecessarily while hurting batch throughput.

Fortunately, we can leverage the UMON to accurately determine when an application has made up for its lost performance. UMON tags are not flushed when the app goes idle, so UMONs can already track (through hit counters [42]) how many misses the *current request* would have incurred if we had not downsized its partition. Therefore, we simply add a counter that uses UMON events to track this; when the count exceeds the current number of misses (plus a guard to account for the small UMON sampling error [42]), the application has made up for its losses. This triggers an interrupt, and the Ubik runtime de-boosts the app and gives the space back to batch apps.

#### 5.1.2. Managing batch applications

Ubik manages batch app partitions at two granularities. First, as in UCP, Ubik repartitions the cache space available to batch apps (but not latency-critical apps) at periodic, coarse-grained intervals (e.g., 50 ms) using the Lookahead algorithm. Second, whenever a latency-critical app partition is resized (e.g., on an *idle→active* transition), Ubik takes space from or gives it to batch apps. Using the Lookahead algorithm on these frequent resizings would be too expensive. Additionally, it is infeasible to precompute batch partition sizes for all cases, as it is done in OnOff, because there are many more possibilities.

Instead, on each coarse-grained reconfiguration interval,

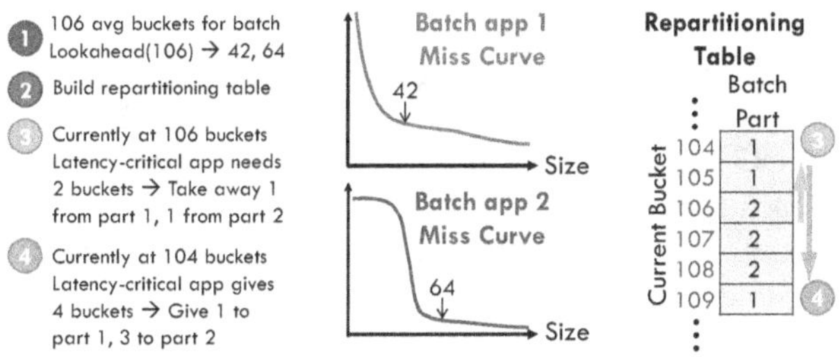


Figure 8: Building and using the repartitioning table, which provides fast incremental reallocations for batch workloads.

the Ubik runtime computes the average cache space that was available to batch apps in the previous interval, and performs Lookahead on this average size to determine the baseline batch allocations. Then, it builds a *repartitioning table* that stores what partitions to give space to or take space from when the space available to batch apps changes. We quantize partition sizes to "buckets", $1/B^{th}$s of cache size ($B = 256$ in our evaluation), so the table has $B$ entries. The table is built greedily: for each possible batch budget, growing a latency-critical partition takes space away from the batch app that gets the lowest marginal utility from its allocation. Figure 8 shows how this table is built and used. When the runtime needs to resize a latency-critical partition, it walks this table from the current to the target buckets to find what batch partitions to take space from or give it to. This makes repartitions fast, and, despite the shortcomings of greedy partitioning with non-convex miss curves [4, 42], it works well in practice because the space available to batch apps is often close to the average.

#### 5.1.3. Putting it all together

Ubik is mostly implemented as a software runtime, requiring minimal hardware extensions over conventional partitioning schemes, namely the MLP profilers and the accurate de-boosting mechanism. Periodically, the runtime reads the UMONs and performance counters, computes the best idle and boost sizes for latency-critical apps (Section 5.1.1), finds the batch app sizes using Lookahead, and builds the repartitioning table (Section 5.1.2). Overall, this process takes a few tens of thousands of cycles. Since this happens at a coarse granularity (every 50 ms), it incurs minimal overheads. Latency-critical apps call into the Ubik runtime when they become idle and active (this does not happen after every request; an app only idles when it runs out of requests to process). On each such event, Ubik resizes the latency-critical partition (to $s_{idle}$ or $s_{boost}$) and uses the repartitioning table to find the batch apps to give or take space from. On an idle-active transition, the runtime also arms the accurate de-boosting circuit, which triggers an interrupt when the cost of the transient has been recovered. Ubik then downsizes the app to $s_{active}$, and gives the space to batch apps using the repartitioning table. These resizings are fast (hundreds of cycles), imposing negligible overheads.

Overall, hardware costs from partitioning are small. For the six-core CMP in Figure 3, Vantage adds a 3-bit partition ID to each LLC tag (0.52% state overhead), 256 bits of state per partition and bank (0.009% state overhead for 2 MB banks), and minimal, off-the-critical-path logic for the replacement process [45]. Each UMON adds 2 KB (256 tags) of state, and is rarely accessed (only one in 768 accesses is inserted into the UMON). Ubik's accurate de-boosting mechanism requires minimal changes to UMONs: a comparator, an MSR to control it, and an input to the interrupt controller.

### 5.2. Ubik with Slack

Ubik as described so far takes conservative decisions to avoid degrading tail latency. Some applications have little to gain from sizes larger than the target size, and in this case, strict Ubik is conservative, often not downsizing at all. However, often these applications also have little to lose from having less space. For example, Figure 2a shows that, at 2 MB, `moses` barely gets any LLC hits, despite being memory-intensive. For these cases, by slightly relaxing the tail latency requirement, we can free a large amount of space. This enables Ubik to smoothly trade off tail latency degradation for higher batch app throughput.

We relax the tail latency requirements by allowing a configurable amount of tail latency degradation, expressed as a fraction of the strict deadline, which we call the slack. Ubik uses this slack on tail latency to determine a *miss slack*, i.e., a bound on the additional misses that can be sustained in the course of a request while maintaining the tail latency within the desired slack. The miss slack is computed adaptively using a simple proportional feedback controller that accepts individual request latencies as input.

Given a miss slack, Ubik uses the miss curve to set $s_{active}$ to a value lower than the given target size such that the additional misses incurred at this size are within the miss slack. $s_{boost}$ and $s_{idle}$ are then determined relative to this new $s_{active}$ as in Section 5.1.1. Since the sizing of $s_{active}$ relative to the target size is contrained only by the relative difference in miss rates but not by any transient lengths, $s_{active}$ can be much lower than the target for apps that are not cache-sensitive, even if they are not very cache-intensive.

Unfortunately, with slack, rare requests that might not impact the miss curve much can suffer significantly, especially since $s_{active}$ may be much smaller than in the no-slack case. To detect these requests, we add a low watermark to the de-boosting circuit: if, after reaching $s_{boost}$, the current misses outgrow the UMON-measured misses by a factor of $(1 + miss\ slack)$, we trigger an interrupt and conservatively use the no-slack $s_{boost}$ and $s_{active}$. This avoids catastrophic degradation for these cases. Further, the adaptive miss slack mechanism mentioned earlier allows Ubik to quickly adapt $s_{active}$ in response to changing application behavior.

## 6. Methodology

**Modeled system:** As in Section 3, we use zsim [46] to model CMPs with 6 cores and a 3-level cache hierarchy, shown in Figure 3, with parameters given in Table 2. This configuration closely models a Westmere-EP processor. We use out-of-order

| Cores | 6 x86-64 cores, Westmere-like OOO [46], 3.2 GHz |
|---|---|
| L1 caches | 32 KB, 4-way set-associative, split D/I, 1-cycle latency |
| L2 caches | 256 KB private per-core, 16-way set-associative, inclusive, 7-cycle latency |
| L3 cache | 6 banks, 2 MB/bank (12 MBs total), 4-way 52-candidate zcache, 20 cycles, inclusive |
| Coherence protocol | MESI protocol, 64B lines, in-cache directory, no silent drops; TSO |
| Memory | 200-cycle latency |

Table 2: Configuration of the simulated 6-core CMP.

core models by default (validated against a real Westmere system [46]), and also include results with simple core models.

Since we focus on cache capacity partitioning and dealing with the effects of performance inertia, we model a fixed-latency LLC and main memory, which do not include bandwidth contention. Bandwidth has no inertia, so Ubik should be easy to combine with bandwidth partitioning techniques for real-time systems [21]. We leave such an evaluation to future work. The memory latency matches a Xeon W3670 running at 3.2 GHz with 3 DDR3-1066 channels at minimal load.

**LLC configurations:** We use private per-core 2 MB LLCs (which provide perfect isolation) as a baseline, and evaluate a shared 12 MB LLC with different schemes: LRU (without partitioning), UCP, StaticLC, OnOff (Section 4), and Ubik. All partitioning policies use Vantage configured as in [45], reconfigure every 50 ms, use 32-way, 256-line UMONs (2 KB each), and linearly interpolate the 32-point UMON miss curves to 256 points for finer granularity.

**Workload mixes:** We simulate mixes of latency-critical and batch apps. Each six-core mix has three latency-critical and three batch apps. Apps are pinned to cores. We use the five latency-critical apps described in Section 3. First, we run each app alone with a 2 MB LLC, and find the request rates that produce 20% and 60% loads. We then use each app in two configurations: with the 20% request rate to simulate a low-load case, and the 60% rate to simulate a high-load case. We test each case with a wide and representative set of batch apps. Each mix has three instances of the same latency-critical workload, with each instance serving a different set of requests. Both requests and arrival times are different for each instance.

To produce a wide variety of batch app mixes, we use a methodology similar to prior partitioning work [42, 45]. We classify all 29 SPEC CPU2006 workloads into four types according to their cache behavior: insensitive (`n`), cache-friendly (`f`), cache-fitting (`t`), and streaming (`s`) as in [45, Table 2], and build random mixes of all the 20 possible combinations of three workload types (e.g., `nnn`, `nnf`, `nft`, and so on). We generate two mixes per possible combination, for a total of 40 mixes. We then simulate all combinations of the 10 three-application latency-critical mixes and the 40 three-application batch mixes to produce 10×40=400 six-application mixes.

To run each mix, we fast-forward each application to the beginning of its *region of interest* (ROI). For each latency-critical app, the ROI starts after processing a fixed number of warmup requests, and covers the number of requests in Table 1. This number has been chosen so that, at 20% load, the ROI takes around 5 billion cycles. For batch apps, we first run each app in isolation with a 2 MB LLC, and measure the number of instructions $I_i$ executed in 5 billion cycles. The ROI starts after fast-forwarding 10 billion instructions, and covers $I_i$ instructions. In each experiment we simulate the full mix until all apps have executed their ROIs, and keep all apps running. We only consider each app's ROI when reporting aggregate metrics. Though involved, this multiprogrammed methodology is *fixed-work* and *minimizes sample imbalance*, allowing unbiased comparisons across schemes [19].

**Metrics:** For each mix, we report two metrics. For latency-critical apps, we report *tail latency degradation*, defined as the $95^{th}$ percentile tail latency (Section 3.2) across all three app instances, normalized to the latency of the same instances running in isolation. For batch apps, we report weighted speedup, $(\sum_i IPC_i/IPC_{i,alone\, on\, 2MB\, LLC})/N_{apps}$ [42, 51], which represents the multiprogrammed speedup that batch applications achieve vs having private LLCs. To achieve statistically significant results, we introduce small amounts of non-determinism [2], randomize request arrival times, and perform enough runs to achieve 95% confidence intervals ≤3% on all individual runs. Most individual runs and all aggregate metrics have confidence intervals within 1%.

As discussed in Section 3, measuring tail latencies accurately requires many runs, making our evaluation compute-intensive. For example, Figure 9 summarizes 145 trillion simulated instructions. For this reason, we evaluate Ubik on small CMPs. Ubik should apply to large-scale CMPs with tens to hundreds of cores, but we leave that evaluation to future work.

## 7. Evaluation

### 7.1. Comparison of LLC Management Schemes

Figure 9 shows the distributions of both tail latency degradation for the latency-critical apps (lower is better) and weighted speedup for the batch apps (higher is better) in each mix. Figure 9a contains the mixes with low-load latency-critical apps, and Figure 9b contains the high-load mixes. On each graph, each line represents a single scheme. For each scheme, mixes are sorted from worst to best (ascending weighted speedups, descending tail latency degradations). Mixes are sorted independently for each line, so these graphs concisely summarize each scheme, but should not be used for mix-by-mix comparisons. In this section, Ubik runs with a slack of 5% (Section 7.2 explores other slack values).

Figure 9a shows that LRU, UCP, and OnOff severely degrade tail latency on a large fraction of the mixes: LRU and OnOff suffer significant degradation for about 20% of the mixes, with many of these being in excess of 2×. While UCP maintains tail latencies within acceptable bounds for a larger fraction of mixes, the worst case degradations for it are just as bad as in LRU and OnOff, about 2.2×. These severe deadline violations make these policies unsuitable for

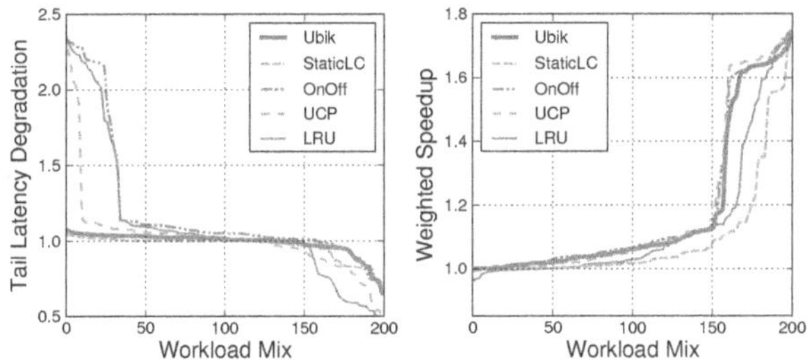


(a) Low load.

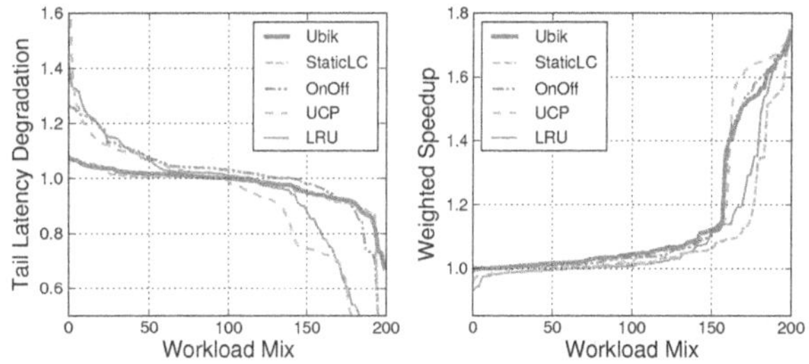


(b) High load.

Figure 9: Distribution of tail latency degradation (latency-critical apps, lower is better) and weighted speedup (batch apps, higher is better) for all schemes vs a private LLC baseline, for the 400 mixes simulated, split into low and high loads (200 mixes each).

| | LRU | UCP | OnOff | StaticLC | Ubik |
|---|---|---|---|---|---|
| Low load | 13.1% | 18.3% | 18.3% | 8.9% | 17.1% |
| High load | 9.8% | 14.7% | 14.5% | 8.3% | 14.8% |

Table 3: Average weighted speedups (%) for all schemes.

latency-critical workloads. In contrast, our proposed StaticLC and Ubik schemes have negligible latency degradation. Most mixes match the tail latency of private LLCs, and some are slightly worse [3]. Moreover, as expected, Ubik's tail latencies are within 3% of StaticLC's (consistent with Ubik's 5% slack).

Tail latencies for the high-load mixes look similar, with Ubik and StaticLC maintaining a tight upper bound on tail latency degradation, while LRU, UCP, and OnOff experience significant degradation: up to 60% for UCP, and 40% for both LRU and OnOff. Though still unacceptably high, these degradations are *better* than in the low-load mixes. Two competing effects are at play here: on one hand, tail latency is more sensitive to performance at high load (Section 3); on the other hand, at higher utilization, latency-critical apps "defend" their cache working sets better in LRU and OnOff, and UCP sees higher average utility, giving them larger partitions. Overall, the second effect dominates, and running latency-critical apps at higher loads gives more stable (albeit higher) tail latencies with these best-effort schemes. As we will see later, which effect dominates depends on the specific latency-critical app.

Figure 9 also shows the distributions of weighted speedups for batch apps, and Table 3 reports their averages. OnOff and UCP perform best for batch apps. LRU enjoys the extra capacity stolen from latency-critical apps, but cannot use it as effectively due to the lack of partitioning among batch apps, performing sensibly worse than OnOff and UCP. StaticLC achieves the smallest weighted speedups, as it always limits batch apps to half of the cache (though, by using UCP on batch apps, StaticLC improves throughput over private LLCs). Finally, Ubik has weighted speedups competitive with OnOff and UCP, and outperforms LRU, *while still meeting deadlines.* Overall, weighted speedups are modest because many batch apps in our mixes are not memory-intensive. As Figure 9 shows, about 23% of the mixes enjoy weighted speedups of over 30%, with improvements of up to 74%.

**Per-application results:** To gain more insights into these results, Figure 10 shows the tail latency degradation and average weighted speedup separately for each latency-critical workload in their low and high load scenarios. In the tail latency graph, each bar shows the tail latency degradation across all 40 batch mixes for a specific latency-critical app and load, and the whisker shows the mix with the worst tail degradation. Intuitively, these graphs can be interpreted as follows. Suppose we have a 40-machine cluster. We run three instances of the same latency-critical app in every machine, and spread the 40 batch app mixes across machines. We then issue requests to all the latency-critical apps uniformly, and measure the tail latency of all response times from all the machines considered together. Each bar shows how much worse the *global* tail latency is vs having private LLCs, and the whisker shows the tail latency of the worst-performing machine. The weighted speedup plots show the additional batch throughput vs having private LLCs, over the whole cluster.

Figure 10 shows large differences across latency-critical apps. First, `xapian` has very low LLC intensity (Section 3), so in the low-load case, all techniques achieve similar tail latency. UCP and Ubik achieve the highest weighted speedups by aggressively downsizing `xapian` partitions. StaticLC is excessively conservative, but even OnOff is wasteful, as it gives `xapian` its full allocation when it's on. However, at high loads `xapian` becomes very sensitive to performance changes (Figure 1a shows its tail latency has a steep slope beyond 60%), and UCP degrades `xapian`'s tail latency by up to 20% in some cases. `masstree` is mildly memory-intensive and has cross-request reuse, but has high MLP as well, which somewhat mitigates its tail latency degradation under LRU, UCP, and OnOff. The three best-effort schemes suffer deadline violations of up to 20% in the low-load case and up to 35% in the high-load case. `moses` is very memory-intensive and has no reuse at 2 MB, but starts to have significant reuse at around 4 MB. Interestingly, UCP detects this and gives `moses` a large fraction of the cache, and with LRU, `moses` naturally grabs the space from batch apps. Both schemes achieve tail laten-

[3] These differences are an artifact of our baseline being private caches instead of a statically sized partition. Because a Vantage partition has very high associativity [45], these differences are overall positive.

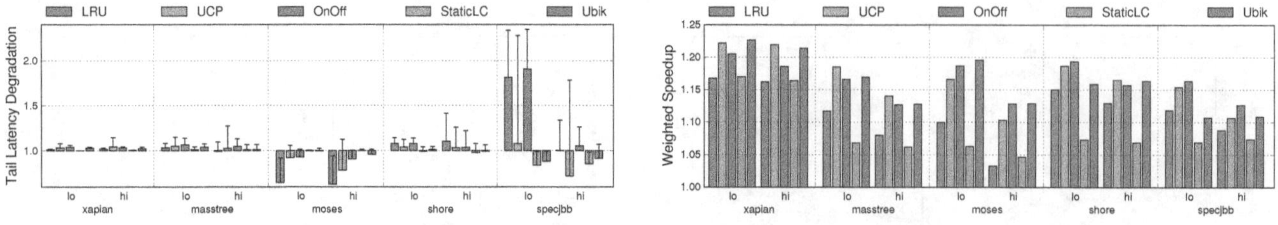


Figure 10: Tail latency degradation (lower is better) and weighted speedup (higher is better) of all schemes vs a private LLC baseline, for the 400 mixes simulated, split by latency-critical app and load, using OOO cores. The left graph shows both overall (bar) and worst-mix (whisker) tail latencies; the right graph shows average weighted speedups.

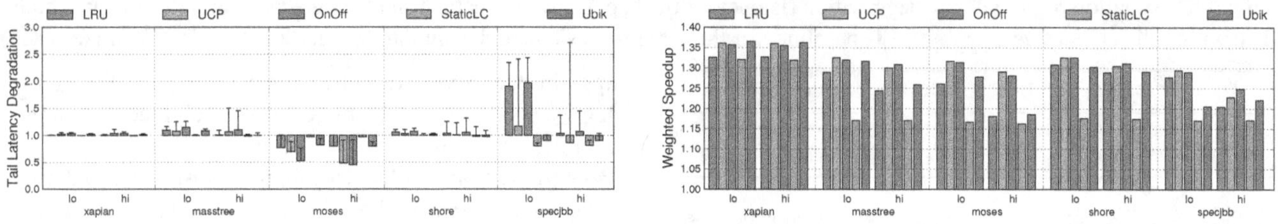


Figure 11: Results with simple in-order (IPC=1) cores: tail latency degradation (lower is better) and weighted speedup (higher is better) of all schemes vs a private LLC baseline, for the 400 mixes simulated, split by latency-critical app and load.

cies well below our target, which is unnecessary and degrades batch throughput. Additionally, UCP also suffers occasional deadline violations of up to 20%. Ubik, on the other hand, maintains `moses`'s target tail latency, and achieves the highest batch throughput of all schemes. Finally, `shore-mt` and `specjbb` have significant cross-request reuse (Figure 2) and are memory-intensive. LRU, OnOff, and UCP experience severe deadline violations for these two apps. On the other hand, StaticLC and Ubik maintain their tail latencies by protecting their working sets when they go idle. Both UCP and OnOff achieve high weighted speedups, but these come at the cost of significant tail latency degradation. Even in these sensitive cases, Ubik achieves significant throughput improvements over StaticLC by exploiting transients and boosting.

In summary, Ubik achieves the best balance between maintaining tail latency and improving batch throughput of all the schemes. Ubik achieves the highest batch throughput of all schemes on `xapian` and `moses`, and achieves a somewhat smaller throughput than UCP and OnOff on `masstree`, `shore-mt`, and `specjbb`, but unlike UCP, OnOff, and LRU, it maintains their tail latency.

**Utilization:** Our end goal is to improve datacenter utilization. With a few conservative assumptions, we can approximate the utilization gains of StaticLC and Ubik. First, since low tail latencies are often critical [11], assume the datacenter executes latency-critical apps at 20% (low) load. Current CMPs implement LRU, so to avoid high tails, the conventional approach is to not coschedule any batch applications. Assume we can use half of the cores without degrading the tail much (which is somewhat optimistic, since in many cases even two latency-critical applications will interfere with each other). In this case, we achieve 10% utilization, which matches reported numbers from industry [35]. In contrast, StaticLC and Ubik can safely schedule mixes across all the machines, achieving 60% utilization, 6× higher than LRU. Beyond utilization, both schemes significantly improve throughput for batch applications.

**In-order cores:** Many datacenter workloads have vast request-level parallelism, so using simpler cores can be a sensible way to improve datacenter efficiency [43, 50, 56]. To see if our proposed techniques apply to simpler cores, Figure 11 shows tail latencies and weighted speedups when using simple in-order core models (IPC=1 except on L1 misses) instead of OOO cores. In-order cores are more sensitive to memory access latency, as they cannot hide stalls. Therefore, LRU, UCP, and OnOff degrade tail latency more severely, being up to 2.7× worse. In contrast, StaticLC and Ubik both avoid significant tail latency degradation despite the higher sensitivity. The added sensitivity to cache misses also translates into higher weighted speedups across all schemes: StaticLC achieves an average weighted speedup of 20%, while Ubik significantly outperforms it with a weighted speedup of 28%. LRU, UCP, and OnOff achieve weighted speedups of 27%, 30%, and 30%, respectively. All schemes also achieve higher maximum weighted speedups (2.44×).

### 7.2. Sensitivity to Slack

As discussed in Section 5, by introducing slack, Ubik can smoothly trade off tail latency for batch throughput. Figure 12 shows tail latencies and weighted speedups when Ubik uses slacks of 0%, 1%, 5%, and 10% (so far, we have discussed results using a 5% slack). Note that the scale on the y-axis for the tail latency degradation chart in Figure 12 is much smaller than in Figure 11 and Figure 10. With no slack, Ubik strictly maintains tail latency and achieves an average weighted speedup of 9.9%. Larger slacks improve batch throughput while maintaining tail latencies within the specified bounds. With slack

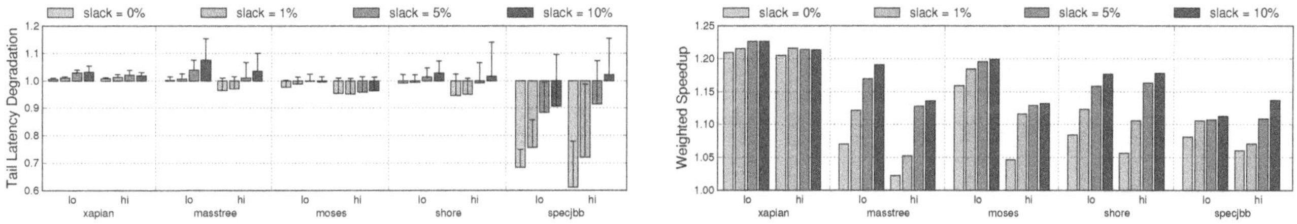


Figure 12: Results for Ubik with 0%, 1%, 5% and 10% slack: tail latency degradation (lower is better) and weighted speedup (higher is better) vs a private LLC baseline, for the 400 mixes simulated, split by latency-critical app and load, using OOO cores.

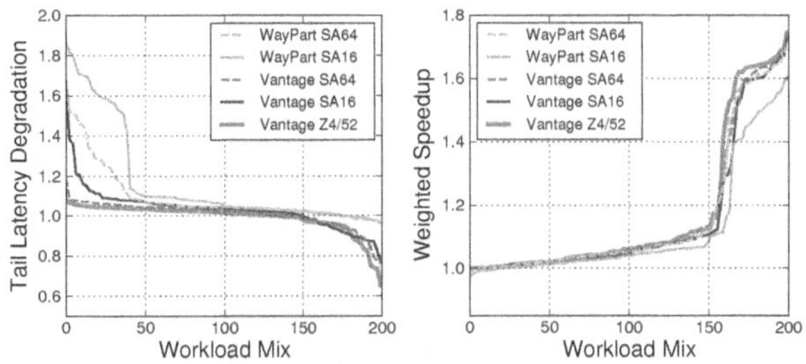


(a) Low load.

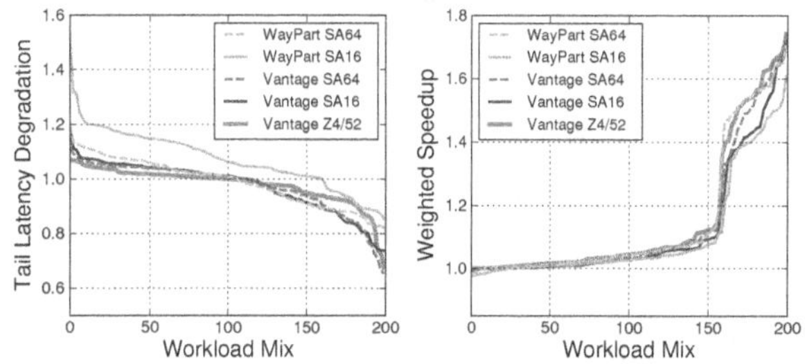


(b) High load.

Figure 13: Distribution of tail latency degradation (latency-critical apps, lower is better) and weighted speedup (batch apps, higher is better) vs a private LLC baseline for Ubik (5% slack) with different partitioning schemes and arrays: way-partitioning and Vantage on set-associative caches of 16 (SA16) and 64 (SA64) ways, and Vantage on the default 4-way 52-candidate zcache.

values of 1%, 5% and 10%, weighted speedup improves to 13.1%, 16.0% and 17.0%, respectively. Therefore, with an adjustable slack, Ubik dominates all the other schemes evaluated. We find that, in practice, a small value of slack (e.g., 5%) achieves a good trade-off between maintaining tail latencies and improving batch performance.

### 7.3. Sensitivity to Partitioning Scheme

Ubik relies on fine-grained partitioning with fast, analyzable transients. So far, we have presented results using Vantage on a 4-way, 52-candidate zcache, which satisfies both properties. Figure 13 characterizes Ubik using way-partitioning and Vantage on 16 and 64-way set-associative caches (SA16/SA64).

Way-partitioning suffers from three problems: lower associativity, coarse-grained partitions, and longer transients. With the way-partitioned 16-way cache, Ubik has limited choice in partition sizes and observes much longer transients, so tail latencies and weighted speedup are significantly degraded. The 64-way cache ameliorates the associativity and granularity problems, resulting in comparable throughput to Vantage on zcaches. However, transients are still longer and unpredictable, so tail latencies are still worse by up to 60%.

Ubik works better with Vantage on set-associative caches. Vantage works well in set-associative arrays, but it loses its analytical guarantees [45] and becomes a soft partitioning scheme. On the 16-way cache, frequent forced evictions hurt both tail latency (by up to 45%) and batch throughput. However, with 64 ways, Vantage has enough associativity to achieve almost the same throughputs and tail latencies as with a zcache. Though rare, the 64-way cache still suffers from occasional tail latency degradation of up to 20%.

In conclusion, while Ubik misses deadlines with way-partitioning due to its lack of predictability, Ubik is usable with set-associative caches partitioned with Vantage, although at the cost of high associativity and occasional deadline violations.

## 8. Conclusions

We have identified the problem of performance inertia, and characterized its impact in latency-critical applications. We have shown that, in systems that execute mixes of batch and latency-critical applications, prior cache partitioning techniques can be adapted to provide capacity isolation and improve cache utilization, but ignoring inertia sacrifices significant batch performance to guarantee isolation of latency-critical workloads. We have used these insights to design Ubik, a partitioning technique that leverages transient behavior to dynamically manage the allocations of latency-critical workloads without degrading their tail latencies, providing both high cache utilization and strict QoS guarantees on mixes of latency-critical and batch workloads.

## Acknowledgments

We sincerely thank Nathan Beckmann, Christopher Fletcher, and the anonymous reviewers for their helpful feedback on prior versions of this manuscript. This work was supported in part by DARPA PERFECT under contract HR0011-13-2-0005 and by NSF grant CCF-1318384.

## References

[1] A. Agarwal, J. Hennessy, and M. Horowitz. An analytical cache model. *ACM Transactions on Computer Systems*, 7(2), 1989.

[2] A. Alameldeen and D. Wood. IPC considered harmful for multiprocessor workloads. *IEEE Micro*, 26(4), 2006.

[3] L. Barroso and U. Hölzle. The case for energy-proportional computing. *IEEE Computer*, 40(12):33–37, 2007.

[4] N. Beckmann and D. Sanchez. Jigsaw: Scalable Software-Defined Caches. In *Proc. PACT-22*, 2013.

[5] S. Bird and B. Smith. PACORA: Performance aware convex optimization for resource allocation. In *Proc. HotPar-3*, 2011.

[6] E. Blem, J. Menon, and K. Sankaralingam. Power Struggles: Revisiting the RISC vs CISC Debate on Contemporary ARM and x86 Architectures. In *Proc. HPCA-16*, 2013.

[7] R. Brain, A. Baran, N. Bisnik, et al. A 22nm High Performance Embedded DRAM SoC Technology Featuring Tri-Gate Transistors and MIMCAP COB. In *Proc. of the Symposium on VLSI Technology*, 2013.

[8] B. D. Bui, M. Caccamo, L. Sha, and J. Martinez. Impact of cache partitioning on multi-tasking real time embedded systems. In *Proc. RTCSA-14*, 2008.

[9] D. Chiou, P. Jain, L. Rudolph, and S. Devadas. Application-specific memory management for embedded systems using software-controlled caches. In *Proc. DAC-37*, 2000.

[10] H. Cook, M. Moreto, S. Bird, et al. A hardware evaluation of cache partitioning to improve utilization and energy-efficiency while preserving responsiveness. In *Proc. ISCA-40*, 2013.

[11] J. Dean and L. A. Barroso. The tail at scale. *Communications of the ACM*, 56(2):74–80, 2013.

[12] C. Delimitrou and C. Kozyrakis. Paragon: QoS-Aware Scheduling for Heterogeneous Datacenters. In *Proc. ASPLOS-18*, 2013.

[13] E. Ebrahimi, C. J. Lee, O. Mutlu, and Y. N. Patt. Fairness via source throttling: A configurable and high-performance fairness substrate for multi-core memory systems. In *Proc. ASPLOS-15*, 2010.

[14] S. Eyerman, L. Eeckhout, T. Karkhanis, and J. E. Smith. A performance counter architecture for computing accurate CPI components. In *Proc. ASPLOS-12*, 2006.

[15] M. Ferdman, A. Adileh, O. Kocberber, et al. Clearing the clouds: a study of emerging scale-out workloads on modern hardware. In *Proc. ASPLOS-17*, 2012.

[16] B. Grot, J. Hestness, S. W. Keckler, and O. Mutlu. Kilo-NOC: a heterogeneous network-on-chip architecture for scalability and service guarantees. In *Proc. ISCA-38*, 2011.

[17] F. Guo, Y. Solihin, L. Zhao, and R. Iyer. A framework for providing quality of service in chip multi-processors. In *Proc. MICRO-40*, 2007.

[18] N. Hardavellas, M. Ferdman, B. Falsafi, and A. Ailamaki. Reactive NUCA: near-optimal block placement and replication in distributed caches. In *Proc. ISCA-36*, 2009.

[19] A. Hilton, N. Eswaran, and A. Roth. FIESTA: A sample-balanced multi-program workload methodology. In *MoBS*, 2009.

[20] R. Iyer, L. Zhao, F. Guo, et al. QoS policies and architecture for cache/memory in CMP platforms. In *Proc. SIGMETRICS*, 2007.

[21] M. K. Jeong, M. Erez, C. Sudanthi, and N. Paver. A QoS-aware memory controller for dynamically balancing GPU and CPU bandwidth use in an MPSoC. In *Proc. DAC-49*, 2012.

[22] N. Jiang, D. Becker, G. Michelogiannakis, and W. Dally. Network congestion avoidance through speculative reservation. In *Proc. HPCA-18*, 2012.

[23] R. Johnson, I. Pandis, N. Hardavellas, et al. Shore-MT: A scalable storage manager for the multicore era. In *Proc. EDBT-12*, 2009.

[24] R. Kapoor, G. Porter, M. Tewari, et al. Chronos: predictable low latency for data center applications. In *Proc. SoCC-3*, 2012.

[25] Y. Kim, M. Papamichael, O. Mutlu, and M. Harchol-Balter. Thread cluster memory scheduling: Exploiting differences in memory access behavior. In *Proc. MICRO-43*, 2010.

[26] P. Koehn, H. Hoang, A. Birch, et al. Moses: Open source toolkit for statistical machine translation. In *Proc. ACL-45*, 2007.

[27] N. Kurd, S. Bhamidipati, C. Mozak, et al. Westmere: A family of 32nm IA processors. In *Proc. ISSCC*, 2010.

[28] B. Lesage, I. Puaut, and A. Seznec. PRETI: Partitioned REal-TIme shared cache for mixed-criticality real-time systems. In *Proc. ICRTNS-20*, 2012.

[29] B. Li, L. Zhao, R. Iyer, et al. CoQoS: Coordinating QoS-aware shared resources in NoC-based SoCs. *Journal of Parallel and Distributed Computing*, 71(5), 2011.

[30] X. Lin and R. Balasubramonian. Refining the utility metric for utility-based cache partitioning. In *Proc. WDDD*, 2011.

[31] R. Liu, K. Klues, S. Bird, et al. Tessellation: Space-time partitioning in a manycore client OS. In *Proc. HotPar-1*, 2009.

[32] Y. Mao, E. Kohler, and R. T. Morris. Cache craftiness for fast multicore key-value storage. In *Proc. EuroSys-7*, 2012.

[33] J. Mars, L. Tang, R. Hundt, et al. Bubble-Up: Increasing Utilization in Modern Warehouse Scale Computers via Sensible Co-locations. In *Proc. MICRO-44*, 2011.

[34] D. Meisner and T. F. Wenisch. Stochastic queuing simulation for data center workloads. *EXERT*, 2010.

[35] D. Meisner, B. Gold, and T. Wenisch. PowerNap: Eliminating server idle power. *Proc. ASPLOS-14*, 2009.

[36] J. Mogul and K. Ramakrishnan. Eliminating receive livelock in an interrupt-driven kernel. In *Proc. USENIX ATC*, 1996.

[37] M. Moreto, F. J. Cazorla, A. Ramirez, et al. FlexDCP: A QoS framework for CMP architectures. *SIGOPS Operating Systems Review*, 43(2), 2009.

[38] K. Nesbit, N. Aggarwal, J. Laudon, and J. Smith. Fair queuing memory systems. In *Proc. MICRO-39*, 2006.

[39] K. J. Nesbit, J. Laudon, and J. E. Smith. Virtual private caches. In *Proc. ISCA-34*, 2007.

[40] J. Ousterhout, P. Agrawal, D. Erickson, et al. The case for RAMClouds: scalable high-performance storage entirely in DRAM. *SIGOPS Operating Systems Review*, 43(4), 2010.

[41] I. Puaut and C. Pais. Scratchpad memories vs locked caches in hard real-time systems: a quantitative comparison. In *Proc. DATE*, 2007.

[42] M. Qureshi and Y. Patt. Utility-based cache partitioning: A low-overhead, high-performance, runtime mechanism to partition shared caches. In *Proc. MICRO-39*, 2006.

[43] V. Reddi, B. Lee, T. Chilimbi, and K. Vaid. Web search using mobile cores: quantifying and mitigating the price of efficiency. In *Proc. ISCA-37*, 2010.

[44] D. Sanchez and C. Kozyrakis. The ZCache: Decoupling Ways and Associativity. In *Proc. MICRO-43*, 2010.

[45] D. Sanchez and C. Kozyrakis. Vantage: Scalable and Efficient Fine-Grain Cache Partitioning. In *Proc. ISCA-38*, 2011.

[46] D. Sanchez and C. Kozyrakis. ZSim: Fast and Accurate Microarchitectural Simulation of Thousand-Core Systems. In *Proc. ISCA-40*, 2013.

[47] M. Schoeberl. Time-predictable computer architecture. *EURASIP Journal on Embedded Systems*, 2009.

[48] A. Seznec. A case for two-way skewed-associative caches. In *Proc. ISCA-20*, 1993.

[49] A. Sharifi, S. Srikantaiah, A. Mishra, et al. METE: meeting end-to-end QoS in multicores through system-wide resource management. In *Proc. SIGMETRICS*, 2011.

[50] J. Shin, K. Tam, D. Huang, et al. A 40nm 16-core 128-thread CMT SPARC SoC processor. In *ISSCC*, 2010.

[51] A. Snavely and D. M. Tullsen. Symbiotic jobscheduling for a simultaneous multithreading processor. In *Proc. ASPLOS-8*, 2000.

[52] S. Srikantaiah, M. Kandemir, and Q. Wang. SHARP control: Controlled shared cache management in chip multiprocessors. In *MICRO-42*, 2009.

[53] W. D. Strecker. Transient behavior of cache memories. *ACM Transactions on Computer Systems*, 1(4), 1983.

[54] L. Tang, J. Mars, W. Wang, et al. ReQoS: Reactive Static/Dynamic Compilation for QoS in Warehouse Scale Computers. In *Proc. ASPLOS-18*, 2013.

[55] G. Tene, B. Iyengar, and M. Wolf. C4: The continuously concurrent compacting collector. In *Proc. ISMM*, 2011.

[56] Tilera. TILE-Gx 3000 Series Overview. Technical report, 2011.

[57] X. Vera, B. Lisper, and J. Xue. Data caches in multitasking hard real-time systems. In *Proc. RTSS-24*, 2003.

[58] D. Wendel, R. Kalla, R. Cargoni, et al. The implementation of POWER7: A highly parallel and scalable multi-core high-end server processor. In *ISSCC*, 2010.

[59] Y. Xie and G. H. Loh. PIPP: promotion/insertion pseudo-partitioning of multi-core shared caches. In *Proc. ISCA-36*, 2009.

[60] H. Yang, A. Breslow, J. Mars, and L. Tang. Bubble-Flux: Precise Online QoS Management for Increased Utilization in Warehouse Scale Computers. In *Proc. ISCA-40*, 2013.

[61] X. Zhang, S. Dwarkadas, and K. Shen. Hardware execution throttling for multi-core resource management. In *Proc. of USENIX ATC*, 2009.

# Architectural Support for Address Translation on GPUs

## Designing Memory Management Units for CPU/GPUs with Unified Address Spaces

Bharath Pichai* Lisa Hsu† Abhishek Bhattacharjee*
*Department of Computer Science
Rutgers University
{bsp57, abhib}@cs.rutgers.edu
†Qualcomm Research
Qualcomm, Inc.
hsul@qti.qualcomm.com

## Abstract

The proliferation of heterogeneous compute platforms, of which CPU/GPU is a prevalent example, necessitates a manageable programming model to ensure widespread adoption. A key component of this is a shared unified address space between the heterogeneous units to obtain the programmability benefits of virtual memory.

To this end, we explore GPU Memory Management Units (MMUs) consisting of Translation Lookaside Buffers (TLBs) and page table walkers (PTWs) in unified heterogeneous systems. We show the challenges posed by GPU warp schedulers on TLBs accessed in parallel with L1 caches, which provide many well-known programmability benefits. In response, we propose modest TLB and PTW augmentations that recover most of the performance lost by introducing L1-parallel TLB access. We also show that a little TLB-awareness can make other GPU performance enhancements (e.g., cache-conscious warp scheduling and dynamic warp formation on branch divergence) feasible in the face of cache-parallel address translation, bringing overheads in the range deemed acceptable for CPUs (10-15% of runtime). We presume this initial design leaves room for improvement but anticipate the bigger insight, that a little TLB-awareness goes a long way in GPUs, will spur further work in this area.

***Categories and Subject Descriptors*** C.1.2 [*Processor Architectures*]: Multiple Data Stream Architectures

***Keywords*** GPUs, MMUs, TLBs, Unified address space

## 1. Introduction

The computer systems community has recently proposed many heterogeneous systems where CPUs are aided by accelerators targeting, among others, massive multidimensional data-sets [58], common signal processing operations [50], object caching [38], and spatially-programmed architectures [47]. To ensure widespread adoption of accelerators, their programming models must be efficient and easy to use.

A key determinant of programming model efficacy is how main memory is addressed by CPUs and accelerators. Traditionally, acceleration technologies like graphics processing units (GPUs) [13, 17, 45, 46] have maintained separate virtual and physical address spaces from CPUs. Main memory may be physically shared but is usually partitioned or allows unidirectional coherence (e.g., ARM CPU/GPUs allow accelerators to snoop CPU memory partitions but not the other way around [55]). There is, however, increasing evidence that processor vendors are shifting towards unified virtual and physical address spaces between CPUs and accelerators because of their programmability benefits. Among other advantages, unified address spaces make data structures and pointers globally visible among compute units, obviating the need for expensive memory copies between CPUs and accelerators. They also unburden CPUs from pinning data pages for accelerators in main memory, improving memory efficiency. As a result, vendors like Intel, AMD, ARM, Qualcomm, and Samsung are embracing integrated CPU/GPUs with fully unified address space support, as detailed in the Heterogeneous Systems Architecture (HSA) [37] specifications. AMD's upcoming Berlin processor, for example, commits fully to HSA with its heterogeneous uniform memory access (hUMA) technology [51].

A key requirement for unified address spaces is effective hardware support for GPU virtual-to-physical address translation. In the CPU world, address translation is achieved using per-core Memory Management Units (MMUs) with Translation Lookaside Buffers (TLBs) and page table walkers (PTWs) to access frequently-used address translations from operating system (OS) page tables. Commercial CPU TLBs and PTWs are usually accessed before (or in parallel with) hardware caches, making caches physically-addressed. While this organization imposes stringent access time requirements on TLBs, it also efficiently supports multiple contexts, dynamically-linked libraries, and cache coherence.


*ASPLOS '14*, March 1–5, 2014, Salt Lake City, Utah, USA.

http://dx.doi.org/10.1145/10.1145/2541940.2541942

In this work, we study address translation for accelerators and its role in the impending unified address space programming paradigm. We focus on general-purpose programming on GPUs because of their ubiquity and relative research maturity [18, 19, 29, 39, 43, 52, 54]. To realize the same programmability benefits as for CPUs, we target designing TLBs and PTWs accessed before (or in parallel with) the GPU's hardware caches. Our high-level insight is that the GPU's warp-based execution model and its scheduler have a critical impact on MMU performance. In particular, we find that implementing a strawman CPU-like TLB and PTW degrades GPU performance severely. Furthermore, we find that previously-proposed warp scheduling enhancements like cache-conscious wavefront scheduling and dynamic warp formation lose most of their effectiveness with naively-designed CPU-like MMUs. Fortunately however, we also show that modest optimizations recover most of this lost performance. Overall, our approaches reduce GPU TLB overheads to levels deemed acceptable in the CPU world (5-15% [6, 7, 9, 10, 16]), showing that a little TLB-awareness goes a long way in GPU design. More specifically, our contributions are:

First, we show that a CPU-like design which places TLBs and PTWs before (or in parallel with) cache access degrades performance by 20-50%. This is because: (1) cache-parallel accesses mean latency (and thus sizing) is restricted; and (2) multiple warp threads execute in lock-step, meaning that a TLB miss from a single thread can stall all warp threads, magnifying miss penalties. In response, we redesign MMUs to better match GPU execution models, finding that modest changes recover most lost performance.

Second, we show the impact of TLBs on cache-conscious warp/wavefront scheduling (CCWS) [52], recently proposed to boost GPU cache hit rates. While naively adding TLBs offsets CCWS, simple modifications yield close to ideal CCWS performance. We also study TLB-based CCWS schemes that are simpler *and* higher-performance.

Third, we show how TLBs affect dynamic warp formation for branch divergence. Using thread block compaction (TBC) [18], we find that dynamically assimilating threads from disparate warps increases memory divergence and TLB misses. Though naive designs degrade performance by over 20%, adding TLB-awareness mitigates these overheads, boosting performance close to ideal TBC.

Overall, this work shows that while GPUs do require careful TLB and PTW designs to ensure reasonable performance, their architecture presents non-drastic changes from the CPU world. We therefore conclude that a little TLB-awareness is highly effective in GPUs, opening up the possibility of much follow-up research in this fruitful area.

## 2. Background

### 2.1 Address Translation on CPUs

CPU TLB design and performance have long been studied by the academic community [6, 7, 9, 10, 30, 48]. Most CPUs currently access TLBs prior to (or in parallel with) L1 cache access, realizing physically-addressed caches. This approach dominates commercial systems (over virtually-addressed caches [14, 35]) because of programmability benefits. Physically-addressed caches prevent coherence problems from address synonyms (multiple virtual addresses mapping to the same physical address) and homonyms (a single virtual address mapping to multiple physical addresses) [14]. This efficiently supports multiple contexts, dynamically-linked libraries, cache coherence among multiple cores and with direct memory access (DMA) engines.

### 2.2 Address Translation on CPU/GPUs

Current heterogeneous systems use rigid programming models that require separate page tables, data replication, and manual data movement between the CPU and GPU. This is especially problematic for pointer-based data structures (e.g., linked lists, trees)[1]. Recent work tries to address this using various smarter memory management schemes [20, 21, 25, 26]. Furthermore, latest CUDA releases permit limited CPU/GPU virtual address sharing [57]. However, none solve the problem using as general and flexible an approach as unified address spaces.

A critical step to unified address spaces is to implement address translation in GPUs. As a first step, Intel and AMD equip today's GPUs with Input Output Memory Management Units [1, 2, 23] (IOMMUs) with their own page tables, TLBs, and PTWs. These IOMMUs have large TLBs and are placed in the memory controller, making GPU caches virtually-addressed.

## 3. Our Approach

Our goal is to provide to the GPU the same programmability benefits enjoyed by the CPU. This implies that GPU address translation must support physically-addressed caches. Therefore, we study GPU MMUs where TLBs are accessed in parallel with the L1 cache. Figure 1 shows our approach, with per shader core TLBs and PTWs. Like CPUs, we assume that L1 caches are virtually-indexed and physically-tagged, allowing TLB access to overlap with L1 cache access. This contrasts with past academic work ignoring address translation [18, 19, 52] or using IOMMUs resident in the memory controller.

This approach has many benefits. First, cache-parallel TLB access eliminates the current need for CPUs to initialize, copy, pin data pages (in main memory), duplicate page tables for GPU IOMMUs, and set up IOMMU TLB entries [11]. It also allows GPUs to support page faults (using traditional or non-traditional techniques that do not support precise exceptions [34, 40]) and access memory mapped files, features desired in hUMA specifications [51] (though their

[1] Some platforms provide pinning mechanisms that do not need data transfers. Both CPU and GPU maintain pointers to the pinned data and the offset arithmetic is the same; however, the pointers are distinct. This suffers overheads from pinning and pointer replication (which can lead to buggy code).

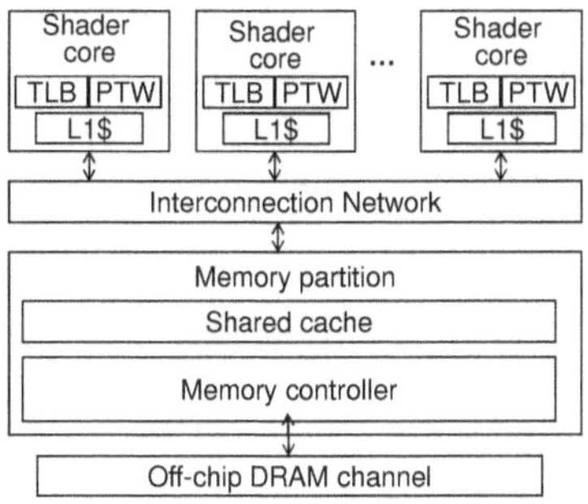


**Figure 1.** Our approach embeds a TLB and PTW per shader core so that all caches become physically-addressed.

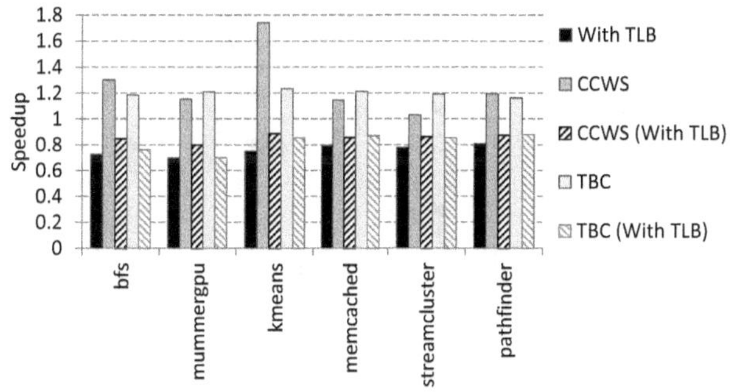


**Figure 2.** Compared to a baseline architecture without TLBs, speedup of naive, 3-ported TLBs per shader core, with and without cache-conscious wavefront scheduling, with and without thread block compaction. Naive TLBs degrade performance in every case.

feasibility requires a range of hardware/software studies beyond the scope of this work).

Second, physically-addressed caches support multiple contexts (one of the goals of HSA [37]) more efficiently. Virtually-addressed caches struggle due to incoherence from address synonyms [35]. Workarounds like cache flushing on context switches can ensure correct functionality, but do so at a performance and complexity cost versus physically-addressed caches.

Third, address translation placement that allows physically-addressed caches also efficiently supports application libraries (mentioned by HSA as a design goal). Traditional virtually-addressed GPU caches suffer from address homonyms [14], which can arise when executing libraries.

Finally, cache coherence between CPU and GPU caches has long been deemed desirable [32, 37, 54]. In general, cache coherence is greatly simplified if GPU caches are physically-addressed, in tandem with CPU caches.

## 4. Understanding the Impact of Warp Scheduling on MMU Design

For all its programmability benefits, address translation at the L1-level is challenging because it constrains TLB access times, and hence, size. Figure 2 shows that naive designs that do not consider the distinguishing characteristics of GPUs can severely degrade performance. The plots show speedups (values higher and lower than 1 are improvements and degradations) of general purpose GPU benchmarks using naive 128-entry, 3-port TLBs with 1 PTW per shader core (`With TLB`). Not only do naive TLBs degrade performance, they also lose 30-50% performance versus conventional cache-conscious wavefront scheduling and thread block compaction [18, 52]. These degradations far exceed the 5-15% overheads deemed acceptable for CPUs and may be attributed to the critical affect that warp-level execution and scheduling has on GPU MMU performance. Specifically, this occurs because:

Default GPU round robin warp scheduling interleaves the memory accesses of individual threads such that their effective temporal locality is stretched beyond the ability of the caches and TLBs to contain them. The graph on the left in Figure 3 quantifies this by plotting: (1) the number of memory references in each workload as a percentage of the total instructions; and (2) miss rates of 128-entry TLBs. While the number of memory references are generally low compared to CPUs (under 25% for all benchmarks), TLB miss rates are very high (ranging from 22% to 70%).

Second, shader cores run warps with multiple threads in lock-step in warps/wavefronts [18, 19, 39]. Therefore, a TLB miss on one warp thread effectively stalls all warp threads, magnifying the miss penalty. Furthermore, multiple warp threads often TLB miss in tandem, stressing conventional PTWs that serialize TLB miss handling. The graph on the right in Figure 3 shows this effect by plotting page divergence (the number of distinct translations requested by a warp). We show both average page divergence and the maximum page divergence of any warp through execution. As shown, the average page divergence for some benchmarks (`bfs` and `mummergpu`) is more than 4 and 8, meaning that multiple translations are needed for a warp to progress, increasing the likelihood of multiple TLB misses. Furthermore, the maximum page divergence is consistently high, magnifying TLB miss latencies. Figure 4 quantifies these effects, comparing the latency of a GPU L1 cache miss to a TLB miss. As shown, TLB misses are about twice as expensive as L1 cache misses because they involve multiple memory references to walk the page table and because separate TLB misses are serialized using a single PTW. This, with high miss rates, explains why naive blocking GPU TLBs degrade performance.

Third, Figure 2 shows that sophisticated warp scheduling techniques beyond the traditional round robin approach lose much of their effectiveness with naively designed MMUs. Consider, for example, cache conscious wavefront scheduling [52], which introduces cache-awareness in the traditional warp scheduler to boost cache hit rates. Figure 2 compares the speedup of CCWS with and without TLBs versus a baseline setup with no TLBs. One may initially expect that warp schedulers that boost cache hit rates also improve TLB performance substantially. While CCWS with TLBs does improve performance over a baseline round-robin warp scheduler with TLBs, it still underperforms a baseline GPU with-

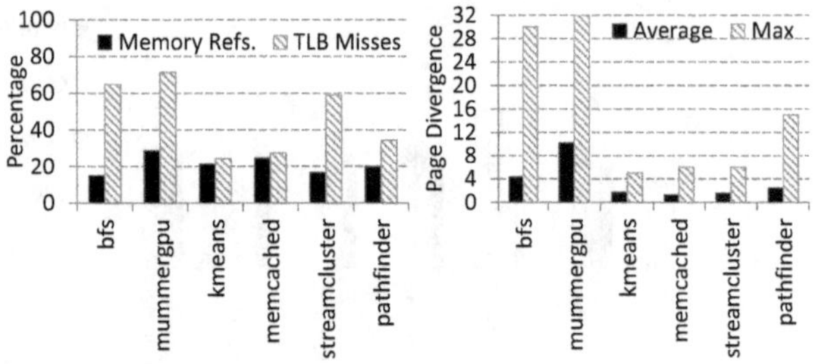


**Figure 3.** The left diagram shows the percentage of total instructions that are memory references and TLB miss rates; the right diagram shows the average number of distinct translations requested per warp (page divergence) and the maximum number of translations requested by any warp through the execution.

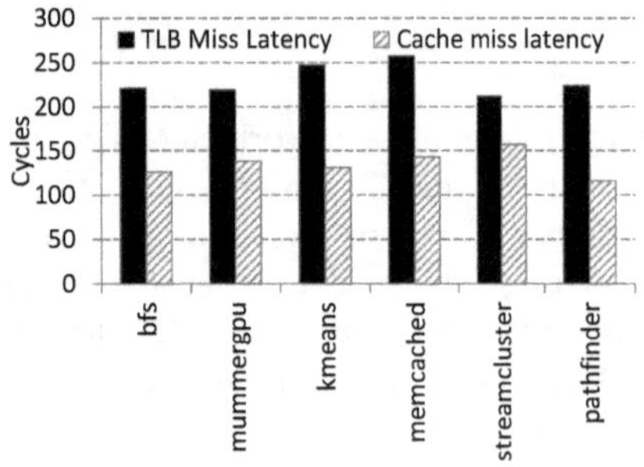


**Figure 4.** Average cycles per TLB miss, compared to L1 cache misses. TLB miss penalties are typically twice as long as L1 cache miss penalties.

out TLBs. The performance gap is even higher (30-50%) compared to CCWS without TLBs. As we will show, the CCWS warp scheduler must be adjusted with some notion of the relative penalties of TLB misses and cache misses to recover this lost performance.

Finally, Figure 2 also shows that warp schedulers that dynamically form warps with threads with similar control flow also lose their effectiveness with cache-parallel TLB access. Specifically, we compare thread block compaction with and without TLBs. We find that performance differences in excess of 20-25% are common between the two cases. We will show that this occurs because TBC dynamically compacts threads which access data in wildly disparate locations, increasing page divergence and hence both TLB miss rates and latencies. Specifically, we have found that TBC increases page divergence by an average of 2-4 in our workloads, and TLB miss rates by 5-10%.

The remainder of this paper refashions MMUs to match warp scheduling characteristics and improve GPU performance. Modest but informed modifications significantly reduces the degradations of Figure 2 to address translation overheads of 5-15% of system runtime (just like CPUs).

## 5. Methodology

### 5.1 Evaluation Workloads

We use server workloads from past studies on control-flow divergence and cache scheduling [18, 52]. From the Rodinia benchmarks [15], we use `bfs` (graph traversal), `kmeans` (data clustering), `streamcluster` (data mining), `mummergpu` (DNA sequence alignment), and `pathfinder` (grid dynamic programming). In addition, we use `memcached`, a key-value store and retrieval system, stimulated with a representative portion of the Wikipedia traces [22]. Our baseline versions of these benchmarks have memory footprints greater than 1GB.

Ideally, we would run benchmarks targeted at future integrated CPU/GPU platforms. Unfortunately, there is a dearth of such workloads because of the lack of abstractions that ease CPU/GPU programming (like unified address spaces themselves). We do include applications like `memcached` which will likely run on these systems but expect that future workloads supporting braided parallelism (a mix of task and data parallelism from a single source) [41] will particularly benefit from unified address spaces. Our studies enable these applications and provide insights, albeit indirectly, on how GPU address translation may affect their performance.

### 5.2 Evaluation Infrastructure

We use GPGPU-Sim [4] with parameters similar to past work [18, 52]. We assume 30 SIMT cores, 32-thread warps, and a pipeline width of 8. We have per core, 1024 threads, 16KB shared memory, and 32KB L1 data caches (with 128 byte lines and LRU). We also use 8 memory channels with 128KB of unified L2 cache space per channel. We run binaries with CPU and GPU portions, but report timing results for the GPU part. GPGPU-Sim uses single instruction multiple data (SIMD) pipelines, grouping SIMD cores into core clusters, each of which has a port to the interconnection network with a unified L2 cache and the memory controller.

Most of our results focus on 4KB pages due to the additional challenge imposed by small page size; however, we also present initial results for large 2MB pages later in the paper. Note that large pages, while effective, don't come for free and can have their own overheads in certain situations [3, 7, 44]. As a result, many applications are restricted to 4KB page sizes; it is important for our GPUs with address translation to be compatible with them.

## 6. Address Translation for GPUs

We now consider GPU MMU design with baseline warp scheduling. We first study the space of TLB and page table walker design options, and show their interaction with traditional round-robin warp scheduling techniques. We then present GPU-appropriate modifications to MMUs to recover much of the lost performance.

### 6.1 Address Translation Design Space

We consider the following address translation design points.

*Number and placement of TLBs:* CPUs traditionally place a TLB in each processor core so that pipelines enjoy fast TLB lookup. One might consider the same option for each GPU shader core. It is possible to implement one TLB per SIMD lane; this provides the highest performance, at the cost of power and area (e.g., we assume 240 SIMD lanes, so this approach requires 240 TLBs per shader core). Instead, we assume a more power- and area-frugal approach, with one TLB per shader core (shared among lanes).

*TLB sizes and port counts:* While larger TLBs have higher hit rates, they also require more area and access latency. Since TLB access must complete by the time the L1 cache set is selected (for virtually-indexed, physically-tagged caches), overly-lengthy hit times degrade performance. Furthermore, since TLBs use power-hungry content-addressable memories [8], their sizes must be carefully chosen. Finally, more TLB ports permit parallel address translation, which can be crucial in high-throughput shader cores. Unfortunately, they also consume area and power.

*Blocking versus non-blocking TLBs:* One way of reducing the impact of TLB misses is to overlap them with useful work. Traditional approaches involve augmenting TLBs to support hits under the original miss or additional misses under the miss. Both approaches improve performance, but require additional hardware like Miss Status Holding Registers (MSHRs) and access ports.

*Page table walker management, counts, and placement:* It is possible to implement page table walking with either hardware or software (where the operating system is interrupted on a TLB miss [27]). Hardware approaches require more area but are typically perform better [27], as they obviate the need to run an interrupt handler. When using hardware PTWs, it is possible to implement one or many per TLB. While a single PTW per TLB saves area, multiple PTWs can potentially provide higher performance if multiple TLB misses occur. Finally, placing PTWs with TLBs encourages faster miss handling; alternately, using a single shared PTW saves area at the cost of performance.

*Page table walk scheduling:* Each page table walk requires multiple memory references (four in x86 [5]) to find the desired PTE, some of which may hit in caches. In multicore systems, it is possible that more than one core concurrently experience TLB misses. In response, one option (which has not been studied to date) is to consider the page table walks of the different cores and see if some of their memory references are to the same locations or cache lines. In response, it is possible to interleave PTW memory references from different cores to reduce the number of memory references and boost cache hit rates (while retaining functional correctness).

*System-level issues (TLB shootdowns, page faults):* The adoption of unified address spaces means that there are many options for handling TLB shootdowns and page faults. In one possibility, we interrupt a CPU to execute the shootdown code or page fault handler on the GPU's behalf. This CPU could be the one that launched the GPU kernel or any other idle core. Alternately, GPUs could themselves run the shootdown code or the page fault handler, as suggested by hUMA [51]. Moreover, recent work shows ways of achieving this without precise exception support [34, 40].

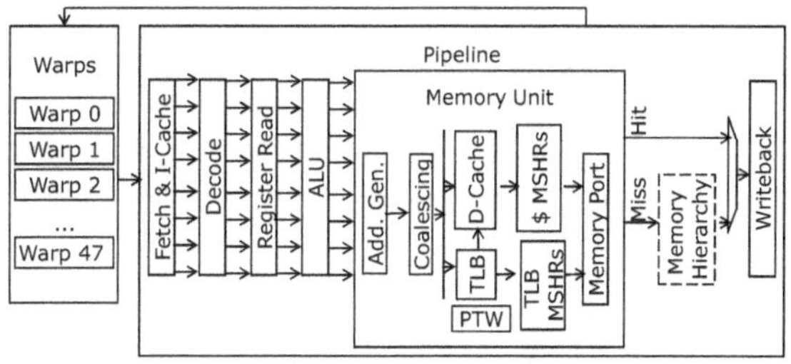


**Figure 5.** Shader core pipeline with address translation. We assume that L1 data caches are virtually-indexed and physically-tagged (allowing TLB lookup in parallel with cache access). All caches are physically-addressed.

### 6.2 Mirroring CPU Address Translation in GPUs

We begin with the natural question of how CPU-style TLBs perform in GPUs. Understanding its benefits and limitations with regard to the warp scheduler provides insights on how to better tailor MMUs for GPUs.

Figure 5 shows our initial strawman design. Each shader core maintains a TLB/PTW and has 48 warps (the minimum scheduling unit) per shader core. Threads of a warp execute the same instruction in lock-step. Instructions are fetched from an I-cache and operands read from a banked register file. Loads and stores access the memory unit.

The memory unit's address generator calculates virtual addresses, which are coalesced into unique cache line references. We enhance this logic by also coalescing multiple intra-warp requests to the same virtual page (and hence PTE). This reduces TLB access traffic and port counts. At this point, two sets of accesses are available: (1) unique cache accesses; and (2) unique PTE accesses. These are presented in parallel to the TLB and data cache. Note that we implement virtually-indexed, physically-tagged L1 caches. We now elaborate on the design space options from Section 6.1, referring to Figure 5 when necessary.

*Number and placement of TLBs:* We assume 1 TLB per shader core shared among SIMD lanes, to save power and area. This is similar to the CPU approach approach of maintaining per-core TLBs.

*TLB sizes and port counts:* Commercial CPUs currently implement 64-512 entry TLBs per core [9, 24]. These sizes are typically picked to be substantially smaller and lower-latency than CPU L1 caches. Using a similar methodology with CACTI [42], we have found that 128-entry TLBs are the are the largest possible structures that do not increase the access time of 32KB GPU L1 data caches. We use 128-entry TLBs in our baseline GPU design, studying other sizes later.

*Blocking versus non-blocking TLBs:* There is evidence that that some CPU TLBs do support hits under misses because of their relatively simple hardware support [28]. However, most commercial CPUs typically use blocking TLBs [6, 48] because of their high hit rates. We therefore assume blocking TLBs in our baseline GPU design. This means that similar to cache misses, TLB misses prompt the scheduler to swap another warp into the SIMD pipeline. Swapped-in warps executing non-memory instructions proceed unhindered (until the original warp's page table walks finish and it completes the `Writeback` stage). Swapped-in threads with memory references, however, do not proceed in this naive design as they require non-blocking support.

Figure 5 shows that TLBs have their own (MSHRs). We assume, like both GPU caches and past work on TLBs [39], that there is one TLB MSHR per warp thread (32 in total). MSHR allocation triggers page table walks, which inject memory requests to the shared caches and main memory.

*Page table walker mechanisms, counts, and placement:* Our GPU assumes hardware PTWs because: (1) they achieve higher performance than software-managed TLBs [27]; and (2) they do not need to run OS code (which GPUs cannot currently execute), unlike software-managed TLBs.

CPUs usually place PTWs close to each TLB so that page table walks can be quickly initiated on misses. We use the same logic to place PTWs next to TLBs. Finally, while it is possible to consider multiple PTWs per GPU TLB, our baseline design mirrors CPUs (which have 1 PTW per core) and has one PTW per shader core. We investigate the suitability of this decision in subsequent sections.

*Page table walk scheduling:* CPU PTWs do not typically interleave memory references from multiple concurrent TLB misses for increased cache hit rate and reduced memory traffic. This is because the low incidence of concurrent TLB misses on CPUs [10] isn't worth the complexity and area overheads of such logic (though this is likely to require relatively-simple combinational logic). Similarly, our naive baseline GPU also doesn't include PTW scheduling logic.

*System-level issues (shootdowns, page faults):* CPUs usually shootdown TLBs on remote cores when its own TLB updates an entry, using software inter-processor interrupts (IPIs). We assume the same approach for GPUs (i.e., if the CPU that initiated the GPU modifies its TLB entries, GPU TLBs are flushed). Similarly, we assume that a page fault interrupts a CPU to run the handler. In practice, our performance was not affected by these decisions (because shootdowns and page faults almost never occur on our workloads). If these become a problem, as detailed in hUMA, future GPUs may be able to run dedicated OS code for shootdowns and page faults without interrupting CPUs. We leave this for future work.

Unfortunately, we have already seen in Figure 2 that this basic design suffers from performance degradations. In response, the next section proposes a set of low-overhead optimizations to recover this lost performance.

### 6.3 Augmenting Address Translation for GPUs

As we have noted, the primary challenge with GPU MMUs is the nature of warp-based execution. Our baseline design assumes a warp width of 32, so it is possible for multiple threads (in the worst case, 32 threads) to demand different address translations. In the pathological case, this results in 32 simultaneous TLB misses. This section shows, however, that not only do modest TLB and PTW augmentations overcome these problems, they can actually exploit the fact that warps have threads operating in lock-step.

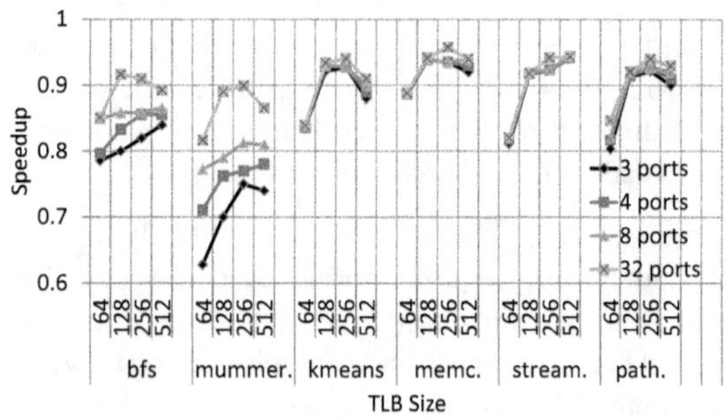


**Figure 6.** Performance for TLB size and port counts, assuming fixed access times. Note that TLBs larger than 128 entries and 4 ports are impractical to implement and actually have much higher access times that degrade performance.

*TLB size and port counts:* An ideal (but impractical) TLB is large, low-latency, and heavily multi-ported, with one port per warp thread (32 in total). While more ports facilitate quick lookups and miss detection, they also significantly increase area and power. Figure 6 sheds light on size, access time, and port count tradeoffs for naive baseline GPU address translation. We vary TLB sizes from 64 to 512 entries (the range of CPU TLB sizes) and port count from 3 (like L1 CPU TLBs) to an ideal number of 32. We present speedups versus against the no-TLB case (speedups are under 1 since adding TLBs degrades performance). We use CACTI to assess access time increases with size.

Figure 6 shows that larger sizes and more ports greatly improve GPU TLB performance. In general, 128-entry TLBs perform best; beyond this, increased access times reduce performance. Figure 6 also shows that while port counts do impact performance (particularly for `mummergpu` and `bfs`), modestly increasing from 3 ports (in our naive baseline) to 4 ports recovers much of this lost performance. This matches results from the page divergence plots of Figure 3, which showed that warps usually request far less than their maximum of 32 translations. This is because coalescing logic before TLBs reduce requests to the same PTE into a single lookup. Only `bfs` and `mummergpu` have average page divergence higher than 4. While this does mean that some warps have higher lookup time (e.g., when `mummergpu` encounters its maximum page divergence of 32), simply augmenting the port count of the naive implementation to 4 recovers much of the lost performance.

*Blocking versus non-blocking TLBs:* Using blocking TLBs, the only way to overlap miss penalties with useful work is to execute alternate warps which do not have memory references and hence do not need access to the MMU. Unfortunately however, GPU TLB miss penalties are extremely long. Therefore, GPU address translation requires more aggressive non-blocking facilities. Specifically, we investigate:

(1) Hits from one warp under misses from another warp: In this approach, the swapped-in warp executes even if it has

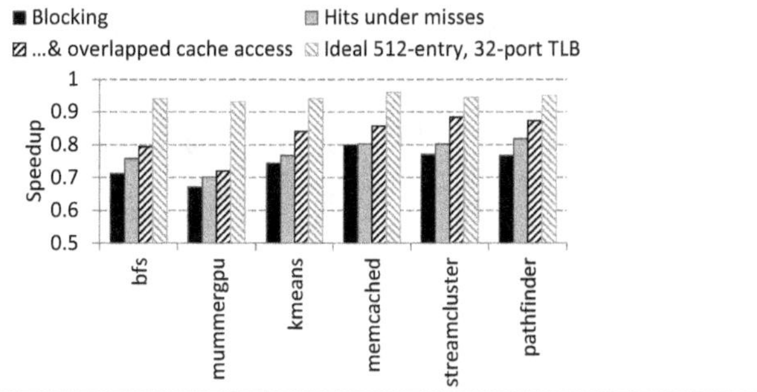


**Figure 7.** On a 128-entry, 4-port TLB, adding non-blocking support improves performance closer to an ideal (no increasing access latency) 32-port, 512-entry TLB.

memory references, as long as they are all TLB hits. When swapped-in thread TLB misses, it too must be swapped out. This approach leverages already-existing TLB MSHRs and requires only simple combinatorial logic updates to the warp scheduler. In fact, hardware costs are similar to CPU TLBs which already support hits under misses [28]. We leave more aggressive miss under miss support for future work.

(2) Overlapping TLB misses with cache accesses within a warp: Beyond overlapping a warp's TLB miss penalty with the execution of other warps, it is also possible to overlap TLB misses with work from the *warp that originally missed.* Since warps have multiple threads, even when some miss, others may hit in the TLB. Since hits immediately yield physical addresses, it is possible to look up the L1 cache with these addresses without waiting for the warp's TLB misses to be resolved. This boosts cache hit rates since this warp's data is likelier to be in the cache before a swapped-in warp evicts its data. Furthermore if these early cache accesses do miss, subsequent cache miss penalties can be overlapped with the TLB miss penalties of the warp.

In this approach, threads that hit in the TLB immediately look up the cache even if the same warp has a TLB miss on a different thread. Data found in the cache is buffered in the standard warp context state in register files (from past work [19, 52]) before the warp is swapped out. This approach requires only simple combinational logic in the PTW and MSHRs to allow TLB hits to proceed for cache lookup.

Results: Figure 7 quantifies the benefits of non-blocking TLBs, normalized to a baseline without TLBs. We first permit hits under misses, then also allow TLB hits to access the cache without waiting for all misses from the same warp to be resolved. We compare these to an *impractical* 512-entry TLB with 32 ports *without increased access latencies.*

While hits under misses improve performance, immediately looking up the cache for threads that TLB hit and PTW scheduling is even more effective. For example, `streamcluster` gains an additional 8% performance from overlapped cache access. We will show how additional enhancement further bring performance close to the impractical, ideal case.

*Page table walk scheduling:* Our page divergence results show that GPUs execute warps that can suffer TLB misses

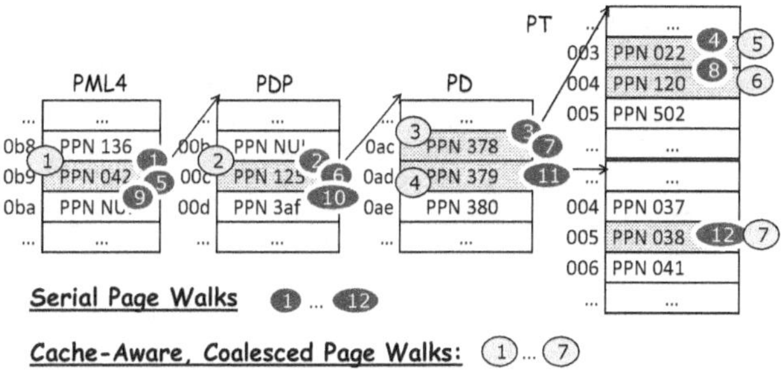


**Figure 8.** Three threads from a warp TLB miss on addresses (`0xb9, 0x0c, 0xac, 0x03`), (`0xb9, 0x0c, 0xac, 0x04`), and (`0xb9, 0x0c, 0xad, 0x05`). A conventional page table walker carries out three serial page walks (shown with dark bubbles) , making references to (1-4), (5-8), and (9-12), a total of 12 loads. Our cache-aware coalesced page walker (shown with light bubbles) reduces this to 7 and achieves better cache hit rate.

on multiple threads, often to distinct PTEs. Consider the example in Figure 8, which shows three concurrent x86 page walks. x86 page table walks require a memory reference to the the Page Map Level 4 (PML4), Page Directory Pointer (PDP), Page Directory (PD), and Page Table (PT). A `CR3` register provides the base physical address of the PML4. A nine bit index (bits 47 to 39 of the virtual address) is concatenated with the base physical address to generate a memory reference to the PML4. This finds the base physical address of the PDP. Bits 38-30 of the virtual address are then used to look up the PDP. Bits 29-21, and 20-12 are similarly used for the PD and PT (which has the desired translation).

Figure 8 shows multilevel page lookups for a warp that has three threads missing on virtual pages (`0xb9, 0x0c, 0xac, 0x03`), (`0xb9, 0x0c, 0xac, 0x04`), and (`0xb9, 0x0c, 0xad, 0x05`). We present addresses in groups of 9-bit indices as these correspond directly to the page table lookups. Naive baseline GPU PTWs perform the three page table walks serially (shown with dark bubbles). This means that each page table walk requires four memory references; (1-4) for (`0xb9, 0x0c, 0xac, 0x03`), (5-8) for (`0xb9, 0x0c, 0xac, 0x04`), and (9-12) for (`0xb9, 0x0c, 0xad, 0x05`). Each of the references hits in the shared cache (several tens of cycles) or main memory. We now exploit commonality in the accesses of these different page table walks in two ways to improve performance:

(1) Reducing the number of page table walk memory references: Higher order virtual address bits tend to remain unchanged across memory references. For example, bits 47-39, and 38-30 of the virtual address change infrequently as lower-order bits (29 to 0) cover 1GB. Since these bits index the PML4 and PDP during page table walks, multiple page table walks usually traverse similar paths. In Figure 8, all three page walks read the same PML4 and PDP locations. We therefore remember PML4 and PDP reads so that they can be reused among page walks. This means that three PML4 and PDP reads are replaced by a single read.

(2) Increasing page table walk cache hit rates: 128-byte cache lines hold 16 consecutive 8-byte PTEs. Therefore,

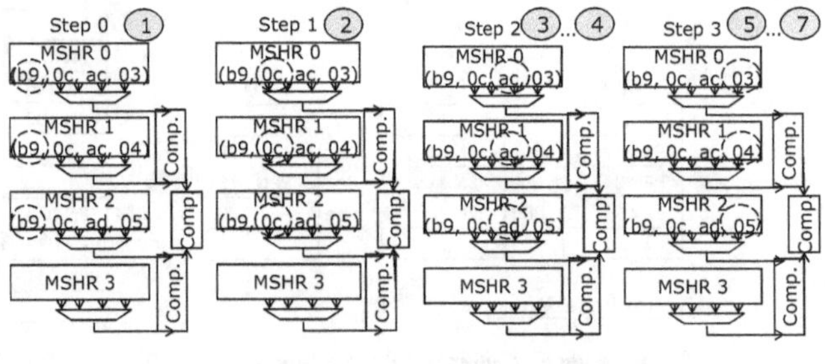


**Figure 9.** Our page table walk scheduler attempts to reduce the number of memory references and increase cache hit rate. The highlighted entries show what memory references in the page walks are performed and in what order. This hardware assumes a mux per MSHR, with a tree-based comparator circuit. We show 4 MSHRs though this approach generalizes to 32 MSHRs.

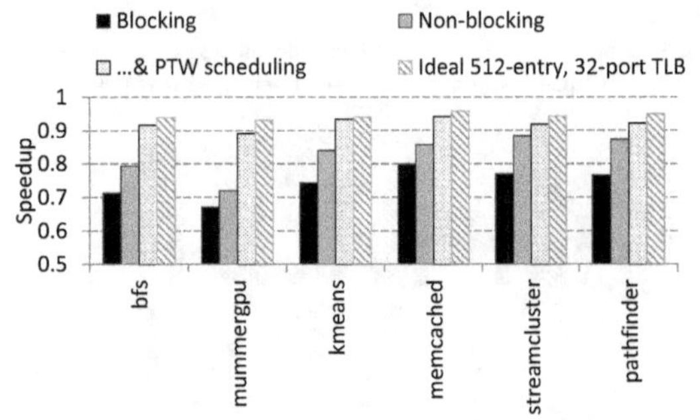


**Figure 10.** On a 128-entry, 4-port TLB, adding non-blocking and PTW scheduling logic achieves close to the performance of an ideal (no increasing access latency) 32-port, 512-entry TLB.

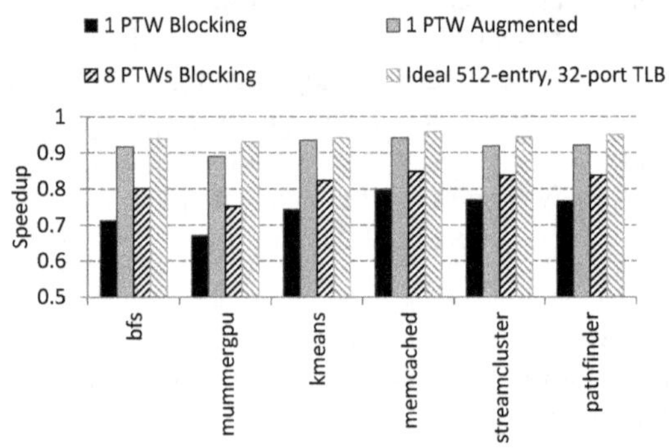


**Figure 11.** Our augmented TLB (with hits under misses and overlapped cache accesses), with 1 PTW outperforms 8 PTWs.

cache lines may be reused across distinct page table walks. For example, in Figure 8, two PD entries from the same cache line are used for all walks. Similarly, the PT entries for virtual pages (`0xb9, 0x0c, 0xac, 0x03`) and (`0xb9, 0x0c, 0xac, 0x04`) are on the same cache line. To exploit this, we interleave memory references from different page table walks (shown in lighter bubbles). In Figure 8, references 3 and 4 (from three different page table walks) are handled successively, as are references 5 and 6 (from page walks for virtual pages (`0xb9, 0x0c, 0xac, 0x03`) and (`0xb9, 0x0c, 0xac, 0x04`)), boosting hit rates.

Implementation: Figure 9 shows PTW scheduling. MSHRs store the virtual page numbers causing TLB misses. We propose combinational hardware that scans the MSHRs, extracting, in four consecutive steps, PML4, PDP, PD, and PT indices. Each stage checks whether the memory accesses for its level are amenable to coalescing (they are repeated) or lie on the same cache line. The PTW then injects references (for each step, we show the matching reference from Figure 8).

Figure 9 shows that a comparator tree matches indices in each stage of the algorithm. It scans the PML4 indices looking for a match in bits 47-44 because both a repeated memory reference and PTEs within the same cache line share all but the bottom 4 index bits. Once the comparator discovers that all the page walks can be satisfied from the same cache line in step 0, a memory reference for PML4 commences. In parallel with this memory reference, the same comparator tree now compares the upper 5 bits of the PDP indices (bits 38-34). Again, all indices match, meaning that in step 1, only one PDP reference is necessary. In step 2, PD indices are studied (in parallel with the PDP memory reference). We find that the top 5 bits match but that the bottom 4 bits don't (indicating that they are multiple accesses to the same cache line). Therefore step 2 injects two memory references (3 and 4) successively. Step 3 uses similar logic to complete the page walks for (`0xb9, 0x0c, 0xac, 0x03`), (`0xb9, 0x0c, 0xac, 0x04`), and (`0xb9, 0x0c, 0xad, 0x05`).

To reduce hardware, we use a comparator tree rather than comparators between every pair of MSHRs (which provides maximum performance). We have found that this achieves close to pairwise comparator performance. Furthermore, we share one comparator tree with multiplexers for all page table levels. This is possible because MSHRs scans can proceed in parallel with loads from the previous step.

Results: Figure 10 shows that PTW scheduling significantly boosts GPU performance. For example, `bfs` and `mummergpu` gain from PTW scheduling because they have a higher page divergence (so there are more memory references from different TLB misses to schedule). We find that PTW scheduling achieves its performance by completely eliminating 10-20% of the PTW memory references and boosting PTW cache hit rates by 5-8% across the workloads. Consequently the number of idle cycles (due in large part to TLB misses) reduces from 5-15% to 4-6%, boosting performance.

Overall, Figure 10 shows that thoughtful non-blocking and PTW scheduling extensions to naive baseline GPUs boosts performance to the extent that it is within 1% of an ideal, impractical, large and heavily-ported 512-entry, 32-port TLB with no access latency penalties. In fact, all the techniques reduce GPU address translation overheads under 10% for all benchmarks, well within the 5-15% range considered acceptable on CPUs.

*Multiple PTWs:* Multiple PTWs are an alternative to PTW scheduling. Unfortunately, their higher performance comes

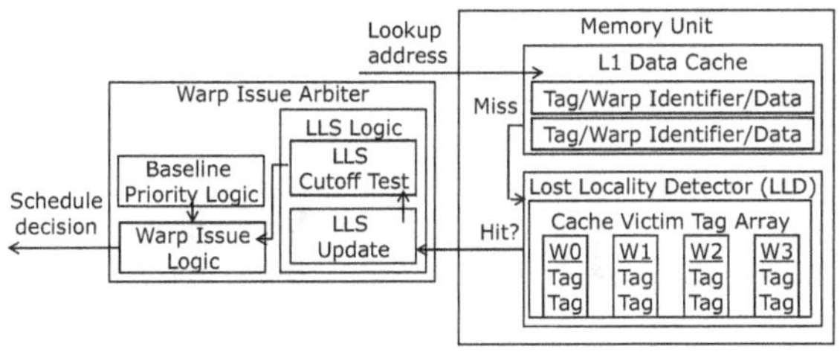


**Figure 12.** Conventional CCWS, with a cache victim tag array.

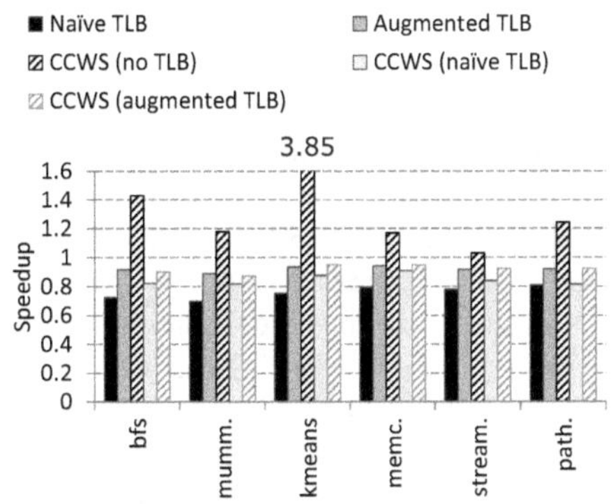


**Figure 13.** Compared to a baseline GPU without TLBs, speedup of naive, 4-ported TLBs per shader core, augmented TLBs and PTWs (non-blocking TLBs with PTW scheduling and cache access overlap), CCWS without TLBs, CCWS with naive TLBs and PTWs, and CCWS with augmented TLBs and PTWs.

with far higher area and power overheads. In our studies, we have found that a single PTW with augmented TLBs (4-ports with non-blocking extensions, PTW scheduling, overlapped cache access) consistently outperform naive TLBs with more PTWs. Specifically, Figure 11 shows a 10% performance gap between the augmented 1 PTW approach and 8 naive PTWs. For the rest of this paper, we therefore use a single lower-overhead PTW with non-blocking support (hit under miss and cache overlap) and PTW scheduling.

# 7. Cache Conscious Warp Scheduling

Our optimizations have, to this point, targeted better MMU designs for typical warp-based round-robin scheduling. There are, however, more advanced scheduling schemes that have been proposed to improve GPU cache behavior and performance on control flow divergence. In this section, we focus on the relationship between cache-conscious wavefront scheduling (CCWS) [52] and MMU design.

## 7.1 Baseline Cache-Conscious Wavefront Scheduling

*Basic operation:* CCWS observes that conventional warp scheduling (e.g., round robin) is oblivious to intra-warp locality, touching data from enough threads to thrash the L1 cache [52]. Carefully limiting the warps that overlap with one another promotes better cache reuse and boosts performance. CCWS accomplishes this using the baseline hardware shown in Figure 13. The cache holds tags and data, but also an identifier for the warp that allocated the cache line. A lost locality detector (LLD) maintains per-warp, set-associative cache victim tag arrays (VTAs), which store the tags of evicted cache lines. The LLD, with lost locality scoring (LLS), identifies warps that share cache working sets and those that increase cache thrashing. CCWS scheduling logic encourages warps that share working sets to run together.

We now explain how CCWS operates. Suppose a warp issues a memory reference. After coalescing, the address is presented to the data cache. On a cache miss, CCWS logic is invoked to determine whether multiple warps are thrashing the cache. The victim tag array of the current warp is probed to see if the desired cache line was recently evicted. A hit indicates the possibility of inter-warp interference. If the warp making the current request were prioritized by the scheduler, intra-warp reuse would be promoted and cache misses reduced. This information is communicated to the LLD, which maintains a counter per warp. A VTA hit increments the warp counter; whenever this happens, lost locality scoring logic sums all counter values. The LLS cutoff logic checks if the total is larger than a predefined cutoff; if so, warps with the highest counter values are prioritized since they hit most in VTAs, indicating that their lines are most-recently evicted and hence most likely to gain if not swapped out. We refer readers to the CCWS paper [52] for more details and sensitivity studies on the update and cutoff values, LLS, and LLD hardware overheads. The remainder of our work, like the original CCWS studies, assumes 16-entry, 8-way victim VTAs per warp.

*Performance of basic approach:* While baseline CCWS ignored address translation [52], one might expect that boosting cache hit rate should also increase TLB hit rates. Figure 13 quantifies the speedup (against a baseline without TLBs) of (1) naive blocking 128-entry, 4-port TLBs with one PTW (no non-blocking or PTW scheduling); (2) augmented TLBs that overlap misses with cache access and allow hits under misses (non-blocking), with PTW scheduling; (3) CCWS without TLBs; (4) CCWS with naive TLBs; and (5) CCWS with augmented TLBs.

Baseline CCWS (without TLBs) consistently improves performance by at least 20%. However, adding CCWS to naive TLBs and augmented TLBs outperform vanilla naive and augmented versions by only 5-10%. Also, the gap between CCWS with and without TLBs remains large (even augmented TLBs and PTWs have a 50-120% difference).

## 7.2 Adding Address Translation Awareness

In response to the limitations of standard CCWS, we now propose two schemes which better design MMUs to cooperate with cache aware warp scheduling.

*TLB-aware CCWS (TA-CCWS):* CCWS loses performance when integrating TLBs (even augmented non-blocking ones with cache overlap and PTW scheduling) because it treats all cache misses equivalently. In reality, some cache misses are

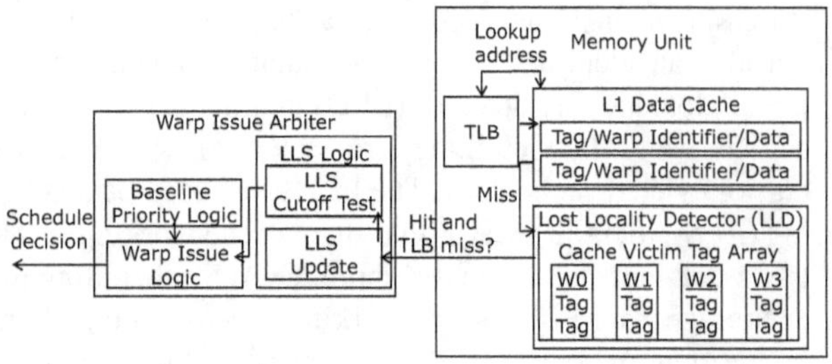


**Figure 14.** TLB-aware cache conscious wavefront scheduling updates locality scores with TLB misses.

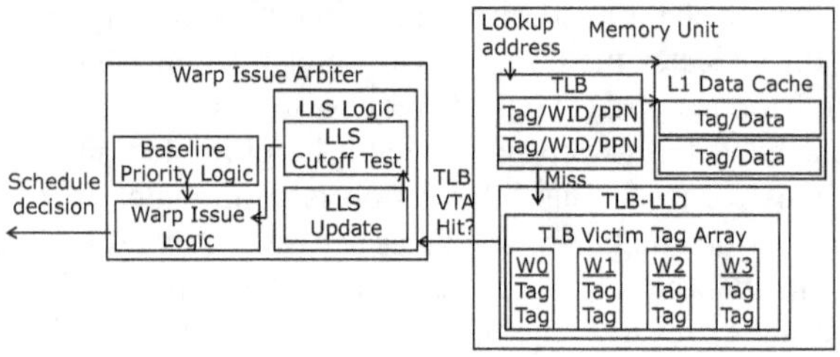


**Figure 15.** TLB conscious warp scheduling, which replaces cache VTAs with TLB VTAs to outperform TA-CCWS, despite using less hardware.

accompanied by TLB misses, others with TLB hits. Baseline CCWS should be modified so that lost locality scoring logic weighs cache misses with TLB misses more heavily than those with TLB hits. TA-CCWS does exactly this, prompting more frequent TLB misses to cause the LLS counter sum to go over the threshold faster. This in turn ensures that the final pool of warps identified as scheduling candidates enjoys intra-warp cache *and intra-warp TLB reuse*.

Figure 14 shows TA-CCWS hardware, with minimal changes to CCWS. We consider only TLB weights that are multiples of 2 so that shifters perform counter updates.

*TLB conscious warp scheduling (TCWS)*: TCWS goes beyond TA-CCWS by observing that TLB and cache behavior are highly correlated. For example, TLB misses are frequently accompanied by cache misses because a TLB miss indicates that cache lines from its physical page were referenced long ago. Therefore, it is possible to subsume cache access behavior by analyzing the intra-warp locality lost on TLB behavior. TCWS exploits this correlation by replacing cache line based victim tag arrays with smaller, lower-overhead, yet more performance-efficient TLB-based VTAs.

Figure 15 illustrates TWCS with TLB-based VTAs containing virtual address tags. VTAs are now looked up on TLB misses rather than cache misses. VTA hits are communicated to lost locality scoring logic, where per-warp counters are updated (similar to baseline CCWS). When the sum of the counters exceeds the prefedined cutoff, warps with the highest LLS counters are prioritized.

This initial approach uses baseline CCWS but with TLB VTAs. There is, however, one problem with this approach.

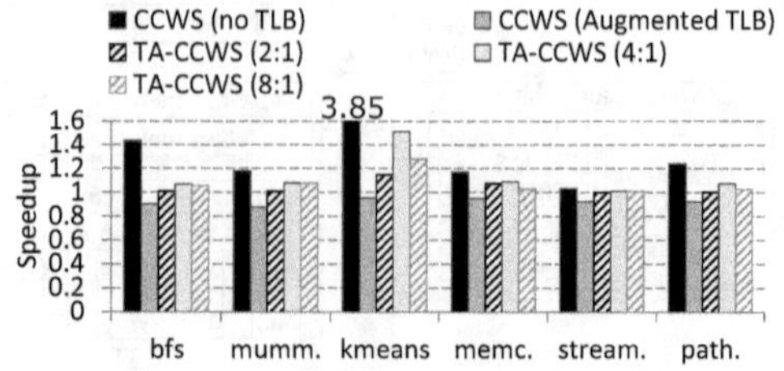


**Figure 16.** TLB-aware CCWS performance for varying weights of TLB misses versus cache misses. TA-CCWS (x:y) indicates that the TLB miss is weighted x times as much as y by LLS logic.

As described, we now update LLS scores only on TLB misses so warp scheduling decisions are relatively infrequent compared to conventional CCWS, which updates scores on cache misses. This makes CCWS less rapidly-adaptive, possibly degrading performance. Therefore, we force more frequent scheduling decisions by also updating LLS counters on TLB hits. We update by observing that each TLB set has an LRU stack (logically) of PTEs. This study assumes 128-entry, 4-way associative GPU TLBs. To update LLS logic sufficiently often, we track the LRU depth of TLB hits. Then, we update the LLS scoring logic, weighting a deeper hit more heavily since it indicates that the PTEs are closer to eviction (and TLBs/caches are likelier to suffer thrashing). A key parameter is how to vary weights with LRU depth.

Note that TCWS actually requires less hardware than CCWS. Since TCWS VTAs maintain tags for 4KB pages, fewer of them are necessary compared to cache line VTAs. TLB-based VTAs in TCWS require half the area overhead of cache line-based CCWS.

### 7.3 Performance of CCWS with TLB Information

*TLB-aware cache conscious scheduling results*: Figure 16 shows that updating LLS scoring logic with not just cache misses but also TLB miss information improves performance substantially. The graph separates the speedups of baseline CCWS (no TLB) and CCWS with augmented TLBs with non-blocking and PTW scheduling logic. It then shows TA-CCWS, with ratios of how much a TLB miss is weighted versus a cache miss. Clearly, weighting TLB misses more heavily improves performance. When they are weighted 4 times as much as cache misses, TA-CCWS achieves within 5-10% of CCWS without TLBs for four benchmarks (`mummergpu`, `memcached`, `streamcluster` and `pathfinder`). While `bfs` and `kmeans` still suffer degradations, we will show that TLB conscious cache scheduling boosts performance even for these benchmarks significantly.

*TLB conscious cache scheduling results*: Figure 17 varies the number of entries per warp (EPW) in the TLB VTA, showing how it affects performance (note that this graph isolates the impact of EPWs alone without LRU depth weighting). Typically, 8 EPWs per warp VTA does best, consistently outperforming TA-CCWS.

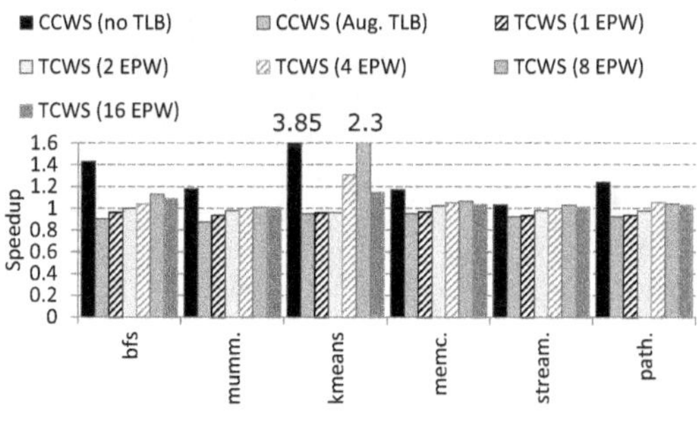


**Figure 17.** TLB conscious warp scheduling achieves within 5-15% of baseline CCWS without TLBs. We show TCWS as the number of entries per warp (EPW) in the VTA is varied.

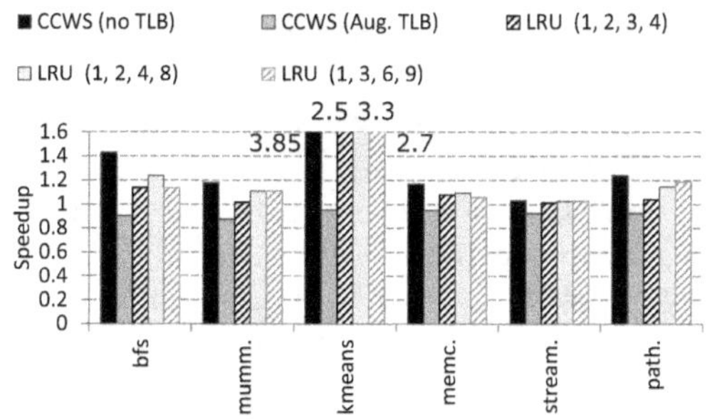


**Figure 18.** TLB conscious warp scheduling with LRU depth weights to added to lost locality scoring.

Figure 18 then shows how updating LLS scores based on the depth of the hit in the TLB set's LRU stack improves performance. We consider many LRU stack weights but only show three of them due to space constraints. The first scheme weights hits on the first entry of the set (MRU) with a score of 1, the second a score of 2, the third a score of 3, and the fourth a score of 4 (`LRU(1, 2, 3, 4)`). Similarly, we also show `LRU(1, 2, 4, 8)` and `LRU(1, 3, 6, 9)`. TLB misses that result in TLB VTA hits are scored as before.

`LRU(1, 2, 4, 8)` typically performs best, consistently getting within 1-15% of the baseline CCWS performance without TLBs. In fact, *not only does TCWS require only half the hardware of TA-CCWS or even CCWS, it outperforms TA-CCWS consistently*.

At a high-level, our graphs provide two insights. First, warp scheduling schemes that improve cache hit rates are intimately affected by TLB hit rates too. Second, overheads from this can be effectively countered with simple, thoughtful TLB and PTW awareness. Our approach, like CPU address translation, consistently reduces overheads to 5-15% of runtime.

# 8. Thread Block Compaction

Our final contribution is to show how address translation affects mechanims to reduce branch divergence overheads. Traditionally, SIMD architectures have supported divergent branch execution by masking vector lanes and stack reconvergence [12, 19], significantly reducing SIMD throughput. Proposed solutions have included stream programming language extensions [31], allowing vector lanes to execute scalar codes for short durations [36], or more recently, dynamic warp formation techniques [19] which assimilate threads with similar control flow paths to form new warps. While address translation affects all of these approaches, we focus on the best known dynamic warp formation scheme, Thread Block Compaction (TBC) [18].

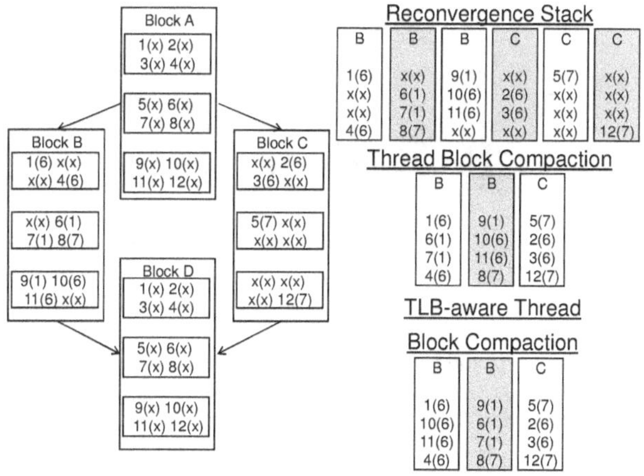


**Figure 19.** Comparison of warp execution when using reconvergence stacks, thread block compaction, and TLB-aware thread block compaction. While TLB-TBC may execute more warps, its higher TLB hit rate provides higher overall performance.

## 8.1 Baseline Thread Block Compaction

*Basic operation:* We now briefly outline the operation of baseline thread block compaction. We refer readers to the original paper for complete details [18]. In CUDA and OpenCL, threads are issued to SIMD cores in units of thread blocks. Warps within a thread block can communicate through shared memory. TBC essentially also proposes control flow locality within a thread block and is implemented using block-wide reconvergence stacks for divergence handling [18]. At a divergent branch, all warps of a thread block synchronize. TBC hardware scans the thread block's threads (which can be across multiple warps) to identify which ones follow the same control flow path. Threads are compacted into new dynamic warps according to branch outcomes and executed until the next branch or reconvergence point (where they are synchronized again for compaction). Overall, this approach increases SIMD utilization.

Unfortunately, blindly adding address translation has problems. Dynamically assimilating threads from different warps into new warps increases both TLB miss rates and warp page divergence (which amplifies the latency of one thread's TLB miss on all warp threads). Consider, for example, the control flow graph of Figure 19. In this example, each thread block contains three warps of 4 threads. Each thread is given a number, along with the virtual page it is accessing if it is a memory operation. For example, 1(6) refers to thread 1 accessing virtual page 6, 1(x) means that thread 1

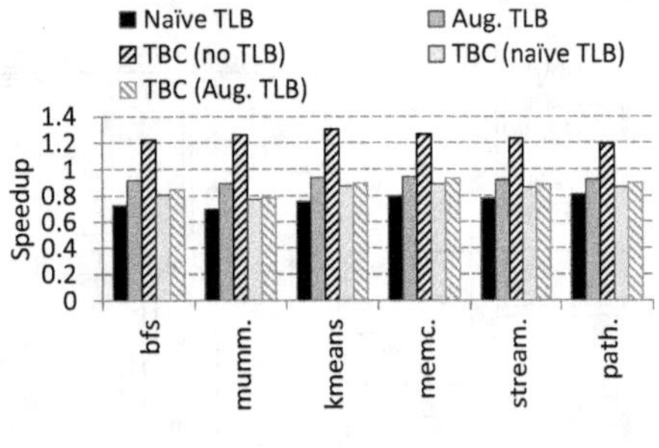

**Figure 20.** Performance of TBC without TLBs versus TBC when using naive 128-entry, 4-port blocking TLBs, and when augmenting TLBs with nonblocking and PTW scheduling facilities.

is execution a non-memory instruction, and x(x) means that the thread is masked off through branching.

All threads execute blocks A and D but only threads 2, 3, 5, and 12 execute block C due to a branch divergence at the end of A (the rest execute block B). Blocks B and C consist of a memory operation. Figure 19 shows the order in which warps execute blocks B and C, using conventional stack reconvergence. Since there is no dynamic warp formation, it takes six distinct warp fetches to execute both branch paths. Instead, Figure 19 shows that forming TBC reduces warp fetches to just three, fully utilizing SIMD pipelines.

Address translation poses some unique problems on TBC. For example, the first dynamic warp now requires virtual pages 1 and 6. If we consider a 1-entry TLB which is initially empty, the first warp takes 2 TLB misses, the second 3, and the third 2. Instead, Figure 19 shows a TLB-aware scheme that potentially performs better by forming a first dynamic warp with threads requiring only virtual page 6 and a second warp requesting virtual page 1. Now, the first two warps suffer 2 TLB misses as opposed to 5 (for baseline, TLB-agnostic TBC), without sacrificing SIMD utilization.

*Performance of basic approach:* Figure 20 quantifies the performance of baseline TBC with TLBs. Against a baseline without TLBs, we plot the speedup of TBC without TLBs, TBC with naive 128-entry, 4-port TLBs (blocking, no PTW scheduling), TBC with augmented TLBs (nonblocking, overlap misses with cache access, PTW scheduling). We also show naive TLBs and augmented TLBs without TBC. There is a significant performance gap between TBC with and without TLBs. Even with augmented TLBs, an average of 20% performance is lost compared to ideal TBC (without TLBs). *In fact, augmented TLBs without TBC actually outperform augmented TLBs with TBC.* We have found that this occurs primarily because TBC increases per-warp page divergence (by an average of 2-4 for our workloads). This further increases TLB miss rates by 5-10%. In response, we study TLB-aware TBC, assuming block-wide reconvergence stacks and age-based scheduling [18].

### 8.2 Address Translation Awareness

*Hardware details:* Figure 21 shows TBC-aware address translation with minimal additional hardware. The diagram shows the basic SIMD pipeline, with red dotted arrows

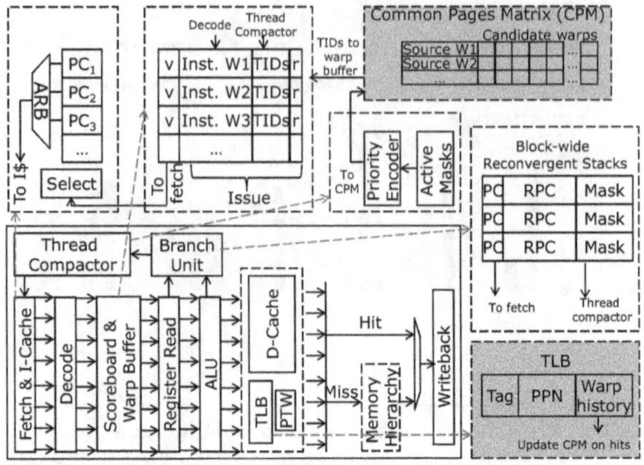

**Figure 21.** Hardware implementation of TLB-aware TBC. We add only the combinational logic in the common page matrix (CPM) and a warp history field per TLB entry. The red dotted arrows zoom into different hardware modules.

zooming on specific modules. We add only the shaded hardware to baseline TBC from [18].

In baseline TBC, on a divergent branch, a branch unit generates active masks based on branch outcomes. A block-wide active mask is sent to the thread compactor and is stored in multiple buffers. Each cycle, a priority encoder selects at most one thread from its corresponding inputs and sends its ID to the warp buffer. Bits corresponding to the selected threads are reset, allowing encoders to select from remaining threads in subsequent cycles. At the end of this step, threads have been formed into dynamic warps based on branch outcomes. When these dynamic warps becomes ready (indicated by the *r* bit per warp buffer entry) they are sent to the fetch unit, which stores program counters and initiates warp fetch. We refer readers to the TBC paper [18] for details on how the priority encoder and compactor assimilate dynamic warps.

Our contribution is to modify this basic design and encourage dynamic warp formation among warps that have historically accessed similar TLB PTEs and are hence likely to do so in the future, minimizing page divergence and miss rates. We use a table called the Common Page Matrix (CPM). Each CPM row holds a tag and multiple saturating counters. The CPM maintains a row for every warp (48 rows for our SIMD cores), each of which has a counter for every other warp (47). Each counter essentially indicates how often the warp ID associated with the row and the column have accessed the same PTEs in the past. We use this structure in tandem with the priority encoder. Threads are compacted into the warp buffer *only if the thread's original warp had accessed PTEs that threads already compacted in the new dynamic warp also accessed.* This information is easily extracted in the CPM when compacting threads; we choose a CPM row with the thread's original warp number. Then, we look up the counters using the original warp numbers of the threads that have already been compacted into the target dynamic warp. We compact the candidate thread into the dynamic warp only if the counters are at maximum value.

Figure 21 shows that CPM counters are updated on TLB hits. Each TLB entry records warp numbers that previously

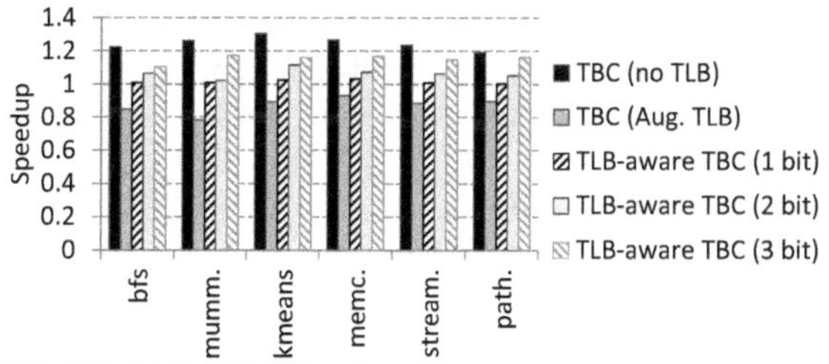


**Figure 22.** Performance of TLB-aware TBC, as the number of bits per CPM counter is varied. With 3-bits per counter, TLB-aware TBC achieves performance within 3-12% of TBC without TLBs.

accessed it. Every time a warp hits on the entry, it selects a CPM row and updates the counters corresponding to the warps in the history list. To ensure that CPM continues to adapt to program behavior, the table is periodically flushed (a flush every 500 cycles suffices).

*Hardware overheads:* TLB-aware TBC adds little hardware to baseline TBC. We track PTE access similarity between warps rather than between threads to reduce hardware costs and because original warps (not dynamic ones) usually have modest page divergence. Warp access patterns provides most of the benefits of per-thread information, but with far less overhead. The CPM has 48x47 entries; we find that 3-bit counters perform well, for a total CPM of 0.8KB. In addition, we use a history length of 2 per TLB; this requires 12 bits (since warp identifier is 6 bits). Fortunately, we observe that PTEs do not actually use full 64-bit address spaces yet, leaving 18 bits unused. We use 12 of these 18 bits to maintain history. All CPM updates and flushes occur off the critical path of dynamic warp formation.

### 8.3 Performance of TLB-Aware TBC

Figure 22 shows the performance of TLB-aware TBC against baseline TLB-agnostic TBC without TLBs, and with augmented TLBs. We assume 1, 2, and 3 bits per CPM counter; more bits provide greater confidence in detecting whether warps access the same PTEs. Even 1 bit counters drastically improves performance over TLB-agnostic TBC with augmented TLBs (15-20% on average). 3 bits boost performance within 5-12% of baseline TBC *without TLBs*, well within the typical 5-15% range deemed acceptable on CPUs. Like CCWS, these results mean that even though address translation tests conventional dynamic warp formation, simple tweaks recovers most lost performance.

## 9. Discussion and Future Work

**Broad applicability.** Our work is applicable to throughput-oriented architectures beyond GPUs like Intel's Many Integrated Core architecture [53], and accelerators like Rigel [33] and vector-thread architectures [36].

**Large pages.** Past work [3, 7, 44, 56] has shown that large pages (2MB/1GB) can potentially improve TLB performance. However, in some cases, their overheads can become an issue; for example, they require specialized OS code, can increase paging traffic, and may require pinning in physical memory (e.g., in Windows). We leave a detailed analysis of the pros and cons of large pages to future work. We do, however, present initial insights on 2MB pages. Specifically, one may, at first blush, expect large pages to dramatically reduce page divergence since it is much likelier that 32 warp threads request the same 2MB chunk rather than the same 4KB chunk. Though this is usually true, we have found that some benchmarks, `mummer` and `bfs`), still suffer high page divergences of 6 and 3. Warp threads in these benchmarks have such far-flung accesses that they essentially span 12MB and 6MB of the address space. We therefore believe that a careful design space study of superpages is a natural next step in the envolution of this work.

**Concurrent research on GPU MMUs.** Concurrent with our work, Power, Hill, and Wood also study memory management unit design for GPUs [49]. Like our work, theirs shows that naively, CPU-style TLB and page table walkers can degrade GPGPU performance substantially. While we focus on the role of the warp scheduler in prudent TLB and page table walker design, Power, Hill, and Wood study the interplay between scratchpad memories, coalescing, TLBs, and eventually study schemes that provide a TLB per compute unit but then share a highly threaded page table walker and page walk cache among compute units. Our results are complementary, showing that a little TLB-awareness in GPU design can recover most of the original lost performance.

## 10. Conclusion

This work examines address translation in CPU/GPUs because of industry trends toward fully-coherent unified virtual address spaces in heterogeneous platforms. This unification simplifies programming models and the burden on programmers to manage memory; however, their implications on architecture remains to be studied. We find that adding address translation at the L1-level of the GPUs does degrade performance; the design of GPU address translation should not be naively borrowed from CPUs (even though CPU address translation is a relatively mature technology) because the resulting overheads are untenable. We conclude that the wide adoption of heterogeneous systems, which rely on a manageable programming model, hinges upon thoughtful GPU-aware address translation. Overall, mindful implementation of TLB-awareness in the GPU execution pipeline is not complicated, thus enabling manageable performance degradation in exchange for the industry-driven desire for enhanced programmability. Therefore, we expect there is a body of low-hanging fruit yet to be plucked for enhancing address translation in heterogeneous systems.

## 11. Acknowledgments

We thank the anonymous reviewers for their feedback on this work. This material is based upon work supported by the National Science Foundation under Grant No. 1337147 and 1253700.

## References


[1] AMD, "AMD I/O Virtualization Technology (IOMMU) Specification," 2006.

[2] N. Amit, M. B. Yehuda, and B.-A. Yassour, "IOMMU: Strategies for Mitigating the IOTLB Bottleneck," *WIOSCA*, 2010.

[3] Andrea Arcangeli, "Transparent Hugepage Support," *KVM Forum*, 2010.

[4] A. Bakhoda, G. Yuan, W. Fung, H. Wong, and T. Aamodt, "Analyzing CUDA Workloads Using a Detailed GPU Simulator," *ISPASS*, 2009.

[5] T. Barr, A. Cox, and S. Rixner, "Translation Caching: Skip, Don't Walk (the Page Table)," *ISCA*, 2010.

[6] ——, "SpecTLB: A Mechanism for Speculative Address Translation," *ISCA*, 2011.

[7] A. Basu, J. Gandhi, J. Chang, M. Swift, and M. Hill, "Efficient Virtual Memory for Big Memory Servers," *ISCA*, 2013.

[8] A. Basu, M. Hill, and M. Swift, "Reducing Memory Reference Energy with Opportunistic Virtual Caching," *ISCA*, 2012.

[9] A. Bhattacharjee, D. Lustig, and M. Martonosi, "Shared Last-Level TLBs for Chip Multiprocessors," *HPCA*, 2010.

[10] A. Bhattacharjee and M. Martonosi, "Inter-Core Cooperative TLB Prefetchers for Chip Multiprocessors," *ASPLOS*, 2010.

[11] P. Boudier and G. Sellers, "Memory System on Fusion APUs," *Fusion Developer Summit*, 2012.

[12] W. Bouknight, S. Denenberg, D. McIntyre, J. Randall, A. Sameh, and D. Slotnick, "The Illiac IV System," *Proceedings of the IEEE*, vol. 60, no. 4, pp. 369–388, April 1972.

[13] I. Buck, T. Foley, D. Horn, J. Sugerman, K. Fatahalian, M. Houston, and P. Hanrahan, "Brook for GPUs: Stream Computing on Graphics Hardware," *SIGGRAPH*, 2004.

[14] M. Cekleov and M. Dubois, "Virtual-Addressed Caches," *IEEE Micro*, 1997.

[15] S. Che, M. Boyer, J. Meng, D. Tarjan, J. Sheaffer, S. ha Lee, and K. Skadron, "Rodinia: A Benchmark Suite for Heterogeneous Computing," *IISWC*, 2009.

[16] D. Clark and J. Emer, "Performance of the VAX-11/780 Translation Buffers: Simulation and Measurement," *ACM Transactions on Computer Systems*, vol. 3, no. 1, 1985.

[17] W. Dally, P. Hanrahan, M. Erez, T. Knight, F. Labonte, J.-H. Ahn, N. Jayasena, U. Kapasi, A. Das, J. Gummaraju, and I. Buck, "Merrimac: Supercomputing with Streams," *SC*, 2003.

[18] W. Fung and T. Aamodt, "Thread Block Compaction for Efficient SIMT Control Flow," *HPCA*, 2011.

[19] W. Fung, I. Sham, G. Yuan, and T. Aamodt, "Dynamic Warp Formation and Scheduling for Efficient GPU Control Flow," *MICRO*, 2007.

[20] I. Gelado, J. Cabezas, N. Navarro, J. Stone, S. Patel, and W. mei Hwu, "An Asymmetric Distributed Shared Memory Model for Heterogeneous Parallel Systems," *ASPLOS*, 2010.

[21] B. Hechtman and D. Sorin, "Evaluating Cache Coherent Shared Virtual Memory for Heterogeneous Multicore Chips," *ISPASS*, 2013.

[22] T. Hetherington, T. Rogers, L. Hsu, M. O'Connor, and T. Aamodt, "Characterizing and Evaluating a Key-Value Store Application on Heterogeneous CPU-GPU Systems," *ISPASS*, 2012.

[23] Intel, "Intel Virtualization Technology for Directed I/O Architecture Specification," 2006.

[24] Intel Corporation, "TLBs, Paging-Structure Caches and their Invalidation," *Intel Technical Report*, 2008.

[25] T. Jablin, J. Jablin, P. Prabhu, F. Liu, and D. August, "Dynamically Managed Data for CPU-GPU Architectures," *CGO*, 2012.

[26] T. Jablin, P. Prabhu, J. Jablin, N. Johnson, S. Beard, and D. August, "Automatic CPU-GPU Communication Management and Optimization," *PLDI*, 2011.

[27] B. Jacob and T. Mudge, "A Look at Several Memory Management Units: TLB-Refill, and Page Table Organizations," *ASPLOS*, 1998.

[28] A. Jaleel and B. Jacob, "In-Line Interrupt Handling for Software-Managed TLBs," *ICCD*, 2001.

[29] A. Jog, O. Kayiran, N. CN, A. Mishra, M. Kandemir, O. Mutlu, R. Iyer, and C. Das, "OWL: Cooperative Thread Array Aware Scheduling Techniques for Improving GPGPU Performance," *ASPLOS*, 2013.

[30] G. Kandiraju and A. Sivasubramaniam, "Going the Distance for TLB Prefetching: An Application-Driven Study," *ISCA*, 2002.

[31] U. Kapasi, W. Dally, S. Rixner, P. Mattson, J. Owens, and B. Khailany, "Efficient Conditional Operations for Data-Parallel Architectures," *MICRO*, 2000.

[32] S. Kaxiras and A. Ros, "A New Perspective for Efficient Virtual-Cache Coherence," *ISCA*, 2013.

[33] J. Kelm, D. Johnson, M. Johnson, N. Crago, W. Tuohy, A. Mahesri, S. Lumetta, M. Frank, and S. Patel, "Rigel: An Architecture and Scalable Programming Interface for a 1000-core Accelerator," *ISCA*, 2008.

[34] H. Kim, "Supporting Virtual Memory in GPGPU Without Supporting Precise Exceptions," *Workshop on Memory Systems Performance and Correctness in conjunction with PLDI*, 2012.

[35] J. Kim, S. L. Min, S. Jeon, B. Ahn, D.-K. Jeong, and C. S. Kim, "U-Cache: A Cost-Effective Solution to the Synonym Problem," *HPCA*, 1995.

[36] R. Krashinsky, C. Batten, M. Hampton, S. Gerding, B. Pharris, J. Casper, and K. Asanovic, "The Vector-Thread Architecture," *ISCA*, 2004.

[37] G. Kyriazis, "Heterogeneous System Architecture: A Technical Review," *Whitepaper*, 2012.

[38] K. Lim, D. Meisner, A. Saidi, P. Ranganathan, and T. Wenisch, "Thin Servers with Smart Pipes: Designing SoC Accelerators for Memcached," *ISCA*, 2013.

[39] J. Meng, D. Tarjan, and K. Skadron, "Dynamic Warp Subdivison for Integrated Branch and Memory Divergence," *ISCA*, 2010.

[40] J. Menon, M. de Kruijf, and K. Sankaralingam, "iGPU: Exception Support and Speculative Execution on GPUs," *ISCA*, 2012.

[41] G. Morris, B. Gaster, and L. Howes, "Kite: Braided Parallelism for Heterogeneous Systems," 2012.

[42] N. Muralimanohar, R. Balasubramonian, and N. Jouppi, "CACTI 6.0: A Tool to Model Large Caches," *MICRO*, 2007.

[43] V. Narasiman, M. Shebanow, C. J. Lee, R. Miftakhudinov, O. Mutlu, and Y. Patt, "Improving GPU Performance via Large Warps and Two-Level Warp Scheduling," *MICRO*, 2011.

[44] J. Navarro, S. Iyer, P. Druschel, and A. Cox, "Practical, Transparent Operating System Support for Superpages," *OSDI*, 2002.

[45] J. Owens, M. Houston, D. Luebke, S. Green, J. Stone, and J. Phillips, "GPU Computing," *IEEE*, vol. 96, no. 5, 2008.

[46] J. Owens, D. Luebke, N. Govindaraju, M. Harris, J. Kruger, A. Lefohn, and T. Purcell, "A Survey of General-Purpose Computation on Graphcis Hardware," *EUROGRAPHICS*, vol. 26, no. 1, 2007.

[47] A. Parashar, M. Pellauer, M. Adler, B. Ahsan, N. Crago, D. Lustig, V. Pavlov, A. Zhai, M. Gambhir, A. Jaleel, R. Allmon, R. Rayess, S. Maresh, and J. Emer, "Triggered Instructions: A Control Paradigm for Spatially-Programmed Architectures," *ISCA*, 2013.

[48] B. Pham, V. Vaidyanathan, A. Jaleel, and A. Bhattacharjee, "CoLT: Coalesced Large Reach TLBs," *MICRO*, 2012.

[49] J. Power, M. Hill, and D. Wood, "Supporting x86-64 Address Translation for 100s of GPU Lanes," *HPCA*, 2014.

[50] W. Qadeer, R. Hameed, O. Shacham, P. Venkatesan, C. Kozyrakis, and M. Horowitz, "Convolution Engine: Balancing Efficiency and Flexibility in Specialized Computing," *ISCA*, 2013.

[51] P. Rogers, "AMD Heterogeneous Uniform Memory Access," *AMD*, 2013.

[52] T. Rogers, M. O'Connor, and T. Aamodt, "Cache Conscious Wavefront Scheduling," *MICRO*, 2012.

[53] L. Seiler, D. Carmean, E. Sprangle, T. Forsyth, M. Abrash, P. Dubey, S. Junkins, A. Lake, J. Sugerman, R. Cavin, R. Espasa, E. Grochowski, T. Juan, and P. Hanrahan, "Larrabee: A Many-Core x86 Architecture for Visual Computing," *SIGGRAPH*, 2008.

[54] I. Singh, A. Shriraman, W. Fung, M. O'Connor, and T. Aamodt, "Cache Coherence for GPU Architecture," *HPCA*, 2013.

[55] S. Steele, "ARM GPUs Now and in the Future," 2011.

[56] M. Talluri and M. Hill, "Surpassing the TLB Performance of Superpages with Less Operating System Support," *ASPLOS*, 1994.

[57] N. Wilt, "The CUDA Handbook," 2012.

[58] L. Wu, R. Barker, M. Kim, and K. Ross, "Navigating Big Data with High-Throughput, Energy-Efficient Data Partitioning," *ISCA*, 2013.

# Author Index

www.ingramcontent.com/pod-product-compliance
Lightning Source LLC
LaVergne TN
LVHW080106011026
849160LV00013B/1038